DISCOVERING
PSYCHOLOGY

DISCOVERING
PSYCHOLOGY

SANDRA E. HOCKENBURY | SUSAN A. NOLAN | DON H. HOCKENBURY

Seventh Edition

worth publishers
Macmillan Learning
New York

Publisher: Rachel Losh
Executive Acquisitions Editor: Daniel McDonough
Developmental Editor: Marna Miller
Senior Marketing Manager: Lindsay Johnson
Marketing Assistant: Allison Greco
Media Producer: Elizabeth Dougherty
Media Editor: Jessica Lauffer
Editorial Assistant: Kimberly Morgan-Smith
Photo Editor: Christine Buese
Photo Researcher: Jacquelyn Wong
Director, Content Management Enhancement: Tracey Kuehn
Managing Editor: Lisa Kinne
Project Editor: Ed Dionne, MPS North America LLC
Production Manager: Stacey B. Alexander
Art Director: Diana Blume
Design Manager: Vicki Tomaselli
Cover and Interior Designer: Charles Yuen
Art Manager: Matthew McAdams
Art Illustrators: Todd Buck, Anatomical Art; TSI evolve
Composition: MPS Limited
Printing and Binding: RR Donnelley
Cover Photos: RGB Ventures/SuperStock/Alamy (background), Patrick Foto/
    Getty Images (left), Image Source/Getty Images (right)

Library of Congress Preassigned Control Number: 2015955442

ISBN-13: 978-1-4641-7105-5
ISBN-10: 1-4641-7105-X

Printed in the United States of America

First printing

Worth Publishers
One New York Plaza
Suite 4500
New York, NY 10004-1562
www.worthpublishers.com

To Laura, for the love and laughter
along the way—S.E.H.

For Mira, Sophie, and Julie—S.A.N.

ABOUT THE AUTHORS

Sandra E. Hockenbury is a science writer who specializes in psychology. Sandy received her B.A. from Shimer College and her M.A. from the University of Chicago, where she was also a research associate at the Institute of Social and Behavioral Pathology. Prior to co-authoring *Psychology* and *Discovering Psychology*, Sandy worked for several years as a psychology editor in both academic and college textbook publishing. Sandy has also taught as an adjunct faculty member at Tulsa Community College.

Sandy's areas of interest include positive psychology, cross-cultural psychology, and the intersection of Buddhist philosophy, neuroscience, and psychology. She is a member of the American Psychological Association (APA), the Association for Psychological Science (APS), and the American Association for the Advancement of Science (AAAS). An avid hiker, Sandy has twice served as a volunteer with Nomads Clinic, a nonprofit organization that brings medical care to remote areas in the Himalayan regions of Nepal and the Tibetan Plateau.

Susan A. Nolan is Professor of Psychology at Seton Hall University in New Jersey. Susan researches interpersonal consequences of mental illness, and the role of gender in science careers. Her research has been funded by the National Science Foundation. Susan is Past President of the Eastern Psychological Association (EPA) and a Fellow of the EPA, the American Psychological Association (APA), and the Association for Psychological Science. She holds an A.B. from the College of the Holy Cross and a Ph.D. from Northwestern University.

Susan is fascinated by the applications of psychology to the "real world," both locally and globally. She served as a representative from the APA to the United Nations for five years, and is the Vice President for Diversity and International Relations of the Society for the Teaching of Psychology and a 2015-2016 U.S. Fulbright Scholar in Bosnia and Herzegovina. She is an avid traveler. Susan uses the examples she encounters through these experiences in the classroom, in this textbook, and in the statistics textbooks that she co-authors.

Don H. Hockenbury recently retired after 36 years of teaching psychology at Tulsa Community College's Northeast Campus. As one of the founding faculty that opened the Northeast Campus in the fall of 1978, more than 10,000 students experienced Don's enthusiastic teaching style over the ensuing decades. Beginning in 1989, Don's classroom expanded to a national level as he and Sandy Hockenbury began the exciting—but daunting—task of writing the first edition of *Psychology*. In doing so, Don and Sandy were committed to creating an introductory psychology text that actively engaged diverse students in much the same way that Don shared his passion for psychology in the classroom. After seven years of almost nonstop work, the first edition of Hockenbury & Hockenbury *Psychology* was published in December 1996, followed a year later by the first edition of *Discovering Psychology*. In co-authoring the first five editions of *Psychology* and *Discovering Psychology*, Don and Sandy's texts were used by millions of students. Although Don is no longer actively involved in classroom teaching, his passion for teaching others about the most exciting science that exists remains as strong as ever.

BRIEF CONTENTS

To the Instructor **xx**
To the Student: Learning from *Discovering Psychology* **xlviii**

SECTION 1 INTRODUCING PSYCHOLOGY
CHAPTER 1 Introduction and Research Methods **1**

SECTION 2 PSYCHOBIOLOGICAL PROCESSES
CHAPTER 2 Neuroscience and Behavior **40**
CHAPTER 3 Sensation and Perception **84**
CHAPTER 4 Consciousness and Its Variations **132**

SECTION 3 BASIC PSYCHOLOGICAL PROCESSES
CHAPTER 5 Learning **180**
CHAPTER 6 Memory **226**
CHAPTER 7 Thinking, Language, and Intelligence **270**
CHAPTER 8 Motivation and Emotion **312**

SECTION 4 THE DEVELOPMENT OF THE SELF
CHAPTER 9 Lifespan Development **356**
CHAPTER 10 Personality **412**

SECTION 5 THE PERSON IN SOCIAL CONTEXT
CHAPTER 11 Social Psychology **452**

SECTION 6 PSYCHOLOGICAL PROBLEMS, DISORDERS, AND TREATMENT
CHAPTER 12 Stress, Health, and Coping **496**
CHAPTER 13 Psychological Disorders **532**
CHAPTER 14 Therapies **584**

APPENDIX A Statistics: Understanding Data **A-1**
APPENDIX B Industrial/Organizational Psychology **B-1**

Glossary **G-1**
References **R-1**
Name Index **NI-1**
Subject Index **SI-1**

CONTENTS

xx To the Instructor

xlviii To the Student: Learning from *Discovering Psychology*

Introduction and Research Methods

lii PROLOGUE: The First Exam

2 Introduction: What Is Psychology?

Psychology's Origins: The Influence of Philosophy and Physiology **3** ▪ Wilhelm Wundt: The Founder of Psychology **4** ▪ Edward B. Titchener: Structuralism **4** ▪ William James: Functionalism **5** ▪ Sigmund Freud: Psychoanalysis **7** ▪ John B. Watson: Behaviorism **8** ▪ Carl Rogers: Humanistic Psychology **9**

9 Contemporary Psychology

Major Perspectives in Psychology **10** ▪ Specialty Areas in Psychology **14**

15 The Scientific Method

The Steps in the Scientific Method: Systematically Seeking Answers **16** ▪ Building Theories: Integrating the Findings from Many Studies **19**

21 Descriptive Research

Naturalistic Observation: The Science of People- and Animal-Watching **22** ▪ Case Studies: Details, Details, Details **22** ▪ Surveys: (A) Always (B) Sometimes (C) Never (D) Huh? **23** ▪ Correlational Studies: Looking at Relationships and Making Predictions: Can Eating Curly Fries Make You Smarter? **24**

26 Experimental Research

Experimental Design: Studying the Effects of Testing **26** ▪ Experimental Controls **28** ▪ Limitations of Experiments and Variations in Experimental Design **29**

34 Ethics in Psychological Research

35 Closing Thoughts

35 PSYCH FOR YOUR LIFE Successful Study Techniques

37 CHAPTER REVIEW: KEY PEOPLE AND KEY TERMS

38 CONCEPT MAP

David Engelhardt/age fotostock

12 🌐 CULTURE AND HUMAN BEHAVIOR
What Is Cross-Cultural Psychology?

20 📊 SCIENCE VERSUS PSEUDOSCIENCE
What Is a Pseudoscience?

31 💬 CRITICAL THINKING
How to Think Like a Scientist

32 🧠 FOCUS ON NEUROSCIENCE
Psychological Research Using Brain Imaging

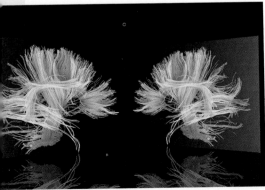

Alfred Pasieka/Science Source

Neuroscience and Behavior

40 PROLOGUE: Asha's Story

42 Introduction: Neuroscience and Behavior

54 🔍 IN FOCUS
Traumatic Brain Injury: From
Concussions to Chronic Traumatic
Encephalopathy

61 📊 SCIENCE VERSUS PSEUDOSCIENCE
Phrenology: The Bumpy Road to
Scientific Progress

62 🧠 FOCUS ON NEUROSCIENCE
Mapping the Pathways of the Brain

63 🧠 FOCUS ON NEUROSCIENCE
Juggling and Brain Plasticity

72 💬 CRITICAL THINKING
"His" and "Her" Brains?

77 📊 SCIENCE VERSUS PSEUDOSCIENCE
Brain Myths

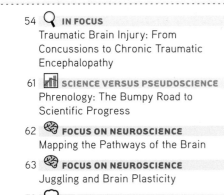

Shahril KHMD/Shutterstock

89 📊 SCIENCE VERSUS PSEUDOSCIENCE
Subliminal Perception

95 🧠 FOCUS ON NEUROSCIENCE
Vision, Experience, and the Brain

103 🔍 IN FOCUS
Do Pheromones Influence Human
Behavior?

112 💬 CRITICAL THINKING
ESP: Can Perception Occur Without
Sensation?

115 🌐 CULTURE AND HUMAN BEHAVIOR
Ways of Seeing: Culture and Top-Down
Processes

122 🔍 IN FOCUS
The Dress That Broke the Internet

126 🌐 CULTURE AND HUMAN BEHAVIOR
Culture and the Müller-Lyer Illusion:
The Carpentered-World Hypothesis

43 The Neuron: The Basic Unit of Communication
Characteristics of the Neuron 43 ▪ Glial Cells 44 ▪ Communication Within
the Neuron: The Action Potential 45 ▪ Communication Between Neurons:
Bridging the Gap 47 ▪ Neurotransmitters and Their Effects 49 ▪ How Drugs
Affect Synaptic Transmission 51

53 The Nervous System and the Endocrine System:
Communication Throughout the Body
The Central Nervous System 53 ▪ The Peripheral Nervous System 55
▪ The Endocrine System 58

60 A Guided Tour of the Brain
The Dynamic Brain: Plasticity and Neurogenesis 62 ▪ The Brainstem:
Hindbrain and Midbrain Structures 65 ▪ The Forebrain 66

71 Specialization in the Cerebral Hemispheres
Language and the Left Hemisphere: The Early Work of Broca and Wernicke 73
▪ Cutting the Corpus Callosum: The Split Brain 74

78 Closing Thoughts

79 PSYCH FOR YOUR LIFE Maximizing Your Brain's Potential

81 CHAPTER REVIEW: KEY PEOPLE AND KEY TERMS

82 CONCEPT MAP

3

Sensation and Perception

84 PROLOGUE: Learning to See

86 Introduction: What Are Sensation and Perception?
Basic Principles of Sensation 87

90 Vision: From Light to Sight
What We See: The Nature of Light 90 ▪ How We See: The Human Visual
System 91 ▪ Processing Visual Information 93 ▪ Color Vision 94

98 Hearing: From Vibration to Sound
What We Hear: The Nature of Sound 98 ▪ How We Hear: The Path of
Sound 99

102 The Chemical and Body Senses: Smell,
Taste, Touch, and Position
How We Smell (Don't Answer That!) 103 ▪ Taste 105 ▪ The Skin and Body
Senses 106

110 Perception
The Perception of Shape: What Is It? 112 ▪ Depth Perception: How Far Away
Is It? 117 ▪ The Perception of Motion: Where Is It Going? 120 ▪ Perceptual
Constancies 121

123 Perceptual Illusions
The Müller-Lyer Illusion **123** ■ The Moon Illusion **124**

125 The Effects of Experience on Perceptual Interpretations

127 Closing Thoughts

127 **PSYCH FOR YOUR LIFE** Strategies to Control Pain

129 **CHAPTER REVIEW: KEY PEOPLE AND KEY TERMS**

130 **CONCEPT MAP**

4

Consciousness and Its Variations

132 PROLOGUE: A Knife in the Dark

134 Introduction: Consciousness: Experiencing the "Private I"
Attention: The Mind's Spotlight **135** ■ The Perils of Multitasking **137**

137 Biological and Environmental "Clocks" That Regulate Consciousness
The Suprachiasmatic Nucleus: The Body's Clock **138**

139 Sleep
The Dawn of Modern Sleep Research **140** ■ The Onset of Sleep and Hypnagogic Hallucinations **140** ■ The First 90 Minutes of Sleep and Beyond **141** ■ Why Do We Sleep? **144**

147 Dreams and Mental Activity During Sleep
Dream Themes and Imagery **148** ■ The Significance of Dreams **149**

152 Sleep Disorders
Insomnia **153** ■ Obstructive Sleep Apnea: Blocked Breathing During Sleep **153** ■ Narcolepsy: Blurring the Boundaries Between Sleep and Wakefulness **153** ■ The Parasomnias: Undesired Arousal or Actions During Sleep **154**

156 Hypnosis
Effects of Hypnosis **156** ■ Explaining Hypnosis: Consciousness Divided? **157**

160 Meditation
Scientific Studies of the Effects of Meditation **161**

164 Psychoactive Drugs
Common Effects of Psychoactive Drugs **164** ■ The Depressants: Alcohol, Barbiturates, Inhalants, and Tranquilizers **165** ■ The Opioids: From Poppies to Demerol **169** ■ The Stimulants: Caffeine, Nicotine, Amphetamines, and Cocaine **170** ■ Psychedelic Drugs: Mescaline, LSD, and Marijuana **173** ■ Designer "Club" Drugs: Ecstasy and the Dissociative Anesthetic Drugs **174**

175 Closing Thoughts

Alexandr79/Shutterstock

141 🔍 **IN FOCUS**
What You Really Want to Know About Sleep

146 🧠 **FOCUS ON NEUROSCIENCE**
The Sleep-Deprived Emotional Brain

148 🧠 **FOCUS ON NEUROSCIENCE**
The Dreaming Brain

152 🔍 **IN FOCUS**
What You Really Want to Know About Dreams

158 💬 **CRITICAL THINKING**
Is Hypnosis a Special State of Consciousness?

163 🧠 **FOCUS ON NEUROSCIENCE**
Meditation and the Brain

166 🧠 **FOCUS ON NEUROSCIENCE**
The Addicted Brain: Diminishing Rewards

173 🧠 **FOCUS ON NEUROSCIENCE**
How Methamphetamines Erode the Brain

176 PSYCH FOR YOUR LIFE Overcoming Insomnia

177 **CHAPTER REVIEW: KEY PEOPLE AND KEY TERMS**

178 **CONCEPT MAP**

Learning

180 PROLOGUE: The Killer Attic

182 Introduction: What Is Learning?

183 Classical Conditioning: Associating Stimuli

Principles of Classical Conditioning **183** ■ Factors That Affect
Conditioning **184** ■ From Pavlov to Watson: The Founding of Behaviorism **187**
■ Conditioned Emotional Reactions **188** ■ Other Classically Conditioned
Responses **191**

192 Contemporary Views of Classical Conditioning

Cognitive Aspects of Classical Conditioning: Reliable Signals **192**
■ Evolutionary Aspects of Classical Conditioning: Biological Predispositions
to Learn **193**

196 Operant Conditioning: Associating Behaviors
and Consequences

Thorndike and the Law of Effect **197** ■ B.F. Skinner and the Search for
"Order in Behavior" **197** ■ Reinforcement: Increasing Future Behavior **198**
■ Punishment: Using Aversive Consequences to Decrease Behavior **200**
■ Discriminative Stimuli: Setting the Occasion for Responding **203** ■ Shaping
and Maintaining Behavior **205** ■ Applications of Operant Conditioning **209**

209 Contemporary Views of Operant Conditioning

Cognitive Aspects of Operant Conditioning: Rats! I Thought *You* Had the
Map! **209** ■ Learned Helplessness: Expectations of Failure and Learning to
Quit **211** ■ Operant Conditioning and Biological Predispositions: Misbehaving
Chickens **213**

214 Observational Learning: Imitating the Actions of Others

Applications of Observational Learning **217**

221 Closing Thoughts

221 PSYCH FOR YOUR LIFE Using Learning Principles
to Improve Your Self-Control

223 **CHAPTER REVIEW: KEY PEOPLE AND KEY TERMS**

224 **CONCEPT MAP**

Juha Saastamoinen/Shutterstock

190 🔍 **IN FOCUS**
Watson, Classical Conditioning,
and Advertising

195 🔍 **IN FOCUS**
Evolution, Biological Preparedness, and
Conditioned Fears: What Gives You the
Creeps?

202 🔍 **IN FOCUS**
Changing the Behavior of Others:
Alternatives to Punishment

204 💬 **CRITICAL THINKING**
Is Human Freedom Just an Illusion?

217 🧠 **FOCUS ON NEUROSCIENCE**
Mirror Neurons: Imitation in the Brain

219 💬 **CRITICAL THINKING**
Does Exposure to Media Violence *Cause*
Aggressive Behavior?

Kornev Andrii/Shutterstock

237 **CULTURE AND HUMAN BEHAVIOR**
Culture's Effects on Early Memories

246 **IN FOCUS**
Déjà Vu Experiences: An Illusion of
Memory?

254 **CRITICAL THINKING**
The Memory Wars: Recovered or False
Memories?

258 **FOCUS ON NEUROSCIENCE**
Assembling Memories: Echoes and
Reflections of Perception

264 **FOCUS ON NEUROSCIENCE**
Mapping Brain Changes in Alzheimer's
Disease

6

Memory

226 PROLOGUE: The Drowning

228 Introduction: What Is Memory?
The Stage Model of Memory **228** ▪ Sensory Memory: Fleeting Impressions
of the World **229** ▪ Short-Term, Working Memory: The Workshop of
Consciousness **231** ▪ Long-Term Memory **234**

238 Retrieval: Getting Information from Long-Term Memory
The Importance of Retrieval Cues **239** ▪ The Encoding Specificity
Principle **241** ▪ Flashbulb Memories: Vivid Events, Accurate Memories? **241**

242 Forgetting: When Retrieval Fails
Hermann Ebbinghaus: The Forgetting Curve **243** ▪ Why Do We Forget? **244**

248 Imperfect Memories: Errors, Distortions,
and False Memories
Forming False Memories: From the Plausible to the Impossible **251**

256 The Search for the Biological Basis of Memory
The Search for the Elusive Memory Trace **256** ▪ The Role of Neurons in
Long-Term Memory **257** ▪ Processing Memories in the Brain: Clues from
Amnesia **259**

265 Closing Thoughts

265 **PSYCH FOR YOUR LIFE** Ten Steps to Boost Your Memory

267 **CHAPTER REVIEW: KEY PEOPLE AND KEY TERMS**

268 **CONCEPT MAP**

7

Thinking, Language, and Intelligence

270 PROLOGUE: The Movie Moment

273 Introduction: Thinking, Language, and Intelligence
The Building Blocks of Thought: Mental Imagery and Concepts **273**

277 Solving Problems and Making Decisions
Problem-Solving Strategies **277** ▪ Obstacles to Solving Problems: Thinking
Outside the Box **280** ▪ Decision-Making Strategies **281** ▪ Decisions Involving
Uncertainty: Estimating the Probability of Events **282**

284 Language and Thought
The Characteristics of Language **285** ▪ The Bilingual Mind: Are Two
Languages Better Than One? **288** ▪ Animal Communication and Cognition **288**

Leoray Francis/hemis.fr/Getty Images

274 **FOCUS ON NEUROSCIENCE**
Seeing Faces and Places in the Mind's Eye

284 **CRITICAL THINKING**
The Persistence of Unwarranted Beliefs

286 **CULTURE AND HUMAN BEHAVIOR**
The Effect of Language on Perception

293 **IN FOCUS**
Does a High IQ Score Predict Success in Life?

298 **IN FOCUS**
Neurodiversity: Beyond IQ

304 **CULTURE AND HUMAN BEHAVIOR**
Performing with a Threat in the Air: How Stereotypes Undermine Performance

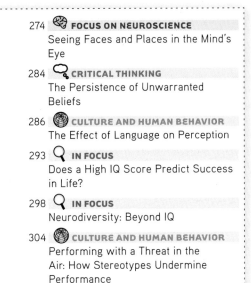

Dmitry Bodyaev/Shutterstock

322 **CRITICAL THINKING**
Has Evolution Programmed Us to Overeat?

324 **FOCUS ON NEUROSCIENCE**
Dopamine Receptors and Obesity

339 **IN FOCUS**
Detecting Lies

342 **FOCUS ON NEUROSCIENCE**
Emotions and the Brain

344 **CRITICAL THINKING**
Emotion in Nonhuman Animals: Laughing Rats, Silly Elephants, and Smiling Dolphins?

290 Measuring Intelligence
The Development of Intelligence Tests **290** ■ Principles of Test Construction: What Makes a Good Test? **294**

295 The Nature of Intelligence
Theories of Intelligence **295** ■ The Roles of Genetics and Environment in Determining Intelligence **300** ■ Cross-Cultural Studies of Group Discrimination and IQ Differences **305**

307 Closing Thoughts

308 **PSYCH FOR YOUR LIFE** A Workshop on Creativity

309 **CHAPTER REVIEW: KEY PEOPLE AND KEY TERMS**

310 **CONCEPT MAP**

8

Motivation and Emotion

312 PROLOGUE: One Step, One Breath

314 Introduction: Motivation and Emotion
Instinct Theories: Inborn Behaviors as Motivators **315** ■ Drive Theories: Biological Needs as Motivators **315** ■ Incentive Motivation: Goal Objects as Motivators **316** ■ Arousal Theory: Optimal Stimulation as a Motivator **316** ■ Humanistic Theory: Human Potential as a Motivator **317**

317 Hunger and Eating
Energy Homeostasis: Calories Consumed = Calories Expended **318** ■ Short-Term Signals That Regulate Eating **318** ■ Long-Term Signals That Regulate Body Weight **319** ■ Excess Weight and Obesity **321**

324 Human Sexuality
First Things First: The Stages of Human Sexual Response **324** ■ What Motivates Sexual Behavior? **326** ■ Sexual Orientation: The Elusive Search for an Explanation **327**

331 Psychological Needs as Motivators
Maslow's Hierarchy of Needs **331** ■ Deci and Ryan's Self-Determination Theory **333** ■ Competence and Achievement Motivation **334**

335 Emotion
The Functions of Emotion **336** ■ The Subjective Experience of Emotion **337** ■ The Neuroscience of Emotion **338** ■ The Expression of Emotion: Making Faces **343**

346 Theories of Emotion: Explaining Emotion
The James–Lange Theory of Emotion: Do You Run Because You're Afraid? Or Are You Afraid Because You Run? **347** ■ Cognitive Theories of Emotion **350**

351 Closing Thoughts

351 **PSYCH FOR YOUR LIFE** Turning Your Goals into Reality

353 **CHAPTER REVIEW: KEY PEOPLE AND KEY TERMS**

354 **CONCEPT MAP**

9

Lifespan Development

356 PROLOGUE: People Are People

358 Introduction: People Are People

360 Genetic Contributions to Development
Your Unique Genotype **361** ■ From Genotype to Phenotype **361**

363 Prenatal Development
The Germinal and Embryonic Periods **363** ■ Prenatal Brain Development **364**
■ The Fetal Period **365**

365 Development During Infancy and Childhood
Physical Development **366** ■ Social and Personality Development **367**
■ Language Development **371** ■ Gender Development: Blue Bears and Pink
Bunnies **374** ■ Cognitive Development **380**

386 Adolescence
Physical and Sexual Development **386** ■ Social Development **390**
■ Identity Formation: Erikson's Theory of Psychosocial Development **391**
■ The Development of Moral Reasoning **393**

396 Adult Development
Emerging Adulthood **396** ■ Physical Changes in Adulthood **398**
■ Social Development in Adulthood **399**

402 Late Adulthood and Aging
Cognitive Changes **403** ■ Social Development **405**

405 The Final Chapter: Dying and Death

406 Closing Thoughts

407 **PSYCH FOR YOUR LIFE** Raising Psychologically Healthy
Children

409 **CHAPTER REVIEW: KEY PEOPLE AND KEY TERMS**

410 **CONCEPT MAP**

TFoxFoto/Shutterstock

368 **CULTURE AND HUMAN BEHAVIOR**
Where Does the Baby Sleep?

372 **SCIENCE VERSUS PSEUDOSCIENCE**
Can a DVD Program Your Baby to Be a
Genius?

388 **FOCUS ON NEUROSCIENCE**
The Adolescent Brain: A Work in
Progress

397 **IN FOCUS**
Hooking Up on Campus

401 **CRITICAL THINKING**
The Effects of Child Care on
Attachment and Development

404 **FOCUS ON NEUROSCIENCE**
Boosting the Aging Brain

10

Personality

412 PROLOGUE: The Secret Twin

414 Introduction: What Is Personality?

OKcamera/Shutterstock

430 **CRITICAL THINKING**
Freud Versus Rogers on Human Nature

440 **FOCUS ON NEUROSCIENCE**
The Neuroscience of Personality: Brain Structure and the Big Five

443 **SCIENCE VERSUS PSEUDOSCIENCE**
Graphology: The "Write" Way to Assess Personality?

415 The Psychoanalytic Perspective on Personality
The Life of Sigmund Freud **416** ▪ Freud's Dynamic Theory of Personality **417** ▪ Personality Development: The Psychosexual Stages **421** ▪ The Neo-Freudians: Freud's Descendants and Dissenters **424** ▪ Evaluating Freud and the Psychoanalytic Perspective on Personality **427**

428 The Humanistic Perspective on Personality
The Emergence of the "Third Force" **429** ▪ Carl Rogers: On Becoming a Person **429** ▪ Evaluating the Humanistic Perspective on Personality **432**

432 The Social Cognitive Perspective on Personality
Albert Bandura and Social Cognitive Theory **433** ▪ Evaluating the Social Cognitive Perspective on Personality **434**

435 The Trait Perspective on Personality
Surface Traits and Source Traits **436** ▪ Two Representative Trait Theories: Raymond Cattell and Hans Eysenck **436** ▪ Sixteen Are Too Many, Three Are Too Few: The Five-Factor Model **438** ▪ Personality Traits and Behavioral Genetics: Just a Chip Off the Old Block? **439** ▪ Evaluating the Trait Perspective on Personality **441**

442 Assessing Personality: Psychological Tests
Projective Tests: Like Seeing Things in the Clouds **442** ▪ Self-Report Inventories: Does Anyone Have an Eraser? **444**

447 Closing Thoughts

447 **PSYCH FOR YOUR LIFE** Possible Selves: Imagine the Possibilities

449 **CHAPTER REVIEW: KEY PEOPLE AND KEY TERMS**

450 **CONCEPT MAP**

11

Social Psychology

452 PROLOGUE: The "Homeless" Man

454 Introduction: What Is Social Psychology?

454 Person Perception: Forming Impressions of Other People
Social Categorization: Using Mental Shortcuts in Person Perception **456**

458 Attribution: Explaining Behavior
The Self-Serving Bias: Using Explanations to Meet Our Needs **460**

461 The Social Psychology of Attitudes
The Effect of Attitudes on Behavior **462** ▪ The Effect of Behavior on Attitudes: Fried Grasshoppers for Lunch?! **462**

Art by: Distort & Mustart http://g.reenvillain.com

458  **FOCUS ON NEUROSCIENCE**
Brain Reward When Making Eye
Contact with Attractive People

460 **CULTURE AND HUMAN BEHAVIOR**
Explaining Failure and Murder: Culture
and Attributional Biases

463 **IN FOCUS**
Interpersonal Attraction and Liking

480 **CRITICAL THINKING**
Abuse at Abu Ghraib: Why Do Ordinary
People Commit Evil Acts?

465 Understanding Prejudice
From Stereotypes to Prejudice: In-Groups and Out-Groups **466**
■ Overcoming Prejudice **470**

471 Conformity: Following the Crowd
Factors Influencing Conformity **473** ■ Culture and Conformity **473**

474 Obedience: Just Following Orders
Milgram's Original Obedience Experiment **474** ■ The Results of Milgram's
Original Experiment **476** ■ Making Sense of Milgram's Findings: Multiple
Influences **476** ■ Conditions That Undermine Obedience: Variations on a
Theme **477** ■ Asch, Milgram, and the Real World: Implications of the Classic
Social Influence Studies **479**

482 Altruism and Aggression: Helping and Hurting Behavior
Factors That Increase the Likelihood of Bystanders Helping **484** ■ Factors
That Decrease the Likelihood of Bystanders Helping **485** ■ Aggression:
Hurting Behavior **486**

490 Closing Thoughts

491 **PSYCH FOR YOUR LIFE** The Persuasion Game

493 **CHAPTER REVIEW: KEY PEOPLE AND KEY TERMS**

494 **CONCEPT MAP**

12

Stress, Health, and Coping

496 PROLOGUE: Fire and Ash

499 Introduction: Stress and Health Psychology
Sources of Stress **501**

507 Physical Effects of Stress: The Mind–Body Connection
Stress and the Endocrine System **507** ■ Stress, Chromosomes, and Aging:
The Telomere Story **509** ■ Stress and the Immune System **511**

513 Individual Factors That Influence the Response to Stress
Psychological Factors **514** ■ Social Factors: A Little Help From Your
Friends **519**

522 Coping: How People Deal with Stress
Problem-Focused Coping Strategies: Changing the Stressor **523** ■ Emotion-
Focused Coping Strategies: Changing Your Reaction to the Stressor **523**
■ Culture and Coping Strategies **526**

527 Closing Thoughts

527 **PSYCH FOR YOUR LIFE** Minimizing the Effects of Stress

529 **CHAPTER REVIEW: KEY PEOPLE AND KEY TERMS**

530 **CONCEPT MAP**

Jenn Huls/Shutterstock

506 **CULTURE AND HUMAN BEHAVIOR**
The Stress of Adapting to a New
Culture

512 **FOCUS ON NEUROSCIENCE**
The Mysterious Placebo Effect

518 **CRITICAL THINKING**
Do Personality Factors Cause Disease?

521 **IN FOCUS**
Providing Effective Social Support

525 **IN FOCUS**
Gender Differences in Responding to
Stress: "Tend-and-Befriend" or "Fight-
or-Flight"?

NorGal/Shutterstock

13

Psychological Disorders

532 PROLOGUE: "I'm Flying! I've Escaped!"

534 Introduction: Understanding Psychological Disorders
What Is a Psychological Disorder? **535** ■ The Prevalence of Psychological
Disorders: A 50–50 Chance? **538**

541 Fear and Trembling: Anxiety Disorders, Posttraumatic
Stress Disorder, and Obsessive–Compulsive Disorder
Generalized Anxiety Disorder: Worrying About Anything and Everything **541**
■ Panic Attacks and Panic Disorders: Sudden Episodes of Extreme Anxiety **542**
■ The Phobias: Fear and Loathing **543** ■ Posttraumatic Stress Disorder and
Obsessive–Compulsive Disorder: Anxiety and Intrusive Thoughts **546**

550 Depressive and Bipolar Disorders: Disordered Moods
and Emotions
Major Depressive Disorder: More Than Ordinary Sadness **550** ■ Bipolar
Disorder: An Emotional Roller Coaster **552** ■ Explaining Depressive
Disorders and Bipolar Disorders **554**

558 Eating Disorders: Anorexia, Bulimia,
and Binge-Eating Disorder

562 Personality Disorders: Maladaptive Traits
Antisocial Personality Disorder: Violating the Rights of Others—Without Guilt or
Remorse **563** ■ Borderline Personality Disorder: Chaos and Emptiness **565**

566 The Dissociative Disorders: Fragmentation of the Self
Dissociative Amnesia and Dissociative Fugue: Forgetting and Wandering **567**
■ Dissociative Identity Disorder: Multiple Personalities **567**

569 Schizophrenia: A Different Reality
Symptoms of Schizophrenia **570** ■ Schizophrenia Symptoms and Culture **572**
■ The Prevalence and Course of Schizophrenia **573**
■ Explaining Schizophrenia **573**

579 Closing Thoughts

579 **PSYCH FOR YOUR LIFE** Understanding and Helping to Prevent
Suicide

581 **CHAPTER REVIEW: KEY PEOPLE AND KEY TERMS**

582 **CONCEPT MAP**

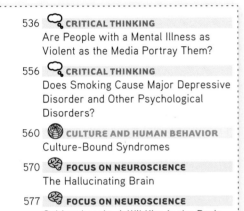

536 **CRITICAL THINKING**
Are People with a Mental Illness as
Violent as the Media Portray Them?

556 **CRITICAL THINKING**
Does Smoking Cause Major Depressive
Disorder and Other Psychological
Disorders?

560 **CULTURE AND HUMAN BEHAVIOR**
Culture-Bound Syndromes

570 **FOCUS ON NEUROSCIENCE**
The Hallucinating Brain

577 **FOCUS ON NEUROSCIENCE**
Schizophrenia: A Wildfire in the Brain

R. Gina Santa Maria/Shutterstock

Therapies

584 PROLOGUE: "A Clear Sense of Being Heard . . ."

586 Introduction: Psychotherapy and Biomedical Therapy

588 Psychoanalytic Therapy
Sigmund Freud and Psychoanalysis **588** ■ Short-Term Dynamic Therapies **589**

590 Humanistic Therapy
Carl Rogers and Client-Centered Therapy **591**

593 Behavior Therapy
Techniques Based on Classical Conditioning **594** ■ Techniques Based on Operant Conditioning **597**

599 Cognitive Therapies
Albert Ellis and Rational-Emotive Behavior Therapy **599** ■ Aaron Beck and Cognitive Therapy **601** ■ Cognitive-Behavioral Therapy and Mindfulness-Based Therapies **603**

605 Group and Family Therapy
Group Therapy **605** ■ Family and Couple Therapy **608**

609 Evaluating the Effectiveness of Psychotherapy
Is One Form of Psychotherapy Superior? **610** ■ What Factors Contribute to Effective Psychotherapy? **611**

614 Biomedical Therapies
Antipsychotic Medications **614** ■ Antianxiety Medications **617** ■ Lithium **618** ■ Antidepressant Medications **619** ■ Electroconvulsive Therapy **622**

625 Closing Thoughts

625 PSYCH FOR YOUR LIFE What to Expect in Psychotherapy

627 CHAPTER REVIEW: KEY PEOPLE AND KEY TERMS

628 CONCEPT MAP

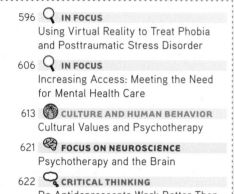

596 🔍 IN FOCUS
Using Virtual Reality to Treat Phobia and Posttraumatic Stress Disorder

606 🔍 IN FOCUS
Increasing Access: Meeting the Need for Mental Health Care

613 🌐 CULTURE AND HUMAN BEHAVIOR
Cultural Values and Psychotherapy

621 🧠 FOCUS ON NEUROSCIENCE
Psychotherapy and the Brain

622 💬 CRITICAL THINKING
Do Antidepressants Work Better Than Placebos?

APPENDIX A

Statistics: Understanding Data

A-1 PROLOGUE: The Tables Are Turned: A Psychologist Becomes a Research Participant

A-2 Descriptive Statistics
Frequency Distribution **A-2** ■ Measures of Central Tendency **A-4** ■ Measures of Variability **A-5** ■ z Scores and the Normal Curve **A-7** ■ Correlation **A-8**

A-10 Inferential Statistics

A-12 Endnote

A-13 **APPENDIX REVIEW: KEY TERMS**

A-14 **CONCEPT MAP**

APPENDIX B

Industrial/Organizational Psychology

B-1 What Is Industrial/Organizational Psychology?

B-3 History of I/O Psychology

B-3 Industrial (Personnel) Psychology

Job Analysis **B-3** ■ A Closer Look at Personnel Selection **B-4**

B-7 Organizational Behavior

Job Satisfaction **B-7** ■ Leadership **B-8**

B-10 Workplace Trends and Issues

Workforce Diversity: Recruiting and Retaining Diverse Talent **B-11** ■ Telework and Telecommuting: The Best Retention Tool **B-12** ■ Internet Recruiting: Using the Web to Recruit Top Talent **B-12** ■ Work–Life Balance: Engaging and Retaining Employees with Families **B-12**

B-13 Employment Settings, Type of Training, Earnings, and Employment Outlook

B-15 **APPENDIX REVIEW: KEY TERMS**

B-16 **CONCEPT MAP**

G-1 Glossary

R-1 References

NI-1 Name Index

SI-1 Subject Index

B-10 Q **IN FOCUS**
Servant Leadership: When It's Not All About You

B-11 Q **IN FOCUS**
Name, Title, Generation

TO THE INSTRUCTOR

Welcome to the seventh edition of *Discovering Psychology!*

We've been gratified by the enthusiastic response to the six previous editions of *Discovering Psychology*. We've especially enjoyed the e-mails and letters we've received from students who felt that our book was speaking directly to them. Students and faculty alike have told us how much they appreciated *Discovering Psychology's* distinctive voice, its inviting learning environment, the engaging writing style, and the clarity of its explanations—qualities we've maintained in the seventh edition.

But as you'll quickly see, this new edition is marked by exciting new changes: a fresh new look, a stronger and more explicit emphasis on scientific literacy, a digital experience that is more tightly integrated for both students and instructors, and—most important—a new co-author! More about these features later.

Before we wrote the first word of the first edition, we had a clear vision for this book: Combine the scientific authority of psychology with a narrative that engages students and relates to their lives. Drawing from decades (yes, it really has been decades) of teaching experience, we've written a book that weaves cutting-edge psychological science with real-life stories that draw students of all kinds into the narrative.

While there is much that is new, this edition of *Discovering Psychology* reflects our continued commitment to the goals that have guided us as teachers and authors. Once again, we invite you to explore every page of the new edition of *Discovering Psychology*, so you can see firsthand how we:

- Communicate both the scientific rigor and the personal relevance of psychology
- Encourage and model critical and scientific thinking
- Show how classic psychological studies help set the stage for today's research
- Clearly explain psychological concepts and the relationships among them
- Present controversial topics in an impartial and evenhanded fashion
- Expand students' awareness of cultural and gender influences
- Create a student-friendly, personal learning environment
- Provide an effective pedagogical system that helps students develop more effective learning strategies

What's New in the Seventh Edition: Big Changes!

We began the revision process with the thoughtful recommendations and feedback we received from hundreds of faculty using the text, from reviewers, from colleagues, and from students. We also had face-to-face dialogues with our own students as well as groups of students across the country. As you'll quickly see, the seventh edition marks a major step in the evolution of *Discovering Psychology*. We'll begin by summarizing the biggest changes to this edition—starting with the most important: a new co-author!

Introducing . . . Susan Nolan

We are very excited and pleased to introduce **Susan A. Nolan** as our new co-author. When the time came to search for a new collaborator, we looked for someone who was an accomplished researcher, a dedicated teacher, and an engaging writer with a passion for communicating psychological science to a broad audience. A commitment to gender equality and cultural sensitivity, and, of course, a good sense of humor were also requirements, as were energy and enthusiasm. We found that rare individual in Susan A. Nolan, Professor of Psychology at Seton Hall University.

Susan made several valuable contributions to the sixth edition of *Discovering Psychology,* and the success of that collaboration prompted our decision to make her a full co-author with this new edition. Reflecting her expertise in clinical, personality, and social psychology, and her background in gender, culture, and diversity studies, Susan revised Chapter 7, Thinking, Language, and Intelligence; Chapter 9, Lifespan Development; Chapter 10, Personality; Chapter 11, Social Psychology; Chapter 12, Stress, Health, and Coping; Chapter 13, Psychological Disorders; and Chapter 14, Therapies. And, she participated fully in our text-wide decisions about design, photographs, art, and content. Beyond the text, she's been fully involved in the development of some exciting new digital resources for the new edition. But more on that below.

New Emphasis on Scientific Literacy

As psychology instructors well know, students come to psychology with many preconceived ideas, some absorbed from popular culture, about the human mind and behavior. These notions are often inaccurate. Complicating matters is the fact that for many students, introductory psychology may be their first college-level science course—meaning that students sometimes have only the vaguest notion of the nature of scientific methodology and evidence. Thus, one important goal for introductory psychology is to teach students how to distinguish fact from opinion, and research-based, empirical findings from something heard from friends or encountered on the Internet.

The importance of this objective is reinforced by the 2013 revision of the APA Guidelines for the Undergraduate Psychology Major. Scientific Literacy and Critical Thinking is identified as one of its five key goals. Psychology educators agree that the skills students learn in psychology can be as important as the content. Scientific literacy and critical thinking skills can help students in a variety of careers, a variety of majors, and can help ensure that students become critical consumers of scientific information in the world around them.

Since the first edition, a hallmark of *Discovering Psychology* and its sister publication, *Psychology,* has always been their emphasis on critical and scientific thinking. *Psychology* was the first introductory psychology textbook to formally discuss and define pseudosciences and to distinguish pseudoscience from science. Our trademark *Science Versus Pseudoscience* boxes, which take a critical look at the evidence for and against phenomena as diverse as graphology, educational videos for infants, and ESP research have proved very popular among instructors and students alike.

In this new edition, we decided to make the **scientific literacy** theme even more explicit. These new features are described below.

New *Think Like a Scientist* Model and Immersive Learning Activities

To help students develop their scientific thinking skills and become critical consumers of information, a unique feature of the seventh edition is a set of **Think Like a Scientist** Immersive Learning Activities found in LaunchPad. Developed for *Psychology* and *Discovering Psychology* by co-authors Susan Nolan and Sandy Hockenbury, each activity provides students with the opportunity to apply their critical thinking and scientific thinking skills. These active learning exercises combine video, audio, text, games, and assessment to help students master scientific literacy skills they will use well beyond the introductory course. In these activities, students are invited to critically explore questions they encounter in everyday life, such as "Can you learn to tell when someone is lying?" and "Are some people 'left-brained' and some people 'right-brained'?"

These activities employ the four-step model introduced in the new Critical Thinking box "How to Think Like a Scientist" in Chapter 1. These four steps include:

1. Identify the Claim

2. Evaluate the Evidence

3. Consider Alternative Explanations

4. Consider the Source of the Research or Claim

Think Like a SCIENTIST

Can you be classified as right-brained or left-brained? Go to LaunchPad: Resources to **Think Like a Scientist** about **The Right Brain Versus the Left Brain.**

LaunchPad

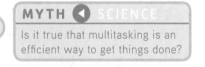

MYTH ◀ SCIENCE

Is it true that multitasking is an efficient way to get things done?

The *Think Like a Scientist* Immersive Learning Activities are designed to teach and develop a skill set that will persist long after the final exam grades are recorded. We hope to develop a set of transferable skills that can be applied to analyzing dubious claims in any subject area—from advertisements to politics. We think students will enjoy completing these activities, and that instructors will value them. The seventh edition of *Discovering Psychology* includes the following *Think Like a Scientist* Immersive Learning Activities:

- Contagious Online Emotions (Chapter 1)
- The Right Brain Versus the Left Brain (Chapter 2)
- ESP (Chapter 3)
- Multitasking (Chapter 4)
- Positive and Negative Reinforcement (Chapter 5)
- Eyewitness Testimony (Chapter 6)
- Brain Exercises (Chapter 7)
- Lie Detection (Chapter 8)
- Learning Environments (Chapter 9)
- Employment-Related Personality Tests (Chapter 10)
- Online Dating (Chapter 11)
- Coping with Stress (Chapter 12)
- Tracking Mental Illness Online (Chapter 13)
- Ketamine (Chapter 14)

New *Myth or Science?* Feature

Students often come to the introductory psychology course with misperceptions about psychological science. Our new **Myth or Science?** feature will help dispel some of these popular but erroneous beliefs.

Each chapter begins with a list of "Is It True?" questions that reflect popular myths about human behavior. These statements were tested with market research to see what percentage of students actually endorsed them. In some cases, agreement reached astonishing levels. For example, in one survey, more than 85% of students agreed that "the right brain is creative and intuitive, and the left brain is analytic and logical" and that "some people are left-brained and some people are right-brained." More than 70% of students agreed that "flashbulb memories are more accurate than normal memories" and that "most psychologists agree with Freud's personality theory." And, more than 90% of surveyed students agreed that "dying people go through five predictable stages." Even frequently debunked statements like "you only use 10% of your brain" received a high rate of agreement.

After being posed at the beginning of the chapter, each question is answered in the body of the chapter. A margin note signals the student to find the explanation and indicates whether the statement is "myth" or "science."

New Data Presentation Program

Our new co-author Susan Nolan brought her expertise in data analysis and presentation to the fully revised graphic art program. We've redesigned our graphs more closely in line with graphing expert Edward Tufte's (1997) guidelines for clear, consistent data visualizations. Graphs are simpler than in previous editions. Most now use fewer colors per graph, and fewer and lighter background gridlines, to allow the representations of data—the bars, for example—to emerge as the most important element. We have used plain bar graphs whenever possible, starting the y axes at 0. When the variable is a percentage, we extended the y axis to 100% whenever possible. We hope that the simpler, more streamlined graphs will allow students to more readily "see" and accurately interpret data.

New Research Methods Section in Chapter 1

Introductory chapters have a reputation for being dry and boring. Instructors, though, know that there are few alternatives: history and methods need to be taught before plunging into content-heavy chapters. For this edition, the section on research methods has been completely rewritten to highlight *psychological science on the topic of student success*. New research examples—such as the impact of social media on well-being, the effect of multitasking on studying, the testing effect, and measures of student well-being—were chosen for their relevance to today's students' lives.

The new end-of-chapter application, **Psych for Your Life: Successful Study Techniques**, provides six research-based strategies to maximize student success. In other words, rather than waiting for the Learning or Memory chapters to introduce study skills tips, we've incorporated these important findings right into Chapter 1—and used them to demonstrate the relevance of psychological research in students' everyday lives and academic success. Along with demonstrating to students *how* psychological research can be used to improve everyday life, the new application gives them a solid foundation of research-based study skills and tips.

All-New Digitally Integrated Package

Today's college students are digital natives. They are accustomed to going online to seek answers and to connect with friends, fellow students, and their instructors. Past editions of *Discovering Psychology* provided a wealth of online resources for students, but the new seventh edition marks a step to a new level of digital integration with **LaunchPad**.

LaunchPad, our new course space, combines an interactive e-Book with high-quality multimedia content and ready-made assessment options, including LearningCurve adaptive quizzing. Pre-built, curated units are easy to assign or adapt with your own material, such as readings, videos, quizzes, discussion groups, and more. LaunchPad also provides access to Gradebook, which offers a window into your students' performance—either individually or as a whole. While a streamlined interface helps students focus on what's due next, social commenting tools let them engage, make connections, and learn from each other. Use LaunchPad on its own or integrate it with your school's learning management system so your class is always on the same page.

The Latest Psychological Science

As was the case with previous editions, we have extensively updated every chapter with the latest research. We have pored over dozens of journals and clicked through thousands of Web sites to learn about the latest in psychological science. As a result, this new edition features scores of new topics. Just to highlight a few additions, the seventh edition includes brand-new sections on scientific thinking and factors contributing to college success (Chapter 1); traumatic brain injury and concussion (Chapter 2); evolutionary and interactionist theories of gender development (Chapter 9), transgender identity (Chapter 9); aggression and violence (Chapter 11); and a critical look at the effectiveness of antidepressants compared to placebo treatments (Chapter 14). And, there are four new prologues (Chapters 1, 8, 9, and 13).

In addition, we have significantly updated coverage of neuroscience and expanded our coverage of culture, gender, and diversity throughout the text. DSM-5 terminology and criteria have been fully integrated into the new edition.

As of our last count, there are over 1,000 new references in the seventh edition of *Discovering Psychology,* more than half of which are from 2013, 2014, or 2015. These new citations reflect the many new and updated topics and discussions in the seventh edition of *Discovering Psychology.* From the effects of social media and multitasking on student success to the latest discoveries about oxytocin, aggression, stress and telomeres, or the effectiveness of meditation in controlling pain and improving attention, our goal is to present students with interesting, clear explanations of psychological science. Later in this preface, you'll find a list of the updates by chapter.

Michael J. Minardi/Getty Images

Dave Duerson Hockey players Derek Boogaard and Bob Probert. Football players John Grimsley, Chris Henry, and Junior Seau. Wrestler Chris Benoit. What do these men have in common? Like Dave Duerson and dozens of other former NFL players, all are professional athletes whose brains, after their deaths, displayed telltale signs of chronic traumatic encephalopathy, or CTE (Gavett & others, 2011; Tartaglia & others, 2014).

New Design, New Photos

Created with today's media-savvy students in mind, the clean, modern, new look of *Discovering Psychology* showcases the book's cutting-edge content and student-friendly style. Carefully chosen photographs—more than 50 percent of them new—apply psychological concepts and research to real-world situations. Accompanied by information-rich captions that expand upon the text, vivid and diverse photographs help make psychology concepts come alive, demonstrating psychology's relevance to today's students.

Connections to the American Psychological Association's Guidelines for the Undergraduate Psychology Major

The American Psychological Association has developed the *APA Guidelines for the Undergraduate Psychology Major: Version 2.0* to provide "optimal expectations for performance" by undergraduate psychology students. The *APA Guidelines* include five broad goals, which are summarized below. This table shows how Hockenbury, Nolan, and Hockenbury's *Discovering Psychology*, Seventh Edition, helps instructors and students achieve these goals.

Goal 1: Knowledge Base in Psychology

APA Learning Objectives:

1.1—Describe key concepts, principles, and overarching themes in psychology
- *Discovering Psychology* covers the full range of psychology's subject areas: history of the field, biological psychology, experimental and cognitive psychology, developmental psychology, social psychology, personality and clinical psychology
- Chapter 1, Introduction and Research Methods, provides an overview of the history and the scope of contemporary psychological science

1.2—Develop a working knowledge of psychology's content domains
- *Discovering Psychology* provides a comprehensive, up-to-date survey of the full range of psychology's subject areas
- Thousands of research citations, with more than 500 from research no older than 2013
- In Focus and Focus on Neuroscience boxes provide in-depth looks at particular topics
- Chapter 1, Introduction and Research Methods

1.3—Describe applications of psychology
- Psych for Your Life end-of-chapter sections (see full list of titles on page xli) show students how they can apply psychological principles to improve their own lives
- "Specialty Areas in Psychology" in Chapter 1, Introduction and Research Methods
- Appendix B, Industrial/Organizational Psychology

Goal 2: Scientific Inquiry and Critical Thinking

APA Learning Objectives:

2.1—Use scientific reasoning to interpret psychological phenomena
- Chapter 1, Introduction and Research Methods, especially the "How to Think Like a Scientist" model introduced on page 31 and discussion of pseudoscience characteristics on pages 20–21.
- Critical Thinking boxes (see full list of titles on page xxxvi)
- Science Versus Pseudoscience boxes (see full list of titles on pages xxxv–xxxvi)
- Myth or Science feature (see description on page xxii)
- *Think Like a Scientist* Immersive Learning Activities, accessible on LaunchPad
- Focus on Neuroscience boxes (see full list on pages xxxix and xli)
- PsychSim 6.0, Concept Practice, Video Activities, and Labs, accessible on LaunchPad

2.2—Demonstrate psychology information literacy
- Chapter 1, Introduction and Research Methods
- Appendix A, Statistics: Understanding Data
- Box on "Psychological Research Using Brain Imaging" (pages 32–33) explains the utility and limitations of brain-imaging research
- Focus on Neuroscience boxes show students how to evaluate research findings based on brain-imaging techniques
- Science versus Pseudoscience boxes teach students how to critically evaluate media claims
- *Think Like a Scientist* Immersive Learning Activities, accessible on LaunchPad
- PsychSim 6.0, Concept Practice, Video Activities, and Labs, accessible on LaunchPad

2.3—Engage in innovative and integrative thinking and problem solving
- "Solving Problems and Making Decisions" in Chapter 7, Thinking, Language, and Intelligence
- Psych for Your Life feature "A Workshop on Creativity"
- *Think Like a Scientist* Immersive Learning Activities, accessible on LaunchPad
- PsychSim 6.0, Concept Practice, Video Activities, and Labs, accessible on LaunchPad

2.4—Interpret, design, and conduct basic psychological research
- Chapter 1, Introduction and Research Methods, describes the range of psychological research strategies, including examples related to student success
- Appendix A, Statistics: Understanding Data

2.5—Incorporate sociocultural factors in scientific inquiry
- Multiple chapters include the impact of sociocultural factors on behavior and psychological processes, especially Chapter 9, Lifespan Development; Chapter 11, Social Psychology; Chapter 12, Stress, Health and Coping; Chapter 13, Psychological Disorders; and Chapter 14, Therapies.
- Culture and Human Behavior boxes (see full list of titles on pages xxxvii and xxxix)
- See list of cultural coverage topics integrated within the main narrative on pages xxxvii–xxxviii
- See list of gender coverage topics integrated within the main narrative on page xl

Goal 3: Ethical and Social Responsibility in a Diverse World	
APA Learning Objectives: 3.1—Apply ethical standards to evaluate psychological science and practice • "Ethics in Psychological Research" in Chapter 1, Introduction and Research Methods • Discussions of obedience, conformity, the study known as the Stanford Prison Experiment, altruism, aggression, and deindividuation in Chapter 11, Social Psychology • *Think Like a Scientist* Immersive Learning Activity "Contagious Online Emotions," accessible on LaunchPad 3.2—Build and enhance interpersonal relationships • Psych for Your Life features "Raising Psychologically Healthy Children," "Reducing Conflict in Intimate Relationships," "Understanding and Helping to Prevent Suicide" • "Social Support" in Chapter 12, Stress, Health, and Coping • See list of gender coverage topics integrated within the main narrative on page xl • Culture and Human Behavior boxes (see full list of titles on pages xxxvii and xxxix)	3.3—Adopt values that build community at local, national, and global levels • Discussions of gender in Chapter 9, Lifespan Development; prejudice, obedience, conformity, the study known as the Stanford Prison Experiment, altruism, and aggression in Chapter 11, Social Psychology; stigma of obesity in Chapter 8, Motivation and Emotion; and of mental illness in Chapters 13, Psychological Disorders, and 14, Therapies • See list of cultural coverage topics integrated within the main narrative on pages xxxvii–xxxviii • See list of gender coverage topics integrated within the main narrative on page xl • Culture and Human Behavior boxes (see full list of titles on pages xxxvii and xxxix)

Goal 4: Communication	
APA Learning Objectives: 4.1—Demonstrate effective writing for different purposes • "The Scientific Method" in Chapter 1 (Introduction and Research Methods) • Questions in Critical Thinking boxes (see full list of titles on page xxxvi) • Response features in *Think Like a Scientist* Immersive Learning Activities, accessible on LaunchPad • Essay questions in Test Bank, which is aligned with APA objectives	4.2—Exhibit effective presentation skills for different purposes • Instructor's Resource Manual with classroom activities that work to develop oral presentation skills, accessible on LaunchPad 4.3—Interact effectively with others • Psych for Your Life features "Raising Psychologically Healthy Children," "Reducing Conflict in Intimate Relationships," "The Persuasion Game," and "Understanding and Helping to Prevent Suicide" • Instructor's Resource Manual with classroom exercises that promote skills for working in a group, accessible on LaunchPad

Goal 5: Professional Development	
APA Learning Objectives: 5.1—Apply psychological content and skills to career goals • "Specialty Areas in Psychology" in Chapter 1, Introduction and Research Methods • Focus on psychological research on student success and study skills in Chapter 1, Introduction and Research Methods • Psych for Your Life features "Successful Study Techniques" and "Turning Your Goals into Reality" • Appendix B, Industrial/Organizational Psychology 5.2—Exhibit self-efficacy and self-regulation • "Introduction" and "Psychological Needs as Motivators" in Chapter 8 (Motivation and Emotion) • "Individual Factors That Influence the Response to Stress" and "Coping" in Chapter 12, Stress, Health, and Coping • Psych for Your Life features (see full list of titles on page xli) • *Think Like a Scientist* Immersive Learning Activities "Multitasking" and "Positive and Negative Reinforcement," accessible on LaunchPad	5.3—Refine project-management skills • "Solving Problems and Making Decisions" in Chapter 7, Thinking, Language, and Intelligence • Psych for Your Life features "A Workshop on Creativity" and "Turning Your Goals into Reality" • Appendix B, Industrial/Organizational Psychology 5.4—Enhance teamwork capacity • Appendix B, Industrial/Organizational Psychology

Major Chapter Revisions

As you page through our new edition, you will encounter new examples, boxes, photos, and illustrations in every chapter. Below are highlights of some of the most significant changes:

CHAPTER 1, INTRODUCTION AND RESEARCH METHODS

- New Prologue, "The First Exam," focusing on test experiences and student study strategies
- New chapter introduction incorporating psychology's goals
- New photo example of the topics that psychologists study
- New photo examples of the biological perspective and studying behavior from different psychological perspectives

- New summary table and graphs showing specialty areas and employment settings for psychologists
- "What Is Cross-Cultural Psychology?" box streamlined and updated with new discussion of rice-cultivation versus wheat-cultivation cultures in China
- New student-focused research examples and photo illustrations of concepts in research methods, including forming a hypothesis and meta-analysis
- New example of how to read a journal reference
- Revised and updated Science Versus Pseudoscience box
- New example of naturalistic observation
- New student-focused example of survey research using the National Survey of Student Engagement, including results comparing study habits of different majors
- New section on correlational studies, using research on Facebook likes and student study behaviors and strategies to illustrate correlations
- New explanation of experimental methods, using an experiment on the testing effect to illustrate the key terms and important concepts of experimental design
- New Critical Thinking box, "How to Think Like a Scientist," introducing a four-step model for scientific thinking that students can apply to any claim or belief
- New photo example of functional magnetic resonance imaging
- Discussion of use of animals in research moved into main text, illustrated with new photo example
- Entirely new "Psych for Your Life" application that provides six research-based study techniques to enhance student success. Along with providing helpful information right at the beginning of the semester, the application demonstrates the value and relevance of psychological research.

CHAPTER 2, NEUROSCIENCE AND BEHAVIOR

- Added information in Figure 2.1 about the structure of sensory neurons
- New photo of neuron and new research on the functions of glial cells and myelin
- Streamlined discussions of communication within the neuron, the action potential, and communication between neurons
- New photo of electrical impulses in the brain
- Discussion of important neurotransmitters expanded to include glutamate, now a boldfaced key term
- Endorphins discussion integrated into main text and illustrated with photo rather than discussed in a separate Focus on Neuroscience box
- New photo examples of botox, dopamine, and Parkinson's Disease
- New photo showing cross section of peripheral nerve
- Expanded discussion of oxytocin, now a boldfaced key term, with coverage of research on its diverse effects on social motivation and behavior
- Coverage of "The 10% Myth" now integrated into text
- Updated and streamlined discussion of plasticity and neurogenesis, now integrated into a single section and including 2013 research on carbon-14 dating of new neuron
- New photo and updated research on Phineas Gage's injury
- Simplified illustration of cerebral cortex lobes
- Revised and updated Critical Thinking box, "'His' and 'Her' Brains?"
- Revised and updated Science Versus Pseudoscience box, "Brain Myths," includes new research on brain lateralization
- Updated research and new photo in Psych for Your Life: Maximizing Your Brain's Potential

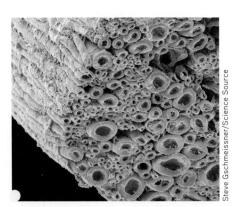

Steve Gschmeissner/Science Source

Nerves and Neurons Are Not the Same A cross section of a peripheral nerve is shown in this electron micrograph. The nerve is composed of bundles of axons (blue) wrapped in the myelin sheath (yellow). In the peripheral nervous system, myelin is formed by a type of glial cell called *Schwann cells,* shown here as a pinkish coating around the axons.

CHAPTER 3, SENSATION AND PERCEPTION

- Streamlined and updated box on subliminal perception
- Focus on Neuroscience "Vision, Experience, and the Brain" revised and updated with 2015 research
- New photo example of color blindness
- Revised figure clarifying human auditory structures and process of hearing
- Added discussion of cochlear implants, with photo illustration
- Added information about the dangers of noise exposure in everyday life and from personal music players
- New example of how frogs without outer ears detect sound
- New cross-cultural research on the language of smell in non-Western groups
- Revised In Focus box "Do Pheromones Influence Human Behavior?" that includes new 2013 and 2014 research on human chemosignals
- New cross-cultural research on effects of ethnicity and culture on pain perception, illustrated with photo
- Revised and updated Critical Thinking box, "ESP: Can Perception Occur Without Sensation?"
- Added discussion of color constancy, now a boldfaced term
- New In Focus box, "The Dress That Broke the Internet" explains why some people see "The Dress" as blue and black and others as gold and white
- New drawings illustrating the Müller-Lyer illusion and the Shepard Tables illusion
- Dramatic new photos illustrating Gestalt principles of organization, monocular cues, stroboscopic motion, and the moon illusion
- Updated Psych for Your Life, including new research on the effectiveness of acupuncture in pain control

CHAPTER 4, CONSCIOUSNESS AND ITS VARIATIONS

- Streamlined discussion of circadian rhythms and the suprachiasmatic nucleus
- Updated research on multitasking, including 2014 data on cell phone usage contributing to motor vehicle accidents
- New research and photo on the effects of artificial light, including computer and tablet screens, on circadian rhythms
- Streamlined In Focus box, "What You Really Want to Know About Sleep"
- Updated section, "Why Do We Sleep?"
- New section on "Sleep and Memory Formation"
- Updated, reorganized, and streamlined discussion of "Dreams and Mental Activity During Sleep"
- Condensed Focus on Neuroscience, "The Dreaming Brain"
- Updated information on the perils of driving while drowsy
- Streamlined coverage of sleep disorders and hypnosis
- New photo and caption tells the story of a young woman with narcolepsy
- New coverage of exploding head syndrome
- Updated and condensed Critical Thinking box on theories of hypnosis
- Discussion of meditation updated with new research, including 2015 research on the effects on working memory and attention in U.S. military personnel
- "Drug abuse" has been changed to "Substance Abuse Disorder" and definition has been revised to conform with DSM-5 language; requirement that legal problems be present has been dropped, and requirement that craving be present has been added

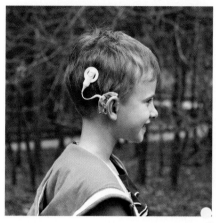

Life in View/Science Source

Restoring Hearing Cochlear implants are electronic devices that are surgically implanted behind the ear. A microphone picks up sounds from the environment, which are converted into electrical impulses that directly stimulate the auditory nerve via electrodes implanted in the cochlea. Cochlear implants do *not* restore normal hearing (Farris-Trimble & others, 2014). However, their use, especially when implanted in early childhood, can allow hearing-impaired individuals to perceive speech and other everyday sounds (Clark & others, 2013; O'Donoghue, 2013).

- Updated data noting that most overdose deaths are now due to legal prescription drugs rather than illegal drugs
- New photos of emergency medical workers, illustrating the dangers of alcohol abuse, and Cory Monteith, illustrating the dangers of depressant drugs
- The term *opiates* replaced with the more accurate term *opioids*
- Updated 2015 research on the surge in heroin and prescription opioid overdose deaths
- New discussion of e-cigarettes, including photo example
- Updated 2014 research on the therapeutic use of psychedelic drugs and ketamine
- Updated information on the legal use of medical marijuana, including 2014 research on data showing fewer opioid overdose deaths in states with legal access to medical marijuana for pain treatment
- Added 2015 research on long-term mental health effects of psychedelic drug use
- Psych for Your Life section retitled "Overcoming Insomnia"

CHAPTER 5, LEARNING

- New photo examples of learning, Ivan Pavlov, primary and conditioned reinforcers, media response to Skinner's work, superstitious rituals, learned helplessness, applications of operant conditioning, and observational learning
- Streamlined discussion of John B. Watson and introduction to behaviorism
- New contemporary photo example of classical conditioning in advertising
- 2014 research suggesting a second identification for the infant in the famous "Little Albert" study, Albert Barger Martin
- Condensed and simplified presentation of Robert Rescorla's classic research
- Revised section on taste aversions
- Replaced reinforcement example of hitting a vending machine with pushing the coin-return lever
- In text and tables, replaced the terms "punishment by application" and "punishment by removal" with "positive punishment" and "negative punishment"
- Revised graphs showing schedules of reinforcement and response patterns
- New historical photo of Keller and Marian Breland
- Streamlined and updated Focus on Neuroscience, "Mirror Neurons: Imitation in the Brain"
- New 2013 research example of observational learning in animals
- New 2014 research on media effects on behavior, identifying a correlational link between a decrease in teen birth rates and viewership of an MTV reality series showing the struggles of teenage parents
- Revised and updated Critical Thinking Box, "Does Exposure to Media Violence *Cause* Aggressive Behavior?" includes 2015 research on the effects of violent video games

CHAPTER 6, MEMORY

- Revised art demonstrating Baddeley's model of working memory
- New tip-of-the-tongue examples
- Revised discussion of flashbulb memories updated with 2015 research and new photo illustration
- Revised graph showing the Ebbinghaus forgetting curve
- New photo examples of the the interaction of memory stages in everyday life, types of information stored in long-term memory, retrieval cues, culture's effects on early memory, "tip-of-the-fingers" experience, and motivated forgetting

Motivated Forgetting Car accidents, serious illnesses, surgeries, and other traumatic events are painful to relive in memory. Some researchers believe that by voluntarily directing our attention away from memories of such traumatic events, we can eventually *suppress* our memory of the experiences, making them difficult or impossible to consciously retrieve (Anderson & others, 2011).

Taxi/Getty Images

- Updated example of eyewitness misidentification, with new illustration
- New 2013 research, conducted by the online magazine *Slate,* showing how faked news photographs can produce false memories about political events
- New coverage of false confessions includes 2015 research and real-world data from the Innocence Project
- New photo of David Snowden with an elderly participant in the Nun Study of Aging and Alzheimer's Disease
- New photos of Suzanne Corkin, Henry Molaison (the famous "H.M."), and of a virtual model of H.M.'s damaged brain based on new 2014 research
- In Focus box "H.M. and Famous People" eliminated
- Fully revised Psych for Your Life application, "Ten Steps to Boost Your Memory" and new photo of memory superstar and journalist Joshua Foer

CHAPTER 7, THINKING, LANGUAGE, AND INTELLIGENCE

- The new term *autism spectrum disorder* has replaced *autism* and *Asperger's syndrome* in the Prologue and throughout the chapter to conform to the DSM-5 classification
- Critical Thinking box "The Persistence of Unwarranted Beliefs" updated with 2015 research
- Culture and Human Behavior box "The Effect of Language on Perception" updated with 2015 research
- New 2014 research example added to discussion of animal cognition
- The term *intellectual disability* has replaced *mental retardation* in the In Focus box "Neurodiversity: Beyond IQ" to conform to new DSM-5 terminology
- Updated research on problem-solving strategies
- New extended example of functional fixedness—repurposing plastic bags and bottles into useful objects—illustrated with new photo
- Confirmation bias introduced as a boldfaced term
- Updated discussion of practical intelligence
- New photo examples of items that don't match the prototype, decision-making strategies, sign language, and Gardner's theory of multiple intelligences
- Updated discussion of stereotype threat
- New photo example of creativity: Steve Jobs

CHAPTER 8, MOTIVATION AND EMOTION

- New prologue, "One Step, One Breath," about one of the authors' experiences as a volunteer trekking through a remote region of the Himalayas
- Revised, condensed, and streamlined introduction to motivational theories
- New photo examples of sensation seekers, achievement motivation, emotion, arousal and intense emotion, the facial feedback hypothesis, and appraisal and emotion
- Condensed, simplified, and updated section on hunger and eating
- New examples of how culture shapes food choices
- New information about body mass index and alternative measures of obesity
- New data on the role that globalization plays in the increase in obesity in developing countries worldwide
- Updated Critical Thinking box "Has Evolution Programmed Us to Overeat?" including 2014 research on stigma associated with obesity
- 2014 research on the decrease in physical activity levels in the United States over the past decade
- New photo of Masters and Johnson

Sandy Hockenbury

The Many Functions of Emotion
Two friends share news, smiles, and laughter as they patiently wait their turns at the medical clinic in an isolated village in Tsum Valley, Nepal. Emotions play an important role in relationships and social communication.

- Evolution and mate preferences now covered within the main text in Chapter 9, Lifespan Development
- Focus on Neuroscience, "Romantic Love and the Brain" no longer included in chapter
- Revised introduction to "Psychological Needs as Motivators" section
- Updated research on self-determination theory
- New example of achievement motivation
- Updated research on the functions of emotion and emotional intelligence
- Streamlined and updated discussion of the subjective experience of emotion and the neuroscience of emotion, including new photo example
- Gender and emotion now covered within the main text in the retitled section, "Culture, Gender, and Emotional Experience"
- New figure based on 2014 cross-cultural research on the association of different emotions with specific physical sensations
- New photo of William James
- Updated research on cognitive theories of emotion

CHAPTER 9, LIFESPAN DEVELOPMENT

- New prologue about a young transgender man, James, growing up in a small town in rural New York
- Revised introduction, with new discussion of longitudinal and cross-sectional research designs; longitudinal design and cross-sectional design are new key terms
- New photo examples of continuity and change over the lifespan
- New photo of X and Y chromosomes
- Expanded and updated discussion of research on the epigenetic effects of early life stress in human subjects
- New photo and discussion of Harry Harlow's classic "contact comfort" research and its role in attachment
- New photos of Mary Ainsworth and Erik Erikson
- Fully revised section on theories of gender-role development now includes evolutionary and interactionist theories
- New photo examples of gender-stereotyped toys
- Mate preferences now covered here
- New section on gender identity
- New photo examples of cognitive development and Piagetian stages
- Updated statistics on U.S. households, including changes in family structure
- New discussion of the new phenomenon of "boomerang kids"

CHAPTER 10, PERSONALITY

- New photo of Carl Jung and streamlined discussion of archetypes
- Streamlined discussion of Freud and his theory drops bolded terms Eros and Thanatos
- Discussion of Alfred Adler's theory of personality updated with new research
- Many new photo examples, including Freud's influence on popular culture, establishing the superego, sublimation, the Oedipus complex, the question of innate good or evil, the TAT, and self-efficacy
- New cross-cultural photo illustration for Critical Thinking box, "Freud Versus Rogers on Human Nature"
- Slightly shortened discussion of the humanistic perspective

Challenging Expectations What makes weight lifting a "male" activity? Eleven-year-old weight lifter Charley Craig, the youngest female weight lifter in the United Kingdom, engages in athletic pursuits that many might not expect for a girl. Are biological constraints a factor here?

Laurentiu Garofeanu/Barcroft M/Getty Images

- Streamlined and updated Science Versus Pseudoscience box on graphology
- Streamlined Focus on Neuroscience, "The Neuroscience of Personality"
- In Focus box, "Explaining Those Amazing Identical Twin Similarities," dropped from chapter
- Streamlined discussion of self-efficacy with new student-centered example
- New 2014 and 2015 research on the trait perspective
- Section on self-report inventories updated with 2015 research

CHAPTER 11, SOCIAL PSYCHOLOGY

- Discussion of person perception updated with new research on the role of person perception in social media
- New photo example of implicit personality theory
- Streamlined Focus on Neuroscience, "Brain Reward When Making Eye Contact with Attractive People"
- Revised introduction to attribution
- New photo example of blaming the victim—the story of Elizabeth Smart
- Condensed Culture and Human Behavior box, "Explaining Failure and Murder"
- Revised discussion of cognitive dissonance, with new examples and research on cognitive dissonance in preschoolers and capuchin monkeys
- Updated In Focus box, "Interpersonal Attraction and Liking"
- Revised and updated discussion of in-group bias; ethnocentricity no longer a bolded key term
- Updated discussion of implicit attitudes, including 2015 research
- Expanded and updated discussion of prejudice, incorporating new research and neuroscience evidence
- Revised and updated section on Milgram's obedience study, including new discussion of contemporary replication
- Updated and revised Critical Thinking box, "Abuse at Abu Ghraib," including critiques of Zimbardo's study known as the Stanford Prison Experiment
- New section, "Altruism and Aggression," includes expanded coverage of Latané and Darley's research on bystander intervention, additional factors that increase the likelihood of bystanders helping, and entirely new section on aggression
- New figures on aggression and the brain, and the influence of sociocultural factors on aggression
- New photos and captions provide contemporary examples of the self-serving bias, the effect of attitudes on behavior, research linking prejudice and negative emotion, destructive obedience of authority, prosocial behavior, coming to the aid of a stranger, road rage, and the rule of reciprocity

CHAPTER 12, STRESS, HEALTH, AND COPING

- New photo examples of stress and appraisal, uncontrollable events, explanatory style, Type A behavior pattern, and providing social support
- Introduction now includes data from an APA survey on stress in America
- "Sources of Stress" updated with 2013, 2014, and 2015 research
- Streamlined Culture and Human Behavior box
- Introduction to "Physical Effects of Stress" updated with 2014 research
- "Stress, Chromosomes, and Aging" updated with 2014 and 2015 research
- Revised and updated discussion of psychological factors in the response to stressors

Establishing the Superego As children, we learn many rules and values from parents and other authorities. The internalization of such values is what Freud called the superego—the inner voice that is our conscience. When we fail to live up to its moral ideals, the superego imposes feelings of guilt, shame, and inferiority.

Thanasis Zovoilis/Getty Images

- New research example demonstrating the importance of relationships in the ability to deal with stressors
- New prologue example in the In Focus box, "Providing Effective Social Support"
- Streamlined and updated introduction to "Coping"
- Streamlined In Focus box, "Gender Differences in Responding to Stress"
- New cross-cultural photo examples of major life events, daily hassles and stress, daily hassles, the benefits of social support, and problem-focused coping
- Photos of Richard Lazarus and Janice Kiecolt-Glaser dropped

CHAPTER 13, PSYCHOLOGICAL DISORDERS

- New Prologue about the psychotic break and successful life of a woman with schizophrenia—Elyn Saks
- Expanded coverage of the DSM-5, presenting a history of the manual, including critiques
- Sample DSM diagnostic criteria figure dropped
- New coverage of the World Health Organization's *International Classification of Diseases*
- New photo example demonstrates the importance of context in differentiating normal and abnormal behavior
- Critical Thinking box updated with new research on violence and mental illness
- Updated cross-cultural research on prevalence of psychological disorders and treatment rates in developing countries
- Revised Table of Key Diagnostic Categories, incorporating DSM-5 terminology and criteria
- Revised introduction to "Anxiety Disorders," incorporating DSM-5 criteria for posttraumatic stress disorder and obsessive-compulsive disorder
- New evolutionary discussion of phobias
- New phobia example—Oprah Winfrey's fear of chewing gum
- Section on social phobia retitled "Social Anxiety Disorder" to conform to DSM-5 terminology, and criteria updated with new research, including cross-cultural research
- Reorganized and updated sections on postraumatic stress disorder and obsessive-compulsive disorder, incorporating DSM-5 criteria
- New cross-cultural research on posttraumatic stress disorder in children living in the Middle East
- New research on how posttraumatic stress disorder symptoms can be triggered by reports in the news media and by events unrelated to the original trauma
- Updated research on the role played by pre-existing vulnerability in the development of posttraumatic stress disorder
- Section on "Mood Disorders" retitled as "Disordered Moods and Emotions: Depressive Disorder and Bipolar Disorder" to conform to new DSM-5 terminology
- New discussion of DSM-5's controversial removal of "the bereavement exclusion" that excluded symptoms caused by bereavement as criteria for depression
- Updated longitudinal research on the prevalence and recurrence of major depressive disorder over the lifespan
- Section on major depressive disorder updated with new examples and 2014 and 2015 research
- New research on cultural differences related to major depressive disorder
- New example to introduce bipolar disorder
- Updated 2014 and 2015 research on the causes of depressive and bipolar disorders
- Updated Critical Thinking box "Does Smoking Cause Depression and Other Psychological Disorders?" includes revised graph

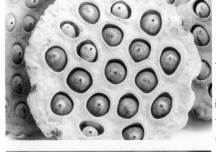

An Evolutionary Fear of Holes Some people are afraid of a certain pattern of holes like those you might see in a chocolate bar, in soap bubbles, or on a lotus seed head like the one shown here. This condition is called trypophobia. Researchers Geoff Cole and Arnold Wilkins (2013) found striking similarities between the visual pattern that triggers fear in trypophobics and the markings on poisonous animals, like certain snakes or the poison dart frog shown here. They speculate that an ability to quickly notice a poisonous creature gave people an evolutionary advantage, even if it sometimes led them to fear harmless objects.

- Revised table of depressive and bipolar disorders, incorporating DSM-5 terminology and criteria
- "Eating Disorders" section expanded and updated to incorporate DSM-5 terminology and criteria, including a new section on the newly described disorder "binge-eating disorder"
- Updated discussion of personality disorders introduces second approach to classification
- New discussion of the differences among the categories *psychopath, sociopath*, and *antisocial personality disorder*, with new photo examples
- Updated research on borderline personality disorder
- Updated 2014 research on the controversy surrounding the authenticity of dissociative identity disorder
- Revised table of dissociative disorders, incorporating DSM-5 terminology and criteria
- Fully revised section on schizophrenia, including new examples, extended coverage of variations of symptoms across cultures, and a cross-cultural look at prevalence
- New photo example of the Truman Show delusion as a culturally-specific symptom of schizophrenia
- New photo examples of people with major depressive disorder, bipolar disorder, and schizophrenia
- Psych for Your Life application on understanding and helping to prevent suicide updated with new statistics

CHAPTER 14, THERAPIES

- Terminology revised throughout to reflect DSM-5 criteria and diagnostic labels
- Streamlined discussion of short-term dynamic therapies
- Discussion of EMDR and exposure therapies moved into main text, in retitled section "Systematic Desensitization and Exposure Therapies"
- Updated 2013 and 2014 research on token economies and contingency management therapies
- Discussion of Albert Ellis's work updated to note "rational-emotive therapy" now renamed "rational-emotive behavior therapy"
- Updated coverage of cognitive therapy
- Updated section "Cognitive-Behavioral Therapy and Mindfulness-Based Therapies," including 2014 research on the use of cognitive-behavioral therapy with clients with schizophrenia to help treat psychotic symptoms
- New In Focus box, "Increasing Access: Meeting the Need for Mental Health Care," introduces the role of paraprofessionals and lay counselors worldwide, plus technology-driven solutions
- Expanded and updated discussion, "Evaluating the Effectiveness of Psychotherapy," includes criteria to evaluate new therapies
- Updated research on antipsychotic medications, including information from the newest edition of the *Primer of Drug Action*
- Updated table on antidepressant medications
- New Critical Thinking box, "Do Antidepressants Work Better Than Placebos?", examines the effectiveness of antidepressants
- New discussions of the experimental use of MDMA to treat anxiety disorders and PTSD and of ketamine to treat major depressive disorder, incorporating 2014 research
- All-new Focus on Neuroscience, "Psychotherapy and the Brain," presents research comparing the effect of antidepressant and psychotherapy treatment on brain activity in people with major depressive disorder
- Updated research on electroconvulsive therapy and new, experimental treatments

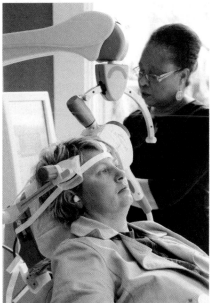

JOE SONGER/AL.COM/Landov

Transcranial Magnetic Stimulation Tammy, an Alabama woman suffering from depression, receives Transcranial Magnetic Stimulation (TMS) under the oversight of a nurse. TMS involves stimulating brain regions with magnetic pulses. Tammy is able to receive this noninvasive treatment in her doctor's office as opposed to in a hospital.

• New photo examples of the varied workplaces of psychologists, Native American healing, transcranial magnetic stimulation, mindfulness-based stress reduction, the stigma associated with psychological problems, and technology-based solutions to expanding access to mental health care

APPENDIX B: INDUSTRIAL/ORGANIZATIONAL PSYCHOLOGY

• New photo examples of human factors involved in the use of workplace equipment, matching job and applicant, leadership, different work styles, work–life balance, and teleworking

Features of *Discovering Psychology*

For all that is new in the seventh edition, we were careful to maintain the unique elements that have been so well received in the previous editions. Every feature and element in our text was carefully developed and serves a specific purpose. From comprehensive surveys, input from reviewers, and our many discussions with faculty and students, we learned what elements people wanted in a text and why they thought those features were important tools that enhanced the learning process. We also surveyed the research literature on text comprehension, student learning, and memory. In the process, we acquired many valuable insights from the work of cognitive and educational psychologists. Described below are the main features of *Discovering Psychology* and a discussion of how these features enhance the learning process.

The Narrative Approach

As you'll quickly discover, our book has a very distinctive voice. From the very first page of this text, the reader comes to know us as people and teachers through carefully selected stories and anecdotes. Some of our friends and relatives have also graciously allowed us to share stories about their lives. The stories are quite varied—some are funny, others are dramatic, and some are deeply personal. All of them are true.

The stories we tell reflect one of the most effective teaching methods: the *narrative approach*. In addition to engaging the reader, each story serves as a pedagogical springboard to illustrating important concepts and ideas. Every story is used to connect new ideas, terms, and ways of looking at behavior to information with which the student is already familiar.

Prologues

As part of the narrative approach, every chapter begins with a **Prologue,** a true story about ordinary people with whom most students can readily identify. The Prologue stories range from the experiences of a teenager with Autism Spectrum Disorder to people struggling with the aftereffects of a devastating wildfire to the story of a man who regained his sight after decades of blindness. Each Prologue effectively introduces the chapter's themes and lays the groundwork for explaining why the topics treated by the chapter are important. The Prologue establishes a link between familiar experiences and new information—a key ingredient in facilitating learning. Later in the chapter, we return to the people and stories introduced in the Prologue, further reinforcing the link between familiar experiences and new ways of conceptualizing them.

Logical Organization, Continuity, and Clarity

As you read the chapters in *Discovering Psychology,* you'll see that each one tells the story of a major topic in a logical way that flows continually from beginning to end. Themes are clearly established in the first pages of the chapter. Throughout the chapter, we come back to those themes as we present subtopics and specific research

Associate the new with the old in some natural and telling way, so that the interest, being shed along from point to point, fully suffuses the entire system of objects. . . . Anecdotes and reminiscences [should] abound in [your] talk; and the shuttle of interest will shoot backward and forward, weaving the new and the old together in a lively and entertaining way.

—*William James,*
Talks to Teachers (1899)

studies. Chapters are thoughtfully organized so that students can easily see how ideas are connected. The writing is carefully paced to maximize student interest and comprehension. Rather than simply mentioning terms and findings, we explain concepts clearly. And we use concrete analogies and everyday examples, rather than vague or flowery metaphors, to help students grasp abstract concepts and ideas.

Paradoxically, one of the ways that we maintain narrative continuity throughout each chapter is through the use of in-text boxes. The boxes provide an opportunity to explore a particular topic in depth without losing the narrative thread of the chapter. The **In Focus** boxes do just that—they focus on interesting topics in more depth than the chapter's organization would allow. These boxes highlight interesting research, answer questions that students commonly ask, or show students how psychological research can be applied in their own lives. The seventh edition of *Discovering Psychology* includes the following In Focus boxes:

- Traumatic Brain Injury: From Concussions to Chronic Traumatic Encephalopathy, p. 54
- Do Pheromones Influence Human Behavior?, p. 103
- The Dress That Broke the Internet, p. 122
- What You Really Want to Know About Sleep, p. 141
- What You Really Want to Know About Dreams, p. 152
- Watson, Classical Conditioning, and Advertising, p. 190
- Evolution, Biological Preparedness, and Conditioned Fears: What Gives You the Creeps?, p. 195
- Changing the Behavior of Others: Alternatives to Punishment, p. 202
- Déjà-Vu Experiences: An Illusion of Memory?, p. 246
- Does a High IQ Score Predict Success in Life?, p. 293
- Neurodiversity: Beyond IQ, p. 298
- Detecting Lies, p. 339
- Hooking Up on Campus, p. 397
- Interpersonal Attraction and Liking, p. 463
- Providing Effective Social Support, p. 521
- Gender Differences in Responding to Stress: "Tend-and-Befriend" or "Fight-or-Flight?," p. 525
- Using Virtual Reality to Treat Phobia and Posttraumatic Stress Disorder, p. 596
- Increasing Access: Meeting the Need for Mental Health Care, p. 606
- Servant Leadership: When It's Not All About You, p. B-10
- Name, Title, Generation, p. B-11

An Anxiety-Reducing Game
Psychologists Tracy Dennis and Laura O'Toole (2014) found that playing a video game based on a treatment called *cognitive bias modification* resulted in a decrease in symptoms of anxiety. People earn points when they direct their attention away from anxiety-provoking targets, like the scary cartoon character, and toward the friendly-looking characters.

Tracy A. Dennis

Scientific Emphasis

Many first-time psychology students walk into the classroom operating on the assumption that psychology is nothing more than common sense or a collection of personal opinions. Clearly, students need to walk away from an introductory psychology course with a solid understanding of the scientific nature of the discipline. To help you achieve that goal, in every chapter we show students how the scientific method has been applied to help answer different kinds of questions about behavior and mental processes.

Because we carefully guide students through the details of specific experiments and studies, they develop a solid understanding of how scientific evidence is gathered and the interplay between theory and research. And because we rely on original rather than secondary sources, students get an accurate presentation of both classic and contemporary psychological studies.

One unique way that we highlight the scientific method in *Discovering Psychology* is with our trademark **Science Versus Pseudoscience** boxes. In these boxes, students see the importance of subjecting various claims to the standards of scientific evidence.

These boxes promote and encourage scientific thinking by focusing on topics that students frequently ask about in class. The seventh edition of *Discovering Psychology* includes the following Science Versus Pseudoscience boxes:

- What Is a Pseudoscience?, pp. 20–21
- Phrenology: The Bumpy Road to Scientific Progress, p. 61
- Brain Myths, p. 77
- Subliminal Perception, p. 89
- Can a DVD Program Your Baby to Be a Genius?, pp. 372–373
- Graphology: The "Write" Way to Assess Personality?, p. 443

Critical Thinking Emphasis

Another important goal of *Discovering Psychology* is to encourage the development of critical thinking skills. To that end, we do not present psychology as a series of terms, definitions, and facts to be skimmed and memorized. Rather, we try to give students an understanding of how particular topics evolve. In doing so, we also demonstrate the process of challenging preconceptions, evaluating evidence, and revising theories based on new evidence. In short, every chapter shows the process of psychological research—and the important role played by critical thinking in that enterprise.

Because we do not shrink from discussing the implications of psychological findings, students come to understand that many important issues in contemporary psychology are far from being settled. Even when research results are consistent, how to interpret those results can sometimes be the subject of considerable debate. As the authors of the text, we very deliberately try to be evenhanded and fair in presenting both sides of controversial issues. In encouraging students to join these debates, we often challenge them to be aware of how their own preconceptions and opinions can shape their evaluation of the evidence.

Beyond discussions in the text proper, every chapter includes one or more **Critical Thinking** boxes. These boxes are carefully designed to encourage students to think about the broader implications of psychological research—to strengthen and refine their critical thinking skills by developing their own positions on questions and issues that don't always have simple answers. Each Critical Thinking box ends with two or three questions that you can use as a written assignment or for classroom discussion. The seventh edition of *Discovering Psychology* includes the following Critical Thinking boxes:

- How to Think Like a Scientist, p. 31
- "His" and "Her" Brains?, p. 72
- ESP: Can Perception Occur Without Sensation?, p. 112
- Is Hypnosis a Special State of Consciousness?, pp. 158–159
- Is Human Freedom Just an Illusion?, p. 204
- Does Exposure to Media Violence *Cause* Aggressive Behavior?, p. 219
- The Memory Wars: Recovered or False Memories?, pp. 254–255
- The Persistence of Unwarranted Beliefs, pp. 284–285
- Has Evolution Programmed Us to Overeat?, p. 322
- Emotion in Nonhuman Animals: Laughing Rats, Silly Elephants, and Smiling Dolphins?, pp. 344–345
- The Effects of Child Care on Attachment and Development, p. 401
- Freud Versus Rogers on Human Nature, p. 430
- Abuse at Abu Ghraib: Why Do Ordinary People Commit Evil Acts?, pp. 480–481
- Do Personality Factors Cause Disease?, p. 518
- Are People with a Mental Illness as Violent as the Media Portray Them?, pp. 536–537
- Does Smoking Cause Major Depressive Disorder and Other Psychological Disorders?, pp. 556–557
- Do Antidepressants Work Better Than Placebos?, pp. 622–623

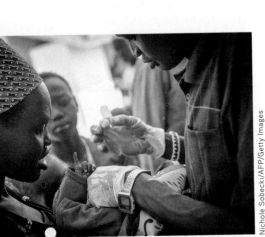

Nichole Sobecki/AFP/Getty Images

Are People Innately Good . . . or Innately Evil? A member of Doctors Without Borders administers polio vaccines to children who are among the tens of thousands of refugees fleeing civil war in South Sudan. Doctors Without Borders is an international group of medical workers that won the Nobel Peace Prize for its work in helping the victims of violence and disasters all over the world. On the one hand, violence motivated by political or ethnic hatred seems to support Freud's contentions about human nature. On the other hand, the selfless behavior of those who help others, often at a considerable cost to themselves, seems to support Rogers's view. Which viewpoint do you think more accurately describes the essence of human nature?

Cultural Coverage

As you can see in Table 1, we weave cultural coverage throughout many discussions in the text. But because students are usually unfamiliar with cross-cultural psychology, we also highlight specific topics in **Culture and Human Behavior** boxes. These boxes increase student awareness of the importance of culture in many areas of human experience. They are unique in that they go beyond simply describing

TABLE 1

Integrated Cultural Coverage

In addition to the topics covered in the Culture and Human Behavior boxes, cultural influences are addressed in the following discussions.

Page(s)	Topic	Page(s)	Topic
11–13	Cross-cultural perspective in contemporary psychology	305–306	Cross-cultural studies of group discrimination and IQ
11–13	Culture, social loafing, and social striving	307	Role of culture in tests and test-taking behavior
53	Effect of traditional Chinese acupuncture on endorphins	317–318	Culture's effect on food preference and eating behavior
102	Cross-cultural research on the language of smell in non-Western groups	321	Role of globalization in the increase of obesity in developing countries worldwide
108	Cross-cultural research on effects of ethnicity and culture on pain perception	322	Rates of sedentary lifestyles worldwide
127–128	Use of acupuncture in traditional Chinese medicine for pain relief	323	Obesity rates in cultures with different levels of economic development
160–162	Meditation in different cultures	335	Culture and achievement motivation
162	Research collaboration between Tibetan Buddhist monks and Western neuroscientists	337	Culturally universal emotions
165	Racial and ethnic differences in drug metabolism rate	337–338	Culture and emotional experience
173	Peyote use in religious ceremonies in other cultures	337–338	Cross-cultural research on gender and emotional expressiveness
174	Medicinal use of marijuana in ancient China, Egypt, India, Greece, and other countries	340	Cross-cultural studies of psychological arousal associated with emotions
175	Rave culture and drug use in Great Britain and Europe	340	Cross-cultural research on association of different emotions with different physical sensations
204	Clash of B. F. Skinner's philosophy with American cultural ideals and individualistic orientation	346	Universal facial expressions
218–220	Cross-cultural application of observational learning principles in entertainment-education programming in Mexico, Latin America, Asia, and Africa	344–346	Culture, cultural display rules, and emotional expression
240	Cross-cultural research on the tip-of-the-tongue phenomenon	368	Cross-cultural research on co-sleeping
287	Spontaneous development of sign languages in a Nicaraguan school and a Bedouin village as cross-cultural evidence of innate human predisposition to develop language	369	Cultural influences on temperament
288	Estimated rate of bilingualism worldwide	370	Cross-cultural studies of attachment
292	Historical misuse of IQ tests to evaluate immigrants	371	Native language and infant language development
292	Wechsler's recognition of the importance of culture and ethnicity in developing the WAIS intelligence test	371	Cross-cultural research on infant-directed speech
296–297	Role of culture in Gardner's definition and theory of intelligence	371	Culture and patterns of language development
297, 300	Role of culture in Sternberg's definition and theory of intelligence	378	Cross-cultural research on mate preferences
303–304	IQ and cross-cultural comparison of educational differences	385	Influence of culture on cognitive development
304–305	Rapid gains in IQ scores in different nations	391	Cultural influences on timing of adolescent romantic relationships

Page(s)	Topic	Page(s)	Topic
395	Culture and moral reasoning	516–517	Cross-cultural research on the effect of expressing positive and negative emotions
402	Data on aging in the world population	526–527	Effect of culture on coping strategies
408	Cultural differences in the effectiveness of different parenting styles	535	Role of culture in distinguishing between normal and abnormal behavior
415–416	Freud's impact on Western culture	536	Description of the World Health Organization's *International Classification of Diseases*
416–417	Cultural influences on Freud's psychoanalytic theory	538–539	Global rates of mental illness
424–425	Cultural influences on Jung's personality theory	539	Cultural differences in rates of mental health treatment
425	Jung on archetypal images, including mandalas, in different cultures	543	Cultural variants of panic disorder
425–426	Cultural influences on the development of Horney's personality theory	544	*Taijin kyofusho*, a culture-specific disorder related to social phobia
430	Rogers on cultural factors in the development of antisocial behavior	546–547	PTSD in children living in a war zone in the Middle East and in child soldiers in Uganda and Congo
435–436	Findings from a German study on the tendency to describe others in terms of traits	548–549	Cultural influences in obsessions and compulsions
438	Cross-cultural research on the universality of the five-factor model of personality	552	Cultural differences related to major depressive disorder
457–458	Cultural conditioning and the "what is beautiful is good" myth	560–561	Culture-bound syndromes
460	Attributional biases in individualistic versus collectivistic cultures	561	Western cultural ideals of beauty and prevalence rates of eating disorders
463	Cultural differences in interpersonal attraction	565	Cultural differences in rates of borderline personality disorder
466–469	Stereotypes, prejudice, and group identity	566	Role of culture in dissociative experiences
469–470	Use of IAT to study social preferences and stereotypes worldwide	570–573	Cultural variations in schizophrenia symptoms
471	Application of lessons from Robbers Cave and jigsaw classroom to reduce prejudice and conflict among ethnic and religious groups worldwide	573	Prevalence and differences in outcome of schizophrenia in different cultures
479	Cross-cultural comparisons of destructive social influence	578–579	Findings from the Finnish Adoptive Family Study of Schizophrenia
480–481	Role of cultural differences in abuse at Abu Ghraib prison in Iraq	590	Use of interpersonal therapy to treat depression in Uganda
489–490	Culture and aggression	606–607	Mechanisms for increasing access to mental health care worldwide
501	Cross-cultural research on life events and stress	612–613	Impact of cultural differences on effectiveness of psychotherapy
505–506	Cultural differences as source of stress	614–615	Efficacy of traditional herbal treatment for psychotic symptoms in India
514	Cross-cultural research on the benefits of perceived control		

cultural differences in behavior. They show students how cultural influences shape behavior and attitudes, including the students' own behavior and attitudes. The seventh edition of *Discovering Psychology* includes the following Culture and Human Behavior boxes:

- What Is Cross-Cultural Psychology?, p. 12
- Ways of Seeing: Culture and Top-Down Processes, p. 115
- Culture and the Müller-Lyer Illusion: The Carpentered-World Hypothesis, p. 126
- Culture's Effects on Early Memories, p. 237

- The Effect of Language on Perception, pp. 286-287
- Performing with a Threat in the Air: How Stereotypes Undermine Performance, pp. 304–305
- Where Does the Baby Sleep?, p. 368
- Explaining Failure and Murder: Culture and Attributional Biases, p. 460
- The Stress of Adapting to a New Culture, p. 506
- Culture-Bound Syndromes, pp. 560–561
- Cultural Values and Psychotherapy, p. 613

Gender Coverage

Gender influences and gender differences are described in many chapters. Table 2 on the following page shows the integrated coverage of gender-related issues and topics in *Discovering Psychology*. To help identify the contributions made by female researchers, the full names of researchers are provided in the References section at the end of the text. When researchers are identified using initials instead of first names (as APA style recommends), many students automatically assume that the researchers are male.

Neuroscience Coverage

Psychology and neuroscience have become intricately intertwined. Especially in the last decade, the scientific understanding of the brain and its relation to human behavior has grown dramatically. The imaging techniques of brain science—PET scans, MRIs, and functional MRIs—have become familiar terminology to many students, even if they don't completely understand the differences between them. To reflect that growing trend, we have increased our neuroscience coverage to show students how understanding the brain can help explain the complete range of human behavior, from the ordinary to the severely disturbed. Each chapter contains one or more **Focus on Neuroscience** discussions that are designed to complement the broader chapter discussion. Here is a complete list of the Focus on Neuroscience features in the seventh edition:

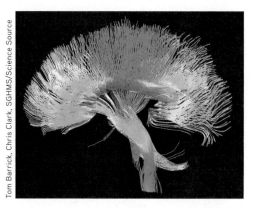

Tom Barrick, Chris Clark, SGHMS/Science Source

- Psychological Research Using Brain Imaging, pp. 32–33
- Mapping the Pathways of the Brain, p. 62
- Juggling and Brain Plasticity, p. 63
- Vision, Experience, and the Brain, p. 95
- The Sleep-Deprived Emotional Brain, p. 146
- The Dreaming Brain, p. 148
- Meditation and the Brain, p. 163
- The Addicted Brain: Diminishing Rewards, p. 166
- How Methamphetamines Erode the Brain, p. 173
- Mirror Neurons: Imitation in the Brain, p. 217
- Assembling Memories: Echoes and Reflections of Perception, p. 258
- Mapping Brain Changes in Alzheimer's Disease, p. 264
- Seeing Faces and Places in the Mind's Eye, p. 274
- Dopamine Receptors and Obesity, p. 324
- Emotions and the Brain, p. 342
- The Adolescent Brain: A Work in Progress, p. 388
- Boosting the Aging Brain, p. 404
- The Neuroscience of Personality: Brain Structure and the Big Five, p. 440
- Brain Reward When Making Eye Contact with Attractive People, p. 458
- The Mysterious Placebo Effect, p. 512
- The Hallucinating Brain, p. 570

TABLE 2

Integrated Gender Coverage

Page(s)	Topic	Page(s)	Topic
4	Titchener's inclusion of female graduate students in his psychology program in the late 1800s	399	Gender differences in single-parent, head-of-household status
6	Contributions of Mary Whiton Calkins to psychology	400, 402	Gender and patterns of career development and parenting responsibilities
6–7	Contributions of Margaret Floy Washburn to psychology	402	Gender differences in life expectancy
60	Endocrine system and effects of sex hormones	422–423	Freud's contention of gender differences in resolving the Oedipus complex
72	Sex differences and the brain	425–426	Horney's critique of Freud's view of female psychosexual development
97	Gender differences in incidence of color blindness	428	Critique of sexism in Freud's theory
103	Gender differences in responses to human chemosignals (pheromones)	463	Gender similarities and differences in interpersonal attraction
108	Gender differences in the perception of pain	466–467	Misleading effect of gender stereotypes
148–149	Gender differences in dream content	476	Gender similarities in results of Milgram's obedience studies
149	Gender and nightmare frequency	489–490	Gender and aggression
153	Gender differences in incidence of obstructive sleep apnea	503–504	Gender differences in frequency and source of daily hassles
167	Gender and rate of metabolism of alcohol	520–522	Gender differences in providing social support and effects of social support
167	Gender and binge drinking among college students	522	Gender differences in susceptibility to the stress contagion effect
184	Women as research assistants in Pavlov's laboratories	525	Gender differences in responding to stress—the "tend-and-befriend" response
304–305	Test performance and the influence of gender stereotypes	537	Gender bias as one critique of DSM-5
322	Gender differences in sedentary lifestyles	541	Gender differences in prevalence of anxiety, posttraumatic stress, and obsessive-compulsive disorders
323	Gender differences in metabolism	544	Gender differences in prevalence of specific phobias
325	Sex differences in the pattern of human sexual response	544	Gender differences in prevalence of social anxiety disorder
326–327	Sex differences in hormonal influences on sexual motivation	546	Gender differences in prevalence of posttraumatic stress disorder
328	Gender differences in reported rates of homosexual behavior	551	Gender differences in prevalence of seasonal affective disorder
338	Gender similarities and differences in experience and expression of emotion	552	Gender differences in prevalence of major depressive disorder
361	Sex differences in genetic transmission of recessive characteristics	554	Lack of gender differences in prevalence of bipolar disorder
374	Definitions of gender and gender role	559	Gender differences in effect of malnutrition caused by anorexia
374–376	Gender differences in childhood behavior	560	Gender differences in prevalence of *hikikomori*
376–379	Theories of gender-role development	561	Gender differences in prevalence of eating disorders
379–380	Gender identity	564	Gender differences in incidence of antisocial personality disorder
386–387	Gender differences in timing of the development of primary and secondary sex characteristics	565	Gender differences in incidence of borderline personality disorder
388–389	Gender and accelerated puberty in father-absent homes	575	Paternal age and incidence of schizophrenia
389–390	Gender differences in effects of early and late maturation	579	Gender differences in number of suicide attempts and in number of suicide deaths
395	Gender differences in moral reasoning	627	Gender differences in sexual contact between therapists and clients
396–398	Average age of first marriage and higher education attainment	B–12	Gender differences in reasons for wanting to telecommute
398–399	Gender differences in response to end of reproductive capabilities		

- Schizophrenia: A Wildfire in the Brain, p. 577
- Psychotherapy and the Brain, p. 621

Psych for Your Life

Among all the sciences, psychology is unique in the degree to which it speaks to our daily lives and applies to everyday problems and concerns. The **Psych for Your Life** feature at the end of each chapter presents the findings from psychological research that address a wide variety of problems and concerns. In each of these features, we present research-based information in a form that students can use to enhance everyday functioning. As you can see in the following list, topics range from improving self-control to overcoming insomnia:

- Successful Study Techniques, pp. 35–37
- Maximizing Your Brain's Potential, pp. 79–81
- Strategies to Control Pain, pp. 127–129
- Overcoming Insomnia, pp. 176–177
- Using Learning Principles to Improve Your Self-Control, pp. 221–222
- Ten Steps to Boost Your Memory, pp. 265–267
- A Workshop on Creativity, pp. 308–309
- Turning Your Goals into Reality, pp. 351–353
- Raising Psychologically Healthy Children, pp. 407–408
- Possible Selves: Imagine the Possibilities, pp. 447–449
- The Persuasion Game, pp. 491–492
- Minimizing the Effects of Stress, pp. 527–529
- Understanding and Helping to Prevent Suicide, pp. 579–581
- What to Expect in Psychotherapy, pp. 625–627

The Pedagogical System

The pedagogical system in *Discovering Psychology* was carefully designed to help students identify important information, test for retention, and learn how to learn. It is easily adaptable to an SQ3R approach, for those instructors who have had success with that technique. As described in the following discussion, the different elements of this text form a pedagogical system that is very student-friendly, straightforward, and effective.

We've found that it appeals to diverse students with varying academic and study skills, enhancing the learning process without being gimmicky or condescending. A special student preface titled **To the Student** on pages xlviii to li, immediately before Chapter 1, describes the complete pedagogical system and demonstrates how students can make the most of it.

The pedagogical system has four main components: (1) Advance Organizers, (2) Chapter Reviews, (3) Concept Maps, and (4) LaunchPad for *Discovering Psychology*, Seventh Edition. (You'll learn more about the many features available in LaunchPad in the next section, "Multimedia to Support Teaching and Learning.") Major sections are introduced by an **Advance Organizer** that identifies the section's *Key Theme* followed by a bulleted list of *Key Questions*. Each Advance Organizer mentally primes the student for the important information that is to follow and does so in a way that encourages active learning. Students often struggle with trying to determine what's important to learn in a particular section or chapter. As a pedagogical technique, the Advance Organizer provides a guide that directs the student toward the most important ideas, concepts, and information in the section. It helps students identify main ideas and distinguish them from supporting evidence and examples.

Merlijn Doomernik/Hollandse Hoogte/Redux

Memory Superstar Joshua Foer
Journalist Joshua Foer (2011) visited a memory competition expecting to find people with special memory abilities. Instead, he encountered a group of "mental athletes"—people with ordinary minds who had trained their memories to accomplish incredible feats, such as reciting hundreds of random digits or pages of poetry. Told that anyone could develop an expert memory with training, he set out to prove it and devoted months to training his own memory. A year later, he won the USA Memory Championship and even set a new U.S. record by memorizing the position of a deck of cards in one minute, 40 seconds. Joshua's secret? Mnemonic techniques, like the method of loci—and lots and lots of practice. Foer explains his method in his Ted Talk, available at http://www.ted.com/talks/joshua_foer_feats_of_memory_anyone_can_do

Several other in-chapter pedagogical aids support the Advance Organizers. A clearly identified **Chapter Outline** provides an overview of topics and organization. Within the chapter, **key terms** are set in boldface type and defined in the margin. *Pronunciation guides* are included for difficult or unfamiliar words. Because students often have trouble identifying the most important theorists and researchers, names of **key people** are set in boldface type within the chapter. The **Chapter Review** provides a page-referenced list of key people and key terms at the end of each chapter.

Concept Maps are visual reviews that encourage students to review and check their learning at the end of the chapter. The hierarchical layout shows how themes, concepts, and facts are related to one another. Chapter photos are included as visual cues to important chapter information.

Multimedia to Support Teaching and Learning

LaunchPad with LearningCurve Quizzing

A comprehensive Web resource for teaching and learning psychology, LaunchPad combines Worth Publishers' awarding-winning media with an innovative platform for easy navigation. For students, it is the ultimate online study guide with rich interactive tutorials, videos, e-Book, and the LearningCurve adaptive quizzing system. For instructors, LaunchPad is a full-course space where class documents can be posted, quizzes are easily assigned and graded, and students' progress can be assessed and recorded. Whether you are looking for the most effective study tools or a robust platform for an online course, LaunchPad is a powerful way to enhance your class. You can preview LaunchPad to accompany *Discovering Psychology* at **launchpadworks.com**

Discovering Psychology and LaunchPad can be ordered together with LP ISBN-10: 1-4641-7692-2 LP ISBN-13: 978-1-4641-7692-0

LaunchPad for *Discovering Psychology* includes all the following resources:

- The **LearningCurve** quizzing system was designed based on the latest findings from learning and memory research. It combines adaptive question selection, immediate and valuable feedback, and a game-like interface to engage students in a learning experience that is unique to them. Each LearningCurve quiz is fully integrated with other resources in LaunchPad through the Personalized Study Plan, so students will be able to review with Worth's extensive library of videos and activities. And state-of-the-art question-analysis reports allow instructors to track the progress of individual students as well as their class as a whole.

- The **interactive e-Book** allows students to highlight and bookmark the text, and to make their own notes, just as they would with a consumable printed textbook.

- **Think Like a Scientist** Immersive Learning Activities, authored by Susan Nolan and Sandy Hockenbury, place students in real-world scenarios, asking them to think critically about scientific claims in the world around them. These active learning exercises combine video, audio, text, games, and assessment to help students hone and develop the scientific literacy skills they will use well beyond the introductory course.

- **Concept Practice,** created by award-winning multimedia author Thomas Ludwig (Hope College), helps students solidify their understanding of key concepts. With these in-depth tutorials, students explore a variety of important topics, often in an experimental context in the role of either researcher or subject. Tutorials combine animations, video, illustrations, and self-assessment.

Think Like a Scientist: Lie Detection
Can you learn to tell if someone is lying? In the *Think Like a Scientist* feature for Chapter 8, students will watch videos and decide whether people are lying or telling the truth. It's an engaging activity that invites students to think critically about the claims and the research on lie detection.

- **PsychSim 6.0,** thoroughly re-imagined and retooled for the mobile web, is the new release of *PsychSim* by Thomas Ludwig (Hope College), using interactive videos, charts, and simulations to immerse students in the world of psychological research and placing them in the role of scientist or subject in activities that highlight important concepts, processes, and experimental approaches.

- **Video Activities** include more than 100 engaging video modules that instructors can easily assign and customize for student assessment. Videos cover classic experiments, current news footage, and cutting-edge research, all of which are sure to spark discussion and encourage critical thinking.

- **Labs** offer interactive experiences that fortify the most important concepts and content of introductory psychology. In these activities, students participate in classic and contemporary experiments, generating real data and reviewing the broader implications of those findings. A virtual host makes this a truly interactive experience.

- The *Scientific American* **News Feed** delivers weekly articles, podcasts, and news briefs on the very latest developments in psychology from the first name in popular science journalism.

- **Deep Integration** is available between LaunchPad products and Blackboard, Brightspace by D2L, Canvas, and Moodle. These deep integrations offer educators single sign-on and Gradebook sync now with auto-refresh. Also, these best-in-class integrations offer deep linking to all Macmillan digital content at the chapter and asset level, giving professors ultimate flexibility and customization capability within their LMS.

Instructor Supplements, Videos, and Presentation Resources

- The **Downloadable Instructor's Resource Manual** was prepared by Heather Jennings of Mercer County Community College, and revised by Matthew Isaak of University of Louisiana at Lafayette, with past contributions from Edna Ross, University of Louisville; Skip Pollock, Mesa Community College; Claudia Cochran-Miller, El Paso Community College; Beth Finders, St. Charles Community College; Beverly Drinnin, Des Moines Area Community College; Wayne Hall, San Jacinto College—Central Campus; Nancy Melucci, Los Angeles Community College District; Paul DeMarco, University of Louisville; Julie Gurner, Community College of Philadelphia; Anne McCrea, Sinclair Community College; and Rachel Rogers, Community College of Rhode Island. Arranged topically rather than by chapter for this edition, the Downloadable Instructor's Resource Manual includes an abundance of materials to aid instructors in planning their courses, including classroom demonstrations and activities, student exercises, advice on teaching the nontraditional student, popular video suggestions, and "Psychology in the News" topics. The lecture guides contain chapter objectives and outlines and suggestions on how to approach your lecture.

- The **Downloadable Diploma Test Bank** was written by Don and Sandra Hockenbury with the assistance of Cornelius Rea. This edition's test bank was expertly revised by Sara Harris, Illinois State University. This enhanced Test Bank includes over 6,000 multiple-choice, true-false, and short-answer essay questions, plus Learning Objectives for each chapter that correspond to those in the Instructor's Resource Manual. Questions have also been keyed to several APA guidelines and learning outcomes for the undergraduate psychology major. Available for both Windows and Macintosh, the Test Bank files can be downloaded at **macmillanhighered.com/Catalog/product/discoveringpsychology -seventhedition-hockenbury/instructorresources#tab**

  Diploma is versatile dual-platform test-generating software that allows instructors to edit, add, or scramble questions from the *Discovering Psychology,* Seventh Edition, Test Bank and to format tests, drag and drop questions to create quizzes quickly and easily, and then print them for an exam. The computerized Test Bank will also allow instructors to export into a variety of formats that are compatible with many Internet-based testing products. For more information on Diploma, please visit Blackboard's Web site: **https://blackboard.secure.force.com**

- Interactive Presentation Slides are another great way to introduce Worth's dynamic media into the classroom without lots of advance preparation. Each presentation covers a major topic in psychology and integrates Worth's high-quality videos and animations for an engaging teaching and learning experience. These interactive presentations are complementary to adopters of Discovering Psychology and are perfect for technology novices and experts alike.

- The **Video Anthology for Introductory Psychology** includes over 150 unique video clips to bring lectures to life. Provided free of charge to adopters of *Discovering Psychology,* this rich collection includes clinical footage, interviews, animations, and news segments that vividly illustrate topics across the psychology curriculum.

- The **i>Clicker Classroom Response System** is a versatile polling system developed by educators and for educators that makes class time more efficient and interactive. i>Clicker allows you to ask questions and instantly record your students' responses, take attendance, and gauge students' understanding and opinions. i>Clicker is available at a 10% discount when packaged with *Discovering Psychology.*

Acknowledgments

Many talented people contributed to this project. First, thanks to Elissa S. Epel, University of California, San Francisco, for her expert advice on the section on telomeres and stress. We would also like to acknowledge the efforts of our supplements team that created materials specifically devoted to our book. Our thanks to:

- **Scott Cohn,** Western State Colorado University, for contributing to the development of two *Think Like a Scientist* Immersive Learning Activities, "ESP" and "Multitasking."

- **Matthew Isaak** at the University of Louisiana at Lafayette for his expert revisions on the Instructor's Resource Manuals, Summative Quizzes, and Lecture Guides.

- **Paul DeMarco,** University of Louisville; **Julie Gurner,** Community College of Philadelphia; **Anne McCrea,** Sinclair Community College; and **Rachel Rogers,** Community College of Rhode Island for contributing activities to the Instructor's Resources.

- **Sara Harris,** Illinois State University, for carefully updating the Test Bank for this edition.

- **Claudia Cochran-Miller** at El Paso Community College and **Marie Waung** at the University of Michigan at Dearborn for their exceptional appendix on industrial/organizational psychology.

- **Marie D. Thomas** at California State University, San Marcos, for updating the student-friendly statistics appendix.

- **Megan McLaughlin** at 9 Speed Creative for her excellent work on the revisions and design of the Lecture Slides.

- **Carolyn Ensley** of Wilfrid Laurier University—Waterloo, for her expert revisions of the LearningCurve chapters and Clicker Questions.

- **Mallory Malkin** of Mississippi University for Women for her strong work on revisions for the Critical Thinking Exercises.

As colleagues who care as much as we do about teaching, they have our gratitude for their hard work and commitment to excellence.

We are indebted to our colleagues who acted as reviewers throughout the development of the seventh edition of *Discovering Psychology.* Their thoughtful suggestions and advice helped us refine and strengthen this edition.

To our February 2013 Introductory Psychology Symposium attendees, we are indebted to you for your input and guidance:

- **Jim Cuellar,** Indiana University
- **Paul DeMarco,** University of Louisville
- **Jerry Green,** Tarrant County College
- **Raymond Kilduff,** Community College of Rhode Island
- **Tera Letzring,** Idaho State University
- **Dan Muhwezi,** Butler Community College
- **Brian Parry,** Colorado Mesa University
- **Edna Ross,** University of Louisville
- **Laura Sherrick,** Front Range Community College

To our Hockenbury, Nolan, & Hockenbury Advisory Board, thank you for your feedback, reviews, and ideas. Your contributions have influenced the seventh edition greatly:

Sherry J. Ash, San Jacinto Community College
Rosenna Bakari, Des Moines Area Community College
Thomas Baker, University of Texas, San Antonio
Shirley A. Bass-Wright, St. Philip's College
Andrea Brown, Montgomery College, Rockville
Sabrina Brown, Pearl River Community College
Kate Byerwalter, Grand Rapids Community College
Jessica K. Carpenter, Elgin Community College
Jenel T. Cavazos, Cameron University
Barbara Corbisier, Blinn College
Ronald E. Diehl, Sinclair Community College
Daniel J. Dickman, Ivy Tech Community College, Evansville
Stan Friedman, Texas State University
Carrie Hall, Miami University
John Haworth, Chattanooga State University
Richard Helms, Central Piedmont Community College
Cynthia Ingle, Bluegrass Community & Technical College
Brandon J. Jablonski, Sinclair Community College
Joan B. Jensen, Central Piedmont Community College
Richard Kandus, Mt. St. Jacinto College
Jennifer S. Lee, Cabrillo College
Elsa Mason, College of Southern Nevada
Stefanie Mitchell, San Jacinto Community College
John Raacke, Fort Hays State University
Vicki Ritts, St. Louis Community College at Meramec
Mahbobeh Yektaparast, Central Piedmont Community College
A. Clare Zaborowski, San Jacinto Community College

The remarkable people who make up Worth Publishers have a well-earned reputation for producing college textbooks and supplements of the highest quality. Special thanks to our publisher, Rachel Losh, for her enthusiasm, creativity, humor, and unfailing support of our project, always with a smile. Rachel, we couldn't have done it without you! We have already greatly benefited from the energy and insights of our new executive acquisitions editor, Daniel McDonough, and welcome him to our team. Next up is our developmental editor, Marna Miller (aka "Wonder Woman"), whose talent, dedication, and unflappable good humor are truly remarkable. Marna is more than "just" a gifted editor—she is a wonderful human being. Developmental editor Michael Kimball also contributed to the *Think Like a Scientist* Immersive Learning Activities. We are grateful he was available to step in. His helpful, often innovative contributions were very valuable. Also contributing to the development of *Think Like a Scientist* activities was Gayle Yamazaki, Senior Educational Technology Advisor for Macmillan Learning. We greatly value her creative perspective. Thanks also go to editorial assistant Kimberly Morgan-Smith, who expertly and cheerfully kept track of countless details, stacks of paper, and electronic files. The incredible new design for the seventh edition reflects the creative talents of senior design manager Vicki Tomaselli. We never cease to be impressed by designer Charles Yuen's ability to create the seamless interaction of text, graphics, boxes, and features that you see on every page of *Discovering Psychology*. The stunning graphics of this edition represent the combined talents of illustrator Todd Buck, art manager Matthew McAdams, photo editor Christine Buese, and photo researcher Jacqueline Wong, whose creative efforts to find just the right image are greatly appreciated.

By any standard, Director, Content Management Enhancement Tracey Kuehn is an unbelievably talented and dedicated person. For the last six editions, Tracey's expertise, creativity, and delightful sense of humor have kept our project—and us—on track. Managing editor Lisa Kinne effectively tackled and resolved the inevitable problems that accompany a project of this complexity. Our heartfelt thanks also to Stacey Alexander, who coordinated a bewildering array of technical details to bring the book to press.

Perhaps the greatest unsung heroes in college textbook publishing are the supplements and media editors. At Worth Publishers, those editors work tirelessly to set the standard by which all other publishers are judged. With conscientious attention to a multitude of details, media editors Lauren Samuelson, Laura Burden, and Jessica Lauffer have expertly assembled the integrated program of print, video, and Internet supplements that accompanies our text. Lauren also coordinated the development of the *Think Like a Scientist* Immersive Learning Activities with creativity, expertise, and enthusiasm.

Senior marketing manager Lindsay Johnson helped launch the seventh edition with her expertly coordinated advertising, marketing, and sales support efforts.

A few personal acknowledgments are in order. Several friends and family members kindly allowed us to share their stories with you. Sadly, Fern, Erv, and Ken are no longer with us, but they live on in our memories, as well as in the personal stories that we continue to tell about them. Sandy and Don deeply miss Fern and Erv's unflagging support, and the kindness, love, and seemingly endless supply of funny stories that we so relied on over the years of writing and revising the six previous editions of *Psychology* and *Discovering Psychology*. We are grateful to James and to Gene Fischer for connecting us with him, and to our good friends Andi, Hawk, and Wyncia; Asha and Paul; Tom and Lynn, and their children, Will, and Lily; and especially Marcia, for allowing us to tell their stories in our book. Sandy would also like to thank Bruce, Kat, Maureen, Alison, Peggy, and Steve for their openhearted presence and companionship on the path. Last but surely not least, Sandy and Don's daughter Laura has lived with this project since birth. Laura, thank you for your idealism, your generous spirit, and for being true to yourself.

Susan is immensely grateful to her husband, Ivan Bojanic, and their families—the Nolan and Bojanic clans—for their love and support, and for patiently enduring endless tales of fascinating psychology research. She also thanks Tom Heinzen for instigating her passion for writing psychology textbooks, and Monica De Iorio, Andrew Giachetti, Marjorie Levinstein, Michelle Magno, Katherine Moen, and Inga

Schowengerdt for their invaluable research assistance. Susan thanks, too, her Seton Hall colleagues as well as the many students whose reactions to the material covered in the Introduction to Psychology class have shaped her teaching and writing. Finally, Susan is indebted to Seton Hall Department of Psychology secretary, Willie Yaylaci, for her generous help and support throughout the writing of this edition.

An Invitation

We hope that you will let us know how you and your students like the seventh edition of *Discovering Psychology*. And, as always, we welcome your thoughts, comments, and suggestions. You can write to us in care of Worth Publishers/Macmillan, One New York Plaza, Suite 4500, New York, NY 10004-1562, or contact us via e-mail at **Hockenbury.Psychology@gmail.com.**

Above all, we hope that your class is an enjoyable and successful one as you introduce your students to the most fascinating and personally relevant science that exists.

Learning from *Discovering Psychology*

Welcome to psychology! Our names are **Sandy Hockenbury, Susan Nolan,** and **Don Hockenbury,** and we're the authors of your textbook. Every semester, we teach several sections of introductory psychology. We wrote this text to help you succeed in the class you are taking. Every aspect of this book has been carefully designed to help you get the most out of your introductory psychology course. Before you begin reading, you will find it well worth your time to take a few minutes to familiarize yourself with the special features and learning aids in this book.

Learning Aids in the Text

KEY THEME

You can enhance your chances for success in psychology by using the learning aids that have been built in to this textbook.

KEY QUESTIONS

> What are the functions of the Prologue, "Myth or Science?" questions, Advance Organizers, Key Terms, Key People, and Concept Maps?

> What are the functions of the different types of boxes in this text, and why should you read them?

> Where can you go to access a virtual study guide at any time of the day or night, and what study aids are provided?

First, read and think about the "Myth or Science?" questions at the beginning of each chapter. These questions reflect common ideas about some of the topics we'll cover. How many of these statements have you heard before? In the course of reading the chapter you'll find out which statements are popular myths—and which are actually true and based on scientific evidence.

Next, take a look at the **Chapter Outline** at the beginning of each chapter. The Chapter Outline provides an overview of the main topics that will be covered in the chapter. You might also want to flip through the chapter and browse a bit so you have an idea of what's to come.

Then, read the chapter **Prologue.** The Prologues are true stories about real people. Some of the stories are humorous, some dramatic. We think you will enjoy this special feature, but it will also help you to understand the material in the chapter that follows and why the topics are important and relevant to your life. In each chapter, we return to the people and stories introduced in the Prologue to illustrate important themes and concepts.

As you begin reading the chapter, you will notice several special elements. **Major Sections** are easy to identify because the heading is in blue type. The beginning of each major section also includes an **Advance Organizer**—a short section preview that looks like the one above.

The **Key Theme** provides you with a preview of the material in the section to come. The **Key Questions** will help you focus on some of the most important material in the section. Keep the questions in mind as you read the section. They will help you identify important points in the chapter. After you finish reading each section, look again at the Advance Organizer. Make sure that you can confidently answer each question before you go on to the next section. If you want to maximize your understanding of the material, write out the answer to each question. You can also use the questions in the Advance Organizer to aid you in taking notes or in outlining chapter sections, both of which are effective study strategies.

Photograph: Gene Fischer "James, Teen Shelter", 2013 www.genefischer.com

James A young man living in a rural area in upstate New York, James is an avid gardener, writer, and artist. He's a volunteer and an activist in his community. He's also transgender. James wants people to realize that there are many parts of his identity as a person. He told your author Susan that people "shouldn't really be focused on this term transgender because a lot of people seem to stick us in a category." He wants people to see beyond the label and get to know him as a person.

Notice that some terms in the chapter are printed in **boldface,** or darker, type. Some of these key terms may already be familiar to you, but most will be new. The darker type signals that the term has a specialized meaning in psychology. Each key term is formally defined within a sentence or two of being introduced. The key terms are also defined in the margins, usually on the page on which they appear in the text. Some key terms include a **pronunciation guide** to help you say the word correctly.

Occasionally, we print words in *italic type* to signal either that they are boldfaced terms in another chapter or that they are specialized terms in psychology.

Certain names also appear in boldface type. These are the **key people**—the researchers or theorists who are especially important within a given area of psychological study. Typically, key people are the psychologists or other researchers whose names your instructor will expect you to know.

You'll also notice notations at the end of major sections inviting you to 〉 Test your understanding with **LEARNING***Curve*. This notation signals that the material you have just finished reading is covered by a comprehensive quiz in LaunchPad. (You can find instructions on how to access LaunchPad in the section titled "LaunchPad for *Discovering Psychology,* Seventh Edition" on the next page.)

In the margins of every chapter, you will find callouts directing you to LaunchPad activities. Some of these LaunchPad activities expand upon topics introduced in the text, while others will help you review and better comprehend the text's information. Many of the activities incorporate video footage or simulations, but all of them were chosen for their relevance to the chapter material.

Also in LaunchPad are the **Think Like a Scientist** Immersive Learning Activities. These activities were created by your authors to help you develop your scientific thinking skills. This special feature provides an interactive, fun, and interesting activity to apply what you've learned to a new topic or claim. Whenever you see a *Think Like a Scientist* callout in the margin of your textbook, check out the activity to explore questions like "Can you learn to tell when someone is lying?" and "Do you have psychic powers?"

Think you're good at paying attention? Try **Video Activity: Attention.**

Can you learn to tell when someone is lying? Go to LaunchPad: Resources to **Think Like a Scientist** about **Lie Detection.**

Reviewing for Examinations

The **Chapter Review** at the end of each chapter includes several elements to help you review what you have learned. All the chapter's **key people** and **key terms** are listed, along with the pages on which they appear and are defined. The key terms are also boldfaced in the chapter summary so you can see their use in context. You can check your knowledge of the key people by describing in your own words why each scientist is important. You will also want to define each key term in your own words, then compare your definition to information on the page where it is discussed. The visual **Concept Maps** at the end of the chapter give you a hierarchical layout showing how themes, concepts, and facts are related to one another. The photos in each Concept Map should provide additional visual cues to help you consolidate your memory of important chapter information. Use the visual Concept Maps to review the information in each section.

Special Features in the Text

Each chapter in *Discovering Psychology* has several boxes that focus on different kinds of topics. Take the time to read the boxes because they are an integral part of each chapter. They also present important information that you may be expected to know for class discussion or tests. There are five types of boxes:

- **Critical Thinking** boxes ask you to stretch your mind a bit by presenting issues that are provocative or controversial. They will help you actively question the implications of the material that you are learning.

- **Science Versus Pseudoscience** boxes examine the evidence for various popular pseudosciences—from subliminal persuasion to *Baby Einstein* videos and graphology. These discussions will help teach you how to think scientifically and to critically evaluate claims in many different fields—not just psychology.

- **Culture and Human Behavior** boxes are another special feature of this text. Many students are unaware of the importance of cross-cultural research in contemporary psychology. These boxes highlight cultural differences in thinking and behavior. They will also sensitize you to the ways in which people's behavior, including your own, has been influenced by cultural factors.

- **In Focus** boxes present interesting information or research. Think of them as sidebar discussions. They deal with topics as diverse as human pheromones, whether animals dream, and why snakes and spiders give so many people the creeps.

- **Focus on Neuroscience** sections provide clear explanations of intriguing studies that use brain-imaging techniques to study psychological processes. Among the topics that are highlighted: schizophrenic hallucinations, mental images, drug addiction, and romantic love and the brain.

The **Psych for Your Life** section at the end of each chapter provides specific suggestions to help apply chapter information to help you deal with real-life concerns. These suggestions are based on psychological research, rather than opinions, anecdotes, or pop psych self-help philosophies.

Especially important is the Psych for Your Life section at the end of Chapter 1, which provides a list of research-based study techniques that you can use to help you succeed in psychology and other courses as well. In addition, the Psych for Your Life sections for Chapters 5, 6, and 8 deal with setting and achieving goals and enhancing motivation and memory, so you may want to skip ahead and read them after you finish this To the Student section. We hope that all of the Psych for Your Life sections make a difference in your life.

There are two special appendices at the back of the text. The **Statistics: Understanding Data** appendix discusses how psychologists use statistics to summarize and draw conclusions from the data they have gathered. The **Industrial/Organizational Psychology** appendix describes the branch of psychology that studies human behavior in the workplace. Your instructor may assign one or both of these appendices, or you may want to read them on your own.

Also at the back of this text is a **Glossary** containing the definitions for all **key terms** in the book and the pages on which they are discussed in more detail. You can use the **Subject Index** to locate discussions of particular topics and the **Name Index** to locate particular researchers. Finally, interested students can look up the specific studies we cite in the **References** sections.

LAUNCHPAD FOR *DISCOVERING PSYCHOLOGY*, SEVENTH EDITION

Get the most out of *Discovering Psychology*, Seventh Edition, with **LaunchPad**, which combines an interactive e-Book with high-quality multimedia content and activities that give you immediate feedback on your performance. Throughout the book you will see callouts that signal you to go to LaunchPad to access this online content.

- **Fully Interactive e-Book:** The LaunchPad e-Book for *Discovering Psychology*, Seventh Edition, comes with powerful study tools. You can search, highlight, and bookmark, making it easier to study.

- **Multimedia Content:** Access videos, simulations, tutorials, and *Think Like a Scientist* activities that help you understand and master the material.

- **LearningCurve:** These game-like quizzes adapt to what you already know and help you master the concepts you need to learn.

To learn more about LaunchPad for *Discovering Psychology,* Seventh Edition, or to request access, go to **launchpadworks.com**.

That's it! We hope you enjoy reading and learning from the seventh edition of *Discovering Psychology.* If you want to share your thoughts or suggestions for the next edition of this book, you can write to us at the following address:

Sandy Hockenbury, Susan Nolan, and Don Hockenbury
c/o Worth Publishers
One New York Plaza
Suite 4500
New York, NY 10004-1562

Or you can contact us at our e-mail address:

Hockenbury.Psychology@gmail.com

Have a great semester!

MYTH OR SCIENCE

Is it true . . .

○ That the field of psychology focuses primarily on treating people with psychological problems and disorders?

○ That Sigmund Freud was the first psychologist?

○ That when two behaviors are "linked," "related," or tend to occur together, it's safe to assume that one behavior caused the other?

○ That reading something over and over is the most effective way to prepare for a test?

○ That psychologists are not allowed to trick you into taking part in a study?

○ That brain scans can pinpoint the exact, single part of the brain that causes a complex behavior?

THE FIRST EXAM

PROLOGUE

YOU DON'T NEED TO BE A PSYCHOLOGIST to notice that the classroom atmosphere can be a little tense the day after the first exam. As we handed back the test results, several faces fell. Many of the students were freshmen and not yet accustomed to the self-paced learning required in a college course. But there were also several older adults, including two military vets, one recently returned from Afghanistan.

"So let's go over these test questions," your author Sandy began. "I noticed a lot of you had trouble with the difference between independent and dependent variables. Maybe we should talk about that again before we go on to Chapter 2."

Jacob frowned. "I can't understand why I did so badly," he said. "I mean, I read the chapter! Look." He held up his textbook. The pages were heavily underlined and covered with highlight colors—yellow, blue, and green.

It isn't unusual for students to have trouble with their first real exam in college. Knowing that, we usually take some time to talk about study skills after exams are returned. "How did you prepare for the exam?" your author Susan asked the class.

"I made flashcards," Latisha said. "But it didn't seem to help that much. I only got a B-, and I thought I really knew this stuff."

"Flashcards can be a great technique," Sandy said, "if you use them correctly."

Latisha looked puzzled. "What do you mean? I used them the way everybody uses flashcards. I tested myself and if I knew the answer, I set the card aside. I kept running through the ones I missed until they were all gone and I knew them all."

"Well, believe it or not," Sandy said, "psychologists have done a lot of research on learning new material, and it turns out that that's *not* the most effective way to use flashcards."

Introduction and Research Methods

IN THIS CHAPTER:

> **INTRODUCTION:** What Is Psychology?

> Contemporary Psychology

> The Scientific Method

> Descriptive Research

> Experimental Research

> Ethics in Psychological Research

> Closing Thoughts

> **PSYCH FOR YOUR LIFE:** Successful Study Techniques

"What is, then?" Latisha asked.

"Stay tuned," Sandy said with a smile. "We're going to talk about it in today's class."

Jenna broke in. "I always freeze on tests. They stress me out so bad my mind goes blank."

"I do too," Tyler piped up. "So my girlfriend gave me this bracelet to wear for exams. She swears by hers. Do you think it helps?"

"What is that?" Sandy said. Tyler handed the heavy metal bracelet to Sandy. "What's it supposed to do?"

"It's made of some kind of special metal—maybe titanium?" Tyler said. "It's magnetic. Oh, and the Web site said it generated a negative ion field,

or maybe it neutralizes positive ions. It didn't make a whole lot of sense to me. But my girlfriend said that a lot of famous baseball players and golfers wear one. It's supposed to help with pain but it's also supposed to help you concentrate and give you a better memory. I figured it couldn't hurt, so why not try it?"

"I'm not aware of any research on using magnets for concentration or memory," Sandy said carefully. "But we can certainly look it up and let you know what we find out."

Later in the chapter, we'll share what we found out about magnetic jewelry—and more important, what psychologists have discovered about the most effective ways to study. You'll also see how psychological research can help you critically evaluate new ideas and claims that you encounter outside the classroom.

As you'll discover, psychology has a lot to say about many of the questions that are of interest to college students. In this introductory chapter, we'll explore the scope of contemporary psychology as well as psychology's historical origins. The common theme connecting psychology's varied topics is its reliance on a solid foundation of scientific evidence. By the end of the chapter, you'll have a better appreciation of the scientific methods that psychologists use to answer questions, big and small, about behavior and mental processes.

Welcome to psychology! □

INTRODUCTION:
What Is Psychology?

KEY THEME
Today, psychology is defined as the science of behavior and mental processes, a definition that reflects psychology's origins and history.

KEY QUESTIONS
> What are the goals and scope of contemporary psychology?
> What roles did Wundt and James play in establishing psychology?
> What were the early schools of thought and approaches in psychology, and how did their views differ?

psychology The scientific study of behavior and mental processes.

Psychology is formally defined as *the scientific study of behavior and mental processes.* But this definition is deceptively simple. As you'll see in this chapter, the scope of contemporary psychology is very broad—ranging from the behavior of a single brain cell to the behavior of a crowd of people or even entire cultures.

Many people think that psychologists are primarily—or even exclusively—interested in studying and treating psychological disorders and problems. But as this chapter will show, psychologists are just as interested in "normal," everyday behaviors and mental processes—topics like learning and memory, emotions and motivation, relationships and loneliness. And, psychologists seek ways to use the knowledge that they discover through scientific research to optimize human performance and potential in many different fields, from classrooms to offices to the military.

MYTH ◄ SCIENCE

Is it true that the field of psychology focuses primarily on treating people with psychological problems and disorders?

What Do Psychologists Study? It's International Pillow Fight Day and these young members of a flash mob join the fun in Vancouver, British Columbia. What motivated them to show up? What kind of emotions might they be feeling? How does the presence of like-minded others affect their behavior? Whether studying the behavior of a crowd of people or a single brain cell, psychologists rely on the scientific method to guide their investigations.

Carmine Marinelli/ZUMA Press/Newscom

The four basic goals of psychology are to *describe, predict, explain,* and *control* or *influence* behavior and mental processes. To illustrate how these goals guide psychological research, think about our classroom discussion. Most people, like Jenna in the Prologue, have an intuitive understanding of what the word *stress* refers to. Psychologists, however, seek to go beyond intuitive or "common sense" understandings of human experience.

Here's how psychology's goals might help guide research on stress:

1. *Describe:* Trying to objectively *describe* the experience of stress, Dr. Garcia studies the sequence of emotional responses that occur during stressful experiences.

2. *Predict:* Dr. Kiecolt investigates responses to different kinds of challenging events, hoping to be able to *predict* the kinds of events that are most likely to evoke a stress response.

3. *Explain:* Seeking to *explain* why some people are more vulnerable to the effects of stress than others, Dr. Lazarus studies the different ways in which people respond to natural disasters.

4. *Control or Influence:* After studying the effectiveness of different coping strategies, Dr. Folkman helps people use those coping strategies to better *control* their reactions to stressful events.

How did psychology evolve into today's diverse and rich science? We begin this introductory chapter by stepping backward in time to describe the early origins of psychology and its historical development. As you become familiar with how psychology began and developed, you'll have a better appreciation for how it has come to encompass such diverse subjects. Indeed, the early history of psychology is the history of a field struggling to define itself as a separate and unique scientific discipline. The early psychologists debated such fundamental issues as:

- What is the proper subject matter of psychology?

- What methods should be used to investigate psychological issues?

- Should psychological findings be used to change or enhance human behavior?

These debates helped set the tone of the new science, define its scope, and set its limits. Over the past century, the shifting focus of these debates has influenced the topics studied and the research methods used.

Psychology's Origins
THE INFLUENCE OF PHILOSOPHY AND PHYSIOLOGY

The earliest origins of psychology can be traced back several centuries to the writings of the great philosophers. More than 2,000 years ago, the Greek philosopher Aristotle wrote extensively about topics such as sleep, dreams, the senses, and memory. Many of Aristotle's ideas remained influential until the beginnings of modern science in the seventeenth century (Kheriaty, 2007).

At that time, the French philosopher René Descartes (1596–1650) proposed a doctrine called *interactive dualism*—the idea that mind and body were separate entities that interact to produce sensations, emotions, and other conscious experiences. Today, psychologists continue to explore the relationship between mental activity and the brain.

Philosophers also laid the groundwork for another issue that would become central to psychology, the *nature–nurture issue.* For centuries, philosophers debated which was more important: the inborn *nature* of the individual or the environmental influences that *nurture* the individual. This debate was sometimes framed as nature *versus* nurture. Today, however, psychologists understand that "nature" and "nuture" are impossible to completely disentangle (Sameroff, 2010). So, while some psychologists do investigate the relative influences of *heredity versus environmental factors* on behavior, today's researchers also focus on studying the dynamic *interaction* between environmental factors and genetic heritage (Dick & others, 2015; Szyf, 2013).

Ted Spiegel/Corbis

Aristotle (384–322 B.C.E.) The first Western thinker to study psychological topics, Aristotle combined the logic of philosophy with empirical observation. His best-known psychological work, *De Anima,* is regarded as the first systematic treatise on psychology. Its topics included such basic psychological processes as the senses, perception, memory, thinking, and motivation. Aristotle's writings on psychology anticipated topics and theories that would be central to scientific psychology centuries later.

David Sacks/Getty Images

Nature or Nurture? Both father and daughter are clearly enjoying the experience of making art together. Is the child's interest in art an expression of her natural tendencies, or is it the result of her father's encouragement and teaching? Originally debated by philosophers hundreds of years ago, the relationship between heredity and environmental factors continues to interest psychologists today (Dick & others, 2015).

structuralism Early school of psychology that emphasized studying the most basic components, or structures, of conscious experiences.

Wilhelm Wundt (1832–1920) German physiologist Wilhelm Wundt is generally credited as being the founder of psychology as an experimental science. In 1879, he established the first psychology research laboratory. By the early 1900s, Wundt's research had expanded to include such topics as cultural psychology and developmental psychology (Wong, 2009).

Bettmann/Corbis

Edward B. Titchener (1867–1927) In contrast to the psychology programs at both Harvard and Columbia at the time, Edward Titchener welcomed women into his graduate program at Cornell. In fact, more women completed their psychology doctorates under Titchener's direction than under any other male psychologist of his generation (Evans, 1991).

Archives of the History of American Psychology, The University of Akron. Color added by publisher

Such philosophical discussions influenced the topics that would be considered in psychology. But the early philosophers could advance the understanding of human behavior only to a certain point. Their methods were limited to intuition, observation, and logic.

The eventual emergence of psychology as a science hinged on advances in other sciences, particularly physiology. *Physiology* is a branch of biology that studies the functions and parts of living organisms, including humans. In the 1600s, physiologists were becoming interested in the human brain and its relation to behavior. By the early 1700s, it was discovered that damage to one side of the brain produced a loss of function in the opposite side of the body. By the early 1800s, the idea that different brain areas were related to different behavioral functions was being vigorously debated. Collectively, the early scientific discoveries made by physiologists were establishing the foundation for an idea that was to prove critical to the emergence of psychology—namely, that scientific methods could be applied to answering questions about behavior and mental processes.

Wilhelm Wundt
THE FOUNDER OF PSYCHOLOGY

By the second half of the 1800s, the stage had been set for the emergence of psychology as a distinct scientific discipline. The leading proponent of this idea was a German physiologist named **Wilhelm Wundt** (Gentile & Miller, 2009). Wundt used scientific methods to study fundamental psychological processes, such as mental reaction times in response to visual or auditory stimuli. For example, Wundt tried to measure precisely how long it took a person to consciously detect the sight and sound of a bell being struck.

A major turning point in psychology occurred in 1874, when Wundt outlined the connections between physiology and psychology in his landmark text, *Principles of Physiological Psychology* (Diamond, 2001). He also promoted his belief that psychology should be established as a separate scientific discipline that would use experimental methods to study mental processes. In 1879, Wundt realized that goal when he opened the first psychology research laboratory at the University of Leipzig. Many mark this event as the formal beginning of psychology as an experimental science (Kohls & Benedikter, 2010).

Wundt defined psychology as the study of consciousness and emphasized the use of experimental methods to study and measure it. Until he died in 1920, Wundt exerted a strong influence on the development of psychology as a science (Wong, 2009). Two hundred students from around the world traveled to Leipzig to earn doctorates in experimental psychology under Wundt's direction. Over the years, some 17,000 students attended Wundt's afternoon lectures on general psychology, which often included demonstrations of devices he had developed to measure mental processes (Blumenthal, 1998).

Edward B. Titchener
STRUCTURALISM

One of Wundt's most devoted students was a young Englishman named **Edward B. Titchener.** After earning his doctorate in Wundt's laboratory, Titchener began teaching at Cornell University in New York. There he established a psychology laboratory that ultimately spanned 26 rooms.

Titchener shared many of Wundt's ideas about the nature of psychology. Eventually, however, Titchener developed his own approach, which he called *structuralism*. **Structuralism** became the first major school of thought in psychology. Structuralism held that even our most complex conscious experiences could be broken down into elemental *structures*, or component parts, of sensations and feelings. To identify these structures of conscious thought, Titchener trained subjects in a procedure called *introspection*. The subjects would view a simple stimulus, such as a book, and then try to reconstruct their sensations and feelings immediately after viewing it. (In psychology, a *stimulus* is anything perceptible to the senses, such as a sight, sound, smell, touch, or taste.) They might first report on the colors they saw, then the smells, and so on, in the attempt to create a total description of their conscious experience (Titchener, 1896).

In addition to being distinguished as the first school of thought in early psychology, Titchener's structuralism holds the dubious distinction of being the first school to disappear. Titchener's death in 1927 essentially marked the end of structuralism as an influential school of thought in psychology. But even before Titchener's death, structuralism was often criticized for relying too heavily on the method of introspection.

As noted by Wundt and other scientists, introspection had significant limitations. First, introspection was an unreliable method of investigation. Different subjects often provided very different introspective reports about the same stimulus. Even subjects well trained in introspection varied in their responses to the same stimulus from trial to trial.

Second, introspection could not be used to study children or animals. Third, complex topics, such as learning, development, mental disorders, and personality, could not be investigated using introspection. Ultimately, the methods and goals of structuralism were simply too limited to accommodate the rapidly expanding interests of the field of psychology.

William James
FUNCTIONALISM

By the time Titchener arrived at Cornell University, psychology was already well established in the United States. The main proponent of American psychology was one of Harvard's most outstanding teachers—**William James.** James had become intrigued by the emerging science of psychology after reading one of Wundt's articles. But there were other influences on the development of James's thinking.

Like many other scientists and philosophers of his generation, James was fascinated by the idea that different species had evolved over time (Menand, 2001). Many nineteenth-century scientists in England, France, and the United States were *evolutionists*—that is, they believed that species had not been created all at once but rather had changed over time (Caton, 2007).

In the 1850s, British philosopher Herbert Spencer had published several works arguing that modern species, including humans, were the result of gradual evolutionary change. In 1859, **Charles Darwin's** groundbreaking work, *On the Origin of Species,* was published. James and his fellow thinkers actively debated the notion of evolution, which came to have a profound influence on James's ideas (Richardson, 2006). Like Darwin, James stressed the importance of adaptation to environmental challenges.

In the early 1870s, James began teaching a physiology and anatomy class at Harvard University. An intense, enthusiastic teacher, James was prone to changing the subject matter of his classes as his own interests changed (B. Ross, 1991). By the late 1870s, James was teaching classes devoted exclusively to the topic of psychology.

At about the same time, James began writing a comprehensive textbook of psychology, a task that would take him more than a decade. James's *Principles of Psychology* was finally published in 1890. Despite its length of more than 1,400 pages, *Principles of Psychology* quickly became the leading psychology textbook.

William James (1842–1910) Harvard professor William James was instrumental in establishing psychology in the United States. In 1890, James published a highly influential text, *Principles of Psychology.* James's ideas became the basis of another early school of psychology, called *functionalism,* which stressed studying the adaptive and practical functions of human behavior.

Bettmann/Corbis

Charles Darwin (1809–1882) Naturalist Charles Darwin had a profound influence on the early development of psychology. Darwin was not the first scientist to propose that complex organisms evolved from simpler species (Caton, 2007). However, Darwin's book, *On the Origin of Species,* published in 1859, gathered evidence from many different scientific fields to present a compelling account of evolution through the mechanism of natural selection. Darwin's ideas have had a lasting impact on scientific thought (Dickins, 2011; Pagel, 2009).

functionalism Early school of psychology that emphasized studying the purpose, or function, of behavior and mental experiences.

G. Stanley Hall (1844–1924) G. Stanley Hall helped organize psychology in the United States. Among his many achievements was the establishment of the first psychology research laboratory in the United States. Hall also founded the American Psychological Association.

Corbis

Mary Whiton Calkins (1863–1930) Under the direction of William James, Mary Whiton Calkins completed all the requirements for a Ph.D. in psychology. Calkins had a distinguished professional career. She established a psychology laboratory at Wellesley College and became the first woman president of the American Psychological Association.

In it, James discussed such diverse topics as brain function, habit, memory, sensation, perception, and emotion.

James's ideas became the basis for a new school of psychology, called functionalism. **Functionalism** stressed the importance of how behavior *functions* to allow people and animals to adapt to their environments. Unlike structuralists, functionalists did not limit their methods to introspection. They expanded the scope of psychological research to include direct observation of living creatures in natural settings. They also examined how psychology could be applied to areas like education, child rearing, and the work environment.

Both the structuralists and the functionalists thought that psychology should focus on the study of conscious experiences. But the functionalists had very different ideas about the nature of consciousness and how it should be studied. Rather than trying to identify the essential structures of consciousness at a given moment, James saw consciousness as an ongoing stream of mental activity that shifts and changes.

Like structuralism, functionalism no longer exists as a distinct school of thought in contemporary psychology. Nevertheless, functionalism's twin themes of the importance of the adaptive role of behavior and the application of psychology to enhance human behavior are still important in modern psychology.

WILLIAM JAMES AND HIS STUDENTS

Like Wundt, James profoundly influenced psychology through his students, many of whom became prominent American psychologists. Two of James's most notable students were G. Stanley Hall and Mary Whiton Calkins.

In 1878, **G. Stanley Hall** received the first Ph.D. in psychology awarded in the United States. Hall founded the first psychology research laboratory in the United States at Johns Hopkins University in 1883. He also began publishing the *American Journal of Psychology,* the first U.S. journal devoted to psychology. Most important, in 1892, Hall founded the American Psychological Association and was elected its first president (Anderson, 2012). Today, the American Psychological Association (APA) is the world's largest professional organization of psychologists, with approximately 150,000 members. (The Association for Psychological Science, founded in 1988, has about 26,000 members.)

In 1890, **Mary Whiton Calkins** was assigned the task of teaching experimental psychology at a new women's college—Wellesley College. Calkins studied with James at nearby Harvard University. She completed all the requirements for a Ph.D. in psychology. However, Harvard refused to grant her the Ph.D. degree because she was a woman and at the time Harvard was not a coeducational institution (Pickren & Rutherford, 2010).

Although never awarded the degree she had earned, Calkins made several notable contributions to psychology. She conducted research in dreams, memory, and personality. In 1891, she established a psychology laboratory at Wellesley College. At the turn of the twentieth century, she wrote a well-received textbook, titled *Introduction to Psychology.* In 1905, Calkins was elected president of the American Psychological Association—the first woman, but not the last, to hold that position.

For the record, the first American woman to earn an official Ph.D. in psychology was **Margaret Floy Washburn,** Edward Titchener's first doctoral student at Cornell University. Washburn strongly advocated the scientific study of the mental processes of different animal species. In 1908, she published an influential text, titled *The Animal Mind.* Her book summarized research on sensation, perception, learning, and other "inner experiences" of different animal species. In 1921, Washburn became the second woman elected president of the American Psychological Association (Viney & Burlingame-Lee, 2003).

Finally, one of G. Stanley Hall's notable students was **Francis C. Sumner.** Sumner was the first African American to receive a Ph.D. in psychology, awarded by Clark University in 1920. After teaching at several southern universities,

Margaret Floy Washburn (1871–1939)
After becoming the first American woman to earn an official Ph.D. in psychology, Washburn went on to a distinguished career. Despite the discrimination against women that was widespread in higher education during the early twentieth century, Washburn made many contributions to psychology. She was the second woman to be elected president of the American Psychological Association.

Archives of the History of American Psychology, The University of Akron. Color added by publisher

Francis C. Sumner (1895–1954) Francis Sumner studied under G. Stanley Hall at Clark University. In 1920, he became the first African American to earn a Ph.D. in psychology. Sumner later joined Howard University in Washington, D.C., and helped create a strong psychology program that led the country in training African American psychologists (Belgrave & Allison, 2010).

Sigmund Freud (1856–1939) In 1909, Freud *(front left)* and several other psychoanalysts were invited by G. Stanley Hall *(front center)* to participate in Clark University's twentieth-anniversary celebration in Worcester, Massachusetts (Hogan, 2003). Freud delivered five lectures on psychoanalysis. Listening in the audience was William James, who later wrote to a friend that Freud struck him as "a man obsessed with fixed ideas" (Rosenzweig, 1997). Carl Jung *(front right)*, who later developed his own theory of personality, also attended this historic conference.

Sumner moved to Howard University in Washington, D.C. While at Howard, he published papers on a wide variety of topics and chaired a psychology department that produced more African American psychologists than all other American colleges and universities combined (Guthrie, 2000, 2004). One of Sumner's most famous students was **Kenneth Bancroft Clark.** Clark's research on the negative effects of discrimination was instrumental in the U.S. Supreme Court's 1954 decision to end segregation in schools (Jackson, 2006). In 1970, Clark became the first African American president of the American Psychological Association (Belgrave & Allison, 2010).

Clark University

Sigmund Freud
PSYCHOANALYSIS

Wundt, James, and other early psychologists emphasized the study of conscious experiences. But at the turn of the twentieth century, new approaches challenged the principles of both structuralism and functionalism.

In Vienna, Austria, a physician named **Sigmund Freud** was developing an intriguing theory of personality based on uncovering causes of behavior that were *unconscious,* or hidden from the person's conscious awareness. Freud's school of thought, called **psychoanalysis,** emphasized the role of unconscious conflicts in determining behavior and personality. Freud himself was a neurologist, *not* a psychologist. Nevertheless, psychoanalysis had a strong influence on psychological thinking in the early part of the century.

Freud's psychoanalytic theory of personality and behavior was based largely on his work with his patients and on insights derived from self-analysis. Freud believed that

MYTH ◀ SCIENCE

Is it true that Sigmund Freud was the first psychologist?

psychoanalysis Personality theory and form of psychotherapy that emphasizes the role of unconscious factors in personality and behavior.

behaviorism School of psychology and theoretical viewpoint that emphasizes the study of observable behaviors, especially as they pertain to the process of learning.

human behavior was motivated by unconscious conflicts that were almost always sexual or aggressive in nature. Past experiences, especially childhood experiences, were thought to be critical in the formation of adult personality and behavior. According to Freud (1904), glimpses of these unconscious impulses are revealed in everyday life in dreams, memory blocks, slips of the tongue, and spontaneous humor. Freud believed that when unconscious conflicts became extreme, psychological disorders could result.

Freud's psychoanalytic theory of personality also provided the basis for a distinct form of psychotherapy. Many of the fundamental ideas of psychoanalysis, such as the importance of unconscious influences and early childhood experiences, continue to influence psychologists and other professionals in the mental health field. We'll explore Freud's theory in more depth in Chapter 10 on personality and Chapter 14 on therapies.

John B. Watson
BEHAVIORISM

The course of psychology changed dramatically in the early 1900s when another approach, called **behaviorism,** emerged as a dominating force. Behaviorism rejected the emphasis on consciousness promoted by structuralism and functionalism. It also flatly rejected Freudian notions about unconscious influences, claiming that such ideas were unscientific and impossible to test. Instead, behaviorism contended that psychology should focus its scientific investigations strictly on *overt behavior*—observable behaviors that could be objectively measured and verified.

Behaviorism is another example of the influence of physiology on psychology. Behaviorism grew out of the pioneering work of a Russian physiologist named **Ivan Pavlov.** Pavlov demonstrated that dogs could learn to associate a neutral stimulus, such as the sound of a bell, with an automatic behavior, such as reflexively salivating to food. Once an association between the sound of the bell and the food was formed, the sound of the bell alone would trigger the salivation reflex in the dog. Pavlov enthusiastically believed he had discovered the mechanism by which all behaviors were learned.

In the United States, a young, dynamic psychologist named **John B. Watson** shared Pavlov's enthusiasm. Watson (1913) championed behaviorism as a new school of psychology. Structuralism was still an influential perspective, but Watson strongly objected to both its method of introspection and its focus on conscious mental processes. As Watson (1924) wrote in his classic book, *Behaviorism:*

> Behaviorism, on the contrary, holds that the subject matter of human psychology *is the behavior of the human being.* Behaviorism claims that consciousness is neither a definite nor a usable concept. The behaviorist, who has been trained always as an experimentalist, holds, further, that belief in the existence of consciousness goes back to the ancient days of superstition and magic.

Behaviorism's influence on American psychology was enormous. The goal of the behaviorists was to discover the fundamental principles of *learning*—how behavior is acquired and modified in response to environmental influences. For the most part, the behaviorists studied animal behavior under carefully controlled laboratory conditions.

Although Watson left academic psychology in the early 1920s, behaviorism was later championed by an equally forceful proponent—the famous American psychologist **B. F. Skinner.** Like Watson, Skinner believed that psychology should restrict itself to studying outwardly observable behaviors that could be measured and verified. In compelling experimental demonstrations, Skinner systematically used reinforcement or punishment to shape the behavior of rats and pigeons.

Three Key Scientists in the Development of Behaviorism Building on the pioneering research of Russian physiologist Ivan Pavlov, American psychologist John B. Watson founded the school of behaviorism. Behaviorism advocated that psychology should study observable behaviors, not mental processes. Following Watson, B. F. Skinner continued to champion the ideas of behaviorism. Skinner became one of the most influential psychologists of the twentieth century. Like Watson, he strongly advocated the study of observable behaviors rather than mental processes.

Ivan Pavlov (1849–1936)

John B. Watson (1878–1958)   **B. F. Skinner (1904–1990)**

Between Watson and Skinner, behaviorism dominated American psychology for almost half a century. During that time, the study of conscious experiences was largely ignored as a topic in psychology (Baars, 2005). In Chapter 5 on learning, we'll look at the lives and contributions of Pavlov, Watson, and Skinner in greater detail.

humanistic psychology School of psychology and theoretical viewpoint that emphasizes each person's unique potential for psychological growth and self-direction.

Carl Rogers
HUMANISTIC PSYCHOLOGY

For several decades, behaviorism and psychoanalysis were the perspectives that most influenced the thinking of American psychologists. In the 1950s, a new school of thought emerged, called **humanistic psychology.** Because humanistic psychology was distinctly different from both psychoanalysis and behaviorism, it was sometimes referred to as the "third force" in American psychology (Waterman, 2013; Watson & others, 2011).

Carl Rogers (1902–1987)

Abraham Maslow (1908–1970)

Humanistic psychology was largely founded by American psychologist **Carl Rogers** (Elliott & Farber, 2010). Like Freud, Rogers was influenced by his experiences with his psychotherapy clients. However, rather than emphasizing unconscious conflicts, Rogers emphasized the *conscious* experiences of his clients, including each person's unique potential for psychological growth and self-direction. In contrast to the behaviorists, who saw human behavior as being shaped and maintained by external causes, Rogers emphasized self-determination, free will, and the importance of choice in human behavior (Elliott & Farber, 2010; Kirschenbaum & Jourdan, 2005).

Abraham Maslow was another advocate of humanistic psychology. Maslow developed a theory of motivation that emphasized psychological growth, which we'll discuss in Chapter 8. Like psychoanalysis, humanistic psychology included not only influential theories of personality but also a form of psychotherapy, which we'll discuss in later chapters.

Two Leaders in the Development of Humanistic Psychology Carl Rogers and Abraham Maslow were key figures in establishing humanistic psychology. Humanistic psychology emphasized the importance of self-determination, creativity, and human potential (Serlin, 2012). The ideas of Carl Rogers have been particularly influential in modern psychotherapy. Abraham Maslow's theory of motivation emphasized the importance of psychological growth.

By briefly stepping backward in time, you've seen how the debates among the key thinkers in psychology's history shaped the development of psychology as a whole. Each of the schools that we've described had an impact on the topics and methods of psychological research. As you'll see throughout this textbook, that impact has been a lasting one. In the next sections, we'll touch on some of the more recent developments in psychology's evolution. We'll also explore the diversity that characterizes contemporary psychology.

❯ Test your understanding of **The Origins of Psychology** with **LEARNING**Curve.

Contemporary Psychology

KEY THEME
As psychology has developed as a scientific discipline, the topics it investigates have become progressively more diverse.

KEY QUESTIONS
❯ How do the perspectives in contemporary psychology differ in emphasis and approach?
❯ How do psychiatry and psychology differ, and what are psychology's major specialty areas?

Over the past half-century, the range of topics in psychology has become progressively more diverse. And, as psychology's knowledge base has increased, psychology itself has become more specialized. Rather than being dominated by a particular approach or school of thought, today's psychologists tend to identify themselves according to: (1) the *perspective* they emphasize in investigating psychological topics and (2) the *specialty area* in which they have been trained and practice.

neuroscience The study of the nervous system, especially the brain.

Major Perspectives in Psychology

Any given topic in contemporary psychology can be approached from a variety of perspectives. Each perspective discussed here represents a different emphasis or point of view that can be taken in studying a particular behavior, topic, or issue. As you'll see in this section, the influence of the early schools of psychology is apparent in the first four perspectives that characterize contemporary psychology.

THE BIOLOGICAL PERSPECTIVE

As we've already noted, physiology has played an important role in psychology since it was founded. Today, that influence continues, as is shown by the many psychologists who take the biological perspective. The *biological perspective* emphasizes studying the physical bases of human and animal behavior, including the nervous system, endocrine system, immune system, and genetics. More specifically, **neuroscience** refers to the study of the nervous system, especially the brain. Sophisticated brain-scanning techniques, including the *PET scan, MRI scan,* and *functional MRI (fMRI) scan*, allow neuroscientists to study the structure and activity of the intact, living brain in increasing detail. Later in the chapter, we'll describe these brain-imaging techniques and explain how psychologists use them as research tools.

THE PSYCHODYNAMIC PERSPECTIVE

The key ideas and themes of Freud's landmark theory of psychoanalysis continue to be important among many psychologists, especially those working in the mental health field. As you'll see in Chapter 10 on personality, and Chapter 14 on therapies, many of Freud's ideas have been expanded or modified by his followers. Today, psychologists who take the *psychodynamic perspective* may or may not follow Freud or take a psychoanalytic approach. However, they do tend to emphasize the importance of unconscious influences, early life experiences, and interpersonal relationships in explaining the underlying dynamics of behavior or in treating people with psychological problems.

THE BEHAVIORAL PERSPECTIVE

Watson and Skinner's contention that psychology should focus on observable behaviors and the fundamental laws of learning is evident today in the *behavioral perspective*. Contemporary psychologists who take the behavioral perspective continue to study

The Biological Perspective The physiological aspects of behavior and mental processes are studied by biological psychologists. Psychologists and other scientists who specialize in the study of the brain and the rest of the nervous system are called neuroscientists. Here, Swiss neuroscientist Juliane Britz uses a device called an *electroencephalogram* to monitor brain wave activity in a research participant. Dr. Britz studies the brain processes involved in sensation, perception, and awareness (Britz & others, 2014).

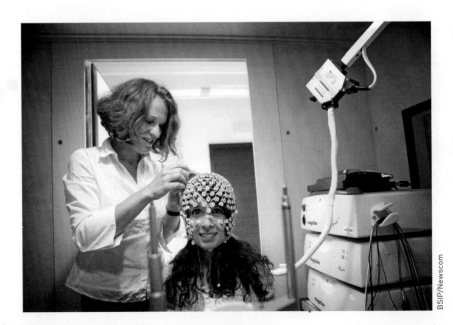

BSIP/News.com

how behavior is acquired or modified by environmental causes. Many psychologists who work in the area of mental health also emphasize the behavioral perspective in explaining and treating psychological disorders. In Chapter 5 on learning, and Chapter 14 on therapies, we'll discuss different applications of the behavioral perspective.

THE HUMANISTIC PERSPECTIVE

The influence of the work of Carl Rogers and Abraham Maslow continues to be seen among contemporary psychologists who take the humanistic perspective (Serlin, 2012; Waterman, 2013). The *humanistic perspective* focuses on the motivation of people to grow psychologically, the influence of interpersonal relationships on a person's self-concept, and the importance of choice and self-direction in striving to reach one's potential. Like the psychodynamic perspective, the humanistic perspective is often emphasized among psychologists working in the mental health field. You'll encounter the humanistic perspective in the chapters on motivation (8), personality (10), and therapies (14).

THE POSITIVE PSYCHOLOGY PERSPECTIVE

The humanistic perspective's emphasis on psychological growth and human potential contributed to the recent emergence of a new perspective. **Positive psychology** is a field of psychological research and theory focusing on the study of positive emotions and psychological states, positive individual traits, and the social institutions that foster those qualities in individuals and communities (Csikszentmihalyi & Nakamura, 2011; Peterson, 2006; Seligman & others, 2005). By studying the conditions and processes that contribute to the optimal functioning of people, groups, and institutions, positive psychology seeks to counterbalance psychology's traditional emphasis on psychological problems and disorders (McNulty & Fincham, 2012).

Topics that fall under the umbrella of positive psychology include personal happiness, optimism, creativity, resilience, character strengths, and wisdom. Positive psychology is also focused on developing therapeutic techniques that increase personal well-being rather than just alleviating the troubling symptoms of psychological disorders (Snyder & others, 2011). Insights from positive psychology research will be evident in many chapters, including the chapters on motivation and emotion (8); personality (10); stress, health, and coping (12); and therapies (14).

THE COGNITIVE PERSPECTIVE

During the 1960s, psychology experienced a return to the study of how mental processes influence behavior. Often referred to as "the cognitive revolution" in psychology, this movement represented a break from traditional behaviorism. Cognitive psychology focused once again on the important role of mental processes in how people process and remember information, develop language, solve problems, and think.

The development of the first computers in the 1950s contributed to the cognitive revolution. Computers gave psychologists a new model for conceptualizing human mental processes—human thinking, memory, and perception could be understood in terms of an information-processing model. We'll consider the cognitive perspective in several chapters, including Chapter 7 on thinking, language, and intelligence. The cognitive perspective has also influenced other areas of psychology, including personality (Chapter 10) and psychotherapy (Chapter 14).

THE CROSS-CULTURAL PERSPECTIVE

More recently, psychologists have taken a closer look at how cultural factors influence patterns of behavior—the essence of the *cross-cultural perspective*. By the late 1980s, *cross-cultural psychology* had emerged in full force as large numbers of

Studying Behavior from Different Psychological Perspectives Psychologists can study a particular behavior, topic, or issue from different perspectives. For example, taking the biological perspective, a psychologist might study whether there are biological differences between rock climbers and other people, such as the ability to stay calm and focused in the face of dangerous situations. A psychologist taking the behavioral perspective might look at how people learn to climb and the types of rewards that reinforce their climbing behavior. And, a psychologist who took the positive psychology perspective might investigate how meeting the challenge of climbing a difficult and dangerous route contributed to self-confidence and personal growth.

Greg Epperson/Getty Images

positive psychology The study of positive emotions and psychological states, positive individual traits, and the social institutions that foster positive individuals and communities.

CULTURE AND HUMAN BEHAVIOR

What Is Cross-Cultural Psychology?

People around the globe share many attributes: We all eat, sleep, form families, seek happiness, and mourn losses. Yet the *way* in which we express our human qualities can vary considerably among cultures (Triandis, 2005). *What* we eat, *where* we sleep, and *how* we form families, define happiness, and express sadness can differ greatly in different cultures.

Culture refers to the attitudes, values, beliefs, and behaviors shared by a group of people and communicated from one generation to another (Cohen, 2009, 2010). Studying the differences among cultures and the influences of culture on behavior are the fundamental goals of **cross-cultural psychology.**

Cultural identity is influenced by many factors, including ethnicity, nationality, race, religion, and language. As we grow up within a given culture, we learn our culture's *norms,* or unwritten rules of behavior. And, we tend to act in accordance with those internalized norms without thinking. For example, according to the dominant cultural norms in the United States, babies usually sleep separately from their parents. But in many cultures around the world, it's taken for granted that babies will sleep in the same bed as their parents (Mindell & others, 2010a, b). Members of these other cultures are often surprised and even shocked at the U.S. practice of separating babies from their parents at night. (In Chapter 9 on lifespan development, we discuss this topic at greater length.)

The tendency to use your own culture as the standard is called **ethnocentrism.** Ethnocentrism may be a natural tendency, but it can prevent us from understanding the behaviors of others (Bizumic & others, 2009). Ethnocentrism may also prevent us from being aware of how our behavior has been shaped by our own culture.

Extreme ethnocentrism can lead to intolerance toward other cultures. If we believe that our way of seeing things or behaving is the only proper one, other ways of behaving and thinking may seem laughable, inferior, wrong, or even immoral.

In addition to influencing how we behave, culture affects how we define our sense of self (Markus & Kitayama, 1991, 1998, 2010). For the most part, the dominant cultures of the United States, Canada, Australia, New Zealand, and Europe can be described as individualistic cultures. **Individualistic cultures** emphasize the needs and goals of the individual over the needs and goals of the group (Henrich, 2014; Markus & Kitayama, 2010). In individualistic societies, the self is seen as *independent,* autonomous, and distinctive. Personal identity is defined by individual achievements, abilities, and accomplishments.

In contrast, **collectivistic cultures** emphasize the needs and goals of the group over those of the individual. Social behavior is more heavily influenced by cultural norms and social context than by individual preferences and attitudes (Owe & others, 2013; Talhelm & others, 2014).

In a collectivistic culture, the self is seen as being much more *interdependent* with others. Relationships with others and identification with a larger group, such as the family or tribe, are key components of personal identity. The cultures of Asia, Africa, Mexico, and Central and South America tend to be collectivistic. About two-thirds of the world's population live in collectivistic cultures (Triandis, 2005).

The distinction between individualistic and collectivistic societies is useful in cross-cultural psychology. However, most cultures are neither completely individualistic nor completely collectivistic, but fall somewhere between the two extremes. And, psychologists are careful not to assume that these generalizations are true of every member or every aspect of a given culture (Kitayama & Uskul, 2011). Psychologists also recognize that there is a great deal of individual variation among the members of every culture (Heine & Norenzayan, 2006). It's important to keep that qualification in mind when cross-cultural findings are discussed.

The Culture and Human Behavior boxes that we have included in this book will help you learn about human behavior in other cultures. They will also help you understand how culture affects *your* behavior, beliefs, attitudes, and values as well.

Dave Stamboulis/age fotostock

The Roots of Collectivistic Culture?   Even within a given society, people's cultural values may vary. Thomas Talhem and his colleagues (2014) found that Chinese from northern China, where wheat is traditionally grown, are more individualistic than Chinese from southern China, where rice is grown, despite sharing the same ethnic, educational, and socioeconomic background. The explanation? As this photo of villagers in southwest China harvesting rice shows, rice farming requires an extraordinary level of cooperation and coordination among villagers, characteristics that are highly valued in collectivistic cultures. In contrast, wheat farmers can succeed without help from their neighbors.

psychologists began studying the diversity of human behavior in different cultural settings and countries (Kitayama & Uskul, 2011; P. Smith, 2010). In the process, psychologists discovered that some well-established psychological findings were not as universal as they had thought.

For example, one well-established psychological finding was that people exert more effort on a task when working alone than

KIM KYUNG-HOON/Reuters/Corbis

Cultural Differences in Everyday Behavior Our everyday behavior reflects *cultural norms*—unspoken standards of social behavior. For example, imagine the behavior of commuters on a subway platform in any large U.S. city. Contrast that behavior with that of commuters in Japan. White-gloved conductors obligingly "assist" passengers in boarding by shoving them in from behind, cramming as many people into the subway car as possible.

when working as part of a group, a phenomenon called *social loafing*. First demonstrated in the 1970s, social loafing was a consistent finding in several psychological studies conducted with American and European subjects. But when similar studies were conducted with Chinese participants, the opposite was found to be true (Hong & others, 2008). Chinese participants worked harder on a task when they were part of a group than when they were working alone, a phenomenon called *social striving*.

Today, psychologists are keenly attuned to the influence of cultural factors on behavior (Heine, 2010; Henrich & others, 2010). Although many psychological processes *are* shared by all humans, it's important to keep in mind that there are cultural variations in behavior. Thus, we have included Culture and Human Behavior boxes throughout this textbook to help sensitize you to the influence of culture on behavior—including your own. We describe cross-cultural psychology in more detail in the Culture and Human Behavior box on page 12.

THE EVOLUTIONARY PERSPECTIVE

Evolutionary psychology refers to the application of the principles of evolution to explain psychological processes and phenomena (Buss, 2009, 2011b). The *evolutionary perspective* reflects a renewed interest in the work of English naturalist Charles Darwin. As noted previously, Darwin's (1859) first book on evolution, *On the Origin of Species,* played an influential role in the thinking of many early psychologists.

The theory of evolution proposes that the individual members of a species compete for survival. Because of inherited differences, some members of a species are better adapted to their environment than are others. Organisms that inherit characteristics that increase their chances of survival in their particular habitat are more likely to survive, reproduce, and pass on their characteristics to their offspring. But individuals that inherit less useful characteristics are less likely to survive, reproduce, and pass on their characteristics. This process reflects the principle of *natural selection*: The most adaptive characteristics are "selected" and perpetuated in the next generation.

Psychologists who take the evolutionary perspective assume that psychological processes are also subject to the principle of natural selection. As David Buss (2008) writes, "An evolved psychological mechanism exists in the form that it does because it solved a specific problem of survival or reproduction recurrently over evolutionary history." That is, psychological processes that helped individuals adapt to their environments also helped them survive, reproduce, and pass those abilities

culture The attitudes, values, beliefs, and behaviors shared by a group of people and communicated from one generation to another.

cross-cultural psychology Branch of psychology that studies the effects of culture on behavior and mental processes.

ethnocentrism The belief that one's own culture or ethnic group is superior to all others and the related tendency to use one's own culture as a standard by which to judge other cultures.

individualistic cultures Cultures that emphasize the needs and goals of the individual over the needs and goals of the group.

collectivistic cultures Cultures that emphasize the needs and goals of the group over the needs and goals of the individual.

evolutionary psychology The application of principles of evolution, including natural selection, to explain psychological processes and phenomena.

Keren Su/Corbis

Steve Prezant/Corbis

The Evolutionary Perspective The evolutionary perspective analyzes behavior in terms of how it increases a species' chances to survive and reproduce. Comparing behaviors across species can often lead to new insights about the adaptive function of a particular behavior. For example, close bonds with caregivers are essential to the primate infant's survival—whether that infant is a golden monkey at a wildlife preserve in northern China or a human infant at a family picnic in Norway. As you'll see in later chapters, the evolutionary perspective has been applied to many different areas of psychology, including human relationships, eating behaviors, and emotional responses (Confer & others, 2010; Scott-Phillips & others, 2011).

on to their offspring (Confer & others, 2010). However, as you'll see in later chapters, some of those processes may not necessarily be adaptive in our modern world (Loewenstein, 2010; Tooby & Cosmides, 2008).

Specialty Areas in Psychology

Many people think that psychologists primarily diagnose and treat people with psychological problems or disorders. In fact, psychologists who specialize in *clinical psychology* are trained in the diagnosis, treatment, causes, and prevention of psychological disorders, leading to a doctorate in clinical psychology.

In contrast, **psychiatry** is a medical specialty. A psychiatrist has earned a medical degree, either an M.D. or D.O., followed by several years of specialized training in the treatment of mental disorders. As physicians, psychiatrists can hospitalize people, order biomedical therapies such as *electroconvulsive therapy (ECT)*, and prescribe medications. Clinical psychologists are not medical doctors and cannot order medical treatments. However, a few states have passed legislation allowing clinical psychologists to prescribe medications after specialized training (Riding-Malon & Werth, 2014).

As you'll learn, contemporary psychology is a very diverse discipline that ranges far beyond the treatment of psychological problems. This diversity is reflected in Figure 1.1, which shows the range of specialty areas and employment settings for

FIGURE 1.1 Specialty Areas and Employment Settings The graph on the left shows the specialty areas of individuals who recently received their doctorates in psychology. The category "Other" includes such specialty areas as health psychology, forensic psychology, and sports psychology. The right graph shows psychologists' primary places of employment.

Source: Data from Finno & others (2006); NSF/NIH/USED/USDA/NEH/NASA, 2009 Survey of Earned Doctorates.

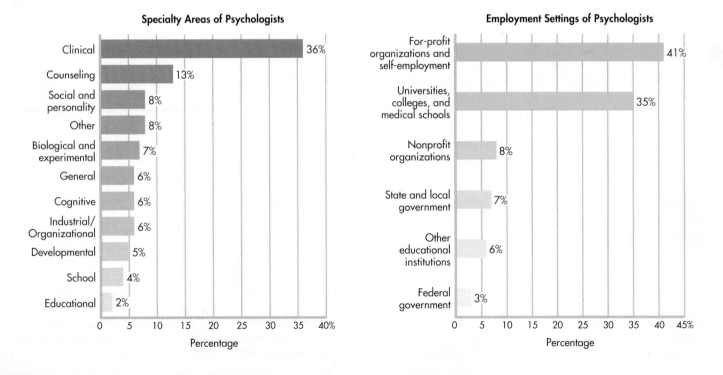

Specialty Areas of Psychologists

Specialty	Percentage
Clinical	36%
Counseling	13%
Social and personality	8%
Other	8%
Biological and experimental	7%
General	6%
Cognitive	6%
Industrial/Organizational	6%
Developmental	5%
School	4%
Educational	2%

Percentage

Employment Settings of Psychologists

Setting	Percentage
For-profit organizations and self-employment	41%
Universities, colleges, and medical schools	35%
Nonprofit organizations	8%
State and local government	7%
Other educational institutions	6%
Federal government	3%

Percentage

TABLE 1.1

Major Specialties in Psychology

Specialty	Major Focus
Biological psychology	Relationship between psychological processes and the body's physical systems; *neuroscience* refers specifically to the study of the brain and the rest of the nervous system.
Clinical psychology	Causes, diagnosis, treatment, and prevention of psychological disorders.
Cognitive psychology	Mental processes, including reasoning and thinking, problem solving, memory, perception, mental imagery, and language.
Counseling psychology	Helping people adjust, adapt, and cope with personal and interpersonal challenges; improving well-being, alleviating distress and maladjustment, and resolving crises.
Developmental psychology	Physical, social, and psychological changes that occur at different ages and stages of the life span.
Educational psychology	Applying psychological principles and theories to methods of learning.
Experimental psychology	Basic psychological processes, including sensation and perception, and principles of learning, emotion, and motivation.
Health psychology	Psychological factors in the development, prevention, and treatment of illness; stress and coping; promoting health-enhancing behaviors.
Industrial/Organizational psychology	The relationship between people and work.
Personality psychology	The nature of human personality, including the uniqueness of each person, traits, and individual differences.
Social psychology	How an individual's thoughts, feelings, and behavior are affected by social environments and the presence of other people.
School psychology	Applying psychological principles and findings in primary and secondary schools.
Applied psychology	Applying the findings of basic psychology to diverse areas; examples include sports psychology, media psychology, forensic psychology, rehabilitation psychology, and military psychology.

psychologists. Table 1.1 provides a brief overview of psychology's most important specialty areas.

› Test your understanding of **Contemporary Psychology** with *LEARNINGCurve*.

The Scientific Method

KEY THEME

The scientific method is a set of assumptions, attitudes, and procedures that guides all scientists, including psychologists, in conducting research.

KEY QUESTIONS

› What assumptions and attitudes are held by psychologists?

› What characterizes each step of the scientific method?

› How does a hypothesis differ from a theory?

Whatever their approach or specialty, psychologists who do research are scientists. And, like other scientists, they rely on the scientific method to guide their research. The **scientific method** refers to a set of assumptions, attitudes, and procedures that

psychiatry Medical specialty area focused on the diagnosis, treatment, causes, and prevention of mental and behavioral disorders.

scientific method A set of assumptions, attitudes, and procedures that guide researchers in creating questions to investigate, in generating evidence, and in drawing conclusions.

empirical evidence Verifiable evidence that is based upon objective observation, measurement, and/or experimentation.

hypothesis (high-POTH-uh-sis) A tentative statement about the relationship between two or more variables; a testable prediction or question.

variable A factor that can vary, or change, in ways that can be observed, measured, and verified.

operational definition A precise description of how the variables in a study will be manipulated or measured.

guide researchers in creating questions to investigate, in generating evidence, and in drawing conclusions.

Like all scientists, psychologists are guided by the basic scientific assumption that *events are lawful.* When this scientific assumption is applied to psychology, it means that psychologists assume that behavior and mental processes follow consistent patterns. Psychologists are also guided by the assumption that *events are explainable.* Thus, psychologists assume that behavior and mental processes have a cause or causes that can be understood through careful, systematic study.

Psychologists are also *open-minded.* They are willing to consider new or alternative explanations of behavior and mental processes. However, their open-minded attitude is tempered by a *healthy sense of scientific skepticism.* That is, psychologists critically evaluate the evidence for new findings, especially those that seem contrary to established knowledge.

The Steps in the Scientific Method
SYSTEMATICALLY SEEKING ANSWERS

Like any science, psychology is based on verifiable or **empirical evidence**—evidence that is the result of objective observation, measurement, and experimentation. As part of the overall process of producing empirical evidence, psychologists follow the four basic steps of the scientific method. In a nutshell, these steps are:

• Formulate a specific question that can be tested.

• Design a study to collect relevant data.

• Analyze the data to arrive at conclusions.

• Report the results.

Following the basic guidelines of the scientific method does not guarantee that valid conclusions will always be reached. However, these steps help guard against bias and minimize the chances for error and faulty conclusions. Let's look at some of the key concepts associated with each step of the scientific method.

STEP 1. FORMULATE A TESTABLE HYPOTHESIS

Once a researcher has identified a question or an issue to investigate, he or she must formulate a hypothesis that can be tested empirically. Formally, a **hypothesis** is a tentative statement that describes the relationship between two or more *variables.* A hypothesis is often stated as a specific prediction that can be empirically tested, such as "strong social networks are associated with greater well-being in college students."

A **variable** is simply a factor that can *vary,* or change. These changes must be capable of being observed, measured, and verified. The psychologist must provide an operational definition of each variable to be investigated. An **operational definition** defines the variable in very specific terms as to how it will be measured, manipulated, or changed. Operational definitions are important because many of the concepts that psychologists investigate—such as memory, happiness, or stress—can be defined and measured in more than one way.

For example, how would you test the hypothesis that "strong social networks are associated with greater well-being in college students"? To test that specific prediction, you would need to formulate an operational definition of each variable. How could you operationally define *social networks? Well-being?* What could you objectively observe and measure?

To investigate the impact of social networks on college students, Adriana Manago and her colleagues (2012) used Facebook data. They operationally defined *network size* as the *participant's number of Facebook friends.* They asked participants to classify their Facebook friends into different categories, such as "close friends," "acquaintances," and "online only" friends. Figure 1.2 shows the percentage of each type of friend in the participants' social networks.

How was *well-being* operationally defined? Manago and her colleagues (2012) used a standard scale that measured life satisfaction. Students rated their agreement on a 5-point scale for nine statements such as "I have a good life" and "I like the way things are going for me." And what did Manago and her colleagues find? Students with larger networks were significantly happier with their lives.

STEP 2. DESIGN THE STUDY AND COLLECT THE DATA

This step involves deciding which research method to use for collecting data. There are two basic types of designs used in research—*descriptive* and *experimental*. Each research approach answers different kinds of questions and provides different kinds of evidence.

Descriptive research includes research strategies for observing and describing behavior, including identifying the factors that seem to be associated with a particular phenomenon. The study by Adriana Manago and her colleagues (2012) on social networks and student well-being is just one example of descriptive research. Descriptive research answers the *who, what, where,* and *when* kinds of questions about behavior. Who engages in a particular behavior? What factors or events seem to be associated with the behavior? Where does the behavior occur? When does the behavior occur? How often does the behavior occur? In the next section, we'll discuss commonly used descriptive methods, including *naturalistic observation, surveys, case studies,* and *correlational studies.*

In contrast, *experimental research* is used to show that one variable causes change in a second variable. In an experiment, the researcher deliberately varies one factor, then measures the changes produced in a second factor. Ideally, all experimental conditions are kept as constant as possible except for the factor that the researcher systematically varies. Then, if changes occur in the second factor, those changes can be attributed to the variations in the first factor.

Are Hands-Free Cell Phones Safer to Use than Regular Cell Phones? Hypotheses are often generated from everyday observations. Many people assume that hands-free devices are safe to use while driving, since they don't require the driver to actually look at the phone or take their hands off the wheel to operate them. But are they? Several studies have found that talking on a hands-free cell phone was just as distracting as talking on a hand-held cell phone (Baumeister & others, 2011; Strayer & others, 2006). Hands-free or not, talking on a cell phone or operating speech-to-text devices while driving were much more distracting than listening to the radio, conversing with a passenger, or listening to music (Strayer & others, 2013). You'll learn why in the discussion of multitasking in Chapter 4.

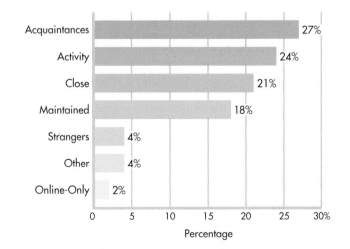

FIGURE 1.2 College Students' Facebook Networks This graph illustrates the percentage of each type of friend in college students' Facebook networks. "Activity" friends were people who shared some activity, such as teammates or co-workers; "maintained" friends were friends from high school or a previous romantic partner. Adriana Manago and her colleagues (2012) found that the proportion of close friends to acquaintances did not make a difference to college students' satisfaction with their lives, but the *number* of friends did. Students with more friends were more satisfied with their lives.

Source: Data from Manago & others (2012).

Ellis Bronte/age fotostock

Success in College: Meta-Analysis Reveals the Most Important Factors Although many factors are implicated in college success, a meta-analysis of over 200 research studies pointed to motivational factors as the strongest predictor of college success (Richardson & others, 2012). The belief that you have the skills and abilities to succeed in college, a trait called *performance self-efficacy,* was more important than high school grades, test scores, and social or economic status.

statistics A branch of mathematics used by researchers to organize, summarize, and interpret data.

statistically significant A mathematical indication that research results are not very likely to have occurred by chance.

meta-analysis A statistical technique that involves combining and analyzing the results of many research studies on a specific topic in order to identify overall trends.

replicate To repeat or duplicate a scientific study in order to increase confidence in the validity of the original findings.

STEP 3. ANALYZE THE DATA AND DRAW CONCLUSIONS

Once observations have been made and measurements have been collected, the raw data need to be analyzed and summarized. Researchers use the methods of a branch of mathematics known as **statistics** to analyze, summarize, and draw conclusions about the data they have collected.

Researchers rely on statistics to determine whether their results support their hypotheses. They also use statistics to determine whether their findings are statistically significant. If a finding is **statistically significant,** it means that the results are not very likely to have occurred by chance. As a rule, statistically significant results confirm the hypothesis. Appendix A provides a more detailed discussion of the use of statistics in psychology research.

Keep in mind that even though a finding is statistically significant, it may not be practically significant. If a study involves a large number of participants, even small differences among groups of subjects may result in a statistically significant finding. But the actual average differences may be so small as to have little practical significance or importance.

For example, Reynol Junco (2012) surveyed nearly two thousand college students and found a statistically significant relationship between grade point average (GPA) and amount of time spent on Facebook: Students who spent a lot of time on Facebook tended to have lower grades than students who spent less time. However, the practical, *real-world* significance of this relationship was low: It turned out that a student had to spend 93 minutes per day more than the average of 106 minutes for the increased time to have even a small (.12 percentage points) impact on GPA. So remember that a statistically significant result is simply one that is not very likely to have occurred by chance. Whether the finding is significant in the everyday sense of being important is another matter altogether.

A statistical technique called *meta-analysis* is sometimes used in psychology to analyze the results of many research studies on a specific topic. **Meta-analysis** involves pooling the results of several studies into a single analysis. By creating one large pool of data to be analyzed, meta-analysis can help reveal overall trends that may not be evident in individual studies.

Meta-analysis is especially useful when a particular issue has generated a large number of studies with inconsistent results. For example, many studies have looked at the factors that predict success in college. British psychologist Michelle Richardson and her colleagues (2012) pooled the results of over 200 research studies investigating personal characteristics that were associated with success in college. "Success in college" was operationally defined as cumulative GPA. They found that *motivational factors* were the strongest predictor of college success, outweighing test scores, high school grades, and socioeconomic status. Especially important was a trait they called *performance self-efficacy,* the belief that you have the skills and abilities to succeed at academic tasks. We'll talk more about self-efficacy in Chapter 8 on motivation and emotion.

STEP 4. REPORT THE FINDINGS

For advances to be made in any scientific discipline, researchers must share their findings with other scientists. In addition to reporting their results, psychologists provide a detailed description of the study itself, including who participated in the study, how variables were operationally defined, how data were analyzed, and so forth.

Describing the precise details of the study makes it possible for other investigators to *replicate,* or repeat, the study. Replication is an important part of the scientific process. When a study is **replicated** and the same basic results are obtained again, scientific confidence that the results are accurate is increased. Conversely, if the replication of a study fails to produce the same basic findings, confidence in the original findings is reduced.

Psychologists present their research at academic conferences or write a paper summarizing the study and submit it to one of the many psychology journals for publication. Before accepting papers for publication, most psychology journals send the paper to other knowledgeable psychologists to review and evaluate. If the study conforms to the principles of sound scientific research and contributes to the existing knowledge base, the paper is accepted for publication.

Throughout this text, you'll see citations that look like the one you encountered in the discussion above on social networks and well-being: "(Manago & others, 2012)." These citations identify the sources of the research and ideas that are being discussed. The citation tells you the author or authors (Manago & others) of the study and the year (2012) in which the study was published. You can find the complete reference in the alphabetized References section at the back of this text. The complete reference lists the authors' full names, the article title, the journal or book in which the article was published, and the DOI, or digital object identifier. The DOI is a permanent Internet "address" for journal articles and other digital works posted on the Internet.

Figure 1.3 shows you how to decipher the different parts of a typical journal reference.

Building Theories
INTEGRATING THE FINDINGS FROM MANY STUDIES

As research findings accumulate from individual studies, eventually theories develop. A **theory,** or *model,* is a tentative explanation that tries to account for diverse findings on the same topic. Note that theories are *not* the same as hypotheses. A hypothesis is a specific question or prediction to be tested. In contrast, a theory integrates and summarizes numerous research findings and observations on a particular topic. Along with explaining existing results, a good theory often generates new predictions and hypotheses that can be tested by further research (Higgins, 2004).

As you encounter different theories, try to remember that theories are *tools* for explaining behavior and mental processes, not statements of absolute fact. Like any

Shawn P. Calhoun

Claude Steele Presenting His Research Along with writing up their research for publication, psychologists also often discuss their research at psychology conferences. Here, Stanford University professor Claude Steele presents his research at the annual meeting of the Association of Psychological Science (APS). Steele's research centers on *stereotype threat,* which refers to the ways that negative stereotypes can affect the performance of people who belong to stigmatized groups. We discuss Steele's influential research in Chapter 7.

theory A tentative explanation that tries to integrate and account for the relationship of various findings and observations.

FIGURE 1.3 How to Read a Journal Reference Using the References section at the back of this text, you can find the complete source for each citation that appears in a chapter. This figure shows the different components of a typical journal reference. In the chapter itself, the citation for this particular reference reads "(Manago & others, 2012)."

Year study published   Authors   Title of study

Manago, Adriana M.; Taylor, Tamara; & Greenfield, Patricia M. (2012). Me and my 400 friends: The anatomy of college students' Facebook networks, their communication patterns, and well-being. *Developmental Psychology,* 48, 369–380. DOI:10.1037/a0026338

Title of scientific journal   Volume number   Page numbers   Digital object identifier

SCIENCE VERSUS PSEUDOSCIENCE

What Is a Pseudoscience?

The word *pseudo* means "fake" or "false." Thus, a pseudoscience is a fake science. More specifically, a **pseudoscience** is a theory, method, or practice that promotes claims in ways that appear to be scientific and plausible even though supporting empirical evidence is lacking or nonexistent (Matute & others, 2011). Surveys have found that pseudoscientific beliefs are common among the general public (National Science Board, 2010).

Do you remember Tyler from our Prologue? He wanted to know whether a magnetic bracelet could help him concentrate or improve his memory. We'll use what we learned about magnet therapy to help illustrate some of the common strategies used to promote pseudosciences.

Magnet Therapy: What's the Attraction?

The practice of applying magnets to the body to supposedly treat various conditions and ailments is called *magnet therapy*. Magnet therapy has been around for centuries. Today, Americans spend an estimated $500 million each year on magnetic bracelets, belts, vests, pillows, and mattresses. Worldwide, the sale of magnetic devices is estimated to be $5 billion per year (Winemiller & others, 2005).

The Internet has been a bonanza for those who market products like magnet therapy. Web sites hail the "scientifically proven healing benefits" of magnet therapy for everything from improving concentration and athletic prowess to relieving stress and curing Alzheimer's disease and schizophrenia (see Johnston, 2008; Parsons, 2007). Treating pain is the most commonly marketed use of magnet therapy. However, reviews of scientific research on magnet therapy consistently conclude that there is no evidence that magnets can relieve pain (National Standard, 2009: National Center for Complementary and Alternative Medicine, 2009).

But proponents of magnet therapy, like those of other pseudoscientific claims, use very effective strategies to create the illusion of scientifically validated products or procedures. Each of

the ploys below should serve as a warning sign that you need to engage your critical and scientific thinking skills.

Strategy 1: Testimonials rather than scientific evidence

Pseudosciences often use testimonials or personal anecdotes as evidence to support their claims. Although they may be sincere and often sound compelling, testimonials are not acceptable scientific evidence. Testimonials lack the basic controls used in scientific research. Many different factors, such as the simple passage of time, could account for a particular individual's response.

Strategy 2: "Sciencey" presentation without scientific substance

Pseudoscientific claims are often peppered with scientific jargon or data to make their claims seem more credible, such as "these

Magnets for concentration and pain relief? Many people use magnetic bracelets to relieve pain or improve focus and concentration. Retired Major League baseball player Ivan "Pudge" Rodriguez credited his magnetic bracelet for helping him keep his balance on the ballfield and relieving the muscle aches that come from a rigorous schedule. How could such claims be empirically tested?

MLB Photos via Getty Images

---

tool, the value of a theory is determined by its usefulness. A useful theory is one that furthers the understanding of behavior, allows testable predictions to be made, and stimulates new research. Often, more than one theory proves to be useful in explaining a particular area of behavior or mental processes, such as the development of personality or the experience of emotion.

It's also important to remember that theories often reflect the *self-correcting nature of the scientific enterprise*. In other words, when new research findings challenge established ways of thinking about a phenomenon, theories are expanded, modified, and even replaced. Thus, as the knowledge base of psychology evolves and changes, theories evolve and change to produce more accurate and useful explanations of behavior and mental processes.

While the conclusions of psychology rest on empirical evidence gathered using the scientific method, the same is not true of *pseudoscientific* claims (J. C. Smith, 2010). As you'll read in the Science Versus Pseudoscience box above, *pseudosciences* often claim to be scientific while ignoring the basic rules of science.

pseudoscience Fake or false science that makes claims based on little or no scientific evidence.

magnets increased biomagnetic balance 84% when worn as directed!" And "sciencey" graphs and technical terms *can* be persuasive, especially to people who value scientific research, making information *seem* true (Tal & Wansink, 2014). Rather than being taken in by scientific-looking graphs or scientific-sounding terms, look for the actual scientific support for the claim that is being made.

Strategy 3: Combining established scientific knowledge with unfounded claims

Pseudosciences often mention well-known scientific facts to add credibility to their unsupported claims. For example, the magnet therapy spiel often starts by referring to the properties of the earth's magnetic field, the fact that blood contains minerals like iron that are attracted to magnets, and so on. Unfortunately, it turns out that the iron in red blood cells is *not* attracted to magnets (Ritchie & others, 2012). Established scientific procedures may also be mentioned, such as magnetic resonance imaging (MRI). For the record, MRI does not use static magnets, which are the type that are found in magnetic jewelry.

Strategy 4: Irrefutable or nonfalsifiable claims

Consider this claim: "Magnet therapy restores the natural magnetic balance required by the body's healing process." How could you test that claim? An *irrefutable* or *nonfalsifiable claim* is one that cannot be disproved or tested in any meaningful way. The irrefutable claims of pseudosciences typically take the form of broad or vague statements that are essentially meaningless.

Strategy 5: Confirmation bias

Scientific conclusions are based on converging evidence from multiple studies, not a single study. Pseudosciences ignore this process and instead trumpet the findings of a single study that seems to support their claims. In doing so, they do *not* mention all the other studies that tested the same thing but yielded results that failed to support the claim. This illustrates **confirmation bias**—the tendency to seek out evidence that confirms an existing belief while ignoring evidence that contradicts or undermines the belief (J. C. Smith, 2010). When disconfirming evidence is pointed out, it is ignored, rationalized, or dismissed.

Strategy 6: Shifting the burden of proof

In science, the responsibility for proving the validity of a claim rests with the person making the claim. Many pseudosciences, however, *shift the burden of proof* to the skeptic. If you express skepticism about a pseudoscientific claim, the pseudoscience advocate will challenge you to *disprove* their claim.

Strategy 7: Multiple outs

What happens when pseudosciences fail to deliver on their promised benefits? Typically, multiple excuses are offered. Privately, Tyler admitted that he hadn't noticed any improvement in his ability to concentrate while wearing the bracelet his girlfriend gave him. But his girlfriend insisted that he simply hadn't worn the bracelet long enough for the magnets to "clear his energy field." Other reasons given when magnet therapy fails to work:

- Magnets act differently on different body parts.
- The magnet was placed in the wrong spot.
- The magnets were the wrong type, size, shape, etc.

One of our goals in this text is to help you develop your scientific thinking skills so you're better able to evaluate claims about behavior or mental processes, especially claims that seem far-fetched or too good to be true. In this chapter, we'll look at the scientific methods used to test hypotheses and claims. And in the Science Versus Pseudoscience boxes in later chapters, you'll see how various pseudoscience claims have stood up to scientific scrutiny. We hope you enjoy this feature!

Descriptive Research

KEY THEME

Descriptive research is used to systematically observe and describe behavior.

KEY QUESTIONS

> What are naturalistic observation and case study research, and why and how are they conducted?

> What is a survey, and why is random selection important in survey research?

> What are the advantages and disadvantages of each descriptive method?

Descriptive research designs include strategies for observing and describing behavior. Using descriptive research designs, researchers can answer important questions, such as when certain behaviors take place, how often they occur, and whether they are related to other factors, such as a person's age, ethnic group, or educational level. As you'll see in this section, descriptive research can provide a wealth of information about behavior, especially behaviors that would be difficult or impossible to study experimentally.

confirmation bias The tendency to seek out evidence that confirms an existing belief while ignoring evidence that might contradict or undermine the belief.

descriptive research Scientific procedures that involve systematically observing behavior in order to describe the relationship among behaviors and events.

Naturalistic Observation: Studying Humans and Animals in Their Natural Settings

Left: In 1980, a single humpback whale was first seen whacking the water with his tail, a foraging technique called "lobtail feeding." Researchers used naturalistic observation to track the spread of this feeding technique throughout a humpback whale population (Allen & others, 2013; de Waal, 2013).

Right: After media reports of aggressive behavior by adult spectators at Canadian youth hockey games, psychologist Anne Bowker and five other observers (2009) systematically recorded the comments of adult spectators at youth hockey games. They found that two-thirds of the comments were directed at the players rather than the officials, and that most comments were positive and encouraging rather than critical.

LaunchPad

Try your hand at collecting and analyzing data by completing **Lab: Naturalistic Observation.**

naturalistic observation The systematic observation and recording of behaviors as they occur in their natural setting.

case study An intensive study of a single individual or small group of individuals.

Naturalistic Observation

THE SCIENCE OF PEOPLE- AND ANIMAL-WATCHING

When psychologists systematically observe and record behaviors as they occur in their natural settings, they are using the descriptive method called **naturalistic observation.** Usually, researchers engaged in naturalistic observation try to avoid being detected by their subjects, whether people or nonhuman animals. The basic goal of naturalistic observation is to detect the behavior patterns that exist naturally—patterns that might not be apparent in a laboratory or if the subjects knew they were being watched.

As you might expect, psychologists very carefully define the behaviors that they will observe and measure before they begin their research. Often, to increase the accuracy of the observations, two or more observers are used. In some studies, observations are recorded so that the researchers can carefully analyze the details of the behaviors being studied.

One advantage of naturalistic observation is that it allows researchers to study human behaviors that cannot ethically be manipulated in an experiment. For example, suppose that a psychologist wants to study bullying behavior in children. It would not be ethical to deliberately create a situation in which one child is aggressively bullied by another child. However, it *would* be ethical to study bullying by observing aggressive behavior in children on a crowded school playground (Drabick & Baugh, 2010).

As a research tool, naturalistic observation can be used wherever patterns of behavior can be openly observed—from the rain forests of the Amazon to restaurants, city streets, and classrooms. Because the observations occur in the natural setting, the results of naturalistic observation studies can be generalized to real-life situations with more confidence than can the results of studies using artificially manipulated or staged situations.

Case Studies

DETAILS, DETAILS, DETAILS

A **case study** is an intensive, in-depth investigation of an individual, a family, or some other social unit. Case studies involve compiling a great deal of information from numerous sources to construct a detailed picture of the person. The individual may be extensively interviewed, and his or her friends, family, and co-workers may be interviewed as well. Psychological and biographical records, neurological and medical records, and even school or work records may be examined. Other sources of information can include psychological testing and observations of the person's behavior. Clinical psychologists and other mental health specialists routinely use case studies to develop a complete profile of a psychotherapy client.

Case studies are also used in psychological research investigating rare, unusual, or extreme conditions. These kinds of case studies often provide psychologists with information that can be used to help understand normal behavior. For example, the Chapter 3 Prologue features the story of Mike May, who partially regained his sight after being blind since early childhood. You'll read how the information gained from extensive testing of Mike's brain and visual abilities has provided insights into brain and visual development in normally sighted individuals.

While case studies can provide invaluable information, they also have limitations. The most important limitation is that the findings on people with rare or unusual conditions might not apply to people in the broader population.

survey A questionnaire or interview designed to investigate the opinions, behaviors, or characteristics of a particular group.

sample A selected segment of the population used to represent the group that is being studied.

representative sample A selected segment that very closely parallels the larger population being studied on relevant characteristics.

random selection Process in which subjects are selected randomly from a larger group such that every group member has an equal chance of being included in the study.

Surveys
(A) ALWAYS (B) SOMETIMES (C) NEVER (D) HUH?

How much time do you spend studying and preparing for class? Is it more, less, or about the same amount of time as other students at your college? Do students in some majors study more than students in other majors?

How could you find out the answers to such questions? A direct way to find out about the behavior, attitudes, and opinions of people is simply to ask them. In a **survey,** people respond to a structured set of questions about their experiences, beliefs, behaviors, or attitudes. One key advantage offered by survey research is that information can be gathered from a much larger group of people than is possible with other research methods.

Typically, surveys involve carefully constructed questionnaires. Questionnaires may be paper, Internet-based, computer-based, or administered in person or over the telephone by a trained interviewer.

Surveys are seldom administered to everyone within the particular group or population under investigation. Instead, researchers usually select a **sample**—a segment of the group or population. Selecting a sample that is representative of the larger group is the key to getting accurate survey results. A **representative sample** very closely parallels, or matches, the larger group on relevant characteristics, such as age, sex, race, marital status, and educational level.

How do researchers select participants so that their sample is representative of the larger group? The most common strategy is to *randomly select* the sample participants. **Random selection** means that every member of the larger group has an equal chance of being selected for inclusion in the sample. To illustrate, let's look at the *National Survey of Student Engagement* (2012), a survey of almost 300,000 U.S. college students and 22,000 Canadian college students. The NSSE surveys college freshmen and seniors about the nature and quality of their educational experience. Table 1.2 shows how the randomly selected sample surveyed in the NSSE compares to the broader population of U.S. undergraduates enrolled in four-year institutions.

What did the NSSE find? Among other findings, they discovered that first-year female students studied more than male students, and online students studied more than on-campus students. Engineering

TABLE 1.2

Comparing a Sample to the Larger Population

	U.S. 4-Year-College Population	NSSE Sample
Enrollment Status		
Full-time	84%	89%
Part-time	16%	14%
Gender		
Female	56%	55%
Male	44%	45%
Race/Ethnicity		
African American/Black	13%	13%
American Indian/Alaska native	1%	1%
Asian/Asian American/Pacific Islander	6%	5%
Caucasian/White	63%	65%
Hispanic	12%	10%
Other	n/a	1%
Multiracial/Multiethnic	3%	3%
International	3%	2%

Source: Data from NSSE, 2012.

How closely did the NSSE sample match important characteristics of U.S. undergraduates enrolled at four-year institutions as a whole? You can see for yourself by comparing the two columns in this table. Clearly, the random selection process used in the NSSE resulted in a sample that very closely approximated the characteristics of the larger population.

correlational study A research strategy that allows the precise calculation of how strongly related two factors are to each other.

correlation coefficient A numerical indication of the magnitude and direction of the relationship (the *correlation*) between two variables.

majors spent the most time preparing for class, while business majors spent the least. The researchers also surveyed faculty about their perceptions of student study habits. Interestingly, students studied *less* than instructors expected but *more* than their instructors believed that they did.

One potential problem with surveys and questionnaires is that people do not always answer honestly, especially when they are asked questions about sexual activity, drug or alcohol use, or illegal activities. The tendency to respond in socially desirable ways can be addressed in a carefully designed survey. One strategy is to rephrase the question and ask for the same information in a different way at different points during the survey. Researchers can then compare the responses to make sure that the participant is responding honestly and consistently. There is some evidence that participants are more likely to respond honestly to Internet or computer-administered surveys than to surveys that are administered in person (Dennis & Li, 2007).

Correlational Studies
LOOKING AT RELATIONSHIPS AND MAKING PREDICTIONS: CAN EATING CURLY FRIES MAKE YOU SMARTER?

KEY THEME

Correlational studies show how strongly two factors are related.

KEY QUESTIONS

> What is a correlation coefficient?

> What is the difference between a positive correlation and a negative correlation?

> Why can't correlational studies be used to demonstrate cause-and-effect relationships?

Along with answering the *who, what, where,* and *when* questions, the data gathered by descriptive research techniques can be analyzed to show how various factors are related. A **correlational study** examines how strongly two variables are related to, or associated with, each other. Correlations can be used to analyze the data gathered by any type of descriptive method, and are also used to analyze the results of experiments.

To illustrate, let's look at a correlational study conducted by psychologists Marissa K. Hartwig and John Dunlosky (2012). Hartwig and Dunlosky were interested in identifying the study habits most strongly linked to academic success. They surveyed 324 college students at a large state university. They used self-reported GPA as the operational definition of *academic achievement*. Figure 1.4 shows some of the survey results. Once the data were collected, Hartwig and Dunlosky used a statistical procedure to calculate a figure called a *correlation coefficient*.

A **correlation coefficient** is a numerical indicator of the strength of the relationship between two factors. A correlation coefficient always falls in the range from

FIGURE 1.4 Study Strategies and Grade-Point Average The graph shows the percentages of students reporting regular use of self-testing, according to grade-point average (GPA). The most common reason for self-testing was to determine how well information had been learned.

Source: Data from Hartwig & Dunlosky, 2012.

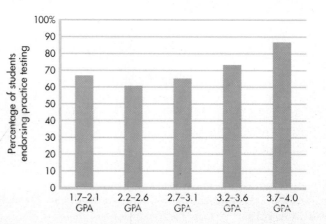

−1.00 to +1.00. The correlation coefficient has two parts—the number and the sign. The number indicates the *strength* of the relationship, and the sign indicates the *direction* of the relationship between the two variables.

More specifically, the closer a correlation coefficient is to 1.00, whether it is positive or negative, the stronger the correlation or association is between the two factors. Hence, a correlation coefficient of +.90 or −.90 represents a very strong association, meaning that the two factors almost always occur together. A correlation coefficient of +.10 or −.10 represents a very weak correlation, meaning that the two factors seldom occur together. (Correlation coefficients are discussed in greater detail in Appendix A on statistics, at the back of this book.)

Notice that correlation coefficients do not function like the algebraic number line. A correlation of −.80 represents a stronger relationship than does a correlation of +.10. The plus or minus sign in a correlation coefficient simply tells you the direction of the relationship between the two variables.

A **positive correlation** is one in which the two factors vary in the *same* direction. That is, the two factors increase or decrease together. For example, Hartwig and Dunlosky (2012) found that there was a strong positive correlation between GPA and use of self-testing as a study strategy. That is, as the use of self-testing *increased,* so did GPA. Other study strategies, such as using flashcards, rereading, or highlighting, were *not* associated with an increase in GPA. Wondering why not? Stay tuned—we'll discuss that very question in the Psych for Your Life section at the end of the chapter.

In contrast, a **negative correlation** is one in which the two variables move in opposite directions: As one factor decreases, the other increases. In a study investigating the relationship between multitasking and GPA, Reynol Junco and Shelia Cotten (2012) found that there was a *negative correlation* between time spent sending text messages while studying and GPA: As time spent texting while studying *increased,* GPA *decreased*.

What can we conclude about the relationship between academic achievemen and sending texts while studying? Or GPA and self-testing? Does the evidence allow us to conclude that texting while studying *causes* a decrease in grade-point average? Or that using self-testing as a study strategy *causes* people to achieve higher GPAs?

Not necessarily. Consider the negative correlation between GPA and time spent texting while studying. It could be that a third variable was responsible for the associations between texting and GPA. Perhaps students who send texts while studying do so because they lack academic motivation, or are uninterested in the subject matter. In other words, it might be that a lack of academic motivation or interest, rather than sending texts, was actually responsible for the lower grades.

Similarly, consider the positive correlation between self-testing and GPA. We cannot conclude that using self-tests in itself *causes* an increase in GPA. It's entirely possible that people who are more academically motivated are also more likely to actively test their mastery of class material, which after all, takes more effort than simply rereading or highlighting material in a textbook. Thus, it could be that highly motivated students are more likely to use self-testing as a study strategy than students who are less motivated.

Here is the critical point: Even if two factors are very strongly correlated, *correlation does not necessarily indicate causality.* A correlation tells you only that two factors seem to be related or that they co-vary in a systematic way. Although two factors may be very strongly correlated, correlational studies cannot be used to demonstrate a true cause-and-effect relationship. As you'll see in the next section, the experimental method is the only scientific strategy that can provide compelling evidence of a cause-and-effect relationship between two variables.

❯ Test your understanding of **The Scientific Method and Descriptive Research Methods** with *LEARNINGCurve*.

positive correlation A finding that two factors vary systematically in the same direction, increasing or decreasing together.

negative correlation A finding that two factors vary systematically in opposite directions, one increasing as the other decreases.

Will Eating Curly Fries Make You Intelligent? British psychologists Michal Kosinski and his colleagues (2013) studied 58,000 Facebook users who had agreed to share their preferences, and found some interesting correlations between Facebook "likes" and personality traits. Some associations were not surprising, such as a strong association between being outgoing and liking dancing. But what about the strong positive correlation between intelligence and liking curly fries and Morgan Freeman's voice? Can you conclude that eating curly fries or listening to Morgan Freeman causes high intelligence? No. Even though a strong positive correlation exists, you cannot conclude that one causes the other.

James McQuillan/Getty Images

experimental research A method of investigation used to demonstrate cause-and-effect relationships by purposely manipulating one factor thought to produce change in another factor.

independent variable The purposely manipulated factor thought to produce change in an experiment; also called the *treatment variable.*

dependent variable The factor that is observed and measured for change in an experiment, thought to be influenced by the independent variable; also called the *outcome variable.*

confounding variable A factor or variable other than the ones being studied that, if not controlled, could affect the outcome of an experiment; also called an *extraneous variable.*

random assignment The process of assigning participants to experimental conditions so that all participants have an equal chance of being assigned to any of the conditions or groups in the study.

control group or control condition In an experiment, the group of participants who are exposed to all experimental conditions, except the independent variable; the group against which changes in the experimental group are compared.

experimental group or experimental condition In an experiment, the group of participants who are exposed to all experimental conditions, including the independent variable.

Experimental Research

KEY THEME

The experimental method is used to demonstrate a cause-and-effect relationship between two variables.

KEY QUESTIONS

> What roles do the independent variable and dependent variable play in an experiment?
> What is the testing effect?
> How can experimental controls help minimize the effects of confounding variables?

In this chapter, we've noted a number of factors that are associated with higher or lower college grades. But all of these factors—such as time spent sending texts and on Facebook—are *correlational,* meaning that while they are linked, they do not necessarily indicate that the two factors are causally related.

In contrast to descriptive research and correlational studies, **experimental research** is used to demonstrate a cause-and-effect relationship between changes in one variable and the effect that is produced on another variable. Conducting an experiment involves deliberately varying one factor, which is called the **independent variable,** sometimes called the *treatment variable.* The researcher then measures the changes, if any, that are produced in a second factor, called the **dependent variable,** also called the *outcome variable.* The dependent variable is so named because changes in it "depend on" variations in the independent variable.

To the greatest degree possible, all other conditions in the experiment are kept exactly the same for all participants. Thus, when the data are analyzed, any changes that are measured in the dependent variable can be attributed to the deliberate manipulation of the independent variable. In this way, an experiment can provide evidence of a cause-and-effect relationship between the independent and dependent variables.

In designing experiments, psychologists try to anticipate and control for **confounding variables.** Also called *extraneous variables,* these factors are *not* the focus of the experiment. However, confounding variables might produce inaccurate experimental results by influencing changes in the dependent variable. Confounding variables in a psychology experiment could include unwanted variability in such factors as age, gender, ethnic background, race, health, occupation, personal habits, education, and so on.

To illustrate how experimental research works, let's look at a topic of interest to most college students: What types of study strategies are most effective?

In most educational settings, learning is thought to take place during study, instruction, and practice. Tests, in contrast, are neutral experiences and simply assess what has been learned. But some studies seemed to suggest that being tested on new information helped students learn and remember it better than simply studying it (see Roediger & Butler, 2011). Psychologists Henry Roediger and Jeffrey Karpicke (2006) set out to investigate the effects of testing on learning and memory.

Experimental Design
STUDYING THE EFFECTS OF TESTING

How could you design an experiment to show a difference between learning due to studying and learning due to testing? Roediger and Karpicke (2006) designed an experiment that compared the effects of repeated testing with the effects of repeated study periods. They predicted that students who repeatedly took tests after studying would have better long-term memory of the new information than students who repeatedly studied, but were not tested on, the same material. The hypothesis, then, was that "repeated testing improves learning more than repeated studying."

The participants were 60 college under-graduates, aged 18 to 24. The researchers used *random assignment* to assign participants to one of two groups: either the *experimental group* or the *control group*. **Random assignment** means that all the participants have an equal chance of being assigned to any of the experimental conditions. Random assignment helps ensure that any potential differences among the participants are spread out evenly across all experimental conditions. Random assignment also helps minimize the possibility of bias because the same criteria are used to assign all participants to the different experimental conditions.

In any well-designed experiment, there is at least one control group. The **control group** serves as a baseline against which changes in the experimental group can be compared. In a typical experiment, the participants assigned to the control group go through all the experimental phases but are *not* exposed to the independent variable. Only the participants in the **experimental group** are exposed to the *independent variable*. In this study, the independent variable was *repeated testing*. The *dependent variable* was the score earned on a final test.

Here's how the experiment was conducted. All of the participants were given a short prose passage to study. Participants in the *control group* read the passage for five minutes, and took a two-minute break. They then studied the passage again for five minutes before taking another two-minute break. They repeated this process for a total of four consecutive study periods. Note that this is the standard test-preparation method: to repeatedly study the same material until you feel certain that you have mastered it.

Participants in the *experimental group* were given the same prose passage to learn. They were also allotted five minutes to study the passage, and then took a two-minute break. But rather than restudying the passage, they took a test on the material: They were given a blank sheet of paper and were allowed ten minutes to write down as much information from the prose passage as they could remember. After another two-minute break, without studying the material again, they were given the same test, followed by a two-minute break. This procedure was followed for a total of one study period and three test periods. Figure 1.5 shows the setup of the experiment.

At the end of the session, all of the participants filled out a short questionnaire asking them to predict how well they would remember the material in a week. A week later, all participants were tested on the material.

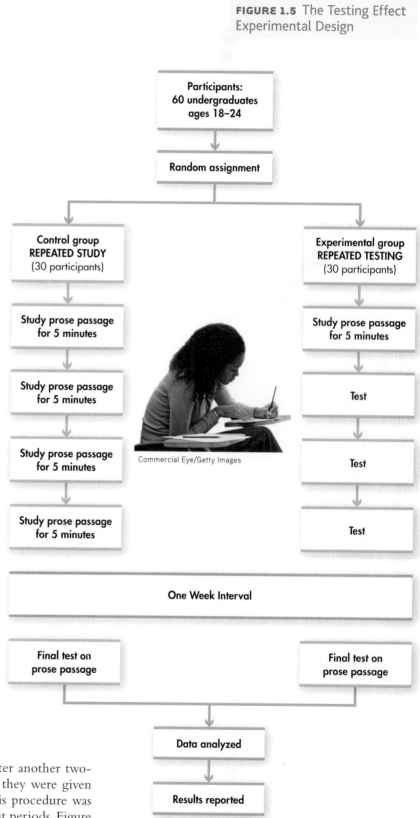

FIGURE 1.5 The Testing Effect Experimental Design

Commercial Eye/Getty Images

FIGURE 1.6 Effects of Testing on Retention: Experimental Results
One week after the experimental sessions concluded, participants were tested to see how much they retained from material they had studied. As you can see, the participants who were repeatedly tested remembered much more of the information than the students who had repeatedly studied the same material.

Source: Data from Roediger & Karpicke, 2006.

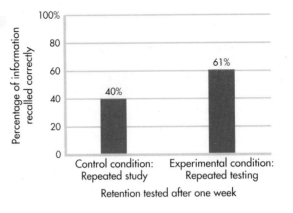

MYTH ◀ SCIENCE
Is it true that reading something over and over is the most effective way to prepare for a test?

How do you think the two groups would compare on a test of their retention of the material a week later? Conventional wisdom would suggest that the control group members, who studied the material in four periods for a total of twenty minutes, would have learned the material much better than the participants in the experimental group, who, after all, had only studied the material for a total of five minutes.

Figure 1.6 shows the results on the test one week later. Despite having studied the material only one-fourth as long as the control group, the experimental group trounced the control group: They remembered 61% of the material in the passage while the control group remembered only 40%. Interestingly, the control group participants were much more confident of their ability to remember the information than the experimental group.

Were you surprised by the results? In fact, the basic results have been replicated by many different researchers (see Bjork & others, 2013; Rowland, 2014). Multiple studies have supported what has been dubbed the **testing effect:** the finding that practicing retrieval of information from memory produces better retention than restudying the same information for an equivalent amount of time. In other words, testing—rather than simply being a neutral assessment of what has been learned—is a powerful learning tool in its own right (Carpenter, 2012; Roediger & Nestojiko, 2015).

We'll discuss some of the reasons for the testing effect in Chapter 6, Memory. In Psych for Your Life at the end of this chapter, we'll describe some of the other ways in which the testing effect has been explored. And, we'll discuss additional ways in which you can use psychological research to improve your own memory for new information.

Experimental Controls

Some experiments involve extra controls to increase the reliability of their findings. One important safeguard is the **double-blind technique,** which is often used when researchers are testing the effectiveness of a procedure or drug treatment. In a double-blind study, both the participants and the researchers interacting with them are *blind,* or unaware of the treatment or condition to which the participants have been assigned.

Using a double-blind technique helps guard against the possibility that the researcher inadvertently becomes an extraneous or confounding variable in the study. This can happen when a researcher, without realizing it, displays **demand characteristics.** These are subtle cues or signals that can bias the outcome of the study by communicating the behavior or response that is expected of the participants. A behavior as subtle as the researcher slightly smiling or frowning when dealing with some participants, but not others, could bias the outcome of a study.

testing effect The finding that practicing retrieval of information from memory produces better retention than restudying the same information for an equivalent amount of time.

double-blind technique An experimental control in which neither the participants nor the researchers interacting with the participants are aware of the group or condition to which the participants have been assigned.

demand characteristics In a research study, subtle cues or signals expressed by the researcher that communicate the kind of response or behavior that is expected from the participant.

Such studies also often involve the use of a **placebo,** which is a so-called "sugar pill" or other inactive substance or procedure. Although it is inactive, a placebo can produce real effects (see Wager & Atlas, 2015). A **placebo effect** is any change that can be attributed to beliefs and expectations rather than to an actual drug, treatment, or procedure.

For example, one student in our class asked us whether we believed that the herb ginkgo biloba could improve memory. To test that notion, psychologist Paul Solomon and his colleagues (2002) used a placebo in a double-blind study to test whether ginkgo biloba improved memory and concentration in older adults. Participants in the experimental group took the manufacturer's recommended daily dosage of ginkgo biloba for six weeks, while those in the control group took an identical dosage of placebo capsules.

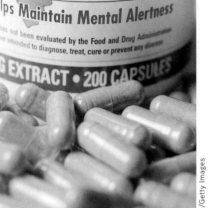

Joe Raedle/Getty Images

Can Ginkgo Biloba Enhance Your Mental Abilities? The herbal supplement *ginkgo biloba* is marketed as a "cognitive enhancer" that supposedly improves memory, alertness, and concentration, especially in older adults. However, studies of ginkgo don't support those claims (see Canter & Ernst, 2007; Daffner, 2010; Snitz & others, 2009).

The researchers who interacted with the participants did not know which participants received the real and which received the fake ginkgo biloba. The researchers who did know the group assignments did *not* interact with or evaluate the participants. Memory and other cognitive abilities were assessed at the beginning and end of the six-week study.

Can you predict the results of the ginkgo biloba experiment? At the end of the six-week study, the test scores of *both* groups rose. However, there were no significant differences between the improvement in the ginkgo biloba and placebo groups. So why did both groups improve? The researchers concluded that it was probably due to the *practice effect*. The participants' experience with the tests—the practice they got by simply taking the mental ability tests twice—was the most likely reason that test scores improved in both groups. This experiment illustrates the importance of the control group: Without a control group to compare, the improvement in the experimental group might have been attributed to the drug. But since the control group participants *also* improved, there must have been another explanation.

Limitations of Experiments and Variations in Experimental Design

A well-designed and carefully executed experiment can provide convincing evidence of a cause-and-effect relationship between the independent and dependent variables. But experiments do have limitations. Because experiments are often conducted in highly controlled laboratory situations, they are sometimes criticized for having little to do with actual behavior. That is, the results may not *generalize* well, meaning that the results cannot be applied to real-world situations or to more general populations beyond the participants in the study. To minimize this, experiments are sometimes carried out in natural settings, rather than in a laboratory. A second potential limitation is that the phenomena the researchers want to study may be impossible or unethical to control experimentally

But researchers are sometimes able to take advantage of naturally occurring events or conditions. In a **natural experiment,** researchers carefully observe and measure the impact of a naturally occurring event or condition on their study participants

placebo A fake substance, treatment, or procedure that has no known direct effects.

placebo effect Any change attributed to a person's beliefs and expectations rather than to an actual drug, treatment, or procedure.

natural experiment A study investigating the effects of a naturally occurring event on the research participants.

Using a Natural Experiment to Study the "Freshman Fifteen" Research shows that many college freshman *do* gain weight, although it is typically closer to five pounds than fifteen (Holm-Denoma & others, 2008). Kandice Kapinos and Olga Yakusheva (2011) used a natural experiment to study the effect of environmental factors on weight gain in college freshmen. Not surprisingly, freshman students who lived in a dorm with an on-site snack bar or cafeteria were more likely to eat more and gain weight than freshmen who had to walk across campus for meals and snacks.

Suzanne DeChillo/The New York Times/Redux

Think Like a SCIENTIST

Could you have been part of an experiment without realizing it? Go to LaunchPad: Resources to **Think Like a Scientist** about **Contagious Online Emotions.**

LaunchPad

critical thinking The active process of minimizing preconceptions and biases while evaluating evidence, determining the conclusions that can reasonably be drawn from evidence, and considering alternative explanations for research findings or other phenomena.

(Rutter, 2008). Although not true experiments, psychologists can use natural experiments to study the effects of disasters, epidemics, or other events.

Sometimes natural experiments involve everyday settings. Psychologists Kandice Kapinos and Olga Yakusheva (2011) were interested in better understanding the relationship between environmental factors and weight gain. Previous research had shown that environmental factors, such as high concentrations of fast-food restaurants, *are* correlated with the average weight of nearby residents (Inagami & others, 2009). However, since the research was correlational, it wasn't possible to conclude that proximity of fast-food restaurants *caused* weight gain. It could be that people with unhealthy eating habits were more likely to choose to live in neighborhoods with easy access to fast food.

Of course, researchers can't randomly assign large numbers of participants to long-term living situations. But Kapinos and Yakusheva identified a naturally occurring situation in which people *are* randomly assigned to housing—college dormitories.

College freshmen do tend to gain weight during their first year away from home—the so-called "freshman fifteen"—although the weight gain is typically closer to five pounds (Holm-Denoma & others, 2008). Kapinos and Yakusheva took advantage of the naturally occurring conditions on their own college campus by comparing weight changes in freshmen who lived in dorms with on-site cafeterias and snack bars with weight changes in freshman who lived in dorms that did *not* have on-site food services. Since freshmen were randomly assigned to the dormitories, the researchers could safely assume that there wasn't some other factor that might cause differences between the two groups.

What did Kapinos and Yakusheva (2011) find? Female students who were assigned to dormitories with on-site dining facilities gained more weight and exercised less than students who were assigned to dormitories without food services. Male students assigned to dormitories with food services reported eating more meals and more snacks, but did not report gaining weight. Kapinos and Yakusheva (2011) concluded that campus design *did* play a significant role in influencing healthy—and unhealthy—behaviors in college students.

Before leaving the topic of research methods, one contemporary trend deserves special mention: the increasing use of brain-imaging techniques in virtually every area of psychology. To help highlight the importance of neuroscience, every chapter includes a special "Focus on Neuroscience" feature. This chapter's Focus on Neuroscience explores brain-imaging techniques and discusses their increasing use in psychological research (see pp. 34–35).

This brief introduction to research methods will give you some idea of how psychologists conduct research. But we hope it also illustrates some of the ways in which scientists—and others—evaluate claims and evidence. In the Critical Thinking box "Think Like a Scientist," we offer several suggestions to help you evaluate claims that you encounter both inside and outside the classroom.

How to Think Like a Scientist

Do violent video games make people aggressive? Are some people "right-brained" and others "left-brained"? What's the best way to lose weight? Do "educational" DVDs and TV shows improve children's language abilities or help them learn how to read?

How can you evaluate the claims you encounter? Both in class and out, it's important to engage in **critical thinking,** *actively questioning* statements rather than blindly accepting them.

Critical thinkers are open to new information, ideas, and claims. However, this open-mindedness is tempered by a healthy sense of skepticism (J. C. Smith, 2010). The critical thinker consistently asks, "What evidence supports this claim?"

In this chapter, we've detailed the ways that psychologists conduct research, including the different ways they test hypotheses. You can think of the claims you encounter in print or in online media, on TV shows, or in conversation as hypotheses, too. In other words, when you encounter an idea or statement that is presented as factual, try to *think like a scientist.*

Like a scientist, you can follow these four steps to determine the validity of a particular claim:

1. Identify the Claim

Some claims are so vague that they are impossible to be tested scientifically. For example, take the statement that "you use only 10% of your brain." Superficially, it *sounds* convincing, but can you imagine an experiment that would actually test this claim? Try to restate the claim in terms of a hypothesis that could be supported or disproved by empirical evidence. How would you define the variables that could be objectively measured?

2. Evaluate the Evidence

As you have learned, the scientific method includes key safeguards in experimental design, such as random assignment, the presence of a control group, and researchers who are "blind" to participants' conditions. So when evidence is offered in support of a particular position, scrutinize it and look for those basic safeguards.

MYTH ◄ SCIENCE

Is it true that when two behaviors are "linked," "related," or tend to occur together it's safe to assume that one behavior caused the other?

Consider also the nature of the evidence that may be offered. When words like "link," "tie," or "association" are used, the evidence is probably correlational, rather than experimental. But remember the distinction between correlation and causation. As you have learned, just because two events are correlated does not mean that they are causally linked. For example, consider a recent study that found a positive correlation between the number of outdoor signs and billboards advertising food and non-alcoholic beverages and the rate of obesity in particular urban neighborhoods (Lesser & others, 2013). As the number of outdoor food ads increased, so did the obesity rate. One Internet headline read, "Billboards Make You Fat!" Some commentators advised that policy makers consider restricting outdoor food advertising as a way of reducing obesity in urban areas.

But is such a conclusion justified? *No.* You cannot conclude that the correlation found between obesity and advertisements occurred because the higher prevalence of advertising caused higher rates of obesity. The evidence does not support that conclusion. In fact, it could just as likely be that advertisers are more likely to place ads for food in areas where they believe there are higher numbers of obese people (Chabris & Simons, 2013).

Similarly, remember that *testimonials are not evidence* (Coltheart & MacArthur, 2012). Distinguish between empirical evidence that can be objectively observed, measured, and shared—and private opinions, based on feelings or personal experience. For example, the fact that a relative's child had a terrible experience in day care is not evidence that day care is generally bad for all children.

3. Consider Alternative Explanations

Especially if a claim is highly unusual, seems to contradict accepted scientific theories, or has no plausible explanation, *consider alternative explanations.* A claim demonstrating improvement in a condition or skill could, in fact, have many different explanations. For example, suppose a friend's cold disappeared after he took a special herbal supplement recommended by another friend. The improvement *could* be due to the herbs. But it could also be due to the placebo effect (page 29) or to the natural healing that often takes place with the simple passage of time. A child's improvement in paying attention in class *might* be due to the new, sugar-restricted diet she started. But it could also be the result of normal maturation, or the extra attention she received from her teacher after her parents expressed their concerns.

4. Consider the Source of the Research or Claim

Typically, scientific research is reported in a peer-reviewed scientific journal or at an academic conference *before* the results are released to the media. So, when research is reported in the popular media or on the Internet, consider the source of the research. While publication in a scientific journal is no guarantee that the results will prove valid over time, you can at least be certain that the research has been carefully evaluated by other scientists in the field. When a claim has no apparent ties to legitimate educational or scientific enterprises, you should be especially cautious. In general, it's worth considering the researchers' motives. If the people or company making the claim have the potential to profit from its use, the source may not be objective.

Whether the claims you encounter come from friends, instructors, or pundits, remember these four steps—and think like a scientist before blindly accepting them.

CRITICAL THINKING QUESTIONS

- Why might other people want to discourage you from thinking critically?

- In what situations is it probably most difficult or challenging for you to exercise critical thinking skills? Why?

- What can you do or say to encourage others to use critical thinking in evaluating questionable claims or assertions?

Psychological Research Using Brain Imaging

Brain-scan images have become so commonplace in news articles and popular magazines that it's easy to forget just how revolutionary brain-imaging technology has been in the field of psychology (Mather & others, 2013a, b). Here, we'll look at three commonly used brain-imaging techniques and examine how they're used in psychological research.

Positron emission tomography, abbreviated **PET,** is based on the fact that increased activity in a particular brain region is associated with increased blood flow and energy consumption. A small amount of radioactively tagged glucose, oxygen, or other substance is injected into the person's bloodstream. Then, the person lies in a PET scanner while performing some mental task. For several minutes, the PET scanner tracks the amounts of radioactive substance used in thousands of different brain regions. A computer analyzes the data, producing color-coded images of the brain's activity.

Magnetic resonance imaging (MRI) does not involve invasive procedures such as injections of radioactive substances. Instead, while the person lies inside a magnetic tube, powerful but harmless magnetic fields bombard the brain. A computer analyzes the electromagnetic signals generated by brain-tissue molecules in response to the magnetic fields. The result is a series of digital images, each a detailed "slice" of the brain's structures. MRI scans are routinely used to produce detailed images of other body parts, such as joints, spine, or organs.

Functional MRI (fMRI) combines the ability to produce a detailed image of the brain's structures with the capacity to track the brain's activity or functioning (K. Smith, 2012). While the person lies in the MRI scanner, a powerful computer tracks the electromagnetic signals that are generated by changes in the brain's metabolic activity, such as increased blood flow to a particular brain region. By measuring the ebb and flow of oxygenated blood in the brain, an fMRI produces a series of scans that show detailed moment-by-moment "movies" of the brain's changing activity in specific structures or regions.

In the study of brain activity, fMRI has several advantages over PET scan technology. Because fMRI is a noninvasive procedure and the magnetic waves are harmless, research participants can safely undergo repeated fMRI scans. Also, fMRI produces a much sharper image than PET scans and can detail much smaller brain structures. Another advantage of fMRI is that it provides a picture of brain activity averaged over seconds rather than the several minutes required by PET scans.

How Psychologists Use Brain-Imaging Technology

Brain imaging is used for both descriptive and experimental research. A descriptive study using brain scans might compare the brain structure or functioning of one carefully defined group of people with another.

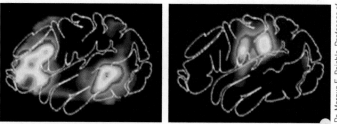

Unpracticed   Practiced

Positron Emission Tomography (PET) PET scans provide color-coded images of the brain's activity. This example shows the comparison between subjects learning a new language task (left) and performing the language task after it has been well learned (right). Red and yellow colors highlight areas with the highest level of activity, while green and blue colors indicate lower levels of brain activity. As you can see, the process of practicing and learning a new language task involves more and different brain areas before becoming established.

For example, MRI scans were used to compare London taxi drivers with matched participants who were not taxi drivers (Maguire & others, 2000, 2006). In order to be licensed, London taxi drivers are required to have an encyclopedic knowledge of the city streets. The MRI scans showed that a brain structure involved in spatial memory, the *hippocampus,* was significantly larger in the experienced taxi drivers than in the control subjects (see MRI scans on the next page). And, the size of the hippocampus was also positively correlated with the length of time the participants had been driving taxis in London: The longer the individual had been driving a taxi, the larger the hippocampus (Woollett & others, 2009). In Chapter 2, Neuroscience and Behavior, we'll look at how the brain changes in response to learning and environmental influences.

Brain-imaging technology can also be used in experimental research, such as a study of the effects of sleep deprivation that we'll discuss in Chapter 4 (see pages 146–147). In a typical experiment, brain scans are taken while research participants are exposed to the experimental treatment or task. These scans are compared to scans taken of control group participants. The differences between the two sets of scans are assumed to be due to the experimental treatment or condition. When multiple participants are compared, researchers combine results to produce a composite scan showing the average differences among the experimental groups.

Limitations of Brain-Imaging Studies

Images are becoming even more detailed as brain-imaging technology advances. Nevertheless, brain-imaging research has several limitations (Miller, 2010; Satel & Lilienfeld, 2013). When you consider the results of brain-imaging studies, including those presented in this textbook, keep the following points in mind:

positron emission tomography (PET) scan An invasive imaging technique that provides color-coded images of brain activity by tracking the brain's use of a radioactively tagged compound, such as glucose, oxygen, or a drug.

magnetic resonance imaging (MRI) A noninvasive imaging technique that produces highly detailed images of the body's structures and tissues, using electromagnetic signals generated by the body in response to magnetic fields.

Hippocampus, Vol. 16, 2006, p. 1097. Reprinted with permission of Wiley-Liss, Inc., a subsidiary of John Wiley & Sons, Inc.

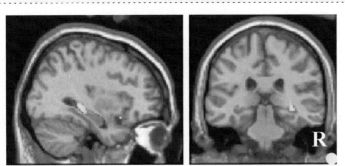

Magnetic Resonance Imaging (MRI) MRI scans produce a highly detailed image of the brain, showing "slices" of the brain from different angles. The yellow dots highlight the brain region that was significantly larger in experienced London taxi drivers, known for their encyclopedic memory of London streets, as compared to control subjects (Maguire & others, 2000, 2006). This region, called the *hippocampus*, is known to be involved in forming new memories. This landmark study provided solid evidence for the once-revolutionary idea that structures in the adult brain change in response to experience and learning.

1. *Brain-imaging studies usually involve a small number of subjects.* Because of the limited availability and the high cost of the technology, many brain-imaging studies have fewer than a dozen participants. With any research involving a small number of participants, caution must be exercised in generalizing results to a wider population (Button & others, 2013).

2. *Brain imaging studies tend to focus on simple aspects of behavior.* Even seemingly simple tasks involve the smooth coordination of multiple brain regions. As Jerome Kagan (2008) observes, "An event as simple as the unexpected sound of a whistle activates 24 different brain areas." Thus, it's naïve to think that complex psychological or behavioral functions can be mapped to a single brain center (Coltheart, 2013; Mather & others, 2013b).

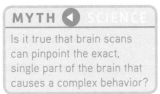

MYTH ◀ SCIENCE

Is it true that brain scans can pinpoint the exact, single part of the brain that causes a complex behavior?

3. *Brain imaging may not increase understanding of a psychological process.* For example, although brain imaging might point to a particular brain structure as being involved in, say, fear or romantic love, knowing this may not advance our understanding of the psychological experience of fear or romantic love (Decety & Cacioppo, 2010).

4. *Brain imaging is not necessarily a more "scientific" explanation.* As psychologist Paul Bloom (2006) points out, "Functional MRI seems more like 'real' science than many of the other things that psychologists are up to. It has all the trappings of work with great laboratory credibility: big, expensive, and potentially dangerous machines, hospitals and medical centers, and a lot of people in white coats." To be truly

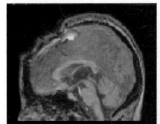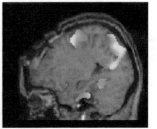

Patient

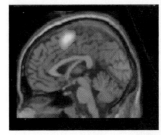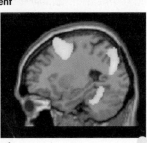

Controls

Owen, A.M., et al. "Detecting awareness in the vegetative state." Science 313 (2006):1402. Reprinted with permission from AAAS.

Functional Magnetic Resonance Imaging (fMRI) fMRI combines highly detailed images of brain structures with moment-by-moment tracking of brain activity. Here, fMRI was used to record the brain activity of a 23-year-old woman who had been unresponsive to external stimuli for five months following an auto accident (Owen & others, 2006). Researchers asked her to first imagine playing tennis, and then to imagine walking through her house. The scans above compare her brain activity to that of normal volunteers ("controls") performing the same tasks. In both the patient and the controls, regions known to be involved in movement and spatial navigation were active. The fMRI scans confirmed that the patient was conscious of her surroundings and able to respond to spoken commands.

useful, brain-activity snapshots of a particular behavior must be accurately interpreted within the context of existing psychological knowledge about the behavior (Beck, 2010; Kihlstrom, 2010).

Looking at Brain-Scan Images

What should you notice when you look at the brain-scan images in this text? First, read the text description so you understand the task or condition being measured. Second, read the brain-scan caption for specific details or areas to notice. Third, carefully compare the treatment scan with the control scan if both are shown. Fourth, keep the limitations of brain-scan technology in mind. Finally, remember that human experience is much too complex to be captured by a single snapshot of brain activity (Miller, 2010).

functional magnetic resonance imaging (fMRI) A noninvasive imaging technique that uses magnetic fields to map brain activity by measuring changes in the brain's blood flow and oxygen levels.

comparative psychology The branch of psychology that studies the behavior of different animal species.

Ethics in Psychological Research

KEY THEME

Psychological research conducted in the United States is subject to ethical guidelines developed by the American Psychological Association (APA).

KEY QUESTIONS

❯ What are five key provisions of the APA ethics code for research involving humans?

❯ Why do psychologists sometimes conduct research with nonhuman animal subjects?

You might wonder what would happen if you were to volunteer to participate in a psychology experiment or study. Are psychologists allowed to manipulate or control you without your knowledge or consent? Could a psychologist force you to reveal your innermost secrets? Could he or she administer electric shocks?

The answer to all of these questions is "no." The American Psychological Association (APA) has developed a strict code of ethics for conducting research with both human and animal subjects. This code is contained in a document called *Ethical Principles of Psychologists and Code of Conduct* (APA, 2002, 2010). You can download a copy of the document at the Web site www.apa.org/ethics.

In general, psychologists must respect the dignity and welfare of participants. Psychologists cannot deceptively expose research participants to conditions that might cause either physical or emotional harm. At most institutions, any psychological research using human or animal subjects is scrutinized by an institutional review board before approval is granted (Fisher & Vacanti-Shova, 2012).

Here are highlights of five key provisions in the most recent APA ethical principles regulating research with human participants:

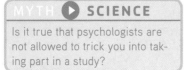

MYTH ▶ SCIENCE

Is it true that psychologists are not allowed to trick you into taking part in a study?

- **Informed consent and voluntary participation.** The psychologist must inform the participants of the purpose of the research, including significant factors that might influence a person's willingness to participate in the study, such as potential risks, discomfort, or unpleasant emotional experiences. The psychologist must also explain that participants are free to decline to participate or to withdraw from the research at any time.

- **Students as research participants.** When research participation is a course requirement or an opportunity for extra credit, the student must be given the choice of an alternative activity to fulfill the course requirement or earn extra credit.

- **The use of deception.** Psychologists can use deceptive techniques as part of the study only when two conditions have been met: (1) when it is not feasible to use alternatives that do not involve deception and (2) when the potential findings justify the use of deception because of their scientific, educational, or applied value.

- **Confidentiality of information.** In their writing, lectures, or other public forums, psychologists may not disclose personally identifiable information about research participants.

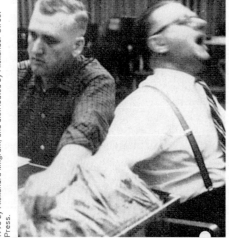

From the film Obedience (c) 1968 by Stanley Milgram, (c)renewed 1993 by Alexandra Milgram; and distributed by Alexander Street Press.

The Shocking Treatment of Research Participants? Could a psychologist ethically conduct an experiment in which research participants were instructed to shock another person for giving incorrect answers on a memory test? This photo is taken from an actual psychology experiment conducted by Stanley Milgram in the early 1960s. To find out more, stay tuned: We discuss Milgram's research in detail in Chapter 11, Social Psychology. Today's psychologists are required to follow stringent ethical guidelines developed by the American Psychological Association.

- **Information about the study and debriefing.** All participants must be provided with the opportunity to obtain information about the nature, results, and conclusions of the research. Psychologists are also obligated to *debrief* the participants and to correct any misconceptions that participants may have had about the research.

What about research involving nonhuman animal subjects? Only a fraction of psychological research studies conducted in a given year involve animal subjects—typically about 7 to 8 percent. About 90 percent of those studies involve rodents or birds, typically rats, mice, and pigeons. Why are animals used in psychological research? A few of the main reasons are listed below.

1. **Many psychologists are interested in the study of animal behavior for its own sake.**

The branch of psychology that focuses on the study of the behavior of nonhuman animals is called **comparative psychology.** Some psychologists also do research in *animal cognition,* which is the study of animal learning, memory, thinking, and language (Wasserman & Zentall, 2006). And research is also pursued for its potential to the animals themselves. For example, psychological research on animal behavior has been used to improve the quality of life of animals in zoos and to increase the likelihood of survival of endangered species in the wild (Blumstein & Fernandez-Juricic, 2010; Goulart & others, 2009).

2. Animal subjects are sometimes used for research that could not feasibly be conducted on human subjects.

There are many similarities between human and animal behavior, but animal behavior tends to be less complex. Thus, it is sometimes easier to identify basic principles of behavior by studying animals. Psychologists can also observe some animals throughout their entire lifespan. To track such changes in humans would take decades of research. Finally, psychologists can exercise greater control over animal subjects than over human subjects. If necessary, researchers can control every aspect of the animals' environment and even their genetic background (Ator, 2005).

The use of nonhuman animal subjects in psychological research is also governed by specific ethical guidelines (APA, 2011; Perry & Dess, 2012). The American Psychological Association publishes the *Guidelines for Ethical Conduct in the Care and Use of Animals,* which you can read at http://www.apa .org/science/leadership/care/guidelines.aspx. The APA guidelines for animal care have been praised as being the most comprehensive set of guidelines of their kind. In addition, psychologists must adhere to federal and state laws governing the use and care of research animals.

❯ Test your understanding of **The Experimental Method and Ethics** with **LEARNING**Curve.

Zhang Jun Xinhua News Agency/Newscom.

Psychological Research Helping Animals Comparative psychologist Rebecca Snyder is the curator of giant panda research and management at Zoo Atlanta. Collaborating with scientists at Chengdu Zoo in Sichuan province in China, Snyder and her colleagues have studied topics as diverse as spatial memory in adult giant pandas, play behavior in cubs, and reproductive behavior (Charlton & others, 2010; Perdue & others, 2009; M. Wilson & others, 2009). Knowledge gained from such research not only improves the quality of life of pandas in zoos, but also can be applied to conservation efforts in the wild (Perdue & others, 2013). Many zoos consult comparative psychologists to help design appropriate housing and enrichment activities for all sorts of animals. For more on the psychological and behavioral research at Zoo Atlanta, visit: http://www.zooatlanta.org/home /research_projects

Closing Thoughts

Remember the students in the chapter Prologue who wanted help with studying for tests? Many students come to psychology courses with questions about personal experiences, seeking help for common problems or explanations for common and uncommon behaviors. As you'll see throughout this book, psychological research has produced many useful insights into behavior and mental processes. At the end of each chapter, we present research-based strategies that *you* can implement to improve your everyday life.

At several points in this chapter, we've described research on factors affecting academic success in college. Fortunately, psychologists have identified several techniques that anyone can use to improve their mastery of new information. We discuss these techniques in the next section, "Psych for Your Life."

PSYCH FOR YOUR LIFE

Successful Study Techniques

Psychologists have conducted literally thousands of research studies investigating learning and memory. In Chapter 6, you'll learn some strategies to improve your memory for specific tasks, such as memorizing lists of items. For now, here are six research-based suggestions that you can use to help you study more effectively—and succeed in this course and others.

1. Focus your attention

Many students think they are good multitaskers. But do you remember the correlational research on multitasking during studying? The psychological research is clear: Attention is a limited resource (Chun & others, 2011). So, when you sit down to study, put your cell phone on "silent" and try to avoid going online except for topic-related material. If you find it hard to stay on task, set a timer and challenge yourself to read for 30 minutes without interruption. You'll be amazed at how much more efficient your studying is.

2. Engage your mind: Be an active reader

One of the most common study techniques used by students is to highlight or underline text in handouts and textbooks. Highlighting and underlining can be helpful, but *only* if done properly (Dunlosky & others, 2013).

Research has found that you're more likely to remember text marked by highlighting or underlining. The problem is that you are *less* likely to remember material that you don't mark. Thus, if you highlight the wrong material, highlighting may be more harmful than helpful. It's also a problem if you highlight *too much* material. If your textbook looks like your younger brother's coloring book, you're probably doing it wrong. One early study found a negative correlation (see p. 25 if you don't remember what that means) between the amount of text highlighted and the scores on tests covering the material: The more material students highlighted, the lower their test scores (Fowler & Barker, 1974).

How can you use highlighting and underlining to improve learning? Be an active reader—and a selective highlighter, highlighting only the most important information. If you have a tendency to highlight entire paragraphs, instead choose no more than one or two points per paragraph to highlight. In this textbook, the "Key Questions" at the beginning of each section will help you identify the most important points.

3. *In the classroom, take notes by hand, not on your laptop*

Many students take notes on a laptop or tablet, but a recent study conclusively showed that using handwriting to take notes increases both conceptual understanding and factual retention of the material (Mueller & Oppenheimer, 2014). Students also had higher test scores when they studied from their handwritten notes versus studying from typed notes, even though their typed notes included more information. The explanation? Students who typed on a laptop tended to simply transcribe verbatim what they heard. In contrast, note-takers using longhand had to listen, digest, and summarize the information in their own words. Doing so required them to deeply engage with the material, which led to better memory for the material (Mueller & Oppenheimer, 2014). Paying attention pays off!

4. *Practice retrieval: The testing effect*

Hundreds of experiments have shown that tests do more than simply assess learning; they are powerful tools in their own right (see Dunlosky & others, 2013; Bjork & others, 2013). Earlier in the chapter, we described an experiment that demonstrated the power of the *testing effect*—the finding that retrieving information from memory produces better retention than restudying the same information (Roediger & Karpicke, 2006; Roediger & Butler, 2011).

Are practice tests helpful only for factual material? Does the testing effect only enhance rote memorization? No. Practice tests need not be multiple-choice or short-answer tests. Essay questions or other tasks that require you to retrieve information from your memory also produce improved retention (Roediger, Putnam, & Smith, 2011; Roediger, Agarwal, & others, 2011).

And, studies have shown that practice tests enhance memory for all types of information. Some examples include spatial information, such as map-learning, and even the learning of new skills like CPR (Dunlosky & others, 2013; Kromann & others, 2009). Research also shows that material learned via retrieval practice transfers to novel situations, when the material is tested in other ways. Thus, it represents more than "teaching to the test" (Roediger, Finn, & Weinstein, 2012).

Why is practice testing such a powerful study technique? One reason may be that practice tests counteract the *fluency effect*. When you reread text or review your notes, the material seems familiar and easy to understand, so the tendency is to assume that you know the material. But often we mistake familiarity for knowledge. Practice testing allows you to identify the gaps that exist in your knowledge so that you can better allocate your study time (Roediger, Putnam, & Smith, 2011).

Practice tests also allow you to practice the very skills that you will need to succeed—retrieving information you've learned from memory (Roediger, Finn, & Weinstein, 2012). And, some research suggests that repeatedly retrieving information seems to help you organize that information in memory, making it easier to remember in the future.

How can you incorporate practice tests into your own studying? Take advantage of any practice quizzes that may be offered by your professor, in study guides, or in your textbook. Challenge yourself to write out the definitions for each of the boldfaced key terms in each section of your text. Even simpler, duplicate the procedure used in the experiment described on pages 26–28. After you finish reading a section of material, close your book and write down ten key points that were in the section you just read. Make sure you go back and check your work against the material you are trying to master; correct any inaccurate information, and fill in any missing ideas.

5. *Use flashcards and practice tests correctly*

Millions of schoolchildren have been taught how to use flashcards: Quiz yourself, and if you answer an item correctly, set the card aside. Keep quizzing yourself on the remaining cards until all cards have been set aside, at which point you can conclude that you have successfully mastered the information.

But *is* this an effective study technique? *Should* students skip material that they have learned in order to focus their effort on material that they have not learned? Let's take a look at a clever experiment that tested this notion.

Jeffrey Karpicke & Henry Roediger (2008) gave participants a list of 40 Swahili words and their English translations. All of the participants studied and were tested on the complete list in the first study session. Then, the participants were divided into four groups and tested a week later after completing three study/test sessions (see figure). The results:

- Students who *studied and were tested on the entire list* in each study period scored 80% on the test a week later.

- Participants who *studied only the items they missed but were tested on the entire list* also scored 80% on the test a week later.

- Participants who studied *all the items but were only tested on items they missed* scored 36% on the test one week later.

- Participants who, like the traditional flashcard user, *only studied and were tested on items they missed* scored 33% on the final test.

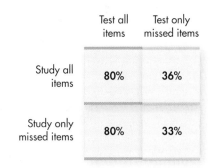

	Test all items	Test only missed items
Study all items	80%	36%
Study only missed items	80%	33%

Effects of Flashcard Strategy on Retention Karpicke and Roediger (2008) found that repeated study has no effect on final test performance—but repeated testing did.
Source: Data from Karpicke & Roediger (2008).

In other words, repeated study had no effect on final test performance—but repeated testing did. How can you apply this finding to your own study habits? For any type of practice test, *don't* stop practicing items that you've answered correctly. Especially if you are using flashcards, don't drop those cards once you think you have mastered the information—keep testing yourself on them.

6. *Space out your study time: The benefits of distributed vs. massed practice*

Psychologists call it "massed practice." Students call it "cramming." A common strategy for time-challenged students, massed practice involves trying to study as much as possible in a short period of time, typically right before an exam. Interestingly, massed practice *is* effective—but *only* in the short term (Bjork & others, 2013). Typically, information learned through cramming is forgotten very quickly.

A much more effective study strategy is what psychologists call *distributed practice*, which means that you learn the information over several sessions, separated in time. Countless studies have shown that information learned over distributed sessions is much better retained than information learned in a single session (see Dunlosky & Rawson, 2015; Soderstrom & Bjork, 2015). One reason may be that the time between sessions gives you a chance to organize and incorporate new information into your memory (Carpenter & others, 2012).

We hope you find these suggestions helpful, both in psychology and in your other courses. Welcome to psychology!

CHAPTER REVIEW

KEY PEOPLE AND KEY TERMS

Mary Whiton Calkins, p. 6
Kenneth Bancroft Clark, p. 7
Charles Darwin, p. 5
Sigmund Freud, p. 7

G. Stanley Hall, p. 6
William James, p. 5
Abraham Maslow, p. 9
Ivan Pavlov, p. 8

Carl Rogers, p. 9
B. F. Skinner, p. 8
Francis C. Sumner, p. 7
Edward B. Titchener, p. 4

Margaret Floy Washburn, p. 7
John B. Watson, p. 8
Wilhelm Wundt, p. 4

psychology, p. 2
structuralism, p. 4
functionalism, p. 6
psychoanalysis, p. 7
behaviorism, p. 8
humanistic psychology, p. 9
neuroscience, p. 10
positive psychology, p. 11
culture, p. 12
cross-cultural psychology, p. 12
ethnocentrism, p. 12
individualistic cultures, p. 12
collectivistic cultures, p. 12
evolutionary psychology, p. 13
psychiatry, p. 14

scientific method, p. 15
empirical evidence, p. 16
hypothesis, p. 16
variable, p. 16
operational definition, p. 16
statistics, p. 18
statistically significant, p. 18
meta-analysis, p. 18
replicate, p. 18
theory, p. 19
pseudoscience, p. 20
confirmation bias, p. 21
descriptive research, p. 21
naturalistic observation, p. 22
case study, p. 22

survey, p. 23
sample, p. 23
representative sample, p. 23
random selection, p. 23
correlational study, p. 24
correlation coefficient, p. 24
positive correlation, p. 25
negative correlation, p. 25
experimental research, p. 26
independent variable, p. 26
dependent variable, p. 26
confounding variable, p. 26
random assignment, p. 27
control group (control condition), p. 27

experimental group (experimental condition), p. 27
testing effect, p. 28
double-blind technique, p. 28
demand characteristics, p. 28
placebo, p. 29
placebo effect, p. 29
natural experiment, p. 29
critical thinking, p. 30
positron emission tomography (PET) scan, p. 32
magnetic resonance imaging (MRI), p. 32
functional magnetic resonance imaging (fMRI), p. 33
comparative psychology, p. 34

Origins of Psychology

Psychology: The scientific study of behavior and mental processes
Psychology's goals: To describe, explain, predict, and influence behavior and mental processes

The work of early philosophers and psychologists provided a foundation for the birth of psychology as an experimental science.

Wilhelm Wundt (1832–1920)
Founded psychology as experimental science

William James (1842–1910)
Functionalism: Adaptive role of behavior

Edward B. Titchener (1867–1927)
Structuralism: Structures of thought; introspection

Sigmund Freud (1856–1939)
Psychoanalysis: Unconscious influences on behavior

Ivan Pavlov (1849–1936)
John B. Watson (1878–1958)
B. F. Skinner (1904–1990)
Behaviorism: Observable behaviors that can be objectively measured and verified

Carl Rogers (1902–1987)
Abraham Maslow (1908–1970)
Humanistic psychology: Psychological growth, human potential, self-direction

Contemporary Psychology

Perspectives:
- Biological
- Psychodynamic
- Behavioral
- Humanistic
- **Positive psychology**
- Cognitive
- **Cross-cultural**
- **Evolutionary psychology**

Specialty areas:
- Biological
- Clinical
- Cognitive
- Counseling
- Developmental
- Educational
- Experimental
- Health
- Industrial/Organizational
- Personality
- Social
- School
- Applied

The Scientific Method

Systematic procedure to collect **empirical evidence**

1. Generate an empirically testable **hypothesis; operationally define** all **variables**
2. Design study and collect data
3. Analyze data and draw conclusions
4. Report the findings

Use **statistics** to analyze findings and determine whether they are **statistically significant**; use **meta-analysis** to combine and analyze data from multiple studies.

Publish details of study design so that study can be **replicated.**

Develop **theories** to integrate and explain various findings and observations.

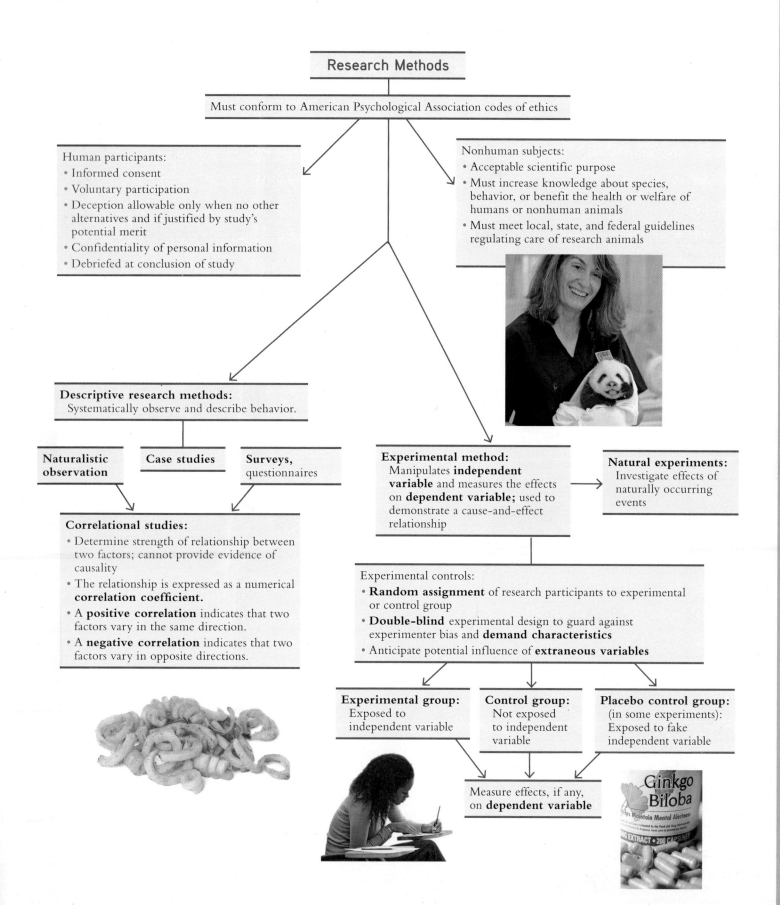

Research Methods

Must conform to American Psychological Association codes of ethics

Human participants:
- Informed consent
- Voluntary participation
- Deception allowable only when no other alternatives and if justified by study's potential merit
- Confidentiality of personal information
- Debriefed at conclusion of study

Nonhuman subjects:
- Acceptable scientific purpose
- Must increase knowledge about species, behavior, or benefit the health or welfare of humans or nonhuman animals
- Must meet local, state, and federal guidelines regulating care of research animals

Descriptive research methods:
Systematically observe and describe behavior.

Naturalistic observation

Case studies

Surveys, questionnaires

Correlational studies:
- Determine strength of relationship between two factors; cannot provide evidence of causality
- The relationship is expressed as a numerical **correlation coefficient.**
- A **positive correlation** indicates that two factors vary in the same direction.
- A **negative correlation** indicates that two factors vary in opposite directions.

Experimental method:
Manipulates **independent variable** and measures the effects on **dependent variable;** used to demonstrate a cause-and-effect relationship

Natural experiments:
Investigate effects of naturally occurring events

Experimental controls:
- **Random assignment** of research participants to experimental or control group
- **Double-blind** experimental design to guard against experimenter bias and **demand characteristics**
- Anticipate potential influence of **extraneous variables**

Experimental group:
Exposed to independent variable

Control group:
Not exposed to independent variable

Placebo control group:
(in some experiments): Exposed to fake independent variable

Measure effects, if any, on **dependent variable**

MYTH (OR) SCIENCE?

Is it true . . .

- That oxytocin is the "love hormone," making people more trusting and empathic?
- That even simple behaviors and abilities involve the activation of multiple parts of the brain?
- That you only use 10% of your brain?
- That because their brains are wired differently, men and women think, feel, and behave differently?
- That the right brain is creative and intuitive, and the left brain is analytic and logical, but that left-brained people can educate their right brain?
- That the brain is essentially "hardwired" by adolescence?

ASHA'S STORY

PROLOGUE

THE HEADACHES BEGAN WITHOUT WARNING. A pounding, intense pain just over Asha's left temple. Asha just couldn't seem to shake it—the pain was unrelenting. She was uncharacteristically tired, too.

But our friend Asha, a 32-year-old university professor, chalked up her constant headache and fatigue to stress and exhaustion. After all, the end of her demanding first semester of teaching and research was drawing near. Still, Asha had always been very healthy and usually tolerated

stress well. She didn't drink or smoke. And no matter how late she stayed up working on her lectures and research proposals, she still got up at 5:30 every morning to work out at the university gym.

There were other, more subtle signs that something was wrong. Asha's husband, Paul, noticed that she had been behaving rather oddly in recent weeks. For example, at Thanksgiving dinner, Asha had picked up a knife by the wrong end and tried to cut her turkey with the handle instead of the blade. A few hours later, Asha had made the same mistake trying to use scissors: She held the blades and tried to cut with the handle.

Asha laughed these incidents off, and for that matter, so did Paul. They both thought she was simply under too much stress. And when Asha occasionally got her words mixed up, neither Paul nor anyone else was terribly surprised. Asha was born in India, and her first language was Tulu. Although Asha was extremely fluent in English, she often got English phrases slightly wrong—like the time she said that Paul was a "straight dart" instead of a "straight arrow." Or when she said that it was "storming cats and birds" instead of "raining cats and dogs."

There were other odd lapses in language. "I would say something, thinking

Neuroscience and Behavior

IN THIS CHAPTER:

> **INTRODUCTION:** Neuroscience and Behavior

> The Neuron: The Basic Unit of Communication

> The Nervous System and the Endocrine System: Communication Throughout the Body

> A Guided Tour of the Brain

> Specialization in the Cerebral Hemispheres

> **PSYCH FOR YOUR LIFE:** Maximizing Your Brain's Potential

it was correct," Asha re-called, "and people would say to me, 'What are you saying?' I wouldn't realize I was saying something wrong. I would open my mouth and just nonsense would come out. But it made perfect sense to me. At other times, the word was on the tip of my tongue—I knew I knew the word, but I couldn't find it. I would fumble for the word, but it would come out wrong. Sometimes I would slur words, like I'd try to say 'Saturday,' only it would come out 'salad day'."

On Christmas morning, Paul and Asha were with Paul's family, opening presents. Asha walked over to Paul's father to look at the pool cue he had received as a gift. As she bent down, she fell forward onto her father-in-law. At first, everyone thought Asha was just joking around. But then she fell to the floor, her body stiff. Seconds later, it was apparent that Asha had lost consciousness and was having a seizure.

Asha remembers nothing of the seizure or of being taken by ambulance to the hospital intensive care unit. She floated in and out of consciousness for the first day and night. A CAT scan showed some sort of blockage in Asha's brain. An MRI scan revealed a large white spot on the left side of her brain. At only 32 years of age, Asha had suffered a stroke—brain damage caused by a disruption of the blood flow to the brain.

She remained in the hospital for 12 days. It was only after Asha was transferred out of intensive care that both she and Paul began to realize just how serious the repercussions of the stroke were. Asha couldn't read or write and had difficulty comprehending what was being said. Although she could speak, she could not name even simple objects, such as a tree, a clock, or her doctor's tie. In this chapter, you will discover why the damage to Asha's brain impaired her ability to perform simple behaviors, like naming common objects. □

INTRODUCTION:
Neuroscience and Behavior

biological psychology The specialized branch of psychology that studies the relationship between behavior and bodily processes and systems; also called *biopsychology* or *psychobiology*.

neuroscience The study of the nervous system, especially the brain.

As we discussed in Chapter 1, **biological psychology** is the scientific study of the biological bases of behavior and mental processes. Biological psychology is one of the scientific disciplines that make important contributions to **neuroscience**—the scientific study of the nervous system. Other scientific disciplines that contribute to neuroscience include biology, physiology, genetics, and neurology.

Neuroscience and biological psychology are not limited to the study of the brain and the nervous system. Throughout this textbook, you'll notice the many questions that have been studied by neuroscientists. Here are some examples:

- How do you tell the difference between red and blue, sweet and sour, loud and soft? (Chapter 3)
- What happens in the brain when you sleep, dream, or meditate? (Chapter 4)
- What exactly is a memory, and how are memories stored in the brain? (Chapter 6)
- Why do you get hungry? How do emotions occur? (Chapter 8)
- How do emotions and personality factors affect your vulnerability to infection and disease? (Chapter 12)
- How does heredity influence your development? What role does genetics play in personality traits and psychological disorders? (Chapters 9, 10, and 13)
- What role does abnormal brain chemistry play in psychological disorders? How do medications alleviate the symptoms of serious psychological disorders? (Chapters 13 and 14)

Neuroscience and Behavior Even simple behaviors, such as laughing and talking while skating with a friend, involve the harmonious integration of multiple internal signals and body processes. What kinds of questions might neuroscientists ask about the common behaviors shown here?

Sam Edwards/age fotostock

This chapter will lay an important foundation for the rest of this book by helping you develop a broad appreciation of the *nervous system*—the body's primary communication network. We'll start by looking at *neurons,* the basic cells of the nervous system. We'll consider the organization of the nervous system and a closely linked communication network, the *endocrine system.* We'll then move on to a guided tour of the brain. We'll look at how certain brain areas are specialized to handle different functions, such as language, vision, and touch. In Psych for Your Life, at the end of the chapter, we'll describe how the brain responds to environmental stimulation by literally altering its physical structure. And we'll return to Asha's story and tell you how she fared after her stroke.

The Neuron

THE BASIC UNIT OF COMMUNICATION

KEY THEME

Information in the nervous system is transmitted by specialized cells, called neurons.

KEY QUESTIONS

> What are the basic components of the neuron, and what are their functions?
> What are glial cells, and what is their role in the nervous system?
> What is an action potential, and how is it produced?

Communication throughout the nervous system takes place via **neurons**—cells that are highly specialized to receive and transmit information from one part of the body to another. Most neurons, especially those in your brain, are extremely small. A bit of brain tissue no larger than a grain of rice contains about 10,000 neurons! Your entire brain contains an estimated 100 *billion* neurons.

Neurons vary greatly in size and shape, reflecting their specialized functions (see Figure 2.1). There are three basic types of neurons, each communicating different kinds of information. **Sensory neurons** convey information about the environment, such as light or sound, from specialized receptor cells in the sense organs to the brain. Sensory neurons also carry information from the skin and internal organs to the brain. **Motor neurons** communicate information to the muscles and glands of the body. Simply blinking your eyes activates thousands of motor neurons. Finally, **interneurons** communicate information *between* neurons. By far, most of the neurons in the human nervous system are interneurons. Many interneurons connect to other interneurons.

One type of neuron deserves special mention. *Mirror neurons* are not structurally different from other motor neurons. They are a distinct type of motor neuron that becomes activated both when individuals perform a motor act *and* when they observe the same motor act done by another individual (Cook & others, 2014; Rizzolatti & Sinigaglia, 2008). We discuss mirror neurons in greater detail in Chapter 5, Learning (see p. 217).

Characteristics of the Neuron

Most neurons have three basic components: a *cell body, dendrites,* and an *axon* (see Figure 2.2 on the next page). The **cell body,** also called the *soma,* contains structures that manufacture proteins and process nutrients, providing the energy the neuron needs to function. The cell body also contains the *nucleus,* which in turn contains the cell's genetic material—twisted strands of DNA called *chromosomes.*

Short, branching fibers, called **dendrites,** extend from the cell bodies of most neurons. The term *dendrite* comes from a Greek word meaning "tree." And, the intricate branching of the dendrites does often resemble the branches of a tree. Dendrites *receive* messages from other neurons or specialized cells. Dendrites with many branches have a greater surface area, which increases the amount of information the neuron can receive. Some neurons have thousands of dendrites.

The **axon** is a single, elongated tube that extends from the cell body in most, though not all, neurons. (Some neurons do not have axons.) Axons carry information *from* the neuron *to* other cells in the body, including other neurons, glands, and muscles. In contrast to the potentially large number of dendrites, a neuron has only one axon exiting from the cell body. However, many axons have branches near their tips that allow the neuron to communicate information to more than one target.

FIGURE 2.1 Types of Neurons
Neurons differ in size, shape, and complexity. The distinctive shapes of neurons reflect their specialized functions. Shown here are a few representative neuron types. Virtually all neurons have three basic parts: a *cell body,* an *axon,* and *dendrites.* In most neurons, the dendrites project from the cell body, but in sensory neurons, the dendrites extend from the opposite end of the axon, as shown here.

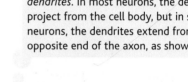

Sensory Neurons
Communicate information *from* the environment *to* the central nervous system

■ Dendrites
■ Cell body
■ Axon

Motor Neurons
Communicate information *from* the central nervous system *to* the muscles

Interneurons
Communicate information from one neuron to another

neuron A highly specialized cell that communicates information in electrical and chemical form; a nerve cell.

sensory neuron The type of neuron that conveys information to the brain from specialized receptor cells in sense organs and internal organs.

motor neuron The type of neuron that signals muscles to relax or contract.

interneuron The type of neuron that communicates information from one neuron to the next.

cell body The part of a cell that processes nutrients and provides energy for the neuron to function; contains the cell's nucleus; also called the *soma.*

dendrites The multiple short fibers that extend from a neuron's cell body and receive information from other neurons or from sensory receptor cells.

axon The long, fluid-filled tube that carries a neuron's messages to other body areas.

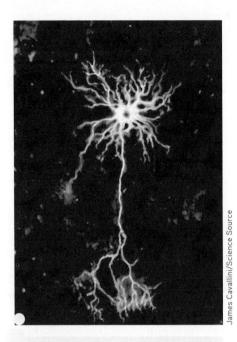

FIGURE 2.2 The Parts of a Typical Neuron The drawing at right shows the location and function of key parts of a neuron. The photograph above, taken with a specialized microscope, clearly shows multiple dendrites and a single long axon projecting from the cell body.

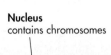

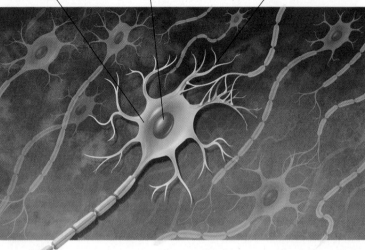

Cell body
processes nutrients and provides energy for neuron

Nucleus
contains chromosomes

Dendrites
receive information from other neurons and sensory receptors

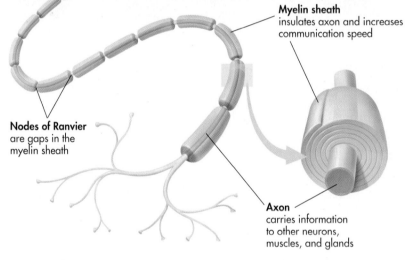

Myelin sheath
insulates axon and increases communication speed

Nodes of Ranvier
are gaps in the myelin sheath

Axon
carries information to other neurons, muscles, and glands

---

glial cells or **glia** (GLEE-ull) The support cells that assist neurons by providing structural support, nutrition, and removal of cell wastes; glial cells manufacture myelin.

myelin sheath (MY-eh-lin) A white, fatty covering wrapped around the axons of some neurons that increases their communication speed.

action potential A brief electrical impulse by which information is transmitted along the axon of a neuron.

stimulus threshold The minimum level of stimulation required to activate a particular neuron.

resting potential The state in which a neuron is prepared to activate and communicate its message if it receives sufficient stimulation.

Axons can vary enormously in length. Most axons are very small; some are no more than a few thousandths of an inch long. Other axons are quite long. For example, the longest axon in your body is that of the motor neuron that controls your big toe. This axon extends from the base of your spine into your foot. If you happen to be a seven-foot-tall basketball player, this axon could be four feet long! For most of us, though, this axon is closer to three feet long.

Glial Cells

Along with neurons, the human nervous system is made up of other specialized cells, called **glial cells** or simply **glia** (see photo on the next page). Glial cells are the most abundant cells in the human brain, outnumbering neurons by about 10 to 1. *Glia* is Greek for "glue," and although they don't actually glue neurons together, glia do provide structural support for neurons throughout the nervous system.

There are several different kinds of glial cells, each with its own specialized function (Fields, 2013). *Microglia* remove waste products from the nervous system, including dead and damaged neurons. *Astrocytes,* shown in the photo on the next page, provide connections between neurons and blood vessels. Astrocytes are also involved in brain development and the communication of information among neurons (Clarke & Barres, 2013).

Two other types of glial cells, *oligodendrocytes* in the brain and *Schwann cells* in the rest of the nervous system, form the **myelin sheath,** a white fatty covering that is wrapped around the axons of some, but not all, neurons. In much the same way that insulating plastic on electrical wires prevents interference when wires contact each other, myelin helps insulate one axon from the axons of other neurons. Rather than forming a continuous coating of the axon, however, the myelin sheath occurs in segments that are separated by small gaps. The small gaps are called the *nodes of Ranvier,* or simply *nodes* (see Figure 2.2). Neurons whose axons are wrapped in myelin communicate their messages up to 50 times faster than do unmyelinated neurons (Fields, 2013). Myelin formation may also be involved in learning new motor behaviors (Long & Corfas, 2014; McKenzie & others, 2014).

The importance of myelin becomes readily apparent when it is damaged. For example, *multiple sclerosis* is a disease that involves the degeneration of patches of the myelin sheath. This degeneration causes the transmission of neural messages to be slowed or interrupted, resulting in disturbances in sensation and movement. Muscle weakness, loss of coordination, and speech and visual disturbances are some of the symptoms that characterize multiple sclerosis.

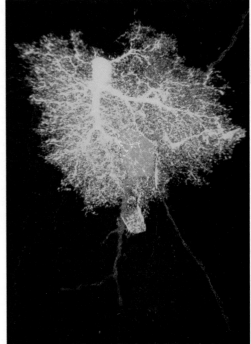

Communication Within the Neuron
THE ACTION POTENTIAL

Essentially, the function of neurons is to transmit information throughout the nervous system. But exactly *how* do neurons transmit information? We'll first describe communication *within* a neuron, and then, in the following section, we'll describe communication *between* neurons.

In general, messages are gathered by the dendrites and cell body and then transmitted along the axon in the form of a brief electrical impulse called an **action potential.** The action potential is produced by the movement of electrically charged particles, called *ions,* across the membrane of the axon. Some ions are negatively charged, while others are positively charged.

Think of the axon membrane as a gatekeeper that carefully controls the balance of positive and negative ions on the interior and exterior of the axon. As the gatekeeper, the axon membrane opens and closes *ion channels* that allow ions to flow into and out of the axon.

Each neuron requires a minimum level of stimulation from other neurons or sensory receptors to activate it. This minimum level of stimulation is called the neuron's **stimulus threshold.** While waiting for sufficient stimulation to activate it, the neuron is said to be *polarized.* This means that there is a difference in the electrical charge between the inside and the outside of the axon.

More specifically, there is a greater concentration of negative ions inside the neuron. Thus, the axon's interior is more negatively charged than is the exterior fluid surrounding the axon. The negative electrical charge is about −70 millivolts (thousandths of a volt) (see Figure 2.4 on page 47). The −70 millivolts is referred to as the neuron's **resting potential.**

In this polarized, negative-inside/positive-outside condition, there are different concentrations of two particular ions: sodium and potassium. While the neuron is in resting potential, the fluid surrounding the axon contains a larger concentration of *sodium* ions than does the fluid within the axon. The fluid within the axon contains a larger concentration of *potassium* ions than is found in the fluid outside the axon.

An *action potential* is triggered when the neuron is sufficiently stimulated by other neurons or sensory receptors. First, the neuron *depolarizes:* At each successive axon

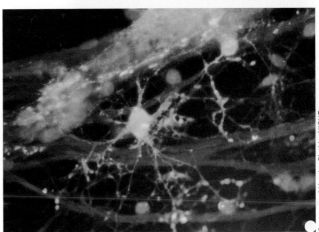

Glial Cells Top: Glial cells, or *glia*, play an active role in brain functioning (Fields, 2013). This colored micrograph shows a star-shaped *astrocyte* (green) surrounding a neuron (red). Astrocytes provide connections between neurons and blood vessels in the brain and also help regulate communication among neurons.

Bottom: This colored micrograph shows the first stages of myelin formation by an *oligodendrocyte* (green). Like a spider spinning a web, the oligodendrocyte sends tendrils out to neighboring axons (red) and wraps layers of myelin around them in a spiral-shaped pattern.

segment, sodium ion channels open for a mere thousandth of a second. The sodium ions rush to the axon interior from the surrounding fluid, and then the sodium ion channels close. Less than a thousandth of a second later, the potassium ion channels open, allowing potassium to flow out of the axon and into the fluid surrounding it. Then the potassium ion channels close (see Figure 2.3). This sequence of depolarization and ion movement continues down the entire length of the axon.

As this ion exchange occurs, the relative balance of positive and negative ions separated by the axon membrane changes. The electrical charge on the inside of the axon momentarily changes to a positive charge of about +30 millivolts. The result is a brief positive electrical impulse that progressively occurs at each segment down the axon—the *action potential*.

Although it's tempting to think of the action potential as traveling in much the same way as electricity travels through a wire, that's *not* what takes place in the neuron. The axon is actually a poor conductor of electricity. At each successive segment of the axon, the action potential is *regenerated* in the same way in which it was generated in the

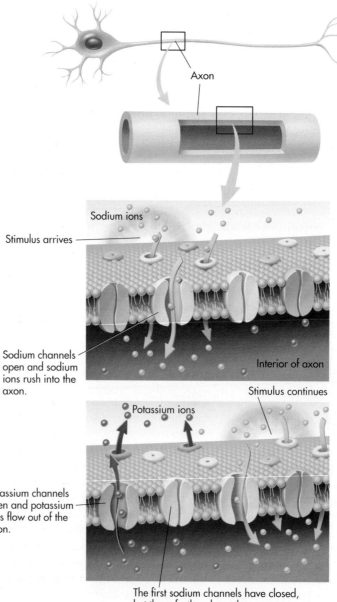

Axon

Sodium ions

Stimulus arrives

Sodium channels open and sodium ions rush into the axon.

Interior of axon

Stimulus continues

Potassium ions

Potassium channels open and potassium ions flow out of the axon.

The first sodium channels have closed, but those farther down the axon open, continuing the process of depolarization along the axon.

FIGURE 2.3 Communication Within the Neuron: The Action Potential These drawings depict the ion channels in the membrane of a neuron's axon. When sufficiently stimulated, the neuron depolarizes and an action potential begins. At each progressive segment of the axon's membrane, sodium ion channels open and sodium ions rush into the interior of the axon. A split second later, the sodium ion channels close and potassium channels open, allowing potassium ions to flow out of the axon. As this sequence occurs, there is a change in the relative balance of positive and negative ions separated by the axon membrane. The electrical charge on the interior of the axon briefly changes from negative to positive. Once started, an action potential is self-sustaining and continues to the end of the axon. Following the action potential, the neuron repolarizes and reestablishes its negative electrical charge.

previous segment—by depolarization and the movement of ions.

Once the action potential is started, it is *self-sustaining* and continues to the end of the axon. In other words, there is no such thing as a partial action potential. Either the neuron is sufficiently stimulated and an action potential occurs, or the neuron is not sufficiently stimulated and an action potential does not occur. This principle is referred to as the *all-or-none law.*

After the action potential, the neuron enters a *refractory period,* lasting a thousandth of a second or less, during which the neuron cannot fire. Instead, the neuron *repolarizes* and reestablishes the negative-inside/positive-outside condition. Like depolarization, repolarization occurs progressively at each segment down the axon. This process reestablishes the *resting potential* conditions so that the neuron is capable of firing again. The graph in Figure 2.4 depicts the complete sequence from resting potential to action potential and back to resting potential.

Action potentials are generated in mere thousandths of a second. Thus, a single neuron can potentially generate hundreds of neural impulses per second. Just how fast do neural impulses zip around your body? The fastest neurons in your body communicate at speeds of up to 270 miles per hour. In the slowest neurons, messages creep along at about 2 miles per hour. This variation in communication speed is due to two factors: the axon diameter and the myelin sheath. The larger the axon's diameter, the faster it conducts action potentials. And, myelinated neurons communicate much faster than unmyelinated neurons because the action potential "jumps" from node to node rather than progressing down the entire length of the axon.

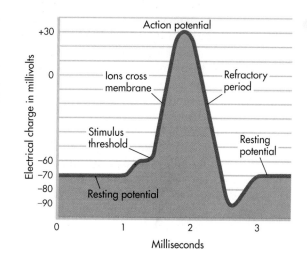

FIGURE 2.4 Electrical Changes During an Action Potential This graph shows the changing electrical charge of the neuron during an action potential. When the neuron depolarizes and ions cross the axon membrane, the result is a brief positive electrical impulse of +30 millivolts—the action potential. During the refractory period, the neuron reestablishes the resting potential negative charge of −70 millivolts and then is ready to activate again.

Communication Between Neurons
BRIDGING THE GAP

KEY THEME

Communication between neurons takes place at the synapse, the junction between two adjoining neurons.

KEY QUESTIONS

> How is information communicated at the synapse?
> What is a neurotransmitter, and what is its role in synaptic transmission?
> What are seven important neurotransmitters, and how do psychoactive drugs affect synaptic transmission?

The primary function of a neuron is to communicate information to other cells, most notably other neurons. The point of communication between two neurons is called the **synapse.** At this communication junction, the message-*sending* neuron is referred to as the *presynaptic neuron.* The message-*receiving* neuron is called the *postsynaptic neuron.* For cells that are specialized to communicate information, neurons have a surprising characteristic: They don't touch each other. The presynaptic and postsynaptic neurons are separated by a tiny, fluid-filled space, called the **synaptic gap,** which is only 20 to 40 nanometers wide. How small is that? For comparison, the thickness of a single sheet of paper is about 100,000 nanometers.

How do neurons communicate? In most cases, when the presynaptic neuron is activated, it generates an action potential that travels to the end of the axon. At

The Brain Capturing a Thought In the brain, as in the rest of the nervous system, information is transmitted by electrical impulses that speed from one neuron to the next (Kim & others, 2012). In this striking image, you can clearly see the synaptic connections (bright yellow dots) between the axons of the presynaptic or "sending" neurons (blue) and the dendrites of the postsynaptic or "receiving" neurons (red).

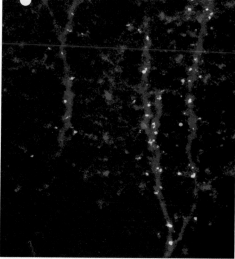

Courtesy of Jinhyun Kim

synapse (SIN-aps) The point of communication between two neurons.

synaptic gap (sin-AP-tick) The tiny space between the axon terminal of one neuron and the dendrite of an adjoining neuron.

axon terminals The branches at the end of the axon that contain tiny pouches, or sacs, called synaptic vesicles.

synaptic vesicles (sin-AP-tick VESS-ick-ullz) The tiny pouches or sacs in axon terminals that contain chemicals called neurotransmitters.

neurotransmitters Chemical messengers manufactured by a neuron.

synaptic transmission (sin-AP-tick) The process through which neurotransmitters are released by one neuron, cross the synaptic gap, and affect adjoining neurons.

reuptake The process by which neurotransmitter molecules detach from a postsynaptic neuron and are reabsorbed by a presynaptic neuron so they can be recycled and used again.

the end of the axon are several small branches called **axon terminals.** Floating in the interior fluid of the axon terminals are tiny sacs called **synaptic vesicles** (see Figure 2.5). The synaptic vesicles hold special chemical messengers manufactured by the neuron, called **neurotransmitters.**

When the action potential reaches the axon terminals, some of the synaptic vesicles "dock" on the axon terminal membrane and then release their neurotransmitters into the synaptic gap. These chemical messengers cross the synaptic gap and attach to *receptor sites* on the dendrites of the receiving or postsynaptic neuron. This journey across the synaptic gap takes just a few millionths of a second. The entire process of transmitting information at the synapse is called **synaptic transmission.**

What happens to the neurotransmitter molecules after they've attached to the receptor sites of the postsynaptic neuron? Most often, they detach from the receptor and are reabsorbed by the presynaptic neuron so they can be recycled and used again. This process is called **reuptake.** Reuptake also occurs with many of the neurotransmitters that failed to attach to a receptor and were left floating in the synaptic gap. Neurotransmitter molecules that are not reabsorbed or that remain attached to the receptor site are broken down or destroyed by enzymes.

Some neurons produce only one type of neurotransmitter, but others manufacture three or more. Each neurotransmitter has a chemically distinct shape. Like a key

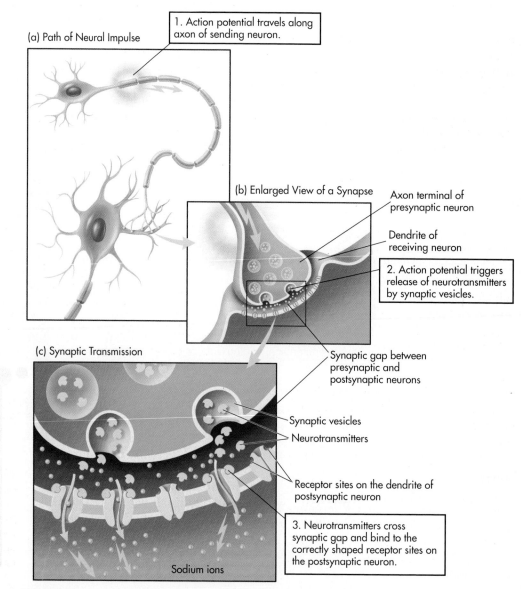

FIGURE 2.5 Communication Between Neurons: The Process of Synaptic Transmission As you follow the steps in this progressive graphic, you can trace the sequence of synaptic transmission in which neurotransmitters are released by the sending, or presynaptic, neuron, cross the tiny fluid-filled space called the synaptic gap, and attach to receptor sites on the receiving, or postsynaptic, neuron.

(a) Path of Neural Impulse

1. Action potential travels along axon of sending neuron.

(b) Enlarged View of a Synapse

Axon terminal of presynaptic neuron

Dendrite of receiving neuron

2. Action potential triggers release of neurotransmitters by synaptic vesicles.

(c) Synaptic Transmission

Synaptic gap between presynaptic and postsynaptic neurons

Synaptic vesicles

Neurotransmitters

Receptor sites on the dendrite of postsynaptic neuron

3. Neurotransmitters cross synaptic gap and bind to the correctly shaped receptor sites on the postsynaptic neuron.

Sodium ions

in a lock, a neurotransmitter's shape must precisely match that of a receptor site on the postsynaptic neuron for the neurotransmitter to affect that neuron (see Figure 2.6). And, the postsynaptic neuron can have many differently shaped receptor sites on its dendrites and other surfaces. Thus, a given neuron may be able to receive several different neurotransmitters.

Depending upon the receptor to which it binds, a neurotransmitter communicates either an excitatory or an inhibitory message to a postsynaptic neuron. An *excitatory message* increases the likelihood that the postsynaptic neuron will activate and generate an action potential. An *inhibitory message* decreases the likelihood that the postsynaptic neuron will activate.

When released by a presynaptic neuron, neurotransmitters cross hundreds, even thousands, of synaptic gaps and affect the intertwined dendrites of adjacent neurons. Because the receiving neuron can have thousands of dendrites that intertwine with the axon terminals of many presynaptic neurons, the number of potential synaptic interconnections between neurons is truly mind-boggling. Each neuron in the brain communicates directly with an average of 1,000 other neurons (Hyman, 2005). However, some specialized neurons have as many as 100,000 connections with other neurons. Thus, there are up to 100 *trillion* synaptic interconnections in your brain (Eroglu & Barres, 2010). That's the number 10 followed by 13 zeros!

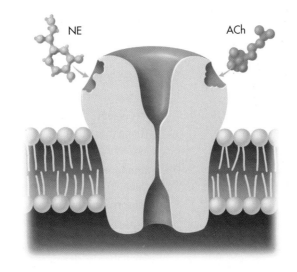

NE   ACh

Neurotransmitters and Their Effects

Your ability to perceive, feel, think, move, act, and react depends on the delicate balance of neurotransmitters in your nervous system. Yet neurotransmitters are present in only infinitesimal amounts in brain tissue—roughly equivalent to a pinch of salt dissolved in an Olympic-sized swimming pool.

Researchers have linked abnormal levels of specific neurotransmitters to various physical and behavioral problems (see Table 2.1 on the next page). However, the connection between a particular neurotransmitter and a particular effect is *not* a simple one-to-one relationship. Most behaviors are the result of the complex interaction of different neurotransmitters. Further, neurotransmitters sometimes have different effects in different areas of the brain.

IMPORTANT NEUROTRANSMITTERS

Acetylcholine, the first neurotransmitter discovered, is found in all motor neurons. It stimulates muscles to contract, including the heart and stomach muscles. Whether it is as simple as the flick of an eyelash or as complex as a back flip, all movement involves acetylcholine.

acetylcholine (uh-seet-ull-KO-leen) Neurotransmitter that causes muscle contractions and is involved in learning and memory.

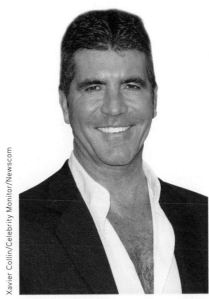

Xavier Collin/Celebrity Monitor/Newscom

Turning Back the Clock with Botox Simon Cowell became famous for judging talent on *American Idol*, *America's Got Talent*, *The X Factor*, and similar shows. In his late fifties, he cheerfully admits to using Botox to make him look much younger than his years. How does Botox eliminate facial wrinkles? Botox injections contain very minute amounts of *botulinum*, a toxin that causes muscle paralysis around the injection site by blocking the release of acetylcholine from motor neurons. Because the muscles can't contract, the skin smooths out, and facial wrinkles are diminished or eliminated.

TABLE 2.1

Summary of Important Neurotransmitters

Neurotransmitter	Primary Roles	Associated Disorder
Acetylcholine	Learning, memory Muscle contractions	Alzheimer's disease
Dopamine	Movement Thought processes Rewarding sensations	Parkinson's disease Schizophrenia Drug addiction
Serotonin	Emotional states Sleep Sensory perception	Depression
Norepinephrine	Physical arousal Learning, memory Regulation of sleep	Depression, stress
Glutamate	Excitatory messages	Seizures Alzheimer's disease
GABA	Inhibitory messages	Anxiety disorders
Endorphins	Pain perception Positive emotions	Opioid addiction

Acetylcholine is also found in many neurons in the brain, and it is important in memory, learning, and general intellectual functioning. People with *Alzheimer's disease,* which is characterized by progressive loss of memory and deterioration of intellectual functioning, have a severe depletion of several neurotransmitters in the brain, most notably acetylcholine.

The neurotransmitter **dopamine** is involved in movement, attention, learning, and pleasurable or rewarding sensations. Evidence suggests that the addictiveness of many drugs, including cocaine and nicotine, is related to their ability to increase dopamine activity in the brain (Volkow & others, 2011a, b).

The degeneration of the neurons that produce dopamine in one brain area causes *Parkinson's disease,* which is characterized by rigidity, muscle tremors, poor balance,

dopamine (DOPE-uh-meen)
Neurotransmitter involved in the regulation of bodily movement, thought processes, and rewarding sensations.

Dopamine and Parkinson's Disease
Parkinson's disease affects approximately 1.5 million Americans, with an estimated 60,000 new cases diagnosed each year. Parkinson's disease usually affects older adults, but Michael J. Fox was diagnosed with Parkinson's at the age of 30. To help ease his symptoms, Fox takes medications containing L-dopa, which temporarily increases brain levels of dopamine.

Astrid Stawiarz/Getty Images

and difficulty in initiating movements. Symptoms can be allevi-ated by a drug called *L-dopa,* which converts to dopamine in the brain.

Excessive brain levels of dopamine are sometimes involved in the hallucinations and perceptual distortions that characterize the severe mental disorder called *schizophrenia.* Some antipsy-chotic drugs that relieve schizophrenic symptoms work by blocking dopamine receptors and reducing dopamine activ-ity in the brain. Unfortunately, because the drugs reduce dopamine in several different areas of the brain, long-term use sometimes produces symptoms that are very similar to those of Parkinson's disease. In the chapters on psychological disorders (Chapter 13) and therapies (Chapter 14), we'll discuss schizophrenia, dopamine, and antipsychotic drugs in more detail.

The neurotransmitters **serotonin** and **norepinephrine** are found in many different brain areas. Serotonin is involved in sleep, sensory perceptions, moods, and emotional states, includ-ing depression (Deneris & Wyler, 2012). Some antidepressant drugs, like *Prozac,* increase the availability of serotonin in certain brain regions. Norepinephrine is implicated in the activation of neurons throughout the brain and helps the body gear up in the face of danger or threat. Norepinephrine also plays a key role in the regulation of sleep, learning, and memory retrieval (McCarley, 2007). Like serotonin and dopamine, norepinephrine dysfunction is implicated in some psychological disorders, especially depression (Goddard & others, 2010).

The most abundant neurotransmitters in the brain are two closely related neurotransmitters, **glutamate** and **gamma-aminobutyric acid,** abbreviated **GABA.** In a delicate balancing act, glutamate conveys *excitatory* messages and GABA communicates *inhibitory* messages. Like a dimmer switch, GABA regulates the level of neural activity in the brain. Too much GABA impairs learning, motivation, and move-ment, but too little GABA can lead to seizures (McCarthy, 2007). Alcohol makes people feel relaxed and less inhibited partly by increasing GABA activity and decreasing glutamate, reducing overall brain activity.

Glutamate is involved in learning, memory, and sensory processes (Morris, 2013). Too much glutamate can overstimulate the brain, causing seizures and cell death. Glutamate is also implicated in Alzheimer's disease, neurological diseases, and schizophrenia.

Endorphins are another important class of neurotransmitter. Chemically similar to morphine, heroin, and other opioid drugs, endorphins are hundreds of times more potent and are released in response to stress, trauma, and pain. Endorphins are impli-cated in the pain-reducing effects of *acupuncture,* an ancient Chinese medical tech-nique that involves inserting needles at various locations in the body (Kemmer, 2007; Zhao, 2008). Also associated with positive mood, endorphins may cause "runner's high" (see photo).

How Drugs Affect Synaptic Transmission

Much of what is known about different neurotransmitters has been learned from observing the effects of drugs and other substances. Many drugs, especially those that affect moods or behavior, work by interfering with the normal functioning of neurotransmitters in the synapses (Volkow & others, 2011a, b).

Some drugs increase or decrease the amounts of neurotransmitters released by neurons. For example, the venom of a black widow spider bite causes ace-tylcholine to be released continuously by motor neurons, causing severe muscle

Kirby Lee/Image of Sport-USA TODAY Sports

The "Endorphin Rush" of Runner's High "Runner's high" is the rush of euphoria that many people experi-ence after intense aerobic exercise, especially running or cycling. In an ingenious experiment by German neuroscientist Henning Boecker and his colleagues (2008), elite male runners were injected with a radioactively tagged chemical that bonded to opioid receptors in the brain. After two hours of endurance running, PET scans showed the highest levels of natural endorphin production in brain regions known to be involved in positive emotions. The scans also showed that endorphin activity was positively correlated with subjective experience: The more intense the euphoria experienced by the individual runner, the higher the level of endorphin activity in his brain.

serotonin (ser-uh-TONE-in) Neurotransmitter involved in sensory perceptions, sleep, and emotions.

norepinephrine (nor-ep-in-EF-rin) Neurotransmitter involved in learning, memory, and regulation of sleep; also, a hormone manufactured by adrenal glands.

glutamate Neurotransmitter that usually communicates an excitatory message.

GABA (gamma-aminobutyric acid) Neurotransmitter that usually communicates an inhibitory message.

endorphins (en-DORF-inz) Neurotransmitters that regulate pain perceptions.

FIGURE 2.7 How Drugs Affect Synaptic Transmission Drugs affect brain activity by interfering with neurotransmitter functioning in the synapse. Drugs may also affect synaptic transmission by increasing or decreasing the amount of a particular neurotransmitter that is produced.

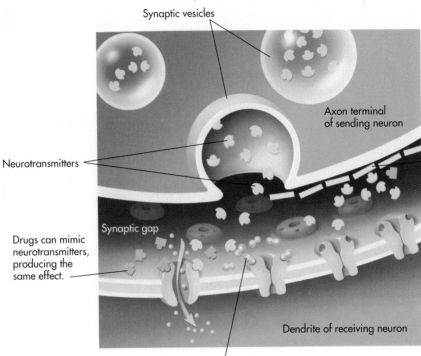

Synaptic vesicles

Axon terminal of sending neuron

Neurotransmitters

Drugs can block reuptake of the neurotransmitter, increasing the neurotransmitter's effect.

Drugs can mimic neurotransmitters, producing the same effect.

Synaptic gap

Dendrite of receiving neuron

Drugs can block receptor sites on the receiving neuron, preventing the neurotransmitter's effect.

agonist Drug or other chemical substance that binds to a receptor site and triggers a response in the cell.

antagonist A drug or other chemical substance that blocks a receptor site and inhibits or prevents a response in the receiving cell.

LaunchPad

Review the process of neural communication by completing the **Video Activity: The Neuron: Basic Units of Communication.**

spasms. Drugs may also affect the length of time the neurotransmitters remain in the synaptic gap, either increasing or decreasing the amount available to the postsynaptic receptor.

One way in which drugs can prolong the effects of the neurotransmitters is by blocking the reuptake of the neurotransmitters by the sending neuron. For example, there is a category of antidepressant medications that are referred to as SSRIs, which stands for *selective serotonin reuptake inhibitors.* SSRIs include such medications as *Prozac, Zoloft,* and *Paxil.* Each of these medications inhibits the reuptake of serotonin, increasing the availability of serotonin in the brain. Similarly, the illegal drug cocaine produces its exhilarating rush by interfering with the reuptake of dopamine (Volkow & others, 2011a, b).

Drugs can also mimic specific neurotransmitters. An **agonist** is a drug or other chemical that binds to a receptor. Agonist drugs are chemically similar to a specific neurotransmitter and produce the same effect. For example, nicotine is a stimulant because it is chemically similar to acetylcholine. It occupies acetylcholine receptor sites, stimulating skeletal muscles and causing the heart to beat more rapidly.

Alternatively, a drug can act as an **antagonist** by *blocking* the effect of neurotransmitters. A drug may fit into receptor sites and prevent neurotransmitters from acting. For example, the drug *curare* blocks acetylcholine receptor sites, causing virtually instantaneous paralysis. The brain sends signals to the motor neurons, but the muscles can't respond because the motor neuron receptor sites are blocked by the curare. Similarly, the drug *naloxone* is an opioid antagonist. By blocking endorphin receptors, it can quickly reverse the effects of heroin, oxycodone, or other opioid drugs (Rich & others, 2011). Figure 2.7 summarizes the effects of drugs on synaptic transmission.

❯ Test your understanding of **Introduction to Neuroscience and the Neuron** with **LEARNING***Curve.*

The Nervous System and the Endocrine System

COMMUNICATION THROUGHOUT THE BODY

KEY THEME

Two major communication systems in the body are the nervous system and the endocrine system.

KEY QUESTIONS

› What are the divisions of the nervous system, and what are their functions?

› How is information transmitted in the endocrine system, and what are its major structures?

› How do the nervous and endocrine systems interact to produce the fight-or-flight response?

Specialized for communication, up to 1 *trillion* neurons are linked throughout your body in a complex, organized communication network called the **nervous system.** The human nervous system is divided into two main divisions: the *central nervous system* and the *peripheral nervous system* (see Figure 2.8). For even simple behaviors to occur, such as curling your toes or scratching your nose, these two divisions must function as a single, integrated unit. Yet each of these divisions is highly specialized and performs different tasks.

The neuron is the most important transmitter of messages in the central nervous system. In the peripheral nervous system, communication occurs along **nerves.** Nerves and neurons are not the same thing. Nerves are made up of large bundles of neuron axons. Unlike neurons, many nerves are large enough to be seen easily with the unaided eye.

The Central Nervous System

The **central nervous system (CNS)** includes the brain and the spinal cord. The central nervous system is so critical to your ability to function that it is entirely protected by bone—the brain by your skull and the spinal cord by your spinal column. Surrounding and protecting the brain and the spinal cord are three layers of membranous tissues, called the *meninges.* As an added measure of protection, the brain and spinal cord are suspended in *cerebrospinal fluid* to protect them from being jarred. Cerebrospinal fluid also fills four hollow cavities in the brain, called *ventricles.* The inner surfaces of the ventricles are lined with *neural stem cells,* specialized cells that generate neurons in the developing brain.

The central nervous system is aptly named. It is central to all your behaviors and mental processes. And it is the central processing center—every action, thought, feeling, and sensation you experience is processed through the central nervous system.

The most important element of the central nervous system is, of course, the brain, which acts as the command center. We'll take a tour of the human brain in a later section.

The spinal cord handles both incoming and outgoing messages. Sensory receptors send messages along sensory nerves to the spinal cord, then up to the brain. To activate muscles, the brain sends signals down the spinal cord which are relayed out along motor nerves to the muscles.

nervous system The primary internal communication network of the body; divided into the central nervous system and the peripheral nervous system.

nerves Bundles of neuron axons that carry information in the peripheral nervous system.

central nervous system (CNS) The division of the nervous system that consists of the brain and spinal cord.

FIGURE 2.8 The Nervous System
The nervous system is a complex, organized communication network that is divided into two main divisions: the central nervous system (shown in blue) and the peripheral nervous system (shown in yellow).

PhotoAlto/Frederic Cirou/Getty Images

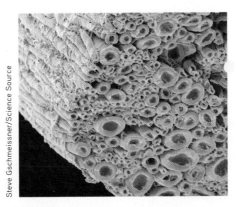

Steve Gschmeissner/Science Source

Nerves and Neurons Are Not the Same A cross section of a peripheral nerve is shown in this electron micrograph. The nerve is composed of bundles of axons (blue) wrapped in the myelin sheath (yellow). In the peripheral nervous system, myelin is formed by a type of glial cell called *Schwann cells,* shown here as a pinkish coating around the axons.

Traumatic Brain Injury: From Concussions to Chronic Traumatic Encephalopathy

Although encased in bone and cushioned by cerebrospinal fluid, the brain is highly susceptible to injury. Just a quarter inch of bone and membranes protect the brain from harm. A sharp blow to the head or body can cause the brain to literally crash into the skull. The shock wave from an explosion, such as a bomb blast, can also violently jar the brain, even when the head is protected by a helmet or other protective headgear. Thus, someone who experiences a close encounter with an intense explosion may *appear* to be unhurt, yet still have a severe brain injury (Sponheim & others, 2011).

When such an event disrupts normal brain functioning, a *traumatic brain injury* (or *TBI*) may be diagnosed. A *concussion* is the most common, and mildest, type of TBI, affecting more than 1 million people every year in the United States alone (Rabinowitz & others, 2014). Along with bomb blasts experienced by people in war zones, other common causes of concussion are auto accidents, falls, and sports injuries.

Traditionally, concussion has been defined as a disruption of normal functioning that occurs in the absence of any discernible structural or physical damage to the brain. However, we know now that concussions can cause physical damage and disrupt many aspects of brain function. As the brain twists or bounces, axons are sheared, myelin damaged, and brain chemistry disrupted. Although damage may not be evident on a CAT or MRI scan, it's obvious in the behavioral manifestations of concussion: loss of consciousness, dizziness, blurred or double vision, slurred speech and memory loss, among others (Rabinowitz & others, 2014).

Most people recover from concussions without complications. However, repeated concussions can lead to a serious brain disease called *chronic traumatic encephalopathy, or CTE.* CTE is a progressive, degenerative brain disease that can only be diagnosed after death. Symptoms include depression and anxiety, poor judgment and lack of impulse control, and problems with memory, concentration, and attention. Ultimately, CTE leads to dementia and death (Gavett & others, 2011).

Increasingly, CTE has been diagnosed in professional athletes, especially football and hockey players. For example, consider the case of Dave Duerson (see photo). After leaving the NFL, Dave Duerson became a successful businessman and spokesperson for the NFL players union. But as the years went by, his emotions

Dave Duerson Hockey players Derek Boogaard and Bob Probert. Football players John Grimsley, Chris Henry, and Junior Seau. Wrestler Chris Benoit. What do these men have in common? Like Dave Duerson and dozens of other former NFL players, all are professional athletes whose brains, after their deaths, displayed telltale signs of chronic traumatic encephalopathy, or CTE (Gavett & others, 2011; Tartaglia & others, 2014).

Michael J. Minardi/Getty Images

and behavior became more erratic. His business failed and so did his once-stable marriage. Troubled by severe headaches, memory problems, depression, and impulses he couldn't control, Duerson suspected he might have developed CTE (Nowinski, 2013).

Just before shooting himself in the chest, Duerson texted his ex-wife. He asked her to donate his brain to the "NFL Brain Bank," meaning the Boston University Center for the Study of Traumatic Encephalopathy. Months later, it was confirmed: Duerson had advanced CTE, which probably contributed to his depression and suicide.

Duerson and the other pro athletes with CTE were known to have suffered multiple concussions. But some researchers now suspect that CTE can result from milder brain injuries. Thomas Owens was a popular, academically successful 21-year-old college football player with no history of depression who committed suicide after complaining of stress. Owens had never been diagnosed with a concussion or head injury, but his brain showed clear signs of CTE. Neurologists believe that it was caused by the thousands of low-impact hits his brain had absorbed over years of playing middle school, high school, and college football.

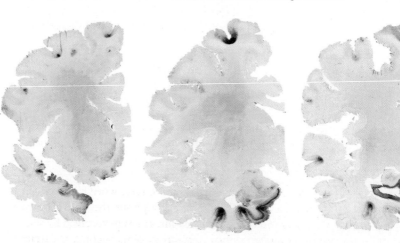

The Ravages of CTE Researchers at the Boston University Center for the Study of Traumatic Encephalopathy found the telltale signs of brain damage (brown coloring) in several regions of Dave Duerson's brain, slices of which are shown here (McKee & others, 2013).

Ann C McKee, MD Professor of Neurology and Pathology, VA Boston Healthcare System and Boston University School of Medicine

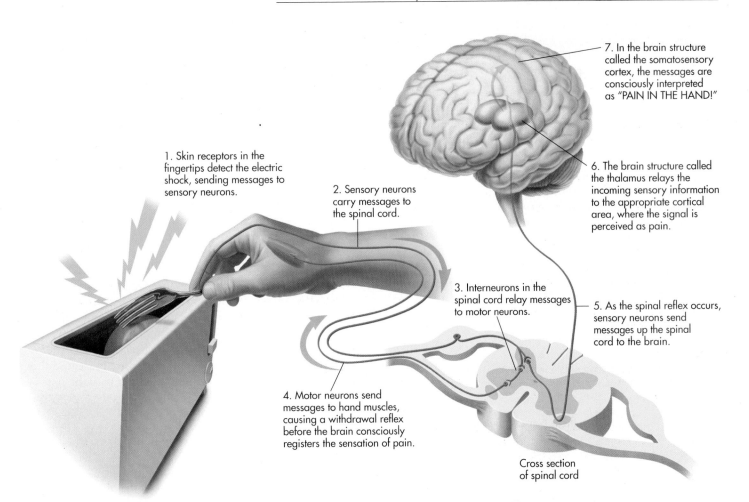

1. Skin receptors in the fingertips detect the electric shock, sending messages to sensory neurons.

2. Sensory neurons carry messages to the spinal cord.

3. Interneurons in the spinal cord relay messages to motor neurons.

4. Motor neurons send messages to hand muscles, causing a withdrawal reflex before the brain consciously registers the sensation of pain.

5. As the spinal reflex occurs, sensory neurons send messages up the spinal cord to the brain.

6. The brain structure called the thalamus relays the incoming sensory information to the appropriate cortical area, where the signal is perceived as pain.

7. In the brain structure called the somatosensory cortex, the messages are consciously interpreted as "PAIN IN THE HAND!"

Cross section of spinal cord

Most behaviors are controlled by your brain. However, the spinal cord can produce **spinal reflexes**—simple, automatic behaviors that occur without any brain involvement. For example, the *withdrawal reflex* occurs when you touch a painful stimulus, such as something hot, electrified, or sharp. As you can see in Figure 2.9, this simple reflex involves a loop of rapid communication among *sensory neurons,* which communicate sensation to the spinal cord; *interneurons,* which relay information within the spinal cord; and *motor neurons,* which signal the muscles to react.

Spinal reflexes are crucial to your survival. The additional few seconds that it would take you to consciously process sensations and decide how to react could result in serious injury. Spinal reflexes are also important as indicators that the neural pathways in your spinal cord are working correctly. That's why physicians test spinal reflexes during neurological examinations by tapping just below your kneecap for the knee-jerk spinal reflex or scratching the sole of your foot for the toe-curl spinal reflex.

The Peripheral Nervous System

The **peripheral nervous system** is the other major division of your nervous system. The word *peripheral* means "lying at the outer edges." Thus, the *peripheral* nervous system comprises all the nerves outside the central nervous system that extend to the outermost borders of your body, including your skin. The communication functions of the peripheral nervous system are handled by its two subdivisions: the *somatic nervous system* and the *autonomic nervous system.*

The **somatic nervous system** takes its name from the Greek word *soma,* which means "body." It plays a key role in communication throughout the entire body. First, the somatic nervous system communicates sensory information received by sensory receptors along sensory nerves *to* the central nervous system. Second, it carries

FIGURE 2.9 A Spinal Reflex A spinal reflex is a simple, involuntary behavior that is processed in the spinal cord without brain involvement. If you accidentally shock yourself by using a metal fork to pry a bagel out of a plugged-in toaster, you'll instantly pull your hand away from the painful stimulus—an example of the withdrawal reflex. The sequence shown here illustrates how the withdrawal reflex can occur before the brain processes the conscious perception of pain.

spinal reflexes Simple, automatic behaviors that are processed in the spinal cord.

peripheral nervous system (per-IF-er-ull) The division of the nervous system that includes all the nerves lying outside the central nervous system.

somatic nervous system The subdivision of the peripheral nervous system that communicates sensory information to the central nervous system and carries motor messages from the central nervous system to the muscles.

autonomic nervous system (aw-toe-NAHM-ick) The subdivision of the peripheral nervous system that regulates involuntary functions.

FIGURE 2.10 The Sympathetic and Parasympathetic Branches of the Autonomic Nervous System
Hikers in the southern United States memorize a simple rhyme to distinguish the venomous coral snake (red stripes touch yellow stripes) from its harmless mimic, a scarlet king snake (red stripes touch black stripes). Arousal of the sympathetic nervous system (left) prepares the hiker to fight or flee from the dangerous snake. When the hiker realizes that the snake is harmless (right), the parasympathetic nervous system calms the body and gradually restores normal functioning.

messages *from* the central nervous system along motor nerves to perform voluntary muscle movements. All the different sensations that you're experiencing right now are being communicated by your somatic nervous system to your spinal cord and on to your brain. When you perform a voluntary action, such as turning a page of this book, messages from the brain are communicated down the spinal cord, and then out to the muscles via the somatic nervous system.

The other subdivision of the peripheral nervous system is the **autonomic nervous system.** The word *autonomic* means "self-governing." Thus, the autonomic nervous system regulates *involuntary* functions, such as heartbeat, blood pressure, breathing, and digestion. These processes occur with little or no conscious involvement. This is fortunate, because if you had to mentally command your heart to beat or your stomach to digest the food you had for lunch, it would be difficult to focus your attention on anything else.

However, the autonomic nervous system is not completely self-regulating. By engaging in physical activity or purposely tensing or relaxing your muscles, you can increase or decrease autonomic activity. Emotions and mental imagery also influence your autonomic nervous system. Vividly imagining a situation that makes you feel angry, frightened, or even sexually aroused can dramatically increase your heart rate and blood pressure. A peaceful mental image can lower many autonomic functions.

The involuntary functions regulated by the autonomic nervous system are controlled by two different branches: the *sympathetic* and *parasympathetic nervous systems.* These two systems control many of the same organs in your body but cause them to respond in opposite ways (see Figure 2.10). In general, the sympathetic nervous

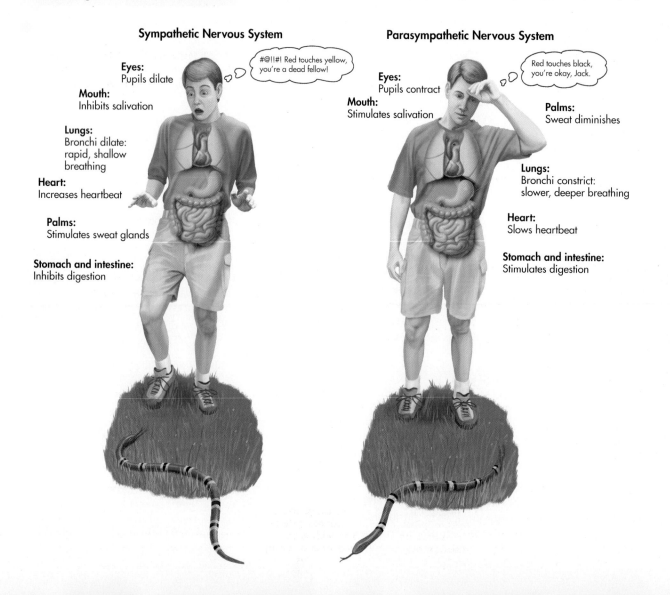

system arouses the body to expend energy, and the parasympathetic nervous system helps the body conserve energy.

The **sympathetic nervous system** is the body's emergency system, rapidly activating bodily systems to meet threats or emergencies. When you are frightened, your breathing accelerates, your heart beats faster, digestion stops, and the bronchial tubes in your lungs expand. All these physiological responses increase the amount of oxygen available to your brain and muscles. Your pupils dilate to increase your field of vision, and your mouth becomes dry, because salivation stops. You begin to sweat in response to your body's expenditure of greater energy and heat. These bodily changes collectively represent the *fight-or-flight response*—they physically prepare you to fight or to flee from a perceived danger. We'll discuss the fight-or-flight response in greater detail in Chapter 8 on emotion and Chapter 12 on stress.

Life on white/Alamy

Whereas the sympathetic nervous system mobilizes your body's physical resources, the **parasympathetic nervous system** conserves and maintains your physical resources. It calms you down after an emergency. Acting much more slowly than the sympathetic nervous system, the parasympathetic nervous system gradually returns your body's systems to normal. Heart rate, breathing, and blood pressure level out. Pupils constrict back to their normal size. Saliva returns, and the digestive system begins operating again.

Although the sympathetic and parasympathetic nervous systems produce opposite effects, they act together, keeping the nervous system in balance (see Figure 2.11). Each division handles different functions, yet the whole nervous system works in unison so that both automatic and voluntary behaviors are carried out smoothly.

Activating the Sympathetic Nervous System When the sympathetic nervous system activates in humans, tiny muscles in the skin contract, which elevates your hair follicles, producing the familiar sensation of "goose bumps" and making your hair stand on end. A similar process takes place in many mammals, making the fur or hair bristle, with rather spectacular results in this kitten.

sympathetic nervous system The branch of the autonomic nervous system that produces rapid physical arousal in response to perceived emergencies or threats.

parasympathetic nervous system The branch of the autonomic nervous system that maintains normal bodily functions and conserves the body's physical resources.

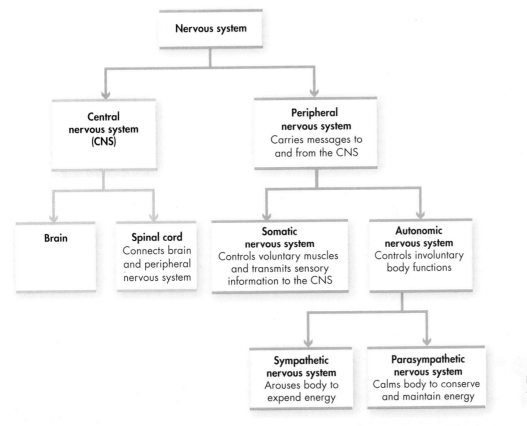

FIGURE 2.11 Organization of the Nervous System

endocrine system (EN-doe-krin) The system of glands, located throughout the body, that secrete hormones into the bloodstream.

hormones Chemical messengers secreted into the bloodstream primarily by endocrine glands.

The Endocrine System

As you can see in Figure 2.12, the **endocrine system** is made up of glands that are located throughout the body. Like the nervous system, the endocrine system uses chemical messengers to transmit information from one part of the body to another. Although the endocrine system is not part of the nervous system, it interacts with the nervous system in some important ways.

Endocrine glands communicate information from one part of the body to another by secreting messenger chemicals called **hormones** into the bloodstream. The hormones circulate throughout the bloodstream until they reach specific hormone receptors on target organs or tissue. Hormones regulate physical processes and influence behavior in a variety of ways. Metabolism, growth rate, digestion, blood pressure, and sexual development and reproduction are just some of the processes that are regulated by the endocrine hormones. Hormones are also involved in emotional response and your response to stress.

Endocrine hormones are closely linked to the workings of the nervous system. For example, the release of hormones may be stimulated or inhibited by certain parts of the nervous system. In turn, hormones can promote or inhibit the generation of nerve impulses. Finally, some hormones and neurotransmitters are chemically identical. The same molecule can act as a hormone in the endocrine system and as a neurotransmitter in the nervous system.

In contrast to the rapid speed of information transmission in the nervous system, communication in the endocrine system takes place much more slowly.

FIGURE 2.12 The Endocrine System The endocrine system and the nervous system are directly linked by the hypothalamus in the brain, which controls the pituitary gland. In turn, the pituitary releases hormones that affect the hormone production of several other endocrine glands. In the male and female figures shown here, you can see the location and main functions of several important endocrine glands.

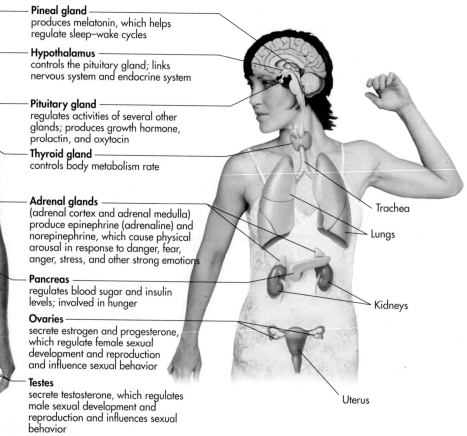

Pineal gland
produces melatonin, which helps regulate sleep–wake cycles

Hypothalamus
controls the pituitary gland; links nervous system and endocrine system

Pituitary gland
regulates activities of several other glands; produces growth hormone, prolactin, and oxytocin

Thyroid gland
controls body metabolism rate

Adrenal glands
(adrenal cortex and adrenal medulla) produce epinephrine (adrenaline) and norepinephrine, which cause physical arousal in response to danger, fear, anger, stress, and other strong emotions

Pancreas
regulates blood sugar and insulin levels; involved in hunger

Ovaries
secrete estrogen and progesterone, which regulate female sexual development and reproduction and influence sexual behavior

Testes
secrete testosterone, which regulates male sexual development and reproduction and influences sexual behavior

Trachea

Lungs

Kidneys

Uterus

Radius Images/Getty Images

Image Source/Glow Images

Hormones rely on the circulation of the blood to deliver their chemical messages to target organs, so it may take a few seconds or longer for the hormone to reach its target organ after it has been secreted by the originating gland.

The signals that trigger the secretion of hormones are regulated by the brain, primarily by a brain structure called the *hypothalamus.* (You'll learn more about the hypothalamus later in the chapter.) The hypothalamus serves as the main link between the endocrine system and the nervous system. The hypothalamus directly regulates the release of hormones by the **pituitary gland,** a pea-sized gland just under the brain. The pituitary's hormones, in turn, regulate the production of other hormones by many of the glands in the endocrine system. This is why the pituitary gland is often referred to as the body's master gland. Under the direction of the hypothalamus, the pituitary gland controls hormone production in other endocrine glands.

The pituitary gland also produces some hormones that act directly. For example, the pituitary produces *growth hormone,* which stimulates normal skeletal growth during childhood. The pituitary gland can also secrete endorphins to reduce the perception of pain. In nursing mothers, the pituitary produces *prolactin,* the hormone that stimulates milk production.

Another important hormone, **oxytocin,** is produced by the hypothalamus and released into the bloodstream by the pituitary gland. Oxytocin is the hormone that produces the let-down reflex, in which stored milk is "let down" into the nipple. Breast-feeding is a good example of the complex interaction among behavior, the nervous system, and the endocrine system (see Figure 2.13). Along with stimulating the release of milk for nursing, oxytocin also signals the uterus to contract during childbirth. *Pitocin,* given to women to induce labor, is a synthetic form of oxytocin.

Oxytocin also has psychological effects (Carter, 2014). It promotes bonding between reproductive partners and between parent and infant, and even between dogs and owners (Nagasawa & others, 2015). Early research found that it also promotes empathy, trust among group members, and sensitivity to social cues (see Miller, 2013). These findings gave oxytocin the reputation as "the love hormone."

But the effects of oxytocin are not that simple. Subsequent research found that in some circumstances, oxytocin can promote aggression or other antisocial behavior (de Dreu & others, 2011; Olff & others, 2013). For example, studies have shown that oxytocin increases bonding among group members but increases dishonest or hostile behavior toward non-group members (Shalvi & de Dreu, 2014; Stallen & others, 2012). And, other researchers have found that some people respond to oxytocin with increased social anxiety, rather than increased feelings of trust (Bartz & others, 2011; Olff & others, 2013). Thus, oxytocin is involved in *many* different aspects of social motivation and behavior.

Another set of glands, called the **adrenal glands,** is of particular interest to psychologists. The adrenal glands consist of the **adrenal cortex,** which is the outer gland, and the **adrenal medulla,** which is the inner gland. Both the adrenal cortex and the adrenal medulla produce hormones that are involved in the human stress response. As you'll see in Chapter 12 on stress, hormones secreted by the adrenal cortex also interact with the *immune system,* the body's defense against invading viruses or bacteria.

The adrenal medulla plays a key role in the fight-or-flight response, described earlier. When aroused, the sympathetic nervous system stimulates the adrenal medulla. In turn, the adrenal medulla produces *epinephrine* and *norepinephrine.*

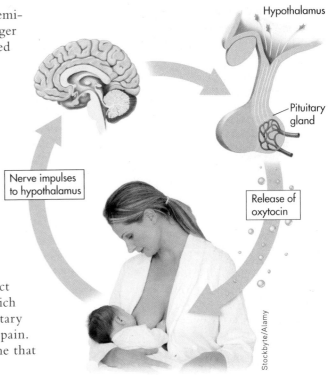

FIGURE 2.13 Interacting Systems Breast-feeding is an example of the complex interaction among the nervous system, the endocrine system, and behavior. Nerve impulses from sensory receptors in the mother's skin are sent to the brain. The hypothalamus signals the release of oxytocin by the pituitary gland, which causes the mother's milk to let down and begin flowing.

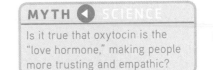

Is it true that oxytocin is the "love hormone," making people more trusting and empathic?

pituitary gland (pih-TOO-ih-tare-ee) The endocrine gland attached to the base of the brain that secretes hormones affecting the function of other glands as well as hormones that act directly on physical processes.

oxytocin Hormone involved in reproduction, social motivation, and social behavior.

adrenal glands The pair of endocrine glands that are involved in the human stress response.

adrenal cortex The outer portion of the adrenal glands.

adrenal medulla The inner portion of the adrenal glands, which secretes epinephrine and norepinephrine.

gonads The endocrine glands that secrete hormones that regulate sexual characteristics and reproductive processes; *ovaries* in females and *testes* in males.

phrenology (freh-NAHL-uh-jee) A pseudoscientific theory of the brain that claimed that personality characteristics, moral character, and intelligence could be determined by examining the bumps on a person's skull.

cortical localization The notion that different functions are located or localized in different areas of the brain; also called *localization of function.*

(You may be more familiar with the word *adrenaline,* which is another name for epinephrine.)

As they circulate through the bloodstream to the heart and other target organs, epinephrine and norepinephrine complement and enhance the effects of the sympathetic nervous system. These hormones also act as neurotransmitters, stimulating activity at the synapses in the sympathetic nervous system. The action of epinephrine and norepinephrine is a good illustration of the long-lasting effects of hormones. If you've noticed that it takes a while for you to calm down after a particularly upsetting or stressful experience, it's because of the lingering effects of epinephrine and norepinephrine in your body.

Also important are the **gonads,** or sex organs—the *ovaries* in women and the *testes* in men. In women, the ovaries secrete the hormones *estrogen* and *progesterone.* In men, the testes secrete male sex hormones called *androgens,* the most important of which is *testosterone.* Testosterone is also secreted by the adrenal glands in both males and females. In both males and females, the sex hormones influence sexual development, sexual behavior, and reproduction. They also affect brain structure and function (Lombardo & others, 2012; McEwen & others, 2012).

❯ Test your understanding of **The Nervous and Endocrine Systems** with **LEARNING***Curve.*

A Guided Tour of the Brain

KEY THEME

The brain is a highly complex, integrated, and dynamic system of interconnected neurons.

KEY QUESTIONS

❯ What are neural pathways, and why are they important?

❯ What are functional and structural plasticity?

❯ What is neurogenesis, and what is the evidence for its occurrence in the adult human brain?

> The human brain produces in 30 seconds as much data as the Hubble Space Telescope has produced in its lifetime.
>
> —*Konrad Kording (2013)*

Think about it: The most complex mass of matter in the universe sits right behind your eyes and between your two ears—your brain. Not even the Internet can match the human brain for speed and sophistication of information transmission. On average, the human brain represents only about 2 percent of the body's weight, yet consumes 20 percent of the body's energy.

In this part of the chapter, we'll take you on a guided tour of the human brain. As your tour guides, our goal here is not to tell you everything that is known or suspected about the human brain. Such an endeavor would take stacks of books rather than a single chapter in a college textbook. Instead, our first goal is to familiarize you with the basic organization and structures of the brain. Our second goal is to give you a general sense of how the brain works. In later chapters, we'll add to your knowledge of the brain as we discuss the brain's involvement in specific psychological processes.

The Human Brain Weighing roughly three pounds, the human brain is about the size of a small cauliflower and has the consistency of tofu. Although your brain makes up only about 2 percent of your total body weight, it uses some 20 percent of the oxygen your body needs while at rest (Magistretti, 2009). The oxygen is used in breaking down glucose to supply the brain with energy.

To begin, it's important to note that the brain generally does not lend itself to simple explanations. One early, simplistic approach to mapping the brain is discussed in Science Versus Pseudoscience, "Phrenology: The Bumpy Road to Scientific

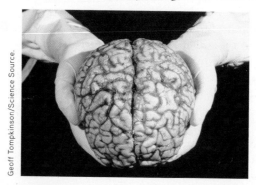

Geoff Tompkinson/Science Source.

SCIENCE VERSUS PSEUDOSCIENCE

Phrenology: The Bumpy Road to Scientific Progress

Are people with large foreheads smarter than people with small foreheads? Does the shape of your head provide clues to your personality? Such notions were at the core of **phrenology,** a popular pseudoscience founded in the 1800s by German physician Franz Gall.

Mary Evans Picture Library/ The Image Works

After studying the anatomy of human and animal brains, Gall became convinced that the size and shape of the cortex were reflected in the size and shape of the skull. Suspecting that variations in the size and shape of the human skull might reflect individual differences in abilities, character, and personality, he went to prisons, hospitals, and schools to study the association between personal characteristics and any distinctive bulges or bumps on the person's skull. Eventually, Gall devised elaborate maps showing the location of the personality characteristics, or "faculties," that he believed were reflected in the shape of the head (see image).

When Gall's theory of phrenology was ridiculed by other scientists for lack of adequate evidence, Gall took his ideas to the general public. He lectured widely and gave "readings" in which he provided a personality description based on measuring the bumps on a person's head. Phrenology continued to be popular with both physicians and the general public well into the 1900s (Sokal, 2001). At the height of phrenology's popularity, some physicians even used leeches to drain blood from areas of the head that were believed to correspond to overdeveloped characteristics, such as "combativeness" or "amativeness" (McCoy, 2000).

Despite its pseudoscientific nature, phrenology helped advance the scientific study of the human mind and brain (Eghigian, 2011). It triggered scientific interest in the possibility of **cortical localization,** or *localization of function*—the idea that specific psychological and mental functions are located (or localized) in specific brain areas (Livianos-Aldano & others, 2007; van Wyhe, 2000).

Today, sophisticated brain-imaging techniques like fMRI and PET scans have demonstrated that some cognitive and perceptual abilities *are* localized in different brain areas. So although Franz Gall and the phrenologists were wrong about the significance of bumps on the skull, they were on target about the general idea of cortical localization.

The Psycograph Invented in the early 1900s, the psycograph stamped out brief summaries of the phrenological "faculties" measured, such as "You are fairly secretive but can improve." The machines were popular attractions in department stores and theater lobbies throughout the United States (McCoy, 1996, 2000).

Getty Images

Progress," above. Although we will identify the functions that seem to be associated with particular brain regions, always remember that specific functions seldom correspond neatly to a single, specific brain site. Most psychological processes, especially complex ones, involve *multiple* brain structures and regions. Even seemingly simple tasks—such as carrying on a conversation, catching a ball, or watching a movie—involve the smoothly coordinated synthesis of information among many different areas of your brain (Turk-Browne, 2013). Thus, contrary to what some people claim, it's *not* true that you "use only 10 percent of your brain." Imagine how well you would function if you lost even a third of your brain tissue, much less 90 percent. As neuroscientist Barry Gordon (2008) observes, "we use virtually every part of the brain, and the brain is active almost all the time."

How is information communicated and shared among these multiple brain regions? Even though we'll talk about brain centers and structures that are involved in different aspects of behavior, the best way to think of the brain is as an *integrated system*.

MYTH ▶ SCIENCE
Is it true that even simple behaviors and abilities involve the activation of multiple parts of the brain?

MYTH ◀ SCIENCE
Is it true that you only use 10% of your brain?

FOCUS ON NEUROSCIENCE

Mapping the Pathways of the Brain

The *Human Connectome Project* has an ambitious goal: to map the millions of miles of neural connections among the 100 billion neurons in the human brain (Sporns, 2011a, b). The **connectome** is nothing less than the complete map of all the neural connections in the brain (Seung, 2012). Launched in 2009 by the National Institutes of Health, the Human Connectome Project aims to combine brain-imaging data from hundreds of participants into a three-dimensional map of the brain's information highways (Margulies & others, 2013).

New brain-scanning techniques called *diffusion spectrum imaging* (DSI) and *diffusion tensor imaging* (DTI) allow neuroscientists to produce three-dimensional images of the neural pathways that connect one part of the brain to another (see Chi, 2014). These pathways, sometimes called *tracts*, are made up of *white matter*, the bundles of myelinated axons. Diffusion imaging tracks the movement of water molecules in brain tissue along the axons.

To give you an idea of the complexity of the Connectome Project's task, imagine a one-millimeter cube of brain tissue about the size of a grain of sugar. To store the images needed to form a picture of all of the neural connections in this tiny cube of brain tissue would require one petrobyte—one million gigabytes—of computer memory. And to put *that* figure in perspective, one petrobyte is roughly the amount of data space that Facebook uses to store 40 billion photos (Vance, 2010).

Each fiber in the photo represents hundreds of thousands of individual axons, which are too minuscule to be distinguished in a brain scan. Blue colors show the bundled axons that form the neural pathway stretching from the top to the bottom of the brain. Green represents pathways from the front (left) to the back (right) of the brain. Red shows the *corpus callosum*, the pathway *between*

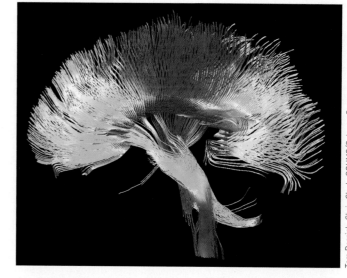

Tom Barrick, Chris Clark, SGHMS/Science Source

the right- and left-brain hemispheres. (You'll read about the corpus callosum later in the chapter.)

Neuroscientists have become increasingly aware of the importance of the brain's network connections (Seung, 2012). And, faulty network connections have been implicated in several brain disorders, including Alzheimer's disease, schizophrenia, and autism (Braskie & others, 2011; Lynall & others, 2010). It may be years before the findings of the Connectome Project yield practical applications, but even preliminary images, like the one shown here, reveal the dynamic intricacy of the most complex object in the universe—the human brain.

Many brain functions involve the activation of *neural pathways* that link different brain structures (Jbabdi & Behrens, 2012; Park & Friston, 2013). Neural pathways are formed by groups of neuron cell bodies in one area of the brain that project their axons to other brain areas (Seung, 2012). These neural pathways form communication networks and circuits that link different brain areas. Mapping the information highways of the human brain is the ambitious goal of *The Human Connectome Project,* which is described in the Focus on Neuroscience above.

The Dynamic Brain
PLASTICITY AND NEUROGENESIS

Before embarking on our tour, we need to describe one last important characteristic of the brain: its remarkable capacity to change in response to experience. Until the mid-1960s, neuroscientists believed—and taught—that by early adulthood the brain's physical structure was *hardwired* or fixed for life. But today it's known that the brain's physical structure is literally sculpted by experience (Knobloch & Jessberger, 2011). The brain's ability to change function and structure is referred to as *neuroplasticity,* or simply *plasticity.* (The word *plastic* originally comes from a Greek word, *plastikos,* which means the quality of being easily shaped or molded.)

One form of plasticity is **functional plasticity,** which refers to the brain's ability to shift functions from damaged to undamaged brain areas. Depending on

connectome Map of neural connections in the brain

functional plasticity The brain's ability to shift functions from damaged to undamaged brain areas.

the location and degree of brain damage, stroke or accident victims often need to "relearn" once-routine tasks such as speaking, walking, and reading. If the rehabilitation is successful, undamaged brain areas gradually assume the ability to process and execute the tasks (Pascual-Leone & others, 2005).

But the brain can do more than just shift functions from one area to another. **Structural plasticity** refers to the brain's ability to physically change its structure in response to learning, active practice, or environmental stimulation. It is now known that even subtle changes in your environment or behavior can lead to structural changes in the brain (Bryck & Fisher, 2012; Jacobs, 2004). In the Focus on Neuroscience, "Juggling and Brain Plasticity," below, we describe an ingenious experiment that dramatically demonstrated structural plasticity in the human brain.

An even more dramatic example of the brain's capacity to change is **neurogenesis**—the development of new neurons. For many years, scientists believed that people and most animals did not experience neurogenesis after birth (Kempermann, 2012a). With the exception of birds, tree shrews, and some rodents, it was thought that the mature brain could lose neurons but could not grow new ones. But new studies offered compelling evidence that challenged that dogma.

First, research by psychologist Elizabeth Gould and her colleagues (1998) showed that adult marmoset monkeys were generating a significant number of new neurons every day in the *hippocampus*, a brain structure that plays a critical role in the ability to

> One of the great conceptual leaps of modern neuroscience has been the notion of neuroplasticity. . . . Scientists now know that even modest changes in the internal or external world can lead to structural changes in the brain.
>
> —*Barry L. Jacobs (2004)*

structural plasticity The brain's ability to change its physical structure in response to learning, active practice, or environmental influences.

neurogenesis The development of new neurons.

FOCUS ON NEUROSCIENCE

Juggling and Brain Plasticity

What happens to the brain when you learn a new, challenging skill? Does learning affect the brain's physical structure?

German researcher Bogdan Draganski and his colleagues (2004, 2006) showed that learning a new skill produces structural changes in the human brain. In their study, 24 young adults were assigned to either a "jugglers" or "nonjugglers" group. A baseline MRI scan indicated that there were no significant regional brain differences between the two groups at the beginning of the study.

Then the juggling group members were given three months to master a basic juggling routine. A second brain scan taken after this period indicated that the jugglers showed a 3 to 4 percent increase in gray matter in two brain regions that are involved in perceiving, remembering, and anticipating complex visual motions. These two regions are shown in yellow in the composite MRI scans shown on the right. In comparison, there were *no* brain changes in the scans of the nonjugglers over the same three-month period.

A third brain scan was performed three months after participants in the juggling group were told to stop practicing. Now, the same regions that had grown while the jugglers were practicing their skills every day had *decreased* in size. While still larger than before the participants had learned to juggle, the regions were 1 to 2 percent smaller than when the participants were juggling

every day. In comparison, the same regions in the nonjuggling control group remained unchanged.

In a later study, novice jugglers showed changes in brain regions within just seven days after learning to juggle (Driemeyer & others, 2008). And, demonstrating the plasticity of even the aging brain, similar changes were found in a group of senior citizens after they learned to juggle (Boyke & others, 2008).

Wondering how long it might take for learning to translate into structural changes in the brain? A new study by Yaniv Sagi and his colleagues (2012) detected tiny structural changes in the hippocampus after study participants spent just *two hours* playing a new video game that involved spatial learning and memory.

Reprinted by permission from Macmillan Publishers Ltd: Nature 427, 311–312 (22 January 2004), copyright 2004 Courtesy of Dr. Arne May

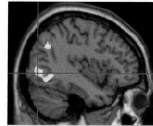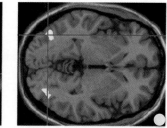

Learning a New Skill Makes Its Mark on the Brain The yellow in these MRIs indicates the brain areas that temporarily increased by 3 to 4 percent in size in those participants who learned to juggle. These brain regions are involved in the ability to perceive, remember, and anticipate complex visual motions.

Robert Crum/Shutterstock

Zela PF/Alamy

We've always known that our brains control our behavior, but not that our behavior could control and change the structure of our brains.

—*Fred Gage (2007)*

Neurogenesis in the Adult Human Brain New neurons, shown in green, can be seen amid already established neurons, shown in red. In one area of the adult hippocampus, researchers found that each cubic centimeter of brain tissue contained from 100 to 300 new neurons (Eriksson & others, 1998). A later study by Kristy Spalding and her colleagues (2013) confirmed that more than a thousand new neurons are generated *each day*, even in older adults.

form new memories. Gould's groundbreaking research provided the first demonstration that new neurons could develop in an adult primate brain. Could it be that the *human* brain also has the capacity to generate new neurons in adulthood?

Researchers Peter Eriksson, Fred Gage, and their colleagues (1998) provided the first evidence that it does. The subjects were five adult cancer patients, whose ages ranged from the late fifties to the early seventies. These patients were all being given a drug used in cancer treatments to determine whether tumor cells are multiplying. The drug is incorporated into newly dividing cells, coloring them. Using fluorescent lights, this chemical tracer can be detected in the newly created cells. Eriksson and Gage reasoned that if new neurons were being generated, the drug would be present in their genetic material.

Within hours after each patient died, an autopsy was performed and the hippocampus was removed and examined. The results were unequivocal. In each patient, *hundreds* of new neurons had been generated since the drug had been administered,

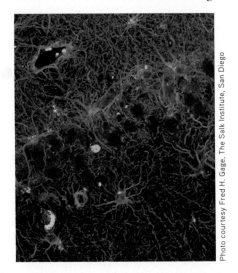

Photo courtesy Fred H. Gage, The Salk Institute, San Diego

even though all the patients were over 50 years old (see accompanying photo).

Some neuroscientists were still skeptical, but a recent study provides definitive proof of neurogenesis in the adult human brain. Swedish neuroscientist Kirsty Spalding and her colleagues (2013) used carbon dating to measure the growth of new neurons in the brains of people aged 19 to 92. More than 50 years ago, aboveground testing of nuclear bombs released carbon-14, or C-14, into the atmosphere. Since these nuclear tests were banned in 1963, levels of C-14 in the atmosphere have declined at a regular and well-known rate. Measuring the amount of C-14 concentration in neurons therefore provided a "time-stamp" for the neurons, allowing researchers to determine when the neurons had been generated.

The carbon-14 signature was unmistakable: Spalding and her colleagues found clear evidence of neurogenesis after birth and, in fact, throughout the lifespan. They were also able to calculate the *rate* of neurogenesis in a specific region of the brain, called the *hippocampus,* a brain region involved in learning and memory. It turned out that an average of 1,400 new neurons were being generated each day. The rate declined only slightly with age. Other regions of the brain, however, did *not* show evidence of neurogenesis.

Research on neurogenesis in humans and animals has uncovered a number of intriguing findings. It is now generally accepted that newborn neurons develop into mature functioning neurons in at least two regions of the human brain—the hippocampus and the *olfactory bulb,* responsible for odor perception (Lee & others, 2012). These newly generated neurons are incorporated into existing neural networks, possibly playing a key role in learning and memory (Kempermann, 2012b; Marin-Burgin & others, 2012). In nonhuman animals, such as macaque monkeys, newborn neurons migrate to multiple brain regions (Gould, 2007). Environmental factors also affect neurogenesis. Stress, exercise, environmental complexity, and even social status have been shown to influence the rate of neurogenesis in monkeys, rodents, and birds (Glasper & others, 2012). In laboratory animals, learning new behaviors enhances the survival of new neurons (Shors, 2014).

In the next section, we'll begin our guided tour of the brain. Following the general sequence of the brain's development, we'll start with the structures at the base of the brain and work our way up to more complicated brain regions, which are responsible for complex mental activity.

The Brainstem
HINDBRAIN AND MIDBRAIN STRUCTURES

KEY THEME

The brainstem includes the hindbrain and midbrain, located at the base of the brain.

KEY QUESTIONS

› Why does damage to one side of the brain affect the opposite side of the body?
› What are the key structures of the hindbrain and midbrain, and what are their functions?

The major regions of the brain are illustrated in Figure 2.14, which can serve as a map to keep you oriented during our tour. At the base of the brain lie the hindbrain and, directly above it, the midbrain. Combined, the structures of the hindbrain and midbrain make up the brain region called the **brainstem.**

THE HINDBRAIN

The **hindbrain** connects the spinal cord with the rest of the brain. Sensory and motor pathways pass through the hindbrain to and from regions that are situated higher up in the brain. Sensory information coming in from one side of the body crosses over at the hindbrain level, projecting to the opposite side of the brain. And outgoing motor messages from one side of the brain also cross over at the hindbrain level, controlling movement and other motor functions on the opposite side of the body. This is referred to as *contralateral organization.*

Contralateral organization accounts for why people who suffer strokes on one side of the brain experience muscle weakness or paralysis on the opposite side of the body. Our friend Asha, for example, suffered only minor damage to motor control areas in her brain. However, because the stroke occurred on the *left* side of her brain, what muscle weakness she did experience was localized on the *right* side of her body, primarily in her right hand.

Three structures make up the hindbrain—the medulla, the pons, and the cerebellum. The **medulla** is situated at the base of the brain directly above the spinal cord. It is at the level of the medulla that ascending sensory pathways and descending motor pathways crisscross to the contralateral side of the body.

brainstem A region of the brain made up of the hindbrain and the midbrain.

hindbrain A region at the base of the brain that contains several structures that regulate basic life functions.

medulla (muh-DOOL-uh) A hindbrain structure that controls vital life functions such as breathing and circulation.

FIGURE 2.14 Major Regions of the Brain Situated at the base of the brain, the hindbrain's functions include coordinating movement and posture, regulating alertness, and maintaining vital life functions. The midbrain helps process sensory information. In combination, the hindbrain and the midbrain comprise the brainstem. The forebrain is the largest brain region and is involved in more sophisticated behaviors and mental processes.

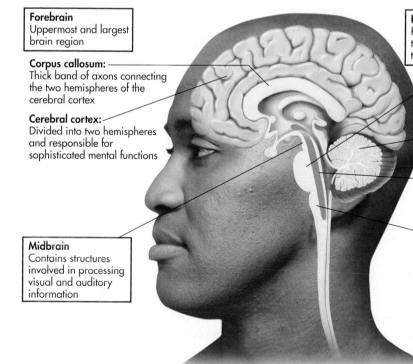

Forebrain
Uppermost and largest brain region

Corpus callosum:
Thick band of axons connecting the two hemispheres of the cerebral cortex

Cerebral cortex:
Divided into two hemispheres and responsible for sophisticated mental functions

Midbrain
Contains structures involved in processing visual and auditory information

Hindbrain
Region at base of brain that connects the brain to the spinal cord

Pons:
Helps coordinate movements on left and right sides of body

Cerebellum:
Coordinates movement, balance, and posture

Reticular formation:
Helps regulate attention and alertness

Medulla:
Controls breathing, heartbeat, and other vital life functions

Jupiter Images/Photos.com/Alamy

pons A hindbrain structure that connects the medulla to the two sides of the cerebellum; helps coordinate and integrate movements on each side of the body.

cerebellum (sair-uh-BELL-um) A large, two-sided hindbrain structure at the back of the brain; responsible for muscle coordination and maintaining posture and equilibrium.

reticular formation (reh-TICK-you-ler) A network of nerve fibers located in the center of the medulla that helps regulate attention, arousal, and sleep; also called the *reticular activating system*.

midbrain The middle and smallest brain region, involved in processing auditory and visual sensory information.

substantia nigra (sub-STAN-she-uh NYE-gruh) An area of the midbrain that is involved in motor control and contains a large concentration of dopamine-producing neurons.

forebrain The largest and most complex brain region, which contains centers for complex behaviors and mental processes; also called the *cerebrum*.

The medulla plays a critical role in basic life-sustaining functions. It contains centers that control such vital autonomic functions as breathing, heart rate, and blood pressure. The medulla also controls a number of vital reflexes, including swallowing, coughing, vomiting, and sneezing. Because the medulla is involved in such critical life functions, damage to this brain region can rapidly prove fatal.

Above the medulla is a swelling of tissue called the **pons,** which represents the uppermost level of the hindbrain. Bulging out behind the pons is the large **cerebellum.** On each side of the pons, a large bundle of axons connects it to the cerebellum. The word *pons* means "bridge," and the pons is a bridge of sorts: Information from various other brain regions located higher up in the brain is relayed to the cerebellum via the pons. The pons also contains centers that play an important role in regulating breathing.

The cerebellum functions in the control of balance, muscle tone, and coordinated muscle movements. It is also involved in the learning of habitual or automatic movements and motor skills, such as typing, writing, or backhanding a tennis ball.

Jerky, uncoordinated movements can result from damage to the cerebellum. Simple movements, such as walking or standing upright, may become difficult or impossible. The cerebellum is also one of the brain areas affected by alcohol consumption, which is why a person who is intoxicated may stagger and have difficulty walking a straight line or standing on one foot. (This is also why a police officer will ask a suspected drunk driver to execute these normally effortless movements.)

At the core of the medulla and the pons is a network of neurons called the **reticular formation,** or the *reticular activating system,* which is composed of many groups of specialized neurons that project up to higher brain regions and down to the spinal cord. The reticular formation plays an important role in regulating attention and sleep.

THE MIDBRAIN

The **midbrain** is an important relay station that contains centers involved in the processing of auditory and visual sensory information. Auditory sensations from the left and right ears are processed through the midbrain, helping you orient toward the direction of a sound. The midbrain is also involved in processing visual information, including eye movements, helping you visually locate objects and track their movements. After passing through the midbrain level, auditory information and visual information are relayed to sensory processing centers farther up in the forebrain region, which will be discussed shortly.

A midbrain area called the **substantia nigra** is involved in motor control and contains a large concentration of dopamine-producing neurons. *Substantia nigra* means "dark substance," and as the name suggests, this area is darkly pigmented. The substantia nigra is part of a larger neural pathway that helps prepare other brain regions to initiate organized movements or actions. In the section on neurotransmitters, we noted that Parkinson's disease involves symptoms of abnormal movement, including difficulty initiating a particular movement. Many of those movement-related symptoms are associated with the degeneration of dopamine-producing neurons in the substantia nigra.

The Forebrain

KEY THEME
The forebrain includes the cerebral cortex and the limbic system structures.

KEY QUESTIONS
› What are the four lobes of the cerebral cortex, and what are their functions?
› What is the limbic system?
› What functions are associated with the thalamus, hypothalamus, hippocampus, and amygdala?

Situated above the midbrain is the largest region of the brain: the **forebrain.** In humans, the forebrain represents about 90 percent of the brain. In Figure 2.15, you can see how the size of the forebrain has increased during evolution, although the

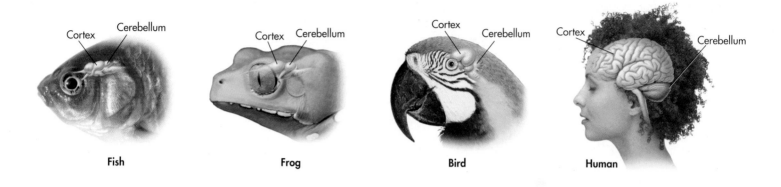

Fish

Frog

Bird

Human

general structure of the human brain is similar to that of other species (Clark & others, 2001). Many important structures are found in the forebrain region, but we'll begin by describing the most prominent—the cerebral cortex.

THE CEREBRAL CORTEX

The outer portion of the forebrain, the **cerebral cortex,** is divided into two **cerebral hemispheres.** The word *cortex* means "bark," and much like the bark of a tree, the cerebral cortex is the outer covering of the forebrain. A thick bundle of axons, called the **corpus callosum,** connects the two cerebral hemispheres, as shown in Figure 2.16. The corpus callosum serves as the primary communication link between the left and right cerebral hemispheres.

The cerebral cortex is only about a quarter of an inch thick. It is composed mainly of glial cells and neuron cell bodies and axons, giving it a grayish appearance—which is why the cerebral cortex is sometimes described as being composed of *gray matter.* Extending inward from the cerebral cortex are white myelinated axons that are sometimes referred to as *white matter.* These myelinated axons connect the cerebral cortex to other brain regions.

Numerous folds, grooves, and bulges characterize the human cerebral cortex. The purpose of these ridges and valleys is easy to illustrate. Imagine a flat, three-foot-by-three-foot piece of paper. You can compact the surface area of this piece of paper by scrunching it up into a wad. In much the same way, the grooves and bulges of the cerebral cortex allow about three square feet of surface area to be packed into the small space of the human skull.

Look again at Figure 2.14 on page 65. The drawing of the human brain is cut through the center to show how the cerebral cortex folds above and around the rest of the brain. In contrast to the numerous folds and wrinkles of the human cerebral cortex, notice the smooth appearance of the cortex in fish, amphibians, and birds in Figure 2.15. Mammals with large brains—such as cats, dogs, and nonhuman primates—also have wrinkles and folds in the cerebral cortex, but to a lesser extent than humans (Jarvis & others, 2005).

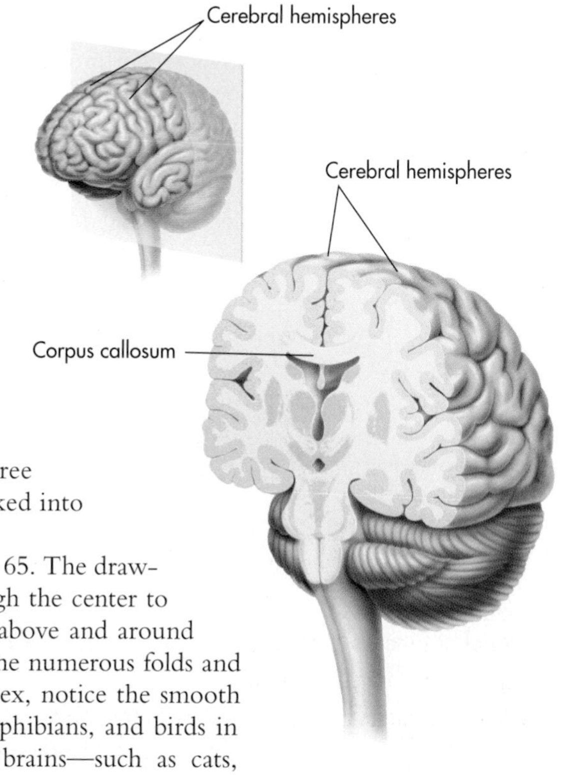

Cerebral hemispheres

Cerebral hemispheres

Corpus callosum

FIGURE 2.15 Evolution and the Cerebral Cortex The brains of these different animal species have many structures in common, including a cerebellum and cortex. However, the proportion devoted to the cortex is much greater in mammals than in species that evolved earlier, such as fish and amphibians. The relative sizes of the different structures reflects their functional importance.

[a] Tracy Kahn/Corbis [b] DLILLC/Corbis [c] Photodisc/Getty Images [d] Corbis Photography/Veer

FIGURE 2.16 The Cerebral Hemispheres and the Corpus Callosum The two hemispheres of the cerebral cortex can be clearly seen in this side-to-side cross-sectional view of the brain. The main communications link connecting the two cerebral hemispheres is the corpus callosum, a thick, broad bundle of some 300 million myelinated neuron axons.

cerebral cortex (suh-REE-brull or SAIR-uh-brull) The wrinkled outer portion of the forebrain, which contains the most sophisticated brain centers.

cerebral hemispheres The nearly symmetrical left and right halves of the cerebral cortex.

corpus callosum A thick band of axons that connects the two cerebral hemispheres and acts as a communication link between them.

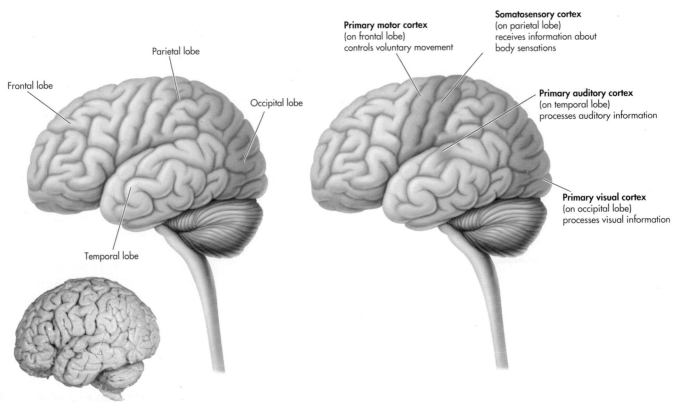

Primary motor cortex
(on frontal lobe)
controls voluntary movement

Somatosensory cortex
(on parietal lobe)
receives information about
body sensations

Primary auditory cortex
(on temporal lobe)
processes auditory information

Primary visual cortex
(on occipital lobe)
processes visual information

Parietal lobe

Frontal lobe

Occipital lobe

Temporal lobe

FIGURE 2.17 Lobes of the Cerebral Cortex Each hemisphere of the cerebral cortex can be divided into four regions, or *lobes*. Each lobe is associated with distinct functions. The association areas, also called the *association cortex*, make up most of the rest of the cerebral cortex.

Hossler, PhD/Custom Medical Stock Photo

Each cerebral hemisphere can be roughly divided into four regions, or *lobes:* the *temporal, occipital, parietal,* and *frontal lobes* (see Figure 2.17). Each lobe is associated with distinct functions. Located near your temples, the **temporal lobe** contains the *primary auditory cortex,* which receives auditory information. At the very back of the brain is the **occipital lobe.** The occipital lobe includes the *primary visual cortex,* where visual information is received.

The **parietal lobe** is involved in processing bodily, or *somatosensory,* information, including touch, temperature, pressure, and information from receptors in the muscles and joints. A band of tissue on the parietal lobe, called the *somatosensory cortex,* receives information from touch receptors in different parts of the body.

Each part of the body is represented on the somatosensory cortex, but this representation is not equally distributed (see Figure 2.18). Instead, body parts are

Focus on the Frontal Lobes: The Famous Case of Phineas Gage
Early interest in the frontal lobes was sparked by the famous case of Phineas Gage, a railroad foreman who suffered a horrendous accident in 1848. A freak explosion shot a three-foot-long iron bar through Gage's skull, piercing his brain and exiting out the top of his head. Gage, shown here holding the iron bar, miraculously recovered, but after the accident the formerly conscientious and soft-spoken foreman became bad-tempered and irresponsible.

After Gage's death in 1861, his physician proposed that Gage's personality changes were caused by damage to his frontal lobes (Harlow, 1869). More than a century later, contemporary neuroscientists studying Gage's skull confirmed that Gage's left frontal lobe had been severely damaged (Damasio & others, 1994; Ratiu & Talos, 2004). More recently, models created by neuroscientist John Van Horn and his colleagues (2012) point to probable damage to the white matter connections between Gage's frontal lobe and other brain regions associated with emotion and memory. This disconnection may have contributed to Gage's personality changes and lack of emotional control after the accident.

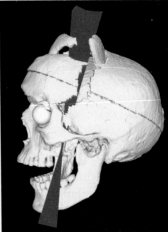

Image courtesy of John Darrell Van Horn, Ph.D., Institute of Neuroimaging and Informatics, University of Southern California. Mapping Connectivity Damage in the Case of Phineas Gage, PLoS One, May 2012, vol 7, issue 5.

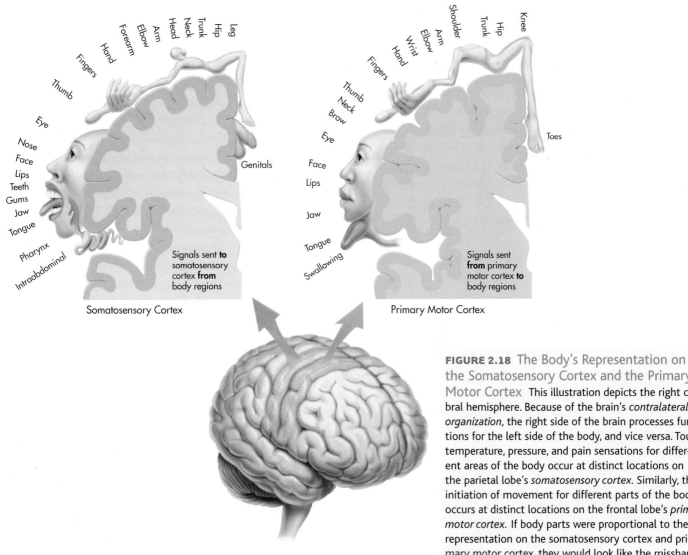

FIGURE 2.18 The Body's Representation on the Somatosensory Cortex and the Primary Motor Cortex This illustration depicts the right cerebral hemisphere. Because of the brain's *contralateral organization*, the right side of the brain processes functions for the left side of the body, and vice versa. Touch, temperature, pressure, and pain sensations for different areas of the body occur at distinct locations on the parietal lobe's *somatosensory cortex*. Similarly, the initiation of movement for different parts of the body occurs at distinct locations on the frontal lobe's *primary motor cortex*. If body parts were proportional to their representation on the somatosensory cortex and primary motor cortex, they would look like the misshapen human figures on the outer edges of the drawings.

represented in proportion to their sensitivity to somatic sensations. For example, on the left side of Figure 2.18, you can see that your hands and face, which are very responsive to touch, have much greater representation on the somatosensory cortex than do the backs of your legs, which are far less sensitive to touch.

The **frontal lobe** is the largest lobe of the cerebral cortex, and damage to this area of the brain can affect many different functions. The frontal lobe is involved in planning, initiating, and executing voluntary movements. The movements of different body parts are represented in a band of tissue on the frontal lobe called the primary motor cortex. The degree of representation on the *primary motor cortex* for a particular body part reflects the diversity and precision of its potential movements, as shown on the right side of Figure 2.18. Thus, it's not surprising that almost one-third of the primary motor cortex is devoted to the hands and another third is devoted to facial muscles. The disproportionate representation of these two body areas on the primary motor cortex is reflected in the human capacity to produce an extremely wide range of hand movements and facial expressions.

The primary sensory and motor areas found on the different lobes represent just a small portion of the cerebral cortex. The remaining bulk of the cerebral cortex consists mostly of *association areas,* also called the *association cortex.* These areas are generally thought to be involved in processing and integrating sensory and motor

temporal lobe An area on each hemisphere of the cerebral cortex, near the temples, that is the primary receiving area for auditory information.

occipital lobe (ock-SIP-it-ull) An area at the back of each cerebral hemisphere that is the primary receiving area for visual information.

parietal lobe (puh-RYE-ut-ull) An area on each hemisphere of the cerebral cortex located above the temporal lobe that processes somatic sensations.

frontal lobe The largest lobe of each cerebral hemisphere; processes voluntary muscle movements and is involved in thinking, planning, and emotional control.

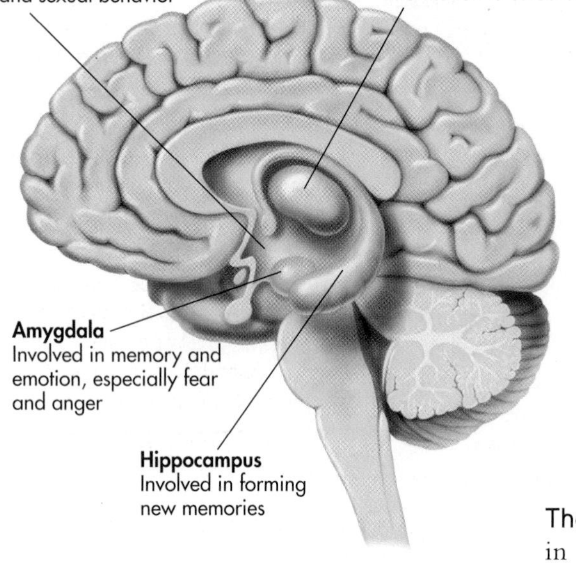

Hypothalamus
Links brain and endocrine system; regulates hunger, thirst, sleep, and sexual behavior

Thalamus
Processes and integrates sensory information; relays sensory information to cerebral cortex

Amygdala
Involved in memory and emotion, especially fear and anger

Hippocampus
Involved in forming new memories

FIGURE 2.19 Key Structures of the Forebrain and Limbic System In the cross-sectional view shown here, you can see the locations and functions of four important subcortical brain structures. In combination, these structures make up the *limbic system,* which regulates emotional control, learning, and memory.

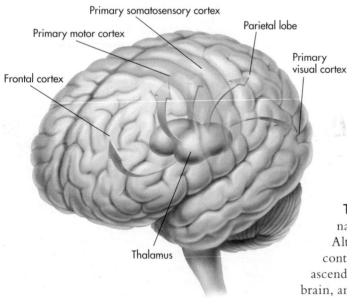

Primary somatosensory cortex

Primary motor cortex

Parietal lobe

Frontal cortex

Primary visual cortex

Thalamus

FIGURE 2.20 The Thalamus Almost all sensory and motor information going to and from the cerebral cortex is processed through the thalamus. This figure depicts some of the neural pathways from different regions of the thalamus to specific lobes of the cerebral cortex.

information. For example, the *prefrontal association cortex,* situated in front of the primary motor cortex, is involved in the planning of voluntary movements. Another association area includes parts of the temporal, parietal, and occipital lobes. This association area is involved in the formation of perceptions and in the integration of perceptions and memories.

THE LIMBIC SYSTEM

Beneath the cerebral cortex are several other important forebrain structures, which are components of the **limbic system.** The word *limbic* means "border," and as you can see in Figure 2.19, the structures that make up the limbic system form a border of sorts around the brainstem. In various combinations, the limbic system structures form complex neural circuits that play critical roles in learning, memory, and emotional control.

Next, we'll briefly consider some key limbic system structures and the roles they play in behavior.

The Hippocampus The **hippocampus** is a large structure embedded in the temporal lobe in each cerebral hemisphere (see Figure 2.19). The word *hippocampus* comes from a Latin word meaning "sea horse." If you have a vivid imagination, the hippocampus does look a bit like the curved tail of a sea horse. The hippocampus plays an important role in your ability to form new memories of events and information. As noted earlier, neurogenesis takes place in the adult hippocampus. The possible role of new neurons in memory formation is an active area of neuroscience research (see Gould, 2007; Livneh & Mizrahi, 2012). In Chapter 6, we'll take a closer look at the role of the hippocampus and other brain structures in memory.

The Thalamus The word *thalamus* comes from a Greek word meaning "inner chamber." And indeed, the **thalamus** is a rounded mass of cell bodies located within each cerebral hemisphere. The thalamus processes and distributes motor information and sensory information (except for smell) going to and from the cerebral cortex. Figure 2.20 depicts some of the neural pathways going from the thalamus to the different lobes of the cerebral cortex. However, the thalamus is more than just a sensory relay station. The thalamus is also thought to be involved in regulating levels of awareness, attention, motivation, and emotional aspects of sensations.

The Hypothalamus *Hypo* means "beneath" or "below." As its name implies, the **hypothalamus** is located below the thalamus. Although it is only about the size of a peanut, the hypothalamus contains more than 40 neural pathways. These neural pathways ascend to other forebrain areas and descend to the midbrain, hindbrain, and spinal cord. The hypothalamus is involved in so many different functions, it is sometimes referred to as "the brain within the brain."

The hypothalamus regulates both divisions of the autonomic nervous system, increasing and decreasing such functions as heart rate and blood pressure. It also helps regulate a variety of behaviors related to survival, such as eating, drinking, frequency of sexual activity, fear, and aggression.

One area of the hypothalamus, called the *suprachiasmatic nucleus* (SCN), plays a key role in regulating daily sleep–wake cycles and other rhythms of the body. We'll take a closer look at the SCN in Chapter 4.

The hypothalamus exerts considerable control over the secretion of endocrine hormones by directly influencing the pituitary gland. The *pituitary gland* is situated just below the hypothalamus and is attached to it by a short stalk. The hypothalamus produces both neurotransmitters and hormones that directly affect the pituitary gland. As we noted in the section on the endocrine system, the pituitary gland releases hormones that influence the activity of other glands.

The Amygdala The **amygdala** is an almond-shaped clump of neuron cell bodies at the base of the temporal lobe. The amygdala is involved in a variety of emotional responses, including fear, anger, and disgust. Animal studies have shown that electrical stimulation of the amygdala can produce behaviors associated with fear or rage, while destruction of the amygdala reduces or disrupts such behaviors.

It's long been known that the amygdala is involved in the detection of threatening stimuli, but neuroscientists have discovered that the amygdala has a broader role. Brain imaging studies have shown that the amygdala responds to many different types of emotional stimuli, appealing as well as upsetting (Cunningham & Brosch, 2012). For example, hungry participants showed increased amygdala activation in response to pictures of food when they were hungry, but not when they were satiated (Mohanty & others, 2008). Thus, some neuroscientists now believe that the amygdala aids in detecting and responding to environmental stimuli that are relevant to an organism's goals.

The amygdala is also involved in learning and forming memories, especially those with a strong emotional component (Phelps, 2006). In Chapters 6 and 8, we'll take a closer look at the amygdala's role in memory and emotion.

Specialization in the Cerebral Hemispheres

KEY THEME

Although they have many functions in common, the two hemispheres of the cerebral cortex are specialized for different tasks.

KEY QUESTIONS

> How did Broca, Wernicke, and Sperry contribute to our knowledge of the brain?

> Why would the corpus callosum be surgically severed, and what effects would that produce?

> How do the functions of the right and left cerebral hemispheres differ?

If you hold a human brain in your hand, the two cerebral hemispheres would appear to be symmetrical. Although the left and right hemispheres are very similar in appearance, they are not identical. Anatomically, one hemisphere may be slightly larger than the other. There are also subtle differences in the sizes of particular structures, in the distribution of gray matter and white matter, and in the patterns of folds, bulges, and grooves that make up the surface of the cerebral cortex (Ocklenburg & Güntürkün, 2012).

What about differences in the functions of the two hemispheres? In many cases, the functioning of the left and right hemispheres is symmetrical, meaning that the same functions are located in roughly the same places on each hemisphere. Examples of such functional symmetry include the primary motor cortex and the somatosensory cortex, which we discussed in the previous section. With regard to other important processes, however, the left and right cerebral hemispheres do differ—each cerebral hemisphere is specialized for particular abilities.

Here's a rough analogy. Imagine two computers that are linked through a network. One computer is optimized for handling word processing, the other for handling graphic design. Although specialized for different functions, the two computers actively share information and can communicate with each other across the network. In this analogy, the two computers correspond to the left and right cerebral hemispheres, and the network that links them is the corpus callosum.

limbic system A group of forebrain structures that form a border around the brainstem and are involved in emotion, motivation, learning, and memory.

hippocampus A curved forebrain structure that is part of the limbic system and is involved in learning and forming new memories.

thalamus (THAL-uh-muss) A forebrain structure that processes sensory information for all senses except smell, relaying that information to the cerebral cortex.

hypothalamus (hi-poe-THAL-uh-muss) A peanut-sized forebrain structure that is part of the limbic system and that regulates behaviors related to survival, such as eating, drinking, and sexual activity.

amygdala (uh-MIG-dull-uh) An almond-shaped cluster of neurons in the brain's temporal lobe, involved in memory and emotional responses, especially fear.

Review the structures of the brain with **PsychSim6: Brain and Behavior.**

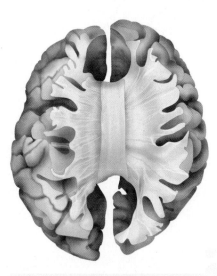

The Corpus Callosum In the drawing, the top of the brain has been cut away, exposing the thick fibers of the corpus callosum, which connect the left and right hemispheres.

CRITICAL THINKING

"His" and "Her" Brains?

Do men and women have fundamentally different brains? Some popular authors claim men's and women's brains are "hardwired" by hormones and genes to produce "separate realities" (Brizendine, 2006, 2010). According to this view, there are innate differences between the brains of males and females, differences that cause gender differences in behaviors, attitudes, personality traits, and skills (Fine, 2012, 2014). But what are these differences? Do they cause men and women to "think, feel, and behave differently," as some headlines and popular books claim? Let's look at the scientific research.

MYTH ◄ SCIENCE

Is it true that because their brains are wired differently, men and women think, feel, and behave differently?

A case in point is a recent study that used diffusion tensor imaging (see p. 62) to compare the neural pathways, or *connectomes*, of over 900 children and young adults. Madhura Ingalhalikar and her colleagues (2014) concluded that the scans of the adolescent and young adult participants showed "fundamental sex differences in the structural architecture in the human brain." On average, males had significantly more neural connections *within* the left and right hemispheres than females. And, females had significantly more neural connections *between* the left and right hemispheres than males.

The media jumped on the findings as evidence that sex differences were "hardwired" in the brain. Going well beyond the study's findings, print articles and online blogs claimed that the findings explained many supposed sex differences, such as why men were better at map-reading, physical coordination, and tasks requiring single-minded focus and why women were better at multitasking and were more socially competent (see O'Connor & Joffe, 2014). For the record, these behaviors were *not* measured in the participant pool.

But just how definitive were the study's results? First, while statistically significant, the differences identified in the study were still quite small (Cossins, 2015; Joel & Tarrasch, 2014). Second, the differences were *quantitative* rather than *qualitative*: that is, the differences were a matter of degree, not kind. Although the average number of connections differed, the general pattern of connections was the same in male and female participants (Fine, 2014).

And, critics noted that male brains are, on average, about 10% larger than female brains. Thus, the differences could have been associated with *brain size* rather than *brain sex*. A later study found that larger brains tend to have more interhemispheric connectivity than smaller brains, *regardless* of sex. In men's and women's brains that were the same size, there were no differences in the pattern of connections: the apparent sex effect disappeared (Hänggi & others, 2014).

Finally, the analysis did not take into account the participants' past experience, such as participation in sports or hobbies (Fine, 2014). Yet, as we've shown in this chapter, experience changes the brain.

Thinking Critically About Brain Differences

How should you interpret media sound bites about profound sex differences in the brain? Or claims that certain personality traits or behaviors are "hardwired in the brain"?

First, it's important to *think critically* about media claims. Unlike reporters, scientists are usually careful to qualify their conclusions and describe the limitations of their research. These limitations are rarely mentioned in media reports. For example, brain studies are typically based on small groups of participants, who may or may not be representative of the wider population of men and women. And, while findings of sex differences in brain structure or function tend to be

Sex Differences and the Brain Subtle gender differences in brain function and structure make headlines, often implying or stating outright that men and women "think differently."

Tasia12/Shutterstock

widely reported in the media, findings of *no difference* go unreported. So, often, does the failure of studies to be replicated by other researchers (Eliot, 2011; Fine, 2013a, 2013b). In other words, the findings of individual research studies are rarely as earth-shattering as reported.

Second, most sex differences amount to minor variations in the size of a particular brain region or to statistical differences in the average level of activation of particular brain regions. Brain structures and functioning are essentially the *same* in men and women—including in the study highlighted above (Fine, 2014; Rippon & others, 2014). As you'll see in later chapters, when it comes to personality traits, abilities, and attitudes, *men and women are much more similar than they are different.*

> The hardwiring paradigm erases the effect of the social world in producing sex/gender differences, so that sex/gender hierarchies appear natural. Neuroscientific explanations of sex/gender differences have added a new allure to an old fashioned sexism.
>
> —*Rebecca Jordan-Young & Raffaella I. Rumiati (2012)*

Finally, it's important to remember that even differences that are biological in origin are not necessarily fixed, permanent, or inevitable (Fine, 2014; Hyde, 2014). Brain development and function *are* affected by biological influences, such as exposure to the sex hormones produced both before birth and throughout your life (Lombardo & others, 2012). However, these biological factors *themselves* are strongly influenced by environmental factors, ranging from the food we eat to the stressful circumstances we experience. As we've emphasized throughout this chapter, both brain function and structure are highly responsive to environmental influences (Fine & others, 2013). Thus, sex differences in structures or function might well be the *result* of the different life experiences of men and women, rather than the cause (Rippon & others, 2014).

CRITICAL THINKING QUESTIONS

- Why are sweeping claims about fundamental sex differences in the human brain misleading?

- What is wrong with the statement that certain behaviors or personality traits are "hardwired" in the male or female brain?

- How might claims that sex differences are "hardwired" or innate affect attitudes or behavior?

- Why is the notion that sex differences might be due to brain differences so appealing to many people?

As you'll see in this section, the first discoveries about the differing abilities of the two brain hemispheres were made more than a hundred years ago by two important pioneers in brain research, Pierre Paul Broca and Karl Wernicke.

Language and the Left Hemisphere
THE EARLY WORK OF BROCA AND WERNICKE

By the end of the 1700s it had already been well established that injury to one side of the brain could produce muscle paralysis or loss of sensation on the opposite side of the body. By the early 1800s, animal experiments had shown that specific functions would be lost if particular brain areas were destroyed. And, as discussed in the Science Versus Pseudoscience box on page 61, phrenology triggered scientific debates about **cortical localization,** or *localization of function*—the idea that particular brain areas are associated with specific functions.

In the 1860s, more compelling evidence for cortical localization was presented by a French surgeon and neuroanatomist named **Pierre Paul Broca.** Broca treated a series of patients who had great difficulty speaking but could comprehend written or spoken language. Subsequent autopsies of these patients revealed a consistent finding—brain damage to an area on the *lower left frontal lobe.* Today, this area on the left hemisphere is referred to as *Broca's area,* and it is known to play a crucial role in speech production (Figure 2.21).

About a decade after Broca's discovery, a young German neurologist named **Karl Wernicke** discovered another area in the left hemisphere that, when damaged, produced a different type of language disturbance. Unlike Broca's patients, Wernicke's patients had great difficulty understanding spoken or written communications. They could speak quickly and easily, but their speech sometimes made no sense. They sometimes used meaningless words or even nonsense syllables, though their sentences seemed to be grammatical. In response to the question "How are you feeling?" a patient might say something like, "Don't glow glover. Yes, uh, ummm, bick, bo chipickers the dallydoe mick more work mittle." Autopsies of these patients' brains revealed consistent damage to an area on the *left temporal lobe* that today is called *Wernicke's area* (see Figure 2.21).

The discoveries of Broca and Wernicke provided the first compelling clinical evidence that language and speech functions are performed primarily by the left cerebral hemisphere. If similar brain damage occurs in the exact same locations on the *right* hemisphere, these severe disruptions in language and speech are usually *not* seen.

The notion that one hemisphere exerts more control over or is more involved in the processing of a particular psychological function is termed **lateralization of function.** Speech and language functions are *lateralized* on the left hemisphere. Generally, the left hemisphere exerts greater control over speech and language abilities in virtually all right-handed and the majority of left-handed people.

Pierre Paul Broca (1824–1880): Evidence for the Localization of Speech Pierre Paul Broca was already a famous scientist and surgeon when he announced in 1861 that he had discovered solid evidence for the localization of language functions in the human brain. His patient was an unpleasant middle-aged man universally known as Tan because that was the only word he could speak—aside from a single swear word when angered. Of normal intelligence, Tan could comprehend the speech of others but could not produce language himself. After Tan's death, an autopsy revealed a distinct lesion on the lower left frontal lobe. This area is still known as *Broca's area.*

Images from the History of Medicine, National Library of Medicine

Karl Wernicke (1848–1905): Evidence for the Localization of Language Comprehension Psychiatrist and neurologist Karl Wernicke was only 26 when he published his findings on a type of aphasia that differed from that identified by Pierre Paul Broca. Wernicke's patients were unable to comprehend written or spoken language, although they could produce speech.

Images from the History of Medicine, National Library of Medicine

cortical localization The notion that different functions are located or localized in different areas of the brain; also called *localization of function.*

lateralization of function The notion that specific psychological or cognitive functions are processed primarily on one side of the brain.

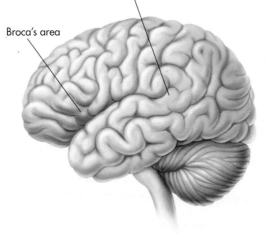

Wernicke's area

Broca's area

FIGURE 2.21 Broca's and Wernicke's Areas of the Cerebral Cortex Broca's area, located on the lower frontal lobe, is involved in the production of speech. Wernicke's area, found in the temporal lobe, is important in the comprehension of written or spoken language. Damage to either of these areas will produce different types of speech disturbances, or aphasia. In most people, both areas are found in the left hemisphere.

Left-Handed Orangutans Like humans, many animals also display a preference for one hand or paw (Ocklenburg & Güntürkün, 2012). Unlike humans, who are predominantly right-handed, animals tend to vary by species, population, and task (Hopkins & Cantalupo, 2005; Grant, 2014). For example, orangutans, like the one shown above, tend to be left-handed, but gorillas, chimpanzees, and bonobos tend to be right-handed (Hopkins & others, 2011). Handedness is discussed in more detail in the Science Versus Pseudoscience box, "Brain Myths," on page 77.

Courtesy of Dr. William D. Hopkins/
Georgia State University

aphasia (uh-FAYZH-yuh) The partial or complete inability to articulate ideas or understand spoken or written language because of brain injury or damage.

split-brain operation A surgical procedure that involves cutting the corpus callosum.

The language disruptions demonstrated by Broca's and Wernicke's patients represent different types of aphasia. **Aphasia** refers to the partial or complete inability to articulate ideas or understand spoken or written language because of brain injury or damage. There are many different types of aphasia.

People with *Broca's aphasia* find it difficult or impossible to produce speech, which is why it is often referred to as *expressive aphasia*. Despite their impairments in speaking, their comprehension of verbal or written words is relatively unaffected.

People with *Wernicke's aphasia* have great difficulty comprehending written or spoken communication, which is why it is often referred to as *receptive aphasia*. Although they can speak, they often have trouble finding the correct words.

At the beginning of this chapter, we described the symptoms experienced by our friend Asha in the weeks before and the months following her stroke. Asha, who is right-handed, experienced the stroke in her left hemisphere. About three days after her stroke, an MRI brain scan showed where the damage had occurred: the left temporal lobe. Asha experienced many symptoms of Wernicke's aphasia. Talking was difficult, not because Asha couldn't speak, but because she had to stop frequently to search for the right words. Asha was unable to name even simple objects, like the cup on her hospital dinner tray or her doctor's necktie. She recognized the objects but was unable to say what they were. She had great difficulty following a normal conversation and understanding speech, both in English and in her native language, Tulu.

Asha also discovered that she had lost the ability to read. She could see the words on the page, but they seemed to have no meaning. Her husband, Paul, brought some of their Christmas cards to the hospital. Asha recalls, "When I realized I couldn't read the Christmas cards, I thought my life was over. I just lost it. I remember crying and telling the nurse, 'I have a doctorate and I can't read, write, or talk!'"

When we visited Asha in the hospital, we brought her a Christmas present: a portable music player with headphones and some albums of relaxing instrumental music. Little did we realize how helpful the music would be for her. One album was a recording of Native American flute music called *Sky of Dreams*. The music was beautiful and rather unusual, with intricate melodies and unexpected, complex harmonies. Although it was very difficult for Asha to follow normal speech, listening to *Sky of Dreams* was an entirely different experience. As Asha explained:

> I tried cranking up the music very high and it soothed me. I could sleep. At the time, the flute music seemed to be just perfectly timed with the way my brain was working. It was tuning out all the other noises so I could focus on just one thing and sleep. So I would play the music over and over again at a very high level. I did that for a long time because my mind was so active and jumbled that I couldn't think.

Asha's language functions were severely disrupted, yet she was able to listen to and appreciate instrumental music—even very complex music. Why? At the end of the next section, we'll offer a possible explanation for what seems to have been a disparity in Asha's cognitive abilities following her stroke.

Cutting the Corpus Callosum
THE SPLIT BRAIN

Since the discoveries by Broca and Wernicke, the most dramatic evidence illustrating the independent functions of the two cerebral hemispheres has come from a surgical procedure called the **split-brain operation.** This operation is used to stop or reduce recurring seizures in severe cases of epilepsy that can't be treated in any other fashion. The procedure involves surgically cutting the corpus callosum, the thick band of axons that connects the two hemispheres.

What was the logic behind cutting the corpus callosum? An epileptic seizure typically occurs when neurons begin firing in a disorganized fashion in one region of the brain. The disorganized neuronal firing quickly spreads from one hemisphere to the other via the corpus callosum. If the corpus callosum is cut, seizures should be

Task 1: Information directed to left verbal hemisphere

Experimenter: "What flashed on the screen?"

Nonverbal right hemisphere

Response: "An apple." Verbal left hemisphere

Task 2: Information directed to right nonverbal hemisphere

Experimenter: "What flashed on the screen?"

Experimenter: "Using your left hand, reach under the screen and pick up what you saw."

Nonverbal right hemisphere

Response: "I didn't see anything." Verbal left hemisphere

FIGURE 2.22 Testing a Split-Brain Person As a split-brain person focuses her attention on the middle of the screen, information is briefly flashed to either the left or right side of the midpoint. In Task 1, information is flashed to her right visual field, sending it to her left verbal hemisphere. When asked about the information, she easily names it. In Task 2, information is directed to her left visual field, sending it to her right nonverbal hemisphere. When asked about the information, she is unable to verbally reply with the correct answer. But when asked to use her left hand, which is controlled by the same right nonverbal hemisphere that detected the flashed image, she is able to reach under the screen, feel the different objects, and pick up the correct one (Gazzaniga, 1983; Wolman, 2012).

Source: Research from Sperry (1982).

contained in just one hemisphere, reducing their severity or eliminating them altogether. This is exactly what happened when the split-brain operation was first tried in this country in the 1940s (Wolman, 2012).

Surprisingly, cutting the corpus callosum initially seemed to produce no noticeable effect on the patients, other than reducing their epileptic seizures. Their ability to engage in routine conversations and tasks seemed to be unaffected. On the basis of these early observations, some brain researchers speculated that the corpus callosum served no function whatsoever. One famous psychologist, Karl Lashley, joked that the primary function of the corpus callosum seemed to be to keep the two hemispheres from sagging (Hoptman & Davidson, 1994).

In the 1960s, however, psychologist and neuroscientist **Roger Sperry** and his colleagues began unraveling the puzzle of the left and right hemispheres. Sperry and his colleagues used the apparatus shown in Figure 2.22 to test the abilities of split-brain patients. They would direct a split-brain subject to focus on a point in the middle of a screen, while briefly flashing a word or picture to the left or right of the midpoint.

In this procedure, visual information to the right of the midpoint is projected to the person's *left* hemisphere, and visual information to the left of the midpoint is projected to the *right* hemisphere. Behind the screen several objects were hidden from the split-brain subject. The subject could reach under a partition below the screen to pick up the concealed objects but could not see them (Sperry, 1982).

In a typical experiment, Sperry projected the image of an object concealed behind the screen, such as a hammer, to the left of the midpoint. This is shown in Task 2, Figure 2.22. Thus, the image of the hammer was sent to the right, nonverbal hemisphere. If a split-brain subject was asked to *verbally* identify the image flashed on the screen, she could not do so and often denied that anything had appeared on the screen. Why? Because her verbal left hemisphere had no way of knowing the information that had been sent to her right hemisphere. However, if a split-brain subject was asked to use her left hand to reach under the partition for the object that had been displayed, she would correctly pick up the hammer. This was because her left hand was controlled by the same right hemisphere that saw the image of the hammer.

Sperry's experiments reconfirmed the specialized language abilities of the left hemisphere that Broca and Wernicke had discovered more than a hundred years

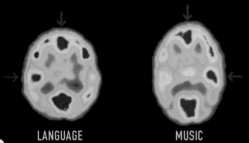

LANGUAGE   MUSIC

Dr. John Mazziotta et al./Science Source

Specialization in the Left and Right Hemispheres The red arrow at the top of each PET scan points to the front of the brain. The red and yellow colors indicate the areas of greatest brain activity. Listening to speech involves a greater degree of activation of the language areas of the left hemisphere. Listening to music involves more activation in right-hemisphere areas. Notice, however, that there is some degree of activity in both hemispheres during these tasks.

Think Like a SCIENTIST

Can you be classified as right-brained or left-brained? Go to LaunchPad: Resources to **Think Like a Scientist** about **The Right Brain Versus the Left Brain.**

 LaunchPad

FIGURE 2.23 Specialized Abilities of the Two Hemispheres Most people are left-hemisphere-dominant for speech and language tasks and right-hemisphere-dominant for visual-spatial tasks. Although the hemispheres display some specialized abilities, many functions are symmetrical and performed the same way on both hemispheres.

earlier. But notice, even though the split-brain subject's right hemisphere could not express itself verbally, it still processed information and expressed itself *nonverbally:* The subject was able to pick up the correct object.

Over the past decades, researchers have gained numerous insights about the brain's lateralization of functions by studying split-brain patients, using brain-imaging techniques with normal subjects, and employing other techniques (Gazzaniga, 2005; Hugdahl & Westerhausen, 2010). On the basis of this evidence, researchers have concluded that—in most people—the left hemisphere is superior in language abilities, speech, reading, and writing.

In contrast, the right hemisphere is more involved in nonverbal emotional expression and visual-spatial tasks (Corballis, 2010). Deciphering complex visual cues, such as completing a puzzle or manipulating blocks to match a particular design, also relies on right-hemisphere processing (Gazzaniga, 1995, 2005). And the right hemisphere excels in recognizing faces and emotional facial cues, reading maps, copying designs, and drawing. Finally, the right hemisphere shows a higher degree of specialization for musical appreciation or responsiveness—but not necessarily for musical ability, which involves the use of the left hemisphere as well (Springer & Deutsch, 2001).

Figure 2.23 summarizes the research findings for the different specialized abilities of the two hemispheres for right-handed people. As you look at the figure, it's important to keep two points in mind. First, the differences between the left and right hemispheres are almost always relative differences, *not* absolute differences. In other words, *both* hemispheres of your brain are activated to some extent as you perform virtually any task (Toga & Thompson, 2003). In the normal brain, the left and right hemispheres function in an integrated fashion, constantly exchanging information (Allen & others, 2007). Thus, Figure 2.23 indicates the hemisphere that typically displays greater activation or exerts greater control over a particular function. Misconceptions about the roles played by the left and right hemispheres are common in

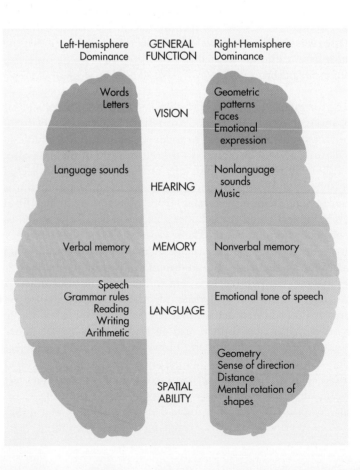

Left-Hemisphere Dominance	GENERAL FUNCTION	Right-Hemisphere Dominance
Words Letters	VISION	Geometric patterns Faces Emotional expression
Language sounds	HEARING	Nonlanguage sounds Music
Verbal memory	MEMORY	Nonverbal memory
Speech Grammar rules Reading Writing Arithmetic	LANGUAGE	Emotional tone of speech
	SPATIAL ABILITY	Geometry Sense of direction Distance Mental rotation of shapes

SCIENCE VERSUS PSEUDOSCIENCE

Brain Myths

Is it true that some people are "right-brained" and other people "left-brained"?

To investigate this question, researchers compared more than a thousand fMRI scans taken while participants rested. There was *no* evidence that participants preferentially relied on networks in the left or right hemisphere, as you would expect if some people were "left-brained" and others "right-brained" (Nielsen & others, 2013).

It certainly *seems* as if some people are more logical, analytical, or detail-oriented than others, especially in the way that they make decisions or tackle problems. But remember that the left and right hemispheres are highly interconnected in the normal, intact human brain. Unless the corpus callosum has been surgically sliced, *all* humans rely on the smooth, integrated functioning of *both* their left and right hemispheres to speak, learn, and generally navigate everyday life. In fact, the more complex the task, the greater the likelihood that *both* hemispheres will be involved in performing it (Allen & others, 2007; Yoshizaki & others, 2007).

What about left-handed people? Is it true that they are right-hemisphere-dominant?

Only about 10 to 13 percent of the population identify themselves as left-handed (Basso, 2007). Unlike right-handed people, who tend to use their right hands for virtually all tasks requiring dexterity, most left-handers actually show a pattern of "mixed" handedness. Strong left-handedness is extremely rare (Wolman, 2005).

It's a myth that left-handers have a fundamentally different brain organization from right-handers. About 75 percent of left-handers are *left-hemisphere-dominant* for language, just like right-handers. The remaining 25 percent are either right-hemisphere-dominant for language or bilateral, using *both* hemispheres for speech and language functions. Just for the record, about 5 percent of *right*-handed people are also either *right*-hemisphere or *bilaterally* specialized for language (Knecht & others, 2000; Ocklenburg & Güntürkün, 2012).

Is the right brain responsible for creativity and intuition? Can you train your right brain?

Although the right hemisphere is specialized for holistic processing, there is no evidence that the right hemisphere is any

MYTH ◀ SCIENCE

Is it true that the right brain is creative and intuitive, and the left brain is analytic and logical, but that left-brained people can educate their right brain?

more "intuitive" or "creative" than the left hemisphere (Gazzaniga, 2005). In fact, a recent study found that a task requiring a *creative* solution involved greater left hemisphere activation than a task that required a

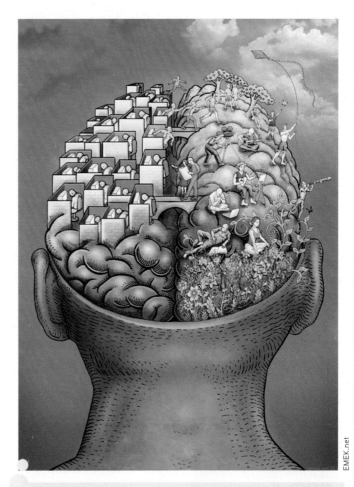

EMEK.net

Left Brain, Right Brain? As this image rather playfully suggests, many people see the two hemispheres as representing diametrically opposed ways of thinking and behaving: the left brain is cold, rational, and analytical; the right brain is emotional, artistic, and free-spirited. But how much truth is there to this myth?

noncreative solution (Aziz-Zadeh & others, 2013). There is also no evidence that any teacher, however skilled, could somehow selectively "educate" one side of your brain in isolation from the other (Goswami, 2006). While it is true that each hemisphere is specialized for different abilities, you rely on the integrated functioning of *both* hemispheres to accomplish most tasks. This is especially true for such cognitively demanding tasks as artistic creativity, musical performance, or finding innovative solutions to complex problems.

the popular media, and even in education (Howard-Jones, 2014). The Science Versus Pseudoscience box, "Brain Myths," explores some of the most common misperceptions about the brain. Second, many functions of the cerebral hemispheres, such as those involving the primary sensory and motor areas, *are* symmetrical. They are located in the same place and are performed in the same way on both the left and the right hemispheres.

Given the basic findings on the laterality of different functions in the two hemispheres, can you speculate about why Asha was unable to read or follow a simple conversation but could easily concentrate on a complex piece of music? Why were her language abilities so disrupted, while her ability to focus on and appreciate music remained intact after her stroke?

A plausible explanation has to do with the location of the stroke's damage on Asha's left temporal lobe. Because language functions are usually localized on the left hemisphere, the stroke produced serious disruptions in Asha's language abilities. However, her *right* cerebral hemisphere sustained no detectable damage. Because one of the right hemisphere's abilities is the appreciation of musical sounds, Asha retained the ability to concentrate on and appreciate music.

❯ Test your understanding of **The Brain** with **LEARNING**Curve.

Closing Thoughts

In our exploration of neuroscience and behavior, we've traveled from the activities of individual neurons to the complex interaction of the billions of neurons that make up the human nervous system, most notably the brain. In the course of those travels, we presented four themes that are crucial to a scientific understanding of brain function: *localization, lateralization, integration,* and *plasticity.*

More than just a historical scientific oddity, phrenology's incorrect interpretation of bumps on the skull helped focus scientific debate on the notion of *localization*—the idea that different functions are localized in different brain areas. Although rejected in the early 1800s when Franz Gall was in his heyday, localization of brain functioning is well established today. The early clinical evidence provided by Broca and Wernicke, and the later split-brain evidence provided by Sperry and his colleagues, confirmed the idea of *lateralization*—that some functions are performed primarily by one cerebral hemisphere.

The ideas of localization and lateralization are complemented by another theme evident in this chapter—*integration.* Although the nervous system is highly specialized, even simple behaviors involve the highly integrated interaction of trillions of synapses. Your ability to process new information and experiences, your memories of previous experiences, your sense of who you are and what you know, your actions and reactions—all depend upon the harmony of the nervous system.

The story of Asha's stroke illustrated what can happen when that harmony is disrupted. Asha survived her stroke, but many people who suffer strokes do not. Of those who do survive a stroke, about one-third are left with severe impairments in their ability to function.

What happened to Asha? Fortunately, her story has a happy ending. Asha was luckier than many stroke victims—she was young, strong, and otherwise healthy. Asha's recovery was also aided by her high level of motivation, willingness to work hard, and sheer will to recover. After being discharged from the hospital, Asha began months of intensive speech therapy. Her speech therapist assigned a great deal of homework that consisted of repeatedly pairing pictures with words, objects with words, and words with objects. Asha was literally rewiring her brain by relearning the correct associations between words and their meanings.

Asha set a very high goal for herself: to return to teaching at the university the following fall semester. With the help of her husband, Paul, and her mother, Nalini, who traveled from India to help coach her back to full recovery, Asha made progressive and significant gains. With remarkable determination, Asha reached the goal she had set for herself. Eight months after her stroke, she returned to the classroom and her research lab.

Today, more than five years after her stroke, the average person would never know that Asha had sustained significant brain damage. Other than an occasional tendency

Asha's Recovery After leaving the hospital, Asha began retraining her brain with speech therapy. Day after day, Asha repeatedly paired words with objects or identified numbers, weekdays, or months. As Asha gradually made progress, her mother began taking her to stores. "She'd tell the clerk I was from India and that my English wasn't very good and ask them to please be patient with me. She basically forced me to talk to the sales clerks." Today, more than five years after the stroke, Asha has completely recovered and resumed teaching.

Courtesy Asha Hegde Niezgoda

to "block" on familiar words—especially when she's very tired—Asha seems to have made a complete recovery.

Thus, Asha's story illustrates a final theme—the brain's remarkable *plasticity*. Next, we take a closer look at how the brain responds to different types of environments. You will also learn how you can use research to enhance your own dendritic potential!

PSYCH FOR YOUR LIFE

Maximizing Your Brain's Potential

It was 1962 when a group of neuroscientists led by psychologist Mark Rosenzweig published the unexpected finding that the brains of rats raised in *enriched environments* were significantly different from the brains of rats raised in *impoverished environments.*

For lab rats, an *enriched environment* is spacious, houses several rats, and has assorted wheels, ladders, tunnels, and objects to explore. The environment is also regularly changed for further variety. Some enriched environments have been designed to mimic an animal's natural environment (see Heyman, 2003). In the *impoverished environment,* a solitary rat lives in a small, bare laboratory cage with only a water bottle and food tray to keep it company.

Decades of research have shown that enrichment increases the number and length of dendrites and dendritic branches, increases the number of glial cells, and enlarges the size of neurons (Cohen, 2003). Enrichment produces more synaptic connections between brain neurons, while impoverishment decreases synaptic connections. With more synapses, the brain has a greater capacity to integrate and process information and to do so more quickly. In young rats, enrichment increases the number of synapses in the cortex by as much as 20 percent. But even the brains of extremely old rats respond to enriched environments. In fact, no matter what the age of the rats studied, environmental enrichment or impoverishment had a significant impact on brain structure (Kempermann & others, 1998).

Enrichment has also been shown to increase the rate of neurogenesis in many different species, from rodents to monkeys (Fan & others, 2007; Nithianantharajah & Hannan, 2006). Both the number and the survival time of new neurons increase in response to enrichment (Gould & Gross, 2002; van Praag & others, 2000). Interestingly, while enriched environments can increase neurogenesis, social isolation and a stressful environment *decrease* neurogenesis (Ming & Song, 2005).

Collectively, these changes result in increased processing and communication capacity in the brain. Behaviorally, enrichment has been shown to enhance performance on tasks designed to measure learning and memory, such as performance in different types of mazes (van Praag & others, 2000).

Who Moved My Exercise Wheel?

Neuroscientists have identified an additional factor that improves brain function, even in aging mammals: exercise (Hillman & others, 2008; Shors, 2014). In one study, just a month of daily exercise helped reverse cognitive declines associated with aging in previously sedentary, elderly mice (van Praag & others, 2005). After having access to an exercise wheel for 30 days, mice that were the rodent equivalent of 70 years old learned to navigate a maze much faster than mice of the same age that did not exercise. They also had better memories of maze locations. Finally, the physically active elderly mice had a greatly increased rate of neurogenesis, and the new neurons functioned as well as new neurons generated in the brains of young mice. As study coauthor Henriette van Praag (2005) points out, "Our findings show that it is never too late in life to start to exercise, and that doing so will likely delay the onset of aging-associated memory loss."

From Animal Studies to Humans

Enrichment studies have been carried out with many other species, including monkeys, cats, birds, honeybees, and even fruit flies. In all cases, enriched environments are associated with striking changes in the brain, however primitive.

An Enriched Environment Primates in the wild, like this marmoset, live in complex, challenging, and ever-changing environments. At psychologist Elizabeth Gould's Princeton lab, marmosets are housed in large enclosures with natural vegetation and novel objects that are changed frequently. In one experiment, synaptic and dendritic connections increased dramatically in marmosets who lived in the enriched environment for just four weeks after being raised in standard laboratory cages (Kozorovitskiy & Gould, 2004).

James Simon/Science Source

Can the conclusions drawn from studies on rats, monkeys, and other animals be applied to human brains? Obviously, researchers cannot directly study the effects of enriched or impoverished environments on human brain tissue as they can with rats.

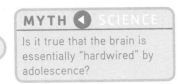

MYTH ◀ SCIENCE

Is it true that the brain is essentially "hardwired" by adolescence?

However, consider a study conducted by Ana Pereira and her colleagues (2007). Male and female participants, aged 21 to 45, were assessed for their overall level of fitness. Using MRI scans, each participant's brain was also mapped for the amount of blood flowing into the hippocampus. Over the next three months, the participants worked out for one hour four times a week. Finally, the same physical and brain measurements were taken again.

As you probably anticipated, all of the participants had significantly improved their overall level of aerobic fitness. More importantly, they had also substantially increased the blood flow to their hippocampuses, in some cases doubling the blood flow as measured prior to the exercise program. In general, the greater the increase in a participant's aerobic fitness, the greater the increase in blood flow to the hippocampus.

Now for the key finding of the study: Along with the human subjects, a group of mice followed a comparable exercise program. In the mice, the exercise program resulted in increased blood flow in the same regions of the hippocampus as in humans. However, the researchers were able to directly examine brain changes in the mice. They found that the increased blood flow to the hippocampus in the mice was *directly* correlated to the birth of new neurons in the same region of the hippocampus. Although neuroscientists tend to be cautious in drawing conclusions, the implication of Pereira's study is obvious: Exercise promotes neurogenesis in the adult human brain just as it does in other mammals. A footnote: The participants in Pereira's study *also* improved their scores on several tests of mental abilities. Later studies have extended and confirmed these findings (Kobilo & others, 2011; Kuzumaki & others, 2011). And, other research has shown that even moderate exercise can increase brain volume in previously sedentary, older adults (Erickson & others, 2011). We describe this study in more depth in Chapter 9.

Neuroscientists have also amassed an impressive array of correlational evidence showing the human benefits from enriched, stimulating environments. For example, several studies have compared symptoms of Alzheimer's disease in elderly individuals with different levels of education (Bennett & others, 2003). Autopsies showed that the more educated individuals had just as much damage to their brain cells as did the poorly educated individuals. However, because the better-educated people had more synaptic connections, their symptoms were much less severe than those experienced by the less-educated people (Melton, 2005).

The results of this study echo those from earlier research on intellectual enrichment: A mentally stimulating, intellectually challenging environment is associated with enhanced cognitive functioning. Just as physical activity strengthens the heart and muscles, mental activity strengthens the brain. Even in late adulthood, remaining mentally and physically active can help prevent or lessen mental decline (Greenwood & Parasuraman, 2012; Hertzog & others, 2009; Hillman & others, 2008).

Pumping Neurons: Exercising Your Brain

So, here's the critical question: Are you a mental athlete—or a cerebral couch potato? Whatever your age, there seems to be a simple prescription for keeping your brain fit. Along with regular physical activity, engaging in any kind of intellectually challenging pursuits will keep those dendrites developing. Enrichment need not involve exotic or expensive pursuits. Novelty and complexity can be as close as your college campus or library. Here are just a few suggestions:

- Get regular aerobic exercise, even if it's no more than a brisk daily walk. If possible, vary your routes and try to notice something new about your surroundings on each walk.

- Don't hide in your room or apartment—seek out social interaction (except when it interferes with studying). Remember, the brain thrives on social stimulation.

- Learn to play a musical instrument. If you can't afford music lessons, join a singing group or choir. If you already play a musical instrument, experiment with a new style or musical genre.

AP Photo/The Juneau Empire, Michael Penn

Keeping the Brain Young Musical training involves many different cognitive, sensory, and motor processes. Thus, it's not surprising that playing a musical instrument is associated with improved cognitive abilities as well as changes in brain structure and function (Zatorre, 2013). Could musical experience over the lifespan also be associated with better cognitive functioning in old age? Brenda Hanna-Pladdy and Alicia MacKay (2011) found that it was. In healthy adults aged 60 to 83, years of active musical participation was directly correlated with better cognitive functioning.

- Take a class in a field outside your college major or in a new area. Experiment by learning something in a field completely new to you.
- Read, and read widely. Buy magazines or check out library books in fields that are new to you.

- Try puzzles of all kinds—word, number, maze, or matching.
- Unplug your television set for two weeks—or longer.

Better yet, take a few minutes and generate your own list of mind-expanding opportunities!

CHAPTER REVIEW

KEY PEOPLE AND KEY TERMS

Pierre Paul Broca, p. 73

Roger Sperry, p. 75

Karl Wernicke, p. 73

biological psychology, p. 42
neuroscience, p. 42
neuron, p. 43
sensory neuron, p. 43
motor neuron, p. 43
interneuron, p. 43
cell body, p. 43
dendrites, p. 43
axon, p. 43
glial cells, p. 44
myelin sheath, p. 44
action potential, p. 44
stimulus threshold, p. 44
resting potential, p. 44
synapse, p. 47
synaptic gap, p. 47
axon terminals, p. 48
synaptic vesicles, p. 48
neurotransmitters, p. 48
synaptic transmission, p. 48
reuptake, p. 48

acetylcholine, p. 49
dopamine, p. 50
serotonin, p. 51
norepinephrine, p. 51
glutamate, p. 51
GABA (gamma-aminobutyric acid), p. 51
endorphins, p. 51
agonist, p. 52
antagonist, p. 52
nervous system, p. 53
nerves, p. 53
central nervous system (CNS), p. 53
spinal reflexes, p. 55
peripheral nervous system, p. 55
somatic nervous system, p. 55
autonomic nervous system, p. 56
sympathetic nervous system, p. 57

parasympathetic nervous system, p. 57
endocrine system, p. 58
hormones, p. 58
pituitary gland, p. 59
oxytocin, p. 59
adrenal glands, p. 59
adrenal cortex, p. 59
adrenal medulla, p. 59
gonads, p. 60
phrenology, p. 61
cortical localization, p. 61
connectome, p. 62
functional plasticity, p. 62
structural plasticity, p. 63
neurogenesis, p. 63
brainstem, p. 65
hindbrain, p. 65
medulla, p. 65
pons, p. 66
cerebellum, p. 66

reticular formation, p. 66
midbrain, p. 66
substantia nigra, p. 66
forebrain, p. 66
cerebral cortex, p. 67
cerebral hemispheres, p. 67
corpus callosum, p. 67
temporal lobe, p. 68
occipital lobe, p. 68
parietal lobe, p. 68
frontal lobe, p. 69
limbic system, p. 70
hippocampus, p. 70
thalamus, p. 70
hypothalamus, p. 70
amygdala, p. 71
cortical localization, p. 73
lateralization of function, p. 73
aphasia, p. 74
split-brain operation, p. 74

Neuroscience and Behavior

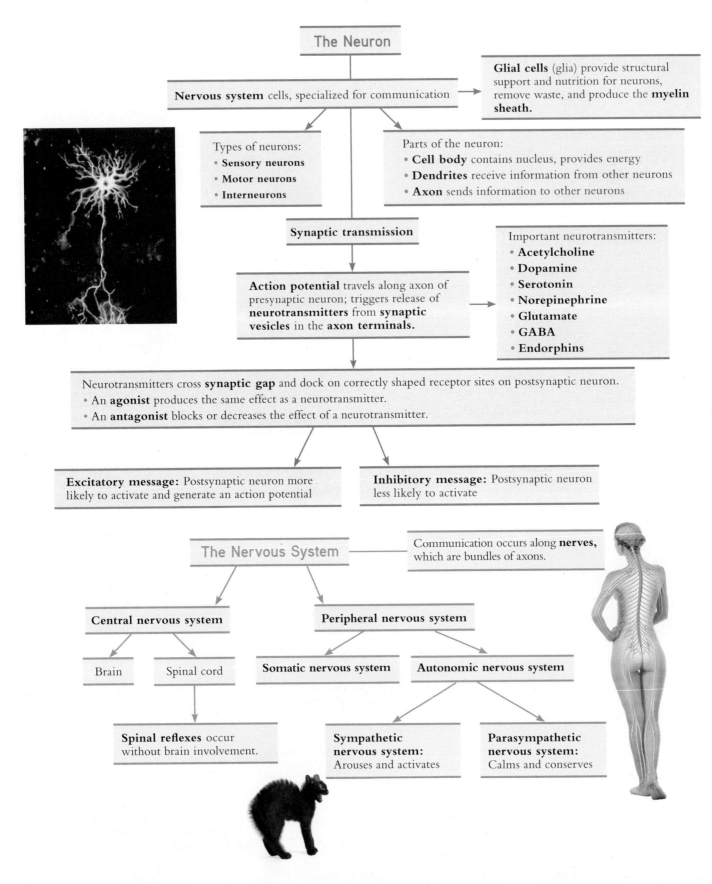

The Neuron

Nervous system cells, specialized for communication

Glial cells (glia) provide structural support and nutrition for neurons, remove waste, and produce the **myelin sheath.**

Types of neurons:
- **Sensory neurons**
- **Motor neurons**
- **Interneurons**

Parts of the neuron:
- **Cell body** contains nucleus, provides energy
- **Dendrites** receive information from other neurons
- **Axon** sends information to other neurons

Synaptic transmission

Action potential travels along axon of presynaptic neuron; triggers release of **neurotransmitters** from **synaptic vesicles** in the **axon terminals.**

Important neurotransmitters:
- **Acetylcholine**
- **Dopamine**
- **Serotonin**
- **Norepinephrine**
- **Glutamate**
- **GABA**
- **Endorphins**

Neurotransmitters cross **synaptic gap** and dock on correctly shaped receptor sites on postsynaptic neuron.
- An **agonist** produces the same effect as a neurotransmitter.
- An **antagonist** blocks or decreases the effect of a neurotransmitter.

Excitatory message: Postsynaptic neuron more likely to activate and generate an action potential

Inhibitory message: Postsynaptic neuron less likely to activate

The Nervous System

Communication occurs along **nerves,** which are bundles of axons.

Central nervous system

Peripheral nervous system

Brain

Spinal cord

Somatic nervous system

Autonomic nervous system

Spinal reflexes occur without brain involvement.

Sympathetic nervous system: Arouses and activates

Parasympathetic nervous system: Calms and conserves

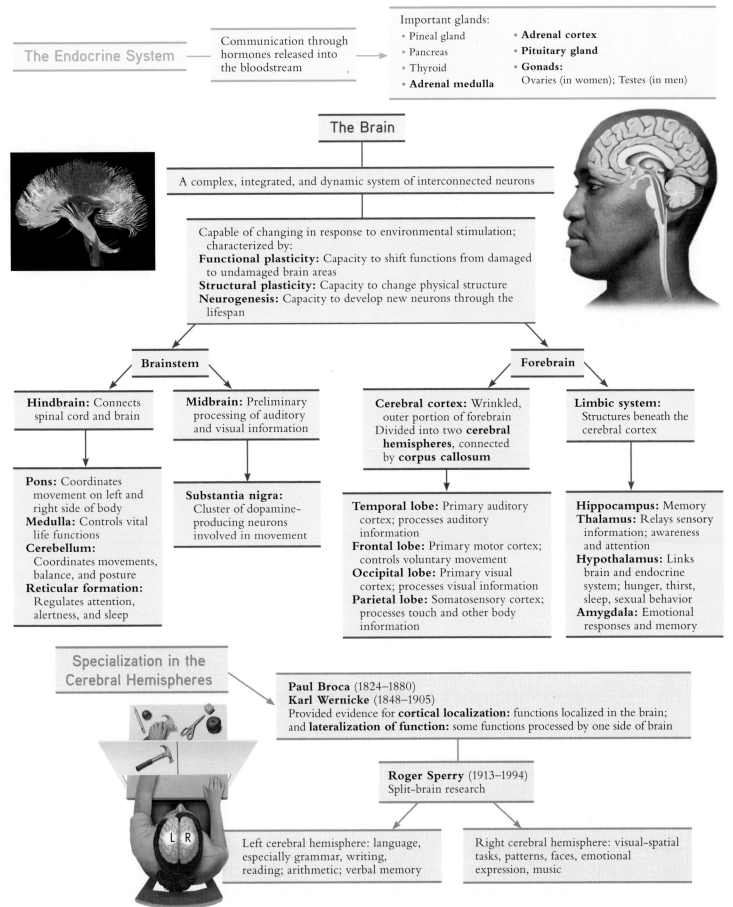

The Endocrine System → Communication through hormones released into the bloodstream →

Important glands:
- Pineal gland
- Pancreas
- Thyroid
- **Adrenal medulla**
- **Adrenal cortex**
- **Pituitary gland**
- **Gonads:**
  Ovaries (in women); Testes (in men)

The Brain

A complex, integrated, and dynamic system of interconnected neurons

Capable of changing in response to environmental stimulation; characterized by:
Functional plasticity: Capacity to shift functions from damaged to undamaged brain areas
Structural plasticity: Capacity to change physical structure
Neurogenesis: Capacity to develop new neurons through the lifespan

Brainstem

Hindbrain: Connects spinal cord and brain

Pons: Coordinates movement on left and right side of body
Medulla: Controls vital life functions
Cerebellum: Coordinates movements, balance, and posture
Reticular formation: Regulates attention, alertness, and sleep

Midbrain: Preliminary processing of auditory and visual information

Substantia nigra: Cluster of dopamine-producing neurons involved in movement

Forebrain

Cerebral cortex: Wrinkled, outer portion of forebrain Divided into two **cerebral hemispheres**, connected by **corpus callosum**

Temporal lobe: Primary auditory cortex; processes auditory information
Frontal lobe: Primary motor cortex; controls voluntary movement
Occipital lobe: Primary visual cortex; processes visual information
Parietal lobe: Somatosensory cortex; processes touch and other body information

Limbic system: Structures beneath the cerebral cortex

Hippocampus: Memory
Thalamus: Relays sensory information; awareness and attention
Hypothalamus: Links brain and endocrine system; hunger, thirst, sleep, sexual behavior
Amygdala: Emotional responses and memory

Specialization in the Cerebral Hemispheres

Paul Broca (1824–1880)
Karl Wernicke (1848–1905)
Provided evidence for **cortical localization:** functions localized in the brain; and **lateralization of function:** some functions processed by one side of brain

Roger Sperry (1913–1994)
Split-brain research

Left cerebral hemisphere: language, especially grammar, writing, reading; arithmetic; verbal memory

Right cerebral hemisphere: visual-spatial tasks, patterns, faces, emotional expression, music

MYTH OR SCIENCE?

Is it true . . .

- That subliminal messages can produce lasting changes in your attitudes and behavior?
- That an object's color is not an intrinsic property of the object?
- That pheromones can make some people irresistible to members of the preferred sex?
- That different tastes are detected on different parts of your tongue?
- That most psychologists study extrasensory perception (ESP)?
- That magnets can relieve pain?

LEARNING TO SEE

PROLOGUE

MIKE WAS JUST THREE YEARS OLD when a jar of chemicals, left in an old storage shed, exploded in his face. The blast destroyed his left eye and severely damaged his right eye. For more than four decades, Mike May was completely blind (Kurson, 2007).

But despite his blindness, Mike experienced—and accomplished—much more than most people ever dream of achieving. Always athletic, Mike played flag football in elementary school and wrestled and played soccer in high school and college. As an adult, he earned a master's degree in international affairs from Johns Hopkins University, went to work for the CIA, and then became a successful businessman.

He also learned to skydive, windsurf, water-ski, and snow-ski. How does a blind person ski down mountains? If you answered, "Very carefully," you'd be wrong—at least in Mike's case. With a guide skiing in front of him shouting "left" or "right" to identify obstacles, Mike hurtled down the most difficult black diamond slopes at speeds up to 65 miles per hour. In fact, Mike has won several medals in national and international championships for blind downhill speed skiing.

It was through skiing that Mike met his wife, Jennifer. An accomplished skier herself, she volunteered to be his guide at a ski slope. Today, Mike and Jennifer and their two sons are all avid skiers (Abrams, 2002).

In the 1990s, Mike started a successful company that develops global positioning devices—along with other mobility devices—for the blind. The portable navigation system gives visually impaired people information about their location, landmarks, streets, and so forth wherever they travel. With his white cane and guide dog, Josh, Mike traveled the world, both as a businessman and a tourist, ever optimistic and open to adventure (Kurson,

Sensation and Perception

3

IN THIS CHAPTER:

> **INTRODUCTION:** What Are Sensation and Perception?

> Vision: From Light to Sight

> Hearing: From Vibration to Sound

> The Chemical and Body Senses: Smell, Taste, Touch, and Position

> Perception

> Perceptual Illusions

> The Effects of Experience on Perceptual Interpretations

> **PSYCH FOR YOUR LIFE:** Strategies to Control Pain

2007). His personal motto: "There is always a way."

But in 1999, Mike's keen sensory world of touch, sounds, and aroma was on the verge of expanding. A new surgical technique became available that offered the chance that Mike's vision might be restored in his right eye. On March 7, 2000, Jennifer held her breath as the bandages were removed. "It was so unexpected— there was just a whoosh! of light blasting into my eye," Mike later recalled (May, 2002). For the first time since he was three years old, Mike May could see.

And what was it like when Mike could see Jennifer for the first time?

"It was incredible," he explained, "but the truth is, I knew exactly what she looked like, so it wasn't all that dramatic to see her. The same with my kids. Now, seeing other people that I can't touch, well, that's interesting because I couldn't see them before."

But what did Mike see? Anatomically, his right eye was now normal. But rather than being 20/20, his vision was closer to 20/1,000. What that means is his view of the world was very blurry. He could see colors, shapes, lines, shadows, light and dark patches. So why wasn't the world crystal clear?

Florence Low

Florence Low

Although the structures of his eye were working, his brain did not know how to interpret the signals it was receiving. As neuropsychologist Ione Fine (2002) explained, "Most people learn the language of vision between the age of birth and two years old. Mike has had to learn it as an adult." Indeed, there is much more to *seeing* than meets the eye.

Faces posed a particular challenge for Mike. During conversations, he found it very distracting to look at people's faces. As Mike wrote in his journal, "I can see their lips moving, eyelashes flickering, head nodding, and hands gesturing. It was easiest to close my eyes or tune out the visual input. This was often necessary in order to pay attention to what they were saying" (May, 2004).

And what was it like the first time he went skiing, just weeks after his surgery? Mike was dazzled by the sight of the tall, dark green trees, the snow, and the distant peaks against the blue sky (May, 2004). But although you might think that vision, even blurry vision, would be a distinct advantage to an expert skier, this was not the case. Mike found it easier to ski with his eyes closed, with Jennifer skiing ahead and shouting out directions. With his eyes open, he was overwhelmed by all the visual stimuli and the frightening sense that objects were rushing toward him. "By the time I thought about and guessed at what the shadows on the snow meant, I would miss the turn or fall on my face. It was best to close my eyes," he explained.

Throughout this chapter, we will come back to Mike's story. We'll also tell you what neuropsychologists Ione Fine and Don MacLeod learned after conducting fMRI scans of Mike's brain. And, later in the chapter, we'll see how well you do, compared to Mike, at deciphering some visual illusions. ☐

INTRODUCTION:
What Are Sensation and Perception?

Glance around you. Notice the incredible variety of colors, shades, shadows, and images. Listen carefully to the diversity of sounds, loud and soft, near and far. Focus on everything that's touching you—your clothes, your shoes, the chair you're sitting on. Now, inhale deeply through your nose and identify the aromas in the air.

With these simple observations, you have exercised four of your senses: vision, hearing, touch, and smell. As we saw in Chapter 2, the primary function of the nervous system is communication—the transmission of information from one part of the body to the other. Where does that information come from? Put simply, your senses are the gateway through which your brain receives all its information about the environment. It's a process that is so natural and automatic that we typically take it for granted until it is disrupted by illness or injury. Nevertheless, as Mike's story demonstrates, people with one nonfunctional sense are amazingly adaptive. Often, they learn to compensate for the missing environmental information by relying on their other senses.

In this chapter, we will explore the overlapping processes of *sensation* and *perception*. **Sensation** refers to the detection and basic sensory experience of environmental stimuli, such as sounds, images, and odors. **Perception** occurs when we integrate, organize, and interpret sensory information in a way that is meaningful. Here's a simple example to contrast the two terms. Your eyes' physical response to light, splotches of color, and lines reflects *sensation*. Integrating and organizing those sensations so that you interpret the light, splotches of color, and lines as a painting, a flag, or some other object reflects *perception*. Mike's visual world reflects this distinction. Although his eye was accurately transmitting visual information from his environment (*sensation*), his brain was unable to make sense out of the information (*perception*).

sensation The process of detecting a physical stimulus, such as light, sound, heat, or pressure.

perception The process of integrating, organizing, and interpreting sensations.

Where does the process of sensation leave off and the process of perception begin? There is no clear boundary line between the two processes as we actually experience them. In fact, many researchers in this area of psychology regard sensation and perception as a single process.

Although the two processes overlap, we will present sensation and perception as separate discussions. In the first half of the chapter, we'll discuss the basics of *sensation*—how our sensory receptors respond to stimulation and transmit that information in usable form to the brain. In the second half of the chapter, we'll explore *perception*—how the brain actively organizes and interprets the signals sent from our *sensory receptors*.

Basic Principles of Sensation

KEY THEME

Sensation is the result of neural impulses transmitted to the brain from sensory receptors that have been stimulated by physical energy from the external environment.

KEY QUESTIONS

> What is the process of transduction?
> What is a sensory threshold, and what are two main types of sensory thresholds?
> How do sensory adaptation and Weber's law demonstrate that sensation is relative rather than absolute?

We're accustomed to thinking of the senses as being quite different from one another. However, all our senses involve some common processes. All sensation is a result of the stimulation of specialized cells, called **sensory receptors,** by some form of *energy*.

Imagine biting into a juicy strawberry. Your experience of hearing the strawberry crunch is a response to the physical energy of vibrations in the air, or *sound waves.* The sweet, slightly tart taste of the strawberry is a response to the physical energy of *dissolvable chemicals* in your mouth, just as the distinctive sharp aroma of the strawberry is a response to *airborne chemical molecules* that you inhale through your nose. The prickly feel of the strawberry's skin is a response to the *pressure* of the strawberry against your hand. And the bright red color of the strawberry is a response to the physical energy of *light waves* reflecting from the irregularly shaped sphere.

Sensory receptors convert these different forms of physical energy into electrical impulses that are transmitted via neurons to the brain. The process by which a form of physical energy is converted into a coded neural signal that can be processed by the nervous system is called **transduction.** These neural signals are sent to the brain, where the perceptual processes of organizing and interpreting the coded messages occur. Figure 3.1 illustrates the basic steps involved in sensation and perception.

Peter Lourenco/Getty Images

Experiencing the World Through Our Senses Imagine biting into a fresh, juicy strawberry. All your senses are involved in your experience—vision, smell, taste, hearing, and touch. Although we're accustomed to thinking of our different senses as being quite distinct, all forms of sensation involve the stimulation of specialized cells called sensory receptors.

sensory receptors Specialized cells unique to each sense organ that respond to a particular form of sensory stimulation.

transduction The process by which a form of physical energy is converted into a coded neural signal that can be processed by the nervous system.

FIGURE 3.1 The Basic Steps of Sensation and Perception

Sensation

Perception

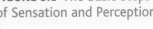

JGI/Blend images/Getty Images

Energy from an environmental stimulus activates specialized receptor cells in the sense organ.

Coded neural messages are sent along a specific sensory pathway to the brain.

These neural messages are decoded and interpreted in the brain as a meaningful perception.

absolute threshold The smallest possible strength of a stimulus that can be detected half the time.

difference threshold The smallest possible difference between two stimuli that can be detected half the time; also called *just noticeable difference*.

Weber's law (VAY-berz) A principle of sensation that holds that the size of the just noticeable difference will vary depending on its relation to the strength of the original stimulus.

sensory adaptation The decline in sensitivity to a constant stimulus.

We are constantly being bombarded by many different forms of energy. For instance, at this very moment radio and television waves are bouncing around the atmosphere and passing through your body. However, sensory receptors are so highly specialized that they are sensitive only to very specific types of energy (which is lucky, or you might be seeing *Friends* reruns in your brain right now). So, for any type of stimulation to be sensed, the stimulus energy must first be in a form that can be detected by our sensory receptor cells. Otherwise, transduction cannot occur.

SENSORY THRESHOLDS

Along with being specialized as to the types of energy that can be detected, our senses are specialized in other ways as well. We do not have an infinite capacity to detect all levels of energy. To be sensed, a stimulus must first be strong enough to be detected—loud enough to be heard, concentrated enough to be smelled, bright enough to be seen. The point at which a stimulus is strong enough to be detected because it activates a sensory receptor cell is called a *threshold*. There are two general kinds of sensory thresholds for each sense—the absolute threshold and the difference threshold.

The **absolute threshold** refers to the smallest possible strength of a stimulus that can be detected half the time. Why just half the time? It turns out that the minimum level of stimulation that can be detected varies from person to person and from trial to trial. Because of this human variability, researchers have arbitrarily set the limit as the minimum level of stimulation that can be detected half the time. Under ideal conditions (which rarely occur in normal daily life), our sensory abilities are far more sensitive than you might think (see Table 3.1). Can stimuli that are below the absolute threshold affect us? We discuss this question in the Science Versus Pseudoscience box, "Subliminal Perception."

The other important threshold involves detecting the *difference* between two stimuli. The **difference threshold** is the smallest possible difference between two stimuli that can be detected half the time. Another term for the difference threshold is *just noticeable difference*, which is abbreviated *jnd*.

The just noticeable difference will *vary* depending on its relation to the original stimulus. This principle of sensation is called *Weber's law*, after the German physiologist Ernst Weber (1795–1878). Imagine holding a pebble (the original stimulus). If a second pebble is placed in your hand, you will notice an increase in weight. But if you start off holding a very heavy rock (the original stimulus), you probably won't detect an increase in weight when the same pebble is balanced on it. **Weber's law** holds that for each sense, the size of a just noticeable difference is a constant proportion of the size of the initial stimulus. So, whether we can detect a change in the strength of a stimulus depends on the intensity of the *original* stimulus.

What Weber's law underscores is that our psychological experience of sensation is *relative*. That is, there is no simple, one-to-one correspondence between the objective characteristics of a physical stimulus, such as the weight of a pebble, and our psychological experience of it.

TABLE 3.1

Absolute Thresholds

Sense	Absolute Threshold
Vision	A candle flame seen from 30 miles away on a clear, dark night
Hearing	The tick of a watch at 20 feet
Taste	One teaspoon of sugar in two gallons of water
Smell	One drop of perfume throughout a three-room apartment
Touch	A bee's wing falling on your cheek from a height of about half an inch

Psychologist Eugene Galanter provided these classic examples of the absolute thresholds for our senses. In each case, people are able to sense these faint stimuli at least half the time.

Source: Information from Galanter (1962).

SENSORY ADAPTATION

Suppose your best friend has invited you over for a spaghetti dinner. As you walk in the front door, you're almost overwhelmed by the odor of onions and garlic cooking on the stove. However, after just a few moments, you no longer notice the smell. Why? Because your sensory receptor cells become less responsive to a constant stimulus. This gradual decline in sensitivity to a constant stimulus is called **sensory adaptation.** Once again, we see that our experience of sensation is relative—in this case, relative to the *duration of exposure*.

Because of sensory adaptation, we become accustomed to constant stimuli, which allows us to quickly notice new or changing stimuli. This makes sense. If we were continually aware of all incoming stimuli, we'd be so overwhelmed with sensory information that we wouldn't be able to focus our attention. So, for example, once you manage to land your posterior on the sofa, you don't need to be constantly reminded that the sofa is beneath you.

subliminal perception The detection of stimuli that are below the threshold of conscious awareness; nonconscious perception.

mere exposure effect The finding that repeated exposure to a stimulus increases a person's preference for that stimulus.

SCIENCE VERSUS PSEUDOSCIENCE

Subliminal Perception

What are subliminal messages? Can they influence people to quit smoking, lose weight, or change their personalities? **Subliminal perception** refers to the detection of stimuli that are below the threshold of conscious perception or awareness. Such stimuli might be rapidly flashed visual images, sounds, or odors that are too faint to be consciously detected. Although not consciously perceived, subliminal stimuli can evoke a brain response (Bahrami & others, 2007; Tamietto & de Gelder, 2010).

The notion that people's behavior could be manipulated by subliminal messages first attracted public attention in 1957. James Vicary, a marketing executive, claimed to have increased concession sales at a New Jersey movie theater by subliminally flashing the words "Eat popcorn" and "Drink Coke" during the movie.

Controlled tests, however, failed to replicate Vicary's claims, and Vicary later admitted that his boast was a hoax to drum up customers for his failing marketing business (Dijksterhuis & others, 2005; Fullerton, 2010). Nevertheless, to this day, many people still believe—and some advertisements claim—that subliminal messages can exert an irresistible, lasting influence.

Can your behavior be profoundly influenced by subliminal self-help CDs, audiotapes, or computer programs? Or by vague images or words embedded in advertisements? No. Numerous studies have shown that subliminal self-help products do *not* produce the changes they claim to produce (Strahan & others, 2005). Likewise, numerous studies on subliminal messages in advertising have shown that they do not influence actual consumer decisions (Simons & others, 2007).

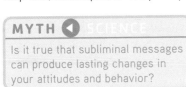

MYTH ◀ SCIENCE

Is it true that subliminal messages can produce lasting changes in your attitudes and behavior?

But do subliminal stimuli have *any* effect? Surprisingly, the answer is a qualified *yes*. For example, consider the **mere exposure effect,** which refers to the well-documented finding that repeated exposure to a particular stimulus leads to increased liking for that stimulus (Zajonc, 2001; Moreland & Topolinski, 2010). The mere exposure effect also holds for subliminally presented stimuli. For example, when people are exposed to subliminal images of a particular geometric shape and, minutes later, are asked to pick the shape they prefer from a group of shapes, they are much more likely to choose the subliminally presented shape.

Subliminal stimuli *can* influence actual behavior—but only under certain conditions. Research suggests that subliminal stimuli are effective *only* when they are relevant to goals that are already held by the observer. So, for example, subliminally flashing the words "Lipton One" made research participants slightly more likely to say that they preferred Lipton One over another brand—but *only* if they were already thirsty. The subliminal stimulus had *no* effect on participants who weren't thirsty (Karremans & others, 2006).

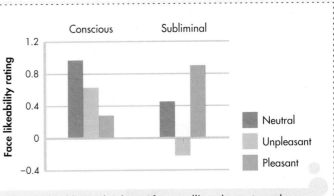

Effects of Subliminal Odors After smelling pleasant, unpleasant, or neutral odors, participants rated photographs of faces on a scale ranging from "extremely unlikeable" to "extremely likeable." Participants' judgments were affected by subliminal odors—but not by odors that they could consciously perceive.
Source: Data from W. Li & others (2007).

Beyond preferences, attitudes and emotions can also be influenced by subliminal stimuli (Smith & others, 2008; Westen & others, 2007). For example, participants were subliminally exposed to faces expressing fear, disgust, or a neutral emotion before being asked to rate the pleasantness of other faces presented on a computer screen. Faces that were preceded by subliminal "fear" stimuli were rated as most unpleasant (Lee & others, 2011).

Can other sensory cues affect us without our awareness? One intriguing study investigated the effect of subliminal odors (W. Li & others, 2007). Participants rated pictures of faces for "likeability" after sniffing either a pleasant, lemony scent; an unpleasant scent (think high school locker room); a neutral scent; or no scent at all (air). The catch was that 75% of the time, the odors were so faint that they could not be consciously detected. Did the subliminal odors affect the likeability ratings?

Yes—but *only* when participants were unaware of which scent they were sniffing. Faces paired with the subliminal pleasant odor received the highest ratings, while faces paired with the subliminal unpleasant odor received the lowest ratings (see graph). However, when participants were aware of an odor, the correlation between likeability and odor pleasantness disappeared.

Why? According to lead researcher Wen Li (W. Li & others, 2007), "People who were conscious of the barely noticeable scents were able to discount that sensory information and just evaluate the faces." But participants who were *not* conscious of the odors attributed their response to the "pleasantness" or "unpleasantness" of the faces they were rating, rather than to the smells that they could *not* consciously perceive.

What can be concluded? Subliminal stimuli *can* briefly influence attitudes, thoughts, preferences, and emotions (Dijksterhuis & Nordgren, 2006). But the key word here is *briefly*. These transient influences are a far cry from the pseudoscientific claims of some subliminal self-help products that promise easy and sweeping changes in behavior, personality, or motivation.

How a Pit Viper Sees a Mouse at Night Does the world look different to other species? In many cases, yes. Each species has evolved a unique set of sensory capabilities. Pit vipers see infrared light, which we sense only as warmth. The mouse here has been photographed through an infrared viewer. The image shows how a pit viper uses its infrared "vision" to detect warm-blooded prey at night (Van Dyke & Grace, 2010). Similarly, many insect and bird species can detect ultraviolet light, which is invisible to humans.

Julius Lab, UCSF

Vision
FROM LIGHT TO SIGHT

KEY THEME

The receptor cells for vision respond to the physical energy of light waves and are located in the retina of the eye.

KEY QUESTIONS

> What is the visible spectrum?
> What are the key structures of the eye and their functions?
> What are rods and cones, and how do their functions differ?

A lone caterpillar on the screen door, the pile of dirty laundry in the corner of the closet, a spectacular autumn sunset, the intricate play of color, light, and texture in a painting by Monet. The sense organ for vision is the eye, which contains receptor cells that are sensitive to the physical energy of *light*. But before we can talk about how the eye functions, we need to briefly discuss some characteristics of light as the visual stimulus.

What We See
THE NATURE OF LIGHT

Light is just one of many different kinds of electromagnetic energy that travel in the form of waves. Other forms of electromagnetic energy include X-rays, the microwaves you use to pop popcorn, and the infrared signals or radio waves transmitted by your TV's remote control. The various types of electromagnetic energy differ in **wavelength,** which is the distance from one wave peak to another.

Humans are capable of seeing only a minuscule portion of the electromagnetic energy range. In Figure 3.2, notice that the visible portion of the electromagnetic energy spectrum can be further divided into different wavelengths. As we'll discuss in more detail later, the different wavelengths of visible light correspond to our psychological perception of different colors.

FIGURE 3.2 The Electromagnetic Spectrum We are surrounded by different kinds of electromagnetic energy waves, yet we are able to see only a tiny portion—less than one percent—of the entire spectrum of electromagnetic energy. Some electronic instruments, like radio and television, are specialized receivers that detect a specific wavelength range. Similarly, the human eye is sensitive to a specific and very narrow range of wavelengths.

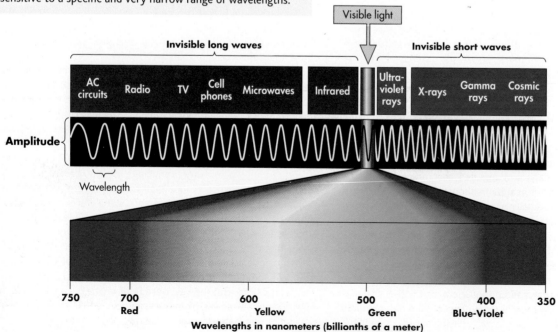

How We See
THE HUMAN VISUAL SYSTEM

Imagine that you're watching your author Susan's cat Milla sunning herself in a nearby window. Simply seeing a brown tabby cat with emerald green eyes involves a complex chain of events. To help understand the visual process, trace the path of light waves through the eye in Figure 3.3 as we describe each step.

First, light waves reflected from the cat enter your eye, passing through the *cornea*, *pupil*, and *lens*. The **cornea,** a clear membrane that covers the front of the eye, helps gather and direct incoming light. The *sclera*, or white portion of the eye, is a tough, fibrous tissue that covers the eyeball except for the cornea. The **pupil** is the black opening in the eye's center. The pupil is surrounded by the **iris,** the colored structure that we refer to when we say that someone has brown eyes. The iris is actually a ring of muscular tissue that contracts or expands to precisely control the size of the pupil and thus the amount of light entering the eye. In dim light, the iris widens the pupil to let light in; in bright light, the iris narrows the pupil.

Behind the pupil is the **lens,** another transparent structure. In a process called **accommodation,** the lens thins or thickens to bend or focus the incoming light so that the light falls on the retina. If the eyeball is abnormally shaped, the lens may not properly focus the incoming light on the retina, resulting in a visual disorder. In nearsightedness, or *myopia*, distant objects appear blurry because the light reflected off the objects focuses in front of the retina. In farsightedness, or *hyperopia*, objects near the eyes appear blurry because light reflected off the objects is focused behind the

wavelength The distance from one wave peak to another.

cornea (CORE-nee-uh) A clear membrane covering the visible part of the eye that helps gather and direct incoming light.

pupil The opening in the middle of the iris that changes size to let in different amounts of light.

iris (EYE-riss) The colored part of the eye, which is the muscle that controls the size of the pupil.

lens A transparent structure, located behind the pupil, that actively focuses, or bends, light as it enters the eye.

accommodation The process by which the lens changes shape to focus incoming light so that it falls on the retina.

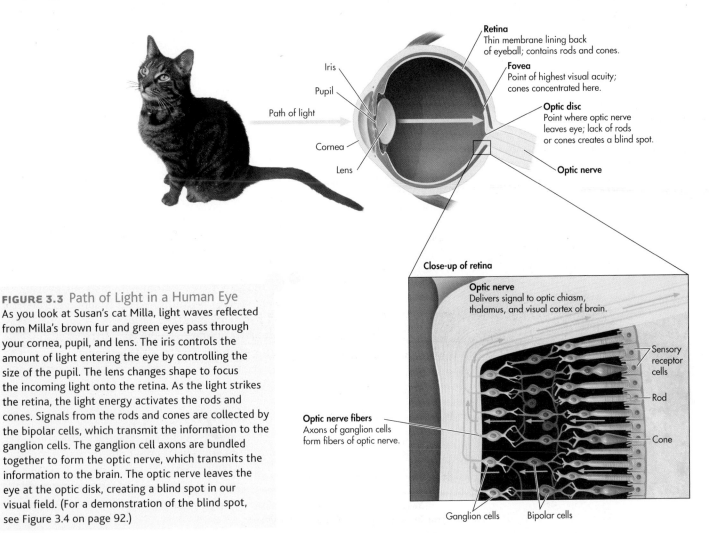

FIGURE 3.3 Path of Light in a Human Eye
As you look at Susan's cat Milla, light waves reflected from Milla's brown fur and green eyes pass through your cornea, pupil, and lens. The iris controls the amount of light entering the eye by controlling the size of the pupil. The lens changes shape to focus the incoming light onto the retina. As the light strikes the retina, the light energy activates the rods and cones. Signals from the rods and cones are collected by the bipolar cells, which transmit the information to the ganglion cells. The ganglion cell axons are bundled together to form the optic nerve, which transmits the information to the brain. The optic nerve leaves the eye at the optic disk, creating a blind spot in our visual field. (For a demonstration of the blind spot, see Figure 3.4 on page 92.)

Ivan Bojanic

Retina
Thin membrane lining back of eyeball; contains rods and cones.

Fovea
Point of highest visual acuity; cones concentrated here.

Optic disc
Point where optic nerve leaves eye; lack of rods or cones creates a blind spot.

Optic nerve

Iris

Pupil

Path of light

Cornea

Lens

Close-up of retina

Optic nerve
Delivers signal to optic chiasm, thalamus, and visual cortex of brain.

Optic nerve fibers
Axons of ganglion cells form fibers of optic nerve.

Sensory receptor cells

Rod

Cone

Ganglion cells   Bipolar cells

Science Source

Slim Rods and Fat Cones The rods and cones in the retina are the sensory receptors for vision. They convert light into electrical impulses that are ultimately transmitted to the brain. Color has been added to this scanning electromicrograph to clearly distinguish the rods and cones. The rods, colored green, are long, thin, and more numerous than the cones, colored blue, which are tapered at one end and shorter and fatter than the rods. As the photo shows, the rods and cones are densely packed in the retina, with many rods surrounding a few cones.

FIGURE 3.4 Demonstration of the Blind Spot Hold this book a few feet in front of you. Close your right eye and stare at the insect spray can with your left eye. Slowly bring the book toward your face. At some point the spider will disappear because you have focused it onto the part of your retina where the blind spot is located. Notice, however, that you still perceive the spider web. That's because your brain has filled in information from the surrounding area (Komatsu, 2006).

retina. During middle age, another form of farsightedness often occurs, called *presbyopia*. Presbyopia is caused when the lens becomes brittle and inflexible. In *astigmatism*, an abnormally curved eyeball results in blurry vision for lines in a particular direction. Corrective glasses remedy these conditions by intercepting and bending the light so that the image falls properly on the retina. Surgical techniques like LASIK correct visual disorders by reshaping the cornea so that light rays focus more directly on the retina.

THE RETINA

RODS AND CONES

The **retina** is a thin, light-sensitive membrane that lies at the back of the eye, covering most of its inner surface (see Figure 3.3). Contained in the retina are the **rods** and **cones.** Because these sensory receptor cells respond to light, they are often called *photoreceptors*. When exposed to light, the rods and cones undergo a chemical reaction that results in a neural signal.

Rods and cones differ in many ways. First, as their names imply, rods and cones are shaped differently. Rods are long and thin, with blunt ends. Cones are shorter and fatter, with one end that tapers to a point. The eye contains far more rods than cones. It is estimated that each eye contains about 7 million cones and about 125 million rods!

Rods and cones are also specialized for different visual functions. Although both are light receptors, rods are much more sensitive to light than are cones. Once the rods are fully adapted to the dark, they are about a thousand times better than cones at detecting weak visual stimuli (Masland, 2001). We therefore rely primarily on rods for our vision in dim light and at night.

Rods and cones also react differently to *changes* in the amount of light. Rods adapt relatively slowly, reaching maximum sensitivity to light in about 30 minutes. In contrast, cones adapt quickly to bright light, reaching maximum sensitivity in about 5 minutes. That's why it takes several minutes for your eyes to adapt to the dim light of a darkened room but only a few moments to adapt to the brightness when you switch on the lights.

You may have noticed that it is difficult or impossible to distinguish colors in very dim light. This difficulty occurs because only the cones are sensitive to the different wavelengths that produce the sensation of color, and cones require much more light than rods do to function effectively. Cones are also specialized for seeing fine details and for vision in bright light.

Most of the cones are concentrated in the **fovea,** which is a region in the very center of the retina. Cones are scattered throughout the rest of the retina, but they become progressively less common toward the periphery of the retina. There are no rods in the fovea. Images that do not fall on the fovea tend to be perceived as blurry or indistinct. For example, focus your eyes on the word "For" at the beginning of this sentence. In contrast to the sharpness of the letters in "For," the words to the left and right are somewhat blurry. The image of the outlying words is striking the peripheral areas of the retina, where rods are more prevalent and there are very few cones.

THE BLIND SPOT

One part of the retina lacks rods and cones altogether. This area, called the **optic disk,** is the point at which the fibers that make up the optic nerve leave the back of the eye and project to the brain. Because there are no photoreceptors in the optic disk, we have a tiny hole, or **blind spot,** in our field of vision. To experience the blind spot, try the demonstration in Figure 3.4.

Why don't we notice this hole in our visual field? The most compelling explanation is that the brain actually fills in the missing background information (Ramachandran, 1992a, 1992b; Weil & Rees, 2010). In effect, signals from neighboring neurons fill in the blind spot with the color and texture of the surrounding visual information (Supèr & Romeo, 2011).

Processing Visual Information

KEY THEME

Signals from the rods and cones undergo preliminary processing in the retina before they are transmitted to the brain.

KEY QUESTIONS

> What are the bipolar and ganglion cells, and how do their functions differ?
> How is visual information transmitted from the retina to the brain?
> What properties of light correspond to color perceptions, and how is color vision explained?

Visual information is processed primarily in the brain. However, before visual information is sent to the brain, it undergoes some preliminary processing in the retina by specialized neurons called **ganglion cells.** This preliminary processing of visual data in the cells of the retina is possible because the retina develops from a bit of brain tissue that "migrates" to the eye during fetal development (Hubel, 1995).

When the numbers of rods and cones are combined, there are over 130 million receptor cells in each retina. However, there are only about 1 million ganglion cells. How do just 1 million ganglion cells transmit messages from 130 million visual receptor cells?

VISUAL PROCESSING IN THE RETINA

Information from the sensory receptors, the rods and cones, is first collected by specialized neurons, called **bipolar cells.** Look back at the lower portion of Figure 3.3. The bipolar cells then funnel the collection of raw data to the ganglion cells. Each ganglion cell receives information from the photoreceptors that are located in its *receptive field* in a particular area of the retina. In this early stage of visual processing, each ganglion cell combines, analyzes, and encodes the information from the photoreceptors in its receptive field before transmitting the information to the brain (Ringach, 2009).

Signals from rods and signals from cones are processed differently in the ganglion. For the most part, a single ganglion cell receives information from only one or two cones but might well receive information from a hundred or more rods. The messages from these many different rods are combined in the retina before they are sent to the brain. Thus, the brain receives less specific visual information from the rods and messages of much greater visual detail from the cones.

As an analogy to how rod information is processed, imagine listening to a hundred people trying to talk at once over the same telephone line. You would hear the sound of many people talking, but individual voices would be blurred. Now imagine listening to the voice of a single individual being transmitted across the same telephone line. Every syllable and sound would be clear and distinct. In much the same way, cones use the ganglion cells to provide the brain with more specific visual information than is received from rods.

Because of this difference in how information is processed, cones are especially important in *visual acuity*—the ability to see fine details. Visual acuity is strongest when images are focused on the fovea because of the high concentration of cones there.

FROM EYE TO BRAIN

How is information transmitted from the ganglion cells of the retina to the brain? The 1 million axons of the ganglion cells are bundled together to form the **optic nerve,** a thick nerve that exits from the back of the eye at the optic disk and extends

LaunchPad

To see how the brain is involved in vision, and to experience your own blind spot, try **Lab: Psychology of Vision.**

retina (RET-in-uh) A thin, light-sensitive membrane, located at the back of the eye that contains the sensory receptors for vision.

rods The long, thin, blunt sensory receptors of the eye that are highly sensitive to light, but not to color, and that are primarily responsible for peripheral vision and night vision.

cones The short, thick, pointed sensory receptors of the eye that detect color and are responsible for color vision and visual acuity.

fovea (FOE-vee-uh) A small area in the center of the retina, composed entirely of cones, where visual information is most sharply focused.

optic disk Area of the retina without rods or cones, where the optic nerve exits the back of the eye.

blind spot The point at which the optic nerve leaves the eye, producing a small gap in the field of vision.

ganglion cells In the retina, the specialized neurons that connect to the bipolar cells; the bundled axons of the ganglion cells form the optic nerve.

bipolar cells In the retina, the specialized neurons that connect the rods and cones with the ganglion cells.

optic nerve The thick nerve that exits from the back of the eye and carries visual information to the visual cortex in the brain.

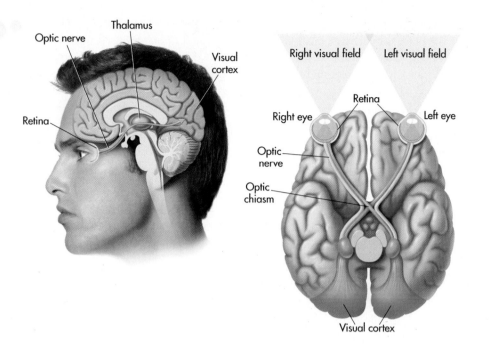

FIGURE 3.5 Neural Pathways from Eye to Brain The bundled axons of the ganglion cells form the optic nerve, which exits the retina at the optic disk. The optic nerves from the left and right eyes meet at the optic chiasm, then split apart. One set of nerve fibers crosses over and projects to the opposite side of the brain, and another set of nerve fibers continues along the same side of the brain. Most of the nerve fibers travel to the thalamus and then on to the visual cortex of the occipital lobe.

ge Source Black/ Alamy

to the brain (see Figure 3.5). The optic nerve has about the same diameter as a pen-cil. After exiting the eyes, the left and right optic nerves meet at the **optic chiasm.** Then the fibers of the left and right optic nerves split in two. One set of axons crosses over and projects to the opposite side of the brain. The other set of axons forms a pathway that continues along the same side of the brain (see Figure 3.5).

From the optic chiasm, most of the optic nerve axons project to the brain structure called the thalamus. (For more on the specific brain structures involved in vision, see Chapter 2). This primary pathway seems to be responsible for processing information about form, color, brightness, and depth. A smaller number of axons follow a detour to areas in the midbrain before they make their way to the thalamus. This secondary pathway seems to be involved in processing information about the location of an object.

Neuroscientists now know that there are several distinct neural pathways in the visual system, each responsible for handling a different aspect of vision (Paik & Ringach, 2011; Purves, 2009). Although specialized, the separate pathways are highly interconnected. From the thalamus, the signals are sent to the visual cortex, where they are decoded and interpreted.

Most of the receiving neurons in the visual cortex of the brain are highly special-ized. Each responds to a particular type of visual stimulation, such as angles, edges, lines, and other forms, and even to the movement and distance of objects (Hubel & Wiesel, 2005; Livingstone & Hubel, 1988). These neurons are sometimes called *feature detectors* because they detect, or respond to, particular features or aspects of more complex visual stimuli. Reassembling the features into a recognizable image involves additional levels of processing in the visual cortex and other regions of the brain, including the frontal lobes.

Understanding exactly how neural responses of individual feature detection cells become integrated into the visual perceptions of faces and objects is a major goal of contemporary neuroscience (Celesia, 2010; Mahon & Caramazza, 2011). Experi-ence also plays an important role in the development of perception, especially visual perception (Huber & others, 2015). In the Focus on Neuroscience, we explore how Mike May's perceptual abilities were affected by his lack of visual experience.

Color Vision

optic chiasm (KY-az-uhm) The point in the brain where the optic nerve fibers from each eye meet and partly cross over to the opposite side of the brain.

We see images of an apple, a banana, and an orange because these objects reflect light waves. But why do we perceive that the apple is red and the banana yellow? What makes an orange orange?

FOCUS ON NEUROSCIENCE

Vision, Experience, and the Brain

After Mike's surgery, his retina and optic nerve were completely normal. Formal testing showed that Mike had excellent color perception and that he could easily identify simple shapes and lines that were oriented in different directions. These abilities correspond to visual pathways that develop very early. Mike's motion perception was also very good. When thrown a ball, he could catch it more than 80 percent of the time.

Perceiving and identifying common objects, however, was difficult. Although Mike could "see" an object, he had to consciously use visual cues to work out its identity. For example, when shown the simple drawing above right, called a "Necker cube," Mike described it as "a square with lines." But when shown the same image as a rotating image on a computer screen, Mike immediately identified it as a cube. Functional MRI scans showed that Mike's brain activity was nearly normal when shown a *moving* object.

What about more complex objects, like faces? Three years after regaining sight, Mike recognized his wife and sons by their hair color, gait, and other clues, *not* by their faces. When tested again, ten years after his surgery, Mike was unable to identify a face as male or female, or its expression as happy or sad (Huber & others, 2015). Despite a decade of visual experience, functional MRI scans revealed that when Mike is shown faces or objects, the part of the brain that is normally activated is still silent.

Necker Cube

Shown a stationary image of a Necker cube, Mike described it as "a square with lines." Only when the image began to rotate did Mike perceive it as a drawing of a cube.

For people with normal vision, recognizing complex three-dimensional objects—like tables, shoes, trees, or pencils—is automatic. But as Mike's story shows, these perceptual conclusions are actually based on experience and built up over time.

Neuroscientist Ione Fine and her colleagues (2003, 2008), who have studied Mike's visual abilities, believe that Mike's case indicates that some visual pathways develop earlier than others. Color and motion perception, they point out, develop early in infancy. But because people will continue to encounter new objects and faces throughout life, areas of the brain that are specialized to process faces and objects show plasticity (Huber & others, 2015). In Mike's case, these brain centers never developed (Levin & others, 2010).

Reprinted by permission from Macmillan Publishers, Ltd: Nature Neuroscience, "Long term deprivation affects visual perception and cortex." By: Fine, Ione, Alex R Wade, Alyssa A Brewer, Michael G May, Daniel F Goodman, Geoffrey M Boynton, Brian A Wandell, and Donald I A Macleod.

Sighted Controls

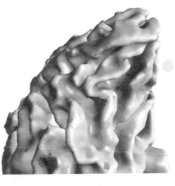

Mike May

Scanning Mike's Brain The red, orange, and yellow colors in the left fMRI scan show the areas of the occipital lobe that are normally activated in response to faces. Blue and purple indicate the typical pattern of brain activity in response to objects. In contrast to a normally sighted individual, Mike's fMRI scan (right), taken three years after his surgery, shows virtually no response to faces and only slight brain activation in response to objects.

THE EXPERIENCE OF COLOR

WHAT MAKES AN ORANGE ORANGE?

Color is *not* a property of an object, but a sensation perceived in the brain (Werner & others, 2007). To explain how we perceive color, we must return to the original visual stimulus—light.

Our experience of **color** involves three properties of the light wave. First, what we usually refer to as color is a property more accurately termed **hue.** Hue varies with the wavelength of light. Look again at Figure 3.2 on page 90. *Different wavelengths correspond to our subjective experience of different colors.* Wavelengths of about 400 nanometers are perceived as violet. Wavelengths of about 700 nanometers are perceived as red. In between are orange, yellow, green, blue, and indigo.

Second, the **saturation,** or *purity,* of the color corresponds to the purity of the light wave. Pure red, for example, produced by a single wavelength, is more *saturated* than pink, which is produced by a combination of wavelengths (red plus white light). In everyday language, saturation refers to the richness of a color. A highly saturated color is vivid and rich; a less saturated color is faded and washed out.

MYTH ▶ SCIENCE

Is it true that an object's color is not an intrinsic property of the object?

color The perceptual experience of different wavelengths of light, involving hue, saturation (purity), and brightness (intensity).

hue The property of wavelengths of light known as color; different wavelengths correspond to our subjective experience of different colors.

saturation The property of color that corresponds to the purity of the light wave.

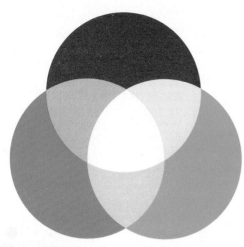

When Red + Blue + Green = White
When light waves of different wavelengths are combined, the wavelengths are added together, producing the perception of a different color. Thus, when green light is combined with red light, yellow light is produced. When the wavelengths of red, green, and blue light are added together, we perceive the blended light as white. If you're wondering why mixing paints together produces a muddy mess rather than pure white, it's because the wavelengths are *subtracted* rather than added. Each color of pigment absorbs a different part of the color spectrum, and each time a color is added, less light is reflected. Thus, the mixed color appears darker. If you mix all three primary colors together, they absorb the entire spectrum—so we perceive the splotch as black.

brightness The perceived intensity of a color, which corresponds to the amplitude of the light wave.

trichromatic theory of color vision The theory that the sensation of color results because cones in the retina are especially sensitive to red light (long wavelengths), green light (medium wavelengths), or blue light (short wavelengths).

color blindness One of several inherited forms of color deficiency or weakness in which an individual cannot distinguish between certain colors.

afterimage A visual experience that occurs after the original source of stimulation is no longer present.

The third property of color is **brightness,** or perceived intensity. Brightness corresponds to the amplitude of the light wave: The higher the amplitude, the greater the degree of brightness.

These three properties of color—hue, saturation, and brightness—are responsible for the amazing range of colors we experience. A person with normal color vision can discriminate from 120 to 150 color differences based on differences in hue, or wavelength, alone. When saturation and brightness are also factored in, we can potentially perceive millions of different colors (Elliot & Maier, 2014).

Many people mistakenly believe that white light contains no color. White light actually contains all wavelengths—and thus all colors—of the visible part of the electromagnetic spectrum. A glass prism placed in sunlight creates a rainbow because it separates sunlight into all the colors of the visible light spectrum.

So we're back to the question: What makes an orange orange? Intuitively, it seems obvious that the color of any object is an inseparable property of the object—unless we spill paint or spaghetti sauce on it. In reality, *color is a sensation perceived in the brain* (Werner & others, 2007).

Our perception of color is primarily determined by the wavelength of light that an object reflects. If your T-shirt is red, it's red because the cloth is *reflecting* only the wavelength of light that corresponds to the red portion of the spectrum. The T-shirt is *absorbing* the wavelengths that correspond to all other colors. An object appears white because it *reflects* all the wavelengths of visible light and absorbs none. An object appears black when it *absorbs* all the wavelengths of visible light and reflects none. Of course, in everyday life, our perceptions of color are also strongly affected by the amount or type of light falling on an object or the textures and colors that surround it (Purves, 2009; Shevell & Kingdom, 2008).

HOW WE SEE COLOR

Color vision has interested scientists for hundreds of years. The first scientific theory of color vision, proposed by Hermann von Helmholtz (1821–1894) in the mid-1800s, was called the *trichromatic theory.* A rival theory, the *opponent-process theory,* was proposed in the late 1800s. Each theory was capable of explaining some aspects of color vision, but neither theory could explain all aspects of color vision. Technological advances in the last few decades have allowed researchers to gather direct physiological evidence to test both theories. The resulting evidence indicates that *both* theories of color vision are accurate. Each theory describes color vision at a different stage of visual processing (Hubel, 1995).

The Trichromatic Theory As you'll recall, only the cones are involved in color vision. According to the **trichromatic theory of color vision,** there are three varieties of cones. Each type of cone is especially sensitive to certain wavelengths—red light (long wavelengths), green light (medium wavelengths), or blue light (short wavelengths). For the sake of simplicity, we will refer to red-sensitive, green-sensitive, and blue-sensitive cones, but keep in mind that there is some overlap in the wavelengths to which a cone is sensitive (Purves, 2009). A given cone will be very sensitive to one of the three colors and only slightly responsive to the other two.

When a color other than red, green, or blue strikes the retina, it stimulates a *combination* of cones. For example, if yellow light strikes the retina, both the red-sensitive and green-sensitive cones are stimulated; purple light evokes strong reactions from red-sensitive and blue-sensitive cones. The trichromatic theory of color vision received compelling research support in 1964, when George Wald showed that different cones were indeed activated by red, blue, and green light.

The trichromatic theory provides a good explanation for the most common form of **color blindness:** red–green color blindness. People with red–green color blindness cannot discriminate between red and green. That's because they have normal blue-sensitive cones, but their other cones are *either* red-sensitive or green-sensitive

(Carroll & others, 2009). Thus, red and green look the same to them. Because red–green color blindness is so common, stoplights are designed so that the location of the light as well as its color provides information to drivers. In vertical stoplights the red light is always on top, and in horizontal stoplights the red light is always on the far left.

The Opponent-Process Theory The trichromatic theory cannot account for all aspects of color vision. One important phenomenon that the theory does not explain is the afterimage. An **afterimage** is a visual experience that occurs after the original source of stimulation is no longer present. To experience an afterimage firsthand, follow the instructions in Figure 3.6. What do you see?

Afterimages can be explained by the opponent-process theory of color vision, which proposes a different mechanism of color detection from the one set forth in the trichromatic theory. According to the **opponent-process theory of color vision,** there are four basic colors, which are divided into two pairs of color-sensitive neurons: red–green and blue–yellow. The members of each pair *oppose* each other. If red is stimulated, green is inhibited; if green is stimulated, red is inhibited. Green and red cannot both be stimulated simultaneously. The same is true for the blue–yellow pair. In addition, black and white act as an opposing pair. Color, then, is sensed and encoded in terms of its proportion of red *or* green and blue *or* yellow.

For example, red light evokes a response of RED-YES–GREEN-NO in the red–green opponent pair. Yellow light evokes a response of BLUE-NO–YELLOW-YES. Colors other than red, green, blue, and yellow activate one member of each of these pairs to differing degrees. Purple stimulates the *red* of the red–green pair plus the *blue* of the blue–yellow pair. Orange activates *red* in the red–green pair and *yellow* in the blue–yellow pair.

Afterimages can be explained when the opponent-process theory is combined with the general principle of sensory adaptation (Jameson & Hurvich, 1989). If you stare continuously at one color, sensory adaptation eventually occurs and your visual receptors become less sensitive to that color. What happens when you subsequently stare at a white surface?

If you remember that white light is made up of the wavelengths for *all* colors, you may be able to predict the result. The receptors for the original color have adapted to the constant stimulation and are temporarily "off duty." Thus, they do not respond to that color. Instead, only the receptors for the opposing color will be activated, and you perceive the wavelength of only the *opposing* color. For example, if you stare at a patch of green, your green receptors eventually become "tired." The wavelengths for both green and red light are reflected by the white surface, but since the green receptors are "off," only the red receptors are activated. Staring at the green, black, and yellow flag in Figure 3.6 should have produced an afterimage of opposing colors: a red, white, and blue American flag.

opponent-process theory of color vision The theory that color vision is the product of opposing pairs of color receptors: red–green, blue–yellow, and black–white; when one member of a color pair is stimulated, the other member is inhibited.

(both) PicturesWild/Shutterstock

The Most Common Form of Color Blindness To someone with the most common form of red–green color blindness, these two photographs look almost exactly the same. People with this type of color blindness have normal blue-sensitive cones, but their other cones are sensitive to either red *or* green. Because of the way red–green color blindness is genetically transmitted, it is much more common in men than in women. About 8 percent of the male population is born with red–green color deficiency, and about a quarter of these males experience only the colors coded by the blue–yellow cones. People who are completely color blind and see the world only in shades of black, white, and gray are extremely rare (Shevell & Kingdom, 2008).

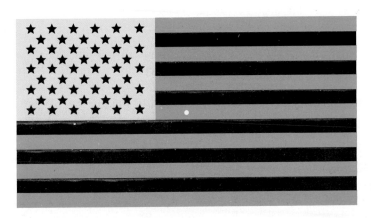

FIGURE 3.6 Experiencing an Afterimage
Stare at the white dot in the center of this oddly colored flag for about 30 seconds, and then look at a white wall or white sheet of paper. What do you see?

An Integrated Explanation of Color Vision At the beginning of this section, we said that current research has shown that *both* the trichromatic theory and the opponent-process theory of color vision are accurate. How can both theories be right? It turns out that each theory correctly describes color vision at a *different level* of visual processing.

As described by the *trichromatic theory,* the cones of the retina do indeed respond to and encode color in terms of red, green, and blue. But recall that signals from the cones and rods are partially processed in the ganglion cells before being transmitted along the optic nerve to the brain. Researchers now believe that an additional level of color processing takes place in the ganglion cells (Demb & Brainard, 2010).

As described by the *opponent-process theory,* the ganglion cells respond to and encode color in terms of opposing pairs (DeValois & DeValois, 1975; Solomon & Lennie, 2007). In the brain, the thalamus and visual cortex also encode color in terms of opponent pairs. Consequently, both theories contribute to our understanding of the process of color vision. Each theory simply describes color vision at a different stage of visual processing (Hubel, 1995; Werner & others, 2007).

> Test your understanding of **Sensation vs. Perception; Vision** with *LEARNINGCurve.*

Hearing
FROM VIBRATION TO SOUND

KEY THEME

Auditory sensation, or hearing, results when sound waves are collected in the outer ear, amplified in the middle ear, and converted to neural messages in the inner ear.

KEY QUESTIONS

> How do sound waves produce different auditory sensations?

> What are the key structures of the ear and their functions?

> How do place theory and frequency theory explain pitch perception?

Your author Sandy has hiked in a desert area that was so quiet she could hear the whir of a single grasshopper's wings in the distance. And she has waited on a subway platform where the screech of metal wheels against metal rails forced her to cover her ears.

The sense of hearing, or **audition,** is capable of responding to a wide range of sounds, from faint to blaring, simple to complex, harmonious to discordant. The ability to sense and perceive very subtle differences in sound is important to physical survival, social interactions, and language development. Most of the time, all of us are bathed in sound—so much so that moments of near-silence, like Sandy's experience in the desert, can seem almost eerie.

What We Hear
THE NATURE OF SOUND

Whether it's the ear-splitting screech of metal on metal or the subtle whir of a grasshopper's wings, *sound waves* are the physical stimuli that produce our sensory experience of sound. Usually, sound waves are produced by the rhythmic vibration of air molecules, but sound waves can be transmitted through other media, such as water, too. Our perception of sound is directly related to the physical properties of sound waves (see Figure 3.7).

One of the first things that we notice about a sound is how loud it is. **Loudness** is determined by the intensity, or **amplitude,** of a sound wave and is measured in units called **decibels.** Zero decibels represents the loudness of the softest sound that humans can hear, or the absolute threshold for hearing. As decibels increase, perceived loudness increases.

Pitch refers to the relative "highness" or "lowness" of a sound. Pitch is determined by the frequency of a sound wave. **Frequency** refers to the rate of vibration,

audition The technical term for the sense of hearing.

loudness The intensity (or amplitude) of a sound wave, measured in decibels.

amplitude The intensity or amount of energy of a wave, reflected in the height of the wave; the amplitude of a sound wave determines a sound's loudness.

decibel (DESS-uh-bell) The unit of measurement for loudness.

pitch The relative highness or lowness of a sound, determined by the frequency of a sound wave.

frequency The rate of vibration, or the number of sound waves per second.

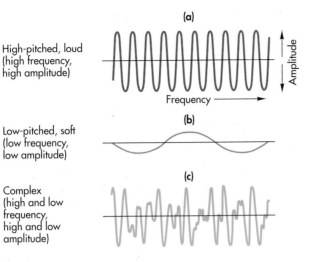

(a)

High-pitched, loud (high frequency, high amplitude)

Amplitude

Frequency →

(b)

Low-pitched, soft (low frequency, low amplitude)

(c)

Complex (high and low frequency, high and low amplitude)

FIGURE 3.7 Characteristics of Sound Waves The length of a wave, its height, and its complexity determine the loudness, pitch, and timbre that we hear. The sound produced by **(a)** would be high-pitched and loud. The sound produced by **(b)** would be soft and low. The sound in **(c)** is complex, like the sounds we usually experience in the natural world.

or number of waves per second, and is measured in units called *hertz*. Hertz simply refers to the number of wave peaks per second. The faster the vibration, the higher the frequency, the closer together the waves are—and the higher the tone produced. If you pluck the high E and the low E strings on a guitar, you'll notice that the low E vibrates far fewer times per second than does the high E.

Most of the sounds we experience do not consist of a single frequency but are *complex,* consisting of several sound-wave frequencies. This combination of frequencies produces the distinctive quality, or **timbre,** of a sound, which enables us to distinguish easily between the same note played on a saxophone and on a piano. Every human voice has its own distinctive timbre, which is why you can immediately identify a friend's voice on the telephone from just a few words, even if you haven't talked to each other for years.

How We Hear

THE PATH OF SOUND

The ear is made up of the outer ear, the middle ear, and the inner ear. Sound waves are *collected* in the outer ear, *amplified* in the middle ear, and *transduced,* or *transformed into neural messages,* in the inner ear (see Figure 3.8 on the next page).

The **outer ear** includes the *pinna,* the *ear canal,* and the *eardrum.* The pinna is that oddly shaped flap of skin and cartilage that's attached to each side of your head. The pinna helps us pinpoint the location of a sound. But the pinna's primary role is to catch sound waves and funnel them into the ear canal. The sound wave travels down the ear canal and then bounces into the **eardrum,** a tightly stretched membrane. When the sound wave hits the eardrum, the eardrum vibrates, matching the vibrations of the sound wave in intensity and frequency.

The eardrum separates the outer ear from the **middle ear.** The eardrum's vibration is transferred to three tiny bones in the middle ear—the *hammer,* the *anvil,* and the *stirrup.* Each bone sets the next bone in motion. The joint action of these three bones almost doubles the amplification of the sound. The innermost bone, the stirrup, transmits the amplified vibration to the *oval window.* If the tiny bones of the middle ear are damaged or become brittle, as they sometimes do in old age, *conduction deafness* may result. Conduction deafness can be helped by a hearing aid, which amplifies sounds.

Like the eardrum, the oval window is a membrane, but it is many times smaller than the eardrum. The oval window separates the middle ear from the **inner ear.** As the oval window vibrates, the vibration is next relayed to an inner structure called the **cochlea,** a fluid-filled tube that's coiled in a spiral. The word *cochlea* comes from the Greek word for "snail," and the spiral shape of the cochlea does resemble a snail's shell. Although the cochlea is a very complex structure, it is quite tiny—no larger than a pea.

timbre (TAM-ber) The distinctive quality of a sound, determined by the complexity of the sound wave.

outer ear The part of the ear that collects sound waves; consists of the pinna, the ear canal, and the eardrum.

eardrum A tightly stretched membrane at the end of the ear canal that vibrates when hit by sound waves.

middle ear The part of the ear that amplifies sound waves; consists of three small bones: the hammer, the anvil, and the stirrup.

inner ear The part of the ear where sound is transduced into neural impulses; consists of the cochlea and semicircular canals.

cochlea (COKE-lee-uh) The coiled, fluid-filled inner-ear structure that contains the basilar membrane and hair cells.

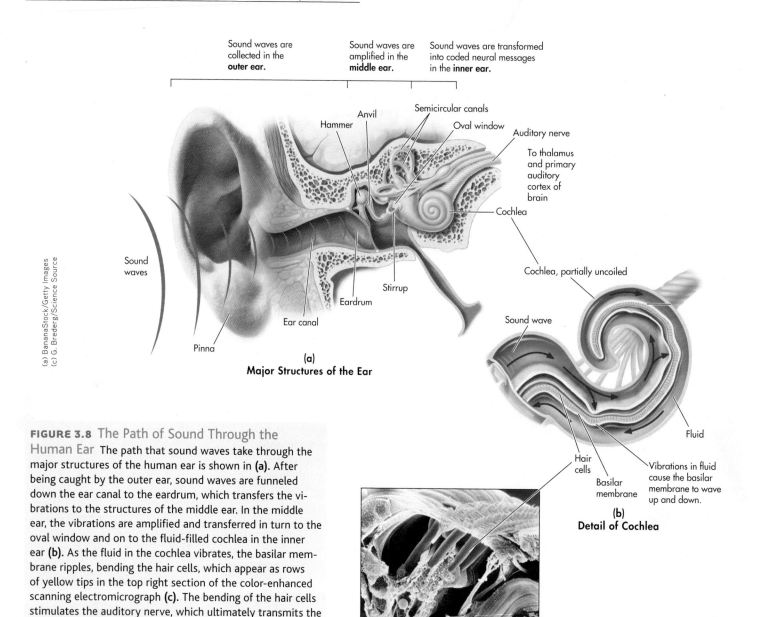

Sound waves are collected in the **outer ear.**

Sound waves are amplified in the **middle ear.**

Sound waves are transformed into coded neural messages in the **inner ear.**

Hammer
Anvil
Semicircular canals
Oval window
Auditory nerve
To thalamus and primary auditory cortex of brain
Cochlea
Sound waves
Pinna
Ear canal
Eardrum
Stirrup

(a)
Major Structures of the Ear

(a) BananaStock/Getty Images
(c) G. Brederg/Science Source

Cochlea, partially uncoiled
Sound wave
Hair cells
Basilar membrane
Fluid
Vibrations in fluid cause the basilar membrane to wave up and down.

(b)
Detail of Cochlea

(c)

FIGURE 3.8 The Path of Sound Through the Human Ear The path that sound waves take through the major structures of the human ear is shown in **(a)**. After being caught by the outer ear, sound waves are funneled down the ear canal to the eardrum, which transfers the vibrations to the structures of the middle ear. In the middle ear, the vibrations are amplified and transferred in turn to the oval window and on to the fluid-filled cochlea in the inner ear **(b)**. As the fluid in the cochlea vibrates, the basilar membrane ripples, bending the hair cells, which appear as rows of yellow tips in the top right section of the color-enhanced scanning electromicrograph **(c)**. The bending of the hair cells stimulates the auditory nerve, which ultimately transmits the neural messages to the auditory cortex in the brain.

Restoring Hearing Cochlear implants are electronic devices that are surgically implanted behind the ear. A microphone picks up sounds from the environment, which are converted into electrical impulses that directly stimulate the auditory nerve via electrodes implanted in the cochlea. Cochlear implants do *not* restore normal hearing (Farris-Trimble & others, 2014). However, their use, especially when implanted in early childhood, can allow hearing-impaired individuals to perceive speech and other everyday sounds (Clark & others, 2013; O'Donoghue, 2013).

Life in View/Science Source

As the fluid in the cochlea ripples, the vibration in turn is transmitted to the **basilar membrane,** which runs the length of the coiled cochlea. Embedded in the basilar membrane are the sensory receptors for sound, called **hair cells,** which have tiny, projecting fibers that look like hairs. Damage to the hair cells or auditory nerve can result in *nerve deafness.* Exposure to loud noise can cause nerve deafness (see Table 3.2). Hearing aids are of no use in this form of deafness because the neural messages cannot reach the brain. However, nerve deafness *can,* in some cases, be treated with a *cochlear implant,* which is an electronic device surgically implanted behind the ear (see photo).

The hair cells bend as the basilar membrane ripples. It is here that transduction finally takes place: The physical vibration of the sound waves is converted into neural

TABLE 3.2

Decibel Levels of Some Common Sounds

Decibels	Examples	Exposure Danger
180	Rocket launching pad	Hearing loss inevitable
140	Shotgun blast, jet plane	Any exposure is dangerous
120	Speakers at rock concert, sandblasting, thunderclap	Immediate danger
100	Chain saw, pneumatic drill	2 hours
90	Truck traffic, noisy home appliances, lawn mower	Less than 8 hours
80	Subway, heavy city traffic, alarm clock at 2 feet	More than 8 hours
70	Busy traffic, noisy restaurant	Critical level begins with constant exposure
60	Air conditioner at 20 feet, conversation, sewing machine	
50	Light traffic at a distance, refrigerator	
40	Quiet office, living room	
30	Quiet library, soft whisper	
0	Lowest sound audible to human ear	

Comstock/Getty Images

Noise exposure, not age, is the leading cause of hearing loss. Many adolescents and young adults are unaware of the potential for permanent hearing loss due to exposure to loud noise. Damage to the delicate hair cells of the inner ear is cumulative. One survey found that 12–15% of school-age children have some hearing deficits due to noise exposure (Harrison, 2012). While rock concerts have long been known for excessively loud music, people are also exposed to unhealthy levels of noise in restaurants, athletic stadiums, and in spin and other exercise classes. iPods and other personal music players can also expose the listener to dangerously high levels of noise (Breinbauer & others, 2012). As a general rule, if other people can hear what you are listening to, the sound is turned up too high.

impulses. As the hair cells bend, they stimulate the cells of the auditory nerve, which carries the neural information to the thalamus and the auditory cortex in the brain (Hackett & Kaas, 2009; Recanzone & Sutter, 2008).

DISTINGUISHING PITCH

How do we distinguish between the low-pitched throb of a bass guitar and the high-pitched tones of a piccolo? Remember, pitch is determined by the *frequency* of a sound wave. The basilar membrane is a key structure involved in our discrimination of pitch. Two complementary theories describe the role of the basilar membrane in the transmission of differently pitched sounds.

According to **frequency theory,** the basilar membrane vibrates at the *same* frequency as the sound wave. Thus, a sound wave of about 100 hertz would excite each hair cell along the basilar membrane to vibrate 100 times per second, and neural impulses would be sent to the brain at the same rate. However, there's a limit to how fast neurons can fire. Individual neurons cannot fire faster than about 1,000 times per second. But we can sense sounds with frequencies that are many times higher than 1,000 hertz. A child, for example, can typically hear pitches ranging from about 20 to 20,000 hertz.

So how can higher-frequency sounds be transmitted? A partial explanation involves the *volley principle,* which draws upon a military strategy developed before the development of modern firearms. To deal with the problem of slow reload times, different groups of soldiers would fire in sequence to minimize the amount of time between "volleys" of bullets launched at the enemy.

The volley principle holds that hair cells also fire in "volleys." Imagine three groups of neurons, each of which can fire at a rate of 1,000 times per second. But rather than firing in unison, the neuron groups take turns, each group firing in rapid succession while the other groups are in the resting state. In this way, impulses can be sent to the brain at rates that exceed 1,000 impulses per second.

Charles Barsotti The New Yorker Collection/The Cartoon Bank

"And only you can hear this whistle?"

basilar membrane (BAZ-uh-ler or BAYZ-uh-ler) The membrane within the cochlea of the ear that contains the hair cells.

hair cells The hair-like sensory receptors for sound, which are embedded in the basilar membrane of the cochlea.

frequency theory The view that the basilar membrane vibrates at the same frequency as the sound wave.

Can Snakes and Frogs Hear? Snakes and frogs have functional inner ears, but they don't have outer ears. So how do snakes hear? With their jaws. When a desert viper rests its head on the ground, a bone in its jaw picks up minute vibrations in the sand. From the jaw, these vibrations are transmitted along a chain of tiny bones to the cochlea in the inner ear, allowing the snake to "hear" the faint footsteps of a mouse or other prey (Freidel & others, 2008). Similarly, a tiny frog found only in the Seychelles Islands lacks a middle ear yet is not deaf. Sound waves are amplified by tiny bones in the frog's mouth and transmitted to the inner ear (Boistel & others, 2013).

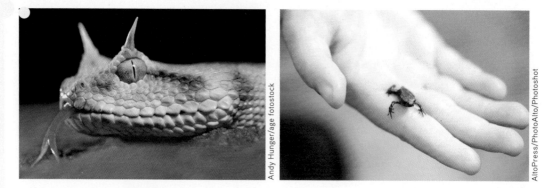

What Does Popcorn Smell Like? English and other European languages have many abstract words that can be used to describe sights, tastes, and textures, but very few words that specifically apply to odors. Typically, odors are described as "smelling like" other objects, such as "smells moldy" or "smells lemony."

The same is not true of all languages, however. Two hunter-gatherer groups, the Jahai in Malaysia and the Mani in Thailand, have rich odor vocabularies, with specific terms to describe precise odor categories (Majid & Burenhult, 2014; Wnuk & Majid, 2014). For example, the Jahai word *p?us* (pronounced pa-OOS) is used to describe the smell of old huts, day-old food, and cabbage (Majid, 2014). Given an odor identification test, the Jahai easily outscored English-speaking participants. Psychologist Asifa Majid, who has studied both tribes, believes that their olfactory expertise reflects the importance of smells in their culture and environment.

So how do we hear higher-pitched sounds above 3,000 hertz? According to **place theory,** different frequencies cause larger vibrations at different *locations* along the basilar membrane. High-frequency sounds, for example, cause maximum vibration near the stirrup end of the basilar membrane. Lower-frequency sounds cause maximum vibration at the opposite end. Thus, different pitches excite different hair cells along the basilar membrane. Higher-pitched sounds are interpreted according to the place where the hair cells are most active.

Both frequency theory and place theory are involved in explaining our discrimination of pitch (Kaas & others, 2013). Frequency theory helps explain our discrimination of low frequencies. Place theory helps explain our discrimination of higher-pitched sounds. For intermediate frequencies or midrange pitches, both place and frequency are involved.

The Chemical and Body Senses
SMELL, TASTE, TOUCH, AND POSITION

KEY THEME

Chemical stimuli produce the sensations of smell and taste, while pressure and other stimuli are involved in touch, pain, position, and balance sensations.

KEY QUESTIONS

> How do airborne molecules result in the sensation of an odor?
> What are the primary tastes, and how does the sensation of taste arise?
> How do fast and slow pain systems differ, and what is the gate-control theory of pain?
> How are body sensations of movement, position, and balance produced?

The senses of smell and taste are closely linked. If you've ever temporarily lost your sense of smell because of a bad cold, you've probably noticed that your sense of taste was also disrupted. Even a hot fudge sundae tastes bland.

Smell and taste are linked in other ways, too. Unlike vision and hearing, which involve sensitivity to different forms of energy, the sensory receptors for taste and smell are specialized to respond to different types of *chemical* substances. That's why smell, or **olfaction,** and taste, or **gustation,** are sometimes called the "chemical senses" (Travers & Travers, 2009).

People can get along quite well without a sense of smell. A surprisingly large number of people are unable to smell specific odors or lack a sense of smell completely, a condition called *anosmia*. Fortunately, humans gather most of their information about the world through vision and hearing. However, many animal species depend on chemical signals as their primary source of information.

Even for humans, smell and taste can provide important information about the environment. Tastes help us determine whether a particular substance is to be savored or spat out. Smells, such as the odor of a smoldering fire, leaking gas, or spoiled food, alert us to potential dangers.

How We Smell (Don't Answer That!)

The sensory stimuli that produce our sensation of an odor are *molecules in the air.* These airborne molecules are emitted by the substance we are smelling. We inhale them through the nose and through the opening in the palate at the back of the throat. In the nose, the molecules encounter millions of *olfactory receptor cells* located high in the nasal cavity. Many species use airborne chemical signals, called *pheromones,* to communicate information about territory, mating strategies, and so forth. What about humans? The In Focus box "Do Pheromones Influence Human Behavior?" explores this question.

Unlike the sensory receptors for hearing and vision, the olfactory receptors are constantly being replaced. Each cell lasts for only about 30 to 60 days. Neuroscientists Linda Buck and Richard Axel won the 2004 Nobel Prize for their identification of the odor receptors that are present on the hair-like fibers of the olfactory neurons. Like synaptic receptors, each odor receptor seems to be specialized to respond to molecules of a different chemical structure. When these olfactory receptor cells are stimulated by the airborne molecules, the stimulation is converted into neural messages that pass along their axons, bundles of which make up the *olfactory nerve.*

place theory The view that different frequencies cause larger vibrations at different locations along the basilar membrane.

olfaction Technical name for the sense of smell.

gustation Technical name for the sense of taste.

pheromones Chemical signals released by an animal that communicate information and affect the behavior of other animals of the same species.

IN FOCUS

Do Pheromones Influence Human Behavior?

Many animals, including primates, communicate by releasing **pheromones**, chemical signals that have evolved for communication with other members of the same species (Drea, 2015; Wyatt, 2015). Pheromones may mark territories, advertise sexual status, or serve as warning signals. From insects to mammals, pheromones are used to communicate aggression, alarm, and fearful states (Radulescu & Mujica-Parodi, 2013). Pheromones are also extremely important in regulating sexual attraction, mating, and reproductive behavior in many animals (Wyatt, 2009). A lusty male cabbage moth, for example, can detect pheromones released from a sexually receptive female cabbage moth that is several miles away.

Do humans produce pheromones as other animals do? Early evidence for the existence of human pheromones comes from studies of the female menstrual cycle by University of Chicago biopsychologist Martha McClintock (1992). While still a college student, McClintock (1971) set out to scientifically investigate the folk notion that women who live in the same dorm eventually develop synchronized menstrual periods. McClintock was able to show that the more time women spent together, the more likely their cycles were to be in sync.

Later research showed that smelling an unknown chemical substance in underarm sweat from female donors synchronized the recipients' menstrual cycles with the donors' cycles (Preti & others, 1986; Stern & McClintock, 1998).

Since this finding, McClintock and her co-researchers have made a number of discoveries in their quest to identify human pheromones, which they prefer to call *human chemosignals.* Their search has narrowed to chemicals found in steroid compounds that are naturally produced by the human body and found in sweat, armpit hair, blood, and semen. One study in McClintock's lab showed that exposure to a chemical compound in the perspiration of breast-feeding mothers significantly increased sexual motivation in other non-breastfeeding women (Spencer & others, 2004). The study's authors speculate that the presence of breast-feeding women acts as a social signal—an indicator that the social and physical environment is one in which pregnancy and breast-feeding will be supported.

The Scent of Attraction Some perfume manufacturers claim that their products contain human pheromones that will make you "irresistible" to members of the opposite sex. But is there any evidence that pheromones affect human sexual attraction?

Jose Luis Pelaez Inc /Getty Images

There is evidence that human chemosignals are also involved in communicating emotional states, including stress, anxiety, and fear (see Radulescu & Mujica-Parodi, 2013). Consider a recent study by Jasper de Groot and his colleagues (2012). Sweat was collected from men while they watched either a scary film or a disgusting film. Women watching a neutral video were then exposed to either the "fear sweat" or the "disgust sweat." Although the women could not consciously perceive any odor, the women who were exposed to the "disgust sweat" produced more disgusted facial expressions and the women exposed to the "fear sweat" produced more fearful facial expressions (de Groot & others, 2012).

In another study, women watched either a frightening video or a neutral video while being exposed to either "neutral sweat" or "fear sweat." Regardless of which video the women watched, women who were exposed to the "fear sweat" were more likely to react with fearful expressions than the women who were exposed to the neutral sweat (de Groot & others, 2014).

Pheromones may not make people irresistible to the preferred sex, as they do in other animal species. Instead, it may be that these consciously undetectable chemosignals play an important role in communicating and synchronizing emotional states among people in groups (de Groot & others, 2014).

MYTH ◀ SCIENCE

Is it true that pheromones can make some people irresistible to members of the preferred sex?

olfactory bulb (ole-FACK-tuh-ree) The enlarged ending of the olfactory cortex at the front of the brain where the sensation of smell is registered.

taste buds The specialized sensory receptors for taste that are located on the tongue and inside the mouth and throat.

So far, hundreds of different odor receptors have been identified (Gottfried, 2010). We don't have a separate receptor for each of the estimated 10,000 different odors that we can detect, however. Rather, each receptor is like a letter in an olfactory alphabet. Just as different combinations of letters in the alphabet are used to produce recognizable words, different combinations of olfactory receptors produce the sensation of distinct odors. Thus, the airborne molecules activate specific combinations of receptors. In turn, the brain identifies an odor by interpreting the *pattern* of olfactory receptors that are stimulated (Shepherd, 2006).

As shown in Figure 3.9, the olfactory nerves directly connect to the **olfactory bulb** in the brain, which is actually the enlarged ending of the *olfactory cortex* at the front of the brain. Axons from the olfactory bulb form the *olfactory tract*. These neural pathways project to different brain areas, including the temporal lobe and structures in the limbic system (Gottfried, 2010; Shepherd, 2006). The projections to the *temporal lobe* are thought to be part of the neural pathway involved in our conscious recognition of smells. The projections to the *limbic system* are thought to regulate our emotional response to odors.

The direct connection of olfactory receptor cells to areas of the cortex and limbic system is unique to our sense of smell. As discussed in Chapter 2, all other bodily sensations are first processed in the thalamus before being relayed to the higher brain centers in the cortex. Olfactory neurons are unique in another way, too. They are the only neurons that *directly* link the brain and the outside world. The axons of the sensory neurons that are located in your nose extend directly into your brain!

As with the other senses, we experience sensory adaptation to odors when exposed to them for a period of time. In general, we reach maximum adaptation to an odor in less than a minute. We continue to smell the odor, but we have become about 70 percent less sensitive to it.

Olfactory function tends to decline with age. About half of those aged 65 to 80 have a significant loss of olfactory function, a number that increases to two-thirds of people aged 80 and above (Lafreniere & Mann, 2009; Rawson, 2006). At any age, air pollution, smoking, and exposure to some industrial chemicals can decrease the ability to smell. Loss of olfactory function is also associated with several diseases—including Parkinson's disease, schizophrenia, and multiple sclerosis—and may be an early marker of Alzheimer's disease (J. Wang & others, 2010; R. Wilson & others, 2009).

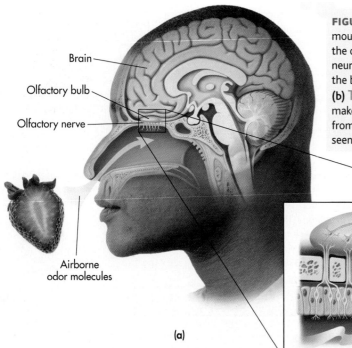

Brain

Olfactory bulb

Olfactory nerve

Airborne odor molecules

(a)

FIGURE 3.9 (a) The Olfactory System Inhaled through the nose or the mouth, airborne molecules travel to the top of the nasal cavity and stimulate the olfactory receptors. When stimulated, these receptor cells communicate neural messages to the olfactory bulb, which is part of the olfactory cortex of the brain, where the sense of smell is registered.
(b) The Olfactory Receptor Cells More than 5 million olfactory neurons make up the moist, mucus-bathed tissue at the back of the nose. Projecting from the olfactory neurons are the fiberlike olfactory hairs, which can be clearly seen in this photograph. Olfactory neurons are replaced every month or two.

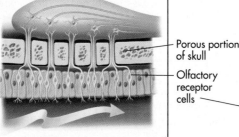

Porous portion of skull

Olfactory receptor cells

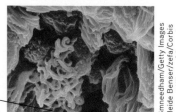

(b)

Although humans are highly sensitive to odors, many animals display even greater sensitivity. Dogs, for example, have about 200 million olfactory receptor cells, compared with the approximately 12 million receptors that humans have (Sela & Sobel, 2010). However, humans are more sensitive to smell than most people realize (Shepherd, 2004).

In fact, people can train their sense of smell (see photo). In a fascinating study, Wen Li and her colleagues (2006) showed that with repeated exposure to a particular class of odors (floral or minty), participants improved in their ability to distinguish subtle differences among the different scents. They also became more sensitive to the odors. These behavioral changes were accompanied by changes in the brain: fMRI scans showed increased activation in the olfactory cortex. The moral? Stop and smell the flowers often enough, and you will improve your ability to discriminate a geranium from a marigold.

Courtesy Noam Sobel

Can Humans Track a Scent? Dogs are famous for their ability to track a scent. Humans? Not so much. However, it turns out that people are better trackers than you might think. Berkeley scientist Jess Porter and colleagues (2007) embedded a long line of chocolate-scented twine into the ground and then tested whether human undergraduates could find and track the scent using their olfactory sense alone. To block all other sensory cues, the college students wore opaque eye masks, earmuffs, and thick knee pads, elbow pads, and work gloves. Although the human trackers were able to locate and follow the trail, their average speed was only about one inch per second. However, after only a few days of practice, the trackers' speed doubled, improving to two inches per second.

Taste

Our sense of taste, or *gustation,* results from the stimulation of special receptors in the mouth. The stimuli that produce the sensation of taste are chemical substances in whatever you eat or drink. These substances are dissolved by saliva, allowing the chemicals to activate the **taste buds.** Each taste bud contains about 50 receptor cells that are specialized for taste.

The surface of the tongue is covered with thousands of little bumps with grooves in between (see Figure 3.10). These grooves are lined with the taste buds. Taste buds are also located on the insides of your cheeks, on the roof of your mouth, and in your throat. Contrary to popular belief, there is no "tongue map" in which different regions of the tongue

FIGURE 3.10 Taste Buds

(a) Embedded in the surface of the tongue are thousands of taste buds, the sensory receptor organs for taste. Taste buds are located in the grooves of the bumps on the surface of the tongue. Each taste bud contains an average of 50 taste receptor cells. When activated, the taste receptor cells send messages to adjoining sensory neurons, which relay the information to the brain. Taste buds, like the olfactory neurons, are constantly being replaced. The life expectancy of a particular taste bud is only about 10 days. **(b)** The photograph shows the surface of the tongue magnified hundreds of times.

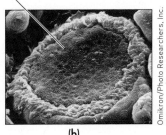

Omikron/Photo Researchers, Inc.
Whitemann/Corbis

Bump on the surface of the tongue

(a)

(b)

Taste buds

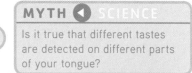

MYTH ◀ SCIENCE

Is it true that different tastes are detected on different parts of your tongue?

Expensive Taste Although wine experts may be able to discern subtle differences among wines, amateurs may not be as objective. To determine the effect of *price* on perceived quality, Hilke Plassmann and her colleagues (2008) asked participants to decide which tasted better: wine poured from a bottle labeled as costing $90 or from a bottle that cost $10. Although the wine in the two bottles was identical, participants overwhelmingly thought the $90 bottle tasted better. Their subjective, verbal rating was confirmed by brain scans: Activity in a brain region associated with pleasant sensations was much higher when they sipped the wine that they thought cost $90 a bottle than when they sipped the same wine from a bottle that supposedly cost $10. The moral: Many different factors affect taste, not the least of which is your expectation of just how good something is likely to taste.

Ken Seet/age fotostock

---

are specialized to respond to sweet, sour, salty, and bitter tastes. Instead, responsiveness to the five basic tastes is present in all tongue areas (Chandrashekar & others, 2006). Each taste bud shows maximum sensitivity to one particular taste and lesser sensitivity to other tastes (Chandrashekar & others, 2006). When activated, special receptor cells in the taste buds send neural messages along pathways to the thalamus in the brain. In turn, the thalamus directs the information to several regions in the cortex (Shepherd, 2006).

There were long thought to be four basic taste categories: sweet, salty, sour, and bitter. However, scientists identified the receptor cells for a fifth basic taste, *umami* (Chaudhari & others, 2000). Loosely translated, *umami* means "yummy" or "delicious" in Japanese. *Umami* is the distinctive taste of monosodium glutamate and is associated with meat and other protein-rich foods. It's also responsible for the savory flavor of Parmesan and other aged cheeses, mushrooms, and seaweed.

From an evolutionary view, these five basic tastes supply the information we need to seek out nutrient-rich foods and avoid potentially hazardous substances (Chandrashekar & others, 2006; Eisenstein, 2010). Sweet tastes attract us to energy-rich foods, *umami* to protein-rich nutrients. Bitter or sour tastes warn us to avoid many toxic or poisonous substances (Peyrot des Gachons & others, 2011). Sensitivity to salty-tasting substances helps us regulate the balance of electrolytes in our diets.

Most tastes are complex and result from the activation of different combinations of basic taste receptors. Taste is just one aspect of *flavor,* which involves several sensations, including the aroma, temperature, texture, and appearance of food (Shepherd, 2006).

The Skin and Body Senses

While vision, hearing, smell, and taste provide you with important information about your environment, another group of senses provides you with information that comes from a source much closer to home: your own body. In this section, we'll first consider the *skin senses,* which provide essential information about your physical status and your physical interaction with objects in your environment. We'll next consider the *body senses,* which keep you informed as to your position and orientation in space.

TOUCH

We usually don't think of our skin as a sense organ. But the skin is in fact the largest and heaviest sense organ. The skin of an average adult covers about 20 square feet of surface area and weighs about six pounds.

There are many different kinds of sensory receptors in the skin. Some of these sensory receptors are specialized to respond to just one kind of stimulus, such as pressure, warmth, or cold (McGlone & Reilly, 2010). Other skin receptors respond to more than one type of stimulus (Delmas & others, 2011).

One important receptor involved with the sense of touch, called the *Pacinian corpuscle,* is located beneath the skin. When stimulated by pressure, the Pacinian corpuscle converts the stimulation into a neural message that is relayed to the brain. If a pressure is constant, sensory adaptation takes place. The Pacinian corpuscle either reduces the number of signals sent or quits responding altogether (which is fortunate, or you'd be unable to forget the fact that you're wearing underwear).

Sensory receptors are distributed unevenly among different areas of the body, which is why sensitivity to touch and temperature varies from one area of the body to another. Your hands, face, and lips, for example, are much more sensitive to touch than are your back, arms, and legs. That's because your hands, face, and lips are much more densely packed with sensory receptors.

PAIN

From the sharp sting of a paper cut to the dull ache of a throbbing headache, a wide variety of stimuli can trigger pain. **Pain** can be defined as an unpleasant sensory and emotional experience associated with actual or potential tissue damage (Gatchel & others, 2011). As unpleasant as it can be, pain helps you survive. Pain warns you about potential or actual injury, prompting you to pay attention and stop what you

---

pain The unpleasant sensation of physical discomfort or suffering that can occur in varying degrees of intensity.

are doing. Sudden pain can trigger the withdrawal reflex—you jerk back from the object or stimulus that is injuring you. (We discussed the withdrawal reflex and other spinal reflexes in Chapter 2.)

Your body's pain receptors are called **nociceptors.** Nociceptors are actually small sensory fibers, called *free nerve endings,* in the skin, muscles, or internal organs. You have millions of nociceptors throughout your body, mostly in your skin (see Table 3.3). For example, your fingertips may have as many as 1,200 nociceptors per square inch. Your muscles and joints have fewer nociceptors, and your internal organs have the smallest number of nociceptors.

Fast and Slow Pain Systems To help illustrate pain pathways, imagine this scene: Your author Don was trying to close a stuck window in his office. As he wrapped his left hand on the top of the window and used his right hand to push down the lower edge, it suddenly came free and slammed shut, jamming his left fingertips between the upper and lower windows. As pain shot through him, he jerked the window back up to dislodge his mangled fingers and then headed to the kitchen for ice.

Don took little comfort in knowing that his injury had triggered two types of nociceptors: *A-delta fibers* and *C fibers.* The myelinated A-delta fibers represent the fast pain system. A-delta fibers transmit the sharp, intense, but short-lived pain of the immediate injury. The smaller, unmyelinated C fibers represent the slow pain system. As the sharp pain subsides, C fibers transmit the longer-lasting throbbing, burning pain of the injury (Guindon & Hohmann, 2009). The throbbing pain carried by the C fibers gradually diminishes as a wound heals over a period of days or weeks.

As shown in Figure 3.11, both the fast A-delta fibers and the slow C fibers transmit their messages to the spinal cord. Several neurotransmitters are involved in processing pain signals, but most C fibers produce a pain enhancer called substance P. **Substance P** stimulates free nerve endings at the site of the injury and also increases pain messages within the spinal cord (Linnman, 2013).

Most of these messages from C fibers and A-delta fibers cross to the other side of the spinal cord, then to the brain. The fast pain messages travel to the thalamus, then to the somatosensory cortex, where the sensory aspects of the pain message are interpreted, such as the location and intensity of the pain. Interestingly, morphine and other opiates have virtually no effect on the fast pain system.

TABLE 3.3

Sensitivity of Different Body Areas to Pain

Most Sensitive	Least Sensitive
Back of the knee	Tip of the nose
Neck region	Sole of the foot
Bend of the elbow	Ball of the thumb

Source: Information from Geldard (1972).

nociceptors Specialized sensory receptors for pain that are found in the skin, muscles, and internal organs.

substance P A neurotransmitter that is involved in the transmission of pain messages to the brain.

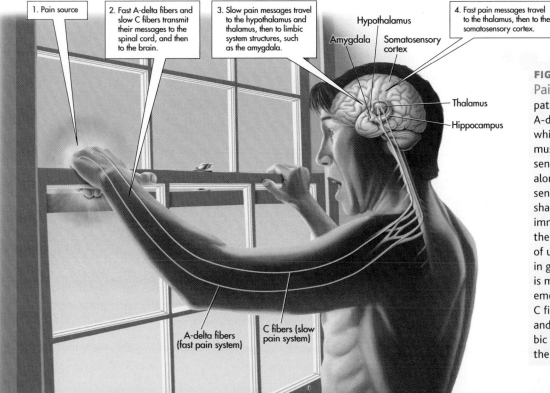

1. Pain source

2. Fast A-delta fibers and slow C fibers transmit their messages to the spinal cord, and then to the brain.

3. Slow pain messages travel to the hypothalamus and thalamus, then to limbic system structures, such as the amygdala.

4. Fast pain messages travel to the thalamus, then to the somatosensory cortex.

Hypothalamus

Amygdala

Somatosensory cortex

Thalamus

Hippocampus

A-delta fibers (fast pain system)

C fibers (slow pain system)

FIGURE 3.11 Fast and Slow Pain Pathways The fast pain pathway consists of myelinated A-delta fibers, shown in purple, which project first to the thalamus and then on to the somatosensory cortex. Signals carried along this pathway produce the sensory aspects of pain—the sharp but short-lived pain of an immediate injury. In contrast, the slow pain pathway consists of unmyelinated C fibers, shown in green. The slow pain pathway is much more involved with the emotional aspects of pain. The C fibers project to the thalamus and hypothalamus, then to limbic system structures, including the amygdala.

For an entertaining demonstration of how expectations influence perception, including pain perception, try the **Video Activity: Pickpockets, Placebos, and Pain: The Role of Expectations.**

Individual differences in pain perception and tolerance People respond to pain very differently (Denk & others, 2014). Women tend to have a lower pain threshold than men, rating pain as more unpleasant and displaying more intense physiological responses to painful stimuli (Jarrett, 2011). Racial differences also influence pain response. Several studies have found that African Americans, Hispanic Americans, and Asians tend to have a lower pain threshold than white Americans. On the other hand, Native Americans have a much higher pain threshold than white Americans, possibly reflecting cultural beliefs that pain should be endured without complaint (Palit & others, 2013). Such differences appear to reflect cultural beliefs about the meaning of pain, social expectations about how people express their experience of pain, and actual physiological differences among ethnic groups (Rahim-Williams & others, 2012).

gate-control theory of pain The theory that pain is a product of both physiological and psychological factors that cause spinal gates to open and relay patterns of intense stimulation to the brain, which perceives them as pain.

In contrast, slow pain messages follow a different route in the brain. From the spinal cord, the slow pain messages travel first to the hypothalamus and thalamus, and then to limbic system structures, such as the amygdala. Its connections to the limbic system suggest that the slow pain system is more involved in the emotional aspects of pain. Morphine and other opiates very effectively block painful sensations in the slow pain system (Guindon & Hohmann, 2009).

Factors That Influence Pain "Gates" There is considerable individual variation in the experience of pain (Jensen & Turk, 2014; Denk & others, 2014). When sensory pain signals reach the brain, the sensory information is integrated with psychological and situational information. According to the **gate-control theory of pain,** depending on how the brain interprets the pain experience, it regulates pain by sending signals down the spinal cord that either open or close pain "gates," or pathways (Melzack & Wall, 1965, 1996). If, because of psychological, social, or situational factors, the brain signals the gates to open, pain is experienced or intensified. If for any of the same reasons the brain signals the gates to close, pain is reduced.

Anxiety, fear, and a sense of helplessness are just a few of the psychological factors that can intensify the experience of pain (Edwards & others, 2009). So do feelings of depression and sadness (Berna & others, 2010). And, neuroscientists have found that manipulating people's moods by exposing them to different odors can affect their experience of pain (Villemure & Bushnell, 2009). Pleasant smells, like violets, evoke a good mood *and* a reduced sense of pain. But unpleasant smells, like rotten food, put people in a bad mood and heighten their sense of pain.

Along with positive moods, a sense of control can reduce the perception of pain. As one example, consider the athlete who has conditioned himself to minimize pain during competition. The experience of pain is also influenced by social and

doable/amanaimages/Corbis

situational factors, along with cultural beliefs about the meaning of pain and the appropriate response to pain (Bosch & Cano, 2013; Gatchel & others, 2011). We discuss some helpful strategies that you can use to minimize pain in the Psych for Your Life section at the end of the chapter.

Psychological factors can also influence the release of *endorphins* and *enkephalins,* the body's natural painkillers (see Chapter 2). Endorphins and enkephalins are produced in the brain and spinal cord. They are released as part of the body's overall response to physical pain or stress. In the brain and spinal cord, endorphins and enkephalins inhibit the transmission of pain signals, including the release of substance P.

Sensitization: Unwarranted Pain One of the most frustrating aspects of pain management is that it can continue even after an injury has healed, such as after recovering from a spinal cord injury or severe burns. A striking example of this phenomenon is *phantom limb pain,* in which a person continues to experience intense painful sensations in a limb that has been amputated (Wolff & others, 2011).

How can phantom limb pain be explained? Basically, the neurons involved in processing the pain signals undergo *sensitization.* Earlier in the chapter, we discussed *sensory adaptation,* in which sensory receptors become gradually less responsive to steady stimulation over time. Sensitization is the opposite of adaptation. In sensitization, pain pathways in the brain become increasingly *more* responsive over time. It's like a broken volume-control knob on your stereo that you can turn up but not down or off.

As the pain circuits undergo sensitization, pain begins to occur in the absence of any sensory input. The result can be the development of persistent, *chronic pain* that continues even after the injury has healed (Denk & others, 2014; Wolff & others, 2011). In the case of phantom limb pain, sensitization has occurred in the pain transmission pathways from the site of the amputation. The sensitized pathways produce painful sensations that mentally feel as though they are coming from a limb that is no longer there.

MOVEMENT, POSITION, AND BALANCE

The phone rings. Without looking up from your textbook, you reach for the phone, pick it up, and guide it to the side of your head. You have just demonstrated your **kinesthetic sense**—the sense that involves the location and position of body parts in relation to one another. (The word *kinesthetics* literally means "feelings of motion.") The kinesthetic sense involves specialized sensory neurons, called **proprioceptors,** which are located in the muscles and joints. The proprioceptors constantly communicate information to the brain about changes in body position and muscle tension.

Closely related to the kinesthetic sense is the **vestibular sense,** which provides a sense of balance, or equilibrium, by responding to changes in gravity, motion, and body position. The two sources of vestibular sensory information, the *semicircular canals* and the *vestibular sacs,* are both located in the ear (see Figure 3.12). These structures are filled with fluid and lined with hair-like receptor cells that shift in response to motion, changes in body position, or changes in gravity (Eatock & Songer, 2011).

kinesthetic sense (kin-ess-THET-ick) The technical name for the sense of location and position of body parts in relation to one another.

proprioceptors (pro-pree-oh-SEP-terz) Sensory receptors, located in the muscles and joints, that provide information about body position and movement.

vestibular sense (vess-TIB-you-ler) The technical name for the sense of balance, or equilibrium.

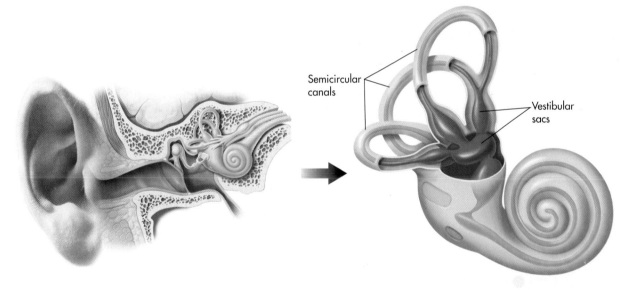

Semicircular canals

Vestibular sacs

When you experience environmental motion, like the rocking of a boat in choppy water, the fluids in the semicircular canals and the vestibular sacs are affected. Changes in your body's position, such as falling backward in a heroic attempt to return a volleyball serve, also affect the fluids. Your vestibular sense supplies the critical information that allows you to compensate for such changes and quickly reestablish your sense of balance.

Maintaining equilibrium also involves information from other senses, particularly vision. Under normal circumstances, this works to our advantage. However, when information from the eyes conflicts with information from the vestibular system, the result can be dizziness, disorientation, and nausea. These are the symptoms commonly experienced in motion sickness, the bane of many travelers in cars, on planes, on boats, and even in space. One strategy that can be used to combat motion sickness is to minimize sensory conflicts by focusing on a distant point or an object that is fixed, such as the horizon.

FIGURE 3.12 The Vestibular Sense The vestibular sense provides our sense of balance, or equilibrium. Shown here are the two sources of vestibular sensory information, both located in the ear: the semicircular canals and the vestibular sacs. Both structures are filled with fluids that shift in response to changes in body position, gravity, or motion.

TABLE 3.4

Summary Table of the Senses

Sense	Stimulus	Sense Organ	Sensory Receptor Cells
Hearing (audition)	Sound waves	Ear	Hair cells in cochlea
Vision	Light waves	Eye	Rods and cones in retina
Color vision	Different wave-lengths of light	Eye	Cones in retina
Smell (olfaction)	Airborne odor molecules	Nose	Hair-like receptor cells at top of nasal cavity
Taste (gustation)	Chemicals dissolved in saliva	Mouth, tongue	Taste buds
Touch	Pressure	Skin	Pacinian corpuscle
Pain	Tissue injury or damage; varied	Skin, muscles, and organs	Nociceptors
Movement (kinesthetic sense)	Movement of the body	None; muscle and joint tissue	Proprioceptors in muscle and joint tissue
Balance (vestibular sense)	Changes in position, gravity	Semicircular canals and vestibular sacs	Hair-like receptor cells in semicircular canals and vestibular sacs

In the first part of this chapter, we've described how the body's senses respond to stimuli in the environment. Table 3.4 summarizes these different sensory systems. To make use of this raw sensory data, the brain must organize and interpret the data and relate them to existing knowledge. Next, we'll look at the process of perception—how we make sense out of the information that we receive from our environment. One long-standing question in psychology is whether information can be perceived *without* the involvement of normal sensory systems, a process called *extrasensory perception,* or *ESP.* We take a close look at this issue in the Critical Thinking box on pages 112–113, "ESP: Can Perception Occur Without Sensation?"

❯ Test your understanding of **The Nonvisual Senses** with *LEARNINGCurve.*

Perception

KEY THEME

Perception refers to the process of integrating, organizing, and interpreting sensory information into meaningful representations.

KEY QUESTIONS

❯ What are bottom-up and top-down processing, and how do they differ?
❯ What is Gestalt psychology?
❯ What Gestalt principles explain how we perceive objects and their relationship to their surroundings?

As we've seen, our senses are constantly registering a diverse range of stimuli from the environment and transmitting that information to the brain. But to make use of this raw sensory data, we must organize, interpret, and relate the data to existing knowledge.

bottom-up processing Information processing that emphasizes the importance of the sensory receptors in detecting the basic features of a stimulus in the process of recognizing a whole pattern; analysis that moves from the parts to the whole; also called *data-driven processing.*

top-down processing Information processing that emphasizes the importance of the observer's knowledge, expectations, and other cognitive processes in arriving at meaningful perceptions; analysis that moves from the whole to the parts; also called *conceptually driven processing.*

Gestalt psychology (geh-SHTALT) School of psychology that maintained sensations are actively processed according to consistent perceptual rules, producing meaningful whole perceptions, or *gestalts.*

Psychologists sometimes refer to this flow of sensory data from the sensory receptors to the brain as **bottom-up processing.** Also called *data-driven processing,* bottom-up processing is often at work when we're confronted with an ambiguous stimulus. For example, imagine trying to assemble a jigsaw puzzle one piece at a time, without knowing what the final picture will be. To accomplish this task, you would work with the individual puzzle pieces to build the image from the "bottom up," that is, from its constituent parts.

But as we interact with our environment, many of our perceptions are shaped by **top-down processing,** which is also referred to as *conceptually driven processing.* Top-down processing occurs when we draw on our knowledge, experiences, expectations, and other cognitive processes to arrive at meaningful perceptions, such as people or objects in a particular context. Cultural experiences also affect perceptual processes, as discussed in the Culture and Human Behavior box on page 115, "Ways of Seeing: Culture and Top-Down Processes."

Both top-down and bottom-up processing are involved in our everyday perceptions. Look at the photograph above. Top-down processing was involved as you reached a number of perceptual conclusions about the image. You quickly perceived a little girl holding a black cat—Sandy and Don's daughter Laura when she was three, holding her cat, Nubbin. You also perceived a child as a whole object even though the cat is actually blocking a good portion of the view of Laura.

But now look at the background in the photograph, which is more ambiguous. Deciphering these images involves both bottom-up and top-down processing. Bottom-up processes help you determine that behind the little girl looms a large, dark green object with brightly colored splotches on it. But what is it?

To identify the mysterious object, you must interpret the sensory data. Top-down processes help you identify the large green blotch as a Christmas tree—a conclusion that you probably would *not* reach if you had no familiarity with the way many Americans celebrate the Christmas holiday. The Christmas tree branches, ornaments, and lights are just fuzzy images, but other images work as clues—a happy child, a stuffed bear with a red-and-white stocking cap. Learning experiences create a conceptual knowledge base from which we can identify and interpret many objects, including kids, cats, and Christmas trees.

Clearly, bottom-up and top-down processing are both necessary to explain how we arrive at perceptual conclusions. But whether we are using bottom-up or top-down processing, a useful way to think about perception is to consider the basic perceptual questions we must answer in order to survive. We exist in an ever-changing environment that is filled with objects that may be standing still or moving, just like ourselves. Whether it's a bulldozer or a bowling ball, we need to be able to identify objects, locate objects in space, and, if they are moving, track their motion. Thus, our perceptual processes must help us organize our sensations to answer three basic, important questions: (1) What is it? (2) How far away is it? and (3) Where is it going?

In the next few sections, we will look at what psychologists have learned about the principles we use to answer these perceptual questions. Much of our discussion reflects the work of an early school of psychology called **Gestalt psychology,** which was founded by German psychologist **Max Wertheimer** in the early 1900s

Courtesy of the authors

Organizing Sensations into Meaningful Perceptions With virtually no conscious effort, the psychological process of perception allows you to integrate, organize, and interpret the lines, colors, and contours in this image as meaningful objects—a laughing child holding a panicky black cat in front of a Christmas tree. How did you reach those perceptual conclusions?

Max Wertheimer (1880–1943) Arguing that the whole is always greater than the sum of its parts, Wertheimer founded Gestalt psychology. Wertheimer and other Gestalt psychologists began by studying the principles of perception but later extended their approach to other areas of psychology.

Bettmann/Corbis

CRITICAL THINKING

ESP: Can Perception Occur Without Sensation?

ESP, or **extrasensory perception,** means the detection of information by some means other than through the normal processes of sensation.

Do you believe in ESP? If you do, you're not alone (Ridolfo & others, 2010). Recent surveys conducted by the Associated Press and the Gallup Poll have found that close to 50 percent of American adults "believe in ESP" (Fram, 2007; D. Moore, 2005).

Forms of ESP include *telepathy,* which is the *direct* communication between the minds of two individuals; *clairvoyance,* the perception of a remote object or event, such as "sensing" that a friend has been injured in a car accident; *psychokinesis,* the ability to influence a physical object without touching it; and *precognition,* the ability to predict future events.

The general term for such unusual abilities is *paranormal phenomena. Paranormal* means "outside the range of normal experience." Thus, these phenomena cannot be explained by known laws of science and nature. **Parapsychology** refers to the scientific investigation of claims of various paranormal phenomena. Contrary to what many people think, very few psychologists conduct any kind of parapsychological research.

> **MYTH** ◀ SCIENCE
>
> Is it true that most psychologists study extrasensory perception (ESP)?

Have you ever felt as if you had just experienced ESP? Consider this example: Some years ago, Sandy had a vivid dream that her cat Nubbin got lost. The next morning, Nubbin sneaked out the back door, went for an unauthorized stroll in the woods, and was gone for three days. Did Sandy have a precognitive dream?

Such common instances are sometimes used to "prove" that ESP exists. However, two less extraordinary concepts can explain both occurrences: coincidence and the fallacy of positive instances. *Coincidence* describes an event that occurs simply by chance. For example, you have over a thousand dreams per year, most of which are about familiar people and situations. By mere chance, *some* aspect of *some* dream will occasionally correspond with reality.

The *fallacy of positive instances* is the tendency to remember coincidental events that seem to confirm our belief about unusual phenomena and to forget all the instances that do not. For example, think of the number of times you've had a dream that did *not* come true. Such situations are far more common than their opposites, but we quickly forget about the hunches that are not confirmed.

Why do people attribute chance events to ESP? Research has shown that believers in ESP are less likely to accurately estimate the probability of an event occurring by chance alone. Nonbelievers tend to be more realistic about the probability of events being the result of simple coincidence or chance (Dagnall & others, 2007; Rogers & others, 2009).

Parapsychologists attempt to study ESP in the laboratory under controlled conditions. Many initially convincing demonstrations of ESP are later shown to be the result of research design problems or of the researcher's unintentional cuing of the subject. Another problem involves *replication.* To be considered valid, experimental results must be able to be replicated, or repeated, by other scientists under identical laboratory conditions. Skeptics claim, and most psychologists agree, that to date, no parapsychology experiment claiming to show evidence of the existence of ESP has been successfully replicated (Hyman, 2010).

One active area of parapsychological research is the study of clairvoyance using an experimental procedure called the *ganzfeld procedure* (J. Palmer, 2003; Westerlund & others, 2006). (*Ganzfeld* is a German word that means "total field.") In a ganzfeld study, a "sender" in one room attempts to communicate the content of pictures or short video clips to a receiver in a separate room. Isolated from all contact and wearing goggles and headphones to block external sensory stimuli, the "receiver" attempts to detect the image that is being sent.

Summarizing dozens of ganzfeld studies conducted over 15 years, Lance Storm and his colleagues (2010, 2013) showed a "hit" rate that was well above chance, implying that some sort

Think Like a SCIENTIST

Do you have psychic powers? Go to LaunchPad: Resources to **Think Like a Scientist** about **ESP.**

📡 **LaunchPad**

ESP (extrasensory perception)
Perception of information by some means other than through the normal processes of sensation.

parapsychology The scientific investigation of claims of paranormal phenomena and abilities.

(Wertheimer, 1923/2009). The Gestalt psychologists emphasized that we perceive whole objects or figures (*gestalts*) rather than isolated bits and pieces of sensory information. Roughly translated, the German word *gestalt* means a unified whole, form, or shape. Although the Gestalt school of psychology no longer formally exists, the pioneering work of the Gestalt psychologists established many basic perceptual principles (S. Palmer, 2002).

The Perception of Shape

WHAT IS IT?

When you look around your world, you don't see random edges, curves, colors, or splotches of light and dark. Rather, you see countless distinct objects against a variety of backgrounds. Although to some degree we rely on size, color, and texture to determine what an object might be, we rely primarily on an object's *shape* to identify it.

The Ganzfeld Technique
Clairvoyance and telepathy experiments often involve use of the *ganzfeld* technique. The research subject lies in a quiet room, with his eyes covered by ping-pong balls cut in half. White noise plays through the headphones covering his ears. Along with blocking extraneous sensory stimuli, this technique can induce mild hallucinations in some subjects (Wackerman & others, 2008).

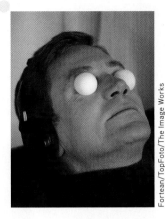

Fortean/TopFoto/The Image Works

of transfer of information had taken place between sender and receiver. These results, published in a well-respected psychology journal, *Psychological Bulletin,* led some psychologists to speculate that there might be something to extrasensory perception after all—and that the ganzfeld procedure might be the way to detect it. But other psychologists dispute the statistical techniques used and argue that these studies do *not* offer conclusive proof that ESP has been demonstrated (Hyman, 2010; Rouder & others, 2013).

The latest salvo in the ESP debate was fired by psychologist Daryl Bem (2011), who tested precognition in a series of nine experiments involving more than a thousand participants. Bem's ingenious strategy was to "time-reverse" standard psychological tasks, changing the normal order of cause-and-effect.

For example, practicing a list of words makes the words easier to remember. In one experiment, participants taking a memory test better remembered words that they practiced *after* taking the test. In another experiment, participants predicted the location of a target image on a computer screen *before* they saw it.

In all, eight of Bem's nine experiments showed small but statistically significant effects in favor of precognition. These, and similar findings from Bem's series of experiments, cannot be easily explained (Judd & Gawronski, 2011).

Bem's research sparked a flurry of media attention, including an appearance on *The Colbert Report.* It also triggered a firestorm of reaction from psychologists and other scientists (Alcock, 2011; Shermer, 2011). Much of the criticism focuses on the statistical methods used to analyze the data (Fiedler & Krueger, 2013; Rouder & Morey, 2011; Wagenmakers & others, 2011). So far, replication attempts have been mostly unsuccessful (Barušs & Rabier, 2014; Galak & others, 2012; Ritchie & others, 2012). Undaunted, Bem and his colleagues (2014) published their own meta-analysis of 90 replication attempts, concluding that the results showed solid support for the existence of precognition.

Of course, the history of science is filled with examples of phenomena that were initially scoffed at and later found to be real, such as the notion that moods affect health and immune system functioning. So keep an open mind about ESP, but also maintain a healthy sense of scientific skepticism. It is entirely possible that some day convincing experimental evidence will demonstrate the existence of ESP abilities (see French & others, 2010; Schlitz & others, 2006). In the final analysis, all psychologists, including those who accept the possibility of ESP, recognize the need for evidence that meets the requirements of the scientific method.

CRITICAL THINKING AND QUESTIONS

- Why do you think that people who believe in ESP are less likely to attribute events to chance than people who don't think ESP is a real phenomenon?

- Can you think of any reasons why replication might be particularly elusive in research on extrasensory perception?

- Why is replication important in all psychological research, but particularly so in studies attempting to prove extraordinary claims, like the existence of ESP?

FIGURE–GROUND RELATIONSHIP

How do we organize our perceptions so that we see an object as separate from other objects? The early Gestalt psychologists identified an important perceptual principle called the **figure–ground relationship,** which describes how this works. When we view a scene, we automatically separate the elements of that scene into the *figure,* which is the main element of the scene, and the *ground,* which is its background.

You can experience the figure–ground relationship by looking at a coffee cup on a table. The coffee cup is the figure, and the table is the ground. Notice that usually the figure has a definite shape, tends to stand out clearly, and is perceptually meaningful in some way. In contrast, the ground tends to be less clearly defined, even fuzzy, and usually appears to be behind and farther away from the figure.

The early Gestalt psychologists noted that figure and ground have vastly different perceptual qualities (N. Rubin, 2001). As Gestalt psychologist Edgar Rubin (1921) observed, "In a certain sense, the ground has no shape." We notice the shape of the

figure–ground relationship Gestalt principle stating that a perception is automatically separated into the *figure,* which clearly stands out, from its less distinct background, the *ground.*

Survival and Figure–Ground Relationships The importance of figure–ground relationships in nature is illustrated by animals that rely on camouflage for survival, like this Eastern screech owl (left) and the pygmy seahorse, barely a half-inch long, which lives only in a specific type of coral in Indonesia (right). When an animal's coloring and markings blend with its background, a predator cannot distinguish the animal (the *figure*) from its surroundings (the *ground*).

Rolf Nussbaumer Photography/Alamy

Michael Patrick O'Neill/Science Source

FIGURE 3.13 Figures Have Shape, but Ground Doesn't Which shape in **(b)** can also be found in **(a)**? The answer is that both shapes are in **(a)**. It's easy to spot the top shape because it corresponds to one of the shapes perceived as a *figure* in **(a)** The bottom shape is harder to find because it is part of the *ground* or background of the total scene. Because we place more importance on figures, we're more likely to notice their shape while ignoring the shape of background regions (N. Rubin, 2001).

Source: Information from N. Rubin (2001).

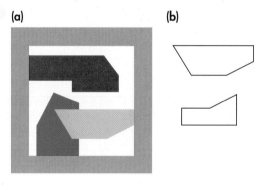

(a)   **(b)**

figure but *not* the shape of the background, even when that ground is used as a well-defined frame (see Figure 3.13). It turns out that brain neurons *also* respond differently to a stimulus that is perceived as a figure versus a stimulus that is part of the ground (Baylis & Driver, 2001). Particular neurons in the cortex that responded to a specific shape when it was the shape of the figure did *not* respond when the same shape was presented as part of the background.

The separation of a scene into figure and ground is not a property of the actual elements of the scene at which you're looking. Rather, your ability to separate a scene into figure and ground is a psychological accomplishment. To illustrate, look at the classic example shown in Figure 3.14. This perception of a single image in two different ways is called a *figure–ground reversal*.

FIGURE 3.14 A Classic Example of Figure–Ground Reversal Figure–ground reversals illustrate the psychological nature of our ability to perceptually sort a scene into the main element and the background. If you perceive the white area as the figure and the dark area as the ground, you'll perceive a vase. If you perceive the dark area as the figure, you'll perceive two faces.

Ways of Seeing: Culture and Top-Down Processes

Do people in different cultures perceive the world differently? In Chapter 1, we described two types of cultures. Unlike people in *individualistic* cultures, who tend to emphasize independence, people in *collectivistic* cultures see humans as being enmeshed in complex relationships. This social perspective is especially pronounced in the East Asian cultures of Korea, Japan, and China, where a person's sense of self is highly dependent upon his or her social context (Beins, 2011). Consequently, East Asians pay much closer attention to the social context in which their own actions, and the actions of others, occur (Nisbett, 2007; Varnum & others, 2010).

The Cultural Eye of the Beholders

Do these cultural differences in social perspective influence visual perception and memory? Take a few seconds to look at the photo on the right. Was your attention drawn by the tiger? Or its surroundings?

In one study, Hannah Faye Chua and her colleagues (2005) used sophisticated eye-tracking equipment to monitor the eye movements of U.S. and Chinese students while they looked at similar photographs that showed a single focal object against a realistic, complex background. The results showed that their eye movements differed: The U.S. students looked sooner and longer at the focal object in the foreground than the Chinese students did. In contrast, the Chinese students spent more time looking at the background than the U.S. students did. And, the Chinese students were also less likely to recognize the foreground objects when they were placed in front of a new background.

Rather than separating the object from its background, the Chinese students tended to see—and remember—object and background as a single perceptual image. Many psychologists believe that this pattern of results reflects the more "holistic" perceptual style that characterizes collectivistic cultures (Boduroglu & others, 2009; Boland & others, 2008).

Similarly, Joshua Goh and his colleagues (2009) compared the visual response of U.S. and East Asian participants to *changes* in photographs. They found that U.S. participants paid more attention to changes in the objects, but East Asian participants paid more attention to changes in the background. The U.S. participants also tended to focus their attention on the object alone, while the East Asian participants alternated looking at the object and the background, paying more attention to the *relationship* between the object and background. "Culture," the researchers observed, "may operate as a top-down mechanism that guides and interacts with basic neuro-perceptual processes."

Cultural Comfort Zones and Brain Functioning

Many psychologists now believe that these cultural differences in social and perceptual style also influence brain function (Park & Huang, 2010). For example, psychologist Trey Hedden and his colleagues (2008) compared brain functioning in East Asian and U.S. participants while they made rapid perceptual judgments comparing two images of a square with an embedded line as shown in this image on the right.

The *relative* task involved determining whether the lines in the two images were in the same proportion to the surrounding squares. The *absolute* task involved determining whether the two lines were the same absolute length, regardless of the size of the squares (see figure). Each participant made these judgments while his or her brain activity was tracked by an fMRI scanner.

Both groups were equally proficient at the task and used the same brain regions in making the simple perceptual judgments. However, the *pattern* of brain activation differed.

James Warwick/Getty Images

Which do you notice first—the tiger or its rocky surroundings?

The individualistic U.S. participants showed greater brain activation while making relative judgments, meaning they had to exert more mental effort. The collectivistic East Asians showed the opposite pattern, devoting greater brain effort to making absolute judgments that required them to ignore the context. Essentially, all participants had to work harder at making perceptual judgments that were outside their cultural comfort zones.

The bottom line? People from different cultures use the same neural processes to make perceptual judgments. But, their culture trains them to use them in different ways. As John Gabrieli (2008) points out, "The way in which the brain responds to these simple drawings reflects, in a predictable way, how the individual thinks about independent or interdependent social relationships." People from different cultures may not literally see the world differently—but they notice different things and think differently about what they *do* see.

Relative task: Is the proportion of the vertical line to the box the same in both images?

Absolute task: Is the absolute length of the two vertical lines the same?

Hedden, Trey; Ketay, Sarah; Aron, Arthur; Markus, Hazel Rose; & Gabrieli, John D. E., Psychological Science, 19:1, pp. 12-17, copyright © 2008 by SAGE Publications. Reprinted by Permission of SAGE Publications.

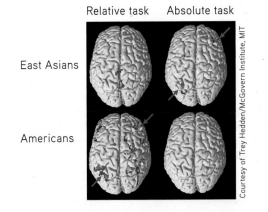

Relative task   Absolute task

East Asians

Americans

Courtesy of Trey Hedden/McGovern Institute, MIT

PERCEPTUAL GROUPING

Many of the forms we perceive are composed of a number of different elements that seem to go together (Glicksohn & Cohen, 2011). It would be more accurate to say that we actively organize the elements to try to produce the stable perception of well-defined, whole objects. This is what perceptual psychologists refer to as "the urge to organize" (see image below). What principles do we follow when we attempt to organize visual elements?

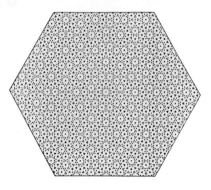

The Perceptual Urge to Organize As you scan this image, you'll experience firsthand the strong psychological tendency to organize visual elements to arrive at the perception of whole figures, forms, and shapes. Notice that as you shift your gaze across the pattern, you momentarily perceive circles, squares, and other geometric forms.

MATLIN, MARGARET W.; FOLEY, HUGH J., SENSATION AND PERCEPTION, 3rd Edition, © 1992. Reprinted by permission of Pearson Education, Inc., Upper Saddle River, NJ

The Gestalt psychologists studied how the perception of visual elements becomes organized into patterns, shapes, and forms. They identified several laws, or principles, that we tend to follow in grouping elements together to arrive at the perception of forms, shapes, and figures. These principles include *similarity, closure, good continuation,* and *proximity.* Examples and descriptions of these perceptual laws are shown in Figure 3.15.

The Gestalt psychologists also formulated a general principle called the *law of Prägnanz,* or the *law of simplicity.* This law states that when several perceptual organizations of an assortment of visual elements are possible, the perceptual interpretation that occurs will be the one that produces the "best, simplest, and most stable shape" (Koffka, 1935). For an illustration, look at Figure 3.16 on the next page. Do you perceive the image as two six-sided objects and one four-sided object? If you are following the law of Prägnanz, you don't. Instead, you perceptually organize the elements in the most cognitively efficient and simple way, perceiving them as three overlapping squares.

FIGURE 3.15 The Gestalt Principles of Organization

(a) *The law of similarity* is the tendency to perceive objects of a similar size, shape, or color as a unit or figure. Thus, you perceive rows of tomatoes, avocados, lemons, and so forth rather than a mixed array of fruits and vegetables.

(b) The *law of closure* is the tendency to fill in the gaps in an incomplete image. Thus, you perceive the fence rails as continuous straight lines even though the image is interrupted by the cowboy boots.

(c) The *law of good continuation* is the tendency to group elements that appear to follow in the same direction as a single unit or figure. Thus, you tend to see the straight and curved sections of the Chicago L-tracks as separate but continuous units.

(d) The *law of proximity* is the tendency to perceive objects that are close to one another as a single unit. Thus, you perceive these three puffins as two distinct units—one puffin standing apart from a puffin pair—rather than as a single group of three puffins.

(a) The Law of Similarity

Air Images/Shutterstock

(b) The Law of Closure

David Stoecklein/age fotostock

(c) The Law of Good Continuation

Laura A. Hockenbury

(d) The Law of Proximity

Rolf Hicker/All Canada Photos/age fotostock

According to the Gestalt psychologists, the law of Prägnanz encompasses all the other Gestalt principles, including the figure–ground relationship. The implication of the law of Prägnanz is that our perceptual system works in an economical way to promote the interpretation of stable and consistent forms (Pinna & Reeves, 2009). The ability to efficiently organize elements into stable objects helps us perceive the world accurately. In effect, we actively and automatically construct a perception that reveals "the essence of something," which is roughly what the German word *Prägnanz* means.

FIGURE 3.16 The Law of Prägnanz: What Do You See? The most fundamental Gestalt principle is the *law of Prägnanz*, or simplicity. It refers to our tendency to efficiently organize the visual elements of a scene in a way that produces the simplest and most stable forms or objects. You probably perceived this image as three overlapping squares rather than as two six-sided objects and one four-sided object.

Depth Perception

HOW FAR AWAY IS IT?

KEY THEME

Perception of distance and motion helps us gauge the position of stationary objects and predict the path of moving objects.

KEY QUESTIONS

> What are the monocular and binocular cues for distance or depth perception, and how does binocular disparity explain our ability to see three-dimensional forms in two-dimensional images?

> What visual cues help us perceive distance and motion?

> Why do we perceive the size and shape of objects as unchanging despite changes in sensory input?

Being able to perceive the distance of an object has obvious survival value, especially regarding potential threats, such as snarling dogs or oncoming trains. But simply walking through your house or apartment also requires that you accurately judge the distance of furniture, walls, other people, and so forth. Otherwise, you'd be constantly bumping into doors, walls, and tables. The ability to perceive the distance of an object as well as the three-dimensional characteristics of an object is called **depth perception.**

MONOCULAR CUES

We use a variety of cues to judge the distance of objects. **Monocular cues** require the use of only one eye (*mono* means "one"). When monocular cues are used by artists to create the perception of distance or depth in paintings or drawings, they are called *pictorial cues.* After familiarizing yourself with these cues, look at the photographs on the next page. Try to identify the monocular cues you used to determine the distance of the objects in each photograph.

1. *Relative size.* If two or more objects are assumed to be similar in size, the object that appears larger is perceived as being closer.
2. *Overlap.* When one object partially blocks or obscures the view of another object, the partially blocked object is perceived as being farther away. This cue is also called *interposition.*
3. *Aerial perspective.* Faraway objects often appear hazy or slightly blurred by the atmosphere.
4. *Texture gradient.* As a surface with a distinct texture extends into the distance, the details of the surface texture gradually become less clearly defined. The texture

depth perception The use of visual cues to perceive the distance or three-dimensional characteristics of objects.

monocular cues (moe-NOCK-you-ler) Distance or depth cues that can be processed by either eye alone.

of the surface seems to undergo a gradient, or continuous pattern of change, from crisp and distinct when close to fuzzy and blended when farther away.

5. *Linear perspective.* Parallel lines seem to meet in the distance. For example, if you stand in the middle of a railroad track and look down the rails, you'll notice that the parallel rails seem to meet in the distance. The closer together the lines appear to be, the greater the perception of distance.

6. *Motion parallax.* When you are moving, you use the speed of passing objects to estimate the distance of the objects. Nearby objects seem to zip by faster than do distant objects. When you are riding on a commuter train, for example, houses and parked cars along the tracks seem to whiz by, while the distant downtown skyline seems to move very slowly.

Another monocular cue is *accommodation.* Unlike pictorial cues, accommodation utilizes information about changes in the shape of the lens of the eye to help us estimate distance. When you focus on a distant object, the lens is flat, but focusing on a nearby object causes the lens to thicken. Thus, to some degree, we use information provided by the muscles controlling the shape of the lens to judge depth. In general, however, we rely more on pictorial cues than on accommodation for depth perception.

Texture Gradient, Overlap, and Aerial Perspective Monocular cues are used to judge the distance of objects in a photograph. The poppies in the foreground are crisp, but the mass of lavender flowers becomes increasingly fuzzy in the background, an example of texture gradient. Similarly, the hills and sky at the top of the image are just blurs of color, creating an impression of even greater distance through aerial perspective. And, the orange-red poppies are perceived as being closer than the lavender flowers that they overlap.

Relative Size and Linear Perspective Monocular cues provide depth cues that create the illusion of a palm tree-lined road receding into the distance. Linear perspective is evident in the near-convergence of the palm trees as the road narrows. And, the palm trees appear to decrease in size, an example of relative size contributing to the perception of distance.

Motion Parallax This photograph of waiters in India passing a tray from one train car to the next captures the visual flavor of motion parallax. Objects that whiz by faster are perceptually judged as being closer, as in the case here of the blurred ground and grass. Objects that pass by more slowly are judged as being farther away, as conveyed by the clearer details of the distant buildings and trees.

BINOCULAR CUES

Binocular cues for distance or depth perception require information from both eyes. One binocular cue is *convergence*—the degree to which muscles rotate your eyes to focus on an object. The more the eyes converge, or rotate inward, to focus on an object, the greater the strength of the muscle signals and the closer the object is perceived to be. For example, if you hold a dime about six inches in front of your nose, you'll notice the slight strain on your eye muscles as your eyes converge to focus on the coin. If you hold the dime at arm's length, less convergence is needed. Perceptually, the information provided by these signals from your eye muscles is used to judge the distance of an object.

Another binocular distance cue is *binocular disparity*. Because our eyes are set a couple of inches apart, a slightly different image of an object is cast on the retina of each eye. When the two retinal images are very different, we interpret the object as being close by. When the two retinal images are more nearly identical, the object is perceived as being farther away (Parker, 2007).

Here's a simple example that illustrates how you use binocular disparity to perceive distance. Hold a pencil just in front of your nose. Close your left eye, then your right.

These images are quite different—that is, there is a great deal of binocular disparity between them. Thus, you perceive the pencil as being very close. Now focus on another object across the room and look at it first with one eye closed, then the other. These images are much more similar. Because there is less binocular disparity between the two images, the object is perceived as being farther away. Finally, notice that with both eyes open, the two images are fused into one.

A *stereogram* is a picture that uses the principle of binocular disparity to create the perception of a three-dimensional image (Kunoh & Takaoki, 1994). Look at the stereogram shown below. When you first look at it, you perceive a two-dimensional picture of leaves. Although the pictorial cues of overlap and texture gradient provide some sense of depth to the image, the elements in the picture appear to be roughly the same distance from you.

However, a stereogram is actually composed of repeating columns of carefully arranged visual information. If you focus as if you are looking at some object that is farther away from the stereogram, the repeating columns of information will present a slightly different image to each eye. This disparate visual information then fuses into a single image, enabling you to perceive a three-dimensional image—three rabbits! To see the rabbits, follow the directions in the caption.

binocular cues (by-NOCK-you-ler) Distance or depth cues that require the use of both eyes.

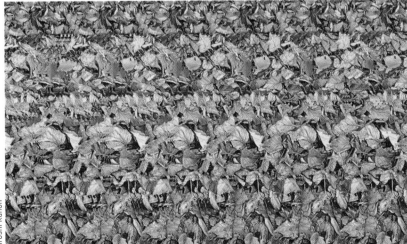

Hiroshi Kunoh

Binocular Disparity and the Perception of Depth in Stereograms This stereogram, *Rustling Hares*, was created by artist Hiroshi Kunoh (Kunoh & Takaoki, 1994). To see the three-dimensional images, first hold the picture close to your face. Focus your eyes as though you are looking at an object that is beyond the book and farther away. Without changing your focus, slowly extend your arms and move the picture away from you. The image of the leaves will initially be blurry, then details will come into focus and you should see three rabbits. The three-dimensional images that can be perceived in stereograms occur because of binocular disparity—each eye is presented with slightly different visual information.

Florence Low

Mike and Motion Perception Catching a ball involves calculating an array of rapidly changing bits of visual information, including the ball's location, speed, and trajectory. Mike was especially appreciative of his newly regained motion perception. As Mike wrote in his journal, "Top on my list is being able to catch a ball in the air. This is pretty hard to do if you are totally blind, and now I can play ball with my boys and catch the ball 80 percent of the time it is thrown to me. I have spent half my life chasing a ball around in one way or another, so this is a big deal."

The Perception of Motion
WHERE IS IT GOING?

In addition to the ability to perceive the distance of stationary objects, we need the ability to gauge the path of moving objects, whether it's a baseball whizzing through the air, a falling tree branch, or an egg about to roll off the kitchen counter. How do we perceive movement?

As we follow a moving object with our gaze, the image of the object moves across the retina. Our eye muscles make microfine movements to keep the object in focus. We also compare the moving object to the background, which is usually stationary. When the retinal image of an object enlarges, we perceive the object as moving toward us. Our perception of the speed of the object's approach is based on our estimate of the object's rate of enlargement (Harris & others, 2008). Neural pathways in the brain combine information about eye-muscle activity, the changing retinal image, and the contrast of the moving object with its stationary background. The end result? We perceive the object as moving.

Neuroscientists do not completely understand how the brain's visual system processes movement. It's known that some neurons are highly specialized to detect motion in one direction but not in the opposite direction. Other neurons are specialized to detect motion at one particular speed. Research also shows that different neural pathways in the cerebral cortex process information about the depth of objects, movement, form, and color (Regan & Gray, 2009; Zeki, 2001).

Psychologically, we tend to make certain assumptions when we perceive movement. For example, we typically assume that the *object,* or figure, moves while the background, or frame, remains stationary (Rock, 1995). Thus, as you visually follow a bowling ball down the alley, you perceive the bowling ball as moving and not the alley, which serves as the background.

Because we have a strong tendency to assume that the background is stationary, we sometimes experience an illusion of motion called *induced motion.* Induced motion was first studied by Gestalt psychologist **Karl Duncker** (1903–1940) in the 1920s (King & others, 2003). Duncker (1929) had subjects sit in a darkened room and look at a luminous dot that was surrounded by a larger luminous rectangular frame. When the *frame* slowly moved to the right, the subjects perceived the *dot* as moving to the left.

Why did subjects perceive the dot as moving? Part of the explanation has to do with top-down processing. Perceptually, Duncker's subjects *expected* to see the smaller dot move within the larger rectangular frame, not the other way around. If you've ever looked up at a full moon on a windy night when the clouds were moving quickly across its face, you've probably experienced the induced motion effect. The combination of these environmental elements makes the moon appear to be racing across the sky.

Another illusion of apparent motion is called *stroboscopic motion.* First studied by Gestalt psychologist Max Wertheimer in the early 1900s, stroboscopic motion creates an illusion of movement with two carefully timed flashing lights (Wertheimer, 1912). A light briefly flashes at one location, followed about a tenth of a second later by another light briefly flashing at a second location. If the time interval and distance between the two flashing lights are just right, a very compelling illusion of movement is created.

What causes the perception of stroboscopic motion? Although different theories have been proposed, researchers aren't completely sure. The perception of motion typically involves the movement of an image across the retina. However, during stroboscopic motion the image does *not* move across the surface of the retina. Rather, the two different flashing lights are detected at two different points on the surface of the retina. Somehow, the brain's visual system combines this rapid sequence of visual information to arrive at the perceptual conclusion of motion, even though no movement has occurred. The perception of smooth motion in a movie is also due to stroboscopic motion.

Perceptual Constancies

Consider this scenario. As you're driving on a flat stretch of highway, a red SUV zips past you and speeds far ahead. As the distance between you and the SUV grows, its image becomes progressively smaller until it is no more than a dot on the horizon. Yet, even though the image of the SUV on your retinas has become progressively smaller, you don't perceive the vehicle as shrinking. Instead, you perceive its shape, size, and brightness as unchanged.

Jean-Marc FavreE/vandystadt/Science Source

Stroboscopic Motion and Movies The perception of smooth movements in a movie is due to stroboscopic motion. Much like this image composed of superimposed, still photographs of French gymnast Yann Cucherat performing a complex move on the horizontal bar, a motion picture is actually a series of static photographs that are projected onto the screen at the rate of 24 frames per second, producing the illusion of smooth motion.

This tendency to perceive objects, especially familiar objects, as constant and unchanging despite changes in sensory input is called **perceptual constancy.** Without this perceptual ability, our perception of reality would be in a continual state of flux. If we simply responded to retinal images, our perceptions of objects would change as lighting, viewing angle, and distance from the object changed from one moment to the next. Instead, color, size, and shape constancy promote a stable view of the world. *Color constancy* may help explain the otherwise puzzling phenomenon described in the In Focus box on the next page, "The Dress That Broke the Internet."

perceptual constancy The tendency to perceive objects, especially familiar objects, as constant and unchanging despite changes in sensory input.

size constancy The perception of an object as maintaining the same size despite changing images on the retina.

SIZE AND SHAPE CONSTANCY

Size constancy is the perception that an object remains the same size despite its changing image on the retina. When our distance from an object changes, the image of the object that is cast on the retinas of our eyes also changes, yet we still perceive it to be the same size. The example of the red SUV illustrates the perception of size constancy. As the distance between you and the red SUV increased, you could eventually block out the retinal image of the vehicle with your hand, but you don't believe that your hand has suddenly become larger than the SUV. Instead, your brain automatically adjusts your perception of the vehicle's size by combining information about retinal image size and distance.

An important aspect of size constancy is that if the retinal image of an object does *not*

Bruno Ehrs/Getty Images

The Doors of Perception Each door in the photograph is positioned at a different angle and thus produces a differently shaped image on your retinas. Nevertheless, because of the perceptual principle of shape constancy, you easily identify all five shapes as rectangular doors.

FIGURE 3.17 How Many Right Angles Do You See? Most people find 12 right angles in this drawing of a slightly tilted cube. But look again. There are *no* right angles in the drawing. Shape constancy leads you to perceive an image of a cube with right angles, despite the lack of sensory data to support that perception.

shape constancy The perception of a familiar object as maintaining the same shape regardless of the image produced on the retina.

color constancy The perception of a familiar object as being the same color under different light conditions.

change but the perception of its distance *increases,* the object is perceived as larger. To illustrate, try this: Stare at a 75-watt light bulb for about 10 seconds. Then focus on a bright, distant wall. You should see an afterimage of the light bulb on the wall that will look several times larger than the original light bulb. Why? When you looked at the wall, the lingering afterimage of the light bulb on your retina remained constant, but your perception of distance increased. When your brain combined and interpreted this information, your perception of the light bulb's size increased. Remember this demonstration. We'll mention it again when we explain how some perceptual illusions occur.

Shape constancy is the tendency to perceive familiar objects as having a fixed shape regardless of the image they cast on our retinas. Try looking at a familiar object, such as a door, from different angles, as in the photograph on the left. Your perception of the door's rectangular shape remains constant despite changes in its retinal image. Shape constancy has a greater influence on your perceptions than you probably realize (see Figure 3.17).

IN FOCUS

The Dress That Broke the Internet

It all started with a Facebook post showing a dress worn at a wedding on a tiny Scottish island. Picked up by a blogger and then by Buzzfeed, the photo blazed across the Internet, racking up an incredible 28 million views within 48 hours. The burning question: *What color is the dress?*

The dress in a photo from Caitlin McNeill's Tumblr site.

Even celebrities got into the "#The Dress" game. Kim Kardashian tweeted, "What color is that dress? I see white & gold. Kanye sees black & blue, who is color blind?"

Some suggested that subtle differences in the cones of the retina were involved. Others blamed the different types of screen displays, but that didn't explain why people looking at the photo on the same screen saw radically different colors.

The most likely explanation seems to involve the phenomenon of **color constancy** (Novella, 2015; Pinker, 2015).

As you've learned, color perception is the result of a complex interaction between the light waves reflected off of an object and your brain's interpretation of those signals. But in determining the color of an object, your brain takes additional factors into account, such as the amount and brightness of background illumination. The brain automatically compensates for shadows and other changing light conditions to perceive the color of familiar objects as unchanging.

For the record, the *actual* dress is blue and black. But in the photo, the light conditions are ambiguous. Is the dress in shadow or bright light? Those who made the unconscious assumption that the dress was in shadow or dim light saw it as white and gold, because white tends to look blue in dim light. But those who assumed that the dress was in bright light saw it as blue and black—the actual colors (Pinker, 2015).

#The Dress is entertaining, but it also makes an important point about top-down processes in perception. As neuroscientist Steven Novella (2015) wrote, "this is not just an isolated weird case. This is how our brains work all the time. What we perceive is a constructed illusion, based upon algorithms that make reasonable assumptions about distance, shading, size, movement, and color—but they are assumptions, none the less, and sometimes they can be wrong or misleading."

Perceptual Illusions

KEY THEME

Perceptual illusions underscore the idea that we actively construct our perceptual representations of the world according to psychological principles.

KEY QUESTIONS

> How can the Müller-Lyer and moon illusions be explained?

> What do perceptual illusions reveal about perceptual processes?

> What roles do perceptual sets, learning experiences, and culture play in perception?

Our perceptual processes are largely automatic and unconscious. On the one hand, this arrangement is mentally efficient. With a minimum of cognitive effort, we decipher our surroundings, answering important perceptual questions and making sense of the environment. On the other hand, because perceptual processing is largely automatic, we can inadvertently arrive at the wrong perceptual conclusion. When we misperceive the true characteristics of an object or an image, we experience a **perceptual illusion.**

During the past century, well over 200 perceptual illusions have been discovered. One famous perceptual illusion is shown in Figure 3.18. The perceptual contradictions of illusions are not only fascinating but can also shed light on how the normal processes of perception guide us to perceptual conclusions. Given the basics of perception that we've covered thus far, you're in a good position to understand how and why some famous illusions seem to occur.

perceptual illusion The misperception of the true characteristics of an object or an image.

Müller-Lyer illusion A famous visual illusion involving the misperception of the identical length of two lines, one with arrows pointed inward, one with arrows pointed outward.

FIGURE 3.18 Illusory Contours: How Many Triangles Do You See? The Gestalt principles of perceptual organization contribute to the illusion of triangular contours in this image. When you look at this ambiguous image, you instantly reverse figure and ground so that the black circular regions become the ground while the white region is visually favored as the figure. The Gestalt principles of closure and good continuation contribute to the perceptual construction of a solid white triangle covering three black disks and an inverted triangle. The images produce a second intriguing illusion: The pure white illusory triangle seems brighter than the surrounding white paper.

The Müller-Lyer Illusion

Look at the center line made by the corners of the walls in (a) and (c) in Figure 3.19. Which line is longer? If you said (c), then you've just experienced the **Müller-Lyer illusion.** In fact, the two center lines are the same length, even though they *appear* to have different lengths. You can confirm that they are the same length by measuring them. The same illusion occurs when you look at a simple line drawing of the Müller-Lyer illusion, shown in parts (b) and (d) of Figure 3.19.

The Müller-Lyer illusion is caused in part by visual depth cues that promote the perception that the center line in (c) is *farther* from you (Gregory, 1968; Rock, 1995). When you look at (c), the center line is that of a wall jutting away from you. When you look at drawing (d), the outward-pointing arrows create much the same visual effect—a corner jutting away from you. In Figure 3.19 (a) and (b), visual depth cues promote the perception of *lesser* distance—a corner that is jutting toward you.

FIGURE 3.19 The Müller-Lyer Illusion Compare the two drawings of buildings. Which *corner* line is longer? Now compare the two line drawings. Which *center* line is longer? In reality, the center lines in the buildings and the line drawings are all exactly the same length, which you can prove to yourself with a ruler.

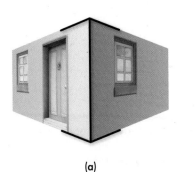
(a)

(b)

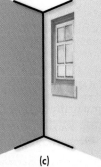
(c)

(d)

moon illusion A visual illusion involving the misperception that the moon is larger when it is on the horizon than when it is directly overhead.

Size constancy also seems to play an important role in the Müller–Lyer illusion. Because they are the same length, the two center lines in the photographs and the line drawings produce retinal images that are the same size. However, as we noted in our earlier discussion of size constancy, if the retinal size of an object stays the same but the perception of its distance increases, we will perceive the object as being larger. Previously, we demonstrated this with the afterimage of a light bulb that seemed much larger when viewed against a distant wall.

The same basic principle seems to apply to the Müller–Lyer illusion. Although all four center lines produce retinal images that are the same size, the center lines in images (c) and (d) are embedded in visual depth cues that make you perceive them as farther away. Hence, you perceive the center lines in these images as being longer, just as you perceived the afterimage of the light bulb as being larger when viewed on a distant wall.

Keep in mind that the arrows pointing inward or outward are responsible for creating the illusion in the Müller–Lyer illusion. Take away those potent depth cues and the Müller–Lyer illusion evaporates. You perceive the two lines just as they are—the same length.

The Moon Illusion

Another famous illusion is one you've probably experienced firsthand—the **moon illusion.** When a full moon is rising on a clear, dark night, it appears much larger when viewed on the horizon against buildings and trees than it does when viewed in the clear sky overhead. But the moon, of course, doesn't shrink as it rises. In fact, *the retinal size of the full moon is the same in all positions.* Still, if you've ever watched the moon rise from the horizon to the night sky, it does *appear* to shrink in size. What causes this illusion?

Part of the explanation has to do with our perception of the distance of objects at different locations in the sky (Ozkan & Braunstein, 2010). Researchers have found that people perceive objects on the horizon as farther away than objects that are directly overhead in the sky. The horizon contains many familiar distance cues, such as buildings, trees, and the smoothing of the texture of the landscape as it fades into the distance. The moon on the horizon is perceived as being *behind* these depth cues, so the depth perception cue of overlap adds to the perception that the moon on the horizon is farther away.

DARRYL WEBB/Reuters/Corbis

The Moon Illusion Why does the moon appear to be much larger when it's viewed on the horizon than when it's viewed higher in the sky?

The moon illusion also involves the misapplication of the principle of size constancy. Like the afterimage of the glowing light bulb, which looked larger on a distant wall, the moon looks larger when the perception of its distance increases. Remember, the retinal image of the moon is the *same* in all locations, as was the afterimage of the light bulb. Thus, even though the retinal image of the moon remains constant, we perceive the moon as being larger because it seems farther away on the horizon (Kaufman & others, 2007).

If you look at a full moon on the horizon through a cardboard tube, you'll remove the distance cues provided by the horizon. The moon on the horizon shrinks immediately—and looks the same size as it does when directly overhead.

MIKE AND PERCEPTUAL ILLUSIONS

Perceptual illusions underscore the fact that what we see is *not* merely a simple reflection of the world, but rather our subjective perceptual interpretation of it. We've been developing and refining our perceptual interpretations from infancy onward. But what about Mike, who regained low vision after more than four decades of blindness?

Psychologist Ione Fine and her colleagues (2003) assessed Mike's perceptual processing with a couple of perceptual illusions. For example, Mike was presented with an image containing illusory contours, shown on the right. It's much like the more complex image we discussed in Figure 3.18. When asked, "What is the 'hidden' shape outlined by the black apertures?" Mike had no response. However, when the form was outlined in red, Mike immediately perceived the red square.

Now look at Figure 3.20. Which tabletop is longer? If you used your keen perceptual skills and confidently said (b), you'd be wrong. If you responded as Mike did and said that the two tabletops are of identical size and shape, you'd be correct. You can use a ruler or tracing paper to verify this. This illusion is referred to as the *Shepard Tables,* named after its creator, psychologist Roger Shepard (1990).

Why wasn't Mike susceptible to this compelling visual illusion? Partly, it's because he does not automatically use many of the depth perception cues we discussed earlier (Gregory, 2003). As psychologist Donald MacLeod explained, "Mike is impressively free from some illusions that beset normal vision, illusions that reflect the constructive processes involved in the perception of three-dimensional objects" (Abrams, 2002).

Although seeing is said to be believing, in the case of illusions, believing can lead to seeing something that isn't really there. Like any psychological process, perception can be influenced by many factors, including our expectations. In the final section of this chapter, we'll consider how prior experiences and cultural factors can influence our perceptions of reality.

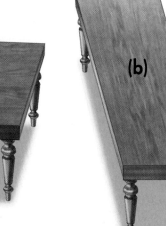

FIGURE 3.20 Which Tabletop Is Longer? The *Shepard Tables* illusion consists of two tables that are oriented in different directions. It capitalizes on our automatic use of depth perception cues to perceive what is really a two-dimensional drawing as three-dimensional objects. By relying on these well-learned depth perception cues, most people pick (b) as being the longer tabletop. In contrast, Mike May was oblivious to the perceptual illusion. He correctly responded that the two tabletops were the same size and shape (Fine & others, 2003). You can verify this with a ruler.

Source: Information from Shepard (1990).

The Effects of Experience on Perceptual Interpretations

Our educational, cultural, and life experiences shape what we perceive. As a simple example, consider a climbing wall in a gym. If your knowledge of climbing is limited, the posts, ropes, arrows, and lines look like a meaningless jumble of equipment. But if you are an expert climber, you see handgrips and footgrips, belays, overhangs, and routes of varying difficulty. Our different perceptions of a climbing wall are shaped by our prior learning experiences.

Learning experiences can vary not just from person to person but also from culture to culture. The Culture and Human Behavior box on page 126, "Culture and the Müller-Lyer Illusion," discusses the important role that unique cultural experiences can play in perception.

Perception can also be influenced by an individual's expectations, motives, and interests. The term **perceptual set** refers to the tendency to perceive objects or situations from a particular frame of reference. Perceptual sets usually lead us to reasonably accurate conclusions. If they didn't, we would develop new perceptual sets that were more accurate. But sometimes a perceptual set can lead us astray. For example, someone with an avid interest in UFOs might readily interpret unusual cloud formations as a fleet of alien spacecraft. Sightings of Bigfoot, mermaids, and the Loch Ness monster that turn out to be brown bears, manatees, or floating logs are all examples of perceptual sets.

People are especially prone to seeing *faces* in ambiguous stimuli, as in the photos shown on previous page. Why? One reason is that the brain is wired to be uniquely responsive to faces or face-like stimuli (Leopold & Rhodes,

perceptual set The tendency to perceive objects or situations from a particular frame of reference.

CULTURE AND HUMAN BEHAVIOR

Culture and the Müller–Lyer Illusion: The Carpentered-World Hypothesis

Since the early 1900s, it has been known that people in industrialized societies are far more susceptible to the Müller-Lyer illusion than are people in some nonindustrialized societies (Matsumoto & Juang, 2008; Phillips, 2011). How can this difference be explained?

Cross-cultural psychologist Marshall Segall and his colleagues (1963, 1966) proposed the *carpentered-world hypothesis*. They suggested that people living in urban, industrialized environments have a great deal of perceptual experience in judging lines, corners, edges, and other rectangular, manufactured objects. Thus, people in carpentered cultures would be more susceptible to the Müller-Lyer illusion, which involves arrows mimicking a corner that is jutting toward or away from the perceiver.

In contrast, people who live in noncarpentered cultures more frequently encounter natural objects. In these cultures, perceptual experiences with straight lines and right angles are relatively rare. Segall predicted that people from these cultures would be less susceptible to the Müller-Lyer illusion.

To test this idea, Segall and his colleagues (1963, 1966) compared the responses of people living in carpentered societies, such as Evanston, Illinois, with those of people living in noncarpentered societies, such as remote areas of Africa. The results confirmed their hypothesis. The Müller-Lyer illusion was stronger for those living in carpentered societies. Could the difference in illusion susceptibility be due to some sort of biological difference rather than a cultural difference? To address this issue, psychologist V. Mary Stewart (1973) compared groups of white and African American schoolchildren living in Evanston, Illinois. Regardless of race, all of the children living in the city were equally susceptible to the Müller-Lyer illusion. Stewart also compared groups of black African children in five different areas of Zambia—ranging from the very carpentered capital city of Lusaka to rural, noncarpentered areas of the country. Once again, the African children living in the carpentered society of Lusaka were just as susceptible to

David Poole/Robert Harding Picture Library Ltd/Alamy

A Noncarpentered Environment People who live in urban, industrialized environments have a great deal of perceptual experience with straight lines, edges, and right angles. In contrast, people who live in a noncarpentered environment, like the village shown here, have little experience with right angles and perfectly straight lines (Phillips, 2011). Are people who grow up in a noncarpentered environment equally susceptible to the Müller-Lyer illusion?

the illusion as the Evanston children, but the African children living in the noncarpentered countryside were not.

These findings provided some of the first evidence for the idea that culture could shape perception. As Segall (1994) later concluded, "Every perception is the result of an interaction between a stimulus and a perceiver shaped by prior experience." Thus, people who grow up in very different cultures might well perceive aspects of their physical environment differently.

The $28,000 Grilled Cheese Sandwich: What Do You See? Is that Madonna on that grilled cheese sandwich? Ten years after she first noticed what she thought was the face of the Virgin Mary on her grilled cheese sandwich, Diana Duyser auctioned it off on eBay. The winning bid? Duyser got $28,000 for her carefully preserved (and partially eaten) relic. Why are we so quick to perceive human faces in ambiguous stimuli?

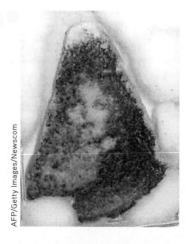

AFP/Getty Images/Newscom

2010; Pascalis & Kelly, 2009). Research by Doris Tsao and her colleagues (Tsao, 2006; Tsao & others, 2006) showed that the primate brain contains individual brain neurons that respond exclusively to faces or face-like images. This specialized face-recognition system allows us to identify an individual face out of the thousands that we can recognize (Kanwisher & Yovel, 2009).

But this extraordinary neural sensitivity also makes us more liable to false positives, seeing faces that aren't there. Vague or ambiguous images with face-like blotches and shadows can also trigger the brain's face-recognition system. Thus, we see faces where they don't exist at all—except in our own minds.

› Test your understanding of **Perception and Perceptual Illusions** with *LEARNINGCurve*.

Closing Thoughts

From reflections of light waves to perceptual illusions, the world you perceive is the result of complex interactions among distinctly dissimilar elements—environmental stimuli, sensory receptor cells, neural pathways, and brain mechanisms. Equally important are the psychological and cultural factors that help shape your perception of the world. As Mike's story illustrated, the world we experience relies not only on the functioning of our different sensory systems but also on neural pathways sculpted by years of learning experiences from infancy onward (Huber & others, 2015).

Alyson Aliano

"I Am Mike May...." "By getting some sight, I gained some new elements of my personality and lifestyle without rejecting the blindness. I am not a blind person or a sighted person. I am not even simply a visually impaired person. I am Mike May with his quirky sense of humor, graying hair, passion for life, and rather unusual combination of sensory skills."

Although he spent more than four decades totally blind, Mike never seemed to lack vision. With conviction, humor, and curiosity, he sought out a life of change and adventure. And he found it. Rather than expecting his surgery to fundamentally change his life, he simply welcomed the opportunity for new experiences. Throughout his life, Mike wrote, "I have sought change and thrive on it. I expected new and interesting experiences from getting vision as an adult but not that it would change my life" (May, 2004). As Mike points out, "My life was incredibly good before I had my operation. I've been very fortunate and had incredible opportunities, and so I can say that life was incredible. It was fantastic as a non-seeing person, and life is still amazing now that I have vision. That's been consistent between not seeing and seeing. Experiencing life to its fullest doesn't depend on having sight" (May, 2002).

We hope that learning about Mike's experiences has provided you with some insights as to how your own life experiences have helped shape your perceptions of the world. In the next section, we'll provide you with some tips that we think you'll find useful in influencing your perceptions of painful stimuli.

biofeedback Technique that involves using auditory or visual feedback to learn to exert voluntary control over involuntary body functions, such as heart rate, blood pressure, blood flow, and muscle tension.

acupuncture Traditional Chinese medical procedure involving the insertion and manipulation of fine needles into specific locations on the body to alleviate pain and treat illness; modern acupuncture sometimes involves sending electrical current through the needles rather than manipulating them.

PSYCH FOR YOUR LIFE

Strategies to Control Pain

Pain specialists use a variety of techniques to control pain, including *hypnosis* and *painkilling drugs* (Flor, 2014). We'll discuss both of these topics in the next chapter. Two other pain-relieving strategies are **biofeedback** and **acupuncture.**

Biofeedback is a process of learning voluntary control over largely automatic body functions, such as heart rate, blood pressure, blood flow, and muscle tension. Using sensitive equipment that signals subtle changes in a specific bodily function, people can learn to become more aware of their body's internal state. With the auditory or visual feedback provided by the biofeedback instrument, the person learns how to exercise conscious control over a particular bodily process.

For example, an individual who experiences chronic tension headaches might use biofeedback to learn to relax shoulder, neck, and facial muscles. Numerous studies have shown that

Peggy Peattie/San Diego Union-Tribune/ZUMA Press

Acupuncture for Pain Relief Dr. Kristin Bell is a primary care physician who uses acupuncture to treat veterans for chronic pain and other conditions. According to Bell, many of her patients "have been able to lower their meds, or even go off chronic narcotics altogether" (Steele, 2012). Along with pain relief, some patients report improvements in mood and sleep quality.

biofeedback is effective in helping people who experience tension headaches, migraine headaches, jaw pain, and back pain (deCharms & others, 2005; Nestoriuc & Martin, 2007).

Acupuncture is a pain-relieving technique that has been used in traditional Chinese medicine for thousands of years. In the United States, acupuncture has been practiced for about 200 years. Currently, about 3 million Americans each year seek acupuncture treatment for various types of pain (National Center for Complementary and Alternative Medicine, 2011).

Acupuncture involves inserting tiny, sterile needles at specific points in the body. The needles are then twirled, heated, or stimulated with a mild electrical current. Exactly how this stimulation diminishes pain signals or the perception of pain has yet to be completely explained (Moffet, 2008, 2009). Some research has shown that acupuncture stimulates the release of endorphins in the brain and may also inhibit the production of substance P (Field, 2009; Lee & others, 2009). Evidence suggests that psychological factors also play a significant role in the pain-relieving effects of acupuncture. Some early clinical studies found that true acupuncture was only slightly more effective than sham acupuncture in relieving pain (Madsen & others, 2009; Moffet, 2009). However, a meta-analysis of dozens of studies found that acupuncture was significantly more effective than sham acupuncture or usual-care treatment in relieving pain associated with chronic headaches, arthritis, and chronic back, neck, and shoulder pain (Avins, 2012; Vickers & others, 2012).

Along with pain relief, acupuncture is being scientifically evaluated as a treatment for other conditions, including anxiety, depression, fatigue related to cancer and other illnesses, and insomnia (see Barnett & others, 2014).

But what about everyday pain, such as the pain that accompanies a sprained ankle or a trip to the dentist? There are several simple techniques that you can use to help cope with minor pain.

Self-Administered Strategies

1. Distraction

By actively focusing your attention on some nonpainful task, you can often reduce pain (Edwards & others, 2009). For example, you can mentally count backward by sevens from 901, multiply pairs of two-digit numbers, draw different geometric figures in your mind, or count ceiling tiles. You can also focus on the details of a picture or other object.

Or try our favorite technique, which we'll dub the "iPod pain relief strategy." Intently listening to an interesting podcast or calming music can reduce discomfort (Loewy & Spintge, 2011; North & Hargreaves, 2009).

2. Imagery

Creating a vivid mental image can help control pain (Pincus & Sheikh, 2009). Usually people create a pleasant and progressive scenario, such as walking along the beach or hiking in the mountains. Try to imagine all the different sensations involved, including the sights, sounds, aromas, touches, and tastes. The goal is to become so absorbed in your fantasy that you distract yourself from sensations of pain.

3. Relaxation and meditation

Deep relaxation can be a very effective strategy for deterring pain sensations (Edwards & others, 2009; Turk & Winter, 2006). One simple relaxation strategy is deep breathing: Inhale deeply, then exhale very slowly and completely, releasing tension throughout your body. As you exhale, consciously note the feelings of relaxation and warmth you've produced in your body.

Several studies have shown that practicing meditation is an effective way to minimize pain (see Flor, 2014; Grant & others, 2010, 2011). Meditation may reduce the subjective experience of pain through multiple pathways, including relaxation, distraction, and inducing a sense of detachment from the painful experience. Apparently, you do not need to be an expert or long-term meditator to benefit from meditation's pain-relieving effects. Fadel Zeidan and his colleagues (2011) found that after just four 20-minute training sessions in a simple meditation technique, participants' ratings of the unpleasantness of a painful stimulus dropped by 57% and ratings of its intensity dropped by 40%. (We'll discuss meditation in more detail in the next chapter.)

4. Positive self-talk and reappraisal

This strategy involves making positive coping statements, either silently or out loud, during a painful episode or procedure. Examples of positive self-talk include statements such as, "It hurts, but I'm okay, I'm in control" and "I'm uncomfortable, but I can handle it."

Self-talk can also include reappraising or redefining the pain (Edwards & others, 2009). Substituting realistic and constructive thoughts about the pain experience for threatening or helpless thoughts can significantly reduce pain. For example, an athlete in training might say, "The pain means my muscles are getting stronger." Or consider the Marine Corps slogan: "Pain is weakness leaving the body."

Can Magnets Relieve Pain?

Our students frequently ask us about different *complementary and alternative medicines (CAMs).* Complementary and alternative medicines are a diverse group of health care systems, practices, or products that are *not* currently considered to be part of conventional medicine. Scientific evidence exists for some CAM therapies, such as the benefits of massage (Moyer & others, 2004). Therapies that are scientifically proven to be safe and effective usually become adopted by the mainstream health care system. However, the effectiveness and safety of many CAMs have not been proven by well-designed scientific studies.

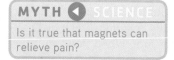

Magnets are one popular CAM that have been used for many centuries to treat pain. But can magnets relieve pain? To date, there is *no* evidence supporting the idea that magnets relieve pain (National Standard Monographs, 2009). The pain relief that some people experience could be due to a placebo effect or expectations that pain will decrease. Or the relief could come from whatever holds the magnet in place, such as a warm bandage or the cushioned insole (Weintraub & others, 2003).

One final note: The techniques described here are *not* a substitute for seeking appropriate medical attention, especially when pain is severe, recurring, or of unknown origin. If pain persists, seek medical attention.

CHAPTER REVIEW

KEY PEOPLE AND KEY TERMS

Max Wertheimer, p. 111

sensation, p. 86

perception, p. 86

sensory receptors, p. 87

transduction, p. 87

absolute threshold, p. 88

difference threshold, p. 88

Weber's law, p. 88

sensory adaptation, p. 88

subliminal perception, p. 89

mere exposure effect, p. 89

wavelength, p. 90

cornea, p. 91

pupil, p. 91

iris, p. 91

lens, p. 91

accommodation, p. 91

retina, p. 92

rods, p. 92

cones, p. 92

fovea, p. 92

optic disk, p. 92

Karl Duncker, p. 120

blind spot, p. 92

ganglion cells, p. 93

bipolar cells, p. 93

optic nerve, p. 93

optic chiasm, p. 94

color, p. 95

hue, p. 95

saturation, p. 95

brightness, p. 96

trichromatic theory of color vision, p. 96

color blindness, p. 96

afterimage, p. 97

opponent-process theory of color vision, p. 97

audition, p. 98

loudness, p. 98

amplitude, p. 98

decibel, p. 98

pitch, p. 98

frequency, p. 98

timbre, p. 99

outer ear, p. 99

eardrum, p. 99

middle ear, p. 99

inner ear, p. 99

cochlea, p. 99

basilar membrane, p. 100

hair cells, p. 100

frequency theory, p. 101

place theory, p. 102

olfaction, p. 102

gustation, p. 102

pheromones, p. 103

olfactory bulb, p. 104

taste buds, p. 105

pain, p. 106

nociceptors, p. 107

substance P, p. 107

gate-control theory of pain, p. 108

kinesthetic sense, p. 109

proprioceptors, p. 109

vestibular sense, p. 109

bottom-up processing, p. 111

top-down processing, p. 111

Gestalt psychology, p. 111

ESP (extrasensory perception), p. 112

parapsychology, p. 112

figure–ground relationship, p. 113

depth perception, p. 117

monocular cues, p. 117

binocular cues, p. 119

perceptual constancy, p. 121

size constancy, p. 121

shape constancy, p. 122

color constancy, p. 122

perceptual illusion, p. 123

Müller-Lyer illusion, p. 123

moon illusion, p. 124

perceptual set, p. 125

biofeedback, p. 127

acupuncture, p. 127

Sensation and Perception

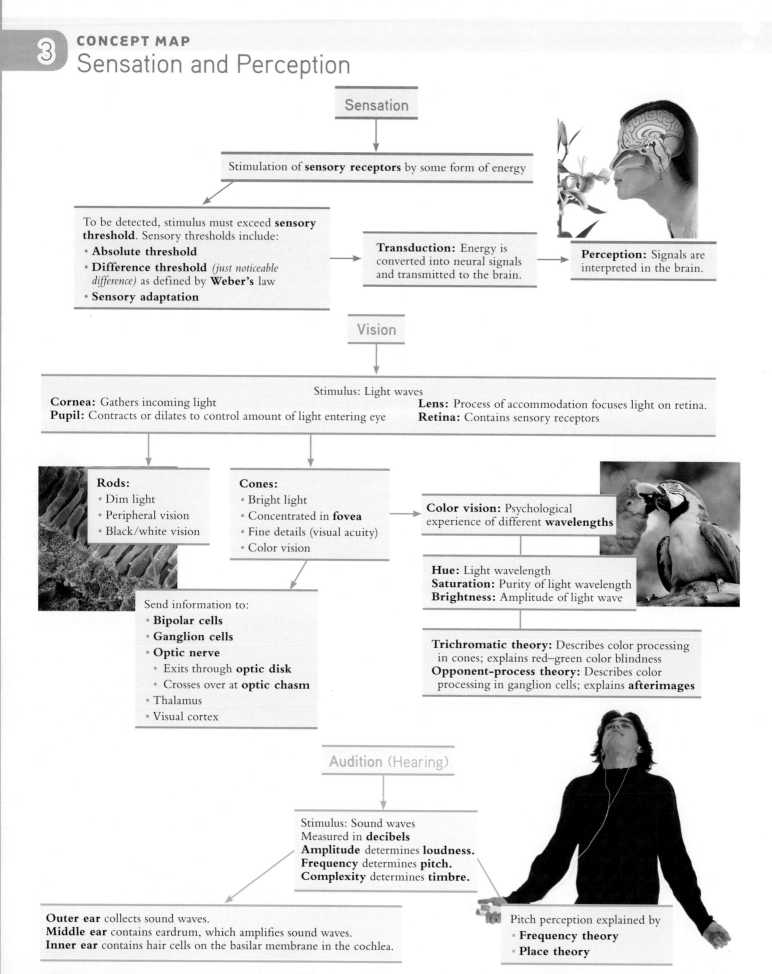

Sensation

Stimulation of **sensory receptors** by some form of energy

To be detected, stimulus must exceed **sensory threshold**. Sensory thresholds include:
- **Absolute threshold**
- **Difference threshold** (*just noticeable difference*) as defined by **Weber's law**
- **Sensory adaptation**

Transduction: Energy is converted into neural signals and transmitted to the brain.

Perception: Signals are interpreted in the brain.

Vision

Stimulus: Light waves

Cornea: Gathers incoming light
Pupil: Contracts or dilates to control amount of light entering eye
Lens: Process of accommodation focuses light on retina.
Retina: Contains sensory receptors

Rods:
- Dim light
- Peripheral vision
- Black/white vision

Cones:
- Bright light
- Concentrated in **fovea**
- Fine details (visual acuity)
- Color vision

Color vision: Psychological experience of different **wavelengths**

Hue: Light wavelength
Saturation: Purity of light wavelength
Brightness: Amplitude of light wave

Send information to:
- **Bipolar cells**
- **Ganglion cells**
- **Optic nerve**
  - Exits through **optic disk**
  - Crosses over at **optic chasm**
- Thalamus
- Visual cortex

Trichromatic theory: Describes color processing in cones; explains red–green color blindness
Opponent-process theory: Describes color processing in ganglion cells; explains **afterimages**

Audition (Hearing)

Stimulus: Sound waves
Measured in **decibels**
Amplitude determines **loudness**.
Frequency determines **pitch**.
Complexity determines **timbre**.

Outer ear collects sound waves.
Middle ear contains eardrum, which amplifies sound waves.
Inner ear contains hair cells on the basilar membrane in the cochlea.

Pitch perception explained by
- **Frequency theory**
- **Place theory**

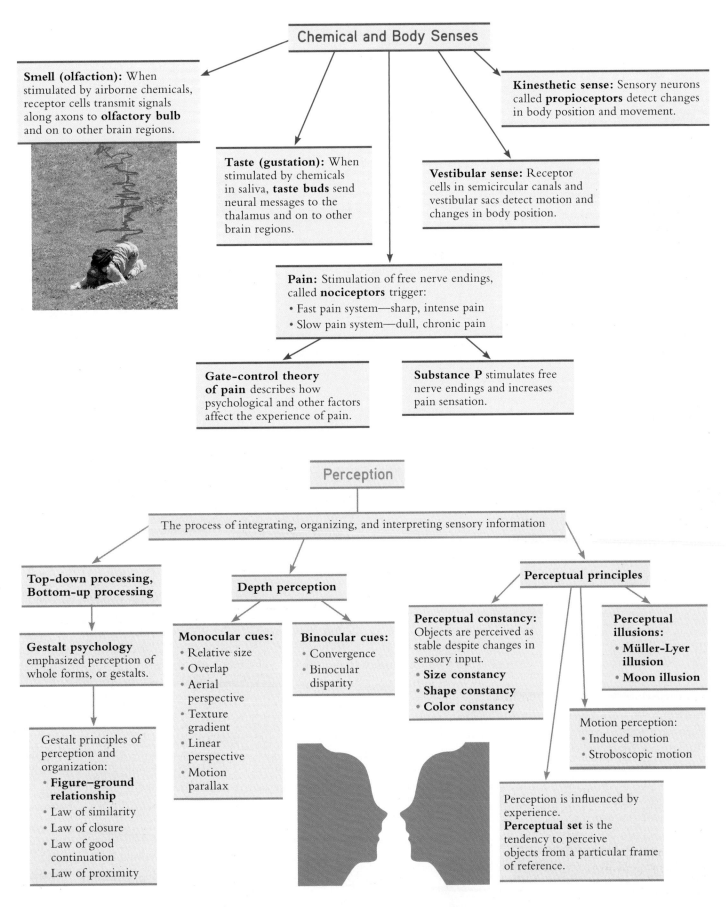

Chemical and Body Senses

Smell (olfaction): When stimulated by airborne chemicals, receptor cells transmit signals along axons to **olfactory bulb** and on to other brain regions.

Taste (gustation): When stimulated by chemicals in saliva, **taste buds** send neural messages to the thalamus and on to other brain regions.

Kinesthetic sense: Sensory neurons called **propioceptors** detect changes in body position and movement.

Vestibular sense: Receptor cells in semicircular canals and vestibular sacs detect motion and changes in body position.

Pain: Stimulation of free nerve endings, called **nociceptors** trigger:
- Fast pain system—sharp, intense pain
- Slow pain system—dull, chronic pain

Gate-control theory of pain describes how psychological and other factors affect the experience of pain.

Substance P stimulates free nerve endings and increases pain sensation.

Perception

The process of integrating, organizing, and interpreting sensory information

Top-down processing, Bottom-up processing

Gestalt psychology emphasized perception of whole forms, or gestalts.

Gestalt principles of perception and organization:
- **Figure–ground relationship**
- Law of similarity
- Law of closure
- Law of good continuation
- Law of proximity

Depth perception

Monocular cues:
- Relative size
- Overlap
- Aerial perspective
- Texture gradient
- Linear perspective
- Motion parallax

Binocular cues:
- Convergence
- Binocular disparity

Perceptual principles

Perceptual constancy: Objects are perceived as stable despite changes in sensory input.
- **Size constancy**
- **Shape constancy**
- **Color constancy**

Perceptual illusions:
- **Müller-Lyer illusion**
- **Moon illusion**

Motion perception:
- Induced motion
- Stroboscopic motion

Perception is influenced by experience.
Perceptual set is the tendency to perceive objects from a particular frame of reference.

MYTH (OR) SCIENCE?

Is it true . . .

- That multitasking is an efficient way to get things done?
- That you can have coherent conversations with people who are talking in their sleep?
- That sleeping pills are an effective way to treat chronic insomnia?
- That it can be dangerous to wake a sleepwalker?
- That you can be hypnotized against your will?
- That meditation is a drowsy, trancelike state that is no different from simple relaxation?
- That alcohol is a stimulant?

A KNIFE IN THE DARK

PROLOGUE

SCOTT HAD SOME SLEEPWALKING episodes as he was growing up, but his parents weren't overly concerned about them. Sleepwalking is pretty common among kids. "I remember Scott getting dressed at midnight, glassy-eyed, saying he had to go to school," Scott's mother recalled. Scott wasn't the only sleepwalker in the family. Two of his younger siblings were also sleepwalkers.

Scott's sister, Laura, remembers another sleepwalking incident. At the time, she was 15 and Scott was five years older. "Scott was getting ready to get married that June and he was coming up on college finals, and he was stressing," Laura recalled. Scott wandered into the kitchen with a glazed facial expression. As he reached the back door and began fumbling with the doorknob, Laura realized that her older brother was sleepwalking. She quickly leaned around him to lock the deadbolt. That's when Scott grabbed her. "He kind of lifted me up and tossed me," Laura recalls. "His face looked almost demonic when he reacted to me. It really scared the hell out of me."

Scott eventually married his high school sweetheart, Yarmila, and had two children. The family settled in Phoenix and Scott worked as a managing engineer for a technology company. By all accounts, Scott and Yarmila's marriage was happy, revolving around their children and Scott's involvement with a teen ministry program at their church.

During most of 1996, Scott was under tremendous pressure at work. A new product line that Scott's team had been developing—a hard-drive chip—was not living up to its promise.

Consciousness and Its Variations

IN THIS CHAPTER:

> **INTRODUCTION:** Consciousness: Experiencing the "Private I"

> Biological and Environmental "Clocks" That Regulate Consciousness

> Sleep

> Dreams and Mental Activity During Sleep

> Sleep Disorders

> Hypnosis

> Meditation

> Psychoactive Drugs

> **PSYCH FOR YOUR LIFE:** Overcoming Insomnia

But abandoning the project would also eliminate his co-workers' jobs. It was a no-win situation.

The work pressure continued. Scott often went for night after night with three hours of sleep or less. To stay alert and focused at work, he resorted to taking caffeine tablets, 200 milligrams a pop. After several nights in a row with very little sleep, Scott would "crash" early to catch up on his sleep.

Finally, Scott got into a heated exchange with his boss. It was decided that the following day Scott would meet with his work group and explain that their project would probably be cancelled.

At dinner that night, Scott discussed the troubling work situation with his family. Around 9:00 P.M., after the kids were in bed, Scott went out to the backyard to work on the broken swimming pool pump but eventually gave up.

Back in the house, Yarmila had fallen asleep on the couch in the family room, the television still on. It was close to 10:00 P.M. Scott kissed her goodnight, went upstairs, changed into his pajama bottoms, and "crashed."

Less than an hour later, Scott was startled awake by the sound of their two dogs barking wildly. Disoriented and confused, he rushed downstairs.

Two police officers, guns drawn, yelled at him to get facedown on the floor.

"What's going on?" Scott asked as he complied.

For an hour, Scott sat handcuffed in the back of a police car. He caught bits and pieces of the comments being made by the police officers and emergency personnel. At first he thought that Yarmila had been seriously hurt and that the police were searching for the person who had done it. But then he realized he was wrong. Yarmila was dead.

It was almost 2:00 A.M. when a Phoenix Police Department detective began interrogating Scott. "What set this thing off, got it going?" the detective asked.

As he sat huddled in the corner of the interrogation room, Scott replied, "Obviously, you think I killed her. I don't know what makes you think that."

"Because a neighbor watched you do it, that's why."

"I'm sorry. I don't remember doing it," Scott answered, then paused. "How did she die?"

"Well, the neighbor says you stabbed her and dragged her over to the pool and held her under the water. From what people are telling me about you guys, you spend a lot of time in the church. A quiet family, so this is really out of character. I want to know what went on, what would lead to something like this? What did she do to set you off like that?"

"Nothing."

"Okay, then what did *you* do to set yourself off like that? Something set you off, Scott."

"I'm sorry, I just don't know."

"Nothing went wrong?"

"I love my wife. I love my kids."

Scott had stabbed Yarmila 44 times, then left her floating facedown in the pool. But he had no memory of his actions.

Could Scott have unknowingly committed such violent acts while he was sleepwalking? Is it possible for someone to carry out complex actions, like driving, while asleep?

1-17-97 FRI
1:57:33 AM
PHOENIX POLICE DEPT.

In this chapter, we'll tackle those questions and others as we explore variations in our experience of consciousness. As you'll see, psychologists have learned a great deal about our daily fluctuations of consciousness. Psychologists have also gained insight into the different ways that alterations in consciousness can be induced, such as through the use of hypnosis, meditation, or psychoactive drugs. We'll return to Scott's story to help illustrate some of these concepts. □

Capturing the Stream of Consciousness One thought, memory, or fantasy seems to blend seamlessly into another.

INTRODUCTION:

Consciousness

EXPERIENCING THE "PRIVATE I"

KEY THEME

Consciousness refers to your immediate awareness of mental activity, internal sensations, and external stimuli.

KEY QUESTIONS

> What did William James mean by the phrase "stream of consciousness"?

> What are the functions of consciousness?

> How is attention defined, and how do the limitations of attention affect human thought and behavior?

Its nature is difficult to define precisely. For our purposes, we'll use a simple definition: **Consciousness** is your immediate awareness of your internal states—your thoughts, sensations, memories—and the external world around you.

Take a few moments to pay attention to your own experience of consciousness. You'll notice that the contents of your awareness shift from one moment to the next. Among other activities, your mental experience might include *focused attention* on this textbook; *awareness of internal sensations*, such as hunger or a throbbing headache; or *planning* and *active problem-solving*, such as mentally rehearsing an upcoming meeting with your adviser.

Even though your conscious experience is constantly changing, you don't experience your personal consciousness as disjointed. Rather, the subjective experience of consciousness has a sense of continuity. This characteristic of consciousness led the influential American psychologist **William James** (1892) to describe consciousness as a "stream" or "river." Despite the changing focus of our awareness, our experience of consciousness as an unbroken "stream" helps provide us with a sense of personal identity that has continuity from one day to the next.

Consciousness allows us to integrate past, present, and future behavior, guide future actions, and maintain a stable sense of self (Baumeister & Masicampo, 2010; Baumeister & others, 2011). And, it gives us the ability to plan and execute long-term, complex goals and communicate with others.

Our definition of consciousness refers to waking awareness. However, psychologists also study other types of conscious experience, which we'll consider later in the chapter. But first, we'll take a closer look at the nature of awareness.

Attention
THE MIND'S SPOTLIGHT

Lost in your thoughts, you don't notice when your instructor calls on you in class. "Pay attention!" your professor says impatiently.

But what *is* attention? In reality, you are always "paying attention" to *something*—just not always the stimuli that you're *supposed* to be paying attention to. For example, when your mind "wanders," you are focusing on your internal environment—your daydreams or thoughts—rather than your external environment (Smilek & others, 2010).

Like consciousness, *attention* is one of the oldest topics in psychology (Raz, 2009). And, like consciousness, attention is difficult to define precisely.

For our purposes, we'll define **attention** as the capacity to selectively focus senses and awareness on particular stimuli or aspects of the environment (Chun & others, 2011; Posner & Rothbart, 2007). Most of the time, we are able to deliberately control our attentional processes, which helps us regulate our thoughts and feelings. For example, we may deliberately turn our attention to a pleasant thought or memory when troubled by a painful memory (Baumeister & Masicampo, 2010; Baumeister & others, 2011).

Psychologists have identified a number of characteristics of attention, some of which have important implications for our daily life. These are:

1. *Attention has a limited capacity.*

At any given moment we are faced with more information than we can effectively process. We cannot pay attention to *all* of the sights, sounds, or other sensations in our external environments. Similarly, the range of potential thoughts, memories, or fantasies available to us at any given time is overwhelming. Thus, we focus our attention on the information that is most relevant to our immediate or long-term goals (Ristic & Enns, 2015).

2. *Attention is selective.*

Attention is often compared to a *spotlight* that we shine on particular external stimuli or internal thoughts. Like a spotlight, we focus on certain areas of our experience while ignoring others (Dijksterhuis & Aarts, 2010).

A classic example of the selective nature of attention is the *cocktail party effect* (Hill & Miller, 2010). If you're at a crowded, noisy party, you're literally engulfed in a sea of auditory stimuli. But, you are able to attend to one stream of speech while ignoring others that compete for your attention (Koch & others, 2011).

Although you can monitor multiple streams of information, you can only truly pay attention to one stream of speech at a time. So, at the same party, you are *somewhat* aware of information that is going on in the background, even though you're not actively paying attention to it (Raz, 2009). For example, if you hear your name mentioned by someone in a different conversational group, you will probably shift your attention to the other conversation and strain your ears to hear what is being said about you.

Alamy

Consciousness, then, does not appear to itself chopped up in bits. . . . It is nothing jointed; it flows. A "river" or a "stream" are the metaphors by which it is most naturally described. In talking of it hereafter, let us call it the stream of thought, or consciousness, of subjective life.

—*William James (1892)*

Everyone knows what attention is. It is the taking possession by the mind, in clear and vivid form, of one out of what seem several simultaneously possible objects or trains of thought. . . . It implies withdrawal from some things in order to deal effectively with others.

—*William James (1890)*

consciousness Personal awareness of mental activities, internal sensations, and the external environment.

attention The capacity to selectively focus awareness on particular stimuli in your external environment or on your internal thoughts or sensations.

Did You See That Clown? Do you think you would notice if a unicycling clown crossed your path? Probably—unless you were using a cell phone! Fully three-quarters of students who were talking on cell phones did not see this clown as they walked across a busy campus square—an example of *inattentional blindness* (Hyman & others, 2010).

Photo courtesy Ira Hyman. © John Wiley & Sons, Ltd

LaunchPad

Worth Publishers

Think you're good at paying attention? Try **Video Activity: Attention.**

FIGURE 4.1(A) Can We Read Your Mind? We'd like you to participate in a mind-reading experiment. Please follow all directions as carefully as you can. First, pick one of the six cards below and remember it.

3. *Attention can be "blind."*

Given the limited, selective nature of attention, you shouldn't be surprised to learn that we often completely miss what seem to be obvious stimuli in our field of vision or hearing. For example, magicians exploit the limited, selective nature of attention with a strategy called *misdirection* (Lamont & others, 2010). They deliberately draw the audience's attention away from the "method," or secret action, and toward the "effect," which refers to what the magician wants the audience to perceive (Macknik & others, 2008). To experience a bit of magic firsthand, direct your attention to Figure 4.1.

Magicians also exploit a basic human tendency known as *inattentional blindness,* which occurs when we simply don't notice some significant object or event that is in our clear field of vision (Mack & Rock, 2000). Because we have a limited capacity for attention, the more attention we devote to one task, the less we have for another. Thus, when we are engaged in one task that demands a great deal of our attention, we may fail to notice an event or object, especially if it is unexpected or unusual.

For example, if a clown on a unicycle crossed your path while you were walking across campus, do you think you would notice? Psychologist Ira Hyman enlisted a student to dress up as a clown and slowly unicycle across a busy campus square (Hyman & others, 2010). Researchers later stopped people whose paths had crossed with the unicycling clown and asked them whether they had seen him. Most of the people who were walking alone, in pairs, or who were listening to iPods *did* notice the clown. However, only one-quarter of those talking on cell phones noticed the clown.

We can also experience *inattentional deafness* (Macdonald & Lavie, 2011). Most of us have been so engrossed in a book or video that we failed to hear a roommate's question.

Say its name aloud several times so you won't forget it. Once you're sure you'll remember it, circle one of the eyes in the row to the right. Then turn to page 138.

Finally, *change blindness* is also relatively common. Change blindness refers to not noticing when something changes, such as when a friend gets a haircut or shaves his beard (Rosielle & Scaggs, 2008). Were you fooled by the magic trick in Figure 4.1? If so, you can blame change blindness.

The Perils of Multitasking

Multitasking refers to paying attention to two or more sources of stimuli at once—such as doing homework while watching television, or talking on the phone while cooking dinner. In essence, Multitasking involves the *division of attention*. When attention is divided among different tasks, each task receives less attention than it would normally (Borst & others, 2010; Lavie, 2010). Some people *are* better at handling multiple tasks than others (Seegmiller & others, 2011). However, people generally underestimate the costs of multitasking. When you attempt to do two things at once—such as talk on the phone while studying—your performance on *both* tasks is impaired (Finley & others, 2014).

In general, tasks that are very different are less likely to interfere with each other. There is evidence that visual and auditory tasks draw on independent, different attention resources—at least for simple, well-rehearsed tasks. For example, listening to the radio (an auditory task) interferes less with driving (a visual task) than would a second visual task (Borst & others, 2010). However, this is *not* the case when one of the tasks requires a great deal of concentration. Absorption in a visual task can produce inattentional deafness, and absorption in an auditory task can produce inattentional blindness (Macdonald & Lavie, 2011).

The perils of divided attention are especially obvious when people use cell phones. As demonstrated by the unicycling clown study, using a cell phone seems to absorb a great deal of attentional resources. Partly because cell phone conversations can be so absorbing, they are especially likely to produce inattentional blindness (Chabris & Simons, 2010). One study found that driving was more impaired when drivers were talking on a cell phone than when the same drivers were legally drunk (Strayer & others, 2006). And, it turns out, using a headset or Bluetooth device while driving does not improve safety. It's the *attention* devoted to the conversation that is dangerously distracting to drivers (see Baumeister & others, 2011; Drews & others, 2008). In fact, the National Safety Council (2014) found that cell phone use was involved in more than a quarter of motor vehicle crashes in 2012—that's *1.5 million* accidents!

Distractions are just one factor that affects the quality of awareness. We'll begin our exploration of variations in consciousness by looking at the biological rhythms that help determine the nature and quality of our daily conscious experience.

Biological and Environmental "Clocks" That Regulate Consciousness

KEY THEME

Many body functions, including mental alertness, are regulated by circadian rhythms, which systematically vary over a 24-hour period.

KEY QUESTIONS

> How do light, the suprachiasmatic nucleus, and melatonin regulate the sleep–wake cycle?

> What is jet lag, and what causes it?

Throughout the course of each day, consciousness ebbs and flows in a natural rhythm. Along with our daily cycle of wakefulness and sleep, researchers have identified more than 100 processes that rhythmically peak and dip at consistent times each day. These variations in physiological or behavioral activities are called *circadian rhythms.*

MYTH ◄ SCIENCE
Is it true that multitasking is an efficient way to get things done?

Think Like a SCIENTIST
Are *you* good at working on several tasks at once? Go to LaunchPad: Resources to **Think Like a Scientist** about **Multitasking**.

LaunchPad

The Emergence of Circadian Rhythms Consistent daily variations in movement, heart rate, and other variables are evident during the fifth month of gestation in the human fetus. After birth, the synchronization of infants' circadian rhythms to a day–night cycle usually occurs by 2 or 3 months of age (Mistlberger & Rusak, 2005). Daytime exposure to bright light helps establish these regular rest–activity circadian rhythms.

Camille Tokerud/Getty Images

circadian rhythm (ser-KADE-ee-en) A cycle or rhythm that is roughly 24 hours long; the cyclical daily fluctuations in biological and psychological processes.

suprachiasmatic nucleus (SCN) (soup-ruh-kye-az-MAT-ick) A cluster of neurons in the hypothalamus in the brain that governs the timing of circadian rhythms.

melatonin (mel-uh-TONE-in) A hormone manufactured by the pineal gland that produces sleepiness.

TABLE 4.1

Examples of Human Circadian Rhythms

Function	Typical Circadian Rhythm
Peak mental alertness and memory	Two daily peaks: around 9:00 A.M. and 9:00 P.M.
Lowest body temperature	About 97°F around 4:00 A.M.
Highest body temperature	About 99°F around 4:00 P.M.
Peak hearing, visual, taste, and smell sensitivity	Two daily peaks: around 3:00 A.M. and 6:00 P.M.
Lowest sensitivity to pain	Around 4:00 P.M.
Peak sensitivity to pain	Around 4:00 A.M.
Peak degree of sleepiness	Two daily peaks: around 3:00 A.M. and 3:00 P.M.
Peak melatonin hormone in blood	Between 1:00 A.M. and 3:00 A.M.

SOURCES: Information from Campbell (1997); Czeisler & Dijk (2001); Refinetti (2000); M. Young (2000).

Want to Sleep Better? Turn Off That Screen! Smartphone, tablet, and laptop screens all emit blue light, which mimics daylight, increasing alertness and suppressing melatonin. A recent study by Anne-Marie Chang and her colleagues (2015) compared the effects of reading a print book with reading a light-emitting e-book two hours before bedtime. They found that the e-book readers took longer to fall asleep, had disrupted sleep patterns, and were less alert the next day than the print book readers. Melatonin production was also lower in the e-book users.

leungchopan/Shutterstock

The word *circadian* combines the Latin words for "about" and "day." So, the term **circadian rhythm** refers to a biological or psychological process that systematically varies over the course of each day. Table 4.1 lists examples of circadian rhythms.

The Suprachiasmatic Nucleus
THE BODY'S CLOCK

Your many circadian rhythms are controlled by a master biological clock—a tiny cluster of neurons in the *hypothalamus* in the brain. This cluster of neurons is called the **suprachiasmatic nucleus,** abbreviated **SCN** (see Figure 4.2). The SCN is the internal pacemaker that governs the timing of circadian rhythms, including the sleep–wake cycle.

Environmental cues are also involved in keeping the circadian rhythms synchronized. The most important of these cues is bright light, especially sunlight, but exposure to artificial light, including that generated by computer or tablet screens, also influences circadian rhythms (Dijk & others, 2012; Münch & others, 2012). In humans, light detected by special photoreceptors in the eye sends signals via the optic nerve to the SCN in the hypothalamus (Drouyer & others, 2007).

As the sun sets, the decrease in available light is detected by the SCN through its connections with the visual system. In turn, the SCN triggers an increase in the production of a hormone called **melatonin.** Melatonin is manufactured by the *pineal gland,* an endocrine gland located in the brain.

Increased blood levels of melatonin help make you sleepy and reduce activity levels. Blood levels of melatonin rise at night, peaking between 1:00 and 3:00 A.M. Shortly before sunrise, the pineal gland all but stops producing melatonin, and you soon wake up. As the sun rises, exposure to sunlight and other bright light suppresses melatonin levels, and they remain very low throughout the day. In this way, sunlight regulates, or *entrains,* the SCN so that it keeps your circadian cycles synchronized and operating on a 24-hour schedule.

FIGURE 4.1(B) Take a close look. Is your card missing? If so, we correctly identified the card you chose! Did we successfully read your mind? Or could there be another explanation? If you can't figure out how we performed this magic trick, you can find the solution on page 177.

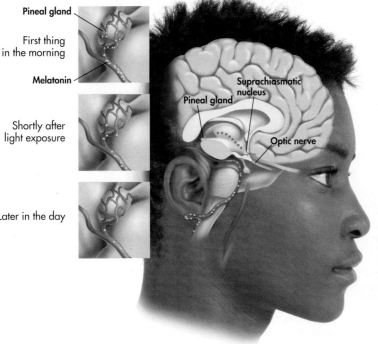

Pineal gland

First thing in the morning

Melatonin

Shortly after light exposure

Later in the day

Suprachiasmatic nucleus

Pineal gland

Optic nerve

Image Source/ Punchstock

FIGURE 4.2 The Biological Clock Special photoreceptors in the retina regulate the effects of light on the body's circadian rhythms (Menaker, 2003). In response to morning light, signals from these special photoreceptors are relayed via the optic nerve to the suprachiasmatic nucleus. In turn, the suprachiasmatic nucleus reduces the pineal gland's production of melatonin, a hormone that causes sleepiness. As blood levels of melatonin decrease, mental alertness increases. Daily exposure to bright light, especially sunlight, helps keep the body's circadian rhythms synchronized and operating on a 24-hour schedule.

In the absence of external time cues, our internal body clock drifts to its natural—or *intrinsic*—rhythm. Interestingly, our intrinsic circadian rhythm is about 24.2 hours, or slightly *longer* than a day (Czeisler & Gooley, 2007). When there are no external time cues, our normally coordinated circadian rhythms become desynchronized.

Exposure to environmental time signals is necessary for us to stay precisely synchronized, or *entrained,* to a 24-hour day. When environmental signals are out of sync with your internal body clock, such as when you travel and cross multiple time zones, you may experience symptoms of *jet lag.* You experience physical and mental fatigue, confusion or problems concentrating, depression or irritability, and disrupted sleep (Eastman & others, 2005). For many people, it can take up to a week or longer to readjust to an extreme time change. People who work the night shift or swing shift can also experience jet lag symptoms.

〉 Test your understanding of **Consciousness and Biological Clocks** with **LEARNING***Curve*.

Sleep

KEY THEME

Modern sleep research began with the invention of the electroencephalograph and the discovery that sleep is marked by distinct physiological processes and stages.

KEY QUESTIONS

〉 What characterizes sleep onset, the NREM sleep stages, and REM sleep?

〉 What is the typical progression of sleep cycles? How do sleep patterns change over the lifespan?

〉 What evidence suggests that we have a biological need for sleep?

From Aristotle to Shakespeare to Freud, history is filled with examples of scholars, writers, and scientists who have been fascinated by sleep and dreams. But prior to the twentieth century, there was no objective way to study the internal processes that might be occurring during sleep. Instead, sleep was largely viewed as a period of restful inactivity in which dreams sometimes occurred.

Tony Savino/The Image Works

Circadian Rhythms and People Who Are Blind This college student, who has been blind since birth, confidently navigates her college campus with the help of her guide dog. Many people with total blindness have desynchronized circadian rhythms because they're unable to detect the sunlight that normally sets the body's internal biological clock, the SCN. Like sighted people deprived of all environmental time cues, blind people can experience desynchronized melatonin, body temperature, and sleep–wake circadian cycles. Consequently, about 60 percent of blind people suffer from recurring bouts of insomnia and other sleep problems (Arendt & others, 2005; Mistlberger & Skene, 2005).

electroencephalograph (e-lec-tro-en-SEFF-uh-low-graph) An instrument that uses electrodes placed on the scalp to measure and record the brain's electrical activity.

EEG (electroencephalogram) The graphic record of brain activity produced by an electroencephalograph.

REM sleep Type of sleep during which rapid eye movements (REM) and dreaming usually occur and voluntary muscle activity is suppressed; also called *active sleep* or *paradoxical sleep*.

NREM sleep Quiet, typically dreamless sleep in which rapid eye movements are absent; divided into four stages; also called *quiet sleep*.

beta brain waves Brain-wave pattern associated with alert wakefulness.

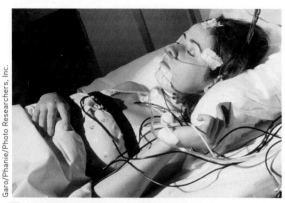

Garo/Phanie/Photo Researchers, Inc.

Wired for Sleep Using electrodes pasted to the scalp, the *electroencephalogram* (EEG) detects changes in the brain's electrical activity. Other instruments record eye and muscle movements, respirations, heart rate, and airflow. Although it may look uncomfortable, most people involved in sleep studies become oblivious to the electrodes and wires as they drift into sleep (Carskadon & Rechtschaffen, 2005).

The Dawn of Modern Sleep Research

The invention of the **electroencephalograph** by German psychiatrist Hans Berger in the 1920s gave sleep researchers an important tool for measuring the rhythmic electrical activity of the brain (Stern, 2001). These rhythmical patterns of electrical activity are referred to as *brain waves.* The electroencephalograph produces a graphic record called an **EEG,** or **electroencephalogram.** By studying EEGs, sleep researchers firmly established that brain-wave activity systematically changes throughout sleep.

Along with brain activity, today's sleep researchers monitor a variety of other physical functions during sleep. Eye movements, muscle movements, breathing rate, airflow, pulse, blood pressure, amount of exhaled carbon dioxide, body temperature, and breathing sounds are just some of the body's functions that are measured in contemporary sleep research (Carskadon & Dement, 2005).

What happens during sleep? Most people tend to think of sleep as an "either/or" condition—the brain is *either* awake and active *or* asleep and idle. In fact, sleep researchers know that the sleeping brain doesn't just shut down during sleep. The sleeping brain remains active, although its patterns of activity are distinctly different from the patterns displayed by the waking brain.

Research also disputes the notion that sleep is a global, brain-wide state (Colwell, 2011). It turns out that during sleep, some brain areas, and even some brain neurons, remain active, while others do not (Nir & others, 2011; Vyazovskiy & others, 2011).

Sleep researchers distinguish between two basic types of sleep. **REM sleep,** or *rapid-eye-movement sleep,* is often called *active sleep* or *paradoxical sleep* because it is associated with heightened body and brain activity during which dreaming consistently occurs. **NREM sleep,** or *non-rapid-eye-movement sleep,* is often referred to as *quiet sleep* because the body's physiological functions and brain activity slow down during this period of slumber. Usually pronounced as "non-REM sleep," it is further divided into four stages, as we'll describe shortly.

The Onset of Sleep and Hypnagogic Hallucinations

Awake and reasonably alert as you prepare for bed, your brain generates small, fast brain waves, called **beta brain waves.** After your head hits the pillow and you close your eyes, your muscles relax. Your brain's electrical activity gradually gears down, generating slightly larger and slower **alpha brain waves.**

During this drowsy, presleep phase, you may experience odd but vividly realistic sensations. You may hear your name called or a loud crash, feel as if you're falling, floating, or flying, or see kaleidoscopic patterns or an unfolding landscape. These brief, vivid sensory phenomena that occasionally occur during the transition to light sleep are called **hypnagogic hallucinations.** Some hypnagogic hallucinations can be so vivid or startling that they cause a sudden awakening (Vaughn & D'Cruz, 2005). Hypnagogic imagery may also reflect daily activities and preoccupations. For example, about a third of participants who learned a new video game, *Alpine Racer II,* reported hypnagogic images related to the skiing game (Schwartz, 2010; Wamsley & others, 2010).

IN FOCUS

What You Really Want to Know About Sleep

Why do I yawn?

Researchers aren't certain. But the notion that too little oxygen or too much carbon dioxide causes yawning is not supported by research. Some evidence suggests that yawning regulates and increases your level of arousal. Yawning is typically followed by an *increase* in activity level. Hence, you frequently yawn after waking up in the morning, while attempting to stay awake in the late evening, or when you're bored.

Is yawning contagious?

Seeing, hearing, or thinking about yawning can trigger a yawn. More than half of adults will yawn when they're shown videos of other people yawning. Blind people will yawn more frequently in response to audio recordings of yawning. Some psychologists believe that contagious yawning is related to our ability to feel empathy for others. (Have you yawned yet?) Interestingly, chimpanzees and macaques, both highly social animals, display contagious yawning. And so do domestic dogs, which in a recent study were shown to "catch" yawns from human strangers. From an evolutionary perspective, such observations lend support to the idea that contagious yawning may have evolved as an adaptive social cue, allowing groups to signal and coordinate times of activity and rest. In support of that view, a new study found that chimpanzees yawn more after viewing iTouch videos of other chimpanzees yawning—but *only* if the chimps were members of their own social group.

Mark Wilson/Getty Images

Why do I get sleepy?

A naturally occurring compound in the body called *adenosine* may be the culprit. In studies with cats, prolonged wakefulness sharply increases adenosine levels, which reflect energy used for brain and body activity. As adenosine levels shoot up, so does the need for sleep. Slow-wave NREM sleep reduces adenosine levels. In humans, the common stimulant drug caffeine blocks adenosine receptors, promoting wakefulness.

Sometimes in the morning when I first wake up, I can't move. I'm literally paralyzed! Is this normal?

REM sleep is characterized by paralysis of the voluntary muscles, which keeps you from acting out your dreams. In a relatively common phenomenon called **sleep paralysis,** the paralysis of REM sleep carries over to the waking state for up to 10 minutes. If preceded by an unpleasant dream or hypnagogic experience, this sensation can be frightening. Sleep paralysis can also occur as you're falling asleep. In either case, the sleep paralysis lasts for only a few minutes. So, if this happens to you, relax—voluntary muscle control will soon return.

Do deaf people who use sign language sometimes "sleep-sign" during sleep?

Yes.

Do the things people say when they talk in their sleep make any sense?

Sleeptalking typically occurs during NREM stages 3 and 4. There are many anecdotes of spouses who have supposedly engaged their sleeptalking mates in extended conversations, but sleep researchers

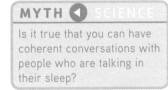

MYTH • SCIENCE

Is it true that you can have coherent conversations with people who are talking in their sleep?

have been unsuccessful in having extended dialogues with people who chronically talk in their sleep. As for the truthfulness of the sleeptalker's utterances, they're reasonably accurate insofar as they reflect whatever the person is responding to while asleep. By the way, not only do people talk in their sleep, but they can also sing or laugh in their sleep. In one case we know of, a little boy sleep-sang "Frosty the Snowman."

SOURCES: Campbell & de Waal (2011); Campbell & others (2009); Cartwright (2004); Empson (2002); Joly-Mascheroni & others (2008); Landolt (2008); Platek & others (2005); Pressman (2007); Rétey & others (2005); Romero & others, 2013; Takeuchi & others (2002).

Probably the most common hypnagogic hallucination is the vivid sensation of falling, which is often accompanied by a *myoclonic jerk*—an involuntary muscle spasm of the whole body that jolts the person completely awake. Also known as *sleep starts,* these experiences can seem really weird (or embarrassing) when they occur, but they are normal events that sometimes occur during sleep onset (Mahowald, 2005).

The First 90 Minutes of Sleep and Beyond

The course of a normal night's sleep follows a relatively consistent cyclical pattern. As you drift off to sleep, you enter NREM sleep and begin a progression through

alpha brain waves Brain-wave pattern associated with relaxed wakefulness and drowsiness.

hypnagogic hallucinations (hip-na-GAH-jick) Vivid sensory phenomena that occur during the onset of sleep.

sleep paralysis A temporary condition in which a person is unable to move upon awakening in the morning or during the night.

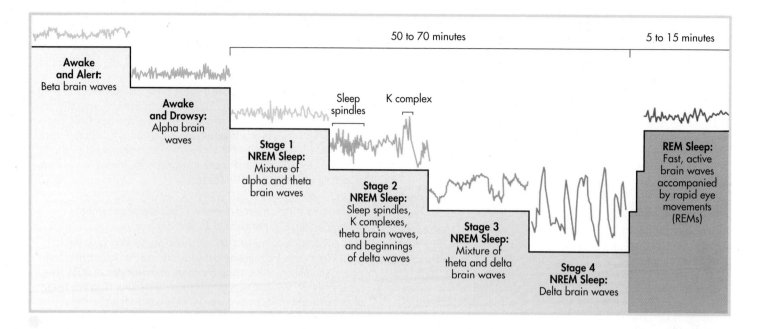

FIGURE 4.3 The First 90 Minutes of Sleep From wakefulness to the deepest sleep of stage 4 NREM, the brain's activity, measured by EEG recordings, progressively diminishes, as demonstrated by larger and slower brain waves. The four NREM stages occupy the first 50 to 70 minutes of sleep. Then, in a matter of minutes, the brain cycles back to smaller, faster brain waves, and the sleeper experiences the night's first episode of dreaming REM sleep, which lasts 5 to 15 minutes. During the rest of the night, the sleeper continues to experience 90-minute cycles of alternating NREM and REM sleep.

Source: Data from Carskadon & Dement (2005).

the four NREM sleep stages (see Figure 4.3). Each progressive NREM sleep stage is characterized by corresponding decreases in brain and body activity. On average, the progression through the first four stages of NREM sleep occupies the first 50 to 70 minutes of sleep.

STAGE 1 NREM

As the alpha brain waves of drowsiness are replaced by even slower *theta brain waves*, you enter the first stage of sleep. Lasting only a few minutes, stage 1 is a transitional stage during which you gradually disengage from the sensations of the surrounding world. During stage 1 NREM, you can quickly regain conscious alertness if needed. Although hypnagogic experiences can occur in stage 1, less vivid mental imagery is common, such as imagining yourself engaged in some everyday activity.

STAGE 2 NREM

Stage 2 represents the onset of true sleep. Stage 2 sleep is defined by the appearance of **sleep spindles,** brief bursts of brain activity that last a second or two, and **K complexes,** single high-voltage spikes of brain activity (see Figure 4.3). Other than these occasional sleep spindles and K complexes, brain activity continues to slow down. Theta waves are predominant in stage 2, but larger, slower brain waves, called *delta brain waves,* also begin to emerge. During the 15 to 20 minutes initially spent in stage 2, delta brain-wave activity gradually increases.

STAGE 3 AND STAGE 4 NREM

In combination, stages 3 and 4 are often referred to as *slow-wave sleep* (SWS). Both stages are defined by the amount of delta brain-wave activity. When delta brain waves represent more than 20 percent of total brain activity, the sleeper is said to be in stage 3 NREM. When delta brain waves exceed 50 percent of total brain activity, the sleeper is said to be in stage 4 NREM.

During the 20 to 40 minutes spent in the night's first episode of stage 4 NREM, delta waves eventually come to represent 100 percent of brain activity. At that point, heart rate, blood pressure, and breathing rate drop to their lowest levels. Not surprisingly, the sleeper is almost completely oblivious to the world. Noises as loud as 90 decibels may fail to wake him. However, his muscles are still capable of movement. For example, sleepwalking typically occurs during stage 4 NREM sleep.

It can easily take 15 minutes or longer to regain full waking consciousness from stage 4. It's even possible to answer your cell phone or respond to a text message, carry

sleep spindles Short bursts of brain activity that characterize stage 2 NREM sleep.

K complex Single but large high-voltage spike of brain activity that characterizes stage 2 NREM sleep.

on a conversation for several minutes, and hang up without ever leaving stage 4 sleep—and without remembering having done so the next day. When people are briefly awakened by sleep researchers during stage 4 NREM and asked to perform some simple task, they often don't remember it the next morning.

Thus far, the sleeper is approximately 70 minutes into a typical night's sleep and immersed in deeply relaxed stage 4 NREM sleep. At this point, the sequence reverses. In a matter of minutes, the sleeper cycles back from stage 4 to stage 3 to stage 2 and enters a dramatic new phase: the night's first episode of REM sleep.

REM SLEEP

During REM sleep, the brain becomes more active, generating smaller and faster brain waves. Visual and motor neurons in the brain activate repeatedly, just as they do during wakefulness. Dreams usually occur during REM sleep. Although the brain is very active, voluntary muscle activity is suppressed, which prevents the dreaming sleeper from acting out her dreams.

REM sleep is accompanied by considerable physiological arousal. The sleeper's eyes dart back and forth behind closed eyelids—the rapid eye movements. Heart rate, blood pressure, and respirations can fluctuate up and down, sometimes extremely. Muscle twitches occur. In both sexes, sexual arousal may occur, which is not necessarily related to dream content.

This first REM episode tends to be brief, about 5 to 15 minutes. From the beginning of stage 1 NREM sleep through the completion of the first episode of REM sleep, about 90 minutes have elapsed.

BEYOND THE FIRST 90 MINUTES

Throughout the rest of the night, the sleeper cycles between NREM and REM sleep. Each sleep cycle lasts about 90 minutes on average, but the duration of cycles may vary from 70 to 120 minutes. Usually, four more 90-minute cycles of NREM and REM sleep occur during the night. Just before and after REM periods, the sleeper typically shifts position.

The progression of a typical night's sleep cycles is depicted in Figure 4.4. Stages 3 and 4 REM, slow-wave sleep, usually occur only during the first two 90-minute cycles. As the night

Synchronized Sleepers As these time-lapse photographs show, couples who regularly sleep in the same bed tend to have synchronized sleep cycles. Since bed partners fall asleep at about the same time, they are likely to have similarly timed NREM–REM sleep cycles. The movements of this couple are also synchronized. Both sleepers shift position just before and after episodes of REM sleep.

FIGURE 4.4 The 90-Minute Cycles of Sleep During a typical night, you experience five 90-minute cycles of alternating NREM and REM sleep. The deepest stages of NREM sleep, stages 3 and 4, occur during the first two 90-minute cycles. Dreaming REM sleep episodes become progressively longer as the night goes on. Shifts in sleep position, indicated by the dots, usually occur immediately before and after REM episodes.

Source: Data from Hobson (2004).

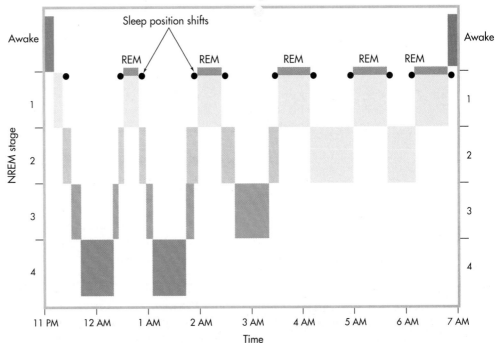

progresses, REM sleep episodes become increasingly longer, and less time is spent in NREM sleep. During the last two 90-minute sleep cycles before awakening, NREM sleep is composed primarily of stage 2 sleep and periods of REM sleep that can last as long as 40 minutes. In a later section, we'll look at dreaming and REM sleep in more detail.

Sleep-Deprived Adolescents Circadian rhythms shift in adolescence. Adolescents tend to fall asleep later and wake up later. Few teenagers get the 8.5 to 9 hours of sleep that they need to feel fully rested. In the U.S., more than two-thirds of teenagers report that they get less than 7 hours of sleep on school nights, which is probably why they tend to sleep about 2 hours longer on weekends. Consequences of regular sleep loss include poor school performance, increased risk of accidents and injuries, and depressed mood (Colrain & Baker, 2011).

CHANGING SLEEP PATTERNS OVER THE LIFESPAN

As any parent knows, sleep patterns change throughout childhood and adolescence. Circadian rhythms seem to develop before birth. Consistent daily variations in movement, heart rate, and other variables are evident by the fifth month of prenatal development. During the third trimester of prenatal development, active (REM) and quiet (NREM) sleep cycles emerge. In the final weeks, REM and NREM sleep are clearly distinguishable in the fetus (Mirmiran & others, 2003).

The newborn sleeps about 16 hours a day, though not all at once. Up to 8 hours—or 50 percent—of the newborn's sleep time is spent in REM sleep. The rest is spent in quiet sleep that is very similar to NREM stages 1 and 2. It's not until about the third month of life that the deep, slow-wave sleep of NREM stages 3 and 4 appears.

The typical 90-minute sleep cycles gradually emerge over the first few years of life. The infant's sleep during the first months of life is characterized by shorter 60-minute sleep cycles, producing up to 13 sleep cycles per day. By age 2, the toddler is experiencing 75-minute sleep cycles. By age 5, the typical 90-minute sleep cycles of alternating REM and NREM sleep are established (Grigg-Damberger & others, 2007).

From childhood through late adulthood, the pattern of a typical night's sleep evolves and changes (see Figure 4.5). Total sleep time decreases, as does the percentage of a night's sleep spent in deeper slow-wave sleep. This is offset by gradual increases in the percentage of time spent each night in lighter NREM stages 1 and 2. The percentage of a night's sleep devoted to REM sleep increases during childhood and adolescence, remains stable throughout adulthood, and then decreases during late adulthood (Ohayon & others, 2004).

Why Do We Sleep?

It may seem obvious: We sleep because we're tired and need rest. Thus, it may surprise you to learn that sleep researchers aren't really sure *why* we sleep. Recent research by Lulu Xie and her colleagues (2013) revealed that sleep initiates a process

FIGURE 4.5 Sleep over the Lifespan
Sleep quality changes significantly over the lifespan. In particular, notice that slow-wave sleep decreases over the lifespan, as does total sleep time. By middle adulthood, people are more likely to experience wakefulness after sleep onset. Adults aged 55 years and older often take longer to fall asleep, which is technically called *sleep latency* (Bootzin & Epstein, 2011).

Source: Republished with permission of American Academy of Sleep Medicine, from Ohayon, M. M.; Carskadon, M. A.; Guilleminault, C.; & Vitiello, M. V. (2004). Meta-analysis of quantitative sleep parameters from childhood to old age in healthy individuals: Developing normative sleep values across the human lifespan. Sleep, 27(7), 1255–1273; permission conveyed through Copyright Clearance Center, Inc.

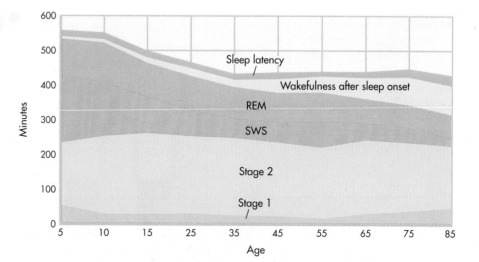

Wayne R Bilenduke/Getty Images

Nature Production/Nature Picture Library

that clears metabolic waste products from the brain. But sleep serves other functions as well (see Underwood, 2013). Along with providing needed rest to muscles and body, sleep is thought to maintain immune system function, improve brain function, enhance learning and consolidate memory, and help regulate moods and emotion (Roth & others, 2010; Walker & Van der Helm, 2009).

However, these explanations don't account for the enormous variability in sleep patterns across different species. Some researchers take the view that the sleep patterns exhibited by different animals, including humans, are the result of *evolutionary adaptation* (Roth & others, 2010; Siegel, 2009). According to this view, different sleep patterns evolved as a way of conserving energy and preventing a particular species from interacting with the environment when doing so is most hazardous.

For example, animals with few natural predators, such as gorillas and lions, sleep as much as 15 hours a day. In contrast, grazing animals, such as cattle and horses, tend to sleep in short bursts that total only about 4 hours per day (Siegel, 2005). Lions, much like their evolutionary cousins, the domestic cat, sleep long and deeply, but giraffes, their prey, sleep very little. Similarly, hibernation patterns also reflect evolutionary adaptation, coinciding with periods during which food is relatively scarce and environmental conditions pose the greatest threat to survival.

Rather than an all-encompassing theory explaining why we sleep, today's sleep researchers recognize that sleep serves a host of vital functions. Studying sleep from multiple perspectives—psychological, physiological, and neurological—yields a dynamic understanding of how sleep occurs and is regulated, and how it contributes to optimal functioning (Datta & MacLean, 2007).

Question: When Does an 800-Pound Predator Sleep? Answer: Any time it wants to! Sleep patterns vary widely across species. For example, sleep duration in mammals varies from a low of 3 hours a day in horses to up to 20 hours a day in bats (Siegel, 2005, 2009). One explanation is that sleep patterns result from evolutionary adaptation to a particular ecological niche. Thus, animals with few predators, like polar bears, have the luxury of sleeping long hours out in the open and even taking daytime naps after a meal. In contrast, giraffes take short naps throughout the day, often keeping one eye open to stay alert for predators.

SLEEP AND MEMORY FORMATION
LET ME SLEEP ON IT!

One important function of sleep deserves special mention. Sleep plays a critical role in strengthening new memories and in integrating new memories with existing memories (Walker, 2009, 2010). Sleep seems to be especially important in preserving emotional memories and memories of details that are relevant to personal goals and preoccupations (Pace-Schott & others, 2015; Stickgold & Walker, 2013).

Sleep researchers are finding that the strengthening and enhancement of new memories during sleep is a very active process. That process seems to work like this: New memories formed during the day are *reactivated* during the 90-minute cycles of sleep that occur throughout the night. This process of repeatedly reactivating these newly encoded memories during sleep strengthens the neuronal connections that contribute to forming long-term memories (Wamsley & others, 2010; Yang & others, 2014). And, along with helping solidify new memories, sleep is also critical to integrating the new memories into existing networks of memories (Stickgold & Walker, 2013).

THE EFFECTS OF SLEEP DEPRIVATION

The importance of sleep is demonstrated by *sleep deprivation studies.* After being deprived of sleep for just one night, research subjects develop *microsleeps,* which are episodes of sleep lasting only a few seconds that occur during wakefulness. People who go without sleep for a day or more also experience disruptions in mood, mental abilities, reaction time, perceptual skills, and complex motor skills (Bonnet, 2005).

But what about getting *less* than your usual amount of sleep? *Sleep restriction studies* reduce the amount of time that people are allowed to sleep to as little as four hours per night.

Sleep restriction produces numerous impairments and changes, not the least of which is an increased urge to sleep. Concentration, vigilance, reaction time, memory skills, and the ability to gauge risks are diminished (Ma & others, 2015). Motor skills—including driving skills—decrease, producing a greater risk of accidents. As discussed in the Focus on Neuroscience box "The Sleep-Deprived Emotional Brain," moods, especially negative moods, become much more volatile (Harvey, 2011). Harmful changes occur in hormone levels, including stress hormone levels (Balbo & others, 2010). The immune system's effectiveness is diminished, increasing susceptibility to colds and infections (Irwin, 2015). Finally, metabolic changes occur, including changes linked to obesity and diabetes (Van Cauter & others, 2008).

When sleep-deprived, people tend to consume more calories and gain weight (Markwald & others, 2013). One explanation is that sleep deprivation tends to increase the appeal of high-calorie foods. As compared to food choices made when they were well rested, people who were sleep-deprived tended to prefer high-caloric

FOCUS ON NEUROSCIENCE

The Sleep-Deprived Emotional Brain

Whether they are children or adults, people often react with greater emotionality when they're not getting adequate sleep (Ma & others, 2015; Zohar & others, 2005). Is this because they're simply tired, or do the brain's emotional centers become more reactive in response to sleep deprivation?

To study this question, researcher Seung-Schik Yoo and his colleagues (2007) deprived some participants of sleep for 35 hours while other participants slept normally. Then, all of the participants observed a series of images ranging from emotionally neutral to very unpleasant and disturbing images while undergoing an fMRI brain scan.

Compare the two fMRI scans shown here. The orange and yellow areas indicate the degree of activation in the *amygdala,* a key component of the brain's emotional centers. Compared to the adequately rested participants, the amygdala activated 60 percent more strongly when the sleep-deprived participants looked at the aversive images.

Yoo's research clearly shows that the sleep-deprived brain is much more prone to strong emotional reactions to negative stimuli. And, new research shows that sleep deprivation also affects how we respond to *positive* stimuli. The same team of researchers found that sleep-deprived participants responded with heightened activity in the brain's reward circuits to images of *pleasant* scenes, such as cute bunnies or ice cream sundaes (Gujar & others, 2011). The implication? Unrealistically positive responses may lead sleep-deprived people to engage in risky or addictive behavior.

As sleep scientist Matthew Walker (2011) observes, "When functioning correctly, the brain finds the sweet spot on the mood spectrum. But the sleep-deprived brain will swing to both extremes, neither of which is optimal for making wise decisions."

So, when you're consistently operating on too little sleep, monitor your emotional reactions so that you don't overreact and say or do something that you will regret later—such as after you've caught up on your sleep.

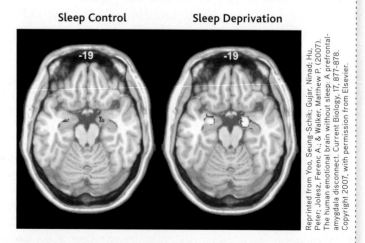

Sleep Control   Sleep Deprivation

treats like potato chips and desserts over nourishing but low-calorie foods like apple slices (Greer & others, 2013).

If sleep restriction continues for multiple nights, all of these changes become more pronounced. Unfortunately most people are *not* good at judging the extent to which their performance is impaired by inadequate sleep. People tend to think they are performing adequately, but in fact, their abilities and reaction time are greatly diminished (M. Walker, 2008).

Sleep researchers have also selectively deprived people of different components of normal sleep. To study the effects of *REM deprivation,* researchers wake sleepers whenever the monitoring instruments indicate that they are entering REM sleep. After several nights of being selectively deprived of REM sleep, the subjects are allowed to sleep uninterrupted. What happens? They experience **REM rebound**—the amount of time spent in REM sleep increases by as much as 50 percent. Similarly, when people are selectively deprived of NREM stages 3 and 4, they experience *NREM rebound,* spending more time in NREM sleep (Borbély & Achermann, 2005; Tobler, 2005). Thus, it seems that the brain needs to experience the full range of sleep states, making up for missing sleep components when given the chance.

Dreams and Mental Activity During Sleep

KEY THEME

A dream is an unfolding sequence of perceptions, thoughts, and emotions that is experienced as a series of actual events during sleep.

KEY QUESTIONS

> How does brain activity change during dreaming sleep, and how are those changes related to dream content?

> What do people dream about, and why don't we remember many of our dreams?

> How do the psychoanalytic, activation-synthesis, and neurocognitive models explain the nature and function of dreams?

Dreams have fascinated people since the beginning of time. By adulthood, about 25 percent of a night's sleep, or almost two hours every night, is spent dreaming. So, assuming you live to a ripe old age, you'll devote more than 50,000 hours, or about six years of your life, to dreaming.

Although dreams may be the most interesting brain productions during sleep, they are not the most common. More prevalent is **sleep thinking,** also called *sleep mentation.* Sleep thinking usually occurs during NREM slow-wave sleep and consists of vague, bland, thoughtlike ruminations about real-life events (McCarley, 2007). Sometimes, sleep thinking interferes with sleep, such as when anxious students toss and turn, reviewing terms and concepts during the night before an important exam.

In contrast to sleep thinking, a **dream** is an unfolding sequence of perceptions, thoughts, and emotions during sleep that is experienced as a series of real-life events (Domhoff, 2005a, 2005b). However bizarre the details or illogical the events, the dreamer accepts them as reality.

Most dreams happen during REM sleep, although dreams also occur during NREM sleep (Foulkes & Domhoff, 2014; Domhoff, 2011). When awakened during active REM sleep, people report a dream about 90 percent of the time, even people who claim that they never dream. The dreamer is usually the main participant in these events, and at least one other person is involved in the dream story. But sometimes the dreamer is simply the observer of the unfolding dream story.

Leo Cullum The New Yorker Collection/The Cartoon Bank

"It's that same dream, where I'm drowning in a bowl of noodles."

sleep thinking Vague, bland, thoughtlike ruminations about real-life events that typically occur during NREM sleep; also called *sleep mentation.*

dream An unfolding sequence of thoughts, perceptions, and emotions that typically occurs during REM sleep and is experienced as a series of real-life events.

![Focus on Neuroscience]

FOCUS ON NEUROSCIENCE

The Dreaming Brain

PET scans and other neuroimaging studies have revealed that the brain's activity during REM sleep is distinctly different from its activity as compared to wakefulness (PET scan *a*) and NREM slow-wave sleep (PET scan *b*). To help orient you, the top of each PET scan corresponds to the front of the brain and the bottom to the back of the brain. The PET scans are color-coded: Bluish purple indicates areas of decreased brain activity and yellow-red indicates areas of increased brain activity.

Compared to wakefulness, PET scan *a* reveals that REM sleep involves decreased activity in the frontal lobes, which are involved in rational thinking. Also decreased is the activity of the primary visual cortex, which normally processes external visual stimuli. In effect, the dreamer is cut off from the reality-testing functions of the frontal lobes—a fact that no doubt contributes to the weirdness of some dreams. The yellow-red areas in PET scan *a* indicate increased activity in association areas of the visual cortex. This brain activation gives rise to the visual images occurring in a dream.

Compared to slow-wave sleep, the yellow-red areas in PET scan *b* indicate that REM sleep is characterized by a sharp increase in limbic system brain areas associated with emotion, motivation, and memory, including the amygdala and hippocampus. The activation of limbic system brain areas reflects the dream's emotional qualities, which can sometimes be intense (Braun & others, 1998; Nofzinger, 2005).

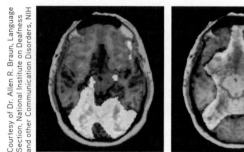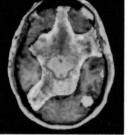

Courtesy of Dr. Allen R. Braun, Language Section, National Institute on Deafness and other Communication Disorders, NIH

(*a*) REM sleep compared to wakefulness

(*b*) REM sleep compared to slow-wave sleep

People usually have four or five dreaming episodes each night. The first REM episode of the night is the shortest, lasting only about 10 minutes. Subsequent REM episodes average around 30 minutes and tend to get longer as the night continues. Early morning dreams, which can last 40 minutes or longer, are the dreams most likely to be recalled.

PET and fMRI scans have revealed that the brain's activity during REM sleep is distinctly different from its activity during either wakefulness or NREM slow-wave sleep (Fuller & others, 2006; Nofzinger, 2006). These differences and the roles they play in dream content are explored in the Focus on Neuroscience box, "The Dreaming Brain."

Dream Themes and Imagery

Although almost everyone can remember having had a bizarre dream, research on dream content shows that bizarre dream stories tend to be the exception, not the rule. As dream researcher William Domhoff (2007) points out, dreams tend be "far more coherent, patterned, and thoughtful than is suggested by the usual image of them." *Most* dreams are about everyday settings, people, activities, and events. Common, however, are abrupt scene changes and unusual juxtapositions of images and actors.

In reviewing studies of dream content, Domhoff (2005b, 2010) has concluded that so-called common dream themes, like being naked in a public place, flying, or failing an exam, are actually quite rare in dream reports. And, dream emotions are usually appropriate in the context of the dream story (Domhoff, 2011). Analyzing thousands of dream reports, Domhoff (2007, 2011) found that negative feelings were more common than positive feelings. Apprehension and fear were the most frequently reported emotions, followed by happiness and confusion. Instances of aggression were more common than instances of friendliness, and the dreamer was more likely to be the victim of aggression than the aggressor. Women were more likely to

Dream Images The hit film *Inception,* starring Leonardo DiCaprio, used compelling dream sequences in its tale of corporate espionage accomplished by invading the dreams of unsuspecting competitors. People tend to emphasize visual imagery when describing their dreams, but sounds and physical sensations are also commonly present. Sensations of falling, flying, spinning, or trying to run may be experienced. We tend to dream of familiar people and places, but the juxtapositions of characters, objects, and events are often illogical, and sometimes bizarre (Nielsen & Stenstrom, 2005). Nevertheless, dreamers rarely question a dream's details—until they wake up!

Warner Bros/The Kobal Collection at Art Resource, NY

experience emotions in their dreams, and men more likely to experience physical aggression.

The emotional tone of the average dream pales in comparison with the intensity of a **nightmare**, a vivid and disturbing dream that often awakens the sleeper. Typically, the dreamer feels helpless or powerless in the face of being aggressively attacked or pursued. Although fear, anxiety, and even terror are the most commonly experienced emotions, some nightmares involve intense feelings of sadness, anger, disgust, or embarrassment (Nielsen & Zadra, 2005).

Nightmares are most common in childhood, but about 5 to 10 percent of adults report that they experience nightmares at least weekly. Women report more frequent nightmares than men. Daytime stress, anxiety, and emotional difficulties are often associated with nightmares. As a general rule, nightmares are *not* indicative of a psychological or sleep disorder unless they occur frequently, cause difficulties returning to sleep, or cause daytime distress (Levin & Nielsen, 2007; Nielsen & others, 2006).

Charles Saxon The New Yorker Collection/The Cartoon Bank

"Off with his head! Off with his head!"

The Significance of Dreams

Why do we dream? Do dreams contain symbolic or hidden messages? In this section, we will look at three models of the nature and function of dreaming. We'll start with the most famous one—the psychoanalytic explanation proposed by Sigmund Freud.

SIGMUND FREUD
DREAMS AS FULFILLED WISHES

In the chapters on personality and therapies (Chapters 10 and 14), we'll look in detail at the ideas of **Sigmund Freud,** the founder of psychoanalysis. As we discussed in Chapter 1, Freud believed that sexual and aggressive instincts are the motivating forces that dictate human behavior. Because these instinctual urges are so consciously unacceptable, sexual and aggressive thoughts, feelings, and wishes are pushed into the unconscious, or *repressed*. However, Freud believed that these repressed urges and wishes could surface in dream imagery.

In his landmark work, *The Interpretation of Dreams* (1900), Freud wrote that dreams are the "disguised fulfillments of repressed wishes" and provide "the royal road to a knowledge of the unconscious mind." In fact, he contended that "wish-fulfillment is the meaning of each and every dream." According to the psychoanalytic view of dreaming, then, dreams function as a sort of psychological "safety valve" for the release of unconscious and unacceptable urges (see Yu, 2011).

Freud (1904) believed that dreams have two components: the **manifest content,** or the dream images themselves, and the **latent content,** the disguised psychological meaning of the dream. For example, Freud (1911) believed that dream images of sticks, swords, brooms, and other elongated objects were *phallic symbols,* representing the penis. Dream images of cupboards, boxes, and ovens supposedly symbolized the vagina.

In some types of psychotherapy today, especially those that follow Freud's ideas, dreams are still seen as an important source of information about psychological conflicts (Auld & others, 2005; Pesant & Zadra, 2004). However, Freud's belief that dreams

AKG/Science Source

Sigmund Freud on the Meaning of Dreams Dream interpretation played an important role in *psychoanalysis*, the psychotherapy Freud developed. Freud believed that because psychological defenses are reduced during sleep, frustrated sexual and aggressive wishes are expressed symbolically in dreams. "In every dream an instinctual wish has to be represented as fulfilled," Freud (1933) wrote.

nightmare A vivid and frightening or unpleasant anxiety dream that occurs during REM sleep.

manifest content In Freud's psychoanalytic theory, the elements of a dream that are consciously experienced and remembered by the dreamer.

latent content In Freud's psychoanalytic theory, the unconscious wishes, thoughts, and urges that are concealed in the manifest content of a dream.

activation–synthesis model of dreaming
The theory that brain activity during sleep produces dream images (*activation*), which are combined by the brain into a dream story (*synthesis*).

> Both emotional salience and the cognitive mishmash of dreams are the undisguised read-out of the dreaming brain's unique chemistry and physiology. This doesn't mean that dreams make no psychological sense. On the contrary, dreams are dripping with emotional salience. Dreams can and should be discussed for their informative messages about the emotional concerns of the dreamer.
>
> —*J. Allan Hobson (1999)*

represent the fulfillment of repressed wishes has not been substantiated by psychological research. Furthermore, research does not support Freud's belief that the dream images themselves—the manifest content of dreams—are symbols that disguise the dream's true psychological meaning (Domhoff, 2003, 2011).

THE ACTIVATION–SYNTHESIS MODEL OF DREAMING

Researchers **J. Allan Hobson** and **Robert W. McCarley** first proposed a new model of dreaming in 1977. Called the **activation–synthesis model of dreaming,** this model maintains that dreaming is our subjective awareness of the brain's internally generated signals during sleep. Since it was first proposed, the model has evolved as new findings have been reported (see McCarley, 2007; Pace-Schott, 2005). Hobson's most recent model, called the *Activation-Input-Modulation (AIM) Model,* is a more comprehensive attempt to relate dreaming to waking awareness with specific reference to the balance of neurotransmitters (Hobson, 2009).

According to the activation–synthesis model, dreams occur when brainstem circuits at the base of the brain activate and trigger higher brain regions, including visual, motor, and auditory pathways (see Figure 4.6). As noted earlier in the Focus on Neuroscience box "The Dreaming Brain," limbic system structures involved in emotion, such as the amygdala and hippocampus, are also activated during REM sleep. When we're awake, these brain structures and pathways are involved in registering stimuli from the external world. But rather than responding to stimulation from the external environment, the dreaming brain is responding to its own internally generated signals (Hobson, 2005).

In the absence of external sensory input, the activated brain combines, or *synthesizes,* these internally generated sensory signals and imposes meaning on them. The dream story itself is derived from a hodgepodge of memories, emotions, and sensations that are triggered by the brain's activation and chemical changes during sleep. According to this model, then, dreaming is essentially the brain synthesizing and integrating memory fragments, emotions, and sensations that are internally triggered (Hobson & others, 1998, 2011).

The activation–synthesis theory does *not* contend that dreams are completely meaningless. But if there is a meaning to dreams, that meaning lies in the deeply personal way in which the images are organized, or synthesized. In other words, the meaning is to be found not by decoding the dream symbols, but by analyzing

Dream Researcher J. Allan Hobson Neuroscientist J. Allan Hobson developed the activation–synthesis model of dreaming with his colleague Robert McCarley. Although Hobson believes that dreams are the by-products of physiological processes in the brain, he does not believe that dreams are meaningless.

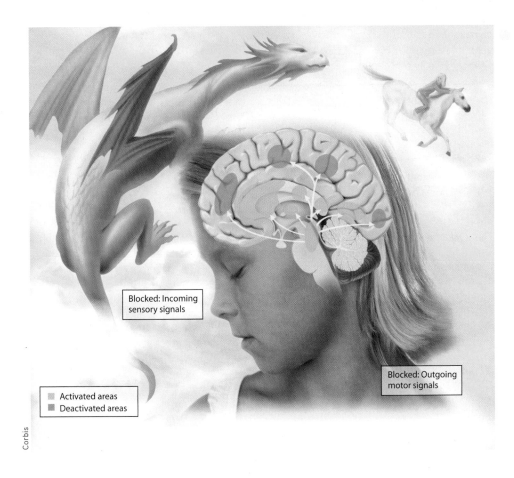

Blocked: Incoming
sensory signals

Blocked: Outgoing
motor signals

■ Activated areas
■ Deactivated areas

Corbis

FIGURE 4.6 The Activation–Synthesis Model of Dreaming According to the activation–synthesis model of dreaming, dreaming is our subjective awareness of the brain's internally generated signals during sleep. Dreaming is initiated when brainstem circuits arouse brain areas involved in emotions, memories, movements, and sensations. These activated brain areas, shown in green, give rise to dreaming consciousness and the dream imaginings of sensations, perceptions, movements, and feelings. The activated brain synthesizes, or combines, these elements, drawing on previous experiences and memories to impose a personal meaning on the dream story (Hobson, 2005; McCarley, 2007).

Other brain areas, highlighted in purple, are deactivated or blocked during dreaming. Outgoing motor signals and incoming sensory signals are blocked, keeping the dreamer from acting out the dream or responding to external stimuli (Pace-Schott, 2005). The logical, rational, and planning functions of the prefrontal cortex are suspended. Hence, dream stories can evolve in ways that seem disjointed or illogical. And because the prefrontal cortex is involved in processing memories, most nightly dream productions evaporate with no lingering memories of having had these experiences (Muzur & others, 2002).

Sources: Research from Hobson (2005); Pace-Schott (2005).

the way the dreamer, once awake, makes sense of the progression of chaotic dream images.

THE NEUROCOGNITIVE THEORY OF DREAMING

In contrast to the activation–synthesis model, the **neurocognitive model of dreaming** emphasizes the *continuity between waking and dreaming cognition.* According to William Domhoff (2005a, 2010, 2011), dreams are not a "cognitive mishmash" of random fragments of memories, images, and emotions generated by lower brainstem circuits, as the activation–synthesis model holds. Rather, dreams reflect our interests, personality, and individual worries (Nir & Tononi, 2010).

Further, the activation–synthesis model rests on the assumption that dreams result from brain activation during REM sleep. However, as Domhoff and other dream researchers point out, people also dream during NREM sleep, at sleep onset, and even experience dreamlike episodes while awake but drowsy (Foulkes & Domhoff, 2014; Nir & Tononi, 2010).

Like dreams, Domhoff (2011) notes, waking thought can also be marked by spontaneous mental images, rapid shifts of scene or topic, and unrealistic or fanciful thoughts. Thus, dreams are not as foreign to our waking experience as the activation–synthesis model claims. Instead, dreams mirror our waking concerns, and do so in a way that is remarkably similar to normal thought processes (Foulkes & Domhoff, 2014).

❯ Test your understanding of **Sleep and Dreams** with *LEARNINGCurve.*

neurocognitive model of dreaming Model of dreaming that emphasizes the continuity of waking and dreaming cognition, and states that dreaming is like thinking under conditions of reduced sensory input and the absence of voluntary control.

IN FOCUS

What You Really Want to Know About Dreams

If I fall off a cliff in my dreams and don't wake up before I hit the bottom, will I die?
The first obvious problem with this bit of folklore is that if you did die before you woke up, how would anyone know what you'd been dreaming about? Beyond this basic contradiction, studies have shown that about a third of dreamers can recall a dream in which they died or were killed.

Do animals dream?
Virtually all mammals and birds experience sleep cycles in which REM sleep alternates with slow-wave NREM sleep. Animals clearly demonstrate perception and memory. They also communicate using vocalizations, facial expressions, posture, and gestures to show territoriality and sexual receptiveness. Thus, it's quite reasonable to conclude that the brain and other physiological changes that occur during animal REM sleep are coupled with mental images.

What do blind people "see" when they dream?
People who become totally blind before the age of 5 typically do not have visual dreams as adults. Even so, their dreams are just as complex and vivid as sighted people's dreams; they just involve other sensations—of sound, taste, smell, and touch.

Is it possible to control your dreams?
Yes, if you have lucid dreams. A *lucid dream* is one in which you become aware that you are dreaming while you are still asleep. About half of all people can recall at least one lucid dream, and some people frequently have lucid dreams. The dreamer can often consciously guide the course of a lucid dream, including backing it up and making it go in a different direction. New research suggests that lucid dreamers may be more aware of their thoughts while awake, too.

Can you predict the future with your dreams?
History is filled with stories of dream prophecies. Over the course of your life, you will have over 100,000 dreams. Simply by chance, it's not surprising that every now and then a dream contains elements that coincide with future events.

Are dreams in color or black and white?
Up to 80 percent of our dreams contain color. When dreamers are awakened and asked to match dream colors to standard color charts, soft pastel colors are frequently chosen.

SOURCES: Empson (2002); Filevich & others, 2015; Hobson & Voss (2010); Hurovitz & others (1999); Voss & others (2009, 2014).

The Perils of Driving While Drowsy According to studies reported by the National Highway Traffic Safety administration (2011), drowsiness is blamed for tens of thousands of traffic accidents each year—and 1,500 deaths. The best way to avoid an accident if you're sleepy? Get off the road and rest. Opening windows and turning up the radio and air conditioning are *not* effective ways to maintain alertness (Centers for Disease Control, 2013).

Peshkova/Shutterstock

Sleep Disorders

KEY THEME

Sleep disorders are surprisingly common, take many different forms, and interfere with a person's daytime functioning.

KEY QUESTIONS

> What are the two broad categories of sleep disorders?

> What are insomnia, sleep apnea, and narcolepsy?

> What kinds of behavior are displayed in the different parasomnias?

Data from the National Sleep Foundation's annual polls indicate that about 7 out of 10 people experience regular sleep disruptions. Such disruptions become a **sleep disorder** when: (1) abnormal sleep patterns consistently occur, (2) they cause subjective distress, and (3) they interfere with a person's daytime functioning (Thorpy, 2005; Thorpy & Plazzi, 2010).

Sleep disorders fall into two broad categories. **Dyssomnias** are sleep disorders involving disruptions in the amount, quality, or timing of sleep. *Obstructive sleep apnea* and *narcolepsy* are examples of dyssomnias. The **parasomnias** are sleep disorders involving undesirable physical arousal, behaviors, or events during sleep or sleep transitions.

Insomnia

Insomnia is not defined solely based on how long a person sleeps. Why? Put simply, because people vary in how much sleep they need to feel refreshed. Rather, **insomnia** is diagnosed when people repeatedly: (1) are dissatisfied with the quality or duration of their sleep; (2) experience *onset insomnia,* meaning that they have difficulty falling asleep, or *maintenance insomnia,* meaning they have difficulty staying asleep; or (3) wake before it is time to get up. Regularly taking 30 minutes or longer to fall asleep is considered to be a symptom of insomnia. These disruptions must also produce daytime sleepiness, fatigue, impaired social or occupational performance, or mood disturbances (Bootzin & Epstein, 2011).

Insomnia is the most common sleep complaint among adults. Although many people occasionally have trouble falling asleep, about 10% of adults experience *chronic insomnia* for a month or longer (Mahowald & Schenck, 2005).

One common cause of insomnia is hyperarousal (Salas & others, 2014). Excitement about an upcoming event or the use of stimulants, like nicotine and caffeine, can make it hard to fall asleep. Most commonly, insomnia can be traced to anxiety over stressful life events, such as job, school, or relationship difficulties. Sometimes, worry about inadequate sleep can itself cause insomnia. Creating a vicious circle, concerns about the inability to sleep make disrupted sleep even more likely, further intensifying anxiety and worry over personal difficulties, producing more sleep difficulties, and so on (Perlis & others, 2005).

Although the *occasional* use of prescription "sleeping pills" can be helpful to treat transient insomnia, frequent use, or use for chronic insomnia, is problematic. Along with having harmful side effects, they do not offer a long-term solution to the problem, since the insomnia returns if the pills are not used. In Psych for Your Life, we'll describe one effective behavioral treatment for insomnia and give you several suggestions to improve the quality of your sleep.

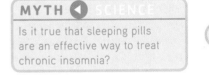

MYTH ◀ SCIENCE

Is it true that sleeping pills are an effective way to treat chronic insomnia?

Obstructive Sleep Apnea
BLOCKED BREATHING DURING SLEEP

Excessive daytime sleepiness is a key symptom of the second most common sleep disorder. In **obstructive sleep apnea (OSA),** the sleeper's airway becomes narrowed or blocked, causing very shallow breathing or repeated pauses in breathing. Each time breathing stops, oxygen blood levels decrease and carbon dioxide blood levels increase, triggering a momentary awakening. Over the course of a night, 300 or more sleep apnea episodes can occur (Schwab & others, 2005).

Obstructive sleep apnea disrupts the quality and quantity of a person's sleep, causing daytime grogginess, poor concentration, memory and learning problems, and irritability (Weaver & George, 2005). Sleep apnea can also cause physical health problems, including weight gain, high blood pressure, and diabetes. Although OSA can occur in any age group, including small children, it becomes more common as people age. It is also more common in men than women.

Sleep apnea can often be treated with lifestyle changes, such as avoiding alcohol or losing weight (Hoffstein, 2005; Powell & others, 2005). Moderate to severe cases of sleep apnea are usually treated with *continuous positive airway pressure* (CPAP), using a device that increases air pressure in the throat so that the airway remains open (Grunstein, 2005).

Narcolepsy
BLURRING THE BOUNDARIES BETWEEN SLEEP AND WAKEFULNESS

Even with adequate nighttime sleep, people with **narcolepsy** experience overwhelming bouts of excessive daytime sleepiness and brief, uncontrollable episodes of sleep. These involuntary sleep episodes, called *sleep attacks* or *microsleeps,* typically last from a few seconds to several minutes.

sleep disorders Serious and consistent sleep disturbances that interfere with daytime functioning and cause subjective distress.

dyssomnias (dis-SOM-nee-uz) A category of sleep disorders involving disruptions in the amount, quality, or timing of sleep; includes insomnia, obstructive sleep apnea, and narcolepsy.

parasomnias (pare-uh-SOM-nee-uz) A category of sleep disorders characterized by arousal or activation during sleep or sleep transitions; includes *sleepwalking, sleep terrors, sleepsex,* and *sleep-related eating disorder.*

insomnia A condition in which a person regularly experiences an inability to fall asleep, to stay asleep, or to feel adequately rested by sleep.

obstructive sleep apnea (APP-nee-uh) A sleep disorder in which the person repeatedly stops breathing during sleep.

narcolepsy (NAR-ko-lep-see) A sleep disorder characterized by excessive daytime sleepiness and brief lapses into sleep throughout the day.

Life with Narcolepsy College student Kailey Profeta was diagnosed with narcolepsy when she was 9 years old. She was home-schooled for years until doctors developed a combination of medications that would keep her awake during the day and let her sleep at night. She graduated from high school at the top of her class, but life with narcolepsy is not easy. "What I feel like on a regular day is what a normal person would feel after not sleeping for 7 days—that's how tired narcoleptics feel. Narcolepsy affects my life a lot, but I'm still me," Kailey says. To listen to Kailey's story and to hear more first-person accounts of life with narcolepsy, go to http://www.nytimes.com/interactive/2009/08/26/health/TE_NARCOLEPSY.html

David Walter Banks for The New York Times/Redux

Most people with narcolepsy—about 70 percent—experience regular episodes of **cataplexy,** which is the sudden loss of voluntary muscle control, lasting from several seconds to several minutes. Such episodes are usually triggered by a sudden, intense emotion, such as laughter, anger, fear, or surprise. In more severe episodes of cataplexy, the person may completely lose muscle control, knees buckling as he or she collapses. Although unable to move or speak, the person is conscious and aware of what is happening.

The Parasomnias
UNDESIRED AROUSAL OR ACTIONS DURING SLEEP

We tend to think of sleep as an "either/or" phenomenon—we are either asleep or we are awake. But as the *parasomnias* show, sometimes sleep and waking states overlap or "bleed" into one another (Colwell, 2011; Mahowald & Schenk, 2005). In the parasomnias, some parts of the brain—like those involved in judging, thinking, or forming new memories—are asleep, but other, more primitive parts of the brain become activated (Cartwright, 2010). The brain is *partially* awake—awake enough to carry out the actions, but not awake enough to be consciously aware of performing the actions (Cartwright, 2010).

The parasomnias are a collection of sleep disorders that are characterized by undesirable physical arousal, behaviors, or events during sleep or sleep transitions (Mahowald & Schenk, 2005; Schenck, 2007). A key characteristic of all of the parasomnias is first, the lack of awareness while performing the actions and second, total amnesia for the behaviors or events upon awakening.

Parasomnias occur during NREM stages 3 and 4 slow-wave sleep during the first half of a night's sleep. They can be triggered by a wide range of stimuli, including sleep deprivation, stress, erratic sleep schedules, sleeping medications, stimulants, pregnancy, and tranquilizers.

The parasomnias were once thought to be extremely rare, especially in adults. However, sleep researchers have discovered that some parasomnias—like sleeptalking, described on page 141, and sleepwalking—are relatively common (Bjorvatn & others, 2010). We'll look at some specific parasomnias next.

SLEEP TERRORS

Also called *night terrors,* **sleep terrors** begin with a sharp increase in physiological arousal—restlessness, sweating, and a racing heart. The person abruptly sits up in bed and may let out a panic-stricken scream. Sleep terrors usually involve the terrifying sensation that one is being choked or crushed or is falling. Although the sufferer may appear to be awake, he is terrified and disoriented, and usually impossible to calm (Mahowald & Schenck, 2005). Sleep terrors are most common in children, but a small percentage of adults also experience them.

cataplexy A sudden loss of voluntary muscle strength and control that is usually triggered by an intense emotion.

sleep terrors A sleep disturbance characterized by an episode of increased physiological arousal, intense fear and panic, frightening hallucinations, and no recall of the episode the next morning; typically occurs during stage 3 or stage 4 NREM sleep; also called *night terrors.*

sleepwalking A sleep disturbance characterized by an episode of walking or performing other actions during stage 3 or stage 4 NREM sleep; also called *somnambulism.*

sleep-related eating disorder (SRED) A sleep disorder in which the sleeper will sleepwalk and eat compulsively.

sleepsex A sleep disorder involving abnormal sexual behaviors and experiences during sleep; also called *sexsomnia.*

SLEEPWALKING AND OTHER COMPLEX BEHAVIORS DURING SLEEP

The Prologue story about Scott described several key features of another parasomnia—**sleepwalking,** or *somnambulism*. Fairly common in childhood, sleepwalking can occur in adulthood, too. About 4 percent of adults regularly sleepwalk (Hughes, 2007). Surprisingly, a sleepwalker can engage in elaborate and complicated behaviors, such as unlocking locks, opening windows, dismantling equipment, using tools, and even driving. Recall that Scott's attack had occurred early in the night, shortly after he had "crashed," or fallen asleep, as is most commonly the case with sleepwalking. The attack had no apparent motive, and as is characteristic of the parasomnias, he had no memory of it when he was awakened by the police (Cartwright, 2004).

It's difficult to rouse sleepwalkers from deep sleep. Occasionally, sleepwalkers can respond aggressively if touched or interrupted (Pressman, 2007). Scott reacted violently to being interrupted while sleepwalking at least once while he was growing up, and his attack on his wife may have been caused by her trying to wake him up and guide him back to the house (Cartwright, 2004, 2007). In most cases, though, sleepwalkers respond to verbal suggestions and can be gently led back to bed without incident.

Sleepwalking is also involved in **sleep-related eating disorder,** which involves sleepwalking nightly to the kitchen, eating compulsively, and then awakening the next morning with no memory of having done so. Although sweet-tasting foods like candy or cake are most commonly consumed, the sleepwalker can also voraciously eat bizarre items, like raw bacon, dry pancake mix, salt sandwiches, coffee grounds, or cat food sandwiches. Interestingly, alcoholic beverages are hardly ever consumed during a sleepeating episode.

Also called *sexsomnia,* **sleepsex** involves abnormal sexual behaviors and experiences during sleep. Without realizing what they are doing, sleepers initiate some kind of sexual behavior, such as masturbation, groping or fondling their bed partner's genitals, or even sexual intercourse (Trajanovic & Shapiro, 2010). Although sometimes described as loving or playful, more often sleepsex behavior is characterized as "robotic," aggressive, and impersonal. Whether affectionate or forceful, sleepsex behavior is usually depicted as being out of character with the individual's sexual behavior when awake (Schenck & others, 2007). As is the case in other parasomnias, the person typically has no memory of his actions the next day (Schenck, 2007).

Finally, no discussion of the parasomnias would be complete without at least a mention of the colorfully titled *exploding head syndrome*. As its name implies, the unfortunate sufferer reports the sensation of loud noises that sound like gunshots or a

> **MYTH ▶ SCIENCE**
> Is it true that it can be dangerous to wake a sleepwalker?

For more information about sleep disorders, visit the American Academy of Sleep Medicine's Web site, www.SleepEducation.com, or the National Sleep Foundation's Web site, www.SleepFoundation.org.

Warning: May Cause Sleep-Driving and Sleep-Eating *Ambien*®, a widely prescribed sleeping pill, was originally marketed as being less addictive and having fewer side effects than older medications. But Ambien users have reported waking up to find the oven turned on and food strewn around the kitchen and in their bed. Other Ambien users have reported driving while asleep, waking up only after being arrested on the side of the road (Saul, 2007a, 2007b). In general, Ambien appears to increase the odds of experiencing parasomnias (Ben-Hamou & others, 2011). The U.S. Food and Drug Administration now requires that Ambien and other sleeping medications warn of sleep-driving, sleep-eating, and sleepwalking as potential side effects.

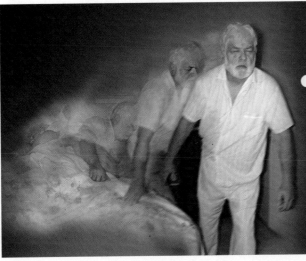

Carol and Mike Werner/Phototake

bomb exploding inside his head while falling asleep or waking up (Sharpless, 2015a). Although painless, episodes are usually accompanied by extreme arousal and fear. Exploding head syndrome was once thought to be extremely rare, but a recent survey found that about one in five college students had experienced one or more episodes. The cause is unknown, but psychologist and exploding head syndrome researcher Brian Sharpless (2015b) likens it to a "brain hiccup." He speculates that the sensation occurs when auditory neurons fire rather than shut down as the brain transitions between sleep and wakefulness.

❯ Test your understanding of **Sleep Disorders** with **LEARNING***Curve*.

Hypnosis

KEY THEME

During hypnosis, people respond to suggestions with changes in perception, memory, and behavior.

KEY QUESTIONS

❯ What characteristics are associated with responsiveness to hypnotic suggestions?

❯ What are some important effects of hypnosis?

❯ How has hypnosis been explained?

What is hypnosis? **Hypnosis** can be defined as a cooperative social interaction in which the hypnotized participant responds to suggestions made by the hypnotist. These suggestions for imaginative experiences can produce changes in perception, memory, thoughts, and behavior (American Psychological Association, 2005a).

For many people the word *hypnosis* conjures up the classic but sinister image of a hypnotist slowly swinging a pocket watch back and forth. But, as psychologist John Kihlstrom (2001) explains, "The hypnotist does not hypnotize the individual. Rather, the hypnotist serves as a sort of coach or tutor whose job is to help the person become hypnotized."

The word *hypnosis* is derived from the Greek *hypnos,* meaning "sleep." However, rather than being a sleeplike trance, hypnosis produces a highly focused, absorbed state of attention that minimizes competing thoughts and attention (Oakley & Halligan, 2013). It is also characterized by increased responsiveness to suggestions, vivid images and fantasies, and a willingness to accept distortions of logic or reality. During hypnosis, people temporarily suspend their sense of initiative and voluntarily accept and follow the hypnotist's instructions (Hilgard, 1986a). However, they typically remain aware of who they are, where they are, and the events that are transpiring.

People vary in their responsiveness to hypnotic suggestions (see Nash, 2008). About 15 percent of adults are highly susceptible to hypnosis, and 10 percent are difficult or impossible to hypnotize. Children tend to be more responsive to hypnosis than are adults (Rhue, 2010).

The best candidates for hypnosis are individuals who approach the experience with positive, receptive attitudes. The expectation that you will be responsive to hypnosis also plays an important role (Silva & others, 2005). People who are highly susceptible to hypnosis have the ability to become deeply absorbed in fantasy and imaginary experience. For instance, they easily become absorbed in reading fiction, watching movies, and listening to music (Kihlstrom, 2007; Milling & others, 2010).

Effects of Hypnosis

Deeply hypnotized subjects sometimes experience profound changes in their subjective experience of consciousness. They may report feelings of detachment from

hypnosis (hip-NO-sis) A cooperative social interaction in which the hypnotized person responds to the hypnotist's suggestions with changes in perception, memory, and behavior.

posthypnotic suggestion A suggestion made during hypnosis asking a person to carry out a specific instruction following the hypnotic session.

posthypnotic amnesia The inability to recall specific information because of a hypnotic suggestion.

their bodies, profound relaxation, or sensations of timelessness. Often, they will later report that carrying out the hypnotist's suggestions seemed to happen by itself, as if the action occurred without effort or conscious control (Polito & others, 2014).

Sensory changes that can be induced through hypnosis include hallucinations, temporary blindness, deafness, or a complete loss of sensation in some part of the body (Kihlstrom, 2007). For example, when the suggestion is made to a highly responsive subject that her arm is numb and cannot feel pain, she will not consciously experience the pain of a pinprick or of having her arm immersed in ice water. This property of hypnosis has led to its use as a technique in pain control (Adachi & others, 2014; Jensen & Patterson, 2014). Painful dental and medical procedures, including surgery, have been successfully performed with hypnosis as the only anesthesia (Hilgard & others, 1994; Salazar & others, 2010).

Hypnosis can also influence behavior outside the hypnotic state. When a **posthypnotic suggestion** is given, the person will carry out that specific suggestion after the hypnotic session is over. For example, under hypnosis, a student was given the posthypnotic suggestion that the number 5 no longer existed. He was brought out of hypnosis and then asked to count his fingers. He counted 11 fingers! Counting again, the baffled young man was at a loss to explain his results.

Some posthypnotic suggestions have been reported to last for months, but most last only a few hours or days. So, even if the hypnotist does not include some posthypnotic signal to cancel the posthypnotic suggestion, the suggestion will eventually wear off.

Memory can be significantly affected by hypnosis (see Kihlstrom, 2007). **Posthypnotic amnesia** is produced by a hypnotic suggestion that suppresses the memory of specific information, such as the subject's name, address, or phone number. The effects of posthypnotic amnesia are usually temporary, disappearing either spontaneously or when a posthypnotic signal is suggested by the hypnotist. When the signal is given, the information floods back into the subject's mind.

Can hypnosis enhance memory, allow you to "zoom in" on details of a crime that have been forgotten, or recover long-forgotten memories? No. Compared with regular police interview methods, hypnosis does *not* significantly enhance memory or improve the accuracy of memories (Mazzoni & others, 2010). In contrast, efforts to enhance memories with hypnosis can produce distorted and inaccurate recollections. In fact, one effect of hypnosis is to greatly increase confidence in *incorrect* memories. False memories, also called *pseudomemories,* can be inadvertently created when hypnosis is used to aid recall, a topic discussed in greater detail in Chapter 6 on memory (Lynn & others, 2003; Mazzoni & Scoboria, 2007).

Explaining Hypnosis
CONSCIOUSNESS DIVIDED?

How can hypnosis be explained? Psychologist **Ernest R. Hilgard** (1986a, 1991, 1992) believed that the hypnotized person experiences **dissociation**—the splitting of consciousness into two or more

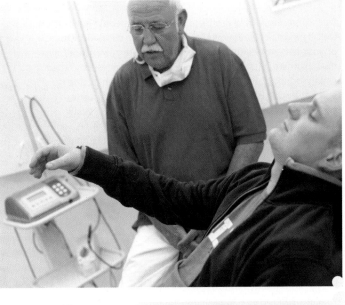

Stephan Elleringmann/laif/Redux

How Is the Hypnotic State Produced? In a willing volunteer, hypnosis can be induced in many different ways, but swinging a pocket watch is usually not one of them. Most often, hypnosis is induced by speaking in a calm, monotonous voice, suggesting that the person is becoming drowsy, sleepy, and progressively more relaxed. This dentist is hypnotizing a patient so that he will be relaxed and pain-free during treatment.

dissociation The splitting of consciousness into two or more simultaneous streams of mental activity.

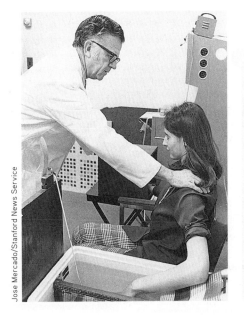

Jose Mercado/Stanford News Service

Hypnotic Suppression of Pain In this classic photo taken at the Stanford Laboratory of Hypnosis Research, psychologist Ernest Hilgard (1904–2001) instructs this hypnotized young woman that she will feel no pain in her arm. Her arm is then immersed in circulating ice water for several minutes, and she reports that she does not experience any pain. In contrast, a nonhypnotized subject perceives the same experience as extremely painful and can keep his arm in the ice water for no more than a few seconds.

Age Regression Through Hypnosis? Some people believe that hypnosis can allow you to reexperience an earlier stage of your life—a phenomenon called *age regression*. Under hypnosis, some adults *do* appear to relive experiences from their childhood, confidently displaying childlike speech patterns and behaviors. However, when attempts are made to verify specific details of the experiences, the details are usually inaccurate (Spanos, 1987–1988). Just as actual deafness and blindness are not produced by hypnotic suggestion, neither is a true return to childhood. Instead, hypnotic subjects combine fragments of actual memories with fantasies and ideas about how children of a particular age should behave.

Cultura/Robyn Breen Shinn/Getty Images

neodissociation theory of hypnosis
Theory proposed by Ernest Hilgard that explains hypnotic effects as being due to the splitting of consciousness into two simultaneous streams of mental activity, only one of which the hypnotic participant is consciously aware during hypnosis.

hidden observer Hilgard's term for the hidden, or dissociated, stream of mental activity that continues during hypnosis.

simultaneous streams of mental activity. According to Hilgard's **neodissociation theory of hypnosis,** a hypnotized person consciously experiences one stream of mental activity that complies with the hypnotist's suggestions. But a second, dissociated stream of mental activity is also operating, processing information that is unavailable to the consciousness of the hypnotized subject. Hilgard (1986a, 1992) referred to this second, dissociated stream of mental activity as the **hidden observer.** (The phrase *hidden observer* does *not* mean that the hypnotized person has multiple personalities.)

CRITICAL THINKING

Is Hypnosis a Special State of Consciousness?

Are the changes in perception, thinking, and behaviors that occur during hypnosis the result of a "special" or "altered" state of consciousness? Here, we'll consider the evidence for three competing points of view on this issue.

The State View: Hypnosis Involves a Special State

The "state" explanation contends that hypnosis is a unique state of consciousness, distinctly different from normal waking consciousness (Wagstaff, 2014). The state view is perhaps best represented by Hilgard's *neodissociation theory of hypnosis*. According to this view, consciousness is split into two simultaneous streams of mental activity during hypnosis. One stream of mental activity remains conscious, but a second stream of mental activity—the one responding to the hypnotist's suggestions—is "dissociated" from awareness (Sadler & Woody, 2010). So according to the neodissociation theory, the hypnotized young woman shown on page 157 reported no pain because the painful sensations were dissociated from awareness.

The Non-State View: Ordinary Psychological Processes

Some psychologists reject the notion that hypnotically induced changes involve a "special" state of consciousness. According to the *social-cognitive view of hypnosis,* subjects are responding to the *social demands* of the hypnosis situation. They act the way they think good hypnotic subjects are supposed to act, conforming to

the expectations of the hypnotist, their own expectations, and situational cues (Lynn & Green, 2011). In this view, the "hypnotized" young woman on page 157 reported no pain because that's what she expected to happen during the hypnosis session.

To back up the social cognitive theory of hypnosis, Nicholas Spanos (1991, 1994, 2005) and his colleagues amassed an impressive array of evidence showing that highly motivated people often perform just as well as hypnotized subjects in demonstrating pain reduction, amnesia, age regression, and hallucinations. Studies of people who simply *pretended* to be hypnotized have shown similar results. On the basis of such findings, non-state theorists contend that hypnosis can be explained in terms of rather ordinary psychological processes, including imagination, situational expectations, role enactment, compliance, and conformity (Wagstaff & Cole, 2005).

The Imaginative Suggestibility View

Challenging the social cognitive view, however, are the results of numerous brain-imaging studies showing that hypnosis can produce alterations in brain function (see Oakley & Halligan, 2013). For example, in one study, hypnotized participants were given instructions to "drain" color from a visual image made up of colored rectangles or, conversely, to "add color" to a visual image made up of gray rectangles, like those shown to the right. The brain function of hypnotized participants reflected the hypnosis-induced visual hallucination—*not* the actual images that participants viewed (Kosslyn & others, 2000).

Some theorists do not agree that hypnotic phenomena are due to dissociation, divided consciousness, or a hidden observer. Alternative theories include the *social cognitive* and *imaginative suggestibility* theories. We discuss this controversy in the Critical Thinking box, "Is Hypnosis a Special State of Consciousness?"

LIMITS AND APPLICATIONS OF HYPNOSIS

Although the effects of hypnosis can be dramatic, there are limits to the behaviors that can be influenced by hypnosis. First, contrary to popular belief, you cannot be hypnotized against your will. Second, hypnosis cannot make you perform behaviors that are contrary to your morals and values. Thus, you're very unlikely to commit criminal or immoral acts under the influence of hypnosis—unless, of course, you find such actions acceptable (Hilgard, 1986b).

Third, hypnosis cannot make you stronger than your physical capabilities or bestow new talents. However, hypnosis *can* enhance physical skills or athletic ability by increasing self-confidence and concentration (Barker & Jones, 2006; Morgan, 2002). Table 4.2 provides additional examples of how hypnosis can be used to help people.

Can hypnosis be used to help you lose weight, stop smoking, or stop biting your nails? Hypnosis is not a magic bullet. However, research *has* shown that hypnosis can be helpful in modifying problematic behaviors, especially when used as part of a structured treatment program (Lynn & others, 2010). For example, when combined with cognitive-behavioral therapy or other supportive treatments, hypnosis has been shown to help motivated people quit smoking (Elkins & others, 2006; Green & others, 2006; Lynn & Kirsch, 2006). In children and adolescents, hypnosis can be an effective treatment for such habits as thumb-sucking, nail-biting, and compulsive hair-pulling (Rhue, 2010).

MYTH ◀ SCIENCE
Is it true that you can be hypnotized against your will?

Psychologists Irving Kirsch and Wayne Braffman (2001) dismiss the social cognitive view that hypnotized subjects are merely acting. But they also contend that brain-imaging studies don't necessarily prove that hypnosis is a unique state. Rather, Kirsch and Braffman maintain that such studies emphasize individual differences in *imaginative suggestibility*—the degree to which a person is able to experience an imaginary state of affairs as if it were real (Kirsch, 2014; Kirsch & others, 2011).

Braffman and Kirsch (1999) have shown that many highly suggestible participants were just as responsive to suggestions when they had *not* been hypnotized as when they had been hypnotized. "Hypnotic responses reveal an astounding capacity that some people have to alter their experience in profound ways," Kirsch and Braffman (2001) write. "Hypnosis is only one of the ways in which this capacity is revealed. It can also be evoked—and almost to the same extent—without inducing hypnosis."

Supporting this approach is a new study that duplicated the brain-imaging research described above with one important difference: All of the participants were given the suggestions to alter their color perception of the image of rectangles, but only half of them were formally hypnotized (McGeown & others, 2012). Half of the participants scored high in hypnotic suggestibility, and half scored low in suggestibility. The results showed that *whether or not they were hypnotized,* highly suggestible participants were able to "see" the visual hallucinations, and low-suggestible participants were *not*. Hypnosis slightly increased the vividness of the subjective perception of the hallucination in the highly suggestible participants, but it had no effect at all on the low-suggestible participants.

Despite the controversy over how best to explain hypnotic effects, psychologists do agree that hypnosis can be a highly effective therapeutic technique (Lynn & others, 2010). And, increasingly, cognitive neuroscientists are using hypnosis as a tool to manipulate subjective awareness (Oakley & Halligan, 2013).

CRITICAL THINKING QUESTIONS

- Does the fact that highly motivated subjects can "fake" hypnotic effects invalidate the notion of hypnosis as a unique state of consciousness? Why or why not?

- What kinds of evidence could prove or disprove the notion that hypnosis is a unique state of consciousness?

Colored rectangles   Grey rectangles

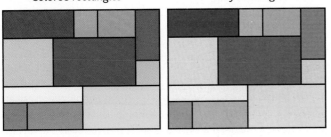

TABLE 4.2

Help Through Hypnosis

Research has demonstrated that hypnosis can effectively:

- Reduce pain and discomfort associated with cancer, rheumatoid arthritis, burn wounds, and other chronic conditions
- Reduce pain and discomfort associated with childbirth
- Reduce the use of narcotics to relieve postoperative pain
- Improve the concentration, motivation, and performance of athletes
- Lessen the severity and frequency of asthma attacks
- Eliminate recurring nightmares
- Enhance the effectiveness of psychotherapy in the treatment of obesity, hypertension, and anxiety
- Remove warts
- Eliminate or reduce stuttering
- Suppress the gag reflex during dental procedures

SOURCES: Research from DuBreuil & Spanos (1993); Covino & Pinnell (2010); Ginandes (2006); Lynn & others (2006b); Nash & others (2009); Stegner & Morgan (2010).

Meditation

KEY THEME

Meditation involves using a mental or physical technique to induce a state of focused attention and heightened awareness.

KEY QUESTIONS

> What are two general types of meditation?
> What are some effects of meditation?

Meditation refers to a group of techniques that induce an altered state of focused attention and heightened awareness. Taking many forms, meditation has been an important part of religious practices throughout the world for thousands of years (Nelson, 2001; Wallace, 2009). However, meditation can also be practiced as a secular technique, independent of any religious tradition or spiritual context (Carmody, 2015).

Common to all forms of meditation is the goal of *controlling or training attention* (Davis & Thompson, 2015; Tang & Posner, 2015). There are literally hundreds of different meditation techniques, but they can be divided into two general categories (Slagter & others, 2011). *Focused attention techniques* involve focusing awareness on a visual image or an object; the sensation of breathing; or a sound, word, or phrase. Sometimes a short word or religious phrase, called a *mantra,* is repeated mentally.

Focused attention techniques involve monitoring and regulating the quality of attention. It may sound simple, but try it: Sit quietly and try to focus your attention on a simple stimulus in your own environment—perhaps a pebble or even a blank Post-it note. You'll quickly realize how hard it is to maintain focus on the object, to notice when your attention is distracted by thoughts or other environmental stimuli, and to return your focus to the chosen object.

In contrast, *open monitoring techniques* involve monitoring the content of experience from moment to moment (Slagter & others, 2011). Rather than concentrating on an object, sound, or activity, the meditator engages in present-centered awareness of the "here and now." When distracting thoughts arise—as they surely will—the practitioner notes the thought and returns to a state of open, nonreflective awareness.

meditation Any one of a number of sustained concentration techniques that focus attention and heighten awareness.

Meditation in Different Cultures (Left) Like this group in Hanoi, Vietnam, many people throughout Asia begin their day with *tai chi,* often meeting in parks and other public places. Tai chi is a form of meditation that involves a structured series of slow, smooth movements. Sometimes described as "meditation in motion," tai chi has been practiced for over 2,000 years.

(Right) These young Americans are practicing *zazen,* or "just sitting," a form of open monitoring meditation (Austin, 2009). Originating in China, Zen is found in many Asian countries, especially Japan, Korea, and Vietnam. Over the past few decades, Zen Buddhism has become increasingly popular in the United States and other Western countries.

Mindfulness, a meditation technique that has become increasingly popular in psychological research and clinical practice, is a form of open monitoring meditation. Definitions vary, but in simple terms, mindfulness mediation involves focusing attention on the present experience with nonjudgmental acceptance (Kabat-Zinn, 2013; Quaglia & others, 2015).

In practice, focused attention and open monitoring techniques often overlap, especially when people are just learning to meditate. For example, beginning mindfulness meditation often starts with focused attention on your breath to calm or "settle" the mind and reduce distractions (Shapiro & Carlson, 2009). Only gradually do practitioners transition to a more open attentiveness to whatever occurs in awareness, whether it be a sensation, thought, or feeling.

Many people assume that meditation involves entering a sort of trancelike state that resembles drowsiness or hypnosis. In fact, mindfulness meditators report the *opposite* effect—a state of heightened awareness and sensitivity to thoughts, internal sensations, and external stimuli such as sounds and smells (Davis & Thompson, 2015; Ricard, 2010).

MYTH ◀ SCIENCE

Is it true that meditation is a drowsy, trancelike state that is no different than simple relaxation?

Scientific Studies of the Effects of Meditation

Much of the early research on meditation investigated its use as a relaxation technique that relieved stress and improved cardiovascular health. The meditation technique that was most widely used in this early research was *transcendental meditation,* or *TM,* a focused attention technique that involved mentally repeating a mantra given to the practitioner by a teacher. Many studies showed that even beginning meditators practicing TM experienced a state of lowered physical arousal, including a decrease in heart rate, lower blood pressure, and changes in brain waves associated with relaxation (Alexander & others, 1994; Benson, 2010).

Contemporary research on meditation is more wide-ranging. Much of this research has been sponsored by the Mind and Life Institute and the 14th Dalai Lama (see photo on page 162). Since the late 1980s, the Mind and Life Institute has fostered a unique scientific collaboration among meditation practitioners, psychologists, and other scientists (Engle, 2011; Ricard & others, 2014). Today, researchers

Jeff Miller/University of Wisconsin-Madison

Studying the Well-Trained Mind
Neuroscientist and psychologist Richard Davidson confers with Buddhist monk Matthieu Ricard during an EEG study that monitored brain waves during different meditative practices (Lutz & others, 2004). Ricard, a former molecular biologist, helped design the studies, held under the auspices of the Mind and Life Institute (www.mindandlife.org). The 14th Dalai Lama has been instrumental in encouraging such collaborations between Western scientists and Tibetan Buddhist practitioners (Ekman & others, 2005; Ricard & others, 2014). As the Dalai Lama wrote, "Buddhists have a 2,500-year history of investigating the workings of the mind" (Gyatso, 2003). Using imaging devices that show what occurs in the brain during meditation, Dr. Davidson has been able to study the effects of Buddhist practice for cultivating compassion, equanimity, or mindfulness.

hope to learn more about the nature of conscious experience as well as meditation's effects on attention, emotional control, health, and the brain (van Vugt, 2015; Tang & others, 2015).

One difficulty in studying meditation is that there are literally hundreds of different meditation techniques (Sedlmeier & others, 2012). Many of today's research studies involve mindfulness techniques, partly because they can be easily taught in a secular context (Davidson, 2010). But even mindfulness-based practices can vary a great deal (Chiesa & Malinowski, 2011). And, study participants may range from novice meditators to people who have practiced meditation for decades. These qualifications need to be kept in mind. However, carefully controlled studies have found that meditation can:

- improve concentration, perceptual discrimination, and attention (Baird & others, 2014; Lutz & others, 2009; Maclean & others, 2010).

- increase working memory and attention in U.S. military personnel before deployment (Jha & others, 2010, 2015).

- improve emotional control and well-being (Arch & Landy, 2015; Davidson, 2005; Farb & others, 2010; Sahdra & others, 2011).

- reduce the symptoms of stress, anxiety, and depression (Shapiro & Jazaieri, 2015; Hayes-Skelton & Wadsworth, 2015; Irving & others, 2015).

Are years of disciplined practice needed to experience the benefits of meditation practice? *No.* In one study, college students with no prior meditation experience learned mindfulness meditation and practiced it for just 20 minutes a day for four days (Zeidan & others, 2010). As compared to a matched control group of students who listened to an audiobook recording of *The Hobbit,* the meditation group significantly improved on several cognitive tasks, such as a memory test. But the most striking result was on a task that required concentration and sustained attention. The meditators, but not the *Hobbit* listeners, sharply improved their ability to focus and sustain attention.

In a similar study, just four days of practice allowed new meditators to reduce their ratings of a painful stimulus's intensity by 40% and unpleasantness by 57%. The pain relief produced by meditation was greater than that produced by morphine or other powerful painkillers, which typically reduce pain ratings by about 25% (Zeidan & others, 2011). Functional MRI scans of the meditators' brains showed a steep reduction of activity in the *primary somatosensory cortex,* which processes sensations of pain, touch, and pressure.

Scientific interest in meditation has dramatically increased in recent years (Jha, 2013). Some psychologists are using meditation to study how intensive mental training affects basic psychological processes, such as attention and memory (Slagter & others, 2011; Ricard & others, 2014). Brain-imaging technology has allowed neuroscientists to document brain changes *during* meditation and brain changes that seem to result as an *effect* of meditation (Tang & others, 2015; Zeidan, 2015). As described in the Focus on Neuroscience box "Meditation and the Brain," meditation has also been used to study *neuroplasticity*—how mental training affects the brain's structure.

FOCUS ON NEUROSCIENCE

Meditation and the Brain

Research on *neuroplasticity*—the brain's capacity to change with experience—has conclusively shown that learning a new skill, such as juggling, changes the physical structure of the brain (Draganski & others, 2004, 2006). So, it turns out, does acquiring new *mental* skills or even just new information. For example, after just two hours of training, adults who learned new color names showed measurable brain changes (Kwok & others, 2011). These changes involved increases in *gray matter*—that is, increases in the size and density of cell bodies and dendrites of neurons in the cortex.

Does meditation, like other forms of mental practice or training, also affect brain structure? One of the earliest findings that meditation was associated with changes in the brain came from the lab of Harvard neuroscientist Sara Lazar. Lazar and her colleagues (2005) recruited a group of 20 experienced insight meditation practitioners. *Insight meditation* is an advanced form of mindfulness meditation, combining traditional mindfulness practice with focused attention on internal experience. The meditation practitioners had an average of nine years of meditation experience, but all were typical Western practitioners, incorporating their daily practice into a busy schedule of family and work responsibilities.

MRI scans showed that several cortical areas were thicker in the meditators' brains than in the brains of a control group of non-meditators who were matched for gender and age. More specifically, the meditators had more gray matter in regions associated with attention, emotion, and sensory processing.

Interestingly, in two regions, thickness was correlated with years of meditation experience—the longer the participants had been meditating, the thicker the cortical regions. And, the differences were *most* pronounced among the older participants. Some cortical areas in the meditators were as thick as corresponding areas in control participants who were 20 years younger. Normally, the cortex gradually shrinks with age, so one intriguing implication of this study was that meditation might help prevent or even reverse the normal age-related thinning of the cortex.

Because this study was correlational, however, it was not possible to attribute the cortical differences to meditation alone. Some other factor could have contributed to the differences between the experienced meditators and the nonmeditating controls. A recent experimental study, however, overcame that limitation (Hölzel & others, 2011). MRI scans were taken of participants two weeks before and two weeks after they learned to meditate in an eight-week

Meditation Matters A study by Sara Lazar and her colleagues (2005) found that cortical areas shown in red and yellow were significantly thicker in meditators than in a matched control group. The somatosensory cortex and insula are both associated with sensory awareness, with the insula specifically linked to awareness of internal body sensations and signals. According to the researchers, the particular region of the prefrontal cortex that was thicker in the meditators than the controls is thought to be associated with the integration of thoughts and feelings.

Labels on image: Somatosensory cortex, Prefrontal cortex, Insula. Credit: Courtesy Dr. Sara Lazar

stress-reduction course. These scans were compared against scans of control group participants who did *not* meditate. The new meditators, but not the controls, showed gray-matter-density increases in several cortical areas, including the hippocampus, cerebellum, and other areas associated with memory, emotion, and awareness.

As researchers continue to investigate the beneficial effects of meditation, neuroscientists hope to uncover some of the neural changes that might underlie changes in behavior, emotion, and cognition. Meditation techniques are also increasingly used as a scientific tool to study neuroplasticity in the adult brain (Tang & others, 2015; Zeidan, 2015). So far, no single pattern of brain changes has been found to be associated with meditation, but that is not surprising given the diversity of techniques and meditation experience among participants in different research studies. As neuroscientist Richard Davidson (2011) notes, the term "meditation" is like the term "sports"—it includes a vast range of different activities, skills, and varying levels of individual expertise and behavior.

Increasingly, meditative practice is also incorporated into psychotherapy (Davis & Hayes, 2011). Today, many psychologists are studying the use of meditation techniques to help tackle psychological problems ranging from eating disorders and substance abuse to major depressive disorder, anxiety, and even more serious disorders (see Bown & others, 2015; Didonna, 2009; Williams & others, 2014). We return to the topic of meditation in Chapter 12 on stress and health, and discuss mindfulness-based therapies in Chapter 14.

If you would like to try a simple meditation technique, turn to page 529 in Chapter 12.

> Test your understanding of **Hypnosis and Meditation** with *LEARNING*Curve.

psychoactive drug A drug that alters consciousness, perception, mood, and behavior.

physical dependence A condition in which a person has physically adapted to a drug so that he or she must take the drug regularly in order to avoid withdrawal symptoms.

drug tolerance A condition in which increasing amounts of a physically addictive drug are needed to produce the original, desired effect.

withdrawal symptoms Unpleasant physical reactions, combined with intense drug cravings, that occur when a person abstains from a drug on which he or she is physically dependent.

drug rebound effect Withdrawal symptoms that are the opposite of a physically addictive drug's action.

Psychoactive Drugs

KEY THEME

Psychoactive drugs alter consciousness by changing arousal, mood, thinking, sensations, and perceptions.

KEY QUESTIONS

> What are four broad categories of psychoactive drugs?
> What are some common properties of psychoactive drugs?
> What factors influence the effects, use, and abuse of drugs?

Psychoactive drugs are chemical substances that can alter arousal, mood, thinking, sensation, and perception. In this section, we will look at the characteristics of four broad categories of psychoactive drugs:

1. *Depressants*—drugs that depress, or inhibit, brain activity.

2. *Opioids*—drugs that are chemically similar to morphine and that relieve pain and produce euphoria.

3. *Stimulants*—drugs that stimulate, or excite, brain activity.

4. *Psychedelic drugs*—drugs that distort sensory perceptions.

Common Effects of Psychoactive Drugs

Addiction is a broad term that refers to a condition in which a person feels psychologically and physically compelled to take a specific drug. People experience **physical dependence** when their body and brain chemistry have physically adapted to a drug. Many physically addictive drugs gradually produce **drug tolerance,** which means that increasing amounts of the drug are needed to gain the original, desired effect.

When a person becomes physically dependent on a drug, abstaining from the drug produces withdrawal symptoms. **Withdrawal symptoms** are unpleasant physical reactions to the lack of the drug, plus an intense craving for it. Withdrawal symptoms are alleviated by taking the drug again. Often, the withdrawal symptoms are opposite to the drug's action, a phenomenon called the **drug rebound effect.** For example, withdrawing from stimulating drugs, like the caffeine in coffee, may produce depression and fatigue. Withdrawal from depressant drugs, such as alcohol, may produce excitability.

Each psychoactive drug has a distinct biological effect. Psychoactive drugs may influence many different bodily systems, but their consciousness-altering effects are primarily due to their effect on the brain. Typically,

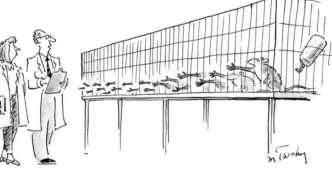

Mike Twohy The New Yorker Collection/ The Cartoon Bank

"At this point, we know it's addictive."

BURGER/PHANIE/age fotostock

Psychoactive Drugs Around the World How pervasive is the use of psychoactive drugs? At an outdoor café in Amsterdam, these young adults meet to socialize and people-watch— accompanied by cigarettes and alcohol. Along with caffeine, nicotine and alcohol are the most widely used psychoactive substances in the world, although they're not used in every culture.

AP Photo/Dima Gavrysh, File

Deadly Additive Drug Effects Having already been nominated for an Academy Award for the 2005 movie *Brokeback Mountain,* actor Heath Ledger was receiving advance critical acclaim for his portrayal of "The Joker" in the 2008 movie *The Dark Knight.* But in January of 2008, Ledger died from an accidental overdose in his New York apartment. In the weeks before his death, Ledger had complained about severe sleeping difficulties. The medical examination found multiple prescription drugs in his body, including two kinds of narcotic painkillers, two kinds of antianxiety drugs, and two kinds of sleeping medications. All of the medications had been legally prescribed, and none had been taken in excess. Even so, the combination produced a lethal additive drug effect, depressing his brain's vital life functions to the point that respiratory failure occurred. Heath Ledger was 28.

these drugs influence brain activity by altering synaptic transmission among neurons. As we discussed in Chapter 2, drugs affect synaptic transmission by increasing or decreasing neurotransmitter amounts or by blocking, mimicking, or influencing a particular neurotransmitter's effects (see Figure 2.7). Chronic drug use can also produce long-term changes in brain structures and functions, as discussed in the Focus on Neuroscience box on page 166, "The Addicted Brain: Diminishing Rewards."

The biological effects of a drug can vary considerably from person to person. An individual's race, gender, age, and weight may influence the intensity of a particular drug's effects. For example, many Asians and Asian Americans have a specific genetic variation that makes them much more responsive to alcohol's effects. In turn, this heightened sensitivity to alcohol is associated with significantly lower rates of alcohol dependence seen among people of Asian heritage as compared to other races (Cook & others, 2005; Kufahl & others, 2008).

Psychological and environmental factors can also influence a drug's effects. An individual's response to a drug can be greatly affected by his or her personality characteristics, mood, expectations, and experience with the drug, as well as the setting in which the drug is taken (Kufahl & others, 2008).

In contrast, **drug abuse,** more formally termed *substance use disorder,* refers to recurrent drug use that involves difficulty controlling the use of the substance, the disruption of normal social, occupational, and interpersonal functioning, and the development of craving, tolerance, and withdrawal symptoms (American Psychiatric Association, 2013). In the United States, alcohol is, by far, the most widely abused substance (Substance Abuse and Mental Health Services Administration, 2009).

The effects of psychoactive drugs are especially unpredictable when combined. At one time, most fatal drug overdoses were caused by illegal narcotics. Today, however, most of the 38,000 drug overdose deaths that occur in the United States each year are caused by prescription drugs, including painkillers, antianxiety medications, and antidepressant medications (Jones & others, 2013).

The Depressants
ALCOHOL, BARBITURATES, INHALANTS, AND TRANQUILIZERS

KEY THEME

Depressants inhibit central nervous system activity, while opioids are addictive drugs that relieve pain and produce euphoria.

KEY QUESTIONS

› What are the physical and psychological effects of alcohol?

› How do barbiturates, inhalants, and tranquilizers affect the body?

› What are the effects of opioids and how do they affect the brain?

The **depressants** are a class of drugs that depress or inhibit central nervous system activity. In general, depressants produce drowsiness, sedation, or sleep. Depressants also relieve anxiety and lower inhibitions. All depressant drugs are potentially

drug abuse (formally called *substance use disorder*) Recurrent substance use that involves impaired control, disruption of social, occupational, and interpersonal functioning, and the development of craving, tolerance, and withdrawal symptoms.

depressants A category of psychoactive drugs that depress or inhibit brain activity.

FOCUS ON NEUROSCIENCE

The Addicted Brain: Diminishing Rewards

Addictive drugs include alcohol, cocaine, heroin, nicotine, and the amphetamines. Although their effects are diverse, these addictive drugs share one thing in common: They all activate dopamine-producing neurons in the brain's reward system (Volkow & others, 2009). The initial dopamine surge in response to an addictive drug is a powerful brain reward, one that prompts the person to repeat the drug-taking behavior (Self, 2005).

The brain's reward system evolved to reinforce behaviors that promote survival, such as eating and sexuality. Many pleasurable activities, including exercising, listening to music, and even looking at an attractive person, can cause a temporary increase in dopamine.

In contrast to naturally rewarding activities and substances, addictive drugs hijack the brain's reward system. Initially, the drug produces the intense dopamine-induced feelings of euphoria. But with repeated drug use, the brain's reward pathways *adapt* to the high dopamine levels. One result is that the availability of dopamine receptors is down-regulated or greatly reduced (Volkow & others, 2011b). Along with decreased dopamine activity, other biochemical changes dampen or inhibit the brain's reward circuits, reducing the pleasurable effects of the abused substance. These adaptations create the conditions for *drug tolerance*—more of the substance is now needed to produce a response that is similar to the drug's original effect (Nestler & Malenka, 2004).

As the brain's reward circuits down-regulate to counter the dopamine surge, another change occurs. The normally reinforcing experiences of everyday life are no longer satisfying or pleasurable. Emotionally, the addict experiences depression, boredom, and apathy (Little & others, 2003).

While lying in a PET scanner and viewing images of laughing children or other pleasurable scenes, the cocaine addict's brain shows little or no dopamine response. But when shown images associated with cocaine use—a coke spoon, the neighborhood where the drugs were bought—the brain's reward circuit "lights up like a Christmas tree" (Hoffman & Froemke, 2007). Thus, everyday experiences are no longer enjoyable. The addicted person needs the substance not to get high but just to feel "normal."

Because the neurons in the brain's reward system have physically changed, they can remain hypersensitive to such cues associated with the abused substance for months and even years after drug use has ended. Simply being exposed to drug-related stimuli or stressful life events can trigger craving—and relapse (Volkow & others, 2006, 2011b).

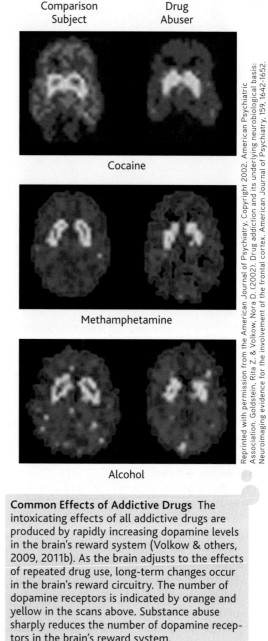

Comparison Subject   Drug Abuser

Cocaine

Methamphetamine

Alcohol

Reprinted with permission from the American Journal of Psychiatry, Copyright 2002. American Psychiatric Association. Goldstein, Rita Z. & Volkow, Nora D. (2002). Drug addiction and its underlying neurobiological basis: Neuroimaging evidence for the involvement of the frontal cortex. American Journal of Psychiatry, 159, 1642-1652.

Common Effects of Addictive Drugs The intoxicating effects of all addictive drugs are produced by rapidly increasing dopamine levels in the brain's reward system (Volkow & others, 2009, 2011b). As the brain adjusts to the effects of repeated drug use, long-term changes occur in the brain's reward circuitry. The number of dopamine receptors is indicated by orange and yellow in the scans above. Substance abuse sharply reduces the number of dopamine receptors in the brain's reward system.

---

physically addictive. Further, the effects of depressant drugs are *addictive*, meaning that the sedative effects are increased when depressants are combined.

ALCOHOL

Weddings, parties, and other social gatherings often include alcohol, a tribute to its relaxing and social lubricating properties. Used in small amounts, alcohol reduces tension and anxiety. But even though it is legal for adults and readily available, alcohol also has a high potential for abuse. Partly because of its ready availability, many drug experts consider alcohol to have the highest social cost of all the addictions (Hawkey & others, 2011; Nutt & others, 2010). Consider these points:

- Excessive alcohol consumption accounts for an estimated 90,000 deaths annually in the United States (Stahre & others, 2014). And, it is a factor in the deaths of over 1,400 U.S. college students each year (Chavez & others, 2011; Wechsler & Nelson, 2008).

- Alcohol is involved in more than half of all assaults, homicides, and motor vehicle accidents (Advokat, Comaty, & Julien, 2014). Intoxicated drivers are the cause of more than 17,000 traffic deaths each year.

- Alcohol intoxication is often a factor in domestic and partner violence, child abuse, and public violent behavior (Easton & others, 2007; Shepherd, 2007).

- Drinking during pregnancy is a leading cause of birth defects. It is the most common cause of intellectual disability—and the only preventable one (Niccols, 2007).

An estimated 17 million Americans are either dependent upon alcohol or have serious alcohol problems. They drink heavily on a regular basis and suffer social, occupational, and health problems as a result (Substance Abuse and Mental Health Services Administration, 2009).

However, the numerous adverse health and social consequences associated with excessive drinking—health problems, injuries, accidents, violence—are not limited to those who are alcohol-dependent. In fact, most of those who periodically drink heavily or drive while intoxicated do *not* meet the formal criteria for alcohol dependence (Woerle & others, 2007).

What Are Alcohol's Psychological Effects? People are often surprised that alcohol is classified as a depressant. Initially, alcohol produces a mild euphoria, talkativeness, and feelings of good humor and friendliness, leading many people to think of alcohol as a stimulant. But these subjective experiences occur because alcohol *lessens inhibitions* by depressing the brain centers responsible for judgment and self-control. Reduced inhibitions and self-control contribute to the aggressive and violent behavior sometimes associated with alcohol abuse. And, impaired judgment and poor impulse control create deadly results when an intoxicated person gets behind the wheel of a car. However, the loss of inhibitions affects individuals differently, depending on their environment and expectations regarding alcohol's effects.

How Does Alcohol Affect the Body? As a general rule, it takes about one hour to metabolize the alcohol in one drink, which is defined as 1 ounce of 80-proof whiskey, 4 ounces of wine, or 12 ounces of beer. All three drinks contain the same amount of alcohol; the alcohol is simply more diluted in beer than in hard liquor.

Factors such as body weight, gender, food consumption, and the rate of alcohol consumption also affect blood alcohol levels. A slender person who quickly consumes three drinks on an empty stomach will become more than twice as intoxicated as a heavier person who consumes three drinks with food. Women metabolize alcohol more slowly than do men. If a man and a woman of equal weight consume the same number of drinks, the woman will become more intoxicated. Table 4.3 on the next page shows the behavioral effects and impairments associated with different blood alcohol levels.

Binge drinking is a particularly risky practice. *Binge drinking* is defined as five or more drinks in a row for men, or four or more drinks in a row for women (Cooke & others, 2010). Every year, several college students die of alcohol poisoning after ingesting large amounts of liquor in a short amount of time. Less well publicized are the other negative effects associated with binge drinking, including aggression, sexual assaults, accidents, and property damage (Mitka, 2009; Wechsler & Nelson, 2008).

MYTH ◀ SCIENCE

Is it true that alcohol is a stimulant?

A Deadly Drug Binge-drinking can lead to tragedy: Acute alcohol poisoning kills six people in the United States every day. Only a third of those who die from overdosing on alcohol were dependent on alcohol. Although the alcohol-related deaths of binge-drinking college students tend to receive the most notice, most alcohol overdoses occur among middle-aged, non-Hispanic white men (Centers for Disease Control and Prevention, 2015a).

Lucy Young /eyevine/Redux

TABLE 4.3

Behavioral Effects of Blood Alcohol Levels

Blood Alcohol Level	Behavioral Effects
0.05%	Lowered alertness; release of inhibitions; impaired judgment
0.10%	Slowed reaction times; impaired motor function; less caution
0.15%	Large, consistent increases in reaction time
0.20%	Marked depression in sensory and motor capability; obvious intoxication
0.25%	Severe motor disturbance; staggering; sensory perceptions greatly impaired
0.30%	Stuporous but conscious; no comprehension of the world around them
0.35%	Surgical anesthesia; minimal level causing death
0.40%	About half of those at this level die

Peopleimages/Getty Images

This Is Fun? According to a national survey of college students, more than half "drank to get drunk" in the previous year (Wechsler & Nelson, 2008). Despite the deaths from alcohol poisoning of several college students each year, binge drinking and public drunkenness remain common at spring break celebrations. College students currently spend $5.5 billion a year on alcohol, more than they spend on textbooks, soft drinks, tea, milk, juice, and coffee combined (Nelson & others, 2005).

In a person who is addicted to alcohol, withdrawal causes rebound hyperexcitability in the brain. The severity of the withdrawal symptoms depends on the level of physical dependence. With a low level of dependence, withdrawal may involve disrupted sleep, anxiety, and mild tremors ("the shakes"). At higher levels of physical dependence on alcohol, withdrawal may involve confusion, hallucinations, and severe tremors or seizures. Collectively, these severe symptoms are called *delirium tremens,* or the *DTs.* In cases of extreme physical dependence, alcohol withdrawal, in the absence of medical supervision, can cause seizures, convulsions, and even death.

INHALANTS

Inhalants are chemical substances that are inhaled to produce an alteration in consciousness. Paint solvents, spray paint, gasoline, and aerosol sprays are just a few of the substances that are abused in this way. Inhalant abuse is most prevalent among adolescent and young adult males.

Although psychoactive inhalants do not have a common chemical structure, they generally act as central nervous system depressants. At low doses, they may cause relaxation, giddiness, and reduced inhibition. At higher doses, inhalants can lead to hallucinations and a loss of consciousness.

Inhalants are very dangerous. Suffocation is one hazard, but many inhaled substances are also toxic to the liver and other organs. Chronic abuse also leads to neurological and brain damage. One study compared cognitive functioning in cocaine and inhalant abusers. Both groups scored well below the normal population, but inhalant users scored even below the cocaine abusers on problem-solving and memory tests. MRI scans showed that the inhalant users also had more extensive brain damage than the cocaine users (Mathias, 2002; Rosenberg & others, 2002).

BARBITURATES AND TRANQUILIZERS

Barbiturates are powerful depressant drugs that reduce anxiety and promote sleep, which is why they are sometimes called "downers." Barbiturates depress activity in the brain centers that control arousal, wakefulness, and alertness. They also depress the brain's respiratory centers.

Like alcohol, barbiturates at low doses cause relaxation, mild euphoria, and reduced inhibitions. Larger doses produce a loss of coordination, impaired mental

inhalants Chemical substances that are inhaled to produce an alteration in consciousness.

barbiturates (barb-ITCH-yer-its) A category of depressant drugs that reduce anxiety and produce sleepiness.

functing, and depression. High doses can produce unconsciousness, coma, and death. Because of the additive effect of depressants, barbiturates combined with alcohol are particularly dangerous. Common barbiturates include the prescription sedatives *Seconal* and *Nembutal*. The illegal drug *methaqualone* (street name *quaalude*) is almost identical chemically to barbiturates and has similar effects.

Barbiturates produce both physical and psychological dependence. Withdrawal from low doses of barbiturates produces irritability and REM rebound nightmares. Withdrawal from high doses of barbiturates can produce hallucinations, disorientation, restlessness, and life-threatening convulsions.

Tranquilizers are depressants that relieve anxiety. Commonly prescribed tranquilizers include *Xanax, Valium, Librium,* and *Ativan.* Chemically different from barbiturates, tranquilizers produce similar, although less powerful, effects. We will discuss these drugs in more detail in Chapter 14 on therapies.

Victor Decolongon/Getty Images

The Dangers of Depressant Drugs Cory Monteith, the popular "singing jock" on the hit television show *Glee*, had battled drug addiction off and on since his teens. A few months after he was released from rehab, he was found dead in a Vancouver hotel room, having overdosed on a potent mixture of heroin and alcohol. Also found in his system were morphine and codeine—making for a deadly combination of depressant drugs. The talented star was just 31.

The Opioids
FROM POPPIES TO DEMEROL

Also called *narcotics* or *opiates,* the **opioids** are a group of addictive drugs that are chemically similar to morphine and that relieve pain and produce feelings of euphoria. Natural opioids include *opium,* which is derived from the opium poppy; *morphine,* the active ingredient in opium; and *codeine,* which can be derived from either opium or morphine. Synthetic and semisynthetic opioids include *heroin, methadone, oxycodone,* and the prescription painkillers *OxyContin, Vicodin, Percodan, Demerol,* and *Fentanyl.*

Opioids produce their powerful effects by mimicking the brain's own natural painkillers, called *endorphins.* Opioids occupy endorphin receptor sites in the brain. When used medically, opioids alter an individual's reaction to pain not by acting at the pain site but by reducing the brain's perception of pain. It was once believed that people who took medically prescribed opioids rarely developed drug tolerance or addiction. Today, physicians and researchers are more aware of the addictive potential of these drugs. Most patients do *not* abuse prescription pain pills or develop physical dependence or addiction (Noble & others, 2008; Volkow & others, 2011a).

Among the most dangerous opioids is *heroin.* When injected into a vein, heroin reaches the brain in seconds, creating an intense rush of euphoria that is followed by feelings of contentment, peacefulness, and warmth. Withdrawal is not life-threatening, but it does produce unpleasant drug rebound symptoms. Withdrawal symptoms include an intense craving for heroin, fever, chills, muscle cramps, and gastrointestinal problems.

Heroin is not the most commonly abused opioid. That distinction belongs to the prescription pain pills, especially *OxyContin,* which combines the synthetic opioid *oxycodone* with a time-release mechanism. Street users discovered that crushing the OxyContin tablets easily destroyed the time-release mechanism. The resulting powder can be snorted, smoked, or diluted in water and injected—resulting in a rapid, intense high.

The synthetic opioids are now the most commonly prescribed class of medications in the United States (Volkow & others, 2011a, 2011b). Abuse of OxyContin and similar prescription pain pills such as hydrocodone and oxycodone has skyrocketed in recent years. In fact, in terms of frequency of illicit use, prescription pain pills are

tranquilizers Depressant drugs that relieve anxiety.

opioids (OH-pee-oidz) A category of psychoactive drugs that are chemically similar to morphine and have strong pain-relieving properties; also called *opiates* or *narcotics.*

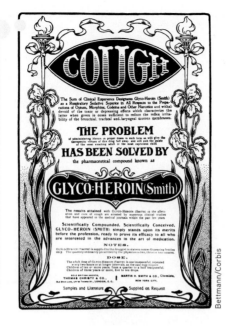

Heroin Cough Syrup
Opium and its derivatives, including heroin, morphine, and codeine, were legal in the United States until 1914. In the late nineteenth and early twentieth centuries, opioids were commonly used in over-the-counter medications for a variety of ailments from sleeplessness to "female problems" (Musto, 1991). This ad for "Glyco-Heroin" cough syrup appeared in 1904. Codeine is still used in some prescription cough syrups.

second only to marijuana (Savage, 2005). Prescription pain pills are especially dangerous when mixed with other drugs, such as alcohol or barbiturates. Deaths from accidental overdose of opioids quadrupled between 1999 and 2010, and prescription opioids accounted for most of this increase (Volkow & others, 2014).

As access to prescription opioids has become more strictly controlled, heroin use and overdose deaths have climbed (Hedegaard & others, 2015; Kolodny & others, 2015). Much of the increase is due to people turning to heroin—a cheaper and more potent high—after first becoming addicted to prescription painkillers (Cicero & others, 2014). Once an urban phenomenon, heroin today is increasingly found in rural small towns and suburbs. Opioid overdose is now the second leading cause of accidental death in the United States, second only to motor vehicle accidents (Volkow & McLellan, 2011; Centers for Disease Control and Prevention, 2015b).

The Stimulants

CAFFEINE, NICOTINE, AMPHETAMINES, AND COCAINE

KEY THEME

Stimulant drugs increase brain activity, while the psychedelic drugs create perceptual distortions, alter mood, and affect thinking.

KEY QUESTIONS

> What are the general effects of stimulants and the specific effects of caffeine, nicotine, amphetamines, and cocaine?

> What are the effects of mescaline, LSD, and marijuana?

> What are the "club drugs," and what are their effects?

Stimulants vary in legal status, the strength of their effects, and the manner in which they are taken. All stimulant drugs, however, are at least mildly addicting, and all tend to increase brain activity.

CAFFEINE AND NICOTINE

Caffeine is the most widely used psychoactive drug in the world and is found in such common sources as coffee, tea, cola drinks, chocolate, and certain over-the-counter medications (see Table 4.4). Caffeine promotes wakefulness, mental alertness, vigilance, and faster thought processes by stimulating the release of dopamine in the brain's prefrontal cortex.

Caffeine also produces its mentally stimulating effects by blocking *adenosine* receptors in the brain. *Adenosine* is a naturally occurring compound in your body that influences the release of several neurotransmitters in the central nervous system. As noted earlier, adenosine levels gradually increase the longer a person is awake. When adenosine levels reach a certain level in your body, the urge to sleep greatly intensifies. Caffeine staves off the urge and promotes alertness by blocking adenosine's sleep-inducing effects (Roehrs & Roth, 2008). Caffeine's adenosine-blocking ability has another effect—it stimulates *indirect* and mild dopamine release in the brain's reward system.

Yes, coffee drinkers, there is ample scientific evidence that caffeine is physically addictive. However, because the brain-reward effects of caffeine are mild, coffee junkies are not likely to ransack the nearest Starbucks or take hostages if deprived of their favorite espresso. However, they will experience withdrawal symptoms if they abruptly stop their caffeine intake. Headaches, irritability, drowsiness, and fatigue can last a week or longer (Juliano & Griffiths, 2004; Reissig & others, 2009).

stimulants A category of psychoactive drugs that increase brain activity, arouse behavior, and increase mental alertness.

caffeine (kaff-EEN) A stimulant drug found in coffee, tea, cola drinks, chocolate, and many over-the-counter medications.

TABLE 4.4

Common Sources of Caffeine

Item	Milligrams Caffeine
Coffee (short, 8 ounces)	85–250
Coffee (grande, 16 ounces)	220–550
Tea (8 ounces)	16–60
Chocolate (semisweet, baking; 1 ounce)	25
Soft drinks (12 ounces)	35–70
Energy drinks (8 ounces, Red Bull, Jolt)	40–80
Caffeinated waters (8 ounces, Water Joe, Avitae)	60–125
Over-the-counter stimulants (NoDoz, Vivarin)	200
Over-the-counter analgesics (Anacin, Midol)	25–130
Over-the-counter cold remedies (Triaminicin, Coryban-D)	30

SOURCE: Information from National Sleep Foundation (2004b).

nicotine A stimulant drug found in tobacco products.

Taken to excess, caffeine can produce anxiety, restlessness, and increased heart rate, and can disrupt normal sleep patterns. Excessive caffeine use can also contribute to the incidence of sleep disorders, including the NREM parasomnias, like sleepwalking (Cartwright, 2004). Recall that Scott, whose story we told in the Prologue, had been taking caffeine pills for several weeks before his sleepwalking episode. Because Scott never drank coffee or other caffeinated beverages, his caffeine tolerance would have been low. Especially when combined with sleep deprivation, irregular sleep schedules, and high levels of stress—all of which Scott experienced—excessive caffeine intake can trigger sleepwalking and other NREM parasomnias. At least one sleep expert believes that Scott's high caffeine use may have contributed to his outburst of sleep violence (Cartwright, 2007).

For some people, a cup of coffee and a cigarette go hand in hand. Cigarettes contain **nicotine,** another potent and addictive stimulant. Nicotine is found in all tobacco products.

Like caffeine, nicotine increases mental alertness and reduces fatigue or drowsiness. Brain-imaging studies show that nicotine increases neural activity in many brain areas, including the frontal lobes, thalamus, hippocampus, and amygdala (Rose & others, 2003). Thus, it's not surprising that smokers report that tobacco enhances mood, attention, and arousal.

When cigarette smoke is inhaled, nicotine reaches the brain in seconds. But over the next hour or two, nicotine's desired effects diminish. For the addicted person, smoking becomes a finely tuned and regulated behavior that maintains steady brain levels of nicotine. At regular intervals ranging from about 30 to 90 minutes, the smoker lights up, avoiding the withdrawal effects that are starting to occur. For the pack-a-day smoker, that averages out to some 70,000 "hits" of nicotine every year.

A new development in nicotine delivery is "vaping," or the use of electronic or "e-cigarettes" (Dawkins & Corcoran, 2014). E-cigarettes are battery-powered devices that heat liquid nicotine and mimic the look and feel of smoking, from a glowing tip to the hazy, smokelike vapor that is inhaled. The e-cigarette market is exploding, both in the United States and globally. There are more than 250 e-cigarette brands, with sales reaching more than 1.7 billion in the United States alone. One worrisome development is the increasing popularity of "vaping" by teenagers (see photo). Some people turn to e-cigarettes as an aid to quitting smoking, but others see them as a safer alternative to tobacco products (Fairchild & others, 2014). And, some people use both conventional and electronic cigarettes (DeAngelis, 2014).

E-Cigarettes: More Popular Than Tobacco? E-cigarette flavor additives like cotton candy, bubble gum, and gummy bear seem to be designed to attract young users. As tobacco use has fallen, "vaping" has increased: In 2014, more middle and high school students used e-cigarettes than tobacco products. A recent survey found that the use of e-cigarettes increased from 1.1 percent in 2013 to 3.9 percent in 2014 among middle school students, and from 4.5 percent to 13.4 percent among high school students. That translates to a total of 450,000 middle school students and 2 million high school students (Arrazola & others, 2015). Many health experts are concerned about the long-term effects of e-cigarettes and their addictive potential, especially among young users (Kandel & Kandel, 2014).

Diego Cervo/Getty Images

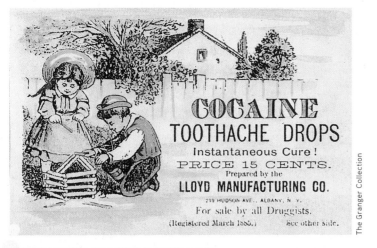

The Granger Collection

Cocaine Toothache Drops? Cocaine was legal in the United States until 1914. Like the opioids, it was widely used as an ingredient in over-the-counter medicines (Jonnes, 1999). Cocaine derivatives, such as novocaine and lidocaine, are used medically as anesthetics. Cocaine was also part of Coca-Cola's original formula in 1888. It was replaced in 1903 with another stimulant, caffeine.

amphetamines (am-FET-uh-meenz) A class of stimulant drugs that arouse the central nervous system and suppress appetite.

cocaine A stimulant drug derived from the leaves of the coca tree.

psychedelic drugs (sy-kuh-DEL-ick) A category of psychoactive drugs that create sensory and perceptual distortions, alter mood, and affect thinking.

mescaline (MESS-kuh-lin) A psychedelic drug derived from the peyote cactus.

LSD A synthetic psychedelic drug.

Whitney Houston: Chronic Cocaine Abuse and Heart Disease Singer Whitney Houston was found facedown in less than a foot of water in a hotel bathtub. The autopsy showed that years of cocaine abuse had badly damaged Houston's heart and circulatory system. Because of its powerful effects on the sympathetic nervous system, chronic cocaine abuse damages the heart, liver, and other organs.

AP Photo/Mark J. Terrill

The use of e-cigarettes is controversial. Some public health researchers support their use because they believe that e-cigarettes are less harmful than regular cigarettes, especially if people use e-cigarettes to help them quit smoking. But others point out that nicotine in any form is highly addictive, that dangerous chemicals may be present in the vapor, and that the long-term effects are unknown (Fairchild & Bayer, 2015).

People who start smoking or vaping for nicotine's stimulating properties often continue to avoid the withdrawal symptoms. Along with an intense craving for nicotine, withdrawal symptoms include jumpiness, irritability, tremors, headaches, drowsiness, "brain fog," and light-headedness.

AMPHETAMINES AND COCAINE

Like caffeine and nicotine, amphetamines and cocaine are addictive substances that affect brain dopamine and stimulate brain activity, increasing mental alertness and reducing fatigue (Wang & others, 2015). However, amphetamines and cocaine also elevate mood and produce a sense of euphoria. When abused, both drugs can produce severe psychological and physical problems.

Sometimes called "speed" or "uppers," **amphetamines** suppress appetite and were once widely prescribed as diet pills. *Benzedrine* and *Dexedrine* are prescription amphetamines. Tolerance to the appetite-suppressant effects occurs quickly, so progressive increases in amphetamine dosage are required to maintain the effect. Consequently, amphetamines are rarely prescribed today for weight control.

Using any type of amphetamines for an extended period of time is followed by "crashing"—withdrawal symptoms of fatigue, deep sleep, intense mental depression, and increased appetite. This is another example of a drug rebound effect. Users also become psychologically dependent on the drug for the euphoric state, or "rush," that it produces, especially when injected.

Cocaine is an illegal stimulant derived from the leaves of the coca plant, which is found in South America. (The coca plant is not the source of cocoa or chocolate, which is made from the beans of the *cacao* tree.) Psychologically, cocaine produces intense euphoria, mental alertness, and self-confidence. These psychological responses occur because cocaine blocks the reuptake of three different neurotransmitters—dopamine, serotonin, and norepinephrine. Blocking reuptake *potentiates,* or increases the effects of, these neurotransmitters.

The effects of cocaine depend partly on the form in which it is taken. A concentrated form of cocaine, called "crack," is smoked. When smoked or injected, cocaine reaches the brain in seconds and effects peak in about five minutes. If inhaled or "snorted," cocaine takes several minutes to be absorbed through the nasal membranes, and peak blood levels are reached in 30 to 60 minutes.

Chronic cocaine use produces a wide range of psychological disorders. Of particular note, the prolonged use of amphetamines or cocaine can result in *stimulant-induced psychosis,* also called *amphetamine-induced psychosis* or *cocaine-induced psychosis.* Schizophrenia-like symptoms develop, including auditory hallucinations of voices and bizarrely paranoid ideas. In response to imagined threats, the psychotic person can become highly aggressive and dangerous.

Methamphetamine, also known as *meth,* is an illegal drug that can be easily manufactured in home or street laboratories.

FOCUS ON NEUROSCIENCE

How Methamphetamines Erode the Brain

Researcher Paul Thompson and his colleagues (2004) used MRI scans to compare the brains of chronic methamphetamine users to those of healthy adults. In the composite scan shown here, red indicates areas with tissue loss from 5 to 10 percent. Green indicates 3 to 5 percent tissue loss, and blue indicates relatively intact brain regions. Thompson found that meth abusers experienced up to 10 percent tissue loss in limbic system areas involved in emotion and reward. Significant tissue loss also occurred in hippocampal regions involved in learning and memory.

"We expected some brain changes, but we didn't expect so much brain tissue to be destroyed," Thompson said. Not surprisingly, methamphetamine abusers performed more poorly on memory tests as compared to healthy people the same age (Thompson & others, 2004).

Thompson, P.M., et. al. "Structural abnormalities in the brains of human subjects who use methamphetamine." The Journal for Neuroscience (2004) 24:Fig. 1.

Areas of Greatest Loss
— Emotion, reward (limbic system)
— Memory (hippocampus)

Providing an intense high that is longer-lasting and less expensive than that of cocaine, methamphetamine use has spread from the western United States to the rest of the country, including small towns in the rural Midwest and South.

Methamphetamine is highly addictive and can cause extensive brain damage and tissue loss, as discussed in the Focus on Neuroscience box, "How Methamphetamines Erode the Brain." Even after months of abstinence, PET scans of former meth users showed significant reductions in the number of dopamine receptors (Volkow & others, 2001).

Extensive neurological damage, especially to the frontal lobes, adds to the cognitive and social skill deficits that are evident in heavy methamphetamine users (Homer & others, 2008). Depression, emotional instability, and impulsive and violent behavior are also common. Finally, some research suggests that it may take years for the brain to recover from damage caused by methamphetamine abuse (Bamford & others, 2008).

Psychedelic Drugs
MESCALINE, LSD, AND MARIJUANA

The term **psychedelic drug** was coined in the 1950s to describe a group of drugs that create profound perceptual distortions, alter mood, and affect thinking. *Psychedelic* literally means "mind manifesting."

MESCALINE AND LSD

Naturally occurring psychedelic drugs have been used in religious rituals for thousands of years. **Mescaline** is derived from the peyote cactus. Another psychedelic drug, called *psilocybin,* is derived from *Psilocybe* mushrooms, which are sometimes referred to as "magic mushrooms" or "shrooms."

In contrast to these naturally occurring psychedelics, **LSD** (*lysergic acid diethylamide*) is a powerful psychedelic drug that was first synthesized in the late 1930s. LSD is far more potent than mescaline or psilocybin. Just 25 micrograms, or one-millionth of an ounce, of LSD can produce profound psychological effects with relatively few physiological changes.

LSD and psilocybin are very similar chemically to the neurotransmitter *serotonin,* which is involved in regulating moods and sensations (see Chapter 2). LSD and psilocybin mimic serotonin in the brain, stimulating serotonin receptor sites in the somatosensory cortex and other brain regions (Carhart-Harris & others, 2014; Kupferschmidt, 2014a).

The effects of a psychedelic experience vary greatly, depending on an individual's personality, current emotional state, surroundings, and the other people present. A "bad trip"

Peyote-Inspired Visions The Huichol Indians of Mexico have used peyote in religious ceremonies for hundreds of years. Huichol yarn paintings, like the one shown here, often depict imagery and scenes inspired by traditional peyote visions. These visions resemble the geometric shapes and radiating patterns of hallucinations induced by psychedelic drugs. Today, peyote is used as a sacrament in the religious ceremonies of the Native American Church, a religion with more than 300,000 members (Swan & Big Bow, 1995). Such ritual use of peyote is not generally associated with psychological or cognitive problems (see Halpern & others, 2005).

John Mitchell/Alamy

marijuana A psychoactive drug derived from the hemp plant.

MDMA or **ecstasy** Synthetic club drug that combines stimulant and mild psychedelic effects.

can produce extreme anxiety, panic, and even psychotic episodes. Tolerance to psychedelic drugs may occur after heavy use. However, even heavy users of LSD do not develop physical dependence, nor do they experience withdrawal symptoms if the drug is not taken.

One large-scale mental health survey of nearly 20,000 participants who had used psychedelic drugs found no increased risk of developing psychological problems (Johansen & Krebs, 2015). However, adverse reactions to LSD can include flashbacks (recurrences of the drug's effects), depression, long-term psychological instability, and prolonged psychotic reactions (Advokat, Comaty, & Julien, 2014). In a psychologically unstable or susceptible person, even a single dose of LSD can precipitate a psychotic reaction. On the other hand, some clinical trials have shown that LSD, psilocybin, or other psychedelic drugs, given under carefully controlled conditions, may be helpful in the treatment of anxiety, addiction, and chronic depression (see Kupferschmidt, 2014a). Such treatments are still highly experimental, however.

MARIJUANA

The common hemp plant, *Cannabis sativa,* is used to make rope and cloth. But when its leaves, stems, flowers, and seeds are dried and crushed, the mixture is called **marijuana,** one of the most widely used illegal drugs. Marijuana's active ingredient is the chemical *tetrahydrocannabinol,* abbreviated *THC.* When marijuana is smoked, THC reaches the brain in less than 30 seconds. One potent form of marijuana, *hashish,* is made from the resin of the hemp plant. Hashish is sometimes eaten.

To lump marijuana with the highly psychedelic drugs mescaline and LSD is somewhat misleading. At high doses, marijuana can sometimes produce sensory distortions that resemble a mild psychedelic experience. Low to moderate doses of THC typically produce a sense of well-being, mild euphoria, and a dreamy state of relaxation. Senses become more focused and sensations more vivid. Taste, touch, and smell may be enhanced; time perception may be altered.

In the early 1990s, researchers discovered receptor sites in the brain that are specific for THC. They also discovered a naturally occurring brain chemical, called *anandamide,* that is structurally similar to THC and that binds to the THC receptors in the brain (Devane & others, 1992; Mechoulam & others, 2014). Anandamide appears to be involved in regulating the transmission of pain signals and may reduce painful sensations. Active ingredients in marijuana have been shown to be involved in several psychological processes, including mood, memory, cognition, appetite, and neurogenesis (see Mechoulam & Parker, 2013).

Marijuana and its active ingredient, THC, have been shown to be helpful in the treatment of pain, epilepsy, hypertension, nausea, glaucoma, arthritis, and asthma (Mechoulam & others, 2014). In cancer patients, THC can prevent the nausea and vomiting caused by chemotherapy.

On the negative side, marijuana interferes with muscle coordination and perception and may impair driving ability. When marijuana and alcohol use are combined, marijuana's effects are intensified—a dangerous combination for drivers. Marijuana has also been shown to interfere with learning, memory, and cognitive functioning (Harvey & others, 2007). New research suggests that marijuana may interfere with memory and cognition by disrupting communication between the hippocampus and the prefrontal cortex (Kucewicz & others, 2011).

Most marijuana users do not develop physical dependence. Chronic users of high doses can develop some tolerance to THC and may experience withdrawal symptoms when its use is discontinued (Budney & others, 2007; Nocon & others, 2006). Such symptoms include irritability, restlessness, insomnia, tremors, and decreased appetite.

Medical Marijuana Marijuana has been used as a medicine for thousands of years in ancient China, Egypt, India, Greece, and other countries. By 2015, 23 states and the District of Columbia had legalized medical marijuana, with similar legislation pending in other states. Four states and the District of Columbia had legalized recreational use for adults. Marijuana can relieve certain types of chronic pain, inflammation, muscle spasms, nausea, vomiting, and other symptoms caused by such illnesses as multiple sclerosis, cancer, and AIDS (see Bostwick, 2012; Mechoulam & others, 2014). One unexpected finding: the average death rate for opioid overdose was 25% lower in states with legalized medical marijuana than in states without legal access to marijuana, suggesting that the availability of medical marijuana for chronic pain may be associated with lower use—and abuse—of narcotic painkillers (Bachhuber & others, 2014).

Jim Wilson/The New York Times/Redux

Designer "Club" Drugs
ECSTASY AND THE DISSOCIATIVE ANESTHETIC DRUGS

Some drugs don't fit into neat categories. The "club drugs" are a loose collection of psychoactive drugs that are popular at dance clubs, parties, and the all-night dance parties called "raves." Many of these drugs are *designer drugs,* meaning that they were synthesized in a laboratory rather than derived from naturally occurring compounds. In this section, we'll take a look at three of the most popular club drugs—*ecstasy, ketamine,* and *PCP.*

The initials **MDMA** stand for the long chemical name of the quintessential club drug better known as **ecstasy.** At low doses, MDMA acts as a stimulant, but at high doses it has mild psychedelic effects. Its popularity, however, results from its emotional effects: Feelings of euphoria, friendliness, and increased well-being are common (Bedi & others, 2010). Ecstasy's side effects hint at the problems that can be associated with its use: dehydration, rapid heartbeat, tremors, muscle tension and involuntary teeth-clenching, and hyperthermia (abnormally high body temperature). Rave partygoers who take MDMA in crowded, hot surroundings are particularly at risk for collapse or death from dehydration and hyperthermia.

The "love drug" effects of ecstasy may result from its unique effect on serotonin in the brain. Along with causing neurons to release serotonin, MDMA also blocks serotonin reuptake, amplifying and prolonging serotonin effects (Braun, 2001). While flooding the brain with serotonin may temporarily enhance feelings of emotional well-being, there are adverse trade-offs.

First, the "high" of MDMA is often followed by depression when the drug wears off. More ominously, studies have shown that moderate or heavy use of ecstasy can damage serotonin nerve endings in the brain (Croft & others, 2001; Reneman & others, 2006). Damage to the brain's serotonin system may account for the depression, anxiety, and sleep and mood disturbances that are associated with long-term use of ecstasy (Benningfield & Cowan, 2013). However, MDMA is also being studied as a potential treatment for posttraumatic stress disorder (see Kupferschmidt, 2014b).

Another class of drugs found at dance clubs and raves is the **dissociative anesthetics,** including phencyclidine, better known as *PCP* or *angel dust,* and *ketamine* (street name *Special K*). Rather than producing actual hallucinations, PCP and ketamine produce marked feelings of dissociation and depersonalization. Feelings of detachment from reality—including distortions of space, time, and body image—are common. Generally, PCP has more intense and longer effects than ketamine does. Ketamine has also shown some promise in the treatment of depression (Fond & others, 2014; McGirr & others, 2015). We discuss the experimental use of ketamine for treatment-resistant depression in Chapter 14 on therapies.

PCP can be eaten, snorted, or injected, but it is most often smoked. The effects are unpredictable, and a PCP trip can last for several days. Some users of PCP report feelings of invulnerability and exaggerated strength. PCP users can become severely disoriented, violent, aggressive, or suicidal. High doses of PCP can cause hyperthermia, convulsions, and death. PCP affects levels of the neurotransmitter *glutamate,* indirectly stimulating the release of dopamine in the brain. Thus, PCP is highly addictive. Memory problems and depression are common effects of long-term use.

❯ Test your understanding of **Psychoactive Drugs** with *LEARNINGCurve.*

Closing Thoughts

Internal biological rhythms and external environmental factors influence the natural ebb and flow of your consciousness over the course of any given day. Beyond those natural oscillations, hypnosis and meditation are techniques that can profoundly alter your experience of consciousness. Meditation, in particular, produces numerous benefits that can help you cope more effectively with life's demands. Some psychoactive drugs, including widely available substances like caffeine, can also influence your experience of consciousness in beneficial ways. But other psychoactive substances, while producing dramatic alterations in consciousness, do so with the potential risk of damaging the finely tuned balance of the brain's neurotransmitters and reward system.

Both natural and deliberate factors seem to have played a role in the extreme breach of consciousness that Scott Falater claimed to experience. Severe disruptions in his normal sleep patterns, his out-of-character use of caffeine, and intense work-related

Scott Houston/Sygma/Corbis

Rave Culture All-night dance parties, called raves, originated in Great Britain and quickly spread to other European countries and to the United States. Raves may draw anywhere from a few hundred to a few thousand people or more. Highly caffeinated "energy drinks," amphetamines, methamphetamine, and other stimulants may be consumed to maintain the energy needed to dance all night. Rave culture also helped popularize the use of *ecstasy,* a synthetic drug.

dissociative anesthetics Class of drugs that reduce sensitivity to pain and produce feelings of detachment and dissociation; includes the club drugs phencyclidine (PCP) and ketamine.

Life in Prison Scott Falater could have received the death penalty after being convicted by a Phoenix jury of first-degree murder in the death of his wife, Yarmila. But during the presentencing investigation, Falater's two children, and even Yarmila's mother, pleaded to spare his life. The sentencing judge agreed, and sentenced Falater to life in prison with no possibility for parole.

Getty Images

stimulus control therapy Insomnia treatment involving specific guidelines to create a strict association between the bedroom and rapid sleep onset.

stresses combined to trigger sleepwalking, a parasomnia that Scott had demonstrated when he was younger. And that Scott reacted violently when his wife tried to guide him back to bed also had precedent: Scott had reacted aggressively earlier in his life when his sister tried to intervene during one of his sleepwalking episodes.

Scott Falater's trial for murdering his wife drew international attention. In the end, the Arizona jury convicted Falater of first-degree, premeditated murder. Falater was sentenced to life in prison with no possibility of parole. Today, Scott Falater is incarcerated in the Arizona State Prison Complex at Yuma, where he works as an educational aide and library clerk.

Overcoming Insomnia

In this section, we'll provide some simple tips to help you minimize sleep problems. If you frequently suffer from insomnia, we'll also describe a very effective treatment that you can implement on your own—**stimulus control therapy.**

Preventing Sleep Problems

You may not realize the degree to which your daily habits can contribute to or even create sleeping difficulties. The following four strategies can help you consistently get a good night's sleep.

1. *Monitor your intake of stimulants.*

Many people don't realize how much caffeine they're ingesting. Coffee, tea, soft drinks, chocolate, and many over-the-counter medications contain significant amounts of caffeine (see Table 4.4). Monitor your caffeine intake, and avoid caffeine products for at least 4 hours before going to bed. Some people are very sensitive to caffeine's stimulating effects and may need to avoid caffeine for up to 10 hours before bedtime. Beyond caffeine, some herbal teas and supplements contain ginseng, ephedrine, or other stimulants that can keep you awake.

2. *Establish a quiet bedtime routine.*

Avoid stimulating mental or physical activity for at least an hour before your bedtime. That means no suspenseful television shows, violent videos, exciting video games, or loud arguments right before bedtime. Ditto for strenuous exercise. Although regular exercise is an excellent way to improve your sleep, exercising within 3 hours of bedtime may keep you awake. Finally, soaking in a very warm bath shortly before bed promotes deep sleep by raising your core body temperature.

3. *Create the conditions for restful sleep.*

Your bedroom should be quiet, cool, and dark. If you live in a noisy environment, invest in a pair of earplugs or some sort of "white noise" source, such as a fan, for your bedroom. Turn off or mute all devices that can potentially disrupt your sleep, including cell phones and computers. And, limit your exposure to all types of electronic screens before bedtime. Remember, the blue light emitted by tablets, laptops, and smartphones can trick your brain into thinking it's morning, triggering alertness rather than sleepiness (Chang & others, 2015).

4. *Establish a consistent sleep–wake schedule.*

While this is probably the single most effective strategy to achieve high-quality sleep, it's also the most challenging for a lot of college students. Try to go to bed at about the same time each night and get up at approximately the same time every morning so that your circadian rhythms stay in sync. Exposure to bright lights or sunlight shortly after awakening in the morning helps keep your internal clock set.

Many students try to "catch up" on their sleep by sleeping in on the weekends. Unfortunately, this strategy can work against you by producing a case of the "Monday morning blues," which is a self-induced case of jet lag caused by resetting your circadian rhythms to the later weekend schedule.

If you've tried all these suggestions and are still troubled by frequent insomnia, you may need to take a more systematic approach, as outlined in the next section.

Stimulus Control Therapy

Without realizing it, you can sabotage your ability to sleep by associating mentally arousing activities and stimuli with your bedroom, such as watching TV, text messaging, reading, surfing the Internet, eating, listening to music, doing homework or paperwork, and so on. Over time, your bed and bedroom become stimuli that trigger arousal rather than drowsiness and the rapid onset of sleep. In turn, this increases the amount of time that you're lying in bed awake, thrashing around, and trying to force yourself to sleep.

Stimulus control therapy is designed to help you (1) establish a consistent sleep–wake schedule and (2) associate your bedroom and bedtime with falling asleep rather than other activities (Morin & others, 2006). To achieve improved sleep, you must commit to the following rules with *no* exceptions for at least two weeks:

- Only sleep and sex are allowed in your bedroom. None of the sleep-incompatible activities mentioned above are allowed in your bed or bedroom.

- Only go to bed when you are sleepy, not tired or wiped out, but *sleepy.*

- Once in bed, if you're still awake after 15 minutes, don't try to force yourself to go to sleep. Instead, get out of bed and go sit in another room. Only go back to bed when you get sleepy.

- Get up at the *same* time *every* morning, including weekends, regardless of how much sleep you got the night before.
- No daytime napping. None. Zip. Nada. Zilch.

Strictly adhering to these rules can be challenging given the realities of work, family, school, and other personal commitments. However, those situations are much easier to manage when you are adequately rested.

Keeping a *sleep diary* can help you track your sleep and sleep-related behaviors. It will also increase your awareness of your sleep habits and the factors that interfere with restorative sleep. You can go to www.sleepfoundation.org/insomnia/content/treatment to download a sleep log from the National Sleep Foundation. Other sleep diaries can easily be found with an Internet search. Sleep well!

VEGAN INSOMNIA

Eric Lewis The New Yorker Collection/The Cartoon Bank

CHAPTER REVIEW

KEY PEOPLE AND KEY TERMS

William James, p. 135
Sigmund Freud, p. 149

J. Alan Hobson, p. 150
Robert W. McCarley, p. 150

Ernest R. Hilgard, p. 157

consciousness, p. 134
attention, p. 135
circadian rhythm, p. 138
suprachiasmatic nucleus (SCN), p. 138
melatonin, p. 138
electroencephalograph, p. 140
EEG (electroencephalogram), p. 140
REM sleep, p. 140
NREM sleep, p. 140
beta brain waves, p. 140
alpha brain waves, p. 140
hypnagogic hallucinations, p. 140
sleep paralysis, p. 141
sleep spindles, p. 142
K complex, p. 142
REM rebound, p. 147

sleep thinking, p. 147
dream, p. 147
nightmare, p. 149
manifest content, p. 149
latent content, p. 149
activation–synthesis model of dreaming, p. 150
neurocognitive model of dreaming, p. 151
sleep disorders, p. 152
dyssomnias, p. 152
parasomnias, p. 152
insomnia, p. 153
obstructive sleep apnea (OSA), p. 153
narcolepsy, p. 153
cataplexy, p. 154
sleep terrors, p. 154
sleepwalking, p. 155

sleep-related eating disorder, (SRED) p. 155
sleepsex, p. 155
hypnosis, p. 156
posthypnotic suggestion, p. 157
posthypnotic amnesia, p. 157
dissociation, p. 157
neodissociation theory of hypnosis, p. 158
hidden observer, p. 158
meditation, p. 160
psychoactive drug, p. 164
physical dependence, p. 164
drug tolerance, p. 164
withdrawal symptoms, p. 164
drug rebound effect, p. 164
drug abuse, p. 165
depressants, p. 165

inhalants, p. 168
barbiturates, p. 168
tranquilizers, p. 169
opioids, p. 169
stimulants, p. 170
caffeine, p. 170
nicotine, p. 171
amphetamines, p. 172
cocaine, p. 172
psychedelic drugs, p. 173
mescaline, p. 173
LSD, p. 173
marijuana, p. 174
MDMA (ecstasy), p. 175
dissociative anesthetics, p. 175
stimulus control therapy, p. 176

SOLUTION TO FIGURE 4.1

Figure 4.1: Can We Read Your Mind? Explanation: Look once more at the six cards on page 136, and then compare them with the five cards pictured on page 138. Notice any differences? If the act of circling an eye distracted you and you fell for the trick—as most people do—you have just experienced *change blindness*.

Consciousness and Its Variations

Consciousness

The immediate awareness of internal and external stimuli

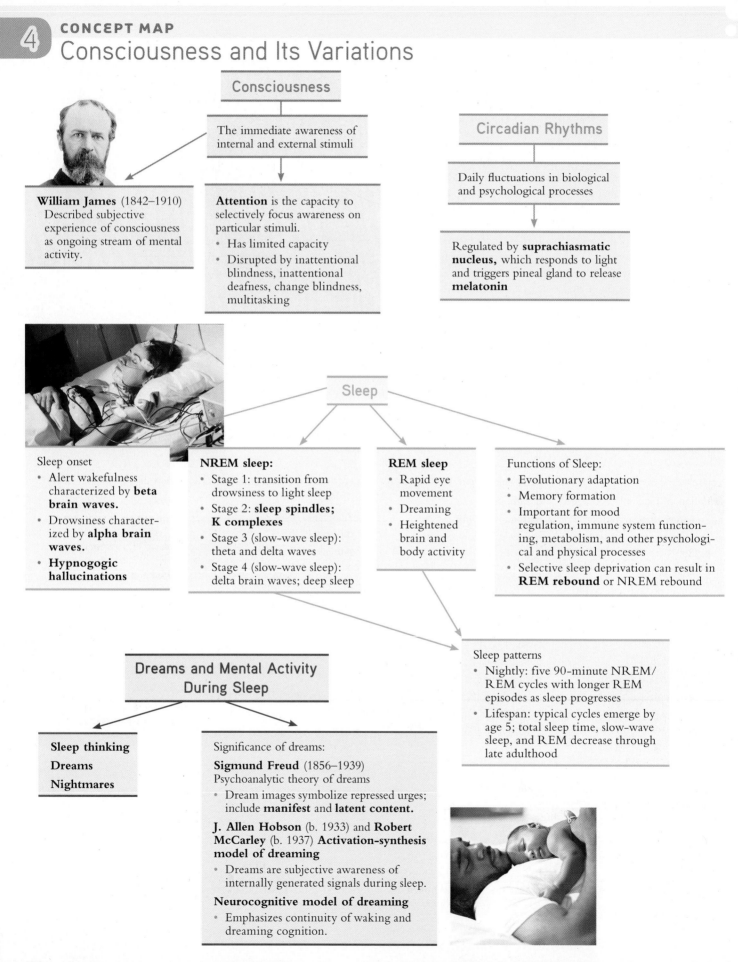

William James (1842–1910) Described subjective experience of consciousness as ongoing stream of mental activity.

Attention is the capacity to selectively focus awareness on particular stimuli.
- Has limited capacity
- Disrupted by inattentional blindness, inattentional deafness, change blindness, multitasking

Circadian Rhythms

Daily fluctuations in biological and psychological processes

Regulated by **suprachiasmatic nucleus,** which responds to light and triggers pineal gland to release **melatonin**

Sleep

Sleep onset
- Alert wakefulness characterized by **beta brain waves.**
- Drowsiness characterized by **alpha brain waves.**
- **Hypnogogic hallucinations**

NREM sleep:
- Stage 1: transition from drowsiness to light sleep
- Stage 2: **sleep spindles; K complexes**
- Stage 3 (slow-wave sleep): theta and delta waves
- Stage 4 (slow-wave sleep): delta brain waves; deep sleep

REM sleep
- Rapid eye movement
- Dreaming
- Heightened brain and body activity

Functions of Sleep:
- Evolutionary adaptation
- Memory formation
- Important for mood regulation, immune system functioning, metabolism, and other psychological and physical processes
- Selective sleep deprivation can result in **REM rebound** or NREM rebound

Sleep patterns
- Nightly: five 90-minute NREM/ REM cycles with longer REM episodes as sleep progresses
- Lifespan: typical cycles emerge by age 5; total sleep time, slow-wave sleep, and REM decrease through late adulthood

Dreams and Mental Activity During Sleep

Sleep thinking
Dreams
Nightmares

Significance of dreams:

Sigmund Freud (1856–1939) Psychoanalytic theory of dreams
- Dream images symbolize repressed urges; include **manifest** and **latent content.**

J. Allen Hobson (b. 1933) and **Robert McCarley** (b. 1937) **Activation-synthesis model of dreaming**
- Dreams are subjective awareness of internally generated signals during sleep.

Neurocognitive model of dreaming
- Emphasizes continuity of waking and dreaming cognition.

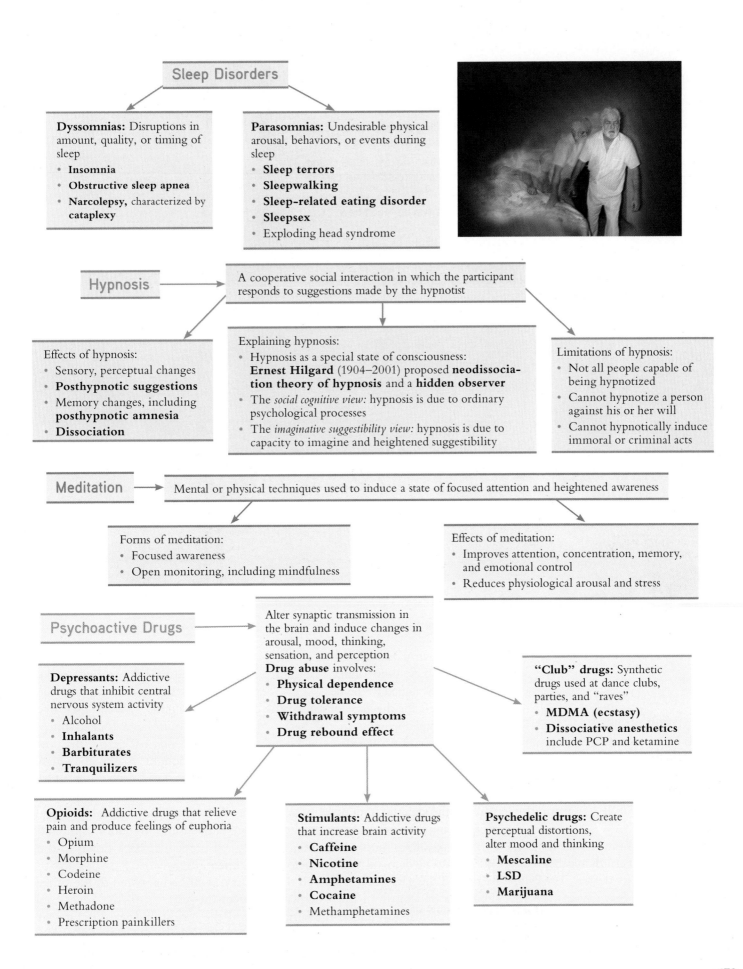

Sleep Disorders

Dyssomnias: Disruptions in amount, quality, or timing of sleep
- **Insomnia**
- **Obstructive sleep apnea**
- **Narcolepsy,** characterized by **cataplexy**

Parasomnias: Undesirable physical arousal, behaviors, or events during sleep
- **Sleep terrors**
- **Sleepwalking**
- **Sleep-related eating disorder**
- **Sleepsex**
- Exploding head syndrome

Hypnosis

A cooperative social interaction in which the participant responds to suggestions made by the hypnotist

Effects of hypnosis:
- Sensory, perceptual changes
- **Posthypnotic suggestions**
- Memory changes, including **posthypnotic amnesia**
- **Dissociation**

Explaining hypnosis:
- Hypnosis as a special state of consciousness: **Ernest Hilgard** (1904–2001) proposed **neodissociation theory of hypnosis** and a **hidden observer**
- The *social cognitive view:* hypnosis is due to ordinary psychological processes
- The *imaginative suggestibility view:* hypnosis is due to capacity to imagine and heightened suggestibility

Limitations of hypnosis:
- Not all people capable of being hypnotized
- Cannot hypnotize a person against his or her will
- Cannot hypnotically induce immoral or criminal acts

Meditation

Mental or physical techniques used to induce a state of focused attention and heightened awareness

Forms of meditation:
- Focused awareness
- Open monitoring, including mindfulness

Effects of meditation:
- Improves attention, concentration, memory, and emotional control
- Reduces physiological arousal and stress

Psychoactive Drugs

Alter synaptic transmission in the brain and induce changes in arousal, mood, thinking, sensation, and perception

Drug abuse involves:
- **Physical dependence**
- **Drug tolerance**
- **Withdrawal symptoms**
- **Drug rebound effect**

Depressants: Addictive drugs that inhibit central nervous system activity
- Alcohol
- **Inhalants**
- **Barbiturates**
- **Tranquilizers**

"Club" drugs: Synthetic drugs used at dance clubs, parties, and "raves"
- **MDMA (ecstasy)**
- **Dissociative anesthetics** include PCP and ketamine

Opioids: Addictive drugs that relieve pain and produce feelings of euphoria
- Opium
- Morphine
- Codeine
- Heroin
- Methadone
- Prescription painkillers

Stimulants: Addictive drugs that increase brain activity
- **Caffeine**
- **Nicotine**
- **Amphetamines**
- **Cocaine**
- Methamphetamines

Psychedelic drugs: Create perceptual distortions, alter mood and thinking
- **Mescaline**
- **LSD**
- **Marijuana**

Is it true . . .

- That Pavlov taught dogs to drool at the sound of a bell by rewarding them with food?
- That you can develop a long-lasting aversion to a food or beverage if you get sick after eating or drinking it?
- That people are more likely to fear snakes, spiders, and heights than more realistic threats like speeding cars or lightning?
- That punishment is an effective way to teach new behaviors?
- That the most effective way to teach a new behavior is to reward it each time it is performed?
- That viewing violent media is not related to aggression?

(inset) kurhan/Shutterstock
(bkgrd) Juha Saastamoinen/Shutterstock

THE KILLER ATTIC

PROLOGUE

YOUR AUTHOR SANDY'S PARENTS, ERV AND FERN, were married for more than 50 years.

Sometimes it seems truly amazing that they managed to stay together for so long, as you'll see from this true story.

It was a warm summer morning in Chicago. Erv and Fern drank their coffee and made plans for the day. The lawn needed mowing, the garage needed cleaning, and someone had to go to the post office to buy stamps. Fern, who didn't like driving, said that she would mow the lawn if Erv would go to the post office. Erv, who didn't like yard work, readily agreed to the deal.

As Erv left for the post office, Fern started cutting the grass in the backyard. When Erv returned, he parked the car around the corner under some large shade trees so that it would stay cool while he puttered around in the garage. Walking through the front door to drop off the stamps, he noticed that the attic fan was squeaking loudly. Switching it off, Erv decided to oil the fan before he tackled the garage. He retrieved the stepladder and oil from the basement, propped the ladder under the attic's trapdoor, and gingerly crawled up into the attic, leaving the trapdoor open.

Meanwhile, Fern was getting thirsty. As she walked past the garage on the way into the house, she noticed the car was still gone. "Why isn't Erv back yet? He must have stopped somewhere on the way back from the post office," she thought. As she got a glass of water, she noticed the stepladder and the open attic door. Muttering that Erv never put anything away, Fern latched the trapdoor shut and dragged the ladder back down to the basement.

Erv, who had crawled to the other side of the attic to oil the fan, never heard the attic trapdoor shut. It was very hot in the well-insulated, airless attic, so he tried to work fast. After

Learning

IN THIS CHAPTER:

› **INTRODUCTION:** What Is Learning?

› Classical Conditioning: Associating Stimuli

› Contemporary Views of Classical Conditioning

› Operant Conditioning: Associating Behaviors and Consequences

› Contemporary Views of Operant Conditioning

› Observational Learning: Imitating the Actions of Others

› **PSYCH FOR YOUR LIFE:** Using Learning Principles to Improve Your Self-Control

oiling the fan, he crawled back to the trapdoor—only to discover that it was latched shut from the outside! "Fern," he hollered, "open the door!" But Fern was already back outside, mowing away, and couldn't hear Erv over the noise of the lawn mower. Erv, dripping with sweat, kept yelling and pounding on the trapdoor.

Outside, Fern was getting hot, too. She stopped to talk to a neighbor, leaving the lawn mower idling. He offered Fern a cold beer, and the two of them leaned over the fence, laughing and talking. From a small, sealed attic window, Erv watched the whole scene. Jealousy was now added to his list of discomforts. He

was also seriously beginning to think that he might sweat to death in the attic heat. He could already see the tabloid headlines in the supermarket checkout line: LAUGHING WIFE DRINKS BEER WHILE HUSBAND COOKS IN ATTIC!

Finally, Fern went back to mowing, wondering what in the world had happened to Erv. Meanwhile, up in the attic, Erv was drenched with sweat and his heart was racing. He promised God he'd never complain about Chicago winters again. At last, Fern finished the lawn and walked back to the house. Hearing the back door open, Erv began to yell and pound on the trapdoor again.

"Hey, Fern! Fern!"

Fern froze in her tracks.

"Fern, let me out! I'm going to suffocate up here!"

"Erv! Is that you? Where are you?" she called, looking around.

"I'm in the attic! Let me out!"

"What are you doing in the attic? I thought you were at the store!"

"What do you *think* I'm doing? Let me out of here! Hurry!"

Once Fern was reassured that Erv had suffered no ill effects from being trapped in the attic, she burst out laughing. Later that day, still grumbling about Fern's harebrained sense of humor, Erv removed the latch from the attic door and replaced it with a handle. Ever since, whenever Erv went up into the attic, he posted a sign on the ladder that read MAN IN THE ATTIC! In fact, for years afterward, Erv got nervous whenever he had to go up into the attic.

For her part, Fern began carefully checking on Erv's whereabouts before closing the attic door. But she still laughs when she tells the story of the "killer attic"—which she does frequently, as it never fails to crack up her listeners. Luckily, Erv was a good sport and was used to Fern's sense of humor.

Erv and Fern both learned from their experience, as is reflected in the changes in their behavior. Learning new behaviors can occur in many ways, but it almost always helps us adapt to changing circumstances, as you'll see in this chapter. □

INTRODUCTION:
What Is Learning?

KEY THEME

Learning refers to a relatively enduring change in behavior or knowledge as a result of experience.

KEY QUESTIONS

> What is conditioning?

> What are three basic types of learning?

What do we mean when we say that Fern and Erv have "learned" from their experience with the killer attic? In the everyday sense, *learning* often refers to formal methods of acquiring new knowledge or skills, such as learning in the classroom or learning to play the flute.

In psychology, however, the topic of learning is much broader. In general, psychologists formally define **learning** as a process that produces a relatively enduring change in behavior or knowledge as a result of an individual's experience. For example, Erv has learned to feel anxious and uncomfortable whenever he needs to enter the attic. He's also learned to take simple precautions, such as posting his MAN IN THE ATTIC! sign, to avoid getting locked in the attic again. As Erv's behavior demonstrates, the learning of new behaviors often reflects adapting to your environment. As the result of experience, you acquire new behaviors or modify old behaviors so as to better cope with your surroundings.

In this broad sense of the word, learning occurs in every setting, not just in classrooms. And learning takes place at every age. Further, the psychological study of learning is not limited to humans. From alligators to zebras, learning is an important aspect of the behavior of virtually all animals.

Psychologists have often studied learning by observing and recording the learning experiences of animals in carefully controlled laboratory situations. Using animal subjects, researchers can precisely control the conditions under which a particular behavior is learned. The goal of much of this research has been to identify the general principles of learning that apply across a wide range of species, including humans.

Much of this chapter will focus on a very basic form of learning, called *conditioning*. **Conditioning** is the process of learning associations between environmental events and behavioral responses. This description may make you think conditioning has only a limited application to your life. In fact, however, conditioning is reflected in most of your everyday behavior, from simple habits to emotional reactions and complex skills.

Conditioning, Learning, and Behavior Through different kinds of experiences, people and animals acquire enduring changes in their behaviors. Psychologists have identified general principles of learning that explain how we acquire new behaviors. These principles apply to simple responses, but they can also help explain how we learn complex skills, such as the proper way to swing a golf club, as these young boys are learning in Beijing, China.

STR/AFP/Getty Images

In this chapter, we'll look at basic types of conditioning—classical conditioning and operant conditioning. As you'll see in the next section, *classical conditioning* explains how certain stimuli can trigger a reflexive, automatic response, as the attic now triggers mild anxiety in Erv. And, as you'll see in a later section, *operant conditioning* is useful in understanding how we acquire new, voluntary actions, such as Erv's posting his sign whenever he climbs into the attic. Finally, toward the end of the chapter, we'll consider the process of *observational learning,* or how we acquire new behaviors by observing the actions of others.

Classical Conditioning
ASSOCIATING STIMULI

KEY THEME

Classical conditioning is a process of learning associations between stimuli.

KEY QUESTIONS

> How did Pavlov discover and investigate classical conditioning?

> How does classical conditioning occur?

> What factors can affect classical conditioning?

One of the major contributors to the study of learning was not a psychologist but a Russian physiologist who was awarded a Nobel Prize for his work on digestion (Miyata, 2009). **Ivan Pavlov** was a brilliant scientist who directed several research laboratories in St. Petersburg, Russia, at the turn of the twentieth century. Pavlov's involvement with psychology began as a result of an observation he made while investigating the role of saliva in digestion, using dogs as his experimental subjects.

In order to get a dog to produce saliva, Pavlov (1904) put food on the dog's tongue. After he had worked with the same dog for several days in a row, Pavlov noticed something curious. The dog began salivating *before* Pavlov put the food on its tongue. In fact, the dog began salivating when Pavlov entered the room or even at the sound of his approaching footsteps. But salivating is a *reflex*—a largely involuntary, automatic response to an external stimulus. (As we've noted in previous chapters, a *stimulus* is anything perceptible to the senses, such as a sight, sound, smell, touch, or taste.) The dog should salivate only *after* the food is presented, not before. Why would the reflex occur before the stimulus was presented? What was causing this unexpected behavior?

If you own a dog, you've probably observed the same basic phenomenon. Your dog gets excited and begins to slobber when you shake a box of dog biscuits, even before you've given him a doggie treat. In everyday language, your pet has learned to anticipate food in association with some signal—namely, the sound of dog biscuits rattling in a box.

Pavlov's extraordinary gifts as a researcher enabled him to recognize the important implications of what had at first seemed a problem—a reflex (salivation) that occurred *before* the appropriate stimulus (food) was presented. He also had the discipline to systematically study how such associations are formed. In fact, Pavlov abandoned his research on digestion and devoted the remaining 30 years of his life to investigating different aspects of this phenomenon. Let's look at what he discovered in more detail.

Principles of Classical Conditioning

The process of conditioning that Pavlov discovered was the first to be extensively studied in psychology. Thus, it's called *classical conditioning* (Hilgard & Marquis, 1940). It's also known as *Pavlovian conditioning* (Lattal, 2013). **Classical conditioning** deals with behaviors that are elicited automatically by some stimulus. *Elicit* means "draw

learning A process that produces a relatively enduring change in behavior or knowledge as a result of past experience.

conditioning The process of learning associations between environmental events and behavioral responses.

classical conditioning The basic learning process that involves repeatedly pairing a neutral stimulus with a response-producing stimulus until the neutral stimulus elicits the same response.

Ivan Pavlov (1849–1936) In his laboratory, Pavlov was known for his meticulous organization, keen memory, and attention to details (Windholz, 1990). But outside his lab, Pavlov was absent-minded, forgetful, and impractical, especially regarding money. He often forgot to pick up his paycheck, and he sometimes lent money to people with hard-luck stories who couldn't possibly pay him back (Fancher, 1996). On a trip to New York City, Pavlov carried his money so carelessly that he had his pocket picked in the subway, and his American hosts had to take up a collection to pay his expenses (Skinner, 1966).

Popperfoto/Getty Images

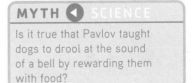

MYTH ◀ SCIENCE

Is it true that Pavlov taught dogs to drool at the sound of a bell by rewarding them with food?

Sovfoto/UIG via Getty Images

Life in Pavlov's Laboratories During Pavlov's four decades of research, more than 140 scientists and students worked in the two laboratories under his direction. Twenty of his co-researchers were women, including his daughter, V. I. Pavlova. Pavlov, who had an extraordinary memory for details, carefully supervised the procedures of dozens of ongoing research projects. Nevertheless, he acknowledged that the scholarly achievements produced by his laboratories represented the collective efforts of himself and his co-workers (Windholz, 1990).

out" or "bring forth." That is, the stimulus doesn't produce a new behavior but rather *causes an existing behavior to occur.*

Classical conditioning almost always involves some kind of reflexive behavior. Remember, a reflex is a relatively simple, unlearned behavior, governed by the nervous system, that occurs *automatically* when the appropriate stimulus is presented. In Pavlov's (1904) original studies of digestion, the dogs salivated reflexively when food was placed on their tongues. But when the dogs began salivating in response to the sight of Pavlov or to the sound of his footsteps, a new, *learned* stimulus elicited the salivary response. Thus, in classical conditioning, a *new* stimulus–response sequence is learned.

How does this kind of learning take place? Essentially, classical conditioning is a process of learning an *association between two stimuli.* Classical conditioning involves pairing a *neutral* stimulus (e.g., the sight of Pavlov) with an *unlearned, natural* stimulus (food in the mouth) that automatically elicits a reflexive response (the dog salivates). If the two stimuli (Pavlov + food) are repeatedly paired, eventually the neutral stimulus (Pavlov) elicits the same basic reflexive response as the natural stimulus (food)—even in the absence of the natural stimulus. So, when the dog in the laboratory started salivating at the sight of Pavlov *before* the food was placed on its tongue, it was because the dog had formed a new, *learned association* between the sight of Pavlov and the food.

Pavlov used special terms to describe each element of the classical conditioning process. The natural stimulus that reflexively produces a response without prior learning is called the **unconditioned stimulus** (abbreviated **UCS**). In this example, the unconditioned stimulus is the food in the dog's mouth. The unlearned, reflexive response is called the **unconditioned response** (or **UCR**). The unconditioned response is the dog's salivation.

To learn more about his discovery, Pavlov (1927) controlled the stimuli that preceded the presentation of food. For example, in one set of experiments, he used a bell as a neutral stimulus—neutral because dogs don't normally salivate to the sound of a ringing bell. Pavlov first rang the bell and then gave the dog food. After this procedure was repeated several times, the dog began to salivate when the bell was rung, before the food was put in its mouth. At that point, the dog was *classically conditioned* to salivate to the sound of a bell alone. That is, the dog had *learned a new association* between the sound of the bell and the presentation of food.

Pavlov called the sound of the bell the *conditioned stimulus.* The **conditioned stimulus** (or **CS**) is the stimulus that is originally neutral but comes to elicit a reflexive response. He called the dog's salivation to the sound of the bell the **conditioned response** (or **CR**), which is the *learned* reflexive response to a previously neutral stimulus. The steps of Pavlov's conditioning process are outlined in Figure 5.1.

Classical conditioning terminology can be confusing. You may find it helpful to think of the word *conditioned* as having the same meaning as "learned." Thus, the "conditioned stimulus" refers to the "learned stimulus," the "unconditioned response" refers to the "unlearned response," and so forth.

It's also important to note that, in this case, the unconditioned response and the conditioned response describe essentially the same behavior—the dog's salivating. Which label is applied depends on which stimulus elicits the response. If the dog is salivating in response to a *natural* stimulus that was not acquired through learning, the salivation is an *unconditioned* response. If, however, the dog has learned to salivate to a *neutral* stimulus that doesn't normally produce the automatic response, the salivation is a *conditioned* response.

Factors That Affect Conditioning

Over the three decades that Pavlov (1928) spent studying classical conditioning, he discovered many factors that could affect the strength of the conditioned response

BIZARRO © 2002 Dan Piraro, Dist. by King Features

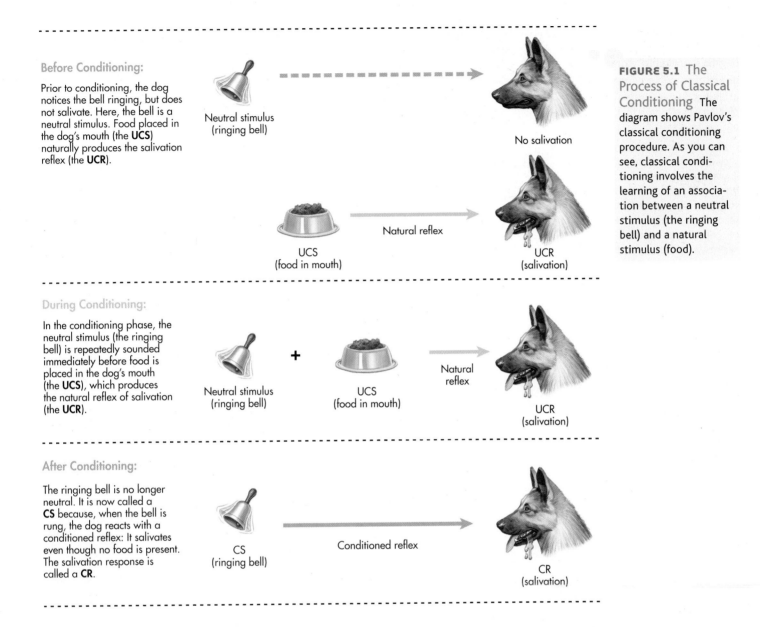

Before Conditioning:

Prior to conditioning, the dog notices the bell ringing, but does not salivate. Here, the bell is a neutral stimulus. Food placed in the dog's mouth (the **UCS**) naturally produces the salivation reflex (the **UCR**).

Neutral stimulus
(ringing bell)

No salivation

UCS
(food in mouth)

Natural reflex

UCR
(salivation)

FIGURE 5.1 The Process of Classical Conditioning The diagram shows Pavlov's classical conditioning procedure. As you can see, classical conditioning involves the learning of an association between a neutral stimulus (the ringing bell) and a natural stimulus (food).

During Conditioning:

In the conditioning phase, the neutral stimulus (the ringing bell) is repeatedly sounded immediately before food is placed in the dog's mouth (the **UCS**), which produces the natural reflex of salivation (the **UCR**).

Neutral stimulus
(ringing bell)

+

UCS
(food in mouth)

Natural reflex

UCR
(salivation)

After Conditioning:

The ringing bell is no longer neutral. It is now called a **CS** because, when the bell is rung, the dog reacts with a conditioned reflex: It salivates even though no food is present. The salivation response is called a **CR**.

CS
(ringing bell)

Conditioned reflex

CR
(salivation)

(Bitterman, 2006). For example, he discovered that the more frequently the conditioned stimulus and the unconditioned stimulus were paired, the stronger was the association between the two.

Pavlov also discovered that the *timing* of stimulus presentations affected the strength of the conditioned response. He found that conditioning was most effective when the conditioned stimulus was presented immediately *before* the unconditioned stimulus. In his early studies, Pavlov found that a half-second was the optimal time interval between the onset of the conditioned stimulus and the beginning of the unconditioned stimulus. Later, Pavlov and other researchers found that the optimal time interval could vary in different conditioning situations but was rarely more than a few seconds.

STIMULUS GENERALIZATION AND DISCRIMINATION

Pavlov (1927) noticed that once a dog was conditioned to salivate to a particular stimulus, new stimuli that were similar to the original conditioned stimulus could also elicit the conditioned salivary response. For example, Pavlov conditioned a dog to salivate to a low-pitched tone. When he sounded a slightly higher-pitched tone,

unconditioned stimulus (UCS) The natural stimulus that reflexively elicits a response without the need for prior learning.

unconditioned response (UCR) The unlearned, reflexive response that is elicited by an unconditioned stimulus.

conditioned stimulus (CS) A formerly neutral stimulus that acquires the capacity to elicit a reflexive response.

conditioned response (CR) The learned, reflexive response to a conditioned stimulus.

stimulus generalization The occurrence of a learned response not only to the original stimulus but to other, similar stimuli as well.

stimulus discrimination The occurrence of a learned response to a specific stimulus but not to other, similar stimuli.

higher order conditioning (also called *second-order conditioning*) A procedure in which a conditioned stimulus from one learning trial functions as the unconditioned stimulus in a new conditioning trial; the second conditioned stimulus comes to elicit the conditioned response, even though it has never been directly paired with the unconditioned stimulus.

the conditioned salivary response would also be elicited. Pavlov called this phenomenon *stimulus generalization*. **Stimulus generalization** occurs when stimuli that are similar to the original conditioned stimulus also elicit the conditioned response, even though they have never been paired with the unconditioned stimulus. If you own a dog that tends to salivate and get excited when you shake a box of dog biscuits, you may have noticed that your dog also drools when you shake a bag of cat food. If so, that would be an example of stimulus generalization.

Just as a dog can learn to respond to similar stimuli, so it can learn the opposite—to *distinguish* between similar stimuli. For example, Pavlov repeatedly gave a dog some food following a high-pitched tone but did not give the dog any food following a low-pitched tone. The dog learned to distinguish between the two tones, salivating to the high-pitched tone but not to the low-pitched tone. This phenomenon, **stimulus discrimination,** occurs when a particular conditioned response is made to one stimulus but not to other, similar stimuli. So, if your dog eventually stops salivating when you shake a bag of cat food, stimulus discrimination has taken place.

HIGHER ORDER CONDITIONING

In further studies of his classical conditioning procedure, Pavlov (1927) found that a conditioned stimulus could itself function as an unconditioned stimulus in a new conditioning trial. This phenomenon is called **higher order conditioning** or *second-order conditioning.* Pavlov paired a ticking metronome with food until the sound of the ticking metronome became established as a conditioned stimulus. Then Pavlov repeatedly paired a new unconditioned stimulus, a black square, with the ticking metronome—but no food. After several pairings, would the black square alone produce salivation? It did, even though the black square had never been directly paired with food. The black square had become a *new* conditioned stimulus, simply by being repeatedly paired with the first conditioned stimulus: the ticking metronome. Like the first conditioned stimulus, the black square produced the conditioned response: salivation.

It is important to note that in higher order conditioning, the new conditioned stimulus has *never* been paired with the unconditioned stimulus. The new conditioned stimulus acquires its ability to produce the conditioned response by virtue of being paired with the first conditioned stimulus (Hussaini & others, 2007; Jara & others, 2006).

Consider this example: Like most children, your authors Don and Sandy's daughter, Laura, received several rounds of immunizations when she was an infant. Each painful injection (the UCS) elicited distress and made her cry (the UCR). After only the *second* vaccination, Laura developed a strong classically conditioned response—just the sight of a nurse's white uniform (the CS) triggered an emotional outburst of fear and crying (the CR). Interestingly, Laura's conditioned fear generalized to a wide range of white uniforms, including a pharmacist's white smock, a veterinarian's white lab coat, and even the white jacket of a cosmetics saleswoman in a department store.

To illustrate higher order conditioning, imagine that baby Laura reacted fearfully when she saw a white-jacketed cosmetics saleswoman in a department store. Imagine further that the saleswoman compounded Laura's reaction by spraying her mother, Sandy, with a new perfume fragrance and handing Sandy a free perfume sample to take home. If Laura responded with fear the next time she smelled the fragrance, higher order conditioning would have taken place. The perfume scent had never been paired with the original UCS, the painful injection. The scent became a new CS by virtue of being paired with the first CS, the white jacket.

Classical Conditioning in Early Life: White Coats and Doctor Visits Most infants receive several vaccinations in their first few years of life. The painful injection (a UCS) elicits fear and distress (a UCR). After a few office visits, the clinic, nurse, or even the medical staff's white lab coats can become a conditioned stimulus (CS) that elicits fear and distress—even in the absence of a painful injection.

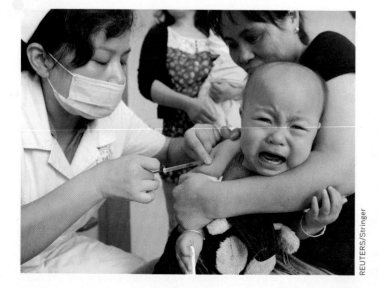

REUTERS/Stringer

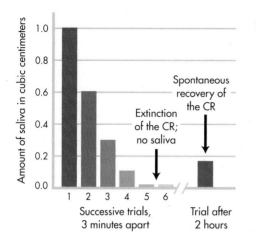

FIGURE 5.2 Extinction and Spontaneous Recovery in Pavlov's Laboratory This demonstration involved a dog that had already been conditioned to salivate (the CR) to just the sight of the meat powder (the CS). During the extinction phase, the CS was repeatedly presented at three-minute intervals and held just out of the dog's reach. As you can see in the graph, over the course of six trials the amount of saliva secreted by the dog quickly decreased to zero. This indicates that *extinction* had occurred. After a two-hour rest period, the CS was presented again. At the sight of the meat powder, the dog secreted saliva once more, evidence for the *spontaneous recovery* of the conditioned response.

Source: Data from Pavlov (1927).

EXTINCTION AND SPONTANEOUS RECOVERY

Once learned, can conditioned responses be eliminated? Pavlov (1927) found that conditioned responses could be gradually weakened. If the conditioned stimulus (the ringing bell) was repeatedly presented *without* being paired with the unconditioned stimulus (the food), the conditioned response seemed to gradually disappear. Pavlov called this process of decline and eventual disappearance of the conditioned response **extinction.**

Pavlov also found that the dog did not simply return to its unconditioned state following extinction (see Figure 5.2). If the animal was allowed a period of rest (such as a few hours) after the response was extinguished, the conditioned response would reappear when the conditioned stimulus was again presented. This reappearance of a previously extinguished conditioned response after a period of time without exposure to the conditioned stimulus is called **spontaneous recovery.** The phenomenon of spontaneous recovery demonstrates that extinction is not unlearning. That is, the learned response may seem to disappear, but it is *not* eliminated or erased (Archbold & others, 2010; Rescorla, 2001).

extinction (in classical conditioning) The gradual weakening and apparent disappearance of conditioned behavior. In classical conditioning, extinction occurs when the conditioned stimulus is repeatedly presented without the unconditioned stimulus.

spontaneous recovery The reappearance of a previously extinguished conditioned response after a period of time without exposure to the conditioned stimulus.

behaviorism School of psychology and theoretical viewpoint that emphasizes the study of observable behaviors, especially as they pertain to the process of learning.

From Pavlov to Watson
THE FOUNDING OF BEHAVIORISM

KEY THEME

Behaviorism was founded by John Watson, who redefined psychology as the scientific study of behavior.

KEY QUESTIONS

> What were the fundamental assumptions of behaviorism?

> How did Watson use classical conditioning to explain and produce conditioned emotional responses?

> How did Watson apply classical conditioning techniques to advertising?

Over the course of three decades, Pavlov systematically investigated different aspects of classical conditioning. Pavlov believed he had discovered the mechanism by which all learning occurs, but he did not apply his findings to human behavior. That task was to be taken up by a young psychologist, **John B. Watson.**

Watson believed that the early psychologists were following the wrong path by focusing on the study of subjective mental processes, which could not be objectively observed (Berman & Lyons, 2007). Instead, Watson (1913) strongly advocated that psychology should be redefined as *the scientific study of behavior,* which, unlike mental processes, *could* be objectively observed. As described in Chapter 1, Watson founded a new school, or approach, in psychology, called **behaviorism.** Pavlov's discovery of

Let us limit ourselves to things that can be observed, and formulate laws concerning only those things. Now what can we observe? We can observe *behavior—what the organism does or says.*

—*John B. Watson (1924)*

John Broadus Watson (1878–1958)
Watson founded behaviorism in the early 1900s, emphasizing the scientific study of observable behaviors rather than the study of subjective mental processes (Hall, 2009). His influence spread far beyond the academic world. After a scandal ended his academic career, Watson went into advertising. He also wrote many books and articles for the general public on child rearing and other topics, popularizing the findings of the "new" science of psychology (Rilling, 2000).

Archives of the History of American Psychology, The University of Akron. Color added by publisher.

the conditioned reflex provided the model Watson had been seeking to investigate and explain human behavior (Evans & Rilling, 2000; Watson, 1916).

Watson believed that virtually *all* human behavior is a result of conditioning and learning—that is, due to past experience and environmental influences. In a characteristically bold statement, Watson (1924) proclaimed:

> I should like to go one step further now and say, "Give me a dozen healthy infants, well-formed, and my own specified world to bring them up in and I'll guarantee to take any one at random and train him to become any type of specialist I might select—doctor, lawyer, artist, merchant-chief and yes, even beggar-man and thief, regardless of his talents, penchants, tendencies, abilities, vocations, and race of his ancestors." I am going beyond my facts and I admit it, but so have the advocates of the contrary and they have been doing it for many thousands of years.

Needless to say, Watson never actually carried out such an experiment, and his boast clearly exaggerated the role of the environment to make his point. Nevertheless, Watson's influence on psychology cannot be overemphasized. Behaviorism was to dominate psychology in the United States for more than 50 years. And, as you'll see in the next section, Watson did carry out a famous and controversial experiment to demonstrate how human behavior could be classically conditioned.

Conditioned Emotional Reactions

Watson believed that, much as Pavlov's dogs reflexively salivated to food, human emotions could be thought of as reflexive responses involving the muscles and glands. In studies with infants, Watson (1919) identified three emotions that he believed represented inborn and natural unconditioned reflexes—fear, rage, and love. According to Watson, each of these innate emotions could be reflexively triggered by a small number of specific stimuli. For example, he found two stimuli that could trigger the reflexive fear response in infants: a sudden loud noise and a sudden dropping motion.

THE FAMOUS CASE OF LITTLE ALBERT

Watson's interest in the role of classical conditioning in emotions set the stage for one of the most famous and controversial experiments in the history of psychology. In 1920, Watson and a graduate student named Rosalie Rayner set out to demonstrate that classical conditioning could be used to deliberately establish a conditioned emotional response in a human subject. Their subject was a baby, whom they called "Albert B.," but who is now more popularly known as "Little Albert." Little Albert lived with his mother in the Harriet Lane Hospital in Baltimore, where his mother was employed.

Watson and Rayner (1920) first assessed Little Albert when he was only nine months old. Little Albert was a healthy, unusually calm baby who showed no fear when presented with a tame white rat, a rabbit, a dog, and a monkey. He was also unafraid of cotton, masks, and even burning newspapers! But, as with other infants whom Watson had studied, fear could be triggered in Little Albert by a sudden loud sound—clanging a steel bar behind his head. In this case, the sudden clanging noise is the unconditioned stimulus, and the unconditioned response is fear.

Two months after their initial assessment, Watson and Rayner attempted to condition Little Albert to fear the tame white rat (the conditioned stimulus). Watson stood behind Little Albert. Whenever Little Albert reached toward the rat, Watson clanged the steel bar with a hammer. Just as before, of course, the unexpected loud CLANG! (the unconditioned stimulus) startled and scared the daylights out of Little Albert (the unconditioned response).

During the first conditioning session, Little Albert experienced two pairings of the white rat with the loud clanging sound. A week later, he experienced five more pairings of the two stimuli. After only these seven pairings of the loud noise and the

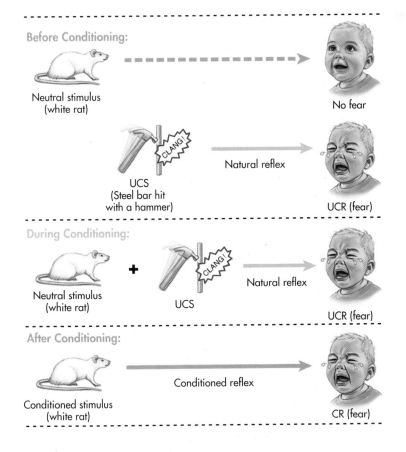

Before Conditioning:

Neutral stimulus
(white rat)

No fear

UCS
(Steel bar hit
with a hammer)

Natural reflex

UCR (fear)

During Conditioning:

Neutral stimulus
(white rat)

+

UCS

Natural reflex

UCR (fear)

After Conditioning:

Conditioned stimulus
(white rat)

Conditioned reflex

CR (fear)

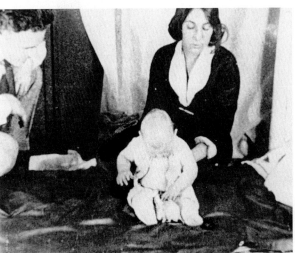

FIGURE 5.3 A Classically Conditioned Fear Response In the photograph below, Rosalie Rayner holds Little Albert as John Watson looks on. Little Albert is petting the tame white rat, clearly not afraid of it. But, after being repeatedly paired with the UCS (a sudden, loud noise), the white rat becomes a CS. After conditioning, Little Albert is terrified of the tame rat. His fear generalized to other furry objects, including rabbits, cotton, Rayner's fur coat, and Watson in a Santa Claus beard.

Benjmain Harris

white rat, the white rat alone triggered the conditioned response—extreme fear—in Little Albert (see Figure 5.3).

Watson and Rayner also found that stimulus generalization had taken place. Along with fearing the rat, Little Albert was now afraid of other furry animals, including a dog and a rabbit. He had even developed a classically conditioned fear response to a variety of fuzzy objects—a sealskin coat, cotton, Watson's hair, and a white-bearded Santa Claus mask!

Although the Little Albert study has attained legendary status in psychology, it had several problems (Harris, 1979, 2011; Paul & Blumenthal, 1989). One criticism is that the experiment was not carefully designed or conducted. For example, Albert's fear and distress were not objectively measured but were subjectively evaluated by Watson and Rayner.

The experiment is also open to criticism on ethical grounds. Watson and Rayner (1920) did not extinguish Little Albert's fear of furry animals and objects, even though they believed that such conditioned emotional responses would "persist and modify personality throughout life." Such an experiment could not ethically be conducted today.

Whether Watson and Rayner had originally intended to extinguish the fear is not completely clear (see Paul & Blumenthal, 1989). Watson (1930) later wrote that he and Rayner could not try to eliminate Albert's fear response because the infant had been adopted by a family in another city shortly after the experiment had concluded.

Generations of psychologists have wondered what happened to Little Albert. After years of detective work, psychologist Hall P. Beck and his colleagues (2009, 2010) identified Albert as Douglas Merritt, the son of a woman working at the hospital where the experiment was conducted. However, psychologist Russell A. Powell and his colleagues (2014) proposed a different candidate: Albert Barger, the infant son of another woman working at the hospital. Like Douglas Merritt, Albert Barger would have been the same age as the "Little Albert B." in Watson and Rayner's study. Unlike Douglas, however, who died at age 6 of a neurological disease, Albert lived to the ripe old age of 88.

IN FOCUS

Watson, Classical Conditioning, and Advertising

From shampoos to soft drinks, advertising campaigns often use sexy models to promote their products. Today, we take this advertising tactic for granted. But it's actually yet another example of Watson's influence.

Shortly after the Little Albert experiment, Watson's wife discovered that he was having an affair with his graduate student Rosalie Rayner. Following a scandalous and highly publicized divorce, Watson was fired from his academic position. Despite his international fame as a scientist, no other university would hire him (Benjamin & others, 2007). Banned from academia, Watson married Rayner and joined the J. Walter Thompson advertising agency (Buckley, 1989; Carpintero, 2004).

Watson was a pioneer in the application of classical conditioning principles to advertising. "To make your consumer react," Watson told his colleagues at the ad agency, "tell him something that will tie him up with fear, something that will stir up a mild rage, that will call out an affectionate or love response, or strike at a deep psychological or habit need" (quoted in Buckley, 1982).

Watson applied this technique to ad campaigns for Johnson & Johnson Baby Powder and Pebeco toothpaste in the 1920s. For the baby powder ad, Watson intentionally tried to stimulate an anxiety response in young mothers by creating doubts about their ability to care for their infants.

The Pebeco toothpaste campaign targeted the newly independent young woman who smoked. The ad raised the fear that attractiveness might be diminished by the effects of smoking—and Pebeco toothpaste was promoted as a way of increasing sexual attractiveness. One ad read, "Girls! Don't worry any more about smoke-stained teeth or tobacco-tainted breath. You can smoke and still be lovely if you'll just use Pebeco twice a day." Watson also developed ad campaigns for Pond's cold cream, Maxwell House coffee, and Camel cigarettes.

While Watson may have pioneered the strategy of associating products with "sex appeal," modern advertising has taken this technique to an extreme. Similarly, some ad campaigns pair products with images of adorable babies, cuddly kittens, happy families, or other "natural" stimuli that elicit warm, emotional responses. If

Charles Guerin/ABACAUSA.COM/Newscom

Classical Conditioning in Contemporary Advertising Taking a cue from John Watson, classical conditioning is widely used in today's commercials and print ads, pairing emotion-evoking images with otherwise neutral stimuli, like soft drinks or new cars. See if you can identify the UCS, UCR, CS, and CR in this striking billboard.

classical conditioning occurs, the product by itself will also elicit a warm, emotional response.

Are such procedures effective? In a word, yes. Attitudes toward a product or a particular brand can be influenced by advertising and marketing campaigns that use classical conditioning methods (W. Hofmann & others, 2010).

You can probably think of situations, objects, or people that evoke a strong classically conditioned emotional reaction in you, such as fear or anger. For example, you might become classically conditioned to cues associated with a person whom you strongly dislike, such as a demeaning boss or an ex-lover. After repeated negative experiences (the UCS) with the person eliciting anger (the UCR), a wide range of cues can become conditioned stimuli (CSs)—the person's name, the sight of the person, locations associated with the person, and so forth—and elicit a strong negative emotional reaction (the CR) in you. Just hearing the person's name can send your heart rate and blood pressure soaring. Other emotional responses, such as feelings of fear, happiness, or sadness, can also be classically conditioned.

In this chapter's Prologue, we saw that Erv became classically conditioned to feel anxious whenever he entered the attic. The attic (the original neutral stimulus) was coupled with being trapped in extreme heat (the UCS), which produced fear (the UCR). Following the episode, Erv found that going into the attic (now a CS) triggered mild fear and anxiety (the CR). Like Erv, many people experience a conditioned fear response to objects, situations, or locations that are associated with some kind of traumatic experience or event. In fact, despite their knowledge of classical conditioning, your authors are not immune to this effect (see photo).

Other Classically Conditioned Responses

Under the right conditions, virtually any automatic response can become classically conditioned. For example, some aspects of sexual responses can become classically conditioned, sometimes inadvertently. To illustrate, suppose that a neutral stimulus, such as the scent of a particular cologne, is regularly paired with the person with whom you are romantically involved. You, of course, are most aware of the scent when you are physically close to your partner in sexually arousing situations. After repeated pairings, the initially neutral stimulus—the particular cologne scent—can become a conditioned stimulus. Now, the scent of the cologne evokes feelings of romantic excitement or mild sexual arousal even in the absence of your lover or, in some cases, long after the relationship has ended. And, in fact, a wide variety of stimuli can become "sexual turn-ons" through classical conditioning.

Classical conditioning can also influence drug responses. For example, if you are a regular coffee drinker, you may have noticed that you begin to feel more awake and alert after just a few groggy sips of your first cup of coffee in the morning. However, it takes at least 20 minutes for the caffeine from the coffee to reach significant levels in your bloodstream. If you're feeling more awake *before* blood levels of caffeine rise, it's probably because you've developed a classically conditioned response to the sight, smell, and taste of coffee (see Figure 5.4). Confirming that everyday experience, such conditioned responses to caffeine-associated stimuli have also been demonstrated experimentally (see Flaten & Blumenthal, 1999; Mikalsen & others, 2001).

Once this classically conditioned drug effect becomes well established, the smell or taste of coffee—even decaffeinated coffee—can trigger the conditioned response of increased arousal and alertness (Attwood & others, 2010).

Conditioned drug effects seem to be involved in at least some instances of placebo response (Benedetti & others, 2010; Stewart-Williams & Podd, 2004). Also called

Classically Conditioned Emotional Reactions After being involved in a serious auto accident, many people develop a conditioned emotional response to the scene of the accident. Your author Don is no exception. He still shudders when he drives through the intersection of 10th and Cincinnati streets near the downtown campus of Tulsa Community College. His car (shown here) was crumpled by an SUV that sped up through a red light and smashed into the driver's side, spinning the car almost 180 degrees. (Fortunately, the entire sequence of events was witnessed by the Tulsa police officer in the car directly behind Don.) Although Don wasn't seriously hurt, just looking at the photo of the intersection (and his totaled car) makes his neck tighten up and his heart race. In this example, can you identify the UCS, UCR, CS, and CR?

"Your magazine smells fabulous. May I kiss you?"

FIGURE 5.4 Classically Conditioned Drug Effects: Does Just the Smell of a Starbucks Espresso Perk You Up? If it does, classical conditioning is at work! Pavlov (1927) suggested that administering a drug could be viewed as a conditioning trial. Just like pairing the sound of a bell with the presentation of food, if specific environmental cues are repeatedly paired with a drug's administration, they can become conditioned stimuli that eventually elicit the drug's effect. For a regular coffee drinker, the sight, smell, and taste of freshly brewed coffee are the original neutral stimuli that, after being repeatedly paired with caffeine (the UCS), eventually become conditioned stimuli, producing the CR: increased arousal and alertness.

placebo response An individual's psychological and physiological response to what is actually a fake treatment or drug; also called *placebo effect*.

placebo effect, a **placebo response** occurs when an individual has a psychological and physiological reaction to what is actually a fake treatment or drug. We'll discuss this phenomenon in more detail in Chapter 12.

Contemporary Views of Classical Conditioning

KEY THEME

Contemporary learning researchers acknowledge the importance of both cognitive factors and evolutionary influences in classical conditioning.

KEY QUESTIONS

> How has the involvement of cognitive processes in classical conditioning been demonstrated experimentally?

> What is meant by the phrase "the animal behaves like a scientist" in classical conditioning?

> How do taste aversions challenge the basic conditioning principles, and what is biological preparedness?

The traditional behavioral perspective holds that classical conditioning results from a simple association of the conditioned stimulus and the unconditioned stimulus. Mental or cognitive processes such as thinking, anticipating, or deciding were not needed to explain the conditioning process. However, according to the *cognitive perspective* (see Chapter 1), mental processes as well as external events are important components in the learning of new behaviors. In the next section, we'll look at research on cognitive processes in classical conditioning.

Cognitive Aspects of Classical Conditioning
RELIABLE SIGNALS

In a series of experiments, learning theorist **Robert Rescorla** demonstrated that classical conditioning involves more than learning the simple association of two stimuli. In a classic study, one group of rats heard a tone (the conditioned stimulus) that was paired 20 times with a brief electric shock (the unconditioned stimulus). A second group of rats experienced the *same* number of tone–shock pairings, but this group also experienced an *additional* 20 shocks with *no* tone (Rescorla, 1968). Then Rescorla tested for the conditioned fear response by presenting the tone alone to each group of rats. Because each group had received 20 tone-shock pairings, both groups should have displayed the same levels of conditioned fear. However, the rats in the first group displayed a much stronger fear response to the tone than did the rats in the second group. Why?

According to Rescorla (1988), classical conditioning depends on the *information* the conditioned stimulus provides about the unconditioned stimulus. For learning to occur, the conditioned stimulus must be a *reliable signal* that predicts the presentations of the unconditioned stimulus. For the first group of rats, that was certainly the situation. Every time the tone sounded, a shock followed. But for the second group, the tone was an unreliable signal. Sometimes the tone preceded the shock, and sometimes the shock occurred without warning.

Rescorla concluded that the rats in both groups were *actively processing information* about the reliability of the signals they encountered. Rather than merely associating two closely paired stimuli, as Pavlov suggested,

Pavlovian conditioning is a sophisticated and sensible mechanism by which organisms represent the world. Our current understanding of Pavlovian conditioning leads to its characterization as a mechanism by which the organism encodes relationships between events in the world. The conditioned stimulus and the unconditioned stimulus are simply two events, and the organism can be seen as trying to determine the relationship between them.

—*Robert A. Rescorla (1997)*　Courtesy of Dr. Robert Rescorla

the animals assess the *predictive value* of stimuli. Applying this interpretation to classical conditioning, we can conclude that Pavlov's dogs learned that the bell was a signal that *reliably predicted* that food would follow.

According to this view, animals use cognitive processes to draw inferences about the signals they encounter in their environments. To Rescorla (1988), classical conditioning "is not a stupid process by which the organism willy-nilly forms associations between any two stimuli that happen to co-occur." Rather, his research suggests that "the animal behaves like a scientist, detecting causal relations among events and using a range of information about those events to make the relevant inferences" (Rescorla, 1980). Put simply, classical conditioning seems to involve *learning the relationships between events* (Rescorla, 1988, 2003).

Evolutionary Aspects of Classical Conditioning
BIOLOGICAL PREDISPOSITIONS TO LEARN

According to Darwin's *theory of evolution by natural selection,* both the physical characteristics and the natural behavior patterns of any species have been shaped by evolution to maximize adaptation to the environment. Thus, just as physical characteristics vary from one species to another, so do natural behavior patterns. Some psychologists wondered whether an animal's natural behavior patterns, as shaped by evolution, would also affect how it learned new behaviors, especially behaviors important to its survival.

According to traditional behaviorists, the general principles of learning applied to virtually all animal species and all learning situations. Thus, they argued that the general learning principles of classical conditioning would be the same regardless of the species or the response being conditioned. However, in the 1960s, some researchers began to report "exceptions" to the well-established principles of classical conditioning (Lockard, 1971; Seligman, 1970). As you'll see in this section, one important exception involved a phenomenon known as a *taste aversion.* The study of taste aversions contributed to a new awareness of the importance of the organism's natural behavior patterns in classical conditioning.

TASTE AVERSIONS AND CLASSICAL CONDITIONING
SPAGHETTI? NO, THANK YOU!

A few years ago, our friend Tom ate a large plateful of spaghetti at a highly rated Italian restaurant. But in the middle of the night, Tom came down with a nasty stomach virus. As a result, Tom developed a **taste aversion**—he avoided eating spaghetti and felt queasy whenever he smelled tomato sauce.

Such learned taste aversions are relatively common. Our students have told us about episodes of motion sickness, morning sickness, or illness that resulted in taste aversions to foods as varied as cotton candy, strawberries, and tacos. In some cases, a taste aversion can persist for years.

At first glance, it seems as if taste aversions can be explained by classical conditioning. In Tom's case, a neutral stimulus (spaghetti) was paired with an unconditioned stimulus (a stomach virus), which produced an unconditioned response (nausea). Now a conditioned stimulus, the spaghetti sauce alone elicited the conditioned response of nausea.

But notice that this explanation seems to violate two basic principles of classical conditioning. First, the conditioning did not require repeated pairings. Conditioning occurred in a *single pairing* of the conditioned stimulus and the unconditioned stimulus. Second, the time span between these two stimuli was *several hours,* not a matter of seconds. Is this possible? The anecdotal reports of people who develop specific taste aversions seem to suggest it is. But such reports lack the objectivity and systematic control that a scientific explanation of behavior requires.

Ken Canning/Getty Images

Classical Conditioning and Survival Animals quickly learn the signals that predict the approach of a predator. In classical conditioning terms, they learn to associate the approach of a predator (the unconditioned stimuli) with particular sounds, smells, or sights (the originally neutral stimuli that become conditioned stimuli). To survive, animals that are vulnerable to predators, such as this alert deer, must be able to use environmental signals to predict events in their environment. A rustle in the underbrush, the faint whiff of a mountain lion, or a glimpse of a human tells the animal that it's time to flee.

taste aversion A classically conditioned dislike for and avoidance of a particular food that develops when an organism becomes ill after eating the food.

biological preparedness In learning theory, the idea that an organism is innately predisposed to form associations between certain stimuli and responses.

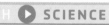

MYTH ▶ SCIENCE

Is it true that you can develop a long-lasting aversion to a food or beverage if you get sick after eating or drinking it?

John Garcia (b. 1917) John Garcia grew up working on farms in northern California. In his late 20s, Garcia enrolled at a community college. At the age of 48, Garcia earned his Ph.D. in psychology from the University of California, Berkeley (Garcia, 1997). Garcia was one of the first researchers to experimentally demonstrate the existence of taste aversions and other "exceptions" to the general laws of classical conditioning. His research emphasized the importance of the evolutionary forces that shape the learning process.

Enter psychologist **John Garcia,** who demonstrated that taste aversions could be produced in laboratory rats under controlled conditions (Garcia & others, 1966). Garcia's procedure was straightforward. Rats first drank saccharin-flavored water (the neutral stimulus). Hours later, the rats were injected with a drug (the unconditioned stimulus) that produced gastrointestinal distress (the unconditioned response). After the rats recovered from their illness, they refused to drink the flavored water again. The rats had developed a taste aversion to the saccharin-flavored water, which had become a conditioned stimulus.

At first, many psychologists were skeptical of Garcia's findings because they seemed to violate the basic principles of classical conditioning (Davis & Riley, 2010). Several leading psychological journals refused to publish Garcia's research, saying the results were unconvincing or downright impossible (Garcia, 1981, 2003). But Garcia's results have been replicated many times. In fact, later research showed that taste aversions could develop even when a full 24 hours separated the presentation of the flavored water and the drug that produced illness (Davis & Riley, 2010).

Conditioned taste aversions also challenged the notion that virtually any stimulus can become a conditioned stimulus. As Pavlov (1928) wrote, "Any natural phenomenon chosen at will may be converted into a conditioned stimulus . . . any visual stimulus, any desired sound, any odor, and the stimulation of any part of the skin." After all, Pavlov had demonstrated that dogs could be classically conditioned to salivate to a ringing bell, a ticking metronome, and even the sight of geometric figures.

But if this were the case, then why didn't Tom develop an aversion to other stimuli he encountered between the time he ate the spaghetti and when he got sick? Why was it that only the spaghetti sauce became a conditioned stimulus that triggered nausea, not the restaurant, the tablecloth, or his dining companions?

Contrary to what Pavlov suggested, Garcia and his colleagues demonstrated that the particular conditioned stimulus that is used *does* make a difference in classical conditioning (Garcia & Koelling, 1966). In another series of experiments, Garcia found that rats did *not* learn to associate a taste with a painful event, such as a shock. Nor did they learn to associate a flashing light and noise with illness. Instead, rats were much more likely to associate a *painful stimulus,* such as a shock, with *external stimuli,* such as flashing lights and noise. And rats were much more likely to associate a *taste stimulus* with *internal stimuli*—the physical discomfort of illness. Garcia and Koelling (1966) humorously suggested that a sick rat, like a sick person, speculates, "It must have been something I ate."

Why is it that certain stimuli are more easy to associate than others? One factor that helps explain Garcia's results is **biological preparedness**—the idea that an organism is innately predisposed to form associations between certain stimuli and responses (Freeman & Riley, 2009). If the particular stimulus and response combination is *not* one that an animal is biologically prepared to associate, then the association may not occur or may occur only with great difficulty (see the In Focus box, "Evolution, Biological Preparedness, and Conditioned Fears: What Gives You the Creeps?").

When this concept is applied to taste aversions, rats (and people) seem to be biologically prepared to associate an illness with a taste rather than with a location, a person, or an object. Hence, Tom developed an aversion to the spaghetti sauce and not to the fork he had used to eat it. Apparently, both humans and rats are biologically prepared to learn taste aversions relatively easily. Thus, taste aversions can be classically conditioned more readily than can more arbitrary associations, such as that between a ringing bell and a plate of food.

Associations that are easily learned may reflect the evolutionary history and survival mechanisms of the particular animal species (Freeman & Riley, 2009). For example, rats in the wild eat a wide variety of foods. If a rat eats a new food and gets sick several hours later, it's likely to survive longer if it learns from this experience to avoid that food in the future (Kalat, 1985; Seligman, 1970).

IN FOCUS

Evolution, Biological Preparedness, and Conditioned Fears: What Gives You the Creeps?

Do these photographs make you somewhat uncomfortable?

A *phobia* is an extreme, irrational fear of a specific object, animal, or situation. It was once believed that all phobias were acquired through classical conditioning, as was Little Albert's fear of the rat and other furry objects. But many people develop phobias without having experienced a traumatic event in association with the object of their fear. Obviously, other forms of learning, such as observational learning, are involved in the development of some fears (Bruchey & others, 2010).

Maria Dryfhout/Shutterstock

When people do develop conditioned fears as a result of traumatic events, they are more likely to associate fear with certain stimuli rather than others. Erv, not surprisingly, has acquired a conditioned fear response to the "killer attic." But why doesn't Erv shudder every time he hears a lawn mower or sees a ladder, the clothes he was wearing when he got trapped, or his can of oil?

Psychologist Martin Seligman (1971) noticed that phobias seem to be quite selective. Extreme, irrational fears of snakes, spiders, heights, and small enclosed places (like Erv and Fern's attic) are relatively common. But very few people have phobias of stairs, ladders, electrical outlets or appliances, or sharp objects, even though these things are far more likely to be associated with accidents or traumatic experiences.

Seligman proposed that humans are biologically prepared to develop fears of objects or situations—such as snakes, spiders, and heights—that may once have posed a threat to humans' evolutionary ancestors. As Seligman (1971) put it, "The great majority of phobias are about objects of natural importance to the survival of the species." According to this view, people don't commonly develop phobias of knives, stoves, or cars because they're not biologically prepared to do so.

Support for this view is provided by early studies that tried to replicate Watson's Little Albert research. Elsie Bregman (1934) was unable to produce a conditioned fear response to wooden blocks and curtains, although she followed Watson's procedure carefully. And Horace English (1929) was unable to produce a conditioned fear of a wooden duck. Perhaps we're more

Stockbrokerxtra Images/ Photolibrary

biologically prepared to learn a fear of furry animals than of wooden ducks, blocks, or curtains!

More recent experimental evidence supports an evolutionary explanation for the most common phobias (Coelho & Purkis, 2009; Öhman, 2009). People seem to be biologically prepared to rapidly detect snakes and spiders. Several studies have shown that people are faster at detecting a single snake or spider image among photos of flowers or other non-threatening objects than they are at detecting a single flower image among pictures of snakes or spiders (see LoBue, 2010; LoBue & others, 2010). One study showed that monkeys also more quickly detect images of a snake than of a flower (Shibasaki & Kawai, 2009). And, both humans and monkeys acquire conditioned fear responses to pictures of snakes and spiders more rapidly than they do to neutral objects, like mushrooms and flowers (Öhman & Mineka, 2001, 2003).

Are such findings the result of frightening experiences with snakes or spiders? Or perhaps learned responses to the knowledge that snakes and spiders are dangerous? Apparently not. Research has shown that preschoolers and even infants are faster at spotting images of snakes and spiders among photos of flowers, frogs, or caterpillars (LoBue, 2010; LoBue & DeLoache, 2008, 2010). They are also more likely to associate snakes and spiders with fearful stimuli, like angry faces or voices (DeLoache & LoBue, 2009; Rakison, 2009).

> MYTH ▶ SCIENCE
>
> Is it true that people are more likely to fear snakes, spiders, and heights than more realistic threats like speeding cars or lightning?

Öhman and Mineka (2003) suggest that because poisonous snakes, reptiles, and insects have been associated with danger throughout the evolution of mammals, there is an evolved "fear module" in the brain that is highly sensitized to such evolutionarily relevant stimuli. According to this explanation, individuals who more rapidly detected such dangerous animals would have been more likely to learn to avoid them and survive to reproduce and pass on their genes to future generations (Coelho & Purkis, 2009; Öhman & others, 2007). For more on how evolved brain mechanisms might be involved in fearful responses, see Chapter 8.

That different species form some associations more easily than others also probably reflects the unique sensory capabilities and feeding habits that have evolved as a matter of environmental adaptation. Bobwhite quail, for instance, rely primarily on vision for identifying potential meals. In contrast, rats have relatively poor eyesight and rely primarily on taste and odor cues to identify food. Given these species differences, it shouldn't surprise you that quail, but not rats, can easily be conditioned to develop an aversion to blue-colored water—a *visual* stimulus. On the other hand, rats learn more readily than quail to associate illness with sour water—a *taste* stimulus

Saving an Endangered Species by Creating a Conditioned Taste Aversion The endangered northern quoll is a small Australian marsupial that seems to have a particular fondness for cane toads, a highly invasive, nonnative species. Quolls and other native species have been decimated by cane toads, whose skin, glands, and internal organs contain a deadly poison.

University of Sydney ecologist Stephanie O'Donnell and her colleagues (2010) successfully created a conditioned taste aversion to teach quolls to avoid eating cane toads. They fed young quolls tiny, dead cane toads that were laced with a nausea-inducing drug. The juvenile cane toads, weighing less than a tenth of an ounce, did not contain enough poison to kill the quolls, but the drug made the quolls extremely nauseous. Did a taste aversion develop? Yes, and the quolls with taste aversions survived up to five times longer in the wild than control group quolls who were *not* exposed to the sickness-inducing toads.

Ultimately, the scientists hope to develop ways to produce cane-toad taste aversions in entire populations of quolls and other endangered species whose survival is imperiled by their habit of munching on the poisonous toads. One idea is to spread drug-laced toad carcasses over a wide area, possibly from the air by plane or helicopter.

Dr Jonathan Webb

(Wilcoxon & others, 1971). In effect, quail are biologically prepared to associate visual cues with illness, while rats are biologically prepared to associate taste cues with illness.

Taste aversion research emphasizes that the study of learning must consider the unique behavior patterns and capabilities of different species. As the result of evolution, animals have developed unique forms of behavior to adapt to their natural environments (Bolles, 1985). These natural behavior patterns and unique characteristics ultimately influence what an animal is capable of learning—and how easily it can be conditioned to learn a new behavior.

❯ Test your understanding of **Introduction to Learning and Classical Conditioning** with *LEARNING*Curve.

Operant Conditioning
ASSOCIATING BEHAVIORS AND CONSEQUENCES

> **KEY THEME**

Operant conditioning deals with the learning of active, voluntary behaviors that are shaped and maintained by their consequences.

> **KEY QUESTIONS**

❯ How did Edward Thorndike study the acquisition of new behaviors, and what conclusions did he reach?

❯ What were B.F. Skinner's key assumptions?

❯ How are positive reinforcement and negative reinforcement similar, and how are they different?

Classical conditioning can help explain the acquisition of many learned behaviors, including emotional and physiological responses. However, recall that classical conditioning involves reflexive behaviors that are automatically elicited by a specific stimulus. Most everyday behaviors don't fall into this category. Instead, they involve nonreflexive, or *voluntary,* actions that can't be explained with classical conditioning.

The investigation of how voluntary behaviors are acquired began with a young American psychology student named Edward L. Thorndike. A few years before Pavlov began his extensive studies of classical conditioning, Thorndike was using cats, chicks, and dogs to investigate how voluntary behaviors are acquired. Thorndike's pioneering studies helped set the stage for the later work of another American psychologist named B.F. Skinner. It was Skinner who developed *operant conditioning,* another form of conditioning that explains how we acquire and maintain voluntary behaviors.

Edward Lee Thorndike (1874–1949) As a graduate student, Thorndike became fascinated by psychology after taking a class taught by William James at Harvard University. Interested in the study of animal behavior, Thorndike conducted his first experiments with baby chicks. When his landlady protested about the chickens in his room, Thorndike moved his experiments, chicks and all, to the cellar of William James's home—much to the delight of the James children. Following these initial experiments, Thorndike constructed his famous "puzzle boxes" to study learning in cats. Later in life, Thorndike focused his attention on improving educational materials. Among his contributions was the *Thorndike-Barnhart Junior Dictionary* for children, which is still published today (Thorndike & Barnhart, 1997; R. L. Thorndike, 1991).

Humanities and Social Sciences Library/New York Public Library/Science Photo Library

Thorndike and the Law of Effect

Edward L. Thorndike was the first psychologist to systematically investigate animal learning and how voluntary behaviors are influenced by their consequences. At the time, Thorndike was only in his early 20s and a psychology graduate student. He conducted his pioneering studies to complete his dissertation and earn his doctorate in psychology.

Thorndike's dissertation focused on the issue of whether animals, like humans, use reasoning to solve problems (Dewsbury, 1998). In an important series of experiments, Thorndike (1898) put hungry cats in specially constructed cages that he called "puzzle boxes." A cat could escape the cage by a simple act, such as pulling a loop or pressing a lever that would unlatch the cage door. A plate of food was placed just outside the cage, where the hungry cat could see and smell it.

Thorndike found that when the cat was first put into the puzzle box, it would engage in many different, seemingly random behaviors to escape. For example, the cat would scratch at the cage door, claw at the ceiling, and try to squeeze through the wooden slats (not to mention complain at the top of its lungs). Eventually, however, the cat would accidentally pull on the loop or step on the lever, opening the door latch and escaping the box. After several trials in the same puzzle box, a cat could get the cage door open very quickly.

Thorndike (1898) concluded that the cats did *not* display any humanlike insight or reasoning in unlatching the puzzle box door. Instead, he explained the cats' learning as a process of *trial and error* (Chance, 1999). The cats gradually learned to associate certain responses with successfully escaping the box and gaining the food reward. According to Thorndike, these successful behaviors became "stamped in," so that a cat was more likely to repeat these behaviors when placed in the puzzle box again. Unsuccessful behaviors were gradually eliminated.

Thorndike's observations led him to formulate the **law of effect**: Responses followed by a "satisfying state of affairs" are "strengthened" and more likely to occur again in the same situation. Conversely, responses followed by an unpleasant or "annoying state of affairs" are "weakened" and less likely to occur again.

Thorndike's description of the law of effect was an important first step in understanding how active, voluntary behaviors can be modified by their consequences. Thorndike, however, never developed his ideas on learning into a formal model or system (Hearst, 1999). Instead, he applied his findings to education, publishing many books on educational psychology (Mayer & others, 2003). Some 30 years after Thorndike's famous puzzle-box studies, the task of further investigating how voluntary behaviors are acquired and maintained would be taken up by another American psychologist, B.F. Skinner (Rutherford, 2012).

Thorndike's Puzzle Box Shown here is one of Thorndike's puzzle boxes, which were made mostly out of wood slats and wire mesh. Thorndike constructed a total of 15 different puzzle boxes, which varied in how difficult they were for a cat to escape from. In a simple box like this one, a cat merely had to step on a treadle at the front of the cage to escape. More complex boxes required the cat to perform a chain of three responses—step on a treadle, pull on a string, and push a bar up or down (Chance, 1999).

law of effect Learning principle, proposed by Thorndike, in which responses followed by a satisfying effect become strengthened and are more likely to recur in a particular situation, while responses followed by a dissatisfying effect are weakened and less likely to recur in a particular situation.

Burrhus Frederick Skinner (1904–1990) As a young adult, Skinner had hoped to become a writer. When he graduated from college, he set up a study in the attic of his parents' home and waited for inspiration to strike. After a year of "frittering" away his time, he decided that there were better ways to learn about human nature (Moore, 2005a). As Skinner (1967) later wrote, "A writer might portray human behavior accurately, but he did not understand it. I was to remain interested in human behavior, but the literary method had failed me; I would turn to the scientific. . . . The relevant science appeared to be psychology, though I had only the vaguest idea of what that meant."

B.F. Skinner and the Search for "Order in Behavior"

From the time he was a graduate student in psychology until his death, the famous American psychologist **B.F. Skinner** searched for the "lawful processes" that would explain "order in behavior" (Skinner, 1956, 1967). Like John Watson, Skinner was a staunch behaviorist. Skinner strongly believed that psychology should restrict itself to studying only phenomena that could be objectively measured and verified—outwardly observable behavior and environmental events.

Skinner acknowledged that Pavlov's classical conditioning could explain the learned association of stimuli in certain reflexive responses (Iversen, 1992). But classical conditioning was limited to existing behaviors that were reflexively elicited. To Skinner, the most important form of learning was demonstrated by *new* behaviors

operant Skinner's term for an actively emitted (or voluntary) behavior that operates on the environment to produce consequences.

operant conditioning The basic learning process that involves changing the probability that a response will be repeated by manipulating the consequences of that response.

reinforcement The occurrence of a stimulus or event following a response that increases the likelihood of that response being repeated.

positive reinforcement A situation in which a response is followed by the addition of a reinforcing stimulus, increasing the likelihood that the response will be repeated in similar situations.

that were actively *emitted* by the organism, such as the active behaviors produced by Thorndike's cats in trying to escape the puzzle boxes.

Skinner (1953) coined the term **operant** to describe any "active behavior that operates upon the environment to generate consequences." In everyday language, Skinner's principles of operant conditioning explain how we acquire the wide range of *voluntary* behaviors that we perform in daily life. But as a behaviorist who rejected mentalistic explanations, Skinner avoided the term *voluntary* because it would imply that behavior was due to a conscious choice or intention.

Skinner defined operant conditioning concepts in very objective terms and he avoided explanations based on subjective mental states (Moore, 2005b). We'll closely follow Skinner's original terminology and definitions.

Reinforcement
INCREASING FUTURE BEHAVIOR

In a nutshell, Skinner's **operant conditioning** explains learning as a process in which behavior is shaped and maintained by its consequences. One possible consequence of a behavior is reinforcement. **Reinforcement** is said to occur when a stimulus or an event follows an operant and increases the likelihood of the operant being repeated. Notice that reinforcement is defined by the effect it produces—increasing or strengthening the occurrence of a behavior in the future.

Let's look at reinforcement in action. Suppose you put your money into a soft-drink vending machine and push the button. Nothing happens. You push the button again. Nothing. You try the coin-return lever. A shower of coins is released. In the future, if another vending machine swallows your money without giving you what you want, what are you likely to do? Hit the coin-return lever, right?

In this example, pushing the coin return lever is the *operant*—the active response you emitted. The shower of coins is the *reinforcing stimulus,* or *reinforcer*—the stimulus or event that is sought in a particular situation. In everyday language, a reinforcing stimulus is typically something desirable, satisfying, or pleasant. Skinner, of course, avoided such terms because they reflected subjective emotional states.

POSITIVE AND NEGATIVE REINFORCEMENT

There are two forms of reinforcement: *positive reinforcement* and *negative reinforcement.* Both affect future behavior, but they do so in different ways (see Table 5.1). It's easier to understand these differences if you note at the outset that Skinner did not use the terms *positive* and *negative* in their everyday sense of meaning "good" and "bad" or "desirable" and "undesirable." Instead, think of the words *positive* and *negative* in terms of their mathematical meanings. *Positive* is the equivalent of a plus sign (+), meaning that something is added. *Negative* is the equivalent of a minus sign (−), meaning that something is subtracted or removed. If you keep that distinction in mind, the principles of positive and negative reinforcement should be easier to understand.

Positive reinforcement involves following an operant with the addition of a reinforcing stimulus. In positive reinforcement situations, a response is strengthened because something is *added* or presented. Everyday examples of positive reinforcement in action are easy to identify. Here are some examples:

- Your backhand return of the tennis ball (the operant) is low and fast, and your tennis coach yells "Excellent!" (the reinforcing stimulus).
- You watch a student production of *Hamlet* and write a short paper about it (the operant) for 10 bonus points (the reinforcing stimulus) in your literature class.

TABLE 5.1

Comparing Positive and Negative Reinforcement

Process	Operant Behavior	Consequence	Effect on Behavior
Positive reinforcement	Studying to make dean's list	Make dean's list	Increase studying in the future
Negative reinforcement	Studying to avoid losing academic scholarship	Avoid loss of academic scholarship	Increase studying in the future

Both positive and negative reinforcement increase the likelihood of a behavior being repeated. Positive reinforcement involves a behavior that leads to a reinforcing or rewarding event. In contrast, negative reinforcement involves behavior that leads to the avoidance of or escape from an aversive or punishing event. Ultimately, both positive and negative reinforcement involve outcomes that strengthen future behavior.

- You reach your sales quota at work (the operant) and you get a bonus check (the reinforcing stimulus).

In each example, if the addition of the reinforcing stimulus has the effect of making you more likely to repeat the operant in similar situations in the future, then positive reinforcement has occurred.

It's important to point out that what constitutes a *reinforcing stimulus* can vary from person to person, species to species, and situation to situation. While gold stars and stickers may be reinforcing to a third-grader, they would probably have little reinforcing value to your average high school student.

It's also important to note that the reinforcing stimulus is not necessarily something we usually consider positive or desirable. For example, most teachers would not think of a scolding as being a reinforcing stimulus to children. But to children, adult attention can be a powerful reinforcing stimulus. If a child receives attention from the teacher only when he misbehaves, then the teacher may unwittingly be reinforcing misbehavior. The child may actually increase disruptive behavior in order to get the sought-after reinforcing stimulus—adult attention—even if it's in the form of being scolded. To reduce the child's disruptive behavior, the teacher would do better to reinforce the child's appropriate behavior by paying attention to him when he's *not* being disruptive, such as when he is working quietly.

Negative reinforcement involves an operant that is followed by the removal of an aversive stimulus. In negative reinforcement situations, a response is strengthened because something is being *subtracted* or removed. Remember that the word *negative* in the phrase *negative reinforcement* is used like a mathematical minus sign (−).

For example, you take two aspirin (the operant) to remove a headache (the aversive stimulus). Thirty minutes later, the headache is gone. Are you now more likely to take aspirin to deal with bodily aches and pain in the future? If you are, then negative reinforcement has occurred.

Aversive stimuli typically involve physical or psychological discomfort that an organism seeks to escape or avoid. Consequently, behaviors are said to be negatively reinforced when they let you either: (1) *escape* aversive stimuli that are already present or (2) *avoid* aversive stimuli before they occur. That is, we're more likely to repeat the same escape or avoidance behaviors in similar situations in the future. The headache example illustrates the negative reinforcement of *escape behavior.* By taking two aspirin, you "escaped" the headache. Paying your electric bill on time to avoid a late charge illustrates the negative reinforcement of *avoidance behavior.* Here are some more examples of negative reinforcement involving escape or avoidance behavior:

- You make backup copies of important computer files (the operant) to avoid losing the data if the computer's hard drive should fail (the aversive stimulus).
- You dab some hydrocortisone cream on an insect bite (the operant) to escape the itching (the aversive stimulus).
- You install a new battery (the operant) in the smoke detector to escape the annoying beep (the aversive stimulus).

In each example, if escaping or avoiding the aversive event has the effect of making you more likely to repeat the operant in similar situations in the future, then negative reinforcement has taken place.

negative reinforcement A situation in which a response results in the removal of, avoidance of, or escape from a punishing stimulus, increasing the likelihood that the response will be repeated in similar situations.

Think Like a SCIENTIST

Can wearable technology help you break a bad habit or form a good one? Go to LaunchPad: Resources to **Think Like a Scientist** about **Positive and Negative Reinforcement.**

 LaunchPad

Negative Reinforcement What behavior is being negatively reinforced? If you're having trouble answering this question, first identify the aversive stimulus.

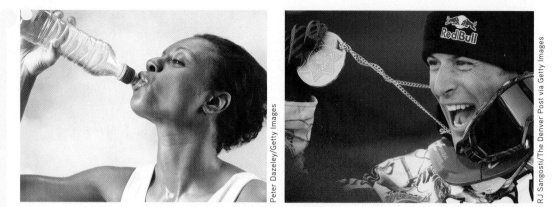

Peter Dazeley/Getty Images

RJ Sangosti/The Denver Post via Getty Images

Types of Reinforcers Primary reinforcers, like water when you're thirsty, are naturally reinforcing—you don't have to learn their value. In contrast, the value of conditioned reinforcers, like grades and awards, has to be learned through their association with primary reinforcers. But conditioned reinforcers can be just as reinforcing as primary reinforcers. As proof, champion snowmobiler Levi LaVallee beams as he shows off the gold medal he won in the Snowmobile Long Jump event at the 2014 Winter X games.

PRIMARY AND CONDITIONED REINFORCERS

Skinner also distinguished two kinds of reinforcing stimuli: primary and conditioned. A **primary reinforcer** is one that is *naturally* reinforcing for a given species. That is, even if an individual has not had prior experience with the particular stimulus, the stimulus or event still has reinforcing properties. For example, food, water, adequate warmth, and sexual contact are primary reinforcers for most animals, including humans.

A **conditioned reinforcer,** also called a *secondary reinforcer,* is one that has acquired reinforcing value by being associated with a primary reinforcer. The classic example of a conditioned reinforcer is money. Money is reinforcing not because those flimsy bits of paper and little pieces of metal have value in and of themselves, but because we've learned that we can use them to acquire primary reinforcers and other conditioned reinforcers. Awards, frequent-flyer points, and college degrees are just a few other examples of conditioned reinforcers.

Conditioned reinforcers need not be as tangible as money or college degrees. Conditioned reinforcers can be as subtle as a smile, a touch, or a nod of recognition. Looking back at the Prologue, for example, Fern was reinforced by the laughter of her friends and relatives each time she told "the killer attic" tale—so she kept telling the story!

Punishment
USING AVERSIVE CONSEQUENCES TO DECREASE BEHAVIOR

KEY THEME

Punishment is a process that decreases the future occurrence of a behavior.

KEY QUESTIONS

> How does punishment differ from negative reinforcement?
> What factors influence the effectiveness of punishment?
> What effects are associated with the use of punishment to control behavior, and what are some alternative ways to change behavior?
> What are discriminative stimuli?

Positive and negative reinforcement are processes that *increase* the frequency of a particular behavior. The opposite effect is produced by punishment. **Punishment** is a process in which a behavior is followed by an aversive consequence that *decreases* the likelihood of the behavior's being repeated. Many people tend to confuse punishment and negative reinforcement, but these two processes produce entirely different effects on behavior (see Table 5.2). Negative reinforcement *always increases* the likelihood that an operant will be repeated in the future. Punishment *always decreases* the future performance of an operant.

Skinner (1953) identified two types of aversive events that can act as punishment. **Positive punishment,** also called *punishment by application,* involves a response being followed by the presentation of an aversive stimulus. The word *positive* in the phrase *positive punishment* signifies that something is added or presented in the situation. In

primary reinforcer A stimulus or event that is naturally or inherently reinforcing for a given species, such as food, water, or other biological necessities.

conditioned reinforcer A stimulus or event that has acquired reinforcing value by being associated with a primary reinforcer; also called a *secondary reinforcer.*

punishment The presentation of a stimulus or event following a behavior that acts to decrease the likelihood of the behavior being repeated.

positive punishment A situation in which an operant is followed by the presentation or addition of an aversive stimulus; also called *punishment by application.*

TABLE 5.2

Comparing Punishment and Negative Reinforcement

Process	Operant	Consequence	Effect on Behavior
Punishment	Wear a warm but unstylish flannel shirt	A friend makes the hurtful comment, "Nice shirt. Whose couch did you steal to get the fabric?"	Decrease wearing the shirt in the future
Negative reinforcement	Wear a warm but unstylish flannel shirt	Avoid feeling cold and uncomfortable all day	Increase wearing the shirt in the future

Punishment and negative reinforcement are two different processes that produce *opposite* effects on a given behavior. Punishment *decreases* the future performance of the behavior, while negative reinforcement *increases* it.

this case, it's an aversive stimulus. Here are some everyday examples of punishment by application:

- An employee wears shorts to work (the operant) and is reprimanded by his supervisor for dressing inappropriately (the punishing stimulus).
- Your dog jumps up on a visitor (the operant), and you smack him with a rolled-up newspaper (the punishing stimulus).
- You are late to class (the operant), and your instructor responds with a sarcastic remark (the punishing stimulus).

In each of these examples, if the presentation of the punishing stimulus has the effect of decreasing the behavior it follows, then punishment has occurred. Although the punishing stimuli in these examples were administered by other people, punishing stimuli also occur as natural consequences for some behaviors. Inadvertently touching a live electrical wire, a hot stove, or a sharp object (the operant) can result in a painful injury (the punishing stimulus).

The second type of punishment is **negative punishment,** also called *punishment by removal.* The word *negative* indicates that some stimulus is subtracted or removed from the situation (see Table 5.3). In this case, it is the loss or withdrawal of a reinforcing stimulus following a behavior. That is, the behavior's consequence is the loss of some privilege, possession, or other desirable object or activity. Here are some everyday examples of punishment by removal:

- After she speeds through a red light (the operant), her drivers' license is suspended (loss of reinforcing stimulus).
- Because he was flirting with another woman (the operant), a guy gets dumped by his girlfriend (loss of reinforcing stimulus).

In each example, if the behavior decreases in response to the removal of the reinforcing stimulus, then punishment has occurred. It's important to stress that, like reinforcement, punishment is defined by the effect it produces. In everyday usage, people often refer to a particular consequence as a punishment when, strictly speaking, it's not. Why? Because the consequence has *not* reduced future occurrences of the behavior. Hence, many consequences commonly thought of as punishments—being sent to prison, fined, reprimanded, ridiculed, or fired from a job—fail to reduce a particular behavior.

Why is it that aversive consequences don't always function as effective punishments? Skinner (1953) as well as other researchers have noted that several factors influence the effectiveness of punishment (Horner, 2002). For example, punishment is more effective if it immediately follows a response than if it is delayed. Punishment is also more effective if it consistently, rather than occasionally, follows a response (Lerman & Vorndran, 2002; Spradlin, 2002). Though speeding tickets and prison sentences are commonly referred to as punishments, these aversive consequences are inconsistently applied and often administered only after a long delay. Thus, they don't always effectively decrease specific behaviors.

negative punishment A situation in which an operant is followed by the removal or subtraction of a reinforcing stimulus; also called *punishment by removal.*

TABLE 5.3

Types of Reinforcement and Punishment

	Reinforcing stimulus	Aversive stimulus
Stimulus presented	Positive reinforcement	Positive punishment
Stimulus removed	Negative punishment	Negative reinforcement

To identify the type of reinforcement or punishment that has occurred, determine whether the stimulus is *aversive* or *reinforcing* and whether it was *presented* or *removed* following the operant.

MYTH ◀ SCIENCE

Is it true that punishment is an effective way to teach new behaviors?

The Effects of Spanking Defined as hitting a child on the buttocks with an open hand without causing a bruise or physical harm, *spanking* is a common form of discipline in the United States (Kazdin & Benjet, 2003). Some researchers believe that mild and occasional spanking is not necessarily harmful, especially when used as a backup for other forms of discipline (Oas, 2010).

However, many studies have demonstrated that physical punishment is associated with increased aggressiveness, delinquency, and antisocial behavior in the child (Gershoff, 2002; Knox, 2010; MacKenzie & others, 2012). In one study of almost 2,500 children, those who had been spanked at age three were more likely to be more aggressive at age five (Taylor & others, 2010). Other negative effects include poor parent–child relationships and an increased risk that parental disciplinary tactics might escalate into physical abuse (Gershoff, 2002; B. Smith, 2012). As Skinner (1974) cautioned, gaining immediate compliance through punishment must be weighed against punishment's negative long-term effects.

Jupiterimages/Banana Stock/Alamy

Even when punishment works, its use has several drawbacks (see B. Smith, 2012). First, punishment may decrease a specific response, but it doesn't necessarily teach or promote a more appropriate response to take its place. Second, punishment that is intense may produce undesirable results, such as complete passivity, fear, anxiety, or hostility (Lerman & Vorndran, 2002). Finally, the effects of punishment are likely to be temporary (Estes & Skinner, 1941; Skinner, 1938). A child who is sent to her room for teasing her little brother may well repeat the behavior when her mother's back is turned. As Skinner (1971) noted, "Punished behavior is likely

IN FOCUS

Changing the Behavior of Others: Alternatives to Punishment

Although punishment may temporarily decrease the occurrence of a problem behavior, it doesn't promote more desirable or appropriate behaviors in its place. Throughout his life, Skinner remained strongly opposed to the use of punishment. Instead, he advocated the greater use of positive reinforcement to strengthen desirable behaviors (Dinsmoor, 1992; Skinner, 1971). Here are four strategies that can be used to reduce undesirable behaviors without resorting to punishment.

Strategy 1: Reinforce an Incompatible Behavior
The best method to reduce a problem behavior is to reinforce an *alternative* behavior that is both constructive and incompatible with the problem behavior. For example, if you're trying to decrease a child's whining, respond to her requests (the reinforcer) only when she talks in a normal tone of voice.

Strategy 2: Stop Reinforcing the Problem Behavior
Technically, this strategy is called *extinction*. The first step in effectively applying extinction is to observe the behavior carefully and identify the reinforcer that is maintaining the problem behavior. Then eliminate the reinforcer.

Suppose a friend keeps interrupting you while you are trying to study, asking you if you want to play a video game or just hang out. You want to extinguish his behavior of interrupting your studying. In the past, trying to be polite, you've responded to his behavior by acting interested (a reinforcer). You could eliminate the reinforcer by acting uninterested and continuing to study while he talks.

It's important to note that when the extinction process is initiated, the problem behavior often *temporarily* increases. This situation is more likely to occur if the problem behavior has only occasionally

Stretch Photography/Blend Images/Corbis

Using Reinforcement in the Classroom Teachers at all levels use positive reinforcement to increase desired behaviors. Often, conditioned reinforcers, like stickers or gold stars, can be exchanged for other, more tangible rewards, like a new pencil or classroom privileges.

been reinforced in the past. Thus, once you begin, be consistent in nonreinforcement of the problem behavior.

Strategy 3: Reinforce the Non-occurrence of the Problem Behavior
This strategy involves setting a specific time period after which the individual is reinforced if the unwanted behavior has *not* occurred.

to reappear after the punitive consequences are withdrawn." For some suggestions on how to change behavior without using a punishing stimulus, see the In Focus box, "Changing the Behavior of Others: Alternatives to Punishment."

Discriminative Stimuli
SETTING THE OCCASION FOR RESPONDING

Another component of operant conditioning is the **discriminative stimulus**—the specific stimulus in the presence of which a particular operant is more likely to be reinforced. For example, a ringing phone is a discriminative stimulus that sets the occasion for a particular response—picking up the telephone and speaking.

This example illustrates how we've learned from experience to associate certain environmental cues or signals with particular operant responses. We've learned that we're more likely to be reinforced for performing a particular operant response when we do so in the presence of the appropriate discriminative stimulus. Thus, you've learned that you're more likely to be reinforced for screaming at the top of your lungs at a football game (one discriminative stimulus) than in the middle of class (a different discriminative stimulus).

In this way, according to Skinner (1974), behavior is determined and controlled by the stimuli that are present in a given situation. In Skinner's view, an individual's behavior is *not* determined by a personal choice or a conscious decision. Instead, individual behavior is determined by environmental stimuli and the person's reinforcement history in that environment. Skinner's views on this point have some very controversial implications, which are discussed in the Critical Thinking box on the next page, "Is Human Freedom Just an Illusion?"

discriminative stimulus A specific stimulus in the presence of which a particular response is more likely to be reinforced, and in the absence of which a particular response is not likely to be reinforced.

Image Source Black/Alamy

Is Maria's preference for this blue sweater based on classical or operant conditioning? Try **Concept Practice: Conditioning in Daily Life.**

For example, if you're trying to reduce bickering between children, set an appropriate time limit, and then provide positive reinforcement if they have *not* squabbled during that interval.

Strategy 4: Remove the Opportunity to Obtain Positive Reinforcement

It's not always possible to identify and eliminate all the reinforcers that maintain a behavior. For example, a child's obnoxious behavior might be reinforced by the social attention of siblings or classmates.

In a procedure called *time-out from positive reinforcement*, the child is removed from the reinforcing situation for a short time, so that the access to reinforcers is eliminated. When the undesirable behavior occurs, the child is immediately sent to a time-out area that is free of distractions and social contact. The time-out period begins as soon as the child's behavior is under control. For children, a good rule of thumb is one minute of time-out per year of age.

Enhancing the Effectiveness of Positive Reinforcement

Often, these four strategies are used in combination. However, remember the most important behavioral principle: *Positively*

reinforce the behaviors that you want to increase. There are several ways in which you can enhance the effectiveness of positive reinforcement:

- Make sure that the reinforcer is *strongly* reinforcing to the individual whose behavior you're trying to modify.
- The positive reinforcer should be delivered *immediately* after the preferred behavior occurs.
- The positive reinforcer should initially be given *every* time the preferred behavior occurs. When the desired behavior is well established, *gradually reduce the frequency of reinforcement.*
- Use a *variety* of positive reinforcers, such as tangible items, praise, special privileges, recognition, and so on. Minimize the use of food as a positive reinforcer.
- Capitalize on what is known as the *Premack principle*—a more preferred activity (e.g., painting) can be used to reinforce a less preferred activity (e.g., picking up toys).
- Encourage the individual to engage in *self-reinforcement* in the form of pride, a sense of accomplishment, and feelings of self-control.

BABY BLUES ©2004 Baby Blues Partnership Dist. By King Features Syndicate

CRITICAL THINKING

Is Human Freedom Just an Illusion?

Skinner was intensely interested in human behavior and social problems (Bjork, 1997). He believed that operant conditioning principles could, and *should*, be applied on a broad scale to help solve society's problems. Skinner's most radical—and controversial—belief was that such ideas as free will, self-determination, and individual choice are just illusions.

Skinner argued that behavior is not simply influenced by the environment but is *determined* by it. Control the environment, he said, and you will control human behavior. As he bluntly asserted in his controversial best-seller, *Beyond Freedom and Dignity* (1971), "A person does not act upon the world, the world acts upon him."

Such views did not sit well with the American public (Rutherford, 2003). Following the publication of *Beyond Freedom and Dignity,* one member of Congress denounced Skinner for "advancing ideas which threaten the future of our system of government by denigrating the American tradition of individualism, human dignity, and self-reliance" (quoted in Rutherford, 2000). Why the uproar?

Beyond Freedom and Dignity
The impact of the publication of *Beyond Freedom and Dignity* in August 1971, can be measured by the flurry of media attention that accompanied its release. Skinner appeared on the cover of *Time* magazine, was interviewed by the *New York Times,* and appeared on many national television shows, including the *Today* show. The *Time* cover headline read, "We Can't Afford Freedom" and showed Skinner surrounded by some of his famous creations, including a pigeon pecking a ping-pong ball and a rat pressing a lever in a Skinner box.

New York Times Co./Getty Images

Skinner's ideas clashed with the traditional American ideals of personal responsibility, individual freedom, and self-determination. Skinner labeled such notions the "traditional prescientific view" of human behavior. According to Skinner, "A scientific analysis [of behavior] shifts both the responsibility and the achievement to the environment." Applying his ideas to social problems, such as alcoholism and crime, Skinner (1971) wrote, "It is the environment which is 'responsible' for objectionable behavior, and it is the environment, not some attribute of the individual, which must be changed."

To understand Skinner's point of view, it helps to think of society as a massive, sophisticated Skinner box. From the moment of birth, the environment shapes and determines your behavior through reinforcing or punishing consequences. Taking this view, you are no more personally responsible for your behavior than is a rat in a Skinner box pressing a lever to obtain a food pellet. Just like the rat's behavior, your behavior is simply a response to the unique patterns of environmental consequences to which you have been exposed. On the one hand, it may seem convenient to blame your history of environmental consequences for your failures and mistakes. On the other hand, that means you can't take any credit for your accomplishments and good deeds, either!

Skinner (1971) proposed that "a technology of behavior" be developed, one based on a scientific analysis of behavior. He believed that society could be redesigned using operant conditioning principles to produce more socially desirable behaviors—and happier citizens (Goddard, 2014). He described such an ideal, utopian society in *Walden Two,* a novel he published in 1948.

Critics charged Skinner with advocating a totalitarian state. They asked who would determine which behaviors were shaped and maintained (Rutherford, 2000; Todd & Morris, 1992). As Skinner pointed out, however, human behavior is *already* controlled by various authorities: parents, teachers, politicians, religious leaders, employers, and so forth. Such authorities regularly use reinforcing and punishing consequences to shape and control

the behavior of others. Skinner insisted that it is better to control behavior in a rational, humane fashion than to leave the control of behavior to the whims and often selfish aims of those in power.

Skinner's ideas may seem radical or far-fetched. But some contemporary thinkers are already developing new ideas about how operant conditioning principles can be used to meet socially desirable goals. A movement called *gamification* advocates turning daily life into a kind of virtual reality game, in which "points" or other conditioned reinforcers are awarded to reward healthy or productive behaviors (Campbell, 2011). For example, some businesses give reductions on health insurance premiums to employees who rack up enough points on a specially equipped pedometer that monitors their daily activity level. The danger? Marketing professionals are already studying ways to use gamification to influence consumer preferences and buying decisions (Schell, 2010).

CRITICAL THINKING QUESTIONS

- If Skinner's vision of a socially engineered society using operant conditioning principles were implemented, would such changes be good or bad for society?

- Are human freedom and personal responsibility illusions? Or is human behavior fundamentally different from a rat's behavior in a Skinner box? If so, how?

- Is your behavior almost entirely the product of environmental conditioning? Think about your answer carefully. After all, exactly why are you reading this box?

NON SEQUITUR © 1996 Wiley Ink, Inc. Dist. by UNIVERSAL UCLICK. Reprinted with permission. All rights reserved.

TABLE 5.4

Components of Operant Conditioning

	Discriminative Stimulus	Operant Response	Consequence	Effect on Future Behavior
Definition	The environmental stimulus that precedes an operant response	The actively emitted or voluntary behavior	The environmental stimulus or event that follows the operant response	Reinforcement increases the likelihood of operant being repeated; punishment or lack of reinforcement decreases the likelihood of operant being repeated.
Examples	Wallet on college sidewalk	Give wallet to security	$50 reward from wallet's owner	Positive reinforcement: More likely to turn in lost items to authorities
	Gas gauge almost on "empty"	Fill car with gas	Avoid running out of gas	Negative reinforcement: More likely to fill car when gas gauge shows empty
	Informal social situation at work	Tell an off-color, sexist joke	Formally reprimanded for sexism and inappropriate workplace behavior	Positive punishment: Less likely to tell off-color, sexist jokes in workplace
	ATM	Insert bank card	Broken ATM machine eats your bank card and doesn't dispense cash	Negative punishment: Less likely to use that ATM in the future

We have now discussed all three fundamental components of operant conditioning (see Table 5.4). In the presence of a specific environmental stimulus (the *discriminative stimulus*), we emit a particular behavior (the *operant*), which is followed by a consequence (*reinforcement* or *punishment*). If the consequence is either positive or negative reinforcement, we are *more* likely to repeat the operant when we encounter the same or similar discriminative stimuli in the future. If the consequence is some form of punishment, we are *less* likely to repeat the operant when we encounter the same or similar discriminative stimuli in the future.

Next, we'll build on the basics of operant conditioning by considering how Skinner explained the acquisition of complex behaviors.

The examples given here illustrate the three key components involved in operant conditioning. The basic operant conditioning process works like this: In the presence of a specific discriminative stimulus, an operant response is emitted, which is followed by a consequence. Depending on the consequence, we are either more or less likely to repeat the operant when we encounter the same or a similar discriminative stimulus in the future.

operant chamber or Skinner box The experimental apparatus invented by B.F. Skinner to study the relationship between environmental events and active behaviors.

Shaping and Maintaining Behavior

KEY THEME

New behaviors are acquired through shaping and can be maintained through different patterns of reinforcement.

KEY QUESTIONS

> How does shaping work?
> What is the partial reinforcement effect, and how do the four schedules of reinforcement differ in their effects?
> What is behavior modification?

To scientifically study the relationship between behavior and its consequences in the laboratory, Skinner invented the **operant chamber,** more popularly known as the **Skinner box.** An operant chamber is a small cage with a food dispenser. Attached to the cage is a device that automatically records the number of operants made by an experimental animal, usually a rat or pigeon. For a rat, the typical operant is pressing a bar; for a pigeon, it is pecking at a small disk. Food pellets are usually used for positive reinforcement. Often, a light in the cage functions as a discriminative stimulus. When the light is on, pressing the bar or pecking the disk is reinforced with a food pellet. When the light is off, these responses do not result in reinforcement.

When a rat is first placed in a Skinner box, it typically explores its new environment, occasionally nudging or pressing the bar in the process. The researcher can accelerate the rat's bar-pressing behavior through a process

Time & Life Pictures/Getty Images

The Skinner Box Popularly called a Skinner box after its inventor, an operant chamber is used to experimentally study operant conditioning in laboratory animals.

Operant Conditioning at Sea-World This sequence shows a SeaWorld trainer using operant conditioning principles with a dolphin that has already been shaped to perform somersaults. **(a)** The trainer gives the dolphin two discriminative stimuli—a distinct vocal sound and a specific hand gesture. **(b)** The dolphin quickly responds with the correct operant—a perfect somersault in the air. **(c)** The operant is positively reinforced with a piece of fish. The same basic techniques are also used to teach seals, sea lions, walruses, and killer whales to perform different tricks on cue.

(a)   (b)   (c)

Courtesy of the authors

called shaping. **Shaping** involves reinforcing successively closer approximations of a behavior until the correct behavior is displayed. For example, the researcher might first reinforce the rat with a food pellet whenever it moves to the half of the Skinner box in which the bar is located. Other responses would be ignored. Once that response has been learned, reinforcement is withheld until the rat moves even closer to the bar. Then the rat might be reinforced only when it touches the bar. Step by step, the rat is reinforced for behaviors that correspond ever more closely to the final goal behavior—pressing the bar.

Skinner believed that shaping could explain how people acquire a wide variety of abilities and skills—everything from tying shoes to operating sophisticated computer programs. Athletic coaches, teachers, parents, and child-care workers all use shaping techniques.

THE PARTIAL REINFORCEMENT EFFECT
BUILDING RESISTANCE TO EXTINCTION

Once a rat had acquired a bar-pressing behavior, Skinner found that the most efficient way to strengthen the response was to immediately reinforce *every* occurrence of bar pressing. This pattern of reinforcement is called **continuous reinforcement.** In everyday life, of course, it's common for responses to be reinforced only sometimes— a pattern called **partial reinforcement.** For example, practicing your basketball skills isn't followed by putting the ball through the hoop on every shot. Sometimes you're reinforced by making a basket, and sometimes you're not.

Now suppose that despite all your hard work, your basketball skills are dismal. If practicing free throws was *never* reinforced by making a basket, what would you do? You'd probably eventually quit playing basketball. This is an example of **extinction.** In operant conditioning, when a learned response no longer results in reinforcement, the likelihood of the behavior's being repeated gradually declines.

Skinner (1956) first noticed the effects of partial reinforcement when he began running low on food pellets one day. Rather than reinforcing every bar press, Skinner tried to stretch out his supply of pellets by rewarding responses only periodically. He found that the rats not only continued to respond, but actually increased their rate of bar pressing.

One important consequence of partially reinforcing behavior is that partially reinforced behaviors tend to be more resistant to extinction than are behaviors conditioned using continuous reinforcement. This phenomenon is called the **partial reinforcement effect.** For example, when Skinner shut off the food-dispensing

shaping The operant conditioning procedure of selectively reinforcing successively closer approximations of a goal behavior until the goal behavior is displayed.

continuous reinforcement A schedule of reinforcement in which every occurrence of a particular response is followed by a reinforcer.

partial reinforcement A situation in which the occurrence of a particular response is only sometimes followed by a reinforcer.

extinction (in operant conditioning) The gradual weakening and disappearance of conditioned behavior. In operant conditioning, extinction occurs when an emitted behavior is no longer followed by a reinforcer.

partial reinforcement effect The phenomenon in which behaviors that are conditioned using partial reinforcement are more resistant to extinction than behaviors that are conditioned using continuous reinforcement.

Christian Petersen/Getty Images

Superstitious Rituals: Behaviors Shaped by Accidental Reinforcement LeBron James is one of the many professional athletes who has developed a superstitious pregame routine (Wargo, 2008). Basketball fans are familiar with "The Ritual," a complex sequence that includes carefully choreographed handshakes with teammates and culminates with James tossing chalk high into the air in front of cheering (or jeering) spectators.

Skinner (1948b) pointed out that superstitions may result when a behavior is accidentally reinforced—that is, when reinforcement is just a coincidence. So although it was really just a fluke that wearing your "lucky" shirt was followed by a win, the illusion of reinforcement can shape and strengthen behavior. And, adding to their reinforcing qualities, Lysann Damisch and her colleagues (2010) found that engaging in superstitious behaviors actually improved performance, probably because doing so enhanced self-confidence.

mechanism, a pigeon conditioned using continuous reinforcement would continue pecking at the disk 100 times or so before the behavior decreased significantly, indicating extinction. In contrast, a pigeon conditioned with partial reinforcement continued to peck at the disk thousands of times! If you think about it, this is not surprising. When pigeons, rats, or humans have experienced partial reinforcement, they've learned that reinforcement may yet occur, despite delays and nonreinforced responses, if persistent responses are made.

In everyday life, the partial reinforcement effect is reflected in behaviors that persist despite the lack of reinforcement. Gamblers may persist despite a string of losses, writers will persevere in the face of repeated rejection slips, and the family dog will continue begging for the scraps of food that it has only occasionally received at the dinner table in the past.

MYTH ◀ SCIENCE

Is it true that the most effective way to teach a new behavior is to reward it each time it is performed?

THE SCHEDULES OF REINFORCEMENT

Skinner (1956) found that specific preset arrangements of partial reinforcement produced different patterns and rates of responding. Collectively, these different reinforcement arrangements are called **schedules of reinforcement.** As we describe the four basic schedules of reinforcement, it will be helpful to refer to Figure 5.5 on the next page, which shows the typical pattern of responses produced by each schedule.

With a **fixed-ratio (FR) schedule,** reinforcement occurs after a fixed number of responses. A rat on a 10-to-1 fixed-ratio schedule (abbreviated FR-10) would have to press the bar 10 times in order to receive one food pellet. Fixed-ratio schedules typically produce a high rate of responding that follows a burst–pause–burst pattern. In everyday life, the fixed-ratio schedule is reflected in any activity that requires a precise number of responses in order to obtain reinforcement. Piecework—work for which you are paid for producing a specific number of

schedule of reinforcement The delivery of a reinforcer according to a preset pattern based on the number of responses or the time interval between responses.

fixed-ratio (FR) schedule A reinforcement schedule in which a reinforcer is delivered after a fixed number of responses has occurred.

variable-ratio (VR) schedule A
reinforcement schedule in which a reinforcer
is delivered after an average number of
responses, which varies unpredictably from
trial to trial.

fixed-interval (FI) schedule A
reinforcement schedule in which a reinforcer
is delivered for the first response that
occurs after a preset time interval has
elapsed.

variable-interval (VI) schedule A
reinforcement schedule in which a reinforcer
is delivered for the first response that
occurs after an average time interval, which
varies unpredictably from trial to trial.

items, such as being paid $1 for every 100 envelopes you stuff—is an example of
an FR-100 schedule.

With a **variable-ratio (VR) schedule,** reinforcement occurs after an *average*
number of responses, which *varies* from trial to trial. A rat on a variable-ratio-20
schedule (abbreviated VR-20) might have to press the bar 25 times on the first trial
before being reinforced and only 15 times on the second trial before reinforcement.
Although the number of responses required on any specific trial is *unpredictable,* over
repeated trials the ratio of responses to reinforcers works out to the predetermined
average.

Variable-ratio schedules of reinforcement produce high, steady rates of responding with hardly any pausing between trials or after reinforcement. Gambling is the
classic example of a variable-ratio schedule in real life (Schüll, 2012). Each spin of
the roulette wheel, toss of the dice, or purchase of a lottery ticket could be the big
one, and the more often you gamble, the more opportunities you have to win (and
lose, as casino owners are well aware).

On a **fixed-interval (FI) schedule,** a reinforcer is delivered for the first
response emitted *after* the preset time interval has elapsed. A rat on a two-minute
fixed-interval schedule (abbreviated FI-2 minutes) would receive no food pellets
for any bar presses made during the first two minutes. But the first bar press *after*
the two-minute interval had elapsed would be reinforced.

Fixed-interval schedules typically produce a scallop-shaped pattern of responding
in which the number of responses tends to increase as the time for the next reinforcer draws near. For example, if your instructor gives you a test every four weeks,
your studying behavior would probably follow the same scallop-shaped pattern of
responding as the rat's bar-pressing behavior. As the end of the four-week interval
draws near, studying behavior increases. After the test, studying behavior drops off
until the end of the next four-week interval approaches.

On a **variable-interval (VI) schedule,** reinforcement occurs for the first
response emitted after an *average* amount of time has elapsed, but the interval varies
from trial to trial. Hence, a rat on a VI-30 seconds schedule might be reinforced
for the first bar press after only 10 seconds have elapsed on the first trial, for the
first bar press after 50 seconds have elapsed on the second trial, and for the first bar
press after 30 seconds have elapsed on the third trial. This works out to an average
of one reinforcer every 30 seconds.

Generally, the unpredictable nature of variable-interval schedules tends to
produce moderate but steady rates of responding, especially when the average
interval is relatively short. In daily life, we experience variable-interval schedules
when we have to wait for events that follow an approximate, rather than a precise, schedule. For example, parents often unwittingly reinforce a whining child
on a variable interval schedule. From the child's perspective, the whining usually
results in the desired request, but how long the child has to whine before getting
reinforced can vary. Thus, the child learns that persistent whining will eventually pay off.

Applications of Operant Conditioning

The In Focus box on alternatives to punishment earlier in the chapter described how operant conditioning principles can be applied to reduce and eliminate problem behaviors. These examples illustrate **behavior modification,** the application of learning principles to help people develop more effective or adaptive behaviors. Most often, behavior modification involves applying the principles of operant conditioning bring about changes in behavior.

avior modification techniques have been successfully applied in many dif-
tings (see Kazdin, 2008). Coaches, parents, teachers, and employers all
se operant conditioning. For example, behavior modification has been
ce public smoking by teenagers (Jason & others, 2009), improve student
school cafeterias (McCurdy & others, 2009), reduce problem behaviors
ildren (Dunlap & others, 2010; Schanding & Sterling-Turner, 2010), and
cial skills and reduce self-destructive behaviors in people with autism and
orders (Makrygianni & Reed, 2010).

sses also use behavior modification. For example, one large retailer increased
ity by allowing employees to choose their own reinforcers. A casual dress
flexible work hours proved to be more effective reinforcers than money
others, 2006). In each of these examples, the systematic use of reinforcement,
, and extinction increased the occurrence of desirable behaviors and decreased
cidence of undesirable behaviors. In Chapter 14 on therapies, we'll look at
ior modification techniques in more detail.

he principles of operant conditioning have also been used in the specialized
ing of animals, such as the Labrador shown at right, to help people who are
ically challenged. Other examples are Seeing Eye dogs and capuchin monkeys
assist people who are severely disabled.

Training Helping Animals with Operant Conditioning Dogs for the Disabled, a British nonprofit organization, is one of many groups that use operant conditioning to train helper animals. During "sneeze training," shown here, a trainer uses hand signals and a clicker to teach a young Labrador to bring tissues when needed. Dogs are taught to open and close doors, help people dress and undress, and even empty a washing machine. Intensive training lasts for about 8 months before young dogs are ready to be placed with an owner.

ontemporary Views of
perant Conditioning

ontrast to Skinner, today's psychologists acknowledge the importance of both cogni-
s and evolutionary factors in operant conditioning.

QUESTIONS

did Tolman's research demonstrate the involvement of cognitive processes
on rning?

ple, e cognitive maps, latent learning, and learned helplessness?

or an animal's natural behavior patterns affect the conditioning of operant
this ?

ssion of classical conditioning, we noted that contemporary psycholo-
ledge the important roles played by cognitive factors and biological
in classical conditioning. The situation is much the same with oper-
ng. The basic principles of operant conditioning have been confirmed
f studies. However, our understanding of operant conditioning has
d by the consideration of cognitive factors and the recognition of the
natural behavior patterns.

e Aspects of Operant Conditioning

UGHT *YOU* HAD THE MAP!

I view, operant conditioning did not need to invoke cognitive factors to
ex cquisition of operant behaviors. Words such as *expect, prefer, choose,* and

behavior modification The application of learning principles to help people develop more effective or adaptive behaviors.

Edward Chace Tolman (1898–1956)
Although he looks rather solemn in this photo, Tolman was known for his openness to new ideas, energetic teaching style, and playful sense of humor. During an important speech, he showed a film of a rat in a maze with a short clip from a Mickey Mouse cartoon spliced in at the end (Gleitman, 1991). Tolman's research demonstrated that cognitive processes are an important part of learning, even in the rat.

Archives of the History of American Psychology, The University of Akron

Sam Gross The New Yorker Collection/ The Cartoon Bank

"Well, you don't look like an experimental psychologist to me."

cognitive map Tolman's term for the mental representation of the layout of a familiar environment.

decide could not be used to explain how behaviors were acquired, maintained, or extinguished. Similarly, Thorndike and other early behaviorists believed that complex, active behaviors were no more than a chain of stimulus–response connections that had been "stamped in" by their effects.

However, not all learning researchers agreed with Skinner and Thorndike. **Edward C. Tolman** firmly believed that cognitive processes played an important role in the learning of complex behaviors—even in the lowly laboratory rat. According to Tolman, although such cognitive processes could not be observed directly, th[ey] could still be experimentally verified and inferred by careful observation of o[?] behavior (Tolman, 1932).

Much of Tolman's research involved rats in mazes. When Tolman [began] research in the 1920s, many studies of rats in mazes had been done. [In an] experiment, a rat would be placed in the "start" box. A food reward wou[ld await in] the "goal" box at the end of the maze. The rat would initially make man[y errors] in running the maze. After several trials, it would eventually learn to ru[n it] quickly and with very few errors.

But what had the rats learned? According to traditional behaviorists, th[ey] learned a *sequence of responses,* such as "first corner—turn left; second cor[ner—turn] left; third corner—turn right," and so on. Each response was associated [with the] "stimulus" of the rat's position in the maze. And the entire sequence of respo[nses was] "stamped in" by the food reward at the end of the maze.

Tolman (1948) disagreed with that view. He noted that several investigato[rs had] reported as incidental findings that their maze-running rats had occasionally [found] their own shortcuts to the food box. In one case, an enterprising rat had knocke[d the] cover off the maze, climbed over the maze wall and out of the maze, and scamp[ered] directly to the food box (Lashley, 1929; Tolman & others, 1946). To Tolman, [these] reports indicated that the rats had learned more than simply the sequence of respo[nses] required to get to the food. Tolman believed instead that the rats eventually b[uilt] up, through experience, a **cognitive map** of the maze—a mental representation [of] its layout.

As an analogy, think of the route you typically take to get to your psycholog[y] classroom. If a hallway along the way were blocked off for repairs, yo[u] would use your cognitive map of the building to come up with a[n] alternative route to class. Tolman showed experimentally th[at] rats, like people, seem to form cognitive maps (Tolma[n,] 1948). And, like us, rats can use their cognitive ma[ps] to come up with an alternative route to a goal wh[en] the customary route is blocked (Tolman & Honz[ik,] 1930a).

Tolman challenged the prevailing behaviorist model [on] another important point. According to Thorndike, for exam[ple,] learning would not occur unless the behavior was "strengthened," [or] "stamped in," by a rewarding consequence. But Tolman showed that [this] was not necessarily the case. In a classic experiment, three groups of rats were p[ut in] the same maze once a day for several days (Tolman & Honzik, 1930b). For grou[p 1,] a food reward awaited the rats at the end of the maze. Their performance in the [maze] steadily improved; the number of errors and the time it took the rats to reach the [goal] box showed a steady decline with each trial. The rats in group 2 were placed i[n the] maze each day with *no* food reward. They consistently made many errors, and [their] performance showed only slight improvement. The performance of the rats in g[roups] 1 and 2 was exactly what the traditional behaviorist model would have predic[ted.]

Now consider the behavior of the rats in group 3. These rats were placed [in the] maze with no food reward for the first 10 days of the experiment. Like the [rats in] group 2, they made many errors as they wandered about the maze. But, beg[inning] on day 11, they received a food reward at the end of the maze. As you ca[n see in] Figure 5.6, there was a dramatic improvement in group 3's performance fr[om]

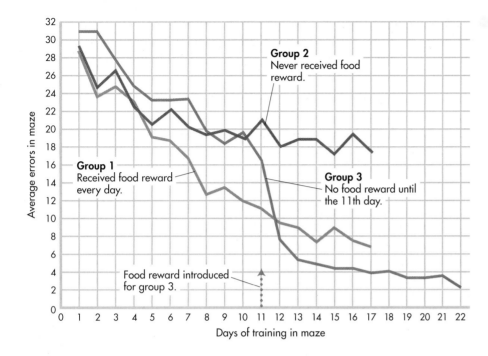

FIGURE 5.6 Latent Learning
Beginning with day 1, the rats in group 1 received a food reward at the end of the maze, and the number of errors they made steadily decreased each day. The rats in group 2 never received a food reward; they made many errors as they wandered about in the maze. The rats in group 3 did not receive a food reward on days 1 through 10. Beginning on day 11, they received a food reward at the end of the maze. Notice the sharp decrease in errors on day 12 and thereafter. According to Tolman, the rats in group 3 had formed a cognitive map of the maze during the first 11 days of the experiment. Learning had taken place, but this learning was not demonstrated until reinforcement was present—a phenomenon that Tolman called *latent learning*.

Data from Tolman & Honzik (1930b).

11 to day 12. Once the rats had discovered that food awaited them at the end of the maze, they made a beeline for the goal. On day 12, the rats in group 3 ran the maze with very few errors, improving their performance to the level of the rats in group 1 that had been rewarded on every trial!

Tolman concluded that *reward*—or reinforcement—is *not necessary* for learning to take place (Tolman & Honzik, 1930b). The rats in group 3 had learned the layout of the maze and formed a cognitive map of the maze simply by exploring it for 10 days. However, they had not been motivated to *demonstrate* that learning until a reward was introduced. Rewards, then, seem to affect the *performance* of what has been learned rather than learning itself. To describe learning that is not immediately demonstrated in overt behavior, Tolman used the term **latent learning** (Soderstrom & Bjork, 2015).

From these and other experiments, Tolman concluded that learning involves the acquisition of knowledge rather than simply changes in outward behavior. According to Tolman (1932), an organism essentially learns "what leads to what." It learns to "expect" that a certain behavior will lead to a particular outcome in a specific situation.

Tolman is now recognized as an important forerunner of modern cognitive learning theorists (Gleitman, 1991; Olton, 1992). Many contemporary cognitive learning theorists follow Tolman in their belief that operant conditioning involves the *cognitive representation* of the relationship between a behavior and its consequence. Today, operant conditioning is seen as involving the cognitive *expectancy* that a given consequence will follow a given behavior (Bouton, 2007; Dickinson & Balleine, 2000).

Learned Helplessness
EXPECTATIONS OF FAILURE AND LEARNING TO QUIT

Cognitive factors, particularly the role of expectation, are involved in another learning phenomenon, called *learned helplessness*. Learned helplessness was discovered by accident. Psychologists were trying to find out if classically conditioned responses would affect the process of operant conditioning in dogs. The dogs were strapped into harnesses and then exposed to a tone (the neutral stimulus) paired with an unpleasant but harmless electric shock (the UCS), which elicited fear (the UCR). After conditioning, the tone alone—now a CS—elicited the conditioned response of fear.

latent learning Tolman's term for learning that occurs in the absence of reinforcement but is not behaviorally demonstrated until a reinforcer becomes available.

learned helplessness A phenomenon in which exposure to inescapable and uncontrollable aversive events produces passive behavior.

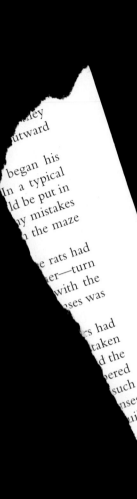

Martin E. P. Seligman: From Learned Helplessness to Positive Psychology
Seligman (b. 1942) began his research career by studying learned helplessness in dogs, and later, in humans. He applied his findings to psychological problems, including depression. Seligman developed techniques to teach people to overcome feelings of helplessness, habitual pessimism, and depression (Seligman & others, 2011; Seligman, 2005). Elected president of the American Psychological Association in 1996, Seligman helped launch *positive psychology*, which emphasized research on human strengths (see Chapter 1). As Seligman (2004) explained, "It became my mission in life to help create a positive psychology whose mission would be the understanding and building of positive emotion, of strength and virtue, and of positive institutions."

Courtesy of The Positive Psychology Center

In the classical conditioning setup, the dogs were unable to escape or avoid the shock. But the next part of the experiment involved an operant conditioning procedure in which the dogs *could* escape the shock. The dogs were transferred to a special kind of operant chamber called a *shuttlebox,* which has a low barrier in the middle that divides the chamber in half. In the operant conditioning setup, the floor on one side of the cage became electrified. To escape the shock, all the dogs had to do was learn a simple escape behavior: Jump over the barrier when the floor was electrified. Normally, dogs learn this simple operant very quickly.

However, when the classically conditioned dogs were placed in the shuttlebox and one side became electrified, the dogs did *not* try to jump over the barrier. Rather than perform the operant to escape the shock, they just lay down and whined. Why?

To Steven F. Maier and **Martin Seligman,** two young psychology graduate students at the time, the explanation of the dogs' passive behavior seemed obvious. During the tone–shock pairings in the classical conditioning setup, the dogs *had learned that shocks were inescapable.* No active behavior that they engaged in—whether whining, barking, or struggling in the harness—would allow them to avoid or escape the shock. In other words, the dogs had "learned" to be helpless: They had developed the *cognitive expectation* that their behavior would have no effect on the environment.

To test this idea, Seligman and Maier (1967) designed a simple experiment. Dogs were arranged in groups of three. The first dog received shocks that it could escape by pushing a panel with its nose. The second dog was "yoked" to the first and received the same number of shocks. However, nothing the second dog did could stop the shock—they stopped only if the first dog pushed the panel. The third dog was the control and got no shocks at all.

After this initial training, the dogs were transferred to the shuttlebox. As Seligman and Maier had predicted, the first and third dogs quickly learned to jump over the barrier when the floor became electrified. But the second dog, the one that had learned that nothing it did would stop the shock, made no effort to jump over the barrier. Because the dog had developed the cognitive expectation that its behavior would have no effect on the environment, it had become passive (Seligman & Maier, 1967). The name of this phenomenon is **learned helplessness**—a phenomenon in which exposure to inescapable and uncontrollable aversive events produces passive behavior (Maier & others, 1969).

Since these early experiments, learned helplessness has been demonstrated in many different species, including primates, cats, rats, and fish (LoLordo, 2001). Even cockroaches demonstrate learned helplessness in a cockroach-sized shuttlebox after being exposed to inescapable shock (G.E. Brown & others, 1999).

In humans, numerous studies have found that exposure to uncontrollable, aversive events can produce passivity and learned helplessness. For example, college students who have experienced failure in previous academic settings may feel that academic tasks and setbacks are beyond their control. Thus, when faced with the demands of exams, papers, and studying, rather than rising to the challenge, they may experience feelings of learned helplessness (Au & others, 2010). If a student believes that academic tasks are unpleasant, unavoidable, and beyond her control, even the slightest setback can trigger a sense of helpless passivity. Such students may be prone to engage in self-defeating responses, such as procrastinating or giving up prematurely.

How can learned helplessness be overcome? In their early experiments, Seligman and Maier discovered that if they forcibly dragged the dogs over the shuttlebox barrier when the floor on one side became electrified, the dogs would eventually overcome their passivity and begin to jump over the barrier on their own (LoLordo, 2001; Seligman, 1992). For students who experience academic learned helplessness, establishing a sense of control over their schoolwork is the first step. Seeking knowledge about course requirements and assignments and setting goals, however modest, that can be successfully met can help students begin to acquire a sense of mastery over environmental challenges (Glynn & others, 2005).

Since the early demonstrations of learned helplessness in dogs, the notion of learned helplessness has undergone several revisions and refinements (Abramson & others, 1978; Gillham & others, 2001). Learned helplessness has been shown to play a role in

Learned Helplessness on the Field In humans, learned helplessness can be produced when negative events are perceived as uncontrollable. Even highly trained athletes can succumb to feelings of learned helplessness in the face of persistent defeats. Athletes who believe that they have no control over the factors that led to their loss or poor performance are less likely to believe that they can succeed in the future (Coffee & others, 2009). They're also less likely to persist in the face of failure (Le Foll & others, 2008).

psychological disorders, particularly depression, and in the ways that people respond to stressful events. Learned helplessness has also been applied in such diverse fields as management, sales, and health psychology (Wise & Rosqvist, 2006). In Chapter 12 on stress, health, and coping, we will take up the topic of learned helplessness again.

Operant Conditioning and Biological Predispositions

MISBEHAVING CHICKENS

Skinner and other behaviorists firmly believed that the general laws of operant conditioning applied to all animal species—whether they were pecking pigeons or bar-pressing rats. As Skinner (1956) wrote:

> Pigeon, rat, monkey, which is which? It doesn't matter. Of course, these species have behavioral repertoires which are as different as their anatomies. But once you have allowed for differences in the ways in which they make contact with the environment, and in the ways in which they act upon the environment, what remains of their behavior shows astonishingly similar properties.

However, psychologists studying operant conditioning, like those studying classical conditioning, found that an animal's natural behavior patterns *could* influence the learning of new behaviors. Consider the experiences of Keller and Marian Breland, two of Skinner's students at the University of Minnesota. The Brelands established a successful business training animals for television commercials, trade shows, fairs, and even displays in department stores (Breland & Breland, 1961). Using operant conditioning, the Brelands trained thousands of animals of many different species to perform all sorts of complex tricks (Bihm & others, 2010a, b).

But the Brelands weren't always successful in training the animals. For example, they tried to train a chicken to play baseball. The chicken learned to pull a loop that activated a swinging bat. After hitting the ball, the chicken was supposed to run to first base. The chicken had little trouble learning to pull the loop, but instead of running to first base, the chicken would chase the ball.

Keller and Marian Breland's "IQ Zoo" B.F. Skinner's students Keller and Marian Breland opened their animal training business in Hot Springs, Arkansas, in 1951. By the 1960s, the Brelands' "IQ Zoo" was one of the most popular roadside attractions in the United States. Among its stars were basketball-playing raccoons, reindeer who operated a printing press, ducks who played the piano, and chickens who danced, walked a tightrope, and played tic-tac-toe. Beyond entertainment, the Brelands were pioneers in the development of animal training and behavior modification techniques. Marian Breland was one of the first psychologists to use positive reinforcement to teach basic self-help skills to people with developmental disabilities and also helped train marine mammals for the U.S. Navy (Bihm & others, 2010a, b).

TABLE 5.5

Comparing Classical and Operant Conditioning

	Classical Conditioning	Operant Conditioning
Type of behavior	Reflexive, involuntary behaviors	Nonreflexive, voluntary behaviors
Source of behavior	Elicited by stimulus	Emitted by organism
Basis of learning	Associating two stimuli: CS + UCS	Associating a response and the consequence that follows it
Responses conditioned	Physiological and emotional responses	Active behaviors that operate on the environment
Extinction process	Conditioned response decreases when conditioned stimulus is repeatedly presented alone	Responding decreases with elimination of reinforcing consequences
Cognitive aspects	Expectation that CS reliably predicts the UCS	Performance of behavior influenced by the expectation of reinforcement or punishment
Evolutionary influences	Innate predispositions influence how easily an association is formed between a particular stimulus and response	Behaviors similar to natural or instinctive behaviors are more readily conditioned

The Brelands also tried to train a raccoon to pick up two coins and deposit them into a metal box. The raccoon easily learned to pick up the coins but seemed to resist putting them into the box. Like a furry little miser, it would rub the coins together. And rather than dropping the coins in the box, it would dip the coins in the box and take them out again. As time went on, this behavior became more persistent, even though the raccoon was not being reinforced for it. In fact, the raccoon's "misbehavior" was actually *preventing* it from getting reinforced for correct behavior (Bailey & Bailey, 1993).

The Brelands noted that such nonreinforced behaviors seemed to reflect innate, instinctive responses. The chicken chasing the ball was behaving like a chicken chasing a bug. Raccoons in the wild instinctively clean and moisten their food by dipping it in streams or rubbing it between their forepaws. These natural behaviors interfered with the operant behaviors the Brelands were attempting to condition—a phenomenon called **instinctive drift** (Bailey & Bailey, 1993).

The biological predisposition to perform such natural behaviors was strong enough to overcome the lack of reinforcement. These instinctual behaviors also *prevented the animals from engaging in the learned behaviors that would result in reinforcement*. Clearly, reinforcement is not the sole determinant of behavior. And, inborn or instinctive behavior patterns can interfere with the operant conditioning of arbitrary responses.

Before you go on to the next section, take a few minutes to review Table 5.5 and make sure you understand the differences between classical and operant conditioning.

❭ Test your understanding of **Operant Conditioning** with *LEARNING*Curve.

Observational Learning
IMITATING THE ACTIONS OF OTHERS

> KEY THEME

In observational learning, we learn through watching and imitating the behaviors of others.

> KEY QUESTIONS

❭ How did Albert Bandura demonstrate the principles of observational learning?

❭ What four mental processes are involved in observational learning?

❭ How has observational learning been shown in nonhuman animals?

instinctive drift The tendency of an animal to revert to instinctive behaviors that can interfere with the performance of an operantly conditioned response.

observational learning Learning that occurs through observing the actions of others.

Classical conditioning and operant conditioning emphasize the role of direct experiences in learning, such as directly experiencing a reinforcing or punishing stimulus following a particular behavior. But much human learning occurs *indirectly*, by watching what others do, then imitating it. In **observational learning,** learning takes place through observing the actions of others.

Humans develop the capacity to learn through observation at a very early age. Studies of infants, some as young as 2 to 3 days, have shown that they will imitate a variety of actions, including opening their mouths, sticking out their tongues, and making other facial expressions (Leighton & Heyes, 2010). In fact, even newborn infants can imitate adult expressions when they are less than an hour old (Meltzoff, 2007; Meltzoff & Moore, 1989). Toddlers and preschoolers can use observational learning to figure out how to solve complex problems like extracting a toy from a puzzle box (Flynn & Whiten, 2010). The Focus on Neuroscience on page 217 describes new research that may shed some light on the brain mechanisms that support our ability to learn through observation.

Albert Bandura is the psychologist most strongly identified with observational learning. Bandura (1974) believes that observational learning is the result of cognitive processes that are "actively judgmental and constructive," not merely "mechanical copying." To illustrate his theory, let's consider his famous experiment involving the imitation of aggressive behaviors (Bandura, 1965). In the experiment, four-year-old children separately watched a short film showing an adult playing aggressively with a Bobo doll—a large, inflated balloon doll that stands upright because the bottom is weighted with sand. All the children saw the adult hit, kick, and punch the Bobo doll in the film.

Time & Life Pictures/Getty Images

Albert Bandura (b. 1925) Bandura contends that most human behavior is acquired through observational learning rather than through trial and error or direct experience of the consequences of our actions. Watching and processing information about the actions of others, including the consequences that occur, influence the likelihood that the behavior will be imitated.

However, there were three different versions of the film, each with a different ending. Some children saw the adult *reinforced* with soft drinks, candy, and snacks after performing the aggressive actions. Other children saw a version in which the aggressive adult was *punished* for the actions with a scolding and a spanking by another adult. Finally, some children watched a version of the film in which the aggressive adult experienced *no consequences*.

After seeing the film, each child was allowed to play alone in a room with several toys, including a Bobo doll. The playroom was equipped with a one-way window so that the child's behavior could be observed. Bandura found that the consequences the children observed in the film made a difference. Children who watched the film in which the adult was punished were much less likely to imitate the aggressive behaviors than were children who watched either of the other two film endings.

Then Bandura added an interesting twist to the experiment. Each child was asked to show the experimenter what the adult did in the film. For every behavior they could imitate, the child was rewarded with snacks and stickers. Virtually all the children imitated the adult's behaviors they had observed in the film, including the aggressive behaviors. The particular version of the film the children had seen made no difference.

Bandura (1965) explained these results much as Tolman explained latent learning. Reinforcement is *not* essential for learning to occur. Rather, the *expectation of reinforcement* affects the *performance* of what has been learned.

Bandura (1986) suggests that four cognitive processes interact to determine whether imitation will occur. First, you must pay *attention* to the other person's behavior. Second, you must *remember* the other person's behavior so that you can perform it at a later time. That is, you must form and store a mental representation of the behavior to be imitated. Third, you must be able to transform this mental representation into *actions that you are capable of reproducing*. These three factors—attention, memory, and motor skills—are necessary for learning to take place through observation.

Fourth, there must be some *motivation* for you to imitate the behavior. This factor is crucial to the actual performance of the learned behavior. You are more likely to imitate a behavior if there is some expectation that doing so will produce reinforcement or reward. Thus, all the children were capable of imitating the adult's

Courtesy of Albert Bandura

LaunchPad

To view video clips of Bandura's classic study, try **Concept Practice: Bandura's Bobo Doll Experiment.**

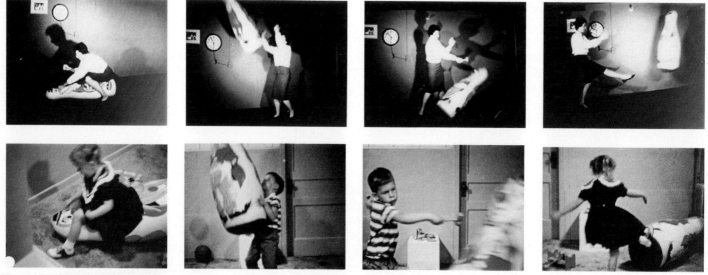

Courtesy Albert Bandura, Stanford University

The Classic Bobo Doll Experiment
Bandura demonstrated the powerful influence of observational learning in a series of experiments conducted in the early 1960s. Children watched a film showing an adult playing aggressively with an inflated Bobo doll. If they saw the adult rewarded with candy for the aggressive behavior or experience no consequences, the children were much more likely to imitate the behavior than if they saw the adult punished for the aggressive behavior (Bandura, 1965; Bandura & others, 1963).

aggressive behavior. But the children who saw the aggressive adult being rewarded were much more likely to imitate the aggressive behavior than were the children who saw the adult punished. Table 5.6 summarizes other factors that increase the likelihood of imitation.

TABLE 5.6

Factors That Increase Imitation

You're more likely to imitate:
- People who are rewarded for their behavior
- Warm, nurturing people
- People who have control over you or have the power to influence your life
- People who are similar to you in terms of age, sex, and interests
- People you perceive as having higher social status
- When the task to be imitated is not extremely easy or difficult
- If you lack confidence in your own abilities in a particular situation
- If the situation is unfamiliar or ambiguous
- If you've been rewarded for imitating the same behavior in the past

Source: Research from Bandura (1977, 1986, 1997).

Many nonhuman animals have been shown to learn new behaviors through observation and imitation (Reader & Biro, 2010). The ability to learn a novel behavior through observation has been demonstrated in many different species of animals from hamsters to ring-tailed lemurs (Lupfer & others, 2003; Kendal & others, 2010). Even guppies can learn foraging behavior and escape routes from other guppies (Reader & others, 2003).

Chimpanzees, apes, and other primates are quite adept at learning through observation. Just as with humans, motivational factors influence observational learning. One study involved imitative behavior of free-ranging orangutans in a preserve located in central Indonesia (Russon & Galdikas, 1995). The orangutans imitated the behavior of both humans and other orangutans, but they were more likely to imitate high-status or dominant models than low-status models. The orangutans were also more likely to imitate models with whom they had close relationships, such as biological parents, siblings, or their human caregivers. Human strangers were virtually never imitated.

FOCUS ON NEUROSCIENCE

Mirror Neurons: Imitation in the Brain

Psychologists have only recently begun to understand the neural underpinnings of the human ability to imitate behavior (Glenberg, 2011). The first clue emerged from an accidental discovery in a lab in Palermo, Italy, in the mid-1990s. Neuroscientist Giacomo Rizzolatti and his colleagues were studying neurons in the premotor cortex of macaque monkeys. Using tiny electrodes to record the activity of individual neurons, Rizzolatti's team had painstakingly identified the specific motor neurons involved in simple behaviors, such as picking up a peanut or grabbing a toy (see Rizzolatti & Sinigaglia, 2008).

As one of the wired-up monkeys watched a lab assistant pick up a peanut, a neuron fired in the monkey's brain—the *same* neuron that fired when the monkey itself picked up a peanut. At first, the researchers thought that the monkey must be making tiny muscle movements, and that these movements were responsible for the motor neuron activity. But the monkey was sitting perfectly still. The researchers were baffled because a motor neuron was thought to fire only if a motor behavior was occurring.

The explanation? Rizzolatti's team had discovered a new class of specialized neurons, which they dubbed **mirror neurons**. Mirror neurons are neurons that fire both when an action is performed and when the action is simply perceived (Iacoboni, 2009). It's important to note that mirror neurons are *not* a new physical type of neurons. As described in Chapter 2, a mirror neuron is defined by its *function*, not its physical structure. In effect, these neurons imitate or "mirror" the observed action as though the observer were actually carrying out the action.

A decade of research has shown that mirror neurons do not simply reflect visual processing, but are also involved in mentally representing and interpreting the actions of others (Glenberg, 2011; Michael & others, 2014). For example, Evelyne Kohler and her colleagues (2002) showed that the same neurons that activated when a monkey cracked open a peanut shell also activated when a monkey simply *heard* a peanut shell breaking.

Following their discovery in the motor cortex, mirror neurons have since been identified in many other brain regions (see Hunter & others, 2013; Iacoboni, 2009). Today, many psychologists use the term *mirror neuron system* to describe mirroring in the brain. That's because even simple behaviors and sensations often involve groups of mirror neurons firing together rather than single neurons firing separately (Cattaneo & Rizzolatti, 2009).

Evidence of Human Mirror Neurons

Brain imaging studies like the one illustrated at right have provided *indirect* evidence of mirror neurons in the human brain (see Oberman & Ramachandran, 2007; Slack, 2007). New studies have provided direct evidence for the existence of mirror neurons in humans (see Molenberghs & others, 2012; Mukamel & others, 2010).

Beyond imitation and observational learning, the mirror neuron system may play a role in empathy, language, and social cognition (Gallese & others, 2011; Lago-Rodriguez & others, 2013). And, some neuroscientists believe that dysfunctions in the mirror neuron system may contribute to autism and other disorders that are associated with impaired social functioning (Perkins & others, 2010). Although these speculations are intriguing, more scientific evidence is needed before such conclusions can be drawn (Decety, 2010; Fan & others, 2010).

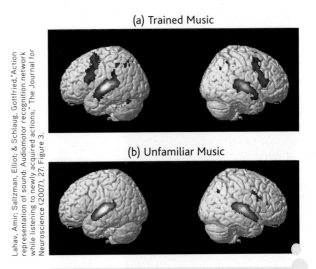

(a) Trained Music

(b) Unfamiliar Music

Lahav, Amir; Saltzman, Elliot; & Schlaug, Gottfried,"Action representation of sound: Audiomotor recognition network while listening to newly acquired actions," The Journal for Neuroscience (2007), 27; Figure 3.

Musical Mirror Neurons Nonmusicians were trained to play a piece of music by ear on a piano keyboard, then underwent a series of fMRI scans (Lahav & others, 2007). Panel (a) shows the participants' brain activity as they listened to the same music they had already learned to play. Even though they were not moving as they lay in the scanner, motor areas of the brain were activated (dark red). The brighter red/yellow color indicates activation in the brain's auditory areas. Panel (b) shows participants' brain activity while they listened to unfamiliar music utilizing the same musical notes but in a different sequence.

As you compare the scans in (a) and (b), notice the extensive activation in motor-related brain regions when the participants listened to the music that they had already learned to play, as in (a). However, these motor areas were *not* activated when they listened to the unfamiliar music that they had never played, as in (b).

Applications of Observational Learning

Bandura's finding that children will imitate film footage of aggressive behavior has more than just theoretical importance. One obvious implication has to do with the effects of negative behaviors that are depicted in films and television shows. Is there any evidence that television and other media can increase negative or destructive behaviors in viewers?

mirror neurons Neurons that activate both when an action is performed and when the same action is perceived.

Animal Culture and Observational Learning Chimpanzee tribes in the wild develop their own unique "cultures" or behavioral differences in tool use, foraging skills, and even courtship rituals (Hopper & others, 2007). Other species, too, acquire and transmit distinct behavior patterns through observational learning (Allen & others, 2013; van de Waal & others, 2013). For example, consider a clever field experiment by psychologist Erica van de Waal and her colleagues (2013). Wild adult vervet monkeys developed a preference for pink corn over blue corn after the researchers treated the blue corn with a bitter-tasting substance. The colors were switched for nearby vervet monkey groups, who quickly became partial to the *blue* corn. After several months, the researchers stopped treating the corn, but the monkeys still ate only the preferred color of corn. And, so did infant monkeys who had never been exposed to bitter-tasting corn of either color. Imitating their mothers, they ate the same color corn that she did, and ignored the other corn.

Erica van de Waal

John Birdsall/The Image Works

Television and Teen Pregnancy: Influencing Behavior Researchers Melissa Kearney and Phillip Levine (2014) found that Internet searches and social media posts about contraception spiked after the airing of episodes of the MTV docu-series *16 and Pregnant*. They also documented a 5.7% decline in teen birth rates in the areas where viewership of the gritty docu-series was highest. The research is correlational, so it can't be used to establish a direct cause-and-effect relationship between viewing the program and the decline in teen pregnancy. However, as researcher Melissa Kearney (2014) comments, "we think the biggest takeaway from this study is that what teenagers are watching can make a really big difference in what they think and, ultimately, how they behave and really important life decisions."

One recent study conducted by psychologist Rebecca Collins and her colleagues (2004) examined the impact of television portrayals of sexual activity on the behavior of U.S. adolescents between the ages of 12 and 17. Over the two-year period of the study, researchers found that adolescents who watched large amounts of television containing sexual content, such as *Friends* and *That '70s Show,* were twice as likely to begin engaging in sexual intercourse in the following year as adolescents who were the same age but watched the least amount of sexually oriented programming.

What about exposure to more explicit sexual content, such as pornographic or sexually explicit Web sites on the Internet? One study found that adolescents who visited such sites were more likely to have multiple sexual partners and to have used alcohol or drugs during their most recent sexual experience (Braun-Courville & Rojas, 2009).

Another important implication of Bandura's research relates to the effects of media depictions of violence on behavior. In the Critical Thinking box, we take an in-depth look at the relationship between media portrayals of violence and aggressive behavior.

Given the potential impact of negative media images, let's look at the flip side. Is there any evidence that television and other media can encourage socially desirable behavior?

Consider the widely viewed MTV reality series, *16 and Pregnant,* which features the struggles of pregnant teens and young mothers. Some commentators feared that the show was glamorizing teenage pregnancy. However, researchers Melissa S. Kearney and Phillip B. Levine (2014) found that teen birth rates in areas where the show was aired dropped 5.7 percent in the 18 months after its introduction. They also surveyed Google searches and social media. They found thousands of tweets and large spikes in Google searches for information about birth control shortly after each episode aired. It's important to note that the study is *correlational,* so it's impossible to say that viewing the TV show directly caused a drop in teen pregnancy. However, the findings highlight ways in which media can influence social outcomes in positive ways.

A remarkably effective application of observational learning has been the use of television and radio dramas to promote social change and healthy behaviors in Asia, Latin America, and Africa (Population Communications International, 2004). Pioneered by Mexican television executive Miguel Sabido, the first such attempt was a long-running serial drama that used observational learning principles to promote literacy among adults. The main storyline centered on the experiences of a group of people in a literacy self-instruction group. Millions of viewers faithfully watched the series. In the year before the televised series, about 90,000 people were enrolled in such literacy groups. In the year during the series, enrollment jumped to 840,000 people (Bandura, 1997).

Does Exposure to Media Violence *Cause* Aggressive Behavior?

Bandura's early observational learning studies showed preschoolers enthusiastically mimicking the movie actions of an adult pummeling a Bobo doll. His research provided a powerful paradigm to study the effects of "entertainment" violence. Bandura found that observed actions were most likely to be imitated when:

- They were performed by a high-status, attractive model.
- The model is rewarded for his or her behavior.
- The model is not punished for his or her actions.

Over the past five decades, more than 1,000 studies have investigated the relationship between media depictions of violence and increases in aggressive behavior in the real world (see Bushman & Anderson, 2007; Bushman & others, 2014). We'll highlight some key findings here.

How Prevalent Is Violence in the Media?

An alarming amount of violence is depicted on American television and in movies. On average, American youth witness 1,000 rapes, murders, and assaults on television annually (Parents Television Council, 2007). More troubling, much of the violent behavior is depicted in ways that are known to *increase* the likelihood of imitation. For example, violent behavior is not punished and is often perpetrated by the "good guys." The long-term consequences of violence are rarely shown.

Is Exposure to Media Violence Linked to Aggressive Behavior?

Numerous research studies show that exposure to media violence produces short-term increases in laboratory measures of aggressive thoughts and behavior. And, hundreds of correlational studies demonstrate a link between exposure to violent media and aggressive behavior (see Anderson & others, 2010; Bushman & others, 2014; Murray, 2008).

Reviewing the accumulation of decades of research evidence, the American Academy of Pediatrics, the American Psychological Association, and the American Medical Association have all issued versions of the following conclusion: "Extensive research evidence indicates that media violence can contribute to aggressive behavior, desensitization to violence, nightmares, and fear of being harmed" (AAP Council on Communications Media, 2009).

MYTH ◀ SCIENCE

Is it true that viewing violent media is not related to aggression?

What About Violent Video Games?

Many people wonder about the effects of violent digital games, especially "first-person shooter" games. Two comprehensive meta-analyses concluded that violent digital games increased aggressive

thoughts, feelings, and behavior (Anderson & others, 2010; Grietemeyer & Mügge, 2014).

But other researchers strongly disagree with these conclusions (Ferguson & Kilbourn, 2010; Ivory & others, 2015). For example, some researchers have *not* found an increase in aggression when violent and non-violent games are carefully matched in terms of competitiveness and other factors (see Przybylski & others, 2014; Engelhardt & others, 2015). And, during the era in which video games increased in popularity and graphic violence, violent crime steadily *declined*, rather than increased, as you would expect if digital games were as dangerous as some claim (Ferguson, 2014).

So Does Violent Media *Cause* Violent Behavior?

Based on their review of the evidence, some psychologists, like Brad Bushman and his colleagues (2009) flatly concluded that "Exposure to violent media increases aggression and violence." But many other psychologists are more cautious in their conclusions (Elson & Ferguson, 2014a, 2014b; Ivory & others, 2015).

It's important to note that the vast majority of studies on media violence and aggressive behavior are *correlational* (Ferguson & Kilbourn, 2009; Savage & Yancey, 2008). As you learned in Chapter 1, correlation does not necessarily imply causation. Even if two factors are strongly correlated, some other variable could be responsible for the association between the two factors. Experimental studies, on the other hand, *are* designed to demonstrate causality. However, most experimental studies involve artificial measures of aggressive behavior, which may *not* accurately measure the likelihood that a participant will act aggressively in real life.

Psychologists on both sides of the debate agree on one important point: Violent behavior is a complex phenomenon that is unlikely to have a single cause. They also generally agree that some viewers *are* highly susceptible to the negative effects of media violence (see Huesmann & others, 2013). Some researchers think that the time has come to go beyond the question of *whether* media violence causes aggressive behavior and focus instead on investigating the factors that are most likely to be associated with its harmful effects (Feshbach & Tangney, 2008 ; Ferguson & Konijn, 2015).

CRITICAL THINKING QUESTIONS

- Given the evidence, what conclusions can you draw about the effect of violent media and digital games on aggressive behavior?

- Why is it so difficult to design an experimental study that would demonstrate that violent media *causes* aggressive behavior?

- Given the general conclusion that some, but not all, viewers are likely to become more aggressive after viewing violent media, what should be done about media violence?

Makutano Junction Regularly watched by over 7 million viewers in Kenya alone, *Makutano Junction* is an award-winning weekly television drama that teaches as it entertains. Set in a small Kenyan town, the soap opera uses compelling dramatic stories, humor, and appealing characters to educate viewers about such serious topics as mental and physical health, family life and relationships, government corruption, and even modern farming practices. One unique aspect of *Mankutano Junction* is that viewers can use their cell phones to send text messages to request additional information about topics covered on the show, such as how to prevent malaria or how to live with HIV or AIDS (P. Smith, 2010). Some 30,000 text messages are received every year. You can watch episodes online at YouTube or at the Kenya TV Web site: http://kenyawebtv.com/index.php/shows/makutano-junction

Mediae Company Ltd.

The serials dramatize the everyday problems people struggle with and model functional strategies and solutions to them. This approach succeeds because it informs, enables, motivates, and guides people for personal and social changes that improve their lives.

—*Albert Bandura (2004a)*

Since the success of this program, the nonprofit group Population Communications International (2004) has developed over 240 "entertainment-education programs" in 27 different countries. Each series is developed with the input of local advisers and is written, produced, and performed by creative talent in the country of the intended audience. The long-running programs feature characters with whom the average viewer can easily identify. While the storylines are dramatic, they also reflect everyday challenges. Based on Bandura's observational learning paradigm, these serial dramas motivate individuals to adopt new attitudes and behavior by modeling behaviors that promote family health, stable communities, and a sustainable environment.

Education-entertainment programs are designed to fulfill the optimal conditions for observational learning to occur (Bandura, 2002). The dramatic intensity, highly involving plot lines, and engaging characters ensure that viewers will become involved in the dramas and pay *attention*. To ensure that the modeled messages are *remembered*, an epilogue at the conclusion of each episode summarizes the key points and issues of the episode. To enhance the viewers' *ability* to carry out the modeled behaviors, a variety of support programs and groups are put in place when the series airs. And *motivating* people to change their behaviors in line with the modeled behaviors is accomplished by depicting the benefits of doing so. Research studies have confirmed the highly successful impact of these extremely popular dramas (see Gesser-Edelsburg & others, 2010; Singhal & others, 2004).

Entertainment-education programs have also aired in the United States. For example, the radio program *Entrelazado,* which is Spanish for "Entwined," was developed in Birmingham, Alabama, to encourage healthy behaviors, including prevention of obesity and tobacco use, among the local Hispanic population (Media for Health, 2011).

Beyond the effects of media depictions on behavior, observational learning has been applied in a wide variety of settings. The fields of education, vocational and job training, psychotherapy, counseling, and medicine use observational learning to help teach appropriate behaviors.

❯ Test your understanding of **Observational Learning** with **LEARNING***Curve*.

Closing Thoughts

One theme throughout this chapter has been the quest to discover general laws of learning that would apply across virtually all species and situations. Watson was convinced that these laws were contained in the principles of classical conditioning. Skinner contended that they were to be found in the principles of operant conditioning. In a sense, they were both right. Thousands of experiments have shown that behavior can be reliably and predictably influenced by classical and operant conditioning procedures. By and large, the general principles of classical and operant conditioning hold up quite well across a wide range of species and situations.

But you've also seen that the general principles of classical and operant conditioning are just that—general, not absolute. Such researchers as John Garcia and Marian and Keller Breland recognized the importance of a species' evolutionary and biological heritage in acquiring new behaviors. Other researchers, such as Edward Tolman and Robert Rescorla, drew attention to the important role played by cognitive processes in learning. And Albert Bandura's investigations of observational learning underscored that classical and operant conditioning principles could not account for all learning.

Another prominent theme has been the adaptive nature of learning. Faced with an ever-changing environment, an organism's capacity to learn is critical to adaptation and survival. Clearly, there are survival advantages in being able to learn that a neutral stimulus can signal an important upcoming event, as in classical conditioning. An organism also enhances its odds of survival by being responsive to the consequences of its actions, as in operant conditioning. And, by observing the actions and consequences experienced by others, behaviors can be acquired through imitation. Thus, it is probably because these abilities are so useful in so many environments that the basic principles of learning are demonstrated with such consistency across so many species.

In the final analysis, it's probably safe to say that the most important consequence of learning is that it promotes the adaptation of many species, including humans, to their unique environments. Were it not for the adaptive nature of learning, Erv would probably have gotten trapped in the attic again!

PSYCH FOR YOUR LIFE

Using Learning Principles to Improve Your Self-Control

Self-control often involves choosing between two reinforcers: (1) a *long-term reinforcer* that will provide gratification at some point in the future or (2) a *short-term reinforcer* that provides immediate gratification but gets in the way of obtaining a long-term reinforcer. Objectively, the benefits of the long-term reinforcer typically far outweigh the benefits associated with the short-term, immediate reinforcer. Yet despite our commitment to the long-term goal, sometimes we choose a short-term reinforcer that conflicts with it. Why?

The Shifting Value of Reinforcers

The key is that *the relative value of reinforcers can shift over time* (Ainslie, 1975, 1992; Rachlin, 1974, 2000). Let's use an example to illustrate this principle. Suppose you sign up for an 8:00 A.M. class that meets every Tuesday morning. On Monday night, the short-term reinforcer (getting extra sleep on Tuesday morning) and the long-term reinforcer (getting a good course grade at the end of the semester) are both potential future reinforcers. Neither reinforcer is immediately available. So, when you compare these two future reinforcers, the value of making a good grade easily outweighs the value of getting

extra sleep on Tuesday morning. That's why you duly set the alarm clock for 6:00 A.M. so you will get to class on time.

Consequently, when your alarm goes off on Tuesday morning, the situation is fundamentally different. The short-term reinforcer is now immediately available: staying in that warm, comfy bed. Compared with Monday night when you set the alarm, the subjective value of extra sleep has increased significantly. Although making a good grade in the course is still important to you, its subjective value has not increased on Tuesday morning. After all, that long-term reinforcer is still in the distant future.

At the moment you make your decision, you choose whichever reinforcer has the greater apparent value to you. At that moment, if the subjective value of the short-term reinforcer outweighs that of the long-term reinforcer, you're very likely to choose the short-term reinforcer (Fishbach & others, 2010). In other words, you'll probably stay in bed.

When you understand how the subjective values of reinforcers shift over time, the tendency to impulsively cave in to available short-term reinforcers starts to make more sense. The availability of an immediate, short-term reinforcer can temporarily outweigh the subjective value of a long-term reinforcer in the distant future (Steel, 2007). How can you counteract these momentary surges in the subjective value of short-term reinforcers? Fortunately, there are several strategies that can help you overcome the temptation of short-term reinforcers and improve your self-control (Fishbach & others, 2010; Kruglanski & others, 2010).

Strategy 1: Precommitment

Precommitment involves making an advance commitment to your long-term goal, one that will be difficult to change when a conflicting reinforcer becomes available (Fujita & Roberts, 2010). In the case of getting to class on time, a precommitment could involve setting multiple alarms and putting them far enough away that you will be forced to get out of bed to shut each of them off. Or you could ask an early-rising friend to call you on the phone and make sure you're awake.

Strategy 2: Self-Reinforcement

Sometimes long-term goals seem so far away that your sense of potential future reinforcement seems weak compared with immediate reinforcers. One strategy to increase the subjective value of the long-term reinforcer is to use self-reinforcement for current behaviors related to your long-term goal (Fishbach & others, 2010). For example, promise yourself that if you spend two hours studying in the library, you'll reward yourself by watching a movie.

It's important, however, to reward yourself only *after* you perform the desired behavior. If you say to yourself, "Rather than study tonight, I'll go to this party and make up for it by studying tomorrow," you've blown it. You've just reinforced yourself for *not* studying! This would be akin to trying to increase bar-pressing behavior in a rat by giving the rat a pellet of food *before* it pressed the bar. Obviously, this contradicts the basic principle of positive reinforcement in which behavior is *followed* by the reinforcing stimulus.

Strategy 3: Stimulus Control

Remember, environmental stimuli can act as discriminative stimuli that "set the occasion" for a particular response (Kruglanski & others, 2010). In effect, the environmental cues that precede a behavior can acquire some control over future occurrences of that behavior. So be aware of the environmental cues that are likely to trigger unwanted behaviors, such as studying in the kitchen (a cue for eating) or in an easy chair in the living room (a cue for watching television). Then replace those cues with others that will help you achieve your long-term goals.

For example, always study in a specific location, whether it's in the library, in an empty classroom, or at a table or desk in a

certain corner of your apartment. Over time, these environmental cues will become associated with the behavior of studying.

Strategy 4: Focus on the Delayed Reinforcer

The cognitive aspects of learning also play a role in choosing behaviors associated with long-term reinforcers (Mischel, 1996; Mischel & others, 2004). When faced with a choice between an immediate and a delayed reinforcer, focus your attention on the delayed reinforcer. You'll be less likely to impulsively choose the short-term reinforcer (Kruglanski & others, 2010).

Practically speaking, this means that if your goal is to save money for school, don't fantasize about a new car or expensive shoes. Focus instead on the delayed reinforcement of achieving your long-term goal (Kross & others, 2010). Imagine yourself proudly walking across the stage and receiving your college degree. Visualize yourself fulfilling your long-term career goals. The idea in selectively focusing on the delayed reinforcer is to mentally bridge the gap between the present and the ultimate attainment of your future goal. One of our students, a biology major, put a picture of a famous woman biologist next to her desk to help inspire her to study.

Strategy 5: Observe Good Role Models

Observational learning is another strategy you can use to improve self-control (Maddux & others, 2010). In a series of classic studies, psychologist Walter Mischel found that children who observed others choose a delayed reinforcer over an immediate reinforcer were more likely to choose the delayed reinforcer themselves (Kross & others, 2010; Mischel, 1996). So look for good role models. Observing others who are currently behaving in ways that will ultimately help them realize their long-term goals can make it easier for you to do the same.

CHAPTER REVIEW

KEY PEOPLE AND KEY TERMS

Albert Bandura, p. 215

John Garcia, p. 194

Ivan Pavlov, p. 183

Robert A. Rescorla, p. 192

Martin Seligman, p. 212

B.F. Skinner, p. 197

Edward L. Thorndike, p. 197

Edward C. Tolman, p. 210

John B. Watson, p. 187

learning, p. 182

conditioning, p. 182

classical conditioning, p. 183

unconditioned stimulus (UCS), p. 184

unconditioned response (UCR), p. 184

conditioned stimulus (CS), p. 184

conditioned response (CR), p. 184

stimulus generalization, p. 186

stimulus discrimination, p. 186

higher order conditioning (second-order conditioning), p. 186

extinction (in classical conditioning), p. 187

spontaneous recovery, p. 187

behaviorism, p. 187

placebo response, p. 192

taste aversion, p. 193

biological preparedness, p. 194

law of effect, p. 197

operant, p. 198

operant conditioning, p. 198

reinforcement, p. 198

positive reinforcement, p. 198

negative reinforcement, p. 199

primary reinforcer, p. 200

conditioned reinforcer, p. 200

punishment, p. 200

positive punishment, p. 200

negative punishment, p. 201

discriminative stimulus, p. 203

operant chamber (Skinner box), p. 205

shaping, p. 206

continuous reinforcement, p. 206

partial reinforcement, p. 206

extinction (in operant conditioning), p. 206

partial reinforcement effect, p. 206

schedule of reinforcement, p. 207

fixed-ratio (FR) schedule, p. 207

variable-ratio (VR) schedule, p. 208

fixed-interval (FI) schedule, p. 208

variable-interval (VI) schedule, p. 208

behavior modification, p. 209

cognitive map, p. 210

latent learning, p. 211

learned helplessness, p. 212

instinctive drift, p. 214

observational learning, p. 214

mirror neurons, p. 217

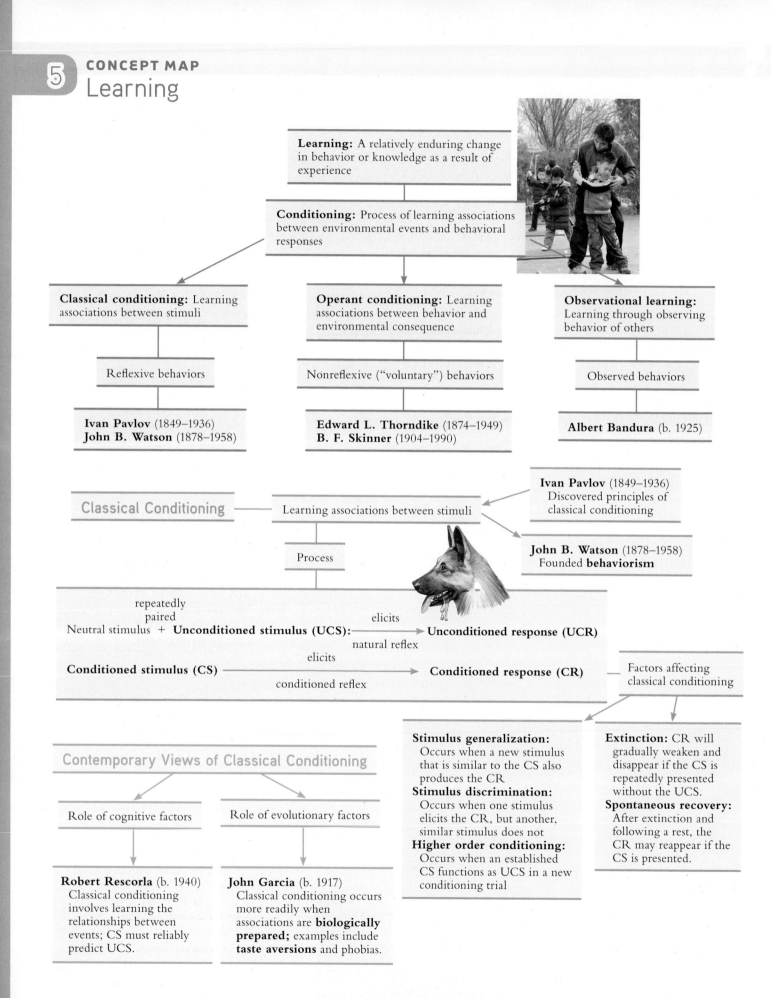

Learning: A relatively enduring change in behavior or knowledge as a result of experience

Conditioning: Process of learning associations between environmental events and behavioral responses

Classical conditioning: Learning associations between stimuli

Operant conditioning: Learning associations between behavior and environmental consequence

Observational learning: Learning through observing behavior of others

Reflexive behaviors

Nonreflexive ("voluntary") behaviors

Observed behaviors

Ivan Pavlov (1849–1936)
John B. Watson (1878–1958)

Edward L. Thorndike (1874–1949)
B. F. Skinner (1904–1990)

Albert Bandura (b. 1925)

Classical Conditioning — Learning associations between stimuli

Ivan Pavlov (1849–1936) Discovered principles of classical conditioning

Process

John B. Watson (1878–1958) Founded **behaviorism**

repeatedly paired
Neutral stimulus + **Unconditioned stimulus (UCS):**   elicits   **Unconditioned response (UCR)**
natural reflex

elicits
Conditioned stimulus (CS) ———————→ **Conditioned response (CR)**
conditioned reflex

Factors affecting classical conditioning

Contemporary Views of Classical Conditioning

Role of cognitive factors

Role of evolutionary factors

Robert Rescorla (b. 1940) Classical conditioning involves learning the relationships between events; CS must reliably predict UCS.

John Garcia (b. 1917) Classical conditioning occurs more readily when associations are **biologically prepared;** examples include **taste aversions** and phobias.

Stimulus generalization: Occurs when a new stimulus that is similar to the CS also produces the CR
Stimulus discrimination: Occurs when one stimulus elicits the CR, but another, similar stimulus does not
Higher order conditioning: Occurs when an established CS functions as UCS in a new conditioning trial

Extinction: CR will gradually weaken and disappear if the CS is repeatedly presented without the UCS.
Spontaneous recovery: After extinction and following a rest, the CR may reappear if the CS is presented.

Operant Conditioning

Learning associations between behaviors and their consequences

Process

Discriminative stimulus sets the occasion. → **Operant** is emitted. → Consequence

Primary reinforcer: Naturally reinforcing
Conditioned reinforcer: Becomes reinforcing by being associated with a primary reinforcer

Reinforcement: Increases the likelihood that a behavior will be repeated

Punishment: Decreases the likelihood that a behavior will be repeated

Types of Reinforcement:
Positive reinforcement: Addition of a reinforcing stimulus *strengthens* an operant response.
Negative reinforcement: Removal of an aversive stimulus *strengthens* an operant response.

Types of Punishment:
Positive punishment: Addition of a punishing stimulus *weakens* an operant response.
Negative punishment: Removal of a reinforcing stimulus *weakens* an operant response.

New behaviors can be acquired through **shaping,** which involves reinforcing progressively closer approximations of a goal behavior.

Behaviors on a **partial reinforcement** schedule are more resistant to **extinction** than behaviors on a **continuous reinforcement** schedule.
Schedules of reinforcement:
• **Fixed-ratio (FR)**
• **Variable-ratio (VR)**
• **Fixed-interval (FI)**
• **Variable-interval (VI)**

Contemporary Views of Operant Conditioning

Role of cognitive factors

Role of evolutionary factors

Observational Learning

Edward C. Tolman (1898–1956) Discovery of **cognitive maps** and **latent learning** provided evidence that learning involves the cognitive representation of the relationship between a behavior and its consequence.
Martin Seligman (b. 1942) Discovery of **learned helplessness** provided evidence for the role of cognitive expectations in learning.

Instinctive drift provided evidence for the importance of natural behavior patterns in learning.

Learning that occurs through observing the actions of others and the consequences of those actions

Albert Bandura (b. 1925) Bobo doll experiment demonstrated that reinforcement is not necessary for learning to occur; expectation of reinforcement affects the performance of what has been learned.

Processes necessary for imitation to occur:
1. **Attention:** pay attention to the model's behavior
2. **Memory:** remember the behavior so that it can be performed later
3. **Motor skill:** ability to transform the mental representation into action
4. **Motivation:** expectation that the behavior will be reinforced

Is it true . . .

○ That "flashbulb memories," the vivid memories you form after an important, dramatic event, are no more accurate than other memories?

○ That déjà vu experiences are a type of ESP, and may be examples of precognition or memories from a previous lifetime?

○ That memory is like a video recorder—it preserves a perfect record of your experience?

○ That eyewitness testimony is the most reliable form of courtroom evidence?

○ That once formed, memories can't change?

○ That it's common to completely repress memories of traumatic events, but that such events can be accurately remembered under hypnosis?

○ That all memories, even complex ones, are located in a single part of the brain?

THE DROWNING

PROLOGUE

ELIZABETH WAS ONLY 14 YEARS OLD when her mother drowned. Although Elizabeth remembered many things about visiting her Uncle Joe's home in Pennsylvania that summer, her memory of the details surrounding her mother's death had always been hazy. As she explained:

In my mind I've returned to that scene many times, and each time the memory gains weight and substance. I can see the cool pine trees, smell their fresh tarry breath, feel the lake's algae-green water on my skin, taste Uncle Joe's iced tea with fresh-squeezed lemon. But the death itself was always vague and unfocused. I never saw my mother's body, and I could not imagine her dead. The last memory I have of my mother was her tiptoed visit the evening before her death, the quick hug, the whispered, "I love you."

Some 30 years later, at her Uncle Joe's 90th birthday party, Elizabeth learned from a relative that she had been the one to discover her mother's body in Uncle Joe's swimming pool. With this realization, memories that had eluded Elizabeth for decades began to come back.

The memories began to drift back, slow and unpredictable, like the crisp piney smoke from the evening camp-fires. I could see myself, a thin, dark-haired girl, looking into the flickering blue-and-white pool. My mother, dressed in her nightgown, is floating face down. "Mom? Mom?" I ask the question several times, my voice rising in terror. I start screaming. I remember the police cars, their lights flashing, and the stretcher with the clean, white blanket tucked in around the edges of the body. The memory had been there all along, but I just couldn't reach it.

As the memory crystallized, it suddenly made sense to Elizabeth why she had always felt haunted by her vague memories of the circumstances

Memory

IN THIS CHAPTER:

› **INTRODUCTION:** What Is Memory?

› Retrieval: Getting Information from Long-Term Memory

› Forgetting: When Retrieval Fails

› Imperfect Memories: Errors, Distortions, and False Memories

› The Search for the Biological Basis of Memory

› **PSYCH FOR YOUR LIFE:** Ten Steps to Boost Your Memory

surrounding her mother's death. And it also seemed to explain, in part, why she had always been so fascinated by the topic of memory.

However, several days later, Elizabeth learned that the relative had been wrong—it was *not* Elizabeth who discovered her mother's body, but her Aunt Pearl. Other relatives confirmed that Aunt Pearl had been the one who found Elizabeth's mother in the swimming pool. Yet Elizabeth's memory had seemed so real.

The Elizabeth in this true story is Elizabeth Loftus, a psychologist who is nationally recognized as the leading expert on the distortions that can occur in the memories of eyewitnesses. Loftus shares this personal story in her book *The Myth of Repressed Memory: False Memories and Allegations of Sexual Abuse.*

In this chapter, we'll consider the psychological and biological processes that underlie how memories are formed and forgotten. As you'll see, memory distortions such as the one Elizabeth Loftus experienced are relatively common. By the end of this chapter, you'll have a much better understanding of the memory process, including the reason that Elizabeth's "memory" of finding her mother's body seemed so real. □

Memories Can Involve All Your Senses
Think back to a particularly memorable experience from your high school years. Can you conjure up vivid memories of smells, tastes, sounds, or emotions associated with that experience? In the years to come, these friends may remember many sensory details associated with this impromptu water fight.

memory The mental processes that enable you to retain and retrieve information over time.

encoding The process of transforming information into a form that can be entered into and retained by the memory system.

FIGURE 6.1 Overview of the Stage Model of Memory

INTRODUCTION:
What Is Memory?

KEY THEME

Memory is a group of related mental processes that are involved in acquiring, storing, and retrieving information.

KEY QUESTIONS

› What are encoding, storage, and retrieval?
› What is the stage model of memory?
› What are the nature and function of sensory memory?

Like Elizabeth's memories of her uncle's home, memories can be vivid and evoke intense emotions. We can conjure up distinct memories that involve all our senses, including smells, sounds, and even tactile sensations. For example, close your eyes and try to recall the feeling of rain-soaked clothes against your skin, the smell of popcorn, and the sound of the half-time buzzer during a high school basketball game.

Memory refers to the mental processes that enable us to acquire, retain, and retrieve information. Rather than being a single process, memory involves three fundamental processes: *encoding, storage,* and *retrieval.*

Encoding refers to the process of transforming information into a form that can be entered and retained by the memory system. For example, to memorize the definition of a key term that appears on a textbook page, you would visually *encode* the patterns of lines and dots on the page as meaningful words that could be retained by your memory. **Storage** is the process of retaining information in memory so that it can be used at a later time. **Retrieval** involves recovering the stored information so that we are consciously aware of it.

The Stage Model of Memory

No single model has been shown to capture all aspects of human memory (Baddeley & others, 2009; Tulving, 2007). However, one very influential model, the **stage model of memory,** is useful in explaining the basic workings of memory. In this model, shown in Figure 6.1, memory involves three distinct stages: *sensory memory, short-term memory,* and *long-term memory* (Atkinson & Shiffrin, 1968; Shiffrin & Atkinson, 1969). The stage model is based on the idea that information is *transferred* from one memory stage to another.

The first stage of memory is called *sensory memory.* **Sensory memory** registers a great deal of information from the environment and holds it for a very brief period of time (Treisman & Lages, 2013). After three seconds or less, the information fades. Think of your sensory memory as an internal camera that continuously takes "snapshots" of your surroundings. With each snapshot, you momentarily focus your attention on specific details. Almost instantly, the snapshot fades, only to be replaced by another.

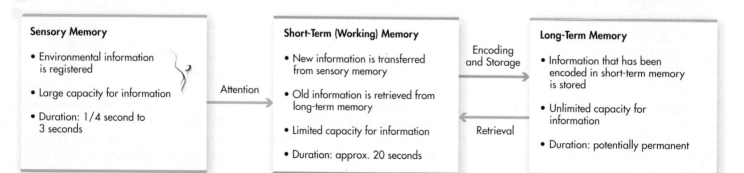

Sensory Memory

• Environmental information is registered

• Large capacity for information

• Duration: 1/4 second to 3 seconds

Attention →

Short-Term (Working) Memory

• New information is transferred from sensory memory

• Old information is retrieved from long-term memory

• Limited capacity for information

• Duration: approx. 20 seconds

Encoding and Storage →

Retrieval ←

Long-Term Memory

• Information that has been encoded in short-term memory is stored

• Unlimited capacity for information

• Duration: potentially permanent

During the very brief time the information is held in sensory memory, you "select," or pay *attention* to, just a few aspects of all the environmental information that's being registered. While studying, for example, you focus your attention on one page of your textbook, ignoring other environmental stimuli. The information you select from sensory memory is important because this information is transferred to the second stage of memory, *short-term memory.*

Short-term memory refers to the active, working memory system. Your short-term memory temporarily holds all the information you are currently thinking about or consciously aware of. That information is stored briefly in short-term memory—for up to about 20 seconds. Because you use your short-term memory to actively process conscious information in a variety of ways, short-term memory is often referred to as *working memory* (Baddeley, 1995, 2007, 2010). Imagining, remembering, and conscious problem solving all take place in short-term memory.

Over the course of any given day, vast amounts of information flow through your short-term memory. Most of this information quickly fades and is forgotten in a matter of seconds. However, some of the information that is actively processed in short-term memory may be encoded for storage in long-term memory.

Long-term memory, the third memory stage, represents what most people typically think of as memory—the long-term storage of information, potentially for a lifetime. It's important to note that the transfer of information between short-term and long-term memory goes two ways. Not only does information flow from short-term memory to long-term memory, but much information also flows in the other direction, from long-term memory to short-term memory.

If you think about it, this makes a great deal of sense. Consider a routine cognitive task, such as carrying on a conversation. Such tasks involve processing current sensory data and retrieving relevant stored information, such as the meaning of individual words. In the next few sections, we'll describe each of the stages of memory in more detail.

PeopleImages/Getty Images

The Interaction of Memory Stages in Everyday Life Imagine cooking a favorite dish from memory. How might each of your memory stages be involved in the food preparation? What kinds of information would be transferred from sensory memory and retrieved from long-term memory?

Sensory Memory
FLEETING IMPRESSIONS OF THE WORLD

Has something like this ever happened to you? You're engrossed in watching a suspenseful movie. From another room, your roommate calls out, "Where'd you put my car keys?" You respond with, "What?" Then, a split second later, the question registers in your mind. Before the other person can repeat the question, you reply, "Oh. They're on your desk."

You were able to answer the question because your *sensory memory* registered and preserved the other person's words for a few fleeting seconds—just long enough for you to recall what had been said to you while your attention was focused on the movie. Sensory memory stores a detailed record of a sensory experience, but only for a few seconds at the most.

THE DURATION OF SENSORY MEMORY
IT WAS THERE JUST A SPLIT SECOND AGO!

The characteristics of visual sensory memory, also called *iconic memory,* were first identified largely through the research of psychologist **George Sperling** in 1960. In his experiment, Sperling flashed the images of 12 letters on a screen for one-twentieth of a second. The letters were arranged in four rows of 3 letters each. Subjects focused their attention on the screen and, immediately after the screen went blank, reported as many letters as they could remember.

storage The process of retaining information in memory so that it can be used at a later time.

retrieval The process of recovering information stored in memory so that we are consciously aware of it.

stage model of memory A model describing memory as consisting of three distinct stages: sensory memory, short-term memory, and long-term memory.

sensory memory The stage of memory that registers information from the environment and holds it for a very brief period of time.

short-term memory The active stage of memory in which information is stored for up to about 20 seconds.

long-term memory The stage of memory that represents the long-term storage of information.

FIGURE 6.2 Sperling's Experiment Demonstrating the Duration of Sensory Memory This figure depicts George Sperling's classic 1960 experiment. (1) Subjects stared at a screen on which rows of letters were projected for just one-twentieth of a second, then the screen went blank. (2) After intervals varying up to one second, a tone was sounded that indicated the row of letters the subject should report. (3) If the tone was sounded within about one-third of a second, subjects were able to report the letters in the indicated row because the image of *all* the letters was still in sensory memory.

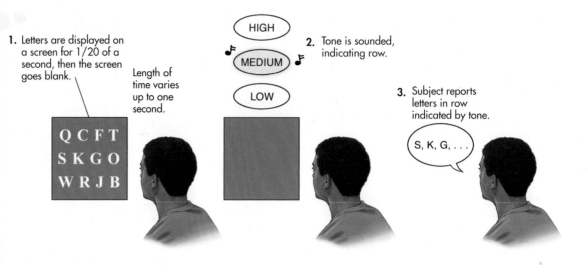

1. Letters are displayed on a screen for 1/20 of a second, then the screen goes blank.

Length of time varies up to one second.

HIGH

MEDIUM

LOW

2. Tone is sounded, indicating row.

3. Subject reports letters in row indicated by tone.

S, K, G, . . .

QCFT
SKGO
WRJB

On average, subjects could report only 4 or 5 of the 12 letters. However, several subjects claimed that they had actually seen *all* the letters but that the complete image had faded from their memory as they spoke, disappearing before they could verbally report more than 4 or 5 letters.

On the basis of this information, Sperling tried a simple variation on the original experiment (see Figure 6.2). He arranged the 12 letters in three rows of 4 letters each. Then, immediately *after* the screen went blank, he sounded a high-pitched, medium-pitched, or low-pitched tone. If the subjects heard the high-pitched tone, they were to report the letters in the top row; the medium-pitched tone signaled the middle row; and the low-pitched tone signaled the bottom row. If the subjects actually did see all the letters, Sperling reasoned, then they should be able to report the letters in a given row by focusing their attention on the indicated row *before* their visual sensory memory faded.

This is exactly what happened. If the tone followed the letter display in under one-third of a second, subjects could accurately report about 3 of the 4 letters in whichever row was indicated by the tone. However, if the interval between the screen going blank and the sound of the tone was more than one-third of a second, the accuracy of the reports decreased dramatically. By the time one second had elapsed, the image in the subject's visual sensory memory had already faded beyond recall.

Sperling's classic experiment demonstrated that our visual sensory memory holds a great deal of information very briefly, for about half a second. This information is available just long enough for us to pay attention to specific elements that are significant to us at that moment. This meaningful information is then transferred from the very brief storage of sensory memory to the somewhat longer storage of short-term memory.

TYPES OF SENSORY MEMORY
PICK A SENSE, ANY SENSE!

Memory researchers believe there is a separate sensory memory for each sense—vision, hearing, touch, smell, and so on (Werkhoven & van Erp, 2013). Of the different senses, however, visual and auditory sensory memories have been the most thoroughly studied. *Visual sensory memory* is sometimes referred to as *iconic memory* because it is the brief memory of an image, or *icon*. *Auditory sensory memory* is sometimes referred to as *echoic memory,* meaning a brief memory that is like an *echo*.

Researchers have found slight differences in the duration of sensory memory for visual and auditory information. Your visual sensory memory typically holds an image of your environment for about one-quarter to one-half second before it is replaced by yet another overlapping "snapshot." This is easy to demonstrate. Quickly wave a pencil back and forth in front of your face. Do you see the fading image of the pencil trailing behind it? That's your visual sensory memory at work. It momentarily holds the snapshot of the environmental image you see before it is almost instantly replaced by another overlapping image.

Your auditory sensory memory holds sound information a little longer, up to three or four seconds. This brief auditory sensory trace for sound allows you to hear speech as continuous words, or a series of musical notes as a melody, rather than as disjointed sounds. It also explains why you are able to "remember" something that you momentarily don't "hear," as in the example of your roommate asking you where the car keys are.

An important function of sensory memory is to very briefly store sensory impressions so that they overlap slightly with one another. Thus, we perceive the world around us as continuous, rather than as a series of disconnected visual images or disjointed sounds.

Short-Term, Working Memory
THE WORKSHOP OF CONSCIOUSNESS

Travis Morisse/The Hutchinson News

Perception and Sensory Memory Traces Because your visual sensory memory holds information for a fraction of a second before it fades, rapidly presented stimuli overlap and appear continuous. Thus, you perceive the separate blades of a rapidly spinning windmill as a smooth blur of motion. Similarly, you perceive a lightning bolt streaking across the sky as continuous even though it is actually three or more separate bolts of electricity.

KEY THEME

Short-term memory provides temporary storage for information transferred from sensory and long-term memory.

KEY QUESTIONS

> What are the duration and capacity of short-term memory?
> How can you overcome the limitations of short-term memory?
> What are the main components of Baddeley's model of working memory?

You can think of *short-term memory,* or *working memory,* as the "workshop" of consciousness. It is the stage of memory in which information transferred from sensory memory *and* information retrieved from long-term memory become conscious. When you recall a past event or mentally add two numbers, the information is temporarily held and processed in your short-term memory. Your short-term memory also allows you to make sense out of this sentence by holding the beginning of the sentence in active memory while you read the rest of the sentence. Thus, short-term, working memory provides temporary storage for information that is currently being used in some conscious cognitive activity.

THE DURATION OF SHORT-TERM MEMORY
GOING, GOING, GONE!

Information in short-term memory lasts longer than information in sensory memory, but its duration is still very short. Estimates vary, but generally you can hold most types of information in short-term memory up to about 20 seconds before it's forgotten (Peterson & Peterson, 1959). However, information can be maintained in short-term memory if it is *rehearsed,* or repeated, over and over. Because consciously rehearsing information will maintain it in short-term memory, this process is called **maintenance rehearsal.** For example, suppose that you decide to order a pizza for yourself and some friends. You look up the number and mentally rehearse it until you can dial the phone.

Information that is *not* actively rehearsed is rapidly lost. Why? One possible explanation is that information that is not maintained by rehearsal simply fades away, or *decays,* with the passage of time. Another potential cause of forgetting in short-term memory is *interference* from new or competing information (Baddeley, 2002; Nairne, 2002). For example, if you are distracted by one of your friends asking you a question before you dial the pizza place, your memory of the phone number will quickly evaporate. Interference may also explain the irritating experience of forgetting someone's name just moments after you're introduced to him or her. If you engage the new acquaintance in conversation without rehearsing his or her name, the conversation may "bump" the person's name out of your short-term memory.

maintenance rehearsal The mental or verbal repetition of information in order to maintain it beyond the usual 20-second duration of short-term memory.

Row 1 — 8 7 4 6
Row 2 — 3 4 9 6 2
Row 3 — 4 2 7 7 1 6
Row 4 — 5 1 4 0 8 1 3
Row 5 — 1 8 3 9 5 5 2 1
Row 6 — 2 1 4 9 7 5 2 4 8
Row 7 — 9 3 7 1 0 4 2 8 9 7
Row 8 — 7 1 9 0 4 2 6 0 4 1 8

Demonstration of Short-Term Memory Capacity

UAVFCIDBDSAI

THE CAPACITY OF SHORT-TERM MEMORY
SO THAT'S WHY THERE WERE SEVEN DWARFS!

Along with having a relatively short duration, short-term memory also has a relatively limited capacity. This is easy to demonstrate. Take a look at the numbers in the margin. If you've got a friend handy who's willing to serve as your research subject, simply read the numbers out loud, one row at a time, and ask your friend to repeat them back to you in the same order. Try to read the numbers at a steady rate, about one per second. Note each row that he correctly remembers.

How many numbers could your friend repeat accurately? Most likely, he could correctly repeat between five and nine numbers. That's what psychologist George Miller (1956) described as the limits of short-term memory in a classic paper titled "The Magical Number Seven, Plus or Minus Two." Miller believed that the capacity of short-term memory is limited to about seven items, or bits of information, at one time. It's no accident that local telephone numbers are seven digits long (Cowan & others, 2004).

So what happens when your short-term memory store is filled to capacity? New information *displaces,* or bumps out, currently held information. Maintenance rehearsal is one way to avoid the loss of information from short-term memory. By consciously repeating the information you want to remember, you keep it active in short-term memory and prevent it from being displaced by new information.

Although the capacity of your short-term memory is limited, there are ways to increase the amount of information you can hold in short-term memory at any given moment. To illustrate this point, let's try another short-term memory demonstration. Read the sequence of letters in the margin, then close your eyes and try to repeat the letters out loud in the same order.

How many letters were you able to remember? Unless you have an exceptional short-term memory, you probably could not repeat the whole sequence correctly. Now try this sequence of letters: D V D F B I U S A C I A.

You probably managed the second sequence with no trouble at all, even though it is made up of exactly the same letters as the first sequence. The ease with which you handled the second sequence demonstrates **chunking**—the grouping of related items together into a single unit. The first letter sequence was perceived as 12 separate items and probably exceeded your short-term memory's capacity. But the second letter sequence was perceived as only four "chunks" of information, which you easily remembered: DVD, FBI, USA, and CIA. Thus, chunking can increase the amount of information held in short-term memory. But to do so, chunking also often involves the retrieval of meaningful information from *long-term memory,* such as the meaning of the initials FBI (Baddeley & others, 2010).

The basic principle of chunking is incorporated into many numbers that we need to remember. Long strings of identification numbers, such as Social Security numbers or credit card numbers, are usually broken up by hyphens or spaces so that you can chunk them easily.

Not every memory researcher accepts that short-term memory is limited to exactly seven items, plus or minus two. Over the half-century since the publication of Miller's classic article, researchers have challenged the seven-item limit (Cowan & others, 2007; Jonides & others, 2008). Current research suggests that the true "magical number" is more likely to be *four plus or minus one* rather than *seven plus or minus two* (Cowan & others, 2007; Cowan, 2010).

Cognitive psychologist Nelson Cowan (2001, 2005, 2010) believes that the type of stimuli used in many short-term memory tests has led researchers to overestimate its capacity. Typically, such memory tests use lists of letters, numbers, or words. According to Cowan, many people *automatically* chunk such stimuli to help remember them. For example, even seemingly random numbers may be easily associated with a date, an address, or another familiar number sequence.

To overcome this tendency, Jeffrey Rouder and his colleagues (2008) used a simple visual stimulus instead of a sequence of numbers, letters, or words. The memory task?

chunking Increasing the amount of information that can be held in short-term memory by grouping related items together into a single unit, or *chunk.*

Remembering the position of colored squares on a computer screen. In this and similar studies, participants were able to hold only three or four items in their short-term memory at a time. Thus, most researchers today believe that the capacity of working memory is no more than about three to four items at a time when chunking is not an option (Cowan, 2010; Mandler, 2013).

Whether the "magic number" is four or seven, the point remains: Short-term memory has a limited number of mental "slots" for information. Chunking can increase the amount of information held in each slot, but the number of slots is still limited.

FROM SHORT-TERM MEMORY TO WORKING MEMORY

Our discussion of the short-term memory store has so far focused on just one type of information—verbal or acoustic codes, that is, speech-like stimuli that we can mentally recite. Lists of numbers, letters, words, or other items fall into this category. However, if you think about it, we also use our short-term memory to temporarily store and manipulate other types of stimuli, such as visual images. For example, suppose you're out shopping with a close friend who asks you whether you think a particular chair will match her living room furniture. Before you respond, you need to call up and hold a mental image of her living room. You are surely using your short-term memory as you consider her question, but how?

In this example, you are actively processing information in a short-term memory system that is often referred to as working memory. Although the terms *working memory* and *short-term memory* are sometimes used interchangeably, **working memory** refers to the active, conscious manipulation of temporarily stored information. You use your working memory when you engage in problem solving, reasoning, language comprehension, and mental comparisons. Short-term memory is more likely to be used when the focus is on simpler memory processes, such as rehearsing lists of syllables, words, or numbers (Baddeley, 2010). And, in contrast to short-term memory, working memory is more likely to involve the recall and manipulation of information held in long-term memory (Corkin, 2013).

The best-known model of working memory was developed by British psychologist Alan Baddeley. In Baddeley's (1992, 2007) model of working memory, there are three main components, each of which can function independently (see Figure 6.3). One component, called the *phonological loop,* is specialized for verbal material, such as lists of numbers or words. This is the aspect of working memory that is often tested by standard memory tasks (Mueller & others, 2003). The second component, called the *visuospatial sketchpad,* is specialized for spatial or visual material, such as remembering the layout of a room or city.

The third component is what Baddeley calls the *central executive,* which controls attention, integrates information, and manages the activities of the phonological loop and the visuospatial sketchpad. The central executive also initiates retrieval and decision processes as necessary and integrates information coming into the system.

working memory The temporary storage and active, conscious manipulation of information needed for complex cognitive tasks, such as reasoning, learning, and problem solving.

FIGURE 6.3 Baddeley's Model of Working Memory: How Do I Get to Marty's House? Suppose you are trying to figure out the fastest way to get to a friend's house. In Baddeley's model of working memory, you would use the *phonological loop* to verbally recite the directions. Maintenance rehearsal helps keep the information active in the phonological loop. You would use the *visuospatial sketchpad* to imagine your route and any landmarks along the way. The *central executive* actively processes and integrates information from the phonological loop, the visuospatial sketchpad, and long-term memory.

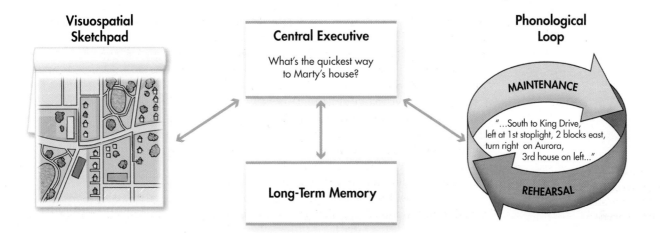

Visuospatial Sketchpad

Central Executive

What's the quickest way to Marty's house?

Long-Term Memory

Phonological Loop

MAINTENANCE

"...South to King Drive, left at 1st stoplight, 2 blocks east, turn right on Aurora, 3rd house on left..."

REHEARSAL

elaborative rehearsal Rehearsal that involves focusing on the meaning of information to help encode and transfer it to long-term memory.

"Did you ever start to do something and then forget what the heck it was?"

Long-Term Memory

KEY THEME

Once encoded, an unlimited amount of information can be stored in long-term memory, which has different memory systems.

KEY QUESTIONS

> What are ways to improve the effectiveness of encoding?
> How do procedural, episodic, and semantic memories differ, and what are implicit and explicit memory?
> How does the semantic network model explain the organization of long-term memory?

Long-term memory refers to the storage of information over extended periods of time. Technically, any information stored longer than the roughly 20-second duration of short-term memory is considered to be stored in long-term memory. In terms of maximum duration, some long-term memories last a lifetime.

In contrast to the limited capacities of sensory and short-term memory, the amount of information that can be held in long-term memory is limitless. Granted, it doesn't always feel limitless, but consider this: Every day, you remember the directions to your college; the names of hundreds of friends, relatives, and acquaintances; and how to start your car. Retrieving information from long-term memory happens quickly and with little effort—most of the time.

ENCODING LONG-TERM MEMORIES

How does information get "into" long-term memory? One very important function that takes place in short-term memory is *encoding,* or transforming the new information into a form that can be retrieved later (see Figure 6.4). As a student, you may have tried to memorize dates, facts, or definitions by simply repeating them to yourself over and over. This strategy reflects an attempt to use maintenance rehearsal to encode material into long-term memory. However, maintenance rehearsal is *not* a very effective strategy for encoding information into long-term memory.

A much more effective encoding strategy is **elaborative rehearsal,** which involves focusing on the *meaning* of information to help encode and transfer it to long-term memory. With elaborative rehearsal, you relate the information to other

FIGURE 6.4 The Role of Sensory and Short-Term Memory in the Stage Model of Memory

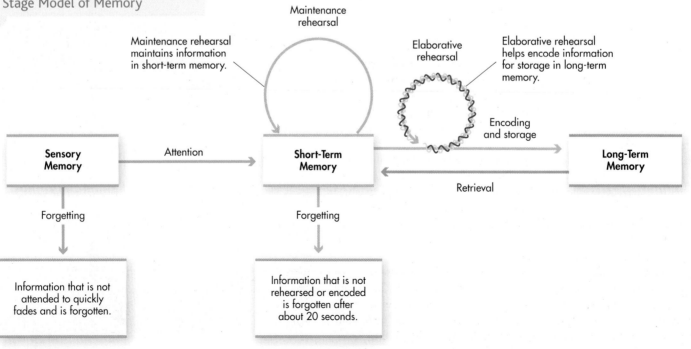

Charles Barsotti The New Yorker Collection/ The Cartoon Bank

information you already know. That is, rather than simply repeating the information, you *elaborate* on the new information in some meaningful way.

Elaborative rehearsal significantly improves memory for new material. This point is especially important for students, because elaborative rehearsal is a helpful study strategy. Here's an example of how you might use elaborative rehearsal to improve your memory for new information. In Chapter 2 we discussed three brain structures that are part of the limbic system: the *hypothalamus,* the *hippocampus,* and the *amygdala.* If you tried to memorize the definitions of these structures by reciting them over and over to yourself, you engaged in the not-so-effective memory strategy of maintenance rehearsal.

But if you elaborated on the information in some meaningful way, you would be more likely to recall it. For example, you could think about the limbic system's involvement in emotions, memory, and motivation by constructing a simple story. "I knew it was lunchtime because my hypothalamus told me I was *hungry, thirsty,* and cold. My hippocampus helped me remember a new restaurant that opened on *campus,* but when I got there I had to wait in line and my amygdala reacted with anger." The story may be a bit silly, but many studies have shown that elaborative rehearsal leads to better retention (Lockhart & Craik, 1990).

Creating this simple story to help you remember the limbic system illustrates two additional factors that enhance encoding. First, applying information to yourself, called the *self-reference effect,* improves your memory for information. Second, the use of *visual imagery,* especially vivid images, also enhances encoding (Kesebir & Oishi, 2010; Paivio, 2007).

The fact that elaborative rehearsal results in more effective encoding and better memory of new information has many practical applications for students. As you study:

- Make sure you understand the new information by restating it in your own words.
- Actively question new information.
- Think about the potential applications and implications of the material.
- Relate the new material to information you already know, searching for connections that make the new information more meaningful.
- Generate your own examples of the concept, especially examples from your own experiences.

At the end of the chapter, in Psych for Your Life, we'll give you more suggestions for strategies you can use to improve your memory.

TYPES OF INFORMATION IN LONG-TERM MEMORY

There are three major categories of information stored in long-term memory (Tulving, 1985, 2002). **Procedural memory** refers to the long-term memory of how to perform different skills, operations, and actions. Typing, riding a bike, running, and making scrambled eggs are all examples of procedural information stored in long-term memory. We begin forming procedural memories early in life when we learn to walk, talk, feed ourselves, and so on.

Often, we can't recall exactly when or how we learned procedural information. And usually it's difficult to describe procedural memories in words. For example, try to describe *precisely* and *exactly* what you do when you blow-dry your hair, play the guitar, or ride a bicycle. A particular skill may be easy to demonstrate but very difficult to describe.

In contrast to procedural memory, **episodic memory** refers to your long-term memory of specific events or episodes, including the time and place that they occurred (Gallo & Wheeler, 2013; Tulving, 2002). Your memory of attending a friend's wedding or your first day at college would both be examples of episodic memories.

procedural memory Category of long-term memory that includes memories of different skills, operations, and actions.

episodic memory Category of long-term memory that includes memories of particular events.

Types of Information Stored in Long-Term Memory A memorable volleyball game involves all three types of long-term memory. Remembering how to return and spike a volleyball are examples of *procedural memory.* Knowing the rules of the game would be an example of *semantic memory.* And, the vivid memory of an epic volleyball match played on a beach vacation would be an example of an *episodic memory.*

semantic memory Category of long-term memory that includes memories of general knowledge, concepts, facts, and names.

explicit memory Information or knowledge that can be consciously recollected; also called *declarative memory*.

implicit memory Information or knowledge that affects behavior or task performance but cannot be consciously recollected; also called *non-declarative memory*.

clustering Organizing items into related groups during recall from long-term memory.

The third category of long-term memory is **semantic memory**—general knowledge that includes facts, names, definitions, concepts, and ideas. Semantic memory represents your personal encyclopedia of accumulated data and trivia stored in your long-term memory. Typically, you store semantic memories in long-term memory *without* remembering when or where you originally acquired the information. For example, can you remember when or where you learned that there are different time zones across the United States? Or when you learned that there are nine innings in a baseball game?

Closely related to episodic memory is *autobiographical memory,* which refers to the events of your life—your personal life history (Fivush, 2011). Your autobiographical memory includes your episodic memories about your life. But it also includes the semantic memories that relate to your life story, such as knowing when and where your parents met or when and where you were born (Tulving & Szpunar, 2009). Autobiographical memory plays a key role in your sense of self (Ross & Wang, 2010). Does culture affect autobiographical memory? In the Culture and Human Behavior box, we examine the impact of culture on people's earliest memories.

IMPLICIT AND EXPLICIT MEMORY
TWO DIMENSIONS OF LONG-TERM MEMORY

Studies with patients who have suffered different types of amnesia as a result of damage to particular brain areas have led memory researchers to recognize that long-term memory is *not* a simple, unitary system. Instead, long-term memory appears to be composed of separate but interacting subsystems and abilities (Slotnick & Schacter, 2007).

What are these subsystems? One basic distinction that has been made is between *explicit memory* and *implicit memory.* **Explicit memory** is *memory with awareness*— information or knowledge that can be consciously recollected, including episodic and semantic information. Thus, remembering what you did last New Year's Day or the topics discussed in your last psychology class are both examples of explicit memory. Explicit memories are also called *declarative memories* because, if asked, you can "declare" the information.

In contrast, **implicit memory** is *memory without awareness.* Implicit memories cannot be consciously recollected, but they still affect your behavior, knowledge, or performance of some task. For example, let's assume that you are a pretty good typist. Imagine that we asked you to type the following phrase with your eyes closed: "most zebras cannot be extravagant." Easy, right? Now, without looking at a typewriter or computer keyboard, try reciting, from left to right, the seven letters of the alphabet that appear on the bottom row of a keyboard. Can you do it? Your authors are both expert typists, and neither one of us could do this. Chances are, you can't either. (In case you're wondering, the letters are *ZXCVBNM.*)

Here's the point: Your ability to type the phrase "most zebras cannot be extravagant" without looking demonstrates that you *do* know the location of the letters *Z, X, C, V, B, N,* and *M.* But your inability to recite that knowledge demonstrates that your memory of each key's location cannot be consciously recollected. Even though you're not consciously aware of the memory, it still affects your behavior. Implicit memories are also called *nondeclarative memories* because you're unable to "declare" the information. Procedural memories, including skills and habits, typically reflect implicit memory processes. Figure 6.5 summarizes the different types of long-term memory.

FIGURE 6.5 Types of Long-Term Memory

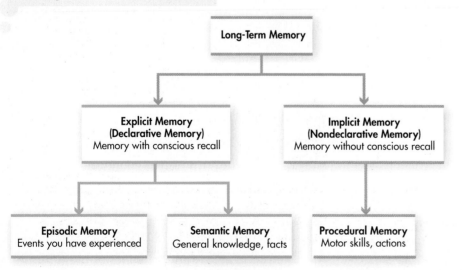

Culture's Effects on Early Memories

For most adults, earliest memories are for events that occurred between the ages of 2 and 4. These early memories mark the beginning of autobiographical memory, which provides the basis for the development of an enduring sense of self (Fivush, 2011; Markowitsch & Staniloiu, 2011). Do cultural differences in the sense of self influence the content of our earliest memories?

Comparing the earliest memories of European American college students and Taiwanese and Chinese college students, developmental psychologist Qi (pronounced "chee") Wang (2001, 2006) found a number of significant differences. First, the average age for earliest memory was much earlier for the U.S.-born students than for the Taiwanese and Chinese students.

Wang also found that the Americans' memories were more likely to be discrete, one-point-in-time events reflecting individual experiences or feelings, such as "I remember getting stung by a bee when I was 3 years old. I was scared and started crying." In contrast, the earliest memories of both the Chinese and Taiwanese students were of general, routine activities with family, schoolmates, or community members, such as playing in the park or eating with family members.

For Americans, Wang notes, the past is like a drama in which the self plays the lead role. Themes of self-awareness and individual autonomy were more common in the American students' memories, which tended to focus on their own experiences, emotions, and thoughts.

In contrast, Chinese students were more likely to include other people in their memories. Rather than focusing exclusively on their own behavior and thoughts, their earliest memories were typically brief accounts that centered on collective activities. For the Chinese students, the self is not easily separated from its social context.

Wang (2013) believes that cultural differences in autobiographical memory are formed in very early childhood, through interaction with family members. For example, *shared reminiscing*—the way that mothers talk to their children about their past experiences—differs in Eastern and Western cultures (Fivush, 2011). When Asian mothers reminisce with their children, they tend to talk about group settings or situations, and to de-emphasize emotions, such as anger, that might separate the child from the group. In comparison, Western mothers tend to focus more on the child's individual activities, accomplishments, and emotional reactions (Ross & Wang, 2010). As Katherine Nelson and Robyn Fivush (2004) observe, such conversations about the personal past "provide children with information about how to be a 'self' in their culture."

Culture and Earliest Memories Psychologist Qi Wang (2013) found that the earliest memories of Chinese and Taiwanese adults tended to focus on routine activities that they shared with other members of their family or social group rather than individual events. Perhaps years from now, these children will remember practicing martial arts with their preschool friends.

Although much of the memory research covered in this chapter centers on explicit memory, psychologists and neuroscientists have become increasingly interested in implicit memory. As we'll see in a later section, there is growing evidence that implicit memory and explicit memory involve different brain regions (Eichenbaum, 2009; Thompson, 2005). Some memory theorists believe that implicit memory and explicit memory are two distinct memory systems (Kihlstrom & others, 2007; Tulving, 2002).

THE ORGANIZATION OF INFORMATION IN LONG-TERM MEMORY

Exactly how information is organized in long-term memory is not completely understood by memory researchers. Nonetheless, memory researchers know that information in long-term memory is *clustered* and *associated*.

Clustering means organizing items into related groups, or *clusters,* during recall. Before reading further, try the demonstration in Figure 6.6. Even though the words are presented in random order, you probably recalled groups of vehicles, fruits, and furniture. In other words, you organized the bits of information by clustering them into related categories.

chair	apple
boat	car
footstool	airplane
orange	lamp
pear	banana
peach	dresser
bed	sofa
bus	bookcase
train	truck
plum	table
grapes	strawberry
motorcycle	bicycle

FIGURE 6.6 Clustering Demonstration Study the words on this list for one minute. Then count backward by threes from 108 to 0. When you've completed that task, write down as many of the words from the list as you can remember.

semantic network model A model that describes units of information in long-term memory as being organized in a complex network of associations.

retrieval The process of recovering information stored in memory so that we are consciously aware of it.

retrieval cue A clue, prompt, or hint that helps trigger recall of a given piece of information stored in long-term memory.

retrieval cue failure The inability to recall long-term memories because of inadequate or missing retrieval cues.

Different bits and pieces of information in long-term memory are also logically linked, or associated. For example, what's the first word that comes to your mind in response to the word *red*? When we asked our students that same question, their top five responses were "blue," "apple," "color," "green," and "rose." Even if you didn't answer with one of the same associations, your response was based on some kind of logical association that you could explain if asked.

Memory researchers have developed several models to show how information is organized in long-term memory. One of the best-known models is called the **semantic network model** (Collins & Loftus, 1975). When one concept is activated in the semantic network, it can *spread* in any number of directions, *activating* other associations in the semantic network. For example, the word *red* might activate "blue" (another color), "apple," "fire truck" (objects that are red), or "alert" (as in the phrase, "red alert"). In turn, these associations can activate other concepts in the network.

The semantic network model is a useful way of conceptualizing how information is organized in long-term memory. However, keep in mind that it is just a metaphor, not a physical structure in the brain. Nevertheless, the fact that information *is* organized in long-term memory has important implications for the retrieval process, as you'll see in the next section.

❯ Test your understanding of **What Is Memory?** with *LEARNINGCurve*.

Retrieval

GETTING INFORMATION FROM LONG-TERM MEMORY

KEY THEME

Retrieval refers to the process of accessing and retrieving stored information in long-term memory.

KEY QUESTIONS

❯ What are retrieval cues and how do they work?

❯ What do tip-of-the-tongue experiences tell us about the nature of memory?

❯ How is retrieval tested, and what is the serial position effect?

So far, we've discussed some of the important factors that affect encoding and storing information in memory. In this section, we will consider factors that influence the retrieval process. Before you read any further, try the demonstration in Figure 6.7. After completing part (a), turn the page and try part (b). We'll refer to this demonstration

FIGURE 6.7(a)
Demonstration of Retrieval Cues

Source: Research from Bransford & Stein (1993).

Instructions: Spend 3 to 5 seconds reading each of the following sentences, and read through the list only once. As soon as you are finished, cover the list and write down as many of the sentences as you can remember (you need not write "can be used" each time). Please begin now.

A brick can be used as a doorstop.
A ladder can be used as a bookshelf.
A wine bottle can be used as a candleholder.
A pan can be used as a drum.
A fork can be used to comb hair.
A guitar can be used as a canoe paddle.
A leaf can be used as a bookmark.
An orange can be used to play catch.
A newspaper can be used to swat flies.
A T-shirt can be used as a coffee filter.
A sheet can be used as a sail.
A boat can be used as a shelter.
A bathtub can be used as a punch bowl.

A flashlight can be used to hold water.
A rock can be used as a paperweight.
A knife can be used to stir paint.
A pen can be used as an arrow.
A barrel can be used as a chair.
A rug can be used as a bedspread.
A CD can be used as a mirror.
A scissors can be used to cut grass.
A board can be used as a ruler.
A balloon can be used as a pillow.
A shoe can be used to pound nails.
A dime can be used as a screwdriver.
A lampshade can be used as a hat.

Now that you've recalled as many sentences as you can, turn to Figure 6.7(b) on page 240.

throughout this section, so please take a shot at it. After you've completed both parts of the demonstration, continue reading.

The Importance of Retrieval Cues

Retrieval refers to the process of accessing, or *retrieving,* stored information. There's a vast difference between what is stored in our long-term memory and what we can actually access. In many instances, our ability to retrieve stored memory hinges on having an appropriate retrieval cue. A **retrieval cue** is a clue, prompt, or hint that can help trigger recall of a stored memory. If your performance on the demonstration experiment in Figure 6.7 was like ours, the importance of retrieval cues should have been vividly illustrated.

Let's compare results. How did you do on the first part of the demonstration, in Figure 6.7(a)? After generating a number of answers, you probably reached a point at which you were unable to remember any more pairs. At that point, you experienced **retrieval cue failure,** which refers to the inability to recall long-term memories because of inadequate or missing retrieval cues.

You should have done much better on the demonstration in Figure 6.7(b). Why the improvement? In part (b) you were presented with retrieval cues that helped you access your stored memories.

This exercise demonstrates the difference between information that is *stored* in long-term memory versus the information that you can *access.* Many of the items on the list that you could not recall in part (a) were not forgotten. They were simply inaccessible—until you had a retrieval cue to help jog your memory. This exercise illustrates that many memories only *appear* to be forgotten. With the right retrieval cue, you can often access stored information that seemed to be completely unavailable.

COMMON RETRIEVAL GLITCHES
THE TIP-OF-THE-TONGUE EXPERIENCE

Quick—what is the name of the actor who stars in the *Ironman* film series? How about the four "houses" at Hogwarts in the Harry Potter books? If popular culture isn't your thing, how about this question: Who wrote the words to "The Star-Spangled Banner"?

Did any of these questions leave you feeling as if you knew the answer but just couldn't quite recall it? If so, you experienced a common, and frustrating, form of retrieval failure, called the **tip-of-the-tongue (TOT) experience.** The TOT experience is the inability to get at a bit of information that you're certain is stored in your memory. Subjectively, it feels as if the information is very close, but just out of reach—or on the tip of your tongue (Schwartz, 2002, 2011).

TOT experiences appear to be universal, and the "tongue" metaphor is used to describe the experience in many cultures (Brennen & others, 2007; Schwartz, 1999, 2002). On average, people have about one TOT experience per week, and TOT experiences with particular words tend to recur (D'Angelo & Humphreys, 2015). Although people of all ages experience such word-finding memory glitches, TOT experiences tend to be more common among older adults than younger adults (Farrell & Abrams, 2011).

When experiencing this sort of retrieval failure, people can almost always dredge up partial responses or related bits of information from their memory. About half the time, people can accurately identify the first letter of the target word and the number of syllables in it. They can also often produce words with similar meanings or sounds. While momentarily frustrating, about 90 percent of TOT experiences are eventually resolved, often within a few minutes.

Tip-of-the-tongue experiences illustrate that retrieving information is not an all-or-nothing process. Often, we remember bits and pieces of what we want

Reminders and Retrieval Cues Smartphone reminders can be potent retrieval cues, triggering recall of a bit of information held in long-term memory, like a pending appointment or the deadline for an assignment.

tip-of-the-tongue (TOT) experience
A memory phenomenon that involves the sensation of knowing that specific information is stored in long-term memory, but being temporarily unable to retrieve it.

Loretta Hostettler/Getty Images

A "Tip-of-the-Fingers" Experience
American Sign Language (ASL) users sometimes have a "tip-of-the-fingers" experience when they are sure they know a sign but can't retrieve it. During a TOT experience, people are often able to remember the first letter or sound of the word they're struggling to remember. Similarly, ASL users tend to remember the hand shape, which appears as the signer begins to make the sign, rather than later parts of the sign, like the hand movement. For words that are finger-spelled, ASL users were more likely to recall the first letters than later letters (Thompson & others, 2005).

Instructions: *Do not* look back at the list of sentences in Figure 6.7(a). Use the following list as retrieval cues, and now write as many sentences as you can. Be sure to keep track of how many you can write down.

flashlight	lampshade
sheet	shoe
rock	guitar
CD	scissors
boat	leaf
dime	brick
wine bottle	knife
board	newspaper
pen	pan
balloon	barrel
ladder	rug
T-shirt	orange
fork	bathtub

FIGURE 6.7(b) Demonstration of Retrieval Cues

Source: Research from Bransford & Stein (1993).

recall A test of long-term memory that involves retrieving information without the aid of retrieval cues; also called *free recall*.

cued recall A test of long-term memory that involves remembering an item of information in response to a retrieval cue.

recognition A test of long-term memory that involves identifying correct information out of several possible choices.

serial position effect The tendency to remember items at the beginning and end of a list better than items in the middle.

to remember. In many instances, information is stored in memory but is not accessible without the right retrieval cues. TOT experiences also emphasize that information stored in memory is *organized* and connected in relatively logical ways. As you mentally struggle to retrieve the blocked information, logically connected bits of information are frequently triggered. In many instances, these related tidbits of information act as additional retrieval cues, helping you access the desired memory.

TESTING RETRIEVAL

RECALL, CUED RECALL, AND RECOGNITION

The first part of the demonstration in Figure 6.7 illustrated the use of recall as a strategy to measure memory. **Recall,** also called *free recall,* involves producing information using no retrieval cues. This is the memory measure that's used on essay tests. Other than the essay questions themselves, an essay test provides no additional retrieval cues to help jog your memory.

The second part of the demonstration used a different memory measurement, called **cued recall.** Cued recall involves remembering an item of information in response to a retrieval cue. Fill-in-the-blank and matching questions are examples of cued-recall tests.

A third memory measurement is **recognition,** which involves identifying the correct information from several possible choices. Multiple-choice tests involve recognition as a measure of long-term memory. The multiple-choice question provides you with one correct answer and several wrong answers. If you have stored the information in your long-term memory, you should be able to recognize the correct answer.

Cued-recall and recognition tests are clearly to the student's advantage. Because these kinds of tests provide retrieval cues, the likelihood that you will be able to access stored information is increased.

THE SERIAL POSITION EFFECT

Notice that the first part of the demonstration in Figure 6.7 did not ask you to recall the sentences in any particular order. Instead, the demonstration tested *free recall*—you could recall the items in any order. Take another look at your answers to Figure 6.7(a). Do you notice any sort of pattern to the items that you did recall?

Most people are least likely to recall items from the middle of the list. This pattern of responses is called the **serial position effect,** which refers to the tendency to retrieve information more easily from the beginning and the end of a list rather than from the middle. There are two parts to the serial position effect. The tendency to recall the first items in a list is called the *primacy effect,* and the tendency to recall the final items in a list is called the *recency effect.*

The primacy effect is especially prominent when you have to engage in *serial recall,* that is, when you need to remember a list of items in their original order. Remembering speeches, telephone numbers, and directions are a few examples of serial recall.

The Encoding Specificity Principle

KEY THEME

According to the encoding specificity principle, re-creating the original learning conditions makes retrieval easier.

KEY QUESTIONS

› How can context and mood affect retrieval?

› What role does distinctiveness play in retrieval, and how accurate are flashbulb memories?

One of the best ways to increase access to information in memory is to re-create the original learning conditions. This simple idea is formally called the **encoding specificity principle** (Tulving, 1983). As a general rule, the more closely retrieval cues match the original learning conditions, the more likely it is that retrieval will occur.

For example, have you ever had trouble remembering some bit of information during a test but immediately recalled it as you entered the library where you normally study? When you intentionally try to remember some bit of information, such as the definition of a term, you often encode much more into memory than just that isolated bit of information. As you study in the library, at some level you're aware of all kinds of environmental cues. These cues might include the sights, sounds, and aromas within that particular situation. *The environmental cues in a particular context can become encoded as part of the unique memories you form while in that context.* These same environmental cues can act as retrieval cues to help you access the memories formed in that context.

This particular form of encoding specificity is called the context effect. The **context effect** is the tendency to remember information more easily when the retrieval occurs in the same setting in which you originally learned the information. Thus, the environmental cues in the library where you normally study act as additional retrieval cues that help jog your memory. Of course, it's too late to help your test score, but the memory was there.

A different form of encoding specificity is called **mood congruence**—the idea that a given mood tends to evoke memories that are consistent with that mood. In other words, a specific emotional state can act as a retrieval cue that evokes memories of events involving the same emotion. So, when you're in a positive mood, you're more likely to recall positive memories. When you're feeling blue, you're more likely to recall negative or unpleasant memories.

Flashbulb Memories

VIVID EVENTS, ACCURATE MEMORIES?

If you rummage around your own memories, you'll quickly discover that highly unusual, surprising, or even bizarre experiences are easier to retrieve from memory than are routine events (Geraci & Manzano, 2010). Such memories are said to be characterized by a high degree of *distinctiveness.* That is, the encoded information represents a unique, different, or unusual memory.

Various events can create vivid, distinctive, and long-lasting memories that are sometimes referred to as *flashbulb memories* (Brown & Kulik, 1982). Just as a camera flash captures the specific details of a scene, a **flashbulb memory** is thought to

Jamie Squire/Getty Images

A Demonstration of the Serial Position Effect: "With white stripes and . . . ummm . . ." Christina Aguilera infamously botched the middle of "The Star-Spangled Banner" when she performed at the 2011 Super Bowl. But without singing them, try to recite the words of "The Star-Spangled Banner." Most Americans correctly remember the words at the beginning and the end of "The Star-Spangled Banner" but—like Aguilera—have difficulty recalling the words and phrases in the middle. An embarrassed Aguilera later apologized, saying "I got so caught up in the moment of the song that I lost my place" (Chen, 2011). Even seasoned performers are not immune to the serial position effect!

encoding specificity principle The principle that when the conditions of information retrieval are similar to the conditions of information encoding, retrieval is more likely to be successful.

context effect The tendency to recover information more easily when the retrieval occurs in the same setting as the original learning of the information.

mood congruence An encoding specificity phenomenon in which a given mood tends to evoke memories that are consistent with that mood.

flashbulb memory The recall of very specific images or details surrounding a vivid, rare, or significant personal event; details may or may not be accurate.

Peggy Peattie/ZUMA Press/Newscom

Flashbulb Memories? Can you remember where you were when you learned of the death of Robin Williams? Of the bombing at the Boston Marathon? Supposedly, shocking national or international events can trigger highly accurate, long-term flashbulb memories. But meaningful personal events, such as your high school graduation or wedding day, are also said to produce vivid flashbulb memories.

> Flashbulb memories are not immune to forgetting, nor are they uncommonly consistent over time. Instead, exaggerated belief in memory's accuracy at long delays is what may have led to the conviction that flashbulb memories are more accurate than everyday memories.
>
> —*Jennifer Talarico and David Rubin (2003)*

MYTH ▶ SCIENCE

Is it true that "flashbulb memories," the vivid memories you form after an important, dramatic event, are no more accurate than other memories?

involve the recall of very specific details or images surrounding a significant, rare, or vivid event.

Do flashbulb memories literally capture specific details, like the details of a photograph, that are unaffected by the passage of time? Emotionally charged national events have provided a unique opportunity to study flashbulb memories. On September 12, 2001, a day after the World Trade Center attacks, psychologists Jennifer Talarico and David Rubin (2003, 2007) asked university students to complete questionnaires about how they learned about the terrorist attacks. For comparison, students also described an ordinary, everyday event that had recently occurred.

Over the next year, students were periodically asked to again describe their memories of the 9/11 attacks and of the ordinary event. When the researchers compared these accounts to the original, September 12 reports, they discovered that both the flashbulb and everyday memories had decayed over time, with an increasing number of inconsistent details. But when asked to rate the vividness and accuracy of both memories, only the ratings for the ordinary memory declined. Despite being just as inconsistent as the ordinary memories, the students perceived their flashbulb memories of 9/11 as being more accurate.

A similar pattern was observed in a 10-year, longitudinal study involving three thousand participants in seven different U.S. cities who described how they learned of the 9/11 attacks (Hirst & others, 2015). Within the first year after the attack, participants rapidly forgot details. Despite inconsistencies between original reports and memories of the event, participants' confidence in the accuracy of their memories remained high. Interestingly, proximity to the attacks was not associated with more accurate memories, but was associated with confidence levels. People who lived in New York at the time of the attacks had much higher levels of confidence in their memories, but their memories were no more accurate than those of non-New Yorkers.

Although flashbulb memories can seem incredibly vivid, they appear to function just as normal, everyday memories do (Talarico & Rubin, 2009; Hirst & others, 2015). We remember some details, forget some details, and think we remember some details. What does seem to distinguish flashbulb memories from ordinary memories is the high degree of confidence the person has in the accuracy of these memories. But clearly, confidence in a memory is *no* guarantee of accuracy. We'll come back to that important point shortly.

❯ Test your understanding of **Memory** with **LEARNING***Curve*.

Forgetting
WHEN RETRIEVAL FAILS

KEY THEME

Forgetting is the inability to retrieve information that was once available.

KEY QUESTIONS

❯ What discoveries were made by Hermann Ebbinghaus?

❯ How do encoding failure, interference, and decay contribute to forgetting, and how can prospective memory be improved?

❯ What is repression and why is the topic controversial?

Forgetting is so common that life is filled with reminders to safeguard against forgetting important information. Cars are equipped with beeping tones so you don't forget to fasten your seatbelt or turn off your headlights. Dentists thoughtfully send brightly colored postcards and call you the day before your scheduled appointment so that it doesn't slip your mind.

Although forgetting can be annoying, it does have adaptive value. Our minds would be cluttered with mountains of useless information if we remembered the name of every person we'd ever met, or every word of every conversation we'd ever had (Kuhl & others, 2007; Roediger & others, 2010).

Psychologists define **forgetting** as the inability to remember information that was previously available. Note that this definition does not refer to the "loss" or "absence" of once-remembered information. While it's tempting to think of forgetting as simply the gradual loss of information from long-term memory over time, you'll see that this intuitively compelling view of forgetting is much too simplistic. And although psychologists have identified several factors that are involved in forgetting, exactly how—and why—forgetting occurs is still being actively researched (Della Sala, 2010; Wixted, 2004).

forgetting The inability to recall information that was previously available.

Hermann Ebbinghaus
THE FORGETTING CURVE

German psychologist **Hermann Ebbinghaus** began the scientific study of forgetting in the 1870s. Because there was a seven-year gap between obtaining his doctorate and his first university teaching position, Ebbinghaus couldn't use university students for experimental subjects (Erdelyi, 2010; Fancher, 1996). So to study forgetting, Ebbinghaus had to rely on the only available research subject: himself.

Ebbinghaus's goal was to determine how much information was forgotten after different lengths of time. But he wanted to make sure that he was studying the memory and forgetting of completely new material, rather than information that had preexisting associations in his memory. To solve this problem, Ebbinghaus (1885) created new material to memorize: thousands of nonsense syllables. A *nonsense syllable* is a three-letter combination, made up of two consonants and a vowel, such as WIB or MEP. It almost sounds like a word, but it is meaningless.

Ebbinghaus carefully noted how many times he had to repeat a list of 13 nonsense syllables before he could recall the list perfectly. To give you a feeling for this task, here's a typical list:

DIS, ROH, LEZ, SUW, QOV, XAR, KUF, WEP, BIW, CUL, TIX, QAP, WEJ, ZOD

Once he had learned the nonsense syllables, Ebbinghaus tested his recall of them after varying amounts of time, ranging from 20 minutes to 31 days. He plotted his results in the now-famous Ebbinghaus *forgetting curve,* shown in Figure 6.8 on the next page.

The Ebbinghaus forgetting curve reveals two distinct patterns in the relationship between forgetting and the passage of time. First, much of what we forget is lost relatively soon after we originally learned it. How quickly we forget material depends on several factors, such as how well the material was encoded in the first place, how meaningful the material was, and how often it was rehearsed.

Hermann Ebbinghaus (1850–1909) After earning his Ph.D. in philosophy in 1873, Ebbinghaus worked as a private tutor for several years. It was during this time that he conducted his famous research on the memory of nonsense syllables. In 1885, he published his results in *Memory: A Contribution to Experimental Psychology.* Ebbinghaus observed, "Left to itself, every mental content gradually loses its capacity for being revived. Facts crammed at examination time soon vanish, if they were not sufficiently grounded by other study and later subjected to a sufficient review."

Bettmann/Corbis

DON'T YOU JUST HATE IT WHEN YOU WALK INTO A ROOM AND FORGET WHAT YOU CAME IN FOR?

SURGERY

Non Sequitur: © 2002 Wiley Miller
Dist. By Universal Press Syndicate

FIGURE 6.8 The Ebbinghaus Forgetting Curve Ebbinghaus's research demonstrated the basic pattern of forgetting: relatively rapid loss of some information, followed by stable memories of the remaining information.

Source: Data from Ebbinghaus (1885/1987).

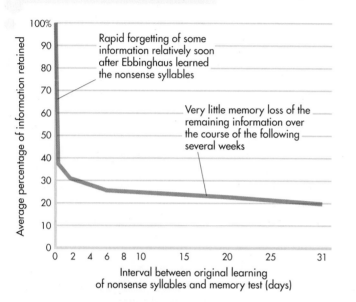

In general, if you learn something in a matter of minutes on just one occasion, most forgetting will occur very soon after the original learning—also in a matter of minutes. However, if you spend many sessions over days or weeks encoding new information into memory, the period of most rapid forgetting will be the first several weeks or months after such learning.

Second, the Ebbinghaus forgetting curve shows that the amount of forgetting eventually levels off. In fact, there's very little difference between how much Ebbinghaus forgot eight hours later and a month later. The information that is *not* quickly forgotten seems to be remarkably stable in memory over long periods of time.

Ebbinghaus's work with nonsense syllables and his forgetting curve have achieved legendary status in psychology. However, it turns out that the pattern of forgetting that Ebbinghaus identified is *not* universal. Under some conditions, memory for new information actually *improves* over time (Erdelyi, 2010; Roediger, 2008).

One well-documented way to increase memory for new information over time is to frequently practice retrieving the information. More specifically, repeatedly *testing* yourself for the new information is a reliable way to improve your memory for that information (Karpicke & Roediger, 2008). One explanation is that retrieving the information on a test reactivates and strengthens the original memory (Hardt & others, 2010). Another possibility is that you learn more effective retrieval cues as you repeatedly test yourself over the same material (Pyc & Rawson, 2010).

Why Do We Forget?

Ebbinghaus was a pioneer in the study of memory. His major contribution was to identify a basic pattern of forgetting: rapid forgetting of some information relatively soon after the original learning, followed by stability of the memories that remain. But what causes forgetting? Psychologists have identified several factors that contribute to forgetting, including encoding failure, decay, interference, and motivated forgetting.

FIGURE 6.9 Test for Memory of Details of a Common Object Which of these drawings is an accurate picture of a real penny?

ENCODING FAILURE
IT NEVER GOT TO LONG-TERM MEMORY

Without rummaging through your loose change, take a look at Figure 6.9. Circle the drawing that accurately depicts the face of a U.S. penny. Now, check your answer against a real penny. Were you correct?

When this task was presented to participants in one study, fewer than half of them picked the correct drawing (Nickerson & Adams, 1982). The explanation? Unless you're a coin collector, you've probably never looked carefully at a penny. Even though you may have handled thousands of pennies, chances are that you've encoded only the most superficial characteristics of a penny—its size, color, and texture—into your long-term memory.

In a follow-up study, William Marmie and Alice Healy (2004) allowed participants to study an unfamiliar coin for short periods of time, ranging from 15 seconds to 60 seconds. Even with only 15 seconds devoted to focusing on the coin's appearance, participants were better able to remember the details of the *unfamiliar* coin

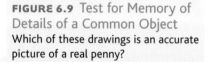

than the all-too-familiar penny. In effect, Marmie and Healy (2004) confirmed that lack of attention at the time of encoding was responsible for the failure to accurately remember the appearance of a penny.

As these simple demonstrations illustrate, one of the most common reasons for forgetting is called **encoding failure**—we never encoded the information into long-term memory in the first place. Encoding failure explains why you forget a person's name two minutes after being introduced to her: The information was momentarily present in your short-term memory, but was never encoded into long-term memory.

Encoding failure can also help explain everyday memory failures due to *absent-mindedness*. Absentmindedness occurs because you don't pay enough attention to a bit of information at the time when you should be encoding it, such as in which aisle you parked your car at the airport. Absentminded memory failures often occur because your attention is *divided*. Rather than focusing your full attention on what you're doing, you're also thinking about other matters (McVay & Kane, 2010).

Research has shown that divided attention at the time of encoding tends to result in poor memory for the information (Craik & others, 1996; Riby & others, 2008; Smallwood & others, 2007). Such absentminded memory lapses are especially common when you're performing habitual actions that don't require much thought, such as parking your car in a familiar parking lot or setting down your cell phone, keys, and wallet or purse when you come home. In some situations, divided attention might even contribute to déjà vu experiences, as we discuss in the In Focus box on the next page.

Absentmindedness is also implicated in another annoying memory problem—forgetting to do something in the future, such as returning a library book or taking a medication on schedule. Remembering to do something in the future is called **prospective memory.** In contrast to other types of memories, the crucial component of a prospective memory is *when* something needs to be remembered, rather than *what*.

Rather than encoding failure, prospective memory failures are due to *retrieval cue failure*—the inability to recall a memory because of missing or inadequate retrieval cues. For example, you forget to submit your credit card payment on time and incur a late fee. The problem with this sort of scenario is that there is no strong, distinctive retrieval cue embedded in the situation. This is why ovens are equipped with timers that buzz and why reminder programs are popular smart phone apps. Such strategies provide distinctive retrieval cues that will hopefully trigger those prospective memories at the appropriate moment. Table 6.1 lists additional suggestions to help minimize prospective memory failures.

DECAY THEORY
FADING WITH THE PASSAGE OF TIME

According to **decay theory,** we forget memories because we don't use them and they fade away over time as a matter of normal brain processes. The idea is that when a new memory is formed, it creates a *memory trace*—a distinct structural or chemical change in the brain. Over time, the normal metabolic processes of the brain are thought to erode the memory trace, especially if it is not "refreshed" by frequent rehearsal. The gradual fading of memories, then, would be similar to the fading of letters on billboards or newsprint exposed to environmental elements, such as sunlight.

Although decay theory makes sense intuitively, too much evidence contradicts it (Jonides & others, 2008). Look again at the Ebbinghaus forgetting curve on page 244. If memories simply faded over time, you would expect to see a steady decline in the amount of information remembered with the passage of time. Instead, once the information held in memory stabilizes, it changes very little over time. In other words, the *rate* of forgetting actually *decreases* over time (Wixted, 2004).

Why Elephants Never Forget...

Dan Reynolds/www.CartoonStock.com

encoding failure The inability to recall specific information because of insufficient encoding of the information for storage in long-term memory.

prospective memory Remembering to do something in the future.

decay theory The view that forgetting is due to normal metabolic processes that occur in the brain over time.

TABLE 6.1

Eight Suggestions for Avoiding Prospective Memory Failure

1	Be proactive! Create a reminder the instant you realize that you need to do something in the future.
2	Make reminder cues and make sure that they tell you *what* you are supposed to remember to do.
3	Make reminder cues **obvious** by posting them where you will definitely see them, such as on your mirror, refrigerator or coffeepot, front or back door, computer monitor, and so on.
4	Put a notepad or Post-it notes and a pencil in lots of convenient places (your dresser, your car, the kitchen counter, etc.).
5	For tasks you need to remember to do in the next few hours, buy small battery-operated kitchen timers.
6	Leave yourself a voice mail message with the reminder at home or at work.
7	Use the calendar reminder and follow-up features on your computer or use a free Internet reminder service (e.g., www.memotome.com).
8	Smart phone users, check out the many reminder apps that are available for iPhone, Android, or other models.

IN FOCUS

Déjà Vu Experiences: An Illusion of Memory?

The term *déjà vu* is French for "already seen." A **déjà vu experience** involves brief but intense feelings of familiarity in a new situation (Gerrans, 2012). Psychology's interest in déjà vu extends back to the late 1800s, when the famous American psychologist William James (1890, 1902) wrote about these experiences.

Déjà Vu Characteristics

Déjà vu experiences are common. Psychologist Alan Brown (2004) analyzed the results of more than 30 surveys and found that about two-thirds of individuals (68 percent) reported having had one or more déjà vu experiences in their life. Psychologists Arthur Funkhouser and Michael Schredl (2010) surveyed students at three German universities and found that over 95 percent had experienced a recent déjà vu incident. This confirms previous research indicating that young adults seem to experience déjà vu more frequently than other age groups.

Although typically triggered by a visual scene, déjà vu experiences can involve any of the senses. For example, blind people can also experience déjà vu (O'Connor & Moulin, 2006). Interestingly, there is a higher incidence of déjà vu experiences in people who are well educated, travel frequently, often watch movies, and regularly remember their dreams (Brown, 2003; Cleary, 2008). We'll come back to that last point shortly.

Because déjà vu experiences can be so compelling, people sometimes assume that the experience must have been an instance of clairvoyance, telepathy, a memory of a past life experience, or some other paranormal experience. But rather than paranormal explanations, contemporary psychologists believe that déjà vu can provide insights into basic memory processes (Brown & Marsh, 2010).

Explaining Déjà Vu

Let's suppose that you have an intense déjà vu experience as you enter Chicago's Shedd Aquarium. You *know* you've never visited the Shedd Aquarium before, so there is *no* memory source you can identify for the intense feeling of recognition.

Ariel Molvig The New Yorker Collection/
The Cartoon Bank

"Whoa. Déjà vu."

Psychologist Anne Cleary (2008) believes this sense of familiarity suddenly arises when features in the current situation trigger the sensation of matching features already contained in an old memory. You recognize some details of the memory as familiar, but can't pinpoint a *source* for that familiarity (Cleary & others, 2012). This is what memory researchers refer to as a disruption in **source memory** or **source monitoring**—your ability to remember the original details or features of a memory, including when, where, and how you acquired the information or had the experience. Interestingly, people who are more sensitive to similarities in their surroundings are also more likely to have déjà vu experiences (Sugimori & Kusumi, 2014).

Most likely, your déjà vu experience was due to *source amnesia:* You have *indirectly* experienced this scene or situation before, but you've forgotten the memory's source. Earlier we noted that people who are well educated, travel a lot, often watch movies, and remember their dreams are more prone to déjà vu experiences (Cleary, 2008). Each of these is a potential gold mine of memory retrieval clue fragments that can match elements of the current scene, triggering a sense of familiarity. Of course, had you immediately recalled the previous source from a little over two years ago—a magazine article about the aquarium—you probably wouldn't have had a déjà vu experience.

Another memory explanation for déjà vu involves a form of *encoding failure* called *inattentional blindness*, which we discussed in Chapter 4. According to the inattentional blindness explanation, déjà vu can be produced when you're not really paying attention to your surroundings (Brown, 2005; Brown & Marsh, 2010). So, suppose you're oblivious to your surroundings while chatting on your cell phone as you walk toward the Shedd Aquarium. As the call ends, you glance up at the entrance to the Shedd Aquarium and bang! *A déjà vu experience!* In this case, the feeling that you have been there before is due to the fact that you really *have* been there before—a split

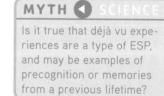

MYTH ◀ SCIENCE

Is it true that déjà vu experiences are a type of ESP, and may be examples of precognition or memories from a previous lifetime?

second ago. While talking on your cell phone, you were nonconsciously processing information about your surroundings. But when you ended the call and shifted your attention, suddenly your surroundings were consciously perceived as familiar.

A different explanation comes from the brain itself. Neurological evidence suggests that at least some instances of déjà vu are related to brain dysfunction (Bartolomei & others, 2012). In particular, it has long been known that déjà vu experiences can be triggered by temporal lobe disruptions (see Brázdil & others, 2012). For many people with epilepsy, the seizures often originate in the temporal lobe. In these people, a déjà vu experience sometimes occurs just prior to a seizure (Lytton, 2008). For most people, however, déjà vu experiences probably involve the common memory processes of *source amnesia* and *inattentional blindness*.

Beyond that point, many studies have shown that information can be remembered decades after it was originally learned, even though it has not been rehearsed or recalled since the original memory was formed (Custers & Ten Cate, 2011). As we discussed earlier, the ability to access memories is strongly influenced by the kinds of retrieval cues provided when memory is tested. If the memory trace simply decayed over time, the presentation of potent retrieval cues should have no effect on the retrieval of information or events experienced long ago—but it does!

So have contemporary memory researchers abandoned decay theory as an explanation of forgetting? Not completely. Although decay is not regarded as the primary cause of forgetting, many of today's memory researchers believe that it contributes to forgetting (Altmann, 2009; Portrat & others, 2008).

INTERFERENCE THEORY
MEMORIES INTERFERING WITH MEMORIES

According to the **interference theory** of forgetting, forgetting is caused by one memory competing with or replacing another memory. The most critical factor is the similarity of the information. The more similar the information is in two memories, the more likely it is that interference will be produced.

There are two basic types of interference. **Retroactive interference** is backward-acting memory interference. It occurs when a *new* memory (the combination for the new lock you just bought for your bicycle) interferes with remembering an *old* memory (the combination for the lock you've been using at the gym).

Proactive interference is forward-acting memory interference. It occurs when an *old* memory (your previous zip code) interferes with remembering a *new* memory (your new zip code). A rather embarrassing example of proactive interference occurs when someone uses the name of a previous partner in referring to a current partner. Such spontaneous memory glitches can occur in the rapid-fire verbal exchange of a heated argument or in the thralls of passion (hopefully not both).

MOTIVATED FORGETTING
FORGETTING UNPLEASANT MEMORIES

Motivated forgetting refers to the idea that we forget because we are motivated to forget, usually because a memory is unpleasant or disturbing. One form of motivated forgetting, called **suppression,** involves the deliberate, conscious effort to forget information. For example, after seeing a disturbing report of a horrendous crime or massacre on the evening news, you consciously avoid thinking about it, turning your attention to other matters. According to some researchers, over time and with repeated effort, pushing an unwanted memory out of awareness may make the memory less accessible (M. C. Anderson & Levy, 2009; Meier & others, 2011).

Another form of motivated forgetting is fundamentally different and much more controversial. **Repression** can be defined as motivated forgetting that occurs unconsciously (Langnickel & Markowitsch, 2006). With repression, all memory of a distressing event or experience is blocked from conscious awareness.

Taxi/Getty Images

Motivated Forgetting Car accidents, serious illnesses, surgeries, and other traumatic events are painful to relive in memory. Some researchers believe that by voluntarily directing our attention away from memories of such traumatic events, we can eventually *suppress* our memory of the experiences, making them difficult or impossible to consciously retrieve (Anderson & others, 2011).

déjà vu experience A memory illusion characterized by brief but intense feelings of familiarity in a situation that has never been experienced before.

source memory or source monitoring Memory for when, where, and how a particular experience or piece of information was acquired.

interference theory The theory that forgetting is caused by one memory competing with or replacing another.

retroactive interference Forgetting in which a new memory interferes with remembering an old memory; backward-acting memory interference.

proactive interference Forgetting in which an old memory interferes with remembering a new memory; forward-acting memory interference.

suppression Motivated forgetting that occurs consciously; a deliberate attempt to not think about and remember specific information.

repression Motivated forgetting that occurs unconsciously; a memory that is blocked and unavailable to consciousness.

As we'll discuss in greater detail in Chapters 10 (Personality) and 14 (Therapies), the idea of repression is a cornerstone of *psychoanalysis*, Sigmund Freud's famous theory of personality and psychotherapy (Knafo, 2009). Freud (1904) believed that psychologically threatening emotions, feelings, conflicts, and urges, especially those that originated in early childhood, become repressed. Even though they are blocked and unavailable to consciousness, the repressed conflicts continue to unconsciously influence the person's behavior, thoughts, and personality, often in maladaptive or unhealthy ways.

Among clinical psychologists who work with psychologically troubled people, the notion that behavior can be influenced by repressed memories is accepted, but not as widely as it once was (Gleaves & others, 2004; Patihis & others, 2014). Among the general public, many people believe that we are capable of repressing memories of unpleasant events. However, trying to scientifically confirm and study the influence of memories that a person does not remember is tricky, if not impossible.

One obvious problem is determining whether a memory has been "repressed" or simply forgotten. For example, several studies have found that people are better able to remember positive life experiences than negative life experiences (Lambert & others, 2010). Is that because unhappy experiences have been "repressed"? Or is it simply that people are less likely to think about, talk about, dwell on, or rehearse unhappy memories?

Among psychologists, repression is an extremely controversial topic (see Erdelyi, 2006a, 2006b). At one extreme are those who believe that true repression *never* occurs (Hayne & others, 2006). At the other extreme are those who are convinced that repressed memories are at the root of many psychological problems, particularly repressed memories of childhood sexual abuse (Gleaves & others, 2004). This latter contention gave rise to a form of psychotherapy involving the recovery of repressed memories. Later in the chapter, we'll explore this controversy in the Critical Thinking box "The Memory Wars: Recovered or False Memories?"

Imperfect Memories
ERRORS, DISTORTIONS, AND FALSE MEMORIES

KEY THEME

Memories can be easily distorted so that they contain inaccuracies. Confidence in a memory is no guarantee that the memory is accurate.

KEY QUESTIONS

> What is the misinformation effect?

> What is source confusion, and how can it distort memories?

> What are schemas and scripts, and how can they contribute to memory distortions?

Although people usually remember the general gist of what they experience, the fallibility of human memory is disturbing. Human memory does *not* function like a camera or digital recorder that captures a perfect copy of visual or auditory information (Schacter & Loftus, 2013). Instead, memory details can change over time. Without your awareness, details can be added, subtracted, exaggerated, or downplayed. In fact, each of us has the potential to confidently and vividly remember the details of some event—and be completely *wrong*. Confidence in a memory is no guarantee that the memory is accurate.

How do errors and distortions creep into memories? A new memory is not simply recorded, but *actively constructed*. To form a new memory, you actively organize and encode different types of information—visual, auditory, tactile, and so on. When you later attempt to retrieve those details, you actively *reconstruct*, or rebuild, the details of the memory (Bartlett, 1932; Stark & others, 2010). In the process of actively constructing or reconstructing a memory, various factors can contribute to errors and distortions in what you remember—or, more accurately, what you *think* you remember.

At the forefront of research on memory distortions is **Elizabeth Loftus,** whose story we told in the Prologue. Loftus is one of the most widely recognized authorities on eyewitness memory and the different ways it can go awry. She has not only conducted extensive research on this topic, but also testified as an expert witness in many high-profile cases (see Loftus, 2007, 2011).

Courtesy Elizabeth Loftus

Psychological studies have shown that it is virtually impossible to tell the difference between a real memory and one that is a product of imagination or some other process. Our job as researchers in this area is to understand how it is that pieces of experience are combined to produce what we experience as "memory."

—Elizabeth Loftus (2002)

MYTH ◀ SCIENCE

Is it true that memory is like a video recorder—it preserves a perfect record of your experience?

THE MISINFORMATION EFFECT
THE INFLUENCE OF POST-EVENT INFORMATION ON MISREMEMBERING

Let's start by considering a Loftus study that has become a classic piece of research. Loftus and co-researcher John C. Palmer (1974) had subjects watch a film of an automobile accident, write a description of what they saw, and then answer a series of questions. There was one critical question in the series: "About how fast were the cars going when they contacted each other?" Different subjects were given different versions of that question. For some subjects, the word *contacted* was replaced with *hit*. Other subjects were given the words *bumped, collided,* or *smashed*.

Depending on the specific word used in the question, subjects gave very different speed estimates. As shown in Table 6.2, the subjects who gave the highest speed estimates got *smashed* (so to speak). Clearly, how a question is worded can influence what is remembered.

A week after seeing the film, the subjects were asked another series of questions. This time, the critical question was "Did you see any broken glass?" Although *no* broken glass was shown in the film, the majority of the subjects whose question had used the word *smashed* a week earlier said "yes." Notice what happened: Following the initial memory (the film of the automobile accident), new information (the word *smashed*) distorted the reconstruction of the memory (remembering broken glass that wasn't really there).

The use of suggestive questions is but one example of how the information a person gets *after* an event can change what the person later remembers about the event. Literally hundreds of studies have demonstrated the different ways that the **misinformation effect** can be produced (Loftus, 1996, 2005). Basically, the research procedure involves three steps. First, participants are exposed to a simulated event, such as an automobile accident or a crime. Next, after a delay, half of the participants receive misinformation, while the other half receive no misinformation. In the final step, all of the participants try to remember the details of the original event.

In study after study, Loftus as well as other researchers have confirmed that post-event exposure to misinformation can distort the recollection of the original event by eyewitnesses (see Davis & Loftus, 2007; Frenda & others, 2011). People have recalled stop signs as yield signs, normal headlights as broken, barns along empty country roads, a blue vehicle as being white, and Minnie Mouse when they really saw Mickey Mouse! Whether it is in the form of suggestive questions, misinformation, or other exposure to conflicting details, such post-event experiences can distort eyewitness memories (Brewer & Wells, 2011).

AP Photo/Chuck Burton

SOURCE CONFUSION
MISREMEMBERING THE SOURCE OF A MEMORY

Have you ever confidently remembered hearing something on television only to discover that it was really a friend who told you the information? Or mistakenly remembered doing something that you actually only *imagined* doing? Or confidently remembered that an event happened at one time and place only to learn later that it really happened at a *different* time and place?

If so, you can blame your faulty memories on a phenomenon called source confusion. **Source confusion** arises when the true source of the memory is forgotten or when a memory is attributed to the wrong source (Johnson & others, 2012; Lindsay, 2008). The notion of source confusion can help explain the misinformation

---

TABLE 6.2

Estimated Speeds

Word Used In Question	Average Speed Estimate
smashed	41 m.p.h.
collided	39 m.p.h.
bumped	38 m.p.h.
hit	34 m.p.h.
contacted	32 m.p.h.

SOURCE: Research from Loftus & Palmer (1974).

misinformation effect A memory-distortion phenomenon in which your existing memories can be altered if you are exposed to misleading information.

source confusion A memory distortion that occurs when the true source of the memory is forgotten.

MYTH ◀ SCIENCE

Is it true that eyewitness testimony is the most reliable form of courtroom evidence?

Eyewitness Misidentification: Convicting the Innocent Ronald Cotton spent more than ten years serving a life-plus-54-years sentence for raping a college student, Jennifer Thompson-Cannino, in her North Carolina apartment. When she first saw Cotton in a police line-up, Thompson-Cannino was not certain that he was the rapist. But by the time of the trial, after repeated questioning by the police, Thompson-Cannino was "absolutely sure" that Cotton was the rapist (Garrett, 2011). So certain was she, that when shown the *actual* perpetrator, who had confessed the crime to another inmate, she said she had never seen him before in her life. Ten years after Cotton's conviction, he was freed when DNA evidence conclusively proved that he had not committed the crime and identified the other prisoner as the rapist. Today, Cotton and Thompson-Cannino are close friends and fellow activists, writing a memoir together and speaking widely to educate law enforcement personnel and others about eyewitness testimony and wrongful convictions (Thompson-Cannino & Cotton, 2009). Scores of studies have shown that eyewitness misidentification is the leading cause of wrongful conviction (see Loftus, 2013; Smalarz & Wells, 2015; The Innocence Project, 2015).

Stuart Franklin/Magnum Photos

Stuart Franklin/Magnum Photos and courtesy of Elizabeth Loftus and Dario Sacchi

Which Is the Real Photo? The photograph of an unknown young man bravely defying oncoming tanks in an antigovernment protest in China's Tiananmen Square has become an iconic image of individual courage and the global struggle for human rights. But after people who remembered the original image correctly were shown the doctored image on the right, their memories changed to incorporate the crowds of onlookers in the fake photo (Sacchi & others, 2007).

In essence, all memory is false to some degree. Memory is inherently a reconstructive process, whereby we piece together the past to form a coherent narrative that becomes our autobiography. In the process of reconstructing the past, we color and shape our life's experiences based on what we know about the world.

—*Daniel M. Bernstein &*
Elizabeth F. Loftus, 2009

false memory A distorted or fabricated recollection of something that did not actually occur.

schema (SKEE-muh) An organized cluster of information about a particular topic.

script A schema for the typical sequence of an everyday event.

effect: False details provided *after* the event become confused with the details of the original memory. For example, in one classic study, participants viewed images showing the use of a screwdriver in a burglary (Loftus & others, 1989). Later, they read a written account of the break-in, but this account featured a hammer instead of a screwdriver. When tested for their memory of the images, 60 percent said that a hammer (the post-event information), rather than a screwdriver (the original information), had been used in the burglary. And they were just as confident of their *false* memories as they were when recalling their *accurate* memories of other details of the original event.

More recently, photographs have been used to demonstrate how false details presented after an original event can become confused with the authentic details of the original memory (Henkel, 2011; Strange & others, 2011). For example, after participants in a study were shown digitally doctored photos of famous news events, such as the violent 1989 Tiananmen Square protests in Beijing, China, details from the *fake* photos were incorporated into participants' original memories of the actual news event (Sacchi & others, 2007).

Elizabeth's story in the Prologue also demonstrated how confusion about the source of a memory can give rise to an extremely vivid, but inaccurate, recollection. Vivid and accurate memories of her uncle's home, such as the smell of the pine trees and the feel of the lake water, became blended with Elizabeth's fantasy of finding her mother's body. The result was a **false memory,** which is a distorted or fabricated recollection of something that did not actually happen. Nonetheless, the false memory subjectively feels authentic and is often accompanied by all the emotional impact of a real memory.

SCHEMAS, SCRIPTS, AND MEMORY DISTORTIONS
THE INFLUENCE OF EXISTING KNOWLEDGE ON WHAT IS REMEMBERED

Given that information presented after a memory is formed can change the contents of that memory, let's consider the opposite effect: Can the knowledge you had *before* an event occurred influence your later memory of the event? If so, how?

Since you were a child, you have been actively forming mental representations called **schemas**—organized clusters of knowledge and information about particular topics. The topic can be almost anything—an object (e.g., a wind chime), a setting (e.g., a movie theater), or a concept (e.g., freedom). One kind of schema, called a **script,** involves the typical sequence of actions and behaviors at a common event, such as eating in a restaurant or taking a plane trip.

Schemas are useful in organizing and forming new memories. Using the schemas you already have stored in long-term memory allows you to quickly integrate new experiences into your knowledge base. For example, consider your schema for "phone." No longer just a utilitarian communication device, phones can be used to play games, take photographs, and play music or videos. As the capabilities of phones expanded, your schema has changed to incorporate these new attributes. Thus, your schema for "phone" includes smart phones that can send email, cruise the Internet, and provide directions. As new applications become available, you can quickly integrate those functions into your existing schema for "phone."

Although useful, schemas can also contribute to memory distortions. In the classic "psychology professor's office" study described in the photo caption on the right, students erroneously remembered objects that were not actually present but were consistent with their schema of a professor's office (Brewer & Treyens, 1981). The schemas we have developed can promote memory errors by prompting us to fill in missing details with schema-consistent information.

But what if a situation contains elements that are *inconsistent* with our schemas or scripts for that situation? Are inconsistent items more likely to stand out in our minds and be better remembered? In a word, yes. Numerous studies have demonstrated that items that are inconsistent with our expectations tend to be better recalled and recognized than items that are consistent with our expectations (see Kleider & others, 2008; Lampinen & others, 2001).

For example, University of Arkansas psychologist James Lampinen and his colleagues (2000) had participants listen to a story about a guy named Jack who performed some everyday activities, like washing his car and taking his dog to the veterinarian for shots. In each scene, Jack performed some actions that would have been consistent with the script (e.g., filling a bucket with soapy water, filling out forms at the vet's office) and some behaviors that were *not* part of a typical script for the activity (e.g., spraying the neighbor's kid with the hose, flirting with the vet's receptionist). When tested for details of the story, participants were more likely to recognize and remember the atypical actions than the consistent actions.

Much like the subjects in the professor's office study, participants in Lampinen's study also experienced compelling *false memories*. Almost always, the false memories were for actions that would have been consistent with the script—if they had actually happened in the story. For example, some participants vividly remembered that Jack rinsed the car off with a hose or that he put a leash on the dog before taking him to the vet's office. Neither of those actions occurred in the story.

Later research by psychologists Brent Strickland and Frank Keil (2011) showed that pre-existing schemas can distort memories for events within *seconds* of viewing them. Study participants watched videos showing athletes kicking, throwing, or hitting a ball. In some videos, the actual point of contact was *not* shown, just the ball flying into the distance. Nevertheless, within seconds of viewing the video, participants believed that they had seen the causal action that had only been implied by the film. Essentially, they "filled in" the missing moment of contact because, based on prior experience, that interpretation simply made sense.

Forming False Memories
FROM THE PLAUSIBLE TO THE IMPOSSIBLE

KEY THEME

A variety of techniques can create false memories for events that never happened.

KEY QUESTIONS

> What is the *lost-in-the-mall* technique, and how does it produce false memories?

> What is imagination inflation, and how has it been demonstrated?

> What factors contribute to the formation of false memories?

Up to this point, we've talked about how misinformation, source confusion, and the mental schemas and scripts we've developed can change or add details to a memory that already exists. However, memory researchers have gone beyond

False Memories of a Psychology Professor's Office After briefly waiting in the psychology professor's office shown above, participants were taken to another room and asked to recall details of the office—the real purpose of the study. Many participants falsely remembered objects that were not actually in the office, such as books, a filing cabinet, a telephone, a lamp, pens, pencils, and a coffee cup. Why? The details that the participants erroneously remembered were all items that would be consistent with a typical professor's office (Brewer & Treyens, 1981). Schemas can cause memory errors by prompting us to fill in missing details with schema-consistent information (Kleider & others, 2008).

LaunchPad

wake

| This word was presented in the original list. | This word is new (not presented in the original list). |

Test the effects of schemas on your memory with **Concept Practice: How Reliable Is Your Memory?**

Worth Publishers

"And here I am at two years of age. Remember? Mom? Pop? No? Or how about this one. My first day of school. Anyone?"

How easily can memories be manipulated? To find out, watch **Video Activity: Creating False Memories: A Laboratory Study.**

changing a few details here and there. Since the mid-1990s, an impressive body of research has accumulated showing how false memories can be created for events that *never* happened (Frenda & others, 2011; Loftus & Cahill, 2007). We'll begin with another Loftus study that has become famous—the *lost-in-the-mall* study.

IMAGINATION INFLATION
REMEMBERING BEING LOST IN THE MALL

In a classic experiment, Loftus and Jacqueline Pickrell (1995) gave each of 24 participants written descriptions of four childhood events that had been provided by a parent or other older relative. Three of the events had really happened, but the fourth was a *pseudoevent*—a false story about the participant getting lost in a shopping mall. Here's the gist of the story: At about the age of 5 or 6, the person got lost for an extended period of time in a shopping mall, became very upset and cried, was rescued by an elderly person, and ultimately was reunited with the family. (Family members verified that the participant had never actually been lost in a shopping mall or department store as a child.)

After reading the four event descriptions, the participants wrote down as many details as they could remember about each event. About two weeks later, participants were interviewed and asked to recall as many details as they could about each of the four events. Approximately one to two weeks after that, participants were interviewed a second time and asked once again what they could remember about the four events.

By the final interview, 6 of the 24 participants had created either full or partial memories of being lost in the shopping mall. How entrenched were the false memories for those who experienced them? Even after being debriefed at the end of the study, some of the participants continued to struggle with the vividness of the false memory. "I totally remember walking around in those dressing rooms and my mom not being in the section she said she'd be in," one participant said (Loftus & Pickrell, 1995).

The research strategy of using information from family members to help create or induce false memories of childhood experiences has been dubbed the *lost-in-the-mall technique* (Loftus, 2003). By having participants remember real events along with imagining pseudoevents, researchers have created false memories for a wide variety of events. For example, participants have been led to believe that as a child they had been saved by a lifeguard from nearly drowning (Heaps & Nash, 2001). Or that they had knocked over a punch bowl on the bride's parents at a wedding reception (Hyman & Pentland, 1996).

Being lost in a mall or knocking over a punchbowl are relatively mundane events. Could false memories of more serious events, such as committing and getting arrested for a crime, also be created? Psychologists Julia Shaw and Stephen Porter (2015) showed that they could—and relatively easily. Just three 40-minute sessions of suggestive questioning were sufficient to convince fully 70 percent of participants that they had committed a serious crime—assault, assault with a weapon, or theft—during adolescence. The memories themselves were vivid and rich in complex detail.

Such findings have an important, real-world application (Howe & Knott, 2015). The Innocence Project (2015), a nonprofit group that investigates false convictions, found that false confessions are a common problem. More than 25 percent of the time when DNA evidence showed someone had been wrongly convicted, false confessions were involved. Many of these confessions had been obtained through interrogations that incorporated strategies that are now known to produce false memories (Shaw & Porter, 2015).

Clearly, then, research has demonstrated that people can develop beliefs and memories for events that definitely did not happen to them. One key factor in the creation of false memories is the power of imagination. Put simply, *imagining the past as different from what it was can change the way you remember it.* Several studies have shown that vividly imagining an event markedly increases confidence that the event actually

Richard Hutchings/PhotoEdit

occurred in childhood, an effect called **imagination inflation** (Garry & Polaschek, 2000; Thomas & others, 2003).

How does imagining an event—even one that never took place—help create a memory that is so subjectively compelling? Several factors seem to be involved. First, repeatedly imagining an event makes the event seem increasingly *familiar*. People then misinterpret the sense of familiarity as an indication that the event really happened (Sharman & others, 2004).

Second, coupled with the sense of increased familiarity, people experience *source confusion*. That is, subtle confusion can occur as to whether a retrieved "memory" has a real event—or an imagined event—as its source. Over time, people may misattribute their memory of *imagining* the pseudoevent as being a memory of the *actual* event.

Third, the more vivid and detailed the imaginative experience, the more likely it is that people will confuse the imagined event with a real occurrence (Thomas & others, 2003). Vivid sensory and perceptual details can make the imagined events feel more like real events.

Simple manipulations, such as suggestions and imagination exercises, can increase the incidence and realism of false memories. So can vivid memory cues and family photos. Table 6.3 summarizes factors known to contribute to the formation of false memories.

TABLE 6.3

Factors Contributing to False Memories

Factor	Description
Misinformation effect	When erroneous information received after an event leads to distorted or false memories of the event
Source	Forgetting or misremembering the true source of a memory
Schema distortion	False or distorted memories caused by the tendency to fill in missing memory details with information that is consistent with existing knowledge about a topic
Imagination inflation	Unfounded confidence in a false or distorted memory caused by vividly imagining the pseudoevent
False familiarity	Increased feelings of familiarity due to repeatedly imagining an event
Blending fact and fiction	Using vivid, authentic details to add to the legitimacy and believability of a pseudoevent
Suggestion	Hypnosis, guided imagery, or other highly suggestive techniques that can inadvertently or intentionally create vivid false memories

Think Like a SCIENTIST

If you saw a crime take place, would you be a good witness? Go to LaunchPad: Resources to **Think Like a Scientist** about **Eyewitness Testimony**.

 LaunchPad

imagination inflation A memory phenomenon in which vividly imagining an event markedly increases confidence that the event actually occurred.

CRITICAL THINKING

The Memory Wars: Recovered or False Memories?

Repressed memory therapy, recovery therapy, recovered memory therapy, trauma therapy—these are some of the names of a therapy introduced in the 1990s and embraced by many psycho-therapists, counselors, social workers, and other mental health workers. Proponents of the therapy claimed they had identified the root cause of a wide assortment of psychological problems: repressed memories of sexual abuse that had occurred during childhood.

This therapeutic approach assumed that incidents of sexual and physical abuse experienced in childhood, especially when perpetrated by a trusted caregiver, were so psychologically threatening that the victims repressed all memories of the experience (Gleaves & others, 2004; McNally & Geraerts, 2009). Despite being repressed, these unconscious memories of unspeakable traumas continued to cause psychological and physical problems, ranging from low self-esteem to eating disorders, substance abuse, and major depressive disorder.

The goal of repressed memory therapy was to help adult incest survivors "recover" their repressed memories of childhood sexual abuse. Reliving these painful experiences would help them begin "the healing process" of working through their anger and other intense emotions (Bass & Davis, 1994). Survivors were encouraged to confront their abusers and, if necessary, break all ties with their abusive families.

The Controversy: The "Recovery" Methods

The validity of the memories recovered in therapy became the center of a highly charged public controversy that has been dubbed "the memory wars" (Loftus, 2004; Patihis & others, 2014). A key issue was the methods used to help people unblock, or recover, repressed memories. Some recovered memory therapists used hypnosis, dream analysis, guided imagery, intensive group therapy, and other highly suggestive techniques to recover the long-repressed memories (Thayer & Lynn, 2006).

Many patients supposedly recovered memories of repeated incidents of physical and sexual abuse, sometimes beginning in early infancy, ongoing for years, and involving multiple victimizers. Even more disturbing, some patients recovered vivid memories of years of alleged ritual satanic abuse involving secret cults practicing cannibalism, torture, and ritual murder (Loftus & Davis, 2006; Sakheim & Devine, 1992).

In more than twenty-five years of doing several hundred studies involving perhaps 20,000 people, we had distorted a significant portion of the subjects' memories. And the mechanism by which we can convince people they were lost, frightened, and crying in a mall is not so different than the mechanism by which therapists might unwittingly encourage memories of sexual abuse.

—*Elizabeth Loftus (2003)*

The Critical Issue: Recovered or False Memories?

Are traumatic memories likely to be repressed? It is well established that in documented cases of trauma, most survivors are troubled by the *opposite* problem—they cannot forget their traumatic memories (Berntsen & Rubin, 2014). Rather than being unable to remember the experience, trauma survivors suffer from recurring flashbacks, intrusive thoughts and memories of the trauma, and nightmares. This pattern is a key symptom of

The ease with which false memories can be implanted is more than just an academic question. It also has some powerful real-world implications. For example, a recent study by Steven Frenda and his colleagues (2013) showed just how easily people's memories of actual political events could be changed. The online magazine *Slate* invited readers to participate in a survey about political events (Saletan, 2010). As part of the survey, five photographs were shown. In each set of five photos, one had been doctored so that it showed an event that had never actually occurred. For example, one phony photo showed Barack Obama shaking hands with Iran president Mahmoud Ahmadinejad. (In reality, Obama has never been in the same room with Ahmadinejad.)

Over 5,000 *Slate* readers participated in the study. When asked how they felt about each of the five political events depicted, fully 50% reported that they remembered the false event happening—and more than half of this group said that they remembered seeing it on the news! As the researchers wrote, "*Slate* readers became participants in the largest false memory experiment ever conducted"—one which demonstrated how easy it is to create false memories for events that never happened.

posttraumatic stress disorder (PTSD), which we'll discuss in Chapter 13.

While it is relatively common for a person to be unable to remember *some* of the specific details of a traumatic event or to be troubled by memory problems after the traumatic event, such memory problems do *not* typically include difficulty in remembering the trauma itself (McNally, 2007a). Memory researchers agree that a person might experience amnesia for a single traumatic incident but are skeptical that anyone could repress *all* memories of *repeated* incidents of abuse, especially when those incidents occurred over a period of several years (McNally & Geraerts, 2009).

Critics of repressed memory therapy contend that many of the supposedly "recovered" memories are actually *false memories* that were produced by the well-intentioned but misguided use of suggestive therapeutic techniques (Davis & Loftus, 2009). Memory experts object to the use of hypnosis and other highly suggestive techniques to recover repressed memories (Gerrie & others, 2004; McNally & Geraerts, 2009). Understandably so. As you've seen in this chapter, compelling research shows the ease with which misinformation, suggestion, and imagination can create vivid—but completely *false*—memories.

> **MYTH ◀ SCIENCE**
>
> Is it true that it's common to completely repress memories of traumatic events, but that such events can be accurately remembered under hypnosis?

What Conclusions Can Be Drawn?

After years of debate, some areas of consensus have emerged (Allen, 2005; Colangelo, 2007). First, there is no question that physical and sexual abuse in childhood is a serious social problem that also contributes to psychological problems in adulthood (Hillberg & others, 2011).

Second, some psychologists contend it is *possible* for memories of childhood abuse to be completely forgotten, only to surface many years later in adulthood (Colangelo, 2007). Nevertheless, it's clear that repressed memories that have been recovered in psychotherapy need to be regarded with caution (Piper & others, 2008).

Third, the details of memories can be distorted with disturbing ease (Herndon & others, 2014). Consequently, the use of highly suggestive techniques to recover memories of abuse raises serious concerns about the accuracy of such memories. As we have noted repeatedly in this chapter, a person's confidence in a memory is no guarantee that the memory is indeed accurate. False or fabricated memories can seem just as detailed, vivid, and real as accurate ones (Gerrie & others, 2004; Lampinen & others, 2005).

Fourth, keep in mind that every act of remembering involves reconstructing a memory. Remembering an experience is not like replaying a movie captured with your cell phone. Memories can change over time. Without our awareness, memories can grow and evolve, sometimes in unexpected ways.

Finally, psychologists and other therapists have become more aware of the possibility of inadvertently creating false memories in therapy (Davis & Loftus, 2009). Guidelines have been developed to help mental health professionals avoid unintentionally creating false memories in clients (American Psychological Association Working Group, 1998; Colangelo, 2007).

CRITICAL THINKING QUESTIONS

- Why is it difficult to determine the accuracy of a "memory" that is recovered in therapy?

- How could the phenomenon of source confusion be used to explain the production of false memories?

Can the same be true of memories for personal, rather than political, history? We explore this question in the Critical Thinking box on a highly charged controversy that has been dubbed "the memory wars."

However, we don't want to leave you with the impression that *all* memories are highly unreliable. In reality, most memories tend to be quite accurate for the gist of what occurred. When memory distortions occur spontaneously in everyday life, they usually involve limited bits of information.

Still, the surprising ease with which memory details can become distorted is unnerving. Distorted memories can ring true and feel just as real as accurate memories (Bernstein & Loftus, 2009; Clifasefi & others, 2007). In the chapter Prologue, you saw how easily Elizabeth Loftus created a false memory. You also saw how quickly she became convinced of the false memory's authenticity and the strong emotional impact it had on her. Rather than being set in stone, human memories are more like clay: They can change shape with just a little bit of pressure.

> **MYTH ◀ SCIENCE**
>
> Is it true that once formed, memories can't change?

❯ Test your understanding of **Forgetting** and **Imperfect Memories** with *LEARNINGCurve*.

memory trace or engram The hypothetical brain changes associated with a particular stored memory.

The Search for the Biological Basis of Memory

KEY THEME

Early researchers believed that memory was associated with physical changes in the brain, but these changes were discovered only in the past few decades.

KEY QUESTIONS

> How are memories both localized and distributed in the brain?

> How do neurons change when a memory is formed?

Does the name *Ivan Pavlov* ring a bell? We hope so. As you should recall from Chapter 5, Pavlov was the Russian physiologist who classically conditioned dogs to salivate to the sound of a bell and other neutral stimuli. Without question, learning and memory are intimately connected. Learning an adaptive response depends on our ability to form new memories in which we associate environmental stimuli, behaviors, and consequences.

Pavlov (1927) believed that the memory involved in learning a classically conditioned response would ultimately be explained as a matter of changes in the brain. However, Pavlov only speculated about the kinds of brain changes that would produce the memories needed for classical conditioning to occur. Other researchers would take up the search for the physical changes associated with learning and memory. In this section, we look at some of the key discoveries that have been made in trying to understand the biological basis of memory.

The Search for the Elusive Memory Trace

An American physiological psychologist named **Karl Lashley** set out to find evidence for Pavlov's speculations. In the 1920s, Lashley began the search for the **memory trace,** or **engram**—the brain changes that were presumed to occur in forming a long-term memory (see photo caption). Guiding Lashley's research was his belief that memory was *localized*, meaning that a particular memory was stored in a specific brain area.

Lashley searched for the specific location of the memory trace that a rat forms for running a maze. Lashley (1929) suspected that the specific memory was localized at a specific site in the *cerebral cortex*, the outermost covering of the brain that contains the most sophisticated brain areas. Once a rat had learned to run the maze, Lashley surgically removed tiny portions of the rat's cortex. After the rat recovered, Lashley tested the rat in the maze again. Obviously, if the rat could still run the maze, then the portion of the brain removed did not contain the memory.

Over the course of 30 years, Lashley systematically removed different sections of the cortex in trained rats. The result of Lashley's painstaking research? No matter which part of the cortex he removed, the rats were still able to run the maze (Lashley, 1929, 1950). At the end of his professional career, Karl Lashley concluded that memories are not localized in specific locations but instead are *distributed*, or stored, throughout the brain.

Lashley was wrong, but not completely wrong. Some memories *do* seem to be localized at specific spots in the brain. Some 20 years after Lashley's death, psychologist **Richard F. Thompson** and his colleagues resumed the search for the location of the memory trace that would confirm Pavlov's speculations.

Thompson classically conditioned rabbits to perform a very simple behavior—an eye blink. By repeatedly pairing a tone with a puff of air administered to the rabbit's eye, he classically conditioned rabbits to blink reflexively in response to the tone alone (Thompson, 1994, 2005).

Thompson discovered that after a rabbit had learned this simple behavior, there was a change in the brain activity in a small area of the rabbit's *cerebellum,* a lower brain structure involved in physical movements. When this tiny area of the cerebellum was removed, the rabbit's memory of the learned response disappeared. It no

Karl S. Lashley (1890–1958) Lashley was trained as a zoologist but turned to psychology after he became friends with John B. Watson, the founder of behaviorism. Interested in discovering the physical basis of the conditioned reflex, Lashley focused his research on how learning and memory were represented in the brain. After years of frustrating research, Lashley (1950) humorously concluded, "This series of experiments has yielded a good bit of information about what and where memory is not. It has discovered nothing directly of the real nature of the engram. I sometimes feel in reviewing the evidence on the localization of the memory trace, that the necessary conclusion is that learning just is not possible."

Archives of the History of American Psychology, The University of Akron. Color added by the publisher.

longer blinked at the sound of the tone. However, the puff of air still caused the rabbit to blink reflexively, so the reflex itself had not been destroyed.

Thompson and his colleagues had confirmed Pavlov's speculations. The long-term memory trace of the classically conditioned eye blink was formed and stored in a very localized region of the cerebellum.

So why had Karl Lashley failed? Unlike Thompson, Lashley was working with a relatively complex behavior. Running a maze involves the use of several senses, including vision, smell, and touch. In contrast, Thompson's rabbits had learned a very simple reflexive behavior—a classically conditioned eye blink.

Thus, part of the reason Lashley failed to find a specific location for a rat's memory of a maze was that the memory was not a single memory. Instead, the rat had developed a complex set of *interrelated memories* involving information from multiple senses. These interrelated memories were processed and stored in different brain areas. As a result, the rat's memories were *distributed* and stored across multiple brain locations. Hence, no matter which small brain area Lashley removed, the rat could still run the maze. So Lashley was right in suggesting that some memories are distributed throughout the brain.

Combined, the findings of Lashley and Thompson indicate that memories have the potential to be *both localized* and *distributed*. Very simple memories may be localized in a specific area, whereas more complex memories are distributed throughout the brain. A complex memory involves clusters of information, and each part of the memory may be stored in the brain area that originally processed the information (Greenberg & Rubin, 2003).

Adding support to Lashley's and Thompson's findings, brain imaging technology has confirmed that many kinds of memories are distributed in the human brain. When we are performing a relatively complex memory task, multiple brain regions are activated—evidence of the distribution of memories involved in complex tasks (Frankland & Bontempi, 2005; Khan & Muly, 2011).

The Focus on Neuroscience on the next page describes a clever study that looked at how memories involving different sensory experiences are assembled when they are retrieved.

The Role of Neurons in Long-Term Memory

What exactly is it that is localized or distributed? The notion of a memory trace suggests that some change must occur in the workings of the brain when a new long-term memory is stored. Logically, two possible changes could occur. First, the *functioning* of the brain's neurons could change. Second, the *structure* of the neurons could change. Given those two possibilities, the challenge for memory researchers has been to identify the specific neurons involved in a given memory, a task that is virtually impossible with the human brain because of its enormous complexity. What this task required was a creature with a limited number of neurons that is also capable of learning new memories.

Enter *Aplysia*, a gentle, seaweed-munching sea snail that resides off the California coast. The study of *Aplysia* over the past 30 years has given memory researchers important insights into the brain changes involved in memory. Why *Aplysia*? Because *Aplysia* has only about 20,000 good-sized neurons. That was a key reason why memory researcher **Eric Kandel** (2006, 2009) chose this unassuming creature to study the neuronal changes that occur when a new memory is formed for a simple classically conditioned response.

Richard F. Thompson (1930–2014) Like Karl Lashley, Richard Thompson (1994, 2005) sought to discover the neurobiological basis for learning and memory. But, unlike Lashley, Thompson (2005) decided to use a very simple behavior—a classically conditioned eye blink—as a model system to locate a memory trace in the brain. He succeeded, identifying the critical region in the cerebellum where the memory of the learned behavior was stored.

Jacques Cornell/Happening Photos

MYTH ◀ SCIENCE

Is it true that all memories, even complex ones, are located in a single part of the brain?

Aplysia, **the Supersnail of Memory Research** Eric Kandel (b. 1929) used *Aplysia*, a sea snail with only about 20,000 neurons, to study how neurons change when simple behaviors are learned and remembered. Kandel, pictured here in his laboratory, was awarded the Nobel Prize in 2000 for his discoveries on the neural basis of memory.

Gaby Gerster/laif/Redux

FOCUS ON NEUROSCIENCE

Assembling Memories: Echoes and Reflections of Perception

If we asked you to remember the theme from *Sesame Street,* you would "hear" the song in your head. Conjure up a memory of your high school cafeteria, and you "see" it in your mind. Memories can include a great deal of sensory information—sounds, sights, and even odors, textures, and tastes. How are such rich sensory aspects of an experience incorporated into a memory that is retrieved?

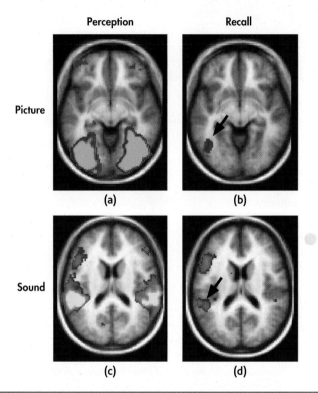

Perception   **Recall**

Picture

(a)   (b)

Sound

(c)   (d)

Researchers set out to investigate this question using a simple memory task and fMRI (Wheeler & others, 2000). Participants studied names for common objects that were paired with either a picture or a sound associated with the word. For example, the word "dog" was either paired with a picture of a dog or the sound of a dog barking. The researchers then used fMRI to measure brain activity when the volunteers were instructed to recall the words they'd memorized.

The results? Retrieving the memory activated a subset of the same brain areas that were involved in perceiving the sensory stimulus. Participants who had memorized the word *dog* with a *picture* of a dog showed a high level of activation in the *visual cortex* when they retrieved the memory. And participants who had memorized the word *dog* with the *sound* of a barking dog showed a high level of activation in the *auditory cortex* when they retrieved the memory.

Of course, many of our memories are highly complex, involving not just sensations but also thoughts and emotions. Neuroscientists assume that such complex memories involve traces that are widely distributed throughout the brain. However, they still don't understand how all these neural records are bound together and interrelated to form a single, highly elaborate memory (Khan & Muly, 2011).

Retrieving the Memory of a Sensory Experience Top row: (a) Perceiving a picture activates areas of the visual cortex. (b) When the memory of the picture is recalled, it reactivates some of the same areas of the visual cortex *(arrow)* that were involved in the initial perception of the picture. Bottom row: (c) Perceiving a sound activates areas of the auditory cortex. (d) When the memory of the sound is recalled, it reactivates some of the same areas of the auditory cortex *(arrow)* that were involved in the initial perception of the sound.

Courtesy of Mark E. Wheeler, Randy L. Buckner, and Steven E. Petersen

If you give *Aplysia* a gentle squirt with a WaterPik, followed by a mild electric shock to its tail, the snail reflexively withdraws its gill flap. When the process is repeated several times, *Aplysia* wises up and acquires a new memory of a classically conditioned response—it withdraws its gill when squirted with the WaterPik alone. This learned gill-withdrawal reflex seems to involve a circuit of just three neurons: one that detects the water squirt, one that detects the tail shock, and one that signals the gill-withdrawal reflex (see Figure 6.10).

When *Aplysia* acquires this new memory through repeated training trials, significant changes occur in the three-neuron circuit (Kandel, 2001). First, the *function* of the neurons is altered: There is an increase in the amount of the neurotransmitters produced by the neurons. Second, the *structure* of the snail's neurons changes: The number of interconnecting branches between the neurons increases, as does the number of synapses, or communication points, on each branch. These changes allow the neurons involved in the particular memory circuit to communicate more easily. Collectively, these changes are called **long-term potentiation,** which refers to a long-lasting increase in synaptic strength (Baudry & others, 2011; Lisman & others, 2012).

The same kinds of brain changes have been observed in more sophisticated mammals. Chicks, rats, and rabbits also show structural and functional neuron changes associated with new learning experiences and memories. And, as you may recall from Psych for Your Life in Chapter 2, there is ample evidence that the same kinds of changes occur in the human brain.

long-term potentiation A long-lasting increase in synaptic strength between two neurons.

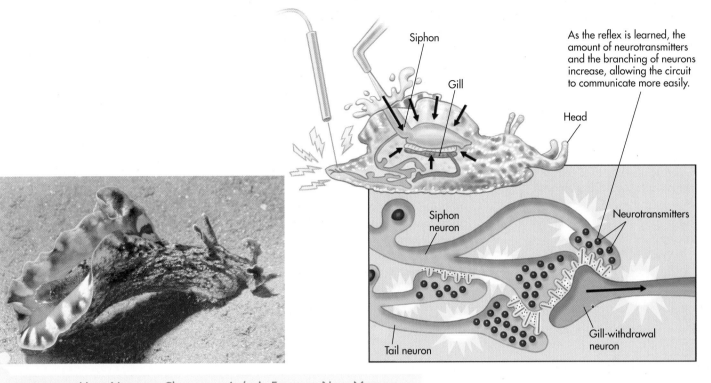

FIGURE 6.10 How Neurons Change as *Aplysia* Forms a New Memory
When *Aplysia* is repeatedly squirted with water, and each squirt is followed by a mild shock to its tail, the snail learns to withdraw its gill flap if squirted with the water alone. Conditioning leads to structural and functional changes in the three neurons involved in the memory circuit.

In terms of our understanding of the memory trace, what do these findings suggest? Although there are vast differences between the nervous system of a simple creature such as *Aplysia* and the enormously complex human brain, some tentative generalizations are possible. Forming a memory seems to produce distinct functional and structural changes in specific neurons. These changes create a memory circuit. Each time the memory is recalled, the neurons in this circuit are activated. As the structural and functional changes in the neurons strengthen the communication links in this circuit, the memory becomes established as a long-term memory (Kandel, 2006, 2009).

Processing Memories in the Brain
CLUES FROM AMNESIA

KEY THEME

Important insights into the brain structures involved in normal memory have been provided by case studies of people with amnesia caused by damaged brain tissue.

KEY QUESTIONS

> Who was H.M. and what did his case reveal about normal memory processes?

> What brain structures are involved in normal memory?

> What are dementia and Alzheimer's disease?

Prior to the advent of today's sophisticated brain imaging technology, researchers studied individuals who had sustained a brain injury or

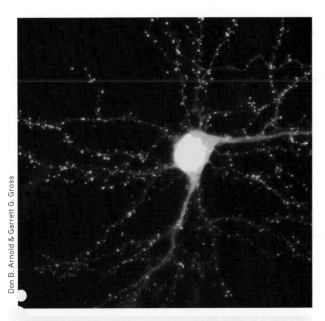

Making Memories in the Brain: Changing Synaptic Connections Forming a new memory involves physical changes in the brain. New synaptic connections are created, and old synaptic connections are weakened or eliminated. This photo shows a single rat neuron (Gross & others, 2013). The bright green and red spots dotting the dendrites extending from the cell body are synapses. As the brain processes information, synapses change. Ultimately, new memories are reflected in the evolving patterns of synaptic structure.

amnesia (am-NEE-zha) Severe memory loss.

retrograde amnesia Loss of memory, especially for episodic information; backward-acting amnesia.

memory consolidation The gradual, physical process of converting new long-term memories to stable, enduring memory codes.

anterograde amnesia Loss of memory caused by the inability to store new memories; forward-acting amnesia.

Disrupting the Consolidation of Memories Head injuries are common in football and many other sports. For example, Seattle Seahawks defensive end Cliff Avril (#56), below, was diagnosed with a concussion and forced to leave the Super Bowl after a collision with a New York Patriots player. In one study, football players who were questioned immediately after a concussion or other head injury could remember how they were injured and the name of the play just performed. But if questioned 30 minutes later for the same information, they could not. Because the head injury had disrupted the memory consolidation process, the memories were permanently lost (Yarnell & Lynch, 1970).

AP Photo/Kevin Terrell

had part of their brain surgically removed for medical reasons. Often, such individuals experienced **amnesia,** or severe memory loss. By relating the type and extent of amnesia to the specific damaged brain areas, researchers uncovered clues as to how the human brain processes memories.

RETROGRADE AMNESIA
DISRUPTING MEMORY CONSOLIDATION

One type of amnesia is retrograde amnesia. *Retrograde* means "backward moving." People who have **retrograde amnesia** are unable to remember some or all of their past, especially episodic memories for recent events. Retrograde amnesia often results from a blow to the head. Boxers sometimes suffer such memory losses after years of fighting. Head injuries from automobile and motorcycle accidents are another common cause of retrograde amnesia. Typically, memories of the events that immediately preceded the injury are completely lost, as in the case of accident victims who cannot remember details about what led up to the accident.

Apparently, establishing a long-term memory is like creating a Jell-O mold—it needs time to "set" before it becomes solid. This process of "setting" a new memory permanently in the brain is called memory consolidation (Dudai & others, 2011). More specifically, **memory consolidation** is the gradual, physical process of converting new long-term memories to stable, enduring memory codes (Medina & others, 2008). If memory consolidation is disrupted before the process is complete, the vulnerable memory may be lost (Dudai, 2004).

In humans, memory consolidation can be disrupted by brain trauma, such as a sudden blow, concussion, electric shock, or encephalitis (Riccio & others, 2003). Similarly, many drugs, such as alcohol and the benzodiazepines, interfere with memory consolidation. In contrast, stimulants and the stress hormones that are released during emotional arousal tend to *enhance* memory consolidation (Nielson & Lorber, 2009).

ANTEROGRADE AMNESIA
DISRUPTING THE FORMATION OF EXPLICIT MEMORIES

Another form of amnesia is **anterograde amnesia**—the inability to form *new* memories. *Anterograde* means "forward moving." The most famous case study of anterograde amnesia lasted over 50 years. It was of a man who for years was known only by his initials—H.M. But the need to protect H.M.'s privacy ended when Henry Molaison died at the age of 82 on December 2, 2008.

In 1953, Henry was 27 years old and had a 10-year history of severe, untreatable epileptic seizures. Henry's doctors located the brain area where the seizures seemed to originate. With no other options available at the time, the decision was made to surgically remove portions of the *medial* (inner) *temporal lobe* on each side of Henry's brain, including the brain structure called the *hippocampus* (Scoville & Milner, 1957). Portions of the left and right *amygdala* were also removed (Annese & others, 2014).

After the experimental surgery, the frequency and severity of Henry's seizures were greatly reduced. However, it was quickly discovered that Henry's ability to form new memories of events and information had been destroyed. Although the experimental surgery had treated H.M.'s seizures, it also dramatically revealed the role of the hippocampus in forming new explicit memories for episodic and semantic information.

Psychologists **Brenda Milner** (1970) and **Suzanne Corkin** (2013) studied Henry extensively over the past 50 years. If you had had the chance to meet Henry, he would have appeared normal enough. He had a good vocabulary and social skills, normal intelligence, and a delightful

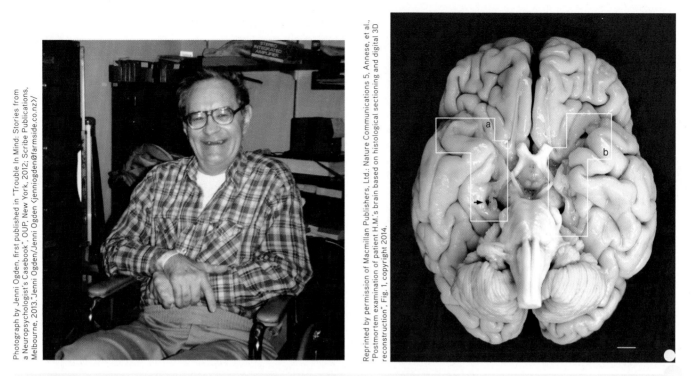

Henry Gustav Molaison: The Real H.M. (1926–2008) At the age of 9, Henry was hit by a bicyclist and jarred his head badly. Not long after, he began experiencing seizures. By early adulthood, Henry's seizures had increased in both severity and frequency. In an effort to control the seizures, an experimental surgery was performed, removing the hippocampus and amygdala on each side of Henry's brain.

Because of the profound anterograde amnesia caused by the surgery, Henry became one of the most intensive case studies in psychology and neuroscience. Over the next half century, Henry participated in hundreds of studies that fundamentally altered the scientific understanding of memory.

Henry died on December 2, 2008, but his contributions to science continue. Neuroscientist Jacopo Annese and his team (2014) dissected Henry's brain, slicing it into 2,400 micro-thin slices in a marathon, 3-day session that was streamed online. Photographs of each slice were taken to create a virtual 3-D digital model of Henry's brain. The white boxes (a) and (b) show where portions of the hippocampus and amygdala on the left and right side of Henry's brain were removed. The researchers also discovered a previously unknown small lesion on Henry's left frontal lobe, which they speculate is probably scar tissue from the original surgery. You can watch a short video of the dissection at http://thebrainobservatory.ucsd.edu/hm_live.php

sense of humor. And he was well aware of his memory problem. When Suzanne Corkin (2002) once asked him, "What do you do to try to remember?" Henry quipped, "Well, that I don't know because I don't remember [chuckle] what I tried."

Despite superficially appearing normal, Henry lived in the eternal present. Had you talked with Henry for 15 minutes, then left the room for 2 or 3 minutes before coming back, he wouldn't remember having met you before. Although some of the psychologists and doctors had treated Henry for years, even decades, Henry was meeting them for the first time on each occasion he interacted with them (Corkin, 2013; MacKay, 2014).

For the most part, Henry's short-term memory worked just fine. In fact, he could fool you. If Henry actively repeated or rehearsed information, he could hold it in short-term memory for an hour or more (Nader & Wang, 2006). Yet just moments after he switched his attention to something else and stopped rehearsing the information, it was gone forever. However, Henry's long-term memory was partially intact. He could retrieve long-term memories from *before* the time he was 16 years old, when the severe epileptic seizures began.

In general, Henry was unable to acquire new long-term memories of events (episodic information) or general knowledge (semantic information). Still, every now and then, Henry

Suzanne Corkin Since the mid-1960s, MIT neuropsychologist Suzanne Corkin (2013) has evaluated different aspects of Henry's memory abilities. In looking back on Henry's life, Corkin (2002) commented, "We all understand the rare opportunity we have had to work with him, and we are grateful for his dedication to research. He has taught us a great deal about the cognitive and neural organization of memory. We are in his debt."

Writer Pictures via AP Images

surprised his doctors and visitors with some bit of knowledge that he acquired after the surgery.

Henry's case suggests that the hippocampus is not involved in most short-term memory tasks, nor is it the storage site for already established long-term memories. Instead, the critical role played by the hippocampus seems to be the *encoding* of new memories for events and information and the *transfer* of those new memories from short-term to long-term memory.

Implicit and Explicit Memory in Anterograde Amnesia Henry's case and those of other patients with anterograde amnesia have contributed greatly to our understanding of implicit versus explicit memories. To refresh your memory, *implicit memories* are memories without conscious awareness. In contrast, *explicit memories* are memories with conscious awareness.

Henry could not form new episodic or semantic memories, which reflects the explicit memory system. But he *could* form new procedural memories, which reflects the implicit memory system. For example, when given the same logical puzzle to solve several days in a row, Henry was able to solve it more quickly each day. This improvement showed that he *implicitly* "remembered" the procedure involved in solving the puzzle. But if you asked Henry if he had ever seen the puzzle before, he would answer "no" because he could not consciously (or *explicitly*) remember having learned how to solve the puzzle. This suggests that the hippocampus is less crucial to the formation of new implicit memories, such as procedural memories, than it is to the formation of new explicit memories.

Were Henry's memory anomalies an exception? Not at all. Studies conducted with other people who have sustained damage to the hippocampus and related brain structures showed the same anterograde amnesia (see Bayley & Squire, 2002). Like Henry, these patients are unable to form new explicit memories, but their performances on implicit memory tasks, which do not require conscious recollection of the new information, are much closer to normal. Such findings indicate that implicit and explicit memory processes involve different brain structures and pathways.

BRAIN STRUCTURES INVOLVED IN MEMORY

Along with the hippocampus, several other brain regions involved in memory include the cerebellum, the amygdala, and the frontal cortex (see Figure 6.11). As you saw earlier, the *cerebellum* is involved in classically conditioning simple reflexes, such as the eye-blink reflex. The cerebellum is also involved in procedural memories and other motor skill memories.

The *amygdala*, which is situated very close to the hippocampus, is involved in encoding and storing the emotional qualities associated with particular memories, such as fear or anger (Hamann, 2009; McGaugh, 2004). For example, normal monkeys are afraid of snakes. But if the amygdala is damaged, a monkey loses its fear of snakes and other natural predators.

The *frontal lobes* are involved in retrieving and organizing information that is associated with autobiographical and episodic memories (Greenberg & Rubin, 2003). The *prefrontal cortex* seems to play an important role in working memory (D'Esposito & Postle, 2015; McNab & Klingberg, 2008).

The *medial temporal lobes*, like the frontal lobes, do not actually store the information that comprises our autobiographical memories. Rather, they are involved in encoding complex memories, by forming links among the information stored in multiple brain regions (Greenberg & Rubin, 2003; Shrager & Squire, 2009). As we described in the Focus on Neuroscience, "Assembling Memories," on page 258, retrieving a memory activates the same brain regions that were involved in initially encoding the memory.

---

dementia Progressive deterioration and impairment of memory, reasoning, and other cognitive functions as the result of disease, injury, or substance abuse.

Alzheimer's disease (AD) A progressive disease that destroys the brain's neurons, gradually impairing memory, thinking, language, and other cognitive functions, resulting in the complete inability to care for oneself; the most common cause of *dementia*.

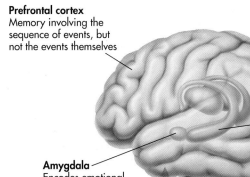

Prefrontal cortex
Memory involving the sequence of events, but not the events themselves

Hippocampus
Encodes and transfers new explicit memories to long-term memory

Amygdala
Encodes emotional aspects of memories

Medial temporal lobe
(not visible) Encodes and transfers new explicit memories to long-term memory

Cerebellum
Memories involving movement

FIGURE 6.11 Brain Structures Involved in Human Memory Shown here are some of the key brain structures involved in encoding and storing memories.

ALZHEIMER'S DISEASE
GRADUALLY LOSING THE ABILITY TO REMEMBER

Understanding how the brain processes and stores memories has important implications. **Dementia** is a broad term that refers to the decline and impairment of memory, reasoning, language, and other cognitive functions. These cognitive disruptions occur to such an extent that they interfere with the person's ability to carry out daily activities. Dementia is not a disease itself. Rather, it describes a group of symptoms that often accompany a disease or a condition.

The most common cause of dementia is **Alzheimer's disease (AD)**. It is estimated that about 5.4 million Americans suffer from AD. That number is expected to dramatically escalate as more and more "baby boomers" reach age 65. The disease usually doesn't begin until after age 60, but the risk goes up with age. About 6 percent of men and women in the 65–74 age group have AD. Among adults age 85 and older, about half may have Alzheimer's disease (Alzheimer's Association, 2011).

Steve Liss/Time Life Pictures/Getty Images

The Nun Study of Aging and Alzheimer's Disease Neurologist David Snowdon is shown here having a laugh during a card game with Sister Esther, who is 106 years old. Since 1986, Snowdon (2002, 2003) has studied 678 elderly Roman Catholic nuns, an ideal research group because their lifestyles and environment are so similar. Although the study is ongoing, several findings have already emerged (see K. P. Riley & others, 2005; Tyas & others, 2007a, 2007b).

For example, the outward signs of Alzheimer's disease (AD) and the degree of brain damage evident at death are not perfectly correlated. Although some nuns had clear brain evidence of AD, they did not display observable cognitive and behavior declines prior to their deaths. Other nuns had only mild brain evidence of AD but showed severe cognitive and behavioral declines.

Interestingly, the sisters who displayed better language abilities when they were young women were less likely to display AD symptoms. This held true regardless of how much brain damage was evident at the time of their death (Iacono & others, 2009). As researcher Diego Iacono (2009) commented, "It's the first time that we're shown that a complex cognitive activity, like language ability, is connected with a neurodegenerative disease."

Mapping Brain Changes in Alzheimer's Disease

The hallmark of Alzheimer's disease is its relentless, progressive destruction of neurons in the brain, turning once-healthy tissue into a tangled, atrophied mass. This progressive loss of brain tissue is dramatically revealed in the MRI images shown below. Created by neuroscientist Paul Thompson and his colleagues (2003), these high-resolution "brain maps" represent composite images of the progressive effects of Alzheimer's disease (AD) in 12 patients over the course of two years. In these color-coded images, blue corresponds to normal tissue (no loss), red indicates up to 10 percent tissue loss, and white indicates up to 20 percent tissue loss.

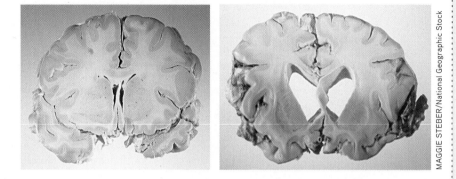

MAGGIE STEBER/National Geographic Stock

Thompson likens the progression of AD to that of molten lava flowing around rocks—the disease leaves islands of brain tissue

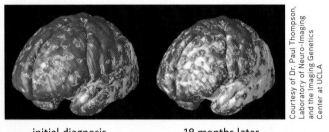

initial diagnosis   18 months later

Courtesy of Dr. Paul Thompson, Laboratory of Neuro-Imaging, and the Imaging Genetics Center at UCLA

unscathed. The disease first attacks the temporal lobes, affecting areas involved in memory, especially short-term memory. Next affected are the frontal areas, which are involved in thinking, reasoning, self-control, and planning ahead. You can also see significant internal loss in limbic areas, which are involved in regulating emotion. At this point in the progression of AD, there is very little loss in sensory and visual brain areas. Eventually the disease engulfs the entire brain. The photos above contrast cross sections of a normal brain (left) and the brain of a person who died of Alzheimer's disease (right). In the normal brain, the temporal lobes are intact. The ventricles, which hold the cerebral spinal fluid, are slender. In the brain ravaged by Alzheimer's, the gaping ventricles extend into the space left by the death of brain cells in the temporal lobes.

Although the cause or causes of Alzheimer's disease are still unknown, it is known that the brains of AD patients develop an abundance of two abnormal structures—*beta-amyloid plaques* and *neurofibrillary tangles* (Ballard & others, 2011). The *plaques* are dense deposits of protein and other cell materials outside and around neurons. The plaques interfere with the ability of neurons to communicate, damaging the neurons to the point that they die. The *tangles* are twisted fibers that build up inside the neuron and interrupt the flow of nourishment to the neuron, ultimately causing the neuron to die. Although most older people develop some plaques and tangles in their brains, the brains of AD patients have them to a much greater extent (Petersen, 2002). The Focus on Neuroscience shown above vividly portrays the progressive loss of neurons that is the root cause of Alzheimer's disease.

In the early stages of AD, the symptoms of memory impairment are often mild, such as forgetting the names of familiar people, forgetting the location of familiar places, or forgetting to do things. But as the disease progresses, memory loss and confusion become more pervasive. The person becomes unable to remember what month it is or the names of family members. Frustrated and disoriented by the inability to retrieve even simple information, the person can become agitated and moody. In the last stage of AD, internal brain damage has become widespread. The person no longer recognizes loved ones and is unable to communicate in any meaningful way. All sense of self and identity has vanished. At the closing stages, the person becomes completely incapacitated. Ultimately, Alzheimer's disease is fatal (Alzheimer's Association, 2011).

Some 14.9 million Americans provide unpaid care for a person with Alzheimer's disease or other dementia. These unpaid caregivers are primarily family members but also include friends and neighbors. In 2010, these caregivers provided 17 billion hours of unpaid care (Alzheimer's Association, 2011). Not only is there a financial toll, but families and caregivers struggle with great physical and emotional stress as they try to cope with the mental and physical changes occurring in their loved one. The average number of hours of unpaid care provided for a relative or friend with Alzheimer's increases as the person's condition worsens.

Numerous resources, such as the Alzheimer's Disease Education & Referral Center (www.alzheimers.org) and the Alzheimer's Association (www.alz.org), are available to help support families and other caregivers.

❭ Test your understanding of the **Biological Basis of Memory** with
LEARNINGCurve.

Closing Thoughts

Human memory is at once both perfectly ordinary and quite extraordinary. With next to no mental effort, you form and recall countless memories as you go through daily life. Psychologists have made enormous progress in explaining how those memories are encoded, stored, retrieved, and forgotten.

Perhaps the most fascinating aspect of human memory is its fallibility. Memory is surprisingly susceptible to errors and distortions. Under some conditions, completely false memories can be experienced, such as Elizabeth Loftus's memory of discovering her mother's body in the swimming pool. Such false memories can be so subjectively compelling that they feel like authentic memories, yet confidence in a memory is not proof of the memory's truth.

Many mysteries of human memory remain, including exactly how memories are stored in and retrieved from the brain. Nevertheless, reliable ways of improving memory in everyday life have been discovered. In the Psych for Your Life feature, we provide several suggestions to enhance your memory for new information.

PSYCH FOR YOUR LIFE

Ten Steps to Boost Your Memory

There are many simple and effective strategies that can help boost your memory for important information. Before reading further, flip back to Chapter 1 and review the research-based study strategies described there. (You *do* remember those suggestions, don't you?) Knowing what you now know about human memory, you should have a better understanding of *why* those strategies are effective. To recap, those strategies included the following:

- Focus your attention
- Be an active reader
- Practice retrieval
- Use flashcards and practice tests correctly
- Space out your study time

Want to improve your memory? Read on for ten simple and effective memory-boosting techniques.

1. Commit the necessary time.

The more time you spend learning material, the better you will understand it and the longer you will remember it. Budget enough time to read the assigned material carefully. If you read material faster than you can comprehend it, you not only won't understand the material, you also won't remember it.

2. Organize the information.

We have a strong natural tendency to organize information in long-term memory into categories. You can capitalize on this tendency by actively organizing information you want to remember. One way to accomplish this is by outlining chapters or your lecture notes. Use the chapter headings and subheadings as categories, or, better yet, create your own categories. Under each category, list and describe the relevant terms, concepts, and ideas. This strategy can double the amount of information you can recall.

3. Elaborate on the material.

You've probably noticed that virtually every term or concept in this text is formally defined in just a sentence or two. But we also spend a paragraph or more explaining what the concept means. To remember the information you read, you have to do the same thing—engage in *elaborative rehearsal* and actively process the information for meaning (see pages 234–235). Actively question new information and think about its implications. Form memory associations by relating the material to what you already know. Try to come up with examples that relate to your own life.

4. Explain it to a friend.

After you read a section of material, stop and summarize what you have read in your own words. When you think you understand it, try explaining the information to a friend or family member. As you'll quickly discover, it's hard to explain material that you don't really understand! Memory research has shown that explaining new material in your own words forces you to integrate the new information into your existing knowledge base—an excellent way to solidify new information in your memory (Kornell, 2008).

5. Use visual imagery.

Two memory codes are better than one (Paivio, 1986). Rather than merely encoding the information verbally, use mental imagery (Carretti & others, 2007; Sadoski, 2005). Much of the information in this text easily lends itself to visual imagery. Use the photographs and other illustrations to help form visual memories of the information.

6. Reduce interference within a topic.

If you occasionally confuse related terms and concepts, it may be because you're experiencing *interference* in your memories for similar information. To minimize memory interference for related information, first break the chapter into manageable sections, then learn the key information one section at a time. As you encounter new concepts, compare them with previously learned concepts, looking for differences and similarities. By building distinct memories for important information as you progress through a topic, you're more likely to distinguish between concepts so they don't get confused in your memory.

7. Counteract the serial position effect.

The *serial position effect* is the tendency to have better recall of information at the beginning and end of a sequence. To counteract this effect, spend extra time learning the information that falls in the middle. Once you've mastered a sequence of material, start at a different point each time you review or practice the information.

8. Use contextual cues to jog memories.

Ideally, study in the setting in which you're going to be tested. If that's not possible, when you're taking a test and a specific memory gets blocked, imagine that your books and notes are in front of you and that you're sitting where you normally study. Simply imagining the surroundings where you learned the material can help jog those memories.

9. Use a mnemonic device for remembering lists.

A *mnemonic device* is a method or strategy to aid memory. Some of the most effective mnemonic devices use visual imagery (Foer, 2011). For example, the *method of loci* is a mnemonic device in which you remember items by visualizing them at specific locations in a familiar setting, such as the different rooms in your house or at specific locations on your way to work or school. To recall the items, mentally revisit the locations and imagine the specific item at that location.

Another mnemonic that involves creating visual associations is the *peg-word method*. First, you learn an easily remembered list containing the peg words, such as: 1 is bun, 2 is shoe, 3 is tree, 4 is door, 5 is hive, 6 is sticks, 7 is heaven, 8 is gate, 9 is vine, 10 is a hen, and you can keep going as needed. Then, you create a vivid mental image associating the first item you want to remember with the first peg word, the next item with the next peg word, and so on. To recall the list, use each successive peg word to help retrieve the mental image.

10. Finally, sleep on it to help consolidate those memories.

As we discussed in Chapter 4 (see pages 145–146), numerous studies have demonstrated that sleep helps you consolidate new memories. (Don't try this as an excuse in class.) A good night's sleep also helps you integrate new memories into existing networks, making it more likely that you'll recall the new information when you need to (Stickgold & Walker, 2013). In other words, all-night cram sessions just before an exam are one of the *least* effective ways to learn new material.

Merlijn Doomernik/Hollandse Hoogte/Redux

Memory Superstar Josh Foer Journalist Josh Foer (2011) visited a memory competition expecting to find people with special memory abilities. Instead, he encountered a group of "mental athletes"—people with ordinary minds who had trained their memories to accomplish incredible feats, such as reciting hundreds of random digits or pages of poetry. Told that anyone could develop an expert memory with training, he set out to prove it and devoted months to training his own memory. A year later, he won the USA Memory Championship and even set a new U.S. record by memorizing the position of a deck of cards in one minute, 40 seconds. Josh's secret? Mnemonic techniques, like the *method of loci*—and lots and lots of practice. Foer explains his method in his Ted Talk, available at http://www.ted.com/talks/joshua_foer_feats_of_memory_anyone_can_do

CHAPTER REVIEW

KEY PEOPLE AND KEY TERMS

Suzanne Corkin, p. 260
Hermann Ebbinghaus, p. 243

memory, p. 228
encoding, p. 228
storage, p. 228
retrieval, p. 228
stage model of memory, p. 228
sensory memory, p. 228
short-term memory, p. 229
long-term memory, p. 229
maintenance rehearsal, p. 231
chunking, p. 232
working memory, p. 233
elaborative rehearsal, p. 234
procedural memory, p. 235
episodic memory, p. 235
semantic memory, p. 236

Eric Kandel, p. 257
Karl Lashley, p. 256

explicit memory, p. 236
implicit memory, p. 236
clustering, p. 237
semantic network model, p. 238
retrieval, p. 239
retrieval cue, p. 239
retrieval cue failure, p. 239
tip-of-the-tongue (TOT) experience, p. 239
recall, p. 240
cued recall, p. 240
recognition, p. 240
serial position effect, p. 240
encoding specificity principle, p. 241

Elizabeth F. Loftus, p. 248
Brenda Milner, p. 260

context effect, p. 241
mood congruence, p. 241
flashbulb memory, p. 241
forgetting, p. 243
encoding failure, p. 245
prospective memory, p. 245
decay theory, p. 245
déjà vu experience, p. 246
source memory (source monitoring), p. 246
interference theory, p. 247
retroactive interference, p. 247
proactive interference, p. 247
suppression, p. 247
repression, p. 247

George Sperling, p. 229
Richard F. Thompson, p. 256

misinformation effect, p. 249
source confusion, p. 249
false memory, p. 250
schema, p. 250
script, p. 250
imagination inflation, p. 253
memory trace (engram), p. 256
long-term potentiation, p. 258
amnesia, p. 260
retrograde amnesia, p. 260
memory consolidation, p. 260
anterograde amnesia, p. 260
dementia, p. 263
Alzheimer's disease (AD), p. 263

6 Memory

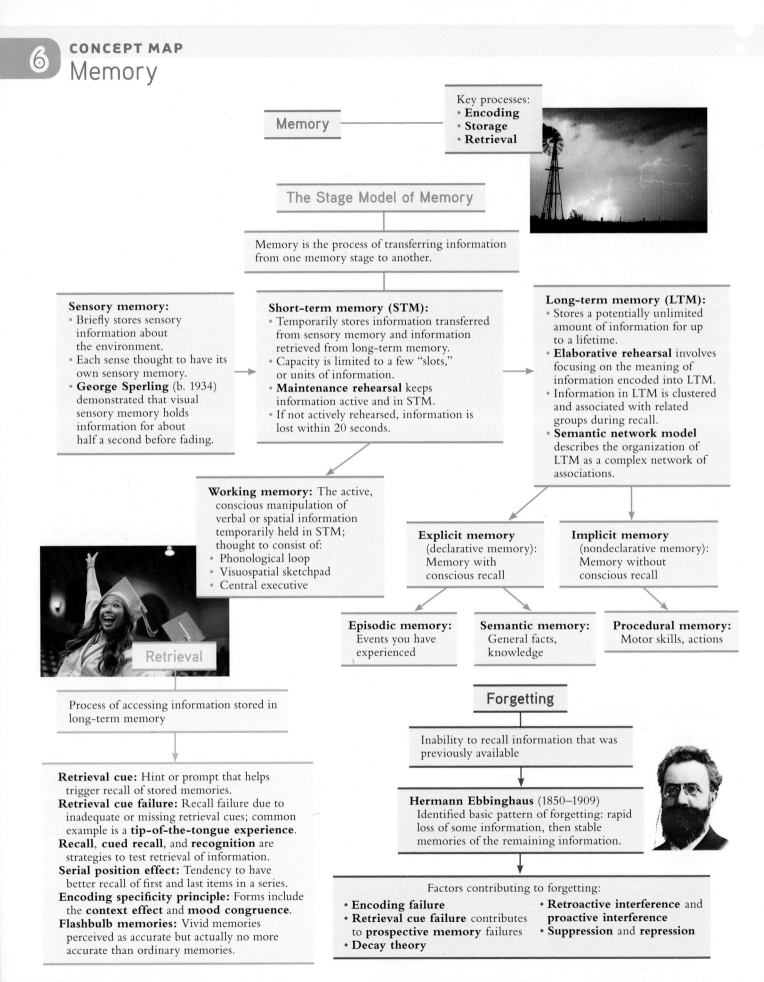

Memory

Key processes:
- **Encoding**
- **Storage**
- **Retrieval**

The Stage Model of Memory

Memory is the process of transferring information from one memory stage to another.

Sensory memory:
- Briefly stores sensory information about the environment.
- Each sense thought to have its own sensory memory.
- **George Sperling** (b. 1934) demonstrated that visual sensory memory holds information for about half a second before fading.

Short-term memory (STM):
- Temporarily stores information transferred from sensory memory and information retrieved from long-term memory.
- Capacity is limited to a few "slots," or units of information.
- **Maintenance rehearsal** keeps information active and in STM.
- If not actively rehearsed, information is lost within 20 seconds.

Long-term memory (LTM):
- Stores a potentially unlimited amount of information for up to a lifetime.
- **Elaborative rehearsal** involves focusing on the meaning of information encoded into LTM.
- Information in LTM is clustered and associated with related groups during recall.
- **Semantic network model** describes the organization of LTM as a complex network of associations.

Working memory: The active, conscious manipulation of verbal or spatial information temporarily held in STM; thought to consist of:
- Phonological loop
- Visuospatial sketchpad
- Central executive

Explicit memory (declarative memory): Memory with conscious recall

Implicit memory (nondeclarative memory): Memory without conscious recall

Episodic memory: Events you have experienced

Semantic memory: General facts, knowledge

Procedural memory: Motor skills, actions

Retrieval

Process of accessing information stored in long-term memory

Retrieval cue: Hint or prompt that helps trigger recall of stored memories.
Retrieval cue failure: Recall failure due to inadequate or missing retrieval cues; common example is a **tip-of-the-tongue experience**.
Recall, **cued recall**, and **recognition** are strategies to test retrieval of information.
Serial position effect: Tendency to have better recall of first and last items in a series.
Encoding specificity principle: Forms include the **context effect** and **mood congruence**.
Flashbulb memories: Vivid memories perceived as accurate but actually no more accurate than ordinary memories.

Forgetting

Inability to recall information that was previously available

Hermann Ebbinghaus (1850–1909) Identified basic pattern of forgetting: rapid loss of some information, then stable memories of the remaining information.

Factors contributing to forgetting:
- **Encoding failure**
- **Retrieval cue failure** contributes to **prospective memory** failures
- **Decay theory**
- **Retroactive interference** and **proactive interference**
- **Suppression** and **repression**

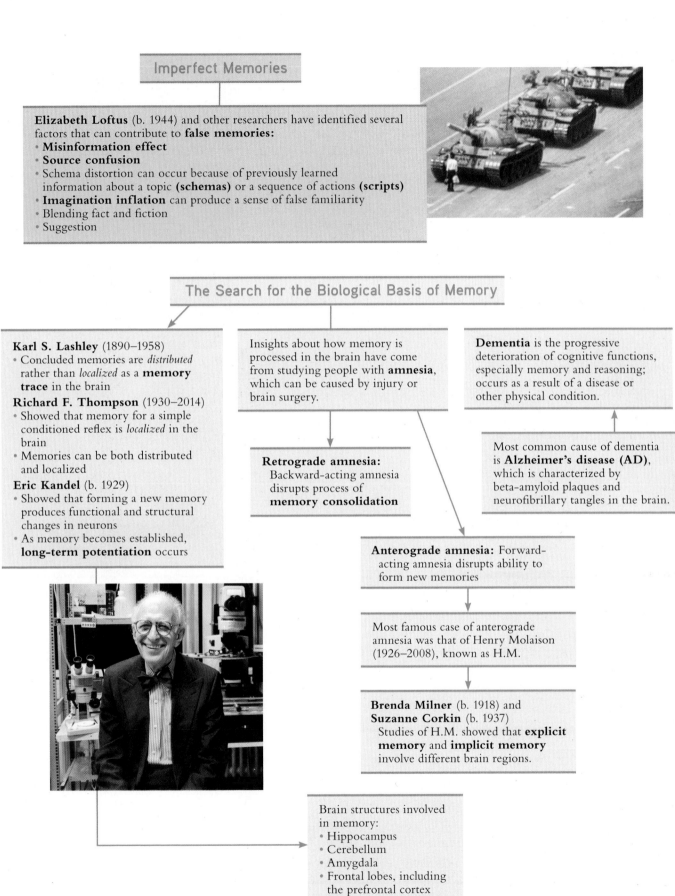

Imperfect Memories

Elizabeth Loftus (b. 1944) and other researchers have identified several factors that can contribute to **false memories:**
- **Misinformation effect**
- **Source confusion**
- Schema distortion can occur because of previously learned information about a topic **(schemas)** or a sequence of actions **(scripts)**
- **Imagination inflation** can produce a sense of false familiarity
- Blending fact and fiction
- Suggestion

The Search for the Biological Basis of Memory

Karl S. Lashley (1890–1958)
- Concluded memories are *distributed* rather than *localized* as a **memory trace** in the brain

Richard F. Thompson (1930–2014)
- Showed that memory for a simple conditioned reflex is *localized* in the brain
- Memories can be both distributed and localized

Eric Kandel (b. 1929)
- Showed that forming a new memory produces functional and structural changes in neurons
- As memory becomes established, **long-term potentiation** occurs

Insights about how memory is processed in the brain have come from studying people with **amnesia**, which can be caused by injury or brain surgery.

Retrograde amnesia: Backward-acting amnesia disrupts process of **memory consolidation**

Dementia is the progressive deterioration of cognitive functions, especially memory and reasoning; occurs as a result of a disease or other physical condition.

Most common cause of dementia is **Alzheimer's disease (AD)**, which is characterized by beta-amyloid plaques and neurofibrillary tangles in the brain.

Anterograde amnesia: Forward-acting amnesia disrupts ability to form new memories

Most famous case of anterograde amnesia was that of Henry Molaison (1926–2008), known as H.M.

Brenda Milner (b. 1918) and **Suzanne Corkin** (b. 1937) Studies of H.M. showed that **explicit memory** and **implicit memory** involve different brain regions.

Brain structures involved in memory:
- Hippocampus
- Cerebellum
- Amygdala
- Frontal lobes, including the prefrontal cortex
- Medial temporal lobes

MYTH OR SCIENCE?

Is it true . . .

○ That people tend to cling to their beliefs even when they are presented with solid evidence that contradicts those beliefs?

○ That, unlike English speakers, Eskimos have dozens of words for snow?

○ That nonhuman animals do not possess high-level cognitive abilities?

○ That most people with an autism spectrum disorder have special mental abilities?

○ That intelligence is primarily determined by heredity?

○ That you're either creative or you're not—there's nothing you can do to increase creativity?

THE MOVIE MOMENT

PROLOGUE

MOUNT MAGAZINE STATE PARK WAS an easy three-hour drive, so when friends invited your author Sandy to join them for the evening in the hilltop cabin they'd rented, she jumped at the chance. The family was lined up to greet Sandy as she pulled up to their cabin in her dusty Subaru. Lynn and Will, relaxed and smiling, were happy to be on vacation with their two teenagers in such a beautiful location. Lily, laughing and talkative, was excited about starting college in the fall. And Tom, Lily's younger brother, was standing off to one side, looking away.

"Tom," Lynn prompted, "Tom, say hello to Sandy."

Ducking his head, Tom looked out from beneath his baseball cap. "Helloooooooo," he said with an odd, singsongy voice, then quickly turned away.

"Good to see you, Tom," Sandy replied. If you didn't know Tom, you might think he was being rude. But Sandy was well aware of Tom's "oddball habits," as he called them, which were most noticeable when he interacted with other people.

Later, as they all hiked to the top of Mount Magazine and savored the incredible view of the river valley below, Sandy thought of some of the conversations that she and Lynn had had over the years about Tom. When Tom was three, a preschool teacher had recommended that he be screened for vague "developmental delays." She wrote, "Tom doesn't interact with the other children." Sometimes, she said, he was "unresponsive," and seemed "lost in his own world." But Lynn and Will thought Tom was just shy.

Tom was unusual in other ways, too. He was smart—very smart. At the age of four, Tom had the reading

Thinking, Language, and Intelligence

7

IN THIS CHAPTER:

› **INTRODUCTION:** Thinking, Language, and Intelligence

› Solving Problems and Making Decisions

› Language and Thought

› Measuring Intelligence

› The Nature of Intelligence

› **PSYCH FOR YOUR LIFE:** A Workshop on Creativity

and writing abilities of a child twice his age. Although he seldom talked, when Tom *did* talk, you couldn't help but do a double-take in response to his large vocabulary. And like lots of little boys, Tom would become obsessed with a particular topic. On one of Sandy's yearly visits, it was volcanoes; on another, construction equipment. But *unlike* lots of other little boys, Tom had little interest in anything other than his obsessions.

As Tom got older, it became harder to minimize the differences between him and his peers. In middle school, while other kids were joining sports teams and expanding their social circles, Tom's only

friends were online chat room acquaintances. Lynn and Will signed Tom up for scouts, tennis lessons, and other group activities, but Tom would sit on the sidelines.

Tom was in the eighth grade when Will experienced what he later called "the movie moment." He was reading a magazine article about artists who shared several unusual personality characteristics. An obsessive interest in a single topic or object. High intelligence. Unusual speech patterns. An inability to "read" other people's emotions or facial expressions. Poor social skills.

"Wow," Will exclaimed. "This sounds like Tom!"

The View from Mount Magazine

Photo courtesy of Arkansas.com

The article explained that these characteristics reflected a condition called *Asperger's syndrome,* named after the Austrian pediatrician who first described it. Considered a mild form of autism, Asperger's was sometimes called the "geek syndrome" because it seemed to be more common among engineers and computer experts—people who were technologically brilliant but socially inept. Eventually, Tom was evaluated by a pediatric neurologist, who agreed that Tom had Asperger's. Since Tom's diagnosis, the term "Asperger's syndrome" has been eliminated as a formal diagnosis by the psychiatric community. Instead, Asperger's is now included in the more general diagnosis of *autism spectrum disorder.*

When Sandy asked Tom if he would share his experiences for this Prologue, she knew that conversations with him could be difficult. Tom often doesn't pick up on the verbal and nonverbal "signals" that most people use to regulate their interactions with others. So Tom and Sandy agreed that she would interview him using instant messaging.

Sandy: Tell me how you felt when you were given the diagnosis of Asperger's.

Tom: I felt that I finally had something to pin my weirdness on.

S: How did you feel weird?

T: Because I wasn't "normal" and making friends like the rest of my peers.

T: I mean, I'm not schizoid. . . . I get lonely like anyone else.

S: What is it about Asperger's that makes social interaction so difficult?

T: Well, I suppose it's because of a lack of understanding on the part of the person with Asperger's we don't understand some aspects of politeness, for example.

T: Sometimes I don't understand why people would be hurt by something.

It's hard for Tom to be tactful because he has trouble interpreting other people's emotional states. He doesn't intend to be rude; he is simply being honest. For example, consider this exchange:

S: I have one more question if that's ok?

T: Okay. Just one?

S: I'm afraid you might be getting bored. See, that's me being polite. ☺

T: Well, it's not like I have anything better to do.

Tom's intellectual gifts have helped him compensate for his social deficits. By the end of his freshman year of high school, Tom ranked first in his class of over 800 students. He also scored so highly on the SAT that he was admitted to a special school for gifted students.

Although some of his fellow students envy his intellectual abilities, Tom is well aware of the special challenges he faces. For example, Tom can get "stuck" on a math problem or writing assignment, reworking it endlessly and unable to complete his homework because it doesn't meet his own standards for perfection.

S: Okay, so here's the last question: You can tell thousands of college students whatever you want to say about Asperger's. What would you say?

T: Well, I could try being a smart aleck and say "We're not as smart as the shrinks say we are. Be thankful you're normal."

S: What's to be thankful for?

T: You can turn in work that's less than perfect. You can make friends.

We'll come back to Tom's story as we discuss the different mental abilities involved in thinking, language, and intelligence. We'll also provide more information about autism and autism spectrum disorder. As you'll see, there is more to "intelligence" than just academic ability. □

INTRODUCTION:
Thinking, Language, and Intelligence

KEY THEME

Thinking is a broad term that refers to how we use knowledge to analyze situations, solve problems, and make decisions.

KEY QUESTIONS

> What are some of the basic characteristics of mental images?

> How do we manipulate mental images?

> What are concepts, and how are they formed?

Cognition is a general term that refers to the mental activities involved in acquiring, retaining, and using knowledge. In previous chapters, we've looked at fundamental cognitive processes such as perception, learning, and memory. These processes are critical in order for us to acquire and retain new knowledge.

In this chapter, we will focus on how we *use* that knowledge to analyze situations, solve problems, make decisions, and use language. As you'll see, such cognitive abilities are widely regarded as key dimensions of *intelligence*—a concept that we will also explore.

The Building Blocks of Thought
MENTAL IMAGERY AND CONCEPTS

In the most general sense, *thinking* is involved in all conscious mental activity, whether it is acquiring new knowledge, reasoning, planning ahead, or daydreaming. More narrowly, we can say that **thinking** involves manipulating mental representations of information in order to draw inferences and conclusions. Thinking, then, involves active mental processes and is often directed toward some goal, purpose, or conclusion.

What exactly is it that we think *with*? Two important forms of mental representations are *mental images* and *concepts*. We'll look first at mental images.

MENTAL IMAGES

When you read the Prologue, did you form a mental image of the view from the deck of a cabin perched above a river valley? Or of a steep hiking trail, lined with wildflowers and butterflies? Or Sandy and Tom sitting in front of their computers and exchanging instant messages? The stories we tell in our prologues typically lend themselves to the creation of mental images. Formally, a **mental image** is a mental representation of objects or events that are not physically present. Does the brain process mental images in the same way that it processes physical perceptions? We discuss this question in the Focus on Neuroscience on page 274, "Seeing Faces and Places in the Mind's Eye."

We often rely on mental images to accomplish some cognitive task. For example, try reciting the letters of the alphabet that consist of only curved lines. To accomplish this task, you have to mentally visualize and then inspect an image of each letter of the alphabet.

Typically, the term *mental images* refers to visual "pictures." However, people can also form mental representations that involve senses other than vision (Cattaneo & Vecchi, 2008; Kollndorfer & others, 2015; Palmiero & others, 2009). For example, you can probably easily create a mental representation for the taste of a chocolate milk shake, the smell of freshly popped popcorn, or the feel of cold, wet clothing sticking to your skin. Nonetheless, most research on mental images has looked at how we manipulate visual images, and we'll focus on visual images in our discussion here.

cognition The mental activities involved in acquiring, retaining, and using knowledge.

thinking The manipulation of mental representations of information in order to draw inferences and conclusions.

mental image A mental representation of objects or events that are not physically present.

Thinking What types of cognitive activities might be required to plan and implement a new clothing line? South African actor and award-winning fashion designer Nkhensani Nkosi, shown here, is highly creative. But she must also be able to draw on existing knowledge, analyze new information, effectively solve problems, and make good decisions.

Per-Anders Pettersson/Getty Images

FOCUS ON NEUROSCIENCE

Seeing Faces and Places in the Mind's Eye

Until the advent of sophisticated brain-scanning techniques, studying mental imagery relied on cognitive tasks, such as measuring how long participants reported it took to scan a mental image (see Kosslyn & others, 2001). Today, however, psychologists are using brain-imaging techniques to study mental imagery. One important issue is whether mental images activate the same brain areas that are involved in perception. Remember, perception takes place when the brain registers information that is received directly from sensory organs.

Previously, researchers found that perceiving certain types of scenes or objects activates specific brain areas. For example, when we look at *faces,* specific brain areas such as the *fusiform facial area (FFA)* are activated (Epstein & Kanwisher, 1998; Pitcher & others, 2011). When we look at pictures of *places,* a different brain area, called the *parahippocampal place area,* or *PPA,* is activated (Cant & Goodale, 2011; Kanwisher, 2001). Given these findings, the critical question is this: If we simply *imagine* faces or places, will the same brain areas be activated?

To answer that question, psychologists Kathleen O'Craven and Nancy Kanwisher (2000) used fMRI to compare brain activity during perception and imagery. Study participants underwent fMRI scans while they looked at photographs of familiar faces and places (scenes from their college campus). Next, the participants were asked to close their eyes and form a vivid mental image of each of the photographs they had just viewed.

Three key findings emerged from the study. First, as you can see from the fMRI scans of two participants shown here, *imagining* a face or place activated the same brain region that is activated when *perceiving* a face or a place. More specifically, forming a mental image of a place activated the parahippocampal place area. And, forming a mental image of a face activated the fusiform facial area.

Second, compared to imagining a face or place, actually perceiving a face or place evoked a stronger brain response, as indicated by the slightly larger red and yellow areas in the perception fMRIs (upper row). Third, because the brain responses between the two conditions were so distinctive, O'Craven and Kanwisher could determine what the participants were imagining—faces or places—simply from looking at the fMRI scans.

Other neuroscientists have confirmed that there is considerable overlap in the brain areas involved in visual perception and mental images (Ganis & others, 2004; Reddy & others, 2010). Clearly, perception and imagination share common brain mechanisms. So, at least as far as the brain is concerned, "the next best thing to being there" might just be closing your eyes . . . and going there in your mind's eye.

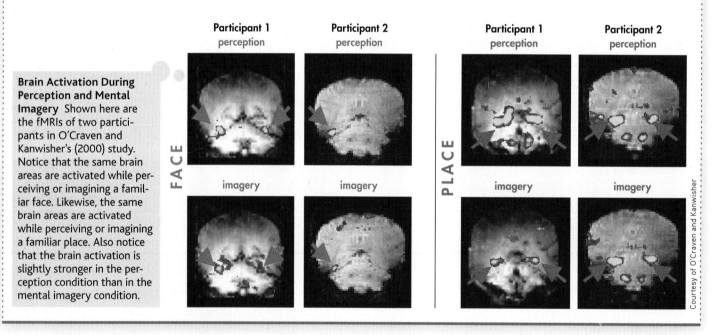

Brain Activation During Perception and Mental Imagery Shown here are the fMRIs of two participants in O'Craven and Kanwisher's (2000) study. Notice that the same brain areas are activated while perceiving or imagining a familiar face. Likewise, the same brain areas are activated while perceiving or imagining a familiar place. Also notice that the brain activation is slightly stronger in the perception condition than in the mental imagery condition.

Courtesy of O'Craven and Kanwisher

Do people manipulate mental images in the same way that they manipulate their visual images of actual objects? Suppose we gave you a map of the United States and asked you to visually locate San Francisco. Then suppose we asked you to fix your gaze on another city. If the other city was far away from San Francisco (like New York), it would take you longer to visually locate it than if it was close by (like Los Angeles). If you were scanning a *mental* image rather than an actual map, would it also take you longer to scan across a greater distance?

In a classic study by Stephen Kosslyn and his colleagues (1978), participants first viewed and memorized a map of a fictitious island with distinct locations, such as a lake, a hut, a rock, and grass (see Figure 7.1). After the map was removed, participants were asked to imagine a specific location on the island, such as the sandy beach. Then a second location, such as the rock, was named. The participants mentally scanned across their mental image of the map and pushed a button when they reached the rock.

The researchers found that the amount of time it took to mentally scan to the new location was directly related to the distance between the two points. The greater the distance between the two points, the longer it took to scan the mental image of the map (Kosslyn & others, 1978). It seems, then, that we tend to scan a mental image in much the same way that we visually scan an actual image (Kosslyn & Thompson, 2000).

However, we don't simply look at mental images in our minds. Sometimes thinking involves the *manipulation* of mental images. For example, try the problem in Figure 7.2 at the bottom of the page, and then continue reading.

It probably took you longer to determine that the 3 in the middle was backward than to determine that the 3 on the far left was backward. Determining which 3s were backward required you to mentally *rotate* each one to an upright position. Just as it takes time to rotate a physical object, it takes time to mentally rotate an image. Furthermore, the greater the degree of rotation required, the longer it takes you to rotate the image mentally and the greater the brain activity that occurs (Seurinck & others, 2011; Wohlschläger & Wohlschläger, 1998). Thus, it probably took you longer to mentally rotate the 3 in the middle, which you had to rotate 180 degrees, than it did to mentally rotate the 3 on the far left, which you had to rotate only 60 degrees.

Collectively, research seems to indicate that we manipulate mental images in much the same way we manipulate the actual objects they represent (Gardony & others, 2014; Rosenbaum & others, 2001). However, mental images are not perfect duplicates of our actual sensory experience. The mental images we use in thinking have some features in common with actual visual images, but they are not like photographs. Instead, they are *memories* of visual images. And, like other memories, visual images are actively constructed and potentially subject to error (Cattaneo & Vecchi, 2008).

CONCEPTS

Along with mental images, thinking also involves the use of concepts. A **concept** is a mental category we have formed to group objects, events, or situations that share similar features or characteristics. Concepts provide a kind of mental shorthand, economizing the cognitive effort required for thinking and communicating.

Using concepts makes it easier to communicate with others, remember information, and learn new information. For example, the concept "food" might include anything from a sardine to a rutabaga. Although very different, we can still group rutabagas and sardines together because they share the central feature of being edible. If someone introduces us to a new delicacy and tells us it is *food,* we immediately know that it is something to eat—even if it is something we've never seen before.

Adding to the efficiency of our thinking is our tendency to organize the concepts we hold into orderly hierarchies composed of main categories and subcategories (Markman & Gentner, 2001; Voorspoels & others, 2011). Thus, a very general concept, such as "furniture," can be mentally divided into a variety of subcategories: tables, chairs, lamps, and so forth. As we learn the key properties that define general concepts, we also learn how members of the concept are related to one another.

How are concepts formed? When we form a concept by learning the *rule* or *features* that define the particular concept, it is called a **formal concept.** Children are taught

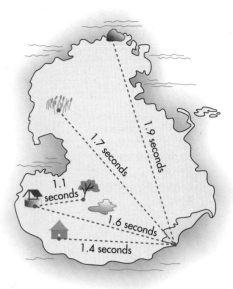

FIGURE 7.1 Mentally Scanning Images This is a reduced version of the map used by Stephen Kosslyn and his colleagues (1978) to study the scanning of mental images. After participants memorized the map, the map was removed. Participants then mentally visualized the map and scanned from one location to another. As you can see by the average scanning times, it took participants longer to scan greater distances on their mental images of the map, just as it takes longer to scan greater distances on an actual map.

Source: Data from Kosslyn & others (1978).

concept A mental category of objects or ideas based on properties they share.

formal concept A mental category that is formed by learning the rules or features that define it.

FIGURE 7.2 Manipulating Mental Images Two of these threes are backward. Which ones?

Are These Mammals? The more closely an item matches the prototype of a concept, the more quickly we can identify the item as being an example of that concept. Because bats, dolphins, and the rather peculiar-looking African long-tailed pangolin don't fit our prototype for a mammal, it takes us longer to decide whether they belong to the category "mammal" than it does to classify animals that are closer to the prototype.

(l) George Steinmetz/Corbis
(c) Michael Krabs/age fotostock
(r) ArchMan/Shutterstock

TABLE 7.1

From Prototypes to Atypical Examples

Vehicles	Fruit
car	orange
truck	apple
bus	banana
motorcycle	peach
train	pear
trolley car	apricot
bicycle	plum
airplane	grape
boat	strawberry
tractor	grapefruit
cart	pineapple
wheelchair	blueberry
tank	lemon
raft	watermelon
sled	honeydew
horse	pomegranate
blimp	date
skates	coconut
wheelbarrow	tomato
elevator	olive

SOURCE: Reprinted from Cognitive Psychology, Vol 7, Rosch, Eleanor H.; & Mervis, Carolyn B., Family Resemblances: Studies in the Internal Structure of Categories, 573–605, Copyright 1975, with permission from Elsevier.

The first items listed under each general concept are the ones most people tend to think of as the prototype examples of that concept. As you move down the list, the items become progressively less similar to the prototype examples.

the specific rules or features that define many simple formal concepts, such as geometric shapes. These defining rules or features can be simple or complex. In either case, the rules are logical but rigid. If the defining features, or *attributes,* are present, then the object is included as a member or example of that concept. For some formal concepts, this rigid all-or-nothing categorization procedure works well. For example, a substance can be categorized as a solid, liquid, or gas. The rules defining these formal concepts are very clear-cut.

However, as psychologist Eleanor Rosch (1973) pointed out, the features that define categories of natural objects and events in everyday life are seldom as clear-cut as the features that define formal concepts. A **natural concept** is a concept formed as a result of everyday experience rather than by logically determining whether an object or event fits a specific set of rules. Rosch suggested that, unlike formal concepts, natural concepts have "fuzzy boundaries." That is, the rules or attributes that define natural concepts are not always sharply defined.

Because natural concepts have fuzzy boundaries, it's often easier to classify some members of natural concepts than others (Rosch & Mervis, 1975). To illustrate this point, think about the defining features or rules that you usually associate with the natural concept "vehicle." With virtually no hesitation, you can say that a car, truck, and bus are all examples of this natural concept. How about a sled? A wheelbarrow? A raft? An elevator? It probably took you a few seconds to determine whether these objects were also vehicles. Why are some members of natural concepts easier to classify than others?

According to Rosch (1978), some members are better representatives of a natural concept than are others. The "best," or most typical, instance of a particular concept is called a **prototype** (Mervis & Rosch, 1981; Rosch, 1978). According to prototype theories of classification, we tend to determine whether an object is an instance of a natural concept by comparing it to the prototype we have developed rather than by logically evaluating whether the defining features are present or absent (Minda & Smith, 2001, 2011).

The more closely an item matches the prototype, the more quickly we can identify it as being an example of that concept (Rosch & Mervis, 1975). For example, it usually takes us longer to identify an olive or a coconut as being a fruit because they are so dissimilar from our prototype of a typical fruit, like an apple or an orange (see Table 7.1).

Some researchers believe that we don't classify a new instance by comparing it to a single "best example" or prototype. Instead, they believe that we store memories of individual instances, called **exemplars,** of a concept (Nosofsky & Zaki, 2002; Voorspoels & others, 2008). Then, when we encounter a new object, we compare it to the exemplars that we have stored in memory to determine whether it belongs to that category (Nosofsky & others, 2011). So, if you're trying to decide whether a coconut is a fruit, you compare it to your memories of other items that you know to be fruits. Is it like an apple? An orange? How about a peach? Or a cantaloupe?

Bizarro ©Dan Piraro. King Feature Syndicate

Concepts, Exemplars, and Humor What makes this cartoon funny? One source of humor is *incongruity*—the juxtaposition of two concepts, especially when an unexpected similarity between the concepts is revealed (Martin, 2007). Here, the joke relies on the juxtaposition of cats and the familiar exemplar for a barbershop—the striped pole outside the door, plate glass window, and chairs and magazines for clients waiting their turn. Exemplars are often used in cartoons to communicate a situation or concept to the audience. If you didn't share the exemplar for *barbershop*, you probably wouldn't find the joke to be very funny.

As the two building blocks of thinking, mental images and concepts help us impose order on the phenomena we encounter and think about. We often rely on this knowledge when we engage in complex cognitive tasks, such as solving problems and making decisions, which we'll consider next.

Solving Problems and Making Decisions

KEY THEME

Problem solving refers to thinking and behavior directed toward attaining a goal that is not readily available.

KEY QUESTIONS

> What are some advantages and disadvantages of each problem-solving strategy?

> What is insight, and how does intuition work?

> How can functional fixedness and mental set interfere with problem solving?

From fixing flat tires to figuring out how to pay for college classes, we engage in the cognitive task of problem solving so routinely that we often don't even notice the processes we follow. Formally, **problem solving** refers to thinking and behavior directed toward attaining a goal that is not readily available (Novick & Bassok, 2005; Wang & Chiew, 2010).

Before you can solve a problem, you must develop an accurate understanding of the problem. Correctly identifying the problem is a key step in successful problem solving (Bransford & Stein, 1993). If your representation of the problem is flawed, your attempts to solve it will also be flawed.

Problem-Solving Strategies

As a general rule, people tend to attack a problem in an organized or systematic way. Usually, the strategy you select is influenced by the nature of the problem and your degree of experience, familiarity, and knowledge about the problem you are confronting (Chrysikou, 2006; Leighton & Sternberg, 2013). In this section, we'll look at some of the common strategies used in problem solving.

TRIAL AND ERROR
A PROCESS OF ELIMINATION

The strategy of **trial and error** involves actually trying a variety of solutions and eliminating those that don't work. When there is a limited range of possible solutions, trial and error can be a useful problem-solving strategy. If you were trying to develop a new spaghetti sauce recipe, for example, you might use trial and error to fine-tune the seasonings.

When the range of possible answers or solutions is large, however, trial and error can be very time-consuming. For example, your author Sandy has a cousin who hates reading written directions, especially for projects like assembling Ikea furniture or making minor household repairs. Rather than taking the time to read through the directions, he'll spend hours trying to figure out how the pieces fit together.

natural concept A mental category that is formed as a result of everyday experience.

prototype The most typical instance of a particular concept.

exemplars Individual instances of a concept or category, held in memory.

problem solving Thinking and behavior directed toward attaining a goal that is not readily available.

trial and error A problem-solving strategy that involves attempting different solutions and eliminating those that do not work.

Trial and Error Even an expert chef like Eugenio Gonzalez of the Philippines needs to "adjust the seasonings"— tasting the food before serving to make sure that the flavors are just right. Recipes are often developed through a process of trial and error.

REUTERS/Cheryl Ravelo

"Yup, I'm guessing here's your problem."

ALGORITHMS
GUARANTEED TO WORK

Unlike trial and error, an **algorithm** is a procedure or method that, when followed step by step, always produces the correct solution. Mathematical formulas are examples of algorithms. For instance, the formula used to convert temperatures from Celsius to Fahrenheit (multiply C by 9/5, then add 32) is an algorithm.

Even though an algorithm may be guaranteed to eventually produce a solution, using an algorithm is not always practical. For example, imagine that while rummaging in a closet you find a combination lock with no combination attached. Using an algorithm will eventually produce the correct combination. You can start with 0–0–0, then try 0–0–1, followed by 0–0–2, and so forth, and systematically work your way through combinations to 36–36–36. But this solution would take a while, because there are 46,656 potential combinations to try. So, although using an algorithm to generate the correct combination for the combination lock is guaranteed to work eventually, it's not a very practical approach to solving this particular problem.

HEURISTICS
RULES OF THUMB

In contrast to an algorithm, a **heuristic** is a general rule-of-thumb strategy that may or may not work. Although heuristic strategies are not guaranteed to solve a given problem, they tend to simplify problem solving because they let you reduce the number of possible solutions. With a more limited range of solutions, you can use trial and error to eventually arrive at the correct one. In this way, heuristics may serve an adaptive purpose by allowing us to use patterns of information to solve problems quickly and accurately (Gigerenzer & Gaissmeier, 2011; Gigerenzer & Goldstein, 2011).

Here's an example. Creating footnotes is described somewhere in the onscreen "Help" documentation for a word-processing software program. If you use the algorithm of scrolling through every page of the Help program, you're guaranteed to solve the problem eventually. But you can greatly simplify your task by using the heuristic of entering "footnotes" in the Help program's search box. This strategy does not guarantee success, however, because the search term may not be indexed.

One common heuristic is to break a problem into a series of *subgoals*. This strategy is often used in writing a term paper. Choosing a topic, locating information about the topic, organizing the information, and so on become a series of subproblems. As you solve each subproblem, you move closer to solving the larger problem. Another useful heuristic involves *working backward* from the goal. Starting with the end point, you determine the steps necessary to reach your final goal. For example, when making a budget, people often start off with the goal of spending no more than a certain total each month, then work backward to determine how much of the target amount they will allot for each category of expenses.

Perhaps the key to successful problem solving is *flexibility*. A good problem solver is able to recognize that a particular strategy is unlikely to yield a solution—and knows to switch to a different approach (Bilalić & others, 2008; Ionescu, 2012). And, sometimes, the reality is that a problem may not have a single "best" solution.

Remember Tom, whose story we told in the Prologue? One characteristic of many people with autism spectrum disorder is cognitive rigidity and inflexible thinking (Kleinhans & others, 2005; Leung & Zakzanis, 2014; Toth & King, 2008). Like Tom, many people can become frustrated when they are "stuck" on a problem. Unlike Tom, most people are able to sense when it's time to switch to a new strategy, take a break for a few hours, seek assistance from

Heuristics at Work Tackling a remodeling job, even a simple one like repainting a room, requires effective problem solving. What heuristics might this young couple use to improve their chances of success?

experts or others who may be more knowledgeable—or accept defeat and give up. In Tom's case, rather than give up on a problem or seek a different approach to solving it, Tom will persevere in his attempt to solve it. For example, faced with a difficult homework problem in an advanced mathematics class, Tom often stayed up until 2:00 or 3:00 A.M., struggling to solve a single problem until he literally fell asleep at his desk.

Similarly, successful problem solving sometimes involves accepting a less-than-perfect solution to a particular problem—knowing when a solution is "good enough," even if not perfect. But to many with autism spectrum disorder, things are either right or wrong—there is no middle ground (Toth & King, 2008). So when Tom got a 98 rather than 100 on a difficult math test, he was inconsolable. When he ranked in the top five in his class, he was upset because he wasn't first. Tom would sometimes be unable to write an essay because he couldn't think of a perfect opening sentence, or turn in an incomplete essay because he couldn't think of the perfect closing sentence.

"Sometimes it's easier if you break the work up into little chunks."

INSIGHT AND INTUITION

The solution to some problems seems to arrive in a sudden realization, or flash of **insight,** that happens after you mull a problem over (Ohlsson, 2010; Öllinger & others, 2008). Sometimes an insight will occur when you recognize how the problem is similar to a previously solved problem. Or an insight can involve the sudden realization that an object can be used in a novel way. Try your hand at the two problems in Figure 7.3. The solution to each of those problems is often achieved by insight.

Insights rarely occur through the conscious manipulation of concepts or information. In fact, you're usually not aware of the thought processes that lead to an insight. Increasingly, cognitive psychologists and neuroscientists are investigating nonconscious processes, including unconscious problem solving, insight, and intuition (Hogarth, 2010; Horr & others, 2014). **Intuition** means coming to a conclusion or making a judgment without conscious awareness of the thought processes involved.

One influential model of intuition is the two-stage model (Bowers & others, 1990; Hodgkinson & others, 2008). In the first stage, called the *guiding stage,* you perceive a pattern in the information you're considering, but not consciously. The perception of such patterns is based on your expertise in a given area and your memories of related information.

In the second stage, the *integrative stage,* a representation of the pattern becomes conscious, usually in the form of a hunch or hypothesis. At this point, conscious analytic thought processes take over. You systematically attempt to prove or disprove the hypothesis. For example, an experienced doctor might integrate both obvious and subtle cues to recognize a pattern in a patient's symptoms, a pattern that takes the form of a hunch or an educated guess. Once the hunch is consciously formulated, she might order lab tests to confirm or disprove her tentative diagnosis.

An intuitive hunch, then, is a new idea that integrates new information with existing knowledge stored in long-term memory. Such hunches are likely to be accurate only in contexts in which you already have a broad base of knowledge and experience (Jones, 2003; M. Lieberman, 2000).

algorithm A problem-solving strategy that involves following a specific rule, procedure, or method that inevitably produces the correct solution.

heuristic A problem-solving strategy that involves following a general rule of thumb to reduce the number of possible solutions.

insight The sudden realization of how a problem can be solved.

intuition Coming to a conclusion or making a judgment without conscious awareness of the thought processes involved.

Problem 1	Six drinking glasses are lined up in a row. The first three are full of water, the last three are empty. By handling and moving only one glass, change the arrangement so that no full glass is next to another full one, and no empty glass is next to another empty one.
Problem 2	A man who lived in a small town married 20 different women in that same town. All of them are still living, and he never divorced any of them. Yet he broke no laws. How could he do this?

FIGURE 7.3 A Demonstration of Insightful Solutions The solutions to these problems are often characterized by sudden flashes of insight. See if you have the "That's it!" experience in solving these problems without looking at the solutions on page 281.

Source: Problem 1 information from Ashcraft (1994); Problem 2 information from Sternberg (1986).

FIGURE 7.4 Overcoming Functional Fixedness Here's a classic problem for you to solve. You have two candles, some thumbtacks, and a box of matches. Using just these objects, try to figure out how to mount the candles on a wall. (The solution is on page 282.)

Source: Research from Duncker (1945).

Overcoming Functional Fixedness: Repurposing The goal of *repurposing* is to find new uses for objects that would otherwise end up clogging waterways, littering sidewalks and roads, or accumulating in landfills. Using liter-sized water bottles and inexpensive solar-powered bulbs, Filipino architect Rodelon Ramos and Iliac Diaz developed a durable, cheap light fixture that can be used to light a home for as long as five hours. Successful repurposing involves finding new uses for familiar objects—the essence of overcoming functional fixedness.

AP Photo/Bullit Marquez

Obstacles to Solving Problems
THINKING OUTSIDE THE BOX

Sometimes, past experience or expertise in a particular domain can actually interfere with effective problem solving. If we're used to always doing something in a particular way, we may not be open to new or better solutions. When we can't move beyond old, inappropriate heuristics, ideas, or problem-solving strategies, *fixation* can block the generation of new, more effective approaches (Moss & others, 2011; Storm & Angello, 2010).

When we view objects as functioning only in the usual or customary way, we're engaging in a tendency called **functional fixedness.** Functional fixedness often prevents us from seeing the full range of ways in which an object can be used. To get a feel for how functional fixedness can interfere with your ability to find a solution, try the problem in Figure 7.4.

For example, consider the problem of disposing of plastic bags, which take decades to centuries to degrade and clog landfills and waterways. Hundreds of U.S. cities have dealt with the problem by passing ordinances banning or restricting their use. Functional fixedness kept people from thinking of the bags as anything but trash. But it turns out that the indestructible nature of these single-use bags can be advantageous: the bags can be turned into "plarn," a plastic yarn that can be repurposed to create durable, waterproof sleeping mats for the homeless. A Chicago-based group, New Life for Old Bags, estimates that it takes between 600 and 700 plastic bags to create one six-by-two foot sleeping mat. The finished mats are distributed to homeless shelters throughout the city (Stuart, 2013).

Another common obstacle to problem solving is **mental set**—the tendency to persist in solving problems with solutions that have worked in the past (Öllinger & others, 2008). Obviously, if a solution has worked in the past, there's good reason to consider using it again. However, if we approach a problem with a rigid mental set, we may not see other possible solutions (Kershaw & Ohlsson, 2004).

Ironically, mental set is sometimes most likely to block insight in areas in which you are already knowledgeable or well trained. Before you read any further, try solving the simple arithmetic problems in Figure 7.5. If you're having trouble coming up with the answer, it's probably because your existing training in solving arithmetic problems is preventing you from seeing the equations from a different perspective than what you have been taught (Knoblich & Öllinger, 2006; Öllinger & others, 2008).

Mental sets can sometimes suggest a useful heuristic. But they can also prevent us from coming up with new, and possibly more effective, solutions. If we try to be flexible in our thinking and overcome the

FIGURE 7.5 Mental Set The equations on the right, expressed in Roman numerals, are obviously incorrect. Your task is to transform each incorrect equation into a correct equation by moving ONE matchstick in each equation. The matchstick can only be moved once. Only Roman numerals and the three arithmetic operators +, −, or = are allowed. Take your best shot at solving the equations before looking at the solutions on page 283. Remember, in the Roman numeral system, I = 1; II = 2; III = 3; IV = 4; V = 5.

Source: Research from Duncker (1945).

tendency toward mental sets, we can often identify simpler solutions to many common problems.

Decision-Making Strategies

KEY THEME

Different cognitive strategies are used when making decisions, depending on the type and number of options available to us.

KEY QUESTIONS

> What are the single-feature model, the additive model, and the elimination-by-aspects model of decision making?

> Under what conditions is each strategy most appropriate?

> How do we use the availability and representativeness heuristics to help us estimate the likelihood of an event?

Who hasn't felt like flipping a coin when faced with an important or complicated decision? Fortunately, most of the decisions we make in everyday life are relatively minor. But every now and then we have to make a decision where much more is at stake. When a decision is important or complex, we're more likely to invest time, effort, and other resources in considering different options.

The decision-making process becomes complicated when each option involves the consideration of several features. It's rare that one alternative is superior in every category. So, what do you do when each alternative has pros and cons? In this section, we'll describe three common decision-making strategies.

THE SINGLE-FEATURE MODEL

One decision-making strategy is called the *single-feature model*. In order to simplify the choice among many alternatives, you base your decision on a single feature. When the decision is a minor one, the single-feature model can be a good decision-making strategy. For example, faced with an entire supermarket aisle of laundry detergents, you could simplify your decision by deciding to buy the cheapest brand. When a decision is important or complex, however, making decisions on the basis of a single feature can increase the riskiness of the decision.

THE ADDITIVE MODEL

A better strategy for complex decisions is to systematically evaluate the important features of each alternative. One such decision-making model is called the *additive model*.

In this model, you first generate a list of the factors that are most important to you. For example, suppose you need off-campus housing. Your list of important factors might include cost, proximity to campus, compatibility with roommates, or having a private bathroom. Then, you rate each alternative for each factor using an arbitrary scale, such as from −5 to +5. If a particular factor has strong advantages or appeal, such as compatible roommates, you give it the maximum rating (+5). If a particular factor has strong drawbacks or disadvantages, such as distance from campus, you give it the minimum rating (−5). Finally, you add up the ratings for each alternative. This strategy can often reveal the best overall choice. If the decision involves a situation in which some factors are more important than others, you can emphasize the more important factors by multiplying the rating.

Taking the time to apply the additive model to important decisions can greatly improve your decision making. By allowing you to evaluate the features of one alternative at a time, then comparing the alternatives, the additive model provides a logical strategy for identifying the most acceptable choice from a range of possible decisions. Although we seldom formally calculate the subjective value of individual features for different options, we often informally use the additive model by

| Problem 1 | Pour the water in glass number 2 into glass number 5. |
| Problem 2 | The man is a minister. |

Solutions to Figure 7.3

Philippe Turpin/Getty Images

Decisions, Decisions There are literally hundreds of different styles, sizes, and colors of athletic shoes available. What strategies do you use when you buy a new pair of shoes?

functional fixedness The tendency to view objects as functioning only in their usual or customary way.

mental set The tendency to persist in solving problems with solutions that have worked in the past.

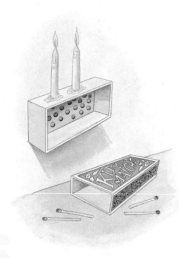

Solution to Figure 7.4

comparing two choices feature by feature. The alternative with the "best" collection of features is then selected.

THE ELIMINATION-BY-ASPECTS MODEL

Psychologist Amos Tversky (1972) proposed another decision-making model called the *elimination-by-aspects model.* Using this model, you evaluate all of the alternatives one characteristic at a time, typically starting with the feature you consider most important. If a particular alternative fails to meet that criterion, you scratch it off your list of possible choices, even if it possesses other desirable attributes. As the range of possible choices is narrowed down, you continue to compare the remaining alternatives, one feature at a time, until just one alternative is left.

For example, suppose you want to buy a new laptop. You might initially eliminate all the models that aren't powerful enough to run the software you need to use, then the models outside your budget, and so forth. Continuing in this fashion, you would progressively narrow down the range of possible choices to the one choice that satisfies all your criteria.

Good decision makers adapt their strategy to the demands of the specific situation. If there are just a few choices and features to compare, people tend to use the additive method, at least informally. However, when the decision is complex, involving the comparison of many choices that have multiple features, people often use *more than one* strategy. That is, we usually begin by focusing on the critical features, using the elimination-by-aspects strategy to quickly narrow down the range of acceptable choices. Once we have narrowed the list of choices down to a more manageable short list, we tend to use the additive model to make a final decision. Of course, it's not always as straightforward as this. Other factors, such as our emotions, play in to our decision making, too (Lerner & others, 2015).

Vivid Images and the Availability Heuristic: Shark! Almost every summer, shark attacks make the headlines in newspapers and online. But how likely are you to die in a shark attack? In 2010, there were *two* deaths due to shark attack. In contrast, 33 people were killed by dog attacks, 29 people were killed by lightning—and 630 people were killed in bicycle accidents (International Shark Attack File, 2010). How does the availability heuristic explain why people are afraid to go to the beach after a well-publicized shark sighting?

Decisions Involving Uncertainty
ESTIMATING THE PROBABILITY OF EVENTS

Some decisions involve a high degree of uncertainty. In these cases, you need to make a decision, but you are unable to predict with certainty that a given event will occur. Instead, you have to estimate the probability of an event occurring. But how do you actually make that estimation?

For example, imagine that you're running late for a very important appointment. You may be faced with this decision: "Should I risk a speeding ticket to get to the appointment on time?" In this case, you would have to estimate the probability of a particular event occurring—getting pulled over for speeding.

In such instances, we often estimate the likelihood that certain events will occur, then gamble. In deciding what the odds are that a particular gamble will go our way, we tend to rely on two rule-of-thumb strategies to help us estimate the likelihood of events: the *availability heuristic* and the *representativeness heuristic* (Tversky & Kahneman, 1982; Kahneman, 2003).

THE AVAILABILITY HEURISTIC

When we use the **availability heuristic,** we estimate the likelihood of an event on the basis of how readily

Watt Jim/Getty Images

available other instances of the event are in our memory. When instances of an event are easily recalled, we tend to consider the event as being more likely to occur. So, we're less likely to exceed the speed limit if we can readily recall that a friend recently got a speeding ticket.

However, when a rare event makes a vivid impression on us, we may overestimate its likelihood (Tversky & Kahneman, 1982). State lottery commissions capitalize on this cognitive tendency by running many TV commercials showing that lucky person who won the $100 million Powerball. A vivid memory is created, which leads viewers to an inaccurate estimate of the likelihood that the event will happen to them.

The key point here is that the less accurately our memory of an event reflects the actual frequency of the event, the less accurate our estimate of the event's likelihood will be. That's why the lottery commercials don't show the other 50 million people staring dejectedly at their TV screens because they did *not* win the $100 million.

THE REPRESENTATIVENESS HEURISTIC

The other heuristic we often use to make estimates is called the **representativeness heuristic** (Kahneman & Tversky, 1982; Kahneman, 2003). Here, we estimate an event's likelihood by comparing how similar its essential features are to our prototype of the event. Remember, a *prototype* is the most typical example of an object or an event.

To go back to our example of deciding whether to speed, we are more likely to risk speeding if we think that we're somehow significantly different from the prototype of the driver who gets a speeding ticket. If our prototype of a speeder is a teenager driving a flashy, high-performance car, and we're an adult driving a minivan with a baby seat, then we will probably estimate the likelihood of our getting a speeding ticket as low.

Like the availability heuristic, the representativeness heuristic can lead to inaccurate judgments. Consider the following description:

Maria is a perceptive, sensitive, introspective woman. She is very articulate, but measures her words carefully. Once she's certain she knows what she wants to say, she expresses herself easily and confidently. She has a strong preference for working alone.

On the basis of this description, is it more likely that Maria is a successful fiction writer or that Maria is a registered nurse? Most people guess that she is a successful fiction writer. Why? Because the description seems to mesh with what many people think of as the typical characteristics of a writer.

However, when you compare the number of registered nurses (which is very large) to the number of successful female fiction writers (which is very small), it's actually much more likely that Maria is a nurse. Thus, the representativeness heuristic can produce faulty estimates if: (1) we fail to consider possible variations from the prototype or (2) we fail to consider the approximate number of prototypes that actually exist.

What determines which heuristic is more likely to be used? Research suggests that the availability heuristic is most likely to be used when people rely on information held in their long-term memory to determine the likelihood of events occurring. On the other hand, the representativeness heuristic is more likely to be used when people compare different variables to make predictions (Harvey, 2007).

The Critical Thinking box "The Persistence of Unwarranted Beliefs" on the next page discusses some of the other psychological factors that can influence the way in which we evaluate evidence, make decisions, and draw conclusions.

> Test your understanding of **Introduction to Thinking, Language and Intelligence; Solving Problems; and Making Decisions** with **LEARNING**Curve.

availability heuristic A strategy in which the likelihood of an event is estimated on the basis of how readily available other instances of the event are in memory.

representativeness heuristic A strategy in which the likelihood of an event is estimated by comparing how similar it is to the prototype of the event.

Solution to Figure 7.5 Most people try to correct the equations in Figure 7.5 by moving a matchstick that changes one of the numbers. Why? Because solving the math problems that we are assigned in school almost always involves manipulating the numbers, not the arithmetic signs. While this assumption is a useful one in solving the vast majority of math problems—especially the ones that you are assigned as homework—it is an example of a mental set that can block you from arriving at new, creative solutions to problems.

The Persistence of Unwarranted Beliefs

Throughout this text, we show that many pseudoscientific claims fail when subjected to scientific scrutiny. However, once a belief in a pseudoscience or paranormal phenomenon is established, the presentation of contradictory evidence often has little impact (Lester, 2000). Ironically, contradictory evidence can actually *strengthen* a person's established beliefs (Lord & others, 1979). For example, in one study, participants were given the accurate information that the flu vaccine does not cause the flu (Nyhan & Reifler, 2015). Those who were already worried about getting the flu from the vaccine were not reassured. In fact, they were even *less* likely to say they would get the flu vaccine after learning this information. How do psychologists account for this phenomenon?

Several psychological studies have explored how people deal with evidence, especially evidence that contradicts their beliefs (see Ross & Anderson, 1982; Zusne & Jones, 1989). The four obstacles to logical thinking described here can account for much of the persistence of unwarranted beliefs in pseudosciences or other areas (Risen & Gilovich, 2007).

Obstacle 1: The Belief-Bias Effect

The *belief-bias effect* occurs when people accept only the evidence that conforms to their belief, rejecting or ignoring any evidence that does not. For example, in a classic study conducted by Warren Jones and Dan Russell (1980), ESP believers and ESP disbelievers watched two attempts at telepathic communication.

"What's nice about working in this place is we don't have to finish any of our experiments."

© 2002, Sidney Harris

In each attempt, a "receiver" tried to indicate what card the "sender" was holding.

In reality, both attempts were rigged. One attempt was designed to appear to be a successful demonstration of telepathy, with a significant number of accurate responses. The other attempt was designed to convincingly demonstrate failure. In this case, the number of accurate guesses was no more than chance and could be produced by simple random guessing.

Following the demonstration, the participants were asked what they believed had taken place. Both believers and disbelievers indicated that ESP had occurred in the successful attempt. But only the believers said that ESP had also taken place in the clearly *unsuccessful* attempt. In other words, the ESP believers ignored or discounted the evidence in the failed attempt. This is the essence of the belief-bias effect.

Language and Thought

Language is a system for combining arbitrary symbols to produce an infinite number of meaningful statements.

> What are the characteristics of language?

> What are the effects of bilingualism?

> What has research found about the cognitive abilities of nonhuman animals?

The human capacity for language is surely one of the most remarkable of all our cognitive abilities. With little effort, you produce hundreds of new sentences every day. And you're able to understand the vast majority of the thousands of words contained in this chapter without consulting a dictionary.

Human language has many special qualities—qualities that make it flexible, versatile, and complex. **Language** can be formally defined as a system for combining arbitrary symbols to produce an infinite number of meaningful statements. We'll begin our discussion of the relationship between language and thought by describing these special characteristics of language. In Chapter 9, we'll discuss language development in children.

language A system for combining arbitrary symbols to produce an infinite number of meaningful statements.

confirmation bias The tendency to seek out evidence that confirms an existing belief while ignoring evidence that might contradict or undermine that belief.

Obstacle 2: Confirmation Bias

Confirmation bias is the strong tendency to search for information or evidence that confirms a belief, while making little or no effort to search for information that might disprove the belief (Gilovich, 1997; Masnick & Zimmerman, 2009). For example, we tend to visit Web sites that support our own viewpoints and read blogs and editorial columns written by people who interpret events from our perspective. At the same time, we avoid the Web sites, blogs, and columns written by people who don't see things our way (Ruscio, 1998).

People also tend to believe evidence that confirms what they *want* to believe is true, a bias that is sometimes called the *wishful thinking bias* (Bastardi & others, 2011). Faced with evidence that seems to contradict a hoped-for finding, people may object to the study's methodology. And, evaluating evidence that seems to confirm a wished-for finding, people may overlook flaws in the research or argument. For example, parents with children in day care may be motivated to embrace research findings that emphasize the benefits of day care for young children and discount findings that emphasize the benefits of home-based care.

Obstacle 3: The Fallacy of Positive Instances

The *fallacy of positive instances* is the tendency to remember uncommon events that seem to confirm our beliefs and to forget events that disconfirm our beliefs. Often, the occurrence is really nothing more than coincidence. For example, you find yourself thinking of an old friend. A few moments later, the phone rings and it's him. You remember this seemingly telepathic event but forget all the times that you've thought of your old friend and he did not call. In other words, you remember the positive instance but fail to notice the negative instances when the anticipated event did not occur (Gilovich, 1997).

Obstacle 4: The Overestimation Effect

The tendency to overestimate the rarity of events is referred to as the *overestimation effect*. Suppose a "psychic" comes to your class of 23 students. Using his psychic abilities, the visitor "senses" that two people in the class were born on the same day. A quick survey finds that, indeed, two people share the same month and day of birth. This is pretty impressive evidence of clairvoyance, right? After all, what are the odds that two people in a class of 23 would have the same birthday?

When we perform this "psychic" demonstration in class, our students usually estimate that it is very unlikely that 2 people in a class of 23 will share a birthday. In reality, the odds are *1 in 2*, or 50–50 (Martin, 1998). Our students' overestimation of the rarity of this event is an example of the *overestimation effect*.

Thinking Critically About the Evidence

On the one hand, it is important to keep an open mind. Simply dismissing an idea as impossible shuts out the consideration of evidence for new and potentially promising ideas or phenomena. At one time, for example, scientists thought it impossible that rocks could fall from the sky (Hines, 2003).

On the other hand, the obstacles described here underscore the importance of choosing ways to gather and think about evidence that will help us avoid unwarranted beliefs and self-deception.

The critical thinking skills we described in Chapter 1 are especially useful in this respect. The boxes "What Is a Pseudoscience?" and "How to Think Like a Scientist" provided guidelines that can be used to evaluate all claims, including pseudoscientific or paranormal claims. In particular, it's important to stress again that good critical thinkers strive to evaluate *all* the available evidence before reaching a conclusion, not just the evidence that supports what they want to believe.

CRITICAL THINKING QUESTIONS

- How can using critical thinking skills help you avoid these obstacles to logical thinking?

- Beyond the logical fallacies described here, what might motivate people to maintain beliefs in the face of contradictory evidence?

The Characteristics of Language

The purpose of language is to communicate—to express meaningful information in a way that can be understood by others. To do so, language requires the use of *symbols*. These symbols may be sounds, written words, or, as in American Sign Language, formalized gestures.

A few symbols may be similar in form to the meaning they signify, such as the English words *boom* and *pop*. However, for most words, the connection between the symbol and the meaning is completely *arbitrary* (Pinker, 1995, 2007). For example, *ton* is a small word that stands for a vast quantity, whereas *nanogram* is a large word that stands for a very small quantity. Because the relationship between the symbol and its meaning is arbitrary, language is tremendously flexible (Pinker, 1994, 2007). New words can be invented, such as *selfie*, *podcast*, and *crowdfund*. And the meanings of words can change and evolve, such as *spam*, *troll*, and *catfish*.

AP Photo/Al Behrman

Sign Language Sign language, used by hearing-impaired people, meets all the formal requirements for language, including syntax, displacement, and generativity. The similarities between spoken language and sign language have been confirmed by brain-imaging studies. The same brain regions are activated in hearing people when they speak as in deaf people when they use sign language (Hickok & others, 2001; Lubbadeh, 2005).

CULTURE AND HUMAN BEHAVIOR

The Effect of Language on Perception

Professionally, Benjamin Whorf (1897–1941) was an insurance company inspector. But his passion was the study of languages, particularly Native American languages. In the 1950s, Whorf proposed an intriguing theory that became known as the *Whorfian hypothesis.*

Whorf (1956) believed that a person's language determines the very structure of his or her thought and perception. Your language, he claimed, determines how you perceive and "carve up" the phenomena of your world. He argued that people who speak very different languages have completely different worldviews. More formally, the Whorfian hypothesis is called the **linguistic relativity hypothesis**—the notion that differences among languages cause differences in the thoughts of their speakers.

To illustrate his hypothesis, Whorf contended that the Eskimos had many different words for "snow." But English, he pointed out, has only the word *snow.* According to Whorf (1956):

> We have the same word for falling snow, snow on the ground, snow packed hard like ice, slushy snow, wind-driven flying snow—whatever the situation may be. To an Eskimo, this all-inclusive word would be almost unthinkable; he would say that falling snow, slushy snow, and so on are sensuously and operationally different, different things to contend with; he uses different words for them and for other kinds of snow.

Whorf's example would be compelling except for one problem: The Eskimos do *not* have dozens of different words for "snow." Rather, they have just a few words for "snow" (Pinker, 2007). Beyond that minor sticking point, think carefully about Whorf's example. Is it really true that English-speaking people have a limited capacity to describe snow? Or do not discriminate between different types of snow? The English language includes *snowflake, snowfall, slush, sleet, flurry, blizzard,* and *avalanche.* Avid skiers have many additional words to describe snow, from *powder* to *mogul* to *hardpack.*

MYTH ◀ SCIENCE

Is it true that, unlike English speakers, Eskimos have dozens of words for snow?

More generally, people with expertise in a particular area tend to perceive and make finer distinctions than nonexperts do. Experts are also more likely to know the specialized terms that reflect those distinctions (Pinker, 1994, 2007). To the knowledgeable bird-watcher, for example, there are distinct differences between a cedar waxwing and a bohemian waxwing. To the nonexpert, they're just two brownish birds with yellow tail feathers.

Despite expert/nonexpert differences in noticing and naming details, we don't claim that the expert "sees" a different reality than a nonexpert. In other words, our perceptions and thought processes influence the language we use to describe those perceptions (Rosch, 1987; Pinker, 2007). Notice that this conclusion is the exact *opposite* of the linguistic relativity hypothesis.

Whorf also pointed out that many languages have different color-naming systems. English has names for 11 basic colors: *black, white, red, green, yellow, blue, brown, purple, pink, orange,* and *gray.* However, some languages have only a few color terms. Navajo, for example, has only one word to describe both blue and green, but two different words for black (Fishman, 1960). Would people who had just a few words for colors "carve up" and perceive the electromagnetic spectrum differently?

Eleanor Rosch set out to answer this question (Heider & Olivier, 1972). The Dani-speaking people of New Guinea have words for only two colors. *Mili* is used for the dark, cool colors of black, green, and blue. *Mola* is used for light, warm colors, such as white, red, and yellow. According to the Whorfian hypothesis,

---

The meaning of these symbols is *shared* by others who speak the same language. That is, speakers of the same language agree on the connection between the sound and what it symbolizes. Consequently, a foreign language sounds like a stream of meaningless sounds because we do not share the memory of the connection between the arbitrary sounds and the concrete meanings they symbolize.

Further, language is a highly structured system that follows specific rules. Every language has its own unique *syntax,* or set of rules for combining words. Although you're usually unaware of these rules as you're speaking or writing, you immediately notice when a rule has been violated.

The rules of language help determine the meaning that is being communicated. For example, word-order rules are very important in determining the meaning of an English phrase. "The boy ate the giant pumpkin" has an entirely different meaning from "The giant pumpkin ate the boy." In other languages, meaning may be conveyed by different rule-based distinctions, such as specific pronouns, the class or category of words, or word endings.

Another important characteristic of language is that it is creative, or *generative.* That is, you can generate an infinite number of new and different phrases and sentences.

A final important characteristic of human language is called *displacement.* You can communicate meaningfully about ideas, objects, and activities that are not physically present. You can refer to activities that will take place in the future, that took place in the past, or that will take place only if certain conditions are met

linguistic relativity hypothesis The hypothesis that differences among languages cause differences in the thoughts of their speakers.

Can You Count Without Number Words? Cognitive neuroscientist Edward Gibson traveled to a remote Amazon village to confirm previous research by anthropologist and linguist Daniel Everett (2005, 2008) that showed the Pirahã people lacked the ability to count and had no comprehension of numbers. Gibson found that rather than identifying quantities by exact numbers, the Pirahã research participants used only relative terms like "few," "some," and "many." According to Gibson, the Pirahã are capable of learning to count, but did not develop a number system because numbers are simply not useful in their culture (Frank & others, 2008).

the people of New Guinea, with names for only two classes of colors, should perceive color differently than English-speaking people, with names for 11 basic colors.

Rosch showed Dani speakers a brightly colored chip and then, 30 seconds later, asked them to pick out the color they had seen from an array of other colors. Despite their lack of specific words for the colors they had seen, the Dani did as well as English

speakers on the test. The Dani people used the same word to label red and yellow, but they still distinguished between the two. Rosch concluded that the Dani people perceived colors in much the same way as English-speaking people.

Other research on color-naming in different languages has arrived at similar conclusions: Although color *names* may vary, color *perception* does not appear to depend on the language used (Delgado, 2004; Kay & Regier, 2007; Lindsey & Brown, 2004). The bottom line? Whorf's strong contention that language *determines* perception and the structure of thought has not been supported. However, cultural and cognitive psychologists today are actively investigating the ways in which language can *influence* perception, thought, and memory (Fausey & others, 2010; Frank & others, 2008; Majid & others, 2004).

A striking demonstration of the influence of language comes from recent studies of remote indigenous peoples living in the Amazon region of Brazil (Everett, 2005, 2008). The language of the Pirahã people, an isolated tribe of fewer than 200 members, has no words for specific numbers (Frank & others, 2008). Their number words appear to be restricted to words that stand for "few," "more," and "many" rather than exact quantities such as "three," "five," or "twenty." Similarly, the Mundurukú language, spoken by another small Amazon tribe, has words only for quantities one through five (Pica & others, 2004). Above that number, they used such expressions as "some," "many," or "a small quantity." In both cases, individuals were unable to complete simple arithmetic tasks (Gordon, 2004).

Such findings do not, by any means, confirm Whorf's belief that language *determines* thinking or perception (Deutscher, 2010; Gelman & Gallistel, 2004). Rather, they demonstrate how language categories can affect *how* individuals think about particular concepts. And most researchers today discuss thinking and language as interacting, each influencing the other and both being influenced by culture (ojalehto & Medin, 2015).

("If I take on extra shifts at work, maybe I can go on spring break with my friends"). You can also carry on a vivid conversation about abstract ideas ("What is justice?") or strictly imaginary topics ("If you were going to spend a year in a space station orbiting Neptune, what would you bring along?").

All your cognitive abilities are involved in understanding and producing language. Using learning and memory, you acquire and remember the meaning of words. You interpret the words you hear or read (or see, in the case of American Sign Language and other sign languages) through the use of perception. You use language to help you reason, represent and solve problems, and make decisions (Polk & Newell, 1995).

Giving Birth to a New Language In 1977, a special school for deaf children opened in Managua, Nicaragua. The children quickly developed a system of gestures for communicating with one another. Since then, the system of gestures has evolved into a unique new language with its own grammar and syntax— *Idioma de Signos Nicaragense* (Senghas & others, 2004; Siegal, 2004). The birth of Nicaraguan Sign Language is not a unique event. Linguists Wendy Sandler and her colleagues (2005) at the University of Haifa have documented the spontaneous development of another unique sign language, this one in a remote Bedouin village where a large number of villagers share a form of hereditary deafness (Fox, 2008). Like Nicaraguan Sign Language, *Al-Sayyid Bedouin Sign Language* has its own syntax and grammatical rules, which differ from other languages in the region. The spontaneous evolution of these two unique sign languages vividly demonstrates the human predisposition to develop rule-based systems of communication (Meir & others, 2010).

bilingualism Fluency in two or more languages.

The Bilingual Mind: Are Two Languages Better Than One?

How many languages can you speak fluently? In many countries, **bilingualism,** or fluency in two or more languages, is the norm. In fact, estimates are that about two-thirds of children worldwide are raised speaking two or more languages (Bialystok & others, 2009).

At one time, especially in the United States, raising children as bilingual was discouraged. Educators believed that children who simultaneously learned two languages would be confused and not learn either language properly. Such confusion, they believed, could lead to delayed language development, learning problems, and lower intelligence (see Garcia & Náñez, 2011).

But new research has found that bilingualism has many cognitive benefits (Kroll & others, 2014). This is true particularly in the case of *balanced proficiency,* when speakers are equally proficient in two languages (Garcia & Náñez, 2011). Several studies have found that bilingual speakers are better able to control attention and inhibit distracting information than are monolinguals—people who are fluent in just a single language (Bialystok, 2011). Why? It turns out that *both* languages are constantly active to some degree in the brain of a bilingual speaker, even in a situation where only one language is spoken. Thus, the bilingual speaker must be a "mental juggler," and the resulting cognitive workout pays off in increased mental agility.

This cognitive flexibility may also have social benefits: Research suggests that bilinguals are better at taking the perspective of others, such as imagining how another person might view a particular situation (Rubio-Fernández & Glucksberg, 2012). One explanation is that from an early age, bilinguals must monitor and evaluate the language knowledge of conversational partners (Costa & Sebastián-Gallés, 2014).

Bilingualism also seems to pay off in preserving brain function in old age (Alladi & others, 2013; Bialystok & others, 2012). One clue came from findings in elderly patients diagnosed with *Alzheimer's disease* or *dementia,* whose symptoms include deterioration in memory and other cognitive functions (Bialystok & others, 2007; Craik & others, 2010). Bilingual patients tended to develop symptoms four to five years later than a control group of patients matched for age, socioeconomic status, and other factors. Like education, exercise, and mental stimulation, speaking two (or more) languages fluently seems to build up what researchers call a *cognitive reserve* that can help protect against cognitive decline in late adulthood (Bialystok & others, 2012; Costa & Sebastián-Gallés, 2014).

Animal Communication and Cognition

Chimpanzees "chutter" to warn of snakes and "chirp" to let others know that a leopard is nearby. Prairie dogs make different sounds to warn of approaching coyotes, dogs, hawks, and even humans wearing blue shirts versus humans wearing yellow shirts (Slobodchikoff & others, 2009). Even insects have complex communication systems. For example, honeybees perform a "dance" to report information about the distance, location, and quality of a pollen source to their hive mates (J. Riley & others, 2005).

Clearly, animals communicate with one another, but are they capable of mastering language? Some of the most promising results have come from the research of psychologists Sue Savage-Rumbaugh and Duane Rumbaugh (Lyn & others, 2006). These researchers began working with a rare chimpanzee species called the *bonobo* in the mid-1980s (Savage-Rumbaugh & Lewin, 1994).

The bonobo named Kanzi was able to learn symbols and also to comprehend spoken English. Altogether, Kanzi understands elementary syntax and more than 500 spoken English words. And, Kanzi can respond to new, complex spoken commands, such as "Put the ball on the pine needles" (Segerdahl & others, 2006). Because these commands are spoken by an assistant out of Kanzi's view, he cannot be responding to nonverbal cues.

Prairie Dogs Prairie dogs use a sophisticated system of vocal communication to describe predators. Their high-pitched calls contain specific information about what the predator is, how big it is, and how fast it is approaching (Slobodchikoff & others, 2009).

Chuck Haney/DanitaDelimont.com

Irene Pepperberg with Alex When Alex died suddenly in September 2007, the story was reported in newspapers around the world, including the *New York Times* (Carey, 2007; Talbot, 2008). Over 30 years of research, Pepperberg and Alex revolutionized ideas about avian intelligence and animal communication. Along with his remarkable language abilities, Alex also displayed an understanding of simple concepts, including an understanding of bigger and smaller, similarity and difference. Shown a green block and a green ball and asked "What's the same?" Alex responds, "Color." Alex could even accurately label quantities up to the number six (Pepperberg, 2007). To learn more about Pepperberg's ongoing research with gray parrots Griffin and Athena, visit www.alexfoundation.org.

© Arlene Levin-Rowe

Research evidence suggests that nonprimates also can acquire limited aspects of language. For example, Louis Herman (2002) trained bottle-nosed dolphins to respond to sounds and gestures, each of which stands for a word. This artificial language incorporates syntax rules, such as those that govern word order.

Finally, consider Alex, an African gray parrot. Trained by Irene Pepperberg (1993, 2000), Alex could answer spoken questions with spoken words and identify and categorize objects by color, shape, and material (Pepperberg, 2007). Alex also used many simple phrases, such as "Come here" and "Want to go back."

Going beyond language, psychologists today study many aspects of animal behavior, including memory, problem solving, planning, cooperation, and even deception. Collectively, such research reflects an active area of psychological research that is referred to as **animal cognition** or **comparative cognition** (Shettleworth, 2010; Wasserman & Zentall, 2006).

And, rather than focusing on whether nonhuman animals can develop human capabilities, such as language, comparative psychologists today study a wide range of cognitive abilities in many different species (Emery & Clayton, 2009; Santos & Rosati, 2015). For example:

- Western scrub jays can, apparently, remember the past and anticipate the future (Clayton & others, 2003). They survive harsh winters by remembering precisely where they stored the food they gathered months earlier (Raby & others, 2007; van der Vaart & others, 2011).

- Black-capped chickadees are able to remember the outcome of a foraging expedition and use that memory to prospectively plan where to seek food in the future (Feeney & others, 2011).

- Pinyon jays can use logic to determine the social status of other birds by watching how a stranger bird interacts with birds whose social status is already known to them (Paz-y-Miño & others, 2004).

- Bengalese finches detect differences in the "syntax" of different bird calls, noticing when the sequencing of phrases differs from songs previously heard (Abe & Watanabe, 2011; Bloomfield & others, 2011).

- Dogs are able to distinguish between people who are stingy with food rewards and people who are generous with food rewards (Bray & others, 2014). They remember this information, and later will approach the generous person even if that person clearly has less food to offer than the stingy person.

- Elephants, highly social animals, seem to understand the nature of cooperation, as reflected in their ability to coordinate their efforts with other elephants in order to reach a food reward (Plotnik & others, 2011).

animal cognition or **comparative cognition** The study of animal learning, memory, thinking, and language.

LaunchPad

Video material is provided by BBC Worldwide Learning and CBS News Archives and produced by Princeton Academic Resources

For a fascinating look at a study of animal cognition, try **Video Activity: Can Chimpanzees Plan Ahead?**

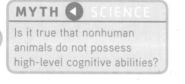

Lending a Trunk In this experiment, Asian elephants had to pull two ends of the same rope simultaneously to drag a bucket of tasty corn within reach. Researchers found that the elephants quickly learned to coordinate their efforts, and would wait at their rope end as long as 45 seconds for an elephant partner. They also appeared to understand that there was no point to pulling if the partner lacked access to the rope (Plotnik & others, 2011).

Think Elephants International, Inc. (www.thinkelephants.org)

MYTH ◄ SCIENCE

Is it true that nonhuman animals do not possess high-level cognitive abilities?

intelligence The global capacity to think rationally, act purposefully, and deal effectively with the environment.

Think Like a SCIENTIST

Can online brain games make you smarter? Go to LaunchPad: Resources to **Think Like a Scientist** about **Brain Exercises**.

LaunchPad

Can nonhuman animals "think"? Do they consciously reason? Such questions may be unanswerable (Premack, 2007). More important, many comparative psychologists today take a different approach. Rather than trying to determine whether animals can reason, think, or communicate like humans, these researchers are interested in the specific cognitive capabilities that different species have evolved to best adapt to their ecological niche (de Waal & Ferrari, 2010; Shettleworth, 2010).

❯ Test your understanding of **Language and Thought** with **LEARNING**Curve.

Measuring Intelligence

KEY THEME

Intelligence is defined as the global capacity to think rationally, act purposefully, and deal effectively with the environment.

KEY QUESTIONS

❯ What roles did Binet, Terman, and Wechsler play in the development of intelligence tests?

❯ How did Binet, Terman, and Wechsler differ in their beliefs about intelligence and its measurement?

❯ Why are standardization, validity, and reliability important components of psychological tests?

Up to this point, we have talked about a broad range of cognitive abilities—the use of mental images and concepts, problem solving and decision making, and the use of language. All these mental abilities are aspects of what we commonly call *intelligence*.

What exactly is intelligence? We will rely on a formal definition developed by psychologist David Wechsler. Wechsler (1944, 1977) defined **intelligence** as the global capacity to think rationally, act purposefully, and deal effectively with the environment. Although many people commonly equate intelligence with "book smarts," notice that Wechsler's definition is much broader. To Wechsler, intelligence is reflected in effective, rational, and goal-directed behavior.

The Development of Intelligence Tests

Can intelligence be measured? If so, how? Intelligence tests attempt to measure general mental abilities, rather than accumulated knowledge or aptitude for a specific subject or area. In the next several sections, we will describe the evolution of intelligence tests, including the qualities that make any psychological test scientifically acceptable.

ALFRED BINET
IDENTIFYING STUDENTS WHO NEEDED SPECIAL HELP

In the early 1900s, the French government passed a law requiring all children to attend school. Faced with the need to educate children from a wide variety of backgrounds, the French government commissioned psychologist **Alfred Binet** to develop procedures to identify students who might require special help.

With the help of French psychiatrist Théodore Simon, Binet devised a series of tests to measure different mental abilities. Binet deliberately did not test abilities, such as reading or mathematics, that the students might have been taught. Instead, he focused on elementary mental abilities, such as memory, attention, and the ability to understand similarities and differences.

Binet arranged the questions on his test in order of difficulty, with the simplest tasks first. He found that brighter children performed like older children. That is, a bright 7-year-old might be able to answer the same number of questions as an average 9-year-old, while a less capable 7-year-old might do only as well as an average 5-year-old.

This observation led Binet to the idea of a mental level, or **mental age,** that was different from a child's chronological age. An "advanced" 7-year-old might have a mental age of 9, while a "slow" 7-year-old might demonstrate a mental age of 5.

It is somewhat ironic that Binet's early tests became the basis for modern intelligence tests. First, Binet did *not* believe that he was measuring an inborn or permanent level of intelligence (Foschi & Cicciola, 2006; Kamin, 1995). Rather, he believed that his tests could help identify "slow" children who could benefit from special help (Newton & McGrew, 2010).

Second, Binet believed that intelligence was too complex a quality to describe with a single number (Siegler, 1992). He steadfastly refused to rank "normal" children on the basis of their scores, believing that such rankings would be unfair. He recognized that many individual factors, such as a child's level of motivation, might affect the child's score. Finally, Binet noted that an individual's score could vary from time to time (Gould, 1993; Kaufman, 2009).

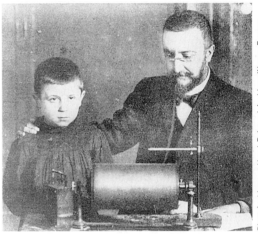

Alfred Binet French psychologist Alfred Binet (1857–1911) is shown here with an unidentified child and an instrument from his laboratory that was used to measure his young participants' breathing rates while they performed different tasks (Cunningham, 1997). Although Binet developed the first systematic intelligence tests, he did not believe that he was measuring innate ability. Instead, he believed that his tests could identify schoolchildren who could benefit from special help.

Binet Archives, at Henri-Poincaré Archives (Nancy, France, CNRS/University of Lorraine)

To judge well, to comprehend well, to reason well, these are the essential activities of intelligence.

—Alfred Binet and Théodore Simon (1905)

LEWIS TERMAN AND THE STANFORD–BINET INTELLIGENCE TEST

There was enormous interest in Binet's test in the United States. The test was translated and adapted by Stanford University psychologist **Lewis Terman.** Terman's revision was called the *Stanford–Binet Intelligence Scale.* First published in 1916, the Stanford–Binet was for many years the standard for intelligence tests in the United States.

Terman adopted the suggestion of a German psychologist that scores on the Stanford–Binet test be expressed in terms of a single number, called the **intelligence quotient,** or **IQ.** This number was derived by dividing the individual's mental age by the chronological age and multiplying the result by 100. Thus, a child of average intelligence, whose mental age and chronological age were the same, would have an IQ score of 100. A "bright" 10-year-old child with a mental age of 13 would have an IQ of 130 (13/10 × 100). A "slow" child with a chronological age of 10 and a mental age of 7 would have an IQ of 70 (7/10 × 100). It was Terman's use of the intelligence quotient that resulted in the popularization of the phrase "IQ test."

WORLD WAR I AND GROUP INTELLIGENCE TESTING

When the United States entered World War I in 1917, the U.S. military was faced with the need to rapidly screen 2 million army recruits. Using a group intelligence test designed by one of Terman's students, army psychologists developed the Army Alpha and Beta tests. The *Army Alpha* test was administered in writing, and the *Army Beta* test was administered orally to recruits and draftees who could not read.

mental age A measurement of intelligence in which an individual's mental level is expressed in terms of the average abilities of a given age group.

intelligence quotient (IQ) A measure of general intelligence derived by comparing an individual's score with the scores of others in the same age group.

Testing Immigrants at Ellis Island This photograph, taken in 1917, shows an examiner administering a mental test to a newly arrived immigrant at the U.S. immigration center on Ellis Island. According to one intelligence "expert" of the time, 80 percent of the Hungarians, 79 percent of the Italians, and 87 percent of the Russians were "feeble-minded" (see Kamin, 1995). The new science of "mental testing" was used to argue for restrictions on immigration.

David Wechsler Born in Romania, David Wechsler (1896–1981) emigrated with his family to New York when he was six years old. Like Binet, Wechsler believed that intelligence involved a variety of mental abilities. He also strongly believed that IQ scores could be influenced by personality, motivation, and cultural factors (Matarazzo, 1981).

After World War I ended, the Army Alpha and Army Beta group intelligence tests were adapted for civilian use. The result was a tremendous surge in the intelligence-testing movement. Group intelligence tests were designed to test virtually all ages and types of people, including preschool children, prisoners, and newly arriving immigrants (Anastasi & Urbina, 1997; Kamin, 1995). However, the indiscriminate use of the tests also resulted in skepticism and hostility.

For example, immigrants were screened as they arrived at Ellis Island. The result was sweeping generalizations about the intelligence of different nationalities and races. During the 1920s, a few intelligence testing experts even urged the U.S. Congress to limit the immigration of certain nationalities to keep the country from being "overrun with a horde of the unfit" (see Kamin, 1995).

Despite concerns about the misuse of the so-called IQ tests, the tests quickly became very popular. Lost was Binet's belief that intelligence tests were useful only to identify those who might benefit from special educational help. Contrary to Binet's contention, it soon came to be believed that the IQ score was a fixed, inborn characteristic that was resistant to change (Gould, 1993).

Terman and other American psychologists believed that a high IQ predicted more than success in school. To investigate the relationship between IQ and success in life, Terman (1926) identified 1,500 California schoolchildren with "genius" IQ scores. He set up a longitudinal research study to follow their careers throughout their lives. Some of the findings of this landmark study are described in the In Focus box "Does a High IQ Score Predict Success in Life?" on the next page.

DAVID WECHSLER AND THE WECHSLER INTELLIGENCE SCALES

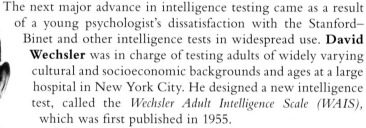

The next major advance in intelligence testing came as a result of a young psychologist's dissatisfaction with the Stanford–Binet and other intelligence tests in widespread use. **David Wechsler** was in charge of testing adults of widely varying cultural and socioeconomic backgrounds and ages at a large hospital in New York City. He designed a new intelligence test, called the *Wechsler Adult Intelligence Scale (WAIS),* which was first published in 1955.

The WAIS had two advantages over the Stanford–Binet. First, the WAIS was specifically designed for adults, rather than for children. Second, Wechsler's test provided scores on 11 subtests measuring different abilities. The subtest scores were grouped to provide an overall verbal score and performance score. The *verbal score* represented scores on subtests of vocabulary, comprehension, knowledge of general information, and other verbal tasks. The *performance score* reflected scores on largely nonverbal subtests, such as identifying the missing part in incomplete pictures, arranging pictures to tell a story, or arranging blocks to match a given pattern.

The design of the WAIS reflected Wechsler's belief that intelligence involved a variety of mental abilities. Because the WAIS provided an individualized profile of the participants' strengths and weaknesses on specific tasks, it marked a return to the attitudes and goals of Alfred Binet (Fancher, 1996; Sternberg, 1990).

The subtest scores on the WAIS also proved to have practical and clinical value. For example, a pattern of low scores on some subtests combined with high scores on other subtests might indicate a specific learning disability (Kaufman, 1990). Researchers have observed a particular pattern in the WAIS scores of people with autism spectrum disorder (Kanai & others, 2012). And someone who did well on the performance subtests but poorly on the verbal subtests might be unfamiliar with the culture rather than deficient in these skills (Aiken, 1997). That's because many items included on the verbal subtests draw on cultural knowledge.

IN FOCUS

Does a High IQ Score Predict Success in Life?

In 1921, Lewis M. Terman identified 1,500 California girls and boys between the ages of 8 and 12 who had IQs above 140, the minimum IQ score for genius-level intelligence. Terman's goal was to track these children by conducting periodic surveys and interviews to see how genius-level intelligence would affect the course of their lives.

Within a few years, Terman (1926) showed that the highly intelligent children tended to be socially well adjusted, as well as taller, stronger, and healthier than average children, with fewer illnesses and accidents. Not surprisingly, those children performed exceptionally well in school.

But how did Terman's "gifted" children fare in the real world as adults? As a group, they showed an astonishing range of accomplishments (Terman & Oden, 1947, 1959). In 1955, when average income was $5,000 a year, the average income for the group was $33,000. Two-thirds had graduated from college, and a sizable proportion had earned advanced academic or professional degrees.

However, not all of Terman's participants were so successful. To find out why, Terman's colleague Melita Oden compared the 100 most successful men (the "A" group) and the 100 least successful men (the "C" group) in Terman's sample. Despite their high IQ scores, only a handful of the C group were professionals, and, unlike the A group, the Cs were earning only slightly above the national average income. In terms of their personal lives, the Cs were less healthy, had higher rates of alcoholism, and were three times more likely to be divorced than the As (Terman & Oden, 1959).

Given that the IQ scores of the A and C groups were essentially the same, what accounted for the difference in their levels of accomplishment? Terman noted that, as children, the As were much more likely to display "prudence and forethought, will power, perseverance, and the desire to excel." As adults, the As were rated differently from the Cs on only three traits: They were more goal oriented, had greater perseverance, and had greater self-confidence. Overall, the As seemed to have greater ambition and a greater drive to achieve. In other words, *personality factors* seemed to account for the differences in level of accomplishment between the A group and the C group (Terman & Oden, 1959).

Stanford University Archives

"With the exception of moral character, there is nothing as significant for a child's future as his grade of intelligence."

—Lewis M. Terman (1916)

As the general success of Terman's gifted children demonstrates, high intelligence can certainly contribute to success in life. But intelligence alone is not enough. Although IQ scores do reliably predict academic success, success in school is no guarantee of success beyond school. Many different personality factors are involved in achieving success: motivation, emotional maturity, commitment to goals, creativity, and—perhaps most important—a willingness to work hard (Duckworth & others, 2007; Furnham, 2008). None of these attributes are measured by traditional IQ tests.

Wechsler's test also provided an overall, global IQ score, but he changed the way that the IQ score was calculated. On the Stanford–Binet and other early tests, the IQ represented the mental age divided by chronological age. But this approach makes little sense when applied to adult participants. Although a 12-year-old is typically able to answer more questions than an 8-year-old because of developmental differences, such year-by-year age differences lose their meaning in adulthood.

Instead, Wechsler calculated the IQ by comparing an individual's score with the scores of others in the same general age group, such as young adults. The average score for a particular age group was statistically fixed at 100. The range of scores is statistically defined so that two-thirds of all scores fall between 85 and 115—the range considered to indicate "normal" or "average" intelligence. This procedure proved so successful that it was adopted by the administrators of other tests, including the current version of the Stanford–Binet. Today, IQ scores continue to be calculated by this method.

The WAIS was revised in 1981, 1997, and most recently, in 2008. The fourth edition of the WAIS is known as WAIS-IV. Since the 1960s, the WAIS has remained the most commonly administered intelligence test. Wechsler also developed two tests for children: the *Wechsler Intelligence Scale for Children (WISC)* and the *Wechsler Preschool and Primary Scale of Intelligence (WPPSI)*.

LaunchPad

Performance Subtests   Back   Next

Worth Publishers

Try your hand at questions that are much like the Wechsler Adult Intelligence Scale (WAIS) items in **Concept Practice: Wechsler Intelligence Tasks.**

achievement test A test designed to measure a person's level of knowledge, skill, or accomplishment in a particular area.

aptitude test A test designed to assess a person's capacity to benefit from education or training.

standardization The administration of a test to a large, representative sample of people under uniform conditions for the purpose of establishing norms.

Principles of Test Construction

WHAT MAKES A GOOD TEST?

Many kinds of psychological tests measure various aspects of intelligence or mental ability. **Achievement tests** are designed to measure a person's level of knowledge, skill, or accomplishment in a particular area, such as mathematics or a foreign language. In contrast, **aptitude tests** are designed to assess a person's capacity to benefit from education or training. The overall goal of an aptitude test is to predict your ability to learn certain types of information or perform certain skills.

Any psychological test must fulfill certain requirements to be considered scientifically acceptable. The three basic requirements of good test design are standardization, reliability, and validity. Let's briefly look at what each of those requirements entails.

STANDARDIZATION

If you answer 75 of 100 questions correctly, what does that score mean? Is it high, low, or average? For an individual's test score to be interpreted, it has to be compared against some sort of standard of performance.

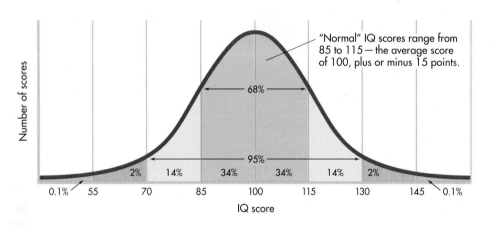

"Normal" IQ scores range from 85 to 115 — the average score of 100, plus or minus 15 points.

Standardization means that the test is given to a large number of participants who are representative of the group of people for whom the test is designed. All the participants take the same version of the test under uniform conditions. The scores of this group establish the *norms,* or the standards against which an individual score is compared and interpreted.

For IQ tests, such norms closely follow a pattern of individual differences called the **normal curve,** or **normal distribution.** In this bell-shaped pattern, most scores cluster around the average score. As scores become more extreme, fewer instances of the scores occur. In Figure 7.6, you can see the normal distribution of IQ scores on the WAIS-IV. About 68 percent of participants taking the WAIS-IV will score between 85 and 115, the IQ range for "normal" intelligence. Less than one-tenth of 1 percent of the population have extreme scores that are above 145 or below 55.

FIGURE 7.6 The Normal Curve of Distribution of IQ Scores The distribution of IQ scores on the WAIS-IV in the general population tends to follow a bell-shaped normal curve, with the average score defined as 100. Notice that 68 percent of the scores fall within the "normal" IQ range of 85 to 115. Ninety-five percent of the general population score between 70 and 130, while only one-tenth of 1 percent score lower than 55 or higher than 145. (Because of rounding, percentages add up to more than 100%.)

RELIABILITY

A good test must also have **reliability.** That is, it must consistently produce similar scores on different occasions. How do psychologists determine whether a psychological test is reliable? One method is to administer two similar, but not identical, versions of the test at different times. Another procedure is to compare the scores on one half of the test with the scores on the other half of the test. A test is considered reliable if the test and retest scores are highly similar when such strategies are used.

VALIDITY

Finally, a good test must demonstrate **validity,** which means that the test measures what it is supposed to measure. One way to establish the validity of a test is by demonstrating its predictive value. For example, if a test is designed to measure mechanical aptitude, people who received high scores should ultimately prove more successful in mechanical jobs than people who received low scores.

❯ Test your understanding of **Measuring Intelligence** with *LEARNINGCurve.*

The Nature of Intelligence

KEY THEME

Psychologists do not agree about the basic nature of intelligence, including whether it is a single, general ability and whether it includes skills and talents as well as mental aptitude.

KEY QUESTIONS

> What is *g*, and how did Spearman and Thurstone view intelligence?
> What is Gardner's theory of multiple intelligences?
> What is Sternberg's triarchic theory of intelligence?

The Wechsler Adult Intelligence Scale and the Stanford–Binet Intelligence Scale are standardized, reliable, and valid. But do they adequately measure intelligence? The question is not as simple as it sounds. There is considerable disagreement among psychologists about the nature of intelligence, including how intelligence should best be defined and measured (Gardner, 2011; Neisser & others, 1996).

Take another look at the chapter Prologue about Tom and his family. In terms of the type of intelligence that is measured by IQ and other standardized tests, Tom is highly intelligent. But despite his high IQ, Tom can find it extremely difficult to carry out many activities that those with a more "normal" or average intelligence can perform almost effortlessly. Applying for an after-school job, joining a conversation that is already in progress, or even knowing why—or whether—a particular joke is funny are very difficult, if not impossible, tasks for Tom. As you'll see in the next section, psychologists have struggled with the challenge of how to define intelligence for over a century.

Theories of Intelligence

Much of the controversy over the definition of *intelligence* centers on two key issues. First, is intelligence a single, general ability, or is it better described as a cluster of different mental abilities? And second, should the definition of intelligence be restricted to the mental abilities measured by IQ and other intelligence tests? Or should intelligence be defined more broadly?

Although these issues have been debated for more than a century, they are far from being resolved. In this section, we'll describe the views of four influential psychologists on both issues.

CHARLES SPEARMAN
INTELLIGENCE IS A GENERAL ABILITY

Some psychologists believe that a common factor, or general mental capacity, is at the core of different mental abilities. This approach originated with British psychologist **Charles Spearman.** Although Spearman agreed that an individual's scores could vary on tests of different mental abilities, he found that the scores on different tests tended to be similar. That is, people who did well or poorly on a test of one mental ability, such as verbal ability, tended also to do well or poorly on the other tests.

Spearman recognized that particular individuals might excel in specific areas. However, Spearman (1904) believed that a factor he called **general intelligence,** or the ***g* factor,** was responsible for their overall performance on tests of mental ability. Psychologists who follow this approach today think that intelligence can be described as a single measure of general cognitive ability, or *g* factor (Gottfredson, 1998). Thus, general mental ability could accurately be expressed by a single number, such as the IQ score. Lewis Terman's approach to measuring and defining intelligence as a single, overall IQ score was in the tradition of Charles Spearman. In terms of Spearman's model, Tom would undoubtedly score very highly on any test that measured *g* factor or general intelligence. For example, when he took the SAT as a high school junior, he scored in the top 3 percent in math and received a perfect score on the writing section.

normal curve or **normal distribution** A bell-shaped distribution of individual differences in a normal population in which most scores cluster around the average score.

reliability The ability of a test to produce consistent results when administered on repeated occasions under similar conditions.

validity The ability of a test to measure what it is intended to measure.

***g* factor** or **general intelligence** The notion of a general intelligence factor that is responsible for a person's overall performance on tests of mental ability.

Charles Spearman (1863–1945) British psychologist Charles Spearman (1904) believed that a single factor, which he called the *g* factor, underlies many different kinds of mental abilities. To Spearman, a person's level of general intelligence was equivalent to his or her level of "mental energy."

Louis L. Thurstone (1887–1955)
American psychologist Louis Thurstone studied electrical engineering and was an assistant to Thomas Edison before he became interested in the psychology of learning. Thurstone was especially interested in the measurements of people's attitudes and intelligence, and was an early critic of the idea of "mental age," believing that intelligence was too diverse to be quantified in a single number or IQ score.

Archives of the History of American Psychology, The University of Akron. Color added by publisher

LOUIS L. THURSTONE
INTELLIGENCE IS A CLUSTER OF ABILITIES

Psychologist **Louis L. Thurstone** disagreed with Spearman's notion that intelligence is a single, general mental capacity. Instead, Thurstone believed that there were seven different "primary mental abilities," each a relatively independent element of intelligence. Verbal comprehension, numerical ability, reasoning, and perceptual speed are examples Thurstone gave of independent "primary mental abilities."

To Thurstone, the so-called *g* factor was simply an overall average score of such independent abilities and consequently was less important than an individual's specific *pattern* of mental abilities (Thurstone, 1937). David Wechsler's approach to measuring and defining intelligence as a pattern of different abilities was very similar to Thurstone's approach.

HOWARD GARDNER
"MULTIPLE INTELLIGENCES"

More recently, **Howard Gardner** has expanded Thurstone's basic notion of intelligence as different mental abilities that operate independently. However, Gardner has stretched the definition of intelligence (Gardner & Taub, 1999). Rather than analyzing intelligence test results, Gardner (1985, 1993) looked at the kinds of skills and products that are valued in different cultures. He also studied individuals with brain damage, noting that some mental abilities are spared when others are lost. To Gardner, this phenomenon implies that different mental abilities are biologically distinct and controlled by different parts of the brain.

Tania A3/Contrasto/Redux

Howard Gardner and His Theory of Multiple Intelligences According to Howard Gardner (above), many mental abilities are not adequately measured by traditional intelligence tests. As Gardner (2003) explains, "Different tasks call on different intelligences or combinations of intelligence. To perform music intelligently involves a different set of intelligences than preparing a meal, planning a course, or resolving a quarrel." Examples might include the spatial intelligence reflected in the sculptures of this talented Cambodian artist, the extraordinary bodily-kinesthetic intelligence of U.S. soccer player Carli Lloyd, and the musical intelligence of Japanese pianist Hiromi.

Like Thurstone, Gardner has suggested that such mental abilities are independent of each other and cannot be accurately reflected in a single measure of intelligence. Rather than one intelligence, Gardner (1993, 1998a) believes there are "multiple intelligences." To Gardner, "an intelligence" is the ability to solve problems, or to create products, that are valued within one or more cultural settings. Thus, he believes that intelligence must be defined within the context of a particular culture (1998b, 2011). Gardner's theory includes eight distinct, independent intelligences, which are summarized in Figure 7.7. Gardner (2011) has identified a ninth possible intelligence, called *existential intelligence,* but is awaiting further research before formalizing it as a ninth intelligence. Existential intelligence, or *spiritual intelligence,* refers to the capacity to reflect upon "ultimate issues," such as the meaning of life.

Ariadne Van Zandbergen/Alamy

Steven Kingsman/Icon Sportswire

Frank Hoensch/Redferns via Getty Images

Linguistic intelligence	Adept use of language: poet, writer, public speaker, native storyteller
Logical-mathematical intelligence	Logical, mathematical, and scientific ability: scientist, mathematician, navigator, surveyor
Musical intelligence	Ability to create, synthesize, or perform music: musician, composer, singer
Spatial intelligence	Ability to mentally visualize the relationships of objects or movements: sculptor, painter, expert chess player, architect
Bodily-kinesthetic intelligence	Control of bodily motions and capacity to handle objects skillfully: athlete, dancer, craftsperson
Interpersonal intelligence	Understanding of other people's emotions, motives, intentions: politician, salesperson, clinical psychologist
Intrapersonal intelligence	Understanding of one's own emotions, motives, and intentions: essayist, philosopher
Naturalist intelligence	Ability to discern patterns in nature: ecologist, zoologist, botanist

FIGURE 7.7 Gardner's Multiple Intelligences

According to Gardner's model of intelligence, everyone has a different pattern of strengths and weaknesses. How would Tom rate? In terms of linguistic, logical-mathematical, and spatial intelligence, Tom would measure very highly. What about an "intelligence" that wouldn't be measured by a standard IQ test, such as musical intelligence? When I asked Tom what type of music he liked, he couldn't tell me.

If I like a song, I like it.
If I don't, I stop listening.
I really can't categorize it.
It's not within my power.

Although lacking musical intelligence probably doesn't affect your ability to function in our culture, other "intelligences" are much more crucial. Without question, Tom's biggest shortcoming falls in the realm of interpersonal intelligence. Understanding and relating to other people is extremely difficult for him.

In most cultures, the ability to effectively navigate social situations is crucial to at least one aspect of Wechsler's definition of intelligence: "the ability to deal effectively with the environment." Although people with mild symptoms of autism spectrum disorder may not be intellectually disabled, their inability to successfully interact with others leads to even mild forms of autism spectrum disorder being labeled as a disability. However, not everyone agrees with this characterization. Is autism spectrum disorder a disability—or is it a difference? We consider this topic in the In Focus box "Neurodiversity: Beyond IQ," on page 298.

Some of the abilities emphasized by Gardner, such as logical-mathematical intelligence, might be tapped by a standard intelligence test. However, other abilities, such as bodily-kinesthetic intelligence or musical intelligence, do not seem to be reflected on standard intelligence tests. Yet, as Gardner points out, such abilities are recognized and highly valued in many different cultures, including our own.

ROBERT STERNBERG
THREE FORMS OF INTELLIGENCE

Robert Sternberg (2012, 2014b) agrees with Gardner that intelligence is a much broader quality than is reflected in the narrow range of mental abilities measured by a conventional IQ test. However, Sternberg (1988, 1995) disagrees with Gardner's notion of multiple, independent intelligences. He believes that some of Gardner's intelligences are more accurately described as specialized talents, whereas intelligence is a more general quality. Sternberg (1988) points out that you would be able to manage just fine if you were tone-deaf and lacked "musical intelligence" in most societies. However, if you didn't have the ability to reason and plan ahead, you would be unable to function in any culture.

Robert Sternberg (b. 1949) Steinberg first became interested in studying intelligence after he did poorly on a sixth-grade intelligence test. He later realized that test anxiety had interfered with his performance. Throughout his college years, Sternberg did poorly in courses that required rote learning—including his first psychology course at Yale. However, Sternberg persevered. He went on to win many awards for his research and, in 2003, was elected president of the American Psychological Association. Much of Sternberg's career has been devoted to studying nontraditional types of intelligence, such as creativity and wisdom, and developing new ways to measure these qualities (Kaufman & others, 2009; Sternberg, 2014a).

Courtesy Robert Sternberg/Tufts University

IN FOCUS

Neurodiversity: Beyond IQ

Can intelligence be summarized by an IQ score? Do standard intelligence tests adequately measure intelligence? Although the questions seem very abstract, their answers can have very real consequences. To give these questions a human face, consider the case of people with autistic symptoms.

Tom, whose story you read in the Prologue, has a very high IQ as measured on standard intelligence tests. However, his inability to navigate social situations makes him less competent in many everyday activities than people with lower IQ scores.

Such difficulties are a hallmark of **autism spectrum disorder.** The symptoms of autism spectrum disorder cover a broad range, from individuals—like Tom—who require very little support to other people who require a great deal of assistance navigating the demands of everyday life. Regardless of symptom severity, autism spectrum disorder is characterized by two core symptoms: (1) deficits in social communication and social interaction and (2) restricted, repetitive behaviors, interests, and activities. Thus, autistic individuals may be unresponsive to social interaction, engage in repetitive or odd motor behaviors, and have very narrow interests and inflexible behavior and routines (Toth & King, 2008).

What about the cognitive abilities of people with autism spectrum disorder? At the mild end of the spectrum, people like Tom have normal language development and have an IQ in the normal or even genius range. But it's a common misconception that most people on the

MYTH ◀ SCIENCE

Is it true that most people with an autism spectrum disorder have special mental abilities?

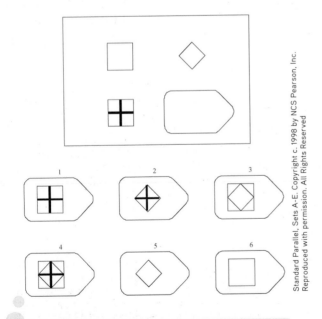

Sample Items from the Raven's Progressive Matrices Test The Raven's test consists of matrix problems that become progressively more difficult. The instructions are simple: Choose the item that best completes the pattern. The test was developed to test general mental ability and is thought to be the "purest" measure of Charles Spearman's *g* factor (Holyoak, 2005)

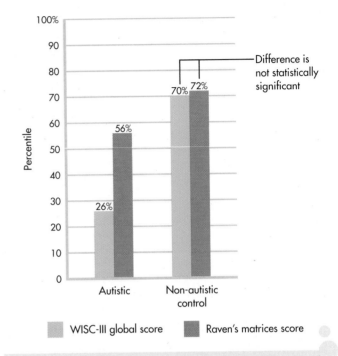

Measuring Intelligence On the average, autistic children scored fully 30 percentile points higher on the nonverbal Raven's Progressive Matrices Test than they did on the WISC-III, which depends heavily on oral instruction and responses. In contrast, a matched control group of non-autistic children received scores that were essentially identical. Adult participants showed a similar pattern. Although a small-scale study, such results suggest that traditional intelligence tests may underestimate intelligence in autistic children and adults. In fact, one-third of the autistic children scored above the 90th percentile on the Raven's, but none did so on the WISC-III. One child raised his score 70 percentile points from 24 to 94 percent—putting him in the "highly intelligent" range rather than the "low-functioning" range.

autistic spectrum are *autistic savants,* like the character "Raymond" played by Dustin Hoffman in the movie *Rainman.* Autistic savants have some extraordinary talent or ability, usually in a very limited area such as math, music, or art. In reality, only about 1 in 10 autistic people are savants (see Dawson & others, 2008; Treffert & Wallace, 2002). However, fewer than 1 in 2,000 non-autistic people have such exceptional abilities.

Another common assumption is that most people with autism are intellectually disabled (e.g., Brown & others, 2008). **Intellectual disability** is a condition in which individuals generally have an IQ of 70 or below and, because of their deficit in mental abilities, are unable to function independently.

Are most people with autism spectrum disorder intellectually disabled? Surveying decades of research, psychologist Meredyth Edelson (2006) found that there was little empirical research to support the claim that the majority of autistic people are intellectually disabled. In fact, because their symptoms vary so much, it's very difficult to generalize about the cognitive abilities of people with autistic spectrum disorders (Sigman & others, 2006).

It is also hard to accurately *measure* intelligence in people who lack the ability to communicate or who are not good at social interaction. In children, for example, intelligence is most commonly measured by Wechsler-based tests, like the WISC-III. But is the WISC-III, which relies heavily on verbal instruction and oral communication, an appropriate instrument for measuring intelligence in autistic children?

To address this question, Michelle Dawson and her colleagues (2007) used the *Raven's Progressive Matrices Test* to measure intelligence in autistic children and adults (see sample items). A *nonverbal* test of logic and higher-level abstract thinking, the test was developed by John Raven, one of Spearman's students. Because the test does not rely upon previously learned information, many cognitive psychologists regard it as an especially pure test of Spearman's *g* factor (Holyoak, 2005).

In Dawson's study, children and adults with autism spectrum disorder took both the Wechsler and the Raven's tests. How did they do? On average, the autistic children scored at the 26th percentile on the Wechsler—a score that would label them as intellectually disabled or low-functioning and well below an average score of 50 percent. In contrast, their average score on the Raven's was 56 percent, *fully 30 percentile points higher,* a difference that moved many children from the low-functioning or intellectually disabled range to the normal range. A similar pattern was found in autistic adults.

Did nonautistic participants also show a big difference in scores on the Wechsler versus the Raven's? No. Members of the non-autistic control groups received very similar scores on the Wechsler and Raven's tests (see graph).

Many autistics affirm that it would be impossible to segregate the part of them that is autistic. To take away their autism is to take away their personhood. . . . Like their predecessors in human rights, many autistics don't want to be cured; they want to be accepted. And like other predecessors in civil rights, many autistics don't want to be required to imitate the majority just to earn their rightful place in society.

—Morton Ann Gernsbacher, 2004

There's an interesting twist to this story. The lead author, Michelle Dawson—who planned the study, handled the data collection, supervised the statistical analysis, and wrote the first draft—is herself autistic. Dawson can't cook, drive, take public transportation, or handle many other everyday tasks. However, Dawson has a phenomenal memory and a razor-sharp logical mind. According to her co-researcher, University of Montreal psychiatrist Laurent Mottron (2008), Dawson also has a remarkable gift for scientific analysis.

It was Dawson who came up with the idea for the study (Gernsbacher, 2007). As Dawson (2007) observes, testing autistic kids' intelligence in a way that requires them to verbally interact with a stranger "is like giving a blind person an intelligence test that requires him to process visual information." On intelligence tests, the assumption has always been that when someone doesn't answer a question, it's because they don't know the answer. But there is another possibility: Perhaps they simply can't express what they know (Gernsbacher, 2004; Gernsbacher & others, 2008).

Why are such findings so important? Well, what happens to children who are labeled as "intellectually disabled," "low-functioning," or "uneducable"? As Laurent Mottron (2006) points out, "If we classify children as intellectually deficient, then that is how they will be treated. They will be denied a host of opportunities."

Today, many researchers, parents, and people "on the spectrum" are embracing a new approach to spectrum disorders. Called *neurodiversity,* it is the recognition that people with autistic spectrum symptoms process information, communicate, and experience their social and physical environment differently than *neurotypical* people who don't have autistic symptoms. Rather than viewing autism as a *disorder* or *disease,* advocates of this viewpoint believe that it should be viewed as a *disability,* like deafness, or a *difference,* like left-handedness (see Jaarsma & Welin, 2012; Kapp & others, 2013).

Neurodiversity advocates do *not* deny that autistic people need special training and support (Baron-Cohen, 2000, 2005). Autism rights activists Amy Roberts and Gareth Nelson (2005) suggest that rather than trying to "cure" autistic people and make them more like nonautistic people, researchers should emphasize giving autistic children and adults the tools that they need to survive in a world that is designed for nonautistic people.

Disorder, disease, disability, or difference? We'll give noted researcher Simon Baron-Cohen (2007) the last word:

Autism is both a disability and a difference. We need to find ways of alleviating the disability while respecting and valuing the difference.

Tyrel Featherston/Ottawa Citizen. Republished by permission.

Michelle Dawson Michelle Dawson readily admits that coping with many everyday challenges is beyond her. Yet, according to her colleague Laurent Mottron (2008), "Michelle is someone who will change the way an entire sector of humanity is considered." Dawson met neuroscientist and autism researcher Mottron when they both appeared on a documentary about autism. Recognizing Dawson's intelligence, Mottron asked her to read some of his scientific papers. When she responded with an insightful critique of his methodology, Mottron took her on as a research collaborator. Since that time, Dawson has co-authored several papers with Mottron and other scientists, including Morton Ann Gernsbacher, former president of the Association for Psychological Science.

autism spectrum disorder
Neurodevelopmental disorder characterized by: (1) deficits in social communication and social interaction and (2) restricted, repetitive behaviors, interests, and activities.

intellectual disability Formerly called *mental retardation.* Neurodevelopmental disorder characterized by deficits in general mental abilities which result in impairments of adaptive functioning, such that the individual fails to meet standards of personal independence and social responsibility.

triarchic theory of intelligence Robert Sternberg's theory that there are three distinct forms of intelligence: analytic, creative, and practical.

Sternberg's **triarchic theory of intelligence** emphasizes both the universal aspects of intelligent behavior and the importance of adapting to a particular social and cultural environment. More specifically, Sternberg (1997, 2012) has proposed a different conception of intelligence, which he calls *successful intelligence.* Successful intelligence involves three distinct types of mental abilities: analytic, creative, and practical.

Analytic intelligence refers to the mental processes used in learning how to solve problems, such as picking a problem-solving strategy and applying it. Although conventional intelligence tests measure mental abilities, they do not evaluate the strategies used to solve problems, which Sternberg considers important in determining analytic intelligence. In the Prologue, Tom's ability to solve complex mathematical equations reflects analytical intelligence.

Creative intelligence is the ability to deal with novel situations by drawing on existing skills and knowledge. The intelligent person effectively draws on past experiences to cope with new situations, which often involves finding an unusual way to relate old information to new. We'll explore the topic of creativity in more detail in the Psych for Your Life section at the end of the chapter.

Practical intelligence involves the ability to adapt to the environment and often reflects what is commonly called "street smarts." Sternberg notes that what is required to adapt successfully in one particular situation or culture may be very different from what is needed in another situation or culture. He stresses that the behaviors that reflect practical intelligence can vary depending on the particular situation, environment, or culture.

How would Tom fare by Sternberg's criteria? Although Tom ranks high in most measures of analytic intelligence, Tom would probably not rank very high in creative or practical intelligence. Successful adaptation involves the flexibility to choose the best problem-solving strategy or to know when to change strategies.

What about practical intelligence? As shown in the Prologue, dealing with the social and academic environment of high school is not easy for Tom. However, many people with autism spectrum disorder find a compatible niche in workplaces in which their ability to focus their attention on a particular technical problem, their preoccupation with details, and other unusual abilities are highly valued, such as in computer programming or engineering firms. In such an environment, their lack of social skills might actually be advantageous (Mayor, 2008). Some companies have figured this out. For example, the German-based international company SAP has committed to hiring 650 people with autism—1 percent of all of their employees—by 2020 (Wang, 2014). They are clear that this is not a charitable initiative; rather, they have found that some people with autism are able to work very methodically and carefully, without zoning out like most of us do. This makes them excel at certain jobs, like debugging computer software. As Sternberg's theory would predict, behaviors that are deemed "intelligent" in one environment—such as a software development firm like SAP—might well be maladaptive in another environment, like a high school cafeteria (Sternberg, 2008).

The exact nature of intelligence will no doubt be debated for some time. However, the intensity of this debate pales in comparison with the next issue we consider: the origins of intelligence.

The Roles of Genetics and Environment in Determining Intelligence

KEY THEME

Both genes and environment contribute to intelligence, but the relationship is complex.

KEY QUESTIONS

> How are twin studies used to measure genetic and environmental influences on intelligence?

> What is a heritability estimate, and why can't it be used to explain differences between groups?

> How do social, cultural, and psychological factors affect performance on intelligence tests?

Given that psychologists do not agree on the definition or nature of intelligence, it probably won't surprise you to learn that psychologists also do not agree on the *origin of intelligence*. On the surface, the debate comes down to this: Do we essentially *inherit* our intellectual potential from our parents, grandparents, and great-grandparents? Or is our intellectual potential primarily determined by our *environment* and upbringing?

Virtually all psychologists agree that *both* heredity and environment are important in determining intelligence level. Where psychologists disagree is in identifying how much of intelligence is determined by heredity and how much by environment. The implications of this debate have provoked some of the most heated arguments in the history of psychology.

Let's start with some basic points about the relationship between genes and the environment. It was once believed that genes provided an unchanging, permanent blueprint for human development. As we'll discuss in Chapter 9, the "genes as blueprint" metaphor has today been replaced by a "genes as data bank" metaphor (Marcus, 2004). It's now known that environmental factors influence *which* of the many genes we inherit are "expressed," meaning actually switched on, or activated. As psychologist Bernard Brown (1999) writes, "Genes are not destiny. There are many places along the gene–behavior pathway where genetic expression can be regulated."

Take the example of height. You inherit a potential *range* for height, rather than an absolute number of inches. Environmental factors influence how close you come to realizing that genetic potential. If you are healthy and well-nourished, you may reach the maximum of your genetic height potential. But if you are poorly nourished and not healthy, you probably won't.

To underscore the interplay between heredity and environment, consider the fact that the average height of Americans has increased by several inches in the past half-century. The explanation for this increase is that nutritional and health standards have steadily improved, not that the genetic heritage of Americans has fundamentally changed. However, heredity does play a role in establishing *limits* on height. If you're born with "short" genes, you're unlikely to reach six foot four, no matter how good your nutrition. (For more on genetics, see Chapter 9.)

The roles of heredity and environment in determining intelligence and personality factors are much more complex than the simple examples of height or eye color (Plomin, 2003; Johnson, 2010). However narrowly intelligence is defined, the genetic range of intellectual potential is influenced by *many* genes, not by one single gene (Plomin & Spinath, 2004; Nisbett & others, 2012). No one knows how many genes might be involved. Given the complexity of genetic and environmental influences, how do scientists estimate how much of intelligence is due to genetics and how much to environment?

> The nature-versus-nurture debate is now informed by current research on molecular biology that moves the question from which factor is more important to how and when expression of the human genome is triggered and maintained. The basic behavior genetics issue has become how environment influences gene expression.
>
> —*Bernard Brown (1999)*

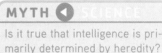
MYTH ◀ SCIENCE
Is it true that intelligence is primarily determined by heredity?

TWIN STUDIES
SORTING OUT THE INFLUENCE OF GENETICS VERSUS ENVIRONMENT

One way this issue has been explored is by comparing the IQ scores of individuals who are genetically related to different degrees. *Identical twins* share exactly the same genes because they developed from a single fertilized egg that split into two. Hence, any dissimilarities between them must be due to environmental factors rather than hereditary differences. *Fraternal twins* are like any other pair of siblings because they develop from two different fertilized eggs.

As you can see in Figure 7.8 on the next page, comparing IQ scores in this way shows the effects of both heredity and environment. Identical twins raised together have very similar IQ scores, whereas fraternal twins raised together have IQs that are less similar (Plomin & Spinath, 2004).

Hero Images/Corbis

Genetics or Environment? These identical twins have a lot in common—including a beautiful smile. Twins are often used in studies of the relative contributions that heredity and environment make to personality and other characteristics.

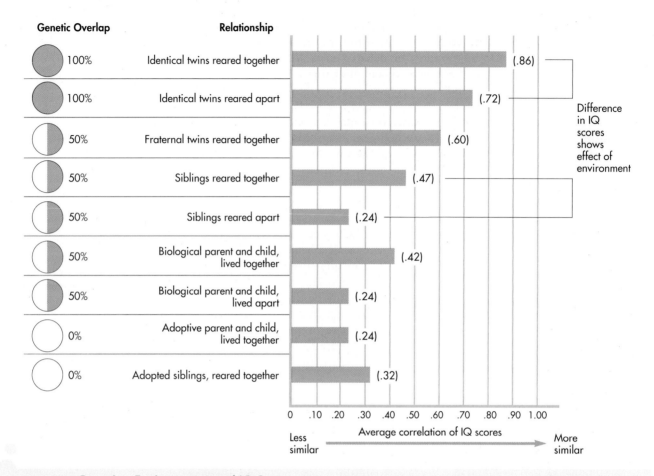

FIGURE 7.8 Genetics, Environment, and IQ Scores This graph shows the average correlations of IQ scores for individuals who are genetically related to different degrees. The graph is based on research by psychologists Thomas Bouchard and Matt McGue, who summarized the results from more than 100 separate studies on over 100,000 pairs of relatives (McGue & others, 1993). The data show that both genetics and environment have an effect on IQ scores. The more closely two individuals are related genetically, the more similar their IQ scores: Identical twins reared together are more alike than are fraternal twins reared together. However, the same data also show the importance of environmental influences: Identical twins reared together are more alike than are identical twins reared apart, and siblings who are reared together are more alike than are siblings reared in different homes.

Source: Research from McGue & others (1993).

However, notice that identical twins raised in separate homes have IQs that are slightly less similar, indicating the effect of different environments. And, although fraternal twins raised together have less similar IQ scores than do identical twins, they show more similarity in IQs than do nontwin siblings. Recall that the degree of genetic relatedness between fraternal twins and nontwin siblings is essentially the same. But because fraternal twins are the same age, their environmental experiences are likely to be more similar than are those of siblings who are of different ages.

Thus, *both* genetic *and* environmental influences are important. Genetic influence is shown by the fact that the closer the genetic relationship, the more similar the IQ scores. Environmental influences are demonstrated by two findings: First, two people who are genetically identical but are raised in different homes have different IQ scores. And second, two people who are genetically unrelated but are raised in the same home have IQs that are much more similar than are those of two unrelated people from randomly selected homes.

Using studies based on degree of genetic relatedness and using sophisticated statistical techniques to analyze the data, researchers have scientifically estimated **heritability**—the percentage of variation within a given population that is due to heredity. The currently accepted *heritability estimate* is about 50 percent for the general population (see Plomin, 2003; Plomin & Spinath, 2004).

heritability The percentage of variation within a given population that is due to heredity.

In other words, approximately 50 percent of the difference in IQ scores *within* a given population is due to genetic factors. But there is disagreement even over this figure, depending on the statistical techniques, data sources used, and age and social class of the population (Deary & others, 2009; Nisbett & others, 2012).

It is important to stress that the 50 percent figure does *not* apply to a single individual's IQ score. If Mike's IQ is 120, it does not mean that 60 IQ points are due to Mike's environment and 60 points are genetically inherited. Instead, the 50 percent heritability estimate means that approximately 50 percent of the difference in IQ scores *within a specific group of people* is due to differences in their genetic makeup. More on this key point shortly.

DIFFERENCES *WITHIN* GROUPS VERSUS DIFFERENCES *BETWEEN* GROUPS

Some group differences in average IQ scores do exist (Ceci & Williams, 2009). In many societies, including the United States, the average IQ scores of minority groups tend to be lower than the average IQ scores of the dominant or majority groups. There also are differences among countries when national estimates of intelligence are determined (Hunt, 2012). And countries with higher overall intelligence tend to have better economic and health outcomes. The question is how to explain such differences. Heritability cannot be used to explain group differences. Although it is possible to estimate the degree of difference *within* a specific group that is due to genetics, it makes no sense to apply this estimate to the differences *between* groups (Rose, 2009). Why? A classic analogy provided by geneticist Richard Lewontin (1970) may help you understand this important point (see Ceci & Williams, 2009).

Suppose you have a 50-pound bag of corn seeds and two pots. A handful of seeds is scooped out and planted in pot A, which has rich, well-fertilized soil. A second handful is scooped out and planted in pot B, which has poor soil with few nutrients (see Figure 7.9).

Because the seeds are not genetically identical, the plants *within group A* will vary in height. So will the plants *within group B*. Given that the environment (the soil) is

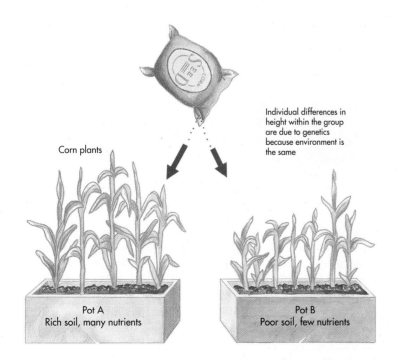

Corn plants

Individual differences in height within the group are due to genetics because environment is the same

Pot A
Rich soil, many nutrients

Pot B
Poor soil, few nutrients

Difference in average height between groups is due to environment

FIGURE 7.9 The Two Pots Analogy
Because the two environments are very different, no conclusions can be drawn about possible overall genetic differences between the plants in pot A and the plants in pot B.

stereotype threat A psychological predicament in which fear that you will be evaluated in terms of a negative stereotype about a group to which you belong creates anxiety and self-doubt, lowering performance in a particular domain that is important to you.

the same for all the plants in one particular pot, this variation within each group of seeds is *completely* due to heredity—nothing differs but the plants' genes.

However, when we compare the average height of the corn plants in the two pots, pot A's plants have a higher average height than pot B's. Can the difference in these average heights be explained in terms of overall genetic differences between the seeds in each pot? No. The overall differences can be attributed to the two different environments, the good soil and the poor soil. In fact, because the environments are so different, it is impossible to estimate what the overall genetic differences are between the two groups of seeds.

Note also that even though, on the average, the plants in pot A are taller than the plants in pot B, some of the plants in pot B are taller than some of the plants in pot A. In other words, the average differences *within a group* of plants tell us nothing about whether an *individual* member of that group is likely to be tall or short.

The same point can be extended to the issue of average IQ differences between racial groups. Unless the environmental conditions of two racial groups are virtually identical, it is impossible to estimate the overall genetic differences between the two groups. Even if intelligence were *primarily* determined by heredity, which is not the case, IQ differences between groups could still be due entirely to the environment.

Other evidence for the importance of the environment in determining IQ scores derives from the improvement in average IQ scores that has occurred in several

CULTURE AND HUMAN BEHAVIOR

Performing with a Threat in the Air: How Stereotypes Undermine Performance

Your anxiety intensifies as you walk into the testing center. You know how much you've prepared for this test. You should feel confident, but you can't ignore the nagging awareness that not everyone expects you to do well. Can your performance be influenced by your awareness of those expectations?

Standardized testing situations are designed so that everyone is treated as uniformly as possible. Nevertheless, some factors, such as the attitudes and feelings that individuals bring to the testing situation, can't be standardized. Among the most powerful of these factors are the expectations that you think other people might hold about your performance.

As psychologist **Claude Steele** (1997) discovered, if those expectations are negative, being aware of that fact can cause you to perform below your actual ability level. Steele coined the term **stereotype threat** to describe this phenomenon. It's a response that occurs when members of a group are aware of a negative stereotype about their group and fear they will be judged in terms of that stereotype. Even more unsettling is the fear that you might somehow confirm the stereotype, even when you know that the negative beliefs are false.

For example, one common stereotype is that women perform poorly in math, especially advanced mathematics. Multiple studies have shown that when women are reminded of their gender before taking an advanced mathematics test, their scores are lower than would be expected (see Steele & others, 2007). Even mathematically gifted women show a drop in scores when they are made aware of gender stereotypes (Good & others, 2008; Kiefer & Sekaquaptewa, 2007).

What about positive stereotypes, such as the racial stereotype that Asians are good at advanced mathematics? In a related phenomenon, called *stereotype lift*, awareness of *positive* expectations

can actually improve performance on tasks (Rydell & others, 2009; Walton & Cohen, 2003).

Psychologist Margaret Shih and her colleagues (1999, 2006) showed how easily gender and racial stereotypes can be manipulated to affect test performance. In one study, mathematically gifted Asian American female college students were randomly assigned to three groups. Group 1 filled out a questionnaire about their Asian background, designed to remind them of their Asian identity. Group 2 filled out a questionnaire designed to remind them of their female identity. Group 3 was the control group and filled out a neutral questionnaire.

The results? The students who were reminded of their racial identity as Asians scored significantly higher on the exam than the students who were reminded of their gender as women. The control group of female students who filled out the neutral questionnaire scored in the middle of the other two groups.

In another study, Shih and her colleagues (2006) assessed the performance of Asian American women on a test of *verbal* ability, an area in which women are stereotypically expected to excel but Asians are not. In this study, the women scored *higher* on the verbal test when reminded of their *gender*, but scored *lower* on the test when reminded of their *race*.

Members of virtually any group can experience a decline in performance due to stereotype threat (Schmader & others, 2008). For example:

• When a test was described as measuring "problem-solving skills," African American students did just as well as white students. But when told that the same test measured "intellectual ability," African American students scored lower than white students (Aronson & others, 2002; Steele & Aronson, 1995).

cultures and countries during the past few generations, a phenomenon called the *Flynn Effect* (Flynn, 2009; Nisbett & others, 2012).

Surveying intelligence test scores around the world, James R. Flynn found that 14 nations showed significant gains in average IQ scores in just one generation (Flynn, 1994, 1999). Subsequent research by Flynn and other researchers documented similar gains in IQ scores in over 30 different countries worldwide (Flynn, 2009). The average IQ score in the United States has also steadily increased over the past century (Flynn, 2007a, 2007b; Weiss, 2010). Such changes in a population can be accounted for only by environmental changes because the amount of time involved is far too short for genetically influenced changes to have occurred.

Cross-Cultural Studies of Group Discrimination and IQ Differences

The effect of social discrimination on intelligence test scores has been shown in numerous cross-cultural studies (see Ogbu, 1986, 2008). In many different societies, average IQ is lower for members of a discriminated-against minority group, even when that group is not racially different from the dominant group. The Culture and Human Behavior box "Performing with a Threat in the Air" explains how belonging to a stigmatized group can affect performance on tests of many different abilities.

- When reminded of their racial identity, white men did worse on a math test when they thought they were competing with Asian men (Aronson & others, 1999). And, when reminded of their gender, men performed worse than women on a test that was described as measuring "social sensitivity," but not when the test was described as measuring "complex information processing" (Koenig & Eagly, 2005).

- When tests were described as measuring intelligence, Hispanic students performed more poorly than white students (Gonzales & others, 2002); children from a low socioeconomic background performed more poorly than students from higher socioeconomic backgrounds (Croizet & Claire, 1998); and social science majors scored lower than natural science majors (Croizet & others, 2004).

- When reminded of the stereotype of the "elderly as forgetful," older adults scored lower on a memory test than did a matched group not given that reminder (Levy, 1996). Conversely, even taking a memory test or just hearing the instructions for a memory test made older adults feel several years older (Hughes & others, 2013).

How does being reminded of a negative stereotype undermine a person's performance? First, there's the fear that you might confirm the stereotype, which creates psychological stress, self-doubt, and anxiety (Schmader & others, 2009). In turn, physiological arousal and distracting thoughts interfere with concentration, memory, and problem-solving abilities (Mrazek & others, 2011; Schmader, 2010). And, ironically, those individuals who are most highly motivated to perform well are the ones most likely to be affected by stereotype threat (Good & others, 2008).

Hundreds of psychological studies have demonstrated that individual performance on tests—even tests that are carefully designed to be fair and objective—is surprisingly susceptible to stereotype threat (Good & others, 2008; Kiefer & Sekaquaptewa, 2007; Walton & Spencer, 2009).

How can stereotype threat be counteracted? Some research has shown that simply being aware of how stereotype threat can affect your performance helps minimize its negative effects (Johns & others, 2005, 2008; Nadler & Clark, 2011). Reminding yourself of *positive* aspects of your social identity, such as your identity as a college student, can boost performance (Shih & others, 2012). Also effective are *self-affirmation* activities, in which you remind yourself of valued aspects of your personal and social identity—characteristics, skills, beliefs, or roles that you value or view as important (Shapiro & others, 2013; Sherman & others, 2013). Such interventions have had lasting effects in a variety of student populations (Bowen & others, 2013; Cohen & others, 2012).

"Stereotype threat is a situational threat—a threat in the air—that, in general form, can affect the members of any group about whom a negative stereotype exists, whether it's skateboarders, older adults, white men, or gang members. Where bad stereotypes about these groups apply, members of these groups can fear being reduced to that stereotype."
—*Claude Steele (1997)*

Linda A. Cicero/Stanford News Service

Defying Centuries of Discrimination
Members of the Buraku Liberation League sing a traditional Buraku lullaby on a rooftop in Japan. They chose a lullaby, the group's leader said, "to sing this as a song for protecting children while reflecting our suffering, sadness and wishes, all of which are conveyed in the song." Overt discrimination against the estimated 1 million Buraku people is technically illegal in Japan, yet they remain the poorest group in Japan, and discrimination persists in employment, marriage, and other areas (Ikeda, 2001).

TABLE 7.2

The Effects of Discrimination on IQ Scores in Japan

Range of IQ Scores	Percentage of Children Scoring in a Given Range	
	Non-Burakumin	Burakumin
Above 125	23.3	2.6
124–109	31.8	19.5
108–93	23.3	22.1
92–77	11.7	18.2
Below 76	9.9	37.6

SOURCE: Data from DeVos & Wagatsuma (1967).

The Burakumin of Japan are not racially different from other Japanese, but they have suffered from generations of discrimination. Their average IQ scores are about 10 to 15 points below those of mainstream Japanese (Ogbu, 1986). In many other cultures, a similar gap in IQ scores exists between the discriminated-against minority and the dominant group.

Take the case of the Burakumin people of Japan. Americans typically think of Japan as relatively homogeneous, and indeed the Burakumin are not racially different from other Japanese. They look the same and speak the same language. However, the Burakumin are the descendants of an outcast group that for generations worked as tanners and butchers. Because they handled dead bodies and killed animals, the Burakumin were long considered unclean and unfit for social contact. For centuries, they were forced to live in isolated enclaves, apart from the rest of Japanese society (DeVos, 1992; DeVos & Wagatsuma, 1967).

Today, there are about 3 million Burakumin in Japan. Although the Burakumin were legally emancipated from their outcast status many years ago, substantial social discrimination against them persists (Ikeda, 2001; Payton, 1992). Because there is no way to tell if a Japanese citizen is of Burakumin descent, there are dozens of private detective agencies in Tokyo and other Japanese cities that openly specialize in tracking Burakumin who are trying to "pass" and hide their background from employers or prospective marriage partners.

The Burakumin are the poorest people in Japan. They are only half as likely as other Japanese to graduate from high school or attend college. Although there are no racial differences between the Burakumin and the other Japanese, the average IQ scores of the Burakumin are well below those of other Japanese. As shown in Table 7.2, their average IQ scores are about 10 to 15 points below those of mainstream Japanese. But, when Burakumin families immigrate to the United States, they are treated like any other Japanese. The children do just as well in school—and on IQ tests—as any other Japanese Americans (Ogbu, 1986).

Of course, Japan is not the only society that discriminates against a particular social group. Many societies discriminate against specific minority groups, such as the Harijans in India (formerly called the untouchables), West Indians in Great Britain, Maoris in New Zealand, and Jews of non-European descent in Israel.

Children belonging to these minority groups score 10 to 15 points lower on intelligence tests than do children belonging to the dominant group in their societies. Children of the minority groups are often one or two years behind dominant-group children in basic reading skills and mathematical skills. Minority-group children are overrepresented in remedial programs and in school dropout rates. They are also under-represented in higher education. The impact of discrimination on group differences in IQ remains even when the minority-group and dominant-group members are of similar socioeconomic backgrounds (Ogbu, 1986, 2008). In many ways, the educational experiences of these minority groups seem to parallel those of minority groups around the world, providing a cross-cultural perspective on the consistent effects of discrimination in many different societies.

ARE IQ TESTS CULTURALLY BIASED?

Another approach to explaining group differences in IQ scores has been to look at cultural bias in the tests themselves. If standardized intelligence tests reflect white, middle-class cultural knowledge and values, minority-group members might do poorly on the tests not because of lower intelligence, but because of unfamiliarity with the white, middle-class culture.

Researchers have attempted to create tests that are "culture-fair" or "culture-free." However, it is now generally recognized that it is virtually impossible to design a test that is completely culture-free (Greenfield, 2003). As cross-cultural psychologist Patricia Greenfield (1997) argues, ability tests "reflect the values, knowledge, and communication strategies of their culture of origin." Within that culture, the intelligence test may be a valid measure. Thus, a test will tend to favor the people from the culture in which it was developed.

Cultural differences may also be involved in *test-taking behavior* (Sternberg, 1995, 2012). People from different cultural backgrounds may use strategies in solving problems or organizing information that are different from those required on standard intelligence tests (Miller-Jones, 1989). In addition, such cultural factors as motivation, attitudes toward test taking, and previous experiences with tests can affect performance and scores on tests.

> Test your understanding of **The Nature of Intelligence** with **LEARNING**Curve.

Testing, Testing, Testing . . . Virtually all college students will be evaluated with standardized tests at some point in their college careers. Although great pains are taken to make tests as unbiased and objective as possible, many factors, both personal and situational, can affect performance on tests. Cultural factors, familiarity with the testing process, and anxiety or nervousness are just a few of the factors that can skew test results. So perhaps the best way to view standardized tests is as just one of many possible indicators of a student's level of knowledge—and of his or her potential to learn.

Closing Thoughts

So, what conclusions can we draw about the debates surrounding intelligence, including the role of heredity in mental ability?

First, it's clear that the IQ score of any individual—regardless of his or her racial, social, or economic group—is the result of a complex interaction among genetic and environmental factors. Second, environmental factors are much more likely than genetic factors to account for average IQ differences among distinct groups of people (Ceci & Williams, 2009; Nisbett & others, 2012). Third, within *any* given group of people, IQ differences among people are due at least as much to environmental influences as they are to genetic influences (Plomin & Spinath, 2004). And finally, IQ scores reflect what IQ tests are designed to measure—a particular group of mental abilities.

As we've seen throughout this chapter, we draw on *many* different types of mental abilities to solve problems, adapt to our environment, and communicate with others. Our culture tends to define "intelligence" in terms of intellectual ability. However, as Tom's story in the Prologue illustrates, social intelligence is an important ingredient in everyday life. Cognitive flexibility and creative thinking also contribute to our ability to successfully adapt to our particular environment. Can you learn to be more creative? We invite you to attend "A Workshop on Creativity" in the Psych for Your Life section on the next page.

PSYCH FOR YOUR LIFE

A Workshop on Creativity

Creativity can be defined as a group of cognitive processes used to generate useful, original, and novel ideas or solutions to problems (Hennessey & Amabile, 2010; Runco, 2007). Notice that usefulness, along with originality, is involved in judging creativity. An idea can be highly original, but if it lacks usefulness, it is not regarded as creative.

Although we typically think of creativity in terms of artistic expression, the act of creativity is almost always linked to the process of solving some problem. In that sense, creativity can occur in virtually any area of life.

Can you learn to be more creative? In general, creativity experts agree that you can. Although there is no simple formula that guarantees creative success, a few basic ingredients are central to the process of creative thinking. Here are several suggestions that can enhance your ability to think creatively.

1. Choose the goal of creativity.

Psychologists have found that virtually everyone possesses the intelligence and cognitive processes needed to be creative (Weisberg, 1988, 1993). But the creative individual values creativity as a personal goal. Without the personal goal of creativity, the likelihood of doing something creative is slim (Hennessey, 2010).

2. Reinforce creative behavior.

People are most creative when motivated by their own interest, the enjoyment of a challenge, and a personal sense of satisfaction and fulfillment (Amabile, 1996, 2001; Gilson & Madjar, 2011). This is called *intrinsic motivation.* In contrast, when people are motivated by external rewards, such as money or grades, they are displaying *extrinsic motivation.*

Researchers used to believe that extrinsic rewards made creative behavior much less likely. New research, however, seems to demonstrate that rewards can increase creative behavior in a person who has some training in generating creative solutions to problems (Eisenberger & others, 1998). When people know that creative behavior will be rewarded, they are more likely to behave in a creative way (Eisenberger & Cameron, 1996).

3. Engage in problem finding.

In many cases, the real creative leap involves recognizing that a problem exists. This is referred to as *problem finding* (Kaufman & Sternberg, 2010). We often overlook creative opportunities by dismissing trivial annoyances rather than recognizing them as potential problems to be solved.

For example, consider the minor annoyance experienced by a man named Art Fry. Fry, a researcher for 3M Corporation, regularly sang in his church choir. To locate the hymns quickly during the Sunday service, Fry used little scraps of paper to mark their places. But the scraps of paper would sometimes fall out when Fry stood up to sing, and he'd have to fumble to find the right page (Kaplan, 1990).

creativity A group of cognitive processes used to generate useful, original, and novel ideas or solutions to problems.

"Never, ever, think outside the box."

While sitting in church, Fry recognized the "problem" and came up with a relatively simple solution. If you put a substance that is sticky, but not *too* sticky, on the scraps of paper, they'll stay on the page and you can take them off when they are not needed anymore.

If you haven't already guessed, Art Fry invented Post-it notes. The formula for the adhesive had been discovered years earlier at 3M, but nobody could imagine a use for a glue that did not bond permanently. The mental set of the 3M researchers was to find *stronger* glues, not weaker ones. Fry's story demonstrates the creative value of recognizing problems instead of simply dismissing them.

A technique called *bug listing* is one useful strategy to identify potential problems. Bug listing involves creating a list of things that annoy, irritate, or bug you or other people. Such everyday annoyances are problems in need of creative solutions.

4. Acquire relevant knowledge.

Creativity requires a good deal of preparation (Weisberg, 1993). Acquiring a solid knowledge base increases your potential for recognizing how to creatively extend your knowledge or apply it in a new way. As the famous French chemist Louis Pasteur said, "Chance favors the prepared mind."

5. Try different approaches.

Creative people are flexible in their thinking. They step back from problems, turn them over, and mentally play with possibilities. By being flexible and imaginative, people seeking creative solutions generate many different responses. This is called *divergent thinking* because it involves moving away (or diverging) from the problem and considering it from a variety of perspectives (Baer, 1993).

Looking for analogies is one technique to encourage divergent thinking. In problem solving, an *analogy* is the recognition of some similarity or parallel between two objects or events that are not usually compared. Similarities can be drawn in terms of the objects' operations, functions, purposes, materials, or other characteristics.

MYTH ◀ SCIENCE

Is it true that you're either creative or you're not—there's nothing you can do to increase creativity?

For example, consider inventor Dean Kamen's ingenious "self-balancing human transporter," the *Segway*, which is modeled on the human body. As Kamen (2001) explains, "There's a gyroscope that acts like your inner ear, a computer that acts like your brain, motors that act like your muscles, and wheels that act like your feet." Rather than using brakes, an engine, or a steering wheel, sophisticated sensors detect subtle shifts in body weight to maintain direction, speed, and balance. Designed for riding on sidewalks, the Segway can move at speeds up to 17 mph and can carry the average rider for a full day.

6. Exert effort and expect setbacks.

Flashes of insight or inspiration can play a role in creativity, but they usually occur only after a great deal of work. Whether you're trying to write a brilliant term paper or design the next *Angry Birds* video game, creativity requires effort and persistence.

Finally, the creative process is typically filled with obstacles and setbacks. The best-selling novelist Stephen King endured years of rejection of his manuscripts before his first book was published. Thomas Edison tried thousands of filaments before he created the first working light bulb. In the face of obstacles and setbacks, the creative person perseveres.

To summarize our workshop on creativity, we'll use the letters of the word *create* as an acronym. Thus, the basic ingredients of *creativity* are:

Choose the goal of creativity.

Reinforce creative behavior.

Engage in problem finding.

Acquire relevant knowledge.

Try different approaches.

Exert effort and expect setbacks.

AP Photo/Paul Sakuma

An Icon of Creativity: "Think Different" Steve Jobs, founder of Apple Computers, was responsible for groundbreaking products like the iPod, iPhone, and iPad that revolutionized entire industries. He was also the founder of Pixar, the animation studio that created *Toy Story*, *Wall-E*, and other hits. In a 1995 interview, Jobs said, "Creativity is just connecting things. When you ask creative people how they did something, they feel a little guilty because they didn't really *do* it, they just *saw* something. . . . They were able to connect experiences they've had and synthesize new things. . . . A lot of people in our industry haven't had very diverse experiences. So they don't have enough dots to connect, and they end up with very linear solutions without a broad perspective on the problem. The broader one's understanding of the human experience, the better design we will have."

CHAPTER REVIEW

KEY PEOPLE AND KEY TERMS

Alfred Binet, p. 291

Howard Gardner, p. 296

cognition, p. 273

thinking, p. 273

mental image, p. 273

concept, p. 275

formal concept, p. 275

natural concept, p. 276

prototype, p. 276

exemplars, p. 276

problem solving, p. 277

trial and error, p. 277

algorithm, p. 278

heuristic, p. 278

Charles Spearman, p. 295

Claude Steele, p. 304

insight, p. 279

intuition, p. 279

functional fixedness, p. 280

mental set, p. 280

availability heuristic, p. 282

representativeness heuristic, p. 283

confirmation bias, 285

language, p. 284

linguistic relativity hypothesis, p. 286

bilingualism, p. 288

Robert Sternberg, p. 297

Lewis Terman, p. 291

animal cognition (comparative cognition), p. 289

intelligence, p. 290

mental age, p. 291

intelligence quotient (IQ), p. 291

achievement test, p. 294

aptitude test, p. 294

standardization, p. 294

normal curve (normal distribution), p. 294

reliability, p. 294

Louis L. Thurstone, p. 296

David Wechsler, p. 292

validity, p. 294

g factor (general intelligence), p. 295

autism spectrum disorder, p. 298

intellectual disability, p. 298

triarchic theory of intelligence, p. 300

heritability, p. 302

stereotype threat, p. 304

creativity, p. 308

Thinking, Language, and Intelligence

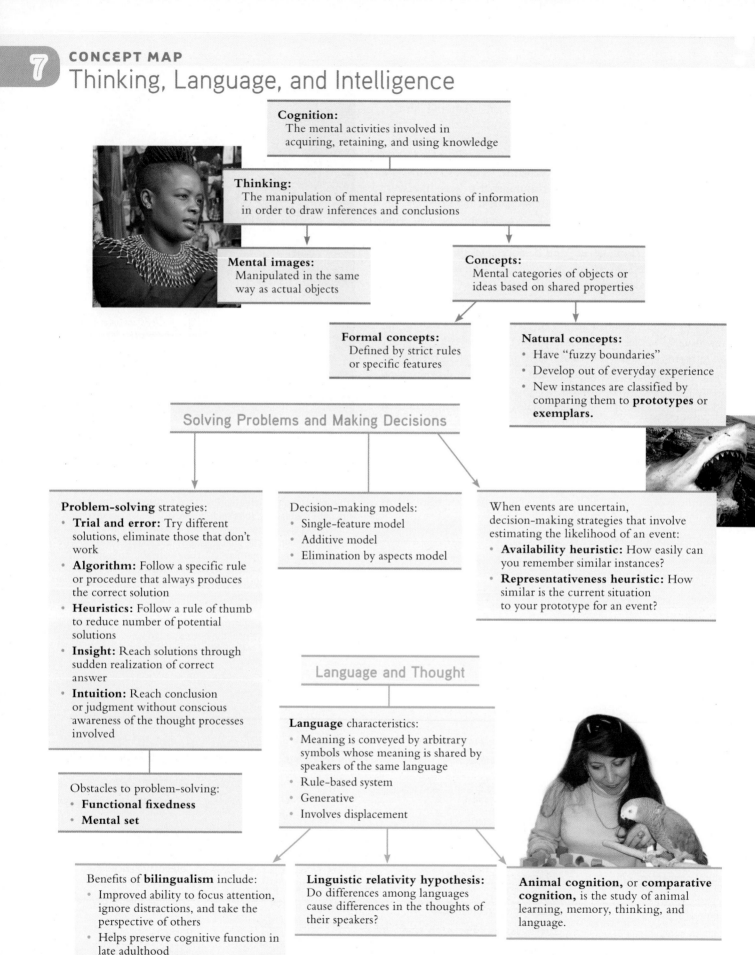

Cognition:
The mental activities involved in acquiring, retaining, and using knowledge

Thinking:
The manipulation of mental representations of information in order to draw inferences and conclusions

Mental images:
Manipulated in the same way as actual objects

Concepts:
Mental categories of objects or ideas based on shared properties

Formal concepts:
Defined by strict rules or specific features

Natural concepts:
- Have "fuzzy boundaries"
- Develop out of everyday experience
- New instances are classified by comparing them to **prototypes** or **exemplars.**

Solving Problems and Making Decisions

Problem-solving strategies:
- **Trial and error:** Try different solutions, eliminate those that don't work
- **Algorithm:** Follow a specific rule or procedure that always produces the correct solution
- **Heuristics:** Follow a rule of thumb to reduce number of potential solutions
- **Insight:** Reach solutions through sudden realization of correct answer
- **Intuition:** Reach conclusion or judgment without conscious awareness of the thought processes involved

Obstacles to problem-solving:
- **Functional fixedness**
- **Mental set**

Decision-making models:
- Single-feature model
- Additive model
- Elimination by aspects model

When events are uncertain, decision-making strategies that involve estimating the likelihood of an event:
- **Availability heuristic:** How easily can you remember similar instances?
- **Representativeness heuristic:** How similar is the current situation to your prototype for an event?

Language and Thought

Language characteristics:
- Meaning is conveyed by arbitrary symbols whose meaning is shared by speakers of the same language
- Rule-based system
- Generative
- Involves displacement

Benefits of **bilingualism** include:
- Improved ability to focus attention, ignore distractions, and take the perspective of others
- Helps preserve cognitive function in late adulthood

Linguistic relativity hypothesis: Do differences among languages cause differences in the thoughts of their speakers?

Animal cognition, or **comparative cognition,** is the study of animal learning, memory, thinking, and language.

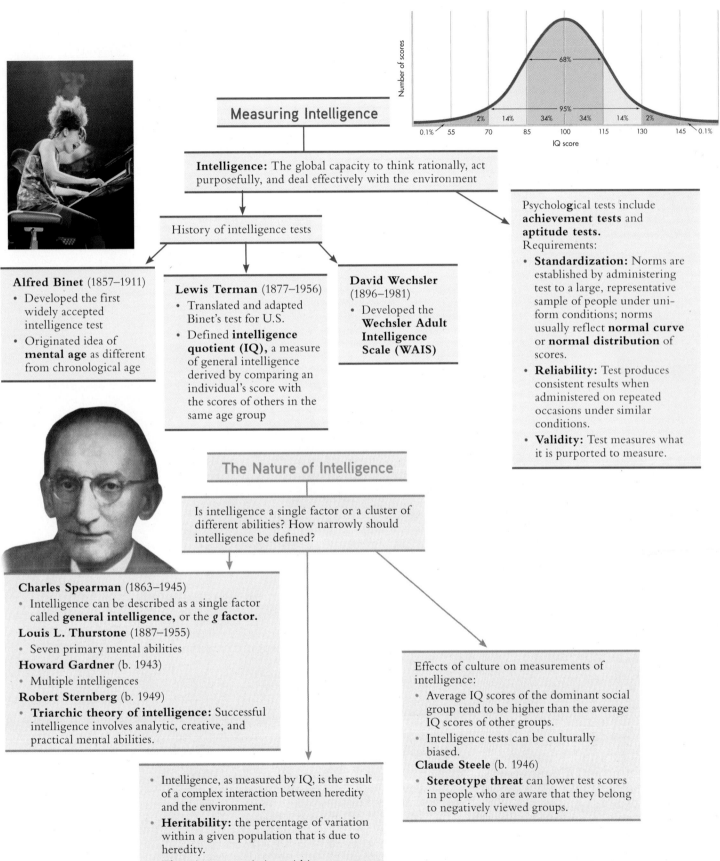

Measuring Intelligence

Intelligence: The global capacity to think rationally, act purposefully, and deal effectively with the environment

History of intelligence tests

Alfred Binet (1857–1911)
- Developed the first widely accepted intelligence test
- Originated idea of **mental age** as different from chronological age

Lewis Terman (1877–1956)
- Translated and adapted Binet's test for U.S.
- Defined **intelligence quotient (IQ),** a measure of general intelligence derived by comparing an individual's score with the scores of others in the same age group

David Wechsler (1896–1981)
- Developed the **Wechsler Adult Intelligence Scale (WAIS)**

Psychological tests include **achievement tests** and **aptitude tests.**
Requirements:
- **Standardization:** Norms are established by administering test to a large, representative sample of people under uniform conditions; norms usually reflect **normal curve** or **normal distribution** of scores.
- **Reliability:** Test produces consistent results when administered on repeated occasions under similar conditions.
- **Validity:** Test measures what it is purported to measure.

The Nature of Intelligence

Is intelligence a single factor or a cluster of different abilities? How narrowly should intelligence be defined?

Charles Spearman (1863–1945)
- Intelligence can be described as a single factor called **general intelligence,** or the **g factor.**

Louis L. Thurstone (1887–1955)
- Seven primary mental abilities

Howard Gardner (b. 1943)
- Multiple intelligences

Robert Sternberg (b. 1949)
- **Triarchic theory of intelligence:** Successful intelligence involves analytic, creative, and practical mental abilities.

- Intelligence, as measured by IQ, is the result of a complex interaction between heredity and the environment.
- **Heritability:** the percentage of variation within a given population that is due to heredity.
- There is more variation within groups than between groups.

Effects of culture on measurements of intelligence:
- Average IQ scores of the dominant social group tend to be higher than the average IQ scores of other groups.
- Intelligence tests can be culturally biased.

Claude Steele (b. 1946)
- **Stereotype threat** can lower test scores in people who are aware that they belong to negatively viewed groups.

Is it true . . .

- That obesity is primarily due to genetics?
- That people are either homosexual or heterosexual?
- That people need to satisfy basic needs before they can try to achieve higher needs, like artistic expression?
- That women are more emotional than men?
- That polygraphs, or lie detector tests, are a valid way to detect lying?
- That facial expressions, such as smiles, are learned and vary from one culture to another?
- That if you "put on a happy face," you will actually feel happier?

(inset) iko/Shutterstock
(bkgrd) Dmitry Bodyaev/Shutterstock

ONE STEP, ONE BREATH

PROLOGUE

A STEEP STAIRCASE HEWN OUT OF solid rock, the trail seemed to rise straight up the Himalayan mountainside. To the left, the canyon walls dripped with moisture. To the right, the trail dropped sharply to the roaring Budhi Gandaki river hundreds of feet below. The rocky trail was coated with mud, and in some spots, fast-running water that could only be crossed by leaping from one rock to another.

Dismayed, your author Sandy gazed up the trail. Her jacket and hiking boots were soaked through. Her wet hair was matted to her forehead. And she was tired from long days of trekking through rain, mud, and sleet. But there was no way back. The only option was to go forward.

"What am I *doing* here?" she said out loud. Sandy thought about the previous weeks. It was her second trip to Nepal as a non-medical volunteer with a small group of doctors and nurses holding health clinics in remote Himalayan villages in Nepal. There were no roads here. Transportation was on foot, and all supplies were carried by donkeys, by yaks, or on human backs.

Many of Sandy's friends thought she was crazy to spend her vacation making this strenuous trek. But Sandy is never happier than when she is on a hiking trail, the more remote the better. On her last trip to Nepal, the weather was perfect for the rigorous trails. But this trek was to be different.

For several days it had rained, soaking through "waterproof" duffels and raingear purchased in the States, no match for a Himalayan deluge. Determined, Sandy and her group had trekked on, despite their discomfort and fatigue. Clinics were scheduled and villagers waiting.

Guides reassured the group that the rain would dissipate once higher,

Motivation and Emotion

IN THIS CHAPTER:

- **INTRODUCTION:** Motivation and Emotion
- Hunger and Eating
- Human Sexuality
- Psychological Needs as Motivators
- Emotion
- Theories of Emotion: Explaining Emotion
- **PSYCH FOR YOUR LIFE:** Turning Your Goals into Reality

8

drier altitudes were reached. And for a few days, sunny weather allowed clothes, tents, boots, and sleeping bags to dry out. Moods lifted with the clouds, as clear skies revealed that these deep valleys were surrounded by stunning, snow-covered peaks.

The last clinic was held in the stone buildings of a school in Samagaon, near Nepal's border with Tibet. Even at 12,000 feet, the village is dwarfed by the still higher peaks that surround it. Villagers began lining up at dawn—young men in jeans, children in school uniforms, women in traditional Tibetan *chubas* and aprons, some holding infants. Their weathered faces marked by curiosity, trepidation,

or friendly grins, the older villagers waited patiently while the children shrieked with excitement. When the clinic finally closed, nearly 350 villagers had been treated. Exhausted but proud of the work they'd done, the volunteers ate a hasty dinner and crawled into sleeping bags.

But the next day brought more rain. Unable to go forward over a high pass as planned, the volunteers had to retrace their steps, covering rapidly in four days what was originally covered in seven. The trails were even more treacherous, some nearly washed out by landslides. Falling rocks and unstable ground added to the danger. The volunteers pushed

313

Sandy Hockenbury

"Never look at the top! If you do, you will lose heart. Just look two steps ahead, and the way will be easy. One step at a time."

"One step, one breath, at a time," Sandy said out loud, and thought about the dozens of similar trails they'd already climbed in the previous weeks. Carefully, the group worked their way up the staircase, testing wet rocks with trekking poles to make sure they were stable, helping one another cross rushing water that was sometimes ankle-deep.

Sandy topped the staircase with relief. But from the short stretch of level ground, she saw the next section of trail winding even more steeply up the mountainside. For a moment, her courage faltered. The sun was already beginning to set behind the canyon walls. Giving up was *not* an option. She could make it. She *would* make it.

on, overcoming their apprehension and even fear as sherpas warned of falling rocks and trails crumbled beneath their feet.

Although no steeper than many previous stretches, this particular staircase was especially daunting. The trail was narrow and slippery, the river below running fast and loud. "I'll never make it," Sandy thought. From halfway up the trail, Pasang, a guide and translator, called

encouragement: "Come, we must hurry! You can do it!"

Pasang is an experienced mountain climber who had already summited Everest. And, she was the first Nepali woman to earn an international mountain climbing guide certification from a prestigious climbing school in France, no mean feat for a young woman from a small village in the Khumbu region near Everest. Sandy remembered Pasang's advice.

Why would people leave their comfortable homes to travel to a remote part of the world as volunteers? And what kept them going despite fear and fatigue? These are the types of questions that we'll cover in this chapter in our exploration of the two closely linked topics, *motivation* and *emotion*. And as we do, we'll tell you more about Sandy's adventure. □

INTRODUCTION:
Motivation and Emotion

KEY THEME

Motivation refers to the forces acting on or within an organism to initiate and direct behavior.

KEY QUESTIONS

> What three characteristics are associated with motivation?
> How is emotion related to the topic of motivation?
> How do instinct, drive, incentive, arousal, and humanistic theories explain the general principles of motivation?

Why did your author Sandy travel halfway around the globe to make such a difficult journey? For that matter, what motivated you to sign up for college? Or to enroll in this class?

The topic of **motivation** includes the biological, emotional, cognitive, or social forces that act on or within you, initiating and directing your behavior. There are three basic characteristics commonly associated with motivation: activation, persistence, and intensity.

motivation The biological, emotional, cognitive, or social forces that activate and direct behavior.

instinct theories The view that certain human behaviors are innate and due to evolutionary programming.

drive theories The view that behavior is motivated by the desire to reduce internal tension caused by unmet biological needs.

homeostasis (home-ee-oh-STAY-sis) The idea that the body monitors and maintains internal states, such as body temperature and energy supplies, at relatively constant levels; in general, the tendency to reach or maintain equilibrium.

Activation is demonstrated by the initiation or production of behavior, such as Sandy's decision to travel to the Himalayas as a medical volunteer. *Persistence* is demonstrated by continued efforts or the determination to achieve a particular goal, often in the face of obstacles, as evidenced by the volunteers slogging their way up steep, muddy trails, despite cold rain and wet equipment. Finally, *intensity* is seen in the greater vigor of responding that usually accompanies motivated behavior.

Motivation is closely tied to emotional processes, and vice versa. Emotions can drive a behavior, such as when we lash out in anger or, motivated by sympathy or compassion, reach out to help a child. Similarly, most of the volunteers made the arduous trek through the Himalayas because of the joy and satisfaction they experienced when they helped heal a sick woman or an injured child. We'll take a detailed look at emotion in the second half of the chapter.

Many theories have been proposed to explain the general topic of motivation (Fiske, 2008; Forbes, 2011). We'll begin our exploration of motivation with a brief survey of the most influential theories.

"Could you give me a little push?"

Instinct Theories
INBORN BEHAVIORS AS MOTIVATORS

Inspired by Charles Darwin's landmark theory of evolution, early psychologists, like William James (1890) and William McDougall (1908), proposed that people were primarily driven by *instincts*. According to **instinct theories,** people are motivated to engage in certain behaviors because of evolutionary programming. Just as animals display automatic and innate instinctual behavior patterns called *fixed action patterns,* such as migration or mating rituals, human behavior was also thought to be motivated by inborn instinctual behavior patterns.

Table 8.1 lists some of the human instincts that William James (1890) included in his famous text, *Principles of Psychology.* By the early 1900s, thousands of instincts had been proposed in one expert's list or another to account for just about every conceivable human behavior (Bernard, 1924). (The early instinct theorists were, no doubt, motivated by a "listing instinct.") But what does it mean to say that an assertive person has a "self-assertion instinct"?

The obvious problem with the early instinct theories was that merely describing and labeling behaviors did not explain them. By the 1920s, instinct theories had fallen out of favor as an explanation of human motivation primarily because of their lack of explanatory power. But the more general idea that some human behaviors are innate and genetically influenced remained an important element in the overall understanding of motivation. Today, psychologists taking the *evolutionary perspective* consider how our evolutionary heritage may influence patterns of many different human behaviors, including motivation (Cosmides & Tooby, 2013).

Drive Theories
BIOLOGICAL NEEDS AS MOTIVATORS

Beginning in the 1920s, instinct theories were replaced by **drive theories.** In general, drive theories asserted that behavior is motivated by the desire to reduce internal tension caused by unmet biological needs, such as hunger or thirst. The basic idea was that these unmet biological needs "drive" or "push" us to behave in certain ways that will lead to a reduction in the drive.

Leading drive theorists, including psychologists Robert S. Woodworth (1918, 1921) and Clark L. Hull (1943, 1952), believed that drives are triggered by the internal mechanisms of homeostasis. The principle of **homeostasis** states that the body monitors and maintains relatively constant levels of internal states, such as body temperature, fluid levels, and energy supplies. If any of these internal conditions deviates very far from the optimal level, the body initiates processes to bring the condition back to the normal or optimal range. Thus, the body automatically tries to maintain

TABLE 8.1

James's List of Human Instincts

Attachment	Resentment
Fear	Curiosity
Disgust	Shyness
Rivalry	Sociability
Greediness	Bashfulness
Suspicion	Secretiveness
Hunting	Cleanliness
Play	Modesty
Shame	Love
Anger	Parental Love

In his famous text, *Principles of Psychology,* William James (1890) devoted a lengthy chapter to the topic of instinct. With an air of superiority, James noted that "no other mammal, not even the monkey, shows so large an array of instincts" as humans. The table shows some of the human instincts identified by James.

Sharon King Grimm

a "steady state," which is what *homeostasis* means. According to drive theorists, when an internal imbalance is detected by homeostatic mechanisms, a **drive** to restore balance is produced. The drive activates behaviors to reduce the need and to reestablish the balance of internal conditions.

Today, the drive concept remains useful in explaining motivated behaviors that clearly have biological components, such as hunger, thirst, and sexuality. However, drive theories also have limitations. For example, eating behavior can be motivated by factors other than the biological drive of hunger: People often eat when they're not hungry and don't eat when they *are* hungry. And how could drive theories account for the motivation to buy a lottery ticket, run a marathon, or leave home and family to volunteer for a month's medical mission in a remote Himalayan village?

Motivation and Drive Theories
According to drive theories of motivation, behavior is motivated by biological drives to maintain *homeostasis,* or an optimal internal balance. After a long soccer practice on a hot day, these high school students are motivated to rest, cool off, and drink water. Drive theories of motivation are useful in explaining biological motives like hunger, thirst, and fatigue, but are less useful in explaining psychological motives. For example, how could we explain their motivation to play competitive soccer?

Incentive Motivation
GOAL OBJECTS AS MOTIVATORS

Building on the base established by drive theories, incentive theories emerged in the 1940s and 1950s. **Incentive theories** proposed that behavior is motivated by the "pull" of external goals, such as rewards, money, or recognition.

Incentive theories drew heavily from well-established learning principles, such as *reinforcement,* and the work of influential learning theorists, such as Pavlov, Watson, Skinner, and Tolman (see Chapter 5).

When combined, drive and incentive theories account for a broad range of the "pushes" and "pulls" motivating many of our behaviors. But even in combination, drive and incentive explanations of motivation still had limitations. In some situations, such as playing a rapid-response video game, our behavior seems to be directed toward *increasing* tension and physiological arousal. If you think about it, Sandy's decision to travel to Nepal was not motivated by either an internal, biological drive or an external incentive.

drive A need or internal motivational state that activates behavior to reduce the need and restore homeostasis.

incentive theories The view that behavior is motivated by the pull of external goals, such as rewards.

arousal theory The view that people are motivated to maintain a level of arousal that is optimal—neither too high nor too low.

sensation seeking The degree to which an individual is motivated to experience high levels of sensory and physical arousal associated with varied and novel activities.

Arousal Theory
OPTIMAL STIMULATION AS A MOTIVATOR

Racing your car along a barren stretch of highway, watching a suspenseful movie, shooting down the Super Slide at a water park—none of these activities seems to involve tension reduction, the satisfaction of some biological need, or the lure of some reward. Rather, performing the activity itself seems to motivate us. Why?

Arousal theory is based on the observation that people experience both very high levels of arousal and very low levels of arousal as being quite unpleasant. When arousal is too low, we experience boredom and become motivated to *increase* arousal by seeking out stimulating experiences (Berlyne, 1960, 1971). But when arousal is too high, we seek to *reduce* arousal in a less stimulating environment. In other words, people are motivated to maintain an *optimal* level of arousal, one that is neither too high nor too low (Hebb, 1955).

Sensation Seeking: Extreme Skiing
Aptly called "extreme sports," they include such diverse activities as hang gliding, ice climbing, white-water kayaking, bungee jumping, and parachuting. People who enjoy such high-risk activities are usually sensation seekers. For them, the rush of adrenaline they feel when they push the outer limit is an exhilarating and rewarding experience.

Joma/Actionplus/Newscom

That the optimal level of arousal varies from person to person is especially evident in *sensation seekers,* who find the heightened arousal of novel experiences very pleasurable. According to psychologist Marvin Zuckerman (1979, 2007, 2009), people who rank high on the dimension of **sensation seeking** have a need for varied, complex, and unique sensory experiences.

No doubt your author Don ranks high on this dimension, since he has tried skydiving and aerobatic flying. (He also once ate a handful of biodegradable packing peanuts, much to the horror of a college secretary.) Although such experiences can sometimes involve physical or social risks, sensation seekers aren't necessarily drawn to danger—but rather to the experience of novelty or excitement. For example, college students who study abroad score significantly higher on sensation seeking than college students who stay in their country of origin (Schroth & McCormack, 2000).

Like people, animals also seem to seek out novel environmental stimulation. Rats, cats, dogs, and other animals actively explore a new environment. In a series of classic studies, psychologist Harry Harlow (1953a, 1953b) showed that a monkey will spend hours trying to open a complicated lock, even when there is no incentive or reward for doing so. And, when kept in a boring cage, a monkey will "work" for the opportunity to open a window to peek into another monkey's cage or to watch an electric train run (Butler & Harlow, 1954).

Humanistic Theory
HUMAN POTENTIAL AS A MOTIVATOR

In the late 1950s, **humanistic theories of motivation** were championed by psychologists Carl Rogers and Abraham Maslow. Although not discounting the role of biological and external motivators, humanistic theories emphasized psychological and cognitive components in human motivation (Sheldon, 2008). Motivation was thought to be affected by how we perceive the world, how we think about ourselves and others, and our beliefs about our abilities and skills (Rogers, 1961, 1977).

According to the humanistic perspective, people are innately motivated to realize their highest personal potential. Although innate and universal, the motivation to strive toward your highest potential could be jeopardized by the absence of a supportive environment—personal, social, and cultural (King, 2008). Later in the chapter, we'll consider the most famous humanistic model of motivation, Maslow's *hierarchy of needs*.

❯ Test your understanding of **Introduction and Motivational Concepts and Theories** with **LEARNING**Curve.

Seeking Stimulation Like humans, animals are also motivated to seek out stimulation and explore novel environments. In his research with monkeys, Harry Harlow (1953c) found that arousal was a powerful motive. These young monkeys are trying to open a complicated lock, despite the lack of an incentive or reward for their behavior.

Harlow Primate Laboratory, University of Wisconsin

Hunger and Eating

KEY THEME

Hunger is a biological motive, but eating behavior is motivated by a complex interaction of biological, social, and psychological factors.

KEY QUESTIONS

❯ What is energy homeostasis, and how is food converted to energy?

❯ What are the short-term signals that regulate eating behavior?

❯ What chemical signals are involved in the long-term regulation of a stable body weight?

❯ What factors contribute to long-term weight gain?

It seems simple: You're hungry, so you eat. But even a moment's reflection will tell you that eating behavior is not that straightforward. When, what, how much, and how often you eat is influenced by an array of psychological, biological, social, and cultural factors.

For example, think about what you ate yesterday. Now contrast your choices with food preferences in other cultures. A typical diet for the Dusan of northern Borneo in Southeast Asia includes anteater, gibbon (a small ape), snake, mouse, and rat meat. After these meats have spoiled to the point of being liquefied, the Dusan consume them with rice. South American Indians eat head lice, bees, iguanas, and monkeys.

Not one man in a billion, when taking his dinner, ever thinks of utility. He eats because the food tastes good and makes him want more.

—*William James*
Principles of Psychology *(1890)*

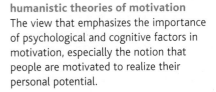

humanistic theories of motivation The view that emphasizes the importance of psychological and cognitive factors in motivation, especially the notion that people are motivated to realize their personal potential.

JORGE UZON/AFP/Newscom

Delicious or Disgusting? The need to eat is a universal human motive. However, culture influences *what* we eat, *when* we eat, and *how* we eat (Rozin, 1996, 2007). This upscale restaurant in Mexico City serves *chapulines* (grasshoppers, left) and *gusanos del maguey* (caterpillars). High in protein and readily available, insects are standard fare in many countries.

The Guianese of South America eat pebbles as a regular part of their diet, while the Vedda of Sri Lanka like rotted wood (see Fieldhouse, 1986). In Nepal, the trekkers were often offered Tibetan butter tea, a thick brew of strong tea, salt, yak butter, and yak milk. Clearly, cultural experience shapes our food choices (Rozin, 2006, 2007).

In the next several sections, we look at what researchers have learned about the factors that trigger hunger and motivate eating behavior.

Energy Homeostasis
CALORIES CONSUMED = CALORIES EXPENDED

How is food converted to energy in the body? The food that you eat is broken down by enzymes, gradually absorbed in your intestines, and converted into amino acids, fatty acids, and simple sugars. The simple sugar **glucose** provides the main source of energy for all mammals, including humans. The hormone **insulin,** secreted by the pancreas, helps control blood levels of glucose and promotes the uptake of glucose by the muscles and other body tissues. Insulin also helps in regulating eating behavior and maintaining a stable body weight.

About one-third of your body's energy is expended for the routine physical activities of daily life, such as walking, brushing your teeth, and digesting the food you eat. The remaining two-thirds of your body's energy is used for continuous bodily functions that are essential to life, such as generating body heat, heartbeat, respiration, and brain activity. When you are lying down and resting, the rate at which your body uses energy for vital body functions is referred to as your **basal metabolic rate (BMR).** Energy that is not needed to meet your immediate bodily needs is stored in the form of body fat, called *adipose tissue.* Your liver, which monitors glucose levels in your bloodstream, can utilize this stored energy if necessary.

Often, there is considerable daily variation in what, when, how often, and how much we eat. Yet despite this variability in eating behavior, our body weight tends to stay relatively constant (Bessesen, 2011). Your typical or average body weight is called your *baseline body weight,* which is maintained by a process called *energy homeostasis.*

But what if you eat more—or less—food than you need? If the number of calories you eat matches the number of calories you expend for energy, your body weight tends to remain stable. If you eat more than you need, the excess glucose is converted into reserve energy—fat. Conversely, if you eat fewer calories than you expend for energy, body fat stores shrink as the reserve energy in fat cells is used for physical activity and metabolic functions. Sandy and most of her fellow volunteers were several pounds lighter at the end of the trek than when they started. Despite constant refueling with high-calorie trail mix and other snacks, the strenuous physical activity required more energy than they were able to replenish.

Short-Term Signals That Regulate Eating

Why do we eat? About 30 minutes before you eat, you experience a *slight* increase in blood levels of insulin and a *slight* decrease in blood levels of glucose. In experimental studies with both humans and rats, these small changes reliably predict the initiation of eating (Chaput & Tremblay, 2009). Once the meal is begun, blood glucose levels return to their baseline level. Interestingly, glucose returns to its baseline level well *before* the food is actually digested and absorbed.

A more important internal signal is *ghrelin,* a hormone manufactured by cells lining the stomach (Kojima, 2011; Olszweski & others, 2008). Ghrelin was dubbed "the

glucose Simple sugar that provides energy and is primarily produced by the conversion of carbohydrates and fats; commonly called *blood sugar.*

insulin Hormone produced by the pancreas that regulates blood levels of glucose and signals the hypothalamus, regulating hunger and eating behavior.

basal metabolic rate (BMR) When the body is at rest, the rate at which it uses energy for vital functions, such as heartbeat and respiration.

hunger hormone" when research showed that it strongly stimulates appetite. Blood levels of ghrelin rise sharply before and fall abruptly after meals (Cummings, 2006; Cummings & others, 2002). It also seems to be involved in the long-term regulation of energy balance and weight. When people diet and lose weight, ghrelin levels—and feelings of hunger—increase.

Eating is also triggered by psychological factors. Both *classical conditioning* and *operant conditioning,* described in Chapter 5, affect eating behavior. For example, in much the same way as Pavlov's dogs were conditioned to salivate at the sound of a bell, your feelings of hunger have probably been classically conditioned by years of experience. Time of day or other stimuli, such as the setting in which you normally eat or just the sight of food utensils, can become associated with the anticipation of eating and trigger the physiological signals that increase your sense of hunger (Davidson, 2000).

Operant conditioning and *positive reinforcement* play a role in eating, too. Voluntary eating behaviors are followed by a *reinforcing stimulus*—the taste of food. Because of prior reinforcement experiences, people develop preferences for certain tastes, especially sweet, salty, and fatty tastes. Hence, your motivation to eat is influenced by prior learning experiences that have shaped your expectations, especially the anticipated pleasure of eating certain foods.

Let's consider a different question: Why do we *stop* eating? *Satiation* is the feeling of fullness and diminished desire to eat that follows eating. But what triggers the sense of satiation? One satiation signal involves *stretch receptors* in the stomach that communicate sensory information to the brainstem. The sensitivity of the stomach's stretch receptors is increased by a hormone secreted by the small intestines, called *cholecystokinin,* which is thankfully abbreviated as *CCK.* In the brain, CCK acts as a neurotransmitter (Delzenne & others, 2010).

Psychological factors play a role in satiation, too. As you eat a meal, food becomes less appealing, especially the specific food that you are eating. By the fourth piece of pizza, the pizza's appeal begins to diminish. This phenomenon is termed *sensory-specific satiety* (Havermans & others, 2009; Maier & others, 2007). Of course, if a *different* appealing food becomes available, your willingness to eat might return. Restaurants are well aware of this, which is why servers will bring a tempting platter of scrumptious desserts to your table after you've finished a large and otherwise satisfying dinner.

Long-Term Signals That Regulate Body Weight

Psychologists and other researchers have discovered many different chemical messengers that monitor and help us maintain a stable body weight over time. Three of the best-documented internal signals are *leptin, insulin,* and *neuropeptide Y.*

Leptin is a hormone secreted by the body's adipose tissue into the bloodstream. The amount of leptin that is secreted is directly correlated with the amount of body fat. The brain receptor sites for leptin are located in several areas of the hypothalamus. Neurons in the stomach and the gut also have leptin receptor sites.

Leptin is a key element in the feedback loop that regulates energy homeostasis. When fat stores increase, so do blood levels of leptin. When the leptin level in the brain increases, food intake is reduced and the body's

Remi Banali

leptin Hormone produced by fat cells that signals the hypothalamus, regulating hunger and eating behavior.

Ob/ob **Mice, Before and After Leptin** Leptin is a hormone produced by body fat. Because of a genetic mutation, these mice, dubbed *ob/ob* mice, lack the ability to produce leptin. Consequently, *ob/ob* mice behave as though their brains were telling them that their body fat reserves are completely depleted and that they are starving. *Ob/ob* mice have voracious appetites and five times as much body fat as normal-weight mice. Yet they display the characteristics of starving animals, including decreased immune system functioning, low body temperatures, and lack of energy. When the *ob/ob* mouse on the right was given supplemental leptin, it lost the excess fat and began eating normally. Its body temperature, immune system, and metabolism also became normal (Friedman & Halaas, 1998). Unfortunately, what worked for obese mice has not worked as easily for obese people, although researchers remain hopeful (Morrison, 2008).

neuropeptide Y (NPY) Neurotransmitter found in several brain areas, most notably the hypothalamus, that stimulates eating behavior and reduces metabolism, promoting positive energy balance and weight gain.

set-point theory Theory that proposes that humans and other animals have a natural or optimal body weight, called the *set-point weight,* that the body defends from becoming higher or lower by regulating feelings of hunger and body metabolism.

fat stores shrink over time. When fat stores shrink, blood levels of leptin decrease, triggering eating behavior.

The hormone *insulin* is also involved in brain mechanisms controlling food intake and body weight. The amount of insulin secreted by the pancreas is directly proportional to the amount of body fat. In the brain, insulin receptors are located in the same hypothalamus areas as leptin receptors. Increased brain levels of insulin are also associated with a reduction in food intake and body weight.

Abbreviated **NPY, neuropeptide Y** is a neurotransmitter manufactured throughout the brain, including the hypothalamus. During periods of weight loss, decreased leptin and insulin levels promote the secretion of NPY by the hypothalamus (Powley, 2009). In turn, increased brain levels of neuropeptide Y trigger eating behavior, reduce body metabolism, and promote fat storage. Conversely, if weight gain occurs, neuropeptide Y activity decreases.

In combination, the long-term and short-term eating-related signals we've discussed provide a feedback loop that is monitored by the hypothalamus (see Figure 8.1). As the hypothalamus detects changes in leptin, insulin, neuropeptide Y, ghrelin, CCK, and other internal signals, food intake and BMR are adjusted to promote or hinder weight gain. The end result? Over time, your average weight stays stable because the number of calories you consume closely matches the number of calories you expend for energy.

According to **set-point theory,** the body has a natural or optimal weight, called the *set-point weight,* that it is set to maintain. Your body vigorously defends this set-point weight from becoming lower or higher by regulating feelings of hunger and body metabolism (Major & others, 2007). But most people tend to drift to a heavier average body weight as they get older. In the next few sections, we'll consider some of the factors that contribute to the upward drift of body weight.

FIGURE 8.1 Regulating Appetite and Body Weight Multiple signals interact to regulate your appetite and energy expenditure so that you maintain a stable body weight over time. As summarized in this drawing, your appetite is stimulated (+) by increased levels of ghrelin and neuropeptide Y. In contrast, your appetite is suppressed (−) by increased levels of leptin, insulin, and CCK.

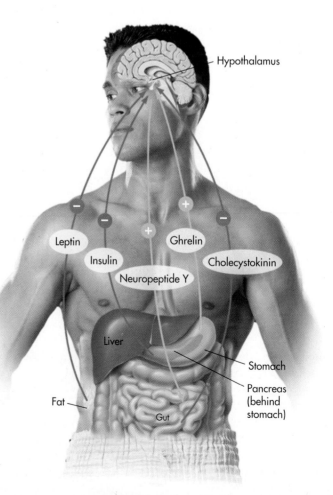

Excess Weight and Obesity

KEY THEME

Many different factors contribute to the high rates of overweight and obesity in the United States and other countries.

KEY QUESTIONS

> What is BMI?

> What factors contribute to excess weight and obesity?

The "thin ideal" is pervasive in American culture. In fact, over the past decades, actresses, models, Miss America Pageant winners, *Playboy* centerfolds, and even cartoon characters have become progressively thinner (Grabe & others, 2008).

But there is an enormous gap between the cultural *ideal* of a slender body and the cultural *reality* of the expanding American waistline. Far from conforming to the "thin ideal," more than two-thirds of American adults and almost one-third of children are above their healthy weight (Flegal & others, 2013; Lobstein & others, 2015).

How is healthy weight determined? For statistical purposes, the most widely used measure of weight status is **body mass index,** abbreviated **BMI.** For adults, the body mass index provides a single numerical value that reflects your weight in relation to your height. A healthy BMI falls between 18 and 25. Generally, people with a BMI between 25 and 29.9 are considered *overweight,* unless their high BMI is due to muscle or bone rather than fat. Thus, it is possible to have a high BMI and still be very healthy, as are many athletes or bodybuilders. In contrast, people who are **obese** have a BMI of 30 or greater *and* an abnormally high proportion of body fat.

Another simple measure of obesity is waist circumference. According to this measure, an adult male's waist should be no more than 40 inches in circumference, and an adult woman's waist should be no more than 35 inches. Some researchers prefer this as a measure of obesity because it indicates the amount of abdominal fat tissue, which is considered to be most damaging to physical health.

More than one-third of the adult U.S. population is considered to be overweight. But another third of adults—over 72 million people—are considered medically obese, weighing in with a BMI of 30 or above (Levi & others, 2011). Beyond the United States, rapidly increasing rates of obesity have become a global health problem. One and a half billion adults are overweight, and about 500 million of these are clinically obese (World Health Organization, 2011). In developing countries, the percentage of obesity has quadrupled since 1980 (Keats & Wiggins, 2014). The most likely culprit? A shift from traditional diets of cereals and grains to a modern, Western diet that is high in fat, sugar, salt, and animal products. Globalization may also be a factor, contributing to the popularization of Western-style processed foods and calorie-dense snacks, soft drinks, and fast food.

body mass index (BMI) A numerical scale indicating adult height in relation to weight; calculated as (703 × weight in pounds)/ (height in inches)².

obese Condition characterized by excessive body fat and a body mass index equal to or greater than 30.0.

Robert Llewellyn/Getty Images

Calculating Your BMI: Where Do You Weigh In?
You can calculate your BMI (body mass index) using the handy calculator at this Web site:

http://tinyurl.com/b53foz

BMI is often used as a "quick and dirty" measure of obesity because it can be easily calculated. However, many researchers prefer measures of waist circumference as a measure of obesity, because it indicates the amount of abdominal fat—which is considered to be the most damaging to physical health. According to this measure, an adult male's waist should be no more than 40 inches in circumference, and an adult woman's waist should be no more than 35 inches.

FACTORS INVOLVED IN BECOMING OVERWEIGHT

In the simplest terms, people become overweight when they habitually take in more calories than the amount of energy they expend. That said, multiple factors affect how much people eat and how the calories are metabolized. These factors include:

1. **The "Supersize It" Syndrome: Overeating** In the past two decades, average daily caloric intake has increased nearly 10 percent for men and 7 percent for women (Piernas & Popkin, 2011). Children, too, have significantly increased their caloric intake over the same period (Lobstein & others, 2015).

CRITICAL THINKING

Has Evolution Programmed Us to Overeat?

The negative consequences of obesity are well known. Along with health problems, people who are overweight or obese are stigmatized in our society—bullied in school, discriminated against at work, and perceived as "lazy" or weak-willed (Puhl & Peterson, 2014). So *why* do so many people overeat?

Psychologist Bruce King (2013) believes that the evolutionary perspective provides several insights. For animals in the wild, food sources are often sporadic and unpredictable. When animals do find food, competition for it can be fierce, even deadly. If an animal waited to eat until it was hungry and its energy reserves were significantly diminished, it would run the risk of starving or falling prey to another animal. Thus, the eating patterns of many animals have evolved so that they readily eat even if not hungry (Berthoud, 2007; Zheng & others, 2009).

Similarly, our prehistoric human ancestors, relying upon the availability of wild game or plant foods, would have also experienced periods of both plentiful food and food shortages. According to King (2013), as a survival mechanism, prehistoric humans would have consumed as much food as possible during times of abundance. Overeating when food is available ensures ample energy reserves to survive times when food is *not* available.

But for most people living in food-abundant societies, foraging for your next meal is usually about as demanding as waiting your turn in a fast-food drive-through lane. There is also evidence that in

Christian Heinrich/imageBROKER/age fotostock

food-rich societies, people are *not* simply motivated to eat because they are hungry or because their bodies are suffering from depleted energy resources. Rather, we are enticed by the anticipated pleasure of highly palatable foods (King, 2013). When a food with a high positive incentive value is readily available, we eat, and often overeat (Mok, 2010).

But unlike our evolutionary ancestors who had to hunt game or forage for seeds, nuts, and fruits, today's humans simply don't need to expend physical energy to acquire the food they need to meet their physical needs. As Pinel and his colleagues (2000) explain, "The increases in the availability of high positive-incentive value foods that have occurred over the past few decades in industrialized nations—increases that have been much too rapid to produce adaptive evolutionary change—have promoted levels of consumption that are far higher than those that are compatible with optimal health and long life."

CRITICAL THINKING QUESTIONS

- How might the behavior of overeating be explained by instinct, drive, incentive, and arousal theories?

- How could the insights provided by the evolutionary explanation be used to resist the temptation to overeat?

---

2. **Positive Incentive Value: Highly Palatable Foods** Rather than being motivated by hunger, we are often enticed to eat by the *positive incentive value* of the available foods and the anticipated pleasures of consuming those highly palatable foods (Carr & Epstein, 2011; Epstein & others, 2007).

3. **The Cafeteria Diet Effect: Variety = More Consumed** We consume more food when offered a variety of highly palatable foods, such as at a cafeteria or an all-you-can-eat buffet (Epstein & others, 2010). This is sometimes called the *cafeteria diet effect*.

4. **Sedentary Lifestyles** One recent study of almost 300,000 people living in 76 countries found that approximately 1 in 5 persons worldwide leads a sedentary lifestyle, engaging in less than 30 minutes of moderate activity on most days of the week (Dumith & others, 2011). Sedentary lifestyles are more common in urbanized, developed countries than in less developed or more rural countries. And, in the United States, people have become increasingly *less* active over the past few decades: From 1994 to 2010, the number of women who reported *no* physical activity during their leisure hours jumped from about 20% to over 50%. For men, the percentage rose from about 11% to 43% (Ladabaum & others, 2014).

5. **Too Little Sleep: Disrupting Hunger Hormones** Multiple studies have shown that not getting adequate sleep disrupts metabolism, including the hunger-related hormones leptin and ghrelin (Taheri & others, 2004). People who sleep fewer than seven hours a night have higher BMIs than people who sleep nine hours or more,

and are much more likely to be overweight or obese (Paunio, 2012; Watson & others, 2012). And, when sleep-deprived, people tend to prefer calorie-rich foods like chocolate and potato chips over healthier fare (Greer & others, 2013).

6. **Individual Differences and Lifespan Changes** Finally, not everyone who overeats gains excess weight. One reason is that people vary greatly in their basal metabolic rate, which accounts for about two-thirds of your energy expenditure. On average, women have a metabolic rate that is 3 to 5 percent lower than men's. Metabolism also decreases with age, so that less food is required to meet your basic energy needs. Consequently, it's not surprising that many people, upon reaching early adulthood, must begin to watch how much they eat.

Of the six factors we've covered here, you can exert control over five of them—all except BMR—to counteract becoming or remaining overweight. And, as explained in the Focus on Neuroscience on page 324, the brain's dopamine system can also be involved in overeating.

FACTORS INVOLVED IN OBESITY

Especially in the past decade, there has been intensive research investigating the causes of obesity—and for good reason. Regardless of how it develops, a BMI of 30 or above has life-threatening consequences (Abdullah & others, 2011; Flegal & others, 2013). Annually, about 300,000 adult deaths in the United States are *directly* attributable to obesity.

Several variables derail the normal mechanisms of energy homeostasis in obesity. First, genetics plays a role. Current research suggests that multiple genes on multiple chromosomes are involved in creating susceptibility to obesity (Friedman, 2009). People with a family history of obesity are two to three times more likely than people with no such family history to become obese. And, the more closely related two people are genetically, the more likely they are to have similar body mass indexes (Bell & others, 2005).

But genetics is *not* destiny. Even though someone may be genetically predisposed to obesity, environmental factors play an important role. If an individual is genetically susceptible and lives in a high-risk environment, obesity is more likely to occur (Rosenquist & others, 2015). And what constitutes a high-risk environment for obesity? An environment characterized by ample and easily obtainable high-fat, high-calorie, palatable foods. A real-world example of this interaction is the sharp increase in obesity in developing countries: As countries develop stable economies and food supplies, the prevalence of obesity rapidly escalates (Keats & Wiggins, 2014).

Once a person is overweight, metabolic factors are also important. For example, many obese people experience *leptin resistance,* in which the normal mechanisms through which leptin regulates body weight and energy balance are disrupted (Enriori & others, 2006; Morrison, 2008).

Eating habits, of course, affect weight. And while any diet that reduces caloric intake will result in weight loss, the more difficult challenge is to maintain the lower weight. Many overweight or obese dieters experience *weight cycling,* or *yo-yo dieting*—the weight lost through dieting is regained in weeks or months and maintained until the next attempt at dieting.

One reason this occurs is because the human body is much more effective at vigorously defending against weight *loss* than it is at protecting against weight *gain* (Keel & others, 2007). As caloric intake is reduced and fat cells begin to shrink, the body actively defends against weight loss by decreasing metabolism rate and energy level. With energy expenditure reduced, far fewer calories are needed to maintain the excess weight. In effect, the body is using energy much more efficiently. If dieters continue to restrict caloric intake, weight loss will plateau in a matter of weeks. When they go off the diet, their now more energy-efficient bodies quickly utilize the additional calories, and they regain the weight they lost.

> Test your understanding of **Hunger and Eating** with *LEARNING*Curve.

MYTH ◀ SCIENCE

Is it true that obesity is primarily due to genetics?

LaunchPad

Is this chapter making you hungry? **Video Activity: Hunger and Eating** explores the factors that cue eating behavior and contribute to weight gain.

Worth Publishers

FOCUS ON NEUROSCIENCE

Dopamine Receptors and Obesity

Eating to Stimulate Brain Reward?

In Chapter 2, we noted that dopamine brain pathways are involved in the reinforcing feelings of pleasure and satisfaction. In Chapter 4, we also noted that many addictive drugs produce their pleasurable effects by increasing brain dopamine levels. These pleasurable effects are most reinforcing in people who have low levels of dopamine brain receptors (Volkow & others, 2007, 2011b). Given that eating can be highly reinforcing and produces pleasurable sensations, could the same mechanisms also play a role in obesity?

In a landmark study, researchers compared dopamine receptors in normal-weight and obese individuals. As shown in the scans here, obese individuals had significantly fewer dopamine receptors, colored red, than the normal-weight individuals. And, among the obese people in the study, the number of dopamine receptors *decreased* as BMI *increased* (Wang & others, 2001, 2004). Thus, it could be that compulsive or binge eating compensates for reduced dopamine function by stimulating the brain's reward system (Volkow & Wise, 2005).

But is the lower number of dopamine receptors a *cause* or a *consequence* of obesity? In a recent study, one group of rats was allowed to eat as much as they wanted of rat chow—a nutritionally complete but boring diet (Johnson & Kenny, 2010). Another group of rats, genetically identical to the first group, was offered a "cafeteria diet" of high-fat, sugary foods that are freely available in the modern American diet: sausage, bacon, cheesecake, pound cake, chocolate, and frosting.

The rats on the junk-food diet rapidly became overweight, eating up to twice as many calories as the rats fed only the boring rat chow. Refusing nutritious, low-calorie food, the rats became compulsive eaters. Like drug addicts seeking a high despite negative consequences, they would eat the junk food even when it was paired with a mild electric shock.

Even more interesting was what happened to the rats' brain chemistry. Much like the brain changes associated with drug addiction, dopamine response in the junk-food-addicted rats was significantly reduced. In other words, rats who pigged out (so to speak) on sugary, fatty foods experienced the same changes in brain chemistry that are associated with addiction to drugs like cocaine, heroin, and alcohol.

Can overeating lead to brain changes in humans, too? Neuroscientist Eric Stice and his colleagues (2010) used fMRI to scan the brains of overweight women while they drank a rich chocolate milkshake. Six months later, the women returned to the lab and repeated the experience. Some of the women had gained a few pounds, and others had not. The researchers found that there was no difference in the response to the milkshake in the women whose weight had remained stable. But women who had gained weight showed a significant reduction in the response of their brain reward system to the milkshake: the more weight gained, the greater the reduction in dopamine response to the milkshake as compared to six months previously.

Such results imply that obesity can be a vicious circle: People eat more to compensate for reduced brain rewards, but overeating reduces the dopamine reward system levels even further. These findings help explain why people continue to overeat despite suffering the unhealthy consequences of obesity.

Obese   Normal

Courtesy of Dr. Gene-Jack Wang, Brookhaven National Laboratory

---

Obsessed with Sex? Sexual themes and images are often used to sell products, market movies, and boost TV ratings. How accurate are media images of human sexuality?

Richard Levine/Alamy

Human Sexuality

KEY THEME

Multiple factors are involved in understanding human sexuality.

KEY QUESTIONS

> What are the four stages of human sexual response?

> How does sexual motivation differ among animal species?

> What biological factors are involved in sexual motivation?

Psychologists consider the drive to have sex a basic human motive. But what exactly motivates that drive? Obviously, there are differences between sex and other basic motives, such as hunger. Engaging in sexual intercourse is essential to the survival of the human species, but it is not essential to the survival of any specific person. In other words, you'll die if you don't eat, but you won't die if you don't have sex.

First Things First

THE STAGES OF HUMAN SEXUAL RESPONSE

The human sexual response cycle was first mapped by sex research pioneers **William Masters** and **Virginia Johnson** during the 1950s and

Pioneers of Sex Research: William Masters (1915–2001) and Virginia Johnson (1925–2013) In 1966 Masters and Johnson, shown here interviewing a couple, broke new ground in the scientific study of sexual behavior when they published *Human Sexual Response*. In that book they provided the first extensive laboratory data on the anatomy and physiology of the male and female sexual response. Although intended for clinicians, the book became a best-seller that was translated into over 30 languages. Some critics felt the Masters and Johnson research had violated "sacred ground" and dehumanized sexuality. But others applauded *Human Sexual Response* for advancing the understanding of human sexuality and dispelling misconceptions. The techniques they developed are still widely used in sex therapy today.

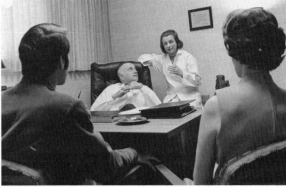

George Tames/The New York Times/Redux

1960s. In the name of science, Masters and Johnson observed hundreds of people engage in more than 10,000 episodes of sexual activity in their laboratory. Their findings, published in 1966, indicated that the human sexual response could be described as a cycle with four stages. Although it is simplified somewhat, Figure 8.2 depicts the basic patterns of sexual response for men and women.

STAGE 1: EXCITEMENT

The *excitement phase* marks the beginning of sexual arousal. Sexual arousal can occur in response to sexual fantasies or other sexually arousing stimuli, physical contact with another person, or masturbation. In both sexes, the excitement stage is accompanied by a variety of bodily changes in anticipation of sexual interaction.

STAGE 2: PLATEAU

In the second phase, the *plateau phase,* physical arousal builds. The penis becomes fully erect and sometimes secretes a few drops of fluid, which may contain active sperm. The testes increase in size. The clitoris withdraws under the clitoral hood but remains very sensitive to stimulation. The vaginal entrance tightens, putting pressure on the penis during intercourse. During the excitement and plateau stages, the degree of arousal may fluctuate up and down (Masters & others, 1995).

STAGE 3: ORGASM

Orgasm is the third and shortest phase of the sexual response cycle. The muscles in the vaginal walls and the uterus contract rhythmically, as do the muscles in and around the penis as the male ejaculates. Both men and women describe the subjective experience of orgasm in similar—and very positive—terms.

The vast majority of men experience one intense orgasm. But many women are capable of experiencing multiple orgasms. If sexual stimulation continues following orgasm, women may experience additional orgasms within a short period of time (King & others, 2010).

STAGE 4: RESOLUTION

Following orgasm, both sexes tend to experience a warm physical "glow" and a sense of well-being. Arousal slowly subsides and returns to normal levels in the *resolution*

FIGURE 8.2 The Male and Female Sexual Response Cycles The figure on the left depicts the three basic variations of the female sexual response. Pattern 1 shows multiple orgasms. Pattern 2 shows sexual arousal that reaches the plateau stage but not orgasm, followed by a slow resolution. Pattern 3 depicts brief reductions in arousal during the excitement stage, followed by rapid orgasm and resolution. The figure on the right depicts the most typical male sexual response, in which orgasm is followed by a refractory period.

Source: Masters, William H.; & Johnson, Virginia E. (1966). Human sexual response. Boston: Little, Brown. Reproduced with permission from Ishi Press.

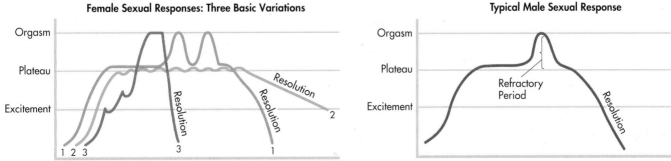

phase. The male experiences a *refractory period,* during which he is incapable of having another erection or orgasm.

What Motivates Sexual Behavior?

In most animals, sexual behavior is biologically determined and triggered by hormonal changes in the female. During the cyclical period known as *estrus,* a female animal is fertile and receptive to male sexual advances. Roughly translated, the Greek word *estrus* means "frantic desire." Indeed, the female animal will often actively signal her willingness to engage in sexual activity—as any owner of an unneutered female cat or dog that's "in heat" can testify. In many, but not all, species, sexual activity takes place only when the female is in estrus.

As you go up the evolutionary scale, moving from relatively simple to more sophisticated animals, sexual behavior becomes less biologically determined and more subject to learning and environmental influences. Sexual behavior also becomes less limited to the goal of reproduction (Buss, 2007a, 2007b). For example, in some primate species, such as monkeys and apes, sexual activity can occur at any time, not just when the female is fertile. In these species, sexual interaction serves important social functions, defining and cementing relationships among the members of the primate group.

The Bonobos of the Congo Bonobos demonstrate a wide variety of sexual interactions, including face-to-face copulation, kissing, and sexual interaction among same-sex pairs (Fruth & Hohmann, 2006; Parish & de Waal, 2000). Sexual behavior is not limited to reproduction; it seems to play an important role in maintaining peaceful relations among members of the bonobo group. As Frans de Waal (1995) wrote, "For these animals, sexual behavior is indistinguishable from social behavior."

FINBARR O'REILLY/Reuters/Corbis

One rare species of chimplike apes, the bonobos of the Democratic Republic of the Congo, exhibits a surprising variety of sexual behaviors (de Waal, 2007; Parish & de Waal, 2000). Although most animals *copulate,* or have sex, with the male mounting the female from behind, bonobos often copulate face to face. Bonobos also engage in oral sex and intense tongue kissing. And bonobos seem to like variety. Along with having frequent heterosexual activity, whether the female is fertile or not, bonobos also engage in homosexual and group sex.

Emory University psychology professor Frans de Waal (1995, 2007), who has extensively studied bonobos, observes that their frequent and varied sexual behavior seems to serve important social functions. Sexual behavior is not limited to fulfilling the purpose of reproduction. Among the bonobos, sexual interaction is used to increase group cohesion, avoid conflict, and decrease tension that might be caused by competition for food. According to de Waal (1995), the bonobos' motto seems to be "Make love, not war."

In humans, of course, sexual behavior is not limited to a female's fertile period (Buss, 2007a, 2007b). And, motives for sexual behavior are not limited to reproduction (Meston & Buss, 2007, 2009). Some women experience monthly fluctuations in sexual interest and motivation that are related to the hormonal cycles that also regulate fertility. However, these changes are highly influenced by social and psychological factors, such as relationship quality (Gangestad & others, 2007; Thornhill, 2007). Even when a woman's ovaries, which produce the female sex hormone *estrogen,* are surgically removed or stop functioning during menopause, there is little or no drop in sexual interest. In many nonhuman female mammals, however, removal of the ovaries results in a complete loss of interest in sexual activity. If injections of estrogen and other female sex hormones are given, the female animals' sexual interest returns.

In male animals, removal of the testes (castration) typically causes a steep drop in sexual activity and interest, although the decline is more gradual in sexually experienced animals. Castration causes a significant decrease in levels of *testosterone,* the hormone responsible for male sexual development. When human males experience lowered levels of testosterone because of illness or castration, a similar drop in sexual interest tends to occur, although the effects vary among individuals (Wrobel & Karasek, 2008). Some men continue to lead a normal sex life for years, but others

quickly lose all interest in sexual activity. In castrated men who experience a loss of sexual interest, injections of testosterone restore the sexual drive.

Testosterone is also involved in female sexual motivation (Davis & others, 2008). Most of the testosterone in a woman's body is produced by her adrenal glands. If these glands are removed or malfunction, causing testosterone levels to become abnormally low, sexual interest often wanes. When supplemental testosterone is administered, the woman's sex drive returns. Thus, in *both* men and women, sexual motivation is biologically influenced by the levels of the hormone testosterone in the body. Of course, sexual behavior is greatly influenced by many different factors— social, cultural, and more.

Sexual Orientation
THE ELUSIVE SEARCH FOR AN EXPLANATION

KEY THEME

Sexual orientation refers to whether a person is attracted to members of the opposite sex, the same sex, or both sexes.

KEY QUESTIONS

> Why is sexual orientation sometimes difficult to identify?
> What factors have been associated with sexual orientation?

Given that biological factors seem to play an important role in motivating sexual desire, it seems only reasonable to ask whether biological factors also play a role in sexual orientation. **Sexual orientation** refers to whether a person is sexually aroused by members of the same sex, the opposite sex, or both sexes. A *heterosexual* person is sexually attracted to individuals of the other sex, a *homosexual* person to individuals of the same sex, and a *bisexual* person to individuals of both sexes. Technically, the term *homosexual* can be applied to either males or females. However, female homosexuals are usually called *lesbians.* Male homosexuals typically use the term *gay* to describe their sexual orientation. Some researchers have posited an additional orientation— *asexual.* Asexuality refers to people who are not sexually attracted to people of either sex, regardless of their actual sexual behavior (Bogaert, 2006).

Sexual orientation is not nearly as cut and dried as many people believe. Some people *are* exclusively heterosexual or homosexual, but others are less easy to categorize. Some people explicitly identify as "mostly," but not exclusively, heterosexual or homosexual (Vrangalova & Savin-Williams, 2012). Some people who consider themselves heterosexual have had a homosexual experience at some point in their

Famous Gay Couples Comedian and popular talk show host Ellen DeGeneres struggled for many years to come to grips with her sexual orientation before publicly coming out as a lesbian. As DeGeneres (2005) recalled, "To be 37 years old and be feeling this sense of shame, that nobody would like me if they found out I was gay, it was a pretty emotional thing to expose yourself to." In 1997, she made television history when she "outed" herself and her character in her television series *Ellen.* But by 2008, Ellen's marriage to long-time companion Portia deRossi, a few months after same-sex marriage became legal in California, was covered like any other celebrity wedding ceremony.

Pictured on the right are "power couple" Chris Hughes, one of Facebook's founders and editor-in-chief of *The New Republic,* and his spouse, Sean Eldridge, an investor and political activist. Hughes (2011) says that "having a partner who has similar intensity in his days, a passion for work in the same way, it makes a difference to come home at night and have an intellectual partner."

sexual orientation The direction of a person's emotional and erotic attraction toward members of the opposite sex, the same sex, or both sexes.

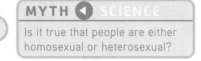

"You know, statistically speaking, at least one of these gingerbread men is gay."

U.S. Senator Tammy Baldwin: "I Ran to Make a Difference." The first openly gay U.S. Senator, Baldwin was elected by Wisconsin voters in 2012. Upon her election, Baldwin stressed that she defined herself by more than just her sexual orientation. As she said, "I didn't run to make history; I ran to make a difference," reiterating her support for all citizens of Wisconsin, including families, seniors, and veterans. Her election is certainly a historic one, but it also demonstrates that sexual orientation is not the only characteristic that voters consider.

lives. In the same vein, many people who identify as homosexuals have had heterosexual experiences (Malcolm, 2008; Rieger & others, 2005). Other people consider themselves to be homosexual but have been involved in long-term, committed heterosexual relationships. Still others are asexual but engage in romantic or sexual relationships. The key points are that there is a range of sexual identity and there is not always a perfect correspondence between a particular person's sexual identity, sexual desires, and sexual behaviors.

Determining the number of people who are homosexual, heterosexual, bisexual, or asexual is challenging. First, survey results vary depending on how the researchers define the terms *homosexual, heterosexual, bisexual,* and *asexual* (Bogaert, 2006; Savin-Williams & Hope, 2009). Where the survey is conducted, how survey participants are selected, and how the survey questions are worded also affect the results.

Depending upon how sexual orientation is defined, estimates of the prevalence rate of homosexuality in the general population range from 1 percent to 21 percent (Savin-Williams, 2006). More important than the exact number of gays and lesbians is the recognition that gays and lesbians constitute a significant segment of the adult population. According to the most recent estimates, about 7% of women and 5% of men in the United States report having ever engaged in homosexual behavior (F. Xu & others, 2010a, 2010b). Asexuality has been studied much less than homosexuality. However, one study of over 18,000 people living in the United Kingdom found that about 1% of people reported no sexual attraction to either men or women (Bogaert, 2004).

WHAT DETERMINES SEXUAL ORIENTATION?

Despite considerable research on this question, psychologists and other researchers cannot say with certainty why people become homosexual or bisexual. For that matter, psychologists don't know exactly why people become *heterosexual* either. Still, research on sexual orientation has pointed toward several general conclusions, especially with regard to homosexuality.

Evidence from multiple studies shows that genetics plays a role in determining sexual orientation (Rodriguez-Larralde & Paradisi, 2009). Most studies compare the incidence of homosexuality among pairs of identical twins (who have identical genes), fraternal twins (who are genetically as similar as any two nontwin siblings), and nontwin siblings. In both males and females, research has shown that the closer the degree of genetic relationship, the more likely it is that when one sibling is homosexual, the other would also be homosexual. Such studies have shown that genetics contributes to homosexual orientation in both men and women, although to a much lesser degree in women than men (Alanko & others, 2010; Långström & others, 2010).

However, genetics is only a partial explanation. In the largest twin studies to date, Swedish researchers showed that *both* genetic and nonshared environmental factors were involved in sexual orientation (Långström & others, 2008, 2010). What are "nonshared" environmental factors? Influences that are experienced by one, but not both, twins. More specifically, these are social and biological factors, rather than upbringing or family environment.

Sexual orientation does seem to be at least partly influenced by genetics (Hyde, 2005). However, that genetic influence is likely to be complex, involving the interaction of multiple genes, not a single "gay gene" (see Vilain, 2008). Beyond heredity, there is also evidence that sexual orientation may be influenced by other biological factors, such as prenatal exposure to sex hormones or other aspects of the prenatal environment (Hines, 2010).

William Haefeli The New Yorker Collection/The Cartoon Bank.

Chip Somodevilla/Getty Images

For example, one intriguing finding is that the more older brothers a man has, the more likely he is to be homosexual (Blanchard, 2008; Blanchard & Lippa, 2008). Could a homosexual orientation be due to psychological factors, such as younger brothers being bullied or indulged by older male siblings? Or being treated differently by their parents or some other family dynamic?

No. Collecting data on men who grew up in adoptive or blended families, Anthony Bogaert (2006a) found that only the number of biologically related older brothers predicted homosexual orientation. Living with older brothers who were *not* biologically related had no effect at all. As Anthony Bogaert (2007b) explains, "It's not the brothers you lived with; it's the environment within the same womb—sharing the same mom." Researchers don't have an explanation for the effect, which has been replicated in multiple studies (see Bogaert, 2007a). One suggestion is that carrying successive male children might trigger some sort of immune response in the mother that, in turn, influences brain development in the male fetus (James, 2006).

Finally, a number of researchers have discovered differences in brain function or structure among gay, lesbian, and heterosexual men and women (see LeVay, 2007; Savic & Lindström, 2008). However, most of these studies have proved small or inconclusive. It's also important to note that there is no way of knowing whether brain differences are the *cause* or the *effect* of different patterns of sexual behavior.

In general, the only conclusion we can draw from these studies is that some biological factors are *correlated* with a homosexual orientation (Mustanski & others, 2002). As we've stressed, correlation does not necessarily indicate causality, only that two factors *seem* to occur together. So stronger conclusions about the role of genetic and biological factors in determining sexual orientation await more definitive research findings.

In an early study involving in-depth interviews with over 1,000 gay men and lesbian women, Alan Bell and his colleagues (1981) found that homosexuality was *not* the result of disturbed or abnormal family relationships. They also found that sexual orientation was determined before adolescence and long before the beginning of sexual activity. Gay men and lesbian women typically became aware of homosexual feelings about three years before they engaged in any such sexual activity. In this regard, the pattern was very similar to that of heterosexual children, in whom heterosexual feelings are aroused long before the child expresses them in some form of sexual behavior.

Several researchers now believe that sexual orientation is established as early as age 6 (Strickland, 1995). Do children who later grow up to be homosexual differ from children who later grow up to be heterosexual? In at least one respect, there seems to be a difference.

Typically, boys and girls differ in their choice of toys, playmates, and activities from early childhood. However, evidence suggests that homosexual males and homosexual females are less likely to have followed the typical pattern of gender-specific behaviors in childhood (Bailey & others, 2000; Lippa, 2008; Rieger & others, 2008). Compared to heterosexual men, gay men recall engaging in more cross-sex-typed behavior during childhood. For example, they remembered playing more with girls than with other boys, preferring girls' toys over boys' toys, and disliking rough-and-tumble play. Lesbians are also more likely to recall cross-gender behavior in childhood. One study suggests that lesbians show an even greater degree of gender nonconformity than gays (Lippa, 2008).

A potential problem with such *retrospective studies* is that the participants may be biased in their recall of childhood events. One way to avoid that problem is by conducting a prospective study. A *prospective study* involves systematically observing a group of people over time to discover what factors are associated with the development of a particular trait, characteristic, or behavior.

One influential prospective study was conducted by Richard Green (1985, 1987). Green followed the development of sexual orientation in two groups of boys. The first

I heard this on the news: "For every older brother a man has, the chances of him being gay increase by one-third." I got a few problems with this theory. Specifically, Jimmy, Eddie, Billy, Tommy, Jay, Paul, and Peter. Those are my older brothers—seven brothers. By their math, I should be 233 percent gay. That's getting up there.

—*Stephen Colbert*—The Colbert Report

Hear two sets of twins talk about their differences in **Video Activity: Homosexuality and the Nature-Nurture Debate.**

"Back when we were in college, and occasionally sleeping together, I never thought I'd be here, toasting you at your wedding to a woman."

group of boys had been referred to a mental health clinic because of their "feminine" behavior. He compared the development of these boys to a matched control group of boys who displayed typically "masculine" behavior in childhood. When all the boys were in their late teens, Green compared the two groups. He found that approximately 75 percent of the previously feminine boys were either bisexual or homosexual, as compared to only 4 percent of the control group.

Less is known about girls who are referred to clinics because of cross-gender behavior, partly because girls are less likely to be referred to clinics for "tomboy" behavior (Zucker & Cohen-Kettenis, 2008). However, Kelley Drummond and her colleagues (2008) found that cross-gender behavior in girls was also associated with the later development of bisexual or homosexual orientation, although at a lower rate than was true for boys.

Once sexual orientation is established, whether heterosexual or homosexual, it is highly resistant to change (Drescher & Zucker, 2006). The vast majority of homosexuals would be unable to change their orientation even if they wished to, just as the majority of heterosexuals would be unable to change their orientation if *they* wished to. Thus, it's a mistake to assume that homosexuals have deliberately chosen their sexual orientation any more than heterosexuals have.

It seems clear that no single factor determines whether people identify themselves as homosexual, heterosexual, or bisexual (Patterson, 2008). Psychological, biological, social, and cultural factors are undoubtedly involved in determining sexual orientation. However, researchers are still unable to pinpoint exactly what those factors are and how they interact. As psychologist Bonnie Strickland (1995) has pointed out, "Sexual identity and orientation appear to be shaped by a complexity of biological, psychological, and social events. Gender identity and sexual orientation, at least for most people, especially gay men, occur early, are relatively fixed, and are difficult to change." Whether we are homosexual, bisexual, or heterosexual, changing our sexual orientation is simply not possible.

Homosexuality has not been considered a sexual disorder by clinical psychologists or psychiatrists since 1973 (American Psychiatric Association, 1994; Silverstein, 2009). Many research studies have also found that homosexuals who are comfortable with their sexual orientation are just as well adjusted as are heterosexuals (see Strickland, 1995). Indeed, in 2009 the American Psychological Association issued a resolution stating that there is no evidence to support therapies that aim to change sexual orientation. Furthermore, it has been found that such therapies can lead to serious psychological outcomes for some people (Shidlo & Schroeder, 2002). As a result, in the United States, some states have banned such therapies through the legal system (Eckholm, 2013).

Like heterosexuals, gays and lesbians can be found in every occupation and at every socioeconomic level in our society. And, like heterosexuals, many gays and lesbians are involved in long-term, committed, and caring relationships (Roisman & others, 2008). Over 25 years of research suggests that children who are raised by gay or lesbian parents are as well adjusted as children who are raised by heterosexual parents (Perrin & others, 2013; Wainwright & Patterson, 2008). Finally, children who are raised by gay or lesbian parents are no more likely to be gay or lesbian in adulthood than are children who are raised by heterosexual parents (Anderssen & others, 2002; Bailey & others, 1995; Regnerus, 2012).

Same-Sex Couples and Their Children Research on same-sex couples in committed, long-term relationships shows that their relationships are quite similar to those of heterosexual couples in most ways (Balsam & others, 2008). One exception: Lesbian couples were better than heterosexual or gay couples at harmonious problem solving (Roisman & others, 2008). What about their children? Research consistently has shown that the children of same-sex parents are very similar to the children of heterosexual parents (Patterson, 2006, 2008). And, contrary to popular belief, teenagers with same-sex parents have peer relationships and friendships that are much like those of teenagers with heterosexual or single parents (Wainwright & Patterson, 2008; Rivers & others, 2008).

❯ Test your understanding of **Human Sexuality** with *LEARNINGCurve*.

Psychological Needs as Motivators

hierarchy of needs Maslow's hierarchical division of motivation into levels that progress from basic physical needs to psychological needs to self-fulfillment needs.

KEY THEME

According to the motivation theories of Maslow and of Deci and Ryan, psychological needs must be fulfilled for optimal human functioning.

KEY QUESTIONS

> How does Maslow's hierarchy of needs explain human motivation?
> What are some important criticisms of Maslow's theory?
> What are the basic premises of self-determination theory?

Why did you enroll in college? What motivates you to study long hours for an important exam? To push yourself to achieve a new "personal best" at a favorite sport? Rather than being motivated by a biological need or drive like hunger, such behaviors are more likely motivated by the urge to satisfy *psychological needs.*

In this section, we'll first consider two theories that attempt to explain psychological motivation: Abraham Maslow's famous *hierarchy of needs* and the more recently developed *self-determination theory* of Edward L. Deci and Richard M. Ryan.

Maslow's Hierarchy of Needs

A major turning point in the discussion of human needs occurred when humanistic psychologist **Abraham Maslow** developed his model of human motivation in the 1940s and 1950s. Maslow acknowledged the importance of biological needs as motivators. But once basic biological needs are satisfied, he believed, "higher" psychological needs emerge to motivate human behavior.

The centerpiece of Maslow's (1954, 1968) model of motivation was his famous **hierarchy of needs,** summarized in Figure 8.3. Maslow believed that people are motivated to satisfy the needs at each level of the hierarchy before moving up to the next level. As people progressively move up the hierarchy, they are ultimately motivated by the desire to achieve self-actualization. The lowest levels of Maslow's hierarchy emphasize fundamental biological and safety needs. At the higher levels,

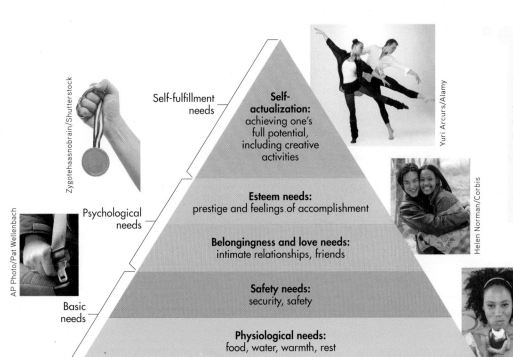

Self-fulfillment needs

Self-actualization: achieving one's full potential, including creative activities

Psychological needs

Esteem needs: prestige and feelings of accomplishment

Belongingness and love needs: intimate relationships, friends

Basic needs

Safety needs: security, safety

Physiological needs: food, water, warmth, rest

FIGURE 8.3 Maslow's Hierarchy of Needs Abraham Maslow believed that people are innately motivated to satisfy a progression of needs, beginning with the most basic physiological needs. Once the needs at a particular level are satisfied, the individual is motivated to satisfy the needs at the next level, steadily progressing upward. The ultimate goal is self-actualization, the realization of personal potential.

Source: Research from Maslow (1970).

the needs become more social and psychologically growth-oriented, culminating in the need to achieve *self-actualization.*

What exactly is self-actualization? Maslow (1970) himself had trouble defining the term, saying that self-actualization is "a difficult syndrome to describe accurately." Nonetheless, Maslow defined **self-actualization** in the following way:

> It may be loosely described as the full use and exploitation of talents, capacities, potentialities, etc. Such people seem to be fulfilling themselves and to be doing the best that they are capable of doing. . . . They are people who have developed or are developing to the full stature of which they are capable.

Maslow identified several characteristics of self-actualized people, which are summarized in Table 8.2.

Maslow's model of motivation generated considerable research, especially during the 1970s and 1980s. Some researchers found support for Maslow's ideas (see Graham & Balloun, 1973). Others, however, criticized his model on several points (see Fox, 1982; Neher, 1991; Wahba & Bridwell, 1976).

First, Maslow's notion that we must satisfy needs at one level before moving to the next level has *not* been supported by empirical research (Sheldon & others, 2001). Second, Maslow's concept of self-actualization is very vague and almost impossible to define in a way that would allow it to be tested scientifically. And, Maslow's initial studies on self-actualization were based on limited samples with questionable reliability. For example, Maslow (1970) often relied on the life stories of acquaintances whose identities were never revealed. He also studied the biographies and autobiographies of famous historical figures he believed had achieved self-actualization, such as Eleanor Roosevelt, Abraham Lincoln, and Albert Einstein.

There is a more important criticism. Despite the claim that self-actualization is an inborn motivational goal toward which all people supposedly strive, most people do *not* experience or achieve self-actualization. Maslow (1970) himself wrote that self-actualization "can seem like a miracle, so improbable an event as to be awe-inspiring." Maslow explained this basic contradiction in a number of different ways. For instance, he suggested that few people experience the supportive environment that is required to achieve self-actualization.

MYTH ◀ SCIENCE

Is it true that people need to satisfy basic needs before they can try to achieve higher needs, like artistic expression?

It is quite true that man lives by bread alone—where there is no bread. But what happens to man's desires when there is plenty of bread and when his belly is chronically filled? At once other (and "higher") needs emerge and these, rather than physiological hungers, dominate the organism. And when these in turn are satisfied, again new (and still "higher") needs emerge, and so on. That is what we mean by saying that the basic human needs are organized into a hierarchy of relative prepotency.

—Abraham Maslow (1943)

Courtesy of Robert D. Farber University
Archives at Brandeis University

TABLE 8.2

Maslow's Characteristics of Self-Actualized People

Realism and acceptance	Self-actualized people have accurate perceptions of themselves, others, and external reality.
Spontaneity	Self-actualized people are spontaneous, natural, and open in their behavior and thoughts. However, they can easily conform to conventional rules and expectations when necessary.
Problem centering	Self-actualized people focus on problems outside themselves. They often dedicate themselves to a larger purpose in life.
Autonomy	Although they accept and enjoy other people, self-actualized individuals have a strong need for privacy and independence.
Continued freshness of appreciation	Self-actualized people continue to appreciate the simple pleasures of life with awe and wonder.
Peak experiences	Self-actualized people commonly have *peak experiences,* or moments of intense ecstasy, wonder, and awe during which their sense of self is lost or transcended.

SOURCE: Research from Maslow (1970).

Perhaps Maslow's most important contribution was to encourage psychology to focus on the motivation and development of psychologically healthy people (King, 2008). In advocating that idea, he helped focus attention on psychological needs as motivators.

Deci and Ryan's Self-Determination Theory

Self-determination theory, abbreviated **SDT,** is a contemporary theory of motivation developed by University of Rochester psychologists **Edward L. Deci** and **Richard M. Ryan** (2000, 2012a, 2012b). Much like Maslow's theory, SDT's premise is that people are actively growth oriented and that they move toward a unified sense of self and integration with others. To realize optimal psychological functioning and growth throughout the life span, Ryan and Deci contend that three innate and universal psychological needs must be satisfied:

- *Autonomy*—the need to determine, control, and organize one's own behavior and goals so that they are in harmony with one's own interests and values.

- *Competence*—the need to learn and master appropriately challenging tasks.

- *Relatedness*—the need to feel attached to others and experience a sense of belongingness, security, and intimacy.

Like Maslow, Deci and Ryan view the need for social relationships as a fundamental psychological motive. The benefits of having strong, positive social relationships are well documented (Leary & Allen, 2011). Another well-established psychological need is having a sense of competence or mastery (Bandura, 1997; White, 1959).

One subtle difference in Maslow's views compared to those of Deci and Ryan has to do with the definition of *autonomy.* Deci and Ryan's definition of *autonomy* emphasizes the need to feel that your activities are self-chosen and self-endorsed (Ryan & Deci, 2011; Niemiec & others, 2010). This reflects the importance of self-determination in Deci and Ryan's theory. In contrast, Maslow's view of *autonomy* stressed the need to feel independent and focused on your own potential (see Table 8.2 on the previous page).

How does a person satisfy the needs for autonomy, competence, and relatedness? In a supportive social, psychological, and physical environment, an individual will pursue interests, goals, and relationships that tend to satisfy these psychological needs. In turn, this enhances the person's psychological growth and intrinsic motivation (Sheldon & Ryan, 2011). **Intrinsic motivation** is the desire to engage in tasks that the person finds inherently satisfying and enjoyable, novel, or optimally challenging. The doctors, nurses, and other volunteers who traveled to Nepal in the Prologue story displayed intrinsic motivation, taking time away from work and family to contribute their efforts to helping others in a distant land.

In contrast, **extrinsic motivation** consists of external influences on behavior, such as rewards, social evaluations, rules, and responsibilities. Of course, much of our behavior in daily life is driven by extrinsic motivation (Ryan & La Guardia, 2000). According to SDT, the person who has satisfied the needs for competence, autonomy, and relatedness actively *internalizes* and *integrates* different external motivators as part of his or her identity and values (Ryan & Deci, 2012). In effect, the person incorporates societal expectations, rules, and regulations as values or rules that he or she personally endorses.

What if one or more of the psychological needs are thwarted by an unfavorable environment, one that is overly challenging, controlling, rejecting, punishing, or even abusive? According to SDT, the person may compensate with substitute needs, defensive behaviors, or maladaptive behaviors. For example, if someone is frustrated in satisfying the need for relatedness, he or she may compensate by chronically seeking the approval of others or by pursuing substitute goals, such as accumulating money or material possessions.

self-actualization Defined by Maslow as a person's "full use and exploitation of talents, capacities, and potentialities."

self-determination theory (SDT) Deci and Ryan's theory that optimal human functioning can occur only if the psychological needs for autonomy, competence, and relatedness are satisfied.

intrinsic motivation The desire to engage in tasks that are inherently satisfying and enjoyable, novel, or optimally challenging; the desire to do something for its own sake.

extrinsic motivation External factors or influences on behavior, such as rewards, consequences, or social expectations.

THE WORLD'S #1 MOTIVATIONAL SPEAKER

competence motivation The desire to direct your behavior toward demonstrating competence and exercising control in a situation.

achievement motivation The desire to direct your behavior toward excelling, succeeding, or outperforming others at some task.

Thematic Apperception Test (TAT) A projective personality test, developed by Henry Murray and colleagues, that involves creating stories about ambiguous scenes.

For more on the historic climb by Pasang and her teammates, visit http://www.k2expedition2014.org/

Extraordinary Achievement Motivation Thousands of students from 120 countries compete each year in the Google Science Fair. Showing off their trophies —and their grins—are the 2013 winners: 14-year-old Viney Kumar, from Australia, who invented a signalling system for emergency vehicles; 15-year-old Ann Makosinski, from Canada, who designed a flashlight without batteries or moving parts; 16-year-old Elif Bilgin, from Turkey, who developed a method to create bioplastics from banana peels; and 17-year-old Eric Chen, from the U.S., who discovered a new approach to finding better anti-flu medications.

In support of self-determination theory, Deci and Ryan have compiled an impressive array of studies, including cross-cultural studies (Deci & Ryan, 2000, 2012a, 2012b). Taking the evolutionary perspective, they also argue that the needs for autonomy, competence, and relatedness have adaptive advantages. For example, the need for relatedness promotes resource sharing, mutual protection, and the division of work, increasing the likelihood that both the individual and the group will survive.

Competence and Achievement Motivation

KEY THEME

Competence and achievement motivation are important psychological motives.

KEY QUESTIONS

> How does competence motivation differ from achievement motivation, and how is achievement motivation measured?

> What characteristics are associated with a high level of achievement motivation, and how does culture affect achievement motivation?

In self-determination theory, Deci and Ryan identified *competence* as a universal motive. You are displaying **competence motivation** when you strive to use your cognitive, social, and behavioral skills to be capable and exercise control in a situation (White, 1959). Competence motivation provides much of the motivational "push" to prove to yourself that you can successfully tackle new challenges, such as striving to do well in this class or making it to the top of a steep trail.

A step beyond competence motivation is **achievement motivation**—the drive to excel, succeed, or outperform others at some task. For example, in the chapter Prologue, Pasang clearly displayed a high level of achievement motivation. Climbing Everest and becoming an internationally certified mountaineering guide are just two examples of Pasang's drive to achieve. In fact, in late July 2014, Pasang summited K-2, the second-highest and, some say, most dangerous mountain in the world. Pasang and her two Nepali teammates were the first all-female team to successfully conquer K-2. Their mission's avowed purpose was to bring attention to the importance of climate change and to encourage sustainable development in the Himalayas.

In the 1930s, Henry Murray identified 20 fundamental human needs or motives, including achievement motivation. Murray (1938) defined the "need to achieve" as the tendency "to overcome obstacles, to exercise power, [and] to strive to do something difficult as well and as quickly as possible." Also in the 1930s, Christiana Morgan and Henry Murray (1935) developed a test to measure human motives called the **Thematic Apperception Test (TAT).** The TAT consists of a series of ambiguous pictures. The person being tested is asked to make up a story about each picture, and the story is then coded for different motivational themes, including achievement. In Chapter 10, on personality, we'll look at the TAT in more detail.

In the 1950s, David McClelland, John Atkinson, and their colleagues (1953) developed a specific TAT scoring system to measure the *need for achievement,* often abbreviated *nAch.* Other researchers developed questionnaire measures of achievement motivation (Spangler, 1992; Ziegler & others, 2010).

Over the next four decades, McClelland and his associates investigated many different aspects of achievement motivation, especially its application in work settings. In cross-cultural studies, McClelland explored how differences in achievement motivation at the national level have influenced economic development (McClelland, 1961, 1976; McClelland & Winter, 1971). He also studied organizational leadership and *power motivation*—the urge to control or influence the behavior of other people or groups (McClelland, 1975, 1989).

Hundreds of studies have shown that measures of achievement motivation generally correlate well with various areas of success, such as school grades, job performance, and worker output (Senko & others, 2008). This is understandable, since people who score high in achievement motivation expend their greatest efforts when faced with moderately challenging tasks. In striving to achieve the task, they often choose to work long hours and have the capacity to delay gratification and focus on the goal. They also tend to display original thinking, seek expert advice, and value feedback about their performance (McClelland, 1985).

ACHIEVEMENT MOTIVATION AND CULTURE

When it is broadly defined as "the desire for excellence," achievement motivation is found in many, if not all, cultures. In individualistic cultures, like those that characterize North American and European countries, the need to achieve emphasizes personal, individual success rather than the success of the group. In these cultures, achievement motivation is also closely linked with succeeding in competitive tasks (Markus & others, 2006; Morling & Kitayama, 2008).

In collectivistic cultures, like those of many Asian countries, achievement motivation tends to have a different focus. Instead of being oriented toward the individual, achievement orientation is more *socially* oriented (Bond, 1986; Kitayama & Park, 2007). For example, students in China felt that it was unacceptable to express pride for personal achievements but that it was acceptable to feel proud of achievements that benefited others (Stipek, 1998). The person strives to achieve not to promote himself or herself but to promote the status or well-being of other members of the relevant social group, such as family members (Matsumoto & Juang, 2008).

Individuals in collectivistic cultures may persevere or aspire to do well in order to fulfill the expectations of family members and to fit into the larger group. For example, the Japanese student who strives to do well academically is typically not motivated by the desire for personal recognition. Rather, the student's behavior is more likely to be motivated by the desire to enhance the social standing of his or her family by gaining admission to a top university (Kitayama & Park, 2007).

❯ Test your understanding of **Psychological Needs as Motivators** with **LEARNING**Curve.

Kiyoshi Ota/Getty Images

Celebrating Achievement in a Collectivistic Culture Does achievement motivation look the same in every culture? Comparing statements by Japanese and American athletes during the Olympics, Hazel Rose Markus found that Japanese emphasized the importance of their supportive relationships, but Americans tended to see their wins as an individual achievement (Markus & others, 2006). Here, Japanese track star Satomi Kubokura celebrates after winning a gold medal in the 19th Asian Athletics Championship in Kobe, Japan.

Emotion

KEY THEME

Emotions are complex psychological states that serve many functions in human behavior and relationships.

KEY QUESTIONS

❯ What are the three components of emotion, and what functions do emotions serve?

❯ How do evolutionary psychologists view emotion?

❯ What are the basic emotions?

The exhilaration of reaching the top of a steep trail. The fear and worry when a friend is late coming in to camp, and the relief and joy when he finally shows up, safe and sound. Emotions color our life from the earliest days of infancy throughout old age. But what, exactly, *is* emotion?

emotion A complex psychological state that involves a subjective experience, a physiological response, and a behavioral or expressive response.

emotional intelligence The capacity to understand and manage your own emotional experiences and to perceive, comprehend, and respond appropriately to the emotional responses of others.

basic emotions The most fundamental set of emotion categories, which are biologically innate, evolutionarily determined, and culturally universal.

The Many Functions of Emotion
Two friends share news, smiles, and laughter as they patiently wait their turns at the medical clinic in an isolated village in Tsum Valley, Nepal. Emotions play an important role in relationships and social communication.

Sandy Hockenbury

Emotion is a complex psychological state that involves three distinct components: a *subjective experience,* a *physiological response,* and a *behavioral* or *expressive response.* How are emotions different from moods? Generally, emotions are intense but rather short-lived. Emotions are also more likely to have a specific cause, to be directed toward some particular object, and to motivate a person to take some sort of action. In contrast, a *mood* involves a milder emotional state that is more general and pervasive, such as gloominess or contentment. Moods may last for a few hours or even days (Gendolla, 2000).

The Functions of Emotion

Emotional processes are closely tied to motivational processes. Like the word *motivation,* the root of the word *emotion* is the Latin word *movere,* which means "to move." Often emotions do move us to act. For example, consider the anger that motivates you to seek out a new job when you feel you've been treated unfairly by your manager or co-workers. Emotions often *motivate* behavior (Damasio & Carvalho, 2013).

Emotions help us to set goals, but emotional states can also be goals in themselves. We seek out romantic partners to enjoy the bliss of falling in love or we practice hard to experience the exhilaration of winning a sports competition. And most of us direct our lives so as to maximize the experience of positive emotions and minimize the experience of negative emotions (Gendolla, 2000).

At one time, psychologists considered emotions to be disruptive forces that interfered with rational behavior (Cacioppo & Gardner, 1999). Emotions were thought of as primitive impulses that needed to be suppressed or controlled.

Today, psychologists are much more attuned to the importance of emotions in many different areas of behavior, *including* rational decision making, purposeful behavior, and setting appropriate goals (Lerner & others, 2015; Mikels & others, 2011). Most of our choices are guided by our feelings, sometimes without our awareness (Kouider & others, 2011). But consider the fate of people who have lost the capacity to feel emotion because of damage to specific brain areas. Despite having an intact ability to reason, such people tend to make disastrous decisions (Damasio, 2004; Rilling & Sanfey, 2011).

Similarly, people who are low in what is termed **emotional intelligence** may have superior reasoning powers, but they sometimes experience one failure in life after another (Mayer & others, 2004; Van Heck & den Oudsten, 2008). Why? Because they lack the ability to manage their own emotions, comprehend the emotional responses of others, and respond appropriately to the emotions of other people. In contrast, people who are high in emotional intelligence possess these abilities, and they are able to understand and use their emotions (Mayer & others, 2008; Telle & others, 2011).

EVOLUTIONARY EXPLANATIONS OF EMOTION

One of the earliest scientists to systematically study emotions was **Charles Darwin.** Darwin published *The Expression of the Emotions in Man and Animals* in 1872, 13 years after he had laid out his general theory of evolution in *On the Origin of Species by Means of Natural Selection* (1859) and only a year after his book on the evolution of humans, *The Descent of Man* (1871). Darwin (1872) described the facial expressions, body movements, and postures used to express specific emotions in animals and humans. He argued that emotions reflect evolutionary adaptations to the problems of survival and reproduction.

Like Darwin, today's evolutionary psychologists believe that emotions are the product of evolution (Damasio & Carvalho, 2013; Cosmides & Tooby, 2013). Emotions help us solve adaptive problems posed by our environment. They "move" us *toward* potential resources, and they move us *away from* potential dangers. Fear prompts us to flee an attacker or evade a threat. Anger moves us to turn and fight a rival. Love propels us to seek out a mate and care for our offspring. Disgust prompts us to avoid a sickening stimulus. Obviously, the capacity to feel and be moved by emotion has adaptive value: An organism that is able to quickly respond to rewards or threats is more likely to survive and successfully reproduce.

Darwin (1872) also pointed out that emotional displays serve the important function of informing other organisms about an individual's internal state. When facing an aggressive rival, the snarl of a baboon signals its readiness to fight. A wolf rolling submissively on its back telegraphs its willingness to back down and avoid a fight.

Emotions are also important in situations that go well beyond physical survival. Virtually all human relationships are heavily influenced by emotions. Our emotional experience and expression, as well as our ability to understand the emotions of others, are crucial to the maintenance of social relationships (Reis & others, 2000).

In the next several sections, we'll consider each of the components of emotion in turn, beginning with the component that is most familiar: the subjective experience of emotion.

The Subjective Experience of Emotion

Most emotion researchers today agree that there are a limited number of **basic emotions** that all humans, in every culture, experience. These basic emotions are thought to be biologically determined, the products of evolution. And what are these basic emotions? As shown in Table 8.3, fear, disgust, surprise, happiness, anger, and sadness are most commonly cited as the basic emotions (Ekman & Cordaro, 2011; Matsumoto & Hwang, 2011a).

Many psychologists contend that each basic emotion represents a sequence of responses that is innate and hard-wired in the brain (Tooby & Cosmides, 2000; Vytal & Hamann, 2010). But your emotional experience is not limited to pure forms of each basic emotion. Rather, each basic emotion represents a family of related emotional states (Ekman & Cordaro, 2011). For example, consider the many types of angry feelings, which can range from mild annoyance to bitter resentment or fierce rage.

Furthermore, psychologists recognize that emotional experience can be complex and multifaceted. People often experience a *blend* of emotions. In more complex situations, people may experience *mixed emotions,* in which very different emotions are experienced simultaneously or in rapid succession (Larsen & McGraw, 2011).

CULTURE, GENDER, AND EMOTIONAL EXPERIENCE

In diverse cultures, psychologists have found general agreement regarding the subjective experience and meaning of different basic emotions. Canadian psychologist James Russell (1991) compared emotion descriptions by people from several different cultures. He found that emotions were most commonly classified according to two dimensions: (1) the degree to which the emotion is *pleasant* or *unpleasant* and (2) the level of *activation,* or arousal, associated with the emotion. For example, joy and contentment are both pleasant emotions, but joy is associated with a higher degree of activation (Feldman Barrett & Russell, 1999).

While these may be the most fundamental dimensions of emotion, cultural variations in classifying emotions do exist. For example, Hazel Rose Markus and Shinobu Kitayama (1991, 1994) found that Japanese subjects classified emotions in terms of not two but three important dimensions. Along with the pleasantness and activation dimensions, they also categorized emotions along a dimension of **interpersonal engagement.** This dimension reflects the idea that some emotions result from your connections and interactions with other people (Kitayama & others, 2000). Japanese participants rated anger and shame as being about the same in terms of unpleasantness and activation, but they rated shame as being much higher than anger on the dimension of interpersonal engagement.

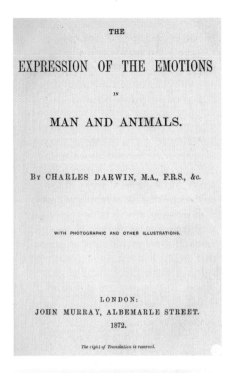

THE

EXPRESSION OF THE EMOTIONS

IN

MAN AND ANIMALS.

By CHARLES DARWIN, M.A., F.R.S., &c.

WITH PHOTOGRAPHIC AND OTHER ILLUSTRATIONS.

LONDON:
JOHN MURRAY, ALBEMARLE STREET.
1872.

The right of Translation is reserved.

Darwin and Emotion Published in 1872, *The Expression of the Emotions in Man and Animals* was the first scientific book to use the new technology of photography. Charles Darwin was one of the first scientists to systematically study emotional expressions. He hoped to show the continuity of emotional expressions among nonhuman animals and humans—additional evidence for his evolutionary theory.

TABLE 8.3

The Basic Emotions

Fear	Disgust
Surprise	Happiness
Anger	Sadness

Most emotion researchers today agree that the six emotions shown above best represent the universal set of basic emotions. Other possible candidates are contempt or disdain, pride, and excitement.

interpersonal engagement Emotion dimension reflecting the degree to which emotions involve a relationship with another person or other people.

MYTH ◄ SCIENCE

Is it true that women are more emotional than men?

Why would the Japanese emphasize interpersonal engagement as a dimension of emotion? Japan is a collectivistic culture, so a person's identity is seen as interdependent with those of other people, rather than independent, as is characteristic of the more individualistic cultures. Thus, social context is an important part of private emotional experience (Kitayama & Park, 2007).

What about gender differences in emotional experience? Both men and women tend to believe that women are "more emotional" than men (Barrett & Bliss-Moreau, 2009; Vigil, 2009). However, many studies have shown that men and women don't really differ in either frequency or intensity of emotional experience (see Kring & Gordon, 1998; Thunberg & Dimberg, 2000).

Rather, the sexes differ in the expression of emotions. In a nutshell, women tend to be more emotionally expressive (Langer, 2010; Keltner & Horberg, 2015). Women tend to be much more at ease expressing their emotions, thinking about emotions, and recalling emotional experiences (Feldman Barrett & others, 2000).

The Neuroscience of Emotion

KEY THEME

Emotions are associated with distinct patterns of responses by the sympathetic nervous system and in the brain.

KEY QUESTIONS

❯ How is the sympathetic nervous system involved in intense emotional responses?

❯ What brain structures are involved in emotional experience, and what neural pathways make up the brain's fear circuit?

❯ How does the evolutionary perspective explain the dual brain pathways for transmitting fear-related information?

Psychologists have long studied the physiological aspects of emotion. Early research focused on the autonomic nervous system's role in triggering physiological arousal. More recently, brain imaging techniques have identified specific brain regions involved in emotions. In this section, we'll look at both areas of research.

EMOTION AND THE SYMPATHETIC NERVOUS SYSTEM
HOT HEADS AND COLD FEET

The pounding heart, rapid breathing, trembling hands and feet, and churning stomach that occur when you experience an intense emotion like fear reflect the activation of the sympathetic branch of the *autonomic nervous system.* When you are threatened, the *sympathetic nervous system* triggers the *fight-or-flight response,* a rapidly occurring series of automatic physical reactions. Breathing and heart rate accelerate, and blood pressure surges. You perspire, your mouth goes dry, and the hairs on your skin may stand up, giving you the familiar sensation of goose bumps. Your pupils dilate, allowing you to take in a wider visual field. Blood sugar levels increase, providing a burst of energy. Digestion stops as blood is diverted from the stomach and intestines to the brain and skeletal muscles, sometimes causing the sensations of light-headedness or "butterflies" fluttering in your stomach. The polygraph, or "lie detector," measures these physiological reactions associated with emotional arousal (see the In Focus box, "Detecting Lies").

The sympathetic nervous system is also activated by other intense emotions, such as excitement, passionate love, or extreme joy. If you've ever ridden an exciting roller coaster, self-consciously given a speech in front of your peers, or been reunited with a loved one after a long absence, you've experienced the high levels of physiological arousal that can be produced by other types of emotions. Obviously, not all emotions involve intense physical reactions. And some emotions, such as contentment, are characterized by decreased physical arousal and the slowing of some body processes (Levenson & others, 1990, 1992).

Research has shown that there are differing patterns of physiological arousal for different emotions (Ekman, 2003). In one series of studies, psychologist Robert W. Levenson (1992) found that fear, anger, and sadness are all associated with accelerated

Think Like a SCIENTIST

Can you learn to tell when someone is lying? Go to LaunchPad: Resources to **Think Like a Scientist** about **Lie Detection.**

 LaunchPad

IN FOCUS

Detecting Lies

The *polygraph,* commonly called a *lie detector,* doesn't really detect lies or deception. Rather, a polygraph measures physiological changes associated with emotions like fear, tension, and anxiety. Heart rate, blood pressure, respiration, and other indicators are monitored during a polygraph interview. The polygraph is based on the assumption that lying is accompanied by anxiety, fear, and stress. When people show arousal patterns typically associated with anxiety or fear, lying is inferred (Grubin, 2010; Meijer & Verschuere, 2010).

There are many potential problems with using a polygraph to detect lying. First, there is no unique pattern of physiological arousal associated specifically with lying (Vrij & others, 2010). Second, some people can lie without experiencing anxiety or arousal. This produces a false negative result—the liar is judged to be telling the truth. Third, people may be innocent of any wrongdoing but still be fearful or anxious when asked incriminating questions—especially if they believe that they are suspected of a crime. Truth-tellers can be as nervous as liars, especially if they have reason to believe that negative consequences will follow if

Greg Gayne/© Fox/Courtesy: Everett Collection

MYTH ◀ SCIENCE

Is it true that polygraphs, or lie detector tests, are a valid way to detect lying?

they are disbelieved (Vrij & others, 2010). This can lead to false positive results—innocent people are judged as being guilty. In fact, polygraph tests are more likely to wrongly identify innocent people as guilty than guilty people as innocent (Bashore & Rapp, 1993; National Research Council, 2003).

Finally, interpreting polygraph results can be highly subjective. In one study, polygraph results were compared to later confessions of guilt in criminal cases. Lying was accurately detected by the polygraph examiners at a rate just slightly better than flipping a coin (Phillips, 1999).

In the scientific community, it is generally agreed that polygraphs are not a valid method to detect lies and that their results should not

Catching Liars Actor Tim Roth played psychologist and professional lie detector Dr. Cal Lightman in the critically acclaimed TV series "*Lie to Me,*" a drama loosely based on the scientific work of emotion researcher Paul Ekman, who served as a scientific consultant on the program. Like Ekman, the fictional Lightman is an expert on reading microexpressions, although he also uses other lie detection methods. However, Lightman's highly unconventional—and often unethical—methods have little in common with Ekman's scientific research. "Dr. Lightman, in less than 45 minutes, accomplishes things that take me weeks, if not months, to figure out," Ekman (2009) commented. "But I suppose if they really showed what I do, people would change the channel because it would be too slow."

be used as evidence (National Research Council, 2003). Because of the polygraph's high error rate, many states do not allow polygraph tests as evidence in court. However, the U.S. government uses polygraph testing in several agencies, including the CIA and the Department of Energy (Holden, 2001).

Microexpressions: Fleeting Indicators of Deceit

Emotion researcher Paul Ekman (2003) has found that deception is associated with a variety of nonverbal cues, such as fleeting facial expressions, vocal cues, and nervous body movements. Especially revealing are the fleeting facial expressions, called *microexpressions,* that last about 1/25 of a second. When people lie and try to control their facial expressions, microexpressions of fear, guilt, or anxiety often "leak" through (Ekman & O'Sullivan, 2006). Even so, no single nonverbal cue indicates that someone is lying, and not all researchers have found evidence that deception is revealed in microexpressions (Vrij, 2015). However, people who are skilled at decoding nonverbal cues—like clinical psychologists—are better than other people at detecting deception (Bond, 2008; Ekman & others, 1999).

Arousal and Intense Emotion A young woman sheds tears of joy at reuniting with her fiance, who holds an engagement ring. Many intense emotions involve the activation of the sympathetic nervous system. Although emotions like extreme joy, fear, and grief subjectively feel very different, they all involve increases in heart rate, breathing, and blood pressure.

Eric Engman/Fairbanks Daily News-Miner/ZUMAPRESS.com/Newscom

amygdala (uh-MIG-dull-uh) An almond-shaped cluster of neurons in the brain's temporal lobe, involved in memory and emotional responses, especially fear.

heart rate. But comparing anger and fear showed differences that confirm everyday experience. Anger produces greater increases in blood pressure than fear. And while anger produces an increase in skin temperature, fear produces a *decrease* in skin temperature. Perhaps that's why when we are angry, we speak of "getting hot under the collar," and when fearful, we feel clammy and complain of having "cold feet."

Levenson (1992, 2003) believes that these differing patterns of sympathetic nervous system activation are universal, reflecting biological responses to the basic emotions that are hard-wired by evolution into all humans. Supporting this contention, Levenson found that male and female subjects, as well as young and elderly subjects, experience the *same* patterns of autonomic nervous system activity for different basic emotions. These distinctive patterns of emotional physiological arousal were also found in members of a remote culture in western Sumatra, an island in Indonesia (Levenson & others, 1992).

Broader surveys of different cultures have also demonstrated that the basic emotions are associated with distinct patterns of autonomic nervous system activity (Levenson, 2003; Scherer & Wallbott, 1994). It seems that people in different cultures associate certain patterns of physical sensations with certain emotions. When asked to describe the way that basic emotions such as fear, anger, sadness, and happiness "felt" in the body, Finnish psychologist Lauri Nummenmaa and his colleagues (2014) found a high degree of agreement in participants from Finland, Sweden, and Taiwan (see Figure 8.4).

THE EMOTIONAL BRAIN

FEAR AND THE AMYGDALA

Sophisticated brain imaging techniques have led to an explosion of new knowledge about the brain's role in emotion (Kemp & others, 2015). Of all the emotions, the brain processes involved in *fear* have been most thoroughly studied. Many brain areas are implicated in emotional responses, but the brain structure called the **amygdala** has long been known to be especially important. As described in Chapter 2, the amygdala is an almond-shaped cluster of neurons located deep in the temporal lobe on each side of the brain. The amygdala is part of the *limbic system,* a group of brain structures involved in emotion, memory, and basic

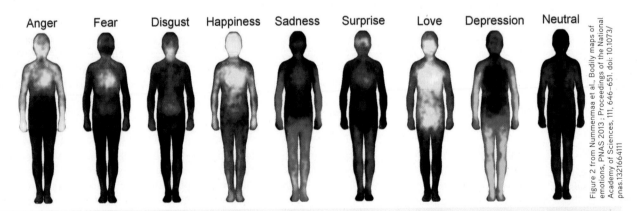

Anger   Fear   Disgust   Happiness   Sadness   Surprise   Love   Depression   Neutral

Figure 2 from Nummenmaa et al., Bodily maps of emotions, PNAS 2013.; Proceedings of the National Academy of Sciences, 111, 646–651. doi: 10.1073/pnas.1321664111

FIGURE 8.4 Mapping Emotions in the Body As expressions like "cold feet" or "butterflies in the stomach" reflect, emotions are often associated with physical sensations. Finnish psychologist Lauri Nummenmaa and his colleagues (2014) investigated this phenomenon in a clever study. Participants were shown blank silhouettes of bodies and, in response to emotion-evoking words, images, or films, they were asked to color in the areas of their body where sensations became stronger or weaker. The body maps show regions where activation increased (warm colors) and decreased (cool colors) when each emotion was felt. While the number of participants is not large enough to draw sweeping conclusions, the results do hint that there may be culturally universal associations of specific emotions with specific body areas. Try this exercise yourself the next time you feel or happy or when you experience another strong emotion. Do the "body maps" found in this research agree with your own experience of different emotions?

If you'd like to participate in the experiment, you can try it here: http://becs.aalto.fi/~lnummen/participate.htm

motivational drives, such as hunger, thirst, and sex. Neural pathways connect the amygdala with many other brain structures (Cunningham & Brosch, 2012; Pessoa & Adolphs, 2010).

Several studies have shown that the amygdala is a key brain structure in the emotional response of fear in humans (LeDoux, 2007). For example, brain imaging techniques have demonstrated that the amygdala activates when you view threatening or fearful faces, or hear people make nonverbal sounds expressing fear (Morris & others, 1999; Öhman & others, 2007). Even when people simply anticipate a threatening stimulus, the amygdala activates as part of the fear circuit in the brain (Phelps & others, 2001).

In rats, amygdala damage disrupts the neural circuits involved in the fear response. For example, rats with a damaged amygdala can't be classically conditioned to acquire a fear response (LeDoux, 2007). In humans, damage to the amygdala also disrupts elements of the fear response. For example, people with amygdala damage lose the ability to distinguish between friendly and threatening faces (Adolphs & others, 1998).

Activating the Amygdala: Direct and Indirect Neural Pathways

Let's use an example to show how the amygdala participates in the brain's fear circuit. Imagine that your sister's eight-year-old son sneaks up behind you at a family picnic and pokes you in the back with a long stick. As you quickly wheel around, he shouts, "Look what I found in the woods!" Dangling from the stick is a wriggling, slimy-looking, three-foot-long snake. He tosses the snake into your face, and you let out a yell and jump two feet into the air. As he bursts into hysterical laughter, you quickly realize that the real-looking snake is made of rubber, your nephew is a twit, and your sister is laughing as hard as her son.

Even if you don't know any obnoxious eight-year-old boys, you've probably experienced a sudden fright in which you instantly reacted to a threatening stimulus, like a snake, a spider, or an oncoming car. Typically, you respond instinctively, without taking time to consciously or deliberately evaluate the situation.

So how can we respond to potentially dangerous stimuli before we've had time to think about them? Let's stay with our example. When you saw the dangling snake, the visual stimulus was first routed to the *thalamus* (see Figure 8.5). As we explained in Chapter 2, all incoming sensory information, with the exception of olfactory sensations, is processed in the thalamus before being relayed to sensory centers in the cerebral cortex.

However, the neuroscientist Joseph LeDoux (1996, 2000) discovered that there are *two* neural pathways for sensory information that project from the thalamus. One leads to the cortex, as previously described, but the other leads directly to the amygdala, bypassing the cortex. When we are faced with a potential threat, sensory information about the threatening stimulus is routed simultaneously along both pathways.

LeDoux (1996) describes the direct thalamus→amygdala pathway as a "short-cut" from the thalamus to the amygdala. This is a "quick-and-dirty" route that transmits crude, almost archetypal, information about the stimulus directly to the amygdala. This rapid transmission allows the brain to start to respond to

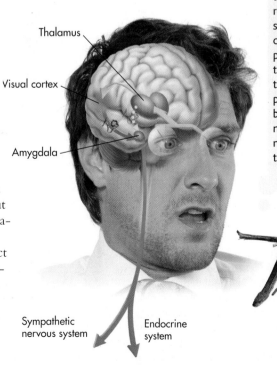

Thalamus

Visual cortex

Amygdala

Sympathetic nervous system

Endocrine system

FIGURE 8.5 Fear Circuits in the Brain When you're faced with a potentially threatening stimulus—like a snake dangling from a stick—information arrives in the thalamus and is relayed simultaneously along two pathways. Crude, archetypal information rapidly travels the direct route to the amygdala, triggering an almost instantaneous fear response. More detailed information is sent along the pathway to the visual cortex, where the stimulus is interpreted. If the cortex determines that a threat exists, the information is relayed to the amygdala along the longer, slower pathway. The amygdala triggers other brain structures, such as the hypothalamus, which activate the sympathetic nervous system and the endocrine system's release of stress hormones.

Source: Research from LeDoux (1994a, 1994b).

(l) Westend61/age fotostock
(r) PhotoSpin, Inc/Alamy

the possible danger represented by a writhing, curved snake dangling from a stick *before* you have time to consciously think about the stimulus. The amygdala activates and triggers the brain's alarm system.

What happens next? The amygdala sends information along neural pathways that project to other brain regions that make up the rest of the brain's fear circuit. One pathway leads to an area of the *hypothalamus,* then on to the *medulla* at the base of the brain. In combination, the hypothalamus and medulla trigger arousal of the sympathetic nervous system. Another pathway projects from the amygdala to a different hypothalamus area that, in concert with the *pituitary gland,* triggers the release of stress hormones (LeDoux, 1995, 2000).

The result? You respond instantly to the threat—"SNAKE!"—by leaping backward, heartbeat and breathing accelerating. But even as you respond to the threat, information is speeding along the other neural pathway that reaches the amygdala by traveling through the cortex. The thalamus sends information to the visual cortex, which creates a detailed and more accurate representation of the visual stimulus. You can also reevaluate the signal that prompted the initial instinctive response. Now you realize that the "snake" is actually just a rubber toy. The cortex sends the "false alarm" message to the amygdala. But note that information traveling the thalamus→cortex→amygdala route takes about twice as long to reach the amygdala as the information traveling along the direct thalamus→amygdala route. Thus, the alarm reaction is already in full swing before signals from the cortex reach the amygdala.

LeDoux believes these dual alarm pathways serve several adaptive functions. The direct thalamus→amygdala pathway rapidly triggers an emotional response to threats that, through evolution, we are biologically prepared to fear, such as snakes, snarling animals, or rapidly moving, looming objects. In contrast, the indirect pathway allows

---

FOCUS ON NEUROSCIENCE

Emotions and the Brain

Do Different Emotions Activate Different Brain Areas?

The idea that different combinations of brain regions are activated by different emotions received considerable support in a brain imaging study by neuroscientist Antonio Damasio and his colleagues (2000). In the study, participants were scanned using positron emission tomography (PET) while they recalled emotionally charged memories to generate feelings of sadness, happiness, anger, and fear.

Each of the four PET scans shown here is an averaged composite of all 39 participants in the study. Significant areas of brain activation are indicated in red, while significant areas of deactivation are indicated in purple. Notice that sadness, happiness, anger, and fear each produced a distinct pattern of brain activation and deactivation. These findings confirmed the idea that each emotion involves distinct neural circuits in the brain. Other research has produced similar findings (Dalgleish, 2004; Vytal & Hamann, 2010).

One interesting finding in the Damasio study was that the emotional memory triggered autonomic nervous system activity and physiological arousal *before* the volunteers signaled that they were subjectively "feeling" the target emotion. Areas of the somatosensory cortex, which processes sensory information from the skin, muscles, and internal organs, were also activated. These sensory signals from the body's peripheral nervous system contributed to

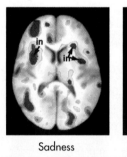
Sadness

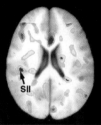
Happiness

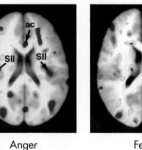
Anger   Fear

Courtesy of Antonio Damasio, University of Southern California

the overall subjective "feeling" of a particular emotion. Remember Damasio's findings because we'll refer to this study again when we discuss theories of emotion.

more complex stimuli to be evaluated in the cortex before triggering the amygdala's alarm system. So, for example, the gradually dawning awareness that your job is in jeopardy as your boss starts talking about the need to reduce staff in your department probably has to travel the thalamus→cortex→amygdala pathway before you begin to feel the cold sweat break out on your palms.

In situations of potential danger, it is clearly advantageous to be able to respond quickly. According to LeDoux (1995, 2000), the direct thalamus→amygdala connection represents an adaptive response that has been hard-wired by evolution into the human brain. From the point of view of survival, as LeDoux (1996) remarks, "The time saved by the amygdala in acting on the thalamic interpretation, rather than waiting for the cortical input, may be the difference between life and death."

In support of this evolutionary explanation, Swedish psychologist Arne Öhman and his colleagues (Öhman & Mineka, 2001; Schupp & others, 2004) have found that people detect and react more quickly to angry or threatening faces than they do to friendly or neutral faces. Presumably, this reflects the faster processing of threatening stimuli via the direct thalamus→amygdala route (Lundqvist & Öhman, 2005).

The Expression of Emotion
MAKING FACES

KEY THEME

The behavioral components of emotion include facial expressions and nonverbal behavior.

KEY QUESTIONS

> What evidence supports the idea that facial expressions for basic emotions are universal?
> How does culture affect the behavioral expression of emotion?
> How can emotional expression be explained in terms of evolutionary theory?

Every day, we witness the behavioral components of emotions in ourselves and others. We laugh with pleasure, slam a door in frustration, or frown at a clueless remark. But of all the ways that we express and communicate our emotional responses, facial expressions are the most important.

In *The Expression of the Emotions in Man and Animals,* Darwin (1872) argued that human emotional expressions are innate and culturally universal. He also noted the continuity of emotional expression between humans and many other species, citing it as evidence of the common evolutionary ancestry of humans and other animals. But do nonhuman animals actually experience emotions? We explore this question in the Critical Thinking box, "Emotion in Nonhuman Animals: Laughing Rats, Silly Elephants, and Smiling Dolphins?"

Of course, humans are the animals that exhibit the greatest range of facial expressions. Psychologist **Paul Ekman** has studied the facial expression of emotions for more than four decades. Ekman (1980) estimates that the human face is capable of creating more than *7,000* different expressions. This enormous flexibility allows us considerable versatility in expressing emotion in all its subtle variations.

To study facial expressions, Ekman and his colleague Wallace Friesen (1978) coded different facial expressions by painstakingly analyzing the facial muscles involved in producing each expression. In doing so, they precisely classified the facial expressions that characterize the basic emotions of happiness, sadness, surprise, fear, anger, and disgust. When shown photographs of these facial expressions, research participants were able to correctly identify the emotion being displayed (Ekman, 1982, 1992, 1993).

Ekman concluded that facial expressions for the basic emotions are innate and probably hard-wired in the brain. Further evidence comes from children who are born blind and deaf. Despite their inability to observe or hear others, they express joy, anger, and pleasure using the same expressions as sighted and

Which Is the "True" Smile? Psychologist and emotion researcher Paul Ekman demonstrates the difference between a fake smile *(left)* and the true smile *(right)*. If you were able to pick out the true smile, it was because you, like most people, are able to decipher the subtle differences in the facial muscles, especially around the eyes and lips. In fact, research has found that people instinctively respond to true smiles with genuine smiles of their own. Polite smiles are more likely to elicit the same (Heerey & Crossley, 2013).

Paul Ekman, Ph.D./Paul Edman Group, LLC.

Emotion in Nonhuman Animals: Laughing Rats, Silly Elephants, and Smiling Dolphins?

Do animals experience emotions? If you've ever frolicked with a playful puppy or shared the contagious contentment of a cat purring in your lap, the answer seems obvious. But before you accept that answer, remember that emotion involves three components: physiological arousal, behavioral expression, and subjective experience. In many animals, fear and other "emotional" responses appear to involve physiological and brain processes that are similar to those involved in human emotional experience. In mammals, it's also easy to observe behavioral responses when an animal is menaced by a predator or by the anger in aggressive displays. But what about subjective experience?

Darwin on Animal Emotions

Charles Darwin never doubted that animals experienced emotions. In his landmark work *The Expression of the Emotions in Man and*

Universal Images Group/age fotostock

Foxes in Love? Rather than living in a pack like coyotes or wolves, their evolutionary relatives, red foxes form a monogamous pair bond and often mate for life. They live, play, and hunt together and share in the care of their offspring. It's tempting, but unscientific, to label their bond as "love."

Argument/Getty Images

Laughing Rats? Rats are sociable, playful creatures. They emit distinct, high-pitched chirps when they play, anticipate treats, and during positive social interactions. They also chirp when they're tickled by researchers like neuroscientist Jaak Panksepp (2000, 2007). But when infant rats are separated from their mothers, or when they're cold, they emit a distress cry that is much lower in frequency than the ultrasonic chirps that are associated with pleasant experiences.

Animals, Darwin (1872) contended that differences in emotional experience between nonhuman animals and humans are a matter of degree, not kind. "The lower animals, like man, manifestly feel pleasure and pain, happiness and misery," he wrote in *The Descent of Man* in 1871. From Darwin's perspective, the capacity to experience emotion is yet another evolved trait that humans share with lower animals (Bekoff, 2007).

One problem in establishing whether animals experience emotion is the difficulty of determining the nature of an animal's subjective experience (Kuczaj, 2013). Even Darwin (1871) readily acknowledged this problem, writing, "Who can say what cows feel, when they surround and stare intently on a dying or dead companion?"

Anthropomorphism: Happy Dolphins?

Despite the problem of knowing just what an animal is feeling, we often *think* that we do. For example, one reason that dolphins are

---

hearing children (Goodenough, 1932; Matsumoto & Hwang, 2011b). Similarly, the spontaneous facial expressions of children and young adults who were born blind do not differ from those of sighted children and adults (Galati & others, 1997, 2003).

CULTURE AND EMOTIONAL EXPRESSION

Facial expressions for the basic emotions seem to be universal across different cultures (Waller & others, 2008). Ekman (1982) and other researchers showed photographs of facial expressions to people in 21 different countries. Despite their different cultural experiences, all the participants identified the emotions being expressed with a high degree of accuracy (see Ekman, 1998). Even the inhabitants of remote, isolated villages in Papua New Guinea, who had never been exposed to movies or other aspects of Western culture, were able to identify the emotions being expressed. Other research has confirmed and extended Ekman's original findings (see Elfenbein & Ambady, 2002; Frank & Stennett, 2001).

Other aspects of emotional expression, such as tone of voice and nonverbal expression, also seem to be easily understood across widely different cultures. As anyone who has ever been the target of a sarcastic remark is well aware, the human voice very effectively conveys emotional messages. Several studies have

Video material is provided by BBC Worldwide Learning and CBS News Archives and produced by Princeton Academic Resources

LaunchPad

To view footage of Paul Ekman and his groundbreaking research on facial expression in Papua New Guinea, go to **Video Activity: Emotion and Facial Expression.**

so appealing is the wide, happy grin they seem to wear. But the dolphin's "smile" is *not* a true facial expression—it's simply the bony curvature of its mouth. If you comment on the friendly, happy appearance of the dolphins frolicking at SeaWorld or another aquarium, you're *projecting* those human emotions onto the dolphins.

You also just committed **anthropomorphism**—you attributed human traits, qualities, or behaviors to a nonhuman animal. The tendency of people to be anthropomorphic is understandable when you consider how extensively most of us were conditioned as children via books, cartoons, and Disney characters to believe that animals are just like people, only with fur or feathers.

From a scientific perspective, anthropomorphism can hinder progress in understanding animal emotions. By assuming that an animal thinks and feels as we do, we run the risk of distorting or obscuring the reality of the animal's own unique experience (de Waal, 2011; Hauser, 2000). Instead, we must acknowledge that other animals are not happy or sad in the same way that humans subjectively experience happiness or sadness.

Animals clearly demonstrate diverse emotions—fear, anger, surprise. But to understand how they subjectively *experience* such feelings—and, indeed, whether they do at all—raises questions that cannot be fully answered at this time. Nonetheless, it seems safe to assume that more primitive animals, like fish, turtles, and snakes, probably do not possess a level of self-awareness that would allow them to experience complex emotions like grief, empathy, or altruism (Hauser, 2000). For more sophisticated animals, like dolphins, primates, and elephants, the evidence is more compelling (Bekoff, 2007; Lyn & Savage-Rumbaugh, 2013; Kuczaj & others, 2013).

One subjective aspect of the scientific method is how to interpret evidence and data. In the case of the evidence for animal emotions, the scientific debate is far from over. Although the lack of a definitive answer can be frustrating, keep in mind that such scientific debates play an important role in avoiding erroneous conclusions and shaping future research.

Martin Harvey/Getty Images

Silly Elephants Elephants form tightly knit family groups. When reunited after a long separation, elephants perform an elaborate greeting ceremony—trumpeting, flapping their ears, and exuberantly intertwining their trunks. Even adult elephants play, sometimes with great enthusiasm, which veteran researcher Cynthia Moss (2000) describes as "elephants acting silly." Female elephants are intensely devoted to their offspring, and family members often touch one another with what looks like affection (Bradshaw & others, 2005).

CRITICAL THINKING QUESTIONS

- What evidence would lead you to conclude that primates, dolphins, or elephants experience emotions?

- Would you accept different evidence to conclude that a 6-month-old human infant can experience emotions? If so, why?

- Is it possible to be completely free of anthropomorphic tendencies in studying animal emotions?

---

found that people from different cultures can accurately identify the emotion being expressed by tone of voice alone, even when the actual words used were unintelligible (Russell & others, 2003; Scherer & others, 2001). Similarly, people from different cultures were able to accurately evaluate the emotional content of video clips depicting an emotional conversation between two people, even though the dialogue was scrambled (Sneddon & others, 2011). And, some body language seems to be universal.

However, some specific nonverbal gestures, which are termed *emblems,* vary across cultures. For example, shaking your head means "no" in the United States but "yes" in southern India and Bulgaria. Nodding your head means "yes" in the United States, but in Japan it could mean "maybe" or even "no way!"

In many situations, you adjust your emotional expressions to make them appropriate in that particular social context. For example, even if you are deeply angered by your supervisor's comments at work, you might consciously restrain yourself and maintain a neutral facial expression. How, when, and where we display our emotional expressions are strongly influenced by cultural norms. Cultural differences in the management of facial expressions are called **display rules** (Ekman & others, 1987; Ambady & others, 2006).

anthropomorphism The attribution of human traits, motives, emotions, or behaviors to nonhuman animals or inanimate objects.

display rules Social and cultural regulations governing emotional expression, especially facial expressions.

Happiness

Surprise

Sadness

Anger

Disgust

Fear

Basic Emotions and Universal Facial Expressions
Paul Ekman and his colleagues have precisely calibrated the muscles used in facial expressions for basic emotions. Ekman showed that people in a wide variety of cultures—even those with no experience of Western culture—were able to identify facial expressions for each of the basic emotions. You can test your own ability to recognize facial expressions of emotion at http://www.emotionwisegroup.org/emotion-test

From Matsumoto, D., & Ekman, P. (1989) Japanese and Caucasian Facial Expressions of Emotion. JACFEE. Photographs courtesy of David Matsumoto and Humintell, LLC.

MYTH ◀ SCIENCE

Is it true that facial expressions, such as smiles, are learned and vary from one culture to another?

Consider a classic experiment in which a hidden camera recorded the facial expressions of Japanese and Americans as they watched films that showed grisly images of surgery, amputations, and so forth (Ekman & others, 1987; Friesen, 1972). When they watched the films alone, the Japanese and American participants displayed virtually identical facial expressions, grimacing with disgust and distaste at the gruesome scenes. But when a scientist was present while the participants watched the films, the Japanese masked their negative facial expressions of disgust or fear with smiles. Why? In Japan an important display rule is that you should not reveal negative emotions in the presence of an authority figure so as not to offend the higher-status individual.

Display rules can also vary for different groups within a given culture. For example, recall our earlier discussion about gender differences in emotional expression. In many cultures, including the United States, women are allowed a wider range of emotional expressiveness and responsiveness than men (Fischer & others, 2004). For example, for men, it's considered "unmasculine" to be too open in expressing certain emotions, such as sadness (Johnson & others, 2011). Crying is especially taboo (Vingerhoets & others, 2000).

So what overall conclusions emerge from the research findings on emotional expressions? First, Paul Ekman and other researchers have amassed considerable evidence that facial expressions for the basic emotions—happiness, sadness, anger, fear, surprise, and disgust—are hard-wired into the brain. They also contend that the basic emotions are biologically determined, the result of evolutionary processes. Second, these emotional expressions serve the adaptive function of communicating internal states to friends and enemies. Like the survival of other social animals, human survival depends on being able to recognize and respond quickly to the emotional state of others. Third, although facial expressions for the basic emotions may be biologically programmed, cultural conditioning, gender-role expectations, and other learning experiences shape how, when, and whether emotional responses are displayed.

Theories of Emotion
EXPLAINING EMOTION

KEY THEME

Emotion theories emphasize different aspects of emotion, but all have influenced the direction of emotion research.

KEY QUESTIONS

❯ What are the basic principles and key criticisms of the James–Lange theory of emotion?

❯ How do the facial feedback hypothesis and other contemporary research support aspects of the James–Lange theory?

❯ What are the two-factor theory and the cognitive appraisal theory of emotion, and how do they emphasize cognitive factors in emotion?

For more than a century, American psychologists have actively debated theories to explain emotion (Manstead, 2015; Reisenzein, 2015). Like many controversies in psychology, the debate helped shape the direction of psychological research. And, in fact, the

"Is that one of the emotions people talk about?"

Charles Barsotti The New Yorker Collection/The Cartoon Bank

earliest psychological theory of emotion, proposed by William James more than a century ago, continues to influence psychological research (Dalgleish, 2004; Russell, 2014).

In this section, we'll look at the most influential theories of emotion. As you'll see, theories of emotion differ in terms of *which* component of emotion receives the most emphasis—subjective experience, physiological arousal, or expressive behavior.

The James–Lange Theory of Emotion

DO YOU RUN BECAUSE YOU'RE AFRAID?
OR ARE YOU AFRAID BECAUSE YOU RUN?

Imagine that you're walking to your car through the deserted college parking lot late at night. Suddenly, a shadowy figure emerges from behind a parked car. As he starts to move toward you, you walk more quickly. "Hey, what's your hurry?" he calls out, and he picks up his pace.

Your heart starts pounding as you break into a run. Reaching your car, you fumble with the keys, then jump in and lock the doors. Your hands are trembling so badly you can barely get the key into the ignition, but somehow you manage, and you hit the accelerator, zooming out of the parking lot and onto a main street. Still feeling shaky, you ease off the accelerator pedal a bit, wipe your sweaty palms on your jeans, and will yourself to calm down. After several minutes, you breathe a sigh of relief.

In this example, all three emotion components are clearly present. You experienced a subjective feeling that you labeled as "fear." You experienced physical arousal—trembling, sweating, pounding heart, and rapid breathing. And you expressed the fear, both in your facial expression and by bolting into a run. What caused this constellation of effects that you experienced as fear?

The common sense view of emotion would suggest that you (1) recognized a threatening situation and (2) reacted by feeling fearful. This subjective experience of fear (3) activated your sympathetic nervous system and (4) triggered fearful behavior. In one of the first psychological theories of emotion, **William James** (1884) disagreed with this commonsense view, proposing a very different explanation of emotion. Danish psychologist Carl Lange proposed a very similar theory at about the same time (see James, 1894; Lange & James, 1922). Thus, this theory, illustrated in Figure 8.6, is known as the **James–Lange theory of emotion.**

Consider our example again. According to the James–Lange theory, your heart didn't pound and you didn't run because you were afraid. Rather, the James–Lange

James–Lange theory of emotion
The theory that emotions arise from the perception of body changes.

Pictorial Press Ltd/Alamy

Common sense says we lose our fortune, are sorry and weep; we meet a bear, are frightened and run; we are insulted by a rival, are angry and strike. The hypothesis here to be defended says that this order of sequence is incorrect, that the one mental state is not immediately induced by the other, that the bodily manifestations must first be interposed between, and that the more rational statement is that we feel sorry because we cry, angry because we strike, afraid because we tremble.

—*William James (1894)*

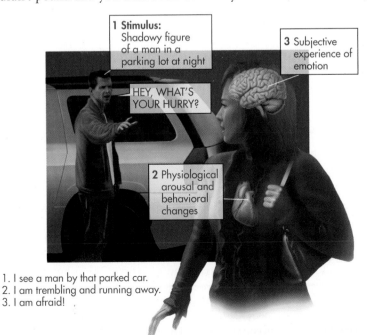

1 **Stimulus:** Shadowy figure of a man in a parking lot at night

HEY, WHAT'S YOUR HURRY?

3 Subjective experience of emotion

2 Physiological arousal and behavioral changes

1. I see a man by that parked car.
2. I am trembling and running away.
3. I am afraid!

FIGURE 8.6 The James–Lange Theory of Emotion
According to William James, we don't tremble and run because we are afraid, we are afraid because we tremble and run. James believed that body signals trigger emotional experience. These signals include physiological arousal and feedback from the muscles involved in behavior.

theory holds that you felt afraid *because* your heart pounded and you ran. Feedback from your physiological arousal and from the muscles involved in your behavior caused your subjective feeling of fearfulness. Thus, James believed that emotion follows this sequence: (1) We perceive a stimulus; (2) physiological and behavioral changes occur, which (3) we experience as a particular emotion.

The James–Lange theory stimulated a great deal of research, much of it consisting of attempts to disprove the theory. In 1927, the famous American physiologist **Walter Cannon** challenged the James–Lange theory (Dror, 2014). First, Cannon pointed out that body reactions are similar for many emotions, yet our subjective experience of various emotions is very different. For example, both fear and rage are accompanied by increased heart rate, but we have no difficulty distinguishing between the two emotions.

Second, Cannon (1927) argued that our emotional reaction to a stimulus is often faster than our physiological reaction. Here's an example to illustrate this point: Sandy's car started to slide out of control on a wet road. She felt fear as the car began to skid, but it was only *after* the car was under control, a few moments later, that her heart began to pound and her hands started to tremble. Cannon correctly noted that it can take several seconds for the physiological changes caused by activation of the sympathetic nervous system to take effect, but the subjective experience of emotion is often virtually instantaneous.

Third, artificially inducing physiological changes does not necessarily produce a related emotional experience. In one early test of the James–Lange theory, Spanish psychologist Gregorio Marañon (1924) injected several subjects with the hormone *epinephrine,* more commonly known as *adrenaline.* Epinephrine activates the sympathetic nervous system. When asked how they felt, the subjects simply reported the physical changes produced by the drug, saying, "My heart is beating very fast." Some reported feeling "as if" they should be feeling an emotion, but they said they did not feel the emotion itself: "I feel *as if* I were afraid."

James (1894) also proposed that if a person were cut off from feeling body changes, he would not experience true emotions. If he felt anything, he would experience only intellectualized, or "cold," emotions. To test this hypothesis, Cannon and his colleagues (1927) disabled the sympathetic nervous system of cats. But the cats still reacted with catlike rage when barking dogs were present: They hissed, growled, and lifted one paw to defend themselves.

What about humans? The sympathetic nervous system operates via the spinal cord. Thus, it made sense to James (1894) that people with spinal cord injuries would experience a decrease in emotional intensity because they would not be aware of physical arousal or other bodily changes.

Once again, however, research has not supported the James–Lange theory. For example, Dutch psychologist Bob Bermond and his colleagues (1991) found that individuals with spinal cord injuries reported that their experience of fear, anger, grief, sentimentality, and joyfulness had either increased in intensity or was unchanged since their injury. Other researchers have reported similar results (see Cobos & others, 2004; Deady & others, 2010).

EVIDENCE SUPPORTING THE JAMES–LANGE THEORY

On the one hand, you'd think that the James–Lange theory of emotion should be nothing more than a historical artifact at this point. Cannon's critique certainly seemed to demolish it. On the other hand, the brilliance of William James is reflected in the fact that researchers keep finding research support for key points in his theory of emotion (Deigh, 2014; Laird & Lacasse, 2014).

For example, look back at the Focus on Neuroscience on page 342 describing the PET scan study by Antonio Damasio and his colleagues (2000). It showed that each of the basic emotions produced a distinct pattern of brain activity, a finding that lends support to the James–Lange theory. To generate a particular basic emotion, the participants were asked to recall an emotionally charged memory and then to signal the researcher when they began subjectively "feeling" the target emotion.

Say "Cheese!" Here's a simple test of the facial feedback hypothesis. In a clever study by Fritz Strack and his colleagues (1988), participants who held a pen between their teeth (*left*) thought that cartoons were funnier than participants who held a pen between their lips (*right*) were. How does this finding support the facial feedback hypothesis?

The PET scans showed that areas of the brain's *somatosensory cortex,* which processes sensory information from the skin, muscles, and internal organs, were activated during emotional experiences. Interestingly, these internal changes were registered in the somatosensory cortex *before* the participants reported "feeling" the emotion. Along with demonstrating the importance of internal physiological feedback in emotional experience, Damasio's study supports another basic premise of the James–Lange theory: that physiological changes occur *before* we subjectively experience an emotion.

Other contemporary research has supported James's contention that the perception of internal bodily signals is a fundamental ingredient in the subjective experience of emotion (Dalgleish, 2004; Laird & Lacasse, 2014). For example, in a study by Hugo Critchley and his colleagues (2004), participants who were highly sensitive to their own internal body signals were more likely to experience anxiety and other negative emotions than people who were less sensitive.

Research on the **facial feedback hypothesis** also supports the notion that our bodily responses affect our subjective experience. The facial feedback hypothesis states that expressing a specific emotion, especially facially, causes us to subjectively experience that emotion (Soussignan, 2004; Winkielman & others, 2015). Supporting this are studies showing that when people mimic the facial expressions characteristic of a given emotion, such as anger or fear, they tend to report *feeling* the emotion (Laird & Lacasse, 2014; Schnall & Laird, 2003).

The basic explanation for this phenomenon is that the facial muscles send feedback signals to the brain. In turn, the brain uses this information to activate and regulate emotional experience, intensifying or lessening emotion (Izard, 1990a, 1990b). In line with this explanation, Paul Ekman and Richard Davidson (1993) demonstrated that deliberately creating a "happy" smile produces brain-activity changes similar to those caused by spontaneously producing a happy smile in response to a real event.

A new wrinkle in facial feedback research comes from the popularity of Botox injections to paralyze selected facial muscles to produce a more youthful appearance. Once paralyzed, the targeted muscles no longer send feedback to the brain. Botox injections can dampen emotional experience, although they don't appear to eliminate it completely (Davis & others, 2010; Havas & others, 2010). However, an ingenious study by David Deal and Tanya Chartrand (2011) demonstrated that paralyzing facial muscles with Botox may make people less able to recognize emotional expressions in *other* people. The explanation? We tend to automatically mimic the facial expressions of other people. Although we're not aware of it, feedback from our facial muscles helps us to better understand their emotional displays.

Collectively, the evidence for the facial feedback hypothesis adds support for aspects of the James–Lange theory.

MYTH ▶ SCIENCE

Is it true that if you "put on a happy face," you will actually feel happier?

facial feedback hypothesis The view that expressing a specific emotion, especially facially, causes the subjective experience of that emotion.

two-factor theory of emotion Schachter and Singer's theory that emotion is the interaction of physiological arousal and the cognitive label that we apply to explain the arousal.

cognitive appraisal theory of emotion The theory that emotional responses are triggered by a cognitive evaluation.

Cognitive Theories of Emotion

A second theory of emotion, proposed by Stanley Schachter and Jerome Singer, was influential for a short time. Schachter and Singer (1962) agreed with James that physiological arousal is a central element in emotion. But they also agreed with Cannon that physiological arousal is very similar for different emotions. Thus, arousal alone would not produce an emotional response.

Instead, Schachter and Singer proposed that we cognitively label physiological arousal as a given emotion based on our appraisal of a situation. Thus, according to the **two-factor theory of emotion,** illustrated in Figure 8.7, emotion is the result of the *interaction* of physiological arousal and the cognitive label we use to explain our stirred-up state.

Schachter and Singer (1962) tested their theory in a clever, but flawed, experiment. Male volunteers were injected with epinephrine, which produces sympathetic nervous system arousal: accelerated heartbeat, rapid breathing, trembling, and so forth. One group was informed that their symptoms were caused by the injection, but the other group was not given this explanation.

One at a time, the volunteers experienced a situation that was designed to be either irritating or humorous. Schachter and Singer predicted that the subjects who were *informed* that their physical symptoms were caused by the drug injection would be less likely to attribute their symptoms to an emotion caused by the situation. Conversely, the subjects who were *not informed* that their physical symptoms were caused by the drug injection would label their symptoms as an emotion produced by the situation.

The results partially supported their predictions. The subjects who were not informed tended to report feeling either happier or angrier than the informed subjects.

Schachter and Singer's theory inspired a flurry of research. The bottom line of those research efforts? The two-factor theory of emotion received little support (Reisenzein, 1983). Nevertheless, Schachter and Singer's theory stimulated a new line of research on the importance of cognition in emotion (Moors, 2009).

To help illustrate the final theory of emotion that we'll consider, let's go back to the shadowy figure lurking in your college parking lot. Suppose that as the guy called out to you, "Hey, what's your hurry?" you recognized his voice as that of a good friend. Your emotional reaction, of course, would be very different. This simple observation is the basic premise of the **cognitive appraisal theory of emotion.**

Developed by Richard Lazarus and Craig Smith (1988), the cognitive appraisal theory of emotion asserts that the most important aspect of an emotional experience

FIGURE 8.7 The Two-Factor Theory of Emotion According to Stanley Schachter and Jerome Singer, emotional experience requires the interaction of two separate factors: (1) physiological arousal and (2) a cognitive *label* for that arousal.

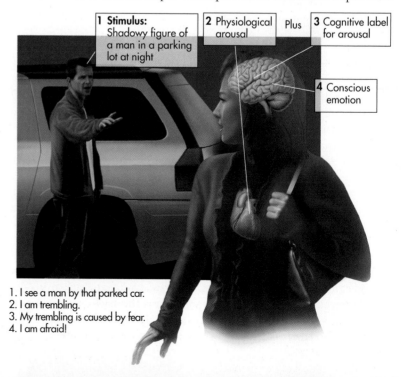

1 **Stimulus:** Shadowy figure of a man in a parking lot at night

2 Physiological arousal   Plus   3 Cognitive label for arousal

4 Conscious emotion

1. I see a man by that parked car.
2. I am trembling.
3. My trembling is caused by fear.
4. I am afraid!

is your cognitive interpretation, or *appraisal,* of the situation or stimulus. That is, emotions result from our appraisal of the *personal meaning* of events and experiences. Thus, the same situation might elicit very different emotions in different people (Moors, 2009; C. Smith & others, 2006).

So, in the case of the shadowy figure in the parking lot, your relief that you were not on the verge of being attacked by a mugger could quickly turn to another emotion. If it's a good friend you hadn't seen for a while, your relief might turn to pleasure, even joy. If it's someone that you'd prefer to avoid, relief might transform itself into annoyance or even anger.

At first glance, the cognitive appraisal theory and the Schachter–Singer two-factor theory seem very similar. Both theories emphasize the importance of cognitive appraisal. However, the two-factor theory says that emotion results from physiological arousal *plus* a cognitive label. In contrast, some appraisal theorists stressed that cognitive appraisal *is* the essential trigger for an emotional response (Lazarus, 1995).

Some critics of the cognitive appraisal approach objected that emotional reactions to events were virtually instantaneous—too rapid to allow for the process of cognitive appraisal. Instead, Robert Zajonc (1998, 2000) suggested, *we feel first and think later.* However, today's appraisal theorists recognize that emotions can be triggered in *multiple* ways (Moors & others, 2013; Scherer, 2013). Complex stimuli—like social situations or personal interactions—must be consciously appraised before an emotion is generated. And complex emotional responses—like mixed emotions, pride, shame, or guilt—are likely to involve conscious, cognitive processes (Izard, 2007).

On the other hand, some emotional responses are virtually instantaneous, bypassing conscious consideration. As Joseph LeDoux and other neuroscientists have demonstrated, the human brain can respond to biologically significant threats *without* involving conscious cognitive processes (Kihlstrom & others, 2000). So at least in some instances, we do seem to feel first and think later.

❯ Test your understanding of **Emotion** with **LEARNING***Curve.*

Christopher Lee/Getty Images

Appraisal and Emotion A Colombia fan rejoices among dejected Japan fans as Colombia wins a decisive match 4-1 at the 2014 World Cup games in Brazil. As cognitive appraisal theory predicts, the emotion determined by any particular event is determined by the way you cognitively appraise that event. For Colombia, the winning goal was an occasion for joy and pride; for Japan, it triggered sadness and a sense of loss.

Closing Thoughts

Psychologists have been interested in the topics of motivation and emotion since the very beginning of psychology as a science. Today, psychologists are acutely aware that all motives reflect the dynamic interaction of biological, psychological, and social factors, including cultural forces. Like any complex undertaking, Sandy's experiences in Nepal reflected many different motivational forces, from the desire to help others to her drive to challenge herself in a difficult and unfamiliar environment.

Emotions, too, reflect the interaction among biological factors shaped by evolution and personal, cultural, and social factors. As you've read this chapter, we hope you've thought about the multiple factors that influence your own motives and emotional responses in different areas of your life. Finally, in Psych for Your Life, we'll show you how you can use psychological research to help you achieve *your* goals and aspirations.

self-efficacy The beliefs that people have about their ability to meet the demands of a specific situation; feelings of self-confidence.

PSYCH FOR YOUR LIFE

Turning Your Goals into Reality

Most people can identify different aspects of their lives they'd like to change. Identifying goals we'd like to achieve is usually easy. Successfully accomplishing these goals is the tricky part. Fortunately, psychological research has identified several strategies and suggestions that can help you get motivated, act, and achieve your goals.

Self-Efficacy: Optimistic Beliefs About Your Capabilities

Your motivation to strive for achievement is closely linked to what you believe about your ability to produce the necessary or desired results in a situation. This is what psychologist Albert Bandura (1997, 2006) calls **self-efficacy**—the degree to which you are convinced of your ability to effectively meet the demands of a particular situation.

Bandura (1997, 2006) has found that if you have an optimistic sense of self-efficacy, you will approach a difficult task as a challenge to be mastered. You will also exert strong motivational effort, persist in the face of obstacles, and look for creative ways to overcome obstacles. If you see yourself as competent and capable, you are more likely to strive for higher personal goals (Bayer & Gollwitzer, 2007; Wood & Bandura, 1991).

People tend to avoid challenging situations or tasks that they *believe* exceed their capabilities (Bandura, 2008). If self-doubts occur, motivation quickly dwindles because the task is perceived as too difficult or threatening. So how do you build your sense of self-efficacy, especially in situations in which your confidence is shaky?

According to Bandura (1991, 2006), the most effective way to strengthen your sense of self-efficacy is through *mastery experiences*—experiencing success at moderately challenging tasks in which you have to overcome obstacles and persevere. As you tackle a challenging task, you should strive for progressive improvement rather than perfection on your first attempt. Understand that setbacks serve a useful purpose in teaching that success usually requires sustained effort. If you experienced only easy successes, you'd be more likely to become disappointed and discouraged and to abandon your efforts when you did experience failure.

A second strategy is *social modeling,* or *observational learning.* In some situations, the motivation to succeed is present, but you lack the knowledge of exactly how to achieve your goals. In such circumstances, it can be helpful to observe and imitate the behavior of someone who is already competent at the task you want to master (Bandura, 1986, 1990). For example, if you're not certain how to prepare effectively for a test or a class presentation, talk with fellow students who *are* successful in doing this. Ask how they study and what they do when they have difficulty understanding material. Knowing what works is often the critical element in ensuring success.

Implementation Intentions: Turning Goals into Actions

Suppose your sense of self-efficacy is strong, but you still have trouble putting your intentions into action. For example, have you ever made a list of New Year's resolutions and looked back at it six months later? If you're like most people, you'll wonder what went wrong.

How can you bridge the gap between good intentions and effective, goal-directed behavior? German psychologist Peter Gollwitzer (1999) points out that many people have trouble *initiating* the actions required to fulfill their goals and then *persisting* in these behaviors until the goals are achieved. Gollwitzer and his

colleagues (2008, 2010) have identified some simple yet effective techniques that help people translate their good intentions into actual behavior.

Step 1: Form a goal intention.

This step involves translating vague, general intentions ("I'm going to do my best") into a specific, concrete, and binding goal. Express the specific goal in terms of "I intend to achieve _____," filling in the blank with the particular behavior or outcome that you wish to achieve. For example, suppose you resolve to exercise more regularly. Transform that general goal into a much more specific goal intention, such as "I intend to work out at the campus gym on Monday, Wednesday, and Friday." Forming the specific goal intention enhances your sense of personal commitment to the goal, and it also heightens your sense of obligation to realize the goal.

Step 2: Create implementation intentions.

This step involves *making a specific plan for turning your good intention into reality.* The trick is to specify exactly where, when, and how you will carry out your intended behavior. Mentally link the intended behaviors to specific situational cues, such as saying, "After my psychology class, I will go to the campus athletic center and work out for 45 minutes." By linking the behavior to specific situational cues, you're more likely to initiate the goal behavior when the critical situation is encountered (Webb & Sheeran, 2007). The ultimate goal of implementation intentions is to create a new automatic link between a specific situation and the desired behavior—and ultimately, to create new habits or routines in your life (Adriaanse & others, 2011).

GARFIELD

As simple as this seems, research has demonstrated that forming specific implementation intentions is very effective (Gollwitzer & Sheeran, 2006; Parks-Stamm & others, 2007). For example, one study involved student volunteers with no enticement for participating in the research, such as money or course credit. Just before the students left for the holidays, they were instructed to write an essay describing how they spent Christmas Eve. The essay had to be written and mailed within two days after Christmas Eve.

Half of the participants were instructed to write out specific implementation intentions describing exactly when and where they would write the report during the critical 48-hour period. They were also instructed to visualize the chosen opportunity and mentally commit themselves to it.

The other half of the participants were not asked to identify a specific time or place, but just instructed to write and mail the report within the 48 hours. The results? Of those in the implementation intention group, 71 percent wrote and mailed the report by the deadline. Only 32 percent of the other group did so (Gollwitzer & Brandstätter, 1997).

Mental Rehearsal: Visualize the Process

The mental images you create in anticipation of a situation can strongly influence your sense of self-efficacy and self-control as well as the effectiveness of your implementation intentions (Knäuper & others, 2009). For example, students sometimes undermine their own performance by vividly imagining their worst fears, such as becoming overwhelmed by anxiety during a class presentation or going completely blank during a test. However, the opposite is also possible. Mentally visualizing yourself dealing *effectively* with a situation can enhance your performance (Conway & others, 2004; Libby & others, 2007). Athletes, in particular, are aware of this and mentally rehearse their performance prior to competition.

So strive to control your thoughts in an optimistic way by mentally focusing on your capabilities and a positive outcome, not your limitations and worst fears. The key here is not just imagining a positive outcome. Instead, imagine and mentally rehearse the *process*—the skills you will effectively use and the steps you will take—to achieve the outcome *you* want. Go for it!

CHAPTER REVIEW

KEY PEOPLE AND KEY TERMS

Walter Cannon, p. 348

Charles Darwin, p. 336

Edward L. Deci, p. 333

motivation, p. 314

instinct theories, p. 315

drive theories, p. 315

homeostasis, p. 315

drive, p. 316

incentive theories, p. 316

arousal theory, p. 316

sensation seeking, p. 316

humanistic theories of motivation, p. 317

glucose, p. 318

insulin, p. 318

Paul Ekman, p. 343

William James, p. 347

Virginia Johnson, p 324

basal metabolic rate (BMR), p. 318

leptin, p. 319

neuropeptide Y (NPY), p. 320

set-point theory, p. 320

body mass index (BMI), p. 321

obese, p. 321

sexual orientation, p. 327

hierarchy of needs, p. 331

self-actualization, p. 332

self-determination theory (SDT), p. 333

Abraham Maslow, p. 331

William Masters, p. 324

Richard M. Ryan, p. 333

intrinsic motivation, p. 333

extrinsic motivation, p. 333

competence motivation, p. 334

achievement motivation, p. 334

Thematic Apperception Test (TAT), p. 334

emotion, p. 336

emotional intelligence, p. 336

basic emotions, p. 337

interpersonal engagement, p. 337

amygdala, p. 340

anthropomorphism, p. 345

display rules, p. 345

James–Lange theory of emotion, p. 347

facial feedback hypothesis, p. 349

two-factor theory of emotion, p. 350

cognitive appraisal theory of emotion, p. 350

self-efficacy, p. 351

Motivation and Emotion

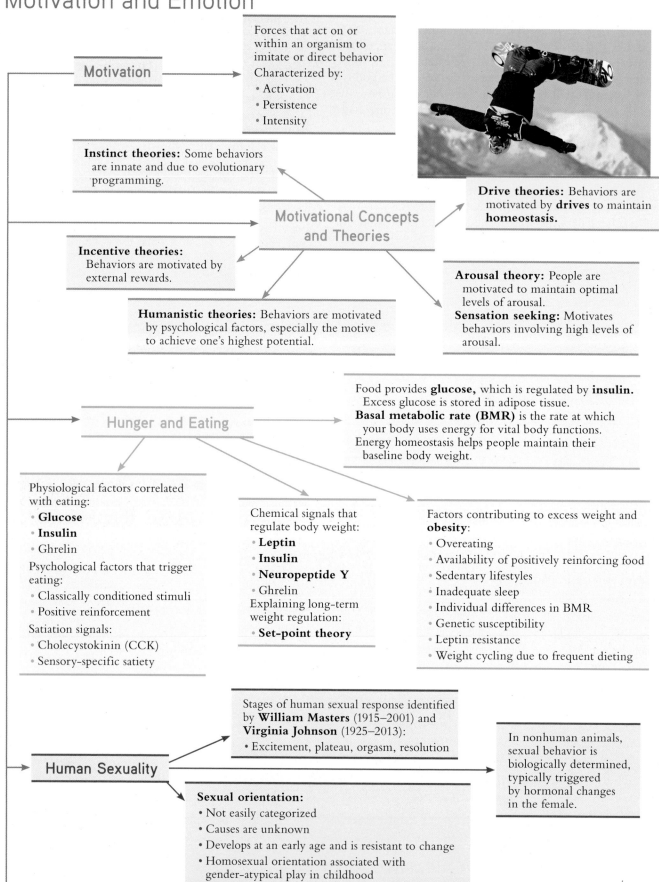

Motivation → Forces that act on or within an organism to imitate or direct behavior
Characterized by:
- Activation
- Persistence
- Intensity

Motivational Concepts and Theories

Instinct theories: Some behaviors are innate and due to evolutionary programming.

Drive theories: Behaviors are motivated by **drives** to maintain **homeostasis.**

Incentive theories: Behaviors are motivated by external rewards.

Arousal theory: People are motivated to maintain optimal levels of arousal.
Sensation seeking: Motivates behaviors involving high levels of arousal.

Humanistic theories: Behaviors are motivated by psychological factors, especially the motive to achieve one's highest potential.

Hunger and Eating

Food provides **glucose,** which is regulated by **insulin.** Excess glucose is stored in adipose tissue.
Basal metabolic rate (BMR) is the rate at which your body uses energy for vital body functions.
Energy homeostasis helps people maintain their baseline body weight.

Physiological factors correlated with eating:
- **Glucose**
- **Insulin**
- Ghrelin

Psychological factors that trigger eating:
- Classically conditioned stimuli
- Positive reinforcement

Satiation signals:
- Cholecystokinin (CCK)
- Sensory-specific satiety

Chemical signals that regulate body weight:
- **Leptin**
- **Insulin**
- **Neuropeptide Y**
- Ghrelin

Explaining long-term weight regulation:
- **Set-point theory**

Factors contributing to excess weight and **obesity:**
- Overeating
- Availability of positively reinforcing food
- Sedentary lifestyles
- Inadequate sleep
- Individual differences in BMR
- Genetic susceptibility
- Leptin resistance
- Weight cycling due to frequent dieting

Human Sexuality

Stages of human sexual response identified by **William Masters** (1915–2001) and **Virginia Johnson** (1925–2013):
- Excitement, plateau, orgasm, resolution

In nonhuman animals, sexual behavior is biologically determined, typically triggered by hormonal changes in the female.

Sexual orientation:
- Not easily categorized
- Causes are unknown
- Develops at an early age and is resistant to change
- Homosexual orientation associated with gender-atypical play in childhood

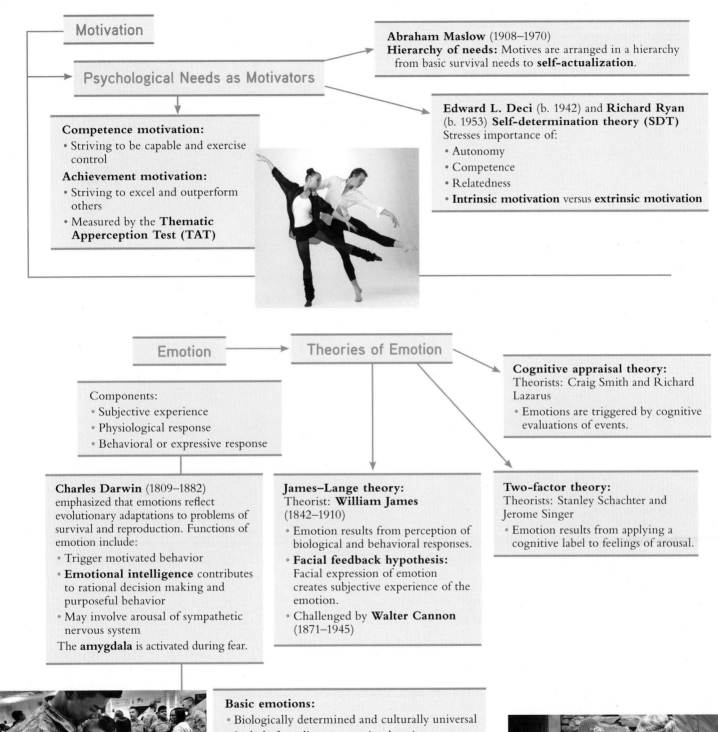

Motivation

Psychological Needs as Motivators

Abraham Maslow (1908–1970)
Hierarchy of needs: Motives are arranged in a hierarchy from basic survival needs to **self-actualization**.

Edward L. Deci (b. 1942) and **Richard Ryan** (b. 1953) **Self-determination theory (SDT)**
Stresses importance of:
• Autonomy
• Competence
• Relatedness
• **Intrinsic motivation** versus **extrinsic motivation**

Competence motivation:
• Striving to be capable and exercise control
Achievement motivation:
• Striving to excel and outperform others
• Measured by the **Thematic Apperception Test (TAT)**

Emotion

Theories of Emotion

Cognitive appraisal theory:
Theorists: Craig Smith and Richard Lazarus
• Emotions are triggered by cognitive evaluations of events.

Components:
• Subjective experience
• Physiological response
• Behavioral or expressive response

Charles Darwin (1809–1882) emphasized that emotions reflect evolutionary adaptations to problems of survival and reproduction. Functions of emotion include:
• Trigger motivated behavior
• **Emotional intelligence** contributes to rational decision making and purposeful behavior
• May involve arousal of sympathetic nervous system
The **amygdala** is activated during fear.

James–Lange theory:
Theorist: **William James** (1842–1910)
• Emotion results from perception of biological and behavioral responses.
• **Facial feedback hypothesis:** Facial expression of emotion creates subjective experience of the emotion.
• Challenged by **Walter Cannon** (1871–1945)

Two-factor theory:
Theorists: Stanley Schachter and Jerome Singer
• Emotion results from applying a cognitive label to feelings of arousal.

Basic emotions:
• Biologically determined and culturally universal
• Include fear, disgust, surprise, happiness, anger, and sadness
Culture and emotion:
• Collectivistic cultures emphasize emotions involving **interpersonal engagement.**
• Emotional expression is regulated by cultural **display rules.**
Paul Ekman (b. 1934):
• Analyzed facial expressions
• Demonstrated that facial expressions for basic emotions are culturally universal

MYTH OR SCIENCE?

Is it true . . .

○ That the genes you inherit provide an unchanging "blueprint" that determines your physical characteristics, abilities, and personality traits?

○ That talking "baby talk" to infants and toddlers won't harm their language development?

○ That educational videos, like *Baby Einstein*, help babies learn how to talk?

○ That transgender people are homosexual?

○ That most adolescents have poor relationships with their parents?

○ That many middle-aged people experience a "midlife crisis"?

○ That dying people go through five predictable stages—denial, anger, bargaining, depression, and acceptance?

PEOPLE ARE PEOPLE

PROLOGUE

JAMES IS THE KIND OF GUY PEOPLE ARE DRAWN TO—extraverted, smart, funny, caring. James is the center of his large group of friends, and his cell phone buzzed with incessant calls and texts as he and your author Susan talked in the bustling coffee shop in his hometown, a rural village in upstate New York. A talented writer and artist, James works at the local food pantry and manages the town's community garden. You know the type: He's the caretaker, the peacemaker, the organizer.

James is also transgender. He is biologically female, but he identified as male very early in life. In fact, he can't even remember a time when he didn't feel like a male. "I remember being a little kid and trying to get my friends to refer to me as a boy," he says. His early identification as male evoked a range of reactions. His friends awkwardly attempted to ignore it. His father was angry. His mother was conflicted. Both parents insisted he call himself a "tomboy" instead of a boy, firmly correcting him again and again. Lacking any other way to describe his feelings, James soon began parroting his parents: "I am not a girl; I am a tomboy."

But even though James faced unusual challenges growing up, his childhood was in other ways no different from that of other children. Through his childhood and adolescence, James progressed through the typical stages of development that we'll learn about in this chapter.

It wasn't until middle school that James first heard the term *transgender,* but at the time he didn't apply it to himself. James just wanted to live his life in accord with his sense of self—as a boy, not a girl. Although he sometimes tried dressing and acting

Lifespan Development

9

IN THIS CHAPTER:

› **INTRODUCTION:** People Are People

› Genetic Contributions to Development

› Prenatal Development

› Development During Infancy and Childhood

› Adolescence

› Adult Development

› Late Adulthood and Aging

› **THE FINAL CHAPTER:** Dying and Death

› **PSYCH FOR YOUR LIFE:** Raising Psychologically Healthy Children

as a female, he just felt more comfortable with "boy stuff."

A turning point came a few years ago, when James was 22 years old. Dressed in women's clothes—"a figure-fitting tank top and everything"—James was working at the community garden. A young boy, trying to be chivalrous, offered to shovel for him. James blew up. "Don't treat me like a woman," he screamed.

Later that day, another staff member who overhead James's extreme reaction asked James point-blank if he had ever thought he might be transgender. Thoughtful, James went home and did some research. "Oh my God," he realized, "this explains everything!"

But rather than being shocked or exhilarated by his discovery, James was simply relieved to learn that there was a term for his experience—and to learn that it was one that he shared with many other people. It helped him in the development of his overall sense of self—not just his gender identity. Matter-of-factly, he began to live as a man, first swapping out his female clothes for male clothes, then slowly but surely coming out as transgender to his friends and family. And he continued to work toward his career goal— to help other young people dealing with the same issues he has faced.

Someday, James hopes to be able to afford to have surgery to alter some of

Photograph: Gene Fischer "James, Teen Shelter", 2013 www.genefischer.com

James A young man living in a rural area in upstate New York, James is an avid gardener, writer, and artist. He's a volunteer and an activist in his community. He's also transgender. James wants people to realize that there are many parts of his identity as a person. He told your author Susan that people "shouldn't really be focused on this term transgender because a lot of people seem to stick us in a category." He wants people to see beyond the label and get to know him as a person.

his female sex characteristics to more closely match his identity as male. For now, he is developing a life living as a man.

As is true for all of us, James's relationships with friends and family are an important part of his life. When James became comfortable telling people that he was transgender, the news elicited a range of reactions from anger and confusion to complete acceptance. His brother was among those who accepted James unconditionally. He said, "Well, I never really saw you as a sister in the first place, so I don't think anything is changing other than pronouns."

In addition to acceptance of his gender identity, James shares the same kinds of dreams many of us have during early adulthood. He would like a home in the woods, and a family of his own. "I'd like to have a kid. Or two. I'd probably pick adoption if I could." And James also wants to be a part of a broader community. "I don't like being around only people who are similar to me. That's boring. I like a range of people. And I guess my message is we really need to start viewing people as people. Not by their skin tone. Not by their LGBTQ status. And not by their gender. People are people."

What James's story illustrates is that who we become in this life—our ongoing development—is not determined by any single characteristic or quality. James is transgender, but that's not the only part of James's development as a person. Like you, James is defined by more than a single characteristic. Nonetheless, James's story illustrates that gender identity is a potent force that shapes and directs the overall development of each of our lives, including the relationships we form. In this chapter, we'll explore the many aspects of human development, including how gender identity and gender roles affect all of our lives. Throughout the chapter, we'll come back to James's story. □

developmental psychology The branch of psychology that studies how people change over the lifespan.

longitudinal design Research strategy in which a variable or group of variables are studied in the same group of participants over time.

cross-sectional design Research strategy in which individuals of different ages or developmental stages are directly compared.

INTRODUCTION:
People Are People

KEY THEME

Developmental psychology is the study of how people change over the lifespan.

KEY QUESTIONS

❯ What are the nine basic stages of the lifespan?

❯ What are some of the key themes in developmental psychology?

One way to look at the overall development of your life is to think of your life as a story. You, of course, are the main character. Your life story so far has had a distinct plot, occasional subplots, and a cast of supporting characters, including family, friends, and lovers.

Like every other person's life story, yours has been influenced by factors beyond your control. One such factor is the unique combination of genes you inherited from your biological mother and father. Another is the historical era during which you grew up. James's life story, for example, will be shaped by the fact that he is living

Continuity and Change over the Lifespan The twin themes of continuity and change throughout the lifespan are evident in the changing nature of relationships. Childhood friendships center on sharing activities, while peer relationships in adolescence emphasize sharing thoughts and feelings. Early adulthood brings the challenge of forming intimate relationships and, for some, beginning a family. Close relationships with friends and family continue to contribute to psychological well-being in middle and late adulthood.

in an era in which more people are learning about and accepting transgender people. Your individual development has also been shaped by the cultural, social, and family contexts within which you were raised.

The patterns of your life story, and the life stories of countless other people, are the focus of **developmental psychology**—the study of how people change physically, cognitively, and socially throughout the lifespan. Developmental psychologists investigate the influence of biological, environmental, social, cultural, and behavioral factors on development at every age and stage of life.

The impact of these factors on individual development is greatly influenced by attitudes, perceptions, and personality characteristics. For example, the adjustment to middle school may be a breeze for one child but a nightmare for another. Gender identity, too, can affect individual development, as we saw in James's story. So, although we are influenced by the events we experience, we also shape the meaning and consequences of those events.

Along with studying common patterns of growth and change, developmental psychologists look at the ways in which people *differ* in their development and life stories. As we'll note several times in this chapter, the typical, or "normal," pattern of development can also vary across cultures (Kagan, 2011; Molitor & Hsu, 2011).

Developmental psychologists use varied research methods, but two research strategies are particularly important in understanding how people develop: *longitudinal* and *cross-sectional designs* (Karmiloff-Smith & others, 2014). Research that utilizes a **longitudinal design** tracks a particular variable or group of variables in the *same* group of participants over time, sometimes for years. For example, a longitudinal study of the effects of day care might compare the social development of a matched group of participants, half of whom attended day care and half of whom didn't, from infancy through high school graduation.

In contrast, research using a **cross-sectional design** studies a variable or group of variables among a group of participants at different ages or developmental stages. For example, to study the effect of aging on cognitive processes, developmental psychologists might compare memory abilities in 45-year-old, 55-year-old, and 65-year-old participants, looking for age-related differences.

Developmental psychologists often conceptualize the lifespan in terms of basic *stages* of development (see Table 9.1). Traditionally, the stages of the lifespan

TABLE 9.1

Major Stages of the Lifespan

Stage	Age Range
Prenatal	Conception to birth
Infancy and toddlerhood	Birth to 2 years
Early childhood	2 to 6 years
Middle childhood	6 to 12 years
Adolescence	12 to 18 years
Emerging adulthood	18 to 25 years
Young adulthood	25 to 40 years
Middle adulthood	40 to 65 years
Late adulthood	65 years to death

The Chapters in Your Life Story If you think of your life as an unfolding story, then the major stages of the human lifespan represent the different "chapters" of your life. Each chapter is characterized by fundamentally different physical, cognitive, and social transitions, challenges and opportunities, demands and adjustments. Comparing different life stories reveals many striking similarities in the developmental themes of any given stage. Nevertheless, every life story is unique.

zygote The single cell formed at conception from the union of the egg cell and sperm cell.

chromosome A long, thread-like structure composed of twisted parallel strands of DNA; found in the cell nucleus.

deoxyribonucleic acid (DNA) The double-stranded molecule that encodes genetic instructions; the chemical basis of heredity.

are defined by age, which implies that we experience relatively sudden, age-related changes as we move from one stage to the next. Indeed, some of life's transitions *are* rather abrupt, such as entering the workforce, becoming a parent, or retiring. And some aspects of development, such as prenatal development and language development, are closely tied to *critical periods,* which are periods during which a child is maximally sensitive to environmental influences.

Still, most of our physical, cognitive, and social changes occur gradually. As we trace the typical course of human development in this chapter, the theme of *gradually unfolding changes* throughout the ages and stages of life will become more evident. Another important theme in developmental psychology is the *interaction between heredity and environment.* Traditionally, this was called the *nature–nurture* issue. Although we are born with a specific genetic potential that we inherit from our biological parents, our environment influences how, when, and whether that potential is expressed. In turn, our genetic inheritance influences the ways in which we experience and interact with the environment (Diamond, 2009; Meaney, 2010).

Genetic Contributions to Development

KEY THEME

Your genotype consists of the chromosomes inherited from your biological parents, but your phenotype—the actual characteristics you display—results from the interaction of genetics and environmental factors.

KEY QUESTIONS

› What are DNA, chromosomes, and genes?
› What role does the environment play in the relationship between genotype and phenotype?
› What is epigenetics?

You began your life as a **zygote,** a single cell no larger than the period at the end of this sentence. Packed in that tiny cell was the unique set of genetic instructions that you inherited from your biological parents. Today, that same set of genetic information is found in the nucleus of nearly every cell of your body.

What form do these genetic data take? The genetic data you inherited from your biological parents is encoded in the chemical structure of the **chromosomes** that are found in the cell nucleus. As depicted in Figure 9.1, each chromosome is a long, thread-like structure composed of twisted parallel strands of **deoxyribonucleic acid,** abbreviated **DNA.** Put simply, DNA stores the inherited information that guides the development of all living organisms.

FIGURE 9.1 Chromosomes, Genes, and DNA Each chromosome contains thousands of genes, and each gene is a unit of DNA instructions. Incredibly fine, the strands of DNA in a single human cell would be more than three inches long if unraveled. If the DNA present in one person were unraveled, it would stretch from Earth to Pluto and back—*twice!*

Packed in the nucleus of the cell are the 23 pairs of chromosomes that represent your unique genotype.

A gene is a segment of the DNA that contains the genetic instructions for making a particular protein.

Each gene is a segment of DNA. The twisted strands that make up a DNA molecule resemble a spiral staircase.

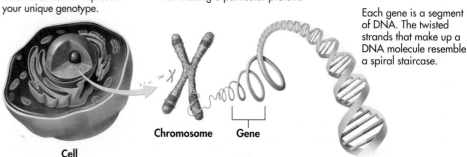

Cell   Chromosome   Gene   DNA

Each of your chromosomes has thousands of DNA segments, called **genes,** that are strung like beads along its length. Each gene is a unit of DNA code for making a particular protein molecule. Interestingly, genes actually make up less than 2 percent of human DNA (Human Genome Project, 2008). Determining the functions of the rest of the DNA is an active area of investigation. This DNA was once referred to as "junk DNA," but most researchers today believe that it is involved in regulating gene functioning (McDaniell & others, 2010; Parker & others, 2009).

What do genes do? In a nutshell, genes direct the manufacture of proteins. Proteins are used in virtually all of your body's functions—from building cells to manufacturing hormones to regulating brain activity. Your body requires hundreds of thousands of different proteins to function. Each protein is formed by a specific combination of amino acids, and that combination is encoded in a particular gene.

Your Unique Genotype

At fertilization, your biological mother's egg cell and your biological father's sperm cell each contributed 23 chromosomes. This set of 23 chromosome pairs represents your unique **genotype,** or genetic makeup. With the exception of the reproductive cells (sperm or eggs), every cell in your body contains a complete, identical copy of your genotype.

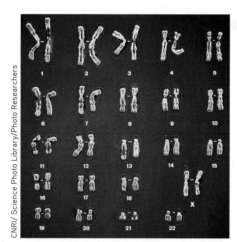

In recent years, scientists mapped out the *human genome*—the complete set of DNA in the human organism (Lander & others, 2001; Venter & others, 2001). One unexpected discovery was that the complete human genome contains only about 20,000 to 25,000 protein-coding genes, far fewer than previous estimates that put the number as high as 100,000 genes.

Although all humans have the same basic set of genes, these genes can come in different versions, called *alleles*. As a general rule, your genotype contains two copies of each gene—one inherited from each biological parent. These genes may be identical or different. The range of potential alleles varies for individual genes (Ku & others, 2010). Some genes have just a few different versions, while other genes have 50 or more possible alleles. It is this unique combination of alleles that helps make your genotype—and you—unique.

The best-known, although not the most common, pattern of allele variation is the simple dominant–recessive gene pair. For example, the development of freckles appears to be controlled by a single gene, which can be either dominant or recessive (Sulem & others, 2007). If you inherit a dominant version of the freckles gene from either or both of your biological parents, you'll have the potential to display freckles. But to be freckle-free, you would have to inherit two recessive "no freckles" genes, one from each biological parent.

Unlike freckles, most characteristics involve the interaction of *multiple* genes (Buchanan & others, 2009). For these characteristics, each gene contributes only a small amount of influence to a particular characteristic.

From Genotype to Phenotype

While the term *genotype* refers to an organism's unique genetic makeup, the term **phenotype** refers to the characteristics that are actually observed in an organism. At one time, the genotype was

---

gene A unit of DNA on a chromosome that encodes instructions for making a particular protein molecule; the basic unit of heredity.

genotype (JEEN-oh-type) The genetic makeup of an individual organism.

sex chromosomes Chromosomes, designated as X or Y, that determine biological sex; the 23rd pair of chromosomes in humans.

phenotype (FEEN-oh-type) The observable traits or characteristics of an organism as determined by the interaction of genetics and environmental factors.

The 23 Pairs of Human Chromosomes Each person's unique genotype is represented in the 23 pairs of chromosomes found in the nucleus of almost all human body cells. This photograph, taken through a microscope, depicts a *karyotype*, which shows one cell's complete set of chromosomes. By convention, the chromosomes are arranged in pairs from largest to smallest, numbered from 1 to 22. The 23rd pair of chromosomes, called the **sex chromosomes**, determines a person's biological sex. The sex chromosomes in this karyotype are XX, indicating a female. A male karyotype would have an XY combination.

Human Sex Chromosomes: X and Y Biological sex is determined by the 23rd pair of chromosomes, the *sex chromosomes*. While every egg cell has one X chromosome, every sperm cell has either one X or one Y chromosome. Whether a zygote develops into a male or a female depends on whether the egg is fertilized by a sperm cell with a Y chromosome (XY, resulting in a male) or by a sperm cell with an X chromosome (XX, resulting in a female). Notice that the X chromosome (*left*) is larger and has more genes than the Y chromosome (*right*). This confers some protection against certain genetic disorders for females. Why? Because by having two X chromosomes, females with a disease-producing allele are more likely to also have a normal allele to override it. This is why males are more likely to display various genetic disorders, such as red–green color blindness and hemophilia.

Most of the genes in each person are dormant. Experience affects which genes are turned on (and off), and when. Thus, the environment participates in sculpting expression of the genome.

—Adele Diamond (2009)

The old "nature versus nurture" debate has long since receded into scientific irrelevance. Instead, the frontier lies in understanding the mechanisms by which environmental factors—whether experiential, metabolic, microbiological, or pharmacologic—interact with the genome to influence brain development and to produce diverse forms of neural plasticity over the lifetime.

—Steven E. Hyman (2009)

epigenetics The study of the cellular mechanisms that control gene expression and of the ways that gene expression impacts health and behavior.

commonly described as a "genetic blueprint," which implied that the genotype was a fixed, master plan, like an architectural blueprint. It was thought that a person's inherited genotype directed and controlled virtually all aspects of development as it unfolded over the lifespan (Dar-Nimrod & Heine, 2011). But research has shown that the genetic blueprint analogy is *not* accurate.

The first problem with the genotype-as-blueprint analogy is that genes don't *directly* control development, traits, or behaviors (Zhang & Meaney, 2010). Rather, as explained earlier, genes direct the production of the thousands of different proteins that are the building blocks of all body tissues and structures—which ultimately *do* influence your development and behavior.

Second, environmental factors influence the phenotype you display. For example, even if your genotype contains a copy of the dominant "freckles" gene, you will *not* develop freckles unless the expression of that dominant gene is triggered by a specific environmental factor: sunlight. On the other hand, if you carry two recessive "no freckles" genes, you won't develop freckles no matter how much time you spend in the sunlight.

Here's the important point: *Different genotypes react differently to environmental factors* (Masterpasqua, 2009). Thus, psychologists and other scientists often speak of *genetic predispositions* to develop in a particular way (Champagne & Mashoodh, 2009). In other words, people with a particular genetic configuration will be more or less sensitive to particular environmental factors. For example, think of people you know who sunburn easily, such as redheads or people with very fair skin. Their genotype is especially sensitive to the effects of ultraviolet light. One person's freckle factory is another person's light tan—or searing sunburn.

THE NEW SCIENCE OF EPIGENETICS

Each of us started life as a single-celled zygote that divided and multiplied. Each new cell contained the exact same set of genetic instructions. Yet some of those cells developed into bones, hair, eyes, joints, lungs, or other specialized tissues. Why, then, are cells so different? How does the single-celled zygote develop into a complex, differentiated organism with kidneys, eyelashes, kneecaps, and a navel?

The dramatic differences among the size, shape, and function of cells are due to *which* genes are "expressed," or activated to participate in protein production. Put simply, cells develop differently because different genes are activated at different times. Some genes are active for just a few hours, others for a lifetime. Many genes are *never* expressed. For example, humans carry all of the genes to develop a tail, but we don't develop a tail because those genes are never activated.

What triggers a gene to activate? Gene expression can be triggered by the activity of *other* genes, internal chemical changes, or by external environmental factors, such as sunlight in our earlier freckles example. Thus, gene expression is *flexible,* responsive to both internal and external factors (Meaney, 2010; Szyf, 2013).

Scientists have only recently begun to understand the processes that regulate gene expression. This new field is called **epigenetics**—the study of the mechanisms that control gene expression and its effects on behavior and health (Meaney, 2010; Zhang & Meaney, 2010). For any given cell, it's the epigenetic "settings" that determine whether it will become a skin cell, a nerve cell, or a heart muscle cell. Thus, epigenetics investigates how gene activity is regulated within a cell, such as identifying the signals that switch genes to "on" or "off."

To help illustrate epigenetic influences, consider identical twins, who develop from a single zygote. Each twin inherits exactly the same set of genes. Yet, as twins develop, differences in physical and psychological characteristics become evident. These differences are due to epigenetic changes—differences in the expression of each twin's genes, *not* to their underlying DNA, which is still identical (Champagne & Mashoodh, 2009; Fraga & others, 2005).

Epigenetic research is providing new insights into *how* the environment affects gene expression and the phenotype (Champagne, 2010; Szyf & Bick, 2013). For example, consider the groundbreaking series of experiments conducted by teams led by Canadian neuroscientist Michael Meaney (2001, 2010). He showed that newborn rats that were genetically predisposed to be skittish, nervous, and high-strung would develop into calm, exploratory, and stress-resistant adult rats when raised by genetically unrelated, attentive mother rats. Conversely, newborn rats that were genetically predisposed to be calm and stress resistant grew up to be nervous, high-strung, and easily stressed out when they were raised by *inattentive,* genetically unrelated mother rats.

The important point is that although the rats' DNA did *not* change, the chemical tags that control gene expression *did* change. The rats' upbringing set in motion a cascade of epigenetic changes that changed their brain chemistry and literally "reprogrammed" their future behavior (see Hyman, 2009; Sapolsky, 2004). Surprisingly, the influence of their upbringing extended to the *next* generation: The calm, stress-resistant rats grew up to be attentive mothers to their own offspring.

Psychologists and other scientists are beginning to identify epigenetic influences in humans. One area of active study is the impact of early stress (see Champagne, 2010; Jensen, 2014). Would childhood stress or adversity produce a recognizable pattern of epigenetic changes in adult *humans,* as it does in adult rats? One study found that suicide victims who had been abused as children had distinct epigenetic marks in brain tissue that were *not* found in the brains of control subjects or in suicide victims who had not been abused as children (McGowan & others, 2009). The pattern of epigenetic marks was consistent with that shown in studies of rat pups who had experienced early stress, such as being separated from their mothers (Hyman, 2009). The research suggested that early childhood adversity had created long-lasting epigenetic changes in the brain.

Interactions among genes, and between the genotype and environmental influences, are two critical factors in the relationship between genotype and phenotype. Beyond these factors, genes can also *mutate,* or spontaneously change, from one generation to the next. Further, DNA itself can be damaged by environmental factors, such as exposure to ultraviolet light, radiation, or chemical toxins. Just as a typo in a recipe can ruin a favorite dish, errors in the genetic code can disrupt the production of the correct proteins and lead to birth defects or genetic disorders.

Prenatal Development

During the prenatal stage, the single-celled zygote develops into a full-term fetus.

> What are the three stages of prenatal development?
> How does the brain develop?
> What are teratogens?

At conception, chromosomes from the biological mother and father combine to form a single cell—the fertilized egg, or *zygote.* Over the relatively brief span of nine months, that single cell develops into the estimated trillion cells that make up a newborn baby. This **prenatal stage** has three distinct phases: the germinal period, the embryonic period, and the fetal period (see photos).

The Germinal and Embryonic Periods

The **germinal period,** also called the *zygotic period,* represents the first two weeks of prenatal development. During this time, the zygote undergoes rapid cell division before becoming implanted on the wall of the mother's uterus. Some of the zygote's cells will eventually form the structures that house and protect the developing fetus and provide nourishment from the mother. By the end of the two-week germinal period, the single-celled zygote has developed into a cluster of cells called the *embryo.*

prenatal stage The stage of development before birth; divided into the germinal, embryonic, and fetal periods.

germinal period The first two weeks of prenatal development.

Prenatal Development Although it is less than an inch long, the beginnings of arms, legs, and fingers can already be distinguished in the 7-week-old embryo (*top left*). The amniotic sac can be clearly seen in this photograph. The fetus at 4 months (*top right*) measures 6 to 10 inches long, and the mother may be able to feel the fetus's movements. Notice the well-formed umbilical cord. Near full term (*bottom*), the 8-month-old fetus gains body fat to help the newborn survive outside the mother's uterus.

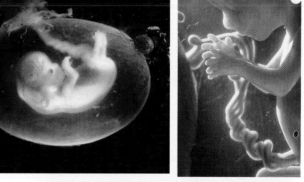

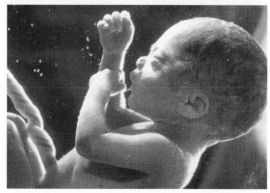

(a) Dr. G. Moscoso/Science Source
(b) and (c) Petit Format/Nestle/Science Source

embryonic period The second period of prenatal development, extending from the third week through the eighth week.

teratogens Harmful agents or substances that can cause malformations or defects in an embryo or fetus.

stem cells Undifferentiated cells that can divide and give rise to cells that can develop into any one of the body's different cell types.

The **embryonic period** begins with week 3 and extends through week 8. During this time of rapid growth and intensive cell differentiation, the organs and major systems of the body form. Genes on the sex chromosomes and hormonal influences also trigger the initial development of the sex organs.

Protectively housed in the fluid-filled *amniotic sac,* the embryo's lifeline is the umbilical cord. Extending from the placenta on the mother's uterine wall to the embryo's abdominal area, the *umbilical cord* delivers nourishment, oxygen, and water, and carries away carbon dioxide and other wastes. The *placenta* is actually a disk-shaped, vascular organ that prevents the mother's blood from directly mingling with that of the developing embryo. Acting as a filter, the placenta prevents many harmful substances that might be present in the mother's blood from reaching the embryo.

The placenta cannot, however, filter out all harmful agents from the mother's blood. Harmful agents or substances that can cause abnormal development or birth defects are called **teratogens.** Generally, the greatest vulnerability to teratogens occurs during the embryonic stage, when major body systems are forming. But many substances, including cocaine, prescription and over-the-counter drugs, cigarette smoke, and alcohol, can damage the developing fetus at *any* stage before birth. Known teratogens include the following:

- Exposure to radiation
- Toxic chemicals and metals, such as mercury, PCBs, and lead
- Viruses and bacteria, such as German measles (rubella), syphilis, genital herpes, and human immunodeficiency virus (HIV)
- Prescription painkillers and other prescription and nonprescription drugs
- Addictive drugs, including heroin, sedatives, cocaine, amphetamines, and methamphetamine
- Maternal smoking and exposure to secondhand smoke
- Alcohol

Alcohol deserves special mention. Although drinking alcohol at any point during pregnancy can harm the fetus, the greatest risk is during the first trimester of prenatal development, when the brain and major organs are developing. Excessive drinking can cause *fetal alcohol syndrome,* which is characterized by physical and mental problems (Bakoyiannis, 2014; Sokol & others, 2003). Symptoms include abnormal facial features, poor coordination, learning disabilities, behavior problems, and intellectual disability. Binge drinking is especially harmful to the developing fetus, but most researchers believe that there is *no* safe level of alcohol use during pregnancy.

Finally, the mother's psychological state can affect the unborn child. Chronic stress, depression, and anxiety are associated with low birth weight and premature birth (see Dunkel Schetter, 2011). Poor nutrition, lack of sleep, and other unhealthy behaviors can also affect the unborn child's growth and development.

By the end of the embryonic period, the embryo has grown from a cluster of a few hundred cells no bigger than the head of a pin to over an inch in length. Now weighing about an ounce, the embryo looks distinctly human, even though its head accounts for about half its body size.

Prenatal Brain Development

By three weeks after conception, a sheet of primitive neural cells has formed. Just as you might roll a piece of paper to make a tube, this sheet of neural cells curls to form the hollow *neural tube.* The neural tube is lined with **stem cells,** which are cells that can divide indefinitely, renew themselves, and give rise to a variety of other types of cells. At four weeks, this structure is about the size of a grain of salt. At seven weeks it is about a quarter-inch long.

The neural stem cells divide and multiply, producing other specialized cells that eventually give rise to neurons and glial cells. Gradually, the top of the neural tube thickens into three bulges that will eventually form the three main regions of the brain: the *hindbrain, midbrain,* and *forebrain* (see Figure 9.2). As the neural tube expands, it develops the cavities, called *ventricles,* that are found at the core of the fully developed brain. The ventricles are filled with cerebrospinal fluid, which cushions and provides nutrients for the brain and spinal cord.

During peak periods of brain development, new neurons are being generated at the rate of 250,000 per minute (McDonald, 2009). The developing brain cells multiply, differentiate, and begin their migration to their final destination. Guided by the fibers of a special type of glial cell, the newly generated neurons travel to specific locations (Bystron & others, 2008). They join with other developing neurons and begin forming the structures of the developing nervous system.

The Fetal Period

The third month heralds the beginning of the **fetal period**—the final and longest stage of prenatal development. The main task during the next seven months is for body systems to grow and reach maturity in preparation for life outside the mother's body. By the end of the third month, the fetus can move its arms, legs, mouth, and head. The fetus becomes capable of reflexive responses, such as fanning its toes if the sole of the foot is stroked and squinting if its eyelids are touched. During the fourth month, the mother experiences *quickening*—she can feel the fetus moving.

The fetal brain is constantly changing, forming as many as 2 million synaptic connections per second. Connections that are used are strengthened, while connections that remain unused are eventually *pruned* or eliminated. The fetus now has distinct sleep–wake cycles and periods of activity (Mirmiran & others, 2003). During the sixth month, the fetus's brain activity becomes similar to that of a newborn baby.

During the final two months of the fetal period, the fetus will double in weight, gaining an additional three to four pounds of body fat. This additional body fat will help the newborn adjust to changing temperatures outside the womb. It also contributes to the newborn's chubby appearance. As birth approaches, growth slows and the fetus's body systems become more active.

At birth, the newborn's brain is only about one-fourth the size of an adult brain, weighing less than a pound. After birth, the neurons grow in size and continue to develop new dendrites and interconnections with other neurons. *Myelin* forms on axons in key areas of the brain, such as those involved in motor control (Jakovcevski & others, 2009). Axons also grow longer, and the branching at the ends of the axons becomes more dense. But the process of neural development has only begun. The development of dendrites and synapses, as well as the extension of axons, continues throughout the lifespan.

❯ Test your understanding of **Genetics and Prenatal Development** with **LEARNING***Curve.*

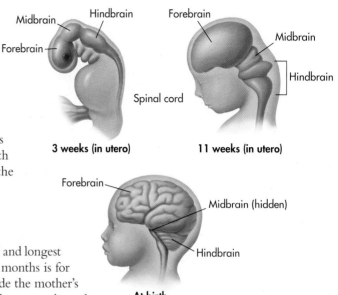

FIGURE 9.2 The Sequence of Fetal Brain Development The human brain begins as a fluid-filled neural tube at about three weeks after conception. The hindbrain structures are the first to develop, followed by midbrain structures. The forebrain structures develop last, eventually coming to surround and envelop the hindbrain and midbrain structures.

Development During Infancy and Childhood

KEY THEME

Although physically helpless, newborn infants are equipped with reflexes and sensory capabilities that enhance their chances for survival.

KEY QUESTIONS

❯ How do the senses and the brain develop after birth?

❯ What roles do temperament and attachment play in social and personality development?

❯ What are the stages of language development?

The newly born infant enters the world with an impressive array of physical and sensory capabilities. Initially, his behavior is mostly limited to reflexes that enhance his

fetal period The third and longest period of prenatal development, extending from the ninth week until birth.

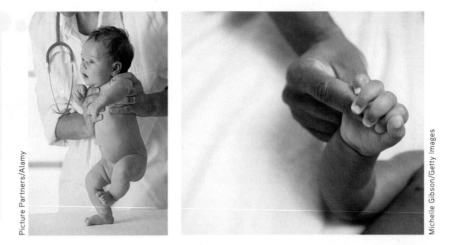

Picture Partners/Alamy

Michelle Gibson/Getty Images

Newborn Reflexes When this 2-week-old baby (*left*) is held upright with her feet touching a flat surface, she displays the *stepping reflex,* moving her legs as if trying to walk. Another reflex that is present at birth is the *grasping reflex* (*right*). The infant's grip is so strong that he can support his own weight. Thought to enhance the newborn's chances for survival, these reflexive responses drop out during the first few months of life as the baby develops voluntary control over movements.

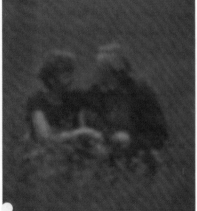

Anthony Young

The Nearsighted Newborn Classic research by psychologist Robert Fantz and his colleagues (1962) showed that the newborn comes into the world very nearsighted, having approximately 20/300 vision. The newborn's ability to detect the contrast of object edges and boundaries is also poorly developed (Stephens & Banks, 1987). As this image illustrates, even by age 3 months, the infant's world is still pretty fuzzy.

Photographs copyright of Anthony Young From *First Glances* by Davida Y. Teller, Journal of Investigative Opthalmology and Visual Science, Vol. 38, 1997, pp. 2183–2203.

chances for survival. Touching the newborn's cheek triggers the *rooting reflex*—the infant turns toward the source of the touch and opens his mouth. Touching the newborn's lips evokes the *sucking reflex*. If you put a finger on each of the newborn's palms, he will respond with the *grasping reflex*—the baby will grip your fingers so tightly that he can be lifted upright. As motor areas of the infant's brain develop over the first year of life, the rooting, sucking, and grasping reflexes are replaced by voluntary behaviors.

The newborn's senses—vision, hearing, smell, and touch—are keenly attuned to people. In a classic study, Robert Fantz (1961) demonstrated that the image of a human face holds the newborn's gaze longer than do other images. Other researchers have also confirmed the newborn's visual preference for the human face (Pascalis & Kelly, 2009). Newborns only 10 *minutes* old will turn their heads to continue gazing at the image of a human face as it passes in front of them, but they will not visually follow other images (Turati, 2004).

And, newborns quickly learn to differentiate between their mothers and strangers. Within just hours of their birth, newborns display a preference for their mother's voice and face over that of a stranger (Bushnell, 2001). For their part, mothers become keenly attuned to their infant's appearance, smell, and even skin texture. Fathers, too, are able to identify their newborn from a photograph after just minutes of exposure (Bader & Phillips, 2002).

Vision is the least developed sense at birth. A newborn infant is extremely nearsighted, meaning she can see close objects more clearly than distant objects. The optimal viewing distance for the newborn is about 6 to 12 inches, the perfect distance for a nursing baby to focus easily on her mother's face and make eye contact. Nevertheless, the infant's view of the world is pretty fuzzy for the first several months, even for objects that are within close range.

The interaction between adults and infants seems to compensate naturally for the newborn's poor vision. When adults interact with very young infants, they almost always position themselves so that their face is about 8 to 12 inches away from the baby's face. Adults also have a strong natural tendency to exaggerate head movements and facial expressions, such as smiles and frowns, again making it easier for the baby to see them.

Physical Development

By the time infants begin crawling, at about 7 to 8 months of age, their view of the world, including distant objects, will be as clear as that of their parents. The increasing maturation of the infant's visual system reflects the development of her brain. At birth, her brain is an impressive 25 percent of its adult weight. In contrast, her birth weight is only about 5 percent of her eventual adult weight. During infancy, her brain will grow to about 75 percent of its adult weight, while her body weight will reach only about 20 percent of her adult weight.

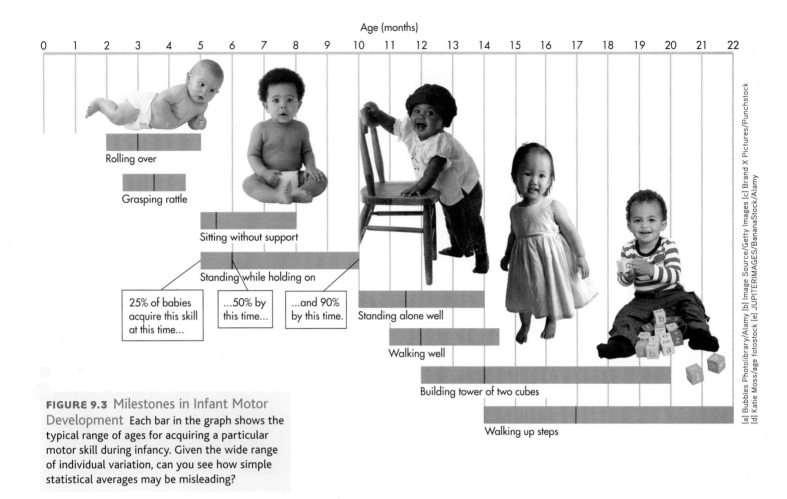

Age (months)

0 1 2 3 4 5 6 7 8 9 10 11 12 13 14 15 16 17 18 19 20 21 22

Rolling over

Grasping rattle

Sitting without support

Standing while holding on

25% of babies acquire this skill at this time...

...50% by this time...

...and 90% by this time.

Standing alone well

Walking well

Building tower of two cubes

Walking up steps

[a] Bubbles Photolibrary/Alamy [b] Image Source/Getty Images [c] Brand X Pictures/Punchstock [d] Katie Moss/age fotostock [e] JUPITERIMAGES/BananaStock/Alamy

FIGURE 9.3 Milestones in Infant Motor Development Each bar in the graph shows the typical range of ages for acquiring a particular motor skill during infancy. Given the wide range of individual variation, can you see how simple statistical averages may be misleading?

During the prenatal period, the top of the body develops faster than the bottom. For example, the head develops before the legs. If you've ever watched a 6-week-old baby struggling to lift her head up, or a 3-month-old baby pulling herself along the floor by her arms, you've probably noticed that an infant's motor skills also develop unevenly, and follow the same general pattern. The word *cephalocaudal* literally means "head to tail," and the term *cephalocaudal pattern* refers to the fact that physical and motor skill development tends to follow a "top to bottom" sequence. The infant develops control over her head, chest, and arms before developing control over the lower part of her body and legs (Kopp, 2011).

A second pattern is the *proximodistal trend,* which refers to the tendency of infants to develop motor control from the center of their bodies outwards. Babies gain control over their abdomen before they gain control over their elbows, knees, hands, or feet.

The basic *sequence* of motor skill development is universal, but the *average ages* can be a little deceptive (see Figure 9.3). As any parent knows, infants vary a great deal in the ages at which they master each skill. For example, virtually all infants are walking well by 15 months of age, but some infants will walk as early as 10 months. Each infant has her own timetable of physical maturation and developmental readiness to master different motor skills.

Social and Personality Development

From birth, forming close social and emotional relationships with caregivers is essential to the infant's physical and psychological well-being. Although physically helpless, the young infant does not play a passive role in forming these relationships. As you'll see in this section, the infant's individual traits play an important role in the development of the relationship between infant and caregiver.

CULTURE AND HUMAN BEHAVIOR

Where Does the Baby Sleep?

In most U.S. families, infants sleep in their own beds (Mindell & others, 2010a). It may surprise you to discover that the United States is very unusual in this respect. In one survey of 100 societies, the United States was the *only one* in which babies slept in separate rooms. Another survey of 136 societies found that in two-thirds of the societies, infants slept in the same beds as their mothers. In the remainder, infants generally slept in the same room as their mothers (Morelli & others, 1992).

In one of the few in-depth studies of co-sleeping in different cultures, Gilda Morelli and her colleagues (1992) compared the sleeping arrangements of several middle-class U.S. families with those of Mayan families in a small town in Guatemala. They found that babies in the Mayan families slept with their mothers until they were 2 or 3, usually until another baby was about to be born. At that point, toddlers moved to the bed of another family member, usually the father or an older sibling. Children continued to sleep with other family members throughout childhood.

Mayan mothers were shocked when the American researchers told them that infants in the United States slept alone and often in a different room from their parents. They believed that the practice was cruel and unnatural, and would have negative effects on the infant's development.

When infants and toddlers sleep alone, bedtime marks a separation from their families. To ease the child's transition to sleeping, "putting the baby to bed" often involves lengthy bedtime rituals, including rocking, singing lullabies, or reading stories (Morrell & Steele, 2003). Small children take comforting items, such as a favorite blanket or teddy bear, to bed with them to ease the stressful transition to falling asleep alone. The child may also use his "security blanket" or "cuddly" to comfort himself when he wakes up in the night, as most small children do.

In contrast, the Mayan babies did not take cuddly items to bed, and no special routines marked the transition between wakefulness and sleep. Mayan parents were puzzled by the very idea. Instead, the Mayan babies simply went to bed when their parents did or fell asleep in the middle of the family's social activities. Morelli and her colleagues (1992) found that the different sleeping customs of the U.S. and Mayan families reflect different cultural values.

Some of the U.S. babies slept in the same room as their parents when they were first born, which the parents felt helped foster feelings of closeness and emotional security in the newborns. Nonetheless, most of the U.S. parents moved their babies to a separate room when they felt that the babies were ready to sleep alone, usually by the time they were 3 to 6 months of age. These parents explained their decision by saying that it was time for the baby to learn to be "independent" and "self-reliant."

In contrast, the Mayan parents felt that it was important to develop and encourage the infant's feelings of *interdependence* with other members of the family. Thus, in both Mayan and U.S. families, sleeping arrangements reflect cultural goals for child rearing and cultural values for relations among family members.

MARIA STENZEL/National Geographic Society

Culture and Co-Sleeping Throughout the world, cultural and ethnic differences influence family decisions about sleeping arrangements for infants and young children (Li & others, 2008; Worthman & Brown, 2007). Among the indigenous Nenets people of Siberia, shown above, *co-sleeping* or *shared sleeping* is common, at least partly for the pragmatic reason of staying warm. Even in the United States, sleeping arrangements vary by racial and ethnic groups. Stephanie Milan and her colleagues (2007) found that Latino and African American preschoolers were more likely to sleep with a sibling or parent than were white preschoolers.

Temperamental Patterns Most babies can be categorized into one of three broad temperamental patterns. An "easy" baby is usually easy to soothe, calm, cheerful, and readily adapts to new situations. "Slow-to-warm-up" babies tend to adapt to new situations and experiences very slowly, but once they adapt, they're fine. "Difficult" babies are more likely to be emotional, irritable, and fussy. Which category do you think the baby shown here might fit into? Why?

ImageSource/age fotostock

TEMPERAMENTAL QUALITIES
BABIES ARE DIFFERENT!

Infants come into the world with very distinct and consistent behavioral styles. Some babies are consistently calm and easy to soothe. Other babies are fussy, irritable, and hard to comfort. Some babies are active and outgoing; others seem shy and wary of new experiences. Psychologists refer to these inborn predispositions to consistently behave and react in a certain way as an infant's **temperament.**

Interest in infant temperament was triggered by a classic longitudinal study launched in the 1950s by psychiatrists Alexander Thomas and Stella Chess. The focus of the study was on how temperamental qualities influence adjustment throughout life. Chess and Thomas rated young infants on a variety of characteristics, such as activity level, mood, regularity in sleeping and eating, and attention span. They found that about two-thirds of the babies could be classified into one of three broad temperamental patterns: *easy, difficult,* and *slow-to-warm-up.*

The remaining third of the infants were characterized as *average* babies because they did not fit neatly into one of these three categories (Thomas & Chess, 1977).

Easy babies readily adapt to new experiences, generally display positive moods and emotions, and have regular sleeping and eating patterns. *Difficult* babies tend to be intensely emotional, are irritable and fussy, and cry a lot. They also tend to have irregular sleeping and eating patterns. *Slow-to-warm-up* babies have a low activity level, withdraw from new situations and people, and adapt to new experiences very gradually. After studying the same children from infancy through childhood, Thomas and Chess (1986) found that these broad patterns of temperamental qualities are remarkably stable.

Other temperamental patterns have been identified. For example, after decades of research, Jerome Kagan (2010a, 2010b) classified temperament in terms of *reactivity*. *High-reactive* infants react intensely to new experiences, strangers, and novel objects. They tend to be tense, fearful, and inhibited. At the opposite pole are *low-reactive* infants, who tend to be calmer, uninhibited, and bolder. Sociable rather than shy, low-reactive infants are more likely to show interest than fear when exposed to new people, experiences, and objects.

Virtually all temperament researchers agree that individual differences in temperament have a genetic and biological basis (Gagne & others, 2009; Zentner & Shiner, 2012). However, researchers also agree that environmental experiences can modify a child's basic temperament (Stack & others, 2010). As Kagan (2004) points out, "Temperament is not destiny. Many experiences will affect high and low reactive infants as they grow up. Parents who encourage a more sociable, bold persona and discourage timidity will help their high reactive children develop a less-inhibited profile."

Because cultural attitudes affect child-rearing practices, infant temperament can also be affected by cultural beliefs (Kagan, 2010a, 2010b). For example, cross-cultural studies of temperament have found that infants in the United States generally displayed more positive emotion than Russian or Asian infants (Molitor & Hsu, 2011). Why? U.S. parents tend to value and encourage expressions of positive emotions, such as smiling and laughing, in their babies. In contrast, parents in other cultures, including those of Russia and many Asian countries, place less emphasis on the importance of positive emotional expression. Thus, the development of temperamental qualities is yet another example of the complex interaction among genetic and environmental factors.

ATTACHMENT
FORMING EMOTIONAL BONDS

Not long after World War II, Austrian psychiatrist Rene Spitz dramatically showed the detrimental effects of institutionalization on children who were deprived of a relationship with a warm, loving caregiver. Although provided with adequate nutrition, many infants failed to thrive. Psychologist Harry Harlow (1905–1981) showed that it wasn't just human children who suffered from the lack of care. Infant rhesus monkeys who were raised in isolation from other monkeys showed severe pathology. When offered the choice between a wire figure holding bottled milk and a cloth-covered figure, the monkeys would cling to the cloth-covered figure even though it did not provide food. The conclusion: All primates, including human primates, seek out what Harlow (1958) termed *contact comfort* (see photo).

Harlow's findings helped stimulate research on the emotional bond that forms between infants and their caregivers, especially parents, during the first year of life, which is called **attachment**. As conceptualized by attachment theorist John Bowlby (1969, 1988) and psychologist **Mary D. Salter Ainsworth** (1979), attachment relationships serve important functions throughout infancy and, indeed, the lifespan. Ideally, the parent or caregiver functions as a *secure base* for the infant, providing a sense of comfort and security—a safe haven from which the infant can explore and learn about the environment. According to attachment theory, an infant's ability to thrive physically and psychologically depends in large part on the quality of attachment (Ainsworth & others, 1978).

Generally, when parents are consistently warm, responsive, and sensitive to their infant's needs, the infant develops a *secure attachment* to her parents (Belsky, 2006). The infant's expectation that her needs will be met by her caregivers is the most essential ingredient in forming a secure attachment to them. And, studies have confirmed that

temperament Inborn predispositions to consistently behave and react in a certain way.

attachment The emotional bond that forms between an infant and caregiver(s), especially his or her parents.

The importance of "contact comfort" in infancy Rhesus monkeys who were separated in infancy from their mothers preferred cloth mothers over wire mothers—even when the wire mothers provided nourishment through an attached feeding bottle. As American psychologist Harry Harlow (1958) concluded, such findings demonstrated the importance of physical contact or "contact comfort" in infacy. (Such studies would be considered unethical and not allowed today.)

Leen/Time Life Pictures/Getty Images

Mary D. Salter Ainsworth (1913–1999)
Best known for developing the *Strange Situation* procedure to measure attachment, Mary D. Salter Ainsworth originated the concept of the *secure base*. She was also the first researcher in the United States to make extensive, systematic, naturalistic observations of mother–infant interactions in their own homes. Her findings often surprised contemporary psychologists. For example, Ainsworth provided the first evidence demonstrating the importance of the caregiver's responsiveness to the infant's needs (Bretherton & Main, 2000).

The Importance of Attachment Secure attachment in infancy forms the basis for emotional bonds in later childhood. At one time, attachment researchers focused only on the relationship between mothers and infants. Today, the importance of the attachment relationship between fathers and children is also recognized (Lucassen & others, 2011).

sensitivity to the infant's needs is associated with secure attachment across diverse cultures (van IJzendoorn & Sagi-Schwartz, 2008; Vaughn & others, 2007).

In contrast, *insecure attachment* may develop when an infant's parents are neglectful, inconsistent, or insensitive to his moods or behaviors. Insecure attachment seems to reflect an ambivalent or detached emotional relationship between an infant and his parents (Ainsworth, 1979; Isabella & others, 1989).

How do researchers measure attachment? The most commonly used procedure, called the *Strange Situation,* was devised by Ainsworth. The Strange Situation is typically used with infants who are between 1 and 2 years old (Ainsworth & others, 1978). In this technique, the baby and his mother are brought into an unfamiliar room with a variety of toys. A few minutes later, a stranger enters the room. The mother stays with the baby for a few moments, then departs, leaving the baby alone with the stranger. After a few minutes, the mother returns, spends a few minutes in the room, leaves, and returns again. Through a one-way window, observers record the infant's behavior throughout this sequence of separations and reunions.

Psychologists assess attachment by observing the child's behavior toward his mother during the Strange Situation procedure. When his mother is present, the *securely attached* baby will use her as a "secure base" from which to explore the new environment, periodically returning to her side. He will show distress when his mother leaves the room and will greet her warmly when she returns. A securely attached baby is easily soothed by his mother (Ainsworth & others, 1978; Lamb & others, 1985).

In contrast, an *insecurely attached* infant is less likely to explore the environment, even when her mother is present. In the Strange Situation, insecurely attached infants may appear either very anxious or completely indifferent. Such infants tend to ignore or avoid their mothers when they are present. Some insecurely attached infants become extremely distressed when their mothers leave the room. When insecurely attached infants are reunited with their mothers, they are hard to soothe and may resist their mothers' attempts to comfort them.

In studying attachment, psychologists have typically focused on the infant's bond with the mother, since the mother is often the infant's primary caregiver. Still, it's important to note that most fathers are also directly involved with the basic care of their infants and children. As is the case with mothers, children are more likely to be securely attached to fathers who are involved with their care and sensitive to their needs (Brown & others, 2012). In homes where both parents are present, children who are attached to one parent are usually also attached to the other (Furman & Simon, 2004). Finally, infants are capable of forming attachments to other consistent caregivers in their lives, such as relatives or workers at a day-care center. Thus, an infant can form *multiple* attachments.

The quality of attachment during infancy is associated with a variety of long-term effects (Bornstein, 2014; Malekpour, 2007). Preschoolers with a history of being securely attached tend to be more prosocial, empathic, and socially competent than are preschoolers with a history of insecure attachment (Rydell & others, 2005). In middle childhood, children with a history of secure attachment in infancy are better adjusted and have higher levels of social and cognitive development than do children who were insecurely attached in infancy (Kerns & others, 2007; Kerns & Richardson, 2005; Stams & others, 2002). Adolescents who were securely attached in infancy have fewer problems, do better in school, and have more successful relationships with their peers than do adolescents who were insecurely attached in infancy (Laible, 2007; Sroufe, 2002; Sweeney, 2007). And college students in Iran who reported secure attachments to their parents and friends were more likely to also report feeling empathy toward others and having an ability to understand another person's perspective (Teymoori & Shahrazad, 2012).

Because attachment in infancy seems to be so important, psychologists have extensively investigated the impact of day care on attachment. Later in the chapter, we'll take a close look at this issue (see p. 401).

Language Development

Probably no other accomplishment in early life is as astounding as language development. By the time a child reaches 3 years of age, he will have learned thousands of words and the complex rules of his language.

According to linguist Noam Chomsky (1965), every child is born with a biological predisposition to learn language—*any* language. In effect, children possess a "universal grammar"—a basic understanding of the common principles of language organization. Infants are innately equipped not only to understand language but also to extract grammatical rules from what they hear. The key task in the development of language is to learn a set of grammatical rules that allows the child to produce an unlimited number of sentences from a limited number of words.

At birth, infants can distinguish among the speech sounds of all the world's languages, no matter what language is spoken in their homes (Kuhl, 2004; Werker & Desjardins, 1995). And shortly after birth, infants prefer speech over other sounds that humans make (Shultz & others, 2014). But infants lose the ability to distinguish among all possible speech sounds by 10 to 12 months of age. Instead, they can distinguish only among the speech sounds that are present in the language to which they have been exposed (Kuhl & others, 1992; Yoshida & others, 2010). Thus, during the first year of life, infants begin to master the sound structure of their own native language.

ENCOURAGING LANGUAGE DEVELOPMENT

Just as infants seem to be biologically programmed to learn language, parents are predisposed to encourage language development by the way they speak to infants and toddlers. People in every culture, especially parents, use a style of speech called *motherese, parentese,* or *infant-directed speech,* with babies (Bryant & Barrett, 2007; Kuhl, 2004). Characteristics of infant-directed speech appear to be universal. For example, researchers studied a remote culture in Kenya that had no exposure to Western languages like English (Bryant & others, 2012). The Kenyan adults were reliably able to identify when recorded English speakers were communicating with a child versus an adult, even though they couldn't understand the words being said. Furthermore, the Kenyan adults often understood the general intent of what was being said to the child. For example, they could tell when a parent was trying to get an infant's attention.

Infant-directed speech is characterized by very distinct pronunciation, a simplified vocabulary, short sentences, high pitch, and exaggerated intonation and expression. Content is restricted to topics that are familiar to the child, and "baby talk" is often used—simplified words such as "go bye-bye" and "night-night." Often, questions are asked, encouraging a response from the infant (Fernald, 1992).

The adult use of infant-directed speech seems to be instinctive. Deaf mothers who use sign language modify their hand gestures when they communicate with infants and toddlers in a way that is very similar to the infant-directed speech of hearing mothers (Koester & Lahti-Harper, 2010).

And, infants seem to prefer infant-directed speech to a more adult conversational style. The positive response from the young child makes adults more likely to use parentese (Fernald, 1985; Smith & Trainor, 2008). As infants mature, the speech patterns of parents change to fit the child's developing language abilities (McRoberts & others, 2009).

THE COOING AND BABBLING STAGE OF LANGUAGE DEVELOPMENT

As with many other aspects of development, the stages of language development appear to be universal (Kuhl, 2004). In virtually every culture, infants follow the same sequence of language development and at roughly similar ages.

At about 3 months of age, infants begin to "coo," repeating vowel sounds such as *ahhhhh* or *ooooo,* varying the pitch up or down. At about 5 months of age, infants begin to *babble.* They add consonants to the vowels

Romilly Lockyer

> **MYTH ▶ SCIENCE**
>
> Is it true that talking "baby talk" to infants and toddlers won't harm their language development?

Deaf Babies Babble with Their Hands Deaf babies whose parents use American Sign Language (ASL) babble with their hands, rather than their voices (Petitto & others, 2001; Petitto & Marentette, 1991). Just as hearing babies repeat the same syllables over and over, deaf babies repeat the same simple hand gestures. Hearing babies born to deaf parents who are exposed only to sign language also babble with their hands (Petitto & others, 2004). Here, a baby repeats the sign for "A."

comprehension vocabulary The words that are understood by an infant or child.

production vocabulary The words that an infant or child understands and can speak.

and string the sounds together in sometimes long-winded productions of babbling, such as *ba-ba-ba-ba, de-de-de-de,* or *ma-ma-ma-ma.*

When infants babble, they are not simply imitating adult speech. Infants all over the world use the *same* sounds when they babble, including sounds that do not occur in the language of their parents and other caregivers. At around 9 months of age, babies begin to babble more in the sounds specific to their language. Babbling, then, seems to be a biologically programmed stage of language development (Gentilucci & Dalla Volta, 2007; Petitto & others, 2004).

THE ONE-WORD STAGE OF LANGUAGE DEVELOPMENT

Long before babies become accomplished talkers, they understand much of what is said to them. Before they are a year old, most infants can understand simple commands, such as "Bring Daddy the block," even though they cannot *say* the words *bring, Daddy,* or *block.* This reflects the fact that an infant's **comprehension vocabulary** (the words she understands) is much larger than her **production vocabulary** (the words she can say). Generally, infants acquire comprehension of words more than twice as fast as they learn to speak new words.

Somewhere around their first birthday, infants produce their first real words. First words usually refer to concrete objects or people that are important to the child, such

---

SCIENCE VERSUS PSEUDOSCIENCE

Can a DVD Program Your Baby to Be a Genius?

It's a marketing phenomenon: Videos developed specifically for infants and very young toddlers, with catchy titles like *Smart Baby, Brainy Baby,* and *Baby Einstein.* When the first *Baby Einstein* video was released in 1997, ads claimed that it promoted infant brain development (Bronson & Merryman, 2009).

Although the makers of *Baby Einstein* no longer feature such explicit claims in their advertising, most companies that market baby media either imply or state outright that their products are educational and will help infants learn (Wartella & others, 2010). No doubt fueled by the hope that viewing such media would benefit their babies, parents spend hundreds of millions of dollars annually on baby video products in the United States alone (DeLoache & others, 2010; Rideout, 2007).

But how effective are such videos? Do infants learn from watching them? Let's look at the evidence.

The first surprise came from a large study that showed that viewing baby media was actually *negatively correlated* with vocabulary growth in infants. Developmental psychologist Frederick J. Zimmerman and his colleagues (2007) found that babies who *never* watched "educational" videos knew more words than babies who did. In fact, the more time infants spent watching baby media, the fewer words they knew.

Interestingly, the deficit in language skills was associated *only* with watching media designed for infant learning—and not other types of television or video. Baby media, the researchers pointed out, have short scenes, anonymous voice-overs rather than talking characters, and visually engaging but disconnected images. In contrast, shows like *Sesame Street,* which feature recognizable characters and a rich narrative context, *have* been shown to have educational benefits (Richert & others, 2011; Zimmerman & others, 2007).

One potential drawback of this study was that it was *correlational* and relied heavily on parent surveys. So, developmental psychologist Judy DeLoache and her colleagues (2010) designed a rigorously controlled experiment in which the infants would be objectively tested for their knowledge of the specific words that were taught on a popular video.

Encouraging Language Development Research shows that one of the most effective ways to enhance a child's cognitive development is to read to her—even in infancy (Robb & others, 2009). Rather than spending money on expensive videos, buy books or check them out from your local library.

Twelve- to 18-month-old infants were randomly assigned to four groups:

• In the *video-with-no-interaction* condition, the children watched the DVD alone at least five times a week over a 4-week period.

• In the *video-with-interaction* condition, the children watched the DVD with a parent for the same amount of time.

• In the *parent-teaching condition,* the children had no exposure to the video at all. Instead, the parents were given a list of the 25 common words featured on the video and were instructed to "try to teach your child as many of these words as you can in whatever way seems natural to you."

Ruby Washington/The New York Times/Redux

as *mama, daddy,* or *ba-ba* (bottle). First words are also often made up of the syllables that were used in babbling.

During the *one-word stage,* babies use a single word and vocal intonation to stand for an entire sentence. With the proper intonation and context, *baba* can mean "I want my bottle!" "There's my bottle!" or "Where's my bottle?"

Many new parents, eager to accelerate their young children's language and cognitive development, purchase DVDs or videos that claim to educate as well as entertain the growing child. But what do babies learn from baby videos? We take a critical look at this question in the Science Versus Pseudoscience box, "Can a DVD Program Your Baby to Be a Genius?"

THE TWO-WORD STAGE OF LANGUAGE DEVELOPMENT

Around their second birthday, toddlers begin putting words together. During the *two-word stage,* they combine two words to construct a simple "sentence," such as "Mama go," "Where kitty?" and "No potty!" During this stage, the words used are primarily content words—nouns, verbs, and sometimes adjectives or adverbs. Articles (*a, an, the*) and prepositions (such as *in, under, on*) are omitted. Two-word sentences reflect the first understandings of grammar. Although these utterances include only the most essential words, they basically follow a grammatically correct sequence.

- Finally, in the *control condition,* the children were not exposed to the video and the parents were not instructed to try to teach them the words. Instead, they were simply tested for their word knowledge before and after the 4-week period.

Why was including a control condition so important? Put simply, because children naturally learn a lot of words during this period of development. Thus, the control condition provided a benchmark of normal vocabulary growth against which the experimental groups could be compared.

What were the results? As shown in the graph, babies learned the most words from interacting with their parents. In contrast, despite extensive exposure to a video designed to teach them specific words, infants in the video groups did not learn any more new words than did children with no exposure to the video at all.

MYTH ◄ SCIENCE

Is it true that educational videos, like *Baby Einstein,* help babies learn how to talk?

Was it because the infants found the videos boring, or didn't pay attention to them? No. Parents reported that their babies were mesmerized by the program. However, in an interesting twist, DeLoache and her colleagues (2010) found that there was no correlation between how much the parents thought their child learned from the video and how much their child had actually learned. However, the more *parents* liked the video, the more they thought their child had learned from it.

This finding may help explain the many enthusiastic testimonials in marketing materials for baby media. Even though there was no difference in how many words were learned, parents who had a favorable attitude toward the video thought that their children had learned more because of viewing it. One possible explanation is illusory correlation: Parents may misattribute normal developmental progress to the child's exposure to the video.

Since the research on baby media began to be published, some companies, like the producers of *Baby Einstein,* have revised their marketing materials to emphasize the "engaging" nature of the media rather than its "educational" nature. The research is clear: Interacting with a parent or other caregiver is by far the most effective way to increase an infant's cognitive and, especially, language skills.

The bottom line: Save your money and talk to your baby. Better yet, read to him! Several studies have found that the best predictor of infant language is the amount of time that parents spend reading to their children (Robb & others, 2009).

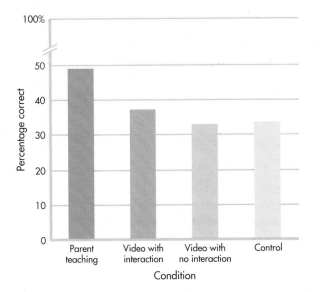

What Do Infants Learn from Baby Videos? Apparently, not much. After four weeks of viewing a best-selling video featuring common words and household objects, babies hadn't learned any more words than infants who had never watched the video. As the researchers conclude, "Significantly more learning occurred in the context of everyday parent-child interactions than in front of television screens."

Source: DeLoache, Judy S.; Chiong, Cynthia; Sherman, Kathleen; Islam, Nadia; Vanderborght, Mieke; Troseth, Georgene L.; Strouse, Gabrielle A.; & O'Doherty, Katherine, Psychological Science, 21:11, pp. 1570–1574, copyright © 2010 by SAGE Publications. Reprinted by Permission of SAGE Publications.

At around 2½ years of age, children move beyond the two-word stage. They rapidly increase the length and grammatical complexity of their sentences. There is a dramatic increase in the number of words they can comprehend and produce. By the age of 3, the typical child has a production vocabulary of more than 3,000 words. Acquiring about a dozen new words per day, a child may have a production vocabulary of more than 10,000 words by school age (Bjorklund, 1995).

Gender Development
BLUE BEARS AND PINK BUNNIES

KEY THEME

Gender refers to the social and cultural aspects associated with being male or female.

KEY QUESTIONS

> What gender differences develop during childhood?
> What are the major theories that explain gender development?

Because the English language is less than precise, we need to clarify a few terms before we begin our discussion of gender development. First, we'll use the term **gender** to refer to the cultural and social meanings that are associated with maleness and femaleness. Thus, **gender role** describes the behaviors, attitudes, and personality traits that a given culture designates as either "masculine" or "feminine" (Wood & Eagly, 2009). Finally, **gender identity** refers to a person's psychological sense of being male or female (Egan & Perry, 2001). When the biological categories of "male" and "female" are being discussed, we'll use the term *sex*.

Being male or female does make a vast difference in most societies. In the United States, newborn babies are often "color-coded" within moments of their birth. When Sandy and Don's daughter was born, she was immediately wrapped in a pink blanket with bunnies, just like the other female infants in the nursery. The male infants were also color-coded by gender—they had blue blankets with little bears. That, of course, is just the beginning of life in a world strongly influenced by gender (see Denny & Pittman, 2007). Many parents may try to raise their children in a "gender-neutral" fashion. However, research shows that even 1-year-olds are already sensitive to subtle gender differences in behavior and mannerisms (Poulin-Dubois & Serbin, 2006). The sections that follow present gender development for typically developing children.

GENDER DIFFERENCES IN CHILDHOOD BEHAVIOR
SPIDER-MAN VERSUS BARBIE

Most toddlers begin using gender labels between the ages of 18 and 21 months. And, roughly between the ages of 2 and 3, children can identify themselves and other children as boys or girls, although the details are still a bit fuzzy to them (Zosuls & others, 2009). Preschoolers don't yet understand that sex is determined by physical characteristics. This is not surprising, considering that the biologically defining sex characteristics—the genitals—are hidden from view most of the time. Instead, young children identify the sexes in terms of external attributes, such as hairstyle, clothing, and activities.

From about the age of 18 months to the age of 2 years, sex differences in behavior begin to emerge (Miller & others, 2006). These differences become more pronounced throughout early childhood. Toddler girls play more with soft toys and dolls, and ask for help from adults more than toddler boys do. Toddler boys play more with blocks and transportation toys, such as trucks and wagons. They also play more actively than do girls (see Ruble & others, 2006).

SW Productions/Getty Images

Color-Coding and Gender Little girls and little boys have a lot in common. Both of these children are clearly excited to be outside riding their scooters. Nevertheless, the little boy's scooter and helmet are blue, and the little girl's scooter and helmet are pink. Why? Is there something "innate" about color preference? Vanessa LoBue and Judy DeLoache (2011) found that little girls don't acquire their preference for pink objects—and little boys their aversion for pink objects—until they are between the ages of 2½ and 3 years old. That's also the age at which they are becoming aware of gender labels and their own gender identity, suggesting that their color preferences are shaped by social expectations.

Liza Donnelly The New Yorker Collection/The Cartoon Bank

*"I don't see liking trucks as a boy thing.
I see it as a liking-trucks thing."*

Paul Bradbury/Getty Images

Stuart Fox/Getty Images

Roughly between the ages of 2 and 3, preschoolers start acquiring gender-role stereotypes for toys, clothing, household objects, games, and work. From the age of about 3 on, there are consistent gender differences in preferred toys and play activities. Boys play more with balls, blocks, and toy vehicles. Girls play more with dolls and domestic toys and engage in more dressing up and art activities. By the age of 3, children have developed a clear preference for toys that are associated with their own sex. This tendency continues throughout childhood (Berenbaum & others, 2008; Freeman, 2007). An exception to this pattern is seen in many transgender children. For example, James, whom you met in the Prologue, always identified as a boy. He described having a "split wardrobe" as a child. This included the girls' clothing that others expected him to wear and the boys' clothing he preferred.

Children also develop a strong preference for playing with members of their own sex—girls with girls and boys with boys (Egan & Perry, 2001; Fridell & others, 2006). It's not uncommon to hear boys refer to girls as "icky" and girls refer to boys as "mean" or "rough." And, in fact, preschool boys *do* play more roughly than girls, cover more territory, and play in larger groups. Throughout the remainder of childhood, boys and girls play primarily with members of their own sex (Hoffmann & Powlishta, 2001; Martin & Ruble, 2010).

According to psychologist Carole Beal (1994), boys and girls seem to almost create separate "social worlds," each with its own style of interaction. They also learn particular ways of interacting that work well with peers of the same sex. For example, boys learn to assert themselves within a group of male friends. Girls tend to establish very close bonds with one or two friends. Girls learn to maintain their close friendships through compromise, conciliation, and verbal conflict resolution.

Children are far more rigid than adults in their beliefs in gender-role stereotypes. Children's strong adherence to gender stereotypes may be a necessary step in developing a gender identity (Halim & Ruble, 2009). Boys are far more rigid than girls in their preferences for toys associated with their own sex. Their attitudes about the sexes are also more rigid than are those held by girls. As girls grow older, they become even more flexible in their views of sex-appropriate activities and attributes, but boys become even less flexible (Schmalz & Kerstetter, 2006).

Girls' more flexible attitude toward gender roles may reflect society's greater tolerance of girls who cross gender lines in attire and behavior. A girl who plays with boys, or who plays with boys' toys, may develop the grudging respect of both sexes. But a boy who plays with girls or with girls' toys may be ostracized by both sexes. Girls are often proud to be labeled a "tomboy," but for many boys, being called a "sissy" is still the ultimate insult (Thorne, 1993). This helps to explain why James's parents were fine with him calling himself a tomboy, a socially acceptable term for girls.

James has observed others' expectations from the vantage point of having lived as both female and male at different points in his life. As a guy, James frequently fields questions about why he is not into stereotypically masculine activities, such as weight lifting. James explains that he hates stereotypes, noting, "I'm not the geek/nerd

Separate Worlds? In early childhood, boys tend to play in groups and favor competitive games and team sports. In contrast, girls tend to establish close relationships with one or two other girls and to cement their friendships by sharing thoughts and feelings. How might such gender differences affect intimate relationships in adolescence and adulthood?

gender The cultural, social, and psychological meanings that are associated with masculinity or femininity.

gender roles The behaviors, attitudes, and personality traits that are designated as either masculine or feminine in a given culture.

gender identity A person's psychological sense of being male or female.

 LaunchPad

Worth Publishers

What causes this girl to choose a particular toy? Watch **Video Activity: Gender Development.**

Are Males More Interested in Sports than Females Are? Anyone who's watched a closely matched girls' basketball game can attest to the fact that girls can be just as competitive in sports as boys. Contrary to what some people think, there is no evidence to support the notion that girls are inherently less interested in sports than boys. During the middle childhood years, from ages 6 to 10, boys and girls are equally interested in sports (Women's Sports Foundation, 2007). Participating in sports enhances the self-esteem of girls as much as it does boys, especially during adolescence (Slutzky & Simpkins, 2009).

Larry Dale Gordon/Getty Images

social learning theory of gender-role development The theory that gender roles are acquired through the basic processes of learning, including reinforcement, punishment, and modeling.

gender schema theory The theory that gender-role development is influenced by the formation of schemas, or mental representations, of masculinity and femininity.

Children are gender detectives who search for cues about gender—who should or should not engage in a particular activity, who can play with whom, and why girls and boys are different. Cognitive perspectives on gender development assume that children are actively searching for ways to find meaning in and make sense of the social world that surrounds them, and they do so by using the gender cues provided by society to help them interpret what they see and hear.

—*Carol Lynn Martin and Diane Ruble (2004)*

stereotype. But, if you are going to stick me in a category, I'm that one. I'm not a jock." And he hates expectations about how he should dress: "Like you are not allowed to wear bright colors anymore because you're a man?"

EXPLAINING GENDER DIFFERENCES
CONTEMPORARY THEORIES

Many theories have been proposed to explain the differing patterns of male and female behavior in our culture and in other cultures (see Reid & others, 2008). Gender theories have included findings and opinions from anthropology, sociology, neuroscience, medicine, philosophy, political science, economics, and religion. (Let's face it, you probably have a few opinions on the issue yourself.) We won't even attempt to cover the full range of ideas. Instead, we'll describe three categories of influential psychological theories.

Historically, Alice Eagly and Wendy Wood (2013) observed, most psychologists have explained gender differences with a focus mostly on sociocultural explanations or mostly on biological explanations. Eagly and Wood argue that *both* viewpoints are important. Based on Eagly and Wood's premise, we will discuss some explanations based primarily on sociocultural factors including social learning theory and gender schema theory, some explanations based primarily on biological factors including evolutionary theory, and interactionist theories that combine both approaches. In Chapter 10 on personality we will discuss Freud's ideas on the development of gender roles.

Social Learning Theory: Learning Gender Roles Based on the principles of learning, the **social learning theory of gender-role development** (also called cognitive social learning theory) contends that gender roles are learned through *reinforcement, punishment,* and *modeling* (Bussey & Bandura, 2004; Hyde, 2014). According to this theory, from a very young age, children are reinforced or rewarded when they display gender-appropriate behavior and punished when they do not.

How do children acquire their understanding of gender norms? Children are exposed to many sources of information about gender roles, including television, video games, books, films, and observation of same-sex adult role models. Children also learn gender differences through *modeling*: They observe and then imitate the sex-typed behavior of significant adults and older children (Bronstein, 2006; Leaper & Friedman, 2007). By observing and imitating such models—whether it's Mom cooking, Dad fixing things around the house, or a male superhero rescuing a helpless female on television—children come to understand that certain activities and attributes are considered more appropriate for one sex than for the other (Martin & Ruble, 2010).

Gender Schema Theory: Constructing Gender Categories Gender schema theory, developed by **Sandra Bem,** incorporates some aspects of social learning theory (Renk & others, 2006; Martin & others, 2004). However, Bem (1981) approached gender-role development from a more strongly cognitive perspective. In contrast to the relatively passive role played by children in social learning theory, **gender schema theory** contends that children *actively* develop mental categories (or *schemas*) for masculinity and femininity (Martin & Ruble, 2004). That is, children actively organize information about other people and appropriate behavior, activities, and attributes into gender categories. Saying that "trucks are for boys and dolls are for girls" is an example of a gender schema. According to gender schema theory, children, like many adults, look at the world through "gender lenses" (Bem, 1987). Gender schemas influence how people pay attention to, perceive, interpret, and remember gender-relevant behavior. Gender schemas also seem to lead children to perceive members of their own sex more favorably than members of the opposite sex (Martin & others, 2002, 2004).

Like schemas in general (see Chapter 6), children's gender schemas do seem to influence what they notice and remember. For example, in a classic experiment, 5-year-olds were shown pictures of children engaged in activities that violated common gender stereotypes, such as girls playing with trucks and boys playing with dolls (Martin & Halverson, 1981, 1983). A few days later, the 5-year-olds "remembered" that the *boys* had been playing with the trucks and the *girls* with the dolls!

Children also readily assimilate new information into their existing gender schemas (Miller & others, 2006). In another classic study, 4- to 9-year-olds were given boxes of gender-neutral gadgets, such as hole punches (Bradbard & others, 1986). But some gadgets were labeled as "girl toys" and some as "boy toys." The boys played more with the "boy" gadgets, and the girls played more with the "girl" gadgets. A week later, the children easily remembered which gadgets went with each sex. They also remembered more information about the gadgets that were associated with their own sex. Simply labeling the objects as belonging to boys or to girls had powerful consequences for the children's behavior and memory—evidence of the importance of gender schemas in learning and remembering new information.

Gender schemas can be subtle. For example, a carefully designed study of almost 60 different children's coloring books found that gender stereotypes were widespread. Males were more likely to be depicted as animals, adults, and superheroes. Females, on the other hand, were more likely to be depicted as children and humans (Fitzpatrick & McPherson, 2010).

Given the gender-schematized world we grow up in, it's not surprising that gender stereotypes remain so pervasive and influential.

Evolutionary Theories Some researchers use primarily biological explanations to explain gender differences in behavior and personality. Perhaps the most prominent of the biological explanations are those that cite evolution as the primary cause of many gender differences. According to the evolutionary approach, gender differences are the result of generations of the dual forces of sexual selection and parental investment (Hyde, 2014). Physical and psychological characteristics—related to either the choice of a mate or the investment in raising one's children—that increased the likelihood of reproductive success tend to become more common. According to evolutionary psychology, behavior and traits are adaptive to the degree that they further the transmission of one's genes to the next generation and beyond.

Evolutionary explanations have been explored for gender differences in a number of areas, including the expression of anger (see Archer, 2004). Specifically, gender

You've Come a Long Way, Baby?
Children's toys continue to reinforce gender stereotypes, sometimes in subtle ways, but also in obvious ways as in these Lego displays.

BIZARRO © 2000 Dan Piraro, Dist. by King Features

ONE SECOND BEFORE THE BLIND DATE

Dist. by Universal Press Synd.

Gender Differences in Mate Preferences? Did the cartoon make you laugh—or at least smile? If it did, it's because you recognized a cultural pattern—the belief that men seek a beautiful, youthful partner, while women are more likely to value financial security and wealth. Cartoons and jokes aside, is there any merit to this observation? *Do* men and women differ in what they look for in a mate?

Challenging Expectations What makes weight lifting a "male" activity? Eleven-year-old weight lifter Charley Craig, the youngest female weight lifter in the United Kingdom, engages in athletic pursuits that many night not expect for a girl. She can lift almost her own body weight! Are biological constraints a factor here?

Laurentiu Garofeanu/Barcroft M/Getty Images

differences in the expression of aggressive tendencies have been observed even in very young children, a suggestion that they may be genetic. Why might this occur? In many species of mammals, including humans, aggression has served a useful evolutionary purpose, increasing the odds that a male will best his fellow males in competition to mate with the females of the species.

We also see evolutionary explanations for behaviors in adulthood, including for mate preferences (Schmitt & others, 2012). To investigate mate preferences, psychologist David Buss (1994, 2009) coordinated a large-scale survey of more than 10,000 people in 37 different cultures. Across all cultures, Buss found, men were more likely than women to value youth and physical attractiveness in a potential mate. In contrast, women were more likely than men to value financial security, access to material resources, high status and education, and good financial prospects.

Buss, an evolutionary psychologist, interprets these gender differences as reflecting the different "mating strategies" of men and women (1995a, 2009, 2011). He contends that men and women face very different "adaptive problems" in selecting a mate. According to Buss (1995b, 1996), the adaptive problem for men is to identify and mate with women who are likely to be successful at bearing their children. Thus, men are more likely to place a high value on youth, because it is associated with fertility, and physical attractiveness, because it signals that the woman is probably physically healthy and has high-quality genes. Women also seek "good" genes, and thus, they value men who are healthy and attractive. But women, on the other hand, have a more pressing need: making sure that the children they do bear survive to carry their genes into future generations (Buss, 2011). Thus, they seek men who possess the resources that the women and their offspring will need to survive.

The evolutionary explanation of sex differences, whether in mate preferences or other areas, is controversial (Confer & others, 2010). Some psychologists argue that it is overly deterministic and does not sufficiently acknowledge the role of culture, gender-role socialization, and other social factors (Eagly & Wood, 2011; Pedersen & others, 2010).

With respect to his research on mate preferences, Buss (2011) reported that his extensive survey also found that men and women in all 37 cultures agreed that the *most* important factor in choosing a mate was mutual attraction and love. And both sexes rated kindness, intelligence, emotional stability, health, and a pleasing personality as more important than a prospective mate's financial resources or good looks.

Buss also flatly states that explaining some of the reasons that might underlie sexual inequality does *not* mean that sexual inequality is natural, correct, or justified. Rather, evolutionary psychologists believe that we must understand the conditions that foster sexual inequality in order to overcome or change those conditions (Buss & Schmitt, 2011).

Interactionist Theories Eagly and Wood (2013) point out that there are many areas of agreement between those who favor sociocultural explanations and those who favor biological explanations. They encourage the development of interactionist theories that explain a given observation using a combination of explanations.

Let's look at one example highlighted by Eagly and Wood (2013)—the division of labor along gender lines. Eagly and Wood observe that men tend to be physically larger and stronger than women and that women are biologically responsible for reproduction. These biological differences mean that it can be more efficient for men and boys to be responsible for some activities—say, those that involve heavy lifting—and women and girls to be responsible for others—say, those that involve nurturing an infant. Eagly and Wood also point out that there are social and psychological factors that create expectations in society that make the "division of labor seem natural and inevitable" (2013). These expectations often start in childhood.

For example, since James began living as a man, several people have wondered why he does not engage in masculine athletic feats. "You should lift weights," he's been told as a man, but not as a woman. This suggestion draws on gender role beliefs about what women and men *should* do, rather than examining James's biological abilities—or his preferences! Indeed, James's biological abilities just before and after his transition to living as a man would have been the same. Conversely, your author Susan has seen girls tasked with caring for younger siblings because the boys were thought biologically incapable of soothing a baby.

Biology plays a role in what women and men do, but both women and men might be prevented from taking part in certain activities for reasons other than biological or physical limitations. Psychological and socially driven beliefs about talents and abilities can also limit opportunities and choices. From the interactionist perspective, it is the interplay of biological constraints and psychological and social constraints that drives the division of labor.

Eagly and Wood (2013) admit that it is challenging to incorporate the many biological and sociocultural influences that might drive any given behavior. However, they see attempts at integrating explanations from the two categories as essential to gaining a fuller understanding of the psychology of sex and gender.

GENDER IDENTITY

As we have seen in this section of the chapter, boys and girls and men and women are different, but they are not polar opposites. Instead, there is a great deal of overlap between them. Rather than being black and white, personality and biological differences more often reflect shades of gray. But whether those shades of gray tend to be light or dark, most people develop a clear sense of gender identity as either male *or* female. And, for most people, their sense of gender identity is consistent with their physical anatomy. But for a significant minority of people, including James, gender identity and physical anatomy are not consistent. In an increasingly visible variation on gender identity, **transgender** individuals are anatomically "normal"—they are biologically male or female. However, their gender identity is in conflict with their biological sex (Sohn & Bosinski, 2007). A *transgender man,* such as James, is an anatomical female who identifies with or wishes to become male. A *transgender woman* is an anatomical male who identifies with or wishes to become female. And, a *cisgender man* or *woman* refers to a person whose anatomy matches their gender identity, such as a biological woman who identifies as a woman. Because this situation is viewed as the norm, the term is infrequently used.

Like James, the typical transgender person has the strong feeling, often present since childhood, of having been born in the body of the wrong sex (Cohen-Kettenis & Pfafflin, 2010; Zucker & Cohen-Kettenis, 2008). Gender identity is distinct from sexual orientation. A transgender person may be homosexual, heterosexual, or bisexual. James, for example, identifies as a straight man, and is romantically interested in women.

Transgender individuals, including James, continue to face discrimination and prejudice many aspects of their lives. Elsa, a young transgender girl living in Colorado, hated when people called her a boy. When she tried to correct them, she was teased. She told her parents, "I wish I didn't exist" (Brown, 2015). But some would argue that the lives of transgender people are not all that different from those of people with a more conventional gender identity. Remember that James, like others at his stage of development, wants a house and a family. He is an emerging adult, a stage we will discuss later in this chapter, and is actively trying to find his place in the world. Being transgender is just one part of his development.

MYTH ◀ SCIENCE

Is it true that transgender people are homosexual?

transgender Condition in which a person's psychological gender identity conflicts with his or her biological sex.

Cognitive Development

KEY THEME

According to Piaget's theory, children progress through four distinct cognitive stages, and each stage marks a shift in how they think and understand the world.

KEY QUESTIONS

› What are Piaget's four stages of cognitive development?

› What are three criticisms of Piaget's theory?

› How do Vygotsky's ideas about cognitive development differ from Piaget's theory?

Just as children advance in motor skill and language development, they also develop increasing sophistication in cognitive processes—thinking, remembering, and processing information. The most influential theory of cognitive development is that of Swiss psychologist **Jean Piaget.** Originally trained as a biologist, Piaget (1961) combined a boundless curiosity about the nature of the human mind with a gift for scientific observation (Boeree, 2006).

Piaget (1952, 1972) believed that children *actively* try to make sense of their environment rather than passively soaking up information about the world. To Piaget, many of the "cute" things children say actually reflect their sincere attempts to make sense of their world. In fact, Piaget carefully observed his own three children in developing his theory and published three books about them (Boeree, 2006).

According to Piaget, children progress through four distinct cognitive stages: the *sensorimotor stage,* from birth to age 2; the *preoperational stage,* from age 2 to age 7; the *concrete operational stage,* from age 7 to age 11; and the *formal operational stage,* which begins during adolescence and continues into adulthood. As a child advances to a new stage, his thinking is *qualitatively different* from that of the previous stage. In other words, each new stage represents a fundamental shift in *how* the child thinks and understands the world.

Piaget saw this progression of cognitive development as a continuous, gradual process. As a child develops and matures, she does not simply acquire more information. Rather, she develops a new understanding of the world in each progressive stage, building on the understandings acquired in the previous stage (Piaget, 1961). As the child *assimilates* new information and experiences, she eventually changes her way of thinking to *accommodate* new knowledge (Piaget, 1961).

Piaget (1971) believed that these stages were biologically programmed to unfold at their respective ages. He also believed that children in every culture progressed through the same sequence of stages at roughly similar ages. However, Piaget also recognized that hereditary and environmental differences could influence the rate at which a given child progressed through the stages.

For example, a "bright" child may progress through the stages faster than a child who is less intellectually capable. A child whose environment provides ample and varied opportunities for exploration is likely to progress faster than a child who has limited environmental opportunities. Thus, even though the sequence of stages is universal, there can be individual variation in the rate of cognitive development.

Bill Anderson/Science Source

Jean Piaget Swiss psychologist Jean Piaget (1896–1980) viewed the child as a little scientist, actively exploring his or her world. Much of Piaget's theory was based on his careful observation of individual children, especially his own children.

THE SENSORIMOTOR STAGE

The **sensorimotor stage** extends from birth until about 2 years of age. During this stage, infants acquire knowledge about the world through actions that allow them to directly experience and manipulate objects. Infants discover a wealth of very practical sensory knowledge, such as what objects look like and how they taste, feel, smell, and sound.

Infants in this stage also expand their practical knowledge about motor actions— reaching, grasping, pushing, pulling, and pouring. In the process, they gain a basic

sensorimotor stage In Piaget's theory, the first stage of cognitive development, from birth to about age 2; the period during which the infant explores the environment and acquires knowledge through sensing and manipulating objects.

understanding of the effects their own actions can produce, such as pushing a button to turn on the television or knocking over a pile of blocks to make them crash and tumble.

At the beginning of the sensorimotor stage, the infant's motto seems to be "Out of sight, out of mind." An object exists only if she can directly sense it. For example, if a 4-month-old infant knocks a ball underneath the couch and it rolls out of sight, she will not look for it. Piaget interpreted this response to mean that to the infant, the ball no longer exists.

However, by the end of the sensorimotor stage, children acquire a new cognitive understanding, called object permanence. **Object permanence** is the understanding that an object continues to exist even if it can't be seen. Now the infant will actively search for a ball that she has watched roll out of sight (Mash & others, 2006). Infants gradually acquire an understanding of object permanence as they gain experience with objects, as their memory abilities improve, and as they develop mental representations of the world, which Piaget called *schemas* (Perry & others, 2008).

This Tastes Different! During the sensorimotor stage, infants and toddlers rely on their basic sensory and motor skills to explore and make sense of the world around them. Piaget believed that infants and toddlers acquire very practical understandings about the world as they touch, feel, taste, push, pull, twist, turn, and manipulate the objects they encounter.

THE PREOPERATIONAL STAGE

The **preoperational stage** lasts from roughly age 2 to age 7. In Piaget's theory, the word *operations* refers to logical mental activities. Thus, the "preoperational" stage is a prelogical stage.

The hallmark of preoperational thought is the child's capacity to engage in symbolic thought. **Symbolic thought** refers to the ability to use words, images, and symbols to represent the world. One indication of the expanding capacity for symbolic thought is the child's impressive gains in language during this stage.

The child's increasing capacity for symbolic thought is also apparent in her use of fantasy and imagination while playing. A discarded box becomes a spaceship, a house, or a fort as children imaginatively take on the roles of different characters. Some children even create an imaginary companion (Taylor & others, 2009). One study of children's role playing documented both imaginary friends like "Pajama Sam," who has "rainbow hair, blue and yellow eyes, [and] sometimes has a bird on his head" and objects that come to life, such as "Marshmallow," who is "a stuffed dog with orange hair who is afraid of the dark, [and] likes to ride in cars, and go camping" (Taylor & others, 2013).

Still, the preoperational child's understanding of symbols remains immature. A 2-year-old shown a picture of a flower, for example, may try to smell it. A young child may be puzzled by the notion that a map symbolizes an actual location—as in the cartoon on page 382. In short, preoperational children are still actively figuring out the relationship between symbols and the actual objects they represent.

The thinking of preoperational children often displays **egocentrism.** By *egocentrism,* Piaget did not mean selfishness or conceit. Rather, egocentric children lack the ability to consider events from another person's point of view. Thus, the young child genuinely thinks that Grandma would like a new Lego set or a video game for her upcoming birthday because that's what *he* wants. Egocentric thought is also operating when the child silently nods his head in answer to Grandpa's question on the telephone.

The preoperational child's thought is also characterized by irreversibility and centration. **Irreversibility** means that the child cannot

object permanence The understanding that an object continues to exist even when it can no longer be seen.

preoperational stage In Piaget's theory, the second stage of cognitive development, which lasts from about age 2 to age 7; characterized by increasing use of symbols and prelogical thought processes.

symbolic thought The ability to use words, images, and symbols to represent the world.

egocentrism In Piaget's theory, the inability to take another person's perspective or point of view.

irreversibility In Piaget's theory, the inability to mentally reverse a sequence of events or logical operations.

Preoperational Thinking: Manipulating Mental Symbols The young child's increasing capacity for symbolic thought is delightfully reflected in symbolic play and deferred imitation. In *symbolic play,* one object stands for another. A box can become a bus, a house, or a rocket ship. *Deferred imitation* is the capacity to repeat an action observed earlier, such as pretending to steer a car or feed a doll.

centration In Piaget's theory, the tendency to focus, or *center*, on only one aspect of a situation and ignore other important aspects of the situation.

conservation In Piaget's theory, the understanding that two equal quantities remain equal even though the form or appearance is rearranged, as long as nothing is added or subtracted.

FOR BETTER OR FOR WORSE

When Laura was almost 3, your author Sandy and her daughter Laura were investigating the tadpoles in the creek behind their home. "Do you know what tadpoles become when they grow up? They become frogs," Sandy explained. Laura looked very serious. After considering this new bit of information for a few moments, she asked, "Laura grow up to be a frog, too?"

mentally reverse a sequence of events or logical operations back to the starting point. For example, the child doesn't understand that adding "3 plus 1" and adding "1 plus 3" refer to the same logical operation. **Centration** refers to the tendency to focus, or center, on only one aspect of a situation, usually a perceptual aspect. In doing so, the child ignores other relevant aspects of the situation.

The classic demonstration of both irreversibility and centration involves a task devised by Piaget. When Sandy and Don's daughter Laura was 5, they tried this task with her. First, they showed her two identical glasses, each containing exactly the same amount of liquid. Laura easily recognized the two amounts of liquid as being the same.

Then, while Laura watched intently, Sandy poured the liquid from one of the glasses into a third container that was much taller and narrower than the others. "Which container," Sandy asked, "holds more liquid?" Like any other preoperational child, Laura answered confidently, "The taller one!" Even when the procedure was repeated, reversing the steps over and over again, Laura remained convinced that the taller container held more liquid than did the shorter container.

This classic demonstration illustrates the preoperational child's inability to understand conservation. The principle of **conservation** holds that two equal physical quantities remain equal even if the appearance of one is changed, as long as nothing is added or subtracted (Piaget & Inhelder, 1974). Because of *centration*, the child cannot simultaneously consider the height and the width of the liquid in the container. Instead, the child focuses on only one aspect of the situation, the height of the liquid. And because of *irreversibility*, the child cannot cognitively reverse the series of events, mentally returning the poured liquid to its original container. Thus, she fails to understand that the two amounts of liquid are still the same.

THE CONCRETE OPERATIONAL STAGE

With the beginning of the **concrete operational stage**, at around age 7, children become capable of true logical thought. They are much less egocentric in their thinking, can reverse mental operations, and can focus simultaneously on two aspects of

Piaget's Conservation Task A five-year-old compares the liquid in the two short beakers, then watches as liquid is poured into a tall, narrow beaker. When asked which has more, the girl insists that there is more liquid in the tall beaker. As Piaget's classic task demonstrates, the average 5-year-old doesn't grasp this principle of conservation.

a problem. In short, they understand the principle of conservation. When presented with two rows of pennies, each row equally spaced, concrete operational children understand that the number of pennies in each row remains the same even when the spacing between the pennies in one row is increased.

As the name of this stage implies, thinking and use of logic tend to be limited to concrete reality—to tangible objects and events. Children in the concrete operational stage often have difficulty thinking logically about hypothetical situations or abstract ideas. For example, an 8-year-old will explain the concept of friendship in very tangible terms, such as "Friendship is when someone plays with me." In effect, the concrete operational child's ability to deal with abstract ideas and hypothetical situations is limited to his or her personal experiences and actual events.

THE FORMAL OPERATIONAL STAGE

At the beginning of adolescence, children enter the **formal operational stage.** In terms of problem solving, the formal operational adolescent is much more systematic and logical than the concrete operational child (Kuhn & Franklin, 2006). Formal operational thought reflects the ability to think logically even when dealing with abstract concepts or hypothetical situations (Kuhn, 2008; Piaget, 1972; Piaget & Inhelder, 1958). In contrast to the concrete operational child, the formal operational adolescent explains *friendship* by emphasizing more global and abstract characteristics, such as mutual trust, empathy, loyalty, consistency, and shared beliefs (Harter, 1990).

But, like the development of cognitive abilities during infancy and childhood, formal operational thought emerges only gradually. Formal operational thought continues to increase in sophistication throughout adolescence and adulthood. Although an adolescent may deal effectively with abstract ideas in one domain of knowledge, his thinking may not reflect the same degree of sophistication in other areas. Piaget (1973) acknowledged that even among many adults, formal operational thinking is often limited to areas in which they have developed expertise or a special interest. Table 9.2 on the next page summarizes Piaget's stages of cognitive development.

CRITICISMS OF PIAGET'S THEORY

Piaget's theory has inspired hundreds, if not thousands, of research studies, and he is considered one of the most important scientists of the twentieth century (Perret-Clermont & Barrelet, 2008). Generally, scientific research has supported Piaget's most fundamental idea: that infants, young children, and older children use distinctly

Think Like a SCIENTIST

Children's cognition is also affected by environmental factors. For example, what classroom decor better helps kindergarten students learn? Go to LaunchPad: Resources to **Think Like a Scientist** about **Learning Environments**.

 LaunchPad

concrete operational stage In Piaget's theory, the third stage of cognitive development, which lasts from about age 7 to adolescence; characterized by the ability to think logically about concrete objects and situations.

formal operational stage In Piaget's theory, the fourth stage of cognitive development, which lasts from adolescence through adulthood; characterized by the ability to think logically about abstract principles and hypothetical situations.

From Concrete Operations to Formal Operations Logical thinking is evident during the concrete operational stage but develops more fully during the formal operational stage. At about the age of 12, the young person becomes capable of applying logical thinking to hypothetical situations and abstract concepts, such as the principles of molecular bonds in this chemistry class. But, as is true of each of Piaget's stages, new cognitive abilities emerge gradually. Having a tangible model to manipulate helps this student grasp abstract concepts related to the brain.

Fuse/Getty Images

TABLE 9.2

Piaget's Stages of Cognitive Development

Stage	Characteristics of the Stage	Major Change of the Stage
Sensorimotor (0–2 years)	Acquires understanding of object permanence. First understandings of cause-and-effect relationships.	Development proceeds from reflexes to active use of sensory and motor skills to explore the environment.
Preoperational (2–7 years)	Symbolic thought emerges. Language development occurs (2–4 years). Thought and language both tend to be egocentric. Cannot solve conservation problems.	Development proceeds from understanding simple cause-and-effect relationships to prelogical thought processes involving the use of imagination and symbols to represent objects, actions, and situations.
Concrete operations (7–11 years)	Reversibility attained. Can solve conservation problems. Logical thought develops and is applied to concrete problems. Cannot solve complex verbal problems and hypothetical problems.	Development proceeds from prelogical thought to logical solutions to concrete problems.
Formal operations (adolescence through adulthood)	Logically solves all types of problems. Thinks scientifically. Solves complex verbal and hypothetical problems. Is able to think in abstract terms.	Development proceeds from logical solving of concrete problems to logical solving of all classes of problems, including abstract problems.

Try **Concept Practice: Piaget and Conservation** for video demonstrations of Piaget's conservation principles.

different cognitive abilities to construct their understanding of the world. However, other aspects of Piaget's theory have been challenged.

Criticism 1: Piaget underestimated the cognitive abilities of infants and young children.

To test for object permanence, Piaget would show an infant an object, cover it with a cloth, and then observe whether the infant tried to reach under the cloth for the object. Using this procedure, Piaget found that it wasn't until an infant was about 9 months old that she behaved as if the object continued to exist after it was hidden.

But what if the infant "knew" that the object was under the cloth but simply lacked the physical coordination to reach for it? How could you test this hypothesis? Rather than using manual tasks to assess object permanence and other cognitive abilities, **Renée Baillargeon** developed a method based on *visual* tasks. Baillargeon's research is based on the premise that infants, like adults, will look longer at "surprising" events that appear to contradict their understanding of the world (Baillargeon & others, 2011, 2012).

In this research paradigm, the infant first watches an *expected event,* which is consistent with the understanding that is being tested. Then, the infant is shown an *unexpected event.* If the unexpected event violates the infant's understanding of physical principles, he should be surprised and look longer at the unexpected event than the expected event.

Figure 9.4 shows one of Baillargeon's classic tests of object permanence, conducted with Julie DeVos (Baillargeon & DeVos, 1991). If the infant understands that objects continue to exist even when they are hidden, she will be surprised when the tall carrot unexpectedly does *not* appear in the window of the panel.

Using variations of this basic experimental procedure, Baillargeon and her colleagues have shown that infants as young as 2½ months of age display object permanence (Baillargeon & others, 2009; Luo & others, 2009). This is more than six months earlier than the age at which Piaget believed infants first showed evidence of object permanence.

Possible Event   Impossible Event

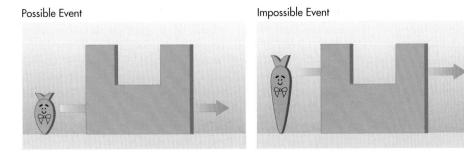

FIGURE 9.4 Testing Object Permanence in Babies How can you test object permanence in infants who are too young to reach for a hidden object? Three-and-a-half-month-old infants initially watched a possible event: The short carrot passes from one side of the panel to the other without appearing in the window. In the impossible event, the tall carrot does the same. Because the infants are surprised and look longer at the impossible event, Baillargeon and DeVos (1991) concluded that the infants had formed a mental representation of the existence, height, and path of each carrot as it moved behind the panel— the essence of object permanence (Baillargeon, 2004).

Piaget's discoveries laid the groundwork for our understanding of cognitive development. However, as developmental psychologists Jeanne Shinskey and Yuko Munakata (2005) observe, today's researchers recognize that "what infants appear to know depends heavily on how they are tested."

Criticism 2: Piaget underestimated the impact of the social and cultural environment on cognitive development.

In contrast to Piaget, the Russian psychologist **Lev Vygotsky** believed that cognitive development is strongly influenced by social and cultural factors. Vygotsky formulated his theory of cognitive development at about the same time Piaget formulated his. However, Vygotsky's writings did not become available in the West until many years after his untimely death from tuberculosis in 1934 (Rowe & Wertsch, 2002; van Geert, 1998).

Vygotsky agreed with Piaget that children may be able to reach a particular cognitive level through their own efforts. However, Vygotsky (1978, 1987) argued that children are able to attain higher levels of cognitive development through the support and instruction that they receive from other people. Researchers have confirmed that social interactions, especially with older children and adults, play a significant role in a child's cognitive development (Psaltis & others, 2009; Wertsch, 2008). Interventions aimed at increasing social interactions seem to be particularly important for children in lower-income countries, who tend to have fewer social interactions than children in higher-income countries do (Aboud & Yousafzai, 2015).

One of Vygotsky's important ideas was his notion of the **zone of proximal development.** This refers to the gap between what children can accomplish on their own and what they can accomplish with the help of others who are more competent (Holzman, 2009). Note that the word *proximal* means "nearby," indicating that the assistance provided goes just slightly beyond the child's current abilities. Such guidance can help "stretch" the child's cognitive abilities to new levels.

Cross-cultural studies have shown that cognitive development is strongly influenced by the skills that are valued and encouraged in a particular environment, such as the ability to weave, hunt, or collaborate with others (Saxe & de Kirby, 2014; Wells, 2009). Such findings suggest that Piaget's stages are not as universal and culture-free as some researchers had once believed (Cole & Packer, 2011).

Criticism 3: Piaget overestimated the degree to which people achieve formal operational thought processes.

Researchers have found that many adults display abstract-hypothetical thinking only in limited areas of knowledge, and that some adults never display formal operational thought processes at all (see Kuhn, 2008; Molitor & Hsu, 2011). College students, for example, may not display formal operational thinking when given problems outside their major, as when an English major is presented with a physics problem (DeLisi & Staudt, 1980). Late in his life, Piaget (1972, 1973) suggested that formal operational thinking might not be a universal phenomenon but, instead, is the product of an individual's expertise in a specific area.

Lev Vygotsky Russian psychologist Lev Vygotsky was born in 1896, the same year as Piaget. He died in 1934 of tuberculosis. Recent decades have seen a resurgence of interest in Vygotsky's theoretical writings, which emphasized the impact of social and cultural factors on cognitive development. According to Vygotsky, cognitive development always takes place within a social and cultural context.

Sovfoto/Eastfoto

zone of proximal development In Vygotsky's theory of cognitive development, the difference between what children can accomplish on their own and what they can accomplish with the help of others who are more competent.

information-processing model of cognitive development The model that views cognitive development as a process that is continuous over the lifespan and that studies the development of basic mental processes such as attention, memory, and problem solving.

adolescence The transitional stage between late childhood and the beginning of adulthood, during which sexual maturity is reached.

puberty The stage of adolescence in which an individual reaches sexual maturity and becomes physiologically capable of sexual reproduction.

primary sex characteristics Sexual organs that are directly involved in reproduction, such as the uterus, ovaries, penis, and testicles.

Girls Get a Head Start These two eighth-graders are the same age! In terms of the progress of sexual and physical maturation, girls are usually about two years ahead of boys.

Rather than distinct stages of cognitive development, some developmental psychologists emphasize the **information-processing model of cognitive development.** This model focuses on the development of fundamental mental processes, such as attention, memory, and problem solving (Munakata & others, 2006). In this approach, cognitive development is viewed as a process of continuous change over the lifespan (Courage & Howe, 2002; Craik & Bialystok, 2006). Through life experiences, we continue to acquire new knowledge, including more sophisticated cognitive skills and strategies. In turn, this improves our ability to process, learn, and remember information.

With the exceptions that have been noted, Piaget's observations of the changes in children's cognitive abilities are fundamentally accurate. His description of the distinct cognitive changes that occur during infancy and childhood ranks as one of the most outstanding contributions to developmental psychology.

❯ Test your understanding of **Infancy and Childhood** with *LEARNING*Curve.

Adolescence

KEY THEME
Adolescence is the stage that marks the transition from childhood to adulthood.

KEY QUESTIONS
❯ What factors affect the timing of puberty?
❯ What characterizes adolescent relationships with parents and peers?
❯ What is Erikson's psychosocial theory of lifespan development?

Adolescence is the transitional stage between late childhood and the beginning of adulthood. Although it can vary by individual, culture, and gender, adolescence usually begins around age 11 or 12. It is a transition marked by sweeping physical, social, and cognitive changes as the individual moves toward independence and adult responsibilities. Outwardly, the most noticeable changes that occur during adolescence are the physical changes that accompany the development of sexual maturity. We'll begin by considering those changes, then turn to the aspects of social development during adolescence. Following that discussion, we'll consider some of the cognitive changes of adolescence, including identity formation.

Physical and Sexual Development

Nature seems to have a warped sense of humor when it comes to **puberty,** the physical process of attaining sexual maturation and reproductive capacity that begins during the early adolescent years. As you may well remember, physical development during adolescence sometimes proceeds unevenly. Feet and hands get bigger before legs and arms do. The torso typically develops last, so shirts and blouses sometimes don't fit quite right. And the left and right sides of the body can grow at different rates. The resulting lopsided effect can be quite distressing: One ear, foot, testicle, or breast may be noticeably larger than the other. Thankfully, such asymmetries tend to even out by the end of adolescence. For transgender people like James, however, puberty offers an additional challenge. Their bodies are developing into the gender that they do not identify with.

Although nature's game plan for physical change during adolescence may seem haphazard, puberty actually tends to follow a predictable sequence for each sex. These changes are summarized in Table 9.3.

PRIMARY AND SECONDARY SEX CHARACTERISTICS

The physical changes of puberty fall into two categories. Internally, puberty involves the development of the **primary sex characteristics,** which are the sex organs that

TABLE 9.3

The Typical Sequence of Puberty

Girls	Average Age	Boys	Average Age
Ovaries increase production of estrogen and progesterone.	9	Testes increase production of testosterone.	10
Internal sex organs begin to grow larger.	9½	External sex organs begin to grow larger.	11
Breast development begins.	10	Production of sperm and first ejaculation	13
Peak height spurt	12	Peak height spurt	14
Peak muscle and organ growth, including widening of hips	12½	Peak muscle and organ growth, including broadening of shoulders	14½
Menarche (first menstrual period)	12½	Voice lowers.	15
First ovulation (release of fertile egg)	13½	Facial hair appears.	16

SOURCE: Data from Brooks-Gunn and Reiter (1990).

secondary sex characteristics Sexual characteristics that develop during puberty and are not directly involved in reproduction but differentiate between the sexes, such as male facial hair and female breast development.

adolescent growth spurt The period of accelerated growth during puberty, involving rapid increases in height and weight.

menarche (meh-NAR-kee) A female's first menstrual period, which occurs during puberty.

are directly involved in reproduction. For example, the female's uterus and the male's testes enlarge in puberty. Externally, development of the **secondary sex characteristics,** which are not directly involved in reproduction, signals increasing sexual maturity. Secondary sex characteristics include changes in height, weight, and body shape; the appearance of body hair and voice changes; and, in girls, breast development.

As you can see in Table 9.3, females are typically about two years ahead of males in terms of physical and sexual maturation. For example, the period of marked acceleration in weight and height gains, called the **adolescent growth spurt,** occurs about two years earlier in females than in males. Much to the chagrin of many sixth- and seventh-grade boys, it's not uncommon for their female classmates to be both heavier and taller than they are.

The statistical averages in Table 9.3 are informative, but—because they are only averages—they cannot convey the normal range of individual variation in the timing of pubertal events (see Ellis, 2004). For example, a female's first menstrual period, termed **menarche,** typically occurs around age 12 or 13, but menarche may take place as early as age 9 or 10 or as late as age 16 or 17. For boys, the testicles typically begin enlarging around age 11 or 12, but the process can begin before age 9 or after age 14.

Thus, it's entirely possible for some adolescents to have already completed physical and sexual maturation before their classmates have even begun puberty. Yet they would all be considered well within the normal age range for puberty (Sun & others, 2002).

Less obvious than the outward changes associated with puberty are the sweeping changes occurring in another realm of physical development: the adolescent's brain. We discuss these developments in the Focus on Neuroscience on page 388.

FACTORS AFFECTING THE TIMING OF PUBERTY

Although you might be tempted to think that the onset of puberty is strictly a matter of biological programming, researchers have found that both genetics and environmental factors play a role in the timing of puberty. Genetic evidence includes the observation that girls usually experience menarche at about the same age their mothers did (Ersoy & others, 2005). And, not surprisingly, the timing of pubertal changes tends to be closer for identical twins than for nontwin siblings (Mustanski & others, 2004).

"Dad, when will I be old enough to shave?"

FOCUS ON NEUROSCIENCE

The Adolescent Brain: A Work in Progress

For many adolescents, the teenage years, especially the early ones, seem to seesaw between moments of exhilaration and exasperation. Impressive instances of insightful behavior are counterbalanced by impulsive decisions made with no consideration of the potential risks or consequences. Many psychologists believe that an important factor in explaining erratic and risky behavior involves the still-developing adolescent brain (Casey, 2015).

To track changes in the developing brain, neuroscientists Jay Giedd, Elizabeth Sowell, Paul Thompson, and their colleagues have used MRI to repeatedly scan the brains of normal kids and teenagers. One striking insight produced by their studies is that the human brain goes through not one but two distinct spurts of brain development—one during prenatal development and one during late childhood just prior to puberty (Giedd, 2008; Gogtay & others, 2004; Lenroot & Giedd, 2006).

Earlier in the chapter, we described how new neurons are produced at an astonishing rate during the first months of prenatal development. By the sixth month of prenatal development, there is a vast overabundance of neurons in the fetal brain. During the final months of prenatal development, neurons that don't make connections are "pruned" or eliminated. During infancy and early childhood, the brain's outer gray matter continues to develop and grow. The tapestry of interconnections between neurons becomes much more intricate as dendrites and axon terminals multiply and branch to extend their reach.

White matter also increases as groups of neurons develop *myelin*, the white, fatty covering that insulates some axons, speeding communication between neurons.

Outwardly, these brain changes are reflected in the increasing cognitive and physical capabilities of the child. But in the brain itself, the "use-it-or-lose-it" principle is at work: Unused neuron circuits are being pruned. While it may seem counterintuitive, the loss of unused neurons and neuronal connections actually improves brain functioning by making the remaining neurons more efficient in processing information.

By 6 years of age, the child's brain is about 95 percent of its adult size. The longitudinal MRI studies of normal kids and adolescents revealed that a *second* wave of gray matter overproduction occurred just prior to puberty. This late childhood surge of cortical gray matter is not due to the production of new neurons. Rather, the size, complexity, and connections among neurons all increase.

ZITS

Environmental factors, such as nutrition and health, also influence the onset of puberty. Generally, well-nourished and healthy children begin puberty earlier than do children who have experienced serious health problems or inadequate nutrition. As living standards and health care have improved, the average age of puberty has steadily been decreasing in many countries over the past century.

For example, 150 years ago the average age of menarche in the United States and other developed countries was about 17 years old. Today it is about 13 years old. Boys, too, are beginning the physical changes of puberty about a year earlier today than they did in the 1960s (Irwin, 2005).

Body size, nutrition, and degree of physical activity are also related to the timing of puberty (Aksglaede & others, 2009; Cheng & others, 2012). In general, heavier children and those with poorer dietary habits begin puberty earlier than do lean children and those who tend to eat healthier food. Girls who are involved in physically demanding athletic activities, such as gymnastics, figure skating, dancing, and competitive running, can experience delays in menarche of up to two years beyond the average age (Brooks-Gunn, 1988; Georgopoulos & others, 2004).

Interestingly, the timing of puberty is also influenced by the absence of the biological father in the home. Several studies have found that girls raised in homes in which the biological father is absent tend to experience puberty earlier than girls raised in homes where the father is present (Bogaert, 2005, 2008; Neberich & others, 2010). In another large study, *both* boys and girls experienced accelerated physical development in homes where fathers were absent (Mustanski & others, 2004).

Why would the absence of a father affect the timing of puberty? A stressful home environment may play a role. In families marked by marital conflict and strife, girls

This increase in gray matter peaks at about age 11 for girls and age 12 for boys (Toga & others, 2006). And this surge is followed by a *second* round of neuronal pruning during the teenage years (Giedd & others, 2009; Toga & others, 2006).

Pruning Gray Matter from Back to Front

The color-coded series of brain images below shows the course of brain development from ages 5 to 20 (Gogtay & others, 2004). Red indicates more gray matter; blue indicates less gray matter.

The MRI images reveal that as the brain matures, neuronal connections are pruned and gray matter diminishes in a back-to-front wave. As pruning occurs, the connections that remain are strengthened and reinforced, and the amount of white matter in the brain steadily increases (Giedd, 2009; Schmithorst & Yuan, 2010). More specifically, the first brain areas to mature are at the extreme front and back of the brain. These areas are involved with very basic functions, such as processing sensations and movement. The next brain areas to mature are the *parietal lobes*, which are involved in language and spatial skills.

The last brain area to experience pruning and maturity is the *prefrontal cortex*. This is significant because the prefrontal cortex plays a critical role in many advanced or "executive" cognitive functions, such as a person's ability to reason, plan, organize, solve problems, and decide. And when does the prefrontal cortex reach full maturity? According to the MRI studies, not until people reach their mid-20s (Gogtay & others, 2004).

This suggests that an adolescent's occasional impulsive or immature behavior is at least partly a reflection of a brain that still has a long way to go to reach full adult maturity (Casey, 2013; Casey & Caudle, 2013). During adolescence, emotions and impulses can be intense and compelling. But the parts of the brain that are responsible for exercising judgment are still maturing (Luna & others, 2013). The result can be behavior that is immature, impulsive, unpredictable—and often risky.

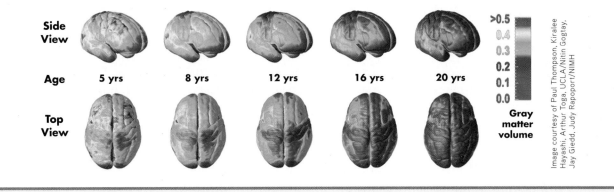

Image courtesy of Paul Thompson, Kiralee Hayashi, Arthur Toga, UCLA/Nitin Gogtay, Jay Giedd, Judy Rapoport/NIMH

enter puberty earlier, regardless of whether the father remains or leaves (Saxbe & Repetti, 2009). And the financial problems that often accompany single parenthood also appear to play a role in early puberty among girls, likely because financial problems are an indicator of a stressful environment (Culpin & others, 2014). In general, negative and stressful family environments are associated with an earlier onset of puberty, while positive family environments are associated with later physical development (Ellis & Essex, 2007; James & others, 2012). Although the mechanisms are not completely clear, it may be that stressful family events increase many of the same hormones that are involved in triggering puberty.

EFFECTS OF EARLY VERSUS LATE MATURATION

Adolescents tend to be keenly aware of the physical changes they are experiencing as well as of the *timing* of those changes compared with their peer group. Most adolescents are "on time," meaning that the maturational changes are occurring at roughly the same time for them as for others in their peer group.

However, some adolescents are "off time," experiencing maturation noticeably earlier or later than the majority of their peers. Generally speaking, off-time maturation is stressful for both boys and girls, who may experience teasing, social isolation, and exclusion from social activities (Conley & Rudolph, 2009).

Being off-time has different effects for girls and boys. Girls who develop early and boys who develop late are most likely to have problems. For example, early-maturing girls tend to be more likely than late-maturing girls to have negative feelings about their body image and pubertal changes, such as menarche (Ge & others,

Effects of Early Versus Late Maturation

As anyone who remembers seventh-grade gym class can attest, the timing of puberty varies widely. Early maturation can have different effects for boys and girls. Early-maturing boys tend to be successful in athletics and popular with their peers, but they are more susceptible to risky behaviors, such as drug, alcohol, or steroid use (McCabe & Ricciardelli, 2004). Early-maturing girls tend to have more negative feelings about the arrival of puberty and body changes, have higher rates of teenage pregnancy, and may be embarrassed or harassed by unwanted attention from older males (Adair & Gordon-Larsen, 2001; Ge & others, 2003).

Courtesy of the authors

2003). Compared to late-maturing girls, early-maturing girls are less likely to have received factual information concerning development. They may also feel embarrassed by unwanted attention from older males (Brooks-Gunn & Reiter, 1990). Early-maturing girls also have higher rates of sexual risk-taking, drug and alcohol use, and delinquent behavior, and are at greater risk for unhealthy weight gain later in life (Adair & Gordon-Larsen, 2001; Belsky & others, 2010).

Early maturation can be advantageous for boys, but it is also associated with risks. Early-maturing boys tend to be popular with their peers. However, although they are more successful in athletics than late-maturing peers, they are also more susceptible to behaviors that put their health at risk, such as steroid use (McCabe & Ricciardelli, 2004). Early-maturing boys are also more prone to feelings of depression, problems at school, and engaging in drug or alcohol use (see Hayatbakhsh & others, 2009; Mendle & Ferrero, 2012).

Social Development

The changes in adolescents' bodies are accompanied by changes in their social interactions, most notably with parents and peers. Contrary to what many people think, parent–adolescent relationships are generally positive. In fact, most teenagers report that they admire their parents and turn to them for advice (Steinberg, 1990, 2001). As a general rule, when parent–child relationships have been good before adolescence, they continue to be relatively smooth during adolescence. Adolescents who perceive their relationships with their parents as being warm and supportive have higher self-esteem and are most likely to follow their parents' guidance and stay out of trouble (Fosco & others, 2012; McElhaney & others, 2008). However, some friction seems to be inevitable as children make the transition to adolescence. And, many developmental psychologists view the increased conflict in early and middle adolescence as healthy, a necessary stage in the adolescent's development of increased autonomy.

MYTH ◀ SCIENCE

Is it true that most adolescents have poor relationships with their parents?

ZITS

ZITS ©2000 Zits Partnership, Dist. By King Features

Although parents remain influential throughout adolescence, relationships with friends and peers become increasingly important (Albert & others, 2013; Somerville, 2013). Adolescents usually encounter greater diversity among their peers as they make the transitions to middle school and high school. To a much greater degree than during childhood, the adolescent's social network, social context, and community influence his or her values, norms, and expectations. In James's case, his interactions with other members of the gay and transgender communities were important influences on his development during adolescence.

Susceptibility to peer influence peaks during early adolescence (Dishion & Tipsord, 2011). As they grow older, adolescents develop resilience against peer influences and increasingly rely on parents' influences regarding appropriate behaviors (Cook & others, 2009; Sumter & others, 2009).

Parents often worry that peer influences will lead to undesirable behavior, but researchers have found that peer relationships tend to *reinforce* the traits and goals that parents fostered during childhood (Steinberg, 2001). This finding is not as surprising as it might seem. Adolescents tend to form friendships with peers who are similar in age, social class, race, and beliefs about drinking, dating, church attendance, and educational goals.

Although peer influence can lead to undesirable behaviors, peers can also influence one another in positive ways (Allen & others, 2008). Friends often exert pressure on one another to study, make good grades, attend college, and engage in prosocial behaviors. This positive influence is especially true for peers who are strong students (Cook & others, 2007).

Peer Relationships in Adolescence
Although parents often worry about the negative impact of peers, peers can also have a positive influence on one another. These boys volunteered to peel potatoes for over 100 Thanksgiving dinners being served to needy families in their Modesto, California, community.

Debbie Noda/Modesto Bee/ZUMAPRESS.com

Romantic and sexual relationships also become increasingly important throughout the adolescent years. One national survey showed that by the age of 12, about one-quarter of adolescents reported having had a "special romantic relationship," although not necessarily a relationship that included sexual intimacy. By age 15, that percentage increased to 50 percent, and reached 70 percent by the age of 18 (Connolly & McIsaac, 2009).

Social and cultural factors influence when, why, and how adolescents engage in romantic and sexual behaviors. The beginning of dating, for example, coincides more strongly with cultural and social expectations and norms, such as when friends begin to date, than with an adolescent's degree of physical maturation (see Collins, 2003). In fact, there are stark cultural differences in the age at which adolescents begin to date. For example, 80 percent of Israeli 14-year-olds report some type of dating, as compared to only 50 percent of North Americans of the same age (Connolly & McIsaac, 2009).

The physical and social developments we've discussed so far are the more obvious changes associated with the onset of puberty. No less important, however, are the cognitive changes that allow the adolescent to think and reason in new, more complex ways.

Identity Formation
ERIKSON'S THEORY OF PSYCHOSOCIAL DEVELOPMENT

When psychologists talk about a person's **identity,** they are referring to her sense of self, including her memories, experiences, and the values and beliefs that guide her behavior. Our sense of personal identity gives us an integrated and continuing sense of self over time.

Identity formation is a process that continues throughout the lifespan. As we embrace new and different roles over the course of our lives, we define ourselves in new and different ways (Erikson & others, 1986; McAdams & Olson, 2010).

For the first time in the lifespan, the adolescent possesses the cognitive skills necessary for dealing with identity issues in a meaningful way (Sebastian & others, 2008).

identity A person's sense of self, including his or her memories, experiences, and the values and beliefs that guide his or her behavior.

Psychoanalyst Erik Erikson (1902–1994) Erikson's landmark theory of psychosocial development stressed the importance of social and cultural influences on personality throughout the stages of life.

Jon Erikson/The Image Works

Beginning in early adolescence, self-definition shifts. Preadolescent children tend to describe themselves in very concrete social and behavioral terms. An 8-year-old might describe himself by saying, "I play with Mark and I like to ride my bike." In contrast, adolescents use more abstract self-descriptions that reflect personal attributes, values, beliefs, and goals (Phillips, 2008). Thus, a 14-year-old might say, "I have strong religious beliefs, love animals, and hope to become a veterinarian."

Some aspects of personal identity involve characteristics over which the adolescent really has no control, such as gender, race, ethnic background, and socioeconomic level. For most people and for most of these characteristics, these identity characteristics are fixed and already internalized by the time an individual reaches the adolescent years. Gender identity is one exception, with some young people like James struggling with the contrast between their bodies and the gender with which they identify.

Beyond such fixed characteristics, the adolescent begins to evaluate herself on several different dimensions. Social acceptance by peers, academic and athletic abilities, work abilities, personal appearance, and romantic appeal are some important aspects of self-definition. Another challenge facing the adolescent is to develop an identity that is independent of her parents while retaining a sense of connection to her family. Thus, the adolescent has not one but several self-concepts that she must integrate into a coherent and unified whole to answer the question, "Who am I?"

The adolescent's task of achieving an integrated identity is one important aspect of psychoanalyst **Erik Erikson**'s influential theory of psychosocial development. Briefly, Erikson (1968) proposed that each of eight stages of life is associated with a particular psychosocial conflict that can be resolved in either a positive or a negative direction (see Table 9.4). Relationships with others play an

TABLE 9.4

Erik Erikson's Psychosocial Stages of Development

Life Stage	Psychosocial Conflict	Positive Resolution	Negative Resolution
Infancy (birth to 18 months)	Trust vs. mistrust	Reliance on consistent and warm caregivers produces a sense of predictability and trust in the environment.	Physical and psychological neglect by caregivers leads to fear, anxiety, and mistrust of the environment.
Toddlerhood (18 months to 3 years)	Autonomy vs. doubt	Caregivers encourage independence and self-sufficiency, promoting positive self-esteem.	Overly restrictive caregiving leads to self-doubt in abilities and low self-esteem.
Early childhood (3 to 6 years)	Initiative vs. guilt	The child learns to initiate activities and develops a sense of social responsibility concerning the rights of others; promotes self-confidence.	Parental overcontrol stifles the child's spontaneity, sense of purpose, and social learning; promotes guilt and fear of punishment.
Middle and late childhood (6 to 12 years)	Industry vs. inferiority	Through experiences with parents and "keeping up" with peers, the child develops a sense of pride and competence in schoolwork and home and social activities.	Negative experiences with parents or failure to "keep up" with peers leads to pervasive feelings of inferiority and inadequacy.
Adolescence	Identity vs. role confusion	Through experimentation with different roles, the adolescent develops an integrated and stable self-definition; forms commitments to future adult roles.	An apathetic adolescent or one who experiences pressures and demands from others may feel confusion about his or her identity and role in society.
Young adulthood	Intimacy vs. isolation	By establishing lasting and meaningful relationships, the young adult develops a sense of connectedness and intimacy with others.	Because of fear of rejection or excessive self-preoccupation, the young adult is unable to form close, meaningful relationships and becomes psychologically isolated.
Middle adulthood	Generativity vs. stagnation	Through child rearing, caring for others, productive work, and community involvement, the adult expresses unselfish concern for the welfare of the next generation.	Self-indulgence, self-absorption, and a preoccupation with one's own needs lead to a sense of stagnation, boredom, and a lack of meaningful accomplishments.
Late adulthood	Ego integrity vs. despair	In reviewing his or her life, the older adult experiences a strong sense of self-acceptance and meaningfulness in his or her accomplishments.	In looking back on his or her life, the older adult experiences regret, dissatisfaction, and disappointment about his or her life and accomplishments.

SOURCE: Research from Erikson (1964a).

important role in determining the outcome of each conflict. According to Erikson, the key psychosocial conflict facing adolescents is *identity versus role confusion.*

To successfully form an identity, adolescents must not only integrate various dimensions of their personality into a coherent whole but also define the roles that they will adopt within the larger society on becoming an adult (Bohn & Berntsen, 2008). To accomplish this, adolescents grapple with a wide variety of issues, such as selecting a potential career and formulating religious, moral, and political beliefs. They must also adopt social roles involving interpersonal relationships, sexuality, and long-term commitments such as marriage and parenthood.

In Erikson's (1968) theory, the adolescent's path to successful identity achievement begins with *role confusion,* which is characterized by little sense of commitment on any of these issues. This period is followed by a *moratorium period,* during which the adolescent experiments with different roles, values, and beliefs. Gradually, by choosing among the alternatives and making commitments, the adolescent arrives at an *integrated identity.*

Psychological research has generally supported Erikson's description of the process of identity formation (Phillips, 2008). However, it's important to keep in mind that identity continues to evolve over the entire lifespan, not just during the adolescent years (Whitbourne & others, 2009). Adolescents and young adults seem to achieve a stable sense of identity in some areas earlier than in others. Far fewer adolescents and young adults have attained a stable sense of identity in the realm of religious and political beliefs than in the realm of vocational choice.

The Development of Moral Reasoning

An important aspect of cognitive development during adolescence is a change in **moral reasoning**—how an individual thinks about moral and ethical decisions. Adolescents and adults often face moral decisions on difficult interpersonal and social issues (Hart, 2005). What is the right thing to do at a given time and place? How is the best possible outcome achieved for all? The adolescent's increased capacities to think abstractly, imagine hypothetical situations, and compare ideals to the real world all affect his thinking about moral issues (Fox & Killen, 2008; Kagan & Sinnott-Armstrong, 2008; Turiel, 2010).

The most influential theory of moral development was proposed by **Lawrence Kohlberg** (1927–1987). Kohlberg's interest in moral development may have been triggered by his experiences as a young adult (see photo on next page). Kohlberg (1976, 1984) used hypothetical moral dilemmas to investigate moral reasoning, such as whether a husband should steal a drug he could not afford to cure his dying wife. Kohlberg analyzed the responses of children, adolescents, and adults to such hypothetical moral dilemmas, focusing on the *reasoning* that they used to justify their answers rather than the answers themselves. He concluded that there are distinct *stages* of moral development. Like Piaget's stages of cognitive development, Kohlberg (1981) believed that moral development unfolded in an age-related, step-by-step fashion.

Kohlberg proposed three distinct *levels* of moral reasoning: *preconventional, conventional,* and *postconventional.* Each level is based on the degree to which a person conforms to conventional standards of society. Furthermore, each level has two *stages* that represent different degrees of sophistication in moral reasoning. Table 9.5 describes the characteristics of the moral reasoning associated with each of Kohlberg's levels and stages.

moral reasoning The aspect of cognitive development that has to do with how an individual reasons about moral decisions.

TABLE 9.5

Kohlberg's Levels and Stages of Moral Development

I. Preconventional Level

Moral reasoning is guided by external consequences. No internalization of values or rules.

Stage 1: Punishment and Obedience

"Right" is obeying the rules simply to avoid punishment because others have power over you and can punish you.

Stage 2: Mutual Benefit

"Right" is an even or fair exchange so that both parties benefit. Moral reasoning guided by a sense of "fair play."

II. Conventional Level

Moral reasoning is guided by conformity to social roles, rules, and expectations that the person has learned and internalized.

Stage 3: Interpersonal Expectations

"Right" is being a "good" person by conforming to social expectations, such as showing concern for others and following rules set by others so as to win their approval.

Stage 4: Law and Order

"Right" is helping maintain social order by doing one's duty, obeying laws simply because they are laws, and showing respect for authorities simply because they are authorities.

III. Postconventional Level

Moral reasoning is guided by internalized legal and moral principles that protect the rights of all members of society.

Stage 5: Legal Principles

"Right" is helping protect the basic rights of all members of society by upholding legalistic principles that promote the values of fairness, justice, equality, and democracy.

Stage 6: Universal Moral Principles

"Right" is determined by self-chosen ethical principles that reflect the person's respect for ideals such as nonviolence, equality, and human dignity. If these moral principles conflict with democratically determined laws, the person's self-chosen moral principles take precedence.

SOURCES: Research from Kohlberg (1981) and Colby & others (1983).

Lawrence Kohlberg (1927–1987) After graduating from high school in 1945, Kohlberg joined the Merchant Marine. In Europe, he witnessed the aftermath of World War II and met many Holocaust survivors. After finishing his service in the Merchant Marine, Kohlberg helped smuggle Jewish refugees into what was then British-controlled Palestine. He was caught and briefly imprisoned by the British but escaped and eventually made his way back to the United States (Schwartz, 2004). Years later, Kohlberg (1988) wrote, "My experience with illegal immigration into Israel raised all sorts of moral questions, issues which I saw as issues of justice. Was using death or violence right or just for a political end? When is it permissible to be involved with violent means for supposedly just ends?" Kohlberg was to be preoccupied with themes of justice and morality for the rest of his life.

Lee Lockwood/Time & Life Pictures/Getty Images

> The hallmark of morality resides less in the ability to resolve abstract moral dilemmas or even figure out how, ideally, others should behave; the hallmark resides more in people's tendency to apply the same moral standards to themselves that they apply to others and to function in accordance with them.
>
> —*Dennis Krebs and Kathy Denton (2006)*

Kohlberg (1984) found that the responses of children under the age of 10 reflected *preconventional* moral reasoning based on self-interest—avoiding punishment and maximizing personal gain. Beginning in late childhood and continuing through adolescence and adulthood, responses typically reflected conventional moral reasoning, which emphasizes social roles, rules, and obligations. Thus, the progression from preconventional to conventional moral reasoning is closely associated with age-related cognitive abilities (Eisenberg & others, 2005; Olthof & others, 2008).

Do people inevitably advance from conventional to postconventional moral reasoning, as Kohlberg once thought? In a 20-year longitudinal study, Kohlberg followed a group of boys from late childhood through early adulthood. Of the 58 participants in the study, only 8 occasionally displayed stage 5 reasoning, which emphasizes respect for legal principles that protect all members of society. *None* of the participants showed stage 6 reasoning, which reflects self-chosen ethical principles that are universally applied (Colby & others, 1983). Kohlberg and his colleagues eventually dropped stage 6 from the theory, partly because clear-cut expressions of "universal moral principles" were so rare (Gibbs, 2003; Rest, 1983).

Kohlberg's original belief that the development of abstract thinking in adolescence naturally and invariably leads people to the formation of idealistic moral principles has not been supported. Only a few exceptional people display the philosophical ideals in Kohlberg's highest level of moral reasoning. The normal course of changes in moral reasoning for most people seems to be captured by Kohlberg's first four stages (Colby & Kohlberg, 1984). By adulthood, the predominant form of moral reasoning is conventional moral reasoning, reflecting the importance of social roles and rules.

Kohlberg's theory has been criticized on several grounds (see Krebs & Denton, 2005, 2006). Probably the most important criticism of Kohlberg's theory is that moral *reasoning* doesn't always predict moral *behavior*. People don't necessarily respond to real-life dilemmas as they do to the hypothetical dilemmas that are used to test moral reasoning. Further, people can, and do, respond at different levels to different kinds of moral decisions. As Dennis Krebs and Kathy Denton (2005) point out, people are *flexible* in their real-world moral behavior: The goals that people pursue affect the types of moral judgments they make.

Similarly, Kohlberg's theory is a theory of cognitive development, focusing on the type of conscious reasoning that people use to make moral decisions. However, as Jonathan Haidt (2007, 2010) points out, moral decisions in the real world are often affected by nonrational

Moral Development: Developing a Sense of Right and Wrong As adolescents develop new cognitive abilities, they become more aware of moral issues in the world. Their newly acquired ability to imagine hypothetical situations and compare abstract ideals to the reality of situations often leads teenagers to question authority or take action against perceived injustices. This 16-year-old protestor is participating in an "Occupy Britain" demonstration in Nottingham, UK.

Press Association via AP Images

processes, such as emotional responses, custom, or tradition. For example, if your beloved dog was killed by a car, would it be morally wrong to cook and eat it? Many people would instinctively say "yes," but probably not because of a well-considered, reasoned argument (Haidt & others, 1993). Haidt (2010) argues that moral decisions are *always* embedded in particular social contexts and influenced, often without our awareness, by emotions and social and cultural beliefs.

GENDER, CULTURE, AND MORAL REASONING

Other challenges to Kohlberg's theory questioned whether it was as universal as its proponents claimed. Psychologist Carol Gilligan (1982) pointed out that Kohlberg's early research was conducted entirely with male subjects, yet it became the basis for a theory applied to both males *and* females. Gilligan also noted that in most of Kohlberg's stories, the main actor who faces the moral dilemma to be resolved is a male. When females are present in the stories, they often play a subordinate role. Thus, Gilligan believes that Kohlberg's model reflects a male perspective that may not accurately depict the development of moral reasoning in women.

To Gilligan, Kohlberg's model is based on an *ethic of individual rights and justice,* which is a more common perspective for men. In contrast, Gilligan (1982) developed a model of women's moral development that is based on an *ethic of care and responsibility.* In her studies of women's moral reasoning, Gilligan found that women tend to stress the importance of maintaining interpersonal relationships and responding to the needs of others, rather than focusing primarily on individual rights (Gilligan & Attanucci, 1988).

But *do* women use different criteria in making moral judgments? In a meta-analysis of studies on gender differences in moral reasoning, Sara Jaffee and Janet Shibley Hyde (2000) found only slight differences between male and female responses. Instead, evidence suggested that *both* men and women used a mix of care and justice perspectives. Thus, while disputing Gilligan's idea that men and women had entirely different approaches to moral reasoning, Jaffe and Hyde found empirical support for Gilligan's larger message: that Kohlberg's theory did *not* adequately reflect the way that humans actually experienced moral decision making.

"I'm sorry, but I'm morally and politically opposed to hangman."

Despite Kohlberg's belief that the stages of moral development were universal, culture also affects moral reasoning (Graham & others, 2011; Haidt, 2007). Kohlberg's moral decisions focus on issues of harm, fairness, and justice. In many cultures, however, other domains are equally deemed to be morally important. For example, religious or spiritual purity, loyalty to one's family or social group, respect for those in authority, and respect for tradition may also be seen as issues of morality. From this perspective, Kohlberg's theory is narrowly focused on just one area of morality—harm, fairness, and justice.

Some cross-cultural psychologists also argue that Kohlberg's stories and scoring system reflect a Western emphasis on *individual* rights and justice that is not shared in many cultures (Shweder & others, 1997). For example, Kohlberg's moral stages do not reflect the sense of interdependence and the concern for the overall welfare of the group that is more common in collectivistic cultures. Cultural psychologist Harry Triandis (1994) reports an example of a response that does not fit into Kohlberg's moral scheme. In response to the scenario in which the husband steals the drug to save his wife's life, a man in New Guinea said, "If nobody helped him, I would say that *we* had caused the crime." Thus, there are aspects of moral reasoning in other cultures that do not seem to be reflected in Kohlberg's theory (Haidt, 2007; Shweder & Haidt, 1993).

❯ Test your understanding of **Adolescence** with **LEARNING***Curve*.

Adult Development

Development throughout adulthood is marked by exploration, physical changes, and the adoption of new social roles.

> What is emerging adulthood?

> What physical changes take place in adulthood?

> What are some general patterns of adult social development?

Emerging Adulthood According to Jeffrey Jensen Arnett (2004, 2010), the years from 18 to the mid- to late-20s are a time of exploration in relationships as well as vocational choices and social roles. Marriage is often postponed until the late 20s or even the 30s, after education is complete and careers are established.

You can think of the developmental changes you experienced during infancy, childhood, and adolescence as early chapters in your life story. Those early life chapters helped set the tone for the primary focus of your life story—adulthood. During the half-century or more that constitutes adulthood, self-definition evolves as people achieve independence and take on new roles and responsibilities.

In his theory of psychosocial development, Erik Erikson (1982) described the two fundamental themes that dominate adulthood: love and work. According to Erikson (1964b, 1968), the primary psychosocial task of early adulthood is to form a committed, mutually enhancing, intimate relationship with another person. During middle adulthood, the primary psychosocial task is *generativity*—to contribute to future generations through your children, your career, and other meaningful activities. In this section, we'll consider both themes as we continue our journey through the lifespan.

Emerging Adulthood

At one time, adolescence marked the end of childhood and the beginning of adulthood. Even as recently as the mid-1970s, most young people moved into the adult roles of stable work, marriage, and parenthood shortly after high school (Arnett, 2000, 2004). In the United States and other industrialized countries today, however, most young adults do not fully transition to adult roles until their late 20s. One reason is the need for additional education or training before entering the adult workforce. And in James's case, he has the added transition to his chosen gender to contend with. According to developmental psychologist Jeffrey Jensen Arnett (2000, 2004, 2010), the period from the late teens until the mid- to late-20s is a distinct stage of the lifespan, called **emerging adulthood.**

According to Erikson's (1964) theory, the identity conflict should be fully resolved by the end of adolescence. However, Arnett (2010) contends that in today's industrialized cultures, identity is not fully resolved until the mid- or late-20s, as has been the case with James. Instead, Arnett writes, "It is during emerging adulthood, not adolescence, that most young people explore the options available to them in love and work and move towards making enduring choices."

Many emerging adults feel "in between": they are no longer adolescents, but not quite adults. Although some find this instability unsettling and disorienting, several studies have found that well-being and self-esteem steadily rise over the course of emerging adulthood for most people (Galambos & others, 2006; Schulenberg & Zarrett, 2006).

While some emerging adults establish long-term, stable relationships, in general relationships during emerging adulthood are characterized by exploration. "Hooking up" during the college and post-college years is common (see the In Focus box on page 397). Compared to their parents and grandparents, today's emerging adults are waiting much longer to get married. As Figure 9.5 shows, in 1970 the median age for a first marriage was 23 for men and 21 for women. By 2010 that figure had increased to 28 for men and 26 for women. Many emerging adults postpone marriage until

emerging adulthood In industrialized countries, the stage of lifespan from approximately the late teens to the mid- to late-20s, which is characterized by exploration, instability, and flexibility in social roles, vocational choices, and relationships.

Cultura RM/JAG IMAGES/Getty Images

IN FOCUS

Hooking Up on Campus

Pop culture and the news media alike have been abuzz about today's hook-up culture. Katy Perry sings, "There's a stranger in my bed, there's a pounding in my head," in her number one *Billboard* hit, "Last Friday Night (T.G.I.F.)" (Perry & others, 2011). And reporter Kate Taylor (2013) of *The New York Times* wrote a long piece about the "hook-up" culture on U.S. university campuses. "It is by now pretty well understood," Taylor wrote, "that traditional dating in college has mostly gone the way of the landline" (2013).

Although there's nothing new about casual sex among young adults, hooking up does differ in some key ways from casual sex. Casual sex refers, by definition, to sexual intercourse, with or without an emotional or friendly relationship. In a "friends with benefits" relationship, the sexual relationship is presumed to be secondary to the friendship. In contrast, "hooking up" refers to a no-strings-attached, sexual encounter that can range from kissing and cuddling to sexual intercourse. The actual sexual behaviors may vary, but the common thread is that the sexual intimacy is not accompanied by the expectation of a committed relationship or even future interactions (Owen & others, 2010; Reiber & Garcia, 2010). Indeed, one college junior told Taylor about her regular hook-up: "We don't really like each other in person, sober," and observed that "we literally can't sit down and have coffee" (Taylor, 2013).

On many college campuses, hooking up is very common. Studies have shown that about 80 percent of students reported hooking up at least once while they were in college, and more than half had hooked up during the previous year (Owen & others, 2010; Reiber & Garcia, 2010). In one study, about 60 percent of students reported that their most recent hook-up partner was a new partner, and of those who had oral, anal, or vaginal sex, less than half said that they used a condom (Lewis & others, 2012). College men generally hold more permissive attitudes toward casual sex than women, and hooking up is no exception (Petersen & Hyde, 2010). Perhaps not surprisingly, alcohol use is strongly implicated in hooking up behavior. Alcohol precedes almost two-thirds of hook-ups (Fielder & Carey, 2010; Vander Ven & Beck, 2009).

THE DAY THE COMPUTER AND THE COFFEE MAKER HOOKED UP.

Liza Donnelly The New Yorker Collection/The Cartoon Bank

Male college students have more favorable attitudes toward hooking up than female college students, although the sexes may not be as far apart as some people think (Bradshaw & others, 2010). As compared to men, women tend to report more negative emotional reactions after hooking up than men (Lewis & others, 2012). However, *both* men and women reported that hooking up had overall been a more positive than negative experience (Lewis & others, 2012; Owen & Fincham, 2010).

Although hooking up is widely accepted on college campuses, both sexes overestimate the degree to which the opposite sex is comfortable with hooking up (Reiber & Garcia, 2010). Today's young adults haven't given up on the hope of creating a long-term committed relationship. Indeed, one college senior quoted in Taylor's news article described how a romantic relationship she had during a study-abroad experience made her hopeful that she would one day have such a relationship back home (Taylor, 2013). However, college students appear to have embraced what appears to be a larger cultural shift toward more flexible, less clearly defined relationships (Bisson & Levine, 2009).

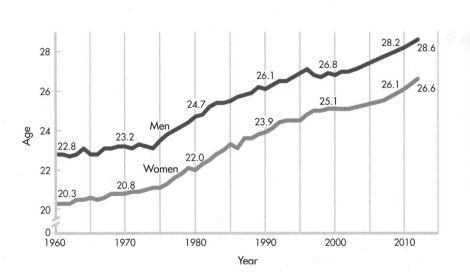

FIGURE 9.5 The Median Age at First Marriage The average age at first marriage is five years older for young adults today than it was in the 1970s. Part of the explanation for this trend is that more people are postponing marriage in order to complete a college education. Among young adults in the 25-to-34 age range, 26 percent of men and 33 percent of women have earned a bachelor's degree or higher.

Sources: Data from U.S. Census Bureau (2008a, 2008b, 2008c); Vespa & others, 2013.

their late 20s or early 30s so they can finish their education and become established in a career (Bernstein, 2010). When planning their futures, emerging adults, especially young women, also consider the potential difficulties in achieving a balance between work and family (Coyle & others, 2015).

Emerging adults also actively explore different career options (Hamilton & Hamilton, 2006). On average, emerging adults hold down an average of seven different jobs during their 20s (Arnett, 2004).

Is emerging adulthood a universal period of development? The answer appears to be no. According to Arnett (2011), emerging adulthood exists only in cultures in which adult responsibilities and roles are postponed until the 20s. This pattern occurs most typically in industrialized or post-industrialized countries. Even within industrialized countries, however, emerging adulthood may not characterize the developmental trajectory of all young adults. For example, members of minority groups, immigrants, and young adults who enter directly into the workforce rather than seeking college or university education are all less likely to experience emerging adulthood as a distinct period of exploration and change.

Physical Changes in Adulthood

Your unique genetic heritage greatly influences the unfolding of certain physical changes during adulthood, such as when your hair begins to thin and turn gray. Such genetically influenced changes can vary significantly from one person to another.

However, genetic heritage is *not* destiny. The lifestyle choices that people make in young and middle adulthood influence the aging process. Staying physically and mentally active, avoiding tobacco products and other harmful substances, and eating a healthy diet can both slow and minimize the physical declines that are typically associated with aging.

Another potent environmental force is simply the passage of time. Decades of use and environmental exposure take a toll on the body. Wrinkles begin to appear as we approach the age of 40, largely because of a loss of skin elasticity combined with years of making the same facial expressions. With each decade after age 20, the efficiency of various body organs declines. For example, lung capacity decreases, as does the amount of blood pumped by the heart, though these changes are usually not noticeable until late adulthood.

Physical strength typically peaks in *early adulthood,* the 20s and 30s. By *middle adulthood,* roughly from the 40s to the mid-60s, physical strength and endurance gradually decline. Physical and mental reaction times also begin to slow during middle adulthood. During *late adulthood,* from the mid-60s on, physical stamina and reaction time tend to decline further and faster.

Significant reproductive and hormonal changes also occur during adulthood. In women, **menopause,** the cessation of menstruation, signals the end of reproductive capacity and occurs anytime from the late 30s to the early 50s. For some women, menopause involves unpleasant symptoms, such as *hot flashes,* which are rapid and extreme increases in body temperature (Umland, 2008). Other symptoms may include night sweats and disturbances in sex drive, sleep, eating, weight, and motivation. Emotional symptoms may include depression, sadness, and emotional instability (E. Freeman, 2010).

Cultural stereotypes reinforce the notion that menopause is mostly a negative experience (APA, 2007). However, many women experience "postmenopausal zest." Freed of menstruation, childbearing, and worries about becoming pregnant, many women feel a renewed sense of energy, freedom, and happiness. Postmenopausal women often develop a new sense of identity, become more assertive, and pursue new aspirations (Fahs, 2007). In many cultures, postmenopausal women are valued for their experience and wisdom (Robinson, 2002).

Middle-aged men do not experience an abrupt end to their reproductive capability. However, they do experience a gradual decline in testosterone levels, a condition

---

Emerging adulthood is a time of life when many different directions remain possible, when little about the future has been decided for certain, [and] when the scope of independent exploration of life's possibilities is greater for most people than it will ever be at any other period of the life course.

—*Jeffrey Jensen Arnett (2000)*

menopause The natural cessation of menstruation and the end of reproductive capacity in women.

sometimes called *andropause* (Hochreiter & others, 2005). Decreased levels of the hormone testosterone cause changes in physical and psychological health. These changes include loss of lean muscle, increased body fat, weakened bones, reduced sexual motivation and function, and cognitive declines (Harman, 2005). Emotional problems such as depression and irritability may also occur.

Does the loss of reproductive capability trigger a "midlife crisis" in women, or especially, in men? No. Consistently, psychological research has shown that there is no such thing as a midlife crisis (see Clay, 2003; Sneed & others, 2012). Instead, most men and women who experienced a "crisis" of depression or despair during middle age *also* experienced depression, anxiety, and similar crises in young adulthood (Wethington, 2000).

Social Development in Adulthood

The "traditional" track of achieving intimacy in adulthood was once to find a mate, get married, and start and raise a family. Today, however, the structure of American families varies widely (see Figure 9.6). For example, the number of unmarried couples living together has increased dramatically—to well over 8 million couples in 2012 (Vespa & others, 2013). Currently, more than 30 percent of children are being raised by a single parent.

Given that more than half of all first marriages end in divorce, the phenomenon of remarrying and starting a second family later in life is not unusual. As divorce has become more common, the number of single parents and stepfamilies has also risen. And among married couples, some opt for a child-free life together. There are also gay and lesbian couples who, like many heterosexual couples, are committed to a long-term, monogamous relationship (Balsam & others, 2008; Goldberg, 2010; Rothblum & Hope, 2009).

Such diversity in adult relationships reflects the fact that adult social development does not always follow a predictable pattern. As you travel through adulthood, your life story may include many unanticipated twists in the plot and changes in the cast of characters. Just as the "traditional" family structure has its joys and heartaches, so do other configurations of intimate and family relationships. In the final analysis, *any* relationship that promotes the overall sense of happiness and well-being of the people involved is a successful one.

MYTH ◀ SCIENCE

Is it true that many middle-aged people experience a "midlife crisis"?

FIGURE 9.6 The Changing Structure of American Families and Households In a relatively short time, American households have undergone a metamorphosis. Between 1970 and 2012, the number of American households increased from 63 million to 115 million, but the average household size decreased from 3.1 to 2.6 persons. As the living arrangements of American families have become more diversified, the U.S. Census Bureau modified the categories it uses to classify households. Hence, the two pie charts differ slightly. Notice that single-parent family groups have doubled. Today, single mothers or fathers represent 9 percent of all households. In contrast, the number of married couples with children has sharply decreased.

Sources: Data from Kreider, 2008; U.S. Census Bureau, 2008c, 2008d; Vespa & others, 2013.

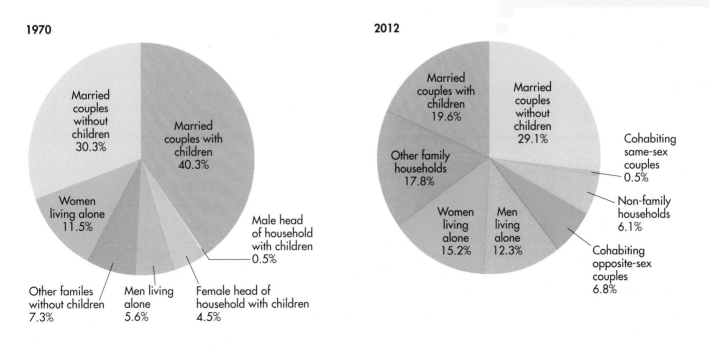

1970

- Married couples without children 30.3%
- Married couples with children 40.3%
- Women living alone 11.5%
- Male head of household with children 0.5%
- Other familes without children 7.3%
- Men living alone 5.6%
- Female head of household with children 4.5%

2012

- Married couples with children 19.6%
- Married couples without children 29.1%
- Other family households 17.8%
- Cohabiting same-sex couples 0.5%
- Women living alone 15.2%
- Men living alone 12.3%
- Non-family households 6.1%
- Cohabiting opposite-sex couples 6.8%

"O.K., now—on three, I'm going to toss a second job in there!"

Danny Shanahan The New Yorker Collection/The Cartoon Bank

Single-Parent Families Today, more than 30 percent of all children are being raised by a single parent. Many single parents provide their children with a warm, stable, and loving environment. In terms of school achievement and emotional stability, children in stable, single-parent households do just as well as children with two parents living in the same home (Dawson, 1991).

Ronnie Kaufman/Larry Hirshowitz/Getty Images

THE TRANSITION TO PARENTHOOD
KIDS 'R' US?

Although it is commonly believed that children strengthen the marital bond, marital satisfaction and time together tend to decline after the birth of the first child (Doss & others, 2009; Lawrence & others, 2010). For all the joy that can be derived from watching a child grow and experience the world, the first child's arrival creates a whole new set of responsibilities, pushes, and pulls on the marital relationship.

Without question, parenthood fundamentally alters your identity as an adult. With the birth or adoption of your first child, you take on a commitment to nurture the physical, emotional, social, and intellectual well-being of the next generation. This change in your identity can be a struggle, especially if the transition to parenthood was more of a surprise than a planned event (Grussu & others, 2005).

Parenthood is further complicated by the fact that children are not born speaking fluently, so you can't immediately enlighten them about the constraints of adult schedules, deadlines, finances, and physical energy. Instead, you must continually strive to adapt lovingly and patiently to your child's needs while managing all the other priorities in your life.

Not all couples experience a decline in marital satisfaction after the birth of a child. The hassles and headaches of child rearing can be minimized if the marital relationship is warm and positive, and if both husband and wife share household and child-care responsibilities (Tsang & others, 2003). The transition to parenthood is also smoother if you're blessed with a child who is born with a good disposition. Parents of babies with an "easy" temperament find it less difficult to adjust to their new role and maintain a healthy marital relationship (Mehall & others, 2009).

That many couples are marrying at a later age and waiting until their 30s to start a family also seems to be advantageous. Becoming a parent at an older age and waiting longer after marriage to start a family may ease the adjustment to parenthood. Why? Largely because the couple is more mature, the marital relationship is typically more stable, and finances are more secure (Hatton & others, 2010; Nelson & others, 2014).

In developed societies, dual-career families have become increasingly common. However, the career tracks of men and women often differ if they have children. Although today's fathers are more actively involved in child rearing than were fathers in previous generations, women still tend to have primary responsibility for child care (Meier & others, 2006). Thus, married women with children are much more likely than are single women or childless women to interrupt their careers, leave their jobs, or switch to part-time work because of child-rearing responsibilities. As a consequence, women with children tend to earn less than childless women (Gangl & Ziefle, 2009).

Many working parents are concerned about the effects of nonparental care on their children. Earlier in the chapter, we discussed the importance of attachment relationships between young children and their primary caregivers. In the Critical Thinking box on the next page, we take a close look at what psychologists have learned about the effects of day care on attachment and other aspects of development.

CRITICAL THINKING

The Effects of Child Care on Attachment and Development

The majority of children under the age of 5 in the United States—more than 11 million children—are in some type of child care (Phillips & Lowenstein, 2011). On average, the infants, toddlers, and pre-schoolers of working parents spend 36 hours a week in child care (NACCRRA, 2010). Does extensive day care during the first years of life create insecurely attached infants and toddlers? Does it produce negative effects in later childhood? Let's look at the evidence.

Developmental psychologist Jay Belsky (1992, 2001, 2002) sparked considerable controversy when he first published studies showing that infants under a year old were more likely to demonstrate insecure attachment if they experienced over 30 hours of day care per week. Based on his research, Belsky contended that children who entered full-time day care before their first birthday were "at risk" to be insecurely attached to their parents. He also claimed that extensive experience with nonmaternal care was linked to aggressive behavior in preschool and kindergarten.

However, reviewing the data in Belsky's and other early studies, psychologist Alison Clarke-Stewart (1989, 1992) pointed out that the actual difference in attachment was quite small when infants experiencing day care were compared with infants cared for by a parent. The proportion of insecurely attached infants in day care is only slightly higher than the proportion typically found in the general population (Lamb & others, 1992).

In other words, *most* of the children who had started day care in infancy were securely attached, just like most of the children who had not experienced extensive day care during infancy (Phillips & Lowenstein, 2011). Similarly, a large, long-term study of the effects of child care on attachment found that spending more hours per week in day care was associated with insecure attachment only in pre-schoolers who also experienced less sensitive and less responsive maternal care (NICHD, 2006). Preschoolers whose mothers were sensitive and responsive showed no greater likelihood of being insecurely attached, regardless of the number of hours spent in day care.

Researchers agree that the *quality* of child care is a key factor in facilitating secure attachment in early childhood and preventing problems in later childhood (NICHD, 2003a, 2003b; Vandell & others, 2010). Many studies have found that children who experience high-quality child care tend to be more sociable, better adjusted, and more academically competent than children who experience low-quality care, even well into their teens (Belsky & others, 2007; Vandell & others, 2010). They also have fewer behavior problems than children who experience lower-quality care (McCartney & others, 2010).

Child care is just one aspect of a child's developmental environment. Sensitive parenting and the quality of caregiving in the child's home have been found to have an even greater influence on social, emotional, and cognitive development than the quality of child care (Belsky & others, 2007).

Clearly, then, day care in and of itself does not necessarily lead to undesirable outcomes (Belsky, 2009). The critical factor is the *quality* of care (Phillips & Lowenstein, 2011). High-quality day care can benefit children, even when it begins in early infancy. In contrast, low-quality care can contribute to social and academic problems in later childhood (Muenchow & Marsland, 2007). Unfortunately, in many areas of the United States, high-quality day care is not readily available or is prohibitively expensive (Phillips & Lowenstein, 2011).

Brian Summers/Getty Images

Individual Attention and Learning Activities High-quality child-care centers offer a variety of age-appropriate (and fun!) activities, toys, and experiences that help nurture a child's motor, cognitive, and social skills. Individual attention from consistent caregivers or teachers helps foster the young child's sense of predictability and security in the care setting.

Characteristics of High-Quality Child Care

- The setting meets state and local standards, and is accredited by a professional organization, such as the National Association for the Education of Young Children.
- Warm, responsive caregivers encourage children's play and learning.
- Groups of children and adults are consistent over time, helping foster stable, positive relationships. Low staff turnover is essential.
- Groups are small enough to provide the individual attention that very young children need.
- A minimum of two adults care for no more than 8 infants, 12 toddlers, or 20 four- and five-year-olds.
- Caregivers are trained in principles of child development and learning.
- Developmentally appropriate learning materials and toys are available that offer interesting, safe, and achievable activities.

SOURCES: National Institute of Child Health and Human Development, 2006; National Association for the Education of Young Children, 2009; National Association of Child Care Resource & Referral Agencies (NACCRRA), 2010.

CRITICAL THINKING QUESTIONS

- Why is it difficult to definitively measure the effects of day care on children?
- Given the benefits of high-quality child care, should the availability of affordable, high-quality care be a national priority?

Do adults, particularly women, experience greater stress because of the conflicting demands of career, marriage, and family? Not necessarily. Generally, multiple roles seem to provide both men and women with a greater potential for increased feelings of self-esteem, happiness, and competence (Cinamon & others, 2007). The critical factor seems to be not the *number* of roles that people take on but the *quality* of their experiences on the job, in marriage, and as a parent (Lee & Phillips, 2006; Plaisier & others, 2008). When experiences in different roles are positive and satisfying, psychological well-being is enhanced. However, when work is dissatisfying, finding high-quality child care is difficult, and making ends meet is a never-ending struggle, stress can escalate and psychological well-being can plummet—for either sex (Bakker & others, 2008).

Although marital satisfaction declines when people first become parents, it rises again after children leave home (Gorchoff & others, 2008). Thus, most parents do *not* experience feelings of sadness, emptiness, and loss when their last child leaves home, often called the "empty nest syndrome" (Bouchard, 2014). Successfully launching your children into the adult world represents the attainment of the ultimate parental goal. There is also more time to spend in leisure activities with your spouse. Not surprisingly, then, marital satisfaction tends to increase steadily once children are out of the nest and flying on their own. Relatively recent is the new phenomenon of *boomerang kids*—adult children returning home after a brief period on their own because of economic pressures. Just as children's departure positively affects marital satisfaction, the return of those same children can have a negative impact on the marital relationship (Bouchard, 2014; Umberson & others, 2005).

Late Adulthood and Aging

KEY THEME

Late adulthood does not necessarily involve a steep decline in physical or cognitive capabilities.

KEY QUESTIONS

› What cognitive changes take place in late adulthood?

› What factors influence social development in late adulthood?

"This next one is a hard-rockin', kick-ass, take-no-prisoners tune we wrote about turning sixty."

The average life expectancy for men in the United States is currently about 76 years, and for women, about 81 years (Xu & others, 2009). Thus, the stage of late adulthood can easily last a decade or more. It has been projected that by 2050, the number of United States residents over the age of 65 will double, going from 40 million today to 89 million (U.S. Census Bureau, 2009). The world population is aging, too. Globally, the number of people aged 80 and older is expected to grow from 69 million in 2014 to 379 million in 2050 (Harper, 2014).

Although we experience many physical and sensory changes throughout adulthood, that's not to say that we completely fall apart when we reach our 60s, 70s, or even 80s. Contrary to many young people's misconceptions of late adulthood, *most* older adults live healthy, active, and self-sufficient lives (National Institute on Aging, 2007; Wurtele, 2009). Even adults 85 years and older report good health and functioning despite increasing prevalence of disease and impairment (Collerton & others, 2009). For many people, good health and well-being reaches well into the latest stages of adulthood (Charles & Carstensen, 2010).

Cognitive Changes

During which decade of life do you think people reach their intellectual peak? If you answered the 20s or 30s, you may be surprised by the results of research. There is a lot of variability in terms of the age at which different cognitive abilities are at their peak (Hartshorne & Germine, 2015). One study of business executives found that older executives performed more poorly than younger executives on some measures of cognitive ability but performed better on others (Klein & others, 2015).

Decades of work by K. Warner Schaie (1995, 2005) and his colleagues has shown that mental abilities remain relatively stable until about the age of 60. And in terms of mental abilities related to what we do—our jobs and our hobbies—we might even see improved cognitive functioning as we age (Ackerman, 2014). After age 60, slight declines begin to appear on tests of general intellectual abilities, such as logical reasoning, math skills, word recall, and the ability to mentally manipulate images (Alwin, 2009; Siegler & others, 2009).

But even after age 60, most older adults maintain their previous levels of ability. A longitudinal study of adults in their 70s, 80s, and 90s found that there were slight but significant declines in memory, perceptual speed, and fluency. However, measures of knowledge, such as vocabulary, remained stable up to age 90 (Singer & others, 2003; Zelinski & Kennison, 2007). Similarly, the ability to speak and understand language tends to remain stable as people age (Shafto & Tyler, 2014). When declines in mental abilities occur during old age, Schaie (2005) found that the explanation is often simply a lack of practice or experience with the kinds of tasks used in mental ability tests. Even just a few hours of training on mental skills can improve test scores for most older adults.

Some research suggests that physiological functioning of the brain begins to slow with age (Salthouse, 2009). Neurons appear to become less efficient at communicating with one another, and this seems to result in slowed and sometimes inhibited cognitive performance (Bucur & others, 2008). According to one hypothesis, older brains appear to *compensate* for this decline in processing speed by outsourcing some of the work to other parts of the brain (Dennis & Cabeza, 2008). However, the need to recruit more regions of the brain comes at a price—slower processing.

Is it possible to minimize declines in mental and physical abilities in old age? In a word, *yes.* Consistently, research has found that those who are better educated and engage in physical, mental, and social activities throughout older adulthood show the smallest declines in mental abilities (Boron & others, 2007; Colcombe & Kramer, 2003; Lindenberger, 2014). However, dysfunctional social relationships can have *negative* effects. In one study of more than 10,000 people living in the United Kingdom, close relationships that caused worry and stress predicted a decline in mental abilities eight years later (Liao & others, 2014). Aerobic exercise, however, has strong research

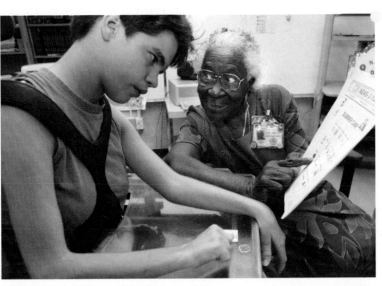

MICHAEL FRANCIS MCELROY/KRT/Newscom

A Lifetime of Experience to Share Like many other senior adults, Lillian Williams derives great personal satisfaction from her work as a volunteer "Foster Grandparent," shown here reading to a student at a school in Fort Lauderdale, Florida. Contributing to their communities, taking care of others, and helping people both younger and older than themselves are important to many older adults.

FOCUS ON NEUROSCIENCE

Boosting the Aging Brain

Dozens of studies have shown that exercise, especially aerobic exercise, improves cognitive functioning in old age (Colcombe & Kramer, 2003; Hillman & others, 2008). Many studies have also shown that remaining mentally and physically active decreases age-related risks for cognitive impairment and Alzheimer's disease (Hertzog & others, 2009; Yaffe & others, 2009).

However, most human studies on brain structure have been *correlational,* rather than experimental, making it difficult to pin down causation. Does staying physically active improve cognitive functioning and brain health in old age? Or are people with better cognitive functioning and brain health more likely to stay physically active?

Psychologist Kirk Erickson and his colleagues (2011) set out to answer this question by designing an experiment to test whether aerobic exercise could improve brain health and cognitive functioning in older adults who were in good physical health but otherwise sedentary. And by sedentary, they meant *sedentary:* One requirement for participating in the study was that the participant had not been physically active for more than 30 minutes in the past six months.

The 120 participants, aged 55 to 80, were randomly assigned to two groups that met three times a week for a year. The *stretching and toning* group attended classes where they engaged in nonaerobic exercise, including muscle-toning exercises, resistance training, and yoga. This group also served as a control condition.

The *aerobic exercise group* started slowly. They began by walking around a track for just 10 minutes a session. Every week, the time spent walking was increased by just 5 minutes. By week 7, the participants were walking 40 minutes per session, three times a week.

What were the findings? After a year of regular exercise, *both* groups improved on measures of spatial memory, which is good news for those who engage in less-active exercise programs. It's also possible that all the participants benefited from the social interaction during their respective exercise classes.

Were there any structural effects on the elderly brains? Because of its involvement in memory (see Chapter 6), researchers looked for changes in the *hippocampus.* The stretching and toning group showed, on average, a 1.4 percent decline in hippocampal volume over the one-year study period, which is about average for this age group.

Thinkstock/Getty Images

In contrast, participants in the aerobic exercise group *increased* the volume of their hippocampus by an average of 2 percent. Two percent may not sound like a large increase. However, because the hippocampus typically shrinks about 1–2 percent annually in older adults, a 2 percent gain is roughly equivalent to reversing two years of tissue loss.

This study is notable for several reasons. First, it showed that even in late adulthood, behavioral interventions can affect brain structure. Second, it showed that aerobic exercise is *neuroprotective*—it helps keep the brain healthy and may protect brain tissue from age-related deterioration. And third, it showed that a very moderate, simple exercise program can significantly improve cognitive abilities and brain health—even in late adulthood.

The bottom line: Declines in cognitive abilities and brain functions are neither inevitable nor unalterable (Voss & others, 2010). As Erickson (2011) points out, you don't have to be a highly conditioned athlete to reap the benefits of aerobic exercise. You don't need to join a gym, hire a trainer, or purchase expensive equipment. All you need is a good pair of shoes and a safe place to walk.

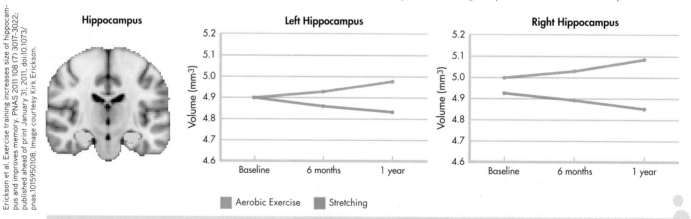

Erickson et al. Exercise training increases size of hippocampus and improves memory. PNAS 2011 108 (7) 3017-3022; published ahead of print January 31, 2011, doi:10.1073/pnas.1015950108. Image courtesy Kirk Erickson.

Effects of Aerobic Exercise on the Hippocampus in Late Adulthood After one year of regular aerobic exercise—simply walking three times a week—elderly participants (purple line) increased the size of their left and right hippocampus (brain region, highlighted in yellow) by an average of 2 percent. In contrast, the stretching-and-toning group (orange line) showed about a 1.5 percent decline in the hippocampal volume, which is normal for this age group.

Source: Erickson, Kirk I.; Voss, Michelle W.; Prakash, Ruchika S.; Basak, Chandramallika; Szabo, Amanda; Chaddock, Laura; & others. (2011). Exercise training increases size of hippocampus and improves memory. Proceedings of the National Academy of Sciences, 108, 3017-3022.

support for its effectiveness in improving cognitive functioning in late adulthood (Hertzog & others, 2009). The Focus on Neuroscience "Boosting the Aging Brain" provides a look at a new experiment that demonstrated the remarkable effects of a moderate exercise program on the brains of elderly adults.

In contrast, the greatest intellectual declines tend to occur in older adults with unstimulating lifestyles, such as people who live alone, are dissatisfied with their lives, and engage in few activities (see Calero-Garcia & others, 2007; Newson & Kemps, 2005).

Social Development

One theory of social development in late adulthood holds that older adults gradually "disengage," or withdraw, from vocational, social, and relationship roles as they face the prospect of their lives ending (Lange & Grossman, 2010). But consider your author Sandy's father, Erv. Even after Erv was well into his 80s, he bowled in a league every Tuesday night and would join about a dozen other retired men in their 70s and 80s for lunch and a monthly poker game.

What Erv and his buddies epitomized is the activity theory of aging. According to the **activity theory of aging,** life satisfaction in late adulthood is highest when you maintain your previous level of activity, either by continuing old activities or by finding new ones (Lange & Grossman, 2010).

Just like younger adults, older adults differ in the level of activity they find personally optimal. Some older adults pursue a busy lifestyle of social activities, travel, college classes, and volunteer work. Other older adults are happier with a quieter lifestyle: reading, pursuing hobbies, or simply puttering around their homes. Such individual preferences reflect lifelong temperamental and personality qualities that continue to be evident as a person ages.

For many older adults, caregiving responsibilities can persist well into late adulthood. Sandy's mother, Fern, for example, spent a great deal of time helping out with her young grandchildren and caring for some of her older relatives. She was not unusual in that respect. Many older adults who are healthy and active find themselves taking care of other older adults who are sick or have physical limitations.

Along with satisfying social relationships, the prescription for psychological well-being in old age includes achieving what Erik Erikson called *ego integrity*—the feeling that one's life has been meaningful (Erikson & others, 1986). Older adults experience ego integrity when they look back on their lives and feel satisfied with their accomplishments, accepting whatever mistakes or missteps they may have made (Torges & others, 2008, 2009).

In contrast, those who are filled with regrets or bitterness about past mistakes, missed opportunities, or bad decisions experience *despair*—a deep sense of disappointment in life. Often the theme of ego integrity versus despair emerges as older adults engage in a *life review,* thinking about or retelling their life story to others (Bohlmeijer & others, 2007; Kunz & Soltys, 2007).

❯ Test your understanding of **Adulthood** with *LEARNING*Curve.

The Final Chapter

DYING AND DEATH

KEY THEME

Attitudes toward dying and death are as diverse in late adulthood as they are throughout the lifespan.

KEY QUESTIONS

❯ How did Kübler-Ross describe the stages of dying?

❯ What are some individual variations in attitudes toward death and dying?

It is tempting to view death as the special province of the very old. Of course, death can occur at any point during the lifespan. It's also tempting to assume that older adults have come to a special understanding about death—that they view the prospect of dying

activity theory of aging The psychosocial theory that life satisfaction in late adulthood is highest when people maintain the level of activity they displayed earlier in life.

with wisdom and serenity. In reality, attitudes toward death in old age show the same diversity that is reflected in other aspects of adult development. Not all older adults are accepting of death, even when poor health has severely restricted their activities (Jun & others, 2010).

As psychologist Robert Kastenbaum (1992) wrote, "Everyone lives in relationship to death at every point in the lifespan." In other words, long before encountering old age, each individual has a personal history of thinking about death. Some people are obsessed with issues of life and death from adolescence or early adulthood onward, while others, even in advanced old age, take more of a one-day-at-a-time approach to living. And, feelings about and attitudes toward death are also influenced by cultural, philosophical, and religious beliefs (Gire, 2011; Rosenblatt, 2007).

In general, worries about death tend to peak in middle adulthood, then *decrease* in late adulthood (Neimeyer & others, 2004; Russac & others, 2007). At any age, people respond with a wide variety of emotions when faced with the prospect of imminent death, such as when they are diagnosed with a terminal illness.

The scientific study of death and dying owes much to pioneering psychiatrist Elisabeth Kübler-Ross (1926–2004). Based on interviews with hundreds of terminally ill patients, Kübler-Ross (1969) proposed that the dying go through five stages. First, they *deny* that death is imminent, perhaps insisting that their doctors are wrong or denying the seriousness of their illness. Second, they feel and express *anger* that they are dying. Third, they *bargain*—they try to "make a deal" with doctors, relatives, or God, promising to behave in a certain way if only they may be allowed to live. Fourth, they become *depressed*. Finally, they *accept* their fate.

MYTH ◀ SCIENCE

Is it true that dying people go through five predictable stages—denial, anger, bargaining, depression, and acceptance?

Although Kübler-Ross's research did much to sensitize the public and the medical community to the emotional experience of dying, it now seems clear that dying individuals do *not* necessarily progress through the predictable sequence of stages that she described (Kastenbaum, 2000, 2005).

Rather, dying is as individual a process as living is. People cope with the prospect of dying much as they have coped with other stresses in their lives. Faced with impending death, some older adults react with passive resignation, others with bitterness and anger. Some people plunge into activity and focus their attention on external matters, such as making funeral arrangements, disposing of their property, or arranging for the care of other family members. And others turn inward, searching for the meaning of their life's story as the close of the final chapter draws near (Kastenbaum, 2000).

But even in dying, our life story doesn't just end. Each of us leaves behind a legacy of memories in the minds of those who survive us. As we live each day, we are building our legacy through our words, our actions, and the many choices we make along the way.

Each of us began life being completely dependent on others for our survival. Over the course of our lifespan, others come to depend on us. It is those people whose lives we have touched in some way, whether for good or for ill, who will remember us. In this sense, the final chapter of our lives will be written not by us, but by those whose life stories have intersected with our own.

SHNS photo by Pam Panchak/Pittsburgh Post-Gazette

The Last Lecture People vary greatly in how they cope with impending death. At the age of 45, Dr. Randy Pausch, a computer science professor at Carnegie Mellon University, learned that he had pancreatic cancer and was given just a few months to live. Pausch reacted by delivering his now famous "Last Lecture," written in response to the question, "What would you say if you knew you were going to die?" Titled *Really Achieving Your Childhood Dreams,* Pausch's lecture was upbeat, humorous, and inspirational, and has since been viewed by millions online. Pausch died about 10 months after giving his speech, which you can view at http://www.cmu.edu/randyslecture

Closing Thoughts

Traditionally, development in childhood has received the most attention from developmental psychologists. Yet, as we have emphasized throughout this chapter, development is a lifelong process.

Throughout this chapter, you've seen that every life is a unique combination of universal and individualized patterns of development. Although some aspects of development unfold in a predictable fashion, every life story, including yours, is influenced by unexpected events and plot twists. Despite predictable changes, the wonderful thing about the developmental process is that you never *really* know what the next chapter of your life story may hold.

Raising Psychologically Healthy Children

Unfortunately, kids don't come with owners' manuals. Maybe that's why if you walk into any bookstore and head for the "parenting" section, you'll see shelves of books offering advice on topics ranging from "how to toilet-train your toddler" to "how to talk to your teenager." We're not going to attempt to cover that range here. However, we will present some basic principles of parenting that have been shown to foster the development of children who are psychologically well-adjusted, competent, and in control of their own behavior.

Basic Parenting Styles and Their Effects on Children

Psychologist Diana Baumrind (1971, 1991, 2005) has described three basic parenting styles: authoritarian, permissive, and authoritative. These parenting styles differ in terms of: (1) parental control and (2) parental responsiveness to the child's needs and wishes.

Parents with an **authoritarian parenting style** are demanding but unresponsive to their children's needs or wishes. Authoritarian parents believe that they should shape and control the child's behavior so that it corresponds to an absolute set of standards. Put simply, they expect children to obey the rules, no questions asked. Rules are made without input from the child, and they are enforced by punishment, often physical.

At the opposite extreme are two **permissive parenting styles** (Maccoby & Martin, 1983). *Permissive-indulgent parents* are responsive, warm, and accepting of their children but impose few rules and rarely punish their children. *Permissive-indifferent parents* are both unresponsive and uncontrolling. Establishing firm rules and consistently enforcing them is simply too much trouble for permissive-indifferent parents. If taken to an extreme, the lack of involvement of permissive-indifferent parenting can amount to child neglect.

The third style is the **authoritative parenting style.** Authoritative parents are warm, responsive, and involved with their children. They set clear standards for mature, age-appropriate behavior and expect their children to be responsive to parental demands. However, authoritative parents also feel a *reciprocal* responsibility to consider their children's reasonable demands and points of view. Thus, there is considerable give-and-take between parent and child. Rules are firm and consistently enforced, but the parents discuss the reasons for the rules with the child.

How do these different parenting styles affect young children? Baumrind (1971) found that the children of authoritarian parents are likely to be moody, unhappy, fearful, withdrawn, unspontaneous, and irritable. The children of permissive parents tend to be more cheerful than the children of authoritarian parents, but they are more immature, impulsive, and aggressive. In contrast, the children of authoritative parents are likely to be cheerful, socially competent, energetic, and friendly. They show high levels of self-esteem, self-reliance, and self-control (Buri & others, 1988). They also tend to be happier and have better overall mental health (Raboteg-Saric & Sakic, 2014; Uji & others, 2014).

Decades of research has shown that parenting styles affect children's competence, adjustment, delinquent behavior, and self-esteem (Heaven & Ciarrochi, 2008; Simons & Conger, 2007). Consistently, research has shown that authoritative parenting is associated with higher grades, lower rates of delinquent behavior, and lower rates of substance abuse than authoritarian or permissive parenting (Grusec, 2011; Turner & others, 2009).

Why does an authoritative parenting style provide such clear advantages over other parenting styles? First, when children perceive their parents' requests as fair and reasonable, they are more likely to comply with the requests. Second, the children are more likely to *internalize* (or accept as their own) the reasons for behaving in a certain way and thus to achieve greater self-control (Martinez & Garcia, 2008).

In contrast, authoritarian parenting tends to promote rebellion and resentment. Because compliance is based on external control and punishment, children may not learn to control their own behavior (Gershoff, 2002). In a study that included participants from China, India, Italy, Kenya, Thailand, and the Philippines, authoritarian parenting produced anxiety and aggression in children (Gershoff & others, 2010).

authoritarian parenting style Parenting style in which parents are demanding and unresponsive toward their children's needs or wishes.

permissive parenting style Parenting style in which parents are extremely tolerant and not demanding; permissive-indulgent parents are responsive to their children, while permissive-indifferent parents are unresponsive.

authoritative parenting style Parenting style in which parents set clear standards for their children's behavior but are also responsive to their children's needs and wishes.

Finally, the child with permissive parents may never learn self-control. And because permissive parents have low expectations, the child may well live up to those expectations by failing to strive to fulfill his or her potential (Baumrind, 1971). However, there is some evidence that the permissive parenting style has benefits in some cultures, including countries in South America and Southern Europe (see Garcia & Gracia, 2009; Martinez & Garcia, 2008). So, it may be that the effectiveness of particular parenting styles, like many other aspects of development, are affected by culture.

How to Be an Authoritative Parent: Some Practical Suggestions

Authoritative parents are high in both responsiveness and control. How can you successfully achieve that balance? Here are several suggestions based on psychological research.

1. Let your children know that you love them.

Attention, hugs, and other demonstrations of physical affection, coupled with a positive attitude toward your child, are *some* of the most important aspects of parenting, aspects that have enduring effects (Steinberg, 2001). Children who experience warm, positive relationships with their parents are more likely to become happy adults with stable marriages and good relationships with friends (Hardy & others, 2010). So the question is simple: Have you hugged your kids today?

2. Listen to your children.

Let your children express their opinions, and respect their preferences when it's reasonable to do so. In making rules and decisions, ask for their input and give it genuine consideration. Strive to be fair and flexible, especially on issues that are less than earthshaking, such as which clothes they wear to school.

3. Use induction to teach as you discipline.

The most effective form of discipline is called **induction** because it *induces* understanding in the child. Induction combines controlling a child's behavior with *teaching* (Hoffman, 1977). Put simply, induction involves consistently explaining (a) the reason for prohibiting or performing certain behaviors, (b) the *consequences* of the action for the child, and (c) the *effect* of the child's behavior on others. When parents use induction, the child begins to learn that his parents' actions are not completely arbitrary or unfair. The child is also more likely to

internalize the reasoning and apply it in new situations (Kerr & others, 2004; Sorkhabi, 2010).

4. Work with your child's temperamental qualities.

Think back to our earlier discussion of temperamental qualities. Be aware of your child's natural temperament and work with it, not against it. If your child is very active, for example, it is unrealistic to expect him to sit quietly during a four-hour plane or bus trip. Knowing that, you can increase the likelihood of positive experiences by planning ahead. Bring coloring books, picture books, or small toys to occupy the young child in a restaurant or at a family gathering. Take frequent "exercise stops" on a long car trip. If your child is unusually sensitive, shy, or "slow-to-warm-up," give her plenty of time to make the transition to new situations and provide lots of preparation so that she knows what to expect.

5. Understand your child's age-related cognitive abilities and limitations.

Some parents make the mistake of assuming that children think in the same way adults do. They may see a toddler or even an infant as purposely "misbehaving," "being naughty," or "rebelling" when the little one is simply doing what one-year-olds or three-year-olds do. Your expectations for appropriate behavior should be geared to the child's age and developmental stage. Having a thorough understanding of the information in this chapter is a good start. You might also consider taking a developmental psychology or child development class. Or go to your college library and check out some of the developmental psychology texts. By understanding your child's cognitive abilities and limitations at each stage of development, you're less likely to misinterpret behavior or to place inappropriate demands on him.

6. Don't expect perfection, and learn to go with the flow.

Accidents happen. Mistakes occur. Children get cranky or grumpy, especially when they're tired or hungry. Don't get too bent out of shape when your child's behavior is less than perfect. Be patient. Moments of conflict with children are a natural, inevitable, and healthy part of growing up. Look at those moments as part of the process by which a child achieves autonomy and a sense of self.

Finally, effective parenting is an ongoing process in which you, as the parent, should be regularly assessing your impact on your child. It's not always easy to combine responsiveness with control, or flexibility with an appropriate level of firmness. When you make a mistake, admit it not just to yourself, but also to your child. In doing so, you'll teach your child how to behave when she makes a mistake. As you'll discover, children are remarkably forgiving—and also resilient.

---

induction A discipline technique that combines parental control with explaining why a behavior is prohibited.

CHAPTER REVIEW

KEY PEOPLE AND KEY TERMS

Mary D. Salter Ainsworth, p. 369

Renée Baillargeon, p. 384

developmental psychology, p. 359

longitudinal design, p. 359

cross-sectional design, p. 359

zygote, p. 360

chromosome, p. 360

deoxyribonucleic acid (DNA), p. 360

gene, p. 361

genotype, p. 361

sex chromosomes, p. 361

phenotype, p. 361

epigenetics, p. 362

prenatal stage, p. 363

germinal period, p. 363

embryonic period, p. 364

teratogens, p. 364

Sandra Bem, p. 377

Erik Erikson, p. 392

stem cells, p. 364

fetal period, p. 365

temperament, p. 368

attachment, p. 369

comprehension vocabulary, p. 372

production vocabulary, p. 372

gender, p. 374

gender roles, p. 374

gender identity, p. 374

social learning theory of gender-role development, p. 376

gender schema theory, p. 377

transgender, p. 379

sensorimotor stage, p. 380

object permanence, p. 381

preoperational stage, p. 381

Lawrence Kohlberg, p. 393

Jean Piaget, p. 380

symbolic thought, p. 381

egocentrism, p. 381

irreversibility, p. 381

centration, p. 382

conservation, p. 382

concrete operational stage, p. 382

formal operational stage, p. 383

zone of proximal development, p. 385

information-processing model of cognitive development, p. 386

adolescence, p. 386

puberty, p. 386

primary sex characteristics, p. 387

Lev Vygotsky, p. 385

secondary sex characteristics, p. 387

adolescent growth spurt, p. 387

menarche, p. 387

identity, p. 391

moral reasoning, p. 393

emerging adulthood, p. 396

menopause, p. 398

activity theory of aging, p. 405

authoritarian parenting style, p. 407

permissive parenting style, p. 407

authoritative parenting style, p. 407

induction, p. 408

Lifespan Development

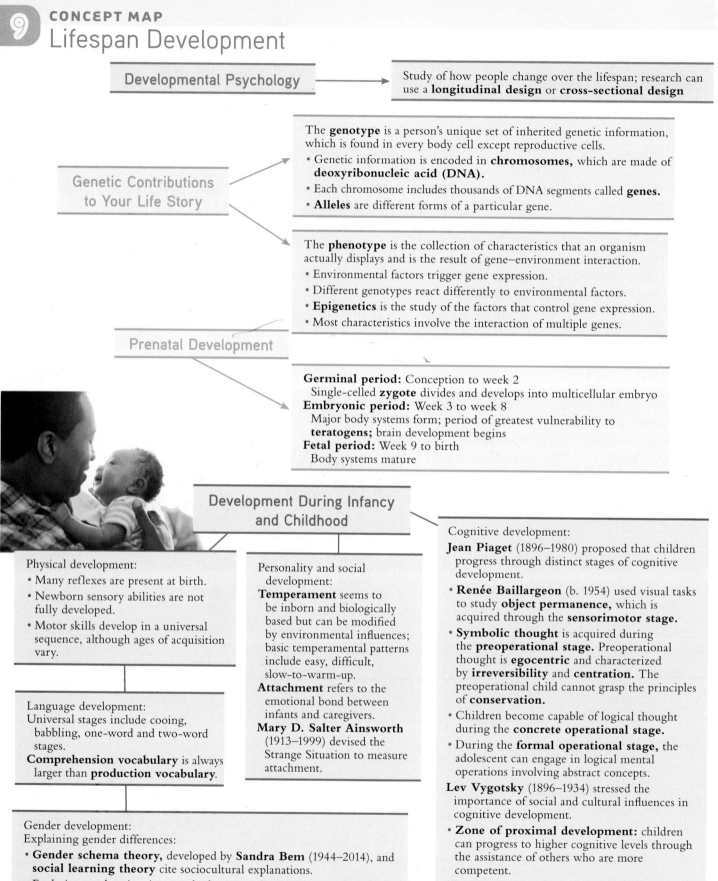

Developmental Psychology → Study of how people change over the lifespan; research can use a **longitudinal design** or **cross-sectional design**

Genetic Contributions to Your Life Story

The **genotype** is a person's unique set of inherited genetic information, which is found in every body cell except reproductive cells.
- Genetic information is encoded in **chromosomes,** which are made of **deoxyribonucleic acid (DNA).**
- Each chromosome includes thousands of DNA segments called **genes.**
- **Alleles** are different forms of a particular gene.

The **phenotype** is the collection of characteristics that an organism actually displays and is the result of gene–environment interaction.
- Environmental factors trigger gene expression.
- Different genotypes react differently to environmental factors.
- **Epigenetics** is the study of the factors that control gene expression.
- Most characteristics involve the interaction of multiple genes.

Prenatal Development

Germinal period: Conception to week 2
  Single-celled **zygote** divides and develops into multicellular embryo
Embryonic period: Week 3 to week 8
  Major body systems form; period of greatest vulnerability to **teratogens;** brain development begins
Fetal period: Week 9 to birth
  Body systems mature

Development During Infancy and Childhood

Physical development:
- Many reflexes are present at birth.
- Newborn sensory abilities are not fully developed.
- Motor skills develop in a universal sequence, although ages of acquisition vary.

Language development:
Universal stages include cooing, babbling, one-word and two-word stages.
Comprehension vocabulary is always larger than **production vocabulary**.

Gender development:
Explaining gender differences:
- **Gender schema theory,** developed by **Sandra Bem** (1944–2014), and **social learning theory** cite sociocultural explanations.
- Evolutionary theories cite sexual selection and parental investment.
- Interactionist theories combine sociocultural and biological explanations.
For **transgender** people, **gender identity** conflicts with biological sex.

Personality and social development:
Temperament seems to be inborn and biologically based but can be modified by environmental influences; basic temperamental patterns include easy, difficult, slow-to-warm-up.
Attachment refers to the emotional bond between infants and caregivers.
Mary D. Salter Ainsworth (1913–1999) devised the Strange Situation to measure attachment.

Cognitive development:
Jean Piaget (1896–1980) proposed that children progress through distinct stages of cognitive development.
- **Renée Baillargeon** (b. 1954) used visual tasks to study **object permanence,** which is acquired through the **sensorimotor stage.**
- **Symbolic thought** is acquired during the **preoperational stage.** Preoperational thought is **egocentric** and characterized by **irreversibility** and **centration.** The preoperational child cannot grasp the principles of **conservation.**
- Children become capable of logical thought during the **concrete operational stage.**
- During the **formal operational stage,** the adolescent can engage in logical mental operations involving abstract concepts.
Lev Vygotsky (1896–1934) stressed the importance of social and cultural influences in cognitive development.
- **Zone of proximal development:** children can progress to higher cognitive levels through the assistance of others who are more competent.
The **information-processing model of cognitive development** emphasizes basic mental processes and stresses that cognitive development is a process of continuous change.

Adolescence

Physical development:
- **Puberty** involves the development of **primary** and **secondary sex characteristics,** including **menarche** in girls.
- Girls experience the **adolescent growth spurt** at a younger age than boys.

Erik Erikson (1902–1994) proposed a theory of psychosocial development stressing that every stage of life is marked by a particular psychosocial conflict. **Identity** versus role confusion is associated with adolescence.

Development of moral reasoning:
Lawrence Kohlberg (1927–1987) proposed a theory of moral development in which children progressed from preconventional to conventional and ultimately postconventional moral reasoning. Criticisms of Kohlberg's theory include:
- Moral decisions are often affected by emotional or other nonrational factors.
- Carol Gilligan theorized that males and females reason differently about moral dilemmas, but evidence shows that the **moral reasoning** of men and women does not differ.
- Kohlberg's theory emphasizes individual rights, a perspective that is not shared by cultures that emphasize interdependence.

Emerging adulthood and adulthood:

Key developmental tasks are forming committed, intimate relationships and *generativity*—which means contributing to future generations through work and family life.
- In industrialized countries, **emerging adulthood** lasts from the late teens to the mid- to late 20s and is characterized by exploration of social roles, vocational choices, and relationships.
- U.S. families are increasingly diverse.
- Marital satisfaction often declines after children are born but often rises after they leave home.

Adult Development

Late adulthood and aging:
- Mental abilities begin to decline slightly at around age 60.
- Cognitive decline can be minimized when older adults are better educated, physically healthy, and engage in physical and mental activity.
- **Activity theory of aging:** life satisfaction in late adulthood is highest when people maintain their previous levels of activity.
- Erikson identified ego integrity versus despair as the key psychosocial conflict of old age.

Dying and death:
- Elisabeth Kübler-Ross proposed a five-stage model of dying: denial, anger, bargaining, depression, and acceptance.
- Individuals respond in diverse ways to impending death.

MYTH OR SCIENCE?

Is it true . . .

- That most psychologists today agree with Sigmund Freud's personality theory?
- That personality traits change quite a bit over the course of our lives?
- That personality is not influenced by genetics, but is primarily shaped by your upbringing?
- That handwriting analysis provides insights into your personality and predicts occupational success?
- That projective tests, like the famous Rorschach inkblot test, accurately reveal personality traits and unconscious conflicts?
- That there are ways to tell if you fake an answer on a personality test?
- That if you can imagine yourself taking the steps to become successful, you're more likely to actually become successful?

THE SECRET TWIN

PROLOGUE

THE TWINS, KENNETH AND JULIAN, were born a few years after the turn of the last century. At first, their parents, Gertrude and Henry, thought they were identical. Both had dark hair and deep brown eyes. Many years later, Kenneth's son, your author Don, would inherit these qualities.

But Gertrude and Henry quickly learned to tell the twins apart. Kenneth was slightly larger than Julian, and, even as infants, their personalities were distinctly different. In the photographs of Kenneth and Julian as children, Julian smiles broadly, almost merrily, his head cocked slightly. But Kenneth always looks straight at the camera, his expression thoughtful, serious, more intense.

We don't know much about Julian's childhood. Kenneth kept Julian's existence a closely guarded secret for more than 50 years. In fact, it was only a few years before his own death that Kenneth revealed that he had once had a twin brother named Julian.

Still, it's possible to get glimpses of Julian's early life from the letters the boys wrote home from summer camp in 1919 and 1920. Kenneth's letters to his mother were affectionate and respectful, telling her about their daily activities and reassuring her that he would look after his twin brother. "I reminded Julian about the boats and I will watch him good," Kenneth wrote in one letter. Julian's letters were equally affectionate, but shorter and filled with misspelled words. Julian's letters also revealed glimpses of his impulsive nature. He repeatedly promised his mother, "I will not go out in the boats alone again."

Julian's impulsive nature was to have a significant impact on his life. When he was 12 years old, Julian darted in front of a car and was seriously injured, sustaining a concussion. In retrospect, Kenneth believed that that was when Julian's problems began. Perhaps it was, because not long after the accident Julian got into serious trouble for the first time: He got caught red-handed stealing money from the "poor box" at church.

Although Kenneth claimed that Julian had always been the smarter twin, Julian fell behind in high school and graduated a year later than Kenneth. After high school, Kenneth left the quiet farming community of Grinnell, Iowa, and moved to Minneapolis. He quickly became self-sufficient, taking a job managing newspaper carriers. Julian stayed in Grinnell and became apprenticed to learn typesetting. Given Julian's propensity for adventure, it's not

surprising that he found typesetting monotonous. So in the spring of 1928, Julian quit typesetting. He also decided to leave Iowa and head east to look for more interesting possibilities.

He found them in Tennessee. A few months after Julian left Iowa, Henry received word that Julian had been arrested for armed robbery and sentenced to 15 years in a Tennessee state prison. Though Kenneth was only 22 years old, Henry gave him a large sum of money and the family car and sent him to try to get Julian released.

Kenneth's conversation with the judge in Knoxville was the first of

IN THIS CHAPTER:

INTRODUCTION: What Is Personality?

The Psychoanalytic Perspective on Personality

The Humanistic Perspective on Personality

The Social Cognitive Perspective on Personality

The Trait Perspective on Personality

Assessing Personality: Psychological Tests

PSYCH FOR YOUR LIFE: Possible Selves: Imagine the Possibilities

many times that he would deal with the judicial system on someone else's behalf. After much negotiation, the judge agreed: If Julian promised to leave Tennessee and never return, and Kenneth paid the cash "fines," Julian would be released from prison.

When Julian walked through the prison gates the next morning, Kenneth stood waiting with a fresh suit of clothes. "Mother and Father want you to come back to Grinnell," he told Julian. But Julian would not hear of it, saying that instead he wanted to go to California to seek his fortune.

"I can't let you do that, Julian," Kenneth said, looking hard at his twin brother.

"You can't stop me, brother," Julian responded, with a cocky smile. Reluctantly, Kenneth kept just enough money to buy himself a train ticket back to Iowa. He gave Julian the rest of the money and the family car.

Julian got as far as Phoenix, Arizona, before he met his destiny. In broad daylight, he robbed a drugstore at gunpoint. As he backed out of the store, a policeman spotted him. A gun battle followed, and Julian was shot twice. Somehow he managed to escape and holed up in a hotel room. Alone and untended, Julian died two days later from the bullet wounds. Once again, Kenneth was sent to retrieve his twin brother.

On a bitterly cold November morning in 1928, Julian's immediate

The Twins Julian *(left)* and Kenneth *(right)*, with their father, Henry, when they were about 10 years old. As boys, Kenneth and Julian were inseparable.

Courtesy of Don Hockenbury

family laid him to rest in the family plot in Grinnell. On the one hand, Kenneth felt largely responsible for Julian's misguided life. "I should have tried harder to help Julian," Kenneth later reflected. On the other hand, Julian had disgraced the family. From the day Julian was buried, the family never spoke of him again, not even in private.

Kenneth took it upon himself to atone for the failings of his twin brother. In the fall of 1929, he entered law school in Tennessee—the same state from which he had secured Julian's release from prison. Three

years later, at the height of the Great Depression, Kenneth established himself as a lawyer in Sioux City, Iowa, where he would practice law for more than 50 years.

As an attorney, Kenneth Hockenbury was known for his integrity, his intensity in the courtroom, and his willingness to take cases regardless of the client's ability to pay. "Someone must defend the poor," he said repeatedly. In lieu of money, he often accepted labor from a working man or produce from farmers.

Almost sixty years after Julian's death, Kenneth died. But unlike the sparse gathering that had attended Julian's burial, scores of people came to pay their last respects to Kenneth Hockenbury. "Your father helped me so much," stranger after stranger told Don at Kenneth's funeral. Without question, Kenneth had devoted his life to helping others.

Why did Kenneth and Julian turn out so differently? Two boys, born on the same day into the same middle-class family. Kenneth the conscientious, serious one; Julian the laughing boy with mischief in his eyes. How can we explain the fundamental differences in their personalities?

No doubt your family, too, is made up of people with very different personalities. By the end of this chapter, you'll have a much greater appreciation for how psychologists explain such personality differences. □

INTRODUCTION:
What Is Personality?

KEY THEME

Personality is defined as an individual's unique and relatively consistent patterns of thinking, feeling, and behaving.

KEY QUESTION

› What are the four major theoretical perspectives on personality?

That you already have an intuitive understanding of the word *personality* is easy to demonstrate. Just from reading this chapter's Prologue, you could easily describe different aspects of Kenneth's and Julian's personalities. Indeed, we frequently toss around the word *personality* in everyday conversations. "He's very competent, but he has an abrasive personality." "She's got such a delightful personality, you can't help liking her."

Your intuitive understanding of personality is probably very similar to the way that psychologists define the concept. **Personality** is defined as an individual's unique and relatively consistent patterns of thinking, feeling, and behaving. A **personality theory** is an attempt to describe and explain how people are similar, how they are different, and why every individual is unique. In short, a personality theory ambitiously tries to explain the *whole person*. At the outset, it's important to stress that no single theory can adequately explain *all* of the aspects of human personality. Every personality theory has its unique strengths and limitations.

Personality theories often reflect the work of a single individual or of a few closely associated individuals. Thus, it's not surprising that many personality theories bear the distinct personal stamp of their creators to a much greater degree than do other kinds of psychological theories. Consequently, we've tried to let the personality theorists speak for themselves. Throughout this chapter, you'll encounter carefully chosen quotations from the theorists' own writings. These quotations will give you brief glimpses into the minds of some of the most influential thinkers in psychology.

There are many personality theories, but they can be roughly grouped under four basic perspectives: the psychoanalytic, humanistic, social cognitive, and trait perspectives. In a nutshell, here's what each perspective emphasizes:

- The *psychoanalytic perspective* emphasizes the importance of unconscious processes and the influence of early childhood experience.

- The *humanistic perspective* represents an optimistic look at human nature, emphasizing the self and the fulfillment of a person's unique potential.

- The *social cognitive perspective* emphasizes learning and conscious cognitive processes, including the importance of beliefs about the self, goal setting, and self-regulation.

- The *trait perspective* emphasizes the description and measurement of specific personality differences among individuals.

After looking at some of the major personality theories that reflect each perspective, we'll consider a closely related topic—how personality is measured and evaluated. And yes, we'll talk about the famous inkblots. But for the inkblots to make sense, we need to trace the evolution of modern personality theories. We'll begin with the tale of a bearded, cigar-smoking gentleman from Vienna of whom you just may have heard—Sigmund Freud.

Colouria/Alamy

Explaining Personality Some people are outgoing, expressive, and fun-loving, like this father and his young son. Other people consistently display the opposite qualities. Are such personality differences due to early childhood experiences? Genetics? Social environment? Personality theories attempt to account for the individual differences that make each one of us unique.

The Psychoanalytic Perspective on Personality

KEY THEME

Freud's psychoanalysis stresses the importance of unconscious forces, sexual and aggressive instincts, and early childhood experience.

KEY QUESTIONS

> What were the key influences on Sigmund Freud's thinking?

> How are unconscious influences revealed?

> What are the three basic structures of personality, and what are the defense mechanisms?

Sigmund Freud, one of the most influential figures of the twentieth century, was the founder of psychoanalysis. **Psychoanalysis** is a theory of personality that stresses the influence of unconscious mental processes, the importance of sexual and aggressive instincts, and the enduring effects of early childhood experience on personality.

personality An individual's unique and relatively consistent patterns of thinking, feeling, and behaving.

personality theory A theory that attempts to describe and explain similarities and differences in people's patterns of thinking, feeling, and behaving.

psychoanalysis (in personality) Sigmund Freud's theory of personality, which emphasizes unconscious determinants of behavior, sexual and aggressive instinctual drives, and the enduring effects of early childhood experiences on later personality development.

Freud the Outsider Sigmund Freud (1856–1939) is shown with his wife, Martha, and youngest child, Anna, at their Vienna home in 1898. Freud always considered himself to be an outsider. First, he was a Jew at a time when anti-Semitism was strong in Europe. Second, Freud's belief that expressions of sexuality are reflected in the behavior of infants and young children was controversial and shocking to his contemporaries. To some degree, however, Freud enjoyed his role as the isolated scientist—it served him well in trying to set himself, and his ideas on personality, apart from other researchers (Gay, 2006).

Freud the Leader In 1909, Freud visited the United States to lecture on his ideas at Clark University in Massachusetts. A year later, Freud and his many followers founded the International Psychoanalytic Association.

Because so many of Freud's ideas have become part of our common culture, it is difficult to imagine just how radical he seemed to his contemporaries. The following biographical sketch highlights some of the important influences that shaped Freud's ideas and theory.

The Life of Sigmund Freud

Sigmund Freud was born in 1856 in what is today Pribor, Czech Republic. When he was 4 years old, his family moved to Vienna, where he lived until the last year of his life.

Freud was extremely intelligent and intensely ambitious. He studied medicine, became a physician, and then proved himself to be an outstanding physiological researcher. Early in his career, Freud was among the first investigators of a new drug that had anesthetic and mood-altering properties—cocaine. However, one of Freud's colleagues received credit for the discovery of the anesthetic properties of cocaine, which left Freud bitter. Adding to his disappointment, Freud's enthusiasm for the medical potential of cocaine quickly faded when he recognized that the drug was addictive (Fancher, 1973; Gay, 2006).

Prospects for an academic career in scientific research were very poor, especially for a Jew in Vienna, which was intensely anti-Semitic at that time. So when he married Martha Bernays in 1886, Freud reluctantly gave up physiological research for a private practice in neurology. The income from private practice would be needed: Sigmund and Martha had six children. One of Freud's daughters, Anna Freud, later became an important psychoanalytic theorist.

INFLUENCES IN THE DEVELOPMENT OF FREUD'S IDEAS

Freud's theory evolved gradually during his first 20 years of private practice. He based his theory on observations of his patients as well as on self-analysis. An early influence on Freud was Joseph Breuer, a highly respected physician. Breuer described to Freud the striking case of a young woman with an array of puzzling psychological and physical symptoms. Breuer found that if he first hypnotized this patient, then asked her to talk freely about a given symptom, forgotten memories of traumatic events emerged. After she freely expressed the pent-up emotions associated with the event, her symptom disappeared. Breuer called this phenomenon *catharsis* (Freud, 1925).

At first, Freud embraced Breuer's technique, but he found that not all of his patients could be hypnotized. Eventually, Freud dropped the use of hypnosis and developed his own technique of **free association** to help his patients uncover forgotten memories. Freud's patients would spontaneously report their uncensored thoughts, mental images, and feelings as they came to mind. From these "free associations," the thread that led to the crucial long-forgotten memories could be unraveled. Breuer and Freud described several of their case studies in their landmark book, *Studies on Hysteria*. Its publication in 1895 marked the beginning of psychoanalysis.

In 1900, Freud published what many consider his most important work, *The Interpretation of Dreams*. By the early 1900s, Freud had developed the basic tenets of his psychoanalytic theory and was no longer the isolated scientist. He was gaining international recognition and developing a following.

In 1904, Freud published what was to become one of his most popular books, *The Psychopathology of Everyday Life*. He described how unconscious thoughts, feelings, and wishes are often reflected in acts of forgetting, inadvertent slips of the tongue, accidents, and errors. By 1909, Freud's influence was also felt in the United States, when he and other psychoanalysts were invited to lecture at Clark University in

Massachusetts. For the next 30 years, Freud continued to refine his theory, publishing many books, articles, and lectures.

The last two decades of Freud's life were filled with many personal tragedies. The terrible devastation of World War I weighed heavily on his mind. In 1920, one of his daughters died. In the early 1920s, Freud developed cancer of the jaw, a condition for which he would ultimately undergo more than 30 operations. And during the late 1920s and early 1930s, the Nazis were steadily gaining power in Germany.

Given the climate of the times, it's not surprising that Freud came to focus on humanity's destructive tendencies. For years he had asserted that sexuality was the fundamental human motive, but now he added aggression as a second powerful human instinct. During this period, Freud wrote *Civilization and Its Discontents* (1930), in which he applied his psychoanalytic perspective to civilization as a whole. The central theme of the book is that human nature and civilization are in basic conflict—a conflict that cannot be resolved.

Freud's extreme pessimism was undoubtedly a reflection of the destruction he saw all around him. By 1933, Adolf Hitler had seized power in Germany. Freud's books were banned and publicly burned in Berlin. Five years later, the Nazis marched into Austria, seizing control of Freud's homeland. Although Freud's life was clearly threatened, it was only after his youngest daughter, Anna, had been detained and questioned by the Gestapo that Freud reluctantly agreed to leave Vienna. Under great duress, Freud moved his family to the safety of England. A year later, his cancer returned. In 1939, Freud died in London at the age of 83 (Gay, 2006).

This brief sketch cannot do justice to the richness of Freud's life and the influence of his culture on his ideas. Today, Freud's legacy continues to influence psychology, philosophy, literature, art, and psychotherapy (Merlino & others, 2008; O'Roark, 2007).

Bettmann/Corbis

Freud the Exile In the spring of 1938, Freud fled Nazi persecution for the safety of London on the eve of World War II. Four of Freud's sisters who remained behind later died in the Nazi extermination camps. He is shown arriving in England, his eldest daughter, Mathilde, at his side. Freud died in London on September 23, 1939.

Freud's Dynamic Theory of Personality

Freud (1940) saw personality and behavior as the result of a constant interplay among conflicting psychological forces. These psychological forces operate at three different levels of awareness: the conscious, the preconscious, and the unconscious. All the thoughts, feelings, and sensations that you're aware of at this particular moment represent the *conscious* level. The *preconscious* contains information that you're not currently aware of but can easily bring to conscious awareness, such as memories of recent events or your street address.

However, the conscious and preconscious are merely the visible tip of the iceberg of the mind. The bulk of this psychological iceberg is made up of the **unconscious,** which lies submerged below the waterline of the preconscious and conscious (see Figure 10.1 on the next page). You're not directly aware of these submerged thoughts, feelings, wishes, and drives, but the unconscious exerts an enormous influence on your conscious thoughts and behavior.

Although it is not directly accessible, Freud (1904) believed that unconscious material often seeps through to the conscious level in distorted, disguised, or symbolic forms. Like a detective searching for clues, Freud carefully analyzed his patients' reports of dreams and free associations for evidence of unconscious wishes, fantasies, and conflicts. Dream analysis was particularly important to Freud. "The interpretation of dreams is the royal road to a knowledge of the unconscious activities of the mind," he wrote in *The Interpretation of Dreams* (1900). Beneath the surface images, or *manifest content,* of a dream lies its *latent content*—the true, hidden, unconscious meaning that is disguised in the dream symbols (see Chapter 4).

Freud (1904, 1933) believed that the unconscious can also be revealed in unintentional actions, such as accidents, mistakes, instances of forgetting, and inadvertent slips of the tongue, which are often referred to as "Freudian slips."

free association A psychoanalytic technique in which the patient spontaneously reports all thoughts, feelings, and mental images that arise, revealing unconscious thoughts and emotions.

unconscious In Freud's theory, a term used to describe thoughts, feelings, wishes, and drives that are operating below the level of conscious awareness.

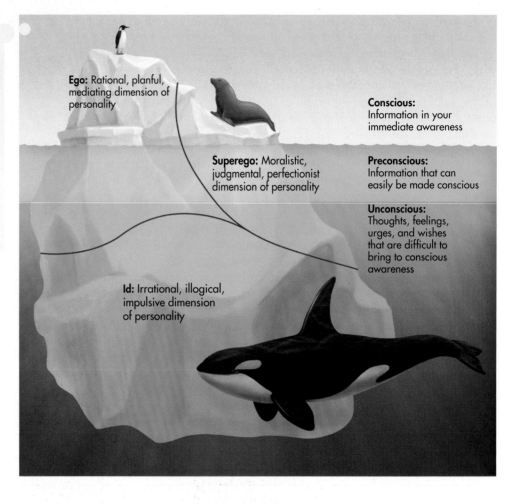

FIGURE 10.1 Levels of Awareness and the Structure of Personality Freud believed that personality is composed of three psychological processes—the id, the ego, and the superego—that operate at different levels of awareness. If you think of personality as being like an iceberg, the bulk of this psychological iceberg is represented by the irrational, impulsive id, which lies beneath the waterline of consciousness. Unlike the entirely unconscious id, the rational ego and the moralistic superego are at least partially conscious.

Ego: Rational, planful, mediating dimension of personality

Conscious: Information in your immediate awareness

Superego: Moralistic, judgmental, perfectionist dimension of personality

Preconscious: Information that can easily be made conscious

Unconscious: Thoughts, feelings, urges, and wishes that are difficult to bring to conscious awareness

Id: Irrational, illogical, impulsive dimension of personality

id Latin for *the it*; in Freud's theory, the completely unconscious, irrational component of personality that seeks immediate satisfaction of instinctual urges and drives; ruled by the pleasure principle.

libido The psychological and emotional energy associated with expressions of sexuality; the sex drive.

pleasure principle The motive to obtain pleasure and avoid tension or discomfort; the most fundamental human motive and the guiding principle of the id.

ego Latin for *I*; in Freud's theory, the partly conscious rational component of personality that regulates thoughts and behavior, and is most in touch with the demands of the external world.

reality principle The capacity to accommodate external demands by postponing gratification until the appropriate time or circumstances exist.

superego In Freud's theory, the partly conscious, self-evaluative, moralistic component of personality that is formed through the internalization of parental and societal rules.

THE STRUCTURE OF PERSONALITY

According to Freud (1933), each person possesses a certain amount of psychological energy. This psychological energy develops into the three basic structures of personality—the id, the ego, and the superego (see Figure 10.1). Understand that these are *not* separate identities or brain structures. Rather, they are distinct psychological processes.

The **id,** the most primitive part of the personality, is entirely unconscious and present at birth. The id is completely immune to logic, values, morality, danger, and the demands of the external world. It is the original source of psychological energy, parts of which will later evolve into the ego and superego (Freud, 1933, 1940).

The id is connected to the biological urges that perpetuate the existence of the individual and the species—hunger, thirst, physical comfort, and, most important, sexuality. Freud (1915c) used the word **libido** to refer specifically to sexual energy or motivation.

The id is ruled by the **pleasure principle**—the relentless drive toward immediate satisfaction of the instinctual urges, especially sexual urges (Freud, 1920). Thus, the id strives to increase pleasure, reduce tension, and avoid pain. Even though it operates unconsciously, Freud saw the pleasure principle as the most fundamental human motive.

Equipped only with the id, the newborn infant is completely driven by the pleasure principle. When cold, wet, hungry, or uncomfortable, the newborn wants his needs addressed immediately. As the infant gains experience with the external world, however, he learns that his caretakers can't or won't always immediately satisfy those needs.

Thus, a new dimension of personality develops from part of the id's psychological energy—the **ego.** Partly conscious, the ego represents the organized, rational, and planning dimensions of personality (Freud, 1933). As the mediator between the id's instinctual demands and the restrictions of the outer world, the ego operates on the reality principle. The **reality principle** is the capacity to postpone gratification until the appropriate time or circumstances exist in the external world (Freud, 1940).

As the young child gains experience, she gradually learns acceptable ways to satisfy her desires and instincts, such as waiting her turn rather than pushing another child off a playground swing. Hence, the ego is the pragmatic part of the personality that learns various compromises to reduce the tension of the id's instinctual urges. If the ego can't identify an acceptable compromise to satisfy an instinctual urge, such as a sexual urge, it can *repress* the impulse, or remove it from conscious awareness (Freud, 1915a).

In early childhood, the ego must deal with external parental demands and limitations. Implicit in those demands are the parents' values and morals, their ideas of the right and wrong ways to think, act, and feel. Eventually, the child encounters other advocates of society's values, such as teachers and religious and legal authorities (Freud, 1926). Gradually, these social values move from being externally imposed demands to being *internalized* rules and values.

By about age 5 or 6, the young child has developed an internal, parental voice that is partly conscious—the **superego.** As the internal representation of parental and societal values, the superego evaluates the acceptability of behavior and thoughts, then praises or admonishes. Put simply, your superego represents your conscience, issuing demands "like a strict father with a child" (Freud, 1926). It judges your own behavior as right or wrong, good or bad, acceptable or unacceptable. And, should you fail to live up to these morals, the superego can be harshly punitive, imposing feelings of inferiority, guilt, shame, self-doubt, and anxiety. If we apply Freud's terminology to the twins described in the chapter Prologue, Kenneth's superego was clearly stronger than Julian's.

THE EGO DEFENSE MECHANISMS
UNCONSCIOUS SELF-DECEPTIONS

The ego has a difficult task. It must be strong, flexible, and resourceful to successfully mediate conflicts among the instinctual demands of the id, the moral authority of the superego, and external restrictions. According to Freud (1923), everyone experiences an ongoing daily battle among these three warring personality processes.

When the demands of the id or superego threaten to overwhelm the ego, *anxiety* results (Freud, 1915b). If instinctual id impulses overpower the ego, a person may act impulsively and perhaps destructively. Using Freud's terminology, you could say that Julian's id was out of control when he stole from the church and tried to rob the drugstore. In contrast, if superego demands overwhelm the ego, an individual may suffer from guilt, self-reproach, or even suicidal impulses for failing to live up to the superego's moral standards (Freud, 1936). Using Freudian terminology again, it is probably safe to say that Kenneth's feelings of guilt over Julian were inspired by his superego.

If a realistic solution or compromise is not possible, the ego may temporarily reduce anxiety by *distorting* thoughts or perceptions of reality through processes that

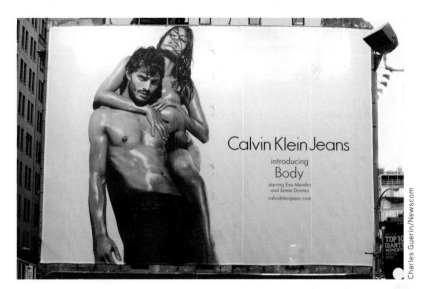

Charles Guerin/Newscom

Appealing to the Id How would Freud explain the appeal of this billboard? In Freud's theory, the id is ruled by the pleasure principle—the instinctual drive to increase pleasure, reduce tension, and avoid pain.

Thanasis Zovoilis/Getty Images

Establishing the Superego As children, we learn many rules and values from parents and other authorities. The internalization of such values is what Freud called the superego—the inner voice that is our conscience. When we fail to live up to its moral ideals, the superego imposes feelings of guilt, shame, and inferiority.

ego defense mechanisms Largely unconscious distortions of thoughts or perceptions that act to reduce anxiety.

repression (in psychoanalytic theory of personality and psychotherapy) The unconscious exclusion of anxiety-provoking thoughts, feelings, and memories from conscious awareness; the most fundamental ego defense mechanism.

displacement The ego defense mechanism that involves unconsciously shifting the target of an emotional urge to a substitute target that is less threatening or dangerous.

sublimation An ego defense mechanism that involves redirecting sexual urges toward productive, socially acceptable, nonsexual activities; a form of displacement.

Freud called **ego defense mechanisms** (A. Freud, 1946; Freud, 1915c). By resorting to these largely unconscious self-deceptions, the ego can maintain an integrated sense of self while searching for a more acceptable and realistic solution to a conflict between the id and superego.

The most fundamental ego defense mechanism is **repression** (Freud, 1915a, 1936). To some degree, repression occurs in every ego defense mechanism. In simple terms, repression is unconscious forgetting. Anxiety-producing thoughts, feelings, or impulses are pushed out of conscious awareness into the unconscious. Common examples include traumatic events, past failures, embarrassments, disappointments, the names of disliked people, episodes of physical pain or illness, and unacceptable urges.

Repression, however, is not an all-or-nothing psychological process. As Freud (1939) explained, "The repressed material retains its impetus to penetrate into consciousness." In other words, if you encounter a situation that is very similar to one you've repressed, bits and pieces of memories of the previous situation may begin to resurface. In such instances, the ego may employ other defense mechanisms that allow the urge or information to remain partially conscious.

This is what occurs with the ego defense mechanism of displacement. **Displacement** occurs when emotional impulses are redirected to a substitute object or person, usually one less threatening or dangerous than the original source of conflict (A. Freud, 1946). For example, an employee angered by a supervisor's unfair treatment may displace his hostility onto family members when he comes home from work. The employee consciously experiences anger but directs it toward someone other than its true target, which remains unconscious.

Freud (1930) believed that a special form of displacement, called *sublimation,* is largely responsible for the productive and creative contributions of people and even of whole societies. **Sublimation** involves displacing sexual urges toward "an aim other than, and remote from, that of sexual gratification" (Freud, 1914). In effect, sublimation channels sexual urges into productive, socially acceptable, nonsexual activities (Cohen & others, 2014).

The major defense mechanisms are summarized in Table 10.1. In Freud's view, the drawback to using any defense mechanism is that maintaining these self-deceptions requires psychological energy. Freud (1936) pointed out that this "continuous expenditure of effort" depletes psychological energy that is needed to cope effectively with the demands of daily life.

The use of defense mechanisms is very common. And, when ego defense mechanisms are used in limited areas and on a short-term basis, psychological energy is not seriously depleted. But when defense mechanisms delay or interfere with our use of more constructive coping strategies, they can be counterproductive.

"Look, call it denial if you like, but I think what goes on in my personal life is none of my own damn business."

Robert Mankoff The New Yorker Collection/ The Cartoon Bank

Sublimation In Freud's view, creative or productive behaviors represent the rechanneling of sexual energy, or libido—an ego defense mechanism he termed *sublimation.* Freud believed that civilization's greatest achievements are the result of the sublimation of instinctual energy into socially acceptable activities, like the work of this sculptor. Later personality theorists criticized Freud's refusal to consider creativity a drive in its own right.

Hero Images/Corbis

TABLE 10.1

The Major Ego Defense Mechanisms

Defense	Description	Example
Repression	The complete exclusion from consciousness of anxiety-producing thoughts, feelings, or impulses; the most basic defense mechanism.	Three years after being hospitalized for back surgery, a man can remember only vague details about the event.
Displacement	The redirection of emotional impulses toward a substitute person or object, usually one less threatening or dangerous than the original source of conflict.	Angered by a neighbor's hateful comment, a mother spanks her daughter for accidentally spilling her milk.
Sublimation	A form of displacement in which sexual urges are rechanneled into productive, nonsexual activities.	A graduate student works on her thesis 14 hours a day while her husband is on an extended business trip.
Rationalization	Justifying one's actions or feelings with socially acceptable explanations rather than consciously acknowledging one's true motives or desires.	After being rejected by a prestigious university, a student explains that he is glad because he would be happier at a smaller, less competitive college.
Projection	The attribution of one's own unacceptable urges or qualities to others.	A married woman who is sexually attracted to a co-worker accuses him of flirting with her.
Reaction formation	Thinking or behaving in a way that is the extreme opposite of unacceptable urges or impulses.	Threatened by his awakening sexual attraction to girls, an adolescent boy goes out of his way to tease and torment adolescent girls.
Denial	The failure to recognize or acknowledge the existence of anxiety-provoking information.	Despite having multiple drinks every night, a man says he is not an alcoholic because he never drinks before 5 P.M.
Undoing	A form of unconscious repentance that involves neutralizing or atoning for an unacceptable action or thought with a second action or thought.	A woman who gets a tax refund by cheating on her taxes makes a larger-than-usual donation to the church collection on the following Sunday.
Regression	Retreating to a behavior pattern characteristic of an earlier stage of development.	After her parents' bitter divorce, a 10-year-old girl refuses to sleep alone in her room, crawling into bed with her mother.

Personality Development

THE PSYCHOSEXUAL STAGES

KEY THEME

The psychosexual stages are age-related developmental periods, and each stage represents a different focus of the id's sexual energies.

KEY QUESTIONS

> What are the five psychosexual stages, and what are the core conflicts of each stage?
> What is the consequence of fixation?
> What role does the Oedipus complex play in personality development?

According to Freud (1905), people progress through five psychosexual stages of development. The foundations of adult personality are established during the first five years of life, as the child progresses through the *oral, anal,* and *phallic* psychosexual stages. The *latency stage* occurs during late childhood, and the fifth and final stage, the *genital stage,* begins in adolescence.

Each psychosexual stage represents a different focus of the id's sexual energies. Freud (1940) contended that "sexual life does not begin only at puberty, but starts with clear manifestations after birth." This statement is often misinterpreted. Freud was *not* saying that an infant experiences sexual urges in the same way that an adult does. Instead, Freud believed that the infant or young child expresses primitive sexual urges by seeking sensual pleasure from different areas of the body. Thus, the **psychosexual stages** are age-related developmental periods in which sexual impulses are focused on different bodily zones and are expressed through the activities associated with these areas.

Over the first five years of life, the expression of primitive sexual urges progresses from one bodily zone to another in a distinct order: the mouth, the anus, and the

psychosexual stages In Freud's theory, age-related developmental periods in which the child's sexual urges are focused on different areas of the body and are expressed through the activities associated with those areas.

genitals. The first year of life is characterized as the *oral stage*. During this time the infant derives pleasure through the oral activities of sucking, chewing, and biting. During the next two years, pleasure is derived through elimination and acquiring control over elimination—the *anal stage.* In the *phallic stage,* pleasure seeking is focused on the genitals.

FIXATION
UNRESOLVED DEVELOPMENTAL CONFLICTS

At each psychosexual stage, Freud (1905) believed, the infant or young child is faced with a developmental conflict that must be successfully resolved in order to move on to the next stage. The heart of this conflict is the degree to which parents either frustrate or overindulge the child's expression of pleasurable feelings. Hence, Freud (1940) believed that parental attitudes and the timing of specific child-rearing events, such as weaning or toilet training, leave a lasting influence on personality development.

If frustrated, the child will be left with feelings of unmet needs characteristic of that stage. If overindulged, the child may be reluctant to move on to the next stage. In either case, the result of an unresolved developmental conflict is *fixation* at a particular stage. The person continues to seek pleasure through behaviors that are similar to those associated with that psychosexual stage. For example, the adult who constantly chews gum, smokes, or bites her fingernails may have unresolved oral psychosexual conflicts.

THE OEDIPUS COMPLEX
A PSYCHOSEXUAL DRAMA

The most critical conflict that the child must successfully resolve for healthy personality and sexual development occurs during the phallic stage (Freud, 1923, 1940). As the child becomes more aware of pleasure derived from the genital area, Freud believed, the child develops a sexual attraction to the opposite-sex parent and hostility toward the same-sex parent. This is the famous **Oedipus complex,** named after the protagonist of a Greek myth. Abandoned at birth, Oedipus does not know the identity of his parents. As an adult, he unknowingly kills his father and marries his mother.

According to Freud, this attraction to the opposite-sex parent plays out as a sexual drama in the child's mind, a drama with different plot twists for boys and for girls. For boys, the Oedipus complex unfolds as a confrontation with the father for the affections of the mother. The little boy feels hostility and jealousy toward his father, but he realizes that his father is more physically powerful. The boy experiences *castration anxiety,* or the fear that his father will punish him by castrating him (Freud, 1933).

To resolve the Oedipus complex and these anxieties, the little boy ultimately joins forces with his former enemy by resorting to the defense mechanism of **identification.** That is, he imitates and internalizes his father's values, attitudes, and mannerisms. There is, however, one strict limitation in identifying with the father. Only the father can enjoy the sexual affections of the mother. This limitation becomes internalized as a taboo against incestuous urges in the boy's developing superego, a taboo that is enforced by the superego's use of guilt and societal restrictions (Freud, 1905, 1923).

Girls also ultimately resolve the Oedipus complex by identifying with the same-sex parent and developing a strong superego taboo against incestuous urges. But the underlying sexual drama in girls follows different themes. The little girl discovers that little boys have a penis and that she does not. She feels a sense of deprivation and loss that Freud termed *penis envy.*

"He has a few things to work through, but we're good together."

Oedipus complex In Freud's theory, a child's unconscious sexual desire for the opposite-sex parent, usually accompanied by hostile feelings toward the same-sex parent.

identification In psychoanalytic theory, an ego defense mechanism that involves reducing anxiety by imitating the behavior and characteristics of another person.

According to Freud (1940), the little girl blames her mother for "sending her into the world so insufficiently equipped." Thus, she develops contempt for and resentment toward her mother. However, in her attempt to take her mother's place with her father, she also *identifies* with her mother. Like the little boy, the little girl internalizes the attributes of the same-sex parent.

Freud's views on female sexuality, particularly the concept of penis envy, are among his most severely criticized ideas. Perhaps recognizing that his explanation of female psychosexual development rested on shaky ground, Freud (1926) admitted, "We know less about the sexual life of little girls than of boys. But we need not feel ashamed of this distinction. After all, the sexual life of adult women is a 'dark continent' for psychology."

JGI/Jamie Grill/Getty Images

Competing with Mom for Dad? According to Freud, the child identifies with the same-sex parent as a way of resolving sexual attraction toward the opposite-sex parent—the Oedipus complex. Freud believed that imitating the same-sex parent also plays an important role in the development of gender identity and, ultimately, of healthy sexual maturity.

THE LATENCY AND GENITAL STAGES

Freud felt that because of the intense anxiety associated with the Oedipus complex, the sexual urges of boys and girls become repressed during the *latency stage* in late childhood. Outwardly, children in the latency stage express a strong desire to associate with same-sex peers, a preference that strengthens the child's sexual identity.

The final resolution of the Oedipus complex occurs in adolescence, during the *genital stage.* As incestuous urges start to resurface, they are prohibited by the moral ideals of the superego as well as by societal restrictions. Thus, the person directs sexual urges toward socially acceptable substitutes, who often resemble the person's opposite-sex parent (Freud, 1905).

In Freud's theory, a healthy personality and sense of sexuality result when conflicts are successfully resolved at each stage of psychosexual development (summarized in Table 10.2). Successfully negotiating the conflicts at each psychosexual stage results in the person's capacity to love and in productive living through one's work, child rearing, and other accomplishments.

> It often happens that a young man falls in love seriously for the first time with a mature woman, or a girl with an elderly man in a position of authority; this is a clear echo of the [earlier] phase of development that we have been discussing, since these figures are able to re-animate pictures of their mother or father.
>
> —*Sigmund Freud (1905)*

TABLE 10.2

Freud's Psychosexual Stages

Age	Stage	Description
Birth to age 1	Oral	The mouth is the primary focus of pleasurable and gratifying sensations, which the infant achieves via feeding and exploring objects with his or her mouth.
Ages 1 to 3	Anal	The anus is the primary focus of pleasurable sensations, which the young child derives through developing control over elimination via toilet training.
Ages 3 to 6	Phallic	The genitals are the primary focus of pleasurable sensations, which the child derives through sexual curiosity, masturbation, and sexual attraction to the opposite-sex parent.
Ages 7 to 11	Latency	Sexual impulses become repressed and dormant as the child develops same-sex friendships with peers and focuses on school, sports, and other activities.
Adolescence	Genital	As the adolescent reaches physical sexual maturity, the genitals become the primary focus of pleasurable sensations, which the person seeks to satisfy in heterosexual relationships.

collective unconscious In Jung's theory, the hypothesized part of the unconscious mind that is inherited from previous generations and that contains universally shared ancestral experiences and ideas.

archetypes (AR-kuh-types) In Jung's theory, the inherited mental images of universal human instincts, themes, and preoccupations that are the main components of the collective unconscious.

The Neo-Freudians
FREUD'S DESCENDANTS AND DISSENTERS

KEY THEME

The neo-Freudians followed Freud in stressing the importance of the unconscious and early childhood, but they developed their own personality theories.

KEY QUESTIONS

> How did the neo-Freudians generally depart from Freud's ideas?
> What were the key ideas of Jung, Horney, and Adler?
> What are three key criticisms of Freud's theory and of the psychoanalytic perspective?

Freud's ideas were always controversial. But by the early 1900s, he had attracted a number of followers, many of whom went to Vienna to study with him. Although these early followers developed their own personality theories, they still recognized the importance of many of Freud's basic notions, such as the influence of unconscious processes and early childhood experiences. In effect, they kept the foundations that Freud had established but offered new explanations for personality processes. Hence, these theorists are often called *neo-Freudians* (the prefix *neo* means "new"). The neo-Freudians and their theories are considered part of the psychoanalytic perspective on personality.

In general, the neo-Freudians disagreed with Freud on three key points. First, they took issue with Freud's belief that behavior was primarily motivated by sexual urges. Second, they disagreed with Freud's contention that personality is fundamentally determined by early childhood experiences. Instead, the neo-Freudians believed that personality can also be influenced by experiences throughout the lifespan. Third, the neo-Freudian theorists departed from Freud's generally pessimistic view of human nature and society.

In Chapter 9 on lifespan development, we described the psychosocial theory of one famous neo-Freudian, Erik Erikson. In this chapter, we'll look at the basic ideas of three other important neo-Freudians: Carl Jung, Karen Horney, and Alfred Adler.

CARL JUNG
ARCHETYPES AND THE COLLECTIVE UNCONSCIOUS

Born in a small town in Switzerland, **Carl Jung** (1875–1961) was fascinated by the myths, folktales, and religions of his own and other cultures. After studying medicine, Jung was drawn to the relatively new field of psychiatry because he believed it could provide deeper insights into the human mind (Jung, 1963).

Intrigued by Freud's ideas, Jung began a correspondence with him. At their first meeting, the two men were so compatible that they talked for 13 hours nonstop. Freud felt that his young disciple was so promising that he called him his "adopted son" and his "crown prince." It would be Jung, Freud decided, who would succeed him and lead the international psychoanalytic movement. However, Jung was too independent to relish his role as Freud's unquestioning disciple. As Jung continued to put forth his own ideas, his close friendship with Freud ultimately ended in bitterness (Solomon, 2003).

Jung rejected Freud's belief that human behavior is fueled by the instinctual drives of sex and aggression. Instead, Jung believed that people are motivated by a more general psychological energy that pushes them to achieve psychological growth, self-realization, and psychic wholeness and harmony. Jung (1963) also believed that personality continues to develop in significant ways throughout the lifespan.

In studying different cultures, Jung was struck by the universality of many images and themes, which also surfaced in his patients' dreams and preoccupations. These observations led to some of Jung's most intriguing ideas, the notions of the collective unconscious and archetypes.

Jung (1936) believed that the deepest part of the individual psyche is the **collective unconscious,** which is shared by all people and reflects humanity's collective evolutionary history. He described the collective unconscious as containing "the whole

What we properly call instincts are physiological urges, and are perceived by the senses. But at the same time, they also manifest themselves in fantasies and often reveal their presence only by symbolic images. These manifestations are what I call the archetypes. They are without known origin; and they reproduce themselves in any time or in any part of the world.

—*Carl Jung (1964)*

spiritual heritage of mankind's evolution, born anew in the brain structure of every individual" (Jung, 1931).

Contained in the collective unconscious are the **archetypes,** the mental images of universal human instincts, themes, and preoccupations (Jung, 1964). Common archetypal themes that are expressed in virtually every culture are the hero, the powerful father, the nurturing mother, the witch, the wise old man, the innocent child, and death and rebirth.

Not surprisingly, Jung's concepts of the collective unconscious and shared archetypes have been criticized as being unscientific or mystical. As far as we know, individual experiences cannot be genetically passed down from one generation to the next. Regardless, Jung's ideas make more sense if you think of the collective unconscious as reflecting shared human experiences. The archetypes, then, can be thought of as symbols that represent the common, universal themes of the human life cycle. These universal themes include birth, achieving a sense of self, parenthood, the spiritual search, and death.

Although Jung's theory never became as influential as Freud's, some of his ideas have gained wide acceptance. For example, Jung (1923) was the first to describe two basic personality types: *introverts,* who focus their attention inward, and *extraverts,* who turn their attention and energy toward the outside world. We will encounter these two basic personality dimensions again when we look at trait theories later in this chapter. Finally, Jung's emphasis on the drive toward psychological growth and self-realization anticipated some of the basic ideas of the humanistic perspective on personality, which we'll look at shortly.

KAREN HORNEY

BASIC ANXIETY AND "WOMB ENVY"

Trained as a Freudian psychoanalyst, **Karen Horney** (1885–1952) (pronounced HORN-eye) emigrated from Germany to the United States during the Great Depression in the 1930s. Horney noticed distinct differences between her American and her German patients. While Freud traced psychological problems to sexual conflicts, Horney found that her American patients were much more worried about their jobs and economic problems than their sex lives. Thus, Horney came to stress the importance of cultural and social factors in personality development—matters that Freud had largely ignored (Horney, 1945).

Archetypes in Popular Culture According to Jung, archetypal images are often found in popular myths, novels, and even films. Consider the classic film *The Wizard of Oz.* The motherless child, Dorothy, is on a quest for self-knowledge and selfhood, symbolized by the circular Emerald City. She is accompanied by her symbolic helpers, the Cowardly Lion (seeking courage), the Tin Woodsman (seeking love), and the Scarecrow (seeking wisdom).

The Mandala Carl Jung (1974) believed that the mandala was the archetypal symbol of the self and psychic wholeness. Mandala images are found in cultures throughout the world. Shown here are three examples from cultures separated by both time and distance: a reconstructed Aztec solar calendar from Mexico (left); a 14th-century rose window from a cathedral in the United Kingdom (center); and the centuries-old image of the *Bhavacakra,* or Buddhist Wheel of Life, from Tibet (right).

(bl) Gianni Dagli Orti/The Art Archive at Art Resource, NY
(c) Bridgeman Images
(br) Topham/The Image Works

Corbis

Man, [Freud] postulated, is doomed to suffer or destroy. . . . My own belief is that man has the capacity as well as the desire to develop his potentialities and become a decent human being, and that these deteriorate if his relationship to others and hence to himself is, and continues to be, disturbed. I believe that man can change and go on changing as long as he lives.

—Karen Horney (1945)

Horney also stressed the importance of social relationships, especially the parent–child relationship, in the development of personality. She believed that disturbances in human relationships, not sexual conflicts, were the cause of psychological problems. Such problems arise from the attempt to deal with *basic anxiety,* which Horney (1945) described as "the feeling a child has of being isolated and helpless in a potentially hostile world."

Horney (1945) described three patterns of behavior that the individual uses to defend against basic anxiety: moving toward, against, or away from other people. Those who move *toward* other people have an excessive need for approval and affection. Those who move *against* others have an excessive need for power, especially power over other people. They are often competitive, critical, and domineering, and they need to feel superior to others. Finally, those who move *away from* other people have an excessive need for independence and self-sufficiency, which often makes them aloof and detached from others.

Horney contended that people with a healthy personality are *flexible* in balancing these different needs, for there are times when each behavior pattern is appropriate. As Horney (1945) wrote, "One should be capable of giving in to others, of fighting, and keeping to oneself. The three can complement each other and make for a harmonious whole." But when one pattern becomes the predominant way of dealing with other people and the world, psychological conflict and problems can result.

Horney also sharply disagreed with Freud's interpretation of female development, especially his notion that women suffer from penis envy. What women envy in men, Horney (1926) claimed, is not their penis, but their superior status in society. In fact, Horney contended that men often suffer *womb envy,* envying women's capacity to bear children. Neatly standing Freud's view of feminine psychology on its head, Horney argued that *men* compensate for their relatively minor role in reproduction by constantly striving to make creative achievements in their work (Gilman, 2001). As Horney (1945) wrote, "Is not the tremendous strength in men of the impulse to creative work in every field precisely due to their feelings of playing a relatively small part in the creation of living beings, which constantly impels them to an overcompensation in achievement?"

Horney shared Jung's belief that people are not doomed to psychological conflict and problems. Also like Jung, Horney believed that the drive to grow psychologically and achieve one's potential is a basic human motive.

ALFRED ADLER

FEELINGS OF INFERIORITY AND STRIVING FOR SUPERIORITY

Born in Vienna, **Alfred Adler** (1870–1937) was an extremely sickly child. Yet through determination and hard work, he overcame his physical weaknesses. After studying medicine, he became associated with Freud. But from the beginning of Adler's interest in psychoanalysis, he disagreed with Freud on several issues. In particular, Adler placed much more emphasis on the importance of conscious thought processes and social motives (West & Bubenzer, 2012). Eventually, Adler broke away from Freud to establish his own theory of personality.

Adler (1933b) believed that the most fundamental human motive is *striving for superiority*—the desire to improve oneself, master challenges, and move toward self-perfection and self-realization. Striving toward superiority arises from universal *feelings of inferiority* that are experienced during infancy and childhood, when the child is helpless and dependent on others. These feelings motivate people to *compensate* for their real or imagined weaknesses by emphasizing their talents and abilities and by working hard to improve themselves (R. Watts, 2012). Hence, Adler (1933a) saw the universal human feelings of inferiority as ultimately constructive and valuable.

However, when people are unable to compensate for specific weaknesses or when their feelings of inferiority are excessive, they can develop an *inferiority complex*—a general sense of inadequacy, weakness, and helplessness. People with an inferiority complex are often unable to strive for mastery and self-improvement.

Corbis

To be a human being means to have inferiority feelings. One recognizes one's own powerlessness in the face of nature. One sees death as the irrefutable consequence of existence. But in the mentally healthy person this inferiority feeling acts as a motive for productivity, as a motive for attempting to overcome obstacles, to maintain oneself in life.

—Alfred Adler (1933a)

At the other extreme, people can *overcompensate* for their feelings of inferiority and develop a *superiority complex*. Behaviors caused by a superiority complex might include exaggerating one's accomplishments and importance in an effort to cover up weaknesses and denying the reality of one's limitations (Adler, 1954).

Like Horney, Adler believed that humans were motivated to grow and achieve their personal goals. And, like Horney, Adler emphasized the importance of cultural influences and social relationships (Carlson & others, 2008; West & Bubenzer, 2012).

Evaluating Freud and the Psychoanalytic Perspective on Personality

Like it or not, Sigmund Freud's ideas have had a profound and lasting impact on our culture and on our understanding of human nature (see Merlino & others, 2008). Today, opinions on Freud span the entire spectrum. Some see him as a genius who discovered brilliant, lasting insights into human nature. Others contend that Freud was a deeply neurotic, driven man who successfully foisted his twisted personal view of human nature onto an unsuspecting public (Crews, 1984, 1996, 2006).

The truth, as you might suspect, lies somewhere in between. Although Freud has had an enormous impact on psychology and on society, there are several valid criticisms of Freud's theory and, more generally, of the psychoanalytic perspective. We'll discuss three of the most important problems next.

INADEQUACY OF EVIDENCE

Freud's theory relies wholly on data derived from his relatively small number of patients and from self-analysis. Most of Freud's patients were relatively well-to-do, well-educated members of the middle and upper classes in Vienna at the beginning of the twentieth century. Freud (1916, 1919, 1939) also analyzed the lives of famous historical figures, such as Leonardo da Vinci, and looked to myth, religion, literature, and evolutionary prehistory for confirmation of his ideas. Any way you look at it, this is a small and rather skewed sample from which to draw sweeping generalizations about human nature.

Furthermore, it is impossible to objectively assess Freud's "data." Freud did not take notes during his private therapy sessions. And, of course, when Freud did report a case in detail, it was still his own interpretation of the case that was recorded. For Freud, proof of the validity of his ideas depended on his uncovering similar patterns in different patients. So the critical question is this: Was Freud imposing his own ideas onto his patients, seeing only what he expected to see? Some critics think so (see Grünbaum, 2006, 2007).

LACK OF TESTABILITY

Many psychoanalytic concepts are so vague and ambiguous that they are impossible to objectively measure or confirm (Crews, 2006; Grünbaum, 2006). For example, how might you go about proving the existence of the id or the superego? Or how could you operationally define and measure the effects of the pleasure principle, the life instinct, or the Oedipus complex?

Psychoanalytic "proof" often has a "heads I win, tails you lose" style to it. In other words, psychoanalytic concepts are often impossible to *dis*prove because even seemingly contradictory information can be used to support Freud's theory. For example, if your memory of childhood doesn't jibe with Freud's description of the psychosexual stages or the Oedipus complex, well, that's because you've repressed it. Freud himself was not immune to this form of reasoning (Robinson, 1993). When one of Freud's patients reported dreams that didn't seem to reveal a hidden wish, Freud interpreted the dreams as betraying the patient's hidden wish to disprove Freud's dream theory!

Sony Pictures/Everett Collection

A Century of Influence One indicator of Freud's influence is his continuing presence in popular culture. He appeared on the cover of *Time* magazine four different times, most recently in 1999 as part of a special issue commemorating the 100 greatest scientists and thinkers of the twentieth century. Freud has also been featured as a character in dozens of films and even television shows—from *Saturday Night Live* to *Star Trek*. Recently, Viggo Mortenson (above) played Sigmund Freud as a character in the movie *A Dangerous Method*, about the relationship between Freud, Jung, and a young patient, Sabine Spielrien, played by Kiera Knightley.

For good or ill, Sigmund Freud, more than any other explorer of the psyche, has shaped the mind of the 20th century. The very fierceness and persistence of his detractors are a wry tribute to the staying power of Freud's ideas.

—*Peter Gay (1999)*

Step by step, we are learning that Freud has been the most overrated figure in the entire history of science and medicine—one who wrought immense harm through the propagation of false etiologies, mistaken diagnoses, and fruitless lines of inquiry.

—*Frederick Crews (2006)*

Corbis

Anna Freud (1895–1982) Freud's youngest daughter, Anna, became his chief disciple and was herself the founder of a psychoanalytic school. Expanding on her father's theory, she applied psychoanalysis to therapy with children. She is shown here addressing a debate on psychoanalysis at the Sorbonne University in Paris in 1950.

MYTH ◀ SCIENCE

Is it true that most psychologists today agree with Sigmund Freud's personality theory?

As Freud acknowledged, psychoanalysis is better at explaining *past* behavior than at predicting future behavior (Gay, 1989). Indeed, psychoanalytic interpretations are so flexible that a given behavior can be explained by any number of completely different motives. For example, a man who is extremely affectionate toward his wife might be exhibiting displacement of a repressed incestuous urge (he is displacing his repressed affection for his mother onto his wife), reaction formation (he actually hates his wife intensely, so he compensates by being overly affectionate), or fixation at the oral stage (he is overly dependent on his wife).

Nonetheless, several key psychoanalytic ideas *have* been substantiated by empirical research (Cogan & others, 2007; Westen, 1990, 1998). Among these are the ideas that: (1) much of mental life is unconscious; (2) early childhood experiences have a critical influence on interpersonal relationships and psychological adjustment; and (3) people differ significantly in the degree to which they are able to regulate their impulses, emotions, and thoughts toward adaptive and socially acceptable ends.

SEXISM

Many people feel that Freud's theories reflect a sexist view of women. Because penis envy produces feelings of shame and inferiority, Freud (1925) claimed, women are more vain, masochistic, and jealous than men. He also believed that women are more influenced by their emotions and have a lesser ethical and moral sense than men.

As Horney and other female psychoanalysts have pointed out, Freud's theory uses male psychology as a prototype. Women are essentially viewed as a deviation from the norm of masculinity (Horney, 1926; Thompson, 1950). Perhaps, Horney suggested, psychoanalysis would have evolved an entirely different view of women if it were not dominated by the male point of view.

To Freud's credit, women were quite active in the early psychoanalytic movement. Several female analysts became close colleagues of Freud (Freeman & Strean, 1987; Roazen, 1999, 2000). And, it was Freud's daughter Anna, rather than any of his sons, who followed in his footsteps as an eminent psychoanalyst. Ultimately, Anna Freud became her father's successor as leader of the international psychoanalytic movement.

The weaknesses in Freud's theory and in the psychoanalytic approach to personality are not minor problems. As you'll see in Chapter 14 on therapies, very few psychologists practice Freudian psychoanalysis today. All the same, Freud made some extremely significant contributions to modern psychological thinking. Most important, he drew attention to the existence and influence of mental processes that occur outside conscious awareness, an idea that continues to be actively investigated by today's psychological researchers.

❯ Test your understanding of **Personality and the Psychoanalytic Perspective** with **LEARNING**Curve.

The Humanistic Perspective on Personality

KEY THEME

The humanistic perspective emphasizes free will, self-awareness, and psychological growth.

KEY QUESTIONS

❯ What roles do the self-concept, the actualizing tendency, and unconditional positive regard play in Rogers's personality theory?

❯ What are key strengths and weaknesses of the humanistic perspective?

By the 1950s, the field of personality was dominated by two completely different perspectives: Freudian psychoanalysis and B.F. Skinner's brand of behaviorism (see Chapter 5). While Freud's theory of personality proposed elaborate and complex internal states, Skinner believed that psychologists should focus on observable behaviors and on the environmental factors that shape and maintain those behaviors (see Rogers & Skinner, 1956). As Skinner (1971) wrote, "A person does not act upon the world, the world acts upon him."

The Emergence of the "Third Force"

Another group of psychologists had a fundamentally different view of human nature. In opposition to both psychoanalysis and behaviorism, they championed a "third force" in psychology, which they called humanistic psychology. **Humanistic psychology** is a view of personality that emphasizes human potential and such uniquely human characteristics as self-awareness and free will (Cain, 2002).

In contrast to Freud's pessimistic view of people as being motivated by unconscious sexual and destructive instincts, the humanistic psychologists saw people as being innately good. Humanistic psychologists also differed from psychoanalytic theorists by their focus on the *healthy* personality rather than on psychologically troubled people.

In contrast to the behaviorist view that human and animal behavior is due largely to environmental reinforcement and punishment, the humanistic psychologists believed that people are motivated by the need to grow psychologically. They also doubted that laboratory research with rats and pigeons accurately reflected the essence of human nature, as the behaviorists claimed. Instead, humanistic psychologists contended that the most important factor in personality is the individual's *conscious, subjective perception of his or her self* (Purkey & Stanley, 2002).

The two most important contributors to the humanistic perspective were Carl Rogers and Abraham Maslow. In Chapter 8 on motivation, we discussed **Abraham Maslow**'s famous *hierarchy of needs* and his concept of self-actualization. Like Maslow, Rogers emphasized the tendency of human beings to strive to fulfill their potential and capabilities (Kirschenbaum, 2004; Kirschenbaum & Jourdan, 2005).

Carl Rogers
ON BECOMING A PERSON

Carl Rogers (1902–1987) grew up in a large, close-knit family in a suburb of Chicago. His parents were highly religious and instilled a moral and ethical atmosphere in the home, which no doubt influenced Rogers's early decision to become a minister. After studying theology, Rogers decided that the ministry was not for him. Instead, he turned to the study of psychology, ultimately enjoying a long, productive, and distinguished career as a psychotherapist, writer, and university professor.

Like Freud, Rogers developed his personality theory from his clinical experiences with his patients. Rogers referred to his patients as "clients" to emphasize their active and voluntary participation in therapy. In marked contrast to Freud, Rogers was continually impressed by his clients' drive to grow and develop their potential.

These observations convinced Rogers that the most basic human motive is the **actualizing tendency**—the innate drive to maintain and enhance the human organism (Bohart, 2007; Bozarth & Wang, 2008). According to Rogers, all other human motives, whether biological or social, are secondary. He compared the actualizing tendency to a child's drive to learn to walk despite early frustration and falls. To get a sense of the vastly different views of Rogers and Freud, read the Critical Thinking box on the next page, "Freud Versus Rogers on Human Nature."

THE SELF-CONCEPT

Rogers (1959) was struck by how frequently his clients in therapy said, "I'm not really sure who I am" or "I just don't feel like myself." This observation helped form the cornerstone of Rogers's personality theory: the idea of the self-concept. The **self-concept** is the set of perceptions and beliefs that you have about yourself, including your nature, your personal qualities, and your typical behavior.

humanistic psychology (theory of personality) The theoretical viewpoint on personality that generally emphasizes the inherent goodness of people, human potential, self-actualization, the self-concept, and healthy personality development.

actualizing tendency In Rogers's theory, the innate drive to maintain and enhance the human organism.

self-concept The set of perceptions and beliefs that you hold about yourself.

At bottom, each person is asking, "Who am I, really? How can I get in touch with this real self, underlying all my surface behavior? How can I become myself?"

—*Carl Rogers (1961)*

LaunchPad

What's *your* self-concept? For some insight, try **Lab: Personality Psychology.**

CRITICAL THINKING

Freud Versus Rogers on Human Nature

Freud's view of human nature was deeply pessimistic. He believed that the human aggressive instinct was innate, persistent, and pervasive. Were it not for internal superego restraints and external societal restraints, civilization as we know it would collapse: The destructive instincts of humans would be unleashed. As Freud (1930) wrote in *Civilization and Its Discontents:*

> Men are not gentle creatures who want to be loved, and who at the most can defend themselves if they are attacked; they are, on the contrary, creatures among whose instinctual endowments is to be reckoned a powerful share of aggressiveness. As a result, their neighbor is for them not only a potential helper or sexual object, but also someone who tempts them to satisfy their aggressiveness on him, to exploit his capacity for work without compensation, to use him sexually without his consent, to seize his possessions, to humiliate him, to cause him pain, to torture and to kill him. *Man is a wolf to man.*

In Freud's view, then, the essence of human nature is destructive. Control of these destructive instincts is necessary. Yet societal, cultural, religious, and moral restraints also make people frustrated, neurotic, and unhappy. Why? Because the strivings of the id toward instinctual satisfaction *must* be frustrated if civilization and the human race are to survive. Hence, as the title of Freud's book emphasizes, civilization is inevitably accompanied by human "discontent."

A pretty gloomy picture, isn't it? Yet if you watch the evening news or read the newspaper, you may find it hard to disagree with Freud's negative image of human nature. People *are* often exceedingly cruel and selfish, committing horrifying acts of brutality against strangers and even against loved ones.

However, you might argue that people can also be extraordinarily kind, self-sacrificing, and loving toward others. Freud would agree with this observation. Yet according to his theory, "good" or "moral" behavior does not disprove the essentially destructive nature of people. Instead, he explains good or moral behavior in terms of superego control, sublimation of the instincts, displacement, and so forth.

But is this truly the essence of human nature? Carl Rogers disagreed strongly. "I do not discover man to be well characterized in his basic nature by such terms as *fundamentally hostile, antisocial, destructive, evil,*" Rogers (1957a) wrote. Instead, Rogers believed that people are more accurately described as *"positive, forward-moving, constructive, realistic, trustworthy."*

If this is so, how can Rogers account for the evil and cruelty in the world? Rogers didn't deny that people can behave destructively and cruelly. Yet throughout his life, Rogers insisted that people are innately good. Rogers (1981) attributed the existence of evil to cultural factors:

> The rough manner of childbirth, the infant's mixed experience with the parents, the constricting, destructive influence of our educational system, the injustice of our distribution of wealth, our cultivated prejudices against individuals who are different—all these elements and many others warp the human organism in directions which are antisocial.

In sharp contrast to Freud, Rogers (1964) said we should *trust* the human organism because the human who is truly free to choose

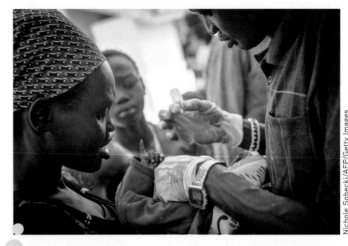

Nichole Sobecki/AFP/Getty Images

Are People Innately Good . . . or Innately Evil? A member of Doctors Without Borders administers polio vaccines to children who are among the tens of thousands of refugees fleeing civil war in South Sudan. Doctors Without Borders is an international group of medical workers that won the Nobel Peace Prize for its work in helping the victims of violence and disasters all over the world.

On the one hand, violence motivated by political or ethnic hatred seems to support Freud's contentions about human nature. On the other hand, the selfless behavior of those who help others, often at a considerable cost to themselves, seems to support Rogers's view. Which viewpoint do you think more accurately describes the essence of human nature?

will naturally gravitate toward behavior that serves to perpetuate the human race and improve society as a whole:

> I dare to believe that when the human being is inwardly free to choose whatever he deeply values, he tends to value those objects, experiences, and goals that will make for his own survival, growth, and development, and for the survival and development of others. . . . The psychologically mature person as I have described him has, I believe, the qualities which would cause him to value those experiences which would make for the survival and enhancement of the human race.

Two great thinkers, two diametrically opposed views of human nature. Now it's your turn to critically evaluate their views.

CRITICAL THINKING QUESTIONS

- Are people inherently driven by aggressive instincts, as Freud claimed? Must the destructive urges of the id be restrained by parents, culture, religion, and society if civilization is to continue? Would an environment in which individuals were unrestrained inevitably lead to an unleashing of destructive instincts?

- Or are people naturally good, as Rogers claimed? If people existed in a truly free and nurturing environment, would they invariably make constructive choices that would benefit both themselves and society as a whole?

The self-concept begins evolving early in life. Because they are motivated by the actualizing tendency, infants and young children naturally gravitate toward self-enhancing experiences. But as children develop greater self-awareness, there is an increasing need for positive regard. *Positive regard* is the sense of being loved and valued by other people, especially one's parents (Bozarth, 2007; Farber & Doolin, 2011).

Rogers (1959) maintained that most parents provide their children with **conditional positive regard**—the sense that the child is valued and loved only when she behaves in a way that is acceptable to others. The problem with conditional positive regard is that it causes the child to learn to deny or distort her genuine feelings. For example, if little Amy's parents scold and reject her when she expresses angry feelings, her strong need for positive regard will cause her to deny her anger, even when it's justified or appropriate. Eventually, Amy's self-concept will become so distorted that genuine feelings of anger are denied because they are inconsistent with her self-concept as "a good girl who never gets angry." Because of the fear of losing positive regard, she cuts herself off from her true feelings.

"To this day, I can hear my mother's voice—harsh, accusing. 'Lost your mittens? You naughty kittens! Then you shall have no pie!'"

Donald Reilly The New Yorker Collection/The Cartoon Bank

Like Freud, Rogers believed that feelings and experiences could be driven from consciousness by being denied or distorted. But Rogers believed that feelings become denied or distorted not because they are threatening but because they contradict the self-concept. In this case, people are in a state of *incongruence:* Their self-concept conflicts with their actual experience (Rogers, 1959). Such a person is continually defending against genuine feelings and experiences that are inconsistent with his self-concept. As this process continues over time, a person progressively becomes more "out of touch" with his true feelings and his essential self, often experiencing psychological problems as a result.

How is incongruence to be avoided? In the ideal situation, a child experiences a great deal of unconditional positive regard from parents and other authority figures. **Unconditional positive regard** refers to the child's sense of being unconditionally loved and valued, even if she doesn't conform to the standards and expectations of others. In this way, the child's actualizing tendency is allowed its fullest expression. However, Rogers did *not* advocate permissive parenting. He thought that parents were responsible for controlling their children's behavior and for teaching them acceptable standards of behavior. Rogers maintained that parents can discipline their child without undermining the child's sense of self-worth.

For example, parents can disapprove of a child's specific *behavior* without completely rejecting the *child herself.* In effect, the parent's message should be, "I do not value your behavior right now, but I still love and value *you.*" In this way, according to Rogers, the child's essential sense of self-worth can remain intact.

Rogers (1957b) believed that it is through consistent experiences of unconditional positive regard that one becomes a psychologically healthy, fully functioning

conditional positive regard In Rogers's theory, the sense that you will be valued and loved only if you behave in a way that is acceptable to others; conditional love or acceptance.

unconditional positive regard In Rogers's theory, the sense that you will be valued and loved even if you don't conform to the standards and expectations of others; unconditional love or acceptance.

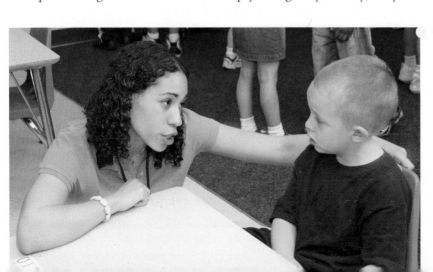

Ellen B. Senisi

Unconditional Positive Regard Rogers contended that healthy personality development is the result of being unconditionally valued and loved as a person (Bozarth, 2007). He advised parents and teachers to control a child's inappropriate behavior without rejecting the child himself. Such a style of discipline teaches acceptable behaviors without diminishing the child's sense of self-worth.

person. The *fully functioning person* has a flexible, constantly evolving self-concept. She is realistic, open to new experiences, and capable of changing in response to new experiences.

Rather than defending against or distorting her own thoughts or feelings, the person experiences *congruence:* Her sense of self is consistent with her emotions and experiences (Farber, 2007). The actualizing tendency is fully operational, and she makes choices that move her in the direction of greater growth and fulfillment of potential. Rogers (1957b, 1964) believed that the fully functioning person is likely to be creative and spontaneous, and to enjoy harmonious relationships with others.

Evaluating the Humanistic Perspective on Personality

The humanistic perspective has been criticized on two particular points. First, humanistic theories are hard to validate or test scientifically. Humanistic theories tend to be based on philosophical assumptions or clinical observations rather than on empirical research. For example, concepts like the self-concept, unconditional positive regard, and the actualizing tendency are very difficult to define or measure objectively.

Second, many psychologists believe that humanistic psychology's view of human nature is *too* optimistic (Bohart, 2013). For example, if self-actualization is a universal human motive, why are self-actualized people so hard to find? And, critics claim, humanistic psychologists have minimized the darker, more destructive side of human nature. Can we really account for all the evil in the world by attributing it to a restrictive upbringing or society?

The influence of humanistic psychology has waned since the 1960s and early 1970s (Cain, 2003). Nevertheless, it has made lasting contributions, especially in the realms of psychotherapy, counseling, education, and parenting (Farber, 2007; Joseph & Murphy, 2013). And the importance of subjective experience and the self-concept has become widely accepted in different areas of psychology (Sheldon, 2008; Sleeth, 2007).

The Social Cognitive Perspective on Personality

KEY THEME

The social cognitive perspective stresses conscious thought processes, self-regulation, and the importance of situational influences.

KEY QUESTIONS

> What is the principle of reciprocal determination?
> What is the role of self-efficacy beliefs in personality?
> What are the key strengths and weaknesses of the social cognitive perspective?

Have you ever noticed how different your behavior and sense of self can be in different situations? Consider this example: You feel pretty confident as you enter your college algebra class. After all, you're pulling an A, and your prof nods approvingly every time you participate in class, which you do frequently. In contrast, your English composition class is a disaster. You're worried about passing the course, and you feel so shaky about your writing skills that you're afraid to even ask a question, much less participate in class. Even a casual observer would notice how differently you behave in the two different situations—speaking freely and confidently in one class, staring at your desk in hopes that your instructor won't notice you in the other.

I am quite aware that out of defensiveness and inner fear individuals can and do behave in ways which are incredibly cruel, horribly destructive, immature, regressive, antisocial, and hurtful. Yet one of the most refreshing and invigorating parts of my experience is to work with such individuals and to discover the strongly positive directional tendencies which exist in them, as in all of us, at the deepest levels.

—*Carl Rogers (1961)*

The idea that a person's conscious thought processes in different situations strongly influence his or her actions is one important characteristic of the *social cognitive perspective* on personality (Cervone & others, 2011). According to the social cognitive perspective, people actively process information from their social experiences. This information influences their goals, expectations, beliefs, and behavior, as well as the specific environments they choose.

The social cognitive perspective differs from psychoanalytic and humanistic perspectives in several ways. First, rather than basing their approach on self-analysis or insights derived from psychotherapy, social cognitive personality theorists rely heavily on experimental findings. Second, the social cognitive perspective emphasizes conscious, self-regulated behavior rather than unconscious mental influences and instinctual drives. And third, as in our algebra-versus-English-class example, the social cognitive approach emphasizes that our sense of self can vary, depending on our thoughts, feelings, and behaviors in a given situation.

Albert Bandura and Social Cognitive Theory

Although several contemporary personality theorists have embraced the social cognitive approach to explaining personality, probably the most influential is **Albert Bandura** (b. 1925). We examined Bandura's classic research on *observational learning* in Chapter 5. In Chapter 8, we encountered Bandura's more recent research on self-efficacy. Here, you'll see how Bandura's ideas on both these topics are reflected in his personality theory, called social cognitive theory. **Social cognitive theory** emphasizes the social origins of thoughts and actions but also stresses active cognitive processes and the human capacity for *self*-regulation (Bandura, 2004b, 2006).

As Bandura's early research demonstrated, we learn many behaviors by observing, and then imitating, the behavior of other people. But, as Bandura (1997) has pointed out, we don't merely observe people's actions. We also observe the *consequences* that follow people's actions, the *rules* and *standards* that apply to behavior in specific situations, and the ways in which people *regulate their own behavior*. Thus, environmental influences are important, but conscious, self-generated goals and standards also exert considerable control over thoughts, feelings, and actions (Bandura, 2001).

For example, consider your own goal of getting a college education. No doubt many social and environmental factors influenced your decision. In turn, your conscious decision to attend college determines many aspects of your current behavior, thoughts, and emotions. And your goal of attending college classes determines which environments you choose.

Bandura (1986, 1997) explains human behavior and personality as being caused by the interaction of behavioral, cognitive, and environmental factors. He calls this process **reciprocal determinism** (see Figure 10.2). According to this principle, each factor both influences the other factors and is influenced by the other factors. Thus, in Bandura's view, our environment influences our thoughts and actions, our thoughts influence our actions and the environments we choose, our actions influence our thoughts and the environments we choose, and so on in a circular fashion.

Courtesy of Albert Bandura

The capacity to exercise control over the nature and quality of life is the essence of humanness. Unless people believe they can produce desired results and forestall detrimental ones by their actions, they have little incentive to act or persevere in the face of difficulties.

—*Albert Bandura (2001)*

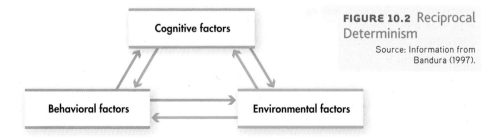

FIGURE 10.2 Reciprocal Determinism

Source: Information from Bandura (1997).

Cognitive factors

Behavioral factors

Environmental factors

social cognitive theory Albert Bandura's theory of personality, which emphasizes the importance of observational learning, conscious cognitive processes, social experiences, self-efficacy beliefs, and reciprocal determinism.

reciprocal determinism A model proposed by psychologist Albert Bandura that explains human functioning and personality as caused by the interaction of behavioral, cognitive, and environmental factors.

Self-Efficacy We acquire a strong sense of self-efficacy by meeting challenges and mastering new skills specific to a particular situation. By encouraging his son and helping him learn how to use a knife properly, this father is fostering the young boy's sense of self-efficacy.

Zero Creatives/Getty Images

The most effective way of developing a strong sense of efficacy is through mastery experiences. Successes build a robust belief in one's efficacy. Failures undermine it. A second way is through social modeling. If people see others like themselves succeed by sustained effort, they come to believe that they, too, have the capacity to do so. Social persuasion is a third way of strengthening people's beliefs in their efficacy. If people are persuaded that they have what it takes to succeed, they exert more effort than if they harbor self-doubts and dwell on personal deficiencies when problems arise.

—*Albert Bandura (2004b)*

self-efficacy The beliefs that people have about their ability to meet the demands of a specific situation; feelings of self-confidence.

BELIEFS OF SELF-EFFICACY

Collectively, a person's cognitive skills, abilities, and attitudes represent the person's *self-system*. According to Bandura (2001), it is our self-system that guides how we perceive, evaluate, and control our behavior in different situations. Bandura (2004b) has found that the most critical elements influencing the self-system are our beliefs of self-efficacy. **Self-efficacy** refers to the degree to which you are subjectively convinced of your own capabilities and effectiveness in meeting the demands of a particular situation.

For example, suppose you were faced with the problem of filling out paperwork for financial aid. Your sense of self-efficacy about finances and paperwork would affect your behavior and your fears of failure or hopes of success (Bandura, 1992; Ozer & Bandura, 1990). If you completely lacked a sense of self-efficacy in this arena, you might even quit before you began, regardless of whether you were actually capable of completing the paperwork. Bandura's concept of self-efficacy makes it easier to understand why people often fail to perform optimally at certain tasks, even though they possess the necessary skills.

However, our self-system is very flexible. How we regard ourselves and our abilities varies depending on the situations or tasks we're facing. In turn, our beliefs influence the tasks we are willing to try and how persistent we'll be in the face of obstacles (Bandura, 1996, 2004b).

We can acquire new behaviors and strengthen our beliefs of self-efficacy in particular situations through observational learning and *mastery experiences* (Bandura, 2001, 2004b). When we perform a task successfully, our sense of self-efficacy becomes stronger. When we fail to deal effectively with a particular task or situation, our sense of self-efficacy is undermined.

From very early in life, children develop feelings of self-efficacy from their experiences in dealing with different tasks and situations, such as athletic, social, and academic activities (Bandura & others, 2003). As Bandura (1992) has pointed out, developing self-efficacy begins in childhood, but it continues as a lifelong process. Each stage of the lifespan presents new challenges.

Evaluating the Social Cognitive Perspective on Personality

A key strength of the social cognitive perspective on personality is its grounding in empirical, laboratory research (Bandura, 2004a). The social cognitive perspective is built on research in learning, cognitive psychology, and social psychology, rather than on clinical impressions. And, unlike vague psychoanalytic and humanistic concepts, the concepts of social cognitive theory are scientifically testable—that is, they can be operationally defined and measured. For example, psychologists can study beliefs of self-efficacy by comparing subjects who are low in self-efficacy in a given situation with subjects who are high in self-efficacy (see Ozer & Bandura, 1990). Not surprisingly, then, the social cognitive perspective has had a major impact on the study of personality.

However, some psychologists feel that the social cognitive approach to personality applies *best* to laboratory research. In the typical laboratory study, the relationships among a limited number of very specific variables are studied. In everyday life, situations are far more complex, with multiple factors converging to affect behavior and personality. Thus, an argument can be made that clinical data, rather than laboratory data, may be more reflective of human personality.

The social cognitive perspective also ignores unconscious influences, emotions, or conflicts. Some psychologists argue that the social cognitive theory focuses on very limited areas of personality—learning, the effects of situations, and the effects of beliefs about the self. Thus, it seems to lack the richness of psychoanalytic and humanistic theories, which strive to explain the *whole* person, including the unconscious, irrational, and emotional aspects of personality (McAdams & Pals, 2006; Westen, 1990).

Nevertheless, by emphasizing the reciprocal interaction of mental, behavioral, and situational factors, the social cognitive perspective recognizes the complex combination of factors that influence our everyday behavior. By emphasizing the important role of learning, especially observational learning, the social cognitive perspective offers a developmental explanation of human functioning that persists throughout one's lifetime. Finally, by emphasizing the self-regulation of behavior, the social cognitive perspective places most of the responsibility for our behavior—and for the consequences we experience—squarely on our own shoulders.

trait A relatively stable, enduring predisposition to consistently behave in a certain way.

trait theory A theory of personality that focuses on identifying, describing, and measuring individual differences in behavioral predispositions.

The Trait Perspective on Personality

KEY THEME

Trait theories of personality focus on identifying, describing, and measuring individual differences.

KEY QUESTIONS

> What are traits, and how do surface traits and source traits differ?
> What are three influential trait theories, and how might heredity affect personality?
> What are the key strengths and weaknesses of trait theories of personality?

Suppose we asked you to describe the personality of a close friend. How would you begin? Would you describe her personality in terms of her unconscious conflicts, the congruence of her self-concept, or her level of self-efficacy? Probably not. Instead, you'd probably generate a list of her personal characteristics, such as "outgoing," "cheerful," and "generous." This rather commonsense approach to personality is shared by the trait theories. The trait approach to personality is very different from the theories we have encountered thus far. The psychoanalytic, humanistic, and social cognitive theories emphasize the *similarities* among people. They focus on discovering the universal processes of motivation and development that explain human personality (Revelle, 1995, 2007). Although these theories do deal with individual differences, they do so only indirectly. In contrast, the trait approach to personality *focuses primarily on describing individual differences* (Funder & Fast, 2010).

"Oh, God! Here comes little Miss Perky."

Trait theorists view the person as being a unique combination of personality characteristics or attributes, called *traits*. A **trait** is formally defined as a relatively stable, enduring predisposition to behave in a certain way. A **trait theory** of personality, then, is one that focuses on identifying, describing, and measuring individual differences in behavioral predispositions. Think back to our description of the twins, Kenneth and Julian, in the chapter Prologue. You can probably readily identify some of their personality traits. For example, Julian was described as impulsive, cocky, and adventurous, while Kenneth was serious, intense, and responsible. And people tend to describe others in terms of traits. Participants in a recent study in Germany were

TABLE 10.3

Cattell's 16 Personality Factors

1 Reserved, unsociable	⟷	Outgoing, sociable
2 Less intelligent, concrete	⟷	More intelligent, abstract
3 Affected by feelings	⟷	Emotionally stable
4 Submissive, humble	⟷	Dominant, assertive
5 Serious	⟷	Happy-go-lucky
6 Expedient	⟷	Conscientious
7 Timid	⟷	Venturesome
8 Tough-minded	⟷	Sensitive
9 Trusting	⟷	Suspicious
10 Practical	⟷	Imaginative
11 Forthright	⟷	Shrewd, calculating
12 Self-assured	⟷	Apprehensive
13 Conservative	⟷	Experimenting
14 Group-dependent	⟷	Self-sufficient
15 Undisciplined	⟷	Controlled
16 Relaxed	⟷	Tense

Raymond Cattell believed that personality could be described in terms of 16 source traits, or basic personality factors. Each factor represents a dimension that ranges between two extremes.

Raymond Cattell (1905–1998) Cattell was a strong advocate of the trait approach to personality. His research led to the development of the Sixteen Personality Factor Questionnaire, one of the most widely used psychological tests for assessing personality.

Courtesy of Mary Cattell

asked to describe people they knew (Leising & others, 2014). Across all participants, 624 adjectives were generated. Among these, the adjectives most frequently used were those that were more "traitlike," such as extraverted and honest. It seems that it's natural for us to think in this way.

People possess traits to different degrees. For example, a person might be extremely shy, somewhat shy, or not shy at all. Hence, a trait is typically described in terms of a range from one extreme to its opposite. Most people fall in the middle of the range (average shyness), while fewer people fall at opposite poles (extremely shy or extremely outgoing).

Surface Traits and Source Traits

Most of the terms that we use to describe people are **surface traits**—traits that lie on "the surface" and can be easily inferred from observable behaviors. Examples of surface traits include attributes like "happy," "exuberant," "spacey," and "gloomy." The list of potential surface traits is extremely long. Personality researcher Gordon Allport combed through an English-language dictionary and discovered more than 4,000 words that described specific personality traits (Allport & Odbert, 1936).

Source traits are thought to be more fundamental than surface traits. As the most basic dimension of personality, a source trait can potentially give rise to a vast number of surface traits. Trait theorists believe that there are relatively few source traits. Thus, one goal of trait theorists has been to identify the most basic set of universal source traits that can be used to describe all individual differences (Pervin, 1994).

Two Representative Trait Theories
RAYMOND CATTELL AND HANS EYSENCK

How many source traits are there? Not surprisingly, trait theorists differ in their answers. Pioneer trait theorist **Raymond Cattell** reduced Allport's list of 4,000 terms to about 171 characteristics by eliminating terms that seemed to be redundant or uncommon (see John, 1990). Cattell collected data on a large sample of people, who were rated on each of the 171 terms. He then used a statistical technique called *factor analysis* to identify the traits that were most closely related to one another. After further research, Cattell eventually reduced his list to 16 key personality factors, which are listed in Table 10.3.

Cattell (1994) believed that these 16 personality factors represent the essential source traits of human personality. To measure these traits, Cattell developed what has become one of the most widely used personality tests, the *Sixteen Personality Factor Questionnaire* (abbreviated *16PF*). We'll discuss the 16PF in more detail later in the chapter.

An even simpler model of universal source traits was proposed by British psychologist **Hans Eysenck** (1916–1997). Eysenck's methods were similar to Cattell's, but his conception of personality includes just three dimensions. The first dimension is *introversion–extraversion,* which is the degree to which a person directs his energies outward toward the environment and other people versus inward toward his inner and self-focused experiences. A person who is high on the dimension of *introversion* might be quiet, solitary, and reserved, avoiding new experiences. A person high on the *extraversion* scale would be outgoing and sociable, enjoying new experiences and stimulating environments.

Eysenck's second major dimension is *neuroticism–emotional stability*. *Neuroticism* refers to a person's predisposition to become emotionally upset, while *stability* reflects a person's predisposition to be emotionally even. Surface traits associated with neuroticism are anxiety, tension, depression, and guilt. At the opposite end, emotional stability is associated with the surface traits of being calm, relaxed, and even-tempered.

Eysenck believed that by combining these two dimensions, people can be classified into four basic types: introverted–neurotic, introverted–stable, extraverted–neurotic, and extraverted–stable. Each basic type is associated with a different combination of surface traits, as shown in Figure 10.3.

In later research, Eysenck identified a third personality dimension, called *psychoticism* (Eysenck, 1990; Eysenck & Eysenck, 1975). A person high on this trait is antisocial, cold, hostile, and unconcerned about others. A person who is low on psychoticism is warm and caring toward others. In the chapter Prologue, Julian might be described as above average on psychoticism, while Kenneth was extremely low on this trait.

Eysenck (1990) believed that individual differences in personality are due to biological differences among people. For example, Eysenck proposed that an introvert's nervous system is more easily aroused than is an extravert's nervous system. Assuming that people tend to seek out an optimal level of arousal (see Chapter 8), extraverts would seek stimulation from their environment more than introverts would. And, because introverts would be more uncomfortable than extraverts in a highly stimulating environment, introverts would be much less likely to seek out stimulation.

Do introverts and extraverts actually prefer different environments? In a clever study, John Campbell and Charles Hawley (1982) found that extraverted students tended to study in a relatively noisy, open area of a college library, where there were ample opportunities for socializing with other students. Introverted students preferred to study in a quiet section of the library, where individual carrels and small tables were separated by tall bookshelves. As Eysenck's theory predicts, the introverts preferred study areas that minimized stimulation, while the extraverts preferred studying in an area that provided stimulation.

Eysenck's proposal is backed by findings from neuroscience research. Among extraverts, PET scans showed increased activity in regions of the brain associated

surface traits Personality characteristics or attributes that can easily be inferred from observable behavior.

source traits The most fundamental dimensions of personality; the broad, basic traits that are hypothesized to be universal and relatively few in number.

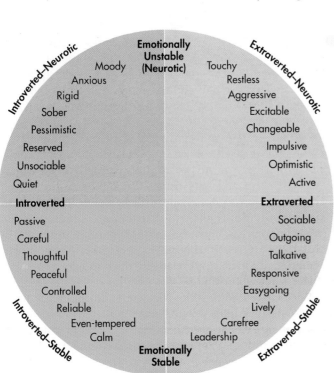

FIGURE 10.3 Eysenck's Theory of Personality Types Hans Eysenck's representation of the four basic personality types. Each type represents a combination of two basic personality dimensions: extraversion–introversion and neuroticism–emotional stability. Note the different surface traits in each quadrant that are associated with each basic personality type.

Source: Research from Eysenck (1982).

TABLE 10.4

The Five-Factor Model of Personality

Low ⟷	High
Factor 1: Neuroticism	
Calm	Worrying
Even-tempered, unemotional	Temperamental, emotional
Hardy	Vulnerable
Factor 2: Extraversion	
Reserved	Affectionate
Loner	Joiner
Quiet	Talkative
Factor 3: Openness to Experience	
Down-to-earth	Imaginative
Conventional, uncreative	Original, creative
Prefer routine	Prefer variety
Factor 4: Agreeableness	
Antagonistic	Acquiescent
Ruthless	Softhearted
Suspicious	Trusting
Factor 5: Conscientiousness	
Lazy	Hardworking
Aimless	Ambitious
Quitting	Persevering

Source: Research from McCrae & Costa (1990).

This table shows the five major personality factors, according to Big Five theorists Robert McCrae and Paul Costa, Jr. Listed below each major personality factor are surface traits that are associated with it. Note that each factor represents a dimension or range between two extreme poles. Most people will fall somewhere in the middle between the two opposing poles.

Use the acronym OCEAN to help you remember the five factors.

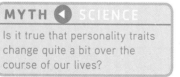

MYTH ◀ SCIENCE

Is it true that personality traits change quite a bit over the course of our lives?

with the processing of sensory information, as compared with introverts (Johnson & others, 1999). The researchers speculated that the increased activity in certain areas of the brain in extraverts "may underlie these individuals' high drive for sensory and emotional stimulation."

Sixteen Are Too Many, Three Are Too Few

THE FIVE-FACTOR MODEL

Many trait theorists felt that Cattell's trait model was too complex and that his 16 personality factors could be reduced to a smaller, more basic set of traits. Yet Eysenck's three-dimensional trait theory seemed too limited, failing to capture other important dimensions of human personality (see Block, 1995).

Today, the consensus among many trait researchers is that the essential building blocks of personality can be described in terms of five basic personality dimensions, which are sometimes called "the Big Five" (Funder, 2001). According to the **five-factor model of personality,** these five dimensions represent the structural organization of personality traits (McCrae & Costa, 1996, 2003).

What are the Big Five? Different trait researchers describe the five basic traits somewhat differently. However, the most commonly accepted five factors are neuroticism, extraversion, openness to experience, agreeableness, and conscientiousness. Table 10.4 summarizes the Big Five traits as defined by personality theorists Robert McCrae and Paul Costa, Jr. Note that Factor 1, neuroticism, and Factor 2, extraversion, are essentially the same as Eysenck's first two personality dimensions.

Does the five-factor model describe the universal structure of human personality? According to ongoing research by Robert McCrae and his colleagues (2004, 2005), the answer appears to be yes. In one wide-ranging study, trained observers rated the personality traits of representative individuals in 50 different cultures, including Arab cultures like those in Kuwait and Morocco and African cultures like those in Uganda and Ethiopia (McCrae & others, 2005). With few exceptions, people could be reliably described in terms of the five-factor structure of personality. Other research has shown that people in European, African, Arab, and Asian cultures describe personality using terms that are consistent with the five-factor model (Allik & McCrae, 2004; Rossier & others, 2005). Based on abundant cross-cultural research, trait theorists Jüri Allik and Robert McCrae (2002, 2004, 2013) believe that the Big Five personality traits are basic features of the human species, universal, and probably biologically based. Some personality researchers, however, are unconvinced, pointing out that there are culturally specific patterns of behavior that do not easily fit the five-factor model (Carlo & others, 2014). And, recent evidence suggests that the five-factor model may not apply as well to pre-industrial, preliterate indigenous tribes and developing countries (Gurven & others, 2013, 2014). However, these findings seem to be the exception, not the rule.

How can we account for the apparent universality of the five-factor structure? Psychologist David Buss (1991, 1995a) has one intriguing explanation. Buss thinks we should look at the utility of these factors from an evolutionary perspective. He believes that the Big Five traits reflect the personality dimensions that are the most important in the "social landscape" to which humans have had to adapt. Being able to identify who has social power (extraversion), who is likely to share resources (agreeableness), and who is trustworthy (conscientiousness) enhances our likelihood of survival.

Research has shown that traits are remarkably stable over time. A young adult who is very extraverted, emotionally stable, and relatively open to new experiences is likely to grow into an older adult who could be described in much the same way (Edmonds & others, 2013; McCrae & Costa, 2006; McCrae & others, 2000). However, this is not to say that personality traits don't change at all. Longitudinal data suggest that some general trends are evident over the lifespan. These include a slight decline in neuroticism, an increase in agreeableness and conscientiousness, and stability in extraversion and openness to experience from early to late adulthood (Soto & others, 2011; Kandler, 2012). In other words, most people become more agreeable, conscientious, and emotionally stable as they mature psychologically (Caspi & others, 2005; Roberts & others, 2006).

Traits are also generally consistent across different situations. However, situational influences may affect the expression of personality traits. Situations in which your behavior is limited by social "rules" or expectations may limit the expression of your personality characteristics. For example, even the most extraverted person may be subdued at a funeral. In general, behavior is most likely to reflect personality traits in familiar, informal, or private situations with few social rules or expectations (A. H. Buss, 1989, 2001).

Given the consistency of traits over time and across situations, many psychologists think that traits may be associated with specific patterns of brain activity or structure (Canli, 2004, 2006; Sampaio & others, 2014). We discuss a recent attempt to investigate the relationship between brain structure and personality traits in the Focus on Neuroscience box on the next page, "The Neuroscience of Personality: Brain Structure and the Big Five."

Keep in mind, however, that human behavior is the result of a complex *interaction* between traits and situations (Mischel, 2004; Mischel & Shoda, 2010; Sherman & others, 2015). People *do* respond, sometimes dramatically, to the demands of a particular situation. But the situations that people choose, and the characteristic way in which they respond to similar situations, are likely to be consistent with their individual personality dispositions (Mischel & Shoda, 1995; Mischel & others, 2002).

Personality Traits and Behavioral Genetics
JUST A CHIP OFF THE OLD BLOCK?

Do personality traits run in families? Are personality traits determined by genetics? Many trait theorists, such as Raymond Cattell and Hans Eysenck, believed that traits are at least partially genetic in origin. For example, Sandy and Don's daughter, Laura, has always been outgoing and sociable, traits that she shares with both her parents. But is she outgoing because she inherited that trait? Or is she outgoing because outgoing behavior was modeled and reinforced? Is it even possible to sort out the relative influence that genetics and environmental experiences have on personality traits?

The field of **behavioral genetics** studies the effects of genes and heredity on behavior. Most behavioral genetics studies on humans involve measuring similarities and differences among members of a large group of people who are genetically related to different degrees. The basic research strategy is to compare the degree of difference among subjects to their degree of genetic relatedness. If a trait is genetically influenced, then the more closely two people are genetically related, the more you would expect them to be similar on that trait (see Chapter 7).

Such studies may involve comparisons between identical twins and fraternal twins or comparisons between identical twins reared apart and identical twins reared together. Adoption studies, in which adopted children are compared to their biological and adoptive relatives, are also used in behavioral genetics.

Evidence gathered from twin studies and adoption studies shows that certain personality traits *are* substantially influenced by genetics (Amin & others, 2011; de Moor & others, 2010; McCrae & others, 2010). The evidence for genetic influence is particularly strong for extraversion and neuroticism, two of the Big

The Continuity of Traits Over the Lifespan Kenneth's conscientiousness was a trait that was evident throughout his life. Because he was too old to join the military when the United States entered World War II, Kenneth volunteered his legal expertise to the American Red Cross.

Courtesy of Don Hockenbury

behavioral genetics An interdisciplinary field that studies the effects of genes and heredity on behavior.

five-factor model of personality A trait theory of personality that identifies extraversion, neuroticism, agreeableness, conscientiousness, and openness to experience as the fundamental building blocks of personality.

Heredity or Environment? Along with sharing common genes, many identical twins share common interests and talents—like concert pianists Alvin *(left)* and Alan Chow. As students at the University of Maryland, they graduated with identical straight-A averages—and shared the stage as co-valedictorians. Both studied piano at Juilliard, and today they are both music professors with active performance schedules. In addition to performing solo, they frequently perform together in recital. However, the Chow twins were reared together, so it would be difficult to determine the relative importance of environmental and genetic influences on their talents and career paths.

© Lisa Kohler

FOCUS ON NEUROSCIENCE

The Neuroscience of Personality: Brain Structure and the Big Five

Many personality theorists, like Hans Eysenck, believed that personality traits are associated with characteristic biological differences among people (DeYoung & Gray, 2009). Some studies have confirmed this belief, identifying distinct patterns of brain activity associated with different personality traits (Canli, 2004, 2006). For example, brain-imaging studies showed that people who were high in extraversion (Factor 2) showed higher levels of brain activation in response to positive images than people who were low in extraversion. Similarly, people who score high on neuroticism (Factor 1) show more activation in response to negative images than people who score low on neuroticism (Canli & others, 2001).

Are personality traits also associated with brain structure? Psychologist Colin DeYoung and his colleagues had over 100 male and female participants undergo MRI scans and also take the *NEO-Personality Inventory*, a personality test that is used to measure the Big Five. The researchers then compared the brain scans and the personality test results. They found:

- *Extraversion* was associated with larger brain tissue volume in the *medial orbitofrontal cortex*, a brain region that is associated with sensitivity to rewarding stimuli.

- *Agreeableness* was associated with increased volume in the *posterior cingulate cortex*, a brain region associated with understanding the beliefs of others (Saxe & Powell, 2006). It was also associated with greater volume in the *fusiform gyrus*, an area of the cortex specialized for perceiving faces (see Chapters 3 and 7).

- *Conscientiousness* was associated with a large region of the frontal cortex called the *middle frontal gyrus*, which is known to be involved in planning, working memory, and self-regulation.

But not all personality traits had such clear correlations. *Neuroticism* was associated with a mixed pattern of brain structure differences. And DeYoung and his colleagues found no significant pattern of brain differences associated with openness to experience (Factor 5). They observed a slightly greater brain volume in one region that is associated with working memory and attention, but the difference was not statistically significant.

Are such studies merely phrenology with a modern face? These findings, while still preliminary, do suggest that there are biological influences on personality. It's important to note, though, that the findings are *correlational*. It's entirely possible that the brain differences are caused by different patterns of behavior rather than the other way around.

Further, unlike the phrenologists (see Chapter 2), today's researchers are well aware that both brain differences and personality traits are shaped by the complex interaction of environmental, genetic, and biological influences. As DeYoung (2010) says, the ultimate goal is to use the methods of neuroscience to help generate a new theory of personality—one in which personality is seen as a "system of dynamic, interacting elements that generates the ongoing flux of behavior and experience."

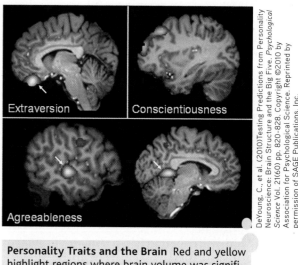

DeYoung, C., et al. (2010)Testing Predictions from Personality Neuroscience: Brain Structure and the Big Five. *Psychological Science* Vol. 21t6O) pp. 820-828. Copyright ©2010 by Association for Psychological Science. Reprinted by permission of SAGE Publications, Inc.

Personality Traits and the Brain Red and yellow highlight regions where brain volume was significantly associated with specific personality traits. The lighter the color, the stronger the association (DeYoung & others, 2010).

MYTH ◀ SCIENCE

Is it true that personality is not influenced by genetics, but is primarily shaped by your upbringing?

Genes confer dispositions, not destinies.

—Danielle Dick & Richard Rose (2002)

Five personality traits (Plomin & others, 1994, 2001; Weiss & others, 2008). Twin studies have also found that openness to experience, conscientiousness, and agreeableness are also influenced by genetics, although to a lesser extent (Bouchard, 2004; Harris & others, 2007).

So is personality completely determined by genetics? Not at all. As behavioral geneticists Robert Plomin and Essi Colledge (2001) explain, "Individual differences in complex psychological traits are due at least as much to environmental influences as they are to genetic influences. Behavioral genetics research provides the best available evidence for the importance of the environment." In other words, the influence of environmental factors on personality traits is at least equal to the influence of genetic factors (Rowe, 2003). For example, researchers have found that early experiences, such as having a parent with an anxiety disorder, affect whether a genetic vulnerability actually turns into a neurotic personality later in life (Barlow & others, 2014). Further underscoring this point is the fact that identical twins are most alike in early life. As the twins grow up, leave home, and encounter different experiences and environments, their personalities become more different (Bouchard, 2004; McCartney & others, 1990).

Evaluating the Trait Perspective on Personality

Although psychologists continue to disagree on how many basic traits exist, they do generally agree that people can be described and compared in terms of basic personality traits. But like the other personality theories, the trait approach has its weaknesses (Block, 1995).

One criticism is that trait theories don't really explain human personality (Epstein, 2010; Pervin, 1994). Instead, they simply label general predispositions to behave in a certain way. Second, trait theorists don't attempt to explain how or why individual differences develop (Boyle, 2008). After all, saying that trait differences are due partly to genetics and partly to environmental influences isn't saying much.

A third criticism is that trait approaches generally fail to address other important personality issues, such as the basic motives that drive human personality, the role of unconscious mental processes, how beliefs about the self influence personality, or how psychological change and growth occur (Block, 2010; McAdams & Walden, 2010). Conspicuously absent are the grand conclusions about the essence of human nature that characterize the psychoanalytic and humanistic theories. So, although trait theories are useful in describing individual differences and predicting behavior, there are limitations to their usefulness.

As you've seen, each of the major perspectives on personality has contributed to our understanding of human personality. The four perspectives are summarized in Table 10.5.

Our discussion of personality would not be complete without a description of how personality is formally evaluated and measured. In the next section, we'll briefly survey the tests that are used in personality assessment.

❭ Test your understanding of **Different Perspectives on Personality** with **LEARNING**Curve.

Jessie Jean/Getty Images

Why Are Siblings So Different? Although two children may grow up in the same home, they experience the home environment in very different ways. Even an event that affects the entire family, such as divorce, unemployment, or a family move, may be experienced quite differently by each child in the family. Children are also influenced by varied experiences outside the home, such as their relationships with teachers, classmates, and friends. Illness and accidents are other nonshared environmental influences. Of course, sibling relationships are themselves a potential source of influence on personality development.

TABLE 10.5

The Major Personality Perspectives

Perspective	Key Theorists	Key Themes and Ideas
Psychoanalytic	Sigmund Freud	Influence of unconscious psychological processes; importance of sexual and aggressive instincts; lasting effects of early childhood experiences
	Carl Jung	The collective unconscious, archetypes, and psychological wholeness
	Karen Horney	Importance of parent–child relationship; defending against basic anxiety; womb envy
	Alfred Adler	Striving for superiority, compensating for feelings of inferiority
Humanistic	Carl Rogers	Emphasis on the self-concept, psychological growth, free will, and inherent goodness
	Abraham Maslow	Behavior as motivated by hierarchy of needs and striving for self-actualization
Social Cognitive	Albert Bandura	Reciprocal interaction of behavioral, cognitive, and environmental factors; emphasis on conscious thoughts, self-efficacy beliefs, self-regulation, and goal setting
Trait	Raymond Cattell	Emphasis on measuring and describing individual differences; 16 source traits of personality
	Hans Eysenck	Three basic dimensions of personality: introversion–extraversion, neuroticism–emotional stability, and psychoticism
	Robert McCrae, Paul Costa, Jr.	Five-factor model, five basic dimensions of personality: neuroticism, extraversion, openness to experience, agreeableness, and conscientiousness

psychological test A test that assesses a person's abilities, aptitudes, interests, or personality on the basis of a systematically obtained sample of behavior.

projective test A type of personality test that involves a person's interpreting an ambiguous image; used to assess unconscious motives, conflicts, psychological defenses, and personality traits.

Rorschach Inkblot Test A projective test using inkblots, developed by Swiss psychiatrist Hermann Rorschach in 1921.

Thematic Apperception Test (TAT) A projective personality test, developed by Henry Murray and colleagues, that involves creating stories about ambiguous scenes.

graphology A pseudoscience that claims to assess personality, social, and occupational attributes based on a person's distinctive handwriting, doodles, and drawing style.

Assessing Personality
PSYCHOLOGICAL TESTS

KEY THEME

Tests to measure and evaluate personality fall into two basic categories: projective tests and self-report inventories.

KEY QUESTIONS

> What are the most widely used personality tests, and how are they administered and interpreted?
> What are some key strengths and weaknesses of projective tests and self-report inventories?

When we discussed intelligence tests in Chapter 7, we described the characteristics of a good psychological test. Beyond intelligence tests, there are literally hundreds of **psychological tests** that can be used to assess abilities, aptitudes, interests, and personality (Spies & others, 2010). Any psychological test is useful insofar as it achieves two basic goals:

1. It accurately and consistently reflects a person's characteristics on some dimension.

2. It predicts a person's future psychological functioning or behavior.

In this section, we'll look at the very different approaches used in the two basic types of personality tests—projective tests and self-report inventories. After looking at some of the most commonly used tests in each category, we'll evaluate the strengths and weaknesses of each approach.

What Do You See in the Inkblot? Intrigued by Freud's and Jung's theories, Swiss psychiatrist Hermann Rorschach (1884–1922) set out to develop a test that would reveal the contents of the unconscious. Rorschach believed that people were more likely to expose their unconscious conflicts, motives, and defenses in their descriptions of the ambiguous inkblots than they would be if the same topics were directly addressed. Rorschach published a series of 10 inkblots with an accompanying manual in a monograph titled *Psychodiagnostics: A Diagnostic Test Based on Perception* in 1921. Because he died the following year, Rorschach never knew how popular his projective test would become. Although the validity of the test is questionable, the Rorschach Inkblot Test is still the icon most synonymous with psychological testing in the popular media.

Projective Tests
LIKE SEEING THINGS IN THE CLOUDS

Projective tests developed out of psychoanalytic approaches to personality. In the most commonly used projective tests, a person is presented with a vague image, such as an inkblot or an ambiguous scene, then asked to describe what she "sees" in the image. The person's response is thought to be a projection of her unconscious conflicts, motives, psychological defenses, and personality traits. Notice that this idea is related to the defense mechanism of *projection,* which was described in Table 10.1 earlier in the chapter. The first projective test was the famous **Rorschach Inkblot Test,** published by Swiss psychiatrist Hermann Rorschach in 1921 (Hertz, 1992).

The Rorschach test consists of 10 cards, 5 that show black-and-white inkblots and 5 that depict colored inkblots. One card at a time, the person describes whatever he sees in the inkblot. The examiner records the person's responses verbatim and also observes his behavior, gestures, and reactions.

Numerous scoring systems exist for the Rorschach. Interpretation is based on such criteria as whether the person reports seeing animate or inanimate objects, human or animal figures, and movement, and whether the person deals with the whole blot or just fragments of it (Exner, 2007; Exner & Erdberg, 2005).

A more structured projective test is the **Thematic Apperception Test,** abbreviated **TAT,** which we discussed in Chapter 8. In the TAT, the person looks at a series of cards, each depicting an ambiguous scene. The person is asked to create a story about the scene, including what the characters are feeling and how the

The Granger Collection, New York

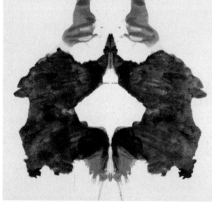

Spencer Grant/Photo Edit

SCIENCE VERSUS PSEUDOSCIENCE

Graphology: The "Write" Way to Assess Personality?

Does the way that you shape your *d*'s, dot your *i*'s, and cross your *t*'s reveal your true inner nature? That's the basic premise of **graphology,** a pseudoscience that claims that your handwriting reveals your temperament, personality traits, intelligence, and reasoning ability. If that weren't enough, graphologists also claim that they can accurately evaluate a job applicant's honesty, reliability, leadership potential, ability to work with others, and so forth (Beyerstein, 2007; Beyerstein & Beyerstein, 1992).

Handwriting analysis is very popular throughout North America and Europe. There are dozens of graphology organizations around the world, each promoting its own specific methods of analyzing handwriting (Imberman & Rifkin, 2008). Many different types of agencies and institutions use graphology. For example, the CIA used graphology to help their agents recruit and manage spies until the early 2000s (Brandon, 2011).

Over the years, graphology has been especially popular in the business world, and it is still widely used in Europe, particularly in France, Germany, and the United Kingdom (Ellin, 2004). According to one estimate, over 80 percent of European companies use graphology in personnel matters (Greasley, 2000; see Simner & Goffin, 2003).

When subjected to scientific evaluation, how does graphology fare? Consider a study by Anthony Edwards and Peter Armitage (1992) that investigated graphologists' ability to distinguish among people in three different groups:

- Successful versus unsuccessful secretaries
- Successful business entrepreneurs versus librarians and bank clerks
- Actors and actresses versus monks and nuns

In designing their study, Edwards and Armitage enlisted the help of leading graphologists and incorporated their suggestions into the study design. The graphologists preapproved the study's format and indicated that they felt it was a fair test of graphology. The graphologists also predicted they would have a high degree of success in discriminating among the people in each group. One graphologist stated that the graphologists would have close to a 100 percent success rate. Remember that prediction.

The three groups—successful/unsuccessful secretaries, entrepreneurs/librarians, and actors/monks—represented a combined total of 170 participants. As requested by the graphologists, all participants indicated their age, sex, and hand preference. Each person also produced 20 lines of spontaneous handwriting on a neutral topic.

Four leading graphologists independently evaluated the handwriting samples. For each group, the graphologists tried to assign each handwriting sample to one category or the other. Two control measures were built into the study: (1) The handwriting samples were also analyzed by four ordinary people with *no* formal training in graphology or psychology; and (2) a *typewritten* transcript of the handwriting samples was evaluated by four psychologists. The psychologists made their evaluations on the basis of the *content* of the transcripts rather than on the handwriting itself.

In the accompanying table, you can see how well the graphologists fared as compared to the untrained evaluators and the psychologists. Clearly, the graphologists fell far short of the nearly perfect accuracy they predicted they would demonstrate. In fact, in one case, the *untrained* assessors actually *outperformed* the graphologists—they were slightly better at identifying successful versus unsuccessful secretaries.

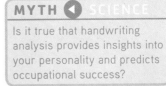

MYTH ◀ SCIENCE

Is it true that handwriting analysis provides insights into your personality and predicts occupational success?

Overall, the completely inexperienced judges achieved a success rate of 59 percent correct. The professional graphologists achieved a slightly better success rate of 65 percent. Obviously, this is not a great difference.

Hundreds of other studies have cast similar doubts on the ability of graphology to identify personality characteristics and to predict job performance from handwriting samples (Bangerter & others, 2009; Dazzi & Pedrabissi, 2009). In a global review of the evidence, psychologist Barry Beyerstein (1996) wrote, "Graphologists have unequivocally failed to demonstrate the validity or reliability of their art for predicting work performance, aptitudes, or personality. . . . If graphology cannot legitimately claim to be a scientific means of measuring human talents and leanings, what is it really? In short, it is a pseudoscience."

How do graphologists respond to the scientific evidence? Many just ignore it. One search company executive pointed to the high satisfaction of his clients at the companies for which he uses graphology (Schofield, 2013). He said, "just because we cannot measure its success rate using mathematics or statistics—that doesn't mean it is not a valid tool." Another admitted "I have no idea how it works, but to me it is obvious: the handwriting of a marketing guy is not the same as the handwriting of a sales guy." For firm believers, no scientific evidence will convince them that graphology is, in the words of one team of researchers, a "potentially rather useless procedure" (König & others, 2010).

Success Rates by Type of Assessor

Group Assessed	Graphologists	Untrained Assessors	Psychologists
Good/bad secretaries	67%	70%	56%
Entrepreneurs/librarians	63%	53%	52%
Actors/monks	67%	58%	53%
Overall success rate	65%	59%	54%

DILBERT

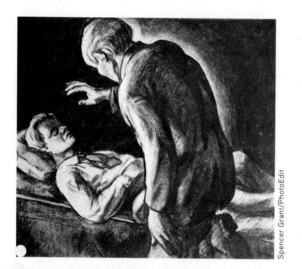

Spencer Grant/PhotoEdit

Lewis J. Merrim/Photo Researchers, Inc.

The Thematic Apperception Test
Developed by psychologists Christiana Morgan and Henry Murray (1935), the TAT involves creating a story about a highly evocative, ambiguous scenes, like the ones shown in the photograph on the left and on the card held by the young boy on the right. The person is thought to project his own motives, conflicts, and other personality characteristics into the story he creates. According to Murray (1943), "Before he knows it, he has said things about an invented character that apply to himself, things which he would have been reluctant to confess in response to a direct question."

MYTH ◄ SCIENCE

Is it true that projective tests, like the famous Rorschach inkblot test, accurately reveal personality traits and unconscious conflicts?

self-report inventory A type of psychological test in which a person's responses to standardized questions are compared to established norms.

Minnesota Multiphasic Personality Inventory (MMPI) A self-report inventory that assesses personality characteristics and psychological disorders; used to assess both normal and disturbed populations.

story turns out. The stories are scored for the motives, needs, anxieties, and conflicts of the main character and for how conflicts are resolved (Bellak, 1993; Langan-Fox & Grant, 2006; Moretti & Rossini, 2004). As with the Rorschach, interpreting the TAT involves the subjective judgment of the examiner.

STRENGTHS AND LIMITATIONS OF PROJECTIVE TESTS

Although sometimes used in research, projective tests are mainly used in counseling and psychotherapy. According to many clinicians, the primary strength of projective tests is that they provide a wealth of qualitative information about an individual's psychological functioning, information that can be explored further in psychotherapy.

However, there are several drawbacks to projective tests. First, the testing situation or the examiner's behavior can influence a person's responses. Second, the scoring of projective tests is highly subjective, requiring the examiner to make numerous judgments about the person's responses. Consequently, two examiners may test the same individual and arrive at different conclusions. Third, projective tests often fail to produce consistent results. If the same person takes a projective test on two separate occasions, very different results may be found. Finally, projective tests are poor at predicting future behavior.

The bottom line? Despite their widespread use, hundreds of studies of projective tests seriously question their *validity*—that the tests measure what they purport to measure—and their *reliability*—the consistency of test results (Hunsley & others, 2015; Weiner & Meyer, 2009). Nonetheless, projective tests remain very popular, especially among clinical, counseling, and school psychologists (Leichtman, 2004; Lilienfeld & others, 2012).

Self-Report Inventories
DOES ANYONE HAVE AN ERASER?

Self-report inventories typically use a paper-and-pencil format and take a direct, structured approach to assessing personality. People answer specific questions or rate themselves on various dimensions of behavior or psychological functioning. Often called *objective personality tests,* self-report inventories contain items that have been shown by previous research to differentiate among people on a particular personality characteristic. Unlike projective tests, self-report inventories are objectively scored by comparing a person's answers to standardized norms collected on large groups of people.

The most widely used self-report inventory is the **Minnesota Multiphasic Personality Inventory (MMPI)** (Butcher, 2010). First published in the 1940s and revised in the 1980s, the current version is referred to as the *MMPI-2*. The MMPI consists of over 500 statements. The person responds to each statement with "True," "False," or "Cannot say." Topics include social, political, religious, and sexual attitudes; physical and psychological health; interpersonal relationships; and abnormal thoughts and behaviors (Delman & others, 2008; Graham, 1993; McDermut & Zimmerman, 2008). Items similar to those used in the MMPI are shown in Table 10.6.

The MMPI is widely used by clinical psychologists and psychiatrists to assess patients. It is also used to evaluate the mental health of candidates for such occupations as police officers, doctors, nurses, and professional pilots. What keeps people from simply answering items in a way that makes them look psychologically healthy? Like many other self-report inventories, the MMPI has special scales to detect whether a person is answering honestly and consistently (Butcher, 2010; Pope & others, 2006). For example, if someone responds "True" to items such as "I *never* put off until tomorrow what I should do today" and "I *always* pick up after myself," it's probably a safe bet that she is inadvertently or intentionally distorting her other responses.

The MMPI was originally designed to assess mental health and detect psychological symptoms. In contrast, the California Psychological Inventory and the Sixteen Personality Factor Questionnaire are personality inventories that were designed to assess normal populations (Boer & others, 2008; Megargee, 2009). Of the over 400 true–false items on the long version of the **California Psychological Inventory (CPI),** nearly half are drawn from the MMPI. The CPI provides measures on such characteristics as interpersonal effectiveness, self-control, independence, and empathy. Profiles generated by the CPI are used to predict such things as high school and college grades, delinquency, and job performance (see Crites & Taber, 2002).

The **Sixteen Personality Factor Questionnaire (16PF)** was originally developed by Raymond Cattell and is based on his trait theory. The 16PF uses a forced-choice format in which the person must respond to each item by choosing one of three alternatives. Just as the test's name implies, the results generate a profile on Cattell's 16 personality factors. Each personality factor is represented as a range, with a person's score falling somewhere along the continuum between the two extremes (see Figure 10.4). The 16PF is widely used for career counseling, marital counseling, and evaluating employees and executives (H. E. P. Cattell & Mead, 2008; Clark & Blackwell, 2007).

TABLE 10.6

Simulated MMPI-2 Items

Most people will use somewhat unfair means to gain profit or an advantage rather than lose it.

I am often very tense on the job.

The things that run through my head sometimes are horrible.

Sometimes there is a feeling like something is pressing in on my head.

Sometimes I think so fast I can't keep up.

I am worried about sex.

I believe I am being plotted against.

I wish I could do over some of the things I have done.

Source: MMPI-2®.

MYTH ▶ SCIENCE

Is it true that there are ways to tell if you fake an answer on a personality test?

California Psychological Inventory (CPI) A self-report inventory that assesses personality characteristics in normal populations.

Sixteen Personality Factor Questionnaire (16PF) A self-report inventory developed by Raymond Cattell that generates a personality profile with ratings on 16 trait dimensions.

FIGURE 10.4 The 16PF: Example Questions and Profiles The 16PF, developed by Raymond Cattell, is a self-report inventory that contains 185 items like those shown in part (a). When scored, the 16PF generates a personality profile. In part (b), personality profiles of airline pilots and writers are compared. Cattell (1973) found that pilots are more controlled, more relaxed, more self-assured, and less sensitive than writers.

Source: Cattell, Raymond B.; Cattell, Karen S.; & Cattell, Heather E P (1993) 16PF questionnaire (5th ed.) ©1993 by the Institute for Personality and Ability Testing, Inc. (IPAT), Champaign, Illinois, USA. 16PF® is a registered trade mark of IPAT, a wholly owned subsidiary of OPP Ltd., Oxford, England. Reproduced from the US 16PF Administrators Manual 5th edition with the permission of the copyright holder.

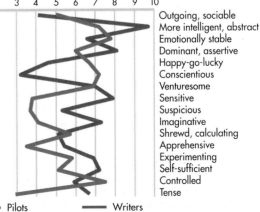

(a) **EXAMPLE QUESTIONS**

1. I often like to watch team games.
   a. true
   b. ?
   c. false
2. I prefer friends who are:
   a. quiet
   b. ?
   c. lively
3. Adult is to child as cat is to:
   a. kitten
   b. dog
   c. baby

Note: The person taking the test is instructed to answer "b. ?" only when neither *a* nor *c* is a better choice for him or her.

(b)

Reserved, unsociable	Outgoing, sociable
Less intelligent, concrete	More intelligent, abstract
Affected by feelings	Emotionally stable
Submissive, humble	Dominant, assertive
Serious	Happy-go-lucky
Expedient	Conscientious
Timid	Venturesome
Tough-minded	Sensitive
Trusting	Suspicious
Practical	Imaginative
Forthright	Shrewd, calculating
Self-assured	Apprehensive
Conservative	Experimenting
Group-dependent	Self-sufficient
Undisciplined	Controlled
Relaxed	Tense

—— Pilots   —— Writers

Another widely used personality test is the *Myers–Briggs Type Indicator* (abbreviated *MBTI*). The MBTI was developed by Isabel Briggs Myers and Katharine Cook Briggs (see Gladwell, 2004; Quenk, 2009). Myers and Briggs were intrigued by Carl Jung's personality theory and his proposal that people could be categorized into discrete personality "types." The Myers–Briggs test differs from other self-report tests in that it is designed to assess personality *types* rather than measure personality *traits*.

The notion of personality types is fundamentally different from personality traits. According to trait theory, people display traits, such as introversion/extraversion, to varying degrees. If you took the 16PF or the CPI, your score would place you somewhere along a continuum from low (very introverted) to high (very extraverted). However, most people would fall in the middle or average range on this trait dimension. But according to type theory, a person is *either* an extrovert *or* an introvert—that is, one of two distinct categories that don't overlap (Arnau & others, 2003; Wilde, 2011).

The MBTI arrives at personality type by measuring a person's *preferred* way of dealing with information, making decisions, and interacting with others. There are four basic categories of these preferences, which are assumed to be *dichotomies*—that is, opposite pairs. These dichotomies are: *Extraversion/Introversion; Sensing/Intuition; Thinking/Feeling;* and *Perceiving/Judging.*

There are 16 possible combinations of scores on these four dichotomies. Each combination is considered to be a distinct personality type. An individual personality type is described by the initials that correspond to the person's preferences as reflected in her MBTI score. For example, an ISFP combination would be a person who is *introverted, sensing, feeling,* and *perceiving,* while an ESTJ would be a person who is *extroverted, sensing, thinking,* and *judging.*

Despite the MBTI's widespread use in business, counseling, and career guidance settings, research has pointed to several problems with the MBTI. One problem is *reliability*—people can receive different MBTI results on different test-taking occasions. Equally significant is the problem of *validity.* For example, research does not support the claim of a relationship between MBTI personality types and occupational success (Pittenger, 2005). More troubling is the lack of evidence supporting the existence of 16 distinctly different personality types (Hunsley & others, 2003). Thus, most researchers in the field of psychological testing advise that caution be exercised in interpreting MBTI results, especially in applying them to vocational choices or predictions of occupational success (see Pittenger, 2005). In fact, after summarizing the research on the general ineffectiveness of the MBTI, a reporter concluded that the test was only useful as "a fun, interesting activity, like a BuzzFeed quiz" (Stromberg, 2015).

Think Like a SCIENTIST

Can an assessment of your personality predict job success? Go to LaunchPad: Resources to **Think Like a Scientist** about **Employment-Related Personality Tests.**

LaunchPad

STRENGTHS AND LIMITATIONS OF SELF-REPORT INVENTORIES

The two most important strengths of self-report inventories are their *standardization* and their *use of established norms* (see Chapter 7). Each person receives the same instructions and responds to the same items. The results of self-report inventories are objectively scored and compared to norms established by previous research. In fact, the MMPI, the CPI, and the 16PF can all be scored by computer.

As a general rule, the reliability and validity of self-report inventories are far greater than those of projective tests. Literally thousands of studies have demonstrated that the MMPI, the CPI, and the 16PF provide accurate, consistent results that can be used to generally predict behavior (Anastasi & Urbina, 1997; Archer & Smith, 2014). For example, self-report ratings have been shown to match up with our tendency to "like" things on Facebook. As Wu Youyou and his colleagues report (2015), "participants with high openness to experience tend to like Salvador Dali, meditation, or TED talks; participants with high extraversion tend to like partying, Snookie (reality show star), or dancing." Aspects of personality, as measured by inventories like the MMPI, the CPI, and the 16PF, have even been shown to predict later physical health, including cognitive functioning in old age, chronic illnesses, and risk of dying (Chapman & others, 2012; Jackson & others, 2015; Vedhara & others, 2015).

Self-report inventories also seem to fit with other measures of personality. For example, many studies have shown that our own self-report ratings of our personalities correlate with our friends' or family members' ratings of our personalities on the same personality inventories (Connelly & Ones, 2010; Watson & others, 2000).

However, self-report inventories also have their weaknesses. First, despite the inclusion of items designed to detect deliberate deception, there is considerable evidence that people can still successfully fake responses and answer in socially desirable ways (Anastasi & Urbina, 1997; Holden, 2008). Second, some people are prone to responding in a set way. They may consistently pick the first alternative or answer "True" whether the item is true for them or not. And some tests, such as the MMPI and CPI, include hundreds of items. Taking these tests can become quite tedious, and people may lose interest in carefully choosing the most appropriate response.

Third, people are not always accurate judges of their own behavior, attitudes, or attributes. And some people defensively deny their true feelings, needs, and attitudes, even to themselves (Cousineau & Shedler, 2006; Shedler & others, 1993). For example, a person might indicate that she enjoys parties, even though she actually avoids social gatherings whenever possible.

To sum up, personality tests are generally useful strategies that can provide insights about the psychological makeup of people. But no personality test, by itself, is likely to provide a definitive description of a given individual. In practice, psychologists and other mental health professionals usually combine personality test results with behavioral observations and background information, including interviews with family members, co-workers, or other significant people in the person's life.

❭ Test your understanding of **Assessing Personality** with *LEARNINGCurve*.

Closing Thoughts

Over the course of this chapter, you've encountered firsthand some of the most influential contributors to modern psychological thought. As you'll see in Chapter 14, the major personality perspectives provide the basis for many forms of psychotherapy. Clearly, the psychoanalytic, humanistic, social cognitive, and trait perspectives each provide a fundamentally different way of conceptualizing personality. That each perspective has strengths and limitations underscores the point that no single perspective can explain all aspects of human personality. Indeed, no one personality theory could explain why Kenneth and Julian were so different. And, given the complex factors involved in human personality, it's doubtful that any single theory ever will capture the essence of human personality in its entirety. Even so, each perspective has made important and lasting contributions to the understanding of human personality.

> **possible selves** The aspect of the self-concept that includes images of the selves that you hope, fear, or expect to become in the future.

PSYCH FOR YOUR LIFE

Possible Selves: Imagine the Possibilities

Some psychologists believe that a person's self-concept is not a singular mental self-image, as Carl Rogers proposed, but a *multifaceted system* of related images and ideas (Hermans, 1996; Markus & Kunda, 1986). This collection of related images about yourself reflects your goals, values, emotions, and relationships (Markus & Cross, 1990; Markus & Wurf, 1987; Unemori & others, 2004).

According to psychologist Hazel Markus and her colleagues, an important aspect of your self-concept has to do with your images of the selves that you *might* become—your **possible selves**. Possible selves are highly personalized, vivid, futuristic images of the self that reflect hopes, fears, and fantasies. As Markus and co-researcher Paula Nurius (1986) wrote, "The possible selves that are hoped for might include the successful self, the creative self, the rich self, the thin self, or the loved and admired self, whereas the dreaded possible selves could be the alone self, the depressed self, the incompetent self, the alcoholic self, the unemployed self, or the bag lady self."

The Influence of Hoped-For and Dreaded Possible Selves

Possible selves are more than just idle daydreams or wishful fantasies. In fact, possible selves influence our behavior in important ways (Markus & Nurius, 1986; Oyserman & James, 2011). We're

often not aware of the possible selves that we have incorporated into our self-concepts. Nevertheless, they can serve as powerful forces that either activate or stall our efforts to reach important goals. Your incentive, drive, and motivation are greatly influenced by your possible selves, and so are your decisions and choices about future behavior (Hoyle & Sherrill, 2006; Robinson & others, 2003).

Imagine that you harbor a hoped-for possible self of becoming a professional musician. You would probably practice with greater regularity and intensity than someone who does not hold a vivid mental picture of performing solo at Carnegie Hall or being named Performer of the Year at the American Country Music Awards.

Dreaded possible selves can also influence behavior, whether they are realistic or not. Consider your author Don's father, Kenneth. Although never wealthy, Kenneth was financially secure throughout his long life. Yet Kenneth had lived through the Great Depression and witnessed firsthand the financial devastation that occurred in the lives of countless people. Kenneth seems to have harbored a dreaded possible self of becoming penniless. When Kenneth died, the family found a $100 bill tucked safely under his mattress.

A positive possible self, even if it is not very realistic, can protect an individual's self-esteem in the face of failure (Markus & Nurius, 1986). A high school girl who thinks she is unpopular with her classmates may console herself with visions of a possible self as a famous scientist who snubs her intellectually inferior classmates at her 10-year class reunion.

Possible Selves, Self-Efficacy Beliefs, and Motivation

Self-efficacy beliefs are closely connected to the idea of possible selves. Performing virtually any task involves the construction of a possible self that is capable and competent of performing the action required (Ruvolo & Markus, 1992).

Thus, people who vividly imagine possible selves

MYTH ▶ **SCIENCE**

Is it true that if you can imagine yourself taking the steps to become successful, you're more likely to actually become successful?

as "successful because of hard work" persist longer and expend more effort on tasks than do people who imagine themselves as "unsuccessful despite hard work" (Ruvolo & Markus, 1992). The motivation to achieve academically increases when your possible selves include a future self who is successful because of academic achievement (Oyserman & James, 2011; Oyserman & others, 2015). To be most effective, possible selves should incorporate concrete strategies for attaining goals. For example, students who visualized themselves taking specific steps to improve their grades—such as doing homework daily or signing up for tutoring—were more successful than students who simply imagined themselves doing better in school (Oyserman & others, 2004).

Applying the Research: Assessing Your Possible Selves

How can you apply these research findings to *your* life? First, it's important to stress again that we're often unaware of how the possible selves we've mentally constructed influence our beliefs, actions, and self-evaluations. Thus, the first step is to consciously assess the role that your possible selves play in your life (Oyserman & James, 2011).

Take a few moments and jot down the "possible selves" that are active in your working self-concept. To help you in this task, write three responses to each of the following questions:

1. Next year, I expect to be . . .

2. Next year, I am afraid that I will be . . .

3. Next year, I want to avoid becoming . . .

After focusing on the short-term future, take these same questions and extend them to 5 years from now or even 10 years from now. Most likely, certain themes and goals will consistently emerge. Now the critical questions:

• How are your possible selves affecting your *current* motivation, goals, feelings, and decisions?

• Are your possible selves even remotely plausible?

• Are they pessimistic and limiting?

• Are they unrealistically optimistic?

Finally, ask yourself honestly: What realistic strategies are you using to try to become the self that you want to become? To avoid becoming the selves that you dread?

How can you improve the likelihood that you will achieve some of your possible selves? One approach is to link your expectations and hopes to concrete strategies about how to behave to reach your desired possible self (Oyserman & others, 2004).

These questions should help you gain some insight into whether your possible selves are influencing your behavior in productive, constructive ways. If they are not, now is an excellent time to think about replacing or modifying the possible selves that operate most powerfully in your own self-concept. Why is this so important? Because to a large extent, who we become is guided by who we *imagine* we'll become. Just imagine the possibilities of who *you* could become!

CHAPTER REVIEW

KEY PEOPLE AND KEY TERMS

Alfred Adler, p. 426
Albert Bandura, p. 433
Raymond Cattell, p. 436

Hans Eysenck, p. 436
Sigmund Freud, p. 415

Karen Horney, p. 425
Carl G. Jung, p. 424

Abraham Maslow, p. 429
Carl Rogers, p. 429

personality, p. 415
personality theory, p. 415
psychoanalysis (in personality), p. 415
free association, p. 416
unconscious, p. 417
id, p. 418
libido, p. 418
pleasure principle, p. 418
ego, p. 419
reality principle, p. 419
superego, p. 419
ego defense mechanisms, p. 420

repression (in psychoanalytic theory of personality and psychotherapy), p. 420
displacement, p. 420
sublimation, p. 420
psychosexual stages, p. 421
Oedipus complex, p. 422
identification, p. 422
collective unconscious, p. 424
archetypes, p. 425
humanistic psychology (theory of personality), p. 429
actualizing tendency, p. 429
self-concept, p. 429

conditional positive regard, p. 431
unconditional positive regard, p. 431
social cognitive theory, p. 433
reciprocal determinism, p. 433
self-efficacy, p. 434
trait, p. 435
trait theory, p. 435
surface traits, p. 436
source traits, p. 436
five-factor model of personality, p. 438
behavioral genetics, p. 439

psychological test, p. 442
projective test, p. 442
Rorschach Inkblot Test, p. 442
Thematic Apperception Test (TAT), p. 442
graphology, p. 443
self-report inventory, p. 444
Minnesota Multiphasic Personality Inventory (MMPI), p. 444
California Personality Inventory (CPI), p. 445
Sixteen Personality Factor Questionnaire (16PF), p. 445
possible selves, p. 447

Personality

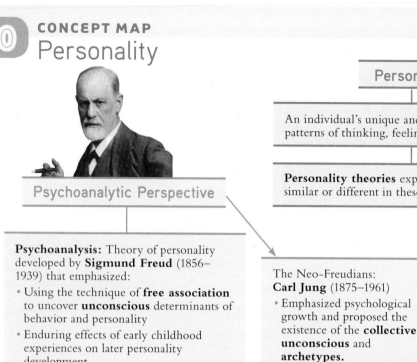

Personality

An individual's unique and relatively consistent patterns of thinking, feeling, and behaving

Personality theories explain how people are similar or different in these patterns.

Psychoanalytic Perspective

Psychoanalysis: Theory of personality developed by **Sigmund Freud** (1856–1939) that emphasized:

- Using the technique of **free association** to uncover **unconscious** determinants of behavior and personality
- Enduring effects of early childhood experiences on later personality development

Freud contended that personality consists of three conflicting psychological forces:

- The **id**—irrational, impulsive personality dimension ruled by the **pleasure principle**
- The **ego**—rational, mediating personality dimension that operates according to the **reality principle**
- The **superego**—moralistic, self-evaluative personality component consisting of internalized parental and societal values and rules

Ego defense mechanisms: Unconscious distortions of reality that temporarily reduce anxiety, including:

- **Repression**
- **Sublimation**
- Projection
- Denial
- Regression
- **Displacement**
- Rationalization
- Reaction formation
- Undoing

Psychosexual stages: Freud's five age-related developmental periods in which sexual impulses are expressed through different bodily zones: oral, anal, phallic, latency, and genital

- During phallic stage, child must resolve **Oedipus complex** through **identification** with same-sex parent.
- Fixation at a particular stage may result if the developmental conflicts are not successfully resolved.

The Neo-Freudians:
Carl Jung (1875–1961)
- Emphasized psychological growth and proposed the existence of the **collective unconscious** and **archetypes.**

Karen Horney (1885–1952)
- Emphasized role of social relationships in protecting against anxiety.

Alfred Adler (1870–1937)
- Believed the most fundamental human motive was to strive for superiority.

Humanistic Perspective

Humanistic psychology emphasizes:

- Inherent goodness of people
- **Self-concept,** self-awareness, and free will
- Human potential and psychological growth
- Healthy personality development

Carl Rogers (1902–1987) proposed that:

- The **actualizing tendency** is the inborn drive to maintain and enhance the organism
- People are motivated to maintain a consistent **self-concept**
- **Conditional positive regard** by parents leads to incongruence so that self-concept conflicts with experience
- **Unconditional positive regard** by parents leads to congruence

Abraham Maslow (1908–1970) contended that:

- People are motivated by hierarchy of needs
- People strive for self-actualization

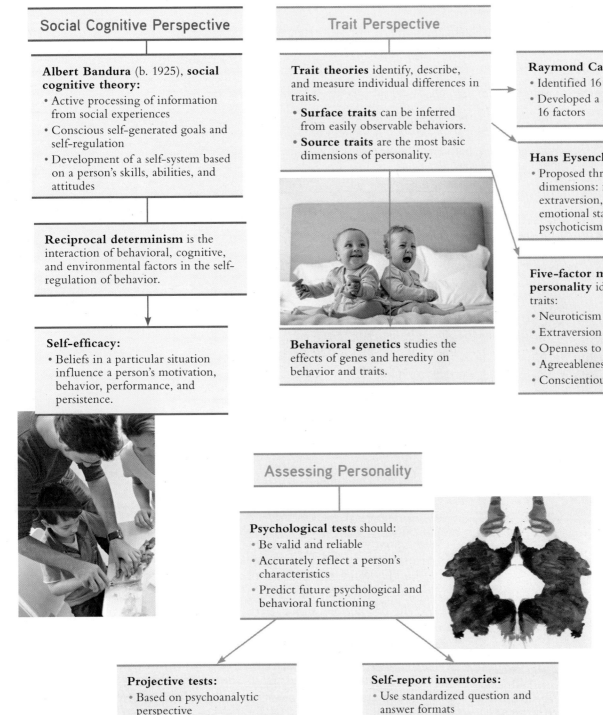

Social Cognitive Perspective

Albert Bandura (b. 1925), **social cognitive theory:**
- Active processing of information from social experiences
- Conscious self-generated goals and self-regulation
- Development of a self-system based on a person's skills, abilities, and attitudes

Reciprocal determinism is the interaction of behavioral, cognitive, and environmental factors in the self-regulation of behavior.

Self-efficacy:
- Beliefs in a particular situation influence a person's motivation, behavior, performance, and persistence.

Trait Perspective

Trait theories identify, describe, and measure individual differences in traits.
- **Surface traits** can be inferred from easily observable behaviors.
- **Source traits** are the most basic dimensions of personality.

Behavioral genetics studies the effects of genes and heredity on behavior and traits.

Raymond Cattell (1905–1998)
- Identified 16 personality factors
- Developed a test to measure the 16 factors

Hans Eysenck (1916–1997)
- Proposed three basic personality dimensions: introversion–extraversion, neuroticism–emotional stability, and psychoticism.

Five-factor model of personality identified five source traits:
- Neuroticism
- Extraversion
- Openness to experience
- Agreeableness
- Conscientiousness

Assessing Personality

Psychological tests should:
- Be valid and reliable
- Accurately reflect a person's characteristics
- Predict future psychological and behavioral functioning

Projective tests:
- Based on psychoanalytic perspective
- Person responds to vague stimulus
- Subjectively scored
- Include **Rorschach Inkblot Test** and **Thematic Apperception Test (TAT)**

Self-report inventories:
- Use standardized question and answer formats
- Are objectively scored with results compared to established norms
- Include the **Minnesota Multiphasic Personality Inventory (MMPI), California Personality Inventory (CPI), Sixteen Personality Factor Inventory (16 PF),** and Myers–Briggs Trait Inventory

Is it true . . .

○ That you judge yourself more harshly than you judge other people when something goes wrong?

○ That if you believe you are not prejudiced, you will not behave in prejudiced ways?

○ That if you're sure of your answer, you'll almost always stick to it even if others disagree with you?

○ That most people will not harm another person if ordered to do so?

○ That people are more likely to help others if they are the only ones available to help?

○ That there is a link between aggression and listening to violent music lyrics?

○ That people who say no to a large request are more easily able to say no to smaller requests that follow?

(inset) Yuri_Arcurs/Getty Images
(bkgrd) Art by Distort & Mustart http://g.reenvillain.com

THE "HOMELESS" MAN

PROLOGUE

REMEMBER ERV AND FERN, Sandy's parents, from Chapter 5? A few years ago, Fern and Erv got two free plane tickets when they were bumped from an overbooked flight. They decided to visit a city they had always wanted to see—San Francisco. Even though Fern was excited about the trip, she was also anxious about visiting the earthquake zone. Erv wasn't especially worried about earthquakes, but he was worried about whether his old army buddy could still beat him at penny poker. Mostly, they both wanted to see the famous sights, eat seafood, wander through shops, and explore used bookstores, which was Erv's favorite hobby.

As it turned out, Fern and Erv were both quite taken by the beauty and charm of San Francisco. But they were also disturbed by the number of homeless people they saw on the city streets, sometimes sleeping in the doorways of expensive shops and restaurants. This was especially disturbing to Fern, who has a heart of gold and is known among her family and friends for her willingness to help others, even complete strangers.

On the third morning of their San Francisco visit, Erv and Fern were walking along one of the hilly San Francisco streets near the downtown area. That's when Fern saw a scruffy-looking man in faded jeans sitting on some steps, holding a cup. Something about his facial expression struck Fern as seeming lost, maybe dejected. Surely this was one of San Francisco's less fortunate, Fern thought to herself. Without a moment's hesitation, Fern rummaged through her purse, walked over to the man, and dropped a handful of quarters in his cup.

"Hey, lady! What the hell d'ya think you're doing!?!" the man exclaimed, jumping up.

Social Psychology

IN THIS CHAPTER:

> **INTRODUCTION:** What Is Social Psychology?

> Person Perception: Forming Impressions of Other People

> Attribution: Explaining Behavior

> The Social Psychology of Attitudes

> Understanding Prejudice

> Conformity: Following the Crowd

> Obedience: Just Following Orders

> Altruism and Aggression: Helping and Hurting Behavior

> Closing Thoughts

> **PSYCH FOR YOUR LIFE:** The Persuasion Game

"Oh, my! Aren't you homeless!?" Fern asked, mortified and turning bright red.

"Lady, this *is* my home," the man snapped, motioning with his thumb to the house behind him. "I live here! And that's my cup of coffee you just ruined!"

Fortunately, the "homeless" man also had a sense of humor. After fishing Fern's quarters out of his coffee and giving them back to her, he chatted with the out-of-towners, enlightening them on the extraordinary cost of San Francisco real estate. As they parted, the not-so-homeless man ended up recommending a couple of his favorite seafood restaurants.

Like Fern, we all try to make sense out of our social environments. As we navigate the world, we constantly make judgments about the traits, motives, and goals of other people. And, like Fern, sometimes we make mistakes!

In this chapter, we will look at how we interpret our social environment, including how we form impressions of other people and explain their behavior. We'll explore how our own behavior, including the likelihood that we will help or harm others, is influenced by the social environment and other people. In the process, we'll come back to Erv and Fern's incident with the "homeless" man to illustrate several important concepts. □

INTRODUCTION:
What Is Social Psychology?

Why did Fern think the man on the steps was homeless? How did the "homeless" man initially interpret Fern's efforts to help him? And in contrast to Fern, not everyone who feels compassion toward homeless people acts in accordance with that attitude. Why did Fern do so?

These are the kinds of issues that social psychologists study. **Social psychology** investigates how your thoughts, feelings, and behavior are influenced by the presence of other people and by the social and physical environment. The social situations can include being alone, in the presence of others, or in front of a crowd of onlookers.

Like other psychology specialty areas, social psychology emphasizes certain concepts. For example, one important social psychology concept is that of your *self.* Your **sense of self** involves you as a social being who has been shaped by your interactions with others and by the social environments, including the culture, in which you operate. Thus, your sense of self plays a key role in how you perceive and react to others.

Some social behaviors, such as helping others, are displayed *universally*—that is, they take a consistent form in diverse cultures. When a specific social behavior is universal, social psychologists will often use insights from evolutionary psychology to understand how the behavior is adaptive.

As we discussed in Chapter 1, *evolutionary psychology* is based on the premise that certain psychological processes and behavior patterns evolved over hundreds of thousands of years. Those patterns evolved because in some way they were adaptive, increasing the odds of survival for humans who displayed those qualities. In turn, this survival advantage increased the genetic transmission of those patterns to subsequent generations (see Buss, 2008; Neuberg & others, 2010).

Social psychology research focuses on many different topics. In this chapter, we'll focus on two key research areas in social psychology. We'll start with an area that has been greatly influenced by the experimental methods and findings of *cognitive psychology,* which we discussed in Chapter 7. **Social cognition** refers to how we form impressions of other people, how we interpret the meaning of other people's behavior, and how our behavior is affected by our attitudes (Bodenhausen & others, 2003; Frith & Frith, 2012).

Later in the chapter, we'll look at **social influence,** which focuses on how our behavior is affected by other people and by situational factors. The study of social influence includes such questions as why we conform to group norms, what compels us to obey an authority figure, under what circumstances we will help a stranger, and what leads us to behave in ways that intentionally harm other people.

Person Perception
FORMING IMPRESSIONS OF OTHER PEOPLE

KEY THEME

Person perception refers to the mental processes we use to form judgments about other people.

KEY QUESTIONS

› What four principles are followed in the person perception process?
› How do social categorization, implicit personality theories, and physical attractiveness affect person perception?

Consider the following scenario. You're attending college in a big city and you commute from your apartment to campus via the subway. Today the subway is more than half full. If you want to sit down, you'll have to share a seat with some other passenger. In a matter of seconds, you must decide which stranger you'll share your ride home with, elbow to elbow, thigh to thigh. How will you decide?

---

social psychology Branch of psychology that studies how a person's thoughts, feelings, and behavior are influenced by the presence of other people and by the social and physical environment.

sense of self An individual's unique sense of identity that has been influenced by social, cultural, and psychological experiences; your sense of who you are in relation to other people.

social cognition The mental processes people use to make sense of their social environments.

social influence The effect of situational factors and other people on an individual's behavior.

person perception The mental processes we use to form judgments and draw conclusions about the characteristics and motives of other people.

social norms The "rules," or expectations, for appropriate behavior in a particular social situation.

Whether it's a seat on the subway or in a crowded movie theater, this is a task that most of us confront almost every day: On the basis of very limited information, we must quickly draw conclusions about the nature and likely behavior of people who are complete strangers to us. How do we arrive at these conclusions?

Person perception refers to the mental processes we use to form judgments and draw conclusions about the characteristics of other people. Person perception is an active, subjective process that always occurs in some *interpersonal context*—that is, situations that involve interactions between two or more people (Macrae & Quadflieg, 2010; Smith & Collins, 2009).

In the interpersonal context of a subway car, you evaluate people based on minimal interaction. You form very rapid *first impressions* largely by looking at other people's faces, regardless of their actual personalities (Ames & others, 2009; Bar & others, 2006; Zebrowitz & Montepare, 2008). In a mere tenth of a second, you evaluate the other person's attractiveness, likeability, competence, trustworthiness, and aggressiveness (Willis & Todorov, 2006).

Four key principles guide person perception and influence your decision (see Ambady & Skowronski, 2008; Zebrowitz & Montepare, 2006). Let's illustrate those principles using the subway scenario.

Making Split-Second Decisions About Strangers Deciding where to sit in a subway car or on a bus involves rapidly evaluating people who are complete strangers. What kinds of factors affect your first impressions of other people? Do your impressions of others seem to result from deliberate or automatic thoughts? Are your first impressions generally accurate?

> **Principle 1. Your reactions to others are determined by your perceptions of them, not by who they really are.** On the subway, you quickly choose not to sit next to the big guy with a scowl on his face. Why? Because *you* perceive him as threatening. Of course, he could be a florist who's surly because he's getting home late.

> **Principle 2. Your self-perception also influences how you perceive others and how you act on your perceptions.** Your decision about where to sit is also influenced by how you perceive yourself (Macrae & Quadflieg, 2010). For example, if you think of yourself as looking intimidating, you may not mind sitting next to the big guy with a scowl.

> **Principle 3. Your goals in a particular situation determine the amount and kinds of information you collect about others.** If your goal is to share a subway seat with someone who will basically leave you alone, you will look for characteristics that are relevant to that goal—perhaps someone wearing telltale white earbuds who is obviously listening to music (Goodwin & others, 2002; Hilton, 1998).

> **Principle 4. In every situation, you evaluate people partly in terms of how you expect them to act within that particular context.** Whether you're in a classroom, restaurant, or public restroom, your behavior is governed by **social norms**—the unwritten "rules," or expectations, for appropriate behavior in that particular social situation (Milgram, 1992). On the subway, for example, you don't sit next to someone else when empty seats are available, and you don't read your seatmate's text messages. Violating these social norms will draw attention from others, as in the cartoon to the right!

What these four guiding principles demonstrate is that person perception is based on an interaction among four components: the perceptions we have of others, our self-perceptions, our goals, and the social norms for that context.

How does person perception play out in the online world of social media? Social psychologists have turned their attention to person perception in online contexts. For example, a Facebook profile photograph is more important than text in driving our perceptions. Even a comment about enjoying hanging out with a big group of friends doesn't outweigh a photo depicting a loner on a park bench. This person would be perceived as introverted (Van Der Heide & others, 2012).

As another example, a person's list of Facebook friends, part of the specific context in the Facebook environment, plays a role in how that person will be perceived. People are perceived to be more physically attractive if they have attractive Facebook

"Goodbye everybody."

social categorization The mental process of categorizing people into groups (or *social categories*) on the basis of their shared characteristics.

explicit cognition Deliberate, conscious mental processes involved in perceptions, judgments, decisions, and reasoning.

implicit cognition Automatic, nonconscious mental processes that influence perceptions, judgments, decisions, and reasoning.

implicit personality theory A network of assumptions or beliefs about the relationships among various types of people, traits, and behaviors.

Think Like a SCIENTIST

What factors in an online dating profile make you want to meet someone? Go to LaunchPad: Resources to **Think Like a Scientist** about **Online Dating**.

LaunchPad

Using Social Categories We often use superficial cues such as clothing and context to assign people to social categories and draw conclusions about their behavior. What sorts of social categories are evident here?

Brent Winebrenner/Getty Images

friends (Antheunis & Schouten, 2011). The more Facebook friends a person has, the more socially attractive they are perceived to be (Tong & others, 2008). But this is true only up to about 300 "friends." After that, perceptions of social attractiveness decrease perhaps because it doesn't seem that all of these people are actually friends.

On a short subway ride, after a quick glance at a Facebook profile, or in other transient situations, you'll probably never learn whether your first impressions were accurate or not. But first impressions are often wrong (Olivola & Todorov, 2010). And even if we have further encounters with a person, it takes a while for our impressions to change. Our first impression can color our overall impression of a person, something called the *halo effect* (Nisbett & Wilson, 1977). Initial information tends to create a "halo" around a person, and it becomes harder to notice new information that might conflict with the initial judgment. Thus, many professors grade work anonymously—they don't want their previous impressions of you affecting their evaluation of your current work (Malouff & others, 2013). Fortunately, in situations that involve long-term relationships with other people, such as in a classroom or at work, we do start to fine-tune our impressions as we acquire additional information about the people we come to know (Smith & Collins, 2009).

Social Categorization
USING MENTAL SHORTCUTS IN PERSON PERCEPTION

Along with person perception, the subway scenario illustrates our natural tendency to group people into categories. **Social categorization** is the mental process of classifying people into groups on the basis of common characteristics.

So how do you socially categorize people who are complete strangers, such as the other passengers on the subway? To a certain extent, you consciously focus on easily observable features, such as the other person's gender, age, or clothing (Kinzler & others, 2010; Miron & Branscomben, 2008). With a quick glance, you might socially categorize someone as "Asian male, 20-something, fraternity sweatshirt, probably a college student." Social psychologists use the term **explicit cognition** to refer to these deliberate, conscious mental processes involved in perceptions, judgments, decisions, and reasoning.

However, your social perceptions are not always completely conscious considerations. In many situations, you react to another person with automatic social perceptions, categorizations, and attitudes. Social psychologists use the term **implicit cognition** to describe the mental processes associated with automatic, nonconscious social evaluations (Gawronski & Payne, 2010).

Prior experiences and beliefs about different social categories can trigger implicit social reactions ranging from very positive to very negative (Nosek & others, 2007). Without consciously realizing it, your reaction to another person can be swayed by characteristics such as ethnicity, weight, sexual orientation, or religious beliefs. There also may be evolutionary origins for our automatic reactions to others. For example, facial features perceived as attractive are similar across cultures (Chatterjee, 2011). And people of all ages tend to agree on facial attractiveness. Babies less than a week old spend more time looking at attractive faces than unattractive faces (Slater & others, 1998, 2010).

We often assume that certain types of people share certain traits and behaviors. This is referred to as an **implicit personality theory.** Different models exist to explain how implicit personality theories develop and function (see Critcher & Dunning, 2009; Ybarra, 2002). But in general terms, your previous social and cultural experiences influence the cognitive *schemas,* or mental frameworks, you hold about the traits and behaviors associated with different "types" of people. So when you perceive someone to be a particular "type," you assume that the person will display those traits and behaviors (see Uleman & others, 2008).

Physical appearance cues play an important role in person perception and social categorization (Olivola & Todorov, 2010). Particularly influential is the implicit personality theory that most people have for physically attractive people, particularly with respect to their faces (see Lemay & others, 2010; Todorov & others, 2015). Starting in childhood, we are bombarded with the cultural message that "what is beautiful is good." In myths, fairy tales, cartoons, movies, and games, heroes are handsome, heroines are beautiful, and the evil villains are ugly (Bazzini & others, 2010). As a result of such cultural conditioning, most people have an implicit personality theory that associates physical attractiveness with a wide range of desirable characteristics.

Decades of research have shown that good-looking people are perceived as being more intelligent, happier, and better adjusted than other people (Eagly & others, 1991; Lorenzo & others, 2010). In an extensive meta-analysis, Judith Langlois and her colleagues (2000) found that people tend to attribute a wide range of positive qualities to attractive individuals, viewing them as being more intelligent, strong, sensitive, honest, sociable, assertive, and emotionally stable. One study even found differences among the same people before and after plastic surgery (Reilly & others, 2015). Participants evaluated photos of women either before or after plastic surgery. The same women were judged to be more attractive, feminine, likable, and socially skilled after plastic surgery than they were before plastic surgery. In addition to attractive people being perceived more positively, Genevieve Lorenzo and her colleagues (2010) found that they are also perceived more accurately, perhaps because people paid more attention to their traits. Lorenzo observed that "people do judge a book by its cover, but a beautiful cover prompts a closer reading" (2010).

But are beautiful people *actually* happier, smarter, or more successful than the rest of us? Economists Daniel Hamermesh and Jason Abrevya (2011) analyzed data from surveys conducted in four countries and concluded that more attractive people *do* tend to be happier, primarily because they also tended to have improved economic outcomes, such as higher salaries and more successful spouses.

Some studies have found that attractive people also tend to have higher self-esteem, intelligence, and other desirable personality traits than people of more average appearance (Langlois & others, 2000; Sheppard & others, 2011). Why? One possibility is that, throughout their lives, they receive more favorable treatment from other people, such as parents, teachers, employers, and peers (Langlois & others, 1995; Sheppard & others, 2011). The attention that they receive may also be due to the positive emotional responses they evoke (Lemay & others, 2010). The Focus on Neuroscience on the next page discusses evidence demonstrating that there may be a brain-based reason for the greater social success of beautiful people.

Obviously, the social categorization process has both advantages and disadvantages. Relegating someone to a social category on the basis of superficial information ignores that person's unique qualities. Sometimes these conclusions are wrong, as Fern's was when she categorized the scruffy-looking San Francisco man with a cup in his hand as homeless.

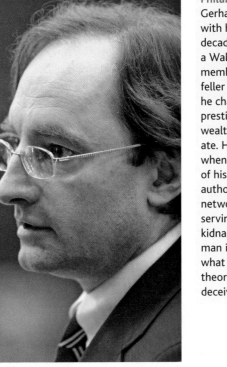

AP Photo/CJ Gunther, Pool

Philanthropist or Criminal? Christian Gerhartsreiter fooled countless people with his aliases (Seal, 2009). Over decades, he posed as British royalty, a Wall Street high roller, and finally, a member of the famously wealthy Rockefeller family. With an upper-crust accent, he charmed his way into exclusive clubs, prestigious jobs, and even marriage to a wealthy Harvard Business School graduate. His con artist life came to an end when, after he divorced and lost custody of his daughter, he kidnapped her. As the authorities closed in, they uncovered his network of lies. Gerhartsreiter is now serving 27 years to life for the kidnapping— and for the murder of a man in the 1980s (Deutsch, 2013). In what ways could implicit personality theory explain how Gerhartsreiter deceived so many people?

What Is Beautiful Is Good We are culturally conditioned to associate beauty with goodness and evil with ugliness— an implicit personality theory that has been dubbed the "what is beautiful is good" myth (Sheppard & others, 2011). For example, in this scene from the Disney film *Enchanted*, the sweet, innocent princess is beautifully dressed and perfectly groomed, but the wicked stepmother is disguised as an old woman, complete with a wart on her chin.

Disney Enterprises/The Kobal Collection at Art Resource, NY

FOCUS ON NEUROSCIENCE

Brain Reward When Making Eye Contact with Attractive People

How does physical attractiveness contribute to social success? A study by neuroscientists Knut Kampe and his colleagues (2001) at University College London may offer some insights. In a functional magnetic resonance imaging (fMRI) study, participants were scanned while they looked at color photographs of 40 different faces, some looking directly at the viewer (eye contact) and some glancing away (non–eye contact). After the fMRI scanning session, participants rated the attractiveness of the faces they had seen.

The results showed that when we make direct eye contact with a physically attractive person, an area on each side of the brain called the *ventral striatum* is activated (yellow areas in fMRI scan). When the attractive person's eye gaze is shifted away from the viewer, activity in the ventral striatum decreases. What makes this so interesting is that the ventral striatum is a brain area that predicts reward (Bray & O'Doherty, 2007). Neural activity in the

ventral striatum increases when an unexpected reward, such as food or water, suddenly appears. Conversely, activity in the ventral striatum decreases when an expected reward fails to appear.

As Kampe (2001) explains, "What we've shown is that when we make eye contact with an attractive person, the brain area that predicts reward starts firing. If we see an attractive person but cannot make eye contact with that person, the activity in this region goes down, signaling disappointment. This is the first study to show that the brain's ventral striatum processes rewards in the context of human social interaction."

Other neuroscientists have identified additional brain reward areas, including the *orbital frontal cortex*, the *nucleus accumbens*, and the *amygdala*, that are responsive to facial attractiveness (see Chatterjee, 2011; Cloutier & others, 2008). This suggests that viewing attractive faces tends to activate many of the same brain areas that are involved in processing other types of pleasurable stimuli.

Eye-Contact Face   **Non–Eye-Contact Face**

Reprinted by permission from Macmillan Publishers Ltd: NATURE 413, Kampe et al. Psychology: Reward value of attractiveness and gaze, Fig. 1, copyright 2001. Courtesy Knut Kampe, University College London

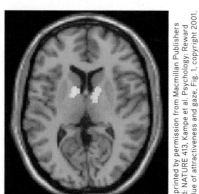

Reprinted by permission from Macmillan Publishers Ltd: NATURE 413, Kampe et al. Psychology: Reward value of attractiveness and gaze, Fig. 1, copyright 2001. Courtesy Knut Kampe, University College London

"Facial beauty evokes a widely distributed neural network involving perceptual, decision-making, and reward circuits. [It] may serve as a neural trigger for the pervasive effects of attractiveness in social interactions," writes neuroscientist Anjan Chatterjee and his colleagues (2009). Apparently, the social advantages associated with facial attractiveness are reinforced by reward processing in the brain.

On the other hand, relying on social categories is a natural, adaptive, and efficient cognitive process. Social categories provide us with considerable basic information about other people. And from an evolutionary perspective, the ability to make rapid judgments about strangers is probably an evolved characteristic that conferred survival value in our evolutionary past.

Attribution

EXPLAINING BEHAVIOR

attribution The mental process of inferring the causes of people's behavior, including one's own. Also refers to the explanation made for a particular behavior.

fundamental attribution error The tendency to attribute the behavior of others to internal, personal characteristics, while ignoring or underestimating the effects of external, situational factors; an attributional bias that is common in individualistic cultures.

KEY THEME

Attribution refers to the process of explaining your own behavior and the behavior of other people.

KEY QUESTIONS

> What are the fundamental attribution error and the self-serving bias?

> How do attributional biases affect our judgments about the causes of behavior?

> How does culture affect attributional processes?

On the first day of class, you sit down and turn to say hi to the classmate next to you. She ignores you and focuses on her phone. You think to yourself, "What a jerk."

Why did you arrive at that conclusion? After all, it's completely possible that your classmate is having a very bad day and just doesn't feel up to talking or is responding to an urgent text message.

Attribution is the process of inferring the cause of someone's behavior, including your own. Psychologists also use the word *attribution* to refer to the explanation you make for a particular behavior. The attributions you make strongly influence your thoughts and feelings about other people.

If your explanation for the silent classmate is that she is just an unpleasant, unfriendly person, you demonstrated a common cognitive bias. The **fundamental attribution error** is the tendency to spontaneously attribute the behavior of others to internal, personal characteristics, while ignoring or underestimating the role of external, situational factors (Ross, 1977). Even though it's entirely possible that situational forces were behind another person's behavior, we tend to automatically assume that the cause is an internal, personal characteristic (Bauman & Skitka, 2010; Zimbardo, 2007).

Notice, however, that when it comes to explaining our *own* behavior, we tend to be biased in the opposite direction, a tendency called the **actor–observer bias**. Rather than internal, personal attributions, we're more likely to explain our own behavior using *external, situational* attributions. She ignored you because she's not nice; you ignored a classmate because you had to text your roommate to check the stove you think you left on. Some jerk pulled out in front of your car because she's a reckless, inconsiderate moron; you pulled out in front of her car because an over-grown hedge blocked your view (Hennessy & others, 2005). And so on.

Why the discrepancy in accounting for the behavior of others as compared to our own behavior? Part of the explanation is that we simply have more information about the potential causes of our own behavior than we do about the causes of other people's behavior. When you observe another driver turn directly into the path of your car, that's typically the only information you have on which to judge his or her behavior. But when *you* inadvertently pull in front of another car, you perceive your own behavior in the context of the various situational factors, such as road conditions, that influenced your action. You also know what motivated your behavior and how differently you have behaved in similar situations in the past. Thus, you're much more aware of the extent to which your behavior has been influenced by situational factors (Jones, 1990).

The fundamental attribution error plays a role in a common explanatory pattern called **blaming the victim.** The innocent victim of a crime, disaster, or serious illness is blamed for having somehow caused the misfortune or for not having taken steps to prevent it. For example, many people blame the poor for their dire straits, the sick for bringing on their illnesses, and victims of domestic violence or rape for somehow "provoking" their attackers.

The blaming the victim explanatory pattern is reinforced by another common cognitive bias. **Hindsight bias** is the tendency, after an event has occurred, to overestimate one's ability to have foreseen or predicted the outcome (Roese & Vohs, 2012). In everyday conversations, this is the person who confidently proclaims *after* the event, "I could have told you that would happen." In the case of blaming the victim, hindsight bias makes it seem as if the victim should have been able to predict—and prevent—what happened (Goldinger & others, 2003).

Why do people often resort to blaming the victim? People have a strong need to believe that the world is fair—that "we get what we deserve and deserve what we get." Social psychologist Melvin Lerner (1980) calls this the **just-world hypothesis.**

actor–observer bias The tendency to attribute our *own* behavior to external, situational characteristics, while ignoring or underestimating the effects of internal, personal factors.

blaming the victim The tendency to blame an innocent victim of misfortune for having somehow caused the problem or for not having taken steps to avoid or prevent it.

hindsight bias The tendency to overestimate one's ability to have foreseen or predicted the outcome of an event.

just-world hypothesis The assumption that the world is fair and that therefore people get what they deserve and deserve what they get.

MYTH ◀ SCIENCE

Is it true that you judge yourself more harshly than you judge other people when something goes wrong?

Blaming the Victim Elizabeth Smart is shown here talking about her experiences during captivity. At age 14, Smart was kidnapped at knifepoint from her bedroom and held captive for nine months. She was deprived of food and raped multiple times every day. After she was rescued, many people asked why she hadn't done more to escape. After all, they pointed out, her captor often brought a veiled Smart out in public. Fighting back against victim blaming, Smart explained that she was terrified by her captor's threats against her family: "You can never judge a child or a victim of any crime on what they should have done, because you weren't there and you don't know" (Serrano, 2013). Why do people often "blame the victim" after crimes, accidents, or other tragedies?

Blaming the victim reflects the belief that, because the world is just, the victim must have done something to deserve his or her fate (Maes & others, 2012). Collectively, these cognitive biases and explanatory patterns help psychologically insulate us from the uncomfortable thought "It could have just as easily been me" (Alves & Correia, 2008; IJzerman & Van Prooijen, 2008).

The Self-Serving Bias
USING EXPLANATIONS TO MEET OUR NEEDS

If you've ever listened to other students react to their grades on an important exam, you've seen the **self-serving bias** in action. When students do well on a test, they tend to congratulate themselves and to attribute their success to how hard they studied, their intelligence, and so forth—all *internal* attributions. But when a student bombs a test, the *external* attributions fly left and right: "They were all trick questions!" "I couldn't concentrate because the guy behind me kept coughing" (Kruger & Gilovich, 2004).

In a wide range of situations, people tend to credit themselves for their success and to blame their failures on external circumstances (Krusemark & others, 2008; Mezulis & others, 2004). Psychologists explain the self-serving bias as resulting from an attempt to save face and protect self-esteem in the face of failure (Kurman, 2010; Kwan & others, 2008). Some evolutionary psychologists argue that the self-serving bias leads people to feel and appear more confident than might be justified in a particular situation (von Hippel & Trivers, 2011). If others then perceive us as more confident, we may have more access to resources that allow us to survive and pass on our genes.

Explaining Misfortune: The Self-Serving Bias Given the self-serving bias, are these NASCAR drivers—including Dale Earnhardt, Jr., in car #88—likely to explain their accident by listing internal factors such as their own carelessness or recklessness? Or are they more likely to blame external factors, such as another driver's poor handling of his vehicle or slick conditions on the Daytona International Speedway?

Jamie Squire/Getty Images

🌐 CULTURE AND HUMAN BEHAVIOR

Explaining Failure and Murder: Culture and Attributional Biases

Although the self-serving bias is common in individualistic cultures such as Australia and the United States, it is far from universal. In many collectivistic cultures, an opposite attributional bias is often demonstrated (Mezulis & others, 2004; Uskul & Kitayama, 2011). Called the *self-effacing bias* or *modesty bias,* it involves blaming failure on internal, personal factors, while attributing success to external, situational factors.

For example, compared to American students, Japanese and Chinese students are more likely to attribute academic failure to personal factors, such as lack of effort, instead of situational factors (Dornbusch & others, 1996). Thus, a Japanese student who does poorly on an exam is likely to say, "I didn't study hard enough." In contrast, Japanese and Chinese students tend to attribute academic *success* to *situational factors.* For example, they might say, "The exam was very easy" or "There was very little competition this year" (Stevenson & others, 1986).

One study asked participants to rate people who were answering questions about their achievements (Chen & Jing, 2012). Collectivistic participants tended to prefer the people who gave modest answers, whereas individualistic participants tended to like people who boasted in their answers.

Cross-cultural differences are also evident with the fundamental attribution error. In general, members of collectivistic cultures are less likely to commit the fundamental attribution error than are members of individualistic cultures (M. Bond & Smith, 1996; Koenig & Dean, 2011). That is, collectivists are more likely to attribute the causes of another person's behavior to external, situational factors rather than to internal, personal factors—the exact *opposite* of the attributional bias that is demonstrated in individualistic cultures (Uskul & Kitayama, 2011).

To test this idea in a naturally occurring context, psychologists Michael Morris and Kaiping Peng (1994) compared articles reporting the same mass murders in Chinese-language and English-language newspapers. In one case, the murderer was a Chinese graduate student attending a U.S. university. In the other case, the murderer was a U.S. postal worker. Regardless of whether the murderer was American or Chinese, the news accounts were fundamentally different depending on whether the *reporter* was American or Chinese.

The American reporters were more likely to explain the killings by making personal, internal attributions. For example, American reporters emphasized the postal worker's "history of being mentally unstable." In contrast, the Chinese reporters emphasized situational factors, such as the fact that the postal worker had recently been fired from his job.

Clearly, then, how we account for our successes and failures, as well as how we account for the actions of others, is yet another example of how human behavior is influenced by cultural conditioning.

Haughtiness invites ruin; humility receives benefits.

—Chinese Proverb

TABLE 11.1

Common Attributional Biases and Explanatory Patterns

Bias	Description
Fundamental attribution error	We tend to explain the behavior of other people by attributing their behavior to internal, personal characteristics, while underestimating or ignoring the effects of external, situational factors. The pattern is reversed when accounting for our own behavior.
Actor–observer bias	We tend to explain our *own* behavior by attributing our actions to external, situational characteristics, while underestimating or ignoring the effects of internal, personal factors. The pattern is reversed when accounting for others' behavior.
Blaming the victim	We tend to blame the victims of misfortune for causing their own misfortune or for not taking steps to prevent or avoid it. This is partly due to the *just-world hypothesis.*
Hindsight bias	After an event has occurred, we tend to overestimate the extent to which we could have foreseen or predicted the outcome.
Self-serving bias	We have a tendency to take credit for our successes by attributing them to internal, personal causes, along with a tendency to distance ourselves from our failures by attributing them to external, situational causes. The self-serving bias is more common in individualistic cultures.
Self-effacing (or modesty) bias	We tend to blame ourselves for our failures, attributing them to internal, personal causes, while downplaying our successes by attributing them to external, situational causes. The self-effacing bias is more common in collectivistic cultures.

Although common in many societies, the self-serving bias is far from universal, as cross-cultural psychologists have discovered (see the Culture and Human Behavior box). The various attributional biases are summarized in Table 11.1.

❯ Test your understanding of **Person Perception and Attribution** with **LEARNING**Curve.

The Social Psychology of Attitudes

KEY THEME

An attitude is a learned tendency to evaluate objects, people, or issues in a particular way.

KEY QUESTIONS

❯ What are the three components of an attitude?

❯ Under what conditions are attitudes most likely to determine behavior?

❯ What is cognitive dissonance?

Should high school graduation requirements include a class on basic sex education, birth control methods, and safe sex? Should there be a compulsory military or community service requirement for all young adults? Should the government be doing more to prepare for climate change?

On these and many other subjects, you've probably formed an attitude. Psychologists formally define an **attitude** as a learned tendency to evaluate some object, person, or issue in a particular way (Banaji & Heiphetz, 2010; Bohner & Dickel, 2011). Attitudes are typically positive or negative, but they can also be *ambivalent,* as when you have mixed feelings about an issue, person, or group (Costarelli, 2011).

As shown in Figure 11.1 on the next page, attitudes can include three components. First, an attitude may have a *cognitive component:* your thoughts about a given topic or object. For example, Emil is an art lover. He often tells his friends that, in his opinion, visiting galleries and museums encourages people to be more open to new experiences. Second, an attitude may have an emotional or *affective component,* as when Emil talks excitedly about how energized he is after seeing an exhibition of Jeff Koons' art. Finally, an attitude may have a *behavioral component,* in which attitudes are

self-serving bias The tendency to attribute successful outcomes of one's own behavior to internal causes and unsuccessful outcomes to external, situational causes.

attitude A learned tendency to evaluate some object, person, or issue in a particular way; such evaluations may be positive, negative, or ambivalent.

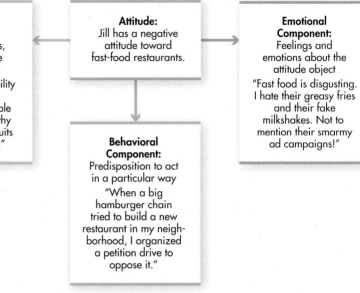

FIGURE 11.1 The Components of Attitudes An attitude is a positive or negative evaluation of an object, person, or idea. An attitude may have cognitive, emotional, and behavioral components.

Cognitive Component:
Beliefs, thoughts, ideas about the attitude object
"The easy availability of fast food discourages people from eating healthy food, like fresh fruits and vegetables."

Attitude:
Jill has a negative attitude toward fast-food restaurants.

Emotional Component:
Feelings and emotions about the attitude object
"Fast food is disgusting. I hate their greasy fries and their fake milkshakes. Not to mention their smarmy ad campaigns!"

Behavioral Component:
Predisposition to act in a particular way
"When a big hamburger chain tried to build a new restaurant in my neighborhood, I organized a petition drive to oppose it."

reflected in action, as when Emil donates to an organization that introduces schoolchildren to the arts.

Along with forming attitudes toward objects, ideas, or political campaigns, we also form attitudes about people. The In Focus box "Interpersonal Attraction and Liking" discusses some of the factors that affect the thoughts and feelings that we develop about other people.

The Effect of Attitudes on Behavior

Intuitively, you probably assume that your attitudes tend to guide your behavior. But social psychologists have consistently found that people don't always act in accordance with their attitudes. For example, you might disapprove of cheating yet find yourself peeking at a classmate's exam paper when the opportunity presents itself.

When are your attitudes likely to influence or determine your behavior? Social psychologists have found that you're most likely to behave in accordance with your attitudes when:

- You anticipate a favorable outcome or response from others for behaving that way.
- Your attitudes are extreme or are frequently expressed (Ajzen, 2001).
- You are very knowledgeable about the subject (Fabrigar & Wegener, 2010).
- You have a vested interest in the subject and personally stand to gain or lose something on a specific issue (Thornton & Tizard, 2010).

Clearly, your attitudes do influence your behavior in many instances. Now, consider the opposite question: Can your behavior influence your attitudes?

The Effect of Behavior on Attitudes
FRIED GRASSHOPPERS FOR LUNCH?!

Suppose you have volunteered to participate in a psychology experiment. At the lab, a friendly experimenter asks you to indicate your degree of preference for a variety of foods, including fried grasshoppers, which you rank pretty low on the list. During the experiment, the experimenter instructs you to eat some fried grasshoppers. You manage to swallow three of the crispy critters. At the end of the experiment, your attitudes toward grasshoppers as a food source are surveyed again.

Attitudes and Behavior These student protesters in Gauhati, India, are calling for an end to all large dam projects in their country. The students believe that large dams have a negative environmental impact, particularly on parts of the country downriver from the dams. People who hold strong opinions and express them openly, like these protestors, are most likely to behave in ways that are consistent with their attitudes.

AP Photo/Anupam Nath

Interpersonal Attraction and Liking

In psychology, *attraction* refers to feeling drawn to other people—having positive thoughts and feelings about them. Often, attraction motivates us to interact with or develop a relationship with the attractive person.

What makes one person more attractive than another? Personal characteristics such as warmth and trustworthiness, adventurousness, and social status influence judgments of attractiveness (Finkel & Baumeister, 2010; Sprecher & Felmlee, 2008). But physical appearance, especially facial features, is probably the most significant factor in attraction. Studies reveal that wide smiles, high eyebrows, dilated pupils, and full lips are judged as attractive by both men and women, and that these preferences are consistent across many cultures (Chatterjee, 2011; Perrett, 2010). Some evolutionary psychologists argue that we associate attractive facial features with health, a desirable characteristic in a mating partner (Fink & Penton-Voak, 2002). However, the sexes do differ in some respects. For example, in online dating, women tend to prefer men who are taller than average, but men tend to prefer women who are of short or average height (Hitsch & others, 2010).

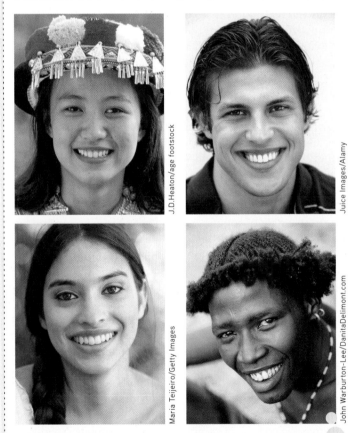

Ideals of Beauty Around the World Large eyes, a wide smile, and full lips are attractive in cultures around the world. The beautiful smiles of a Hmong woman from Thailand, a young Hispanic American man, a woman from Chile, and a man from the Omo Delta in East Africa would be considered attractive by any cultural standard.

Some aspects of attraction are *interpersonal*. For example, we are more attracted to people whom we perceive as being like us—in physical characteristics, personality traits, attitudes, and even psychological health (Finkel & Baumeister, 2010). Although similarity is a powerful predictor of attraction in most Western cultures, cross-cultural research has shown that it is less important in some Eastern cultures, such as Japan (Heine & others, 2009).

Familiarity is another predictor of attraction and liking. In general, the more we interact with a person, the more we tend to like that person. Why? One explanation is that *most* interactions with other people are relatively pleasant (Reis & others, 2011). So, unless a person is particularly obnoxious or *un*pleasant, frequent interactions lead to more feelings of mutual pleasure, understanding, and acceptance.

The situations in which we interact with people also affect attraction. When happy, intoxicated, or physically aroused by exercise or exertion, we are more likely to rate others as attractive (Finkel & Baumeister, 2010). And, if we anticipate that attractive people are likely to be attracted to or like *us,* we're more likely to be attracted to them, to like them, and to behave warmly toward them (Stinson & others, 2009).

Finally, feelings of attraction can be influenced by the socioeconomic and cultural environment. For example, cross-cultural research has shown that men in societies in which food and resources are in short supply tend to prefer heavier women (Swami & Tovée, 2006; Tovée & others, 2006). Conversely, a preference for thinner women is more common in societies where resources are abundant (Swami & others, 2010).

But is it culture or hunger that shapes a preference for heavier women? In a clever study, Leif Nelson and Evan Morrison (2005) compared the preferences of college students as they were entering and leaving a campus dining hall at dinnertime. The presumably hungry men *entering* the dining hall preferred heavier women than the satiated men *exiting* the dining hall. (Having an empty or full stomach didn't affect the female college students' ratings of an ideal body shape.) The moral of the story: Culture affects body shape preference, but may do so through processes that are not culture-specific but rather situational.

Researchers have also observed a preference for specific body proportions that is consistent across cultures (Singh & others, 2010). Whether heavy or thin, a woman with a waist that is a good deal smaller than her hips seems to be universally viewed as attractive. This is true even among men who are blind; without ever having seen images of women considered beautiful, they preferred this proportion when they felt female mannequins (Karremans & others, 2010). Why? This body proportion has been shown to predict both lower risk for a range of diseases, including diabetes and cancer, and increased reproductive success (Singh & Singh, 2011). Evolutionary researchers suggest that this preference makes perfect sense, as a healthy reproductive partner increases the chance of genes being passed on. (The research on mate preferences is discussed further on page 378 in Chapter 9.)

p.studio66/Shutterstock

Fried Grasshoppers: Tasty or Disgusting? Most Americans do not rate fried grasshoppers as one of their favorite foods. Suppose you agreed to eat a handful of grasshoppers after being asked to do so by a rude, unfriendly experimenter. Do you think your attitude toward fried grasshoppers would improve more than that of a person who ate grasshoppers after being asked to do so by a friendly, polite experimenter? Why or why not?

Karen Ballard/Redux Pictures

Social Psychologist Philip Zimbardo (b. 1933) Zimbardo grew up in an immigrant family in a poor neighborhood in the South Bronx, an experience that sensitized him to the power of situational influences and the destructive nature of stereotypes and prejudice (Zimbardo, 2005, 2007).

Zimbardo's research has ranged from attitude change to shyness, prison reform, and the psychology of evil. As Zimbardo (2000b) observes, "The joy of being a psychologist is that almost everything in life is psychology, or should be, or could be." Later in the chapter, we'll encounter Zimbardo's most famous—and controversial—research: a study known as the "Stanford Prison Experiment."

Later in the day, you talk to a friend who also participated in the experiment. You mention how friendly and polite you thought the experimenter was. But your friend had a different experience. He thought the experimenter was an arrogant, rude jerk.

Here's the critical question: Whose attitude toward eating fried grasshoppers is more likely to change in a positive direction? Given that you interacted with a friendly experimenter, most people assume that *your* feelings about fried grasshoppers are more likely to have improved than your friend's attitude. In fact, it is your friend—who encountered the obnoxious experimenter—who is much more likely to hold a more positive attitude toward eating fried grasshoppers than you.

At first glance, this finding seems to go against the grain of common sense. So how can we explain this outcome? The fried grasshoppers story represents the basic design of a classic experiment by social psychologist **Philip Zimbardo** and his colleagues (1965). Zimbardo's experiment underscored the importance of cognitive dissonance, a phenomenon first identified by social psychologists Leon Festinger and J. Merrill Carlsmith (1959). **Cognitive dissonance** is an unpleasant state of psychological tension (*dissonance*) that occurs when there's an inconsistency between two thoughts or perceptions (*cognitions*). This state of dissonance is so unpleasant that we are strongly motivated to reduce it (Festinger, 1957, 1962; Gawronski, 2012).

Cognitive dissonance commonly occurs in situations in which you become uncomfortably aware that your behavior and your attitudes are in conflict (Cooper, 2012). In these situations, you are simultaneously holding two conflicting cognitions: your original attitude versus the realization that your behavior contradicts that attitude. If you can easily rationalize your behavior to make it consistent with your attitude, then any dissonance you might experience can be quickly and easily resolved. But when your behavior *cannot* be easily justified, how can you resolve the contradiction and eliminate the unpleasant state of dissonance? Since you can't go back and change the behavior, *you change your attitude to make it consistent with your behavior.*

Let's take another look at the results of the grasshopper study, this time from the perspective of cognitive dissonance theory. Your attitude toward eating grasshoppers did *not* change. Why? Because you could easily rationalize the conflict between your attitude ("Eating grasshoppers is disgusting") and your behavior (eating three grasshoppers). You probably justified your behavior by saying something like, "I ate the grasshoppers because I wanted to help out the nice experimenter." However, your friend, who encountered the rude experimenter, can't use that rationalization. Thus, he experiences an uncomfortable state of cognitive dissonance. Since he can't go back and change his behavior, he is left with the only part of the equation that can be changed—his attitude (see Figure 11.2). "You know, eating those grasshoppers wasn't *that* bad," your friend comments. "In fact, they were kind of crunchy." Notice how his change in attitude reduces the dissonance between his previous attitude and his behavior. And he might not have even realized that his attitude had changed.

Research from social neuroscience suggests that cognitive dissonance can lead to attitude change quickly, perhaps without us even realizing that the process is occurring. Difficult decisions are often followed by an attitude change that favors the object or outcome chosen. Brain scans show changes in the parts of the brain associated with distress, arousal, emotion, and conflict within seconds after a person makes a difficult decision, which may indicate the discomfort produced by the change in attitude (Jarcho & others, 2010; van Veen & others, 2009).

This response to cognitive dissonance does not seem to be unique to adults or even humans. Louisa Egan and her colleagues (2007) have seen dissonance among four-year-old children who are forced to choose between two stickers—a dolphin sticker and a dragonfly sticker, for example—that they previously liked equally. They also observed the same effect among capuchin monkeys who were forced to choose between two colors of M&Ms that they previously liked equally. After choosing one, the monkeys preferred the chosen M&M color from then on. In both cases, it was not just that they were familiar with the chosen sticker or chosen M&M. Even when the researchers made the choice, the children and chimps preferred the chosen stickers and M&M color over the other options.

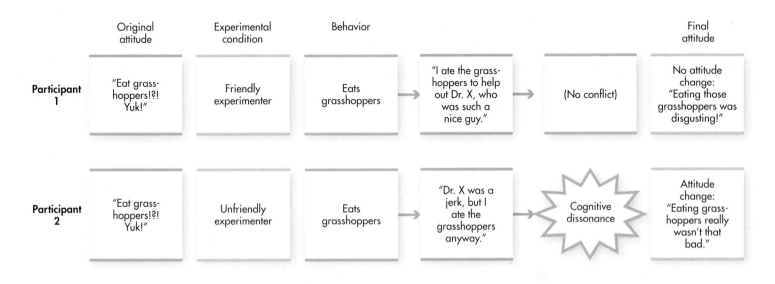

	Original attitude	Experimental condition	Behavior			Final attitude
Participant 1	"Eat grass-hoppers!?! Yuk!"	Friendly experimenter	Eats grasshoppers	"I ate the grass-hoppers to help out Dr. X, who was such a nice guy."	(No conflict)	No attitude change: "Eating those grasshoppers was disgusting!"
Participant 2	"Eat grass-hoppers!?! Yuk!"	Unfriendly experimenter	Eats grasshoppers	"Dr. X was a jerk, but I ate the grasshoppers anyway."	Cognitive dissonance	Attitude change: "Eating grass-hoppers really wasn't that bad."

FIGURE 11.2 How Cognitive Dissonance Leads to Attitude Change When your behavior conflicts with your attitudes, an uncomfortable state of tension is produced. However, if you can rationalize or explain your behavior, the conflict (and the tension) is eliminated or avoided. If you *can't* explain your behavior, you may change your attitude so that it is in harmony with your behavior.

Attitude change due to cognitive dissonance is quite common in everyday life. For example, consider the person who impulsively buys a new leather coat that she really can't afford. "It was too good a bargain to pass up," she rationalizes. Similarly, researchers have found that people who quit smoking offered fewer rationalizations for smoking. But if they started smoking again, they started rationalizing again. For example, some said, "You've got to die of something, so why not enjoy yourself and smoke" (Fotuhi & others, 2013).

Cognitive dissonance also influences how we frame decisions we have made when we have chosen between two alternatives, such as which college to attend. *After* you make a choice, you emphasize the negative features of the choice you've rejected, which is commonly called a "sour grapes" rationalization. You also emphasize the positive features of the choice to which you have committed yourself—a "sweet lemons" rationalization.

Understanding Prejudice

KEY THEME

Prejudice refers to a negative attitude toward people who belong to a specific social group, while stereotypes are clusters of characteristics that are attributed to people who belong to specific social categories.

KEY QUESTIONS

> What is the function of stereotypes, and how do they relate to prejudice?

> What are in-groups and out-groups, and how do they influence social judgments?

> What are implicit attitudes, and how are they measured?

In this section, you'll see how person perception, attribution, and attitudes come together in explaining **prejudice**—a negative attitude toward people who belong to a specific social group.

Prejudice is ultimately based on the exaggerated notion that members of other social groups are very different from members of our own social group. So as you read this discussion, it's important for you to keep two well-established points in mind. First, *people from different groups, such as from different racial and ethnic groups, are far more alike than they are different* (Mallett & Wilson, 2010; Wagner & others, 2011). And second, any differences that may exist *between* members of different groups are far smaller than differences *among* various members of the same group (Bodenhausen & Richeson, 2010).

It also is important to observe that conversations about prejudice often focus on race and ethnicity. But prejudice can occur with respect to many different kinds of social groups. There can be prejudice based on sexual orientation, gender identity, religion, or age. There can also be prejudice based on a person's identification with

cognitive dissonance An unpleasant state of psychological tension or arousal *(dissonance)* that occurs when two thoughts or perceptions *(cognitions)* are inconsistent; typically results from the awareness that attitudes and behavior are in conflict.

prejudice A negative attitude toward people who belong to a specific social group.

stereotype A cluster of characteristics that are associated with all members of a specific social group, often including qualities that are unrelated to the objective criteria that define the group.

multiple groups (Herek & McLemore, 2013; Kang & Bodenhausen, 2015; Newheiser & others, 2013; North & Fiske, 2013). For example, one study found that older people were perceived more negatively than middle-aged or younger people when they acted in unexpected ways, such as listening to Rihanna and other pop singers. Although younger people and middle-aged people could act in ways that were unexpected for their age, older people could not do so without consequences (North & Fiske, 2013). Older people did not have the same freedom to have the same range of interests that younger people had.

From Stereotypes to Prejudice
IN-GROUPS AND OUT-GROUPS

As we noted earlier, using social categories to organize information about other people seems to be a natural cognitive tendency. Many social categories can be defined by relatively objective characteristics, such as age, language, religion, and skin color. A specific kind of social category is a **stereotype**—a cluster of characteristics that are attributed to members of a specific social group or category. Stereotypes are based on the assumption that people have certain characteristics *because* of their membership in a particular group.

Stereotypes typically include qualities that are unrelated to the objective criteria that define a given category (Crawford & others, 2011). For example, we can objectively sort people into different categories by age. But our stereotypes for different age groups may include qualities that have little or nothing to do with "number of years since birth." Associations of "impulsive and irresponsible" with teenagers, or "boring and conservative" with middle-aged adults are examples of associating unrelated qualities with age groups—that is, stereotyping.

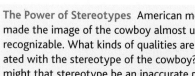

"I had to do it, Jeb. He was grilling zucchini."

Like our use of other social categories, our tendency to stereotype social groups seems to be a natural cognitive process. Stereotypes simplify social information so that we can sort out, process, and remember information about other people more easily (Bodenhausen & Richeson, 2010). But like other mental shortcuts we've discussed in this chapter, relying on stereotypes can cause problems. Attributing a stereotypic cause for an outcome or event can blind us to the true causes of events (Johnston & Miles, 2007). For example, a parent who assumes that a girl's poor computer skills are due to her gender rather than a lack of instruction might never encourage her to overcome her problem.

Research by psychologist Claude Steele (1997, 2003, 2011) has demonstrated another detrimental effect of negative stereotypes, which he calls *stereotype threat*. As we discussed in Chapter 7, simply being aware that your social group is associated with a particular stereotype can negatively impact your performance on tests or tasks that measure

The Power of Stereotypes American movies have made the image of the cowboy almost universally recognizable. What kinds of qualities are associated with the stereotype of the cowboy? How might that stereotype be an inaccurate portrayal of a person working on a cattle ranch today?

abilities that are thought to be associated with that stereotype (Schmader, 2010; Shapiro & others, 2013). For example, even mathematically gifted women tend to score lower on difficult math tests when told that the test tended to produce gender differences than when told that such tests did not produce gender differences (Forbes & Schmader, 2010; Rydell & others, 2010). (On pages 304–305 in Chapter 7, you'll find some suggestions for counteracting the effects of stereotype threat.)

Once they are formed, stereotypes are hard to shake. Sometimes stereotypes have a kernel of truth, making them easy to confirm, especially when you see only what you expect to see. Even so, there's a vast difference between a kernel and the cornfield. When stereotypic beliefs become expectations that are applied to *all* members of a given group, stereotypes can be both misleading and damaging (Dovidio & Gaertner, 2010).

Consider the stereotype that men are more assertive than women and that women are more nurturing than men. This stereotype does have evidence to support it, but only in terms of the *average* difference between men and women (Wood & Eagly, 2010). Thus, it would be unfair and often inaccurate to automatically apply this stereotype to every individual man and woman.

Equally important, when confronted by evidence that contradicts a stereotype, people tend to discount that information in a variety of ways (Phelan & Rudman, 2010; Rudman & Fairchild, 2004). For example, suppose you are firmly convinced that all "Zeegs" are dishonest, sly, and untrustworthy. One day you absent-mindedly leave your wallet on a store's checkout counter. As you walk into the parking lot, you hear a voice calling, "Hey, you forgot your wallet!" It's a Zeeg running after you to return your wallet.

Will this experience change your stereotype of Zeegs as dishonest, sly, and untrustworthy? Probably not. It's more likely that you'll conclude that this individual Zeeg is an *exception* to the stereotype. If you run into more than one honest Zeeg, you may create a mental subgroup for individuals who belong to the larger group but depart from the stereotype in some way (Queller & Mason, 2008; Sherman & others, 2005). By creating a subcategory of "honest, hardworking Zeegs," you can still maintain your more general stereotype of Zeegs as dishonest, sly, and untrustworthy.

Creating exceptions allows people to maintain stereotypes in the face of contradictory evidence. Typical of this exception-that-proves-the-rule approach is the person who says, "Hey, I'm not prejudiced! In fact, I've got a couple of good friends who are Zeegs."

Stereotypes are closely related to another tendency in person perception. People have a strong tendency to perceive others in terms of two very basic social categories: "us" and "them." More precisely, the **in-group** ("us") refers to the group or groups to which we belong, and the **out-group** ("them") refers to groups of which we are not a member. Preferences for the in-group start early (Rhodes & Chalik, 2013). One study conducted in the U.S. and in Taiwan found that as soon as the children in the racial majority were able to categorize people according to race, preferences for their own race emerged (Dunham & others, 2013). Among children

in-group A social group to which one belongs.

out-group A social group to which one does not belong.

Overcoming and Combating Prejudice
The self-described "son of a black man from Kenya and a white woman from Kansas," Barack Obama seemed an unlikely presidential candidate. Obama's ability to build a political coalition among people of different racial, ethnic, economic, and age groups led to his winning the White House—twice. In a speech on racial politics in the United States, Obama declared, "I believe deeply that we cannot solve the challenges of our time unless we solve them together—unless we perfect our union by understanding that we may have different stories, but we hold common hopes; that we may not look the same and we may not have come from the same place, but we all want to move in the same direction—towards a better future for our children and our grandchildren."

SAUL LOEB/AFP/Getty Images

Emotions and Prejudice Psychologists Lasana Harris and Susan Fiske (2006) examined the link between prejudice and negative emotions. They used fMRI to examine the brains of participants viewing images of people often stereotyped as incompetent, such as the elderly or disabled. Participants who viewed these images showed higher levels of activity in the prefrontal cortex, as indicated here by the orange spot circled in red. This is a pattern associated with the experience of pity.

as young as three and four years old, white Americans preferred white faces over black or Asian faces, and Asians in Taiwan preferred Asian faces over white faces.

In-groups and out-groups aren't necessarily limited to racial, ethnic, or religious boundaries. Virtually any characteristic can be used to make in-group and out-group distinctions: Mac versus PC users, Cubs versus White Sox fans, and even, it seems, graham cracker lovers versus green bean lovers. Both 9-month-old and 14-month-old infants liked a rabbit puppet better when it shared their preference for either graham crackers or green beans (Hamlin & others, 2013).

THE OUT-GROUP HOMOGENEITY EFFECT
THEY'RE ALL THE SAME TO ME

Two important patterns characterize our views of in-groups versus out-groups. First, when we describe the members of our *in-group,* we typically see them as being quite varied, despite having enough features in common to belong to the same group. In other words, we notice the diversity within our own group.

Second, we tend to see members of the *out-group* as much more similar to one another, even in areas that have little to do with the criteria for group membership. This tendency is called the **out-group homogeneity effect.** (The word *homogeneity* means "similarity" or "uniformity.")

For example, what qualities do you associate with the category of "engineering major"? If you're *not* an engineering major, you're likely to see engineering majors as a rather similar crew: male, logical, analytical, conservative, and so forth. However, if you *are* an engineering major, you're much more likely to see your in-group as quite *heterogeneous,* or varied (Dovidio & Gaertner, 2010). You might even come up with several subgroups, such as studious engineering majors versus party-animal engineering majors, and electrical engineering majors versus chemical engineering majors.

IN-GROUP BIAS
WE'RE TACTFUL—*THEY'RE* SNEAKY

In-group bias is our tendency to make favorable, positive attributions for behaviors by members of our in-group and unfavorable, negative attributions for behaviors by members of out-groups. We succeeded because we worked hard; they succeeded because they lucked out. We failed because of circumstances beyond our control; they failed because they're stupid and incompetent. We're thrifty; they're stingy. And so on.

In combination, stereotypes and in-group/out-group bias form the *cognitive* basis for prejudicial attitudes. But, as with many attitudes, prejudice also has a strong *emotional* component (Jackson, 2011). In the case of prejudice, the emotions are intensely negative—and evident in brain scans. In one study, participants viewing images of low-status people—such as homeless people or drug addicts—showed increased activity in the amygdala and insula, an indication of disgust (Harris & Fiske, 2006).

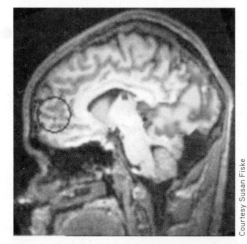

Courtesy Susan Fiske

The same researchers examined participants' responses to images of people often stereotyped as incompetent, such as people who are elderly or disabled. Participants viewing these images showed increased activity in the prefrontal cortex, activity that accompanies pity (see photo at left). *Behaviorally,* prejudice can be displayed in some form of *discrimination*—behaviors ranging from sneering at to physically attacking members of an out-group (Dovidio & Gaertner, 2010).

How can we account for the extreme emotions that often characterize prejudice against out-group members? One theory holds that prejudice and intergroup hostility increase when different groups are competing for scarce resources, whether jobs, acreage, oil, water, or political power (see Pratto & Glasford, 2008). Prejudice and intergroup hostility are also likely to increase during times of social change (Brewer, 1994; Staub, 1996). However, policies that promote diversity can *decrease* prejudice, even when groups are in conflict (Guimond & others, 2013).

But prejudice often exists in the absence of direct competition for resources, changing social conditions, or even contact with members of a particular out-group. What accounts for prejudice in such situations? One explanation is that people are often prejudiced against groups that are perceived as threatening important in-group norms and values (Esses & others, 2005; Louis & others, 2013). For example, a person might be extremely prejudiced against gays and lesbians because he feels that they threaten his in-group's cherished values, such as a strong commitment to traditional sex roles and family structure. This explanation is supported by several neuroscience studies that observed increased activity in the amygdala when participants viewed someone of a different race (Cikara & Van Bavel, 2014). The amygdala is associated with responses related to fear.

IMPLICIT ATTITUDES

Most people today agree that prejudice and racism are wrong. Blatant displays of racist, sexist, or homophobic speech or behavior are no longer socially acceptable. However, some psychologists now believe that overt forms of prejudice have been replaced by more subtle forms of prejudice (Hewstone & others, 2002; Sritharan & Gawronski, 2010).

Sometimes people who are not *consciously* prejudiced against particular groups nevertheless respond in prejudiced ways (Plant & Devine, 2009). For example, a man who consciously strives to be nonsexist may be reluctant to consult a female surgeon, or when he hears a news story that mentions a police officer, he may assume the officer is a man. Such biased responses can sometimes affect behavior in ways that we neither intend nor realize (Devine, 2001; Stanley & others, 2011). And many of these effects can be harmful. For black Americans, for example, implicit attitudes about race have been linked to difficulties getting hired or receiving lifesaving medical treatment, to higher rates of discipline in school, and to an increased likelihood of being the victim of police violence (Okonofua & Eberhardt, 2015; Richardson, 2015).

How can such responses be explained? In contrast to *explicit* attitudes, of which you are consciously aware, **implicit attitudes** are evaluations that are automatic, unintentional, and difficult to control (Bohner & Dickel, 2011). They are sometimes, but not always, unconscious (Sritharan & Gawronski, 2010).

Our implicit attitudes often differ from our explicit attitudes, especially when social and cultural norms prohibit negative attitudes regarding race, gender, or sexual orientation (Bodenhausen & Richeson, 2010). If people won't admit or aren't consciously aware of implicit attitudes, how can they be detected and measured? The most widely used test to measure implicit attitudes and preferences is the *Implicit Association Test,* or *IAT,* developed by psychologist Anthony Greenwald and his colleagues (1998).

The IAT is a computer-based test that measures the degree to which you associate particular groups of people with specific characteristics or attributes. The IAT is based on the assumption that people can sort images and words more easily when concepts seem to "match" or go together. So, for example, the Age IAT measures the speed with which you classify pairings of "good" or "bad" words with photographs of people of different ages. Similarly, the Race–Weapons IAT measures the degree to which participants associate photographs of black or white faces with weapons (like a gun or a sword) or harmless objects (a camera or water bottle).

Other IATs measure implicit attitudes toward sexual orientation, weight, disability, and racial and ethnic groups. IATs have also been developed to measure the strength of stereotyped associations, such as the strength of associations between gender and career or family. You can try the IAT yourself online at: https://implicit.harvard.edu.

out-group homogeneity effect The tendency to see members of out-groups as very similar to one another.

in-group bias The tendency to judge the behavior of in-group members favorably and out-group members unfavorably.

implicit attitudes Preferences and biases toward particular groups that are automatic, spontaneous, unintentional, and often unconscious; measured with the *Implicit Associations Test* (IAT).

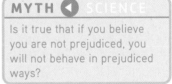

MYTH ◄ SCIENCE

Is it true that if you believe you are not prejudiced, you will not behave in prejudiced ways?

LaunchPad

stevecoleimages/Getty Images

What factors affect whether you see this behavior as violent? Try **Lab: Stereotyping.**

The IAT has been completed by over 10 million people around the world (Banaji & Heiphetz, 2010). The results suggest that implicit preferences are quite pervasive. As Brian Nosek and his colleagues (2007) concluded, "With few exceptions, across domains and demographic categories, participants showed implicit and explicit social preferences and stereotypes. Men and women, young and old, conservative and liberal, Black, White, Asian, and Hispanic—all groups have social preferences for some groups over others, and hold stereotypic associations or beliefs. Social preferences are not possessed exclusively by a privileged few—they are a general characteristic of human social cognition."

Although in wide use, the IAT is controversial (see Amodio & Mendoza, 2010; Azar, 2008). For example, some researchers argue that the ease with which certain associations are made may reflect familiarity with cultural stereotypes, rather than personal bias or prejudice (Blanton & others, 2009). Other researchers have demonstrated that brief training can reduce prejudice as measured by the IAT (Calanchini & others, 2013). And, the degree to which *implicit* attitudes affect *actual* behavior is still an open question, although some studies suggest that they do (see Greenwald & others, 2009; Stanley & others, 2011).

Despite controversies about the IAT, there is evidence that implicit attitudes can be changed. For example, psychologists agree that becoming *aware* of our biased attitudes, whether implicit or explicit, is an important step toward overcoming them (Devine & others, 2012; Paluck & Green, 2009). Also, mindfulness meditation, introduced in the chapter on consciousness, has been shown to reduce implicit bias based on both age and race (Lueke & Gibson, 2015). We turn to the topic of overcoming prejudice in the next section.

Overcoming Prejudice

KEY THEME

Prejudice can be overcome when people cooperate to achieve a common goal.

KEY QUESTIONS

> How has this finding been applied in the educational system?

> What other conditions are essential to reducing tension between groups?

How can prejudice be combated? A classic series of studies headed by psychologist **Muzafer Sherif** helped clarify the conditions that produce intergroup conflict *and* harmony. Sherif and his colleagues (1961) studied a group of 11-year-old boys in an unlikely setting for a scientific experiment: a summer camp located at Robbers Cave State Park in Oklahoma.

THE ROBBERS CAVE EXPERIMENT

Pretending to be camp counselors and staff, the researchers observed the boys' behavior under carefully orchestrated conditions. The boys were randomly assigned to two groups. The groups arrived at camp in separate buses and were headquartered in different areas of the camp. One group of boys dubbed themselves the Eagles, the other the Rattlers. After a week of separation, the researchers arranged for the groups to meet in a series of competitive games. A fierce rivalry quickly developed, demonstrating the ease with which mutually hostile groups could be created.

The rivalry became increasingly bitter. The Eagles burned the Rattlers' flag. In response, the Rattlers trashed the Eagles' cabin. Somewhat alarmed, the researchers tried to diminish the hostility by bringing the two groups together under peaceful circumstances and on an equal basis—having them go to the movies together, and so forth. But contact alone did not mitigate the hostility. For example, when the Rattlers and Eagles ate together in the same dining hall, a massive food fight erupted!

How could harmony between the groups be established? Sherif and his fellow researchers created a series of situations in which the two groups would need to *cooperate*

Creating Conflict Between Groups Psychologist Muzafer Sherif and his colleagues demonstrated how easily hostility and distrust could be created between two groups. Competitive situations, like this tug-of-war, increased tension between the Rattlers and the Eagles.

From Sherif, Muzafer; Harvey, O. J.; White, B. Jack; Hood, William R.; & Sherif, Carolyn W. (1961/1988). The Robbers Cave Experiment: Intergroup Conflict and Cooperation. Middletown, CT: Wesleyan University Press.

to achieve a common goal. For example, the researchers secretly sabotaged the water supply. Working together, the Eagles and the Rattlers managed to fix it. After a series of such joint efforts, the rivalry diminished and the groups became good friends (Sherif, 1956; Sherif & others, 1961).

Sherif successfully demonstrated how hostility between groups could be created and, more important, how that hostility could be overcome. However, other researchers questioned whether these results would apply to other intergroup situations. After all, these boys were very homogeneous: white, middle class, Protestant, and carefully selected for being healthy and well-adjusted (Fiske & Ruscher, 1993; Sherif, 1966). In other words, there were no *intrinsic* differences between the Rattlers and the Eagles; there was only the artificial distinction created by the researchers.

THE JIGSAW CLASSROOM
PROMOTING COOPERATION

Social psychologist Elliot Aronson (1990, 1992) tried adapting the results of the Robbers Cave experiments to a very different group situation—a newly integrated elementary school. Realizing that mere contact between black and white children was not dissipating tension and prejudice, Aronson reasoned that perhaps the competitive schoolroom atmosphere was partly at fault.

Aronson and his colleagues tried a teaching technique that stressed cooperative, rather than competitive, learning situations (see Aronson, 1990; Aronson & Bridgeman, 1979). Dubbed the *jigsaw classroom technique,* this approach brought together students in small, ethnically diverse groups to work on a mutual project. Like the pieces of a jigsaw puzzle, each student became an expert on one aspect of the overall project and had to teach it to the other members of the group. Thus, interdependence and cooperation replaced competition.

The results? Children in the jigsaw classrooms had higher self-esteem and a greater liking for children in other ethnic groups than did children in traditional classrooms. They also demonstrated a lessening of negative stereotypes and prejudice, and a reduction in intergroup hostility (see Aronson, 1987, 1995; Aronson & Bridgeman, 1979). As Aronson (1999) points out, "Cooperation changes our tendency to categorize the out-group from 'those people' to 'us people'."

Lessons from Robbers Cave and the jigsaw classroom have been used to reduce prejudice and conflict among ethnic and religious groups around the world (Aboud & others, 2012). For example, a number of programs have been developed to promote cooperation between Israelis and Palestinians through joint projects in which members of both groups work together to stage a play, conduct scientific studies, or play on a soccer team (Maoz, 2012).

❯ Test your understanding of **The Psychology of Attitudes and Prejudice** with **LEARNING***Curve.*

From Sherif, Muzafer; Harvey, O. J.; White, B. Jack; Hood, William R.; & Sherif, Carolyn W. (1961/1988). *The Robbers Cave Experiment: Intergroup Conflict and Cooperation.* Middletown, CT: Wesleyan University Press.

Overcoming Group Conflict To decrease hostility between the Rattlers and the Eagles at Robbers Cave, the researchers created situations that required the joint efforts of both groups to achieve a common goal, such as fixing the water supply. These cooperative tasks helped the boys recognize their common interests and become friends.

Conformity
FOLLOWING THE CROWD

KEY THEME

Social influence involves the study of how behavior is influenced by other people and by the social environment.

KEY QUESTIONS

❯ What factors influence the degree to which people will conform?

❯ Why do people conform?

❯ How does culture affect conformity?

As we noted earlier, *social influence* is the psychological study of how our behavior is influenced by the social environment and other people. For example, if you

Life in society requires consensus as an indispensable condition. But consensus, to be productive, requires that each individual contribute independently out of his experience and insight. When consensus comes under the dominance of conformity, the social process is polluted and the individual at the same time surrenders the powers on which his functioning as a feeling and thinking being depends.

—*Solomon Asch (1955)*

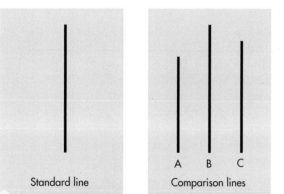

Standard line   Comparison lines

FIGURE 11.3 The Line Judgment Task Used in the Asch Conformity Studies In Asch's classic studies on conformity, participants were asked to pick the comparison line that matched the standard line.

Source: Asch (1957).

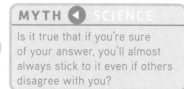

MYTH ◀ **SCIENCE**

Is it true that if you're sure of your answer, you'll almost always stick to it even if others disagree with you?

typically contribute to class discussions, you've probably felt the power of social influence in classes where nobody else said a word (Stowell & others, 2010). No doubt you found yourself feeling at least slightly uncomfortable every time you ventured a comment.

If you changed your behavior to mesh with that of your classmates, you demonstrated conformity. **Conformity** occurs when you adjust your opinions, judgment, or behavior so that it matches that of other people, or the norms of a social group or situation (Hogg, 2010).

There's no question that all of us conform to group or situational norms to some degree. The more critical issue is *how far* we'll go to adjust our perceptions and opinions so that they're in sync with the majority opinion—an issue that intrigued social psychologist **Solomon Asch.** Asch (1951) posed a straightforward question: Would people still conform to the group if the group opinion was clearly wrong?

To study this question experimentally, Asch (1955) chose a simple, objective task with an obvious answer (Figure 11.3). A group of people sat at a table and looked at a series of cards. On one side of each card was a standard line. On the other side were three comparison lines. All each person had to do was publicly indicate which comparison line was the same length as the standard line.

Asch's experiment had a hidden catch. All the people sitting around the table were actually in cahoots with the experimenter, except for one—the real participant. Had you been the real participant in Asch's (1956) experiment, here's what you would have experienced. The first card is shown, and the five people ahead of you respond, one at a time, with the obvious answer: "Line B." Now it's your turn, and you respond the same. The second card is put up. Again, the answer is obvious and the group is unanimous. So far, so good.

Then the third card is shown, and the correct answer is just as obvious: Line C. But the first person confidently says, "Line A." And so does everyone else, one by one. Now it's your turn. To you it's clear that the correct answer is Line C. But the five people ahead of you have already publicly chosen Line A. How do you respond? You hesitate. Do you go with the flow or with what you know?

The real participant was faced with the uncomfortable situation of disagreeing with a unanimous majority on 12 of 18 trials in Asch's experiment. Notice, there was no direct pressure to conform—just the implicit, unspoken pressure of answering differently from the rest of the group.

Over 100 participants experienced Asch's experimental dilemma. Not surprisingly, participants differed in their degree of conformity. Nonetheless, the majority of Asch's participants (76 percent) conformed with the group judgment on at least one of the critical trials. When the data for all participants were combined, the participants followed the majority and gave the wrong answer on *37 percent* of the critical trials (Asch, 1955, 1957). In comparison, a control group of participants who responded alone instead of in a group accurately chose the matching line 99 percent of the time.

Although the majority opinion clearly exerted a strong influence, it's also important to stress the flip side of Asch's results. On almost two-thirds of the trials in which the majority named the wrong line, the participants stuck to their guns and gave the correct answer, despite being in the minority (see Friend & others, 1990; Hodges & Geyer, 2006). And 95 percent defied the majority and gave the correct response at least once. In fact, some researchers argue that these results show more independence than conformity (Griggs, 2015).

Even those who conform may not have experienced a lasting change in their perception or opinion. One study observed conformity with respect to people's opinions about others' attractiveness (Huang & others, 2014). In follow-up studies, however, any change in opinion due to conformity was present after three days, but not after seven days.

Factors Influencing Conformity

The basic model of Asch's classic experiment has been used in hundreds of studies exploring the dynamics of conformity (Bond, 2005). It's even been examined in online contexts, where people are making decisions based on the responses of anonymous, unseen others (Rosander & Eriksson, 2012; Zhu & others, 2012). Why do we sometimes find ourselves conforming to the larger group? There are two basic reasons.

First is our desire to be liked and accepted by the group, which is referred to as **normative social influence.** Interestingly, the power of social influence may apply uniquely to humans. One study found that two-year-old humans, but not chimpanzees or orangutans, conformed to the behavior of their peers (Haun & others, 2014). Second is our desire to be right. When we're uncertain or doubt our own judgment, we may look to the group as a source of accurate information, which is called **informational social influence** (Turner, 2010).

Asch and other researchers identified several conditions that promote conformity, which are summarized in Table 11.2. But Asch also discovered that conformity *decreased* under certain circumstances. For example, having an ally seemed to counteract the social influence of the majority. Participants were more likely to go against the majority view if just one other participant did so, even if the other person's dissenting opinion is wrong (Allen & Levine, 1969; Packer, 2008b). Conformity also lessens even if the other dissenter's competence is questionable, as in the case of a dissenter who wore thick glasses and complained that he could not see the lines very well (Allen & Levine, 1971; Turner, 2010).

REUTERS/Lucy Nicholson

Adolescents and Conformity
Conformity to group norms peaks in early adolescence, as illustrated by the similarities in appearance among this group of friends. Think back to your own adolescence. Do you remember how important it was to you to fit in with other adolescents, especially those in your peer group?

TABLE 11.2

Factors That Promote Conformity

You're more likely to conform to group norms when:

- You are facing a unanimous group of at least four or five people
- You must give your response in front of the group
- You have not already expressed commitment to a different idea or opinion
- You find the task to be ambiguous or difficult
- You doubt your abilities or knowledge in the situation
- You are strongly attracted to a group and want to be a member of it

SOURCES: Asch (1955); Campbell & Fairey (1989); Deutsch & Gerard (1955); Gerard & others (1968); Tanford & Penrod (1984).

Culture and Conformity

Do patterns of conformity differ in other cultures? The answer seems to be yes. A survey of more than 80,000 people from 62 countries found that the value placed on conformity varied widely across cultures (Fischer & Schwartz, 2011). How might conformity vary across cultures? British psychologists Rod Bond and Peter Smith (1996) found in a wide-ranging meta-analysis that conformity is generally higher in collectivistic cultures than in individualistic cultures. Because individualistic cultures tend to emphasize independence, self-expression, and standing out from the crowd, the whole notion of conformity tends to carry a negative connotation.

In collectivistic cultures, however, publicly conforming while privately disagreeing tends to be regarded as socially appropriate tact or sensitivity. Publicly challenging the judgments of others, particularly the judgment of members of one's in-group, would be considered rude, tactless, and insensitive to the feelings of others.

conformity Adjusting your opinions, judgments, or behaviors so that they match the opinions, judgments, or behaviors of other people, or the norms of a social group or situation.

normative social influence Behavior that is motivated by the desire to gain social acceptance and approval.

informational social influence Behavior that is motivated by the desire to be correct.

Social Psychologist Stanley Milgram (1933–1984) Milgram is best known for his obedience studies, but his creative research skills went far beyond the topic of obedience. To study the power of social norms, for example, Milgram sent his students out into New York City to intrude into waiting lines or ask subway passengers to give up their seats. Milgram often capitalized on the "texture of everyday life" to "examine the way in which the social world impinges on individual action and experience" (Milgram, 1974a).

Photo by Eric Kroll, Courtesy of Alexandra Milgram

The individual who is commanded by a legitimate authority ordinarily obeys. Obedience comes easily and often. It is a ubiquitous and indispensable feature of social life.

—Stanley Milgram (1963)

Obedience
JUST FOLLOWING ORDERS

KEY THEME

Stanley Milgram conducted a series of controversial studies on obedience, which is behavior performed in direct response to the orders of an authority.

KEY QUESTIONS

> What were the results of Milgram's original obedience experiments?
> What experimental factors were shown to increase the level of obedience?
> What experimental factors were shown to decrease the level of obedience?

Stanley Milgram was one of the most creative and influential researchers that social psychology has known (Blass, 2004, 2009; A. G. Miller, 2009). He is best known for his experimental investigations of obedience. **Obedience** is the performance of a behavior in response to a direct command. Typically, an authority figure or a person of higher status, such as a teacher or supervisor, gives the command.

Milgram was intrigued by Asch's discovery of how easily people could be swayed by group pressure. But Milgram wanted to investigate behavior that had greater personal significance than simply judging line lengths on a card (Milgram, 1963). Thus, Milgram posed what he saw as the most critical question: Could a person be pressured by others into committing an immoral act, some action that violated his or her own conscience, such as hurting a stranger? In his efforts to answer that question, Milgram embarked on one of the most systematic and controversial investigations in the history of psychology: to determine how and why people obey the destructive dictates of an authority figure (Blass, 2009; Russell, 2011).

Milgram's Original Obedience Experiment

Milgram was only 28 years old and a new faculty member at Yale University when he conducted his first obedience experiments. He recruited participants through direct-mail solicitations and ads in the local paper. Milgram's participants represented a wide range of occupational and educational backgrounds. Postal workers, high school teachers, white-collar workers, engineers, and laborers participated in the study.

Outwardly, it appeared that two participants showed up at the same time at Yale University to take part in the psychology experiment, but the second participant was actually an accomplice working with Milgram. The role of the experimenter, complete with white lab coat, was played by a high school biology teacher. When both participants arrived, the experimenter greeted them and gave them a plausible explanation of the study's purpose: to examine the effects of punishment on learning.

Both participants drew slips of paper to determine who would be the "teacher" and who the "learner." However, the drawing was rigged so that the real participant was always the teacher and the accomplice was always the learner. The learner was actually

The "Electric Chair" With the help of the real participant, who had been assigned to the role of "teacher," the experimenter straps the "learner" into the electric chair. Unbeknownst to the real participant, the learner was actually a 47-year-old accountant who had been carefully rehearsed for his part in the experimental deception. The experimenter told both participants, "Although the shocks can be extremely painful, they cause no permanent tissue damage."

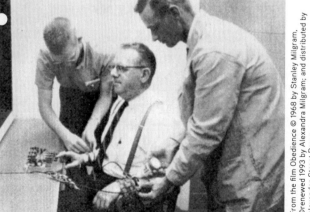

From the film Obedience © 1968 by Stanley Milgram, ©renewed 1993 by Alexandra Milgram; and distributed by Alexander Street Press.

a mild-mannered, 47-year-old accountant who had been carefully rehearsed for his part in the drama. Assigned to the role of the teacher, the real participant would be responsible for "punishing" the learner's mistakes by administering electric shocks.

Immediately after the drawing, the teacher and learner were taken to another room, where the learner was strapped into an "electric chair." The teacher was then taken to a different room, from which he could hear but not see the learner. Speaking into a microphone, the teacher tested the learner on a simple word-pair memory task. In the other room, the learner pressed one of four switches to indicate with which alternative the word had previously been paired. The learner's response was registered in an answer box positioned on top of the "shock generator" in front of the teacher. Each time the learner answered incorrectly, the teacher was to deliver an electric shock.

Just in case there was any lingering doubt in the teacher's mind about the legitimacy of the shock generator, the *teacher* was given a sample jolt using the switch marked 45 volts. In fact, this sample shock was the only real shock given during the course of the staged experiment.

The first time the learner answered incorrectly, the teacher was to deliver an electric shock at the 15-volt level. With each subsequent error, the teacher was told to progress to the next level on the shock generator. The teacher was also told to announce the voltage level to the learner before delivering the shock.

At predetermined voltage levels, the learner vocalized first his discomfort, then his pain, and, finally, agonized screams. Some of the learner's vocalizations at the different voltage levels are shown in Table 11.3. After 330 volts, the learner's script called for him to fall silent. If the teacher protested that he wished to stop or that he was worried about the learner's safety, the experimenter would say, "The experiment requires that you continue" or "You have no other choice, you *must* continue."

According to the script, the experiment would be halted when the teacher refused to obey the experimenter's orders to continue. Alternatively, if the teacher obeyed the experimenter, the experiment would be halted once the teacher had progressed all the way to the maximum shock level of 450 volts.

Courtesy of Alexandra Milgram

Milgram's "Shock Generator" A young Stanley Milgram sits next to his "shock generator." Milgram went to great lengths to make the shock generator look as authentic as possible. The front panel of the bogus shock generator had been engraved by professional industrial engravers. Whenever the teacher pressed a shock switch, the red light above the switch went on, a buzzing and clicking sound was heard, and the needle on the voltage meter swung to the right.

TABLE 11.3

The Learner's Schedule of Protests in Milgram's Obedience Experiment

120 volts → Ugh! Hey, *this* really hurts.

150 volts → Ugh!!! Experimenter! That's all. Get me out of here. I told you I had heart trouble. My heart's starting to bother me now. Get me out of here, please. My heart's starting to bother me. I refuse to go on. Let me out.

210 volts → Ugh!! Experimenter! Get me out of here. I've had enough. I *won't* be in the experiment any more.

270 volts → (*Agonized scream.*) Let me out of here. Let me out of here. Let me out of here. Let me out. Do you hear? Let me out of here.

300 volts → (*Agonized scream.*) I absolutely refuse to answer any more. Get me out of here. You can't hold me here. Get me out. Get me out of here.

315 volts → (*Intensely agonized scream.*) I told you I refuse to answer. I'm no longer part of this experiment.

330 volts → (*Intense and prolonged agonized scream.*) Let me out of here. Let me out of here. My heart's bothering me. Let me out, I tell you. (*Hysterically.*) Let me out of here. Let me out of here. You have no right to hold me here. Let me out! Let me out! Let me out! Let me out of here! Let me out! Let me out!

Source: Milgram (1974a).

This table shows examples of the learner's protests at different voltage levels. If the teacher administered shocks beyond the 330-volt level, the learner's agonized screams were replaced with an ominous silence.

obedience The performance of a behavior in response to a direct command.

Either way, after the experiment, the teacher was interviewed and it was explained that the learner had not actually received dangerous electric shocks. To underscore this point, a "friendly reconciliation" was arranged between the teacher and the learner, and the true purpose of the study was explained to the participant.

The Results of Milgram's Original Experiment

Can you predict how Milgram's participants behaved? Of the 40 participants, how many obeyed the experimenter and went to the full 450-volt level? On a more personal level, how do you think *you* would have behaved had you been one of Milgram's participants?

Milgram himself asked psychiatrists, college students, and middle-class adults to predict how participants would behave (see Milgram, 1974a). All three groups predicted that *all* of Milgram's participants would refuse to obey at some point. *None* of those surveyed thought that any of Milgram's participants would go to the full 450 volts.

As it turned out, they were all wrong. *Two-thirds of Milgram's participants—26 of the 40—were fully compliant and went to the full 450-volt level.* And of those who defied the experimenter, *not one stopped before the 300-volt level.* Table 11.4 on the next page shows the results of Milgram's original obedience study.

Surprised? Milgram himself was stunned by the results, never expecting that the majority of subjects would administer the maximum voltage. Were his results a fluke? Did Milgram inadvertently assemble a sadistic group of New Haven residents who were all too willing to inflict extremely painful, even life-threatening, shocks on a complete stranger?

The answer to both these questions is no. Milgram's obedience study has been repeated many times in the United States and other countries (see Blass, 2000, 2012). And, in fact, Milgram (1974a) replicated his own study on numerous occasions, using variations of his basic experimental procedure.

In one replication, for instance, Milgram's participants were 40 women. The results were identical. Confirming Milgram's results since then, eight other studies also found no sex differences in obedience to an authority figure (see Blass, 2000, 2004; Burger, 2009).

Perhaps Milgram's participants saw through his elaborate experimental hoax, as some critics have suggested (Orne & Holland, 1968). Was it possible that the participants did not believe that they were really harming the learner? Again, the answer seems to be no. Most of Milgram's participants seemed totally convinced that the situation was authentic. And they did not behave in a cold-blooded, unfeeling way. Far from it. As the experiment progressed, many participants showed signs of extreme tension and conflict.

In describing the reaction of one participant, Milgram (1963) wrote, "I observed a mature and initially poised businessman enter the laboratory smiling and confident. Within 20 minutes he was reduced to a twitching, stuttering wreck, who was rapidly approaching a point of nervous collapse." Extreme reactions like this one have led people to question the ethics of Milgram's experiment (Perry, 2013).

Making Sense of Milgram's Findings
MULTIPLE INFLUENCES

Milgram, along with other researchers, identified several aspects of the experimental situation that had a strong impact on the participants (see Blass, 1992, 2000; Milgram, 1965). Overall, he demonstrated that the rate of obedience rose or fell depending upon the situational variables the participants experienced (Zimbardo, 2007). Here are some of the forces that influenced participants to continue obeying the experimenter's orders:

- **A previously well-established mental framework to obey.** Having volunteered to participate in a psychology experiment, Milgram's participants arrived

MYTH ◀ SCIENCE

Is it true that most people will not harm another person if ordered to do so?

The Aftereffects of Milgram's Study: Were Subjects Harmed? Milgram's findings were disturbing. But some psychologists found his methods equally upsetting. To psychologist Diana Baumrind (1964), it was unethical for Milgram to subject his participants to that level of emotional stress, humiliation, and loss of dignity. But Milgram (1964) countered that he had not set out to create stress in his participants. It was his unanticipated *results,* not his *methods,* that disturbed people. Who would object to his experiment, he asked, "if everyone had broken off at 'slight shock' or at the first sign of the learner's discomfort?" Concerns were also expressed that participants would experience serious aftereffects from the experiment. However, in a follow-up questionnaire, 84 percent of participants in Milgram's experiment indicated that they were "glad to have taken part in the experiment," and only about 1 percent regretted participating (Milgram, 1974b).

From the film Obedience © 1968 by Stanley Milgram; © renewed 1993 by Alexandra Milgram; and distributed by Alexander Street Press.

at the lab with the mental expectation that they would obediently follow the directions of the person in charge—the experimenter.

- **The situation, or context, in which the obedience occurred.** The participants were familiar with the basic nature of scientific investigation, believed that scientific research was worthwhile, and were told that the goal of the experiment was to "advance the scientific understanding of learning and memory" (Milgram, 1974a). All these factors predisposed the subjects to trust and respect the experimenter's authority (Darley, 1992).

- **The gradual, repetitive escalation of the task.** At the beginning of the experiment, the participant administered a very low level of shock—15 volts. Participants could easily justify using such low levels of electric shock in the service of science. The shocks, like the learner's protests, escalated only gradually.

- **The experimenter's behavior and reassurances.** Many participants asked the experimenter who was responsible for what might happen to the learner. In every case, the teacher was reassured that the *experimenter* was responsible for the learner's well-being. Thus, the participants could believe that they were not responsible for the consequences of their actions.

- **The physical and psychological separation from the learner.** Several "buffers" distanced the participant from the pain that he was inflicting on the learner. First, the learner was in a separate room and not visible. Only his voice could be heard. Second, punishment was depersonalized: The participant simply pushed a switch on the shock generator. Finally, the learner never appealed directly to the teacher to stop shocking him. The learner's pleas were always directed toward the *experimenter,* as in "Experimenter! Get me out of here!" Undoubtedly, this contributed to the participant's sense that the experimenter, rather than the participant, was ultimately in control of the situation, including the teacher's behavior.

- **Confidence that the learner was actually receiving shocks.** There is evidence suggesting that at least some of Milgram's participants suspected that the learner was not receiving shocks. Milgram (1965) reported that only 56.1% of participants "fully believed the learner was getting painful shocks." Others had doubts to varying degrees, and as doubts increased, the likelihood of obeying also increased. Conversely, those most confident that the learner was actually receiving shocks were *less* likely to obey. Psychologist Gina Perry (2013) spent several years immersing herself in the archives at Yale and interviewing many researchers and participants associated with Milgram's studies. She discovered unpublished data, compiled by Milgram's research assistant, Taketo Murata. Across the 23 variations of Milgram's experiments, Murata found that participants were more likely to disobey if they believed the learner was actually receiving shocks.

Conditions That Undermine Obedience
VARIATIONS ON A THEME

In a lengthy series of experiments, Milgram systematically varied the basic obedience paradigm. To give you some sense of the enormity of Milgram's undertaking, approximately *1,000* participants, each tested individually, experienced some variation of Milgram's obedience experiment.

TABLE 11.4

The Results of Milgram's Original Study

Shock Level	Switch Labels and Voltage Levels	Number of Subjects Who Refused to Administer a Higher Voltage Level
Slight Shock		
1	15	
2	30	
3	45	
4	60	
Moderate Shock		
5	75	
6	90	
7	105	
8	120	
9	135	
10	150	
11	165	
12	180	
Very Strong Shock		
13	195	
14	210	
15	225	
16	240	
Intense Shock		
17	255	
18	270	
19	285	
20	300	
Extreme Intensity Shock		
21	315	5
22	330	
23	345	4
24	360	2
Danger: Severe Shock		1
25	375	1
26	390	
27	405	1
28	420	
XXX		
29	435	
30	450	26

SOURCE: Data from Milgram (1974a).

Contrary to what psychiatrists, college students, and middle-class adults predicted, the majority of Milgram's subjects did not refuse to obey by the 150-volt level of shock. As this table shows, 14 of Milgram's 40 participants (35 percent) refused to continue at some point after administering 300 volts to the learner. However, 26 of the 40 participants (65 percent) remained obedient to the very end, administering the full 450 volts to the learner.

By varying his experiments, Milgram identified several conditions that decreased the likelihood of destructive obedience, which are summarized in Figure 11.4. For example, willingness to obey diminished sharply when the buffers that separated the teacher from the learner were lessened or removed, such as when both of them were in the same room.

If Milgram's findings seem to cast an unfavorable light on human nature, there are two reasons to take heart. First, when teachers were allowed to act as their own authority and freely choose the shock level, 95 percent of them did not venture beyond 150 volts—the first point at which the learner protested. Clearly, Milgram's participants were not responding to their own aggressive or sadistic impulses, but rather to orders from an authority figure (see Reeder & others, 2008).

Second, Milgram found that people were more likely to muster up the courage to defy an authority when they saw others do so. When Milgram's participants observed what they thought were two other participants disobeying the experimenter, the real participants followed their lead 90 percent of the time and refused to continue. Like the participants in Asch's experiment, Milgram's participants were more likely to stand by their convictions when they were not alone in expressing them. Despite these encouraging notes, the overall results of Milgram's obedience research painted a bleak picture of human nature.

Many people wonder whether Milgram would get the same results if his experiments were repeated today. Are people still as likely to obey an authority figure? There have been several replications or partial replications in recent years, including one by psychologist Jerry Burger and several by entertainment or news media including on the Discovery Channel show *Curiosity,* a BBC documentary, and *DatelineNBC* (BBC News, 2008; Burger, 2009; Lowry, 2011; Perry, 2013).

In one example, using methods similar to Milgram's, French researchers found high levels of obedience in a game-show setting in a TV studio where participants obeyed a television host (Beauvois & others, 2012). In the show, called *Game of Death,*

FIGURE 11.4 Factors That Decrease Destructive Obedience By systematically varying his basic experimental design, Milgram identified several factors that diminish the likelihood of destructive obedience. In this graph, you can see the percentage of participants who administered the maximum shock in different experimental variations. For example, when Milgram's subjects observed what they thought were two other participants disobeying the experimenter, the real subjects followed their lead 90 percent of the time and refused to continue.

Source: Data from Milgram (1974a).

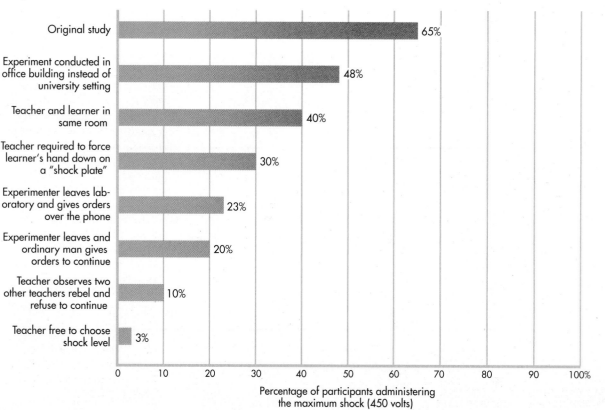

Experimental Variations

Percentage of participants administering the maximum shock (450 volts)

the researchers used all the trappings of a television production to convince participants that the situation was real—a glamorous and well-known host, professional cameras, spotlights, a comedian to warm up the audience, and a live audience naïve to the actual goal of the situation.

The researchers recruited 76 participants from Paris, having excluded anyone who was aware of Milgram's research. Participants were asked to shock another "contestant" every time he answered a question incorrectly. (As in Milgram's study, the "contestant" was an actor who was not actually receiving shocks.) The game show host used prompts similar to those used by Milgram's experimenter, and she had an added encouragement available to her—having the audience intervene. The researchers explained that "in power-based and situation-based terms, the host-questioner rapport in the present study was very close to the researcher-professor situation in Milgram's study" (Beauvois & others, 2012).

So, what do you think happened? Eighty-one percent of participants obeyed, a figure higher than, although not statistically different from, Milgram's findings. Importantly, unlike in Milgram's era, there was an immediate international outcry about the ethics of putting unwitting participants in such a situation.

More than 40 years after the publication of Milgram's research, the moral issues that his findings highlighted are still with us. We discuss a contemporary instance of destructive obedience in the Critical Thinking box on the next page, "Abuse at Abu Ghraib: Why Do Ordinary People Commit Evil Acts?"

Asch, Milgram, and the Real World
IMPLICATIONS OF THE CLASSIC SOCIAL INFLUENCE STUDIES

The scientific study of conformity and obedience has produced some important insights. The first is the degree to which our behavior is influenced by situational factors (see Benjamin & Simpson, 2009; Zimbardo, 2007). Being at odds with the majority or with authority figures is very uncomfortable for most people—enough so that our judgment and perceptions can be distorted and we may act in ways that violate our conscience.

More important, perhaps, is the insight that each of us *does* have the capacity to resist group or authority pressure (Bocchiaro & Zimbardo, 2010). Because the

AP Photo/Christophe Ena

The Game of Death Television producer Christophe Nick was one of the creators of *Game of Death*, a 2010 recreation of Stanley Milgram's experiment. Shown on French television, the show demonstrated that high levels of obedience still can occur. Eighty-one percent of the "contestants" on *Game of Death* obeyed the host's order to shock another contestant who had answered a question incorrectly. In an interview, Nick explained, "Most of us think we have free thinking and so we are responsible for our acts. This experience shows that in certain circumstances, a power—the TV in this case—is able to make you do something you don't want to do." Contestant Jerome Pasanau agreed with Nick's assertion. He said, "I wanted to stop the whole time, but I just couldn't. I didn't have the will to do it. And that goes against my nature. I haven't really figured out why I did it" (Beardsley, 2010).

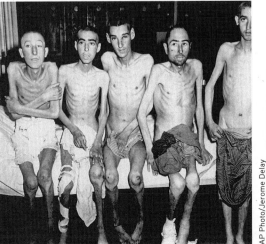

United States Holocaust Memorial Museum, courtesy of Tibor Vince

AP Photo/Jerome Delay

Destructive Obedience and Prejudice Blind obedience to authority combined with ethnic prejudice in Germany during World War II led to the slaughter of millions of Jews in concentration camps. When questioned after the war, Nazi officials and soldiers claimed that they were "just following orders." In the almost 70 years since the end of World War II, genocide, ethnic cleansing, and politically inspired mass killings have occurred in Cambodia, Bosnia and Herzegovina, Rwanda, and the Sudanese Darfur. As of 2015, in the Central African Republic, up to 6,000 people have been killed and more than 500,000 people were currently displaced from their homes (Nichols, 2015; UNHCR, 2015).

central findings of these studies are so dramatic, it's easy to overlook the fact that some participants refused to conform or obey despite considerable social and situational pressure (Packer, 2008a). Consider the response of a participant in one of Milgram's later studies (Milgram, 1974a). A 32-year-old industrial engineer named Jan Rensaleer protested when he was commanded to continue at the 255-volt level:

CRITICAL THINKING

Abuse at Abu Ghraib: Why Do Ordinary People Commit Evil Acts?

When the first photos appeared from Abu Ghraib prison near Baghdad, Iraq, people around the world were shocked. The photos graphically depicted Iraqi prisoners being humiliated, abused, and beaten by U.S. military personnel. In one photo, an Iraqi prisoner stood naked with feces smeared on his face and body. Smiling American soldiers, both male and female, posed alongside the corpse of a beaten Iraqi prisoner, giving the thumbs-up sign for the camera.

In the international uproar that followed, U.S. political leaders and Defense Department officials scrambled, damage control their priority. "A few bad apples" was the official pronouncement—just isolated incidents of sadistic soldiers run amok. The "bad apples" were identified and arrested: nine members of an Army Reserve unit based in Maryland.

Why would ordinary Americans mistreat people like that? How can normal people commit such cruel, immoral acts?

Unless we learn the dynamics of "why," we will never be able to counteract the powerful forces that can transform ordinary people into evil perpetrators.

—*Philip Zimbardo, (2004b)*

Would You Have Obeyed? "I was instructed by persons in higher rank to 'stand there, hold this leash, look at the camera,'" Lynndie England (2005) said. Among those calling the shots was Corporal Charles Graner, the alleged ringleader who was sentenced to 10 years in prison for his attacks on Iraqi detainees. Graner, England, and one other reservist were convicted of mistreatment and given prison sentences. No officers were court-martialed or charged with any criminal offense.

What actually happened at Abu Ghraib?

At its peak population in early 2004, the Abu Ghraib prison complex housed more than 6,000 Iraqis who had been detained during the American invasion and occupation of Iraq (James, 2008).

There had been numerous reports of mistreatment at Abu Ghraib, including official complaints by the International Red Cross. However, most Americans had no knowledge of the prison conditions until photographs documenting shocking incidents of abuse were shown in the national media (Hersh, 2004a, 2004b).

What factors contributed to the events that occurred at Abu Ghraib prison?

Multiple elements combined to create the conditions for brutality, including *in-group versus out-group thinking, negative stereotypes, dehumanization,* and *prejudice.* The Iraqi prisoners were of a different culture, ethnic group, and religion than the prison guards, none of whom spoke Arabic. Categorizing the prisoners as a dangerous and threatening out-group allowed the American guards to *dehumanize* the detainees (Fiske & others, 2004).

The worst incidents took place in a cell block that held the prisoners who had been identified as potential "terrorists" or "insurgents" (Hersh, 2005). The guards were led to believe that it was their patriotic duty to mistreat these potential terrorists in order to help extract useful information (Kelman, 2005; Post, 2011; Taguba, 2004). Thinking in this way also helped reduce any *cognitive dissonance* the soldiers might have been experiencing by *justifying* the aggression.

Is what happened at Abu Ghraib similar to what happened in Milgram's studies?

Milgram's controversial studies showed that even ordinary citizens will obey an authority figure and commit acts of destructive obedience. Some of the accused soldiers, like Army Reserve Private Lynndie England, did claim that they were "just following orders." Photographs of England, especially the one in which she was holding a naked male prisoner on a leash, created international outrage and revulsion. But England (2004) testified that her superiors praised the photos, saying, "Hey, you're doing great, keep it up."

But were the guards "just following orders"?

During the court-martials, soldiers who were called as witnesses for the prosecution testified that no *direct* orders were given to mistreat prisoners (Zernike, 2004). However, as a classic and controversial study by Stanford University psychologist Philip Zimbardo and his colleagues (1973) showed, *implied* social norms and roles can be just as powerful as explicit orders.

The study that became known as the Stanford Prison Experiment was conducted in 1971 (Haney & others, 1973). Twenty-four male college students were randomly assigned to be either prisoners or prison guards. They played their roles in a makeshift but realistic prison that had been set up in the basement of a Stanford University building. All of the participants had been evaluated and judged to be psychologically healthy, well-adjusted individuals.

Experimenter: It is absolutely essential that you continue.

Mr. Rensaleer: Well, I won't—not with the man screaming to get out.

Experimenter: You have no other choice.

Mr. Rensaleer: I *do* have a choice. *(Incredulous and indignant)* Why don't I have a choice? I came here on my own free will. I thought I could help in a research project. But if I have

---

Originally, the study was slated to run for two weeks. But after just six days, the situation was spinning out of control. As Zimbardo (2005) recalls, "Within a few days, [those] assigned to the guard role became abusive, red-necked prison guards. . . . Within 36 hours the first prisoner had an emotional breakdown, crying, screaming, and thinking irrationally." In all, five participants had emotional breakdowns (Drury & others, 2012). Prisoners who did not have extreme stress reactions became passive and depressed.

While Milgram's experiments showed the effects of *direct authority pressure,* the Stanford Prison Experiment demonstrated the powerful influence of *situational roles* and *conformity to implied social rules and norms.* These influences are especially pronounced in vague or novel situations where *normative social influence* is more likely (Zimbardo, 2007). When people are not certain what to do, they tend to rely on cues provided by others and to conform their behavior to that of those in their immediate group (Fiske & others, 2004).

It's important to note, however, that researchers have questioned whether it was only normative social influence that guided the behavior of the Stanford Prison Experiment participants (Griggs, 2014). For example, some psychologists noted that Zimbardo and his colleagues had been very directive with the guards (Reicher & Haslam, 2006). In 2002, a new study conducted in the United Kingdom was filmed for a show by the British Broadcasting Corporation. In this study, called the BBC Prison Experiment, the guards were *not* given directions as to how to treat the prisoners. What happened? The guards did not act abusively toward the prisoners. Thus, the researchers concluded that demand characteristics in the form of guidance from the Stanford researchers may have played a role in the abuse in the Stanford study. As you learned in the introduction and research methods chapter, *demand characteristics* are cues that suggest to participants how they should respond. The psychologists concluded that similar cues may have been present in the "culture" of the Abu Ghraib prison.

At Abu Ghraib, the accused soldiers received no special training and were ignorant of regulations regarding the treatment of civilian detainees or enemy prisoners of war (see James, 2008; Zimbardo, 2007). Guards apparently took their cues from one another and from the military intelligence personnel who encouraged them to "set the conditions" for interrogation (Hersh, 2005; Taguba, 2004).

Other factors might also be at play in situations like Abu Ghraib. For example, researchers found that participants who signed up for a study described to be about prison were more likely to have qualities related to the potential to abuse others—such as aggression, narcissism, and dominance—than those signing up for other studies (Carnahan & McFarland, 2007). These researchers noted that this self-selection was likely to be true in military contexts, such as Abu Ghraib, as well.

Are people helpless to resist destructive obedience in a situation like Abu Ghraib prison?

No. As Milgram demonstrated, *people can and do resist pressure to perform evil actions.* Not all military personnel at Abu Ghraib

Accepting Responsibility At her trial, Lynndie England, the file clerk from a small town in West Virginia, apologized for her actions. In an interview after her conviction, England (2005) said that she would always feel guilty "for doing the wrong thing, posing in pictures when I shouldn't have, degrading [the prisoners] and humiliating them—and not saying anything to anybody else to stop it."

went along with the pressure to mistreat prisoners (Hersh, 2005; Taguba, 2004). Consider these examples:

- Master-at-Arms William J. Kimbro, a Navy dog handler, adamantly refused to participate in improper interrogations using dogs to intimidate prisoners despite being pressured by military intelligence personnel (Hersh, 2004b).

- When handed a CD filled with digital photographs depicting prisoners being abused and humiliated, Specialist Joseph M. Darby turned it over to the Army Criminal Investigation Division. It was Darby's conscientious action that finally prompted a formal investigation of the prison.

At the court-martials, army witnesses testified that the abusive treatment would never be allowed under any stretch of the normal rules for handling inmates in a military prison (Zernike, 2004).

In fact, as General Peter Pace, chairman of the Joint Chiefs of Staff, stated forcefully in a November 2005 press conference, "It is absolutely the responsibility of every U.S. service member, if they see inhumane treatment being conducted, to intervene to stop it."

Finally, it's important to point out that understanding the factors that contributed to the events at Abu Ghraib does *not* excuse the perpetrators' behavior or absolve them of individual responsibility. And, as Milgram's research shows, the action of even one outspoken dissenter can inspire others to resist unethical or illegal commands from an authority figure (Packer, 2008a).

CRITICAL THINKING QUESTIONS

- How might the fundamental attribution error lead people to blame "a few bad apples" rather than noticing situational factors that contributed to the Abu Ghraib prison abuse?

- Who should be held responsible for the inhumane conditions and abuse that occurred at Abu Ghraib prison?

TABLE 11.5

Resisting an Authority's Unacceptable Orders

- Verify your own discomfort by asking yourself, "Is this something I would do if I were controlling the situation?"

- Express your discomfort. It can be as simple as saying, "I'm really not comfortable with this."

- Resist even slightly objectionable commands so that the situation doesn't escalate into increasingly immoral or destructive obedience.

- If you realize you've already done something unacceptable, stop at that point rather than continuing to comply.

- Find or create an excuse to get out of the situation and validate your concerns with someone who is not involved with the situation.

- Question the legitimacy of the authority. Most authorities have legitimacy only in specific situations. If authorities are out of their legitimate context, they have no more authority in the situation than you do.

- If it is a group situation, find an ally who also feels uncomfortable with the authority's orders. Two people expressing dissent in harmony can effectively resist conforming to the group's actions.

Sources: Information from American Psychological Association, 2005b; Asch, 1956, 1957; Blass, 1991, 2004; Haney & others, 1973; Milgram, 1963, 1974a; Zimbardo, 2000a, 2004a, 2007.

to hurt somebody to do that, or if I was in his place, too, I wouldn't stay there. I can't continue. I'm very sorry. I think I've gone too far already, probably.

Like some of the other participants in the obedience and conformity studies, Rensaleer effectively resisted the situational and social pressures that pushed him to obey. As did Army Sergeant Joseph M. Darby, who triggered the investigation of abuses at the Abu Ghraib prison camp in Iraq by turning over a CD with photos of the abuse to authorities. As Darby said, the photos "violated everything that I personally believed in and everything that I had been taught about the rules of war." Table 11.5 summarizes several strategies that can help people resist the pressure to conform or obey in a destructive, dangerous, or morally questionable situation.

How are such people different from those who conform or obey? Unfortunately, there's no satisfying answer to that question. No specific personality trait consistently predicts conformity or obedience in experimental situations such as those Asch and Milgram created (see Blass, 2000, 2004; Burger, 2009). In other words, the social influences that Asch and Milgram created in their experimental situations can be compelling even to people who are normally quite independent.

Finally, we need to emphasize that conformity and obedience are not completely bad in and of themselves. Quite the contrary. Conformity and obedience are necessary for an orderly society, which is why such behaviors were instilled in all of us as children. The critical issue is not so much whether people conform or obey, because we all do so every day of our lives. Rather, the critical issue is whether the norms we conform to, or the orders we obey, reflect values that respect the rights, well-being, and dignity of others.

❯ Test your understanding of **Factors Influencing Conformity and Obedience** with **LEARNING**Curve.

Altruism and Aggression
HELPING AND HURTING BEHAVIOR

KEY THEME

Prosocial behavior describes any behavior that helps another person, including altruistic acts. Aggression describes behavior that is intended to harm another person.

KEY QUESTIONS

❯ What factors increase the likelihood that people will help a stranger?

❯ What factors decrease the likelihood that people will help a stranger?

❯ How can the lack of bystander response in the Genovese murder case be explained in light of psychological research on helping behavior?

❯ What factors increase the likelihood that people will harm another person?

Kitty Genovese (1935–1964) Known as Kitty by her friends, Genovese had grown up in Brooklyn. As a young woman, she managed a sports bar in Queens, shown here.

New York Daily News Archive/Getty Images

It was about 3:20 A.M. on Friday, March 13, 1964, when 28-year-old Kitty Genovese returned home from her job managing a bar. Like other residents in her middle-class New York City neighborhood, she parked her car at an adjacent railroad station. Her apartment entrance was only 100 feet away.

As she got out of her car, she noticed a man at the end of the parking lot. When the man moved in her direction, she began walking toward a nearby police call box, which was under a streetlight in front of a bookstore. On the opposite side of the street was a 10-story apartment building. As she neared the streetlight, the man grabbed her and she screamed. Across the street, lights went on in the apartment building. "Oh, my God! He stabbed me! Please help me! Please help me!" she screamed.

"Let that girl alone!" a man yelled from one of the upper apartment windows. The attacker looked up, then walked off, leaving Kitty on the ground, bleeding.

The street became quiet. Minutes passed. One by one, lights went off. Struggling to her feet, Kitty made her way toward her apartment. As she rounded the corner of the building moments later, her assailant returned, stabbing her again. "I'm dying! I'm dying!" she screamed.

Again, lights went on. Windows opened and people looked out. This time, the assailant got into his car and drove off. It was now 3:35 A.M. Fifteen minutes had passed since Kitty's first screams for help. A New York City bus passed by. Staggering, then crawling, Kitty moved toward the entrance of her apartment. She never made it. Her attacker returned, searching the apartment entrance doors. At the second apartment entrance, he found her, slumped at the foot of the steps. This time, he stabbed her to death.

Edward Hausner/The New York Times Pictures/Redux

It was 3:50 A.M. when someone first called the police. The police took just two minutes to arrive at the scene. About half an hour later, an ambulance carried Kitty Genovese's body away. Only then did people come out of their apartments to talk to the police.

Over the next two weeks, police investigators learned that a total of 38 people had witnessed Kitty's murder—a murder that involved three separate attacks over a period of about 30 minutes. Why didn't anyone try to help her? Or call the police when she first screamed for help?

When *The New York Times* interviewed various experts, they seemed baffled, although one expert said it was a "typical" reaction (Mohr, 1964). If there was a common theme in their explanations, it seemed to be "apathy." The occurrence was simply representative of the alienation and depersonalization of life in a big city, people said (see Rosenthal, 1964a, 1964b).

Not everyone bought this pat explanation. In the first place, it wasn't true. As social psychologists **Bibb Latané** and **John Darley** (1970) later pointed out in their landmark book, *The Unresponsive Bystander: Why Doesn't He Help?*:

> People often help others, even at great personal risk to themselves. For every "apathy" story, one of outright heroism could be cited. . . . People sometimes help and sometimes don't. What determines when help will be given?

That's the critical question, of course. When do people help others? And why do people help others?

When we help another person with no expectation of personal benefit, we're displaying **altruism** (Batson & others, 2011). An altruistic act is fundamentally selfless—the individual is motivated purely by the desire to help someone in need. Everyday life is filled with little acts of altruistic kindness, such as Fern giving the "homeless" man a handful of quarters or the stranger who thoughtfully holds a door open for you as you juggle an armful of packages.

Altruistic actions fall under the broader heading of **prosocial behavior,** which describes any behavior that helps another person, whatever the underlying motive. Note that prosocial behaviors are not necessarily altruistic. Sometimes we help others out of guilt. And, sometimes we help others in order to gain something, such as recognition, rewards, increased self-esteem, or having the favor returned (Batson & others, 2011). Whatever the reason, there is evidence from neuroscience research that some

altruism Helping another person with no expectation of personal reward or benefit.

prosocial behavior Any behavior that helps another, whether the underlying motive is self-serving or selfless.

AP Photo/Bill Haber

Prosocial Behavior in Action Many people volunteer their time and energy to help others. In New Orleans, University students Ty Gonzalez and Melissa Santos worked with other volunteers after Hurricane Katrina. They collected wood from damaged homes that could be reused for rebuilding efforts.

TopPhoto via AP Images

Coming to the Aid of a Stranger Everyday life is filled with examples of people who come to the aid of a stranger in distress, like the man shown here in Ningbo, China. He bravely scaled three stories of a building to save a three-year-old boy. The boy was dangling dangerously in the air, his head stuck between security bars over his window. The man climbed up to the boy and held him until he could be rescued by firefighters.

forms of prosocial behavior lead to activation in the brain structures associated with rewards (Kurzban & others, 2015). Researchers suggest that such findings highlight possible evolutionary causes for altruistic behavior.

Factors That Increase the Likelihood of Bystanders Helping

Kitty Genovese's death triggered hundreds of investigations into the conditions under which people will help others (Dovidio, 1984; Dovidio & others, 2006). Those studies began in the 1960s with the pioneering efforts of Bibb Latané and John Darley, who conducted a series of ingenious experiments in which it appears that help is needed. For example, in one study, participants believed they were overhearing an epileptic seizure (Darley & Latané, 1968). In another study, participants were in a room that started to fill with smoke (Latané & Darley, 1968). Based on these studies, Latané and Darley concluded that people must pass through three stages before they offer help. First, they must notice an emergency situation. Second, they must interpret it as a situation that actually requires help. Third, they must decide that it is their responsibility to offer help (Latané & Darley, 1968).

Other researchers joined the effort to understand what factors influence a person's decision to help another (see Dovidio & others, 2006; Fischer & others, 2011; Zaki & Mitchell, 2013). Some of the most significant factors that increase the likelihood of helping include:

- **The "feel good, do good" effect.** People who feel good, successful, happy, or fortunate are more likely to decide to help others (see Forgas & others, 2008; C. Miller, 2009). Those good feelings can be due to virtually any positive event, such as succeeding at a task or even just enjoying a warm, sunny day.

- **Feeling guilty.** We tend to be more helpful when we're feeling guilty. For example, after telling a lie or inadvertently causing an accident, people were more likely to decide to help others (Basil & others, 2006; Cohen & others, 2012; de Hooge & others, 2011).

- **Seeing others who are willing to help.** Whether it's donating blood or helping a stranded motorist change a flat tire, we're more likely to decide to help if we observe others do the same (Fischer & others, 2011). This is true even when we are the recipient of help (Tsvetkova & Macy, 2014).

- **Perceiving the other person as deserving help.** We're more likely to decide to help people who are in need of help through no fault of their own. For example, people are twice as likely to give some change to a stranger if they believe the stranger's wallet has been stolen than if they believe the stranger has simply spent all his money (Burn, 2009; Laner & others, 2001; Latané & Darley, 1970). Similarly, people are more likely to support welfare programs if they believe that the welfare recipients are actively trying to find a job (Petersen & others, 2012).

- **Knowing how to help.** Research has confirmed that knowing what to do and being physically capable of helping contributes greatly to the decision to help someone else (Fischer & others, 2011; Steg & de Groot, 2010). In line with this, some universities have implemented bystander training to give students skills to intervene, for example, to prevent a sexual assault (Hua, 2013; University of Arizona, n.d.).

- **A personalized relationship.** When people have any sort of personal relationship with another person, even at the level of simply making eye contact with someone, they're more likely to decide to help that person (Solomon & others, 1981; Vrugt & Vet, 2009). This might explain why researchers have observed that people are less likely to help in anonymous online contexts than in the "real world" (Barlińska & others, 2013). When online interactions are *not* anonymous, a personal relationship makes people more likely to help, for example in cyberbullying situations (Macháčková & others, 2013).

- **A dangerous situation.** People also are more likely to decide to help in dangerous situations—those that are clearly an emergency, those when the perpetrator is present, and those that present a physical risk to the helper (Fischer & others, 2011). Even in an online context, bystanders are more likely to intervene in cyberbullying when it is more severe (Bastiaensens, & others, 2014). These findings might seem surprising, but it may be that these are situations in which it is clear that help is needed.

Factors That Decrease the Likelihood of Bystanders Helping

Unfortunately, instances in which bystanders fail to intervene are still regularly reported. For example, during spring break revels on a Florida beach, police reported a gang rape that occurred while hundreds of people watched (Southall, 2015). And in Philadelphia, when a woman on a bus passed out, evidently from drug or alcohol use, bystanders just filmed the situation while her young daughter tried to rouse her (Gambacorta, 2014). A police official said, "There's very little reason why 15 calls to 9-1-1 weren't received."

Given examples like these and many others, it's important to consider influences that decrease the likelihood of helping behavior. As we look at some of the key findings, we'll also note how each factor might have played a role in the death of Kitty Genovese.

- **The presence of other people.** In general, people are much more likely to decide to help when they are alone (Fischer & others, 2011; Latané & Nida, 1981). If other people are present or imagined, helping behavior declines—a phenomenon called the **bystander effect.** This effect has even been observed in five-year-old children. One study found that children were more likely to help a teacher when they were alone or when the only other children present were behind a barrier and physically unable to help (Plötner & others, 2015).

There seem to be two major reasons for the bystander effect. First, the presence of other people creates a **diffusion of responsibility.** The responsibility to intervene is *shared* (or *diffused*) among all the onlookers. Because no one person feels all the pressure to respond, each bystander becomes less likely to help.

Ironically, the sheer number of bystanders seemed to be the most significant factor working against Kitty Genovese. Remember that when she first screamed, a man yelled down, "Let that girl alone!" With that, each observer instantly knew that he or she was not the only one watching the events on the street below. Hence, no single individual felt the full responsibility to help.

Second, the bystander effect seems to occur because each of us is motivated to some extent by the desire to behave in a socially acceptable way (*normative social influence*) and to appear correct (*informational social influence*). In the case of Kitty Genovese, the lack of intervention by any of the witnesses may have signaled the others that intervention was not appropriate, wanted, or needed.

- **Being in a big city or a very small town.** Kitty Genovese was attacked late at night in one of the biggest cities in the world. Research by Robert Levine and his colleagues (2008) confirmed that people are less likely to decide to help

Reyer Boxem/Hollandse Hoogte/Redux

The Bystander Effect: What Would You Do? What would you do if you came across a man lying crumpled on the ground on a college campus? Would you stop to help him, call campus security, or look away and hurry past? What factors in the scene shown in the photograph make it more or less likely that the woman will stop to try to help a stranger?

bystander effect A phenomenon in which the greater the number of people present, the less likely each individual is to help someone in distress.

diffusion of responsibility A phenomenon in which the presence of other people makes it less likely that any individual will help someone in distress because the obligation to intervene is shared among all the onlookers.

aggression Verbal or physical behavior intended to cause harm to other people.

strangers in big cities, but other aspects of city life, like crowding and economic status, also affect helping. On the other hand, people are *also* less likely to help a stranger in towns with populations under 5,000 (Steblay, 1987).

- **Vague or ambiguous situations.** When situations are ambiguous and people are not certain that help is needed, they're less likely to decide to offer help (Solomon & others, 1978). The ambiguity of the situation may also have worked against Kitty Genovese. The people in the apartment building saw a man and a woman struggling on the street below but had no way of knowing whether the two were acquainted. "We thought it was a lovers' quarrel," some of the witnesses later said (Gansberg, 1964). Researchers have found that people are especially reluctant to intervene when the situation appears to be a domestic dispute, because they are not certain that assistance is wanted (Gracia & others, 2009). In a recent incident in Jersey City, NJ, a woman was fatally stabbed by her ex-boyfriend. A neighbor who heard the attack reportedly "went back to bed, not wanting to get involved" in what he likely perceived as a domestic dispute (Villanova, 2014).

- **When the personal costs for helping outweigh the benefits.** As a general rule, we tend to weigh the costs as well as the benefits of helping in deciding whether to act. If the potential costs outweigh the benefits, it's less likely that people will help (Fischer & others, 2006, 2011). The witnesses in the Genovese case may have felt that the benefits of helping Genovese were outweighed by the potential hassles and danger of becoming involved in the situation.

On a small yet universal scale, the murder of Kitty Genovese dramatically underscores the power of situational and social influences to affect our behavior. Although social psychological research has provided insights about the factors that influenced the behavior of those who witnessed the Genovese murder, it should not be construed as a justification for the inaction of the bystanders. After all, Kitty Genovese's death probably could have been prevented by a single phone call. If we understand the factors that decrease helping behavior, we can recognize and overcome those obstacles when we encounter someone who needs assistance. If *you* had been Kitty Genovese—or if Kitty Genovese had been your sister, friend, or classmate—how would *you* have hoped other people would react?

Aggression
HURTING BEHAVIOR

The flip side of helping behavior is hurting behavior, or **aggression**—any verbal or physical behavior intended to cause harm to other people. To be classified as aggression, the aggressor must believe that their behavior is harmful to the other person, and the other person must not wish to be harmed (Anderson & Bushman, 2002). A child who hits her little brother, a mugger who threatens his victim, a boss who screams at her subordinates, or a terrorist who fires shots in a crowded mall—all are engaged in acts of aggression. But the doctor who knowingly inflicts pain while setting a broken arm is not.

Have you ever wondered about the wide variation in aggressive tendencies? Why does one friend threaten a fistfight when provoked, while another calmly walks away? Like helping behavior, hurting behavior is driven by a range of factors—biological, psychological, and sociocultural.

THE INFLUENCE OF BIOLOGY ON AGGRESSION

Researchers have long thought that our tendency to behave aggressively has a biological component. Biological theories of aggression include genetic, structural, and biochemical explanations.

The Influence of Genes and Brain Structure When someone behaves aggressively, how do we know if that is driven, even in part, by inborn personality characteristics? There have been a number of studies that tried to separate the effects of genes and

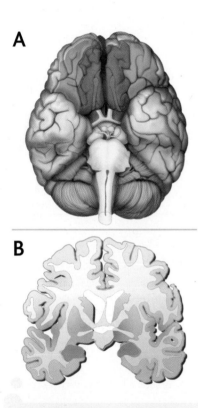

A

B

Aggression and the Brain Some researchers offer a biological explanation for aggression. They suggest that aggression occurs when people have trouble regulating their emotions. And, in fact, some of the brain patterns that researchers observe for aggression are similar to those that they observe for the regulation of emotion. The colored parts of the brain in this figure are involved in both emotion regulation and aggression. Psychologist Richard Davidson and his colleagues (2000) saw similar activity for both emotion regulation and aggression in parts of the prefrontal cortex (A) and the amygdala (B).

environmental influences in rates of aggression. For example, one study found that identical twins had similar aggressive tendencies whether or not they were raised together. Because twins share 100% of their genes, this finding indicates a strong genetic influence on aggressive behavior (Bouchard & others, 1990; Segal, 2012). Two meta-analyses that explored studies on heredity and aggression concluded that genetics played a significant role in people's levels of aggressiveness (Ferguson, 2010; Miles & Carey, 1997).

The presence of behaviors that appear to be driven, at least in part, by genetics leads to questions about whether these behaviors have an evolutionary basis. That is, are there adaptive benefits to having a genetic predisposition toward aggression, at least in certain contexts? Evolutionary theorists say yes (Ferguson & Beaver, 2009). Aggression, they assert, can help people to acquire or secure resources for themselves and for those who share their genes (Buss & Duntley, 2006).

Another biological explanation for aggression points to differences in the parts of the brain that regulate emotion, including the amygdala, the prefrontal cortex, and the limbic system (Bobes & others, 2013; Davidson & others, 2000; Meyer-Lindenberg & others, 2006). For example, researchers have observed differences in the prefrontal cortex of people who are prone to aggressive and angry outbursts (Best & others, 2002).

Biochemical Influences Biochemical influences on aggression include the hormone testosterone and alcohol abuse. For example, Irene van Bokhoven and her colleagues (2006) followed 96 boys from kindergarten through age 21. They found that boys who had higher levels of testosterone over this period were more likely to have criminal records as adults. This tendency is not limited to men. Both male and female college students who had committed acts of violence or engaged in drug use were found to have higher rates of testosterone (Banks & Dabbs, 1996). And a link between testosterone and aggression has been found among female prisoners (Dabbs & Hargrove, 1997).

However, it's important not to overstate the link between testosterone and aggression. In a meta-analysis of 45 studies, Angela Book and her colleagues (2001) found only a weak relationship between the two. Further, some researchers point out that high testosterone can also have positive effects. For example, it may be linked to good negotiation and leadership skills (Yildirim & Derksen, 2012).

Although most people who consume alcohol are not violent, the rate of violence is higher among those under the influence of alcohol than among those who have not consumed alcohol (Duke & others, 2011; Pedersen & others, 2014). This effect has been established in both laboratory and everyday settings (Chermack & Taylor, 1995; Exum, 2006; Graham & others, 2006). One research team bravely spent over 1,000 nights in over 100 bars in Toronto, Canada, and logged more than 1,000 violent incidents. As the crowd became more intoxicated, aggressive incidents were more likely to occur. And, the aggressive person's level of intoxication was generally related to the severity of the violent act (Graham & others, 2006).

PSYCHOLOGICAL INFLUENCES ON AGGRESSION

While it's clear that there are biological influences on aggression, there also are psychological influences. For example, a great deal of aggressive behavior is learned. In addition, there are situational factors that can increase people's tendency to be aggressive.

Learning People who are violent are often mimicking behavior they have seen, a form of observational learning. For example, in Chapter 5, you read about Albert Bandura's classic Bobo Doll experiments in which children learned to behave aggressively toward a large balloon doll by watching a brief video in which an adult did the same. Exposure to violence may also lead to aggression over the longer term. Researchers have

Bar Fight The rate of violence tends to be higher among people who have consumed alcohol. Research conducted in bars found a positive correlation between levels of intoxication and the frequency and intensity of violent incidents (Graham & others, 2006).

ACE STOCK LIMITED/Alamy

found that both women and men exposed to violence in their families while growing up were more likely to abuse their partners and their children as adults (Heyman & Smith Slep, 2002). But a higher likelihood is not a guarantee that the family pattern of violence will be repeated. In fact, most people who were exposed to violence as children *do not* grow up to be abusers themselves.

There also is evidence that exposure to violence in the media—whether in a film, a video game, or music lyrics—might increase the likelihood that someone will behave aggressively, perhaps imitating the violence they viewed (Greitemeyer & Mügge, 2014). For example, one experiment found that people randomly assigned to watching reality television shows that depicted aggression, such as *The Jersey Shore,* were more likely to then act in aggressive ways than people randomly assigned to watch non-aggressive reality TV or crime dramas like *CSI* (Gibson & others, 2014). (On the flip side, exposure to prosocial TV shows, movies, and video games—in which people helped one another—was related to increased helping behaviors (Prot & Others, 2014).)

In the Critical Thinking box "Does Exposure to Media Violence *Cause* Aggressive Behavior" in Chapter 5, you read about the evidence that viewing media violence is related to aggressive behavior (see Bushman & others, 2009). Viewing pornography, especially pornography depicting sexual violence, also has been linked to increased aggressive attitudes toward women (Hald & others, 2010). Although there is a strong link, it's important to note that much of the research connecting media violence to actual aggressive behavior is correlational. Remember from Chapter 1 that correlational studies cannot tell us whether one variable, such as viewing pornography, causes another, such as aggression. The research that is experimental and could show causal links is primarily in artificial situations (Ferguson & Kilbourn, 2009).

Other forms of violent media, like violent video games, also have been linked to increased aggression. For example, one study followed more than 1,000 boys and girls throughout their high school years, and found that students who played violent video games throughout this time showed increases in aggressive behavior over the four years of the study (Willoughby & others, 2012). Listening to violent music lyrics—from heavy metal, rap, and rock songs—led participants in one study to be more aggressive. Compared with participants who listened to the same music without lyrics, they doled out larger amounts of a painful hot sauce for another (fictional) participant to consume (Brummert Lennings & Warburton, 2011). Because this was an experiment, we can safely conclude that listening to the violent lyrics *caused* the higher levels of aggressive behavior.

Frustration Aggression can be learned, but it can also be driven by situational factors that are annoying or frustrating. For example, researchers have identified high temperatures as a source for frustration-linked aggression (Anderson & Bushman, 2002). Violence in Minneapolis increased as nighttime temperatures increased (Bushman & others, 2005). Even exposure to words associated with hotter temperatures—*sunburn* or *sweats,* for example—leads to increased hostility as compared with neutral or colder words (DeWall & Bushman, 2009). Temperature is also linked to violence on a global scale. As climate change leads to warmer temperatures globally, increased rates of conflict between individuals and between groups are being reported (Hsiang & others, 2013).

When frustrated by a stressful situation or an annoying person, people can react aggressively (Anderson & Bushman, 2002). Jodi Whitaker and her colleagues (2013) conducted an experiment in which they created a situation that would be incredibly frustrating to their student participants. The students were invited to take an extremely difficult history test that could earn them desirable snacks for a top performance. Some students were then "mistakenly" given access to the answers—but were frustrated by

MYTH ▶ SCIENCE

Is it true that there is a link between aggression and listening to violent music lyrics?

Road Rage Aggression can result from the frustration we feel in a stressful situation. For example, "road rage" can stem from frustration experienced while driving, perhaps because we have been cut off by another driver or have encountered an unexpected detour.

Stuart Pearce/age fotostock

having the answers, and the chance to cheat, quickly taken away. After taking the test, students were asked to rate a series of violent and nonviolent video games. Students who were frustrated rated their desire to play violent video games higher than students who never had a chance to cheat or who never had their chance to cheat taken away.

When's the last time you got really frustrated or angry? If you drive, it might have been behind the wheel. About one third of us admit to having been the aggressor in a road rage situation, and that's particularly true of younger drivers and male drivers (Smart & others, 2003). Road rage results from a number of factors, especially frustration—the frustration that results when we perceive inappropriate or reckless driving behavior, when there is heavy traffic, or when we're running late (Wickens & others, 2013). These factors are even more frustrating—and even more likely to lead to aggression—when we're already stressed out for other reasons (Wickens & others, 2013).

GENDER, CULTURE, AND AGGRESSION

Quick—which gender do you think is more likely to engage in aggressive behavior? In this case, the stereotype that males are the more aggressive gender is true, on average. (But just on average. As with every psychology finding, there are lots of exceptions.) Psychologist John Archer (2004) conducted a meta-analysis of aggression in real-world settings. He concluded that "Direct, especially physical, aggression was more common in males than females at all ages sampled, was consistent across cultures, and occurred from early childhood on, showing a peak between 20 and 30 years." Research suggests, however, that girls and women are just as aggressive as boys in *indirect* aggression, which refers to aggression related to interactions, such as gossiping and spreading rumors (Archer & Coyne, 2005).

Why are men more likely than women to behave in physically aggressive ways? There may be biological reasons. Evolutionary theorists suggest that the gender difference is due to the fact that men are more likely to reproduce if they have access to desirable mating partners, something that is more likely for men with resources—which can be acquired through aggression (Buss & Duntley, 2006). In addition, men are more likely to use aggression in the context of mating. For example, in an experiment, men who thought about sexual topics were more likely to behave aggressively than men who thought about topics related to happiness (Ainsworth & Maner, 2012).

But there also are environmental explanations. The ways in which girls and boys exhibit aggression are influenced by the reactions of others. Children learn aggression-related scripts—or guides for how they should act—by responding to input from peers and teachers, parents and other family members, and the media (Ostrov & Godleski, 2010).

Cultural factors also influence aggressive behavior and attitudes. Aggression and violence seem to be more common in certain types of societies (Bond, 2004). These include societies that are less economically developed, that have higher levels of economic inequality, and that are *not* democracies (Bond, 2004). Researchers have also found that there are regional and national differences in certain types of aggression based on the concept of a culture of honor (Vandello & others, 2008). A *culture of honor* is one in which actions perceived as damaging your reputation must be addressed (Vandello & Cohen, 2004). In some countries, such as Turkey, the culture of honor is focused on offenses against one's family (Cihangir, 2013; van Osch & others, 2013).

In the Americas, especially the southern United States and Latin America, the culture of violence tends to be based on masculine honor. Psychologist Joseph Vandello and his colleagues (2008) describe masculine honor as having "an emphasis on masculinity and male toughness." In such cultures, violence that is seen as helping a man restore his reputation is more acceptable. For example, if a man is mocked at a sporting event, a violent response might be seen as reasonable or even admirable (Vandello & Cohen, 2003). Masculine honor culture, although usually regional, can also be contextual. Some researchers have observed an aggression-inducing culture of masculine honor in North American bars (Graham & Wells, 2003).

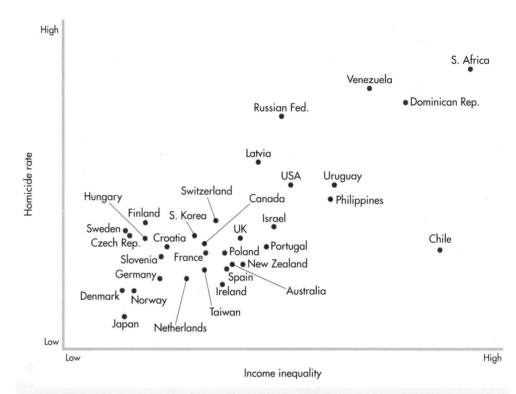

FIGURE 11.5 Income Inequality and Murder A study of 33 countries found a very strong link between the level of income inequality in a country and the homicide rate (Elgar & Aitken, 2010). As you can see in this graph, many countries, such as Japan, are low in both inequality and homicide, whereas others, such as South Africa, are very high in both. The United States is above average for both measures. The correlation between these two measures demonstrates that sociocultural factors, in addition to biological and psychological factors, are important predictors of aggression.

Source: Data from Elgar & Aitken (2010).

Cultures with significant income inequality also have higher rates of aggression. Researchers have identified a strong link between income inequality and violence, particularly murder (Nivette, 2011; Wilkinson & Pickett, 2009). For example, a study of 33 countries found a very high correlation of 0.80 between the level of income inequality in a country and the homicide rate (Elgar & Aitken, 2010; see Figure 11.5). From Chapter 1, you may remember that the highest possible correlation is 1.00, indicating that two variables are perfectly related. A correlation of 0.80 is close to the highest you would see in social science research. Just the fact that this important cultural element is so tightly bound with extreme violence is an indication that sociocultural factors, in addition to biological and psychological factors, are important predictors of violence.

❭ Test your understanding of **Altruism and Aggression** with *LEARNINGCurve*.

Closing Thoughts

We began this chapter with a prologue about Fern trying to help a stranger in a strange city. As it turned out, Fern's social perceptions of the man were inaccurate: He was not a homeless person living on the streets of San Francisco. As simple as this incident was, it underscored a theme that was repeatedly echoed throughout our subsequent discussions of person perception, attribution, and attitudes. Our subjective impressions, whether they are accurate or not, play a pivotal role in how we perceive and think about other people.

A different theme emerged in our later discussions of conformity, obedience, helping behavior, and hurting behavior. Social and situational factors, especially the behavior of others in the same situation, can have powerful effects on how we act at a given moment. But like Fern, each of us has the freedom to choose how we respond in a given situation. When we're aware of the social forces that influence us, it can be easier for us to choose wisely.

In the final analysis, we are social animals who often influence one another's thoughts, perceptions, and actions, sometimes in profound ways. In the following Psych for Your Life section, we'll look at some of the ways that social psychological insights have been applied by professional persuaders—and how you can counteract attempts to persuade you.

persuasion The deliberate attempt to influence the attitudes or behavior of another person in a situation in which that person has some freedom of choice.

PSYCH FOR YOUR LIFE

The Persuasion Game

At the time, Sandy's and Don's daughter, Laura, was only 3 1/2 years old, happily munching her Cheerios and doodling pictures in the butter on her bread. Don sat across from her at the kitchen table, reading a draft of this chapter. "Don't play with your food, Laura," Don said without looking up.

"Okay, Daddy," she chirped. "Daddy, are you in a happy mood?" Don paused. "Yes, I'm in a happy mood, Laura," he said thoughtfully. "Are you in a happy mood?"

"Yes, Daddy," Laura replied as she made the banana peel dance around her placemat. "Daddy, will you get me a Mermaid Barbie doll for my birthday?"

Ah, so young and so clever! From very early in life, we learn the basics of **persuasion**—the deliberate attempt to influence the attitudes or behavior of another person in a situation in which that person has some freedom of choice. Clearly, Laura had figured out one basic rule: She's more likely to persuade Mom or Dad when they're in "a happy mood."

Professional persuaders often manipulate people's attitudes and behavior using techniques based on two fundamental social norms: the rule of reciprocity and the rule of commitment (Cialdini & Sagarin, 2005). Here we'll provide you with some practical suggestions to avoid being taken in by persuasion techniques.

The Rule of Reciprocity

The *rule of reciprocity* is a simple but powerful social norm (Burger & others, 2009; Shen & others, 2011). If someone gives you something or does you a favor, you feel obligated to return the favor. So after a classmate lets you copy her lecture notes for the class session you missed, you feel obligated to return a favor when she asks for one.

The "favor" can be almost anything freely given, such as a free food sample in a grocery store, a free gardening workshop at your local hardware store, or a free guide, booklet, planning kit, or trial. The rule of reciprocity is part of the sales strategy used by companies that offer "free" in-home trials of their products. It's also why department stores that sell expensive cosmetics offer "free" makeovers.

Technically, you are under "no obligation" to buy anything. Nonetheless, the tactic often creates an uncomfortable sense of obligation, so you do feel pressured to reciprocate by buying the product (Cialdini, 2009).

One strategy that uses the rule of reciprocity is called the *door-in-the-face technique* (Turner & others, 2007). First, the persuader makes a large request that you're certain to refuse. For example, Joe asks to borrow $500. You figuratively "slam the door in his face" by quickly turning him down. But then Joe, apologetic, appears to back off and makes a much smaller request—to borrow $20. From your perspective, it appears that Joe has made a concession to you and is trying to be reasonable. This puts you in the position of reciprocating with a concession of your own. "Well, I can't lend you $500," you grumble, "but I guess I could lend you 20 bucks." Of course, the persuader's real goal was to persuade you to comply with the second, smaller request.

The rule of reciprocity is also operating in the *that's-not-all technique* (Burger, 2011). First, the persuader makes an offer. But before you can accept or reject it, the persuader appears to throw in something extra to make the

> **MYTH ⊙ SCIENCE**
> Is it true that people who say no to a large request are more easily able to say no to smaller requests that follow?

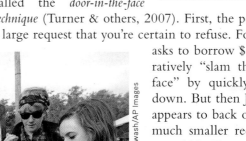

The Rule of Reciprocity It's not altruism that prompted Procter and Gamble to give away free Scope mouthwash at the VOODOO music festival in New Orleans. Many companies employ young marketing representatives, often college students, to host promotional events at music festivals, on campus, or wherever young people congregate, hoping to inspire brand loyalty. American businesses spend an estimated $20 billion a year on promotional products, hoping that the "rule of reciprocity" will make recipients feel obligated to respond by purchasing their brands in the future.

Cheryl Gerber/Invision for SCOPE Mouthwash/AP Images

deal even more attractive to you. So as you're standing there mulling over the price of the more expensive high-definition, flat-panel television, the salesperson says, "Listen, I'm offering you a great price but that's not all I'll do—I'll throw in some top-of-the-line HDMI connector cables at no charge." From your perspective, it appears as though the salesperson has just done you a favor by making a concession you did not ask for. This creates a sense of obligation for you to reciprocate by buying the "better" package.

The Rule of Commitment

Another powerful social norm is the *rule of commitment*. Once you make a public commitment, there is psychological and interpersonal pressure on you to behave consistently with your earlier commitment. The *foot-in-the-door technique* is one strategy that capitalizes on the rule of commitment (Guéguen & others, 2008; Rodafinos & others, 2005). Here's how it works.

First, the persuader makes a small request that you're likely to agree to. For example, she might stop you on the street and ask you to sign a petition supporting some social cause. By agreeing to do so, you've made a small *commitment* to the social cause. At that point, she has gotten her "foot in the door." Next, the persuader asks you to comply with a second, larger request, such as making a donation to the group she represents. Because of your earlier commitment, you feel psychologically pressured to behave consistently by now agreeing to the larger commitment (Cialdini, 2009).

The rule of commitment is also operating in the *low-ball technique*. First, the persuader gets you to make a commitment by deliberately understating the cost of the product you want. He's thrown you a "low ball," one that is simply too good to turn down. In reality, the persuader has no intention of honoring the artificially low price.

Here's an example of the low-ball technique in action: You've negotiated an excellent price (the "low ball") on a used car and filled out the sales contract. The car salesman shakes your hand and beams, then takes your paperwork into his manager's office for approval. Ten minutes pass—enough time for you to convince yourself that you've made the right decision and solidify your commitment to it.

At that point, the salesman comes back from his manager's office looking dejected. "I'm terribly sorry," the car salesman says. "My manager won't let me sell the car at that price because we'd lose too much money on the deal. I told him I would even take a lower commission, but he won't budge."

Notice what has happened. The attractive low-ball price that originally prompted you to make the commitment has been pulled out from under your feet. What typically happens? Despite the loss of the original inducement to make the purchase—the low-ball price—people often feel compelled to keep their commitment to make the purchase even though it is at a higher price (Cialdini, 2009).

Defending Against Persuasion Techniques

It is increasingly important to be aware that persuasive messages can impact your attitudes and behavior. For several years now, online advertisers have targeted messages directly to you based on your online behavior, such as your browsing history (Ur & others, 2012). But they may now also be targeting you based on your personality.

Researchers at the University of Cambridge teamed up with researchers at Microsoft and found that some of your personality traits, such as how outgoing or anxious you are, can be predicted from your Facebook profile (Bachrach & others, 2012). Related to this, other researchers found improved persuasion when ads were matched to personality (Hirsh & others, 2012). Specifically, for an ad for a cell phone, outgoing people responded best when they were promised "you'll always be where the excitement is," and anxious people responded best when they were told that the phone would help them "stay safe and secure."

So, in a world where you are increasingly targeted, how can you reduce the likelihood that you'll be manipulated into making a decision that may not be in your best interest? Here are three practical suggestions.

1. Sleep on it.

Persuasive transactions typically occur quickly. Part of this is our own doing. We've finally decided to go look at a new laptop, automobile, or whatever, so we're psychologically primed to buy the product. The persuader uses this psychological momentum to help coax you into signing on the dotted line right then and there. It's only later, of course, that you sometimes have second thoughts. So when you think you've got the deal you want, tell the persuader that you always sleep on important decisions before making a final commitment.

The sleep-on-it rule often provides an opportunity to discover whether the persuader is deliberately trying to pressure or manipulate you. If the persuader responds to your sleep-on-it suggestion by saying something like "This offer is good for today only," then it's likely that he or she is afraid that your commitment to the deal will crumble if you think about it too carefully or look elsewhere.

2. Play devil's advocate.

List all of the reasons why you should *not* buy the product or make a particular commitment (Albarracín & Vargas, 2010; Crano & Prislin, 2006). Arguing *against* the decision will help activate your critical thinking skills. It's also helpful to discuss important decisions with a friend, who might be able to point out disadvantages that you have overlooked.

3. When in doubt, do nothing.

Learn to trust your gut feelings when something doesn't feel quite right. If you feel that you're being psychologically pressured or cornered, you probably are. As a general rule, if you feel any sense of hesitation, lean toward the conservative side and do nothing. If you take the time to think things over, you'll probably be able to identify the source of your reluctance.

CHAPTER REVIEW

Solomon Asch, p. 472

John M. Darley, p. 483

social psychology, p. 454

sense of self, p. 454

social cognition, p. 454

social influence, p. 454

person perception, p. 455

social norms, p. 455

social categorization, p. 456

explicit cognition, p. 456

implicit cognition, p. 456

implicit personality theory, p. 456

Bibb Latané, p. 483

Stanley Milgram, p. 474

attribution, p. 459

fundamental attribution error, p. 459

actor-observer bias, p. 459

blaming the victim, p. 459

hindsight bias, p. 459

just-world hypothesis, p. 459

self-serving bias, p. 460

attitude, p. 461

cognitive dissonance, p. 464

prejudice, p. 465

Muzafer Sherif, p. 470

Philip G. Zimbardo, p. 464

stereotype, p. 466

in-group, p. 467

out-group, p. 467

out-group homogeneity effect, p. 468

in-group bias, p. 468

implicit attitudes, p. 469

conformity, p. 472

normative social influence, p. 473

informational social influence, p. 473

obedience, p. 474

altruism, p. 483

prosocial behavior, p. 483

bystander effect, p. 485

diffusion of responsibility, p. 485

aggression, p. 486

persuasion, p. 491

Social Psychology

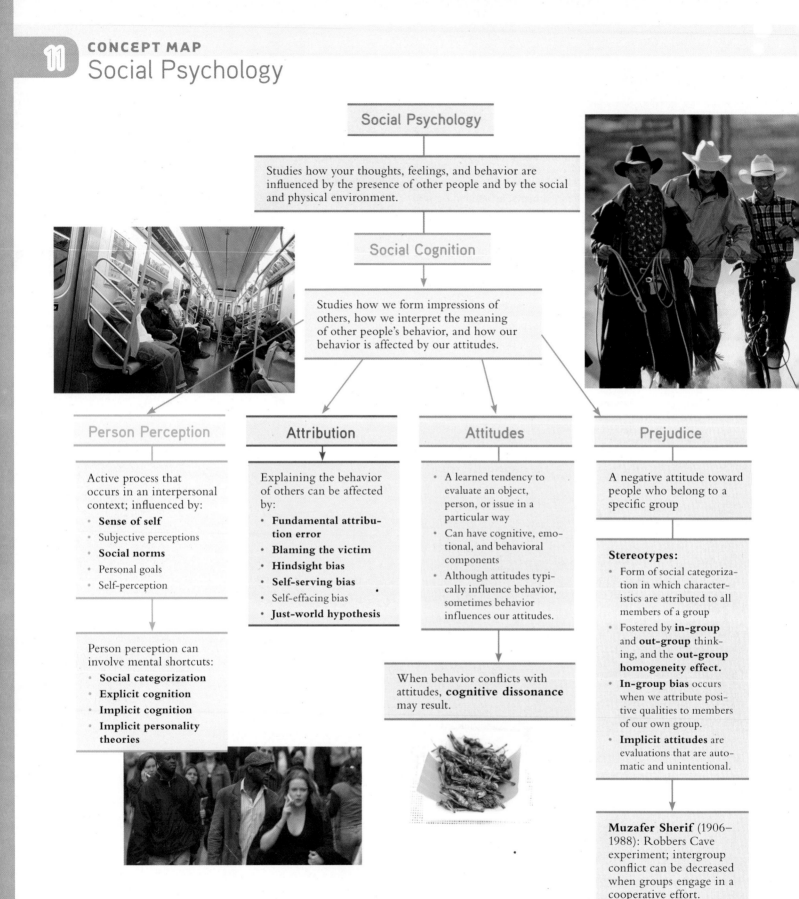

Social Psychology

Studies how your thoughts, feelings, and behavior are influenced by the presence of other people and by the social and physical environment.

Social Cognition

Studies how we form impressions of others, how we interpret the meaning of other people's behavior, and how our behavior is affected by our attitudes.

Person Perception

Active process that occurs in an interpersonal context; influenced by:
- **Sense of self**
- Subjective perceptions
- **Social norms**
- Personal goals
- Self-perception

Person perception can involve mental shortcuts:
- **Social categorization**
- **Explicit cognition**
- **Implicit cognition**
- **Implicit personality theories**

Attribution

Explaining the behavior of others can be affected by:
- **Fundamental attribution error**
- **Blaming the victim**
- **Hindsight bias**
- **Self-serving bias**
- Self-effacing bias
- **Just-world hypothesis**

Attitudes

- A learned tendency to evaluate an object, person, or issue in a particular way
- Can have cognitive, emotional, and behavioral components
- Although attitudes typically influence behavior, sometimes behavior influences our attitudes.

When behavior conflicts with attitudes, **cognitive dissonance** may result.

Prejudice

A negative attitude toward people who belong to a specific group

Stereotypes:
- Form of social categorization in which characteristics are attributed to all members of a group
- Fostered by **in-group** and **out-group** thinking, and the **out-group homogeneity effect.**
- **In-group bias** occurs when we attribute positive qualities to members of our own group.
- **Implicit attitudes** are evaluations that are automatic and unintentional.

Muzafer Sherif (1906–1988): Robbers Cave experiment; intergroup conflict can be decreased when groups engage in a cooperative effort.

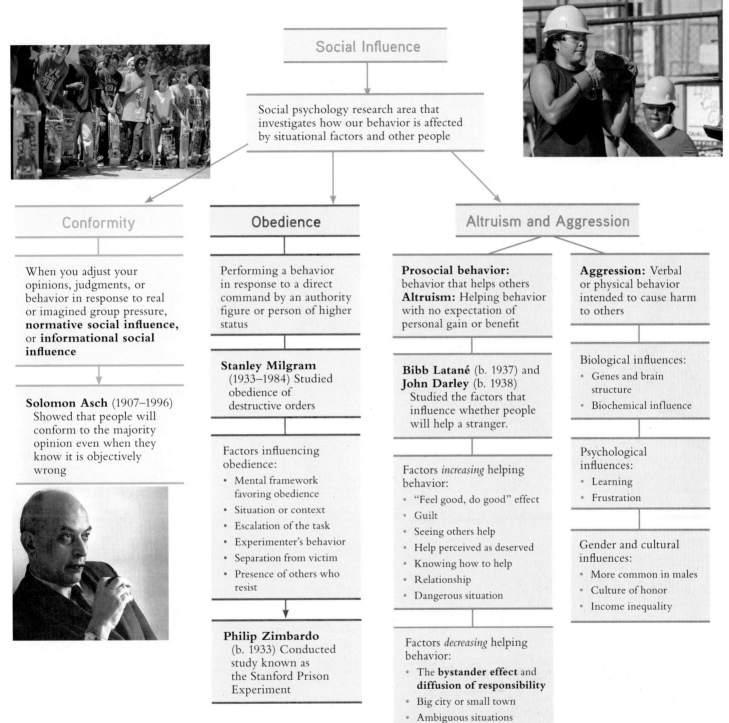

Social Influence

Social psychology research area that investigates how our behavior is affected by situational factors and other people

Conformity

When you adjust your opinions, judgments, or behavior in response to real or imagined group pressure, **normative social influence,** or **informational social influence**

Solomon Asch (1907–1996) Showed that people will conform to the majority opinion even when they know it is objectively wrong

Obedience

Performing a behavior in response to a direct command by an authority figure or person of higher status

Stanley Milgram (1933–1984) Studied obedience of destructive orders

Factors influencing obedience:
- Mental framework favoring obedience
- Situation or context
- Escalation of the task
- Experimenter's behavior
- Separation from victim
- Presence of others who resist

Philip Zimbardo (b. 1933) Conducted study known as the Stanford Prison Experiment

Altruism and Aggression

Prosocial behavior: behavior that helps others
Altruism: Helping behavior with no expectation of personal gain or benefit

Bibb Latané (b. 1937) and **John Darley** (b. 1938) Studied the factors that influence whether people will help a stranger.

Factors *increasing* helping behavior:
- "Feel good, do good" effect
- Guilt
- Seeing others help
- Help perceived as deserved
- Knowing how to help
- Relationship
- Dangerous situation

Factors *decreasing* helping behavior:
- The **bystander effect** and **diffusion of responsibility**
- Big city or small town
- Ambiguous situations
- Personal costs outweigh benefits

Aggression: Verbal or physical behavior intended to cause harm to others

Biological influences:
- Genes and brain structure
- Biochemical influence

Psychological influences:
- Learning
- Frustration

Gender and cultural influences:
- More common in males
- Culture of honor
- Income inequality

MYTH OR SCIENCE?

Is it true . . .

- That most people exposed to severe trauma will develop PTSD or other serious psychological problems?
- That all stress is bad for you?
- That stress is linked to premature aging?
- That pessimists handle stress better because they expect bad things to happen?
- That high-achieving people who work long hours are setting themselves up for a heart attack?
- That women derive more health benefits from marriage than men do?
- That the best way to comfort stressed-out friends or relatives is to give them advice and show them that the problem is not as bad as it seems?

FIRE AND ASH

PROLOGUE

HAWK WOKE UP, LUNGS AND EYES burning. Her friend's smoking always bothered her, but this couldn't just be cigarette smoke.

Pulling on her boots, Hawk went outside. Everything was saturated in a sickly, orange light. The air was filled with smoke, obscuring the sky and burning her throat. What was going on?

Hawk answered her ringing cell phone. "Hawk!" her mother said forcefully. "You need to come home, NOW. There's a fire over in Fourmile Canyon. We have to evacuate! Get up here right away and pack up whatever stuff you want to take with you."

Hawk's mind started racing. It was her last summer in the small house high in the pines above Boulder, Colorado, where she had lived her entire life. She had enlisted in the Air Force right after finishing high school and was due to report for boot camp in just a few weeks. Her stomach tightened as she realized that she might not have a home to return to.

Feeling numb, Hawk sped to the edge of town. The road up the mountain was blocked off, and a man wearing a Boulder County sheriff's uniform stopped her. "This area is closed now," he barked. "You should have come earlier!" But Hawk hadn't earned her nickname by being easily cowed. No one even noticed as she drove right up the mountain behind one of the fire department SUVs.

Standing in the doorway to her room, Hawk looked around blankly. She started grabbing items—clothes, sketchpads, her laptop. She panicked when she couldn't find the little box that held her father's medals and photos from his Marine service in Vietnam. She grabbed the flag that the Air Force had given her grandmother when her grandfather died.

"Hawk, come on, we need to leave," her mother called. Taking one last look around her room, Hawk reluctantly

Stress, Health, and Coping

IN THIS CHAPTER:

> **INTRODUCTION:** Stress and Health Psychology

> Physical Effects of Stress: The Mind–Body Connection

> Individual Factors That Influence the Response to Stress

> Coping: How People Deal with Stress

> **PSYCH FOR YOUR LIFE:** Minimizing the Effects of Stress

ran back down the stairs to her car. Most of their neighbors had already left. Chalk marked the doors to show that the sheriff had checked to make sure that no one was left inside.

Almost 1,500 miles away, Andi had just returned from kayaking along the Washington coast. It was Labor Day, the last day of her vacation before she headed home to Colorado. Late that afternoon, she checked her e-mail.

To: Andi
Subject: Fourmile fire
Hi Andi,
Wanted to let you know of a fire that may be headed toward your house. They are evacuating Fourmile and Sunshine Canyons, and Sugarloaf, too. I know you're not home so you're safe but wanted to let you know.
Andrea

Andi called her house. Four rings, and then the answering machine picked up. That meant the power was still on—and her house was still standing.

Meanwhile, back in Colorado, your author Sandy was anxiously monitoring the situation. Although nowhere near the path of the fire, she could see and smell the thick plumes of black smoke that filled the sky. When darkness came, brilliant orange flames

Partick Cullis

flickered all over the distant foothills, punctuated by occasional bursts of light when the fire flared up. Online, there were emergency bulletins, Twitter feeds, and even a Facebook page with posts about the fire, but there was nothing that could tell her whether her friends' homes had survived the fast-moving flames. No one knew anything other than that the fire was out of control and spreading rapidly.

Thousands of mountain residents had been forced to evacuate, some fleeing flames that reached 200 feet into the air. One man reported that his car bumper had melted in the intense heat as he drove through the fire.

Andi called home again. This time, her call went straight to voicemail. "At that moment," Andi said, "I knew my house was gone." All she had left was her car, one suitcase of clothes, her laptop, her kayak, and her dog, Nellie.

For days, the hot, dry winds blew, and the wildfires burned out of control. Firefighters fought to contain the fire and protect as many homes as they could. Trees and houses continued to explode. New fires broke out all over the rugged canyons and hills northwest of Boulder. "BOULDER ON EDGE," the headlines read. An

additional 9,000 people were told to prepare to evacuate their homes.

A few people illegally hiked into the burn area to see if their homes were still standing. Rumors flew, and the evacuees clamored for information at public meetings. But authorities were too busy fighting the fire to survey areas that were already destroyed.

Five days after the fire began, Hawk was able to return to her home, smoke-damaged but thankfully still standing. Six thousand acres had burned, and 169 homes were completely destroyed. Andi's house, where she had lived for 20 years, had burned to the ground.

Your author Sandy was one of a small group of friends who accompanied Andi in a caravan up to her land. The long dirt road to her property went through a blackened, barren, almost lunar-looking landscape.

And Andi's house? The main floor had completely collapsed into the lower floor, where we could make out the blackened outlines of her toppled

woodstove and dishwasher. Twisted pipes. Chunks of melted glass and metal, pieces of exploded pottery. There was nothing left—nothing but a six-inch-deep pile of rubble and ashes. "Wow," someone said softly.

Andi sucked in her breath and swallowed hard. She tried to say something cheerful, but it was all she could do to hold back tears. She had steeled herself to expect the worst, but nothing had prepared her for such complete devastation.

Most members of the community breathed a sigh of relief when the fires were finally out, when people could return home, when life could go back to normal. But for the nearly 200 families who had lost their homes, "normal" was just a memory. Where to live? How to begin replacing not just a house or a few lost treasures, but . . . *everything*?

It took days for Hawk and her mother to wash the soot off their windows, floors, and walls. But for Andi and the others who had lost their homes in the Colorado firestorm, the toughest challenges were ahead of them. As we explore the nature of stress and health psychology, we'll return to their stories. □

Cathy Steiner

INTRODUCTION:
Stress and Health Psychology

KEY THEME

When events are perceived as exceeding your ability to cope with them, you experience an unpleasant emotional and physical state called stress.

KEY QUESTIONS

❯ What is health psychology, and what is the biopsychosocial model?

❯ How do life events, traumatic events, daily hassles, and burnout contribute to stress?

❯ What are some social and cultural sources of stress?

As the fires raged on, the word *stress* seemed to be on everyone's lips. A major disaster in a small city has an impact that spreads far beyond those who are immediately affected. Even people whose homes were nowhere near the fire were tense, preoccupied, and worried. We all seemed to be holding our collective breath, and it wasn't just because of the thick, acrid smoke that made breathing difficult. People developed coughs, headaches, insomnia, and nightmares.

A wildfire raging through a densely populated area is an obvious source of psychological stress. However, most sources of stress are more mundane. As a college student, you are undoubtedly very familiar with feeling "stressed out." Juggling the demands of classes, work, friends, and family can be challenging. And, many of us report high levels of stress. An American Psychological Association survey of more than 2,000 Americans found that 20 percent reported extreme levels of stress—rating their stress an 8, 9, or 10 on a 10-point scale (APA, 2013).

What exactly is *stress*? It's one of those words that is frequently used but is hard to define precisely. Early stress researchers, who mostly studied animals, defined stress in terms of the physiological response to harmful or threatening events (see Selye, 1956). However, people are far more complex than animals in their response to potentially stressful events. Two people may respond very differently to the same potentially stressful event. And, as you'll see, not all stress is unhealthy.

Today, **stress** is generally defined as a negative emotional state occurring in response to events that are perceived as taxing or exceeding a person's resources or ability to cope. This definition emphasizes the important role played by a person's evaluation, or *appraisal*, of events in the experience of stress. According to the **cognitive appraisal model** developed by **Richard Lazarus,** whether we experience stress depends largely on our *cognitive appraisal* of an event and the resources we have to deal with the event (Lazarus & Folkman, 1984; Smith & Kirby, 2011).

If we think that we have adequate resources to deal with a situation, it will probably create little or no stress in our lives. But if we perceive our resources as being inadequate to deal with a situation we see as threatening, challenging, or even harmful, we'll experience the effects of stress. If our coping efforts are effective, stress will decrease. If they are ineffective, stress will increase. Figure 12.1 on the next page depicts the relationship between stress and appraisal.

In this chapter, we'll take a close look at stress and its effects. We'll also explore the intricate connections between mind and body—or, more accurately, among emotions, thoughts, behavior, physical responses, and health.

To illustrate how thoughts and feelings can affect physical reactions, try this thought experiment. As vividly as you can, recall a time when a close friend said something that made you angry or hurt your feelings. As you remember the details, note any physical sensations that arise. Can you feel your shoulders tensing, your stomach tightening, or a lump in your throat? Has your heart started beating faster or has your face flushed? If so, your thoughts alone produced a fleeting but concrete physical response.

stress A negative emotional state occurring in response to events that are perceived as taxing or exceeding a person's resources or ability to cope.

cognitive appraisal model of stress Developed by Richard Lazarus, a model of stress that emphasizes the role of an individual's evaluation (*appraisal*) of events and situations and of the resources that he or she has available to deal with the event or situation.

"Your mother and I are feeling overwhelmed, so you'll have to bring yourselves up."

David Sipress The New Yorker Collection/ The Cartoon Bank

FIGURE 12.1 **Stress and Appraisal** According to Richard Lazarus (1999), events are not stressful in and of themselves. Instead, the experience of stress is determined by your subjective response to external events or circumstances. If you believe you have the resources necessary to meet a challenge, you'll experience little or no stress. We evaluate—and re-evaluate—our coping responses as we deal with stressful circumstances. If our coping efforts are successful, stress will decrease. If unsuccessful, stress will increase.

Aleksandar Stojkovic/Shutterstock

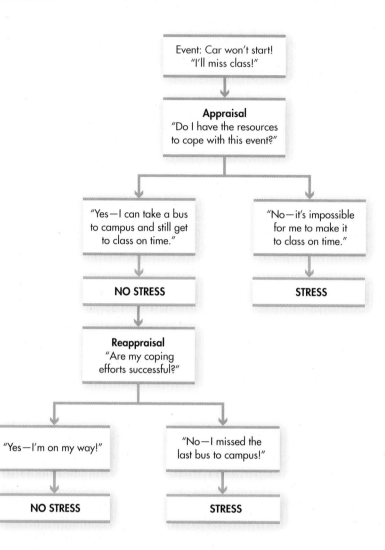

health psychology The branch of psychology that studies how biological, behavioral, and social factors influence health, illness, medical treatment, and health-related behaviors.

Can positive thoughts and memories also cause physical changes? To answer this, try another thought experiment. Rather than thinking of a painful incident, make a list of people, circumstances, or items for which you are thankful. The items can be as trivial as finding a parking space or as significant as good health. The content of your list doesn't matter, but don't stop until you have managed to come up with at least 10 items, no matter how inconsequential they might seem.

As you become more absorbed in this task, called a *gratitude list,* note how your body sensations begin to change. Many people begin to experience feelings of relaxation and calmness when they focus their attention on the things in their life for which they are thankful (Emmons & McCullough, 2003; Seligman & others, 2005). If you did, too, you've just seen how manipulating your thoughts can produce a positive effect on your body. In fact, studies have shown that actively expressing gratitude is linked to better physical health, better relationships, and lower levels of stress and depression (Emmons & Stern, 2013; Wood & others, 2008).

The relationship between mind and body is a key element in the field of **health psychology,** one of the most rapidly growing specialty areas in psychology. Health psychologists are interested in how psychological, social, emotional, and behavioral factors influence health, illness, and treatment.

Decades of research have confirmed that psychological and social factors make major contributions to physical health—and disease (G. E. Miller & others, 2009; Williams & others, 2011). Social factors that contribute to poor health include poverty, discrimination, and lack of access to medical and psychological care. Psychological factors like stress and depression, and other psychological disorders, also contribute to poor health outcomes. Finally, unhealthy behaviors—such as smoking, substance abuse, and sedentary lifestyles—are themselves leading causes of disability, disease, and death in modern society (Adler, 2009). Thus, health psychologists, with their knowledge of the principles of behavior and behavior change, have an important role to play in encouraging the development of healthy lifestyles—and discouraging unhealthy behaviors.

Along with developing strategies to foster emotional and physical well-being, health psychologists investigate issues such as the following:

- How to promote health-enhancing behaviors
- How people respond to being ill
- How people respond in the patient–health practitioner relationship

Health psychologists work with many different health care professionals, including physicians, nurses, social workers, and occupational and physical therapists. In their research and clinical practice, health psychologists are guided by the **biopsychosocial model.** According to this model, health and illness are determined by the complex interaction of *biological factors,* such as genetic predispositions; *psychological factors,* like health beliefs and attitudes; and *social factors,* like family relationships and cultural influences (G. E. Miller & others, 2009). In this chapter, we'll look closely at the roles that different biological, psychological, and social factors play in our experience of health and illness.

Sources of Stress

Life is filled with potential **stressors**—events or situations that produce stress. Virtually any event or situation can be a source of stress if you question your ability or resources to deal effectively with it (Cooper & Dewe, 2007; Lazarus & Folkman, 1984). In this section, we'll survey some of the most important and common sources of stress.

LIFE EVENTS AND CHANGE
IS *ANY* CHANGE STRESSFUL?

Early stress researchers Thomas Holmes and Richard Rahe (1967) believed that any change that required you to adjust your behavior and lifestyle would cause stress. In an attempt to measure the amount of stress people experienced, they developed the *Social Readjustment Rating Scale (SRRS).* The scale included 43 life events that are likely to require some level of adaptation. Each life event was assigned a numerical rating of its relative impact, ranging from 11 to 100 *life change units* (see Table 12.1). Cross-cultural studies have shown that people in many different cultures tend to rank the magnitude of stressful events in a similar way (McAndrew & others, 1998; Wong & Wong, 2006).

According to the life events approach, *any* change, whether positive or negative, is inherently stress-producing. Holmes and Rahe found that people who had accumulated more than 150 life change units within a year had an increased rate of physical or psychological illness (Holmes & Masuda, 1974; Rahe, 1972).

The original life events scale has been revised and updated so that it better weighs the influences of gender, age, marital status, and other individual characteristics (Hobson & Delunas, 2001). New scales have also been developed for specific groups (Dohrenwend, 2006). For instance, the College Student Stress Scale measures unique experiences of college student life that contribute to stress, such as "flunking a class" and "difficulties with parents" (Feldt, 2008).

Despite its popularity, there are several problems with the life events approach. First, the link between scores on the SRRS and the development of physical and psychological problems is relatively weak. In fact, researchers have found that most people weather major life events without developing serious physical or psychological problems (Monroe & Reid, 2009).

Second, the SRRS assumes that a given life event will have the same impact on virtually everyone. But clearly, the stress-producing potential of

biopsychosocial model The belief that physical health and illness are determined by the complex interaction of biological, psychological, and social factors.

stressors Events or situations that are perceived as harmful, threatening, or challenging.

TABLE 12.1

The Social Readjustment Rating Scale: Sample Items

Life Event	Life Change Units
Death of spouse	100
Divorce	73
Marital separation	65
Death of close family member	63
Major personal injury or illness	53
Marriage	50
Fired at work	47
Retirement	45
Pregnancy	40
Change in financial state	38
Death of close friend	37
Change to different line of work	36
Mortgage or loan for major purchase	31
Foreclosure on mortgage or loan	30
Change in work responsibilities	29
Outstanding personal achievement	28
Begin or end school	26
Trouble with boss	23
Change in work hours or conditions	20
Change in residence	20
Change in social activities	18
Change in sleeping habits	16
Vacation	13
Christmas	12
Minor violations of the law	11

SOURCE: Holmes & Rahe (1967).

The Social Readjustment Rating Scale, developed by Thomas Holmes and Richard Rahe (1967), was an early attempt to quantify the amount of stress experienced by people in a wide range of situations.

Major Life Events and Stress
Would the birth of a child or losing your home in a fire both produce damaging levels of stress? According to the life events approach, any event that required you to change or adjust your lifestyle would produce significant stress—whether the event was positive or negative, planned or unexpected. How was the life events approach modified by later research?

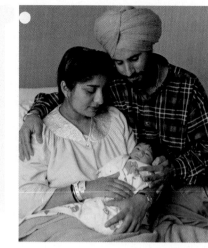

Jennifer Leigh Sauer/Getty Images

daily hassles Everyday minor events that annoy and upset people.

MYTH ◀ SCIENCE

Is it true that most people exposed to severe trauma will develop PTSD or other serious psychological problems?

FIGURE 12.2 Whatever Doesn't Kill You Makes You Stronger Psychologist Mark Seery and his colleagues (2010) found that people who had experienced *some* adversity in their lives handled new stressors better than people who had experienced either a high level of adversity or none at all. After experiencing a significant negative event, they were less distressed and experienced fewer posttraumatic stress symptoms. Even more important, they were generally happier with their lives than people whose lives had been either very hard or relatively carefree.

Source: Data from Seery & others (2010).

an event might vary widely from one person to another. For example, if you are in a marriage that is filled with conflict, getting divorced (73 life change units) might be significantly less stressful than remaining married.

Third, the life events approach assumes that change in itself, whether good or bad, produces stress. However, researchers have found that negative life events have a more adverse effect on health than positive events (Hatch & Dohrenwend, 2007). Today, most researchers agree that undesirable events are significant sources of stress but that change in itself is not *necessarily* stressful.

TRAUMATIC EVENTS

One category of life events deserves special mention. *Traumatic events* are events or situations that are negative, severe, and far beyond our normal expectations for everyday life or life events (Robinson & Larson, 2010). Witnessing or surviving a violent attack, serious accident, and experiences associated with combat, war, or major disasters are examples of the types of events that are typically considered to be traumatic.

Traumatic events are surprisingly common, especially among young adults. One large survey of college students found that 85 percent reported having been exposed to a traumatic event during their lifetime (Frazier & others, 2009). The most common traumatic events experienced by college students were the unexpected death of a loved one, sexual assault, and family violence.

Traumatic events, even relatively mild ones like a minor car accident, can be very stressful. When traumas are intense or repeated, some psychologically vulnerable people may develop *posttraumatic stress disorder* (abbreviated *PTSD*). As we will see in Chapter 13, PTSD is a disorder that involves intrusive thoughts of the traumatic event, emotional numbness, and symptoms of anxiety, such as nervousness, sleep disturbances, and irritability. However, it's important to note that *most* people recover from traumatic events without ever developing PTSD (Seery & others, 2010). For example, research shows that less than 30 percent of those who experience major disasters—such as floods, earthquakes, and hurricanes—develop PTSD (Bonanno & others, 2011). In reality, most people are remarkably resilient—a topic we discuss next.

DEVELOPING RESILIENCE

There's a famous saying that "whatever doesn't kill you makes you stronger." Psychologist Mark Seery and his colleagues (2010) set out to test that hypothesis in a multi-year, longitudinal study of the relationship between well-being and exposure to negative life events. They carefully measured health outcomes and *cumulative adversity*—defined as the total amount of negative events experienced over a lifetime—in a large, representative sample of U.S. adults.

Seery and his colleagues (2010) found that, as expected, *high* levels of cumulative adversity were associated with poor health outcomes. But, it turned out, so were very *low*

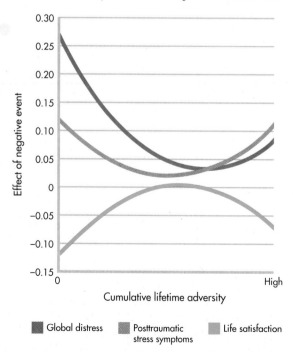

Cumulative lifetime adversity

■ Global distress   ■ Posttraumatic stress symptoms   ■ Life satisfaction

levels of adversity. As shown in Figure 12.2, faring best of all were people with a *moderate* level of adversity. They were not only healthier, but also better able to cope with recent misfortune than people who had experienced either very low or high levels of adversity. Experiencing *some* stress was healthier than experiencing no stress at all.

Why might experiencing some adversity be healthier, in the long run, than living a charmed, stress-free life? Seery argues that people who are *never* exposed to stressful, difficult events don't develop the ability to cope with adversity when it does occur—as it eventually does. So, even minor setbacks can be perceived as overwhelming.

In contrast, people who have had to cope with a moderate level of adversity develop *resilience*—the ability to cope with stress and adversity, to adapt to negative or unforeseen circumstances, and to rebound after negative experiences. Just as moderate exercise builds muscle and aerobic capacity, leading to physical fitness, moderate experience of adversity builds resilience.

DAILY HASSLES
THAT'S NOT WHAT I ORDERED!

What made you feel "stressed out" in the past week? Chances are, it was not a major life event. Instead, it was probably some unexpected but minor annoyance, such as splotching ketchup on your new T-shirt, misplacing your keys, or getting into an argument with your roommate.

Stress researcher Richard Lazarus and his colleagues suspected that such ordinary irritations in daily life might be an important source of stress. To explore this idea, they developed a scale measuring **daily hassles**—everyday occurrences that annoy and upset people (DeLongis & others, 1982; Kanner & others, 1981). Table 12.2 lists examples from the original Daily Hassles Scale and from other scales developed for specific populations.

The frequency of daily hassles, as well as a tendency to react more negatively to hassles, are linked to mental and physical illness, unhealthy behaviors, and decreased well-being (Charles & others, 2013; O'Connor & others, 2008). Some researchers have found that the number of daily hassles people experience is a better predictor of physical illness and symptoms than is the number of major life events experienced (Almeida & others, 2005). And, experiencing daily hassles as a child is predictive of poorer health as an adult (Odgers & Jaffee, 2013).

Why do daily hassles take such a toll? One explanation is that such minor stressors are *cumulative* (Grzywacz & Almeida, 2008). Each hassle may be relatively unimportant in itself, but after a day or two filled with minor hassles, the effects add up. People feel drained, grumpy, and stressed out.

Daily hassles also contribute to the stress produced by major life events. Any major life change can create a ripple effect, generating a host of new daily hassles (Maybery & others, 2007). For example, people who lost their homes in the wildfire had to scramble to find temporary housing, navigate insurance paperwork, and purchase all the essentials of everyday life that we take for granted. As Andi said, "Imagine if you picked up your house, turned it upside down, and shook it. Now imagine having to describe each and every item that fell out, including where you got it and how much it cost. Think about doing that for every towel, sock, pair of jeans, plate and coffee cup and rug and T-shirt and dog toy that you own. It's a nightmare."

Are there gender differences in the experience of daily hassles? Interpersonal conflict is the most common source of daily stress for *both* men and women (Almeida & others, 2005). However, women are more likely to report daily stress that is associated with friends and family, while men are more likely to feel hassled by stressors that are school- or work-related (Zwicker & DeLongis, 2010). For both sexes, stress at work or school tends to affect home life (Bodenmann & others, 2010).

MYTH ◄ SCIENCE

Is it true that all stress is bad for you?

TABLE 12.2

Examples of Daily Hassles

Daily Hassles Scale
- Concern about weight
- Concern about health of family member
- Not enough money for housing
- Too many things to do
- Misplacing or losing things
- Too many interruptions
- Don't like current work duties
- Traffic
- Car repairs or transportation problems

College Daily Hassles Scale
- Increased class workload
- Troubling thoughts about your future
- Fight with boyfriend/girlfriend
- Concerns about meeting high standards
- Wasting time
- Computer problems
- Concerns about failing a course
- Concerns about money

Acculturative Daily Hassles for Children
- It bothers me when people force me to be like everyone else.
- Because of the group I'm in, I don't get the grades I deserve.
- I don't feel at home here in the United States.
- People think I'm shy, when I really just have trouble speaking English.
- I think a lot about my group and its culture.

SOURCES: Research from Blankstein & Flett, 1992; Kanner & others, 1981; Ross & others, 1999; Staats & others, 2007; Suarez-Morales & others, 2007.

Arguing that "daily hassles" could be just as stress-inducing as major life events, Richard Lazarus and his colleagues constructed a 117-item Daily Hassles Scale. Later, other researchers developed daily hassles scales for specific groups.

Major Life Events, Daily Hassles, and Stress: Kathmandu, 2015 A major earthquake struck Nepal in April 2015, forcing thousands of Nepalis from homes rendered unsafe by the initial quake and the frequent aftershocks. For weeks, people lived in tents and other makeshift shelters, waiting for the ground to stop shaking. Here, Kathmandu residents and others evacuated from nearby villages wait in long lines for food and water. The daily hassles created by major disasters add to the high level of stress felt by all those affected.

The Yomiuri Shimbun via AP Images

For women, daily stress tends to spill over into their interactions with their partners. Men, on the other hand, are more likely to simply withdraw. In fact, one study found that the most likely place to find a father after a stressful day at work was sitting alone in a room (Repetti & others, 2009).

WORK STRESS AND BURNOUT
IS IT QUITTING TIME YET?

Jason Patterson The New Yorker Collection/The Cartoon Bank

Whether due to concerns about job security, unpleasant working conditions, difficult co-workers and supervisors, or unreasonable demands and deadlines, *work stress* can produce a pressure cooker environment that takes a significant toll on your physical health (Nakao, 2010). It can also increase the likelihood of unhealthy behaviors. For example, college students who experienced high levels of work stress also consumed more alcohol than other students (Butler & others, 2010).

When work stress is prolonged and becomes chronic, it can produce a stress response called **burnout.** There are three key components of burnout (Maslach & Leiter, 2005, 2008). First, people feel *exhausted,* as if they've used up all of their emotional and physical resources. Second, people experience feelings of *cynicism,* demonstrating negative or overly detached attitudes toward the job or work environment. People also often feel unappreciated (Demerouti & others, 2010). Third, people feel a sense of *failure or inadequacy.* They may feel incompetent and unproductive and have a sharply reduced sense of accomplishment. In fact, some researchers have observed a great deal of overlap between the symptoms of burnout and the symptoms of major depressive disorder (Bianchi & others, 2015). (We'll learn more about major depressive disorder in Chapter 13 on psychological disorders.)

One workplace condition that commonly produces burnout is work *overload,* when the demands of the job exceed the worker's ability to meet them (Maslach & Leiter, 2008). A second is *lack of control.* Generally, the more control you have over your work and work environment, the less stressful it is (Q. Wang & others, 2010). Complex, demanding jobs are much less likely to produce feelings of overload, burnout, or stress when workers have control over how they perform those jobs (Chung-Yan, 2010).

However, even in high-stress occupations or demanding work environments, burnout can be prevented. Burnout is least likely to occur when there is a sense of *community* in the workplace (Maslach & Leiter, 2008; Woodhead & others, 2014). Supportive co-workers, a sense of teamwork, and a positive work environment can all buffer workplace stress and prevent burnout.

burnout An unhealthy condition caused by chronic, prolonged work stress that is characterized by exhaustion, cynicism, and a sense of failure or inadequacy.

SOCIAL AND CULTURAL SOURCES OF STRESS

For disadvantaged groups exposed to crowding, crime, poverty, and substandard housing, everyday living conditions can be a significant source of stress (Gallo & others, 2009; Haushofer & Fehr, 2014; King & Ogle, 2014). People who live under difficult or unpleasant conditions often experience ongoing, or *chronic,* stress (Adler & Rehkopf, 2008).

Chronic stress is also associated with lower *socioeconomic status* (SES), which is a measure of overall status in society (Chandola & Marmot, 2011). The core components of SES are income, education, and occupation. One finding that has been consistent over time and across multiple cultures is the strong association of physical health and longevity with SES (Adler, 2009).

People in lower SES groups tend to experience more negative life events *and* more daily hassles than people in more privileged groups (Hatch & Dohrenwend, 2007). People in less privileged groups also tend to have fewer resources to help them cope with the stressors that they do experience. Thus, it's not surprising that people in the lowest socioeconomic levels tend to have the highest levels of psychological distress, illness, and premature death (Braveman & others, 2010).

Beyond these external factors, low social status is in itself highly stressful (Hackman & others, 2010). Many studies have shown that perceiving yourself as being of low social status is associated with poorer physical health—*regardless* of your objective social status as measured by traditional SES measures (Adler, 2009; Derry & others, 2013).

The powerful effects of perceived social status were convincingly demonstrated in a study by Sheldon Cohen and his colleagues (2008). Volunteers were exposed to a cold virus (see Figure 12.3). The volunteers who saw themselves as being low on the social status totem pole had higher rates of infection than volunteers who *objectively* matched them on social status measures but *subjectively* did not see themselves as being of low status (Cohen & others, 2008).

Racism and discrimination are other important sources of chronic stress for many people (Brondolo & others, 2011; Ong & others, 2009). In one survey, for example, more than three-quarters of African American adolescents reported being treated as incompetent or dangerous—or both—because of their race (Sellers & others, 2006). Such subtle instances of racism, called *microaggressions,* take a cumulative toll (Schmitt & others, 2014; Sue & others, 2008). Whether it's subtle or blatant, racism significantly contributes to the chronic stress often experienced by members of minority groups. Racism can also increase the risk for stress-related health problems such as hypertension (Hicken & others, 2014).

Stress can also result when cultures clash. For refugees, immigrants, and their children, adapting to a new culture can be extremely stress-producing (Berry, 2003; Jamil & others, 2007). The Culture and Human Behavior box "The Stress of Adapting to a New Culture" on the next page describes factors that influence the degree of stress experienced by people encountering a new culture.

FIGURE 12.3 Subjective Socioeconomic Status and Health The *objective* socioeconomic status of a group of volunteers was assessed in terms of income level and education. The volunteers' *subjective* social status was assessed by showing them a picture of a ladder and asking them to indicate where they thought they stood relative to their fellow Americans in terms of income, education, and occupation. All the volunteers were then exposed to a cold virus. Even after controlling for factors such as smoking and other risk factors, Sheldon Cohen and his colleagues (2008) found that subjective, rather than objective, social status was associated with susceptibility to infection. Regardless of their objective socioeconomic status, participants who perceived themselves as being lower in social status were more susceptible to infection than those who did not.

Source: Data from Cohen & others (2008).

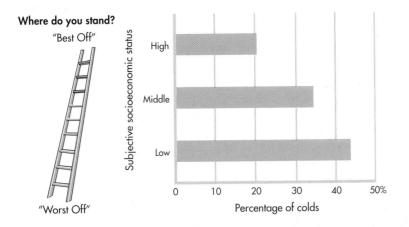

CULTURE AND HUMAN BEHAVIOR

The Stress of Adapting to a New Culture

Refugees, immigrants, and even international students are often unprepared for the dramatically different values, language, food, customs, and climate that await them in their new land. The process of changing one's values and customs as a result of contact with another culture is referred to as *acculturation*. **Acculturative stress** is the stress that results from the pressure of adapting to a new culture (Sam & Berry, 2010).

Cross-cultural psychologist John Berry (2003, 2006) has found that a person's attitudes are important in determining how much acculturative stress is experienced (Sam & Berry, 2010). When people encounter a new cultural environment, they are faced with two questions: (1) Should I seek positive relations with the dominant society? (2) Is my original cultural identity of value to me, and should I try to maintain it?

The answers produce one of four possible patterns of acculturation: integration, assimilation, separation, or marginalization (see the diagram). Each pattern represents a different way of coping with the stress of adapting to a new culture (Berry, 1994, 2003).

Integrated individuals continue to value their original cultural customs but also seek to become part of the dominant society. They embrace a *bicultural* identity (Huynh & others, 2011). Biculturalism is associated with higher self-esteem and lower levels of depression, anxiety, and stress, suggesting that the bicultural identity may be the most adaptive acculturation pattern (Schwartz & others, 2010). In fact, a meta-analysis of 83 studies showed that biculturalism had the strongest association with psychological and social adjustment (Nguyen & Benet-Martínez, 2013). The successfully integrated individual's level of acculturative stress will be low (Lee, 2010).

Assimilated individuals give up their old cultural identity and try to become part of the new society. They adopt the customs and social values of the new environment, and abandon their original cultural traditions.

Assimilation usually involves a moderate level of stress, partly because it involves a psychological loss—one's previous cultural identity. People who follow this pattern also face the possibility of being rejected either by members of the majority culture or by members of their original culture (Schwartz & others, 2010). The process of learning new behaviors and suppressing old behaviors can also be moderately stressful.

Joe Raedle/Getty Images

Acculturative Stress Acculturative stress can be reduced when immigrants learn the language and customs of their newly adopted home. Here, two friends, one from China, one from Cuba, help each other in an English class in Miami, Florida.

Individuals who follow the pattern of *separation* maintain their cultural identity and avoid contact with the new culture. They may refuse to learn the new language, live in a neighborhood that is primarily populated by others of the same ethnic background, and socialize only with members of their own ethnic group.

In some cases, separation is not voluntary, but is due to the dominant society's unwillingness to accept the new immigrants. Thus, it can be the result of discrimination. Whether voluntary or involuntary, the level of acculturative stress associated with separation tends to be high.

Finally, *marginalized* people lack cultural and psychological contact with *both* their traditional cultural group and the culture of their new society. By taking the path of marginalization, they lost the important features of their traditional culture but have not replaced them with a new cultural identity.

Although rare, the path of marginalization is associated with the greatest degree of acculturative stress. Marginalized individuals are stuck in an unresolved conflict between their traditional culture and the new society, and may feel as if they don't really belong anywhere. Fortunately, only a small percentage of immigrants fall into this category (Schwartz & others, 2010).

	Question 1: Should I seek positive relations with the dominant society?	
	Yes	**No**
Question 2: Is my original cultural identity of value to me, and should I try to maintain it? **Yes**	Integration	Separation
No	Assimilation	Marginalization

Patterns of Adapting to a New Culture According to cross-cultural psychologist John Berry, there are four basic patterns of adapting to a new culture (Sam & Berry, 2010). Which pattern is followed depends on how the person responds to the two key questions shown.

Source: Research from Sam & Berry (2010).

Physical Effects of Stress
THE MIND–BODY CONNECTION

KEY THEME

Stress affects physical health through its effects on the endocrine system, the immune system, and chromosomes.

KEY QUESTIONS

› What endocrine pathways are involved in the fight-or-flight response and the general adaptation syndrome?

› What are telomeres, and how are they affected by acute and chronic stress?

› What is psychoneuroimmunology, and how does the immune system interact with the nervous system?

From headaches to heart attacks, stress contributes to a wide range of disorders, especially when it is long-term, or chronic. Basically, stress appears to undermine physical well-being in two ways: indirectly and directly.

First, stress can *indirectly* affect a person's health by prompting behaviors that jeopardize physical well-being, such as not eating or sleeping properly or failing to get enough exercise (Habhab & others, 2009; Mezick & others, 2009; Stults-Kolehmainen & Sinha, 2014). High levels of stress can also interfere with cognitive abilities, such as attention, concentration, memory, and decision making (McNeil & Morgan, 2010; Thompson, 2010). In turn, such cognitive disruptions can increase the likelihood of accidents and injuries.

Second, stress can *directly* affect physical health by altering body functions, leading to physical symptoms, illness, or disease (Zachariae, 2009). For example, people who are under a great deal of stress often tighten their neck and head muscles, resulting in tension headaches. Even stress experienced early in life can lead to cancer or diabetes later in life (Fagundes & Way, 2014). But exactly how do stressful events influence bodily processes, such as muscle contractions?

Stress and the Endocrine System

To explain the connection between stress and health, researchers have focused on how the nervous system, including the brain, interacts with two other important body systems: the endocrine and immune systems. We'll first consider the role of the endocrine system in our response to stressful events and then look at the connections between stress and the immune system.

WALTER CANNON
STRESS AND THE FIGHT-OR-FLIGHT RESPONSE

Any kind of immediate threat to your well-being is a stress-producing experience that triggers a cascade of changes in your body. As we've noted in previous chapters, this rapidly occurring chain of internal physical reactions is called the **fight-or-flight response.** Collectively, these changes prepare us either to fight or to take flight from an immediate threat.

The fight-or-flight response was first described by American physiologist **Walter Cannon,** one of the earliest contributors to stress research. Cannon (1932) found that the fight-or-flight response involved both the sympathetic nervous system and the endocrine system (see Chapter 2).

With the perception of a threat, the hypothalamus and lower brain structures activate the sympathetic nervous system (see left side of Figure 12.4 on the next page). The sympathetic nervous system stimulates the adrenal medulla to secrete hormones called **catecholamines,** including *adrenaline* and *noradrenaline.* Circulating through the blood, catecholamines trigger the rapid and intense bodily changes associated with the fight-or-flight response. Once the threat is removed, the high level of bodily arousal subsides gradually, usually within about 20 to 60 minutes.

acculturative stress (uh-CUL-chur-uh-tiv) The stress that results from the pressure of adapting to a new culture.

fight-or-flight response A rapidly occurring chain of internal physical reactions that prepare people to either fight or take flight from an immediate threat.

catecholamines (cat-uh-COLE-uh-meenz) Hormones secreted by the adrenal medulla that cause rapid physiological arousal, including adrenaline and noradrenaline.

Walter B. Cannon (1875–1945) Cannon made many lasting contributions to psychology, including an influential theory of emotion, which we discussed in Chapter 8. During World War I, Cannon's research on the effects of stress and trauma led him to identify the body's response to threatening circumstances—the *fight-or-flight response.*

Edgar Fahs Smith Collection, University of Pennsylvania Library

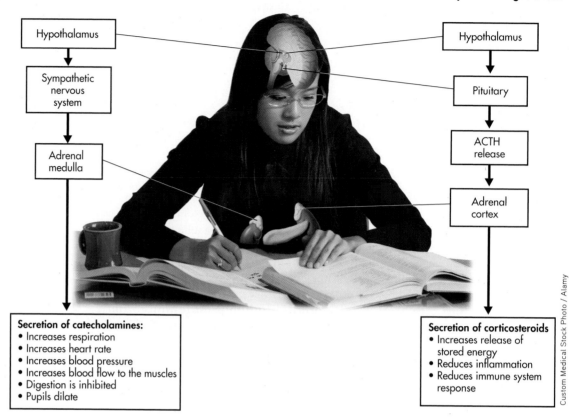

Pathway 1: Acute stress

Pathway 2: Prolonged stress

FIGURE 12.4
Endocrine System Pathways in Stress Two different endocrine system pathways are involved in the response to stress (Joëls & Baram, 2009). Walter Cannon identified the endocrine pathway shown on the left side of this diagram. This is the pathway involved in the fight-or-flight response to immediate threats. Hans Selye identified the endocrine pathway shown on the right. This second endocrine pathway plays an important role in dealing with prolonged, or chronic, stressors.

Hypothalamus

Sympathetic nervous system

Adrenal medulla

Hypothalamus

Pituitary

ACTH release

Adrenal cortex

Secretion of catecholamines:
• Increases respiration
• Increases heart rate
• Increases blood pressure
• Increases blood flow to the muscles
• Digestion is inhibited
• Pupils dilate

Secretion of corticosteroids:
• Increases release of stored energy
• Reduces inflammation
• Reduces immune system response

Custom Medical Stock Photo / Alamy

As a short-term reaction, the fight-or-flight response helps ensure survival by swiftly mobilizing internal physical resources to defensively attack or flee an immediate threat. Without question, the fight-or-flight response is very useful if you're suddenly faced with a life-threatening situation, such as having to flee your house when you see a wall of flame come over the ridge. However, if exposure to a threat is prolonged, the intense arousal of the fight-or-flight response can also become prolonged. And humans often experience intense and prolonged stress even in situations that are not life-threatening. As researcher Robert Sapolsky points out, "No zebra on earth, running for its life, would understand why fear of speaking in public would cause you to secrete the same hormones that it's doing at that point to save its life" (National Geographic, 2008). Under these conditions, Cannon believed, the fight-or-flight response could prove harmful to physical health.

HANS SELYE

STRESS AND THE GENERAL ADAPTATION SYNDROME

A Pioneer in Stress Research With his tie off and his feet up, Canadian endocrinologist Hans Selye (1907–1982) looks the picture of relaxation. Selye documented the physical effects of exposure to prolonged stress. His popular book *The Stress of Life* (1956) helped make *stress* a household word.

Time & Life Pictures/Getty Images

Cannon's suggestion that prolonged stress could be physically harmful was confirmed by Canadian endocrinologist **Hans Selye.** Most of Selye's pioneering research was done with rats that were exposed to prolonged stressors, such as electric shock, extreme heat or cold, or forced exercise. Regardless of the condition that Selye used to produce prolonged stress, he found the same pattern of physical changes in the rats. First, the adrenal glands became enlarged. Second, stomach ulcers and loss of weight occurred. And third, there was shrinkage of the thymus gland and lymph glands, two key components of the immune system. Selye believed that these distinct physical changes represented the essential effects of stress—the body's response to any demand placed on it.

Selye (1956, 1976) found that prolonged stress activates a second endocrine pathway (see Figure 12.4) that involves the hypothalamus, the pituitary gland, and the adrenal cortex. In response to a stressor, the hypothalamus signals the pituitary gland to secrete a hormone called *adrenocorticotropic hormone,* abbreviated *ACTH.* In turn, ACTH stimulates the adrenal cortex to release stress-related hormones called **corticosteroids,** the most important of which is *cortisol.*

In the short run, the corticosteroids provide several benefits, helping protect the body against the harm caused by stressors. For example, corticosteroids reduce inflammation of body tissues and enhance muscle tone in the heart and blood vessels. However, unlike the effects of catecholamines, which tend to diminish rather quickly, corticosteroids have long-lasting effects. If a stressor is prolonged, continued high levels of corticosteroids can weaken important body systems, lowering immunity and increasing susceptibility to physical symptoms of illness.

Selye (1976) showed that the devastating effects of prolonged stress developed in three progressive stages, producing what he termed the **general adaptation syndrome.** These stages include:

1. *Alarm stage:* Catecholamines are released by the adrenal medulla. Intense arousal occurs, and the body mobilizes internal physical resources to meet the demands of the stress-producing event.

2. *Resistance stage:* As the body tries to adapt to the continuing stressful situation, physiological arousal lessens but remains above normal. Resistance to new stressors is impaired.

3. *Exhaustion stage:* If the stress-producing event persists, the symptoms of the alarm stage reappear, only now irreversibly. The body's energy reserves become depleted and adaptation begins to break down, leading to exhaustion, physical disorders, and, potentially, death.

Selye's description of the general adaptation syndrome firmly established some of the critical biological links between stress-producing events and their potential impact on physical health. There is mounting evidence that chronic stress can lead to increased vulnerability to acute and chronic physical diseases, as well as psychological problems (Hammen, 2005; G. E. Miller & others, 2009). And, as we'll see in the next section, there is new evidence explaining the link between chronic stress and premature aging.

Stress, Chromosomes, and Aging
THE TELOMERE STORY

Diseases associated with aging and even premature aging itself have long been associated with chronic stress (Epel, 2009a; Kiecolt-Glaser & Glaser, 2010). But how might psychological stress affect physical aging?

One part of the answer may ultimately be found in the chromosomes. **Telomeres** are repeated, duplicate DNA sequences that are found at the very tips of chromosomes (see Figure 12.5). Like the plastic tips that protect shoelaces from fraying, telomeres

corticosteroids (core-tick-oh-STER-oydz) Hormones released by the adrenal cortex that play a key role in the body's response to long-term stressors.

general adaptation syndrome Hans Selye's term for the three-stage progression of physical changes that occur when an organism is exposed to intense and prolonged stress. The three stages are alarm, resistance, and exhaustion.

telomeres Repeated, duplicate DNA sequences that are found at the very tips of chromosomes and that protect the chromosomes' genetic data during cell division.

For an overview of stress and its effects on the brain, try the **Video Activity: Stress**.

FIGURE 12.5 Telomeres As shown in the drawing, *telomeres* are short, repeated DNA sequences that are found at the very tips of chromosomes (Epel, 2009b). In the photo, the telomeres are the fluorescent tips on the blue-stained human chromosomes. Like the plastic tips that protect shoelaces from fraying, telomeres protect the genetic data in the chromosomes from being broken or scrambled during cell division. With each cell division, the telomeres get shorter. However, an enzyme called *telomerase* can protect and even lengthen telomeres. Psychologists today are actively studying the environmental factors that affect telomere length, including behavioral interventions that increase telomerase activity (Blackburn & Epel, 2012; Jacobs & others, 2011).

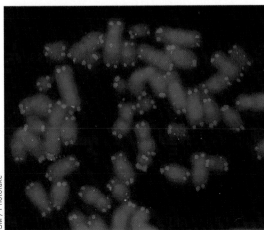

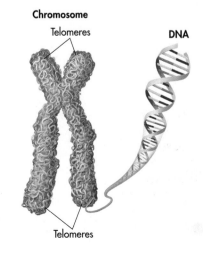

Chromosome

Telomeres

DNA

Telomeres

protect the genetic data in the chromosomes from being broken or scrambled during cell division. With each cell division, the string of telomeres gets shorter. When telomeres become too short, the cell can no longer divide and may die or atrophy, causing tissue damage or loss. A growing body of literature has linked shorter telomeres with aging, age-related diseases, and mortality (Blackburn & Epel, 2012; Révész & others, 2014).

Although telomere length is roughly reflective of a cell's age, the story is not that simple. Surprisingly, telomeres can also *lengthen* in response to physiological changes (Epel, 2009b). An enzyme called *telomerase* has the capacity to add DNA to shortened telomeres, rebuilding and extending the length of telomeres (Epel & others, 2010).

Could telomeres be implicated in the link between stress and premature aging? The tentative answer seems to be *yes*. First, several studies have linked elevated levels of stress hormones cortisol and the catecholamines to shorter telomeres (see Epel, 2009b). Second, researchers have discovered that people who are under chronic stress tend to have shortened telomeres (Schutte & Malouff, 2014).

In a groundbreaking study that compared mothers of chronically ill children with mothers of healthy children, Elissa Epel and her colleagues (2004) found that caring for a chronically ill child was inversely associated with telomere length. That is, the longer the caregiving time, the shorter were the telomeres. Further, telomeres were shortest in mothers who perceived themselves as being under a great deal of stress, regardless of whether their children were healthy or ill (see Figure 12.6). Subsequent research has found that many types of chronic stress are associated with unusually short telomeres (Blackburn & Epel, 2012). For example, 9-year-old boys living in a stressful family environment had telomeres that were, on average, 40 percent shorter than those in 9-year-old boys living in nurturing family environments (Mitchell & others, 2014).

A clever study by Elissa Epel and colleagues (2010) provides the strongest evidence to date for a direct link between psychological stress and telomere length. Telomerase activity in "chronic-stress" older women who were caregivers for people with dementia was compared with telomerase activity in a "low-stress" matched control group. At the beginning of the study, telomerase activity was measured and found to be lower in the chronic-stress women than in the low-stress women.

All of the participants were exposed to an acute laboratory stressor: Each had to deliver an impromptu speech in front of stony-faced judges and then take a math test. How did telomerase respond to acute stress? Within 90 minutes of experiencing the acute stress, telomerase activity increased by almost 20 percent in both groups of women. And, those participants who perceived the laboratory stressor as most threatening had the highest telomerase response (see Figure 12.7).

FIGURE 12.6 Perceived Stress and Telomere Length In a ground-breaking study, psychologist Elissa Epel and her colleagues (2004) compared telomere length in mothers of chronically ill children with telomere length in mothers of healthy children. Even after controlling for chronological age and other biological factors, telomeres were significantly shorter in women who perceived themselves as being under a great deal of stress than in those who did not. How significant was the difference? The reduction in telomere length in the highly stressed women was roughly equivalent to more than a decade of normal aging (Epel & others, 2004).

Source: Data from Epel & others (2004).

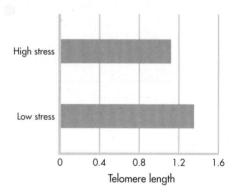

FIGURE 12.7 Effects of Chronic and Acute Stress on Telomerase Activity *Telomerase* is an enzyme that protects and lengthens telomeres. In an experiment by Elissa Epel and her colleagues (2010), telomerase activity was lower in women who were under chronic stress ("caregivers") than it was in a control group of women who were not under stress. In response to an acute stressor in the laboratory, telomerase activity rose sharply in both groups. Even at its peak, however, telomerase activity in the chronic stress group remained significantly below that of the control group.

Data from Epel & others (2010).

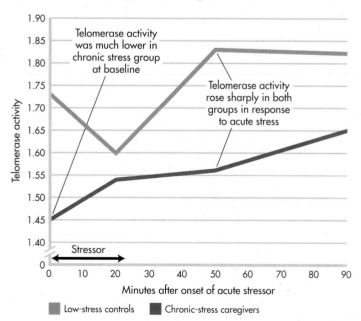

Epel's research is the first experimental demonstration that telomerase activity is directly affected by acute psychological stress. Acute, short-term stress produced a positive, *adaptive* effect on telomerase activity; chronic stress had a negative, *maladaptive* effect on telomerase activity.

Although research on telomeres and telomerase activity is still in its infancy, new findings suggest potential interventions that might someday be used to target telomeres to improve health and prevent age-related degenerative diseases. For example, research suggests that engaging in healthy behaviors—such as eating well, exercising, and getting enough sleep—helps protect telomeres from the effects of stress (Puterman & others, 2010; Puterman & others, 2015). Researchers are also actively investigating the impact of factors like stress management, meditation, and diet on telomeres (Epel & others, 2009; Jacobs & others, 2011; Ornish & others, 2008).

immune system Body system that produces specialized white blood cells that protect the body from viruses, bacteria, and tumor cells.

lymphocytes (LIMF-oh-sites) Specialized white blood cells that are responsible for immune defenses.

psychoneuroimmunology An interdisciplinary field that studies the interconnections among psychological processes, nervous and endocrine system functions, and the immune system.

Stress and the Immune System

The **immune system** is your body's surveillance system. It detects and battles foreign invaders, such as bacteria, viruses, and tumor cells. Your immune system comprises several organs, including bone marrow, the spleen, the thymus, and the lymph nodes (see Figure 12.8). The most important elements of the immune system are **lymphocytes**—the specialized white blood cells that fight bacteria, viruses, and other foreign invaders. Lymphocytes are initially manufactured in the bone marrow. From the bone marrow, they migrate to other immune system organs, such as the thymus and spleen, where they develop more fully and are stored until needed.

Lymphocytes in Action This color-enhanced photo shows white blood cells, or lymphocytes, attacking and ingesting the beadlike chain of streptococcus bacteria, which can cause pneumonia.

PSYCHONEUROIMMUNOLOGY

Until the 1970s, the immune system was thought to be completely independent of other body systems, including the nervous and endocrine systems. Thus, most scientists believed that psychological processes could not influence the immune system response.

However, research in a new interdisciplinary field called *psychoneuroimmunology* helped establish that there are many interconnections among these systems, including the brain (Ader, 1993). **Psychoneuroimmunology** is the scientific study of the connections among psychological processes *(psycho-)*, the nervous system *(-neuro-)*, and the immune system *(-immunology)*.

First, the central nervous system and the immune system are *directly* linked via sympathetic nervous system fibers, which influence the production and functioning of lymphocytes.

Second, the surfaces of lymphocytes contain receptor sites for neurotransmitters and hormones, including catecholamines and cortisol. Thus, rather than operating independently, the activities of lymphocytes and the immune system are directly influenced by neurotransmitters, hormones, and other chemical messengers from the nervous and endocrine systems.

Third, psychoneuroimmunologists have discovered that lymphocytes themselves *produce* neurotransmitters and hormones. These neurotransmitters and hormones, in turn, influence the nervous and endocrine systems. In other words, there is ongoing interaction and communication among the nervous system, the endocrine system, and the immune system (Kendall-Tackett, 2010). Each system influences *and* is influenced by the other systems (Kiecolt-Glaser, 2009).

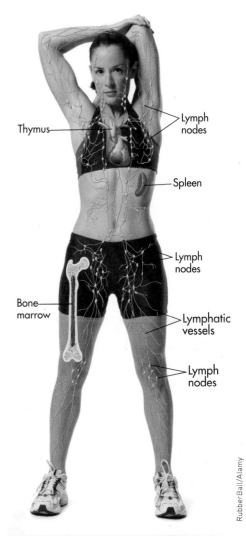

FIGURE 12.8 The Immune System Your immune system battles bacteria, viruses, and other foreign invaders that try to set up housekeeping in your body. The specialized white blood cells that fight infection are manufactured in the bone marrow and are stored in the thymus, spleen, and lymph nodes until needed.

STRESSORS THAT CAN INFLUENCE THE IMMUNE SYSTEM

When researchers began studying how stress affects the immune system, they initially focused on extremely stressful events, such as the reentry of returning astronauts or being forced to stay awake for days (see Kiecolt-Glaser & Glaser, 1993). These highly stressful events, it turned out, were associated with reduced immune system functioning.

Subsequent research found that immune system functioning was also affected by more common stresses. For example, the stress caused by the end or disruption of important interpersonal relationships impairs immune function, putting people at greater risk for health problems (Kiecolt-Glaser & others, 2009; Wright & Loving, 2011). And perhaps not surprisingly, chronic stressors that continue for years, such as caring for a family member with Alzheimer's disease, also diminish immune system functioning (Jeckel & others, 2010). Even ordinary stressors, such as marital arguments or the pressure of exams, can adversely affect the immune system (Lester & others, 2010).

What are the practical implications of reduced immune system functioning? One consistent finding is that psychological stress increases the length of time it takes for a wound to heal. In one study, dental students volunteered to receive two small puncture wounds on the roofs of their mouths (Marucha & others, 1998). To compare the impact of stress on wound healing, the students received the first wound when they were on summer vacation and the second wound three days before their first major exam during the fall term. The results? The wounds inflicted before the major test healed an average of 40 percent more slowly—an extra three days—than the wounds inflicted on the same volunteers during summer vacation. Other studies have shown similar findings (Glaser & Kiecolt-Glaser, 2005; Gouin & Kiecolt-Glaser, 2012).

FOCUS ON NEUROSCIENCE

The Mysterious Placebo Effect

The *placebo effect* is perhaps one of the most dramatic examples of how the mind influences the body. A *placebo* is an inactive substance with no known effects, such as a sugar pill or an injection of sterile water. Placebos are often used in biomedical research to help gauge the effectiveness of an actual medication or treatment. But after being given a placebo, many research participants, including those suffering from pain or diseases, experience benefits from the placebo treatment (Klinger & others, 2014). How can this be explained?

In Chapter 2, we noted that one possible way that placebos might reduce pain is by activating the brain's own natural painkillers—the *endorphins*. (The endorphins are structurally similar to opioid painkillers, like morphine.) One reason for believing this is that a drug called *naloxone,* which blocks the brain's endorphin response, also blocks the painkilling effects of placebos (Price & others, 2008). Might placebos reduce pain by activating the brain's natural opioid network?

A brain imaging study by Swedish neuroscientist Predrag Petrovic and his colleagues (2002) tackled this question. In the study, painfully hot metal was placed on the back of each volunteer's hand. Each volunteer was then given an injection of either an actual opioid painkiller or a saline solution placebo. About 30 seconds later, positron emission tomography (PET) was used to scan the participants' brain activity.

Both the volunteers who received the painkilling drug *and* the volunteers who received the placebo treatment reported that the injection provided pain relief. In the two PET scans shown here, you can see that the genuine painkilling drug *(left)* and the placebo *(right)* activated the same brain area, called the *anterior cingulate cortex* (marked by the cross). The anterior cingulate cortex is known to contain many opioid receptors. Interestingly,

From Science, 295, 1737-1740. Petrovic, Predrag; Kalso, Eija; Petersson, Karl M.; and Ingvar, Martin. Placebo and opioid analgesia--Imaging shared neuronal network. Reprinted with permission from AAAS

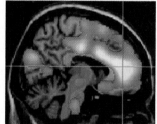 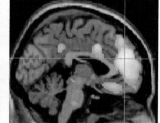

Received opioid painkiller   **Received placebo**

the level of brain activity was directly correlated with the participants' subjective perception of pain relief. The PET scan on the right shows the brain activity of those participants who had strong placebo responses.

Many questions remain about exactly how placebos work, but studies by Petrovic (2010) and others have substantiated the biological reality of the placebo effect. For example, Jon-Kar Zubieta and his colleagues (2005) showed that a placebo treatment activated opioid receptors in several brain regions associated with pain. Further, the greater the activation, the higher the level of pain individual volunteers were able to tolerate. As these studies show, cognitive expectations, learned associations, and emotional responses can have a profound effect on the perception of pain. Research has also demonstrated that placebos produce measurable effects on other types of brain processes, including those of people experiencing Parkinson's disease or major depressive disorder (de la Fuente-Fernández, 2009; Hunter & others, 2009).

What about the relationship between stress and infection? In a series of carefully controlled studies, psychologist Sheldon Cohen and his colleagues (2006; 2012) demonstrated that people who are experiencing high levels of stress are more susceptible to infection by a cold virus than people who are not under stress (see Figure 12.9). Participants who experienced *chronic* stressors that lasted a month or longer were *most* likely to develop colds after being exposed to a cold virus. One reason may be that chronic stress triggers the secretion of corticosteroids, which affect immune system functioning. Other research has shown that stress interferes with the effectiveness of influenza vaccinations (Pedersen & others, 2009).

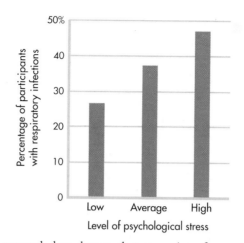

FIGURE 12.9 Stress and the Common Cold Are you more likely to catch a cold if you're under a great deal of stress? In a classic series of studies, Sheldon Cohen and his colleagues (1991, 1993) measured levels of psychological stress in healthy volunteers, then exposed them to a cold virus. They found an almost perfect relationship between the level of stress and the rate of infection. The higher the volunteers' psychological stress level, the higher the rate of respiratory infection.

Source: Cohen & others (1993).

Health psychologists have found that a wide variety of stressors are associated with diminished immune system functioning, increasing the risk of health problems and slowing recovery times (see Kiecolt-Glaser, 2009). However, while stress-related decreases in immune system functioning may heighten our susceptibility to health problems, exposure to stressors does not automatically translate into poorer health.

First, although prolonged, chronic stress impairs immune functioning, remember that acute, short-term stress actually enhances immune functioning (Dhabhar, 2011; Groer & others, 2010). Second, physical health is affected by the interaction of many factors, including heredity, nutrition, health-related habits, and access to medical care. Of course, your level of exposure to bacteria, viruses, and other sources of infection or disease will also influence your likelihood of becoming sick.

Finally, the simple fact is that some people are more vulnerable to the negative effects of stress than others. Why? As you'll see in the next section, researchers have found that a wide variety of psychological factors can influence people's reactions to stressors (Pedersen & others, 2011).

Courtesy Janice Kiecolt-Glaser

How do stressful events and negative emotions influence the immune system, and how big are the effects? This broad question has been intensely interesting to psychoneuroimmunology (PNI) researchers over the last three decades, and the consequent discoveries have substantially changed the face of health psychology.

—*Janice Kiecolt-Glaser (2009)*

> Test your understanding of **Introduction: Stress and Health Psychology** and **Physical Effects of Stress** with **LEARNING**Curve.

Individual Factors That Influence the Response to Stress

KEY THEME

Psychologists have identified several psychological factors that can modify an individual's response to stress and affect physical health.

KEY QUESTIONS

> How do feelings of control, explanatory style, and negative emotions influence stress and health?

> What is Type A behavior, and what role does hostility play in the relationship between Type A behavior and health?

People vary a great deal in the way they respond to a distressing event, whether it's a parking ticket or a bad grade on a crucial exam. In part, individual differences in reacting to stressors result from how people appraise an event and their resources for coping with the event. However, psychologists and other researchers have identified several factors that influence an individual's response to stressful events. In this section, we'll take a look at some of the most important psychological and social factors that seem to affect an individual's response to stress.

Psychological Factors

It's easy to demonstrate the importance of psychological factors in the response to stressors. For example, sit in a crowded waiting room and watch how differently people react to news of delays or cancelled appointments. Some people take the news calmly, while others become enraged and indignant. Psychologists have confirmed what common sense suggests: Psychological processes play a key role in determining the level of stress experienced.

PERSONAL CONTROL

For five days the fires raged. Every night, Hawk sat in front of her friend's TV watching the news, wondering whether the house she was born in was still standing but knowing that there was absolutely nothing she could do to help protect it. Despite the nonstop coverage, there was no new information—just more images of burnt houses and flames flickering all over the mountainsides. Hawk had never felt so helpless in her entire life.

Whether it be a wildfire threatening your home or a cancelled airline flight, situations that you perceive as being beyond your control are highly stressful. In contrast, having a sense of control over a stressful situation *reduces* the impact of stressors and decreases feelings of anxiety and depression (Dulin & others, 2013; Thompson, 2009). People who can control a stress-producing event often show no more psychological distress or physical arousal than people who are not exposed to the stressor at all.

Psychologists Judith Rodin and Ellen Langer (1977) first demonstrated the importance of a sense of control in a classic series of studies with nursing home residents. One group of residents—the "high-control" group—was given the opportunity to make choices about their daily activities and to exercise control over their environment. In contrast, residents assigned to the "low-control" group had little control over their daily activities. Decisions were made for them by the nursing home staff. Eighteen months later, the high-control residents were more active, alert, sociable, and healthier than the low-control residents. And, twice as many of the low-control residents had died (Langer & Rodin, 1976; Rodin & Langer, 1977).

How does a sense of control affect health? If you feel that you can control a stressor by taking steps to minimize or avoid it, you will experience less stress, both subjectively and physiologically (Heth & Somer, 2002; Heth & others, 2004). Having a sense of personal control also enhances positive emotions, such as self-confidence and feelings of self-efficacy, autonomy, and self-reliance. In contrast, feeling a lack of control over events produces all the hallmarks of the stress response. Levels of catecholamines and corticosteroids increase, and the effectiveness of immune system functioning decreases (see Maier & Watkins, 2000).

Further, not everyone benefits from feelings of enhanced personal control. Cross-cultural studies have shown that a sense of control is more highly valued in individualistic, Western cultures than in collectivistic, Eastern cultures (Thompson, 2009). Comparing Japanese and British participants, Darryl O'Connor and Mikiko Shimizu (2002) found that a heightened sense of personal control *was* associated with a lower level of perceived stress—but *only* among the British participants.

EXPLANATORY STYLE
OPTIMISM VERSUS PESSIMISM

We all experience defeat, rejection, or failure at some point in our lives. Yet despite repeated failures, rejections, or defeats, some people persist in their efforts.

Uncontrollable Events Every morning, local authorities in Boulder, Colorado, held a public information meeting for the anxious mountain residents who had been forced to evacuate their homes. Only firefighters and emergency personnel were allowed in the dangerous area where the fire was still raging. Many shared Hawk's sentiments, who said, "Not knowing whether my home was still standing or not—and not being able to do anything about it one way or the other—was the hardest part. All I could do was wait." Psychological research has shown that events and situations that are perceived as being beyond your control are especially likely to cause stress (Heth & Somer, 2002). Given that, how might you be able to lessen the stressful impact of such situations?

Craig F. Walker/The Denver Post via Getty Images

In contrast, some people give up in the face of failure and setbacks—the essence of *learned helplessness,* which we discussed in Chapter 5. What distinguishes between those who persist and those who give up?

According to psychologist **Martin Seligman** (1990, 1992), how people characteristically explain their failures and defeats makes the difference. People who have an **optimistic explanatory style** tend to use *external, unstable,* and *specific* explanations for negative events. In contrast, people who have a **pessimistic explanatory style** use *internal, stable,* and *global* explanations for negative events. Pessimists are also inclined to believe that no amount of personal effort will improve their situation. Not surprisingly, pessimists tend to experience more stress than optimists.

Let's look at these two explanatory styles in action. Optimistic Olive sees an attractive guy at a party and starts across the room to introduce herself and strike up a conversation. As she approaches him, the guy glances at her, then abruptly turns away. Hurt by the obvious snub, Optimistic Olive retreats to the buffet table. Munching on some fried zucchini, she mulls the matter over in her mind. At the same party, Pessimistic Pete sees an attractive female across the room and approaches her. He, too, gets a cold shoulder and retreats to the chips and clam dip. Standing at opposite ends of the buffet table, here is what each of them is thinking:

> OPTIMISTIC OLIVE: *What's* his *problem?* (External explanation: The optimist blames other people or external circumstances.)

> PESSIMISTIC PETE: *I must have said the wrong thing. She probably saw me stick my elbow in the clam dip before I walked over.* (Internal explanation: The pessimist blames self.)

> OPTIMISTIC OLIVE: *I'm really not looking my best tonight. I've just got to get more sleep.* (Unstable, temporary explanation)

> PESSIMISTIC PETE: *Let's face it, I'm a pretty boring guy and really not very good-looking.* (Stable, permanent explanation)

> OPTIMISTIC OLIVE: *He looks pretty preoccupied. Maybe he's waiting for his girlfriend to arrive. Or his boyfriend!* (Specific explanation)

> PESSIMISTIC PETE: *Women never give me a second look, probably because I dress like a nerd and I never know what to say to them.* (Global, pervasive explanation)

> OPTIMISTIC OLIVE: *Whoa! Who's that guy over there?! Okay, Olive, turn on the charm! Here goes!* (Perseverance after a rejection)

> PESSIMISTIC PETE: *Maybe I'll just hold down this corner of the buffet table . . . or go home and soak up some TV.* (Passivity and withdrawal after a rejection)

Most people, of course, are neither as completely optimistic as Olive nor as totally pessimistic as Pete. Instead, they fall somewhere along the spectrum of optimism and pessimism. Further, explanatory style may vary somewhat in different situations (Fosnaugh & others, 2009). Even so, a person's characteristic explanatory style, particularly for negative events, is relatively stable across the lifespan (Abela & others, 2008).

Explanatory style is linked to health consequences (Brummett & others, 2006; Wise & Rosqvist, 2006). For example, men with an optimistic explanatory style at age 25 were significantly healthier at age 50 than men with a pessimistic explanatory style (Peterson & Park, 2007). Other studies have shown that a pessimistic explanatory style is associated with poorer physical health (Peterson & Steen, 2009). For example, first-year law school students who had an optimistic, confident, and generally positive outlook had significantly higher levels of lymphocytes, T cells, and helper T cells. Explaining the positive relationship between optimism and good health, Suzanne Segerstrom and her colleagues (2003) suggest that optimists are more

Roz Chast The New Yorker Collection/The Cartoon Bank

How Do You Explain Your Setbacks and Failures? No one is thrilled to receive a failing grade on an important paper or exam. However, everyone experiences setbacks, rejection, and failure at some point. The way you *explain* your setbacks has a significant impact on motivation and on mental and physical health.

mediaphotos/Getty Images

MYTH ◀ SCIENCE

Is it true that pessimists handle stress better because they expect bad things to happen?

optimistic explanatory style Accounting for negative events or situations with external, unstable, and specific explanations.

pessimistic explanatory style Accounting for negative events or situations with internal, stable, and global explanations.

inclined to persevere in their efforts to overcome obstacles and challenges. Optimism has even been shown to help people cope with pain (Boselie & others, 2014; Goodin & Bulls, 2013). Optimists are also more likely to cope effectively with stressful situations than pessimists (Iwanaga & others, 2004).

"Officer, everything in the world is bothering me."

CHRONIC NEGATIVE EMOTIONS

THE HAZARDS OF BEING GROUCHY

Some people seem to have been born with a sunny, cheerful disposition. But other people almost always seem to be unhappy campers—they frequently experience bad moods and negative emotions like anger, irritability, worry, or sadness (D. J. Miller & others, 2009). Are people who are prone to chronic negative emotions more likely to suffer health problems?

Many studies have found a strong link between negative emotions and poor health (see Lahey, 2009). For example, a meta-analysis of more than 100 studies found that people who are habitually anxious, depressed, angry, or hostile *are* more likely to develop a chronic disease such as arthritis or heart disease (Friedman & Booth-Kewley, 2003).

This effect also can be seen geographically. Johannes Eichstaedt and his colleagues (2015) studied Twitter feeds in over 1,000 counties in the United States. They found that counties where tweets were more likely to include negative emotions, such as hostility, relationship tensions, or boredom, tended to have higher death rates from heart disease.

How might chronic negative emotions predispose people to develop disease? Not surprisingly, tense, angry, and unhappy people experience more stress than do happier people. They also report more daily hassles than people who are generally in a positive mood (McIntyre & others, 2008). And, they react much more intensely, and with far greater distress, to stressful events (Lahey, 2009).

Of course, everyone occasionally experiences bad moods or has a bad day. Are these fluctuations in mood associated with health risks? Some studies suggest that even transient increases in negative mood are associated with unhealthy cardiovascular and hormone responses (Daly & others, 2010; Jacobs & others, 2007).

It is also important to consider the role of culture. For example, although expressing anger is predictive of ill health, such as heart disease, among Americans, expressing anger actually seems to be protective among Japanese people (Kitayama & others, 2015). The researchers suspect that this cultural difference is because the expression of anger indicates the presence of stressful experiences among Americans. But in Japan, anger is more commonly related to power and a sense of control, because most Japanese do not feel free to openly express anger.

POSITIVE EMOTIONS

If negative emotions are associated with poor health, are positive emotions associated with good health? First, positive emotions are *not* just the absence of negative emotions (Larsen & others, 2009). The health benefits of experiencing positive emotions go beyond merely dampening or eliminating negative emotions (Stellar & others, 2015).

Research has shown that positive emotions are associated with increased resistance to infection, decreased illnesses, fewer reports of illness symptoms, less pain, and longevity (Pressman & Cohen, 2005; Steptoe & others, 2009). One large Canadian study found that people who experienced high levels of positive emotion were less likely to develop heart disease than people who reported low levels of positive emotions (Davidson & others, 2010).

Like negative emotions, positive emotions also seem to be predictive of health in social media studies. In the Twitter study described above, counties where tweets more often contained positive emotions, like optimism, tended to have lower death rates from heart disease (Eichstaedt & others, 2015). This effect was found at an international level as well. Countries whose residents reported higher levels of positive emotions also tended to have higher reported levels of physical health (Pressman & others, 2013). This was true among wealthier countries like Ireland, as well as among lower-income countries like Haiti.

How might positive emotions affect health? First, positive emotions bring calming and health protective effects to the cardiovascular, endocrine, and immune systems (Brummett & others, 2009). Second, positive emotions are associated with health-promoting behaviors, such as regular exercise, eating a healthy diet, and not smoking. Finally, individuals who frequently experience positive emotions tend to have more friends and stronger social networks than people who don't (Steptoe & others, 2009).

TYPE A BEHAVIOR AND HOSTILITY

The concept of Type A behavior originated about 35 years ago, when two cardiologists, Meyer Friedman and Ray Rosenman (1974), noticed that many of their patients shared certain traits. The original formulation of the **Type A behavior pattern** included a cluster of three characteristics: (1) an exaggerated sense of time urgency, often trying to do more and more in less and less time; (2) a general sense of hostility, frequently displaying anger and irritation; and (3) intense ambition and competitiveness. In contrast, people who were more relaxed and laid back were classified as displaying the *Type B behavior pattern*. After tracking the health of more than 3,000 middle-aged, healthy men, they found that those classified as Type A were twice as likely to develop heart disease as those classified as Type B. This held true even when the Type A men did not display other known risk factors for heart disease, such as smoking, high blood pressure, and elevated levels of cholesterol in their blood.

The Type A Behavior Pattern The original formulation of the Type A behavior pattern included hostility, ambition, and a sense of time urgency. Type A people hate wasting time and often try to do two or more things at once. However, later research showed that hostility, anger, and cynicism were far more damaging to physical health than ambition or time urgency (Suls & Bunde, 2005).

Although early results linking the Type A behavior pattern to heart disease were impressive, studies soon began to appear in which Type A behavior did *not* reliably predict the development of heart disease (see Krantz & McCeney, 2002; Myrtek, 2007). These findings led researchers to question whether the different components of the Type A behavior pattern were equally hazardous to health. After all, many people thrive on hard work, especially when they enjoy their jobs. And, high achievers don't necessarily suffer from health problems.

When researchers focused on the association between heart disease and each separate component of the Type A behavior pattern—time urgency, hostility, and achievement striving—an important distinction began to emerge. Feeling a sense of time urgency and being competitive or achievement oriented did *not* seem to be associated with the development of heart disease. Instead, the critical component that emerged as the strongest predictor of cardiac disease was *hostility* (Chida & Steptoe, 2009; J. E. Williams, 2010). Hostile people are much more likely than other people to develop heart disease, even when other risk factors are taken into account (Niaura & others, 2002; J. E. Williams, 2010). These findings fit with the research we talked about in the previous section describing a link between negative emotions like hostility and poor health outcomes across counties and countries.

How does hostility predispose people to heart disease and other health problems? *Hostility* refers to the tendency to feel anger, annoyance, resentment, and contempt, and to hold cynical and negative beliefs about human nature in general. Hostile people are also prone to believing that the disagreeable behavior of others is intentionally directed against them. Thus, hostile people tend to be suspicious, mistrustful, cynical, and pessimistic.

MYTH ◀ SCIENCE

Is it true that high-achieving people who work long hours are setting themselves up for a heart attack?

Type A behavior pattern A behavioral and emotional style characterized by a sense of time urgency, hostility, and competitiveness.

Thus, hostile Type As tend to react more intensely to a stressor than other people do (Chida & Hamer, 2008). They experience greater increases in blood pressure and heart rate. Because of their attitudes and behavior, hostile men and women also tend to *create* more stress in their own lives (Suls & Bunde, 2005). They also tend to experience more frequent, and more severe, negative life events and daily hassles than other people.

In general, the research evidence demonstrating the role of personality factors in the development of stress-related disease is impressive. Nevertheless, it's important to keep this evidence in perspective: Personality characteristics are just *some* of the many factors involved in the overall picture of health and disease. We look at this issue in more detail in the Critical Thinking box below. And, in Psych for Your Life, at the end of this chapter, we describe some of the steps you can take to help you minimize the effects of stress on your health.

CRITICAL THINKING

Do Personality Factors Cause Disease?

- You overhear a co-worker saying, "I'm not surprised he had a heart attack—the guy is a workaholic!"

- An acquaintance casually remarks, "She's been so depressed since her divorce. No wonder she got cancer."

- A tabloid headline hails, "New Scientific Findings: Use Your Mind to Cure Cancer!"

Statements like these make health psychologists, psychoneuroimmunologists, and physicians extremely uneasy. Why? Throughout this chapter, we've presented scientific evidence that emotional states can affect the functioning of the endocrine system and the immune system. Both systems play a significant role in the development of various physical disorders. We've also shown that personality factors, such as hostility and pessimism, are associated with an increased likelihood of developing poor health. But saying that "emotions affect the immune system" is a far cry from making such claims as "a positive attitude can cure cancer."

Psychologists and other scientists are cautious in the statements they make about the connections between personality and health for several reasons. First, many studies investigating the role of psychological factors in disease are *correlational*. That is, researchers have statistical evidence that two factors happen together so often that the presence of one factor reliably predicts the occurrence of the other. However, correlation does not necessarily indicate causality—it indicates only that two factors occur together. It's completely possible that some third, unidentified factor may have caused the other two factors to occur.

Second, personality factors might indirectly lead to disease via poor health habits. Low conscientiousness, high sensation seeking, and high extraversion are each associated with poor health habits (Atherton & others, 2014; Lodi-Smith & others, 2010; Miller & Quick, 2010). In turn, poor health habits are associated with higher rates of illness. That's why psychologists who study the role of personality factors in disease are typically careful to measure and consider the possible influence of the participants' health practices.

Third, it may be that the disease influences a person's emotions, rather than the other way around (Spezzaferri & others, 2009). After being diagnosed with advanced cancer or heart disease, most people would probably find it difficult to feel cheerful, optimistic, or in control of their lives.

"What do you mean, I have an ulcer? I give ulcers, I don't get them!"

One way that researchers try to disentangle the relationship between personality and health is to conduct carefully controlled prospective studies. A *prospective study* starts by assessing an initially healthy group of participants on variables thought to be risk factors, such as certain personality traits. Then the researchers track the health, personal habits, health habits, and other important dimensions of the participants' lives over a period of months, years, or decades. In analyzing the results, researchers can determine the extent to which each risk factor contributed to the health or illness of the participants. Thus, prospective studies provide more compelling evidence than do studies that are based on people who are already in poor health.

CRITICAL THINKING QUESTIONS

- Given that health professionals frequently advise people to change their health-related behaviors to improve physical health, should they also advise people to change their psychological attitudes, traits, and emotions? Why or why not?

- What are the advantages and disadvantages of correlational studies? Prospective studies?

Social Factors

A LITTLE HELP FROM YOUR FRIENDS

KEY THEME

Social support refers to the resources provided by other people.

KEY QUESTIONS

> How has social support been shown to benefit health?

> How can relationships and social connections sometimes increase stress?

> What gender differences have been found in social support and its effects?

Psychologists have become increasingly aware of the importance that close relationships play in our ability to deal with stressors and, ultimately, in our physical health (Uchino & Birmingham, 2011). Consider the following research evidence:

- Analyzing 148 studies that included over 300,000 participants, Julianne Holt-Lunstad and her colleagues (2010) found that people who were socially isolated were twice as likely to die over a given period than people with strong social relationships—a risk factor that is roughly equivalent to smoking 15 cigarettes a day.

- In a study begun in the 1950s, college students rated their parents' level of love and caring. A half-century later, 87 percent of those who had rated their parents as being "low" in love and caring had been diagnosed with a serious physical disease. In contrast, only 25 percent of those who had rated their parents as being "high" in love and caring had been diagnosed with a serious physical disease (Shaw & others, 2004).

- Evidence from animal research suggests that social isolation in nonhuman animals has similar consequences as those for loneliness in humans (Cacioppo & others, 2015b). There may be an evolutionary mechanism that leads to increased vigilance as a way of increasing chances of survival in human and nonhuman animals alike. This focus on self-preservation may cause stress and worsened physical and mental health. This evolutionary explanation is supported by research suggesting that loneliness is, to some degree, an inherited quality (Goossens & others, 2015).

These are just a few of the hundreds of studies exploring how interpersonal relationships influence our health and ability to tolerate stress (Cohen, 2004; Uchino, 2009). To investigate the role played by personal relationships in stress and health, psychologists measure the level of **social support**—the resources provided by other people in times of need.

Decades of psychological research have shown that socially isolated people have poorer health and higher death rates than people who have many social contacts or relationships (Holt-Lunstad & others, 2015). In fact, social isolation seems to be as potent a health risk as smoking, alcohol abuse, obesity, or physical inactivity (Holt-Lunstad & others, 2010; Steptoe & others, 2013).

Beyond social isolation, researchers have found that the more *diverse* your social network, the more pronounced the health benefits (Cohen & Janicki-Deverts, 2009). That is, prospective studies have shown that the people who live longest are those who have more *different types* of relationships—such as being married; having close relationships with family members, friends, and neighbors; and belonging to social, political, or religious groups (Berkman & Glass, 2000; Ellwardt & others, 2015b). In fact, researchers have found that people who live in such diverse social networks have:

- greater resistance to upper respiratory infections (Cohen, 2005)

- lower incidence of stroke and cardiovascular disease among women in a high-risk group (Rutledge & others, 2004, 2008)

- lower incidence of dementia and cognitive loss in old age (Desai & others, 2010; Ellwardt & others, 2015a)

social support The resources provided by other people in times of need.

The Benefits of Social Support Social support from your community can buffer the effects of stress, especially during natural disasters. Here, young Nepali volunteers work together to help clear the rubble from homes in their neighborhood after a 7.9-magnitude earthquake struck Nepal in April, 2015.

The Asahi Shimbun via Getty Images

Pets as a Source of Social Support
Pets can provide both companionship and social support, especially for people with limited social contact. Studies have found that the presence of a pet cat or dog can lower blood pressure and lessen the cardiovascular response to acute stress (Allen & others, 2002).

Joe Carini/ The Image Works

RICH ADDICKS/The New York Times/Redux

The Health Benefits of Companionship
Marteen and Wiley Blankenship celebrated their 48th wedding anniversary by working as volunteers in Alabama, helping people in a small town devastated by a violent tornado. Many studies have shown that couples and married people tend to live longer than people who are single, divorced, or widowed. In fact, adults who never marry are about 58% more likely to die early than those who are married and living with their spouse (Kaplan & Kronick, 2006).

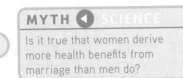

MYTH ◄ SCIENCE

Is it true that women derive more health benefits from marriage than men do?

HOW SOCIAL SUPPORT BENEFITS HEALTH

Social support may benefit our health and improve our ability to cope with stressors in several ways (Feeney & Collins, 2014; Uchino, 2009). First, the social support of friends and relatives can modify our appraisal of a stressor's significance, including the degree to which we perceive it as threatening or harmful. Simply knowing that support and assistance are readily available may make the situation seem less threatening.

Second, the presence of supportive others seems to decrease the intensity of physical reactions to a stressor (Uchino & others, 2010). Thus, when faced with a painful medical procedure or some other stressful situation, many people find the presence of a supportive friend to be calming.

Third, social support can influence our health by making us less likely to experience negative emotions (Cohen, 2004). Given the well-established link between chronic negative emotions and poor health, a strong social support network can promote positive moods and emotions, enhance self-esteem, and increase feelings of personal control. In contrast, loneliness and depression are unpleasant emotional states that increase levels of stress hormones and adversely affect immune system functioning (Cacioppo & others, 2015a; Irwin & Miller, 2007).

The flip side of the coin is that relationships with others can also be a significant *source* of stress (Rook & others, 2011; Lund & others, 2014). In fact, negative interactions with other people are sometimes more effective at creating psychological distress than positive interactions are at improving well-being (Rafaeli & others, 2008). And, although married people tend to be healthier than unmarried people overall, marital conflict has been shown to have adverse effects on physical health, especially for women (Robles, 2014; Whisman & others, 2010).

Clearly, the quality of interpersonal relationships is an important determinant of whether those relationships help or hinder our ability to cope with stressful events (Rook, 2015). When other people are perceived as being judgmental, their presence may increase the individual's physical reaction to a stressor. In two clever studies, psychologist Karen Allen and her colleagues (1991, 2002) demonstrated that the presence of a favorite dog or cat was more effective than the presence of a spouse or friend in lowering reactivity to a stressor. Why? Perhaps because the pet was perceived as being nonjudgmental, non-evaluative, and unconditionally supportive. Unfortunately, the same is not always true of friends, family members, and partners.

Stress may also increase when well-meaning friends or family members offer unwanted or inappropriate social support. The In Focus box offers some suggestions on how to provide helpful social support and avoid inappropriate support behaviors.

GENDER DIFFERENCES IN THE EFFECTS OF SOCIAL SUPPORT

Who do you turn to when you are in need of help? In general, men tend to rely heavily on a close relationship with their spouse or partner. Women, in contrast, are more likely to list close friends along with their spouse as confidants (Ackerman & others, 2007; Coventry & others, 2004). Because men tend to have a much smaller network of intimate others, they may be particularly vulnerable to social isolation, especially if their spouse dies. That may be one reason that the health benefits of being married are more pronounced for men than for women (Zwicker & DeLongis, 2010).

When stressful events strike, women tend to reach out to one another for support and comfort (Taylor & Master, 2011). For example, Andi's many friends rallied around her when she returned to Boulder, helping her find a place to live, and bringing food and groceries to her rental cottage. And, rather than face her burned-out home for the first time alone, Andi recruited your author Sandy and a few other close friends to go with her.

On the other hand, women can be particularly vulnerable to some of the problematic aspects of social support, for a couple of reasons. First, women are more likely than men to serve as *providers* of support, which can be a very stressful role (Ekwall & Hallberg, 2007).

IN FOCUS

Providing Effective Social Support

A close friend turns to you for help in a time of crisis or personal tragedy. What should you do or say? As we've noted in this chapter, appropriate social support can help people weather crises and can significantly reduce the amount of distress that they feel. Inappropriate support, in contrast, may only make matters worse (Uchino, 2009).

Researchers generally agree that there are several broad categories of social support. Three are most commonly studied: emotional, tangible, and informational. Each provides different beneficial functions (Lett & others, 2009).

Emotional support includes expressions of concern, empathy, and positive regard. *Tangible support* involves direct assistance, such as providing transportation, lending money, or helping with meals, child care, or household tasks. When people offer helpful suggestions, advice, or possible resources, they are providing *informational support.*

It's possible that all three kinds of social support might be provided by the same person, such as a relative, spouse, or very close friend. More commonly, we turn to different people for different kinds of support (Masters & others, 2007).

Psychologists have identified several support behaviors that are typically perceived as helpful by people under stress (Goldsmith, 2004; Hobfoll & others, 1992). In a nutshell, you're most likely to be perceived as helpful if you:

- are a good listener and show concern and interest
- ask questions that encourage the person under stress to express his or her feelings and emotions
- express understanding about why the person is upset
- express affection for the person, whether with a warm hug or simply a pat on the arm
- are willing to invest time and attention in helping
- can help the person with practical tasks, such as housework, transportation, or responsibilities at work or school

Just as important is knowing what *not* to do or say. Andi in the Prologue story frequently expressed frustration about well-meaning comments that simply made her feel worse. A prime example were statements beginning with the words "At least . . . ," as when people said, "Well, your house and all your belongings are destroyed, but at least you're safe." As Andi said, "If your sentence starts with 'at least,' don't say it at all!" Here are several behaviors that, however well intentioned, are often perceived as unhelpful:

- Giving advice that the person under stress has not requested.
- Telling the person, "I know exactly how you feel." It's a mistake to think that you have experienced distress identical to what the other person is experiencing.

Nicolas McComber/Getty Images

- Talking about yourself or your own problems.
- Minimizing the importance of the person's problem by saying things like, "Hey, don't make such a big deal out of it," "It could be a lot worse," or "Don't worry, everything will turn out okay."
- Joking or acting overly cheerful.
- Offering your philosophical or religious interpretation of the stressful event by saying things like, "It's fate," "It's God's will," or "It's your karma."
- Making a big deal out of the support and help you do provide, which may make the recipient feel even more anxious or vulnerable. In fact, "invisible support," in which the recipient isn't aware of your help, is one of the most effective forms of social support (Bolger & Amarel, 2007; Howland & Simpson, 2010). For example, asking a question in class because you know that a classmate doesn't understand the material would be an example of invisible support.

Finally, remember that although social support is helpful, it is *not* a substitute for counseling or psychotherapy. If a friend seems overwhelmed by problems or emotions, or is having serious difficulty handling the demands of everyday life, you should encourage him or her to seek professional help. Most college campuses have a counseling center or a health clinic that can provide referrals to qualified mental health workers. Sliding fee schedules, based on ability to pay, are usually available, and many campus counseling centers are free of charge for students. Thus, you can assure the person that cost need not be an obstacle to getting help—or an additional source of stress!

> **MYTH ◄ SCIENCE**
>
> Is it true that the best way to comfort stressed-out friends or relatives is to give them advice and show them that the problem is not as bad as it seems?

coping Behavioral and cognitive responses used to deal with stressors; involves our efforts to change circumstances, or our interpretation of circumstances, to make them more favorable and less threatening.

problem-focused coping Coping efforts primarily aimed at directly changing or managing a threatening or harmful stressor.

emotion-focused coping Coping efforts primarily aimed at relieving or regulating the emotional impact of a stressful situation.

Second, women may be more likely to suffer from the *stress contagion effect,* becoming upset about negative life events that happen to other people whom they care about (Dalgard & others, 2006). Since women tend to have larger and more intimate social networks than men, they have more opportunities to become distressed by what happens to people who are close to them. And women are more likely than men to be upset about negative events that happen to their relatives and friends. In contrast, men are more likely to be distressed only by negative events that happen to their immediate family—their wives and children (Rosenfield & Smith, 2010).

⟩ Test your understanding of **Individual Factors That Influence the Response to Stress** with **LEARNING***Curve*.

Coping
HOW PEOPLE DEAL WITH STRESS

KEY THEME

Coping refers to the ways in which we try to change circumstances, or our interpretation of circumstances, to make them less threatening.

KEY QUESTIONS

⟩ What are the two basic forms of coping, and when is each form typically used?
⟩ What are some of the most common coping strategies?
⟩ How does culture affect coping style?

Think about some of the stressful periods that have occurred in your life. What kinds of strategies did you use to deal with those distressing events? Which strategies seemed to work best? Did any of the strategies end up working against your ability to reduce the stressor? If you had to deal with the same events again today, would you do anything differently?

For example, imagine that you discovered that you weren't allowed to register for classes because the financial aid office had lost your paperwork. How would you react? What would you do?

The strategies that you use to deal with distressing events are examples of coping. **Coping** refers to the ways in which we try to change circumstances, or our interpretation of circumstances, to make them more favorable and less threatening (Folkman, 2009).

When coping is effective, we adapt to the situation and stress is reduced. Unfortunately, coping efforts do not always help us adapt. Maladaptive coping can involve thoughts and behaviors that intensify or prolong distress, or that produce self-defeating outcomes (Thompson & others, 2010). The rejected lover who continually dwells on his former companion, passing up opportunities to form new relationships and letting his studies slide, is demonstrating maladaptive coping. Maladaptive coping can also include maladaptive behaviors. People of all ages sometimes engage in unhealthy coping behaviors. But one survey found that millenials are significantly more likely than those of other generations to cope by eating more or by becoming a couch potato—for example, playing video games or spending too much time online (APA, 2013).

Adaptive coping responses serve many functions (Folkman, 2009; Folkman & Moskowitz, 2007). Most important, adaptive coping involves realistically evaluating the situation and determining what can be done to minimize the impact of the stressor. But adaptive coping also involves dealing with the emotional aspects of the situation. In other words, adaptive coping often includes developing emotional tolerance for negative life events, maintaining self-esteem, and keeping emotions in balance. Finally, adaptive coping efforts are directed toward preserving important relationships.

Ways of Coping Like the stress response itself, adaptive coping is a dynamic and complex process. Imagine that your landlord told you that you had to move in 10 days. What types of coping strategies might prove most helpful?

Ben Sklar/The New York Times/Redux

Traditionally, coping has been broken down into two major categories: *problem-focused* and *emotion-focused* (Folkman & Moskowitz, 2004). As you'll see in the next sections, each type of coping serves a different purpose. However, people are flexible in the coping styles they adopt, often relying on different coping strategies for different stressors (Bonanno & Burton, 2013; Kammeyer-Mueller & others, 2009).

Problem-Focused Coping Strategies
CHANGING THE STRESSOR

Problem-focused coping is aimed at managing or changing a threatening or harmful stressor. Problem-focused coping strategies tend to be most effective when you can exercise some control over the stressful situation or circumstances (Kammeyer-Mueller & others, 2009; Park & others, 2004).

Sandy's friend Wyncia, whose own house narrowly escaped the flames, demonstrated the value of problem-focused coping. A member of the volunteer fire department, she received the call to mobilize just minutes after she saw the thick cloud of black smoke and realized that the fire was nearby. Grabbing her emergency kit, Wyncia raced to the fire station, leaving her husband to pack up their dog and whatever else he could hurriedly stuff into their car as the flames drew near.

Wyncia said, "When you experience that gut 'fight-or-flight reaction,' and there's no one to fight, and nowhere to run, you just melt down. But when you're with the fire department, instead of melting down, you get up and do your job. Joining the fire department as a volunteer was the best thing I could have done. Instead of just sitting at the bottom of the hill and waiting for news, and looking at the horrible smoke and wondering whether my house was still there, I was actually involved with the people who were working on the problem."

Planful problem solving involves efforts to rationally analyze the situation, identify potential solutions, and then implement them. In effect, you take the attitude that the stressor represents a problem to be solved. Once you assume that mental stance, you follow the basic steps of problem solving (see Chapter 7).

When people tackle a problem head on, they are engaging in *confrontive coping*. Ideally, confrontive coping is direct and assertive but not hostile or angry. When it is hostile or aggressive, confrontive coping may well generate negative emotions in the people being confronted, damaging future relations with them (Folkman & Lazarus, 1991). However, if you recall our earlier discussion of hostility, then you won't be surprised to find that hostile individuals often engage in confrontive coping (Vandervoort, 2006).

Emotion-Focused Coping Strategies
CHANGING YOUR REACTION TO THE STRESSOR

When the stressor is one over which we can exert little or no control, we often focus on the dimension of the situation that we *can* control—the emotional impact of the stressor on us. When people think that nothing can be done to alter a situation, they tend to rely on **emotion-focused coping.**

Ziv Koren/Polaris/Newscom

Problem-Focused and Emotion-Focused Coping Strategies Dealing with the devastation that follows major disasters requires multiple coping strategies. Thousands of people were killed, and hundreds of thousands of homes destroyed or damaged in the major earthquake that hit Nepal in April, 2015. Along with coping with the emotional impact of losing homes, friends, and family members, people must also call upon problem-focused strategies to deal with the challenges of rebuilding shattered communities. This woman is sifting through the rubble of her home in historic Durbar Square in Kathmandu, searching for whatever belongings she can salvage.

Cathy Steiner

Coping Through Humor: Everybody Say "Argh!" Humor is one helpful way to distance yourself, at least temporarily, from the emotional impact of a difficult situation. As we planned our trip to Andi's burned-out home to see what might be salvaged, Andi joked that we would be like a band of pirates looking for buried treasure. But the house was completely destroyed—there was to be no loot for these pirates. Laughing through tears, Andi led us in a rousing chorus of "Argh!" and then bravely planted the pirate flag on the only thing left standing—her charred exercise bicycle.

They direct their efforts toward relieving or regulating the emotional impact of the stressful situation (Scott & others, 2010). Although emotion-focused coping doesn't change the problem, it can help you feel better about it.

When you shift your attention away from the stressor and toward other activities, you're engaging in the emotion-focused coping strategy called *escape–avoidance*. As the name implies, the basic goal is to escape or avoid the stressor and neutralize distressing emotions. Excessive sleeping and the use of drugs and alcohol are maladaptive forms of escape–avoidance, as are escaping into fantasy or wishful thinking. More constructive escape–avoidance strategies include exercising or immersing yourself in your studies, hobbies, or work.

Because you are focusing your attention on something other than the stressor, escape–avoidance tactics provide emotional relief in the short run. Thus, avoidance strategies can be helpful when you are facing a stressor that is brief and has limited consequences. But avoidance strategies such as wishful thinking tend to be counterproductive when the stressor is a severe or long-lasting one, like a serious or chronic disease (Wolf & Mori, 2009).

In the long run, escape–avoidance tactics are associated with poor adjustment and feelings of depression and anxiety (Murberg & Bru, 2005; Woodhead & others, 2013). That's not surprising if you think about it. After all, the problem *is* still there. And if the problem is one that needs to be dealt with promptly, such as academic problems, the delays caused by escape–avoidance strategies can make the stressful situation worse.

Seeking social support is the coping strategy that involves turning to friends, relatives, or other people for emotional, tangible, or informational support. As we discussed earlier in the chapter, having a strong network of social support can help buffer the impact of stressors (Uchino, 2009). Confiding in a trusted friend gives you an opportunity to vent your emotions and better understand the stressful situation.

When you acknowledge the stressor but attempt to minimize or eliminate its emotional impact, you're engaging in the coping strategy called *distancing*. Having an attitude of joy and lightheartedness in daily life, and finding the humor in life's absurdities or ironies, is one form of distancing (Kuhn & others, 2010; McGraw & others, 2013). Sometimes people emotionally distance themselves from a stressor by discussing it in a detached, depersonalized, or intellectual way.

For example, when Andi planned her first trip up to her burned-out house to see what could be salvaged, she joked that we would be like pirates looking for booty in the wreckage. The admittedly silly joke caught on. Along with the pile of donated shovels, rakes, screens, face masks and heavy work gloves, one friend brought a handmade pirate flag and another a stuffed parrot! When we got to Andi's home-site, she planted the flag on top of the only item of furniture that was still standing—her charred exercise bicycle.

In certain high-stress occupations, distancing can help workers cope with painful human problems. Clinical psychologists, social workers, rescue workers, police officers, and medical personnel often use distancing to some degree to help them deal with distressing situations without falling apart emotionally themselves.

In contrast to distancing, *denial* is a refusal to acknowledge that the problem even exists. Like escape–avoidance strategies, denial can compound problems in situations that require immediate attention.

Perhaps the most constructive emotion-focused coping strategy is *positive reappraisal*. When we use positive reappraisal, we try not only to minimize the negative emotional aspects of the situation but also to create positive meaning by focusing on personal growth (Folkman, 2009). Even in the midst of deeply disturbing situations, positive reappraisal can help people experience positive emotions and minimize the potential for negative aftereffects (Nowlan & others, 2015; Weiss & Berger, 2010).

Positive Reappraisal: Transcending Tragedy Model Petra Nemcova was vacationing with her fiancé when a tsunami struck Thailand. Swept up in the powerful currents of debris and destruction, Nemcova lost sight of her fiancé in the swirling waters but managed to grab hold of a partly submerged palm tree. Suffering from a shattered pelvis and internal injuries, Nemcova clung to the tree for eight hours before being rescued. Three months later, her fiancé's body was found.

Nemcova founded Happy Hearts Fund, an international foundation that has raised tens of millions of dollars and founded schools and clinics in areas hit by natural disasters around the world, including Thailand, Sri Lanka, Pakistan, Cambodia, and Vietnam. Nemcova is shown here at the opening of a kindergarten in an Indonesian village that was devastated by a powerful earthquake.

AP Photo/Purwowiyoto

For example, as Andi said, "Your life is terrible and wonderful at the same time. It's terrible because you've lost everything you own. But it's wonderful because you see the incredible kindness of strangers."

Some people turn to their religious or spiritual beliefs to help them cope with stress. *Positive religious coping* includes seeking comfort or reassurance in prayer or from a religious community, or believing that your personal experience is spiritually meaningful. Positive religious coping is generally associated with lower levels of stress and anxiety, improved mental and physical health, and enhanced well-being (Ano & Vasconcelles, 2005).

On the other hand, religious beliefs can also lead to a less positive outcome. Individuals who respond with *negative religious coping,* in which they become angry, question their religious beliefs, or believe that they are being punished, tend to experience increased levels of distress, poorer health, and decreased well-being (Ano & Vasconcelles, 2005; Smith & others, 2005).

For many people, religious coping offers a sense of control or certainty during stressful events or circumstances (Hogg & others, 2010; Kay & others, 2010). For example,

---

IN FOCUS

Gender Differences in Responding to Stress: "Tend-and-Befriend" or "Fight-or-Flight"?

Physiologically, men and women show the same hormonal and sympathetic nervous system activation that Walter Cannon (1932) described as the "fight-or-flight" response to stress. Yet *behaviorally,* the two sexes react very differently.

To illustrate, consider this finding: When men come home after a stressful day at work, they tend to withdraw from their families, wanting to be left alone—an example of the "flight" response (Repetti & others, 2009). After a stressful workday, however, women tend to seek out interactions with their marital partners (Schulz & others, 2004). And, women tend to be more nurturing toward their children, rather than less (Campos & others, 2009).

As we have noted in this chapter, women tend to be much more involved in their social networks than men. And, as compared to men, women are much more likely to seek out and use social support when they are under stress. Throughout their lives, women tend to mobilize social support—especially from other women—in times of stress (Zwicker & DeLongis, 2010).

Why the gender difference in coping with stress? Health psychologists Shelley Taylor and her colleagues (Taylor & others, 2000; Taylor & Gonzaga, 2007) believe that evolutionary theory offers some insight. According to the evolutionary perspective, the most adaptive response in virtually any situation is one that promotes the survival of both the individual and the individual's offspring (Taylor & Master, 2011). Given that premise, neither fighting nor fleeing is likely to have been an adaptive response for females, especially females who were pregnant, nursing, or caring for their offspring. According to Taylor (2006), "Tending to offspring in times of stress would be vital to ensuring the survival of the species." Rather than fighting or fleeing, they argue, women developed a *tend-and-befriend* behavioral response to stress.

What is the "tend-and-befriend" pattern of responding? *Tending* refers to "quieting and caring for offspring and blending into the environment," Taylor and her colleagues (2000) write. That is, rather than confronting or running from the threat, females take cover and protect their young. Evidence supporting this behavior pattern includes studies showing that many female animals adopt a "tending" strategy when faced by a threat (Taylor, 2006; Trainor & others, 2010).

The "befriending" side of the equation relates to women's tendency to seek social support during stressful situations. *Befriending* is the creation and maintenance of social networks that provide resources and protection for the female and her offspring under conditions of stress (Taylor & Master, 2011).

However, both males and females show the same neuroendocrine responses to an acute stressor—the sympathetic nervous system activates, stress hormones pour into the bloodstream, and, as those hormones reach different organs, the body kicks into high gear. So why do women "tend and befriend" rather than "fight or flee," as men do? Taylor points to the effects of another hormone, *oxytocin.* Higher in females than in males, oxytocin is associated with maternal behaviors in all female mammals, including humans. Oxytocin has been demonstrated to increase people's willingness to talk about their emotions, which is linked with bonding between people (Lane & others, 2013). Oxytocin also tends to have a calming effect on both males and females (see Southwick & others, 2005).

In combination, all of these oxytocin-related changes seem to help turn down the physiological intensity of the fight-or-flight response for women. And perhaps, Taylor suggests, they also promote the tend-and-befriend response.

"I'm somewhere between O. and K."

Edward Koren The New Yorker Collection/ The Cartoon Bank

Think Like a SCIENTIST

Can you reduce your stress level by watching cute animal videos? Go to LaunchPad: Resources to **Think Like a Scientist** about **Coping with Stress**.

🅜 LaunchPad

some people find strength in the notion that adversity is a test of their religious faith or that they have been given a particular challenge in order to fulfill a higher moral purpose. For some people, religious or spiritual beliefs can increase resilience, optimism, and personal growth during times of stress and adversity (Pargament & Cummings, 2010).

Finally, it's important to note that there is no single "best" coping strategy. In general, the most effective coping is flexible, meaning that we fine-tune our coping strategies to meet the demands of a particular stressor (Carver, 2011; Cheng, 2009). And, people often use multiple coping strategies, combining problem-focused and emotion-focused forms of coping. In the initial stages of a stressful experience, we may rely on emotion-focused strategies to help us step back emotionally from a problem. Once we've regained our equilibrium, we may use problem-focused coping strategies to identify potential solutions.

Although it's virtually inevitable that you'll encounter stressful circumstances, there are coping strategies that can help you minimize their health effects. We suggest several techniques in the Psych for Your Life section at the end of the chapter.

Culture and Coping Strategies

Culture can influence the choice of coping strategies (Chun & others, 2006). Americans and other members of individualistic cultures tend to emphasize personal autonomy and personal responsibility in dealing with problems. Thus, they are *less* likely to seek social support in stressful situations than are members of collectivistic cultures, such as Asian cultures (Wong & Wong, 2006). Members of collectivistic cultures tend to be more oriented toward their social group, family, or community and toward seeking help with their problems (Kuo, 2013).

Individualists also tend to emphasize the importance and value of exerting control over their circumstances, especially circumstances that are threatening or stressful (O'Connor & Shimizu, 2002). Thus, they favor problem-focused strategies, such as confrontive coping and planful problem solving. These strategies involve directly changing the situation to achieve a better fit with their wishes or goals (Wong & Wong, 2006).

Culture and Coping This young boy lost his legs in a devastating earthquake that killed almost 100,000 people in southwest China. Do coping strategies differ across cultures? According to some researchers, people in China, Japan, and other Asian cultures are more likely to rely on emotional coping strategies than people in individualistic cultures (Heppner, 2008; Yeh & others, 2006). Coping strategies that are particularly valued in collectivistic cultures include emotional self-control, gracefully accepting one's fate and making the best of a bad situation, and maintaining harmonious relationships with family members.

Imaginechina via AP Images

In collectivistic cultures, however, a greater emphasis is placed on controlling your personal reactions to a stressful situation rather than trying to control the situation itself (Zhou & others, 2012). According to some researchers, people in China, Japan, and other Asian cultures are more likely to rely on emotional coping strategies than people in individualistic cultures. Coping strategies that are particularly valued in collectivistic cultures include emotional self-control, gracefully accepting one's fate and making the best of a bad situation, and maintaining harmonious relationships with family members (Heppner, 2008; Yeh & others, 2006). This emotion-focused coping style emphasizes gaining control over inner feelings by accepting and accommodating yourself to existing realities (O'Connor & Shimizu, 2002).

For example, the Japanese emphasize accepting difficult situations with maturity, serenity, and flexibility (Gross, 2007). Common sayings in Japan are "The true tolerance is to tolerate the intolerable" and "Flexibility can control rigidity." Along with controlling inner feelings, many Asian cultures also stress the goal of controlling the outward expression of emotions, however distressing the situation (Park, 2010).

These cultural differences in coping underscore the point that there is no formula for effective coping in all situations. That we use multiple coping strategies throughout almost every stressful situation reflects our efforts to identify what will work best at a given moment in time. To the extent that any coping strategy helps us identify realistic alternatives, manage our emotions, and maintain important relationships, it is adaptive and effective.

> Test your understanding of **Coping: How People Deal with Stress** with **LEARNING**Curve.

Closing Thoughts

From disasters and major life events to the minor hassles and annoyances of daily life, stressors come in all sizes and shapes. Stress is an unavoidable part of life. If prolonged or intense, stress can adversely affect both our physical and psychological well-being. Fortunately, most of the time people deal effectively with the stresses in their lives. But effective coping can minimize the effects of even the most intense stressors, like losing your home in a fire.

Ultimately, the level of stress that we experience is due to a complex interaction of psychological, biological, and social factors. We hope that reading this chapter has given you a better understanding of how stress affects your life and how you can reduce its impact on your physical and psychological well-being. In Psych for Your Life, we'll suggest some concrete steps you can take to minimize the harmful impact of stress in *your* life.

Greg Lefcourt

The Poetry of Loss: Making Meaning from Tragedy Andi had never thought of herself as a writer. However, facing the loss of everything she owned, she wrote long e-mails to her large network of friends. The e-mails turned into essays, which turned into a blog, www.burningdownthehouseblog.com. Through her blog, Andi shares her experiences with hundreds of readers on what she calls "the poetry of loss." Despite the pain and the anger, Andi says, there is a new sense of "wonder, and exploration, and learning, and excitement"—the "terrible gift" of great loss (O'Conor, 2011). Andi also did a TEDx talk about her experiences, which you can watch at http://tinyurl.com/pv9f96r. Can you identify the different coping strategies that Andi used?

PSYCH FOR YOUR LIFE

Minimizing the Effects of Stress

Sometimes stressful situations persist despite our best efforts to resolve them. Knowing that chronic stress can jeopardize your health, what can you do to minimize the adverse impact of stress on your physical well-being? Here are four practical suggestions.

Suggestion 1: Avoid or Minimize the Use of Stimulants

In dealing with stressful situations, people often turn to stimulants to help keep them going, such as coffee or caffeinated energy drinks. If you know someone who smokes, you've probably observed that most smokers react to stress by increasing their smoking (Ng & Jeffery, 2003; Todd, 2004). The

problem is that common stimulants like caffeine and nicotine actually work *against* you in coping with stress. They increase the physiological effects of stress by raising heart rate and blood pressure. In effect, users of stimulant drugs are already primed to respond with greater reactivity, exaggerating the physiological consequences of stress (Klein & others, 2010).

The best advice? Avoid stimulant drugs altogether. If that's not possible, make a conscious effort to monitor your use of stimulants, especially when you're under stress. You'll find it easier to deal with stressors when your nervous system is not already in high gear because of caffeine, nicotine, or other stimulants. Minimizing your use of stimulants will also make it easier for you to implement the next suggestion.

Westend61/Getty Images

Suggestion 2: Exercise Regularly

Numerous studies all point to the same conclusion: Regular exercise, particularly aerobic exercise like walking, swimming, or running, is one of the best ways to reduce the impact of stress (Edenfield & Blumenthal, 2011; Thøgersen-Ntoumani & others, 2015). The key word here is *regular*. Try walking briskly for 20 minutes four or five times a week. It will improve your physical health and help you cope with stress. In fact, just about any kind of physical exercise helps buffer the negative effects of stress. (Rapidly right-clicking your computer mouse doesn't count.) Compared to sofa slugs, physically fit people are less physiologically reactive to stressors and produce lower levels of stress hormones (Hamer & others, 2006). Psychologically, regular exercise reduces anxiety and depressed feelings, and increases self-confidence and self-esteem.

Suggestion 3: Get Enough Sleep

With the ongoing push to get more and more done, people often stretch their days by short-changing themselves on sleep. But sleep deprivation just adds to your feelings of stress. "Without sufficient sleep it is more difficult to concentrate, make careful decisions, and follow instructions," explains researcher Mark Rosekind (2003). "You are more likely to make mistakes or errors, and are more prone to being impatient and lethargic. And, your attention, memory and reaction time are all adversely affected."

The stress–sleep connection also has the potential to become a vicious cycle. School, work, or family-related pressures contribute to reduced or disturbed sleep, leaving you less than adequately rested and making efforts to deal with the situation all the more taxing and distressing (Akerstedt & others, 2009). And inadequate sleep, even for just a few nights, takes a physical toll on the body, leaving us more prone to health problems (Cohen & others, 2009).

Fortunately, research indicates that the opposite is also true: Getting adequate sleep promotes resistance and helps buffer the effects of stress (Lange & others, 2010). For some suggestions to help promote a good night's sleep, see the Psych for Your Life section at the end of Chapter 4.

Suggestion 4: Practice a Relaxation or Meditation Technique

You can significantly reduce stress-related symptoms by regularly using any one of a variety of relaxation techniques (Benson, 2010). *Meditation* is one effective stress reduction strategy. As discussed in Chapter 4 (see pp. 160–163), there are many different meditation techniques, but they all involve focusing mental attention, heightening awareness, and quieting internal chatter. Most meditation techniques are practiced while sitting quietly, but others involve movement, such as yoga and walking meditation. Many studies have demonstrated the physical and psychological benefits of meditation, including lessening the effects of stress (Chiesa & Serretti, 2009; Ludwig & Kabat-Zinn, 2008).

One form of meditation that has been receiving a great deal of attention in psychology is called *mindfulness meditation*. Mindfulness techniques were developed as a Buddhist practice more than 2,000 years ago, but modern psychologists and other health practitioners have adapted these practices for use in a secular context (Didonna, 2008). Mindfulness practice has been shown to be helpful in both preventing and relieving stress (Creswell & Lindsay, 2014; Jha & others, 2010; Weinstein & others, 2009).

Definitions of mindfulness are as varied as the practices associated with it. It's important to note, also, that strictly speaking, *mindfulness* refers to an approach to everyday life as well as a formal meditation technique (Shapiro & Carlson, 2009). However, for our purposes, **mindfulness meditation** can be defined as a technique in which practitioners focus *awareness* on *present experience* with *acceptance* (Siegel & others, 2008).

Advocates of mindfulness practice believe that most psychological distress is caused by our *reactions* to events and circumstances—our emotions, thoughts, and judgments. As psychologist Mark Williams points out, "We are always explaining the world to ourselves, and we react emotionally to these explanations rather than to the facts. . . . Thoughts are not facts" (Williams & others, 2007). Mindfulness practice is a way to correct that habitual perspective, clearing and calming the mind in the process. David Ludwig and Jon Kabat-Zinn (2008) explain:

> Mindfulness can be considered a universal human capacity proposed to foster clear thinking and open-heartedness. As such, this form of meditation requires no particular religious or cultural belief system. The goal of mindfulness is to maintain awareness moment by moment, disengaging oneself from strong attachment to beliefs, thoughts, or emotions, thereby developing a greater sense of emotional balance and well-being.

In other words, mindfulness meditation involves paying attention to your ongoing mental experience in a nonjudgmental, nonreactive manner (Ludwig & Kabat-Zinn, 2008;

mindfulness meditation A technique in which practitioners focus *awareness* on *present experience* with *acceptance*.

Shapiro & Carlson, 2009). The *mindfulness of breathing* technique is a simple mindfulness practice that is often recommended for beginners.

Mindfulness of Breathing

- Find a comfortable place to sit quietly. Assume a sitting posture that is relaxed yet upright and alert. Close your eyes and allow the muscles in your face, neck, and shoulders to slowly relax.

- Focus on your breath as your primary object of attention, feeling the breathing in and breathing out, the rise and fall of your abdomen, the sensation of air moving across your upper lip and in your nostrils, and so forth.

- Whenever some other phenomenon arises in the field of awareness, note it, and then gently bring the mind back to the breathing. As thoughts, feelings, or images arise in your mind, simply note their presence and go back

to focusing your attention on the physical sensation of breathing.

- To maintain attention on your breathing, it's sometimes helpful to count your breaths. Inhale gently, exhale, and then speak the word "one" in your mind. Inhale gently, exhale, and mentally speak the word "two." Do the same up until the count of four, and then start over again. Remember, focus on the physical sensation of breathing, such as the feeling of air moving across your nostrils and upper lip, the movement of your chest and abdomen, and so forth.

How long should you meditate? Many meditation teachers advise that you begin with a short, easily attainable goal, such as meditating for five minutes without taking a break. As you become more comfortable in your practice, gradually work your way up to longer periods of time, ideally 20 to 30 minutes per session.

Sources: Shapiro & Carlson, 2009; Wallace, 2009; Williams & others, 2007.

CHAPTER REVIEW

KEY PEOPLE AND KEY TERMS

Walter B. Cannon, p. 507

stress, p. 499

cognitive appraisal model, p. 499

health psychology, p. 500

biopsychosocial model, p. 501

stressors, p. 501

daily hassles, p. 503

burnout, p. 504

Richard Lazarus, p. 499

acculturative stress, p. 506

fight-or-flight response, p. 507

catecholamines, p. 507

corticosteroids, p. 509

general adaptation syndrome, p. 509

telomeres, p. 509

Martin Seligman, p. 515

immune system, p. 511

lymphocytes, p. 511

psychoneuroimmunology, p. 511

optimistic explanatory style, p. 515

pessimistic explanatory style, p. 515

Hans Selye, p. 508

Type A behavior pattern, p. 517

social support, p. 519

coping, p. 522

problem-focused coping, p. 523

emotion-focused coping, p. 523

mindfulness meditation, p. 528

Stress, Health, and Coping

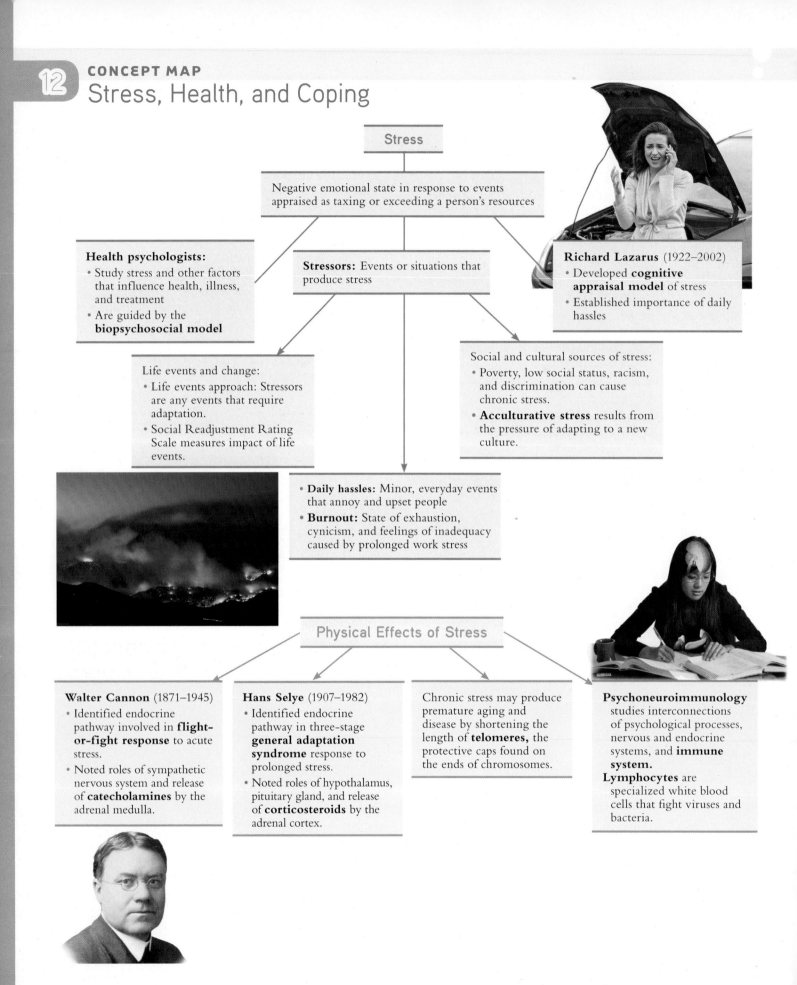

Stress

Negative emotional state in response to events appraised as taxing or exceeding a person's resources

Health psychologists:
• Study stress and other factors that influence health, illness, and treatment
• Are guided by the **biopsychosocial model**

Stressors: Events or situations that produce stress

Richard Lazarus (1922–2002)
• Developed **cognitive appraisal model** of stress
• Established importance of daily hassles

Life events and change:
• Life events approach: Stressors are any events that require adaptation.
• Social Readjustment Rating Scale measures impact of life events.

Social and cultural sources of stress:
• Poverty, low social status, racism, and discrimination can cause chronic stress.
• **Acculturative stress** results from the pressure of adapting to a new culture.

• **Daily hassles:** Minor, everyday events that annoy and upset people
• **Burnout:** State of exhaustion, cynicism, and feelings of inadequacy caused by prolonged work stress

Physical Effects of Stress

Walter Cannon (1871–1945)
• Identified endocrine pathway involved in **flight-or-fight response** to acute stress.
• Noted roles of sympathetic nervous system and release of **catecholamines** by the adrenal medulla.

Hans Selye (1907–1982)
• Identified endocrine pathway in three-stage **general adaptation syndrome** response to prolonged stress.
• Noted roles of hypothalamus, pituitary gland, and release of **corticosteroids** by the adrenal cortex.

Chronic stress may produce premature aging and disease by shortening the length of **telomeres,** the protective caps found on the ends of chromosomes.

Psychoneuroimmunology studies interconnections of psychological processes, nervous and endocrine systems, and **immune system.**
Lymphocytes are specialized white blood cells that fight viruses and bacteria.

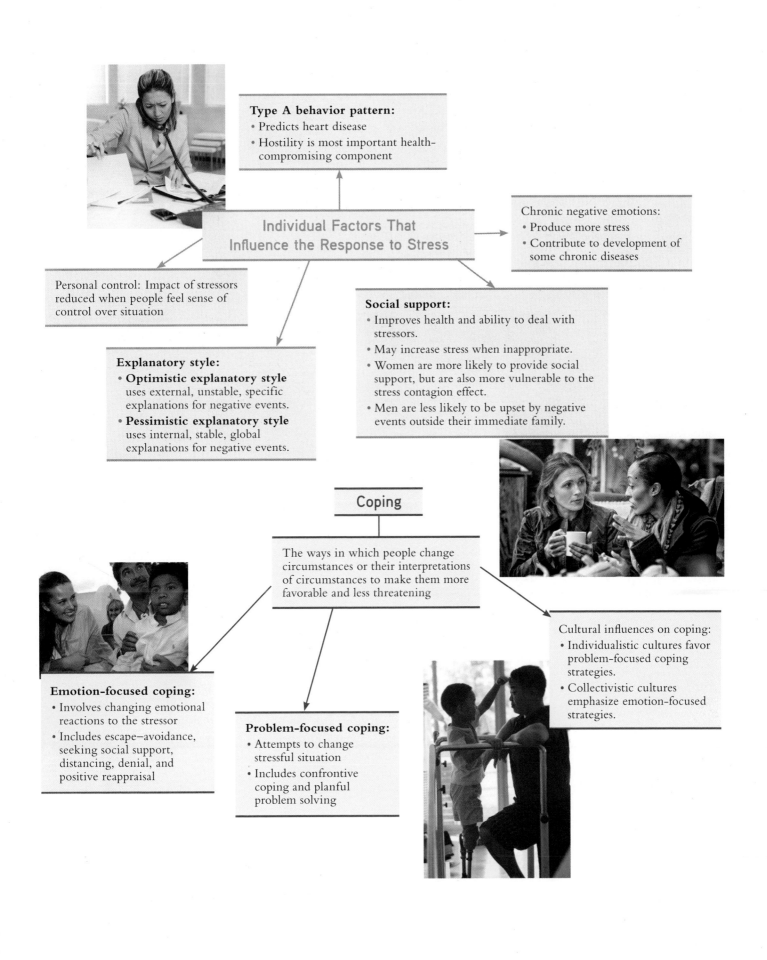

Type A behavior pattern:
- Predicts heart disease
- Hostility is most important health-compromising component

Individual Factors That Influence the Response to Stress

Chronic negative emotions:
- Produce more stress
- Contribute to development of some chronic diseases

Personal control: Impact of stressors reduced when people feel sense of control over situation

Social support:
- Improves health and ability to deal with stressors.
- May increase stress when inappropriate.
- Women are more likely to provide social support, but are also more vulnerable to the stress contagion effect.
- Men are less likely to be upset by negative events outside their immediate family.

Explanatory style:
- **Optimistic explanatory style** uses external, unstable, specific explanations for negative events.
- **Pessimistic explanatory style** uses internal, stable, global explanations for negative events.

Coping

The ways in which people change circumstances or their interpretations of circumstances to make them more favorable and less threatening

Cultural influences on coping:
- Individualistic cultures favor problem-focused coping strategies.
- Collectivistic cultures emphasize emotion-focused strategies.

Emotion-focused coping:
- Involves changing emotional reactions to the stressor
- Includes escape–avoidance, seeking social support, distancing, denial, and positive reappraisal

Problem-focused coping:
- Attempts to change stressful situation
- Includes confrontive coping and planful problem solving

MYTH OR SCIENCE?

Is it true . . .

○ That most people with a psychological disorder are violent?

○ That psychological disorders are rare?

○ That the less anxiety you have, the better?

○ That people who are perfectionists probably have obsessive–compulsive disorder?

○ That many psychological disorders run in families?

○ That the types of psychological disorders are pretty much the same in every culture?

○ That people with schizophrenia have a split personality?

(inset) Piotr Marcinski/Shutterstock
(bkgrd) NorGal/Shutterstock

"I'M FLYING! I'VE ESCAPED!"

PROLOGUE

ELYN SAKS, VANDERBILT UNIVERSITY FRESHMAN, was hosting a high school student considering Vanderbilt in her dorm room. Elyn had become increasingly anxious during her first semester. With the arrival of a stranger, her agitation spiked. And she snapped.

With no warning, Elyn ran into the wintry Nashville night. A blanket that she had impulsively wrapped around her head traced her path into the dark. She darted around the snowy campus, extending her arms as if in flight. The high school student, frightened and confused, pleaded for Elyn to come back inside. But Elyn couldn't stop herself. "Even though I heard her," Elyn later wrote, "even though I registered the genuine fear in her voice, I continued to run, as though powered by some kind of engine. 'No one can get me!' I shouted. 'I'm flying! I've escaped!'" (Saks, 2008).

Elyn ran farther and faster. The night hid the details around her, and sound was muffled. It felt like total and perfect silence, a silence that ended only when she recognized her visitor's voice begging her to calm down. Slowly, she began to ask herself where she was and what she was doing. Eventually, Elyn decided that she could stop.

This wasn't the first time that Elyn had lost touch with reality or behaved irrationally. One night she ordered her friends to dare her to do something. At first, they played along, telling her to sing a song, then dance. But Elyn took it further, "You want me to swallow this whole bottle of aspirin?" She did, frightening her friends, who rushed her to the emergency room. Other times, she would go days without eating, sleeping, or bathing. And she wasn't always able

Psychological Disorders

to distinguish what was real from what was not. After a tumultuous freshman year, Elyn asked her parents to help her find a therapist. It was the first time she sought treatment for her symptoms. Eventually, she would be diagnosed with *schizophrenia,* a serious psychological disorder in which sufferers are often disconnected from the world around them.

Elyn's outbursts in college were early indicators of the series of psychotic breaks she would eventually suffer. Over the years, even as she remained in school, she experienced delusional beliefs, such as thinking that her therapist wanted to kill her. She also often exhibited strange speech patterns, like telling her therapist, "I won't let you go. Throw. So." And she frequently had hallucinations—for example, hearing her name being called when she was alone.

Elyn sometimes found it hard to mask these and other symptoms in public. One time, for example, while working on a group project, Elyn casually asked her fellow students whether they had ever killed anyone. When they expressed concern, she responded with disjointed words, "You know. Heaven and hell. Who's what, what's who." Then, climbing out onto the roof, Elyn waved her arms and yelled, "This is the real me" (Saks, 2008).

IN THIS CHAPTER:

> **INTRODUCTION:** Understanding Psychological Disorders

> Fear and Trembling: Anxiety Disorders, Posttraumatic Stress Disorder, and Obsessive-Compulsive Disorder

> Depressive and Bipolar Disorders: Disordered Moods and Emotions

> Eating Disorders: Anorexia, Bulimia, and Binge-Eating Disorder

> Personality Disorders: Maladaptive Traits

> The Dissociative Disorders: Fragmentation of the Self

> Schizophrenia: A Different Reality

> **PSYCH FOR YOUR LIFE:** Understanding and Helping to Prevent Suicide

Over many difficult years, Elyn struggled with her condition and tried a number of different treatments. She sometimes lost touch with reality for months at a time and spent extended periods in inpatient psychiatric hospitals. Although about half of people with schizophrenia experience either a single episode or a less severe version of the disorder, Elyn's experience predicted a grim future. She was told she would never be able to live and work on her own.

Throughout these struggles, however, Elyn actively sought treatment for her symptoms and continued to work very hard in school. And with help from skilled clinicians, her effort paid off. She graduated from Vanderbilt first in her class and went on to earn a Master's at Oxford University in England and a law degree at Yale University. Today, Elyn's schizophrenia is well controlled by medication and therapy, treatments you'll learn about in Chapter 14. Elyn describes her emergence from her symptoms of

schizophrenia as "daylight dawning after a long night."

Elyn is now happily married and has a startlingly successful academic career. In 2009, Elyn won a MacArthur Foundation fellowship, popularly known as a "Genius Grant." Elyn decided to use her MacArthur funding to found an institute for studying ethics related to mental health. But this meant publicly sharing her diagnosis. Elyn was worried, and family and friends fueled her unease. One colleague challenged her, "You want to be known as the schizophrenic with a job?" (Carey, 2011). But to Elyn's surprise, "coming out" as a successful person with schizophrenia was widely applauded. In fact, it motivated many others to share similar stories.

In her memoir, Elyn observes that she will always need treatment to control the symptoms of her illness. But Elyn has benefited from advances in our understanding of mental illnesses such as schizophrenia, and she is hopeful that the story of her success

will spur mental health professionals to reconsider the assumption that people with schizophrenia are unlikely to ever live productive, successful lives.

In this chapter, you'll learn about the symptoms that characterize some of the most common psychological disorders, including schizophrenia, the disorder experienced by Elyn. The symptoms of many psychological disorders are not as outwardly severe as those that Elyn experienced for years. And there is a wide range of psychological disorders that differ in symptoms, severity, and prognosis. But whether the psychological symptoms are obvious or not, they can seriously impair a person's ability to function. You'll also learn in this chapter about some of the underlying causes of psychological disorders. As you'll see, biological, psychological, and environmental factors have been implicated as contributing to many psychological disorders. Later in the chapter, we'll come back to Elyn's story. □

INTRODUCTION:
Understanding Psychological Disorders

KEY THEME

Understanding psychological disorders includes considerations of their origins, symptoms, and development, as well as how behavior relates to cultural and social norms.

KEY QUESTIONS

› What is a psychological disorder, and what differentiates abnormal behavior from normal behavior?
› What is DSM-5, and how was it developed?
› How prevalent are psychological disorders?

Does the cartoon on the left make you smile? The cartoon is humorous, but it's actually intended to make some serious points. It reflects several common misconceptions about psychological disorders that we hope to dispel in this chapter.

First, there's the belief that "crazy" behavior is very different from "normal" behavior. Granted, sometimes it is, like Elyn's bizarre pronouncements from the roof in front of her classmates. But as you'll see throughout this chapter, the line that divides "normal" and "crazy" behavior is often not as sharply defined as most people think. In many instances, the difference between normal and abnormal behavior is a matter of degree. For example, as you leave your apartment or house, it's normal to check or

Leo Cullum The The New Yorker Collection/ The Cartoon Bank

*"I'm going to be late, dear.
It's total craziness here."*

even double-check that the door is securely locked. However, if you feel compelled to go back and check the lock 50 times, it would be considered abnormal behavior.

The dividing line between normal and abnormal behavior is also often determined by the social or cultural context in which a particular behavior occurs. For example, among traditional Hindus in India, certain dietary restrictions are followed as part of the mourning process. It would be a serious breach of social norms if an Indian widow ate fish, meat, onions, garlic, or any other "hot" foods within six months of her husband's death. A Catholic widow in the United States would consider such restrictions absurd.

Second, when we encounter people whose behavior strikes us as weird, unpredictable, or baffling, it's easy to simply dismiss them as "crazy," as in the cartoon. Although convenient, such a response is too simplistic, not to mention unkind. It could also be wrong. Sometimes, unconventional people are labeled as crazy when they're actually just creatively challenging the conventional wisdom with new ideas.

Even if a person's behavior is seriously disturbed, labeling that person as "crazy" tells us nothing meaningful. What are the person's specific symptoms? What might be the cause of the symptoms? How did they develop? How long can they be expected to last? And how might the person be helped? The area of psychology and medicine that focuses on these questions is called **psychopathology**—the scientific study of the origins, symptoms, and development of psychological disorders. In this chapter and the next, we'll take a closer look at psychological disorders and their treatment.

Finally, there is still a strong social stigma attached to suffering from a psychological disorder (Ben-Zeev & others, 2010; Tucker & others, 2013). Because of the social stigma that can be associated with psychological disorders, people are often reluctant to seek the help of mental health professionals (Bathje & Pryor, 2011; Corrigan & others, 2014). People who *are* under the care of a mental health professional often hide the fact, telling only their closest friends—and understandably so. Being labeled "crazy" carries all kinds of implications, most of which reflect negative stereotypes about people with mental illness (Wirth & Bodenhausen, 2009). For example, University of Michigan professor Peter Railton spoke about how he hid his depression for years because of nagging questions: "Would people think less of me? Would I seem to be tainted, reduced in their eyes, someone with an inner failing whom no one would want to hire or with whom no one would want to marry or have children?" (Flaherty, 2015). In the Critical Thinking box "Are People with a Mental Illness as Violent as the Media Portray Them?", we discuss the accuracy of such stereotypes in more detail.

psychopathology The scientific study of the origins, symptoms, and development of psychological disorders.

psychological disorder or **mental disorder** A pattern of behavioral and psychological symptoms that causes significant personal distress, impairs the ability to function in one or more important areas of life, or both.

DSM-5 Abbreviation for the *Diagnostic and Statistical Manual of Mental Disorders*, Fifth Edition; the book published by the American Psychiatric Association that describes the specific symptoms and diagnostic guidelines for different psychological disorders.

Crazy Behavior? If you saw one of these costumed people walking down the street on an average day, you might think she was "crazy." But if you knew she was enjoying herself on International Zombie Day, you might just wish you were taking part, too. The social norms of a particular situation affect our perceptions of what is abnormal behavior.

Christian Aslund/Getty Images

What Is a Psychological Disorder?

What exactly are we talking about when we say that someone has a psychological or mental disorder? A **psychological disorder** or **mental disorder** can be defined as a pattern of behavioral or psychological symptoms that causes significant personal distress, impairs the ability to function in one or more important areas of life, or both (DSM-5, 2013). An important qualification is that the pattern of behavioral or psychological symptoms must represent a serious departure from the prevailing social and cultural norms. Hence, the behavior of a traditional Hindu woman who refuses to eat onions, garlic, or other "hot" foods following the death of her husband is perfectly normal because that norm is part of the Hindu culture.

What determines whether a given pattern of symptoms or behaviors qualifies as a psychological disorder? Throughout this chapter, you'll notice numerous references to DSM-5. **DSM-5** stands for *Diagnostic and Statistical Manual of Mental Disorders*, Fifth Edition, which was published by the American Psychiatric Association in 2013.

DSM-5 describes more than 260 specific psychological disorders, plus numerous additional conditions, like child physical abuse and educational problems. It provides codes for each disorder, and includes the symptoms, the criteria that must be met to make a diagnosis, and the frequency, typical course, and risk factors for each disorder. It also includes issues related to gender and culture for each disorder. DSM-5 provides mental health professionals with both a common language for labeling disorders and comprehensive guidelines for diagnosing them. DSM-5 also increasingly matches the disorders outlined in a similar manual utilized internationally, the World Health Organization's *International Classification of Diseases (ICD)*. Beginning in October 2015, mental health clinicians in the United States have been required to use codes from the ICD when seeking reimbursement through health insurance companies (Chamberlin, 2014).

The first edition of the *Diagnostic and Statistical Manual* was published in 1952. With each new edition, the number of distinct disorders has progressively increased—from fewer than a hundred in the first edition to more than three times that number in recent editions, including DSM-5 (Frances & Widiger, 2012; Horwitz, 2002; Houts, 2002). Some disorders that are relatively well known today, such as eating disorders, attention-deficit/hyperactivity disorder, and social anxiety disorder, were not added until later editions. And, some behavior patterns that were categorized as "disorders" in early editions, such as homosexuality, have been dropped from later editions because they are no longer considered to be psychological disorders.

CRITICAL THINKING

Are People with a Mental Illness as Violent as the Media Portray Them?

Are people with a psychological disorder more violent than other people? When a heinous crime occurs, such as a mass shooting in a public place, people tend to react by assuming that the perpetrator "must be crazy." Such statements may reflect the belief that mental illness and violent crime are closely linked. As Mary Camp and her colleagues (2010) write, "those categorized as mad are expected to be violent, unpredictable, or antisocial."

In *some* cases, such as the 2012 shootings in an elementary school in Newtown, Connecticut, or the 2014 shootings near the University of California, Santa Barbara, the killers do have symptoms of mental disturbance. Yet the vast majority of violent crimes, even heinous ones, are committed by people who are *not* mentally ill. And another study found that symptoms of mental illness were not a strong predictor of criminal behavior (Peterson & others, 2014).

Multiple studies have found that people with a major mental illness belong to the most stigmatized group in modern society (Hinshaw & Stier, 2008; Schomerus & others, 2012). Substantial progress has been made in the understanding and treatment of psychological disorders. However, in much of the popular media, people with psychological disorders are still portrayed in highly negative, stereotyped ways (Klin & Lemish, 2008; Nairn & others, 2011). One stereotype is that of the mentally disturbed person as a helpless victim. The other stereotype is that of the mentally disordered person as an evil villain who is unpredictable, dangerous, and violent (Camp & others, 2010). For example, many of the criminals in the Batman series, including the Joker and the Riddler, end up imprisoned in the fictional Arkham Asylum for the Criminally Insane after they are captured (Daniels, 2008).

One comprehensive survey found that although 5 percent of "normal" television characters are murderers, 20 percent of "mentally ill" characters are killers (Gerbner, 1998). The same survey found that about 40 percent of "normal" characters were violent,

but 70 percent of characters labeled as mentally ill were violent. This trend is also apparent in stories about real people. A study of Canadian news stories in 20 major newspapers over five years found that 40 percent of articles that discussed mental illness put it in the context of "danger, violence, or criminality" (Whitley & Berry, 2013). These media stereotypes reflect and reinforce the

Warner Bros./Courtesy Everett Collection

Hollywood Villains Heath Ledger, who played the Joker in *The Dark Knight,* described him as "a psychopathic, mass-murdering, schizophrenic clown." The film was criticized for perpetuating negative stereotypes about mental illness, but the "insane killer" is a standard plot device in many films and television dramas (Camp & others, 2010). Sometimes horrific events seem to confirm the stereotype, such as when a mentally disturbed young man shot 70 people at a midnight screening of *The Dark Knight Rises.* But research shows that most people with a mental illness are *not* violent.

It's important to understand that DSM-5 was not written by a single person or even a small group of experts. Rather, DSM-5 represents the *consensus* of hundreds of mental health professionals, mostly psychiatrists and clinical psychologists, representing many different organizations and perspectives. DSM-5 was developed over twelve years. Teams of mental health professionals conducted extensive reviews of the research findings for each category of mental disorder and conducted field trials, studies that examined how well the DSM worked in clinical settings. The APA also developed a Web site to allow both professionals and the public to provide feedback.

Despite these efforts, DSM-5 has many critics (see Frances, 2012; Frances & Widiger, 2012; Wakefield, 2013a; G. Watts, 2012). More specifically, it has been criticized for:

- inclusion of some conditions that are too "normal" to be considered disorders, such as extreme sadness related to bereavement (Maj, 2012; Wakefield, 2013b; G. Watts, 2012)

- use of arbitrary cutoffs to draw the line between people with and without a particular disorder, and even between different diagnoses (Caspi & others, 2014; J. Cohen & others, 2011; Insel, 2013; Laceulle & others, 2015)

- gender bias (Marecek & Gavey, 2013; Yonkers & Clarke, 2011)

- possible bias resulting from the financial ties of many DSM-5 authors to the pharmaceutical industry, which might benefit from the expansion of mental illness categories or loosening of criteria for diagnoses (Cosgrove & Krimsky, 2012)

---

widespread belief among Americans that most people with mental illness are violent and threatening (Diefenbach & West, 2007).

This public perception that people with a mental illness are dangerous contributes to the stigma of mental illness (Fazel & others, 2009; Torrey, 2011). But let's look at the evidence. *Are* people with mental disorders more violent than other people?

One groundbreaking study by psychologist Henry Steadman and his colleagues (1998) monitored the behavior of more than 1,000 former mental patients in the year after they were discharged from psychiatric facilities. For their control group, they also monitored a matched group of people who were not former mental patients but were living in the same neighborhood.

The researchers found that, overall, the former mental patients did *not* have a higher rate of violence than the comparison group. Former mental patients who demonstrated symptoms of substance use disorder were the most likely to engage in violent behavior. However, the same was also true of the control group. In other words, substance use disorder was associated with more violent behavior in *all* participants, whether they had a history of mental illness or not. The study also found that the violent behavior that *did* occur was most frequently aimed at friends and family members, not at strangers.

MYTH ◄ SCIENCE

Is it true that most people with a psychological disorder are violent?

Recent meta-analytic research reviews have confirmed the general finding that substance abuse greatly increases the risk of violent behavior by people who have been diagnosed with a severe mental illness, such as schizophrenia (see Douglas & others, 2009; Fazel & others, 2009). Beyond substance abuse, there is evidence that people with severe mental disorders who are experiencing extreme psychological symptoms, such as bizarre delusional ideas and hallucinated voices, do display a *slightly* higher level of violent and illegal behavior than do "normal" people (Bucci & others, 2013; Malla & Payne, 2005). However, the person with a mental disorder who is *not* suffering from such symptoms is no more likely than the average person to be involved in violent or illegal behavior. Other factors, such as a family history of violence, living in impoverished neighborhoods, and abusing drugs or alcohol, are stronger predictors of violence (Nederlof & others, 2013; Norko & Baranoski, 2005; Singh & others, 2012). It also is important to point out that people with some kinds of mental illness are a good deal more likely to be the victims of a violent crime than other people (Short & others, 2013).

Canadian psychologist Kevin Douglas and his colleagues (2009) emphasize that the overall size of the association between psychosis and violence is relatively small. As they point out, "Most violent individuals are not psychotic, and most psychotic individuals are not violent."

Clearly, the incidence of violent behavior among current or former mental patients is exaggerated in media portrayals. In turn, the exaggerated fear of violence from people with a psychological disorder contributes to the stigma of mental illness (Fazel & others, 2009). As psychologists Stephen Hinshaw and Andrea Stier (2008) emphasize, "Media depictions that routinely and inevitably link all forms of mental disorder with physical violence are stereotypic and inaccurate. Indeed, empirical data reveal that people with mental illness are far more likely to be victims of violent crime than are other individuals, and far more likely to be victims than to be perpetrators of violence."

CRITICAL THINKING QUESTIONS

- Can you think of any reasons why people with psychological disorders are more likely to be depicted as villains than members of other social groups?

- Can you think of any television shows or movies in which characters with a severe psychological disorder were shown in a sympathetic light? If so, are such depictions more or less common than depictions of people with a mental illness as dangerous or violent?

- What evidence could you cite to challenge the notion that people with psychological disorders are dangerous?

Finally, many critics believe that DSM-5 blurs the distinction between everyday normal unhappiness and "mental illness" (G. Watts, 2012). If the threshold for diagnosing mental disorders is set too low, some critics argue, too many people will be diagnosed with a "mental disorder" (Angell, 2011; Frances, 2010).

Despite its flaws, DSM-5 is the most comprehensive and authoritative set of guidelines available for diagnosing psychological disorders. Thus, we'll refer to the DSM often in this chapter.

The Prevalence of Psychological Disorders
A 50–50 CHANCE?

Just how common are psychological disorders? To investigate that question, researcher Ronald C. Kessler and his colleagues (2005a, 2005b) conducted a nationally representative survey of more than 9,000 Americans, ages 18 and older. Called the National Comorbidity Survey Replication (NCS-R), the survey involved more than two years of face-to-face interviews throughout the country. Participants were asked if they had experienced specific symptoms of psychological disorders: (1) during the previous 12 months and (2) at any point in their lives. They were also asked about possible risk factors associated with mental disorders, such as substance use.

The NCS-R results reconfirmed many of the findings of previous national surveys, including the finding that psychological disorders are much more prevalent than many people believe (Kessler & others, 2005c). Specifically, the NCS-R found that one out of four respondents (26 percent) reported experiencing the symptoms of a psychological disorder during the previous year (Kessler & others, 2005b). The NCS-R and other surveys like it also reveal a high degree of *comorbidity,* which means that people diagnosed with one disorder are also frequently diagnosed with another disorder as well.

Figure 13.1 shows the typical age of onset for some of the common mental disorders reported by the NCS-R respondents at any point in their life. As you can see in the left-hand graph, the different categories of mental disorders vary significantly in the median age of onset. Anxiety disorders and impulse-control disorders tend to begin at a much earlier age—around age 11—as compared to substance abuse disorders or mood disorders. In the right-hand graph, you can see the lifetime prevalence of the same categories of mental disorders. Like the original National Comorbidity Survey, the NCS-R found that almost one out of two adults (46%) had experienced the symptoms of a psychological disorder at some point thus far in their lives.

Rates of mental illness are high not just in the United States, but also globally. In a large-scale study conducted in conjunction with the World Health Organization, researchers surveyed about 85,000 people in 17 countries from almost every continent (Kessler & others, 2007). The lifetime rate of mental illness is about one third, with rates varying across countries—from about 12% in Nigeria to almost 50% in the United States (Wang & others, 2011). But estimates for countries with the lowest rates, like Nigeria, are likely to be biased because of a cultural stigma against disclosing symptoms of psychological disorders (Gureje & others, 2006).

Although it might initially seem disturbing to think that one-third to one-half of the adult population in the United States will experience the symptoms of a mental disorder,

MYTH ◄ SCIENCE
Is it true that psychological disorders are rare?

How Prevalent Are Psychological Disorders? Psychological disorders are far more common than most people think. According to the National Comorbidity Survey Replication (NCS-R), about one in four American adults has experienced the symptoms of some type of psychological disorder during the previous year. However, most people who experience such symptoms do not receive treatment (Wang & others, 2005).

Massimo Pizzotti/age fotostock

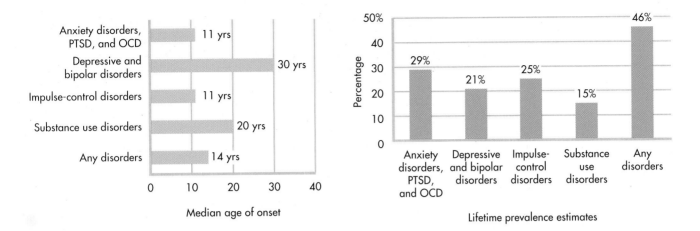

FIGURE 13.1 Age of Onset and the Lifetime Prevalence of Psychological Disorders The graph on the left shows the median age of onset for common categories of psychological disorders in the National Comorbidity Survey Replication (NCS-R). While the onset of anxiety, posttraumatic stress, and obsessive–compulsive disorders or impulse-control disorders tends to occur in the preteen years, the onset of depressive and bipolar disorders typically occurs around age 30, well into young adulthood. The graph on the right shows the lifetime prevalence for the same categories. The NCS-R reconfirmed that the lifetime prevalence of experiencing a psychological disorder is almost one out of two. The bars in the graph on the right add up to more than 100% because some people are diagnosed with more than one disorder.

lead researcher Ronald C. Kessler (2003b) helps put these findings into perspective, pointing out that:

> It wouldn't surprise anyone if I said that 99.9% of the population had been physically ill at some time in their life. Why, then, should it surprise anyone that 50% of the population has been mentally ill at some time in their life? The reason, of course, is that we invest the term "mentally ill" with excess meaning. A number of common mental illnesses, like adjustment disorders and brief episodes of depression, are usually mild and self-limiting. Many people experience these kinds of disorders at some time in their lives.

The NCS-R found that most people in the United States with the symptoms of a mental disorder (59 percent) received no treatment during the past year. Of those who did receive some kind of treatment, it was usually provided by a general medical practitioner, psychiatrist, or mental health specialist. Even so, the treatment provided was often inadequate, falling short of established treatment guidelines (Wang & others, 2005). These trends are shared globally. People in developing countries are even less likely than those in developed countries to seek treatment (Wang & others, 2011).

It seems clear that many people who could benefit from mental health treatment don't receive it. Several factors contribute to this unmet need, including lack of insurance, low income, and lack of access to mental health care, such as in developing countries or rural areas of developed countries (Santiago & others, 2013; Wang & others, 2011). Some people lack awareness about psychological disorders or shun treatment for fear of being stigmatized for seeking help with troubling psychological symptoms.

On the other hand, it also seems clear that most people manage to weather psychological symptoms without becoming completely debilitated and needing professional intervention (Mojtabai & others, 2011). One explanation for this is that people use a variety of coping strategies—some more effective than others—to manage psychological symptoms.

But it's important to remember that even ineffective strategies can appear to be effective. Why? Because the symptoms of many psychological disorders, especially those involving mild to moderate symptoms, diminish with the simple passage of

Think Like a SCIENTIST

Tracking the incidence of mental health problems is challenging. Can Internet searches reveal trends? Go to LaunchPad: Resources to **Think Like a Scientist** about **Tracking Mental Illness Online.**

 LaunchPad

time or with improvements in the person's overall situation. Nevertheless, there are many effective treatments available for psychological disorders that can produce improvements that occur much more quickly and endure longer. We'll look at the different types of therapies used to treat psychological disorders in the next chapter.

For the remainder of this chapter, we'll focus on psychological disorders in six DSM-5 categories: anxiety, posttraumatic stress, and obsessive-compulsive disorders; depressive and bipolar disorders; eating disorders; personality disorders; dissociative disorders; and schizophrenia. Along with being some of the most common disorders encountered by mental health professionals, they're also the ones that our students ask about most often. To help you distinguish between normal and maladaptive behaviors, we'll start the discussion of each mental disorder category by describing behavior that falls within the normal range of psychological functioning, such as normal feelings of anxiety or normal variations in mood.

Table 13.1 describes other categories of mental disorders contained in the DSM-5. Some of these disorders have been discussed in previous chapters. In the Psych for Your Life section at the end of this chapter, we'll look at what you can do to help prevent one of the most disturbing consequences of psychological problems—suicide.

❯ Test your understanding of **Understanding Psychological Disorders** with **LEARNING***Curve*.

This table includes some of the main diagnostic categories that are *not* covered in this chapter. We cover the major classes of psychological disorders in this chapter. Other important, but less common, diagnostic categories are shown here.

TABLE 13.1

Some Additional Diagnostic Categories in DSM-5

Diagnostic Category	Core Features	Examples of Specific Disorders
Neurodevelopmental disorders	Includes a wide range of developmental, behavioral, learning, and communication disorders that are usually first diagnosed in infancy, childhood, or adolescence. Symptoms of a particular disorder may vary depending on a child's age and development level.	**Autistic spectrum disorder:** Onset of symptoms prior to age of 3. Characterized by: (1) deficits in social communication and social interaction and (2) restricted, repetitive behaviors, interests, and activities; diagnosed according to level of symptom of severity, ranging from "requiring support" to "requiring very substantial support." **Tourette's disorder:** Onset prior to age of 18. Characterized by motor tics, such as recurring spasmodic movements of the head or arms, and vocal tics, such as recurring and sudden clicking, grunting, or snorting sounds. Sometimes involves uncontrollable utterances of profane or obscene words.
Substance-related and addictive disorders (see Chapter 4)	Characterized by a cluster of cognitive, behavioral, and physiological symptoms indicating that the individual continues using the substance or behavior despite significant problems related to the substance or behavior.	**Substance use disorder:** Recurrent substance use that involves impaired control, disruption of social, occupational, and interpersonal functioning, and the development of craving, tolerance, and withdrawal symptoms. **Gambling disorder:** Persistent gambling that disrupts personal, family, and/or vocational pursuits.
Somatic symptom and related disorders	Characterized by persistent, recurring complaints of bodily (or *somatic*) symptoms that are accompanied by abnormal thoughts, feelings, and behaviors in response to these symptoms.	**Somatic symptom disorder:** Characterized by excessive worry or distress that is out of proportion to the seriousness of physical symptoms that are present. **Illness anxiety disorder:** Excessive preoccupation with one's health and worry about illness despite the absence of serious physical symptoms.
Disruptive, impulse-control, and conduct disorders	Varied group of disorders involving problems in the self-control of emotions and behaviors and that are manifested in behaviors that harm or violate the rights of others.	**Kleptomania:** The recurrent failure to resist impulses to steal items that are not needed for personal use or for their monetary value. **Pyromania:** Deliberately setting fires on more than one occasion, accompanied by pleasure, gratification, or relief of tension.

Source: American Psychiatric Association (2013).

Fear and Trembling
ANXIETY DISORDERS, POSTTRAUMATIC STRESS DISORDER, AND OBSESSIVE–COMPULSIVE DISORDER

KEY THEME

Intense anxiety that disrupts normal functioning is an essential feature of the anxiety disorders, posttraumatic stress disorder, and obsessive–compulsive disorder.

KEY QUESTIONS

› How does pathological anxiety differ from normal anxiety?
› What characterizes generalized anxiety disorder and panic disorder?
› What are the phobias, and how have they been explained?

Anxiety is a familiar emotion to all of us—that feeling of tension, apprehension, and worry that often hits during personal crises and everyday conflicts. Although it is unpleasant, anxiety is sometimes helpful. Think of anxiety as your personal, internal alarm system that tells you that something is not quite right. When it alerts you to a realistic threat, anxiety is adaptive and normal. For example, anxiety about your grades may motivate you to study harder.

Anxiety has both physical and mental effects. As your internal alarm system, anxiety puts you on *physical alert,* preparing you to defensively "fight" or "flee" potential dangers. Anxiety also puts you on *mental alert,* making you focus your attention squarely on the threatening situation. You become extremely vigilant, scanning the environment for potential threats. When the threat has passed, your alarm system shuts off and you calm down. But even if the problem persists, you can normally put your anxious thoughts aside temporarily and attend to other matters.

In the **anxiety disorders,** however, the anxiety is *maladaptive,* disrupting everyday activities, moods, and thought processes. It's as if you've triggered a faulty car alarm that activates at the slightest touch and has a broken "off " switch.

Three features distinguish normal anxiety from pathological anxiety. First, pathological anxiety is *irrational.* The anxiety is provoked by perceived threats that are exaggerated or nonexistent, and the anxiety response is out of proportion to the actual importance of the situation. Second, pathological anxiety is *uncontrollable.* The person can't shut off the alarm reaction, even when he or she knows it's unrealistic.

And third, pathological anxiety is *disruptive.* It interferes with relationships, job or academic performance, or everyday activities. In short, pathological anxiety is unreasonably intense, frequent, persistent, and disruptive (Beidel & Stipelman, 2007; Woo & Keatinge, 2008).

As a symptom, anxiety occurs in many different psychological disorders. In the anxiety disorders, however, anxiety is the *main* symptom, although it is manifested differently in each of the disorders. Other disorders with anxiety as a symptom include posttraumatic stress disorder (PTSD) and obsessive–compulsive disorder (OCD). In this section, we'll talk about anxiety disorders, PTSD, and OCD, but we'll first focus on the anxiety disorders.

Disorders that include anxiety—the anxiety disorders, PTSD, and OCD—are among the most common of all psychological disorders. According to some estimates, they will affect about one in four people in the United States during their lifetimes (Kessler & others, 2005b; McGregor, 2009). Evidence of disabling anxiety has been found in virtually every culture studied, although symptoms may vary from one cultural group to another (Chentsova-Dutton & Tsai, 2007; Good & Hinton, 2009). Most of these disorders are much more common in women than in men (McLean & others, 2011).

Generalized Anxiety Disorder
WORRYING ABOUT ANYTHING AND EVERYTHING

Global, persistent, chronic, and excessive apprehension is the main feature of **generalized anxiety disorder (GAD).** People with this disorder are constantly tense

Roz Chast The New Yorker Collection/The Cartoon Bank

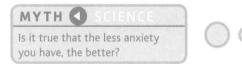

MYTH ◀ SCIENCE

Is it true that the less anxiety you have, the better?

anxiety An unpleasant emotional state characterized by physical arousal and feelings of tension, apprehension, and worry.

anxiety disorders A category of psychological disorders in which extreme anxiety is the main diagnostic feature and causes significant disruptions in the person's cognitive, behavioral, or interpersonal functioning.

generalized anxiety disorder (GAD) An anxiety disorder characterized by excessive, global, and persistent symptoms of anxiety; also called *free-floating anxiety.*

and anxious, and their anxiety is pervasive. They feel anxious about a wide range of life circumstances, sometimes with little or no apparent justification (Craske & Waters, 2005; Sanfelippo, 2006). The more issues about which a person worries excessively, the more likely it is that he or she suffers from generalized anxiety disorder (DSM-5, 2013).

Normally, anxiety quickly dissipates when a threatening situation is resolved. In generalized anxiety disorder, however, when one source of worry is removed, another quickly moves in to take its place. The anxiety can be attached to virtually any object or to none at all. Because of this, generalized anxiety disorder is sometimes referred to as *free-floating anxiety.*

EXPLAINING GENERALIZED ANXIETY DISORDER

What causes generalized anxiety disorder? As is true with most psychological disorders, environmental, psychological, and genetic as well as other biological factors are probably involved in GAD (Payne & others, 2014; Stein & Steckler, 2010). For example, a brain that is "wired" for anxiety can give a person a head start toward developing GAD in later life, but problematic relationships and stressful experiences can make the possibility more likely. Signs of problematic anxiety can be evident from a very early age, such as in the example of a child with a very shy temperament who consistently feels overwhelming anxiety in new situations or when separated from his parents. In some cases, such children develop anxiety disorders such as GAD in adulthood (Creswell & O'Connor, 2011; Weems & Silverman, 2008).

Panic Attacks and Panic Disorders
SUDDEN EPISODES OF EXTREME ANXIETY

Generalized anxiety disorder is like the dull ache of a sore tooth—a constant, ongoing sense of uneasiness, distress, and apprehension. In contrast, a **panic attack** is a sudden episode of extreme anxiety that rapidly escalates in intensity. The most common symptoms of a panic attack are a pounding heart, rapid breathing, breathlessness, and a choking sensation. Accompanying the intense, escalating surge of physical arousal are feelings of terror and the belief that one is about to die, go crazy, or completely lose control. A panic attack typically peaks within 10 minutes of onset and then gradually subsides. Nevertheless, the physical symptoms of a panic attack are so severe and frightening that it's not unusual for people to rush to an emergency room, convinced they are having a heart attack, stroke, or seizure (Buccelletti & others, 2013; Craske & Barlow, 2008).

Sometimes panic attacks occur after a stressful experience, such as an injury or illness, or during a stressful period of life, such as while changing jobs or during a period of marital conflict (Moitra & others, 2011). Experiences of bereavement, separation from significant others, and interpersonal loss are among the experiences most often associated with triggering panic attacks (Klauke & others, 2010). In other cases, however, panic attacks seem to come from nowhere.

When panic attacks occur *frequently* and *unexpectedly,* the person is said to be suffering from **panic disorder.** In this disorder, the frequency of panic attacks is highly variable and quite unpredictable. One person may have panic attacks several times a month. Another person may go for months without an attack and then experience panic attacks for several days in a row. Understandably, people with panic disorder are quite apprehensive about when and where the next panic attack will hit (Craske & Waters, 2005; Good & Hinton, 2009).

Some panic disorder sufferers go on to develop agoraphobia. **Agoraphobia** involves fear of suffering a panic attack or other embarrassing or incapacitating symptoms in a place from which escape would be difficult or impossible (DSM-5, 2013). For example, some agoraphobia sufferers fear falling, getting lost, or becoming incontinent in a public place where help might not be available and escape might be impossible. Crowds, stores, elevators, public transportation, or even traveling in a car may be avoided. Many people with agoraphobia, imprisoned by their fears, never leave their homes.

Adele and Anxiety Disorders Singer Adele has long suffered from debilitating anxiety while touring. She described having regular "anxiety attacks" that limit how often she plays to large audiences. Adele also gets anxious around other celebrities. She told a reporter, "I was about to meet Beyoncé and I had a full-blown anxiety attack" (Fisher, 2012).

MARIO ANZUONI/Reuters/Landov

panic attack A sudden episode of extreme anxiety that rapidly escalates in intensity.

panic disorder An anxiety disorder in which the person experiences frequent and unexpected panic attacks.

agoraphobia An anxiety disorder involving extreme fear of experiencing a panic attack or other embarrassing or incapacitating symptoms in a public situation where escape is impossible and help is unavailable.

Your author Susan treated a number of people with agoraphobia while working in an outpatient clinic for people with panic disorders. For example, Anya, a 32-year-old accountant, experienced infrequent but intense attacks of anxiety and fearfulness. Heart pounding and perspiring heavily, she felt as though she couldn't breathe. More than once, Anya called an ambulance because she was convinced she was having a heart attack. As her panic attacks increased in frequency and severity, Anya quit her job, fearful that she might have a panic attack while driving to work, riding the elevator to her office, or meeting with clients.

EXPLAINING PANIC DISORDER

People with panic disorder are often hypersensitive to the signs of physical arousal (Schmidt & Keough, 2010; Zvolensky & Smits, 2008). The fluttering heartbeat or momentary dizziness that the average person barely notices signals disaster to the panic-prone. Researchers have suggested that this oversensitivity to physical arousal is one of three important factors in the development of panic disorder. This *triple vulnerabilities model* of panic states that a biological predisposition toward anxiety, a low sense of control over potentially life-threatening events, and an oversensitivity to physical sensations combine to make a person vulnerable to panic (Bentley & others, 2013; Craske & Barlow, 2008).

People with panic disorder may also be victims of their own illogical thinking. According to the *catastrophic cognitions theory,* people with panic disorder are not only oversensitive to physical sensations, they also tend to *catastrophize* the meaning of their experience (Good & Hinton, 2009; Hinton & Hinton, 2009). A few moments of increased heart rate after climbing a flight of stairs is misinterpreted as the warning signs of a heart attack. Such catastrophic misinterpretations simply add to the physiological arousal, creating a vicious circle in which the frightening symptoms intensify.

Syndromes resembling panic disorder have been reported in many cultures (Chentsova-Dutton & Tsai, 2007; Hinton & Hinton, 2009). For example, the Spanish phrase *ataque de nervios* literally means "attack of nerves." It's a disorder reported in many Latin American cultures, in Puerto Rico, and among Latinos in the United States. *Ataque de nervios* has many symptoms in common with panic disorder—heart palpitations, dizziness, and the fear of dying, going crazy, or losing control. However, the person experiencing *ataque de nervios* also becomes hysterical. She may scream, swear, strike out at others, and break things. *Ataque de nervios* typically follows a severe stressor, especially one involving a family member. Funerals, accidents, or family conflicts often trigger such attacks. Because *ataque de nervios* tends to elicit immediate social support from others, it seems to be a culturally shaped, acceptable way to respond to severe stress.

The Phobias
FEAR AND LOATHING

A **phobia** is a persistent and irrational fear of a specific object, situation, or activity. In the general population, *mild* irrational fears that don't significantly interfere with a person's ability to function are very common. Many people are fearful of certain animals, such as dogs or snakes, or are moderately uncomfortable in particular situations, such as flying in a plane or riding in a glass elevator. Nonetheless, many people cope with such fears without being overwhelmed with anxiety. As long as the fear doesn't interfere with their daily functioning, they would not be diagnosed with a psychological disorder.

phobia A persistent and irrational fear of a specific object, situation, or activity.

Roz Chast The New Yorker Collection/The Cartoon Bank

TABLE 13.2

Some Unusual Phobias

Amathophobia	Fear of dust
Anemophobia	Fear of wind
Aphephobia	Fear of being touched by another person
Bibliophobia	Fear of books
Catotrophobia	Fear of breaking a mirror
Ergophobia	Fear of work or responsibility
Erythrophobia	Fear of red objects
Gamophobia	Fear of marriage
Hypertrichophobia	Fear of growing excessive amounts of body hair
Levophobia	Fear of things being on the left side of your body
Phobophobia	Fear of acquiring a phobia
Phonophobia	Fear of the sound of your own voice
Triskaidekaphobia	Fear of the number 13

In comparison, people with **specific phobia,** formerly called *simple phobia,* are more than just terrified of a particular object or situation. In some people, encountering the feared situation or object can provoke a full-fledged panic attack. Importantly, the incapacitating terror and anxiety interfere with the person's ability to function in daily life. Some people with phobias realize that their fears are irrational or excessive, but still will go to great lengths to avoid the feared object or situation. Consider the case of Antonio, who has a phobia of dogs. He works in a pizza parlor, making pizzas and taking orders. He could make more money if he took a job as a delivery person, but he won't even consider it because he is too afraid he might encounter a dog while making deliveries.

About 13 percent of the general population experiences a specific phobia at some time in their lives (Kessler & others, 2005a). More than twice as many women as men suffer from specific phobia. Occasionally, people have unusual phobias. (See Table 13.2). Oprah Winfrey, for example, has been afraid of chewing gum since she was a child, when her grandmother left used gum around the house. In an interview with Jamie Foxx, she told him: "When I saw you chewing on Oscar night, I freaked out" (O Magazine, 2005). Generally, the objects or situations that produce specific phobias tend to fall into four categories:

- Fear of particular situations, such as flying, driving, tunnels, bridges, elevators, crowds, or enclosed places
- Fear of features of the natural environment, such as heights, water, thunderstorms, or lightning
- Fear of injury or blood, including the fear of injections, needles, and medical or dental procedures
- Fear of animals and insects, such as snakes, spiders, dogs, cats, slugs, or bats

SOCIAL ANXIETY DISORDER
FEAR OF BEING JUDGED IN SOCIAL SITUATIONS

A second type of phobia also deserves additional comment. **Social anxiety disorder** is one of the most common psychological disorders and is more prevalent among women than men (Altemus, 2006; Kessler & others, 2005b). Social anxiety disorder goes well beyond the shyness that everyone sometimes feels at social gatherings. Rather, the person with social anxiety disorder is paralyzed by fear of social situations in which she may be judged by others. Eating a meal in public, making small talk at a party, or using a public restroom can be agonizing for the person with social anxiety disorder.

The core of social anxiety disorder seems to be an irrational fear of being critically evaluated by others. Some, but not all, people with social anxiety disorder recognize that their fear is excessive and irrational. Even so, they approach social situations with tremendous dread and anxiety (Kashdan & others, 2013). In severe cases, they may even suffer a panic attack in social situations. When the fear of being judged by others in social situations significantly interferes with daily life, social anxiety disorder may be present (DSM-5, 2013).

As with panic attacks, cultural influences can add some novel twists to social anxiety disorder. Consider *taijin kyofusho,* a disorder that usually affects young Japanese males. It has several features in common with social anxiety disorder, including extreme social anxiety and avoidance of social situations. However, the person with *taijin kyofusho* is not worried about being embarrassed in public. Rather, reflecting the cultural emphasis of concern for others, the person with *taijin kyofusho* fears that his appearance or smell, facial expression, or body language will offend, insult, or embarrass other people (Iwamasa, 1997; Norasakkunkit & others, 2012).

Social Anxiety Disorder About one out of eight adults in the United States has experienced social anxiety disorder at some point in his or her life (Kessler & others, 2005a). Social anxiety disorder is far more debilitating than everyday shyness. People with social anxiety disorder are intensely fearful of being watched or judged by others. Even ordinary activities, such as eating lunch in a public café, can cause unbearable anxiety.

Hemis/Alamy

EXPLAINING PHOBIAS
LEARNING THEORIES

The development of some phobias can be explained in terms of basic learning principles (Craske & Waters, 2005). *Classical conditioning* may well be involved in the development of a specific phobia that can be traced back to some sort of traumatic event. In Chapter 5 on learning, we saw how psychologist John Watson classically conditioned "Little Albert" to fear a tame lab rat that had been paired with loud noise. Following the conditioning, the infant's fear generalized to other furry objects.

More recently, researchers demonstrated the role of classical conditioning in the development of phobias by pairing something new, like an invented cartoon character named Spardi, with something frightening, like a picture of a woman being mugged at knife-point. Participants rated Spardi as more frightening in this circumstance than when the character was paired with something pleasant, like a picture of a sunset (Vriends & others, 2012). In much the same way, your author Sandy's neighbor Michelle has been extremely phobic of dogs ever since she was bitten by a German shepherd when she was 4 years old. In effect, Michelle developed a *conditioned response* (fear) to a *conditioned stimulus* (the German shepherd) that has *generalized* to similar stimuli—any dog.

Operant conditioning can also be involved in the avoidance behavior that characterizes phobias. In Michelle's case, she quickly learned that she could reduce her anxiety and fear by avoiding dogs altogether. To use operant conditioning terms, her *operant response* of avoiding dogs is *negatively reinforced* by the relief from anxiety and fear that she experiences.

Observational learning can also be involved in the development of phobias. Some people learn to be phobic of certain objects or situations by observing the fearful reactions of someone else who acts as a *model* in the situation. The child who observes a parent react with sheer panic to the sight of a spider or mouse may imitate the same behavioral response. People can also develop phobias from observing vivid media accounts of disasters, as when some people become afraid to fly after watching graphic TV coverage of a plane crash.

We also noted in Chapter 5 that humans seem *biologically prepared* to acquire fears of certain animals or situations, such as snakes or heights, which were survival threats in human evolutionary history (Workman & Reader, 2008).

People also seem to be predisposed to develop phobias toward creatures that arouse disgust, like slugs, maggots, or cockroaches. Instinctively, it seems, many people find such creatures repulsive, possibly because they are associated with disease, infection, or filth. Such phobias may reflect a fear of contamination or infection that is also based on human evolutionary history (Cisler & others, 2007).

Yuck! It's hard to suppress a shudder of disgust at the sight of a slug sliming its way across the sidewalk . . . or a cockroach scuttling across the kitchen floor. Are such responses instinctive? Why are people more likely to develop phobias for slugs, maggots, and cockroaches than for mosquitoes or grasshoppers?

(tl) Vassiliy Vishnevskiy/iStockphoto
(tr) Fotosearch

specific phobia An excessive, intense, and irrational fear of a specific object, situation, or activity that is actively avoided or endured with marked anxiety.

social anxiety disorder An anxiety disorder involving the extreme and irrational fear of being embarrassed, judged, or scrutinized by others in social situations.

ilovezion/Shutterstock

John Arnold/Shutterstock

An Evolutionary Fear of Holes Some people are afraid of a certain pattern of holes like those you might see in a chocolate bar, in soap bubbles, or on a lotus seed head like the one shown here. This condition is called trypophobia. Researchers Geoff Cole and Arnold Wilkins (2013) found striking similarities between the visual pattern that triggers fear in trypophobics and the markings on poisonous animals, like certain snakes or the poison dart frog shown here. They speculate that an ability to quickly notice a poisonous creature gave people an evolutionary advantage, even if it sometimes led them to fear harmless objects.

posttraumatic stress disorder (PTSD)
A disorder triggered by exposure to a highly traumatic event that results in recurrent, involuntary, and intrusive memories of the event; avoidance of stimuli and situations associated with the event; negative changes in thoughts, moods, and emotions; and a persistent state of heightened physical arousal.

Posttraumatic Stress Disorder and Obsessive–Compulsive Disorder

ANXIETY AND INTRUSIVE THOUGHTS

KEY THEME

Extreme anxiety and intrusive thoughts are symptoms of both posttraumatic stress disorder (PTSD) and obsessive–compulsive disorder (OCD).

KEY QUESTIONS

> What is PTSD, and what causes it?
> What is obsessive–compulsive disorder?
> What are the most common types of obsessions and compulsions?

Posttraumatic stress disorder (PTSD) is a long-lasting disorder that develops in response to an extreme physical or psychological trauma. Extreme traumas are events that produce intense feelings of horror and helplessness, such as a serious physical injury or threat of injury to yourself or to loved ones. Although not classified as an anxiety disorder, some of the same patterns of emotion, cognition, and behavior mark both PTSD and anxiety disorders.

Originally, PTSD was primarily associated with direct experiences of military combat. Veterans of military conflict in Afghanistan and Iraq, like veterans of earlier wars, have a higher prevalence of PTSD than nonveterans (E. Cohen & others, 2011; Fontana & Rosenheck, 2008). However, it's now known that PTSD can *also* develop in survivors of other sorts of extreme traumas, such as natural disasters, physical or sexual assault, or terrorist attacks (McNally, 2003). Rescue workers, relief workers, and emergency service personnel can also develop PTSD symptoms (Berger & others, 2012; Eriksson & others, 2001). Simply witnessing the injury or death of others can be sufficiently traumatic for PTSD to occur. And some researchers have documented PTSD symptoms in people who were exposed to trauma in the media, such as graphic images related to terrorism or war on television (Garfin & others, 2015; Silver & others, 2013).

In any given year, it's estimated that more than 5 million American adults experience PTSD. There is also a significant gender difference—more than twice as many women as men experience PTSD after exposure to trauma (Olff & others, 2007). Children can also experience the symptoms of PTSD. For example, PTSD has been observed in children living in a war zone in the Middle East and children living in New Orleans after Hurricane Katrina (Fasfous & others, 2013; Langley & others, 2014).

Chris Hondros/Getty Images

Invisible Wounds: PTSD Among U.S. Veterans of the Iraq and Afghanistan Wars Infantry scout Jesus Bocanegra witnessed suffering and death firsthand in Iraq. After returning home to the U.S., Bocanegra suffered from frequent flashbacks, nightmares, nervousness, and felt emotionally numb. Like Bocanegra, some 300,000 veterans have been diagnosed with PTSD or major depressive disorder (Tanielian, 2008). The high rate of PTSD and suicide may be related to unique aspects of the Iraq and Afghanistan conflicts. As Veterans Affairs physician Karen Seal and her colleagues (2008) observed, "The majority of military personnel experience high-intensity guerrilla warfare and the chronic threat of roadside bombs and improvised explosive devices. Some soldiers endure multiple tours of duty, many experience traumatic injury, and more of the wounded survive than ever before."

Four core clusters of symptoms characterize PTSD (DSM-5, 2013). First, the person *frequently recalls the event*, replaying it in his mind. Such recollections are often *intrusive*, meaning that they are unwanted and interfere with normal thoughts. Recollections can even be triggered by unrelated events. After the Boston Marathon bombings in 2013, almost 40 percent of a sample of military veterans in Boston who already suffered from PTSD reported increased emotional distress (Miller & others, 2013). Second, the person *avoids stimuli* or *situations* that tend to trigger memories of the experience. Third, he may experience *negative alterations in thinking, moods, and emotions*. He may feel alienated from others, blame himself or others for the traumatic event, and feel a persistent sense of guilt, fear, or anger. Some people are unable to recall key features of the traumatic event. Fourth, the person experiences *increased physical arousal.* He may be easily startled, experience sleep disturbances, have problems concentrating and remembering, and be prone to irritability or angry outbursts (DSM-5, 2013).

Posttraumatic stress disorder is somewhat unusual in that the source of the disorder is the traumatic event itself, rather than a cause that lies within the individual. Even well-adjusted and psychologically healthy

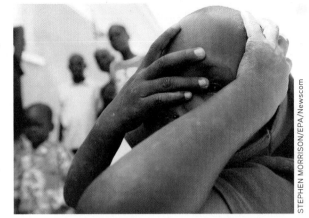

STEPHEN MORRISON/EPA/Newscom

people may develop PTSD when exposed to an extremely traumatic event (Ozer & others, 2003). Among Vietnam veterans in the United States, for example, exposure to combat and involvement in actions that harmed civilians or prisoners of war played a bigger role in the development of PTSD than a soldier's preexisting psychological vulnerability (Dohrenwend & others, 2013).

Terrorist attacks, because of their suddenness and intensity, are particularly likely to produce posttraumatic stress disorder in survivors, rescue workers, and observers (Neria & others, 2011). For example, four years after the bombing of the Murrah Building in Oklahoma City, more than a third of the survivors suffered from posttraumatic stress disorder (North & others, 1999). Seven years after the bombing, more than a quarter still had PTSD (North & others, 2011). Similarly, five years after the 9/11 terrorist attacks, more than 11 percent of rescue and recovery workers met formal criteria for PTSD—a rate comparable to that of soldiers returning from active duty in Iraq and Afghanistan (Stellman & others, 2008). Among people who had directly witnessed the attacks, over 16 percent had PTSD symptoms four years after the attacks (Farfel & others, 2008; Jayasinghe & others, 2008).

However, it's also important to note that no stressor, no matter how extreme, produces posttraumatic stress disorder in everyone. Why is it that some people develop PTSD while others don't? Several factors influence the likelihood of developing posttraumatic stress disorder. First, there is evidence that a vulnerability to PTSD can be inherited (Wilker & Kolassa, 2013). Second, people with a personal or family history of psychological disorders are more likely to develop PTSD when exposed to an extreme trauma (Amstadter & others, 2009; Koenen & others, 2008). Third, the magnitude of the trauma plays an important role. More extreme stressors are more likely to produce PTSD. Frequency of exposure is a factor as well. When people undergo *multiple* traumas, the incidence of PTSD can be quite high. One study even observed PTSD symptoms among journalists who never left the newsroom but were frequently exposed to traumatic images (Feinstein & others, 2014).

OBSESSIVE-COMPULSIVE DISORDER
CHECKING IT AGAIN . . . AND AGAIN

When you leave your home, you probably check to make sure all the doors are locked. You may even double-check just to be on the safe side. But once you're confident that the door is locked, you don't think about it again. Some people trivialize the term "obsessive–compulsive disorder" or "OCD," saying "I'm so OCD" to describe this behavior or a tendency to be extremely neat, for example (Pavelko & Myrick, 2015). But most people who say this probably do not have an actual diagnosis. Some people with an actual diagnosis of OCD find the casual use of the term offensive, including author Alison Dotson who points out, "OCD isn't cute" (Tipu, 2015).

Here's a sense of what OCD is really like. Imagine you've checked the door *30* times. Yet you're still not quite sure that the door is really locked. You know the feeling is irrational, but you feel compelled to check again and again. Imagine you've *also* had to repeatedly check that the coffeepot was unplugged, that the stove was turned

The Ravages of War: Child Soldiers An estimated quarter-million children serve as unwilling combatants in wars today, most of them kidnapped from their families and forced to serve as soldiers. Child soldiers not only suffer torture and violence, they are also often forced to commit atrocities against others. Not surprisingly, these children suffer from very high rates of posttraumatic stress disorder (Bayer & others, 2007; Kohrt & others, 2008). One survey of former child soldiers in refugee camps in Uganda found that 97 percent of the children suffered from PTSD symptoms (see J. Dawson, 2007; Derluyn & others, 2004). Rehabilitation centers have been established throughout Uganda and the Democratic Republic of Congo, where many of these children live, but more assistance is desperately needed (Ursano & Shaw, 2007). This girl hides her eyes during a role-playing game at a rehabilitation center. Role-playing is used to help children cope with the trauma of the violence that they saw or took part in.

MYTH ◀ SCIENCE

Is is true that people who are perfectionists probably have obsessive–compulsive disorder?

Howard Hughes and Obsessive–Compulsive Disorder Shown at the controls of his Spruce Goose aircraft, Hughes was an extraordinary aviator, engineer, inventor, and film producer and director. But Hughes was also tormented by his obsessive fear of germs, which could be traced back to his childhood. Hughes's mother was constantly fearful that her son would catch polio or be sickened by germs. As an adult, Hughes developed increasingly extreme and bizarre compulsions, such as sitting naked for weeks in "germ free zones" in darkened hotel rooms and wearing tissue boxes on his feet. By the time Hughes died, he was a mentally ill recluse, emaciated, and a drug addict (Bartlett & Steele, 2004; Dittman, 2005).

off, and so forth. Finally, imagine that you got only two blocks away from home before you felt compelled to turn back and check *again*—because you still were not certain.

Sound agonizing? This is the psychological world of the person who suffers from one form of obsessive–compulsive disorder. **Obsessive–compulsive disorder (OCD)** is a disorder in which a person's life is dominated by repetitive thoughts (*obsessions*) and behaviors (*compulsions*). Like PTSD, OCD is not classified as an anxiety disorder, but shares similar symptom patterns.

Obsessions are repeated, intrusive, uncontrollable thoughts or mental images that cause the person great anxiety and distress. Obsessions are not the same as everyday worries. Normal worries typically have some sort of factual basis, even if they're somewhat exaggerated. In contrast, obsessions have little or no basis in reality and are often extremely far-fetched. One common obsession is an irrational fear of dirt, germs, and other forms of contamination. Another common theme is pathological doubt about having accomplished a simple task, such as shutting off appliances (Antony & others, 2007; Renshaw & others, 2010).

A **compulsion** is a repetitive behavior that a person feels driven to perform. Typically, compulsions are ritual behaviors that must be carried out in a certain pattern or sequence. Compulsions may be *overt physical behaviors,* such as repeatedly washing your hands, checking doors or windows, or entering and reentering a doorway until you walk through exactly in the middle. Or they may be *covert mental behaviors,* such as counting or reciting certain phrases to yourself. But note that the person does not compulsively wash his hands because he enjoys being clean. Rather, he washes his hands because to *not* do so causes extreme anxiety. If the person tries to resist performing the ritual, unbearable tension, anxiety, and distress result (Mathews, 2009).

Obsessions and compulsions tend to fall into a limited number of categories. About three-fourths of patients with obsessive–compulsive disorder suffer from multiple obsessions, and slightly more than half report more than one type of compulsion (Rasmussen & Eisen, 1992). The most common obsessions and compulsions are shown in Table 13.3.

Many people with obsessive–compulsive disorder have the irrational belief that failure to perform the ritual action will lead to a catastrophic or disastrous outcome (MacDonald & Davey, 2005). Research suggests that many people with OCD, especially those with checking or counting compulsions, are particularly prone to superstitious or "magical" thinking (Einstein & Menzies, 2004; Kingdon & others, 2012). Even though the person knows that her obsessions are irrational or her compulsions absurd, she is unable to resist their force.

People may experience either obsessions or compulsions. More commonly, obsessions and compulsions are *both* present. Often, the obsessions and compulsions are linked in some way. For example, a man who was obsessed with the idea that he might have lost an important document felt compelled to pick up every scrap of paper he saw on the street and in other public places.

Other compulsions bear little logical relationship to the feared consequences. For instance, a woman believed that if she didn't get dressed according to a strict pattern, her husband would die in an automobile accident. In all cases, people with obsessive–compulsive disorder feel that something terrible will happen if the compulsive action is left undone (Mathews, 2009).

Interestingly, obsessions and compulsions take a similar shape in different cultures around the world. However, the *content* of the obsessions and compulsions tends to mirror the particular culture's concerns and beliefs. In the United States, compulsive washers are typically preoccupied with obsessional fears of germs and

obsessive–compulsive disorder (OCD) Disorder characterized by the presence of intrusive, repetitive, and unwanted thoughts (obsessions) and repetitive behaviors or mental acts that an individual feels driven to perform (compulsions).

obsessions Repeated, intrusive, and uncontrollable irrational thoughts or mental images that cause extreme anxiety and distress.

compulsions Repetitive behaviors or mental acts that a person feels driven to perform in order to prevent or reduce anxiety and distress, or to prevent a dreaded event or situation.

TABLE 13.3

The Most Common Obsessions and Compulsions

Obsession	Description
Contamination	Irrational fear of contamination by dirt, germs, or other toxic substances. Typically accompanied by cleaning or washing compulsion.
Pathological doubt	Feeling of uncertainty about having accomplished a simple task. Recurring fear that you have inadvertently harmed someone or violated a law. Typically accompanied by checking compulsion.
Violent or sexual thoughts	Fear that you have harmed or will harm another person or have engaged or will engage in some sort of unacceptable behavior. May take the form of intrusive mental images or impulses.

Compulsion	Description
Washing	Urge to repeatedly wash yourself or clean your surroundings. Cleaning or washing may involve an elaborate, lengthy ritual. Often linked with contamination obsession.
Checking	Checking repeatedly to make sure that a simple task has been accomplished. Typically occurs in association with pathological doubt. Checking rituals may take hours.
Counting	Need to engage in certain behaviors a specific number of times or to count to a certain number before performing some action or task.
Symmetry and precision	Need for objects or actions to be perfectly symmetrical or in an exact order or position. Need to do or undo certain actions in an exact fashion.

Source: From Psychiatric Clinics of North America, 15, Rasmussen, Steven A.; & Eisen, Jane L., The epidemiology and clinical features of obsessive–compulsive disorder, 743–758, Copyright Elsevier (1992).

infection. But in rural Nigeria and rural India, compulsive washers are more likely to have obsessional concerns about religious purity rather than germs (Rapoport, 1989; Rego, 2009).

EXPLAINING OBSESSIVE–COMPULSIVE DISORDER

Although the causes of obsessive–compulsive disorder are still being investigated, evidence strongly suggests that biological factors are involved (Chamberlain & Fineberg, 2013). For example, deficiencies in the neurotransmitters norepinephrine and serotonin have been implicated in obsessive–compulsive disorder. When treated with drugs that increase the availability of these substances in the brain, many patients with OCD experience a marked decrease in symptoms. Excess of another neurotransmitter, glutamate, has recently also been implicated in OCD (Maia & Cano-Colino, 2015).

In addition, obsessive–compulsive disorder has been linked with broad deficits in the ability to manage cognitive processes such as attention (Snyder & others, 2014). This may, in turn, be linked to dysfunction in specific brain areas, such as areas involved in the fight-or-flight response, and in the frontal lobes, which play a key role in our ability to think and plan ahead (Anderson & Savage, 2004; Pujol & others, 2011). Another brain area that has been implicated is the *caudate nucleus,* which is involved in regulating movements (Guehl & others, 2008; Maia & others, 2009). Dysfunctions in these brain areas might help account for the overwhelming sense of doubt and the lack of control over thoughts and actions that are experienced in obsessive–compulsive disorder.

The anxiety, posttraumatic stress, and obsessive–compulsive disorders are summarized in Table 13.4.

〉 Test your understanding of **Anxiety Disorders** with *LEARNINGCurve.*

S. Harris/www.CartoonStock.com

TABLE 13.4

Disorders Involving Intense Anxiety

Generalized Anxiety Disorder
- Persistent, chronic, unreasonable worry and anxiety
- General symptoms of anxiety, including persistent physical arousal

Panic Disorder
- Frequent and unexpected panic attacks, with no specific or identifiable trigger

Phobias
- Intense anxiety or panic attack triggered by a specific object or situation
- Persistent avoidance of feared object or situation

Posttraumatic Stress Disorder (PTSD)
- Anxiety triggered by intrusive, recurrent memories of a highly traumatic experience

Obsessive–Compulsive Disorder (OCD)
- Anxiety caused by uncontrollable, persistent, recurring thoughts (obsessions) and/or urges to perform certain actions (compulsions)

major depressive disorder A mood disorder characterized by extreme and persistent feelings of despondency, worthlessness, and hopelessness, causing impaired emotional, cognitive, behavioral, and physical functioning.

Depressive and Bipolar Disorders
DISORDERED MOODS AND EMOTIONS

KEY THEME

In the depressive and the bipolar disorders, disturbed emotions cause psychological distress and impair daily functioning.

KEY QUESTIONS

> What are the symptoms and course of major depressive disorder, persistent depressive disorder, bipolar disorder, and cyclothymic disorder?
> How prevalent are depressive and bipolar disorders?
> What factors contribute to the development of depressive and bipolar disorders?

Let's face it, we all have our ups and downs. When things are going well, we feel cheerful and optimistic. When events take a more negative turn, our mood can sour. We feel miserable and pessimistic. Either way, the intensity and duration of our moods are usually in proportion to the events going on in our lives. That's completely normal.

In the depressive disorders and the bipolar and related disorders, however, emotions violate the criteria of normal moods. In quality, intensity, and duration, a person's emotional state does not seem to reflect what's going on in his or her life. A person may feel a pervasive sadness despite the best of circumstances. Or a person may be extremely energetic and overconfident with no apparent justification. These mood changes persist much longer than the normal fluctuations in moods that we all experience.

Because disturbed moods and emotions are core symptoms in both the depressive and bipolar disorders, they are sometimes called *mood disorders* or *affective disorders*. The word "affect" is synonymous with "emotion" or "feelings." In DSM-5, depressive disorders and bipolar disorders are given their own distinct categories rather than grouped together. In this section, we'll look at depressive disorders first and then turn to bipolar disorders.

Major Depressive Disorder
MORE THAN ORDINARY SADNESS

The intense psychological pain of **major depressive disorder** is hard to convey to those who have never experienced it. Several patients described their struggles with depression to researchers (Smith & Rhodes, 2015). Ravi explained, "You get into a state I think mentally where, you're just like out on an island. And . . . you can see from that island another shore and all these people are there, but there's no way that you can get across." Sally described it as "like part of you gone, your heart. . . . Perhaps half my heart has gone away."

THE SYMPTOMS OF MAJOR DEPRESSIVE DISORDER

The patient quotes above give you a feeling for how the symptoms of depression affect the whole person—emotionally, cognitively, behaviorally, and physically. Take a few minutes to study Figure 13.2, which summarizes the common symptoms of major depressive disorder. Depression is also often accompanied by the physical symptoms of anxiety (Andover & others, 2011). Some depressed people experience a sense of physical restlessness or nervousness, demonstrated by fidgeting or aimless pacing.

Suicide is always a potential risk in major depressive disorder (Brådvik & Berglund, 2010). Thoughts become globally pessimistic and negative about the self, the world, and the future (Beck & others, 1979; Possel

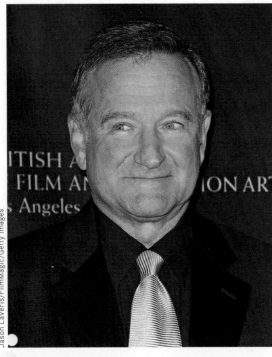

Jason LaVeris/FilmMagic/Getty Images

Robin Williams Famed actor and comedian Robin Williams seemed to have everything: a loving family, a successful Hollywood career, and the admiration of millions of fans. But Williams also had a long history of depression and alcoholism, and had spent time in rehab for his addictions. Even when sober, the depression lingered. Williams once said that, when sober, he is "just as insecure. The demons are still there. The little voice saying 'you're garbage, you're nothing'" (Whitty, 2014). In 2014, Williams hanged himself.

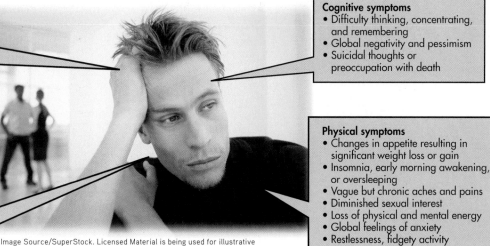

Emotional symptoms
- Feelings of sadness, hopelessness, helplessness, guilt, emptiness, or worthlessness
- Feeling emotionally disconnected from others
- Turning away from other people

Behavioral symptoms
- Dejected facial expression
- Makes less eye contact; eyes downcast
- Smiles less often
- Slowed movements, speech, and gestures
- Tearfulness or spontaneous episodes of crying
- Loss of interest or pleasure in usual activities, including sex
- Withdrawal from social activities

Cognitive symptoms
- Difficulty thinking, concentrating, and remembering
- Global negativity and pessimism
- Suicidal thoughts or preoccupation with death

Physical symptoms
- Changes in appetite resulting in significant weight loss or gain
- Insomnia, early morning awakening, or oversleeping
- Vague but chronic aches and pains
- Diminished sexual interest
- Loss of physical and mental energy
- Global feelings of anxiety
- Restlessness, fidgety activity

Image Source/SuperStock. Licensed Material is being used for illustrative purposes only; person depicted in the licensed Material is a model.

& Winkeljohn Black, 2014). This pervasive negativity and pessimism are often manifested in suicidal thoughts or a preoccupation with death. Approximately 10 percent of those suffering from major depressive disorder attempt suicide (McGirr & others, 2007). Grammy award–winning hip-hop artist Lupe Fiasco described the unshakable negativity that drove his depression and suicidal thoughts in his song *Beautiful Lasers,* "All you see is all my feats; all I see is all my flaws; all I hear is all my demons; even through your applause."

Abnormal sleep patterns are another hallmark of major depressive disorder. The amount of time spent in nondreaming, deeply relaxed sleep is greatly reduced or absent (see Chapter 4). Rather than the usual 90-minute cycles of dreaming, the person experiences sporadic REM periods of varying lengths. Spontaneous awakenings occur repeatedly during the night. Very commonly, the depressed person awakens at 3:00 or 4:00 A.M., then cannot get back to sleep, despite feeling exhausted. Less commonly, some depressed people sleep excessively, sometimes as much as 18 hours a day.

To be diagnosed with major depressive disorder, a person must display most of the symptoms described for two weeks or longer (DSM-5, 2013). In many cases, there doesn't seem to be any external reason for the persistent feeling of depression. In other cases, a person's downward emotional spiral has been triggered by a negative life event, stressful situation, or chronic stress (Gutman & Nemeroff, 2011).

One significant negative event deserves special mention: the death of a loved one. Previous editions of the *Diagnostic and Statistical Manual* stated that depression-like symptoms that might accompany grieving did not qualify as major depression unless those symptoms persisted for two months, rather than two weeks. DSM-5 removes that special treatment for bereavement, based on the reasoning that bereavement is like any other psychosocial event that might trigger a depressive episode. While it is normal to feel a sense of loss and deep sadness when a close friend or family member dies, feelings of worthlessness, self-loathing, and the inability to anticipate happiness or pleasure may indicate that major depressive disorder may be present (DSM-5, 2013).

Although major depressive disorder can occur at any time, some people experience symptoms that intensify at certain times of the year. For people with **seasonal affective disorder (SAD),** repeated episodes of major depressive disorder are as predictable as the changing seasons, especially the onset of autumn and winter when there is the least amount of sunlight. Seasonal affective disorder is more common among women and among people who live in the northern latitudes (Partonen & Pandi-Perumal, 2010).

FIGURE 13.2 The Symptoms of Major Depressive Disorder The experience of major depressive disorder can permeate every aspect of life. This figure shows some of the most common emotional, behavioral, cognitive, and physical symptoms of that disorder.

seasonal affective disorder (SAD) A mood disorder in which episodes of depression typically occur during the fall and winter and subside during the spring and summer.

J. K. Rowling British author J. K. Rowling created a terrifying set of characters in her bestselling *Harry Potter* series: "Dementors are among the foulest creatures that walk this earth. They infest the darkest, filthiest places, they glory in decay and despair, they drain peace, hope, and happiness out of the air around them" (Rowling, 1999). The effect of the fearsome dementors is a lot like the effect of major depressive disorder. In fact, Rowling admits that the dementors were based on her own experience with depression following several stressful life experiences. After her marriage ended while living abroad in Portugal, she moved back to the United Kingdom as a single parent with a young child. "I was definitely clinically depressed," she later said, describing depression aptly: "It's just all the color drained out of life really" (ABC News, 2009).

Some people experience a chronic form of depression called *persistent depressive disorder* that is often less severe than major depressive disorder. **Persistent depressive disorder** may develop after some stressful event or trauma, such as the death of a parent in childhood (DSM-5, 2013). Although the person functions adequately, she has a chronic case of "the blues" that can continue for years.

THE PREVALENCE AND COURSE OF MAJOR DEPRESSIVE DISORDER

Major depressive disorder is often called "the common cold" of psychological disorders, and for good reason: It is among the most prevalent psychological disorders. And in terms of its physical, psychological, and economic impact, it's one of the most devastating of *any* illness worldwide (Ledford, 2014). In any given year, about 7 percent of Americans are affected by major depressive disorder (Kessler & others, 2005b). In terms of lifetime prevalence, many researchers have estimated that about 15 percent of Americans will be affected by major depressive disorder at some point in their lives. However, some researchers suspect that number is too low. In a longitudinal study following more than 800 people for 30 years—from childhood through adulthood—about half of the sample experienced an episode of major depressive disorder at some point (Rohde & others, 2013). In this study, the typical length of an episode was 11 weeks.

Women are about twice as likely as men to be diagnosed with major depressive disorder (Hyde & others, 2008). Why the striking gender difference in the prevalence of major depressive disorder? Research by psychologist Susan Nolen-Hoeksema (2001, 2003) suggests that women are more vulnerable to depression because they experience a greater degree of chronic stress in daily life combined with a lesser sense of personal control than men. The interaction of these factors creates a vicious circle that intensifies and perpetuates depressed feelings in women (Nolen-Hoeksema & Hilt, 2009; Nolen-Hoeksema & others, 2007).

There also are cultural differences related to major depressive disorder. Although depression occurs globally with similar symptom presentation across different countries, people often talk about it differently (Ferrari & others, 2013; Simon & others, 2002). For example, people in Cambodia refer to their experience with depression as "the water in my heart has fallen" (Singh, 2015). And the Haitian word for depression translates to "thinking too much" (Singh, 2015). Such differences in the language and understanding of depression must be taken into account when diagnosing and treating this disorder.

Many people who experience major depressive disorder try to cope with the symptoms without seeking professional help (Edlund & others, 2008; Farmer & others, 2012). Left untreated, the symptoms of major depressive disorder can easily last six months or longer. When not treated, depression may become a recurring mental disorder that becomes progressively more severe. More than half of all people who have been through one episode of major depressive disorder can expect a relapse, usually within two years. With each recurrence, the symptoms tend to increase in severity and the time between major depressive episodes decreases (Hammen, 2005; Roca & others, 2011). However, it's important to note that several effective treatments for depression are available. We will describe many of these treatments in Chapter 14.

Bipolar Disorder
AN EMOTIONAL ROLLER COASTER

Years ago, your author Susan worked as a therapist in a community mental health center. She had been treating a client, a man in his fifties named Henry, who was experiencing symptoms of depression. After several months of appointments, he failed to show up for two weekly appointments in a row. When he returned, he was buoyant. He walked quickly with a bounce to his step, and greeted everyone in the waiting

persistent depressive disorder A disorder involving chronic feelings of depression that is often less severe than major depressive disorder.

room and at the front desk as if they were old friends. Henry entered Susan's office grinning, his eyes wild.

Henry's new mood was not just a decrease in his symptoms of depression. It was a swing in the opposite direction. Henry excitedly told Susan that he had quit his job as an engineer at a small radio station and was putting his savings into an investment scheme that involved medical equipment. He soon changed topics. "I won't be here next week because I'm going to Mexico! I'm staying at a famous resort in Tulum!" He explained that he would connect with Hollywood stars there, and would soon be working on a movie project, maybe as a producer.

Henry spoke loudly and so rapidly that his words often got tangled up with each other. His arms and legs looked as if they were about to get tangled up, too—Henry was in constant motion. His grinning, rapid-fire speech was punctuated with grand, sweeping gestures and exaggerated facial expressions. Before Susan could get a word in edgewise and long before the scheduled end of the therapy session, Henry left, despite Susan's efforts to detain him, explaining that he had to go shopping for new hunting gear.

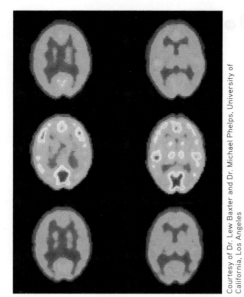

Courtesy of Dr. Lew Baxter and Dr. Michael Phelps, University of California, Los Angeles

Brain Activity During the Extremes of Bipolar Disorder These PET scans record the brain activity of an individual with bipolar disorder as he cycled rapidly from depression to mania and back to depression over a 10-day period. In the top and bottom PET scans, the blue and green colors clearly show the sharp reduction in overall brain activity that coincided with the episodes of depression. In the center PET scans, the bright red, orange, and yellow colors indicate high levels of activity in diverse brain regions during the intervening episodes of mania.

Source: Lewis Baxter and Michael E. Phelps, UCLA School of Medicine.

THE SYMPTOMS OF BIPOLAR DISORDER

Henry displayed classic symptoms of the mental disorder that used to be called *manic depression* and is today called **bipolar disorder.** In contrast to major depressive disorder, bipolar disorder almost always involves abnormal moods at *both* ends of the emotional spectrum. Episodes of incapacitating depression alternate with shorter periods of extreme euphoria, called **manic episodes.** For the vast majority of people with bipolar disorder, a manic episode immediately precedes or follows a bout with major depressive disorder. However, a small percentage of people with bipolar disorder experience only manic episodes (DSM-5, 2013).

Many people use the term "manic" informally to describe people who are in a more energetic mood than normal. But a true manic episode is much more extreme than what we often mean in casual conversation. Manic episodes typically begin suddenly, and symptoms escalate rapidly. During a manic episode, people are uncharacteristically euphoric, expansive, and excited for several days or longer. Although they sleep very little, they have boundless energy. The person's self-esteem is wildly inflated, and he exudes supreme self-confidence. Often, he has grandiose plans for obtaining wealth, power, and fame (Carlson & Meyer, 2006; Miklowitz, 2008). Sometimes the grandiose ideas represent *delusional,* or false, beliefs. Henry's belief that he would make movies with Hollywood stars whom he would meet in Mexico was delusional.

Henry's fast-forward speech was loud and virtually impossible to interrupt. During a manic episode, words are spoken so rapidly, they're often slurred as the person tries to keep up with his own racing thought processes. Attention is easily distracted by virtually anything, triggering a *flight of ideas,* in which thoughts rapidly and loosely shift from topic to topic.

Not surprisingly, the ability to function during a manic episode is severely impaired. Hospitalization is usually required, partly to protect people from the potential consequences of their inappropriate decisions and behaviors. During manic episodes, people can also run up a mountain of bills, disappear for weeks at a time,

bipolar disorder A mood disorder involving periods of incapacitating depression alternating with periods of extreme euphoria and excitement; formerly called *manic depression.*

manic episode A sudden, rapidly escalating emotional state characterized by extreme euphoria, excitement, physical energy, and rapid thoughts and speech.

Russell Brand and Bipolar Disorder British actor and comedian Russell Brand is known as much for his bad behavior, chronicled in the tabloids, as for his performances. Brand has been open about his bouts with mental illness, including heroin addiction and a diagnosis of bipolar disorder. In an interview, he talked about the role that his struggles have played in shaping him and leading to his eventual successes. "I've had a few lucky things, but then I have had the momentum of years of toil, pain, agony and humiliation, which I have endured and single-mindedly continued, when all about me were telling me I was insane" (Barnes, 2006).

become sexually promiscuous, or commit illegal acts. Very commonly, the person becomes agitated or verbally abusive when others question her grandiose claims (Miklowitz & Johnson, 2007).

Some people experience a milder but chronic form of bipolar disorder called cyclothymic disorder. In **cyclothymic disorder,** people experience moderate but frequent mood swings for two years or longer. These mood swings are not severe enough to qualify as either bipolar disorder or major depressive disorder. Often, people with cyclothymic disorder are perceived as being extremely moody, unpredictable, and inconsistent.

THE PREVALENCE AND COURSE OF BIPOLAR DISORDER

As in Henry's case, the onset of bipolar disorder typically occurs in the person's early 20s. The extreme mood swings of bipolar disorder tend to start and stop much more abruptly than the mood changes of major depressive disorder. And while an episode of major depression can easily last for six months or longer, the manic and depressive episodes of bipolar disorder tend to be much shorter— lasting anywhere from a few days to a couple of months (Fagiolini & others, 2013; Solomon & others, 2010). But contrary to what many people think, the cycling between manic and depressive episodes does not occur in minutes, or even hours.

Bipolar disorder is far less common than major depressive disorder. Unlike major depressive disorder, there are no differences between the sexes in the rate at which bipolar disorder occurs. For both men and women, the lifetime risk of developing bipolar disorder is about 1 percent (Merikangas & others, 2007). Bipolar disorder is rarely diagnosed in childhood.

In the vast majority of cases, bipolar disorder is a recurring mental disorder (Jones & Tarrier, 2005). A small percentage of people with bipolar disorder display *rapid cycling,* experiencing four or more manic or depressive episodes every year (Marneros & Goodwin, 2005). More commonly, bipolar disorder tends to recur every couple of years. Often, bipolar disorder recurs when the individual stops taking *lithium,* a medication that helps control the disorder. Susan later learned that this was what had happened with Henry.

Explaining Depressive Disorders and Bipolar Disorders

Multiple factors appear to be involved in the development of depressive and bipolar disorders. First, family, twin, and adoption studies suggest that some people inherit a *genetic predisposition,* or a greater vulnerability, to depressive and bipolar disorders (Kendler & others, 2006; Levinson, 2009; Smoller & Finn, 2003). Researchers have consistently found that both major depressive disorder and bipolar disorder, like most psychological disorders, tend to run in families, although bipolar disorder has much stronger genetic roots than major depressive disorder (Moore & others,

cyclothymic disorder (sie-klo-THY-mick) A mood disorder characterized by moderate but frequent mood swings that are not severe enough to qualify as bipolar disorder.

Creativity, Depressive Disorders, and Bipolar Disorders Although creative people, on average, have better mental health than others, the *most* creative people—"creative geniuses"—are at higher risk for developing a mental illness than other people (Simonton, 2014). Specifically, depressive and bipolar disorders occur more frequently among the most creative writers and artists than among the general population, leading some researchers to propose a biochemical or genetic link between depressive and bipolar disorders and the artistic temperament (Jamison, 1993). Writer Mark Twain (left), novelist Ernest Hemingway (middle), and poet Sylvia Plath all suffered from severe bouts of depression throughout their lives. Both Plath and Hemingway committed suicide.

2013; Sullivan & others, 2012). Personality characteristics associated with these disorders have also been found to have a genetic component, even in children who do not share a parent's diagnosis (Murray & others, 2007). For example, nondepressed children of parents with depressive disorders show the kind of biased thinking and the patterns of brain activity often seen in people who are depressed (Gotlib & others, 2014).

A second factor that has been implicated in the development of depressive and bipolar disorders is differences in the activation of structures in the brain. For example, one study found that people who were depressed showed increased activation in certain parts of the brain when trying to get rid of negative words in their working memory (Foland-Ross & others, 2013). People who were not depressed showed similar activation, an indication of effort, when getting rid of positive words.

Another important factor is disruptions in brain chemistry. Since the 1960s, several medications, called *antidepressants,* have been developed to treat major depressive disorder. Some researchers believe that increased levels in the brain of some neurotransmitters, such as norepinephrine and serotonin, accompany an improvement in the symptoms of depression among people taking antidepressants. Antidepressant medications will be discussed in more detail in Chapter 14.

Abnormal levels of another neurotransmitter may also be involved in bipolar disorder. For decades, it's been known that the drug lithium effectively alleviates symptoms of both mania and depression. Apparently, lithium regulates the availability of a neurotransmitter called *glutamate,* which acts as an excitatory neurotransmitter in many brain areas (Dixon & Hokin, 1998). By normalizing glutamate levels, lithium helps prevent both the excesses that may cause mania and the deficits that may cause depression.

Stress is also implicated in the development of depressive and bipolar disorders (Quinn & Joormann, 2015). First, major depressive disorder and chronic stress lead to remarkably similar changes in the neurochemistry of the brain (Hill & others, 2012).

MYTH ▶ SCIENCE

Is it true that many psychological disorders run in families?

Second, major depressive disorder is often triggered by traumatic and stressful events (Gutman & Nemeroff, 2011). Exposure to recent stressful events is one of the best predictors of episodes of major depressive disorder. This is especially true for people who have experienced previous episodes of depression and who have a family history of depressive disorders or mood disorders. And this is especially true for exposure to stress in relationships with other people (Vrshek-Schallhorn & others, 2013). But even in people with no family or personal history of either disorder, chronic stress can produce major depressive disorder (Muscatell & others, 2009).

Finally, research has uncovered some intriguing links between cigarette smoking and the development of major depressive disorder and other psychological disorders (Munafo & others, 2008). We explore the connection between cigarette smoking and mental illness in the Critical Thinking box "Does Smoking Cause Major Depressive Disorder and Other Psychological Disorders?"

In summary, considerable evidence points to the role of genetic factors, biochemical factors, and stressful life events in the development of both depressive disorders and bipolar disorders (Feliciano & Areàn, 2007). However, exactly how these factors interact to cause these disorders is still being investigated. Table 13.5 summarizes the symptoms of the most important depressive disorders and bipolar disorders.

CRITICAL THINKING

Does Smoking Cause Major Depressive Disorder and Other Psychological Disorders?

Are people with a mental disorder more likely to smoke than other people? Researcher Karen Lasser and her colleagues (2000) assessed smoking rates in American adults with and without psychological disorders. Lasser found that people with mental illness are twice as likely to smoke cigarettes as people with no mental illness. Here are some of the specific findings from Lasser's study:

- Forty-one percent of individuals with a current psychological disorder are smokers, as compared to 22 percent of people who have never been diagnosed with a mental disorder.

- People with a psychological disorder are more likely to be heavy smokers, consuming a pack of cigarettes per day or more.

- People who have been diagnosed with many psychological disorders have higher rates of smoking than people with fewer mental disorders (see the graph on the next page).

What can account for the correlation between smoking and psychological disorders? Subjectively, smokers often report that they experience better attention and concentration, increased energy, lower anxiety, and greater calm after smoking, effects that are probably due to the nicotine in tobacco. So, one possible explanation is that people with a mental illness smoke as a form of self-medication. Notice that this explanation assumes that mental illness *causes* people to smoke.

Nicotine, of course, is a powerful psychoactive drug. It triggers the release of *dopamine* and stimulates key brain structures involved in producing rewarding sensations, including the *thalamus*, the *amygdala*, and the *nucleus accumbens* (Berrendero & others, 2010; Le Foll & Goldberg, 2007; Stein & others, 1998). Nicotine receptors on different neurons also regulate the release of other important neurotransmitters, including *serotonin, acetylcholine, GABA,* and *glutamate* (McGehee & others, 2007). In other words, nicotine affects multiple brain structures and alters the

Nicotine's Effects in the Brain After cigarette smokers were injected with up to two milligrams of nicotine, researchers used fMRI to track the brain areas activated, which included the *nucleus accumbens,* the *amygdala,* and the *thalamus.* Previous research has shown that these brain structures produce the reinforcing, mood-elevating properties of other abused drugs, including cocaine, amphetamines, and opiates (Stein & others, 1998).

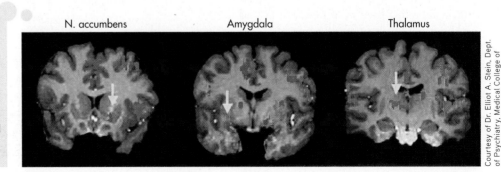

N. accumbens   Amygdala   Thalamus

TABLE 13.5

Depressive Disorders and Bipolar Disorders

Major Depressive Disorder

- Loss of interest or pleasure in almost all activities
- Despondent mood; feelings of emptiness, worthlessness, or excessive guilt
- Preoccupation with death or suicidal thoughts

- Difficulty sleeping or excessive sleeping
- Diminished ability to think, concentrate, or make decisions
- Diminished appetite and significant weight loss

Persistent Depressive Disorder

- Chronic depressed feelings that are often less severe than those that accompany major depressive disorder

Seasonal Affective Disorder (SAD)

- Recurring episodes of depression that follow a seasonal pattern, typically occurring in the fall and winter months and subsiding in the spring and summer months

Bipolar Disorder

- One or more manic episodes characterized by euphoria, high energy, grandiose ideas, flight of ideas, inappropriate self-confidence, and decreased need for sleep
- Usually one or more major depressive episodes
- In some cases, may rapidly alternate between symptoms of mania and major depressive disorder

Cyclothymic Disorder

- Moderate, recurring mood swings that are not severe enough to qualify as major depressive disorder or bipolar disorder

---

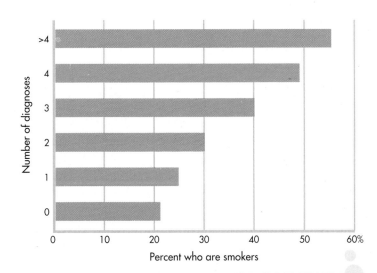

Smoking Rates Compared to the Number of Lifetime Mental Disorder Diagnoses

Source: Data from Lasser & others (2000).

release of many different neurotransmitters. These same brain areas and neurotransmitters are also directly involved in many different psychological disorders.

Although the idea that mental illness causes smoking seems to make sense, some researchers now believe that the arrow of causation points in the *opposite* direction. In the past decade, many studies have suggested that smoking triggers the onset of symptoms in people who are probably already vulnerable to the development of a mental disorder, especially major depressive disorder. Consider just a few studies:

- Several studies focusing on adolescents found that cigarette smoking predicted the onset of depressive symptoms, rather

than the other way around (Beal & others, 2013; Boden & others, 2010; Windle & Windle, 2001).

- In studies of people with bipolar disorder, daily cigarette smokers had worse symptoms and lengthier hospitalizations than nonsmoking patients with bipolar disorder (Dodd & others, 2010; Saiyad & El-Mallakh, 2012).

- A positive association was found between smoking and the severity of symptoms experienced by people with anxiety disorders (McCabe & others, 2004).

- In a study of people with schizophrenia, 90 percent started smoking *before* their illness began (Kelly & McCreadie, 1999). In addition, among adolescent boys, smokers were almost twice as likely as nonsmokers to later develop schizophrenia (Weiser & others, 2004). These studies suggest that smoking may precipitate an initial schizophrenic episode in vulnerable people.

Further research may help disentangle the complex interaction between smoking and mental disorders, but one fact is known: Mentally ill cigarette smokers, like other smokers, are at much greater risk of premature disability and death. So, along with the psychological and personal suffering that accompanies almost all psychological disorders, those with mental illness carry the additional burden of consuming nearly half of all the cigarettes smoked in the United States.

CRITICAL THINKING QUESTIONS

- Is the evidence sufficient to conclude that there is a causal relationship between cigarette smoking and the onset of mental illness symptoms? Why or why not?

- Should tobacco companies be required to contribute part of their profits to the cost of mental health treatment and research?

eating disorder A category of mental disorders characterized by severe disturbances in eating behavior.

anorexia nervosa An eating disorder characterized by excessive weight loss, an irrational fear of gaining weight, and distorted body self-perception.

bulimia nervosa An eating disorder characterized by binges of extreme overeating followed by self-induced vomiting, misuse of laxatives, or other inappropriate methods to purge the excess food and prevent weight gain.

binge-eating disorder An eating disorder characterized by binges of extreme overeating without use of self-induced vomiting or other inappropriate measures to purge the excess food.

Eating Disorders
ANOREXIA, BULIMIA, AND BINGE-EATING DISORDER

KEY THEME

Anorexia nervosa, bulimia nervosa, and binge-eating disorder are psychological disorders characterized by severely disturbed, maladaptive eating behaviors.

KEY QUESTIONS

> What are the symptoms, characteristics, and causes of anorexia nervosa?
> What are the symptoms, characteristics, and causes of bulimia nervosa?
> What are the symptoms, characteristics, and causes of binge-eating disorder?

Eating disorders involve serious and maladaptive disturbances in eating behavior. The DSM-5 category in which eating disorders are included is technically called "Eating and Feeding Disorders," which includes disorders of infancy and childhood. But here we will focus on disorders that tend to begin in adolescence or early adulthood. Eating disorders can include extreme reduction of food intake, severe bouts of overeating, and obsessive concerns about body shape or weight (DSM-5, 2013). The three main types of eating disorders are *anorexia nervosa, bulimia nervosa,* and *binge-eating disorder,* which usually begin during adolescence or early adulthood (see Table 13.6). Ninety to 95 percent of the people who experience an eating disorder are female (Støving & others, 2011). Despite the 10-to-1 gender-difference ratio, the central features of eating disorders are similar for males and females.

TABLE 13.6

Eating Disorders

Anorexia Nervosa
• Severe and extreme disturbance in eating habits and calorie intake
• Body weight that is significantly less than what would be considered normal for the person's age, height, and gender, and refusal to maintain a normal body weight
• Intense fear of gaining weight or becoming fat
• Distorted perceptions about the severity of weight loss and a distorted self-image, such that even an extremely emaciated person may perceive herself as fat
Bulimia Nervosa
• Recurring episodes of binge eating, which is defined as an excessive amount of calories within a two-hour period
• The inability to control or stop the excessive eating behavior
• Recurrent episodes of purging, which is defined as using laxatives, diuretics, self-induced vomiting, or other methods to prevent weight gain
Binge-Eating Disorder
• Recurring episodes of binge eating
• The inability to control or stop the excessive eating behavior
• Not associated with recurrent episodes of purging or other methods to prevent weight gain

 LaunchPad

Video material is provided by BBC Worldwide Learning and CBS News Archives and produced by Princeton Academic Resources

Hear the story of one man's struggle with an eating disorder. Watch Video Activity: Overcoming Anorexia Nervosa.

ANOREXIA NERVOSA
LIFE-THREATENING WEIGHT LOSS

Three key features define **anorexia nervosa.** First, the person refuses to maintain a minimally normal body weight. With a body weight that is significantly below normal, body mass index can drop to 12 or lower. Second, despite being dangerously underweight, the person with anorexia is intensely afraid of gaining weight or becoming fat. Third, she has a distorted perception about the size of her body. Although emaciated, she looks in the mirror and sees herself as fat or obese, denying the seriousness of her weight loss (DSM-5, 2013).

The severe malnutrition caused by anorexia disrupts body chemistry in ways that are very similar to those caused by starvation. Basal metabolic rate decreases, as do blood levels of glucose, insulin, and leptin. Other hormonal levels drop, including the level of reproductive hormones. In women, reduced estrogen may result in the menstrual cycle stopping. In males, decreased testosterone disrupts sex drive and sexual function (Pinheiro & others, 2010). Because the ability to retain body heat is greatly diminished, people with severe anorexia often develop a soft, fine body hair called *lanugo*.

BULIMIA NERVOSA AND BINGE-EATING DISORDER

Like people with anorexia, people with **bulimia nervosa** fear gaining weight. Intense preoccupation and dissatisfaction with their bodies are also apparent. However, people with bulimia stay within a normal weight range or may even be slightly overweight. Another difference is that people with bulimia usually recognize that they have an eating disorder.

People with bulimia nervosa experience extreme periods of binge eating, consuming as many as 50,000 calories on a single binge. Binges typically occur twice a week and are often triggered by negative feelings or hunger. During the binge, the person usually consumes sweet, high-calorie foods that can be swallowed quickly, such as ice cream, cake, and candy. Binges typically occur in secrecy, leaving the person feeling ashamed, guilty, and disgusted by his own behavior. After bingeing, he compensates by purging himself of the excessive food by self-induced vomiting or by misuse of laxatives or enemas. Once he purges, he often feels psychologically relieved. Some people with bulimia don't purge themselves of the excess food. Rather, they use fasting and excessive exercise to keep their body weight within the normal range (American Psychiatric Association, 2000; DSM-5, 2013).

Like anorexia nervosa, bulimia nervosa can take a serious physical toll on the body. Repeated purging disrupts the body's electrolyte balance, leading to muscle cramps, irregular heartbeat, and other cardiac problems, some potentially fatal. Stomach acids from self-induced vomiting erode tooth enamel, causing tooth decay and gum disease. Over time, frequent vomiting can damage the gastrointestinal tract (Powers, 2009).

Like people with bulimia, people with **binge-eating disorder** engage in bingeing behaviors (DSM-5, 2013). Unlike people with bulimia, they do not engage in purging or other behaviors that rid their bodies of the excess food. People with binge-eating disorder experience the same feelings of distress, lack of control, and shame that people with bulimia experience.

Agencia el Universal/El Universal de Mexico/Newscom

Size 0: An Impossible Cultural Ideal? Isabelle Caro, a famous French fashion model, died in 2010 after a decade-long struggle with anorexia. After the anorexia-related deaths of Caro and a Brazilian model, Ana Carolina Reston, France, Germany, and Spain proposed bans on ultra-thin models. But despite periodic outcries, the emaciated, skin-and-bones look continues to be the fashion industry norm. Eating disorders are most prevalent in developed, Western countries, where a slender body is the cultural ideal, especially for women and girls. Many psychologists believe that such unrealistic body expectations contribute to eating disorders (Hawkins & others, 2004; Treasure & others, 2008).

CULTURE AND HUMAN BEHAVIOR

Culture-Bound Syndromes

At several points in this chapter, we've noted ways in which culture shapes the symptoms of psychological disorders. Psychological disorders do not always look the same in every culture. And further, some disorders, called *culture-specific disorders* or *culture-bound syndromes,* appear to be found only in a single culture.

For example, *hikikomori* is a syndrome first identified in Japan in the 1970s in adolescents and young adults (Kato & others, 2011; Teo, 2010). *Hikikomori* involves a pattern of extreme social withdrawal. People suffering from *hikikomori* become virtual recluses, often confining themselves to a single room in their parents' home, sometimes for years. They refuse all social interaction or engagement with the outside world and, in some cases, do not speak even to family members who care for them. Locked away from the world, they spend their time alone in their room, preoccupied with watching television, playing video games, or surfing the Internet.

Most *hikikomori* are young males, but the syndrome has also been identified in women and middle-aged adults (Kato & others, 2012). Once rare, *hikikomori* has become a social phenomenon. Some estimates are that a million or more young Japanese live as *hikikomori* (Watts, 2002).

Hikikomori has symptoms in common with several Western disorders, including social anxiety disorder, major depressive disorder, generalized anxiety disorder, and agoraphobia. However, its specific features are uniquely Japanese, reflecting social pressures and values. Some researchers believe that *hikikomori* is an extreme reaction to the pressure to succeed in school and to conform to social expectations that characterizes Japanese culture (Teo, 2010; Teo & Gaw, 2010). Also implicated is the close, almost symbiotic relationship that is encouraged between mothers and children, especially sons, in

MYTH ◀ SCIENCE

Is it true that the types of psychological disorders are pretty much the same in every culture?

Shutting Themselves In Nineteen-year-old Dai Hasebe has lived as a *hikikomori* or shut-in since he was 11 years old, rarely leaving his family's Tokyo apartment. Like other *hikikomori*, he does not attend school or hold a job. Although *hikikomori* has some features in common with social anxiety disorder, agoraphobia, major depressive disorder, and generalized anxiety disorder, the specific constellation of symptoms appears to be unique to Japanese culture.

Japan. Japanese parents, apparently, are more tolerant of the *hikikomori's* continuing dependency into adulthood than parents in other cultures might be (Wong & Ying, 2006).

Western cultures have culture-bound syndromes, too. Consider the case of anorexia nervosa, discussed on pages 558–559. Isolated cases of self-starvation have been reported throughout history and in many cultures. For the most part, though, these cases of anorexia nervosa were rare and seem to have been associated with religious motives or a desire for spiritual purification (Banks, 2009; Keel & Klump, 2003).

The most common form of anorexia nervosa today has a distinctly different look. Its incidence is highest in the United States, Western Europe, and other "westernized" cultures, where an

CAUSES OF EATING DISORDERS

A COMPLEX PICTURE

Anorexia, bulimia, and binge-eating disorder involve decreases in brain activity of the neurotransmitter *serotonin* (Bailer & Kaye, 2011; Kuikka & others, 2001). Disrupted brain chemistry may also contribute to the fact that eating disorders frequently co-occur with other psychiatric disorders, such as major depressive disorder, substance abuse disorder, personality disorders, obsessive–compulsive disorder, and anxiety disorders (Thompson & others, 2007; Swanson & others, 2011). While chemical imbalances may cause eating disorders, researchers are also studying whether they can result from eating disorders as well (Smolak, 2009).

Family interaction patterns may also contribute to eating disorders. For example, critical comments by parents or siblings about a child's weight, or parental modeling of disordered eating, may increase the odds that an individual develops an eating disorder (Quiles Marcos & others, 2013; Thompson & others, 2007). There also is evidence that other psychological characteristics may be risk factors. For example, having negative beliefs about oneself is associated with having an eating disorder (Yiend & others, 2014). Also, researchers have found that unnaturally slender physique is the cultural ideal (Anderson-Fye, 2009). In these cultures, self-starvation is associated with an intense fear of becoming fat (DSM-5, 2013). There is also a much higher incidence in women than in men, reflecting cultural beliefs about the importance of thinness for women (Keel & Klump, 2003).

Interestingly, researchers are seeing that the global transmission of social trends and information about psychological disorders appear to be contributing to the spread of syndromes that were once limited to a particular culture. For example, Chinese psychiatrist Sing Lee only learned about eating disorders during his training in the United Kingdom in the 1980s. Upon his return home to Hong Kong, he combed through hospital records and interviewed colleagues but could find very few occurrences of anorexia nervosa or other eating disorders in his native country. And, these few cases looked remarkably different from what he had observed in the United Kingdom. In Hong Kong, young women with anorexia did not express a fear of being fat. Instead they attributed their extreme thinness to physical problems such as a bloated stomach or a poor appetite (Lee & others, 1993). Also, unlike patients in the West, Hong Kong patients tended to be from less privileged backgrounds and were less likely to follow fashion and beauty trends.

But that all changed in 1994, when fourteen-year-old schoolgirl Charlene Hsu Chi-Ying, emaciated and weighing only 75 pounds, collapsed and died on a busy street in the heart of Hong Kong (Watters, 2010). The dramatic nature of her death led to breathless media coverage. "Girl Who Died in Street Was a Walking Skeleton" read one headline. Within hours, many people in Hong Kong read about anorexia nervosa for the first time. With no traditional framework for understanding why an honor student would deliberately starve herself to death, the Hong Kong media sought out Western explanations, blaming images of women in the media and the fashion industry. Soon, celebrities were announcing their own battles with anorexia, and reports of anorexia became increasingly common. Over the next decade,

Slimming—A Global Pursuit? Taiwanese pop star Jolin Tsai is widely admired for her singing talent—and for her slender build. The author of a best-selling diet book, Tsai often shares her weight-loss secrets with interviewers. The incidence of eating disorders in many Asian countries has skyrocketed in recent decades. Some researchers attribute this increase to the spread of Western ideals of beauty along with publicity about anorexia nervosa, a disease previously rare in these countries (Watters, 2010). "Slimming" diets, clinics, and drugs are a growing industry across Asia.

TPG/Getty Images

eating disorders in Hong Kong, Japan, and other Asian countries skyrocketed, and patients were much more likely to report a fear of being fat (S. Lee & others, 2010; Pike & Borovoy, 2004).

Many questions about culture-bound syndromes remain unanswered. For example, it is not clear whether culture-bound syndromes like *hikikomori* are distinct disorders, or whether they represent a culturally influenced expression of some more universal underlying pathology. And when a disorder like anorexia nervosa appears to spread across cultures, is the increased incidence actually *caused* by media coverage? Or does it simply reflect an increase in the diagnosis of cases that already existed? These questions are complex and unlikely to have simple answers. As we've seen throughout this chapter, psychological disorders reflect the complex interaction of biological predispositions and psychological factors and are always expressed within a particular social and cultural context. So, it's unlikely that any single factor is responsible for the rate or symptoms of a particular psychological disorder.

a tendency toward perfectionism in childhood—traits like needing to complete schoolwork perfectly and feeling a need to obey rules without question—was associated with a later diagnosis of anorexia (Halmi & others, 2012). *Girls* actor Zosia Mamet explained that her experience with an eating disorder ". . . has never really been about weight or food—that's just the way the monster manifests itself. Really these diseases are about control: control of your life and of your body" (Mamet, 2014).

Although cases of eating disorders have been documented for at least 150 years, contemporary Western cultural attitudes toward thinness and dieting probably contribute to the increased incidence of eating disorders today. This seems to be especially true with anorexia, which occurs predominantly in Western or "westernized" countries (Anderson-Fye, 2009; Cafri & others, 2005). We discuss this issue and the more general topic of culture's effects on psychological disorders in the Culture and Human Behavior box "Culture-Bound Syndromes."

❯ Test your understanding of **Mood Disorders and Eating Disorders** with **LEARNING**Curve.

Personality Disorders

MALADAPTIVE TRAITS

KEY THEME

The personality disorders are characterized by inflexible, maladaptive patterns of thoughts, emotions, behavior, and interpersonal functioning.

KEY QUESTIONS

> How do people with a personality disorder differ from people who are psychologically well adjusted?

> What behaviors and personality characteristics are associated with antisocial and borderline personality disorders?

Like every other person, you have your own unique *personality*—the consistent and enduring patterns of thinking, feeling, and behaving that characterize you as an individual. As we described in Chapter 10, your personality can be described as a specific collection of personality traits. Your *personality traits* are relatively stable predispositions to behave or react in certain ways. In other words, your personality traits reflect different dimensions of your personality.

By definition, personality traits are consistent over time and across situations. But that's not to say that personality traits are etched in stone. Rather, the psychologically well-adjusted person possesses a fair degree of flexibility and adaptiveness. Based on our experiences with others, we are able to modify how we display our personality traits so that we can think, feel, and behave in healthier and more appropriate ways.

Tom Cheney The New Yorker Collection/The Cartoon Bank

In contrast, someone with a **personality disorder** has personality traits that are inflexible and maladaptive across a broad range of situations. However, the behavior of people with personality disorders goes well beyond that of a normal individual who occasionally experiences an emotional meltdown or who is grumpier, more aloof, or more self-centered than most people.

The personality disorders involve pervasive patterns of perceiving, relating to and thinking about the self, other people, and the environment that interfere with long-term functioning (Oltmanns & Balsis, 2011). And, these maladaptive behaviors are not restricted to isolated episodes or specific circumstances. Rather, these maladaptive patterns of emotions, thought processes, and behavior tend to be very stable over time. The patterns also deviate markedly from the social and behavioral expectations of the individual's culture. Usually, personality disorders become evident during adolescence or early adulthood. Personality disorders are evident in about 10 percent of the general population (Lenzenweger, 2008).

Many researchers believe that personality disorders reflect conditions in which "normal" personality traits are taken to an abnormal extreme (Samuel & others, 2010; Trull & Widiger, 2008). For example, it's normal to feel uneasy or sad when separated from a loved one. In a personality disorder, however, these responses reach pathological extremes. Rather than uneasiness, a person might experience intense feelings of desperation and intense anxiety. And rather than sadness, the person might experience unbearably intense feelings of abandonment and emptiness.

Despite the fact that the maladaptive personality traits consistently cause personal or social turmoil, people with personality disorders often blame others for their difficulties. Even if they are aware of their maladaptive personality patterns, they typically don't think there's anything wrong with them. In other words, they are unable to see that their inflexible style of thinking and behaving is at the root of their personal and social difficulties. Consequently, people with personality disorders often don't seek help.

personality disorder Inflexible, maladaptive patterns of thoughts, emotions, behavior, and interpersonal functioning that are stable over time and across situations and that deviate from the expectations of the individual's culture.

TABLE 13.7

Personality Disorders

Odd, Eccentric Cluster	Dramatic, Emotional, Erratic Cluster	Anxious, Fearful Cluster
Paranoid Personality Disorder • Pervasive but unwarranted distrust and suspiciousness; assumes that other people intend to deceive, exploit, or harm them. **Schizoid Personality Disorder** • Pervasive detachment from social relationships; emotionally cold and flat; indifferent to praise or criticism from others; preference for solitary activities; lacking in close friends. **Schizotypal Personality Disorder** • Odd thoughts, speech, emotional reactions, mannerisms, and appearance; impaired social and interpersonal functioning; often superstitious.	**Antisocial Personality Disorder** • Blatantly disregards or violates the rights of others; impulsive, irresponsible, deceitful, manipulative, and lacking in guilt or remorse. **Borderline Personality Disorder** • Intense, unstable relationships, emotions, and self-image; impulsive; desperate efforts to avoid real or imagined abandonment; feelings of emptiness; self-destructive tendencies. **Histrionic Personality Disorder** • Exaggerated, overly dramatic expression of emotions and attention-seeking behavior that often includes sexually seductive or provocative behaviors. **Narcissistic Personality Disorder** • Grandiose sense of self-importance; exaggerates abilities and accomplishments; excessive need for admiration; boastful, pretentious; lacking in empathy.	**Avoidant Personality Disorder** • Extreme social inhibition and social avoidance due to feelings of inadequacy, and hypersensitivity to criticism, rejection, or disapproval. **Dependent Personality Disorder** • Excessive need to be taken care of, leading to submissive, clinging behaviors; fears of separation; and the inability to assume responsibility. **Obsessive–Compulsive Personality Disorder** • Rigid preoccupation with orderliness, personal control, rules, or schedules that interferes with completing tasks; unreasonable perfectionism.

Source: Information from DSM-5 (2013).

DSM-5 identifies ten distinct personality disorders, summarized in Table 13.7. These disorders are organized into three basic clusters: odd, eccentric personality disorders; dramatic, emotional, erratic personality disorders; and anxious, fearful personality disorders. However, this classification system is problematic (American Psychiatric Association, 2012a, 2012b). For example, many people display the characteristics of more than one personality disorder, making diagnosis difficult.

For the first time, DSM-5 includes a second approach to classifying personality disorders. It involves assessing people on two dimensions: (1) a *severity* scale, which assesses the degree of impairment in personality functioning; and (2) a *trait* scale, which rates the person on pathological personality traits, such as the tendency to be antagonistic, emotionally unstable, impulsive, or manipulative. DSM-5 includes both the older and the newer approaches as a compromise between differences of opinion as to which is more useful.

In this section, we'll focus our discussion on two of the more serious personality disorders, antisocial personality disorder and borderline personality disorder. These two disorders are also among the most thoroughly researched. Because clinicians use the older method of diagnosis more commonly than the newer one, we will refer to it throughout our discussion.

Antisocial Personality Disorder
VIOLATING THE RIGHTS OF OTHERS—WITHOUT GUILT OR REMORSE

Often referred to as a *psychopath* or *sociopath*, the individual with **antisocial personality disorder** has the ability to lie, cheat, steal, and otherwise manipulate and harm other people. And when caught, the person shows little or no remorse for having caused pain, damage, or loss to others (Patrick, 2007). It's as though the person has no conscience or sense of guilt. This pattern of blatantly disregarding and violating the rights of others is the central feature of antisocial personality disorder (DSM-5, 2013). Although many people associate violence with antisocial personality disorder, a history of violence is not necessary for the diagnosis (DSM-5, 2013). In fact, there

antisocial personality disorder
A personality disorder characterized by a pervasive pattern of disregarding and violating the rights of others; such individuals are also often referred to as *psychopaths* or *sociopaths*.

HEIKO JUNGE/EPA/Landov

HANDOUT/Reuters/Landov

Sociopath Versus Psychopath Anders Breivik (left), who murdered dozens of children at a summer camp in Norway, would be considered a sociopath, according to neuroscientist Jack Pemment (2013). His horrific acts were in response to his extreme nationalistic beliefs, and he saw himself as a martyr for his country. Breivik seems to have a sense of morality, although it is tragically misguided. The serial killer Israel Keyes (right), who buried weapons and shovels to dispose of bodies all over the U.S. to facilitate his homicides, is likely a psychopath. After his arrest, he told investigators that for most of his life, he thought that people just pretended to be nice. Keyes seems to have no sense of morality whatsoever.

is evidence that some psychopaths succeed in high-status, competitive professions such as in business or politics where a ruthless personality might be useful (Boddy & others, 2010; Lilienfeld & others, 2012). Researchers have also noted a relative lack of anxiety in these individuals, especially those most likely to harm others for their own benefit (De Brito & Hodgins, 2009; Neumann & others, 2013). Approximately 4 percent of the general population displays the characteristics of antisocial personality disorder, with men far outnumbering women (Grant & others, 2004).

More recently, researchers have argued that the definitions of psychopath and sociopath are different from the criteria for antisocial personality disorder, despite the fact that all three are often used interchangeably. For example, Arielle Baskin-Sommers and her colleagues reported two subtypes—those with psychopathy who tend to be more "cold" and "callous," and those with more traditional antisocial traits who tend to be more "hot" or "volatile" (2015). Relatedly, Jack Pemment (2013) explains that sociopaths have a sense of morality, but it differs from that of others in their community. Their particular sense of morality can lead sociopaths to commit deviant, and sometimes criminal, acts. Psychopaths, on the other hand, lack any sense of morality and do not have normal emotional responses. For example, unlike others, psychopaths do not startle when presented with disturbing images, such as a weapon aimed at them or a victim of a violent assault (Levenston & others, 2000).

Evidence of the maladaptive personality patterns associated with antisocial personality disorder is often seen in childhood or early adolescence (Diamantopoulou & others, 2010; Hiatt & Dishion, 2008). In many cases, the child has repeated run-ins with the law or school authorities. Behaviors that draw the attention of authorities can include cruelty to animals, attacking or harming adults or other children, theft, setting fires, and destroying property. During childhood and adolescence, this pattern of behavior is typically diagnosed as *conduct disorder.* The habitual failure to conform to social norms and rules often becomes the person's predominant life theme, which continues into adulthood (Patrick, 2007).

Deceiving and manipulating others for their own personal gain is another hallmark of individuals with antisocial personality disorder. With an uncanny ability to look you directly in the eye and speak with complete confidence and sincerity, they will lie in order to gain money, sex, or whatever their goal may be. Often, they are contemptuous about the feelings or rights of others, blaming the victim for his or her stupidity. This quality makes antisocial personality disorder especially difficult to treat because clients often manipulate and lie to their therapists, too (McMurran & Howard, 2009).

Because they are consistently irresponsible, individuals with antisocial personality disorder often fail to hold a job or meet financial obligations. Their past is often checkered with arrests and jail sentences. High rates of alcoholism and other forms of substance abuse are also strongly associated with antisocial personality disorder (Hasin & others, 2011; Fridell & others, 2008). However, by middle to late adulthood, the antisocial tendencies of such individuals tend to diminish.

Borderline Personality Disorder

CHAOS AND EMPTINESS

> Borderline individuals are the psychological equivalent of third-degree-burn patients. They simply have no emotional skin. Even the slightest touch or movement can create immense suffering.

This is how psychologist Marsha Linehan (2009) describes the chaotic, unstable world of people with **borderline personality disorder (BPD).** Borderline personality disorder is characterized by impulsiveness and chronically unstable emotions, relationships, and self-image. Moods and emotions are intense, fluctuating, and extreme, often vastly out of proportion to the triggering incident, and seemingly uncontrollable. The person with borderline personality disorder unpredictably swings from one mood extreme to another. Inappropriate, intense, and often uncontrollable episodes of anger are another hallmark of this disorder (Berenson & others, 2011).

Relationships with others are as chaotic and unstable as the person's moods. The person with borderline personality disorder has a chronic, pervasive sense of emptiness. Desperately afraid of abandonment, she alternately clings to others and pushes them away. Because her sense of identity is so fragile, she constantly seeks reassurance and self-definition from others. When it is not forthcoming, she may erupt in furious anger or abject despair.

Relationships careen out of control as the person shifts from inappropriately idealizing the newfound lover or friend to viewing them with complete contempt or hostility. She sees herself, and everyone else, as absolutes: ecstatic or miserable, perfect or worthless (Arntz & ten Haaf, 2012; de Montigny-Malenfant & others, 2013).

Often, the deep despair and inner emptiness that people with BPD experience are outwardly expressed in self-destructive behavior (Linehan & Dexter-Mazza, 2008). "Cutting" or other acts of self-mutilation, threats of suicide, and suicide attempts are common, especially in response to perceived rejection or abandonment. Underscoring the seriousness of borderline personality disorder is a grim statistic: As many as 10 percent of those who meet the BPD criteria eventually commit suicide, an extremely high percentage that is about *50 times* the suicide rate for the general population (American Psychiatric Association, 2001; Qin, 2011).

Borderline personality disorder is often considered to be the most serious and disabling of the personality disorders. People with this disorder often also suffer from depression, substance abuse, and eating disorders (Mercer & others, 2009; Walter & others, 2009). And because they often lack control over their impulses, self-destructive, impulsive behavior is common, such as gambling, reckless driving, drug abuse, or sexual promiscuity.

Along with being among the most severe of the personality disorders, borderline personality disorder is also the most commonly diagnosed. A recent survey found that BPD was more prevalent than previously thought. Estimates suggest that BPD affects about 6 percent of the population, or possibly some 18 million Americans (Grant & others, 2008). The researchers also found the highest prevalence of borderline personality disorder among women, people in lower-income groups, and Native American men, while the lowest incidence was among women of Asian descent.

WHAT CAUSES BORDERLINE PERSONALITY DISORDER?

As with the other personality disorders, multiple factors have been implicated. Because people with borderline personality disorder have such intense and chronic fears of abandonment and are terrified of being alone, some researchers believe that a disruption in attachment relationships in early childhood is an important contributing cause (Barone & others, 2011). Dysfunctional family relationships are common: Many borderline patients report having experienced neglect or physical, sexual, or emotional abuse in childhood (Ball & Links, 2009; Watson & others, 2006).

A more comprehensive theory, called the *biosocial developmental theory of borderline personality disorder,* has been proposed by Marsha Linehan (1993; Crowell & others, 2009).

borderline personality disorder
A personality disorder characterized by instability of interpersonal relationships, self-image, and emotions, and marked impulsivity.

Jeff Kravitz/FilmMagic/Getty Images

Inflicting Physical Pain to Relieve Emotional Agony "Cutting"—slicing into your own skin with a razor, knife, or other sharp object—is a common symptom among those diagnosed with borderline personality disorder (Selby & others, 2011; Zanarini & others, 2011). Why would someone intentionally inflict such painful injuries on herself? Singer Amy Winehouse once cut herself with a shard of glass while being interviewed by a Spin magazine reporter. She spoke openly about having cut herself since she was 9 years old. The physical pain of cutting, Winehouse said, helped ease her emotional pain. Winehouse died of acute alcohol poisoning at the age of 27.

dissociative experience A break or disruption in consciousness during which awareness, memory, and personal identity become separated or divided.

dissociative disorders A category of psychological disorders in which extreme and frequent disruptions of awareness, memory, and personal identity impair the ability to function.

Dissociation and Possession A member of the Dongria Kondh tribe in eastern India dances in a trance during a ceremony on top of Niyamgiri mountain, which the community regards as sacred. Such dissociative trance and possession states are common in religions around the world (Krippner, 1994). When dissociative experiences take place within a religious ritual context, they are not considered abnormal. In fact, such experiences may be highly valued (Mulhern, 1991).

According to this view, borderline personality disorder is the outcome of a unique combination of biological, psychological, and environmental factors. Some children are born with a biological temperament that is characterized by extreme emotional sensitivity, a tendency to be impulsive, and the tendency to experience negative emotions. Linehan believes that borderline personality disorder results when such a biologically vulnerable child is raised by caregivers who do not teach him how to control his impulses or help him learn how to understand, regulate, and appropriately express his emotions (Crowell & others, 2009).

In some cases, Linehan believes, parents or caregivers actually shape and reinforce the child's pattern of frequent, intense emotional displays by their own behavior. For example, they may sometimes ignore a child's emotional outbursts and sometimes reinforce them. In Linehan's theory, a history of abuse and neglect may be present but is not a necessary ingredient in the toxic mix that produces borderline personality disorder. Despite the difficulties faced by people suffering from borderline personality disorder, treatments developed by Linehan and her colleagues have been shown to help patients to manage this mental illness (see Bohus & others, 2000).

The Dissociative Disorders
FRAGMENTATION OF THE SELF

KEY THEME

In the dissociative disorders, disruptions in awareness, memory, and identity interfere with the ability to function in everyday life.

KEY QUESTIONS

> What is dissociation, and how do normal dissociative experiences differ from the symptoms of dissociative disorders?
> What are dissociative amnesia, dissociative amnesia with dissociative fugue, and dissociative identity disorder (DID)?
> What is thought to cause DID?

Despite the many changes you've experienced throughout your lifetime, you have a pretty consistent sense of identity. You're aware of your surroundings and can easily recall memories from the recent and distant past. In other words, a normal personality is one in which *awareness, memory,* and *personal identity* are associated and well integrated.

In contrast, a **dissociative experience** is one in which a person's awareness, memory, and personal identity become separated or divided. While that may sound weird, dissociative experiences are not inherently pathological. Mild dissociative experiences are quite common and completely normal (Dalenberg & others, 2009; Wieland, 2011). For example, you become so absorbed in a book or movie that you lose all track of time. While driving, your author Susan is occasionally so preoccupied with her thoughts—often about her class that day—that when she arrives on campus, she remembers next to nothing about the trip. In each of these cases, you've experienced a temporary "break" or "separation" in your memory or awareness—a temporary, mild dissociative experience.

Clearly, then, dissociative experiences are not necessarily abnormal. But in the **dissociative disorders,** the dissociative experiences are much more extreme or more frequent and they severely disrupt everyday functioning. Awareness, or recognition of familiar surroundings, may be completely obstructed. Memories of pertinent personal information may be unavailable to consciousness. Identity may be lost, confused, or fragmented (Dell & O'Neil, 2009).

The category of dissociative disorders consists of two basic disorders: (1) *dissociative amnesia,* which can occur either with or without *dissociative fugue,* and (2) *dissociative identity disorder,* which was previously called *multiple personality disorder.* Until recently, the dissociative disorders were thought to be extremely rare. How rare? An extensive review conducted in the 1940s uncovered a grand total of 76 reported cases of dissociative disorders since the beginnings of modern medicine in the 1700s (Taylor & Martin, 1944). Although a few more cases were reported during the 1950s and 1960s, the clinical picture changed dramatically in the 1970s when a surge of dissociative disorder diagnoses occurred (Kihlstrom, 2005). Later in this discussion, we'll explore some of the possible reasons as well as the controversy surrounding the "epidemic" of dissociative disorders that began in the 1970s.

Dissociative Amnesia and Dissociative Fugue
FORGETTING AND WANDERING

Dissociative amnesia refers to the partial or total inability to recall important information that is not due to a medical condition, such as an illness, an injury, or a drug. Usually the person develops amnesia for personal events and information, rather than for general knowledge or skills. That is, the person may not be able to remember his wife's name but does remember how to read and who Martin Luther King, Jr., was. In most cases, dissociative amnesia is a response to stress, trauma, or an extremely distressing situation, such as combat, marital problems, or physical abuse (McLewin & Muller, 2006).

Some cases of dissociative amnesia involve a condition called **dissociative fugue.** In amnesia with dissociative fugue, the person outwardly appears completely normal. However, the person is confused about her identity. While in the fugue state, she suddenly and inexplicably travels away from her home, wandering to other cities or even countries. In some cases, people in a fugue state adopt a completely new identity.

As is true with other cases of amnesia, dissociative fugues are thought to be associated with traumatic events or stressful periods. However, it's unclear as to *how* a fugue state develops, or *why* a person experiences a fugue state rather than other sorts of symptoms, such as simple anxiety or depression. Interestingly, when the person "awakens" from the fugue state, she may remember her past history but have amnesia for what occurred *during* the fugue state (DSM-5, 2013).

Dissociative Identity Disorder
MULTIPLE PERSONALITIES

Among the dissociative disorders, none is more fascinating—or controversial—than dissociative identity disorder, formerly known as *multiple personality disorder.* **Dissociative identity disorder (DID)** involves extensive memory disruptions for personal information along with the presence of two or more distinct identities, or "personalities," within a single person.

Typically, each personality has her or his own name and is experienced as if it has her or his own personal history and self-image. These alternate personalities, often called *alters* or *alter egos,* may be of widely varying ages and different genders. Alters are not really separate people. Rather, they constitute a "system of mind" (Courtois & Ford, 2009). That is, the alters seem to embody different aspects of the individual's personality that, for some reason, cannot be integrated into the primary personality. The alternate personalities hold memories, emotions, and motives that are not admissible to the individual's conscious mind. At different times, different alter egos take control of the person's experience, thoughts, and behavior. Typically, the primary personality is unaware of the existence of the alternate personalities. However, the alter egos may have knowledge of each other's existence and share memories (see Kong & others, 2008). Sometimes the experiences of one alter are accessible to another alter but not vice versa.

Symptoms of amnesia and memory problems are reported in virtually all cases of DID (Dorahy, 2014). There are frequent gaps in memory for both recent and childhood experiences. Commonly, those with dissociative identity disorder "lose time" and are unable to recall their behavior or whereabouts during specific time periods.

dissociative amnesia A dissociative disorder involving the partial or total inability to recall important personal information.

dissociative fugue (fyoog) A type of dissociative amnesia involving sudden and unexpected travel away from home, extensive amnesia, and identity confusion.

dissociative identity disorder (DID) A dissociative disorder involving extensive memory disruptions along with the presence of two or more distinct identities, or "personalities"; formerly called *multiple personality disorder.*

Dissociative Fugue: "Who Am I Now?" Just before a new school year, 23-year-old teacher Hannah Upp disappeared. Intensive search efforts produced nothing, but then Hannah was seen at a Manhattan Apple store and, later, at a Starbucks. Hannah was finally rescued when a Staten Island Ferry crew saw her swimming almost a mile from shore—three weeks after she had initially disappeared. Hannah had no memories of the events following her disappearance, and was disturbed by her amnesia and flight. In an interview, she asked, "How do you feel guilty for something you didn't even know you did? It's not your fault, but it's still somehow you. So it's definitely made me reconsider everything. Who was I before? Who was I then—is that part of me? Who am I now?" (Marx & Didziulis, 2009) Although psychologists don't understand what causes dissociative amnesia with dissociative fugue, a rare condition, stressful events are often implicated.

Nicole Bengiveno/The New York Times/Redux

"Tell me more about these nine separate and distinct personalities."

In addition to their memory problems, people with DID typically have numerous psychiatric and physical symptoms, along with a chaotic personal history (Cardena & Gleaves, 2007). Symptoms of major depressive disorder, anxiety, posttraumatic stress disorder, substance abuse, sleep disorders, and self-destructive behavior are also very common. Often, the patient with DID has been diagnosed with a variety of other psychological disorders before the DID diagnosis is made (Rodewald & others, 2011).

Not all mental health professionals are convinced that dissociative identity disorder is a genuine psychological disorder (Cardena & Gleaves, 2007; Lynn & others, 2006 a). One reason for skepticism is that reported cases sharply increased in the early 1970s shortly after books, films, and television dramas about multiple personality disorder became popular. As psychologist John Kihlstrom (2005) noted, not only the number of cases but also the number of "alters" showed a dramatic increase. To some psychologists, such findings suggest that patients with DID learned "how to behave like a multiple" from media portrayals of sensational cases or by responding to their therapists' suggestions (Gee & others, 2003; Lynn & others, 2012). People with another mental illness or other vulnerability might be particularly susceptible to such influences (Lynn & others, 2012). And there is research to support this conclusion. Guy Boysen and Alexandra VanBergen reviewed many studies of people with dissociative identity disorder, and concluded that "in terms of key symptoms of the disorder, people taught to simulate DID are largely indistinguishable from people actually diagnosed with DID" (2014).

On the other hand, DID is not the only psychological disorder for which prevalence rates have increased over time. For example, rates of obsessive–compulsive disorder and PTSD have also increased over the past few decades, primarily because mental health professionals have become more aware of these disorders and more likely to screen for symptoms. The dissociative disorders are summarized in Table 13.8.

TABLE 13.8

Dissociative Disorders

Dissociative Amnesia
• Inability to remember important personal information, too extensive to be explained by ordinary forgetfulness

Dissociative Amnesia with Dissociative Fugue
• Sudden, unexpected travel away from home
• Confusion about personal identity or assumption of new identity

Dissociative Identity Disorder
• Presence of two or more distinct identities, each with consistent patterns of personality traits and behavior
• Behavior that is controlled by two or more distinct, recurring identities
• Amnesia; frequent memory gaps

EXPLAINING DISSOCIATIVE IDENTITY DISORDER

According to one explanation, dissociative identity disorder represents an extreme form of dissociative coping (Moskowitz & others, 2009). A very high percentage of patients with DID report having suffered extreme physical or sexual abuse in childhood—over 90 percent in most surveys (Foote & others, 2006; Sar & others, 2007). According to this explanation, to cope with the trauma, the child "dissociates" himself or herself from it, creating alternate personalities to experience the trauma.

Over time, alternate personalities are created to deal with the memories and emotions associated with intolerably painful experiences. Feelings of anger, rage, fear, and guilt that are too powerful for the child to consciously integrate can be dissociated into these alternate personalities. In effect, dissociation becomes a pathological defense mechanism that the person uses to cope with overwhelming experiences.

Although widely accepted among therapists who work with patients with DID, the dissociative coping theory is difficult to test empirically. One problem is that memories of childhood are notoriously unreliable. Since DID is usually diagnosed in adulthood, it is very difficult, and often impossible, to determine whether the reports of childhood abuse are real or imaginary.

Another problem with the "traumatic memory" explanation of dissociative identity disorder is that just the *opposite* effect occurs to most trauma victims—they are bothered by recurring and intrusive memories of the traumatic event. For example, in a study by Gail Goodman and her colleagues (2003), more than 80 percent of young adults with a documented history of childhood sexual abuse remembered the abuse. Of those who didn't report the abuse, reluctance to disclose the abuse and being too young to remember the abuse seemed to be the most likely explanations. Although the scientific debate about the validity of the dissociative disorders is likely to continue for some time, the dissociative disorders are fundamentally different from the last major category of disorders we'll consider—schizophrenia.

> Test your understanding of **Personality and Dissociative Disorders** with **LEARNING**Curve.

AP Photo/John Amis

Herschel Walker and Dissociative Identity Disorder As a professional football player, Walker (2008) was somewhat of an enigma to his teammates because of his diverse pursuits, which ranged from bobsledding to ballet dancing, and because he often referred to himself in the third person. "Herschel played well today," he might say. After retiring from football, Walker began suffering from unexplained violent outbursts, blackouts, and memory loss. Since being diagnosed with dissociative identity disorder, Walker has identified a dozen distinct alters, including "The Warrior," who handled playing football and the pain that went with it, and "The Hero," who made public appearances. With therapy, Walker is learning to manage his symptoms and hopes to educate the public about this rare disorder.

Schizophrenia
A DIFFERENT REALITY

KEY THEME

One of the most serious psychological disorders is schizophrenia, which involves severely distorted beliefs, perceptions, and thought processes.

KEY QUESTIONS

> What are the major symptoms of schizophrenia, and how do positive and negative symptoms differ?
> How does culture affect the symptoms of schizophrenia?
> What factors have been implicated in the development of schizophrenia?

Normally, you've got a pretty good grip on reality. You can easily distinguish between external reality and the different kinds of mental states that you routinely experience, such as dreams or daydreams. But as we negotiate life's many twists and turns, the ability to stay firmly anchored in reality is not a given. Rather, we're engaged in an ongoing process of verifying the accuracy of our thoughts, beliefs, and perceptions.

If any mental disorder demonstrates the potential for losing touch with reality, it's the one that Elyn Saks suffered from, schizophrenia. In media accounts and casual conversation, a person with schizophrenia is often mistakenly described as having "a split personality." Elyn Saks explains the distinction: "the schizophrenic mind is not split, but shattered" (Saks, 2008). **Schizophrenia** is a psychological disorder that involves severely distorted beliefs, perceptions, and thought processes. During a schizophrenic episode, people lose their grip on reality, like Elyn screaming "I'm flying!" in the chapter Prologue. They become engulfed in an entirely different inner world, one that is often characterized by mental chaos, disorientation, and frustration.

MYTH ◀ SCIENCE

Is it true that people with schizophrenia have a split personality?

schizophrenia A psychological disorder in which the ability to function is impaired by severely distorted beliefs, perceptions, and thought processes.

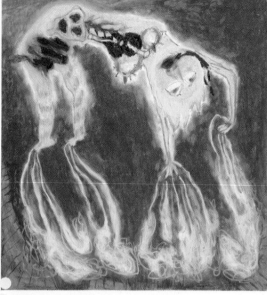

Glimpses of Schizophrenia Artist Karen Sorenson, who manages her schizophrenia with medication, painted "Electricity Makes You Float" shortly after the 9/11 World Trade Center attacks. The painting, she says, grew out of a "psychotic fantasy. . . I thought that I could shoot rays of energy from the palms of my hands and blow up buildings. Somehow I identified with murderers. Making this picture helped free me of the obsessiveness of the idea . . . [by] putting it out there into the brilliance of daylight" (2011).

Courtesy Karen Sorensen

Symptoms of Schizophrenia

The characteristic symptoms of schizophrenia can be described in terms of two broad categories: positive and negative symptoms. **Positive symptoms** reflect an excess or distortion of normal functioning. Positive symptoms includes: (1) *delusions,* or false beliefs; (2) *hallucinations,* or false perceptions; (3) severely disorganized thought processes and speech; and (4) severely disorganized behavior. In contrast, **negative symptoms** reflect an absence or reduction of normal functions, such as greatly reduced motivation, emotional expressiveness, or speech.

According to DSM-5, schizophrenia is diagnosed when two or more of these characteristic symptoms are actively present for a month or longer. At least one symptom must be delusions, hallucinations, or disorganized speech. Usually, schizophrenia also involves a longer personal history, typically six months or more, of odd behaviors, beliefs, perceptual experiences, and other less severe signs of mental disturbance (Keshavan & others, 2011). In Elyn's case, her symptoms lasted for years (Saks, 2008).

Schizophrenia may be diagnosed either with or without catatonia (DSM-5, 2013). *Catatonia* includes symptoms that reflect highly disturbed movements or actions. These may include bizarre postures or grimaces, complete immobility, no speech or very little speech, extremely agitated behavior, the echoing of words just spoken by another person, or imitation of the movements of others. People with catatonia will resist direction from others and may also assume rigid postures to resist being moved.

POSITIVE SYMPTOMS

DELUSIONS, HALLUCINATIONS, AND DISTURBANCES IN SENSATION, THINKING, AND SPEECH

A **delusion** is a false belief that persists despite compelling contradictory evidence. Schizophrenic delusions are not simply unconventional or inaccurate beliefs. Rather, they are bizarre and far-fetched notions. The person may believe that secret agents are poisoning his food or that the next-door neighbors are actually aliens from outer space who are trying to transform him into a remote-controlled robot. At times, Elyn believed that she was an evil person who was capable of committing terrible violent acts, including killing children (Saks, 2008). The delusional person often becomes preoccupied with his erroneous beliefs and ignores any evidence that contradicts them.

Certain themes consistently appear in schizophrenic delusions. *Delusions of reference* reflect the person's false conviction that other people's behavior and ordinary events are somehow personally related to her. For example, she is certain that billboards and advertisements are about her or contain cryptic messages directed at her. In contrast, *delusions of grandeur* involve the belief that the person is extremely powerful, important, or wealthy. In *delusions of persecution,* the basic theme is that others are plotting against or trying to harm the person or someone close to her. *Delusions of being controlled* involve the belief that outside forces—aliens, the government, or random people, for example—are trying to exert control on the individual.

Schizophrenic delusions are often so convincing that they can provoke inappropriate or bizarre behavior. Delusional thinking may lead to dangerous behaviors, as when a person responds to his delusional ideas by hurting himself or attacking others.

Among the most disturbing experiences in schizophrenia are **hallucinations,** which are false or distorted perceptions—usually voices or visual stimuli—that seem vividly real (see Figure 13.3). The content of hallucinations is often tied to the person's delusional beliefs. For example,

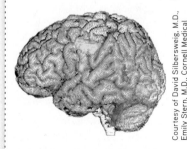

FOCUS ON NEUROSCIENCE

The Hallucinating Brain

Researcher David Silbersweig and his colleagues (1995) used PET scans to take a "snapshot" of brain activity during schizophrenic hallucinations. The scan shown here was recorded at the exact instant a schizophrenic patient hallucinated disembodied heads yelling orders at him. The bright orange areas reveal activity in the left auditory and visual areas of his brain, but not in the frontal lobe, which normally is involved in organized thought processes.

Courtesy of David Silbersweig, M.D., Emily Stern, M.D., Cornell Medical Center

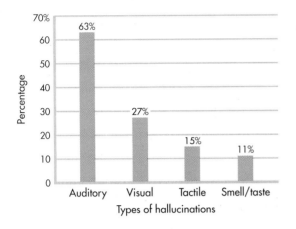

FIGURE 13.3 Incidence of Different Types of Hallucinations in Schizophrenia Schizophrenia-related hallucinations can occur in any sensory modality. Auditory hallucinations, usually in the form of voices, are the most common type of hallucinations that occur in schizophrenia, followed by visual hallucinations.

Source: Data from Mueser & others (1990) and Bracha & others (1989).

if she harbors delusions of grandeur, hallucinated voices may reinforce her grandiose ideas by communicating instructions from God, the devil, or angels. If the person harbors delusions of persecution, hallucinated voices or images may be extremely frightening, threatening, or accusing. The content and experience of hallucinations and delusions may also be influenced by culture and religious beliefs. For example, researchers studied auditory hallucinations of people in the United States, Ghana, and India (Luhrmann & others, 2015). They found that people in the United States were more likely to experience their voices as dark and sometimes vicious, whereas people in Ghana and India were more likely to report having a positive relationship with their voices. As one Indian participant explained while laughing, "I have a companion to talk to" (Khazan, 2014).

When a schizophrenic episode is severe, hallucinations can be virtually impossible to distinguish from objective reality. For example, Elyn reported that she could sometimes hear someone calling her name when she knew she was completely alone (Saks, 2008). When schizophrenic symptoms are less severe, the person may recognize that the hallucination is a product of his own mind. As Elyn reported, she knew that she had to try to control her psychotic thoughts at school and in social settings and was sometimes able to do so.

Other positive symptoms of schizophrenia include disturbances in sensation, thinking, and speech. Visual, auditory, and tactile experiences may seem distorted or unreal. For example, one woman described the sensory distortions in this way:

> Looking around the room, I found that things had lost their emotional meaning. They were larger than life, tense, and suspenseful. They were flat, and colored as if in artificial light. I felt my body to be first giant, then minuscule. My arms seemed to be several inches longer than before and did not feel as though they belonged to me. (Anonymous, 1990)

Along with sensory distortions, the person may experience severely disorganized thinking. It becomes enormously difficult to concentrate, remember, and integrate important information while ignoring irrelevant information (Barch, 2005). The person's mind drifts from topic to topic in an unpredictable, illogical manner, such as the Prologue example of Elyn's ramblings to her classmates. Such disorganized thinking is often reflected in the person's speech (Badcock & others, 2011). Ideas, words, and images are sometimes strung together in ways that seem nonsensical to the listener.

NEGATIVE SYMPTOMS
FLAT AFFECT, ALOGIA, AND AVOLITION

Negative symptoms consist of marked deficits or decreases in behavioral or emotional functioning. One commonly seen negative symptom is referred to as *diminished emotional expression* or flat affect. Regardless of the situation, the person responds in an emotionally "flat" way, showing a dramatic reduction in emotional responsiveness and facial expressions. Speech is slow and monotonous, lacking normal vocal inflections. A closely related negative symptom is *alogia,* or greatly reduced production of speech. In alogia, verbal responses are limited to brief, empty comments.

People with schizophrenia might hear the roars of Satan or the whispers of children. They might move armies with their thoughts and receive instructions from other worlds. They might feel penetrated by scheming parasites, stalked by enemies, or praised by guardian angels. People with schizophrenia might also speak nonsensically, their language at once intricate and impenetrable. And many would push, or be pushed, to the edge of the social landscape, overcome by solitude.

—*R. Walter Heinrichs (2005)*

positive symptoms In schizophrenia, symptoms that reflect excesses or distortions of normal functioning, including delusions, hallucinations, and disorganized thoughts and behavior.

negative symptoms In schizophrenia, symptoms that reflect defects or deficits in normal functioning, including flat affect, alogia, and avolition.

delusion A falsely held belief that persists despite compelling contradictory evidence.

hallucination A false or distorted perception that seems vividly real to the person experiencing it.

FIGURE 13.4 Presence of Symptoms in Schizophrenia This graph shows the incidence of positive and negative symptoms in over 100 people at the time they were hospitalized for schizophrenia. Delusions were the most common positive symptom, and avolition, or apathy, was the most common negative symptom.

Source: Data from Andreasen & Flaum (1991).

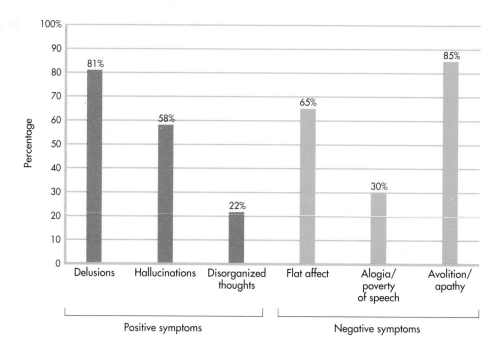

Finally, *avolition* refers to the inability to initiate or persist in even simple forms of goal-directed behaviors, such as dressing, bathing, or engaging in social activities. Instead, the person seems to be completely apathetic, sometimes sitting still for hours at a time. In combination, the negative symptoms accentuate the isolation of the person with schizophrenia, who may appear uncommunicative and completely disconnected from his or her environment. Not everyone with schizophrenia experiences negative symptoms. Elyn Saks wrote of feeling lucky to have escaped experiencing most negative symptoms (Saks, 2008). Figure 13.4 shows the frequency of positive and negative symptoms at the time of hospitalization for schizophrenia.

Schizophrenia Symptoms and Culture

Symptoms of schizophrenia often vary across cultures. For example, there can be cultural variations in delusional themes and the content of hallucinations (Bauer & others, 2011).

Delusions are a prime example of a symptom often rooted in culture. Indeed, some themes that would be considered to be delusional in one culture might be widely held beliefs in another culture. The International Study on Psychotic Symptoms examined data from over 1,000 people with schizophrenia in seven countries: Austria, Georgia, Ghana, Lithuania, Nigeria, Pakistan, and Poland (Stompe & others, 2006). Among the delusions experienced by the people in this sample, 16.8 percent of the content was culturally specific. For example, in Nigeria and Ghana there were relatively high rates of delusions that involved "being an angel or a prophet," concepts that are integral parts of these cultures.

Even within a single culture, the content of delusions changes as the culture shifts. A study of delusions in U.S. inpatient psychiatric patients found that delusions have changed over time. During World War II, delusions tended to center on Nazi soldiers.

A Truly Modern Delusion In cultures where reality television and surveillance technology have become mainstream, the "Truman Show" delusion—the belief that your life is being filmed as a show—is increasingly common. *The Truman Show* is a 1998 hit movie about an insurance salesman who discovered that his entire life was secretly being filmed for broadcast. When experiencing the Truman Show delusion, Ohio college student Nick Lotz even took an acting course to improve his "performance." At first he thought he was angling for a $100 million prize, but later he came to believe that the goal of his delusional reality show was to join the cast of *Saturday Night Live*—a truly culturally specific, modern delusion (Marantz, 2013).

Recently, delusions are more likely to involve technology (Cannon & Kramer, 2012). Joel Gold and Ian Gold (2012) describe a common type of delusion involving technology—people who believe that they are being filmed continuously, with the footage being aired as if they were secretly cast on a television show like *Big Brother*. The Golds refer to this as the "Truman Show" delusion after the 1998 film in which a whole town is secretly filmed for years as global entertainment.

The Prevalence and Course of Schizophrenia

Every year, about 200,000 new cases of schizophrenia are diagnosed in the United States, and annually, approximately 1 million Americans are treated for schizophrenia. All told, about 1 percent of the U.S. population will experience at least one episode of schizophrenia at some point in life (Rado & Janicak, 2009). Worldwide, no society or culture is immune to this mental disorder. Researchers have long believed that most cultures correspond very closely to the 1 percent rate of schizophrenia seen in the United States (Minzenberg & others, 2011). However, a comprehensive review of almost 200 studies concluded that global rates of schizophrenia were closer to 4 percent, meaning that schizophrenia may be far more widespread than once believed (Saha & others, 2005).

The onset of schizophrenia typically occurs during young adulthood, as it did with Elyn (Gogtay & others, 2011). However, the course of schizophrenia is marked by enormous individual variability. Even so, a few global generalizations are possible (Malla & Payne, 2005; Walker & others, 2004). The good news is that about one-quarter of those who experience an episode of schizophrenia recover completely and never experience another episode. Another one-quarter experience recurrent episodes of schizophrenia but often with only minimal impairment in the ability to function.

Now the bad news. For the rest of those who have experienced an episode of schizophrenia—about one-half of the total—schizophrenia becomes a chronic mental illness, and the ability to function may be severely impaired. The people in this last category face the prospect of repeated hospitalizations and extended treatment. Thus, chronic schizophrenia places a heavy emotional, financial, and psychological burden on people with the disorder, their families, and society (Combs & Mueser, 2007). Yet, as Elyn's story shows, a diagnosis of schizophrenia does not mean that a person cannot be successful in his or her career and personal life.

Cultural factors also seem to affect the outcome of schizophrenia. Despite less access to mental health care, people with schizophrenia often have a better outcome in the developing world than in the developed world (Haro & others, 2011; World Health Organization, 1998). For example, the World Health Organization (WHO) found that full recovery after a single episode of psychosis occurred in just 3 percent of cases in the United States but in 54 percent of cases in India. WHO (1998) suggests that people in the developing world might be more accepting of mental illness, and are more likely to have extended family support systems than people in the developed world.

Other studies have qualified these findings. For example, Josep Haro and others (2011) found that people with schizophrenia living in the developing world tended to experience a greater decline in their symptoms over time than those with schizophrenia living in the developed world. But they also fared worse in terms of life skills, such as holding a job and living independently. The decline in symptoms did not coincide with improved life functioning. Clearly, culture is an important factor in the experience and course of schizophrenia.

Explaining Schizophrenia

Schizophrenia is an extremely complex disorder. There is enormous individual variability in the onset, symptoms, and duration of and recovery from schizophrenia. So it shouldn't come as a surprise that the causes of schizophrenia seem to be equally complex. In this section, we'll survey some of the factors that have been implicated in the development of schizophrenia.

Young Adulthood and Schizophrenia The onset of schizophrenia typically occurs between the ages of 18 and 25. Daniel Laitman, however, was diagnosed at age 15 when he showed symptoms that included the disturbed movements of catatonia and auditory hallucinations. Daniel's treatment includes both medications and psychotherapy. He also reports benefitting from long-distance running and the unwavering support of his family. Now in his early 20s, Daniel is a college student and a successful stand-up comedian. He has been open about his diagnosis. "I tell people what it is and if they have questions they can ask me. Schizophrenia is a part of me" (Focus on Family Support, 2010).

Ann Mandel Laitman

GENETIC FACTORS
FAMILY, TWIN, ADOPTION, AND GENE STUDIES

Studies of families, twins, and adopted individuals have firmly established that genetic factors play a significant role in many cases of schizophrenia (Pogue-Geile & Yokley, 2010). First, family studies have consistently shown that schizophrenia tends to cluster in certain families (Choi & others, 2007; Helenius & others, 2012). Second, family and twin studies have consistently shown that the more closely related a person is to someone who has schizophrenia, the greater the risk that she will be diagnosed with schizophrenia at some point in her lifetime (see Figure 13.5). Third, adoption studies have consistently shown that if either *biological* parent of an adopted individual had schizophrenia, the adopted individual is at greater risk to develop schizophrenia (Wynne & others, 2006). And fourth, by studying families that display a high rate of schizophrenia, researchers have consistently found that the presence of certain genetic variations seems to increase susceptibility to the disorder (Fanous & others, 2005; Williams & others, 2005).

Ironically, some of the best evidence that points to genetic involvement in schizophrenia—the almost 50 percent risk rate for a person whose identical twin has schizophrenia—is the same evidence that underscores the importance of environmental factors (Joseph & Leo, 2006; Oh & Petronis, 2008). If schizophrenia were purely a matter of inherited maladaptive genes, then you would expect a risk rate much closer to 100 percent for monozygotic twins. Obviously, nongenetic factors must play a role in explaining why half of identical twins with a schizophrenic twin do *not* develop schizophrenia.

Nevertheless, scientists are getting closer to identifying some of the specific genetic patterns that are associated with an increased risk of developing schizophrenia. New research using sophisticated gene analysis techniques confirms the incredibly complex role that genes play in the development of schizophrenia (Gilman & others, 2012; Rapoport & others, 2012). For example, one study of people with schizophrenia with *no* family history of the disease found that genetic mutations were much higher in the schizophrenic patients than in individuals without schizophrenia (Girard & others, 2011). These mutations were present in many different genes, including genes that had not previously been associated with schizophrenia.

FIGURE 13.5 The Risk of Developing Schizophrenia Among Blood Relatives The risk percentages shown here reflect the collective results of about 40 studies investigating the likelihood of developing schizophrenia among blood relatives. As you can see, the greatest risk occurs if you have an identical twin who has schizophrenia (48 percent lifetime risk) or if both of your biological parents have schizophrenia (46 percent lifetime risk). However, environmental factors are also involved in the development of schizophrenia.

Source: Data from Gottesman (1991).

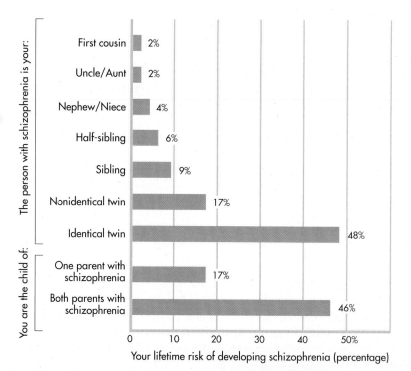

In another large-scale research project, three different research teams compared DNA samples from thousands of people diagnosed with schizophrenia with DNA samples from control groups of people who did *not* have schizophrenia (Purcell & others, 2009; Shi & others, 2009; Stefansson & others, 2009). Some of the people in the control groups had *other* mental or physical disorders, but most were healthy. The researchers were looking for specific genetic variations that were more common in the genomes of people with schizophrenia than in people without schizophrenia.

Collectively, the studies found that schizophrenia was associated with literally *thousands* of common gene variations. Some of the specific variants were quite rare, while others were quite common. Taken individually, none of the gene variants is capable of "causing" schizophrenia. Even in combination, the genetic variants are only associated with an increased *risk* of developing schizophrenia.

As yet, no specific pattern of genetic variation can be identified as the genetic "cause" of schizophrenia. However, three particularly interesting findings stand out. First, some of the same unique genetic patterns associated with schizophrenia have also been found in DNA samples from people with bipolar disorder (Purcell & others, 2009). This finding suggests that bipolar disorder and schizophrenia might share some common genetic origins. Second, also implicated were several chromosome locations that are associated with genes that influence brain development, memory, and cognition. Finally, a large number of the gene variants were found to occur on a specific chromosome that is also known to harbor genes involved in the immune response (Shi & others, 2009). Later in this section, we'll discuss some intriguing links between viral infections and schizophrenia, which suggests that the immune system may be implicated in the development of schizophrenia.

PATERNAL AGE
OLDER FATHERS AND THE RISK OF SCHIZOPHRENIA

Despite the fact that family and twin studies point to the role of genetic factors in the risk of developing schizophrenia, no genetic model thus far explains all of the patterns of schizophrenia occurrence within families (Insel & Lehner, 2007). Adding to the complexity, schizophrenia often occurs in individuals with *no* family history of mental disorders. Elyn, for example, has an uncle who suffered from depression but no close relatives who suffered from schizophrenia or any other serious mental disorders (Saks, 2008).

One explanation for these anomalies is that for each generation, new cases of schizophrenia arise from genetic mutations carried in the sperm of the biological fathers, especially older fathers. As men age, their sperm cells continue to reproduce by dividing. By the time a male is 20, his sperm cells have undergone about 200 divisions; by the time he is 40, there have been about 660 divisions. As the number of divisions increases over time, the sperm cells accumulate genetic mutations that can then be passed on to that man's offspring. Hence, the theory goes, as paternal age increases, the risk of offspring developing schizophrenia also increases (Bajwa & others, 2011). While paternal age is a potential risk factor, it's important to keep in mind that three-quarters of the cases of schizophrenia in this study were *not* associated with older paternal age.

THE IMMUNE SYSTEM
THE VIRAL INFECTION THEORY

Another provocative theory is that schizophrenia might be caused by exposure to an influenza virus or other viral infection during prenatal development or shortly after birth (Carter, 2008; Yudofsky, 2009). A virus might seem an unlikely cause of a serious mental disorder, but viruses *can* spread to the brain and spinal cord by traveling along nerves. According to this theory, exposure to a viral infection during prenatal development or early infancy affects the developing brain, producing changes that make the individual more vulnerable to schizophrenia later in life.

There is growing evidence to support the viral infection theory. In one compelling study, psychiatrist Alan S. Brown and his colleagues (2004) compared stored blood samples of 64 mothers of people who later developed schizophrenia with a matched set of blood samples from women whose children did not develop schizophrenia. Both sets of blood samples had been collected years earlier during the women's pregnancies. After analyzing the blood samples for the presence of influenza antibodies, Brown and his colleagues (2004) found that women who had been exposed to the flu virus during the first trimester had a sevenfold increased risk of bearing a child who later developed schizophrenia. A related finding is that schizophrenia occurs more often in people who were born in the winter and spring months, when upper respiratory infections are most common (Disanto & others, 2012; Torrey & others, 1996).

ABNORMAL BRAIN STRUCTURES
LOSS OF GRAY MATTER

Researchers have found that about half of the people with schizophrenia show some type of brain structure abnormality. The most consistent finding has been the enlargement of the fluid-filled cavities, called *ventricles,* located deep within the brain (Kempton & others, 2010; Meduri & others, 2010). However, researchers are not certain how enlarged ventricles might be related to schizophrenia.

Other differences that have been found are a loss of gray matter tissue and lower overall volume of the brain (Olabi & others, 2011; Vita & others, 2012). As we discussed in Chapter 2, *gray matter* refers to the glial cells, neuron cell bodies, and unmyelinated axons that make up the quarter-inch-thick cerebral cortex. Researchers have found that the loss of gray matter is associated with increased clinical symptoms and decreased cognitive functioning among people with schizophrenia (Asami & others, 2012).

To investigate the neurological development of schizophrenia, neuroscientist Paul M. Thompson and his colleagues (2001) undertook a prospective study of brain structure changes in 12 adolescents with early-onset childhood schizophrenia. The six females and six males had all experienced schizophrenic symptoms, including psychotic symptoms, before the age of 12. The intent of the study was to provide a visual picture of the timing, rates, and anatomical distribution of brain structure changes in adolescents with schizophrenia.

Each of the 12 adolescents was scanned repeatedly with high-resolution MRIs over a five-year period, beginning when they were about 14. The adolescents were carefully matched with healthy teens of the same gender, age, socioeconomic background, and height. The findings of this important study are featured in the Focus on Neuroscience.

Although there is evidence that brain abnormalities are found in schizophrenia, such findings do not prove that brain abnormalities are the sole cause of schizophrenia. First, some people with schizophrenia do *not* show brain structure abnormalities. Second, the evidence is correlational. Researchers are still investigating whether differences in brain structures and activity are the cause or the consequence of schizophrenia. Third, the kinds of brain abnormalities seen in schizophrenia are also seen in other mental disorders. Rather than specifically causing schizophrenia, it's quite possible that brain abnormalities might contribute to psychological disorders in general.

ABNORMAL BRAIN CHEMISTRY
HYPOTHESES RELATED TO NEUROTRANSMITTERS

There are several hypotheses that attribute schizophrenia to imbalances in neurotransmitters. The oldest of these is the dopamine hypothesis, which attributes

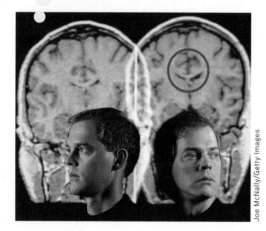

Identical Twins but Not Identical Brains David and Steven Elmore are identical twins, but they differ in one important respect—Steven *(right)* has schizophrenia. Behind each is a CT scan, which reveals that Steven's brain is slightly smaller, with less area devoted to the cortex at the top of the brain. Steven also has larger fluid-filled ventricles, which are circled in red on his brain scan. As researcher Daniel Weinberger (1995) commented, "The part of the cortex that Steven is missing serves as perhaps the most evolved part of the human brain. It performs complicated tasks such as thinking organized thoughts. This might help explain why paranoid delusions and hallucinations are characteristic of schizophrenia."

Joe McNally/Getty Images

FOCUS ON NEUROSCIENCE

Schizophrenia: A Wildfire in the Brain

In a five-year prospective study, neuroscientist Paul Thompson and his colleagues (2001) used high-resolution brain scans to map brain structure changes in normal adolescents and adolescents with early-onset schizophrenia. Thompson found marked differences in the brain development of normal teens and teens with schizophrenia. As expected, the healthy teenagers showed a gradual, small loss of gray matter—about 1 percent—over the five-year study. This loss is due to the normal pruning of unused brain connections that takes place during adolescence (see Chapter 9).

But in sharp contrast to the normal teens, the teenagers with schizophrenia showed a severe loss of gray matter that developed in a specific, wavelike pattern. The loss began in the parietal lobes and, over the five years of the study, progressively spread forward to the temporal and frontal regions. As Thompson (2001) noted, "We were stunned to see a spreading wave of tissue loss that began in a small region of the brain. It moved across the brain like a forest fire, destroying more tissue as the disease progressed."

The brain images show the average rate of gray matter loss over the five-year period. Gray matter loss ranged from about 1 percent (blue) in the normal teens to more than 5 percent (pink) in the schizophrenic teens. One fascinating finding was that the amount of gray matter loss was directly correlated to the teenage patients' clinical symptoms. Psychotic symptoms increased the most in the participants who lost the greatest quantity of gray matter.

Also, the *pattern* of loss mirrored the progression of neurological and cognitive deficits associated with schizophrenia. For example, more rapid gray matter loss in the *temporal lobes* was associated with more severe *positive* symptoms, such as hallucinations and delusions. More rapid loss of gray matter in the *frontal lobes* was strongly correlated with the severity of *negative* symptoms, including flat affect and poverty of speech. When the participants were 18 to 19 years old and the final brain scans were taken, the patterns of gray matter loss were similar to those found in the brains of adult patients with schizophrenia.

Despite the wealth of information generated by Thompson's study, the critical question remains unanswered: What sparks the cerebral forest fire in the schizophrenic brain?

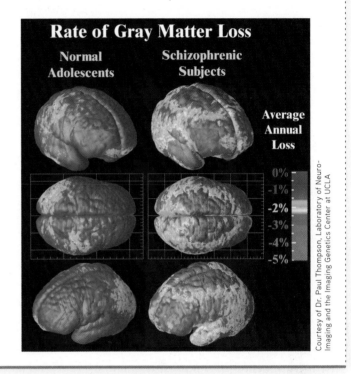

Rate of Gray Matter Loss

Normal Adolescents   Schizophrenic Subjects

Average Annual Loss

0%
-1%
-2%
-3%
-4%
-5%

Courtesy of Dr. Paul Thompson, Laboratory of Neuro-Imaging and the Imaging Genetics Center at UCLA

schizophrenia to excessive activity of the neurotransmitter dopamine in the brain. Two pieces of indirect evidence support this notion. First, antipsychotic drugs, such as Haldol, Thorazine, and Stelazine, *reduce or block dopamine activity in the brain.* These drugs reduce schizophrenic symptoms, especially positive symptoms, in many people. Second, drugs that enhance dopamine activity in the brain, such as amphetamines and cocaine, can produce schizophrenia-like symptoms in normal adults or increase symptoms in people who already have schizophrenia.

However, there is also evidence that contradicts the dopamine hypothesis (Jucaite & Nyberg, 2012). For example, not all individuals who have schizophrenia experience a reduction of symptoms in response to the antipsychotic drugs that reduce dopamine activity in the brain. And for many patients, these drugs reduce some but not all schizophrenic symptoms, and tend to reduce positive symptoms more than negative symptoms (Kendler & Schaffner, 2011). One new theory is that some parts of the brain, such as the limbic system, may have too much dopamine, while other parts of the brain, such as the cortex, may have too little (Combs & Mueser, 2007; Kendler & Schaffner, 2011). There also is increasing evidence that imbalances in other neurotransmitters—glutamate and adenosine—are related to schizophrenia (Boison & others, 2012; Lau & others, 2013; Moghaddam & Javitt, 2011). Thus, the connection between neurotransmitters and schizophrenia symptoms remains unclear.

PSYCHOLOGICAL FACTORS
UNHEALTHY FAMILIES

Researchers have investigated such factors as dysfunctional parenting, disturbed family communication styles, and critical or guilt-inducing parental styles as possible contributors to schizophrenia (Johnson & others, 2001). However, no single psychological factor seems to emerge consistently as causing schizophrenia. Rather, it seems that those who are genetically predisposed to develop schizophrenia may be more vulnerable to the effects of disturbed family environments (Tienari & Wahlberg, 2008).

Strong support for this view comes from a landmark study conducted by Finnish psychiatrist Pekka Tienari and his colleagues (1987, 1994). In the Finnish Adoptive Family Study of Schizophrenia, researchers followed about 150 adopted individuals whose biological mothers had schizophrenia. As part of their study, the researchers assessed the adoptive family's degree of psychological adjustment, including the mental health of the adoptive parents. The study also included a control group of about 180 adopted individuals whose biological mothers did *not* have schizophrenia.

Tienari and his colleagues (1994, 2006; Wynne & others, 2006) found that adopted children with a schizophrenic biological mother had a much higher rate of schizophrenia than did the children in the control group. However, this was true *only* when the children were raised in a psychologically disturbed adoptive home. As you can see in Figure 13.6, when children with a genetic background of schizophrenia were raised in a psychologically healthy adoptive family, they were *no more likely* than the control-group children to develop schizophrenia.

Although adopted children with no genetic history of schizophrenia were less vulnerable to the psychological stresses of a disturbed family environment, they were by no means completely immune to such influences. As Figure 13.6 shows, one-third of the control-group adoptees developed symptoms of a serious psychological disorder if they were raised in a disturbed family environment.

Tienari's study underscores the complex interaction of genetic and environmental factors. Clearly, children who were genetically at risk to develop schizophrenia benefited from being raised in a healthy psychological environment. Put simply, a healthy psychological environment may counteract a person's inherited vulnerability for schizophrenia. Conversely, a psychologically unhealthy family environment can act as a catalyst for the onset of schizophrenia, especially for those individuals with a genetic history of schizophrenia (Tienari & Wahlberg, 2008).

FIGURE 13.6 The Finnish Adoptive Family Study of Schizophrenia   In the Finnish Adoptive Family Study, psychiatrist Pekka Tienari and his colleagues (1994, 2006) tracked the mental health of two groups of adopted individuals: one group with biological mothers who had schizophrenia and a control group whose biological mothers did not have schizophrenia. This graph shows the strong influence of the adoptive family environment on the development of serious mental disorders.

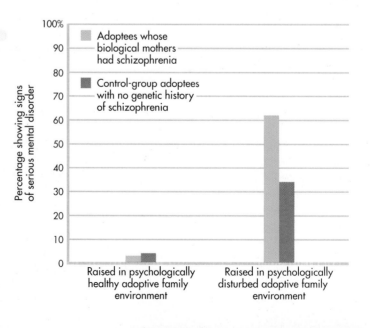

After more than a century of intensive research, schizophrenia remains a baffling disorder. Thus far, no single biological, psychological, or social factor has emerged as the causal agent in schizophrenia. And it's virtually impossible to know what caused schizophrenia in any single individual like Elyn. Nevertheless, researchers are expressing greater confidence that the pieces of the schizophrenia puzzle are beginning to form a more coherent picture.

Even if the exact causes of schizophrenia remain elusive, there is still reason for optimism. In the past few years, new antipsychotic drugs, such as those that Elyn takes, have been developed that are much more effective in treating both the positive and negative symptoms of schizophrenia (Sharif & others, 2007). In the next chapter, we'll take a detailed look at the different treatments and therapies for schizophrenia and other psychological disorders.

> Test your understanding of **Schizophrenia** with **LEARNING**Curve.

Closing Thoughts

In this chapter, we've looked at the symptoms and causes of several psychological disorders. We've seen that some of the symptoms of psychological disorders represent a sharp break from normal experience. The behavior of Elyn Saks in the Prologue is an example of the severely disrupted functioning characteristic of schizophrenia. In contrast, the symptoms of other psychological disorders, such as the anxiety disorders and depressive disorders, differ from normal experience primarily in their degree, intensity, and duration.

Psychologists are only beginning to understand the causes of many psychological disorders. The broad picture that emerges reflects a familiar theme: Biological, psychological, and social factors all contribute to the development of psychological disorders. In the next chapter, we'll look at how psychological disorders are treated.

In the final section, Psych for Your Life, we'll explore one of the most serious consequences of psychological problems—suicide. Because people who are contemplating suicide often turn to their friends before they seek help from a mental health professional, we'll also suggest several ways in which you can help a friend who expresses suicidal intentions.

PSYCH FOR YOUR LIFE

Understanding and Helping to Prevent Suicide

Who Commits Suicide?

Suicide and attempted suicide are all too common. Each year more than 800,000 people around the world take their own lives, including almost 40,000 in the United States (World Health Organization, 2014). For every death by suicide, it's estimated that 25 people have attempted suicide—a total of about 1,000,000 attempts a year in the United States alone (Centers for Disease Control, 2012). In any given year, almost 500,000 people in the United States require emergency room treatment as a result of attempted suicide (CDC, 2012).

On average, someone commits suicide in the United States every 17 minutes. It is estimated that each suicide affects the lives of at least six other people.

Most people don't realize that more than twice as many Americans die each year from suicide as from homicide. In 2009, suicide was the 10th leading cause of death, while homicide ranked 15th (Kochanek & others, 2011). The global numbers are equally surprising. One recent headline read: "More People Die from Suicide Than from Wars, Natural Disasters Combined" (Schlein, 2014).

In the United States, women outnumber men by three to one in the number of suicide attempts. However, men outnumber women by more than four to one in suicide deaths, primarily because men tend to use more lethal methods, such as shooting and hanging (CDC, 2012; Kochanek & Smith, 2004).

Suicide is the third leading cause of death for young people ages 15 to 24, accounting for 20 percent of annual deaths in this age group (CDC, 2012). Over the past four decades, the suicide rate for adolescents and young adults has increased by almost 300 percent (U.S. Public Health Service, 1999). Although this trend has received considerable media attention, the suicide rate of adolescents and young adults is still below that of older adults. In fact, the highest suicide rate consistently occurs in the oldest segments of our population—among those aged 75 and above (Kochanek & Smith, 2004).

A notion that is often perpetuated in the popular press is that there is a significant increase in the number of suicides during the winter holidays. This claim is a myth, plain and simple. However, there are consistent seasonal variations in suicide deaths. In the United States, suicide rates are lower during the fall and winter months and higher during the spring and summer months (Kposowa & D'Auria, 2010).

What Risk Factors Are Associated with Suicidal Behavior?

Hundreds of studies have identified psychosocial and environmental factors associated with an increased risk of suicidal behavior (see L. Brown & others, 2004; Gould & others, 2003; Hawton & others, 2012; Joiner & others, 2005; Lieb & others, 2005; Nock & others, 2013). Factors that increase the risk of suicidal behavior include:

- Feelings of hopelessness and social isolation
- Recent relationship problems or a lack of significant relationships
- Poor coping and problem-solving skills
- Poor impulse control and impaired judgment
- Rigid thinking or irrational beliefs
- A major psychological disorder, especially major depressive disorder, bipolar disorder, or schizophrenia
- Alcohol or other substance abuse
- Childhood physical or sexual abuse
- Prior self-destructive behavior
- A family history of suicide
- Presence of a firearm in the home
- Exposure to bullying, including cyberbullying (Fisher & others, 2012)

Why Do People Attempt or Commit Suicide?

The suicidal person's view of life has become progressively more pessimistic and negative. At the same time, his view of self-inflicted death as an alternative to life becomes progressively more acceptable and positive (Shneidman, 1998, 2004).

Some people choose suicide to escape the pain of a chronic illness or the slow, agonizing death of a terminal disease. Others commit suicide because of feelings of hopelessness, depression, guilt, rejection, failure, humiliation, or shame (Lester, 1997, 2010). The common denominator is that they see suicide as the only escape from their own unbearably painful emotions (Jamison, 2000; Lester, 2010).

When faced with a dilemma, the average person tends to see a range of possible solutions, accepting the fact that none of the solutions may be ideal. In contrast, the suicidal person's thinking and perceptions have become rigid and constricted. She can see only two ways to solve her problems: a magical resolution or suicide. Because she cannot imagine a realistic way of solving her problems, death seems to be the only logical option (Shneidman, 1998, 2004).

How Can You Help Prevent Suicide?

If someone is truly intent on taking his or her own life, it may be impossible to prevent him or her from doing so. But that does not mean that you can't try to help a friend who is expressing suicidal intentions. People often turn to their friends rather than to mental health professionals. If a friend confides that he or she is feeling hopeless and suicidal, these guidelines may help you help your friend.

It's important to stress, however, that these guidelines are meant only to help you provide "psychological first aid" in a crisis situation. They do *not* qualify you as a suicide prevention expert. Your goal is to help your friend weather the immediate crisis so that he or she can be directed to a mental health professional.

Guideline 1: Actively listen as the person talks and vents her feelings.

The majority of those who attempt suicide communicate their intentions to friends or family members (Shneidman, 1998). When a friend is despondent and desperate, you can help by listening, expressing your understanding and compassion, and, if necessary, referring him to a professional counselor or suicide prevention specialist.

The suicidal person often feels isolated or lonely, with few sources of social support (Joiner, 2010). Let the person talk, and try to genuinely empathize with your friend's feelings. An understanding friend who is willing to take the time to listen patiently without passing judgment may provide just the support the person needs to overcome the immediate suicidal feelings.

Guideline 2: Don't deny or minimize the person's suicidal intentions.

Brushing aside suicidal statements with platitudes, like "Don't be silly, you've got everything to live for," or clichés, like "Every cloud has a silver lining," is not a helpful response. This is *not* the time to be glib, patronizing, or superficial. Instead, ask your friend if she wants to talk about her feelings. Try to be matter-of-fact and confirm that she is indeed seriously suicidal, rather than simply exaggerating her frustration or disappointment.

How can you confirm that the person is suicidal? Simply ask, "Are you really thinking about killing yourself?" Talking about specific suicide plans (how, when, and where), giving away valued possessions, and putting one's affairs in order are some indications that a person's suicidal intentions are serious.

Guideline 3: Identify other potential solutions.

The suicidal person is operating with psychological blinders that prevent him from seeing alternative courses of action or other ways of looking at his problems. How can you remove those blinders? Simply saying "Here are some options you may not have thought about" is a good starting point. You might list alternative solutions to the person's problems, helping him to understand that other potential solutions do exist, even though none may be perfect (Shneidman, 1998).

Guideline 4: Ask the person to delay his decision.

Most suicidal people are ambivalent about wanting to die. If your friend did not have mixed feelings about committing suicide, he probably wouldn't be talking to you. If he is still intent on suicide after talking about other alternatives, ask him to *delay* his decision. Even a few days' delay may give the person enough time to psychologically regroup, consider alternatives, or seek help.

> So ubiquitous is the impulse to commit suicide that one out of every two Americans has at some time considered, threatened, or actually attempted suicide.
>
> —David Lester

Guideline 5: Encourage the person to seek professional help.

If the person is seriously suicidal and may harm herself in the near future, do *not* leave her alone. The most important thing you can do is help to get the person referred to a mental health

Learning to Be a Supportive Friend College students contemplating suicide often turn first to a friend or roommate rather than seeking professional help or confiding in an adult (Drum & others, 2009). Many colleges and universities have trained students to help other students who seem to be in distress. If a friend is despondent, you can help by listening empathically, expressing your understanding and compassion, and if necessary, referring him or her to a counselor or suicide prevention resource.

professional for evaluation and treatment. If you don't feel you can do this alone, find another person to help you.

There are any number of resources you can suggest, including local suicide hotlines or mental health associations, the college counseling service, and the person's family doctor or religious adviser. You can also suggest calling 1-800-SUICIDE (1-800-784-2433), which will connect you with a crisis center in your area.

CHAPTER REVIEW

KEY PEOPLE AND KEY TERMS

psychopathology, p. 535

psychological disorder (mental disorder), p. 535

DSM-5, p. 535

anxiety, p. 541

anxiety disorders, p. 541

generalized anxiety disorder (GAD), p. 541

panic attack, p. 542

panic disorder, p. 542

agoraphobia, p. 542

phobia, p. 543

specific phobia, p. 544

social anxiety disorder, p. 544

posttraumatic stress disorder (PTSD), p. 546

obsessive–compulsive disorder (OCD), p. 548

obsessions, p. 548

compulsions, p. 548

major depressive disorder, p. 550

seasonal affective disorder (SAD), p. 551

persistent depressive disorder, p. 552

bipolar disorder, p. 553

manic episode, p. 553

cyclothymic disorder, p. 554

eating disorder, p. 558

anorexia nervosa, p. 558

bulimia nervosa, p. 559

binge-eating disorder, p. 559

personality disorder, p. 562

antisocial personality disorder, p. 563

borderline personality disorder (BPD), p. 565

dissociative experience, p. 566

dissociative disorders, p. 566

dissociative amnesia, p. 567

dissociative fugue, p. 567

dissociative identity disorder (DID), p. 567

schizophrenia, p. 569

positive symptoms, p. 570

negative symptoms, p. 570

delusion, p. 570

hallucination, p. 570

Psychological Disorders

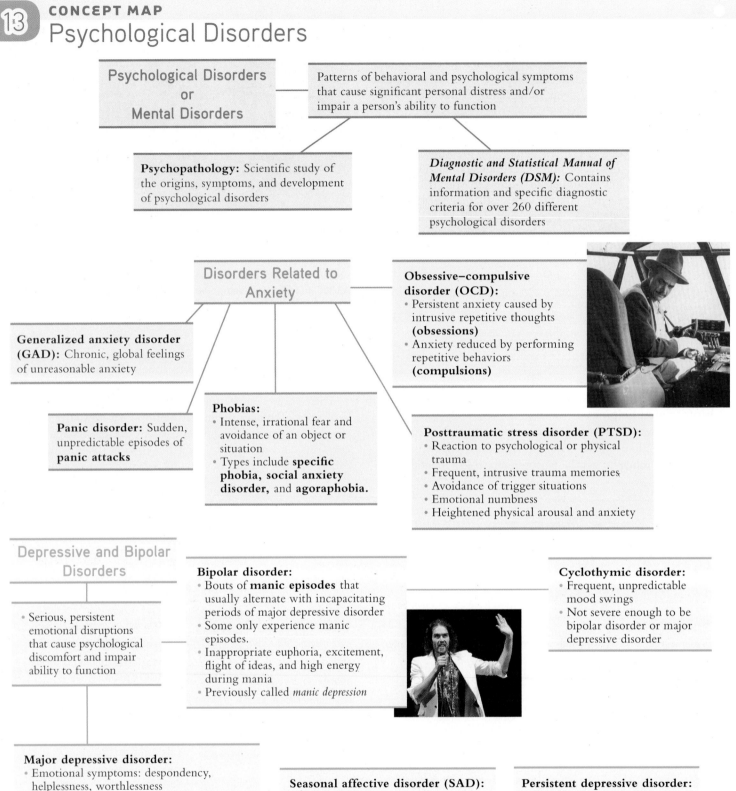

Psychological Disorders or Mental Disorders — Patterns of behavioral and psychological symptoms that cause significant personal distress and/or impair a person's ability to function

Psychopathology: Scientific study of the origins, symptoms, and development of psychological disorders

Diagnostic and Statistical Manual of Mental Disorders (DSM): Contains information and specific diagnostic criteria for over 260 different psychological disorders

Disorders Related to Anxiety

Generalized anxiety disorder (GAD): Chronic, global feelings of unreasonable anxiety

Panic disorder: Sudden, unpredictable episodes of **panic attacks**

Phobias:
- Intense, irrational fear and avoidance of an object or situation
- Types include **specific phobia, social anxiety disorder,** and **agoraphobia.**

Obsessive–compulsive disorder (OCD):
- Persistent anxiety caused by intrusive repetitive thoughts **(obsessions)**
- Anxiety reduced by performing repetitive behaviors **(compulsions)**

Posttraumatic stress disorder (PTSD):
- Reaction to psychological or physical trauma
- Frequent, intrusive trauma memories
- Avoidance of trigger situations
- Emotional numbness
- Heightened physical arousal and anxiety

Depressive and Bipolar Disorders

- Serious, persistent emotional disruptions that cause psychological discomfort and impair ability to function

Bipolar disorder:
- Bouts of **manic episodes** that usually alternate with incapacitating periods of major depressive disorder
- Some only experience manic episodes.
- Inappropriate euphoria, excitement, flight of ideas, and high energy during mania
- Previously called *manic depression*

Cyclothymic disorder:
- Frequent, unpredictable mood swings
- Not severe enough to be bipolar disorder or major depressive disorder

Major depressive disorder:
- Emotional symptoms: despondency, helplessness, worthlessness
- Behavioral symptoms: slowed movements, dejected expressions
- Cognitive symptoms: difficulty thinking, concentrating, and suicidal thoughts
- Physical symptoms: loss of physical and mental energy, appetite and sleep changes

Seasonal affective disorder (SAD):
- Recurring episodes of major depressive disorder during fall and winter months
- Associated with reduced sunlight exposure

Persistent depressive disorder:
- Chronic, low-grade depressed feelings
- Ability to function not seriously impaired

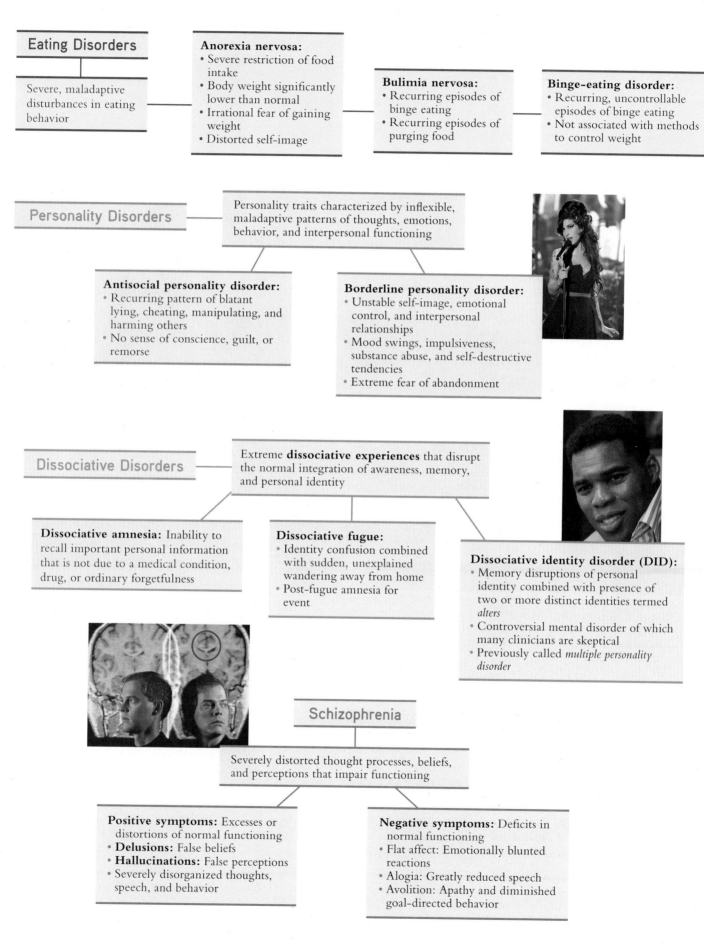

Eating Disorders

Severe, maladaptive disturbances in eating behavior

Anorexia nervosa:
- Severe restriction of food intake
- Body weight significantly lower than normal
- Irrational fear of gaining weight
- Distorted self-image

Bulimia nervosa:
- Recurring episodes of binge eating
- Recurring episodes of purging food

Binge-eating disorder:
- Recurring, uncontrollable episodes of binge eating
- Not associated with methods to control weight

Personality Disorders

Personality traits characterized by inflexible, maladaptive patterns of thoughts, emotions, behavior, and interpersonal functioning

Antisocial personality disorder:
- Recurring pattern of blatant lying, cheating, manipulating, and harming others
- No sense of conscience, guilt, or remorse

Borderline personality disorder:
- Unstable self-image, emotional control, and interpersonal relationships
- Mood swings, impulsiveness, substance abuse, and self-destructive tendencies
- Extreme fear of abandonment

Dissociative Disorders

Extreme **dissociative experiences** that disrupt the normal integration of awareness, memory, and personal identity

Dissociative amnesia: Inability to recall important personal information that is not due to a medical condition, drug, or ordinary forgetfulness

Dissociative fugue:
- Identity confusion combined with sudden, unexplained wandering away from home
- Post-fugue amnesia for event

Dissociative identity disorder (DID):
- Memory disruptions of personal identity combined with presence of two or more distinct identities termed *alters*
- Controversial mental disorder of which many clinicians are skeptical
- Previously called *multiple personality disorder*

Schizophrenia

Severely distorted thought processes, beliefs, and perceptions that impair functioning

Positive symptoms: Excesses or distortions of normal functioning
- **Delusions:** False beliefs
- **Hallucinations:** False perceptions
- Severely disorganized thoughts, speech, and behavior

Negative symptoms: Deficits in normal functioning
- Flat affect: Emotionally blunted reactions
- Alogia: Greatly reduced speech
- Avolition: Apathy and diminished goal-directed behavior

MYTH OR SCIENCE?

Is it true . . .

- That psychologists are never allowed to prescribe medications?
- That therapy is effective only if it is provided by a clinical psychologist or other highly trained therapist?
- That the different types of psychotherapy generally have similar results?
- That, for some disorders, psychotherapy and medications lead to similar changes in brain activity?
- That antidepressants are a much more effective treatment than placebos for the vast majority of cases of depression?
- That electroconvulsive therapy (ECT), once called "shock therapy," causes permanent brain damage and memory loss?
- That it is never ethical for therapists to date clients?

"A CLEAR SENSE OF BEING HEARD . . ."

PROLOGUE

HOW WOULD WE DESCRIBE MARCIA? She's an extraordinarily kind, intelligent woman. Her thoughtfulness and sensitivity are tempered by a ready laugh and a good sense of humor. She's happily married, has a good job as a feature writer for a large suburban newspaper, and has two young children, who only occasionally drive her crazy. If Marcia has a flaw, it's that she tends to judge herself much too harshly. She's too quick to blame herself when anything goes wrong.

Juggling a full-time career, marriage, and parenting is a challenge for anyone, but Marcia always makes it look easy. The last time your author Sandy had dinner at Bill and Marcia's home, the meal featured homegrown vegetables, made-from-scratch bread, and fresh seasonings from the herb pots in the kitchen. Outwardly, Marcia appears to have it all. But a few years ago, she began to experience a pervasive sense of dread and unease—feelings that gradually escalated into a full-scale depressive episode. Marcia describes the onset of her feelings in this way:

Physically, I began to feel as if I were fraying around the edges. I had a constant sense of anxiety and a recurring sense of being a failure. My daughter, Maggie, was going through a rather difficult stage. Andy was still a baby. I felt worn out. I started worrying constantly about my children. Are they safe? Are they sick? What's going to happen? Are my kids going to get hurt? I knew that I really didn't have any reason to worry that much, but I did. It finally struck me that my worrying and my anxiety and my feelings of being a failure were not going to go away on their own.

Marcia decided to seek help. She made an appointment with her therapist, a psychiatrist whom Marcia had

14

IN THIS CHAPTER:

> **INTRODUCTION:** Psychotherapy and Biomedical Therapy

> Psychoanalytic Therapy

> Humanistic Therapy

> Behavior Therapy

> Cognitive Therapies

> Group and Family Therapy

> Evaluating the Effectiveness of Psychotherapy

> Biomedical Therapies

> **PSYCH FOR YOUR LIFE:** What to Expect in Psychotherapy

last seen 10 years earlier, when she had helped Marcia cope with a very difficult time in her life. Marcia summarizes her experience this way:

How has therapy helped me? My feelings before a therapy session may vary greatly, depending on the issue under discussion. However, I always find the sessions cathartic and I invariably feel great relief. I feel a sense of being understood by someone who knows me but who is detached from me. I have a clear sense of being heard, as though my therapist has given me a gift of listening and of allowing me to see myself as the worthwhile and capable person I am. It is as though therapy allows me to see more clearly into a mirror that my problems have obscured.

Over the course of several months, Marcia gradually began to feel better. Today, Marcia is calmer, more confident, and feels much more in control of her emotions and her life. As Marcia's mental health improved, so did her relationships with her children and her husband.

Psychotherapy has also helped me communicate more clearly. It has enabled me to become more resilient after some emotional conflict. It has had a preventive effect in helping me to ignore or manage situations that might under certain circumstances trigger depression, anxiety, or obsessive worry. And it makes me a better parent and marriage partner.

Therapy's negative effects? I'm poorer; it costs money. And therapy poses the risk of becoming an end in itself. Psychotherapy has the attraction of being a safe harbor from the petty assaults of everyday life. There's always the danger of losing sight of the goal of becoming a healthier and more productive person, and becoming stuck in the therapy process.

Marcia's experience with psychotherapy reflects many of the themes we will touch on in this chapter. We'll look at different forms of therapy that psychologists and other mental health professionals use to help people cope with psychological problems. We'll also consider the popularity of newer ways to deliver mental health care—including self-help groups and technology-based treatments—and how they differ from more traditional forms of therapy. Toward the end of the chapter, we'll discuss biomedical approaches to the treatment of psychological disorders. Over the course of the chapter, we'll come back to Marcia's story. □

Fotografía de Pere Chuliá-España/Getty Images

Seeking Help People enter psychotherapy for many different reasons. Some people seek to overcome severe psychological disorders, while others want to learn how to cope better with everyday challenges or relationship problems. And, for some people, the goal of therapy is to attain greater self-knowledge or personal fulfillment.

psychotherapy The treatment of emotional, behavioral, and interpersonal problems through the use of psychological techniques designed to encourage understanding of problems and modify troubling feelings, behaviors, or relationships.

biomedical therapies The use of medications, electroconvulsive therapy, or other medical treatments to treat the symptoms associated with psychological disorders.

MYTH ◀ SCIENCE

Is it true that psychologists are never allowed to prescribe medications?

INTRODUCTION:
Psychotherapy and Biomedical Therapy

KEY THEME

Two forms of therapy are used to treat psychological disorders and personal problems—psychotherapy and biomedical therapies.

KEY QUESTIONS

› What is psychotherapy, and what is its basic assumption?
› What is biomedical therapy, and how does it differ from psychotherapy?

People seek help from mental health professionals for a variety of reasons. Like Marcia, many people seek help because they are suffering from some form of a *psychological disorder*—troubling thoughts, feelings, or behaviors that cause psychological discomfort or interfere with a person's ability to function.

But not everyone who seeks professional help is suffering from a psychological disorder. Many people seek help in dealing with troubled relationships, such as parent–child conflicts or an unhappy marriage. And sometimes people need help with life's transitions, such as coping with the death of a loved one, dissolving a marriage, or adjusting to retirement.

In this chapter, we'll look at the two broad forms of therapy that mental health professionals use to help people: *psychotherapy* and *biomedical therapy*. **Psychotherapy** refers to the use of psychological techniques to treat emotional, behavioral, and interpersonal problems. While there are many different types of psychotherapy, they all share the assumption that psychological factors play a significant role in a person's troubling feelings, behaviors, or relationships. Table 14.1 summarizes the diverse range of mental health professionals who use psychotherapy techniques to help people.

In contrast to psychotherapy, the **biomedical therapies** involve the use of medication or other medical treatments to treat the symptoms associated with psychological disorders. Drugs that are used to treat psychological or mental disorders are termed *psychotropic medications.* The biomedical therapies are based on the assumption that the symptoms of many psychological disorders involve biological factors, such as abnormal brain chemistry. As we saw in Chapter 13, the involvement of biological factors in many psychological disorders is well documented. Treating psychological disorders with a combination of psychotherapy and biomedical therapy, especially psychotropic medications, has become increasingly common (Cuijpers & others, 2009; Sudak, 2011). Until very recently, only licensed physicians were legally allowed to prescribe psychotropic medications.

However, that tradition may be changing. Since the 1990s, a movement to allow specially trained psychologists to prescribe has achieved some success. It began with the U.S. Department of Defense conducting a successful pilot program in which 10 military psychologists were given intensive training in prescribing psychotropic medications to treat psychological disorders (Ax & others, 2008). The success of the Department of Defense program was one of the factors that persuaded New Mexico, Louisiana, and Illinois lawmakers to enact legislation that permitted licensed psychologists to acquire additional training to prescribe psychotropic medications.

TABLE 14.1

Who's Who Among Mental Health Professionals

Clinical psychologist	Holds an academic doctorate (Ph.D., Psy.D., or Ed.D.) and is required to be licensed to practice. Assesses and treats mental, emotional, and behavioral disorders. Has expertise in psychological testing and evaluation, diagnosis, psychotherapy, research, and prevention of mental and emotional disorders. May work in private practice, hospitals, or community mental health centers.
Counseling psychologist	Holds an academic doctorate and must be licensed to practice. Assesses and treats mental, emotional, and behavioral problems and disorders, but usually disorders that are of lesser severity. The distinction between clinical psychologists and counseling psychologists, however, has decreased over the years.
Psychiatrist	Holds a medical degree (M.D. or D.O.) and is required to be licensed to practice. Has expertise in the diagnosis, treatment, and prevention of mental and emotional disorders. Often has training in psychotherapy. May prescribe medications, electroconvulsive therapy, or other medical procedures.
Psychoanalyst	Usually a psychiatrist or clinical psychologist who has received additional training in the specific techniques of psychoanalysis, the form of psychotherapy originated by Sigmund Freud.
Licensed professional counselor	Holds at least a master's degree in counseling, with extensive supervised training in assessment, counseling, and therapy techniques. May be certified in specialty areas. Most states require licensure or certification.
Psychiatric social worker	Holds a master's degree in social work (M.S.W.). Training includes an internship in a social service agency or mental health center. Most states require certification or licensing. May or may not have training in psychotherapy.
Marriage and family therapist	Usually holds a master's degree, with extensive supervised experience in couple or family therapy. May also have training in individual therapy. Many states require licensing.
Psychiatric nurse	Holds an R.N. degree and has selected psychiatry or mental health nursing as a specialty area. Typically works in a hospital psychiatric unit or in a community mental health center. May or may not have training in psychotherapy.

At this time, only a limited number of psychologists are able to prescribe medications. However, an increasing number of clinical psychologists *are* involved in medication treatment decisions or have clients who are taking psychotropic medications. Recognizing this trend, the American Psychological Association (2011) released new guidelines for psychologists regarding prescription medications. Among other points, the guidelines stress that psychologists who are involved in medication decisions should educate themselves about potential benefits and side effects of any medication. Psychologists are also urged to adopt a biopsychosocial approach to treatment, in which they consider psychological and social aspects of each case.

Not all psychologists favor the idea of extending prescription privileges to qualified psychologists (see Heiby, 2010; Heiby & others, 2004). Some argue that clinical psychologists should focus on what they do best: providing psychological interventions and treatments that help people acquire more effective patterns of thinking and behaving. Others are concerned that the safety and well-being of patients could be at risk if psychologists receive inadequate training to prescribe psychotropic medications (Lavoie & Barone, 2006).

We'll begin this chapter by surveying some of the most influential approaches in psychotherapy: psychoanalytic, humanistic, behavioral, and cognitive. Each approach is based on different assumptions about the underlying causes of psychological problems. And each approach uses different strategies to produce beneficial changes in the way a person thinks, feels, and behaves—the ultimate goal of all forms of psychotherapy. After discussing the effectiveness of psychotherapy, we'll look at the most commonly used biomedical treatments for psychological disorders.

The Varied Workplaces of Psychologists Clinical and counseling psychologists work in a wide variety of venues. Prison psychologist Tamara Russell, pictured here, oversees a staff of clinicians at the Washington State Penitentiary in Walla Walla, Washington. She received an award from the American Psychological Association for her innovative and effective work. The creative programming she introduced includes "Kittens in the Klink," a way for inmates to learn altruism by being paired with motherless kittens that they feed and socialize until the kittens are old enough to be adopted. As Russell explains, "A lot of guys never realized they could do something for others" (Hagar, 2013).

AP Photo/Walla Walla Union-Bulletin, Greg Lehman

Psychoanalytic Therapy

KEY THEME

Psychoanalysis is a form of therapy developed by Sigmund Freud and is based on his theory of personality.

KEY QUESTIONS

› What are the key assumptions and techniques of psychoanalytic therapy?

› How do short-term dynamic therapies differ from psychoanalysis, and what is interpersonal therapy?

When cartoonists portray a psychotherapy session, they often draw a person lying on a couch and talking while a bearded gentleman sits behind the patient, passively listening. This stereotype reflects some of the key ingredients of traditional **psychoanalysis,** a form of psychotherapy originally developed by **Sigmund Freud** in the early 1900s. Although psychoanalysis was developed a century ago, its assumptions and techniques continue to influence many psychotherapies today (Borden, 2009; Lerner, 2008; Luborsky & Barrett, 2006).

Sigmund Freud and Psychoanalysis

As a therapy, traditional psychoanalysis is closely interwoven with Freud's theory of personality. As you may recall from Chapter 10 on personality, Freud stressed that early childhood experiences provided the foundation for later personality development. When early experiences result in unresolved conflicts and frustrated urges, these emotionally charged memories are *repressed,* or pushed out of conscious awareness. Although unconscious, these repressed conflicts continue to influence a person's thoughts and behavior, including the dynamics of his relationships with others.

Psychoanalysis is designed to help unearth unconscious conflicts so that the patient attains *insight* into the real source of her problems. Through the intense relationship that develops between the psychoanalyst and the patient, long-standing psychological conflicts are recognized and re-experienced. If the analytic treatment is successful, the conflicts are resolved.

Freud developed several techniques to coax long-repressed memories, impulses, and conflicts to a patient's consciousness (Liff, 1992). In the famous technique called **free association,** the patient spontaneously reports all her thoughts, mental images, and feelings while lying on a couch. The psychoanalyst usually sits out of view, occasionally asking questions to encourage the flow of associations.

Blocks in free association, such as a sudden silence or an abrupt change of topic, were thought to be signs of resistance. **Resistance** is the patient's conscious or unconscious attempts to block the process of revealing repressed memories and conflicts (Luborsky & Barrett, 2006). Resistance is a sign that the patient is uncomfortably close to uncovering psychologically threatening material.

Dream interpretation is another important psychoanalytic technique. Because psychological defenses are reduced during sleep, Freud (1911) believed that unconscious conflicts and repressed impulses were expressed symbolically in dream images. For example, Freud (1900) suggested that a lion in a woman's dream referred to her father who had a "beard which encircled his face like a Mane." Often, the dream images were used to trigger free associations that might shed light on the dream's symbolic meaning.

More directly, the psychoanalyst sometimes makes carefully timed **interpretations,** explanations of the unconscious meaning of the patient's behavior, thoughts, feelings, or dreams. The timing of such interpretations is important. If an interpretation is offered before the patient is psychologically ready to confront an issue, he may

Sigmund Freud and Psychoanalytic Therapy At the beginning of the twentieth century, Sigmund Freud (1856–1939) developed an influential form of psychotherapy called psychoanalysis. Traditional psychoanalysis is not widely practiced today, partly because it is too lengthy and expensive. However, many of the techniques that Freud pioneered, such as free association, dream analysis, and transference, are still commonly used in different forms of psychotherapy.

Bettmann/Corbis

The resistance accompanies the treatment step by step. Every single association, every act of the person under treatment must reckon with the resistance and represents a compromise between the forces that are striving towards recovery and opposing ones.

—*Sigmund Freud (1912)*

psychoanalysis (in psychotherapy)
A type of psychotherapy originated by Sigmund Freud in which free association, dream interpretation, and analysis of resistance and transference are used to explore repressed or unconscious impulses, anxieties, and internal conflicts.

free association A psychoanalytic technique in which the patient spontaneously reports all thoughts, feelings, and mental images that arise, revealing unconscious thoughts and emotions.

Freud's Famous Couch During psychoanalytic sessions, Freud's patients would lie on the couch. Freud himself sat at the head of the couch, out of the patient's view. Freud believed that this arrangement encouraged the patient's free flow of thoughts, feelings, and images. Although some traditional psychoanalysts still have the patient lie on a couch, many psychoanalysts today favor comfortable chairs on which analyst and patient sit, facing each other.

AP Photo

reject the interpretation or respond defensively, increasing resistance (Prochaska & Norcross, 2014).

One of the most important processes that occurs in the relationship between the patient and the psychoanalyst is called transference. **Transference** occurs when the patient unconsciously responds to the therapist as though the therapist were a significant person in the patient's life, often a parent. The psychoanalyst encourages transference by purposely remaining as neutral as possible. In other words, the psychoanalyst does not reveal personal feelings, take sides, make judgments, or actively advise the patient. This therapeutic neutrality is designed to produce "optimal frustration" so that the patient transfers and projects unresolved conflicts onto the psychoanalyst (Magnavita, 2008). These conflicts are then relived and played out in the context of the relationship between the psychoanalyst and the patient.

All of these psychoanalytic techniques are designed to help the patient see how past conflicts influence her current behavior and relationships, including her relationship with the psychoanalyst. Once these kinds of insights are achieved, the psychoanalyst helps the patient work through and resolve long-standing conflicts. As resolutions occur, maladaptive behavior patterns that were previously driven by unconscious conflicts can be replaced with more adaptive emotional and behavioral responses.

The intensive relationship between the patient and the psychoanalyst takes time to develop. The traditional psychoanalyst sees the patient three times a week or more, often for years (Schwartz, 2003; Zusman & others, 2007). Freud's patients were on the couch six days a week (Liff, 1992). Obviously, traditional psychoanalysis is a slow, expensive process that few people can afford. For those who have the time and the money, traditional psychoanalysis is still available.

Short-Term Dynamic Therapies

Most people entering psychotherapy today are not seeking the kind of major personality overhaul that traditional psychoanalysis is designed to produce. Instead, people come to therapy expecting help with specific problems. People also expect therapy to provide beneficial changes in a matter of weeks or months, not years.

Many different forms of **short-term dynamic therapies** based on traditional psychoanalytic notions are now available (Levenson, 2010, 2011). These short-term dynamic therapies have several features in common. Therapeutic contact lasts for no more than a few months. The patient's problems are quickly assessed at the beginning of therapy. The therapist and patient agree on specific, concrete, and attainable goals. In the actual sessions, most psychodynamic therapists are more directive than are traditional psychoanalysts, actively engaging the patient in a dialogue.

As in traditional psychoanalysis, the therapist uses interpretations to help the patient recognize hidden feelings and transferences that may be occurring in important relationships in her life (Kush, 2009).

resistance In psychoanalysis, the patient's unconscious attempts to block the revelation of repressed memories and conflicts.

dream interpretation A technique used in psychoanalysis in which the content of dreams is analyzed for disguised or symbolic wishes, meanings, and motivations.

interpretation A technique used in psychoanalysis in which the psychoanalyst offers a carefully timed explanation of the patient's dreams, free associations, or behaviors to facilitate the recognition of unconscious conflicts or motivations.

transference In psychoanalysis, the process by which emotions and desires originally associated with a significant person in the patient's life, such as a parent, are unconsciously transferred onto the psychoanalyst.

short-term dynamic therapies Type of psychotherapy that is based on psychoanalytic theory but differs in that it is typically time-limited, has specific goals, and involves an active, rather than neutral, role for the therapist.

BIZARRO

> AT THE RISK OF SOUNDING CLICHE, DOCTOR, LET ME SAY THAT I HAVE CERTAIN UN-RESOLVED ISSUES REGARDING MY PARENTS.

One particularly influential short-term psychodynamic therapy is **interpersonal therapy,** abbreviated **IPT**. In contrast to other psychodynamic therapies, interpersonal therapy focuses on *current* relationships and social interactions rather than on past relationships. Originally developed as a brief treatment for major depressive disorder, interpersonal therapy is based on the assumption that psychological symptoms are caused and maintained by interpersonal problems (Gunlicks-Stoessel & Weissman, 2011).

Interpersonal therapy may be brief or long-term, but it is highly structured (Blanco & others, 2006; Teyber, 2009). In the first phase of treatment, the therapist identifies the interpersonal problem that is causing difficulties. In the interpersonal therapy model, there are four categories of personal problems: unresolved grief, role disputes, role transitions, and interpersonal deficits. *Unresolved grief* refers to problems dealing with the death of significant others, while *role disputes* refer to repetitive conflicts with significant others, such as the person's partner, family members, friends, or co-workers. *Role transitions* include problems involving major life changes, such as going away to college, becoming a parent, getting married or divorced, or retiring. *Interpersonal deficits* refer to absent or faulty social skills that limit the ability to start or maintain healthy relationships with others (Mallinckrodt, 2001). During treatment, the therapist helps the person understand his particular interpersonal problem and develop strategies to resolve it.

IPT is used to treat eating disorders and substance use disorders as well as major depressive disorder. It is also effective in helping people deal with interpersonal problems, such as marital conflict, parenting issues, and conflicts at work (Bleiberg & Markowitz, 2008). In one innovative application, IPT was successfully used to treat symptoms of major depressive disorder in villagers in Uganda, demonstrating its effectiveness in a non-Western culture (Bolton & others, 2003). Beyond individual psychotherapy, IPT has proved to be valuable in family and group therapy sessions (Woody, 2008; Zimmerman, 2008).

Even though traditional, lengthy psychoanalysis is uncommon today, Freud's basic assumptions and techniques continue to be influential. Contemporary research has challenged many of Freud's original ideas. However, modern researchers continue to study the specific factors that seem to influence the effectiveness of basic Freudian techniques, such as dream analysis, interpretation, transference, and the role of insight in reducing psychological symptoms (Glucksman & Kramer, 2004; Luborsky & Barrett, 2006).

Humanistic Therapy

KEY THEME

The most influential humanistic psychotherapy is client-centered therapy, which was developed by Carl Rogers.

KEY QUESTIONS

> What are the key assumptions of humanistic therapy, including client-centered therapy?
> What therapeutic techniques and conditions are important in client-centered therapy?
> How do client-centered therapy and psychoanalysis differ?

The *humanistic perspective* in psychology emphasizes human potential, self-awareness, and freedom of choice (see Chapter 10). Humanistic psychologists contend that the most important factor in personality is the individual's conscious, subjective perception of his or her self. They see people as being innately good and motivated by the need to grow psychologically. If people are raised in a genuinely accepting atmosphere and given freedom to make choices, they will develop healthy self-concepts and strive to fulfill their unique potential as human beings (Kirschenbaum & Jourdan, 2005; Pos & others, 2008).

interpersonal therapy (IPT) A brief psychodynamic psychotherapy that focuses on current relationships and is based on the assumption that symptoms are caused and maintained by interpersonal problems.

client-centered therapy A type of psychotherapy developed by humanistic psychologist Carl Rogers in which the therapist is nondirective and reflective, and the client directs the focus of each therapy session; also called *person-centered therapy*.

Carl Rogers and Client-Centered Therapy

The humanistic perspective has exerted a strong influence on psychotherapy (Cain, 2002, 2003; Schneider & Krug, 2009). Probably the most influential of the humanistic psychotherapies is **client-centered therapy,** also called *person-centered therapy,* developed by **Carl Rogers.** In naming his therapy, Rogers (1951) deliberately used the word *client* rather than *patient.* He believed that the medical term *patient* implied that people in therapy were "sick" and were seeking treatment from an all-knowing authority figure who could "heal" or "cure" them. Instead of stressing the therapist's expertise or perceptions of the patient, client-centered therapy emphasizes the *client's* subjective perception of himself and his environment (Cain, 2002; Raskin & Rogers, 2005).

Like Freud, Rogers saw the therapeutic relationship as the catalyst that leads to insight and lasting personality change. But Rogers viewed the nature of this relationship very differently from Freud. According to Rogers (1977), the therapist should not exert power by offering carefully timed "interpretations" of the patient's unconscious conflicts. Advocating just the opposite, Rogers believed that the therapist should be *nondirective.* That is, the therapist must not direct the client, make decisions for the client, offer solutions, or pass judgment on the client's thoughts or feelings. Instead, Rogers believed, change in therapy must be chosen and directed by the client (Bozarth & others, 2002). The therapist's role is to create the conditions that allow the client, not the therapist, to direct the focus of therapy.

What are the therapeutic conditions that promote self-awareness, psychological growth, and self-directed change? Rogers (1957c, 1980) believed that three qualities of the therapist are necessary: *genuineness, unconditional positive regard,* and *empathic understanding.* First, *genuineness* means that the therapist honestly and openly shares her thoughts and feelings with the client. By modeling genuineness, the therapist indirectly encourages the client to exercise this capability more fully in himself.

Second, the therapist must value, accept, and care for the client, whatever her problems or behavior. Rogers called this quality *unconditional positive regard* (Bozarth & Wang, 2008). Rogers believed that people develop psychological problems largely because they have consistently experienced only *conditional acceptance.* That is, parents, teachers, and others have communicated this message to the client: "I will accept you *only if* you conform to my expectations." Because acceptance by significant others has been conditional, the person has cut off or denied unacceptable aspects of herself, distorting her self-concept. In turn, these distorted perceptions affect her thoughts and behaviors in unhealthy, unproductive ways. The therapist who successfully creates a climate of unconditional positive regard fosters the person's natural tendency to move toward self-fulfilling decisions without fear of evaluation or rejection.

Third, the therapist must communicate *empathic understanding* by reflecting the content and personal meaning of the feelings being experienced by the client. In effect, the therapist creates a psychological mirror, reflecting the client's thoughts and feelings as they exist in the client's private inner world. The goal is to help the client explore and clarify his feelings, thoughts, and perceptions. In the process, the client begins to see himself, and his problems, more clearly (Freire, 2007).

Carl Rogers (1902–1987) In his classic text, *On Becoming a Person,* Rogers (1961) described how his own thinking changed as he developed client-centered therapy. He wrote, "In my early professional years, I was asking the question: How can I treat, or cure, or change this person? Now I would phrase the question in this way: How can I provide a relationship which this person may use for his own personal growth?"

Corbis

An empathic way of being with another person has several facets. It means entering the private perceptual world of the other and becoming thoroughly at home in it. It involves being sensitive, moment by moment, to the changing felt meanings which flow in this other person, to the fear or rage or tenderness or confusion or whatever that he or she is experiencing.

—*Carl Rogers (1980)*

Group Therapy Session with Carl Rogers Rogers filmed many of his therapy sessions as part of an ongoing research program to identify the most helpful aspects of client-centered therapy. Shown on the far right, Rogers contended that human potential would flourish in an atmosphere of genuineness, unconditional positive regard, and empathic understanding.

Michael Rougier/Time & Life Pictures/Getty Images

Client-Centered Therapy The client-centered therapist strives to create a warm, accepting climate that allows the client the freedom to explore troubling issues. The therapist engages in active listening, reflecting both the content and the personal meaning of what the client is saying. In doing so, the therapist helps the client develop a clearer perception and understanding of her own feelings and motives.

Empathic understanding requires the therapist to listen *actively* for the personal meaning beneath the surface of what the client is saying (Watson, 2002). Rogers believed that when the therapeutic atmosphere contains genuineness, unconditional positive regard, and empathic understanding, change is more likely to occur. Such conditions foster feelings of being psychologically safe, accepted, and valued. In this therapeutic atmosphere, change occurs as the person's self-concept and worldview gradually become healthier and less distorted. In effect, the client is moving in the direction of *self-actualization*—the realization of his or her unique potentials and talents.

A large number of studies have generally supported the importance of genuineness, unconditional positive regard, and empathic understanding (Elliott & others, 2004; Greene, 2008). Such factors promote trust and self-exploration in therapy. However, these conditions, by themselves, may not be sufficient to help clients change (Cain & Seeman, 2002; Sachse & Elliott, 2002).

MOTIVATIONAL INTERVIEWING: HELPING CLIENTS COMMIT TO CHANGE

Like psychoanalysis, client-centered therapy has evolved and adapted to changing times. It continues to have a powerful impact on therapists, teachers, social workers, and counselors (see Cooper & others, 2013). Of particular note has been the development of motivational interviewing (Miller & Rollnick, 2012). *Motivational interviewing (MI)* is designed to help clients overcome the mixed feelings or reluctance they might have about committing to change. MI is used for a range of psychological problems, but has most frequently been applied to addictions, such as substance use disorders or gambling, or to techniques to improve health, such as through diet or exercise (Cushing & others, 2014; Lundahl & others, 2010). Usually lasting only a session or two, MI is more directive than traditional client-centered therapy (Arkowitz & others, 2007; Hettema & others, 2005).

The main goal of MI is to encourage and strengthen the client's self-motivating statements, or "change talk" (Hayes & others, 2011). These are expressions of the client's need, desire, and reasons for change. Using client-centered techniques, the therapist responds with empathic understanding and reflective listening, helping the client explore his or her own values and motivations for change. When the client expresses reluctance, the therapist acknowledges the mixed feelings and redirects the emphasis toward change (Miller & Rose, 2009). As Jennifer Hettema and her colleagues (2005) explain:

> The counselor seeks to evoke the client's own motivation, with confidence in the human desire and capacity to grow in positive directions. Instead of implying that "I have what you need," MI communicates, "You have what you need." In this way, MI falls squarely within the humanistic "third force" in the history of psychotherapy.

TABLE 14.2

Comparing Psychodynamic and Humanistic Therapies

Type of Therapy	Founder	Source of Problems	Treatment Techniques	Goals of Therapy
Psychoanalysis	Sigmund Freud	Repressed, unconscious conflicts stemming from early childhood experiences	Free association, analysis of dream content, interpretation, and transference	To recognize, work through, and resolve long-standing conflicts
Client-centered therapy	Carl Rogers	Conditional acceptance that causes the person to develop a distorted self-concept and worldview	Nondirective therapist who displays unconditional positive regard, genuineness, and empathic understanding	To develop self-awareness, self-acceptance, and self-determination

Along with being influential in individual psychotherapy, the client-centered approach has been applied to group therapy, marital counseling, parenting, education, business, and even community and international relations (Chen & others, 2011; Henderson & others, 2007; Wagner & Ingersoll, 2012). Table 14.2 compares some aspects of psychoanalysis and client-centered therapy.

> Test your understanding of **Psychotherapy and Humanistic Therapy** with **LEARNING**Curve.

Behavior Therapy

KEY THEME

Behavior therapy uses learning principles to directly change problem behaviors.

KEY QUESTIONS

> What are the key assumptions of behavior therapy?

> What therapeutic techniques are based on classical conditioning, and how are they used to treat psychological disorders and problems?

> What therapy treatments are based on operant conditioning, and how are they used to treat psychological disorders and problems?

Psychoanalysis, client-centered therapy, and other insight-oriented therapies maintain that the road to psychologically healthier behavior is through increased self-understanding of motives and conflicts. As insights are acquired through therapy, problem behaviors and feelings presumably will give way to more adaptive behaviors and emotional reactions.

However, gaining insight into the source of problems does not necessarily result in desirable changes in behavior and emotions. Even though you fully understand *why* you are behaving in counterproductive ways, your maladaptive or self-defeating behaviors may continue. For instance, an adult who is extremely anxious about public speaking may understand that he feels that way because he was raised by a critical and demanding parent. But having this insight into the underlying cause of his anxiety may do little, if anything, to reduce his anxiety or change his avoidance of public speaking.

In sharp contrast to the insight-oriented therapies we discussed in the preceding sections, the goal of **behavior therapy,** also called *behavior modification,* is to modify specific problem behaviors, not to change the entire personality. And, rather than focusing on the past, behavior therapists focus on current behaviors.

Behavior therapists assume that maladaptive behaviors are *learned,* just as adaptive behaviors are. Thus, the basic strategy in behavior therapy involves unlearning maladaptive behaviors and learning more adaptive behaviors in their place. Behavior therapists employ techniques that are based on the learning principles of classical conditioning, operant conditioning, and observational learning to modify the problem behavior.

HAYKIRDI/Getty Images

Behavior Therapy—From Bad Habits to Severe Psychological Disorders Nail biting and cigarette smoking are examples of the kinds of everyday maladaptive behaviors that can be successfully treated with behavior therapy. Behavioral techniques can also be used to treat more severe psychological problems, such as phobias, and to improve functioning in people with severe mental disorders such as schizophrenia and autistic spectrum disorder.

behavior therapy A type of psychotherapy that focuses on directly changing maladaptive behavior patterns by using basic learning principles and techniques; also called *behavior modification.*

Mary Cover Jones (1896–1987) This photograph, taken around 1919, shows Mary Cover Jones as a college student in her early 20s. Although Jones pioneered the use of behavioral techniques in therapy, she did not consider herself a "behaviorist" and ultimately came to disagree with many of Watson's views. Fifty years after she treated Peter, Jones (1975) wrote, "Now I would be less satisfied to treat the fears of a three-year-old . . . in isolation from him as a tantalizingly complex person with unique potentials for stability and change."

counterconditioning A behavior therapy technique based on classical conditioning that involves modifying behavior by conditioning a new response that is incompatible with a previously learned response.

exposure therapy Behavioral therapy for phobias, panic disorder, posttraumatic stress disorder, or related anxiety disorders in which the person is repeatedly exposed to the disturbing object or situation under controlled conditions.

systematic desensitization A type of behavior therapy in which phobic responses are reduced by pairing relaxation with a series of mental images or real-life situations that the person finds progressively more fear-provoking; based on the principle of counterconditioning.

Techniques Based on Classical Conditioning

Just as Pavlov's dogs learned to salivate to a ringing bell that had become associated with food, learned associations can be at the core of some maladaptive behaviors, including strong negative emotional reactions. In the 1920s, psychologist John Watson demonstrated this phenomenon with his famous "Little Albert" study. In Chapter 5, we described how Watson classically conditioned an infant known as Little Albert to fear a tame lab rat by repeatedly pairing the rat with a loud clanging sound. Over time, Albert's conditioned fear generalized to other furry objects, including a fur coat, cotton, and a Santa Claus mask (Watson & Rayner, 1920).

MARY COVER JONES
THE FIRST BEHAVIOR THERAPIST

Watson himself never tried to eliminate Little Albert's fears. But Watson's research inspired one of his students, **Mary Cover Jones,** to explore ways of reversing conditioned fears. With Watson acting as a consultant, Jones (1924a) treated a 3-year-old named Peter who "seemed almost to be Albert grown a bit older." Like Little Albert, Peter was fearful of various furry objects, including a tame rat, a fur coat, cotton, and wool. Because Peter was especially afraid of a tame rabbit, Jones focused on eliminating the rabbit fear. She used a procedure that has come to be known as **counterconditioning**—the learning of a new conditioned response that is incompatible with a previously learned response.

Jones's procedure was very simple (Jones, 1924b; Watson, 1924). The caged rabbit was brought into Peter's view but kept far enough away to avoid eliciting fear (the original conditioned response). With the rabbit visible at a tolerable distance, Peter sat in a high chair and happily munched his favorite snack, milk and crackers. Peter's favorite food was used because, presumably, the enjoyment of eating would naturally elicit a positive response (the desired conditioned response). Such a positive response would be incompatible with the negative response of fear.

Every day for almost two months, the rabbit was inched closer and closer to Peter as he ate his milk and crackers. As Peter's tolerance for the rabbit's presence gradually increased, he was eventually able to hold the rabbit in his lap, petting it with one hand while happily eating with his other hand (Jones, 1924a, 1924b). Not only was Peter's fear of the rabbit eliminated, but he also stopped being afraid of other furry objects, including the rat, cotton, and the fur coat (Watson, 1924).

For her pioneering efforts in the treatment of children's fears, Jones is widely regarded as the first behavior therapist (Gieser, 1993; Rutherford, 2006).

SYSTEMATIC DESENSITIZATION AND EXPOSURE THERAPIES

Mary Cover Jones's pioneering studies in treating children's fears laid the groundwork for the later development of more standardized procedures to treat phobias and other anxiety disorders. **Exposure therapy** describes several techniques that have been recognized as effective treatments for anxiety disorders, posttraumatic stress disorder (PTSD), and obsessive–compulsive disorder (OCD). A person gradually and repeatedly relives a frightening experience under controlled conditions to help him overcome his fear of the dreaded object or situation and establish more adaptive beliefs and cognitions. Using a combination of behavioral and cognitive techniques, exposure therapy has a high rate of success in the treatment of anxiety disorders, PTSD, and OCD (McNally, 2007; Powers & others, 2010; Rosa-Alcázar & others, 2008).

One widely used type of exposure therapy, called *systematic desensitization,* was developed by South African psychiatrist Joseph Wolpe in the 1950s (Wolpe, 1958, 1982). Based on the same premise as counterconditioning, **systematic desensitization** involves learning a new conditioned response (relaxation) that is incompatible with or inhibits the old conditioned response (fear and anxiety).

Three basic steps are involved in systematic desensitization. First, the patient learns *progressive relaxation,* which involves successively relaxing one muscle group after another

Degree of Fear	Imagined Scene
100	Holding mouth open, eyes closed, listening to the sound of the dental drill as a cavity is repaired
95	Holding mouth open in preparation for an oral injection
90	Lying back in dental chair, eyes closed, as dentist examines teeth
85	Lying back in dental chair, mouth open, listening to the sounds of dental equipment as dental technician cleans teeth
80	Lying in dental chair, watching dental technician unwrap sterilized dental tools
75	Being greeted by the dental technician and walking back to dental examination chair
70	Sitting in dentist's waiting room
60	Driving to dentist's office for appointment
50	Looking at the bright yellow reminder postcard on the refrigerator and thinking about dental appointment
40	Listening to a family member talk about her last dental visit
30	Looking at television or magazine advertisements depicting people in a dentist's chair
25	Calling dentist's office to make an appointment
20	Thinking about calling dentist's office to set up an appointment
15	Driving past dentist's office on a workday
10	Driving past dentist's office on a Sunday afternoon

Image Source/Getty Images

FIGURE 14.1 A Sample Anxiety Hierarchy Used in Systematic Desensitization As part of systematic desensitization, the therapist helps the client develop an anxiety hierarchy. The sample anxiety hierarchy shown here illustrates the kinds of scenes that might be listed by a person who is phobic of dental treatment. Starting at the bottom of the hierarchy, relaxation is paired with each scene until the client can calmly visualize the image. Only then does he move to the next scene in the hierarchy.

until a deep state of relaxation is achieved. Second, the behavior therapist helps the patient construct an *anxiety hierarchy,* sometimes called an *exposure hierarchy,* which is a list of anxiety-provoking images associated with the feared situation, arranged in a hierarchy from least to most anxiety-producing (see Figure 14.1). The patient also develops an image of a relaxing *control scene,* such as walking on a secluded beach on a sunny day.

The third step involves the actual process of desensitization through exposure to feared experiences. While deeply relaxed, the patient imagines the least-threatening scene on the anxiety hierarchy. After he can maintain complete relaxation while imagining this scene, he moves to the next. If the patient begins to feel anxiety or tension, the behavior therapist guides him back to imagining the previous scene or the control scene. If necessary, the therapist helps the patient relax again, using the progressive relaxation technique.

Over several sessions, the patient gradually and systematically works his way up the hierarchy, imagining each scene while maintaining complete relaxation. Once mastered with mental images, the desensitization procedure may be continued with exposure to the actual feared situation, which is called *in vivo systematic desensitization.* If the technique is successful, the feared situation no longer produces a conditioned response of fear and anxiety. The In Focus box "Using Virtual Reality to Treat Phobia and Posttraumatic Stress Disorder," on the next page, describes systematic desensitization using a "virtual reality" version of the actual feared situation.

In practice, systematic desensitization is often combined with other techniques, such as *observational learning* (Bandura, 2004b). Let's consider a clinical example that combines systematic desensitization and observational learning. The client is Santiago, a 60-year-old man afraid of flying on airplanes. His behavior therapist first teaches Santiago progressive relaxation so he can induce relaxation in himself. Then, she and Santiago move through the anxiety hierarchy they created. In Santiago's case, the exposure hierarchy starts with imagining airplanes flying above high in the sky, then moves on to viewing pictures of airplanes at a distance, then viewing the interior of airplanes, and ultimately actually boarding an airplane and taking a flight. There were other, smaller steps in the hierarchy as well, to make sure Santiago could progress from step to step without too much of a "jump."

Santiago is able to move through the hierarchy by experiencing relaxation in conjunction with exposure to each consecutive stimulus that might have produced anxiety. Because relaxation and anxiety are incompatible, the relaxation essentially "blocks" Santiago's anxiety about flying, just as Peter's enjoyment of his milk and cookies blocked his anxiety about the rabbit. Another important aspect of the

 LaunchPad

Video material is provided by BBC Worldwide Learning and CBS News Archives and produced by Princeton Academic Resources

To observe the type of exposure therapy used with OCD, watch **Video Activity: Treating OCD: Exposure and Response Prevention.**

IN FOCUS

Using Virtual Reality to Treat Phobia and Posttraumatic Stress Disorder

Virtual reality (VR) therapy consists of computer-generated scenes that you view wearing goggles and a special motion-sensitive headset. Move your head in any direction and an electromagnetic sensor in the helmet detects the movement, and the computer-generated scene you see changes accordingly. Turning a handgrip lets you move forward or backward to explore your artificial world. You can also use a virtual hand to reach out and touch objects, such as an elevator button or a spider.

VR technology was first used in the treatment of specific phobias, including fear of flying, heights, spiders, driving, and enclosed places (Côté & Bouchard, 2008). In the virtual reality scene, patients are progressively exposed to the feared object or situation. For example, psychologist Ralph Lamson used virtual reality as a form of computer-assisted systematic desensitization to help more than 60 patients conquer their fear of heights. Rather than creating mental images, the person experiences computer-generated images that seem almost real. Once the goggles are donned, patients begin a 40-minute journey that starts in a café and progresses to a narrow wooden plank that leads to a bridge.

Although computer-generated and cartoonlike, the scenes of being high above the ground on the plank or bridge are real enough to trigger the physiological indicators of anxiety. Lamson encourages the person to stay in the same spot until the anxiety diminishes. Once relaxed, the person continues the VR journey. By the time the person makes the return journey back over the plank, heart rate and blood pressure are close to normal. After virtual reality therapy, over 90 percent of Lamson's patients successfully rode a glass elevator up to the 15th floor.

Once experimental, virtual reality therapy has become an accepted treatment for specific phobias and is now being extended to other disorders, such as social anxiety disorder, panic disorder, and acrophobia (Meyerbröker & Emmelkamp, 2010; Opriş & others, 2012). One innovative application of VR therapy is in the treatment of posttraumatic stress disorder (PTSD) in veterans of the wars in Vietnam, Iraq, and Afghanistan (McLay & others, 2011). Many PTSD patients are unable or unwilling to mentally re-create the traumatic events that caused their disorder, but the vivid sensory details of the "virtual world" encourage the patient to relive the experience in a controlled fashion.

For example, a young woman who suffered from severe PTSD after witnessing and barely escaping the 9/11 attack on the World Trade Center was finally able to relive the events of the day through controlled, graduated exposure to a virtual reenactment of the events. Similarly, war veterans can be exposed to the sights and sounds of combat in a way that could not be accomplished in the "real world" of a therapist's office or a busy downtown street. Marine veteran Joshua Musser was treated with virtual reality therapy after fighting in Iraq and developing PTSD. Musser told CNN (2011), "It put you back in Iraq where you kind of have one foot here and one foot there. The only thing outside of Iraq that you hear is [the clinical psychologist's] voice, and so when she sees that I'm really starting to stress out . . . she would be in my ear and be pulling me back."

VR therapy is easier and less expensive to administer than graduated exposure to the actual feared object or situation. Another advantage is that the availability of VR may make people who are extremely phobic more willing to seek treatment. In one survey of people who were phobic of spiders, more than 80 percent preferred virtual reality treatment over graduated exposure to real spiders (Garcia-Palacios & others, 2001). And, research suggests that patients will be less likely to refuse treatment or drop out of treatment with virtual exposure than with real-world exposure (Meyerbröker & Emmelkamp, 2010).

Virtual Reality Psychologist Hunter Hoffmann is shown here demonstrating the use of SpiderWorld, a three-dimensional virtual reality program that creates the very realistic sensation of seeing, and even touching, large spiders. Once experimental, virtual reality treatment has been shown to be effective in treating specific phobias and other disorders, including posttraumatic stress disorder in combat veterans and in victims of terrorist attacks (Freedman & others, 2010; Opriş & others, 2012).

behavior therapist's treatment of Santiago involves observational learning: She shows Santiago videos of people calmly boarding and riding on planes. Together, systematic desensitization and observational learning help Santiago overcome his phobia, and he is ultimately able to fly with minimal discomfort.

A newer form of exposure therapy for people suffering from traumatic memories has received a great deal of attention. *Eye movement desensitization reprocessing,* abbreviated *EMDR,* involves patients visually following the waving finger of a therapist while simultaneously holding a mental image of disturbing memories, events, or situations. Early research by its founder, psychologist Francine Shapiro, found that most patients experienced significant relief from their symptoms after just *one* EMDR therapy session (Shapiro, 1989a, 1989b, 2007). This was the beginning of what was to become one of the fastest-growing—and most lucrative—therapeutic techniques of the past decades (Herbert & others, 2000). Numerous studies have shown that patients experience relief from symptoms of anxiety after EMDR (see Davidson & Parker, 2001; Goldstein & others, 2000; Mills & Hulbert-Williams, 2012).

Yet, many elements of EMDR are similar to other treatment techniques, some of them well established and based on well-documented psychological principles. These similarities have led researchers to ask whether EMDR is more effective than exposure therapy or other cognitive-behavioral treatments. And the answer seems to be no. Not only is EMDR no more effective than standard treatments for anxiety disorders, including PTSD, it is actually *less* effective than exposure therapy for PTSD (Albright & Thyer, 2010; Davidson & Parker, 2001; Taylor & others, 2003; Verstrael & others, 2013). In addition, several studies found *no difference* between "real" EMDR and "sham" EMDR, a kind of placebo condition that removed the eye movements from the treatment (Davidson & Parker, 2001; Feske & Goldstein, 1997; Goldstein & others, 2000).

AVERSIVE CONDITIONING

The psychologist John Garcia first demonstrated how taste aversions could be classically conditioned (see Chapter 5). After rats drank a sweet-flavored water, Garcia injected them with a drug that made them ill. The rats developed a strong taste aversion for the sweet-flavored water, avoiding it altogether (Garcia & others, 1966). In much the same way, **aversive conditioning** attempts to create an unpleasant conditioned response to a harmful stimulus, such as cigarette smoking or alcohol consumption. For substance use disorder and addiction, taste aversions are commonly induced with the use of nausea-inducing drugs. For example, a medication called *Antabuse* is used in aversion therapy for alcoholism (Ellis & Dronsfield, 2013). Consuming alcohol while taking Anatabuse produces bouts of extreme, highly unpleasant nausea.

Aversive conditioning techniques have been applied to a wide variety of problem behaviors (Cain & LeDoux, 2008). However, mental health professionals are typically very cautious about the use of such techniques, partly because of their potential to harm or produce discomfort for clients (C. B. Fisher, 2009; Francis, 2009). In addition, aversive techniques are generally not very effective (Emmelkamp, 2004).

Techniques Based on Operant Conditioning

B. F. Skinner's *operant conditioning* model of learning is based on the simple principle that behavior is shaped and maintained by its consequences (see Chapter 5). Behavior therapists have developed several treatment techniques that are derived from operant conditioning. *Shaping* involves reinforcing successive approximations of a desired behavior. Shaping is often used to teach appropriate behaviors to patients who are mentally disabled by autism spectrum disorder, intellectual disability, or severe mental illness. For example, shaping has been used to increase the attention span of hospitalized patients with severe schizophrenia (Combs & others, 2011; Mueser & others, 2013).

Other operant conditioning techniques involve controlling the consequences that follow behaviors. *Positive* and *negative reinforcement* are used to increase the incidence of desired behaviors. *Extinction,* or the absence of reinforcement, is used to reduce the occurrence of undesired behaviors.

Let's illustrate how operant techniques are used in therapy by describing a behavioral program to treat a 4-year-old girl's sleeping problems (Ronen, 1991). The first step in the treatment program was to identify specific problem behaviors and determine their *baseline rate,* or how often each problem occurred before treatment began

Eye Movement Desensitization Reprocessing (EMDR) In EMDR therapy, the client visually follows the therapist's moving finger while mentally focusing on a traumatic memory or vivid mental image of a troubling situation. Supposedly, the rhythmic eye movements help the client to "release" and "integrate" the trauma.

aversive conditioning A relatively ineffective type of behavior therapy that involves repeatedly pairing an aversive stimulus with the occurrence of undesirable behaviors or thoughts.

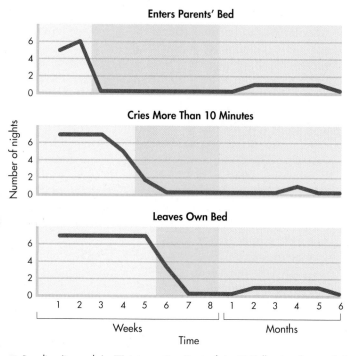

FIGURE 14.2 The Effect of Operant Conditioning Techniques These graphs depict the changes in three specific sleep-related problem behaviors of a 4-year-old girl over the course of behavioral therapy. The intervention for each problem behavior was introduced separately over several weeks. As you can see, behavior therapy produced a rapid reduction in the rate of each problem behavior. The green area shows the maintenance of desired behavior changes over a six-month follow-up.

Source: Data from Ronen (1991).

token economy A form of behavior therapy in which the therapeutic environment is structured to reward desired behaviors with tokens or points that may eventually be exchanged for tangible rewards.

(see Figure 14.2). The baseline rate allowed the therapist to objectively measure the child's progress. The parents next identified several very specific behavioral goals for their daughter. These goals included not crying when she was put to bed, not crying if she woke up in the night, not getting into her parents' bed, and staying in her own bed throughout the night.

The parents were taught operant techniques to decrease the undesirable behaviors and increase desirable ones. For example, to *extinguish* the girl's screaming and crying, the parents were taught to ignore the behavior rather than continue to reinforce it with parental attention. In contrast, desirable behaviors were to be *positively reinforced* with abundant praise, encouragement, social attention, and other rewards. Figure 14.2 shows the little girl's progress for three specific problem behaviors.

Operant conditioning techniques have been applied to many different kinds of psychological problems, from habit and weight control to helping autistic children learn to speak and behave more adaptively.

The **token economy** is another example of the use of operant conditioning techniques to modify behavior. A token economy is a system for strengthening desired behaviors through positive reinforcement in a very structured environment. Basically, tokens or points are awarded as positive reinforcers for desirable behaviors and withheld or taken away for undesirable behaviors. The tokens can be exchanged for other reinforcers, such as special privileges.

Token economies have been most successful in controlled environments in which the behavior of the client is under ongoing surveillance or supervision. Thus, token economies have been used in classrooms, inpatient psychiatric units, and group homes (Field & others, 2004; Kamps & others, 2011; Kokaridas & others, 2013). Although effective, token economies are difficult to implement, especially in community-based outpatient clinics, so they are not in wide use today (R. P. Lieberman, 2000).

A modified version of the token economy has been used with outpatients in treatment programs called *contingency management*. Like the token economy, a contingency management intervention involves carefully specified behaviors that "earn" the individual concrete rewards. Unlike token economies, which cover many behaviors, contingency management strategies are typically more narrowly focused on one or

TABLE 14.3

Behavior Therapy

Type of Therapy	Founder	Source of Problems	Treatment Techniques	Goals of Therapy
Behavior therapy	Based on classical conditioning, operant conditioning, and observational learning	Learned maladaptive behavior patterns	Systematic desensitization, virtual reality, aversive conditioning, reinforcement and extinction, token economy, contingency management interventions, observational learning	To unlearn maladaptive behaviors and replace them with adaptive, appropriate behaviors

a small number of specific behaviors (Prochaska & Norcross, 2014). Contingency management interventions have proved to be especially effective in the outpatient treatment of people who are dependent on heroin, cocaine, alcohol, or multiple drugs (Higgins & others, 2011; Tuten & others, 2012).

Table 14.3 summarizes key points about behavior therapy.

Cognitive Therapies

KEY THEME

Cognitive therapies are based on the assumption that psychological problems are due to maladaptive thinking.

KEY QUESTIONS

> What are rational-emotive behavior therapy and cognitive therapy, and how do they differ?

> What are cognitive-behavioral therapy and mindfulness-based therapies?

While behavior therapy assumes that faulty learning is at the core of problem behaviors and emotions, the **cognitive therapies** assume that the culprit is *faulty thinking*. The key assumption of the cognitive therapies could be put like this: Most people blame their unhappiness and problems on external events and situations, but the real cause of unhappiness is the way the person *thinks* about the events, not the events themselves. Thus, cognitive therapists zero in on the faulty, irrational patterns of thinking that they believe are causing the psychological problems. Once faulty, irrational patterns of thinking have been identified, the next step is to *change* them to more adaptive, healthy patterns of thinking. In this section, we'll look at how this change is accomplished in two influential forms of cognitive therapy: Ellis's *rational-emotive behavior therapy* (REBT) and Beck's *cognitive therapy* (CT).

Albert Ellis and Rational-Emotive Behavior Therapy

Shakespeare said it more eloquently, but psychologist **Albert Ellis** has expressed the same sentiment: "You largely feel the way you think." Ellis was trained as both a clinical psychologist and a psychoanalyst. As a practicing psychoanalyst, Ellis became increasingly disappointed with the psychoanalytic approach to solving human problems. Psychoanalysis simply didn't seem to work: His patients would have insight after insight, yet never get any better.

In the 1950s, Ellis began to take a more active, directive role in his therapy sessions. He developed *rational-emotive therapy*, now called **rational-emotive behavior therapy,** and abbreviated **REBT.** It was renamed to acknowledge that REBT addresses behavior to some degree as well as thoughts. REBT is based on the assumption that "people are not disturbed by things but rather by their view of things" (Ellis, 1991; Ellis & Ellis, 2011). The key premise of REBT is that people's difficulties are caused by their faulty expectations and irrational beliefs. Rational-emotive behavior therapy focuses on changing the patterns of irrational thinking that are believed to be the primary cause of the client's emotional distress and psychological problems (Ellis, 2013).

There is nothing either good or bad, but thinking makes it so.

—*William Shakespeare*, Hamlet

cognitive therapies A group of psychotherapies based on the assumption that psychological problems are due to illogical patterns of thinking; treatment techniques focus on recognizing and altering these unhealthy thinking patterns.

rational-emotive behavior therapy (REBT) A type of cognitive therapy, developed by psychologist Albert Ellis, that focuses on changing the client's irrational beliefs.

FIGURE 14.3 The "ABC" Model in Rational-Emotive Behavior Therapy Common sense tells us that unhappiness and other unpleasant emotions are caused by unpleasant or disturbing events. This view is shown in the top part of the figure. But Albert Ellis (1993) points out that it is really our *beliefs* about the events, not the events themselves, that make us miserable, as diagrammed in the bottom part of the figure.

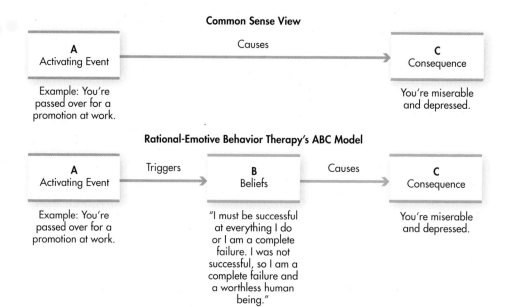

Common Sense View

| A Activating Event | Causes | C Consequence |

Example: You're passed over for a promotion at work.

You're miserable and depressed.

Rational-Emotive Behavior Therapy's ABC Model

| A Activating Event | Triggers | B Beliefs | Causes | C Consequence |

Example: You're passed over for a promotion at work.

"I must be successful at everything I do or I am a complete failure. I was not successful, so I am a complete failure and a worthless human being."

You're miserable and depressed.

Albert Ellis (1913–2007) A colorful and sometimes controversial figure, Albert Ellis developed rational-emotive behavior therapy (REBT). Rational-emotive behavior therapy promotes psychologically healthier thought processes by disputing irrational beliefs and replacing them with more rational interpretations of events.

Photo courtesy of Albert Ellis Institute

Ellis points out that most people mistakenly believe that they become upset and unhappy because of external events. But Ellis (1993; Ellis & Ellis, 2011) would argue that it's not external events that make people miserable—it's their *interpretation* of those events. It's not David's behavior that's really making Carrie miserable—it's Carrie's *interpretation* of the meaning of David's behavior. In rational-emotive behavior therapy, psychological problems are explained by the "ABC" model, as shown in Figure 14.3. According to this model, when an *Activating event* (**A**) occurs, it is the person's *Beliefs* (**B**) about the event that cause emotional *Consequences* (**C**).

Identifying the core irrational beliefs that underlie personal distress is the first step in rational-emotive behavior therapy. Often, irrational beliefs reflect "musts" and "shoulds" that are absolutes, such as the notion that "I should be competent at everything I do." Other common irrational beliefs are listed in Table 14.4.

According to rational-emotive behavior therapy, unhappiness and psychological problems can often be traced to people's irrational beliefs. Becoming aware of these irrational beliefs is the first step toward replacing them with more rational alternatives. Some of the most common irrational beliefs are listed to the right.

TABLE 14.4

Irrational Beliefs

1. It is a dire necessity for you to be loved or approved of by virtually everyone in your community.
2. You must be thoroughly competent, adequate, and achieving in all possible respects if you are to consider yourself worthwhile.
3. Certain people are bad, wicked, or villainous, and they should be severely blamed and punished for their villainy. You should become extremely upset over other people's wrongdoings.
4. It is awful and catastrophic when things are not the way you would very much like them to be.
5. Human unhappiness is externally caused, and you have little or no ability to control your bad feelings and emotions.
6. It is easier to avoid than to face difficulties and responsibilities. Avoiding difficulties whenever possible is more likely to lead to happiness than facing difficulties.
7. You need to rely on someone stronger than yourself.
8. Your past history is an all-important determinant of your present behavior. Because something once strongly affected your life, it should indefinitely have a similar effect.
9. You should become extremely upset over other people's problems.
10. There is a single perfect solution to all human problems, and it is catastrophic if this perfect solution is not found.

Source: Information from Ellis (1991).

The consequences of such thinking are unhealthy negative emotions, like extreme anger, despair, resentment, and feelings of worthlessness. These kinds of irrational cognitive and emotional responses interfere with constructive attempts to change disturbing situations (Ellis & Ellis, 2011; O'Donohue & Fisher, 2009). According to REBT, the result is self-defeating behaviors, anxiety disorders, major depressive disorder, and other psychological problems.

The next step in rational-emotive behavior therapy is for the therapist to vigorously *dispute the irrational beliefs*. In doing so, rational-emotive behavior therapists tend to be very direct and even confrontational (Ellis & Ellis, 2011). Rather than trying to establish a warm, supportive atmosphere, rational-emotive behavior therapists rely on logical persuasion and reason to push the client toward recognizing and surrendering his irrational beliefs (Dryden, 2008). According to Ellis (1991), blunt, harsh language is sometimes needed to push people into helping themselves. Understandably, this therapeutic environment can make REBT challenging for the client.

"Look, making you happy is out of the question, but I can give you a compelling narrative for your misery."

The long-term therapeutic goal of REBT is to teach clients to recognize and dispute their own irrational beliefs in a wide range of situations. However, responding "rationally" to unpleasant situations does not mean denying your feelings (Dryden 2009; Ellis & Bernard, 1985). Ellis believes that it is perfectly appropriate and rational to feel sad when you are rejected or regretful when you make a mistake. Appropriate emotions are the consequences of rational beliefs, such as "I would prefer that everyone like me, but that's not likely to happen." Such healthy mental and emotional responses encourage people to work toward constructively coping with difficult situations (Dryden & Branch, 2008; Ellis & Harper, 1975).

Albert Ellis was a colorful figure whose ideas have been extremely influential in psychotherapy (DeAngelis, 2007). Rational-emotive behavior therapy is a popular approach in clinical practice, partly because it is straightforward and simple. It has been shown to be generally effective in the treatment of major depressive disorder, social anxiety disorder, and certain other anxiety disorders. Rational-emotive behavior therapy is also useful in helping people overcome self-defeating behaviors, such as an excessive need for approval, extreme shyness, and chronic procrastination (David & others, 2009; Ellis, 2013).

cognitive therapy (CT) Therapy developed by Aaron T. Beck that focuses on changing the client's unrealistic and maladaptive beliefs.

Aaron Beck and Cognitive Therapy

Like Albert Ellis, psychiatrist **Aaron T. Beck** was initially trained as a psychoanalyst. Beck's development of **cognitive therapy,** abbreviated **CT,** grew out of his research on depression (Beck, 2004; Beck & others, 1979). Seeking to scientifically validate the psychoanalytic assumption that depressed patients "have a need to suffer," Beck began collecting data on the free associations and dreams of his depressed patients. What he found, however, was that his depressed patients did *not* have a need to suffer. In fact, his depressed patients often went to great lengths to avoid being hurt or rejected by others.

Instead, Beck discovered that depressed people have an extremely negative view of the past, present, and future (Beck & others, 1979). Rather than realistically evaluating their situation, depressed patients have developed a *negative cognitive bias,* consistently distorting their experiences in a negative way. Their negative perceptions of events and situations are shaped by deep-seated, self-deprecating beliefs, such as "I can't do anything right," "I'm worthless," or "I'm unlovable" (Beck, 1991).

Aaron T. Beck (b. 1921) In Aaron Beck's cognitive therapy, clients learn to identify and change their automatic negative thoughts. Originally developed to treat major depressive disorder, cognitive therapy has also been applied to other psychological problems, such as anxiety disorders, phobias, and eating disorders.

Photo courtesy of Beck Institute for Cognitive Behavior Therapy

According to Aaron Beck, people with major depressive disorder perceive and interpret experiences in very negative terms. They are prone to systematic errors in logic, or cognitive biases, which shape their negative interpretation of events. This table shows the most common cognitive biases in major depressive disorder.

TABLE 14.5

Cognitive Biases in Depression

Cognitive Bias (Error)	Description	Example
Arbitrary inference	Drawing a negative conclusion when there is little or no evidence to support it	When Joan calls Jim to cancel their lunch date because she has an important meeting at work, Jim concludes that she is probably going out to lunch with another man.
Selective abstraction	Focusing on a single negative detail taken out of context and ignoring the more important aspects of the situation	During Kaori's annual review, her manager praises her job performance but notes that she could be a little more confident when she deals with customers over the phone. Kaori leaves her manager's office thinking that he is on the verge of firing her because of her poor telephone skills.
Overgeneralization	Drawing a sweeping, global conclusion based on an isolated incident and applying that conclusion to other unrelated areas of life	Tony spills coffee on his final exam. He apologizes to his instructor but can't stop thinking about the incident. He concludes that he is a klutz who will never be able to succeed in a professional career.
Magnification and minimization	Grossly overestimating the impact of negative events and grossly underestimating the impact of positive events so that small, bad events are magnified, but good, large events are minimized	One week after Emily aces all her midterms, she worries about flunking out of college when she gets a B on an in-class quiz.
Personalization	Taking responsibility, blaming oneself, or applying external events to oneself when there is no basis or evidence for making the connection	Andrei becomes extremely upset when his instructor warns the class about plagiarism. He thinks the instructor's warning was aimed at him, and he concludes that the instructor suspects him of plagiarizing parts of his term paper.

Source: Information from Beck & others (1979).

Beck's cognitive therapy essentially focuses on correcting the cognitive biases that underlie major depressive disorder and other psychological disorders (see Table 14.5).

Beck's CT has much in common with Ellis's rational-emotive behavior therapy. Like Ellis, Beck believes that what people think creates their moods and emotions. And like REBT, CT involves helping clients identify faulty thinking and replace unhealthy patterns of thinking with healthier ones.

But in contrast with Ellis's emphasis on "irrational" thinking, Beck believes that major depressive disorder and other psychological problems are caused by *distorted thinking* and *unrealistic beliefs* (Hollon & Beck, 2004; Wright & others, 2011). Rather than logically debating the "irrationality" of a client's beliefs, the CT therapist encourages the client to *empirically test the accuracy of his or her assumptions and beliefs* (Hollon & Beck, 2004; Wills, 2009). Let's look at how this occurs in Beck's CT.

The first step in CT is to help the client learn to recognize and monitor the automatic thoughts that occur without conscious effort or control. Whether negative or positive, automatic thoughts can control your mood and shape your emotional and behavioral reactions to events (Ingram & others, 2007). Because their perceptions are shaped by their negative cognitive biases, depressed people usually have automatic thoughts that reflect very negative interpretations of experience. Not surprisingly, the result of such negative automatic thoughts is a deepened sense of depression, hopelessness, and helplessness.

In the second step of CT, the therapist helps the client learn how to *empirically test* the reality of the automatic thoughts that are so upsetting. For example, to test the belief that "I always say the wrong thing," the therapist might assign the person the task of initiating a conversation with three acquaintances and noting how often he actually said the wrong thing.

Initially, the CT therapist acts as a model, showing the client how to evaluate the accuracy of automatic thoughts. By modeling techniques for evaluating the accuracy of automatic thoughts, the therapist hopes to eventually teach the client to do the same on her own. The CT therapist also strives to create a therapeutic climate of *collaboration* that encourages the client to contribute to the evaluation of the logic and accuracy of automatic thoughts (Beck & others, 1979). This approach contrasts with the confrontational approach used by the REBT therapist, who directly challenges the client's thoughts and beliefs.

Beck's cognitive therapy has been shown to be effective in treating major depressive disorder and other psychological disorders, including anxiety disorders, borderline personality disorders, eating disorders, posttraumatic stress disorder, and relationship problems (Beck & Dozois, 2011; Butler & others, 2006; Dobson & Dobson, 2009; Gaudiano, 2008). Along with effectively treating major depressive disorder, cognitive therapy may also help *prevent* it from recurring, especially if clients learn and then use the skills they have learned in therapy. In one study, high-risk patients who had experienced several episodes of depression in the past were much less likely to relapse when they continued cognitive therapy after their depression had lifted (Beck & Alford, 2009). Beck's cognitive therapy techniques have even been adapted to help treat psychotic symptoms, such as the delusions and disorganized thought processes that often characterize schizophrenia (Beck & others, 2009; van der Gaag & others, 2014). And, it can also improve motivation, self-confidence, and activity levels in people with schizophrenia (Grant & others, 2012; Turkington & Morrison, 2012). Some evidence suggests that cognitive therapy can even reduce symptoms among people with schizophrenia who are not taking medications (Morrison & others, 2014).

Table 14.6 summarizes the key characteristics of Ellis's rational-emotive behavior therapy and Beck's cognitive therapy.

"You only think you're barking at nothing. We're all barking at something."

TABLE 14.6

Comparing Cognitive Therapies

Type of Therapy	Founder	Source of Problems	Treatment Techniques	Goals of Therapy
Rational-emotive behavior therapy (REBT)	Albert Ellis	Irrational beliefs	Very directive: Identify, logically dispute, and challenge irrational beliefs.	Surrender of irrational beliefs and absolutist demands
Cognitive therapy (CT)	Aaron T. Beck	Unrealistic, distorted perceptions and interpretations of events due to cognitive biases	Directive collaboration: Teach client to monitor automatic thoughts; test accuracy of conclusions; correct distorted thinking and perception.	Accurate and realistic perception of self, others, and external events

Cognitive-Behavioral Therapy and Mindfulness-Based Therapies

Although we've presented cognitive and behavioral therapies in separate sections, it's important to note that cognitive and behavioral techniques are often combined in therapy. **Cognitive-behavioral therapy** (abbreviated **CBT**) refers to a group of psychotherapies that incorporate techniques from *both* approaches. CBT is based on the assumption that cognitions, behaviors, and emotional responses are interrelated (Hollon & Beck, 2004). Thus, changes in thought patterns will affect moods and behaviors, and changes in behaviors will affect thoughts and moods. Along with challenging maladaptive beliefs and substituting more adaptive cognitions, the therapist uses

cognitive-behavioral therapy (CBT) Therapy that integrates cognitive and behavioral techniques and that is based on the assumption that thoughts, moods, and behaviors are interrelated.

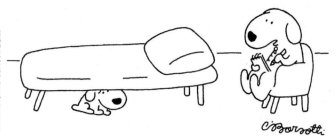

*"And what do you think will happen
if you do get on the couch?"*

behavior modification, shaping, reinforcement, and modeling to teach problem solving and to change unhealthy behavior patterns.

The hallmark of cognitive-behavioral therapy is its pragmatic approach. Therapists design an integrated treatment plan, combining techniques from the behavioral and the cognitive approaches that are most appropriate for specific problems.

Cognitive-behavioral therapy has been used in the treatment of children, adolescents, and the elderly (Dautovich & Gum, 2011; Kazdin, 2004; Weisz & Kazdin, 2010). Studies have shown that cognitive-behavioral therapy is a very effective treatment for many disorders, including major depressive disorder, eating disorders, substance use disorders, and anxiety disorders (Sheldon, 2011).

Cognitive-behavioral therapy can also help decrease the incidence of positive symptoms, such as delusions and hallucinations, in patients with schizophrenia and psychotic symptoms by teaching them how to test the reality of their mistaken beliefs and perceptions (Morrison & others, 2014; Wright & others, 2009). One man with schizophrenia, Peter Bullimore, described such therapy as making his voices seem less frightening. "My relationship with my voices has changed," Bullimore reported. "It has woken me up to a new world" (Wilson, 2014). Variations of cognitive-behavioral therapy for schizophrenia have also been shown to improve cognitive functioning, such as attention and problem solving, and social skills (Bowie & others, 2014; Kurtz & Richardson, 2012; Wykes & others, 2011). So far, however, there is no conclusive evidence that cognitive-behavioral therapy can help negative symptoms as well as positive symptoms (Velthorst & others, 2014).

An emerging approach in cognitive-behavioral therapy involves the use of mindfulness techniques. These new therapies are called *mindfulness-based interventions, mindfulness-based therapies,* or *mindfulness and acceptance therapies* (Chiesa & Malinowski, 2011; Cullen, 2011). As discussed in Chapter 4 on consciousness and Chapter 12 on stress, health, and coping, *mindfulness* is a meditation technique that involves *present-centered awareness without judgment* (Hölzel & others, 2011). Contemporary mindfulness practices are based on Buddhist meditation techniques that originated over two thousand years ago.

Like traditional cognitive-behavioral therapy, the mindfulness-based therapies involve techniques that target both thoughts and behaviors. Unlike cognitive-behavioral therapy, however, mindfulness-based therapies do not seek to challenge, test, or replace the *content* of thoughts. Rather, the goal is to change the *context* in which those thoughts are understood (Hayes & others, 2011). That is, clients are taught to *observe and change their relationship* to maladaptive thoughts and emotions.

The ability to monitor thoughts and feelings without judgment ideally allows people to experience disturbing thoughts and feelings without reacting to them (Walsh, 2011). How? One important technique is called *decentering* (Bieling & others, 2012; Hayes & others, 2011). Individuals are taught to notice, label, and relate to their thoughts and emotions as "just passing events" rather than to identify with them and allow them to shape experience. By increasing mindful awareness of thoughts, impulses, cravings, and emotions, clients are less likely to act on them or be ruled by them.

Mindfulness-based stress reduction (MBSR) was the first mindfulness-based therapy to earn broad acceptance. Developed by Jon Kabat-Zinn (2003, 2013), MBSR involves a structured program of mindfulness meditation, yoga and mindful body practices, and group discussion. The success of MBSR in the treatment of stress and anxiety helped spark the development of other mindfulness-based therapies targeted to specific disorders. For example, *mindfulness-based cognitive therapy (MBCT)* was developed to treat major depressive disorder, although it has been expanded to include other disorders (Coelho & others, 2013; Khoury & others, 2013; Segal & others, 2004, 2013). Mindfulness training has also been incorporated as a

Mindfulness-Based Stress Reduction Participants focus on their balance as part of a Stress Reduction Program in California. Most mindfulness-based programs include meditation, yoga and other body practices, and group discussion to help participants reduce stress.

core element in other cognitive-behavioral treatments, including therapies designed to treat substance use disorder and borderline personality disorder (Hayes & others, 2011; Lynch & others, 2007).

Although a relatively new approach, the mindfulness-based therapies show promise. Two meta-analyses found that mindfulness-based approaches were effective treatments for depressive disorders, although results were mixed for anxiety disorders (S. Hofmann & others, 2010; Strauss & others, 2014). And, one large, carefully controlled study found that MBCT was as effective as antidepressant medications in preventing relapse after an acute episode of major depressive disorder (Bieling & others, 2012; Segal & others, 2010).

Group and Family Therapy

KEY THEME

Group therapy involves one or more therapists working with several clients simultaneously.

KEY QUESTIONS

> What are some key advantages of group therapy?

> What is family therapy, and how do its assumptions and techniques differ from those of individual therapy?

Individual psychotherapy offers a personal relationship between a client and a therapist, one that is focused on a single client's problems, thoughts, and emotions. But individual psychotherapy has certain limitations. The therapist sees the client in isolation, rather than within the context of the client's interactions with others. Hence, the therapist must rely on the client's interpretation of reality and the client's description of relationships with others. Group and family therapy provides the opportunity to overcome these limitations (Norcross & others, 2005; Schachter, 2011).

Group Therapy

Group therapy involves one or more therapists working with several people simultaneously. Group therapy may be provided by a therapist in private practice or at a community mental health clinic. Often, group therapy is an important part of the treatment program for hospital inpatients. Groups may be as small as 3 or 4 people, or as large as 10 or more people (Burlingame & McClendon, 2008).

Virtually any approach—psychodynamic, client-centered, behavioral, or cognitive—can be used in group therapy (Free, 2008; Tasca & others, 2011). And just about any problem that can be handled individually can be dealt with in group therapy (Garvin, 2011).

Group therapy has a number of advantages over individual psychotherapy. First, group therapy is very cost-effective. Because a single therapist can work simultaneously with several people, it is less expensive for the client and less time-consuming for the therapist. Second, rather than relying on a client's self-perceptions about how she relates to other people, the therapist can observe her actual interactions with others. Observing the way clients interact with others in a group may provide unique insights into their personalities and behavior patterns. Sometimes, the group can serve as a microcosm of the client's actual social life (Burlingame & others, 2004; Yalom, 2005).

Third, the support and encouragement provided by the other group members may help a person feel less alone and understand that his or her problems are not unique. For example, a team of family therapists set up group meetings with family

group therapy A form of psychotherapy that involves one or more therapists working simultaneously with a small group of clients.

"So, would anyone in the group care to respond to what Clifford has just shared with us?"

Tom Cheney The New Yorker Collection/The Cartoon Bank

members and co-workers of people who had died in the attacks on the World Trade Center (Boss & others, 2003). The therapists' goals included helping the families come to terms with their loss, especially in cases in which the bodies of their loved ones had not been recovered. One woman, who had lost dozens of co-workers, some of them close friends, explained the impact of the group sessions in this way:

> As I saw the widows dealing with their loss, and believing it a bit more, it helped me to accept it even more. It was easier with sharing together. Strength in numbers. It makes you feel less alone. Out of the thousands of people you bump into, not everyone can understand what you've been through. If I am with any one of the families, I know they will understand what I am going through. We comfort each other. Even a blood sister might not understand as well.

Group therapies in the aftermath of other disasters, including Hurricane Katrina, have provided similar support (Salloum & others, 2009).

🔍 IN FOCUS

Increasing Access: Meeting the Need for Mental Health Care

In the United States, more than two-thirds of people with mental illnesses in the general population go untreated, with even higher rates for African Americans and Hispanic Americans (Kazdin & Blase, 2011). And people are far less likely to get treatment in many other countries, particularly developing countries, where there are far fewer mental health clinicians (Kazdin & Blase, 2011; Kohn, 2014; Wang & others, 2011). Psychologists and other mental health clinicians have been working to address this problem. Some of the most interesting innovations in increasing access involve the use of clinicians without traditional training and technology-driven solutions.

MYTH ◀ SCIENCE

Is it true that therapy is effective only if it is provided by a clinical psychologist or other highly trained therapist?

Paraprofessionals and Lay Counselors

Clinicians who have not received traditional academic training are increasingly delivering mental health care. Worldwide, there are 40 million community health workers, paraprofessionals without extensive medical or psychological training (Rotheram-Borus & others, 2012). Paraprofessionals typically have some kind of training and may earn a certificate in their field, but they do not earn the licensure that a professional, such as a psychologist or licensed clinical social worker, has.

Lay counselors have even less training than paraprofessionals. For example, in a refugee camp in Uganda, Somali and Rwandan refugees with as little as a primary school education received brief training as lay counselors to serve other refugees with PTSD (Neuner & others, 2008). Following treatment, about 30 percent of their fellow refugees met the criteria for PTSD, as compared with more than 60 percent of those who were not treated.

The United States has relatively few mental health paraprofessionals (Rotheram-Borus & others, 2012). A lay counselor model exists, however, in many Latino communities in the United States, which deploy minimally trained mental health care workers called *promotoras* into neighborhoods (Tran & others, 2014). Lay counselors are also used in the United States to provide online or telephone support—"hotlines"—for people who are thinking of suicide, have been sexually assaulted, or are trying to quit smoking. Several studies back the effectiveness of smoking "quitlines," including their ability to reach underserved groups such as African Americans (Kazdin & Blase, 2011). In another example, a program trained youth counselors to help with suicide prevention efforts in a rural community of mostly native Hawaiians (Chung-Do & others, 2014). The program led more people with suicidal thoughts to seek help.

Self-Help Groups

Self-help groups offer another venue for mental health care delivery by nonprofessionals. The best-known self-help group is Alcoholics Anonymous (AA), which follows a 12-step structure. The 12 steps of AA include themes of admitting that you have a problem, seeking help from

Paul Burke/Aristide Foundation

Lay Mental Health Workers In a refugee camp in Port-au-Prince, Haiti, a lay mental health worker teaches relaxation techniques to people who have been displaced from their homes. Studies suggest that people treated by lay mental health workers have better mental health outcomes than people who receive no care (see Neuner & others, 2008).

Fourth, group members may provide each other with helpful, practical advice for solving common problems and can act as models for successfully overcoming difficulties. Finally, working within a group gives people an opportunity to try out new behaviors in a safe, supportive environment (Yalom, 2005). For instance, someone who is very shy and submissive can practice more assertive behaviors and receive honest feedback from other group members.

Group therapy is typically conducted by a mental health professional. In contrast, *self-help groups* and *support groups* are typically conducted by nonprofessionals. Self-help groups and support groups have become increasingly popular in the United States and can be very helpful. As discussed in the In Focus box, "Increasing Access: Meeting the Need for Mental Health Care," the potential of these groups to promote mental health should not be underestimated.

a "higher power," confessing your shortcomings, repairing your relationships with others, and helping other people who have the same problem. These 12 steps have been adapted by many different groups to fit their particular problem.

Just how helpful are self-help groups? Research has shown that self-help groups can be as effective as therapy provided by a mental health professional, at least for some psychological problems (Harwood & L'Abate, 2010). Because self-help groups are typically free, or charge just a nominal fee to cover materials, they may provide a cost-effective alternative for people who cannot afford or do not have access to psychotherapy (Kazdin & Blase, 2011).

Technology-Based Solutions

Research also supports the use of technological solutions to deliver mental and physical health care to underserved areas (Ben-Zeev, 2012; Teachman, 2014). When the technology involves computers or smart phones, this innovation is often called *eHealth*. Psychotherapy delivered via internet technology, such as Skype, is about as effective as face-to-face psychotherapy (Griffiths & others, 2010). Even the old-fashioned telephone has also been demonstrated to be effective, with the bonus of a far higher percentage of people completing treatment than with face-to-face therapy (Hammond & others, 2012; Mohr & others, 2008).

In some cases, technology allows the delivery of mental health treatment without the need for a therapist. For example, one study found that people were more likely to respond honestly in a computer-based clinical interview when they thought they were talking to a virtual human than when they thought they were talking to an actual human (Lucas & others, 2014). In addition, supportive emails or text messages, sent automatically, have been used for conditions ranging from smoking addiction to eating disorders (Bauer & others, 2003; Lenert & others, 2004). In one case, people with schizophrenia were sent more than 800 automatic text messages over several months (Granholm & others, 2012). For example, a text might ask, "What do you do to help cope with voices?" Patients who received these messages were more likely to take their medication regularly, had more social interactions, and had less severe hallucinations than those who did not receive the messages.

Researchers have also examined self-administered cognitive-behavioral therapies that use technology. One treatment, cognitive bias modification (CBM), targets anxiety (Eldar & others, 2012; Lau & Pile, 2015; Teachman, 2014). Patients play a game in which both threatening and nonthreatening targets are presented—for example,

cartoon characters with angry or friendly faces (see photo). To win, players learn to direct their attention to the nonthreatening target (Dennis & O'Toole, 2014; MacLeod & Mathews, 2012). Repeated play has been demonstrated to lead to decreases in symptoms of anxiety, particularly if people have breaks between sessions (Abend & others, 2014; MacLeod & Mathews, 2012).

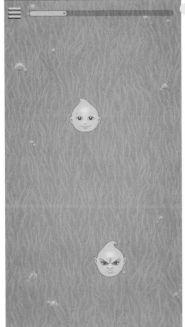

Tracy A. Dennis

An Anxiety-Reducing Game
Psychologists Tracy Dennis and Laura O'Toole (2014) found that playing a video game based on a treatment called *cognitive bias modification* resulted in a decrease in symptoms of anxiety. People earn points when they direct their attention away from anxiety-provoking targets, like the scary cartoon character, and toward the friendly-looking characters.

Increased access to mental health care is an important goal. However, as the use of unconventional resources to deliver treatment increases, the field of psychology will face new challenges. First, just because treatment is available does not mean people in need will use it or that it will be effective (Kazdin & Rabbitt, 2013). And, new ethical considerations have arisen. For example, psychological organizations in many countries are developing ethical standards for those providing therapy by phone or Internet-based technologies (Barnett & Scheetz, 2003; Canadian Psychological Association, 2006). Grappling with the logistical and ethical issues of innovative ways to provide treatment is worth it, however, if access to much-needed care is expanded.

Jodi Jacobson/Getty Images

A Family Therapy Session Family therapists typically work with all the members of a family at the same time, including young children. The family therapist can then directly observe how family members interact, resolve differences, and exert control over one another. As unhealthy patterns of family interactions are identified, they can often be replaced with new patterns that promote the psychological well-being of the family as a whole.

family therapy A form of psychotherapy that is based on the assumption that the family is a system and that treats the family as a unit.

Family and Couple Therapy

Most forms of psychotherapy tend to see a person's problems—and the solutions to those problems—as primarily originating within the individual himself. **Family therapy** operates on a different premise, focusing on the whole family rather than on an individual. The major goal of family therapy is to alter and improve the ongoing interactions among family members. Typically, family therapy involves many members of the immediate family, including children and adults, and may also include important members of the extended family, such as grandparents or in-laws (Nichols, 2012; Sexton & others, 2004).

Family therapy is based on the assumption that the family is a *system,* an interdependent unit, not just a collection of separate individuals. The family is seen as a dynamic structure in which each member plays a unique role. According to this view, every family has certain unspoken "rules" of interaction and communication. Some of these tacit rules revolve around issues such as which family members exercise power and how, who makes decisions, who keeps the peace, and what kinds of alliances members have formed among themselves. As such issues are explored, unhealthy patterns of family interaction can be identified and replaced with new "rules" that promote the psychological health of the family as a unit.

Family therapy is often used to enhance the effectiveness of individual psychotherapy. For example, patients with schizophrenia are less likely to experience relapses when family members are involved in therapy (Kopelowicz & others, 2007; O'Brien & others, 2014). In many cases, the therapist realizes that the individual client's problems reflect conflict and disturbance in the entire family system (Smerud & Rosenfarb, 2011). For the client to make significant improvements, the family as a whole must become psychologically healthier. Family therapy is also indicated when there is conflict among family members or when younger children are being treated for behavior problems, such as truancy or aggressive behavior (Connell & others, 2007).

Many family therapists also provide *marital* or *couple therapy* (Bischoff, 2011). (The term *couple therapy* is preferred today because such therapy is conducted with any couple in a committed relationship, whether they are married or unmarried, heterosexual or homosexual). As is the case with family therapy, there are many different approaches to couple therapy (Lebow, 2008; Snyder & Balderrama-Durbin, 2012). For example, *behavioral couple therapy* is based on the assumption that couples are satisfied when they experience more reinforcement than punishment in their relationship. Thus, it focuses on increasing caring behaviors and teaching couples how to constructively resolve conflicts and problems. In general,

BIZARRO

Not only is he INCREDIBLY MANIPULATIVE, I'm beginning to suspect he's DELUSIONAL.

MARRIAGE COUNSELOR

most couple therapies have the goal of improving communication, reducing negative communication, and increasing intimacy between the pair.

❯ Test your understanding of **Behavior, Cognitive, Group and Family Therapies** with **LEARNING**Curve.

Evaluating the Effectiveness of Psychotherapy

KEY THEME

Decades of research demonstrate that psychotherapy is effective in helping people with psychological disorders.

KEY QUESTIONS

❯ What are the common factors that contribute to successful outcomes in psychotherapy?
❯ What is eclecticism?

Let's start with a simple fact: Most people with psychological symptoms do *not* seek help from mental health professionals (Jagdeo & others, 2009; Kessler & others, 2004). Some people may be reluctant to seek treatment because of the stigma that is still associated with psychological problems (Pescosolido & others, 2013; Wahl, 2012). And, of course, not everyone has access to professional treatment (Kazdin & Blase, 2011). But many people eventually weather their psychological problems without professional intervention, sometimes seeking help and support from friends and family. And some people eventually improve simply with the passage of time, a phenomenon called *spontaneous remission*. Does psychotherapy offer significant benefits over just waiting for the possible "spontaneous remission" of symptoms?

The basic strategy for investigating this issue is to compare people who enter psychotherapy with a carefully selected, matched control group of people who do not receive psychotherapy (Freeman & Power, 2007; Nezu & Nezu, 2008). During the past half-century, hundreds of such studies have investigated the effectiveness of the major forms of psychotherapy (Cooper, 2008; Nathan & Gorman, 2007). To combine and interpret the results of such large numbers of studies, researchers have used a statistical technique called *meta-analysis*. Meta-analysis involves pooling the results of several studies into a single analysis, essentially creating one large study that can reveal overall trends in the data.

When meta-analysis is used to summarize studies that compare people who receive psychotherapy treatment to no-treatment controls, researchers consistently arrive at the same conclusion: *Psychotherapy is significantly more effective than no treatment*. On average, the person who completes psychotherapy treatment is better off than about 80 percent of those in the untreated control group (Cooper, 2008; Lambert & Ogles, 2004).

The benefits of psychotherapy usually become apparent in a relatively short time. As shown in Figure 14.4 on the next page, approximately 50 percent of people show significant improvement by the eighth weekly session of psychotherapy. By the end of six months of weekly psychotherapy sessions, about 75 percent are significantly improved (Baldwin & others, 2009; Lambert & others, 2001).

The gains that people make as a result of psychotherapy also tend to endure long after the therapy has ended, sometimes for years (Lambert & Ogles, 2004; Shedler, 2010). Even brief forms of psychotherapy tend to produce beneficial and long-lasting changes (Beck, 2011; Shapiro & others, 2003). And, multiple meta-analyses have found that individual and group therapy are equally effective in producing significant gains in psychological functioning (Burlingame & others, 2004; Cuijpers & others, 2008).

Lady Gaga: "I'm Not Ashamed" Flamboyant performing artist Lady Gaga has been outspoken about her battles with mental illness, which include eating disorders and depression. She described her 2013 bout with depression as a "deep sadness like an anchor dragging everywhere I go" (Grow, 2014). She shared her experiences because she wants to encourage people to seek treatment for mental illness. Lady Gaga told a reporter, "I've tried therapy. I mean, I have and I'm not ashamed to talk about it." She said that she wanted her fans to "stop acting like we should be embarrassed" to talk about mental health and seeking treatment (CTV News, 2013).

Kevin Mazur/WireImage/Getty Images

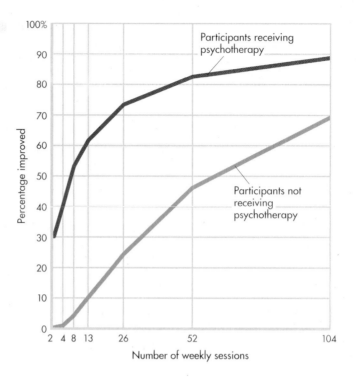

FIGURE 14.4 Psychotherapy Versus No Treatment This graph depicts the rates of improvement for more than 2,000 people in weekly psychotherapy and for 500 people who did not receive psychotherapy. As you can see, after only eight weekly sessions, more than 50 percent of participants receiving psychotherapy improved significantly. After the same length of time, only 4 percent of participants not receiving psychotherapy showed "spontaneous remission" of symptoms. Clearly, psychotherapy accelerates both the rate and degree of improvement for those experiencing psychological problems.

Source: Data from McNeilly & Howard (1991).

Brain imaging technologies are providing another line of evidence demonstrating the power of psychotherapy to bring about change for people with many psychological disorders (Barsaglini & others, 2014; Karlsson, 2011). In one study, PET scans were used to measure brain activity before and after 10 weeks of therapy for obsessive–compulsive disorder (Schwartz & others, 1996; Schwartz & Begley, 2002). The psychotherapy patients who improved showed the same changes in brain function that are associated with effective drug therapy for this disorder.

Similarly, PET scans of patients with major depressive disorder show changes in brain functioning toward more normal levels after 12 weeks of interpersonal therapy (Martin & others, 2001). In other words, psychotherapy alone produces distinct physiological changes in the brain—changes that are associated with a reduction in symptoms (Arden & Linford, 2009; Karlsson, 2011).

Nevertheless, it's important to note that psychotherapy is *not* a miracle cure. While most people experience significant benefits from psychotherapy, not everyone benefits to the same degree. Some people who enter psychotherapy improve only slightly or not at all. Others drop out early, presumably because therapy wasn't working as they had hoped (Barrett & others, 2008). And in some cases, people get worse despite therapeutic intervention (Boisvert & Faust, 2003; Linden, 2013).

Is One Form of Psychotherapy Superior?

Given that the major types of psychotherapy use different assumptions and techniques, does one type of psychotherapy stand out as more effective than the others? In some cases, one type of psychotherapy *is* more effective than another in treating a particular problem (Barlow & others, 2013; Budd & Hughes, 2009). For example, cognitive therapy and interpersonal therapy are effective in treating major depressive disorders (Craighead & others, 2007). Cognitive, cognitive-behavioral, and behavior therapies tend to be more successful than insight-oriented therapies in helping people who are experiencing panic disorder, obsessive–compulsive disorder, phobias, and posttraumatic stress disorder (Clark & others, 2003; Craske & Barlow, 2008;

Foa & others, 2013). And, insight-oriented therapies are also less effective than other therapies in the treatment of disorders characterized by severe psychotic symptoms, such as schizophrenia (Mueser & Glynn, 1993).

However, when meta-analyses are used to assess the collective results of treatment outcome studies, a surprising but consistent finding emerges: *In general, there is little or no difference in the effectiveness of different psychotherapies.* Despite sometimes dramatic differences in psychotherapy techniques, all of the standard psychotherapies have very similar success rates (Cooper, 2008; Luborsky & others, 2002; Wampold, 2001). For example, one meta-analysis examined seven different types of psychotherapy for depression (Barth & others, 2013). All seven were more effective than a control group in which patients received no therapy, and the seven were fairly similar in their effectiveness in reducing symptoms of depression.

One important qualification must be made at this point. In this chapter, we've devoted considerable time to explaining four major approaches to therapy: psychoanalytic and psychodynamic therapy; humanistic therapy; behavior therapy; and cognitive and cognitive-behavioral therapies. While distinct, all of these psychotherapy approaches have in common the fact that they are *empirically supported treatments.* In other words, they are based on known psychological principles, have been subjected to controlled scientific trials, and have demonstrated their effectiveness in helping people with psychological problems (David & Montgomery, 2011).

In contrast, one ongoing issue in contemporary psychotherapy is the proliferation of *untested* psychotherapies (Barlow & others, 2013). The fact that there is little difference in outcome among the empirically supported therapies does *not* mean that any and every form of psychotherapy is equally effective (Dimidjian & Hollon, 2010; Herbert & others, 2000). Too often, untested therapy techniques are heavily marketed and promoted, promising miraculous cures with little or no empirical research to back up their claims (Lazarus, 2000; Lilienfeld, 2007).

Psychologist James D. Herbert and his colleagues (2000) argue that before being put into widespread use, new therapies should provide empirically based answers to the following questions:

- Does the treatment work better than no treatment?
- Does the treatment work better than a placebo?
- Does the treatment work better than standard treatments?
- Does the treatment work through the processes that its proponents claim?

Often, "revolutionary" new therapies are developed, advertised, and marketed directly to the public—and to therapists—*before* controlled scientific studies of their effectiveness have been conducted (Lazarus, 2000). Many of the untested therapies are ineffective or, as in the case of EMDR, discussed on pages 596–597, are no more effective than established therapies (Lilienfeld, 2011; Lohr & others, 2003).

Is it true that the different types of psychotherapy generally have similar results?

Paul Noth The New Yorker Collection/The Cartoon Bank

"The drug has, however, proved more effective than traditional psychoanalysis."

What Factors Contribute to Effective Psychotherapy?

How can we explain the fact that different forms of psychotherapy are basically equivalent in producing positive results? One possible explanation is that the factors that are crucial to producing improvement are present in *all* effective therapies. Researchers have identified a number of common factors that are related to a positive therapy outcome (Bjornsson, 2011; Laska & others, 2013; Sparks & others, 2008).

Spencer Grant/PhotoEdit

Therapeutic Sensitivity to Cultural Differences A therapist's sensitivity to a client's cultural values can affect the ability to form a good working relationship and, ultimately, the success of psychotherapy (V. Thompson & others, 2004). Thus, some clients prefer to see therapists who are from the same ethnic or cultural background, as is the case with the African American therapist and client shown here. In general, therapists have become more attuned to the important role played by culture in effective psychotherapy.

eclecticism (ih-KLEK-tih-siz-um) The pragmatic and integrated use of techniques from different psychotherapies.

S. Harris/www.CartoonStock.com

"I utilize the best from Freud, the best from Jung and the best from my Uncle Marty, a very smart fellow."

First and most important is the quality of the *therapeutic relationship* (Cooper, 2008; Norcross & Lambert, 2011; Norcross & Wampold, 2011a). When psychotherapy is helpful, the therapist–client relationship is characterized by mutual respect, trust, and hope. Working in a cooperative alliance, both people are actively trying to achieve the same goals.

Second, certain *therapist characteristics* are associated with successful therapy. Helpful therapists have a caring attitude and the ability to listen empathically. They are genuinely committed to their clients' welfare (Aveline, 2005). Regardless of approach, they tend to be warm, sensitive, and responsive people, and they are perceived as sincere and genuine (Beutler & others, 2004). Interestingly, however, years of experience as a therapist is not associated with successful therapy (Tracey & others, 2014). Researchers speculate that experience does not lead clinicians to perform better because there is no structure to provide them with ongoing feedback about their patients' improvement.

Third, *client characteristics* are important (Clarkin & Levy, 2004; Knerr & others, 2011). If the client is motivated, committed to therapy, and actively involved in the process, a successful outcome is much more likely (Tallman & Bohart, 1999). Emotional and social maturity and the ability to express thoughts and feelings are important. Clients who are optimistic, who expect psychotherapy to help them with their problems, and who don't have a previous history of psychological disorders are more likely to benefit from therapy (Leon & others, 1999). Finally, *external circumstances,* such as a stable living situation and supportive family members, can enhance the effectiveness of therapy.

Effective therapists are also sensitive to the *cultural differences* that may exist between themselves and their clients (Smith & others, 2011; Sue & Sue, 2008b). As described in the Culture and Human Behavior box on the next page, cultural differences can be a barrier to effective psychotherapy. Increasingly, training in cultural sensitivity and multicultural issues is being incorporated into psychological training programs in the United States (Sammons & Speight, 2008).

Notice that none of these factors are specific to any particular brand of psychotherapy. However, this does not mean that differences between psychotherapy techniques are completely irrelevant. Rather, it's important that there be a good "match" between the person seeking help and the specific psychotherapy techniques used (Norcross & Wampold, 2011b). One person may be very comfortable with psychodynamic techniques, such as exploring childhood memories and free association. Another person might be more open to behavioral techniques, like systematic desensitization. For therapy to be optimally effective, the individual should feel comfortable with both the therapist and the therapist's approach to therapy.

Increasingly, such a personalized approach to therapy is being facilitated by the movement of mental health professionals toward **eclecticism**—the pragmatic and integrated use of diverse psychotherapy techniques (Hollanders, 2007; Lambert & others, 2004). Today, therapists identify themselves as eclectic more often than any other approach (Norcross & others, 2005; Lambert & Ogles, 2004). *Eclectic psychotherapists* carefully tailor the therapy approach to the problems and characteristics of the person seeking help. For example, an eclectic therapist might integrate insight-oriented techniques with specific behavioral techniques to help someone suffering from extreme shyness. A related approach is *integrative* psychotherapy. Integrative psychotherapists also use multiple approaches to therapy, but they tend to blend them together rather than choosing different approaches for different clients (Lazarus, 2008; Stricker & Gold, 2008).

CULTURE AND HUMAN BEHAVIOR

Cultural Values and Psychotherapy

The goals and techniques of many established approaches to psychotherapy tend to reflect European and North American cultural values (McGoldrick & others, 2005; Mutiso & others, 2014; T. B. Smith & others, 2011). In this box, we'll look at how those cultural values can clash with the values of clients from other cultures, diminishing the effectiveness of psychotherapy.

A Focus on the Individual

In Western psychotherapy, the client is usually encouraged to become more assertive, more self-sufficient, and less dependent on others in making decisions. Problems are assumed to have an internal cause and are expected to be solved by the client alone. Therapy emphasizes meeting the client's individual needs, even if those needs conflict with the demands of significant others. In collectivistic cultures, however, the needs of the individual are much more strongly identified with the needs of the group to which he or she belongs (Brewer & Chen, 2007; Pedersen & others, 2008; Sue & Sue, 2008a, 2008b).

For example, traditional Native Americans are less likely than European Americans to believe that personal problems are due to a cause within the individual (Garrett, 2008). Instead, one person's problems may be seen as a problem for the entire community to resolve.

In traditional forms of Native American healing, family members, friends, and other members of the community may be asked to participate in the treatment or healing rituals. One type of therapy, called *network therapy,* is conducted in the person's home and can involve as many as 70 members of the individual's community or tribe (LaFromboise & others, 1993).

Latino cultures, too, emphasize interdependence over independence. In particular, they stress the value of *familismo*—the importance of the extended family network. Because the sense of family is so central to Latino culture, some psychologists recommend that members of the client's extended family, such as grandparents and in-laws, be actively involved in psychological treatment (Garza & Watts, 2010).

Many collectivistic Asian cultures also emphasize a respect for the needs of others (Lee & Mock, 2005). The Japanese psychotherapy called *Naikan therapy* is a good example of how such cultural values affect the goals of psychotherapy (Tanaka-Matsumi, 2004). According to Naikan therapy, being self-absorbed is the surest path to psychological suffering. Thus, the goal of Naikan therapy is to replace the focus on the self with a sense of gratitude and obligation toward others. Rather than talking about how his own needs were not met by family members, the Naikan client is asked to meditate on how he has failed to meet the needs of others. Naikan therapy can be done on an outpatient basis but is often completed over a week spent in seclusion (Sengoku & others, 2010).

The Importance of Insight

Psychodynamic, humanistic, and cognitive therapies all stress the importance of insight or awareness of an individual's thoughts and feelings. But many cultures do *not* emphasize the importance of exploring painful thoughts and feelings in resolving psychological problems. For example, Asian cultures stress that mental health is enhanced by the avoidance of negative thinking. Hence, a depressed or anxious person in China and many other Asian countries would be encouraged to *avoid* focusing on upsetting thoughts (Kim & Park, 2008).

Intimate Disclosure Between Therapist and Client

Many Western psychotherapies are based on the assumption that the clients will disclose their deepest feelings and most private thoughts to their therapists. But in some cultures, intimate details of one's personal life would never be discussed with a stranger. Asians are taught to disclose intimate details only to very close friends. For example, a young Vietnamese student of ours vowed never to return to see a psychologist she had consulted about her struggles with depression. The counselor, she complained, was too "nosy" and asked too many personal questions. In many cultures, people are far more likely to turn to family members or friends than they are to mental health professionals (Leung & Boehnlein, 2005).

The demands for emotional openness may also clash with cultural values. In Asian cultures, people tend to avoid the public expression of emotions and often express thoughts and feelings nonverbally. Native American cultures tend to value the restraint of emotions rather than the open expression of emotions (Garrett, 2006; LaFromboise & others, 1993).

Recognizing the need for psychotherapists to become more culturally sensitive, the American Psychological Association has recommended formal training in multicultural awareness for all psychologists (Fouad & Arredondo, 2007; Tanaka-Matsumi, 2011). The APA (2003) has also published extensive guidelines for psychologists who provide psychological help to culturally diverse populations. Interested students can download a copy of the APA guidelines at www.apa.org/pi/multiculturalguidelines.pdf.

LEZLIE STERLING/MCT/Landov

Drumming Therapy At the Sacramento Native American Health Center in California, several people of Native American descent participate in a healing ritual that involves drumming on traditional instruments. For many Native Americans, healing practices involve the community.

psychotropic medications (sy-ko-TRO-pick) Drugs that alter mental functions, alleviate psychological symptoms, and are used to treat psychological or mental disorders.

⟩ Test your understanding of **Evaluating the Effectiveness of Psychotherapy** with *LEARNINGCurve*.

Biomedical Therapies

KEY THEME

The biomedical therapies are medical treatments for the symptoms of psychological disorders and include medication and electroconvulsive therapy.

KEY QUESTIONS

⟩ What medications are used to treat the symptoms of schizophrenia, anxiety, bipolar disorder, and major depressive disorder, and how do they achieve their effects?

⟩ What is electroconvulsive therapy, and what are its advantages and disadvantages?

Medical treatments for psychological disorders actually predate modern psychotherapy by hundreds of years. In past centuries, patients were whirled, soothed, drenched, restrained, and isolated—all in an attempt to alleviate symptoms of psychological disorders. Today, such "treatments" seem cruel, inhumane, and useless. Keep in mind, however, that these early treatments were based on the limited medical knowledge of the time. As you'll see in this section, some of the early efforts to treat psychological disorders did eventually evolve into treatments that are widely used today.

For the most part, it was not until the twentieth century that effective biomedical therapies were developed to treat the symptoms of mental disorders. Today, the most common biomedical therapy is the use of **psychotropic medications**—prescription drugs that alter mental functions and alleviate psychological symptoms. You can see how medications affect neurotransmitter functioning in the synapses between neurons in Figure 2.7 on page 52. Although often used alone, psychotropic medications are increasingly combined with psychotherapy (Kaut & Dickinson, 2007; Sudak, 2011).

Antipsychotic Medications

For more than 2,000 years, traditional practitioners of medicine in India used an herb derived from the snakeroot plant to diminish the psychotic symptoms commonly associated with schizophrenia: hallucinations, delusions, and disordered thought processes (Bhatara & others, 1997). The same plant was used in traditional Japanese medicine to treat anxiety and restlessness (Jilek, 1993). In the 1930s, Indian physicians discovered that the herb was also helpful in the treatment of high blood pressure. They developed a synthetic version of the herb's active ingredient, called *reserpine*.

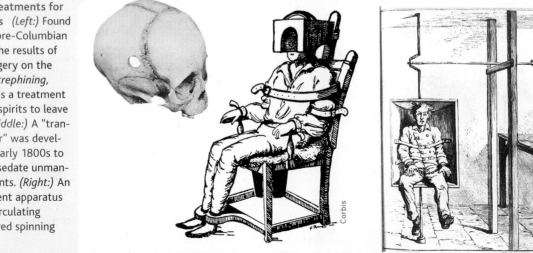

Historical Treatments for Mental Illness *(Left:)* Found in Peru, this pre-Columbian skull shows the results of primitive surgery on the brain, called *trephining*, presumably as a treatment to allow evil spirits to leave the body. *(Middle:)* A "tranquilizing chair" was developed in the early 1800s to restrain and sedate unmanageable patients. *(Right:)* An early treatment apparatus called the "circulating swing" involved spinning patients.

The Granger Collection

Corbis

SPL/Science Source

Reserpine first came to the attention of American researchers as a potential treatment for high blood pressure. But it wasn't until the early 1950s that American researchers became aware of research in India demonstrating the effectiveness of reserpine in treating schizophrenia (Frankenburg, 1994).

It was also during the 1950s that French scientists began investigating the psychoactive properties of another drug, called *chlorpromazine*. Like reserpine, chlorpromazine diminished the psychotic symptoms commonly seen in schizophrenia. Hence, reserpine and chlorpromazine were dubbed **antipsychotic medications.** Because chlorpromazine had fewer side effects than reserpine, it nudged out reserpine as the preferred medication for treating schizophrenia-related symptoms. Since then, chlorpromazine has been better known by its trade name, *Thorazine,* and is still used to treat psychotic symptoms. The antipsychotic drugs are also referred to as *neuroleptic medications,* or simply *neuroleptics.*

How do these drugs diminish psychotic symptoms? Reserpine and chlorpromazine act differently on the brain, but both drugs reduce levels of the neurotransmitter called *dopamine.* Since the development of these early drugs, more than 30 other antipsychotic medications have been developed (see Table 14.7). These antipsychotic medications also act on dopamine receptors in the brain (Abi-Dargham, 2004; Laruelle & others, 2003; Richtand & others, 2007).

The first antipsychotics effectively reduced the *positive symptoms* of schizophrenia—hallucinations, delusions, and disordered thinking (see Chapter 13). This therapeutic effect had a revolutionary impact on the number of people hospitalized for schizophrenia. Until the 1950s, patients with schizophrenia were thought to be incurable. These chronic patients formed the bulk of the population in the "back wards" of psychiatric hospitals. With the introduction of the antipsychotic medications,

The First Antipsychotic Drug More than 2,000 years ago, ancient Hindu medical texts prescribed the use of an herb derived from *Rauwolfia serpentina,* or snakeroot plant, to treat epilepsy, insomnia, and other ailments. But its primary use was to treat *oonmaad*—a Sanskrit term for an abnormal mental condition that included disruptions in "wisdom, perception, knowledge, character, creativity, conduct, and behavior" (Bhatara & others, 1997). Today it is known that the herb has a high affinity for dopamine receptors in the brain.

R Koenig/age fotstock

TABLE 14.7

Antipsychotic Medications

	Generic Name	Trade Name
Typical Antipsychotics	Chlorpromazine	Thorazine
	Fluphenazine	Prolixin
	Trifluoperazine	Stelazine
	Thioridazine	Mellaril
	Thiothixene	Navane
	Haloperidol	Haldol
Atypical Antipsychotics	Clozapine	Clozaril
	Risperidone	Risperdal
	Olanzapine	Zyprexa
	Paliperidone	Invega
	Quetiapine	Seroquel
	Aripiprazole	Abilify
	Amisulpride	Solian

Source: Information from Advokat, Comaty, & Julien (2014).

(bkgrd) JB Reed/Bloomberg via Getty Images

antipsychotic medications (an-tee-sy-KAHT-ick or an-ty-sy-KAHT-ick) Prescription drugs that are used to reduce psychotic symptoms; frequently used in the treatment of schizophrenia; also called *neuroleptics.*

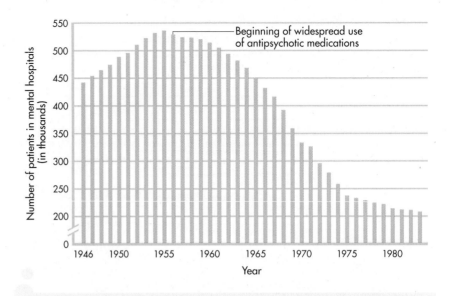

FIGURE 14.5 Change in the Number of Patients Hospitalized for Mental Disorders, 1946–1983 When the first antipsychotic drugs came into wide use in the late 1950s, the number of people hospitalized for mental disorders began to drop sharply.

Source: Data from Julien (2011).

however, the number of patients in mental hospitals decreased dramatically (see Figure 14.5).

DRAWBACKS OF ANTIPSYCHOTIC MEDICATIONS

Even though the early antipsychotic drugs allowed thousands of patients to be discharged from hospitals, these drugs had a number of drawbacks. First, they didn't actually *cure* schizophrenia. Psychotic symptoms often returned if a person stopped taking the medication.

Second, the early antipsychotic medications were not very effective in eliminating the *negative symptoms* of schizophrenia—social withdrawal, apathy, and lack of emotional expressiveness. In some cases, the drugs even made negative symptoms worse.

Third, the antipsychotics often produced unwanted side effects, such as dry mouth, weight gain, constipation, sleepiness, and poor concentration (Stahl, 2009).

Fourth, the fact that the early antipsychotics *globally* altered brain levels of dopamine turned out to be a double-edged sword. Dopamine pathways in the brain are involved not only in psychotic symptoms but also in normal motor movements. Consequently, the early antipsychotic medications could produce motor-related side effects—muscle tremors, rigid movements, a shuffling gait, and a masklike facial expression. This collection of side effects occurred so commonly that mental hospital staff members sometimes informally referred to it as the "Thorazine shuffle."

Even more disturbing, the long-term use of antipsychotic medications causes a small percentage of people to develop a potentially irreversible motor disorder called *tardive dyskinesia*. Tardive dyskinesia is characterized by severe, uncontrollable facial tics and grimaces, chewing movements, and other involuntary movements of the lips, jaw, and tongue.

Closely tied to the various side effects of the first antipsychotic drugs is a fifth problem: the "revolving door" pattern of hospitalization, discharge, and rehospitalization. Schizophrenic patients, once stabilized by antipsychotic medication, were released from hospitals into the community. But because of either the medication's unpleasant side effects or inadequate medical follow-up, or both, many patients eventually stopped taking the medication. When psychotic symptoms returned, the patients were rehospitalized.

THE ATYPICAL ANTIPSYCHOTICS

Beginning around 1990, a second generation of antipsychotic drugs began to be introduced. Called **atypical antipsychotic medications,** these drugs affect brain levels of dopamine and *serotonin.* The first atypical antipsychotics were *clozapine* and *risperidone.* More recent atypical antipsychotics include *olanzapine, sertindole,* and *quetiapine.*

The atypical antipsychotics have several advantages over the older antipsychotic drugs (Advokat, Comaty, & Julien, 2014). First, the new drugs are less likely to cause movement-related side effects. That's because they do not block dopamine receptors in the movement areas of the brain. Instead, they more selectively target dopamine receptors in brain areas associated with psychotic symptoms. The atypical antipsychotics are also much more effective in treating the negative symptoms of schizophrenia—apathy, social withdrawal, and flat emotions (Woo & others, 2009). Some patients who have not responded to the older antipsychotic drugs improve dramatically with the new medications (Turner & Stewart, 2006).

The atypical antipsychotic medications also appear to lessen the incidence of the "revolving door" pattern of hospitalization and rehospitalization. As compared to discharged patients taking the older antipsychotic medications, patients taking risperidone or olanzapine are much less likely to relapse and return to the hospital (Bhanji & others, 2004).

The atypical antipsychotic medications sparked considerable hope for better therapeutic effects, fewer adverse reactions, and greater patient compliance. Although they were less likely to cause movement-related side effects, the second-generation antipsychotics caused some of the same side effects as the first-generation antipsychotics, including weight gain and cardiac problems. The atypical antipsychotic medications are also associated with a sharply increased risk of developing diabetes, especially in patients younger than age 40 (Advokat, Comaty, & Julien, 2014; Angell, 2011). Equally important, large-scale studies have demonstrated that the newer antipsychotic medications do *not* produce greater improvements than the older traditional antipsychotics (Crossley & others, 2010).

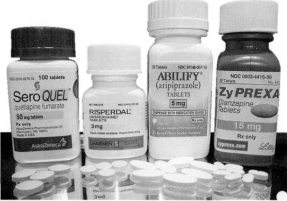

Second-Generation Antipsychotics Sales of antipsychotic medications earn more money than any other group of drugs—almost 15 billion dollars in 2010 (Wilson, 2010). Helping to fuel sales was the development of the new atypical antipsychotic medications, which are much more expensive than the older, traditional antipsychotic drugs. A second factor is the increased off-label use of antipsychotic medications for non-psychotic conditions, including the anxiety disorders and bipolar disorder—despite the fact that there is little evidence to support the use of these powerful drugs to treat the symptoms of these disorders (Alexander & others, 2010; Comer & others, 2011).

atypical antipsychotic medications Newer antipsychotic medications that, in contrast with the early antipsychotic drugs, block dopamine receptors in brain regions associated with psychotic symptoms rather than more globally throughout the brain, resulting in fewer side effects.

antianxiety medications Prescription drugs that are used to alleviate the symptoms of anxiety.

Antianxiety Medications

Anxiety that is intense and persistent can be disabling, interfering with a person's ability to eat, sleep, and function. **Antianxiety medications** are prescribed to help people deal with the problems and symptoms associated with pathological anxiety (see Table 14.8).

The best-known antianxiety drugs are the *benzodiazepines,* which include the trade-name drugs *Valium* and *Xanax.* These antianxiety medications calm jittery feelings, relax the muscles, and promote sleep. They used to go by the name "tranquilizers" because of this effect. They take effect rapidly, usually within an hour or so. In general, the benzodiazepines produce their effects by increasing the level of *GABA,* a neurotransmitter that inhibits the transmission of nerve impulses in the brain and slows brain activity (see Chapter 2).

TABLE 14.8

Antianxiety Medications

	Generic Name	Trade Name
Benzodiazepines	Diazepam	Valium
	Chlordiazepoxide	Librium
	Lorazepam	Ativan
	Triazolam	Halcion
	Alprazolam	Xanax
Non-benzodiazepine	Buspirone	Buspar

Source: Information from Advokat, Comaty, & Julien (2014).

lithium A naturally occurring substance that is used in the treatment of bipolar disorder.

antidepressant medications Prescription drugs that are used to reduce the symptoms associated with major depressive disorder.

Taken for a week or two, and in therapeutic doses, the benzodiazepines can effectively reduce anxiety levels. However, the benzodiazepines have several potentially dangerous side effects. First, they can reduce coordination, alertness, and reaction time. Second, their effects can be intensified when they are combined with alcohol and many other drugs, including over-the-counter antihistamines. Such a combination can produce severe drug intoxication, even death.

Third, the benzodiazepines can be physically addictive if taken in large quantities or over a long period of time. If physical dependence occurs, the person must withdraw from the drug gradually, as abrupt withdrawal can produce life-threatening symptoms. Because of their addictive potential, the benzodiazepines are less widely prescribed today.

An antianxiety drug with the trade name *Buspar* has fewer side effects. Buspar is not a benzodiazepine, and it does not affect the neurotransmitter GABA. In fact, exactly how Buspar works is unclear, but it is believed to affect brain dopamine and serotonin levels (Davidson & others, 2009). Regardless, Buspar relieves anxiety while allowing the individual to maintain normal alertness. It does not cause the drowsiness, sedation, and cognitive impairment that are associated with the benzodiazepines. And Buspar seems to have a very low risk of dependency and physical addiction.

However, Buspar has one major drawback: It must be taken for two to three *weeks* before anxiety is reduced. While this decreases Buspar's potential for abuse, it also decreases its effectiveness for treating acute anxiety.

Another new medication that has been explored as a treatment for anxiety disorders and posttraumatic stress disorder is MDMA, short for methylenedioxymethamphetamine (Baldwin & others, 2014). MDMA is often called "ecstasy" when used as a recreational drug. There is growing evidence that a few doses of MDMA, prescribed and monitored by a physician, can improve the outcome for people undergoing behavioral therapy for these disorders (Johansen & Krebs, 2009). MDMA use can lead to dangerous or unpleasant side effects and has the potential for abuse. It is typically taken only a few times, however, diminishing the likelihood that this will occur (Meyer, 2013; Oehen & others, 2013). Despite the availability of newer treatment options for immediate, short-term relief from anxiety, the benzodiazepines are still regarded as the most effective medications currently available.

Lithium

In Chapter 13, on psychological disorders, we described *bipolar disorder,* previously known as *manic depression.* The medication most commonly used to treat bipolar disorder is **lithium,** a naturally occurring substance. Lithium counteracts manic symptoms, and to a lesser degree depressive symptoms, in bipolar patients (Nivoli & others, 2010; Nivoli & others, 2012). Its effectiveness in treating bipolar disorder has been well established since the 1960s (Preston & others, 2008).

As a treatment for bipolar disorder, lithium can prevent acute manic episodes over the course of a week or two. Once an acute manic episode is under control, the long-term use of lithium can help prevent relapses into either mania or major depressive disorder. The majority of patients with bipolar disorder respond well to lithium therapy. However, lithium doesn't help everyone. Some people on lithium therapy experience relapses (Severus & others, 2009).

Like all other medications, lithium has potential side effects. If the lithium level is too low, manic symptoms persist. If it is too high, lithium poisoning may occur, with symptoms such as vomiting, muscle weakness, and reduced muscle coordination. Consequently, the patient's lithium blood level must be carefully monitored.

How lithium works was once a complete mystery. Lithium's action was especially puzzling because it prevented mood disturbances at the manic end of the emotional spectrum and to some degree at the depressive end as well. It turns out that lithium

Lithium Water Lithium salt, a naturally occurring substance, was used in many over-the-counter medicines before it was discovered to be helpful in the treatment of mania. As this late-nineteenth-century ad shows, small amounts of lithium salt were also added to bottled water. An early version of the soft drink 7-Up included small amounts of lithium (Maxmen & Ward, 1995). Marketed as "lithium soda," one ad campaign claimed that it was the drink that took "the ouch out of the grouch!"

Jay Paull/Getty Images

affects levels of an excitatory neurotransmitter called *glutamate,* which is found in many areas of the brain. Apparently, lithium stabilizes the availability of glutamate within a narrow, normal range, preventing both abnormal highs and abnormal lows (Keck & McElroy, 2009; Malhi & others, 2013).

Bipolar disorder can also be treated with an anticonvulsant medicine called *Depakote.* Originally used to prevent epileptic seizures, Depakote seems to be especially helpful in treating those who rapidly cycle through bouts of bipolar disorder several times a year. It's also useful for treating bipolar patients who do not respond to lithium (Davis & others, 2005).

Antidepressant Medications

The **antidepressant medications** counteract the classic symptoms of major depressive disorder—hopelessness, guilt, dejection, suicidal thoughts, difficulty concentrating, and disruptions in sleep, energy, appetite, and sexual desire. The first generation of antidepressants consists of two classes of drugs, called *tricyclics* and *MAO inhibitors* (see Table 14.9). Tricyclics and MAO inhibitors affect multiple neurotransmitter pathways in the brain. Evidence suggests that these medications alleviate major depressive disorder by increasing the availability of two key brain neurotransmitters, *norepinephrine* and *serotonin.* However, even though brain levels of norepinephrine and serotonin begin to rise within *hours* of taking a tricyclic or MAO inhibitor, it can take up to six *weeks* before depressive symptoms begin to lift (Thase & Denko, 2008).

Tricyclics and MAO inhibitors can be effective in reducing depressive symptoms, but they can also produce numerous side effects (Holsboer, 2009). Tricyclics can cause weight gain, dizziness, dry mouth and eyes, and sedation. And, because tricyclics affect the cardiovascular system, an overdose can be fatal. As for the MAO inhibitors, they can interact with a chemical found in many foods, including cheese, smoked meats, and red wine. Eating or drinking these while taking an MAO inhibitor can result in dangerously high blood pressure, leading to stroke or even death.

The search for antidepressants with fewer side effects led to the development of the second generation of antidepressants. Second-generation antidepressants include *trazodone* and *bupropion,* trade name *Wellbutrin.* Wellbutrin, for example, is a *dopamine-norepinephrine* inhibitor that does not affect serotonin neurons (Advokat, Comaty, & Julien, 2014). Although chemically different from the tricyclics, the second-generation antidepressants were generally no more effective than the first-generation ones, and they turned out to have many of the same side effects.

In 1987, the picture changed dramatically with the introduction of a third group of antidepressants, the **selective serotonin reuptake inhibitors,** abbreviated **SSRIs.** Rather than acting on multiple neurotransmitter pathways, the SSRIs primarily affect the availability of a single neurotransmitter—serotonin. Compared with the earlier antidepressants, the new antidepressants act much more selectively in targeting specific serotonin pathways in the brain. The first SSRI to be released was *fluoxetine,* which is better known by its trade name, *Prozac.* Prozac was quickly followed by its chemical cousins, *Zoloft* and *Paxil.*

TABLE 14.9

Antidepressant Medications

	Generic Name	Trade Name
First-Generation Antidepressants		
Tricyclic antidepressants	Imipramine	Tofranil
	Desipramine	Norpramin
	Amitriptyline	Elavil
MAO inhibitors	Phenelzine	Nardil
	Tranylcypromine	Parnate
Second-Generation Antidepressants	Trazodone	Desyrel
	Bupropion	Wellbutrin
	Venlafaxine	Effexor
Selective Serotonin Reuptake Inhibitors (SSRIs)	Fluoxetine	Prozac
	Sertraline	Zoloft
	Paroxetine	Paxil
	Fluvoxamine	Luvox
	Citalopram	Celexa
	Escitalopram	Lexapro
Dual-Action Antidepressants	Nefazodone	Serzone
	Mirtazapine	Remeron
	Duloxetine	Cymbalta

Source: Information from Advokat, Comaty, & Julien (2014).

selective serotonin reuptake inhibitors (SSRIs) Class of antidepressant medications that increase the availability of serotonin in the brain and cause fewer side effects than earlier antidepressants; they include Prozac, Paxil, and Zoloft.

GOOD SHRINK, BAD SHRINK

Mick Stevens The New Yorker Collection/The Cartoon Bank

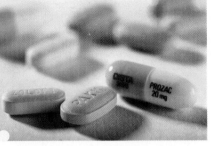

The Most Commonly Prescribed Class of Medication: Antidepressants The number of people treated with antidepressant medication more than doubled from 13 million people in 1996 to 27 million people in 2005 (Olfson & Marcus, 2009). With the exception of African Americans, antidepressant usage increased in virtually every demographic group. Partially fueling the increase is the rise in the number of prescriptions written by physicians who do *not* give the patient a psychiatric diagnosis (Mojtabai & Olfson, 2011). In fact, people with depressive symptoms are less likely to undergo psychotherapy treatment with a psychiatrist, psychologist, or other counselors (Mojtabai & Olfson, 2008).

Think Like a SCIENTIST

How would a "party drug" end up being prescribed for depression? Go to LaunchPad: Resources to **Think Like a Scientist** about **Ketamine**.

LaunchPad

Prozac was specifically designed to alleviate depressive symptoms with fewer side effects than earlier antidepressants. It achieved that goal with considerable success. Although no more effective than tricyclics or MAO inhibitors, Prozac and the other SSRI antidepressants tend to produce fewer, and milder, side effects. But no medication is risk-free. Among Prozac's potential side effects are headaches, nervousness, difficulty sleeping, loss of appetite, and sexual dysfunction (Bresee & others, 2009).

Partly because of its relatively mild side-effect profile Prozac quickly became very popular. By the early 1990s, an estimated *1 million prescriptions per month* were being written for Prozac. By the late 1990s, Prozac had become the best-selling antidepressant in the world. Today, Prozac is available in generic form, greatly reducing its cost. In 2010, sales of antidepressants surpassed $11 billion a year in the United States alone (Hayes, 2011).

Since the original SSRIs were released, several new antidepressants have been developed, including *Serzone* and *Remeron*. These antidepressants, called *dual-action antidepressants,* also affect serotonin levels, but their mechanism is somewhat different from that of the SSRIs.

One promising new treatment is an experimental drug called ketamine (Larkin & Beautrais, 2011). As discussed in Chapter 4, ketamine is used in high doses as an anesthetic, and called Special K when sold as a street drug. In one study, 71% of severely depressed patients who received intravenous ketamine saw a decrease in depressive symptoms within just one day, as compared with 0% of those taking placebo (Zarate & others, 2006). There were some serious side effects from ketamine, such as hallucinations, but none that lasted more than two hours.

Despite its impressive effectiveness, ketamine is likely to be used only in emergency situations, in large part because its effects tend to last no more than a week. However, ketamine's fast response time means that seriously depressed people who visit the ER might be able to forgo inpatient treatment. During the time it takes for ketamine to wear off, more traditional antidepressants and psychotherapy might have time to start working. There also is evidence that the use of ketamine reduces suicide rates (DiazGranados & others, 2010).

Antidepressants are often used in the treatment of disorders other than depression, sometimes in combination with other drugs. For example, the SSRIs are commonly prescribed to treat anxiety disorders, obsessive–compulsive disorder, and eating disorders (Davidson & others, 2009; Lissemore & others, 2014; Mitchell & others, 2013). Wellbutrin is also used to treat a number of other disorders, including anxiety, obesity, and adult attention-deficit hyperactivity disorder (Ahima, 2011; Lee, K.-U., & others, 2009). Under the name Zyban, Wellbutrin is also prescribed to help people stop smoking.

With so many antidepressants available today, which should be prescribed? Many factors, including previous attempts with antidepressants, possible interactions with other medications, and personal tolerance of side effects, can influence this decision. Currently, medications are typically prescribed on a "trial-and-error" basis—people are prescribed different drugs or combinations of drugs in different dosages until they find the regimen that works for them. Thus, patients may need to try multiple medications before finding an effective treatment.

Many researchers believe that genetic differences may explain why people respond so differently to antidepressants and other psychotropic medications (Crisafulli & others, 2011). The new field of *pharmacogenetics* is the study of how genes influence an individual's response to drugs (Nurnberger, 2009). As this field advances, it may help overcome the trial-and-error nature of prescribing not only antidepressants, but other psychotropic medications as well.

How do antidepressants and psychotherapy compare in their effectiveness? Several large-scale studies have found that both cognitive therapy and interpersonal therapy are just as effective as antidepressant medication in producing remission from depressive symptoms (Imel & others, 2008; Thase & others, 2007). Mindfulness-based cognitive therapy has also been shown to be as effective as antidepressant treatment in preventing relapse. Brain imaging studies are just beginning to show how such treatments might change brain activity—a topic that we showcase in the Focus on Neuroscience box below. Despite these findings, more people with depression are treated with antidepressants than with psychotherapy (Marcus & Olfson, 2010).

FOCUS ON NEUROSCIENCE

Psychotherapy and the Brain

As we discussed in Chapter 13, major depressive disorder is characterized by a variety of physical symptoms and includes changes in brain activity (Abler & others, 2007; Kempton & others, 2011). Antidepressants are assumed to work by changing brain chemistry and activity. Does psychotherapy have the same effect?

MYTH ▶ SCIENCE

Is it true that, for some disorders, psychotherapy and medications lead to similar changes in brain activity?

To address this question, fMRI scans were done on 27 people with major depressive disorder and compared to a matched group of 25 normal control subjects who were *not* depressed (Siegle & others, 2007). Compared with the nondepressed adults, the depressed individuals showed altered brain activity following an emotional task and a cognitive task. These tasks were chosen because major depressive disorder tends to affect both people's emotional responses and their thought processes.

For the emotional task, both groups were asked to briefly view negative emotional words that they perceived to be relevant for them personally. The depressed people showed increased activity in the *amygdala*. The control group, made up of people who were not depressed, did not exhibit activity in the amygdala following this task. In addition, after completing a cognitive task in which they were asked to mentally sort a short list of numbers, depressed people showed less activity in the *prefrontal cortex* than did those in the control group.

A sample of nine of the depressed people in this study then completed 14 weeks of cognitive therapy (DeRubeis & others, 2008). After treatment, the brain activity of the people treated for depression resembled that of the control group. The posttreatment brain scan shown here displays the activity in the amygdala in response to viewing the negative emotional word "ugly" for people in the control group or for people treated for depression. The graph highlights the differences among these two groups and a third group, people who have not yet been treated for depression. People who do not suffer from depression are indicated in green; people with depression who have been treated with cognitive therapy are indicated in purple; and people with depression who have not been treated are indicated in turquoise. There is increased brain activation only among the third group, the depressed people before treatment.

Interestingly, the changes in brain activation that result from psychotherapy are similar to changes that result from medications. For example, in a study of people with major depressive disorder, PET scans revealed that patients who took the antidepressant Paxil *and* patients who completed interpersonal therapy

(discussed earlier in this chapter) showed a trend toward more normalized brain functioning (Brody & others, 2001). Activity declined significantly in brain regions that had shown abnormally high activity before treatment began. Similar results were found in a study comparing a different antidepressant, Effexor, and a different type of psychotherapy, cognitive-behavioral therapy (Kennedy & others, 2007).

As these findings emphasize, psychotherapy—and not just antidepressant medication—affects brain chemistry and functioning. Such effects are not limited to depression. Similar changes toward a more normal pattern of brain functioning have also been found in people with panic disorder, posttraumatic stress disorder, obsessive–compulsive disorder, phobias, and other anxiety disorders after psychotherapy treatment (Barsaglini & others, 2014; Karlsson, 2011; Straube & others, 2006).

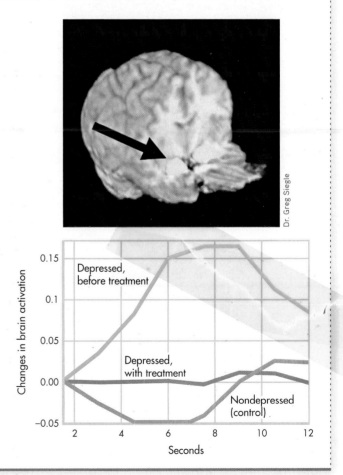

Dr. Greg Siegle

Do Antidepressants Work Better Than Placebos?

Are antidepressants just fancy placebos? Consider this statement by psychologist Irving Kirsch on a 2012 episode of the TV news show *60 Minutes*: "The difference between the effect of the placebo and the effect of an antidepressant is minimal for most people." Interviewer Lesley Stahl was astounded: "So, you're saying if they took a sugar pill, they'd have the same effect?"

Kirsch's surprising statement is based on meta-analyses (Fournier & others, 2010; Kirsch & others, 2008). As discussed in Chapter 1, a meta-analysis combines the results of many studies into a single analysis. The meta-analyses to which Kirsch referred included all studies, published and unpublished, that had been submitted to the U.S. Food and Drug Administration during the process of approval for new antidepressants. It is important that they included unpublished studies because unpublished studies are more likely than published studies to have found no difference between the placebo and the antidepressant. This is because journal editors tend to prefer publishing articles that found some difference rather than articles that found no difference (Turner, 2013).

Placebo Researcher Psychologist Irving Kirsch conducts research at Harvard's Program in Placebo Studies.

60 Minutes/CBS News

Kirsch and his colleagues found that most patients improved with *either* antidepressants or placebos (see graph on next page). Antidepressants were found to work better than placebos for some patients—but only those with very high levels of depression, the area shown in blue. Except in that area, the difference between the lines could have simply occurred by chance. Overall, according to Kirsch and his colleagues, about 80 percent of the improvement from antidepressants seems to be due to a placebo effect.

The placebo effect, as discussed in Chapter 1 on page 29 and Chapter 12 on page 512, has been well documented and is not limited to psychological disorders. Placebos have been demonstrated to lead to improvements in a range of health problems, including the management of pain and the treatment of symptoms related to the gastrointestinal, endocrine, cardiovascular, respiratory, and immune systems (Price & others, 2008). For example, in one study, patients with Parkinson's disease experienced improved movement after taking a placebo. In another study, people who simply held a bottle of ibuprofen reported lower levels of pain than people who did not hold the bottle (Price & others, 2008; Rutchick & Slepian, 2013).

You may now be thinking that the placebo effect means that any improvements are just imaginary. But as described in Chapter 12 on page 512, brain imaging shows that placebos lead to real biological changes (Meissner & others, 2011). In response to a placebo, patients with Parkinson's disease experience increased dopamine activation, pain patients saw less neural activity in the parts of the brain associated with pain, and depressed patients experienced metabolic increases in the same parts of the brain that respond to antidepressants (Price & others, 2008). Interestingly, another study found that the effect of a placebo on Parkinson's symptoms was stronger when patients thought the placebo was expensive than when they thought it was cheap (Espay & others, 2015). Either way, improvements tend to come without the side effects and potentially high costs of "real" medication.

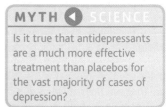

MYTH ◀ SCIENCE

Is it true that antidepressants are a much more effective treatment than placebos for the vast majority of cases of depression?

Electroconvulsive Therapy

As we have just seen, millions of prescriptions are written for antidepressant medications in the United States every year. In contrast, a much smaller number of patients receive **electroconvulsive therapy,** or **ECT,** as a medical treatment for severe cases of major depressive disorder. Also known as *electroshock therapy* or *shock therapy,* electroconvulsive therapy involves using a brief burst of electric current to induce a seizure in the brain, much like an epileptic seizure. Although ECT is most commonly used to treat major depressive disorder, it is occasionally used to treat mania, schizophrenia, and other severe mental disorders (Nahas & Anderson, 2011).

ECT is a relatively simple and quick medical procedure, usually performed in a hospital. The patient lies on a table. Electrodes are placed on one or both of the patient's temples, and the patient is given a short-term, light anesthetic and muscle-relaxing drugs. To ensure adequate airflow, a breathing tube is sometimes placed in the patient's throat.

electroconvulsive therapy (ECT)
A biomedical therapy used primarily in the treatment of major depressive disorder that involves electrically inducing a brief brain seizure; also called *electroshock therapy.*

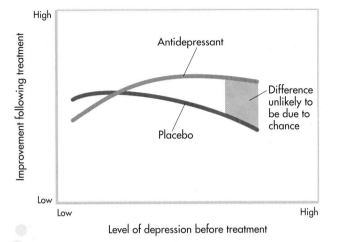

Placebo Versus Antidepressant According to a meta-analysis by psychologist Irving Kirsch and his colleagues (2008), antidepressants work no better than placebos in the treatment of depression for many people. This graph shows improvement for depressed people with varying starting levels of depression—from low depression on the left to high depression on the right. The green line shows improvement for depressed people taking antidepressant medication. The red line shows improvement for depressed people taking placebos. Antidepressants did produce greater improvement for some people, but these differences were only substantial enough to be considered "real" in people with the highest levels of initial depression (area indicated by blue shading).

Source: Data from Kirsch & others (2008).

Kirsch argues that we should question whether it's worth the risk of giving a "real" drug when a placebo is just as effective for some people. But this may be a hard sell to physicians and patients who believe that antidepressants are the most effective treatment for depression. Other researchers view the pharmaceutical industry, which has immense resources, as contributing to exaggerated reports of the effects of medications (Cuijpers & others, 2010). Pharmaceutical companies have billions of dollars at stake in convincing physicians and patients that their medications are effective,

and they spend more than $25 billion each year just in the United States marketing their drugs (Kornfield & others, 2013).

While acknowledging concerns about the influence of the pharmaceutical industry, other researchers have found that antidepressants are superior to placebos. Using different statistical methods, several researchers identified a subset of about 20 percent of patients who benefited from antidepressants over placebos at all levels of depression severity (Horder & others, 2011; Thase & others, 2011). But even these researchers don't entirely dispute Kirsch's findings.

As more is known about the effects of placebos, there is more discussion about how to harness their power. Researchers suggest that clinicians should receive training on ethical ways to openly and successfully prescribe placebos by educating patients about their effectiveness (Brody & Miller, 2011). In the past, clinicians believed that successful treatment with placebos required that the patients believe the placebo was real, but recent research questions this premise. One study on irritable bowel syndrome (IBS) observed improvement in patients even after they were told they were receiving "placebo pills made of an inert substance, like sugar pills, that have been shown in clinical studies to produce significant improvement in IBS symptoms through mind–body self-healing processes" (Kaptchuk & others, 2010).

Research on the placebo effect continues to accumulate. However, despite Kirsch's argument, it's important to remember that many people have been and continue to be helped by antidepressant medication. Other treatment options, such as psychotherapy, may be unavailable. So, if antidepressants are helping you, you should continue to take them as directed by your physician. It can be dangerous to stop taking antidepressant medications without guidance from a physician.

CRITICAL THINKING QUESTIONS

• Why do you think studies that found differences are more likely to be published than studies that found no differences?

• What is the ethical problem with giving a patient a placebo and saying it is an antidepressant?

• Why might simply giving a patient a placebo openly not work without additional education?

While the patient is unconscious, a split-second burst of electricity induces a seizure. The seizure lasts for about a minute. Outwardly, the seizure typically produces mild muscle tremors. After the anesthesia wears off and the patient wakes up, confusion and disorientation may be present for a few hours. Some patients experience a temporary or permanent memory loss for the events leading up to the treatment. To treat major depressive disorder, the patient typically receives two to three treatments per week for two to seven weeks, with less frequent follow-up treatments for several additional months (Fink, 2009).

In the short term, ECT is a very effective treatment for severe cases of major depressive disorder: About 80 percent of patients improve (Rasmussen, 2009). ECT also relieves the symptoms of depression very quickly, typically within days. Author Donald Antrim once described his experience with ECT as "the color came back on" (Sullivan, 2014). And as the symptoms of depression decrease, ECT patients' quality of life tends to increase to a level similar to that in people without depression (McCall & others, 2013).

MYTH ◀ SCIENCE

Is it true that electroconvulsive therapy (ECT), once called "shock therapy," causes permanent brain damage and memory loss?

Because of its rapid therapeutic effects, ECT can be a lifesaving procedure for extremely suicidal or severely depressed patients (Nahas & Anderson, 2011). Such patients may not survive for the several weeks it takes for antidepressant drugs to alleviate symptoms. Antrim, for example, credits ECT with saving his life (Sullivan, 2014).

Typically, ECT is used only after other forms of treatment, including both psychotherapy and medication, have failed to help the patient, especially when depressive symptoms are severe. For some people, such as elderly individuals, ECT may be less dangerous than antidepressant drugs. In general, the complication rate from ECT is very low.

Nevertheless, inducing a brain seizure is not a matter to be taken lightly. ECT has potential dangers. Serious cognitive impairments can occur, such as extensive amnesia and disturbances in language and verbal abilities. However, fears that ECT might produce brain damage have not been confirmed by research (Eschweiler & others, 2007; McDonald & others, 2009).

Perhaps ECT's biggest drawback is that its antidepressive effects can be short-lived. Relapses within four months are relatively common (Glass, 2001). About half the patients treated for major depressive disorder experience a relapse within six months. Today, patients are often treated with long-term antidepressant medication following ECT, which reduces the relapse rate (McCall & others, 2011). In severe, recurrent cases of major depressive disorder, ECT may also be periodically readministered to prevent the return of depressive symptoms.

At this point, you may be wondering why ECT is not in wider use. The reason is that ECT is considered controversial (Dukart & others, 2014; Shorter, 2009). Not everyone agrees that ECT is either safe or effective.

Some have been quite outspoken against it, arguing that its safety and effectiveness are not as great as its supporters have claimed (Andre, 2009). The controversy over ECT is tied to its portrayal in popular media over time. The use of ECT declined drastically in the 1960s and 1970s when it was depicted in many popular books and movies, including *One Flew Over the Cuckoo's Nest,* as a brutal treatment with debilitating side effects (Swartz, 2009). Its use has increased greatly since that time, especially in the past decade or two, with ECT now available in most major metropolitan areas in the United States (Shorter, 2009).

How does ECT work? Despite many decades of research, it's still not known exactly why electrically inducing a convulsion relieves the symptoms of major depressive disorder (Michael, 2009). One theory is that ECT seizures may somehow "reboot" the brain by depleting and then replacing important neurotransmitters (Swartz, 2009).

Some new, experimental treatments suggest that those seizures may not actually be necessary. That is, it may be possible to provide lower levels of electrical current to the brain than traditional ECT delivers and still reduce severe symptoms of depression and other mental illnesses. For example, *transcranial direct current stimulation (tDCS)* is similar to ECT, but uses a small fraction of the electricity (Brunoni & others, 2012; Shiozawa & others, 2014). Another, related treatment is *transcranial magnetic stimulation (TMS),* which involves stimulation of certain regions of the brain with magnetic pulses of various frequencies. Unlike ECT, both tDCS and TMS require no anesthetic, induce no seizures, and can be conducted in a private doctor's office rather than a hospital (Dell'Osso & Altamura, 2014; Janicak & others, 2010; Rosenberg & Dannon, 2009).

Yet another experimental treatment, *vagus nerve stimulation (VNS),* involves the surgical implantation of a device about the size of a pacemaker into the left chest wall. The device provides brief, intermittent electrical stimulation to the left vagus nerve, which runs through the neck and connects to the brain stem (McClintock & others, 2009). Finally, *deep brain stimulation (DBS)* utilizes electrodes surgically implanted in the brain and a battery-powered neurostimulator surgically implanted in the chest. Wires under the skin connect the two implants, and the neurostimulator sends electrical signals to the brain (Fink, 2009; Schläpfer & Bewernick, 2009).

Keep in mind that tDCS, TMS, VNS, and DBS are still experimental, and some of the research findings are mixed (Dougherty & others, in press). And like ECT, the specific mechanism by which they may work is not entirely clear. Still, researchers

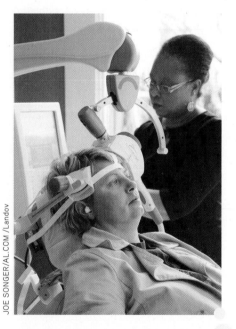

JOE SONGER/AL.COM /Landov

Transcranial Magnetic Stimulation
Tammy, an Alabama woman suffering from depression, receives transcranial magnetic stimulation (TMS) under the oversight of a nurse. TMS involves stimulating brain regions with magnetic pulses. Tammy is able to receive this noninvasive treatment in her doctor's office as opposed to in a hospital.

are hopeful that these techniques will provide additional viable treatment options for people suffering from severe psychological symptoms (McDonald & others, 2009).

❯ Test your understanding of **Biomedical Therapies** with *LEARNINGCurve*.

Closing Thoughts

As you've seen throughout this chapter, a wide range of therapies is available to help people who are troubled by psychological symptoms and disorders. Like our friend Marcia, whose story we told in the Prologue, many people benefit psychologically from psychotherapy. As the first part of the chapter showed, psychotherapy can help people by providing insight, developing more effective behaviors and coping strategies, and changing thought patterns.

The biomedical therapies, discussed in the second part of the chapter, can also help people with psychological problems. This was also true in Marcia's case, when she reluctantly agreed to try an antidepressant medication. For almost a year, Marcia took a low dose of one of the SSRI antidepressant medications. It helped in the short term, lessening the feelings of depression and anxiety and giving her time to work through various issues in therapy and develop greater psychological resilience. Today, people are increasingly being helped by a combination of psychotherapy and one of the psychotropic medications.

As our discussion of the effectiveness of psychotherapy has shown, characteristics of both the therapist and the client are important to the success of psychotherapy. In the Psych for Your Life section at the end of this chapter, we describe the attitudes that should be brought to the therapeutic relationship, discuss some general ground rules of psychotherapy, and dispel some common misunderstandings. The Psych for Your Life section will help you understand the nature of the therapeutic relationship and provide information useful to anyone who may be considering entering psychotherapy.

THE SEVEN DWARFS AFTER THERAPY

Mike Twohy The New Yorker Collection/The Cartoon Bank

What to Expect in Psychotherapy

The cornerstone of psychotherapy is the relationship between the therapist and the person seeking help. But the therapy relationship is different from all other close relationships. On the one hand, the therapist–client relationship is characterized by intimacy and the disclosure of very private, personal experiences. On the other hand, there are distinct boundaries to the therapist–client relationship. To a therapy client, especially one who is undertaking psychotherapy for the first time, the therapy relationship may sometimes seem confusing and contradictory.

The following guidelines should help you understand the special nature of the therapy relationship and develop realistic expectations about the process of psychotherapy.

1. Find a competent, qualified psychotherapist.

Where should you go for help? Most colleges have a student counseling center or medical clinic where you can ask to see a counselor or request a referral to a qualified therapist. You can also ask family members, friends, your family doctor, or a religious leader for suggestions.

If possible, learn more about the therapist before your first visit (APA Help Center, 2012a). What are her qualifications? What approach does she take to treatment? Does she have experience with treating problems like yours?

Along with professional background, personal qualities are also important. When psychotherapists were asked how they chose their own therapists, openness, warmth, and caring were among the top criteria (Nordal, 2010).

Perhaps most importantly, you should feel comfortable with your therapist. Many psychotherapists offer a free initial consultation. So if you don't feel comfortable with the first psychotherapist you meet, don't hesitate to try out a couple of therapists before making your decision (Amada, 2011).

2. Strengthen your commitment to change.

Therapy is not about maintaining the status quo. It is about making changes in terms of how you think, feel, act, and respond. For many people, the idea of change produces mixed feelings. You can increase the likelihood of achieving your goals in therapy by thinking about the reasons you want to change and reminding yourself of your commitment to change (Hettema & others, 2005; Miller & Rose, 2009).

3. Therapy is a collaborative effort.

Don't expect your therapist to do all the work for you. Therapy is a two-way street (APA Help Center, 2012b). If you are going to benefit from psychotherapy, you must actively participate in the therapeutic process. Often, therapy requires effort not only during the therapy sessions but also *outside* them. Many therapists assign "homework" to be completed between sessions. You may be asked to keep a diary of your thoughts and behaviors, read assigned material, rehearse skills that you've learned in therapy, and so forth. Such exercises are important components of the overall therapy process.

4. Don't confuse catharsis with change.

In the chapter Prologue, Marcia mentions the cathartic effect of therapy. *Catharsis* refers to the emotional release that people experience from the simple act of talking about their problems. Although it usually produces short-term emotional relief, catharsis in itself does not resolve the problem. Even so, catharsis is an important element of psychotherapy. Discussing emotionally charged issues with a therapist can lessen your sense of psychological tension and urgency, and can help you explore the problem more rationally and objectively.

5. Don't confuse insight with change.

Despite what you've seen in the movies, developing insight into the sources or nature of your psychological problems does not magically resolve them. Nor does insight automatically translate into healthier thoughts and behaviors. Instead, insight allows you to look at and understand your problems in a new light. The opportunity for change occurs when your therapist helps you use these insights to redefine past experiences, resolve psychological conflicts, and explore more adaptive forms of behavior. Even with the benefit of insight, it takes effort to change how you think, behave, and react to other people.

6. Don't expect your therapist to make decisions for you.

One of the most common misunderstandings about psychotherapy is that your therapist is going to tell you how to run your life. Not so. Virtually all forms of therapy are designed to increase a person's sense of responsibility, confidence, and mastery in dealing with life's problems. Your therapist won't make your decisions for you, but he or she *will* help you explore your feelings about important decisions—including ambivalence or fear. Some people find this frustrating because they want the therapist to tell them what to do. But if your therapist made decisions for you, it would only foster dependency and undermine your ability to be responsible for your own life (Amada, 2011).

7. Expect therapy to challenge how you think and act.

As you confront issues that you've never discussed before or even admitted to yourself, you may find therapy very anxiety-provoking. Moments of psychological discomfort are a normal, even expected, part of the therapy process.

Think of therapy as a psychological magnifying glass. Therapy tends to magnify both your strengths and your weaknesses. Such intense self-scrutiny is not always flattering. Examining how you habitually deal with failure and success, conflict and resolution, and disappointment and joy can be disturbing. You may become

aware of the psychological games you play or of how you use ego defense mechanisms to distort reality. You may have to acknowledge your own immature, maladaptive, or destructive behavior patterns. Although it can be painful, becoming aware that changes are needed is a necessary step toward developing healthier forms of thinking and behavior.

8. Your therapist is not a substitute friend.

Unlike friendship, which is characterized by a mutual give-and-take, psychotherapy is focused solely on *you*. Rather than thinking of your therapist as a friend, think of him or her as an expert consultant—someone you've hired to help you deal better with your problems. The fact that your therapist is not socially or personally involved with you allows him or her to respond objectively and honestly. Part of what allows you to trust your therapist and "open up" emotionally is the knowledge that your therapist is ethically and legally bound to safeguard the confidentiality of what you say.

9. Therapeutic intimacy does not include sexual intimacy.

It's very common for clients to have strong feelings of affection, love, and even sexual attraction toward their therapists (Martin & others, 2011; Pope & Tabachnick, 1993). After all, the most effective therapists tend to be warm, empathic people who are genuinely caring and supportive (Beutler & others, 2004). However, *it is never ethical or appropriate for a therapist to have any form of sexual contact with a client.* There are *no* exceptions to that statement. Sexual contact between a therapist and a client violates the ethical standards of *all* mental health professionals. A psychotherapist who engages in sexual behavior with a client risks losing his or her license to practice psychotherapy.

MYTH ▶ SCIENCE

Is it true that it is never ethical for therapists to date clients?

How often does sexual contact occur? About 9 percent of male therapists and 3 percent of female therapists admit that they have had sexual contact with clients (Pope & others, 2006).

Sexual involvement between client and therapist can be enormously damaging (Norris & others, 2003; Pope & others, 2006b). Not only does it destroy the therapist's professional objectivity, but it also destroys the trust the client has invested in the therapist. When a therapist becomes sexually involved with a client, regardless of who initiated the sexual contact, the client is being exploited.

Rather than exploiting a client's feelings of sexual attraction, an ethical therapist will help the client understand and work through such feelings. Therapy should ultimately help you develop closer, more loving relationships with other people—but *not* with your therapist.

10. Don't expect change to happen overnight.

Change occurs in psychotherapy at different rates for different people. How quickly change occurs depends on many factors, such as the seriousness of your problems, the degree to which you are psychologically ready to make needed changes, and the therapist's skill in helping you implement those changes. As a general rule, most people make significant progress in a few months of weekly therapy sessions (Harnett & others, 2010). You can help create the climate for change by choosing a therapist you feel comfortable working with and by genuinely investing yourself in the therapy process.

CHAPTER REVIEW

KEY PEOPLE AND KEY TERMS

Aaron T. Beck, p. 601

Albert Ellis, p. 599

Sigmund Freud, p.588

Mary Cover Jones, p. 594

Carl Rogers, p. 591

psychotherapy, p. 586

biomedical therapies, p. 586

psychoanalysis (in psychotherapy), p. 588

free association, p. 588

resistance, p. 588

dream interpretation, p. 588

interpretation, p. 588

transference, p. 589

short-term dynamic therapies, p. 589

interpersonal therapy (IPT), p. 590

client-centered therapy, p. 591

behavior therapy, p. 593

counterconditioning, p. 594

exposure therapy, p. 594

systematic desensitization, p. 594

aversive conditioning, p. 597

token economy, p. 598

cognitive therapies, p. 599

rational-emotive behavior therapy (REBT), p. 599

cognitive therapy (CT), p. 601

cognitive-behavioral therapy (CBT), p. 603

group therapy, p. 605

family therapy, p. 608

eclecticism, p. 612

psychotropic medications, p. 614

antipsychotic medications, p. 615

atypical antipsychotic medications, p. 617

antianxiety medications, p. 617

lithium, p. 618

antidepressant medications, p. 619

selective serotonin reuptake inhibitors (SSRIs), p. 619

electroconvulsive therapy (ECT), p. 622

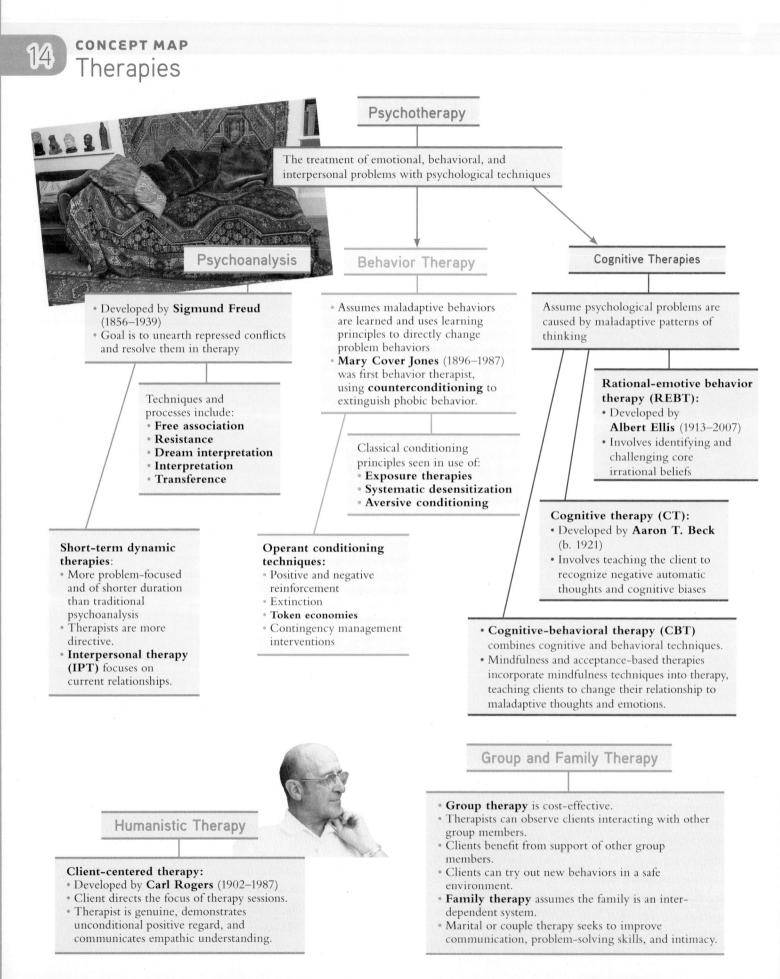

Psychotherapy

The treatment of emotional, behavioral, and interpersonal problems with psychological techniques

Psychoanalysis

- Developed by **Sigmund Freud** (1856–1939)
- Goal is to unearth repressed conflicts and resolve them in therapy

Techniques and processes include:
- **Free association**
- **Resistance**
- **Dream interpretation**
- **Interpretation**
- **Transference**

Short-term dynamic therapies:
- More problem-focused and of shorter duration than traditional psychoanalysis
- Therapists are more directive.
- **Interpersonal therapy (IPT)** focuses on current relationships.

Behavior Therapy

- Assumes maladaptive behaviors are learned and uses learning principles to directly change problem behaviors
- **Mary Cover Jones** (1896–1987) was first behavior therapist, using **counterconditioning** to extinguish phobic behavior.

Classical conditioning principles seen in use of:
- **Exposure therapies**
- **Systematic desensitization**
- **Aversive conditioning**

Operant conditioning techniques:
- Positive and negative reinforcement
- Extinction
- **Token economies**
- Contingency management interventions

Cognitive Therapies

Assume psychological problems are caused by maladaptive patterns of thinking

Rational-emotive behavior therapy (REBT):
- Developed by **Albert Ellis** (1913–2007)
- Involves identifying and challenging core irrational beliefs

Cognitive therapy (CT):
- Developed by **Aaron T. Beck** (b. 1921)
- Involves teaching the client to recognize negative automatic thoughts and cognitive biases

- **Cognitive-behavioral therapy (CBT)** combines cognitive and behavioral techniques.
- Mindfulness and acceptance-based therapies incorporate mindfulness techniques into therapy, teaching clients to change their relationship to maladaptive thoughts and emotions.

Humanistic Therapy

Client-centered therapy:
- Developed by **Carl Rogers** (1902–1987)
- Client directs the focus of therapy sessions.
- Therapist is genuine, demonstrates unconditional positive regard, and communicates empathic understanding.

Group and Family Therapy

- **Group therapy** is cost-effective.
- Therapists can observe clients interacting with other group members.
- Clients benefit from support of other group members.
- Clients can try out new behaviors in a safe environment.
- **Family therapy** assumes the family is an interdependent system.
- Marital or couple therapy seeks to improve communication, problem-solving skills, and intimacy.

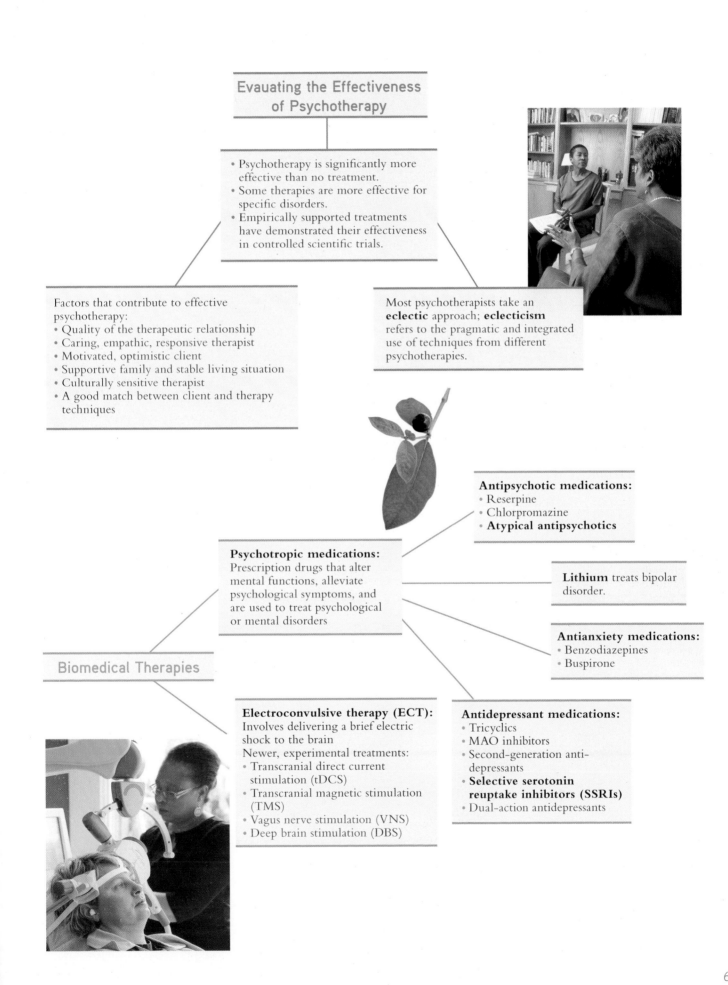

Evauating the Effectiveness of Psychotherapy

- Psychotherapy is significantly more effective than no treatment.
- Some therapies are more effective for specific disorders.
- Empirically supported treatments have demonstrated their effectiveness in controlled scientific trials.

Factors that contribute to effective psychotherapy:
- Quality of the therapeutic relationship
- Caring, empathic, responsive therapist
- Motivated, optimistic client
- Supportive family and stable living situation
- Culturally sensitive therapist
- A good match between client and therapy techniques

Most psychotherapists take an **eclectic** approach; **eclecticism** refers to the pragmatic and integrated use of techniques from different psychotherapies.

Antipsychotic medications:
- Reserpine
- Chlorpromazine
- **Atypical antipsychotics**

Psychotropic medications:
Prescription drugs that alter mental functions, alleviate psychological symptoms, and are used to treat psychological or mental disorders

Lithium treats bipolar disorder.

Antianxiety medications:
- Benzodiazepines
- Buspirone

Biomedical Therapies

Electroconvulsive therapy (ECT):
Involves delivering a brief electric shock to the brain
Newer, experimental treatments:
- Transcranial direct current stimulation (tDCS)
- Transcranial magnetic stimulation (TMS)
- Vagus nerve stimulation (VNS)
- Deep brain stimulation (DBS)

Antidepressant medications:
- Tricyclics
- MAO inhibitors
- Second-generation antidepressants
- **Selective serotonin reuptake inhibitors (SSRIs)**
- Dual-action antidepressants

Statistics: Understanding Data

Marie D. Thomas, *Californis State University, San Marcos*

IN THIS CHAPTER:

❭ Descriptive Statistics

❭ Inferential Statistics

❭ Endnote

THE TABLES ARE TURNED: A PSYCHOLOGIST BECOMES A RESEARCH PARTICIPANT

PROLOGUE

FOR 12 MONTHS I WAS a participant in a research project that was designed to compare the effects of "traditional" and "alternative" diet, exercise, and stress-reduction programs (Riegel & others, 1996). Volunteers who were randomly assigned to the *traditional* program were taught to eat a high-fiber, low-fat diet; do regular aerobic exercise; and practice a progressive muscle relaxation technique. Participants who were randomly assigned to the *alternative* program received instruction in yoga and in a meditation technique, along with a diet based on body type and tastes. I was randomly assigned to the *no-treatment* control group, which was monitored throughout the year for weight and general health but received no diet, exercise, or stress-reduction intervention.

The participants in the study were drawn from a large medical group. Invitations to participate in the study were sent to 15,000 members of the medical group. Out of that initial pool, 124 volunteers were recruited, and about 40 were randomly assigned to each group—the *traditional, alternative,* and *no-treatment control* groups. The participants included men and women between the ages of 20 and 56. A total of 88 participants lasted the full year. The researchers were pleased that so many of us stayed with the project; it isn't easy to get people to commit to a year-long study!

Data collection began even before participants found out the group to which they had been randomly assigned. We were mailed a thick packet of questionnaires covering a wide range of topics. One questionnaire asked about our current health status, use of prescription and over-the-counter medications, use of vitamins, and visits to both physicians and alternative health care practitioners. Another questionnaire focused on self-perceptions of health and well-being. Here we rated our mood, energy level, physical symptoms, and health in general. A lifestyle survey requested information about diet (how often did we eat red meat? how many servings of fruits and vegetables did we consume a day?), exercise

This pie chart shows how much pie I ate while making this chart.

BIZZARRO.COM
Dist. 10 King Features

© BIZZARRO © 2004 Dan Piraro, Dist. By King Features Syndicate.

(how many times per week did we do aerobic exercise?), and behavior (did we smoke cigarettes or consume alcoholic beverages?). The lifestyle survey also assessed psychological variables such as levels of stress and happiness and how well we felt we were coping.

At our first meeting with the researchers, we handed in the questionnaires and were told which of the three groups we had been assigned to. We returned early the next morning to have our blood pressure and weight measured and to have blood drawn for tests of our levels of cholesterol, triglycerides, and glucose. The two intervention groups also received a weekend of training in their respective programs. In addition to daily practice of the techniques they had been taught, people in the *traditional* and *alternative* groups were expected to maintain a "compliance diary"—a daily record of their exercise, diet, and relaxation/meditation activities. The purpose of this diary was to determine whether health outcomes were better for people who practiced the techniques regularly. At first I was disappointed when I was randomly assigned to the control group because I was especially interested in learning the alternative techniques. However, I was relieved later, when I found out how much detailed record keeping the intervention groups had to do!

The researchers accumulated even more data over the year-long period. Every 3 months, our blood pressure and weight were measured.

At 6 and 12 months, the researchers performed blood tests and asked us to fill out questionnaires identical to those we'd completed at the beginning of the project.

The study included many variables. The most important independent variable (the variable that the researcher manipulates) was group assignment: *traditional* program, *alternative* program, or *no-treatment* control. The dependent variables (variables that are not directly manipulated by the researcher but that may change in response to manipulations of the independent variable) included weight, blood pressure, cholesterol level, self-perceptions regarding health, and mood. Since the dependent variables were measured several times, the researchers could study changes in them over the course of the year.

This study can help to answer important questions about the kinds of programs that tend to promote health. But the purpose of describing it here is not just to tell you whether the two intervention programs were effective and whether one worked better than the other. In the next couple of sections, I will use this study to help explain how researchers use **statistics** to (1) summarize the data they have collected and (2) draw conclusions about the data. The job of assessing what conclusions can be drawn from the research findings is the domain of *inferential statistics,* which I'll discuss later in this appendix. We'll begin by exploring how research findings can be summarized in ways that are brief yet meaningful and easy to understand. For this, researchers use descriptive statistics. □

statistics A branch of mathematics used by researchers to organize, summarize, and interpret data.

descriptive statistics Mathematical methods used to organize and summarize data.

frequency distribution A summary of how often various scores occur in a sample of scores. Score values are arranged in order of magnitude, and the number of times each score occurs is recorded.

Descriptive Statistics

The study of programs to promote health generated a large amount of data. How did the researchers make sense of such a mass of information? How did they summarize it in meaningful ways? The answer lies in descriptive statistics. **Descriptive statistics** do just what their name suggests—they describe data. There are many ways to describe information. This appendix will examine four of the most common: frequency distributions, measures of central tendency, measures of variability, and measures of relationships between variables. Since I don't have access to all the data that the health-promotion researchers gathered, I'll use hypothetical numbers to illustrate these statistical concepts.

Frequency Distribution

Suppose that at the start of the health-promotion study 30 people in the traditional group reported getting the following number of hours of aerobic exercise each week:

A table like this is one way of presenting a frequency distribution. It shows at a glance that most of the people in our hypothetical group of 30 were not zealous exercisers before they began their traditional health-promotion program. Nearly two-thirds of them (19 people) engaged in vigorous exercise for two hours or less each week.

TABLE A.1

A Frequency Distribution Table

Hours of Aerobic Exercise per Week	Frequency
0	4
1	7
2	8
3	4
4	3
5	2
6	1
7	1
	30

2, 5, 0, 1, 2, 2, 7, 0, 6, 2, 3, 1, 4, 5, 2, 1, 1, 3, 2, 1, 0, 4, 2, 3, 0, 1, 2, 3, 4, 1

Even with only 30 cases, it is difficult to make much sense of these data. Researchers need a way to organize such *raw scores* so that the information makes sense at a glance. One way to organize the data is to determine how many participants reported exercising zero hours per week, how many reported exercising one hour, and so on, until all the reported amounts are accounted for. If the data were put into a table, the table would look like Table A.1.

This table is one way of presenting a **frequency distribution**—a summary of how often various scores occur. Categories are set up (in this case, the number of hours of aerobic exercise per week), and occurrences of each category are tallied to give the frequency of each one.

What information can be gathered from this frequency distribution table? We know immediately that most of the participants did aerobic exercise less than three hours per week. The number of hours per week peaked at two and declined steadily thereafter. According to the table, the most diligent exerciser worked out about an hour per day.

Some frequency distribution tables include an extra column that shows the percentage of cases in each category. For example, what percentage of participants reported two hours of aerobic exercise per week? The percentage is calculated by dividing the category frequency (8) by the total number of people (30), which yields about 27 percent.

While a table is good for summarizing data, it is often useful to present a frequency distribution visually, with graphs. One type of graph is the **histogram** (Figure A.1). A histogram is like a bar chart with two special features: The bars are always vertical, and they always touch. Categories (in our example, the number of hours of aerobic exercise per week) are placed on the *x* axis (horizontal), and the *y* axis (vertical) shows the frequency of each category. The resulting graph looks something like a city skyline, with buildings of different heights.

Another way of graphing the same data is with a **frequency polygon,** shown in Figure A.2. A mark is made above each category at the point representing its frequency. These marks are then connected by straight lines. In our example, the polygon begins before the "0" category and ends at a category of "8," even though both of these categories have no cases in them. This is traditionally done so that the polygon is a closed figure.

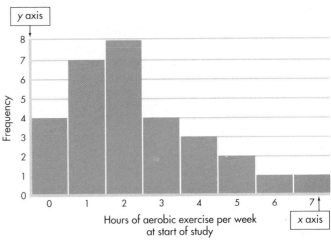

FIGURE A.1 A Histogram This histogram is another way of presenting the data given in Table A.1. Like the table, the histogram shows that most people do, at best, only a moderate amount of aerobic exercise (two hours or less each week). This is immediately clear from the fact that the highest bars on the chart are on the left, where the hours of exercise are lowest.

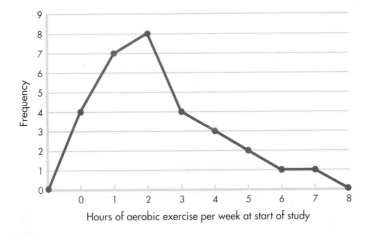

FIGURE A.2 A Frequency Polygon (Positive Skew) Like Table A.1 and Figure A.1, this frequency polygon shows at a glance that the number of hours of aerobic exercise performed weekly is not great for most people. The high points come at one and two hours, which doesn't amount to much more than 10 or 15 minutes of exercise daily. An asymmetrical distribution like this one, which includes mostly low scores, is said to be positively skewed.

Frequency polygons are good for showing the shape of a distribution. The polygon in Figure A.2 looks like a mountain, rising sharply over the first two categories, peaking at 2, and gradually diminishing from there. Such a distribution is asymmetrical, or a **skewed distribution,** meaning that if we drew a line through the middle of the *x* axis (halfway between 3 and 4 hours), more scores would be piled up on one side of the line than on the other. More specifically, the polygon in Figure A.2 represents a *positively skewed* distribution, indicating that most people had low scores. The "tail" of the distribution extends in a positive direction. A *negatively skewed* distribution would

histogram A way of graphically representing a frequency distribution; a type of bar chart that uses vertical bars that touch.

frequency polygon A way of graphically representing a frequency distribution; frequency is marked above each score category on the graph's horizontal axis, and the marks are connected by straight lines.

skewed distribution An asymmetrical distribution; more scores occur on one side of the distribution than on the other. In a *positively* skewed distribution, most of the scores are low scores; in a *negatively* skewed distribution, most of the scores are high scores.

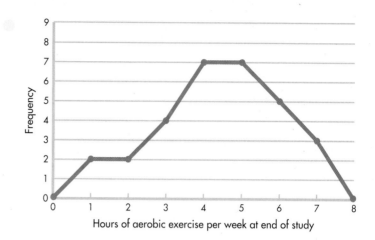

FIGURE A.3 A Frequency Polygon (Negative Skew)
When more scores fall at the high end of a distribution than at the low end, the distribution is said to be negatively skewed. We would expect a negatively skewed distribution if a health-promotion program worked and encouraged more hours of aerobic exercise. The more effective the program, the greater the skew.

have mostly high scores, with fewer scores at the low end of the distribution. In this case, the tail of the distribution extends in a negative direction. For example, if the traditional diet and exercise intervention worked, the 30 participants should, as a group, be exercising more at the end of the study than they had been at the beginning. Perhaps the distribution of hours of aerobic exercise per week at the end of the study would look something like Figure A.3—a distribution with a slight negative skew.

In contrast to skewed distributions, a **symmetrical distribution** is one in which scores fall equally on both halves of the graph. A special case of a symmetrical distribution, the normal curve, is discussed in a later section.

A useful feature of frequency polygons is that more than one distribution can be graphed on the same set of axes. For example, the end-of-study hours of aerobic exercise per week for the *traditional* and *alternative* groups could be compared on a single graph. Doing so would make it possible to see at a glance whether one group was exercising more than the other after a year of their respective programs.

By the way, Figure A.3 is actually a figment of my imagination. According to the diaries kept by the traditional and alternative program participants, compliance with the exercise portion of the program decreased over time. This does not necessarily mean that these participants were exercising *less* at the end of the study than at the beginning, but they certainly did not keep up the program as it was taught to them. Compliance with the prescribed diets was steadier than compliance with exercise; compliance by the alternative group dropped between three months and six months, and then rose steadily over time. There was, however, one major difference between the two intervention groups in terms of compliance. Participants in the alternative group were more likely to be meditating at the end of the study than their traditional group counterparts were to be practicing progressive relaxation.

Measures of Central Tendency

Frequency distributions can be used to organize a set of data and tell us how scores are generally distributed. But researchers often want to put this information into a more compact form. They want to be able to summarize a distribution with a single score that is "typical." To do this, they use a **measure of central tendency.**

THE MODE

The **mode** is the easiest measure of central tendency to calculate. The mode is simply the score or category that occurs most frequently in a set of raw scores or in a frequency distribution. The mode in the frequency distribution shown in Table A.1 is 2; more participants reported exercising two hours per week than any other category. In this example, the mode is an accurate representation of central tendency, but this is not always the case. In the distribution 1, 1, 1, 10, 20, 30, the mode is 1, yet half the scores are 10 and above. This type of distortion is the reason measures of central tendency other than the mode are needed.

symmetrical distribution A distribution in which scores fall equally on both sides of the graph. The normal curve is an example of a symmetrical distribution.

measure of central tendency A single number that presents some information about the "center" of a frequency distribution.

mode The most frequently occurring score in a distribution.

THE MEDIAN

Another way of describing central tendency is to determine the **median,** or the score that falls in the middle of a distribution. If the exercise scores were laid out from lowest to highest, they would look like this:

0, 0, 0, 0, 1, 1, 1, 1, 1, 1, 1, 2, 2, 2, 2, 2, 2, 2, 2, 3, 3, 3, 3, 4, 4, 4, 5, 5, 6, 7
↑

What would the middle score be? Since there are 30 scores, look for the point that divides the distribution in half, with 15 scores on each side of this point. The median can be found between the 15th and 16th scores (indicated by the arrow). In this distribution, the answer is easy: A score of 2 is the median as well as the mode.

THE MEAN

A problem with the mode and the median is that both measures reflect only one score in the distribution. For the mode, the score of importance is the most frequent one; for the median, it is the middle score. A better measure of central tendency is usually one that reflects *all* scores. For this reason, the most commonly used measure of central tendency is the **mean,** or arithmetic average. You have calculated the mean many times. It is computed by summing a set of scores and then dividing by the number of scores that went into the sum. In our example, adding together the exercise distribution scores gives a total of 70; the number of scores is 30, so 70 divided by 30 gives a mean of 2.33.

Formulas are used to express how a statistic is calculated. The formula for the mean is

$$\overline{X} = \frac{\Sigma X}{N}$$

In this formula, each letter and symbol has a specific meaning:

$\overline{X}$ is the symbol for the mean. (Sometimes you'll see M used as the symbol of the mean instead.)

Σ is sigma, the Greek letter for capital S, and it stands for "sum." (Taking a course in statistics is one way to learn the Greek alphabet!)

X represents the scores in the distribution, so the numerator of the equation says, "Sum up all the scores."

N is the total number of scores in the distribution. Therefore, the formula says, "The mean equals the sum of all the scores divided by the total number of scores."

Although the mean is usually the most representative measure of central tendency because each score in a distribution enters into its computation, it is particularly susceptible to the effect of extreme scores. Any unusually high or low score will pull the mean in its direction. Suppose, for example, that in our frequency distribution for aerobic exercise, one exercise zealot worked out 70 hours per week. The mean number of aerobic exercise hours would jump from 2.33 to 4.43. This new mean is deceptively high, given that most of the scores in the distribution are 2 and below. Because of just that one extreme score, the mean has become less representative of the distribution. Frequency tables and graphs are important tools for helping us identify extreme scores *before* we start computing statistics.

Measures of Variability

In addition to identifying the central tendency in a distribution, researchers may want to know how much the scores in that distribution differ from one another. Are they grouped closely together or widely spread out? To answer this question, we need some **measure of variability.** Figure A.4 shows two distributions with the same mean but with different variability.

A simple way to measure variability is with the **range,** which is computed by subtracting the lowest score in the distribution from the highest score. Let's say that there are 15 participants in the traditional diet and exercise group and that their weights at the beginning of the study varied from a low of 95 pounds to a high of 155 pounds. The range of weights in this group would be 155 − 95 = 60 pounds.

median The score that divides a frequency distribution exactly in half so that the same number of scores lie on each side of it.

mean The sum of a set of scores in a distribution divided by the number of scores; the mean is usually the most representative measure of central tendency.

measure of variability A single number that presents information about the spread of scores in a distribution.

range A measure of variability; the highest score in a distribution minus the lowest score.

FIGURE A.4 Distributions with Different Variability Two distributions with the same mean can have very different variability, or spread, as shown in these two curves. Notice how one is more spread out than the other; its scores are distributed more widely.

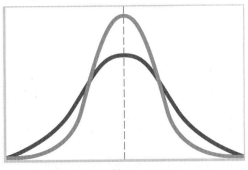

Mean

standard deviation A measure of variability; expressed as the square root of the sum of the squared deviations around the mean divided by the number of scores in the distribution.

As a measure of variability, the range provides a limited amount of information because it depends on only the two most extreme scores in a distribution (the highest and lowest scores). A more useful measure of variability would give some idea of the average amount of variation in a distribution. But variation from what? The most common way to measure variability is to determine how far scores in a distribution vary from the distribution's mean. We saw earlier that the mean is usually the best way to represent the "center" of the distribution, so the mean seems like an appropriate reference point.

What if we subtract the mean from each score in a distribution to get a general idea of how far each score is from the center? When the mean is subtracted from a score, the result is a *deviation* from the mean. Scores that are above the mean would have positive deviations, and scores that are below the mean would have negative deviations. To get an average deviation, we would need to sum the deviations and divide by the number of deviations that went into the sum. There is a problem with this procedure, however. If deviations from the mean are added together, the sum will be 0 because the negative and positive deviations will cancel each other out. In fact, the real definition of the mean is "the only point in a distribution where all the scores' deviations from it add up to 0."

We need to somehow "get rid of" the negative deviations. In mathematics, such a problem is solved by squaring. If a negative number is squared, it becomes positive. So instead of simply adding up the deviations and dividing by the number of scores (N), we first square each deviation and then add together the *squared* deviations and divide by N. Finally, we need to compensate for the squaring operation. To do this, we take the square root of the number just calculated. This leaves us with the **standard deviation.** The larger the standard deviation, the more spread out are the scores in a distribution.

Let's look at an example to make this clearer. Table A.2 lists the hypothetical weights of the 15 participants in the traditional group at the beginning of the study. The mean, which is the sum of the weights divided by 15, is calculated to be 124 pounds, as shown at the bottom of the left-hand column. The first step in computing the standard deviation is to subtract the mean from each score, which gives that score's deviation from

To calculate the standard deviation, you simply add all the scores in a distribution (the left-hand column in this example) and divide by the total number of scores to get the mean. Then you subtract the mean from each score to get a list of deviations from the mean (third column). Next you square each deviation (fourth column), add the squared deviations together, divide by the total number of cases, and take the square root.

TABLE A.2

Calculating the Standard Deviation

Weight X	Mean $\overline{X}$	Weight − Mean $X - \overline{X}$	(Weight − Mean) Squared $(X - \overline{X})^2$
155	124	31	961
149	124	25	625
142	124	18	324
138	124	14	196
134	124	10	100
131	124	7	49
127	124	3	9
125	124	1	1
120	124	−4	16
115	124	−9	81
112	124	−12	144
110	124	−14	196
105	124	−19	361
102	124	−22	484
95	124	−29	841
Sum (Σ) = 1,860		$\Sigma = 0$	$\Sigma = 4,388$
Mean ($\overline{X}$) = 124			

$$SD = \sqrt{\frac{\Sigma(x - \overline{x})^2}{N}} = \sqrt{\frac{4,388}{15}} = 17.10$$

the mean. These deviations are listed in the third column of the table. The next step is to square each of the deviations (done in the fourth column), add the squared deviations ($\Sigma(X - \overline{X})^2 = 4{,}388$), and divide that total by the number of participants ($N = 15$). Finally, we take the square root to obtain the standard deviation ($SD = 17.10$). The formula for the standard deviation (SD) incorporates these instructions:

$$SD = \sqrt{\frac{\Sigma(X - \overline{X})^2}{N}}$$

Notice that when scores have large deviations from the mean, the *standard deviation* is also large.

z Scores and the Normal Curve

The mean and the standard deviation provide useful descriptive information about an entire set of scores. But researchers can also describe the relative position of any individual score in a distribution. This is done by locating how far away from the mean the score is in terms of standard deviation units. A statistic called a **z score** gives us this information:

$$z = \frac{X - \overline{X}}{SD}$$

This equation says that to compute a z score, we subtract the mean from the score we are interested in (that is, we calculate its deviation from the mean) and divide this quantity by the standard deviation. A positive z score indicates that the score is above the mean, and a negative z score shows that the score is below the mean. The larger the z score, the farther away from the mean the score is.

Let's take an example from the distribution found in Table A.2. What is the z score of a weight of 149 pounds? To find out, you simply subtract the mean from 149 and divide by the standard deviation.

$$z = \frac{149 - 124}{17.10} = 1.46$$

A z score of +1.46 tells us that a person weighing 149 pounds falls about one and a half standard deviations above the mean. In contrast, a person weighing 115 pounds has a weight below the mean and would have a negative z score. If you calculate this z score, you will find it is −0.53. This means that a weight of 115 is a little more than one-half a standard deviation below the mean.

Some variables, such as height, weight, and IQ, if graphed for large numbers of people, fall into a characteristic pattern. Figure A.5 shows this pattern, which is called the **standard normal curve** or the **standard normal distribution.** The normal curve is symmetrical (that is, if a line is drawn down its center, one side of the curve is a mirror image of the other side), and the mean, median, and mode fall exactly in the middle. The x axis of Figure A.5 is marked off in standard deviation units, which, conveniently, are also z scores. Notice that most of the cases fall between −1 and +1 SDs, with the number of cases sharply tapering off at either end. This pattern is the reason the normal curve is often described as "bell shaped."

The great thing about the normal curve is that we know exactly what percentage of the distribution falls between any two points on the curve. Figure A.5 shows the percentages of cases between major standard deviation units. For example, 34 percent of the distribution falls between 0 and +1.

z score A number, expressed in standard deviation units, that shows a score's deviation from the mean.

standard normal curve or **standard normal distribution** A symmetrical distribution forming a bell-shaped curve in which the mean, median, and mode are all equal and fall in the exact middle.

FIGURE A.5 The Standard Normal Curve The standard normal curve has several characteristics. Most apparent is its symmetrical bell shape. On such a curve, the mean, the median, and the mode all fall at the same point. But not every curve that is shaped roughly like a bell is a standard normal curve. With a normal curve, specific percentages of the distribution fall within each standard deviation unit from the mean. These percentages are shown on the graph. (Because of rounding, percentages add up to more than 100%.)

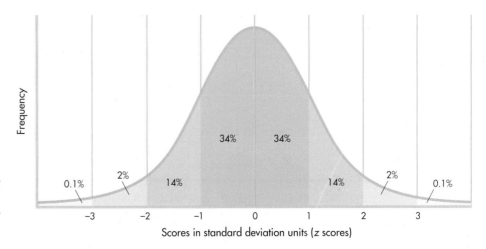

correlation The relationship between two variables.

correlation coefficient A numerical indication of the magnitude and direction of the relationship (the *correlation*) between two variables.

positive correlation A finding that two factors vary systematically in the same direction, increasing or decreasing together.

negative correlation A finding that two factors vary systematically in opposite directions, one increasing as the other decreases.

scatter diagram or **scatter plot** A graph that represents the relationship between two variables.

That means that 84 percent of the distribution falls *below* one standard deviation (the 34 percent that is between 0 and +1, plus the 50 percent that falls below 0). A person who obtains a z score of +1 on some normally distributed variable has scored better than 84 percent of the other people in the distribution. If a variable is normally distributed (that is, if it has the standard bell-shaped pattern), a person's z score can tell us exactly where that person stands relative to everyone else in the distribution.

Correlation

So far, the statistical techniques we've looked at focus on one variable at a time, such as hours of aerobic exercise weekly or pounds of weight. Other techniques allow us to look at the relationship, or **correlation,** between two variables. Statistically, the magnitude and direction of the relationship between two variables can be expressed by a single number called a **correlation coefficient.**

To compute a correlation coefficient, we need two sets of measurements from the same individuals or from pairs of people who are similar in some way. To take a simple example, let's determine the correlation between height (we'll call this the x variable) and weight (the y variable). We start by obtaining height and weight measurements for each individual in a group. The idea is to combine all these measurements into one number that expresses something about the relationship between the two variables, height and weight. However, we are immediately confronted with a problem: The two variables are measured in different ways. Height is measured in inches, and weight is measured in pounds. We need some way to place both variables on a single scale.

Think back to our discussion of the normal curve and z scores. What do z scores do? They take data of any form and put them into a standard scale. Remember, too, that a high score in a distribution always has a positive z score, and a low score in a distribution always has a negative z score. To compute a correlation coefficient, the data from both variables of interest can be converted to z scores. Therefore, each individual will have two z scores: one for height (the x variable) and one for weight (the y variable).

Then, to compute the correlation coefficient, each person's two z scores are multiplied together. All these "cross-products" are added up, and this sum is divided by the number of individuals. In other words, a correlation coefficient is the average (or mean) of the z-score cross-products of the two variables being studied:

$$\text{correlation coefficient} = \frac{\Sigma z_x z_y}{N}$$

A correlation coefficient can range from +1.00 to −1.00. The exact number provides two pieces of information: It tells us about the *magnitude* of the relationship being measured, and it tells us about its *direction*. The magnitude, or degree, of relationship is indicated by the size of the number. A number close to 1 (whether positive or negative) indicates a strong relationship, while a number close to 0 indicates a weak relationship. The sign (+ or −) of the correlation coefficient tells us about the relationship's direction.

A **positive correlation** means that as one variable increases in size, the second variable also increases. For example, height and weight are positively correlated: As height increases, weight tends to increase also. In terms of z scores, a positive correlation means that high z scores on one variable tend to be multiplied by high z scores on the other variable and that low z scores on one variable tend to be multiplied by low z scores on the other. Remember that just as two positive numbers multiplied together result in a positive number, so two negative numbers multiplied together also result in a positive number. When the cross-products are added together, the sum in both cases is positive.

A **negative correlation,** in contrast, means that two variables are *inversely* related. As one variable increases in size, the other variable decreases. For example, professors like to believe that the more hours students study, the fewer errors they will make on exams. In z-score language, high z scores (which are positive) on one variable (more hours of study) tend to be multiplied

by low z scores (which are negative) on the other variable (fewer errors on exams), and vice versa, making negative cross-products. When the cross-products are summed and divided by the number of cases, the result is a negative correlation coefficient.

An easy way to show different correlations is with graphs. Plotting two variables together creates a **scatter diagram** or **scatter plot,** like the ones in Figures A.6, A.7, and A.8. These figures show the relationship between complying with some component of the alternative health-promotion program and some other variable related to health. Although the figures describe relationships actually found in the study, I have made up the specific correlations to illustrate key points.

Figure A.6 shows a moderately strong positive relationship between compliance with the yoga part of the alternative program and a person's energy level. You can see this just by looking at the pattern of the data points. They generally form a line running from the lower left to the upper right. When calculated, this particular correlation coefficient is +.59, which indicates a correlation roughly in the middle between 0 and +1.00. In other words, people who did more yoga tended to have higher energy levels. The "tended to" part is important. Some people who did not comply well with the yoga routine still had high energy levels, while the reverse was also true. A +1.00 correlation, or a *perfect* positive correlation, would indicate that frequent yoga sessions were *always* accompanied by high levels of energy, and vice versa. What would a scatter diagram of a perfect +1.00 correlation look like? It would be a straight diagonal line starting in the lower left-hand corner of the graph and progressing to the upper right-hand corner.

Several other positive correlations were found in this study. Compliance with the alternative diet was positively associated with increases in energy and positive health perceptions. In addition, following the high-fiber, low-fat traditional diet was associated with a higher level of coping and high vitamin intake.

The study also found some negative correlations. Figure A.7 illustrates a *negative* correlation between compliance with the meditation part of the alternative program and cigarette smoking. This correlation coefficient is −.77. Note that the data points fall in the opposite direction from those in Figure A.6, indicating that as the frequency of meditation increased, cigarette smoking decreased. The pattern of points in Figure A.7 is closer to a straight line than is the pattern of points in Figure A.6. A correlation of −.77 shows a relationship of greater magnitude than does a correlation of +.59. But though −.77 is a relatively high correlation, it is not a perfect relationship. A *perfect* negative relationship would be illustrated by a straight diagonal line starting in the upper left-hand corner of the graph and ending at the lower right-hand corner.

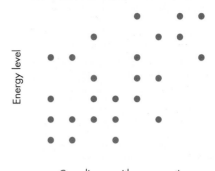

Compliance with yoga routine

FIGURE A.6 Scatter Plot of a Positive Correlation A correlation (or the lack of one) can be clearly shown on a scatter plot. This one shows a moderately strong positive correlation between participants' compliance with the yoga component of the alternative health-promotion program and their energy level. The positive direction of the correlation is indicated by the upward-sloping pattern of the dots, from bottom left to top right. This means that if one variable is high, the other tends to be high, too, and vice versa. That the strength of the relationship is only moderate is indicated by the fact that the data points (each indicating an individual participant's score) are not all positioned along a straight diagonal line.

Compliance with meditation routine

FIGURE A.7 Scatter Plot of a Negative Correlation In general, people who engage in meditation more often tend to smoke less. This negative correlation is indicated by the downward-sloping pattern of dots, from upper left to lower right. Because these dots are clustered somewhat closer together than those in Figure A.6, we can tell at a glance that the relationship here is somewhat stronger.

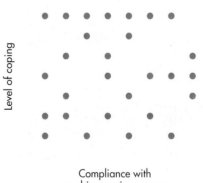

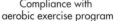

Compliance with aerobic exercise program

FIGURE A.8 Scatter Plot of No Correlation You may be surprised to learn that in this study, compliance with the aerobic exercise portion of the traditional program was not related to level of coping. This scatter plot shows that lack of relationship. The points fall randomly, revealing no general direction or trend and thus indicating the absence of a correlation.

Finally, Figure A.8 shows two variables that are not related to each other. The hypothetical correlation coefficient between compliance with the aerobic exercise part of the traditional program and a person's level of coping is +.03, barely above 0. In the scatter diagram, data points fall randomly, with no general direction to them. From a z-score point of view, when two variables are not related, the cross-products are mixed—that is, some are positive and some are negative. Sometimes high z scores on one variable go with high z scores on the other, and low z scores on one variable go with low z scores on the other. In both cases, positive cross-products result. In other pairs of scores, high z scores on one variable go with low z scores on the other variable (and vice versa), producing negative cross-products. When the cross-products for the two variables are summed, the positive and negative numbers cancel each other out, resulting in a 0 (or close to 0) correlation.

In addition to describing the relationship between two variables, correlation coefficients are useful for another purpose: prediction. If we know a person's score on one of two related variables, we can predict how he or she will perform on the other variable. For example, in a recent issue of a magazine, I found a quiz to rate my risk of heart disease. I assigned myself points depending on my age, HDL ("good") and total cholesterol levels, systolic blood pressure, and other risk factors, such as cigarette smoking and diabetes. My total points (−2) indicated that I had less than a 1 percent risk of developing heart disease in the next five years. How could such a quiz be developed? Each of the factors I rated is correlated to some degree with heart disease. The older you are and the higher your cholesterol and blood pressure, the greater your chance of developing heart disease. Statistical techniques are used to determine the relative importance of each of these factors and to calculate the points that should be assigned to each level of a factor. Combining these factors provides a better prediction than any single factor because none of the individual risk factors correlate perfectly with the development of heart disease.

One thing you cannot conclude from a correlation coefficient is *causality*. In other words, the fact that two variables are highly correlated does not necessarily mean that one variable directly causes the other. Take the meditation and cigarette-smoking correlation. This negative correlation tells us that people in the study who diligently practiced meditation tended to smoke less than those who seldom meditated. Regular meditation may have had a direct effect on the desire to smoke cigarettes, but it is also possible that one or more other variables affected both meditation and smoking. For example, perhaps participation in the study convinced some people that they needed to change their lifestyles completely. Both compliance with the meditation routine and a decreased level of cigarette smoking may have been "caused" by this change in lifestyle. As discussed in Chapter 1, the *experimental method* is the only method that can provide compelling scientific evidence of a cause-and-effect relationship between two or more variables. Can you think of a way to test the hypothesis that regularly practicing meditation causes a reduction in the desire to smoke cigarettes?

Inferential Statistics

Let's say that the mean number of physical symptoms (like pain) experienced by the participants in each of the three groups was about the same at the beginning of the health-promotion study. A year later, the number of symptoms had decreased in the two intervention groups but had remained stable in the control group. This may or may not be a meaningful result. We would expect the average number of symptoms to be somewhat different for each of the three groups because each group consisted of different people. And we would expect some fluctuation in level over time, due simply to chance. But are the differences in the number of symptoms between the intervention groups and the control group large enough *not* to be due to chance alone? If other researchers conducted the same study with different participants, would they be likely to get the same general pattern of results? To answer such questions, we turn to inferential statistics. **Inferential statistics** guide us in determining what inferences, or conclusions, can legitimately be drawn from a set of research findings.

Depending on the data, different inferential statistics can be used to answer questions such as the ones raised in the preceding paragraph. For example, *t* tests are used to compare the means of two groups. Researchers could use a *t* test, for instance, to compare average energy level at the end of the study in the traditional and alternative groups. Another *t* test could compare the average energy level at the beginning and end of the study within the alternative group. If we wanted to compare the means of more than two groups, another technique, *analysis of variance* (often abbreviated as ANOVA), could be used. Each inferential statistic helps us determine how likely a particular finding is to have occurred as a matter of nothing more than chance or random variation. If the inferential statistic indicates that the odds of a particular finding occurring are considerably greater than mere chance, we can conclude that our results are *statistically significant*. In other words, we can conclude with a high degree of confidence that the manipulation of the independent variable, rather than simply chance, is the reason for the results.

To see how this works, let's go back to the normal curve for a moment. Remember that we know exactly what percentage of a normal curve falls between any two *z* scores. If we choose one person at random out of a normal distribution, what is the chance that this person's *z* score is above +2? If you look at Figure A.9 (it's the same as Figure A.5), you will see that about 2.1 percent of the curve lies above a *z* score (or standard deviation unit) of +2. Therefore, the chance, or *probability,* that the person we choose will have a *z* score above +2 is .021 (or 2.1 chances out of 100). That's a pretty small chance. If you study the normal curve, you will see that the majority of cases (about 96 percent) fall between −2 and +2 *SD*s, so in choosing a person at random, that person is not likely to fall above a *z* score of +2.

When researchers test for statistical significance, they usually employ statistics other than *z* scores, and they may use distributions that differ in shape from the normal curve. The logic, however, is the same. They compute some kind of inferential statistic that they compare to the appropriate distribution. This comparison tells them the likelihood of obtaining their results if chance alone is operating.

The problem is that no test exists that will tell us for sure whether our intervention or manipulation "worked"; we always have to deal with probabilities, not certainties. Researchers have developed some conventions to guide them in their decisions about whether or not their study results are statistically significant. Generally, when the probability of obtaining a particular result if random factors alone are operating is less than .05 (5 chances out of 100), the results are considered statistically significant. Researchers who want to be even more sure set their probability value at .01 (1 chance out of 100).

inferential statistics Mathematical methods used to determine how likely it is that a study's outcome is due to chance and whether the outcome can be legitimately generalized to a larger population.

***t* test** Test used to establish whether the means of two groups are statistically different from each other.

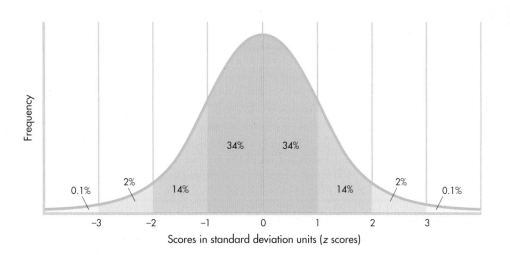

FIGURE A.9 The Standard Normal Curve

Type I error Erroneously concluding that study results are significant.

Type II error Failing to find a significant effect that does, in fact, exist.

population A complete set of something—people, nonhuman animals, objects, or events.

sample A subset of a population.

Because researchers deal with probabilities, there is a small but real possibility of *erroneously* concluding that study results are significant; this is called a **Type I error.** The results of one study, therefore, should never be completely trusted. For researchers to have greater confidence in a particular effect or result, the study should be repeated, or *replicated.* If the same results are obtained in different studies, then we can be more certain that our conclusions about a particular intervention or effect are correct.

There is a second decision error that can be made—a **Type II error.** This is when a researcher fails to find a significant effect, yet that significant effect really exists. A Type II error results when a study does not have enough *power;* in a sense, the study is not strong enough to find the effect the researcher is looking for. Higher power may be achieved by improving the research design and measuring instruments, or by increasing the number of participants being studied.

One final point about inferential statistics. Are the researchers interested only in the changes that might have occurred in the small groups of people participating in the health-promotion study, or do they really want to know whether the interventions would be effective for people in general? This question focuses on the difference between a population and a sample. A **population** is a complete set of something—people, nonhuman animals, objects, or events. The researchers who designed this study wanted to know whether the interventions they developed would benefit *all* people (or, more precisely, all people between the ages of 20 and 56). Obviously, they could not conduct a study on this entire population. The best they could do was choose some portion of that population to serve as participants; in other words, they selected a **sample.** The study was conducted on this sample. The researchers analyzed the sample results, using inferential statistics to make guesses about what they would have found had they studied the entire population. Inferential statistics allow researchers to take the findings they obtain from a sample and apply them to a population.

So what did the health-promotion study find? Did the interventions work? The answer is "yes," sort of. The traditional and alternative treatment groups, when combined, improved more than did the no-treatment control group. At the end of the study, participants in the two intervention programs had, on average, better self-perceptions regarding health, better mood, more energy, and fewer physical symptoms. Compared with the traditional and the no-treatment groups, the alternative group showed greater average improvement in health perceptions and a significant decrease in depression and the use of prescription drugs. Interestingly, participation in the treatment groups did not generally result in changes in health risk, such as lowered blood pressure or decreased weight. The researchers believe that little change occurred because the people who volunteered for the study were basically healthy individuals. The study needs to be replicated with a less healthy sample. In sum, the intervention programs seemed to have a greater effect on health perceptions and psychological variables than on physical variables. The researchers concluded that a health-promotion regimen (either traditional or alternative) is helpful. I'm sure other studies will be conducted to explore these issues further!

Endnote

Although I briefly saw other study participants at each three-month data-collection point, I never spoke to anyone. The last measurement session, however, was also a celebration for our year-long participation in the project. Approximately 30 people attended my session, and participants from each of the three groups were present. After our blood was drawn and our blood pressure and weight readings were taken, we were treated to breakfast. Then one of the principal researchers *debriefed* us: She gave us some background on the study and told us what she hoped to learn. At this point, participants were given the opportunity to talk about how the study had affected their lives. It was

"It's my fervent hope, Fernbaugh, that these are meaningless statistics."

fascinating to hear members of the intervention groups describe the changes they had made over the past year. One woman said that a year ago she could never imagine getting up early to meditate, yet now she looks forward to awakening each morning at 4:00 A.M. for her first meditation session. Other people described the modifications they had made in their diet and exercise patterns and how much better they felt. Although I did not experience either of the interventions, I know that simply being a participant in the study made me more conscious of what I ate and how much I exercised. This could have been a confounding factor; that is, it could have inadvertently changed my behavior even though I was in the control group. In fact, my weight decreased and my level of "good" cholesterol increased over the course of the year.

We were not paid for our participation in this study, but we received small gifts as tokens of the researchers' appreciation. In addition, we were all given the option of taking any or all of the intervention training at no cost (and some courses in alternative techniques could be quite expensive). The most important thing for me was the satisfaction of participation—the fact that I had stayed with the study for an entire year and, in a small way, had made a contribution to science.

APPENDIX REVIEW

KEY TERMS

statistics, p. A-2

descriptive statistics, p. A-2

frequency distribution, p. A-2

histogram, p. A-3

frequency polygon, p. A-3

skewed distribution, p. A-3

symmetrical distribution, p. A-4

measure of central tendency, p. A-4

mode, p. A-4

median, p. A-5

mean, p. A-5

measure of variability, p. A-5

range, p. A-5

standard deviation, p. A-6

z score, p. A-7

standard normal curve (standard normal distribution), p. A-7

correlation, p. A-8

correlation coefficient, p. A-8

positive correlation, p. A-8

negative correlation, p. A-8

scatter diagram (scatter plot), p. A-8

inferential statistics, p. A-11

t test, p. A-11

Type I error, p. A-12

Type II error, p. A-12

population, p. A-12

sample, p. A-12

CONCEPT MAP

Statistics: Understanding Data

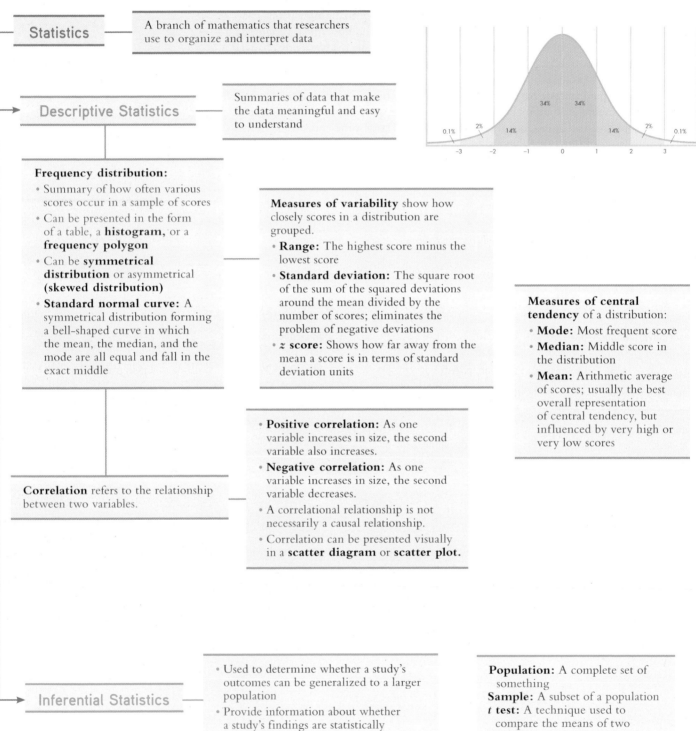

Statistics — A branch of mathematics that researchers use to organize and interpret data

Descriptive Statistics — Summaries of data that make the data meaningful and easy to understand

Frequency distribution:
- Summary of how often various scores occur in a sample of scores
- Can be presented in the form of a table, a **histogram,** or a **frequency polygon**
- Can be **symmetrical distribution** or asymmetrical **(skewed distribution)**
- **Standard normal curve:** A symmetrical distribution forming a bell-shaped curve in which the mean, the median, and the mode are all equal and fall in the exact middle

Measures of variability show how closely scores in a distribution are grouped.
- **Range:** The highest score minus the lowest score
- **Standard deviation:** The square root of the sum of the squared deviations around the mean divided by the number of scores; eliminates the problem of negative deviations
- *z* **score:** Shows how far away from the mean a score is in terms of standard deviation units

Measures of central tendency of a distribution:
- **Mode:** Most frequent score
- **Median:** Middle score in the distribution
- **Mean:** Arithmetic average of scores; usually the best overall representation of central tendency, but influenced by very high or very low scores

Correlation refers to the relationship between two variables.

- **Positive correlation:** As one variable increases in size, the second variable also increases.
- **Negative correlation:** As one variable increases in size, the second variable decreases.
- A correlational relationship is not necessarily a causal relationship.
- Correlation can be presented visually in a **scatter diagram** or **scatter plot.**

Inferential Statistics
- Used to determine whether a study's outcomes can be generalized to a larger population
- Provide information about whether a study's findings are statistically significant

Population: A complete set of something
Sample: A subset of a population
t **test:** A technique used to compare the means of two groups

Industrial/Organizational Psychology

Claudia Cochran-Miller *El Paso Community College*

Marie Waung *University of Michigan, Dearborn*[1]

IN THIS CHAPTER:

> What Is Industrial/Organizational Psychology?

> History of I/O Psychology

> Industrial (Personnel) Psychology

> Organizational Behavior

> Workplace Trends and Issues

> Employment Settings, Type of Training, Earnings, and Employment Outlook

IN THE POPULAR TELEVISION SIT-COM *The Office,* Steve Carrell played Michael Scott, branch office manager of a fictitious paper company. Claiming to be "friend first, boss second," Michael taught viewers exactly what a manager should *not* say or do. In an episode about sexual harassment, for example, Michael reluctantly announced that he was giving up all non-work-related conversations and jokes, only to immediately lapse into coarse sexual innuendo. As a manager, Michael was incompetent, narcissistic, inconsiderate, and blatantly oblivious to any of his deficiencies.

Many of us recognize parts of this character at our own workplaces. And this is probably why the show has been so successful. Today's workplace is governed by standards, policies, rules, and laws—all of which Michael flouted on a daily basis. Leading others

Steve Carrell as Michael Scott in the television sitcom *The Office.*

takes insight, passion, and know-how, none of which Michael possessed. Unfortunately, many managers receive little or no training about assessment, leadership, human relations, human motivation, and the like. Consequently they are often ill-equipped to be effective managers, just like our beloved Michael.

Leadership development has been one of the greatest challenges in the world of industrial and organizational psychology (I/O). This field of psychology also helps build teams, streamline processes, increase job satisfaction, and transform workplace culture, among other objectives. This appendix will introduce you to the many benefits of bringing psychology to the workplace. So, Michael, listen up. ☐

What Is Industrial/ Organizational Psychology?

Industrial/organizational (I/O) psychology is the branch of psychology that focuses on the study of human behavior in the workplace. The "industrial," or "I," side of I/O psychology focuses on measuring human characteristics and matching those characteristics to particular jobs. This process involves applying psychological

industrial/organizational (I/O) psychology The branch of psychology that focuses on the study of human behavior in the workplace.

[1]Claudia Cochran-Miller and Marie Waung contributed equally to this appendix.

personnel psychology A subarea of I/O psychology that focuses on matching people's characteristics to job requirements, accurately measuring job performance, and assessing employee training needs.

organizational behavior A subarea of I/O psychology that focuses on the workplace culture and its influence on employee behavior.

research findings to personnel functions such as pre-employment testing, placement, training and development, and performance management. This specialty, often called **personnel psychology,** helps companies attract, recruit, select, and train the best employees for the organization.

In contrast, the "organizational," or "O," side focuses on the workplace culture and its influence on employee behavior. Organizational psychology helps companies develop a culture that fulfills organizational goals while addressing employee needs. Organizational psychologists, then, apply psychological findings to areas such as leadership development, team building, motivation, ethics training, and wellness planning. The "O" side of I/O psychology is also called **organizational behavior.** In their research and work, I/O psychologists generally concentrate on the content areas described below:

1. **JOB ANALYSIS.** Job analysts must determine the duties of a particular position, as well as the personal characteristics that best match those duties.

2. **SELECTION AND PLACEMENT.** This area includes the development of assessment techniques to help select job applicants most likely to be successful in a given job or organization.

3. **TRAINING AND DEVELOPMENT.** Psychologists in this field may design customized training programs and evaluate the effectiveness of those programs.

4. **PERFORMANCE MANAGEMENT AND EVALUATION.** Companies are often concerned with ways to improve their performance evaluation systems. Performance management systems include teaching managers how to collect evaluation data, how to avoid evaluation errors, and how to communicate the results.

5. **ORGANIZATIONAL DEVELOPMENT.** The goal of organizational development (OD) is to bring about positive change in an organization, through assessment of the organizational social environment and culture.

6. **LEADERSHIP DEVELOPMENT.** Leadership research strives to identify the traits, behaviors, and skills that great leaders have in common. One goal is matching an organization's mission with the optimal leadership profile.

7. **TEAM BUILDING.** Team membership and successful team design are critical to the needs of today's organizations.

8. **QUALITY OF WORK LIFE.** Psychologists in this area study the factors that contribute to a productive and healthy workforce, such as perk packages and employee-centered policies.

9. **ERGONOMICS.** The focus of ergonomics is the design of equipment and the development of work procedures based on human capabilities and limitations. Ergonomics helps employers provide healthier and safer workplaces.

Designing for People One subarea of industrial/organizational psychology is concerned with the human factors involved in the use of workplace procedures and equipment. For example, this factory's procedure for tightening bolts on the wheel of a log skidder requires the mechanic to kneel and heft a heavy wrench—a tiring, painful position. The employer installed a counterbalanced tool that allows the operator to sit level with the wheel and work with his legs and back relaxed.

Time & Life Pictures/Getty Images

History of I/O Psychology

Although I/O psychology is often misperceived as a new field in psychology, it is actually more than a century old. In Chapter 1, you learned about Wilhelm Wundt, generally credited as the founder of psychology. Wundt's first research assistant, James McKeen Cattell, broke new ground in the field of mental testing (Cattell, 1890), thus influencing the job application process as we know it today. If you've ever taken a personality test, an IQ test, or even a state-mandated academic achievement test, then Cattell's concept of mental testing has affected your life. In 1921, Cattell founded the Psychological Corporation, one of the largest publishers of psychological tests. Today, pre-employment testing has become a basic step for screening job applicants, helping many organizations with their hiring decisions.

Hugo Münsterberg (1863–1916) After earning his Ph.D. in psychology at the University of Leipzig in 1887, Münsterberg established himself as a pioneer in applied psychology, extending his research to business, medical, legal, and educational settings. Invited by William James to teach at Harvard University, Münsterberg taught there until his death.

Science Source/Photo Researchers Inc.

Another one of Wundt's students, Hugo Münsterberg, is considered by many to be the father of I/O psychology. His book *Psychology and Industrial Efficiency* (1913) was the field's first textbook. Here, Münsterberg explained the benefits of matching the job to the worker. He believed that successful matches had multiple benefits, including increased job satisfaction, improved work quality, and higher worker productivity.

Industrial (Personnel) Psychology

Three major goals of personnel psychologists are selecting the best applicants for jobs, training employees so that they perform their jobs effectively, and accurately evaluating employee performance. The first step in attaining each of these goals is to perform a job analysis.

Job Analysis

When job descriptions are lacking or inaccurate, employers and employees may experience frustration as tasks are confused and positions are misunderstood or even duplicated. Consequently, I/O psychologists are called upon to conduct job analyses that result in accurate job descriptions, benefiting everyone involved. Outdated or inflated job descriptions may land organizations in legal hot water. More specifically, a job description that indicates more knowledge, skill, or ability than is actually needed to perform well in a job could violate the Americans with Disabilities Act. For example, sewing straight seams may be determined more by one's sense of touch than by perfect vision; thus, if a garment manufacturer required sewing machine operators to have perfect vision, then visually impaired people—some of whom may be able to sew perfect seams—would be excluded unfairly from employment. The Equal Employment Opportunity Commission (EEOC), the Department of Labor (DOL), and the Americans with Disabilities Act (ADA) all endorse job analysis as a precautionary method to avoid legal problems (EEOC, 1999).

Job analysis is a technique that identifies the major responsibilities of a job, along with the human characteristics needed to fill it. Someone performing a job analysis may observe employees at work, interview them, or ask them to complete surveys regarding major job duties and tasks. This information is then used to create or revise

job analysis A technique that identifies the major responsibilities of a job, along with the human characteristics needed to fill it.

FIGURE B.1 A Sample Job Analysis The job analysis is a crucial tool in personnel psychology. A thorough job analysis can be a necessary step not only for selecting job applicants but also in training employees for specific positions and in evaluating their performance. This job analysis is for the job of job analyst itself.

Source: *Dictionary of Occupational Titles* (1991).

JOB ANALYST alternate titles: personnel analyst

Collects, analyzes, and prepares occupational information to facilitate personnel, administration, and management functions of organization; consults with management to determine type, scope, and purpose of study. Studies current organizational occupational data and compiles distribution reports, organization and flow charts, and other background information required for study. Observes jobs and interviews workers and supervisory personnel to determine job and worker requirements. Analyzes occupational data, such as physical, mental, and training requirements of jobs and workers, and develops written summaries, such as job descriptions, job specifications, and lines of career movement. Utilizes developed occupational data to evaluate or improve methods and techniques for recruiting, selecting, promoting, evaluating, and training workers, and administration of related personnel programs. May specialize in classifying positions according to regulated guidelines to meet job classification requirements of civil service system, a specialty known as Position Classifier.

job descriptions, such as the example given in Figure B.1. Sometimes this information can even be used to restructure an organization. Why should an employer invest in this process? When job analysis is the foundation of recruitment, training, and performance management systems, these systems have a better chance of reducing turnover and improving productivity and morale (Felsberg, 2004).

Job analysis is also important for *designing effective training programs*. In 2007, U.S. organizations spent over $58.5 billion on training programs for their employees (*Training,* 2007). I/O psychologists can assist organizations in creating customized and effective training programs that integrate job analysis data with organizational goals. Modern training programs should include collaborative and on-demand methods, such as e-learning, virtual classrooms, and podcasts, so as to maximize training success. "With the younger generation of employees, organizations need to rethink how they deliver learning," explains Karen O'Leonard, analyst and project leader of the "2007 Training Industry Report." "Today the most important trends are toward audio, mobile, and collaborative environments" (*Training,* 2007). The best training results are achieved not only through effective delivery methods but also when the training objectives are directly linked to performance measures.

Finally, job analysis is useful in *designing performance appraisal systems*. Job analysis defines and clarifies job competencies so that performance appraisal instruments may be developed and training results can be assessed. This process helps managers make their expectations and ratings clear and easy to understand. As more companies realize the benefits of job analysis, they will call upon I/O psychologists to design customized performance management systems to better track and communicate employee performance.

A Closer Look at Personnel Selection

Whether you are looking for a job or trying to fill a position at your company, it's helpful to understand the personnel selection process. The more you know about how selection decisions are made, the more likely you are to find a job that fits your needs, skills, and interests—and this benefits employers and employees alike.

The goal in personnel selection is to hire only those applicants who will perform the job effectively. There are many selection devices available for the screening process, including psychological tests, work samples, and selection interviews. With so many devices available, each with strengths and weaknesses, personnel psychologists are often called upon to recommend those devices that might best be used in a particular selection process. Consequently, they must consider **selection device validity,** the extent to which a selection device is successful in distinguishing between those applicants who will become high performers and those who will not.

Matching Job and Applicant A job analysis helps to pinpoint the qualities a person must have to succeed at a particular job. Not everyone has the special combination of compassion and toughness needed to be an effective physical therapist, for instance.

PSYCHOLOGICAL TESTS

Charles Wonderlic, president of the Wonderlic Testing Firm and grandson of the founder, explains why psychological tests are so frequently used in the selection process: "To make better hiring and managing decisions that reduce turnover and improve sales, many store owners add personality profiling tools and other tests to their hiring process because it offers recruiters insight into candidates' traits they may not have even thought to explore" (Wonderlic, 2005). A survey of Fortune 1000 firms ($n = 151$) found that 28 percent of employer respondents use honesty/integrity tests, 22 percent screen for violence potential, and 20 percent screen for personality (Piotrowski & Armstrong, 2006). The survey also reveals that up to a third of employers may soon include online testing as a part of their screening process. Employers want quick, inexpensive, and accurate ways to identify whether applicant qualifications, aptitudes, and personality traits match the position requirements. Common types of psychological tests are integrity/honesty tests, cognitive ability tests, mechanical aptitude tests, motor and sensory ability tests, and personality tests.

Let's first examine the popularity of *integrity tests,* which came about largely because of legislation limiting the use of polygraph tests in the workplace. According to the *2007 National Retail Security Survey* (Hollinger & Adams, 2007), employee theft accounted for approximately half of all retail losses, at $19.5 billion—way ahead of the $13.3 billion cost of shoplifting. The hiring of honest employees is definitely in the company's best interest. Unfortunately, integrity tests are plagued with concerns about validity, reliability, fairness, and privacy (Karren & Zacharias, 2007). Some researchers are working diligently to address issues like high rates of false positives, and the ability to "fake" an honest answer (Marcus & others, 2007). Despite these problems, several million integrity tests are administered in the United States every year (Wanek & others, 2003).

Cognitive ability tests measure general intelligence or specific cognitive skills, such as mathematical or verbal ability. The Wonderlic Personnel Test–Revised (WPT-R) was released in January 2007. This 12-minute test of cognitive ability, or general intelligence, has been taken by more than 125 million people since 1937 (Press Release Newswire, 2007). Sample items from two cognitive ability tests are presented in Figure B.2. *Mechanical ability tests* measure mechanical reasoning and may be used

selection device validity The extent to which a personnel selection device is successful in distinguishing between those who will become high performers at a certain job and those who will not.

(a) 1. RESENT/RESERVE — Do these words
    1 have similar meanings
    2 have contradictory meanings
    3 mean neither the same nor opposite
  2. Paper sells for 21 cents per pad. What will 4 pads cost?

(b)

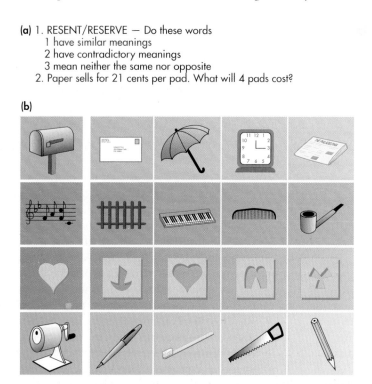

For each item find the picture that goes best with the picture in the first box. Draw a dark line from the upper right corner to the lower left corner in the proper box to show the right answer.

FIGURE B.2 Sample Items from Two Cognitive Ability Tests
Cognitive ability tests can measure either general intelligence or specific cognitive skills, such as mathematical ability. (a) These two items are from the Wonderlic Personnel Test, which is designed to assess general cognitive ability. Employers assume that people who cannot answer most questions correctly would not be good candidates for jobs that require general knowledge and reasoning skills. (b) The chart is from the Non-Verbal Reasoning Test. It assesses reasoning skills apart from the potentially confounding factor of skill with the English language.
Sources: Corsini (1958); Wonderlic (1998).

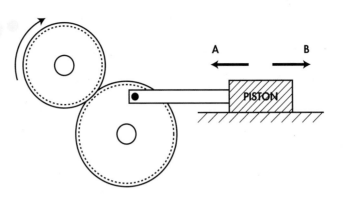

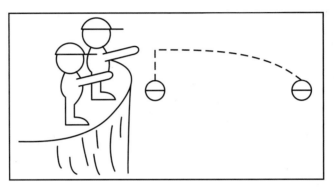

FIGURE B.3 Sample Items from a Mechanical Ability Test Questions such as these from the Resource Associates Mechanical Reasoning Test are designed to assess a person's ability to figure out the physical properties of things. Such a test might be used to predict job performance for carpenters or assembly-line workers.

Courtesy of Resource Associates, Inc.

to predict job performance for engineering, carpentry, and assembly work. Figure B.3 presents sample items from the Resource Associates Mechanical Reasoning Test. *Motor ability tests* include measures of fine dexterity in fingers and hands, accuracy and speed of arm and hand movements, and eye–hand coordination. *Sensory ability tests* include measures of visual acuity, color vision, and hearing.

Personality tests are designed to measure either abnormal or normal personality characteristics. An assessment of abnormal personality characteristics might be appropriate for selecting people for sensitive jobs, such as nuclear power plant operator, police officer, or airline pilot. Tests designed to measure normal personality traits, however, are more popular for the selection of employees (Bates, 2002). Tests based on the Big Five Model allow employers to identify traits such as conscientiousness, extraversion, and agreeableness (Bates, 2002). This information can also be used to understand employee motivation and enhance team building and team placement.

WORK SAMPLES AND SITUATIONAL EXERCISES

Two other kinds of personnel selection devices are work samples and situational exercises. Work samples are typically used for jobs involving the manipulation of objects, while situational exercises are usually used for jobs involving managerial or professional skills. Work samples have been called "high-fidelity simulations" in that they require applicants to complete tasks as if they were on the job (Motowidlo & others, 1997). Companies like Toyota, Quest Diagnostics, and SunTrust Bank have been using interactive job simulations in their selection steps.

At Toyota, applicants must demonstrate their ability to read dials and gauges and spot safety problems in a virtual setting as a part of their "Computer Assembler Audition." Quest Diagnostics is using online video previewing of jobs to educate potential applicants about the typical workday of a phlebotomist. This step helps reduce turnover. Finally, use of an online screening and assessment system allowed SunTrust Bank to shorten the previous two- to four-week pre-employment process down to a single week. Employers are also learning that "[job] simulations can reduce the risk of litigation, since these methods are more closely aligned to the job" (Winkler, 2006).

SELECTION INTERVIEWS

Great news! You passed the pre-employment test and have been called in for an interview. Now it's just a matter of sailing through the objective interview, right? Wrong! Chances are that the company's interviewing methods are subjective, outdated, and non-research based. The Society for Human Resource Management (SHRM) has found that many companies continue to ignore the growing body of research that supports objective selection strategies. In its 2006 survey, SHRM found that as many as 40 percent of responding companies reported continued use of unstructured interviews, sometimes developed "off-the-cuff," as opposed to the structured behavioral interviews recommended by the research. Furthermore, only 24 percent actually used scoring scales to rate the interviewee responses, fostering even greater subjectivity.

"Good boy, what a good boy. You're hired."

In contrast to unstructured interviews, *structured behavioral interviews,* if developed and conducted properly, are adequate predictors of job performance. A structured interview should be based on a job analysis, prepared in advance, standardized for all applicants, and evaluated by a panel of interviewers trained to record and rate the applicant's responses using a numeric rating scale. When these criteria are met, the interview is likely to be an effective selection tool (Krohe, 2006).

Organizational Behavior

Organizational behavior (OB) focuses on how the organization and the social environment in which people work affect their attitudes and behaviors. Job satisfaction is the attitude most thoroughly researched by I/O psychologists, with over 10,000 studies to date. The impact of leadership on attitudes and behaviors is another well-researched OB topic. We will examine both of these topics here.

Job Satisfaction

Lucy and Jane are both engineers who work in the same department of the same company. Lucy is almost always eager to get to work in the morning. She feels that her work is interesting and that she has plenty of opportunities to learn new skills. In contrast, Jane is unhappy because she feels that she doesn't get the recognition she deserves at work. She also complains that the company doesn't give enough vacation time to employees and that it provides inadequate benefits. Jane can't think of many good things about her job. She's even beginning to feel that her job is negatively affecting her personal life.

Fortunately, Lucy is more typical of U.S. workers than Jane is. A recent *International Herald Tribune*/France 24/Harris Interactive survey reported that at least two-thirds of U.S. workers say they are satisfied with the type of work they do and their pay (Harris Interactive, 2007).

Several approaches have been used to explain differences in job satisfaction. An early approach was based on a **discrepancy hypothesis,** which consists of three ideas: (1) that people differ in what they want from a job, (2) that people differ in how they evaluate what they experience at work, and (3) that job satisfaction is based on the difference between what is desired and what is experienced (Lawler, 1973; Locke, 1976). Lucy and Jane, for instance, may not only want different things from their jobs; they may also make different assessments of the same events at work. Although their supervisor may treat them in the same encouraging manner, Lucy may see the boss's encouragement as supportive while Jane may view it as condescending. As a result, one perceives a discrepancy between desires and experiences, whereas the other does not.

discrepancy hypothesis An approach to explaining job satisfaction that focuses on the discrepancy, if any, between what a person wants from a job and how that person evaluates what is actually experienced at work.

trait approach to leader effectiveness
An approach to determining what makes an effective leader that focuses on the personal characteristics displayed by successful leaders.

behavioral theories of leader effectiveness Theories of leader effectiveness that focus on differences in the behaviors of effective and ineffective leaders.

Subsequent research supported the discrepancy hypothesis. For example, negative discrepancies (getting less than desired) were found to be related to dissatisfaction. Interestingly, positive discrepancies (getting more than desired) were also related to dissatisfaction in some cases (Rice & others, 1989). As an example, you might be dissatisfied with a job because it involves more contact with customers than you wanted or expected.

However, other factors have been identified as contributing to job satisfaction. The 2007 SHRM Job Satisfaction Survey lists compensation, benefits, job security, work–life balance, and communication between employees and senior management as the current top five "very important" job satisfaction aspects for employees (Lockwood, 2007).

Leadership

I/O psychologists have invested extensive energy searching for the formula for a great leader. *Leaders* are those who have the ability to direct groups toward the attainment of organizational goals. There are several classic theories that shaped our early views of leadership. The **trait approach to leader effectiveness,** one of the earliest theories, was based on the idea that great leaders are *born,* not made. This approach assumed that leaders possess certain qualities or characteristics resulting in natural abilities to lead others. Some examples of these "natural-born" leaders included John F. Kennedy, Martin Luther King, Jr., and Nelson Mandela. A large number of traits—such as height, physical attractiveness, dominance, resourcefulness, and intelligence—were examined for connections to leader effectiveness. A substantial amount of trait research was initially conducted, much of it showing little connection between personal traits and leader effectiveness (Hollander & Julian, 1969; Stogdill, 1948). Recent trait research continues, with some studies identifying traits, such as emotional intelligence, that can have a positive impact on employee behavior (Rego & others, 2007). Unfortunately, to date, trait researchers still haven't found a comprehensive "leadership recipe."

Consequently the emphasis turned to another explanation for effective leadership. Could leaders be *made*? Could they be taught "leadership behaviors" that would make them more effective? Researchers exploring the **behavioral theories of leader effectiveness** reasoned that the behaviors of effective and ineffective leaders must differ. In 1960, Douglas McGregor published *The Human Side of Enterprise,* in which he outlined Theory X and Theory Y, creating the view that leaders were polarized into those who either cared about the job (X) or cared about the people (Y). Research on these two dimensions found that ineffective managers focused on only one dimension. For example, if your boss cares only about production, then your job satisfaction and morale may decline. In contrast, if your boss is "all heart" but holds no production expectations, your job satisfaction may be high but your productivity low (Bass, 1981; Locke & Schweiger, 1979). A few years after McGregor's book was published, Robert Blake and Jane Mouton expanded upon the theory with their Managerial Grid, claiming it was possible to care about *both* productivity and people. By placing these two variables on a grid, they could plot five primary managerial styles (see Figure B.4). A manager with low ratings in both areas was labeled (1,1), an "Impoverished Manager." In contrast,

What Makes a Leader? Raised by a single mother in a New York City housing project, Ursula Burns credits education and hard work for her rise from summer engineering intern to CEO of Xerox Corporation (Bettex, 2010). Forbes now rates Burns among the most powerful women in the world. Burns includes being authentic as one of her key recommendations for successful leadership. She is known for speaking her mind, whether that means questioning a company's culture or advocating her "pragmatic" approach to work–life balance (Peck, 2011).

Bloomberg via Getty Images

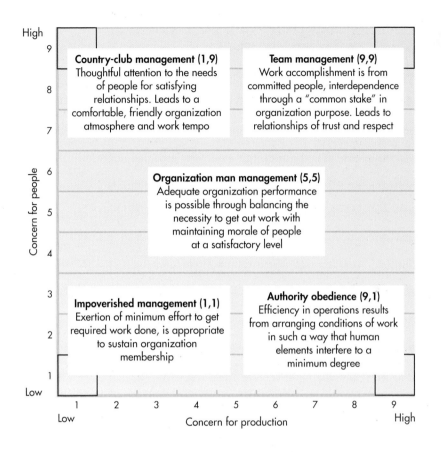

FIGURE B.4 Robert Blake and Jane Mouton's "Managerial Grid" identifies five different leadership styles (1985). With *concern for production* as the *x* axis and *concern for the people* as the *y* axis, managerial styles can be assessed based on whether they rank low or high on these concerns.

Source: Blake, Robert R.; & Mouton, Jane S. (1985). The managerial grid III: The key to leadership excellence. Austin, TX: Grid International, Inc.

one scoring highest on both concern for production and concern for people was labeled (9,9), the "Team Leader" (Blake & Mouton, 1985).

Next to evolve were **situational** (or **contingency**) **theories of leadership,** which stated that there was no one "best" way to manage *every* employee. These theories claimed that good leadership skills depend, or are contingent upon, various situational factors, such as the structure of the task and the willingness of the follower. Accordingly, the best leaders will utilize the leadership style most appropriate for the employee and the situation at hand. These theories tended to be complicated, but they did a better job of explaining leader effectiveness than either the trait approach or behavioral theories.

Much of the research on leadership emphasized the impact of leaders on followers, ignoring the fact that followers also influence leaders. In contrast, a modern approach, called the **leader–member exchange model,** emphasizes two types of relationships that can develop between leaders and employees. Positive leader–member relationships are characterized by mutual trust, respect, and liking. These relationships have numerous benefits, including higher job satisfaction and goal commitment, improved work climate, and lower turnover rates (Gerstner & Day, 1997). Negative leader–member relationships show a lack of trust, respect, and liking. These relationships lead to decreased job satisfaction and job performance, among other consequences (Gomez & Rosen, 2001). This research shows that effective leaders manage to establish positive relationships by setting high expectations and making an effort to build trust and reciprocal respect.

More recently, leadership research has focused on topics such as transformational versus transactional leadership, charismatic leadership, shared leadership, and servant leadership, which is highlighted in the In Focus box on the next page, "Servant Leadership: When It's Not All About You." Although researchers have yet to find the formula for a perfect leader, they have shed a bright light on the optimal conditions for leadership development.

situational (contingency) theories of leadership Leadership theories claiming that various situational factors influence a leader's effectiveness.

leader–member exchange model A model of leadership emphasizing that the quality of the interactions between supervisors and subordinates varies depending on the unique characteristics of both.

IN FOCUS

Servant Leadership: When It's Not All About You

What do Jeffrey Skilling, Bernard Ebbers, and Dennis Kozlowski have in common? They were all entrusted with leadership positions for corporate giants such as Enron, WorldCom, and Tyco. They also failed miserably in their posts as leaders. Ebbers, former CEO of WorldCom, was convicted of fraud and conspiracy and is said to have been personally responsible for the $11 billion loss to WorldCom investors. Formerly CEO of the now-defunct Enron, Jeffrey Skilling went to federal prison after having been found guilty of fraud and insider trading in one of America's notorious cases of corporate corruption. Kozlowski, too, went to prison, convicted of misappropriating $400 million of his company's funds while he was CEO of Tyco.

All three of these individuals are what some researchers call *narcissistic leaders.* Research on selfish leadership demonstrates that narcissistic leaders display certain behaviors that make them more likely to take self-serving risks, inconsiderate of the role of stewardship placed upon them as leaders. One study found that such CEOs focus on themselves at the expense of organizational awareness (Chatterjee & Hambrick, 2007). By featuring their pictures, their names, and their stories on organizational literature, these CEOs demand all the attention, instead of sharing the spotlight with the hardworking "stagehands" behind the scenes.

If you've ever known a highly narcissistic individual, it was probably not by choice. As employees, we like to receive recognition and at least some acknowledgment that what we do is valued. Selfish leaders are unable to fill our needs because of their own need to have their egos stroked on a constant basis. Their belief system includes self-promoting ideas such as, "I am, by far, the most valuable person in this organization," or "Leadership is a solo endeavor, not a group activity" (Chatterjee & Hambrick, 2007).

Enter the servant leader. In 1970, Robert Greenleaf, a retired AT&T corporate executive, was the first to use the term *servant leader.* He defined a servant leader as one who makes service to others, including one's employees, the foremost leadership objective. Greenleaf believed that servant leaders are successful because of their sincere commitment to helping their followers succeed. They invert the organizational chart, placing employee needs above their own (Zandy, 2007). Employee centeredness, where the leader's focus is on employee concerns, allows leaders to roll up their sleeves during crunch times. Most important, servant leaders' humility allows them to recognize their employees as emerging leaders who need organizational support to reach their potential. Humility is the servant leader's most prominent trait, unlike the narcissistic leader's self-promotion.

Warren Buffett, one of the richest men in the world, exemplifies servant leadership. Buffett's financial success often overshadows his generous spirit and humble demeanor; he has pledged to give 99% of his $47 billion fortune to charity. As a leader, he values the development of his staff and colleagues, often acknowledging his own mistakes before announcing their successes. His ethical transparency allows everything to be disclosed. Buffett says, "You don't need to play outside the lines. You can make a lot of money hitting the ball down the middle" (George, 2006). If only Skilling, Ebbers, and Kozlowski had followed his lead.

REUTERS/Krishna Murari Krishan

Empowering Others When Bill Gates co-founded Microsoft in 1975, his vision seemed radical: a computer running Microsoft software in every home. Today, Gates is one of the wealthiest men in the world. Gates found success as a leader who values and supports others' contributions. He said, "As we look ahead into the next century, leaders will be those who empower others" (quoted in Childress & Senn, 1995). Shown here visiting with slum dwellers in Danapur, India, Gates and his wife, Melinda, have extended this humble leadership style into a vast philanthropic mission "guided by the belief that every life has equal value" (Bill & Melinda Gates Foundation, 2015). The Gates Foundation has supported grantees with more than $33 billion as it seeks to reduce poverty, enhance health care, and increase access to education.

Workplace Trends and Issues

The Society for Human Resource Management (SHRM, 2007) has identified the top challenges facing companies today:

1. Succession planning (replacement of retiring leaders)
2. Recruitment and selection of talented employees
3. Engaging and retaining talented employees
4. Providing leaders with the skills to be successful

IN FOCUS

Name, Title, Generation

If you visit Instagram, Facebook, and YouTube as part of your daily routine, you're probably a millennial. If *avatar, blog,* and *Wiki* don't sound like Star Wars characters to you, then you're surely a millennial. So what's a millennial? Google it and you'll find millennials are the Net Generation, born between 1981 and 1999. Millennials, also called Generation Y, are walking around loaded—with gadgets, that is. They are the most technologically savvy generation, and they have entered the workplace. They're great at multitasking, pragmatic thinking, future-looking, team playing, and tech-operating. But they have their faults, too: They wear iPods during meetings, assume everything is public, have narcissistic tendencies, demand immediate praise, and don't like to be criticized, not even constructively (Tyler, 2008).

Generation gaps are challenging employers in many ways. Some employers are seeing as many as four generations of workers walk through their doors. In their book *When Generations Collide: Who They Are. Why They Clash. How to Solve the Generational Puzzle at Work*

(2002), authors Lynne C. Lancaster and David Stillman discuss the generational issues facing the workplace. Multiple age groups means differing values, goals, and perceptions. In one example, they describe the ways the four generations view the process of feedback:

- Traditionalists (born 1900–1945): No news is good news.
- Baby boomers (born 1946–1964): Once a year, with lots of documentation.
- Generation Xers (born 1965–1980): Sorry to interrupt, but how am I doing?
- Millennials (born 1981–1999): Feedback whenever I want it at the push of a button . . . and NOW!

Surely, the workplace of the future must embrace all generations, train them to get along, and build complementary teams. Leaders of the future will need to inspire *all* of their employees, from the traditionalists to the millennials.

AP Photo/The Christian Science Monitor, Ann Hermes

Differing Work Styles Millennials often prefer to work collaboratively and may be most comfortable with the constant interaction that this work environment facilitates.

5. Rising health care costs

6. Creating/maintaining a performance-based culture (rewarding exceptional job performance)

To face these challenges, the workplace of the future is expected to become more dynamic, diversified, flexible, and responsive. Organizations and their employees will need to adapt to the ever-changing world of work, complete with resource limitations and technological innovations. Let's examine how some of these challenges are being addressed.

Workforce Diversity
RECRUITING AND RETAINING DIVERSE TALENT

Changing workforce demographics continue to challenge many employers (see the In Focus box "Name, Title, Generation"). Diverse employees have diverse needs, interests, and expectations. Organizations that can best address these issues will be most likely to attract top candidates. Several organizations are creating excellent perk packages to recruit among the diversified field of top candidates. *Fortune*'s "100 Best Companies to Work For" (2008) shows more companies offering telecommuting (84 percent), compressed workweeks (82 percent), on-site gyms (69 percent), job sharing (63 percent), and on-site child care (29 percent), many of which are highly desirable to different populations such as working parents or older workers. Google, *Fortune*'s

Marilynn K. Yee/The New York Times/Redux

Telework or Telecommuting: Working at Home Kipp Jarecke-Cheng, a director of global public relations and communications for a design and technology consulting company, works from home in order to avoid a long commute. According to the Census Bureau, the typical telecommuter is now a 49-year-old college graduate working for a company with more than 100 employees (Tugend, 2014). For the self-motivated individual with good communication skills, telecommuting offers the advantages of greater autonomy and flexible time management. On the down side, teleworkers are more likely to work in the evenings and on the weekends (Steward, 2000). Men and women vary in their reasons for telecommuting. Being able to earn money and care for their children at the same time is a motivating factor for many women (Sullivan & Lewis, 2001).

Best Company, doesn't stop there. At Google headquarters in Mountain View, California, employees enjoy an amazing variety of on-site services such as gourmet meals, child care, health care, oil changes, car washes, dry cleaning, massage therapy, gyms, hairstylists, and fitness classes, to name just a few. Often called the Google Campus, this laid-back environment has proved successful in attracting the best candidates in the industry.

Telework and Telecommuting
THE BEST RETENTION TOOL

The latest estimates show that 33 million Americans hold jobs that could be performed at home by telecommuting (Fisher, 2008). Telecommuting programs offer advantages such as flexible work schedules, more freedom at work, and less time wasted commuting. One study focused on the best practices of several telework organizations, including Intel Corporation, Hewlett-Packard, and Dow Chemical Corporation. These organizations were identified as having model telework programs in place, with recruitment and retention as the primary organizational benefits (Telework Coalition, 2006). More recently, the 2008–2009 WorldatWork Salary Budget Survey ($n = 2,288$) reported that the number of respondent employers offering telework options to their employees jumped from 30 percent in 2007 to 42 percent in 2008 (WorldatWork, 2008–2009). As with any major change in the workplace, telework poses new challenges to organizations. How does working from home affect performance, workplace relations, and career prospects? A recent meta-analysis asked these and many other questions about the effects of telecommuting (Gajendran & Harrison, 2007). The researchers found telecommuting has predominantly positive effects for both employees and employers, including higher job satisfaction, employee morale and autonomy, and improved supervisor–employee relations. I/O psychologists may guide employers to accept telework as an important solution to many problems.

Internet Recruiting
USING THE WEB TO RECRUIT TOP TALENT

Internet job-search services, such as monster.com, hotjobs.com, and company Web sites, have changed the way in which employees are recruited. In its 2007 survey, the Conference Board, a global business membership and research organization, found that 73 percent of job seekers used the Internet to find information about prospective employers, to post resumes on job boards, and to gain career advice. This surge in Internet job-seeking poses new challenges for employers, such as compliance with new legal requirements for online applicant tracking, or simply how to narrow down the multitude of resume submissions brought on by the ease of resume posting.

Work–Life Balance
ENGAGING AND RETAINING EMPLOYEES WITH FAMILIES

Juggling the demands of both career and family can lead to many conflicts. This struggle, often called *work–family conflict,* results in higher absenteeism, lower morale, and higher turnover in the workplace. Further, results from a meta-analysis reviewing 38 studies found that employee perceptions of family-friendly work culture, along with supportive bosses and spouses, can reduce work–family conflict (Mesmer-Magnus & Viswesvaran, 2006). Therefore, it makes good business sense to help working parents balance the demands of work and family life. Unfortunately, several studies indicate that few U.S. employers have family-friendly policies. A recent *Forbes* survey revealed that the U.S. workplace is not

Juggling Career and Family Women compose nearly half of the total U.S. labor force, and work–family conflict has become a more significant issue for parents of both sexes. This businesswoman must balance her son's child-care schedule against demands at the office.

Ariel Skelley/Getty Images

family-oriented when compared with other industrialized countries (*Forbes,* 2007). The *Forbes* survey found that paid maternity and paternity leave, paid sick days, alternative work schedules, and other such family-friendly policies are lacking in many U.S. companies. Research also shows that "[workplace] policies for families in the U.S. are weaker than those of *all* high-income countries and even many middle- and low-income countries" (Heymann, 2007). Although many companies advertise family-friendly environments, few of them actually offer initiatives such as flexible scheduling. More employers must begin to adopt family-friendly policies and build pro-family cultures to attract and retain this large sector of the workforce.

To keep pace with evolving challenges such as the ones described above, I/O psychologists will constantly need to adjust the focus of their research and its applications. In the future, I/O psychologists will continue to have a significant role in and around the workplace. To explore what it's like to be an I/O psychologist, we'll look at the preparation required for the job, and where you might go from there.

Employment Settings, Type of Training, Earnings, and Employment Outlook

Many I/O psychologists belong to Division 14 of the American Psychological Association (APA), the Society for Industrial and Organizational Psychology (SIOP). The division conducts periodic surveys of its members and, as a result, can supply information on topics such as typical work settings, job duties, and salary levels of I/O psychologists.

The employment settings of I/O psychologists are represented in Figure B.5. Of the I/O psychologists who belong to SIOP and who responded to the 2006 employment

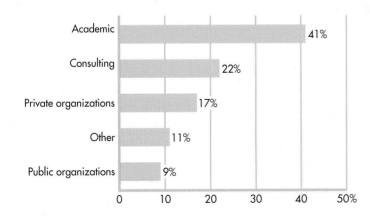

FIGURE B.5 Work Settings of I/O Psychologists Most I/O psychologists work in institutions of higher education. Forty-one percent of the members of the Society for Industrial and Organizational Psychology work in colleges and universities. Next come I/O psychologists who work as consultants to organizations (22 percent). Another substantial percentage (17 percent) are employed by large private corporations, such as insurance companies and consumer-product manufacturers. Public organizations, such as government agencies, employ half as many I/O psychologists as private organizations do (9 percent versus 17 percent).

Source: Data from Khanna & Medsker (2007).

setting survey, 41 percent worked in academic settings (primarily universities and colleges); 22 percent worked as consultants to organizations; 17 percent worked in private organizations; and 9 percent worked for public organizations (Khanna & Medsker, 2007).

Those with bachelor's degrees may find work in fields related to I/O psychology, such as in the administration of training programs or as interviewers. However, a master's (M.A.) or doctorate (Ph.D.) degree is required to work in the field of I/O psychology. Though there are plenty of programs to choose from, with more than 200 master's and doctorate programs available for I/O psychologists in the United States, admission into these programs can be very competitive, especially at the doctoral level.

The majority of SIOP members hold doctorate degrees (87 percent) as opposed to master's degrees (13 percent). When selecting your degree, you must consider the length and requirements of the program. Are you prepared to attend graduate school as a full-time student for five to six years, conduct a detailed research project, and write a dissertation? If your answer to these questions is yes, then a doctorate degree may be for you. This degree qualifies you for I/O psychologist positions at major corporations and research and teaching positions at colleges and universities, and it provides the most credibility to conduct consulting work.

If you would prefer to pursue a degree that allows you to quickly apply your knowledge and skills to the workplace, then a master's degree may be a better fit. Most master's programs require two to three years of graduate course work and the completion of a research project. Having a master's degree allows you to work as an I/O psychologist carrying out I/O duties for private or public organizations, teach at two-year colleges, and take on consulting opportunities.

Finally, a bachelor's degree, attained after four years of undergraduate course work, yields numerous employment opportunities in areas involving I/O psychology. These positions include jobs for personnel, training, and labor-relations specialists. Although these jobs are expected to show faster-than-average job growth through the year 2016, the high number of qualified college graduates and experienced workers will keep these jobs highly competitive (U.S. Bureau of Labor Statistics, 2008).

What's the payoff for all this education and hard work? Salaries for I/O psychologists are dependent upon educational qualifications, the kind of industry, and experience. The 2006 salary survey of SIOP members indicated that the median salary for those with doctorate degrees was $98,500; for those with master's degrees, the median salary was $72,000 (Khanna & Medsker, 2007). It also helps to know that the job market for I/O psychologists has remained strong over the years and is projected to have an above-average growth rate (21 percent) through 2016 (Occupational Outlook Handbook, 2008–2009).

If you would like to learn more about career opportunities in I/O psychology, visit some of the Web sites listed in Table B.1.

TABLE B.1

Below is a list of Web sites that relate to working in the field of industrial/organizational psychology.

www.aomonline.org	Academy of Management
www.dol.gov	U.S. Department of Labor Job Information Site
www.shrm.org	Society for Human Resource Management
www.siop.org	Society for Industrial and Organizational Psychology
www.bls.gov	U.S. Department of Labor, Bureau of Labor Statistics
www.onetcenter.org	Occupational Information Network

APPENDIX REVIEW

KEY TERMS

industrial/organizational (I/O) psychology, p. B-1

personnel psychology, p. B-2

organizational behavior, p. B-2

job analysis, p. B-3

selection device validity, p. B-5

discrepancy hypothesis, p. B-7

trait approach to leader effectiveness, p. B-8

behavioral theories of leader effectiveness, p. B-8

situational (contingency) theories of leadership, p. B-9

leader–member exchange model, p. B-9

Industrial/Organizational Psychology

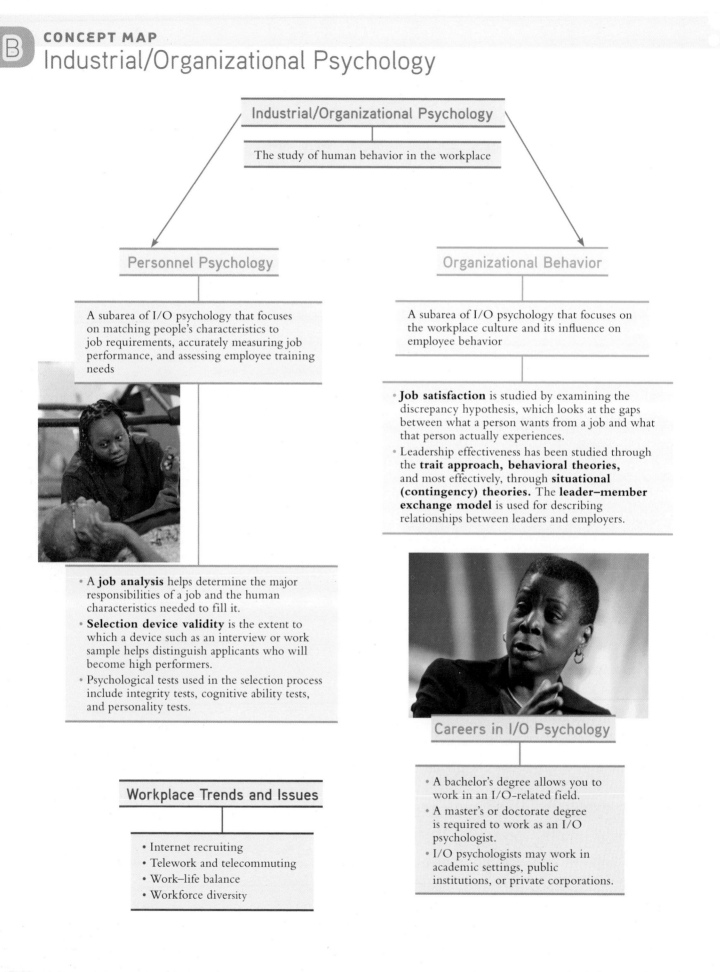

Industrial/Organizational Psychology

The study of human behavior in the workplace

Personnel Psychology

A subarea of I/O psychology that focuses on matching people's characteristics to job requirements, accurately measuring job performance, and assessing employee training needs

- A **job analysis** helps determine the major responsibilities of a job and the human characteristics needed to fill it.
- **Selection device validity** is the extent to which a device such as an interview or work sample helps distinguish applicants who will become high performers.
- Psychological tests used in the selection process include integrity tests, cognitive ability tests, and personality tests.

Organizational Behavior

A subarea of I/O psychology that focuses on the workplace culture and its influence on employee behavior

- **Job satisfaction** is studied by examining the discrepancy hypothesis, which looks at the gaps between what a person wants from a job and what that person actually experiences.
- Leadership effectiveness has been studied through the **trait approach, behavioral theories,** and most effectively, through **situational (contingency) theories.** The **leader–member exchange model** is used for describing relationships between leaders and employers.

Careers in I/O Psychology

- A bachelor's degree allows you to work in an I/O-related field.
- A master's or doctorate degree is required to work as an I/O psychologist.
- I/O psychologists may work in academic settings, public institutions, or private corporations.

Workplace Trends and Issues

- Internet recruiting
- Telework and telecommuting
- Work–life balance
- Workforce diversity

GLOSSARY

A

absolute threshold The smallest possible strength of a stimulus that can be detected half the time. (p. 88)

accommodation The process by which the lens changes shape to focus incoming light so that it falls on the retina. (p. 91)

acculturative stress (uh-CUL-chur-uh-tiv) The stress that results from the pressure of adapting to a new culture. (p. 507)

acetylcholine (uh-seet-ull-KO-leen) Neurotransmitter that causes muscle contractions and is involved in learning and memory. (p. 49)

achievement motivation The desire to direct your behavior toward excelling, succeeding, or outperforming others at some task. (p. 334)

achievement test A test designed to measure a person's level of knowledge, skill, or accomplishment in a particular area. (p. 294)

action potential A brief electrical impulse by which information is transmitted along the axon of a neuron. (p. 44)

activation–synthesis model of dreaming The theory that brain activity during sleep produces dream images (*activation*), which are combined by the brain into a dream story (*synthesis*). (p. 150)

activity theory of aging The psychosocial theory that life satisfaction in late adulthood is highest when people maintain the level of activity they displayed earlier in life. (p. 405)

actor–observer bias The tendency to attribute our own behavior to external, situational characteristics, while ignoring or underestimating the effects of internal, personal factors. (p. 459)

actualizing tendency In Rogers's theory, the innate drive to maintain and enhance the human organism. (p. 429)

acupuncture Traditional Chinese medical procedure involving the insertion and manipulation of fine needles into specific locations on the body to alleviate pain and treat illness; modern acupuncture sometimes involves sending electrical current through the needles rather than manipulating them. (p. 127)

adolescence The transitional stage between late childhood and the beginning of adulthood, during which sexual maturity is reached. (p. 386)

adolescent growth spurt The period of accelerated growth during puberty, involving rapid increases in height and weight. (p. 387)

adrenal cortex The outer portion of the adrenal glands. (p. 59)

adrenal glands The pair of endocrine glands that are involved in the human stress response. (p. 59)

adrenal medulla The inner portion of the adrenal glands, which secretes epinephrine and norepinephrine. (p. 59)

afterimage A visual experience that occurs after the original source of stimulation is no longer present. (p. 96)

aggression Verbal or physical behavior intended to cause harm to other people. (p. 486)

agonist Drug or other chemical substance that binds to a receptor site and triggers a response in the cell. (p. 52)

agoraphobia An anxiety disorder involving extreme fear of experiencing a panic attack or other embarrassing or incapacitating symptoms in a public situation where escape is impossible and help is unavailable. (p. 542)

algorithm A problem-solving strategy that involves following a specific rule, procedure, or method that inevitably produces the correct solution. (p. 279)

alpha brain waves Brain-wave pattern associated with relaxed wakefulness and drowsiness. (p. 141)

altruism Helping another person with no expectation of personal reward or benefit. (p. 483)

Alzheimer's disease (AD) A progressive disease that destroys the brain's neurons, gradually impairing memory, thinking, language, and other cognitive functions, resulting in the complete inability to care for oneself; the most common cause of dementia. (p. 262)

amnesia (am-NEE-zha) Severe memory loss. (p. 260)

amphetamines (am-FET-uh-meenz) A class of stimulant drugs that arouse the central nervous system and suppress appetite. (p. 172)

amplitude The intensity or amount of energy of a wave, reflected in the height of the wave; the amplitude of a sound wave determines a sound's loudness. (p. 98)

amygdala (uh-MIG-dull-uh) An almond-shaped cluster of neurons in the brain's temporal lobe, involved in memory and emotional responses, especially fear. (pp. 71, 340)

animal cognition or comparative cognition The study of animal learning, memory, thinking, and language. (p. 289)

anorexia nervosa An eating disorder characterized by excessive weight loss, an irrational fear of gaining weight, and distorted body self-perception. (p. 558)

antagonist A drug or other chemical substance that blocks a receptor site and inhibits or prevents a response in the receiving cell. (p. 52)

anterograde amnesia Loss of memory caused by the inability to store new memories; forward-acting amnesia. (p. 260)

anthropomorphism The attribution of human traits, motives, emotions, or behaviors to nonhuman animals or inanimate objects. (p. 345)

antianxiety medications Prescription drugs that are used to alleviate the symptoms of anxiety. (p. 617)

antidepressant medications Prescription drugs that are used to reduce the symptoms associated with major depressive disorder. (p. 618)

antipsychotic medications (an-tee-sy-KAHT-ick or an-ty-sy-KAHT-ick) Prescription drugs that are used to reduce psychotic symptoms; frequently used in the treatment of schizophrenia; also called *neuroleptics*. (p. 615)

antisocial personality disorder A personality disorder characterized by a pervasive pattern of disregarding and violating the rights of others; such individuals are also often referred to as *psychopaths* or *sociopaths*. (p. 563)

anxiety An unpleasant emotional state characterized by physical arousal and feelings of tension, apprehension, and worry. (p. 541)

anxiety disorders A category of psychological disorders in which extreme anxiety is the main diagnostic feature and causes significant disruptions in the person's cognitive, behavioral, or interpersonal functioning. (p. 541)

aphasia (uh-FAYZH-yuh) The partial or complete inability to articulate ideas or understand spoken or written language because of brain injury or damage. (p. 74)

aptitude test A test designed to assess a person's capacity to benefit from education or training. (p. 294)

archetypes (AR-kuh-types) In Jung's theory, the inherited mental images of universal human instincts, themes, and preoccupations that are the main components of the collective unconscious. (p. 424)

arousal theory The view that people are motivated to maintain a level of arousal that is optimal—neither too high nor too low. (p. 316)

attachment The emotional bond that forms between an infant and caregiver(s), especially his or her parents. (p. 369)

attention The capacity to selectively focus awareness on particular stimuli in your external environment or on your internal thoughts or sensations. (p. 135)

attitude A learned tendency to evaluate some object, person, or issue in a particular way; such evaluations may be positive, negative, or ambivalent. (p. 461)

attribution The mental process of inferring the causes of people's behavior, including one's own. Also refers to the explanation made for a particular behavior. (p. 458)

atypical antipsychotic medications Newer antipsychotic medications that, in contrast with the early antipsychotic drugs, block dopamine receptors in brain regions associated with psychotic symptoms rather than more globally throughout the brain, resulting in fewer side effects. (p. 617)

audition The technical term for the sense of hearing. (p. 98)

authoritarian parenting style Parenting style in which parents are demanding and unresponsive toward their children's needs or wishes. (p. 407)

authoritative parenting style Parenting style in which parents set clear standards for their children's behavior but are also responsive to their children's needs and wishes. (p. 407)

autism spectrum disorder Neurodevelopmental disorder characterized by: (1) deficits in social communication and social interaction and (2) restricted, repetitive behaviors, interests, and activities. (p. 300)

autonomic nervous system (aw-toe-NAHM-ick) The subdivision of the peripheral nervous system that regulates involuntary functions. (p. 56)

availability heuristic A strategy in which the likelihood of an event is estimated on the basis of how readily available other instances of the event are in memory. (p. 283)

aversive conditioning A relatively ineffective type of behavior therapy that involves repeatedly pairing an aversive stimulus with the occurrence of undesirable behaviors or thoughts. (p. 597)

axon The long, fluid-filled tube that carries a neuron's messages to other body areas. (p. 43)

axon terminals The branches at the end of the axon that contain tiny pouches, or sacs, called synaptic vesicles. (p. 48)

B

barbiturates (barb-ITCH-yer-its) A category of depressant drugs that reduce anxiety and produce sleepiness. (p. 168)

basal metabolic rate (BMR) When the body is at rest, the rate at which it uses energy for vital functions, such as heartbeat and respiration. (p. 318)

basic emotions The most fundamental set of emotion categories, which are biologically innate, evolutionarily determined, and culturally universal. (p. 336)

basilar membrane (BAZ-uh-ler or BAYZ-uh-ler) The membrane within the cochlea of the ear that contains the hair cells. (p. 101)

behavior modification The application of learning principles to help people develop more effective or adaptive behaviors. (p. 209)

behavior therapy A type of psychotherapy that focuses on directly changing maladaptive behavior patterns by using basic learning principles and techniques; also called *behavior modification*. (p. 593)

behavioral genetics An interdisciplinary field that studies the effects of genes and heredity on behavior. (p. 439)

behavioral theories of leader effectiveness Theories of leader effectiveness that focus on differences in the behaviors of effective and ineffective leaders. (p. B-8)

behaviorism School of psychology and theoretical viewpoint that emphasizes the study of observable behaviors, especially as they pertain to the process of learning. (pp. 8, 187)

beta brain waves Brain-wave pattern associated with alert wakefulness. (p. 140)

bilingualism Fluency in two or more languages. (p. 288)

binge-eating disorder An eating disorder characterized by binges of extreme overeating without use of self-induced vomiting or other inappropriate measures to purge the excess food. (p. 558)

binocular cues (by-NOCK-you-ler) Distance or depth cues that require the use of both eyes. (p. 119)

biofeedback Technique that involves using auditory or visual feedback to learn to exert voluntary control over involuntary body functions, such as heart rate, blood pressure, blood flow, and muscle tension. (p. 127)

biological preparedness In learning theory, the idea that an organism is innately predisposed to form associations between certain stimuli and responses. (p. 194)

biological psychology The specialized branch of psychology that studies the relationship between behavior and bodily processes and systems; also called *biopsychology* or *psychobiology*. (p. 42)

biomedical therapies The use of medications, electroconvulsive therapy, or other medical treatments to treat the symptoms associated with psychological disorders. (p. 586)

biopsychosocial model The belief that physical health and illness are determined by the complex interaction of biological, psychological, and social factors. (p. 501)

bipolar cells In the retina, the specialized neurons that connect the rods and cones with the ganglion cells. (p. 93)

bipolar disorder A mood disorder involving periods of incapacitating depression alternating with periods of extreme euphoria and excitement; formerly called manic *depression*. (p. 553)

blaming the victim The tendency to blame an innocent victim of misfortune for having somehow caused the problem or for not having taken steps to avoid or prevent it. (p. 459)

blind spot The point at which the optic nerve leaves the eye, producing a small gap in the field of vision. (p. 93)

body mass index (BMI) A numerical scale indicating adult height in relation to weight; calculated as (703 × weight in pounds)/(height in inches)². (p. 321)

borderline personality disorder A personality disorder characterized by instability of interpersonal relationships, self-image, and emotions, and marked impulsivity. (p. 565)

bottom-up processing Information processing that emphasizes the importance of the sensory receptors in detecting the basic features of a stimulus in the process of recognizing a whole pattern; analysis that moves from the parts to the whole; also called *data-driven processing*. (p. 110)

brainstem A region of the brain made up of the hindbrain and the midbrain. (p. 65)

brightness The perceived intensity of a color, which corresponds to the amplitude of the light wave. (p. 96)

bulimia nervosa An eating disorder characterized by binges of extreme overeating followed by self-induced vomiting, misuse of laxatives, or other inappropriate methods to purge the excess food and prevent weight gain. (p. 558)

burnout An unhealthy condition caused by chronic, prolonged work stress that is characterized by exhaustion, cynicism, and a sense of failure or inadequacy. (p. 504)

bystander effect A phenomenon in which the greater the number of people present, the less likely each individual is to help someone in distress. (p. 485)

C

caffeine (kaff-EEN) A stimulant drug found in coffee, tea, cola drinks, chocolate, and many over-the-counter medications. (p. 170)

California Psychological Inventory (CPI) A self-report inventory that assesses personality characteristics in normal populations. (p. 445)

case study An intensive study of a single individual or small group of individuals. (p. 22)

cataplexy A sudden loss of voluntary muscle strength and control that is usually triggered by an intense emotion. (p. 154)

catecholamines (cat-uh-COLE-uh-meenz) Hormones secreted by the adrenal medulla that cause rapid physiological arousal, including adrenaline and noradrenaline. (p. 507)

cell body The part of a cell that processes nutrients and provides energy for the neuron to function; contains the cell's nucleus; also called the *soma*. (p. 43)

central nervous system (CNS) The division of the nervous system that consists of the brain and spinal cord. (p. 53)

centration In Piaget's theory, the tendency to focus, or center, on only one aspect of a situation and ignore other important aspects of the situation. (p. 382)

cerebellum (sair-uh-BELL-um) A large, two-sided hindbrain structure at the back of the brain; responsible for muscle coordination and maintaining posture and equilibrium. (p. 66)

cerebral cortex (suh-REE-brull or SAIR-uh-brull) The wrinkled outer portion of the forebrain, which contains the most sophisticated brain centers. (p. 67)

cerebral hemispheres The nearly symmetrical left and right halves of the cerebral cortex. (p. 67)

chromosome A long, thread-like structure composed of twisted parallel strands of DNA; found in the cell nucleus. (p. 360)

chunking Increasing the amount of information that can be held in short-term memory by grouping related items together into a single unit, or *chunk*. (p. 232)

circadian rhythm (ser-KADE-ee-en) A cycle or rhythm that is roughly 24 hours long; the cyclical daily fluctuations in biological and psychological processes. (p. 138)

classical conditioning The basic learning process that involves repeatedly pairing a neutral stimulus with a response-producing stimulus until the neutral stimulus elicits the same response. (p. 183)

client-centered therapy A type of psychotherapy developed by humanistic psychologist Carl Rogers in which the therapist is nondirective and reflective, and the client directs the focus of each therapy session; also called *person-centered therapy*. (p. 590)

clustering Organizing items into related groups during recall from long-term memory. (p. 236)

cocaine A stimulant drug derived from the leaves of the coca tree. (p. 172)

cochlea (COKE-lee-uh) The coiled, fluid-filled inner-ear structure that contains the basilar membrane and hair cells. (p. 99)

cognition The mental activities involved in acquiring, retaining, and using knowledge. (p. 273)

cognitive appraisal model of stress Developed by Richard Lazarus, a model of stress that emphasizes the role of an individual's evaluation (*appraisal*) of events and situations and of the resources that he or she has available to deal with the event or situation. (p. 499)

cognitive appraisal theory of emotion The theory that emotional responses are triggered by a cognitive evaluation. (p. 350)

cognitive dissonance An unpleasant state of psychological tension or arousal (*dissonance*) that occurs when two thoughts or perceptions (*cognitions*) are inconsistent; typically results from the awareness that attitudes and behavior are in conflict. (p. 465)

cognitive map Tolman's term for the mental representation of the layout of a familiar environment. (p. 210)

cognitive therapies A group of psychotherapies based on the assumption that psychological problems are due to illogical patterns of thinking; treatment techniques focus on recognizing and altering these unhealthy thinking patterns. (p. 599)

cognitive therapy (CT) Therapy developed by Aaron T. Beck that focuses on changing the client's unrealistic and maladaptive beliefs. (p. 601)

cognitive-behavioral therapy (CBT) Therapy that integrates cognitive and behavioral techniques and that is based on the assumption that thoughts, moods, and behaviors are interrelated. (p. 603)

collective unconscious In Jung's theory, the hypothesized part of the unconscious mind that is inherited from previous generations and that contains universally shared ancestral experiences and ideas. (p. 424)

collectivistic cultures Cultures that emphasize the needs and goals of the group over the needs and goals of the individual. (p. 13)

color The perceptual experience of different wavelengths of light, involving hue, saturation (purity), and brightness (intensity). (p. 95)

color blindness One of several inherited forms of color deficiency or weakness in which an individual cannot distinguish between certain colors. (p. 96)

color constancy The perception of a familiar object as being the same color under different light conditions. (p. 122)

comparative psychology The branch of psychology that studies the behavior of different animal species. (p. 34)

competence motivation The desire to direct your behavior toward demonstrating competence and exercising control in a situation. (p. 334)

comprehension vocabulary The words that are understood by an infant or child. (p. 372)

compulsions Repetitive behaviors or mental acts that a person feels driven to perform in order to prevent or reduce anxiety and distress, or to prevent a dreaded event or situation. (p. 548)

concept A mental category of objects or ideas based on properties they share. (p. 275)

concrete operational stage In Piaget's theory, the third stage of cognitive development, which lasts from about age 7 to adolescence; characterized by the ability to think logically about concrete objects and situations. (p. 383)

conditional positive regard In Rogers's theory, the sense that you will be valued and loved only if you behave in a way that is acceptable to others; conditional love or acceptance. (p. 431)

conditioned reinforcer A stimulus or event that has acquired reinforcing value by being associated with a primary reinforcer; also called a *secondary reinforcer*. (p. 200)

conditioned response (CR) The learned, reflexive response to a conditioned stimulus. (p. 185)

conditioned stimulus (CS) A formerly neutral stimulus that acquires the capacity to elicit a reflexive response. (p. 185)

conditioning The process of learning associations between environmental events and behavioral responses. (p. 183)

cones The short, thick, pointed sensory receptors of the eye that detect color and are responsible for color vision and visual acuity. (p. 93)

confirmation bias The tendency to seek out evidence that confirms an existing belief while ignoring evidence that might contradict or undermine the belief. (p. 21, 284)

conformity   Adjusting your opinions, judgments, or behaviors so that they match the opinions, judgments, or behaviors of other people, or the norms of a social group or situation. (p. 473)

confounding variable   A factor or variable other than the ones being studied that, if not controlled, could affect the outcome of an experiment; also called an *extraneous variable*. (p. 26)

connectome   Map of neural connections in the brain (p. 62)

consciousness   Personal awareness of mental activities, internal sensations, and the external environment. (p. 135)

conservation   In Piaget's theory, the understanding that two equal quantities remain equal even though the form or appearance is rearranged, as long as nothing is added or subtracted. (p. 382)

context effect   The tendency to recover information more easily when the retrieval occurs in the same setting as the original learning of the information. (p. 241)

continuous reinforcement   A schedule of reinforcement in which every occurrence of a particular response is followed by a reinforcer. (p. 206)

control group or **control condition**   In an experiment, the group of participants who are exposed to all experimental conditions, except the independent variable; the group against which changes in the experimental group are compared. (p. 26)

coping   Behavioral and cognitive responses used to deal with stressors; involves our efforts to change circumstances, or our interpretation of circumstances, to make them more favorable and less threatening. (p. 522)

cornea   (CORE-nee-uh) A clear membrane covering the visible part of the eye that helps gather and direct incoming light. (p. 91)

corpus callosum   A thick band of axons that connects the two cerebral hemispheres and acts as a communication link between them. (p. 67)

correlation   The relationship between two variables. (p. A-8)

correlation coefficient   A numerical indication of the magnitude and direction of the relationship (the *correlation*) between two variables. (pp. 24, A-8)

correlational study   A research strategy that allows the precise calculation of how strongly related two factors are to each other. (p. 24)

cortical localization   The notion that different functions are located or localized in different areas of the brain; also called *localization of function*. (pp. 60, 73)

corticosteroids   (core-tick-oh-STER-oydz) Hormones released by the adrenal cortex that play a key role in the body's response to long-term stressors. (p. 509)

counterconditioning   A behavior therapy technique based on classical conditioning that involves modifying behavior by conditioning a new response that is incompatible with a previously learned response. (p. 594)

creativity   A group of cognitive processes used to generate useful, original, and novel ideas or solutions to problems. (p. 308)

critical thinking   The active process of minimizing preconceptions and biases while evaluating evidence, determining the conclusions that can reasonably be drawn from evidence, and considering alternative explanations for research findings or other phenomena. (p. 30)

cross-cultural psychology   Branch of psychology that studies the effects of culture on behavior and mental processes. (p. 13)

cross-sectional design   Research strategy in which individuals of different ages or developmental stages are directly compared. (p. 358)

cued recall   A test of long-term memory that involves remembering an item of information in response to a retrieval cue. (p. 240)

culture   The attitudes, values, beliefs, and behaviors shared by a group of people and communicated from one generation to another. (p. 13)

cyclothymic disorder   (sie-klo-THY-mick) A mood disorder characterized by moderate but frequent mood swings that are not severe enough to qualify as bipolar disorder. (p. 554)

D

daily hassles   Everyday minor events that annoy and upset people. (p. 502)

decay theory   The view that forgetting is due to normal metabolic processes that occur in the brain over time. (p. 245)

decibel   (DESS-uh-bell) The unit of measurement for loudness. (p. 98)

déjà vu experience   A memory illusion characterized by brief but intense feelings of familiarity in a situation that has never been experienced before. (p. 247)

delusion   A falsely held belief that persists despite compelling contradictory evidence. (p. 571)

demand characteristics   In a research study, subtle cues or signals expressed by the researcher that communicate the kind of response or behavior that is expected from the participant. (p. 28)

dementia   Progressive deterioration and impairment of memory, reasoning, and other cognitive functions as the result of disease, injury, or substance abuse. (p. 262)

dendrites   The multiple short fibers that extend from a neuron's cell body and receive information from other neurons or from sensory receptor cells. (p. 43)

deoxyribonucleic acid (DNA)   The double-stranded molecule that encodes genetic instructions; the chemical basis of heredity. (p. 360)

dependent variable   The factor that is observed and measured for change in an experiment, thought to be influenced by the independent variable; also called the *outcome variable*. (p. 26)

depressants   A category of psychoactive drugs that depress or inhibit brain activity. (p. 165)

depth perception   The use of visual cues to perceive the distance or three-dimensional characteristics of objects. (p. 117)

descriptive research   Scientific procedures that involve systematically observing behavior in order to describe the relationship among behaviors and events. (p. 21)

descriptive statistics   Mathematical methods used to organize and summarize data. (p. A-2)

developmental psychology   The branch of psychology that studies how people change over the lifespan. (p. 358)

difference threshold   The smallest possible difference between two stimuli that can be detected half the time; also called *just noticeable difference*. (p. 88)

diffusion of responsibility   A phenomenon in which the presence of other people makes it less likely that any individual will help someone in distress because the obligation to intervene is shared among all the onlookers. (p. 485)

discrepancy hypothesis   An approach to explaining job satisfaction that focuses on the discrepancy, if any, between what a person wants from a job and how that person evaluates what is actually experienced at work. (p. B-7)

discriminative stimulus   A specific stimulus in the presence of which a particular response is more likely to be reinforced, and in the absence of which a particular response is not likely to be reinforced. (p. 203)

displacement   The ego defense mechanism that involves unconsciously shifting the target of an emotional urge to a substitute target that is less threatening or dangerous. (p. 420)

display rules   Social and cultural regulations governing emotional expression, especially facial expressions. (p. 345)

dissociation   The splitting of consciousness into two or more simultaneous streams of mental activity. (p. 157)

dissociative amnesia   A dissociative disorder involving the partial or total inability to recall important personal information. (p. 567)

dissociative anesthetics   Class of drugs that reduce sensitivity to pain and produce feelings of detachment and dissociation; includes the club drugs phencyclidine (PCP) and ketamine. (p. 175)

dissociative disorders   A category of psychological disorders in which extreme and frequent disruptions of awareness, memory, and personal identity impair the ability to function. (p. 566)

dissociative experience   A break or disruption in consciousness during which awareness, memory, and personal identity become separated or divided. (p. 566)

dissociative fugue   (fyoog) A type of dissociative amnesia involving sudden and unexpected travel away from home, extensive amnesia, and identity confusion. (p. 567)

dissociative identity disorder (DID)   A dissociative disorder involving extensive memory disruptions along with the presence of two or more distinct identities, or "personalities"; formerly called multiple *personality disorder*. (p. 567)

dopamine   (DOPE-uh-meen) Neurotransmitter involved in the regulation of bodily movement, thought processes, and rewarding sensations. (p. 50)

double-blind technique   An experimental control in which neither the participants nor the researchers interacting with the participants are aware of the group or condition to which the participants have been assigned. (p. 28)

dream   An unfolding sequence of thoughts, perceptions, and emotions that typically occurs during REM sleep and is experienced as a series of real-life events. (p. 147)

dream interpretation   A technique used in psychoanalysis in which the content of dreams is analyzed for disguised or symbolic wishes, meanings, and motivations. (p. 589)

drive   A need or internal motivational state that activates behavior to reduce the need and restore homeostasis. (p. 316)

drive theories   The view that behavior is motivated by the desire to reduce internal tension caused by unmet biological needs. (p. 314)

drug abuse   (formally called *substance use disorder*) Recurrent substance use that involves impaired control, disruption of social, occupational, and interpersonal functioning, and the development of craving, tolerance, and withdrawal symptoms. (p. 165)

drug rebound effect   Withdrawal symptoms that are the opposite of a physically addictive drug's action. (p. 164)

drug tolerance   A condition in which increasing amounts of a physically addictive drug are needed to produce the original, desired effect. (p. 164)

DSM-5   Abbreviation for the *Diagnostic and Statistical Manual of Mental Disorders*, Fifth Edition; the book published by the American Psychiatric Association that describes the specific symptoms and diagnostic guidelines for different psychological disorders. (p. 535)

dyssomnias   (dis-SOM-nee-uz) A category of sleep disorders involving disruptions in the amount, quality, or timing of sleep; includes insomnia, obstructive sleep apnea, and narcolepsy. (p. 153)

E

eardrum   A tightly stretched membrane at the end of the ear canal that vibrates when hit by sound waves. (p. 99)

eating disorder   A category of mental disorders characterized by severe disturbances in eating behavior. (p. 558)

eclecticism   (ih-KLEK-tih-siz-um) The pragmatic and integrated use of techniques from different psychotherapies. (p. 612)

EEG (electroencephalogram)   The graphic record of brain activity produced by an electroencephalograph. (p. 140)

ego   Latin for *I*; in Freud's theory, the partly conscious rational component of personality that regulates thoughts and behavior, and is most in touch with the demands of the external world. (p. 418)

ego defense mechanisms   Largely unconscious distortions of thoughts or perceptions that act to reduce anxiety. (p. 420)

egocentrism   In Piaget's theory, the inability to take another person's perspective or point of view. (p. 381)

elaborative rehearsal   Rehearsal that involves focusing on the meaning of information to help encode and transfer it to long-term memory. (p. 234)

electroconvulsive therapy (ECT)   A biomedical therapy used primarily in the treatment of major depressive disorder that involves electrically inducing a brief brain seizure; also called *electroshock therapy*. (p. 622)

electroencephalograph   (e-lec-tro-en-SEFF-uh-low-graph) An instrument that uses electrodes placed on the scalp to measure and record the brain's electrical activity. (p. 140)

embryonic period   The second period of prenatal development, extending from the third week through the eighth week. (p. 364)

emerging adulthood   In industrialized countries, the stage of lifespan from approximately the late teens to the mid- to late-20s, which is characterized by exploration, instability, and flexibility in social roles, vocational choices, and relationships. (p. 396)

emotion   A complex psychological state that involves a subjective experience, a physiological response, and a behavioral or expressive response. (p. 336)

emotion-focused coping   Coping efforts primarily aimed at relieving or regulating the emotional impact of a stressful situation. (p. 522)

emotional intelligence   The capacity to understand and manage your own emotional experiences and to perceive, comprehend, and respond appropriately to the emotional responses of others. (p. 336)

empirical evidence   Verifiable evidence that is based upon objective observation, measurement, and/or experimentation. (p. 16)

encoding   The process of transforming information into a form that can be entered into and retained by the memory system. (p. 228)

encoding failure   The inability to recall specific information because of insufficient encoding of the information for storage in long-term memory. (p. 245)

encoding specificity principle   The principle that when the conditions of information retrieval are similar to the conditions of information encoding, retrieval is more likely to be successful. (p. 241)

endocrine system   (EN-doe-krin) The system of glands, located throughout the body, that secrete hormones into the bloodstream. (p. 58)

endorphins   (en-DORF-inz) Neurotransmitters that regulate pain perceptions. (p. 51)

epigenetics   The study of the cellular mechanisms that control gene expression and of the ways that gene expression impacts health and behavior. (p. 362)

episodic memory   Category of long-term memory that includes memories of particular events. (p. 235)

ESP (extrasensory perception)   Perception of information by some means other than through the normal processes of sensation. (p. 112)

ethnocentrism   The belief that one's own culture or ethnic group is superior to all others and the related tendency to use one's own culture as a standard by which to judge other cultures. (p. 13)

evolutionary psychology The application of principles of evolution, including natural selection, to explain psychological processes and phenomena. (p. 13)

exemplars Individual instances of a concept or category, held in memory. (p. 277)

experimental group or **experimental condition** In an experiment, the group of participants who are exposed to all experimental conditions, including the independent variable. (p. 26)

experimental research A method of investigation used to demonstrate cause-and-effect relationships by purposely manipulating one factor thought to produce change in another factor. (p. 26)

explicit cognition Deliberate, conscious mental processes involved in perceptions, judgments, decisions, and reasoning. (p. 456)

explicit memory Information or knowledge that can be consciously recollected; also called *declarative memory.* (p. 236)

exposure therapy Behavioral therapy for phobias, panic disorder, posttraumatic stress disorder, or related anxiety disorders in which the person is repeatedly exposed to the disturbing object or situation under controlled conditions. (p. 594)

extinction (in classical conditioning) The gradual weakening and apparent disappearance of conditioned behavior. In classical conditioning, extinction occurs when the conditioned stimulus is repeatedly presented without the unconditioned stimulus. (p. 187)

extinction (in operant conditioning) The gradual weakening and disappearance of conditioned behavior. In operant conditioning, extinction occurs when an emitted behavior is no longer followed by a reinforcer. (p. 206)

extrinsic motivation External factors or influences on behavior, such as rewards, consequences, or social expectations. (p. 333)

F

facial feedback hypothesis The view that expressing a specific emotion, especially facially, causes the subjective experience of that emotion. (p. 349)

false memory A distorted or fabricated recollection of something that did not actually occur. (p. 250)

family therapy A form of psychotherapy that is based on the assumption that the family is a system and that treats the family as a unit. (p. 608)

fetal period The third and longest period of prenatal development, extending from the ninth week until birth. (p. 365)

fight-or-flight response A rapidly occurring chain of internal physical reactions that prepare people to either fight or take flight from an immediate threat. (p. 507)

figure–ground relationship Gestalt principle stating that a perception is automatically separated into the *figure,* which clearly stands out, from its less distinct background, the *ground.* (p. 113)

five-factor model of personality A trait theory of personality that identifies extraversion, neuroticism, agreeableness, conscientiousness, and openness to experience as the fundamental building blocks of personality. (p. 439)

fixed-interval (FI) schedule A reinforcement schedule in which a reinforcer is delivered for the first response that occurs after a preset time interval has elapsed. (p. 208)

fixed-ratio (FR) schedule A reinforcement schedule in which a reinforcer is delivered after a fixed number of responses has occurred. (p. 207)

flashbulb memory The recall of very specific images or details surrounding a vivid, rare, or significant personal event; details may or may not be accurate. (p. 241)

forebrain The largest and most complex brain region, which contains centers for complex behaviors and mental processes; also called the *cerebrum.* (p. 66)

forgetting The inability to recall information that was previously available. (p. 243)

formal concept A mental category that is formed by learning the rules or features that define it. (p. 275)

formal operational stage In Piaget's theory, the fourth stage of cognitive development, which lasts from adolescence through adulthood; characterized by the ability to think logically about abstract principles and hypothetical situations. (p. 383)

fovea (FOE-vee-uh) A small area in the center of the retina, composed entirely of cones, where visual information is most sharply focused. (p. 93)

free association A psychoanalytic technique in which the patient spontaneously reports all thoughts, feelings, and mental images that arise, revealing unconscious thoughts and emotions. (pp. 417, 588)

frequency The rate of vibration, or the number of sound waves per second. (p. 98)

frequency distribution A summary of how often various scores occur in a sample of scores. Score values are arranged in order of magnitude, and the number of times each score occurs is recorded. (p. A-2)

frequency polygon A way of graphically representing a frequency distribution; frequency is marked above each score category on the graph's horizontal axis, and the marks are connected by straight lines. (p. A-3)

frequency theory The view that the basilar membrane vibrates at the same frequency as the sound wave. (p. 101)

frontal lobe The largest lobe of each cerebral hemisphere; processes voluntary muscle movements and is involved in thinking, planning, and emotional control. (p. 69)

functional fixedness The tendency to view objects as functioning only in their usual or customary way. (p. 281)

functional magnetic resonance imaging (fMRI) A noninvasive imaging technique that uses magnetic fields to map brain activity by measuring changes in the brain's blood flow and oxygen levels. (p. 33)

functional plasticity The brain's ability to shift functions from damaged to undamaged brain areas. (p. 62)

functionalism Early school of psychology that emphasized studying the purpose, or function, of behavior and mental experiences. (p. 6)

fundamental attribution error The tendency to attribute the behavior of others to internal, personal characteristics, while ignoring or underestimating the effects of external, situational factors; an attributional bias that is common in individualistic cultures. (p. 458)

G

g factor or **general intelligence** The notion of a general intelligence factor that is responsible for a person's overall performance on tests of mental ability. (p. 295)

GABA (gamma-aminobutyric acid) Neurotransmitter that usually communicates an inhibitory message. (p. 51)

ganglion cells In the retina, the specialized neurons that connect to the bipolar cells; the bundled axons of the ganglion cells form the optic nerve. (p. 93)

gate-control theory of pain The theory that pain is a product of both physiological and psychological factors that cause spinal gates to open and relay patterns of intense stimulation to the brain, which perceives them as pain. (p. 108)

gender The cultural, social, and psychological meanings that are associated with masculinity or femininity. (p. 375)

gender identity A person's psychological sense of being male or female. (p. 375)

gender roles The behaviors, attitudes, and personality traits that are designated as either masculine or feminine in a given culture. (p. 375)

gender schema theory The theory that gender-role development is influenced by the formation of schemas, or mental representations, of masculinity and femininity. (p. 376)

gene A unit of DNA on a chromosome that encodes instructions for making a particular protein molecule; the basic unit of heredity. (p. 361)

general adaptation syndrome Hans Selye's term for the three-stage progression of physical changes that occur when an organism is exposed to intense and prolonged stress. The three stages are alarm, resistance, and exhaustion. (p. 509)

generalized anxiety disorder (GAD) An anxiety disorder characterized by excessive, global, and persistent symptoms of anxiety; also called *free-floating anxiety.* (p. 541)

genotype (JEEN-oh-type) The genetic makeup of an individual organism. (p. 361)

germinal period The first two weeks of prenatal development. (p. 363)

Gestalt psychology (geh-SHTALT) School of psychology that maintained sensations are actively processed according to consistent perceptual rules, producing meaningful whole perceptions, or *gestalts.* (p. 110)

glial cells or **glia** (GLEE-ull) The support cells that assist neurons by providing structural support, nutrition, and removal of cell wastes; glial cells manufacture myelin. (p. 44)

glucose Simple sugar that provides energy and is primarily produced by the conversion of carbohydrates and fats; commonly called *blood sugar.* (p. 318)

glutamate Neurotransmitter that usually communicates an excitatory message. (p. 51)

gonads The endocrine glands that secrete hormones that regulate sexual characteristics and reproductive processes; *ovaries* in females and *testes* in males. (p. 60)

graphology A pseudoscience that claims to assess personality, social, and occupational attributes based on a person's distinctive handwriting, doodles, and drawing style. (p. 442)

group therapy A form of psychotherapy that involves one or more therapists working simultaneously with a small group of clients. (p. 605)

gustation Technical name for the sense of taste. (p. 103)

H

hair cells The hair-like sensory receptors for sound, which are embedded in the basilar membrane of the cochlea. (p. 101)

hallucination A false or distorted perception that seems vividly real to the person experiencing it. (p. 571)

health psychology The branch of psychology that studies how biological, behavioral, and social factors influence health, illness, medical treatment, and health-related behaviors. (p. 500)

heritability The percentage of variation within a given population that is due to heredity. (p. 302)

heuristic A problem-solving strategy that involves following a general rule of thumb to reduce the number of possible solutions. (p. 279)

hidden observer Hilgard's term for the hidden, or dissociated, stream of mental activity that continues during hypnosis. (p. 158)

hierarchy of needs Maslow's hierarchical division of motivation into levels that progress from basic physical needs to psychological needs to self-fulfillment needs. (p. 331)

higher order conditioning (also called *second-order conditioning*) A procedure in which a conditioned stimulus from one learning trial functions as the unconditioned stimulus in a new conditioning trial; the second conditioned stimulus comes to elicit the conditioned response, even though it has never been directly paired with the unconditioned stimulus. (p. 186)

hindbrain A region at the base of the brain that contains several structures that regulate basic life functions. (p. 65)

hindsight bias The tendency to overestimate one's ability to have foreseen or predicted the outcome of an event. (p. 459)

hippocampus A curved forebrain structure that is part of the limbic system and is involved in learning and forming new memories. (p. 71)

histogram A way of graphically representing a frequency distribution; a type of bar chart that uses vertical bars that touch. (p. A-3)

homeostasis (home-ee-oh-STAY-sis) The idea that the body monitors and maintains internal states, such as body temperature and energy supplies, at relatively constant levels; in general, the tendency to reach or maintain equilibrium. (p. 314)

hormones Chemical messengers secreted into the bloodstream primarily by endocrine glands. (p. 58)

hue The property of wavelengths of light known as color; different wavelengths correspond to our subjective experience of different colors. (p. 95)

humanistic psychology School of psychology and theoretical viewpoint that emphasizes each person's unique potential for psychological growth and self-direction. (p. 9)

humanistic psychology (theory of personality) The theoretical viewpoint on personality that generally emphasizes the inherent goodness of people, human potential, self-actualization, the self-concept, and healthy personality development. (p. 429)

humanistic theories of motivation The view that emphasizes the importance of psychological and cognitive factors in motivation, especially the notion that people are motivated to realize their personal potential. (p. 317)

hypnagogic hallucinations (hip-na-GAH-jick) Vivid sensory phenomena that occur during the onset of sleep. (p. 141)

hypnosis (hip-NO-sis) A cooperative social interaction in which the hypnotized person responds to the hypnotist's suggestions with changes in perception, memory, and behavior. (p. 156)

hypothalamus (hi-poe-THAL-uh-muss) A peanut-sized forebrain structure that is part of the limbic system and that regulates behaviors related to survival, such as eating, drinking, and sexual activity. (p. 71)

hypothesis (high-POTH-uh-sis) A tentative statement about the relationship between two or more variables; a testable prediction or question. (p. 16)

I

id Latin for *the it*; in Freud's theory, the completely unconscious, irrational component of personality that seeks immediate satisfaction of instinctual urges and drives; ruled by the pleasure principle. (p. 418)

identification In psychoanalytic theory, an ego defense mechanism that involves reducing anxiety by imitating the behavior and characteristics of another person. (p. 422)

identity A person's sense of self, including his or her memories, experiences, and the values and beliefs that guide his or her behavior. (p. 391)

imagination inflation A memory phenomenon in which vividly imagining an event markedly increases confidence that the event actually occurred. (p. 253)

immune system Body system that produces specialized white blood cells that protect the body from viruses, bacteria, and tumor cells. (p. 511)

implicit attitudes Preferences and biases toward particular groups that are automatic, spontaneous, unintentional, and often unconscious; measured with the *Implicit Associations Test* (IAT). (p. 469)

implicit cognition Automatic, nonconscious mental processes that influence perceptions, judgments, decisions, and reasoning. (p. 456)

implicit memory Information or knowledge that affects behavior or task performance but cannot be consciously recollected; also called *non-declarative memory*. (p. 236)

implicit personality theory   A network of assumptions or beliefs about the relationships among various types of people, traits, and behaviors. (p. 456)

in-group   A social group to which one belongs. (p. 467)

in-group bias   The tendency to judge the behavior of in-group members favorably and out-group members unfavorably. (p. 469)

incentive theories   The view that behavior is motivated by the pull of external goals, such as rewards. (p. 316)

independent variable   The purposely manipulated factor thought to produce change in an experiment; also called the *treatment variable*. (p. 26)

individualistic cultures   Cultures that emphasize the needs and goals of the individual over the needs and goals of the group. (p. 13)

induction   A discipline technique that combines parental control with explaining why a behavior is prohibited. (p. 408)

industrial/organizational (I/O) psychology   The branch of psychology that focuses on the study of human behavior in the workplace. (p. B-1)

inferential statistics   Mathematical methods used to determine how likely it is that a study's outcome is due to chance and whether the outcome can be legitimately generalized to a larger population. (p. A-11)

information-processing model of cognitive development   The model that views cognitive development as a process that is continuous over the lifespan and that studies the development of basic mental processes such as attention, memory, and problem solving. (p. 386)

informational social influence   Behavior that is motivated by the desire to be correct. (p. 473)

inhalants   Chemical substances that are inhaled to produce an alteration in consciousness. (p. 168)

inner ear   The part of the ear where sound is transduced into neural impulses; consists of the cochlea and semicircular canals. (p. 99)

insight   The sudden realization of how a problem can be solved. (p. 279)

insomnia   A condition in which a person regularly experiences an inability to fall asleep, to stay asleep, or to feel adequately rested by sleep. (p. 153)

instinct theories   The view that certain human behaviors are innate and due to evolutionary programming. (p. 314)

instinctive drift   The tendency of an animal to revert to instinctive behaviors that can interfere with the performance of an operantly conditioned response. (p. 214)

insulin   Hormone produced by the pancreas that regulates blood levels of glucose and signals the hypothalamus, regulating hunger and eating behavior. (p. 318)

intellectual disability   Formerly called *mental retardation*. Neurodevelopmental disorder characterized by deficits in general mental abilities which result in impairments of adaptive functioning, such that the individual fails to meet standards of personal independence and social responsibility. (p. 300)

intelligence   The global capacity to think rationally, act purposefully, and deal effectively with the environment. (p. 290)

intelligence quotient (IQ)   A measure of general intelligence derived by comparing an individual's score with the scores of others in the same age group. (p. 291)

interference theory   The theory that forgetting is caused by one memory competing with or replacing another. (p. 247)

interneuron   The type of neuron that communicates information from one neuron to the next. (p. 43)

interpersonal engagement   Emotion dimension reflecting the degree to which emotions involve a relationship with another person or other people. (p. 337)

interpersonal therapy (IPT)   A brief psychodynamic psychotherapy that focuses on current relationships and is based on the assumption that symptoms are caused and maintained by interpersonal problems. (p. 590)

interpretation   A technique used in psychoanalysis in which the psychoanalyst offers a carefully timed explanation of the patient's dreams, free associations, or behaviors to facilitate the recognition of unconscious conflicts or motivations. (p. 589)

intrinsic motivation   The desire to engage in tasks that are inherently satisfying and enjoyable, novel, or optimally challenging; the desire to do something for its own sake. (p. 333)

intuition   Coming to a conclusion or making a judgment without conscious awareness of the thought processes involved. (p. 279)

iris   (EYE-riss) The colored part of the eye, which is the muscle that controls the size of the pupil. (p. 91)

irreversibility   In Piaget's theory, the inability to mentally reverse a sequence of events or logical operations. (p. 381)

J

James–Lange theory of emotion   The theory that emotions arise from the perception of body changes. (p. 347)

job analysis   A technique that identifies the major responsibilities of a job, along with the human characteristics needed to fill it. (p. B-3)

just-world hypothesis   The assumption that the world is fair and that therefore people get what they deserve and deserve what they get. (p. 459)

K

K complex   Single but large high-voltage spike of brain activity that characterizes stage 2 NREM sleep. (p. 142)

kinesthetic sense   (kin-ess-THET-ick) The technical name for the sense of location and position of body parts in relation to one another. (p. 109)

L

language   A system for combining arbitrary symbols to produce an infinite number of meaningful statements. (p. 284)

latent content   In Freud's psychoanalytic theory, the unconscious wishes, thoughts, and urges that are concealed in the manifest content of a dream. (p. 149)

latent learning   Tolman's term for learning that occurs in the absence of reinforcement but is not behaviorally demonstrated until a reinforcer becomes available. (p. 211)

lateralization of function   The notion that specific psychological or cognitive functions are processed primarily on one side of the brain. (p. 73)

law of effect   Learning principle, proposed by Thorndike, in which responses followed by a satisfying effect become strengthened and are more likely to recur in a particular situation, while responses followed by a dissatisfying effect are weakened and less likely to recur in a particular situation. (p. 197)

leader–member exchange model   A model of leadership emphasizing that the quality of the interactions between supervisors and subordinates varies depending on the unique characteristics of both. (p. B-9)

learned helplessness   A phenomenon in which exposure to inescapable and uncontrollable aversive events produces passive behavior. (p. 212)

learning   A process that produces a relatively enduring change in behavior or knowledge as a result of past experience. (p. 183)

lens   A transparent structure, located behind the pupil, that actively focuses, or bends, light as it enters the eye. (p. 91)

leptin   Hormone produced by fat cells that signals the hypothalamus, regulating hunger and eating behavior. (p. 319)

libido   The psychological and emotional energy associated with expressions of sexuality; the sex drive. (p. 418)

limbic system   A group of forebrain structures that form a border around the brainstem and are involved in emotion, motivation, learning, and memory. (p. 71)

linguistic relativity hypothesis   The hypothesis that differences among languages cause differences in the thoughts of their speakers. (p. 286)

lithium   A naturally occurring substance that is used in the treatment of bipolar disorder. (p. 618)

long-term memory   The stage of memory that represents the long-term storage of information. (p. 229)

long-term potentiation   A long-lasting increase in synaptic strength between two neurons. (p. 258)

longitudinal design   Research strategy in which a variable or group of variables are studied in the same group of participants over time. (p. 358)

loudness   The intensity (or amplitude) of a sound wave, measured in decibels. (p. 98)

LSD   A synthetic psychedelic drug. (p. 172)

lymphocytes   (LIMF-oh-sites) Specialized white blood cells that are responsible for immune defenses. (p. 511)

M

magnetic resonance imaging (MRI)   A noninvasive imaging technique that produces highly detailed images of the body's structures and tissues, using electromagnetic signals generated by the body in response to magnetic fields. (p. 32)

maintenance rehearsal   The mental or verbal repetition of information in order to maintain it beyond the usual 20-second duration of short-term memory. (p. 231)

major depressive disorder   A mood disorder characterized by extreme and persistent feelings of despondency, worthlessness, and hopelessness, causing impaired emotional, cognitive, behavioral, and physical functioning. (p. 550)

manic episode   A sudden, rapidly escalating emotional state characterized by extreme euphoria, excitement, physical energy, and rapid thoughts and speech. (p. 553)

manifest content   In Freud's psychoanalytic theory, the elements of a dream that are consciously experienced and remembered by the dreamer. (p. 149)

marijuana   A psychoactive drug derived from the hemp plant. (p. 174)

MDMA or **ecstasy**   Synthetic club drug that combines stimulant and mild psychedelic effects. (p. 174)

mean   The sum of a set of scores in a distribution divided by the number of scores; the mean is usually the most representative measure of central tendency. (p. A-5)

measure of central tendency   A single number that presents some information about the "center" of a frequency distribution. (p. A-4)

measure of variability   A single number that presents information about the spread of scores in a distribution. (p. A-5)

median   The score that divides a frequency distribution exactly in half so that the same number of scores lie on each side of it. (p. A-5)

meditation   Any one of a number of sustained concentration techniques that focus attention and heighten awareness. (p. 160)

medulla   (muh-DOOL-uh) A hindbrain structure that controls vital life functions such as breathing and circulation. (p. 65)

melatonin   (mel-uh-TONE-in) A hormone manufactured by the pineal gland that produces sleepiness. (p. 138)

memory   The mental processes that enable you to retain and retrieve information over time. (p. 228)

memory consolidation   The gradual, physical process of converting new long-term memories to stable, enduring memory codes. (p. 260)

memory trace or **engram**   The hypothetical brain changes associated with a particular stored memory. (p. 256)

menarche   (meh-NAR-kee) A female's first menstrual period, which occurs during puberty. (p. 387)

menopause   The natural cessation of menstruation and the end of reproductive capacity in women. (p. 398)

mental age   A measurement of intelligence in which an individual's mental level is expressed in terms of the average abilities of a given age group. (p. 291)

mental image   A mental representation of objects or events that are not physically present. (p. 273)

mental set   The tendency to persist in solving problems with solutions that have worked in the past. (p. 281)

mere exposure effect   The finding that repeated exposure to a stimulus increases a person's preference for that stimulus. (p. 89)

mescaline   (MESS-kuh-lin) A psychedelic drug derived from the peyote cactus. (p. 172)

meta-analysis   A statistical technique that involves combining and analyzing the results of many research studies on a specific topic in order to identify overall trends.   (p. 18)

midbrain   The middle and smallest brain region, involved in processing auditory and visual sensory information. (p. 66)

middle ear   The part of the ear that amplifies sound waves; consists of three small bones: the hammer, the anvil, and the stirrup. (p. 99)

mindfulness meditation   A technique in which practitioners focus *awareness* on *present experience* with *acceptance*. (p. 528)

Minnesota Multiphasic Personality Inventory (MMPI)   A self-report inventory that assesses personality characteristics and psychological disorders; used to assess both normal and disturbed populations. (p. 444)

mirror neurons   Neurons that activate both when an action is performed and when the same action is perceived. (p. 217)

misinformation effect   A memory-distortion phenomenon in which your existing memories can be altered if you are exposed to misleading information. (p. 249)

mode   The most frequently occurring score in a distribution. (p. A-4)

monocular cues   (moe-NOCK-you-ler) Distance or depth cues that can be processed by either eye alone. (p. 117)

mood congruence   An encoding specificity phenomenon in which a given mood tends to evoke memories that are consistent with that mood. (p. 241)

moon illusion   A visual illusion involving the misperception that the moon is larger when it is on the horizon than when it is directly overhead. (p. 124)

moral reasoning   The aspect of cognitive development that has to do with how an individual reasons about moral decisions. (p. 393)

motivation   The biological, emotional, cognitive, or social forces that activate and direct behavior. (p. 314)

motor neuron   The type of neuron that signals muscles to relax or contract. (p. 43)

Müller-Lyer illusion   A famous visual illusion involving the misperception of the identical length of two lines, one with arrows pointed inward, one with arrows pointed outward. (p. 123)

myelin sheath   (MY-eh-lin) A white, fatty covering wrapped around the axons of some neurons that increases their communication speed. (p. 44)

N

narcolepsy   (NAR-ko-lep-see) A sleep disorder characterized by excessive daytime sleepiness and brief lapses into sleep throughout the day. (p. 153)

natural concept   A mental category that is formed as a result of everyday experience. (p. 277)

natural experiment   A study investigating the effects of a naturally occurring event on the research participants. (p. 29)

naturalistic observation   The systematic observation and recording of behaviors as they occur in their natural setting. (p. 22)

negative correlation   A finding that two factors vary systematically in opposite directions, one increasing as the other decreases. (pp. 25, A-8)

negative punishment   A situation in which an operant is followed by the removal or subtraction of a reinforcing stimulus; also called *punishment by removal*. (p. 201)

negative reinforcement   A situation in which a response results in the removal of, avoidance of, or escape from a punishing stimulus, increasing the likelihood that the response will be repeated in similar situations. (p. 199)

negative symptoms   In schizophrenia, symptoms that reflect defects or deficits in normal functioning, including flat affect, alogia, and avolition. (p. 571)

neodissociation theory of hypnosis   Theory proposed by Ernest Hilgard that explains hypnotic effects as being due to the splitting of consciousness into two simultaneous streams of mental activity, only one of which the hypnotic participant is consciously aware during hypnosis. (p. 158)

nerves   Bundles of neuron axons that carry information in the peripheral nervous system. (p. 53)

nervous system   The primary internal communication network of the body; divided into the central nervous system and the peripheral nervous system. (p. 53)

neurocognitive model of dreaming   Model of dreaming that emphasizes the continuity of waking and dreaming cognition, and states that dreaming is like thinking under conditions of reduced sensory input and the absence of voluntary control. (p. 151)

neurogenesis   The development of new neurons. (p. 63)

neuron   A highly specialized cell that communicates information in electrical and chemical form; a nerve cell. (p. 43)

neuropeptide Y (NPY)   Neurotransmitter found in several brain areas, most notably the hypothalamus, that stimulates eating behavior and reduces metabolism, promoting positive energy balance and weight gain. (p. 320)

neuroscience   The study of the nervous system, especially the brain. (pp. 10, 42)

neurotransmitters   Chemical messengers manufactured by a neuron. (p. 48)

nicotine   A stimulant drug found in tobacco products. (p. 171)

nightmare   A vivid and frightening or unpleasant anxiety dream that occurs during REM sleep. (p. 149)

nociceptors   Specialized sensory receptors for pain that are found in the skin, muscles, and internal organs. (p. 107)

norepinephrine   (nor-ep-in-EF-rin) Neurotransmitter involved in learning, memory, and regulation of sleep; also, a hormone manufactured by adrenal glands. (p. 51)

normal curve or **normal distribution**   A bell-shaped distribution of individual differences in a normal population in which most scores cluster around the average score. (p. 295)

normative social influence   Behavior that is motivated by the desire to gain social acceptance and approval. (p. 473)

NREM sleep   Quiet, typically dreamless sleep in which rapid eye movements are absent; divided into four stages; also called *quiet sleep*. (p. 140)

O

obedience   The performance of a behavior in response to a direct command. (p. 475)

obese   Condition characterized by excessive body fat and a body mass index equal to or greater than 30.0. (p. 321)

object permanence   The understanding that an object continues to exist even when it can no longer be seen. (p. 381)

observational learning   Learning that occurs through observing the actions of others. (p. 214)

obsessions   Repeated, intrusive, and uncontrollable irrational thoughts or mental images that cause extreme anxiety and distress. (p. 548)

obsessive–compulsive disorder (OCD)   Disorder characterized by the presence of intrusive, repetitive, and unwanted thoughts (obsessions) and repetitive behaviors or mental acts that an individual feels driven to perform (compulsions). (p. 548)

obstructive sleep apnea   (APP-nee-uh) A sleep disorder in which the person repeatedly stops breathing during sleep. (p. 153)

occipital lobe   (ock-SIP-it-ull) An area at the back of each cerebral hemisphere that is the primary receiving area for visual information. (p. 69)

Oedipus complex   In Freud's theory, a child's unconscious sexual desire for the opposite-sex parent, usually accompanied by hostile feelings toward the same-sex parent. (p. 422)

olfaction   Technical name for the sense of smell. (p. 103)

olfactory bulb   (ole-FACK-tuh-ree) The enlarged ending of the olfactory cortex at the front of the brain where the sensation of smell is registered. (p. 104)

operant   Skinner's term for an actively emitted (or voluntary) behavior that operates on the environment to produce consequences. (p. 198)

operant chamber or **Skinner box**   The experimental apparatus invented by B.F. Skinner to study the relationship between environmental events and active behaviors. (p. 205)

operant conditioning   The basic learning process that involves changing the probability that a response will be repeated by manipulating the consequences of that response. (p. 198)

operational definition   A precise description of how the variables in a study will be manipulated or measured. (p. 16)

opioids   (OH-pee-oidz) A category of psychoactive drugs that are chemically similar to morphine and have strong pain-relieving properties; also called *opiates* or *narcotics*. (p. 169)

opponent-process theory of color vision   The theory that color vision is the product of opposing pairs of color receptors: red–green, blue–yellow, and black–white; when one member of a color pair is stimulated, the other member is inhibited. (p. 97)

optic chiasm   (KY-az-uhm) The point in the brain where the optic nerve fibers from each eye meet and partly cross over to the opposite side of the brain. (p. 94)

optic disk   Area of the retina without rods or cones, where the optic nerve exits the back of the eye. (p. 93)

optic nerve   The thick nerve that exits from the back of the eye and carries visual information to the visual cortex in the brain. (p. 93)

optimistic explanatory style   Accounting for negative events or situations with external, unstable, and specific explanations. (p. 515)

organizational behavior   A subarea of I/O psychology that focuses on the workplace culture and its influence on employee behavior. (p. B-2)

out-group   A social group to which one does not belong. (p. 467)

out-group homogeneity effect   The tendency to see members of out-groups as very similar to one another. (p. 469)

outer ear   The part of the ear that collects sound waves; consists of the pinna, the ear canal, and the eardrum. (p. 99)

oxytocin   Hormone involved in reproduction, social motivation, and social behavior. (p. 59)

P

pain The unpleasant sensation of physical discomfort or suffering that can occur in varying degrees of intensity. (p. 106)

panic attack A sudden episode of extreme anxiety that rapidly escalates in intensity. (p. 542)

panic disorder An anxiety disorder in which the person experiences frequent and unexpected panic attacks. (p. 542)

parapsychology The scientific investigation of claims of paranormal phenomena and abilities. (p. 112)

parasomnias (pare-uh-SOM-nee-uz) A category of sleep disorders characterized by arousal or activation during sleep or sleep transitions; includes *sleepwalking, sleep terrors, sleepsex,* and *sleep-related eating disorder.* (p. 153)

parasympathetic nervous system The branch of the autonomic nervous system that maintains normal bodily functions and conserves the body's physical resources. (p. 57)

parietal lobe (puh-RYE-ut-ull) An area on each hemisphere of the cerebral cortex located above the temporal lobe that processes somatic sensations. (p. 69)

partial reinforcement A situation in which the occurrence of a particular response is only sometimes followed by a reinforcer. (p. 206)

partial reinforcement effect The phenomenon in which behaviors that are conditioned using partial reinforcement are more resistant to extinction than behaviors that are conditioned using continuous reinforcement. (p. 206)

perception The process of integrating, organizing, and interpreting sensations. (p. 86)

perceptual constancy The tendency to perceive objects, especially familiar objects, as constant and unchanging despite changes in sensory input. (p. 121)

perceptual illusion The misperception of the true characteristics of an object or an image. (p. 123)

perceptual set The tendency to perceive objects or situations from a particular frame of reference. (p. 125)

peripheral nervous system (per-IF-er-ull) The division of the nervous system that includes all the nerves lying outside the central nervous system. (p. 55)

permissive parenting style Parenting style in which parents are extremely tolerant and not demanding; permissive-indulgent parents are responsive to their children, while permissive-indifferent parents are unresponsive. (p. 407)

persistent depressive disorder A disorder involving chronic feelings of depression that is often less severe than major depressive disorder. (p. 552)

person perception The mental processes we use to form judgments and draw conclusions about the characteristics and motives of other people. (p. 454)

personality An individual's unique and relatively consistent patterns of thinking, feeling, and behaving. (p. 415)

personality disorder Inflexible, maladaptive patterns of thoughts, emotions, behavior, and interpersonal functioning that are stable over time and across situations and that deviate from the expectations of the individual's culture. (p. 562)

personality theory A theory that attempts to describe and explain similarities and differences in people's patterns of thinking, feeling, and behaving. (p. 415)

personnel psychology A subarea of I/O psychology that focuses on matching people's characteristics to job requirements, accurately measuring job performance, and assessing employee training needs. (p. B-2)

persuasion The deliberate attempt to influence the attitudes or behavior of another person in a situation in which that person has some freedom of choice. (p. 491)

pessimistic explanatory style Accounting for negative events or situations with internal, stable, and global explanations. (p. 515)

phenotype (FEEN-oh-type) The observable traits or characteristics of an organism as determined by the interaction of genetics and environmental factors. (p. 361)

pheromones Chemical signals released by an animal that communicate information and affect the behavior of other animals of the same species. (p. 103)

phobia A persistent and irrational fear of a specific object, situation, or activity. (p. 543)

phrenology (freh-NAHL-uh-jee) A pseudoscientific theory of the brain that claimed that personality characteristics, moral character, and intelligence could be determined by examining the bumps on a person's skull. (p. 60)

physical dependence A condition in which a person has physically adapted to a drug so that he or she must take the drug regularly in order to avoid withdrawal symptoms. (p. 164)

pitch The relative highness or lowness of a sound, determined by the frequency of a sound wave. (p. 98)

pituitary gland (pih-TOO-ih-tare-ee) The endocrine gland attached to the base of the brain that secretes hormones affecting the function of other glands as well as hormones that act directly on physical processes. (p. 59)

place theory The view that different frequencies cause larger vibrations at different locations along the basilar membrane. (p. 103)

placebo A fake substance, treatment, or procedure that has no known direct effects. (p. 29)

placebo effect Any change attributed to a person's beliefs and expectations rather than to an actual drug, treatment, or procedure. (p. 29)

placebo response An individual's psychological and physiological response to what is actually a fake treatment or drug; also called *placebo effect.* (p. 192)

pleasure principle The motive to obtain pleasure and avoid tension or discomfort; the most fundamental human motive and the guiding principle of the id. (p. 418)

pons A hindbrain structure that connects the medulla to the two sides of the cerebellum; helps coordinate and integrate movements on each side of the body. (p. 66)

population A complete set of something—people, nonhuman animals, objects, or events. (p. A-12)

positive correlation A finding that two factors vary systematically in the same direction, increasing or decreasing together. (pp. 25, A-8)

positive psychology The study of positive emotions and psychological states, positive individual traits, and the social institutions that foster positive individuals and communities. (p. 11)

positive punishment A situation in which an operant is followed by the presentation or addition of an aversive stimulus; also called *punishment by application.* (p. 200)

positive reinforcement A situation in which a response is followed by the addition of a reinforcing stimulus, increasing the likelihood that the response will be repeated in similar situations. (p. 198)

positive symptoms In schizophrenia, symptoms that reflect excesses or distortions of normal functioning, including delusions, hallucinations, and disorganized thoughts and behavior. (p. 571)

positron emission tomography (PET) scan An invasive imaging technique that provides color-coded images of brain activity by tracking the brain's use of a radioactively tagged compound, such as glucose, oxygen, or a drug. (p. 32)

possible selves The aspect of the self-concept that includes images of the selves that you hope, fear, or expect to become in the future. (p. 447)

posthypnotic amnesia   The inability to recall specific information because of a hypnotic suggestion. (p. 156)

posthypnotic suggestion   A suggestion made during hypnosis asking a person to carry out a specific instruction following the hypnotic session. (p. 156)

posttraumatic stress disorder (PTSD)   A disorder triggered by exposure to a highly traumatic event that results in recurrent, involuntary, and intrusive memories of the event; avoidance of stimuli and situations associated with the event; negative changes in thoughts, moods, and emotions; and a persistent state of heightened physical arousal. (p. 546)

prejudice   A negative attitude toward people who belong to a specific social group. (p. 465)

prenatal stage   The stage of development before birth; divided into the germinal, embryonic, and fetal periods. (p. 363)

preoperational stage   In Piaget's theory, the second stage of cognitive development, which lasts from about age 2 to age 7; characterized by increasing use of symbols and prelogical thought processes. (p. 381)

primary reinforcer   A stimulus or event that is naturally or inherently reinforcing for a given species, such as food, water, or other biological necessities. (p. 200)

primary sex characteristics   Sexual organs that are directly involved in reproduction, such as the uterus, ovaries, penis, and testicles. (p. 386)

proactive interference   Forgetting in which an old memory interferes with remembering a new memory; forward-acting memory interference. (p. 247)

problem solving   Thinking and behavior directed toward attaining a goal that is not readily available. (p. 277)

problem-focused coping   Coping efforts primarily aimed at directly changing or managing a threatening or harmful stressor. (p. 522)

procedural memory   Category of long-term memory that includes memories of different skills, operations, and actions. (p. 235)

production vocabulary   The words that an infant or child understands and can speak. (p. 372)

projective test   A type of personality test that involves a person's interpreting an ambiguous image; used to assess unconscious motives, conflicts, psychological defenses, and personality traits. (p. 442)

proprioceptors   (pro-pree-oh-SEP-terz) Sensory receptors, located in the muscles and joints, that provide information about body position and movement. (p. 109)

prosocial behavior   Any behavior that helps another, whether the underlying motive is self-serving or selfless. (p. 483)

prospective memory   Remembering to do something in the future. (p. 245)

prototype   The most typical instance of a particular concept. (p. 277)

pseudoscience   Fake or false science that makes claims based on little or no scientific evidence. (p. 20)

psychedelic drugs   (sy-kuh-DEL-ick) A category of psychoactive drugs that create sensory and perceptual distortions, alter mood, and affect thinking. (p. 172)

psychiatry   Medical specialty area focused on the diagnosis, treatment, causes, and prevention of mental and behavioral disorders. (p. 15)

psychoactive drug   A drug that alters consciousness, perception, mood, and behavior. (p. 164)

psychoanalysis   Personality theory and form of psychotherapy that emphasizes the role of unconscious factors in personality and behavior. (p. 7)

psychoanalysis (in personality)   Sigmund Freud's theory of personality, which emphasizes unconscious determinants of behavior, sexual and aggressive instinctual drives, and the enduring effects of early childhood experiences on later personality development. (p. 415)

psychoanalysis (in psychotherapy)   A type of psychotherapy originated by Sigmund Freud in which free association, dream interpretation, and analysis of resistance and transference are used to explore repressed or unconscious impulses, anxieties, and internal conflicts. (p. 588)

psychological disorder or **mental disorder**   A pattern of behavioral and psychological symptoms that causes significant personal distress, impairs the ability to function in one or more important areas of life, or both. (p. 535)

psychological test   A test that assesses a person's abilities, aptitudes, interests, or personality on the basis of a systematically obtained sample of behavior. (p. 442)

psychology   The scientific study of behavior and mental processes. (p. 2)

psychoneuroimmunology   An interdisciplinary field that studies the interconnections among psychological processes, nervous and endocrine system functions, and the immune system. (p. 511)

psychopathology   The scientific study of the origins, symptoms, and development of psychological disorders. (p. 535)

psychosexual stages   In Freud's theory, age-related developmental periods in which the child's sexual urges are focused on different areas of the body and are expressed through the activities associated with those areas. (p. 421)

psychotherapy   The treatment of emotional, behavioral, and interpersonal problems through the use of psychological techniques designed to encourage understanding of problems and modify troubling feelings, behaviors, or relationships. (p. 586)

psychotropic medications   (sy-ko-TRO-pick) Drugs that alter mental functions, alleviate psychological symptoms, and are used to treat psychological or mental disorders. (p. 614)

puberty   The stage of adolescence in which an individual reaches sexual maturity and becomes physiologically capable of sexual reproduction. (p. 386)

punishment   The presentation of a stimulus or event following a behavior that acts to decrease the likelihood of the behavior being repeated. (p. 200)

pupil   The opening in the middle of the iris that changes size to let in different amounts of light. (p. 91)

R

random assignment   The process of assigning participants to experimental conditions so that all participants have an equal chance of being assigned to any of the conditions or groups in the study. (p. 26)

random selection   Process in which subjects are selected randomly from a larger group such that every group member has an equal chance of being included in the study. (p. 23)

range   A measure of variability; the highest score in a distribution minus the lowest score. (p. A-5)

rational-emotive behavior therapy (REBT)   A type of cognitive therapy, developed by psychologist Albert Ellis, that focuses on changing the client's irrational beliefs. (p. 599)

reality principle   The capacity to accommodate external demands by postponing gratification until the appropriate time or circumstances exist. (p. 418)

recall   A test of long-term memory that involves retrieving information without the aid of retrieval cues; also called free recall. (p. 240)

reciprocal determinism   A model proposed by psychologist Albert Bandura that explains human functioning and personality as caused by the interaction of behavioral, cognitive, and environmental factors. (p. 433)

recognition   A test of long-term memory that involves identifying correct information out of several possible choices. (p. 240)

reinforcement The occurrence of a stimulus or event following a response that increases the likelihood of that response being repeated. (p. 198)

reliability The ability of a test to produce consistent results when administered on repeated occasions under similar conditions. (p. 295)

REM rebound A phenomenon in which a person who is deprived of REM sleep greatly increases the amount of time spent in REM sleep at the first opportunity to sleep without interruption. (p. 147)

REM sleep Type of sleep during which rapid eye movements (REM) and dreaming usually occur and voluntary muscle activity is suppressed; also called *active sleep* or *paradoxical sleep*. (p. 140)

replicate To repeat or duplicate a scientific study in order to increase confidence in the validity of the original findings. (p. 18)

representative sample A selected segment that very closely parallels the larger population being studied on relevant characteristics. (p. 23)

representativeness heuristic A strategy in which the likelihood of an event is estimated by comparing how similar it is to the prototype of the event. (p. 283)

repression Motivated forgetting that occurs unconsciously; a memory that is blocked and unavailable to consciousness. (p. 247)

repression (in psychoanalytic theory of personality and psychotherapy) The unconscious exclusion of anxiety-provoking thoughts, feelings, and memories from conscious awareness; the most fundamental ego defense mechanism. (p. 420)

resistance In psychoanalysis, the patient's unconscious attempts to block the revelation of repressed memories and conflicts. (p. 589)

resting potential The state in which a neuron is prepared to activate and communicate its message if it receives sufficient stimulation. (p. 44)

reticular formation (reh-TICK-you-ler) A network of nerve fibers located in the center of the medulla that helps regulate attention, arousal, and sleep; also called the *reticular activating system*. (p. 66)

retina (RET-in-uh) A thin, light-sensitive membrane, located at the back of the eye, that contains the sensory receptors for vision. (p. 93)

retrieval The process of recovering information stored in memory so that we are consciously aware of it. (pp. 229, 238)

retrieval cue A clue, prompt, or hint that helps trigger recall of a given piece of information stored in long-term memory. (p. 238)

retrieval cue failure The inability to recall long-term memories because of inadequate or missing retrieval cues. (p. 238)

retroactive interference Forgetting in which a new memory interferes with remembering an old memory; backward-acting memory interference. (p. 247)

retrograde amnesia Loss of memory, especially for episodic information; backward-acting amnesia. (p. 260)

reuptake The process by which neurotransmitter molecules detach from a postsynaptic neuron and are reabsorbed by a presynaptic neuron so they can be recycled and used again. (p. 48)

rods The long, thin, blunt sensory receptors of the eye that are highly sensitive to light, but not to color, and that are primarily responsible for peripheral vision and night vision. (p. 93)

Rorschach Inkblot Test A projective test using inkblots, developed by Swiss psychiatrist Hermann Rorschach in 1921. (p. 442)

S

sample A selected segment of the population used to represent the group that is being studied. (p. 23); a subset of a population. (p. A-12)

saturation The property of color that corresponds to the purity of the light wave. (p. 95)

scatter diagram or **scatter plot** A graph that represents the relationship between two variables. (p. A-8)

schedule of reinforcement The delivery of a reinforcer according to a preset pattern based on the number of responses or the time interval between responses. (p. 207)

schema (SKEE-muh) An organized cluster of information about a particular topic. (p. 250)

schizophrenia A psychological disorder in which the ability to function is impaired by severely distorted beliefs, perceptions, and thought processes. (p. 569)

scientific method A set of assumptions, attitudes, and procedures that guide researchers in creating questions to investigate, in generating evidence, and in drawing conclusions. (p. 15)

script A schema for the typical sequence of an everyday event. (p. 250)

seasonal affective disorder (SAD) A mood disorder in which episodes of depression typically occur during the fall and winter and subside during the spring and summer. (p. 551)

secondary sex characteristics Sexual characteristics that develop during puberty and are not directly involved in reproduction but differentiate between the sexes, such as male facial hair and female breast development. (p. 387)

selection device validity The extent to which a personnel selection device is successful in distinguishing between those who will become high performers at a certain job and those who will not. (p. B-5)

selective serotonin reuptake inhibitors (SSRIs) Class of antidepressant medications that increase the availability of serotonin in the brain and cause fewer side effects than earlier antidepressants; they include Prozac, Paxil, and Zoloft. (p. 619)

self-actualization Defined by Maslow as a person's "full use and exploitation of talents, capacities, and potentialities." (p. 333)

self-concept The set of perceptions and beliefs that you hold about yourself. (p. 429)

self-determination theory (SDT) Deci and Ryan's theory that optimal human functioning can occur only if the psychological needs for autonomy, competence, and relatedness are satisfied. (p. 333)

self-efficacy The beliefs that people have about their ability to meet the demands of a specific situation; feelings of self-confidence. (pp. 351, 434)

self-report inventory A type of psychological test in which a person's responses to standardized questions are compared to established norms. (p. 444)

self-serving bias The tendency to attribute successful outcomes of one's own behavior to internal causes and unsuccessful outcomes to external, situational causes. (p. 461)

semantic memory Category of long-term memory that includes memories of general knowledge, concepts, facts, and names. (p. 236)

semantic network model A model that describes units of information in long-term memory as being organized in a complex network of associations. (p. 238)

sensation The process of detecting a physical stimulus, such as light, sound, heat, or pressure. (p. 86)

sensation seeking The degree to which an individual is motivated to experience high levels of sensory and physical arousal associated with varied and novel activities. (p. 316)

sense of self An individual's unique sense of identity that has been influenced by social, cultural, and psychological experiences; your sense of who you are in relation to other people. (p. 454)

sensorimotor stage In Piaget's theory, the first stage of cognitive development, from birth to about age 2; the period during which the infant explores the environment and acquires knowledge through sensing and manipulating objects. (p. 380)

sensory adaptation   The decline in sensitivity to a constant stimulus. (p. 88)

sensory memory   The stage of memory that registers information from the environment and holds it for a very brief period of time. (p. 229)

sensory neuron   The type of neuron that conveys information to the brain from specialized receptor cells in sense organs and internal organs. (p. 43)

sensory receptors   Specialized cells unique to each sense organ that respond to a particular form of sensory stimulation. (p. 87)

serial position effect   The tendency to remember items at the beginning and end of a list better than items in the middle. (p. 240)

serotonin   (ser-uh-TONE-in) Neurotransmitter involved in sensory perceptions, sleep, and emotions. (p. 51)

set-point theory   Theory that proposes that humans and other animals have a natural or optimal body weight, called the *set-point weight*, that the body defends from becoming higher or lower by regulating feelings of hunger and body metabolism. (p. 320)

sex chromosomes   Chromosomes, designated as X or Y, that determine biological sex; the 23rd pair of chromosomes in humans. (p. 361)

sexual orientation   The direction of a person's emotional and erotic attraction toward members of the opposite sex, the same sex, or both sexes. (p. 327)

shape constancy   The perception of a familiar object as maintaining the same shape regardless of the image produced on the retina. (p. 122)

shaping   The operant conditioning procedure of selectively reinforcing successively closer approximations of a goal behavior until the goal behavior is displayed. (p. 206)

short-term dynamic therapies   Type of psychotherapy that is based on psychoanalytic theory but differs in that it is typically time-limited, has specific goals, and involves an active, rather than neutral, role for the *therapist.* (p. 589)

short-term memory   The active stage of memory in which information is stored for up to about 20 seconds. (p. 229)

situational (contingency) theories of leadership   Leadership theories claiming that various situational factors influence a leader's effectiveness. (p. B-9)

Sixteen Personality Factor Questionnaire (16PF)   A self-report inventory developed by Raymond Cattell that generates a personality profile with ratings on 16 trait dimensions. (p. 445)

size constancy   The perception of an object as maintaining the same size despite changing images on the retina. (p. 121)

skewed distribution   An asymmetrical distribution; more scores occur on one side of the distribution than on the other. In a *positively* skewed distribution, most of the scores are low scores; in a *negatively* skewed distribution, most of the scores are high scores. (p. A-3)

sleep disorders   Serious and consistent sleep disturbances that interfere with daytime functioning and cause subjective distress. (p. 153)

sleep paralysis   A temporary condition in which a person is unable to move upon awakening in the morning or during the night. (p. 141)

sleep spindles   Short bursts of brain activity that characterize stage 2 NREM sleep. (p. 142)

sleep terrors   A sleep disturbance characterized by an episode of increased physiological arousal, intense fear and panic, frightening hallucinations, and no recall of the episode the next morning; typically occurs during stage 3 or stage 4 NREM sleep; also called *night terrors.* (p. 154)

sleep thinking   Vague, bland, thoughtlike ruminations about real-life events that typically occur during NREM sleep; also called *sleep mentation.* (p. 147)

sleep-related eating disorder (SRED)   A sleep disorder in which the sleeper will sleepwalk and eat compulsively. (p. 154)

sleepsex   A sleep disorder involving abnormal sexual behaviors and experiences during sleep; also called *sexsomnia.* (p. 154)

sleepwalking   A sleep disturbance characterized by an episode of walking or performing other actions during stage 3 or stage 4 NREM sleep; also called *somnambulism.* (p. 154)

social anxiety disorder   An anxiety disorder involving the extreme and irrational fear of being embarrassed, judged, or scrutinized by others in social situations. (p. 545)

social categorization   The mental process of categorizing people into groups (or social categories) on the basis of their shared characteristics. (p. 456)

social cognition   The mental processes people use to make sense of their social environments. (p. 454)

social cognitive theory   Albert Bandura's theory of personality, which emphasizes the importance of observational learning, conscious cognitive processes, social experiences, self-efficacy beliefs, and reciprocal determinism. (p. 433)

social influence   The effect of situational factors and other people on an individual's behavior. (p. 454)

social learning theory of gender-role development   The theory that gender roles are acquired through the basic processes of learning, including reinforcement, punishment, and modeling. (p. 376)

social norms   The "rules," or expectations, for appropriate behavior in a particular social situation. (p. 454)

social psychology   Branch of psychology that studies how a person's thoughts, feelings, and behavior are influenced by the presence of other people and by the social and physical environment. (p. 454)

social support   The resources provided by other people in times of need. (p. 519)

somatic nervous system   The subdivision of the peripheral nervous system that communicates sensory information to the central nervous system and carries motor messages from the central nervous system to the muscles. (p. 55)

source confusion   A memory distortion that occurs when the true source of the memory is forgotten. (p. 249)

source memory or **source monitoring**   Memory for when, where, and how a particular experience or piece of information was acquired. (p. 247)

source traits   The most fundamental dimensions of personality; the broad, basic traits that are hypothesized to be universal and relatively few in number. (p. 437)

specific phobia   An excessive, intense, and irrational fear of a specific object, situation, or activity that is actively avoided or endured with marked anxiety. (p. 545)

spinal reflexes   Simple, automatic behaviors that are processed in the spinal cord. (p. 55)

split-brain operation   A surgical procedure that involves cutting the corpus callosum. (p. 74)

spontaneous recovery   The reappearance of a previously extinguished conditioned response after a period of time without exposure to the conditioned stimulus. (p. 187)

stage model of memory   A model describing memory as consisting of three distinct stages: sensory memory, short-term memory, and long-term memory. (p. 229)

standard deviation   A measure of variability; expressed as the square root of the sum of the squared deviations around the mean divided by the number of scores in the distribution. (p. A-6)

standard normal curve or **standard normal distribution**   A symmetrical distribution forming a bell-shaped curve in which the mean, median, and mode are all equal and fall in the exact middle. (p. A-7)

standardization   The administration of a test to a large, representative sample of people under uniform conditions for the purpose of establishing norms. (p. 294)

statistically significant   A mathematical indication that research results are not very likely to have occurred by chance. (p. 18)

statistics   A branch of mathematics used by researchers to organize, summarize, and interpret data. (pp. 18, A-2)

stem cells   Undifferentiated cells that can divide and give rise to cells that can develop into any one of the body's different cell types. (p. 364)

stereotype   A cluster of characteristics that are associated with all members of a specific social group, often including qualities that are unrelated to the objective criteria that define the group. (p. 466)

stereotype threat   A psychological predicament in which fear that you will be evaluated in terms of a negative stereotype about a group to which you belong creates anxiety and self-doubt, lowering performance in a particular domain that is important to you. (p. 304)

stimulants   A category of psychoactive drugs that increase brain activity, arouse behavior, and increase mental alertness. (p. 170)

stimulus control therapy   Insomnia treatment involving specific guidelines to create a strict association between the bedroom and rapid sleep onset. (p. 176)

stimulus discrimination   The occurrence of a learned response to a specific stimulus but not to other, similar stimuli. (p. 186)

stimulus generalization   The occurrence of a learned response not only to the original stimulus but to other, similar stimuli as well. (p. 186)

stimulus threshold   The minimum level of stimulation required to activate a particular neuron. (p. 44)

storage   The process of retaining information in memory so that it can be used at a later time. (p. 229)

stress   A negative emotional state occurring in response to events that are perceived as taxing or exceeding a person's resources or ability to cope. (p. 499)

stressors   Events or situations that are perceived as harmful, threatening, or challenging. (p. 501)

structural plasticity   The brain's ability to change its physical structure in response to learning, active practice, or environmental influences. (p. 63)

structuralism   Early school of psychology that emphasized studying the most basic components, or structures, of conscious experiences. (p. 4)

sublimation   An ego defense mechanism that involves redirecting sexual urges toward productive, socially acceptable, nonsexual activities; a form of displacement. (p. 420)

subliminal perception   The detection of stimuli that are below the threshold of conscious awareness; nonconscious perception. (p. 89)

substance P   A neurotransmitter that is involved in the transmission of pain messages to the brain. (p. 107)

substantia nigra   (sub-STAN-she-uh NYE-gruh) An area of the midbrain that is involved in motor control and contains a large concentration of dopamine-producing neurons. (p. 66)

superego   In Freud's theory, the partly conscious, self-evaluative, moralistic component of personality that is formed through the internalization of parental and societal rules. (p. 418)

suppression   Motivated forgetting that occurs consciously; a deliberate attempt to not think about and remember specific information. (p. 247)

suprachiasmatic nucleus (SCN)   (soup-ruh-kye-az-MAT-ick) A cluster of neurons in the hypothalamus in the brain that governs the timing of circadian rhythms. (p. 138)

surface traits   Personality characteristics or attributes that can easily be inferred from observable behavior. (p. 437)

survey   A questionnaire or interview designed to investigate the opinions, behaviors, or characteristics of a particular group. (p. 23)

symbolic thought   The ability to use words, images, and symbols to represent the world. (p. 381)

symmetrical distribution   A distribution in which scores fall equally on both sides of the graph. The normal curve is an example of a symmetrical distribution. (p. A-4)

sympathetic nervous system   The branch of the autonomic nervous system that produces rapid physical arousal in response to perceived emergencies or threats. (p. 57)

synapse   (SIN-aps) The point of communication between two neurons. (p. 47)

synaptic gap   (sin-AP-tick) The tiny space between the axon terminal of one neuron and the dendrite of an adjoining neuron. (p. 47)

synaptic transmission   (sin-AP-tick) The process through which neurotransmitters are released by one neuron, cross the synaptic gap, and affect adjoining neurons. (p. 48)

synaptic vesicles   (sin-AP-tick VESS-ick-ullz) The tiny pouches or sacs in axon terminals that contain chemicals called neurotransmitters. (p. 48)

systematic desensitization   A type of behavior therapy in which phobic responses are reduced by pairing relaxation with a series of mental images or real-life situations that the person finds progressively more fear-provoking; based on the principle of counterconditioning. (p. 594)

T

t test   Test used to establish whether the means of two groups are statistically different from each other. (p. A-11)

taste aversion   A classically conditioned dislike for and avoidance of a particular food that develops when an organism becomes ill after eating the food. (p. 193)

taste buds   The specialized sensory receptors for taste that are located on the tongue and inside the mouth and throat. (p. 104)

telomeres   Repeated, duplicate DNA sequences that are found at the very tips of chromosomes and that protect the chromosomes' genetic data during cell division. (p. 509)

temperament   Inborn predispositions to consistently behave and react in a certain way. (p. 369)

temporal lobe   An area on each hemisphere of the cerebral cortex, near the temples, that is the primary receiving area for auditory information. (p. 69)

teratogens   Harmful agents or substances that can cause malformations or defects in an embryo or fetus. (p. 364)

testing effect   The finding that practicing retrieval of information from memory produces better retention than restudying the same information for an equivalent amount of time. (p. 28)

thalamus   (THAL-uh-muss) A forebrain structure that processes sensory information for all senses except smell, relaying that information to the cerebral cortex. (p. 71)

Thematic Apperception Test (TAT)   A projective personality test, developed by Henry Murray and colleagues, that involves creating stories about ambiguous scenes. (pp. 334, 442)

theory   A tentative explanation that tries to integrate and account for the relationship of various findings and observations. (p. 19)

thinking   The manipulation of mental representations of information in order to draw inferences and conclusions. (p. 273)

timbre   (TAM-ber) The distinctive quality of a sound, determined by the complexity of the sound wave. (p. 99)

tip-of-the-tongue (TOT) experience   A memory phenomenon that involves the sensation of knowing that specific information is stored in long-term memory, but being temporarily unable to retrieve it. (p. 239)

token economy   A form of behavior therapy in which the therapeutic environment is structured to reward desired behaviors with tokens or points that may eventually be exchanged for tangible rewards. (p. 598)

top-down processing   Information processing that emphasizes the importance of the observer's knowledge, expectations, and other cognitive processes in arriving at meaningful perceptions; analysis that moves from the whole to the parts; also called *conceptually driven processing*. (p. 110)

trait   A relatively stable, enduring predisposition to consistently behave in a certain way. (p. 435)

trait approach to leader effectiveness   An approach to determining what makes an effective leader that focuses on the personal characteristics displayed by successful leaders. (p. B-8)

trait theory   A theory of personality that focuses on identifying, describing, and measuring individual differences in behavioral predispositions. (p. 435)

tranquilizers   Depressant drugs that relieve anxiety. (p. 169)

transduction   The process by which a form of physical energy is converted into a coded neural signal that can be processed by the nervous system. (p. 87)

transference   In psychoanalysis, the process by which emotions and desires originally associated with a significant person in the patient's life, such as a parent, are unconsciously transferred onto the psychoanalyst. (p. 589)

transgender   Condition in which a person's psychological gender identity conflicts with his or her biological sex. (p. 379)

trial and error   A problem-solving strategy that involves attempting different solutions and eliminating those that do not work. (p. 277)

triarchic theory of intelligence   Robert Sternberg's theory that there are three distinct forms of intelligence: analytic, creative, and practical. (p. 300)

trichromatic theory of color vision   The theory that the sensation of color results because cones in the retina are especially sensitive to red light (long wavelengths), green light (medium wavelengths), or blue light (short wavelengths). (p. 96)

two-factor theory of emotion   Schachter and Singer's theory that emotion is the interaction of physiological arousal and the cognitive label that we apply to explain the arousal. (p. 350)

Type A behavior pattern   A behavioral and emotional style characterized by a sense of time urgency, hostility, and competitiveness. (p. 517)

Type I error   Erroneously concluding that study results are significant. (p. A-12)

Type II error   Failing to find a significant effect that does, in fact, exist. (p. A-12)

U

unconditional positive regard   In Rogers's theory, the sense that you will be valued and loved even if you don't conform to the standards and expectations of others; unconditional love or acceptance. (p. 431)

unconditioned response (UCR)   The unlearned, reflexive response that is elicited by an unconditioned stimulus. (p. 185)

unconditioned stimulus (UCS)   The natural stimulus that reflexively elicits a response without the need for prior learning. (p. 185)

unconscious   In Freud's theory, a term used to describe thoughts, feelings, wishes, and drives that are operating below the level of conscious awareness. (p. 417)

V

validity   The ability of a test to measure what it is intended to measure. (p. 295)

variable   A factor that can vary, or change, in ways that can be observed, measured, and verified. (p. 16)

variable-interval (VI) schedule   A reinforcement schedule in which a reinforcer is delivered for the first response that occurs after an average time interval, which varies unpredictably from trial to trial. (p. 208)

variable-ratio (VR) schedule   A reinforcement schedule in which a reinforcer is delivered after an average number of responses, which varies unpredictably from trial to trial. (p. 208)

vestibular sense   (vess-TIB-you-ler) The technical name for the sense of balance, or equilibrium. (p. 109)

W

wavelength   The distance from one wave peak to another. (p. 91)

Weber's law   (VAY-berz) A principle of sensation that holds that the size of the just noticeable difference will vary depending on its relation to the strength of the original stimulus. (p. 88)

withdrawal symptoms   Unpleasant physical reactions, combined with intense drug cravings, that occur when a person abstains from a drug on which he or she is physically dependent. (p. 164)

working memory   The temporary storage and active, conscious manipulation of information needed for complex cognitive tasks, such as reasoning, learning, and problem solving. (p. 233)

Z

z score   A number, expressed in standard deviation units, that shows a score's deviation from the mean. (p. A-7)

zone of proximal development   In Vygotsky's theory of cognitive development, the difference between what children can accomplish on their own and what they can accomplish with the help of others who are more competent. (p. 385)

zygote   The single cell formed at conception from the union of the egg cell and sperm cell. (p. 360)

2007 Training Industry Report. (2007, November/December). *Training, 44,* 8–24.

60 Minutes. (2012). Treating depression: Is there a placebo effect? Retrieved from http://www.cbsnews.com/news/treating-depression-is-there-a-placebo-effect/American Psychological Association. (2013). Guidelines for psychological practice in health care delivery systems. *American Psychologist, 68*(1), 1–6. doi:10.1037/a0029890

AAP Council on Communications Media. (2009). Media Violence. *Pediatrics, 124*(5), 1495–1503. doi:10.1542/peds.2009-2146.

ABC News (2009, July 15). Inside the magical world of Harry Potter author. Retrieved on September 2, 2011 from http://abcnews.go.com/Entertainment/story?id=8081011&page=2

Abdullah, Asnawi; Wolfe, Rory; Stoelwinder, Johannes U; de Courten, Maximilian; Stevenson, Christopher; Walls, Helen L; & Peeters, Anna. (2011). The number of years lived with obesity and the risk of all-cause and cause-specific mortality. *International Journal of Epidemiology 40*(4), 985–996. doi:10.1093/ije/dyr018

Abe, Kentaro, & Watanabe, Dai. (2011). Songbirds possess the spontaneous ability to discriminate syntactic rules. *Nature Neuroscience, 14,* 1067–1074. doi:10.1038/nn.2869

Abela, John R. Z.; Auerbach, Randy P.; & Seligman, Martin E. P. (2008). Dispositional pessimism across the lifespan. In Keith S. Dobson & David J. A. Dozois (Eds.), *Risk factors in depression.* San Diego, CA: Elsevier Academic Press.

Abend, Rany; Pine, Daniel S.; Fox, Nathan A.; & Bar-Haim, Yair. (2014). Learning and memory consolidation processes of attention-bias modification in anxious and nonanxious individuals. *Clinical Psychological Science, 2,* 620–627. doi:10.1177/2167702614526571

Abi-Dargham, Anissa. (2004). Do we still believe in the dopamine hypothesis? New data bring new evidence. *International Journal of Neuropsychopharmacology, 7*(Suppl. 1), S1–S5.

Abler, Birgit; Erk, Susanne; & Herwig, Uwe. (2007). Anticipation of aversive stimuli activates extended amygdala in unipolar depression. *Journal of Psychiatric Research, 41*(6), 511–522.

Aboud, Frances E., & Yousafzai, Aisha K. (2015). Global health and development in early childhood. *Annual Review of Psychology, 66,* 433–457. doi:10.1146/annurev-psych-010814-015128

Aboud, Frances, E.; Tredoux, Colin; Tropp, Linda R.; Brown, Christia S.; Niens, Ulrike; & Noor, Noraini M. (2012). Interventions to reduce prejudice and enhance inclusion and respect for ethnic differences in early childhood: A systematic review. *Developmental Review, 32,* 307–226.

Abrams, Michael. (2002, June). Sight unseen. *Discover, 23,* 54–59.

Abramson, Lyn Y.; Seligman, Martin E. P.; & Teasdale, John D. (1978). Learned helplessness in humans: Critique and reformulation. *Journal of Abnormal Psychology, 87,* 49–74.

Ackerman, Joshua M.; Kenrick, Douglas T.; & Schaller, Mark. (2007). Is friendship akin to kinship? *Evolution and Human Behavior, 28*(5), 365–374.

Ackerman, Phillip L. (2014). Adolescent and adult intellectual development. *Current Directions in Psychological Science, 23,* 246–251. doi:10.1177/0963721414534960

Adachi, Tomonori; Fujino, Haruo; Nakae, Aya; Mashimo, Takashi; & Sasaki, Jun. (2014). A meta-analysis of hypnosis for chronic pain problems: A comparison between hypnosis, standard care, and other psychological interventions. *International Journal of Clinical and Experimental Hypnosis, 62,* 1–28. doi:10.1080/00207144.2013.841471

Adair, Linda S., & Gordon-Larsen, Penny. (2001). Maturational timing and overweight prevalence in US adolescent girls. *American Journal of Public Health, 91,* 642–644.

Ader, Robert. (1993). Conditioned responses. In Bill Moyers & Betty Sue Flowers (Eds.), *Healing and the mind.* New York, NY: Doubleday.

Adler, Alfred. (1933a/1979). Advantages and disadvantages of the inferiority feeling. In Heinz L. Ansbacher & Rowena R. Ansbacher (Eds.), *Superiority and social interest: A collection of later writings.* New York, NY: Norton.

Adler, Alfred. (1933b/1979). On the origin of the striving for superiority and of social interest. In Heinz L. Ansbacher & Rowena R. Ansbacher (Eds.), *Superiority and social interest: A collection of later writings.* New York, NY: Norton.

Adler, Alfred. (1954). *Understanding human nature.* New York, NY: Fawcett.

Adler, Nancy E. (2009). Health disparities through a psychological lens. *American Psychologist, 64*(8), 663–673.

Adler, Nancy E., & Rehkopf, David H. (2008). U.S. disparities in health: Descriptions, causes, and mechanisms. *Annual Review of Public Health, 29,* 235–252.

Adolphs, Ralph; Tranel, Daniel; & Damasio, Antonio R. (1998). The human amygdala in social judgment. *Nature, 393,* 470–474.

Adriaanse, Marieke A.; Gollwitzer, Peter M.; De Ridder, Denise T. D.; de Wit, John B. F.; & Kroese, Floor M. (2011). Breaking habits with implementation intentions: A test of underlying processes. *Personality and Social Psychology Bulletin, 37,* 502. doi:10.1177/0146167211399102

Advokat, Claire D.; Comaty, Joseph E.; & Julien, Robert M. (2014). *Julien's primer of drug action.* (13th ed.). New York, NY: Worth.

Ahima, Rexford S. (2011). Principles of obesity therapy. In Rexford S. Ahima (Ed.), *Metabolic basis of obesity* (pp. 359–379). New York, NY: Springer.

Aiken, Lewis R. (1997). *Psychological testing and assessment* (9th ed.) Boston, MA: Allyn & Bacon.

Ainslie, George. (1975). Specious reward: A behavioral theory of impulsiveness and impulse control. *Psychological Bulletin, 82,* 463–496.

Ainslie, George. (1992). *Picoeconomics: The strategic interaction of successive motivational states within the person.* Cambridge, England: Cambridge University Press.

Ainsworth, Mary D. Salter. (1979). Attachment as related to motherinfant interaction. In Jay S. Rosenblatt, Robert A. Hinde, Colin Beer, & Marie Busnel (Eds.), *Advances in the study of behavior* (Vol. 9). New York, NY: Academic Press.

Ainsworth, Mary D. Salter; Blehar, Mary C.; Waters, Everett; & Wall, Sally. (1978). *Patterns of attachment: A psychological study of the Strange Situation.* Hillsdale, NJ: Erlbaum.

Ainsworth, Sarah E., & Maner, Jon. K. (2012). Sex begets violence: Mating motives, social dominance, and physical aggression in men. *Journal of Personality and Social Psychology, 103*(5), 819–829. doi:10.1037/a0029428

Ajzen, Icek. (2001). Nature and operations of attitudes. *Annual Review of Psychology, 52*(1), 27–58.

Akerstedt, Torbjörn; Nilsson, Peter M.; & Kecklund, Gören. (2009). Sleep and recovery. In Sabine Sonnetag, Pamela L. Perrewé, and Daniel Ganster (Eds.), *Current perspectives on job-stress recovery.* Bingley, England: JAI Press/Emerald Group.

Aksglaede, Lise; Juul, Anders; Olsen, Lina W.; & Sorensen, Thorkild I. (2009). Age at puberty and the emerging obesity epidemic. *PLOS ONE, 4*(12), e8450. doi:10.1371/journal.pone.0008450

Alanko, Katarina; Santtila, Pekka; Harlaar, N.; Witting, Katarina; Varjonen, Markus; Jern, Patrik; Johansson, Ada; von der Pahlen, Bettina; & Sandnabba, N. Kenneth. (2010). Common genetic effects of gender atypical behavior in childhood and sexual orientation in adulthood: A study of Finnish twins. *Archives of Sexual Behavior, 39,* 81–92.

Albarracín, Dolores, & Vargas, Patrick. (2010). Attitudes and persuasion: From biology to social responses to persuasive intent. In S. T. Fiske, D. T. Gilbert & G. Lindzey (Eds.), *Handbook of social psychology, Vol. 1* (pp. 394–427). Hoboken, NJ: Wiley.

Albert, Dustin; Chein, Jason; & Steinberg, Laurence. (2013). The teenage brain: Peer influences on adolescent decision making. *Current Directions in Psychological Science, 22,* 114–120. doi:10.1177/0963721412471347

Albright, David L., & Thyer, Bruce. (2010). Does EMDR reduce posttraumatic stress disorder symptomatology in combat veterans? *Behavioral Interventions, 25,* 1–19.

Alcock, James. (2011). Back from the future: Parapsychology and the Bem Affair. Retrieved from http://www.csicop.org/specialarticles/show/back_from_the_future

Alexander, Charles N.; Robinson, Pat; Orme-Johnson, David W.; & Schneider, Robert H. (1994). The effects of transcendental meditation compared to other methods of relaxation and meditation in reducing risk factors, morbidity, and mortality. *Homeostasis in Health and Disease, 35,* 243–263.

Alexander, G. Caleb; Gallagher, S. A.; A. Mascola, A.; Moloney, R. M.; & Stafford, R. S. (2010). Increasing off-label use of antipsychotic medications in the United States, 1995–2008. *Pharmacoepidemiology and Drug Safety, 20,* 177–184.

Alladi, Suvarna; Bak, Thomas H.; Duggirala, Vasanta; Surampudi, Bapiraju; Shailaja, Mekala; Shukla, Anuj Kumar; Chaudhuri, Jaydip Ray; & Kaul, Subhash. (2013). Bilingualism delays age at onset of dementia, independent of education and immigration status. *Neurology, 81,* 1938–1944. doi:10.1212/01.wnl.0000436620.33155.a4

Allen, Daniel N.; Strauss, Gregory P.; Kemtes, Karen A.; & Goldstein, Gerald. (2007). Hemispheric contributions to nonverbal abstract reasoning and problem solving. *Neuropsychology, 21,* 713–720.

Allen, Jenny; Weinrich, Mason; Hoppitt, Will; & Rendell, Luke. (2013). Network-based diffusion analysis reveals cultural transmission of lobtail feeding in humpback whales. *Science, 340,* 485–488. doi:10.1126/science.1231976

Allen, Jon G. (2005). *Coping with trauma: Hope through understanding* (2nd ed.). Washington, DC: American Psychological Association.

Allen, Karen M.; Blascovich, Jim; & Mendes, Wendy B. (2002). Cardiovascular reactivity and the presence of pets, friends, and spouses: The truth about cats and dogs. *Psychosomatic Medicine, 64,* 727–739.

Allen, Karen M.; Blascovich, Jim; Tomaka, Joe; & Kelsey, Robert M. (1991). Presence of human friends and pet dogs as moderators of autonomic responses to stress in women. *Journal of Personality and Social Psychology, 61,* 582–589.

Allen, Laura B.; McHugh, R. Kathryn; & Barlow, David H. (2008). Emotional disorders: A unified protocol. In David H. Barlow (Ed.), *Clinical handbook of psychological disorders* (4th ed., pp. 216–249). New York, NY: Guilford.

Allen, Vernon L., & Levine, John M. (1969). Consensus and conformity. *Journal of Experimental Social Psychology, 5,* 389–399.

Allen, Vernon L., & Levine, John M. (1971). Social support and conformity: The role of independent assessment of reality. *Journal of Experimental Social Psychology, 7,* 48–58.

Allik, Jüri, & McCrae, Robert R. (2002). A five-factor theory perspective. In Robert R. McCrae & Jüri Allik (Eds.), *The five-factor model of personality across cultures.* New York, NY: Kluwer Academic/Plenum.

Allik, Juri, & McCrae, Robert R. (2004). Toward a geography of personality traits: Patterns of profiles across 36 cultures. *Journal of Cross-Cultural Psychology, 35,* 13–28.

Allik, Jüri, & McCrae, Robert R. (2013). Universality of the five-factor model of personality. In Paul T. Costa; & Thomas A. Widiger (Eds.), *Personality Disorders and the Five Factor Model of Personality.* Washington, DC: American Psychological Association.

Allport, Gordon W., & Odbert, Harold S. (1936). Trait-names: A psycholexical study. *Psychological Monographs, 47*(211).

Almeida, David M.; Neupert, Shevaun D.; Banks, Sean R.; & Serido, Joyce. (2005). Do daily stress processes account for socioeconomic health disparities? *Journal of Gerontology: Series B, 60B,* 34–39.

Altemus, Margaret. (2006). Sex differences in depression and anxiety disorders: Potential biological determinants. *Hormones and Behavior, 50*(4), 534–538.

Altmann, Erik M. (2009). Evidence for temporal decay in short-term episodic memory. *Trends in Cognitive Sciences, 13*(7), 279.

Alves, Hélder, & Correia, Isabel. (2008). On the normativity of expressing the belief in a just world: Empirical evidence. *Social Justice Research, 21,* 106–118.

Alwin, Duane F. (2009). History, cohorts, and patterns of cognitive aging. In Hayden B. Bosworth and Christpher Hertzog (Eds.), *Aging and cognition: Research methodologies and empirical advances* (pp. 9–38). Washington, DC: American Psychological Association.

Alzheimer's Association. (2011). Alzheimer's disease facts and figures. *Alzheimer's & Dementia, 7*(2), 1–63. Retrieved from www.alz.org/downloads/Facts_Figures_2011.pdf

Amabile, Teresa M. (1996). *Creativity in context.* Boulder, CO: Westview Press.

Amabile, Teresa M. (2001). Beyond talent: John Irving and the passionate craft of creativity. *American Psychologist, 56,* 333–336.

Amada, Gerald. (2011). *A guide to psychotherapy.* Lanham, MD: Evans.

Ambady, Nalini, & Skowronski, John J. (2008). *First impressions.* New York, NY: Guilford.

Ambady, Nalini; Chiao, Joan Y.; & Chiu, Pearl. (2006). Race and emotion: Insights from a social neuroscience perspective. In John T. Cacioppo, Penny S. Visser, & Cynthia L. Pickett (Eds.), *Social neuroscience: People thinking about thinking people.* Cambridge, MA: MIT Press.

American Psychiatric Association. (1994). *Diagnostic and statistical manual of mental disorders* (4th ed.). Washington, DC: Author.

American Psychiatric Association. (2000). Practice guidelines for the treatment of patients with eating disorders [Revision]. *American Journal of Psychiatry, 157*(Suppl.).

American Psychiatric Association. (2001). Practice guideline for the treatment of patients with borderline personality disorder. *American Journal of Psychiatry, 158,* 2.

American Psychiatric Association. (2012a). *Personality disorders.* Retrieved on July 10, 2012, from: http://www.dsm5.org/proposedrevision/pages/personalitydisorders.aspx

American Psychiatric Association. (2012b). *Rationale for the proposed changes to the personality disorders classification in DSM-5.* Retrieved on July 10, 2012, from http://www.dsm5.org/Documents/Personality%20Disorders/Rationale 20for%20the%20Proposed%20changes%20to%20the%20Personality%20Disorders%20in%20DSM-5%205-1-12.pdf

American Psychiatric Association. (2013). *Diagnostic and statistical manual of mental disorders, fifth edition* (DSM-5). Washington, DC: American Psychiatric Publishing.

American Psychological Association (APA). (2002). Ethical principles of psychologists and code of conduct. *American Psychologist, 57,* 1060–1073. Retrieved on December 5, 2009 from http://www.apa.org/ETHICS/code2002.html

American Psychological Association (APA). (2003). Guidelines on multicultural education, training, research, practice, and organizational change for psychologists. *American Psychologist, 58,* 377–402. PDF of guidelines available at www.apa.org/pi/multiculturalguidelines.pdf

American Psychological Association (APA). (2005a). New definition: Hypnosis. Washington, DC: American Psychological Association, Division 30, Society for Psychological Hypnosis. Retrieved on December 5, 2009, from http://www.apa.org/divisions/div30/define_hypnosis.html

American Psychological Association (APA). (2005b). Obeying and resisting malevolent orders. Retrieved on November 28, 2005 from http://www.psychologymatters.org/milgram.html

American Psychological Association (APA). (2007). Guidelines for psychological practice with girls and women. *American Psychologist, 62,* 949–979.

American Psychological Association (APA). (2009). Resolution on appropriate affirmative responses to sexual orientation distress and change efforts. Retrieved on July 9, 2013 from http://www.apa.org/about/policy/sexual-orientation.aspx

American Psychological Association (APA). (2010). Ethical principles of psychologists and code of conduct: 2010 Amendments, from http://www.apa.org/ethics/code/index.aspx

American Psychological Association (APA). (2011). Guidelines for Ethical Conduct in the Care and Use of Animals, from http://www.apa.org/ethics/code/index.aspx

American Psychological Association (APA). (2011). Practice guidelines regarding psychologists' involvement in pharmacological issues. *American Psychologist, 66,* 835–849.

American Psychological Association (APA). (2013). *Stress in America: Missing the health care connection.* Washington, DC: Author.

American Psychological Association Working Group on Investigation of Memories of Childhood Abuse. (1998). Final conclusions of the American Psychological Association Working Group on Investigation of Memories of Childhood Abuse. *Psychology, Public Policy, and Law, 4,* 933–940.

Ames, Daniel R.; Kammrath, Lara K.; Suppes, Alexandra; & Bolger, Niall. (2009). Not so fast: The (not-quite-complete) dissociation between accuracy and confidence in thin-slice impressions. *Personality and Social Psychology Bulletin, 36*(2), 264–277. doi:10.1177/0146167209354519

Amin, N.; Schuur, M.; Gusareva, E. S.; Isaacs, A.; Aulchenko, Y. S.; Kirichenko, A. V.; Zorkoltseva, I. V.; & others. (2011). A genome-wide linkage study of individuals with high scores on NEO personality traits. *Molecular Psychiatry.* doi:10.1038/mp.2011.97

Amodio, David M., & Mendoza, Saaid A. (2010). Implicit intergroup bias: Cognitive, affective, and motivational underpinnings. In Bertram Gawronski & B. Keith Payne (Eds.), *Handbook of implicit social cognition: Measurement, theory, and applications.* New York, NY: Guilford.

Amstadter, Ananda B.; Nugent, Nicole R.; & Koenen, Karestan C. (2009). Genetics of PTSD: Fear conditioning as a model for future research. *Psychiatric Annals, 39*(6), 358–367.

Anastasi, Anne, & Urbina, Susana. (1997). *Psychological testing* (7th ed.). Upper Saddle River, NJ: Prentice Hall.

Anderson, Craig A., & Bushman, Brad J. (2002). Human aggression. *Annual Review of Psychology, 53*(1), 27–51.

Anderson, Craig A.; Shibuya, Akik; Ihori, Nobuko; Swing, Edward L.; Bushman, Brad J.; Sakamoto, Akira; Rothstein, Hannah R.; & Saleem, Muniba. (2010). Violent video game effects on aggression, empathy, and prosocial behavior in Eastern and Western countries: A meta-analytic review. *Psychological Bulletin, 136,* 151–173. doi:10.1037/a0018251

Anderson, Karen E., & Savage, Cary R. (2004). Cognitive and neurobiological findings in obsessive-compulsive disorder. *Psychiatric Clinics of North America, 27,* 37–47.

Anderson, Michael C., & Levy, Benjamin J. (2009). Suppressing unwanted memories. *Current Directions in Psychological Science, 18,* 189–194.

Anderson, Michael C.; Reinholz, Julia; & Kuhl, Brice A.; & Mayr, Ulrich. (2011). Intentional suppression of unwanted memories grows more difficult as we age. *Psychology and Aging. 26,* 397–405.

Anderson, Norman B. (2012, January). 120 years strong. *Monitor on Psychology, 43,* 9.

Anderson-Fye, Eileen. (2009). Cross-cultural issues in body image among children and adolescents. In Linda Smolak & J. Kevin Thompson (Eds.), *Body image, eating disorders, and obesity in youth: Assessment, prevention, and treatment* (2nd ed., pp. 113–133). Washington, DC: American Psychological Association.

Anderssen, Norman; Amlie, Christine; & Ytteroy, Erling A. (2002). Outcomes for children with lesbian or gay parents. A review of studies from 1978 to 2000. *Scandinavian Journal of Psychology, 43,* 335–351.

Andover, Margaret S.; Izzo, Genevieve N.; & Kelly, Chris A. (2011). Comorbid and secondary depression. In Dean McKay & Eric A. Storch (Eds.), *Handbook of child and adolescent anxiety disorders* (pp. 135–153). New York, NY: Springer Science + Business Media.

Andre, Linda. (2009). *Doctors of deception: What they don't want you to know about shock treatment.* New Brunswick, NJ: Rutgers University Press.

Andreasen, Nancy C., & Flaum, Michael. (1991). Schizophrenia: The characteristic symptoms. *Schizophrenia Bulletin, 17,* 27–49.

Angell, Marcia. (2011, June 23). The epidemic of mental illness: Why? *New York Review of Books, 58.* Accessed on August 31, 2011 at http://www.nybooks.com/articles/archives/2011/jun/23/epidemicmental-illness-why

Annese, Jacopo; Schenker-Ahmed, Natalie M.; Bartsch, Hauke; Maechler, Paul; Sheh, Colleen; Thomas, Natasha; Kayano, Junya; Ghatan, Alexander; Bresler, Noah; Frosch, Matthew P.; Klaming, Ruth; & Corkin, Suzanne. (2014). Postmortem examination of patient H.M.'s brain based on histological sectioning and digital 3D reconstruction. *Nature Communications, 5,* Article 3122. doi:10.1038/ncomms4122

Ano, Gene G., & Vasconcelles, Erin B. (2005). Religious coping and psychological adjustment to stress: A meta-analysis. *Journal of Clinical Psychology, 61,* 461–480.

Anonymous. (1990). First person account: Birds of a psychic feather. *Schizophrenia Bulletin. 16,* 165–168.

Antheunis, Marjolijn L., & Schouten, Alexander P. (2011). The effects of other-generated and system-generated cues on adolescents' perceived attractiveness on social network sites. *Journal of Computer-Mediated Communication, 16*(3), 391–406. doi:10.1111/j.1083-6101.2011.01545.x

Antony, Martin M.; Purdon, Christine; & Summerfeldt, Laura J. (2007). *Psychological treatment of obsessive compulsive disorders: Fundamentals and beyond.* Washington, DC: American Psychological Association.

APA Help Center. (2012a). *How to choose a psychologist.* Retrieved from http://www.apa.org/helpcenter/choose-therapist.aspx

APA Help Center. (2012b). *How to find help through seeing a psychologist.* Retrieved from http://www.apa.org/helpcenter/therapy.aspx

Arch, Joanna J., & Landy, Lauren N. (2015). Emotional benefits of mindfulness. In Kirk Warren Brown, J. David Creswell, & Richard M. Ryan (Eds.), *Handbook of mindfulness: Theory, research, and practice.* New York, NY: Guilford.

Archbold, Georgina E. B.; Bouton, Mark E.; & Nader, Karim. (2010). Evidence for the persistence of contextual fear memories following immediate extinction. *European Journal of Neuroscience, 31*(7), 1303–1311.

Archer, John. (2004). Sex differences in aggression in real-world settings: A meta-analytic review. *Review of General Psychology, 8*(4), 291–322. doi:10.1037/1089-2680.8.4.291

Archer, John, & Coyne, Sarah M. (2005). An integrated review of indirect, relational, and social aggression. *Personality and Social Psychology Review, 9*(3), 212–230.

Archer, Robert P., & Smith, Steven R. (2014). *Personality assessment* (2nd ed.). New York, NY: Routledge.

Arden, John B., & Linford, Lloyd. (2009). *Brain-based therapy with adults: Evidence-based treatment for everyday practice.* Hoboken, NJ: Wiley.

Arendt, Josephine; Stone, Barbara; & Skene, Debra J. (2005). Sleep disruption in jet lag and circadian rhythm-related disorders. In Meir H. Kryger, Thomas Roth, & William C. Dement (Eds.), *Principles and practice of sleep medicine* (4th ed.). Philadelphia, PA : Elsevier Saunders.

Arkowitz, Hal; Westra, Henny A.; Miller, William R.; & Rollnick, Stephen (Eds.). (2007). *Motivational interviewing in the treatment of psychological problems.* New York, NY: Guilford Press.

Arnau, Randolph C.; Green, Bradley A.; Rosen, David H.; Gleaves, David H.; & Melancon, Janet G. (2003). Are Jungian preferences really categorical? An empirical investigation using taxometric analysis. *Personality and Individual Differences, 34,* 233–251.

Arnett, Jeffrey Jensen. (2000). Emerging adulthood: A theory of development from the late teens through the twenties. *American Psychologist, 55,* 469–480. doi:10.1037/0003-066X.55.5.469

Arnett, Jeffrey Jensen. (2004). *Emerging adulthood: The winding road from the late teens through the twenties.* New York, NY: Oxford University Press.

Arnett, Jeffrey Jensen. (2010). Oh, grow up! Generational grumbling and the new life stage of emerging adulthood—Commentary on

Trzesniewski & Donnellan (2010). *Perspectives on Psychological Science, 5,* 89–92. doi:10.1177/1745691609357016

Arnett, Jeffrey Jensen. (2011). Emerging adulthood(s): The cultural psychology of a new life stage. In Lene Arnett Jensen (Ed.), *Bridging cultural and developmental approaches to psychology: New syntheses in theory, research, and policy.* New York, NY: Oxford University Press.

Arntz, Arnoud, & ten Haaf, José. (2012). Social cognition in borderline personality disorder: Evidence for dichotomous thinking but no evidence for less complex attributions. *Behaviour Research and Therapy, 50,* 707–718.

Aronson, Elliot. (1987). Teaching students what they think they already know about prejudice and desegregation. In Vivian Parker Makosky (Ed.), *G. Stanley Hall Lecture Series* (Vol. 7). Washington, DC: American Psychological Association.

Aronson, Elliot. (1990). Applying social psychology to desegregation and energy conservation. *Personality and Social Psychology Bulletin, 16,* 118–132.

Aronson, Elliot. (1992). The return of the repressed: Dissonance theory makes a comeback. *Psychological Inquiry, 3,* 303–311.

Aronson, Elliot. (1995). *The social animal* (7th ed). New York, NY: Freeman.

Aronson, Elliot. (1999). The power of self-persuasion. *American Psychologist, 54,* 875–883.

Aronson, Elliot, & Bridgeman, Diane. (1979). Jigsaw groups and the desegregated classroom: In pursuit of common goals. *Personality and Social Psychology Bulletin, 5,* 438–466.

Aronson, Joshua; Fried, Carrie B.; & Good, Catherine. (2002). Reducing the effects of stereotype threat on African American college students by shaping theories of intelligence. *Journal of Experimental Social Psychology, 38,* 113–125.

Aronson, Joshua; Lustina, Michael J.; Good, Catherine; Keough, Kelli; Steele, Claude M.; & Brown, Joseph. (1999). When white men can't do math: Necessary and sufficient factors in stereotype threat. *Journal of Experimental Social Psychology, 35,* 29–46.

Arrazola, René A.; Singh, Tushar; Corey, Catherine G.; Husten, Corinne G.; Neff, Linda J.; Apelberg, Benjamin J.; Bunnell, Rebecca E.; Choiniere, Conrad J.; King, Brian A.; Cox, Shanna; McAfee, Tim; & Caraballo, Ralph S. (2015). Tobacco use among middle and high school students—United States, 2011–2014. *Morbidity and Mortality Weekly Report, 64,* 381–385.

Asami, Takeshi; Bouix, Sylvain; Whitford, Thomas J.; Shenton, Martha E.; Salisbury, Dean F.; & McCarley, Robert W. (2012). Longitudinal loss of gray matter volume in patients with first-episode schizophrenia: DARTEL automated analysis and ROI validation. *Neuroimage, 59*(2), 986–996.

Asch, Solomon E. (1951). Effects of group pressure upon the modification and distortion of judgments. In Harold S. Guetzkow (Ed.), *Groups, leadership, and men: Research in human relations. Reports on research sponsored by the Human Relations and Morale Branch of the Office of Naval Research, 1945–1950.* Pittsburgh, PA: Carnegie Press.

Asch, Solomon E. (1955, November). Opinions and social pressure. *Scientific American, 193,* 31–35.

Asch, Solomon E. (1956). Studies of independence and conformity: A minority of one against a unanimous majority. *Psychological Monographs, 70*(9, Whole No. 416).

Asch, Solomon E. (1957). An experimental investigation of group influence. In *Symposium on preventive and social psychiatry.* Washington, DC: U.S. Government Printing Office, Walter Reed Army Institute of Research.

Ashcraft, Mark H. (1994). *Human memory and cognition* (2nd ed.). New York, NY: HarperCollins.

Atherton, Olivia; Robins, Richard; Rentfrow, P. Jason; & Lamb, Michael. (2014). Personality correlates of risky health outcomes: Findings from a large Internet study. *Journal of Research in Personality, 50,* 56–60. doi:10.1016/j.jrp.2014.03.002

Atkinson, Richard C., & Shiffrin, Richard M. (1968). Human memory: A proposed system and its control processes. In Kenneth W. Spence & Janet T. Spence (Eds.), *The psychology of learning and motivation: Advances in research and theory* (Vol. 2). New York, NY: Academic Press.

Ator, Nancy A. (2005). Conducting behavioral research: Methodological and laboratory animal welfare issues. In Chana K. Akins, Sangeeta Panicker, & Christopher L. Cunningham (Eds.), *Laboratory animals in research and teaching: Ethics, care, and methods.* Washington, DC: American Psychological Association.

Attwood, Angela; Terry, Philip; & Higgs, Suzanne. (2010). Conditioned effects of caffeine on performance in humans. *Physiology & Behavior, 99*(3), 286–293.

Au, Raymond C. P.; Watkins, David A.; & Hattie, John A. C. (2010). Academic risk factors and deficits of learned hopelessness: A longitudinal study of Hong Kong secondary school students. *Educational Psychology, 30*(2), 125–138.

Auld, Frank; Hyman, Marvin; & Rudzinski, Donald. (2005). Theory and strategy of dream interpretation. In Frank Auld, Marvin Hyman, & Donald Rudzinski (Eds.), *Resolution of inner conflict: An introduction to psychoanalytic therapy* (2nd ed.). Washington, DC: American Psychological Association.

Austin, James H. (2009). *Selfless insight: Zen and the meditative transformations of consciousness.* Cambridge, MA: MIT Press.

Aveline, Mark. (2005). The person of the therapist. *Psychotherapy Research, 15*(3), 155–164.

Avins, Andrew L. (2012). Needling the status quo: Comment on "Acupuncture for Chronic Pain." *Archives of Internal Medicine, 172*(19), 1–2. doi:10.1001/archinternmed.2012.4198

Ax, Robert K.; Bigelow, Brian J.; Harowski, Kathy; Meredith, James M.; Nussbaum, David; & Taylor, Randy R. (2008). Prescriptive authority for psychologists and the public sector: Serving under-served health care consumers. *Psychological Services, 5,* 184–197.

Azar, B. (2008). IAT: Fad or fabulous? *Monitor on Psychology, 39,* 44.

Aziz-Zadeh, Lisa; S.-L. Liew, Sook-Lei; Dandekar, Francesco. (2013). Exploring the neural correlates of visual creativity. *Social Cognitive and Affective Neuroscience, 8,* 475–480. doi:10.1093/scan/nss021

Baars, Barnard. (2005). Consciousness eclipsed: Jacques Loeb, Ivan P. Pavlov, and the rise of reductionistic biology after 1900. *Consciousness and Cognition, 14,* 219–230.

Bachhuber, Marcus A.; Saloner, Brendan; Cunningham, Chinazo O.; Barry, Colleen L. (2014). Medical cannabis laws and opioid analgesic overdose mortality in the United States, 1999-2010. *JAMA Internal Medicine.* Published online August 25, 2014. doi:10.1001/jamainternmed.2014.4005

Bachrach, Yoram; Kosinski, Michal; Graepel, Thore; Kohli, Pushmeet; & Stillwell, David. (2012, June). Personality and patterns of Facebook usage. In *Proceedings of the 3rd Annual ACM Web Science Conference* (pp. 24–32). ACM.

Badcock, Johanna C.; Dragović, Milan; Garrett, Coleman; & Jablensky, Assen. (2011). Action (verb) fluency in schizophrenia: Getting a grip on odd speech. *Schizophrenia Research, 126*(1–3), 138–143.

Baddeley, Alan D. (1992, January 31). Working memory. *Science, 255*(5044), 556–559.

Baddeley, Alan D. (1995). Working memory. In Michael S. Gazzaniga (Ed.), *The cognitive neurosciences.* Cambridge, MA: MIT Press.

Baddeley, Alan D. (2002). Is working memory still working? *European Psychologist, 7,* 85–97.

Baddeley, Alan D. (2007). *Working memory, thought, and action.* New York, NY: Oxford University Press.

Baddeley, Alan. (2010). Working memory. *Current Biology, 20*(4), R136–R140.

Baddeley, Alan D.; Bäckman, Lars; & Nyberg, Lars. (2010). Long-term and working memory: How do they interact? *Memory, aging and the brain: A Festschrift in honour of Lars-Göran Nilsson.* (pp. 7–23). New York, NY: Psychology Press.

Baddeley, Alan D.; Eysenck, Michael W.; & Anderson, Michael C. (2009). *Memory.* New York, NY: Psychology Press.

Bader, Alan P., & Phillips, Roger D. (2002). Fathers' recognition of their newborns by visual-facial and olfactory cues. *Psychology of Men and Masculinity, 3,* 79–84.

Baer, John. (1993). *Creativity and divergent thinking: A task-specific approach.* Hillsdale, NJ: Erlbaum.

Bahrami, Bahador; Lavie, Nilli; & Rees, Geraint. (2007). Attentional load modulates response of human primary visual cortex to invisible stimuli. *Current Biology, 17,* 509–513.

Bailer, U. F., & Kaye, W. H. (2011). Serotonin: Imaging findings in eating disorders. *Current Topics in Behavioral Neuroscience, 6,* 59–79. doi:10.1007/7854_2010_78

Bailey, J. Michael; Bobrow, David; Wolfe, Marilyn; & Mikach, Sarah. (1995). Sexual orientation of adult sons of gay fathers. *Developmental Psychology, 31,* 124–129.

Bailey, J. Michael; Dunne, Michael P.; & Martin, Nicholas G. (2000). Genetic and environmental influences on sexual orientation and its correlates in an Australian twin sample. *Journal of Personality and Social Psychology, 78,* 524–536.

Bailey, Marian Breland; & Bailey, Robert E. (1993). "Misbehavior": A case history. *American Psychologist, 48,* 1157–1158.

Baillargeon, Renée. (2004). Infants' physical world. *Current Directions in Psychological Science, 13,* 89–94.

Baillargeon, Renée, & DeVos, Julie. (1991). Object permanence in young infants: Further evidence. *Child Development, 62,* 1227–1246.

Baillargeon, Renée; Li, Jie; Gertner, Yael; & Wu, Di. (2011). How do infants reason about physical events? In Usha Goswami (Ed.), *The Wiley-Blackwell Handbook of Childhood and Cognitive Development* (2nd ed.). Hoboken, NJ: Wiley-Blackwell.

Baillargeon, Renée; Stavans, Maayan; Wu, Di; Gertner, Yael; Setoh, Peipei; Kittredge, Audrey K.; & Bernard, Amélie. (2012). Object individuation and physical reasoning in infancy: An integrative account. *Language Learning and Development, 8,* 4–46. doi:10.1080/15475441.2012.630610

Baillargeon, Renée; Wu, Di; Yuan, Sylvia; Li, Jie; & Luo, Yuyan. (2009). Young infants' expectations about self-propelled objects. In B. Hood & L. Santos (Eds.), *The origins of object knowledge* (pp. 285–352). Oxford, England: Oxford University Press.

Baird, Benjamin; Mrazek, Michael D.; Phillips, Dawa T.; Schooler, Jonathan W. (2014). Domain-specific enhancement of metacognitive ability following meditation training. *Journal of Experimental Psychology: General.* Advance online publication. doi:10.1037/a0036882

Bajwa, Ghulam-Murtaza; Hasija, Deepa; Jadapalle, Sree Latha Krishna; Ghaffar, Sadia; & Badr, Amel. (2011). Advanced paternal age and the risk of schizophrenia: A literature review. *Psychiatric Annals, 41*(6), 325–328.

Bakker, Arnold B.; Demerouti, Evangelia; & Dollard, Maureen F. (2008). How job demands affect partners' experience of exhaustion: Integrating work-family conflict and crossover theory. *Journal of Applied Psychology, 93*(4), 901–911.

Bakoyiannis, Ioannis; Gkioka, Eleana; Pergialiotis, Vasileios; Mastroleon, Ioanna; Prodromidou, Anastasia; Vlachos, Georgios D.; & Perrea, Despina. (2014). Fetal alcohol spectrum disorders and cognitive functions of young children. *Reviews in the Neurosciences, 25,* 631–639. doi:10.1515/revneuro-2014-0029

Balbo, Marcella; Leproult, Rachel; & Van Cauter, Eve. (2010). Impact of sleep and its disturbances on hypothalamo-pituitary-adrenal axis activity. *International Journal of Endocrinology.* doi:10.1155/2010/759234

Baldwin, David S.; Anderson, Ian M.; Nutt, David J.; Allgulander, Christer; Bandelow, Borwin; den Boer, Johan A.; Christmas, David M.; & others. (2014). Evidence-based pharmacological treatment of anxiety disorders, post-traumatic stress disorder and obsessive-compulsive disorder: A revision of the 2005 guidelines from the British Association for Psychopharmacology. *Journal of Psychopharmacology, 28*(5), 1–37. doi:0.1177/0269881114525674

Baldwin, Scott A.; Berkelion, Arjan; Atkins, David C.; Olsen, Joseph A.; & Nielsen, Steven L. (2009, April). Rates of change in naturalistic psychotherapy: Contrasting dose-effect and good-enough level models of change. *Journal of Consulting and Clinical Psychology, 77*(2), 203–211.

Ball, J. S, & Links, P. S. (2009). Borderline personality disorder and childhood trauma: Evidence for a causal relationship. *Current Psychiatry Reports, 11*(1), 63–68.

Ballard, Clive; Gauthier, Serge; Corbett, Anne; Brayne, Carol; Aarsland, Dag; & Baudry, Michel; Bi, Xiaoning; Gall, Christine; & Lynch, Gary. (2011). The biochemistry of memory: The 26 year journey of a 'new and specific hypothesis'. *Neurobiology of Learning and Memory, 95*(2), 125–133.

Balsam, Kimberly F.; Beauchaine, Theodore P.; Rothblum, Esther D.; & Solomon, Sondra E. (2008). Three-year follow-up of same-sex couples who had civil unions in Vermont, same-sex couples not in civil unions, and heterosexual married couples. *Developmental Psychology, 44,* 102–116.

Bamford, Nigel S.; Zhang, Hui; Joyce, John A.; Scarlis, Christine A.; & others. (2008, April 10). Repeated exposure to methamphetamine causes long-lasting presynaptic corticostriatal depression that is renormalized with drug readministration. *Neuron, 58,* 89–103. Retrieved on December 6, 2009, from http://www.ncbi.nlm.nih.gov/pmc/articles/PMC2394729

Banaji, Mahzarin R., & Heiphetz, Larisa. (2010). Attitudes. In S. T. Fiske, D. T. Gilbert & G. Lindzey (Eds.), *Handbook of social psychology, Vol. 1,* (pp. 353–393). Hoboken, NJ: Wiley.

Bandura, Albert. (1965). Influence of models' reinforcement contingencies on the acquisition of imitative behaviors. *Journal of Personality and Social Psychology, 1,* 589–595.

Bandura, Albert. (1974). Behavior theory and the models of man. *American Psychologist, 29,* 859–869.

Bandura, Albert. (1977). *Social learning theory.* Englewood Cliffs, NJ: Prentice Hall.

Bandura, Albert. (1986). *Social foundations of thought and action: A social cognitive theory.* Englewood Cliffs, NJ: Prentice Hall.

Bandura, Albert. (1990). Conclusion: Reflections on nonability determinants of competence. In Robert J. Sternberg & John Kolligian, Jr. (Eds.), *Competence considered.* New Haven, CT: Yale University Press.

Bandura, Albert. (1991). Self-regulation of motivation through anticipatory and self-reactive mechanisms. In Richard Dienstbier (Ed.), *Nebraska Symposium on Motivation 1990* (Vol. 38). Lincoln: University of Nebraska Press.

Bandura, Albert. (1992). Exercise of personal agency through the self-efficacy mechanism. In Ralf Schwarzer (Ed.), *Self-efficacy: Thought control of action.* Washington, DC: Hemisphere.

Bandura, Albert. (1996). Failures in self-regulation: Energy depletion or selective disengagement? *Psychological Inquiry, 7,* 20–24.

Bandura, Albert. (1997). *Self-efficacy: The exercise of control.* New York, NY: Freeman.

Bandura, Albert. (2001). Social cognitive theory: An agentic perspective. *Annual Review of Psychology, 52,* 1–26.

Bandura, Albert. (2002). Environmental sustainability by sociocognitive deceleration of population growth. In Peter Schmuck & Wesley P. Schultz (Eds.), *The psychology of sustainable development.* Dordrecht, The Netherlands: Kluwer.

Bandura, Albert. (2004a). Quoted in Population Communications International, "Telling stories, saving lives." Retrieved September 5, 2004, from http://www.population.org/index.shtml

Bandura, Albert. (2004b). Swimming against the mainstream: The early years from chilly tributary to transformative mainstream. *Behaviour Research and Therapy, 42,* 613–630.

Bandura, Albert. (2006). Towards a psychology of human agency. *Perspectives on Psychological Science, 1,* 164–180.

Bandura, Albert. (2008). An agentic perspective on positive psychology. In Shane J. Lopez (Ed.), *Positive psychology: Exploring the best in people.* Westport, CT: Greenwood.

Bandura, Albert; Caprara, Gian Vittorio; Barbaranelli, Claudio; Gerbino, Maria; & Pastorelli, Concetta. (2003). Role of affective selfregulatory efficacy in diverse spheres of psychosocial functioning. *Child Development, 74,* 769–782.

Bandura, Albert; Ross, Dorothea; & Ross, Sheila A. (1963). Imitation of film-mediated aggressive models. *Journal of Abnormal and Social Psychology, 66,* 3–11.

Bangerter, Adrian; König, Cornelius J.; Blatti, Sandrine; & Salvisberg, Alexander. (2009). How widespread is graphology in personnel selection practice? A case study of a job market myth. *International Journal of Selection and Assessment, 17*(2), 219–230.

Banks, Caroline Giles. (2009). 'Culture' in culture-bound syndromes: The case of anorexia nervosa. *Social Science and Medicine, 34,* 867–884.

Banks, Terry, & Dabbs, J. M. (1996). Salivary testosterone and cortisol in a deliquent and violent urban subculture. *Journal of Social Psychology, 136*(1), 49–56.

Bar, Moshe; Neta, Maital; & Linz, Heather. (2006). Very first impressions. *Emotion, 6*(2), 269–278. doi:10.1037/1528-3542.6.2.269

Barch, Deanna M. (2005). The cognitive neuroscience of schizophrenia. *Annual Review of Clinical Psychology, 1,* 321–353.

Barker, Jamie, & Jones, Marc V. (2006). Using hypnosis, technique refinement, and self-modeling to enhance self-efficacy: A case study in cricket. *The Sport Psychologist, 20,* 94–110.

Barlińska, Julia; Szuster, Anna; & Winiewski, Mikolaj. (2013). Cyberbullying among adolescent bystanders: Role of the communication medium, form of violence, and empathy. *Journal of Community & Applied Social Psychology, 23,* 37–51. doi:10.1002/casp.2137

Barlow, David H.; Bullis, Jacqueline R.; Comer, Jonathan S.; & Ametaj, Amantia A. (2013). Evidence-based psychological treatments: An update and a way forward. *Annual Review of Clinical Psychology, 9,* 1–27. doi:10.1146/annurev-clinpsy-050212-185629

Barlow, David H; Ellard, Kristin K.; Sauer-Zavala, Shannon; Bullis, Jaqueline R; & Carl, Jenna R. (2014). The origins of neuroticism. *Perspectives on Psychological Science, 9,* 481–496. doi:10.1177/1745691614544528

Barnes, Anthony. (2006, September 10). Russell Brand's got issues. *The Independent.* Retrieved on February 6, 2014 from http://www.independent.co.uk/news/media/russell-brands-got-issues-415385.html

Barnett, Jeffrey E., & Scheetz, Karin. (2003). Technological advances and telehealth: Ethics, law, and the practice of psychotherapy. *Psychotherapy: Theory, Research, Practice, Training, 40*(1–2), 86–93.

Barnett, Jeffrey E.; Shale, Allison J.; Elkins, Gary; & Fisher, William. (2014). *Complementary and alternative medicine for psychologists: An essential resource.* Washington, DC: American Psychological Association. doi:10.1037/14435-011

Baron-Cohen, Simon. (2000, January 5). Is Asperger's syndrome/high-functioning autism necessarily a disability? Invited submission for Special Millenium Issue of Developmental and Psychopathology. Retrieved on September 18, 2008, from http://www.geocities.com/CapitolHill/7138/lobby/disability.htm

Baron-Cohen, Simon. (2005). Enhanced attention to detail and hyper-systemizing in autism. Commentary on Elizabeth Milne, John Swettenham, & Ruth Campbell, Motion perception in autism: A review. *Current Psychology of Cognition, 23,* 59–64.

Baron-Cohen, Simon (2007, August 8). Quoted in Emine Saner, "It's not a disease, it's a way of life." *The Guardian.* Retrieved on September 15, 2008, from http://www.guardian.co.uk/society/2007/aug/07/health.medicineandhealth

Barone, L.; Fossati, A.; & Guiducci, V. (2011). Attachment mental states and inferred pathways of development in borderline personality disorder: A study using the Adult Attachment Interview. *Attachment and Human Development, 13*(5), 451–469. doi:10.1080/14616734.2011.602245

Barrett, Lisa F., & Bliss-Moreau, Eliza. (2009). She's emotional. He's having a bad day: Attributional explanations for emotion stereotypes. *Emotion, 9,* 649–658.

Barrett, Marna S.; Chua, Wee-Jhong; Crits-Christoph, Paul; Gibbons, Mary Beth; & Thompson, Don. (2008, June). Early withdrawal from mental health treatment: Implications for psychotherapy practice. *Psychotherapy: Theory, Research, Practice, Training, 45*(2), 247–267.

Barsaglini, Alessio; Sartori, Guiseppe; Benetti, Stefania; Pettersson-Yeo, William; & Mechelli, Andrea. (2014). The effects of psychotherapy on brain function: A systematic and critical review. *Progress in Neurobiology, 114,* 1–14. doi:10.1016/j.pneurobio.2013.10.006

Barth, Jürgen; Munder, Thomas; Gerger, Heike; Nüesch, Eveline; Trelle, Sven; Znoj, Hansjörg., ... Cuijpers, Pim. (2013). Comparative efficacy of seven psychotherapeutic interventions for patients with depression: A network meta-analysis. *PLOS Medicine, 10*(5), e1001454.

Bartlett, Donald L., & Steele, James B. (2004). *Howard Hughes: His life and madness.* New York, NY: Norton.

Bartlett, Frederic C. (1932). *Remembering.* Cambridge, England: Cambridge University Press.

Bartolomei, Fabrice; Barbeau, Emmanuel J.; Nguyen, Trung; McGonigal, Aileen; Régis, Jean; Chauvel, Patrick; & Wendling, Fabrice. (2012). Rhinal–hippocampal interactions during déjà vu. *Clinical Neurophysiology, 123*(3), 489–495. doi:10.1016/j.clinph.2011.08.01

Bartz, Jennifer; Simeon, Daphne; Hamilton, Holly; Kim, Suah; Crystal, Sarah; Braun, Ashley; Vicens, Victor; & Hollander, Eric. (2011). Social effects of oxytocin in humans: Context and person matter. *Trends in Cognitive Science, 15,* 301–309.

Baruss, Imants & Rabier, Vanille. (2014). Failure to replicate retrocausal recall. *Psychology of Consciousness: Theory, Research, and Practice, 1,* 82–91. doi:10.1037/cns0000005

Bashore, Theodore R., & Rapp, Paul E. (1993). Are there alternatives to traditional polygraph procedures? *Psychological Bulletin, 113,* 3–22.

Basil, Debra Z.; Ridgway, Nancy M.; & Basil, Michael D. (2006). Guilt appeals: The mediating effect of responsibility. *Psychology & Marketing, 23*(12), 1035–1054.

Baskin-Sommers, Arielle R.; Curtin, John J.; & Newman, Joseph P. (2015). Altering the cognitive-affective dysfunctions of psychopathic and externalizing offender subtypes with cognitive remediation. *Clinical Psychological Sciences, 3,* 45–57. doi:10.1177/2167702614560744

Bass, Bernard M. (1981). *Stogdill's handbook of leadership.* New York, NY: Free Press.

Bass, Ellen, & Davis, Linda. (1994). *The courage to heal* (3rd ed.). New York, NY: HarperPerennial.

Basso, Olga. (2007). Right or wrong? On the difficult relationship between epidemiologists and handedness. *Epidemiology, 18,* 191–193.

Bastardi, Anthony; Uhlmann, Eric L.; & Ross, Lee. (2011). Wishful thinking: Belief, desire, and the motivated evaluation of scientific evidence. *Psychological Science, 22,* 731–732.

Bastiaensens, Sara; Vandebosch, Heidi; Poels, Karolien; Van Cleemput, Katrien; DeSmet, Ann; & De Bourdeaudhuij, Ilse. (2014). Cyberbullying on social network sites: An experimental study into bystanders' behavioural intentions to help the victim or reinforce the bully. *Computers in Human Behavior, 31,* 259–271. doi:10.1016/j.chb.2013.10.036

Bates, Steve. (2002, February). Personality counts. *HR Magazine, 47,* 28.

Bathje, Geoff J., & Pryor, John B. (2011). The relationships of public and self-stigma to seeking mental health services. *Journal of Mental Health Counseling, 33*(2), 161–177.

Batson, C. Daniel; Ahmad, Nadia; & Stocks, E. L. (2011). Four forms of prosocial motivation: Egoism, altruism, collectivism, and principalism. In David Dunning (Ed.), *Social motivation* (pp. 103–126). New York, NY: Psychology Press.

Baudry, Michel; Bi, Xiaoning; Gall, Christine; & Lynch, Gary. (2011). The biochemistry of memory: The 26 year journey of a 'new and specific hypothesis'. *Neurobiology of Learning and Memory, 95*(2), 125–133.

Bauer, Stephanie; Percevic, Robert; Okon, Eberhard; Meermann, Rolf U.; & Kordy, Hans. (2003). Use of text messaging in the aftercare of patients with bulimia nervosa. *European Eating Disorders Review, 11*(3), 279–290.

Bauer, Susanne M.; Schanda, Hans; Karakula, Hanna; Olajossy-Hilkesberger, Luiza; Rudaleviciene, Palmira; Okribelashvili, Nino; Chaudhry, Haroon R.; Idemudia, Sunday E.; Gscheider, Sharon; Ritter, Kristina; & Stompe, Thomas. (2011). Culture and the prevalence of hallucinations in schizophrenia. *Comprehensive Psychiatry, 52*(3), 319–325.

Bauman, Christopher W., & Skitka, Linda J. (2010). Making attributions for behaviors: The prevalence of correspondence bias in the general population. *Basic and Applied Social Psychology, 32*(3), 269–277.

Baumeister, Roy F., & Masicampo, E. J. (2010). Conscious thought is for facilitating social and cultural interactions: How mental simulations serve the animal–culture interface. *Psychological Review, 117*(3), 945–971. doi:10.1037/a0019393

Baumeister, Roy F.; Masicampo, E. J.; & Vohs, Kathleen D. (2011). Do conscious thoughts cause behavior? *Annual Review of Psychology, 62,* 331–61.

Baumrind, Diana. (1964). Some thoughts on ethics of research: After reading Milgram's "Behavioral Study of Obedience." *American Psychologist, 19,* 421–423.

Baumrind, Diana. (1971). Current patterns of parental authority. *Developmental Psychology Monographs, 4,* 1–103.

Baumrind, Diana. (1991). The influence of parenting style on adolescent competence and substance abuse. *Journal of Early Adolescence, 11,* 56–95.

Baumrind, Diana. (2005). Patterns of parental authority and adolescent autonomy. *New Directions for Child & Adolescent Development, 2005*(108), 61–69.

Bayer, Christophe Pierre; Klasen, Fionna; & Adam, Hubertus. (2007). Association of trauma and PTSD symptoms with openness to reconciliation and feelings of revenge among former Ugandan and Congolese child soldiers. *Journal of the American Medical Association, 298,* 555–559.

Bayer, Ute C., & Gollwitzer, Peter M. (2007). Boosting scholastic test scores by willpower: The role of implementation intentions. *Self and Identity, 6,* 1–19.

Bayley, Peter J., & Squire, Larry R. (2002). Medial temporal lobe amnesia: Gradual acquisition of factual information by nondeclarative memory. *Journal of Neuroscience, 22,* 5741–5748.

Baylis, Gordon C., & Driver, Jon. (2001). Shape-coding in IT cells generalizes over contrast and mirror reversal, but not figure-ground reversal. *Nature Neuroscience, 4,* 937–942.

Bazzini, Doris; Curtin, Lisa; Joslin, Serena; Regan, Shilpa; & Martz, Denise. (2010). Do animated Disney characters portray and promote the beauty-goodness stereotype? *Journal of Applied Social Psychology, 40*(10), 2687–2709. doi:10.1111/j.1559-1816.2010.00676.x

BBC News. (2008, December 19). People 'still willing to torture'. *BBC News.* Retrieved from http://news.bbc.co.uk/2/hi/7791278.stm

Beal, Carole R. (1994). *Boys and girls: The development of gender roles.* New York, NY: McGraw-Hill.

Beal, Sarah J.; Negriff, Sonya; Dorn, Lorah D.; Pabst, Stephanie; & Schulenberg, John. (2014). Longitudinal associations between smoking and depressive symptoms among adolescent girls. *Prevention Science, 15,* 506–515. doi:10.1007/s11121-013-0402-x

Beardsley, Eleanor. (2010, March 18). Fake TV game show 'tortures' man, shocks France. *NPR.* Retrieved on June 3, 2014, from http://www.npr.org/templates/story/story.php?storyId=124838091

Beauvois, Jean-Léon; Courbet, Didier; & Oberlé, Dominque. (2012). The prescriptive power of the television host: A transposition of Milgram's obedience paradigm to the context of TV game show. *Revue Européenne de Psychologie Appliquée, 62,* 111–119.

Beck, Aaron T. (1991). Cognitive therapy: A 30-year retrospective. *American Psychologist, 46,* 368–375.

Beck, Aaron T. (2004, March). Quoted in Anita Bowles, "Beck in action." *APS Observer, 17*(3), 7–8.

Beck, Aaron T., & Alford, Brad A. (2009). *Depression: Causes and treatment.* Philadelphia, PA: University of Pennsylvania Press.

Beck, Aaron T., & Dozois, David J. A. (2011). Cognitive Therapy: Current Status and Future Directions. *Annual Review of Medicine, 62*(1), 397–409. doi:10.1146/annurev-med-052209-100032

Beck, Aaron T.; Rector, Neil A.; Stolar, Neal; & Grant, Paul. (2009). *Schizophrenia: Cognitive theory, research, and therapy.* New York, NY: Guilford Press.

Beck, Aaron T.; Rush, A. John; Shaw, Brian F.; & Emery, Gary. (1979). *Cognitive therapy of depression.* New York, NY: Guilford.

Beck, Diane M. (2010). The appeal of the brain in the popular press. *Perspectives on Psychological Science, 5,* 762–766. doi:10.1177/1745691610388779

Beck, Hall P.; Levinson, Sharman; & Irons, Gary. (2009). Finding Little Albert: A journey to John B. Watson's infant laboratory. *American Psychologist, 64*(7), 605–614.

Beck, Hall P.; Levinson, Sharman; & Irons, Gary. (2010). The evidence supports Douglas Merritte as Little Albert. *American Psychologist, 65,* 301–303. doi:10.1037/a0019444

Beck, Judith S. (2011). *Cognitive behavior therapy: Basics and beyond.* New York, NY: Guilford Press.

Bedi, Gillinder; Hyman, David; & de Wit, Harriet. (2010). Is ecstasy an "empathogen"? Effects of ±3,4-methylenedioxymethamphetamine on prosocial feelings and identification of emotional states in others. *Biological Psychiatry, 68,* 1134–1140. doi:10.1016/j.biopsych.2010.08.003

Beidel, Deborah C., & Stipelman, Brooke. (2007). Anxiety disorders. In Michel Hersen, Samuel M. Turner, & Deborah C. Beidel (Eds.), *Adult psychopathology and diagnosis* (5th ed., pp. 349–409). Hoboken, NJ: Wiley.

Beins, Bernard C. (2011). Methodological and conceptual issues in cross-cultural research. In K. D. Keith (Ed.), *Cross-Cultural Psychology: Contemporary Themes and Perspectives* (pp. 37–55). Oxford, England: Wiley-Blackwell.

Bekoff, Marc. (2007). *The emotional lives of animals.* Novato, CA: New World Library.

Belgrave, Faye Z., & Allison, Kevin W. (2010). *African American psychology: From Africa to America.* Thousand Oaks, CA: Sage.

Bell, Alan; Weinberg, Martin; & Hammersmith, Sue. (1981). *Sexual preference: Its development in men and women.* Bloomington: Indiana University Press.

Bell, C. G.; Walley, A. J.; & Froguel, P. (2005). The genetics of human obesity. *Nature Reviews Genetics 6,* 221–34.

Bellak, Leopold. (1993). *The Thematic Apperception Test, the Children's Apperception Test, and the Senior Apperception Technique in clinical use* (5th ed.). Boston, MA: Allyn & Bacon.

Belsky, Jay. (1992). Consequences of child care for children's development: A deconstructionist view. In Alan Booth (Ed.), *Child care in the 1990s: Trends and consequences.* Hillsdale, NJ: Erlbaum.

Belsky, Jay. (2001). Emanuel Miller Lecture: Developmental risks (still) associated with early child care. *Journal of Child Psychology, Psychiatry and Allied Disciplines, 42,* 845–859.

Belsky, Jay. (2002). Quantity counts: Amount of child care and children's socioemotional development. *Journal of Development & Behavioral Pediatrics, 23,* 167–170.

Belsky, Jay. (2006). Determinants and consequences of infant-parent attachment. In Catherine Susan Tamis-LeMonda (Ed.), *Child psychology: A handbook of contemporary issues* (2nd ed., pp. 53–77). New York, NY: Psychology Press.

Belsky, Jay. (2009). Classroom composition, childcare history and social development: Are childcare effects disappearing or spreading? *Social Development, 18*(1), 230–238.

Belsky, Jay; Steinberg, Laurence; Houts, Renate M.; & Halpern-Felsher, Bonnie L. (2010). The development of reproductive strategy in females: Early maternal harshness → earlier menarche → increased sexual risk taking. *Developmental Psychology, 46*(1), 120–128.

Belsky, Jay; Vandell, D. L.; Burchinal, M.; Clarke-Stewart, K. A.; McCartney, K.; & Owen, M. T. (2007). Are there long-term effects of early child care? *Child Development, 78*(2), 681–701.

Bem, Daryl J. (2011). Feeling the future: Experimental evidence for anomalous retroactive influences on cognition and affect. *Journal of Personality and Social Psychology, 100,* 407–425.

Bem, Daryl; Tressoldi, Patrizio E.; Rabeyron, Thomas; & Duggan, Michael. (2014, April 11). Feeling the future: A meta-analysis of 90 experiments on the anomalous anticipation of random future events. Retrieved from http://ssrn.com/abstract=2423692 or http://dx.doi.org/10.2139/ssrn.2423692

Bem, Sandra L. (1981). Gender schema theory: A cognitive account of sex typing. *Psychological Review, 88,* 354–364.

Bem, Sandra L. (1987). Gender schema theory and the romantic tradition. In P. Shaver & C. Hendrick (Eds.), *Sex and gender.* Beverly Hills, CA: Sage.

Benedetti, Fabrizio; Carlino, Elisa; & Pollo, Antonella. (2010). How placebos change the patient's brain. *Neuropsychopharmacology, 36,* 339–354. doi:10.1038/npp.2010.81

Ben-Hamou, Monsif; Marshall, Nathaniel S.; Grunstein, Ronald R.; Saini, Bandana; & Fois, Romano A. (2011). Spontaneous adverse event reports associated with zolpidem in Australia 2001–2008. *Journal of Sleep Research, 20,* 559–568. doi:10.1111/j.1365-2869.2011.00919.x

Benjamin, Ludy T., Jr., & Simpson, Jeffry A. (2009). The power of the situation: The impact of Milgram's obedience studies on personality and social psychology. *American Psychologist, 64*(1), 12–19. doi:10.1037/a0014077

Benjamin, Ludy T.; Whitaker, Jodi L.; Ramsey, Russell M.; & Zeve, Daniel R. (2007). John B. Watson's alleged sex research: An appraisal of the evidence. *American Psychologist, 62,* 131–139.

Bennett, David A.; Wilson, Robert S.; Schneider, Julie A.; Evans, D. A.; Mendes de Leon, C. F.; Arnold, S. E; & others. (2003). Education modifies the relation of Alzheimer's disease pathology to level of cognitive function in older persons. *Neurology, 60,* 1909–1915.

Benningfield, Margaret M., & Cowan, Ronald L. (2013). Brain serotonin function in MDMA (ecstasy) users: Evidence for persisting neurotoxicity. *Neuropsychopharmacology, 38,* 253–255. doi:10.1038/npp.2012.178

Benson, Herbert. (2010). *Relaxation revolution: The science and genetics of mind body healing.* New York, NY: Scribner.

Bentley, Kate H.; Gallagher, Matthew W.; Boswell, James F.; Gorman, Jack M.; Shear, Katherine M.; Woods, Scott W.; & Barlow, David H. (2013). The interactive contributions of perceived control and anxiety sensitivity in panic disorder: A triple vulnerabilities perspective. *Journal of Psychopathology and Behavioral Assessment, 35,* 57–64. doi:10.1007/s10862-012-9311-8

Ben-Zeev, Dror. (2012). Mobile technologies in the study, assessment, and treatment of schizophrenia. *Schizophrenia Bulletin.* Advance online publication. doi:10.1093/schbul/sbr179

Ben-Zeev, D.; Young, M. A.; & Corrigan, P. W. (2010). DSM-V and the stigma of mental illness. *Journal of Mental Health, 19*(4), 318–327. doi:10.3109/09638237.2010.492484

Berenbaum, Sheri A.; Martin, Carol L.; Hanish, Laura D.; Briggs, Philip T.; & Fabes, Richard A. (2008). Sex differences in children's play. In Jill B. Becker, Karen J. Berkley, Nori Geary, Elizabeth Hampson, James P. Herman, & Elizabeth A. Young (Eds.), *Sex differences in the brain: From genes to behavior.* Oxford, England: Oxford University Press.

Berenson, Kathy R.; Downey, Geraldine; Rafaeli, Eshkol; Coifman, Karin G.; & Paquin, Nina Leventhal. (2011). The rejection–rage contingency in borderline personality disorder. *Journal of Abnormal Psychology, 120*(3), 681–690.

Berger, William; Evandro, Silvia F.; Figueira, Ivan; Marques-Portella, Carla; Luz, Mariana P.; Neylan, Thomas C.; Marmar, Charles R.; & Mendlowics, Mauro V. (2012). Rescuers at risk: A systematic review and meta-regression analysis of the worldwide current prevalence and correlates of PTSD in rescue workers. *Social Psychiatry and Psychiatric Epidemiology, 47,* 1001–1011. doi:10.1007/s00127-011-0408-2

Berkman, Lisa F., & Glass, Thomas. (2000). Social integration, social networks, social support, and health. In Lisa F. Berkman & Ichir Kawachi (Eds.), *Social epidemiology* (pp. 137–173). New York, NY: Oxford University Press.

Berlyne, Daniel E. (1960). *Conflict, arousal, and curiosity.* New York, NY: McGraw-Hill.

Berlyne, Daniel E. (1971). *Aesthetics and psychobiology.* New York, NY: Appleton-Century-Crofts.

Berman, David, & Lyons, William. (2007). The first modern battle for consciousness: J. B. Watson's rejection of mental images. *Journal of Consciousness Studies, 14,* 5–26.

Bermond, Bob; Fasotti, L.; Nieuwenhuyse, B.; & Schuerman, J. (1991). Spinal cord lesions, peripheral feedback and intensities of emotional feelings. *Cognition & Emotion, 5,* 201–220.

Berna, Chantal; Leknes, Siri; Holmes, Emily A.; Edwards, Robert R.; Goodwin, Guy M.; & Tracey, Irene. (2010). Induction of depressed mood disrupts emotion regulation neurocircuitry and enhances pain unpleasantness. *Biological Psychiatry, 67,* 1083–1090. doi:10.1073/pnas.0505210102

Bernard, Luther L. (1924). *Instinct: A study in social psychology.* New York, NY: Holt.

Bernstein, Daniel M., & Loftus, Elizabeth F. (2009). How to tell if a particular memory is true or false. *Perspectives on Psychological Science 4,* 370–374.

Bernstein, Robert. (2010). Census bureau reports families with children increasingly face unemployment, from http://www.census.gov/Press-Release/ www/releases/archives/families_households/014540.html doi:10.1136/ adc.2003.038067

Berntsen, Dorthe, & Rubin, David C. (2014). Involuntary memories and dissociative amnesia: Assessing key assumptions in posttraumatic stress. *Clinical Psychological Science, 2,* 174–186. doi:10.1177/2167702613496241

Berrendero, Fernando; Robledo, Patricia; Trigo, José M.; Martin-Garcia, Elena; & Maldonado, Rafael. (2010). Neurobiological mechanisms involved in nicotine dependence and reward: Participation of the endogenous opioid system. *Neuroscience and Biobehavioral Reviews. 35,* 220–231.

Berry, John W. (1994). Acculturative stress. In Walter J. Lonner & Roy Malpass (Eds.), *Psychology and culture.* Boston, MA: Allyn & Bacon.

Berry, John W. (2003). Conceptual approaches to acculturation. In Kevin M. Chun, Pamela Balls Organista, & Gerardo Marín (Eds.), *Acculturation: Advances in theory, measurement and applied research.* Washington, DC: American Psychological Association.

Berry, John W. (2006). Acculturative stress. In Paul T. P. Wong & C. J. Lilian Wong, *Handbook of multicultural perspectives on stress and coping* (pp. 287–298). Dallas, TX: Spring.

Berthoud, Hans-Rudolf. (2007). Interactions between the "cognitive" and "metabolic" brain in the control of food intake. *Physiology and Behavior, 91,* 486–498.

Bessesen, D. H. (2011). Regulation of body weight: What is the regulated parameter? *Physiology and Behavior, 104,*599–607.

Best, Mary; Williams, J. Michael; & Coccaro, Emil F. (2002). Evidence for a dysfunctional prefrontal circuit in patients with an impulsive aggressive disorder. *Proceedings of the National Academy of Sciences, 99*(12), 8448–8453.

Bettex, Morgan. (2010). Xerox CEO Ursula Burns to deliver 2011 commencement address. *MIT News.* Retrieved from http://news.mit.edu/2010/commencement-speaker-burns

Beutler, Larry E.; Malik, Mary; Alimohamed, Shabia; Harwood, T. Mark; Talebi, Hani; Noble, Sharon; & Wong, Eunice. (2004). Therapist variables. In Michael J. Lambert (Ed.), *Bergin and Garfield's handbook of psychotherapy and behavior change* (5th ed.). New York, NY: Wiley.

Beyerstein, Barry L. (1996). Graphology. In Gordon Stein (Ed.), *The encyclopedia of the paranormal.* Amherst, NY: Prometheus Books.

Beyerstein, Barry L. (2007). Graphology—A total write-off. In Sergio Della Sala (Ed.), *Tall tales about the mind & brain: Separating fact from fiction* (pp. 233–270). New York, NY: Oxford University Press.

Beyerstein, Barry L., & Beyerstein, Dale (Eds.). (1992). *The write stuff: Evaluations of graphology—The study of handwriting analysis.* Amherst, NY: Prometheus Books.

Bhanji, Nadeem H.; Chouinard, Guy; & Margolese, Howard C. (2004). A review of compliance, depot intramuscular antipsychotics and the new long-acting injectable atypical antipsychotic risperidone in schizophrenia. *European Neuropsychopharmacology, 14*(2), 87–92.

Bhatara, Vinod S.; Sharma, J. N.; Gupta, Sanjay; & Gupta, Y. K. (1997). *Rauwolfia serpentina:* The first herbal antipsychotic. *American Journal of Psychiatry, 154,* 894.

Bialystok, Ellen. (2011). Reshaping the mind: The benefits of bilingualism. *Canadian Journal of Experimental Psychology, 65,* 229–235. doi:10.1037/a0025406

Bialystok, Ellen; Craik, Fergus I.M.; & Freedman, Morris. (2007). Bilingualism as a protection against the onset of symptoms of dementia. *Neuropsychologia, 45,* 459– 464. doi:10.1016/j.neuropsychologia.2006.10.009

Bialystok, Ellen; Craik, Fergus I.M.; Green, David W.; & Gollan, Tamar H. (2009). Bilingual minds. *Psychological Science in the Public Interest, 10,* 89–129. doi:10.1177/1529100610387084

Bialystok, Ellen; Craik, Fergus I.M.; & Luk, Gigi. (2012). Bilingualism: Consequences for mind and brain. *Trends in Cognitive Sciences, 16,* 240–250. doi:10.1016/j.tics.2012.03.001

Bianchi, Renzo; Schonfeld, Irvin; & Laurent, Eric. (2015). Burnout and depression overlap: A review. *Clinical Psychology Review, 36,* 28–41. doi:10.1016/j.cpr.2015.01.004

Bieling, Peter J., Hawley, Lance L., Bloch, Richard T., Corcoran, Kathleen M., Levitan, Robert D., Young, L. Trevor., . . . Segal, Zindel V. (2012). Treatment-specific changes in decentering following mindfulness-based cognitive therapy versus antidepressant medication or placebo for prevention of depressive relapse. *Journal of Consulting and Clinical Psychology, 80*(3), 365–372.

Bihm, Elson M.; Gillaspy, J. Arthur, Jr.; Abbott, Hannah J.; & Lammers, William J. (2010a). More misbehavior of organisms: A Psi Chi lecture by Marian and Robert Bailey. *The Psychological Record, 60*(3), 505–522.

Bihm, Elson M.; Gillaspy, J. Arthur, Jr.; Lammers, William J.; & Huffman, Stephanie P. (2010b). IQ zoo and teaching operant concepts. *The Psychological Record, 60*(3), 523–526.

Bilalić, Merim; McLeod, Peter; & Gobet, Fernand. (2008). Inflexibility of experts—Reality or myth? Quantifying the Einstellung effect in chess masters. *Cognitive Psychology, 56,* 73–102.

Bill & Melinda Gates Foundation. (2015). *Foundation fact sheet.* Retrieved from http://www.gatesfoundation.org/Who-We-Are/General-Information/Foundation-Factsheet

Binet, Alfred, & Simon, Théodore. (1905). New methods for the diagnosis of the intellectual level of subnormals. *L'Année Psychologique, 11,* 191–244.

Bischoff, Richard J. (2011). The state of couple therapy. In Joseph L. Wetchler (Ed.), *Handbook of clinical issues in couple therapy.* New York, NY: Routledge.

Bisson, Melissa, & Levine, Timothy. (2009). Negotiating a friends with benefits relationship. *Archives of Sexual Behavior, 38*(1), 66–73. doi:10.1007/s10508-007-9211-2

Bitterman, M. E. (2006). Classical conditioning since Pavlov. *Review of General Psychology, 10,* 365–376.

Bizumic, Boris; Duckitt, John; Popadic, Dragan; Dru, Vincent; & Krauss, Stephen. (2009). A cross-cultural investigation into a reconceptualization of ethnocentrism. *European Journal of Social Psychology, 39*(6), 871–899.

Bjork, Daniel W. (1997). *B. F. Skinner: A life.* Washington, DC: American Psychological Association.

Bjork, Robert A.; Dunlosky, John; & Kornell, Nate. (2013). Self-regulated learning: Beliefs, techniques, and illusions. *Annual Review of Psychology, 64,* 417–444. doi:10.1146/annurev-psych-113011-143823

Bjorklund, Barbara R. (1995). Language development and cognition. In David F. Bjorklund (Ed.), *Children's thinking: Developmental function and individual differences* (2nd ed.). Pacific Grove, CA: Brooks/Cole.

Bjornsson, Andri S. (2011). Beyond the "psychological placebo": Specifying the nonspecific in psychotherapy. *Clinical Psychology: Science and Practice, 18*(2), 113–118.

Bjorvatn, Bjørn; Grønli, Janne; & Pallesen, Ståle. (2010). Prevalence of different parasomnias in the general population. *Sleep Medicine, 11,* 1031–1034. doi:10.1016/j.sleep.2010.07.011

Blackburn, Elizabeth, & Epel, Elissa S. (2012). Too toxic to ignore. *Nature, 490,* 169–171. doi:10.1038/490169a

Blake, Robert R., & Mouton, Jane S. (1985). *The managerial grid III: The key to leadership excellence.* Austin, TX: Grid International.

Blanchard, Ray. (2008). Sex ratio of older siblings in heterosexual and homosexual, right-handed and non-right-handed men. *Archives of Sexual Behavior, 37*(6), 977–981.

Blanchard, Ray, & Lippa, Richard A. (2008). The sex ratio of older siblings in non-right-handed homosexual men. *Archives of Sexual Behavior, 37*(6), 970–976.

Blanco, Carlos; Clougherty, Kathleen F.; & Lipsitz, W. Joshua. (2006). Homework in Interpersonal Psychotherapy (IPT): Rationale and practice. *Journal of Psychotherapy Integration, 16*(2) [Special issue: Integration of between-session (homework) activities into psychotherapy], 201–218.

Blankstein, Kirk R., & Flett, Gordon L. (1992). Specificity in the assessment of daily hassles: Hassles, locus of control, and adjustment in college students. *Canadian Journal of Behavioural Science, 24,* 382–398.

Blanton, Hart; Klick, Jonathan; Mitchell, Gregory, Jaccard, Jacques; Mellers, Barbara; & Tetlock, Philip E. (2009). Strong claims and weak evidence: Reassessing the predictive validity of the IAT. *Journal of Applied Psychology, 94,* 567–582.

Blass, Thomas. (1991). Understanding behavior in the Milgram obedience experiment. *Journal of Personality and Social Psychology, 60,* 398–413.

Blass, Thomas. (1992). The social psychology of Stanley Milgram. In Mark P. Zanna (Ed.), *Advances in experimental social psychology* (Vol. 25). San Diego, CA: Academic Press.

Blass, Thomas. (2000). The Milgram Paradigm after 35 years. Some things we now know about obedience to authority. In Thomas Blass (Ed.), *Obedience to authority: Current perspectives on the Milgram paradigm* (pp. 35–59). Mahwah, NJ: Erlbaum.

Blass, Thomas. (2004). *The man who shocked the world: The life and legacy of Stanley Milgram.* New York, NY: Basic Books.

Blass, Thomas. (2009). From New Haven to Santa Clara: A historical perspective on the Milgram obedience experiments. *American Psychologist, 64,* 37–45. doi:10.1037/a0014434

Blass, Thomas. (2012). A cross-cultural comparison of studies of obedience using the Milgram paradigm: A review: Cross-cultural comparison of studies of obedience. *Social and Personality Psychology Compass, 6*(2), 196–205. doi:10.1111/j.1751-9004.2011.00417.x

Bleiberg, Kathryn L., & Markowitz, John C. (2008). Interpersonal psychotherapy for depression. In David H. Barlow (Ed.), *Clinical handbook of psychological disorders: A step-by-step treatment manual* (4th ed.). New York, NY: Guilford Press.

Block, Jack. (1995). A contrarian view of the five-factor approach to personality description. *Psychological Bulletin, 117,* 187–215.

Block, Jack. (2010). The five-factor framing of personality and beyond: Some ruminations. *Psychological Inquiry, 21*(1), 2–25.

Bloom, Paul. (2006, June 27). Seduced by the flickering lights of the brain. *Seed Magazine.* Retrieved on February 22, 2008, from http://seedmagazine.com/news/2006/06/seduced_by_the_flickering_ligh.php

Bloomfield, Tiffany C.; Gentner, Timothy Q.; & Margoliash, Daniel. (2011). What birds have to say about language. *Nature Neuroscience, 14,* 947–948.

Blumenthal, Arthur L. (1998). Leipzig, Wilhelm Wundt, and psychology's gilded age. In Gregory A. Kimble & Michael Wertheimer (Eds.), *Portraits of pioneers in psychology* (Vol. 3). Washington, DC: American Psychological Association.

Blumstein, Daniel T., & Fernandez-Juricic, Esteban. (2010). *A primer of conservation behavior.* Sunderland, MA: Sinauer Associates.

Bobes, Maria A.; Ostrosky, Feggy; Diaz, Karla; Romero, Cesar; Borja, Karina; Santos, Yusniel; & Valdés-Sosa, Mitchell. (2013). Linkage of functional and structural anomalies in the left amygdala of reactive-aggressive men. *Social Cognitive and Affective Neuroscience, 8,* 928–936.

Bocchiaro, Piero, & Zimbardo, Philip G. (2010). Defying unjust authority: An exploratory study. *Current Psychology: A Journal for Diverse Perspectives on Diverse Psychological Issues, 29*(2), 155–170.

Boddy, Clive R.; Ladyshewsky, Richard; & Galvin, Peter. (2010). Leaders without ethics in global business: Corporate psychopaths. *Journal of Public Affairs, 10*(3), 121–138.

Boden, Joseph M.; Fergusson, David M.; & Horwood, L. John. (2010). Cigarette smoking and depression: Tests of causal linkages using a longitudinal birth cohort. *British Journal of Psychiatry, 196,* 440–446.

Bodenhausen, Galen V., & Richeson, Jennifer A. (2010). Prejudice, stereotyping, and discrimination. In R. F. Baumeister & E. J. Finkel (Eds.), *Advanced social psychology: The state of the science* (pp. 341–383). New York, NY: Oxford University Press.

Bodenhausen, Galen V.; Macrae, C. Neil; & Hugenberg, Kurt. (2003). Social cognition. In T. Million & M. J. Lerner (Eds.), *Handbook of psychology: Personality and social psychology, 5,* 257–282. New York, NY: Wiley.

Bodenmann, Guy; Atkins, David C.; Schär, Marcel; & Poffet, Valérie. (2010). The association between daily stress and sexual activity. *Journal of Family Psychology, 24*(3), 271–279.

Boduroglu, Aysecan; Shah, Priti; & Nisbett, Richard E. (2009). Cultural differences in allocation of attention in visual information processing. *Journal of Cross-Cultural Psychology, 40*(3), 349–360. doi:10.1177/0022022108331005

Boecker, Henning; Sprenger, Till; Spilker, Mary E.; Henriksen, Gjermund; Koppenhoefer, Marcus; Wagner, Klaus J.; Valet, Michael; Berthele, Achim; & Tolle, Thomas R. (2008). The runner's high: Opioidergic mechanisms in the human brain. *Cerebral Cortex, 18,* 2523–2531.

Boer, Douglas P.; Starkey, Nicola J.; & Hodgetts, Andrea M. (2008). The California Psychological Inventory—434- and 260-item editions. In Gregory J. Boyle, Gerald Matthews, & Donald H. Saklofske (Eds.), *The SAGE Handbook of Personality Theory and Assessment, Vol. 2. Personality measurement and testing.* Thousand Oaks, CA: Sage.

Boeree, C. George (2006). Jean Piaget. *Personality Theories.* Retrieved from http://www.ship.edu/~cgboeree/piaget.html

Bogaert, Anthony F. (2004). Asexuality: Prevalence and associated factors in a national probability sample. *Journal of Sex Research, 41*(3), 279–287. doi:10.1080/00224490409552235

Bogaert, Anthony F. (2005). Age at puberty and father absence in a national probability sample. *Journal of Adolescence, 28,* 541–546.

Bogaert, Anthony F. (2006). Toward a conceptual understanding of asexuality. *Review of General Psychology, 10*(3), 241–250. doi:10.1037/1089-2680.10.3.241

Bogaert, Anthony F. (2007a). Extreme right-handedness, older brothers, and sexual orientation in men. *Neuropsychology, 21,* 141–148.

Bogaert, Anthony F. (2007b, June 5). Quoted in Michael Abrams, "The real story on gay genes." *Discover,* 424.

Bogaert, Anthony F. (2008). Menarche and father absence in a national probability sample. *Journal of Biosocial Science, 40,* 623–636. doi:10.1017/S0021932007002386

Bohart, Arthur C. (2007). The actualizing person. In Mick Cooper, Maureen O'Hara, Peter F. Schmid, & Gill Wyatt (Eds.), *The handbook of personcentred psychotherapy and counselling.* New York, NY: Palgrave Macmillan.

Bohart, Arthur C. (2013). Darth Vader, Carl Rogers, and self-organizing wisdom. In Arthur C. Bohart, Barbara S. Held, Eward Mendelowitz, & Kirk J. Schneider (Eds.),. *Humanity's dark side: Evil, destructive experience, and psychotherapy.* Washington, DC: American Psychological Association. doi:10.1037/13941-003

Bohlmeijer, Ernst; Roemer, Marte; & Cuijpers, Pim. (2007). The effects of reminiscence on psychological well-being in older adults: A meta-analysis. *Aging & Mental Health, 11*(3), 291–300.

Bohn, Annette, & Berntsen, Dorthe. (2008). Life story development in childhood: The development of life story abilities and the acquisition of cultural life scripts from late middle childhood to adolescence. *Developmental Psychology, 44*(4), 1135–1147.

Bohner, Gerd, & Dickel, Nina. (2011). Attitudes and attitude change. *Annual Review of Psychology, 62,* 391–417.

Bohus, Martin; Haaf, Brigitte; Stiglmayr, Christian; Pohl, Ulrike; Boehme, Renate; & Linehan, Marsha. (2000). Evaluation of inpatient dialectical-behavioral therapy for borderline personality disorder—A prospective study. *Behaviour Research and Therapy, 38*(9), 875–887.

Boison, Detlev; Singer, Philipp; Shen, Hae-Ying; Feldon, Joram; & Yee, Benjamin K. (2012). Adenosine hypothesis of schizophrenia–opportunities for pharmacotherapy. *Neuropharmacology, 62*(3), 1527–1543.

Boistel, Renaud; Aubin, Thierry; Cloetens, Peter; Peyrin, Françoise; Scott, Thierry; Herzog, Philippe; Gerlach, Justin; Polleth, Nicolas; & Aubry, Jean-François. (2013). How minute sooglossid frogs hear without a middle ear. *Proceedings of the National Academy of Sciences, 110,* 15360–15364. doi:10.1073/pnas.1302218110

Boisvert, Charles M., & Faust, David. (2003). Leading researchers' consensus on psychotherapy research findings: Implications for the teaching and conduct of psychotherapy. *Professional Psychology: Research and Practice, 34*(5), 508–513.

Boland, Julie E.; Chua, Hannah Faye; & Nisbett, Richard E. (2008). How we see it: Culturally different eye movement patterns over visual scenes. In Keith Rayner, Deli Shen, Xuejun Bai, & Guoli Yan (Eds.), *Cognitive and cultural influences on eye movements* (pp. 363–378). Tianjin, China: Tianjin People's Publishing House.

Bolger, Niall, & Amarel, David. (2007). Effects of social support visibility on adjustment to stress: Experimental evidence. *Journal of Personality and Social Psychology, 92*(3), 458–475.

Bolles, Robert C. (1985). The slaying of Goliath: What happened to reinforcement theory? In Timothy D. Johnston & Alexandra T. Pietrewicz (Eds.), *Issues in the ecological study of learning.* Hillsdale, NJ: Erlbaum.

Bolton, Paul; Bass, Judith; Neugebauer, Richard; Verdeli, Helen; Clougherty, Kathleen F.; Wickramaratne, Priya; & others. (2003). Group interpersonal psychotherapy for depression in rural Uganda: A randomized controlled trial. *Journal of the American Medical Association, 289,* 3117–3124.

Bonanno, George, & Burton, Charles. (2013). Regulatory flexibility: An individual differences perspective on coping and emotion regulation. *Perspectives on Psychological Science, 8*(6), 591–612. doi:10.1177/1745691613504116

Bonanno, George A.; Westphal, Maren; & Mancini, Anthony D. (2011). Resilience to loss and potential trauma. *Annual Review of Clinical Psychology, 7,* 511–535.

Bond, Charles F. (2008). A few can catch a liar, sometimes. *Applied Cognitive Psychology, 22,* 1298–1300.

Bond, Michael Harris. (1986). *The psychology of the Chinese people.* New York, NY: Oxford University Press.

Bond, Michael Harris. (2004). Culture and aggression—from context to coercion. *Personality and Social Psychology Review, 8,* 62–78.

Bond, Rod, & Smith, Peter B. (1996). Culture and conformity: A meta-analysis of studies using Asch's (1952b, 1956) line judgment task. *Psychological Bulletin, 119,* 111–137.

Bond, Rod. (2005). Group size and conformity. *Group Processes & Intergroup Relations, 8*(4), 331–354.

Bonnet, Michael H. (2005). Acute sleep deprivation. In Meir H. Kryger, Thomas Roth, & William C. Dement (Eds.), *Principles and practice of sleep medicine* (4th ed.). Philadelphia, PA: Elsevier Saunders.

Book, Angela S.; Starzyk, Katherine B.; & Quinsey, Vernon L. (2001). The relationship between testosterone and aggression: A meta-analysis. *Aggression and Violent Behavior, 6*(6), 579–599.

Bootzin, Richard R., & Epstein, Dana R. (2011). Understanding and treating insomnia. *Annual Review of Clinical Psychology, 7,* 435–458.

Borbély, Alexander A, & Achermann, Peter. (2005). Sleep homeostasis and models of sleep regulation. In Meir H. Kryger, Thomas Roth, & William C. Dement (Eds.), *Principles and practice of sleep medicine* (4th ed.). Philadelphia, PA: Elsevier Saunders.

Borden, William. (2009). *Contemporary psychodynamic theory and practice.* Chicago, IL: Lyceum Books.

Bornstein, Marc H. (2014). Human infancy . . . and the rest of the lifespan. *Annual Review of Psychology, 65,* 121–158.

Boron, Julie B.; Turiano, Nicholas A.; Willis, Sherry L.; & Schaie, K. Warner. (2007). Effects of cognitive training on change in accuracy in inductive reasoning ability. *Journals of Gerontology Series B: Psychological Sciences & Social Sciences, 62B*(3), P179–P186.

Borst, Jelmer P.; Taatgen, Niels A.; & van Rijn, Hedderik. (2010). The problem state: A cognitive bottleneck in multitasking. *Journal of Experimental Psychology: Learning, Memory, and Cognition, 26,* 363–382.

Bosch, Jos A., & Cano, Annmarie. (2013) Health Psychology special section on disparities in pain. *Health Psychology, 32,* 1115–1116. doi:10.1037/hea0000041

Boselie, Jantine; Vancleef, Linda; Smeets, Tom; & Peters, Madelon. (2014). Increasing optimism abolishes pain-induced impairments in executive task performance. *Pain, 155*(2), 334–340. doi:10.1016/j.pain.2013.10.014

Boss, Pauline; Beaulieu, Lorraine; Wieling, Elizabeth; Turner, William; & LaCruz, Shulaika. (2003). Healing loss, ambiguity, and trauma: A community-based intervention with families of union workers missing after the 9/11 attack in New York, NY City. *Journal of Marital and Family Therapy, 29,* 455–467.

Bostwick, J. Michael. (2012). Blurred boundaries: The therapeutics and politics of medical marijuana. *Mayo Clinic Proceedings, 87,* 172–186. doi:10.1016/j.mayocp.2011.10.003

Bouchard, Geneviève. (2014). How do parents react when their children leave home? An integrative review. *Journal of Adult Development, 21,* 69–79. doi:10.1007/s10804-013-9180-8

Bouchard, Thomas J., Jr. (2004). Genetic influence on human psychological traits. *Psychological Science, 13,* 148–151.

Bouchard, Thomas J.; Lykken, David T.; McGue, Matthew; Segal, Nancy L.; & Tellegen, Auke. (1990). Sources of human psychological differences: The Minnesota study of twins reared apart. *Science, 250*(4978), 223–228.

Bouton, Mark E. (2007). *Learning and behavior: A contemporary synthesis.* Sunderland, MA: Sinauer.

Bowen, Natasha K.; Wegmann, Kate M.; & Webber, Kristina C. (2013). Enhancing a brief writing intervention to combat stereotype threat among middle-school students. *Journal of Educational Psychology, 10,* 427–435. doi:10.1037/a0031177

Bowen, Sarah; Vieten, Cassandra; Witkiewitz, Katie; & Carroll, Haley. (2015). A mindfulness-based approach to addiction. In Kirk Warren Brown, J. David Creswell, & Richard M. Ryan. *Handbook of mindfulness: Theory, research, and practice.* New York, NY: Guilford.

Bowers, Kenneth S.; Regehr, Glenn; Balthazard, Claude; & Parker, Kevin. (1990). Intuition in the context of discovery. *Cognitive Psychology, 22,* 72–110.

Bowie, Christopher R.; Grossman, Michael; Gupta, Maya; Oyewumi, L. K.; & Harvey, Philip D. (2014). Cognitive remediation in schizophrenia: Efficacy and effectiveness in patients with early versus long-term course of illness. *Early Intervention in Psychiatry, 8,* 32–38. doi:10.1111/eip.12029

Bowker, Anne; Boekhoven, Belinda; Nolan, Amanda; Bauhaus, Stephanie; Glover, Paul; Powell, Tamara; & Taylor, Shannon. (2009). Naturalistic observations of spectator behavior at youth hockey games. *The Sport Psychologist, 23,* 301–316.

Bowlby, John. (1969). *Attachment and Loss: Vol. 1. Attachment.* New York, NY: Basic Books.

Bowlby, John. (1988). *A secure base.* New York, NY: Basic Books.

Boyke, Janina; Driemeyer, Joenna; Gaser, Christian; Büchel, Christian; & May, Arne. (2008). Training-induced brain structure changes in the elderly. *Journal of Neuroscience, 28,* 7031–7035.

Boyle, Gregory J. (2008). Critique of the five-factor model of personality. In Gregory J. Boyle, Gerald Matthews, & Donald H. Saklofske (Eds.), *The SAGE Handbook of Personality Theory and Assessment, Vol. 1. Personality theories and models.* Thousand Oaks, CA: Sage.

Boysen, Guy A., & VanBergen, Alexandra. (2014). Simulation of multiple personalities: A review of research comparing diagnosed and simulated dissociative identity disorder. *Clinical Psychology Review, 34,* 14–28.

Bozarth, Jerold D. (2007). Unconditional positive regard. In Mick Cooper, Maureen O'Hara, Peter F. Schmid, & Gill Wyatt (Eds.), *The handbook of person-centered psychotherapy and counselling.* New York, NY: Palgrave Macmillan.

Bozarth, Jerold D., & Wang, Chun-Chuan. (2008). The "unitary actualizing tendency" and congruence in client-centered therapy. In Brian E. Levitt (Ed.), *Reflections on human potential: Bridging the person-centered approach and positive psychology.* Ross-on-Wye, England: PCCS Books.

Bozarth, Jerold D.; Zimring, Fred M.; & Tausch, Reinhard. (2002). Client-centered therapy: The evolution of a revolution. In David J. Cain & Julius Seeman (Eds.), *Humanistic psychotherapies: Handbook of research and practice.* Washington, DC: American Psychological Association.

Bracha, H. Stefan; Wolkowitz, Owen M.; Lohr, James B.; Karson, Craig N.; & Bigelow, Llewellyn B. (1989). High prevalence of visual hallucinations in research subjects with chronic schizophrenia. *American Journal of Psychiatry, 146,* 526–528.

Bradbard, Marilyn R.; Martin, Carol L.; Endsley, Richard C.; & Halverson, Charles F. (1986). Influence of sex stereotypes on children's exploration and memory: A competence versus performance distinction. *Developmental Psychology, 22,* 481–486.

Bradshaw, Carolyn; Kahn, Arnold S.; & Saville, Bryan K. (2010). To hook up or date: Which gender benefits? *Sex Roles, 62,* 661–669.

Bradshaw, G. A.; Schore, Allan N.; Brown, Janine L.; Poole, Joyce H.; & Moss, Cynthia J. (2005). Elephant breakdown. Social trauma: Early disruption of attachment can affect the physiology, behaviour, and culture of animals and humans over generations. *Nature, 433,* 807.

Brådvik, Louise, & Berglund, Mats. (2010). Depressive episodes with suicide attempts in severe depression: Suicides and controls differ only in the later episodes of unipolar depression. *Archives of Suicide Research, 14*(4), 363–367.

Braffman, Wayne, & Kirsch, Irving. (1999). Imaginative suggestibility and hypnotizability: An empirical analysis. *Journal of Personality and Social Psychology, 77,* 578–587.

Brandon, Susan E. (2011). Impacts of psychological science on national security agencies post-9/11. *American Psychologist, 66,* 495–506. doi:10.1037/a0024818

Bransford, John D., & Stein, Barry S. (1993). *The IDEAL problem solver: A guide for improving thinking, learning, and creativity* (2nd ed.). New York, NY: Freeman.

Braskie, Meredith N.; Jahanshad, Neda; Stein, Jason L.; Barysheva, Marina; McMahon, Katie L.; de Zubicaray, Greig I.; & others. (2011). Common Alzheimer's disease risk variant within the CLU gene affects white matter microstructure in young adults. *Journal of Neuroscience, 31,* 6764. doi:10.1523/jneurosci5794-10.2011

Braun, Allen R.; Balkin, Thomas J.; Wesensten, Nancy J.; Gwadry, Fuad; Carson, Richard E.; Varga, Mary; & others. (1998, January 2). Dissociated patterns of activity in visual cortices and their projections during human rapid eye movement during sleep. *Science, 279,* 91–95.

Braun, Stephen. (2001, Spring). Ecstasy on trial: Seeking insight by prescription. *Cerebrum, 3,* 10–21.

Braun-Courville, Debra K., & Rojas, Mary. (2009). Exposure to sexually explicit web sites and adolescent sexual attitudes and behaviors. *Journal of Adolescent Health, 45*(2), 156–162.

Braveman, Paula A.; Cubbin, Catherine; Egerter, Susan; Williams, David R.; & Pamuk, Elsie. (2010). Socioeconomic disparities in health in the United States: What the patterns tell us. *American Journal of Public Health, 100*(S1), S186–S196.

Bray, Emily E.; MacLean, Evan L; & Hare, Brian A. (2014). Context specificity of inhibitory control in dogs. *Animal Cognition, 17,* 15–31. doi:10.1007/s10071-013-0633-z

Bray, Signe, & O'Doherty, John. (2007). Neural coding of reward-prediction error signals during classical conditioning with attractive faces. *Journal of Neurophysiology, 97*(4), 3036–3045.

Brázdil, Milan; Marecek, Radek; Urbánek, Tomáš; Kašpárek, Tomáš; Mikl, Michal; Rektor, Ivan; Zeman, Adam. (2012). Unveiling the mystery of déjà vu: The structural anatomy of déjà vu. *Cortex, 48,* 1240–1243. doi:10.1016/j.cortex.2012.03.004

Bregman, Elsie O. (1934). An attempt to modify the emotional attitude of infants by the conditioned response technique. *Journal of Genetic Psychology, 45,* 169–198.

Breinbauer, Hayo A.; Anabalón, Jose L.; Gutierrez, Daniela; Cárcamo, Rodrigo; Olivares, Carla; & Caro, Jorge. (2012). Output capabilities of personal music players and assessment of preferred listening levels of test subjects: Outlining recommendations for preventing music-induced hearing loss. *The Laryngoscope, 122,* 2549–2556. doi:10.1002/lary.23596

Breland, Keller, & Breland, Marian. (1961). The misbehavior of organisms. *American Psychologist, 16,* 681–684.

Brennen, Tim; Vikan, Anne; & Dybdahl, Ragnhild. (2007). Are tip-of-the-tongue states universal? Evidence from the speakers of an unwritten language. *Memory, 15*(2), 167–176.

Bresee, Catherine; Gotto, Jennifer; & Rapaport, Mark H. (2009). Treatment of depression. In Alan F. Schatzberg & Charles B. Nemeroff (Eds.), *The American Psychiatric Publishing textbook of psychopharmacology* (4th ed., pp. 1081–1111). Washington, DC: American Psychiatric Publishing.

Bretherton, Inge, & Main, Mary. (2000). Mary Dinsmore Salter Ainsworth (1913–1999). *American Psychologist, 55,* 1148–1149.

Breuer, Josef, & Freud, Sigmund. (1895/1957). *Studies on hysteria* (James Strachey, Ed. & Trans., in collaboration with Anna Freud). New York, NY: Basic Books.

Brewer, Marilyn B. (1994). The social psychology of prejudice: Getting it all together. In Mark P. Zanna & James M. Olson (Eds.), *The psychology of prejudice: The Ontario Symposium* (Vol. 7). Hillsdale, NJ: Erlbaum.

Brewer, Marilynn B., & Chen, Ya-Ru. (2007). Where (who) are collectives in collectivism? Toward conceptual clarification of individualism and collectivism. *Psychological Review, 114*(1), 133–151.

Brewer, Neil, & Wells, Gary L. (2011). Eyewitness identification. *Current Directions in Psychological Science* 20(24). doi:10.1177/0963721410389169

Brewer, William F., & Treyens, James C. (1981). Role of schemata in memory for places. *Cognitive Psychology, 13,* 207–230.

Britz, Juliane; Hernàndez, Laura Díaz; Ro, Tony; & Michel, Christoph M. (2014). EEG-microstate dependent emergence of perceptual awareness. *Frontiers in Behavioral Neuroscience 8,* 2–10. doi:10.3389/fnbeh.2014.00163

Brizendine, Louann. (2006). *The female brain.* New York, NY: Morgan Road Books.

Brizendine, Louann. (2010). *The male brain.* New York, NY: Three Rivers Press/Crown Publishing.

Brock, Timothy C. (2008). Negligible scholarly impact of 38-witnesses parable. *American Psychologist, 63,* 561–562.

Brody, Arthur L.; Saxena, Sajaya; Stoessel, Paula; Gillies, Laurie; Fairbanks, Lynn A.; Alborzian, Shervin; & others. (2001, July). Regional brain metabolic changes in patients with major depression treated with either paroxetine or interpersonal therapy. *Archives of General Psychiatry, 58,* 631–640.

Brody, Howard, & Miller, Franklin G. (2011). Lessons from recent research about the placebo effect—From art to science. *Journal of the American Medical Association, 306*(23), 2612–2613. doi:10.1001/jama.2011.1850

Brondolo, Elizabeth; ver Halen, Nisha Brady; Libby, Daniel; & Pencille, Melissa. (2011). Racism as a psychosocial stressor. In Richard J. Contrada & Andrew Baum (Eds.), *The handbook of stress science: Biology, psychology, and health.* New York, NY: Springer.

Bronson, Po, & Merryman, Ashley. (2009). *NurtureShock: New thinking about children.* New York, NY: Grand Central.

Bronstein, Phyllis. (2006). The family environment: Where gender role socialization begins. In Judith Worell & Carol D. Goodheart (Eds.), *Handbook of girls' and women's psychological health: Gender and well-being across the lifespan* (pp. 262–271). New York, NY: Oxford University Press.

Brooks-Gunn, Jeanne. (1988). Antecedents and consequences of variations of girls' maturational timing. In Melvin D. Levine & Elizabeth R. McAnarney (Eds.), *Early adolescent transitions.* Lexington, MA: Lexington Books.

Brooks-Gunn, Jeanne, & Reiter, Edward O. (1990). The role of pubertal processes. In S. Shirley Feldman & Glen R. Elliott (Eds.), *At the threshold: The developing adolescent.* Cambridge, MA: Harvard University Press.

Broomhall, Elizabeth. (2012). Hayat Sindi interview: A passion for science. Retrieved on May 5, 2014, from http://www.arabianbusiness.com/hayat-sindi-interview—passion-for-science-453690.html

Brown, Alan S. (2003). A review of the déjà vu experience. *Psychological Bulletin, 129,* 394–413.

Brown, Alan S. (2004). *The déjà vu experience: Essays in cognitive psychology.* New York, NY: Psychology Press.

Brown, Alan S. (2005, January 31). Looking at déjà vu for the first time. *The Scientist, 19*(2), 20–21.

Brown, Alan S., & Marsh, Elizabeth J. (2010). Digging into déjà vu: Recent research on possible mechanisms. In B. H. Ross (Ed.), *The psychology of learning and motivation: Advances in research and theory* (Vol. 53) (pp. 33–62). San Diego, CA: Elsevier Academic Press.

Brown, Alan S.; Begg, Melissa D.; Gravenstein, Stefan; Schaefer, Catherine A.; Wyatt, Richard J.; Bresnahan, Michaeline; Babulas, Vicki P.; & Susser, Ezra S. (2004). Serological evidence of prenatal influenza in the etiology of schizophrenia. *Archives of General Psychiatry, 61,* 774–780.

Brown, Bernard. (1999, April). Optimizing expression of the common human genome for child development. *Current Directions in Psychological Science, 8,* 37–41.

Brown, Gary E.; Davis, Eric; & Johnson, Amanda. (1999). Forced exercise blocks learned helplessness in the cockroach (*Periplaneta americana*). *Psychological Reports, 84,* 155–156.

Brown, Geoffrey L.; Mangelsdorf, Sarah C.; & Neff, Cynthia. (2012). Father involvement, paternal sensitivity, and father–child attachment security in the first 3 years. *Journal of Family Psychology, 26,* 421–430. doi:10.1037/a0027836

Brown, Jennifer. (2015). Elsa's story. Retrieved from http://extras.denverpost.com/transgender/elsa.html

Brown, Kirk Warren; Creswell, David J.; & Ryan, Richard M. (2015). Introduction: The evolution of mindfulness science. In Kirk Warren Brown, J. David Creswell, & Richard M. Ryan (Eds.) *Handbook of mindfulness: Theory, research, and practice.* New York, NY: Guilford.

Brown, Lisa M.; Bongar, Bruce; & Cleary, Karin M. (2004). A profile of psychologists' views of critical risk factors for completed suicide in older adults. *Professional Psychology: Research & Practice, 35,* 90–96.

Brown, Roger, & Kulik, James. (1982). Flashbulb memories. In Ulric Neisser (Ed.), *Memory observed: Remembering in natural contexts.* San Francisco, CA: Freeman.

Brown, Ronald T.; Antonuccio, David O.; DuPaul, George J.; Fristad, Mary A.; King, Cheryl A.; Leslie, Laurel K.; McCormick, Gabriele S.; Pelham, William E., Jr.; Piacentini, John C.; & Vitiello, Benedetto. (2008). *Childhood mental health disorders: Evidence base and contextual factors for psychosocial, psychopharmacological, and combined interventions.* Washington, DC: American Psychological Association.

Bruchey, Aleksandra K.; Jones, Carolyn E.; & Monfils, Marie- H. (2010). Fear conditioning by-proxy: Social transmission of fear during memory retrieval. *Behavioural Brain Research, 214*(1), 80–84.

Brummert Lennings, Heidi I., & Warburton, Wayne A. (2011). The effect of auditory versus visual violent media exposure on aggressive behaviour: The role of song lyrics, video clips and musical tone. *Journal of Experimental Social Psychology, 47*(4), 794–799. doi:10.1016/j.jesp.2011.02.006

Brummett, Beverly H.; Boyle, Stephen H.; Kuhn, Cynthia M.; Siegler, Ilene C.; & Williams, Redford B. (2009). Positive affect is associated with cardiovascular reactivity, norepinephrine level, and morning rise in salivary cortisol. *Psychophysiology, 46*(4), 862–869.

Brummett, Beverly H.; Helms, Michael J.; Dahlstrom, W. Grant; & Siegler, Ilene C. (2006). Prediction of all-cause mortality by the Minnesota Multiphasic Personality Inventory Optimism-Pessimism Scale scores: Study of a college sample during a 40-year follow-up period. *Mayo Clinic Proceedings, 81*(12), 1541–1544.

Brunoni, Andre R.; Nitsche, Michael A.; Bolognini, N.; Bikson, M.; Wagner, T.; Merabet, L.; Edwards, Dylan J.; & others. (2012). Clinical research with transcranial direct current stimulation (tDCS): Challenges and future directions. *Brain Stimulation: Basic, Translational, and Clinical Research in Neuromodulation, 5*(3), 175–195. doi:10.1016/j.brs.2011.03.002

Bryant, Gregory A., & Barrett, H. Clark. (2007). Recognizing intentions in infant-directed speech: Evidence for universals. *Psychological Science, 18,* 746–751.

Bryant, Gregory A.; Lienard, Pierre; & Clark Barrett, H. (2012). Recognizing infant-directed speech across distant cultures: Evidence from Africa. *Journal of Evolutionary Psychology, 10,* 47–59. doi:10.1556/jep.10.2012.2.1

Bryck, Richard L., & Fisher, Philip A. (2012). Training the brain: Practical applications of neural plasticity from the intersection of cognitive neuroscience, developmental psychology, and prevention science. *American Psychologist, 67,* 87–100.

Buccelletti, Francesco; Ojetti, Veronica; Carroccia, Annarita; Marsiliani, Davide; Mangiola, F.; Calabro, G.; Iacomini, P.; Zuccala, Giuseppe; & Franceschi, Francesco. (2013). Recurrent use of the emergency department in patients with anxiety disorder. *European Review for Medical and Pharmacological Sciences, 17,* 100–106.

Bucci, Sandra; Birchwood, Max; Twist, Laura; Tarrier, Nicholas; Emsley, Richard; & Haddock, Gillian. (2013). Predicting compliance with command hallucinations: Anger, impulsivity and appraisals of voices' power and intent. *Schizophrenia Research, 147,* 163–168.

Buchanan, Anne V.; Sholtis, S.; Richtsmeier, J.; & Weiss, K. M. (2009). What are genes "for" or where are traits "from"? What is the question? *Bioessays, 31*(2), 198–208. doi:10.1002/bies.200800133

Buckley, Kerry W. (1982). The selling of a psychologist: John Broadus Watson and the application of behavioral techniques to advertising. *Journal of the History of the Behavioral Sciences, 18*, 207–221.

Buckley, Kerry W. (1989). *Mechanical man: John Broadus Watson and the beginnings of behaviorism*. New York, NY: Guilford.

Bucur, Barbara; Madden, David J.; Spaniol, Julia; Provenzale, James M.; Cabeza, Roberto; White, Leonard E.; & Huettel, Scott A. (2008). Age-related slowing of memory retrieval: Contributions of perceptual speed and cerebral white matter integrity. *Neurobiology of Aging, 29*(7), 1070–1079.

Budd, Rick, & Hughes, Ian. (2009). The dodo bird verdict—Controversial, inevitable and important: A commentary on 30 years of meta-analyses. *Clinical Psychology & Psychotherapy, 16*(6), 510–522.

Budney, Alan J.; Roffman, Roger; Stephens, Robert S.; & Walker, Denise. (2007, December). Marijuana dependence and its treatment. *Addiction Science and Clinical Practice, 4*, 4–16.

Burger, Jerry M. (2009). Replicating Milgram: Would people still obey today? *American Psychologist, 64*(1), 1–11.

Burger, Jerry M. (2011). Is that all there is? Reaction to the that's-not-all procedure. In R. M. Arkin (Ed.), *Most underappreciated: 50 prominent social psychologists describe their most unloved work*. New York, NY: Oxford University Press.

Burger, Jerry M.; Sanchez, Jackeline; Imberi, Jenny E.; & Grande, Lucia R. (2009). The norm of reciprocity as an internalized social norm: Returning favors even when no one finds out. *Social Influence, 4*(1), 11–17.

Buri, John R.; Louiselle, Peggy A.; Misukanis, Thomas M.; & Mueller, Rebecca A. (1988). Effects of parental authoritarianism and authoritativeness on self-esteem. *Personality and Social Psychology Bulletin, 14*, 271–282.

Burlingame, Gary M.; & McClendon, Debra T. (2008). Group therapy. In Jay L. Lebow (Ed.), *Twenty-first century psychotherapies: Contemporary approaches to theory and practice* (pp. 347–388). Hoboken, NJ: Wiley.

Burlingame, Gary M.; MacKenzie, K. Roy; & Strauss, Bernhard. (2004). Small group treatment: Evidence for effectiveness and mechanisms of change. In Michael J. Lambert (Ed.), *Bergin and Garfield's handbook of psychotherapy and behavior change* (5th ed.). New York, NY: Wiley.

Burn, Shawn Meghan. (2009). A situational model of sexual assault prevention through bystander intervention. *Sex Roles, 60*(11–12), 779–792.

Bushman, Brad J., & Anderson, Craig A. (2007). Measuring the effect of violent media on aggression. *American Psychologist, 62*, 253–254.

Bushman, Brad J.; Gollwitzer, Mario; & Cruz, Carlos. (2014). There is broad consensus: Media researchers agree that violent media increase aggression in children, and pediatricians and parents concur. *Psychology of Popular Media Culture*, October 6, 2014, no pagination specified. doi:10.1037/ppm0000046

Bushman, Brad J.; Huesmann, L. Rowell; & Whitaker, Jodi L. (2009). Violent media effects. In R. L. Nabi & M. B. Oliver (Eds.), *Media processes and effects* (pp. 361–376). Thousand Oaks, CA: Sage.

Bushman, Brad J.; Wang, Morgan C.; & Anderson, Craig A. (2005). Is the curve relating temperature to aggression linear or curvilinear? Assaults and temperature in Minneapolis reexamined. *Journal of Personality and Social Psychology, 89*(1), 62–66. doi:10.1037/0022-3514.89.1.62

Bushnell, I. W. R. (2001). Mother's face recognition in newborn infants: Learning and memory. *Infant and Child Development, 10*, 67–74.

Buss, Arnold H. (1989). Personality as traits. *American Psychologist, 44*, 1378–1388.

Buss, Arnold H. (2001). *Psychological dimensions of the self*. Thousand Oaks, CA: Sage.

Buss, David M. (1991). Evolutionary personality psychology. *Annual Review of Psychology, 42*, 459–491.

Buss, David M. (1994). *The evolution of desire: Strategies of human mating*. New York, NY: Basic Books.

Buss, David M. (1995a). Evolutionary psychology: A new paradigm for psychological science. *Psychological Inquiry, 6*, 1–31.

Buss, David M. (1995b). Psychological sex differences: Origins through sexual selection. *American Psychologist, 50*, 164–168.

Buss, David M. (1996). Sexual conflict: Evolutionary insights into feminism and into feminism and the "Battle of the Sexes." In David M. Buss & Neil M. Malamuth (Eds.), *Sex, power, conflict: Evolutionary and feminist perspectives*. New York, NY: Oxford University Press.

Buss, David M. (2007a). The evolution of human mating. *Acta Psychologica Sinica, 39*(3) [Special issue: Evolutionary psychology], 502–512.

Buss, David M. (2007b). The evolution of human mating strategies: Consequences for conflict and cooperation. In Steven W. Gangestad & Jeffry A Simpson (Eds.), *The evolution of mind: Fundamental questions and controversies*. New York, NY: Guilford.

Buss, David M. (2008). *Evolutionary psychology: The new science of the mind* (3rd ed.). Boston, MA: Pearson.

Buss, David M. (2009). The great struggles of life: Darwin and the emergence of evolutionary psychology. *American Psychologist, 64*, 140–148.

Buss, David M. (2011). Internet mating strategies. In J. Brockman (Ed.), *How is the Internet changing the way you think?* New York, NY: HarperCollins.

Buss, David M. (2011a). *Evolutionary psychology: The new science of the mind* (4th ed.). Boston, MA: Pearson.

Buss, David M., & Duntley, Joshua D. (2006). The evolution of aggression. In Mark Schaller, Jeffry. A. Simpson, & Douglas. T. Kenrick (Eds.), *Evolution and social psychology* (pp. 263–286). New York, NY: Psychology Press.

Buss, David M., & Schmitt, David P. (2011). Evolutionary psychology and feminism. *Sex Roles, 64*(9–10), 768–787.

Bussey, Kay, & Bandura, Albert. (2004). Social cognitive theory of gender development and functioning. In Alice H. Eagly, Anne E. Beall, & Robert J. Sternberg (Eds.), *The psychology of gender* (2nd ed.). New York, NY: Guilford.

Butcher, James N. (2010). Personality assessment from the nineteenth to the early twenty-first century: Past achievements and contemporary challenges. *Annual Review of Clinical Psychology, 6*, 1–20.

Butler, Adam B.; Dodge, Kama D.; & Faurote, Eric J. (2010). College student employment and drinking: A daily study of work stressors, alcohol expectancies, and alcohol consumption. *Journal of Occupational Health Psychology, 15*(3), 291–303.

Butler, Andrew C.; Chapman, Jason E.; Forman, Evan M.; & Beck, Aaron T. (2006, January). The empirical status of cognitive-behavioral therapy: A review of meta-analyses. *Clinical Psychology Review, 26*(1), 17–31.

Butler, Robert A.; & Harlow, Harry F. (1954). Persistence of visual exploration in monkeys. *Journal of Comparative and Physiological Psychology, 47*, 258–263.

Button, Katherine S.; Ioannidis, John P. A.; Mokrysz, Claire; Nosek, Brian A.; Flint, Jonathan; Robinson Emma S. J.; & Munafò, Marcus R. (2013). Power failure: Why small sample size undermines the reliability of neuroscience. *Nature Reviews Neuroscience 14*, 365–376. doi:10.1038/nrn3475

Bystron, Irina; Blakemore, Colin; & Rakic, Pasko. (2008). Development of the human cerebral cortex: Boulder Committee revisited. *National Review Neuroscience, 9*(2), 110–122. doi:10.1038/nrn2252

Cacioppo, John T., & Gardner, Wendi L. (1999). Emotion. *Annual Review of Psychology, 50*, 191–214.

Cacioppo, John; Cacioppo, Stephanie; Capitanio, John; & Cole, Steven. (2015a). The neuroendocrinology of social isolation. *Annual Review of Psychology, 66*, 733–767. doi:10.1146/annurev-psych-010814-015240

Cacioppo, John; Cacioppo, Stephanie; Cole, Steven; Capitanio, John; Goossens, Luc; & Boomsma, Dorret. (2015b). Loneliness across phylogeny and a call for comparative studies and animal models. *Perspectives on Psychological Science, 10*, 202–212. doi:10.1177/1745691614564876

Cafri, Guy; Yamamiya, Yuko; Brannick, Michael; & Thompson, J. Kevin. (2005). The influence of sociocultural factors on body image: A meta-analysis. *Clinical Psychology: Science and Practice, 12*, 421–433.

Cain, Christopher K., & LeDoux, Joseph E. (2008). Brain mechanisms of Pavlovian and instrumental aversive conditioning. In Robert J. Blanchard, D. Caroline Blanchard, Guy Griebel, & David Nutt (Eds.), *Handbook of Behavioral Neuroscience: Vol. 17. Handbook of anxiety and fear* (pp. 103–124). Amsterdam, The Netherlands: Elsevier.

Cain, David J. (2002). Defining characteristics, history, and evolution of humanistic psychotherapies. In David J. Cain & Julius Seeman (Eds.), *Humanistic psychotherapies: Handbook of research and practice.* Washington, DC: American Psychological Association

Cain, David J. (2003). Advancing humanistic psychology and psychotherapy: Some challenges and proposed solutions. *Journal of Humanistic Psychology, 43,* 10–41.

Cain, David J., & Seeman, Julius (Eds.). (2002). *Humanistic psychotherapies: Handbook of research and practice.* Washington, DC: American Psychological Association.

Calanchini, Jimmy; Gonsalkorale, Karen; Sherman, Jeffrey W.; & Klauer, Karl C. (2013). Counter-prejudicial training reduces activation of biased associations and enhances response monitoring. *European Journal of Social Psychology, 43,* 321–325.

Calero-García, M. D.; Navarro-González, E.; & Muñoz-Manzano, L. (2007). Influence of level of activity on cognitive performance and cognitive plasticity in elderly persons. *Archives of Gerontology and Geriatrics, 45,* 307–318.

Camp, Mary E.; Webster, Cecil R.; Coverdale, Thomas R.; Coverdale, John H.; & Nairn, Ray. (2010). The Joker: A dark night for depictions of mental illness. *Academic Psychiatry, 34,* 145–149.

Campbell, Jennifer D., & Fairey, Patricia J. (1989). Informational and normative routes to conformity: The effect of faction size as a function of norm extremity and attention to the stimulus. *Journal of Personality and Social Psychology, 57,* 457–458.

Campbell, John B., & Hawley, Charles W. (1982). Study habits and Eysenck's theory of extraversion-introversion. *Journal of Research in Personality, 16,* 139–146.

Campbell, MacGregor. (2011). Game on: When work becomes play. *New Scientist,* issue 2794.

Campbell, Matthew W., & de Waal, Frans B. M. (2011). Ingroup-outgroup bias in contagious yawning by chimpanzees supports link to empathy. *PLOS ONE, 6*(4), 10.1371/journal.pone.0018283

Campbell, Matthew W.; Carter, J. Devyn; Proctor, Darby; Eisenberg, Michelle L.; & de Waal, Frans B. M. (2009, September 9). Computer animations stimulate contagious yawning in chimpanzees. *Proceedings of the Royal Society, Biological Sciences.* Advanced online publication. 10.1098/rspb.2009.1087

Campbell, Scott S. (1997). The basics of biological rhythms. In Mark R. Pressman & William C. Orr (Eds.), *Understanding sleep: The evaluation and treatment of sleep disorders.* Washington, DC: American Psychological Association.

Campos, Belinda; Graesch, Anthony P.; Repetti, Rena; Bradbury, Thomas; & Ochs, Elinor. (2009). Opportunity for interaction? A naturalistic observation study of dual-earner families after work and school. *Journal of Family Psychology, 23*(6), 798–807.

Canadian Psychological Association. (2006). Providing psychological services via electronic media: Draft ethical guidelines for psychologists providing psychological services via electronic media. Retrieved from://www.cpa.ca /aboutcpa/committees/ethics/psychserviceselectronically

Canli, Turhan; Zhao, Zuo; Desmond, John E.; Kang, Eunjoo; Gross, James; & Gabrieli, John D. E. (2001). An fMRI study of personality influences on brain reactivity to emotional stimuli. *Behavioral Neuroscience, 115,* 33–42.

Canli, Turhan. (2004). Functional brain-mapping of extraversion and neuroticism: Learning from individual differences in emotion processing. *Journal of Personality, 72,* 1105–1132.

Canli, Turhan. (2006) *Biology of personality and individual differences.* New York, NY: Guilford.

Cannon, Brooke J., & Kramer, Lorraine Masinos. (2012). Delusion content across the 20th century in an American psychiatric hospital. *International Journal of Social Psychiatry, 58*(3), 323–327.

Cannon, Walter B. (1927). The James-Lange theory of emotion: A critical examination and an alternative theory. *American Journal of Psychology, 39,* 106–124.

Cannon, Walter B. (1932). *The wisdom of the body.* New York, NY: Norton.

Cannon, Walter B.; Lewis, J.T.; & Britton, S.W. (1927). The dispensability of the sympathetic division of the autonomic nervous system. *Boston Medical and Surgical Journal, 197,* 514.

Cant, Jonathan S., & Goodale, Melvyn A. (2011). Scratching beneath the surface: New insights into the functional properties of the lateral occipital area and parahippocampal place area. *Journal of Neuroscience, 31*(22), 8248–8258. doi:10.1523/jneurosci.6113-10.2011

Canter, Peter H., & Ernst, Edzard. (2007). *Ginkgo biloba* is not a smart drug: An updated systematic review of randomised clinical trials testing the nootropic effects of *G. biloba* extracts in healthy people. *Human Psychopharmacology: Clinical and Experimental, 22,* 265–278.

Cardena, Etzel, & Gleaves, David H. (2007). Dissociative disorders. In Michel Hersen, Samuel M. Turner, & Deborah C. Beidel (Eds.), *Adult psychopathology and diagnosis* (5th ed., pp. 473–503). Hoboken, NJ: Wiley.

Carey, Benedict. (2007). Brainy parrot dies, emotive to the end. *New York Times.* Retrieved on August 20, 2008, from http://www.nytimes.com/2007 /09/11/science/11parrot.html

Carey, Benedict. (2011, October 22). Memoir about schizophrenia spurs others to come forward. New York Times. Retrieved from http://www.nytimes .com/2011/10/23/health/23livesside.html

Carhart-Harris, Robin; Kaelen, Mendel; & Nutt, David. (2014). How do hallucinogens work on the brain? *The Psychologist, 27,* 662–665.

Carlo, Gustavo; Knight, George P.; Roesch, Scott C.; Opal, Deanna; & Davis, Alexandra. (2014). Personality across cultures: A critical analysis of Big Five research and current directions. In Frederick T. L. Leong, Lillia Comas-Díaz, Gordon C. Nagayama Hall, Vonnie C. McLoyd, & Joseph E. Trimble (Eds.), *APA Handbook of Multicultural Psychology, Vol. 1: Theory and research.* Washington, DC: American Psychological Association. doi:10.1037/14189-015

Carlson, Gabrielle A., & Meyer, Stephanie E. (2006). Phenomenology and diagnosis of bipolar disorder in children, adolescents, and adults: Complexities and developmental issues. *Development and Psychopathology, 18*(4) [Special issue: Developmental approaches to bipolar disorder], 939–969.

Carlson, Jon; Watts, Richard; & Maniacci, Michael. (2008). *Adlerian therapy: Theory and practice.* Washington, DC: American Psychological Association.

Carpenter, Shana K. (2012). Testing enhances the transfer of learning. *Current Directions in Psychological Science, 21,* 279–283.

Carpenter, Shana K.; Cepeda, Nicholas J.; Rohrer, Doug; Kang, Sean H. K; & Pashler, Harold. (2012). Using spacing to enhance diverse forms of learning: Review of recent research and implications for instruction. *Educational Psychology Review 24:* 369–378. doi:10.1007/s10648-012-9205-z

Carpintero, Helio. (2004). Watson's behaviorism: A comparison of the two editions (1925 and 1930). *History of Psychology, 7*(2), 183–202.

Carr, Katelyn A., & Epstein Leonard. (2011). Relationship between food habituation and reinforcing efficacy of food. *Learning and Motivation, 42,* 165–172.

Carretti, Barbara; Borella, Erika; & De Beni, Rossana. (2007). Does strategic memory training improve the working memory performance of younger and older adults? *Experimental Psychology, 54,* 311–320.

Carroll, Joseph; Baraas, Rigmor C.; Wagner-Schuman, Melissa; Rha, Jungtae; Siebe, Cory A.; Sloan, Christina; & others. (2009). Cone photoreceptor mosaic disruption associated with Cys203Arg mutation in the M-cone opsin. *Proceedings of the National Academy of Sciences, 106,* 20948–20953.

Carskadon, Mary A.; & Dement, William C. (2005). Normal human sleep: An overview. In Meir H. Kryger, Thomas Roth, & William C. Dement (Eds.), *Principles and practice of sleep medicine* (4th ed.). Philadelphia, PA: Elsevier Saunders.

Carskadon, Mary A., & Rechtschaffen, Allan. (2005). Monitoring and staging human sleep. In Meir H. Kryger, Thomas Roth, & William C. Dement (Eds.), *Principles and practice of sleep medicine* (4th ed.). Philadelphia, PA: Elsevier Saunders.

Carmody, James. (2015). Reconceptualizing mindfulness: The psychological principles of attending in mindfulness practice and their role in well-being. In Kirk Warren Brown, J. David Creswell, & Richard M. Ryan (Eds.), *Handbook of mindfulness: Theory, research, and practice.* New York, NY: Guilford.

Carnahan, Thomas, & McFarland, Sam. (2007). Revisiting the Stanford prison experiment: Could participant self-selection have led to the cruelty? *Personality and Social Psychology Bulletin, 33*, 603–614. doi:10.1177/0146167206292689

Carter, C. Sue. (2014). Oxytocin pathways and the evolution of human behavior. *Annual Review of Psychology, 65*, 17–39. doi:10.1146/annurev-psych-010213-115110

Carter, Christopher J. (2008). Schizophrenia susceptibility genes directly implicated in the life cycles of pathogens: Cytomegalovirus, influenza, herpes simplex, rubella, and *toxoplasma gondii*. *Schizophrenia Bulletin*. Advanced online publication.doi:10.1093/schbul/sbn054

Cartwright, Rosalind D. (2004). Sleepwalking violence: A sleep disorder, a legal dilemma, and a psychological challenge. *American Journal of Psychiatry, 161*, 1149–1158.

Cartwright, Rosalind D. (2007). Response to M. Pressman: Factors that predispose, prime, and precipitate NREM parasomnias in adults: Clinical and forensic implications. *Sleep Medicine Review, 11*, 5–30.

Cartwright, Rosalind D. (2010). *The twenty-four hour mind: The role of sleep and dreaming in our emotional lives*. New York, NY: Oxford University Press.

Carver, Charles S. (2011). Coping. In Richard J. Contrada & Andrew Baum (Eds.), *The handbook of stress science: Biology, psychology, and health*. New York, NY: Springer.

Casey, B. J. (2013). The teenage brain: An overview. *Current Directions in Psychological Science, 22*, 80–81. doi:10.1177/0963721413486971

Casey, B. J. (2015). Beyond simple models of self-control to circuit-based accounts of adolescent behavior. *Annual Review of Psychology, 66*, 295–319. doi:10.1146/annurev-psych-010814-015156

Casey, B. J., & Caudle, Kristina. (2013). The teenage brain: Self control. *Current Directions in Psychological Science, 22*, 82–87. doi:10.1177/0963721413480170

Caspi, Avshalom; Houtes, Renate M.; Belsky, Daniel W.; Goldman-Mellor, Sidra J.; Harrington, HonaLee; Israel, Salomon; . . . Moffitt, Terrie E. (2014). The p factor: One general psychopathology factor in the structure of psychiatric disorders? *Clinical Psychological Science, 2*, 119–137. doi:10.1177/2167702613497473

Caspi, Avshalom; Roberts, Brent W.; & Shiner, Rebecca L. (2005). Personality development: Stability and change. *Annual Review of Psychology, 56*, 453–484.

Caton, Hiram. (2007). Getting our history right: Six errors about Darwin and his influence. *Evolutionary Psychology, 5*, 52–69.

Cattaneo, Luigi, & Rizzolatti, Giacomo. (2009). The mirror neuron system. *Archives of Neurology, 66*(5), 557–560. doi:10.1001/archneurol.2009.41

Cattaneo, Zaira, & Vecchi, Tomaso. (2008). Supramodality effects in visual and haptic spatial processes. *Journal of Experimental Psychology: Learning, Memory, and Cognition, 34*, 631–642.

Cattell, Heather E. P., & Mead, Alan D. (2008). The Sixteen Personality Factor Questionnaire (16PF). In Gregory J. Boyle, Gerald Matthews, & Donald H. Saklofske (Eds.), *The SAGE Handbook of Personality Theory and Assessment, Vol 2: Personality measurement and testing*. Thousand Oaks, CA: Sage.

Cattell, James McKeen. (1890). Mental tests and measurements. *Mind, 15*, 373–381.

Cattell, Raymond B. (1973, July). Personality pinned down. *Psychology Today*, 40–46.

Cattell, Raymond B. (1994). A cross-validation of primary personality structure in the 16 P.F. by two parcelled factor analysis. *Multivariate Experimental Clinical Research, 10*(3), 181–191.

Cattell, Raymond B.; Cattell, A. Karen S.; & Cattell, Heather E. P. (1993). *16 PF questionnaire* (5th ed.). Champaign, IL: Institute for Personality and Ability Testing.

Ceci, Stephen J., & Williams, Wendy M. (2009). Should scientists study race and IQ? Yes: The scientific truth must be pursued. *Nature, 457*, 788–789.

Celesia, Gastone G. (2010). Visual perception and awareness: A modular system. *Journal of Psychophysiology, 24*(2), 62–67.

Centers for Disease Control and Prevention. (2012). *HIV among youth in the US*. Retrieved from http://www.cdc.gov/vitalsigns/hivamongyouth

Centers for Disease Control. (2012). Suicide: Facts at a Glance. Retrieved from http://www.cdc.gov/violenceprevention/pdf/suicide_datasheet-a.pdf

Centers for Disease Control. (2013). Diagnoses of HIV infection in the United States and dependent areas, 2011. *HIV Surveillance Report, 23*, 1–84.

Centers for Disease Control and Prevention (2015a, January 6). Alcohol poisoning kills 6 people in US each day. Retrieved on May 15, 2015, from http://www.cdc.gov/media/releases/2015/p0106-alcohol-poisoning.html

Centers for Disease Control and Prevention (2015b). National Vital Statistics System mortality data. Retrieved from http://www.cdc.gov/nchs/deaths.htm

Cervone, Daniel; Mor, Nilly; Orom, Heather; Shadel, William G.; & Scott, Walter D. (2011). Self-efficacy beliefs and the architecture of personality: On knowledge, appraisal, and self-regulation. In Kathleen D. Vohs & Roy F. Baumeister (Eds.), *Handbook of self-regulation: Research, theory, and applications*. New York, NY: Guilford.

Chabris, Christopher F., & Simons, Daniel J. (2013, March 8). Does this ad make me fat? Accessed June 14, 2013, from http://www.nytimes.com/2013/03/10/opinion/sunday/does-this-ad-make-me-fat.html

Chabris, Christopher, & Simons, Daniel. (2010). *The invisible gorilla: And other ways our intuitions deceive us*. New York, NY: Crown Publishers/Random House.

Chamberlain, Samuel R., & Fineberg, Naomi, A. (2013). The neurobiology of obsessive-compulsive disorder. In Kevin Oscsner & Stephen M. Kosslyn (Eds.), *The Oxford handbook of cognitive neuroscience*, vol. 2: *The cutting edges* (pp. 463–473). New York, NY: Oxford University Press.

Chamberlin, Jamie. (2014, June). New law moves ICD-10-CM implementation to 2015. *Monitor on Psychology, 45*(6), 12. Retrieved from http://www.apa.org/monitor/2014/06/upfront-icd.aspx

Champagne, Frances A. (2010). Early adversity and developmental outcomes: Interaction between genetics, epigenetics, and social experiences across the life span. *Perspectives on Psychological Science, 5*, 564–574. doi:10.1177/1745691610383494

Champagne, Frances A., & Mashoodh, Robin. (2009). Genes in context: Gene–environment interplay and the origins of individual differences in behavior. *Current Directions in Psychological Science, 18*, 127–131.

Chance, Paul. (1999). Thorndike's puzzle boxes and the origins of the experimental analysis of behavior. *Journal of the Experimental Analysis of Behavior, 72*, 433–440.

Chandola, Tarani, & Marmot, Michael G. (2011). Socioeconomic status and stress. In Richard J. Contrada & Andrew Baum (Eds.), *The handbook of stress science: Biology, psychology, and health*. New York, NY: Springer.

Chandrashekar, Jayaram; Hoon, Mark A.; Ryba, NicholaMays J. P.; & Zuker, Charles S. (2006). The receptors and cells for mammalian taste. *Nature, 444*, 288–294.

Chang, Anne-Marie; Aeschbach, Daniel; Duffy, Jeanne F.; & Czeisler, Charles A. (2015). Evening use of light-emitting eReaders negatively affects sleep, circadian timing, and next-morning alertness. *Proceedings of the National Academy of Sciences, 112*, 1232–1237. doi:10.1073/pnas.1418490112

Chapman, Benjamin; Duberstein, Paul; Tindle, Hilary A; Sink, Kaycee M.; Robbins, John; Tancredi, Daniel J.; & Franks, Peter. (2012). Personality predicts cognitive function over seven years in older persons. *American Journal of Geriatric Psychiatry, 20*, 612–621. doi:10.1097/JGP.0b013e31822cc9cb

Chaput, Jeanne-Paul, & Tremblay, Angelo. (2009) Obesity and physical inactivity: The relevance of reconsidering the notion of sedentariness. *Obesity Facts, 2*, 249–254.

Charles, Susan; Piazza, Jennifer; Mogle, Jaqueline; Sliwinski, Martin; & Almeida, David. (2013). The wear and tear of daily stressors on mental health. *Psychological Science, 24*, 733–741. doi:10.1177/0956797612462222

Charles, Susan T., & Carstensen, Laura L. (2010). Social and emotional aging. *Annual Review of Psychology, 61*, 383–409.

Charlton, Benjamin D.; Zhihe, Zhang; & Snyder, Rebecca J. (2010). Giant pandas perceive and attend to formant frequency variation in male bleats. *Animal Behaviour, 79*, 1221–1227. doi:10.1016/j.anbehav.2010.02.018

Chatterjee, Anjan. (2011). Neuroaesthetics: A coming of age story. *Journal of Cognitive Neuroscience, 23*(1), 53–62.

Chatterjee, Anjan; Thomas, Amy; Smith, Sabrina E.; & Aguirre, Geoffrey K. (2009). The neural response to facial attractiveness. *Neuropsychology, 23,* 135–143.

Chatterjee, Arijit, & Hambrick, Donald C. (2007). It's all about me: Narcissistic chief executive officers and their effects on company strategy and performance. *Administrative Science Quarterly, 52,* 351–386.

Chaudhari, Nirupa; Landin, Ana Marie; & Roper, Stephen D. (2000). A metabotropic glutamate receptor variant functions as a taste receptor. *Nature Neuroscience, 3,* 113–119.

Chavez, Pollyanna R.; Nelson, David E.; Naimi, Timothy S.; & Brewer, Robert D. (2011). Impact of a new gender-specific definition for binge drinking on prevalence estimates for women. *American Journal of Preventive Medicine, 40*(4), Apr 2011, 468–471. doi:10.1016/j.amepre.2010.12.008

Chen, Fang Fang, & Jing, Yiming. (2012). The impact of individualistic and collectivistic orientation on the judgement of self-presentation. *European Journal of Social Psychology, 42,* 470–481. doi:10.1002/ejsp.1872

Chen, Joyce. (2011, February 6). Christina Aguilera National Anthem flub: Singer said "I lost my place" at Super Bowl XLV. *New York Daily News.* Retrieved September 12, 2011, from http://articles.nydailynews.com/2011-02-06/gossip/28537023_1_christina-aguilera-nationalanthem-wardrobe-malfunction-super-bowl-xlv

Chen, Vivian Hsueh Hua, & Wu, Yuehua. (2015). Group identification as a mediator of the effect of players' anonymity on cheating in online games. *Behaviour and Information Technology, 34,* 658–667. doi:10.1080/0144929X.2013.843721

Chen, Xinguang; Murphy, Debra A.; Naar-King, Sylvie & Parsons, Jeffery T. (2011). A clinic-based motivational intervention improves condom use among subgroups of youth living with HIV. *Journal of Adolescent Health, 49*(2), 193–198.

Cheng, C. (2009). Dialectical thinking and coping flexibility: A multimethod approach. *Journal of Personality, 77*(2), 471–494.

Cheng, Guo; Buyken, Anette E.; Shi, Lijie; Karaolis-Danckert, Nadina; Kroke Anja; Wudy, Stefan A.; Degen, Gisela H.; & Remer, Thomas. (2012). Beyond overweight: Nutrition as an important lifestyle factor influencing timing of puberty. *Nutrition Reviews, 70,* 133–152. doi:10.1111/j.1753-4887.2011.00461.x

Chentsova-Dutton, Yulia E., & Tsai, Jeanne L. (2007). Cultural factors influence the expression of psychopathology. In Scott O. Lilienfeld & William T. O'Donohue (Eds.), *The great ideas of clinical science* (pp. 375–396). New York, NY: Routledge.

Chermack, Stephen T., & Taylor, Stuart P. (1995). Alcohol and human physical aggression: Pharmacological versus expectancy effects. *Journal of Studies on Alcohol and Drugs, 56*(4), 449–456.

Chi, Kelly Rae. (2014, November). White's the matter. *The Scientist, 28*(11), 67.

Chida, Yoichi, & Hamer, Mark. (2008). Chronic psychosocial factors and acute physiological responses to laboratory-induced stress in healthy populations: A quantitative review of 30 years of investigations. *Psychological Bulletin, 134*(6), 829–885.

Chida, Yoichi, & Steptoe, Andrew. (2009). The association of anger and hostility with future coronary heart disease: A meta-analytic review of prospective evidence. *Journal of the American College of Cardiology, 53*(11), 936–946.

Chiesa, Alberto, & Malinowski, Peter. (2011). Mindfulness based approaches: Are they all the same? *Journal of Clinical Psychology, 67,* 1–21. doi:10.1002/jclp.20776

Chiesa, Alberto, & Serretti, Alessandro. (2009). Mindfulness-based stress reduction for stress management in healthy people: A review and meta-analysis. *Journal of Alternative and Complementary Medicine, 15*(5), 593–600.

Childress, John R., & Senn, Larry E. (1995). *In the eye of the storm: Reengineering corporate culture.* Los Angeles: Leadership Press.

Choi, Kyeong-Sook; Jeon, Hyun Ok; & Lee, Yu-Sang. (2007). Familial association of schizophrenia symptoms retrospectively measured on a lifetime basis. *Psychiatric Genetics, 17*(2), 103–107.

Chomsky, Noam. (1965). *Aspects of a theory of syntax.* Cambridge, MA: MIT Press.

Chrysikou, Evangelia G. (2006). When shoes become hammers: Goal-derived categorization training enhances problem-solving performance. *Journal of Experimental Psychology: Learning, Memory, and Cognition, 32,* 935–942.

Chua, Hannah Faye; Boland, Julie E.; & Nisbett, Richard E. (2005). Cultural variation in eye movements during scene perception. *Proceedings of the National Academy of Sciences, 102,* 12629–12633.

Chun, Chi-Ah; Moos, Rudolf H.; & Cronkite, Ruth C. (2006). Culture: A fundamental context for the stress and coping paradigm. In Paul T. P. Wong, Lilian Chui Jan Wong, and Walter J. Lonner (Eds.), *Handbook of multicultural perspectives on stress and coping.* Dallas, TX: Spring.

Chun, Marvin M.; Golomb, Julie D.; & Turk-Browne, Nicholas B. (2011). A taxonomy of external and internal attention. *Annual Review of Psychology, 62, 2011* 73–101. doi:10.1146/annurev.psych.093008.100427

Chung-Do, Jane J.; Napoli, Stephanie B.; Hooper, Kealoha; Tydingco, Tasha; Bifulco, Kris; & Goebert, Deborah. (2014, August 12). Youth-led suicide prevention in an indigenous rural community. *Psychiatric Times.* Retrieved from http://www.psychiatrictimes.com/cultural-psychiatry/youth-led-suicide-prevention-indigenous-rural-community

Chung-Yan, Greg A. (2010). The nonlinear effects of job complexity and autonomy on job satisfaction, turnover, and psychological well-being. *Journal of Occupational Health Psychology, 15*(3), 237–251.

Cialdini, Robert B. (2009). Compliance. In D. Sander & K. Scherer (Eds.), *The Oxford companion to emotion and the affective sciences.* Oxford, England: Oxford University Press.

Cialdini, Robert B., & Sagarin, Brad J. (2005). Principles of interpersonal influence. In T. C. Brock & M. C. Green (Eds.), *Persuasion: Psychological insights and perspectives* (pp. 143–169). Thousand Oaks, CA: Sage.

Cicero, Theodore J.; Ellis, Matthew S.; Surratt, Hilary L.; & Kurtz, Steven P. (2014). The changing face of heroin use in the United States: A retrospective analysis of the past 50 years. *JAMA Psychiatry, 71,* 821–826. doi:10.1001/jamapsychiatry.2014.366

Cihangir, Sezgin. (2013). Gender specific honor codes and cultural change. *Group Processes & Intergroup Relations, 16*(3), 319–333. doi:10.1177/1368430212463453

Cikara, Mina, & Van Bavel, Jay J. (2014). The neuroscience of intergroup relations: An integrative review. *Perspectives on Psychological Science, 9,* 245–274. doi:10.1177/1745691614527464

Cinamon, Rachel Gali; Weisel, Amatzia; & Tzuk, Kineret. (2007). Work-family conflict within the family: Crossover effects, perceived parent-child interaction quality, parental self-efficacy, and life role attributions. *Journal of Career Development, 34,* 79–100.

Cisler, Josh M.; Reardon, John M.; & Williams, Nathan L. (2007). Anxiety sensitivity and disgust sensitivity interact to predict contamination fears. *Personality and Individual Differences, 42*(6), 935–946.

Clark, Damon A.; Mitra, Partha P.; & Wang, Samuel S.-H. (2001). Scalable architecture in mammalian brains. *Nature, 411,* 189–193.

Clark, David M.; Ehlers, Anke; McManus, Freda; Hackman, Ann; Fennell, Melanie; Campbell, Helen; Flower, Teresa; Davenport, Clare; & Louis, Beverly. (2003). Cognitive therapy versus fluoxetine in generalized social phobia: A randomized placebo-controlled trial. *Journal of Counseling and Clinical Psychology, 71,* 1058–1067.

Clark, Graeme M.; Clark, Jonathan C. M.; & Furness, John B. (2013). The evolving science of cochlear implants. *Journal of the American Medical Association, 310,* 1225–1226. doi:10.1001/jama.2013.278142

Clark, Wendy L., & Blackwell, Terry L. (2007). 16PF® (5th edition) Personal career development profile: Test review. *Rehabilitation Counseling Bulletin, 50*(4), 247–250.

Clarke, Laura E., & Barres, Ben A. (2013). Emerging roles of astrocytes in neural circuit development. *Nature Reviews Neuroscience 14,* 311–321. doi:10.1038/nrn3484

Clarke-Stewart, K. Alison. (1989). Infant day care: Maligned or malignant? *American Psychologist, 44,* 266–273.

Clarke-Stewart, K. Alison. (1992). Consequences of child care for children's development. In Alan Booth (Ed.), *Child care in the 1990s: Trends and consequences.* Hillsdale, NJ: Erlbaum.

Clarkin, John F., & Levy, Kenneth N. (2004). The influence of client variables on psychotherapy. In Michael J. Lambert (Ed.), *Bergin and Garfield's handbook of psychotherapy and behavior change* (5th ed.). New York, NY: Wiley.

Clay, Rebecca. (2003, April). Researchers replace midlife myths with facts. *Monitor on Psychology, 34,* 38–39. doi:10.1037/e300092003-024

Clayton, Nicola S.; Bussey, Timothy J.; & Dickinson, Anthony. (2003). Can animals recall the past and plan for the future? *Nature Reviews Neuroscience, 4*(8), 685–691. doi:10.1038/nrn1180

Cleary, Anne M. (2008). Recognition memory, familiarity, and déjà vu experiences. *Current Directions in Psychological Science, 17,* 353–357.

Cleary, Anne M.; Brown, Alan S.; Sawyer, Benjamin D.; Nomi, Jason S.; Ajoku, Adaeze C.; & Ryals, Anthony J. (2012). Familiarity from the configuration of objects in 3-dimensional space and its relation to déjà vu: A virtual reality investigation. *Consciousness and Cognition: An International Journal, 21,* 969–975. doi:10.1016/j.concog.2011.12.010

Clifasefi, Seema L.; Garry, Maryanne; & Loftus, Elizabeth. (2007). Setting the record (or video camera) straight on memory: The video camera model of memory and other memory myths. In Sergio Della Sala (Ed.), *Tall tales about the mind and brain: Separating fact from fiction.* New York, NY: Oxford University Press.

Cloutier, Jasmin; Heatherton, Todd F.; Whalen, Paul J.; & Kelley, William M. (2008). Are attractive people rewarding? Sex differences in the neural substrates of facial attractiveness. *Journal of Cognitive Neuroscience, 20*(6), 941–951.

CNN. (Producer). (2011). *Virtual reality battles PTSD* [Video]. Available from http://www.cnn.com/video/#/video/tech/2011/09/23/virtual-reality-battles.cnn

Cobos, Pilar; Sánchez, María; Pérez, Nieves; & Vila, Jaime. (2004). Effects of spinal cord injuries on the subjective component of emotions. *Cognition & Emotion, 18,* 281–287.

Coelho, Carlos M., & Purkis, Helena. (2009). The origins of specific phobias: Influential theories and current perspectives. *Review of General Psychology, 13*(4), 335–348.

Coelho, Helen F.; Canter, Peter H.; & Ernst, E. (2013). Mindfulness-based cognitive therapy: Evaluating current evidence and informing future research. *Psychology of Consciousness: Theory, Research, and Practice, 1*(S), 97–107. doi:10.1037/2326-5523.1.S.97

Coffee, Pete; Rees, Tim; & Haslam, S. Alexander. (2009). Bouncing back from failure: The interactive impact of perceived controllability and stability on self-efficacy beliefs and future task performance. *Journal of Sports Sciences, 27,* 1117–1124.

Cogan, Rosemary; Cochran, Bradley S.; & Velarde, Luis C. (2007). Sexual fantasies, sexual functioning, and hysteria among women: A test of Freud's (1905) hypothesis. *Psychoanalytic Psychology, 24*(4), 697–700.

Cohen, Adam B. (2009). Many forms of culture. *American Psychologist, 64*(3), 194–204.

Cohen, Adam B. (2010). Just how many different forms of culture are there? *American Psychologist, 65*(1), 59–61.

Cohen, Dov; Kim, Emily; & Hudson, Nathan W. (2014). Religion, the forbidden, and sublimation. *Current Directions in Psychological Science, 23,* 208–214. doi:10.1177/0963721414531436

Cohen, Estee; Zerach, Gadi; & Solomon, Zahava. (2011). The implication of combat-induced stress reaction, PTSD, and attachment in parenting among war veterans. *Journal of Family Psychology,* May 30, 2011, No Pagination Specified. doi:10.1037/a0024065. Advance online publication.

Cohen, Geoffrey L.; Purdie-Vaughns, Valerie; & Garcia, Julio. (2012). An identity threat perspective on intervention. In Michael Inzlicht & Toni Schmader (Eds.), *Stereotype threat: Theory, process, and application.* New York, NY: Oxford University Press.

Cohen, Hal. (2003). Creature comforts: Housing animals in complex environments. *The Scientist, 17*(9), 22–24.

Cohen, Jeremy; Mychailyszyn, Matthew; Settipani, Cara; Crawley, Sarah; & Kendall, Philip C. (2011). Issues in differential diagnosis: Considering generalized anxiety disorder, obsessive-compulsive disorder, and post-traumatic stress disorder. In Dean McKay & Eric A. Storch (Eds.), *Handbook of child and adolescent anxiety disorders* (pp. 23–35). New York, NY: Springer Science + Business Media.

Cohen, Sheldon; Janicki-Deverts, Denise; Doyle, William; Miller, Gregory; Frank, Ellen; Rabin, Bruce; & Turner, Ronald. (2012). Chronic stress, glucocorticoid receptor resistance, inflammation, and disease risk. *Proceedings of the National Academy of Sciences, 109*(16), 5995–5999. doi:10.1073/pnas.1118355109

Cohen, Sheldon. (2004). Social relationships and health. *American Psychologist, 59,* 676–684, 547

Cohen, Sheldon; Alper, Cuneyt M.; & Doyle, William J. (2006). Positive emotional style predicts resistance to illness after experimental exposure to rhinovirus or influenza A virus. *Psychosomatic Medicine, 68*(6), 809–815.

Cohen, Sheldon; Alper, Cuneyt M.; Doyle, William J.; Adler, Nancy; Treanor, John J.; & Turner, Ronald B. (2008). Objective and subjective socioeconomic status and susceptibility to the common cold. *Health Psychology, 27,* 268–274.

Cohen, Sheldon; Doyle, William J.; Alper, Cuneyt M.; Janicki-Deverts, Denise; & Turner, Ronald B. (2009). Sleep habits and susceptibility to the common cold. *Archives of Internal Medicine, 169*(1), 62–67.

Cohen, Sheldon, & Janicki-Deverts, Denise. (2009). Can we improve our physical health by altering our social networks? *Perspectives on Psychological Science, 4,* 375–378.

Cohen, Sheldon; Tyrrell, David A. J.; & Smith, Andrew P. (1991). Psychological stress and susceptibility to the common cold. *New England Journal of Medicine, 325,* 606–612.

Cohen, Sheldon; Tyrrell, David A. J.; & Smith, Andrew P. (1993). Negative life events, perceived stress, negative affect, and susceptibility to the common cold. *Journal of Personality and Social Psychology, 64,* 131–140.

Cohen, Sheldon. (2005). Keynote Presentation at the Eight International Congress of Behavioral Medicine: The Pittsburgh common cold studies: Psychosocial predictors of susceptibility to respiratory infectious illness. *International Journal of Behavioral Medicine, 12*(3), 123–131.

Cohen, Taya R.; Panter, Abigail. T.; & Turan, Nazli. (2012). Guilt proneness and moral character. *Current Directions in Psychological Science, 21*(5), 355–359. doi:10.1177/0963721412454874

Cohen-Kettenis, Peggy T., & Pfafflin, Friedemann. (2010). The DSM diagnostic criteria for gender identity disorder in adolescents and adults. *Archives of Sexual Behavior, 39*(2), 499–513.

Colangelo, James J. (2007). Recovered memory debate revisited: Practice implications for mental health counselors. *Journal of Mental Health Counseling, 29*(2), 93–120.

Colby, Anne, & Kohlberg, Lawrence. (1984). Invariant sequence and internal consistency in moral judgment stages. In William M. Kurtines & Jacob L. Gewirtz (Eds.), *Morality, moral behavior, and moral development.* New York, NY: Wiley.

Colby, Anne; Kohlberg, Lawrence; Gibbs, John; & Lieberman, Marcus. (1983). A longitudinal study of moral judgment. *Monographs of the Society for Research in Child Development, 48,* (1–2), 1–124.

Colcombe, Stanley, & Kramer, Arthur F. (2003). Fitness effects on the cognitive function of older adults: A meta-analytic study. *Psychological Science, 14*(2), 125–130.

Cole, Geoff G., & Wilkins, Arnold J. (2013). Fear of holes. *Psychological Science, 24*(10), 1–6. doi:10.1177/0956797613484937

Cole, Michael, & Packer, Martin. (2011). Culture and cognition. In Kenneth D. Keith (Ed.), *Cross-Cultural psychology: Contemporary themes and perspectives.* Chichester, England: Wiley-Blackwell.

Collerton, Joanna.; Davies, Karen; Jagger, Carol; Kingston, Anrew; Bond, John; Eccles, Martin P.; Robinson, Louise A.; & others. (2009). Health and disease in 85 year olds: Baseline findings from the Newcastle 85+ cohort study. *BMJ, 339,* b4904.

Collins, Allan M., & Loftus, Elizabeth F. (1975). A spreading activation theory of semantic processing. *Psychological Review, 82,* 407–428.

Collins, Rebecca L. (2004, September 7). Quoted in "Rand study finds adolescents who watch a lot of TV with sexual content have sex sooner." Retrieved on September 8, 2004, from http://www.rand.org/news/press.04/09.07.html

Collins, W. Andrew. (2003). More than myth: The developmental significance of romantic relationships during adolescence. *Journal of Research on Adolescence, 13,* 1–24.

Colrain, Ian M., & Baker, Fiona C. (2011). Changes in sleep as a function of adolescent development. *Neuropsychology Review, 21,* 5–21. doi:10.1007/s11065-010-9155-5

Coltheart, Max. (2013). How can functional neuroimaging inform cognitive theories? *Perspectives on Psychological Science 8,* 98–103. doi:10.1177/1745691612469208

Coltheart, Max, & McArthur, Genevieve. (2012). Neuroscience, education and educational efficacy research. In Sergio Della Sala & Mike Anderson (Eds.), *Neuroscience in education: The good, the bad, and the ugly.* Oxford, England: Oxford University Press.

Colwell, Christopher S. (2011). Neuroscience: Sleepy neurons? *Nature, 472,* 427–428. doi:10.1038/472427a

Combs, Dennis R., & Mueser, Kim T. (2007). Schizophrenia. In Michel Hersen, Samuel M. Turner, & Deborah C. Beidel (Eds.), *Adult psychopathology and diagnosis* (5th ed., pp. 234–285). Hoboken, NJ: Wiley.

Combs, Dennis R.; Chapman, Dustin; Waguspack, Jace; Basso, Michael R.; & Penn, David L. (2011). Attention shaping as a means to improve emotion perception deficits in outpatients with schizophrenia and impaired controls. *Schizophrenia Research, 127*(1–3), 151–156.

Comer, Jonathan S.; Mojtabai, Ramin; & Olfson, Mark. (2011). National trends in the antipsychotic treatment of psychiatric outpatients with anxiety disorders. *American Journal of Psychiatry, 168,* 1057–1065. doi:10.1176/appi.ajp.2011.11010087

Confer, Jaime C.; Easton, Judith A.; Fleischman, Diana S.; Goetz, Cari D.; Lewis, David M. G.; Perilloux, Carin; & Buss, David M. (2010). Evolutionary psychology: Controversies, questions, prospects, and limitations. *American Psychologist, 65,* 110–126. doi:10.1037/a0018413

Conley, Colleen S., & Rudolph, Karen D. (2009). The emerging sex difference in adolescent depression: Interacting contributions of puberty and peer stress. *Development Psychopathology, 21*(2), 593–620. doi:10.1017/S0954579409000327

Connell, Arin M.; Dishion, Thomas J.; & Yasui, Miwa. (2007). An adaptive approach to family intervention: Linking engagement in family-centered intervention to reductions in adolescent problem behavior. *Journal of Consulting and Clinical Psychology, 75*(4), 568–579.

Connelly, Brian S., & Ones, Deniz S. (2010). Another perspective on personality: Meta-analytic integration of observers' accuracy and predictive validity. *Psychological Bulletin, 136,* 1092–1122. doi:10.1037/a0021212

Connolly, J. A., & McIsaac, C. (2009). Romantic relationships in adolescence. In R. M. Lerner & L. Steinberg (Eds.), *Handbook of Adolescent Psychology, Vol. 2: Contextual influences on adolescent development* (3rd ed.). (pp. 104–151). Hoboken, NJ: Wiley.

Conway, Martin A.; Meares, Kevin; & Standart, Sally. (2004). Images and goals. *Memory, 12,* 525–531.

Cook, Emily C.; Buehler, Cheryl; & Henson, Robert. (2009). Parents and peers as social influences to deter antisocial behavior. *Journal of Youth and Adolescence, 38*(9), 1240–1252.

Cook, Richard; Bird, Geoffrey; Catmur, Caroline; Press, Clare; Heyes, Cecilia. (2014). Mirror neurons: From origin to function. *Behavioral and Brain Sciences, 37,* 177–192. doi:10.1017/S0140525X13000903

Cook, Thomas D.; Deng, Yingding; & Morgano, Emily. (2007). Friendship influences during early adolescence: The special role of friends' grade point average. *Journal of Research on Adolescence, 17*(2), 325–356.

Cook, Travis A. R.; Luczak, Susan E.; Shea, Shoshana H.; Ehlers, Cindy L.; Carr, Lucinda G.; & Wall, Tamara L. (2005). Associations of ALDH2 and ADH1B genotypes with response to alcohol in Asian Americans. *Journal of Studies on Alcohol, 66,* 196–204.

Cooke, Richard; French, David P.; & Sniehotta, Falko F. (2010). Wide variation in understanding about what constitutes 'binge-drinking'. *Drugs: Education, Prevention & Policy, 17*(6), 762–775. doi:10.3109/09687630903246457

Cooper, Cary L., & Dewe, Philip. (2007). Stress: A brief history from the 1950s to Richard Lazarus. In Alan Monat, Richard S. Lazarus, & Gretchen Reevy (Eds.), *The Praeger handbook on stress and coping: Vol. 1.* Westport, CT: Praeger/Greenwood.

Cooper, Joel. (2012). Cognitive dissonance theory. In Paul A. M. Van Lange, Arie W. Kruglanski, & E. Tory Higgins (Eds.), *Handbook of theories of social psychology* (Vol. 1). Thousand Oaks, CA: Sage.

Cooper, Mick. (2008). *Essential research findings in counseling and psychotherapy.* Thousand Oaks, CA: Sage.

Cooper, Mick; O'Hara, Maureen; Schmid, Peter F.; & Wyatt, Gill (Eds.). (2013). *The handbook of person-centred psychotherapy and counselling.* New York, NY: Palgrave Macmillan.

Corballis, Michael C. (2010). Handedness and cerebral asymmetry: An evolutionary perspective. In Kenneth Hugdahl & René Westerhausen, (Eds.), *The two halves of the brain: Information processing in the cerebral hemispheres.* Cambridge, MA: MIT Press.

Corkin, Suzanne. (2002). What's new with the amnesic patient H.M.? *Nature Reviews Neuroscience, 3,* 153–160.

Corkin, Suzanne. (2013). *Present tense: The unforgettable life of the amnesic patient, H. M.* New York, NY: Basic Books.

Corrigan, Patrick W.; Druss, Benjamin G.; & Perlick, Deborah A. (2014). The impact of mental illness stigma on seeking and participating in mental health care. *Psychological Science in the Public Interest, 15*(2), 37–70. doi:10.1177/1529100614531398

Corsini, Raymond J. (1958). *The Nonverbal Reasoning Test: To measure the capacity to reason logically as indicated by solutions to pictorial problems.* Chicago, IL: Pearson Performance Solutions.

Cosgrove, Lisa, & Krimsky, Sheldon. (2012). A comparison of DSM-IV and DSM-5 panel members' financial associations with industry: A pernicious problem persists. *PLOS Medicine, 9*(3), e1001190.

Cosmides, Leda, & Tooby, John. (2013). Evolutionary psychology: New perspectives on cognition and motivation. *Annual Review of Psychology, 64,* 201–209.

Cossins, Daniel (2015, January 16). Crossed wires. *The Scientist, 29.* Retrieved from http://www.the-scientist.com/?articles.view/articleNo/41919/title/Crossed-Wires

Costa, Albert, & Sebastián-Gallés, Núria. (2014). How does the bilingual experience sculpt the brain? *Nature Reviews Neuroscience, 15,* 336–345.

Costarelli, Sandro. (2011). Seeming ambivalent, being prejudiced: The moderating role of attitude basis on experienced affect. *Group Dynamics: Theory, Research, and Practice, 15*(1), 49–59.

Côté, Sophie, & Bouchard, Stéphane. (2008). Virtual reality exposure's efficacy in the treatment of specific phobias: A critical review. *Journal of CyberTherapy and Rehabilitation, 1*(1), 75–91.

Courage, Mary L., & Howe, Mark L. (2002). From infant to child: The dynamics of cognitive change in the second year of life. *Psychological Bulletin, 128,* 250–277.

Courtois, Christine A., & Ford, Julian D. (Eds.). (2009). *Treating complex traumatic stress disorders: An evidence-based guide.* New York, NY: Guilford.

Cousineau, Tara McKee, & Shedler, Jonathan. (2006). Predicting physical health: Implicit mental health measures versus self-report scales. *Journal of Nervous and Mental Disease, 194*(6), 427–432.

Coventry, Will L.; Gillespie, Nathan A.; Heath, A. C.; & Martin, N. G. (2004). Perceived social support in a large community sample—age and sex differences. *Social Psychiatry and Psychiatric Epidemiology, 39*(8), 625–636.

Covino, Nicholas A., & Pinnell, Cornelia M. (2010). Hypnosis and medicine. In Steven Jay Lynn, Judith W. Rhue, & Irving Kirsch (Eds.), *Handbook of clinical hypnosis* (2nd ed.). Washington, DC: American Psychological Association.

Cowan, Nelson. (2001). The magical number 4 in short-term memory: A reconsideration of mental storage capacity. *Behavioral and Brain Sciences, 24,* 87–185.

Cowan, Nelson. (2005). *Working memory capacity: Essays in cognitive psychology.* New York, NY: Psychology Press.

Cowan, Nelson. (2010). The magical mystery four: How is working memory capacity limited, and why? *Current Directions in Psychological Science, 19*(1), 51–57.

Cowan, Nelson; Chen, Zhijian; & Rouder, Jeffrey N. (2004). Constant capacity in an immediate serial-recall task: A logical sequel to Miller (1956). *Psychological Science, 15,* 634–640.

Cowan, Nelson; Morey, Candice C.; & Chen, Zhijian. (2007). The legend of the magical number seven. In Sergio Della Sala (Ed.), *Tall tales about the mind and brain: Separating fact from fiction.* New York, NY: Oxford University Press.

Coyle, Emily F.; Van Leer, Elizabeth; Schroeder, Kingsley, M.; & Fulcher, Megan. (2015). Planning to have it all: Emerging adults' expectations of future work-family conflict. *Sex Roles, 72,* 547–557. doi:10.1007/s11199-015-0492-y

Craighead, W. Edward; Sheets, Erin S.; Brosse, Alisha L.; & Ilardi, Stephen S. (2007). Psychosocial treatments for major depressive disorder. In Peter E. Nathan & James M. Gorman (Eds.), *A guide to treatments that work* (3rd ed., pp. 289–307). New York, NY: Oxford University Press.

Craik, Fergus I. M.; & Bialystok, Ellen. (2006). Cognition through the lifespan: Mechanisms of change. *Trends in Cognitive Sciences, 10,* 131–138.

Craik, Fergus I.M.; Bialystok, Ellen; & Freedman, Morris. (2010). Delaying the onset of Alzheimer disease: Bilingualism as a form of cognitive reserve. *Neurology, 75,* 1726–1729. doi:10.1212/WNL.0b013e3181fc2a1c

Craik, Fergus I. M.; Govoni, Richard; Naveh-Benjamin, Moshe; & Anderson, Nicole D. (1996). The effects of divided attention on encoding and retrieval processes in human memory. *Journal of Experimental Psychology: General, 125,* 159–180.

Crano, William D., & Prislin, R. (2006). Attitudes and persuasion. *Annual Review of Psychology, 57,* 345–374.

Craske, Michelle G., & Barlow, David H. (2008). Panic disorder and agoraphobia. In David H. Barlow (Ed.), *Clinical handbook of psychological disorders* (4th ed., pp. 1–64). New York, NY: Guilford.

Craske, Michelle G., & Waters, Allison M. (2005). Panic disorder, phobias, and generalized anxiety disorder. *Annual Review of Clinical Psychology, 1,* 197–225.

Crawford, Jarret T.; Jussim, Lee; Madon, Stephanie; Cain, Thomas R.; & Stevens, Sean T. (2011). The use of stereotypes and individuating information in political person perception. *Personality and Social Psychology Bulletin.* doi:10.1177/0146167211399473

Creswell, Cathy, & O'Connor, Thomas G. (2011). Interpretation bias and anxiety in childhood: Stability, specificity and longitudinal associations. *Behavioural and Cognitive Psychotherapy, 39*(2), 191–204.

Creswell, J. David, & Lindsay, Emily. (2014). How does mindfulness training affect health? A mindfulness stress buffering account. *Current Directions in Psychological Science, 23,* 401–407. doi:10.1177/0963721414547415

Crews, Frederick. (1984/1986). The Freudian way of knowledge. In *Skeptical engagements.* New York, NY: Oxford University Press.

Crews, Frederick. (1996). The verdict on Freud. *Psychological Science, 7,* 63–68.

Crews, Frederick. (2006). The unknown Freud. In Frederick Crews (Ed.), *Follies of the wise: Dissenting essays.* Emeryville, CA: Shoemaker & Hoard.

Crisafulli, C.; Fabbri, C.; Porcelli, S.; Drago, A.; Spina, E.; De Ronchi, D.; & Serretti, A. (2011). Pharmacogenetics of antidepressants. *Frontiers in Pharmacology, 2,* 6. doi:10.3389/fphar.2011.00006

Critcher, Clayton R., & Dunning, David. (2009). Egocentric pattern projection: How implicit personality theories recapitulate the geography of the self. *Journal of Personality and Social Psychology, 97*(1), 1–16. doi:10.1037/a0015670

Critchley, Hugo D.; Wiens, Stefan; Rotshtein, Pia; Ohman, Arne; & Dolan, Raymond J. (2004). Neural systems supporting interoceptive awareness. *Nature Neuroscience, 7,* 189–195.

Crites, John O., & Taber, Brian J. (2002). Appraising adults' career capabilities: Ability, interest, and personality. In Spencer G. Niles (Ed.), *Adult career development: Concepts, issues and practices* (3rd ed., pp. 120–138). Columbus, OH: National Career Development Association.

Croft, Rodney J.; Klugman, Anthony; Baldeweg, Torsten; & Gruzelier, John H. (2001). Electrophysiological evidence of serotonergic impairment in long-term MDMA ("Ecstasy") users. *American Journal of Psychiatry, 158,* 1687–1692.

Croizet, Jean-Claude, & Claire, Theresa. (1998). Extending the concept of stereotype and threat to social class: The intellectual underperformance of students from low socioeconomic backgrounds. *Personality and Social Psychology Bulletin, 24,* 588–654.

Croizet, Jean-Claude; Després, Gérard; Gauzins, Marie-Eve; Huguet, Pascal; Leyens, Jacques-Philippe; & Méot, Alain. (2004). Stereotype threat undermines intellectual performance by triggering a disruptive mental load. *Personality and Social Psychology Bulletin, 30,* 721–731.

Crossley, Nicolas A.; Constante, Miguel; McGuire, Philip; Power, Paddy. (2010). Efficacy of atypical v. typical antipsychotics in the treatment of early psychosis: Meta-analysis. *British Journal of Psychiatry, 196,* 434–439.

Crowell, Sheila E.; Beauchaine, Theodore P.; & Linehan, Marsha M. (2009). A biosocial developmental model of borderline personality disorder: Elaborating and extending Linehan's theory. *Psychological Bulletin, 135,* 495–510.

Csikszentmihalyi, Mihaly; & Nakamura, Jeanne. (2011). Positive psychology: Where did it come from, where is it going? In Kennon M. Sheldon, Todd B. Kashdan, & Michael F. Steger (Eds.), *Designing positive psychology: Taking stock and moving forward.* New York, NY: Oxford University Press. doi:10.1093/acprof:oso/9780195373585.003.0001

CTV News. (2013, November 10). Lady Gaga used therapy to cope with fame. *CTV News.* Retrieved from http://www.ctvnews.ca/entertainment/lady-gaga-used-therapy-to-cope-with-fame-1.1536107

Cuijpers, Pim; Smit, Filip; Bohlmeijer, Ernst; Hollon, Steven D.; & Andersson, Gerhard. (2010). Efficacy of cognitive-behavioural therapy and other psychological treatments for adult depression: Meta-analytic study of publication bias. *British Journal of Psychiatry, 196,* 173–178. doi:10.1192/bjp.bp.109.066001

Cuijpers, Pim; van Straten, Annemieke; Andersson, Gerhard; & van Oppen, Patricia. (2008). Psychotherapy for depression in adults: A meta-analysis of comparative outcome studies. *Journal of Consulting and Clinical Psychology, 76*(6), 909–922.

Cuijpers, Pim; van Straten, A.; Warmerdam, L.; & Andersson, G. (2009). Psychotherapy versus the combination of psychotherapy and pharmacotherapy in the treatment of depression: A meta-analysis. *Depress Anxiety, 26*(3), 279–288. doi:10.1002/da.20519

Cullen, Margaret. (2011). Mindfulness-based interventions: An emerging phenomenon. *Mindfulness, Mindfulness, 2,* 186–193. doi 10.1007/s12671-011-0058-1

Culpin, Iryana; Heron, Jon; Araya, Ricardo; Melotti, Roberto; Lewis, Glyn; & Joinson, Carol (2014). Father absence and timing of menarche in adolescent girls from a UK cohort: The mediating role of maternal depression and major financial problems. *Journal of Adolescence, 37,* 291–301. doi:10.1016/j.adolescence.2014.02.003

Cummings, David E. (2006). Ghrelin and the short- and long-term regulation of appetite and body weight. *Physiology & Behavior, 89,* 71–84.

Cummings, Donald E.; Weigle, David S.; Frayo, R. Scott; Breen, Patricia A.; Ma, Marina K.; Dellinger, E. Patchen; & Purnell, Jonathan Q. (2002). Plasma ghrelin levels after diet-induced weight loss or gastric bypass surgery. *New England Journal of Medicine, 346,* 1623–1630.

Cunningham, Jacqueline L. (1997). Alfred Binet and the quest for testing higher mental functioning. In Wolfgang G. Bringmann, Helmut E. Lück, Rudolf Miller, & Charles E. Early (Eds.), *A pictorial history of psychology.* Chicago, IL: Quintessence.

Cunningham, William A., & Brosch, Tobias. (2012). Motivational salience: Amygdala tuning from traits, needs, values, and goals. *Current Directions in Psychological Science 21,* 54–59. doi:10.1177/0963721411430832

Cushing, Christopher C.; Jensen, Chad D.; Miller Mary B.; & Leffingwell, Thad R. (2014). Meta-analysis of motivational interviewing for adolescent health behavior: Efficacy beyond substance use. *Journal of Consulting and Clinical Psychology, 82*(6), 1212–1218. doi:10.1037/a0036912

Custers, Eugene J. F. M., & Ten Cate, Olle T. J. (2011). Very long-term retention of basic science knowledge in doctors after graduation. *Medical Education, 45*(4), 422–430. doi:10.1111/j.1365-2923.2010.03889.x

Czeisler, Charles A., & Dijk, Derk-Jan. (2001). Human circadian physiology and sleep-wake regulation. In Joseph Takahashi, Fred W. Turek,

& Robert Y. Moore (Eds.), *Handbook of behavioral neurobiology: Circadian clocks* (Vol. 12). New York, NY: Kluwer/Plenum Press.

Czeisler, Charles A., & Gooley, Joshua J. (2007). Sleep and circadian rhythms in humans. *Cold Spring Harbor Symposia on Quantitative Biology, 72,* 579–597. doi:10.1101/sqb.2007.72.064

Dabbs, James M., & Hargrove, Marian F. (1997). Age, testosterone, and behavior among female prison inmates. *Psychosomatic Medicine, 59*(5), 477–480.

Daffner, Kirk R. (2010). Promoting successful cognitive aging: A comprehensive review. *Journal of Alzheimers Disease, 19*(4), 1101–1122. doi:10.3233/0T1L4201H5104272/JAD-2010-1306

Dagnall, Neil; Parker, Andrew; & Munley, Gary. (2007). Paranormal belief and reasoning. *Personality and Individual Differences, 43*(6), 1406–1415.

Dalenberg, Constance J.; Paulson, Kelsey; Dell, Paul F.; & O'Neil, John A. (2009). The case for the study of 'normal' dissociation processes. In Paul F. Dell & John A. O'Neill (Eds.), *Dissociation and the dissociative disorders: DSM-V and beyond* (pp. 145–154). New York, NY: Routledge/Taylor & Francis Group.

Dalgard, Odd Steffen; Dowrick, Christopher; Lehtinen, Ville; Vazquez-Barquero, Jose Luis; Casey, Patricia; Wilkinson, Greg; & others. (2006). Negative life events, social support and gender difference in depression: A multinational community survey with data from the ODIN study. *Social Psychiatry and Psychiatric Epidemiology, 41*(6), 444–451.

Dalgleish, Tim. (2004). The emotional brain. *Nature Reviews Neuroscience, 5,* 582–589.

Daly, Michael; Delaney, Liam; Doran, Peter P.; Harmon, Colm; & MacLachlan, Malcolm. (2010). Naturalistic monitoring of the affect–heart rate relationship: A day reconstruction study. *Health Psychology, 29*(2), 186–195.

Damasio, Antonio R. (2004). Emotions and feelings: A neurobiological perspective. In Antony S. R. Manstead, Nico Frijda, & Agneta Fischer (Eds.), *Feelings and emotions: The Amsterdam symposium.* New York, NY: Cambridge University Press.

Damasio, Antonio R., & Carvalho, Gil B. (2013). The nature of feelings: Evolutionary and neurobiological origins. *Nature Reviews Neuroscience 14,* 143–152. doi:10.1038/nrn3403

Damasio, Antonio R.; Grabowski, Thomas J.; Bechara, Antoine; Damasio, Hanna; Ponto, Laura L. B.; Parvizi, Josef; & Hichwa, Richard D. (2000). Subcortical and cortical brain activity during the feeling of self-generated emotions. *Nature Neuroscience, 3,* 1049–1056.

Damasio, H., Grabowski, T., Frank, R., Galaburda, A. M. and Damasio, A. R. (1994). The return of Phineas Gage: Clues about the brain from the skull of a famous patient. *Science, 264,* 1102–1105.

Damisch, Lysann; Stoberock, Barbara; & Mussweiler, Thomas. (2010). Keep your fingers crossed! How superstition improves performance. *Psychological Science, 21,* 1014–1020. doi:10.1177/0956797610372631

D'Angelo, Maria, & Humphreys, Karin. (2015). Tip-of-the-tongue states reoccur because of implicit learning, but resolving them helps. *Cognition, 142,* 166–190. doi:10.1016/j.cognition.2015.05.019

Daniels, Bradley J. (2008). Arkham asylum: Forensic psychology and Gotham's (not so) "serious house." In Robin S. Rosenberg (Ed.), *The psychology of superheroes: An unauthorized exploration* (pp. 201–211). Dallas, TX: BenBella Books, pp. 201–211.

Dar-Nimrod, Ilan, & Heine, Steven J. (2011). Genetic essentialism: On the deceptive determinism of DNA. *Psychological Bulletin, 137,* 800–818. doi:10.1037/a0021860.

Darley, John M. (1992). Social organization for the production of evil [Book review essay]. *Psychological Inquiry, 3,* 199–218.

Darley, John. M., & Latané, Bibb. (1968). Bystander intervention in emergencies: Diffusion of responsibility. *Journal of Personality and Social Psychology, 8*(4p1), 377.

Darwin, Charles R. (1859/1998). *On the origin of species by means of natural selection.* New York, NY: Modern Library.

Darwin, Charles R. (1871/1981). *The descent of man, and selection in relation to sex* (Introductions by John T. Bonner and Robert M. May). Princeton, NJ: Princeton University Press.

Darwin, Charles R. (1872/1998). *The expression of the emotions in man and animals* (3rd ed.). New York, NY: Appleton.

Datta, Sublimal; & MacLean, Robert Ross. (2007). Neurobiological mechanisms for the regulation of mammalian sleep–wake behavior: Reinterpretation of historical evidence and inclusion of contemporary cellular and molecular evidence. *Neuroscience and Biobehavioral Reviews, 31,* 775–824.

Dautovich, Natalie D.; Gum, Amber M. (2011). Cognitive behavioral therapy for late-life depression and comorbid psychiatric conditions. In Kristen Sorocco, Kristen Hilliard, & Sean Lauderdale (Eds.), *Cognitive behavior therapy with older adults: Innovations across care settings.* New York, NY: Springer.

David, Daniel; Lynn, Steven J.; & Ellis, Albert (Eds.). (2009). *Rational and irrational beliefs: Research, theory, and clinical practice.* New York, NY: Oxford University Press.

David, Daniel, & Montgomery, Guy H. (2011). The scientific status of psychotherapies: A new evaluative framework for evidence-based psychosocial interventions. *Clinical Psychology: Science and Practice, 18*(2), 89–99.

Davidson, Jonathan R. T.; Connor, Kathryn M.; & Zhang, Wei. (2009). Treatment of anxiety disorders. In Alan F. Schatzberg & Charles B. Nemeroff (Eds.), *The American Psychiatric Publishing textbook of psychopharmacology* (4th ed., pp. 1171–1199). Washington, DC: American Psychiatric Publishing.

Davidson, Karina; Mostofsky, Elizabeth; & Whang, William. (2010). don't worry, be happy: Positive affect and reduced 10-year incident coronary heart disease: The Canadian Nova Scotia Health Survey. *European Heart Journal, 31,* 1065–1070.

Davidson, Paul R., & Parker, Kevin C. H. (2001). Eye movement desensitization and reprocessing (EMDR): A meta-analysis. *Journal of Consulting and Clinical Psychology, 69,* 305–316.

Davidson, Richard J. (2005). Emotion regulation, happiness, and the neuroplasticity of the brain. *Advances in Mind-Body Medicine, 21*(3–4), 25–28.

Davidson, Richard J.; Putnam, Katherine M.; & Larson, Christine L. (2000). Dysfunction in the neural circuitry of emotion regulation—a possible prelude to violence. *Science, 289*(5479), 591–594.

Davidson, Richard R. (2010). Commentary: Empirical explorations of mindfulness: Conceptual and methodological conundrums. *Emotion, 10,* 8–11.

Davidson, Richard R. (2011, June 23). Investigating healthy minds. Radio interview, *On Being,* npr.org. Broadcast 6/23/11. Retrieved on July 19, 2011, from http://being.publicradio.org/programs/2011/healthy-minds

Davidson, Terry L. (2000). Pavlovian occasion setting: A link between physiological change and appetitive behavior. *Appetite, 35,* 271–272.

Davis, Catherine M., & Riley, Anthony L. (2010). Conditioned taste aversion learning. *Annals of the New York Academy of Sciences, 1187*(1), 247–275.

Davis, Daphne M., & Hayes, Jeffrey A. (2011). What are the benefits of mindfulness? A practice review of psychotherapy-related research. *Psychotherapy, 48*(2), 198–208. doi:10.1037/a0022062

Davis, Deborah, & Loftus, Elizabeth F. (2007). Internal and external sources of misinformation in adult witness memory. In Michael P. Toglia, J. Don Read, & R. C. L. Lindsay (Eds.), *The Handbook of Eyewitness Psychology. Vol. I: Memory for events.* Mahwah, NJ: Erlbaum.

Davis, Deborah, & Loftus, Elizabeth. (2009). The scientific status of "repressed" and "recovered" memories of sexual abuse. In J. L. Skeem, K. S. Douglas & S. O. Lilienfeld (Eds.), *Psychological science in the courtroom: Consensus and controversy* (pp. 55–79). New York, NY: Guilford.

Davis, Jake H., & Thompson, Evan. (2015). Developing attention and decreasing affective bias: Toward a cross-cultural cognitive science of mindfulness. In Kirk Warren Brown, J. David Creswell, & Richard M. Ryan (Eds.), *Handbook of mindfulness: Theory, research, and practice.* New York, NY: Guilford.

Davis, Joshua Ian; Senghas, Ann; Brandt, Fredric; & Ochsner, Kevin N. (2010). The effects of BOTOX injections on emotional experience. *Emotion, 10,* 433–440. doi:10.1037/a0018690

Davis, Lori L.; Bartolucci, Al; & Petty, Frederick. (2005). Divalproex in the treatment of bipolar depression: A placebo-controlled study. *Journal of Affective Disorders, 85*(3), 259–266.

Davis, Susan R.; Moreau, Michele; Kroll, Robin; Bouchard, Celine l.; Panay, Nick; Gass, Margery; Braunstein, Glenn D.; Hirschberg, Angelica L.; Rodenberg, Cynthia; Pack, Simon; Koch, Helga; Moufarege, Alain; & Studd, John. (2008). Testosterone for low libido in postmenopausal women not taking estrogen. *New England Journal of Medicine, 359*(19), 2005–2017.

Dawkins, Lynne, & Corcoran, Olivia. (2014). Acute electronic cigarette use: Nicotine delivery and subjective effects in regular users. *Psychopharmacology, 231,* 401–407. doi:10.1007/s00213-013-3249-8

Dawson, Deborah A. (1991). Family structure and children's health and well-being: Data from the 1988 National Health Interview Study on Child Health. *Journal of Marriage and the Family, 53,* 573–584.

Dawson, Jennifer A. (2007). African conceptualisations of posttraumatic stress disorder and the impact of introducing Western concepts. *Psychology, Psychiatry, and Mental Health Monographs, 2,* 101–112.

Dawson, Michelle. (2007, August 20–27). Quoted in Sharon Begley, "The puzzle of human ability." *Newsweek.* Retrieved on August 20, 2008, from http://www.newsweek.com/id/32250

Dawson, Michelle; Mottron, Laurent; & Gernsbacher, Morton Ann. (2008). Learning in autism. In John H. Byrne & Henry Roediger (Eds.), *Learning and memory: A comprehensive reference: Volume 2. Cognitive psychology.* New York, NY: Elsevier.

Dawson, Michelle; Soulieres, Isabelle; Gernsbacher, Morton Ann; & Mottron, Laurent. (2007). The level and nature of autistic intelligence. *Psychological Science, 18,* 657–659.

Dazzi, Carla, & Pedrabissi, Luigi. (2009). Graphology and personality: An empirical study on validity of handwriting analysis. *Psychological Reports, 105*(3, Pt2), 1255–1268.

De Brito, Stéphane A., & Hodgins, Sheilagh. (2009). Antisocial personality disorder. In Mary McMurran & Richard Howard (Eds.), *Personality, personality disorder and violence* (pp. 133–153). Chichester, England: Wiley-Blackwell.

de Dreu, Carsten K. W.; Greer, Lindred L.; Van Kleef, Gerben A.; Shalvi, Shaul; & Michel J. J. Handgraaf. (2011). Oxytocin promotes human ethnocentrism *Proceedings of the National Academy of Sciences, 8,* 1262–1266. doi:10.1073/pnas.1015316108

de Groot, Jasper H. B.; Semin, Gün R.; & Smeets, Monique A. M. (2014). I can see, hear, and smell your fear: Comparing olfactory and audiovisual media in fear communication. *Journal of Experimental Psychology: General, 143*(2), 825–834. doi:10.1037/a0033731

de Groot, Jasper H. B.; Smeets, Monique A. M.; Kaldewaij, Annemarie; Duijndam, Maarten J. A.; & Semin, Gün R. (2012). Chemosignals communicate human emotions. *Psychological Science, 23,* 1417–1424.

de Hooge, Ilona E.; Nelissen, Rob M. A.; Breugelmans, Seger M.; & Zeelenberg, Marcel. (2011). What is moral about guilt? Acting "prosocially' at the disadvantage of others. *Journal of Personality and Social Psychology, 100*(3), 462–473.

de la Fuente-Fernández, Raúll. (2009). The placebo-reward hypothesis: Dopamine and the placebo effect. *Parkinsonism & Related Disorders, 15*(Suppl 3), S72–S74.

de Montigny-Malenfant, Béatrice; Santerre, Marie-Ève; Bouchard, Sébastien; Sabourin, Stéphane; Lazaridès, Ariane; & Bélanger, Claude. (2013). Couples' negative interaction behaviors and borderline personality disorder. *American Journal of Family Therapy, 40,* 259–271. doi:10.1080/01926187.2012.688006

de Moor, Marleen H.; Costa, Paul T.; Terracciano, AAntonio; Krueger, Robert F.; de Geus, Eco J.; Toshiko, Tanaka; Penninx, Brenda W. J. H.; & others. (2010). Meta-analysis of genome-wide association studies for personality. *Molecular Psychiatry.* doi:10.1038/mp.2010.128

de Waal, Frans B. M. (1995, March). Bonobo sex and society. *Scientific American, 271,* 82–88.

de Waal, Frans B. M. (2011). What is an animal emotion? *Annals of the New York Academy of Sciences, 1224, The Year in Cognitive Neuroscience* 191–206. doi:10.1111/j.1749-6632.2010.05912.x

de Waal, Frans B. M. (2013). Animal conformists. *Science, 340,* pp. 437–438.

de Waal, Frans B.M., & Ferrari, Pier Francesco. (2010). Towards a bottom-up perspective on animal and human cognition. *Trends in Cognitive Sciences, (14)*5, 201–207. doi:10.1016/j.tics.2010.03.003

Deady, D. K. , North, N. T. , Allan, D. , Smith; M.J. Law; & O'Carroll, Ronan E. (2010). Examining the effect of spinal cord injury on

emotional awareness, expressivity and memory for emotional material. *Psychology, Health, & Medicine, 15,* 406–419.

DeAngelis, Tori. (2007, October). Goodbye to a legend. *Monitor on Psychology, 38,* 38.

DeAngelis, Tori. (2014, March). Are e-cigarettes a game changer? *Monitor on Psychology, 45,* 48–53. doi:10.1037/e505762014-016

Deary, Ian J.; Johnson, Wendy; & Houlihan, Lorna M. (2009). Genetic foundations of human intelligence. *Human Genetics, 126*(1), 215–232.

Decety, Jean. (2010). To what extent is the experience of empathy mediated by shared neural circuits? *Emotion Review, 2*(3), 204–207.

Decety, Jean, & Cacioppo, John. (2010). Frontiers in human neuroscience: The golden triangle and beyond. *Perspectives on Psychological Science, 5,* 767–771. doi:10.1177/1745691610388780

deCharms, R. Christopher; Maeda, Fumiko; Glover, Gary H.; Ludlow, David; Pauly, John M.; Soneji, Deepak; Gabrieli, John D. E.; & Mackey, Sean C. (2005). Control over brain activation and pain learned by using real-time functional MRI. *Proceedings of the National Academy of Sciences, 102,* 18626–18631.

Deci, Edward L., & Ryan, Richard M. (2000). The "what" and "why" of goal pursuits: Human needs and the self-determination of behavior. *Psychological Inquiry, 11,* 227–268.

Deci, Edward L., & Ryan, Richard M. (2012a). Motivation, personality, and development within embedded social contexts: An overview of self-determination theory. In Richard M. Ryan (Ed.), *The Oxford handbook of human motivation.* New York, NY: Oxford University Press.

Deci, Edward L., & Ryan, Richard M. (2012b). Self-determination theory. In Paul A. M. Van Lange, Arie Kruglanski, & E. Tory Higgins (Eds.), *Handbook of theories of social psychology* (Vol. 1). Thousand Oaks, CA: Sage.

DeGeneres, Ellen. (2005). Quote from interview "The real Ellen story— Coming out party London." Retrieved on February 27, 2005, from http://www.ellen-degeneres.com.

Deigh, John. (2014). William James and the rise of the scientific study of emotion. *Emotion Review, 6,* 4–12. doi:10.1177/1754073913496483

Delgado, Ana R. (2004). Order in Spanish colour words: Evidence against linguistic relativity. *British Journal of Psychology, 95,* 81–90.

DeLisi, Richard, & Staudt, Joanne. (1980). Individual differences in college students' performance on formal operations tasks. *Journal of Applied Developmental Psychology, 1,* 163–174.

Dell, Paul F., & O'Neil, John Allison (Eds.). (2009). *Dissociation and the dissociative disorders: DSM-V and beyond.* New York, NY: Routledge.

Della Sala, Sergio. (2010). *Forgetting.* New York, NY: Psychology Press.

Dell'Osso, Bernardo; & Altamura, A. Carlo. (2014). Transcranial brain stimulation techniques for major depression: Should we extend TMS lessons to tDCS? *Clinical Practice & Epidemiology in Mental Health, 10,* 92–93.

Delman, Howard M.; Robinson, Delbert G.; & Kimmelblatt, Craig A. (2008). General psychiatric symptoms measures. In A. John Rush, Jr., Michael B. First, & Deborah Blacker (Eds.), *Handbook of psychiatric measures* (2nd ed., pp. 61–82). Arlington, VA: American Psychiatric Publishing.

Delmas, P.; Hao, J.; & Rodat-Despoix, L. (2011). Molecular mechanisms of mechanotransduction in mammalian sensory neurons. *Nature Reviews Neuroscience, 12*(3), 139–153.

DeLoache, Judy S.; Chiong, Cynthia; Sherman, Kathleen; Islam, Nadia; Vanderborght, Mieke; Troseth, Georgene L.; Strouse, Gabrielle A.; & O'Doherty, Katherine. (2010). Do babies learn from baby media? *Psychological Science, 21*(11), 1570–1574. doi:10.1177/0956797610384145

DeLoache, Judy S., & LoBue, Vanessa. (2009). The narrow fellow in the grass: Human infants associate snakes and fear. *Developmental Science, 12*(1), 201–207. doi:10.1111/j.1467-7687.2008.00753.x

DeLongis, Anita; Coyne, James C.; Dakof, C.; Folkman, Susan; & Lazarus, Richard S. (1982). Relationship of daily hassles, uplifts, and major life events to health status. *Health Psychology, 1,* 119–136.

Delzenne, Nathalie M.; Blundell, John E.; Brouns, F., Cunningham, K., de Graaf, K., Erkner, A., Lluch, A., & Mars, M., Peters, H.P.F. &

Westerterp-Plantenga, M. (2010). Gastrointestinal targets of appetite regulation in humans. *Obesity Reviews, 11*, 234–250.

Demb, Jonathan B., & Brainard, David H. (2010). Neurons show their true colors. *Nature, 467*, 670–671.

Demerouti, Evangelia; Mostert, Karina; & Bakker, Arnold B. (2010). Burnout and work engagement: A thorough investigation of the independency of both constructs. *Journal of Occupational Health Psychology, 15*(3), 209–222.

Deneris, Evan S., & Wyler, Steven C. (2012). Serotonergic transcriptional networks and potential importance to mental health. *Nature Neuroscience, 15*(4), 519–27. doi:10.1038/nn.3039

Denk, Franziska; McMahon, Stephen B.; & Tracey, Irene. (2014). Pain vulnerability: A neurobiological perspective. *Nature Neuroscience, 17*, 192–200. doi:10.1038/nn.3628

Dennis, J. Michael, & Li, Rick (2007, October 10). More honest answers to Web surveys? A study of data collection mode effects. *Journal of Online Research 10*(7), 1–15.

Dennis, Nancy A., & Cabeza, Roberto. (2008). Neuroimaging of healthy cognitive aging. In F. I. M. Craik and T. A. Salthouse (Eds.), *The handbook of aging and cognition* (pp. 1–54). Mahwah, NJ: Erlbaum.

Dennis, Tracy A., & O'Toole, Laura J. (2014). Mental health on the go: Effects of a gamified attention-bias modification mobile application in trait-anxious adults. *Clinical Psychological Science.* Advance online publication. doi:10.1177/2167702614522228

Denny, Dallas, & Pittman, Cathy. (2007). Gender identity: From dualism to diversity. In Mitchell S. Tepper & Annette Fuglsang Owens (Eds.). *Sexual Health. Vol 1: Psychological foundations. Praeger perspectives: Sex, love, and psychology.* Westport, CT: Praeger/Greenwood.

Derluyn, Ilse; Broekaert, Eric; Schuyten, Gilberte; & De Temmerman, Els. (2004). Post-traumatic stress in former Ugandan child soldiers. *Lancet, 363*(9412), 861–863.

Derry, Heather; Fagundes, Christopher; Andridge, Rebecca; Glaser, Ronald; Malarkey, William; & Kiecolt-Glaser, Janice. (2013). Lower subjective social status exaggerates interleukin-6 responses to a laboratory stressor. *Psychoneuroendocrinology, 38*, 2676–2685. doi:10.1016/j.psyneuen.2013.06.026

DeRubeis, Robert J.; Siegle, Greg J.; & Hollon, Steven D. (2008). Cognitive therapy versus medication for depression: Treatment outcomes and neural mechanisms. *Nature Reviews Neuroscience, 9*(10), 788–796. doi:10.1038/nrn2345

Desai, Abhilash K.; Grossberg, George T.; & Chibnall, John T. (2010). Healthy brain aging: A road map. *Clinics in Geriatric Medicine, 26*(1), 1–16.

D'Esposito, Mark, & Postle, Bradley R. (2015). The cognitive neuroscience of working memory. *Annual review of psychology, 66*, 115–141. doi: 10.1146/annurev-psych-010814-015031

Deutsch, Linda. (2013, August 15). 'Clark Rockefeller' gets 27 years for murder. *Boston Globe.* Retrieved from https://www.bostonglobe.com/news/nation/2013/08/15/clark-rockefeller-sentenced-years-for-calif-murder/9QyCqk3OgTHu5fZzfrrsNL/story.html

Deutsch, Morton, & Gerard, Harold B. (1955). A study of normative and informational social influence upon individual judgment. *Journal of Abnormal and Social Psychology, 51*, 629–636.

Deutscher, Guy. (2010). *Through the language glass: Why the world looks different in other languages.* New York, NY: Metropolitan Books/Holt.

DeValois, Russell L., & DeValois, Karen K. (1975). Neural coding of color. In Edward C. Carterette & Morton P. Friedman (Eds.), *Handbook of perception* (Vol. 5). New York, NY: Academic Press.

Devane, William A.; Hanus, L.; Breuer, A.; Pertwee, R. G.; Stevenson, L. A.; Griffin, G.; & others. (1992). Isolation and structure of a brain constituent that binds to the cannabinoid receptor. *Science, 258*, 1946–1949.

Devine, Patricia G. (2001). Implicit prejudice and stereotyping: How automatic are they? Introduction to the special section. *Journal of Personality and Social Psychology, 81*, 757–759.

Devine, Patricia, G.; Forscher, Patrick S.; Austin, Anthony J.; & Cox, William T.L. (2012). Long-term reduction in implicit race bias: A prejudice habit-breaking intervention. *Journal of Experimental Social Psychology, 48*, 1267–1278. doi:10.1016/j.jesp.2012.06.003

DeVos, George Alphonse. (1992). *Social cohesion and alienation: Minorities in the United States and Japan.* Boulder, CO: Westview Press.

DeVos, George Alphonse; & Wagatsuma, Hiroshi. (1967). *Japan's invisible race: Caste in culture and personality.* Berkeley and Los Angeles: University of California Press.

DeWall, Nathan C., & Bushman, Brad J. (2009). Hot under the collar in a lukewarm environment: Words associated with hot temperature increase aggressive thoughts and hostile perceptions. *Journal of Experimental Social Psychology, 45*(4), 1045–1047. doi:10.1016/j.jesp.2009.05.003

Dewsbury, Donald A. (1998). Celebrating E. L. Thorndike a century after *Animal Intelligence. American Psychologist, 53*, 1121–1124.

DeYoung, Colin G. (2010). Toward a theory of the Big Five. *Psychological Inquiry, 21*, 26–33.

DeYoung, Colin G., & Gray, Jeremy R. (2009). Personality neuroscience: Explaining individual differences in affect, behavior, and cognition. In P. J. Corr & G. Matthews (Eds.), *Cambridge handbook of personality* (pp. 323–346). New York, NY: Cambridge University Press.

DeYoung, Colin G.; Hirsh, Jacob B.; Shane, Matthew S.; Papademetris, Xenophon; Rajeevan, Nallakkandi; & Gray, Jeremy R. (2010). Testing predictions from personality neuroscience: Brain structure and the big five. *Psychological Science, 21*(6), 820–828.

Dhabhar, Firdaus S. (2011). Effects of stress on immune function: Implications for immunoprotection and immunopathology. In Richard J. Contrada & Andrew Baum (Eds.), *The handbook of stress science: Biology, psychology, and health.* New York, NY: Springer.

Diamantopoulou, Sofia; Verhulst, Frank C.; & van der Ende, Jan. (2010). Testing developmental pathways to antisocial personality problems. *Journal of Abnormal Child Psychology: An official publication of the International Society for Research in Child and Adolescent Psychopathology, 38*(1), 91–103.

Diamond, Adele. (2009). The interplay of biology and the environment broadly defined. *Developmental Psychology, 45*, 1–8, 361.

Diamond, Solomon. (2001). Wundt before Leipzig. In Robert W. Rieber & David K. Robinson (Eds.), *Wilhelm Wundt in history: The making of a scientific psychology.* New York, NY: Kluwer Academic/Plenum Publishers.

DiazGranados, Nancy; Ibrahim, Lobna; Brutsche, Nancy; Ameli, Rezvan; Henter, Ioline, D.; Luckenbaugh, David A.; Machado-Vieira, Rodrigo; & others. (2010). Rapid resolution of suicidal ideation after a single infusion of an NMDA antagonist in patients with treatment-resistant major depressive disorder. *Journal of Clinical Psychiatry, 71*(12), 1605–1611. doi:10.4088/JCP.09m05327blu

Dick, Danielle M.; Agrawal, Arpana; Keller, Matthew C.; Adkins, Amy; Aliev, Fazil; Monroe, Scott; Hewitt, John K.; Kendler, Kenneth S.; & Sher, Kenneth J. (2015). Candidate gene–environment interaction research: Reflections and recommendations. *Perspectives on Psychological Science, 10*, 37–59. doi:10.1177/1745691614556682

Dick, Danielle M., & Rose, Richard J. (2002). Behavior genetics: What's new? What's next? *Current Directions in Psychological Science, 11*, 70–74.

Dickins, Thomas E. (2011). Evolutionary approaches to behaviour. In Vren Swami (Ed.), *Evolutionary psychology: A critical introduction.* Oxford, England: Wiley-Blackwell.

Dickinson, Anthony, & Balleine, Bernard W. (2000). Causal cognition and goal-directed action. In Cecilia Heyes & Ludwig Huber (Eds.), *The evolution of cognition.* Cambridge, MA: MIT Press.

Dictionary of Occupational Titles. (1991). Washington, DC: U.S. Government Printing Office.

Didonna, Fabrizio (Ed.). (2008). *Clinical handbook of mindfulness.* New York, NY: Springer.

Didonna, Fabrizio (Ed.). (2009). *Clinical handbook of mindfulness.* New York, NY: Springer.

Diefenbach, Donald L., & West, Mark D. (2007). Television and attitudes toward mental health issues: Cultivation analysis and the third-person effect. *Journal of Community Psychology, 35*(2), 181–195.

Dijk, Derk-Jan; & Lockley, Steven W. (2002). Integration of human sleep-wake regulation and circadian rhythmicity. *Journal of Applied Physiology, 92*, 852–862.

Dijk, Derk-Jan, Duffy, Jeanne F.; Silva, Edward J.; Shanahan, Theresa L.; Boivin, Diane B.; & Czeisler, Charles A. (2012). Amplitude reduction and phase shifts of melatonin, cortisol and other circadian rhythms after a gradual advance of sleep and light exposure in humans. *PLOS ONE, 7*, Article e30037. doi:10.1371/journal.pone.0030037

Dijksterhuis, Ap, & Aarts, Henk. (2010). Goals, attention, and (un)consciousness. *Annual Review of Psychology, 61*, 467–90. doi:10.1146/annurev.psych.093008.100445

Dijksterhuis, Ap; Aarts, Henk; & Smith, Pamela K. (2005). The power of the subliminal: On subliminal persuasion and other potential applications. In Ran R. Hassin, James S. Uleman, & John A. Bargh (Eds.), *The new unconscious.* New York, NY: Oxford University Press.

Dijksterhuis, Ap, & Nordgren, Loran F. (2006). A theory of unconscious thought. *Perspectives on Psychological Science, 1*, 95–109.

Dimidjian, Sona, & Hollon, Steven D. (2010). How would we know if psychotherapy were harmful? *American Psychologist, 65*(1), 21–33.

Dinsmoor, James A. (1992). Setting the record straight: The social views of B.F. Skinner. *American Psychologist, 47*, 1454–1463.

Disanto, Giulio; Morahan, Lacey V.; DeLuca, Gabriele C.; Giovannoni, Gavin; Ebers, George C.; & Ramagopalan, Sreeram V. (2012). Seasonal distribution of psychiatric births in England. *Season of Birth and Psychiatric Disease, 7*, 1–4.

Dishion, Thomas J., & Tipsord, Jessica M. (2011). Peer contagion in child and adolescent social and emotional development. *Annual Review of Psychology, 62*, 189–214. doi:10.1146/annurev.psych.093008.100412

Dittmann, Melissa. (2005, July–August). Fighting phobias: Hughes's germ phobia revealed in psychological autopsy. *Monitor on Psychology, 36*, 102.

Dixon, John F., & Hokin, Lowell E. (1998, July 7). Lithium acutely inhibits and chronically up-regulates and stabilizes glutamate by presynaptic nerve endings in mouse cerebral cortex. *Proceedings of the National Academy of Sciences, USA, 95*, 8363–8368.

Dobson, Deborah, & Dobson, Keith. (2009). *Evidence-based practice of cognitive-behavioral therapy.* New York, NY: Guilford Press.

Dodd, Seetal; Brnabic, Alan J. M.; Berk, Lesley; Fitzgerald, Paul B.; de Castella, Anthony R.; Filia, Sacha, … Berk, Michael. (2010). A prospective study of the impact of smoking on outcomes in bipolar and schizoaffective disorder. *Comprehensive Psychiatry, 51*(5), 504–509.

Dohrenwend, Bruce P. (2006). Inventorying stressful life events as risk factors for psychopathology: Toward resolution of the problem of intracategory variability. *Psychological Bulletin, 132*(3), 477–495.

Dohrenwend, Bruce P.; Yager, Thomas J.; Wall, Melanie M.; & Adams, Ben G. (2013). The roles of combat exposure, personal vulnerability, and involvement in harm to civilian prisoners in Vietnam-war-related posttraumatic stress disorder. *Clinical Psychological Science, 2*, 223–238. doi:10.1177/2167702612469355

Domhoff, G. William. (2003). *The scientific study of dreams: Neural networks, cognitive development, and content analysis.* Washington, DC: American Psychological Association.

Domhoff, G. William. (2005a). Refocusing the neurocognitive approach to dreams: A critique of the Hobson versus Solms debate. *Dreaming, 15*, 3–20.

Domhoff, G. William. (2005b). The content of dreams: Methodologic and theoretical implications. In Meir H. Kryger, Thomas Roth, & William C. Dement (Eds.), *Principles and practice of sleep medicine* (4th ed.). Philadelphia, PA: Elsevier Saunders.

Domhoff, G. William. (2007). Realistic simulation and bizarreness in dream content: Past findings and suggestions for future research. In Deirdre Barrett & Patrick McNamara (Eds.), *The new science of dreaming: Content, recall, and personality characteristics* (Vol. 2). Westport, CT: Praeger Press.

Domhoff, G. William. (2010). The case for a cognitive theory of dreams. Retrieved on July 13, 2011 from http://dreamresearch.net/Library/domhoff_2010.html

Domhoff, G. William. (2011). The neural substrate for dreaming: Is it a subsystem of the default network? *Consciousness and Cognition. 20*(4), 1163–1174. doi:10.1016/j.concog.2011.03.001

Dorahy, Martin J.; Brand, Bethany L.; Sar, Vedat; Kruger, Christa; Stavropoulos, Pam; Martinez-Taboas, Alfonso; … Middleton, Warwick. (2014). Dissociative identity disorder: An empirical overview. *Australian and New Zealand Journal of Psychiatry, 48*, 402–417. doi:10.1177/0004867414527523

Dornbusch, Sanford M.; Glasgow, Kristan L.; & Lin, I-Chun. (1996). The social structure of schooling. *Annual Review of Psychology, 47*, 401–429.

Doss, Brian D.; Rhoades, Galena K.; Stanley, Scott M.; & Markman, Howard J. (2009). The effect of the transition to parenthood on relationship quality: An 8-year prospective study. *Journal of Personality and Social Psychology, 96*(3), 601–619.

Dougherty, Darin D.; Rezai, Ali R.; Carpenter, Linda L.; Howland, Robert H.; Bhati, Mahendra T.; O'Reardon, John P.; … Malone, Donald A., Jr. (2015). A randomized sham-controlled trial of deep brain stimulation of the ventral capsule/ventral striatum for chronic treatment-resistant depression. *Biological Psychiatry, 78*, 240–248. doi:10.1016/j.biopsych.2014.11.023

Douglas, Kevin S.; Gay, Laura S.; & Hart, Stephen D. (2009). Psychosis as a risk factor for violence to others: A meta-analysis. *Psychological Bulletin, 135*, 679–706.

Dovidio, John F. (1984). Helping behavior and altruism: An empirical and conceptual overview. *Advances in Experimental Social Psychology, 17*, 361–427.

Dovidio, John F., & Gaertner, Samuel L. (2010). Intergroup bias. In S. T. Fiske, D. T. Gilbert & G. Lindzey (Eds.), *Handbook of social psychology, Vol. 2* (pp. 1084–1121). Hoboken, NJ: Wiley.

Dovidio, John F.; Piliavin, Jane Allyn; & Schroeder, David A. (2006). *The social psychology of prosocial behavior.* Mahwah, NJ: Erlbaum.

Drabick, Deborah A., & Baugh, David. (2010). A community-based approach to preventing youth violence: What can we learn from the playground? *Progress in Community Health Partnerships, 4*(3), 189–196. doi:10.1353/S1557055X10300052/cpr.2010.0002

Draganski, Bogdan; Gaser, Christian; Busch, Volker; Schuierer, Gerhard; Bogdahn, Ulrich; & May, Arne. (2004). Neuroplasticity: Changes in grey matter induced by training. *Nature, 427*, 311–312.

Draganski, Bogdan; Gaser, Christian; Kempermann, Gerd; Kuhn, H. Georg; Winkler, Jürgen; Büchel, Christian; & May, Arne. (2006). Temporal and spatial dynamics of brain structure changes during extensive learning. *Journal of Neuroscience, 26*(23), 6314–6317.

Drea, Christine M. (2015). D'scent of man: A comparative survey of primate chemosignaling in relation to sex. *Hormones and Behavior, 68*, 117–133. doi:10.1016/j.yhbeh.2014.08.001

Drescher, Jack, & Zucker, Kenneth J. (2006). *Position statement on therapies focused on attempts to change sexual orientation (reparative or conversion therapies).* Binghamton, NY: Harrington Park/Haworth Press.

Drews, Frank A.; Pasupathi, Monisha; & Strayer, David L. (2008). Passenger and cell phone conversations in simulated driving. *Journal of Experimental Psychology: Applied, 14*, 398–400.

Driemeyer, Joenna; Boyke, Janina; Gaser, Christian; Büchel, Christian; & May, Arne. (2008). Changes in gray matter induced by learning—Revisited. *PLOS ONE, 3*, e2669.

Dror, Otniel E. (2014). The Cannon–Bard thalamic theory of emotions: A brief genealogy and reappraisal. *Emotion Review, 6*, 13–20. doi:10.1177/1754073913494898

Drouyer, Elise; Rieux, Camille; Hut, Roelof A.; & Cooper, Howard M. (2007). Responses of suprachiasmatic nucleus neurons to light and dark adaptation: Relative contributions of melanopsin and rod–cone inputs. *Journal of Neuroscience, 27*(36), 9623–9631.

Drum, David J.; Brownson, Chris; Denmark, Adryon Burton; & Smith, Shanna E. (2009). New data on the nature of suicidal crises in college students: Shifting the paradigm. *Professional Psychology: Research and Practice, 40*, 213–222. doi:10.1037/a0014465

Drummond, Kelley D.; Bradley, Susan J.; Peterson-Badali, Michele; & Zucker, Kenneth J. (2008). A follow-up study of girls with gender identity disorder. *Developmental Psychology, 44*, 34–45.

Drury, Scott; Hutchens, Scott A.; Shuttlesworth, Duane E.; & White, Carole L. (2012). Philip G. Zimbardo on his career and the Stanford Prison Experiment's 40th anniversary. *History of Psychology, 15*(2), 161–170. doi:10.1037/a0025884

Dryden, Windy. (2008). *Rational emotive behaviour therapy: Distinctive features.* New York, NY: Routledge.

Dryden, Windy. (2009). *How to think and intervene like an REBT therapist.* New York, NY: Routledge.

Dryden, Windy, & Branch, Rhena. (2008). *Fundamentals of rational emotive behaviour therapy: A training handbook.* Hoboken, NJ: Wiley.

DSM-5. (2013). *Diagnostic and statistical manual of mental disorders* (Fifth edition). Washington, DC: American Psychiatric Association.

DuBreuil, Susan C., & Spanos, Nicholas P. (1993). Psychological treatment of warts. In Judith W. Rhue, Steven Jay Lynn, & Irving Kirsch (Eds). *Handbook of clinical hypnosis.* Washington, DC: American Psychological Association. doi:10.1037/10274-027

Duckworth, Angela L.; Peterson, Christopher; Matthews, Michael D.; & Kelly, Dennis R. (2007). Grit: Perseverance and passion for long-term goals. *Journal of Personality and Social Psychology, 92,* 1087–1101.

Dudai, Yadin. (2004). The neurobiology of consolidations, or, How stable is the engram? *Annual Review of Psychology, 55,* 51–86.

Dudai, Yadin; Nalbantian, Suzanne; Matthews, Paul M.; & McClelland, James L. (2011). The Engram revisited: On the elusive permanence of memory. *The memory process: Neuroscientific and humanistic perspectives* (pp. 29–40). Cambridge, MA: MIT Press.

Dukart, Juergen; Regen, Francesca; Kherif, Ferath; Colla, Michael; Bajbouj, Malek; Heuser, Isabella; Frackowiak, Richard S.; & others. (2014). Electroconvulsive therapy-induced brain plasticity determines therapeutic outcome in mood disorders. *Proceedings of the National Academy of Sciences (PNAS), 111*(3), 1156–1161. doi:10.1073/pnas.1321399111

Dulin, Patrick; Hanson, Bridget; & King, Diane. (2013). Perceived control as a longitudinal moderator of late-life stressors on depressive symptoms. *Aging & Mental Health, 17,* 718–723. doi:10.1080/13607863.2013.784956

Duke, Aaron A.; Giancola, Peter R.; Morris, David H.; Holt, Jerred C. D.; & Gunn, Rachel L. (2011). Alcohol dose and aggression: Another reason why drinking more is a bad idea. *Journal of Studies on Alcohol and Drugs, 72*(1), 34–43.

Dumith, Samuel C.; Hallal, Pedro C.; Reis, Rodrigo S.; & Kohl, Harold W. (2011). Worldwide prevalence of physical inactivity and its association with human development index in 76 countries. *Preventive Medicine, 53,* 24–28.

Duncker, Karl. (1929/1967). Induced motion. In Willis D. Ellis (Ed.), *Source book of Gestalt psychology.* New York, NY: Humanities Press.

Duncker, Karl. (1945). On problem solving. *Psychological Monographs, 58*(Whole No. 270).

Dunham, Yarrow; Chen, Eva E.; & Banaji, Mahzarin R. (2013). Two signatures of implicit intergroup attitudes: Developmental invariance and early enculturation. *Psychological Science, 24*(6), 860–868.

Dunkel Schetter, Christine. (2011). Psychological science on pregnancy: Stress processes, biopsychosocial models, and emerging research issues. *Annual Review of Psychology, 62,* 531–58. doi:10.1146/annurev.psych.031809.130727

Dunlap, Glen; Iovannone, Rose; Wilson, Kelly J.; Kincaid, Donald K.; & Strain, Phillip. (2010). Prevent-teach-reinforce: A standardized model of school-based behavioral intervention. *Journal of Positive Behavior Interventions, 12*(1), 9–22.

Dunlosky, John, & Rawson, Katherine A. (2015). Practice tests, spaced practice, and successive relearning: Tips for classroom use and for guiding students' learning. *Scholarship of Teaching and Learning in Psychology, 1,* 72–78. doi:10.1037/stl0000024

Dunlosky, John; Rawson, Katherine A.; Marsh, Elizabeth J.; Nathan, Mitchell J.; & Willingham, Daniel T. (2013). Improving students' learning with effective learning techniques: Promising directions from cognitive and educational psychology. *Psychological Science in the Public Interest, 14*(1), 4–58. doi:10.1177/1529100612453266

Eagly, Alice H.; Ashmore, Richard. D.; Makhijani, Mona G.; & Longo, Laura C. (1991). What is beautiful is good, but ...: A metaanalytic review of research on the physical attractiveness stereotype. *Psychological Bulletin, 110,* 109–128.

Eagly, Alice H.; & Wood, Wendy (2011). Feminism and the evolution of sex differences and similarities. *Sex Roles, 64,* 758–767. doi:10.1007/s11199-011-9949-9

Eagly, Alice H., & Wood, Wendy. (2013). The nature–nurture debates: 25 years of challenges in understanding the psychology of gender. *Perspectives on Psychological Science, 8*(3), 340–357.

Eastman, Charmane I.; Gazda Clifford J.; Burgess Helen J.; Crowley, Stephanie J.; & Fogg, Louis F. (2005). Advancing circadian rhythms before eastward flight: A strategy to prevent or reduce jet lag. *Sleep, 28,* 33–44.

Easton, Caroline J.; Mandel, Dolores; & Babuscio, Theresa. (2007). Differences in treatment outcome between male alcohol dependent offenders of domestic violence with and without positive drug screens. *Addictive Behaviors, 32,* 2151–2163.

Eatock, Ruth Anne, & Songer, Jocelyn E. (2011) Vestibular hair cells and afferents: Two channels for head motion signals. *Annual Review of Neuroscience. 34,* 501–534. doi:10.1146/annurev-neuro-061010-113710

Ebbinghaus, Hermann. (1885/1987). *Memory: A contribution to experimental psychology* (Henry A. Ruger & Clara E. Bussenius, Trans.). New York, NY: Dover.

Eckholm, E. (2013). Court hears gay "conversion therapy" arguments. *New York Times.* Retrieved on July 9, 2013 from http://www.nytimes.com/2013/04/18/us/day-in-court-for-california-law-banning-conversion-therapy.html

Edelson, Meredyth Goldberg. (2006). Are the majority of children with autism mentally retarded? A systematic evaluation of the data. *Focus on Autism and Other Developmental Disabilities, 21,* 66–83.

Edenfield, Teresa M., & Blumenthal, James A. (2011). Exercise and stress reduction. In Richard J. Contrada & Andrew Baum (Eds.), *The handbook of stress science: Biology, psychology, and health.* New York, NY: Springer.

Edlund, Mark J.; Fortney John C.; Reaves, Christina M.; Pyne, Jeffrey M.; & Mittal, Dinesh. (2008). Beliefs about depression and depression treatment among depressed veterans. *Medical Care, 46,* 581–589.

Edmonds, Grant W.; Goldberg, Lewis R.; Hampson, Sarah E.; & Barckley, Maureen. (2013). Personality stability from childhood to midlife: Relating teachers' assessments in elementary school to observer- and self-ratings 40 years later. *Journal of Research in Personality, 47,* 505–513. doi:10.1016/j.jrp.2013.05.003

Edwards, Anthony G. P., & Armitage, Peter. (1992). An experiment to test the discriminating ability of graphologists. *Personality and Individual Differences, 13,* 69–74.

Edwards, Robert R.; Campbell, Claudia; Jamison, Robert N.; & Wiech, Katja. (2009). The neurobiological underpinnings of coping with pain. *Current Directions in Psychological Science, 18,* 237–241. doi:10.1111/j.1467-8721.2009.01643.x

EEOC. (1999). Uniform guidelines on employee selection procedures, & testing and assessment: An employer's guide to good hiring practices. U.S. Department of Labor, Employment and Training Administration: Author.

Egan, Louisa C.; Santos, Laurie R.; & Bloom, Paul. (2007). The origins of cognitive dissonance: Evidence from children and monkeys. *Psychological Science, 18*(11), 978–983. doi:10.1111/j.1467-9280.2007.02012.x

Egan, Susan K., & Perry, David G. (2001). Gender identity: A multidimensional analysis with implications for psychosocial adjustment. *Developmental Psychology, 37,* 451–463.

Eghigian, Greg. (2011). Voices from the past: Nelson Sizer's forty years in phrenology. *Psychiatric Times,* pp. 1–4. http://www.psychiatrictimes.com/blog/psych-history/content/article/10168/1844972

Eichenbaum, Howard. (2009). Memory. In G. G. Berntson & J. T. Cacioppo (Eds.), *Handbook of neuroscience for the behavioral sciences, Vol. 1* (pp. 552–566). Hoboken, NJ: Wiley.

Eichstaedt, Johannes; Schwartz, Hansen; Kern, Margaret; Park, Gregory; Labarthe, Darwin; Merchant, Raina; Jha, Sneha; Agrawal, Megha; Dziurzynski, Lukasz A.; Sap, Maarten; Weeg, Christopher; & Larson, Emily E. (2015). Psychological language on Twitter predicts county-level heart disease mortality. *Psychological Science, 26,* 159–169. doi:10.1177/0956797614557867

Einstein, Danielle, & Menzies, Ross G. (2004). The presence of magical thinking in obsessive compulsive disorder. *Behaviour Research and Therapy, 42,* 539–549.

Eisenberg, Nancy; Cumberland, Amanda; Guthrie, Ivanna K.; Murphy, Bridget C.; & Shepard, Stephanie A. (2005). Age changes in prosocial responding and moral reasoning in adolescence and early adulthood. *Journal of Research on Adolescence, 15*(3), 235–260.

Eisenberger, Robert; Armeli, Stephen; & Pretz, Jean. (1998). Can the promise of reward increase creativity? *Journal of Personality and Social Psychology, 74,* 704–714.

Eisenberger, Robert, & Cameron, Judy. (1996). Detrimental effects of reward: Reality or myth? *American Psychologist, 51,* 1153–1166.

Eisenstein, Michael. (2010). Taste: More than meets the mouth. *Nature, 468*(7327), S18–S19.

Ekman, Paul. (1980). *The face of man.* New York, NY: Garland.

Ekman, Paul. (1982). *Emotion in the human face* (2nd ed.). New York, NY: Cambridge University Press.

Ekman, Paul. (1992). Facial expressions of emotion: New findings, new questions. *Psychological Science, 3,* 34–38.

Ekman, Paul. (1993). Facial expression and emotion. *American Psychologist, 48,* 384–392.

Ekman, Paul. (1998). Afterword. In Charles Darwin (1872/1998), *The expression of the emotions in man and animals.* New York, NY: Oxford University Press.

Ekman, Paul (2003). *Emotions revealed: Recognizing faces and feelings to improve communication and emotional life.* New York, NY: Holt.

Ekman, Paul. (2009, May). Quoted in Novotney, A. The truth behind 'Lies.' *Monitor on Psychology,* p. 40.

Ekman, Paul, & Cordaro, Daniel. (2011). What is meant by calling emotions basic? *Emotion Review, 3,* 364–370. doi:10.1177/1754073911410740

Ekman, Paul, & Davidson, Richard J. (1993). Voluntary smiling changes regional brain activity. *Psychological Science, 4,* 342–345.

Ekman, Paul; Davidson, Richard J.; Ricard, Matthieu; & Wallace, B. Alan. (2005). Buddhist and psychological perspectives on emotions and well-being. *Current Directions in Psychological Science, 14*(2), 59–63. doi:10.1111/j.0963-7214.2005.00335.x

Ekman, Paul, & Friesen, Wallace V. (1978). *Facial action coding system: A technique for the measurement of facial movement.* Palo Alto, CA: Consulting Psychologists Press.

Ekman, Paul; Friesen, Wallace V.; O'Sullivan, Maureen; Chan, Anthony; Diacoyanni-Tarlatzis, Irene; Heider, Karl; & others. (1987). Universal and cultural differences in the judgments of facial expressions of emotion. *Journal of Personality and Social Psychology, 53,* 712–717.

Ekman, Paul, & O'Sullivan, Maureen. (2006). From flawed self-assessment to blatant whoppers: The utility of voluntary and involuntary behavior in detecting deception. *Behavioral Sciences and the Law, 24,* 673–686.

Ekman, Paul; O'Sullivan, Maureen; & Frank, Mark G. (1999). A few can catch a liar. *Psychological Science, 10,* 263–266.

Ekwall, Anna Kristensson, & Hallberg, Ingalill Rahm. (2007). The association between caregiving satisfaction, difficulties and coping among older family caregivers. *Journal of Clinical Nursing, 16*(5), 832–844.

Eldar, Sharon; Apter, Alan; Lotan, Daniel; Edgar, Koraly Perez; Naim, Reut; Fox, Nathan A.; . . . Bar-Haim, Yair. (2012). Attention bias modification treatment for pediatric anxiety disorders: A randomized controlled trial. *American Journal of Psychiatry, 169*(2), 213–220.

Elfenbein, Hillary Anger, & Ambady, Nalini. (2002). On the universality and specificity of emotion recognition: A meta-analysis. *Psychological Bulletin, 128,* 203–235.

Elgar, Frank J., & Aitken, Nicole. (2010). Income inequality, trust and homicide in 33 countries. *European Journal of Public Health, 21*(2), 241–246. doi:10.1093/eurpub/ckq068

Eliot, Lise. (2011). The trouble with sex differences. *Neuron, 72,* 895–898. doi:10.1016/j.neuron.2011.12.001

Elkins, Gary; Marcus, Joel; & Bates, Jeff. (2006). Intensive hypnotherapy for smoking cessation: A prospective study. *International Journal of Clinical and Experimental Hypnosis, 54,* 303–315.

Ellin, Abby. (2004, July 18). What your handwriting says about your career. *New York Times.* Retrieved from http://www.nytimes.com/2004/07/18/jobs/what-your-handwriting-says-about-your-career.html

Elliot, J. Andrew, & Maier, Markus A. (2014). Color psychology: Effects of perceiving color on psychological functioning in humans. *Annual Review of Psychology, 65,* 95–120. doi:10.1146/annurev-psych-010213-115035

Elliott, Robert, & Farber, Barry A. (2010). Carl Rogers: Idealistic pragmatist and psychotherapy research pioneer. In Louis G. Castonguay, Christopher J. Muran, Lynne Angus, Jeffrey A. Hayes, Nicholas Ladany, & Timothy Anderson (Eds.), *Bringing psychotherapy research to life: Understanding change through the work of leading clinical researchers* (pp. 17–27). Washington, DC: American Psychological Association.

Elliott, Robert; Greenberg, Leslie S.; & Lietaer, Germain. (2004). Research on experiential psychotherapies. In Michael J. Lambert (Ed.), *Handbook of psychotherapy and behavior change* (5th ed.). Hoboken, NJ: Wiley.

Ellis, Albert. (1991). *Reason and emotion in psychotherapy.* New York, NY: Carol.

Ellis, Albert. (1993). Reflections on rational-emotive therapy. *Journal of Consulting and Clinical Psychology, 61,* 199–201.

Ellis, Albert. (2013). *Better, deeper and more enduring brief therapy: The rational emotive behavior therapy approach.* Routledge.

Ellis, Albert, & Bernard, Michael E. (1985). What is rational-emotive therapy (RET)? In Albert Ellis & Michael E. Bernard (Eds.), *Clinical applications of rational-emotive therapy.* New York, NY: Plenum Press.

Ellis, Albert, & Ellis, Debbie Joffe. (2011). *Rational emotive therapy.* Washington, DC American Psychological Association.

Ellis, Albert, & Harper, Robert A. (1975). *A new guide to rational living.* Hollywood, CA: Wilshire Book Company.

Ellis, Bruce J. (2004). Timing of pubertal maturation in girls: An integrated life history approach. *Psychological Bulletin, 130,* 920–958.

Ellis, Bruce J., & Essex, Marilyn J. (2007). Family environments, adrenarche, and sexual maturation: A longitudinal test of a life history model. *Child Development, 78,* 1799–1817.

Ellis, Pete M., & Dronsfield, Alan T. (2013). Antabuse's diamond anniversary: Still sparkling on? *Drug and Alcohol Review, 32,* 342–344. doi:10.1111/dar.12018

Ellwardt, Lea; Van Tilburg, Theo; & Aartsen, Marja. (2015a). The mix matters: Complex personal networks relate to higher cognitive functioning in old age. *Social Science & Medicine, 125,* 107–115. doi:10.1016/j.socscimed.2014.05.007

Ellwardt, Lea; van Tilburg, Theo; Aartsen, Marja; Wittek, Rafael; & Steverink, Nardi. (2015b). Personal networks and mortality risk in older adults: A twenty-year longitudinal study. *PLOS ONE, 10*(3), 11–13. doi:10.1371/journal.pone.0116731

Elson, Malte, & Ferguson, Christopher J. (2014a). Does doing media violence research make one aggressive? The ideological rigidity of social-cognitive theories of media violence and a response to Bushman and Huesmann (2013), Krahé (2013), and Warburton (2013). *European Psychologist, 19,* 68–75. doi:10.1027/1016-9040/a000185

Elson, Malte, & Ferguson, Christopher J. (2014b). Twenty-five years of research on violence in digital games and aggression: Empirical evidence, perspectives, and a debate gone astray. *European Psychologist, 19,* 33–46. doi:10.1027/1016-9040/a000147

Emery, Nathan J., & Clayton, Nicola S. (2009). Comparative social cognition. *Annual Review of Psychology, 60,* 87–113. doi:10.1146/annurev.psych.60.110707.163526

Emmelkamp, Paul M. G. (2004). Behavior therapy with adults. In Michael J. Lambert (Ed.), *Bergin and Garfield's handbook of psychotherapy and behavior change* (5th ed.). New York, NY: Wiley.

Emmons, Robert A., & McCullough, Michael E. (2003). Counting blessings versus burdens: An experimental investigation of gratitude and subjective wellbeing in daily life. *Journal of Personality and Social Psychology, 84,* 377–389.

Emmons, Robert, A., & Stern, Robin. (2013). Gratitude as a psychotherapeutic intervention. *Journal of Clinical Psychology, 69,* 846–855. doi:10.1002/jclp.22020

Empson, Jacob. (2002). *Sleep and dreaming* (3rd ed.). New York, NY: Palgrave/St. Martin's Press.

Engelhardt, Christopher R.; Mazurek, Micah O.; Hilgard, Joseph; Rouder, Jeffrey N.; & Bartholow, Bruce D. (2015). Effects of violent-video-game exposure on aggressive behavior, aggressive-thought accessibility, and aggressive affect among adults with and without autism spectrum disorder. *Psychological Science, 26,* 1187–1200. doi:10.1177/0956797615583038

England, Lynndie. (2004, May 12). Quoted in "Army private 'ordered to pose'." *Cable News Network (CNN).* Accessed on May 12, 2004, from http://www.cnn.com/2004/US/05/12/prisoner.abuse.england.ap/index.html

England, Lynndie. (2005, October 2). Quoted in "Behind the Abu Ghraib photos." *Dateline NBC.* Accessed on November 30, 2005, from http://msnbc.msn.com/id/9532670

Engle, R. Adam. (2011). Personal communication.

English, Horace B. (1929). Three cases of the "conditioned fear response." *Journal of Abnormal and Social Psychology, 24,* 221–225.

Enriori, Pablo J.; Evans, Anne E.; Sinnayah, Puspha; & Cowley, Michael A. (2006). Leptin resistance and obesity. *Obesity, 14*(Suppl. 5), 254S–258S.

Epel, Elissa S. (2009a). Psychological and metabolic stress: A recipe for accelerated cellular aging? *Hormones, 8,* 7–22.

Epel, Elissa S. (2009b). Telomeres in a life-span perspective: A new "psychobiomarker"? *Current Directions in Psychological Science, 18,* 6–10.

Epel, Elissa S.; Blackburn, Elizabeth H.; Lin, Jue; Dhabhar, Firdaus S.; Adler, Nancy E.; Morrow, Jason D.; & Cawthon, Richard M. (2004). Accelerated telomere shortening in response to life stress. *PNAS, 101*(49), 17312–17315.

Epel, Elissa; Daubenmier, Jennifer; Moskowitz, Judith Tedlie; Folkman, Susan; & Blackburn, Elizabeth. (2009). Can meditation slow rate of cellular aging? Cognitive stress, mindfulness, and telomeres. *Annals of the New York Academy of Sciences, 1172,* 34–53.

Epel, Elissa S.; Lin, Jue; Dhabhar, Firdaus S.; Wolkowitz, Owen M.; Puterman, E.; Karan, Lori; & Blackburn, Elizabeth H. (2010). Dynamics of telomerase activity in response to acute psychological stress. *Brain, Behavior, and Immunity, 24,* 531–539. doi:10.1016/j.bbi.2009.11.018

Epstein, Leonard H.; Leddy, John J.; & Temple, Jennifer L. (2007). Food reinforcement and eating: A multilevel analysis. *Psychological Bulletin, 133,* 884–906.

Epstein Leonard H.; Salvy, Sarah J.; Carr, K. A.; Dearing, Kelly K.; & Bickel, W. K. (2010). Food reinforcement, delay discounting and obesity. *Physiology and Behavior, 100,* 438–445.

Epstein, Russell, & Kanwisher, Nancy. (1998). A cortical representation of the local visual environment. *Nature, 392,* 598–601.

Epstein, Seymour. (2010). The big five model: Grandiose ideas about surface traits as the foundation of a general theory of personality. *Psychological Inquiry, 21*(1), 34–39.

Erdelyi, Matthew Hugh. (2006a). The unified theory of repression. *Behavioral and Brain Sciences, 29,* 499–551. doi:10.1017/S0140525X06009113

Erdelyi, Matthew Hugh. (2006b). The return of the repressed. *Behavioral and Brain Sciences, 29*(5), Oct 2006, 535–551. doi:10.1017/S0140525X06479115

Erdelyi, Matthew Hugh. (2010). The ups and downs of memory. *American Psychologist, 65,* 623–633.

Erdelyi, Matthew Hugh. (2014). The interpretation of dreams, and of jokes. *Review of General Psychology, 18,* 115–126. doi:10.1037/gpr0000002

Erickson, Kirk I. (2011, February 7). Quoted in "Fitness: A walk to remember? Study says yes. *New York Times.* Retrieved from http://www.-nytimes.com/2011/02/08/health/research/08fitness.html

Erickson, Kirk I.; Voss, Michelle W.; Prakash, Ruchika S.; Basak, Chandramallika; Szabo, Amanda; Chaddock, Laura; & others. (2011). Exercise training increases size of hippocampus and improves memory. *Proceedings of the National Academy of Sciences, 108*(7), 3017–3022.

Erikson, Erik H. (1964a). *Childhood and society* (Rev. ed.). New York, NY: Norton.

Erikson, Erik H. (1964b). *Insight and responsibility.* New York, NY: Norton.

Erikson, Erik H. (1968). *Identity: Youth and crisis.* New York, NY: Norton.

Erikson, Erik H. (1982). *The life cycle completed: A review.* New York, NY: Norton.

Erikson, Erik H.; Erikson, Joan M.; & Kivnick, Helen Q. (1986). *Vital involvement in old age: The experience of old age in our time.* New York, NY: Norton.

Eriksson, Cynthia B.; Vande Kemp, Hendrika; Gorsuch, Richard; Hoke, Stephen; & Foy, David W. (2001). Trauma exposure and PTSD symptoms in international relief and development personnel. *Journal of Traumatic Stress, 14,* 205–219.

Eriksson, Peter S.; Perfilieva, Ekaterina; Björk-Eriksson, Thomas; Alborn, Ann-Marie; Nordborg, Claes; Peterson, Daniel A.; & Gage, Fred H. (1998). Neurogenesis in the adult hippocampus. *Nature Medicine, 4,* 1313–1317.

Eroglu, Cagla, & Barres, Ben A. (2010). Regulation of synaptic connectivity by glia. *Nature 468,* 223–231. doi:10.1038/nature09612

Ersoy, Betul; Balkan, C.; & Gunnay, T. (2005). The factors affecting the relation between the menarcheal age of mother and daughter. *Child: Care, Health and Development, 31,* 303–308.

Eschweiler, Gerhard W.; Vonthein, Reinhard; & Bode, Ruediger. (2007). Clinical efficacy and cognitive side effects of bifrontal versus right unilateral electroconvulsive therapy (ECT): A short-term randomised controlled trial in pharmaco-resistant major depression. *Journal of Affective Disorders, 101*(1–3), 149–157.

Espay, Alberto J.; Norris, Matthew M.; Eliassen, James C.; Dwivedi, Alok; Smith, Matthew S.; Banks, Chrisi; Allendorfer, Jane B.; Lang, Anthony E.; Fleck, David E.; Linke, Michael J.; & Szaflarski, Jerzy P. (2015). Placebo effect of medication cost in Parkinson disease: A randomized double-blind study. *Neurology, 84,* 1–9.

Esses, Victoria M.; Jackson, Lynne M.; & Dovidio, John F. (2005). Instrumental relations among groups: Group competition, conflict, and prejudice. In John F. Dovidio, John, Peter Glick, & Laurie A. Rudman (Eds.), *On the nature of prejudice: Fifty years after Allport* (pp. 227–243). Malden, MA: Blackwell.

Estes, William K., & Skinner, B. F. (1941). Some quantitative properties of anxiety. *Journal of Experimental Psychology, 29,* 390–400.

Evans, Rand B. (1991). E. B. Titchener on scientific psychology and technology. In Gregory A. Kimble, Michael Wertheimer, & Charlotte White (Eds.), *Portraits of pioneers in psychology* (Vol. 1). Washington, DC: American Psychological Association.

Evans, Rand B., & Rilling, Mark. (2000). How the challenge of explaining learning influenced the origins and development of John B. Watson's behaviorism. *American Journal of Psychology, 113,* 275–301.

Everett, Daniel L. (2005). Cultural constraints on grammar and cognition in Pirahã: Another look at the design features of human language. *Current Anthropology, 46,* 621–646.

Everett, Daniel L. (2008, January 19). Quoted in Liz Else & Lucy Middleton, "Interview: Out on a limb over language." *New Scientist, 2639,* 42–44.

Exner, John E., Jr. (2007). A new U.S. adult nonpatient sample. *Journal of Personality Assessment, 89*(Suppl1), S154–S158.

Exner, John E., Jr., & Erdberg, Philip. (2005). *The Rorschach: A comprehensive system* (3rd ed.). Hoboken, NJ: Wiley.

Exum, M. Lyn. (2006). Alcohol and aggression: An integration of findings from experimental studies. *Journal of Criminal Justice, 34*(2), 131–145.

Eysenck, Hans J. (1982). *Personality, genetics, and behavior.* New York, NY: Praeger.

Eysenck, Hans J. (1990). Biological dimensions of personality. In Lawrence A. Pervin (Ed.), *Handbook of personality: Theory and research.* New York, NY: Guilford.

Eysenck, Hans J., & Eysenck, Sybil B. G. (1975). *Psychoticism as a dimension of personality.* London, England: Hodder & Stoughton.

Fabrigar, Leandre R., & Wegener, Duane T. (2010). Attitude structure. In R.F. Baumeister & E. J. Finkel (Eds.), *Advanced social psychology: The state of the science* (pp. 177–216). New York, NY: Oxford University Press.

Fagiolini, Andrea.; Forgione, Rocco; Maccari, Mauro; Cuomo, Alessandro; Morana, Benedetto; Dell'Osso, Mario C.; . . . Rossi,

Alessandro. (2013). Prevalence, chronicity, burden, and borders of bipolar disorder. *Journal of Affective Disorders, 148,* 161–169.

Fagundes, Christopher, & Way, Baldwin. (2014). Early-life stress and adult inflammation. *Current Directions in Psychological Science, 23,* 277–283. doi:10.1177/0963721414535603

Fahs, Breanne. (2007). Second shifts and political awakenings: Divorce and the political socialization of middle-aged women. *Journal of Divorce & Remarriage, 47*(3–4), 43–66.

Fairchild, Amy L., & Bayer, Ronald. (2015). Smoke and fire over e-cigarettes. *Science, 347,* 375–376. doi:10.1126/science.126071

Fairchild, Amy L.; Bayer, Ronald; & Colgrove, James. (2014). The renormalization of smoking? E-cigarettes and the tobacco "endgame." *New England Journal of Medicine, 370,* 293–295. doi:10.1056/NEJMp1313940

Fan, Yang-Teng; Decety, Jean; Yang, Chia-Yen; Liu, Ji-Lin; & Cheng, Yawei. (2010). Unbroken mirror neurons in autism spectrum disorders. *Journal of Child Psychology and Psychiatry, 51*(9), 981–988. doi:10.1111/j.1469-7610.2010.02269.x

Fan, Yang; Liu, Zhengyan; Weinstein, Philip R.; Fike, John R.; & Liu, Jialing. (2007). Environmental enrichment enhances neurogenesis and improves functional outcome after cranial irradiation. *European Journal of Neuroscience, 25,* 38–46.

Fancher, Raymond E. (1973). *Psychoanalytic psychology: The development of Freud's thought.* New York, NY: Norton.

Fancher, Raymond E. (1996). *Pioneers of psychology* (3rd ed.). New York, NY: Norton.

Fanous, Ayman H.; van den Oord, Edwin J.; Riley, Brien P.; Aggen, Steven H.; Neale, Michael C.; O'Neill, F. Anthony; Walsh, Dermot; & Kendler, Kenneth S. (2005). Relationships between a high-risk haplotype in the *DTNBP1* (dysbindin) gene and clinical features of schizophrenia. *American Journal of Psychiatry, 162,* 1824–1832.

Fantz, Robert L. (1961, May). The origin of form perception. *Scientific American, 204,* 66–72.

Fantz, Robert L.; Ordy, J. M.; & Udelf, M. S. (1962). Maturation of pattern vision in infants during the first six months. *Journal of Comparative and Physiological Psychology, 55,* 907–917.

Farb, Norman A. S.; Anderson, Adam K.; Mayberg, Helen; Bean, Jim; McKeon, Deborah; & Segal, Zindel V. (2010). Minding one's emotions: Mindfulness training alters the neural expression of sadness. *Emotion, 10*(1), 25–33. doi:10.1037/a0017151.supp

Farber, Barry A. (2007). On the enduring and substantial influence of Carl Rogers' not-quite necessary nor sufficient conditions. *Psychotherapy: Theory, Research, Practice, Training, 44,* 289–294.

Farber, Barry A., & Doolin, Erin M. (2011). Positive regard. *Psychotherapy, 48*(1), 58–64.

Farfel, Mark; DiGrande, Laura; Brackbill, Robert; Prann, Angela; Cone, James; Friedman, Stephen; Walker, Deborah J.; Pezeshki, Grant; & others. (2008). An overview of 9/11 experiences and respiratory and mental health conditions among World Trade Center Health Registry enrollees. *Journal of Urban Health, 85,* 880–909.

Farmer, Caroline; Farrand, Paul; & O'Mahen, Heather. (2012). 'I am not a depressed person': How identity conflict affects help-seeking rates for major depressive disorder. *BMC Psychiatry, 12*(164), 1–10.

Farrell, Meagan T., & Abrams, Lise. (2011). Tip-of-the-tongue states reveal age differences in the syllable frequency effect. *Journal of Experimental Psychology: Learning, Memory, and Cognition, 37*(1), 277–285.

Farris-Trimble, Ashley; McMurray, Bob; Cigrand, Nicole; Tomblin, J. Bruce. (2014). The process of spoken word recognition in the face of signal degradation. *Journal of Experimental Psychology: Human Perception and Performance, 40,* 308–327. doi:10.1037/a0034353

Fasfous, Ahmed F.; Peralta-Ramirez, Isabel; & Pérez-García, Miguel. (2013). Symptoms of PTSD among children living in war zones in same cultural context and different situations. *Journal of Muslim Mental Health, 7,* 47–61.

Fausey, Caitlin M.; Long, Bria L.; Inamori, A.; & Boroditsky, L. (2010). Constructing agency: The role of language. *Frontiers in Psychology, 1,* 162. doi:10.3389/fpsyg.2010.00162

Fazel, Seena; Langstrom, Niklas; Hjern, Anders; Grann, Martin; & Lichtenstein, Paul. (2009). Schizophrenia, substance abuse, and violent crime. *Journal of the American Medical Association, 301,* 2016–2023.

Feeney, Brooke, & Collins, Nancy. (2014). A new look at social support: A theoretical perspective on thriving through relationships. *Personality and Social Psychology Review, 19*(2), 113–147. doi:10.1177/1088868314544222

Feeney, Miranda C.; Roberts, William A.; & Sherry, David F. (2011). Black-capped chickadees (*Poecile atricapillus*) anticipate future outcomes of foraging choices. *Journal of Experimental Psychology: Animal Behavior Processes, 37*(1), 30–40. doi:10.1037/a0019908

Feinstein, Anthony; Audet, Blair; & Waknine, Elizabeth. (2014). Witnessing images of extreme violence: A psychological study of journalists in the newsroom. *Journal of the Royal Society of Medicine Open, 5*(8), 1–7. doi:10.1177/2054270414533323

Feldman Barrett, Lisa; Lane, Richard D.; Sechrest, Lee; & Schwartz, Gary E. (2000). Sex differences in emotional awareness. *Personality and Social Psychology Bulletin, 26,* 1027–1035.

Feldman Barrett, Lisa; & Russell, James A. (1999). The structure of current affect: Controversies and emerging consensus. *Current Directions in Psychological Science, 8,* 10–14.

Feldt, Ronald C. (2008). Development of a brief measure of college stress: The College Student Stress Scale. *Psychological Reports, 102*(3), 855–860.

Feliciano, Leilani, & Areán, Patricia A. (2007). Mood disorders: Depressive disorders. In Michel Hersen, Samuel M. Turner, & Deborah C. Beidel (Eds.), *Adult psychopathology and diagnosis* (5th ed., pp. 286–316). Hoboken, NJ: Wiley.

Felsberg, Eric J. (2004). Conducting job analyses and drafting lawful job descriptions under the Americans with Disabilities Act. *Employment Relations Today, 31,* 91–93.

Ferguson, Christopher J. (2010). Genetic contributions to antisocial personality and behavior: A meta-analytic review from an evolutionary perspective. *Journal of Social Psychology, 150*(2), 160–180.

Ferguson, Christopher J. (2014). Is video game violence bad? *The Psychologist, 27,* 324–327.

Ferguson, Christopher J., & Beaver, Kevin M. (2009). Natural born killers: The genetic origins of extreme violence. *Aggression and Violent Behavior, 14*(5), 286–294. doi:10.1016/j.avb.2009.03.005

Ferguson, Christopher J., & Kilbourn, John. (2009). The public health risks of media violence: A meta-analytic review. *Journal of Pediatrics, 154,* 759–763.

Ferguson, Christopher J., & Konijn, Elly A. (2015, January 19). She said/he said: A peaceful debate on video game violence. *Psychology of Popular Media Culture,* no pagination specified. doi:10.1037/ppm0000064

Ferguson, Christopher J., and Kilburn, John. (2010). Much ado about nothing: The misestimation and overinterpretation of violent video game effects in eastern and western nations: Comment on Anderson et al. (2010). *Psychological Bulletin, 136,* 174–178.

Fernald, Anne. (1985). Four-month-old infants prefer to listen to motherese. *Infant Behavior and Development, 8,* 181–182.

Fernald, Anne. (1992). Human maternal vocalizations to infants as biologically relevant signals: An evolutionary perspective. In Jerome H. Barkow, Leda Cosmides, & John Tooby (Eds.), *The adapted mind: Evolutionary psychology and the generation of culture* (pp. 391–428). New York, NY: Oxford University Press.

Ferrari, Alize J.; Somerville, Adele J.; Baxter, Amanda J.; Norman, Rosana; Patten, Scott B.; Vos, Theo; & Whiteford, Harvey A. (2013). Global variation in the prevalence and incidence of major depressive disorder: A systematic review of the epidemiological literature. *Psychological Medicine, 43,* 471–481. doi:10.1017/S0033291712001511

Feshbach, Seymour, & Tangney, June. (2008). Television viewing and aggression: Some alternative perspectives. *Perspectives on Psychological Sciences, 3,* 387–389.

Feske, Ulrike, & Goldstein, Alan J. (1997). Eye movement desensitization and reprocessing treatment for panic disorder: A controlled outcome and partial dismantling study. *Journal of Clinical and Consulting Psychology, 65,* 1026–1035.

Festinger, Leon. (1957). *A theory of cognitive dissonance.* Stanford, CA: Stanford University Press.

Festinger, Leon. (1962). Cognitive dissonance. *Scientific American, 207,* 93–99. (Reprinted in *Contemporary psychology: Readings from Scientific American,* 1971, San Francisco, CA: Freeman.)

Festinger, Leon, & Carlsmith, J. Merrill. (1959). Cognitive consequences of forced compliance. *Journal of Abnormal and Social Psychology, 58,* 203–210.

Fiedler, Klaus, & Krueger, Joachim I. (2013). Afterthoughts on precognition: No cogent evidence for anomalous influences of consequent events on preceding cognition. *Theory and Psychology, 23,* 323–333. doi:10.1177/0959354313485504

Field, Clinton E.; Nash, Heather M.; Handwerk, Michael L.; & Friman, Patrick C. (2004). A modification of the token economy for nonresponsive youth in family-style residential care. *Behavior Modification, 28,* 438–457.

Field, Tiffany. (2009). *Complementary and alternative therapies research.* Washington, DC: American Psychological Association.

Fielder, Robyn L., & Carey, Michael P. (2010). Prevalence and characteristics of sexual hookups among first-semester female college students. *Journal of Sex & Marital Therapy, 36*(4), 346–359.

Fieldhouse, Paul. (1986). *Food and nutrition: Customs and culture.* London, England: Croom Helm.

Fields, R. Douglas. (2013). Map the other brain. *Nature, 501,* 25–27.

Filevich, Elisa; Dresler, Martin; Brick, Timothy R.; & Kühn, Simone. (2015). Metacognitive mechanisms underlying lucid dreaming. *Journal of Neuroscience, 35,* 1082–1088. doi:10.1523/JNEUROSCI.3342-14.2015

Fine, Cordelia. (2012). Explaining, or sustaining, the status quo? The potentially self-fulfilling effects of "hardwired" accounts of sex differences. *Neuroethics, 5,* 285–294. doi:10.1007/s12152-011-9118-4

Fine, Cordelia. (2013a). Neurosexism in functional neuroimaging: From scanner to pseudo-science to psyche. In Michelle K. Ryan & Nyla R. Branscombe, Eds. *The SAGE handbook of gender and psychology.* London, England: Sage.

Fine, Cordelia. (2013b). Is there neurosexism in functional neuroimaging investigations of sex differences? *Neuroethics, 6,* 369–409. doi:10.1007/s12152-012-9169-1

Fine, Cordelia. (2014). His brain, her brain? *Science, 346,* 915–916. doi:10.1126/science.1262061

Fine, Cordelia; Jordan-Young, Rebecca; Kaiser, Anelis; & Rippon, Gina. (2013) Plasticity, plasticity, plasticity … and the rigid problem of sex. *Trends in Cognitive Sciences, 17,* 550–551.

Fine, Ione. (2002). Quoted in *The man who learnt to see.* BB2 Documentary.

Fine, Ione; Rieser, John J.; Ashmead, Daniel H.; Ebner, Ford F.; & Corn, Anne L. (2008). The behavioral and neurophysiological effects of sensory deprivation *Blindness and brain plasticity in navigation and object perception.* (pp. 127–152). Mahwah, NJ: Erlbaum.

Fine, Ione; Wade, Alex R.; Brewer, Alyssa A.; May, Michael G.; Goodman, Daniel F.; Boynton, Geoffrey M.; Wandell, Brian A.; & MacLeod, Donald I. A. (2003). Long-term deprivation affects visual perception and cortex. *Nature Neuroscience, 6,* 915–916.

Fink, Bernhard, & Penton-Voak, Ian. (2002). Evolutionary psychology of facial attractiveness. *Current Directions in Psychological Science, 11*(5), 154–158.

Fink, Max. (2009). *Electroconvulsive therapy: A guide for professionals & their patients.* New York, NY: Oxford University Press.

Finkel, Eli J., & Baumeister, Roy F. (2010). Attraction and rejection. In R. F. Baumeister & E. J. Finkel (Eds.), *Advanced social psychology: The state of the science.* New York, NY: Oxford University Press.

Finley, Jason R.; Benjamin, Aaron S.; & McCarley, Jason S. (2014). Metacognition of multitasking: How well do we predict the costs of divided attention? *Journal of Experimental Psychology: Applied, 20,* 158–165. doi:10.1037/xap0000010

Finno, Ariel A; Salazar, Marcos; Frincke, Jessica L.; Pate, William E., II; & Kohout, Jessica. (2006). *Debt, salary, and career data in psychology: What you need to know.* Center for Psychology Workforce Analysis and Research (CPWAR) Presentations. APA Research Office. Retrieved March 8, 2008, from http://research.apa.org/presentations.html

Fischer, Agneta H.; Rodriguez-Mosquera, Patricia M.; van Vianen, Annelies E. M.; & Manstead, Antony S. R. (2004). Gender and culture differences in emotion. *Emotion, 4,* 87–94.

Fischer, Peter; Greitemeyer, Tobias; Pollozek, Fabian; & Frey, Dieter. (2006). The unresponsive bystander: Are bystanders more responsive in dangerous emergencies? *European Journal of Social Psychology, 36*(2), 267–278.

Fischer, Peter; Krueger, Joachim I.; Greitemeyer, Tobias; Vogrincic, Claudia; Kastenmüller, Andreas; Frey, Dieter; Heene, Moritz; Wicher, Magdalena; & Kainbacher, Martina. (2011). The bystander-effect: A meta-analytic review on bystander intervention in dangerous and non-dangerous emergencies. *Psychological Bulletin, 137*(4), 517–537. doi:10.1037/a0023304

Fischer, Ronald, & Schwartz, Shalom. (2011). Whence differences in value priorities? Individual, cultural, or artifactual sources. *Journal of Cross-Cultural Psychology, 42,* 1127–1144. doi:10.1177/0022022110381429

Fishbach, Ayelet; Converse, Benjamin A.; Hassin, Ran R.; Ochsner, Kevin N.; & Trope, Yaacov. (2010). Walking the line between goals and temptations: Asymmetric effects of counteractive control *Self control in society, mind, and brain.* (pp. 389–407). New York, NY: Oxford University Press.

Fisher, Anne. (2008). Gas prices too high? Your employer might help. *Fortune Magazine.* Retrieved on December 9, 2009, from http://money.cnn.com/2008/06/02/magazines/fortune/annie_gas.fortune/index.htm

Fisher, Celia B., & Vacanti-Shova, Karyn. (2012). The responsible conduct of psychological research: An overview of ethical principles, APA Ethics Code standards, and federal regulations. In Samuel J. Knapp, Michael C. Gottlieb, Mitchell M. Handelsman, Leon D. VandeCreek (Eds.), *APA handbook of ethics in psychology, Vol 2: Practice, teaching, and research.* Washington, DC: American Psychological Association. doi:10.1037/13272-016

Fisher, Celia B. (2009). *Decoding the ethics code: A practical guide for psychologists* (2nd ed.). Thousand Oaks, CA: Sage.

Fisher, Helen L.; Moffitt, Terrie; Housts, Renate M.; Belsky, Daniel W.; Arseneault, Louise; & Caspi, Avshalom. (2012). Bullying victimization and risk of self harm in early adolescence: Longitude cohort study. *British Medical Journal, 344,* 1–9. doi:10.1136/bmj.e2683

Fisher, Luchina. (October 2, 2012). Anxious celebrities: Stars with anxiety. ABCNews. Retrieved on February 6, 2014 from http://abcnews.go.com/Entertainment/george-michael-tops-celebrities-anxiety/story?id=17366705#3

Fisher, Terri D.; Moore, Zachary T.; & Pittenger, Mary-Jo. (2012). Sex on the brain? An examination of frequency of sexual cognitions as a function of gender, erotophilia, and social desirability. *Journal of Sex Research, 49*(1), 69–77.

Fishman, Joshua A. (1960/1974). A systematization of the Whorfian hypothesis. In John W. Berry & P. R. Dasen (Eds.), *Culture and cognition: Readings in cross-cultural psychology.* London, England: Methuen.

Fiske, Susan T. (2008). Core social motivations: Views from the couch, consciousness, classroom, computers, and collectives. In James Y. Shah & Wendi L. Gardner (Eds.), *Handbook of motivation science.* New York, NY: Guilford.

Fiske, Susan T.; Harris, Lasana T.; & Cuddy, Amy J. C. (2004). Why ordinary people torture enemy prisoners. *Science, 306,* 1482–1483.

Fiske, Susan T.; & Ruscher, Janet B. (1993). Negative interdependence and prejudice: Whence the affect? In Diane M. Mackie & David L. Hamilton (Eds.), *Affect, cognition, and stereotyping: Interactive processes in group perception.* San Diego, CA: Academic Press.

Fitzpatrick, Maureen J.; & McPherson, Barbara J. (2010). Coloring within the lines: Gender stereotypes in contemporary coloring books. *Sex Roles, 62*(1–2), 127–137. doi:10.1007/s11199-009-9703-8

Fivush, Robyn. (2011). The development of autobiographical memory. *Annual Review of Psychology, 62*(1), 559–582. doi:10.1146/annurev.psych.121208.131702

Flaherty, Colleen. (2015, February 25). Personal philosophy. *Inside Higher Education* Retrieved from https://www.insidehighered.com/news/2015/02/25/professors-reflections-his-battle-depression-touch-many-recent-disciplinary-meeting

Flaten, Magne Arve, & Blumenthal, Terry D. (1999). Caffeine-associated stimuli elicit conditioned responses: An experimental model of the placebo effect. *Psychopharmacology, 145,* 105–112.

Flegal, Katherine M.; Kit, Brian K.; Orpana, Heather; & Graubard, Barry I. (2013). Association of all-cause mortality with overweight and obesity using standard body mass index categories: A systematic review and meta-analysis. *Journal of the American Medical Association, 309,* 71–82. doi:10.1001/jama.2012.113905

Flor, Herta. (2014). Psychological pain interventions and neurophysiology: Implications for a mechanism-based approach. *American Psychologist, 69,* 188–196. doi:10.1037/a0035254

Flynn, Emma, & Whiten, Andrew. (2010). Studying children's social learning experimentally in the wild. *Learning & Behavior, 38*(3), 284-296. doi:10.3758/lb.38.3.284

Flynn, James R. (1994). IQ gains over time. In Robert J. Sternberg (Ed.), *Encyclopedia of human intelligence.* New York, NY: Macmillan.

Flynn, James R. (1999). Searching for justice: The discovery of IQ gains over time. *American Psychologist, 54,* 5–20.

Flynn, James R. (2007a). Solving the IQ puzzle. *Scientific American Mind, 18,* 24–31.

Flynn, James R. (2007b). What lies behind g(I) and g(ID). *European Journal of Personality, 21,* 722–724.

Flynn, James R. (2009). *What is intelligence? Beyond the Flynn effect.* Cambridge, England: Cambridge University Press.

Foa, Edna B.; Gillihan, Seth J.; & Bryant, Richard A. (2013). Challenges and successes in dissemination of evidence-based treatments for posttraumatic stress: Lessons learned from prolonged exposure therapy for PTSD. *Psychological Science in the Public Interest, 14*(2), 65–111. doi:10.1177/1529100612468841

Focus on Family Support. (2010, September 1). Retrieved from https://bbrfoundation.org/stories-of-recovery/focus-on-family-support

Foer, Joshua. (2011). *Moonwalking with Einstein: The art and science of remembering everything.* Penguin Press.

Foland-Ross, Lara C.; Hamilton, Paul; Joormann, Jutta; Berman, Marc G.; Jonides, John; & Gotlib, Ian H. (2013). The neural basis of difficulties disengaging from negative irrelevant material in major depression. *Psychological Science, 24*(3), 334–44. doi:10.1177/0956797612457380

Folkman, Susan. (2009). Commentary on the special section "Theory-based approaches to stress and coping": Questions, answers, issues, and next steps in stress and coping research. *European Psychologist, 14*(1), 72–77.

Folkman, Susan, & Lazarus, Richard S. (1991). Coping and emotion. In Alan Monat & Richard S. Lazarus (Eds.), *Stress and coping: An anthology* (3rd ed.). New York, NY: Columbia University Press.

Folkman, Susan, & Moskowitz, Judith Tedlie. (2004). Coping: Pitfalls and promise. *Annual Review of Psychology, 55,* 745–774.

Folkman, Susan, & Moskowitz, Judith Tedlie. (2007). Positive affect and meaning-focused coping during significant psychological stress. In Miles Hewstone, Henk A. W. Schut, John B. F. De Wit, Kees Van Den Bos, & Margaret S. Stroebe (Eds.), *The scope of social psychology: Theory and applications* (pp. 193–208). New York, NY: Psychology Press.

Fond, Guillaume; Loundou, Anderson; Rabu, Corentin; Macgregor, Alexandra; Lançon, Christophe; Brittner, Marie; Micoulaud-Franchi, Jean-Arthur; Richieri, Raphaelle; Courtet, Philippe; Abbar, Mocrane; Roger, Matthieu; Leboyer, Marion; & Boyer, Laurent. (2014). Ketamine administration in depressive disorders: A systematic review and meta-analysis. *Psychopharmacology, 231,* 3663–3676. doi:10.1007/s00213-014-3664-5

Fontana, Alan, & Rosenheck, Robert. (2008). Treatment-seeking veterans of Iraq and Afghanistan: Comparison with veterans of previous wars. *Journal of Nervous and Mental Disease, 196*(7), 513–521.

Foote, Brad; Smolin, Yvette; & Kaplan, Margaret. (2006). Prevalence of dissociative disorders in psychiatric outpatients. *American Journal of Psychiatry, 163*(4), 623–629.

Forbes. (2007). Forbes survey revealed that the U.S. workplace is not family-oriented when compared to other industrialized countries. Retrieved on February 15, 2008, from *Forbes,* msn.com.

Forbes, Chad E., & Schmader, Toni. (2010). Retraining attitudes and stereotypes to affect motivation and cognitive capacity under stereotype threat. *Journal of Personality and Social Psychology, 99*(5), 740–754.

Forbes, David L. (2011). Toward a unified model of human motivation. *Review of General Psychology, 15*(2), 85–98.

Forgas, Joseph P.; Dunn, Elizabeth; & Granland, Stacey. (2008). Are you being served …? An unobtrusive experiment of affective influences on helping in a department store. *European Journal of Social Psychology, 38,* 333–342.

Fortune. (2008). 100 Best companies to work for. Retrieved on September 15, 2008, from www.Fortunemagazine.com

Foschi, Renato, & Cicciola, Elisabetta. (2006). Politics and naturalism in the 20th century psychology of Alfred Binet. *History of Psychology, 9,* 267–289.

Fosco, Gregory M.; Stormshak, Elizabeth a.; Dishion, Thomas J.; & Winter, Charlotte (2012). Family relationships and parental monitoring during middle school as predictors of early adolescent problem behavior. *Journal of Clinical Child and Adolescent Psychology, 41,* 202–213. doi:10.1080/15374416.2012.651989

Fosnaugh, Jessica; Geers, Andrew L.; & Wellman, Justin A. (2009). Giving off a rosy glow: The manipulation of an optimistic orientation. *The Journal of Social Psychology, 149*(3), 249–263.

Fotuhi, Omid; Fong, Geoffrey T.; Zanna, Mark P.; Borland, Ron; Yong, Hua H.; & Cummings, K. Michael. (2013). Patterns of cognitive dissonance-reducing beliefs among smokers: A longitudinal analysis from the International Tobacco Control (ITC) Four Country Survey. *Tobacco Control, 22,* 52–58.

Fouad, Nadya A., & Arredondo, Patricia. (2007). Evaluating cultural identity and biases. In Nadya A. Fouad & Patricia Arredondo (Eds.), *Becoming culturally oriented: Practical advice for psychologists and educators* (pp. 15–34). Washington, DC: American Psychological Association.

Foulkes, David, & Domhoff, G. William. (2014). Bottom-up or top-down in dream neuroscience? A top-down critique of two bottom-up studies. *Consciousness and Cognition: An International Journal, 27,* 168–171. doi:10.1016/j.concog.2014.05.002

Fournier, Jay C.; DeRubeis, Robert J.; Hollon, Steven D.; Dimidjian, Sona; Amsterdam, Jay D.; Shelton, Richard C.; & Fawcett, Jan. (2010). Antidepressant drug effects and depression severity: A patient-level meta-analysis. *Journal of the American Medical Association, 303*(1), 47–53. doi:10.1001/jama.2009.1943

Fowler, Robert L., & Barker, Anne S. (1974). Effectiveness of highlighting for retention of text material. *Journal of Applied Psychology, 59*(3), 358–364. doi:10.1037/h0036750

Fox, Margalit. (2008). *Talking hands: What sign language reveals about the mind.* New York, NY: Simon & Schuster.

Fox, Nathan A., & Killen, Melanie. (2008). Morality, culture, and the brain: What changes and what stays the same. In W. Sinnott-Armstrong (Ed.), *Moral Psychology, Vol. 3: The neuroscience of morality: Emotion, brain disorders, and development* (pp. 313–316). Cambridge, MA: MIT Press.

Fox, William M. (1982). Why we should abandon Maslow's need hierarchy theory. *Journal of Humanistic Education and Development, 21,* 29–32.

Fraga, Mario F.; Ballestar, Esteban; Paz, Maria F.; Ropero, Santiago; Setien, Fernando; Ballestar, Maria L.; Heine-Suner, Damia; & others. (2005). Epigenetic differences arise during the lifetime of monozygotic twins. *Proceedings of the National Academy of Sciences, 102,* 10413–10414.

Fram, Alan. (2007). That's the spirit: One-third of people believe in ghosts—and some report seeing one. *Associated Press Archive,* Record No. d8SGT3CG0. Associated Press, Washington, DC.

Frances, Allen. (2010, April 20). DSM-5 plans to loosen criteria for adult ADD. *Psychiatric Times* Accessed at http://www.psychiatrictimes.com/depression/content/article/10168/1556462

Frances, Allen J. (2012). DSM-5 is a guide, not a Bible—Simply ignore its 10 worst changes. *Psychiatric Times.* Retrieved on 10/14/13 from http://www.psychiatrictimes.com/blogs/dsm-5/dsm-5-guide-notbible%E2%80%94simply-ignore-its-10-worst-changes

Frances, Allen J., & Widiger, Thomas. (2012). Psychiatric diagnosis: lessons from the DSM-IV past and cautions for the DSM-5 future. *Annual Review of Clinical Psychology, 8,* 109–130.

Francis, Ronald D. (2009). *Ethics for psychologists* (2nd ed.). Chichester, England: Wiley-Blackwell.

Frank, Mark G., & Stennett, Janine. (2001). The forced-choice paradigm and the perception of facial expressions of emotion. *Journal of Personality and Social Psychology, 80,* 75–85.

Frank, Michael C.; Everett, Daniel L.; Fedorenko, Evelina; & Gibson, Edward. (2008). Number as a cognitive technology: Evidence from Piraha language and cognition. *Cognition, 108,* 819–824.

Frankenburg, Frances R. (1994). History of the development of antipsychotic medication. *Psychiatric Clinics of North America, 17,* 531–540.

Frankland, Paul W., & Bontempi, Bruno. (2005). The organization of recent and remote memories. *Nature Reviews Neuroscience, 6,* 119–130.

Frazier, Patricia; Anders, Samantha; Perera, Sulani; Tomich, Patricia; Tennen, Howard; Park, Crystal; & Tashiro, Ty. (2009). Traumatic events among undergraduate students: Prevalence and associated symptoms. *Journal of Counseling Psychology, 56,* 450–460.

Free, Michael L. (2008). *Cognitive therapy in groups: Guidelines and resources for practice* (2nd ed.). Chichester, England: Wiley.

Freedman, Sara A.; Hoffman, Hunter G.; Garcia-Palacios, Azucena; Weiss, Patrice L. (Tamar); Avitzour, Sara; & Josman, Naomi. (2010). Prolonged exposure and virtual reality–enhanced imaginal exposure for PTSD following a terrorist bulldozer attack: A case study. *Cyberpsychology, Behavior, and Social Networking, 13,* 95–101.

Freeman, Chris, & Power, Mick. (2007). *Handbook of evidence-based psychotherapies: A guide for research and practice.* Chichester, England: Wiley.

Freeman, Ellen W. (2010). Associations of depression with the transition to menopause. *Menopause 17,* 823–827 doi:10.1097/gme.0b013e3181db9f8b

Freeman, Kevin B., & Riley, Anthony L. (2009). The origins of conditioned taste aversion learning: A historical analysis. In S. Reilly & T. Schachtman (Eds.), *Conditioned taste aversion: Behavioral and neural processes* (pp. 9–36). New York, NY: Oxford University Press.

Freeman, Lucy, & Strean, Herbert S. (1987). *Freud and women.* New York, NY: Continuum.

Freeman, Nancy K. (2007). Preschoolers' perceptions of gender appropriate toys and their parents' beliefs about genderized behaviors: Miscommunication, mixed messages, or hidden truths? *Early Childhood Education Journal, 3,* 357–366.

Freidel, Paul; Young, Bruce; & van Hemmen, J. Leo. (2008). Auditory localization of ground-borne vibrations in snakes. *Physical Review Letters, 100,* 048701.

Freire, Elizabeth S. (2007). Empathy. In Mick Cooper, Maureen O'Hara, Peter F. Schmid, & Gill Wyatt (Eds.), *The handbook of person-centered psychotherapy and counseling.* New York, NY: Palgrave Macmillan.

French, Christopher C.; Krippner, Stanley; & Friedman, Harris L. (2010). Reflections of a (relatively) moderate skeptic *Debating psychic experience: Human potential or human illusion?* (pp. 53–64). Santa Barbara, CA: Praeger/ABC-CLIO.

Frenda, Steven J.; Knowles, Eric D.; Saletan, William; Loftus, Elizabeth F. (2013). False memories of fabricated political events. *Journal of Experimental Social Psychology, 49,* 280–286. doi:10.1016/j.jesp.2012.10.013

Frenda, Steven J.; Nichols, Rebecca M.; Loftus, Elizabeth F. (2011). Current issues and advances in misinformation research. *Current Directions in Psychological Science, 20*(1), 20–23. doi:10.1177/0963721410396620

Freud, Anna. (1946). *The ego and mechanisms of defence* (Cecil Baines, Trans.). New York, NY: International Universities Press.

Freud, Sigmund. (1900/1974). The interpretation of dreams. In James Strachey (Ed.), *The standard edition of the complete psychological works of Sigmund Freud* (Vols. 4 & 5). London, England: Hogarth.

Freud, Sigmund. (1904/1965). *The psychopathology of everyday life* (Alan Tyson, Trans., & James Strachey, Ed.). New York, NY: Norton.

Freud, Sigmund. (1905/1975). *Three essays on the theory of sexuality* (James Strachey, Ed.). New York, NY: Basic Books.

Freud, Sigmund. (1911/1989). On dreams. In Peter Gay (Ed.), *The Freud reader.* New York, NY: Norton.

Freud, Sigmund. (1912/1958). The dynamics of resistance. In *The standard edition of the complete psychological works of Sigmund Freud* (Vol. 12, pp. 97–108). London, England: Hogarth.

Freud, Sigmund. (1914/1948). On narcissism: An introduction. In Joan Riviere (Trans.), *Collected papers: Vol. 4. Papers on metapsychology and applied psychoanalysis.* London, England: Hogarth.

Freud, Sigmund. (1915a/1948). Repression. In Joan Riviere (Trans.), *Collected Papers: Vol. 4. Papers on metapsychology and applied psychoanalysis.* London, England: Hogarth.

Freud, Sigmund. (1915b/1959). Analysis, terminable and interminable. In Joan Riviere (Trans.), *Collected Papers: Vol. 5. Miscellaneous papers* (2nd ed.). London, England: Hogarth.

Freud, Sigmund. (1915c/1959). Libido theory. In Joan Riviere (Trans.), *Collected papers: Vol. 5. Miscellaneous papers* (2nd ed.). London, England: Hogarth

Freud, Sigmund. (1916/1964). *Leonardo da Vinci and a memory of his childhood.* (James Strachey, Trans., in collaboration with Anna Freud). New York, NY: Norton.

Freud, Sigmund. (1919/1989). *Totem and taboo: Some points of agreement between the mental lives of savages and neurotics* (James Strachey, Ed. & Trans., with a biographical introduction by Peter Gay). New York, NY: Norton.

Freud, Sigmund. (1920/1961). *Beyond the pleasure principle* (James Strachey, Ed.). New York, NY: Norton.

Freud, Sigmund. (1923/1962). *The ego and the id* (Joan Riviere, Trans., & James Strachey, Ed.). New York, NY: Norton.

Freud, Sigmund. (1925/1989). Some psychical consequences of the anatomical distinction between the sexes. In Peter Gay (Ed.), *The Freud reader.* New York, NY: Norton.

Freud, Sigmund. (1926/1947). *The question of lay analysis: An introduction to psychoanalysis* (Nancy Proctor-Gregg, Trans.). London, England: Imago.

Freud, Sigmund. (1930/1961). *Civilization and its discontents* (James Strachey, Ed. & Trans.). New York, NY: Norton.

Freud, Sigmund. (1933). *New introductory lectures on psychoanalysis* (W. J. H. Sprott, Trans.). New York, NY: Norton.

Freud, Sigmund. (1936). *The problem of anxiety* (Henry Alden Bunker, Trans.). New York, NY: The Psychoanalytic Quarterly Press and Norton.

Freud, Sigmund. (1939/1967). *Moses and monotheism* (Katherine Jones, Trans.). New York, NY: Vintage Books.

Freud, Sigmund. (1940/1949). *An outline of psychoanalysis* (James Strachey, Trans.). New York, NY: Norton.

Fridell, Mats; Hesse, Morten; Jæger, Mads Meier; & Kühlhorn, Eckart. (2008). Antisocial personality disorder as a predictor of criminal behaviour in a longitudinal study of a cohort of abusers of several classes of drugs: Relation to type of substance and type of crime. *Addictive Behaviors, 33*(6), 799–811.

Fridell, Sari R.; Owen-Anderson, Allison; Johnson, Laurel L.; Bradley, Susan J.; & Zucker, Kenneth J. (2006). The playmate and play style preferences structured interview: A comparison of children with gender identity disorder and controls. *Archives of Sexual Behavior, 35,* 729–737.

Friedman, Howard S., & Booth-Kewley, Stephanie. (2003). The 'disease-prone personality': A meta-analytic view of the construct. In Peter Salovey & Alexander J. Rothman (Eds.), *Social psychology of health.* New York, NY: Psychology Press.

Friedman, Jeffrey M. (2009). Causes and control of excess body fat. *Nature, 459,* 340–342.

Friedman, Jeffrey M., & Halaas, Jeffrey L. (1998, October 22). Leptin and the regulation of body weight in mammals. *Nature, 395,* 763–770.

Friedman, Meyer, & Rosenman, Ray H. (1974). *Type A behavior and your heart.* New York, NY: Knopf.

Friend, Ronald; Rafferty, Yvonne; & Bramel, Dana. (1990). A puzzling misinterpretation of the Asch "conformity" study. *European Journal of Social Psychology, 20,* 29–44.

Friesen, Wallace V. (1972). Cultural differences in facial expressions in a social situation: An experimental test of the concept of display rules. Unpublished doctoral dissertation, University of California, San Francisco, CA.

Frith, Chris D., & Frith, Uta. (2012). Mechanisms of social cognition. *Annual Review of Psychology, 63*(1), 287–313. doi:10.1146/annurev-psych-120710-100449

Fruth, Barbara, & Hohmann, Gottfried. (2006). Social grease for females? Same-sex genital contacts in wild bonobos. In Volker Sommer & Paul L. Vasey (Eds.), *Homosexual behaviour in animals: An evolutionary perspective*. New York, NY: Cambridge University Press.

Fujita, Kentaro, & Roberts, Joseph C. (2010). Promoting prospective self-control through abstraction. *Journal of Experimental Social Psychology, 46,* 1049–1054.

Fuller, Patrick M.; Gooley, Joshua J.; & Saper, Clifford B. (2006). Neurobiology of the sleep-wake cycle: Sleep architecture, circadian regulation, and regulatory feedback. *Journal of Biological Rhythms, 21,* 482–493.

Fullerton, Ronald A. (2010). "A virtual social H-bomb": The late 1950s controversy over subliminal advertising. *Journal of Historical Research in Marketing, 2*(2), 166–173.

Funder, David C. (2001). Personality. *Annual Review of Psychology, 52,* 197–221.

Funder, David C., & Fast, Lisa A. (2010). Personality in social psychology. In Susan T. Fiske, Daniel T. Gilbert, & Gardner Lindzey (Eds.), *Handbook of social psychology, Vol 1.* Hoboken, NJ: Wiley.

Funkhouser, Arthur, & Schredl, Michael. (2010). The frequency of déjà vu (déjà rêve) and the effects of age, dream recall frequency and personality factors. *International Journal of Dream Research, 3*(1), 60–64.

Furman, Wyndol, & Simon, Valerie A. (2004). Concordance in attachment states of mind and styles with respect to fathers and mothers. *Developmental Psychology, 40,* 1239–1247.

Furnham, Adam. (2008). *Personality and intelligence at work: Exploring and explaining individual differences at work.* London, England: Routledge.

Gabrieli, John D. E. (2008, January 30). Quoted in Cathryn M. Delude, "Culture influences brain function, study shows." *MIT Tech Talk, 52*(14), 4.

Gage, Fred H. (2007, August 19). Quoted in Gretchen Reynolds, "Lobes of steel." *The New York Times.* Retrieved October 9, 2007, from http://www.nytimes.com/2007/08/19/sports/play-magazine/0819play-brain.htm

Gagne, Jeffrey R.; Vendlinski, Matthew K.; & Goldsmith, H. Hill. (2009). The genetics of childhood temperament. In Yong-Kyu Kim (Ed.), *Handbook of behavior genetics.* (pp. 251–267). New York, NY: Springer Science + Business Media.

Gajendran, Raji V., & Harrison, David A. (2007). The good, the bad, and the unknown about telecommuting: Meta-analysis of psychological mediators and individual consequences. *Journal of Applied Psychology, 92,* 1524–1541.

Galak, Jeff; LeBoeuf, Robyn A.; Nelson, Leif D.; & Simmons, Joseph P. (2012). Correcting the past: Failures to replicate psi. *Journal of Personality and Social Psychology, 103,* 933–948. doi:10.1037/a0029709

Galambos, Nancy L.; Barker, Erin T.; Krahn, Harvey J. (2006). Depression, self-esteem, and anger in emerging adulthood: Seven-year trajectories. *Developmental Psychology, 42,* 350-365. doi:10.1037/0012-1649.42.2.350

Galanter, Eugene. (1962). Contemporary psychophysics. In Roger Brown, Eugene Galanter, Eckhard H. Hess, & George Mandler (Eds.), *New directions in psychology.* New York, NY: Holt, Rinehart & Winston.

Galati, Dario; Scherer, Klaus B.; & Ricci-Bitti, Pio E. (1997). Voluntary facial expression of emotion: Comparing congenitally blind with normally sighted encoders. *Journal of Personality and Social Psychology, 73,* 1363–1379.

Galati, Dario; Sini, Barbara; Schmidt, Susanne; & Tinti, Carla. (2003). Spontaneous facial expressions in congenitally blind and sighted children aged 8–11. *Journal of Visual Impairment and Blindness, 97,* 418–428.

Gallese, Vittori; Gernsbacher, Morton A.; Heyes, Cecilia; Hickock, Gregory; & Iacoboni, Marco. (2011). Mirror neuron forum. *Perspectives on Psychological Science, 6,* 369–407. doi:10.1177/1745691611413392

Gallo, David A., & Wheeler, Mark E. (2013). Episodic memory. In Daniel Reisberg (Ed.), *The Oxford handbook of cognitive psychology.* New York, NY: Oxford University Press.

Gallo, Linda C.; de los Monteros, Karla Espinosa; & Shivpuri, Smriti. (2009). Socioeconomic status and health: What is the role of reserve capacity? *Current Directions in Psychological Science, 18*(5), 269–274.

Gambacorta, David. (2014, March 10). Police, DHS investigate mom after video goes viral. *Philly News.* Retrieved from http://articles.philly.com/2014-03-10/news/48054988_1_facebook-page-bus-driver-bus-stops

Gangestad, Steven W.; Garver-Apgar, Christine E.; Simpson, Jeffry A.; & Cousins, Alita J. (2007). Changes in women's mate preferences across the ovulatory cycle. *Journal of Personality and Social Psychology, 92,* 151–163.

Gangl, Markus, & Ziefle, Andrea (2009). Motherhood, labor force behavior, and women's careers: An empirical assessment of the wage penalty for motherhood in Britain, Germany, and the United States. *Demography, 46*(2), 341–369.

Ganis, Giorgio; Thompson, William; & Kosslyn, Stephen. (2004). Brain areas underlying visual mental imagery and visual perception: An fMRI study. *Cognitive Brain Research, 20,* 226–241.

Gansberg, Martin. (1964, March 27). 37 who saw murder didn't call the police. *New York Times,* pp. 1, 38.

García, Eugene E., & Náñez, José E., Sr. (2011). *Bilingualism and cognition: Informing research, pedagogy, and policy.* Washington, DC: American Psychological Association.

Garcia, Fernando, & Gracia, Enrique (2009). Is always authoritative the optimum parenting style? Evidence from Spanish families. *Family Therapy, 36*(1), 17–47.

Garcia, John. (1981). Tilting at the paper mills of academe. *American Psychologist, 36,* 149–158.

Garcia, John. (1997). Foreword by Robert C. Bolles: From mathematics to motivation. In Mark E. Bouton & Michael S. Fanselow (Eds.), *Learning, motivation, and cognition: The functional behaviorism of Robert C. Bolles.* Washington, DC: American Psychological Association.

Garcia, John. (2003). Psychology is not an enclave. In Robert J. Sternberg (Ed.), *Psychologists defying the crowd: Stories of those who battled the establishment and won.* Washington, DC: American Psychological Association.

Garcia, John; Ervin, Frank R.; & Koelling, Robert A. (1966). Learning with prolonged delay of reinforcement. *Psychonomic Science, 5,* 121–122.

Garcia, John, & Koelling, Robert A. (1966). Relation of cue to consequence in avoidance learning. *Psychonomic Science, 4,* 123–124.

Garcia-Palacios, Azucena; Hoffman, Hunter G.; See, Sheer Kong; Tsai, Amy; & Botella, Cristina. (2001). Redefining therapeutic success with virtual reality exposure therapy. *CyberPsychology and Behavior, 4,* 341–348.

Gardner, Howard. (1985). *Frames of mind: The theory of multiple intelligences.* New York, NY: Basic Books.

Gardner, Howard. (1993). *Frames of mind: The theory of multiple intelligences* (2nd ed.). New York, NY: Basic Books.

Gardner, Howard. (1998a). Are there additional intelligences? The case for naturalist, spiritual, and existential intelligences. In J. Kane (Ed.), *Education, information, and transformation.* Upper Saddle River, NJ: Prentice Hall.

Gardner, Howard. (1998b, Winter). A multiplicity of intelligences. *Scientific American Presents: Exploring Intelligence, 9,* 18–23.

Gardner, Howard. (2003). Three distinct meanings of intelligence. In Robert Sternberg, Jacques Lautrey, & Todd I. Lubert (Eds.), *Models of intelligence: International perspectives.* Washington, DC: American Psychological Association.

Gardner, Howard, & Taub, James. (1999, Fall). Debating "multiple intelligences." *Cerebrum, 1,* 13–36.

Gardner, Michael K. (2011). Theories of intelligence. In M. A. Bray & T. J. Kehle (Eds.), *The Oxford handbook of school psychology* (pp. 79–100). New York, NY: Oxford University Press.

Gardony, Aaron L.; Taylor, Holly A.; & Brunyé, Tad T. (2014). What does physical rotation reveal about mental rotation? *Psychological Science, 25,* 605–612. doi:10.1177/0956797613503174

Garfin, Dana R.; Holman, E. Alison; & Silver, Roxane C. (2015). Cumulative exposure to prior collective trauma and acute stress responses to the Boston, MA Marathon bombings. *Psychological Science, 1–9.* doi:10.1177/0956797614561043

Garrett, Brandon L. (2011). *Convicting the innocent.* Cambridge, MA: Harvard University Press.

Garrett, Michael T. (2006). When Eagle speaks: Counseling Native Americans. In Courtland C. Lee (Ed.), *Multicultural issues in counseling: New approaches to diversity* (3rd. ed., pp. 25–53). Alexandria, VA: American Counseling Association.

Garrett, Michael T. (2008). Native Americans. In Garrett McAuliffe (Ed.), *Culturally alert counseling: A comprehensive introduction* (pp. 220–254). Thousand Oaks, CA: Sage.

Garry, Maryanne, & Polaschek, Devon L. L. (2000). Imagination and memory. *Current Directions in Psychological Science, 9,* 6–10.

Garvin, Charles. (2011). Group work with people who suffer from serious mental illness. In Geoffrey L. Greif & Paul H. Ephross (Eds.), *Group work with populations at risk.* New York, NY: Oxford University Press.

Garza, Yvonne, & Watts, Richard E. (2010). Filial therapy and Hispanic values: Common ground for culturally sensitive helping. *Journal of Counseling & Development, 88*(1), 108–113.

Gatchel, Robert J.; Howard, Krista; & Haggard, Rob. (2011). Pain: The biopsychosocial perspective. In R. J. Contrada & A. Baum (Eds.), *The handbook of stress science: Biology, psychology, and health* (pp. 461–473). New York, NY: Springer.

Gaudiano, Brandon A. (2008). Cognitive-behavioural therapies: Achievements and challenges. *Evidence-Based Mental Health, 11,* 5–7.

Gavett, Brandon E.; Stern, Robert A.; & McKee, Ann C. (2011). Chronic traumatic encephalopathy: A potential late effect of sport-related concussive and subconcussive head trauma. *Clinics in Sports Medicine, 30,* 179–188.

Gawronski, Bertram. (2012). Back to the future of dissonance theory: Cognitive consistency as a core motive. *Social Cognition, 30*(6), 652–668.

Gawronski, Bertram, & Payne, B. Keith. (2010). *Handbook of implicit social cognition: Measurement, theory, and applications.* New York, NY: Guilford.

Gay, Peter (Ed.). (1989). *The Freud reader.* New York, NY: Norton.

Gay, Peter. (1999, March 29). Psychoanalyst: Sigmund Freud. *Time 100 Special Issue: Scientists and Thinkers of the 20th Century, 153*(12), 66–69.

Gay, Peter. (2006). *Freud: A life for our time.* New York, NY: Norton.

Gazzaniga, Michael S. (1983). Right hemisphere language following brain bisection: A 20-year perspective. *American Psychologist, 38,* 526–537.

Gazzaniga, Michael S. (1995). Consciousness and the cerebral hemispheres. In Michael S. Gazzaniga (Ed.), *The cognitive neurosciences.* Cambridge, MA: MIT Press.

Gazzaniga, Michael S. (2005). Forty-five years of split-brain research and still going strong. *Nature Reviews Neuroscience, 6,* 653–659.

Ge, Xiaojia; Kim, Irene J.; Brody, Gene H.; Conger, Rand D.; Simons, Ronald L.; Gibbons, Frederick X.; & Cutrona, Carolyn E. (2003). It's about timing and change: Pubertal transition effects on symptoms of major depression among African American youths. *Developmental Psychology, 39,* 430–439.

Gee, Travis; Allen, Kelly; & Powell, Russell A. (2003). Questioning premorbid dissociative symptomatology in dissociative identity disorder: Comment on Gleaves, Hernandez, and Warner (1999). *Professional Psychology: Research and Practice, 34,* 114–116.

Geldard, Frank A. (1972). *The human senses* (2nd ed.). New York, NY: Wiley.

Gelman, Rochel, & Gallistel, C. R. (2004). Language and the origin of numerical concepts. *Science, 306,* 441–443.

Gendolla, Guido H. E. (2000). On the impact of mood on behavior: An integrative theory and a review. *Review of General Psychology, 4,* 378–408.

Gentile, Barbara F., & Miller, Benjamin O. (2009). *Foundations of psychological thought: A history of psychology.* Thousand Oaks, CA: Sage.

Gentilucci, Maurizio, & Dalla Volta, Riccardo. (2007). The motor system and the relationships between speech and gesture. *Gesture, 7,* 159–177.

George, Bill. (2006, October 30). The master gives it back. *U.S. News & World Report,* 66–68.

Georgopoulos, Neoklis A.; Markou, Kostas B.; Theodoropoulou, Anastasia; Vagenakis, George A.; Mylonas, Panagiotis; & Vagenakis, Apostolos G. (2004). Growth, pubertal development, skeletal maturation and bone mass acquisition in athletes. *Hormones (Athens), 3*(4), 233–243.

Geraci, Lisa, & Manzano, Isabel. (2010). Distinctive items are salient during encoding: Delayed judgements of learning predict the isolation effect. *Quarterly Journal of Experimental Psychology, 63*(1), 50–64.

Gerard, Harold B.; Wilhelmy, Roland A.; & Conolley, Edward S. (1968). Conformity and group size. *Journal of Personality and Social Psychology, 8,* 79–82.

Gerbner, George. (1998). Images of mental illness in the mass media. *Media Development, 2.* Retrieved December 9, 2009, from http://www.waccglobal.org/en/19982-communication-and-disability/885-Images-of-mental-illness-in-the-mass-media—.html.

Gernsbacher, Morton Ann. (2004). Language is more than speech: A case study. *Journal of Developmental and Learning Disorders, 8,* 81–98.

Gernsbacher, Morton Ann. (2007). The true meaning of research participation. *APS Observer, 20.*

Gernsbacher, Morton Ann; Sauer, Eve A.; Geye, Heather M.; Schweigert, Emily K.; & Goldsmith, H. Hill. (2008). Infant and toddler oral and manual-motor skills predict later speech fluency in autism. *Journal of Child Psychology and Psychiatry, 49,* 43–50.

Gerrans, Philip. (2012). Dream experience and a revisionist account of delusions of misidentification. *Consciousness and Cognition: An International Journal, 21*(1), 217–227. doi:10.1016/j.concog.2011.11.003

Gerrie, Matthew P.; Garry, Maryanne; & Loftus, Elizabeth F. (2004). False memories. In Neil Brewer & Kip Williams (Eds.), *Psychology and law: An empirical perspective.* New York, NY: Guilford.

Gershoff, Elizabeth Thompson. (2002). Corporal punishment by parents and associated child behavior and experiences: A meta-analytic and theoretical review. *Psychological Bulletin, 128,* 539–579.

Gershoff, Elizabeth Thompson; Grogan-Kaylor, A.; Lansford, J. E.; Chang, L.; Zelli, A.; Deater-Deckard, K.; & Dodge, K. A. (2010). Parent discipline practices in an International sample: Associations with child behaviors and moderation by perceived normativeness. *Child Development, 81*(2), 487–502.

Gerstner, Charlotte R., & Day, David V. (1997, December). Metaanalytic review of leader-member exchange theory: Correlates and construct issues. *Journal of Applied Psychology, 82,* 827–844.

Gesser-Edelsburg, Anat; Guttman, Nurit; & Israelashvili, Moshe. (2010). An entertainment-education study of secondary delegitimization in the Israeli-Palestinian conflict. *Peace and Conflict: Journal of Peace Psychology, 16*(3), 253–274.

Gibbs, John C. (2003). Moral development and reality: Beyond the theories of Kohlberg and Hoffman. Thousand Oaks, CA: Sage.

Gibson, Bryan; Thompson, Jody; Hou, Beini; & Bushman, Brad J. (2014). Just "harmless entertainment"? Effects of surveillance reality TV on physical aggression. *Psychology of Popular Media Culture.* Retrieved from http://dx.doi.org/10.1037/ppm0000040

Giedd, Jay N. (2008). The teen brain: Insights from neuroimaging. *Journal of Adolescent Health, 42*(4), 335–343. doi:.1016/j.jadohealth.2008.01.007

Giedd, Jay N. (2009, January/February). The teen brain: Primed to learn, primed to take risks. *Cerebrum.* Retrieved on April 13, 2009, from http://www.dana.org/news/cerebrum/detail.aspx?id=19620

Giedd, Jay N.; Lalonde, F. M.; Celano, M. J.; White, S. L.; Wallace, G. L.; Lee, N. R.; & Lenroot, R. K. (2009). Anatomical brain magnetic resonance imaging of typically developing children and adolescents. *Journal of the American Academy of Child and Adolescent Psychiatry, 48*(5), 465–470. doi:10.1097/CHI.0b013e31819f2715

Gieser, Marlon T. (1993). The first behavior therapist as I knew her. *Journal of Behavior Therapy and Experimental Psychiatry, 24,* 321–324.

Gigerenzer, Gerd, & Gaissmaier, Wolfgang. (2011). Heuristic decision making. *Annual Review of Psychology, 62,* 451–458. doi:10.1146/annurev-psych-120709-14534

Gigerenzer, Gerd, & Goldstein, Daniel G. (2011). The recognition heuristic: A decade of research. *Judgment and Decision Making, 6*(1), 100–121.

Gillham, Jane E.; Shatte, Andrew J.; Reivich, Karen J.; & Seligman, Martin E. P. (2001). Optimism, pessimism, and explanatory style. In Edward C. Chang (Ed.), *Optimism and pessimism: Implications for theory, research, and practice.* Washington, DC: American Psychological Association.

Gilligan, Carol A. (1982). *In a different voice: Psychological theory and women's development.* Cambridge, MA: Harvard University Press.

Gilligan, Carol A., & Attanucci, Jane. (1988). Two moral orientations: Gender differences and similarities. In Carol A. Gilligan, Janie Victoria Ward, & Jill Maclean Taylor (Eds.), *Mapping the moral domain: A contribution of women's thinking to psychological theory and education*. Cambridge, MA: Harvard University Press.

Gilman, Sander L. (2001). Images in psychiatry: Karen Horney, M.D., 1885–1952. *American Journal of Psychiatry, 158,* 1205.

Gilman, Sarah R.; Chang, Johnathan; Xu, Bin; Bawa, Tejdeep S.; Gogos, Joseph A.; Karayiorgou, Maria; & Vitkup, Dennis. (2012). Diverse types of genetic variation converge on functional gene networks involved in schizophrenia. *Nature Neuroscience, 15,* 1723–1729. doi:10.1038/nn.3261

Gilovich, Thomas. (1997, March/April). Some systematic biases of everyday judgment. *Skeptical Inquirer, 21,* 31–35.

Gilson, Lucy L., & Madjar, Nora. (2011). Radical and incremental creativity: Antecedents and processes. *Psychology of Aesthetics, Creativity, and the Arts, 5,* 21–28.

Ginandes, Carol. (2006). The strategic integration of hypnosis and CBT for the treatment of mind/body conditions. In Robin A. Chapman (Ed.). *The clinical use of hypnosis in cognitive behavior therapy: A practitioner's casebook.* New York, NY: Springer.

Girard, Simon L.; Gauthier, Julie; Noreau, Anne; Xiong, Lan; Zhou, Sirui; Jouan, Loubna; Dionne-Laporte, Alexandre; & others. (2011). Increased exonic de novo mutation rate in individuals with schizophrenia. *Nature Genetics 43,* 860–863. doi:10.1038/ng.886, 596

Gire, James T. (2011). Cultural variations in perceptions of aging. In Kenneth D. Keith (Ed.), *Cross-cultural psychology: Contemporary themes and perspectives.* Chichester, England: Wiley-Blackwell.

Gladwell, Malcolm. (2004, September 20). Annals of psychology: Personality plus. *The New York,* 42–48.

Glaser, Ronald, & Kiecolt-Glaser, Janice K. (2005). Stress-induced immune dysfunction: Implications for health. *Nature Reviews Immunology, 5,* 243–250.

Glasper, Erica R.; Schoenfeld, Timothy J.; Gould, Elizabeth. (2012). Adult neurogenesis: Optimizing hippocampal function to suit the environment. *Behavioural Brain Research, 227,* 380–383. doi:10.1016/j.bbr.2011.05.013

Glass, Richard M. (2001). Electro convulsive therapy: Time to bring it out of the shadows. *Journal of the American Medical Association, 285,* 1346–1348.

Gleaves, David H.; Smith, Steven M.; Butler, Lisa D.; & Spiegel, David. (2004). False and recovered memories in the laboratory and clinic: A review of experimental and clinical evidence. *Clinical Psychology: Science and Practice, 11,* 3–28.

Gleitman, Henry. (1991). Edward Chace Tolman: A life of scientific and social purpose. In Gregory A. Kimble, Michael Wertheimer, & Charlotte White (Eds.), *Portraits of pioneers in psychology.* Washington, DC: American Psychological Association/Hillsdale, NJ: Erlbaum.

Glenberg, Arthur M. (2011). Positions in the mirror are closer than they appear. *Perspectives on Psychological Science, 6,* 408–410. doi:10.1177/1745691611413393

Glicksohn, Arit, & Cohen, Asher. (2011). The role of Gestalt grouping principles in visual statistical learning. *Attention, Perception, & Psychophysics, 73*(3), 708–713. doi:10.3758/s13414-010-0084-4

Glucksman, Myron L., & Kramer, Milton. (2004). Using dreams to assess clinical change during treatment. *Journal of the American Academy of Psychoanalysis and Dynamic Psychiatry, 32,* 345–358.

Glynn, Shawn M.; Aultman, Lori Price; & Owens, Ashley M. (2005). Motivation to learn in general education programs. *Journal of General Education, 54*(2), 150–170.

Goddard, Andrew W.; Ball, Susan G.; Martinez, James; Robinson, Michael J.; Yang, Charles R.; Russell, James M.; & Shekhar, Anantha. (2010). Current perspectives of the roles of the central norepinephrine system in anxiety and depression. *Depression and Anxiety, 27,* 339–350. doi:10.1002/da.20642

Goddard, Murray J. (2014). Critical psychiatry, critical psychology, and the behaviorism of B. F. Skinner. *Review of General Psychology, 18,* 208-215.

Gogtay, Nitin; Giedd, Jay N.; Lusk, Leslie; Hayashi, Kiraless M.; Rapoport, Judith L.; Thompson, Paul M.; & others. (2004, May 25). Dynamic mapping of human cortical development during childhood through early adulthood. *Proceedings of the National Academy of Sciences, 101,* 8174–8179. Retrieved from http://www.pnas.org/cgi/reprint/101/21/8174

Gogtay, Nitin; Vyas, Nora S.; Testa, Renee; Wood, Stephen J.; & Pantelis, Christos. (2011). Age of onset of schizophrenia: Perspectives from structural neuroimaging studies. *Schizophrenia Bulletin, 37*(3), 504–513.

Goh, Joshua O.; Tan, Jiat C.; & Park, Denise C. (2009). Culture modulates eye-movements to visual novelty. *PLOS ONE, 4*(12), e8238. doi:10.1371/journal.pone.0008238

Gold, Joel, & Gold, Ian. (2012). The "Truman Show" delusion: Psychosis in the global village. *Cognitive Neuropsychiatry, 17*(6), 455–472.

Goldberg, Abbie E. (2010). *Lesbian and gay parents and their children: Research on the family life cycle.* Washington, DC: American Psychological Association.

Goldinger, Stephen D.; Kleider, Heather M.; Azuma, Tamiko; & Beike, Denise R. (2003). "Blame the victim" under memory load. *Psychological Science, 14*(1), 81–85.

Goldsmith, D. J. (2004). *Communicating social support.* New York, NY: Cambridge University Press.

Goldstein, Alan J.; de Beurs, Edwin; Chambless, Dianne L.; & Wilson, Kimberly A. (2000). EMDR for panic disorder with agoraphobia: Comparison with waiting list and credible attention-placebo control condition. *Journal of Consulting and Clinical Psychology, 68,* 947–956.

Gollwitzer, Peter M. (1999). Implementation intentions: Strong effects of simple plans. *American Psychologist, 54,* 493–503.

Gollwitzer, Peter M., & Brandstätter, Veronika. (1997). Implementation intentions and effective goal pursuit. *Journal of Personality and Social Psychology, 73,* 186–199.

Gollwitzer, Peter M.; Gawrilow, Caterina; & Oettingen, Gabriele. (2010). The power of planning: Self-control by effective goal-striving. In R. R. Hassin, K. N. Ochsner, & Y. Trope (Eds.), Self control in society, mind, and brain (pp. 279–296). New York, NY: Oxford University Press.

Gollwitzer, Peter M.; Parks-Stamm, Elizabeth J.; Jaudas, Alexander; & Sheeran, Paschal. (2008). Flexible tenacity in goal pursuit. In James Y. Shah & Wendi L. Gardner (Eds.), *Handbook of motivation science.* New York, NY: Guilford.

Gollwitzer, Peter M., & Sheeran, Paschal. (2006). Implementation intentions and goal achievement: A meta-analysis of effects and processes. *Advances in Experimental Social Psychology, 38,* 249–268.

Gomez, C., & Rosen, B. (2001, December). The leader-member exchange as a link between managerial trust and employee empowerment. *Group & Organization Management, 26,* 512.

Gonzales, Patricia M.; Blanton, Hart; & Williams, Kevin J. (2002). The effects of stereotype threat and double-minority status on the test performance of Latino women. *Personality and Social Psychology Bulletin, 28,* 659–670.

Good, Byron J., & Hinton, Devon E. (2009). Introduction: Panic disorder in cross-cultural and historical perspective. In Devon E. Hinton & Byron J. Good (Eds.), *Culture and panic disorder* (pp. 1–28). Stanford, CA: Stanford University Press.

Good, Catherine; Aronson, Joshua; & Harder, Jayne Ann. (2008). Problems in the pipeline: Stereotype threat and women's achievement in high-level math courses. *Journal of Applied Developmental Psychology, 29,* 17–28.

Goodenough, Florence. (1932). The expression of emotion in a blind-deaf child. *Journal of Abnormal Social Psychology, 27,* 328–333.

Goodin, Burel, & Bulls, Hailey. (2013). Optimism and the experience of pain: Benefits of seeing the glass as half full. *Current Pain and Headache Reports, 17*(5). doi:10.1007/s11916-013-0329-8.

Goodman, Gail S.; Ghetti, Simona; Quas, Jodi A.; Edelstein, Robin S.; Alexander, Kristen Weede; Redlich, Allison D.; Cordon, Ingrid M.; & Jones, David P. H. (2003). A prospective study of memory for child sexual abuse: New findings relevant to the repressed-memory controversy. *Psychological Science, 14,* 113–118.

Goodwin, Stephanie A.; Fiske, Susan T.; Rosen, Lee D.; & Rosenthal, Alisa M. (2002). The eye of the beholder: Romantic goals and impression biases. *Journal of Experimental Social Psychology, 38*(3), 232–241.

Goossens, Luc; van Roekel, Eeske; Verhagen, Maaike; Cacioppo, John; Cacioppo, Stephanie; Maes, Marlies; & Boomsma, Dorret. (2015). The genetics of loneliness: Linking evolutionary theory to genome-wide genetics, epigenetics, and social science. *Perspectives on Psychological Science, 10,* 213–226. doi:10.1177/1745691614564878.

Gorchoff, Sara M.; John, Oliver P.; & Helson, Ravenna. (2008). Contextualizing change in marital satisfaction during middle age: An 18-year longitudinal study. *Psychological Science, 19,* 1194–1200.

Gordon, Barry. (2008, February 7). Quoted in Robynne Boyd, "Do people only use 10 percent of their brains?" *Scientific American.* Retrieved on April 10, 2014, from http://www.scientificamerican.com/article/people-only-use-10-percent-of-brain

Gordon, Peter. (2004, October 15). Numerical cognition without words: Evidence from Amazonia. *Science, 306,* 496–499.

Goswami, Usha. (2006). Neuroscience and education: From research to practice? *Nature Reviews Neuroscience, 7,* 2–7.

Gotlib, Ian H.; Joormann, Jutta; & Folanda-Ross, Lara C. (2014). Understanding familial risk for depression: A 25-year perspective. *Perspectives on Psychological Science, 9*(1), 94–108. doi:10.1177/1745691613513469

Gottesman, Irving I. (1991). *Schizophrenia genesis: The origins of madness.* New York, NY: Freeman.

Gottfredson, Linda S. (1998, Winter). The general intelligence factor. *Scientific American Presents: Exploring Intelligence, 9,* 24–29.

Gottfried, Jay. (2010). Central mechanisms of odour object perception. *Nature Reviews Neuroscience 11,* 628–641. doi:10.1038/nrn2883

Gouin, Jean-Philippe, & Kiecolt-Glaser, Janice. (2012). The impact of psychological stress on wound healing: Methods and mechanisms. *Immunology and Allergy Clinics of North America, 31*(1), 81–93. doi:10.1016/j.iac.2010.09.010

Goulart, Vinícius D.; Azevedo, Pedro G.; van de Schepop, Joanna A.; Teixeira, Camila P.; Barçante, Luciana; Azevedo, Cristiano S.; & Young, Robert J. (2009). GAPs in the study of zoo and wild animal welfare. *Zoo Biology, 28*(6), 561–573.

Gould, Elizabeth. (2007). How widespread is adult neurogenesis in mammals? *Nature Reviews Neuroscience, 8,* 481–488.

Gould, Elizabeth, & Gross, Charles G. (2002). Neurogenesis in adult mammals: Some progress and problems. *Journal of Neuroscience, 22,* 619–623.

Gould, Elizabeth; Tanapat, Patima; McEwen, Bruce S.; Flügge, Gabriele; & Fuchs, Eberhard. (1998, March 17). Proliferation of granule cell precursors in the dentate gyrus of adult monkeys is diminished by stress. *Proceedings of the National Academy of Sciences, USA, 95,* 3168–3171.

Gould, Madelyn S.; Greenberg, Ted; Velting, Drew M.; & Shaffer, David. (2003). Youth suicide risk and preventive interventions: A review of the past 10 years. *Journal of the American Academy of Child & Adolescent Psychiatry, 42,* 386–405.

Gould, Stephen Jay. (1993). *The mismeasure of man* (2nd ed.). New York, NY: Norton.

Grabe, Shelly; Ward, L. Monique; & Hyde, Janet Shibley. (2008). The role of the media in body image concerns among women: A metaanalysis of experimental and correlational studies. *Psychological Bulletin, 134,* 460–476.

Gracia, Enrique; García, Fernando; & Lila, Marisol. (2009). Public responses to intimate partner violence against women: The influence of perceived severity and personal responsibility. *The Spanish Journal of Psychology, 12*(2), 648–656.

Graham, Jesse; Nosek, Brian A.; Haidt, Jonathan; Iyer, Ravi; Koleva; Spassena; & Ditto, Peter H. (2011). Mapping the moral domain. *Journal of Personality and Social Psychology,* Online first publication, January 17, 2011. doi:10.1037/a0021847

Graham, John R. (1993). *MMPI-2: Assessing personality and psychopathology* (2nd ed.). New York, NY: Oxford University Press.

Graham, Kathryn D., & Wells, Samantha. (2003). Sombody's gonna get their head kicked in tonight! Aggression among young males in bars—A question of values? *British Journal of Criminology, 43,* 546–566.

Graham, Kathryn D.; Osgood, D. Wayne; Wells, Samantha.; & Stockwell, Tim. (2006). To what extent is intoxication associated with aggression in bars? A multilevel analysis. *Journal of Studies on Alcohol and Drugs, 67*(3), 382–390.

Graham, William K., & Balloun, Joe. (1973). An empirical test of Maslow's need hierarchy theory. *Journal of Humanistic Psychology, 13,* 97–108.

Granholm, Eric; Ben-Zeev, Dror; Link, Peter C.; Bradshaw, Kristen R.; & Holden, Jason L. (2012). Mobile assessment and treatment for schizophrenia (MATS): A pilot trial of an interactive text-messaging intervention for medication adherence, socialization, and auditory hallucinations. *Schizophrenia Bulletin, 38*(3), 414–425. doi:10.1093/schbul/sbr155

Grant, Bob. (2014, September). On the other hand. *The Scientist, 28.* Retrieved from http://www.the-scientist.com/?articles.view/articleNo/40868/title/On-the-Other-Hand

Grant, Bridget F.; Chou, S. Patricia; Goldstein, Risë B.; Huang, Boji; Stinson, Frederick S.; Saha, Tulshi D.; Smith, Sharon M.; Dawson, Deborah A.; Pulay, Attila J.; Pickering, Roger P.; & Ruan, W. June. (2008, April). Prevalence, correlates, disability, and comorbidity of DSM-IV borderline personality disorder: Results from the Wave 2 National Epidemiologic Survey on Alcohol and Related Conditions. *Journal of Clinical Psychiatry, 69*(4), 533–545.

Grant, Bridget F.; Hasin, Deborah S.; Stinson, Frederick S.; Dawson, Deborah A.; Chou, S. Patricia; Ruan, W. June; & Pickering, Roger P. (2004). Prevalence, correlates, and disability of personality disorders in the United States: Results from the National Epidemiologic Survey on Alcohol and Related Conditions. *Journal of Clinical Psychiatry, 65,* 948–958.

Grant, Joshua A.; Courtemanche, Jérôme; Duerden, Emma G.; Duncan, Gary H.; & Rainville, Pierre. (2010). Cortical thickness and pain sensitivity in zen meditators. *Emotion, 10*(1), 43–53. doi:10.1037/a0018334

Grant, Joshua A.; Courtemanche, Jérôme; Rainville, Pierre. (2011). A non-elaborative mental stance and decoupling of executive and pain-related cortices predicts low pain sensitivity in Zen meditators. *Pain, 152,* 150–156. doi:10.1016/j.pain.2010.10.006

Grant, Paul M.; Huh, Gloria A.; Perivoliotis, Dimitri; Stolar, Neal M.; & Beck, Aaron T. (2012). Randomized trial to evaluate the efficacy of cognitive therapy for low-functioning patients with schizophrenia. *Archives of General Psychiatry, 69,* 121–127. doi:10.1001/archgenpsychiatry.2011.129

Greasley, Peter. (2000). Handwriting analysis and personality assessment: The creative use of analogy, symbolism, and metaphor. *European Psychologist, 5,* 44–51.

Green, Joseph P.; Lynn, Steven Jay; & Montgomery, Guy H. (2006). A meta-analysis of gender, smoking cessation, and hypnosis: A brief communication. *International Journal of Clinical and Experimental Hypnosis, 54,* 224–233.

Green, Richard. (1985). Gender identity in childhood and later sexual orientation: Follow-up of 78 males. *American Journal of Psychiatry, 142,* 339–341.

Green, Richard. (1987). *The "sissy boy syndrome" and the development of homosexuality.* New Haven, CT: Yale University Press.

Greenberg, Daniel L., & Rubin, David C. (2003). The neuropsychology of autobiographical memory. *Cortex, 39,* 687–728.

Greene, Roberta R. (2008). Carl Rogers and the Person-Centered approach. In Roberta R. Greene (Ed.), *Human behavior theory and social work practice* (3rd ed., pp. 113–132). Piscataway, NJ: Transaction Publishers.

Greenfield, Patricia M. (1997). You can't take it with you: Why ability assessments don't cross cultures. *American Psychologist, 52,* 1115–1124.

Greenfield, Patricia M. (2003, February). Quoted in Benson, Etienne. "Intelligence across cultures." *APA Monitor on Psychology, 34,* 56.

Greenwald, Anthony G.; McGhee, Debbie E.; & Schwartz, Jordan L. K. (1998). Measuring individual differences in implicit cognition: The implicit association test. *Journal of Personality and Social Psychology, 74*(6), 1464–1480.

Greenwald, Anthony G.; Poehlman, T. Andrew; Uhlmann, Eric; & Banaji, Mahzarin R. (2009). Understanding and using the Implicit

Association Test: III. Meta-analysis of predictive validity. *Journal of Personality and Social Psychology, 97,* 17–41.

Greenwood, Patricia M., & Parasuraman, Raja. (2012). *Nurturing the older brain and mind.* Cambridge, MA: MIT Press.

Greer, Stephanie M.; Goldstein, Andrea N.; & Walker, Matthew P. (2013). The impact of sleep deprivation on food desire in the human brain. *Nature Communications 4,* Article number: 2259. doi:10.1038/ncomms3259

Gregory, Richard L. (1968, November). Visual illusions. *Scientific American, 212,* 66–76.

Gregory, Richard L. (2003). Seeing after blindness. *Nature Neuroscience, 6,* 909–910.

Greitemeyer, Tobias, & Mügge, Dirk O. (2014). Video games do affect social outcomes: A meta-analytic review of the effects of violent and prosocial video game play. *Personality and Social Psychology Bulletin, 40,* 578–589. doi:10.1177/0146167213520459

Greitermeyer, Tobias, & Mügge, Dirk O. (2014). Video games do affect social outcomes: A meta-analytic review of the effects of violent and prosocial video game play. *Personality and Social Psychology Bulletin, 40,* 578–589. doi:10.1177/0146167213520459

Griffiths, Kathleen M.; Farrer, Louise; & Christensen, Helen. (2010). The efficacy of internet interventions for depression and anxiety disorders: A review of randomised controlled trials. *Medical Journal of Australia, 192*(11), S4–S11. Retrieved from https://www.mja.com.au

Grigg-Damberger, Madeleine; Gozal, David; Marcus, Carole L.; Quan, Stuart F.; Rosen, Carol L.; Chervin, Ronald D.; & others. (2007). Visual scoring of sleep and arousal in infants and children. *Journal of Clinical Sleep Medicine, 3,* 201–240.

Griggs, Richard A. (2014). Coverage of the Stanford prison experiment in introductory psychology textbooks. *Teaching of Psychology, 41,* 195–203. doi:10.1177/009862831453796

Griggs, Richard A. (2015). The disappearance of independence in textbook coverage of Asch's social pressure experiments. *Teaching of Psychology, 42,* 137–142. doi:10.1177/0098628315569939

Groer, Maureen; Meagher, Mary W.; & Kendall-Tackett, Kathleen. (2010). An overview of stress and immunity. In Kathleen Kendall-Tackett (Ed.), *The psychoneuroimmunology of chronic disease: Exploring the links between inflammation, stress, and illness.* Washington, DC: American Psychological Association.

Gross, Garrett G.; Junge, Jason A.; Mora, Rudy J.; Kwon, Hyung-Bae; Olson, C. Anders; Takahashi, Terry T.; Liman, Emily R.; Ellis-Davies, Graham C.R.; Ellis-Davies, Graham C.R.; McGee, Aaron W.; Sabatini, Bernardo L.; Roberts, Richard W.; & Arnold, Don B. (2013). Recombinant probes for visualizing endogenous synaptic proteins in living neurons. *Neuron 78,* 971–985. doi:10.1016/j.neuron.2013.04.017

Gross, James J. (2007). The cultural regulation of emotions. In James J. Gross (Ed.), *Handbook of emotion regulation* (pp. 486–503). New York, NY: Guilford.

Grow, Kory. (2014, February 6). Lady Gaga reveals post-'Artpop' depression: 'I felt like I was dying.' *Rolling Stone.* Retrieved from http://www.rollingstone.com/music/news/lady-gaga-reveals-post-artpop-depression-i-felt-like-i-was-dying-20140206#ixzz3AlkvafWv

Grubin, Don. (2010). Polygraphy. In Jennifer M. Brown & Elizabeth A. Campbell, (Eds.), *The Cambridge handbook of forensic psychology.* New York, NY: Cambridge University Press.

Grünbaum, Adolf. (2006). Is Sigmund Freud's psychoanalytic edifice relevant to the 21st century? *Psychoanalytic Psychology, 23,* 257–284.

Grünbaum, Adolf. (2007). The reception of my Freud-critique in the psychoanalytic literature. *Psychoanalytic Psychology, 24,* 545–576.

Grunstein, Ronald. (2005). Continuous positive airway pressure treatment for obstructive sleep apnea-hypopnea syndrome. In Meir H. Kryger, Thomas Roth, & William C. Dement (Eds.), *Principles and practice of sleep medicine* (4th ed.). Philadelphia, PA: Elsevier Saunders.

Grusec, Joan E. (2011). Socialization processes in the family: Social and emotional development. *Annual Review of Psychology, 62,* 243–69. doi:10.1146/annurev.psych.121208.131650

Grussu, Pietro; Quatraro, Rosa M.; & Nasta, Maria T. (2005). Profile of mood states and parental attitudes in motherhood: Comparing women with planned and unplanned pregnancies. *Birth: Issues in Perinatal Care, 2,* 107–114.

Grzywacz, Joseph G., & Almeida, David M. (2008). Stress and binge drinking: A daily process examination of stressor pile-up and socioeconomic status in affect regulation. *International Journal of Stress Management, 15*(4), 364–380.

Guéguen, Nicolas; Marchand, Marie; Pascual, Alexandre; & Lourel, Marcel. (2008). Foot-in-the-door technique using a courtship request: A field experiment. *Psychological Reports, 103*(2), 529–534.

Guehl, Dominique; Benazzouz, Abdelhamid; Aouizerate, Bruno; Cuny, Emmanuel; Rotge, Jean-Yves; Rougier, Alain; Tignol, Jean; Bioulac, Bernard; & Burbaud, Pierre. (2008, March). Neuronal correlates of obsessions in the caudate nucleus. *Biological Psychiatry, 63*(6), 557–562.

Guimond, Serge; Crisp, Richard J.; De Oliveira, Pierre; Kamiejski, Rodolphe; Kteily, Nour; Kuepper, Beate; . . . Zick, Andreas. (2013). Diversity policy, social dominance, and intergroup relations: Predicting prejudice in changing social and political contexts. *Journal of Personality and Social Psychology, 104*(6), 941–958. doi:10.1037/a0032069

Guindon, José, & Hohmann, Andrea. (2009). Pain: Mechanisms and measurement. In Gary G. Berntson & John T. Cacioppo (Eds.), *Handbook of neuroscience in the behavioral sciences.* Hoboken, NJ: Wiley

Gujar, Ninad; Yoo, Seung-Schik; Hu, Peter; & Walker, Matthew P. (2011). Sleep deprivation amplifies reactivity of brain reward networks, biasing the appraisal of positive emotional experiences. *Journal of Neuroscience, 31*(12): 4466–4474. doi:10.1523/jneurosci.3220-10.2011

Gunlicks-Stoessel, Meredith & Weissman, Myrna M. (2011). Interpersonal psychotherapy (IPT). In Leonard M. Horowitz & Stephen Strack (Eds.), *Handbook of interpersonal psychology: Theory, research, assessment, and therapeutic interventions* (pp. 533–544). Hoboken, NJ: Wiley.

Gureje, Oye; Lasebikan, Victor O.; Kola, Lola; & Makanjuola, Victor A. (2006). Lifetime and 12-month prevalence of mental disorders in the Nigerian survey of mental health and well-being. *British Journal of Psychiatry, 188,* 465–471. doi:10.1192/bjp.188.5.465

Gurven, Michael; von Rueden, Christopher; Massenkoff, Maxim; Kaplan, Hillard; & Lero Vie, Marino. (2013). How universal is the Big Five? Testing the five-factor model of personality variation among forager–farmers in the Bolivian Amazon. *Journal of Personality and Social Psychology, 104,* 354–370. doi:10.1037/a0030841

Gurven, Michael; von Rueden, Christopher; Stieglitz, Jonathan; Kaplan, Hillard; & Rodriguez, Daniel E. (2014). The evolutionary fitness of personality traits in a small-scale subsistence society. *Evolution and Human Behavior, 35,* 17–25. doi:10.1016/j.evolhumbehav.2013.09.002

Guthrie, Robert V. (2000). Francis Cecil Sumner: The first African American pioneer in psychology. In Gregory A. Kimble & Michael Wertheimer (Eds.), *Portraits of pioneers in psychology* (Vol. 4, pp. 180–193). Washington, DC: American Psychological Association.

Guthrie, Robert V. (2004). *Even the rat was white: A historical view of psychology.* Upper Saddle River, NJ: Pearson Education.

Gutman, David A., & Nemeroff, Charles B. (2011). Stress and depression. In Richard J. Contrada & Andrew Baum (Eds.), *The handbook of stress science: Biology, psychology, and health* (pp. 345–357). New York, NY: Springer.

Gyatso, Tenzin. (2003, April 26). The monk in the lab. *The New York Times,* p. A19. Retrieved April 26, 2003, from http://www.nytimes.com/2003/04/26/opinion/26LAMA.html

Habhab, Summar; Sheldon, Jane P; & Loeb, Roger C. (2009). The relationship between stress, dietary restraint, and food preferences in women. *Appetite, 52*(2), 437–444.

Hackett, Troy A., & Kaas, John H. (2009). Audition. In Gary G. Berntson & John T. Cacioppo (Eds.), *Handbook of neuroscience in the behavioral sciences.* Hoboken, NJ: Wiley

Hackman, Daniel A.; Farah, Martha J.; Meaney, Michael J. (2010). Socioeconomic status and the brain: Mechanistic insights from human and animal research. *Nature Reviews Neuroscience, 11,* 651–659.

Hagar, Sheila. (2013). Washington State Penitentiary psychologist earns national acclaim for programs. *Union-Bulletin*. Retrieved from http://union-bulletin.com /news/2013/sep/19/washington-state-penitentiary-psychologist-earns-n

Haidt, Jonathan. (2007). The new synthesis in moral psychology. *Science, 316*, 998–1002.

Haidt, Jonathan. (2010). Moral psychology must not be based on faith and hope: Commentary on Narvaez (2010). *Perspectives on Psychological Science, 5*, 182–184.

Haidt, Jonathan; Koller, Silvia Helena; & Dias, Maria G. (1993). Affect, culture, and morality, or is it wrong to eat your dog? *Journal of Personality and Social Psychology, 65*, 613–628.

Hald, Gert M.; Malamuth, Neil M.; & Yuen, Carlin. (2010). Pornography and attitudes supporting violence against women: Revisiting the relationship in nonexperimental studies. *Aggressive Behavior, 36*(1), 14–20. doi:10.1002/ab.20328

Halim, May Ling, & Ruble, Diane N. (2009). Gender identity and stereotyping in early and middle childhood. In Joan C. Chrisler & Donald R. McCreary (Eds.), *Handbook of Gender Research in Psychology*, New York, NY: Springer.

Hall, Geoffrey. (2009). Watson: The thinking man's behaviourist. *British Journal of Psychology, 100*(1a), 185–187.

Halmi, Katherine A.; Bellace, Dara; Berthod, Samantha; Gosh, Samiran; Berrettini, Wade; Brandt, Harry A.; … Strober, Michael. (2012). An examination of early childhood perfectionism across anorexia nervosa subtypes. *International Journal of Eating Disorders, 45*, 800–807.

Halpern, Diane F.; Beninger, Anna S.; & Straight, Carli A. (2011). Sex differences in intelligence. In Robert J. Sternberg & Scott Barry Kaufman (Eds.), *The Cambridge handbook of intelligence* (pp. 253–270). New York, NY: Cambridge University Press.

Halpern, John H.; Sherwood, Andrea R.; Hudson, James I.; Yurgelun-Todd, Deborah; & Pope, Harrison G. (2005). Psychological and cognitive effects of long-term peyote use among Native Americans. *Biological Psychiatry, 58*, 624–631.

Hamann, Stephan. (2009). The human amygdala and memory. In P. J. Whalen & E. A. Phelps (Eds.), *The human amygdala* (pp. 177–203). New York, NY: Guilford.

Hamer, M.; Taylor, A.; & Steptoe, A. (2006). The effect of acute aerobic exercise on stress related blood pressure responses: A systematic review and meta-analysis. *Biological Psychology, 71*(2), 183–190.

Hamermesh, Daniel S., & Abrevaya, Jason. (2011). Beauty is the promise of happiness? (Discussion Paper No. 5600). Bonn, Germany: The Institute for the Study of Labor (IZA).

Hamilton, S., & Hamilton, M.A. (2006). School, work, and emerging adulthood. In J. J. Arnett & J. L. Tanner (Eds.), *Emerging adults in America: Coming of age in the 21st century*. Washington, DC: American Psychological Association.

Hamlin, J. Kiley; Mahajan, Neha; Liberman, Zoe; & Wynn, Karen. (2013). Not like me = bad: Infants prefer those who harm dissimilar others. *Psychological Science, 24*(4), 589–594. doi:10.1177/0956797612457785

Hammen, Constance. (2005). Stress and depression. *Annual Review of Clinical Psychology, 1*, 293–319.

Hammond, Geoffrey C.; Croudace, Tim J.; Radhakrishnan, Muralikrishnan; Lafortune, Louise; Watson, Alison; McMillan-Shields, Fiona; & Jones, Peter B. (2012). Comparative effectiveness of cognitive therapies delivered face-to-face or over the telephone: An observational study using propensity methods. *PLOS ONE, 7*(9), 1–15. doi:10.1371/journal.pone.0042916

Haney, Craig; Banks, Curtis; & Zimbardo, Philip. (1973). Interpersonal dynamics in a simulated prison. *International Journal of Criminology and Penology, 1*, 69–97.

Hänggi, Jürgen; Fövenyi, Laszlo; Liem, Franziskus; Meyer, Martin; & Jäncke, Lutz. (2014). The hypothesis of neuronal interconnectivity as a function of brain size—a general organization principle of the human connectome. *Frontiers in Human Neuroscience, 8*, 915. doi:10.3389/fnhum.2014.00915

Hanna-Pladdy, Brenda, & MacKay, Alicia. (2011). The relation between instrumental musical activity and cognitive aging. *Neuropsychology, 25*(3), 378–386. doi:10.1037/a0021895

Hardt, Oliver; Wang, Szu-Han; & Nader, Karim. (2010). Storage or retrieval deficit: the yin and yang of amnesia. *Learning and Memory, 16*, 224–230.

Hardy, Sam A.; Bhattacharjee, Amit; Reed, Americus, II; & Aquino, Karl. (2010). Moral identity and psychological distance: The case of adolescent parental socialization. *Journal of Adolescence, 33*(1), 111–123.

Harlow, Harry F. (1953a). Learning by Rhesus monkeys on the basis of manipulation-exploration motives. *Science, 117*, 466–467.

Harlow, Harry F. (1953b). Mice, monkeys, men, and motives. *Psychological Review, 60*, 23–32.

Harlow, Harry F. (1953c). Motivation as a factor in new responses. In *Current theory and research in motivation: A symposium*. Lincoln: University of Nebraska Press.

Harlow, Harry F. (1958) The nature of love. *American Psychologist, 13,* 673–685.

Harlow, John M. (1869). Recovery from passage of an iron bar through the head. (Read before the Massachusetts Medical Society, June 3, 1868.) Boston, MA: David Clapp & Son Medical and Special Journal Office.

Harman, S. Mitchell (2005). Testosterone in older men after the Institute of Medicine Report: Where do we go from here? *Climacteric, 8*, 124–135.

Harnett, Paul; O'Donovan, Analise; & Lambert, Michael J. (2010). The dose response relationship in psychotherapy: Implications for social policy. *Clinical Psychologist, 14*(2), 39–44.

Haro, Josep M.; Novick, Diego; Bertsch, Jordan; Karagiania, Jamie; Dossenbach, Martin; & Jones, Peter B. (2011). Cross-national clinical and functional remission rates: Worldwide schizophrenia outpatient health outcomes (W-SOHO) study. *British Journal of Psychiatry, 199*, 194–201. doi:10.1192/bjp.bp.110.082065

Harper, Sarah. (2014). Economic and social implications of aging societies. *Science, 346*, 587–592.

Harris, Ben. (1979). Whatever happened to Little Albert? *American Psychologist, 34*, 151–160.

Harris, Ben. (2011). Letting go of Little Albert: Disciplinary memory, history, and the uses of myth. *Journal of the History of the Behavioral Sciences, 47*, 1–17. doi:10.1002/jhbs.20470

Harris Interactive. (2007, October 9). Six nation survey finds satisfaction with current job: American workers most likely to feel well-paid and to like their boss. Retrieved from http://www.harrisinteractive.com/news /allnewsbydate.asp?NewsID=1255

Harris, Julie Aitken; Vernon, Philip A.; & Jang, Kerry L. (2007, January). Rated personality and measured intelligence in young twin children. *Personality and Individual Differences, 42*(1), 75–86.

Harris, Julie M.; Nefs, Harold T.; & Grafton, Catherine E. (2008). Binocular vision and motion-in-depth. *Spatial Vision, 21*(6), 531–547. doi:10.1163/156856808786451462

Harris, Lasana T., & Fiske, Susan T. (2006). Dehumanizing the lowest of the low. *Psychological Science, 17*(10), 847–853.

Harrison, Robert V. (2012, December 13). The prevention of noise-induced hearing loss in children. *International Journal of Pediatrics, 2012*, 473–541. doi:10.1155/2012/473541

Hart, Dan. (2005). The development of moral identity. In G. Carlo & C. P. Edwards (Eds.), *Moral motivation through the life span* (pp. 165–196). Lincoln: University of Nebraska Press.

Harter, Susan. (1990). Self and identity development. In S. Shirley Feldman & Glen R. Elliott (Eds.), *At the threshold: The developing adolescent*. Cambridge, MA: Harvard University Press.

Hartshorne, Joshua K., & Germine, Laura T. (2015). When does cognitive functioning peak? The asynchronous rise and fall of different cognitive abilities across the life span. *Psychological Science, 26*, 433–443. doi:10.1177/0956797614567339

Hartwig, Marissa K., & Dunlosky, John. (2012). Study strategies of college students: Are self-testing and scheduling related to achievement? *Psychonomic Bulletin & Review, 19*(1), 126–134. doi:10.3758/s13423-011-0181-y

Harvey, Allison G. (2011). Sleep and circadian functioning: Critical mechanisms in the mood disorders? *Annual Review of Clinical Psychology. 7*, 297–319. doi:10.1146/annurev-clinpsy-032210-104550

Harvey, Megan A.; Sellman, John D.; Porter, Richard J.; & Frampton, Christopher M. (2007). The relationship between non-acute adolescent cannabis use and cognition. *Drug & Alcohol Review, 26*, 309–319.

Harvey, Nigel. (2007, February). Use of heuristics: Insights from forecasting research. *Thinking & Reasoning, 13*(1), 5–24.

Harwood, T. M., & L'Abate, L. (2010). *Self-help in mental health: A critical review.* New York, NY: Springer Science Business Media.

Hasin, Deborah; Fenton, Miriam C.; Skodol, Andrew; Krueger, Rorbert; Keyes, Katherine; Geier, Timothy; ... Grant, Bridget. (2011). Personality disorders and the 3-year course of alcohol, drug, and nicotine use disorders. *Archives of General Psychiatry, 68*(11), 1158–1167.

Hatch, Stephani L., & Dohrenwend, Bruce P. (2007). Distribution of traumatic and other stressful life events by race/ethnicity, gender, SES, and age: A review of the research. *American Journal of Community Psychology, 40*, 313–332.

Hatton, Holly; Conger, Rand D.; Larsen-Rife, Dannelle; & Ontai, Lenna. (2010). An integrative and developmental perspective for understanding romantic relationship quality during the transition to parenthood. In M. S. Schulz, M. K. Pruett, P. K. Kerig & R. D. Parke. (Eds.), *Strengthening couple relationships for optimal child development: Lessons from research and intervention* (pp. 115–129). Washington, DC: American Psychological Association.

Haun, Daniel B.M.; Rekers, Yvonne; & Tomasello, Michael. (2014). Children conform to the behavior of peers; other great apes stick with what they know. *Psychological Science, 25*, 2160–2167. doi:10.1177/0956797614553235

Hauser, Marc D. (2000). *Wild minds: What animals really think.* New York, NY: Holt.

Haushofer, Johannes, & Fehr, Ernst. (2014). On the psychology of poverty. *Science, 344*, 862–867. doi:10.1126/science.1232491

Havas, David A.; Glenberg, Arthur M.; Gutowski, Karol A.; Lucarelli, Mark J.; & Davidson, Richard J. (2010). Cosmetic use of botulinum toxin-A affects processing of emotional language. *Psychological Science, 21*, 895–900. doi:10.1177/0956797610374742

Havermans, Remco C.; Janssen, Tim; Giesen, Janneke, C.A.H.; Roefs, Anne; & Jansen, Anita. (2009) Food liking, food wanting, and sensory-specific satiety. *Appetite, 52*, 222–225.

Hawkey, Chris; Rhodes, Jon; Gilmore, Ian; & Sheron, Nick. (2011). Drugs and harm to society. *Lancet, 377*, 9765, 554. doi:10.1016/ S0140-6736(11)60198-0

Hawkins, Nicole; Richards, P. Scott; Granley, H. Mac; & Stein, David M. (2004). The impact of exposure to the thin-ideal media image on women. *Eating Disorders: The Journal of Treatment and Prevention, 12*, 35–50.

Hawton, Keith; Saunders, Kate E. A.; & O'Connor, Rory C. (2012). Suicide 1: Self-harm and suicide in adolescents. *Lancet, 379*, 2373–2382.

Hayatbakhsh, Mohammad R.; Najman, Jake M.; McGee, Tara R.; Bor, William; & O'Callaghan, Michael J. (2009). Early pubertal maturation in the prediction of early adult substance use: A prospective study. *Addiction, 104*(1), 59–66.

Hayes, Emily. (2011). Nonpsychiatric prescribing fuels rise in antidepressant use. *Internal Medicine News.* Accessed on September 20, 2011, from http://www.internalmedicinenews.com/news/mental-health/single-article/nonpsychiatric-prescribing-fuels-rise-in-antidepressant-use/8a560f9536.html

Hayes, Steven C.; Villatte, Matthieu; Levin, Michael; & Hildebrandt, Mikaela. (2011). Open, aware, and active: Contextual approaches as an emerging trend in the behavioral and cognitive therapies. *Annual Review of Clinical Psychology, 7*, 141–68. doi:10.1146/annurev-clinpsy-032210-104449

Hayes-Skelton, Sarah A., & Wadsworth, Lauren P. (2015). Mindfulness in the treatment of anxiety. In Kirk Warren Brown, J. David Creswell, & Richard M. Ryan. *Handbook of mindfulness: Theory, research, and practice.* New York, NY: Guilford.

Hayne, Harlene; Garry, Maryanne; Loftus, Elizabeth F. (2006). On the continuing lack of scientific evidence for repression. *Behavioral and Brain Sciences, 29*(5), 521–522. doi:10.1017/S0140525X06319115

Heaps, Christopher M., & Nash, Michael. (2001). Comparing recollective experience in true and false autobiographical memories. *Journal of Experimental Psychology: Learning, Memory, and Cognition, 27*, 920–930.

Hearst, Eliot. (1999). After the puzzle boxes: Thorndike in the 20th century. *Journal of the Experimental Analysis of Behavior, 72*, 441–446.

Heaven, Patrick, & Ciarrochi, Joseph. (2008). Parental styles, gender and the development of hope and self-esteem. *European Journal of Personality, 22*(8), 707–724.

Hebb, Donald O. (1955). Drives and the C. N. S. (central nervous system). *Psychological Review, 62*, 243–254.

Hedden, Trey; Ketay, Sarah; Aron, Arthur; Markus, Hazel Rose; & Gabrieli, John D. E. (2008). Cultural influences on neural substrates of attentional control. *Psychological Science, 19*, 12–17.

Hedegaard, Holly; Chen, Li-Hui; & Warner, Margaret. (2015). Drug-poisoning deaths involving heroin: United States, 2000–2013 (NCHS data brief, no. 190). Hyattsville, MD: National Center for Health Statistics.

Heerey, Erin A., & Crossley, Helen M. (2013). Predictive and reactive mechanisms in smile reciprocity. *Psychological Science, 24*, 1446–1455. doi:10.1177/0956797612472203

Heiby, Elaine M. (2010). Concerns about substandard training for prescription privileges for psychologists. *Journal of Clinical Psychology, 66*(1), 104–111. doi:10.1002/jclp.20650

Heiby, Elaine M.; DeLeon, Patrick H.; & Anderson, Timothy. (2004). A debate on prescription privileges for psychologists. *Professional Psychology: Research and Practice, 35*, 336–344.

Heider, Eleanor Rosch, & Olivier, Donald C. (1972). The structure of the color space in naming and memory for two languages. *Cognitive Psychology, 3*, 337–354.

Heine, Steven J. (2010). Cultural psychology. In Roy F. Baumeister & Eli J. Finkel (Eds.), *Advanced social psychology: The state of the science* (pp. 655–696). New York, NY: Oxford University Press.

Heine, Steven J.; Foster, Julie-Ann B.; & Spina, Roy. (2009). Do birds of a feather universally flock together? Cultural variation in the similarity-attraction effect. *Asian Journal of Social Psychology, 12*(4), 247–258.

Heine, Steven J.; & Norenzayan, Ara. (2006). Toward a psychological science for a cultural species. *Perspectives on Psychological Science, 1*, 251–269.

Heinrichs, R. Walter. (2005). The primacy of cognition in schizophrenia. *American Psychologist, 60*, 229–242.

Helenius, Dorte; Munk-Jorgensen, Povl; & Steinhausen, Hans-Christoph. (2012). Family load estimates of schizophrenia and associated risk factors in a nation-wide population study of former child and adolescent patients up to forty years of age. *Schizophrenia Research, 139*, 183–188.

Henderson, Valerie Land; O'Hara, Maureen; Barfield, Gay Leah; & Rogers, Natalie. (2007). Applications beyond the therapeutic context. In Mick Cooper, Maureen O'Hara, Peter F. Schmid, & Gill Wyatt, (Eds.), *The handbook of person-centred psychotherapy and counselling.* New York, NY: Palgrave Macmillan.

Henkel, Linda A. (2011). Photograph-induced memory errors: When photographs make people claim they have done things they have not. *Applied Cognitive Psychology, 25*(1), 78–86.

Hennessey, Beth A. (2010). The creativity-motivation connection. In J.C. Kaufman & R.J. Sternberg (Eds.), *The Cambridge handbook of creativity* (pp. 342–365). New York, NY: Cambridge University Press.

Hennessey, Beth A., & Amabile, Teresa M. (2010). Creativity. *Annual Review of Psychology, 61*, 569–598.

Hennessy, Dwight A.; Jakubowski, Robert; & Benedetti, Alyson J. (2005). The influence of the actor-observer bias on attributions of other drivers. In D. A. Hennessy & D. L. Wiesenthal (Eds.), *Contemporary issues in road user behavior and traffic safety* (pp. 13–20). Hauppauge, NY: Nova Science.

Henrich, Joseph; Heine, Steven J.; & Norenzayan, Ara. (2010). The weirdest people in the world? *Behavioral and Brain Sciences, 33*(2–3), 61–83. doi:10.1017/S0140525X0999152X

Henrich, Joseph. (2014). Rice, psychology, and innovation. *Science, 344*, 593–594. doi:10.1126/science.1253815

Heppner, Puncky Paul. (2008). Expanding the conceptualization and measurement of applied problem solving and coping: From stages and dimensions to the almost forgotten cultural context. *American Psychologist, 63*, 805–816.

Herbert, James D.; Lilienfeld, Scott O.; Lohr, Jeffrey M.; Montgomery, Robert W.; O'Donohue, William T.; Rosen, Gerald M.; & Tolin, David F. (2000). Science and pseudoscience in the development of eye movement desensitization and reprocessing: Implications for clinical psychology. *Clinical Psychology Review, 20*, 945–971.

Herek, Gregory M., & McLemore, Kevin A. (2013). Sexual prejudice. *Annual Review of Psychology, 64*(1), 309–333. doi:10.1146/annurev-psych-113011-143826

Herman, Louis M. (2002). Exploring the cognitive world of the bottle-nosed dolphin. In Marc Bekoff, Colin Allen, & Gordon M. Burghardt (Eds.), *The cognitive animal: Empirical and theoretical perspectives on animal cognition.* Cambridge, MA: MIT Press.

Hermans, Hubert J. M. (1996). Voicing the self: From information processing to dialogical interchange. *Psychological Bulletin, 119*, 31–50.

Herndon, Phillip; Myers, Bryan; Mitchell, Katherine; Kehn, Andre; & Henry, Sarah. (2014). False memories for highly aversive early childhood events: Effects of guided imagery and group influence. *Psychology of Consciousness: Theory, Research, and Practice, 1*, 20–31. doi:10.1037/cns0000011

Hersh, Seymour. (2004a, May 9). Chain of command. *The New York* (Posted online May 9, 2004, print issue of May 17, 2004). Retrieved on November 28, 2004, from http://www.newyorker.com/printablers/fact/040517/fa_fact2

Hersh, Seymour. (2004b, April 30). Torture at Abu Ghraib. *The New Yorker* (Posted online April 30, 2004, issue of May 10, 2004). Retrieved on November 29, 2005, from http://www.newyorker.com/printables/fact/040510fa_fact

Hersh, Seymour. (2005). *Chain of command: The road from 9/11 to Abu Ghraib.* New York, NY: HarperPerennial.

Hertz, Marguerite R. (1992). Rorschach-bound: A 50-year memoir. *Professional Psychology: Research and Practice, 23*, 168–171.

Hertzog, Christopher; Kramer, Arthur F.; Wilson, Robert S.; & Ulman, Lindenberger. (2009). Enrichment effects on adult cognitive development: Can the functional capacity of older adults be preserved and enhanced? *Psychological Science in the Public Interest, 9*, 1–65.

Heth, Josephine Todrank; Schapira, Daniel; & Nahir, A. Menachim. (2004). Controllability Awareness, Perceived Stress and Tolerating Chronic Illness. In Serge P. Shohov (Ed.), *Advances in psychology research, Vol. 28.* Hauppauge, NY: Nova Science.

Heth, Josephine Todrank, & Somer, Eli. (2002). Characterizing stress tolerance "Controllability awareness" and its relationship to perceived stress and reported health. *Personality and Individual Differences, 33*, 883–895.

Hettema, Jennifer; Steele, Julie; & Miller, William R. (2005). Motivational interviewing. *Annual Review of Clinical Psychology, 1*, 91–111.

Hewstone, Miles; Rubin, Mark; & Willis, Hazel. (2002). Intergroup bias. *Annual Review of Psychology, 53*, 575–604.

Heyman, Karen. (2003). The enriched environment. *The Scientist, 17*(9), 24–25.

Heyman, Richard E., & Smith Slep, Amy M. (2002). Do child abuse and interparental violence lead to adulthood family violence? *Journal of Marriage and Family, 64*, 864–870.

Heymann, Jody. (2007, February). The healthy families act: The importance to Americans' livelihoods, families, and health. Written testimony submitted to the U.S. Senate Committee on Health, Education, Labor, and Pensions. Retrieved September 2009 from http://help.senate.gov/Hearings/2007_02_13/Heymann.pdf

Hiatt, Kristina D., & Dishion, Thomas J. (2008). Antisocial personality development. In Theodore P. Beauchaine & Stephen P. Hinshaw (Eds.), *Child and adolescent psychopathology* (pp. 370–404). Hoboken, NJ: Wiley.

Hicken, Margaret; Lee, Hedwig; Morenoff, Jeffrey; House, James; & Williams, David. (2014). Racial/ethnic disparities in hypertension prevalence: Reconsidering the role of chronic stress. *American Journal of Public Health, 104*(1), 117–123. doi:10.2105/ajph.2013.301395

Hickok, Gregory; Bellugi, Ursula; & Klima, Edward S. (2001, June). Sign language in the brain. *Scientific American, 184*, 58–65.

Higgins, E. Tory. (2004). Making a theory useful: Lessons handed down. *Personality and Social Psychology Review, 8*(2), 138–145.

Higgins, Stephen T.; Silverman, Kenneth; & Washio, Yukiko. (2011). Contingency management. In Marc Galanter & Herbert D. Kleber (Eds.), *Psychotherapy for the treatment of substance abuse* (pp. 193–218). Arlington, VA: American Psychiatric Publishing.

Hilgard, Ernest R. (1986a). *Divided consciousness: Multiple controls in human thought and action.* New York, NY: Wiley.

Hilgard, Ernest R. (1986b, January). A study in hypnosis. *Psychology Today, 20*, 23–27.

Hilgard, Ernest R. (1991). A neodissociation interpretation of hypnosis. In Steven J. Lynn & J. Rhue (Eds.), *Theories of hypnosis: Current models and perspectives.* New York, NY: Guilford.

Hilgard, Ernest R. (1992). Divided consciousness and dissociation. *Consciousness and Cognition, 1*, 16–32.

Hilgard, Ernest R.; Hilgard, Josephine R.; & Barber, Joseph. (1994). *Hypnosis in the relief of pain* (Rev. ed.). New York, NY: Brunner/Mazel.

Hilgard, Ernest R., & Marquis, Donald G. (1940). *Conditioning and learning.* New York, NY: Appleton-Century-Crofts.

Hill, Kevin T., & Miller, Lee M. (2010). Auditory attentional control and selection during cocktail party listening. *Cerebral Cortex, 20*(3), 583–590. doi:10.1093/cercor/bhp124

Hill, Matthew N.; Hellemans, Kim G. C.; Verma, Pamela; Gorzalka, Boris B.; & Weinberg, Joanne. (2012). Neurobiology of chronic mild stress: Parallels to major depression. *Neuroscience and Biobehavioral Reviews, 36*, 2085–2117.

Hillberg, Tanja; Hamilton-Giachritsis, Catherine; & Dixon, Louise. (2011). Review of meta-analyses on the association between child sexual abuse and adult mental health difficulties: A systematic approach. *Trauma, Violence, & Abuse, 12*(1), 38–49. doi:10.1177/1524838010386812

Hillman, Charles H.; Erickson, Kirk I.; & Kramer, Arthur F. (2008). Be smart, exercise your heart: Exercise effects on brain and cognition. *Nature Reviews Neuroscience, 9*, 58–65.

Hilton, James L. (1998). Interaction goals and person perception. In John McConnon Darley & Joel Cooper (Eds.), *Attribution and social interaction: The legacy of Edward E. Jones.* Washington, DC: American Psychological Association.

Hines, Melissa. (2010). Sex-related variation in human behavior and the brain. *Trends in Cognitive Science, 14*, 448–456. doi:10.1016/j.tics.2010.07.005

Hines, Terence M. (2003). *Pseudoscience and the paranormal: A critical examination of the evidence* (2nd ed.). Buffalo, NY: Prometheus.

Hinshaw, Stephen P., & Stier, Andrea. (2008). Stigma as related to mental disorders. *Annual Review of Psychology, 4*, 67-93. doi:10.1146/annurev.clinpsy.4.022007.141245

Hinton, Devon E., & Hinton, Susan D. (2009). Twentieth-century theories of panic in the United States. In Devon E. Hinton & Byron J. Good (Eds.), *Culture and panic disorder* (pp. 113–131). Stanford, CA: Stanford University Press.

Hirsh, Jacob B.; Kang, Sonia K.; & Bodenhausen, Galen V. (2012). Personalized persuasion tailoring persuasive appeals to recipients' personality traits. *Psychological Science, 23*(6), 578–581.

Hirst, William; Phelps, Elizabeth A.; Meksin, Robert; Vaidya, Chandan J.; Johnson, Marcia K.; Mitchell, Karen J.; Buckner, Randy L.; Budson, Andrew E.; Gabrieli, John D.E.; Lustig, Cindy; Mather, Mara; Ochsner, Kevin N.; Schacter, Daniel; Simons, Jon S.; Lyle, Keith B.; Cuc, Alexandru F.; & Olsson, Andreas. (2015). A ten-year follow-up of a study of memory for the attack of September 11, 2001: Flashbulb memories and memories for flashbulb events. *Journal of Experimental Psychology: General, 144*, 604–623. doi:10.1037/xge0000055

Hitsch, Günter; Hortaçsu, Ali; & Ariely, Dan. (2010). What makes you click?—Mate preferences in online dating. *Quantitative Marketing and Economics, 8*(4), 393–427. doi:10.1007/s11129-010-9088-6

Hobfoll, Stevan E.; Lilly, Roy S.; & Jackson, Anita P. (1992). Conservation of social resources and the self. In Hans O. F. Veiel & Urs Baumann (Eds.), *The meaning and measurement of social support.* New York, NY: Hemisphere.

Hobson, Charles, J.; & Delunas, Linda. (2001). National norms and lifeevent frequencies for the revised Social Readjustment Rating Scale. *International Journal of Stress Management, 8*, 299–314.

Hobson, J. Allan. (1999). *Consciousness.* New York, NY: Scientific American Library.

Hobson, J. Allan. (2004). *Dreaming: An introduction to the science of sleep.* New York, NY: Oxford University Press.

Hobson, J. Allan. (2005, October 27). Sleep is of the brain, by the brain and for the brain. *Nature, 437,* 1254–1264.

Hobson, J. Allan. (2009). REM sleep and dreaming: Towards a theory of protoconsciousness. *Nature Reviews Neuroscience, 10,* 803–813. doi:10.1038/nrn2716

Hobson, J. Allan, & McCarley, Robert W. (1977). The brain as a dream-state generator: An activation-synthesis hypothesis of the dream process. *American Journal of Psychiatry, 134,* 1335–1348.

Hobson, J. Allan; Sangsanguan, Suchada; Arantes, Henry; & Kahn, David. (2011). Dream logic—The inferential reasoning paradigm. *Dreaming, 21*(1), 1–15. doi:10.1037/a0022860

Hobson, J. Allan; Stickgold, Robert; & Pace-Schott, Edward F. (1998). The neuropsychology of REM sleep dreaming. *NeuroReport, 9*(3), R1–R14.

Hobson, J. Allan, & Voss, Ursula. (2010). Lucid dreaming and the bimodality of consciousness. In Elaine Perry, Daniel Collerton, Fiona LeBeau, & Heather Ashton (Eds.), *New horizons in the neuroscience of consciousness* (pp. 155–165). Amsterdam, The Netherlands: John Benjamins.

Hochreiter, W. W.; Ackermann, D. K.; & Brütsch, H. P. (2005). [Andropause]. *Ther Umsch, 62*(12), 821–826.

Hodges, Bert H., & Geyer, Anne L. (2006). A nonconformist account of the Asch experiments: Values, pragmatics, and moral dilemmas. *Personality and Social Psychology Review, 10*(1), 2–19.

Hodgkinson, Gerard P.; Langan-Fox, Janice; & Sadler-Smith, Eugene. (2008). Intuition: A fundamental bridging construct in the behavioural sciences. *British Journal of Psychology, 99,* 1–27.

Hoffman, John, & Froemke, Susan (Eds.). (2007). *Addiction: Why can't they just stop?* New York, NY: Rodale.

Hoffman, Martin L. (1977). Moral internalization: Current theory and research. In Leonard Berkowitz (Ed.), *Advances in experimental social psychology* (Vol. 10). New York, NY: Academic Press.

Hoffmann, Melissa L., & Powlishta, Kimberly K. (2001, September). Gender segregation in childhood: A test of the interaction style theory. *Journal of Genetic Psychology, 162*(3), 2.

Hoffstein, Victor. (2005). Snoring and upper airway resistance. In Meir H. Kryger, Thomas Roth, & William C. Dement (Eds.), *Principles and practice of sleep medicine* (4th ed.). Philadelphia, PA: Elsevier Saunders.

Hofmann, Stefan G.; Sawyer, Alice T.; Witt, Ashley A.; & Oh, Diana. (2010). The effect of mindfulness-based therapy on anxiety and depression: A meta-analytic review. *Journal of Consulting and Clinical Psychology, 78,* 169–183.

Hofmann, Wilhelm; De Houwer, Jan; Perugini, Marco; Baeyens, Frank; & Crombez, Geert. (2010). Evaluative conditioning in humans: A meta-analysis. *Psychological Bulletin, 136*(3), 390–421.

Hogan, John D. (2003). G. Stanley Hall: Educator, organizer, and pioneer developmental psychologist. In Gregory A. Kimble & Michael Wertheimer (Eds.), *Portraits of pioneers in psychology* (Vol. 5, pp. 18–36). Washington, DC: American Psychological Association.

Hogarth, Robin M. (2010). Intuition: A challenge for psychological research on decision making. *Psychological Inquiry, 21*(4), 338–353.

Hogg, Michael A. (2010). Influence and leadership. In Susan T. Fiske, Daniel Gilbert, & Gardner Lindzey (Eds.), *Handbook of social psychology, Vol. 2* (pp. 1166–1207). Hoboken, NJ: Wiley.

Hogg, Michael A.; Adelman, Janice R.; & Blagg, Robert D. (2010). Religion in the face of uncertainty: An uncertainty-identity theory account of religiousness. *Personality and Social Psychology Review, 14*(1), 72–83.

Holden, Constance. (2001). Polygraph screening: Panel seeks truth in lie detector debate. *Science, 291,* 967.

Holden, Ronald R. (2008, January). Underestimating the effects of faking on the validity of self-report personality scales. *Personality and Individual Differences, 44*(1), 311–321.

Hollander, Edwin P., & Julian, James W. (1969). Contemporary trends in the analysis of the leadership process. *Psychological Bulletin, 71,* 387–397.

Hollanders, Henry. (2007). Integrative and eclectic approaches. In Windy Dryden (Ed.), *Dryden's handbook of individual therapy.* Thousand Oaks, CA, Sage.

Hollinger, Richard C., & Adams, Amanda. (2007). *2007 National Retail Security Survey.* University of Florida–Gainesville: Author.

Hollon, Steven D., & Beck, Aaron T. (2004). Behavior therapy with adults. In Michael J. Lambert (Ed.), *Bergin and Garfield's handbook of psychotherapy and behavior change* (5th ed.). New York, NY: Wiley.

Holm-Denoma, Jill M.; Joiner, Thomas E. Jr.; Vohs, Kathleen D.; & Heatherton, Todd F. (2008). The "freshman fifteen" (the "freshman five" actually): Predictors and possible explanations. *Health Psychology, 27,* No. 1(Suppl.), S3–S9. doi:10.1037/0278-6133.27.1.S3

Holmes, Thomas H., & Masuda, Minoru. (1974). Life change and illness susceptibility. In Barbara Snell Dohrenwend & Bruce P. Dohrenwend (Eds.), *Stressful life events: Their nature and effects.* New York, NY: Wiley.

Holmes, Thomas H., & Rahe, Richard H. (1967). The Social Readjustment Rating Scale. *Journal of Psychosomatic Research, 11,* 213–218.

Holsboer, Florian. (2009). Putative new-generation antidepressants. In Alan F. Schatzberg & Charles B. Nemeroff (Eds.), *The American Psychiatric Publishing textbook of psychopharmacology* (4th ed., pp. 503–529). Washington, DC: American Psychiatric Publishing.

Holt-Lunstad, Julianne; Smith, Timothy B.; & Layton, J. Bradley. (2010). Social relationships and mortality risk: A meta-analytic review. *PLOS Medicine, 7*(7), e1000316.

Holt-Lunstad, Julianne; Smith, Timothy; Baker, Mark; Harris, Tyler; & Stephenson, David. (2015). Loneliness and social isolation as risk factors for mortality: A meta-analytic review. *Perspectives on Psychological Science, 10,* 227–237. doi:10.1177/1745691614568352

Holyoak, Keith J. (2005). Analogy. In Keith J. Holyoak & Robert G. Morrison (Eds.), *The Cambridge handbook of thinking and reasoning.* New York, NY: Cambridge University Press, p. 302

Hölzel, Britta K.; Carmody, James; Vangel, Mark; Congleton, Christina; Yerramsetti, Sita M.; Gard, Tim; & Lazar, Sara W. (2011). Mindfulness practice leads to increases in regional brain gray matter density. *Psychiatry Research, 191,* 36–43.

Holzman, Lois. (2009). *Vygotsky at work and play.* New York, NY: Routledge/Taylor & Francis Group.

Homer, Bruce D.; Solomon, Todd M.; Moeller, Robert W.; Mascia, Amy; DeRaleau, Lauren; & Halkitis, Perry N. (2008). Methamphetamine abuse and impairment of social functioning: A review of the underlying neurophysiological causes and behavioral implications. *Psychological Bulletin, 134,* 301–310.

Hong, Ying-yi; Wyer, Robert S., Jr.; & Fong, Candy P. S. (2008). Chinese working in groups: Effort dispensability versus normative influence. *Asian Journal of Social Psychology, 11*(3), 187–195. doi:10.1111/j.1467-839X.2008.00257.x

Hopkins, William D., & Cantalupo, Claudio. (2005). Individual and setting differences in the hand preferences of chimpanzees (*Pan troglodytes*): A critical analysis and some alternative explanations. *Laterality, 10,* 65–80.

Hopkins, William D.; Phillips, Kimberley A.; Bania, Amanda; Calcutt, Sarah E.; Gardner, Molly; Russell, Jamie; Schaeffer, Jennifer; Lonsdorf, Elizabeth V.; Ross, Stephen R.; & Schapiro, Steven J. (2011). Hand preferences for coordinated bimanual actions in 777 Great Apes: Implications for the evolution of handedness in hominins. *Journal of Human Evolution, 60,* 605–611. doi:10.1016/j.jhevol.2010.12.008

Hopper, Lydia M.; Spiteri, Antoine; Lambeth, Susan P.; Schapiro, Steven J.; Horner, Victoria; & Whiten, Andrew. (2007). Experimental studies of traditions and underlying transmission processes in chimpanzees. *Animal Behaviour, 73,* 1021–1032.

Hoptman, Matthew J., & Davidson, Richard J. (1994). How and why do the two cerebral hemispheres interact? *Psychological Bulletin, 116,* 195–219.

Horder, Jamie; Matthews, Paul; & Waldmann, Robert. (2011). Placebo, Prozac, and PLoS: Significant lessons for psychopharmacology. *Journal of Psychopharmacology, 25*(10), 1277–1288. doi:10.1177/0269881110372544

Horner, Robert H. (2002). On the status of knowledge for using punishment: A commentary. *Journal of Applied Behavior Analysis, 35*(4), 465–467.

Horney, Karen. (1926/1967). The flight from womanhood. In Harold Kelman (Ed.), *Feminine psychology*. New York, NY: Norton.

Horney, Karen. (1945/1972). *Our inner conflicts: A constructive theory of neurosis*. New York, NY: Norton.

Horr, Ninja; Braun, Christoph; & Volz, Kirsten G. (2014). Feeling before knowing why: The role of the orbitofrontal cortex in intuitive judgments—an MEG study. *Cognitive, Affective and Behavioral Neuroscience, 14,* 1271–1285. doi:10.3758/s13415-014-0286-7

Horwitz, Allan V. (2002). *Creating mental illness*. Chicago, IL: University of Chicago Press.

Houts, Arthur C. (2002). Discovery, invention, and the expansion of the modern diagnostic and statistical manuals of mental disorders. In Larry E. Beutler & Mary L. Malik (Eds.), *Rethinking the DSM: A psychological perspective*. Washington, DC: American Psychological Association.

Howard-Jones, Paul A. (2014). Neuroscience and education: Myths and messages. *Nature Reviews Neuroscience, 15,* 817–824. doi:10.1038/nrn3817

Howe, Mark L., & Knott, Lauren M. (2015). The fallibility of memory in judicial processes: Lessons from the past and their modern consequences. *Memory, 23,* 633–656. doi:10.1080/09658211.2015.1010709

Howland, Maryhope, & Simpson, Jeffrey A. (2010). Getting in under the radar: A dyadic view of invisible support. *Psychological Science, 21,* 1827–1834. Published online November 19, 2010. doi:10.1177/0956797610388817

Hoyle, Rick H., & Sherrill, Michelle R. (2006, December). Future orientation in the self-system: Possible selves, self-regulation, and behavior. *Journal of Personality, 74*(6), 1673–1696.

Hsiang, Solomon M.; Burke, Marshall; & Miguel, Edward. (2013). Quantifying the influence of climate on human conflict. *Science, 341*(6151), 1235367.

Hua, Cynthia. (2013, January 24). Mandatory bystander training introduced for sophomores. *The Yale News.* Retrieved from http://yaledailynews.com/blog/2013/01/24/bystander-training-introduced

Huang, Yi; Kendrick, Keith M.; & Yu Rongjun. (2014). Conformity to the opinions of other people lasts for no more than 3 days. *Psychological Science, 25,* 1388–1393. doi:10.1177/0956797614532104

Hubel, David H. (1995). *Eye, brain, and vision*. New York, NY: Scientific American Library.

Hubel, David H., & Wiesel, Torsten N. (2005). *Brain and visual perception: The story of a 25-year collaboration*. New York, NY: Oxford University Press.

Huber, Elizabeth; Webster, Jason M.; Brewer, Alyssa A.; MacLeod, Donald I.A.; Wandell, Brian A.; Boynton, Geoffrey M.; Wade, Alex R.; & Fine, Ione. (2015). A lack of experience-dependent plasticity after more than a decade of recovered sight. *Psychological Science, 26,* 393–401. doi:10.1177/0956797614563957

Huesmann, L. Rowell; Dubow, Eric F.; & Yang, Grace. (2013). Why it is hard to believe that media violence causes aggression. In Karen E. Dill (Ed.), *The Oxford handbook of media psychology*. New York, NY: Oxford University Press.

Hugdahl, Kenneth, & Westerhausen, René (Eds.). (2010). *The Two Halves of the Brain: Information Processing in the Cerebral Hemispheres*. Cambridge, MA: MIT Press.

Hughes, Chris. (2011, April 11). Quoted in Ari Karpel. Forty under forty: Chris Hughes and Sean Eldridge. *The Advocate.* Retrieved on October 2, 2012, from http://www.advocate.com/print-issue/cover-stories/2011/04/11/chris-hughes-and-sean-eldridge

Hughes, John R. (2007). A review of sleepwalking (somnambulism): The enigma of neurophysiology and polysomnography with differential diagnosis of complex partial seizures. *Epilepsy & Behavior, 11,* 483–491.

Hughes, Mathew L.; Geraci, Lisa; & De Forrest, Ross L. (2013). Aging 5 years in 5 minutes: The effect of taking a memory test on older adults' subjective age. *Psychological Science, 24,* 2481–2488. doi:10.1177/0956797613494853

Hull, Clark L. (1943). *Principles of behavior: An introduction to behavior theory*. New York, NY: Appleton-Century-Crofts.

Hull, Clark L. (1952). *A behavior system: An introduction to behavior theory concerning the individual organism*. New Haven, CT: Yale University Press.

Human Genome Project. (2008). *Genomics and its impact on science and society: A primer*. Washington, DC: U.S. Department of Energy, Office of Science. Retrieved on October 4, 2008, from http://www.ornl.gov/sci/techresources/Human_Genome/publicat/primer2001/primer11.pdf

Hunsley, John; Lee, Catherine M.; & Wood, James M. (2003). Controversial and questionable assessment techniques. In Scott O. Lilienfeld, Steven Jay Lynn, & Jeffrey M. Lohr (Eds.), *Science and pseudoscience in clinical psychology*. New York, NY: Guilford.

Hunsley, John; Lee, Catherine M.; Wood, James M.; & Taylor, Whitney. (2015). Controversial and questionable assessment technique. In Scott Lilienfeld, Steven Lynn, Jeffrey Lohr, & Carol Tarvis (Eds.), *Science and Pseudoscience in Clinical Psychology* (2nd ed., pp. 42–82). New York, NY: Guilford.

Hunt, Earl. (2012). What makes nations intelligent? *Perspectives on Psychological Science, 7,* 284–306. doi:10.1177/1745691612442905

Hunter, Aimee M.; Ravikumar, S.; Cook, Ian A.; & Leuchter, Andrew F. (2009). Brain functional changes during placebo lead-in and changes in specific symptoms during pharmacotherapy for major depression. *Acta Psychiatrica Scandinavica, 119*(4), 266–273.

Hunter, Simone; Hurley, Robin A.; & Taber, Katherine H. (2013). A look inside the mirror neuron system. *Journal of Neuropsychiatry and Clinical Neurosciences, 25,* 171–175. doi:10.1176/appi.neuropsych.13060128

Hurovitz, Craig S.; Dunn, Sarah; Domhoff, G. William; & Fiss, Harry. (1999). The dreams of blind men and women: A replication and extension of previous findings. *Dreaming, 9,* 183–193.

Hussaini, Syed Abid; Komischke, Bernhard; Menzel, Randolf; & Lachnit, Harald. (2007). Forward and backward second-order Pavlovian conditioning in honeybees. *Learning & Memory, 14*(10), 678–683.

Huynh, Que-Lam; Nguyen, Angela M. D.; & Benet-Martínez, Verónica. (2011). Bicultural identity integration. In Seth J. Schwartz, Koen Luyckx, & Vivian L. Vignoles (Eds.), *Handbook of identity theory and research*. New York, NY: Springer.

Hyde, Janet Shibley. (2005). The genetics of sexual orientation. In Janet Shibley Hyde (Ed.), *Biological substrates of human sexuality*. Washington, DC: American Psychological Association.

Hyde, Janet Shibley. (2014). Gender similarities and differences. *Annual Review of Psychology, 65,* 373–398.

Hyde, Janet S.; Mezulis, Amy H.; & Abramson, Lyn Y. (2008). The ABCs of depression: Integrating affective, biological, and cognitive models to explain the emergence of the gender difference in depression. *Psychological Review, 115,* 291–313. doi:10.1037/0033-295X.115.2.291

Hyman, Ira E., Jr.; Boss, S. Matthew; Wise, Breanne M.; McKenzie, Kira E.; & Caggiano, Jenna M. (2010). Did you see the unicycling clown? Inattentional blindness while walking and talking on a cell phone. *Applied Cognitive Psychology, 24*(5), 597–607. doi:10.1002/acp.1638

Hyman, Ira E., Jr., & Pentland, Joel. (1996). The role of mental imagery in the creation of false childhood memories. *Journal of Memory & Language, 35,* 101–117.

Hyman, Ray. (2010). Meta-analysis that conceals more than it reveals: Comment on Storm et al. (2010). *Psychological Bulletin, 136*(4), 486–490.

Hyman, Steven E. (2005). Neurotransmitters. *Current Biology, 15,* R154–R158.

Hyman, Steven E. (2009). How adversity gets under the skin. *Nature Neuroscience 12,* 241–243.

Iacoboni, Marco. (2009). Imitation, empathy, and mirror neurons. *Annual Review of Psychology, 60,* 653–670.

Iacono, Diego. (2009, July 8). Quoted in Hadley Leggett, "Nun brains show language skills predict future Alzheimer's risk." *Wired* Online Magazine. Accessed on October 29, 2009 at http://www.wired.com/wiredscience/2009/07/nunstudy

Iacono, Diego; Markesbery, W. R.; Gross, M.; Pletnikova, Olga; Rudow, Gay; Zandi, P.; & Troncoso, Juan C. (2009). The Nun Study: Clinically silent AD, neuronal hypertrophy, and linguistic skills in early life. *Neurology, 73,* 665–673.

Ijzerman, Hans, & Van Prooijen, Jan-Willem. (2008, June). Just world and the emotional defense of self. *Social Psychology, 39*(2), 117–120.

Ikeda, Hiroshi. (2001). Buraku students and cultural identity: The case of a Japanese minority. In Nobuo Shimahara, Ivan Z. Holowinsky, & Saundra Tomlinson-Clarke (Eds.), *Ethnicity, race, and nationality in education: A global perspective.* Mahwah, NJ: Erlbaum.

Imberman, Arlyn, & Rifkin, June. (2008). *Signature for success.* Kansas City, MO: Andrews McMeel.

IMS Health. (2010). Report on the U.S. pharmaceutical market. Danbury, CT: Author. Retrieved in September 2011 from http://www.imshealth.com /portal/site/imshealth/menuitem.a46c6d4df3db4b3d88f611019418c 22a /?vgnextoid=d690a27e9d5b7210VgnVCM100000ed152ca2RCRD

Imel, Zac E.; Malterer, Melanie B.; McKay, Kevin M.; & Wampold, Bruce E. (2008). A meta-analysis of psychotherapy and medication in unipolar depression and dysthymia. *Journal of Affective Disorders, 110,* 197–206.

Ingalhalikar, Madhura; Smith, Alex; Parker, Drew; Satterthwaite, Theodore D.; Elliott, Mark A.; Ruparel, Kosha; Hakonarson, Hakon; Gur, Raquel E.; Gur, Ruben C.; & Verma Ragini. (2014). Sex differences in the structural connectome of the human brain. *Proceedings of the National Academy of Sciences, 111,* 823–828. doi:10.1073/pnas.1316909110

Inagami, Sanae; Cohen, Deborah A.; Brown, Arleen F.; & Asch, Steven M. (2009). Body mass index, neighborhood fast food and restaurant concentration, and car ownership. *Journal of Urban Health, 86,* 683–95.

Ingram, Rick E.; Trenary, Lucy; Odom, Mica; Berry, Leandra; & Nelson, Tyler. (2007). Cognitive, affective and social mechanisms in depression risk: Cognition, hostility, and coping style. *Cognition & Emotion, 21,* 78–94.

Innocence Project. (2015). *False confessions or admissions.* Retrieved on June 17, 2015, from http://www.innocenceproject.org/causes-wrongful-conviction /false-confessions-or-admissions

Insel, Thomas. (2013). Director's blog: Transforming diagnosis. *National Institutes of Mental Health.* Retrieved on October 14, 2013, from http://www .nimh.nih.gov/about/director/2013/transforming-diagnosis.shtml

Insel, Thomas R., & Lehner, Thomas. (2007). A new era in psychiatric genetics? *Biological Psychiatry, 61*(9), 1017–1018.

International Shark Attack File. (2010). *ISAF 2010 worldwide shark attack summary.* University of Florida: Florida Museum of Natural History. Retrieved September 2010, from http://www.flmnh.ufl.edu/fish/sharks /isaf/2010summary. html

Ionescu, Thea. (2012). Exploring the nature of cognitive flexibility. *New Ideas in Psychology, 30*(2), 190–200. doi:10.1016/j.newideapsych.2011.11.001

Irving, Julie Anne; Farb, Norman A. S.; & Segal, Zindel V. (2015). Mindfulness-based cognitive therapy for chronic depression. In Kirk Warren Brown, J. David Creswell, & Richard M. Ryan (Eds.), *Handbook of mindfulness: Theory, research, and practice.* New York, NY: Guilford.

Irwin, Charles E., Jr. (2005). Editorial: Pubertal timing: Is there any new news? *Journal of Adolescent Health, 37,* 343–344.

Irwin, Michael R. (2015). Why sleep is important for health: A psychoneuroimmunology perspective. *Annual Review of Psychology, 66,* 143–172. doi:10.1146/annurev-psych-010213-115205

Irwin, Michael R., & Miller, Andrew H. (2007, May). Depressive disorders and immunity: 20 years of progress and discovery. *Brain, Behavior, and Immunity, 21*(4), 374–383.

Isabella, Russell A.; Belsky, Jay; & von Eye, Alexander. (1989). Origins of infant-mother attachment: An examination of interactional synchrony during the infant's first year. *Developmental Psychology, 25,* 12–21.

Iversen, Iver H. (1992). Skinner's early research: From reflexology to operant conditioning. *American Psychologist, 47,* 1318–1328.

Ivory, James D.; Markey, Patrick M.; Elson, Malte; Colwell, John; Ferguson, Christopher J.; Griffiths, Mark D.; Savage, Joanne; & Williams, Kevin D. (2015). Manufacturing consensus in a diverse field of scholarly opinions: A comment on Bushman, Gollwitzer, and Cruz. *Psychology of Popular Media Culture, 4,* 222–229. doi:10.1037/ppm0000056

Iwamasa, Gayle Y. (1997). Asian Americans. In Steven Friedman (Ed.), *Cultural issues in the treatment of anxiety.* New York, NY: Guilford.

Iwanaga, Makoto; Yokoyama, Hiroshi; & Seiwa, Hidetoshi. (2004). Coping availability and stress reduction for optimistic and pessimistic individuals. *Personality and Individual Differences, 36,* 11–22.

Izard, Carroll E. (1990a). Facial expressions and the regulation of emotions. *Journal of Personality and Social Psychology, 58,* 487–498.

Izard, Carroll E. (1990b). The substrates and functions of emotion feelings: William James and current emotion theories. *Personality and Social Psychology Bulletin, 16,* 626–635.

Izard, Carroll E. (2007). Basic emotions, natural kinds, emotion schemas, and a new paradigm. *Perspectives on Psychological Science, 2,* 260–280.

Jaarsma, P., & Welin, S. (2012). Autism as a natural human variation: Reflections on the claims of the neurodiversity movement. *Health Care Analysis, 20,* 20–30.

Jackson, John P., Jr. (2006). Kenneth B. Clark: The complexities of activist psychology. In Donald A. Dewsbury, Ludy T. Benjamin, & Michael Wertheimer (Eds.), *Portraits of pioneers in psychology* (Vol. VI, pp. 273–286). Washington, DC, and Mahwah, NJ: American Psychological Association and Lawrence Erlbaum Associates.

Jackson, Joshua J.; Connolly, James J.; Garrison, S. Mason; Leveille, Madeleine M.; & Connolly, Seamus L. (2015). Your friends know how long you will live: A 75-year study of peer-rated personality traits. *Psychological Science, 26,* 335–340. doi:10.1177/0956797614561800

Jackson, Lynne M. (2011). Cognitive, affective, and interactive processes of prejudice. *The psychology of prejudice: From attitudes to social action.* Washington, DC: American Psychological Association.

Jacobs, Barry L. (2004). Depression: The brain finally gets into the act. *Current Directions in Psychological Science, 13,* 103–106.

Jacobs, Nele E.; Myin-Germeys, I.; Derom, C.; Delespaul, P.; van Os, J.; & Nicolson, N. A. (2007). A momentary assessment study of the relationship between affective and adrenocortical stress responses in daily life. *Biological Psychology, 74,* 60–66.

Jacobs, Tonya L.; Epel, Elissa S.; Lin, Jue; Blackburn, Elizabeth H.; Wolkowitz, Owen M.; Bridwell, David A.; Zanesco, Anthony P.; & others. (2011). Intensive meditation training, immune cell telomerase activity, and psychological mediators. *Psychoneuroendocrinology, 36*(5), 664–681. doi:10.1016/j.psyneuen.2010.09.010

Jaffee, Sara, & Hyde, Janet Shibley. (2000). Gender differences in moral orientation: A meta-analysis. *Psychological Bulletin, 126,* 703–726.

Jagdeo, Amit; Cox, Brian J.; Stein, Murray B.; & Sareen, Jitender. (2009). Negative attitudes toward help seeking for mental illness in 2 population-based surveys from the United States and Canada. *Canadian Journal of Psychiatry/La Revue canadienne de psychiatrie, 54*(11), 757–766.

Jakovcevski, I.; Filipovic, R.; Mo, Z.; Rakic, S.; & Zecevic, N. (2009). Oligodendrocyte development and the onset of myelination in the human fetal brain. *Frontiers in Neuroanatomy, 3,* 5. doi:10.3389/neuro.05.005.2009

James, Jenée; Ellis, Bruce J.; Schlomer, Gabriel L.; & Garber, Judy. (2012). Sex-specific pathways to early puberty, sexual debut, and sexual risk taking: Tests of an integrated evolutionary-developmental model. *Developmental Psychology, 48,* 687–702. doi:10.1037/a0026427

James, Larry C. (2008). *Fixing hell: An Army psychologist confronts Abu Ghraib.* New York, NY: Grand Central Publishing.

James, William H. (2006). Two hypotheses on the causes of male homosexuality and paedophilia. *Journal of Biosocial Science, 38*(6), 745–761.

James, William. (1884). What is an emotion? *Mind, 9,* 188–205.

James, William. (1890). *Principles of psychology.* New York, NY: Holt.

James, William. (1892). *Psychology, briefer course.* New York, NY: Holt.

James, William. (1894). The physical basis of emotion. *Psychological Review, 1,* 516–529. (Reprinted in the 1994 Centennial Issue of *Psychological Review, 101,* 205–210).

James, William. (1899/1958). *Talks to teachers.* New York, NY: Norton.

James, William. (1902). *The varieties of religious experience: A study in human nature.* New York, NY: Longmans, Green.

Jameson, Dorothea, & Hurvich, Leo M. (1989). Essay concerning color constancy. *Annual Review of Psychology, 40,* 1–22.

Jamil, Hikmet; Nassar-McMillan, Sylvia C.; & Lambert, Richard G. (2007, April). Immigration and attendant psychological sequelae: A comparison of three waves of Iraqi immigrants. *American Journal of Orthopsychiatry, 77*(2), 199–205.

Jamison, Kay Redfield. (1993). *Touched with fire: Manic-depressive illness and the artistic temperament.* New York, NY: Free Press.

Jamison, Kay Redfield. (2000). *Night falls fast: Understanding suicide.* New York, NY: Vintage.

Janicak, Philip G.; Nahas, Ziad; Lisanby, Sarah H.; Solvason, H. B.; Sampson, Shirlene M.; McDonald, William M.; Marangell, Lauren B.; & others. (2010). Durability of clinical benefit with transcranial magnetic stimulation (TMS) in the treatment of pharmacoresistant major depression: Assessment of relapse during a 6-month, multisite, open-label study. *Brain Stimulation, 3,* 187–199. doi:10.1016/j.brs.2010.07.003

Jara, Elvia; Vila, Javier; & Maldonado, Antonio. (2006). Second-order conditioning of human causal learning. *Learning and Motivation, 37,* 230–246.

Jarcho, Johanna M.; Berkman, Elliot T.; & Lieberman, Matthew D. (2010). The neural basis of rationalization: Cognitive dissonance reduction during decision-making. *Social Cognitive and Affective Neuroscience, 6*(4), 460–467. doi:10.1093/scan/nsq054

Jarrett, Christian. (2011). Ouch! The different ways people experience pain. *The Psychologist, 24,* 416–420.

Jarvis, Erich D.; Güntürkün, Onur; Bruce, Laura; Csillag, András; Karten, Harvey; & The Avian Brain Nomenclature Consortium. (2005). Avian brains and a new understanding of vertebrate evolution. *Nature Reviews Neuroscience, 6,* 151–159.

Jason, Leonard A.; Pokorny, Steven B.; Adams, Monica; Topliff, Annie; Harris, Courtney; & Hunt, Yvonne. (2009). Youth tobacco access and possession policy interventions: Effects on observed and perceived tobacco use. *American Journal on Addictions, 18*(5), 367–374.

Jayasinghe, Nimali; Giosan, Cezar; Evans, Susan; Spielman, Lisa; & Difede, JoAnn. (2008, November). Anger and posttraumatic stress disorder in disaster relief workers exposed to the September 11, 2001 World Trade Center disaster: One-year follow-up study. *Journal of Nervous and Mental Disease, 196*(11), 844–846.

Jbabdi, Saad, & Behrens, Timothy E. J. (2012). Specialization: The connections have it. *Nature Neuroscience, 15,* 171–172. doi:10.1038/nn.3031

Jeckel, Christina Moriguchi; Lopes, Rodrigo P.; Berleze, Maria Christina; Luz, Clarice; Feix, Leandro; Argimon, Irani I.; & others. (2010). Neuroendocrine and immunological correlates of chronic stress in 'strictly healthy' populations. *Neuroimmunomodulation, 17*(1), 9–18.

Jensen, Mark P., & Patterson, David R. (2014). Hypnotic approaches for chronic pain management: Clinical implications of recent research findings. *American Psychologist, 69,* 167–177. doi:10.1037/a0035644

Jensen, Mark P., & Turk, Dennis C. (2014). Contributions of psychology to the understanding and treatment of people with chronic pain: Why it matters to ALL psychologists. *American Psychologist, 69,* 105–118. doi:10.1037/a0035641

Jensen, Per. (2014). Behaviour epigenetics—The connection between environment, stress and welfare. *Applied Animal Behaviour Science, 157,* 1–7. doi:10.1016/j.applanim.2014.02.009

Jha, Amishi P. (2013, March/April). Being in the now. *Scientific American Mind,* pp. 26–33.

Jha, Amishi P.; Morrison, Alexandra B; Dainer-Best, Justin; Parker, Suzanne; Rostrup, Nina; & Stanley, Elizabeth A. (2015). Minds "at attention": Mindfulness training curbs attentional lapses in military cohorts. *PLOS ONE, 10,* e0116889. doi:10.1371/journal.pone.0116889

Jha, Amishi P.; Stanley, Elizabeth A.; Kiyonaga, Anastasia; Wong, Ling; & Gelfand, Lois. (2010). Examining the protective effects of mindfulness training on working memory capacity and affective experience. *Emotion, 10,* 54–64. doi:10.1037/a0018438.

Jilek, Wolfgang G. (1993). Traditional medicine relevant to psychiatry. In Norman Sartorius, Giovanni de Girolamo, Gavin Andrews, G. Allen German, & Leon Eisenberg (Eds.), *Treatment of mental disorders: A review of effectiveness.* Washington, DC: World Health Organization/American Psychiatric Press.

Joel, Daphna, & Tarrasch, Ricardo. (2014). On the mis-presentation and misinterpretation of gender-related data: The case of Ingalhalikar's human connectome study. *Proceedings of the National Academy of Sciences, 111,* E637. doi:10.1073/pnas.1323319111

Joëls, Marian, & Baram, Tallie Z. (2009). The neuro-symphony of stress. *Nature Reviews Neuroscience, 10,* 459–466.

Johansen, P. Ø., & Krebs, T. S. (2009). How could MDMA (ecstasy) help anxiety disorders? A neurobiological rationale. *Journal of Psychopharmacology.* Advance online publication. doi:10.1177/0269881109102787

Johansen, Pål-Ørjan, & Krebs, Teri Suzanne. (2015). Psychedelics not linked to mental health problems or suicidal behavior: A population study. *Psychopharmacology, 29,* 270–279. doi:10.1177/0269881114568039

John, Oliver P. (1990). The "Big Five" factor taxonomy: Dimensions of personality in the natural language and in questionnaires. In Lawrence A. Pervin (Ed.), *Handbook of personality: Theory and research.* New York, NY: Guilford.

Johns, Michael; Inzlicht, Michael; & Schmader, Toni. (2008). Stereotype threat and executive resource depletion: Examining the influence of emotion regulation. *Journal of Experimental Psychology: General, 137,* 691–705.

Johns, Michael; Schmader, Toni; & Martens, Andy. (2005). Knowing is half the battle: Teaching stereotype threat as a means of improving women's math performance. *Psychological Science, 16,* 175–179.

Johnson, Debra L.; Wiebe, John S.; Gold, Sherri M.; Andreasen, Nancy C.; Hichwa, Richard D.; Watkins, G. Leonard; & Ponto, Laura L. Boles. (1999). Cerebral blood flow and personality: A positron emission tomography study. *American Journal of Psychiatry, 156,* 252–257.

Johnson, Jeffrey G.; Cohen, Patricia; Kasen, Stephanie; Smailes, Elizabeth M.; & Brook, Judith S. (2001). Association of maladaptive parental behavior with psychiatric disorder among parents and their offspring. *Archives of General Psychiatry, 58,* 453–460.

Johnson, Kerri L.; McKay, Lawrie S.; & Pollick, Frank E. (2011). He throws like a girl (but only when he's sad): Emotion affects sex-decoding of biological motion displays. *Cognition, 119,* 265–280. doi:10.1016/j.cognition.2011.01.016

Johnson, Marcia K.; Raye, Carol L.; Mitchell, Karen J.; & Ankudowich, Elizabeth. (2012). The cognitive neuroscience of true and false memories. In R. F. Belli (Ed.), *True and false recovered memories: Toward a reconciliation of the debate. Vol. 58: Nebraska Symposium on Motivation.* New York, NY: Springer.

Johnson, Paul M., & Kenny, Paul J. (2010). Dopamine D2 receptors in addiction-like reward dysfunction and compulsive eating in obese rats. *Nature Neuroscience, 13,* 635–641. doi:10.1038/nn.2519

Johnson, Wendy. (2010). Understanding the genetics of intelligence: Can height help? Can corn oil? *Current Directions in Psychological Science, 19*(3), 177–182.

Johnston, Laurance. (2008). Magnetic healing: What's the attraction? Retrieved June 21, 2009, from http://www.healingtherapies.info/magnetic_healing.htm

Johnston, Lucy, & Miles, Lynden. (2007). Attributions and stereotype moderation. *New Zealand Journal of Psychology, 36*(1), 13–17.

Joiner, Thomas E.; Brown, Jessica S.; & Wingate, LaRicka R. (2005). The psychology and neurobiology of suicidal behavior. *Annual Review of Psychology, 56,* 287–314.

Joiner, Thomas. (2010). Myths about suicide. Cambridge, MA: Harvard University Press, 2010.

Joly-Mascheroni, Ramiro M.; Senju, Atsushi; & Shepherd, Alex J. (2008). Dogs catch human yawns. *Biology Letters, 4,* 446–448.

Jones, Christopher M.; Mack, Karin A.; & Paulozzi, Leonard J. (2013). Pharmaceutical overdose deaths. *Journal of the American Medical Association, 309,* 657–659.

Jones, Edward E. (1990). *Interpersonal perception.* New York, NY: Freeman.

Jones, Gary. (2003). Testing two cognitive theories of insight. *Journal of Experimental Psychology: Learning, Memory, and Cognition, 29,* 1017–1027.

Jones, Mary Cover. (1924a). The elimination of children's fears. *Journal of Experimental Psychology, 7,* 382–390.

Jones, Mary Cover. (1924b). A laboratory study of fear: The case of Peter. *Pedagogical Seminary* and *Journal of Genetic Psychology, 31,* 308–315.

Jones, Mary Cover. (1975). A 1924 pioneer looks at behavior therapy. *Journal of Behavior Therapy and Experimental Psychiatry, 6,* 181–187.

Jones, Steven H., & Tarrier, Nick. (2005, December). New developments in bipolar disorder. *Clinical Psychology Review, 25*(8) [Special issue: The psychology of bipolar disorder], 1003–1007.

Jones, Warren H., & Russell, Dan W. (1980). The selective processing of belief-discrepant information. *European Journal of Social Psychology, 10,* 309–312.

Jonides, John; Lewis, Richard L.; Nee, Derek Evan; Lustig, Cindy A.; Berman, Marc G.; & Moore, Katherine Sledge. (2008). The mind and brain of short-term memory. *Annual Review of Psychology, 59,* 193–224.

Jonnes, Jill. (1999). *Hep-cats, narcs, and pipe dreams: A history of America's romance with illegal drugs.* Baltimore, MD: Johns Hopkins University Press.

Jordan-Young, Rebecca, & Rumiati, Raffaella I. (2012). Hardwired for sexism? Approaches to sex/gender in neuroscience. *Neuroethics, 5,* 305–315. doi:10.1007/s12152-011-9134-4

Joseph, Jay, & Leo, Jonathan. (2006, Winter). Genetic relatedness and the lifetime risk for being diagnosed with schizophrenia: Gottesman's 1991 figure 10 reconsidered. *Journal of Mind and Behavior, 27*(1), 73–90.

Joseph, Stephen, & Murphy, David. (2013). Person-centered approach, positive psychology, and relational helping: Building bridges. *Journal of Humanistic Psychology, 53,* 26–51.

Jucaite, Aurelija, & Nyberg, Svante. (2012). Dopamine hypothesis of schizophrenia: A historical perspective. In Jeffrey S. Albert & Michael W. Wood (Eds.). *Targets and emerging therapies for schizophrenia.* New York, NY: Wiley.

Judd, Charles M., & Gawronski, Bertram. (2011). Editorial comment. *Journal of Personality and Social Psychology, 100,* 406.

Juliano, Laura M., & Griffiths, Roland R. (2004). A critical review of caffeine withdrawal: Empirical validation of symptoms and signs, incidence, severity, and associated features. *Psychopharmacology, 176,* 1–29.

Julien, Robert M. (2011). *A primer of drug action* (12th ed.). New York, NY: Worth.

Jun, Z.; Stephen, B.; Morag, F.; Ann Louise, K.; Carol, B.; & Jane, F. (2010). The oldest old in the last year of life: Population-based findings from Cambridge City over-75s cohort study participants aged 85 and older at death. *Journal of the American Geriatrics Society, 58*(1), 1–11.

Junco, Reynol. (2012). Too much face and not enough books: The relationship between multiple indices of Facebook use and academic performance. *Computers in Human Behavior, 28*(1), 187–198. doi:10.1016/j.chb.2011.08.026

Junco, Reynol, & Cotten, Shelia R. (2012). No A 4 U: The relationship between multitasking and academic performance. *Computers & Education, 59*(2), 505–514. doi:10.1016/j.compedu.2011.12.023

Jung, Carl G. (1923/1976). Psychological types. In Joseph Campbell (Ed.), *The portable Jung.* New York, NY: Penguin.

Jung, Carl G. (1931/1976). The structure of the psyche. In Joseph Campbell (Ed.), *The portable Jung.* New York, NY: Penguin.

Jung, Carl G. (1936/1976). The concept of the collective unconscious. In Joseph Campbell (Ed.), *The portable Jung.* New York, NY: Penguin.

Jung, Carl G. (1963). *Memories, dreams, reflections* (Richard and Clara Winston, Trans.). New York, NY: Random House.

Jung, Carl G. (1964). *Man and his symbols.* New York, NY: Dell.

Jung, Carl G. (1974). *Dreams* (R. F. C. Hull, Trans.). New York, NY: MJF Books.

Kaas, Jon H.; O'Brien, Barbara M. J.; & Hackett, Troy A. (2013). Auditory processing in primate brains. In Randy J. Nelson, Sheri J.Y. Mizumori, & Irving B. Weiner (Eds.), *Handbook of Psychology, Vol. 3: Behavioral neuroscience* (2nd ed.). New York, NY: Wiley.

Kabat-Zinn, Jon. (2003). Mindfulness-based interventions in context: Past, present, and future. *Clinical Psychology: Science and Practice, 10,* 144–156.

Kabat-Zinn, Jon. (2013). *Full catastrophe living: Using the wisdom of your body and mind to face stress, pain, and illness.* New York, NY: Random House.

Kagan, Jerome. (2004, Winter). New insights into temperament. *Cerebrum, 6,* 51–66.

Kagan, Jerome. (2008). A trio of concerns. *Perspectives on Psychological Science, 2,* 361–376.

Kagan, Jerome. (2010a). Emotions and temperament. In M. Bornstein (Ed.), *Handbook of cultural developmental science* (pp. 175–194). New York, NY: Taylor & Francis.

Kagan, Jerome. (2010b). *The temperamental thread: How genes, culture, time, and luck make us who we are.* Washington, DC: Dana Press.

Kagan, Jerome. (2011). Three lessons learned. *Perspectives on Psychological Science 6,* 107–113, doi:10.1177/1745691611400205

Kagan, Jerome, & Sinnott-Armstrong, W. (2008). Morality and its development. In Walter Sinnott-Armstrong (Ed.), *Moral Psychology, Vol 3: The neuroscience of morality: Emotion, brain disorders, and development* (pp. 297–312). Cambridge, MA: MIT Press.

Kahneman, Daniel. (2003). A perspective on judgment and choice: Mapping bounded rationality. *American Psychologist, 58,* 697–720.

Kahneman, Daniel, & Tversky, Amos. (1982). On the psychology of prediction. In Daniel Kahneman, Paul Slovic, & Amos Tversky (Eds.), *Judgment under uncertainty: Heuristics and biases.* New York, NY: Cambridge University Press.

Kalat, James W. (1985). Taste-aversion learning in ecological perspective. In Timothy D. Johnston & Alexandra T. Pietrewicz (Eds.), *Issues in the ecological study of learning.* Hillsdale, NJ: Erlbaum.

Kamen, Dean. (2001, December 2). Quoted in John Heilemann, "Reinventing the wheel." *Time Online Edition.* Retrieved February 25, 2005, from http://www.time.com/time/business/article/0,8599,186660-1,00.html

Kamin, Leon J. (1995). The pioneers of IQ testing. In Russell Jacoby & Naomi Glauberman (Eds.), *The bell curve debate: History, documents, opinions.* New York, NY: Times Books.

Kammeyer-Mueller, John D.; Judge, Timothy A.; & Scott, Brent A. (2009). The role of core self-evaluations in the coping process. *Journal of Applied Psychology, 94*(1), 177–195.

Kampe, Knut K.W. (2001, October 10). Quoted in *MSNBC Science News,* "When eyes meet, the brain soars." Retrieved on February 27, 2002, from http://stacks.msnbc.com/news/641208.asp

Kampe, Knut K.W.; Frith, Chris D.; Dolan, Raymond J.; & Frith, Uta. (2001, October 11). Reward value of attractiveness and gaze. *Nature, 413,* 589.

Kamps, Debra; Wills, Howard P.; Heitzman-Powell, Linda; Laylin, Jeff; Szoke, Carolyn; Petrillo, Tai & Culey, Amy. (2011). Class-wide function-related intervention teams: Effects of group contingency programs in urban classrooms. *Journal of Positive Behavior Interventions, 13,* 154–167.

Kanai, Chieko; Tani, Masayuki; Hashimoto, Ryuichiro; Yamada, Takashi; Ohta, Haruhisa; & Watanabe, Hiromi. (2012). Cognitive profiles of adults with Asperger's disorder, high-functioning autism, and pervasive developmental disorder not otherwise specified based on the WAIS-III. *Research in Autism Spectrum Disorders, 6,* 58–64. doi:10.1016/j.rasd.2011.09.004

Kandel, Eric R. (2001). The molecular biology of memory storage: A dialogue between genes and synapses. *Science, 294,* 1030–1038.

Kandel, Eric R. (2006). *In search of memory: The emergence of a new science of mind.* New York, NY: Norton.

Kandel, Eric R. (2009). The biology of memory: A forty-year perspective. *Journal of Neuroscience, Vol. 29*(41), 12748–12756. doi:10.1523/jneurosci.3958-09.2009

Kandel, Eric R., & Kandel, Denise B. (2014). A molecular basis for nicotine as a gateway drug. *New England Journal of Medicine, 371,* 932–943. doi:10.1056/NEJMsa1405092

Kandler, Christian. (2012). Nature and nurture in personality development: The case of neuroticism and extraversion. *Current Directions in Psychological Science, 21,* 290–296. doi:10.1177/0963721412452557

Kang, Sonia K., & Bodenhausen, Galen V. (2015). Multiple identities in social perception and interaction: Challenges and opportunities. *Annual Review of Psychology, 66,* 547–574. doi:10.1146/annurev-psych-010814-015025

Kanner, Allen D.; Coyne, James C.; Schaefer, Catherine; & Lazarus, Richard S. (1981). Comparison of two modes of stress management: Daily hassles and uplifts versus major life events. *Journal of Behavioral Medicine, 4,* 1–39.

Kanwisher, Nancy. (2001). Faces and places: Of central (and peripheral) interest. *Nature Neuroscience, 4,* 455–456.

Kanwisher, Nancy, & Yovel, Galit. (2009) Face perception. In Gary G. Berntson & John T. Cacioppo (Eds.), *Handbook of neuroscience in the behavioral sciences.* Hoboken, NJ: Wiley.

Kapinos, Kandice A., & Yakusheva, Olga. (2011). Environmental influences on young adult weight gain: Evidence from a natural experiment. *Journal of Adolescent Health, 48,* 52–58. doi:10.1016/j.jadohealth.2010.05.021

Kaplan, Robert M., & Kronick, Richard G. (2006). Marital status and longevity in the United States population. *Journal of Epidemiology and Community Health, 60,* 760–765.

Kaplan, Steve. (1990). Capturing your creativity. In Michael G. Walraven & Hiram E. Fitzgerald (Eds.), *Annual editions: Psychology: 1990/91.* Guilford, CT: Dushkin.

Kapp, Steven K.; Gillespie-Lynch, Kristen; Sherman, Lauren E.; & Hutman, Ted. (2013). Deficit, difference, or both? Autism and neurodiversity. *Developmental Psychology, 49,* 59–71. doi:10.1037/a0028353

Kaptchuk, Ted J.; Friedlander, Elizabeth; Kelley, John M.; Sanchez, M. N.; Kokkotou, Efi; Singer, Joyce P.; Kowalczykowski, Magda; & others. (2010). Placebos without deception: A randomized controlled trial in irritable bowel syndrome. *PLOS ONE, 5*(12), 1–7. doi:10.1371/journal.pone.0015591

Karlsson, Hasse. (2011). How psychotherapy changes the brain: Understanding the mechanisms. *Psychiatric Times, 28.* Retrieved from http://www.psychiatrictimes.com/psychotherapy/how-psychotherapy-changes-brain

Karmiloff-Smith, Annette; Casey, B. J.; Massand, Esha; Tomalski, Przemyslaw; & Thomas, Michael S. C. (2014). Environmental and genetic influences on neurocognitive development: The Importance of multiple methodologies and time-dependent intervention. *Clinical Psychological Science 2,* 628–637. doi:10.1177/2167702614521188

Karpicke, Jeffrey D., & Roediger, Henry L. (2008). The critical importance of retrieval for learning. *Science, 319,* 966–968. doi:10.1037/a0026252

Karremans, Johan C.; Frankenhuis, Willem E.; & Arons, Sander. (2010). Blind men prefer a low waist-to-hip ratio. *Evolution and Human Behavior, 31*(3), 182–186. doi:10.1016/j.evolhumbehav.2009.10.001

Karremans, Johan C.; Stroebe, Wolfgang; & Claus, Jasper. (2006). Beyond Vicary's fantasies: The impact of subliminal priming and brand choice. *Journal of Experimental Social Psychology, 42*(6), 792–798.

Karren, Ronald J., & Zacharias, Larry. (2007, June). Integrity tests: Critical issues. *Human Resource Management Review, 17,* 221–234.

Kashdan, Todd B.; Farmer, Antonina S.; Adams, Leah M.; Ferssizidis, Patty; McKnight, Patrick E.; & Nezlek, John B. (2013). Distinguishing healthy adults from people with social anxiety disorder: Evidence for the value of experiential avoidance and positive emotions in everyday social interactions. *Journal of Abnormal Psychology, 122*(3), 645–655. doi:10.1037/a0032733

Kastenbaum, Robert. (1992). *The psychology of death.* New York, NY: Springer-Verlag.

Kastenbaum, Robert. (2000). Death attitudes and aging in the 21st century. In Adrian Tomer (Ed.), *Death attitudes and the older adult: Theories, concepts, and applications. Series in death, dying, and bereavement.* New York, NY: Brunner-Routledge.

Kastenbaum, Robert. (2005). Is death better in utopia? *Illness, Crisis, & Loss, 13*(1), 31–48.

Kato, Takahiro A.; Shinfuku, Naotaka; Sartorius, Norman; Kanba, Shigenobu. (2011). Are Japan's *hikikomori* and depression in young people spreading abroad? *Lancet, 378,* 1070. doi:10.1016/S0140-6736(11)61395-0

Kato, Takahiro A.; Tateno, Masaru; Shinfuku, Naotaka; Fujisawa, Daisuke; Teo, Alan R.; Sartorius, Norman; Akiyama, Tsuyoshi; Ishida, Tetsuya; Choi, Tae Young; Balhara, Yatan Pal Singh; Matsumoto, Ryohei; Umene-Nakano, Wakako; Fujimura, Yota; Wand, Anne; Pei-Chen Chang, Jane; Yuan-Feng Chang, Rita; Shadloo, Behrang; Uddin Ahmed, Helal; Lerthattasilp, Tiraya; Kanba, Shigenobu. (2012) Does the "hikikomori" syndrome of social withdrawal exist outside Japan? A preliminary international investigation. *Social Psychiatry and Psychiatric Epidemiology, 47,* 1061–1075.

Kaufman, Alan S. (1990). *Assessing adolescent and adult intelligence.* Boston, MA: Allyn & Bacon.

Kaufman, Alan S. (2009). *IQ testing 101.* New York, NY: Springer.

Kaufman, James C.; Grigorenko, Elena L.; & Sternberg, Robert J. (Eds.). (2009). *The essential Sternberg: Essays on intelligence, psychology, and education.* New York, NY: Springer.

Kaufman, James C., & Sternberg, Robert J. (2010). *The Cambridge handbook of creativity* New York, NY: Cambridge University Press.

Kaufman, Lloyd; Vassiliades, Vassias; & Noble, Richard. (2007). Perceptual distance and the moon illusion. *Spatial Vision, 20,* 155–175.

Kaut, Kevin P., & Dickinson, Josephine A. (2007). The mental health practitioner and psychopharmacology. *Journal of Mental Health Counseling, 29*(3), 204–225.

Kay, Aaron C.; Gaucher, Danielle; McGregor, Ian; & Nash, Kyle. (2010). Religious belief as compensatory control. *Personality and Social Psychology Review, 14*(1), 37–48.

Kay, Paul, & Regier, Terry. (2007). Color naming universals: The case of Berinmo. *Cognition, 102,* 289–298.

Kazdin, Alan E. (2004). Cognitive-behavior modification. In Jerry M. Wiener & Mina K. Dulcan (Eds.), *The American Psychiatric Publishing textbook of child and adolescent psychiatry.* Arlington, VA: American Psychiatric Publishing.

Kazdin, Alan E.. (2008). *Behavior modification in applied settings.* Long Grove, IL: Waveland Press.

Kazdin, Alan E., & Benjet, Corina. (2003). Spanking children: Evidence and issues. *Current Directions in Psychological Science, 12,* 99–103.

Kazdin, Alan E., & Blase, Stacey. (2011). Rebooting psychotherapy research and practice to reduce the burden of mental illness. *Perspectives on Psychological Science, 6*(1), 21–37. doi:10.1177/1745691610393527

Kazdin, Alan E., & Rabbitt, Sarah M. (2013). Novel models for delivering mental health services and reducing the burdens of mental illness. *Clinical Psychological Science, 1*(2), 170–191. doi:10.1177/1745691610393527

Kearney, Melissa. (2014, January 13). Quoted in "Is '16 and Pregnant' an effective form of birth control?" National Public Radio. Accessed from http://www.npr.org/2014/01/13/262175399/is-16-and-pregnant-an-effective-form-of-birth-control

Kearney, Melissa, & Levine, Phillip B. (2014). Media influences on social outcomes: The impact of MTV's *16 and Pregnant* on teen childbearing (Working Paper 19795). Cambridge, MA: National Bureau of Economic Research. Accessed from http://www.nber.org/papers/w19795

Keats, S., & Wiggins, S. (2014). *Future diets: Implications for agriculture and food prices.* ODI Report. London, England: Overseas Development Institute.

Keck, Paul E., Jr., & McElroy, Susan L. (2009). Treatment of bipolar disorder. In Alan F. Schatzberg & Charles B. Nemeroff (Eds.), *The American Psychiatric Publishing textbook of psychopharmacology* (4th ed., pp. 1113–1133). Washington, DC: American Psychiatric Publishing.

Keel, Pamela A.; Baxter, Mark G.; & Heatherton, Todd F. (2007). A 20-year longitudinal study of body weight, dieting, and eating disorder symptoms. *Journal of Abnormal Psychology, 116,* 422–432.

Keel, Pamela K., & Klump, Kelly L. (2003). Are eating disorders culture-bound syndromes? Implications for conceptualizing their etiology. *Psychological Bulletin, 129,* 747–769.

Kelly, Ciara, & McCreadie, Robin. (1999). Smoking habits, current symptoms, and premorbid characteristics of schizophrenic patients in Nithsdale, Scotland. *American Journal of Psychiatry, 156,* 1751–1757.

Kelman, Herbert C. (2005). The policy context of torture: A social-psychological analysis. *International Review of the Red Cross, 87,* 123–134.

Keltner, Dacher, & Horberg, E.J. (2015). Emotion-cognition interactions. In Mario Mikulincer, Phillip R. Shaver, Eugene Borgida, & John A. Bargh (Eds.), *APA Handbook of Personality and Social Psychology, Volume 1: Attitudes and social cognition.* Washington, DC: American Psychological Association. doi:10.1037/14341-020

Kemmer, Susanne. (2007, February/March). Sticking point. *Scientific American Mind,* pp. 64–69.

Kemp, Andrew H.; Krygier, Jonathan; & Harmon-Jones, Eddie. (2015). Neuroscientific perspectives of emotion. In Rafael A. Calvo, Sidney K. D'Mello, Jonathan Gratch, & Arvid Kappas (Eds.), *The Oxford handbook of affective computing.* New York, NY: Oxford University Press. doi:10.1093/oxfordhb/9780199942237.013.016

Kempermann, Gerd. (2012a). New neurons for "survival of the fittest." *Nature Reviews Neuroscience 13,* 727–736. doi:10.1038/nrn3319

Kempermann, Gerd. (2012b). Youth culture in the adult brain. *Science, 335,* 1175–1176. doi:10.1126/science.1219304

Kempermann, Gerd; Kuhn, H. Georg; & Gage, Fred H. (1998, May 1). Experience-induced neurogenesis in the senescent dentate gyrus. *Journal of Neuroscience, 18,* 3206–3212.

Kempton, Matthew J.; Salvador, Zainab; Munafò, Marcus R.; Geddes, John R.; Simmons, Andrew; Frangou, Sophia; & Williams, Steven C. R. (2011). Structural neuroimaging studies in major depressive disorder: Meta-analysis and comparison with bipolar disorder. *Archives of General Psychiatry, 68*(7), 675–690.

Kempton, Matthew J.; Stahl, Daniel; Williams, Steven C. R.; & DeLisi, Lynn E. (2010). Progressive lateral ventricular enlargement in schizophrenia: A meta-analysis of longitudinal MRI studies. *Schizophrenia Research, 120*(1–3), 54–62.

Kendal, Rachel L.; Custance, Deborah M.; Kendal, Jeremy R.; Vale, Gillian; Stoinski, Tara S.; Rakotomalala, Nirina Lalaina; & Rasamimanana, Hantanirina. (2010). Evidence for social learning in wild lemurs (Lemur catta). *Learning & Behavior, 38*(3), 220–234. doi:10.3758/lb.38.3.220

Kendall-Tackett, K. (2010). *The psychoneuroimmunology of chronic disease: Exploring the links between inflammation, stress, and illness.* Washington, DC: American Psychological Association.

Kendler, Kenneth S.; Gatz, Margaret; Gardner, Charles O.; & Pedersen, Nancy L. (2006). A Swedish national twin study of lifetime major depression. *American Journal of Psychiatry, 163,* 109–114.

Kendler, Kenneth S., & Schaffner, Kenneth F. (2011). The dopamine hypothesis of schizophrenia: An historical and philosophical analysis. *Philosophy, Psychiatry, & Psychology, 18*(1), 41–63.

Kennedy, Sidney H.; Konarski, Jakub Z.; Segal, Zindel V.; Lau, Mark A.; Bieling, Peter J.; McIntyre, Roger S.; & Mayberg, Helen S. (2007). differences in brain glucose metabolism between responders to CBT and venlafaxine in a 16-week randomized controlled trial. *American Journal of Psychiatry, 164*(5), 778–788. doi:10.1176/appi.ajp.164.5.778

Kerns, Kathryn A.; Abraham, Michelle M.; & Schlegelmilch, Andrew. (2007). Mother-child attachment in later middle childhood: Assessment approaches and associations with mood and emotion regulation. *Attachment & Human Development, 9,* 33–53.

Kerns, Kathryn A., & Richardson, Rhonda A. (2005). *Attachment in middle childhood.* New York, NY: Guilford.

Kerr, David C. R.; Lopez, Nestor L.; Olson, Sheryl L.; & Sameroff, Arnold J. (2004). Parental discipline and externalizing behavior problems in early childhood: The roles of moral regulation and child gender. *Journal of Abnormal Child Psychology, 32*(4), 369–383.

Kershaw, Trina C., & Ohlsson, Stellan. (2004). Multiple causes of difficulty in insight: The case of the nine-dot problem. *Journal of Experimental Psychology: Learning, Memory, and Cognition, 30,* 3–13.

Kesebir, Selin, & Oishi, Shigehiro. (2010). A spontaneous self-reference effect in memory: Why some birthdays are harder to remember than others. *Psychological Science, 21*(10), 1525–1531.

Keshavan, M. S.; DeLisi, L. E.; & Seidman, L. J. (2011). Early and broadly defined psychosis risk mental states. *Schizophrenia Research, 126*(1–3), 1–10. doi:10.1016/j.schres.2010.10.006

Kessler, Ronald C. (2003b, February). [*In-cites* interview with Dr. Ronald C. Kessler.] *ISI Essential Science Indicators.* Thompson Scientific, Philadelphia, PA. Retrieved on January 9, 2005, from http://www.incites.com/papers/DrRonaldKessler.html

Kessler, Ronald C., & researchers from the World Health Organization. (2004, June 2). World Mental Health Survey Consortium: Prevalence, severity, and unmet need for treatment of mental disorders in the World Health Organization mental health surveys. *Journal of the American Medical Association, 291,* 2581–2590. Retrieved January 9, 2005, from http://jama.ama-assn.org/cgi/reprint/291/21/2581.pdf

Kessler, Ronald C.; Angermeyer, Matthias; Anthony, James C.; De Graaf, Ron; Demyttenaere, Koen; Gasquet, Isabelle; ... Ustun, T. Bedirhan. (2007). Lifetime prevalence and age-of-onset distributions of mental disorders in the World Health Organization's world mental health survey initiative. *World Psychiatry, 6,* 168–176.

Kessler, Ronald C.; Berglund, Patricia; Demler, Olga; Jin, Robert; Koretz, Doreen; Merikangas, Kathleen R.; Rush, A. John; Walters, Ellen E.; & Wang, Philip S. (2003a, June 18). The epidemiology of major depressive disorder: Results from the National Comorbidity Survey Replication (NCS-R). *Journal of the American Medical Association, 289,* 3095–3105.

Kessler, Ronald C.; Berglund, Patricia; Demler, Olga; Jin, Robert; Merikangas, Kathleen R.; & Walters, Ellen E. (2005a). Lifetime prevalence and age-of-onset distributions of DSM-IV disorders in the National Comorbidity Survey Replication. *Archives of General Psychiatry, 62,* 593–602.

Kessler, Ronald C.; Chiu, Wai Tat; Demler, Olga; & Walters, Ellen E. (2005b). Prevalence, severity, and comorbidity of 12-month DSMIV disorders in the National Comorbidity Survey Replication. *Archives of General Psychiatry, 62,* 617–627.

Kessler, Ronald C.; Demler, Olga; Frank, Richard G.; Olfson, Mark; Pincus, Harold Alan; Walters, Ellen E.; Wang, Philip; Wells, Kenneth B.; & Zaslavsky, Alan M. (2005c, June 16). Prevalence and treatment of mental disorders, 1990 to 2003. *New England Journal of Medicine, 352,* 2515–2523.

Khan, Zafar U.; & Muly, E. Chris. (2011). Molecular mechanisms of working memory. *Behavioural Brain Research.* doi:10.1016/j.bbr.2010.12.039

Khazan, Olga. (2014, July 23). When hearing voices is a good thing. *The Atlantic.* Retrieved from http://www.theatlantic.com/health/archive/2014/07/when-hearing-voices-is-a-good-thing/374863

Khanna, Charu, & Medsker, Gina J. (2007). 2006 income and employment survey results for the Society for Industrial and Organizational Psychology. *The Industrial-Organizational Psychologist, 45.*

Kheriaty, Aaron. (2007). The return of the unconscious. *Psychiatric Annals, 37,* 285–287.

Khoury, Bassam; Lecomte, Tania; Fortin, Guillaume; Masse, Marjolaine; Therien, Phillip; Bouchard, Vanessa; Chapleau, Marie-Andrée; & others. (2013). Mindfulness-based therapy: A comprehensive meta-analysis. *Clinical Psychology Review, 33,* 763–771. doi:10.1016/j.cpr.2013.05.005

Kiecolt-Glaser, Janice K. (2009). Psychoneuroimmunology: Psychology's gateway to the biomedical future. *Perspectives on Psychological Science, 4,* 367–369.

Kiecolt-Glaser, Janice K., & Glaser, Ronald. (1993). Mind and immunity. In Daniel Goleman & Joel Gurin (Eds.), *Mind/body medicine: How to use your mind for better health.* Yonkers, NY: Consumer Reports Books.

Kiecolt-Glaser, Janice K., & Glaser, Ronald. (2010). Psychological stress, telomeres, and telomerase. *Brain, Behavior, and Immunology, 24,* 529–530. doi:10.1016/j.bbi.2010.02.002

Kiecolt-Glaser, Janice K; Gouin, Jean-Philippe; & Hantsoo, Liisa. (2009). Close relationships, inflammation, and health. *Neuroscience and Biobehavioral Reviews, 35*(1), 33–37.

Kiefer, Amy K., & Sekaquaptewa, Denise. (2007). Implicit stereotypes, gender identification, and math-related outcomes: A prospective study of female college students. *Psychological Science, 18,* 13–18.

Kihlstrom, John F. (2001). Hypnosis and the psychological unconscious. In Howard S. Friedman (Ed.), *Assessment and therapy: Specialty articles from the encyclopedia of mental health.* San Diego, CA: Academic Press.

Kihlstrom, John F. (2005). Dissociative disorders. *Annual Review of Clinical Psychology, 1,* 227–253.

Kihlstrom, John F. (2007). Consciousness in hypnosis. In Philip David Zelazo, Morris Moscovitch, & Evan Thompson (Eds.), *The Cambridge handbook of consciousness.* New York, NY: Cambridge University Press.

Kihlstrom, John F. (2010). Social neuroscience: The footprints of Phineas Gage. *Social Cognition, 28,* 757–783.

Kihlstrom, John F.; Dorfman, Jennifer; & Park, Lillian. (2007). Implicit and explicit memory and learning. In Max Velmans & Susan Schneider (Eds.), *The Blackwell companion to consciousness.* Malden, MA: Blackwell.

Kihlstrom, John F.; Mulvaney, Shelagh; Tobias, Betsy A.; & Tobias, Irene P. (2000). In Eric Eich, John F. Kihlstrom, Gordon H. Bower, Joseph P. Forgas, & Paula M. Niedenthal (Eds.), *Cognition and emotion.* New York, NY: Oxford University Press.

Kim, Bryan S. K., & Park, Yong S. (2008). East and Southeast Asian Americans. In Garrett McAuliffe (Ed.), *Culturally alert counseling: A comprehensive introduction* (pp. 188–219). Thousand Oaks, CA: Sage.

Kim, Jinhyun; Zhao, Ting; Petralia, Ronald S.; Yu, Yang; Peng, Hanchuan; Myers, Eugene; & Magee, Jeffrey C. (2012). mGRASP enables mapping mammalian synaptic connectivity with light microscopy. *Nature Methods, 9,* 96–102. doi:10.1038/nmeth.1784

King, Bruce M. (2013). The modern obesity epidemic, ancestral hunter-gatherers, and the sensory/reward control of food intake. *American Psychologist, 68,* 88–96.

King, D. Brett; Cox, Michaella; & Wertheimer, Michael. (2003). Karl Duncker: Productive problems with beautiful solutions. *Gestalt Theory, 25*(1–2), 95–110.

King, Katherine, & Ogle, Christin. (2014). Negative life events vary by neighborhood and mediate the relation between neighborhood context and psychological well-being. *PLOS ONE, 9*(4): e93539. doi:10.1371/journal.pone.0093539

King, Laura A. (2008). Personal goals and life dreams: Positive psychology and motivation in daily life. In James Y. Shah & Wendi L. Gardner (Eds.), *Handbook of motivation science.* New York, NY: Guilford.

King, Robert; Belsky Jay; Mah Kenneth; & Binik Yitzchak. (2010). Are there different types of female orgasm? *Archive of Sexual Behavior, 40,* 865–875.

Kingdon, Bianca L.; Egan, Sarah J.; & Rees, Clare S. (2012). The illusory beliefs inventory: A new measure of magical thinking and its relationship with obsessive compulsive disorder. *Behavioural and Cognitive Psychotherapy, 40,* 39–53. doi:10.1017/S1352465811000245

Kinzler, Katherine D.; Shutts, Kristin; & Correll, Joshua. (2010). Priorities in social categories. *European Journal of Social Psychology, 40*(4), 581–592.

Kirsch, Irving. (2014). Wagstaff's definition of hypnosis. *Journal of Mind-Body Regulation, 2,* 124–125.

Kirsch, Irving, & Braffman, Wayne. (2001). Imaginative suggestibility and hypnotizability. *Current Directions in Psychological Science, 10,* 57–61.

Kirsch, Irving; Cardeña, Etzel; Derbyshire, Stuart; Dienes, Zoltan; Heap, Michael; Kallio, Sakari; Mazzoni, Giuliana; Naish, Peter; Oakley, David; Potter, Catherine; Walters, Val; & Whalley, Matthew. (2011). Definitions of hypnosis and hynotizability and their relation to suggestion and suggestibility: A consensus statement. *Contemporary Hypnosis & Integrative Therapy, 28,* 107–115.

Kirsch, Irving; Deacon, Brett J.; Huedo-Medina, Tania B.; Scoboria, Alan; Moore, Thomas J.; & Johnson, Blair T. (2008). Initial severity and antidepressant benefits: A meta-analysis of data submitted to the Food and Drug Administration. *PLOS Medicine 5*(2): e45, 260–268. doi:10.1371/journal.pmed.0050045

Kirschenbaum, Howard. (2004). Carl Rogers's life and work: An assessment on the 100th anniversary of his birth. *Journal of Counseling and Development, 82,* 116–124.

Kirschenbaum, Howard, & Jourdan, April. (2005). The current status of Carl Rogers and the person-centered approach. *Psychotherapy: Theory, Research, Practice, Training, 42,* 37–51.

Kitayama, Shinobu; Markus, Hazel Rose; & Kurokawa, Masaru. (2000). Culture, emotion, and well-being: Good feelings in Japan and the United States. *Cognition & Emotion, 14,* 93–124.

Kitayama, Shinobu, & Park, Hyekyung. (2007). Cultural shaping of self, emotion, and well-being: How does it work? *Social and Personality Psychology Compass, 1,* 202–222., 337

Kitayama, Shinobu; Park, Jiyoung; Boylan, Jennifer; Miyamoto, Yuri; Levine, Cynthia; & Markus, Hazel; et al. (2015). Expression of anger and ill health in two cultures: An examination of inflammation and cardiovascular risk. *Psychological Science, 26,* 211–220. doi:10.1177/0956797614561268

Kitayama, Shinobu; & Uskul, Ayse K. (2011). Culture, mind, and the brain: Current evidence and future directions. *Annual Review of Psychology, 62,* 419–449. doi:10.1146/annurev-psych-120709-145357

Klauke, Benedikt; Deckert, Jürgen; Reif, Andreas; Pauli, Paul; & Domschke, Katharina. (2010). Life events in panic disorder—An update on 'candidate stressors.' *Depression and Anxiety, 27*(8), 716–730.

Kleider, Heather M.; Pezdek, Kathy; Goldinger, Stephen D.; & Kirk, Alice. (2008). Schema-driven source misattribution errors: Remembering the expected from a witnessed event. *Applied Cognitive Psychology, 22,* 1–20.

Klein, Laura C.; Bennett, Jeanette M.; Whetzel, Courtney A.; Granger, Douglas A.; & Ritter, Frank E. (2010). Caffeine and stress after salivary a-amylase activity in young men. *Human Psychopharmacology: Clinical and Experimental, 25*(5), 359–367.

Klein, Rachael M.; Dilchert, Stephan; Ones, Deniz S.; & Dages, Kelly D. (2015, March 30). Cognitive predictors and age-based adverse impact among business executives. *Journal of Applied Psychology, 100,* 1497–1510. doi:10.1037/a0038991

Kleinhans, Natalia; Akshoomoff, Natacha; & Dells, Dean C. (2005). Executive functions in autism and Asperger's disorder: Flexibility, fluency, and inhibition. *Developmental Neuropsychology, 27,* 379–401.

Klin, Anat, & Lemish, Dafna. (2008). Mental disorders stigma in the media: Review of studies on production, content, and influences. *Journal of Health Communication, 13*(5), 434–449.

Klinger, Regine; Colloca, Luana; Bingel, Ulrike; & Flor, Herta. (2014). Placebo analgesia: Clinical applications. *Pain, 155,* 1055–1058. doi:10.1016/j.pain.2013.12.007

Knafo, Danielle. (2009). Freud's memory erased. *Psychoanalytic Psychology, 26*(2), 171–190.

Knäuper, Bärbel; Roseman, Michelle; Johnson, Philip J.; & Krantz, Lillian H. (2009). Using mental imagery to enhance the effectiveness of implementation intentions. *Current Psychology, 28,* 181–186.

Knecht, S.; Dräger, B.; Deppe, M.; Bobe, L.; Lohmann, H.; Flöel, A.; Ringelstein, E.-B.; & Henningsen, H. (2000). Handedness and hemispheric language dominance in healthy humans. *Brain, 123,* 2512–2518. doi:10.1093/brain/123.12.2512

Knerr, Michael; Bartle-Haring, Suzanne; McDowell, Tiffany; Adkins, Katie; Delaney, Robin O.; Gangamma, Rashmi; Glebova, Tatiana; Garfsky, Erika & Meyer, Kevin (2011). The impact of initial factors on therapeutic alliance in individual and couples therapy. *Journal of Marital & Family Therapy, 37*(2), 182–199.

Knoblich, Gunther, & Öllinger, Michael. (2006, October). The Eureka moment. *Scientific American Mind, 17*(5), 38–43.

Knobloch, Marlen, & Jessberger, Sebastian. (2011). Perspectives on adult neurogenesis. *European Journal of Neuroscience, 33*(6), 1013–1017. doi:10.1111/j.1460-9568.2010.07598.x

Knox, Michele. (2010). On hitting children: A review of corporal punishment in the United States. *Journal of Pediatric Health Care, 24*(2), 103–107.

Kobilo, Tali; Yuan, Chunyan; & van Praag, Henriette. (2011). Endurance factors improve hippocampal neurogenesis and spatial memory in mice. *Learning & Memory, 18*(2), 103–107. doi:10.1101/lm.2001611

Koch, Iring; Lawo, Vera; Fels, Janina; & Vorländer, Michael. (2011). Switching in the cocktail party: Exploring intentional control of auditory selective attention. *Journal of Experimental Psychology: Human Perception and Performance.* Advance online publication. doi:10.1037/a0022189

Kochanek, Kenneth D., & Smith, Betty L. (2004, February 11). Deaths: Preliminary data for 2002 (National Vital Statistics Report, 52, No. 13). Atlanta: Centers for Disease Control, Department of Health and Human Services. Retrieved January 7, 2005, from http://www.cdc.gov/nchs/data/nvsr/nvsr52/nvsr5213.pdf

Kochanek, Kenneth, D.; Xu, Jiaquan; Murphy, Sherry, L.; Miniño, Arialdi, M.; & Kung, Hsiang-Ching. (2011). *Deaths: Preliminary data for 2009.* Hyattsville, MD: National Center for Health Statistics.

Koenen, Karestan C.; Amstadter, Ananda B.; & Nugent, Nicole R. (2008). Genetic risk factors for PTSD. In Douglas L. Delahanty (Ed.), *The psychobiology of trauma and resilience across the lifespan* (pp. 23–46). Lanham, MD: Jason Aronson.

Koenig, Anne M., & Dean, Kristy K. (2011). Cross cultural differences and similarities in attribution. In K. D. Keith (Ed.), *Cross-cultural psychology: Contemporary themes and perspectives.* Hoboken, NJ: Wiley-Blackwell.

Koenig, Anne M., & Eagly, Alice H. (2005). Stereotype threat in men on a test of social sensitivity. *Sex Roles, 52,* 489–496.

Koester, Lynne Sanford, & Lahti-Harper, Eve. (2010). Mother-infant hearing status and intuitive parenting during the first 18 months. *American Annals of the Deaf, 155,* 5–18. doi:10.1353/aad.0.0134

Koffka, Kurt. (1935). *Principles of Gestalt psychology.* New York, NY: Harcourt, Brace.

Kohlberg, Lawrence. (1976). Moral stages and moralization: The cognitive developmental approach. In T. Lickona (Ed.), *Moral development and behavior: Theory, research, and social issues.* New York, NY: Holt, Rinehart & Winston.

Kohlberg, Lawrence. (1981). *The Philosophy of Moral Development: Moral Stages and the Idea of Justice: Vol. 1. Essays on moral development.* New York, NY: Harper & Row.

Kohlberg, Lawrence. (1984). *The psychology of moral development.* New York, NY: Harper & Row.

Kohlberg, Lawrence. (1988). Quoted in James W. Fowler, John Snarey, & Karen A. Denicola, *Remembrances of Lawrence Kohlberg.* Atlanta, GA: Center for Research in Faith and Moral Development.

Kohler, Evelyne; Keysers, Christian; Umiltà, M. Allessandra; Fogassi, Leonardo; Gallese, Vittorio; & Rizzolatti, Giacomo. (2002). Hearing sounds, understanding actions: Action representation in mirror neurons. *Science, 297,* 846–848.

Kohls, Niko, & Benedikter, Roland. (2010). The origins of the modern concept of "neuroscience": Wilhelm Wundt between empiricism, and idealism: Implications for contemporary neuroethics. In James J. Giordano, James J. & Bert Gordijn (Eds.), *Scientific and philosophical perspectives in neuroethics* (pp. 37–65). New York, NY: Cambridge University Press.

Kohn, Robert. (2014). Trends, gaps, and disparities in mental health. In S. O. Okpaku (Ed.), *Essentials of global mental health* (pp. 27–38). Cambridge, England: Cambridge University Press.

Kohrt, Brandon A.; Jordans, Mark J. D.; Tol, Wietse A.; Speckman, Rebecca A.; Maharjan, Sujen M.; Worthman, Carol M.; & Komproe, Ivan H. (2008). Comparison of mental health between former child soldiers and children never conscripted by armed groups in Nepal. *Journal of the American Medical Association, 300*(6), 691–702.

Kojima, M. (2011). Mechanism of appetite regulation by ghrelin. *Brain and Development, 43,* 87–90.

Kokaridas, Dimitrios; Maggouritsa, Georgia; Stoforos, Periklis; Patsiaouras, Asterios; Theodorakis, Yiannis; & Diggelidis, Nikolaos. (2013). The effect of a token economy system program and physical activity on improving quality of life of patients with schizophrenia: A pilot study. *American Journal of Applied Psychology, 2*(6), 80–88. doi:10.11648/j.ajap.20130206.13

Kollndorfer, Kathrin; Kowalczyk, Knesia; Nell, Stephanie; Krajnik, Jacqueline; Mueller, Christian; & Schöpf, Veronika. (2015). The inability to self-evaluate smell performance: How the vividness of mental images outweighs awareness of olfactory performance. *Frontiers in Psychology, 6.* doi:10.3389/fpsyg.2015.00627

Kolodny, Andrew; Courtwright, David T.; Hwang, Catherine S.; Kreiner, Peter; Eadie, John L.; Clark, Thomas W., & Alexander, G. Caleb. (2015). The prescription opioid and heroin crisis: A public health approach to an epidemic of addiction. *Annual Review of Public Health, 3,* 559–574. doi:10.1146/annurev-publhealth-031914-122957

Komatsu, Hidehiko. (2006). The neural mechanisms of perceptual filling-in. *Nature Reviews Neuroscience, 7,* 220–231.

Kong, Lauren L.; Allen, John J. B.; & Glisky, Elizabeth L. (2008). Interidentity memory transfer in dissociative identity disorder. *Journal of Abnormal Psychology, 117,* 686–692.

König, Cornelius J.; Klehe, Ute-Christine; Berchtold, Matthias; & Kleinmann, Martin. (2010). Reasons for being selective when choosing personnel selection procedures. *International Journal of Selection and Assessment, 18,* 17–27. doi:10.1111/j.1468-2389.2010.00485.x

Kopelowicz, Alex; Liberman, Robert P.; & Zarate, Roberto. (2007). Psychosocial treatments for schizophrenia. In Peter E. Nathan & Jack M. Gorman (Eds.), *A guide to treatments that work* (3rd ed., pp. 243–269). New York, NY: Oxford University Press.

Kopp, Claire B. (2011). Development in the early years: Socialization, motor development, and consciousness. *Annual Review of Psychology. 62,* 165–87. doi:10.1146/annurev.psych.121208.131625

Kornell, Nate. (2008, February). How to study. *British Psychological Society Research Digest Blog.* Retrieved May 15, 2008, from http://bpsresearch-digest.blogspot.com/2008/02/how-to-study.html

Kornfield, Rachel; Donohue, Julie; Berndt, Ernst R.; & Alexander, G. C. (2013). Promotion of prescription drugs to consumers and providers, 2001–2010. *PLOS ONE, 8*(3), 1–7. doi:10.1371/journal.pone.0055504

Kosinski, Michal; Stillwell, David; & Graepel, Thore. (2013). Private traits and attributes are predictable from digital records of human behavior. *Proceedings of the National Academy of Sciences, 110,* 5802–5805. doi:10.1073/pnas.1218772110.

Kosslyn, Stephen M.; Ball, Thomas M.; & Reiser, Brian J. (1978). Visual images preserve metric spatial information: Evidence from studies of image scanning. *Journal of Experimental Psychology: Human Perception and Performance, 4,* 47–60.

Kosslyn, Stephen M.; Ganis, Giorgio; & Thompson, William L. (2001). Neural foundations of imagery. *Nature Reviews Neuroscience, 2,* 635–642.

Kosslyn, Stephen M., & Thompson, William L. (2000). Shared mechanisms in visual imagery and visual perception: Insights from cognitive neuroscience. In Michael S. Gazzaniga (Ed.), *The new cognitive neurosciences* (2nd ed.). Cambridge, MA: MIT Press.

Kosslyn, Stephen M.; Thompson, William L.; Costantini-Ferrando, Maria F.; Alpert, Nathaniel M.; & Spiegel, David. (2000). Hypnotic visual illusion alters color processing in the brain. *American Journal of Psychiatry, 157,* 1279–1284.

Kouider, Sid; Berthet, Vincent; & Faivre, Nathan. (2011). Preference is biased by crowded facial expressions. *Psychological Science, 22,* 184–189.

Kozorovitskiy, Yevgenia, & Gould, Elizabeth. (2004). Dominance hierarchy influences adult neurogenesis in the dentate gyrus. *Journal of Neuroscience, 24,* 6755–6759.

Kposowa, Augustine, & D'Auria, Stephanie. (2010). Association of temporal factors and suicides in the United States, 2000–2004. *Social Psychiatry and Psychiatric Epidemiology, 45,* 433–445. doi:10.1007/s00127-009-0082-9

Krantz, David S., & McCeney, Melissa K. (2002). Effects of psychological and social factors on organic disease: A critical assessment of research on coronary heart disease. *Annual Review of Psychology, 53,* 341–369.

Krebs, Dennis L., & Denton, Kathy. (2005). Toward a more pragmatic approach to morality: A critical evaluation of Kohlberg's model. *Psychological Bulletin, 112,* 629–649.

Krebs, Dennis L., & Denton, Kathy. (2006). Explanatory limitations of cognitive-developmental approaches to morality. *Psychological Bulletin, 113,* 672–675.

Kreider, Rose M. (2008, March 3). *Improvements to demographic household data in the current population survey: 2007.* Washington, DC: U.S. Census Bureau, Housing and Household Economic Statistics Division.

Kring, Ann M., & Gordon, Albert H. (1998). Sex differences in emotion: Expression, experience, and physiology. *Journal of Personality and Social Psychology, 74,* 686–703.

Krippner, Stanley. (1994). Cross-cultural treatment perspectives of dissociative disorders. In Steven Jay Lynn & Judith W. Rhue (Eds.), *Dissociation: Clinical and theoretical perspectives.* New York, NY: Guilford Press.

Krohe, James. (2006). Are workplace tests worth taking? Only if you do them right—which you probably don't. *Across the Board, 43,* 16–23.

Kromann, Charles B.; Jensen, Morten L.; & Ringsted, Charlotte. (2009). The effect of testing on skills learning. *Medical Education, 43*(1), 21–27. doi:10.1111/j.1365-2923.2008.03245.x

Kroll, Judith F.; Bobb, Susan C.; & Hoshino, Noriko. (2014). Two languages in mind: Bilingualism as a tool to investigate language, cognition, and the brain. *Current Directions in Psychological Science, 23,* 159–163. doi:10.1177/0963721414528511

Kross, Ethan; Mischel, Walter; Hassin, Ran R.; Ochsner, Kevin N.; & Trope, Yaacov. (2010). From stimulus control to self-control: Toward an integrative understanding of the processes underlying willpower *Self control in society, mind, and brain.* (pp. 428–446). New York, NY: Oxford University Press.

Kruger, Justin, & Gilovich, Thomas. (2004). Actions, intentions, and self-assessment: The road to self-enhancement is paved with good intentions. *Personality and Social Psychology Bulletin, 30*(3), 328–329.

Kruglanski, Arie W.; Kapetz, Catalina; Hassin, Ran R.; Ochsner, Kevin N.; & Trope, Yaacov. (2010). Unpacking the self-control dilemma and its modes of resolution *Self control in society, mind, and brain* (pp. 297–311). New York, NY: Oxford University Press.

Krusemark, Elizabeth A.; Campbell, W. Keith; & Clementz, Brett A. (2008, July). Attributions, deception, and event related potentials: An investigation of the self-serving bias. *Psychophysiology, 45*(4), 511–515.

Ku, Chee S.; Loy, En Y.; Salim, Agus; Pawitan, Yudi; & Chia, Kee S. (2010). The discovery of human genetic variations and their use as disease markers: Past, present and future. *Journal of Human Genetics, 55*(7), 403–415. doi:10.1038/jhg.2010.55

Kübler-Ross, Elisabeth. (1969). *On death and dying.* New York, NY: Macmillan.

Kucewicz, Michal T.; Tricklebank, Mark D.; Bogacz, Rafal; Jones, & Matthew W. (2011). Dysfunctional prefrontal cortical network activity and interactions following cannabinoid receptor activation. *Journal of Neuroscience, 31,* 15560–15568.

Kuczaj Stan A., II. (2013). Emotions (and feelings) everywhere. In Shigeru Watanabe & Stan A. Kuczaj (Eds.), *Emotions of animals and humans: Comparative perspectives.* New York, NY: Springer Science + Business Media.

Kuczaj II, Stan A.; Highfill, Lauren E.; Makecha, Radhika N.; & Byerly, Holli C. (2013). Why do dolphins smile? A comparative perspective on dolphin emotions and emotional expressions. In Shigeru Watanabe & Stan A. Kuczaj (Eds.), *Emotions of animals and humans: Comparative perspectives.* New York, NY: Springer Science + Business Media.

Kufahl, Peter; Li, Zhu; Risinger, Robert; Rainey, Charles; Piacentine, Linda; Wu, Gaohong; Bloom, Alan; Yang, Zheng; & Li, Shi-Jiang. (2008). Expectation modulates human brain responses to acute cocaine: A functional magnetic resonance imaging study. *Biological Psychiatry, 63,* 222–230.

Kuhl, Brice A.; Dudukovic, Nicole M.; Kahn, Itamar; & Wagner, Anthony D. (2007). Decreased demands on cognitive control reveal the neural processing benefits of forgetting. *Nature Neuroscience, 10,* 908–914.

Kuhl, Patricia K. (2004). Early language acquisition: Cracking the speech code. *Nature Reviews Neuroscience, 5,* 831–843.

Kuhl, Patricia K.; Williams, Karen A.; Lacerda, Francisco; Stevens, Kenneth N.; & Lindblom, Bjorn. (1992, January 31). Linguistic experience alters phonetic perception in infants by 6 months of age. *Science, 255,* 606–608.

Kuhn, Clifford C.; Nichols, Michael R.; & Belew, Barbara L. (2010). The role of humor in transforming stressful life events. In Thomas W. Miller (Ed.), *Handbook of stressful transitions across the lifespan.* New York, NY: Springer.

Kuhn, Deanna. (2008). Formal Operations from a Twenty-First Century Perspective. *Human Development, 51,* 48–55. doi:10.1159/000113155

Kuhn, Deanna, & Franklin, Sam. (2006). The second decade: What develops (and how)? In D. Kuhn & R. Siegler (Eds.), *Handbook of child psychology. Vol. 2: Cognition, perception, and language* (6th ed.) New York, NY: Wiley.

Kuikka, Jyrki T.; Tammela, Liisa; Karhunen, Leila; Rissanen, Aila; Bergström, Kim A.; Naukkarinen, Hannu; . . . Uusitupa, Matti. (2001). Reduced serotonin transporter binding in binge eating women. *Psychopharmacology, 155*(3), 310–314.

Kunoh, Hiroshi, & Takaoki, Eiji. (1994). *3-D planet: The world as seen through stereograms.* San Francisco, CA: Cadence Books.

Kunz, John A.; & Soltys, Florence G. (2007). *Transformational reminiscence: Life story work.* New York, NY: Springer.

Kuo, Ben. (2013). Collectivism and coping: Current theories, evidence, and measurements of collective coping. *International Journal of Psychology, 48,* 374–388. doi:10.1080/00207594.2011.640681

Kupferschmidt, Kai. (2014a) High hopes. *Science, 345,* 18–23.

Kupferschmidt, Kai. (2014b) Can ecstasy treat the agony of PDSD? *Science, 345,* 22–23.

Kurman, Jenny. (2010). Good, better, best: Between culture and self-enhancement. *Social and Personality Psychology Compass, 4*(6), 379–392.

Kurson, Robert. (2007). *Crashing through.* New York, NY: Random House.

Kurtz, Matthew M., & Richardson, Christi L. (2012). Social cognitive training for schizophrenia: A meta-analytic investigation of controlled research. *Schizophrenia Bulletin, 38*(5), 1092–1104. doi:10.1093/schbul/sbr036

Kurzban, Robert; Burton-Chellew, Maxwell N.; & West, Stuart A. (2015). The evolution of altruism in humans. *Annual Review of Psychology, 66,* 575–599. doi:10.1146/annurev-psych-010814-015355

Kush, Francis R. (2009). Brief psychodynamic and cognitive therapy regarding acute treatment. *Journal of Psychotherapy Integration, 19*(2), 158–172.

Kuzumaki, Naoko; Ikegami, Daigo; Tamura, Rie; Hareyama, Nana; Imai, Satoshi; Narita, Michiko; Torigoe, Kazuhiro; & others. (2011). Hippocampal epigenetic modification at the brain-derived neurotrophic factor gene induced by an enriched environment. *Hippocampus, 21*(2), 127–132. doi:10.1002/hipo.20775

Kwan, Virginia S. Y.; Kuang, Lu Lu; & Zhao, Belinda X. (2008). In search of the optimal ego: When self-enhancement bias helps and hurts adjustment. In H. A. Wayment & J. J. Bauer (Eds.), *Transcending self-interest: Psychological explorations of the quiet ego.* Washington, DC: American Psychological Association.

Kwok, Veronica; Niu, Zhendong; Kay, Paul; Zhou, Ke; Mo, Lei; Jin, Zhen; So, Kwok-Fai; & Tan, Li Hai. (2011). Learning new color names produces rapid increase in gray matter in the intact adult human cortex. *Proceedings of the National Academy of Sciences, 108,* 6686–6688.

Laceulle, Odilia M.; Vollebergh, Wilma A.; & Ormel, Johan. (2015, February 23). The structure of psychopathology in adolescence: Replication of a general psychopathology factor in the TRAILS study. *Clinical Psychological Science.* doi:10.1177/2167702614560750

Ladabaum, Uri; Mannalithara, Ajitha; Myer, Parvathi A.; & Singh, Gurkirpal. (2014). Obesity, abdominal obesity, physical activity, and caloric intake in U.S. adults: 1988-2010. *American Journal of Medicine, 127,* 717–727. e12.doi:10.1016/j.amjmed.2014.02.026

Lafreniere, Denis, & Mann, Norman. (2009). Anosmia: Loss of smell in the elderly. *Otolaryngologic Clinics of North America, 42*(1), 123–131.

LaFromboise, Teresa D.; Trimble, Joseph E.; & Mohatt, Gerald V. (1993). Counseling intervention and American Indian tradition: An integrative approach. In Donald R. Atkinson, George Morten, & Derald Wing Sue (Eds.), *Counseling American minorities: A cross-cultural perspective* (4th ed.). Madison, WI: Brown & Benchmark.

Lago-Rodriguez, Angel; Lopez-Alonso, Virginia; & Fernández-del-Olmo, Miguel. (2013). Mirror neuron system and observational learning: Behavioral and neurophysiological evidence. *Behavioural Brain Research, 248,* 104–113. doi:10.1016/j.bbr.2013.03.033

Lahav, Amir; Saltzman, Elliot; & Schlaug, Gottfried. (2007). Action representation of sound: Audiomotor recognition network while listening to newly acquired actions. *Journal of Neuroscience, 27,* 308–314.

Lahey, Benjamin B. (2009). Public health significance of neuroticism. *American Psychologist, 64*(4), 241–256.

Laible, Deborah. (2007). Attachment with parents and peers in late adolescence: Links with emotional competence and social behavior. *Personality and Individual Differences, 43,* 1185–1197.

Laird, James D., & Lacasse, Katherine. (2014). Bodily influences on emotional feelings: Accumulating evidence and extensions of William James's theory of emotion. *Emotion Review, 6,* 27–34. doi:10.1177/1754073913494899

Lamb, Michael E.; Sternberg, Kathleen J.; & Prodromidis, Margardita. (1992). Nonmaternal care and the security of infant–mother attachment: A reanalysis of the data. *Infant Behavior and Development, 15,* 71–83.

Lamb, Michael E.; Thompson, Ross A.; Gardner, William; & Charnov, Eric L. (1985). Infant–mother attachment: The origins and developmental significance of individual differences in Strange Situation behavior. Hillsdale, NJ: Erlbaum.

Lambert, Anthony J.; Good, Kimberly S.; & Kirk, Ian J. (2010). Testing the repression hypothesis: Effects of emotional valence on memory suppression in the think-No think task. *Consciousness and Cognition: An International Journal, 19*(1), 281–293.

Lambert, Michael J., & Ogles, Benjamin M. (2004). The efficacy and effectiveness of psychotherapy. In Michael J. Lambert (Ed.), *Bergin and Garfield's handbook of psychotherapy and behavior change* (5th ed.). New York, NY: Wiley.

Lambert, Michael J.; Garfield, Sol L.; & Bergin, Allen E. (2004). Overview, trends, and future issues. In Michael J. Lambert (Ed.), *Bergin and Garfield's handbook of psychotherapy and behavior change* (5th ed.). New York, NY: Wiley.

Lambert, Michael J.; Hansen, Nathan B.; & Finch, Arthur E. (2001). Patient-focused research: Using patient outcome data to enhance treatment effects. *Journal of Consulting and Clinical Psychology, 69,* 159–172.

Lamont, Peter; Henderson, John M.; & Smith, Tim J. (2010). Where science and magic meet: The illusion of a "science of magic." *Review of General Psychology, 14*(1), 16–21. doi:10.1037/a0017157

Lampinen, James M.; Copeland, Susann M.; & Neuschatz, Jeffrey S. (2001). Recollections of things schematic: Room schemas revisited. *Journal of Experimental Psychology: Learning, Memory, and Cognition, 27,* 1211–1222.

Lampinen, James M.; Faries, Jeremiah M.; Neuschatz, Jeffrey S.; & Toglia, Michael P. (2000). Recollections of things schematic: The influence of scripts on recollective experience. *Applied Cognitive Psychology, 14,* 543–554.

Lampinen, James M.; Meier, Christopher R.; & Arnal, Jack D. (2005). Compelling untruths: Content borrowing and vivid false memories. *Journal of Experimental Psychology: Learning, Memory, and Cognition, 31,* 954–963.

Lancaster, Lynne C., & Stillman, David. (2002). *When generations collide: Who they are. Why they clash. How to solve the generational puzzle at work.* New York, NY: HarperCollins.

Lander, E. S.; Linton, L. M.; Birren, B.; Nusbaum, C.; Zody, M. C.; Baldwin, J.; Devon, K.; Dewar, K.; & others. (2001). Initial sequencing and analysis of the human genome. *Nature, 409*(6822), 860–921. doi:10.1038/35057062

Lander, Hans Jürgen. (1997). Hermann Ebbinghaus. In Wolfgang G. Bringmann, Helmut E. Lück, Rudolf Miller, & Charles E. Early (Eds.), *A pictorial history of psychology.* Chicago, IL: Quintessence.

Landolt, Hans-Peter. (2008). Sleep homeostasis: A role for adenosine in humans? *Biochemical Pharmacology, 75,* 2070–2079.

Lane, Anthony; Luminet, Oliver; Rimé, Bernard; Gross, James; de Timary, Phillipe; & Mikolajczak, Moïra. (2013). Oxytocin increases willingness to socially share one's emotions. *International Journal of Psychology, 48,* 676–681. doi:10.1080/00207594.2012.677540

Laner, Mary R.; Benin, Mary H.; & Ventrone, Nicole A. (2001). Bystander attitudes toward victims of violence: Who's worth helping? *Deviant Behavior, 22*(1), 23–42.

Langan-Fox, Janice, & Grant, Sharon. (2006). The Thematic Apperception Test: Toward a Standard Measure of the Big Three Motives. *Journal of Personality Assessment, 87*(3), 277–291.

Lange, Carl G., & James, William. (1922). *The emotions* (I. A. Haupt, Trans.). Baltimore, MD: Williams & Wilkins.

Lange, Jean, & Grossman, Sheila. (2010). Theories of aging. In Kristen L. Mauk (Ed.), *Gerontological nursing: Competencies for care* (2nd ed., pp. 50–74). Sudbury, MA: Jones and Bartlett.

Lange, Tanja; Dimitrov, Stoyan; & Born, Jan. (2010). Effects of sleep and circadian rhythm on the human immune system. *Annals of the New York Academy of Sciences, 1193*(1), 48–59.

Langer, Ellen, & Rodin, Judith. (1976). The effects of choice and enhanced personal responsibility for the aged: A field experiment in an institutional setting. *Journal of Personality and Social Psychology, 34,* 191–198.

Langer, Shelby L. (2010). Gender differences in experimental disclosure: Evidence, theoretical explanations, and avenues for future research. *Sex Roles, 63,* 178–183. doi:10.1007/s11199-010-9795-1

Langley, Audra K.; Cohen, Judith A.; Mannarino, Anthony P.; Jaycox, Lisa H.; Schonlau, Matthais; Scott, Molly; ... Gegenheimer, Kate L. (2014). Trauma exposure and mental health problems among school children 15 months post-hurricane Katrina. *Journal of Child and Adolescent Trauma, 6*(3), 143–156. doi:10.1080/19361521.2013.812171

Langlois, Judith H.; Kalakanis, Lisa; Rubenstein, Adam J.; Larson, Andrea; Hallam, Monica; & Smoot, Monica. (2000). Maxims or myths of beauty? A meta-analytic and theoretical review. *Psychological Bulletin, 126*(3), 390–423.

Langlois, Judith H., Ritter, J. M., Casey, R. J., & Sawin, D. B. (1995). Infant attractiveness predicts maternal behaviors and attitudes. *Developmental Psychology, 31,* 464–472.

Langnickel, Robert, & Markowitsch, Hans. (2006). Repression and the unconscious. *Behavioral and Brain Sciences, 29*(5), 524–525. doi:10.1017/S0140525X06359110

Långström, Niklas; Rahman, Qazi; Carlström, Eva; & Lichtenstein, Paul. (2008). Genetic and environmental effects on same-sex sexual behavior: A population study of twins in Sweden. *Archives of Sexual Behavior.* Retrieved on September 2009 from http://www.springerlink. com/content /2263646523551487/?p=5310511181974ce6b6abe 4ac49752533=4

Långström, Niklas; Rahman, Qazi; Carlström, Eva; & Lichtenstein, Paul. (2010). Genetic and environmental effects on same-sex sexual behavior: A population study of twins in Sweden. *Archives of Sexual Behavior, 39*(1), 75–80.

Larkin, Gregory L., & Beautrais, Annette L. (2011). A preliminary naturalistic study of low-dose ketamine for depression and suicide ideation in the emergency department. *International Journal of Neuropsychopharmacology, 14*(8), 1127–1131.

Larsen, Jeff T., & McGraw, A. Peter. (2011). Further evidence for mixed emotions. *Journal of Personality and Social Psychology, 100,* 1095–1110.

Larsen, Jeff T.; Norris, Catherine J.; McGraw, A. Peter; Hawkley, Louise C.; & Cacioppo, John T. (2009). The evaluative space grid: A single-item measure of positivity and negativity. *Cognition and Emotion, 23*(3), 453–480.

Laruelle, Marc; Kegeles, Lawrence S.; & Abi-Dargham, Anissa. (2003). Glutamate, dopamine, and schizophrenia: From pathophysiology to treatment. *Annals of the New York Academy of Sciences, 1003,* 138–158.

Lashley, Karl S. (1929). *Brain mechanisms and intelligence.* Chicago, IL: University of Chicago Press.

Lashley, Karl S. (1950). In search of the engram. *Symposia of the Society for Experimental Biology, 4,* 454–482.

Laska, Kevin M.; Gurman, Alan S.; & Wampold, Bruce E. (2013). Expanding the lens of evidence-based practice in psychotherapy: A common factors perspective. *Psychotherapy.* Advance online publication. doi:10.1037/a0034332

Lasser, Karen; Boyd, J. Wesley; Woolhandler, Steffie; Himmelstein, David U.; McCormick, Danny; & Bor, David H. (2000). Smoking and mental illness: A population-based prevalence study. *Journal of the American Medical Association, 284,* 2606–2610.

Latané, Bibb, & Darley, John M. (1970). *The unresponsive bystander: Why doesn't he help?* New York, NY: Appleton-Century-Crofts.

Latané, Bibb, & Darley, John, M. (1968). Group inhibition of bystander intervention in emergencies. *Journal of Personality and Social Psychology, 10*(3), 215–221.

Latané, Bibb, & Nida, Steve A. (1981). Ten years of research on group size and helping. *Psychological Bulletin, 89,* 308–324.

Lattal, K. Matthew. (2013). Pavlovian conditioning. In Gregory J. Madden, William V. Dube, Timothy D. Hackenberg, Gregory P. Hanley, & Kennon A. Lattal, (Eds.), *APA Handbook of Behavior Analysis, Vol. 1: Methods and principles.* Washington, DC: American Psychological Association. doi:10.1037/13937-013

Lau, Chi-leong; Wang, Han-Cheng; Hsu, Jung-Lung; & Liu, Mu-En. (2013). Does the dopamine hypothesis explain schizophrenia? *Reviews in the Neurosciences, 24*(4), 389–400.

Lau, Jennifer Y.F., & Pile, Victoria. (2014). Can cognitive bias modification of interpretations training alter mood states in children and adolescents? A reanalysis of data from six studies. *Clinical Psychological Science, 3,* 112–125. doi:10.1177/2167702614549596

Lavie, Nilli. (2010). Attention, distraction, and cognitive control under load. *Current Directions in Psychological Science, 19*(3), 143–148. doi:10.1177/0963721410370295

Lavoie, Kim L., & Barone, Silvana. (2006). Prescription privileges for psychologists: A comprehensive review and critical analysis of current issues and controversies. *CNS Drugs, 20*(1), 51–66.

Lawler, Edward E., III. (1973). *Motivation in work organizations.* Pacific Grove, CA: Brooks/Cole.

Lawrence, Erika; Rothman, Alexia D.; Cobb, Rebecca J.; & Bradbury, Thomas N. (2010). Marital satisfaction across the transition to parenthood: Three eras of research. In Marc S. Schulz, Marsha Kline Pruett,

Patricia K. Kerig & Ross D. Parke (Eds.), *Strengthening couple relationships for optimal child development: Lessons from research and intervention.* (pp. 97–114). Washington, DC: American Psychological Association.

Lazar, Sara W.; Kerr, Catherine E.; Wasserman, Rachel H.; Gray, Jeremy R.; Greve, Douglas; Treadway, Michael T.; McGarvey, Metta; & others. (2005). Meditation experience is associated with increased cortical thickness. *NeuroReport, 16,* 1893–1897.

Lazarus, Arnold A. (2000). Will reason prevail? From classic psychoanalysis to New Age therapy. *American Journal of Psychotherapy, 54,* 152–155.

Lazarus, Arnold A. (2008). Technical eclecticism and multimodal therapy. In Jay L. Lebow (Ed.), *Twenty-first century psychotherapies: Contemporary approaches to theory and practice* (pp. 424–452). Hoboken, NJ: Wiley.

Lazarus, Richard S. (1995). Vexing research problems inherent in cognitive-mediational theories of emotion—and some solutions. *Psychological Inquiry, 6,* 183–197.

Lazarus, Richard S. (1999). *Stress and emotion: A new synthesis.* New York, NY: Springer.

Lazarus, Richard S., & Folkman, Susan. (1984). *Stress, appraisal, and coping.* New York, NY: Springer.

Lazarus, Richard S., & Smith, Craig A. (1988). Knowledge and appraisal in the cognition-emotion relationship. *Cognition and Emotion, 2,* 281–300. doi:10.1080/02699938808412701

Le Foll, Bernard, & Goldberg, Steven R. (2007). Targeting the dopamine D-sub-3 receptor for treatment of nicotine dependence. In Tony P. George (Ed.), *Medication treatments for nicotine dependence* (pp. 199–212). Boca Raton, FL: CRC Press.

Le Foll, David; Rascle, Olivier; & Higgins, N. C. (2008). Attributional feedback-induced changes in functional and dysfunctional attributions, expectations of success, hopefulness, and short-term persistence in a novel sport. *Psychology of Sport and Exercise, 9,* 77–101. doi:10.1016/j.psychsport.2007.01.004

Leaper, Campbell, & Friedman, Carly Kay. (2007). The socialization of gender. In Joan E. Grusec & Paul D. Hastings (Eds.), *Handbook of socialization: Theory and research.* New York, NY: Guilford.

Leary, Mark R., & Allen, Ashley Batts. (2011). Personality and persona: Personality process in self-presentation. *Journal of Personality, 79,* 889–916.

Lebow, Jay L. (2008). Couple and family therapy. In Jay L. Lebow (Ed.), *Twenty-first century psychotherapies: Contemporary approaches to theory and practice* (pp. 307–346). Hoboken, NJ: Wiley.

Ledford, Heidi. (2014). If depression were cancer. *Nature, 515,* 182–184.

LeDoux, Joseph E. (1994a, June). Emotion, memory, and the brain. *Scientific American, 270,* 50–57.

LeDoux, Joseph E. (1994b). Memory versus emotional memory in the brain. In Paul Ekman & Richard J. Davisdon (Eds.), *The nature of emotion: Fundamental questions.* New York, NY: Oxford University Press.

LeDoux, Joseph E. (1995). Emotion: Clues from the brain. *Annual Review of Psychology, 46,* 209–235.

LeDoux, Joseph E. (1996). *The emotional brain: The mysterious underpinnings of emotional life.* New York, NY: Simon & Schuster.

LeDoux, Joseph E. (2000). Emotion circuits in the brain. *Annual Review of Neuroscience, 23,* 155–184.

LeDoux, Joseph E. (2007). The amygdala. *Current Biology, 17,* R868–R874.

Lee, Evelyn, & Mock, Matthew R. (2005). Asian families: An overview. In Monica McGoldrick, Joe Giordano, & Nydia Garcia-Petro (Eds.), *Ethnicity & Family Therapy* (3rd ed., pp. 269–289). New York, NY: Guilford.

Lee, Hyo-Jeong J.; Lee, Jae-Ho, Lee, Eun-Ok, Lee, Hyo-Jung; Kim, Kwan-Hyun; Kim, Sun-Hyung; & others. (2009). Substance P and beta endorphin mediate electroacupuncture induced analgesic activity in mouse cancer pain model. *Acupuncture & Electro-Therapeutics Research, 34,* 27–40.

Lee, Jo Ann, & Phillips, Stephen J. (2006). Work and family: Can you have it all? *Psychologist-Manager Journal, 9*(1), 41–75.

Lee, Kyoung-Uk; Bahk, Won-Myong; Jon, Duk-In; Min, Kyung J.; Shin, Young C.; Woo, Young S. & Kim, Chan-Hyung (2009). The prescription pattern and side-effect profile of bupropion. *Clinical Psychopharmacology and Neuroscience, 7*(2), 39–43.

Lee, Sing; Ho, Ting Pong; & Hsu, L. K. George. (1993). Fat phobic and non-fat phobic anorexia nervosa: A comparative study of 70 Chinese patients in Hong Kong. *Psychological Medicine, 23,* 999–1017.

Lee, Sing; Ng, King Lam; Kwok, Kathleen; & Fung, Corina. (2010). The changing profile of eating disorders at a tertiary psychiatric clinic in Hong Kong (1987–2007). *International Journal of Eating Disorders, 43*(4), 307–314. doi:10.1002/eat.20686

Lee, Star W.; Clemenson, Gregory D.; & Gage, Fred H. (2012). New neurons in an aged brain. *Behavioural Brain Research, 227,* 497–507. doi:10.1016/j.bbr.2011.10.00

Lee, Su Young; Kang, Jee In; Lee, Eun; Namkoong, Kee; & An, Suk Kyoon. (2011). Differential priming effect for subliminal fear and disgust facial expressions. *Attention, Perception, & Psychophysics, 73*(2), 473–481.

Lee, Yih-teen. (2010). Home versus host—identifying with either, both, or neither? The relationship between dual cultural identities and intercultural effectiveness. *International Journal of Cross Cultural Management, 10*(1), 55–76.

Leichtman, Martin. (2004). Projective tests: The nature of the task. In Mark J. Hilsenroth & Daniel L. Segal (Eds.), *Comprehensive Handbook of Psychological Assessment, Vol. 2: Personality assessment* (pp. 297–314). Hoboken, NJ: Wiley.

Leighton, Jacqueline P.; & Sternberg, Robert J. (2013). Reasoning and problem solving. In Alice F. Healy, Robert W. Proctor, & Irving B. Weiner (Eds.), *Handbook of Psychology, Vol. 4: Experimental psychology* (2nd ed.). Hoboken, NJ: Wiley.

Leighton, Jane, & Heyes, Cecilia. (2010). Hand to mouth: Automatic imitation across effector systems. *Journal of Experimental Psychology: Human Perception and Performance, 36*(5), 1174–1183.

Leising, Daniel; Scharloth, Joachim; Lohse, Oliver; & Wood, Dustin. (2014). What types of terms do people use when describing an individual's personality? *Psychological Science, 25,* 1787–1794. doi:10.1177/0956797614541285

Lemay, Edward P., Jr.; Clark, Margaret S.; & Greenberg, Aaron. (2010). What is beautiful is good because what is beautiful is desired: Physical attractiveness stereotyping as projection of interpersonal goals. *Personality and Social Psychology Bulletin, 36*(3), 339–353.

Lenert, Leslie; Muñoz, Ricardo F.; Perez, John E.; & Bansod, Aditya. (2004). Automated e-mail messaging as a tool for improving quit rates in an internet smoking cessation intervention. *Journal of the American Medical Informatics Association, 11*(4), 235–240. doi:10.1197/jamia.M1464

Lenroot, Rhoshel K., & Giedd, Jay N. (2006). Brain development in children and adolescents: Insights from anatomical magnetic resonance imaging. *Neuroscience & Biobehavioral Reviews, 30*(6), 718–729.

Lenzenweger, Mark F. (2008). Epidemiology of personality disorders. *Psychiatric Clinics of North America, 31,* 395–403.

Leon, Scott C.; Kopta, S. Mark; Howard, Kenneth I.; & Lutz, Wolfgang. (1999). Predicting patients' responses to psychotherapy: Are some more predictable than others? *Journal of Consulting and Clinical Psychology, 67,* 698–704.

Leopold, David A., & Rhodes, Gillian. (2010). A comparative view of face perception. *Journal of Comparative Psychology, 124*(3), 233–251.

Lerman, Dorothea C.; & Vorndran, Christina M. (2002). On the status of knowledge for using punishment: Implications for treating behavior disorders. *Journal of Applied Behavior Analysis, 35*(4), 431–464.

Lerner, Howard D. (2008). Psychodynamic perspectives. In Michael Hersen & Alan M. Gross (Eds.), *Handbook of Clinical Psychology: Vol. 1. Adults* (pp. 127–160). Hoboken, NJ: Wiley.

Lerner, Jennifer S.; Li, Ye; Valdesolo, Piercarlo; & Kassam, Karin S. (2015). Emotion and decision making. *Annual Review of Psychology, 66,* 799–823. doi:10.1146/annurev-psych-010213-115043

Lerner, Jennifer S.; Li, Ye; Valdesolo, Piercarlo; & Kassam, Karim S. (2015). Emotion and decision making. *Annual Review of Psychology, 66,* 799–823. doi:10.1146/annurev-psych-010213-115043

Lerner, Melvin J. (1980). *The belief in a just world: A fundamental delusion.* New York, NY: Plenum Press.

Lesser, Lenard I.; Zimmerman, Frederick J.; & Cohen, Deborah A. (2013). Outdoor advertising, obesity, and soda consumption: A cross-sectional study. *BMC Public Health, 13*(1): 20. doi:10.1186/1471-2458-13-20

Lester, David. (1997). *Making sense of suicide: An in-depth look at why people kill themselves.* Philadelphia, PA: Charles Press.

Lester, David. (2010). The final hours: A linguistic analysis of the final words of a suicide. *Psychological Reports, 106*(3), 791–797. doi:10.2466/pr0.106.3.791–797

Lester, Gregory W. (2000, November/December). Why bad beliefs don't die. *Skeptical Inquirer, 24,* 40–43.

Lester, S. Reid; Brown, Jason R.; Aycock, Jeffrey. E.; Grubbs, S. Lee; & Johnson, Roger B. (2010). Use of saliva for assessment of stress and its effect on the immune system prior to gross anatomy practical examinations. *Anatomical Sciences Education. Lester: 3,* 160–167.

Lett, Heather S.; Blumenthal, James A.; Babyak, Michael A.; Catellier, Diane J.; Carney, Robert M.; Berkman, Lisa F.; & others. (2009). Dimensions of social support and depression in patients at increased psychosocial risk recovering from myocardial infarction. *International Journal of Behavioral Medicine, 16*(3), 248–258.

Leung, Paul K.; & Boehnlein, James K. (2005). Vietnamese families. In Monica McGoldrick, Joseph Giordano, & Nydia Garcia-Petro (Eds.), *Ethnicity & family therapy* (3rd ed., pp. 363–373). New York, NY: Guilford.

Leung, Rachel C., & Zakzanis, Konstantine K. (2014). Brief report: Cognitive flexibility in autism spectrum disorders: A quantitative review. *Journal of Autism Developmental Disorders, 44,* 2628–2645. doi:10.1007/s10803-014-2136-4

LeVay, Simon. (2007). A difference in hypothalamic structure between heterosexual and homosexual men. In Gillian Einstein (Ed.), *Sex and the brain.* Cambridge, MA: MIT Press.

Levenson, Hanna. (2010). *Brief dynamic therapy.* Washington, DC: American Psychological Association.

Levenson, Hanna. (2011). Time-limited dynamic psychotherapy. In Leonard M. Horowitz & Stephen Strack (Eds.), *Handbook of interpersonal psychology: Theory, research, assessment, and therapeutic interventions* (pp. 545–563). Hoboken, NJ: Wiley.

Levenson, Robert W. (1992). Autonomic nervous system differences among emotions. *Psychological Science, 3,* 23–27.

Levenson, Robert W. (2003). Blood, sweat, and fears: The autonomic architecture of emotion. In Paul Ekman, Joseph Campos, Richard J. Davidson, & Frans B.M. de Waal (Eds.), *Emotions inside out: 130 years after Darwin's: The expression of the emotions in man and animals.* New York, NY: New York University Press.

Levenson, Robert W.; Ekman, Paul; & Friesen, Wallace V. (1990). Voluntary facial action generates emotion-specific autonomic nervous system activity. *Psychophysiology, 27,* 363–384.

Levenson, Robert W.; Ekman, Paul; Heider, Karl; & Friesen, Wallace V. (1992). Emotion and autonomic nervous system activity in the Minangkabau of west Sumatra. *Journal of Personality and Social Psychology, 62,* 972–988.

Levenston, Gary K.; Patrick, Christopher J.; Bradley, Margaret M.; & Lang, Peter J. (2000). The psychopath as observer: Emotion and attention in picture processing. *Journal of Abnormal Psychology, 109*(3), 373–383. doi:10.1037//0021-843X.109J.373

Levi, Jeffrey; Segal, Laura M.; St. Laurent, Rebecca; & Kohn, David. (2011). *F as in fat: How obesity threatens America's future.* Princeton, NJ: Robert Wood Johnson Foundation.

Levin, Netta; Dumoulin, Serge O.; Winawer, Jonathan; Dougherty, Robert F.; & Wandell, Brian A. (2010). Cortical maps and white matter tracts following long period of visual deprivation and retinal image restoration. *Neuron, 65,* 21–31.

Levin, Ross, & Nielsen, Tore A. (2007). Disturbed dreaming, posttraumatic stress disorder, and affect distress: A review and neurocognitive model. *Psychological Bulletin, 133,* 482–528.

LeVine, Elaine S. (2007). Experiences from the frontline: Prescribing in New Mexico. *Psychological Services, 4,* 59–71.

Levine, Robert V.; Reysen, Stephen; & Ganz, Ellen. (2008). The kindness of strangers revisited: A comparison of 24 US cities. *Social Indicators Research, 85*(3), 461–481.

Levinson, Douglas F. (2009). Genetics of major depression. In Ian H. Gotlib & Constance L. Hammen (Eds.), *Handbook of depression* (2nd ed., pp. 165–186). New York, NY: Guilford.

Levy, Becca. (1996). Improving memory in old age through implicit self-stereotyping. *Journal of Personality and Social Psychology, 71,* 1092–1107.

Lewis, Melissa A.; Granato, Hollie; Blayney, Jessica A.; Lostutter, Ty W.; & Kilmer, Jason R. (2012). Predictors of hooking up sexual behaviors and emotional reactions among U.S. college students. *Archives of Sexual Behavior, 41*(5), 1219–1229.

Lewontin, Richard. (1970, March). Race and intelligence. *Bulletin of the Atomic Scientists,* 2–8.

Li, Shenghui; Jin, Xingming; Yan, Chonghuai; Wu, Shenghu; Jiang, Fan; & Shen, Xiaoming. (2008). Bed- and room-sharing in Chinese school-aged children: Prevalence and association with sleep behaviors. *Sleep Medicine, 9,* 555–563.

Li, Wen; Luxenberg, Erin; Parrish, Todd; & Gottfried, Jay A. (2006). Learning to smell the roses: Experience-dependent neural plasticity in human piriform and orbitofrontal cortices. *Neuron, 21,* 1097–1108.

Li, Wen; Moallem, Isabel; Paller, Ken A.; & Gottfried, Jay A. (2007). Subliminal smells can guide social preferences. *Psychological Science, 18,* 1044–1049.

Liao, Jing; Head, Jenny; Kumari, Meena; Stansfeld, Stephen; Kivimaki, Mika; Singh-Manoux, Archana; & Brunner, Eric J. (2014). Negative aspects of close relationships as risk factors for cognitive aging. *American Journal of Epidemiology, 180,* 1118–1125. doi:10.1093/aje/kwu236

Libby, Lisa K.; Shaeffer, Eric M.; Eibach, Richard P.; & Slemmer, Jonathan. (2007). Picture yourself at the polls: Visual perception in mental imagery affects self-perception and behavior. *Psychological Science, 18,* 199–203.

Lick, David J., & Johnson, Kerri L. (2015). The interpersonal consequences of processing ease: Fluency as a metacognitive foundation of prejudice. *Current Directions in Psychological Science, 24,* 143–148. doi:10.1177/0963721414558116

Lieb, Roselind; Bronisch, Thomas; Höfler, Michael; Schreier, Andrea; & Wittchen, Hans-Ulrich. (2005). Maternal suicidality and risk of suicidality in offspring: Findings from a community study. *American Journal of Psychiatry, 162,* 1665–1671.

Lieberman, Matthew D. (2000). Intuition: A social cognitive neuroscience approach. *Psychological Bulletin, 126,* 109–137.

Lieberman, Robert Paul. (2000). The token economy. *American Journal of Psychiatry, 157,* 1398.

Liff, Zanvel A. (1992). Psychoanalysis and dynamic techniques. In Donald K. Freedheim (Ed.), *History of psychotherapy: A century of change.* Washington, DC: American Psychological Association.

Lilienfeld, Scott O. (2007). Psychological treatments that cause harm. *Perspectives on Psychological Science, 2*(1), 53–69.

Lilienfeld, Scott O. (2011). Distinguishing scientific from pseudoscientific psychotherapies: Evaluating the role of theoretical plausibility, with a little help from Reverend Bayes. *Clinical Psychology: Science and Practice, 18,* 105–112. doi:10.1111/j.1468-2850.2011.01241.x

Lilienfeld, Scott O.; Ammirati, Rachel; & David, Michal. (2012). Distinguishing science from pseudoscience in school psychology: Science and scientific thinking as safeguards against human error. *Journal of School Psychology, 50*(1), 7–36. doi:10.1016/j.jsp.2011.09.006

Lilienfeld, Scott O.; Waldman, Irwin D.; Landfield, Kristin; Watts, Ashley L.; Rubenzer, Steven; & Faschingbauer, Thomas R. (2012). Fearless dominance and the U.S. presidency: Implications of psychopathic personality traits for successful and unsuccessful political leadership. *Journal of Personality and Social Psychology, 103*(3), 489–505.

Linden, Michael. (2013). How to define, find and classify side effects in psychotherapy: From unwanted events to adverse treatment reactions. *Clinical Psychology and Psychotherapy, 20,* 286–296. doi:10.1002/cpp.1765

Lindenberger, Ulman. (2014). Human cognitive aging: Corriger la fortune? *Science, 346,* 572–579.

Lindsay, D. Stephen (2008). Source monitoring. In H. L. Roediger, III (Ed.), *Cognitive psychology of memory. Vol. 2 of Learning and Memory: A comprehensive Reference, 4 Vols.* (pp. 325–348). Oxford, England: Elsevier.

Lindsay, D. Stephen; Hagen, Lisa; Read, J. Don; Wade, Kimberley A.; & Garry, Maryanne. (2004a). True photographs and false memories. *Psychological Science, 15,* 149–154.

Lindsay, D. Stephen; Wade, Kimberley A.; Hunter, Michael A.; & Read, J. Don. (2004b). Adults' memories of childhood: Affect, knowing, and remembering. *Memory, 12,* 27–43.

Lindsey, Delwin T., & Brown, Angela M. (2004). Commentary: Sunlight and "blue": The prevalence of poor lexical color discrimination within the "grue" range. *Psychological Science, 15,* 291–294.

Linehan, Marsha M. (1993). *Cognitive-behavioral treatment of borderline personality disorder.* New York, NY: Guilford Press.

Linehan, Marsha M. (2009, May 2). Radical compassion: Translating Zen into psychotherapy. Presented at Meditation and Psychotherapy: Cultivating Compassion and Wisdom, Boston, MA.

Linehan, Marsha M., & Dexter-Mazza, Elizabeth T. (2008). Dialectical behavior therapy for borderline personality disorder. In David H. Barlow (Ed.), *Clinical handbook of psychological disorders* (4th ed., pp. 365–420). New York, NY: Guilford Press.

Linnman, Clas. (2013). New pieces for the substance P puzzle. *Pain, 154,* 966–967. doi:10.1073/pnas.1010654108

Lippa, Richard A. (2008). The relation between childhood gender non-conformity and adult masculinity-femininity and anxiety in heterosexual and homosexual men and women. *Sex Roles, 59*(9–10), 684–693.

Lisman, John; Yasuda, Ryohei; & Raghavachari, Sridhar. (2012). Mechanisms of CaMKII action in long-term potentiation. *Nature Reviews Neuroscience, 13,* 169–182. doi:10.1038/nrn3192

Lissemore, Jennifer I.; Leyton, Marco; Gravel, Paul; Sookman, Debbie; Nordahl, Thomas E.; & Benkalfat, Chawki. (2014). OCD: Serotonergic mechanisms. In R. A. J. O. Dierckx et al. (Eds.), *PET and SPECT in Psychiatry* (pp. 433–450). doi:10.1007/978-3-642-40384-2_17

Little, Karley Y.; Krolewski, David M.; Zhang, Lian; & Cassin, Bader J. (2003). Loss of striatal vesicular monoamine transporter protein (VMAT2) in human cocaine users. *American Journal of Psychiatry, 160,* 47–55.

Livianos-Aldana, Lorenzo; Rojo-Moreno, Luis; & Sierra-San-Miguel, Pilar. (2007). F. J. Gall and the phrenological movement. *American Journal of Psychiatry, 164,* 414.

Livingstone, Margaret, & Hubel, David. (1988, May 6). Segregation of form, color, movement and depth: Anatomy, physiology, and perception. *Science, 240,* 740–749.

Livneh, Yoav, & Mizrahi, Adi. (2012). Experience-dependent plasticity of mature adult-born neurons. *Nature Neuroscience, 15,* 26–28. doi:10.1038/nn.2980

Lobstein, Tim; Jackson-Leach, Rachel; Moodie, Marjory L.; Hall, Kevin D.; Gortmaker, Steven L.; Swinburn, Boyd A.; James, W. Philip T.; Wang, Youfa; & McPherson, Klim. (2015). Child and adolescent obesity: Part of a bigger picture. *Lancet, 385,* 2510–2520. doi:10.1016/S0140-6736(14)61746-3

LoBue, Vanessa. (2010). And along came a spider: An attentional bias for the detection of spiders in young children and adults. *Journal of Experimental Child Psychology, 107*(1), 59–66.

LoBue, Vanessa, & DeLoache, Judy S. (2008). Detecting the snake in the grass: Attention to fear-relevant stimuli by adults and young children. *Psychological Science, 19,* 284–289.

LoBue, Vanessa, & DeLoache, Judy S. (2010). Superior detection of threat-relevant stimuli in infancy. *Developmental Science, 13*(1), 22–228. doi:10.1111/j.1467-7687.2009.00872.x

LoBue, Vanessa, & DeLoache, Judy S. (2011). Pretty in pink: The early development of gender-stereotyped colour preferences. *British Journal of Developmental Psychology, 29,* 656–667. doi:10.1111/j.2044-835X.2011.02027.x

LoBue, Vanessa; Rakison, David H.; & DeLoache, Judy S. (2010). Threat perception across the lifespan: Evidence for multiple converging pathways. *Current Directions in Psychological Science, 19,* 375–379.

Lockard, Robert B. (1971). Reflections on the fall of comparative psychology: Is there a message for us all? *American Psychologist, 26,* 168–179.

Locke, E. A., & Schweiger, D. M. (1979). Participation in decision-making: One more look. *Research in Organizational Behavior, 1,* 265–339.

Locke, Edwin A. (1976). The nature and causes of job satisfaction. In M. D. Dunnette (Ed.), *Handbook of industrial and organizational psychology* (pp. 1297–1349). Chicago, IL: Rand McNally.

Lockhart, Robert S., & Craik, Fergus I. M. (1990). Levels of processing: A retrospective commentary on a framework for memory research. *Canadian Journal of Psychology, 44*(1), 87–112.

Lockwood, Nancy R. (2007, July). Planning for retention. (Future Focus) Survey about job satisfaction of human resource professionals and nonhuman resource employees. *HR Magazine, 52.*

Lodi-Smith, Jennifer; Jackson, Joshua; Bogg, Tim; Walton, Kate; Wood, Dustin; Harms, Peter; & Roberts, Brent W. (2010). Mechanisms of health: Education and health-related behaviours partially mediate the relationship between conscientiousness and self-reported physical health. *Psychology & Health, 25*(3), 305–319.

Loewenstein, George. (2010). Insufficient emotion: Soul-searching by a former indicter of strong emotions. *Emotion Review, 2*(3), 234–239.

Loewy, Joanne V., & Spintge, Ralph. (2011). Music soothes the savage breast. *Music and Medicine, 3,* 69–71. doi:10.1177/1943862111401626

Loftus, Elizabeth F. (1996). *Eyewitness testimony* (Rev. ed.). Cambridge, MA: Harvard University Press.

Loftus, Elizabeth F. (2002). Memory faults and fixes. *Issues in Science and Technology, 18*(4), 41–50.

Loftus, Elizabeth F. (2003). Our changeable memories: Legal and practical implications. *Nature Reviews Neuroscience, 4,* 231–234.

Loftus, Elizabeth F. (2004, 18 December). Dispatch from the (un)civil memory wars. *The Lancet, 364*(Suppl. 1), s20–s21.

Loftus, Elizabeth F. (2005). Planting misinformation in the human mind: A 30-year investigation of the malleability of memory. *Learning and Memory, 12,* 361–366.

Loftus, Elizabeth F. (2007). Memory distortions: Problems solved and unsolved. In Maryanne Garry & Harlene Hayne (Eds.), *Do justice and let the sky fall: Elizabeth Loftus and her contributions to science, law, and academic freedom.* Mahwah, NJ: Erlbaum.

Loftus, Elizabeth F. (2011). How I got started: From semantic memory to expert testimony. *Applied Cognitive Psychology, 25,* 347–348. doi:10.1002/acp.1769

Loftus, Elizabeth F., & Cahill, Larry. (2007). Memory distortion: From misinformation to rich false memory. In James S. Nairne (Ed.), *The foundation of remembering: Essays in honor of Henry L. Roediger, III.* New York, NY: Psychology Press.

Loftus, Elizabeth F., & Davis, Deborah. (2006). Recovered memories. *Annual Review of Clinical Psychology, 2,* 469–498.

Loftus, Elizabeth F., & Palmer, J. C. (1974). Reconstruction of automobile destruction: An example of the interaction between language and memory. *Journal of Verbal Learning and Verbal Behavior, 13,* 585–589.

Loftus, Elizabeth F., & Pickrell, Jacqueline E. (1995). The formation of false memories. *Psychiatric Annals, 25,* 720–725.

Loftus, Elizabeth F.; Donders, Karen; Hoffman, Hunter G.; & Schooler, Jonathan W. (1989). Creating new memories that are quickly accessed and confidently held. *Memory & Cognition, 17,* 607–616.

Lohr, Jeffrey M.; Hooke, Wayne; Gist, Richard; & Tolin, David F. (2003). Novel and controversial treatments for trauma-related stress disorders. In Scott O. Lilienfeld, Steven Jay Lynn, & Jeffrey M. Lohr (Eds.), *Science and pseudoscience in clinical psychology.* New York, NY: Guilford.

LoLordo, Vincent M. (2001). Learned helplessness and depression. In Marilyn E. Carroll & J. Bruce Overmier (Eds.), *Animal research and human health: Advancing human welfare through behavioral science.* Washington, DC: American Psychological Association.

Lombardo, Michael V.; Ashwin, Emma; Auyeung, Bonnie; Chakrabarti, Bhismadev; Taylor, Kevin; Hackett, Gerald; Bullmore, Edward T.; & Baron-Cohen, Simon. (2012). Fetal testosterone influences sexually dimorphic gray matter in the human brain. *Journal of Neuroscience, 32,* 674–680. doi:10.1523/JNEUROSCI.4389-11.2012

Long, Patrick, & Corfas, Gabriel. (2014). To learn is to myelinate. *Science, 346,* 298. doi:10.1126/science.1261127

Lord, Charles G.; Ross, Lee; & Lepper, Mark R. (1979). Biased assimilation and attitude polarization: The effects of prior theories on subsequently considered evidence. *Journal of Personality and Social Psychology, 37,* 2098–2109.

Lorenzo, Genevieve L.; Biesanz, Jeremy C.; & Human, Lauren J. (2010). What is beautiful is good and more accurately understood: Physical attractiveness and accuracy in first impressions of personality. *Psychological Science, 21*(12), 1777–1782.

Lorenzo, Genevieve L.; Biesanz, Jeremy C.; & Human, Lauren J. (2010). What is beautiful is good and more accurately understood: Physical attractiveness and accuracy in first impressions of personality. *Psychological Science, 21*(12), 1777–1782. doi:10.1177/0956797610388048

Louis, Winnifred R.; Esses, Victoria M.; & Lalonde, Richard N. (2013). National identification, perceived threat, and dehumanization as antecedents of negative attitudes toward immigrants in Australia and Canada: Negative attitudes toward immigrants. *Journal of Applied Social Psychology, 43,* 156–165. doi:10.1111/jasp.12044

Lowry, Brian. (October 24, 2011). Eli Roth probes evil on discovery's 'curiosity.' *Variety.* Retrieved from http://variety.com/2011/voices/opinion/roth-probes-nature-of-evil-on-discoverys-curiosity-1200572557

Lubbadeh, Jens. (2005, June). Same brain for speech and sign. *Scientific American Mind, 16*(2), 86–87.

Luborsky, Lester, & Barrett, Marna S. (2006). The history and empirical status of key psychoanalytic concepts. *Annual Review of Clinical Psychology, 2,* 69–78.

Luborsky, Lester; Rosenthal, Robert; Diguer, Louis; Andrusyna, Tomasz P.; Berman, Jeffrey S.; Levitt, Jill T.; Seligman, David A.; & Krause, Elizabeth D. (2002). The dodo bird verdict is alive and well—mostly. *Clinical Psychology: Science and Practice, 9,* 2–12.

Lucas, Gale M.; Gratch, J., King; Aisha; & Morency, Louis-Philippe. (2014). It's only a computer: Virtual humans increase willingness to disclose. *Computers in Human Behavior, 37,* 94–100.

Lucassen, Nicole; Tharner, Anne; van IJzendoorn, Marinus H.; Bakermans-Kranenburg, Marian J.; Volling, Brenda L.; Verhulst, Frank C.; & others. (2011). The association between paternal sensitivity and infant–father attachment security: A meta-analysis of three decades of research. *Journal of Family Psychology, 25,* 986–992.

Ludwig, David S., & Kabat-Zinn, Jon. (2008). Mindfulness in medicine. *Journal of the American Medical Association, 300,* 1350–1352.

Lueke, Adam, & Gibson, Bryan. (2015). Mindfulness meditation reduces implicit age and race bias: The role of reduced automaticity of responding. *Social Psychological and Personality Science, 6,* 284–291. doi:10.1177/1948550614559651

Luhrmann, Tanya Marie; Padvamati, Raman; Tharoor, Hema; & Osei, Akwasi. (2015). Differences in voice-hearing experiences of people with psychosis in the USA, India, and Ghana: Interview-based study. *British Journal of Psychiatry, 206,* 41–44. doi:10.1192/bjp.bp.113.139048

Luna, Beatriz; Paulsen, David J.; Padmanabhan, Aarthi; & Geier, Charles. (2013). The teenage brain: Cognitive control and motivation. *Current Directions in Psychological Science, 22,* 94–100. doi:10.1177/0963721413478416

Lund, Rikke; Christensen, Ulla; Nilsson, Charlotte Juul; Kriegbaum, Margit; & Rod, Naja Hulvej. (2014, in press). Stressful social relations and mortality: A prospective cohort study. *Journal of Epidemiology and Community Health., 68,* 720–727. doi:10.1136/jech-2013-203675

Lundahl, Brad W.; Kunz, Chelsea; Brownell, Cynthia; Tollefson, Derrik; & Burke, Brian L. (2010). A meta-analysis of motivational interviewing: Twenty-five years of empirical studies. *Research on Social Work Practice, 20*(137), 137–160. doi:10.1177/1049731509347850

Lundqvist, Daniel, & Öhman, Arne. (2005). Caught by the evil eye: Nonconscious information processing, emotion, and attention to facial stimuli. In Lisa Feldman Barrett, Paula M. Niedenthal, & Piotr Winkielman (Eds.), *Emotion and consciousness.* New York, NY: Guilford.

Luo, Yuyan; Kaufman, Lisa; & Baillargeon, Renée E. (2009). Young infants' reasoning about physical events involving inert and self-propelled objects. *Cognitive Psychology, 58*(4), 441–486.

Lupfer, Gwen; Frieman, Jerome; & Coonfield, Daniel. (2003). Social transmission of flavor preferences in two species of hamsters (Mesocricetus auratus and Phodopus campbelli). *Journal of Comparative Psychology, 117*(4), 449–455.

Lutz, Antoine; Greischar, Lawrence L.; Rawlings, Nancy B.; Richard, Matthieu; & Davidson, Richard J. (2004, November 16). Long-term meditators self-induce high-amplitude gamma synchrony during mental practice. *Proceedings of the National Academy of Sciences, 101,* 16369–16373.

Lutz, Antoine; Slagter, Heleen A.; Rawlings, Nancy B.; Francis, Andrew D.; Greischar, Lawrence L.; & Davidson, Richard J. (2009) Mental training enhances stability of attention by reducing cortical noise. *Journal of Neuroscience, 29,* 13418–13427.

Lyn, Heidi, & Savage-Rumbaugh, Sue. (2013). The use of emotion symbols in language-using apes. In Shigeru Watanabe & Stan A. Kuczaj (Eds.), *Emotions of animals and humans: Comparative perspectives.* New York, NY: Springer Science + Business Media.

Lyn, Heidi; Greenfield, Patricia; & Savage-Rumbaugh, Sue. (2006). The development of representational play in chimpanzees and bonobos: Evolutionary implications, pretense, and the role of inter-species communication. *Cognitive Development, 21,* 199–213.

Lynall, Mary-Ellen; Bassett, Danielle S.; Kerwin, Robert; McKenna, Peter J.; Kitzbichler, Manfred; Muller, Ulrich & Bullmore, Ed. (2010). Functional connectivity and brain networks in schizophrenia. *Journal of Neuroscience, 30,* 9477–9487.

Lynch, Thomas R.; Trost, William T.; Salsman, Nicholas; & Linehan, Marsha M. (2007). Dialectical behavior therapy for borderline personality disorder. *Annual Review of Clinical Psychology, 3,* 181–205. doi:10.1146/annurev.clinpsy.2.022305.095229

Lynn, Steven Jay, & Green, Joseph P. (2011). The sociocognitive and dissociation theories of hypnosis: Toward a rapprochement. *International Journal of Clinical and Experimental Hypnosis, 59*(3), 277–293.

Lynn, Steven Jay, & Kirsch, Irving. (2006). *Essentials of clinical hypnosis: An evidence-based approach.* Washington, DC: American Psychological Association.

Lynn, Steven Jay; Fassler, Oliver; Joshua A. Knox, Joshau A.; & Lilienfeld, Scott O. (2006a). Dissociation and dissociative identity disorder: Treatment guidelines and cautions. In Jane E. Fisher & William T. O'Donohue (Eds.), *Practitioner's guide to evidence-based psychotherapy.* New York, NY: Springer. doi:10.1007/978-0-387-28370-8_24

Lynn, Steven Jay; Kirsch, Irving; & Koby, Danielle G. (2006b). Pain management, behavioral medicine, and dentistry. In Lynn, Steven Jay, & Kirsch, Irving, Eds. *Essentials of clinical hypnosis: An evidence-based approach.* Washington, DC, : American Psychological Association. doi:10.1037/11365-011

Lynn, Steven Jay; Kirsch, Irving; & Rhue, Judith W. (2010). An introduction to clinical hypnosis. In Steven Jay Lynn, Judith W. Rhue, & Irving Kirsch (Eds.), *Handbook of clinical hypnosis* (2nd ed., pp. 3–18). Washington, DC: American Psychological Association.

Lynn, Steven Jay; Lilienfeld, Scott O.; Mercklebach, Harald; Giesbrecht, Timo; & Van Der Kloet, Dalena. (2012). Dissociation and dissociative disorders: Challenging conventional wisdom. *Current Directions in Psychological Science, 21,* 48–53. doi:10.1177/0963721411429457

Lynn, Steven Jay; Lock, Timothy; Loftus, Elizabeth F.; Krackow, Elisa; & Lilienfeld, Scott O. (2003). The remembrance of things past: Problematic memory recovery techniques in psychotherapy. In Scott O. Lilienfeld, Steven Jay Lynn, & Jeffrey M. Lohr (Eds.), *Science and pseudoscience in clinical psychology.* New York, NY: Guilford.

Lytton, William W. (2008). Computer modeling of epilepsy. *Nature Reviews Neuroscience, 9,* 626–637.

Ma, Ning; Dinges, David F.; Basner, Mathias; & Rao, Hengyi. (2015). How acute total sleep loss affects the attending brain: A meta-analysis of neuroimaging studies. *Sleep: Journal of Sleep and Sleep Disorders Research, 38,* 233–240.

Maccoby, Eleanor E., & Martin, John A. (1983). Socialization in the context of the family: Parent-child interaction. In Paul H. Mussen (Ed.), *Handbook of Child Psychology: Vol. 4. Socialization, personality, and social development.* New York, NY: Wiley.

MacDonald, Benie, & Davey, Graham C. L. (2005). Inflated responsibility and perseverative checking: The effect of negative mood. *Journal of Abnormal Psychology, 114,* 176–182.

Macdonald, James S. P., & Lavie, Nilli. (2011). Visual perceptual load induces inattentional deafness. *Attention, Perception, & Psychophysics, 73*(6), 1780–1789. doi:10.3758/s13414-011-0144-4

Macháková, Hana; Dedkova, Lenka; Sevcikova, Anna; & Cerna, Alena. (2013). Bystanders' support of cyberbullied schoolmates. *Journal of Community and Applied Social Psychology, 23,* 25–36. doi:10.1002/casp.2135

Mack, Arien, & Rock, Irvin. (2000). *Inattentional blindness.* Cambridge, MA: MIT Press.

MacKay, Donald G. (2014, May/June). The engine of memory. *Scientific American Mind, 25,* 30–38.

MacKenzie, Michael J.; Nicklas, Eric; Waldfogel, Jane; & Brooks-Gunn, Jeanne. (2012). Corporal punishment and child behavioural and cognitive outcomes through 5 years of age: Evidence from a contemporary urban birth cohort study. *Infant and Child Development, 21,* 3–33. doi:10.1002/icd.758

Macknik, Stephen L.; King, Mac; Randi, James; Robbins, Apollo; Teller; Thompson, John; & Martinez-Conde, Susana. (2008). Attention and awareness in stage magic: Turning tricks into research. *Nature Reviews Neuroscience, 9,* 871–879.

MacLean, Katherine A.; Ferrer, Emilio; Aichele, Stephen R.; Bridwell, David A.; Zanesco, Anthony P.; Jacobs, Tonya L.; King, Brandon G.; & others. (2010). Intensive meditation training improves perceptual discrimination and sustained attention. *Psychological Science, 21*(6), 829–839.

MacLeod, Colin, & Mathews, Andrew. (2012). Cognitive bias modification approaches to anxiety. *Annual Review of Clinical Psychology, 8,* 189–217. doi:10.1146/annurev-clinpsy-032511-143052

Macrae, C. Neil, & Quadflieg, Susanne. (2010). Perceiving people. In S. T. Fiske, D. T. Gilbert, & G. Lindzey (Eds.), *Handbook of social psychology, Vol. 1* (5th ed., pp. 428–463). Hoboken, NJ: Wiley.

Maddux, James E.; Volkmann, Jeffrey; & Hoyle, Rick H. (2010). Self-efficacy *Handbook of personality and self-regulation* (pp. 315–331). Chichester, England: Wiley-Blackwell.

Madsen, Matias Vested; Gøtzsche, Peter C.; & Hróbjartsson, Asbjørn. (2009, January 27). Acupuncture treatment for pain: Systematic review of randomised clinical trials with acupuncture, placebo acupuncture, and no acupuncture groups. *British Medical Journal, 338,* a3115. Retrieved on July 12, 2009, from http://www.bmj.com/cgi/reprint/338/jan27_2/a3115.pdf

Maes, Jürgen; Tarnai, Christian; & Schuster, Julia. (2012) About is and ought in research on belief in a just world: The Janus-faced just-world motivation. In E. Kals & J. Maes (Eds.), *Justice and Conflict* (pp. 93–106). New York, NY: Springer.

Magistretti, Pierre J. (2009). Low-cost travel in neurons. *Science, 325,* 1349–1351.

Magnavita, Jeffrey J. (2008). Psychoanalytic psychotherapy. In Jay L. Lebow (Ed.), *Twenty-first century psychotherapies: Contemporary approaches to theory and practice* (pp. 206–236). Hoboken, NJ: Wiley.

Maguire, Eleanor A.; Gadian, David G.; Johnsrude, Ingrid S.; Good, Catriona D.; Ashburner, John; Frackowiak, Richard S. J.; & Frith, Christopher D. (2000). Navigation-related structural change in the hippocampi of taxi drivers. *Proceedings of the National Academy of Sciences, USA, 97,* 4398–4403.

Maguire, Eleanor A.; Woollett, Katherine; & Spiers, Hugo J. (2006). London taxi drivers and bus drivers: A structural MRI and neuropsychological analysis. *Hippocampus, 16,* 1091–1101.

Mahon, Bradford Z., & Caramazza, Alfonso. (2011). What drives the organization of object knowledge in the brain? *Trends in Cognitive Sciences, 15*(3), 97–103.

Mahowald, Mark W. (2005). Other parasomnias. In Meir H. Kryger, Thomas Roth, & William C. Dement (Eds.), *Principles and practice of sleep medicine* (4th ed.). Philadelphia, PA: Elsevier Saunders.

Mahowald, Mark W., & Schenck, Carlos H. (2005). Insights from studying human sleep disorders. *Nature, 437,* 1279–1285. doi:10.1038/nature04287

Maia, Tiago V., & Cano-Colino, Maria. (2015). The role of serotonin in orbitofrontal function and obsessive-compulsive disorder. *Clinical Psychological Science, 3,* 46–482. doi:10.1177/2167702614566809

Maia, Tiago V.; Cooney, Rebecca E; & Peterson, Bradley S. (2009). The neural bases of obsessive-compulsive disorder in children and adults. *Development and Psychopathology, 20*(4), 1251–1283.

Maier, Andrea; Vickers, Zata; & Inman, J. Jeffrey (2007). Sensoryspecific satiety, its crossovers, and subsequent choice of potato chip flavors. *Appetite, 49,* 419–428.

Maier, Steven F., & Watkins, Linda R. (2000). The neurobiology of stressor controllability. In Jane E. Gillham (Ed.), *The science of optimism and hope: Research essays in honor of Martin E. P. Seligman.* Philadelphia, PA: Templeton Foundation Press.

Maier, Steven F.; Seligman, Martin E.; & Solomon, Richard L. (1969). Pavlovian fear conditioning and learned helplessness: Effects of escape and avoidance behavior of (a) the CS=UCS contingency, and (b) the independence of the UCS and voluntary responding. In Byron A. Campbell & Russell M. Church (Eds.), *Punishment and aversive behavior.* New York, NY: Appleton-Century-Crofts.

Maj, Mario. (2012). Bereavement-related depression in the DSM-5 and ICD-11. *World Psychiatry, 11(1),* 1–2.

Majid, Asifa. (2014, 13 January). Quoted in Gruber, Karl, "Can you name that smell?" *Science.* Retrieved on February 11, 2014, from: http://news.sciencemag.org/brain-behavior/2014/01/can-you-name-smell

Majid, Asifa; Bowerman, Melissa; Kita, Sotaro; Haun, Daniel B. M.; & Levinson, Stephen C. (2004). Can language restructure cognition? The case for space. *Trends in Cognitive Sciences, 8,* 108–114.

Majid, Asifa, & Burenhult, Niclas. (2014). Odors are expressible in language, as long as you speak the right language. *Cognition, 130,* 266–270. doi:10.1016/j.cognition.2013.11.004

Major, Geneviève C.; Doucet, Eric; & Trayhurn, Paul. (2007). Clinical significance of adaptive thermogenesis. *International Journal of Obesity, 31,* 204–212.

Makrygianni, Maria K., & Reed, Phil. (2010). A meta-analytic review of the effectiveness of behavioural early intervention programs for children with autistic spectrum disorders. *Research in Autism Spectrum Disorders, 4*(4), 577–593.

Malcolm, James P. (2008). Heterosexually married men who have sex with men: Marital separation and psychological adjustment. *Journal of Sex Research, 45*(4), 350–357.

Malekpour, Mokhtar. (2007). Effects of attachment on early and later development. *British Journal of Developmental Disabilities, 53,* 81–95.

Malhi, Gin S.; Tanious, Michelle; Das, Pritha; Coulston, Carissa M.; & Berk, Michael. (2013). Potential mechanisms of action of lithium in bipolar disorder. *CNS Drugs, 27,* 135–153. doi:10.1007/s40263-013-0039-0

Malla, Ashok, & Payne, Jennifer. (2005). First-episode psychosis: Psychopathology, quality of life, and functional outcome. *Schizophrenia Bulletin, 31,* 650–671.

Mallett, Robyn K., & Wilson, Timothy D. (2010). Increasing positive intergroup contact. *Journal of Experimental Social Psychology, 46*(2), 382–387.

Mallinckrodt, Brent. (2001). Interpersonal processes, attachment, and development of social competencies in individual and group psychotherapy. In Barbara R. Sarason & Steve Duck (Eds.), *Personal relationships: Implications for clinical and community psychology.* Chichester, England: Wiley.

Malouff, John M.; Emmerton, Ashley J.; & Schutte, Nicola S. (2013). The risk of a halo bias as a reason to keep students anonymous during grading. *Teaching of Psychology, 40*(3), 233–237. doi:10.1177/0098628313487425

Mamet, Zosia. (n.d.). Zosia Mamet opens up about her personal eating disorder struggles in Glamour's September issue. *Glamour.* Retrieved from http://www.glamour.com/health-fitness/2014/08/zosia-mamet-opens-up-about-her-eating-disorder

Manago, Adriana M.; Taylor, Tamara; & Greenfield, Patricia M. (2012). Me and my 400 friends: The anatomy of college students' Facebook networks, their communication patterns, and well-being. *Developmental Psychology, 48,* 369–380. doi:10.1037/a0026338

Mandler, George. (2013). The limit of mental structures. *Journal of General Psychology, 140,* 243–250. doi:10.1080/00221309.2013.807217

Manning, Rachel; Levine, Mark; & Collin, Alan. (2007). The Kitty Genovese murder and the social psychology of helping: The parable of the 38 witnesses. *American Psychologist, 62,* 555–562.

Manning, Rachel; Levine, Mark; & Collin, Alan. (2008). The legacy of the 38 witnesses and the importance of getting it right. *American Psychologist, 63,* 562–563.

Manstead, Antony S.R., & Parkinson, Brian. (2015). Emotion theories. In Bertram Gawronski & Galen V. Bodenhausen (Eds.), *Theory and explanation in social psychology.* New York, NY: Guilford.

Maoz, Ifat. (2012). Contact and social change in an ongoing asymmetrical conflict: Four social-psychological models of reconciliation-aimed planned encounters between Israeli Jews and Palestinians. In John Dixon & Mark Levine (Eds.). *Beyond prejudice: Extending the social psychology of conflict, inequality and social change* (pp. 269–285). Cambridge, England: Cambridge University Press.

Marañon, Gregorio. (1924). Contribution à l'étude de l'action émotive de l'adrenaline. *Revue Francaise d'Endocrinologie, 2,* 301–325.

Marantz, Andrew. (2013, September 16). Annals of psychology: Unreality star. *The New Yorker.*

Marcus, Bernd; Lee, Kibeom; & Ashton, Michael C. (2007). Personality dimensions explaining relationships between integrity tests and counterproductive behavior: Big Five, or one in addition? *Personnel Psychology, 60,* 1–34.

Marcus, Gary. (2004). *The birth of the mind: How a tiny number of genes creates the complexities of human thought.* New York, NY: Basic Books.

Marcus, Steven C., & Olfson, Mark. (2010). National trends in the treatment for depression from 1998 to 2007. *Archives of General Psychiatry, 67(12),* 1265–1273. doi:10.1001/archgenpsychiatry.2010.151

Marecek, Jeanne; & Gavey, Nicola. (2013). DSM-5 and beyond: A critical feminist engagement with psychodiagnosis. *Feminism & Psychology, 23(1),* 3–9.

Margulies, Daniel S.; Böttger, Joachim; Watanabe, Aimi; & Gorgolewski, Krzysztof J. (2013). Visualizing the human connectome. *NeuroImage, 80,* 445–461. doi:10.1016/j.neuroimage.2013.04.111

Marín-Burgin, Antonia; Mongiat, Lucas A.; Pardi, M. Belén; & Schinder, Alejandro F. (2012). Unique processing during a period of high excitation/inhibition: Balance in adult-born neurons. *Science 335,* 1238. doi:10.1126/science.1214956

Markman, Arthur B., & Gentner, Dedre. (2001). Thinking. *Annual Review of Psychology, 52,* 223–247.

Markowitsch, Hans J., & Staniloiu, Angelica. (2011). Memory, autonoetic consciousness, and the self. *Consciousness and Cognition: An International Journal, 20(1),* 16–39.

Markus, Hazel Rose, & Cross, Susan. (1990). The interpersonal self. In Lawrence A. Pervin (Ed.), *Handbook of personality: Theory and research.* New York, NY: Guilford.

Markus, Hazel Rose, & Kitayama, Shinobu. (1991). Culture and the self: Implications for cognition, emotion, and motivation. *Psychological Review, 98,* 224–253.

Markus, Hazel Rose, & Kitayama, Shinobu. (1994). The cultural construction of self and emotion: Implications for social behavior. In Shinobu Kitayama & Hazel Rose Markus (Eds.), *Emotion and culture: Empirical studies of mutual influence.* Washington, DC: American Psychological Association.

Markus, Hazel Rose, & Kitayama, Shinobu. (1998). The cultural psychology of personality. *Journal of Cross-Cultural Psychology, 29,* 63–87.

Markus, Hazel Rose, & Kitayama, Shinobu. (2010). Culture and selves: A cycle of mutual constitution. *Perspectives on Psychological Science, 5,* 420–430. doi:10.1177/1745691610375557

Markus, Hazel Rose, & Kunda, Ziva. (1986). Stability and malleability of the self-concept. *Journal of Personality and Social Psychology, 51,* 858–866.

Markus, Hazel Rose, & Nurius, Paula. (1986). Possible selves. *American Psychologist, 41,* 954–969.

Markus, Hazel Rose, & Wurf, Elissa. (1987). The dynamic self-concept: A social psychological perspective. *Annual Review of Psychology, 38,* 299–337.

Markus, Hazel Rose; Uchida, Yukiko; Omoregie, Heather; Townsend, Sarah S. M.; & Kitayama, Shinobu. (2006). Going for the gold: Models of agency in Japanese and American contexts. *Psychological Science, 17,* 103–112.

Markwald, Rachel R.; Melanson, Edward L.; Smith, Mark R.; Higgins, Janine; Perreault, Leigh; Eckel, Robert H.; & Kenneth P. Wright, Jr. (2013). Impact of insufficient sleep on total daily energy expenditure, food intake, and weight gain. *Proceedings of the National Academy of Sciences, 110,* 5695–5700. doi:10.1073/pnas.121695111

Marmie, William R., & Healy, Alice F. (2004). Memory for common objects: Brief intentional study is sufficient to overcome poor recall of US coin features. *Applied Cognitive Psychology, 18,* 445–453.

Marneros, Andreas, & Goodwin, Frederick (Eds.). (2005). *Bipolar disorders: Mixed states, rapid cycling, and atypical forms.* Cambridge, England: Cambridge University Press.

Martin, Bruce. (1998, May). Coincidences: Remarkable or random? *Skeptical Inquirer, 22,* 23–28.

Martin, Carol; Godfrey, Mary; Meekums, Bonnie & Madill, Anna (2011). Managing boundaries under pressure: A qualitative study of therapists' experiences of sexual attraction in therapy. *Counseling & Psychotherapy Research, 11(4),* 248–256.

Martin, Carol Lynn, & Halverson, Charles F., Jr. (1981). A schematic processing model of sex typing and stereotyping in children. *Child Development, 52,* 1119–1134.

Martin, Carol Lynn, & Halverson, Charles F., Jr. (1983). The effects of sex-typing schemas on young children's memory. *Child Development, 54,* 563–574.

Martin, Carol Lynn, & Ruble, Diane N. (2004). Children's search for gender cues: Cognitive perspectives on gender development. *Psychological Science, 13,* 67–70.

Martin, Carol Lynn, & Ruble, Diane N. (2010). Patterns of gender development. *Annual Review of Psychology, 61,* 353–381.

Martin, Carol Lynn; Ruble, Diane N.; & Szkrybalo, Joel. (2002). Cognitive theories of early gender development. *Psychological Bulletin, 128,* 903–933.

Martin, Carol Lynn; Ruble, Diane N.; & Szkrybalo, Joel. (2004). Recognizing the centrality of gender identity and stereotype knowledge in gender development and moving toward theoretical integration: Reply to Bandura and Bussey. (2004). *Psychological Bulletin, 130,* 702–710.

Martin, Douglas; Hutchison, Jacqui; Slessor, Gillian; Urquhart, James; Cunningham, Sheila J.; & Smith, Kenny. (2014). The spontaneous formation of stereotypes via cumulative cultural evolution. *Psychological Science, 25,* 1777–1786. doi:10.1177/0956797614541129

Martin, Rod A. (2007). *The psychology of humor: An integrative approach.* Amsterdam, The Netherlands: Elsevier.

Martin, Stephen D.; Martin, Elizabeth; Santoch, S. Rai; Richardson, Mark A.; & Royall, Robert. (2001). Brain blood flow changes in depressed patients treated with interpersonal psychotherapy or venlafaxine hydrochloride. *Archives of General Psychiatry, 58,* 641–648.

Martinez, Isabel, & Garcia, José F. (2008). Internalization of values and self-esteem among Brazilian teenagers from authoritative, indulgent, authoritarian, and neglectful homes. *Family Therapy, 35(1),* 43–59.

Marucha, Phillip T.; Kiecolt-Glaser, Janice K.; & Favagehi, Mehrdad. (1998). Mucosal wound healing is impaired by examination stress. *Psychosomatic Medicine, 60,* 362–365.

Marx, Rebecca Flynt, & Didziulis, Vytenis. (2009, February 27). A life, interrupted. *New York Times.* Retrieved from http://www.nytimes.com/2009/03/01/nyregion/thecity/01miss.html

Mash, Clay; Novak, Elizabeth; Berthier, Neil E.; & Keen, Rachel. (2006). What do two-year-olds understand about hidden-object events? *Developmental Psychology, 42(2),* 263–271.

Maslach, Christina, & Leiter, Michael P. (2005). Stress and burnout: The critical research. In C. L. Cooper (Ed.), *Handbook of stress medicine and health* (2nd ed.). London, England: CRC Press.

Maslach, Christina, & Leiter, Michael P. (2008). Early predictors of job burnout and engagement. *Journal of Applied Psychology, 93,* 498–512.

Masland, Richard H. (2001). The fundamental plan of the retina. *Nature Neuroscience, 4,* 877–886.

Maslow, Abraham H. (1943). A theory of human motivation. *Psychological Review, 50,* 370–396.

Maslow, Abraham H. (1954). *Motivation and personality.* New York, NY: Harper.

Maslow, Abraham H. (1968). *Toward a psychology of being* (2nd ed.). Princeton, NJ: Van Nostrand.

Maslow, Abraham H. (1970). *Motivation and personality* (2nd ed.). New York, NY: Harper & Row.

Masnick, Amy M., & Zimmerman, Corinne. (2009). Evaluating scientific research in the context of prior belief: Hindsight bias or confirmation bias? *Journal of Psychology of Science and Technology, 2*(1), 29–36.

Masterpasqua, Frank (2009). Psychology and epigenetics. *Review of General Psychology, 13*(3), 194–201.

Masters, Kevin S.; Stillman, Alexandra M.; & Spielmans, Glen I. (2007, February). Specificity of social support for back pain patients: Do patients care who provides what? *Journal of Behavioral Medicine, 30*(1), 11–20.

Masters, William H., & Johnson, Virginia E. (1966). *Human sexual response.* Boston, MA: Little, Brown.

Masters, William H.; Johnson, Virginia E.; & Kolodny, Robert C. (1995). *Human sexuality* (5th ed.). New York, NY: HarperCollins.

Matarazzo, Joseph D. (1981). Obituary: David Wechsler (1896–1981). *American Psychologist, 36,* 1542–1543.

Mather, Mara; John T. Cacioppo, John T.; & Kanwisher, Nancy. (2013a). Introduction to the Special Section: 20 Years of fMRI—What Has It Done for Understanding Cognition? *Perspectives on Psychological Science, 8,* 41–43. doi:10.1177/1745691612469036

Mather, Mara; Cacioppo, John T.; & Kanwisher, Nancy. (2013b). How fMRI can inform cognitive theories. *Perspectives on Psychological Science, 8:* 108–113. doi:10.1177/1745691612469037

Mathews, Carol A. (2009). Phenomenology of obsessive-compulsive disorder. In Martin M. Antony & Murray B. Stein (Eds.), *Oxford handbook of anxiety and related disorders* (pp. 56–64). New York, NY: Oxford University Press.

Mathias, Robert. (2002). Chronic solvent abusers have more brain abnormalities and cognitive impairments than cocaine abusers. *NIDA Notes, 17*(4).

Matsumoto, David, & Hwang, Hyl Sung. (2011a, May). Reading facial expressions of emotion. Retrieved on August 3, 2011 from: http://www.apa.org/science/about/psa/2011/05/facial-expressions.aspx

Matsumoto, David, & Hwang, Hyi Sung. (2011b). Culture, emotion, and expression. In Kenneth Keith (Ed.), *Cross-cultural psychology: Contemporary themes and perspectives.* Hoboken, NJ: Wiley-Blackwell.

Matsumoto, David, & Juang, Linda. (2008). *Culture and psychology* (4th ed.). Belmont, CA: Wadsworth.

Matute, Helena; Yarritu, Ion; Vadillo, Miguel A. (2011). Illusions of causality at the heart of pseudoscience. *British Journal of Psychology, 102,* 392–405. doi:10.1348/000712610X532210

Maxmen, Jerrold S., & Ward, Nicholas G. (1995). *Essential psychopathology and its treatment* (2nd ed.). New York, NY: Norton.

May, Mike. (2002, September 26). Quoted in British Broadcasting Corporation (BBC) transcript, September 26, 2002. *LiveChat: The man who learned to see.* Retrieved on August 2, 2004, from http://www.bbc.co.uk/ouch/wyp/mikemayqa.shtml

May, Mike. (2004). Quoted in Sendero Group, "Mike's journal." Retrieved on August 2, 2004, from http#//www.senderogroup.com/mikejournal.htm

Maybery, D. J.; Neale, Jason; Arentz, Alex; & Jones-Ellis, Jenny. (2007, June). The Negative Event Scale: Measuring frequency and intensity of adult hassles. *Anxiety, Stress & Coping, 20*(2), 163–176.

Mayer, John D.; Salovey, Peter; & Caruso, David R. (2004). Emotional intelligence: Theory, findings, and intelligence. *Psychological Inquiry, 15,* 197–215.

Mayer, John D.; Salovey, Peter; & Caruso, David R. (2008). Emotional intelligence: New ability or eclectic traits? *American Psychologist, 63,* 503–517.

Mayer, Richard E.; Zimmerman, Barry J.; & Schunk, Dale H. (2003). E. L. Thorndike's enduring contributions to educational psychology *Educational psychology: A century of contributions* (pp. 113–154). Mahwah, NJ: Erlbaum.

Mayor, Tracy. (2008, April 2). Asperger's and IT: Dark secret or open secret? *Computerworld.* Retrieved on October 23, 2015 from http://www.computerworld.com/article/2536193/it-management-asperger-s-and-it-dark-secret-or-open-secret.html

Mazzoni, Giuliana, & Scoboria, Alan. (2007). False memories. In Francis T. Durso (Ed.), *Handbook of applied social cognition* (2nd ed.). Chichester, England: Wiley.

Mazzoni, Giuliana; Heap, Michael; & Scoboria, Alan. (2010). Hypnosis and memory: Theory, laboratory research, and applications. In Steven Jay Lynn, Judith W. Rhue, & Irving Kirsch, (Eds.) *Handbook of clinical hypnosis* (2nd ed.). Washington, DC: American Psychological Association.

McAdams, Dan P., & Olson, Bradley D. (2010). Personality development: Continuity and change over the life course. *Annual Review of Psychology, 61,* 517–542.

McAdams, Dan P., & Pals, Jennifer L. (2006). A new Big Five: Fundamental principles for an integrative science of personality. *American Psychologist, 61,* 204–217.

McAdams, Dan P., & Walden, Keegan. (2010). Jack Block, the Big Five, and personality from the standpoints of actor, agent, and author. *Psychological Inquiry, 21*(1), 50–56.

McAndrew, Francis T.; Akande, Adebowale; Turner, Saskia; & Sharma, Yadika. (1998). A cross-cultural ranking of stressful life events in Germany, India, South Africa, and the United States. *Journal of Cross-Cultural Psychology, 29,* 717–727.

McCabe, Marita P., & Ricciardelli, Lina A. (2004). A longitudinal study of pubertal timing and extreme body change behaviors among adolescent boys and girls. *Adolescence, 39,* 145–166.

McCabe, Randi E.; Chudzik, Susan M.; Antony, Martin M.; Young, Lisa; Swinson, Richard P.; & Zolvensky, Michael J. (2004). Smoking behaviors across anxiety disorders. *Anxiety Disorders, 18,* 7–18.

McCall, Cade, & Singer, Tania. (2012). The animal and human neuroendocrinology of social cognition, motivation, and behavior. *Nature Neuroscience, 15,* 681–688. doi:10.1038/nn.3084

McCall, W. V.; Reboussin, David; Prudic, Joan; Haskett, Roger F.; Isenberg, Keith; Olfson, Mark; Rosenquist, Peter B.; & others. (2013). Poor health-related quality of life prior to ECT in depressed patients normalizes with sustained remission after ECT. *Journal of Affective Disorders, 147,* 107–111. doi:10.1016/j.jad.2012.10.018

McCall, W. Vaughn; Rosenquist, Peter B.; Kimball, James; Haskett, Roger; Isenberg, Keith; Prudic, Joan; Lasater, Barbara; & Sackeim, Harold A. (2011). Health-related quality of life in a clinical trial of ECT followed by continuation pharmacotherapy: Effects immediately after ECT and at 24 weeks. *Journal of ECT, 27,* 97–102. doi:10.1097/YCT.0b013e318205c7d7

McCarley, Robert W. (2007). Neurobiology of REM and NREM sleep. *Sleep Medicine, 8,* 302–330.

McCarthy, Margaret M. (2007). GABA receptors make teens resistant to input. *Nature Neuroscience, 10,* 397–399.

McCartney, Kathleen; Burchinal, Margaret; Clarke-Stewart, Alison; Bub, Kristen L.; Owen, Margaret T.; & Belsky, Jay (2010). Testing a series of causal propositions relating time in child care to children's externalizing behavior. *Developmental Psychology, 46*(1), 1–17.

McCartney, Kathleen; Harris, Monica J.; & Bernieri, Frank. (1990). Growing up and growing apart: A developmental meta-analysis of twin studies. *Psychological Bulletin, 107,* 226–237.

McClelland, David C. (1961). *The achieving society.* Princeton, NJ: Van Nostrand.

McClelland, David C. (1975). *Power: The inner experience.* New York, NY: Irvington.

McClelland, David C. (1976). *The achieving society* (2nd ed.). Oxford, England: Irvington.

McClelland, David C. (1985). *Human motivation.* Glenview, IL: Scott, Foresman.

McClelland, David C. (1989). Motivational factors in health and disease. *American Psychologist, 44,* 675–683.

McClelland, David C., & Winter, David G. (1971). *Motivating economic achievement.* New York, NY: Free Press.

McClelland, David C., Atkinson, John W.; Clark, Russell A.; & Lowell, Edgar L. (1953). *The achievement motive*. New York, NY: Appleton-Century-Crofts.

McClintock, Martha K. (1971). Menstrual synchrony and suppression. *Nature, 229*, 244–245.

McClintock, Martha K. (1992, October). Quoted in John Easton, "Sex, rats, and videotapes: From the outside in." *The University of Chicago Magazine, 85*(1), 32–36.

McClintock, Shawn M.; Trevino, Kenneth; & Husain, Mustafa M. (2009). Vagus nerve stimulation: Indications, efficacy, and methods. In Conrad M. Swartz (Ed.), *Electroconvulsive and neuromodulation therapies* (pp. 543–555). New York, NY: Cambridge University Press.

McCoy, Bob. (2000). *Quack!: Tales of medical fraud from the Museum of Questionable Medical Devices*. Santa Monica, CA: Santa Monica Press.

McCoy, Robert. (1996). Phrenology. In Gordon Stein (Ed.), *The encyclopedia of the paranormal*. Amherst, NY: Prometheus Books.

McCrae, Robert R., & Costa, Paul T., Jr. (1990). *Personality in adulthood*. New York, NY: Guilford.

McCrae, Robert R., & Costa, Paul T., Jr. (1996). Toward a new generation of personality theories: Theoretical contexts for the five-factor model. In Jerry S. Wiggins (Ed.), *The five-factor model of personality: Theoretical perspectives*. New York, NY: Guilford.

McCrae, Robert R., & Costa, Paul T., Jr. (2003). *Personality in adulthood: A five-factor theory perspective* (2nd ed.). New York, NY: Guilford.

McCrae, Robert R., & Costa, Paul T., Jr. (2006). Cross-cultural perspectives on adult personality trait development. In David K. Mroczek & Todd D. Little (Eds.), *Handbook of personality development*. Mahwah, NJ: Erlbaum.

McCrae, Robert R.; Costa, Paul T., Jr.; Martin, Thomas A.; Oryol, Valery E.; Rukavishnikov, Alexey A.; Senin, Ivan G.; Hrebíckóva, Martina; & Urbánek, Tomás. (2004). Consensual validation of personality traits across cultures. *Journal of Research in Personality, 38*, 179–201.

McCrae, Robert R.; Costa, Paul T., Jr.; Ostendorf, Fritz; Angleitner, Alois; Hrebíckóva, Martina; Avia, Maria D.; & others. (2000). Nature over nurture: Temperament, personality, and life span development. *Journal of Personality and Social Psychology, 78*, 173–186.

McCrae, Robert R.; Scally, Matthew; Terracciano, Antonio; Abecasis, Gonçalo R.; & Costa, Paul T., Jr. (2010). An alternative to the search for single polymorphisms: Toward molecular personality scales for the five-factor model. *Journal of Personality and Social Psychology, 99*(6), 1014–1024. doi:10.1037/a0020964

McCrae, Robert R.; Terracciano, Antonio; & Members of the Personality Profiles of Cultures Project. (2005). Universal features of personality traits from the observer's perspective: Data from 50 cultures. *Journal of Personality and Social Psychology, 88*, 547–561.

McCurdy, Barry L.; Lannie, Amanda L.; & Barnabas, Ernesto. (2009). Reducing disruptive behavior in an urban school cafeteria: An extension of the Good Behavior Game. *Journal of School Psychology, 47*(1), 39–54.

McDaniell, Ryan; Lee, Burn-Kyu; Song, Lingyun; Liu, Zheng; Boyle, Alan P.; Erdos, Michael R.; & others. (2010). Heritable individual-specific and allele-specific chromatin signatures in humans. *Science, 328*(5975), 235–239. doi:10.1126/science.1184655

McDermut, Wilson, & Zimmerman, Mark. (2008). Personality disorders, personality traits, and defense mechanisms measures. In A. John Rush, Jr., Michael B. First, & Deborah Blacker (Eds.), *Handbook of psychiatric measures* (2nd ed., pp. 687–729). Arlington, VA: American Psychiatric Publishing.

McDonald, Ann. (2009). Prenatal development—The DANA Guide. *The DANA Guide to Brain Health* Retrieved 12-31-2009, from http://www.dana .org/news/brainhealth/detail.aspx?id=10050

McDonald, William M.; Meeks, Thomas W.; McCall, W. Vaughan; & Zorumski, Charles F. (2009). Electroconvulsive therapy. In Alan F. Schatzberg & Charles B. Nemeroff (Eds.), *The American Psychiatric Publishing textbook of psychopharmacology* (4th ed., pp. 861–899). Washington, DC: American Psychiatric Publishing.

McDougall, William. (1908). *Introduction to social psychology*. London, England: Methuen.

McElhaney, Kathleen B.; Porter, Maryfrances R.; Thompson, L. Wrenn; & Allen, Joseph P. (2008). Apples and oranges: Divergent meanings of parents' and adolescents' perceptions of parental influence. *Journal of Early Adolescence, 28*(2), 206–229.

McEwen, Bruce S.; Akama, Keith T.; Spencer-Segal, Joanna L.; Milner, Teresa A.; & Waters, Elizabeth M. (2012). Estrogen effects on the brain: Actions beyond the hypothalamus via novel mechanisms. *Behavioral Neuroscience, 126*(1), 4–16. doi:10.1037/a0026708

McGaugh, James L. (2004). The amygdala modulates the consolidation of memories of emotionally arousing experiences. *Annual Review of Neuroscience, 27*, 1–28.

McGehee, Daniel S.; Iacoviello, Michael; & Mitchum, Robert. (2007). Cellular and synaptic effects of nicotine. In Tony P. George (Ed.), *Medication treatments for nicotine dependence* (pp. 25–38). Boca Raton, FL: CRC Press.

McGeown, William J.; Venneri, Annalena; Kirsch, Irving; Nocetti, Luca; Roberts, Kathrine; Foan, Lisa; & Mazzoni, Giuliana. (2012). Suggested visual hallucination without hypnosis enhances activity in visual areas of the brain. *Consciousness and Cognition: An International Journal, 21*, 100–116. doi:10.1016/j.concog.2011.10.015

McGirr, Alexander; Berlim, M.T.; Bond, D.J.; Fleck, M.P.; Yatham, L.N.; & Lam, R.W. (2015). A systematic review and meta-analysis of randomized, double-blind, placebo-controlled trials of ketamine in the rapid treatment of major depressive episodes. *Psychological Medicine, 45*, 693–704. doi:10.1017/S0033291714001603

McGirr, Alexander; Renaud, Johanne; Seguin, Monique; Alda, Martin; Benkelfat, Chawki; Lesage, Alain; & Turecki, Gustavo. (2007). An examination of DSM-IV depressive symptoms and risk for suicide completion in major depressive disorder: A psychological autopsy study. *Journal of Affective Disorders 97*, 203–209.

McGlone, Francis, & Reilly, David. (2010). The cutaneous sensory system. *Neuroscience & Biobehavioral Reviews, 34*(2), 148–159.

McGoldrick, Monica; Giordano, Joseph; & Garcia-Preto, Nydia. (2005). Overview: Ethnicity and family therapy. In Monica McGoldrick, Joseph Giordano, & Nydia Garcia-Preto (Eds.), *Ethnicity & family therapy* (3rd ed., pp. 1–40). New York, NY: Guilford.

McGowan, Patrick O.; Sasaki, Aya; D'Alessio, Ana C.; Dymov, Sergiy; Labonté, Benoit; Szyf, Moshe; Turecki, Gustavo; & Meaney, Michael J. (2009). Epigenetic regulation of the glucocorticoid receptor in human brain associates with childhood abuse. *Nature Neuroscience, 12*, 342–348.

McGraw, Peter; Williams, Lawrence; & Warren, Caleb. (2013). The rise and fall of humor: Psychological distance modulates humorous responses to tragedy. *Social Psychological and Personality Science, 5*, 566–572. doi:10.1177/1948550613515006

McGregor, Douglas. (1960). *The human side of enterprise*. New York: McGraw-Hill.

McGregor, Jacqueline C. (2009). Anxiety disorders. In Robert E. Rakel & Edward T. Bope (Eds.), *Conn's current therapy 2009* (pp. 1111–1115). Philadelphia, PA: Saunders Elsevier.

McGue, Matt; Bouchard, Thomas J., Jr.; Iacono, William G.; & Lykken, David T. (1993). Behavioral genetics of cognitive ability: A lifespan perspective. In Robert Plomin & Gerald E. McClearn (Eds.), *Nature, nurture, and psychology*. Washington, DC: American Psychological Association.

McIntyre, Kevin P.; Korn, James H.; & Matsuo, Hisako. (2008). Sweating the small stuff: How different types of hassles result in the experience of stress. *Stress and Health: Journal of the International Society for the Investigation of Stress, 24*(5), 383–392.

McKee, Ann C.; Stein, Thor D.; Nowinski, Christopher J.; Stern, Robert A.; Daneshvar, Daniel H.; Alvarez, Victor E.; Lee Hyo-Soon; Hall, Garth F.; Wojtowicz, Sydney M.; Baugh, Christine M.; Riley, David O.; Kubilus, Caroline A.; Cormier, Kerry A.; Jacobs, Matthew A.; Martin, Brett R.; Abraham, Carmela R.; Ikezu, Tsuneya; Reichard, Robert Ross; Wolozin, Benjamin L.; Budson, Andrew E.; Goldstein, Lee E.; Kowall, Neil W.; and Cantu, Robert C. (2013). The spectrum of disease in chronic traumatic encephalopathy. *Brain, 136*(Pt 1), 43–64. doi:10.1093/brain/aws307

McKenzie, Ian A.; Ohayon, David; Li, Huiliang; de Faria, Joana Paes; Emery, Ben; Tohyama, Koujiro; & Richardson, William D. (2014). Motor skill learning requires active central myelination. *Science, 346,* 318–322. doi:10.1126/science.1254960

McLay, Robert N.; Wood, Dennis P.; Webb-Murphy, Jennifer A.; Spira, James L.; Wiederhold, Mark D.; Pyne, Jeffrey M.; & Wiederhold, Brenda K. (2011). A randomized, controlled trial of virtual reality-graded exposure therapy for post-traumatic stress disorder in active duty service members with combat-related post-traumatic stress disorder. *Cyberpsychology, Behavior, and Social Networking, 14*(4), 223–229.

McLean, Carmen P.; Asnaani, Anu; Litz, Brett T.; & Hofmann, Stefan G. (2011). Gender differences in anxiety disorders: Prevalence, course of illness, comorbidity and burden of illness. *Journal of Psychiatric Research, 45*(8), 1027–1035.

McLewin, Lise A., & Muller, Robert T. (2006, September–October). Childhood trauma, imaginary companions, and the development of pathological dissociation. *Aggression and Violent Behavior, 11*(5), 531–545.

McMurran, Mary, & Howard, Richard. (2009). Personality, personality disorder and violence: Implications for future research and practice. In Mary McMurran & Richard Howard (Eds.), *Personality, personality disorder and violence* (pp. 299–311). West Sussex, England: Wiley-Blackwell.

McNab, Fiona, & Klingberg, Torkel. (2008). Prefrontal cortex and basal ganglia access in working memory. *Nature Neuroscience, 11,* 103–107.

McNally, Richard J. (2003). Progress and controversy in the study of posttraumatic stress disorder. *Annual Review of Psychology, 54,* 229–252.

McNally, Richard J. (2007a). Dispelling confusion about traumatic dissociative amnesia. *Mayo Clinic Proceedings, 82,* 1083–1087.

McNally, Richard J. (2007b). Mechanisms of exposure therapy: How neuroscience can improve psychological treatments for anxiety disorders. *Clinical Psychology Review, 27*(6), 750–759. doi:10.1016/j.cpr.2007.01.003

McNally, Richard J., & Geraerts, Elke. (2009). A new solution to the recovered memory debate. *Perspectives on Psychological Science, 4*(2), 126–134.

McNeil, Jeffrey A., & Morgan, C. A., III. (2010). Cognition and decision making in extreme environments. In Carrie H. Kennedy & Jeffrey Moore (Eds.), *Military neuropsychology.* New York, NY: Springer.

McNeilly, Cheryl L., & Howard, Kenneth I. (1991). The effects of psychotherapy: A reevaluation based on dosage. *Psychotherapy Research, 1,* 74–78.

McNulty, James K., & Fincham, Frank D. (2012). Beyond positive psychology: Toward a contextual view of psychological processes and wellbeing. *American Psychologist, 67,* 101–110.

McRoberts, Gerald W.; McDonough, Colleen; & Lakusta, Laura. (2009). The role of verbal repetition in the development of infant speech preferences from 4 to 14 months of age. *Infancy, 14*(2), 162–194.

McVay, Jennifer C., & Kane, Michael J. (2010). Adrift in the stream of thought: The effects of mind wandering on executive control and working memory capacity. In A. Gruszka, G. Matthews, & B. Szymura (Eds.), *Handbook of individual differences in cognition: Attention, memory, and executive control* (pp. 321–334). New York, NY: Springer Science + Business Media.

Meaney, Michael J. (2001). Maternal care, gene expression, and the transmission of individual differences in stress reactivity across generations. *Annual Review of Neuroscience, 24,* 1161–1192.

Meaney, Michael J. (2010). Epigenetics and the biological definition of gene × environment interactions. *Child Development, 81,* 41–79. doi:10.1111/j.1467-8624.2009.01381.x

Mechoulam, Raphael; Hanuš, Lumír O.; Pertwee, Roger; & Howlett, Allyn C. (2014). Early phytocannabinoid chemistry to endocannabinoids and beyond. *Nature Reviews Neuroscience, 15,* 757–764. doi:10.1038/nrn3811

Mechoulam, Raphael, & Parker, Linda A. (2013). The endocannabinoid system and the brain. *Annual Review of Psychology, 64,* 21–47. doi:10.1146/annurev-psych-113011-143739

Media for Health. (2011). Our Programs, from http://www.mediaforhealth.org/our_programs.html

Medina, Jorge H.; Bekinschtein, Pedro; Cammarota, Martin; & Izquierdo, Iván. (2008). Do memories consolidate to persist or do they persist to consolidate? *Behavioural Brain Research, 192,* 61–69.

Meduri, Mario; Bramanti, Placido; Ielitro, Giuseppe; Favaloro, Angelo; Milardi, Demetrio; Cutroneo, Giuseppina; & others. (2010). Morphometrical and morphological analysis of lateral ventricles in schizophrenia patients versus healthy controls. *Psychiatry Research: Neuroimaging, 183*(1), 52–58.

Megargee, Edwin I. (2009). The California Psychological Inventory. In James N. Butcher (Ed.), *Oxford handbook of personality assessment* (pp. 323–335). New York, NY: Oxford University Press.

Mehall, Karissa G.; Spinrad, Tracy L.; Eisenberg, Nancy; & Gaertner, Bridget M. (2009). Examining the relations of infant temperament and couples' marital satisfaction to mother and father involvement: A longitudinal study. *Fathering, 7*(1), 2–48.

Meier, Beat; König, Anja; Parak, Samuel; & Henke, Katharina. (2011). Suppressed, but not forgotten. *Swiss Journal of Psychology, 70*(1), 5–11.

Meier, Jo A.; McNaughton-Cassill, Mary; & Lynch, Molly. (2006). The management of household and childcare tasks and relationship satisfaction in dual-earner families. *Marriage & Family Review, 40*(2–3), 61–88.

Meijer, Ewout H., & Verschuere, Bruno. (2010). The polygraph and the detection of deception. *Journal of Forensic Psychology Practice, 10,* 325–338. doi:10.1080/15228932.2010.481237

Meir, Irit, Sandler, Wendy, Padden, Carol; & Aronoff, Mark (2010). Emerging sign languages. In M. Marschark & P. Spencer (Eds.) *Oxford handbook of deaf studies, language, and education* (Vol. 2). Oxford, England: Oxford University Press.

Meissner, Karin; Bingel, Ulrike; Colloca, Luana; Wagner, Tor D.; Watson, Alison; & Flaten, Magne Arve. (2011). The placebo effect: Advances from different methodological approaches. *Journal of Neuroscience, 31*(45), 16117–16124.

Melton, Lisa. (2005, December 17). Use it, don't lose it. *New Scientist, 188,* 32–35.

Meltzoff, Andrew N. (2007). 'Like me': A framework for social cognition. *Developmental Science, 10,* 126–134.

Meltzoff, Andrew N., & Moore, M. Keith. (1989). Imitation in newborn infants: Exploring the range of gestures imitated and the underlying mechanisms. *Developmental Psychology, 25,* 954–962.

Melzack, Ronald, & Wall, Patrick D. (1965). Pain mechanisms: A new theory. *Science, 150,* 971–980.

Melzack, Ronald, & Wall, Patrick D. (1996). *The challenge of pain* (2nd ed.). Harmondworth, England: Penguin.

Menaker, Michael. (2003, January 10). Perspectives: Circadian photoreception. *Science, 299,* 213–214.

Menand, Louis. (2001). *The Metaphysical Club: A story of ideas in America.* New York, NY: Farrar, Straus & Giroux.

Mendle, Jane, & Ferrero, Joseph. (2012). Detrimental psychological outcomes associated with pubertal timing in adolescent boys. *Developmental Review, 32*(1), 49–66. doi:10.1016/j.dr.2011.11.001

Mercer, Deanna; Douglass, Alan B.; & Links, Paul S. (2009, April). Meta-analyses of mood stabilizers, antidepressants and antipsychotics in the treatment of borderline personality disorder: Effectiveness for depression and anger symptoms. *Journal of Personality Disorders, 23*(2), 156–174.

Merikangas, K. R.; Akiskal, H. S.; Angst, J.; Greenberg, P. E.; Hirschfeld, R.; Petukhova, M.; & Kessler, R. C. (2007). Lifetime and 12-month prevalence of bipolar spectrum disorder in the National Comorbidity Survey replication. *Archives of General Psychiatry, 64*(5), 543–552.

Merlino, Joseph P.; Jacobs, Marily S.; Kaplan, Judy Ann; & Moritz, Lynne K. (Eds.). (2008). *Freud at 150: 21st-century essays on a man of genius.* Lanham, MD: Jason Aronson.

Mervis, Carolyn B., & Rosch, Eleanor. (1981). Categorization of natural objects. *Annual Review of Psychology, 32,* 89–115.

Mesmer-Magnus, Jessica R., & Viswesvaran, Chockalingam. (2006). How family-friendly work environments affect work-family conflict: A metaanalytic examination. *Journal of Labor Research, 27,* 555–574.

Meston, Cindy M., & Buss, David M. (2007). Why humans have sex. *Archives of Sexual Behavior, 36*(4), 477–507. doi:10.1007/s10508-007-9175-2

Meston, Cindy M., & Buss, David M. (2009). *Why women have sex: Understanding sexual motivations from adventure to revenge (and everything in between)*. New York, NY: Holt.

Meyer, Jerrold S. (2013). 3,4-methylenedioxymethamphetamine (MDMA): Current perspectives. *Substance Abuse and Rehabilitation, 4,* 83–99. doi:10.2147/SAR.S37258

Meyerbröker, Katharina, & Emmelkamp, Paul M. G. (2010). Virtual reality exposure therapy in anxiety disorders: A systematic review of process-and-outcome studies. *Depression and Anxiety, 27*(10), 933–944.

Meyer-Lindenberg, Andreas; Buckholtz, Joshua W.; Kolachana, Bhaskar.; Hariri, Ahmad R.; Pezawas, Lukas.; Blasi, Giuseppe.; ... Weinberger, Daniel R. (2006). Neural mechanisms of genetic risk for impulsivity and violence in humans. *Proceedings of the National Academy of Sciences, 103*(16), 6269–6274.

Mezick, Elizabeth J.; Matthews, Karen A.; Hall, Martica; Kamarck, Thomas W.; Buysse, Daniel J.; Owens, Jane F.; & Reis, Steven. (2009). Intra-individual variability in sleep duration and fragmentation: Associations with stress. *Psychoneuroendocrinology, 34*(9), 1346–1354.

Mezulis, Amy H.; Abramson, Lyn Y.; & Hyde, Janet S. (2004, September). Is there a universal positivity bias in attributions? A meta-analytic review of individual, developmental, and cultural differences in the self-serving attributional bias. *Psychological Bulletin, 130*(5), 711–747.

Michael, John; Sandberg, Kristian; Skewes, Joshua; Wolf, Thomas; Blicher, Jakob; Overgaard, Morten; & Frith, Chris D. (2014). Understanding continuous theta-burst stimulation demonstrates a causal role of premotor homunculus in action. *Psychological Science, 25,* 963–972. doi:10.1177/0956797613520608

Michael, Nikolaus. (2009). Hypothesized mechanisms and sites of action of electroconvulsive therapy. In Conrad M. Swartz (Ed.), *Electroconvulsive and neuromodulation therapies* (pp. 75–93). New York, NY: Cambridge University Press.

Mikalsen, Anita; Bertelsen, Bård; & Flaten, Magne Arve. (2001). Effects of caffeine, caffeine-associated stimuli, and caffeine-related information on physiological and psychological arousal. *Psychopharmacology, 157,* 373–380.

Mikels, Joseph A.; Maglio, Sam J.; Reed, Andrew E.; & Kaplowitz, Lee J. (2011). Should I go with my gut? Investigating the benefits of emotion-focused decision making. *Emotion, 11,* 743–753.

Miklowitz, David J. (2008). Bipolar disorder. In David H. Barlow (Ed.), *Clinical handbook of psychological disorders* (4th ed., pp. 421–462). New York, NY: Guilford Press.

Miklowitz, David J., & Johnson, Sheri L. (2007). Bipolar disorder. In Michel Hersen, Samuel M. Turner, & Deborah C. Beidel (Eds.), *Adult psychopathology and diagnosis* (5th ed., pp. 317–348). Hoboken, NJ: Wiley.

Milan, Stephanie; Snow, Stephanie; & Belay, Sophia. (2007). The context of preschool children's sleep: Racial/ethnic differences in sleep locations, routines, and concerns. *Journal of Family Psychology, 21*(1), 20–28.

Miles, Donna R., & Carey, Gregory. (1997). Genetic and environmental architecture on human aggression. *Journal of Personality and Social Psychology, 72*(1), 207.

Milgram, Stanley. (1963). Behavioral study of obedience. *Journal of Abnormal Psychology, 67,* 371–378.

Milgram, Stanley. (1964). Issues in the study of obedience: A reply to Baumrind. *American Psychologist, 19,* 848–852.

Milgram, Stanley. (1965/1992). Some conditions of obedience and disobedience to authority. In John Sabini & Maury Silver (Eds.), *The individual in a social world: Essays and experiments* (2nd ed.). New York, NY: McGraw-Hill.

Milgram, Stanley. (1974a). *Obedience to authority: An experimental view.* New York, NY: Harper & Row.

Milgram, Stanley. (1974b, June). Interview by Carol Tavris: The frozen world of the familiar stranger: An interview with Stanley Milgram. *Psychology Today,* pp. 71–80.

Milgram, Stanley. (1992). On maintaining social norms: A field experiment in the subway. In John Sabini & Maury Silver (Eds.), *The individual in a social world: Essays and experiments* (2nd ed.). New York, NY: McGraw-Hill.

Miller, Arthur G. (2009). Reflections on "Replicating Milgram" (Burger, 2009). *American Psychologist, 64*(1), 20–27. doi:10.1037/a0014407

Miller, Christian. (2009). Social psychology, mood, and helping: Mixed results for virtue ethics. *Journal of Ethics, 13*(2), 145–173.

Miller, Cindy Faith; Trautner, Hanns Martin; & Ruble, Diane N. (2006). The role of gender stereotypes in children's preferences and behavior. In Lawrence Balter & Catherine S. Tamis-LeMonda (Eds.), *Child psychology: A handbook of contemporary issues* (2nd ed.). New York, NY: Psychology Press.

Miller, Claude H., & Quick, Brian L. (2010). Sensation seeking and psychological reactance as health risk predictors for an emerging adult population. *Health Communication, 25*(3), 266–275.

Miller, Drew J.; Vachon, David D.; & Lynam, Donald R. (2009). Neuroticism, negative affect, and negative affect instability: Establishing convergent and discriminant validity using ecological momentary assessment. *Personality and Individual Differences, 47*(8), 873–877.

Miller, George A. (1956/1994). The magical number seven, plus or minus two: Some limits on our capacity for processing information [Special centennial issue]. *Psychological Review, 101,* 343–352.

Miller, Greg. (2013). The promise and perils of oxytocin. *Science, 339,* 267–269. doi:10.1126/science.339.6117.267

Miller, Gregory A. (2010). Mistreating psychology in the decades of the brain. *Perspectives on Psychological Science, 5*(6), 716–743. doi:10.1177/1745691610388774

Miller, Gregory E.; Chen, Edith; & Cole, Steve W. (2009). Health psychology: Developing biologically plausible models linking the social world and physical health. *Annual Review of Psychology, 60,* 501–524.

Miller, Mark W.; Wolf, Erika J.; & Hein, Christina. (2013). Psychological effects of the marathon bombing on Boston-area veterans with posttraumatic stress disorder. *Journal of Traumatic Stress, 26,* 1–5.

Miller, William R., & Rollnick, Stephen. (2012). *Motivational interviewing: Preparing people for change* (2nd ed.). New York, NY: Guilford Press.

Miller, William R., & Rose, Gary S. (2009). Toward a theory of motivational interviewing. *American Psychologist, 64*(6), 527–537. doi:10.1037/a0016830

Miller-Jones, Dalton. (1989). Culture and testing. *American Psychologist, 44,* 360–366.

Milling, Leonard S.; Coursen, Elizabeth L.; Shores, Jessica S.; and Waszkiewicz, Jolanta A. (2010). The predictive utility of hypnotizability: The change in suggestibility produced by hypnosis. *Journal of Consulting and Clinical Psychology, 78*(1), 126–130. doi:10.1037/a0017388

Mills, Sarah, & Hulbert-Williams, Lee. (2012). Distinguishing between treatment efficacy and effectiveness in post-traumatic stress disorder (PTSD): Implications for contentious therapies. *Counselling Psychology Quarterly, 25*(3), 319–330.

Milner, Brenda. (1970). Memory and the medial temporal regions of the brain. In Karl H. Pribram & Donald E. Broadbent (Eds.), *Biology of memory.* New York, NY: Academic Press.

Minda, John Paul, & Smith, J. David. (2001). Prototypes in category learning: The effects of category size, category structure, and stimulus complexity. *Journal of Experimental Psychology: Learning, Memory, and Cognition, 27,* 775–799.

Minda, John Paul, & Smith, J. David. (2011). Prototype models of categorization: Basic formulation, predictions, and limitations. In E. M. Pothos & A. J. Wills (Eds.), *Formal approaches in categorization* (pp. 40–64). New York, NY: Cambridge University Press.

Mindell, Jodi A.; Sadeh, Avi; Kohyama, Jun; & How, Ti Hwei. (2010a). Parental behaviors and sleep outcomes in infants and toddlers: A cross-cultural comparison. *Sleep Medicine, 11*(4), 393–399.

Mindell, Jodi A.; Sadeh, Avi; Wiegand, Benjamin; How, Ti Hwei; & Goh, Daniel Y. T. (2010b). Cross-cultural differences in infant and toddler sleep. *Sleep Medicine, 11*(3), 274–280.

Ming, Guo-li, & Song, Hongjun. (2005). Adult neurogenesis in the mammalian nervous system. *Annual Review of Neuroscience, 28,* 223–250.

Minzenberg, Michael J.; Yoon, Jong H.; & Carter, Cameron S. (2011). Schizophrenia. In Robert E. Hales, Stuart C. Yudofsky, & Glen O. Gabbard (Eds.), *Essentials of psychiatry* (3rd ed., pp. 111–150). Arlington, VA: American Psychiatric Publishing.

Mirmiran, Majid; Maas, Yolanda G.; & Ariagno, Ronald L. (2003). Development of fetal and neonatal sleep and circadian rhythms. *Sleep Medicine Reviews, 7*(4), 321–334.

Miron, Anca M., & Branscomben, Nyla R. (2008). Social categorization, standards of justice, and collective guilt. In Arie Nadler, Thomas E. Malloy, & Jeffrey D. Fisher (Eds.), *The social psychology of intergroup reconciliation* (pp. 77–96). New York, NY: Oxford University Press.

Mischel, Walter. (1996). From good intentions to willpower. In Peter M. Gollwitzer & John A. Bargh (Eds.), *The psychology of action: Linking cognition and motivation to behavior.* New York, NY: Guilford.

Mischel, Walter. (2004). Toward an integrative science of the person. *Annual Review of Psychology, 55*, 1–22.

Mischel, Walter, & Shoda, Yuichi. (1995). A cognitive-affective system theory of personality: Reconceptualizing situations, dispositions, dynamics, and invariance in personality structure. *Psychological Review, 102*, 246–268.

Mischel, Walter, & Shoda, Yuichi. (2010). The situated person. In Batja Mesquita, Lisa Feldman Barrett, & Eliot R. Smith (Eds.), *The mind in context.* New York: Guilford.

Mischel, Walter; Ayduk, Ozlem; Baumeister, Roy F.; & Vohs, Kathleen D. (2004). Willpower in a cognitive-affective processing system: The dynamics of delay of gratification *Handbook of self-regulation: Research, theory, and applications.* (pp. 99–129). New York, NY: Guilford.

Mischel, Walter; Shoda, Yuichi; & Mendoza-Denton, Rodolfo. (2002). Situation-behavior profiles as a locus of consistency in personality. *Current Directions in Psychological Science, 11*, 50–54.

Mistlberger, Ralph E., & Rusak, Benjamin. (2005). Circadian rhythms in mammals: Formal properties and environmental influences. In Meir H. Kryger, Thomas Roth, & William C. Dement (Eds.), *Principles and practice of sleep medicine* (4th ed.). Philadelphia, PA: Elsevier Saunders.

Mistlberger, Ralph E., & Skene, Debra J. (2005). Nonphotic entrainment in humans? *Journal of Biological Rhythms, 20*, 339–352.

Mitchell, Colter; Hobcraft, John; McLanahan, Sara S.; Siegel, Susan Rutherford; Berg, Arthur; & Brooks-Gunne, Jeanne; Garfinkel, Irwin; & Notterman, Daniel. (2014). Social disadvantage, genetic sensitivity, and children's telomere length. *Proceedings of the National Academy of Sciences, 111*, 5944–5949. doi:10.1073/pnas.1404293111

Mitchell, James E.; Roerig, James; & Steffen, Kristine. (2013). Biological therapies for eating disorders. *International Journal of Eating Disorders, 46*(5), 470–477. doi:10.1002/eat.22104

Mitka, Mike. (2009). College binge drinking still on the rise. *JAMA, 302*(8), 836–837. doi:10.1001/jama.2009.1154

Miyata, Yo. (2009). Pavlov's Nobel Prize in physiology or medicine. *Japanese Journal of Physiological Psychology and Psychophysiology, 27*(3), 225–2.

Moffet, Howard H. (2008). Traditional acupuncture theories yield null outcomes: A systematic review of clinical trials. *Journal of Clinical Epidemiology, 61*(8), 741–747. doi:10.1016/S0895-4356(08)000632/j.jclinepi.2008.02.013

Moffet, Howard H. (2009). Sham acupuncture may be as efficacious as true acupuncture: A systematic review of clinical trials. *Journal of Alternative and Complementary Medicine, 15*(3), 213–216. doi:10.1089/acm.2008.0356

Moghaddam, Bita, & Javitt, Daniel. (2011). From revolution to evolution: The glutamate hypothesis of schizophrenia and its implication for treatment. *Neuropsychopharmacology, 37*(1), 4–15.

Mohanty, Aprajita; Gitelman, Darren R.; Small, Dana M.; Mesulam, M. Marsel. (2008). The spatial attention network interacts with limbic and monoaminergic systems to modulate motivation-induced attention shifts. *Cerebral Cortex, 18*, 2604–2613. doi:10.1093/cercor/bhn021

Mohr, Charles. (1964, March 28). Apathy is puzzle in Queens killing: Behavioral specialists hard put to explain witnesses' failure to call police. *New York Times*, pp. 21, 40.

Mohr, David C.; Vella, Lea; Hart, Stacey; Heckman, Timothy; & Simon, Gregory. (2008). The effect of telephone-administered psychotherapy on symptoms of depression and attrition: A meta-analysis. *Clinical Psychology (New York, NY), 15*(3), 243–253. doi:10.1111/j.1468-2850.2008.00134.x

Moitra, Ethan; Dyck, Ingrid; Beard, Courtney; Bjornsson, Andri S.; Sibrava, Nicholas J.; Weisberg, Risa B.; & Keller, Martin B. (2011). Impact of stressful life events on the course of panic disorder in adults. *Journal of Affective Disorders.* doi:10.1016/j.jad.2011.05.029

Mojtabai, Ramin, & Olfson, Mark. (2008). National trends in psychotherapy by office-based psychiatrists. *Archives of General Psychiatry, 65*, 962–970.

Mojtabai, Ramin, & Olfson, Mark. (2011). Proportion of antidepressants prescribed without a psychiatric diagnosis is growing. *Health Affairs, 30*, 1434–1442. doi:10.1377/hlthaff.2010.1024

Mojtabai, R.; Olfson, M.; Sampson, N. A.; Jin, R.; Druss, B.; Wang, P. S., & Kessler, R. C. (2011). Barriers to mental health treatment: Results from the National Comorbidity Survey Replication. *Psychological Medicine, 41*(8), 1751–1761. doi:10.1017/S0033291710002291

Mok, Leh Woon. (2010). The effect of variety and dietary restraint on food intake in lean young women: A preliminary study. *Journal of General Psychology, 137*, 63–83.

Molenberghs, Pascal; Cunnington, Ross; & Mattingley, Jasson B. (2012). Brain regions with mirror properties: A meta-analysis of 125 human fMRI studies. *Neuroscience & Biobehavioral Reviews, 36*, 341–349. doi:10.1016/j.neubiorev.2011.07.004

Molitor, Adriana, & Hsu, Hui-Chin. (2011). Child development across cultures. In Kenneth D. Keith (Ed.), *Cross-cultural psychology: Contemporary themes and perspectives.* Chichester, England: Wiley-Blackwell.

Monroe, Scott M., & Reid, Mark W. (2009). Life stress and major depression. *Current Directions in Psychological Science, 18*(2), 68–72.

Moore, David W. (2005, June 15). Three in four Americans believe in paranormal. Gallup News Service. Retrieved February 22, 2008, from http://www.gallup.com/poll/16915/Three-Four-Americans-BelieveParanormal.aspx

Moore, Jay. (2005a). Some historical and conceptual background to the development of B. F. Skinner's "radical behaviorism"—Part 1. *Journal of Mind and Behavior, 26*, 65–94.

Moore, Jay. (2005b). Some historical and conceptual background to the development of B. F. Skinner's "radical behaviorism"—Part 3. *Journal of Mind and Behavior, 26*, 137–160.

Moore, Mollie N.; Salk, Rachel H.; Van Hulle, Carol A.; Abramson, Lyn Y.; Hyde, Janet S.; Lemery-Chalfant, Kathryn.; & Goldsmith, H. Hill. (2013). Genetic and environmental influences on rumination, distraction, and depressed mood in adolescence. *Clinical Psychological Science, 1*(3), 316–322.

Moors, Agnes. (2009). Theories of emotion causation: A review. *Cognition & Emotion, 23*, 625–662.

Moors, Agnes; Ellsworth, Phoebe C.; Scherer, Klaus R.; & Frijda, Nico H. (2013). Appraisal theories of emotion: State of the art and future development. *Emotion Review, 5*, 119–124. doi:10.1177/1754073912468165

Moreland, Richard L., & Topolinski, Sascha. (2010). The mere exposure phenomenon: A lingering melody by Robert Zajonc. *Emotion Review, 2*(4), 329–339.

Morelli, Gilda A.; Rogoff, Barbara; Oppenheim, David; & Goldsmith, Denise. (1992). Cultural variation in infants' sleeping arrangements: Questions of independence. *Developmental Psychology, 28*, 604–613.

Moretti, Robert J., & Rossini, Edward D. (2004). The Thematic Apperception Test (TAT). In Mark J. Hilsenroth & Daniel L. Segal (Eds.), *Comprehensive Handbook of Psychological Assessment, Vol. 2: Personality assessment.* Hoboken, NJ: Wiley.

Morgan, Christiana, & Murray, Henry A. (1935). A method of investigating fantasies: The Thematic Apperception Test. *Archives of Neurology and Psychiatry, 4*, 310–329.

Morgan, William P. (2002). Hypnosis in sport and exercise psychology. In J. L. Van Raalte, & B. W. Brewer (Eds.), *Exploring sport and exercise psychology.* Washington, DC: American Psychological Association.

Morin, Charles M.; Bootzin, Richard R.; Buysse, Daniel J.; Edinger, Jack D.; Espie, Colin A.; & Lichstein, Kenneth L. (2006). Psychological and behavioral treatment of insomnia: Update of the recent evidence (1998–2004). *Sleep, 29*, 1398–1414.

Morling, Beth, & Kitayama, Shinobu. (2008). Culture and motivation. In James Y. Shah & Wendi L. Gardner (Eds.), *Handbook of motivation science.* New York, NY: Guilford.

Morrell, Julian, & Steele, Howard. (2003). The role of attachment security, temperament, maternal perception, and care-giving behavior in persistent infant sleeping problems. *Infant Mental Health Journal, 24,* 447–468.

Morris, John S.; Scott, Sophie K.; & Dolan, Raymond J. (1999). Saying it with feeling: Neural responses to emotional vocalizations. *Neuropsychologia, 37,* 1155–1163.

Morris, Michael W., & Peng, Kaiping. (1994). Culture and cause: American and Chinese attributions for social and physical events. *Journal of Personality and Social Psychology, 67,* 949–971.

Morris, Richard G. (2013). NMDA receptors and memory encoding. *Neuropharmacology, 74,* 32–40. doi:10.1016/j.neuropharm.2013.04.014

Morrison, Anthony P.; Turkington, Douglas; Pyle, Melissa; Spencer, Helen; Brabban, Alison; Dunn, Graham; Christodoulides, Tom; Dudley, Rob; Chapman, Nicola; Callcott, Pauline; Grace, Tim; Lumley, Victoria; Drage, Laura; Tully, Sarah; Irving, Kerry; Cummings, Anna; Byrne, Rory; Davies, Linda M.; & Hutton, Paul. (2014). Cognitive therapy for people with schizophrenia spectrum disorders not taking antipsychotic drugs: A single-blind randomised controlled trial. *Lancet, 383,* 1395–1403. doi:10.1016/S0140-6736(13)62246-1

Morrison, Christopher D. (2008). Leptin resistance and the response to positive energy balance. *Physiology & Behavior, 94,* 660–663.

Moskowitz, Andrew; Schafer, Ingo; & Dorahy, Martin Justin. (2009). *Psychosis, trauma, and dissociation.* New York, NY: Wiley.

Moss, Cynthia. (2000). Elephant memories: Thirteen years in the life of an elephant family. Chicago, IL: University of Chicago Press.

Moss, Jarrod; Kotovsky, Kenneth; & Cagan, Jonathan. (2011). The effect of incidental hints when problems are suspended before, during, or after an impasse. *Journal of Experimental Psychology: Learning, Memory, and Cognition, 37*(1), 140–148. doi:10.1037/a0021206

Motowidlo, Stephan J.; Borman, Walter C.; & Schmit, Mark J. (1997). A theory of individual differences in task and contextual performance. *Human Performance, 10,* 71–83.

Mottron, Laurent. (2006, February 20). Quoted in André Picard, "The postie and the prof dispute perceptions of autism." *Globe and Mail.* Retrieved on February 20, 2006, from http://www.theglobeandmail.com/servlet/story/RTGAM.20060220.wxautism0220/BNStory/specialScienceandHealth/home

Mottron, Laurent. (2008, February 25). Quoted in David Wolman, "The truth about autism: Scientists reconsider what they *think* they know." *Wired Magazine: 16.03.* Retrieved on March 2, 2008, from http://www.wired.com/print/medtech/health/magaine/1603/ff_autism

Moyer, Christopher A.; Rounds, James.; & Hannum, James W. (2004). A meta-analysis of massage therapy research. *Psychological Bulletin, 130,* 3–18.

Mrazek, Michael D.; Chin, Jason M.; Schmader, Toni; Hartson, Kimberly A.; Smallwood, Jonathan; & Schooler, Jonathan W. (2011). Threatened to distraction: Mind-wandering as a consequence of stereotype threat. *Journal of Experimental Social Psychology, 47,* 1243–1248. doi:10.1016/j.jesp.2011.05.011

Mueller, Shane T.; Seymour, Travis L.; Kieras, David E.; & Meyer, David E. (2003). Theoretical implications of articulatory duration, phonological similarity, and phonological complexity in verbal working memory. *Journal of Experimental Psychology: Learning, Memory, and Cognition, 29,* 1353–1380.

Mueller, Pam A., & Oppenheimer, Daniel M. (2014). The pen is mightier than the keyboard: Advantages of longhand over laptop note taking. *Psychological Science, 25,* 1159-1168. doi:10.1177/0956797614524581

Muenchow, Susan, & Marsland, Katherine W. (2007). Beyond baby steps: Promoting the growth and development of U.S. child-care policy. In J. Lawrence Aber, Sandra J. Bishop-Josef, Stephanie M. Jones, Kathryn Taaffe McLearn, & Deborah A. Phillips (Eds.), *Child development and social policy: Knowledge for action* (pp. 97–112). Washington, DC: American Psychological Association.

Mueser, Kim T., & Glynn, Shirley M. (1993). Efficacy of psychotherapy for schizophrenia. In Thomas R. Giles (Ed.), *Handbook of effective psychotherapy.* New York, NY: Plenum Press.

Mueser, Kim T.; Bellack, Alan S.; & Brady, E. U. (1990). Hallucinations in schizophrenia. *Acta Psychiatrica Scandinavica, 82,* 26–29.

Mueser, Kim T.; Deavers, Frances; Penn, David L.; & Cassisi, Jeffrey E. (2013). Psychosocial treatments for schizophrenia. *Annual Review of Clinical Psychology, 9,* 465–497. doi:10.1146/annurev-clinpsy-050212-185620

Mukamel, Roy; Ekstrom, Arne D.; Kaplan, Jonas; Iacoboni, Marco; & Fried, Itzhak. (2010). Single-neuron responses in humans during execution and observation of actions. *Current Biology, 20*(8), 750–756.

Mulhern, Sherrill. (1991). Embodied alternative identities: Bearing witness to a world that might have been. *Psychiatric Clinics of North America, 14,* 769–786.

Munafo, Marcus R.; Hitsman, Brian; Rende, Richard; Metcalfe, Chris; & Niaura, Raymond. (2008, January). Effects of progression to cigarette smoking on depressed mood in adolescents: Evidence from the National Longitudinal Study of Adolescent Health. *Addiction, 103*(1), 162–171.

Munakata, Yuko; Kuhn, D.; Siegler, Robert S.; Damon, William; & Lerner, Robert M. (2006). Information processing approaches to development. In William Damon & Richard M. Lerner (Eds.), *Handbook of Child Psychology: Vol. 2, Cognition, perception, and language* (6th ed., pp. 426–463). Hoboken, NJ: Wiley.

Münch, Mirjam; Linhart, Friedrich; Borisuit, Apiparn; Jaeggi, Susanne M.; & Scartezzini, Jean-Louis. (2012). Effects of prior light exposure on early evening performance, subjective sleepiness, and hormonal secretion. *Behavioral Neuroscience, 126,* 196–203. doi:10.1037/a0026702

Münsterberg, Hugo. (1913). *Psychology and industrial efficiency.* Boston, MA: Houghton Mifflin.

Murberg, Terje A., & Bru, Edvin. (2005). The role of coping styles as predictors of depressive symptoms among adolescents: A prospective study. *Scandinavian Journal of Psychology, 46*(4), 385–393.

Murray, Greg; Goldstone, Eliot; & Cunningham, Everarda. (2007). Personality and the predisposition(s) to bipolar disorder: Heuristic benefits of a two-dimensional model. *Bipolar disorders, 9*(5), 453–461.

Murray, Henry A. (1938). *Explorations in personality.* New York, NY: Oxford University Press.

Murray, Henry A. (1943). *Thematic Apperception Test manual.* Cambridge, MA: Harvard University Press.

Murray, John P. (2008). Media violence: The effects are both real and strong. *American Behavioral Scientist, 51,* 1212–1230.

Muscatell, Keeley A.; Slavich, George M.; Monroe, Scott M.; & Gotlib, Ian H. (2009). Stressful life events, chronic difficulties, and the symptoms of clinical depression. *Journal of Nervous and Mental Disease, 197,* 154–160.

Mustanski, Brian S.; Chivers, Meredith L.; & Bailey, J. Michael. (2002). A critical review of recent biological research on human sexual orientation. *Annual Review of Sex Research, 13,* 89–140.

Mustanski, Brian S.; Viken, Richard J.; Kaprio, Jaakko; Pulkkinen, Lea; & Rose, Richard J. (2004). Genetic and environmental influences on pubertal development: Longitudinal data from Finnish twins at ages 11 and 14. *Developmental Psychology, 40,* 1188–1198.

Musto, David F. (1991, July). Opium, cocaine and marijuana in American history. *Scientific American, 265,* 40–47.

Mutiso, V.N.; Gatonga, P.; Ndeti, D.M.; Gafna, T.; Mbwayo, A.W.; & Khasakhala, L.I. (2014). Collaboration between traditional and Western practitioners. In S. O. Okpaku (Ed.), *Essentials of global mental health* (pp. 135–143). Cambridge, England: Cambridge University Press.

Muzur, Amir; Pace-Schott, Edward F.; & Hobson, J. Allan. (2002). The prefrontal cortex in sleep. *Trends in Cognitive Sciences, 6,* 475–481.

Myrtek, Michael. (2007). Type A behavior and hostility as independent risk factors for coronary heart disease. In Jochen Jordan, Benjamin Bardé, & Andreas Michael Zeiher (Eds.), *Contributions toward evidence-based psychocardiology: A systematic review of the literature* (pp. 159–183). Washington, DC: American Psychological Association.

NACCRRA. (2010). NACCRRA 2009 *Annual report: Making connections: All children, all families, all settings.* Arlington, VA: Author.

Nader, Karim, & Wang, Szu-Han. (2006). Fading in. *Learning & Memory, 13,* 530–535.

Nadler, Joel T., & Clark, M. H. (2011). Stereotype threat: A meta-analysis comparing African Americans to Hispanic Americans. *Journal of Applied Social Psychology, 41*(4), 872–890.

Nagasawa, Miho; Mitsui, Shouhei; En, Shiori; Ohtani, Nobuyo; Ohta, Mitsuaki; Sakuma, Yasuo; Onaka, Tatsushi; Mogi, Kazutaka; & Kikusui, Takefumi. (2015). Oxytocin-gaze positive loop and the coevolution of human–dog bonds. *Science, 348,* 333–336. doi:10.1126/science.1261022

Nahas, Ziad, & Anderson, Berry S. (2011). Brain stimulation therapies for mood disorders: The continued necessity of electroconvulsive therapy. *Journal of the American Psychiatric Nurses Association, 17,* 214–216. doi:10.1177/1078390311409037

Nairn, Ray; Coverdale, Sara; & Coverdale, John H. (2011). A framework for understanding media depictions of mental illness. *Academic Psychiatry, 35,* 202–206.

Nairne, James S. (2002). Remembering over the short-term: The case against the standard model. *Annual Review of Psychology, 53,* 53–81.

Nakao, Mutsuhiro. (2010). Work-related stress and psychosomatic medicine. *BioPsychoSocial Medicine, 4,* 4.

Nash, Michael R. (2008). Foundations of clinical hypnosis. In Michael R. Nash & Amanda J. Barnier (Eds.), *The Oxford handbook of hypnosis: Theory, research, and practice* (pp. 487–502). New York, NY: Oxford University Press.

Nash, Michael R.; Perez, Nicole; Tasso, Anthony; & Levy, Jacob J. (2009). Clinical research on the utility of hypnosis in the prevention, diagnosis, and treatment of medical and psychiatric disorders. *International Journal of Clinical and Experimental Hypnosis, 57,* 443–450. doi:10.1080 /00207140903099153

Nathan, Peter E., & Gorman, Jack M. (Eds.). (2007). *A guide to treatments that work* (3rd ed.). New York, NY: Oxford University Press.

National Association for the Education of Young Children. (2009). *Developmentally appropriate practice in early childhood programs serving children from birth through age 8.* Washington, DC: Author. Retrieved December 8, 2009, from http://www.naeyc.org/files/naeyc/file/positions/PSDAP.pdf

National Center for Complementary and Alternative Medicine. (2009). *Get the facts: Magnets for pain.* Retrieved June 21, 2009, from http:// nccam.nih.gov/health/magnet/D408_GTF.pdf

National Center for Complementary and Alternative Medicine. (2011). Acupuncture: An introduction. Retrieved from https://nccih.nih.gov /health/acupuncture/introduction

National Council on Aging. (1998, September 28). *News: Half of older Americans report they are sexually active and 4 in 10 want more sex, says new survey.* Retrieved on April 12, 1999, from http://www.ncoa.org/news/archives/sexsurvey.htm

National Geographic Society. (2008). *Stress: Portrait of a killer* [Motion picture]. Randy Bean & William Free (Producers) & John Hemingway (Director).

National Highway Traffic Safety Administration. (2011). Traffic safety facts crash stats: Drowsy driving. Washington, DC: Department of Transportation, National Highway Traffic Safety Administration. Retrieved from http:// www.nrd.nhtsa.dot.gov/pubs/811449.pdf

National Institute on Aging. (2007). U.S. Department of Health and Human Services, National Institutes of Health.

National Research Council. (2003). *The polygraph and lie detection.* Washington, DC: National Academies Press.

National Safety Council (2014). NSC releases latest injury and fatality statistics and trends. Retrieved on July 25, 2014, from http://www.nsc.org /Pages/NSC-releases-latest-injury-and-fatality-statistics-and-trends-.aspx

National Science Board. (2010). *Science and engineering indicators: 2010.* (Vol. 1). (NSB 10–01) Arlington, VA: National Science Foundation.

National Sleep Foundation. (2004b). *Got caffeine? Try our caffeine calculator.* Washington, DC: Author. Retrieved on August 20, 2004, from http://www .sleepfoundation.org/caffeine.cfm

National Standard Monographs. (2009). Magnet therapy. Retrieved July 9, 2009, from http://www.naturalstandard.com/naturalstandard/demos /patient-magnet.asp

National Survey of Student Engagement. (2012). *Promoting student learning and institutional improvement: Lessons from NSSE at 13.* Bloomington: Indiana University Center for Postsecondary Research.

Neal, David T., & Chartrand, Tanya L. (2011). Embodied emotion perception: Amplifying and dampening facial feedback modulates emotion perception accuracy. *Social Psychological and Personality Science, 2,* 673–678.

Neberich, Wiebke; Penke, Lars; Lehnart, Lars; & Asendorpf, Jens B. (2010). Family of origin, age at menarche, and reproductive strategies: A test of four evolutionary-developmental models. *European Journal of Developmental Psychology, 7*(2), 153–177.

Nederlof, Angela F.; Muris, Peter; & Hovens, Johannes E. (2013). The epidemiology of violent behavior in patients with a psychotic disorder: A systematic review of studies since 1980. *Aggression and Violent Behavior, 18,* 183–189.

Neher, Andrew. (1991). Maslow's theory of motivation: A critique. *Journal of Humanistic Psychology, 31,* 89–112.

Neimeyer, Robert A.; Wittkowski, Joachim; & Moser, Richard P. (2004). Psychological research on death attitudes: An overview and evaluation. *Death Studies, 28*(4), 309–340.

Neisser, Ulric; Boodoo, Gwyneth; Bouchard, Thomas J., Jr.; Boykin, A. Wade; Brody, Nathan; Ceci, Stephen J.; & others. (1996). Intelligence: Knowns and unknowns. *American Psychologist, 51,* 77–101, 298.

Nelson, Katherine, & Fivush, Robyn. (2004). The emergence of autobiographical memory: A social cultural developmental theory. *Psychological Review, 111,* 486–511.

Nelson, Katherine S.; Kushlev, Kostadin; & Lyubomirsky, Sonja. (2014). The pains and pleasures of parenting: When, why, and how is parenthood associated with more or less well-being? *Psychological Bulletin, 140,* 846–895. doi:10.1037/a0035444

Nelson, Leif D., & Morrison, Evan L. (2005). The symptoms of resource scarcity: Judgments of food and finances influence preferences for potential partners. *Psychological Science, 16,* 167–173.

Nelson, Marcia Z. (2001). *Come and sit: A week inside meditation centers.* Woodstock, VT: Skylight Paths.

Nelson, Toben F.; Naimi, Timothy S.; Brewer, Robert D.; & Wechsler, Henry. (2005). The state sets the rate: The relationship of college binge drinking to state binge drinking rates and selected state alcohol control policies. *American Journal of Public Health, 95,* 441–446.

Neria, Yuval; DiGrande, Laura; & Adams, Ben G. (2011). Posttraumatic stress disorder following the September 11, 2001, terrorist attacks: A review of the literature among highly exposed populations. *American Psychologist, 66*(6), 429–446.

Nestler, Eric J., & Malenka, Robert C. (2004, March). The addicted brain. *Scientific American, 290,* 78–85.

Nestoriuc, Yvonne, & Martin, Alexandra. (2007). Efficacy of biofeedback for migraine: A meta-analysis. *Pain, 128,* 111–127.

Neuberg, Steven L.; Kenrick, Douglas T.; & Schaller, Mark. (2010). Evolutionary social psychology. In S. T. Fiske, D. T. Gilbert & G. Lindzey (Eds.), *Handbook of Social Psychology, Vol. 2.* Hoboken, NJ: John Wiley.

Neumann, Craig S.; Hare, Robert D.; & Johansson, Peter T. (2013). The psychopathy checklist-revised (PCL-R), low anxiety, and fearlessness: A structural equation modeling analysis. *Personality Disorders: Theory, Research, and Treatment, 4*(2), 129–137. doi:10.1037/a0027886

Neuner, Frank; Onyut, Patience L.; Ertl, Verena; Odenwald, Michael; Schauer, Elisabeth; & Elbert, Thomas. (2008). Treatment of posttraumatic stress disorder by trained lay counselors in an African refugee settlement: A randomized controlled trial. *Journal of Consulting and Clinical Psychology, 76*(4), 686–694. doi:10.1037/0022-006X.76.4.686

Newheiser, Anna-Kaisa; Hewstone, Miles; Voci, Alberto; Schmid, Katharina; Zick, Andreas; & Küpper, Beate. (2013). Social-psychological aspects of religion and prejudice: Evidence from survey and experimental research. In Steve Clark, Russell Powell, & Julian Savulescu (Eds.), *Religion, intolerance, and conflict: A scientific and conceptual investigation* (pp. 107–125). Oxford, England: Oxford University Press.

Newson, Rachel S., & Kemps, Eva B. (2005). General lifestyle activities as a predictor of current cognition and cognitive change in older adults: A cross-sectional and longitudinal examination. *Journals of Gerontology, Series B: Psychological Sciences and Social Sciences, 60,* P113–P120.

Newton, Jocelyn H., & McGrew, Kevin S. (2010). Introduction to the special issue: Current research in Cattell–Horn–Carroll–based assessment. *Psychology in the Schools, 47*(7), 621–634.

Nezu, Arthur M., & Nezu, Christine M. (Eds.). (2008). *Evidence-based outcome research: A practical guide to conducting randomized controlled trials for psychosocial interventions.* New York, NY: Oxford University Press.

Ng, Debbie M., & Jeffery, Robert W. (2003). Relationships between perceived stress and health behaviors in a sample of working adults. *Health Psychology, 22,* 638–642.

Nguyen, Angela-MinhTu D., & Benet-Martínez, Verónica. (2013). Biculturalism and adjustment: A meta-analysis. *Journal of Cross-Cultural Psychology, 44,* 122–159. doi:10.1177/0022022111435097

Niaura, Raymond; Todaro, John F.; Stroud, Laura; Spiro, Avron; Ward, Kenneth D.; & Weiss, Scott. (2002). Hostility, the metabolic syndrome, and incident coronary heart disease. *Health Psychology, 21,* 588–593.

Niccols, Alison. (2007). Fetal alcohol syndrome and the developing socio-emotional brain. *Brain and Cognition, 65,* 135–142.

NICHD. (2006). The NICHD Study of Early Child Care and Youth Development (SECCYD): Findings for children up to age 4 1/2 years (Eunice Kennedy Shriver National Institute of Child Health and Human Development, NIH publication no. 05-4318). Washington, DC: U.S. Government Printing Office.

NICHD Early Child Care Research Network. (2003a). Does quality of child care affect child outcomes at age 4 1/2? *Developmental Psychology, 39,* 451–469.

NICHD Early Child Care Research Network. (2003b). Families matter—even for kids in child care. *Journal of Developmental & Behavioral Pediatrics, 24,* 58–62.

Nichols, Michael P. (2012). *Family therapy: Concepts and methods* (10th ed.). Boston, MA: Pearson.

Nichols, Michelle. (2015, January 8). Ethnic cleansing in Central African Republic, no genocide: U.N. inquiry. *Reuters.* G. Crosse (Ed.). Retrieved from http://www.reuters.com/article/2015/01/08/us-centralafrica-inquiry -idUSKBN0KH2BM20150108

Nickerson, Raymond S., & Adams, Marilyn J. (1982). Long-term memory for a common object. In Ulric Neisser (Ed.), *Memory observed: Remembering in natural contexts.* San Francisco, CA: Freeman.

Nielsen, Jared A.; Zielinski, Brandon A.; Ferguson, Michael A.; Lainhart, Janet E.; Anderson, Jeffrey S. (2013) An evaluation of the left-brain vs. right-brain hypothesis with resting state functional connectivity magnetic resonance imaging. *PLOS ONE 8,* e71275. doi:10.1371/journal.pone.0071275

Nielsen, Tore A., & Stenstrom, Philippe. (2005, October 27). What are the memory sources of dreaming? *Nature, 437,* 1286–1289.

Nielsen, Tore A., Stenstrom, Philippe; & Levin, Ross. (2006). Nightmare frequency as a function of age, gender, and September 11, 2001: Findings from an Internet questionnaire. *Dreaming, 16,* 145–158.

Nielsen, Tore A., & Zadra, Antonio. (2005). Nightmares and other common dream disturbances. In Meir H. Kryger, Thomas Roth, & William C. Dement (Eds.), *Principles and practice of sleep medicine* (4th ed.). Philadelphia, PA: Elsevier Saunders.

Nielson, Kristy A., & Lorber, William. (2009). Enhanced post-learning memory consolidation is influenced by arousal predisposition and emotion regulation but not by stimulus valence or arousal. *Neurobiology of Learning and Memory, 92*(1), 70–79. doi:10.1016/j.nlm.2009.03.002

Niemiec, Christopher P.; Ryan, Richard M.; & Deci, Edward L. (2010). Self-determination theory and the relation of autonomy to self-regulatory processes and personality development. In Rick H. Hoyle (Ed.), *Handbook of Personality and Self-Regulation,* 69–191. Hoboken, NJ: Wiley-Blackwell. doi:10.1002/9781444318111

Nir, Yuval, & Tononi, Giulio. (2010). Dreaming and the brain: From phenomenology to neurophysiology. *Trends in Cognitive Science, 14,* 88–100. doi:10.1016/j.tics.2009.12.001

Nir, Yuval; Staba, Richard J.; Andrillon, Thomas; Vyazovskiy Vladyslav V.; Cirelli, Chiara; Fried, Ithak; Tononi, Giulio. (2011). Regional slow waves and spindles in human sleep. *Neuron, 70,* 153–169.

Nisbett, Richard E. (2007). Eastern and Western ways of perceiving the world. In Yuichi Shoda, Daniel Cervone, Geraldine Downey (Eds.), *Persons in context: Building a science of the individual* (pp. 62–83). New York, NY: Guilford.

Nisbett, Richard E.; Aronson, Joshua; Blair, Clancy; Dickens, William; Flynn, James; Halpern, Diane F.; & Turkheimer, Eric. (2012). Intelligence: New findings and theoretical developments. *American Psychologist, 67,* 130–159. doi:10.1037/a0026699

Nisbett, Richard E., & Wilson, Timothy. D. (1977). The halo effect: Evidence for unconscious alteration of judgments. *Journal of Personality and Social Psychology, 35*(4), 250.

Nithianantharajah, Jess, & Hannan, Anthony J. (2006). Enriched environments, experience-dependent plasticity, and disorders of the nervous system. *Nature Reviews Neuroscience, 7,* 697–709.

Nivette, Amy E. (2011). Cross-national predictors of crime: A meta-analysis. *Homicide Studies, 15*(2), 103–131. doi:10.1177/1088767911406397

Nivoli, A. M.; Murru, A.; & Vieta, E. (2010). Lithium: Still a cornerstone in the long-term treatment in bipolar disorder? *Neuropsychobiology, 62*(1), 27–35. doi:10.1159/000314307

Nivoli, Alessandra; Murru, Andrea; Goikolea, José M.; Crespo, José M.; Montes, José M.; González-Pinto, Ana; ... Vieta, Eduard. (2012). New treatment guidelines for acute bipolar mania: A critical review. *Journal of Affective Disorders, 140*(2), 125–141. doi:10.1016/j.jad.2011.10.015

Noble, Meredith; Tregear, Stephen J.; Treadwell, Jonathan R.; & Schoelles, Karen. (2008). Long-term opioid therapy for chronic noncancer pain: A systematic review and meta-analysis of efficacy and safety. *Journal of Pain and Symptom Management, 35,* 214–228.

Nock, Matthew K.; Greif Green, Jennifer; Hwang, Irving; McLaughlin, Katie A.; Sampson, Nancy A.; Zaslavsky, Alan M.; & Kessler, Ronald C. (2013). Prevalence, correlates, and treatment of lifetime suicidal behavior among adolescents. *JAMA Psychiatry, 70*(3), 1–11. doi:10.1001/2013.jamapsychiatry.55

Nocon, Agnes; Wittchen, Hans-Ulrich; Pfister, Hildegard; Zimmermann, Petra; & Lieb, Roselind. (2006). Dependence symptoms in young cannabis users? A prospective epidemiological study. *Journal of Psychiatric Research, 40,* 394–403.

Nofzinger, Eric A. (2005). Neuroimaging and sleep medicine. *Sleep Medicine Review, 9,* 157–172.

Nofzinger, Eric A. (2006). Neuroimaging of sleep and sleep disorders. *Current Neurology and Neuroscience Reports, 6,* 149–155.

Nolen-Hoeksema, Susan. (2001). Gender differences in depression. *Current Directions in Psychological Science, 10,* 173–176.

Nolen-Hoeksema, Susan. (2003). *Women who think too much: How to break free of over-thinking and reclaim your life.* New York, NY: Henry Holt.

Nolen-Hoeksema, Susan, & Hilt, Lori M. (2009). Gender differences in depression. In Ian H. Gotlib & Constance L. Hammen (Eds.), *Handbook of depression* (2nd ed., pp. 386–404). New York, NY: Guilford.

Nolen-Hoeksema, Susan; Stice, Eric; & Wade, Emily. (2007, February). Reciprocal relations between rumination and bulimic, substance abuse, and depressive symptoms in female adolescents. *Journal of Abnormal Psychology, 116*(1), 198–207.

Norasakkunkit, Vinai; Kitayama, Shinobu; & Uchida, Yukiko. (2012). Social anxiety and holistic cognition: Self-focused social anxiety in the United States and other-focused social anxiety in Japan. *Journal of Cross-Cultural Psychology, 43,* 742–757.

Norcross, John C., & Lambert, Michael J. (2011). Psychotherapy relationships that work II. *Psychotherapy, 48*(1), 4–8. doi:10.1037/a0022180

Norcross, John C., & Wampold, Bruce E. (2011a). Evidence-based therapy relationships: Research conclusions and clinical practices. *Psychotherapy, 48*(1), 98–102. doi:10.1037/a0022161

Norcross, John C., & Wampold, Bruce E. (2011b). What works for whom: Tailoring psychotherapy to the person. *Journal of Clinical Psychology: In Session, 67,* 127–132. doi:10.1002/jclp.20764

Norcross, John C.; Karpiak, Christie P.; & Santoro, Shannon O. (2005). Clinical psychologists across the years: The division of clinical psychology from 1960 to 2003. *Journal of Clinical Psychology, 61,* 1467–1483.

Nordal, Katherine C. (2010). Dr. Katherine C. Nordal on how to find a therapist. *American Psychological Association Press Releases.* Retrieved from http://www.apa.org/news/press/releases/2010/05/locate-a-therapist.aspx

Norko, Michael, & Baranoski, Madelon V. (2005, January). The state of contemporary risk assessment research. *Canadian Journal of Psychiatry, 50*(1), 18–26.

Norris, Donna M.; Gutheil, Thomas G.; & Strasburger, Larry H. (2003, April). This couldn't happen to me: Boundary problems and sexual misconduct in the psychotherapy relationship. *Psychiatric Services, 54*(4), 517–522.

North, Adrian C., & Hargreaves, David. (2009). The power of music. *The Psychologist, 22,* 1012–1014.

North, Carol S.; Nixon, Sara Jo.; Shariat, Sheryll; Mallonee, Sue; McMillen, J. Curtis; Spitznagel, Edward L.; & Smith, Elizabeth M. (1999). The psychiatric impact of the Oklahoma City bombing on survivors of the direct blast. *Journal of the American Medical Association, 282,* 755–762.

North, Carol S.; Pfefferbaum, Betty; Kawasaki, A.; Lee, Sungkyu; & Spitznagel, Edward L. (2011). Psychosocial adjustment of directly exposed survivors seven years after the Oklahoma City bombing. *Comprehensive Psychiatry, 52*(1), 1–8. doi:10.1016/j.comppsych.2010.04.003

North, Michael S., & Fiske, Susan T. (2013). Act your (old) age: Prescriptive, ageist biases over succession, consumption, and identity. *Personality and Social Psychology Bulletin, 39*(6), 720–734. doi:10.1177/0146167213480043

Nosek, Brian A.; Greenwald, Anthony G.; & Banaji, Mahzarin R. (2007). The Implicit Association Test at age 7: A methodological and conceptual review. In J. A. Bargh (Ed.), *Automatic Processes in Social Thinking and Behavior.* Psychology Press.

Nosek, Brian A.; Smyth, Frederick L.; Hansen, Jeffrey J.; Devos, Thierry; Lindner, Nicole M.; Ranganath, Kate A.; Smith, Colin Tucker; Olson, Kristina R.; Chugh, Dolly; Greenwald, Anthony G.; & Banaji, Mahzarin R. (2007). Pervasiveness and correlates of implicit attitudes and stereotypes. *European Review of Social Psychology, 18,* 36–88.

Nosofsky, Robert M., & Zaki, Safa R. (2002). Exemplar and prototype models revisited: Response strategies, selective attention, and stimulus generalization. *Journal of Experimental Psychology: Learning, Memory, and Cognition, 28,* 924–940.

Nosofsky, Robert M.; Little, Daniel R.; Donkin, Christopher; & Fific, Mario. (2011). Short-term memory scanning viewed as exemplar-based categorization. *Psychological Review, 118,* 280–315.

Novella, Steven. (2015, February 27). What color is this dress? It's an optical illusion. Retrieved on March 27, 2015, from http://theness.com/neurologicablog/index.php/what-color-is-this-dress-its-an-optical-illusion

Novick, Laura R., & Bassok, Miriam. (2005). Problem solving. In Keith J. Holyoak & Robert G. Morrison (Eds.), *The Cambridge handbook of thinking and reasoning.* New York, NY: Cambridge University Press.

Nowinski, Chris. (2013, February 1). Hit parade: The future of the sports concussion crisis. *Cerebrum.* Accessed April 8, 2014, from http://www.dana.org/Cerebrum/2013/Hit_Parade__The_Future_of_the_Sports_Concussion_Crisis

Nowlan, Jamie S.; Wuthrich, Viviana M.; & Rapee, Ronald M. (2015). Positive reappraisal in older adults: A systematic literature review. *Aging & Mental Health, 19,* 475–484. doi:10.1080/13607863.2014.954528

Nummenmaa, Lauri; Glereana, Enrico; Hari, Riitta; & Hietanend, Jari K. (2014). Bodily maps of emotions. *Proceedings of the National Academy of Sciences, 111,* 646–651. doi:10.1073/pnas.1321664111

Nurnberger, John I. (2009, June). New hope for pharmacogenetic testing. *American Journal of Psychiatry, 166*(6), 635–638.

Nutt, David J.; King, Leslie A; & Phillips, Lawrence D. (2010). Drug harms in the UK: A multicriteria decision analysis. *Lancet, 376,* 1558–1565. doi:10.1016/S0140-6736(10)61462-6

Nyhan, Brendan, & Reifler, Jason. (2015). Does correcting myths about the flu vaccine work? An experimental evaluation of the effects of corrective information. *Vaccine, 33,* 459–464. doi:10.1016/j.vaccine.2014.11.017

O Magazine. (2005, December). Oprah talks to Jamie Foxx. Oprah.com. Retrieved February 17, 2014, from http://www.oprah.com/omagazine/Oprahs-Interview-with-Jamie-Foxx/1

O'Brien, Mary P.; Miklowitz, David J.; Candan, Kristin A.; Marshall, Catherine; Domingues, Isabel; Walsh, Barbara C.; Zinberg, Jamie L.; & others. (2014). A randomized trial of family focused therapy with populations at clinical high risk for psychosis: Effects on interactional behavior. *Journal of Consulting and Clinical Psychology.* Advance online publication. doi:10.1037/a0034667

O'Conor, Andi. (2011, March 2). Quoted in Caroline H. Dworkin, A Colorado blogger on losing her home to a fire. *New York Times.* Retrieved on July 22, 2011, from http://www.nytimes.com/2011/03/03/garden/03qna.html

O'Connor, Akira R., & Moulin, Christopher J. A. (2006). Normal patterns of déjà experience in a healthy, blind male: Challenging optical pathway delay theory. *Brain and Cognition, 62,* 246–249.

O'Connor, Cliodhna, & Joffe, Helene. (2014) Gender on the brain: A case study of science communication in the new media environment. *PLOS ONE, 9,* e110830. doi:10.1371/journal.pone.0110830

O'Connor, Daryl B.; Jones, Fiona; Conner, Mark; McMillan, Brian; & Ferguson, Eamonn. (2008). Effects of daily hassles and eating style on eating behavior. *Health Psychology, 27*(1), S20–S31.

O'Connor, Daryl B., & Shimizu, Mikiko. (2002). Sense of personal control, stress and coping style: A cross-cultural study. *Stress and Health, 18,* 173–183.

O'Craven, Kathleen M., & Kanwisher, Nancy. (2000). Mental imagery of faces and places activates corresponding stimulus-specific brain regions. *Journal of Cognitive Neuroscience, 12,* 1013–1023.

O'Donnell, Stephanie O.; Webb, Jonathan K.; & Shine, Richard. (2010) Conditioned taste aversion enhances the survival of an endangered predator imperilled by a toxic invader. *Journal of Applied Ecology, 47,* 558–565. doi:10.1111/j.1365-2664.2010.01802.x

Odgers, Candace, & Jaffee, Sara. (2013). Routine versus catastrophic influences on the developing child. *Annual Review of Public Health, 34*(1), 29–48. doi:10.1146/annurev-publhealth-031912-114447

O'Donoghue, Gerard. (2013). Cochlear implants—Science, serendipity, and success. *New England Journal of Medicine, 369,* 1190–1193. doi:10.1056/NEJMp1310111

O'Donohue, William T., & Fisher, Jane E. (2009). *Cognitive behavior therapy: Applying empirically supported techniques in your practice* (2nd ed.). Hoboken, NJ: Wiley.

O'Roark, Ann M. (2007). The best of consulting psychology 1900–2000: Insider perspectives. *Consulting Psychology Journal: Practice and Research, 59,* 189–202.

Oakley, David A., & Halligan, Peter W. (2013). Hypnotic suggestion: Opportunities for cognitive neuroscience. *Nature Reviews Neuroscience, 14,* 565–576.

Oas, Peter T. (2010). Current status on corporal punishment with children: What the literature says. *American Journal of Family Therapy, 38*(5), 413–420.

Oberman, Lindsay M., & Ramachandran, Vilayanur S. (2007). The simulating social mind: The role of the mirror neuron system and simulation in the social and communicative deficits of autism spectrum disorders. *Psychological Bulletin, 133,* 310–327.

Occupational Outlook Handbook. (2008–2009) Psychologists. Retrieved on September 23, 2008, from http://www.bls.gov/oco/ocos056.htm:outlook,

Ocklenburg, Sebastian, & Güntürkün, Onur. (2012). Hemispheric asymmetries: The comparative view. *Frontiers in Psychology, 3,* 1–9. doi:10.3389/fpsyg.2012.00005

Oehen, Peter; Traber, Rafael; Widmer, Verena; & Schnyder, Ulrich (2013). A randomized, controlled pilot study of MDMA (±3,4-Methylenedioxymethamphetamine)-assisted psychotherapy for treatment of resistant, chronic post-traumatic stress disorder (PTSD). *Journal of Psychopharmacology, 27*(1), 40–52. doi:10.1177/0269881112464827

Ogbu, John U. (1986). The consequences of the American caste system. In Ulric Neisser (Ed.), *The school achievement of minority children: New perspectives.* Hillsdale, NJ: Erlbaum.

Ogbu, John U. (2008). *Minority status, oppositional culture, and schooling: Sociocultural, political, and historical studies in education.* New York, NY: Routledge.

Oh, G., & Petronis, A. (2008). Environmental studies of schizophrenia through the prism of epigenetics. *Schizophrenia Bulletin, 34*(6), 1122–1129. doi:10.1093/schbul/sbn105

Ohayon, Maurice M.; Carskadon, Mary A.; Guilleminault, Christian; & Vitiello, Michael V. (2004). Meta-analysis of quantitative sleep parameters from childhood to old age in healthy individuals: Developing normative sleep values across the human lifespan. *Sleep, 27*, 1255–1273.

Ohlsson, Stellan. (2010). *Deep learning: How the mind overrides experience.* New York, NY: Cambridge University Press.

Öhman, Arne. (2009). Of snakes and faces: An evolutionary perspective on the psychology of fear. *Scandinavian Journal of Psychology, 50*(6), 543–552. doi:10.1111/j.1467-9450.2009.00784.x

Öhman, Arne; Carlsson, Katrina; & Lundqvist, Daniel. (2007). On the unconscious subcortical origin of human fear. *Physiology & Behavior, 92*, 180–185.

Öhman, Arne, & Mineka, Susan. (2001). Fear, phobias, and preparedness: Toward an evolved module of fear and fear learning. *Psychological Review, 108*, 483–522.

Öhman, Arne, & Mineka, Susan. (2003). The malicious serpent: Snakes as a prototypical stimulus for an evolved module of fear. *Current Directions in Psychological Science, 12*, 5–9.

ojalehto, bethany l., & Medin, Douglas L. (2015). Perspectives on culture and concepts. *Annual Review of Psychology, 66*, 249–275. doi:10.1146/annurev-psych-010814-015120

Okonofua, Jason A., & Eberhardt, Jennifer L. (2015). Two strikes: Race and the disciplining of young students. *Psychological Science, 26*, 617–624. doi:10.1177/0956797615570365

Olabi, B.; Ellison-Wright, I.; McIntosh, A. M.; Wood, S. J.; Bullmore, E.; & Lawrie, S. M. (2011). Are there progressive brain changes in schizophrenia? A meta-analysis of structural magnetic resonance imaging studies. *Biological Psychiatry, 70*(1), 88–96. doi:10.1016/j.biopsych.2011.01.032

Olff, Miranda; Frijling, Jessie L.; Kubzansky, Laura D.; Bradley, Bekh; Ellenbogen, Mark A.; Cardoso, Christopher; Bartz, Jennifer A.; Yee, Jason R.; van Zuiden, Mirjam. (2013). The role of oxytocin in social bonding, stress regulation and mental health: An update on the moderating effects of context and interindividual differences. *Psychoneuroendocrinology, 38*, 1883–94. doi:10.1016/j.psyneuen.2013.06.019

Olff, Miranda; Langeland, Willie; & Draijer, Nel. (2007, March). Gender differences in posttraumatic stress disorder. *Psychological Bulletin, 133*(2), 183–204.

Olfson, Mark, & Marcus, Steven C. (2009). National patterns in antidepressant medication treatment. *Archives of General Psychiatry. 66*, 848–856. doi:10.1001/archgenpsychiatry.2009.81

Olivola, Christopher Y., & Todorov, Alexander. (2010). Fooled by first impressions? Reexamining the diagnostic value of appearance-based inferences. *Journal of Experimental Social Psychology, 46*(2), 315–324. doi:10.1016/j.jesp.2009.12.002

Öllinger, Michael; Jones, Gary; & Knoblich, Günther. (2008). Investigating the effect of mental set on insight problem solving. *Experimental Psychology, 55*, 269–282.

Olszweski, Pawel K.; Schiöth, Helgi B.; & Levine, Allen S. (2008). Ghrelin in the CNS: From hunger to a rewarding and memorable meal? *Brain Research Reviews, 58*, 160–170.

Olthof, Tjeert; Rieffe, Carolien; Terwogt, Mark M.; Lalay-Cederburg, Cindy; Reijntjes, Albert; & Hagenaar, Janneke. (2008). The assignment of moral status: Age-related differences in the use of three mental capacity criteria. *British Journal of Developmental Psychology, 26*(2), 233–247.

Oltmanns, Thomas F., & Balsis, Steve. (2011). Personality disorders in later life: Questions about the measurement, course, and impact of disorders. *Annual Review of Clinical Psychology, 7*, 321–349. doi:10.1146/annurev-clinpsy-090310-120435

Olton, David S. (1992). Tolman's cognitive analysis: Predecessors of current approaches in psychology. *Journal of Experimental Psychology: General, 121*, 427–428.

Ong, Anthony D.; Fuller-Rowell, Thomas; & Burrow, Anthony L. (2009). Racial discrimination and the stress process. *Journal of Personality and Social Psychology, 96*, 1259–1271.

Opriş, David; Pintea, Sebastian; García-Palacios, Azucena; Botella, Cristina; Szamosközi, Ştegan; & David, Daniel. (2012). Virtual reality exposure therapy in anxiety disorders: A quantitative meta-analysis. *Depression and Anxiety, 29*(2), 85-93.

Orne, Martin T., & Holland, Charles H. (1968). On the ecological validity of laboratory deceptions. *International Journal of Psychiatry, 6*, 282–293.

Ornish, Dean; Lin, Jue; Daubenmier, Jennifer; Weidner, Gerdi; Eppel, Elissa; Kemp, Colleen; Magbanua, Mark Jesus M.; & others. (2008). Increased telomerase activity and comprehensive lifestyle changes: A pilot study. *Lancet Oncology, 9*, 1048–1057.

Ostrov, Jamie M., & Godleski, Stephanie A. (2010). Toward an integrated gender-linked model of aggression subtypes in early and middle childhood. *Psychological Review, 117*(1), 233–242. doi:10.1037/a0018070

Owe, Elinor; Vignoles, Vivian L.; Becker, Maja; Brown, Rupert; Smith, Peter B.; Lee, Spike W. S.; . . . Jalal, Baland. (2013). Contextualism as an important facet of individualism-collectivism: Personhood beliefs across 37 national groups. *Journal of Cross-Cultural Psychology, 44*(1), 24–45. doi:10.1177/0022022111430255

Owen, Adrian M.; Coleman, Martin R.; Boly, Melanie; Davis, Matthew H.; Laureys, Steven; Pickard, John D. (2006). Detecting awareness in the vegetative state. *Science, 313*, 1402. doi:10.1126/science.1130197

Owen, Jesse J., & Fincham, Frank. (2010). Young adults' emotional reactions after hooking up encounters. *Archives of Sexual Behavior*, pp. 1–10. doi:10.1007/s10508-010-9652-x

Owen, Jesse J.; Rhoades, G. K.; Stanley, S. M.; & Fincham, F. D. (2010). Hooking up among college students: Demographic and psychosocial correlates. *Archives of Sexual Behavior, 39*(3), 653–663.

Oyserman, Daphna; Bybee, Deborah; Terry, Kathy; & Hart-Johnson, Tamera. (2004). Possible selves as roadmaps. *Journal of Research in Personality, 38*, 130–149.

Oyserman, Daphna; Destin, Mesmin; & Novin, Sheida. (2015). The context-sensitive future self: Possible selves motivate in context, not otherwise. *Self and Identity, 14*, 173–188. doi:10.1080/15298868.2014.965733

Oyserman, Daphna, & James, Leah. (2011). Possible Identities. In Seth J. Schwartz, Koen Luyckx, & Vivian L. Vignoles (Eds.), *Handbook of Identity Theory and Research* (pp. 117–145). New York, NY: Springer.

Ozer, Elizabeth M., & Bandura, Albert. (1990). Mechanisms governing empowerment effects: A self-efficacy analysis. *Journal of Personality and Social Psychology, 58*, 472–486.

Ozer, Emily J.; Best, Suzanne R.; Lipsey, Tami L.; & Weiss, Daniel S. (2003). Predictors of posttraumatic stress disorder and symptoms in adults: A meta-analysis. *Psychological Bulletin, 129*, 52–73.

Ozkan, Kerem, & Braunstein, Myron L. (2010). Background surface and horizon effects in the perception of relative size and distance. *Visual Cognition, 18*(2), 229–254.

Pace-Schott, Edward F. (2005). The neurobiology of dreaming. In Meir H. Kryger, Thomas Roth, & William C. Dement (Eds.), *Principles and practice of sleep medicine* (4th ed.). Philadelphia, PA: Elsevier Saunders.

Pace-Schott, Edward F.; Germain, Anne; & Milad, Mohammed R. (2015, April 20). Effects of sleep on memory for conditioned fear and fear extinction. *Psychological Bulletin, 141*, 835–857. doi:10.1037/bul0000014

Packer, Dominic J. (2008a). Identifying systematic disobedience in Milgram's obedience experiments: A meta-analytic review. *Perspectives on Psychological Science, 3*(4), 301–304.

Packer, Dominic J. (2008b). On being both with us and against us: A normative conflict model of dissent in social groups. *Personality and Social Psychology Review, 12*(1), 50–72.

Pagel, Mark. (2009). Natural selection 150 years on. *Nature, 457*, 808–811.

Paik, Se-Bum, & Ringach, Dario L. (2011). Retinal origin of orientation maps in visual cortex. *Nature Neuroscience, 14*, 919–925. doi:10.1038/nn.2824

Paivio, Allan. (1986). *Mental representations: A dual coding approach.* New York, NY: Oxford University Press.

Paivio, Allan. (2007). *Mind and its evolution: A dual coding theoretical approach.* Mahwah, NJ: Erlbaum.

Palit, Shreela; Kerr, Kara L.; Kuhn, Bethany L.; Terry, Ellen L.; DelVentura, Jennifer L.; Bartley, Emily J.; Shadlow, Joanna O.; & Rhudy, Jamie L. (2013). Exploring pain processing differences in Native Americans. *Health Psychology, 32,* 1127–1136. doi: 10.1037/a0031057

Palmer, John. (2003). ESP in the ganzfeld: Analysis of a debate. *Journal of Consciousness Studies, 10,* 51–58.

Palmer, Stephen E. (2002). Perceptual grouping: It's later than you think. *Current Directions in Psychological Science, 11,* 101–106.

Palmiero, Massimiliano; Olivetti Belardinelli, Marta; Nardo, DAvide; Sestieri, Carlo; Di Matteo, Rosalia; D'Ausilio, Alessandro; & Romani, G. L. (2009). Mental imagery generation in different modalities activates sensory-motor areas. *Cognitive Processing, 10,* 268–271.

Palomares, Nicholas A. (2009). Women are sort of more tentative than men, aren't they? How men and women use tentative language differently, similarly, and counterstereotypically as a function of gender salience. *Communication Research, 36*(4), 538–560.

Paluck, Elizabeth Levy, & Green, Donald P. (2009). Prejudice reduction: What works? A review and assessment of research and practice. *Annual Review of Psychology, 60,* 339–367. doi:10.1146/annurev.psych.60.110707.163607

Panksepp, Jaak. (2000). The riddle of laughter: Neural and psycho-evolutionary underpinnings of joy. *Psychological Science, 9,* 183–186.

Panksepp, Jaak. (2007). Neuroevolutionary sources of laughter and social joy: Modeling primal human laughter in laboratory rats. *Behavioural Brain Research, 182,* 231–244.

Parents Television Council. (2007). *Dying to entertain: Violence on primetime broadcast television 1998-2006.* Los Angeles, CA: Parents Television Council.

Pargament, Kenneth I., & Cummings, Jeremy. (2010). Anchored by faith: Religion as a resilience factor. In John W. Reich, Alex J. Zautra; & John Stuart Hall (Eds.), *Handbook of adult resilience.* New York, NY: Guilford.

Parish, Amy R., & de Waal, Frans B. M. (2000). The other "closest living relative": How bonobos (*Pan paniscus*) challenge traditional assumptions about females, dominance, intra- and intersexual interactions, and hominid evolution. In Dori LeCroy & Peter Moller, (Eds.), *Evolutionary perspectives on human reproductive behavior. Annals of the New York Academy of Sciences, vol. 907.* New York, NY: New York Academy of Sciences.

Park, Crystal L.; Armeli, Stephen; & Tennen, Howard. (2004). Appraisal-coping goodness of fit: A daily Internet study. *Personality and Social Psychology Bulletin, 30,* 558–569.

Park, Denise C., & Huang, Chih-mao. (2010). Culture wires the brain: A cognitive neuroscience perspective. *Perspectives on Psychological Science, 5,* 391–400.

Park, Hae-Jeong, & Friston, Karl. (2013). Structural and functional brain networks: From connections to cognition. *Science, 342,* 1238411. doi:10.1126/science.1238411

Park, S. (2010). The face of the Asian American male client: A clinician's assessment. In William Ming Liu, Derek Kenji Iwamoto, & Mark H. Chae (Eds.), *Culturally responsive counseling with Asian American men.* New York, NY: Routledge/Taylor & Francis Group.

Parker, Andrew J. (2007). Binocular depth perception and the cerebral cortex. *Nature Reviews Neuroscience, 8,* 379–391.

Parker, Stephen C. J.; Hansen, Loren; Abaan, Hatice Ozel; Tullius, Thomas D.; & Margulies, Elliott H. (2009). Local DNA topography correlates with functional noncoding regions of the human genome. *Science, 324,* 389–392.

Parks-Stamm, Elizabeth J.; Gollwitzer, Peter M.; & Oettingen, Gabriele. (2007). Action control by implementation intentions: Effective cue detection and efficient response initiation. *Social Cognition, 25,* 248–266.

Parsons, Dee. (2007, February 21). World of magnets: Magnetic bracelets therapy: Natural pain relief magnet products for arthritis, back pain treatments, fibromyalgia treatment. Retrieved June 22, 2009, from http://www.worldofmagnets.co.uk/

Partonen, Timo, & Pandi-Perumal, S. R. (2010). *Seasonal affective disorder: Practice and research.* New York, NY: Oxford University Press.

Pascalis, Olivier, & Kelly, David J. (2009). The origins of face processing in humans: Phylogeny and ontogeny. *Perspectives on Psychological Science, 4*(2), 200–209.

Pascual-Leone, Alvaro; Amedi, Amir; Fregni, Felipe; & Merabet, Lotfi B. (2005). The plastic human cortex. *Annual Review of Neuroscience, 28,* 377–401.

Patihis, Lawrence; Ho, Lavina Y.; Tingen, Ian W.; Lilienfeld, Scott O.; & Loftus, Elizabeth F. (2014). Are the "memory wars" over? A scientist-practitioner gap in beliefs about repressed memory. *Psychological Science, 25,* 519–530.

Patrick, Christopher J. (2007). Antisocial personality disorder and psychopathy. In William T. O'Donohue, Kevin A. Fowler, & Scott O. Lilienfeld (Eds.), *Personality disorders: Toward the DSM-V* (pp. 109–166). Thousand Oaks, CA: Sage.

Patterson, Charlotte J. (2006). Children of gay and lesbian parents. *Current Directions in Psychological Science, 15,* 241–244.

Patterson, Charlotte J. (2008). Sexual orientation across the life span: Introduction to the special section. *Developmental Psychology, 44,* 1–4.

Paul, Diane B., & Blumenthal, Arthur L. (1989). On the trail of Little Albert. *The Psychological Record, 39,* 547–553.

Paulozzi, Len J. (2008). Recent changes in drug poisoning mortality in the United States by urban-rural status and by drug type. *Pharmacoepidemiology Drug Safety, 17,* 997–1005.

Paulozzi, Len J., & Annest, Joseph L. (2007). U.S. data show sharply rising drug-induced death rates. *Injury Prevention, 13,* 130–132, 167.

Paunio, Tiina. (2012). Sleep modifies metabolism. *Sleep: Journal of Sleep and Sleep Disorders Research, 35,* 589–590.

Pavelko, Rachelle L., & Myrick, Jessica Gail. (2015). That's so OCD: The effects of disease trivialization via social media on user perceptions and impression formation. *Computers in Human Behavior, 49,* 251–258.

Pavlov, Ivan. (1904/1965). On conditioned reflexes. In Richard J. Herrnstein & Edwin G. Boring (Eds.), *A source book in the history of psychology.* Cambridge, MA: Harvard University Press.

Pavlov, Ivan. (1927/1960). *Conditioned reflexes: An investigation of the physiological activity of the cerebral cortex* (G. V. Anrep, Trans.). New York, NY: Dover Books. Retrieved in May 25, 2001, from http://psychclassics.yorku.ca/Pavlov/index.htm

Pavlov, Ivan. (1928). *Lectures on conditioned reflexes.* New York, NY: International Publishers.

Payne, Laura A.; Ellard, Kristen K.; Farchione, T. J.; Fairholme, Christopher P.; & Barlow, David H. (2014). Emotional disorders: A unified transdiagnostic protocol. In David H. Barlow (Ed.), *Clinical handbook of psychological disorders* (5th ed.). New York, NY: Guilford Press.

Payton, Jack R. (1992, May 16). The sad legacy of Japan's outcasts. *Chicago Tribune,* Sect. 1, p. 21.

Paz-y-Miño, C. Guillermo; Bond, Alan B.; Kamil, Alan C. & Balda, Russell P. (2004). Pinyon jays use transitive inference to predict social dominance. *Nature 430,* 778–781.

Peck, Adam. (2011). Ursula Burns shares her views on leadership. *MIT Sloan Blog Archive.* Retrieved from http://mitsloanblog.typepad.com/mba2012/2011/03/ursula-burns-shares-her-views-on-leadership.html

Pedersen, Anette Fischer; Bovbjerg, Dana Howard; & Zachariae, Robert. (2011). Stress and susceptibility to infectious disease. In Richard J. Contrada & Andrew Baum (Eds.), *The handbook of stress science: Biology, psychology, and health.* New York, NY: Springer.

Pedersen, Anette Fischer; Zachariae, Robert; & Bovbjerg, Dana Howard. (2009). Psychological stress and antibody response to influenza vaccination: A meta-analysis. *Brain, Behavior, and Immunity, 23*(4), 427–433.

Pedersen, Paul B.; Crethar, Hugh C.; & Carlson, Jon. (2008). Defining inclusive cultural empathy. In Paul B. Pedersen, Hugh C. Crethar, & Jon Carlson (Eds.), *Inclusive cultural empathy: Making relationships central in counseling and psychotherapy* (pp. 41–44). Washington, DC: American Psychological Association.

Pedersen, William; Putcha-Bhagavatula, Anila; & Miller, Lynn. (2010). Are men and women really that different? Examining some of Sexual Strategies Theory (SST)'s key assumptions about sex-distinct mating mechanisms. *Sex Roles*, 1–15. doi:10.1007/s11199-010-9811-5

Pedersen, William C.; Vasquez, Eduardo A.; Bartholow, Bruce D.; Grosvenor, Marianne; & Truong, Ana. (2014). Are you insulting me? Exposure to alcohol primes increases aggression following ambiguous provocation. *Personality and Social Psychology Bulletin, 40,* 1037–1049. doi:10.1177/0146167214534993

Pemment, Jack. (2013). Psychopathy versus sociopathy: Why the distinction has become crucial. *Aggression and Violent Behavior, 18*(5), 458–461.

Pepperberg, Irene M. (1993). Cognition and communication in an African gray parrot (*Psittacus erithacus*): Studies on a nonhuman, non-primate, nonmammalian subject. In Herbert L. Roitblat, Louis M. Herman, & Paul E. Nachtigall (Eds.), *Language and communication: Comparative perspectives.* Hillsdale, NJ: Erlbaum.

Pepperberg, Irene M. (2000). *The Alex studies: Cognitive and communicative abilities of gray parrots.* Cambridge, MA: Harvard University Press.

Pepperberg, Irene M. (2007). Grey parrots do not always "parrot": The roles of imitation and phonological awareness in the creation of new labels from existing vocalizations. *Language Sciences, 29,* 1–13.

Perdue, Bonnie M.; Snyder, Rebecca J.; Pratte, Jason; Marr, M. Jackson; & Maple, Terry L. (2009). Spatial memory recall in the giant panda (Ailuropoda melanoleuca). *Journal of Comparative Psychology, 123,* 275–279. doi:10.1037/a0016220

Perdue, Bonnie M.; Snyder, Rebecca J.; Wilson, Megan L.; & Maple, Terry L. (2013). Giant panda welfare in captivity. *Journal of Applied Animal Welfare Science, 16,* 394–395. doi:10.1080/10888705.2013.827944

Pereira, Ana C.; Huddleston, Dan H.; Brickman, Adam M.; Sosunov, Alexander A.; Hene, Rene; McKhann, Guy M.; Sloan, Richard; Gage, Fred H.; Brown, Truman R.; & Small, Scott A. (2007). An *in vivo* correlate of exercise-induced neurogenesis in the adult dentate gyrus. *Proceedings of the National Academy of Sciences, 104,* 5638–5643.

Perkins, Tom; Stokes, Mark; McGillivray, Jane; & Bittar, Richard. (2010). Mirror neuron dysfunction in autism spectrum disorders. *Journal of Clinical Neurosciences, 17*(10), 1239–1243. doi:S0967-5868(10)00177-3 [pii]

Perlis, Michael L.; Smith, Michael T.; & Pigeon, Wilfred R. (2005). Etiology and pathophysiology of insomnia. In Meir H. Kryger, Thomas Roth, & William C. Dement (Eds.), *Principles and practice of sleep medicine* (4th ed.). Philadelphia, PA: Elsevier Saunders.

Perrett, David I. (2010). *In your face: The new science of human attraction.* New York, NY: Palgrave Macmillan.

Perret-Clermont, Anne-Nelly, & Barrelet, Jean-Marc. (2008). *Jean Piaget and Neuchatel: The learner and the scholar.* New York, NY: Psychology Press.

Perrin, Ellen C.; Siegel, Benjamin S.; and the Committee on Psychological Aspects of Child and Family Health. (2013). Promoting the well-being of children whose parents are gay or lesbian. *Pediatrics, 131*(4), e1374–e1383.

Perry, Gina. (2013). *Behind the shock machine: The untold story of the notorious Milgram psychology experiment.* Melbourne, Australia: Scribe.

Perry, Jennifer L., & Dess, Nancy K. (2012). Laboratory animal research ethics: A practical, educational approach. In Samuel J. Knapp, Michael C. Gottlieb, Mitchell M. Handelsman, Leon D. VandeCreek (Eds.), *APA handbook of ethics in psychology, Vol. 2: Practice, teaching, and research.* Washington, DC: American Psychological Association. doi:10.1037/13272-020

Perry, Katy; Gottwald, Lukasz; Martin, Max; & McKee, Bonnie. On *Teenage Dream* [CD] Vol. 2010. New York, NY: Capitol Records. (2011). "Last Friday night (T.G.I.F.)" [Recorded by K. Perry]

Perry, Lynn K.; Smith, Linda B.; & Hockema, Stephen A. (2008). Representational momentum and children's sensori-motor representations of objects. *Developmental Science, 11*(3), F17–F23.

Pervin, Lawrence A. (1994). A critical analysis of current trait theory. *Psychological Inquiry, 5,* 103–113.

Pesant, Nicholas, & Zadra, Antonio. (2004). Working with dreams in therapy: What do we know and what should we do? *Clinical Psychology Review, 24,* 489–512.

Pescosolido, Bernice, A.; Medina, Tait R.; Martin, Jack K.; & Long, J. S. (2013). The "backbone" of stigma: Identifying the global core of public prejudice associated with mental illness. *American Journal of Public Health.* Advance online publication. doi:10.2105/AJPH.2012.301147

Pessoa, Luiz, & Adolphs, Ralph. (2010). Emotion processing and the amygdala: From a 'low road' to 'many roads' of evaluating biological significance. *Nature Reviews Neuroscience, 11,* 773–782.

Petersen, Jennifer L., & Hyde, Janet S. (2010). A meta-analytic review of research on gender differences in sexuality, 1993–2007. *Psychological Bulletin, 136*(1), 21–38.

Petersen, Michael B.; Sznycer, Daniel; Cosmides, Leda; & Tooby, John. (2012). Who deserves help? Evolutionary psychology, social emotions, and public opinion about welfare: Who deserves help? *Political Psychology, 33*(3), 395–418. doi:10.1111/j.1467-9221.2012.00883.x

Petersen, Ronald C. (2002). *Mayo Clinic on Alzheimer's disease.* Rochester, MN: Mayo Clinic Press.

Peterson, Christopher. (2006). *A primer in positive psychology.* New York, NY: Oxford University Press.

Peterson, Christopher, & Steen, Tracy A. (2009). Optimistic explanatory style. In Shane J. Lopez & C. R. Snyder (Eds.). *Oxford handbook of positive psychology* (2nd ed.). New York, NY: Oxford University Press.

Peterson, Jillian K.; Skeem, Jennifer; Kennealy, Patrick; Bray, Beth; & Zvonkovic, Andrea. (2014). How often and how consistently do symptoms directly precede criminal behavior among offenders with mental illness? *Law and Human Behavior, 38,* 439–449. doi:10.1037/lhb0000075

Peterson, Lloyd R., & Peterson, Margaret J. (1959). Short-term retention of individual items. *Journal of Experimental Psychology, 58,* 193–198.

Petitto, Laura Ann; Holowka, Siobhan; Sergio, Lauren E.; Levy, Bronna; & Ostry, David J. (2004). Baby hands that move to the rhythm of language: Hearing babies acquiring sign languages babble silently on the hands. *Cognition, 93,* 43–73.

Petitto, Laura Ann; Holowka, Siobhan; Sergio, Lauren E.; & Ostry, David. (2001). Language rhythms in baby hand movements. *Nature, 413,* 35–36.

Petitto, Laura Ann, & Marentette, Paula F. (1991). Babbling in the manual mode: Evidence for the ontogeny of language. *Science, 251,* 1493–1496.

Petrovic, Pedrag. (2010). Placebo analgesia and the brain. In Morten L. Kringelbach & Kent C. Berridge (Eds.), *Pleasures of the brain.* New York, NY: Oxford University Press.

Petrovic, Predrag; Kalso, Eija; Petersson, Karl Magnus; & Ingvar, Martin. (2002, March 1). Placebo and opioid analgesia—Imaging a shared neuronal network. *Science, 295,* 1737–1740.

Peyrot des Gachons, Catherine; Beauchamp, Gary K.; Stern, Robert M.; Koch, Kenneth L.; & Breslin, Paul A. S. (2011). Bitter taste induces nausea. *Current Biology, 21*(7), R247–R248.

Phelan, Julie E., & Rudman, Laurie A. (2010). Reactions to ethnic deviance: The role of backlash in racial stereotype maintenance. *Journal of Personality and Social Psychology, 99*(2), 265–281.

Phelps, Elizabeth A. (2006). Emotion and cognition: Insights from studies of the human amygdala. *Annual Review of Psychology, 57,* 27–53.

Phelps, Elizabeth A.; O'Connor, Kevin J.; Gatenby, J. Christopher; Gore, John C.; Grillon, Christian; & Davis, Michael. (2001). Activation of the left amygdala to a cognitive representation of fear. *Nature Neuroscience, 4,* 237–441.

Phillips, Deborah A., & Lowenstein, Amy E. (2011). Early care, education, and child development. *Annual Review of Psychology, 62,* 483–500.

Phillips, Michael. (1999). Problems with the polygraph. *Science, 15,* 413.

Phillips, Tommy M. (2008). Age-related differences in identity style: A cross-sectional analysis. *Current Psychology, 27*(3), 205–215.

Phillips, William L. (2011). Cross-cultural differences in visual perception of color, illusions, depth, and pictures. In K. D. Keith (Ed.), *Cross-cultural*

psychology: Contemporary themes and perspectives (pp. 160–180). Oxford, England: Wiley-Blackwell.

Piaget, Jean. (1952). *The origins of intelligence in children* (Margaret Cook, Trans.). New York, NY: International Universities Press.

Piaget, Jean. (1961). The genetic approach to the psychology of thought. *Journal of Educational Psychology, 52*(6), 275–281.

Piaget, Jean. (1971/1993). The epigenetic system and the development of cognitive functions. In Mark H. Johnson, Yuko Munakata, & Rick O. Gilmore (Eds.), *Brain development and cognition: A reader* (pp. 31–38). Malden, MA: Blackwell.

Piaget, Jean. (1972). Intellectual evolution from adolescence to adulthood. *Human Development, 15*, 1–12.

Piaget, Jean. (1973). The stages of cognitive development: Interview with Richard I. Evans. In Richard I. Evans (Ed.), *Jean Piaget: The man and his ideas.* New York, NY: Dutton.

Piaget, Jean, & Inhelder, Bärbel. (1974). *The child's construction of quantities: Conservation and atomism.* London, England: Routledge & Kegan Paul.

Piaget, Jean, & Inhelder, Bärbel. (1958). *The growth of logical thinking from childhood to adolescence: An essay on the construction of formal operational structures* (Anne Parsons & Stanley Milgram, Trans.). New York, NY: Basic Books.

Pica, Pierre; Lemer, Cathy; Izard, Veronique; & Dehaene, Stanislas. (2004, October 15). Exact and approximate arithmetic in an Amazonian indigene group. *Science, 306*, 499–503.

Pickren, Wade E., & Rutherford, Alexandra. (2010). *A history of modern psychology in context.* Hoboken, NJ: John Wiley.

Piernas, Carmen, & Popkin, Barry M. (2011). Increased portion sizes from energy-dense foods affect total energy intake at eating occasions in US children and adolescents: Patterns and trends by age group and sociodemographic characteristics, 1977–2006. *American Journal of Clinical Nutrition, 94,* 1324–1332.

Pike, Kathleen M., & Borovoy, Amy. (2004). The rise of eating disorders in Japan: Issues of culture and limitations of the model of "Westernization." *Culture, Medicine, and Psychiatry, 28*, 493–531. doi:10.1007/s11013-004-1066-6

Pincus, David, & Sheikh, Anees A. (2009). *Imagery for pain relief: A scientifically grounded guidebook for clinicians.* New York, NY: Routledge/Taylor & Francis Group.

Pinel, John P. J.; Assanand, Sunaina; & Lehman, Darrin R. (2000). Hunger, eating, and ill health. *American Psychologist, 55*, 1105–1116.

Pinheiro, A. P.; Raney, T. J.; Thornton, L. M.; Fichter, M. M.; Berrettini, W. H.; Goldman, D., . . . Bulik, C. M. (2010). Sexual functioning in women with eating disorders. *International Journal of Eating Disorders, 43*(2), 123–129. doi:10.1002/eat.20671

Pinker, Steven. (1994). *The language instinct: How the mind creates language.* New York, NY: Morrow.

Pinker, Steven. (1995). Introduction: Language. In Michael S. Gazzaniga (Ed.), *The cognitive neurosciences.* Cambridge, MA: MIT Press.

Pinker, Steven. (2007). *The stuff of thought: Language as a window into human nature.* New York, NY: Viking.

Pinker, Steven. (2015, February 28). Quoted in Matthew Herper, "Rock star psychologist Steven Pinker explains why #The Dress looked white not blue. Retrieved on March 27, 2015, from http://www.forbes.com/sites/matthewherper/2015/02/28/psychologist-and-author-stephen-pinker-explains-thedress

Pinna, Baingio, & Reeves, Adam. (2009). From perception to art: How vision creates meaning. *Spatial Vision, 22*(3), 225–272.

Piotrowski, Chris, & Armstrong, Terry. (2006). Current recruitment and selection practices: A national survey of Fortune 1000 firms. *North American Journal of Psychology, 8*, 489–496.

Piper, August; Lillevik, Linda; & Kritzer, Roxanne. (2008). What's wrong with believing in repression?: A review for legal professionals. *Psychology, Public Policy, and Law, 14*(3), 223–242.

Pitcher, David; Dilks, Daniel D.; Saxe, Rebecca R.; Triantafyllou, Christina; & Kanwisher, Nancy. (2011). Differential selectivity for dynamic versus static information in face-selective cortical regions. *NeuroImage, 15*(56), 2356–2363.

Pittenger, David J. (2005). Cautionary comments regarding the Myers- Briggs Type Indicator. *Consulting Psychology Journal: Practice and Research, 57*, 210–221.

Plaisier, I.; Beekman, A. T. F.; de Bruijn, J. G. M.; de Graaf, R.; ten Have, M.; Smit, J. H.; van Dyck, R.; & Penninx, B. W. J. H. (2008). The effect of social roles on mental health: A matter of quantity or quality? *Journal of Affective Disorders, 111*(2–3), 261–270.

Plant, E. Ashby, & Devine, Patricia G. (2009). The active control of prejudice: Unpacking the intentions guiding control efforts. *Journal of Personality and Social Psychology, 96*(3), 640–652. doi:10.1037/a0012960

Plassmann, Hilke; O'Doherty, John; Shiv, Baba; & Rangel, Antonio. (2008). Marketing actions can modulate neural representations of experienced pleasantness. *Proceedings of the National Academy of Sciences, 105,* 1050–1054.

Platek, Steven M.; Mohamed, Feroze B.; & Gallup, Gordon G., Jr. (2005). Contagious yawning and the brain. *Cognitive Brain Research, 23,* 448–452.

Plomin, Robert. (2003). General cognitive ability. In Robert Plomin, John C. DeFries, & Peter McGuffin (Eds.), *Behavioral genetics in the postgenomic era.* Washington, DC: American Psychological Association.

Plomin, Robert, & Colledge, Essi. (2001). Genetics and psychology: Beyond heritability. *European Psychologist, 6*, 229–240.

Plomin, Robert; DeFries, John C.; McClearn, Gerald E.; & McGuffin, Peter. (2001). *Behavioral genetics* (4th ed.). New York, NY: Worth.

Plomin, Robert; Owen, Michael J.; & McGuffin, Peter. (1994). The genetic basis of complex human behaviors. *Science, 264*, 1733–1739.

Plomin, Robert, & Spinath, Frank M. (2004). Intelligence: Genetics, genes, and genomics. *Journal of Personality and Social Psychology, 86*, 112–129.

Plötner, Maria; Over, Harriet; Carpenter, Malinda; & Tomasello, Michael. (2015). Young children show the bystander effect in helping situations. *Psychological Science, 26*, 499–506. doi:10.1177/0956797615569579

Plotnik, Joshua M.; Lair, Richard; Suphachoksahakun, Wirot; & de Waal, Frans B. M. (2011). Elephants know when they need a helping trunk in a cooperative task. *Proceedings of the National Academy of Sciences, 108*(12), 5116–5121. doi:10.1073/ pnas.1101765108

Pogue-Geile, Michael F., & Yokley, Jessica L. (2010). Current research on the genetic contributors to schizophrenia. *Current Directions in Psychological Science, 19*(4), 214–219.

Polito, Vince; Barnier, Amanda J.; Woody, Erik Z.; & Connors, Michael H. (2014). Measuring agency change across the domain of hypnosis. *Psychology of Consciousness: Theory, Research, and Practice, 1*, 3–19. doi:10.1037/ cns0000010

Polk, Thad A., & Newell, Allen. (1995). Deduction as verbal reasoning. *Psychological Review, 102*, 533–566.

Pope, Kenneth S.; Butcher, James N.; & Seelen, Joyce. (2006a). Assessing malingering and other aspects of credibility. In Kenneth S. Pope, James N. Butcher, & Joyce Seelen (Eds.), *The MMPI, MMPI-2, & MMPI-A in court: A practical guide for expert witnesses and attorneys* (3rd. ed., pp. 129–160); Washington, DC: American Psychological Association.

Pope, Kenneth S.; Keith-Spiegel, Patricia; & Tabachnick, Barbara G. (2006b). Sexual attraction to clients: The human therapist and the (sometimes) inhuman training system. *Training and Education in Professional Psychology, S*(2), 96–111.

Pope, Kenneth S., & Tabachnick, Barbara G. (1993). Therapists' anger, hate, fear, and sexual feelings: National survey of therapist responses, client characteristics, critical events, formal complaints, and training. *Professional Psychology: Research and Practice, 24*, 142–152.

Population Communications International. (2004). Telling stories, saving lives. Retrieved on September 5, 2004, from http://www.population.org/index.shtml.

Porter, Jess; Craven, Brent; Khan, Rehan M.; Chang, Shao-Ju; Kang, Irene; Judkewitz, Benjamin; Volpe, Jason; Settles, Gary; & Sobel, Noam. (2007). Mechanisms of scent-tracking in humans. *Nature Neuroscience, 10*, 27–29.

Portrat, Sophie; Barrouillet, Pierre; & Camos, Valérie. (2008). Time-related decay or interference-based forgetting in working memory? *Journal of Experimental Psychology: Learning, Memory, and Cognition, 34*, 1561–1564.

Pos, Alberta E.; Greenberg, Leslie S.; & Elliott, Robert. (2008). Experiential therapy. In Jay L. Lebow (Ed.), *Twenty-first century psychotherapies: Contemporary approaches to theory and practice* (pp. 80–122). Hoboken, NJ: Wiley.

Posner, Michael I., & Rothbart, Mary K. (2007) Research on attention networks as a model for the integration of psychological science. *Annual Review of Psychology, 58,* 1–23.

Possel, Patrick, & Winkeljohn Black, Stephanie. (2014). Testing three different sequential meditational interpretations of Beck's cognitive model of the development of depression. *Journal of Clinical Psychology, 70*(1), 72–94.

Post, Jerrold M. (2011). Crimes of obedience: 'Groupthink' at Abu Ghraib. *International Journal of Group Psychotherapy, 61*(1), 49–66.

Poulin-Dubois, Diane, & Serbin, Lisa A. (2006). La connaissance des catégories de genre et des stéréotypes sexués chez le jeune enfant. = Infants' knowledge about gender stereotypes and categories. *Enfance, 58*(3), 283–310.

Powell, Nelson B.; Riley, Robert W.; & Guilleminault, Christian. (2005). Surgical management of sleep-disordered breathing. In Meir H. Kryger, Thomas Roth, and William C. Dement (Eds.), *Principles and practice of sleep medicine* (4th ed.). Philadelphia, PA: Elsevier Saunders.

Powell, Russell A.; Digdon, Nancy; Harris, Ben; & Smithson, Christopher. (2014). Correcting the record on Watson, Rayner, and Little Albert: Albert Barger as "Psychology's Lost Boy." *American Psychologist, 69,* 600–611.

Powers, Mark B.; Halpern, Jacqueline M.; Ferenschak, Michael P.; Gillihan, Seth J.; Foa, Edna B. (2010). A meta-analytic review of prolonged exposure for posttraumatic stress disorder. *Clinical Psychology Review, 30,* 635–641. doi:10.1016/j.cpr.2010.04.007

Powers, Pauline M. (2009). Bulimia nervosa. In Robert E. Rakel & Edward T. Bope (Eds.), *Conn's current therapy 2009* (pp. 1115–1117). Philadelphia, PA: Saunders Elsevier.

Powley, Terry L. (2009). Hunger. In Gary G. Berntson, John T. Cacioppo (Eds.), *Handbook of neuroscience for the behavioral sciences* (Vol. 2, pp. 659–678) Hoboken, NJ: Wiley.

Pratto, Felicia, & Glasford, Demis E. (2008). Ethnocentrism and the value of a human life. *Journal of Personality and Social Psychology, 95,* 1411–1428.

Premack, David. (2007). Human and animal cognition: Continuity and discontinuity. *Proceedings of the National Academy of Sciences, 104,* 13861–13867. doi_10.1073_pnas.0706147104

Press Release Newswire, PRweb.com. (2007, January). Wonderlic announces release of revised Wonderlic Personnel Test (WPT-R): Update incorporates the latest advances in test development and scoring, accurately measuring intelligence and predicting success on the job. Libertyville, IL: Wonderlic.

Pressman, Mark R. (2007). Disorders of arousal from sleep and violent behavior: The role of physical contact and proximity. *Sleep, 30,* 1039–1047.

Pressman, Sarah D., & Cohen, Sheldon. (2005). Does positive affect influence health? *Psychological Bulletin, 131*(6), 925–971.

Pressman, Sarah; Gallagher, Mathew; & Lopez, Shane. (2013). Is the emotion-health connection a "first-world problem"? *Psychological Science, 24,* 544–549. doi:10.1177/0956797612457382

Preston, John D.; O'Neal, John H.; & Talaga, Mary C. (2008). *Handbook of clinical psychopharmacology for therapists* (5th ed.). Oakland, CA: New Harbinger.

Preti, George; Cutler, Winnifred B.; Garcia, C. R.; Huggins, G. R.; & Lawley, H. J. (1986). Human axillary secretions influence women's menstrual cycles: The role of donor extract of females. *Hormones and Behavior, 20,* 474–482.

Price, Donald D.; Finniss, Damien G.; & Benedetti, Fabrizio. (2008). A comprehensive review of the placebo effect: Recent advances and current thought. *Annual Review of Psychology, 59,* 565–590. doi:10.1146/annurev.psych.59.113006.095941

Prochaska, James O.; & Norcross, John C. (2014). *Systems of psychotherapy: A transtheoretical analysis* (8th ed.). Stamford, CT: Cengage Learning.

Prot, Sara; Gentile, Douglas A.; Anderson, Craig A.; Suzuki, Kanae; Swing, Edward; Ming Lim, Kam; ... Lam, Ben Chun Pan. Long-term relations among prosocial-media use, empathy, and prosocial behavior. *Psychological Science, 25,* 358–368. doi:10.1177/0956797613503854

Przybylski, Andrew K.; Deci, Edward L.; Rigby, C. Scott; & Ryan, Richard M. (2014). Competence-impeding electronic games and players' aggressive feelings, thoughts, and behaviors. *Journal of Personality and Social Psychology, 106,* 441–457. doi:10.1037/a0034820

Psaltis, Charis; Duveen, Gerard; & Perret-Clermont, Anne-Nelly. (2009). The social and the psychological: Structure and context in intellectual development. *Human Development, 52*(5), 291–312.

Puhl, Rebecca M.; & Peterson, Jamie Lee. (2014). The nature, consequences, and public health implications of obesity stigma. In Patrick W. Corrigan (Ed.), *The stigma of disease and disability: Understanding causes and overcoming injustices.* Washington, DC: American Psychological Association. doi:10.1037/14297-010

Pujol, Jesus; Soriano-Mas, Carles; Gispert, Juan D.; Bossa, Matias; Reig, Santiago; Ortiz, Hector; ... Olmos, Salvador. (2011). Variations in the shape of frontobasal brain region in obsessive-compulsive disorder. *Human Brain Mapping, 32,* 1100–1108.

Purcell, Shaun M.; Wray, Naomi R.; Stone, Jennifer L.; Visscher, Peter M.; O'Donovan, Michael C.; Sullivan, Patrick F.; & Sklar, Pamela. (2009). Common polygenic variation contributes to risk of schizophrenia and bipolar disorder. *Nature, 460,* 748–752.

Purkey, William Watson, & Stanley, Paula Helen. (2002). The self in psychotherapy. In David J. Cain & Julius Seeman (Eds.), *Humanistic psychotherapies: Handbook of research and practice.* Washington, DC: American Psychological Association.

Purves, Dale. (2009). Vision. In Gary G. Berntson & John T. Cacioppo (Eds.), *Handbook of neuroscience in the behavioral sciences.* Hoboken, NJ: Wiley.

Puterman, Eli; Lin, Jue; Blackburn, Elizabeth; O'Donovan, Aoife; Adler, Nancy; & Epel, Elissa. (2010). The power of exercise: Buffering the effect of chronic stress on telomere length. *PLOS ONE, 5,* e10837.

Puterman, Eli; Lin, Jue; Krauss, John; Blackburn, Elizabeth; & Epel, Elissa. (2015). Determinants of telomere attrition over 1 year in healthy older women: Stress and health behaviors matter. *Molecular Psychiatry, 20*(4), 529–535. doi:10.1038/mp.2014.70

Pyc, Mary A., & Rawson, Katherine A. (2010, October 15). Why testing improves memory: Mediator effectiveness hypothesis. *Science, 330,* 335. doi:10.1126/science.1191465

Qin, Ping. (2011). The impact of psychiatric illness on suicide: Differences by diagnosis of disorders and by sex and age of subjects. *Journal of Psychiatric Research, 45,* 1445–1452.

Quaglia, Jordan T.; Brown, Kirk Warren; Lindsay, Emily K.; Creswell, J. David; & Goodman, Robert J. (2015). From conceptualization to operationalization of mindfulness. In Kirk Warren Brown, J. David Creswell, & Richard M. Ryan (Eds.), *Handbook of mindfulness: Theory, research, and practice.* New York, NY: Guilford.

Queller, Sarah, & Mason, Winter. (2008). A decision bound categorization approach to the study of subtyping of atypical group members. *Social Cognition, 26*(1), 66–101.

Quenk, Naomi. L. (2009). *Essentials of Myers-Briggs type indicator assessment.* Hoboken, NJ: Wiley.

Quiles Marcos, Yolanda; Quiles Sebastián, María José; Pamies Aubalat, Lidia; Botella Ausina, Juan; & Treasure, Janet. (2013). Peer and family influence in eating disorders: A meta-analysis. *European Psychiatry, 28*(4), 199–206.

Quinn, Meghan E., & Joormann, Jutta. (2015). Stress-induced changes in executive control are associated with depression symptoms: Examining the role of rumination. *Clinical Psychological Science, 3,* 628–636. doi:10.1177/2167702614563930

Rabinowitz, Amanda R.; Li, Xiaoqi; & Levin, Harvey S. (2014). Sport and nonsport etiologies of mild traumatic brain injury: Similarities and differences. *Annual Review of Psychology, 65,* 301–331.

Raboteg-Saric, Zora, & Sakic, Marija. (2013). Relations of parenting styles and friendship quality to self-esteem, life satisfaction and happiness in adolescents. *Applied Research Quality Life, 9,* 749–765. doi:10.1007/s11482-013-9268-0

Raby, Caroline R.; Alexis, Dean M.; Dickinson, Anthony; & Clayton, Nicola S. (2007). Planning for the future by western scrub-jays. *Nature, 445,* 919–921. doi:10.1038/nature05575

Rachlin, Howard. (1974). Self-control. *Behaviorism, 2,* 94–107.

Rachlin, Howard. (2000). *The science of self-control.* Cambridge, MA: Harvard University Press.

Rado, Jeffrey, & Janicak, Philip G. (2009). Schizophrenia. In Robert E. Rakel & Edward T. Bope (Eds.), *Conn's current therapy 2009* (pp. 1128–1131). Philadelphia, PA: Saunders Elsevier.

Radulescu, Anca R.; & Mujica-Parodi, Lilianne R. (2013). Human gender differences in the perception of conspecific alarm chemosensory cues. *PLOS ONE, 8,* e68485. doi:10.1371/journal.pone.0068485

Rafaeli, E., Cranford, J. A., Green, A. S., Shrout, P. E.; & Bolger, N. (2008). The good and bad of relationships: How social hindrance and social support affect relationship feelings in daily life. *Personality and Social Psychology Bulletin, 34*(12), 1703–1718.

Rahe, Richard H. (1972). Subjects' recent life changes and their nearfuture illness reports. *Annals of Clinical Research, 4,* 250–265.

Rahim-Williams, Bridgett; Riley, Joseph L. III; Williams, Ameenah K. K.; & Fillingim, Roger B. (2012). A quantitative review of ethnic group differences in experimental pain response: Do biology, psychology, and culture matter? *Pain Medicine, 13,* 522–540. doi:10.1111/j.1526-4637.2012.01336.x

Raj, John Dilip; Nelson, John Abraham; & Rao, K. S. P. (2006). A study on the effects of some reinforcers to improve performance of employees in a retail industry. *Behavior Modification, 30,* 848–866.

Rakison, David H. (2009). Does women's greater fear of snakes and spiders originate in infancy? *Evolution and Human Behavior, 30,* 438–444. doi:10.1016/j.evolhumbehav.2009.06.002

Ramachandran, Vilayanur S. (1992a, May). Blind spots. *Scientific American, 266,* 86–91.

Ramachandran, Vilayanur S. (1992b). Filling in gaps in perception: Part 1. *Current Directions in Psychological Science, 1,* 199–205.

Rapoport, Judith L. (1989). *The boy who couldn't stop washing: The experience and treatment of obsessive-compulsive disorder.* New York, NY: Dutton.

Rapoport, Judith L.; Giedd, Jay N.; & Gogtay, Nitin. (2012). Neurodevelopmental model of schizophrenia: Update 2012. *Molecular Psychiatry, 17,* 1228–1238.

Raskin, Nathaniel J., & Rogers, Carl R. (2005). Person-centered therapy. In Raymond J. Corsini & Danny Wedding (Eds.), *Current psychotherapies* (7th ed., instr. ed., pp. 130–165). Belmont, CA: Thomson Brooks/Cole.

Rasmussen, Keith G. (2009). Evidence for electroconvulsive therapy efficacy in mood disorders. In Conrad M. Swartz (Ed.), *Electroconvulsive and neuromodulation therapies* (pp. 109–123). New York, NY: Cambridge University Press.

Ratiu, Peter, & Talos, Ion-Florin. (2004). The tale of Phineas Gage, digitally remastered. *New England Journal of Medicine, 351,* e21. doi:10.1056/NEJMicm031024

Rawson, Nancy E. (2006). Olfactory loss in aging. *Science of Aging Knowledge Environment, 5,* pe6., 106.

Raz, Amir. (2009) Varieties of attention: A research-magician's perspective. In G. Bernston & J. Cacioppo (Eds.), *Handbook of neuroscience for the behavioural sciences* (pp. 361–369). Hoboken, NJ: Wiley.

Reader, Simon M., & Biro, Dora. (2010). Experimental identification of social learning in wild animals. *Learning & Behavior, 38*(3), 265–283.

Reader, Simon M.; Kendal, Jeremy R.; & Laland, Kevin N. (2003). Social learning of foraging sites and escape routes in wild Trinidadian guppies. *Animal Behaviour, 66,* 729–739.

Recanzone, Gregg H.; & Sutter, Mitchell L. (2008). The biological basis of audition. *Annual Review of Psychology, 59,* 119–142.

Reddy, Leila; Tsuchiya, Naotsugu; & Serre, Thomas. (2010). Reading the mind's eye: Decoding category information during mental imagery. *Neuroimage, 50,* 818–825. doi:10.1016/j.neuroimage.2009.11.084

Reeder, Glenn D.; Monroe, Andrew E.; & Pryor, John B. (2008). Impressions of Milgram's obedient teachers. Situational cues inform inferences about motives and traits. *Journal of Personality and Social Psychology, 95,* 1–17.

Refinetti, Roberto. (2000). *Circadian physiology.* Boca Raton, FL: CRC Press.

Regan, David, & Gray, Rob. (2009). Binocular processing of motion: Some unresolved questions. *Spatial Vision, 22*(1), 1–43. doi:10.1163/156856809786618501

Regnerus, Mark. (2012). How different are the adult children of parents who have same-sex relationships? Findings from the New Family Structures Study. *Social Science Research, 41*(4), 752–770.

Rego, Arménio; Sousa, Filipa; Pina e Cunha, Miguel; Correia, Anabela; & Saur-Amaral, Irina. (2007). Leader self-reported emotional intelligence and perceived employee creativity: An exploratory study. *Creativity & Innovation Management, 16,* 250–264.

Rego, Simon A. (2009). Culture and anxiety disorders. In Sussie Eshun & Regan A. R. Gurung (Eds.), *Culture and mental health: Socio-cultural influences, theory, and practice* (pp. 197–220). West Sussex, England: Wiley-Blackwell.

Reiber, Chris, & Garcia, Justin R. (2010). Hooking up: Gender differences, evolution, and pluralistic ignorance. *Evolutionary Psychology 8*(3), 390–404.

Reicher, Stephen, & Haslam, Alexander. (2006). Rethinking the psychology of tyranny: The BBC prison study. *British Journal of Social Psychology, 45,* 1–40. doi:10.1348/014466605X48998

Reid, Pamela Trotman; Cooper, Shauna M.; & Banks, Kira Hudson. (2008). Girls to women: Developmental theory, research, and issues. In Florence L. Denmark & Michele A. Paludi (Eds.). *Psychology of women: A handbook of issues and theories* (2nd ed.). Westport, CT: Praeger/Greenwood.

Reilly, Michael J.; Tomsic, Jaclyn A.; Fernandez, Stephen J.; & Davison, Steven, P. (2015). Effect of facial rejuvenation surgery on perceived attractiveness, femininity, and personality. *JAMA Facial Plastic Surgery, 17,* 202–207. doi:10.1001/jamafacial.2015.0158

Reis, Harry T.; Collins, W. Andrew; & Berscheid, Ellen. (2000). The relationship context of human behavior and development. *Psychological Bulletin, 126,* 844–872.

Reisenzein, Rainer. (1983). The Schachter theory of emotion: Two decades later. *Psychological Bulletin, 94,* 239–264.

Reisenzein, Rainer. (2015). A short history of psychological perspectives of emotion. In Rafael A. Calvo, Sidney K. D'Mello, Jonathan Gratch, & Arvid Kappas (Eds.), *The Oxford handbook of affective computing.* New York, NY: Oxford University Press. doi:10.1093/oxfordhb/9780199942237.013.014

Reissig, Chad J.; Strain, Eric C.; & Griffiths, Roland R. (2009). Caffeinated energy drinks—A growing problem. *Drug and Alcohol Dependence, 99,* 1–10.

Reneman, Liesbeth; Schilt, T.; & de Win, Maartje M. (2006). Memory function and serotonin transporter promoter gene polymorphism in ecstasy (MDMA) users. *Journal of Psychopharmacology, 20,* 389–399.

Renk, Kimberly; Donnelly, Reesa; McKinney, Cliff; & Agliata, Allison Kanter. (2006). The development of gender identity: Timetables and influences. In Kam-Shing Yip (Ed.), *Psychology of gender identity: An international perspective.* Hauppauge, NY: Nova Science.

Renshaw, Keith D.; Steketee, Gail; Rodrigues, Camila S.; & Caska, Catherine M. (2010). Obsessive–compulsive disorder. In J. Gayle Beck (Ed.), *Interpersonal processes in the anxiety disorders: Implications for understanding psychopathology and treatment* (pp. 153–177). Washington, DC: American Psychological Association.

Repetti, Rena; Wang, Shu-wen; & Saxbe, Darby. (2009). Bringing it all back home: How outside stressors shape families' everyday lives. *Current Directions in Psychological Science, 18*(2), 106–111.

Rescorla, Robert A. (1968). Probability of shock in the presence and absence of CS in fear conditioning. *Journal of Comparative and Physiological Psychology, 66,* 1–5.

Rescorla, Robert A. (1980). Pavlovian second-order conditioning: Studies in associative learning. Hillsdale, NJ: Erlbaum.

Rescorla, Robert A. (1988). Pavlovian conditioning: It's not what you think it is. *American Psychologist, 43,* 151–160.

Rescorla, Robert A. (1997). Quoted in James E. Freeman, "Pavlov in the classroom. An interview with Robert A. Rescorla." *Teaching of Psychology, 24*, 283–286.

Rescorla, Robert A. (2001). Retraining of extinguished Pavlovian stimuli. *Journal of Experimental Psychology: Animal Behavior Processes, 27*, 115–124.

Rescorla, Robert A. (2003). Contemporary study of Pavlovian conditioning. *The Spanish Journal of Psychology, 6*(2), 185–195.

Rest, James R. (1983). Morality. In Paul H. Mussen, John H. Flavell, & Ellen M. Markman (Eds.), *Handbook of child psychology* (4th ed., Vol. 3). New York, NY: Wiley.

Rétey, Julia V.; Adam, Martin; Honegger, E. Katharina; Khatami, Ramin; Luhmann, U. F. O.; Jung, H. H.; Berger, W.; & Landolt, Hans-Peter. (2005). A functional genetic variation of adenosine deaminase affects the duration and intensity of deep sleep in humans. *Proceedings of the National Academy of Sciences, 102*, 15676–15681.

Revelle, William. (1995). Personality processes. *Annual Review of Psychology, 46*, 295–328, 467.

Revelle, William. (2007). Experimental approaches to the study of personality. In Richard W. Robins, R. Chris Fraley, & Robert F. Krueger (Eds.), *Handbook of research methods in personality psychology* (pp. 37–61). New York, NY: Guilford.

Révész, Dóra; Verhoeven, Josine E.; Milaneschi, Yuri; de Geus, Eco J. C. N.; Wolkowitz, Owen M.; & Penninx, Brenda W. J. H. (2014). Dysregulated physiological stress systems and accelerated cellular aging. *Neurobiology of Aging, 35*, 1422–1430. doi:10.1016/j.neurobiolaging .2013.12.027

Rhodes, Marjorie; & Chalik, Lisa. (2013). Social categories as markers of intrinsic interpersonal obligations. *Psychological Science, 24*(6), 999–1006. doi:10.1177/0956797612466267

Rhue, Judith W. (2010). Clinical hypnosis with children. In Steven Jay Lynn, Judith W. Rhue, & Irving Kirsch (Eds.), *Handbook of clinical hypnosis* (2nd ed.), (pp. 467–491). Washington, DC: American Psychological Association.

Riby, Leigh Martin; Smallwood, Jonathan; & Gunn, Valerie P. (2008). Mind wandering and retrieval from episodic memory: A pilot event-related potential study. *Psychological Reports, 102*(3), 805–818.

Ricard, Matthieu. (2010). *Why meditate? Working with thoughts and emotions.* New York, NY: Hay House.

Ricard, Matthieu; Lutz, Antoine; & Davidson, Richard J. (2014, November). Mind of the meditator. *Scientific American 311,* 38–45. doi:10.1038/ scientificamerican1114-38

Riccio, David C.; Millin, Paula M.; & Gisquet-Verrier, Pascale. (2003). Retrograde amnesia: Forgetting back. *Current Directions in Psychological Science, 12*, 41–44.

Rice, Robert W.; McFarlin, Dean B.; & Bennett, Debbie E. (1989). Standards of comparison and job satisfaction. *Journal of Applied Psychology, 74* (4), 591–598.

Rich, Josiah D.; Green, Traci C.; & McKenzie, Michelle S. (2011). Opioids and deaths. *New England Journal of Medicine, 364*(7), 686. doi:10.1056/NEJMc1014490

Richardson, L. Song. (2015). Police racial violence: Lessons from social psychology. *Fordham Law Review, 6*, 2961–2976.

Richardson, Michelle; Abraham, Charles; & Bond, Rod. (2012). Psychological correlates of university students' academic performance: A systematic review and meta-analysis. *Psychological Bulletin, 138*(2), 353–387. doi:10.1037/a0026838

Richardson, Robert D. (2006). *William James: In the maelstrom of American modernism.* Boston, MA: Houghton Mifflin.

Richert, Rebekah A.; Robb, Michael B.; & Smith, Erin I. (2011). Media as social partners: The social nature of young children's learning from screen media. *Child Development, 82*, 82–95. doi:10.1111/j.1467-8624.2010.01542.x

Richtand, Neil M.; Welge, Jeffrey A.; & Logue, Aaron D. (2007, August). Dopamine and serotonin receptor binding and antipsychotic efficacy. *Neuropsychopharmacology, 32*(8), 1715–1726.

Rideout, V. (2007). *Parents, children and media: A report from the Kaiser Family Foundation.* Menlo Park, CA: Kaiser Family Foundation.

Riding-Malon, Ruth, & Werth, James L., Jr. (2014). Psychological practice in rural settings: At the cutting edge. *Professional Psychology: Research and Practice, 45*, 85–91. doi:10.1037/a0036172

Ridolfo, Heather; Baxter, Amy; Lucas, Jeffrey W. (2010). Social influences on paranormal belief: Popular versus scientific support. *Current Research in Social Psychology, 15*, 33–41.

Riegel, B.; Simon D.; Weaver, J.; Carlson, B.; Clapton, P.; & Gocka, I. (1996). *Ayurvedic medicine demonstration project* (1R21 RR09726-01). Bethesda, MD: Report submitted to the National Institutes of Health, Institute for Alternative Medicine.

Rieger, Gerulf; Chivers, Meredith L.; & Bailey, J. Michael. (2005). Sexual arousal patterns of bisexual men. *Psychological Science, 16*, 579–584.

Rieger, Gerulf; Linsenmeier, Joan A. W.; & Gygax, Lorenz. (2008, January). Sexual orientation and childhood gender nonconformity: Evidence from home videos. *Developmental Psychology, 44*(1), 46–58.

Riley, J. R.; Greggers, U.; Smith, A. D.; Reynolds, D. R.; & Menzel, R. (2005). The flight paths of honeybees recruited by the waggle dance. *Nature, 435*, 205–207.

Riley, Kathryn P.; Snow, David A.; Desrosiers, Mark F.; & Markesbery, William R. (2005). Early life linguistic ability, late life cognitive function, and neuropathology: Findings from the Nun Study. *Neurobiology of Aging, 26*, 341–317.

Rilling, James K., & Sanfey, Alan G. (2011). The neuroscience of social decision-making. *Annual Reviews of Psychology, 62*, 23–48.

Rilling, Mark. (2000). John Watson's paradoxical struggle to explain Freud. *American Psychologist, 55*, 301–312.

Ringach, Dario L. (2009). Wiring of receptive fields and functional maps in primary visual cortex. In Michael S. Gazzaniga (Ed.), *The cognitive neurosciences* (4th ed.). Cambridge, MA: MIT Press.

Rippon, Gina; Jordan-Young, Rebecca; Kaiser, Anelis; & Fine, Cordelia. (2014). Recommendations for sex/gender neuroimaging research: Key principles and implications for research design, analysis and interpretation. *Frontiers in Human Neuroscience, 8,* 650. doi:10.3389/fnhum.2014.00650

Risen, Jane; & Gilovich, Thomas. (2007). Informal logical fallacies. In Robert J. Sternberg, Henry Roediger III, & Diane F. Halpern (Eds.), *Critical thinking in psychology.* New York, NY: Cambridge University Press.

Ristic, Jelena, & Enns, James T. (2015). The changing face of attentional development. *Current Directions in Psychological Science, 24*, 24–31. doi:10.1177/0963721414551165

Ritchie S. J., Wiseman R., & French C.C. (2012). Failing the future: Three unsuccessful attempts to replicate Bem's "Retroactive Facilitation of Recall" effect. *PLOS ONE, 7*(3): e33423. doi:10.1371/journal.pone.0033423

Ritchie, Stuart J.; Chudler, Eric H.; & Della Sala, Sergio. (2012). Don't try this at school: The attraction of 'alternative' educational techniques. In Sergio Della Sala & Mike Anderson (Eds.), *Neuroscience in education: The good, the bad, and the ugly.* Oxford, England: Oxford University Press.

Rivers, Ian; Poteat, V. Paul; & Noret, Nathalie. (2008). Victimization, social support, and psychosocial functioning among children of same-sex and opposite-sex couples in the United Kingdom. *Developmental Psychology, 44*, 127–134.

Rizzolatti, Giacomo, & Sinigaglia, Corrado. (2008). *Mirrors in the brain: How our minds share actions and emotions* (Frances Anderson, Trans.). New York, NY: Oxford University Press.

Roazen, Paul. (1999). *Freud: Political and social thought.* Piscataway, NJ: Transaction.

Roazen, Paul. (2000). *The historiography of psychoanalysis.* Piscataway, NJ: Transaction.

Robb, Michael B.; Richert, Rebekah A.; & Wartella, Ellen A. (2009). Just a talking book? Word learning from watching baby videos. *British Journal of Developmental Psychology, 27*(1), 27–45. doi:10.1348/026151008X320156

Roberts, Amy, & Nelson, Gareth. (2005, June 18). Quoted in Bijal Trevedi, "Autistic and proud of it." *New Scientist, 2504*, 36.

Roberts, Brent W.; Walton, Kate E.; & Viechtbauer, Wolfgang. (2006). Patterns of mean-level change in personality traits across the life course: A meta-analysis of longitudinal studies. *Psychological Bulletin, 132*(1), 1–25.

Robinson, Barbara S.; Davis, Kathleen L.; & Meara, Naomi M. (2003). Motivational attributes of occupational possible selves for low-income rural women. *Journal of Counseling Psychology, 50,* 156–164.

Robinson, Gail. (2002). Cross-cultural perspectives on menopause. In Anne E. Hunter & Carie Forden. *Readings in the psychology of gender: Exploring our differences and commonalities.* (pp. 140–149). Needham Heights, MA: Allyn & Bacon, 393.

Robinson, Jordan S., & Larson, Christine. (2010). Are traumatic events necessary to elicit symptoms of posttraumatic stress? *Psychological Trauma: Theory, Research, Practice, and Policy, 2*(2), 71–76.

Robinson, Paul. (1993). *Freud and his critics.* Berkeley: University of California Press.

Robles, Theodore. (2014). Marital quality and health: Implications for marriage in the 21st century. *Current Directions in Psychological Science, 23*(6), 427–432. doi:10.1177/0963721414549043

Roca, Miquel; Armengol, Silvia; Garcia-Garcia, Margarida; Rodriguez-Bayon, Antonia; Ballesta, Isabel; Serrano, Maria J.; . . . Gili, Margalida. (2011). Clinical differences between first and recurrent episodes in depressive patients. *Comprehensive Psychiatry, 52,* 26–32.

Rock, Irvin. (1995). *Perception.* New York, NY: Scientific American Library.

Rodafinos, Angelo S.; Vucevic, Arso; & Sideridis, Georgios D. (2005). The effectiveness of compliance techniques: Foot in the door versus door in the face. *Journal of Social Psychology, 145*(2), 237–239.

Rodewald, Frauke; Wilhelm-Gößling, Claudia; Emrich, Hinderk M.; Reddemann, Luise; & Gast, Ursula. (2011). Axis-I comorbidity in female patients with dissociative identity disorder and dissociative identity disorder not otherwise specified. *Journal of Nervous and Mental Disease, 199*(2), 122–131.

Rodin, Judith, & Langer, Ellen. (1977). Long-term effects of a control-relevant intervention with the institutionalized aged. *Journal of Personality and Social Psychology, 35,* 897–902.

Rodriguez-Larralde, Alvaro, & Paradisi, Irene. (2009). [Influence of genetic factors on human sexual orientation. Review]. *Investigacion Clinica, 50*(3), 377–391.

Roediger, Henry L. (2008). The cognitive psychology of memory: Introduction. In Henry L. Roediger (Ed.), *Cognitive psychology of memory,* Vol 2 of *Learning and Memory: A comprehensive reference* (pp.1–5), J. Byrne, ed. Oxford, England: Elsevier.

Roediger, Henry L., & Butler, Andrew C. (2011). The critical role of retrieval practice in long-term retention. *Trends in Cognitive Science, 15,* 20–27.

Roediger, Henry L.; Finn, Bridgid; & Weinstein, Yana. (2012). Applications of cognitive science to education. In Sergio Della Sala & Mike Anderson (Eds.), *Neuroscience in education: The good, the bad, and the ugly.* Oxford, England: Oxford University Press.

Roediger, Henry L., III; Agarwal, Pooja K.; McDaniel, Mark A.; & McDermott, Kathleen B. (2011). Test-enhanced learning in the classroom: Long-term improvements from quizzing. *Journal of Experimental Psychology: Applied, 17,* 382–395.

Roediger, Henry L., III; & Karpicke, Jeffrey D. (2006). Test-enhanced learning: Taking memory tests improves long-term retention. *Psychological Science, 17,* 249–255.

Roediger, Henry L. III, & Nestojko, John F. (2015). The relative benefits of studying and testing on long-term retention. In Jeroen G.W. Raaijmakers, Amy H. Criss, Robert L. Goldstone, Robert M. Nosofsky, & Mark Steyvers (Eds.), *Cognitive modeling in perception and memory: A festschrift for Richard M. Shiffrin.* New York, NY: Psychology Press.

Roediger, Henry L., III; Putnam, Adam L.; & Smith, Megan A. (2011). Ten benefits of testing and their applications to educational practice. In Jose P. Mestre & Brian H. Ross (Eds.), *The psychology of learning and motivation (Vol. 55): Cognition in education.* San Diego, CA: Elsevier. doi:10.1016/B978-0-12-387691-1.00001-6

Roediger, Henry L., III; Weinstein, Yana; & Agarwal, Pooja K. (2010). Forgetting: Preliminary considerations. In S. Della Sala (Ed.), *Forgetting* (pp. 1–22). New York, NY: Psychology Press.

Roehrs, Timothy, & Roth, Thomas. (2008). Caffeine: Sleep and daytime sleepiness. *Sleep Medicine Reviews, 12*(2), 153–162.

Roese, Neal J., & Vohs, Kathleen D. (2012). Hindsight bias. *Perspectives on Psychological Science, 7*(5), 411–426. doi:10.1177/1745691612454303

Rogers, Carl R. (1951). *Client-centered psychotherapy.* Boston, MA: Houghton-Mifflin.

Rogers, Carl R. (1957a/1989). A note on "The Nature of Man." In Howard Kirschenbaum & Valerie Land Henderson (Eds.), *The Carl Rogers reader.* Boston, MA: Houghton Mifflin.

Rogers, Carl R. (1957b/1989). A therapist's view of the good life: The fully functioning person. In Howard Kirschenbaum & Valerie Land Henderson (Eds.), *The Carl Rogers reader.* Boston, MA: Houghton Mifflin.

Rogers, Carl R. (1957c). The necessary and sufficient conditions of therapeutic personality change. *Journal of Consulting Psychology, 21,* 95–103.

Rogers, Carl R. (1959). A theory of therapy, personality, and interpersonal relationships, as developed in the client-centered framework. In S. Koch (Ed.), *Psychology: A Study of a Science Vol. 3. Formulations of the person and the social context.* New York, NY: McGraw-Hill.

Rogers, Carl R. (1961). *On becoming a person.* Boston, MA: Houghton Mifflin.

Rogers, Carl R. (1964/1989). Toward a modern approach to values: The valuing process in the mature person. In Howard Kirschenbaum & Valerie Land Henderson (Eds.), *The Carl Rogers reader.* Boston, MA: Houghton Mifflin.

Rogers, Carl R. (1977). *Carl Rogers on personal power: Inner strength and its revolutionary impact.* New York, NY: Delacorte Press.

Rogers, Carl R. (1980). *A way of being.* Boston, MA: Houghton Mifflin.

Rogers, Carl R., (1981/1989). Notes on Rollo May. In Howard Kirschenbaum & Valerie Land Henderson (Eds.), *Carl Rogers: Dialogues.* Boston, MA: Houghton Mifflin.

Rogers, Carl R.; & Skinner, B. F. (1956, November 30). Some issues concerning the control of human behavior: A symposium. *Science, 124,* 1057–1066.

Rogers, Paul; Davis, Tiffany; & Fisk, John. (2009). Paranormal belief and susceptibility to the conjunction fallacy. *Applied Cognitive Psychology, 23*(4), 524–542.

Rohde, Paul; Lewinsohn, Peter M.; Klein, Daniel, N.; Seeley, John R.; & Gau, Jeff M. (2013). Key characteristics of major depressive disorder occurring in childhood, adolescence, emerging adulthood, and adulthood. *Clinical Psychological Science, 1*(1), 41–53.

Roisman, Glenn I.; Clausell, Eric; & Holland, Ashley. (2008, January). Adult romantic relationships as contexts of human development: A multi-method comparison of same-sex couples with opposite-sex dating, engaged, and married dyads. *Developmental Psychology, 44*(1), 91–101.

Romero, Teresa; Konno, Akitsugu; & Hasegawa, Toshikazu. (2013). Familiarity bias and physiological responses in contagious yawning by dogs support link to empathy. (2013). *PLOS ONE, 8,* e71365. doi:10.1371/journal.pone.0071365

Ronen, Tammie. (1991). Intervention package for treating sleep disorders in a four-year-old girl. *Journal of Behavior Therapy and Experimental Psychiatry, 22,* 141–148.

Rook, Karen. (2015). Social networks in later life: Weighing positive and negative effects on health and well-being. *Current Directions in Psychological Science, 24*(1), 45–51. doi:10.1177/0963721414551364

Rook, Karen S.; August, Kristin J.; & Sorkin, Dara H. (2011). Social network functions and health. In Richard J. Contrada & Andrew Baum (Eds.), *The handbook of stress science: Biology, psychology, and health.* New York, NY: Springer.

Rosa-Alcázar, Ana I.; Sánchez-Meca, Julio; Gómez-Conesa, Antonia; & Marín-Martínez, Fulgencio. (2008). Psychological treatment of obsessive–compulsive disorder: A meta-analysis. *Clinical Psychology Review, 28*(8), 1310–1325. doi:10.1016/j.cpr.2008.07.001

Rosander, Michael, & Eriksson, Oskar. (2012). Conformity on the Internet—The role of task difficulty and gender differences. *Computers in Human Behavior, 28*(5), 1587–1595. doi:10.1016/j.chb.2012.03.023

Rosch, Eleanor H. (1973). Natural categories. *Cognitive Psychology, 4,* 328–350.

Rosch, Eleanor H. (1978). Principles of categorization. In Eleanor H. Rosch & Barbara B. Lloyd (Eds.), *Cognition and categorization.* Hillsdale, NJ: Erlbaum.

Rosch, Eleanor H. (1987). Linguistic relativity. *Et Cetera, 44,* 254–279.

Rosch, Eleanor H., & Mervis, Carolyn B. (1975). Family resemblances: Studies in the internal structure of categories. *Cognitive Psychology, 7,* 573–605.

Rose, Jed E.; Behm, Frederique M.; Westman, Eric C.; Mathew, Roy J.; London, Edythe D.; Hawk, Thomas C.; Turkington, Timothy G.; & Coleman, R. Edward. (2003). PET studies of the influences of nicotine on neural systems in cigarette smokers. *American Journal of Psychiatry, 160,* 323–333.

Rose, Steven. (2009). Should scientists study race and IQ? NO: Science and society do not benefit. *Nature, 457,* 786–788.

Rosekind, Mark. (2003, April 8). Quoted in National Sleep Foundation press release, "Sleep is important when stress and anxiety increase, says the National Sleep Foundation." Washington, DC. Retrieved on January 4, 2005, from http://www.sleepfoundation.org/PressArchives/stress.cfm

Rosenbaum, David A.; Carlson, Richard A.; & Gilmore, Rick O. (2001). Acquisition of intellectual and perceptual-motor skills. *Annual Review of Psychology, 52,* 453–470.

Rosenberg, Neil; Grigsby, Jim; Dreisbach, James; Busenbark, David; & Grigsby, Paul. (2002). Neuropsychologic impairment and MRI abnormalities associated with chronic solvent abuse. *Journal of Toxicology: Clinical Toxicology, 40,* 21–34.

Rosenberg, Oded, & Dannon, Pinhas N. (2009). Transcranial magnetic stimulation. In Conrad M. Swartz (Ed.), *Electroconvulsive and neuromodulation therapies* (pp. 527–542). New York, NY: Cambridge University Press.

Rosenblatt, Paul C. (2007). Culture, socialization, and loss, grief, and mourning. In Balk, David; Wogrin, Carol; Thornton, Gordon; Meagher, David (Eds.), *Handbook of thanatology: The essential body of knowledge for the study of death, dying, and bereavement,* New York, NY: Routledge/Taylor & Francis Group.

Rosenfield, Sarah, & Smith, Dena. (2010). Gender and mental health: Do men and women have different amounts or types of problems? In Teresa L. Scheid & Tony N. Brown (Eds.), *A handbook for the study of mental health: Social contexts, theories, and systems* (2nd ed.). New York, NY: Cambridge University Press.

Rosenquist, James Niels; Lehrer, Steven F.; O'Malley, A. James; Zaslavsky, Alan M.; Smoller, Jordan W.; & Christakis, Nicholas A. (2015). Cohort of birth modifies the association between FTO genotype and BMI. *Proceedings of the National Academy of Sciences, 112,* 354–359. doi:10.1073/pnas.1411893111

Rosenthal, Abraham M. (1964a, May 3). Study of the sickness called apathy. *The New York Times Magazine,* Sect. VI, pp. 24, 66, 69–72.

Rosenthal, Abraham M. (1964b). *Thirty-eight witnesses.* New York, NY: McGraw-Hill.

Rosenzweig, Saul. (1997). Freud's only visit to America. In Wolfgang G. Bringmann, Helmut E. Lück, Rudolf Miller, & Charles E. Early (Eds.), *A pictorial history of psychology.* Chicago, IL: Quintessence.

Rosielle, Luke J., & Scaggs, W. Jeffrey. (2008). What if they knocked down the library and nobody noticed? The failure to detect large changes to familiar scenes. *Memory, 16,* 115–124.

Ross, Barbara. (1991). William James: Spoiled child of American psychology. In Gregory A. Kimble, Michael Wertheimer, & Charlotte White (Eds.), *Portraits of pioneers in psychology.* Washington, DC: American Psychological Association.

Ross, Lee. (1977). The intuitive psychologist and his shortcomings: Distortions in the attribution process. In Leonard Berkowitz (Ed.), *Advances in experimental social psychology* (Vol. 10). New York, NY: Academic Press.

Ross, Lee, & Anderson, Craig A. (1982). Shortcomings in the attribution process: On the origins and maintenance of erroneous social assessments. In Daniel Kahneman, Paul Slovic, & Amos Tversky (Eds.), *Judgment under uncertainty: Heuristics and biases.* New York, NY: Cambridge University Press.

Ross, Michael, & Wang, Qi. (2010). Remember: Culture and autobiographical memory. *Perspectives on Psychological Science, 5*(4) 401–409, doi:10.1177/1745691610375555

Ross, Shannon E.; Niebling, Bradley C.; & Heckert, Teresa M. (1999). Sources of stress among college students. *College Student Journal, 33,* 312–317.

Rossier, Jerome; Dahourou, Donatien; & McCrae, Robert R. (2005). Structural and mean level analyses of the five-factor model and locus of control: Further evidence from Africa. *Journal of Cross-Cultural Psychology, 36,* 227–246.

Roth, Thomas; Zammit, Gary; Lankford, Alan; Mayleben, David; Stern, Theresa; Pitman, Verne; Clark, David; & Werth, John L. (2010). Nonrestorative sleep as a distinct component of insomnia. *Sleep, 33,* 449–458.

Rothbaum, Fred; Kakinuma, Miki; Nagaoka, Rika; & Azuma, Hiroshi. (2007). Attachment and AMAE: Parent-child closeness in the United States and Japan. *Journal of Cross-Cultural Psychology, 38,* 465–486.

Rothblum, Esther D., & Hope, Deborah A. (2009). An overview of same-sex couples in relationships: A research area still at sea. In Deborah Hope (Ed.), *Contemporary perspectives on lesbian, gay, and bisexual identities.* (pp. 113–139). New York, NY: Springer Science + Business Media.

Rotheram-Borus, Mary Jane; Swendeman, Dallas; & Chorpita, Bruce F. (2012). Disruptive innovations for designing and diffusing evidence-based interventions. *American Psychologist, 67*(6), 463–476. doi:10.1037/a0028180

Rouder, Jeffrey N., & Morey, Richard D. (2011). A Bayes factor meta-analysis of Bem's ESP claim. *Psychonomic Bulletin & Review.* doi:10.3758/s13423-011-0088-7

Rouder, Jeffrey N.; Morey, Richard D.; Cowan, Nelson; Zwilling, Christopher E.; Morey, Candice C.; & Pratte, Michael S. (2008). An assessment of fixed-capacity models of visual working memory. *Proceedings of the National Academy of Sciences, USA, 105,* 5975–5979.

Rouder, Jeffrey N.; Morey, Richard D.; & Province, Jordan M. (2013). A Bayes factor meta-analysis of recent extrasensory perception experiments: Comment on Storm, Tressoldi, and DiRisio (2010). *Psychological Bulletin, 139,* 241–247. doi:10.1037/a0029008

Rowe, David C. (2003). Assessing genotype-environment interactions and correlations in the postgenomic era. In Robert Plomin, John C. DeFries, Ian W. Craig, & Peter McGuffin (Eds.), *Behavioral genetics in the postgenomic era.* Washington, DC: American Psychological Association.

Rowe, Shawn M., & Wertsch, James V. (2002). Vygotsky's model of cognitive development. In Usha Gowsami (Ed.), *Blackwell handbook of childhood cognitive development.* Malden, MA: Blackwell.

Rowland, Christopher A. (2014). The effect of testing versus restudy on retention: A meta-analytic review of the testing effect. *Psychological Bulletin, 140,* 1432–1463. doi:10.1037/a0037559

Rowling, J. K. (1999). *Harry Potter and the Prisoner of Azkaban.* New York, NY: Scholastic.

Rozin, Paul. (1996). The socio-cultural context of eating and food choice. In H. L. Meiselman & H. J. H. MacFie (Eds.), *Food choice, acceptance and consumption.* London, England: Blackie Academic and Professional.

Rozin, Paul. (2006). About 17 (+/-2) potential principles about links between the innate mind and culture: Preadaptation, predispositions, preferences, pathways, and domains. In Peter Carruthers, Laurence Stephen, & Stephen Stich (Eds.), *The Innate Mind. Vol. 2: Culture and cognition.* New York, NY: Oxford University Press.

Rozin, Paul. (2007). Food and eating. In Shinobu Kitayama & Dov Cohen (Eds.), *Handbook of cultural psychology.* New York, NY: Guilford.

Rubin, Edgar. (1921/2001). Readings in perception. In Steven Yantis (Ed.), *Visual perception: Essential readings.* Philadelphia, PA: Psychology Press.

Rubin, Nava. (2001). Figure and ground in the brain. *Nature Neuroscience, 4,* 857–858.

Rubio-Fernández, Paula, & Glucksberg, Sam. (2012). Reasoning about other people's beliefs: Bilinguals have an advantage. *Journal of Experimental Psychology: Learning, Memory, and Cognition, 38,* 211–217. doi:10.1037/a0025162

Ruble, Diane N.; Martin, Carol Lynn; & Berenbaum, Sheri A. (2006). Gender development. In Nancy Eisenberg, William Damon, & Richard M. Lerner (Eds.), *Handbook of Child Psychology: Vol. 3, Social, emotional, and personality development* (6th ed.). Hoboken, NJ: Wiley.

Rudman, Laurie A., & Fairchild, Kimberly. (2004). Reactions to counterstereotypic behavior: The role of backlash in cultural stereotype maintenance. *Journal of Personality and Social Psychology, 87*(2), 157–176.

Runco, Mark A. (2007). *Creativity: Theories and themes: Research, development, and practice.* San Diego, CA: Elsevier Academic.

Ruscio, John. (1998, November/December). The perils of post-hockery. *Skeptical Inquirer, 22,* 44–48.

Russac, R. J.; Gatliff, Colleen; Reece, Mimi; & Spottswood, Diahann. (2007). Death anxiety across the adult years: An examination of age and gender effects. *Death Studies, 31*(6), 549–561.

Russell, James A. (1991). Culture and the categorization of emotions. *Psychological Bulletin, 110*, 426–450.

Russell, James A. (2014). William James and his legacy. *Emotion Review, 6, 3.* doi:10.1177/1754073913503610

Russell, James A.; Bachorowski, Jo-Anne; & Fernández-Dols, José-Miguel. (2003). Facial and vocal expressions of emotions. *Annual Review of Psychology, 54*, 359–349.

Russell, Nestar John Charles. (2011). Milgram's obedience to authority experiments: Origins and early evolution. *British Journal of Social Psychology, 50*, 140–162. doi:10.1348/014466610X492205

Russon, Anne E., & Galdikas, Birute M. F. (1995). Constraints on great apes' imitation: Model and action selectivity in rehabilitant orangutan (*Pongo pygmaeus*) imitation. *Journal of Comparative Psychology, 109*, 5–17.

Rutchick, Abraham M., & Slepian, Michael. (2013). Handling ibuprofen increases pain tolerance and decreases perceived pain intensity in a cold pressor test. *PLOS ONE, 8*(3), 1–5. doi:10.1371/journal.pone.0056175

Rutherford, Alexandra. (2000). Radical behaviorism and psychology's public: B. F. Skinner in the popular press, 1934–1990. *History of Psychology, 3*, 371–395.

Rutherford, Alexandra. (2003). B. F. Skinner's technology of behavior in American life: From consumer culture to counterculture. *Journal of the History of the Behavioral Sciences, 39*, 1–23.

Rutherford, Alexandra. (2006). Mother of behavior therapy and beyond: Mary Cover Jones and the study of the "whole child." In Donald A. Dewsbury, Lucy T. Benjamin, & Michael Wertheimer (Eds.), *Portraits of pioneers in psychology* (Vol. VI, pp. 189–204). Washington, DC: American Psychological Association.

Rutherford, Alexandra. (2012, March). B. F. Skinner: Scientist, celebrity, social visionary. *APS Observer, 25*. Accessed on April 2, 2014, from http://www.psychologicalscience.org/index.php/publications/observer/2012/march-12/b-f-skinner-scientist-celebrity-social-visionary.html

Rutledge, Thomas; Linke, Sarah E.; Olson, Marian B.; Francis, Jennifer; Johnson, B. Delia; Bittner, Vera; York, Kaki; & others. (2008). Social networks and incident stroke among women with suspected myocardial ischemia. *Psychosomatic Medicine, 70*, 282–287.

Rutledge, Thomas; Reis, Steven E.; Olson, Marian; Owens, Jane; Kelsey, Sheryl F.; Pepine, Carl J.; Mankad, Sunil; Rogers, William J.; & others. (2004). Social networks are associated with lower mortality rates among women with suspected coronary disease: The National Heart, Lung, and Blood Institute–sponsored Women's Ischemia Syndrome Evaluation Study. *Psychosomatic Medicine, 66*, 882–888.

Rutter, Michael. (2008). Proceeding from observed correlation to causal interference: The use of natural experiments. *Perspectives on Psychological Science, 2*, 377–396.

Ruvolo, Ann Patrice, & Markus, Hazel Rose. (1992). Possible selves and performance: The power of self-relevant imagery. *Social Cognition, 10*, 95–124.

Ryan, Richard M., & Deci, Edward L. (2011). Human autonomy in cross-cultural context: Perspectives on the psychology of agency, freedom, and well-being. In Valery I. Chirkov, Richard M. Ryan, Kennon M. Sheldon (Eds.), *Cross-cultural advancements in positive psychology.* New York, NY: Springer.

Ryan, Richard M., & Deci, Edward L. (2012). Multiple identities within a single self: A self-determination theory perspective on internalization within contexts and cultures. In Mark R. Leary & June Price Tangney (Eds.), *Handbook of self and identity* (2nd ed.) (pp. 225–246). New York, NY: Guilford.

Ryan, Richard M., & La Guardia, Jennifer G. (2000). What is being optimized over development? A self-determination theory and basic psychological needs. In Sara Honn Qualls & Norman Abeles (Eds.), *Psychology and the aging revolution: How we adapt to longer life.* Washington, DC: American Psychological Association.

Rydell, Ann-Margaret; Bohlin, Gunilla; & Thorell, Lisa B. (2005). Representations of attachment to parents and shyness as predictors of children's relationships with teachers and peer competence in preschool. *Attachment & Human Development, 7*, 187–204.

Rydell, Robert J.; McConnell, Allen R.; & Beilock, Sian L. (2009). Multiple social identities and stereotype threat: Imbalance, accessibility, and working memory. *Journal of Personality and Social Psychology, 96*(5), 949–966.

Rydell, Robert J.; Rydell, Michael T.; & Boucher, Kathryn L. (2010). The effect of negative performance stereotypes on learning. *Journal of Personality and Social Psychology, 99*(6), 883–896.

Sacchi, Dario L. M.; Agnoli, Franca; & Loftus, Elizabeth F. (2007). Changing history: Doctored photographs affect memory for past public events. *Applied Cognitive Psychology, 21*, 1005–1022.

Sachse, Rainer, & Elliott, Robert. (2002). Process–outcome research on humanistic therapy variables. In David J. Cain & Julius Seeman (Eds.), *Humanistic psychotherapies: Handbook of research and practice.* Washington, DC: American Psychological Association.

Sadler, Pamela, & Woody, Erik. (2010). Dissociation in hypnosis: Theoretical frameworks and psychotherapeutic implications. In Steven Jay Lynn, Judith W. Rhue, & Irving Kirsch (Eds.), *Handbook of clinical hypnosis* (2nd ed.), (pp. 151–178). Washington, DC: American Psychological Association.

Sadoski, Mark. (2005). A dual coding view of vocabulary learning. *Reading & Writing Quarterly, 21*, 221–238.

Sagi, Yaniv; Tavor, Ido; Hofstetter, Shir; Tzur-Moryosef, Shimrit; Blumenfeld-Katzir, Tamar; & Assaf, Yanif. (2012). Learning in the fast lane: New insights into neuroplasticity. *Neuron, 73*(6), 1195–1203.

Saha, Sukanta; Chant, David; Welham, Joy; & McGrath, John. (2005). A systematic review of the prevalence of schizophrenia. *PLOS Medicine, 2*, 413–433.

Sahdra, Baljinder K.; MacLean, Katherine A.; Ferrer, Emilio; Shaver, Phillip R.; Rosenberg, Erika L.; Jacobs, Tonya L.; Zanesco, Anthony P.; & others. (2011). Enhanced response inhibition during intensive meditation training predicts improvements in self-reported adaptive socioemotional functioning. *Emotion, 11*(2), 299–312. doi:10.1037/a0022764

Saiyad, Mohammedlatif, & El-Mallakh, Rif S. (2012). Smoking is associated with greater symptom load in bipolar disorder patients. *Annals of Clinical Psychiatry, 24*(4), 305–309.

Sakheim, David K., & Devine, Susan E. (Eds.). (1992). *Out of darkness: Exploring satanism and ritual abuse.* New York, NY: Lexington Books.

Saks, Elyn. (2008). *The center cannot hold: My journey through madness.* New York, NY: Hyperion.

Salas, Rachel E.; Galea, Joseph M.; Gamaldo, Alyssa A.; Gamaldo, Charlene E.; Allen, Richard P.; Smith, Michael T.; Cantarero, Gabriela; Lam, Barbara D.; & Celnik, Pablo A. (2014). Increased use-dependent plasticity in chronic insomnia. *Sleep 37*, 535–544. doi:10.5665/sleep.3492

Salazar, Gloria Maria Martinez; Faintuch, Salamao; Laser, Eleanor; & Lang, Elvira. (2010). Hypnosis during invasive medical and surgical procedures. In Steven J Lynn, Judith W Rhue, & Irving Kirsch (Eds.), *Handbook of clinical hypnosis* (2nd ed., pp. 575–592). Washington DC: American Psychological Association.

Saletan, William. (2010, May 24). The ministry of truth. *Slate.* Retrieved on May 16, 2014, from http://www.slate.com/articles/health_and_science/the_memory_doctor/2010/05/the_ministry_of_truth.html

Salloum, Alison; Garside, Laura W.; Irwin, C. Louis; Anderson, Adrian D.; & Francois, Anita H. (2009). Grief and trauma group therapy for children after Hurricane Katrina. *Social Work with Groups, 32*(1), 64–79.

Salthouse, Timothy A. (2009). When does age-related cognitive decline begin? *Neurobiology of Aging, 30*(4), 507–514.

Sam, David L., & Berry, John W. (2010). Acculturation: When individuals and groups of different cultural backgrounds meet. *Perspectives on Psychological Science, 5*, 472–481.

Sameroff, Arnold. (2010). A unified theory of development: A dialectic integration of nature and nurture. *Child Development, 81*(1), 6–22.

Sammons, Cynthia C, & Speight, Suzette L. (2008). A qualitative investigation of changes in graduate students associated with multicultural counseling courses. *The Counseling Psychologist, 36*(6), 814–838.

Samuel, Douglas B.; Simms, Leonard J.; Clark, Lee A.; Livesley, W. John; & Widiger, Thomas A. (2010). An item response theory integration of normal and abnormal personality scales. *Personality Disorders: Theory, Research, and Treatment, 1*(1), 5–21. doi:10.1037/a0018136

Sampaio, Adriana; Soares, José M.; Coutinho, Joana; Sousa, Nuno; & Gonçalves, Óscar F. (2013). The Big Five default brain: Functional evidence. *Brain Structure Function, 219,* 1913–1922. doi:10.1007/s00429-013 -0610-y

Sanbonmatsu, David M.; Strayer, David. L.; Medeiros-Ward, Nathan; & Watson, Jason M. (2013). Who multi-tasks and why? Multi-tasking ability, perceived multi-tasking ability, impulsivity, and sensation seeking. *PLOS ONE, 8*(1), e54402. doi:10.1371/journal.pone.0054402

Sandler, Wendy; Meir, Irit; Padden, Carol; & Aronoff, Mark. (2005). The emergence of grammar in a new sign language. *Proceedings of the National Academy of Sciences, 102,* 2661–2665.

Sanfelippo, Augustin J. (2006). *Panic disorders: New research.* Hauppauge, NY: Nova Biomedical Books.

Santiago, Catherine D.; Kaltman, Stacey; & Miranda, Jeanne. (2013). Poverty and mental health: How do low-income adults and children fare in psychotherapy? *Journal of Clinical Psychology, 69*(2), 115–126.

Santos, Laurie R., & Rosati, Alexandra G. (2015). The evolutionary roots of human decision making. *Annual Review of Psychology, 66,* 321–347. doi:10.1146/annurev-psych-010814-015310

Sapolsky, Robert M. (2004). Mothering style and methylation. *Nature Neuroscience, 7,* 791–792.

Sar, Vedat; Koyuncu, Ahmet; & Ozturk, Erdinc. (2007, January– February). Dissociative disorders in the psychiatric emergency ward. *General Hospital Psychiatry, 29*(1), 45–50.

Satel, Sally, & Lilienfeld, Scott O. (2013). *Brainwashed: The seductive appeal of mindless neuroscience.* New York, NY: Basic Books.

Saul, Stephanie. (2007a, March 14). F.D.A. warns of odd effects of sleeping pills. Retrieved on July 14, 2009, from http://www.nytimes.com/2007/03 /14/business/15drugcnd.html

Saul, Stephanie. (2007b, March 15). F.D.A. warns of sleeping pills' strange effects. Retrieved on July 14, 2009, from http://www.nytimes.com/2007/03 /15/business/15drug.ready.html

Savage-Rumbaugh, E. Sue, & Lewin, Roger. (1994, September). Ape at the brink. *Discover, 15,* 91–98.

Savage, Joanne, & Yancey, Christina. (2008). The effects of media violence exposure on criminal aggression: A meta-analysis. *Criminal Justice and Behavior, 35,* 722–791.

Savage, Seddon R. (2005). Critical issues in pain and addiction. *Pain Management Rounds, 2,* 1–6.

Savic, Ivanka, & Lindström, Per. (2008). PET and MRI show differences in cerebral asymmetry and functional connectivity between homo- and heterosexual subjects. *Proceedings of the National Academy of Sciences, 105,* 9403– 9408.

Savin-Williams, Ritch C. (2006). Who's gay? Does it matter? *Current Directions in Psychological Science, 15,* 40–44.

Savin-Williams, Ritch C., & Hope, Debra A. (2009). How many gays are there? It depends. In Debra A. Hope (Ed.), *Contemporary perspectives on lesbian, gay, and bisexual identities* (pp. 5–41). New York, NY: Springer.

Saxbe, Darby E., & Repetti, Rena L. (2009). Brief report: Fathers' and mothers' marital relationship predicts daughters' pubertal development two years later. *Journal of Adolescence, 32*(2), 415–423.

Saxe, Geoffrey, & de Kirby, Kenton. (2014). Cultural context of cognitive development. *WIREs Cognitive Science, 5,* 447–461.

Saxe, Rebecca, & Powell, Lindsay J. (2006). It's the thought that counts: Specific brain regions for one component of theory of mind. *Psychological Science, 17,* 692–699.

Schachter, Robert. (2011). Using the group in cognitive group therapy. *Group, 35*(2), 135–149.

Schachter, Stanley, & Singer, Jerome E. (1962). Cognitive, social, and physiological determinants of emotional state. *Psychological Review, 69,* 379–399.

Schacter, Daniel L., & Loftus, Elizabeth F. (2013). Memory and law: What can cognitive neuroscience contribute? *Nature Neuroscience, 16,* 119–123.

Schaie, K. Warner. (1995). *Intellectual development in adulthood: The Seattle Longitudinal Study.* New York, NY: Cambridge University Press.

Schaie, K. Warner. (2005). *Developmental influences on adult intelligence: The Seattle Longitudinal Study.* New York, NY: Oxford University Press.

Schanding, G. Thomas, Jr., & Sterling-Turner, Heather E. (2010). Use of the mystery motivator for a high school class. *Journal of Applied School Psychology, 26*(1), 38–53.

Schell, Jason. (2010, dd). Design outside the box: Beyond Facebook. Presented at DICE Summit 2011[1].

Schenck, Carlos H. (2007). *Sleep: The mysteries, the problems, and the solutions.* New York, NY: Penguin.

Schenck, Carlos H.; Arnulf, Isabelle; & Mahowald, Mark W. (2007). Sleep and sex: What can go wrong? A review of the literature on sleep related disorders and abnormal sexual behaviors and experiences. *Sleep, 30,* 683–702.

Scherer, Klaus R. (2013). The nature and dynamics of relevance and valence appraisals: Theoretical advances and recent evidence. *Emotion Review, 5,* 150–162. doi:10.1177/1754073912468166

Scherer, Klaus R., & Wallbott, Harald G. (1994). Evidence for universality and cultural variation of differential emotion response patterning. *Journal of Personality and Social Psychology, 66,* 310–328.

Scherer, Klaus R.; Banse, Rainer; & Wallbott, Harald G. (2001). Emotion inferences from vocal expression correlate across languages and cultures. *Journal of Cross-Cultural Psychology, 32,* 76–92.

Schläpfer, Thomas E.; & Bewernick, Bettina H. (2009). Deep brain stimulation: Methods, indications, locations, and efficacy. In Conrad M. Swartz (Ed.), *Electroconvulsive and neuromodulation therapies* (pp. 556–572). New York, NY: Cambridge University Press.

Schlein, Lisa. (2014, September 4). More people die from suicide than from wars, natural disasters combined. *Voice of America.* Retrieved from http:// www.voanews.com/content/more-people-die-from-suicide-than-from-wars -natural-disasters-combined/2438749.html

Schlitz, Marilyn; Wiseman, Richard; & Watt, Caroline. (2006). Of two minds: Sceptic-proponent collaboration within parapsychology. *British Journal of Psychology, 97,* 313–322.

Schmader, Toni. (2010). Stereotype threat deconstructed. *Current Directions in Psychological Science, 19*(1), 14–18. doi:10.1177/0963721409359292

Schmader, Toni; Forbes, Chad E.; Zhang, Shen; & Mendes, Wendy Berry. (2009). A metacognitive perspective on the cognitive deficits experienced in intellectually threatening environments. *Personality and Social Psychology Bulletin, 35*(5), 584–596. doi:10.1177/0146167208330450

Schmader, Toni; Johns, Michael; & Forbes, Chad. (2008). An integrated process model of stereotype threat effects on performance. *Psychological Review, 115,* 236–256.

Schmalz, Dorothy L., & Kerstetter, Deborah L. (2006). Girlie girls and manly men: Children's stigma consciousness of gender in sports and physical activities. *Journal of Leisure Research, 38,* 536–557.

Schmidt, Norman B., & Keough, Meghan E. (2010). Treatment of panic. *Annual Review of Clinical Psychology, 6,* 241–256.

Schmithorst, Vincent J., & Yuan, Weihong. (2010). White matter development during adolescence as shown by diffusion MRI. *Brain and Cognition, 72*(1), 16–25.

Schmitt, David P.; Jonason, Peter K.; Byerley, Garrett J.; Flores, Sandy D.; Illbeck, Brittany E.; O'Leary, Kimberly N.; & Qudrat, Ayesha. (2012). A reexamination of sex differences in sexuality: New studies reveal old truths. *Current Directions in Psychological Science, 21*(2), 135–139.

Schmitt, Michael; Branscombe, Nyla; Postmes, Tom; & Garcia, Amber. (2014). The consequences of perceived discrimination for psychological well-being: A meta-analytic review. *Psychological Bulletin, 140*(4), 921–948. doi:10.1037/a0035754

Schnall, Simone, & Laird, James D. (2003). Keep smiling: Enduring effects of facial expressions and postures on emotional experience and memory. *Cognition & Emotion, 17,* 787–797.

Schneider, Kirk J., & Krug, Orah T. (2009). *Existential-humanistic therapy.* Washington, DC: American Psychological Association.

Schofield, Hugh (2013, April 29). *A French love affair . . . with graphology—BBC News.* Retrieved from http://www.bbc.com/news/magazine-22198554

Schomerus, Georg; Schwahn, Christian; Holzinger, Anita; Corrigan, Patrick. W.; Grabe, H. J.; Carta, Manolo G.; & Angermeyer, Matthais C. (2012). Evolution of public attitudes about mental illness: A systematic review and meta-analysis. *Acta Psychiatrica Scandinavica, 125,* 440–452. doi:10.1111/j.1600-0447.2012.01826.x

Schroth, Marvin L., & McCormack, William A. (2000) Current problems and resolutions—Sensation seeking and need for achievement among study-abroad students. *Journal of Social Psychology, 140,* 533.

Schulenberg, J. E., & Zarrett, N. R. (2006). Mental health during emerging adulthood: Continuity and discontinuity in courses, causes, and functions. In J. J. Arnett & J. L. Tanner (Eds.), *Emerging adults in America: Coming of age in the 21st century.* Washington, DC: American Psychological Association.

Schüll, Natasha Dow. (2012). *Addiction by design: Machine gambling in Las Vegas.* Princeton, NJ: Princeton University Press.

Schulz, Marc S.; Cowan, Philip A.; Cowan, Carolyn Pape; & Brennan, Robert T. (2004). Coming home upset: Gender, marital satisfaction, and the daily spillover of workday experience into couple interactions. *Journal of Family Psychology, 18,* 250–263.

Schupp, Harald T.; Öhman, Arne; Junghöfer, Markus; Weike, Almut I.; Stockburger, Jessica; & Hamm, Alfons O. (2004). The facilitated processing of threatening faces: An ERP analysis. *Emotion, 4,* 189–200.

Schutte, Nicola, & Malouff, John. (2014, November 13). The relationship between perceived stress and telomere length: A meta-analysis. *Stress & Health.* Advance online publication. doi:10.1002/smi.2607

Schwab, Richard J.; Kuna, Samuel T.; & Remmers, John E. (2005). Anatomy and physiology of upper airway obstruction. In Meir H. Kryger, Thomas Roth, & William C. Dement (Eds.), *Principles and practice of sleep medicine* (4th ed.). Philadelphia, PA: Elsevier Saunders.

Schwartz, Bennett L. (1999). Sparkling at the end of the tongue: The etiology of tip-of-the-tongue phenomenology. *Psychonomic Bulletin and Review, 6,* 379–393.

Schwartz, Bennett L. (2002). *Tip-of-the-tongue states: Phenomenology, mechanism, and lexical retrieval.* Mahwah, NJ: Erlbaum.

Schwartz, Bennett L. (2011). The effect of being in a tip-of-the-tongue state on subsequent items. *Memory & Cognition, 39*(2), 245–250.

Schwartz, Charlotte. (2003). A brief discussion on frequency of sessions and its impact upon psychoanalytic treatment. *Psychoanalytic Review, 90,* 179–191.

Schwartz, Earl. (2004, Summer/Fall). Why some ask why: Kohlberg and Milgram. *Judaism, 53,* 230–240.

Schwartz, Jeffrey M., & Begley, Sharon. (2002). *The mind and the brain: Neuroplasticity and the power of mental force.* New York, NY: Regan Books.

Schwartz, Jeffrey M.; Stoessel, Paula W.; & Phelps, Michael E. (1996). Systematic changes in cerebral glucose metabolic rate after successful behavior modification treatment of obsessive–compulsive disorder. *Archives of General Psychiatry, 53,* 109–117.

Schwartz, Seth J.; Unger, Jennifer B.; Zamboanga, Byron L.; & Szapocznik, José. (2010). Rethinking the concept of acculturation: Implications for theory and research. *American Psychologist, 65*(4), 237–251.

Schwartz, Sophie. (2010). Life goes on in dreams. *Sleep, 2010 33*(1), 15–16.

Scott-Phillips, Thomas C.; Dickins, Thomas E.; & West, Stuart A. (2011). Evolutionary theory and the ultimate-proximate distinction in the human behavioral sciences. *Perspectives on Psychological Science, 6,* 38–47. doi:10.1177/1745691610393528

Scott, Samantha L.; Carper, Teresa Marino; Middleton, Melissa; White, Rachel; Renk, Kimberly; & Grills-Taquechel, Amie. (2010). Relationships among locus of control, coping behaviors, and levels of worry following exposure to hurricanes. *Journal of Loss and Trauma, 15*(2), 123–137.

Scoville, William Beecher, & Milner, Brenda. (1957). Loss of recent memory after bilateral hippocampal lesions. *Journal of Neurology, Neurosurgery, and Psychiatry, 20,* 11–21.

Seal, Karen H.; Bertenthal, Daniel; Maguen, Shira; Gima, Kristian; Chu, Anna; & Marmar, Charles R. (2008). Getting beyond "Don't ask, don't tell": An evaluation of U.S. Veterans Administration post-deployment mental health screening of veterans returning from Iraq and Afghanistan. *American Journal of Public Health, 98,* 714–720.

Seal, Mark. (2009). The man in the Rockefeller suit. *Vanity Fair.* Retrieved from http://www.vanityfair.com/style/2009/01/fake_rockefeller200901

Sebastian, Catherine; Burnett, Stephanie; & Blakemore, Sarah-Jayne. (2008). Development of the self-concept during adolescence. *Trends in Cognitive Sciences, 12*(11), 441–446.

Sedlmeier, Peter; Eberth, Juliane; Schwarz, Marcus; Zimmermann, Doreen; Haarig, Frederik; Jaeger, Sonia; & Kunze, Sonja. (2012). The psychological effects of meditation: A meta-analysis. *Psychological Bulletin, 138,* 1139–1171. doi:10.1037/a0028168

Seery, Mark D.; Holman, E. Alison; & Silver, Roxane Cohen. (2010). Whatever does not kill us: Cumulative lifetime adversity, vulnerability, and resilience. *Journal of Personality and Social Psychology, 99*(6), 1025–1041. doi:10.1037/a0021344

Seegmiller, Janelle K.; Watson, Jason M.; & Strayer, David L. (2011). Individual differences in susceptibility to inattentional blindness. *Journal of Experimental Psychology: Learning, Memory, and Cognition, 37,* 785–791. doi:10.1037/a0022474

Segal, Nancy L. (2012). *Born together—reared apart: The landmark Minnesota Twin Study.* Cambridge, MA: Harvard University Press.

Segal, Zindel V.; Bieling, Peter; Young, Trevor; MacQueen, Glenda; Cooke, Robert; Martin, Lawrence; Bloch, Richard; & Levitan, Robert D. (2010). Antidepressant monotherapy vs. sequential pharmacotherapy and mindfulness-based cognitive therapy, or placebo, for relapse prophylaxis in recurrent depression. *Archives of General Psychiatry, 67*(12), 1256–1264.

Segal, Zindel V.; Teasdale, John D.; & Williams, J. Mark G. (2004). Mindfulness-based cognitive therapy: Theoretical rationale and empirical status. In Steven C. Hayes, Victoria M. Follette, & Marsha M. Linehan (Eds.), *Mindfulness and acceptance: Expanding the cognitive-behavioral tradition.* New York, NY: Guilford.

Segal, Zindel V.; Williams, J. Mark G.; & Teasdale, John D. (2013). *Mindfulness-based cognitive therapy for depression: A new approach to preventing relapse* (2nd ed.) New York, NY: Guilford.

Segall, Marshall H. (1994). A cross-cultural research contribution to unraveling the nativist/empiricist controversy. In Walter J. Lonner & Roy Malpass (Eds.), *Psychology and culture.* Boston, MA: Allyn & Bacon.

Segall, Marshall H.; Campbell, Donald T.; & Herskovits, Melville J. (1963). Cultural differences in the perception of geometric illusions. *Science, 193,* 769–771.

Segall, Marshall H.; Campbell, Donald T.; & Herskovits, Melville J. (1966). *The influence of culture on visual perception.* Indianapolis, IN: Bobbs-Merrill.

Segerdahl, Pär; Fields, William; & Savage-Rumbaugh, Sue. (2006). *Kanzi's primal language: The cultural initiation of primates into language.* New York, NY: Palgrave Macmillan.

Segerstrom, Suzanne C.; Castañeda, Jay O.; & Spencer, Theresa E. (2003). Optimism effects on cellular immunity: Testing the affective and persistence models. *Personality and Individual Differences, 35,* 1615–1624.

Sela, Lee, & Sobel, Noam. (2010). Human olfaction: A constant state of change-blindness. *Experimental Brain Research, 205,* 13–29.

Selby, Edward A.; Bender, Theodore W.; Gordon, Kathryn H.; Nock, Matthew K.; & Joiner, Thomas E., Jr. (2011, July 4). Nonsuicidal selfinjury (NSSI) disorder: A preliminary study. *Personality Disorders: Theory, Research, and Treatment.* Advance online publication. doi:10.1037/a0024405

Self, David W. (2005). Neural basis of substance abuse and dependence. In Benjamin J. Sadock & Virginia A. Sadock (Eds.), *Comprehensive textbook of psychiatry* (8th ed.). Baltimore, MD: Lippincott Williams & Wilkins.

Seligman, Martin E.P. (1970). On the generality of the laws of learning. *Psychological Review, 77,* 406–418.

Seligman, Martin E.P. (1971). Phobias and preparedness. *Behavior Therapy, 2,* 307–320.

Seligman, Martin E.P. (1990). *Learned optimism.* New York, NY: Knopf.

Seligman, Martin E.P. (1992). *Helplessness: On development, depression, and death.* New York, NY: Freeman.

Seligman, Martin E.P. (2004). Can happiness be taught? *Daedalus, 133,* 80–87. doi:10.1162/001152604323049424

Seligman, Martin E. P. (2005). Positive psychology, positive prevention, and positive psychotherapy. In C. R. Snyder & Shane J. Lopez (Eds.), *Handbook of positive psychology.* New York, NY: Oxford University Press.

Seligman, Martin E. P.; Steen, Tracy A.; Park, Nansook; & Peterson, Christopher. (2005). Positive psychology progress: Empirical validation of interventions. *American Psychologist, 60,* 410-421. doi:10.1037/0003-066X.60.5.410

Seligman, Martin E.P. (2011). *Flourish: A visionary new understanding of happiness and well-being.* New York: Free Press.

Seligman, Martin E.P., & Maier, Steven F. (1967). Failure to escape traumatic shock. *Journal of Experimental Psychology, 37B,* 1–21.

Seligman, Martin E.P.; Steen, Tracy A.; Park, Nansook; & Peterson, Christopher. (2005). Positive psychology progress: Empirical validation of interventions. *American Psychologist, 60,* 410–421.

Sellers, Robert M.; Copeland-Linder, Nikeea; Martin, Pamela P.; & Lewis, R. L'Heureux. (2006). Racial identity matters: The relationship between racial discrimination and psychological functioning in African American adolescents. *Journal of Research on Adolescence, 16,* 187–216.

Selye, Hans. (1956). *The stress of life.* New York, NY: McGraw-Hill.

Selye, Hans. (1976). *The stress of life* (Rev. ed.). New York, NY: McGraw-Hill.

Senghas, Ann; Kita, Sotaro; & Özyürek, Asli. (2004, September 17). Children creating core properties of language: Evidence from an emerging sign language in Nicaragua. *Science, 305,* 1779–1782.

Sengoku, Mari; Murata, Hiroaki; Kawahara, Takanobu; Imamura, Kaori & Nakagome, Kazuyuki (2010). Does daily naikan therapy maintain the efficacy of intensive naikan therapy against depression?. *Psychiatry and Clinical Neurosciences, 64,* 44–51.

Senko, Corwin; Durik, Amanda M.; & Harackiewicz, Judith M. (2008). Historical perspectives and new directions in achievement goal theory: Understanding the effects of mastery and performance-approach. In James Y. Shah & Wendi L. Gardner (Eds.), *Handbook of motivation science.* New York, NY: Guilford.

Serlin, Ilene. (2012). The history and future of humanistic psychology. *Journal of Humanistic Psychology, 51,* 428–431. doi:10.1177/0022167811412600

Serrano, Zulai. (2013, October 8). Elizabeth Smart book: Kidnapping survivor says don't ask a victim why they didn't escape sooner. http://www.hngn.com/articles/14343/20131008/elizabeth-smart-book-kidnapping-survivor-dont-ask-victim-why-didnt.htm

Seung, Sebastian. (2012). *Connectome: How the brain's wiring makes us who we are.* Boston, MA: Houghton Mifflin.

Seurinck, Ruth; de Lange, Floris P.; Achten, Erik; & Vingerhoets, Guy. (2011). Mental rotation meets the motion after effect: The role of hV5/MT+ in visual mental imagery. *Journal of Cognitive Neuroscience, 2,* 1395–1404. doi:10.1162/jocn.2010.21525

Severus, W. Emanuel; Kleindienst, Nikolaus; Evoniuk, Gary; Bowden, Charles; Möller, Hans-Jürgen; Bohus, Martin; Fangou, Sophia; Greil, Waldemar & Calabrese, Joseph. (2009). Is the polarity of relapse/recurrence in bipolar-I disorder patients related to serum lithium levels? Results from an empirical study. *Journal of Affective Disorders, 115*(3), 466–470.

Sexton, Thomas L.; Alexander, James F.; & Mease, Alyson Leigh. (2004). Levels of evidence for the models and mechanisms of therapeutic change in family and couple therapy. In Michael J. Lambert (Ed.), *Bergin and Garfield's handbook of psychotherapy and behavior change* (5th ed.). New York, NY: Wiley.

Shafto, Meredith A., & Tyler, Lorraine K. (2014). Language in the aging brain: The network dynamics of cognitive decline and preservation. *Science, 346,* 583–587.

Shalvi, Shaul, & de Dreu, Carsten. (2014). Oxytocin promotes group-serving dishonesty. *Proceedings of the National Academy of Sciences, 111,* 5503–5507. doi:10.1073/pnas.1400724111

Shapiro, David A.; Barkham, Michael; Stiles, William B.; Hardy, Gillian E.; Rees, Anne; Reynolds, Shirley; & Startup, Mike. (2003). Time is of the essence: A selective review of the fall and rise of brief therapy research. *Psychology and Psychotherapy: Theory, Research and Practice, 76*(3), 211–235. doi:10.1348/147608303322362460

Shapiro, Francine. (1989a). Efficacy of the eye movement desensitization procedure in the treatment of traumatic memories. *Journal of Traumatic Stress, 2,* 199–223.

Shapiro, Francine. (1989b). Eye movement desensitization: A new treatment for post-traumatic stress disorder. *Journal of Behavior Therapy and Experimental Psychiatry, 20,* 211–217.

Shapiro, Francine. (2007). EMDR and case conceptualization from an adaptive information processing perspective. In Francine Shapiro, Florence W. Kaslow, & Louise Maxfield (Eds.), *Handbook of EMDR and family therapy processes* (pp. 3–34). Hoboken, NJ: Wiley.

Shapiro, Jenessa R.; Williams, Amy M.; & Hambarchyan, Mariam. (2013). Are all interventions created equal? A multi-threat approach to tailoring stereotype threat interventions. *Journal of Personality and Social Psychology, 104*(2), 277–288. doi:10.1037/a0030461

Shapiro, Shauna L., & Carlson, Linda E. (2009). *The art and science of mindfulness: Integrating mindfulness into psychology and the helping professions.* Washington, DC: American Psychological Association.

Shapiro, Shauna L., & Jazaieri, Hooria. (2015). Mindfulness-based stress reduction for healthy stressed adults. In Kirk Warren Brown, J. David Creswell, & Richard M. Ryan (Eds.), *Handbook of mindfulness: Theory, research, and practice.* New York, NY: Guilford.

Sharif, Zafar, Bradford, Daniel; Stroup, Scott; & Lieberman, Jeffrey. (2007) Pharmacological treatments for schizophrenia. In P. Nathan and J. Gorman (Eds.), *A guide to treatments that work* (3rd ed., pp. 203–242). New York, NY: Oxford University Press.

Sharman, Stefanie J.; Garry, Maryanne; & Beuke, Carl J. (2004). Imagination or exposure causes imagination inflation. *American Journal of Psychology, 117,* 157–168.

Sharpless, Brian A. (2015a). Exploding head syndrome is common in college students. *Journal of Sleep Research, 24,* 447–449. doi:10.1111/jsr.12292

Sharpless, Brian A. (2015b, April 3). Quoted in James Hamblin, "How many beliefs are due to sleep deprivation? *The Atlantic.* Retrieved from http://www.theatlantic.com/health/archive/2015/04/how-many-beliefs-are-due-to-sleep-deprivation/389303

Shaw, Benjamin A.; Krause, Neal; Chatters, Linda M.; & Ingersoll-Dayton, Berit. (2004). Emotional support from parents early in life, aging, and health. *Psychology of Aging, 19,* 4–12.

Shaw, Julia, & Porter, Stephen. (2015). Constructing rich false memories of committing crime. *Psychological Science, 26,* 291–301. doi:10.1177/0956797614562862

Shedler, Jonathan. (2010). The efficacy of psychodynamic therapy. *American Psychologist, 95,* 98–109.

Shedler, Jonathan; Mayman, Martin; & Manis, Melvin. (1993). The illusion of mental health. *American Psychologist, 48,* 1117–1131.

Sheldon, B. (2011). *Cognitive-behavioural therapy: Research and practice in health and social care* (2nd ed.). New York, NY: Routledge.

Sheldon, Kennon M. (2008). The interface of motivation science and personology: Self-concordance, quality motivation, and multilevel personality integration. In James Y. Shah & Wendi L. Gardner (Eds.), *Handbook of motivation science.* New York, NY: Guilford.

Sheldon, Kennon M., & Ryan, Richard M. (2011). Positive psychology and self-determination theory: A natural interface. In Valery I. Chirkov, Richard M. Ryan, Kennon M. Sheldon (Eds.), *Human autonomy in cross-cultural context.* New York, NY: Springer.

Sheldon, Kennon M.; Elliot, Andrew J.; Kim, Youngmee; & Kasser, Tim. (2001). What is satisfying about satisfying events? Testing 10 candidate psychological needs. *Journal of Personality and Social Psychology, 80,* 325–339.

Shen, Hao; Wan, Fang; & Wyer, Robert S., Jr. (2011). Cross-cultural differences in the refusal to accept a small gift: The differential influence of reciprocity norms on Asians and North Americans. *Journal of Personality and Social Psychology, 100*(2), 271–281.

Shepard, Roger N. (1990). *Mind sights: Original visual illusions, ambiguities, and other anomalies, with a commentary on the play of mind in perception and art.* New York, NY: Freeman.

Shepherd, Gordon M. (2004). Unsolved mystery: The human sense of smell: Are we better than we think? *PLOS Biology, 2,* 0572–0575.

Shepherd, Gordon M. (2006). Smell images and the flavour system in the human brain. *Nature, 444,* 316–321.

Shepherd, Jonathan. (2007). Preventing alcohol-related violence: A public health approach. *Criminal Behaviour & Mental Health, 17,* 250–264.

Sheppard, Leah D.; Goffin, Richard D.; Lewis, Rhys J.; & Olson, James. (2011). The effect of target attractiveness and rating method on the accuracy of trait ratings. *Journal of Personnel Psychology, 10*(1), 24–33.

Sherif, Muzafer. (1956, November). Experiments in group conflict. *Scientific American, 195,* 33–47.

Sherif, Muzafer. (1966). *In common predicament: Social psychology of intergroup conflict and cooperation.* Boston, MA: Houghton Mifflin, 502.

Sherif, Muzafer; Harvey, O. J.; White, B. Jack; Hood, William R.; & Sherif, Carolyn W. (1961/1988). *The Robbers Cave experiment: Intergroup conflict and cooperation.* Middletown, CT: Wesleyan University Press.

Sherman, David K.; Hartson, Kimberly A.; Binning, Kevin R.; Purdie-Vaughns, Valerie; Garcia, Julio; Taborsky-Barba, Suzanne; Tomassetti, Sarah; Nussbaum, A. David; & Cohen, Geoffrey L. (2013). Deflecting the trajectory and changing the narrative: How self-affirmation affects academic performance and motivation under identity threat. *Journal of Personality and Social Psychology, 104,* 591–618. doi:10.1037/a0031495

Sherman, Jeffrey W.; Stroessner, Steven J.; Conrey, Frederica R.; & Azam, Omar A. (2005). Prejudice and stereotype maintenance processes: Attention, attribution, and individuation. *Journal of Personality and Social Psychology, 89*(4), 607–622.

Sherman, Ryne A.; Rauthmann, John F.; Brown, Nicolas A.; Serfass, David G.; & Jones, Ashley B. (2015, April 27). The independent effects of personality and situations on real-time expressions of behavior and emotion. *Journal of Personality and Social Psychology.* No pagination specified. doi:10.1037/pspp0000036

Shermer, MIchael. (2011, April 19). Extransensory pornception: Doubts about a new paranormal claim. http://www.scientificamerican.com/article/extrasensory-pornception

Shettleworth, Sara J. (2010). *Cognition, evolution, and behavior* (2nd ed.). New York, NY: Oxford University Press.

Shevell, Steven K.; & Kingdom, Frederick A.A. (2008). Color in complex scenes. *Annual Review of Psychology, 5,* 143–166.

Shi, Jianxin; Levinson, Douglas F.; Duan, Jubao; Sanders, Alan R.; Zheng, Yonglan; Pe'er, Itsik; Dudbridge, Frank; & others. (2009). Common variants on chromosome 6p22.1 are associated with schizophrenia. *Nature, 460,* 753–757.

Shibasaki, Masahiro, & Kawai, Nobuyuki. (2009). Rapid detection of snakes by Japanese monkeys (Macaca fuscata): An evolutionarily predisposed visual system. *Journal of Comparative Psychology, 123,* 131–135. doi:10.1037/a0015095

Shidlo, Ariel, & Schroeder, Michael. (2002). Changing sexual orientation: A consumer's report. *Professional Psychology: Research and Practice, 33*(3), 249–259. Special Section: Responding to Sexual Orientation Issues. doi:10.1037/0735-7028.33.3.249

Shiffrin, Richard M., & Atkinson, Richard C. (1969). Storage and retrieval processes in long-term memory. *Psychological Review, 76*(2), 179–193.

Shih, Margaret J.; Pittinsky, Todd L.; & Ambady, Nalini. (1999). Stereotype susceptibility: Identity salience and shifts in quantitative performance. *Psychological Science, 10,* 80–83.

Shih, Margaret J.; Pittinsky, Todd L.; & Ho, Geoffrey C. (2012). Stereotype boost: Positive outcomes from the activation of positive stereotypes. In Michael Inzlicht & Toni Schmader (Eds.), *Stereotype threat: Theory, process, and application.* New York, NY: Oxford University Press.

Shih, Margaret J.; Pittinsky, Todd L.; & Trahan, Amy. (2006). Domain-specific effects of stereotypes on performance. *Self and Identity, 5,* 1–14.

Shinskey, Jeanne L., & Munakata, Yuko. (2005). Familiarity breeds searching: Infants reverse their novelty preferences when reaching for hidden objects. *Psychological Science, 16,* 596–600.

Shiozawa, Pedro; Fregni, Filipe; Benseñor, Isabela M.; Lotufo1, Paulo A.; Berlim, Marcelo T.; Daskalakis, Jeff Z.; Cordeiro, Quirino; & Brunoni, André R. (2014). Transcranial direct current stimulation for major depression: An updated systematic review and meta-analysis. *International Journal of Neuropsychopharmacology, 17,* 1443–1452. doi:10.1017/S1461145714000418

Shneidman, Edwin S. (1998). *The suicidal mind.* New York, NY: Oxford University Press.

Shneidman, Edwin S. (2004). *Autopsy of a suicidal mind.* New York, NY: Oxford University Press.

Shors, Tracey J. (2014). The adult brain makes new neurons, and effortful learning keeps them alive. *Current Directions in Psychological Science, 23,* 311–318. doi:10.1177/0963721414540167

Short, Tasmin B. R.; Thomas, Stuart; Luebbers, Stefan; Mullen, Paul; & Ogloff, James R. P. (2013). A case-linkage study of crime victimization in schizophrenia-spectrum disorders over a period of deinstitutionalization. *BMC Psychiatry, 13*(66), 1–9.

Shorter, Edward. (2009). History of electroconvulsive therapy. In Conrad M. Swartz (Ed.), *Electroconvulsive and neuromodulation therapies* (pp. 167–179). New York, NY: Cambridge University Press.

Shrager, Yael, & Squire, Larry R. (2009). Medial temporal lobe function and human memory. In M. S. Gazzaniga, E. Bizzi, L. M. Chalupa, S. T. Grafton, T. F. Heatherton, C. Koch, J. E. LeDoux, S. J. Luck, G. R. Mangan, J. A. Movshon, H. Neville, E. A. Phelps, P. Rakic, D. L. Schacter, M. Sur & B. A. Wandell (Eds.), *The cognitive neurosciences* (4th ed., pp. 675–690). Cambridge, MA: Massachusetts Institute of Technology.

SHRM. (2007, December). Strategic research on human capital challenges: Executive summary. Alexandria, VA: Author.

Shultz, Sarah; Vouloumanos, Athena; Bennett, Randi H.; & Pelphrey, Kevin. (2014). Neural specialization for speech in the first months of life. *Developmental Science, 17,* 766–774. doi:10.1016/j.neubiorev.2014.10.006

Shweder, R. A.; Much, N. C.; Mahapatra, M.; & Park, L. (1997). The "big three" of morality (autonomy, community, and divinity), and the "big three" explanations of suffering. In A. Brandt & P. Rozin (Eds.), *Morality and health.* New York, NY: Routledge.

Shweder, Richard A., & Haidt, Jonathan. (1993). The future of moral psychology: Truth, intuition, and the pluralist way. *Psychological Science, 4,* 360–365.

Siegal, Michael. (2004, September 17). Signposts to the essence of language. *Science, 305,* 1720–1721.

Siegel, Jerome M. (2005). Clues to the functions of mammalian sleep. *Nature, 437,* 1264–1271. doi:10.1038/nature04285

Siegel, Jerome M. (2009). Sleep viewed as a state of adaptive inactivity. *Nature Reviews Neuroscience 10,* 747–753. doi:10.1038/nrn2697

Siegel, Ronald D.; Gormer, Christopher K.; & Olendzki, Andrew. (2008). Mindfulness: What is it? Where does it come from? In Fabrizio Didonna (Ed.), *Clinical handbook of mindfulness.* New York, NY: Springer.

Siegle, Greg L.; Thompson, Wesley; Carter, Cameron S.; Steinhauer, Stuart R.; & Thase, Michael E. (2007). Increased amygdala and decreased dorsolateral prefrontal BOLD responses in unipolar depression: Related and independent features. *Biological Psychiatry, 61,* 198–209. doi:10.1016/j.biopsych.2006.05.048

Siegler, Irene C.; Poon, Leonard W.; Madden, David J.; Dilworth-Anderson, Peggy; Schaie, K. Warner; Willis, Sherry L.; & Martin, Peter. (2009). Psychological aspects of normal aging. In Dan German Blazer and David C. Steffens (Eds.), *The American Psychiatric Publishing textbook of geriatric psychiatry* (4th ed., pp. 137–155). Arlington, VA: American Psychiatric Publishing.

Siegler, Robert S. (1992). The other Alfred Binet. *Developmental Psychology, 28,* 179–190.

Sigman, Marian; Spence, Sarah J.; & Wang, A. Ting. (2006). Autism from developmental and neuropsychological perspectives. *Annual Review of Clinical Psychology, 2*(3), 327–355.

Silbersweig, David A.; Stern, Emily; & Frackowaik, R. S. J. (1995, November 9). A functional neuroanatomy of hallucinations in schizophrenia. *Nature, 387,* 176–184.

Silva, Christopher; Bridges, K. Robert; & Metzger, Mitchell. (2005). Personality, expectancy, and hypnotizability. *Personality and Individual Differences, 39,* 131–142.

Silver, Roxane Cohen; Holman, Alison E.; Pizarro Anderson, Judith; Poulin, Michael; McIntosh, Daniel N.; & Gil-Rivas, Virginia. (2013). Mental and physical-health effects of acute exposure to media of the September 11, 2001, attacks and the Iraq war. *Association for Psychological Science, 24*(9), 1623–1634. doi:70.7777/0956797612460406

Silverstein, Charles. (2009). The implications of removing homosexuality from the DSM as a mental disorder. *Archives of Sexual Behavior, 38*(2), 161–163.

Simner, Marvin L., & Goffin, Richard D. (2003, December). A position statement by the International Graphonomics Society on the use of graphology in personnel selection testing. *International Journal of Testing, 3*(4), 353–364.

Simon, Gregory; Goldberg, David P.; Von Korff, Michael; & Üstün, T. Bedirhan. (2002). Understanding cross-national differences in depression prevalence. *Psychological Medicine, 32,* 585–594. doi:10.1017/S0033291702005457

Simons, Daniel J.; Hannula, Deborah E.; Warren, David E.; & Day, Steven W. (2007). Behavioral, neuroimaging, and neuropsychological approaches to implicit perception. In Philip David Zelazo, Morris Moscovitch, & Evan Thompson (Eds.), *The Cambridge handbook of consciousness.* New York, NY: Cambridge University Press.

Simons, Leslie Gordon, & Conger, Rand D. (2007). Linking mother–father differences in parenting to a typology of family parenting styles and adolescent outcomes. *Journal of Family Issues, 28*(2), 212–241.

Simonton, Dean Keith. (2014). The mad-genius paradox: Can creative people be more mentally healthy but highly creative people more mentally ill? *Perspectives on Psychological Science, 9,* 470–480. doi:10.1177/1745691614543973

Singer, Tania. (2012). The past, present and future of social neuroscience: A European perspective. *NeuroImage, 61,* 437–449.

Singer, Tania, Seymour, B., O'Doherty, J., Kaube, H., Dolan, R. J.; & Frith, C. D. (2004). Empathy for pain involves the affective but not sensory components of pain. *Science, 303*(5661), 1157–1162.

Singer, Tania, Seymour, B., O'Doherty, J. P., Stephan, K. E., Dolan, R. J.; & Frith, C. D. (2006). Empathic neural responses are modulated by the perceived fairness of others. *Nature, 439,* 466–469.

Singer, Tania; Verhaeghen, Paul; Ghisletta, Paolo; Lindenberger, Ulman; & Baltes, Paul. (2003). The fate of cognition in very old age: Six-year longitudinal findings in the Berlin Aging Study (BASE). *Psychology and Aging, 18,* 318–331.

Singh, Devendra, Dixson, Barnaby. J.; Jessop, Tim. S.; Morgan, Bethan; & Dixson, Alan F. (2010). Cross-cultural consensus for waist–hip ratio and women's attractiveness. *Evolution and Human Behavior, 31*(3), 176–181. doi:10.1016/j.evolhumbehav.2009.09.001

Singh, Devendra; & Singh, Dorian. (2011). Shape and significance of feminine beauty: An evolutionary perspective. *Sex Roles, 64*(9-10), 723–731. doi:201110.1007/s11199-011-9938-z

Singh, Jay P.; Grann, Martin; Lichtenstein, Paul; Långström, Niklas; & Fazel, Seena. (2012). A novel approach to determining violence risk in schizophrenia: Developing a stepped strategy in 13,806 discharged patients. *PLOS ONE, 7*(2), 1–9. doi:10.1371

Singh, Maanvi. (2015, February 2). Why Cambodians never get 'depressed.' *NPR.* Retrieved from http://www.npr.org/blogs/goatsandsoda/2015/02/02/382905977/why-cambodians-never-get-depressed

Singhal, Arvind; Cody, Michael J.; Rogers, Everett M.; & Sabido, Miguel. (Eds.). (2004). *Entertainment-education and social change: History, research, and practice.* Mahwah, NJ: Erlbaum.

Skinner, B. F. (1938). *The behavior of organisms: An experimental analysis.* New York, NY: Appleton-Century-Crofts.

Skinner, B. F. (1948a/1976). *Walden two.* Englewood Cliffs, NJ: Prentice Hall.

Skinner, B. F. (1948b/1992). Superstition in the pigeon. *Journal of Experimental Psychology: General, 121,* 273–274.

Skinner, B. F. (1953). *Science and human behavior.* New York, NY: Macmillan.

Skinner, B. F. (1956). A case history in scientific method. *American Psychologist, 11,* 221–233.

Skinner, B. F. (1961, November). Teaching machines. *Scientific American, 205,* 90–102.

Skinner, B. F. (1966). Some responses to the stimulus "Pavlov." *Conditional Reflex, 1,* 74–78. (Reprinted in 1999 in the *Journal of the Experimental Analysis of Behavior, 72,* 463–465).

Skinner, B. F. (1967). B. F. Skinner . . . an autobiography. In E. G. Boring & G. Lindzey (Eds.), *A history of psychology in autobiography* (Vol. 5). New York, NY: Appleton-Century-Crofts.

Skinner, B. F. (1971). *Beyond freedom and dignity.* New York, NY: Bantam Books.

Skinner, B. F. (1974). *About behaviorism.* New York, NY: Knopf.

Slack, Gordy. (2007, November 12). Source of human empathy found in the brain. *New Scientist, 2629,* 12.

Slagter, Heleen A.; Davidson, Richard A.; & Lutz, Antoine. (2011). Mental training as a tool in the neuroscientific study of brain and cognitive plasticity. *Frontiers in Human Neuroscience, 5,* 1–12. doi:10.3389/fnhum.2011.00017

Slater, Alan; Quinn, Paul C.; Kelly, David J.; Lee, Kang; Longmore, Christopher A.; McDonald, Paula R.; & Pascalis, Olivier. (2010). The shaping of the face space in early infancy: Becoming a native face processor. *Child Development Perspectives, 4*(3), 205–211.

Slater, Alan; Von der Schulenburg, Charlotte; Brown, Elizabeth; Badenoch, Marion; Butterworth, George; Parsons, Sonia; & Samuels, Curtis. (1998). Newborn infants prefer attractive faces. *Infant Behavior and Development, 21*(2), 345–354.

Sleeth, Daniel B. (2007). The self system: Toward a new understanding of the whole person (Part 3). *The Humanistic Psychologist, 35,* 45–66.

Slobodchikoff, C. N.; Paseka, Andrea; & Verdolin, Jennifer L. (2009). Prairie dog alarm calls encode labels about predator colors. *Animal Cognition 12*: 435–439.

Slotnick, Scott D., & Schacter, David L. (2007). The cognitive neuroscience of memory and consciousness. In Philip David Zelazo, Morris Moscovitch, & Evan Thompson (Eds.), *The Cambridge handbook of consciousness.* New York, NY: Cambridge University Press.

Slutzky, Carly B., & Simpkins, Sandra D. (2009). The link between children's sport participation and self-esteem: Exploring the mediating role of sport self-concept. *Psychology of Sport and Exercise, 10*(3), 381–389.

Smalarz, Laura, & Wells, Gary L. (2015). Contamination of eyewitness self-reports and the mistaken-identification problem. *Current Directions in Psychological Science, 24,* 120–124. doi:10.1177/0963721414554394

Smallwood, Jonathan; McSpadden, Merrill; & Schooler, Jonathan W. (2007). The lights are on but no one's home: Meta-awareness and the decoupling of attention when the mind wanders. *Psychonomic Bulletin & Review, 14*(3), 527–533.

Smart, Reginald G.; Mann, Robert E.; & Stoduto, Gina. (2003). The prevalence of road rage: Estimates from Ontario. *Canadian Journal of Public Health, 94*(4), 247–250.

Smerud, Phyllis E., & Rosenfarb, Irwin S. (2011). The therapeutic alliance and family psychoeducation in the treatment of schizophrenia: An exploratory prospective change process study. *Couple and Family Psychology: Research and Practice, 1*(S), 85–91.

Smilek, Daniel; Carriere, Jonathan S. A.; & Cheyne, Allan J. (2010). Out of mind, out of sight: Eye blinking as indicator and embodiment of mind wandering. *Psychological Science, 21,* 78–789.

Smith, Brendan L. (2012, April). The case against spanking. *APA Monitor on Psychology, 43,* 60–63.

Smith, Craig A., & Kirby, Leslie D. (2011). The role of appraisal and emotion in coping and adaptation. In Richard J. Contrada & Andrew Baum (Eds.), *The handbook of stress science: Biology, psychology, and health.* New York, NY: Springer.

Smith, Craig A.; David, Bieke; & Kirby, Leslie D. (2006). Emotion-eliciting appraisals of social situations. In Joseph P. Forgas (Ed.), *Affect in social thinking and behavior.* New York, NY: Psychology Press.

Smith, Eliot R., & Collins, Elizabeth C. (2009). Contextualizing person perception: Distributed social cognition. *Psychological Review, 116,* 343–364.

Smith, Jonathan A., & Rhodes, John E. (2015). Being depleted and being shaken: An interpretative phenomenological analysis of the experiential features of a first episode of depression. *Psychology and Psychotherapy: Theory, Research and Practice, 88,* 197–209.

Smith, Jonathan C. (2010). *Pseudoscience and extraordinary claims: A critical thinker's toolkit.* Malden, MA: Wiley-Blackwell.

Smith, Kerri. (2012). Brain imaging: fMRI 2.0. *Nature, 484,* 24–26 doi:10.1038/484024a

Smith, Nicholas A., & Trainor, Laurel J. (2008). Infant-directed speech is modulated by infant feedback. *Infancy, 13*(4), 410–420.

Smith, Pamela K.; Dijksterhuis, Ap; & Chaiken, Shelly. (2008). Subliminal exposure to faces and racial attitudes: Exposure to whites makes whites like blacks less. *Journal of Experimental Social Psychology, 44,* 50–64.

Smith, Peter B. (2010). Cross-cultural psychology: Some accomplishments and challenges. *Psychological Studies, 55*(2), 89–95.

Smith, Timothy B.; Domenech Rodríguez, Melanie; & Bernal, Guillermo. (2011). Culture. *Journal of Clinical Psychology: In Session, 67,* 166–175. doi:10.1002/jclp.20757

Smith, Timothy B.; McCullough, Michael E.; & Poll, Justin. (2005). Religiousness and depression: Evidence for a main effect and the moderating influence of stressful life events. *Psychological Bulletin, 129,* 614–636.

Smolak, Linda. (2009). Risk factors in the development of body image, eating problems, and obesity. In Linda Smolak & J. Kevin Thompson (Eds.), *Body image, eating disorders, and obesity in youth: Assessment, prevention, and treatment* (2nd ed., pp. 135–155). Washington, DC: American Psychological Association.

Smoller, Jordan W., & Finn, Christopher T. (2003). Family, twin, and adoption studies of bipolar disorder. *American Journal of Medical Genetics, Part C, Seminars in Medical Genetics, 123C*(1), 48–58.

Sneddon, Ian; McKeown, Gary; McRorie, Margaret; Vukicevic, Tijana. (2011). Cross-cultural patterns in dynamic ratings of positive and negative natural emotional behaviour. *PLOS ONE, 6*(2): e14679. doi:10.1371/journal.pone.0014679

Sneed, Joel R.; Whitbourne, Susan Krauss; Schwartz, Seth J.; & Huang, Shi. (2012). The relationship between identity, intimacy, and midlife well-being: Findings from the Rochester Adult Longitudinal Study. *Psychology and Aging, 27,* 318–323. doi:10.1037/a0026378

Snitz, Beth E.; O'Meara, Ellen S.; Carlson, Michelle C.; Arnold, Alice M.; Ives, Diane G.; Rapp, Stephen R.; Saxton, Judith; Lopez, Oscar L.; Dunn, Leslie O.; Sink, Kaycee M.; & DeKosky, Steven T. (2009). Ginkgo biloba for preventing cognitive decline in older adults: A randomized trial. *JAMA: Journal of the American Medical Association, 302*(24), 2663–2670.

Snowdon, David A. (2002). *Aging with grace: What the nun study teaches us about leading longer, healthier, and more meaningful lives.* New York, NY: Bantam.

Snowdon, David A. (2003). Healthy aging and dementia: Findings from the Nun Study. *Annals of Internal Medicine, 139,* 450–454.

Snyder, Charles R.; Lopez, Shane J.; & (Teramoto) Pedrotti, Jennifer T. (2011). *Positive psychology: The scientific and practical explorations of human strengths.* Thousand Oaks, CA: Sage.

Snyder, Hannah R.; Kaiser, Roselinde H.; Warren, Stacie L.; & Heller, Wendy. (2014). Obsessive-compulsive disorder is associated with broad impairments in executive function: A meta-analysis. *Clinical Psychological Science, 3,* 301–330. doi:10.1177/2167702614534210

Snyder, Douglas K., & Balderrama-Durbin, Christina. (2012). Integrative approaches to couple therapy: Implications for clinical practice and research. *Behavior Therapy 43,* 13–24. doi:10.1016/j.beth.2011.03.004

Soderstrom, Nicholas C., & Bjork, Robert A. (2015). Learning versus performance: An integrative review. *Perspectives on Psychological Science, 10,* 176–199. doi:10.1177/1745691615569000

Soderstrom, Nicholas C., & Bjork, Robert A. (2015). Learning versus performance: An integrative review. *Perspectives on Psychological Science, 10,* 176–199. doi:10.1177/1745691615569000

Sohn, Michael, & Bosinski, Hartmut A. G. (2007) Continuing medical education: Gender identity disorders: diagnostic and surgical aspects (CME). *Journal of Sexual Medicine.* 4, 1193–1208.

Sokal, Michael H. (2001). Practical phrenology as psychological counseling in the 19th-century United States. In C. D. Green, M. Shore, & T. Teo (Eds.), *The transformation of psychology: Influences of 19th-century philosophy, technology, and natural science.* Washington, DC: American Psychological Association.

Sokol, Robert J., Jr.; Delaney-Black, Virginia; & Nordstrom, Beth. (2003). Fetal alcohol spectrum disorder. *Journal of the American Medical Association, 290*(22), 2996–2999. doi:10.1001/jama.290.22.2996

Solomon, David A.; Leon, Andrew C.; Coryell, William H.; Endicott, Jean; Li, Chunshan; Fiedorowics, Jess G.; Boyken, Lara; & Keller, Martin B. (2010). Longitudinal course of bipolar I disorder. *Archives of General Psychiatry, 67*(4), 339–347. doi:10.1001/archgenpsychiatry.2010.15

Solomon, Henry; Solomon, Linda Zener; Arnone, Maria M.; Maur, Bonnie J.; Reda, Rosina M.; & Roth, Esther O. (1981). Anonymity and helping. *Journal of Social Psychology, 113,* 37–43. doi:10.1080/00224545.1981.9924347

Solomon, Hester McFarland. (2003). Freud and Jung: An incomplete encounter. *Journal of Analytical Psychology, 48,* 553–569.

Solomon, Linda Zener; Solomon, Henry; & Stone, Ronald. (1978). Helping as a function of number of bystanders and ambiguity of emergency. *Personality and Social Psychology Bulletin, 4,* 318–321.

Solomon, Paul R.; Adams, Felicity; Silver, Amanda; Zimmer, Jill; & De-Veaux, Richard. (2002). Ginkgo for memory enhancement: A randomized controlled trial. *Journal of the American Medical Association, 288,* 835–840.

Solomon, Samuel G., & Lennie, Peter. (2007). The machinery of colour vision. *Nature Reviews Neuroscience, 8*(4), 276–286.

Somerville, Leah H. (2013). The teenage brain: Sensitivity to social evaluation. *Current Directions in Psychological Science, 22,* 121–127. doi:10.1177/0963721413476512

Sorenson, Karen. (2011). [Letter to Sandra Hockenbury]. Copy in possession of Sandra Hockenbury.

Sorkhabi, Nadia. (2010). Sources of parent-adolescent conflict: Content and form of parenting. *Social Behavior & Personality: An International Journal, 38*(6), 761–782.

Soto, Christopher J.; John, Oliver P.; Gosling, Samuel D.; & Potter, Jeff. (2011). Age differences in personality traits from 10 to 65: Big five domains and facets in a large cross-sectional sample. *Journal of Personality and Social Psychology, 100*(2), 330–348.

Soussignan, Robert. (2004). Regulatory function of facial actions in emotion processes. In Serge P. Shohov (Ed.), *Advances in Psychology Research, 31,* 173–198. Hauppauge, NY: Nova Science.

Southall, Ashley. (2015, April 12). 2 Alabama college students charged in spring break sexual assault on Florida beach. *New York Times.* Retrieved from http://www.nytimes.com/2015/04/13/us/2-alabama-college-students-charged-in-sexual-assault-on-florida-beach.html?_r=1

Southwick, Steven M.; Vythilingam, Meena; & Charney, Dennis S. (2005). The psychobiology of depression and resilience to stress: Implications for prevention and treatment. *Annual Review of Clinical Psychology, 1,* 255–291.

Spalding, Kirsty L; Bergmann, Olaf; Alkass, Kanar; Bernard, Samuel; Salehpour, Mehran; Huttner, Hagen B.; Boström, Emil; Westerlund, Isabelle; Vial, Céline; Buchholz, Bruce A.; Possnert, Göran; Mash, Deborah C.; Druid, Henrik; & Frisén, Jonas. (2013). Dynamics of hippocampal neurogenesis in adult humans. *Cell, 153,* 1219–1227.

Spangler, William D. (1992). Validity of questionnaire and TAT measures of need for achievement: Two meta-analyses. *Psychological Bulletin, 112,* 140–154.

Spanos, Nicholas P. (1987–1988, Winter). Past-life hypnotic regression: A critical view. *Skeptical Inquirer, 12,* 174–180.

Sparks, Jacqueline A.; Duncan, Barry L.; & Miller, Scott D. (2008). Common factors in psychotherapy. In Jay L. Lebow (Ed.), *Twenty-first century psychotherapies: Contemporary approaches to theory and practice* (pp. 453–497). Hoboken, NJ: Wiley.

Spearman, Charles E. (1904). "General intelligence" objectively determined and measured. *American Journal of Psychology, 15,* 201–293.

Spencer, Natasha A.; McClintock, Martha K.; Sellergren, Sarah A.; Bullivant, Susan; Jacob, Suma; & Mennella, Julie A. (2004). Social chemosignals from breastfeeding women increase sexual motivation. *Hormones and Behavior, 46,* 362–370.

Sperling, George. (1960). The information available in brief visual presentations. *Psychological Monographs, 74*(48).

Sperry, Roger W. (1982). Some effects of disconnecting the cerebral hemispheres. *Science, 217,* 1223–1226.

Spezzaferri, Rosa; Modica, Maddalena; Racca, Vittorio; Ripamonti, Vittorino; Tavanelli, Monica; Brambilla, Gabriella; & Ferratini, Maurizio. (2009). Psychological disorders after coronary artery by-pass surgery: A one-year prospective study. *Monaldi Archives for Chest Disease, 72*(4), 200–205.

Spies, Robert A.; Carlson, Janet F.; & Geisinger, Kurt F. (2010). *The mental measurements yearbook* (18th ed.), Lincoln: Buros Institute of Mental Measurements/University of Nebraska Press.

Sponheim, Scott R.; McGuire, Kathryn A.; Kang, Seung Suk; Davenport, Nicholas D.; Aviyente, Selin; Bernat, Edward M.; & Lim, Kelvin O. (2011). Evidence of disrupted functional connectivity in the brain after combat-related blast injury. *NeuroImage, 54*(Suppl 1), S21–S29. doi:10.1016/j.neuroimage.2010.09.007

Sporns, Olaf. (2011a). The human connectome: A complex network. *Annals of New York Academy of Science, 1224* (2011) 109–125. doi:10.1111/j.1749-6632.2010.05888.x

Sporns, Olaf. (2011b). *Networks of the brain.* Cambridge, MA: MIT Press.

Spradlin, Joseph E. (2002). Punishment: A primary process. *Journal of Applied Behavior Analysis, 35*(4), 475–477.

Sprecher, Susan, & Felmlee, Diane. (2008). Insider perspectives on attraction. In S. Sprecher, A. Wenzel & J. Harvey (Eds.), *Handbook of relationship initiation.* New York, NY: Psychology Press.

Springer, Sally P., & Deutsch, Georg. (2001). *Left brain, right brain. Perspectives from cognitive neuroscience* (5th ed.). New York, NY: Freeman/Worth.

Sritharan, Rajees, & Gawronski, Bertram. (2010). Changing implicit and explicit prejudice: Insights from the associative-propositional evaluation model. *Social Psychology, 41*(3), 2010, 113–123. doi:10.1027/1864-9335/a000017

Sroufe, L. Alan. (2002). From infant autonomy to promotion of adolescent autonomy: Prospective, longitudinal data on the role of parents in development. In John G. Borkowski & Sharon Landesman Ramey (Eds.), *Parenting and the child's world: Influences on academic, intellectual, and social-emotional development.* Mahwah, NJ: Erlbaum.

Staats, Sara; Cosmar, David; & Kaffenberger, Joshua. (2007). Sources of happiness and stress for college students: A replication and comparison over 20 years. *Psychological Reports, 10,* 685–696.

Stack, Dale M.; Serbin, Lisa A.; Enns, Leah N.; Ruttle, Paula L.; & Barrieau, Lindsey. (2010). Parental effects on children's emotional development over time and across generations. *Infants & Young Children, 23*(1), 52–69. doi:10.1097/IYC.1090b1013e3181c97606

Stahl, Stephen M. (2009). *Stahl's illustrated antipsychotics.* New York, NY: Cambridge University Press.

Stahre, Mandy; Roeber, Jim; Kanny, Dafna; Brewer, Robert D.; & Zhang, Xingyou. (2014). Contribution of excessive alcohol consumption to deaths and years of potential life lost in the United States. *Preventing Chronic Disease, 11,* 130293. doi:10.5888/pcd11.130293

Stallen, Mirre; De Dreu, Carsten K. W.; Shalvi, Shaul; Smidts, Ale; & Sanfey, Alan G. (2012). The herding hormone: Oxytocin stimulates in-group conformity *Psychological Science, 23,* 1288–1292. doi:10.1177/0956797612446026

Stams, Geert-Jan J. M.; Juffer, Femmie; & van IJzendoorn, Marinus H. (2002). Maternal sensitivity, infant attachment, and temperament in early childhood predict adjustment in middle childhood: The case of adopted children and their biologically unrelated parents. *Developmental Psychology, 38,* 806–821.

Stanley, Damian A.; Sokol-Hessner, Peter; Banaji, Mahzarin R.; & Phelps, Elizabeth A. (2011). Implicit race attitudes predict trustworthiness judgments and economic trust decisions. *PNAS 108,* 7710–7715; Advanced online publication, April 25, 2011. doi:10.1073/pnas.1014345108

Stark, Craig E. L.; Okado, Yoko; Loftus, Elizabeth F. (2010). Imaging the reconstruction of true and false memories using sensory reactivation and the misinformation paradigms. *Learning & Memory, 17,* 485–488. doi:10.1101/lm.1845710

Staub, Ervin. (1996). Cultural-societal roots of violence: The examples of genocidal violence and of contemporary youth violence in the United States. *American Psychologist, 51,* 117–132.

Steadman, Henry J.; Mulvey, Edward P.; Monahan, John; Robbins, Pamela Clark; Appelbaum, Paul S.; Grisso, Thomas; & others. (1998). Violence by people discharged from acute psychiatric inpatient facilities and by others in the same neighborhoods. *Archives of General Psychiatry, 55,* 393–401.

Steblay, Nancy Mehrkens. (1987). Helping behavior in urban and rural environments: A meta-analysis. *Psychological Bulletin, 102,* 346–356.

Steel, Piers. (2007). The nature of procrastination: A meta-analytic and theoretical review of quintessential self-regulatory failure. *Psychological Bulletin, 133,* 65–94.

Steele, Claude M. (1997). A threat in the air: How stereotypes shape intellectual identity and performance. *American Psychologist, 52,* 613–629.

Steele, Claude M. (2003). Through the back door to theory. *Psychological Inquiry, 14,* 314–317.

Steele, Claude M. (2011). *Whistling Vivaldi: How stereotypes affect us and what we can do.* New York, NY: Norton.

Steele, Claude M., & Aronson, Joshua. (1995). Stereotype threat and the intellectual performance of African Americans. *Journal of Personality and Social Psychology, 69,* 797–811.

Steele, Jeannette. (2012, January 8). PTSD? Try meditation, yoga. *UT-San Diego.* Retrieved from http://www.utsandiego.com/news/2012/jan/08/ptsd-try-meditation-and-yoga

Steele, Jennifer R.; Reisz, Leah.; Williams, Amanda.; & Kawakami, Kerry. (2007). Women in mathematics: Examining the hidden barriers that gender stereotypes can impose. In Ronald J. Burke & Mary C. Mattis (Eds.), *Women and minorities in science, technology, engineering and mathematics: Upping the numbers.* London, England: Elgar.

Stefansson, Hrein; Ophoff, Roei A.; Steinberg, Stacy; Andreassen, Ole A.; Cichon, Sven; Rujescu, Dan; Werge, Thomas; & others. (2009). Common variants conferring risk of schizophrenia. *Nature, 460,* 744–747.

Steg, Linda, & de Groot, Judith. (2010). Explaining prosocial intentions: Testing causal relationships in the norm activation model. *British Journal of Social Psychology, 49*(4), 725–743.

Stegner, Aaron J., & Morgan, William P. (2010). Hypnosis, exercise, and sport psychology. In Steven Jay Lynn, Judith W. Rhue, & Irving Kirsch (Eds.). (2010). *Handbook of clinical hypnosis* (2nd ed.). Washington, DC: American Psychological Association.

Stein, Elliot A.; Pankiewicz, John; Harsch, Harold H.; Cho, Jung-Ki; Fuller, Scott A.; Hoffmann, Raymond G.; & others. (1998). Nicotine-induced limbic cortical activation in the human brain: A functional MRI study. *American Journal of Psychiatry, 155,* 1009–1015.

Stein, Murray B.; & Steckler, Thomas. (2010). *Behavioral neurobiology of anxiety and its treatment.* New York, NY: Springer Science + Business Media.

Steinberg, Laurence. (1990). Autonomy, conflict, and harmony in the family relationship. In S. Shirley Feldman & Glen R. Elliott (Eds.), *At the threshold: The developing adolescent.* Cambridge, MA: Harvard University Press.

Steinberg, Laurence. (2001). We know some things: Parent–adolescent relationships in retrospect and prospect. *Journal of Research on Adolescence, 11,* 1–19.

Stellar, Jennifer; John-Henderson, Neha; Anderson, Craig; Gordon, Amie; McNeil, Galen; & Keltner, Dacher. (2015). Positive affect and markers of inflammation: Discrete positive emotions predict lower levels of inflammatory cytokines. *Emotion, 15*(2), 129–133. doi:10.1037/emo0000033

Stellman, Jeanne Mager; Smith, Rebecca P.; Katz, Craig L.; Sharma, Vansh; Charney, Dennis S.; Herbert, Robin; Moline, Jacqueline; & others. (2008). Enduring mental health morbidity and social function impairment in World Trade Center rescue, recovery, and cleanup workers: The psychological dimension of an environmental health disaster. *Environmental Health Perspectives, 116,* 1248–1253.

Stephens, Benjamin R., & Banks, Martin S. (1987) Contrast discrimination in human infants. *Journal of Experimental Psychology: Human Perception and Performance, 13,* 558–565.

Steptoe, Andrew; Dockray, Samantha; & Wardle, Jane. (2009). Positive affect and psychobiological processes relevant to health. *Journal of Personality, 77*(6), 1747–1776.

Steptoe, Andrew; Shankar, Aparna; Demakakos, Panayotes; & Wardle, Jane. (2013). Social isolation, loneliness, and all-cause mortality in older men and women. *Proceedings of the National Academy of Sciences, 110,* 5797–5801. doi:10.1073/pnas.1219686110

Stern, Kathleen, & McClintock, Martha K. (1998, March 12). Regulation of ovulation by human hormones. *Nature, 392,* 177.

Stern, Peter. (2001). Sweet dreams are made of this. *Science, 294,* 1047.

Sternberg, Robert J. (1986). *Intelligence applied: Understanding and increasing your intellectual skills.* San Diego, CA: Harcourt Brace Jovanovich.

Sternberg, Robert J. (1988). A three-facet model of creativity. In Robert J. Sternberg (Ed.), *The nature of creativity.* New York, NY: Cambridge University Press.

Sternberg, Robert J. (1990). *Metaphors of mind: Conceptions of the nature of intelligence.* New York, NY: Cambridge University Press.

Sternberg, Robert J. (1995). For whom the bell curve tolls: A review of the bell curve. *Psychological Science, 6,* 257–261.

Sternberg, Robert J. (1997). The concept of intelligence and its role in lifelong learning and success. *American Psychologist, 52,* 1030–1037.

Sternberg, Robert J. (2008). Applying psychological theories to educational practice. *American Educational Research Journal, 45,* 150–165.

Sternberg, Robert J. (2012). Intelligence in its cultural context. In Michele J. Gelfand, Chi-yue Ciu, & Ying-yi Hong (Eds.), *Advances in culture and psychology.* (Vol. 2). New York, NY: Oxford University Press.

Sternberg, Robert J. (2012). The triarchic theory of successful intelligence. In Dawn P. Flanagan & Patti L. Harrison. (Eds.) *Contemporary intellectual assessment: Theories, tests, and issues* (3rd ed.). New York, NY: Guilford.

Sternberg, Robert J. (2014a). I study what I stink at: Lessons learned from a career in psychology. *Annual Review of Psychology, 65,* 2014, 1–16. doi:10.1146/annurev-psych-052913-074851

Sternberg, Robert J. (2014b). Teaching about the nature of intelligence. *Intelligence, 42,* 176–179. doi:10.1016/j.intell.2013.08.010

Stevenson, Harold W.; Lee, Shin-Ying; & Stigler, James W. (1986). Mathematics achievements of Chinese, Japanese, and American children. *Science, 236,* 693–698.

Steward, Barbara. (2000). Changing times: The meaning, measurement and use of time in teleworking. *Time & Society, 9,* 57–74.

Stewart-Williams, Steve, & Podd, John. (2004). The placebo effect: Dissolving the expectancy versus conditioning debate. *Psychological Bulletin, 130,* 324–340.

Stewart, V. Mary. (1973). Tests of the "carpentered world" hypothesis by race and environment. *International Journal of Psychology, 8,* 12–34.

Stice, Eric; Yokum, Sonja; Blum, Kenneth; & Bohon, Cara. (2010). Weight gain is associated with reduced striatal response to palatable food. *Journal of Neuroscience, 30,* 13105–13109.

Stickgold, Robert, & Walker, Matthew P. (2013). Sleep-dependent memory triage: Evolving generalization through selective processing. *Nature Neuroscience, 16,* 139–145.

Stigler, Melissa; Dhavan, Poonam; Van Dusen, Duncan; Arora, Monika; Reddy, K.S.; & Perry, Cheryl L. (2010). Westernization and tobacco use among young people in Delhi, India. *Social Science & Medicine, 71*(5), 891–897.

Stinson, Danu A., Cameron, Jessica J., Wood, Joanne V., Gaucher, Danielle, & Holmes, J. G. (2009). Deconstructing the "reign of error": Interpersonal warmth explains the self-fulfilling prophecy of anticipated acceptance. *Personality and Social Psychology Bulletin, 35,* 1165–1178.

Stipek, Deborah. (1998). Differences between Americans and Chinese in the circumstances evoking pride, shame, and guilt. *Journal of Cross-Cultural Psychology, 29,* 616–629.

Stogdill, Ralph M. (1948). Personal factors associated with leadership: A survey of the literature. *Journal of Psychology, 25,* 35–71.

Stompe, Thomas; Karakula, Hanna; Rudaleviciene, Palmira; Okribelashvili, Nino; Chaudhry, Haroon R.; Idemudia, E. E., & Gscheider, S. (2006). The pathoplastic effect of culture on psychotic symptoms in schizophrenia. *World Cultural Psychiatry Research Review, 1*(3/4), 157–163.

Storm, Benjamin C., & Angello, Genna. (2010). Overcoming fixation: Creative problem solving and retrieval-induced forgetting. *Psychological Science, 21*(9), 1263–1265. doi:10.1177/0956797610379864

Storm, Lance; Tressoldi, Patrizio E.; & Di Risio, Lorenzo. (2010). Meta-analysis of free-response studies, 1992–2008: Assessing the noise reduction model in parapsychology. *Psychological Bulletin, 136*(4), 471–485.

Storm, Lance; Tressoldi, Patrizio E.; & Utts, Jessica. (2013). Testing the Storm et al. (2010) meta-analysis using Bayesian and frequentist approaches: Reply to Rouder et al. (2013). *Psychological Bulletin, 139,* 248–254. doi:10.1037/a0029506

Støving, René Klinkby; Andries, Alin; Brixen, Kim; Bilenberg, Niels; & Hørder, Kirsten. (2011). Gender differences in outcome of eating disorders: A retrospective cohort study. *Psychiatry Research, 186*(2–3), 362–366.

Stowell, Jeffrey R.; Oldham, Terrah; & Bennett, Dan. (2010). Using student response systems ("clickers") to combat conformity and shyness. *Teaching of Psychology, 37*(2), 135–140.

Strack, Fritz; Martin, Leonard L.; & Stepper, Sabine. (1988). Inhibiting and facilitating conditions of the human smile: A non-obtrusive test of the facial-feedback hypothesis. *Journal of Personality and Social Psychology, 54,* 768–777.

Strahan, Erin J.; Spencer, Steven J.; & Zanna, Mark P. (2005). Subliminal priming and persuasion: How motivation affects the activation of goals and the persuasiveness of messages. In Frank R. Kardes, Paul M. Herr, & Jacques Nantel (Eds.), *Applying social cognition to consumer-focused strategy.* Mahwah, NJ: Erlbaum.

Strange, Deryn; Garry, Maryanne; Bernstein, Daniel M.; & Lindsay, D. Stephen. (2011). Photographs cause false memories for the news. *Acta Psychologica, 136*(1), 90–94.

Straube, Thomas; Glauer, Madlen; Dilger, Stefan; Mentzel, Hans-Joachim; & Miltner, Wolfgang H. R. (2006). Effects of cognitive-behavioral therapy on brain activation in specific phobia. *NeuroImage, 29,* 125–135. doi:10.1016/j.neuroimage.2005.07.007

Strauss, Clara; Cavanagh, Kate; Oliver, Annie; & Pettman, Danelle. (2014). Mindfulness-based interventions for people diagnosed with a current episode of an anxiety or depressive disorder: A meta-analysis of randomised controlled trials. *PLOS ONE, 9*(4), 1–13. doi:10.1371/journal.pone.0096110

Strayer, David L.; Cooper, Joel M.; Turrill, Jonna; Coleman, James; Medeiros-Ward, Nate; & Biondi, Francesco. (2013). *Measuring cognitive distraction in the automobile.* Washington, DC: AAA Foundation for Traffic Safety.

Strayer, David L.; Drews, Frank A.; & Crouch, Dennis J. (2006). A comparison of the cell phone driver and the drunk driver. *Human Factors: The Journal of the Human Factors and Ergonomics Society, 48,* 381–391.

Stricker, George, & Gold, Jerold. (2008). Integrative therapy. In Jay L. Lebow (Ed.), *Twenty-first century psychotherapies: Contemporary approaches to theory and practice* (pp. 389–423). Hoboken, NJ: Wiley.

Strickland, Bonnie R. (1995). Research on sexual orientation and human development: A commentary. *Developmental Psychology, 31,* 137–140.

Strickland, Brent, & Keil, Frank. (2011). Event completion: Event based inferences distort memory in a matter of seconds. *Cognition, 121,* 409–415. doi:10.1016/j.cognition.2011.04.007

Stromberg, Joseph. (2015, April 14). Why the Myers-Briggs test is totally meaningless. *Vox.* Retrieved from http://www.vox.com/2014/7/15/5881947/myers-briggs-personality-test-meaningless

Stuart, Gwynedd. (2013, Oct. 19). Show us your . . . sleeping mats for the homeless. *Chicago Reader.* Retrieved from: http://www.chicagoreader.com/chicago/new-life-old-bags-ruth-werstler-homeless-recycle

Stults-Kolehmainen, Matthew, & Sinha, Rajita. (2014). The effects of stress on physical activity and exercise. *Sports Medicine, 44*(1), 81–121. doi:10.1007/s40279-013-0090-5

Suarez-Morales, Lourdes; Dillon, Frank R.; & Szapocznik, Jose. (2007). Validation of the Acculturative Stress Inventory for Children. *Cultural Diversity and Ethnic Minority Psychology, 13,* 216–224.

Substance Abuse and Mental Health Services Administration. (2009). *Results from the 2008 National Survey on Drug Use and Health: National findings* (Office of Applied Studies, NSDUH Series H-36, HHS Publication No. SMA 09-4434). Rockville, MD.

Sudak, Donna M. (2011). *Combining CBT and medication: An evidence-based approach.* Hoboken, NJ: Wiley.

Sue, David, & Sue, Diane M. (2008a). *Foundations of counseling and psychotherapy: Evidence-based practices for a diverse society.* Hoboken, NJ: Wiley.

Sue, Derald Wing; Capodilupo, Christina M.; & Holder, Aisha M. B. (2008). Racial microaggressions in the life experience of black Americans. *Professional Psychology: Research and Practice, 39,* 329–336.

Sue, Derald Wing, & Sue, David. (2008b). *Counseling the culturally diverse: Theory and practice* (5th ed.). Hoboken, NJ: Wiley.

Sugimori, Eriko, & Kusumi, Takashi. (2014). The similarity hypothesis of déjà vu: On the relationship between frequency of real-life déjà vu experiences and sensitivity to configural resemblance. *Journal of Cognitive Psychology, 26,* 48–57. doi:10.1080/20445911.2013.854248

Sulem, Patrick; Gudbjartsson, Daniel F.; Stacey, Simon N.; Helgason, Agnar; Rafnar, Thorunn; Magnusson, Kristinn P.; & others. (2007). Genetic determinants of hair, eye and skin pigmentation in Europeans. *Nature Genetics, 39*(12), 1443–1452.

Sullivan, Cathy, & Lewis, Suzan. (2001). Home-based telework, gender, and the synchronization of work and family: Perspectives of teleworkers and their co-residents. *Gender, Work & Organization, 8,* 123–145.

Sullivan, John Jeremiah. (2014, September 17). Donald Antrim and the art of anxiety. *New York Times Magazine.* Retrieved from http://www.nytimes.com/2014/09/21/magazine/donald-antrim-and-the-art-of-anxiety.html

Sullivan, Patrick F.; Daly, Mark J.; & O'Donovan, Michael. (2012). Genetic architectures of psychiatric disorders: The emerging picture and its implications. *Nature Reviews, 13,* 537–551.

Suls, Jerry, & Bunde, James. (2005). Anger, anxiety, and depression as risk factors for cardiovascular disease: The problems and implications of overlapping affective dispositions. *Psychological Bulletin, 131,* 260–300.

Sumter, Sindy R.; Bokhorst, Caroline L.; Steinberg, Laurence; & Westenberg, P. Michael. (2009). The developmental pattern of resistance to peer influence in adolescence: Will the teenager ever be able to resist? *Journal of Adolescence, 32*(4), 1009–1021.

Sun, Shumei S.; Schubert, Christine M.; Chumlea, William Cameron; Roche, Alex F.; Kulin, Howard E.; Lee, Peter A.; & others. (2002). National estimates of the timing of sexual maturation and racial differences among US children. *Pediatrics, 110,* 911–919.

Supèr, Hans, & Romeo, August. (2011). Rebound spiking as a neural mechanism for surface filling-in. *Journal of Cognitive Neuroscience, 23*(2), 491–501.

Swami, Viren, & Tovée, Martin J. (2006). Does hunger influence judgments of female physical attractiveness? *British Journal of Psychology, 97*(3), 353–363. doi:10.1348/000712605X80713

Swami, Viren; Frederick, David A.; Aavik, Toivo; Alcalay, Lidia; Allik, Jüri; Anderson, Donna; Andrianto, Sonny; & others. (2010). The attractive female body weight and female body dissatisfaction in 26 countries across 10 world regions: Results of the international body project I. *Personality and Social Psychology Bulletin, 36*(3), 309–325. doi:10.1177/0146167209359702

Swan, Daniel C., & Big Bow, Harding. (1995, Fall). Symbols of faith and belief—Art of the Native American Church. *Gilcrease Journal, 3,* 22–43.

Swanson, Sonja A.; Crow, Scott J.; Le Grange, Daniel; Swendsen, Joel; & Merikangas, Kathleen R. (2011). Prevalence and correlates of eating disorders in adolescents. *Archives of General Psychiatry, 68*(7), 1–10.

Swartz, Conrad M. (2009). Preface. In Conrad M. Swartz (Ed.), *Electroconvulsive and neuromodulation therapies* (pp. xvii–xxx). New York, NY: Cambridge University Press.

Sweeney, Gladys M. (2007). Why childhood attachment matters: Implications for personal happiness, families, and public policy. In A. Scott Loveless & Thomas B. Holman (Eds.), *The Family in the New Millennium: World Voices Supporting the "Natural" Clan:, Vol. 1: The place of family in human society* (pp. 332–346). Westport, CT: Praeger/Greenwood.

Szyf, Moshe. (2013). How do environments talk to genes? *Nature Neuroscience, 16,* 2–4. doi:10.1038/nn.3286

Szyf, Moshe, & Bick, Johanna. (2013). DNA methylation: A mechanism for embedding early life experiences in the genome. *Child Development, 84,* 49–57. doi:10.1111/j.1467-8624.2012.01793.x

Taguba, Antonio M. (2004). Article 15–6. Investigation of the 800th Military Police Brigade. Retrieved on December 8, 20055 from: http://www.npr.org/iraq/2004/prison_abuse_report.pdf

Taheri, Shahrad; Lin, Ling; Austin, Diane; Young, Terry; & Mignot, Emmanuel. (2004, December). Short sleep duration is associated with reduced leptin, elevated ghrelin, and increased body mass index. *PLOS Medicine, 1*(3), e62, 001–008. Retrieved on December 8, 2009, from http://www.plosmedicine.org/article/nfo%3Adoi%2F10.1371%2Fjournal.pmed.0010062

Takeuchi, Tomoka; Fukuda, Kazuhiko; Sasaki, Yuka; Inugami, Maki; & Murphy, Timothy I. (2002). Factors related to the occurrence of isolated sleep paralysis elicited during a multi-phasic sleep-wake schedule. *Sleep, 25,* 89–96.

Tal, Aner, & Wansink, Brian. (2014, October 15). Blinded with science: Trivial graphs and formulas increase ad persuasiveness and belief in product efficacy. *Public Understanding of Science.* Advance online publication. doi:10.1177/0963662514549688

Talarico, Jennifer M., & Rubin, David C. (2003). Confidence, not consistency, characterizes flashbulb memories. *Psychological Science, 14,* 455–461.

Talarico, Jennifer M., & Rubin, David C. (2007). Flashbulb memories are special after all; in phenomenology, not accuracy [sic]. *Applied Cognitive Psychology, 21,* 557–578.

Talarico, Jennifer M., & Rubin, David C. (2009). Flashbulb memories result from ordinary memory processes and extraordinary event characteristics. In O. Luminet & A. Curci (Eds.), *Flashbulb memories: New issues and new perspectives* (pp. 79–97). New York, NY: Psychology Press.

Talbot, Margaret. (2008, May 12). Birdbrain: The woman behind the world's chattiest parrots. *The New York,* 64–75.

Talhelm, T.; Zhang, X.; Oishi, S.; Shimin, C.; Duan, D.; Lan, X.; & Kitayama, S. (2014). Large-scale psychological differences within China explained by rice versus wheat agriculture. *Science, 344,* 603–608. doi:10.1126/science.1246850

Tallman, Karen, & Bohart, Arthur C. (1999). The client as a common factor: Clients as self-healers. In Mark A. Hubble, Barry L. Duncan, & Scott D. Miller (Eds.), *The heart and soul of change: What works in therapy.* Washington, DC: American Psychological Association.

Tamietto, Marco, & de Gelder, Beatrice. (2010). Neural bases of the non-conscious perception of emotional signals. *Nature Reviews Neuroscience, 11*(10), 697–709.

Tanaka-Matsumi, Junko. (2004). Japanese forms of psychotherapy: Naikan therapy and morita therapy. In Uwe P. Gielen, Jefferson M. Fish, & Juris G. Draguns (Eds.), *Handbook of culture, therapy, and healing.* Mahwah, NJ: Erlbaum.

Tanaka-Matsumi, Junko. (2011). Culture and psychotherapy: Searching for an empirically supported relationship. In Kenneth D. Keith (Ed.), *Cross-cultural psychology: Contemporary themes and perspectives.* Oxford, England: Wiley-Blackwell.

Tanford, Sarah, & Penrod, Steven. (1984). Social influence model: A formal integration of research on majority and minority influence processes. *Psychological Bulletin, 95,* 189–225.

Tang, Yi-Yuan, & Posner, Michael I. (2015). Mindfulness in the context of the attention system. In Kirk Warren Brown, J. David Creswell, & Richard M. Ryan (Eds.), *Handbook of mindfulness: Theory, research, and practice.* New York, NY: Guilford.

Tang, Yi-Yuan; Hölzel, Britta K.; & Posner, Michael I. (2015). The neuroscience of mindfulness meditation. *Nature Reviews Neuroscience, 16,* 213–225. doi:10.1038/nrn3916

Tanielian, Terri. (2008). Invisible wounds of war: Recommendations for addressing psychological and cognitive injuries. Testimony presented before the House Committee on Veterans' Affairs on June 11, 2008.

Tartaglia, Maria Carmela; Hazrati, Lili-Naz; Davis, Karen D.; Green, Robin E. A.; Wennberg, Richard; Mikulis, David; Ezerins, Leo John; Keightley, Michelle; & Tator, Charles. (2014) Chronic traumatic encephalopathy and other neurodegenerative proteinopathies. *Frontiers of Human Neuroscience, 8,* 30. doi:10.3389/fnhum.2014.00030

Tasca, Giorgio A.; Foot, Meredith; Leite, Catherine; Maxwell, Hilary; Balfour, Louise; & Bissada, Hany. (2011). Interpersonal processes in psychodynamic-interpersonal and cognitive behavioral group therapy: A systematic case study of two groups. *Psychotherapy, 48*(3), 260–273.

Taylor, Catherine A., Manganello, Jennifer A.; Lee, Shawna J.; & Rice, Janet C. (2010). Mothers' spanking of 3-year-old children and subsequent risk of children's aggressive behavior. *Pediatrics, 125*(5), e1057–1065. doi:10.1542/peds.2009-2678

Taylor, Kate. (2013). Sex on campus: She can play that game, too. *New York Times.* Retrieved from *New York Times* on July 12, 2013.

Taylor, Marjorie; Sachet, Alison B.; Maring, Bayta L.; & Mannering, Anne M. (2013). The assessment of elaborated role-play in young children: Invisible friends, personified objects, and pretend identities. *Social Development, 22,* 75–93. doi:10.1111/sode.12011

Taylor, Marjorie; Shawber, A. B.; Mannering, A. M.; Markman, K. D.; Klein, W. M. P.; & Suhr, J. A. (2009). Children's imaginary companions: What is it like to have an invisible friend? *Handbook of imagination and mental simulation.* (pp. 211–224). New York, NY: Psychology Press.

Taylor, Shelley E. (2006). Tend and befriend: Biobehavioral bases of affiliation under stress. *Current Directions in Psychological Science, 15*(6), 273–277.

Taylor, Shelley E., & Gonzaga, Gian C. (2007). Affiliative responses to stress: A social neuroscience model. In Eddie Harmon-Jones & Piotr Winkielman (Eds.), *Social neuroscience: Integrating biological and psychological explanations of social behavior.* New York, NY: Guilford.

Taylor, Shelley E.; Klein, Laura Cousino; Lewis, Brian P.; Gruenewald, Tara L.; Gurung, Regan A.; & Updegraff, John A. (2000). Biobehavioral responses to stress in females: Tend-and-befriend, not fight-or-flight. *Psychological Review, 107,* 411–429.

Taylor, Shelley E., & Master, Sarah L. (2011). Social responses to stress: The tend-and-befriend model. In Richard J. Contrada & Andrew Baum (Eds.), *The handbook of stress science: Biology, psychology, and health.* New York, NY: Springer.

Taylor, Steven; Thordarson, Dana S.; Maxfield, Louise; Fedoroff, Ingrid C.; Lovell, Karina; & Ogrodniczuk, John. (2003). Comparative efficacy, speed, and adverse effects of three PTSD treatments: Exposure therapy, EMDR, and relaxation training. *Journal of Consulting and Clinical Psychology, 71,* 330–338.

Taylor, W. S., & Martin, M. F. (1944). Multiple personality. *Journal of Abnormal and Social Psychology, 39,* 281–300.

Teachman, Bethany A. (2014). No appointment necessary: Treating mental illness outside the therapist's office. *Perspectives on Psychological Science, 9*(1), 85–87. doi:10.1177/1745691613512659

Telework Coalition. (2006, March). *Benchmarking study. Best practices for large-scale implementation in public and private sector organizations.* Washington, DC: Author.

Telle, Nils-Torge; Senior, Carl; & Butler, Michael. (2011). Trait emotional intelligence facilitates responses to a social gambling task. *Personality and Individual Differences, 50*(4), 523–526. doi:10.1016/j.paid.2010.11.010

Teo, Alan R. (2010) A new form of social withdrawal in Japan: A review of hikikomori. *International Journal of Social Psychiatry, 56,* 178–185.

Teo, Alan R., & Gaw, Albert C. (2010). Hikikomori, a Japanese culture-bound syndrome of social withdrawal?: A proposal for DSM-5. *Journal of Nervous and Mental Disease, 198,* 444–449.

Terman, Lewis M. (1916). *Measurement of intelligence.* Boston, MA: Houghton Mifflin.

Terman, Lewis M. (1926). *Genetic studies of genius* (2nd ed., Vol. I). Stanford, CA: Stanford University Press.

Terman, Lewis M., & Oden, Melita H. (1947). *Genetic Studies of Genius: Vol. IV. The gifted child grows up: Twenty-five years' follow-up of a superior group.* Stanford, CA: Stanford University Press.

Terman, Lewis M., & Oden, Melita H. (1959). *Genetic studies of genius: Vol. V. The gifted at mid-life: Thirty-five years' follow-up of the superior child.* Stanford, CA: Stanford University Press.

Teyber, Edward. (2009). *Interpersonal process in therapy: An integrative model* (6th ed.) Pacific Grove, CA: Thomson Brooks/Cole.

Teymoori, Ali, & Shahrazad, Wan. (2012). Relationship between mother, father, and peer attachment and empathy with moral authority. *Ethics & Behavior, 22,* 16–29. doi:10.1080/10508422.2012.638820

Thase, Michael E., & Denko, Timothey. (2008). Pharmacotherapy of mood disorders. *Annual Review of Clinical Psychology, 4,* 53–91.

Thase, Michael E.; Friedman, Edward S.; Biggs, Melanie M.; Wisniewski, Stephen R.; Trivedi, Madhukar H.; Luther, James F.; Fava, Maurizio; & others. (2007). Cognitive therapy versus medication in augmentation and switch strategies as second-step treatments: A STAR★D report. *American Journal of Psychiatry, 164,* 739–752.

Thase, Michael E.; Larsen, Klaus G.; & Kennedy, Sidney H. (2011). Assessing the "true" effect of active antidepressant therapy v. placebo in major depressive disorder: Use of a mixture model. *British Journal of Psychiatry, 199,* 501–507. doi:10.1192/bjp.bp.111.093336

Thayer, Amanda, & Lynn, Steven Jay. (2006). Guided imagery and recovered memory therapy: Considerations and cautions. *Journal of Forensic Psychology Practice, 6,* 63–73.

Thøgersen-Ntoumani, Cecilie; Loughren, Elizabeth; Kinnaflick, Florence-Emilie; Taylor, Ian; Duda, Joan; & Fox, Ken. (2015). Changes in work affect in response to lunchtime walking in previously physically inactive employees: A randomized trial. *Scandinavian Journal of Medicine and Science in Sports.* doi:10.1111/sms.12398

Thomas, Alexander, & Chess, Stella. (1977). *Temperament and development.* New York, NY: Brunner/Mazel.

Thomas, Alexander, & Chess, Stella. (1986). The New York Longitudinal Study: From infancy to early adult life. In Robert Plomin & Judith Dunn (Eds.), *The study of temperament: Changes, continuities, and challenges.* Hillsdale, NJ: Erlbaum.

Thomas, Ayanna K.; Bulevich, John B.; & Loftus, Elizabeth F. (2003). Exploring the role of repetition and sensory elaboration in the imagination inflation effect. *Memory & Cognition, 31,* 630–640.

Thompson, Clara. (1950/1973). Some effects of the derogatory attitude toward female sexuality. In Jean Baker Miller (Ed.), *Psychoanalysis and women.* Baltimore, MD: Penguin Books.

Thompson, Henry L. (2010). *The stress effect: Why smart leaders make dumb decisions—and what to do about it.* San Francisco, CA: Jossey-Bass.

Thompson, J. Kevin; Roehrig, Megan; & Kinder, Bill N. (2007). Eating disorders. In Michel Hersen, Samuel M. Turner, & Deborah C. Beidel (Eds.), *Adult psychopathology and diagnosis* (5th ed., pp. 571–600). Hoboken, NJ: Wiley.

Thompson, Paul. M. (2001, September 25). Quoted in "UCLA Researchers map how schizophrenia engulfs teen brains." University of California–Los Angeles press release. Retrieved on March 6, 2005, from http://www.loni.ucla.edu/~thompson/MEDIA/PNAS/Pressrelease.html

Thompson, Paul M.; Hayashi, Kiralee M.; de Zubicaray, Greig; Janke, Andrew L.; Rose, Stephen E.; Semple, James; Herman, David; Hong, Michael S.; Dittmer, Stephanie S.; Doddrell, David M.; & Toga, Arthur W. (2003). Dynamics of gray matter loss in Alzheimer's disease. *Journal of Neuroscience, 23,* 994–1005. Retrieved on July 10, 2004, from http://www.loni.ucla.edu/~thompson/PDF/ADwave.pdf

Thompson, Paul M.; Hayashi, Kiralee M.; Simon, Sara L.; Geaga, Jennifer A.; Hong, Michael S.; Sui, Yihong; Lee, Jessica Y.; Toga, Arthur W.; Ling, Walter; & London, Edythe D. (2004). Structural abnormalities in the brains of human subjects who use methamphetamine. *Journal of Neuroscience, 24,* 6028–6036.

Thompson, Paul M.; Vidal, Christine; Gledd, Jay N.; Gochman, Peter; Blumenthal, Jonathan; Nicolson, Robert; & others. (2001). Mapping adolescent brain change reveals dynamic wave of accelerated gray matter loss in very early-onset schizophrenia. *Proceedings of the National Academy of Sciences, USA, 98*, 11650–11655.

Thompson, Renee J.; Mata, Jutta; Jaeggi, Susanne M.; Buschkuehl, Martin; Jonides, John; & Gotlib, Ian H. (2010). Maladaptive coping, adaptive coping, and depressive symptoms: Variations across age and depressive state. *Behaviour Research and Therapy, 48*(6), 459–466.

Thompson, Richard F. (1994). Behaviorism and neuroscience. *Psychological Review, 101*, 259–265.

Thompson, Richard F. (2005). In search of memory traces. *Annual Review of Psychology, 56*, 1–23.

Thompson, Robin; Emmorey, Karen; & Gollan, Tamar H. (2005). "Tip of the fingers" experiences by deaf signers. *Psychological Science, 16*, 856–860.

Thompson, Suzanne C. (2009). The role of personal control in adaptive functioning. In Shane J. Lopez & C. R. Snyder (Eds.). *Oxford handbook of positive psychology* (2nd ed.). New York, NY: Oxford University Press.

Thompson, Vetta L. Sanders; Bazile, Anita; & Akbar, Maysa. (2004). African Americans' perceptions of psychotherapy and psychotherapists. *Professional Psychology: Research and Practice, 35*, 19–26.

Thorndike, Edward L. (1898). Animal intelligence: An experimental study of the associative processes in animals. *Psychological Review Monograph Supplement, 2*(Serial No. 8).

Thorndike, Robert L. (1991). Edward L. Thorndike: A professional and personal appreciation. In Gregory A. Kimble, Michael Wertheimer, & Charlotte L. White (Eds.), *Portraits of pioneers in psychology*. Washington, DC: American Psychological Association.

Thorndike, Edward L., & Barnhart, Clarence L. (1997). *Thorndike Barnhart Junior Dictionary*. Glenview, IL: Pearson Scott Foresman.

Thorne, Barrie. (1993). *Gender play: Girls and boys in school*. New Brunswick, NJ: Rutgers University Press.

Thornhill, Randy. (2007). The evolution of women's estrus, extended sexuality, and concealed ovulation, and their implications for human sexuality research. In Steven W. Gangestad & Jeffry A. Simpson (Eds.). *The evolution of mind: Fundamental questions and controversies*. New York, NY: Guilford.

Thornton, Bill, & Tizard, Hayley J. (2010). 'Not in my back yard': Evidence for arousal moderating vested interest and oppositional behavior to proposed change. *Social Psychology, 41*(4), 255–262.

Thorpy, Michael J. (2005). Classification of sleep disorders. In Meir H. Kryger, Thomas Roth, & William C. Dement (Eds.), *Principles and practice of sleep medicine* (4th ed.). Philadelphia, PA: Elsevier Saunders.

Thorpy, Michael J., & Plazzi, Giuseppe. (2010). *The parasomnias and other sleep-related movement disorders*. New York, NY: Cambridge University Press.

Thunberg, Monika, & Dimberg, Ulf. (2000). Gender differences in facial reactions to fear-relevant stimuli. *Journal of Nonverbal Behavior, 24*, 45–51.

Thurstone, Louis L. (1937). *Primary mental abilities*. Chicago, IL: University of Chicago Press.

Tiedt, Hannes O.; Weber, Joachim E.; Pauls, Alfred; Beier, Klaus M.; Lueschow, Andreas. (2013). Sex-differences of face coding: Evidence from larger right hemispheric M170 in men and dipole source modelling. *PLOS ONE 8*, e69107. doi:10.1371/journal.pone.0069107

Tienari, Pekka, & Wahlberg, Karl-Erik. (2008). Family environment and psychosis. In Craig Morgan, Kwame McKenzie, & Paul Fearon (Eds.), *Society and Psychosis*. New York, NY: Cambridge University Press.

Tienari, Pekka; Sorri, Anneli; Lahti, Ilpo; Naarala, Mikko; Wahlberg, Karl-Erik; Moring, Juha; & others. (1987). Genetic and psychosocial factors in schizophrenia: The Finnish Adoptive Family Study. *Schizophrenia Bulletin, 13*, 477–484.

Tienari, Pekka; Wahlberg, Karl-Erik; & Wynne, Lyman C. (2006, Winter). Finnish adoption study of schizophrenia: Implications for family interventions. *Families, Systems, & Health, 24*(4), 442–451.

Tienari, Pekka; Wynne, Lyman C.; Moring, Juha; Lahti, Ilpo; Naarala, Mikko; Sorri, Anneli; & others. (1994). The Finnish Adoptive Family Study of Schizophrenia: Implications for family research. *British Journal of Psychiatry, 164*(Suppl.), 20–26.

Tipu, Fatima. (2015, February 22). OCD is not a quirk. *The Atlantic*. Retrieved from http://www.theatlantic.com/health/archive/2015/02/ocd-is-a-disorder-not-a-quirk/385562

Titchener, Edward B. (1896/2009). An outline of psychology. In Barbara Gentile & Benjamin O. Miller (Eds.), *Foundations of psychological thought: A history of psychology* (pp. 219–236). Thousand Oaks, CA: Sage.

Tobler, Irene. (2005). Phylogeny of sleep regulation. In Meir H. Kryger, Thomas Roth, & William C. Dement (Eds.), *Principles and practice of sleep medicine* (4th ed.). Philadelphia, PA: Elsevier Saunders.

Todd, James T., & Morris, Edward K. (1992). Case histories in the great power of steady misrepresentation. *American Psychologist, 47*, 1441–1453.

Todd, Michael. (2004). Daily processes in stress and smoking: Effects of negative events, nicotine dependence, and gender. *Psychology of Addictive Behaviors, 18*, 31–39.

Todorov, Alexander; Olivola, Christopher Y.; Dotsch, Ron; & Mende-Siedlecki, Peter. (2015). Social attributions from faces: Determinants, consequences, accuracy, and functional significance. *Annual Review of Psychology, 66*, 519–545. doi:10.1146/annurev-psych-113011-143831

Toga, Arthur W., & Thompson, Paul M. (2003). Mapping brain asymmetry. *Nature Reviews Neuroscience, 4*, 37–48.

Toga, Arthur W.; Thompson, Paul M.; & Sowell, Elizabeth R. (2006). Mapping brain maturation. *Trends Neuroscience, 29*(3), 148–159. doi:.1016/j.tins.2006.01.007

Tolman, Edward C. (1932). *Purposive behavior in animals and men*. New York, NY: Appleton-Century-Crofts.

Tolman, Edward C. (1948). Cognitive maps in rats and men. *Psychological Review, 55*, 189–208.

Tolman, Edward C., & Honzik, Charles H. (1930a). "Insight" in rats. *Publications in Psychology, 4*, 215–232.

Tolman, Edward C., & Honzik, Charles H. (1930b). Introduction and removal of reward, and maze performance in rats. University of California, Berkeley, *Publications in Psychology, 4*, 257–275.

Tolman, Edward C.; Ritchie, B. F.; & Kalish, D. (1946/1992). Studies in spatial learning. I. Orientation and the short-cut. *Journal of Experimental Psychology: General, 121*, 429–434.

Tong, Stephanie T.; Van Der Heide, Brandon; Langwell, Lindsey; & Walther, Joseph B. (2008). Too much of a good thing? The relationship between number of friends and interpersonal impressions on Facebook. *Journal of Computer-Mediated Communication, 13*(3), 531–549. doi:10.1111/j.1083-6101.2008.00409.x

Tooby, John, & Cosmides, Leda. (2000). Evolutionary psychology and the emotions. In Michael Lewis & Jeanette M. Haviland-Jones (Eds.), *Handbook of emotions* (2nd ed.). New York, NY: Guilford.

Tooby, John, & Cosmides, Leda. (2008). The evolutionary psychology of the emotions and their relationship to internal regulatory variables. In Michael Lewis, Jeannette M. Haviland-Jones, & Lisa Feldman Barrett (Eds.), *Handbook of emotions* (3rd ed., pp. 114–137). New York, NY: Guilford.

Torges, Cynthia M.; Stewart, A.J.; & Duncan, L.E. (2009). Appreciating life's complexities: Assessing narrative ego integrity in late midlife. *Journal of Research in Personality, 43*(1), 66–74.

Torges, Cynthia M.; Stewart, Abigail J.; & Nolen-Hoeksema, Susan. (2008). Regret resolution, aging, and adapting to loss. *Psychology and Aging, 23*, 169–180.

Torrey, Fuller E. (2011). Stigma and violence: Isn't it time to connect the dots? *Schizophrenia Bulletin, 37*(5), 892–896. doi:10.1093/schbul/sbr05

Torrey, E. Fuller; Rawlings, Robert R.; Ennis, Jacqueline M.; Merrill, Deborah Dickerson; & Flores, Donn S. (1996) Birth seasonality in bipolar disorder, schizophrenia, schizoaffective disorder and stillbirths. *Schizophrenia Research, 21*, 141–149.

Toth, Karen, & King, Bryan Y. (2008). Asperger's syndrome: Diagnosis and treatment. *American Journal of Psychiatry, 165*, 958–963.

Tovée, Martin J.; Swami, Viren; Furnham, Adrian; & Mangalparsad, Roshila. (2006). Changing perceptions of attractiveness as observers are exposed to a different culture. *Evolution and Human Behavior, 27*(6), 443–456.

Tracey, Terence J. G.; Wampold, Bruce E.; Lichtenberg, James W.; & Goodyear, Rodney K. (2014). Expertise in psychotherapy: An elusive goal? *American Psychologist, 69*(3), 218–229. doi:10.1037/a0035099

Trainor, Brian C.; Takahashi, Elizabeth Y.; Silva, Andrea L.; Crean, Katie K.; & Hostetler, Caroline. (2010). Sex differences in hormonal responses to social conflict in the monogamous California mouse. *Hormones and Behavior, 58*(3), 506–512.

Trajanovic, Nikola N., & Shapiro, Colin M. (2010). Sexsomnias. In Michael J. Tharpy & Giuseppe Plazzi (Eds.), *The parasomnias and other sleeprelated movement disorders.* New York, NY: Cambridge University Press.

Tran, Anh N.; Ornelas, India J.; Kim, Mimi; Perez, Georgin;, Green, Melissa; Lyn, Michelle J.; & Corbie-Smith, Giselle. (2014). Results from a pilot promotora program to reduce depression and stress among immigrant Latinas. *Health Promotion Practice, 15*(3), 365–372.

Travers, Susan P., & Travers, Joseph B. (2009). Chemical senses. In G.G. Berntson & J. T. Cacioppo (Eds.), *Handbook of neuroscience for the behavioral sciences, Vol. 1* (pp. 267–305). Hoboken, NJ: Wiley.

Treasure, Janet L.; Wack, Elizabeth R.; & Roberts, Marion E. (2008). Models as a high-risk group: The health implications of a size zero culture. *British Journal of Psychiatry, 192,* 243–244.

Treffert, Darold A., & Wallace, Gregory L. (2002). Islands of genius: Artistic brilliance and a dazzling memory can sometimes accompany autism and other developmental disorders. *Scientific American, 86,* 76–85.

Treisman, Michel, & Lages, Martin. (2013). On the nature of sensory memory. In Charles Chubb, Barbara A. Dosher, Zhong-Lin Lu, Richard M. Shiffrin (Eds.), *Human information processing: Vision, memory, and attention. Decade of behavior.* Washington, DC: American Psychological Association.

Triandis, Harry C. (1994). *Culture and social behavior.* New York, NY: McGraw-Hill.

Triandis, Harry C. (2005). Issues in individualism and collectivism. In Richard M. Sorrentino, Dov Cohen, James M. Olson, & Mark P. Zanna (Eds.), *Cultural and social behavior: The Ontario Symposium, vol. 10.* Mahwah, NJ: Erlbaum.

Trull, Timothy J., & Widiger, Thomas A. (2008). Geology 102: More thoughts on a shift to a dimensional model of personality disorders. *Social and Personality Psychology Compass, 2,* 949–967.

Tsang, Laura Lo Wa; Harvey, Carol D. H.; Duncan, Karen A.; & Sommer, Reena. (2003). The effects of children, dual earner status, sex role traditionalism, and marital structure on marital happiness over time. *Journal of Family and Economic Issues, 24,* 5–26.

Tsao, Doris. (2006). A dedicated system for processing faces. *Science, 314,* 72–73.

Tsao, Doris; Freiwald, Winrich A.; Tootell, Roger B. H.; & Livingstone, Margaret S. (2006). A cortical region consisting entirely of faceselective cells. *Science, 311,* 670–674.

Tsvetkova, Milena, & Macy, Michael W. (2014). The social contagion of generosity. *PLOS ONE, 9*(2), 1–9. doi:10.1371/journal.pone.0087275

Tucker, Jeritt R.; Hammer, Joseph H.; Vogel, David L.; Bitman, Rachel L.; Wade, Nathaniel G.; & Maier, Emily J. (2013). Disentangling self-stigma: Are mental illness and help-seeking self-stigmas different? *Journal of Counseling Psychology, 60*(4), 1–12. doi:10.1037/a0033555

Tufte, Edward R. (1997). *Visual explanations: Images and quantities, evidence and narrative.* Cheshire, CT: Graphics Press.

Tugend, Alina. (2014, March 7). It's unclearly defined, but telecommuting is fast on the rise. *The New York Times.* Retrieved from http://www.nytimes.com/2014/03/08/your-money/when-working-in-your-pajamas-is-more-productive.html?_r=0

Tulving, Endel. (1983). *Elements of episodic memory.* Oxford, England: Clarendon Press/Oxford University Press.

Tulving, Endel. (1985). How many memory systems are there? *American Psychologist, 40,* 385–398.

Tulving, Endel. (2002). Episodic memory: From mind to brain. *Annual Review of Psychology, 53,* 1–25.

Tulving, Endel. (2007). Are there 256 different kinds of memory? In James S. Nairne (Ed.), *The foundations of remembering: Essays in honor of Henry L. Roediger, III.* New York, NY: Psychology Press.

Tulving, Endel, & Szpunar, Karl K. (2009). Episodic memory. *Scholarpedia, 4,* 3332. doi:10.4249/scholarpedia.3332

Turati, Chiara. (2004). Why faces are not special to newborns: An alternative account of the face preference. *Current Directions in Psychological Science, 13,* 5–8.

Turiel, Elliot. (2010). The relevance of moral epistemology and psychology for neuroscience. In P. D. Zelazo, M. Chandler, & E. Crone (Eds.), *Developmental social cognitive neuroscience* (pp. 313–331). New York, NY: Psychology Press.

Turk, Dennis C., & Winter, Frits. (2006). *The pain survival guide: How to reclaim your life.* Washington, DC: American Psychological Association.

Turk-Browne, Nicholas B. (2013). Functional interactions as big data in the brain. *Science, 342,* 580–584.

Turkington, Douglas, & Morrison, Anthony P. (2012). Cognitive therapy for negative symptoms of schizophrenia. *Archive of General Psychiatry, 69,* 119–120. doi:10.1001/archgenpsychiatry.2011.141

Turner, Erick H. (2013). Publication bias, with a focus on psychiatry: Causes and solutions. *CNS Drugs, 27,* 457–468. doi:10.1007/s40263-013-0067-9

Turner, Erlanger A.; Chandler, Megan; & Heffer, Robert W. (2009). The influence of parenting styles, achievement motivation, and self-efficacy on academic performance in college students. *Journal of College Student Development, 50*(3), 337–346.

Turner, John C. (2010). The analysis of social influence. In T. Postmes & N. R. Branscombe (Eds.), *Rediscovering social identity.* NY: Psychology Press.

Turner, Martin S., & Stewart, Duncan W. (2006, November). Review of the evidence for the long-term efficacy of atypical antipsychotic agents in the treatment of patients with schizophrenia and related psychoses. *Journal of Psychopharmacology, 20*(6, Suppl.), 20–37.

Turner, Monique Mitchell; Tamborini, Ron; Limon, M. Sean; & Zuckerman- Hyman, Cynthia. (2007, September). The moderators and mediators of door-in-the-face requests: Is it a negotiation or a helping experience? *Communication Monographs, 74*(3), 333–356.

Tuten, L. Michelle; Jones, Hendree E.; Schaeffer, Cindy M.; & Stitzer, Maxine L. (2012). *Contingency management to improve treatment outcomes.* Washington, DC: American Psychological Association.

Tversky, Amos. (1972). Elimination by aspects: A theory of choice. *Psychological Review, 80,* 281–299.

Tversky, Amos, & Kahneman, Daniel. (1982). Judgment under uncertainty: Heuristics and biases. In Daniel Kahneman, Paul Slovic, & Amos Tversky (Eds.), *Judgment under uncertainty: Heuristics and biases.* New York, NY: Cambridge University Press.

Tyas, Suzanne L.; Salazar, Juan Carlos; Snowdon, David A.; Desrosiers, Mark F.; Riley, Kathryn P.; & others. (2007a). Transitions to mild cognitive impairments, dementia, and death: Findings from the nun study. *American Journal of Epidemiology, 165,* 1231–1238.

Tyas, Suzanne L.; Snow, David A.; Desrosiers, Mark F.; Riley, Kathryn P.; & Markesbery, William R. (2007b). Healthy ageing in the Nun Study: Definition and neuropathologic correlates. *Age and Ageing, 36,* 650–655.

Tyler, Kathryn. (2008, January). Generation gaps: Millennials may be out of touch with workplace behavior. *HR Magazine, 53*(1), 69–73.

U.S. Bureau of Labor Statistics. (2008). Human resources, training, and labor relations managers and specialists profile. *Occupational outlook handbook.* www.bls.gov/OCO

U.S. Census Bureau. (2008a). 2007 American Community Survey 1-year estimates: Marital status. Retrieved on November 4, 2008, from http://factfinder.census.gov

U.S. Census Bureau. (2008b). 2007 American Community Survey 1-year estimates: Ranking table R1204: Median age at first marriage for men. Retrieved on November 4, 2008, from http://factfinder.census.gov

U.S. Census Bureau. (2008c). 2007 American Community Survey 1-year estimates: Ranking table R1205: Median age at first marriage for women. Retrieved on November 4, 2008, from http://factfinder.census.gov

U.S. Census Bureau. (2008d). 2007 American Community Survey 1-year estimates: Table S1501: Educational attainment. Retrieved on November 4, 2008, from http://factfinder.census.gov, 395.

U.S. Census Bureau. (2009). Census Bureau reports world's older population projected to triple by 2050. doi:10.3945/ajcn.2008.26733

U.S. Public Health Service. (1999). *The Surgeon General's call to action to prevent suicide.* Washington, DC: Government Printing Office. Retrieved October 30, 2001, from http://www.surgeongeneral.gov/library/calltoaction/calltoaction.pdf

Uchino, Bert N. (2009). Understanding the links between social support and physical health: A life-span perspective with emphasis on the separability of perceived and received support. *Perspectives on Psychological Science, 4*(3), 236–255.

Uchino, Bert N., & Birmingham, Wendy. (2011). Stress and support processes. In Richard J. Contrada & Andrew Baum (Eds.), *The handbook of stress science: Biology, psychology, and health.* New York, NY: Springer.

Uchino, Bert N.; Carlisle, McKenzie; Birmingham, Wendy; & Vaughn, Allison A. (2010). Social support and the reactivity hypothesis: Conceptual issues in examining the efficacy of received support during acute psychological stress. *Biological Psychology, 86*(2), 137–142.

Uji, Masayo; Sakamoto, Ayuko; Adachi, Keiichiro; & Kitamura, Toshinori. (2013). The impact of authoritative, authoritarian, and permissive parenting styles on children's later mental health in Japan: Focusing on parent and child gender. *Journal of Child and Family Studies, 23,* 293–302. doi:10.1007/s10826-013-9740-3

Uleman, James S.; Saribay, S. Adil; & Gonzalez, Celia M. (2008). Spontaneous inferences, implicit impressions, and implicit theories. *Annual Review of Psychology, 59,* 329–360.

Umberson, Debra; Williams, Kristi; Powers, Daniel A.; Chen, Meichu D.; & Campbell, Anna M. (2005). As good as it gets? A life course perspective on marital quality. *Social Forces, 84,* 493–511. doi:10.1353/sof.2005.0131

Umland, Elena M. (2008). Treatment strategies for reducing the burden of menopause-associated vasomotor symptoms. *Journal of Managed Care Pharmacy, 14*(3 Suppl), 14–19.

Underwood, Emily. (2013). Sleep: The brain's housekeeper? *Science, 342,* 301.

Unemori, Patrick; Omoregie, Heather; & Markus, Hazel Rose. (2004, October–December). Self-portraits: Possible selves in European-American, Chilean, Japanese and Japanese-American cultural contexts. *Self and Identity, 3*(4), 321–328.

UNHCR country operations profile—Central African Republic. (2015). *United Nations High Commissioner for Refugees.* Retrieved on June 16, 2015, from http://www.unhcr.org/pages/49e45c156.html

University of Arizona. (n.d.). *Step UP! Be a Leader, Make a Difference program.* Retrieved from http://stepupprogram.org/about

Ur, Blase; Leon, Pedro Giovanni; Cranor, Lorrie Faith; Shay, R., & Wang, Yang. (2012, July). Smart, useful, scary, creepy: Perceptions of online behavioral advertising. In *Proceedings of the Eighth Symposium on Usable Privacy and Security* (p. 4). New York, NY: ACM.

Ursano, Robert J., & Shaw, Jon A. (2007). Children of war and opportunities for peace. *Journal of the American Medical Association, 298,* 567–568.

Uskul, Ayse K., & Kitayama, Shinobu. (2011). Culture, mind, and the brain: Current evidence and future. *Annual Review of Psychology, 62,* 419–449.

van Bokhoven, Irene.; van Goozen, Stephanie H. M.; van Engeland, Herman.; Schaal, Benoist.; Arseneault, Louise.; Séguin, Jean R.; . . . Tremblay, Richard E. (2006). Salivary testosterone and aggression, delinquency, and social dominance in a population-based longitudinal study of adolescent males. *Hormones and Behavior, 50*(1), 118–125. doi:10.1016/j.yhbeh.2006.02.002

Van Cauter, Eve; Spiegel, Karine; Tasalim Esra; & Leproult, Rachel. (2008). Metabolic consequences of sleep and sleep loss. *Sleep Medicine, 9,* S23–S28.

Van Der Heide, Brandon; D'Angelo, Jonathan D.; & Schumaker, Erin M. (2012). The effects of verbal versus photographic self-presentation on impression formation in Facebook. *Journal of Communication, 62*(1), 98–116. doi:10.1111/j.1460-2466.2011.01617.x

van der Gaag, Mark; Valmaggia, Lucia R.; & Smit, Filip. (2014). The effects of individually tailored formulation-based cognitive behavioural therapy in auditory hallucinations and delusions: A meta-analysis. *Schizophrenia Research.* Retrieved from http://dx.doi.org/10.1016/j.schres.2014.03.016

van der Vaart, Elske; Verbrugge, Rineke; & Hemelrijk, Charlotte K. (2011). Corvid caching: Insights from a cognitive model. *Journal of Experimental Psychology: Animal Behavior Processes, 37*(3), 330–340. doi:10.1037/a0022988

van de Waal, Erica; Borgeaud, Christèle; & Whiten, Andrew. (2013). Potent social learning and conformity shape a wild primate's foraging decisions. *Science 340,* 483–485. doi:10.1126/science.1232769

Van Dyke, James Urban; & Grace, Michael S. (2010). The role of thermal contrast in infrared-based defensive targeting by the copperhead, *Agkistrodon contortrix. Animal Behaviour, 79*(5), 993–999.

van Geert, Paul. (1998). A dynamic systems model of basic developmental mechanisms: Piaget, Vygotsky, and beyond. *Psychological Review, 105,* 634–677.

van Heck, Guus L., & den Oudsten, Brenda L. (2008). Emotional intelligence: Relationships to stress, health, and well-being. In Ad Vingerhoets, Ivan Nyklicek, & Johan Denollet (Eds.), *Emotion regulation: Conceptual and clinical issues.* New York, NY: Springer Science + Business Media.

Van Horn, John Darrell; Irimia, Andrei; Torgerson, Carinna M.; Chambers, Micah C.; Kikinis, Ron; & Toga, Arthur W. (2012). Mapping connectivity damage in the case of Phineas Gage. *PLOS ONE, 7*(5): e37454. doi:10.1371/journal.pone.0037454

van IJzendoorn, Marinus H.; & Sagi-Schwartz, Abraham. (2008). Cross-cultural patterns of attachment: Universal and contextual dimensions. In J. Cassidy & P. R. Shaver (Eds.), *Handbook of attachment: Theory, research, and clinical applications* (2nd ed., pp. 880–905). New York, NY: Guilford.

van Osch, Yvette.; Breugelmans, Seger M.; Zeelenberg, Marcel.; & Boluk, Pinar. (2013). A different kind of honor culture: Family honor and aggression in Turks. *Group Processes & Intergroup Relations, 16*(3), 334–344. doi:10.1177/1368430212467475

van Praag, Henriette; Kempermann, Gerd; & Gage, Fred H. (2000). Neural consequences of environmental enrichment. *Nature Reviews Neuroscience, 1,* 191–198.

van Praag, Henriette. (2005, September 20). Quoted in "Exercise may reverse mental decline brought on by aging." Society for Neurosciences news release. Retrieved September 27, 1995, from http://apu.sfn.org/content/AboutSFN1/NewsReleases/pr_091405.html

van Veen, Vincent; Krug, Marie. K.; Schooler, Jonathan W.; & Carter, Cameron S. (2009). Neural activity predicts attitude change in cognitive dissonance. *Nature Neuroscience, 12*(11), 1469–1474. doi:10.1038/nn.2413

van Vugt, Marieke K. (2015). Cognitive benefits of mindfulness. In Kirk Warren Brown, J. David Creswell, & Richard M. Ryan (Eds.), *Handbook of mindfulness: Theory, research, and practice.* New York, NY: Guilford.

van Wyhe, John. (2000). *The history of phrenology on the Web.* Retrieved January 17, 2000, from http://www.jmvanwyhe.freeserve.co.uk

Vance, Ashlee. (2010, December 27). In pursuit of a mind map, slice by slice. *The New York Times.* Downloaded from http://www.nytimes.com/2010/12/28/science/28brain.html?ref=science

Vandell, Deborah L.; Belsky, Jay; Burchinal, Margaret; Steinberg, Laurence; & Vandergrift, Nathan. (2010). Do effects of early child care extend to age 15 years? Results from the NICHD study of early child care and youth development. *Child Development, 81*(3), 737–756. doi:10.1111/j.1467-8624.2010.01431.x

Vandello, Joseph A., & Cohen, Dov. (2004). When believing is seeing: Sustaining norms of violence in cultures of honor. In Mark Schaller & Christian S. Crandall (Eds.), *The psychological foundatiosn of culture* (pp. 281–304). Mahwah, NJ: Erlbaum.

Vandello, Joseph A.; & Cohen, Dov. (2003). Male honor and female fidelity: Implicit cultural scripts that perpetuate domestic violence.

Journal of Personality and Social Psychology, 84(5), 997–1010. doi:10.1037/0022-3514.84.5.997

Vandello, Joseph A.; Cohen, Dov.; & Ransom, Sean. (2008). U.S. Southern and Northern differences in perceptions of norms about aggression: Mechanisms for the perpetuation of a culture of honor. *Journal of Cross-Cultural Psychology, 39*(2), 162–177. doi:10.1177/0022022107313862

Vander Ven, Thomas, & Beck, Jeffrey. (2009). Getting drunk and hooking up: An exploratory study of the relationship between alcohol intoxication and casual coupling in a university sample. *Sociological Spectrum, 29*(5), 626–648.

Vandervoort, Debra J. (2006). Hostility and health: Mediating Effects of belief systems and coping styles. *Current Psychology, 25*(1), 50–66.

Varnum, Michael E. W.; Grossmann, Igor; Kitayama, Shinobu; & Nisbett, Richard E. (2010). The origin of cultural differences in cognition: The social orientation hypothesis. *Current Directions in Psychological Science, 19,* 9–13.

Vaughn, Bradley V., & D'Cruz, O'Neill F. (2005). Cardinal manifestations of sleep disorders. In Meir H. Kryger, Thomas Roth, & William C. Dement (Eds.), *Principles and practice of sleep medicine* (4th ed.). Philadelphia, PA: Elsevier Saunders.

Vaughn, Brian E.; Coppola, Gabrielle; & Verissimo, Manuela. (2007). The quality of maternal secure-base scripts predicts children's secure-base behavior in three sociocultural groups. *International Journal of Behavioral Development, 31,* 65–76.

Vedhara, Kavita; Gill, Sana; Eldesouky, Lameese; Campbell, Bruce K.; Arevalo, Jesusa M.G.; Ma, Jeffrey; & Cole, Steven W. (2015). Personality and gene expression: Do individual differences exist in the leukocyte transcriptome? *Psychoneuroendocrinology, 52,* 72–82. doi:10.1016/j.psyneuen.2014.10.028

Velthorst, E.; Koeter, M.; van der Gaag, M.; Nieman, D.H.; Fett, A.K.J.; Smit, F.; . . . de Haan, L. (2015). Adapted cognitive–behavioural therapy required for targeting negative symptoms in schizophrenia: Meta-analysis and meta-regression. *Psychological Medicine, 45*(3), 453–465. doi:10.1017/S0033291714001147

Venter, J. Craig; Adams, Mark D.; Myers, Eugene W.; Li, Peter W.; Mural, Richard J.; Sutton, G. Granger; Smith, Hamilton O.; Yandell, Mark; & others. (2001). The sequence of the human genome. *Science, 291*(5507), 1304–1351. doi:10.1126/science.1058040

Verstrael, Sietse; van der Wurff, Peter; & Vermetten, Eric. (2013). Eye movement densensitization and reprocessing (EMDR) as treatment for combat-related PTSD: A meta-analysis. *Military Behavioral Health, 1*(2), 68–73. doi:10.1080/21635781.2013.827088

Vespa, Jonathan; Lewis, Jamie M.; & Kreider, Rose M. (2013). *America's families and living arrangements: 2012, current population reports, P20-570.* Washington, DC.: U.S. Census Bureau.

Vickers, Andrew J.; Cronin, Angel M.; Maschino, Alexandra C.; Lewith, George; MacPherson, Hugh; Foster, Nadine E.; Sherman, Karen J.; Witt, Claudia M.; & Linde, Klaus. (2012). Acupuncture for chronic pain: Individual patient data meta-analysis. *Archives of Internal Medicine, 172,* 1–10. doi:10.1001/archinternmed.2012.3654

Vigil, Jacob M. (2009). A socio-relational framework of sex differences in the expression of emotion. *Behavioral and Brain Sciences, 32*(5), 375–390.

Vilain, Eric J. N. (2008). Genetics of sexual development and differentiation. In David L. Rowland & Luca Incrocci (Eds.), *Handbook of sexual and gender identity disorders.* Hoboken, NJ: Wiley.

Villanova, Patrick. (2014, October 15). Jersey City man charged with fatally stabbing 53-year-old ex-girlfriend, authorities say. *The Jersey Journal.* Retrieved from http://www.nj.com/hudson/index.ssf/2014/10/fatal_stabbing_victim_identified_as_53-year-old_woman_boyfriend_charged_authorities.html

Villemure, Chantal, & Bushnell, M. Catherine. (2009). Mood influences supraspinal pain processing separately from attention. *Journal of Neuroscience, 29,* 705–715. doi:10.1523/jneurosci.3822-08.2009

Viney, Wayne, & Burlingame-Lee, Laura. (2003). Margaret Floy-Washburn: A quest for the harmonies in the context of a rigorous scientific framework. In Gregory A. Kimble & Michael Wertheimer (Eds.), *Portraits of pioneers in psychology.* (Vol.V). Washington, DC: American Psychological Association.

Vingerhoets, Ad J. J. M.; Cornelius, Randolph R.; Van Heck, Guus L.; & Becht, Marleen C. (2000). Adult crying: A model and review of the literature. *Review of General Psychology, 4,* 354–377.

Vita, Antonio; De Peri, Luca; Deste, Giacomo; & Sacchetti, Emilio. (2012). Progressive loss of cortical gray matter in schizophrenia: A meta-analysis and meta-regression of longitudinal MRI studies. *Translational Psychiatry, 2*(11), e190.

Volkow, Nora D.; Chang, Linda; Wang, Gene-Jack; Fowler, Joanna S.; Ding, Yu-Sin; Sedler, Mark; Logan, Jean; & others. (2001). Low level of brain dopamine D2 receptors in methamphetamine abusers: Association with metabolism in the orbitofrontal cortex. *American Journal of Psychiatry, 158,* 2015–2021.

Volkow, Nora D.; Fowler, Joanna S.; Wang, Gene-Jack; Baler, Ruben D.; & Telang, Frank. (2009). Imaging dopamine's role in drug abuse and addiction. *Neuropharmacology, 56*(Suppl. 1), 3–8.

Volkow, Nora D.; Fowler, Joanna S.; Wang, Gene-Jack; Swanson, James M.; & Telang, Frank. (2007). Dopamine in drug abuse and addiction: Results of imaging studies and treatment implications. *Archives of Neurology, 64,* 1575–1579.

Volkow, Nora D., & McLellan, Thomas A. (2011). Curtailing diversion and abuse of opioid analgesics without jeopardizing pain treatment. *JAMA, 305*(13), 1346–1347. doi:10.1001/jama.2011.369

Volkow, Nora D.; McLellan, Thomas A.; Cotto, Jessica H.; Karithanom, Meena; & Weiss, Susan R. B. (2011a). Characteristics of opioid prescriptions in 2009. *JAMA, 305* (13), 1299–1301. doi:10.1001/jama.2011.401

Volkow, Nora D.; Wang, Gene-Jack; Fowler, Joanna S.; Tomasi, Dardo; and Telang, Frank. (2011b). Addiction: Beyond dopamine reward circuitry. *Proceedings of the National Academy of Sciences.* Published online before print March 14, 201. doi:10.1073/pnas.1010654108

Volkow, Nora D.; Wang, Gene-Jack; Telang, Frank; Fowler, Joanna S.; Logan, Jean; Childress, Anna-Rose; Jayne, Millard; Ma, Yeming; & Wong, Christopher. (2006). Cocaine cues and dopamine in dorsal striatum: Mechanism of craving in cocaine addiction. *Journal of Neuroscience, 26,* 6583–6588.

Volkow, Nora D., Frieden, Thomas R.; Hyde, Pamela S.; & Cha, Stephen S. (2014). Medication-assisted therapies—Tackling the opioid-overdose epidemic. *New England Journal of Medicine, 370,* 2063–2066. doi:10.1056/NEJMp1402780

Volkow, Nora D., & Wise, Roy A. (2005). How can drug addiction help us understand obesity? *Nature Neuroscience, 8,* 555–560.

Von Hippel, W., & Trivers, R. (2011). The evolution and psychology of self-deception. *Behavioral and Brain Sciences, 34*(01), 1–16. doi:10.1017/S0140525X10001354

Voorspoels, Wouter; Storms, Gert; & Vanpaemel, Wolf. (2011). Representation at different levels in a conceptual hierarchy. *Acta Psychologica, 138,* 11–18. doi:10.1016/j.actpsy.2011.04.007

Voorspoels, Wouter; Vanpaemel, Wolf; & Storms, Gert. (2008). Exemplars and prototypes in natural language concepts: A typicality-based evaluation. *Psychonomic Bulletin & Review, 15,* 630–637.

Voss, Michelle W.; Prakash, R. S.; Erickson, K. I.; Basak, C.; Chaddock, L.; Kim, J. S.; Alves, H.; & others. (2010). Plasticity of brain networks in a randomized intervention trial of exercise training in older adults. *Frontiers in Aging Neuroscience, 2,* 1–17.

Voss, Ursula; Holzmann, Romain; Hobson, Allan; Paulus, Walter; Koppehele-Gossel, Judith; Klimke, Ansgar; & Nitsche, Michael A. (2014). Induction of self awareness in dreams through frontal low current stimulation of gamma activity. *Nature Neuroscience, 17,* 810–812.

Voss, Ursula; Holzmann, Romain; Tuin, Inka; & Hobson, J. Allan. (2009). Lucid dreaming: A state of consciousness with features of both waking and non-lucid dreaming. *Sleep, 32*(9), 1191–200.

Vrangalova, Zhana, & Savin-Williams, Ritch C. (2012). Mostly heterosexual and mostly gay/lesbian: Evidence for new sexual orientation identities. *Archives of Sexual Behavior, 41*(1), 85–101.

Vriends, Noortje; Michael, Tanja; Schindler, Bettina; & Margraf, Jurgen. (2012). Associative learning in flying phobia. *Journal of Behavior Therapy and Experimental Psychiatry, 43,* 838–843.

Vrij, Aldert. (2015). Deception detection. In Brian L. Cutler & Patricia A. Zapf (Eds.), *APA Handbook of Forensic Psychology, Vol. 2: Criminal investigation, adjudication, and sentencing outcomes.* Washington, DC: American Psychological Association. doi:10.1037/14462-008

Vrij, Aldert; Ennis, Edel; Farman, Sarah; & Mann, Samantha. (2010). People's perceptions of their truthful and deceptive interactions in daily life. *Open Access Journal of Forensic Psychology, 2,* 6–42.

Vrshek-Schallhorn, Suzanne; Mineka, Susan; Zinbarg, Richard E.; Craske, Michelle G.; Griffith, James W.; Sutton, Jonathan; ... Adam, Emma K. (2013). Refining the candidate environment: Interpersonal stress, the serotonin transporter polymorphism, and gene-environment interactions in major depression. *Clinical Psychological Science, 2,* 235–248. doi:10.1177/2167702613499329

Vrugt, Anneke, & Vet, Carolijn. (2009). Effects of a smile on mood and helping behavior. *Social Behavior and Personality, 37*(9), 1251–1258.

Vyazovskiy, Vladyslav V.; Olcese, Umberto; Hanlon, Erin C.; Nir, Yuval; Cirelli, Chiara; & Tononi, Giulio. (2011). Local sleep in awake rats. *Nature, 472,* 443–447. doi:10.1038/nature10009

Vygotsky, Lev S. (1978). Mind in society: The development of higher psychological processes. Cambridge, MA: Harvard University Press.

Vygotsky, Lev S. (1987). *Thinking and speech* (Norris Minick, Trans.). New York, NY: Plenum Press.

Vytal, Katherine., & Hamann, Stephen. (2010). Neuroimaging support for discrete neural correlates of basic emotions: A voxel-based meta-analysis. *Journal of Cognitive Neuroscience, 22,* 2864–2885. doi:10.1162/jocn.2009.21366

Wackerman, Jiri; Pütz, Peter; & Allefeld, Carsten. (2008). Ganzfeld-induced hallucinatory experience, its phenomenology and cerebral electrophysiology. *Cortex, 44,* 1364–1378.

Wagenmakers, Eric-Jan; Wetzels, Ruud; Borsboom, Denny; & van der Maas, Han. (2011). Why psychologists must change the way they analyze their data: The case of psi. *Journal of Personality and Social Psychology, 100,* 426–432.

Wager, Tor D., & Atlas, Lauren Y. (2015). The neuroscience of placebo effects: Connecting context, learning, and health. *Nature Neuroscience, 16,* 403–418. doi:10.1038/nrn3976

Wagner, Christopher C., & Ingersoll, Karen S. (2012). *Motivational interviewing in groups.* Retrieved from http://books.google.com/books?id=WIfzs84A5rcC&printsec=frontcover &dq=motivational+interviewing+in+groups&hl=en&sa=X&ei=4mthU9KmMqWysASJl4CoBw&ved=0CD8Q6AEwAA#v=onepage&q=motivational%20interviewing%20in%20groups&f=false

Wagner, Dana E.; Harrison, Patrick R.; & Mallett, Robyn K. (2011). Understanding the intergroup forecasting error. In L. R. Tropp & R. K. Mallett (Eds.), *Moving beyond prejudice reduction: Pathways to positive intergroup relations.* Washington, DC: American Psychological Association.

Wagstaff, Graham F. (2014). On the centrality of the concept of an altered state to definitions of hypnosis. *Journal of Mind-Body Regulation, 2,* 90–108.

Wagstaff, Graham F., & Cole, Jon. (2005). Levels of explanation and the concept of a hypnotic state. *Contemporary Hypnosis, 22,* 14–17.

Wahba, Mahmoud A., & Bridwell, Lawrence G. (1976). Maslow reconsidered: A review of research on the need hierarchy theory. *Organizational Behavior and Human Decision Processes, 15,* 212–240.

Wahl, Otto F. (2012). Stigma as a barrier to recovery from mental illness. *Trends in Cognitive Science,* 16(1), 9–10.

Wainwright, Jennifer L., & Patterson, Charlotte J. (2008). Peer relations among adolescents with female same-sex parents. *Developmental Psychology, 44,* 117–126.

Wakefield, Jerome C. (2013a). DSM-5: An overview of changes and controversies. *Clinical Social Work Journal, 41,* 139–154.

Wakefield, Jerome C. (2013b). The DSM-5 debate over the bereavement exclusion: Psychiatric diagnosis and the future of empirically supported treatment. *Clinical Psychology Review, 33,* 825–845.

Walker, Elaine; Kestler, Lisa; Bollini, Annie; & Hochman, Karen M. (2004). Schizophrenia: Etiology and course. *Annual Review of Psychology, 55,* 401–430.

Walker, Herschel. (2008). *Breaking free: My life with dissociative identity disorder.* New York, NY: Touchstone.

Walker, Matthew P. (2008, March 23). Interview: KCBS In Depth: Sleep. Retrieved on July 21, 2008, from www.kcbs.com/episode_download.php?contentType=36&contentId=1685669

Walker, Matthew P. (2009). The role of sleep in cognition and emotion. *The Year in Cognitive Neuroscience 2009: Annals of the New York Academy of Sciences, 1156:* 168–197. doi:10.1111/j.1749-6632.2009.04416.x C2009

Walker, Matthew P. (2010). Sleep, memory and emotion. *Progress in Brain Research, 185,* 49–68.

Walker, Matthew P., & van der Helm, Els. (2009). Overnight therapy? The role of sleep in emotional brain processing. *Psychological Bulletin, 135*(5), 731–748. doi:10.1037/a0016570

Walker, Matthew. (2011). Quoted in Yasmin Anwar, "Pulling an all-nighter can bring on euphoria and risky behavior." Retrieved on June 28, 2011, from http://newscenter.berkeley.edu/2011/03/22/pulling-an-all-nighter

Wallace, B. Alan. (2009). *Mind in the balance: Meditation in science, Buddhism, and Christianity.* New York, NY: Columbia University.

Waller, Bridget M.; Cray, James J., Jr.; & Burrows, Anne M. (2008). Selection for universal facial emotion *Emotion, 8,* 435–439.

Walsh, Roger. (2011). Contemplative psychotherapies. In R. J. Corsini & D. Wedding (Eds.), *Current psychotherapies* (9th ed.). Belmont, CA: Brooks/Cole.

Walter, Marc; Gunderson, John G.; Zanarini, Mary C.; Grilo, Carlos M.; Morey, Leslie C.; Stout, Robert L.; Skodol, Andrew E.; Yen, Shirley; McGlashan, Thomas H.; & Sanislow, Charles A. (2009). New onsets of substance use disorders in borderline personality disorder over 7 years of follow-ups: Findings from the Collaborative Longitudinal Personality Disorders Study. *Addiction, 104,* 97–103.

Walton, Gregory M., & Cohen, Geoffrey L. (2003). Stereotype lift. *Journal of Experimental Social Psychology, 39,* 456–467.

Walton, Gregory M., & Spencer, Scott J. (2009). Latent ability: Grades and test scores systematically underestimate the intellectual ability of negatively stereotyped students. *Psychological Science, 20,* 1132–1139.

Wampold, Bruce E. (2001). *The great psychotherapy debate: Models, methods, and findings.* Mahwah, NJ: Erlbaum.

Wamsley, Eric; Perry, Karen; Djonlagic, Ina; Reaven, Laura; & Stickgold, Robert. (2010). Cognitive replay of visuomotor learning at sleep onset: Temporal dynamics and relationship to task performance. *Sleep, 33,* 59–68.

Wanek, James E.; Sackett, Paul R.; & Ones, Deniz S. (2003). Towards an understanding of integrity test similarities and differences: An item-level analysis of seven tests. *Personnel Psychology, 56,* 873–894.

Wang, Gene-Jack; Volkow, Nora D.; Logan, Jean; Pappas, Naomi R.; Wong, Christopher T.; Zhu, W.; Netusil, Noelwah; & Fowler, Joanna S. (2001). Brain dopamine and obesity. *Lancet, 357,* 354–357.

Wang, Gene-Jack; Volkow, Nora D.; Thanos, Panayotis K.; & Fowler, Joanna S. (2004). Similarity between obesity and drug addiction as assessed by neurofunctional imaging: A concept review. *Journal of Addictive Diseases, 23,* 39–53.

Wang, Jianli; Eslinger, Paul J.; Doty, Richard L.; Zimmerman, Erin K.; Grunfeld, Robert; Sun, Xiaoyu; Meadowcroft, Mark D.; Connor, James R.; Price, Joseph L.; Smith, Michael B.; & Yang, Qing X. (2010). Olfactory deficit detected by fMRI in early Alzheimer's disease. *Brain Research, 1357,* 184–194. doi:10.1016/j.brainres.2010.08.018

Wang, Kevin H.; Penmatsa, Aravind; & Gouaux, Eric. (2015). Neurotransmitter and psychostimulant recognition by the dopamine transporter. *Nature, 521,* 322–327. doi:10.1038/nature14431

Wang, Philip S.; Aguilar-Gaxiola, Sergio; Alonso, Jordi; Lee, Sing; Schoenbaum, Michael; Ustun, T. Bedirhan; ... Tsang, Adley. (2011). Assessing mental disorders and service use across countries: The WHO world mental health survey initiative. In Darrel A. Regier, William E. Narrow, Emily A. Kuhl, & David J. Kupfer (Eds.). *The conceptual evolution of DSM-5* (pp. 231–266). Arlington, VA: American Psychiatric Publishing. Retrieved from http://site.ebrary.com/id/10617407?ppg=297

Wang, Philip S.; Lane, Michael; Olfson, Mark; Pincus, Harold A.; Wells, Kenneth B.; & Kessler, Ronald C. (2005). Twelve-month use of mental health services in the United States: Results from the National Co-morbidity Survey Replication. *Archives of General Psychiatry, 62,* 629–640.

Wang, Qi. (2001). Culture effects on adults' earliest childhood recollection and self-description: Implications for the relation between memory and the self. *Journal of Personality and Social Psychology, 81,* 220–223.

Wang, Qi. (2006). Earliest recollections of self and others in European American and Taiwanese young adults. *Psychological Science, 17,* 708–714.

Wang, Qi. (2013). *The autobiographical self in time and culture.* New York, NY: Oxford University Press. doi:10.1093/acprof:oso/9780199737833.001.0001

Wang, Qiang; Bowling, Nathan A.; & Eschleman, Kevin J. (2010). A meta-analytic examination of work and general locus of control. *Journal of Applied Psychology, 95*(4), 761–768.

Wang, Shirley S. (2014, March 27). How autism can help you land a job. *Wall Street Journal.* Retrieved from http://www.wsj.com/articles/SB1000142405270230441840457946556136486855

Wang, Yingxu, & Chiew, Vincent. (2010). On the cognitive process of human problem solving. *Cognitive Systems Research, 11,* 81–92. doi:10.1016/j.cogsys.2008.08.003

Wargo, Eric. (2008). The many lives of superstition. *APS Observer, 21,* 18–24.

Wartella, Ellen; Richert, Rebekah A.; & Robb, Michael B. (2010). Babies, television and videos: How did we get here? *Developmental Review, 30*(2), 116–127. doi:10.1016/j.dr.2010.03.008

Washburn, Margaret Floy. (1908). *The animal mind.* New York, NY: Macmillan.

Wasserman, Edward A., & Zentall, Thomas R. (2006). *Comparative cognition: Experimental explorations of animal intelligence.* New York, NY: Oxford University Press.

Waterman, Alan S. (2013). The humanistic psychology–positive psychology divide: Contrasts in philosophical foundations. *American Psychologist, 68*(3), Apr 2013, 124–133. doi:10.1037/a0032168

Watson, David; Hubbard, Brock; & Wiese, David. (2000). Self-other agreement in personality and affectivity: The role of acquaintanceship, trait visibility, and assumed similarity. *Journal of Personality and Social Psychology, 78,* 546–558. doi:10.1037//0022-3514.78.3.546

Watson, Jeanne C. (2002). Re-visioning empathy. In David J. Cain & Julius Seeman (Eds.), *Humanistic psychotherapies: Handbook of research and practice.* Washington, DC: American Psychological Association.

Watson, Jeanne C.; Goldman, Rhonda N.; & Greenberg, Leslie S. (2011). Humanistic and experiential theories of psychotherapy. In John C. Norcross, Gary R. VandenBos, & Donald K. Freedheim (Eds.), *History of psychotherapy: Continuity and change* (2nd ed., pp. 141–172). Washington, DC: American Psychological Association.

Watson, John B. (1913). Psychology as the behaviorist views it. *Psychological Review, 20,* 158–177.

Watson, John B. (1916). The place of the conditioned-reflex in psychology. *Psychological Review, 23,* 89–116.

Watson, John B. (1919). A schematic outline of the emotions. *Psychological Review, 26,* 165–196.

Watson, John B. (1924/1970). *Behaviorism.* New York, NY: Norton.

Watson, John B. (1930). *Behaviorism* (Rev. ed.). Chicago, IL: University of Chicago Press.

Watson, John B., & Rayner, Rosalie. (1920/2000). Conditioned emotional reactions. *Journal of Experimental Psychology, 3,* 1–14. (Reprinted March 2000: *American Psychologist, 55*(3), 313–317).

Watson, Nathaniel F.; Harden, Kathryn Paige; Buchwald, Dedra; Vitiello, Michael V.; Pack, Allan I.; Weigle, David S.; & Goldberg, Jack. (2012). Sleep duration and body mass index in twins: A gene-environment interaction. *Sleep: Journal of Sleep and Sleep Disorders Research, 3,* 597–603.

Watson, Stuart; Chilton, Roy; & Fairchild, Helen. (2006). Association between childhood trauma and dissociation among patients with borderline personality disorder. *Australian and New Zealand Journal of Psychiatry, 40*(5), 478–481.

Watters, Ethan. (2010). *Crazy like us: The globalization of the American psyche.* New York, NY: Free Press.

Watts, Geoff. (2012). Critics attack DSM-5 for overmedicalising normal human behaviour. *BMJ, 344,* e1020.

Watts Jonathan. (2002). Public health experts concerned about "hikikomori." *Lancet, 359,* 1131.

Watts, Richard E. (2012). On the origin of the striving for superiority and of social interest. In Jon Carlson & Michael P. Maniacci (Eds.), *Alfred Adler revisited.* New York, NY: Routledge/Taylor & Francis Group.

Weaver, Terri E., & George, Charles F. P. (2005). Cognition and performance in patients with obstructive sleep apnea. In Meir H. Kryger, Thomas Roth, & William C. Dement (Eds.), *Principles and practice of sleep medicine* (4th ed.). Philadelphia, PA: Elsevier Saunders.

Webb, Thomas L., & Sheeran, Paschal (2007). How do implementation intentions promote goal attainment? A test of component processes. *Journal of Experimental Social Psychology, 43,* 295–302. doi:10.1016/j.jesp.2006.02.001

Wechsler, David. (1944). *The measurement of adult intelligence* (3rd ed.). Baltimore, MD: Williams & Wilkins.

Wechsler, David. (1977). *Manual for the Wechsler Intelligence Scale for Children* (Rev.). New York, NY: Psychological Corporation.

Wechsler, Henry, & Nelson, Toben F. (2008). What we have learned from the Harvard School of Public Health College Alcohol Study: Focusing attention on college student alcohol consumption and the environmental conditions that promote it. *Journal of Studies on Alcohol and Drugs, 69*(4), 481–490.

Weems, Carl, & Silverman, Wendy. (2008). Anxiety disorders. In Theodore P. Beauchaine & Stephen P. Hinshaw (Eds.), *Child and adolescent psychopathology* (pp. 447–476). Hoboken, NJ: Wiley.

Weil, Rimona S., & Rees, Geraint. (2010). A new taxonomy for perceptual filling-in. *Brain Research Reviews.* doi:10.1016/j.brainresrev.2010.10.004

Weinberger, Daniel R. (1995, June). Quoted in Joel L. Swerdlow, "Quiet miracles of the brain." *National Geographic, 187,* 2–41.

Weiner, Irving B., & Meyer, Gregory J. (2009). Personality assessment with the Rorschach Inkblot Method. In James N. Butcher (Ed.), *Oxford handbook of personality assessment.* New York, NY: Oxford University Press.

Weinstein, N.; Brown, K. W.; & Ryan, R. M. (2009). A multi-method examination of the effects of mindfulness on stress attribution, coping, and emotional well-being. *Journal of Research in Personality, 43,* 374–385. doi:10.1016/j.jrp.2008.12.008

Weintraub, Michael I.; Wolfe, Gil I.; Barohn, Richard A.; Cole, Steven P.; Parry, Gareth J.; Hayat, Ghazala; & others. (2003). Static magnetic field therapy for symptomatic diabetic neuropathy: A randomized, doubleblind, placebo-controlled trial. *Archives of Physical Medicine and Rehabilitation, 84,* 736–746.

Weisberg, Robert W. (1988). Problem solving and creativity. In Robert J. Sternberg (Ed.), *The nature of creativity.* New York, NY: Cambridge University Press.

Weisberg, Robert W. (1993). *Creativity: Beyond the myth of genius.* New York, NY: Freeman.

Weiser, Mark; Reichenberg, Abraham; Grotto, Itamar; Yasvitzky, Ross; Rabinowitz, Jonathan; Lubin, Gad; ... Davidson, Michael. (2004). Higher rates of cigarette smoking in male adolescents before the onset of schizophrenia: A historical-perspective cohort study. *American Journal of Psychiatry, 161*(7), 1219–1223.

Weiss, Alexander; Bates, Timothy C.; & Luciano, Michelle. (2008). Happiness is a personal(ity) thing: The genetics of personality and well-being in a representative sample. *Psychological Science, 19*(3), 205–210.

Weiss, Lawrence G. (2010). Considerations on the Flynn effect. *Journal of Psychoeducational Assessment, 28*(5), 482.

Weiss, Tzipi, & Berger, Roni. (2010). Posttraumatic growth around the globe: Research findings and practice implications. In Tzipi Weiss & Roni Berger (Eds.), *Posttraumatic growth and culturally competent practice: Lessons learned from around the globe.* Hoboken, NJ: Wiley.

Weisz, John R., & Kazdin, Alan E. (2010). *Evidence-based psychotherapies for children and adolescents.* New York, NY: Guilford.

Wells, Gordon. (2009). The social context of language and literacy development. In O. A. Barbarin & B. H. Wasik. *Handbook of early child development and early education: Research to practice.* (pp. 271–302). New York, NY: Guilford.

Werker, Janet, & Desjardins, Renee. (1995). Listening to speech in the 1st year of life: Experiential influences on phoneme production. *Current Directions in Psychological Science, 4,* 76–81.

Werkhoven, Peter, & van Erp, Jan. (2013). Multimodal perception and simulation. In Charles Chubb, Barbara A. Dosher, Zhong-Lin Lu, & Richard M. Shiffrin (Eds.). (2013), *Human information processing: Vision, memory, and attention. Decade of behavior.* Washington, DC: American Psychological Association.

Werner, John S.; Pinna, Baingio; & Spillman, Lothar. (2007, March). Illusory color and the brain. *Scientific American, 296,* pp. 90–95.

Wertheimer, Max. (1912/1965). Experimentelle Studien über das Se-hen von Bewegung. *Zeitschrift für Psychologie, 61,* 162–163, 221–227. (Portions of original publication translated and reprinted in Richard J. Herrnstein & Edwin G. Boring [Eds.], *A source book in the history of psychology* [Don Cantor, Trans.]. Cambridge, MA: Harvard University Press.)

Wertheimer, Max. (1923/2009). Laws of organization in perceptual forms. In Barbara F. Gentile, Barbara F. & Benjamin O. Miller (Eds.), *Foundations of psychological thought: A history of psychology.* (pp. 427–440). Thousand Oaks, CA: Sage.

Wertsch, James V. (2008). From social interaction to higher psychological processes: A clarification and application of Vygotsky's theory. *Human Development, 51*(1), 66–79.

West, John D., & Bubenzer, Donald L. (2012). A basic difference between individual psychology and psychoanalysis. In Jon Carlson & Michael P. Maniacci (Eds.), *Alfred Adler revisited.* New York: Routledge/Taylor & Francis Group.

Westen, Drew; Weinberger, Joel; & Bradley, Rebekah. (2007). Motivation, decision making, and consciousness: From psychodynamics to subliminal priming and emotional constraint satisfaction. In Philip David Zelazo, Morris Moscovitch, & Evan Thompson (Eds.), *The Cambridge handbook of consciousness.* New York, NY: Cambridge University Press.

Westerlund, Joakim; Parker, Adrian; Dalkvist, Jan; & Hadlaczky, Gerga. (2006). Remarkable correspondences between Ganzfeld mentation and target content—A psychical or psychological effect? *Journal of Parapsychology, 70*(1), 23–48.

Wethington, Elaine. (2000). Expecting stress: Americans and the "midlife crisis." *Motivation and Emotion, 24,* 85–103.

Wheeler, Mark E.; Petersen, Steven E.; & Buckner, Randy L. (2000). Memory's echo: Vivid remembering reactivates sensory-specific cortex. *Proceedings of the National Academy of Sciences, USA, 97,* 11125–11129.

Whisman, Mark A.; Uebelacker, Lisa A.; & Settles, Tatiana D. (2010). Marital distress and the metabolic syndrome: Linking social functioning with physical health. *Journal of Family Psychology, 24*(3), 367–370.

Whitaker, Jodi L.; Melzer, Andre.; Steffgen, Georges.; & Bushman, Brad J. (2013). The allure of the forbidden: Breaking taboos, frustration, and attraction to violent video games. *Psychological Science, 24*(4), 507–513. doi:10.1177/0956797612457397

Whitbourne, Susan K.; Sneed, Joel R.; & Sayer, Aline (2009). Psychosocial development from college through midlife: A 34-year sequential study. *Developmental Psychology, 45*(5), 1328–1340.

White, Robert W. (1959). Motivation reconsidered: The concepts of competence. *Psychological Review, 66,* 297–333.

Whitley, Rob, & Berry, Sarah. (2013). Trends in newspaper coverage of mental illness in Canada: 2005–2010. *Canadian Journal of Psychiatry, 58*(2), 107–112.

Whitty, Stephen. (2014). Robin Williams, RIP: 1951–2014. Retrieved from http://www.nj.com/entertainment/movies/index.ssf/2014/08/robin_williams_rip_1951-2014.html

Whorf, Benjamin L. (1956). Science and linguistics. In J. B. Carroll (Ed.), *Language, thought, and reality: Selected papers of Benjamin Lee Whorf.* Cambridge, MA: MIT Press.

Wickens, Christine M.; Mann, Robert E.; & Wiesenthal, David L. (2013). Addressing driver aggression: Contributions from psychological science. *Current Directions in Psychological Science, 22*(5), 386–391. doi:10.1177/0963721413486986

Wieland, Sandra. (2011). Dissociation in children and adolescents: What it is, how it presents, and how we can understand it. In Sandra Wieland (Ed.),

Dissociation in traumatized children and adolescents: Theory and clinical interventions. (pp. 1–27). New York, NY: Routledge/Taylor & Francis Group.

Wilcoxon, Hardy C.; Dragoin, William B.; & Kral, Paul A. (1971). Illness-induced aversions in rat and quail: Relative salience of visual and gustatory cues. *Science, 171,* 826–828.

Wilde, Douglass J. (2011). *Jung's personality theory quantified.* New York, NY: Springer-Verlag.

Wilker, Sarah, & Kolassa, Iris-Tatjana. (2013). The formation of a neural fear network in posttraumatic stress disorder: Insights from molecular genetics. *Clinical Psychological Science, 2*(2), 1–19. doi:10.1177/2167702613479583

Wilkinson, Richard G., & Pickett, Kate E. (2009). Income inequality and social dysfunction. *Annual Review of Sociology, 35,* 493–511.

Williams, J. Mark G.; Crane, Catherine; Barnhofer, Thorsten; Brennan, Kate; Duggan, Danielle S.; Fennell, Melanie J.V.; Hackmann, Ann; Krusche, Adele; Muse, Kate; Von Rohr, Isabelle Rudolf; Shah, Dhruvi; Crane, Rebecca S.; Eames, Catrin; Jones, Mariel; Radford, Sholto; Silverton, Sarah; Sun, Yongzhong; Weatherley-Jones, Elaine; Whitaker, Christopher J.; Russell, Daphne; & Russell, Ian T. (2014). Mindfulness-based cognitive therapy for preventing relapse in recurrent depression: A randomized dismantling trial. *Journal of Consulting and Clinical Psychology, 82,* 275–286. doi:10.1037/a0035036

Williams, Janice E. (2010). Anger/hostility and cardiovascular disease. In Michael Potegal, Gerhard Stemmler, & Charles Spielberger (Eds.), *International handbook of anger: Constituent and concomitant biological, psychological, and social processes.* New York: Springer.

Williams, Mark; Teasdale, John; Segal, Zindel; & Kabat-Zinn, Jon. (2007). *The mindful way through depression: Freeing yourself from chronic unhappiness.* New York, NY: Guilford.

Williams, Nigel M.; O'Donovan, Michael C.; & Owen, Michael J. (2005). Is the dysbindin (DTNBP1) a susceptibility gene for schizophrenia? *Schizophrenia Bulletin, 31,* 800–805.

Williams, Paula G.; Smith, Timothy W.; Gunn, Heather E.; & Uchino, Bert N. (2011). Personality and stress: Individual differences in exposure, reactivity, recovery, and restoration. In Richard J. Contrada & Andrew Baum (Eds.), *The handbook of stress science: Biology, psychology, and health.* New York, NY: Springer.

Willis, Janine, & Todorov, Alexander. (2006). First impressions: Making up your mind after a 100-ms exposure to a face. *Psychological Science, 17,* 592–598. doi:10.1111/j.1467-9280.2006.01750.x

Willoughby, Tina.; Adachi, Paul J. C.; & Good, Marie. (2012). A longitudinal study of the association between violent video game play and aggression among adolescents. *Developmental Psychology, 48*(4), 1044–1057. doi:10.1037/a0026046

Wills, Frank. (2009). *Beck's cognitive therapy: Distinctive features.* New York, NY: Routledge.

Wilson, Clare, (2014). Rethinking schizophrenia: Taming demons without drugs. Retrieved from http://www.newscientist.com/article/dn24992-rethinking-schizophrenia-taming-demons-without-drugs.html?full=true#.Uv6o3PldWSo

Wilson, Duff. (2010, October 2). Side effects may include lawsuits. *The New York Times.* Retrieved from http://www.nytimes.com

Wilson, Megan L.; Snyder, Rebecca J.; Zhang, Zhi H.; Lan, Luo; Li, C. L.; & Maple, Terry L. (2009). Effects of partner on play fighting behavior in giant panda cubs. Play & culture studies. In Cindy Dell Clark (Ed.), *Transactions at play: Play and culture studies.* Lanham, MD: University Press of America.

Wilson, Robert S.; Arnold, Steven E.; Schneider, Julie A.; Boyle, Patricia A.; Buchman, Aron S.; & Bennett, David A. (2009). Olfactory impairment in presymptomatic Alzheimer's disease. *Annals of the New York Academy of Sciences, 1170,* 730–735. doi:10.1111/j.1749-6632.2009.04013.x

Windholz, George. (1990). Pavlov and the Pavlovians in the laboratory. *Journal of the History of the Behavioral Sciences, 26,* 64–73.

Windle, Michael, & Windle, Rebecca C. (2001). Depressive symptoms and cigarette smoking among middle adolescents: Prospective associations and intrapersonal and interpersonal influences. *Journal of Consulting and Clinical Psychology, 69,* 215–226.

Winemiller, Mark H.; Billow, Robert G.; Laskowski, Edward R.; & Harmsen, W. Scott. (2005). Effect of magnetic vs shammagnetic insoles on nonspecific foot pain in the workplace: A randomized, double-blind, placebo-controlled trial. *Mayo Clinic Proceedings, 80,* 1138–1145.

Winkielman, Piotr; Niedenthal, Paula; Wielgosz, Joseph; Eelen, Jiska; & Kavanagh, Liam C. (2015). Embodiment of cognition and emotion. In Mario Mikulincer, Phillip R. Shaver, Eugene Borgida, & John A. Bargh (Eds.), *APA Handbook of Personality and Social Psychology, Vol. 1: Attitudes and social cognition.* Washington, DC: American Psychological Association. doi:10.1037/14341-004

Winkler, Connie. (2006, September). Job tryouts go virtual: Online job simulations provide sophisticated candidate assessments. *HR Magazine, 51*(9), 131–134.

Wirth, James H, & Bodenhausen, Galen V. (2009). The role of gender in mental-illness stigma: A national experiment. *Psychological Science, 20*(2), 169–173.

Wise, Deborah, & Rosqvist, Johan. (2006). Explanatory style and wellbeing. In Jay C. Thomas, Daniel L. Segal, & Michel Hersen (Eds.), *Comprehensive Handbook of Personality and Psychopathology. Vol. 1: Personality and everyday functioning* (pp. 285–305). Hoboken, NJ: Wiley.

Wixted, John T. (2004). The psychology and neuroscience of forgetting. *Annual Review of Psychology, 55,* 235–269.

Wnuk, Ewelina, & Majid, Asifa (2014). Revisiting the limits of language: The odor lexicon of Maniq. *Cognition, 131,* 125–138.

Woerle, Sandra; Roeber, Jim; & Landen, Michael G. (2007). Prevalence of alcohol dependence among excessive drinkers in New Mexico. *Alcoholism: Clinical and Experimental Research, 31,* 293–298.

Wohlschläger, Andreas; & Wohlschläger, Astrid. (1998). Mental and manual rotation. *Journal of Experimental Psychology: Human Perception and Performance, 24,* 397–412.

Wolf, Erika J., & Mori, DeAnna L. (2009). Avoidant coping as a predictor of mortality in veterans with end-stage renal disease. *Health Psychology, 28*(3), 330–337.

Wolff, Andre; Vanduynhoven, Eric; van Kleef, Maarten; Huygen, Frank; Pope, Jason E.; & Mekhail, Nagy. (2011). Phantom pain. *Pain Practice, 11*(4), 403–413. doi:10.1111/j.1533-2500.2011.00454.x

Wolman, David. (2005, November 5). The secrets of human handedness. *New Scientist, 2524,* 36.

Wolman, David. (2012). The split brain: A tale of two halves. *Nature, 483,* 260–263 doi:10.1038/483260a

Wolpe, Joseph. (1958). *Psychotherapy by reciprocal inhibition.* Stanford, CA: Stanford University Press.

Wolpe, Joseph. (1982). *The practice of behavior therapy.* New York, NY: Pergamon Press.

Women's Sports Foundation. (2007). Title IX myths and facts. Retrieved from http://www.womenssportsfoundation.org/home/advocate/title-ix-and-issues/what-is-title-ix/title-ix-myths-and-facts

Wonderlic, Charles. (2005). Pre-employment testing and employee selection. Retrieved on December 7, 2009, from furninfo.com

Wonderlic, E. F. (1998). *Wonderlic personnel test manual.* Libertyville, IL: Wonderlic.

Wong, Paul T. P., & Wong, Lilian C. J. (Eds.). (2006). *Handbook of multicultural perspectives on stress and coping.* New York, NY: Springer.

Wong, V., & Ying, Winnie. (2006). Social withdrawal of young people in Hong Kong: A social exclusion perspective. *Hong Kong Journal of Social Work, 40* (1/2), 61–92.

Wong, Wan-chi. (2009). Retracing the footsteps of Wilhelm Wundt: Explorations in the disciplinary frontiers of psychology and in Völkerpsychologie. *History of Psychology, 12*(4), 229–265.

Woo, Stephanie M., & Keatinge, Carolyn. (2008). *Diagnosis and treatment of mental disorders across the lifespan.* Hoboken, NJ: Wiley.

Woo, Tsung-Ung W.; Canuso, Carla M.; Wojcik, Joanne D.; Brunette, Mary F.; & Green, Alan I. (2009). Treatment of schizophrenia. In Alan F. Schatzberg & Charles B. Nemeroff (Eds.), *The American Psychiatric*

Publishing textbook of psychopharmacology (4th ed., pp. 1135–1169). Washington, DC: American Psychiatric Publishing.

Wood, Alex M.; Maltby, John; Gillett, Raphael; Linley, P. Alex; & Joseph, Stephen. (2008). The role of gratitude in the development of social support, stress, and depression: Two longitudinal studies. *Journal of Research in Personality, 42,* 854–871.

Wood, Robert, & Bandura, Albert. (1991). Social cognitive theory of organizational management. In Richard M. Steers & Lyman W. Porter (Eds.), *Motivation and work behavior.* New York, NY: McGraw-Hill.

Wood, Wendy, & Eagly, Alice H. (2009). Gender identity. In Mark R. Leary & Rick H. Hoyle (Eds.), *Handbook of individual differences in social behavior* (pp. 109–125). New York, NY: Guilford.

Wood, Wendy, & Eagly, Alice H. (2010). Gender. In Susan T. Fiske, Daniel T. Gilbert, & Gardner Lindzey (Eds.), *Handbook of social psychology, 1.* Hoboken, NJ: Wiley.

Woodhead, Erin; Cronkite, Ruth; Moos, Rudolph; & Timko, Christine. (2013). Coping strategies predictive of adverse outcomes among community adults. *Journal of Clinical Psychology, 70,* 1183–1195. doi:10.1002/jclp.21924

Woodhead, Erin; Northrop, Lynn; & Edelstein, Barry. (2014, August 6). Stress, social support, and burnout among long-term care nursing staff. *Journal of Applied Gerontology.* Advance online publication. doi:10.1177/0733464814542465

Woodworth, Robert S. (1918). *Dynamic psychology.* New York, NY: Columbia University Press.

Woodworth, Robert S. (1921). *Psychology: A study of mental life.* New York, NY: Holt.

Woody, Robert Henley. (2008). The evolution and modern practice of interpersonal process family therapy, *American Journal of Family Therapy, 36,* 99–106.

Woollett, Katherine; Spiers, Hugo J.; & Maguire, Eleanor A. (2009). Talent in the taxi: A model system for exploring expertise. *Philosophical Transactions of the Royal Society B: Biological Sciences, 364*(1522), 1407–1416. doi:10.1098/364/1522/1407rstb.2008.0288

Workman, Lance, & Reader, Will. (2008). *Evolutionary psychology: An introduction.* New York, NY: Cambridge University Press.

World Health Organization. (1998). Schizophrenia and public health. Geneva: Author. Retrieved from http://www.who.int/mental_health/media/en/55.pdf

World Health Organization. (2011). Obesity and overweight. Retrieved from http://www.who.int/mediacentre/factsheets/fs311/en

World Health Organization. (2014). *Preventing suicide: A global imperative.* Luxembourg: WHO Library.

WorldatWork. (2008–2009). WorldatWork survey finds telework on the rise in the U.S., Canada: Analysis of employee retention practices shows some cross-border differences. Retrieved on December 7, 2009, from http://www.worldatwork.org/waw/adimLink?id=28062

Worthman, Carol M., & Brown, Ryan A. (2007). Companionable sleep: Social regulation of sleep and cosleeping in Egyptian families. *Journal of Family Psychology, 21,* 124–135.

Wright, Brittany, & Loving, Timothy. (2011). Health implications of conflict in close relationships. *Social and Personality Psychology Compass, 5,* 552–562. doi:10.1111/j.1751-9004.2011.00371.x

Wright, Jesse H.; Thase, Michael E.; & Beck, Aaron T. (2011). Cognitive therapy. In Robert E. Hales, Stuart C. Yudofsky, & Glen O. Gabbard (Eds.), *Essentials of psychiatry.* Arlington, VA: American Psychiatric Publishing.

Wright, Jesse H.; Turkington, Douglas; Kingdon, David G.; & Basco, Monica Ramirez. (2009). *Cognitive-behavior therapy for severe mental illness: An illustrated guide.* Washington, DC: American Psychiatric Publishing.

Wrobel, Beata, & Karasek, Michal. (2008). Human sexuality and sex steroids. *Neuro Endocrinology Letters, 29*(1), 3–10.

Wurtele, Sandy K. (2009). "Activities of older adults" survey: Tapping into student views of the elderly. *Educational Geronotology, 35,* 1026–1031. doi:10.1080/03601270902973557

Wyatt, Tristram D. (2009). Fifty years of pheromones. *Nature, 457,* 262–263.

Wyatt, Tristram D. (2015). The search for human pheromones: The lost decades and the necessity of returning to first principles. *Proceedings of the Royal Society B, 282,* 20142994. doi:10.1098/rspb.2014.2994

Wykes, Til; Huddy, Vyv; Cellard, Caroline; McGurk, Susan R.; & Czobor, Pál. (2011). A meta-analysis of cognitive remediation for schizophrenia: Methodology and effect sizes. *American Journal of Psychiatry, 168*(5), 472–485. doi:10.1176/appi.ajp.2010.10060855

Wynne, Lyman C.; Tienari, Pekka; & Nieminen, P. (2006, December). Genotype-environment interaction in the schizophrenia spectrum: Genetic liability and global family ratings in the Finnish adoption study. *Family Process, 45*(4), 419–434.

Xie, Lulu; Kang, Hongyi; Xu, Qiwu; Chen, Michael J.; Liao, Yonghong; Thiyagarajan, Meenakshisundaram; O'Donnell, John; Christensen, Daniel J.; Nicholson, Charles; Iliff, Jeffrey J.; Takano, Takahiro; Deane, Rashid; & Nedergaard, Maiken. (2013). Sleep drives metabolite clearance from the adult brain. *Science, 342,* 373–377. doi:10.1126/science.124122

Xu, Fujie; Sternberg, Maya R.; & Markowitz, Lauri E. (2010a). Men who have sex with men in the United States: Demographic and behavioral characteristics and prevalence of HIV and HSV-2 infection: Results from national health and nutrition examination survey 2001–2006. *Sexually Transmitted Diseases, 37*(6), 399–405. doi:310.1097/OLQ.1090b1013e3181ce1122b.

Xu, Fujie; Sternberg, Maya R.; & Markowitz, Lauri E. (2010b). Women who have sex with women in the United States: Prevalence, sexual behavior and prevalence of herpes simplex virus type 2 infection-results from national health and nutrition examination survey 2001–2006. *Sexually Transmitted Diseases, 37*(7), 407–413. doi:10.1097/OLQ.0b013e3181db2e18

Xu, Jiaquan Q.; Kochanek, Kenneth D.; & Tejada-Vera, Betzaida. (2009). Deaths: Preliminary data for 2007. *National Vital Statistics Reports, 58*(1). Hyattsville, MD: National Center for Health Statistics.

Yaffe, Kristine; Fiocco, Alexandra J.; Lindquist, K.; Vittinghoff, E.; Simonsick, E. M.; Newman, A. B.; Satterfield, S.; & others. (2009). Predictors of maintaining cognitive function in older adults: The HealthABC study. *Neurology 72,* 2029–2035.

Yalom, Irvin D. (2005). *The theory and practice of group psychotherapy* (5th ed.). New York, NY: Basic Books.

Yamaguchi, Susumu, & Ariizumi, Yukari. (2006). Close interpersonal relationships among Japanese: Amae as distinguished from attachment and dependence. In Uichol Kim, Kuo-Shu Yang, & Kwang-Kuo Hwang (Eds.), *Indigenous and cultural psychology: Understanding people in context.* New York, NY: Springer Science + Business Media.

Yang, Guang; Lai, Cora Sau Wan; Cichon, Joseph; Ma, Lei; Li, Wei; & Gan, Wen-Biao. (2014). Sleep promotes branch-specific formation of dendritic spines after learning. *Science, 344,* 1173–1178.

Yarnell, Phillip R., & Lynch, Steve. (1970, April 25). Retrograde memory immediately after concussion. *Lancet, 1,* 863–865.

Ybarra, Oscar. (2002). Naive causal understanding of valenced behaviors and its implications for social information processing. *Psychological Bulletin, 128,* 421–441.

Yeh, Christine J.; Inman, Arpana C.; Kim, Angela B.; & Okubo, Yuki (2006). Asian American families' collectivistic coping strategies in response to 9/11. *Cultural Diversity and Ethnic Minority Psychology, 12,* 134–148. doi:10.1037/1099-9809.12.1.134

Yiend, Jenny; Parnes, Charlotte; Shepherd, Kirsty; Roche, Mary-Kate; & Cooper, Myra J. (2014). Negative self-beliefs in eating disorders: A cognitive-bias-modification study. *Clinical Psychological Science, 2,* 756–766. doi:10.1177/2167702614528163

Yildirim, Baris O., & Derksen, Jan J. (2012). A review on the relationship between testosterone and life-course persistent antisocial behavior. *Psychiatry Research, 200*(2–3), 984–1010. doi:10.1016/j.psychres.2012.07.044

Yonkers, Kimberly A., & Clarke, Diana E. (2011). Gender and gender-related issues in DSM-5. In Darrel A. Regier, William E. Narrow, Emily A. Kuhl, & David J. Kupfer (Eds.), *The conceptual evolution of DSM-5* (pp. 287–301). Arlington, VA: American Psychiatric Publishing.

Yoo, Seung-Schik; Gujar, Ninad; Hu, Peter; Jolesz, Ferenc A.; & Walker, Matthew P. (2007). The human emotional brain without sleep: A prefrontal-amygdala disconnect. *Current Biology, 17,* 877–878.

Yoshida, Katherine A.; Pons, Ferran; Maye, Jessica; & Werker, Janet F. (2010). Distributional phonetic learning at 10 months of age. *Infancy, 15*(4), 420–433.

Yoshizaki, Kazuhito; Weissman, Daniel H.; & Banich, Marie T. (2007). A hemispheric division of labor aids mental rotation. *Neuropsychology, 21,* 326–336.

Young, Michael W. (2000, March). The tick-tock of the biological clock. *Scientific American, 282*(3), 64–71.

Youyou, Wu; Kosinski, Michal; & Stillwell, David. (2015). Computer-based personality judgments are more accurate than those made by humans. *Proceedings of the National Academy of Sciences, 112,* 1036–1040. doi:10.1073/pnas.1418680112

Yu, Calvin Kai-Ching. (2011). The mechanisms of defense and dreaming. *Dreaming, 21*(1), 51–69. doi:10.1037/a0022867

Yudofsky, Stuart C. (2009). Contracting schizophrenia: Lessons from the influenza epidemic of 1918–1919. *Journal of the American Medical Association, 301*(3), 324–326.

Zachariae, Robert. (2009). Psychoneuroimmunology: A bio-psycho-social approach to health and disease. *Scandinavian Journal of Psychology, 50*(6), 645–651.

Zajonc, Robert B. (1998). Emotions. In Daniel T. Gilbert, Susan T. Fiske, & Gardner Lindzey (Eds.), *Handbook of social psychology* (4th ed.). New York, NY: McGraw-Hill.

Zajonc, Robert B. (2000). Feeling and thinking: Closing the debate over the independence of affect. In Joseph F. Forgas (Ed.), *Feeling and thinking: The role of affect in social cognition.* New York, NY: Cambridge University Press.

Zajonc, Robert B. (2001). Mere exposure: A gateway to the subliminal. *Current Directions in Psychological Science, 10,* 224–228.

Zaki, Jamil, & Mitchell, Jason P. (2013). Intuitive prosociality. *Current Directions in Psychological Science, 22,* 466–470. doi:10.1177/0963721413492764

Zanarini, Mary C.; Horwood, Jeremy; Wolke, Dieter; Waylen, Andrea; Fitzmaurice, Garrett; & Grant, Bridget F. (2011). Prevalence of DSM-IV borderline personality disorder in two community samples: 6,330 English 11-year-olds and 34,653 American adults. *Journal of Personality Disorders, 25,* 607–619.

Zandy, Amy. (2007, July/August). If you want to lead, learn to serve. *Debt Cubed.* Retrieved on September 15, 2008, from http://www.debt3online.com/?page=article&article_id=189

Zarate, Carlos A.; Singh, Jaskaran B.; Carlson, Paul J.; Brutsche, Nancy E.; Ameli, Rezvan; Luckenbaugh, David A.; Charney, Dennis S. & others. (2006). A randomized trial of an N-methyl-D-aspartate antagonist in treatment-resistant major depression. *Archives of General Psychiatry, 63,* 856–864. Retrieved from www.archgenpsychiatry.com

Zatorre, Robert J. (2013). Music, the food of neuroscience? *Nature, 434,* 312–315.

Zebrowitz, Leslie A., & Montepare, Joann M. (2006). The ecological approach to person perception: Evolutionary roots and contemporary offshoots. In Mark Schaller, Jeffry A. Simpson, & Douglas T. Kenrick (Eds.), *Evolution and social psychology* (pp. 81–113). Madison, CT: Psychosocial Press.

Zebrowitz, Leslie A., & Montepare, Joann M. (2008). First impressions from facial appearance cues. In N. Ambady & J. J. Skowronski (Eds.), *First impressions.* New York, NY: Guilford.

Zeidan, Fadel. (2015). The neurobiology of mindfulness meditation. In Kirk Warren Brown, J. David Creswell, & Richard M. Ryan (Eds.), *Handbook of mindfulness: Theory, research, and practice.* New York, NY: Guilford.

Zeidan, Fadel; Johnson, Susan K.; Diamond, Bruce J.; David, Zhanna; & Goolkasian, Paula. (2010). Mindfulness meditation improves cognition: Evidence of brief mental training. *Consciousness and Cognition, 19*(2), 597–605. doi:10.1016/jconcog.2010.03.014

Zeidan, Fadel; Martucci, Katherine T.; Kraft, Robert A.; Gordon, Nakia S.; McHaffie, John G.; & Coghill, Robert C. (2011). Brain mechanisms supporting the modulation of pain by mindfulness meditation. *Journal of Neuroscience, 31,* 5540–5548.

Zeki, Semir. (2001). Localization and globalization in conscious vision. *Annual Review of Neuroscience, 24,* 57–86.

Zelinski, Elizabeth M., & Kennison, Robert F. (2007). Not your parents' test scores: Cohort reduces psychometric aging effects. *Psychology and Aging, 22*(3), 546–557.

Zentner, Marcel, & Shiner, Rebecca L. (2012). *Handbook of temperament.* New York, NY: Guilford.

Zernike, Kate. (2004, August 7). At abuse hearing, no testimony that G.I.'s acted on orders. *New York Times.* Retrieved on August 7, 2004, at http://www.nytimes.com/2004/08/07/international/middleeast/07abuse.html

Zhang, Tie-Yuan, & Meaney, Michael J. (2010). Epigenetics and the environmental regulation of the genome and its function. *Annual Review of Psychology, 61,* 1–28. doi:10.1146/annurev.psych.60.110707.163625

Zhao, Zhi-Qi. (2008). Neural mechanism underlying acupuncture analgesia. *Progress in Neurobiology, 85,* 355–375.

Zheng, Huiyuan; Lenard, Natalie; Shin, Andrew; & Berthoud, Hans- Rudolf. (2009). Appetite control and energy balance regulation in the modern world: Reward-driven brain overrides repletion signals. *International Journal of Obesity, 33,* S8–S13.

Zhou, Xinyue; He, Lingnan; Yang, Qing; Lao, Junpeng; & Baumeister, Roy F. (2012). Control deprivation and styles of thinking. *Journal of Personality and Social Psychology, 102,* 460–478. doi:10.1037/a0026316

Zhu, Haiya; Huberman, Bernardo; & Luon, Yarun. (2012). To switch or not to switch: Understanding social influence in online choices. In *Proceedings of the SIGCHI Conference on Human Factors in Computing Systems,* 2257–2266.

Ziegler, Matthias; Schmukle, Stefan; Egloff, Boris; & Bühner, Markus. (2010). Investigating measures of achievement motivation(s). *Journal of Individual Differences, 31,* 15–21.

Zimbardo, Philip G. (2000a). Prologue: Reflections on the Stanford Prison Experiment: Genesis, transformations, consequences. In Thomas Blass (Ed.), *Obedience to authority: Current perspectives on the Milgram paradigm.* Mahwah, NJ: Erlbaum.

Zimbardo, Philip G. (2000b, Sept./Oct.). Quoted in Christina Maslach, Emperor of the edge. *Psychology Today.* Retrieved on February 23, 2006, from https://www.psychologytoday.com/articles/200009/emperor-the-edge

Zimbardo, Philip G. (2004a). A situationist perspective on the psychology of evil: Understanding how good people are transformed into perpetrators. In Arthur G. Miller (Ed.), *The social psychology of good and evil.* New York, NY: Guilford.

Zimbardo, Philip G. (2004b, May 9). Power turns good soldiers into 'bad apples.' *Boston Globe.* Retrieved on December 5, 2005, from http://www.boston.com/news/globe/editorial_opinion/oped/articles/2004/05/09/power_turns_good_soldiers_into_bad_apples/

Zimbardo, Philip G. (2005, January 19). You can't be a sweet cucumber in a vinegar barrel: A talk with Philip Zimbardo. *Edge: The Third Culture.* Retrieved on October 8, 2005, from http://edge.org/3rd_culture/zimbardo05/zimbardo05_index.html

Zimbardo, Philip G. (2007). *The Lucifer effect: Understanding how good people turn evil.* New York, NY: Random House.

Zimbardo, Philip G.; Banks, W. Curtis; Haney, Craig; & Jaffe, David. (1973, April 8). The mind is a formidable jailer: A Pirandellian prison. *The New York Times Magazine,* pp. 38ff.

Zimbardo, Philip G.; Weisenberg, Matisyohu; Firestone, Ira; & Levy, Burton. (1965). Communicator effectiveness in producing public conformity and private attitude change. *Journal of Personality, 33,* 233–256.

Zimmerman, Federick J.; Christakis, Dmitri; & Meltzoff, Andrew N. (2007). Associations between media viewing and language development in children under age 2 years. *Journal of Pediatrics, 151,* 364–368.

Zimmerman, Isaiah M. (2008). Interpersonal group psychotherapy. In George Max Saiger, Sy Rubenfeld, & Mary D. Dluhy (Eds.), *Windows into today's group therapy: The National Group Psychotherapy Institute of the Washington School of Psychiatry.* New York, NY: Routledge/Taylor & Francis Group.

Zohar, Dov; Tzischinsky, Orna; Epstein, Rachel; & Lavie, Peretz. (2005). The effects of sleep loss on medical residents' emotional reactions to work events: A cognitive-energy model. *Sleep, 28,* 47–54.

Zosuls, Kristina M.; Ruble, Diane N.; Tamis-LeMonda, Catherine S.; Bornstein, Marc H.; Greulich, Faith K.; & Shrout, Patrick E. (2009). The acquisition of gender labels in infancy: Implications for gender-typed play. *Developmental Psychology, 45,* 688–701.

Zubieta, Jon-Kar; Bueller, Joshua A.; Jackson, Lisa R.; Scott, David J.; Xu, Yanjun; Koeppe, Robert A.; Nichols, Thomas E.; & Stohler, Christian S. (2005). Placebo effects mediated by endogenous opioid activity on opioid receptors. *Journal of Neuroscience, 25,* 7754–7762.

Zucker, Kenneth J., & Cohen-Kettenis, Peggy T. (2008). Gender identity disorder in children and adolescents. In David L. Rowland & Luca Incrocci (Eds.), *Handbook of sexual and gender identity disorders.* Hoboken, NJ: Wiley.

Zuckerman, Marvin. (1979). *Sensation seeking: Beyond the optimal level of arousal.* Hillsdale, NJ: Erlbaum.

Zuckerman, Marvin. (2007). *Sensation seeking and risky behavior.* Washington, DC: American Psychological Association.

Zuckerman, Marvin. (2009). Sensation seeking. In Mark R. Leary & Rick H. Hoyle (Eds.), *Handbook of individual differences in social behavior.* (pp. 455–465). New York, NY: Guilford.

Zusman, Jose Alberto; Cheniaux, Elie; & de Freitas, Sergio (2007). Psychoanalysis and change: Between curiosity and faith. *International Journal of Psychoanalysis, 88,* 113–125.

Zusne, Leonard, & Jones, Warren H. (1989). *Anomalistic psychology: A study of magical thinking* (2nd ed.). Hillsdale, NJ: Erlbaum.

Zvolensky, Michael J., & Smits, Jasper A. J. (Eds.). (2008). *Anxiety in health behaviors and physical illness.* New York, NY: Springer.

Zwicker, Amy, & DeLongis, Anita. (2010). Gender, stress, and coping. In J. C. Chrisler & D. R. McCreary (Eds.), *Handbook of gender research in psychology* (pp. 495–512). New York, NY: Springer.

AAP Council on Communications Media, 219
Aarts, Henk, 135
ABC News, 552
Abdullah, Asnawi, 323
Abe, Kentaro, 289
Abela, John R. Z., 515
Abend, Rany, 607
Abi-Dargham, Anissa, 615
Abler, Birgit, 621
Aboud, Frances E., 385, 471
Abrams, Lise, 239
Abrams, Michael, 84, 125
Abramson, Lyn Y., 212
Abrevya, Jason, 457
Achermann, Peter, 147
Ackerman, Joshua M., 520
Ackerman, Phillip L., 403
Adachi, Tomonori, 157
Adair, Linda S., 390
Adams, Amanda, B–5
Adams, Marilyn J., 244
Ader, Robert, 511
Adler, Alfred, 426, 427
Adler, Nancy E., 501, 505
Adolphs, Ralph, 341
Adriaanse, Marieke A., 352
Advokat, Claire D., 167, 174, 615, 617, 619
Agarwal, Pooja K., 36
Ahima, Rexford S., 620
Aiken, Lewis R., 292
Ainslie, George, 221
Ainsworth, Mary D. Salter, 369, 370
Ainsworth, Sarah E., 489
Aitken, Nicole, 490
Ajzen, Icek, 462
Akerstedt, Torbjörn, 528
Aksglaede, Lise, 388
Alanko, Katarina, 328
Albarracín, Dolores, 492
Albert, Dustin, 391
Albright, David L., 597
Alcock, James, 113
Alexander, Charles N., 161
Alexander, G. Caleb, 617
Alford, Brad A., 603
Alladi, Suvarna, 288
Allen, Ashley Batts, 333
Allen, Daniel N., 76, 77
Allen, Jenny, 22, 218
Allen, Jon G., 255
Allen, Karen, 520
Allen, Laura B., 391
Allen, Vernon L., 473
Allik, Jüri, 438
Allison, Kevin W., 7
Allport, Gordon W., 436

Almeida, David M., 503
Altamura, A. Carlo, 624
Altemus, Margaret, 544
Altmann, Erik M., 247
Alves, Hélder, 460
Alwin, Duane F., 403
Alzheimer's Association, 263, 264, 265
Amabile, Teresa M., 308
Amada, Gerald, 626
Amarel, David, 521
Ambady, Nalini, 344, 345, 455
American Psychiatric Association, 165, 330, 540, 559, 563, 565
American Psychological Association, 34, 35, 156, 398, 482, 499, 522, 587, 613
American Psychological Association Working Group, 255
Ames, Daniel R., 455
Amin, N., 439
Amodio, David M., 470
Amstadter, Ananda B., 547
Anastasi, Anne, 292, 446, 447
Anderson, Berry S., 622, 624
Anderson, Craig A., 219, 284, 486, 488
Anderson, Karen E., 549
Anderson, Michael C., 247
Anderson, Norman B., 6
Anderson-Fye, Eileen, 561
Anderssen, Norman, 330
Andover, Margaret S., 550
Andre, Linda, 624
Andreasen, Nancy C., 572
Angell, Marcia, 538, 617
Angello, Genna, 280
Annese, Jacopo, 260, 261
Ano, Gene G., 525
Antheunis, Marjolijn L., 456
Antony, Martin M., 548
APA Help Center, 626
Arch, Joanna J., 162
Archbold, Georgina E. B., 187
Archer, John, 377, 489
Archer, Robert P., 446
Arden, John B., 610
Areàn, Patricia A., 556
Arendt, Josephine, 139
Ariizumi, Yukari, 338
Arkowitz, Hal, 592
Armitage, Peter, 443
Armstrong, Terry, B–5
Arnau, Randolph C., 446
Arnett, Jeffrey Jensen, 396, 398
Arntz, Arnoud, 565
Aronson, Elliot, 471
Aronson, Joshua, 304, 305

Arrazola, René A., 171
Arredondo, Patricia, 613
Asami, Takeshi, 576
Asch, Solomon E., 472, 473, 482
Ashcraft, Mark H., 279
Atherton, Olivia, 518
Atkinson, John, 334
Atkinson, Richard C., 228
Atlas, Lauren Y., 29
Ator, Nancy A., 35
Attanucci, Jane, 395
Attwood, Angela, 191
Au, Raymond C. P., 212
Auld, Frank, 149
Austin, James H., 161
Aveline, Mark, 612
Avins, Andrew L., 128
Ax, Robert K., 586
Azar, B., 470
Aziz-Zadeh, Lisa, 77

Baars, Barnard, 9
Bachhuber, Marcus A., 174
Bachrach, Yoram, 492
Badcock, Johanna C., 571
Bader, Alan P., 366
Baer, John, 308
Bahrami, Bahador, 89
Bailer, U. F., 560
Bailey, J. Michael, 329, 330
Bailey, Marian Breland, 214
Bailey, Robert E., 214
Baillargeon, Renée, 384, 385
Baird, Benjamin, 162
Bajwa, Ghulam-Murtaza, 575
Baker, Fiona C., 144
Bakker, Arnold B., 402
Bakoyiannis, Ioannis, 364
Balbo, Marcella, 146
Balderrama-Durbin, Christina, 608
Baldwin, David S., 618
Baldwin, Scott A., 609
Ball, J. S., 565
Ballard, Clive, 264
Balleine, Bernard W., 211
Balloun, Joe, 332
Balsam, Kimberly F., 330, 399
Balsis, Steve, 562
Bamford, Nigel S., 173
Banaji, Mahzarin R., 461, 470
Bandura, Albert, 215–216, 218, 220, 333, 351, 352, 376, 433, 434, 595
Bangerter, Adrian, 443
Banks, Caroline Giles, 560
Banks, Martin S., 366
Banks, Terry, 487

Bar, Moshe, 455
Baram, Tallie Z., 508
Baranoski, Madelon V., 537
Barch, Deanna M., 571
Barker, Anne S., 36
Barker, Jamie, 159
Barli ska, Julia, 485
Barlow, David H., 440, 542, 543, 610, 611
Barnes, Anthony, 554
Barnett, Jeffrey E., 128, 607
Barnhart, Clarence L., 196
Baron-Cohen, Simon, 299
Barone, L., 565
Barone, Silvana, 587
Barrelet, Jean-Marc, 383
Barres, Ben A., 45
Barrett, H. Clark, 371
Barrett, Lisa Feldman, 338
Barrett, Marna S., 588, 590, 610
Barsaglini, Alessio, 610, 621
Barth, Jürgen, 611
Bartlett, Donald L., 548
Bartlett, Frederic C., 248
Bartolomei, Fabrice, 246
Bartz, Jennifer, 59
Baruss, Imants, 113
Bashore, Theodore R., 339
Basil, Debra Z., 484
Baskin-Sommers, Arielle, 564
Bass, Bernard M., B–8
Bass, Ellen, 254
Basso, Olga, 77
Bassok, Miriam, 277
Bastardi, Anthony, 285
Bastiaensens, Sara, 485
Bates, Steve, B–6
Bathje, Geoff J., 535
Batson, C. Daniel, 483
Baudry, Michel, 258
Bauer, Stephanie, 607
Bauer, Susanne M., 572
Baugh, David, 22
Bauman, Christopher W., 459
Baumeister, Roy F., 17, 135, 137, 463
Baumrind, Diana, 407, 408, 476
Bayer, Christophe Pierre, 547
Bayer, Ronald, 172
Bayer, Ute C., 352
Bayley, Peter J., 262
Baylis, Gordon C., 114
Bazzini, Doris, 457
BBC News, 478
Beal, Sarah J., 557
Beale, Carole, 375
Beardsley, Eleanor, 479
Beautrais, Annette L., 620

Beauvois, Jean-Léon, 478–479
Beaver, Kevin M., 487
Beck, Aaron T., 550, 601–602, 603
Beck, Diane M., 33
Beck, Hall P., 189
Beck, Jeffrey, 397
Beck, Judith S., 609
Bedi, Gillinder, 174
Begley, Sharon, 610
Behrens, Timothy E. J., 62
Beidel, Deborah C., 541
Beins, Bernard C., 115
Bekoff, Marc, 344, 345
Belgrave, Faye Z., 7
Bell, Alan, 329
Bell, C. G., 323
Bellak, Leopold, 444
Belsky, Jay, 369, 390, 401
Bem, Daryl J., 113
Bem, Sandra L., 377
Benedetti, Fabrizio, 191
Benedikter, Roland, 4
Benet-Martínez, Verónica, 506
Ben-Hamou, Monsif, 155
Benjamin, Ludy T., 190
Benjamin, Ludy T., Jr., 479
Benjet, Corina, 202
Bennett, David A., 80
Benningfield, Margaret M., 175
Benson, Herbert, 161, 528
Bentley, Kate H., 543
Ben-Zeev, Dror, 535, 607
Berenbaum, Sheri A., 375
Berenson, Kathy R., 565
Berger, Roni, 524
Berger, William, 546
Berglund, Mats, 550
Berkman, Lisa F., 519
Berlyne, Daniel E., 316
Berman, David, 187
Bermond, Bob, 348
Berna, Chantal, 108
Bernard, Luther L., 315
Bernard, Michael E., 601
Bernstein, Daniel M., 250, 255
Bernstein, Robert, 398
Berntsen, Dorthe, 254, 393
Berrendero, Fernando, 556
Berry, John W., 505, 506
Berry, Sarah, 536
Berthoud, Hans-Rudolf, 322
Bessesen, D. H., 318
Best, Mary, 487
Bettex, Morgan, B-8
Beutler, Larry E., 612, 627
Bewernick, Bettina H., 625
Beyerstein, Barry L., 443
Beyerstein, Dale, 443
Bhanji, Nadeem H., 617
Bhatara, Vinod S., 614
Bialystok, Ellen, 288, 386
Bianchi, Renzo, 504
Bick, Johanna, 362
Bieling, Peter J., 604, 605
Bihm, Elson M., 213
Bilalić, Merim, 278
Bill & Melinda Gates Foundation, B-10

Binet, Alfred, 291
Birmingham, Wendy, 519
Biro, Dora, 216
Bischoff, Richard J., 608
Bisson, Melissa, 397
Bitterman, M. E., 185
Bizumic, Boris, 12
Bjork, Daniel W., 204
Bjork, Robert A., 28, 36, 37, 211
Bjorklund, Barbara R., 374
Bjornsson, Andri S., 611
Blackburn, Elizabeth, 509, 510
Blackwell, Terry L., 445
Blake, Robert, B-8, B-9
Blanchard, Ray, 329
Blanco, Carlos, 590
Blankstein, Kirk R., 503
Blanton, Hart, 470
Blase, Stacey, 606, 607, 609
Blass, Thomas, 474, 476, 482
Bleiberg, Kathryn L., 590
Bliss-Moreau, Eliza, 338
Block, Jack, 438, 441
Bloom, Paul, 33
Bloomfield, Tiffany C., 289
Blumenthal, Arthur L., 4, 189
Blumenthal, James A., 528
Blumenthal, Terry D., 191
Blumstein, Daniel T., 35
Bobes, Maria A., 487
Bocchiaro, Piero, 479
Boddy, Clive R., 564
Boden, Joseph M., 557
Bodenhausen, Galen V., 454, 465, 466, 469, 535
Bodenmann, Guy, 503
Boduroglu, Aysecan, 115
Boecker, Henning, 51
Boehnlein, James K., 613
Boer, Douglas P., 445
Boeree, C. George, 380
Bogaert, Anthony F., 327, 328, 329, 388
Bohart, Arthur C., 429, 432, 612
Bohlmeijer, Ernst, 405
Bohn, Annette, 393
Bohner, Gerd, 461, 469
Bohus, Martin, 566
Boison, Detlev, 577
Boistel, Renaud, 102
Boland, Julie E., 115
Bolger, Niall, 521
Bolles, Robert C., 196
Bolton, Paul, 590
Bonanno, George, 523
Bonanno, George A., 502
Bond, Charles F., 339
Bond, Michael Harris, 335, 473, 489
Bond, Rod, 460, 473
Bonnet, Michael H., 146
Bontempi, Bruno, 257
Book, Angela, 487
Booth-Kewley, Stephanie, 516
Bootzin, Richard R., 144, 153
Borbély, Alexander A., 147
Borden, William, 588

Bornstein, Marc H., 370
Boron, Julie B., 403
Borovoy, Amy, 561
Borst, Jelmer P., 137
Bosch, Jos A., 108
Boselie, Jantine, 516
Bosinski, Hartmut A.G., 379
Boss, Pauline, 606
Bostwick, J. Michael, 174
Bouchard, Geneviève, 402, 440, 441
Bouchard, Stéphane, 596
Bouchard, Thomas, 302, 487
Bouton, Mark E., 211
Bowen, Natasha K., 305
Bowers, Kenneth S., 279
Bowie, Christopher R., 604
Bowker, Anne, 22
Bowlby, John, 369
Boyke, Janina, 63
Boyle, Gregory J., 441
Boysen, Guy A., 568
Bozarth, Jerold D., 429, 431, 591
Bracha, H. Stefan, 571
Bradbard, Marilyn R., 377
Bradshaw, Carolyn, 397
Bradshaw, G. A., 345
Brådvik, Louise, 550
Braffman, Wayne, 159
Brainard, David H., 98
Branch, Rhena, 601
Brandon, Susan E., 443
Brandstätter, Veronika, 353
Branscomben, Nyla R., 456
Bransford, John D., 238, 277
Braskie, Meredith N., 62
Braun, Allen R., 148
Braun, Stephen, 174
Braun-Courville, Debra K., 218
Braunstein, Myron L., 124
Braveman, Paula A., 505
Bray, Emily E., 289
Bray, Signe, 458
Brázdil, Milan, 246
Bregman, Elsie, 195
Breinbauer, Hayo A., 101
Breland, Keller, 213–214
Breland, Marian, 213–214
Brennen, Tim, 239
Bresee, Catherine, 620
Bretherton, Inge, 370
Brewer, Marilyn B., 469
Brewer, Marilynn B., 613
Brewer, Neil, 249
Brewer, William F., 251
Bridgeman, Diane, 471
Bridwell, Lawrence G., 332
Britz, Juliane, 10
Brizendine, Louann, 72
Brock, Timothy C., 483
Brody, Arthur L., 621
Brody, Howard, 623
Brondolo, Elizabeth, 505
Bronson, Po, 372
Bronstein, Phyllis, 376
Brooks-Gunn, Jeanne, 387, 388, 390
Brosch, Tobias, 71, 341
Brown, Alan S., 246, 576
Brown, Angela M., 287

Brown, Bernard, 301
Brown, Gary E., 212
Brown, Geoffrey L., 370
Brown, Jennifer, 379
Brown, Kirk Warren, 163
Brown, Lisa M., 580
Brown, Roger, 241
Brown, Ronald T., 298
Brown, Ryan A., 368
Bru, Edvin, 524
Bruchey, Aleksandra K., 195
Brummert Lennings, Heidi I., 488
Brummett, Beverly H., 515, 517
Brunoni, Andre R., 624
Bryant, Gregory A., 371
Bryck, Richard L., 63
Bubenzer, Donald L., 426, 427
Buccelletti, Francesco, 542
Bucci, Sandra, 537
Buchanan, Anne V., 361
Buckley, Kerry W., 190
Bucur, Barbara, 403
Budd, Rick, 610
Budney, Alan J., 174
Bulls, Hailey, 516
Bunde, James, 517, 518
Burenhult, Niclas, 102
Burger, Jerry M., 476, 478, 482, 491
Buri, John R., 407
Burlingame, Gary M., 605, 609
Burlingame-Lee, Laura, 6
Burn, Shawn Meghan, 484
Burton, Charles, 523
Bushman, Brad J., 219, 486, 488
Bushnell, I. W. R., 366
Bushnell, M. Catherine, 108
Buss, Arnold H., 439
Buss, David M., 13, 326, 378, 438, 454, 487, 489
Bussey, Kay, 376
Butcher, James N., 444, 445
Butler, Adam B., 504
Butler, Andrew C., 26, 36, 603
Butler, Robert A., 317
Button, Katherine S., 33
Bystron, Irina, 365

Cabeza, Roberto, 403
Cacioppo, John, 33, 519, 520
Cacioppo, John T., 336
Cafri, Guy, 561
Cahill, Larry, 252
Cain, Christopher K., 597
Cain, David J., 429, 432, 591, 592
Calanchini, Jimmy, 470
Calero-Garcia, M. D., 405
Cameron, Judy, 308
Camp, Mary E., 536
Campbell, Jennifer D., 473
Campbell, John, 437
Campbell, MacGregor, 204
Campbell, Matthew. W., 141
Campbell, Scott S., 138
Campos, Belinda, 525
Canadian Psychological Association, 607
Canli, Turham, 439, 440
Cannon, Brooke J., 573

Cannon, Walter B., 348, 507, 525
Cano, Annmarie, 108
Cano-Colino, Maria, 549
Cant, Jonathan S., 274
Cantalupo, Claudio, 74
Canter, Peter H., 29
Caramazza, Alfonso, 94
Cardena, Etzel, 568
Carey, Benedict, 289, 534
Carey, Gregory, 487
Carey, Michael P., 397
Carhart-Harris, R., 173
Carlo, Gustavo, 438
Carlsmith, J. Merrill, 464
Carlson, G. A., 553
Carlson, Jon, 427
Carlson, Linda E., 161, 528–529
Carmody, James, 160
Carnahan, Thomas, 481
Carpenter, Shana K., 28, 37
Carpintero, Helio, 190
Carr, Katelyn A., 322
Carretti, Barbara, 266
Carroll, Joseph, 96–97
Carskadon, Mary A., 140, 142
Carstensen, Laura L., 402
Carter, C. Sue, 59
Carter, Christopher J., 575
Cartwright, Rosalind D., 141, 154, 155, 171
Carvalho, Gil B., 336
Carver, Charles S., 526
Casey, B. J., 388, 389
Caspi, Avshalom, 439, 537
Caton, Hiram, 5
Cattaneo, Luigi, 217
Cattaneo, Zaira, 273, 275
Cattell, Heather E. P., 445
Cattell, James McKeen, B–3
Cattell, Karen S., 445
Cattell, Raymond, 436, 445
Caudle, Kristina, 389
Ceci, Stephen J., 303, 307
Celesia, Gastone G., 94
Centers for Disease Control, 152, 579
Centers for Disease Control and Prevention, 167, 170
Cervone, Daniel, 433
Chabris, Christopher F., 31, 137
Chalik, Lisa, 467
Chamberlain, Samuel R., 549
Chamberlin, Jamie, 536
Champagne, Frances A., 362, 363
Chance, Paul, 197
Chandola, Tarani, 505
Chandrashekar, Jayaram, 106
Chang, Anne-Marie, 138, 176
Chapman, Benjamin, 446
Chaput, Jeanne-Paul, 318
Charles, Susan, 503
Charles, Susan T., 402
Charlton, Benjamin D., 35
Chartrand, Tanya, 349
Chatterjee, Anjan, 456, 458, 463
Chatterjee, Arijit, B–10
Chaudhari, Nirupa, 106
Chavez, Pollyanna R., 167

Chen, Fang Fang, 460
Chen, Joyce, 241, 593
Chen, Ya-Ru, 613
Cheng, C., 526
Cheng, Guo, 388
Chentsova-Dutton, Yulia E., 541, 543
Chermack, Stephen T., 487
Chess, Stella, 368–369
Chi, Kelly Rae, 62
Chida, Yoichi, 517, 518
Chiesa, Alberto, 162, 528, 604
Chiew, Vincent, 277
Childress, John R., B–10
Choi, Kyeong-Sook, 574
Chomsky, Noam, 371
Chrysikou, Evangelia G., 277
Chua, Hannah Faye, 115
Chun, Chi-Ah, 526
Chun, Marvin M., 35, 135
Chung-Do, Jane J., 606
Chung-Yan, Greg A., 504
Cialdini, Robert B., 491, 492
Ciarrochi, Joseph, 407
Cicciola, Elisabetta, 291
Cicero, Theodore J., 170
Cihangir, Sezgin, 489
Cikara, Mina, 469
Cinamon, Rachel Gali, 402
Cisler, Josh M., 545
Claire, Theresa, 305
Clark, Damon A., 67
Clark, David M., 610
Clark, Graeme M., 100
Clark, M. H., 305
Clark, Wendy L., 445
Clarke, Diana E., 537
Clarke, Laura E., 45
Clarke-Stewart, K. Alison, 401
Clarkin, John F., 612
Clay, Rebecca, 399
Clayton, Nicola S., 289
Cleary, Anne M., 246
Clifasefi, Seema L., 255
Clotier, Jasmin, 458
CNN, 596
Cobos, Pilar, 348
Coelho, Carlos M., 195
Coelho, Helen F., 604
Cogan, Rosemary, 428
Cohen, Adam B., 12
Cohen, Asher, 116
Cohen, Dov, 420, 489
Cohen, Estee, 546
Cohen, Geoffrey L., 304, 305
Cohen, Hal, 79
Cohen, Jeremy, 537
Cohen, Sheldon, 484, 505, 513, 516, 519, 520, 528
Cohen-Kettenis, Peggy T., 330, 379
Colangelo, James J., 255
Colby, Anne, 393, 394
Colcombe, Stanley, 403, 404
Cole, Geoff G., 545
Cole, Jon, 158
Cole, Michael, 385
Colledge, Essi, 440
Collerton, Joanna, 402
Collins, Allan M., 237

Collins, Elizabeth C., 455, 456
Collins, Nancy, 520
Collins, Rebecca L., 218
Collins, W. Andrew, 391
Colrain, Ian M., 144
Coltheart, Max, 31, 33
Colwell, Christopher S., 140, 154
Comaty, Joseph E., 167, 174, 615, 617, 619
Combs, Dennis R., 573, 577, 597
Comer, Jonathan S., 617
Confer, Jaime C., 14, 378
Conger, Rand D., 407
Conley, Colleen S., 389
Connell, Arin M., 608
Connelly, Brian S., 447
Connolly, J. A., 391
Conway, Martin A., 353
Cook, Emily J., 391
Cook, Richard, 43
Cook, Thomas D., 391
Cook, Travis A. R., 165
Cooke, Richard, 167
Cooper, Cary L., 501
Cooper, Mick, 464, 592, 609, 611, 612
Corballis, Michael C., 76
Corcoran, Olivia, 171
Cordaro, Daniel, 337
Corfas, Gabriel, 45
Corkin, Suzanne, 260, 261
Correia, Isabel, 460
Corrigan, Patrick W., 535
Corsini, Raymond J., B–5
Cosgrove, Lisa, 537
Cosmides, Leda, 14, 315, 336, 337
Cossins, Daniel, 72
Costa, Albert, 288
Costa, Paul, Jr., 438
Costarelli, Sandro, 461
Côté, Sophie, 596
Cotton, Ronald, 249
Courage, Mary L., 386
Courtois, Christine A., 567
Cousineau, Tara McKee, 447
Coventry, Will L., 520
Covino, Nicholas A., 160
Cowan, Nelson, 232, 233
Cowan, Ronald L., 175
Coyle, Emily F., 398
Coyne, Sarah M., 489
Craighead, W. Edward, 610
Craik, Fergus I. M., 235, 245, 288, 386
Crano, William D., 492
Craske, Michelle G., 542, 543, 545, 610
Crawford, Jarret T., 466
Creswell, Cathy, 542
Creswell, J. David, 528
Crews, Frederick, 427, 428
Crisafulli, C., 620
Critcher, Clayton R., 456
Critchley, Hugo D., 349
Crites, John O., 445
Croft, Rodney J., 175
Croizet, Jean-Claude, 305
Cross, Susan, 447

Crossley, Helen M., 343
Crossley, Nicolas A., 617
Crowell, Sheila E., 565, 566
Csikszentmihalyi, Mihaly, 11
CTV News, 609
Cuijpers, Pim, 586, 609, 623
Cullen, Margaret, 604
Culpin, Iryana, 389
Cummings, David E., 319
Cummings, Jeremy, 526
Cunningham, Jacqueline L., 291
Cunningham, William A., 71, 341
Cushing, Christopher C., 592
Custers, Eugene J. F. M., 247
Czeisler, Charles A., 138, 139

Dabbs, James M., 487
Daffner, Kirk R., 29
Dagnall, Neil, 112
Dalenberg, Constance J., 566
Dalgard, Odd Steffen, 522
Dalgleish, Tim, 342, 347, 349
Dalla Volta, Riccardo, 372
Daly, Michael, 516
Damasio, Antonio R., 336, 342, 348
Damasio, H., 68
Damisch, Lysann, 207
D'Angelo, Maria, 239
Daniels, Bradley J., 536
Dannon, Pinhas N., 624
Darley, John, 477, 483, 484
Dar-Nimrod, Ilan, 362
Darwin, Charles, 13, 336, 337, 343, 344
Datta, Sublimal, 145
D'Auria, Stephanie, 580
Dautovich, Natalie D., 604
Davey, Graham C. L., 548
David, Daniel, 601, 611
Davidson, Jonathan R. T., 618, 620
Davidson, Karina, 516
Davidson, Paul R., 597
Davidson, Richard J., 75, 162, 349, 486, 487
Davidson, Richard R., 162, 163
Davidson, Terry L., 319
Davis, Catherine M., 194
Davis, Deborah, 249, 254, 255
Davis, Daphne M., 163
Davis, Jake H., 160, 161
Davis, Joshua I., 349
Davis, Linda, 254
Davis, Lori L., 619
Davis, Susan R., 327
Dawkins, Lynne, 171
Dawson, Deborah A., 400
Dawson, Jennifer A., 547
Dawson, Michelle, 298, 299
Day, David V., B–9
Dazzi, Carla, 443
D'Cruz, O'Neill F., 140
De Brito, Stéphane A., 564
de Dreu, Carsten K. W., 59
de Gelder, Beatrice, 89
de Groot, Jasper H. B., 103
de Groot, Judith, 484
de Hooge, Ilona E., 484
de Kirby, Kenton, 385

de la Fuente-Fernández, Raúll, 512
de Montigny-Malenfant, Béatrice, 565
de Moor, Marleen H., 439
de Waal, Frans B. M., 22, 141, 290, 326, 345
Deady, D. K., 348
Deal, David, 349
Dean, Kristy K., 460
DeAngelis, Tori, 171, 601
Deary, Ian J., 303
Decety, Jean, 33, 217
deCharms, R. Christopher, 128
Deci, Edward L., 333–334
DeGeneres, Ellen, 327
Deigh, John, 348
Delgado, Ana R., 287
DeLisi, Richard, 385
Dell, Paul F., 566
Della Sala, Sergio, 243
Dell'Osso, Bernardo, 624
Delman, Howard M., 445
Delmas, P., 106
DeLoache, Judy S., 195, 372, 373, 374
DeLongis, Anita, 503, 520, 525
Delunas, Linda, 501
Delzenne, Nathalie M., 319
Demb, Jonathan B., 98
Dement, William C., 140, 142
Demerouti, Evangelia, 504
den Oudsten, Brenda L., 336
Deneris, Evan S., 51
Denk, Franziska, 108, 109
Denko, Timothey, 619
Dennis, J. Michael, 24
Dennis, Nancy A., 403
Dennis, Tracy A., 607
Denny, Dallas, 374
Denton, Kathy, 394
Derksen, Jan J., 487
Derluyn, Ilse, 547
Derry, Heather, 505
DeRubeis, Robert J., 621
Desai, Abhilash K., 519
Desjardins, Renee, 371
D'Esposito, Mark, 262
Dess, Nancy K., 35
Deutsch, Georg, 76
Deutsch, Linda, 457
Deutsch, Morton, 473
Deutscher, Guy, 287
DeValois, Karen K., 98
DeValois, Russell L., 98
Devane, William A., 174
Devine, Patricia G., 469, 470
Devine, Susan E., 254
DeVos, George Alphonse, 306
DeVos, Julie, 384, 385
DeWall, Nathan C., 488
Dewe, Philip, 501
Dewsbury, Donald A., 197
Dexter-Mazza, Elizabeth T., 565
DeYoung, Colin G., 440
Dhabhar, Firdaus S., 513
Diamantopoulou, Solomon, 564
Diamond, Adele, 360, 362
Diamond, Solomon, 4
DiazGranados, Nancy, 620

Dick, Danielle M., 3
Dickel, Nina, 461, 469
Dickins, Thomas E., 5
Dickinson, Anthony, 211
Dickinson, Josephine A., 614
Dictionary of Occupational Titles, B–4
Didonna, Fabrizio, 163, 528
Didziulis, Vytenis, 567
Diefenbach, Donald L., 537
Dijk, Derk-Jan, 138
Dijksterhuis, Ap, 89, 135
Dimberg, Ulf, 338
Dimidjian, Sona, 611
Dinsmoor, James A., 202
Disanto, Giulio, 576
Dishion, Thomas J., 391, 564
Dittman, Melissa, 548
Dixon, John F., 555
Dobson, Deborah, 603
Dobson, Keith, 603
Dodd, Seetal, 557
Dohrenwend, Bruce P., 501, 502, 505, 547
Domhoff, G. William, 147, 148, 151
Doolin, Erin M., 431
Dorahy, Martin Justiin, 567
Dornbusch, Sanford M., 460
Doss, Brian D., 400
Dougherty, Darin D., 624
Douglas, Kevin S., 537
Dovidio, John F., 467, 468, 484
Dozois, David J. A., 603
Drabick, Deborah A., 22
Draganski, Bogdan, 63, 163
Drea, Christine M., 103
Drescher, Jack, 330
Drews, Frank A., 137
Driemeyer, Joenna, 63
Driver, Jon, 114
Dronsfield, Alan T., 597
Dror, Otniel E., 348
Drouyer, Elise, 138
Drum, David J., 581
Drummond, Kelley D., 330
Drury, Scott, 481
Dryden, Windy, 601
DSM-5, 535, 542, 544, 546, 547, 551, 552, 553, 558, 559, 561, 563, 567, 570
DuBreuil, Susan C., 160
Duckworth, Angela L., 293
Dudai, Yadin, 260
Dukart, Juergen, 624
Duke, Aaron A., 487
Dulin, Patrick, 514
Dumith, Samuel C., 322
Duncker, Karl, 120, 280
Dunham, Yarrow, 467
Dunkel Schetter, Christine, 364
Dunlap, Glen, 209
Dunlosky, John, 24, 25, 36, 37
Dunning, David, 456
Duntley, Joshua D., 487, 489

Eagly, Alice H., 305, 374, 376, 378–379, 457, 467
Eastman, Charmane I., 139

Easton, Caroline J., 167
Eatock, Ruth Anne, 109
Ebbinghaus, Hermann, 243, 244
Eberhardt, Jennifer L., 469
Eckholm, E., 330
Edelson, Meredyth Goldberg, 298
Edenfield, Teresa M., 528
Edlund, Mark J., 552
Edmonds, Grant W., 438
Edwards, Anthony G. P., 443
Edwards, Robert R., 108, 128
Egan, Louisa C., 464
Egan, Susan K., 375
Eichenbaum, Howard, 237
Eichstaedt, Johannes, 516
Einstein, Danielle, 548
Eisen, Jane L., 548, 549
Eisenberg, Nancy, 394
Eisenberger, Robert, 308
Eisenstein, Michael, 106
Ekman, Paul, 162, 337, 339, 343, 344, 345, 346, 349
Ekwall, Anna Kristensson, 521
Eldar, Sharon, 607
Elfenbein, Hillary Anger, 344
Elgar, Frank J., 490
Eliot, Lise, 72
Elkins, Gary, 159
Ellin, Abby, 443
Elliot, J. Andrew, 96
Elliott, Robert, 9, 592
Ellis, Albert, 599–600, 601
Ellis, Bruce J., 387, 389
Ellis, Pete M., 597
Ellwardt, Lea, 519
El-Mallakh, Rif S., 557
Elson, Malte, 219
Emery, Nathan J., 289
Emmelkamp, Paul M. G., 596, 597
Emmons, Robert A., 500
Empson, Jacob, 141, 152
Engelhardt, Christopher R., 219
England, Lynndie, 480, 481
Engle, R. Adam, 161
English, Horace B., 195
Enns, James T., 135
Enriori, Pablo J., 323
Epel, Elissa S., 509, 510, 511
Epstein, D. R., 144, 153
Epstein, Leonard H., 322
Epstein, Russell, 274
Epstein, Seymour, 441
Equal Employment Opportunity Commission, B–3
Erdberg, Philip, 442
Erdelyi, Matthew Hugh, 243, 244, 248
Erickson, Kirk I., 80, 404
Erikson, Erik H., 391, 392–393, 396, 405
Eriksson, Cynthia B., 546
Eriksson, Oskar, 473
Eriksson, Peter S., 64
Ernst, Edzard, 29
Ersoy, Betul, 387
Eschweiler, Gerhard W., 624
Espay, Alberto J., 622
Esses, Victoria M., 469

Essex, Marilyn J., 389
Estes, William K., 202
Evans, Rand B., 4, 188
Everett, Daniel L., 287
Exner, John E., Jr., 442
Exum, M. Lyn, 487
Eysenck, Hans J., 437
Eysenck, Sybil B. G., 437

Fabrigar, Leandre R., 462
Fagiolini, Andrea, 554
Fagundes, Christopher, 507
Fahs, Breanne, 398
Fairchild, Amy L., 171, 172
Fairchild, Kimberly, 467
Fairey, Patricia J., 473
Fan, Yang, 79
Fan, Yang-Teng, 217
Fancher, Raymond E., 83, 243, 292, 416
Fanous, Ayman H., 574
Fantz, Robert L., 366
Farb, Norman A. S., 162
Farber, Barry A., 9, 431, 432
Farfel, Mark, 547
Farmer, Caroline, 552
Farrell, Meagan T., 239
Farris-Trimble, Ashley, 100
Fasfous, Ahmed F., 546
Fast, Lisa A., 435
Fausey, Caitlin M., 287
Faust, David, 610
Fazel, Seena, 537
Feeney, Brooke, 520
Feeney, Miranda C., 289
Fehr, Ernst, 505
Feinstein, Anthony, 547
Feldman Barrett, Lisa, 337, 338
Feldt, Ronald C., 501
Feliciano, Leilani, 556
Felmlee, Diane, 463
Felsberg, Eric J., B–4
Ferguson, Christopher J., 219, 487, 488
Fernald, Anne, 371
Fernandez-Juricic, Esteban, 35
Ferrari, Alize J., 552
Ferrari, Pier Francesco, 290
Ferrero, Joseph, 390
Feshbach, Seymour, 219
Feske, Ulrike, 597
Festinger, Leon, 464
Fiedler, Klaus, 113
Field, Clinton E., 598
Field, Tiffany, 128
Fielder, Robyn L., 397
Fieldhouse, Paul, 318
Fields, R. Douglas, 44, 45
Filevich, Elisa, 152
Fincham, Frank, 397
Fincham, Frank D., 11
Fine, Cordelia, 72
Fine, Ione, 86, 95, 125
Fineberg, Naomi A., 549
Fink, Bernhard, 463
Fink, Max, 623, 624
Finkel, Eli J., 463
Finley, Jason R., 137

Finn, Bridgid, 36
Finn, Christopher T., 554
Fischer, Peter, 484, 485, 486
Fischer, Ronald, 473
Fishbach, Ayelet, 221, 222
Fisher, Anne, B–12
Fisher, Celia B., 34, 597
Fisher, Jane E., 601
Fisher, Luchina, 542
Fisher, Philip A., 63
Fisher, Terri D., 580
Fishman, Joshua A., 286
Fiske, Susan T., 315, 466, 468, 471, 480, 481
Fitzpatrick, Maureen J., 377
Fivush, Robyn, 236, 237
Flaherty, Colleen, 535
Flaten, Magne Arve, 191
Flaum, M., 572
Flegal, Katherine M., 321, 323
Flett, Gordon L., 503
Flor, Herta, 127, 128
Flynn, Eemma, 215
Flynn, James R., 305
Foa, Edna B., 611
Focus on Family Support, 573
Foer, Joshua, 266, 267
Foland-Ross, Lara C., 555
Folkman, Susan, 499, 501, 522, 523
Fond, Guillaume, 175
Fontana, Alan, 546
Foote, Brad, 568
Forbes, B–13
Forbes, Chad E., 467
Forbes, David L., 315
Ford, Julian D., 567
Forgas, Joseph P., 484
Fortune, B–11
Foschi, Renato, 291
Fosco, Gregory M., 390
Fosnaugh, Jessica, 515
Fotuhi, Omid, 465
Fouad, Nadya A., 613
Foulkes, David, 147, 151
Fournier, Jay C., 622
Fowler, Robert L., 36
Fox, Margalit, 287
Fox, Nathan A., 393
Fox, William M., 332
Fraga, Mario F., 362
Fram, Alan, 112
Frances, Allen, 536, 537, 538
Francis, Ronald D., 597
Frank, Mark G., 344
Frank, Michael C., 287
Frankenburg, Frances R., 615
Frankland, Paul W., 257
Franklin, Sean, 383
Frazier, Patricia, 502
Free, Michael L., 605
Freedman, Sara A., 596
Freeman, Chris, 609
Freeman, Ellen W., 398
Freeman, Kevin B., 194
Freeman, Lucy, 428
Freeman, Nancy K., 375
Freidel, Paul, 102

Freire, Elizabeth S., 591
French, Christopher C., 113
Frenda, Steven J., 249, 252, 254
Freud, Anna, 420
Freud, Sigmund, 8, 149, 248, 416, 417, 418, 419, 420, 421, 422, 423, 427, 428, 430, 588
Fridell, Mats, 564
Fridell, Sari R., 375
Friedman, Carly Kay, 376
Friedman, Howard S., 516
Friedman, Jeffrey M., 319, 323
Friedman, Meyer, 517
Friend, Ronald, 472
Friesen, Wallace V., 343, 346
Friston, Karl, 62
Frith, Chris D., 454
Frith, Uta, 454
Froemke, Susan, 166
Fruth, Barbara, 326
Fuller, Patrick M., 148
Fullerton, Ronald A., 89
Funder, David C., 435, 438
Funkhouser, Arthur, 246
Furman, Wyndol, 370
Furnham, Adam, 293

Gabrieli, John D. E., 115
Gaertner, Samuel L., 467, 468
Gage, Fred H., 64
Gagne, Jeffrey R., 369
Gaissmaier, Wolfgang, 278
Gajendran, Raji V., B–12
Galambos, Nancy L., 396
Galanter, Eugene, 88
Galati, Dario, 344
Galdikas, Birute M. F., 216
Galak, Jeff, 113
Gallese, Vittori, 217
Gallistel, C. R., 287
Gallo, David A., 235
Gallo, Linda C., 505
Gambacorta, David, 485
Gangestad, Steven W., 326
Gangl, Markus, 400
Ganis, Giorgio, 274
Garcia, Eugene E., 288
Garcia, Enrique, 408
Garcia, Fernando, 408
Garcia, John, 194, 597
Garcia, José F., 407, 408
Garcia, Justin R., 397
Garcia-Palacios, Azucena, 596
Gardner, Howard, 296
Gardner, Michael K., 295
Gardner, Wendi L., 336
Gardony, Aaron L., 275
Garfin, Dana R., 546
Garrett, Brandon L., 249
Garrett, Michael T., 613
Garry, Maryanne, 253
Garvin, Charles, 605
Garza, Yvonne, 613
Gatchel, Robert J., 106, 108
Gaudiano, Brandon A., 603
Gavett, Brandon E., 54
Gavey, Nicola, 537
Gaw, Albert C., 560

Gawronski, Bertram, 113, 456, 464, 469
Gay, Peter, 416, 417, 427, 428
Gazzaniga, Michael S., 75, 76, 77
Ge, Xiaojia, 389–390
Gee, Travis, 568
Geldard, Frank A., 107
Gelman, Rochel, 287
Gendolla, Guido H. E., 336
Gentile, Barbara F., 4
Gentilucci, Maurizio, 372
Gentner, Dedre, 275
George, Bill, B–10
George, Charles F. P., 153
Georgopoulos, Neoklis A., 388
Geraci, Lisa, 241
Geraerts, Elke, 254, 255
Gerard, Harold B., 473
Gerbner, George, 536
Germine, Laura T., 403
Gernsbacher, Morton Ann, 299
Gerrans, Philip, 246
Gerrie, Matthew P., 255
Gershoff, Elizabeth T., 202, 407
Gerstner, Charlotte R., B–9
Gesser-Edelsburg, Anat, 220
Geyer, Anne L., 472
Gibbs, John C., 394
Gibson, Bryan, 470, 488
Giedd, Jay N., 388, 389
Gieser, Marlon T., 594
Gigerenzer, Gerd, 278
Gillham, Jane E., 212
Gilligan, Carol A., 395
Gilman, Sander L., 426
Gilman, Sarah R., 574
Gilovich, Thomas, 284, 285, 460
Gilson, Lucy L., 308
Ginandes, Carol, 160
Girard, Simon L., 574
Gire, James T., 406
Gladwell, Malcolm, 446
Glaser, Ronald, 509, 512
Glasford, Dennis E., 469
Glasper, Erica R., 64
Glass, Richard M., 624
Glass, Thomas, 519
Gleaves, David H., 248, 254, 568
Gleitman, Henry, 210, 211
Glenberg, Arthur M., 217
Glicksohn, Arit, 116
Glucksberg, Sam, 288
Glucksman, Myron L., 590
Glynn, Shawn M., 212, 611
Goddard, Andrew W., 51
Goddard, Murray J., 204
Godleski, Stephanie A., 489
Goffin, Richard D., 443
Gogtay, Nitin, 388, 389, 573
Goh, Joshua O., 115
Gold, Ian, 573
Gold, Jerold, 612
Gold, Joel, 573
Goldberg, Abbie E., 399
Goldberg, S R., 556
Goldsmith, D. J., 521
Goldstein, Alan J., 597
Goldstein, Daniel G., 278

Gollwitzer, Peter M., 352, 353
Gomez, C., B–9
Gonzaga, Gian C., 525
Gonzales, Patricia M., 305
Good, Byron J., 541, 543
Good, Catherine, 304, 305
Goodale, Melvyn A., 274
Goodenough, Florence, 344
Goodin, Burel, 516
Goodman, Gail S., 569
Goodwin, Frederick, 554
Goodwin, Stephanie A., 455
Gooley, Joshua J., 139
Goossens, Luc, 519
Gorchoff, Sara M., 402
Gordon, Albert H., 338
Gordon, Barry, 61
Gordon, Peter, 287
Gordon-Larsen, Penny, 390
Gorman, Jack M., 609
Goswami, Usha, 77
Gotlib, Ian H., 555
Gottesman, Irving I., 574
Gottfredson, Linda S., 295
Gottfried, Jay, 104
Gouin, Jean-Philippe, 512
Goulart, Vinicius D., 35
Gould, Elizabeth, 63, 64, 70, 79
Gould, Madelyn S., 580
Gould, Stephen Jay, 291, 292
Grabe, Shelly, 321
Grace, Michael S., 90
Gracia, Enrique, 486
Graham, Jesse, 395
Graham, John R., 445
Graham, Kathryn D., 487, 489
Graham, William K., 332
Granholm, Eric, 607
Grant, Bob, 74
Grant, Bridget F., 564, 565
Grant, Joshua A., 128
Grant, Paul M., 603
Grant, Sharon, 444
Gray, Jeremy R., 440
Gray, Rob, 120
Greasley, Peter, 443
Green, Donald P., 470
Green, Joseph P., 158, 159
Green, Richard, 329–330
Greenberg, Daniel L., 257, 262
Greene, Roberta R., 592
Greenfield, Patricia, 307
Greenwald, Anthony G., 469, 470
Greenwood, Patricia M., 80
Greer, Stephanie M., 147, 323
Greitemeyer, Tobias, 219, 488
Griffiths, Kathleen M., 607
Griffiths, Roland R., 170
Grigg-Damberger, Madeleine, 144
Griggs, Richard A., 472, 481
Groer, Maureen, 513
Gross, Charles G., 79
Gross, Garrett G., 259
Gross, James J., 526
Grossman, Sheila, 405
Grow, Kerry, 609
Grubin, Don, 339

Grünbaum, Adolf, 427
Grunstein, Ronald, 153
Grusec, Joan E., 407
Grussu, Pietro, 400
Grzywacz, Joseph G., 503
Guéguen, Nicolas, 492
Guehl, Dominique, 549
Guimond, Serge, 469
Guindon, José, 107, 108
Gujar, Ninad, 146
Gum, Amber M., 604
Gunlicks-Stoessel, Meredith, 590
Güntürkün, Onur, 71, 74, 77
Gureje, Oye, 538
Gurven, Michael, 438
Guthrie, Robert V., 7
Gutman, David A., 551, 556
Gyatso, Tenzim, 162

Habhab, Summar, 507
Hackett, Troy A., 101
Hackman, Daniel A., 505
Hagar, Sheila, 587
Haidt, Jonathan, 394–395
Halaas, Jeffrey L., 319
Hald, Gert M., 488
Halim, May L., 375
Hall, Geoffrey, 188
Hallberg, Ingalill R., 521
Halligan, Peter W., 156, 158, 159
Halmi, Katherine A., 561
Halpern, John H., 173
Halverson, Charles F., Jr., 377
Hamann, Stephan, 262, 337, 342
Hambrick, Donald C., B–10
Hamer, Marc, 518, 528
Hamermesh, Daniel S., 457
Hamilton, M. A., 398
Hamilton, S., 398
Hamlin, J. Kiley, 468
Hammen, Constance, 509, 552
Hammond, Geoffrey C., 607
Haney, Craig, 480, 482
Hänggi, J rgen, 72
Hannan, Anthony J., 79
Hanna-Pladdy, Brenda, 80
Hardt, Oliver, 244
Hardy, Sam A., 408
Hargreaves, David, 128
Hargrove, Marian F., 487
Harlow, Harry F., 317, 369
Harlow, John M., 68
Harman, S. Mitchell, 399
Harnett, Paul, 627
Haro, Josep M., 573
Harper, Robert A., 601
Harper, Sarah, 402
Harris, Ben, 189
Harris, Julie Aitken, 440
Harris, Julie M., 120
Harris, Lasana T., 468
Harrison, David A., B–12
Harrison, Robert V., 101
Hart, Dan, 393
Harter, Susan, 383
Hartshorne, Joshua K., 403
Hartwig, Marissa K., 24, 25
Harvey, Allison G., 146

Harvey, Megan A., 174
Harvey, Nigel, 283
Harvey, O. J., 470
Harwood, T. M., 607
Hasin, Deborah, 564
Haslam, Alexander, 481
Hatch, Stephani L., 502, 505
Hatton, Holly, 400
Haun, Daniel B. M., 473
Hauser, Marc D., 345
Haushofer, Johannes, 505
Havas, David A., 349
Havermans, Remco C., 319
Hawkey, Chris, 167
Hawkins, Nicole, 559
Hawley, Charles, 437
Hawton, Keith, 580
Hayatbakhsh, Mohammad R., 390
Hayes, Emily, 620
Hayes, Jeffrey A., 163
Hayes, Steven C., 592, 604, 605
Hayes-Skelton, Sarah A., 162
Hayne, Harlene, 248
Healy, Alice, 244–245
Heaps, Christopher M., 252
Hearst, Eliot, 197
Heaven, Patrick, 407
Hebb, Donald O., 316
Hedden, Trey, 115
Hedegaard, Holly, 170
Heerey, Erin A., 343
Heiby, Elaine M., 587
Heider, Eleanor R., 286
Heine, Steven J., 12, 13, 362, 463
Heinrichs, R. Walter, 571
Heiphetz, Larisa, 461, 470
Helenius, Dorte, 574
Henderson, Valerie L., 593
Henkel, Linda A., 250
Hennessey, Beth A., 308
Hennessey, Dwight A., 459
Henrich, Joseph, 12, 13
Heppner, Puncky Paul, 526
Herbert, James D., 597, 611
Herek, Gregory M., 466
Herman, Louis M., 289
Hermans, Hubert J. M., 447
Herndon, Philip, 255
Hersh, Seymour, 480, 481
Hertz, Marguerite R., 442
Hertzog, Christopher, 80, 404, 405
Heth, Josephine Todrank, 514
Hettema, Jennifer, 592, 626
Hewstone, Miles, 469
Heyes, Cecilia, 215
Heyman, Karen, 79
Heyman, Richard E., 488
Heymann, Jody, B–13
Hiatt, Kristina D., 564
Hicken, Margaret, 505
Hickok, Gregory, 285
Higgins, E. Tory, 19
Higgins, Stephen T., 599
Hilgard, Ernest R., 156, 157–158, 159, 183
Hill, Kevin T., 135
Hill, Matthew N., 555
Hillberg, Tanja, 255

Hillman, Charles H., 79, 80, 404
Hilt, Lori M., 552
Hilton, James L., 455
Hines, Melissa, 328
Hines, Terence M., 285
Hinshaw, Stephen, 536, 537
Hinton, Devon E., 541, 543
Hinton, Susan D., 543
Hirsh, Jacob B., 492
Hirst, William, 242
Hitsch, Günter, 463
Hobfoll, Stevan E., 521
Hobson, Charles J., 501
Hobson, J. Allan, 143, 150, 151, 152
Hochreiter, W. W., 399
Hodges, Bert H., 472
Hodgins, Sheilagh, 564
Hodgkinson, Gerard P., 279
Hoffman, John, 166
Hoffman, Martin L., 408
Hoffmann, Melissa L., 375
Hoffstein, Victor, 153
Hofmann, Stefan, 605
Hofmann, Wilhelm, 190
Hogan, John D., 7
Hogarth, Robin M., 279
Hogg, Michael A., 472, 525
Hohmann, Andrea, 107, 108
Hohmann, Gottfried, 326
Hokin, Lowell E., 555
Holden, Constance, 339
Holden, Ronald R., 447
Holland, Charles H., 476
Hollander, Edwin P., B–8
Hollanders, Henry, 612
Hollinger, Richard C., B–5
Hollon, Steven D., 602, 603, 611
Holm-Denoma, Jill M., 30
Holmes, Thomas H., 501
Holsboer, Florian, 619
Holt-Lunstad, Julianne, 519
Holyoak, Keith J., 298, 299
Hölzel, Britta K., 163, 604
Holzman, Lois, 385
Homer, Bruce D., 173
Hong, Ying-yi, 13
Honzik, Charles H., 210–211
Hood, William R., 470
Hope, Deborah A., 328, 399
Hopkins, William D., 74
Hopper, Lydia M., 218
Hoptman, Matthew J., 75
Horberg, E. J., 338
Horder, Jamie, 623
Horner, Robert H., 201
Horney, Karen, 425, 426, 428
Horr, Ninja, 279
Horwitz, Allan V., 536
Houts, Arthur C., 536
Howard, Kenneth I., 610
Howard, Richard, 564
Howard-Jones, Paul A., 77
Howe, Mark L., 252, 386
Howland, M., 521
Hoyle, Rick H., 448
Hsiang, Solomon M., 488
Hsu, Hui-Chin, 359, 369, 385
Hua, Cynthia, 484

Huang, Chih-mao, 115
Huang, Yi, 472
Hubel, David H., 93, 94, 96, 98
Huber, Elizabeth, 94, 95, 127
Huesmann, L. Rowell, 219
Hugdahl, Kenneth, 76
Hughes, Ian, 610
Hughes, John R., 155
Hughes, Mathew L., 305
Hulbert-Williams, L., 597
Hull, Clark L., 315
Human Genome Project, 361
Humphreys, Karin, 239
Hunsley, John, 444, 446
Hunt, Earl, 303
Hunter, Aimee M., 512
Hunter, Simone, 217
Hurovitz, Craig S., 152
Hurvich, Leo M., 97
Hussaini, Syed A., 186
Huynh, Que-Lam, 506
Hwang, Hyl Sung, 337, 344
Hyde, Janet S., 72, 397, 552
Hyde, Janet Shibley, 328, 376, 377, 395
Hyman, Ira E., Jr., 136, 252
Hyman, Ray, 112, 113
Hyman, Steven E., 49, 362, 363

Iacoboni, Marco, 217
Iacono, Diego, 263
Ikeda, Hiroshi, 306
Imberman, Arylin, 443
Imel, Zac E., 620
Inagami, Sanae, 30
Ingalhalikar, Madhura, 72
Ingersoll, K. S., 593
Ingram, Rick E., 602
Inhelder, Bärbel, 382, 383
Innocence Project, The, 249, 252
Insel, Thomas R., 537, 575
Interactive, Harris, B–7
International Shark Attack File, 282
Ionescu, Thea, 278
Irving, Julie Anne, 162
Irwin, Charles E., Jr., 388
Irwin, Michael R., 146, 520
Isabella, Russell A., 370
Iversen, Iver H., 197
Ivory, James D., 219
Iwamasa, Gayle Y., 544
Iwanaga, Makoto, 516
Izard, Carroll E., 349, 351

Jaarsma, P., 299
Jackson, John P., Jr., 7
Jackson, Joshua J., 446
Jackson, Lynne M., 468
Jacobs, Barry L., 63
Jacobs, Nele E., 516
Jacobs, Tonya L., 509, 511
Jaffee, Sara, 395, 503
Jagdeo, Amit, 609
Jakovcevski, I., 365
James, Jenée, 389
James, Larry C., 480, 481

James, Leah, 447, 448
James, William, 135, 246, 315, 317, 347, 348
James, William H., 329
Jameson, Dorothea, 97
Jamil, Hikmet, 505
Jamison, Kay Redfield, 555, 580
Janicak, Philip G., 573, 624
Janicki-Deverts, Denise, 519
Jara, Elvira, 186
Jarcho, Johanna M., 464
Jarrett, Christian, 108
Jarvis, Erich D., 67
Jason, Leonard A., 209
Javitt, Daniel, 577
Jayasinghe, Nimali, 547
Jazaieri, Hooria, 162
Jbabdi, Saad, 62
Jeckel, Christina M., 512
Jeffery, Robert W., 527
Jensen, Mark P., 108, 157
Jensen, Per, 363
Jessberger, Sebastian, 62
Jha, Amishi P., 162, 528
Jilek, Wolfgang G., 614
Jing, Yiming, 460
Joel, Daphna, 72
Joëls, Marian, 508
Joffe, Helene, 72
Johansen, Pål-Ørjan, 174, 618
Johns, Michael, 305
Johnson, Debra L., 438
Johnson, Jeffrey G., 578
Johnson, Kerri L., 346
Johnson, Marcia K., 249
Johnson, Paul M., 324
Johnson, Sheri L., 554
Johnson, Virginia E., 325
Johnson, Wendy, 301
Johnston, Laurance, 20
Johnston, Lucy, 466
Joiner, Thomas E., 580
Joly-Mascheroni, Ramiro M., 141
Jones, Christopher M., 165
Jones, Edward E., 459
Jones, Gary, 279
Jones, Mary Cover, 594
Jones, Marc V., 159
Jones, Steven H., 554
Jones, Warren H., 284
Jonides, John, 232, 245
Jonnes, Jill, 172
Joormann, Jutta, 555
Jordan-Young, Rebecca, 72
Joseph, Jay, 574
Joseph, Stephen, 432
Jourdan, April, 9, 429, 590
Juang, Linda, 126, 335
Jucaite, Aurelija, 577
Judd, Charles M., 113
Julian, James W., B–8
Juliano, Laura M., 170
Julien, Robert M., 167, 174, 615, 616, 617, 619
Jun, Z., 406
Junco, Reynol, 18, 25
Jung, Carl G., 424, 425

Kaas, Jon H., 101, 102
Kabat-Zinn, Jon, 161, 528, 604
Kagan, Jerome, 33, 359, 369, 393
Kahneman, Daniel, 282, 283
Kalat, James W., 194
Kamen, Dean, 309
Kamin, Leon J., 291, 292
Kammeyer-Mueller, John D., 523
Kampe, Knut K. W., 458
Kamps, Debra, 598
Kanai, Chieko, 292
Kandel, Denise B., 171
Kandel, Eric R., 171, 257–258, 259
Kandler, Christian, 438
Kane, Michael J., 245
Kang, Sonia K., 466
Kanner, Allen D., 503
Kanwisher, Nancy, 126, 274
Kapinos, Kandice A., 30
Kaplan, Robert M., 520
Kaplan, Steve, 308
Kapp, Steven K., 299
Kaptchuk, Ted J., 623
Karasek, Michal, 326
Karlsson, Hasse, 610, 621
Karmiloff-Smith, Annette, 359
Karpicke, Jeffrey D., 26, 28, 36, 244
Karremans, Johan C., 89, 463
Karren, Ronald J., B–5
Kashdan, Todd B., 544
Kastenbaum, Robert, 406
Kato, Takahiro A., 560
Kaufman, Alan S., 291, 292
Kaufman, James C., 297, 308
Kaufman, Lloyd, 124
Kaut, Kevin P., 614
Kawai, Nobuyuki, 195
Kay, Aaron C., 525
Kay, Paul, 287
Kaye, W. H., 560
Kazdin, Alan E., 202, 209, 606, 607, 609
Kearney, Melissa, 218
Keatinge, C., 541
Keats, S., 321, 323
Keck, Paul E., Jr., 619
Keel, Pamela A., 323
Keel, Pamela K., 560, 561
Keil, Frank, 251
Kelly, Ciara, 557
Kelly, David J., 126, 366
Kelman, Herbert C., 480
Keltner, Dacher, 338
Kemmer, Susanne, 51
Kemp, Andrew H., 340
Kempermann, Gerd, 63, 64, 79
Kemps, Eva B., 405
Kempton, Matthew J., 576, 621
Kendal, Rachel L., 216
Kendall-Tackett, K., 511
Kendler, Kenneth S., 554, 577
Kennedy, Sidney H., 621
Kennison, Robert F., 403
Kenny, Paul J., 324
Keough, Meghan E., 543
Kerns, Kathryn A., 370
Kerr, David C. R., 408
Kershaw, Trina C., 280

Kerstetter, Deborah L., 375
Kesebir, Selin, 235
Keshavan, M. S., 570
Kessler, Ronald C., 538, 539, 541, 544, 552, 609
Khan, Zafar U., 257, 258
Khanna, Charu, B–13, B–14
Khazan, Olga, 571
Kheriaty, Aaron, 3
Khoury, Bassam, 604
Kiecolt-Glaser, Janice K., 509, 511, 512, 513
Kiefer, Amy K., 304, 305
Kihlstrom, John, 33, 156, 157, 237, 351, 567, 568
Kilbourn, John, 219, 488
Killen, Melanie, 393
Kim, Bryan S. K., 613
Kim, Jinhyun, 47
King, Bruce M., 322
King, Bryan Y., 278, 298
King, D. Brett, 120
King, Katherine, 505
King, Laura A., 317, 333
King, Robert, 325
Kingdom, Frederick A. A. 96
Kingdon, Bianca L., 548
Kinzler, Katherine D., 456
Kirby, Leslie D., 499
Kirsch, Irving, 159, 622, 623
Kirschenbaum, Howard, 9, 429, 590
Kitayama, Shinobu, 12, 13, 335, 337, 338, 460, 516
Klauke, Benedikt, 542
Kleider, Heather M., 251
Klein, Laura C., 527
Klein, Rachael M., 403
Kleinhans, Natalia, 278
Klin, Anat, 536
Klingberg, Torkel, 262
Klinger, Regine, 512
Klump, Kelly L., 560, 561
Knafo, Danielle, 248
Knäuper, Bärbel, 353
Knecht, S., 77
Knerr, Michael, 612
Knoblich, Gunther, 280
Knobloch, Marlen, 62
Knott, Lauren M., 252
Knox, Michele, 202
Knuth, Clifford C., 524
Kobilo, Tali, 80
Koch, Iring, 135
Kochanek, Kenneth D., 579, 580
Koelling, Robert A., 194
Koenen, Karestan C., 547
Koenig, Anne M., 305, 460
Koester, Lynne Sanford, 371
Koffka, Kurt, 116
Kohlberg, Lawrence, 393–394
Kohler, Evelyne, 217
Kohls, Niko, 4
Kohn, Robert, 606
Kohrt, Brandon A., 547
Kojima, M., 318
Kokaridas, Dimitrios, 598
Kolassa, Iris-Tatjana, 547
Kollndorfer, Kathrin, 273
Kolodny, Andrew, 170

Komatsu, Hidehiko, 92
Kong, Lauren L., 567
König, Cornelius J., 443
Konijn, Elly A., 219
Kopelowicz, Alex, 608
Kopp, Claire B., 367
Kording, Konrad, 60
Kornell, Nate, 266
Kornfield, Rachel, 623
Kosinski, Michal, 25
Kosslyn, Stephen, 158, 274–275
Kouider, Sid, 336
Kozorovitskiy, Yevgenia, 79
Kposowa, Augustine, 580
Kramer, Arthur F., 403, 404
Kramer, Lorraine Masinos, 573
Kramer, Milton, 590
Krantz, David S., 517
Krebs, Dennis L., 394
Krebs, Teri Suzanne, 174, 618
Kreider, Rose M., 399
Krimsky, Sheldon, 537
Kring, Ann M., 338
Krippner, Stanley, 566
Krohe, James, B–7
Kroll, Judith F., 288
Kromann, Charles B., 36
Kronick, Richard G., 520
Kross, Ethan, 222
Krueger, Joachim I., 113
Krug, Orah T., 591
Kruger, Justin, 460
Kruglanski, Arie W., 222
Krusemark, Elizabeth A., 460
Ku, Chee S., 361
Kübler-Ross, Elisabeth, 406
Kucewicz, Michal T., 174
Kuczaj, Stan A. II, 344, 345
Kufahl, Peter, 165
Kuhl, Brice A., 243
Kuhl, Patricia K., 371
Kuhn, Clifford C., 524
Kuhn, Deanna, 383, 385
Kuikka, Jyrki T., 560
Kulik, James, 241
Kunda, Ziva, 447
Kunoh, Hiroshi, 119
Kunz, John A., 405
Kuo, Ben, 526
Kupferschmidt, Kai, 173, 174, 175
Kurman, Jenny, 460
Kurson, Robert, 84–85
Kurtz, Matthew M., 604
Kurzban, Robert, 484
Kush, Francis R., 589
Kusumi, T., 246
Kuzumaki, Naoko, 80
Kwan, Virginia S. Y., 460
Kwok, Veronica, 163

L'Abate, L., 607
Lacasse, Katherine, 348, 349
Laceulle, Odilia M., 537
Ladabaum, Uri, 322
Lafreniere, Denis, 104
LaFromboise, Teresa D., 613
Lages, Martin, 228
Lago-Rodriguez, Angel, 217

La Guardia, Jennifer G., 333
Lahav, Amir, 217
Lahey, Benjamin B., 516
Lahti-Harper, Eve, 371
Laible, Deborah, 370
Laird, James D., 348, 349
Lamb, Michael E., 370, 401
Lambert, Anthony J., 248, 609, 612
Lambert, Michael J., 609, 612
Lamont, Peter, 136
Lampinen, James M., 251, 255
Lancaster, Lynne C., B–11
Lander, E. S., 361
Landolt, Hans-Peter, 141
Landy, Lauren N., 162
Lane, Anthony, 525
Laner, Mary R., 484
Langan-Fox, Janice, 444
Lange, Carl G., 347
Lange, Jean, 405
Lange, Tanja, 528
Langer, Ellen, 514
Langer, Shelby L., 338
Langley, Audra K., 546
Langlois, Judith H., 457
Langnickel, Robert, 247
Långström, Niklas, 328
Larkin, Gregory L., 620
Larsen, Jeff T., 337, 516
Larson, Christine, 502
Laruelle, Mark, 615
Lashley, Karl S., 210, 256
Laska, Kevin M., 611
Lasser, Karen, 556, 557
Latané, Bibb, 483, 484, 485
Lattal, K. Matthew, 183
Lau, Chi-leong, 577
Lau, Jennifer Y. F., 607
Lavie, Nilli, 136, 137
Lavoie, Kim L., 587
Lawler, Edward E., III, B–7
Lawrence, Erika, 400
Lazar, Sara W., 163
Lazarus, Arnold A., 611, 612
Lazarus, Richard S., 350, 351, 499, 500, 501, 523
Le Foll, Bernard, 556
Le Foll, David, 213
Leaper, Campbell, 376
Leary, Mark R., 333
Lebow, Jay L., 608
Ledford, Heidi, 552
LeDoux, Joseph E., 341, 342, 343, 597
Lee, Evelyn, 613
Lee, Jo Ann, 402
Lee, Kyoung-Uk, 128, 620
Lee, Sing, 561
Lee, Star W., 64
Lee, Su Young, 89
Lee, Yih-teen, 506
Lehner, Thomas, 575
Leichtman, Martin, 444
Leighton, Jacqueline P., 277
Leighton, Jane, 215
Leiter, Michael P., 504
Lemay, Edward P., Jr., 457
Lemish, Dafna, 536

Lenert, Leslie, 607
Lennie, Peter, 98
Lenroot, Rhoshel K., 388
Lenzenweger, Mark F., 562
Leo, Jonathan, 574
Leon, Scott C., 612
Leopold, David A., 125–126
Lerman, Dorothea C., 201
Lerner, Howard D., 588
Lerner, Jennifer S., 282, 336
Lerner, Melvin J., 459
Lesser, Lenard I., 31
Lester, David, 580
Lester, Gregory W., 284
Lester, S. Reid, 512
Lett, Heather S., 521
Leung, Paul K., 613
Leung, Rachel C., 278
LeVay, Simone, 329
Levenson, Hanna, 589
Levenson, Robert W., 339–340
Levenston, Gary K., 564
Levi, Jeffrey, 321
Levin, Netta, 95
Levin, Ross, 149
Levine, John M., 473
Levine, Phillip, 218
Levine, Robert V., 485
Levine, Timothy, 397
Levinson, Douglas F., 554
Levy, Becca, 305
Levy, Benjamin J., 247
Levy, Kenneth N., 612
Lewin, Roger, 288
Lewis, Melissa A., 397
Lewis, Suzan, B–12
Lewontin, Richard, 303
Li, Rick, 24
Li, Shenghui, 368
Li, Wen, 89, 105
Liao, Jing, 403
Libby, Lisa K., 353
Lieb, Roselind, 580
Lieberman, Matthew, 279
Lieberman, Robert Paul, 598
Liff, Zanvel A., 588, 589
Lilienfeld, Scott O., 32, 444, 611
Linden, Michael, 610
Lindenberger, Ulman, 403
Lindsay, D. Stephen, 249, 253
Lindsay, Emily, 528
Lindsey, Delwin T., 287
Lindström, Per, 329
Linehan, Marsha M., 565–566
Linford, Lloyd, 610
Links, Paul S., 565
Linnman, Clas, 107
Lippa, Richard A., 329
Lisman, John, 258
Lissemore, Jennifer I., 620
Little, Karley Y., 166
Livianos-Aldano, Lorenzo, 61
Livingstone, Margaret, 94
Livneh, Yoav, 70
Lobstein, Tim, 321
LoBue, Vanessa, 195, 374
Lockard, Robert B., 193
Locke, Edwin A., B–7, B–8

Lockhart, Robert S., 235
Lockwood, Nancy R., B–8
Lodi-Smith, Jennifer, 518
Loewenstein, George, 14
Loewy, Joanne V., 128
Loftus, Elizabeth E., 237, 248–249, 250, 252, 254, 255
Lohr, Jeffrey M., 611
LoLordo, Vincent M., 212
Lombardo, Michael V., 60, 72
Long, Patrick, 45
Lorber, William, 260
Lord, Charles G., 284
Lorenzo, Genevieve L., 457
Louis, Winnifred R., 469
Loving, Timothy, 512
Lowenstein, Amy E., 401
Lowry, Brian, 478
Lubbadeh, Jens, 285
Luborsky, Lester, 588, 590, 611
Lucas, Gale M., 607
Lucassen, Nicole, 370
Ludwig, David S., 528
Lueke, Adam, 470
Luhrmann, Tanya Marie, 571
Luna, Beatriz, 389
Lund, Rikke, 520
Lundahl, Brad W., 592
Lundqvist, Daniel, 343
Luo, Yuyan, 384
Lupfer, Gwen, 216
Lutz, Antoine, 162
Lyn, Heidi, 345
Lynall, Mary-Ellen, 62
Lynch, Steve, 260
Lynch, Thomas R., 605
Lynn, Steven J., 157, 158, 159, 160, 254, 568
Lyons, William, 187
Lytton, William W., 246

Ma, Ning, 146
Maccoby, Eleanor E., 407
MacDonald, Bernie, 548
Macdonald, James S. P., 136, 137
Macháčková, Hana, 485
Mack, Arien, 136
MacKay, Alicia, 80
MacKay, Donald G., 261
Mackenzie, Michael J., 202
Macknik, Stephen L., 136
Maclean, Katherine A., 162
MacLean, Robert R., 145
MacLeod, Colin, 607
MacLeod, Donald, 125
Macrae, C. Neil, 455
Macy, Michael W., 484
Maddux, James E., 222
Madjar, Nora, 308
Madsen, Matias V., 128
Maes, Jürgen, 460
Magistretti, Pierre J., 60
Magnavita, Jeffrey J., 589
Maguire, Eleanor A., 32, 33
Mahon, Bradford Z., 94
Mahowald, Mark W., 141, 153, 154
Maia, Tiago V., 549
Maier, Andrea, 319

Maier, Markus A., 96
Maier, Steven F., 212, 514
Main, Mary, 370
Maj, Mario, 537
Majid, Asifa, 102, 287
Major, Geneviève C., 320
Makrygianni, Maria K., 209
Malcolm, James P., 328
Malekpour, Mokhtar, 370
Malenka, Robert C., 166
Malhi, Gin S., 619
Malinowski, Peter, 162, 604
Malla, Ashok, 537, 573
Mallett, Robyn K., 465
Mallinckrodt, Brent, 590
Malouff, John, 510
Malouff, John M., 456
Mamet, Zosia, 561
Manago, Adriana M., 16–17
Mandler, George, 233
Maner, Jon K., 489
Mann, Norman, 104
Manning, Rachel, 483
Manstead, Anthony S. R., 346
Manzano, Isabel, 241
Maoz, Ifat, 471
Marañon, Gregorio, 348
Marantz, Andrew, 572
Marcus, Bernd, B–5
Marcus, Gary, 301
Marcus, Steven C., 620, 621
Marecek, Jeanne, 537
Marentette, Paula F., 371
Margulies, Daniel S., 62
Marín-Burgin, Antonia, 64
Markman, Arthur B., 275
Markowitsch, Hans, 247
Markowitsch, Hans J., 237
Markowitz, John C., 590
Markus, Hazel, 12, 335, 337, 338, 447, 448
Markwald, Rachel R., 146
Marmie, William R., 244–245
Marmot, Michael G., 505
Marneros, Andreas, 554
Marquis, Donald G., 183
Marsh, Elizabeth J., 246
Marsland, Katherine W., 401
Martin, Alexandra, 128
Martin, Bruce, 285
Martin, Carol, 610, 627
Martin, Carol Lynn, 375, 376, 377
Martin, John A., 407
Martin, M. F., 567
Martin, Rod A., 277
Martinez, Isabel, 407, 408
Marucha, Phillip T., 512
Marx, Rebecca Flynt, 567
Mash, Clay, 381
Mashoodh, Robin, 362
Masicampo, E. J., 135
Maslach, Christina, 504
Masland, Richard H., 92
Maslow, Abraham H., 331–332
Masnick, Amy M., 285
Mason, Winter, 467
Master, Sarah L., 520, 525
Masterpasqua, Frank, 362

Masters, Kevin S., 521
Masters, William H., 325
Masuda, Minoru, 501
Matarazzo, Joseph D., 292
Mather, Mara, 32, 33
Mathews, Andrew, 607
Mathews, Carol A., 548
Mathias, Robert, 168
Matsumoto, David, 126, 335, 337, 344, 346
Matute, Helena, 20
Maxmen, Jerold S., 618
May, Mike, 85, 86, 127
Maybery, D. J., 503
Mayer, John D., 336
Mayer, Richard E., 197
Mayor, Tracy, 300
Mazzoni, Giuliana, 157
McAdams, Dan P., 391, 435, 441
McAndrew, Francis T., 501
McArthur, Genevieve, 31
McCabe, Marita P., 390
McCabe, Randi E., 557
McCall, W. Vaughn, 623, 624
McCarley, Robert W., 51, 147, 150, 151
McCartney, Kathleen, 401, 441
McCeney, Melissa K., 517
McClelland, David C., 334, 335
McClendon, Debra T., 605
McClintock, Martha K., 103
McClintock, S. M., 624
McCormack, William A., 317
McCoy, Bob, 61
McCrae, Robert R., 438, 439
McCreadie, Robin, 557
McCullough, Michael E., 500
McCurdy, Berry L., 209
McDaniell, Ryan, 361
McDermut, Wilson, 445
McDonald, Ann, 365
McDonald, William M., 624, 625
McDougall, William, 315
McElhaney, Kathleen B., 390
McElroy, Susan L., 619
McEwen, Bruce S., 60
McFarland, Sam, 481
McGaugh, James L., 262
McGehee, Daniel S., 556
McGeown, William J., 159
McGirr, Alexander, 175, 551
McGlone, Francis, 106
McGoldrick, Monica, 613
McGowan, Patrick O., 363
McGraw, A. Peter, 337
McGraw, Peter, 524
McGregor, Jacqueline C., 541
McGrew, Kevin S., 291
McGue, Matt, 302
McIntyre, Kevin P., 516
McIsaac, C., 391
McKee, Ann C., 54
McKenzie, Ian A., 45
McLay, Robert N., 596
McLean, Carmen P., 541
McLellan, Thomas A., 170
McLemore, Kevin A., 466
McLewin, Lise A., 567

McMurran, Mary, 564
McNab, Fiona, 262
McNally, Richard J., 254, 255, 546, 594
McNeil, Jeffrey A., 507
McNeilly, Cheryl L., 610
McNulty, James K., 11
McPherson, Barbara J., 377
McRoberts, Gerald W., 371
McVay, Jennifer C., 245
Mead, Alan D., 445
Meaney, Michael, 360, 362
Mechoulam, Raphael, 174
Media for Health, 220
Medin, Douglas L., 287
Medina, Jorge H., 260
Medsker, Gina J., B–13, B–14
Meduri, Mario, 576
Megargee, Edwin I., 445
Mehall, Karissa G., 400
Meier, Beat, 247
Meier, Jo A., 400
Meijer, Ewout H., 339
Meir, Irit, 287
Meissner, Karin, 622
Melton, Lisa, 80
Meltzoff, Andrew N., 215
Melzack, Ronald, 108
Menaker, Michael, 139
Menand, Louis, 5
Mendle, Jane, 390
Mendoza, Saaid A., 470
Menzies, Ross G., 548
Mercer, Deanna, 565
Merikangas, K. R., 554
Merlino, Joseph P., 417, 427
Merryman, Ashley, 372
Mervis, Carolyn B., 276
Mesmer-Magnus, Jessica R., B–12
Meston, Cindy M., 326
Meyer, Gregory J., 444
Meyer, Jerold S., 618
Meyer, S. E., 553
Meyerbröker, Katharina, 596
Meyer-Lindenberg, Andreas, 487
Mezick, Elizabeth J., 507
Mezulis, Amy H., 460
Michael, John, 217
Michael, Nikolaus, 624
Mikalsen, Anita, 191
Mikels, Joseph A., 336
Miklowitz, David J., 553, 554
Milan, Stephanie, 368
Miles, Donna R., 487
Miles, L., 466
Milgram, Stanley, 455, 474, 475, 476, 477, 478, 480, 482
Miller, Arthur G., 474
Miller, A. H., 520
Miller, B. O., 4
Miller, Christian, 484
Miller, Cindy F., 374, 377
Miller, Claude H., 518
Miller, Drew J., 516
Miller, Franklin G., 623
Miller, George, 232
Miller, Greg, 59
Miller, Gregory A., 32

Miller, Gregory E., 500, 501, 509
Miller, Lee M., 135
Miller, Mark W., 546
Miller, William R., 592, 626
Miller-Jones, Dalton, 307
Milling, Leonard S., 156
Mills, Sarah, 597
Milner, Brenda, 260
Minda, John Paul, 276
Mindell, Jodi A., 12, 368
Mineka, Susan, 195, 341
Ming, Guo-li, 79
Minzenberg, Michael J., 573
Mirmiran, Majid, 144, 365
Miron, Anca M., 456
Mischel, Walter, 222, 439
Mistlberger, Ralph E., 137, 139
Mitchell, Colter, 510
Mitchell, James E., 620
Mitchell, Jason P., 484
Mitka, Mike, 167
Miyata, Yo, 183
Mizrahi, Adi, 70
Mock, Matthew R., 613
Moffet, Howard H., 128
Moghaddam, Bita, 577
Mohanty, Aprajita, 71
Mohr, Charles, 483
Mohr, David C., 607
Moitra, Ethan, 542
Mojtabai, Ramin, 539, 620
Mok, Leh Woon, 322
Molenberghs, Pascal, 217
Molitor, Adriana, 359, 369, 385
Monroe, Scott M., 501
Montepare, Joann M., 455
Montgomery, Guy H., 611
Moore, David W., 112
Moore, Jay, 108, 197
Moore, M. Keith, 215
Moore, Mollie N., 554–555
Moors, Agnes, 350, 351
Moreland, Richard L., 89
Morelli, Gilda A., 368
Moretti, Robert J., 444
Morey, Richard D., 113
Morgan, C. A., III, 507
Morgan, Christiana, 334, 444
Morgan, William P., 159, 160
Mori, DeAnna L., 524
Morin, Charles M., 176
Morling, Beth, 335
Morrell, Julian, 368
Morris, Edward K., 204
Morris, John S., 341
Morris, Michael W., 460
Morris, Richard G., 51
Morrison, Anthony P., 603, 604
Morrison, Christopher D., 319, 323
Morrison, Evan L., 463
Moskowitz, Andrew, 568
Moskowitz, Judith Tedlie, 522, 523
Moss, Cynthia, 345
Moss, Jarrod, 280
Motowidlo, Stephan J., B–6
Mottron, Laurent, 299
Moulin, Christopher J. A., 246
Mouton, Jane, B–8, B–9

Moyer, Christopher A., 128
Mrazek, Michael D., 305
Mueller, Pam A., 36
Mueller, Shane T., 233
Muenchow, Susan, 401
Mueser, Kim T., 571, 573, 577, 597, 611
Mügge, Dirk O., 219, 488
Mujica-Parodi, Lilianne R., 103
Mukamel, Roy, 217
Mulhern, Sherrill, 566
Muller, Robert T., 567
Muly, E. Chris, 257, 258
Munafo, Marcus R., 556
Munakata, Yuko, 385, 386
Münch, Mirgam, 138
Murata, Taketo, 477
Murberg, Terje A., 524
Murphy, David, 432
Murray, Greg, 555
Murray, Henry A., 334, 444
Murray, John P., 219
Muscatell, Keeley A., 556
Mustanski, Brian S., 329, 387, 388
Musto, David F., 170
Mutiso, V. N., 613
Myrtek, Michael, 517

NACCRRA (National Association of Child Care Resource & Referral Agencies), 401
Nader, Karim, 261
Nadler, Joel T., 305
Nagasawa, Miho, 59
Nahas, Ziad, 622, 624
Nairn, Ray, 536
Nairne, James S., 231
Nakamura, Jeanne, 11
Nakao, Mutsuhiro, 504
Náñez, José E., Sr., 288
Nash, Michael R., 156, 160, 252
Nathan, Peter E., 609
National Association for the Education of Young Children, 401
National Center for Complementary and Alternative Medicine, 20, 128
National Geographic, 508
National Highway Traffic Safety Administration, 152
National Institute on Aging, 402
National Research Council, 339
National Safety Council, 137
National Science Board, 20
National Sleep Foundation, 171
National Standard, 20
National Standard Monographs, 129
National Survey of Student Engagement, 23–24
Neberich, Wiebke, 388
Nederlof, Angela E., 537
Neher, Andrew, 332
Neimeyer, Robert A., 406
Neisser, Ulric, 295
Nelson, Gareth, 299
Nelson, Katherine, 237
Nelson, Katherine S., 400
Nelson, Leif, 463

Nelson, Marcia Z., 160
Nelson, Toben F., 167, 168
Nemeroff, Charles B., 551, 556
Nestler, Eric J., 166
Nestojko, John F., 28
Nestoriuc, Yvonne, 128
Neuberg, Steven L., 454
Neumann, Craig S., 564
Neuner, Frank, 606
Newell, Allen, 287
Newheiser, Anna-Kaisa, 466
Newson, Rachel S., 405
Newton, Jocelyn H., 291
Nezu, Arthur M., 609
Nezu, Christine M., 609
Ng, Debbie M., 527
Nguyen, Angela-MinhTu D., 506
Niccols, Alison, 167
NICHD (National Institute of
    Child Health and Human
    Development), 401
Nichols, Michael P., 608
Nichols, Michelle, 479
Nickerson, Raymond S., 244
Nida, Steve A., 485
Nielsen, Jared A., 77
Nielsen, Tore A., 148, 149
Nielson, Kristy A., 260
Niemiec, Christopher P., 333
Nir, Yuval, 140, 151
Nisbett, Richard E., 115, 301, 303,
    305, 307, 456
Nithianantharajah, Jess, 79
Nivette, Amy E., 490
Nivoli, Alessandra M., 618
Noble, Meredith, 169
Nock, Matthew K., 580
Nocon, Agnes, 174
Nofzinger, Eric A., 148
Nolen-Hoeksema, Susan, 552
Norasakkunkit, Vinai, 544
Norcross, John C., 589, 599, 605,
    612
Nordal, Katherine C., 626
Nordgren, Loran F., 89
Norenzayan, Ara, 12
Norko, Michael, 537
Norris, Donna M., 627
North, Adrian C., 128
North, Carol S., 547
North, Michael S., 466
Nosek, Brian A., 456, 470
Nosofsky, Robert M., 276
Novella, Steven, 122
Novick, Laura R., 277
Nowinski, Chris, 54
Nowlan, Jamie S., 524
Nummenmaa, Lauri, 340
Nurius, Paula, 447, 448
Nurnberger, John I., 620
Nutt, David J., 167
Nyberg, Svante, 577
Nyhan, Brendan, 284

Oakley, David A., 156, 158, 159
Oas, Peter T., 202
Oberman, Lindsay M., 217
O'Brien, Mary P., 608

Occupational Outlook Handbook,
    B–14
Ocklenburg, Sebastian, 71, 74, 77
O'Connor, Akira R., 246
O'Connor, Cliodhna, 72
O'Connor, Daryl B., 503, 514, 526
O'Connor, Thomas G., 542
O'Conor, Andi, 527
O'Craven, Kathleen, 274
Odbert, Harold S., 436
Oden, Melita H., 293
Odgers, Candace, 503
O'Doherty, J., 458
O'Donnell, Stephanie, 196
O'Donoghue, Gerard, 100
O'Donohue, William T., 601
Oehen, Peter, 618
Ogbu, John U., 305, 306, 307
Ogle, Christin, 505
Ogles, Benjamin M., 609, 612
Oh, G., 574
Ohlsson, Stellan, 279, 280
Öhman, Arne, 195, 341, 343
Oishi, Shigehiro, 235
ojalehto, bethany, 287
Okonofua, Jason A., 469
Olabi, B., 576
Olff, Miranda, 59, 546
Olfson, Mark, 620, 621
Olivier, Donald C., 286
Olivola, Christopher Y., 456, 457
Öllinger, Michael, 279, 280
Olson, Bradley D., 391
Olszweski, Pawel K., 318
Olthof, Tjeert, 394
Oltmanns, Thomas F., 562
Olton, David S., 211
O Magazine, 544
O'Neil, John Allison, 566
Ones, Deniz S., 447
Ong, Anthony D., 505
Oppenheimer, Daniel M., 36
Opriş, David, 596
Orne, Martin T., 476
Ornish, Dean, 511
O'Roark, Ann M., 417
Ostrov, Jamie M., 489
O'Sullivan, Maureen, 339
O'Toole, Laura, 607
Owe, Elinore, 12
Owen, Adrian M., 33
Owen, Jesse J., 397
Oyserman, Daphna, 447, 448
Ozer, Elizabeth M., 434
Ozer, Emily J., 547
Ozkan, Kerem, 124

Pace-Schott, Edward F., 145, 150,
    151
Packer, Dominic J., 473, 480, 481
Packer, Martin, 385
Pagel, Mark, 5
Paik, Se-Bum, 94
Paivio, Allan, 235, 266
Palit, Shreela, 108
Palmer, John C., 112, 249
Palmer, Stephen E., 112
Palmiero, Massimiliano, 273

Pals, Jennifer L., 435
Paluck, Elizabeth Levy, 470
Pandi-Perumal, S. R., 551
Panksepp, Jaak, 344
Paradisi, Irene, 328
Parasuraman, Raja, 80
Pargament, Kenneth I., 526
Parish, Amy R., 326
Park, Crystal L., 523
Park, Denise C., 115
Park, Hae-Jeong, 62
Park, Hyekyung, 335, 338
Park, Nansook, 515
Park, S., 527
Park, Yong S., 613
Parker, Andrew J., 119
Parker, Kevin C.H., 597
Parker, Linda A., 174
Parker, Stephen C. J., 361
Parks-Stamm, Elizabeth J., 353
Parsons, Dee, 20
Partonen, Timo, 551
Pascalis, Olivier, 126, 366
Pascual-Leone, Alvaro, 63
Patihis, Lawrence, 248, 254
Patrick, Christopher J., 563, 564
Patterson, Charlotte J., 330
Patterson, David R., 157
Paul, Diane B., 189
Paunio, Tina, 323
Pavlov, Ivan, 183, 184, 185, 186,
    187, 191, 194, 256
Payne, B. Keith, 456
Payne, Jennifer, 537, 573
Payne, Laura A., 542
Payton, Jack R., 306
Paz-y-Miño, C. Guillermo, 289
Peck, Adam, B–8
Pedersen, Anette F., 513
Pedersen, Paul B., 613
Pedersen, William, 378
Pedersen, William C., 487
Pedrabissi, Luigi, 443
Pemment, Jack, 564
Peng, Kaiping, 460
Penrod, Steven, 473
Pentland, Joel, 252
Penton-Voak, Ian, 463
Pepperberg, Irene, 289
Perdue, Bonnie M., 35
Pereira, Ana C., 80
Perkins, Tom, 217
Perlis, Michael L., 153
Perret-Clermont, Anne-Nelly, 383
Perrett, David I., 463
Perrin, Ellen C., 330
Perry, David G., 375
Perry, Gina, 476, 477, 478
Perry, Jennifer L., 35
Perry, Katy, 397
Perry, Lynn K., 381
Pervin, Lawrence A., 441
Pesant, Nicholas, 149
Pescosolido, Bernice A., 609
Pessoa, Luis, 341
Petersen, Jennifer L., 397
Petersen, Michael B., 484

Petersen, Ronald C., 264
Peterson, Christopher, 11, 515
Peterson, Jillian K., 536
Peterson, Jamie Lee, 322
Peterson, Lloyd R., 231
Peterson, Margaret J., 231
Petitto, Laura A., 371, 372
Petronis, A., 574
Petrovic, Predrag, 512
Peyrot des Gachons, Catherine, 106
Pfafflin, F., 379
Phelan, Julie E., 467
Phelps, Elizabeth A., 71, 341
Phillips, Deborah A., 401
Phillips, Michael, 339
Phillips, Roger D., 366
Phillips, Stephen J., 402
Phillips, Tommy M., 392, 393
Phillips, William L., 126
Piaget, Jean, 380, 382, 383, 385
Pica, Pierre, 287
Pickett, Kate E., 490
Pickrell, Jacqueline, 252
Pickren, Wade E., 6
Piernas, Carmen, 321
Pike, Kathleen M., 561
Pile, Victoria, 607
Pincus, David, 128
Pinel, John P. J., 322
Pinheiro, A. P., 559
Pinker, Steven, 122, 285, 286
Pinna, Baingio, 117
Pinnell, Cornelia M., 160
Piotrowski, Chris, B–5
Piper, August, 255
Pitcher, David, 274
Pittenger, David J., 446
Pittman, Cathy, 374
Plaisier, I., 402
Plant, E. A., 469
Plassmann, Hilke, 106
Platek, Steven M., 141
Plazzi, Giuseppe, 152
Plomin, Robert, 301, 302, 307, 440
Plötner, Maria, 485
Plotnik, Joshua M., 289, 290
Podd, John, 191
Pogue-Geile, Michael F., 574
Polaschek, D.L.L., 253
Polito, Vince, 157
Polk, Thad A., 287
Pope, Kenneth S., 445, 627
Popkin, Barry M., 321
Population Communications
    International, 218, 220
Porter, Jess, 105
Porter, Stephen, 252
Portrat, Sophie, 247
Pos, Alberta E., 590
Posner, Michael I., 135, 160
Possel, Patrick, 550–551
Post, Jerrold M., 480
Postle, Bradley R., 262
Poulin-Dubois, D., 374
Powell, Lindsay J., 440
Powell, Nelson B., 153
Powell, Russell A., 189
Power, Mick, 609

Powers, Mark B., 594
Powers, Pauline M., 559
Powley, Terry L., 320
Powlishta, Kimberly K., 375
Pratto, Felicia, 469
Premack, David, 290
Pressman, Mark R., 141, 155
Pressman, Sarah D., 516, 517
Press Release Newswire, B–5
Preston, John D., 618
Preti, George, 103
Price, Donald D., 512, 622
Prislin, R., 492
Prochaska, James O., 589, 599
Prot, Sara, 488
Pryor, John B., 535
Przybylski, Andrew K., 219
Psaltis, Charis, 385
Puhl, Rebecca M., 322
Pujol, Jesus, 549
Purcell, Shaun M., 575
Purkey, William Watson, 429
Purkis, Helena, 195
Purves, Dale, 94, 96
Puterman, Eli, 511
Putnam, Adam L., 36
Pyc, Mary A., 244

Qin, Ping, 565
Quadflieg, Susanne, 455
Quaglia, Jordan T., 161
Queller, Sarah, 467
Quenk, Naomi L., 446
Quick, Brian L., 518
Quiles Marcos, Yolanda, 560
Quinn, Meghan E., 555

Rabbitt, Sarah M., 607
Rabier, Vanille, 113
Rabinowitz, Amanda R., 54
Raboteg-Saric, Zora, 407
Raby, Caroline R., 289
Rachlin, Howard, 221
Rado, Jeffrey, 573
Radulescu, Anca R., 103
Rafaeli, E., 520
Rahe, Richard H., 501
Rahim-Williams, Bridgett, 108
Raj, John Dilip, 209
Rakison, David H., 195
Ramachandran, Vilayanur S., 93, 217
Rapoport, Judith L., 549, 574
Rapp, Paul E., 339
Raskin, Nathaniel J., 591
Rasmussen, Keith G., 623
Rasmussen, Steven A., 548, 549
Ratiu, Peter, 68
Rawson, Katherine A., 37, 244
Rawson, Nancy E., 104
Rayner, Rosalie, 188–189, 594
Raz, Amir, 135
Reader, Simon M., 216
Reader, Will, 545
Recanzone, Gregg H., 101
Rechtschaffen, Allan, 140
Reddy, Leila, 274
Reed, Phil, 209

Reeder, Glenn D., 478
Rees, Geraint, 93
Reeves, Adam, 117
Refinetti, Roberto, 138
Regan, David, 120
Regier, Terry, 287
Regnerus, Mark, 330
Rego, Arménio, 549, B–8
Rehkopf, David H., 505
Reiber, Chris, 397
Reicher, Stephen, 481
Reid, Mark W., 501
Reid, Pamela T., 376
Reifler, Jason, 284
Reilly, David, 106
Reilly, Michael J., 457
Reis, Harry T., 337, 463
Reisenzein, Rainer, 346, 350
Reissig, Chad J., 170
Reiter, Edward O., 387, 390
Reneman, Liesbeth, 175
Renk, Kimberly, 377
Renshaw, Keith D., 548
Repetti, Rena L., 389, 504, 525
Rescorla, Robert, 187, 192–193
Rest, James R., 394
Rétey, Julia V., 141
Revelle, William, 435
Révész, Dóra, 510
Rhodes, Gillian, 125–126
Rhodes, John E., 550
Rhodes, Marjorie, 467
Rhue, Judith W., 156, 159
Riby, Leigh M., 245
Ricard, Matthieu, 161, 162
Ricciardelli, Lina A., 390
Riccio, David C., 260
Rice, Robert W., B–8
Rich, Josiah D., 52
Richardson, Christi L., 604
Richardson, L. Song, 469
Richardson, Michelle, 18
Richardson, Rhonda A., 370
Richardson, Robert D., 5
Richert, Rebekah A., 372
Richeson, Jennifer A., 465, 466, 469
Richtand, Neil M., 615
Rideout, V., 372
Riding-Malon, Ruth, 14
Ridolfo, Heather, 112
Riegel, B., A–1
Rieger, Gerulf, 328, 329
Rifkin, June, 443
Riley, Anthony L., 194
Riley, J. R., 288
Riley, Kathryn P., 263
Rilling, James K., 336
Rilling, Mark, 188
Ringach, Dario L., 93, 94
Rippon, Gina, 72
Risen, Jane, 284
Ristic, Jelena, 135
Rivers, Ian, 330
Rizzolatti, Giacomo, 43, 217
Roazen, Paul, 428
Robb, Michael B., 373
Roberts, Amy, 299

Roberts, Brent W., 439
Robinson, Barbara S., 448
Robinson, Gail, 398
Robinson, Jordan S., 502
Robinson, Paul, 427
Robles, Theodore, 520
Roca, Miquel, 552
Rock, Irvin, 120, 123, 136
Rodafinos, Angelo S., 492
Rodewald, Frauke, 568
Rodin, Judith, 514
Rodriguez-Larralde, Alvaro, 328
Roediger, Henry L., 26, 28, 36, 243, 244
Roese, Neal J., 459
Rogers, Carl R., 317, 429, 430, 431, 432, 591
Rogers, Paul, 112
Rohde, Paul, 552
Roisman, Glenn I., 330
Rojas, Mary, 218
Rollnick, Stephen, 592
Romeo, August, 93
Romero, Teresa, 141
Ronen, Tammmie, 597, 598
Rook, Karen S., 520
Rosa-Alcázar, Ana I., 594
Rosander, Michael, 473
Rosati, Alexandra G., 289
Rosch, Eleanor H., 276, 286–287
Rose, Gary S., 592, 626
Rose, Jed E., 171
Rose, Steven, 303
Rosekind, Mark, 528
Rosen, B., B–9
Rosenbaum, David A., 275
Rosenberg, Neil, 168
Rosenberg, Oded, 624
Rosenblatt, Paul C., 406
Rosenfarb, Irwin S., 608
Rosenfield, Sarah, 522
Rosenheck, Robert, 546
Rosenman, Ray, 517
Rosenquist, James N., 323
Rosenthal, Abraham M., 483
Rosenzweig, Saul, 7
Rosielle, Luke J., 137
Rosqvist, Johan, 213, 515
Ross, Barbara, 5
Ross, Lee, 284, 459
Ross, Michael, 236, 237
Ross, Shannon E., 503
Rossier, Jerome, 438
Rossini, Edward D., 444
Roth, Thomas, 145
Rothbart, Mary K., 135
Rothbaum, Fred, 338
Rothblum, Esther D., 399
Rotheram-Borus, Mary Jane, 606
Rouder, Jeffrey N., 113, 232
Rowe, David C., 440
Rowe, Shawn M., 385
Rowland, Christopher A., 28
Rowling, J. K., 552
Rozin, Paul, 318
Rubin, David C., 242, 254, 257, 262
Rubin, Edgar, 113

Rubin, Nava, 113, 114
Rubio-Fernández, P., 288
Ruble, Diane N., 374, 375, 376, 377
Rudman, Laurie A., 467
Rudolph, Karen D., 389
Rumbaugh, Duane, 288
Rumiati, Raffaella I., 72
Runco, Mark A., 308
Rusak, Benjamin, 137
Ruscher, Janet B., 471
Ruscio, John, 285
Russac, R. J., 406
Russell, Dan, 284
Russell, James A., 337, 345, 347
Russell, Nestar John Charles, 474
Russon, Anne E., 216
Rutchick, Abraham M., 622
Rutherford, Alexandra, 6, 197, 204, 594
Rutledge, Thomas, 519
Rutter, Michael, 30
Ruvolo, Ann Patrice, 448
Ryan, Richard M., 333–334
Rydell, Ann-Margaret, 370
Rydell, Robert J., 304, 467

Sacchi, Dario L. M., 250
Sachse, Rainer, 592
Sadler, Pamela, 158
Sadoski, Mark, 266
Sagarin, Brad J., 491
Sagi, Yaniv, 63
Sagi-Schwartz, A., 370
Saha, Sukanta, 573
Sahdra, Baljinder K., 162
Saiyad, Mohammedlatif, 557
Sakheim, David K., 254
Sakic, Marija, 407
Saks, Elyn, 532, 533, 569, 570, 571, 572, 575
Salas, Rachel E., 153
Salazar, Gloria Maria Martinez, 157
Saletan, William, 254
Salloum, Alison, 606
Salthouse, Timothy A., 403
Sam, David L., 506
Sameroff, Arnold, 3
Sammons, Cynthia C., 612
Sampaio, Adriana, 439
Samuel, Douglas B., 562
Sandler, Wendy, 287
Sanfelippo, Augustin J., 542
Sanfey, Alan G., 336
Santiago, Catherine D., 539
Santos, Laurie R., 289
Sapolsky, Robert M., 363
Sar, Vedat, 568
Satel, Sally, 32
Saul, Stephanie, 155
Savage, Cary R., 549
Savage, Joanne, 219
Savage, Seddon R., 170
Savage-Rumbaugh, Sue, 288, 345
Savic, Ivanka, 329
Savin-Williams, Ritch C., 327, 328
Saxbe, Darby E., 389
Saxe, Rebecca, 385, 440
Scaggs, W. Jeffrey, 137

Schachter, Robert, 605
Schachter, Stanley, 350
Schacter, Daniel L., 236, 248
Schaffner, Kenneth F., 577
Schaie, K. Warner, 403
Schanding, G. Thomas, Jr., 209
Scheetz, Karin, 607
Schell, Jason, 204
Schenck, Carlos H., 153, 154, 155
Scherer, Klaus R., 340, 345, 351
Schläpfer, Thomas E., 625
Schlein, Lisa, 579
Schlitz, Marilyn, 113
Schmader, Toni, 304, 305, 467
Schmalz, Dorothy L., 375
Schmidt, Norman B., 543
Schmithorst, Vincent J., 389
Schmitt, David P., 378
Schmitt, Michael, 505
Schnall, Simone, 349
Schneider, Kirk J., 591
Schofield, Hugh, 443
Schomerus, Georg, 536
Schouten, Alexander P., 456
Schredl, Michael, 246
Schroeder, Michael, 330
Schroth, Marvin L., 317
Schulenberg, J. E., 396
Schüll, Natasha Dow, 208
Schulz, Marc S., 525
Schupp, Harald T., 343
Schutte, Nicola, 510
Schwab, Richard J., 153
Schwartz, Bennett L., 239
Schwartz, Charlotte, 589
Schwartz, Earl, 394
Schwartz, Jeffrey M., 610
Schwartz, Seth J., 506
Schwartz, Shalom, 473
Schwartz, Sophie, 140
Schweiger, D. M., B–8
Scoboria, A., 157
Scott, Samantha L., 524
Scott-Phillips, Thomas C., 14
Scoville, William B., 260
Seal, Karen H., 546
Seal, Mark, 457
Sebastian, Catherine, 391
Sebastián-Gallés, Núria, 288
Sedlmeier, Peter, 162
Seegmiller, Janelle K., 137
Seeman, Julius, 592
Seery, Mark, 502–503
Segal, Nancy L., 487
Segal, Zindel V., 604, 605
Segall, Marshall H., 126
Segerdahl, Pär, 288
Segerstrom, Suzanne C., 515–516
Sekaquaptewa, Denise, 304, 305
Sela, Lee, 105
Selby, Edward A., 565
Self, David W., 166
Seligman, Martin E. P., 11, 193, 194,
    195, 212, 500, 515
Sellers, Robert M., 505
Selye, Hans, 499, 508–509
Senghas, Ann, 287
Sengoku, Mari, 613
Senko, Corwin, 335

Senn, Larry E., B–10
Serbin, Lisa A., 374
Serlin, Ilene, 9, 11
Serrano, Zulai, 459
Serretti, Alessandro, 528
Seung, Sebastian, 62
Seurinck, Ruth, 275
Severus, W. Emanuel, 618
Sexton, Thomas L., 608
Shafto, Meredith A., 403
Shahrazad, Wan, 370
Shalvi, Shaul, 59
Shapiro, Colin M., 155
Shapiro, David A., 609
Shapiro, Francine, 596–597
Shapiro, Jenessa R., 305, 467
Shapiro, Shauna L., 161, 162,
    528–529
Sharif, Zafar, 579
Sharman, Stefanie J., 253
Sharpless, Brian A., 156
Shaw, Benjamin A., 519
Shaw, Jon A., 547
Shaw, Julia, 252
Shedler, Jonathan, 447, 609
Sheeran, Paschal, 352, 353
Sheikh, Anees A., 128
Sheldon, B., 604
Sheldon, Kennon M., 317, 332,
    333, 432
Shelia, Cotten, 25
Shen, Hao, 491
Shepard, Roger, 125
Shepherd, Gordon M., 104, 105,
    106
Shepherd, Jonathan, 167
Sheppard, Leah D., 457
Sherif, Carolyn W., 470
Sherif, Muzafer, 470, 471
Sherman, David K., 305
Sherman, Jeffrey W., 467
Sherman, Ryne A., 439
Shermer, Michael, 113
Sherrill, Michelle R., 448
Shettleworth, Sara J., 289, 290
Shevell, Steven K., 96
Shi, Jianxin, 575
Shibasaki, Masahiro, 195
Shidlo, Ariel, 330
Shiffrin, Richard M., 228
Shih, Margaret, 304, 305
Shimizu, Mikiko, 514, 526
Shiner, Rebecca L., 369
Shinskey, Jeanne, 385
Shneidman, Edwin S., 580, 581
Shoda, Yuichi, 439
Shors, Tracey J., 64, 79
Short, Tasmin B. R., 537
Shorter, Edward, 624
Shrager, Yael, 262
Shultz, Sarah, 371
Shweder, Richard A., 395
Siegal, Michael, 287
Siegel, Jerome M., 145
Siegel, Ronald D., 528
Siegle, Greg L., 621
Siegler, Irene C., 291, 403
Sigman, Marian, 298
Silbersweig, David A., 570

Silva, Christopher, 156
Silver, Roxane Cohen, 546
Silverman, Wendy, 542
Silverstein, Charles, 330
Simner, Marvin L., 443
Simon, Gregory, 552
Simon, Théodore, 291
Simon, Valerie A., 370
Simons, Daniel J., 31, 89, 137
Simons, Leslie Gordon, 407
Simonton, Dean Keith, 555
Simpkins, Sandra D., 376
Simpson, Jeffry A., 479, 521
Singer, Jerome, 350
Singer, Tania, 403
Singh, Devendra, 463
Singh, Dorian, 463
Singh, Jay P., 537
Singh, Maanvi, 552
Singhal, Arvind, 220
Sinha, Rajita, 507
Sinigaglia, Corrado, 43, 217
Sinnott-Armstrong, W., 393
Skene, Debra J., 139
Skinner, B. F., 83, 108, 197, 200,
    201, 202–203, 204, 206, 207,
    208, 429
Skitka, Linda J., 459
Skowronski, John J., 455
Slack, Gordy, 217
Slagter, Heleen A., 160, 162
Slater, Alan, 456
Sleeth, Daniel B., 432
Slepian, Michael, 622
Slobodchikoff, C. N., 288
Slotnick, Scott D., 236
Slutzky, Carly B., 376
Smalarz, Laura, 249
Smallwood, Jonathan, 245
Smart, Reginald G., 489
Smerud, Phyllis E., 608
Smilek, Daniel, 135
Smith, Betty L., 579, 580
Smith, Brendan L., 202
Smith, Craig A., 350–351, 499
Smith, Dena, 522
Smith, Eliot R., 455, 456
Smith, Jonathan A., 550
Smith, Jonathan C., 20, 21, 31
Smith, J. David, 276
Smith, Kerri, 32
Smith, Megan A., 36
Smith, Nicholas A., 371
Smith, Pamela K., 89
Smith, Peter B., 13, 220, 460, 473
Smith, Steven R., 446
Smith, Timothy B., 525, 612, 613
Smith Slep, Amy M., 488
Smits, Jasper A. J., 543
Smolak, Linda, 560
Smoller, Jordan W., 554
Sneddon, Ian, 345
Sneed, Joel R., 399
Snowdon, David A., 263
Snyder, Charles R., 11
Snyder, Douglas K., 608
Snyder, Hannah R., 549
Sobel, Noam, 105

Society for Human Resource
    Management, B–10
Soderstrom, Nicholas C., 37, 211
Sohn, Michael, 379
Sokal, Michael H., 61
Sokol, Robert J., Jr., 364
Solomon, David A., 554
Solomon, Henry, 484
Solomon, Linda Zener, 486
Solomon, Paul, 29
Solomon, Samuel G., 98
Soltys, Florence G., 405
Somer, Eli, 514
Somerville, Leah H., 391
Song, Hongjun, 79
Songer, Jocelyn E., 109
Sorkhabi, Nadia, 408
Soto, Christopher J., 438
Soussignan, Robert, 349
Southall, Ashley, 485
Southwick, Steven M., 525
Sowell, Elizabeth, 388
Spalding, Kirsty L., 64
Spangler, William D., 334
Spanos, Nicholas P., 158, 160
Sparks, Jacqueline A., 611
Spearman, Charles E., 295
Speight, Suzette L., 612
Spencer, Natasha A., 103
Spencer, Scott J., 305
Sperling, George, 229–230
Sperry, Roger, 75
Spezzaferri, Rosa, 518
Spies, Robert A., 442
Spinath, Frank M., 301, 302, 307
Spintge, Ralph, 128
Sponheim, Scott R., 54
Sporns, Olaf, 62
Spradlin, Joseph E., 201
Sprecher, Susan, 463
Springer, Sally P., 76
Squire, Larry R., 262
Sritharan, Rajees, 469
Sroufe, L. Alan, 370
Staats, Sara, 503
Stack, Dale M., 369
Stahl, Stephen M., 616
Stahre, Mandy, 167
Stallen, Mirre, 59
Stams, Geert-Jan J. M., 370
Staniloiu, Angelica, 237
Stanley, Damian A., 469, 470
Stanley, Paula Helen, 429
Stark, Craig E. L., 248
Staub, Ervin, 469
Staudt, Joanne, 385
Steadman, Henry, 537
Steblay, Nancy Mehrkens, 486
Steckler, T., 542
Steel, Piers, 222
Steele, Claude M., 304, 305, 466
Steele, Howard, 368
Steele, James B., 548
Steele, Jeannette, 127
Steen, Tracey A., 515
Stefansson, Hrein, 575
Steg, Linda, 484
Stegner, Aaron J., 160
Stein, Barry S., 238, 277

Stein, Elliot A., 556
Stein, Murray B., 542
Steinberg, Laurence, 390, 391, 408
Stellar, Jennifer, 516
Stellman, Jeanne Mager, 547
Stennett, Janine, 344
Stenstrom, Philippe, 148
Stephens, Benjamin R., 366
Steptoe, Andrew, 516, 517, 519
Sterling-Turner, Heather E., 209
Stern, Kathleen, 103
Stern, Robin, 500
Sternberg, Robert J., 277, 279, 292, 297, 300, 307, 308
Stevenson, Harold W., 460
Steward, Barbara, B–12
Stewart, Duncan W., 617
Stewart, V. Mary, 126
Stewart-Williams, Steve, 191
Stice, Eric, 324
Stickgold, Robert, 145, 146, 266
Stier, Andrea, 536, 537
Stillman, David, B–11
Stinson, Danu A., 463
Stipek, Deborah, 335
Stipelman, Brooke, 541
Stogdill, Ralph M., B–8
Stompe, Thomas, 572
Storm, Benjamin C., 280
Storm, Lance, 112
Støving, René Klinkby, 558
Stowell, Jeffrey R., 472
Strack, Fritz, 349
Strahan, Erin J., 89
Strange, Deryn, 250, 253
Straube, Thomas, 621
Strauss, Clara, 605
Strayer, David L., 17, 137
Strean, Herbert S., 428
Stricker, George, 612
Strickland, Bonnie, 329, 330
Strickland, Brent, 251
Stromberg, Joseph, 446
Stuart, Gwynedd, 280
Stults-Kolehmainen, Matthew, 507
Suarez-Morales, Lourdes, 503
Substance Abuse and Mental Health Services Administration, 165, 167
Sudak, Donna M., 586, 614
Sue, David, 612, 613
Sue, Derald, 505
Sue, Diane, 612, 613
Sugimori, Eriko, 246
Sulem, Patrick, 361
Sullivan, Cathy, B–12
Sullivan, John Jeremiah, 623, 624
Sullivan, Patrick F., 555
Suls, Jerry, 517, 518
Sumter, Sindy R., 391
Sun, Shumei S., 387
Supèr, Hans, 93
Sutter, Mitchell L., 101
Swami, Viren, 463
Swanson, Sonja A., 560
Swartz, Conrad M., 624
Sweeney, Gladys M., 370
Szpunar, Kari K., 236
Szyf, Moshe, 3, 362

Tabachnick, Barbara G., 627
Taber, Brian J., 445
Taguba, Antonio M., 480, 481
Taheri, Shahrad, 322
Takaoki, Eiji, 119
Takeuchi, Tomoka, 141
Tal, Aner, 21
Talarico, Jennifer M., 242
Talbot, Margaret, 289
Talhelm, Thomas, 12
Tallman, Karen, 612
Talos, Ion-Florin, 68
Tamietto, Marcus, 89
Tanaka-Matsumi, Junko, 613
Tanford, Sarah, 473
Tang, Yi-Yuan, 160, 162, 163
Tangney, June, 219
Tanielian, Terri, 546
Tarrasch, Ricardo, 72
Tarrier, Nick, 554
Tasca, Giorgio A., 605
Taub, James, 296
Taylor, Catherine A., 202
Taylor, Kate, 397
Taylor, Margorie, 381
Taylor, Shelley E., 520, 525
Taylor, Steven, 597
Taylor, Stuart P., 487
Taylor, W. S., 567
Teachman, Bethany A., 607
Telework Coalition, B–12
Telle, Nils-Torge, 336
Ten Cate, Olle T. J., 247
ten Haaf, José, 565
Teo, Alan R., 560
Terman, Lewis M., 292, 293
Teyber, Edward, 590
Teymoori, Ali, 370
Thase, Michael E., 619, 620, 623
Thayer, Amanda, 254
Thøgersen-Ntoumani, Cecilie, 528
Thomas, Alexander, 368–369
Thomas, Ayanna K., 253
Thompson, Clara, 428
Thompson, Evan, 160, 161
Thompson, Henry L., 507
Thompson, J. Kevin, 560
Thompson, Paul M., 76, 173, 264, 388, 576, 577
Thompson, Renee J., 522
Thompson, Richard F., 237, 256–257
Thompson, Robin, 240
Thompson, S. C., 514
Thompson, V., 612
Thompson, William L., 275
Thompson-Cannino, Jennifer, 249
Thorndike, Edward L., 196, 197
Thorne, Barrie, 375
Thornhill, Randy, 326
Thornton, Bill, 462
Thorpy, Michael J., 152
Thunberg, Monika, 338
Thurstone, Louis L., 296
Thyer, Bruce, 597
Tienari, Pekka, 578
Tipsord, Jessica M., 391
Tipu, Fatima, 547
Titchener, Edward B., 5
Tizard, Hayley J., 462

Tobler, Irene, 147
Todd, James T., 204
Todd, Michael, 527
Todorov, Alexander, 455, 456, 457
Toga, Arthur W., 76, 389
Tolman, Edward Chase, 210–211
Tong, Stephanie T., 456
Tononi, Giulio, 151
Tooby, John, 14, 315, 336, 337
Topolinski, Sascha, 89
Torges, Cynthia M., 405
Torrey, E. Fuller, 537, 576
Toth, Karen, 278, 298
Tovée, Martin J., 463
Tracey, Terence J. G., 612
Training, B–4
Trainor, Brian C., 525
Trainor, Laurel J., 371
Trajanovic, Nikola N., 155
Tran, Anh N., 606
Travers, Joseph B., 102
Travers, Susan P., 102
Treasure, Janet L., 559
Treffert, Darold A., 298
Treisman, Michel, 228
Tremblay, Angelo, 318
Treyens, James C., 251
Triandis, Harry C., 12, 395
Trivers, R., 460
Trull, Timothy J., 562
Tsai, Jeanne L., 541, 543
Tsang, Laura Lo Wa, 400
Tsao, Doris, 126
Tsvetkova, Milena, 484
Tucker, Jeritt R., 535
Tugend, Alina, B–12
Tulving, Endel, 228, 235, 236, 237, 241
Turati, Chiara, 366
Turiel, Elliot, 393
Turk, Dennis C., 108, 128
Turk-Browne, Nicholas B., 61
Turkington, Douglas, 603
Turner, Erick H., 622
Turner, Erlanger A., 407
Turner, John C., 473
Turner, Martin S., 617
Turner, Monique Mitchell, 491
Tuten, L. Michelle, 599
Tversky, Amos, 282, 283
Tyas, Suzanne L., 263
Tyler, Kathryn, B–11
Tyler, Lorraine K., 403

Uchino, Bert N., 519, 520, 521, 524
Uji, Masayo, 407
Uleman, James S., 457
Umberson, Debra, 402
Umland, Elena M., 398
Underwood, Emily, 145
Unemori, Patrick, 447
UNHCR, 479
University of Arizona, 484
Ur, Blase, 492
Urbina, Susana, 292, 446, 447
Ursano, Robert J., 547
U.S. Bureau of Labor Statistics, B–14
U.S. Census Bureau, 397, 399, 402

Uskul, A. K., 12, 13, 460
U.S. Public Health Service, 580

Vacanti-Shova, Karyn, 34
Van Bavel, Jay J., 469
VanBergen, Alexandra, 568
van Bokhoven, Irene, 487
Van Cauter, Eve, 146
Vance, Ashlee, 62
Vandell, Deborah L., 401
Vandello, Joseph, 489
van der Gaag, Mark, 603
Van Der Heide, Brandon, 455
Van der Helm, Els, 145
van der Vaart, Elske, 289
Vander Ven, Thomas, 397
Vandervoort, Debra J., 523
van de Waal, Erica, 218
Van Dyke, James Urban, 90
van Erp, Jan, 230
van Geert, Paul, 385
Van Heck, Guus L., 336
Van Horn, John, 68
van IJzendoorn, Marinus H., 370
van Osch, Yvette, 489
van Praag, Henriette, 79
van Veen, Vincent, 464
van Vugt, Marieke K., 162
van Wyhe, John, 61
Vargas, Patrick, 492
Varnum, Michael E. W., 115
Vasconcelles, Erin B., 525
Vaughn, Bradley V., 140
Vaughn, Brian E., 370
Vecchi, Tomaso, 273, 275
Vedhara, Kavita, 446
Velthorst, E., 604
Venter, J. Craig, 361
Verschuere, Bruno, 339
Verstrael, Sietse, 597
Vespa, Jonathan, 397, 399
Vet, Carolijn, 484
Vickers, Andrew J., 128
Vigil, Jacob M., 338
Vilain, Eric J. N., 328
Villanova, Patrick, 486
Villemure, Chantal, 108
Viney, Wayne, 6
Vingerhoets, Ad J. J. M., 346
Viswesvaran, Chockalingam, B–12
Vita, Antonio, 576
Vohs, Kathleen D., 459
Volkow, Nora D., 50, 51, 52, 166, 169, 170, 173, 324
von Hippel, W., 460
Voorspoels, Wouter, 275, 276
Vorndran, Christina M., 201
Voss, Michelle W., 404
Voss, Ursula, 152
Vrangalova, Zhana, 327
Vriends, Noortje, 545
Vrij, Aldert, 339
Vrshek-Schallhorn, Suzanne, 556
Vrugt, Anneke, 484
Vyazovskiy, Vladislav V., 140
Vygotsky, Lev S., 385
Vytal, Katherine, 337, 342

Wackerman, Jiri, 113
Wadsworth, Lauren P., 162
Wagatsuma, Hiroshi, 306
Wagenmakers, Eric-Jan, 113
Wager, Tor D., 29
Wagner, Christopher C., 593
Wagner, Dana E., 465
Wagstaff, Graham F., 158
Wahba, Mahmoud A., 332
Wahl, Otto F., 609
Wahlberg, Karl-Erik, 578
Wainwright, Jennifer L., 330
Wakefield, Jerome C., 537
Walden, Keegan, 441
Walker, Elaine, 573
Walker, Herschel, 569
Walker, Matthew P., 145, 146, 147, 266
Wall, Patrick D., 108
Wallace, B. Alan, 160, 529
Wallace, Gregory L., 298
Wallbott, Harald G., 340
Waller, Bridget M., 344
Walsh, Roger, 604
Walter, Marc, 565
Walton, Gregory M., 304, 305
Wampold, Bruce E., 611, 612
Wamsley, Eric, 140, 145
Wanek, James E., B–5
Wang, Chun-Chuan, 429, 591
Wang, Gene-Jack, 324, 538, 606
Wang, Jianli, 104
Wang, Kevin H., 172
Wang, Philip S., 539
Wang, Qi, 236, 237
Wang, Qiang, 504
Wang, Shirley S., 300
Wang, Szu-Han, 261
Wang, Yingxu, 277
Wansink, Brian, 21
Warburton, Wayne A., 488
Ward, Nicholas G., 618
Wargo, Eric, 207
Wartella, Ellen, 372
Wasserman, Edward A., 35, 289
Watanabe, Dai, 289
Waterman, Alan S., 9, 11
Waters, Allison M., 542, 545
Watkins, Linda R., 514
Watson, David, 447
Watson, Jeanne C., 9, 592
Watson, John B., 8, 187, 188–189, 594
Watson, Nathaniel F., 323
Watson, Stuart, 565
Watters, Ethan, 561
Watts, Geoff, 537, 538
Watts, Jonathan, 560
Watts, Richard E., 426, 613
Way, Balwin, 507
Weaver, Terri E., 153
Webb, Thomas L., 352
Wechsler, David, 290
Wechsler, Henry, 167, 168

Weems, Carl, 542
Wegener, Duane T., 462
Weil, Rimona S., 93
Weinberger, Daniel R., 576
Weiner, Irving B., 444
Weinstein, N., 528
Weinstein, Yanna, 36
Weintraub, Michael I., 129
Weisberg, Robert W., 308
Weiser, Mark, 557
Weiss, Alexander, 440
Weiss, Lawrence G., 305
Weiss, Tzipi, 524
Weissman, Myrna M., 590
Welin, S., 299
Wells, Gordon, 385
Wells, Gary L., 249
Wells, Samantha, 489
Werker, Janet, 371
Werkhoven, Peter, 230
Werner, John S., 95, 96, 98
Werth, James L., Jr., 14
Wertheimer, Max, 112, 120
Wertsch, James V., 385
West, John D., 426, 427
West, Mark D., 537
Westen, Drew, 89, 428, 435
Westerhausen, René, 76
Westerlund, Joakim, 112
Wethington, Elaine, 399
Wheeler, Mark E., 235, 258
Whisman, Mark A., 520
Whitaker, Jodi L., 488
Whitbourne, Susan K., 393
White, B. Jack, 470
White, Robert W., 333, 334
Whiten, Andrew, 215
Whitley, Rob, 536
Whitty, Stephen, 550
Whorf, Benjamin, 286
Wickens, Christine M., 489
Widiger, Thomas, 536, 537
Widiger, Thomas A., 562
Wieland, Sandra, 566
Wiesel, Torsten N., 94
Wiggins, S., 321, 323
Wilcoxon, Hardy C., 196
Wilde, Douglas J., 446
Wilker, Sarah, 547
Wilkins, Arnold, 545
Wilkinson, Richard G., 490
Williams, J. Mark G., 163
Williams, Janice E., 517
Williams, Mark, 528, 529
Williams, Nigel M., 574
Williams, Paula G., 500
Williams, Wendy M., 303, 307
Willis, Janine, 455
Willoughby, Tina, 488
Wills, Frank, 602
Wilson, Clare, 604
Wilson, Duff, 617
Wilson, Megan, 35

Wilson, Robert S., 104
Wilson, Timothy D., 456, 465
Windholz, George, 83, 184
Windle, Michael, 557
Windle, Rebecca C., 557
Winemiller, Mark H., 20
Winkeljohn Black, Stephanie, 550–551
Winkielman, Piotr, 349
Winkler, Connie, B–6
Winter, David G., 334
Winter, Frits, 128
Wirth, James H., 535
Wise, Deborah, 213, 515
Wise, Roy A., 324
Wixted, John T., 243, 245
Wnuk, Ewelina, 102
Woerle, Sandra, 167
Wohlschläger, Andreas, 275
Wohlschläger, Astrid, 275
Wolf, Erika J., 524
Wolff, Andre, 108, 109
Wolman, David, 75, 77
Wolpe, Joseph, 594
Women's Sports Foundation, 376
Wonderlic, Charles, B–5
Wong, Lilian C. J., 501, 526
Wong, Paul T. P., 501, 526
Wong, V., 560
Wong, Wan-chi, 4
Woo, Stephanie M., 541
Woo, Tsung-Ung W., 617
Wood, Alex M., 500
Wood, Robert, 352
Wood, Wendy, 374, 376, 378–379, 467
Woodhead, Erin, 504, 524
Woodworth, Robert S., 315
Woody, Erik, 158
Woody, Robert Henley, 590
Woollett, Katherine, 32
Workman, Lance, 545
WorldatWork, B–12
World Health Organization, 321, 573, 579
Worthman, Carol M., 368
Wright, Brittany, 512
Wright, Jesse H., 602, 604
Wrobel, Beata, 326
Wurf, Elissa, 447
Wurtele, Sandy K., 402
Wyatt, Tristram D., 103
Wykes, Til, 604
Wyler, Steven C., 51
Wynne, Lyman C., 574, 578

Xie, Lulu, 144–145
Xu, Fujie, 328
Xu, Jiaquan Q., 402

Yaffe, Kristine, 404
Yakusheva, Olga, 30
Yalom, Irvin D., 605, 607

Yamaguchi, Susumu, 338
Yancey, Christina, 219
Yang, Guang, 145
Yarnell, Phillip R., 260
Ybarra, Oscar, 456
Yeh, Christine J., 526
Yiend, Jenny, 560
Yildirim, Baris O., 487
Ying, Winnie, 560
Yokley, Jessica L., 574
Yonkers, Kimberly A., 537
Yoo, Seung-Schik, 146
Yoshida, Katherine A., 371
Yoshizaki, Kazuhito, 77
Young, Michael W., 138
Yousafzai, Aisha K., 385
Youyou, Wu, 446
Yovel, Galit, 126
Yu, Calvin Kai-Ching, 149
Yuan, Weihong, 389
Yudofsky, Stuart C., 575

Zachariae, Robert, 507
Zacharias, Larry, B–5
Zadra, Antonio, 149
Zajonc, Robert B., 89, 351
Zaki, Jamil, 484
Zaki, Safa R., 276
Zakzanis, Konstantine K., 278
Zanarini, Mary C., 565
Zandy, Amy, B–10
Zarate, Carlos A., 620
Zarrett, N. R., 396
Zatorre, Robert J., 80
Zebrowitz, Leslie A., 455
Zeidan, Fadel, 128, 162, 163
Zeki, Semir, 120
Zelinski, Elizabeth M., 403
Zentall, Thomas R., 35, 289
Zentner, Marcel, 369
Zernike, Kate, 480, 481
Zhang, Tie-Yuan, 362
Zhao, Zhi-Qi, 51
Zheng, Huiyuan, 322
Zhou, Xinyue, 526
Zhu, Haiya, 473
Ziefle, Andrea, 400
Ziegler, Matthias, 334
Zimbardo, Philip G., 459, 464, 476, 479, 480, 481, 482
Zimmerman, Corinne, 285
Zimmerman, Frederick J., 372
Zimmerman, Isiah M., 590
Zimmerman, Mark, 445
Zohar, Dov, 146
Zosuls, Kristina M., 374
Zubieta, Jon-Kar, 512
Zucker, Kenneth J., 330, 379
Zuckerman, Marvin, 316
Zusman, Jose Alberto, 589
Zusne, Leonard, 284
Zvolensky, Michael J., 543
Zwicker, Amy, 503, 520, 525

SUBJECT INDEX

absentmindedness, 245
absolute threshold, 88
Abu Ghraib prison, abuse at, 480–481
access to mental health care, 606–607
accommodation, 91, 118
acculturative stress, 506, 507
acetylcholine, 49–50
achievement motivation, 334–335
achievement tests, 294
ACTH (adrenocorticotropic hormone), 509
action potential, 44, 45–47
activation, 315
Activation-Input-Modulation (AIM) Model, 150
activation-synthesis model of dreaming, 150–151
active reading, 35–36
activity theory of aging, 405
actor-observer bias, 459, 461
actualizing tendency, 429
acupuncture, 51, 127, 128
addiction, 164
additive model, 281–282
Adele, 542
A-delta fibers, 107
adenosine, 141, 170
Adler, Alfred, 426–427
adolescence
  brain in, 388–389
  circadian rhythms in, 144
  defined, 386
  development in, 386–395
  identity formation in, 391–393
  moral reasoning development in, 393–395
  physical and sexual development in, 386–390
  social development in, 390–391
adolescent growth spurt, 387
adrenal cortex, 59
adrenal glands, 58, 59
adrenaline. See epinephrine
adrenal medulla, 59–60
adrenocorticotropic hormone (ACTH), 509
adulthood
  emerging, 396, 398
  physical changes in, 398–399
  social development in, 399–402
advertising and classical conditioning, 190
aerial perspective and depth perception, 117, 118
affective disorders, 550
afterimage, 96, 97

age regression, 158
aggressive behavior
  biological influences on, 486–487
  gender, culture, and, 489–490
  observational learning of, 215–216, 219
  psychological influences on, 487–489
aging and stress, 509–511
agonist, 52
agoraphobia, 542–543
agreeableness, 438, 440
Aguilera, Christina, 241
AIM (Activation-Input-Modulation) Model, 150
alcohol
  aggression and, 487
  as depressant, 166–168
Alcoholics Anonymous, 606–607
algorithms, 278, 279
alleles, 361
all-or-none law, 47
alogia, 571
alpha brain waves, 140, 141, 142
alters or alter egos, 567
altruism, 483
Alzheimer's disease, 262, 263–265
amae, 338
Ambien, 155
American Psychological Association (APA), 6, 34, 35
American Sign Language, 240
amnesia
  anterograde, 260–262
  retrograde, 260
  source, 246
amniotic sac, 364
amphetamines, 172
amplitude, 98
amygdala
  depression and, 621
  facial attractiveness and, 458
  fear and, 340–343
  memory and, 260–261, 262, 263
  nicotine and, 556
  overview, 70, 71
  sleep deprivation and, 146
analogy, 308
anal stage, 422, 423
analysis of variance (ANOVA), A-11
analytic intelligence, 300
androgens, 60
andropause, 399
animal cognition, 289

animals
  classical conditioning, survival, and, 193, 194–195
  communication and cognition in, 288–290
  conditioned taste aversion in, 196
  dreaming and, 152
  emotion in, 344–345
  generalizability of findings from, 80
  handedness in, 74
  hearing of, 102
  learning by, 197
  observational learning by, 216, 218
  odor sensitivity and, 105
  operant conditioning of, 206, 209
  research on, 34–35
  sexual behavior in, 326
  sleep patterns in, 145
  training and behavior modification techniques for, 213–214
  vision of, 90
anorexia nervosa, 558–559, 560–561
anosmia, 102
antagonists, 52
anterior cingulate cortex, 512
anterograde amnesia, 260–262
anthropomorphism, 344–345
antianxiety medication, 617–618
antidepressant medication, 52, 555, 619–621, 622–623
antipsychotic medication, 614–617
antisocial personality disorder, 563–564
anvil, 99, 100
anxiety
  basic anxiety, 426
  ego defense mechanisms, 419–421
anxiety disorders
  generalized anxiety disorder, 541–542
  obsessive-compulsive disorder, 547–549
  overview, 541, 549
  panic attacks and panic disorders, 542–543
  phobias, 543–545
  posttraumatic stress disorder, 546–547
  social anxiety disorder, 544

anxiety hierarchy, 595
APA (American Psychological Association), 6, 34, 35
aphasia, 74
Aplysia (sea snail), 257–259
appraisal
  emotion and, 351
  stress and, 499–500
aptitude tests, 294
archetypes, 424, 425
Aristotle, 3
Army Alpha and Beta tests, 291–292
arousal, emotional, 338–340
arousal theory, 316–317
Asch, Solomon, 472
asexuality, 327–328
Asperger's syndrome, 272
assessment of personality, 442–447
assimilation, 506
association areas, 69–70
astigmatism, 92
astrocytes, 44–45
ataque de nervios, 543
attachment, 369–370, 401
attention
  characteristics of, 135–137
  division of, 137
  encoding failure and, 245
  meditation and, 160
attitudes
  components of, 461–462
  effect of, on behavior, 462
  effect of behavior on, 462, 464–465
  implicit, 469–470
attraction, interpersonal, 463
attractiveness, 458, 463
attribution
  explaining behavior, 458–460
  self-serving bias, 460–461
atypical antipsychotic medications, 617
audition, 98. See also hearing
auditory cortex, 258
auditory sensory memory, 230–231
authoritarian parenting style, 407
authoritative parenting style, 407–408
authority, resisting unacceptable orders from, 482
autism spectrum disorder, 272, 298–299, 300
autistic savants, 298
autistic spectrum disorder, 540
autobiographical memory, 236, 237

autonomic nervous system, 56, 338, 340
autonomy, 333
availability heuristic, 282–283
aversive conditioning, 597
aversive stimulus, 199
avoidance behavior, 199
avolition, 572
Avril, Cliff, 260
axon, 43–44, 53
axon terminals, 48

Baby Boomers, B-11
Baby Einstein videos, 372–373
Baillargeon, Renée, 384
Baldwin, Tammy, 328
Bandura, Albert, 215, 433–434
barbiturates, 168–169
basal metabolic rate, 318
basic anxiety, 426
basic emotions, 336, 337
basilar membrane, 100, 101
BBC Prison Experiment, 481
Beck, Aaron T., 601–603
behavioral genetics, 439–441
behavioral perspective, 10–11
behavioral theories of leader effectiveness, B-8–B-9
behaviorism, 8–9, 187–191
behavior modification/therapy, 209, 593–599
belief-bias effect, 284
beliefs, persistence of unwarranted, 284–285
Bem, Sandra, 377
benzodiazepines, 617
beta-amyloid plaques, 264
beta brain waves, 140, 142
bias
    actor-observer, 459, 461
    confirmation, 21, 284, 285
    cultural, in IQ tests, 307
    in DSM-5, 537
    hindsight, 459, 461
    in-group, 468–469
    self-effacing or modesty, 460, 461
    self-serving, 460–461
    wishful thinking, 285
biculturalism, 506
Big Five personality traits, 438–439, 440
bilingualism, 288
Binet, Alfred, 291
binge drinking, 167
binge-eating disorder, 558
binocular cues, 119
biochemical influences on aggression, 487
biofeedback, 127–128
biological basis of memory
    memory trace, 256–257
    neurons in long-term memory, 257–259
    overview, 256
    processing memories in brain, 259–265
biological clocks, 137–139

biological influences on aggression, 486–487
biological perspective, 10
biological predispositions and operant conditioning, 213–214
biological preparedness, 194–195
biological psychology, 42
biomedical therapies
    antianxiety medications, 617–618
    antidepressant medications, 619–621, 622
    antipsychotic medications, 614–617
    electroconvulsive therapy, 622–625
    lithium, 618–619
    overview, 586
biopsychosocial model, 501
biosocial developmental theory of borderline personality disorder, 565–566
bipolar cells, 91, 93
bipolar disorder, 552–554, 557, 618–619
bisexuality, 327–330
blaming victim, 459–460, 461
Blankenship, Marteen and Wiley, 520
blindness
    circadian rhythms and, 139
    déjà vu experiences and, 246
    dreaming and, 152
blind spot, 92–93
blood alcohol levels, 168
Bobo doll study, 215–216
Bocanegra, Jesus, 546
bodily-kinesthetic intelligence, 297
body mass index (BMI), 321
body senses
    movement, 109–110
    skin, 106–109
boomerang kids, 402
borderline personality disorder, 563, 565–566
Botox, 49
bottom-up processing, 110, 111
brain. *See also specific structures of brain*
    addictive drugs and, 166
    in adolescence, 388–389
    aggression and, 486, 487
    Alzheimer's disease and, 264
    bipolar disorder and, 553
    brainstem, 65–66
    during dreams, 148
    effect of nicotine on, 556–557
    emotions and, 342
    exercise and, 404
    facial attractiveness and, 458
    forebrain, 66–71
    gender and, 72
    improving function of, 79–81
    as integrated system, 61, 78
    mapping pathways of, 62
    meditation and, 163

memory and, 262–263
mental images and, 274
methamphetamine and, 173
neurogenesis, 62–64, 79
plasticity, 62–64, 79
prenatal development of, 364–365
processing memories in, 259–265
psychotherapy and, 621
regions of, 65
"right-brained" and "left-brained" people, 77
specialization in cerebral hemispheres, 71, 73–78
structure of, and Big Five personality traits, 440
weight of, 60
brain chemistry. *See also* neurotransmitters
    in depressive and bipolar disorders, 555
    in schizophrenia, 576–577
brain-imaging techniques in research, 31, 32–33
brainstem, 65–66
brain structures
    in depressive and bipolar disorders, 555
    in schizophrenia, 576, 577
brain waves, 140
Brand, Russell, 554
breathing, mindfulness of, 529
Breivik, Anders, 564
Breland, Keller and Marian, 213–214
Breuer, Joseph, 416
brightness, 96
Broca, Pierre Paul, 73
Broca's aphasia, 74
Broca's area, 73
Buffett, Warren, B-10
bug listing, 308
bulimia nervosa, 558
burnout, 503
Burns, Ursula, B-8
Buspar, 618
bystander effect, 485
bystander intervention, 484–486

cafeteria diet effect, 322
caffeine, 170–171, 191
California Psychological Inventory (CPI), 445
Calkins, Mary Whiton, 6
CAMs (complementary and alternative medicines), 128–129
Cannon, Walter B., 348, 507
capacity of short-term memory, 232–233
Caro, Isabelle, 559
carpentered-world hypothesis, 126
case studies, 22–23
castration anxiety, 422
cataplexy, 154
catastrophic cognitions theory of panic, 543

catatonia, 570
catecholamines, 507
catharsis, 416, 626
Cattell, James McKeen, B-3
Cattell, Raymond, 436
caudate nucleus, 549
CBT (cognitive-behavioral therapy), 603–604
cell body, 43, 44
central executive, 233
central nervous system, 53, 55
centration, 382
cerbrospinal fluid, 53
cerebellum, 65, 66, 256–257, 262, 263
cerebral cortex, 65, 67–70, 256
cerebral hemispheres
    defined, 67
    specialization in, 71, 73–78
C fibers, 107
change blindness, 137
chemicals, disolvable and airborne, 87
chemical senses
    overview, 102
    smell, 103–105
    taste, 105–106
chemosignals, human, 103
child care, 401
childhood. *See* infancy and childhood
Chi-Ying, Charlene Hsu, 561
chlorpromazine, 615
Chow, Alvin and Alan, 439
chromosomes, 43, 360, 361, 509–511
chronic insomnia, 153
chronic pain, 109
chronic traumatic encephalopathy (CTE), 54
chunking, 232
cigarette smoking and psychological disorders, 556–557
circadian rhythms, 137–138, 139, 144
cisgender individuals, 379
citations, 19
clairvoyance, 112
Clark, Kenneth Bancroft, 7
classical conditioning
    behaviorism, 187–188
    conditioned emotional reactions, 188–191
    conditioned responses, 191–192
    contemporary views of, 192–196
    eating behavior and, 318–319
    factors affecting, 184–187
    operant conditioning compared to, 214
    overview, 183
    principles of, 183–184
    process of, 185
    therapy techniques based on, 594–597
client-centered therapy, 590, 591–593
clients, characteristics of, 612

clinical psychology, 14
closure, law of, 116, 123
clustering, 236, 237
cocaine, 172
cochlea, 99–100
cochlear implants, 100
cocktail party effect, 135
cognition
  animals and, 288–290
  explicit and implicit, 456
  intelligence and, 273
  social, 454
cognitive ability tests, B-5
cognitive appraisal model of stress, 499
cognitive appraisal theory of emotion, 350–351
cognitive aspects
  of classical conditioning, 192–193
  of operant conditioning, 209–211
cognitive-behavioral therapy (CBT), 603–604
cognitive biases, 601–602
cognitive bias modification, 607
cognitive development
  in infancy and childhood, 380–386
  in late adulthood, 403, 405
cognitive dissonance, 464–465, 480
cognitive expectations, 212
cognitive maps, 210
cognitive perspective, 11
cognitive theories of emotion, 350–351
cognitive therapies, 599–605
cognitive therapy (CT), 601–603
coincidence, 112
Colbert, Stephen, 329
colds and stress, 513
collective unconscious, 424–425
collectivistic cultures, 12, 13, 115, 460, 526–527
color, 95
color blindness, 96–97
color constancy, 121, 122
color vision, 94–98
communication in animals, 288–290
comparative cognition, 289
comparative psychology, 34
competence, 333
competence motivation, 334
complementary and alternative medicines (CAMs), 128–129
comprehension vocabulary, 372
compulsions, 548, 549
concepts, 275–277
conceptually driven processing, 111
concrete operational stage, 382–383, 384
concussion, 54, 260
conditional positive regard, 431
conditioned reinforcer, 200
conditioned response (CR), 184, 185, 545

conditioned stimulus (CS), 184, 185, 545
conditioning, 182
conduct disorder, 564
conduction deafness, 99
cones, 91, 92, 93
confessions, false, 252
confidentiality of research, 34
confirmation bias, 21, 284, 285
conformity
  Abu Ghraib prison abuse and, 480–481
  culture and, 473
  defined, 473
  factors influencing, 473
  overview, 471–472
  resisting unacceptable orders from authority, 482
confounding variable, 26
congruence, state of, 432
connectome, 62, 72
conscientiousness, 438, 440
conscious experience, 9
consciousness
  attention, 135–137
  biological and environmental clocks that regulate, 137–139
  dreams and mental activity during sleep, 147–152
  hypnosis, 156–160
  meditation, 160–163
  multitasking, perils of, 137
  overview, 134–135
  psychoactive drugs, 164–174
  short-term memory and, 231
  sleep, 139–147
  sleep disorders, 152–156
conservation, 382
contact comfort, 369
contagious yawning, 141
context effect, 241
contingency management, 598–599
continuous positive airway pressure (CPAP), 153
continuous reinforcement, 206
contralateral organization, 65
control, sense of, and stress, 514
control group or condition, 26, 27
controls, experimental, 28–29
control scene for relaxation, 595
convergence, 119
convictions, wrongful, 249
coping strategies
  culture and, 526–527
  emotion-focused, 523–526
  problem-focused, 523
  stress and, 522–523
Corkin, Suzanne, 260–261
cornea, 91
corpus callosum, 62, 65, 67, 71, 75–78
correlation, A-8–A-10
correlational studies, 24–25
correlation coefficient, 24–25, A-8
cortical localization, 60, 61, 73, 78
corticosteroids, 509

co-sleeping, 368
counterconditioning, 594
couple therapy, 608–609
Cowell, Simon, 49
CPAP (continuous positive airway pressure), 153
CPI (California Psychological Inventory), 445
CR (conditioned response), 184, 185, 545
Craig, Charley, 378
creative intelligence, 300
creativity, 308–309
critical periods, 360
critical thinking, 31
cross-cultural perspective, 11–13, 305–307. See also culture
cross-sectional design, 358, 359
CS (conditioned stimulus), 184, 185, 545
CTE (chronic traumatic encephalopathy), 54
cued recall, 240
cultural bias in IQ tests, 307
cultural norms, 13
cultural values and psychotherapy, 613
culture
  achievement motivation and, 335
  aggression and, 489–490
  attributional biases and, 460
  conformity and, 473
  coping strategies and, 526–527
  co-sleeping and, 368
  defined, 12, 13
  early memories and, 237
  emotional expression and, 344–346
  moral reasoning and, 395
  Müller-Lyer illusion and, 126
  outcome of schizophrenia and, 573
  stress of adapting to new, 506
  therapist sensitivity to, 612, 613
  top-down processes and, 115
culture-bound syndromes, 560–561
culture of honor, 489
cumulative adversity, 502–503
curare, 52
"cutting," 565
cyclothymic disorder, 554, 557

daily hassles, 502, 503
Darby, Joseph M., 481, 482
Darwin, Charles, 5, 336–337, 343, 344
data
  analysis of, 18
  collection of, 17
data-driven processing, 111
Dawson, Michelle, 299
deafness
  in infants, 371
  sign language, 285, 287
  "tip-of-the-fingers" experience and, 240
debriefing, 34, A-12

decay theory of memory, 231
decentering, 604
deception in research, 34
Deci, Edward L., 333
decibel, 98, 101
deep brain stimulation, 624
DeGeneres, Ellen, 327
déjà vu experiences, 246
delirium tremens, 168
delta brain waves, 142
delusions, 570, 571, 572
demand characteristics, 28, 481
dementia, 262, 263–265, 288
dendrites, 43, 44
denial, 421, 524
deoxyribonucleic acid (DNA), 360–361
Depakote, 619
dependent variable, 26
depolarized neuron, 45–46
depressant drugs
  alcohol, 166–168
  barbiturates and tranquilizers, 168–169
  inhalants, 168
  overview, 165–166
depressive disorders. See also antidepressant medication
  bipolar disorder, 552–554, 618–619
  brain and, 621
  cognitive biases in, 601–602
  ECT and, 623–624
  explanations for, 554–557
  major depressive disorder, 550–552
  overview, 550, 557
depth perception, 117–119
deRossi, Portia, 327
Descartes, René, 3
descriptive research
  case studies, 22–23
  correlational studies, 24–25
  defined, 17, 21
  naturalistic observation, 22
  surveys, 23–24
descriptive statistics
  correlation, A-8–A-10
  defined, A-2
  frequency distribution, A-2–A-4
  measures of central tendency, A-4–A-5
  measures of variability, A-5–A-7
  z scores and normal curve, A-7–A-8
designer "club" drugs, 174–175
developmental psychology, 358, 359
Diagnostic and Statistical Manual of Mental Disorders, Fifth Edition (DSM-5), 535–538
difference threshold, 88
difficult temperament, 368–369
diffusion of responsibility, 485
diffusion spectrum imaging (DSI), 62
diffusion tensor imaging (DTI), 62

discrepancy hypothesis, B-7–B-8
discrimination
    as chronic source of stress, 505
    IQ differences and, 305–307
    prejudice and, 468
    stimulus, 185–186
discriminative stimulus, 203, 205
displacement characteristic of
        language, 286–287
displacement in psychoanalytic
        theory, 420, 421
display rules, 345
disruptive, impulse-control, and
        conduct disorders, 540
dissociation, 157–158
dissociative amnesia, 567
dissociative anesthetics, 175
dissociative disorders, 566–569
dissociative experience, 566
dissociative fugue, 567
dissociative identity disorder,
        567–569
distraction and pain control, 128
distributed practice, 37
divergent thinking, 308
DNA (deoxyribonucleic acid),
        360–361
DOI (digital object identifier), 19
door-in-the-face technique, 491
dopamine, 50–51, 166, 556,
        577, 615
dopamine receptors and
        obesity, 324
double-blind technique, 28
dream interpretation, 588, 589
dreams
    activation-synthesis model of,
        150–151
    brain during, 148
    neurocognitive theory of, 151
    overview, 147–148
    significance of, 149–150
    themes and imagery, 148–149
drive, 316
drive theories, 314, 315–316
driving while drowsy, 152
drug abuse, 165
drug rebound effect, 164
drug responses and classical
        conditioning, 191–192
drugs. See also psychoactive
        drugs
    antidepressant medication, 52
    effect of on synaptic transmission,
        51–52
drug tolerance, 164, 166
DSI (diffusion spectrum
        imaging), 62
DSM-5 (Diagnostic and Statistical
        Manual of Mental Disorders,
        Fifth Edition), 535–538
DTI (diffusion tensor imaging), 62
Duerson, Dave, 54
Duncker, Karl, 120
duration
    of exposure, 88
    of sensory memory, 229–230
    of short-term memory, 231–232

dying and death, 405–406
dyssomnias, 152, 153

ear
    major structures of, 100
    vestibular sense and, 109
ear canal, 99, 100
eardrum, 99, 100
earnings of I/O psychologists,
        B-14
easy temperament, 368–369
eating disorders
    anorexia nervosa, 558–559
    bulimia nervosa and
        binge-eating disorder, 559
    causes of, 560–561
    overview, 558
    sleep-related, 155
Ebbers, Bernard, B-10
Ebbinghaus, Hermann, 243–244
echoic memory, 230
e-cigarettes, 171–172
eclecticism, 612
ecstasy, 174–175, 618
ECT (electroconvulsive
        therapy), 14
EEG (electroencephalogram), 140
ego, 418, 419
egocentrism, 381
ego defense mechanisms, 419–421
eHealth, 607
Ekman, Paul, 339, 343
elaborative rehearsal, 234–235,
        266
Eldridge, Sean, 327
electroconvulsive therapy (ECT),
        14, 622–625
electroencephalogram (EEG), 140
electroencephalograph, 140
electromagnetic spectrum, 90
elicit, 183–184
elimination-by-aspects model of
        decision-making, 282
Ellis, Albert, 599–601
Elmore, David and Steven, 576
emblems, 345
embryo, 363
embryonic period, 364
emerging adulthood, 396, 398
emotion
    in animals, 344–345
    expression of, 343–346
    functions of, 336–337
    neuroscience of, 338–343
    overview, 335–336
    stress and, 516–518
    subjective experience of,
        337–338
    theories of, 346–351
emotional intelligence, 336
emotionality and sleep
        deprivation, 146
emotional stability, 437
emotional support, 521
emotion-focused coping,
        522, 523–526
empathic understanding, 591
empirical evidence, 16

empirically supported treatments,
        609–611
employment settings of I/O
        psychologists, B-13–B-14
encoding of memory, 228,
        234–235, 246
encoding specificity principle, 241
endocrine system, 42, 58–60,
        507–509
endorphins, 50, 51, 108,
        169, 512
energy and sensory receptors, 87
energy homeostasis, 318
England, Lynndie, 480–481
engram, 256–257
enkephalins, 108
enriched environments, 79–81
environment. See also heredity
        versus environmental factors
    enriched and impoverished,
        79–81
    role of in intelligence, 300–305
environmental clocks, 137–139
epigenetics, 362–363
epilepsy and déjà vu experiences,
        246
epinephrine, 59–60, 348
episodic memory, 235
Erikson, Erik, 392–393
escape behavior, 199
ESP (extrasensory perception),
        112–113, 284
estrogen, 60, 326
estrus, 326
ethics
    in Little Albert study, 189
    in psychotherapy, 627
    in research, 34–35
ethnocentrism, 12, 13
evidence that contradicts beliefs,
        284–285
evolutionary adaptation, 145
evolutionary aspects of classical
        conditioning, 193–196
evolutionary perspective
    on emotion, 336–337
    on gender differences, 377–378
    instinct theories, 315
    on overeating, 322
    overview, 13–14
evolutionary psychology, 454
evolutionists, 5
excitement phase of sexual
        response, 325
exemplars, 276–277
exercise
    aging brain and, 404
    brain function and, 79, 80
    stress and, 528
existential intelligence, 296
expectations of reinforcement,
        215
experience
    conscious, 9
    effects of, on perceptual
        interpretations, 125–126
    vision, brain, and, 95
experimental design, 26–28

experimental group or condition,
        26, 27
experimental research
    defined, 17, 26
    experimental controls, 28–29
    experimental design, 26–28
    limitations of and variations on,
        29–30
explanatory style, 514–516
explicit cognition, 456
explicit memory, 236, 262
exploding head syndrome,
        155–156
exposure therapy, 594
expression of emotion, 343–346
expressive aphasia, 74
extinction, 187, 202, 206, 597–598
extraneous variable, 26
extrasensory perception (ESP),
        112–113
extraversion, 436, 438, 440
extraverts, 425
extrinsic motivation, 308, 333
eye movement desensitization
        reprocessing, 596–597
eyewitness misidentification, 249
Eysenck, Hans, 436–437

Facebook
    networks, 17
    person perception on, 455–456
    satisfaction and, 17
    time on related to GPA, 18, 26
facial attractiveness, 458
facial expression, 343–344, 346
facial feedback hypothesis, 349
factor analysis, 436
Falater, Scott, 132–134, 175–176
fallacy of positive instances, 112,
        285
false memories, 157, 250, 251–255
familismo, 613
family and couple therapy,
        608–609
fast pain system, 107
faulty thinking, 599, 600–601,
        602
fear response
    amygdala and, 340–343
    classically conditioned, 188–189,
        195, 545
feature detectors, 94
fetal alcohol syndrome, 364
fetal period, 365
fight-or-flight response, 57, 338,
        507–508, 525
figure-ground relationship,
        113–114
Finnish Adoptive Family Study of
        Schizophrenia, 578
first impressions, 455
five-factor model of personality,
        438–439
fixation, 422
fixed-interval (FI) schedule, 208
fixed-ratio (FR) schedule, 207–208
flashbulb memories, 241–242
flashcards, 36

flat affect, 571
flavor, 106
flexibility and problem-solving, 278–279
flight of ideas, 553
fluency effect, 36
Flynn Effect, 304–305
fMRI (functional MRI), 32–33
focused attention techniques, 160–161
foot-in-the-door technique, 492
forebrain, 65, 66–71
forgetting
    decay theory of, 245, 247
    as encoding failure, 244–245
    interference theory of, 247
    motivated, 247–248
    overview, 242–243
forgetting curve, 243–244
formal concepts, 275–276
formal operational stage, 383, 384
fovea, 91, 92, 93
fraternal twins, 301
free association, 416, 417, 588
free nerve endings, 107
free recall, 240
free will, 204
frequency, 98–99
frequency distribution, A-2–A-3
frequency polygon, A-3
frequency theory of pitch, 101, 102
Freud, Anna, 416, 417, 428
Freud, Sigmund, 7–8, 149, 415, 416–417, 427, 430, 588–590. See also psychoanalysis
frontal lobe, 68, 69, 73, 262
frustration and aggression, 488–489
fully functioning person, 432
functional fixedness, 280, 281
functionalism, 6
functional MRI (fMRI), 32–33
functional plasticity, 62–63
fundamental attribution error, 458, 459, 461
fusiform facial area, 274

GABA (gamma-aminobutyric acid), 50, 51
Gage, Phineas, 68
Gall, Franz, 61
gambling disorder, 540
Game of Death (TV show), 478–479
gamification, 204
ganglion cells, 91, 93
ganzfeld procedure, 112–113
Garcia, John, 194
Gardner, Howard, 296–297
gate-control theory of pain, 108
Gates, Bill and Melinda, B-10
gender
    aggression and, 489
    defined, 374, 375
    emotional experience and, 338
    moral reasoning and, 395
    perception of pain and, 108
    response to stress and, 525

social support and, 520–522
stereotype threat and, 304–305
gender development in infancy and childhood, 374–379
gender identity, 374, 375, 379
gender role, 374, 375
gender schema theory, 376, 377
gene, 361
general adaptation syndrome, 509
generalization
    defined, 29
    stimulus, 185–186, 189
generalized anxiety disorder, 541–542, 549
generation gaps and employment, B-11
Generation Xers, B-11
generative characteristic of language, 286
genetic predisposition, 362
genetics
    aggression and, 486–487
    behavioral, 439–441
    depressive and bipolar disorders and, 554–555
    development and, 360–363
    intelligence and, 300–305
    schizophrenia and, 574–575
genital stage, 421, 423
genome, 361
genotype, 361
Genovese, Kitty, 482–483
genuineness, 591
Gerhartsreiter, Christian, 457
germinal period, 363
Gestalt psychology, 110, 111–112, 116, 120
g factor (general intelligence), 295
ghrelin, 318–319
Gibson, Edward, 287
ginkgo biloba, 29
glial cells, 44–45
glucose, 318
glutamate, 50, 51, 555, 619
goals, turning into actions, 351–353
gonads, 60
Gonzalez, Eugenio, 277
good continuation, law of, 116, 123
grandeur, delusions of, 570
graphology, 442, 443
grasping reflex, 366
gratitude list, 500
gray matter, 163, 389, 576, 577
Greenleaf, Robert, B-10
group conflict, overcoming, 470–471
group differences in IQ scores, 303–305
group intelligence testing, 291–292
group therapy, 605–607
gustation, 102, 103, 105–106

hair cells, 100–101
Hall, G. Stanley, 6, 7
hallucinations, 570–571
halo effect, 456

hammer, 99, 100
handedness, 74, 77
handwriting analysis, 443
Harlow, Harry, 317, 369
hashish, 174
head injuries, 260
health psychology, 500–501
hearing. See also deafness
    nature of sound, 98–99
    path of sound, 99–101
    pitch, 101–102
Hegde Niezgoda, Asha, 40–42, 74, 78–79
Hemingway, Ernest, 555
heredity versus environmental factors. See also nature-nurture issue
    intelligence, 300–305
    overview, 3
    personality, 439–441
heritability, 303
heroin, 169, 170
heterosexuality, 327–330
heuristics, 278, 279, 282–283
hidden observer, 158
hierarchy of needs, 331–333, 429
higher order conditioning, 186
highlighting information, 35–36
hikikomori, 560, 561
hindbrain, 65–66
hindsight bias, 459, 461
hippocampus
    exercise and, 404
    memory and, 32, 260–262, 263
    neurogenesis and, 63–64
    overview, 70, 71
histogram, A-3
Hockenbury, Kenneth and Julian, 412–414, 439
Hoffmann, Hunter, 596
holes, fear of, 545
homeostasis, 314, 315–316
homosexuality, 327–330
hooking up, 397
hormones, 58–60, 507, 509, 525
Horney, Karen, 425–426, 428
hostility, 517–518
Houston, Whitney, 172
hue, 95–96
Hughes, Chris, 327
Hughes, Howard, 548
Huichol Indians, 173
Hull, Clark L., 315
Human Connectome Project, 62
human development. See also lifespan
    genetic contributions to, 360–363
    prenatal, 363–365
humanistic perspective, 11, 428–432, 441
humanistic psychology, 9
humanistic theories of motivation, 317
humanistic therapy, 590–592

human sexuality
    motivation and, 326–327
    sexual orientation, 327–330
    stages of response, 324–326
humor and coping, 523
hunger and eating
    energy homeostasis, 318
    obesity, 321–324
    overview, 317–318
    regulation of, 318–320
hyperopia, 91–92
hypnagogic hallucinations, 140–141
hypnosis
    age regression through, 158
    effects of, 156–157
    limits and applications of, 159–160
    overview, 156
    theories and views of, 157–159
hypothalamus, 58, 59, 70–71, 138, 342
hypothesis
    defined, 16
    formulating, 16–17
    theory compared to, 19

IAT (Implicit Association Test), 469–470
ICD (International Classification of Diseases), 536
iconic memory, 229, 230
id, 418
identical twins, 301
identification in psychoanalytic theory, 422–423
identity, 392
identity formation, 391–393
illness anxiety disorder, 540
illusions, perceptual, 123–125
imagery and pain control, 128
imagination inflation, 252–255
imaginative suggestibility view of hypnosis, 158–159
imitation of behavior and mirror neurons, 217
immigrants, screening of, 292
immune system
    defined, 511
    hormones and, 59
    schizophrenia and, 575–576
    stress and, 511–513
implementation intentions, 352–353
Implicit Association Test (IAT), 469–470
implicit attitudes, 469–470
implicit cognition, 456
implicit memory, 236, 262
implicit personality theory, 456
impoverished environments, 79
inattentional blindness, 136, 137, 246
inattentional deafness, 136
incentive theories, 316
income inequality and aggression, 490
incongruence, state of, 431

incongruity, 277
independent variable, 26
individualistic cultures, 12, 13, 115
induction, 408
industrial/organizational psychology
    employment settings, training, earnings, and employment outlook, B-13–B-14
    history of, B-3
    job analysis, B-3–B-4
    job satisfaction, B-7–B-8
    leadership, B-8–B-10
    overview, B-1–B-2
    personnel selection, B-4–B-7
    workplace trends and issues, B-10–B-13
infancy and childhood
    cognitive development in, 380–386
    gender development in, 374–379
    language development in, 371–374
    newborns, 365–366
    parenting styles, 407–408
    physical development in, 366–367
    social and personality development in, 367–370
infant-directed speech, 371
inferential statistics, A-10–A-12
inferiority complex, 426
informational social influence, 473, 485
informational support, 521
information-processing model of cognitive development, 386
informed consent, 34
in-group, 467–468
in-group bias, 468–469
inhalants, 168
inhibitory message, 49
inner ear, 99
insight, 279, 588, 613, 626
insight meditation, 163
insomnia, 153, 176–177
instinctive drift, 214
instinct theories, 314
insulin, 318
integrative psychotherapy, 612
integrity tests, B-5
intellectual disability, 298, 300
intelligence
    autism spectrum disorder and, 298–299
    cognition and, 273
    cross-cultural studies of, 305–307
    defined, 290
    development of tests for, 290–294
    measurement of, 298–299
    nature of, 295–297, 300
    roles of genetics and environment in, 300–305

success in life and, 293
intelligence quotient (IQ), 291
intelligence tests
    cultural bias in, 307
    discrimination and, 306–307
    overview, 290–294
    stereotype threat and, 304–305
intensity, aspect of motivation, 315
interactionist theories of gender differences, 378–379
interactive dualism, 3
interference theory of memory, 231
International Classification of Diseases (ICD), 536
Internet recruiting, B-12
interneurons, 43, 55
interpersonal attraction, 463
interpersonal context, 455
interpersonal deficits, 590
interpersonal engagement, 337
interpersonal intelligence, 297
interpersonal therapy, 590
interpretation in psychoanalysis, 588–589
interviews for personnel selection, B-7
intrapersonal intelligence, 297
intrinsic motivation, 308, 333
introspection, 5
introversion, 436
introverts, 425
intuition, 279
in vivo systematic desensitization, 595
ion channels, 45
IQ (intelligence quotient), 291
IQ Zoo, 213
iris, 91
irrational beliefs, 600–601
irreversibility, 381–382

James, LeBron, 207
James, William, 5–7, 135, 196, 315, 347
James-Lange theory of emotion, 347–349
Japan, Burakumin people of, 306
jet lag, 139
jigsaw classroom technique, 471
job analysis, B-3–B-4
Jobs, Steve, 309
job satisfaction, B-7–B-8
Johnson, Virginia, 324–325
Jones, Mary Cover, 594
Jung, Carl, 7, 424–425
just noticeable difference, 88
just-world hypothesis, 459

karyotype, 361
K complex, 142
ketamine, 175, 620
Keyes, Israel, 564
Kimbro, William J., 481
kinesthetic sense, 109
Kirsch, Irving, 622

kleptomania, 540
Kohlberg, Lawrence, 393, 394
Kozlowski, Dennis, B-10
Kubokura, Satomi, 335

Lady Gaga, 609
Laitman, Daniel, 573
Lamson, Ralph, 596
language
    animals and, 288–290
    balanced proficiency in two, 288
    bilingualism, 288
    characteristics of, 285–287
    defined, 284
    effects of, on perception, 286–287
    in infancy and childhood, 371–374
    left hemisphere and, 73–75
Lashley, Karl, 256
late adulthood and aging, 402–405
latency stage, 421, 423
latent content of dreams, 149, 417
latent learning, 211
lateralization of function, 73, 78
law of effect, 197
lay counselors, 606
Lazarus, Richard, 499
L-dopa, 51
leader-member exchange model, B-9
leadership, B-8–B-10
learned helplessness, 211–213
learning
    aggression and, 487–488
    brain plasticity and, 63
    classical conditioning, 183–192
    contemporary views of classical conditioning, 192–196
    contemporary views of operant conditioning, 209–214
    observational, 214–220
    operant conditioning, 196–209
    overview, 182–183
    principles of, 8
    self-control, improving using principles of, 221–222
Ledger, Heath, 165, 536
lens, 91
leptin, 319–320
leptin resistance, 323
libido, 418
lie detection, 339
lifespan. See also infancy and childhood
    adolescence, 386–395
    adulthood, 396–402
    dying and death, 405–406
    late adulthood, 402–405
    sleep patterns over, 144
    stages of, 359–360
light, nature of, 90
light waves, 87
limbic system, 70–71, 104, 340–341. See also amygdala
linear perspective and depth perception, 118

linguistic intelligence, 297
linguistic relativity hypothesis, 286–287
lithium, 618–619
Little Albert case, 188–189, 195
lobes of cerebral cortex, 68
localization of function, 60, 61, 73, 78
Loftus, Elizabeth, 226–227, 249, 250, 255
logical-mathematical intelligence, 297
longitudinal design, 358, 359
long-term memory
    chunking and, 232
    encoding, 234–235
    organization of information in, 237–238
    overview, 229, 234
    role of neurons in, 257–259
    types of, 235–236
long-term potentiation, 258
lost-in-the-mall technique, 252
Lotz, Nick, 572
loudness, 98
low-ball technique, 492
LSD, 172, 173–174
lucid dreams, 152
lymphocytes, 511

magnetic resonance imaging (MRI), 32–33
magnet therapy, 20, 128–129
maintaining behavior, 205–208
maintenance insomnia, 153
maintenance rehearsal, 231
major depressive disorder, 550–552, 557, 621, 623–624
Makutano Junction (TV series), 220
mandala, 425
manic episodes, 553
manifest content of dreams, 149, 417
manipulation of mental images, 275
mantra, 160
MAO inhibitors, 619
marginalization, 506
marijuana, 174
masculine honor culture, 489
Maslow, Abraham, 9, 317, 331–332, 429
massed practice, 37
Masters, William, 324–325
mastery experiences, 352, 434
maturation, early compared to late, 389–390
May, Mike, 23, 84–86, 95, 120, 124–125, 127
McDougall, William, 315
MDMA, 174–175, 618
mean, A-5
measures
    of central tendency, A-4–A-5
    of variability, A-5–A-7

mechanical ability tests, B-5–B-6
media
    for babies, 372–373
    critical thinking about claims
        made by, 72
    depictions of violence and
        mental illness in, 536–537
    observational learning and,
        218–220, 488
medial orbitofrontal cortex, 440
medial temporal lobe, 260, 262,
    263
median, A-5
medical marijuana, 174
meditation
    brain and, 163
    for coping with stress, 528–529
    effects of, 161–163
    overview, 160–161
    pain control and, 128
medulla, 65–66, 342
melatonin, 138, 139
memory
    biological basis of, 256–265
    boosting, 265–266
    culture and, 237
    déjà vu experiences, 246
    distortions of, 250–251
    encoding specificity
        principle, 241
    false memories, 157, 250,
        251–255
    flashbulb, 241–242
    forgetting, 242–248
    hippocampus and, 32–33
    as imperfect, 248–251
    implicit and explicit, 236–237,
        262
    long-term, 234–238
    overview, 228
    perception and, 258
    prospective, 245
    recovered memories, 254–255
    retrieval, 238–242
    sensory, 229–231
    short-term, working, 231–233
    sleep and, 145–146
    stage model of, 228–229, 234
    tip-of-the-tongue experience,
        239–240
memory consolidation, 260
memory trace, 245, 256–257
menarche, 387
meninges, 53
menopause, 398
mental age, 291
mental disorders, 535–536. See
    also psychological disorders
mental health professionals, 587
mental image, 273–275
mental rehearsal for self-
    efficacy, 353
mental sets, 280–281
mere exposure effect, 89
mescaline, 172, 173–174
meta-analysis, 18, 609
methamphetamine, 172–173
method of loci, 266

microaggressions, 505
microexpressions, 339
microglia, 44
microsleeps, 146, 153–154
midbrain, 65, 66
middle ear, 99
middle frontal gyrus, 440
Milgram, Stanley, 474, 475
Millennials, B-11
Miller, Brenda, 260
mindfulness, 161
mindfulness-based therapies,
    604–605, 620–621
mindfulness meditation, 161-163,
    528–529
Minnesota Multiphasic Person-
    ality Inventory (MMPI),
    444–445
mirror neurons, 43, 217
misdirection, 136
misinformation effect, 249
MMPI (Minnesota Multiphasic
    Personality Inventory),
    444–445
mnemonic device, 266
mode, A-4
modeling, 376–377
modesty bias, 460, 461
Molaison, Henry G., 260–262
monocular cues, 117–118
Monteith, Cory, 169
mood congruence, 241
mood disorders, 550
moon illusion, 124
moral reasoning, 393–395
motion parallax, 118
motion perception, 120–122
motivated forgetting, 247–248
motivation
    arousal theory, 316–317
    drive theories, 315–316
    emotion and, 336
    humanistic theories, 317
    incentive theories, 316
    instinct theories, 315
    intrinsic and extrinsic, 308
    overview, 314–315
    possible selves and, 448
    psychological needs and,
        331–335
    sexual behavior and, 326–327
motivational factors, 18
motivational interviewing, 592
motor ability tests, B-6
motor neurons, 43, 55
movement senses, 109–110
MRI (magnetic resonance
    imaging), 32–33
Müller-Lyer illusion, 123–124,
    126
multiple intelligences theory,
    296–297
multiple sclerosis, 45
multitasking, 17, 35, 137
Münsterberg, Hugo, B-3
music, violent lyrics in, 488
musical intelligence, 297
Musser, Joshua, 596

myelin sheath, 44, 45, 53
Myers-Briggs Type Indicator, 446
myoclonic jerk, 141
myopia, 91

Naikan therapy, 613
naloxone, 52
narcissistic leaders, B-10
narcolepsy, 153–154
National Comorbidity Survey
    Replication (NCS-R),
    538–539
natural concepts, 276, 277
natural experiment, 29–30
naturalistic observation, 22
naturalist intelligence, 297
natural selection, 14, 193
nature-nurture issue, 3, 301, 360.
    See also heredity versus
    environmental factors
Necker cube, 95
negative correlation, 25, A-8–
    A-9
negative emotions, 516
negatively skewed distribution,
    A-3–A-4
negative punishment, 201
negative reinforcement, 198–199
negative religious coping, 525
negative symptoms of
    schizophrenia, 570, 577, 616
Nemcova, Petra, 524
neodissociation theory of
    hypnosis, 158
neo-Freudians, 424–427
NEO-Personality Inventory, 440
nerve deafness, 100
nerves, 53
nervous system, 42, 53, 55–57
network therapy, 613
neural pathways, 62, 94
neural stem cells, 53
neural tube, 364
neurocognitive theory of
    dreaming, 151
neurodevelopmental
    disorders, 540
neurodiversity, 299
neurofibrillary tangles, 264
neurogenesis, 63–64, 80
neuroleptic medications, 615
neurons
    characteristics of, 43–44
    communication between,
        47–49
    communication within, 45–47
    defined, 42, 43
    glial cells, 44–45
    in long-term memory, 257–259
    neurotransmitters and, 49–51
    synaptic transmission
        and, 51–52
    types of, 43
neuropeptide Y, 320
neuroplasticity, 62–63, 79, 163
neuroscience
    behavior and, 42
    brain and, 60–71, 78–79

brain imaging and, 32–33
    defined, 10, 42
    gender and, 72
    nervous and endocrine systems,
        53, 55–60
    neurons, 42–52
    specialization in cerebral
        hemispheres, 71, 73–78
    traumatic brain injury, 54
neuroticism, 437, 438, 440
neurotransmitters, 48–51,
    556–557, 576–577. See also
    specific neurotransmitters, such
    as dopamine
Nick, Christophe, 479
nicotine, 171–172, 556–557
nightmares, 149
night terrors, 154
nociceptors, 107
nodes of Ranvier, 44, 45
nondeclarative memory, 236
nondirective therapy, 591
non-rapid-eye-movement
    (NREM) sleep, 140
norepinephrine, 49, 50, 51,
    59–60
normal curve or distribution,
    294, 295
normative social influence,
    473, 485
norms
    cultural, 13
    defined, 12
    implied social, 480–481
    social, 454
    of test, 446
note-taking, 36
NREM rebound, 147
NREM (non-rapid-eye-
    movement) sleep, 140,
    142–144
nucleus, 43, 44
nucleus accumbens, 458, 556

Obama, Barack, 468
obedience
    authority, resisting unacceptable
        orders from, 482
    defined, 475
    factors influencing, 476–479
    Milgram experiment,
        474–476
    results of Milgram experiment,
        476
obesity, 321–324
object permanence, 381, 385
observation, naturalistic, 22
observational learning
    applications of, 217–220
    overview, 214–216
    in phobias, 545
    systematic desensitization
        and, 595
obsessions, 548, 549
obsessive-compulsive disorder,
    547–549
obstructive sleep apnea, 153
occipital lobe, 68, 69

O'Conor, Andi, 497–498, 523, 524, 527
odor
  as molecules in air, 103
  subliminal, 89
  vocabulary for, 102
Oedipus complex, 422
Office, The (TV show), B-1
olfaction, 102, 103–105
olfactory bulb, 64, 104
olfactory cortex, 104
olfactory nerve, 103
olfactory receptors, 103, 104
olfactory tract, 104
oligodendrocytes, 45
one-word stage of language development, 372–373
onset insomnia, 153
open monitoring meditation techniques, 160–161
openness to experience, 438
operant, 198
operant chamber, 205–206, 212
operant conditioning
  applications of, 209
  classical conditioning compared to, 214
  components of, 205
  contemporary views of, 209–214
  discriminative stimuli, 203, 205
  eating behavior and, 318–319
  overview, 196
  phobias and, 545
  punishment, 200–203
  reinforcement, 198–200
  shaping and maintaining behavior, 205–208
  Skinner and order in behavior, 197–198
  therapy techniques based on, 597–599
  Thorndike and law of effect, 197
operational definition, 16
opioids, 169–170
opponent-process theory of color vision, 96, 97–98
optic chiasm, 94
optic disk, 91, 92, 93
optic nerve, 91, 93–94
optimistic explanatory style, 514–516
oral stage, 422, 423
orbital frontal cortex, 458
organizational behavior
  job satisfaction, B-7–B-8
  leadership, B-8–B-10
  overview, B-2
orgasm, 325
outcome variable, 26
outer ear, 99
out-group, 467–468
out-group homogeneity effect, 468, 469
oval window, 99, 100
ovaries, 58, 60
overeating, 321–322

overestimation effect, 285
overlap and depth perception, 117, 118
overt behavior, 8
Owens, Thomas, 54
oxytocin, 59, 525

Pace, Peter, 481
Pacinian corpuscle, 106
pain
  hypnotic suppression of, 157
  sense of, 106–109
  strategies to control, 127–129
pain pills, prescription, 169–170
panic attacks and panic disorders, 542–543, 549
parahippocampal place area, 274
paranormal phenomena, 112
paraprofessionals, 606
parapsychology, 112
parasomnias, 152, 153, 154–156
parasympathetic nervous system, 56, 57
parenthood, transition to, 400, 402
parenting styles, 407–408
parietal lobe, 68, 69, 389
Parkinson's disease, 50–51
partial reinforcement, 206
partial reinforcement effect, 206–207
paternal age and schizophrenia, 575
Pausch, Randy, 406
Pavlov, Ivan, 8, 183
Pavlov, V. I., 184
Pavlovian conditioning, 183. *See also* classical conditioning
Paxil, 52
PCP, 175
peer relationships in adolescence, 391
peg-word method, 266
penis envy, 422–423
perception
  of color, 96
  culture and, 115
  defined, 86–87
  of depth, 117–119
  effects of experience on, 125–126
  effects of language on, 286–287
  ESP, 112–113
  of faces or places, 274
  Gestalt psychology, 111–112
  memories and, 258
  of motion, 120–121
  of pain, 108
  sensory memory trace and, 231
  of shape, 112–117
  steps in, 87
  subliminal, 89
  top-down and bottom-up processing, 110–111
perceptual constancies, 121–122
perceptual grouping, 116–117
perceptual illusions, 123–125
perceptual set, 125

performance and stereotype threat, 304–305
performance appraisal systems, B-4
performance score of WAIS, 292
performance self-efficacy, 18
peripheral nervous system, 53, 55–57
permissive parenting style, 407
persecution, delusions of, 570
persistence, aspect of motivation, 315
persistent depressive disorder, 552, 557
personality
  assessment of, 442–447
  health and, 518
  humanistic perspective on, 428–432
  intelligence and, 293
  overview, 414–415
  psychoanalytic perspective on, 415–428
  social cognitive perspective on, 432–435
  trait perspective on, 435–441
personality disorders
  antisocial, 563–564
  borderline, 565–566
  overview, 562–563
personality tests, B-6
personality theory
  of Freud, 417–423
  implicit, 456–457
  overview, 415
personality types, 446
person-centered therapy, 591–593
personnel psychology
  job analysis, B-3–B-4
  overview, B-2
  selection of personnel, B-4–B-7
personnel selection
  psychological tests, B-5–B-6
  selection device validity, B-4
  selection interviews, B-7
  work samples and situational exercises, B-6
person perception
  impression formation, 455–456
  overview, 454–455
  social categorization, 456–458
persuasion, 491–492
pessimistic explanatory style, 514–516
PET (positron emission tomography), 32–33
pets and social support, 520
peyote, 173
phallic stage, 422, 423
phallic symbols, 149
phantom limb pain, 108–109
pharmacogenetics, 620
phenotype, 361–362
pheromones, 103
phobias, 195, 543–545, 549, 596
phonological loop, 233
photoreceptors, 92
phrenology, 60, 61, 440

physical attractiveness, 458
physical dependence, 164
physical development
  in adolescence, 386–390
  in adulthood, 399–402
  in infancy and childhood, 366–367
physical punishment, 202
physiology, 4
Piaget, Jean
  criticism of theory of, 383–386
  theory of, 380–383
pineal gland, 138
pinna, 99, 100
pitch, 98, 101–102
pituitary gland, 58, 59, 71, 342
placebo, 29, 622–623
placebo effect, 29, 512
placebo response, 191–192
placenta, 364
place theory of pitch, 102, 103
planful problem solving, 523
plaques, beta-amyloid, 264
plateau phase of sexual response, 325
Plath, Sylvia, 555
pleasure principle, 418
polarized neuron, 45
polygraph, 339
pons, 65, 66
population, A-12
positive correlation, 25, A-8, A-9
positive emotions, 516–517
positive incentive value of food, 322
positively skewed distribution, A-3
positive psychology, 11, 212
positive punishment, 200–201
positive reappraisal, 524
positive reinforcement, 198–199, 203, 598
positive religious coping, 525–526
positive self-talk and pain control, 128
positive symptoms of schizophrenia, 570, 572, 577, 615
positron emission tomography (PET), 32–33
possible selves, 447–449
posterior cingulate cortex, 440
posthypnotic amnesia, 156, 157
posthypnotic suggestion, 156, 157
postsynaptic neuron, 47
posttraumatic stress disorder (PTSD)
  development of, 502
  memory and, 254–255
  overview, 546–547, 549
  treatment of, 596
potassium ions, 45–46
power motivation, 334
practical intelligence, 300
practice effect, 29
practice tests, 36
Prägnanz (simplicity), law of, 116–117
precognition, 112, 113

prefrontal association cortex, 70
prefrontal cortex, 262, 263, 389, 621
prejudice
  Abu Ghraib prison abuse and, 480–481
  implicit attitudes, 469–470
  in-group bias, 468–469
  out-group homogeneity effect, 468
  overcoming, 470–471
  overview, 465–466
  stereotypes and, 466–468
Premack principle, 203
prenatal development
  brain and, 364–365
  fetal period, 365
  germinal and embryonic periods, 363–364
prenatal stage, 363
preoperational stage, 381, 384
presbyopia, 92
presynaptic neuron, 47
primacy effect, 241
primary auditory cortex, 68
primary motor cortex, 69, 70
primary reinforcer, 200
primary sex characteristics, 386–387
primary somatosensory cortex, 162
primary visual cortex, 68, 70
proactive interference, 247
probability, A-11
problem finding, 308
problem-focused coping, 522, 523
problem solving
  defined, 277
  obstacles to, 280–281
  strategies for, 277–279
procedural memory, 235
processing memories, 259–265
processing visual information, 93–94, 111, 115, 122
production vocabulary, 372
Profeta, Kailey, 154
progesterone, 60
progressive relaxation, 594–595
projection, 421
projective test, 442, 444
proprioceptors, 109
prosocial behavior, 483
prospective memory, 245
prospective study, 329, 518
prototypes, 276, 277, 283
proximity, law of, 116
Prozac, 51, 52, 619–620
pseudoevents, 252
pseudomemories, 157
pseudoscience, 20–21
  belief bias effect and, 284
  brain myths, 77
  confirmation bias and, 284
  ESP, 112–113, 246, 284
  genius babies through media programs, 372-373
  graphology, 442-443
  magnet therapy, 1-2, 20-21

open-mindedness and, 31, 113, 284
overestimation effect and, 284
phrenology, 61, 73, 78, 440
subliminal perception and, 88-89
unwarranted beliefs and, 284
psilocybin, 173–174
psychedelic drugs, 173–174
psychiatry, 14, 15
psychoactive drugs
  addiction to, 166
  categories, 164
  depressants, 165–169
  designer "club," 174–175
  effects of, 164–165
  opioids, 169–170
  psychedelic, 173–174
  stimulants, 170–173
psychoanalysis, 7–8, 149, 248, 415
psychoanalytic perspective on personality
  dynamic theory, 417–421
  ego defense mechanisms, 419–421
  evaluation of, 427–428
  influences on, 416–417
  neo-Freudians and, 424–427
  overview, 441
  psychosexual stages of development, 421–423
  structure of personality, 418–419
psychoanalytic therapy, 588–590, 593
psychodynamic perspective, 10
psychokinesis, 112
psychological disorders
  age of onset of, 539
  anxiety disorders, 541–549
  cigarette smoking and, 556–557
  culture-specific, 560–561
  depressive and bipolar disorders, 550–557
  diagnosis of, 535–536
  dissociative disorders, 566–569
  eating disorders, 558–561
  overview, 534–535
  personality disorders, 562–566
  prevalence of, 538–540
  schizophrenia, 569–579
  suicide prevention, 579–581
  violence and, 536–537
psychological factors and stress, 514–518
psychological tests, 442, B-5–B-6
psychology. See also biological psychology; clinical psychology; comparative psychology; developmental psychology; evolutionary psychology; Gestalt psychology; health psychology; humanistic psychology; industrial/organizational psychology; parapsychology; personnel psychology; positive psychology; social psychology
  defined, 2
  goals of, 3

major perspectives in, 10–14
origins of, 3–4
specialty areas in, 14–15
psychoneuroimmunology, 511
psychopathology, 535
psychopaths, 564
psychosexual stages of development, 421–423
psychosis, stimulant-induced, 172
psychosocial stages of development, 391–393
psychotherapy
  access to, 606–607
  behavior therapy, 593–599
  brain and, 621
  cognitive, 599–605
  cultural values and, 613
  evaluation of effectiveness of, 609–612, 620–621
  family and couple, 608–609
  group, 605–607
  guidelines for seeking and participating in, 626–627
  humanistic, 590–592
  integrative, 612
  overview, 586–587
  psychoanalytic, 588–590, 593
psychoticism, 437
psychotropic medications, 586, 614
PTSD. See posttraumatic stress disorder
puberty, 386–390
punishment, 200–203
punishment by application, 200–201
punishment by removal, 201
pupil, 91
puzzle box, 197
pyromania, 540

race
  perception of pain and, 108
  stereotype threat and, 304–305
racism, as chronic source of stress, 505
random assignment, 26, 27
random selection, 23
range, A-5–A-6
rapid cycling bipolar disorder, 554
rapid-eye-movement (REM) sleep, 140, 143–144, 147–148
rational-emotive behavior therapy (REBT), 599–601, 603
rationalization, 421
rave culture, 175
Raven's Progressive Matrices Test, 299
raw scored, A-2
Rayner, Rosalie, 188, 189, 190
reaction formation, 421
reactive temperament, 369
reality principle, 418, 419
REBT (rational-emotive behavior therapy), 599–601
recall, 240

recency effect, 241
receptive aphasia, 74
receptive field, 93
receptor sites, 48, 49
reciprocal determinism, 433
recognition, 240
recovered memories, 254–255
reference, delusions of, 570
reference lists, 19
reflex, 183
refractory period, 47
regression, 421
reinforcement
  of alternative incompatible behavior, 202
  elimination of, 202
  incentive motivation and, 316
  long-term and short-term, 221
  of non-occurrence of problem behavior, 202–203
  overview, 198–200
  schedules of, 207–208
  shift in value of, 221–222
reinforcing stimulus, 199
relatedness, 333
relative size and depth perception, 117, 118
relaxation
  coping with stress and, 528
  pain control and, 128
reliability of tests, 294, 295, 444
REM deprivation, 147
REM rebound, 147
REM (rapid-eye-movement) sleep, 140, 143–144, 147–148
Rensaleer, Jan, 480, 482
replicate, 18–19, 112
repolarization of neuron, 47
reporting research findings, 18–19
representativeness heuristic, 283
representative sample, 23
repression
  of memory, 247–248, 254–255, 588
  in psychoanalytic theory, 420, 421, 588
repurposing, 280
Rescorla, Robert, 192
research. See also scientific method; statistics
  on meditation, 161–162
  on sleep, 140, 146–147
research designs, 17
reserpine, 614–615
resilience, 502–503
resistance, 588, 589
resolution phase of sexual response, 325–326
response, unconditioned and conditioned, 184, 185
resting potential, 44, 45, 47
Reston, Ana Carolina, 559
reticular formation, 65, 66
retina, 91, 92, 93
retrieval cue failure, 238, 245
retrieval cues, 238, 239–240

retrieval of memory
cues for, 239–241
encoding specificity principle, 241
overview, 228, 229, 238–239
retroactive interference, 247
retrograde amnesia, 260
retrospective study, 329
reuptake, 48
risk factors for suicidal behavior, 580
road rage, 488
Robbers Cave experiment, 470–471
Rodriguez, Ivan, 20
rods, 91, 92, 93
Rogers, Carl, 9, 317, 429–432, 591–592
role disputes, 590
role models, 222
role transitions, 590
rooting reflex, 366
Rorschach, Hermann, 442
Rorschach Inkblot Test, 442
Rowling, J. K., 552
rule of commitment, 492
rule of reciprocity, 491
runner's high, 51
Ryan, Richard M., 333

Saks, Elyn, 532, 569, 571
sample, 23, A-12
satiation, 318–319
saturation, 95–96
scatter diagram or plot, A-8, A-9
schedules of reinforcement, 207–208
schemas, 250–251, 456
schizophrenia
abnormal brain chemistry in, 576–577
abnormal brain structures in, 576
dopamine and, 51
genetic factors in, 574–575
imaging studies of, 577
immune system and, 575–576
negative symptoms of, 571–572, 616
paternal age and, 575
positive symptoms of, 570–571, 572, 615
prevalence and course of, 573
psychological factors in, 578–579
symptoms and culture in, 572–573
Schwann cells, 53
scientific method
building theories, 19–20
defined, 15–16
steps in, 16–19
sclera, 91
scripts, 250–251
seasonal affective disorder, 551, 557
secondary reinforcer, 200
secondary sex characteristics, 387

second-order conditioning, 186
secure attachment, 369–370
seizures and déjà vu experiences, 246
selection device validity, B-4–B-5
selective serotonin reuptake inhibitors (SSRIs), 52, 619–620
self, sense of, 454
self-actualization, 332, 333, 592
self-affirmation, 305
self-concept, 429, 431, 447–449
self-control, improving, 221–222
self-determination, 204
self-determination theory, 333–334
self-effacing bias, 460, 461
self-efficacy, 351–352, 434
self-efficacy beliefs, 448
self-help groups, 606–607
self-reference effect, 235
self-regulation, 433
self-reinforcement, 203, 222
self-report inventories, 444–447
self-serving bias, 460–461
Seligman, Martin, 212, 515
Selye, Hans, 508
semantic memory, 235, 236
semantic network model, 238
semicircular canals, 109
sensation
basic principles of, 87–89
chemical and body senses, 102–110
defined, 86–87
hearing, 98–102
overview of senses, 110
vision, 90–98
sensation seeking, 316–317
sense of self, 454
sensitization, 108–109
sensorimotor stage, 380–381, 384
sensory adaptation, 88–89, 108
sensory experiences, memories of, 258
sensory memory
duration of, 229–230
overview, 228–229
in stage model of memory, 234
types of, 230–231
sensory neurons, 43
sensory receptors, 87
sensory-specific satiety, 318–319
serial position effect, 240–241, 266
serotonin, 50, 51, 560
servant leaders, B-10
Sesame Street, 372
SES (socioeconomic status) and stress, 505
set-point theory, 320
sex chromosomes, 361
sex differences and brain, 72
sexism of psychoanalytic theory, 428
sexsomnia, 154, 155
sexual abuse, "recovered" memories of, 254–255

sexual contact in psychotherapy, 627
sexual orientation, 327–330
shape constancy, 122
shape perception, 112–114, 116–117
shaping behavior, 205–208, 597
shared characteristic of language, 286
shared reminiscing, 237
Shepard Tables illusion, 125
Sherif, Muzafer, 470
short-term dynamic therapies, 589–590
short-term memory
capacity of, 232–233
duration of, 231
overview, 229, 231
in stage model of memory, 234
working memory and, 233
shuttlebox, 212
sign language, 285, 287
single-feature model, 281
situational exercises, B-6
situational theories of leadership, B-9
16 and Pregnant (docu-series), 218
Sixteen Personality Factor Questionnaire (16PF), 436, 445
size constancy, 121–122, 124
skewed distribution, A-3–A-4
Skilling, Jeffrey, B-10
Skinner, B. F., 8–9, 197–198, 204, 597
Skinner box, 204, 205–206
skin senses, 106–109
sleep. See also sleep disorders
coping with stress and, 528
in infancy and childhood, 368
memory formation and, 145–146, 266
onset of, 140–141
purpose of, 144–145
research on, 140
stages and patterns of, 141–144
weight and, 322–323
sleep attacks, 153–154
sleep deprivation, 146–147
emotional effects of, 146
sleep disorders
defined, 152, 153
insomnia, 153
narcolepsy, 153–154
obstructive sleep apnea, 153
parasomnias, 154–156
sleep paralysis, 141
sleep-related eating disorder, 155
sleepsex, 154, 155
sleep spindles, 142
sleep starts, 141
sleeptalking, 141
sleep terrors, 154
sleep thinking, 147
sleepwalking, 154, 155, 175–176
slow pain system, 107–108
slow-to-warm-up temperament, 368–369

slow-wave sleep, 142, 148
Smart, Elizabeth, 459
smell, 103–105
Snyder, Rebecca, 35
social anxiety disorder, 544
social categorization, 456–458
social cognition, 454
social cognitive perspective
on hypnosis, 158–159
on personality, 432–435, 441
social development
in adulthood, 399–402
in infancy and childhood, 367–370
social influence, 454, 479–480, 482
social learning theory of gender-role development, 376–377
social loafing, 13
social norms, 454, 480–481
social psychology
aggression, 486–491
altruism, 482–486
attitudes, 461–465
attribution, 458–461
conformity, 471–473
obedience, 474–482
overview, 454
person perception, 454–458
persuasion game, 491–492
prejudice, 465–471
Social Readjustment Rating Scale, 501–502
social status, perceived, and health, 505
social striving, 13
social support
defined, 519
gender differences in effects of, 520–522
health benefits of, 520
providing effective, 521
seeking, 524
socioeconomic status (SES) and stress, 505
sociopaths, 564
sodium ions, 45–46
somatic nervous system, 55–56
somatic symptoms and disorders, 540
somatosensory cortex, 68–69, 70, 349
somnambulism, 155
Sorenson, Karen, 570
sound waves, 87, 98–99, 100
source amnesia, 246
source confusion, 249–250, 253
source memory/monitoring, 246, 247
source traits, 436, 437
spanking, 202
spatial intelligence, 297
Spearman, Charles, 295
specific phobia, 544, 545
Sperling, George, 229–230
Sperry, Roger, 75–76
spinal reflexes, 55

split-brain operation, 75–78
spontaneous recovery, 187
spontaneous remission, 609
SSRIs (selective serotonin reuptake inhibitors), 52, 619–620
stage model of memory, 228–229, 234
standard deviation, A-6–A-7
standardization, 294, 446
standard normal curve, A-7
standard normal distribution, A-7
Stanford-Binet Intelligence Scale, 291
Stanford Prison Experiment, 480–481
state view of hypnosis, 158
statistically significant, 18, A-11
statistics
    defined, 18, A-2
    descriptive, A-2–A-10
    inferential, A-10–A-12
Steele, Claude, 19, 305
stem cells, 364
stepping reflex, 366
stereograms, 119
stereotypes
    of mental illness, 536–537
    prejudice and, 466–468
stereotype threat, 19, 304–305
Sternberg, Robert, 297, 299
stigma of mental illness, 536–537
stimulant drugs
    amphetamines and cocaine, 172–173
    caffeine and nicotine, 170–172
    overview, 170
    stress and, 527
stimulus
    aversive, 199
    defined, 5, 183
    discriminative, 203, 205
    reinforcing, 199
    unconditioned and conditioned, 184, 185
stimulus control therapy for overcoming insomnia, 176–177
stimulus generalization and discrimination, 185–186, 189
stimulus threshold, 44, 45
stirrup, 99, 100
storage of memory, 228, 229
Strange Situation, 370
strategies
    to boost memory, 265–266
    to control pain, 127–129
    to improve self-control, 221–222
    for insomnia, 176–177
    to maximize brain potential, 79–81
    for study, 35–37
stream of consciousness, 134, 135
stress
    of adapting to new culture, 506
    appraisal and, 499–500
    chromosomes, aging, and, 509–511
    coping with, 522–527

daily hassles, 503–504
    defined, 499
    depressive and bipolar disorders and, 555–556
    endocrine system and, 507–509
    factors influencing response to, 513–522
    immune system and, 511–513
    life events and change, 501–502
    minimizing effects of, 527–529
    physical effects of, 507–513
    psychological factors and, 514–518
    resilience, 502–503
    social and cultural sources of, 505
    social factors and, 519–522
    traumatic events, 502
    of work, and burnout, 504
stressors, 501
stretch receptors, 318–319
stroboscopic motion, 120–121
structuralism, 4–5, 6
structural plasticity, 63
structured behavioral interviews, B-7
study strategies, 23–24, 25, 35–36
subjective experience of emotion, 337–338
sublimation, 420, 421
subliminal perception, 89
substance P, 107
substance-related and addictive disorders, 540
substance use disorder, 165
substantia nigra, 66
successful intelligence, 300
sucking reflex, 366
suicide, prevention of, 579–581
Sumner, Francis C., 6–7
superego, 418, 419
superiority, striving for, 426
superiority complex, 427
superstitious rituals, 207
support groups, 607
suppression of memory, 247
suprachiasmatic nucleus, 70, 138–139
surface traits, 436, 437
surveys, 23–24
symbolic thought, 381
symmetrical distribution, A-4
sympathetic nervous system, 56–57, 338–340
synapse, 47
synaptic connections and memory, 259
synaptic gap, 47
synaptic transmission
    effect of drugs on, 51–52
    overview, 47–49
synaptic vesicles, 48
synchronized sleep, 143
syntax, 286
systematic desensitization, 594–595

tai chi, 161
tangible support, 521

tangles, neurofibrillary, 264
tardive dyskinesia, 616
taste, 105–106
taste aversion, 193–196
taste buds, 104, 105
TAT (Thematic Apperception Test), 334, 442, 444
TBI (traumatic brain injury), 54
technology-based solutions to mental health care access, 607
telepathy, 112
telework and telecommuting, B-12
telomeres, 509–511
temperament, 368–369
temporal lobe, 68, 69, 577
tend-and-befriend response, 525
teratogens, 364
Terman, Lewis, 291
terrorist attacks and PTSD, 547
testes, 58, 60
testing effect, 26–28, 36
testosterone, 60, 326–327, 487
tests of intelligence. *See* intelligence tests
test-taking behavior, 307
tetrahydrocannabinol (THC), 174
texture gradient and depth perception, 117–118
thalamus, 70, 71, 341, 556
that's-not-all technique, 491–492
Thematic Apperception Test (TAT), 334, 442, 444
theory
    building, 19–20
    defined, 19
    of emotion, 346–351
    of evolution by natural selection, 193
    of gender differences, 376–379
    of intelligence, 295–297, 299
therapeutic relationship, 612, 626–627
therapists, characteristics of, 612, 613
thinking
    concepts, 275–277
    decision making, 281–283
    defined, 273
    mental images, 273–275
    solving problems, 277–281
Thompson, Richard F., 256–257
thorazine, 615
Thorndike, Edward L., 196–197
threshold, 88
Thurstone, Louis L., 296
timbre, 99
time-out from positive reinforcement, 203
tip-of-the-tongue experience, 239–240
Titchener, Edward B., 4–5
token economy, 598
Tolman, Edward C., 210–211
top-down processing, 110, 111, 115, 122
touch, 106

Tourette's disorder, 540
tracts, 62
Traditionalists, B-11
training programs
    for employees, B-4
    for I/O psychologists, B-14
trait, 435
trait approach to leader effectiveness, B-8
trait perspective on personality, 435–441
trait theory, 435
tranquilizers, 168–169
transcendental meditation, 161
transcranial direct current stimulation, 624
transcranial magnetic stimulation, 624
transduction, 87, 100–101
transference, 589
transgender individuals, 379
traumatic brain injury (TBI), 54
traumatic events, 502
treatment variable, 26
trephining, 614
trial and error learning, 197, 277
triarchic theory of intelligence, 300
trichromatic theory of color vision, 96–97, 98
tricyclic antidepressants, 619
triple vulnerabilities model of panic, 543
"Truman Show" delusion, 572
trypophobia, 545
Tsai, Jolin, 561
t test, A-11
Twain, Mark, 555
twin studies of intelligence, 301–303
two-factor theory of emotion, 350
two-stage model of intuition, 279
two-word stage of language development, 373–374
Type A behavior pattern, 517–518
Type I error, A-12
Type II error, A-12

umami, 106
umbilical cord, 364
uncertainty and decision making, 282–283
unconditional positive regard, 431, 591
unconditioned response (UCR), 184, 185
unconditioned stimulus (UCS), 184, 185
unconscious
    collective unconscious, 424–425
    defined, 7
    Freud and, 417
undoing, 421
unresolved grief, 590
unstructured interviews, B-7
Upp, Hannah, 567

vagus nerve stimulation, 624
validity of tests, 294, 295, 444
vaping, 171–172
variable, 16, 26
variable-interval (VI) schedule, 208
variable-ratio (VR) schedule, 208
ventircles, 53
ventral striatum, 458
verbal score of WAIS, 292
vestibular sense, 109
Vicary, James, 89
video games, violent, 219, 488
violence. *See also* aggressive behavior
  child soldiers and, 547
  in media, 219, 536–537
viral infection theory and schizophrenia, 575–576
virtual reality (VR) therapy, 596
vision
  color vision, 94–98
  experience, brain, and, 95
  human visual system, 91–93

nature of light, 90
processing visual information, 93–94
visual cortex, 258
visual imagery, 235
visualization for self-efficacy, 353
visual sensory memory, 230
visuospatial sketchpad, 233
volley principle of pitch, 102
voluntary participation in research, 34
von Helmholtz, Hermann, 96
Vygotsky, Lev, 385

WAIS (Wechsler Adult Intelligence Scale), 292–293
Wald, George, 97
Washburn, Margaret Floy, 6, 7
Watson, John B., 8–9, 187–188, 189, 190
wavelengths, 90, 91, 95–96
Weber, Ernst, 88
Weber's law, 88
Wechsler, David, 292–293

Wechsler Adult Intelligence Scale (WAIS), 292–293
weight
  regulation of, 319–320
  sleep and, 322–323
Wellbutrin, 619, 620
Wernicke, Karl, 73
Wernicke's aphasia, 74
Wernicke's area, 73
Wertheimer, Max, 111–112
"what is beautiful is good" myth, 456
white matter, 62, 67
Whorfian hypothesis, 286–287
Williams, Robin, 550
Winehouse, Amy, 565
wishful thinking bias, 285
withdrawal reflexes, 55
withdrawal symptoms, 164
womb envy, 426
Woodworth, Robert S., 315
workforce diversity, B-11–B-12
working memory, 233
work-life balance, B-12–B-13

workplace trends and issues
  Internet recruiting, B-12
  overview, B-10–B-11
  telework and telecommuting, B-12
  workforce diversity, B-11–B-12
  work-life balance, B-12–B-13
work samples, B-6
work stress, 504
Wundt, Wilhelm, 4, B-3

X chromosome, 361

yawning, 141
Y chromosome, 361

zazen, 161
Zimbardo, Philip, 464
Zoloft, 52
zone of proximal development, 385
z score, A-7
zygote, 360, 363